THEOLOGICAL DICTIONARY

OF THE

NEW TESTAMENT

EDITED BY

GERHARD FRIEDRICH

Translator and Editor

GEOFFREY W. BROMILEY, D. LITT., D. D.

Volume VI

Πε—Ρ

WM. B. EERDMANS PUBLISHING COMPANY

GRAND RAPIDS, MICHIGAN

THEOLOGICAL DICTIONARY OF THE NEW TESTAMENT

Translated from
THEOLOGISCHES WÖRTERBUCH ZUM NEUEN TESTAMENT
Sechster Band Πε-P, herausgegeben von Gerhard Friedrich

Published by
W. KOHLHAMMER VERLAG
Stuttgart, Germany

Printed in the Netherlands
by Henkes-Holland N.V., Haarlem

Preface

After five years another volume of the Theological Dictionary has now been finished. It is bulky, and covers only two letters as compared with the three or four of the earlier volumes. There are several reasons for this, both material and temporal. It is a familiar fact that to be brief is very difficult in a busy period. This affects the preparation of articles for the Dictionary too. Though the editor has often tried to make radical cuts, he has not always succeeded in keeping individual articles within the desired limits.

There are also good material reasons, however, why many articles are longer than originally planned. The Dictionary is so designed as to comprise under one of the words in a group what is theologically significant and characteristic about the group as a whole, so that articles on the other terms in the group have to be confined in the main to a brief sketch of their distinctive features. This plan can be carried out when a work is completed in a short span of time. Since the preparation of the first articles for the Theological Dictionary, however, thirty years have elapsed, and during these thirty years there has been theological advance in spite of political events. The result is that many of the present articles cannot simply refer back to earlier volumes, as originally intended, but have had to make more additions or changes than previously anticipated. This means that the Theological Dictionary will be rather larger than first planned.

As before, I have been assisted during the past years by a whole group of helpers who have in different ways contributed to the reliability and success of the work by sacrificial labour in the checking of manuscripts and the correction of proofs. With gratitude and a high sense of appreciation I mention in particular G. Bertram, J. Betz, A. Böhlig, P. Boendermaker, E. Dammann, A. Debrunner, J. Fichtner, G. Fohrer, D. J. Georgacas, A. Hiller, W. Kasch, P. Katz, H. Kleinknecht, H. Krämer, E. Lohse, W. Lohse, T. W. Manson, C. F. D. Moule, E. Nestle, C. H. Peisker, K. H. Rengstorf, E. Risch, K. H. Schelkle, G. Schlichting, W. Schneemelcher, J. Schreiber, S. Schulz, K. Staab, H. Traub, A. Wanner and K. Zimmermann.

Finally, as editor I should like to make a request of those who use the Dictionary. In the case of any small miscellany it is customary to quote the author as well as the journal. Now many of the articles in the Theological Dictionary are not just summaries of previous works but independent contributions to research with the scope of monographs. It is thus out of place to give only the volume and page numbers in referring to articles of this kind. The authors have a right to be mentioned by name.

For the sixth time thousands of copies of a volume of the Theological Dictionary are going out into the world. The editor trusts that this volume too will render service academically by combining philology and theology, ecumenically by leading beyond the confessions to the Bible, and practically by aiding pastors in their preaching and teaching.

G. Friedrich

Erlangen, June 16, 1959.

Editor's Preface

The post-war volumes of the Theological Dictionary of the New Testament are distinguished from the first four by many special features. Gerhard Friedrich succeeds Gerhard Kittel as editor. The fall of Hitler has made possible wider international contacts, especially with scholars of the English-speaking world. The series begins to benefit not only from newer developments in biblical and theological studies but also from exciting discoveries like the Dead Sea Scrolls.

These changes have certain important implications for the Dictionary. Some of the judgments in earlier articles have had to be reconsidered. A place has had to be found for additional material. Points not originally thought to be significant have had to be discussed. In a work extending over so many decades some of this would have been inevitable in any case. The break between the Kittel and the Friedrich volumes, however, has made an even more imperious demand, even at the risk of adding to the final size of the work.

Naturally the purpose, design and structure of the Dictionary remain the same. Nor is there any change in either its proper use or its enduring value. Added interest is imparted, however, by the fact that the post-war volumes bring us increasingly into the sphere of modern research and debate. Readers of the present version will also profit by the fact that few of even the most important articles in these later volumes have ever been offered previously in English translation.

A great debt is again owed to Professor F. F. Bruce of Manchester University for his invaluable and indefatigable labours in proof reading. If some errors still slip through the net — and we are grateful to readers who call attention to these — there is the consolation that Dr. Bruce in particular has been able to correct not a few errors in the original German.

Pasadena, California, Ascension Day, 1968. *G. W. Bromiley*

Contents

Page

Contents   XIII

Contributors

Editor:

Gerhard Friedrich, Erlangen.

Contributors:

Ernst Bammel, Erlangen.
Otto Bauernfeind, Tübingen.
Friedrich Baumgärtel, Erlangen.
Werner Bieder, Basel.
Hans Bietenhard, Bern.
Günther Bornkamm, Heidelberg.
Herbert Braun, Mainz.
Rudolf Bultmann, Marburg.
Oskar Cullmann, Basel and Paris.
Gerhard Delling, Halle.
Johannes Fichtner, Bethel.
Werner Foerster, Münster.
Leonhard Goppelt, Hamburg.
Heinrich Greeven, Kiel.
Günther Harder, Berlin-Zehlendorf.
Friedrich Hauck, Erlangen.
Claus-Hunno Hunzinger, Göttingen.
Joachim Jeremias, Göttingen.
Wilhelm Kasch, Kiel.
Hermann Kleinknecht, Münster.
Helmut Krämer, Bethel.
Karl Georg Kuhn, Heidelberg.
Friedrich Lang, Tübingen.
Eduard Lohse, Kiel.
Christian Maurer, Bethel.
Rudolf Meyer, Jena.
Wilhelm Michaelis, Bern.
Otto Michel, Tübingen.
Herbert Preisker, Jena.
Bo Reicke, Basel.
Rolf Rendtorff, Berlin-Zehlendorf.
Karl Heinrich Rengstorf, Münster.
Ernst Harald Riesenfeld, Uppsala.
Karl Ludwig Schmidt, Basel.
Carl Schneider, Speyer.
Siegfried Schulz, Erlangen.
Eduard Schweizer, Zürich.
Heinrich Seesemann, Frankfurt a.M.
Erik Sjöberg, Johanneshov (Sweden).

Gustav Stählin, Mainz.
Hermann Strathmann, Erlangen.
Artur Weiser, Tübingen.
Konrad Weiss, Rostock.

| πείθω, πεποίθησις, πειθός, πειθώ, πεισμονή, |
| πειθαρχέω, ἀπειθής, ἀπειθέω, ἀπείθεια |

† πείθω.

1. πείθω in the Active (apart from the Perfect).

a. The act. πείθειν is used in the NT in the customary senses, not always sharply differentiated, which are found in Gk. usage from the time of Homer :[1] "to convince," "to persuade," "to seduce (by persuasion)," "to corrupt." The meaning "to convince" occurs in Plat. Resp., I, 327c; Thuc., III, 31, "to persuade" in Hom. Il., 9, 345; Plat. Resp., II, 364b, "to seduce" in Hom. Il., 6, 360, "to corrupt" in Hdt., VIII, 134; Lys., 21, 10. Indicative of the role of πείθειν among the Gks. is the personification of Πειθώ as a deity, e.g., Hes. Op., 73; Theog., 349. Whereas in Hom. πείθειν appears only in the "determinative" sense "to persuade successfully," "to convince,"[2] in the period which follows the pres. usually expresses intention and the aor. success, though the context decides.

b. The typical Gk. concepts of persuading and convincing are notably absent from the Heb. tongue. In transl. books, therefore, πείθειν and πείθεσθαι (→ 3, 26 ff.) are rare, and there is no true Heb. equivalent. On the other hand πέποιθα, which expresses confidence, is relatively common in the Gk. OT, → 4, 38 ff. Only in books in which the influence of Hellenism is linguistically and materially stronger, and for which there is no Heb., e.g., Macc. and Tob., do we find more instances of πείθειν and πείθεσθαι along with πέποιθα. Indeed, in 4 Macc. we find 13 examples, though πέποιθα does not occur here at all. When the words appear in the transl. books, it is because the LXX renders freely. Thus at 1 S. 24:7 the Mas. has the rare and not very clear verb שסע; שסע בדברים has something of the sense of "to belabour with reproaches" (A.V. "stayed his servants with these words"). The LXX, however has : ἔπεισεν Δαυιδ τοὺς ἄνδρας αὐτοῦ ἐν λόγοις. At Jer. 29(36):8 the close connection between persuading and deceiving finds expression. The HT has here נשא II hi "to deceive," which the LXX often renders by ἀπατᾶν (Gn. 3:13; 2 Ch. 32:15; Is. 36:14; 37:10; Jer. 4:10 twice), but for which it now puts πείθειν or ἀναπείθειν in the sense "to persuade," "to lead," even "to corrupt." The LXX, then, has in view the perverting power of the prophets' words rather than the deceitful images which they present. The concept of the false prophet thus begins to acquire greater precision. πείθειν means "to convince," "to move," in Jdt. 12:11; 2 Macc. 4:34, 45; 7:26; 11:14; 4 Macc. 16:24. "To persuade" on rational grounds is the sense in 4 Macc. 2:6. In Wis. 16:8 it is used of God who convinces by means of miracles. Antiochus IV attempts to lead the Jews into apostasy by persecution, 4 Macc. 8:12, though cf. 9:18.[3]

c. The meaning "to convince" is the most natural at Ac. 18:4 ("he sought to convince"), also Ac. 28:23; Ign. Sm., 5, 1; Dg., 7, 4 (opp. βιάζεσθαι). On the

---

π ε ί θ ω. [1] Liddell-Scott ; Walde-Pok., II, 139.

[2] The basic sense of the stem πειθ- (πιθ-, ποιθ-) is 1. "to have confidence in a statement," "to give credence to it," "to be convinced," then 2. "to have confidence in a command, admonition etc.," hence "to obey," also "to be persuaded." Originally πειθ- was only intr., but a pass. developed out of the intr., and from this was derived 3. the trans. "to convince," "to persuade." Cf. S. Schulz, Die Wurzel ΠΕΙΘ- (ΠΙΘ-) im älteren Gr., Diss. Berne (1952) [Debrunner].

[3] This paragraph is by G. Bertram.

other hand differentiation is difficult at Ac. 19:8. πείθειν means "to persuade" at Mt. 27:20; Ac. 14:19. In both these verses the sense "to seduce" is not far off, also in Ac. 19:26, and certainly in Herm. s., 8, 6, 5, though "to persuade" is alone possible in Ac. 26:28, [4] Mart. Pol., 3, 1; 4; 5, 1; 8, 3. In Ac. 12:20; Mt. 28:14 πείθειν probably means "to bribe," [5] though "to pacify" is also possible at Mt. 28:14, cf. Mart. Pol., 10, 2; Ac. 13:43; Mart. Pol., 8, 2; 9, 2, where πείθειν simply means "to entreat."

The signification is uncertain in the following passages: 2 C. 5:11: εἰδότες οὖν τὸν φόβον τοῦ κυρίου ἀνθρώπους πείθομεν, θεῷ δὲ πεφανερώμεθα. Most natural is to take ἀνθρώπους πείθειν, in the sense "to seek to win men," as a description of the apostolic calling, and possibly Ac. 18:4; 19:8; 28:23 show that πείθειν can be used technically in this sense. But if so, there can hardly be any allusion here to the accusation of opponents. In view of this possibility, [6] one should probably translate: "Of course we seek (as we are charged) to persuade men — yet in such sort that we can answer for it before God, who sees us through and through." On this reading the θεῷ δὲ πεφανερώμεθα is an answer to the accusation of secrecy and insincerity, cf. 4:2. Gl. 1:10: ἄρτι γὰρ ἀνθρώπους πείθω ἢ τὸν θεόν; ἢ ζητῶ ἀνθρώποις ἀρέσκειν; If, as is customary, the two rhetorical questions are regarded as parallel, ἀνθρώπους πείθειν must be taken in the same sense as ἀνθρώποις ἀρέσκειν, and thus means: "to persuade men." Since the second question demands No as its answer, the answer required by the first disjunctive question is "God." [7] Paul is thus disclaiming any attempt to persuade men; he is persuading God. This is quite possible if the later ἀρέσκειν is already in view in the question ἢ τὸν θεόν; and if Paul is consequently saying no more than that he wants to please God rather than men. Nevertheless, can ἀνθρώπους πείθειν be taken in a sense opposed to that in Ac. 18:4; 19:8; 28:23 and even 2 C. 5:11? Is not the reference here also to authentic apostolic preaching? If so, the first question demands the answer "Men," and it is directed against the charge that Paul is seeking to persuade God (by his preaching of freedom from the Law). The second question, then, is not parallel to the first, but answers the different objection that Paul speaks to please men; hence ἀνθρώποις ἀρέσκειν is materially identical with τὸν θεόν (πείθειν).

---

[4] At Ac. 26:28 ℵ B al read ἐν ὀλίγῳ με πείθεις Χριστιανὸν ποιῆσαι (ℜE pl have the smoother γενέσθαι). We might see in this a mixture of two expressions: "Soon thou persuadest me to become a Christian," and: "Soon thou wilt make me a Christian" (Pr.-Bauer), or as a shorter form of ἐν ὀλίγῳ (χρόνῳ) με πείθεις (σεαυτὸν) Χριστιανὸν ποιῆσαί (με): "Thou wilt persuade me that in a twinkling thou hast made me a Christian" (A. Fridrichsen, "Exegetisches zum NT: 3. Act. Apost. 26:28," Symb. Osl., 14 [1935], 49-52; also "Act. 26:28," Coniectanea Neotestamentica, 3 [1938], 13-16), or finally: "Soon thou persuadest me to play the Christian" (so A. Nairne, "ΕΝ ΟΛΙΓΩ ΜΕ ΠΕΙΘΕΙΣ ΧΡΙΣΤΙΑΝΟΝ ΠΟΙΗΣΑΙ — Ac. 26:28," JThSt., 21 [1920], 171 f., also J. H. Ropes in Jackson-Lake, III, 329; K. Lake and J. Cadbury, ibid., IV, 322-324; F. F. Bruce, The Acts of the Apostles [1951], ad loc.). Grammatically Ac. 26:28 can also be understood as follows: There is both a temporal present and an active element in the phrase "thou persuadest me in this moment." Gk. cannot express both these in the one form, however, and so it must disregard either the one or the other (ἔπεισας or πείθεις), cf. A. Debrunner, "Sprachwissenschaft u. klass. Philologie," Indogermanische Forschungen, 48 (1930), 10-13. For further bibl. cf. Pr.-Bauer[4], s.v. and Fridrichsen, loc. cit.
[5] So also 2 Macc. 4:45 and in the pass. 10:20.
[6] Cf. R. Bultmann, "Exegetische Probleme d. 2 K. Zu 2 K. 5:1-5; 5:11-6:10; 10-13; 12:21," Symbolae Biblicae Upsalienses, 9 (1947), 13.
[7] The ἢ τὸν θεόν can hardly mean "and even God!" in mounting emphasis (so W. Bousset in Schr. NT, ad loc.).

Most uncertain is the exposition of 1 Jn. 3:19: ἐν τούτῳ γνωσόμεθα ὅτι ἐκ τῆς ἀληθείας ἐσμὲν καὶ ἔμπροσθεν αὐτοῦ πείσομεν τὴν καρδίαν ἡμῶν κτλ. A first question is whether the ἐν τούτῳ refers forward or backward. The text of v. 19 f. is also uncertain: should there be a καί before ἐν τούτῳ? Should there not be a second ὅτι in v. 20? [8] There can be no doubt that ἔμπροσθεν αὐτοῦ πείσομεν τὴν καρδίαν (vl. τὰς καρδίας) ἡμῶν means "we assure (allay) our heart before him." It could be, then, that v. 20 gives the reason: "For if our heart condemn us, God is greater than our heart and knows all things." This can only mean, then, that God pardons us because He knows us better than we know ourselves. But this is very odd, since v. 21 seems to say almost the very opposite, namely, that we have confidence toward God only when our heart does not condemn us. One would thus expect v. 19 f. to say that if our heart condemn us we cannot assure it before God, and it seems natural to think that the true text must have read: ἔμπροσθεν αὐτοῦ <οὐ> πείσομεν κτλ. On the other hand, this conjecture is not necessary, for it is possible that v. 20 and v. 21 are distinguishing between the two situations: "if our heart condemn us" and "if our heart do not condemn us." [9]

2. πείθομαι.

a. In the NT, as in Gk., πείθομαι means first "to trust," "to rely on" (Hom. Od., 20, 45; Hdt., VII, 144 [τῷ θεῷ!]), also "to be convinced, persuaded" (Soph. Phil., 624; Plat. Prot., 388a), consequently also "to believe" (Hdt., I, 8; Plat. Ap., 25e) or "to follow" (Xenoph. An., VII, 3, 39) (in the sense "to be tractable"); this sense "to follow" can even have the further meaning "to obey" (Hom. Il., 1, 79; Soph. Ant., 67; Plat. Ap., 29d : πείσομαι δὲ μᾶλλον τῷ θεῷ ἢ ὑμῖν).

b. Like the act. (→ 1, 16 ff.), the pass. πείθεσθαι is rare in those books of the LXX which were transl. from the Heb. In Est. 4:4 it is used for the colourless קבל, which means "to take," "receive," "put on," also transf. The true meaning of Est. 4:4 HT is that Mordecai did not accept the clothes sent him by Esther but kept on his mourning garb. The LXX, however, gives the phrase a psychological turn ; Mordecai will not be persuaded by Esther to put off the signs of grief. The ref. in Prv. 26:25 is to the enemy whom one must not trust (הֶאֱמֶן). Here, too, the LXX introduces πείθεσθαι. The verb thus carries with it a suggestion of deception. This is also true in Wis. 13:7. There is for adherents of nature religions a certain explanation and excuse in the fact that men are deceived by the sight of a powerful and beautiful creation. On the other hand πέπεισμαι in Tob. 14:4 BA is par. to πιστεύω in א. It here expresses religious faith. As the context shows, the ref. is more to personal conviction. This is also indicated by the same word in 4 Macc. 5:16, whereas πιστεύω, which is to be regarded as a tendentious alteration of א, is designed to emphasise believing confession. πέπεισμαι is also used in the sense of personal conviction in 2 Macc. 9:27 in an epistolary flourish. τεκμηρίοις πεπεισμένοι, "convinced by proofs," occurs in 3 Macc. 3:24, cf. also the aor. in 4:19 (vl.) with σαφῶς. "To be persuaded, moved," is the meaning of πείθεσθαι in 2 Macc. 4:34; 10:20 (bribery); 3 Macc. 1:11; "to obey" in 4 Macc. 6:4; 8:17, 26; 10:13; 12:4, 5; 15:10; 18:1 (the king, one's mother, the Law). [10]

---

[8] Only the most important variants are noted. For full exposition the comm. should be consulted, cf. C. H. Dodd, *The Johannine Epistles* (1946); R. Schnackenburg, *Die Johannesbriefe, Herders Theol. Kommentar z. NT*, XIII, 3 (1953).

[9] Cf. the comm.

[10] This paragraph is by G. Bertram.

c. πειθόμεθα in Hb. 13:18 (vl. πεποίθαμεν) means "we are convinced"; this is also the meaning of πείθομαι in Herm. s., 8, 11, 12. Ac. 26:26 is weaker: λανθάνειν γὰρ αὐτὸν τούτων οὐ πείθομαι οὐθέν, "I believe that none of these things can be unknown to him." The perf. especially has the sense "I am convinced" in Lk. 20:6; R. 8:38; 14:14 (οἶδα καὶ πέπεισμαι); 15:14; 2 Tm. 1:5, 12; Hb. 6:9; Ign. Tr., 3, 2; Ign. Pol., 2, 3; Pol., 9, 2; Barn., 1, 4. The pass. aor. πεισθῆναι is used similarly, cf. Ac. 5:40 after Gamaliel's speech: ἐπείσθησαν δὲ αὐτῷ, "they were persuaded by him" or "they followed him." πείθεσθαι, like πεισθῆναι, can often mean "to be won over by persuasion," "to follow," Ac. 21:14; 23:21; 27:11; Ign. R., 7, 2; Herm. m., 12, 3, 3. In Lk. 16:31 following is almost obeying; here the οὐδὲ ... πεισθήσονται, which corresponds to the preceding οὐκ ἀκούουσιν, is best translated: "they will not let themselves be told." The meaning can be "to obey" in, e.g., Hb. 13:17: πείθεσθε τοῖς ἡγουμένοις ὑμῶν καὶ ὑπείκετε, Jm. 3:3, of horses which obey the bit, and esp. R. 2:8: τοῖς ... πειθομένοις τῇ ἀδικίᾳ, where the antithesis τοῖς ... ἀπειθοῦσι τῇ ἀληθείᾳ makes the sense perfectly clear. So also Gl. 5:7: ἀληθείᾳ μὴ πείθεσθαι (occasionally interpolated into 3:1 as well).[11] πείθονται τοῖς ὡρισμένοις νόμοις occurs in Dg., 5, 10.

The use of πείθεσθαι is of no great theological significance in any of these passages apart from R. 2:8; Gl. 5:7. Underlying the antithesis of R. 2:8 is the thought that the true relation to God is that of obedience (→ ἀπειθεῖν, 11, 2 ff.; → πίστις).[12] In Gl. 5:7 the πείθεσθαι ἀληθείᾳ is materially though not verbally identical with the ὑπακούειν τῷ εὐαγγελίῳ of R. 10:16, and hence also with πιστεύειν in the Pauline sense (→ πίστις). Reference might also be made to two verses in which πείθεσθαι denotes acceptance of the Christian message: Ac. 17:4; 28:24. That πείθεσθαι here means "to obey" rather than "to be convinced" is shown by passages in which rejection of the message is expressed by ἀπειθεῖν (→ 11, 8 ff.). These formulations are, of course, less significant for the meaning of πείθεσθαι than for the light they throw on the understanding of πιστεύειν, cf. Ac. 28:24, where ἀπιστεῖν is the opposite of πείθεσθαι.[13] Thus in 2 Cl., 17, 5 unbelievers, when it is too late, say: οὐαὶ ἡμῖν, ὅτι ... οὐκ ἐπιστεύομεν καὶ οὐκ ἐπειθόμεθα τοῖς πρεσβυτέροις τοῖς ἀναγγέλλουσιν ἡμῖν περὶ τῆς σωτηρίας ἡμῶν. Similarly, the following of false Messiahs can be described as πείθεσθαι in Ac. 5:36, 37, though πείθεσθαι has here almost the sense "to be seduced."

3. πέποιθα.

a. In the NT, as in the Gk. world, πεποιθέναι means "to have conceived trust," and to persist in a state of confidence, hence "to trust firmly" (Hdt., IX, 88; Soph. Ai., 769), "to rely on" (Hom. Il., 4, 325; Aesch. Eum., 826 [Ζηνί!]).

b. Unlike πείθω, πέποιθα has a solid equivalent in Heb. in בטח (→ II, 521, 20 ff.) and derivates.[14] Acc. to the understanding of the Gk. transl. בטח contains esp. the con-

---

[11] The text of the v. is uncertain. The majority of MSS read: τίς ὑμᾶς ἐνέκοψεν ἀληθείᾳ μὴ πείθεσθαι; "who has hindered you from obeying the truth?" But perhaps one should read with F G latt: τίς ὑμᾶς ἐνέκοψεν; ἀληθείᾳ μὴ πείθεσθαι μηδενὶ πείθεσθε, "who has hindered you? Obey no one in not obeying the truth," cf. Bl.-Debr. § 488, 1b app. and → III, 856, n. 6.

[12] On the concept of obedience towards God in the Gk. world → πειθαρχέω, n. 1.

[13] Cf. how some minuscules add a καὶ πεισθέντες at Hb. 11:13 to denote faith in the promise, elsewhere πίστις in Hb.

[14] This root occurs in all 183 times in the Mas. There are another 10 instances in Sir. In the LXX we find πέποιθα 81 times, καταπέποιθα as a vl. at Ez. 16:15 and πεποίθησις

cepts of confidence and hope, including peace, rest and security. The same linguistic field is covered by the term in both Gk. and English. It is understandable that πέποιθα should also be used for Heb. words which have a secondary meaning along any of the above lines. Thus it is used for חסה, which occurs 37 times in the Mas. and is 20 times transl. by ἐλπίζειν and 10 by πέποιθα. The hapax legomenon חָסוּת in Is. 30:3 and once מַחְסֶה in Is. 28:17, which is elsewhere rendered ἐλπίς, can also be the original of πέποιθα. Thus חסה ("to seek refuge") can include in content the secondary sense of confidence. קוה, "to wait," "to endure," which occurs 48 times in the Mas. and is 28 times transl. by ὑπομένειν, is rendered πέποιθα only at Is. 8:17 and 33:2. שׂבע, 14 times in the Mas., means "to look (for help)"; πέποιθα is used for it 3 times at Is. 17:7, 8; 32:3. From the root נבט ("to look") comes the noun מַבָּט meaning "prospect," "hope," and πέποιθα is used for this in 2 of the 3 instances, Is. 20:5, 6. שׁקט and שָׁקֵט, 38 times and once in the Mas. in the sense "to rest," are 3 times transl. by πέποιθα, Is. 14:7; 30:15 (along with בְּטְחָה); Ιερ. 31(48):11. Again, שַׁאֲנַן (10 [11] times in the Mas.), meaning "peaceful," "without care," "arrogant," often used for a settled economic and social situation and consequently for the resultant sense of security, pride and even arrogance, is 3 times transl. by πλούσιος (Is. 32:9; 33:20) or πλοῦτος (Is. 32:18), but also by πέποιθα at 32:11, where it is taken to be synon. to בטח. שׁען, "to rest on," transf. "to trust," which occurs 22 times in the Mas., is in 8 instances the original of πέποιθα, 2 Ch. 14:10; 16:7 twice; 16:8; Is. 10:20 twice; 30:12; 31:1. The idea of hanging (תלה) is understood similarly when this root is rendered by πέποιθα at Is. 22:24. Here the LXX provides an interpretation and introduces the fig. understanding. False confidence is in view when a verb like סות hi ("to entice, seduce") is transl. by πέποιθα, 2 Ch. 32:15. On the other hand, a word like ענג "to delight in," "to rejoice in sure possession," is used with a religious ref. to God in Is. 58:14, so that the LXX rightly has the religious term πέποιθα for it. In Aram. Da. 3:28 Θ (3:95) also uses πέποιθα for the hithp of רחץ, "to rely on something" (LXX ἐλπίζειν). Finally, the root עזז twice seems to be rendered by πέποιθα in Job. At 31:21 the sense of the HT is correctly given, but there is considerable re-interpretation at 6:13. The LXX goes its own way in introducing πέποιθα, and with it the idea of confidence, in the following passages: Job 27:8; Is. 8:14; 30:32; 32:19; cf. also the variants at Is. 17:8 and Ιερ. 27(50):38; ψ 96:7.

In books written or preserved only in Gk. πέποιθα is none too common; indeed, one has the sense of a certain restriction in its use (Jdt., Wis., Sir., Da., Bar. 11 times; 1-3 Macc. 10 times). The LXX as a whole thus uses πέποιθα 142 times. In the later transl. there seems to be a certain expansion of usage. In particular 'Α and Σ tend to replace ἐλπίζειν by πέποιθα esp. for בטח. Thus in the Ps. there are more expressions of trust in which πέποιθα is employed. Neither linguistically nor materially, however, did the term undergo any new development in either the apocr. or the later translations.

Trust in God is a basic feature in OT religion. This is indicated by the prophetic message. Is. and Jer. in particular demand confidence in God and warn against false confidence in earthly powers. Ez. uses πέποιθα only once at 33:13. The word is also almost completely absent in the minor prophets, though cf. Zeph. 3:2, also Am. 6:1; Hab. 2:18. In the Ps. trust in God is expressed in certain psalms of confidence which are formally a development of the psalm of complaint. [15] This expression of confidence

---

once at 4 Βασ. 18:19. Also common are ἐλπίζειν (48 times), ἐλπίς (30), and ἐπελπίζειν (2), a total of 80 instances. Other renderings are ἀναψυχή at Ιερ. 30:26 (49:31), ἀσφάλεια, ἀσφαλής at Lv. 26:5; Dt. 12:10; Prv. 11:15; Gn. 34:25; εἰρήνη at Job 11:18 (?); Is. 14:30; Ez. 38:8, 11, 14; 39:6, 26, πέποιθα and εἰρήνη as a double transl. at Prv. 3:23, ἐλπίς and εἰρήνη at Ez. 34:27, ἡσυχία, ἡσυχάζειν at Ez. 38:11, and θαρρεῖν at Prv. 31:11 (along with 13 other passages). In the 8 remaining verses the LXX either had a different text, translated arbitrarily, or in 4 instances gave no rendering at all.

[15] Cf. H. Gunkel, *Einl. in die Ps.* (1933), 254-256.

seldom takes the form of prayer. It is more often didactic, and the watchword πέποιθα is common in didactic and wisdom literature. Ps., Job and Prv. offer many instances, and we almost seem to have a comprehensive summary of all religious experience in the addition to Sir. 2:5 אs : ἐν νόσοις καὶ πενίᾳ ἐπ' αὐτῷ πεποιθὼς γείνου. [16]

c. Concerning the occurrence of the term in the NT the following points call for notice. The strong man relies on his armour, Lk. 11:22. The rich rely on their riches, א and D in the addition at Mk. 10:24. The friends of Paul draw confidence from the very fact that Paul is imprisoned, Phil. 1:14: πεποιθότες τοῖς δεσμοῖς μου. Paul trusts in the faithfulness or the right judgment of the community, 2 C. 2:3; Gl. 5:10; 2 Th. 3:4. He also trusts in the ὑπακοή of his friend, Phlm. 21. Construed with the infinitive πεποιθέναι can denote confident conviction, cf. R. 2:19: πέποιθάς τε σεαυτὸν ὁδηγὸν εἶναι τυφλῶν κτλ., 2 C. 10:7: εἴ τις πέποιθεν (Β δοκεῖ πεποιθέναι) ἑαυτῷ Χριστοῦ εἶναι. Similarly with a ὅτι clause, Phil. 1:25 : καὶ τοῦτο πεποιθὼς οἶδα ὅτι μενῶ κτλ.; [17] 2:24 : πέποιθα δὲ ἐν κυρίῳ ὅτι καὶ αὐτὸς ταχέως ἐλεύσομαι.

These passages are of no theological significance for the concept πεποιθέναι. It is worth noting, of course, that for the Christian confidence in someone or something is distinctively qualified by being a πεποιθέναι ἐν κυρίῳ. This is expressly stated in Gl. 5:10 (not B); Phil. 2:24; 2 Th. 3:4, and also in Phil. 1:14 unless ἐν κυρίῳ is here to be related to τῶν ἀδελφῶν. Hereby a certain limit is set on confidence. It does not arise on the ground of human reckoning and it thus renounces human certainty, but in so doing it acquires the distinctive assurance of faith. Materially, then, it does not differ from the confidence in God expressed in Phil. 1:6: πεποιθὼς αὐτὸ τοῦτο ὅτι ὁ ἐναρξάμενος ... ἐπιτελέσει ... Only here and in 2 C. 1:9 (→ 7, 25 ff.) does Paul speak of confidence in God. [18] It is surprising and significant that there are in the NT so few references to the confidence in God which is so characteristic of the OT, esp. the Psalms, → 5, 43 ff. [19] As an aspect of piety we find πεποιθέναι ἐπὶ τῷ θεῷ or τὸν θεόν only in the description of Jesus Himself in Hb. 2:13 (on the basis of Is. 8:17 and 2 Βασ. 22:3) and on the lips of the mockers at the foot of the cross, Mt. 27:43 (on the basis of ψ 21:8). [20]

In the description of genuine Chr. piety in 1 Cl., 58, 1 we read : ἵνα κατασκηνώσωμεν πεποιθότες ἐπὶ τὸ ὁσιώτατον τῆς μεγαλωσύνης αὐτοῦ ὄνομα, which is related

---

[16] These three paragraphs are by G. Bertram.

[17] τοῦτο here can hardly be the obj. of οἶδα, which in this case would be explicated in the ὅτι clause, so that πεποιθώς would characterise οἶδα as a knowledge of confident assurance. It is better to take τοῦτο as the obj. of πεποιθώς; if this is so, τοῦτο must refer back to v. 24. Confidence that Paul's remaining is necessary for the community is then the basis of the knowledge that he will in fact remain. Even better is to take πεποιθὼς οἶδα as a non-logical expression for an εἰδὼς πέποιθα. In this case, too, the τοῦτο (dependent on εἰδώς) relates to v. 24, but the content of v. 24 is what Paul knows and the ὅτι clause tells us of what he is confident.

[18] Lohmeyer (Loh. Phil. on 1:6) thinks that the πεποιθώς of Phil. 1:6 is at most "in you," not "in God." He contests the view that confidence in the Chr. sense can ever be in God. All self-awareness melts away before God. Confidence, which unites equals, and rests on the certainty of one's own power and achievement, is possible only among men. Here NT πεποιθέναι seems to be understood in terms of a modern concept of the relation of confidence.

[19] Cf. Wnd. 2 C. on 1:9b (47); Loh. Phil., 19, n. 2 (on 1:6).

[20] In the par. to 2 Βασ. 22:3 at ψ 17:2 the Heb. אֶחֱסֶה־בּוֹ is rendered by ἐλπιῶ ἐπ' αὐτόν in the LXX. Similarly בָּל at ψ 21:8 is transl. ἤλπισεν in the LXX, → II, 521, 20 ff.

to the preceding quotation from Prv. 1:33 in 57, 7: ὁ δὲ ἐμοῦ ἀκούων κατασκηνώσει ἐπ' ἐλπίδι πεποιθώς. In 1 Cl., 60, 1 God is invoked as (ὁ) χρηστὸς ἐν τοῖς πεποιθόσιν ἐπὶ σέ. In Herm. m., 9, 6 those who pray in faith are described in the words of Paul as πεποιθότες ἐπὶ τὸν κύριον, and similarly Herm. s., 9, 18, 5 refers to the ψυχὴ πεποιθυῖα ἐπὶ τὸν κύριον. Finally, Dg., 1, 1 characterises Christianity very generally as a θεῷ πεποιθέναι and θρησκεύειν αὐτόν. [21]

It is noteworthy that all these references (apart from Dg., 1, 1) are OT quotations or expressions, not original Christian formulations. If there is so little reference to confidence in God in the NT this is because the concern of the NT, as distinct from the Psalms, is not with the individual destiny and need of the worshipper, in face of which the righteous sets his trust in God, but rather with the common distress of mankind and with eschatological salvation. With this reference, however, confidence takes the form of faith. The confidence in God which characterises the relation to Him is subsumed under faith. This also means, however, that confidence in God is taken in the radical sense in which it includes absolute surrender of one's own assurance. It is thus united with obedience, which is free from all autonomy. That πεποιθέναι in the sense of radical relying on God is now caught up in πιστεύειν may be seen from the fact the new relationship to God in faith can be described as the rejection of false πεποιθέναι, cf. esp. Phil. 3:3 f., where πεποιθέναι ἐν σαρκί characterises the Jewish confidence which is grounded in the privileges mentioned in vv. 4-6 and which forms the antithesis to the πίστις Χριστοῦ of v. 9. To differentiate this confidence from the phenomenon of faith Paul likes to use the verb καυχᾶσθαι (→ III, 648, 20 ff.; 649, 8 ff.), and so here in v. 3 καυχᾶσθαι ἐν Χριστῷ is the opposite of πεποιθέναι ἐν σαρκί. We find the same usage in 2 C. 1:9: ... αὐτοὶ ἐν ἑαυτοῖς τὸ ἀπόκριμα τοῦ θανάτου ἐσχήκαμεν, ἵνα μὴ πεποιθότες ὦμεν ἐφ' ἑαυτοῖς ἀλλ' ἐπὶ τῷ θεῷ τῷ ἐγείροντι τοὺς νεκρούς (→ πεποίθησις, 8, 1 ff.). There is an echo of it in Lk. 18:9: Jesus speaks πρός τινας τοὺς πεποιθότας ἐφ' ἑαυτοῖς ὅτι εἰσὶν δίκαιοι, and also in Barn., 9, 4, where in the description of the Jews there is reference to περιτομή, ἐφ' ᾗ πεποίθασιν.

† πεποίθησις.

πεποίθησις, "trust," "confidence," is a later Gk. word rejected by the Atticist Phryn. Ecl., 294. It occurs once each in the LXX (4 Βασ. 18:19 for בִּטָּחוֹן) and Philo (Virt., 226). [1]

In the NT we find it only in the Pauline corpus. The use in 2 C. 1:15; 8:22 is the same as that of πεποιθέναι in 2 C. 2:3; Gl. 5:10; Phlm. 21; 2 Th. 3:4 (→ 6, 9 f.). The πεποίθησις in which Paul hopes to come to Corinth (2 C. 1:15) is confidence in the growing understanding of his conduct on the part of the congregation (v. 14); the πεποίθησις (8:22) of the brother sent by him to Corinth is confidence in the readiness of the church to take part in the collection. If the reference in both

---

[21] In Justin πεποιθέναι ἐπὶ τῷ θεῷ characterises genuine Jews, Dial., 8, 2. This phrase occurs in OT quotations in Apol., 40, 19; Dial., 27, 1.

π ε π ο ί θ η σ ι ς. [1] Cf. Liddell-Scott, Pr.-Bauer⁴, s.v.; Wnd. 2 K. on 1:15 (61). πεποίθησις is derived from the perf. πέποιθα, cf. P. Chantraine, La formations des noms en grec ancien (1933), 289.

instances is to a confidence in certain men in specific situations, the πεποίθησις of Phil. 3:4 is that which shapes the whole of existence, whether as the self-confidence of autonomous man or as the surrender to radical confidence in God, → 7, 17 ff. The καίπερ ἐγὼ ἔχων πεποίθησιν καὶ ἐν σαρκί ("though I myself might also be able to put my trust in the flesh") links up with the preceding οἱ ... οὐκ ἐν σαρκὶ πεποιθότες and describes the Jewish attitude of self-confidence which Paul has abandoned. Its radical opposite, namely, the confidence which man has in God alone when he looks away from himself, is set forth in 2 C. 3:4: πεποίθησιν δὲ τοιαύτην ἔχομεν διὰ τοῦ Χριστοῦ πρὸς τὸν θεόν, as the continuation clearly shows : οὐχ ὅτι ἀφ᾽ ἑαυτῶν κτλ. ² The only difference as compared with Phil. 3:4 is that the reference is not to the confidence proper to Christian faith in general but to the specific self-awareness of the apostle (the τοιαύτην refers to vv. 1-3). There is no material difference between this πεποίθησις and the apostolic παρρησία of 3:12 (→ V, 882, 50 ff.) or the apostolic καύχησις of R. 15:17 (→ III, 650, 22 ff.). This apostolic confidence is also at issue in 2 C. 10:2: δέομαι δὲ τὸ μὴ παρὼν θαρρῆσαι τῇ πεποιθήσει ᾗ λογίζομαι τολμῆσαι ἐπί τινας κτλ.

In the later Pauline corpus πεποίθησις is used in a somewhat weaker sense to single out from πίστις the element of trust or confidence within it, cf. Eph. 3:12 (ἐν Χριστῷ ᾽Ιησοῦ) ἐν ᾧ ἔχομεν τὴν παρρησίαν καὶ προσαγωγὴν ἐν πεποιθήσει διὰ τῆς πίστεως αὐτοῦ. Here ἐν πεποιθήσει is used adjectivally ("full of confidence"), so that προσαγωγὴ ἐν πεποιθήσει and παρρησία are synonymous expressions, in keeping with the tendency in Eph. to heap up synonymous words or phrases.

The position is much the same in the liturgical expressions in 1 Cl., 2, 3 : ἐν ἀγαθῇ προθυμίᾳ μετ᾽ εὐσεβοῦς πεποιθήσεως ἐξετείνετε τὰς χεῖρας ὑμῶν πρὸς τὸν παντοκράτορα θεόν, and 26, 1: τῶν ὁσίως αὐτῷ (sc. θεῷ) δουλευσάντων ἐν πεποιθήσει πίστεως ἀγαθῆς. Acc. to 35, 2 πίστις ἐν πεποιθήσει, with ἀλήθεια ἐν παρρησίᾳ, is one of the δῶρα τοῦ θεοῦ in which the church rejoices. At 1 Cl., 31, 3 πεποίθησις is simple confidence in God (Isaac); at 45, 8 it is the confident hope of the OT saints in eschatological salvation; in 2 Cl., 6, 9 it is the confident hope of Christians. The opposite in Herm. s., 9, 22, 3 is κενὴ πεποίθησις combined with αὐθάδεια, the vain self-confidence of arrogant Christians.

† πειθός, πειθώ.

πειθός or πειθώ occurs in the NT only at 1 C. 2:4. The very different readings [1] in the transmission of this verse may finally be reduced to two possibilities: ἐν πειθοῖς σοφίας λόγοις or ἐν πειθοῖ σοφίας. In the first of these ("with persuasive words of wisdom") Paul is using πειθός ("persuasive") as an adj. for which there is as yet no attestation elsewhere. The formation is correct enough, [2]

---

² The πρὸς τὸν θεόν can hardly be directly dependent on πεποίθησιν, in which case πεποίθησις πρὸς τὸν θεόν would correspond to a πεποιθέναι ἐπὶ τῷ θεῷ (cf. 2 C. 1:9; common in the LXX, where πεποιθέναι is used with ἐπί, εἰς and ἐν, but never with πρός). It is dependent rather on the whole sentence and corresponds to κατέναντι θεοῦ in 2:17; 12:19 and ἐνώπιον τοῦ θεοῦ in 4:2.

π ε ι θ ό ς.   [1] Cf. the comm., esp. Ltzm. K., ad loc.
[2] Bl.-Debr. § 112, App.

and the fathers raise no objections against the word. In the second ("with the persuasive art of wisdom") we have the noun πειθώ,[3] in use from the time of Aesch. and denoting the gift or faculty of persuasion. [4] As far as the interpretation of the sentence is concerned, it makes no difference which reading we accept. In either case Paul is stating that his preaching does not derive its power to convince from the rhetorical art of human wisdom. The antithesis is: ἐν ἀποδείξει πνεύματος καὶ δυνάμεως.

† πεισμονή.

πεισμονή is a late and comparatively rare word which is not attested prior to the NT. It is derived from πείθω or πείθομαι and thus means persuasion in either the active or the passive sense. [1] It occurs in the NT only at Gl. 5:8: ἡ πεισμονὴ οὐκ ἐκ τοῦ καλοῦντος ὑμᾶς. The usual rendering is: "This persuasion (or advice) does not come from him who calls you." On this view πεισμονή is used in the sense of πειθώ. But if in v. 7 we are to read ἀληθείᾳ μὴ πείθεσθαι μηδενὶ πείθεσθε (→ 4, n. 11), the true sense is: "This following, or obedience, does not come . . ." [2] According to this understanding πεισμονή catches up πείθεσθαι, which is quite in keeping with Paul's style.

In Ign. R., 3, 3 we have a rhetorical expression : οὐ πεισμονῆς τὸ ἔργον, ἀλλὰ μεγέθους ἐστὶν ὁ Χριστιανισμός, "Christianity is not a matter of persuasion, but of (true) greatness." [3] Just. Apol., 53, 1 uses the word in the sense of convincing ; the prophecies adduced by him suffice εἰς πεισμονὴν τοῖς τὰ ἀκουστικὰ καὶ νοερὰ ὦτα ἔχουσιν.

† πειθαρχέω.

πειθαρχεῖν, "to obey," is a verb which was used in Gk. from Soph. and Herodot., and which occurs also in LXX and Philo.

In the NT πειθαρχέω denotes obedience due both to men and to God. Tt. 3:1 refers to the former: ὑπομίμνῃσκε αὐτοὺς ἀρχαῖς ἐξουσίαις ὑποτάσσεσθαι, πειθαρχεῖν . . . Rather less forceful is the saying in Ac. 27:21, where the meaning is simply "to heed or follow the admonition": ἔδει μὲν . . . πειθαρχήσαντάς μοι μὴ ἀνάγεσθαι ἀπὸ τῆς Κρήτης. Obedience in the full sense, however, is at issue

---

[3] Attested as a proper name from Hesiod, → 1, 10 f.

[4] Cf. Eur. Hec., 813-820. For further examples, Pr.-Bauer[4], s.v.

π ε ι σ μ ο ν ή. [1] Cf. Liddell-Scott, Pr.-Bauer[4], s.v.; Bl.-Debr. § 488, 1b App. Acc. to H. Collitz, "Zwei Hapax Legomena der Gotischen Bibel," Curme Volume of Linguistic Studies = Language Monographs, 7 (1930), 62-68, πεισμονή is not derived from πείθω but from πείθομαι—*πείσμων ("obedient," "pliant") and thus means "tractability," "subservience." On the other hand cf. Schwyzer, I, 524 for derivation from πειθ-.

[2] So Bl.-Debr. § 488, 1b, App.

[3] Bau. Ign., ad loc.

π ε ι θ α ρ χ έ ω. Liddell-Scott, Pr.-Bauer[4], s.v. The word derives from πείθαρχος (Aesch.), "obeying a superior, the government, an authority." Hence πειθαρχεῖν strictly "obeying a ruler or person in authority" (not "obeying friendly advice" or the like).

in the well-known saying in Ac. 5:29: πειθαρχεῖν δεῖ θεῷ μᾶλλον ἢ ἀνθρώποις,[1] cf. also Ac. 5:32.

πειθαρχεῖν, like πείθεσθαι (→ 4, 23 ff.), can also be used for obedience to Chr. preaching, Pol., 9, 1. Rhetorically the word occurs in Dg., 7, 2 for the obedience of the moon and stars to the Creator.[2]

† ἀπειθής.

ἀπειθής in the sense "disobedient" is found in Gk. from the time of Thucyd.[1] (earlier still in the sense "unworthy of belief"). In the LXX it is used like ἀπειθεῖν to denote the people disobedient to God.[2]

In the NT the use corresponds stylistically to that of ἀπειθεῖν and ἀπείθεια. Along OT lines the mission of the precursor of the Messiah is described in Lk. 1:17 as ἐπιστρέψαι ... ἀπειθεῖς ἐν φρονήσει δικαίων. In the list of vices depicting the sinful walk of pre-Christian mankind in Tt. 3:3 ἀπειθεῖς occurs between ἀνόητοι and πλανώμενοι.[3] False teachers are called ἀπειθεῖς in Tt. 1:16.[4] Rather different is the special use in Ac. 26:19 (οὐκ ἐγενόμην ἀπειθὴς τῇ οὐρανίῳ ὀπτασίᾳ)[5] and also γονεῦσιν ἀπειθεῖς in the lists of vices in R. 1:30 and 2 Tm. 3:2.

† ἀπειθέω.

ἀπειθεῖν (derived from ἀπειθής), "to be disobedient," is found in Gk. from the time of Aesch. In the LXX it is used for various Heb. words, esp. מרה and סרר. Here already it is a significant theological term inasmuch as it denotes the sinful attitude of the people, which in the OT is essentially understood as disobedience against God.[1]

---

[1] Naturally the thought that man has to obey God is not as such alien to the Gk. world. It is developed very impressively in Plat. Ap., 28e ff., cf. esp. 29d: πείσομαι δὲ μᾶλλον τῷ θεῷ ἢ ὑμῖν. For further details cf. Wettstein on Ac. 4:19. Obedience to the Godhead plays a great role in later Stoicism: πείθεσθαι τῷ θεῷ, e.g., Epict. Diss., III, 1, 37: ἄγε οὖν τῷ θεῷ πεισθῶμεν, ἵνα μὴ θεοχόλωτοι ὦμεν, ibid., 24, 97 and 110; IV, 3, 9; 12, 11 (cf. II, 16, 44; III, 1, 16 f.), τοῖς θεοῖς, Epict. Diss., II, 14, 12; IV, 1, 154; Ench., 31, 1. In the Stoic sense this obedience means adjustment to the order of the cosmos, Epict. Diss., II, 23, 42: πείθεσθαι τῇ τοῦ Διὸς διοικήσει, III, 26, 18: τῇ διοικήσει τῶν ὅλων, M. Ant., XI, 20: τῇ τῶν ὅλων διατάξει, though obedience to the ethical demand is part of this. In M. Ant. πειθαρχεῖν is also used in this sense in V, 9: τῷ λόγῳ, X, 14: αὐτῇ sc. τῇ φύσει. Cf. also εὐπειθὴς τῷ λόγῳ, Epict. Diss., III, 12, 13; εὐπειθῶς τῷ θεῷ, IV, 24, 95; εὐπειθὴς θεῷ, M. Ant., VII, 67. ἀπειθεῖν to God or the gods, Epict. Diss., I, 14, 16; III, 24, 101; Ench., 32, 2; τῇ θείᾳ διοικήσει, III, 11, 1; τοῖς θείοις διατάγμασιν, IV, 4, 32; ἀπείθεια with θεομαχία, III, 24, 24; ἀπειθές sc. τοῖς ὅλοις, M. Ant., XI, 20.

[2] Cf. Plat. Tim., 56c; M. Ant., VI, 1; XI, 20.

ἀ π ε ι θ ή ς. [1] → πειθαρχέω, n. 1. ἀπειθής is to be derived from πείθομαι, v. S. Schulz, op. cit., 56.

[2] Is. 30:9; Jer. 5:23; Nu. 20:10.

[3] In Just. Dial., 120, 5 the ἀπειθεῖς καὶ ἀμετάθετοι are the unbelieving Gentiles.

[4] As in the OT the Jews are called a γένος ἄχρηστον καὶ ἀπειθὲς καὶ ἄπιστον in Just. Dial., 130, 3 (cf. 140, 2). At Barn., 12, 4 ἀπειθῇ is a variant for ἀπειθοῦντα in a quotation from Is. 65:2.

[5] Cf. Plat. Ap., 29a: ἀπειθῶν τῇ μαντείᾳ, Phaed., 61ab: μὴ ἀπειθῆσαι or πιθέσθαι τῷ ἐνυπνίῳ.

ἀ π ε ι θ έ ω. [1] Cf. L. Köhler, Theol. d. AT³ (1953), 159 f. and e.g., Is. 3:8; 59:13; 63:10; 65:2; Zech. 7:11; Ex. 23:21; Lv. 26:15; Dt. 1:26; 9:7, 23 f.; 2 Εσδρ. 19:29. The Gk. world also speaks of ἀπειθεῖν against the deity, Eur. Or., 31; Plat. Leg., V, 741d; Ditt. Syll.³, 736, 40; cf. also → 10, n. 1.

The NT adopts this usage. Is. 65:2 is quoted in R. 10:21.[2] Prv. 1:25 appears in 1 Cl., 57, 4. In a backward glance at OT history the wilderness generation is characterised by ἀπειθεῖν in Hb. 3:18, as in the OT. Nevertheless, ἀπειθεῖν is used not merely of Israel or the Jews in their opposition to God. It can also be used of the generation of the flood (1 Pt. 3:20) or of sinners generally, who are disobedient to the ἀλήθεια and obey ἀδικία (R. 2:8). These are called ἀπειθοῦντες in the absolute in 1 Cl., 58, 1. Naturally the Gentiles can be called disobedient in a special sense, Hb. 11:31. Paul reminds Gentile Christians of the time when they were once disobedient to God, R. 11:30. If in so doing (11:30 f.) he sets the present disobedience of the Jews over against the prior disobedience of the Gentiles, ἀπειθεῖν has acquired in relation to the former the sense which is now characteristic, namely, that of refusing to believe the Christian *kerygma*; for faith is obedience to the divinely appointed order of salvation (→ 4, 19 ff.; → πίστις). Hence ἀπειθεῖν often stands in antithesis to πιστεύειν, Ac. 14:1 f.; 1 Pt. 2:7 f.; Jn. 3:36.[3] It is also synonymous with ἀπιστία.[4] Such ἀπειθεῖν can be asserted of either Jews (R. 11:31; 15:31; Ac. 14:2; 17:5 D; 19:9) or Gentiles, or without regard to the nationality of those concerned (1 Pt. 2:7 AP℟, 8; 3:1; 4:17; Jn. 3:36; Ign. Mg., 8, 2). In this sense ἀπειθεῖν can be used in the absolute (R. 11:31; 15:31;[5] Ac. 14:2; 17:5 D; 19:9; 1 Pt. 2:7 AP℟; Ign. Mg., 8, 2), or we may have ἀπειθεῖν τῷ λόγῳ (1 Pt. 2:8; 3:1), τῷ εὐαγγελίῳ (1 Pt. 4:17), τῷ υἱῷ (Jn. 3:36, cf. Pol., 2, 1: αὐτῷ). Rather more specialised is the use in 1 Cl., 59, 1, which refers to the possible ἀπειθεῖν of the readers to what is said in the epistle.

† ἀπείθεια.

ἀπείθεια, derived from ἀπειθής and meaning "disobedience," is used in Gk. from the time of Xenophon.[1] It occurs in the LXX at 4 Macc. 8:9, 18; 12:3.

Its use in the NT corresponds to that of the verb ἀπειθεῖν. The noun, like the verb, denotes disobedience to God, i.e., sin. This is clearly brought out by a comparison of R. 11:32 with Gl. 3:22. Hb. 4:6, 11 speaks of the ἀπείθεια of the wilderness generation, R. 11:30 of that of the Jewish people in general, R. 11:32 of that of mankind before and outside Christ. Hence in Eph. 2:2; 5:6 sinners (obviously not merely from among the Gentiles) are called the υἱοὶ τῆς ἀπειθείας.[2] In Herm. s., 9, 15, 3 the third of the vices personified as virgins in black is Ἀπείθεια.

Bultmann

---

[2] Cf. also Barn., 12, 4; Just. Apol., 35, 3; 38, 1; 49, 3; Dial., 24, 4; 97, 2; 114, 2.
[3] This use has obviously shaped the formulation in 1 Pt. 3:20 as well. The disobedience of the generation of the flood is disobedience to the preaching of Noah, of which we read in Jewish tradition and to which 2 Pt. 2:5 also refers, cf. Wnd. Kath. Br. on 2 Pt. 2:5.
[4] Hb. 3:18 f. ἀπειθεῖν and ἀπιστεῖν as variants, 1 Pt. 2:7.
[5] Though τῷ θεῷ may be supplied here from v. 30.
ἀπείθεια. [1] → πειθαρχεῖν, n. 1.
[2] The phrase in Eph. 5:6 has also made its way into Col. 3:6 in ℌ℟G pl lat sy.

† πεινάω (λιμός)

Contents : A. The Greek-Hellenistic World : 1. The Use of πεινάω (λιμός); 2. The Attitude to the Phenomenon of Hunger. B. The Old Testament and Judaism : I. The Use : 1. of λιμός; 2. of πεινάω. II. The Interpretation of Hunger in the OT. III. The Attitude of Judaism to the Hungry Poor. C. The New Testament : 1. The Synoptic Gospels : a. The Calling of the Hungry Blessed ; b. The Hunger of Jesus and His Disciples for the Sake of their Calling ; c. Mt. 21:18 f. and 25:31-46; 2. The Pauline Epistles ; 3. The Johannine Writings.

A. The Greek-Hellenistic World.

1. The Use of πεινάω (λιμός). [1]

a. πεινάω, "to be hungry," lit. from Hom. (Il., 3, 25 etc.: λέων πεινάων); transf. "avidly to desire something (as necessary to life)," with gen. of obj., [2] e.g., χρημάτων, Xenoph. Sym., 4, 36; Cyrop., VIII, 3, 39 (cf. Vergil Aen., 3, 57: auri sacra fames), συμμάχων, Xenoph. Cyrop., VII, 5, 50, ἐπαίνου, Xenoph. Oec., 13, 9; Plut. Aud., 13 (II, 44c); Suav. Viv. Epic., 18 (II, 1100b), τῆς ὥρας (beauty) καθάπερ ὀπώρας, Plat. Leg., VIII, 837c, τοῦ δακρῦσαί τε καὶ ... ἀποπλησθῆναι, Plat. Resp., X, 606a, cf. (ἡ πείνη) μαθημάτων, τοῦ μανθάνειν, Plat. Phileb., 52a, πτωχοὶ καὶ πεινῶντες (here probably "lacking") ἀγαθῶν ἰδίων, Plat. Resp., VII, 521a.

b. Instead of the less common adj. forms (in the NT only πρόσπεινος at Ac. 10:10) the part. is mostly used. As compared with the noun ἡ πεῖνα, ὁ and ἡ [3] λιμός ("hunger," "famine") expresses a higher degree of want. Plato [4] uses it almost always for fatal lack in a phrase already found in Hom. Od., 12, 342 : λιμῷ (ἀπο)θανεῖν. ἡ πεῖνα, on the other hand, is used by him for the regular "need of nourishment." In keeping with this λιμός in fig. use expresses deprivation or lack rather than desire. Cf. already Eur. El., 371 f.: εἶδον ... λιμόν τ' ἐν ἀνδρὸς πλουσίου φρονήματι, γνώμην τε μεγάλην ἐν πένητι σώματι. Philo refers λιμός allegorically to ἔνδεια and he uses it tig. almost always in this sense, Rer. Div. Her., 289 : παθῶν ἔνδεια καὶ λιμός, Ebr., 148 νηστείαν ... καὶ λιμὸν (φρονήσεως), Det. Pot. Ins., 116 : πολλὰ ... λιμὸς ἀρετῆς ... διέφθειρε. On the other hand, he sees in ἡ πεῖνα (always lit.) the demand which rules man (Agric., 36 with ἐπιθυμία, but 38 λιμός "lack") or which torments him (Congr., 165; Vit. Mos., I, 191). In keeping are the expressions ὑπὸ τοῦ πεινῶντος ἡδονῆς, Migr. Abr., 143; τοὺς διψῶντας καὶ πεινῶντας καλοκἀγαθίας, Fug., 139.

2. The Attitude to the Phenomenon of Hunger.

In the religions of antiquity, esp. in their early stages, the ensuring of nourishment through the fertility of the earth is an important reason for worshipping the gods. [5] This, e.g., is what caused Israel after the conquest repeatedly to adopt the Baals, the

---

π ε ι ν ά ω. [1] Thes. Steph., Pass.-Cr., Liddell-Scott, Preisigke Wört., s.v.
[2] On the acc. in Mt. 5:6 v. Pr.-Bauer⁴, s.v. and Bl.-Debr. § 171, 1.
[3] Bl.-Debr. § 49, 1 and App. § 2.
[4] Cf. F. Ast, Lexicon Platonicum, III (1836), s.v.
[5] Chant. de la Saussaye⁴, I, 69 f., 452, 547 f., 560, 555-558, 634, 642; II, 300-304, 321, 440.

local fertility gods. [6] Bad harvests and famine were everywhere attributed to the wrath of the gods, → V, 388 f. [7]

Furthermore, in antiquity it is a social and political duty of rulers to ensure for all their subjects a subsistence level which will keep them from hunger. [8] The Pharaohs and their high officials boast of their fulfilment of this duty. [9] Because they thus preserve the life of men, rulers are paid divine honours by the Hell. world. [10] In the constitutions of the ancient West the primary concept in this respect is that of social justice, whereas in the Orient, esp. in Egypt, and later in Hellenism, the principle of care or provision is predominant. [11]

Hence the statements of philosophy presuppose first that "in any state or society which is in any sense well organised" an honest man will never fall into such poverty as to suffer hunger, Plat. Leg., XI, 936b c. Plato thus concludes that begging should be forbidden by law, since only the honest man deserves sympathy if he is hungry. Elsewhere Plato speaks of hunger as a natural physiological phenomenon, and deduces herefrom certain anthropological principles concerning this most powerful ἐπιθυμία. [12] When in the imperial period the gulf between the wealthy and the non-propertied masses grew wider even in the West, Stoic philosophy demanded of each member of the body of human society: *cum esuriente panem suum dividat.* [13] At the same time later philosophy sought even more strongly than earlier philosophy to free its adherents from bodily demands. To this end it encouraged a moderate restriction (→ ἐγκράτεια, II, 340, 27 ff.) to bare essentials in food and clothing; in the normal course everyone could expect this. [14] The Stoic sage goes further in maintaining his freedom from external want by regarding it as an adiaphoron, like wealth, which is neither good nor evil; [15] if it becomes too pressing he can escape it by εὔλογος ἐξαγωγή, "well-considered suicide." [16] In Neo-Pythagoreanism and Neo-Platonism this depreciation and suppression of the body and its needs is even stronger. [17] Acc. to Porphyrius everyone should so strive after moderation that his ideal will be complete abstention from nourishment, Abst., I, 27, cf. 37 f.; IV, 20. The real goal of this later philosophy is no longer the freedom of the personality but union with the divine, which is increasingly conceived of in dualistic and Gnostic antithesis to the physical. In Christian Gnosticism we even find the idea that Jesus Himself despised natural nourishment [18] and gave no promises to

---

[6] E. Sellin, *Gesch. des isr.-jüd. Volkes*², I (1935), 123 f.; M. Noth, *Gesch. Israels* (1950), 122-124. Cf. Jer. 44:15-18 and P. Volz, *Der Prophet Jeremia*² (1928), XXVIII f.

[7] Chant. de la Saussaye⁴, I, 599; II, 359 f. In the Gk. world these ideas find expression esp. in the Demeter myth, cf. Hom. Hymn. Cer., 310 f., or the Erysichthon saga, Callim. Hymn., 6, 24-115; Ovid Metam., VIII, 738-878 [Kleinknecht].

[8] H. Bolkestein, *Wohltätigkeit u. Armenpflege im vorchr. Altertum* (1939), 29-33, 248-286, 349-379, 391-400, cf. also R. v. Pöhlmann, *Gesch. d. sozialen Frage u. des Sozialismus in der antiken Welt*³ (1925).

[9] So, e.g., Amenemhet I: "I have given to the poor and sustained the orphan ... There was no hunger in my years, nor any thirst therein," Bolkestein, 10. The actual state of affairs was very different, *op. cit.,* 447-450: Under Ramses III striking labourers declared: "Hunger and thirst have driven us here, we have no clothes ... Tell that to Pharaoh."

[10] Inscr. address them as τοῦ τὸν βίον τῶν ἀνθρώπων ἐπανορθώσαντος, Ditt. Or., 90, 2 or τὸν κοινὸν τοῦ ἀνθρωπίνου βίου σωτῆρα, Ditt. Syll.³, 760, 8 f.; cf. Rev. 13:17.

[11] Bolkestein, 418-484.

[12] Resp., IV, 437d; Lys., 221a; Gorg., 494b; 496c; 497c; Phileb., 54e.

[13] Sen. ad Lucilium, 95, 51, cf. Bolkestein, 470-74.

[14] So esp. the Cynics (Antisthenes acc. to Xenoph. Sym., 4, 34 ff.), also the Stoa, e.g., Sen. ad Lucilium, 17, 9; 18, 6-11.

[15] E.g., Sen. ad Lucilium, 80, 6; 123, 1-6, 16, cf. M. Pohlenz, *Die Stoa,* I (1948), 121-123.

[16] E.g., Sen. ad Lucilium, 12, 10; 17, 9; 51, 9; 70 etc., cf. Pohlenz, 156.

[17] Cf. H. Strathmann, *Gesch. d. frühchr. Askese* (1941), 292-343. In distinction from these ascetic strivings fasting is not designed to free the body from physical wants, → IV, 927.

[18] Valentinus in Cl. Al. Strom., III, 7, 59, 3 (GCS, 15, 223, 12 ff.), cf. W. Bauer, *Das Leben Jesu im Zeitalter der nt.lichen Apokryphen* (1909), 316 f.

those who suffer from physical hunger. [19] On the basis of the advancing Gnostic understanding the vegetation gods, whose previous function had been to still the pangs of
natural hunger, had already been given in the mystery religions the new function of
serving the hunger for abiding life. [20]

In Philo Stoic, Platonic and Gnostic elements are superimposed over the Jewish heritage at this pt. too. Philo also commends ἐγκράτεια and ὀλιγόδεια, a controlled
moderation. For this that which nature provides (Virt., 6), bread and water, is sufficient
nourishment. [21] It should make itself as independent as possible of hunger and thirst,
"strict and terrible masters" (Vit. Mos., I, 191), cf. Vit. Cont., 37; Agric., 36-39. In
particular it must find a place for the much more important satisfying of the soul, Spec.
Leg., II, 201; cf. Migr. Abr., 204. At the same time, more under the influence of Jewish
ideas, Philo calls hunger the "most insupportable of all evils," Spec. Leg., II, 201; cf.
Jos., 156; Poster. C., 142; Vit. Mos., I, 191. He thus rejects the Cynic ἐγκράτεια which
leads to hunger, Det. Pot. Ins., 19, though cf. 34, and extols the fact that fallen man has
to provide against hunger by hard work, Op. Mund., 167. To the Hell. world he offers
an ideal of contemplative moderation in the Therapeutae (Vit. Cont.) and also, like
Joseph. (Bell., 2, 128-133, 150-153), in the Essenes (Omn. Prob. Lib., 75-91).

B. The Old Testament and Judaism.

With unimportant exceptions (Is. 44:12; cf. 1 K. 11:34 → 16, 21 ff.) the OT does not
refer to hunger as the regularly recurring need for food which corresponds to the toil
of earning one's daily bread on an earth marked by the curse. Its reference is simply to
the hunger which arises from the lack or withdrawal of the normal fruits of labour.

I. The Use.

This fact is mirrored already in the usage. In the LXX we never find the noun ἡ
πεῖνα but always ὁ (ἡ) λιμός. In accordance with the intention of the Heb. this is
almost always used for the Heb. רָעָב, and only very occasionally for the equivalents
רְעָבוֹן and כָּפָן; the reverse is also true. For רָעֵב, verb and adj., we normally find πεινᾶν,
but for the hi λιμαγχονεῖν and λιμοκτονεῖν. Conversely, πεινᾶν is used only 5 times
for עָיֵף "weak," "spent" (→ II, 228, n. 11), and once for יָעֵף "exhausted," but it is
regularly used for רָעֵב. πεινᾶν retreats under the shadow of the much more common
λιμός; nevertheless, the two do not become co-extensive in meaning.

1. The Use of λιμός.

a. λιμός denotes first an acute lack of food as a result of the absence of means of
nourishment, i.e, famine, whether through failure of crops due to drought [22] or the cutting

---

[19] Marcion eliminated the twofold νῦν from Lk. 6:21 (Tert. Marc., IV, 14), cf. Tertullian
De Anima, 23 (CSEL, 20, 336).

[20] → IV, 805, 1 ff., cf. R. Bultmann, *Das Urchr. im Rahmen der antiken Religionen* (1949),
176 f.

[21] So in agreement with the Stoic-Cynic diatribe Spec. Leg., I, 173; Vit. Cont., 73; cf.
Act. Thom., 20.

[22] In Palestine the harvest depends on the winter rains coming at the right time and
in sufficient quantity. Lack of rain leads at once to a rise in the price of grain, G. Dalman,
Arbeit u. Sitte in Palästina, II (1932), 331-337. Climatically a complete lack of rain in any
given year is most unusual in Palestine and it is hardly conceivable over a number of years.
When periods of famine lasted for some yrs. in the OT the ref. can only be to periods of
deficient rainfall, Dalman, I, 1 (1928), 195-199. The ancient world already knew how to
make provision against such natural disasters by imports, but this was hardly possible in
South Palestine. Alien rulers were able to meet the two famines mentioned by Joseph. in
the NT period by imports from Egypt, Ant., 15, 299 ff. in 25/24 B.C. and Ant., 3, 317 ff.;
20, 49 ff., 100 ff.; cf. Ac. 11:28 ff. under Tiberius Alexander 46-48 A.D.

off of supplies in war (2 K. 6:25; 7:4; 25:3). Through every natural cause it is a work of God, either as something which shapes history (Ps. 105:16; 2 K. 8:1) or as a visitation (Dt. 11:10-17; 2 S. 21:1; 24:13; 1 Ch. 21:12; cf. 1 K. 17:1; Is. 14:30; Sir. 39:29; 48:2). Hence deliverance from languishing is sought from God (1 K. 8:37; 2 Ch. 6:28; 20:9; Ps. Sol. 5:8) and is experienced as His help by men of God.[23] Later Judaism clings to this understanding, though it lays increasing stress on the concept of retribution, Jos. Ant., 15, 299 f.

b. λιμός is also the subjective result of famine, i.e., hunger, a gnawing lack of that which is necessary to life. In this sense λιμός is in Jer. and Ez., with μάχαιρα and θάνατος (דֶּבֶר), a phenomenon of the divine judgment in salvation history. These three deadly arrows (Dt. 32:23; Ez. 5:16) bring on the rebellious people of the covenant a judgment which is eschatological in character,[24] and which is to be followed by a new beginning as out of death. λιμός is again used along these lines, with sword, pestilence etc., to denote historical judgment in Dt. 32:23 f.; Lv. 26:23-26; Test. Jud. 23; Ps. Sol. 13:2 f.; Philo Vit. Mos., I, 110; Praem. Poen., 127; Ab., 5, 8; b. Ab., 5, 10.

In both these senses λιμός appears occasionally in Jewish[25] and regularly in Christian apocalyptic as one of the signs of the end. The emphasis is sometimes on the fact that the end is not yet (cf. Mt. 24:7 and par.: λιμοί as ἀρχὴ ὠδίνων) and sometimes on the fact that judgment is already here (the image of famine in Rev. 6:5 f. cf. Ez. 4:9-17; Rev. 6:8 cf. Ez. 14:21 → n. 24; the subjective effect in Rev. 18:8).

c. Only rarely in the OT is λιμός the extended, tormenting and distressing lack of adequate nourishment, "hunger" (Is. 5:13; 8:21; Dt. 28:48; Lam. 5:10; Am. 8:11, cf. Tob. 4:13; Sir. 18:25). This is usually expressed by πεινᾶν.

2. The Use of πεινᾶν.

In the first instance πεινᾶν undoubtedly denotes the effect of famine (Gn. 41:55; 2 K. 7:12). It can also be used for the exhaustion caused by a military campaign (Ju. 8:4 f.; 2 S. 17:29 cf. Is. 5:27) or a desert journey (Dt. 25:18; Ps. 107:4-9); in this sense it is often the rendering of the Heb. עָיֵף.[26] Mostly, however, it denotes "persistent hunger" in consequence of national or social distress.

II. The Interpretation of Hunger in the Old Testament.

Hunger as thus defined can be understood in many different ways according to the various interpretations of historical life.[27] In the prophetic demand for repentance, with its attack on attachment to earthly goods, it can be proclaimed as a judgment. Acc. to Is. 5:13; 8:21 the yoke of the enemy will bring hunger, and Dt. 28:47 f. gives the reason : "Because thou servedst not Yahweh, thy God, with joyfulness, and with gladness of heart, for the abundance of all things, therefore shalt thou serve thine enemies ... in hunger, and in thirst ... and in want of all things," cf. Lam. 5:10; Neh. 5:3. This constant deprivation of the essentials of life is an expression of rejection and abandonment by God, Is. 8:21. There thus develops out of hunger for bread the much more terrible λιμός

---

[23] Ps. 105:16 ff.; 1 K. 17:1-16 cf. Lk. 4:25; 2 K. 4:38-44; 6:27; Ps. 33:19; 107:4-9; Prv. 10:3; Job 5:20, 22; Neh. 9:15; Ps. Sol. 13:2; 15:7.

[24] Jer. 14:12 f. (15:2; 16:4;) 21:7, 9; 24:10; 27:8, 13; 29:17; 32:24, 36; 34:17; 38:2; 42:17, 22; 44:13, only the sword and famine : Jer. 5:12; 11:22; 14:13, 15 f. (18); 18:21; 42:16; 44:12, 18, 27; wild beasts are sometimes added to the three punishments in Ez. (5:12; 6:11 f.; 7:15; 12:16), and this gives us the four visitations of Rev. 6:8 : Ez. 14:21 cf. 5:17.

[25] Eth. En. 80:2 f.; 99:5; 4 Esr. 6:22; S. Bar. 27:6; 70:8; (Sib., IV, 150 f.;) Sanh., 97a Bar. and par., Str.-B., IV, 981 f.

[26] At this pt. the term is close to → κοπιάω, III, 828, 8 ff., which is often associated with πεινάω in the LXX (Is. 5:27; 40:28; 46:2; Sir. 16:27).

[27] Cf. E. Sellin, Israels Güter u. Ideale (1897); Eichr. Theol. AT, III³, 63-72.

τοῦ ἀκοῦσαι λόγου κυρίου which Am. 8:11 proclaims as a judgment and which is not a growing religious demand but a gnawing lack of everything that gives life.[28] The transf. use here is not just a general image ; the strict use which is the background of the image may be seen clearly in it.[29]

Along with the proclamation of hunger as a future judgment we find the view that the hunger which overtakes God's people in the present is a salutary abasement. Dt. 8:3 regards the hunger of the people in the wilderness as a historical means of instruction and thus finds for it a significance which positively, too, goes beyond the actual need for bread, cf. Dt. 29:5; Ez. 12:17-20. In contrast Is. 49:10 sets the present humiliation of the people (cf. Is. 49:13) in an eschatological perspective when it says concerning the redemptive return through the desert : οὐ πεινάσουσιν οὐδὲ διψήσουσιν (cf. 'Ιερ. 38:12, 25; Ez. 34:29; 36:29). This is not the removal of natural need by restoration of the primitive state but eschatological deliverance from the lack which arises with the historical guidance of the people and which ultimately discloses the lack of all that is necessary to life. In this historical, not dualistic, sense those who suffer from lack of food and drink are summoned in Is. 55:1 f. not to seek in vain to provide the necessities of life for themselves but to receive them in the form of the divine promise of salvation. Along the same lines the LXX seems to take fig. the promised refreshment of the weary in Jer. 31:25 (→ II, 228, 15 ff.): ἐμέθυσα πᾶσαν ψυχὴν διψῶσαν καὶ πᾶσαν ψυχὴν πεινῶσαν ἐνέπλησα, Ιερ. 38:25. Here, too, πειναν means "to lack" rather than "to strive." Only in Sir. 24:21 does the term become a fig. expression for religious longing : οἱ ἐσθίοντές με (sc. τὴν σοφίαν) ἔτι πεινάσουσιν κτλ., cf. Prv. 9:5. Underlying this is the meaning current in Hell. usage ; πειναν is the regularly recurring demand for food, → n. 31.

With an individual reference hunger denotes saving abasement in the promises of salvation to hungry עֲנִיִּים[30] often in direct association with the declaration of judgment on those who are full. The prophetic admonition to repent, which from the very first bears a reference to the poor who are deprived of their rights, can sometimes speak of these as the hungry.[31] In 1 S. 2:5; Ps. 107:36-41; 146:7 the satisfying of the hungry even in history is extolled as a saving revelation of Him who abases only to exalt. At the same time hunger and thirst are in Is. 65:13 (cf. 1 S. 2:5) proclaimed to the high and mighty as a sign of rejection.[32] These words of promise seek to turn hunger, the most elemental expression of impotence, into waiting upon the only Giver of life.[33] Does this promise live on in Judaism?[34]

---

[28] Cf. A. Weiser, *Das Buch der 12 kleinen Propheten (AT Deutsch)* (1949/50), ad loc. For this reason alone the λιμὸς μεγάλη ... ἐφ᾿ ὅλην τὴν οἰκουμένην of Ac. 11:28 cannot have meant in the source, as Wdt. Ag., ad loc. conjectures, the demand of the world for the proclamation of the word. Even Philo does not use the term in this sense (→ 12, 26 ff., esp. Det. Pot. Ins., 116).

[29] For fig. use elsewhere in the OT cf. Ιερ. 38:25; Sir. 24:21; Job 18:12.

[30] → πτωχός cf. A. Rahlfs, עָנִי u. עָנָו in d. Ps. (1892); Sellin, op. cit. (→ n. 27), 284-295; H. Birkeland, *Ani u. Anaw in d. Ps.* (1933); A. Kuschke, "Arm u. reich im AT," ZAW, 57 (1939), 31-57; A. Weiser, *Die Ps. (AT Deutsch)*[3] (1950), 55 f.

[31] Is. 58:6 f., 9 f., cf. Ez. 18:7, 16; Is. 32:6 f.; Job 22:7; 24:4-11. With some fluidity these admonitions pass over into those of the Wisdom lit., which reach their climax in Prv. 25:21 (= R. 12:20): "If thine enemy be hungry, give him bread to eat ..." (cf. Tob. 1:17; 4:16; Sir. 4:2; Test. Iss. 3, 5, 7; Zeb. 5-8; Slav. En. 9; 42:8; 63:1, → 17, 20 ff.). The ref. is to the benevolence to which those outside the Bible are also summoned (cf. Bolkestein, 6-8), not to the removal of the injustice which causes hunger.

[32] Hunger, as distinct from thirst (→ II, 228, 34 ff.), is not usually a torment of hell in Jewish eschatology, Volz Esch., 322 f.

[33] The life of the עָנִי is characterised by hunger as well as sickness (→ III, 200, 30 ff.), in fluctuating partnership with the unequally harsh animosity of human foes, → II, 812, 16 ff.

[34] A sign of change is that already in Job 5:5 the LXX has δίκαιος for רָעֵב [Bertram].

III. The Attitude of Judaism to the Hungry Poor.

By means of the central prototype, Joseph, who experienced as a test the humiliation of imprisonment, hunger etc., the Test. XII promise exaltation by the Lord. [35] In the pseudepigr. the promise is given to poverty (→ πτωχός), not because it teaches us to expect all things from God and not from our own strength, but (Test. XII) because it is a test of faithfulness, or (Ps. Sol.) because it is a chastisement which leads to the better fulfilment of the Law, [36] the only criterion of standing before God, Ps. Sol. 5:1-12; 10:1-6; 13:7-10; 16:11-14; 18:4. Poverty is no longer the starting-point of the divine relationship but an appendage which broke away completely in the course of the 1st cent. A.D. [37] For Rabbinism poverty is not at all a saving abasement leading to hope in God. It is a misfortune which chastises and at best purifies. [38]

This extinguishing of the promise for the hungry poor (→ n. 43) characterises the growing distinction between the message of Judaism and that of the OT. It is the more surprising, then, that social relations offer more rather than fewer presuppositions for it. Just prior to the coming of Jesus the policies of Herod the Gt. had reduced great masses to a poverty which stood in glaring contradiction to the increasing wealth of the few. [39] At the same time the religious groups which sought to achieve the true community of God either ascetically (→ 14, 15 ff.) or by way of the Law had bound themselves together in close-knit communities which, without making this their goal, ensured all their members of a bare subsistence by mutual inter-aid. [40] Legalistic Judaism of every kind met the poverty which became general after the collapse of the nation by a strongly established and willingly practised public and private benevolence which at least sought to ensure food for all [41] even though it did not turn penury into the promise of blessing.

C. πεινάω in the New Testament.

1. The Synoptic Gospels.

a. The Calling of the Hungry Blessed. According to the common tradition of Mt. 5:6 and Lk. 6:21 Jesus called the hungry blessed. What was originally meant by this may best be seen if we disregard the later [42] explanatory additions in Mt. and turn to the early history of the term (→ 16, 25-17, 13) [43] and the total witness

---

[35] Test. Jos. 1. The sayings in Test. Jud. 25, which contain verbal reminiscences of the Beatitudes, are a Chr. interpolation.

[36] Cf. the newly discovered Hab. Comm. 12:2-10 : the members of the sect, who are elsewhere called "doers of the Law" (7:11; 8:1; 12:4 f.), are described as "the poor" in 12:3, 6, 10; their opponent, the "ungodly priest," betrayed the Law and heaped up riches (8:8-12; 9:5 f.; 12:10, cf. Eth. En. 94:7 f.; 97:8 f.). Cf. also Damasc. 6:15 f.; 19:9 → πλούσιος.

[37] Cf. Moore, II, 156.

[38] Str.-B., I, 818-826.

[39] Jos. Bell., 2, 84 ff.; Ant., 15, 267 ff.; 17, 304 ff.

[40] Irrespective of historical connections, this is true of the Essenes (Jos. Bell., 2, 122 ff.; Philo Omn. Prob. Lib., 85 ff.), the Damascus community (Damasc. 13:11 f.; 14:12-16), the Qumran community (Manual 1:11 ff.; 5:2; 6:2, 18-25; 9:7 f.), perhaps also the circles behind Test. XII if a passage like Jos. 17 refers to a real inner community and not to an ideal of the community as a whole.

[41] Str.-B., II, 643 f.; IV, 536-558; Moore, II, 162-179.

[42] Kittel Probleme, 53 f.; Bultmann Trad., 114.

[43] It is no accident that there is no Jewish par. to the Beatitudes (Str.-B., I, 191 f.). The Rabb. pars. to the first beatitude adduced by P. Fiebig, Jesu Bergpredigt (1924), 1-3 extol the virtue of humility, whereas Jesus calls the needy blessed. The only literary witness to a continuation of the OT promise in pre-Chr. Judaism is the Magnificat at Lk. 1:46-55. In the Ass. Mos., which W. Grundmann, Jesus d. Galiläer u. d. Judt. (1941), 81, adduces as the voice of the Anawim, there is no trace of it (cf. 7:6), and even in Test. XII we catch

of the Synoptic Gospels. The hungry are men who both outwardly and inwardly are painfully deficient in the things essential to life as God meant it to be, and who, since they cannot help themselves, turn to God on the basis of His promise. These men, and these alone, find God's help in Jesus. They are not an existing social or religious group. [44] The beatitude, in basic unity with the promise of the Ps., is a saving word which first brings into being those to whom it applies. The hungry who are blessed are not beggars. They are believers who seek help from Jesus because of their own helplessness.

This original comprehensive sense of the beatitude is given a particular reference in both Gospels. Mt., obviously in the light of the controversy with Judaism, which insists on its own righteousness, [45] construes hunger as a hungering and thirsting after righteousness. This hunger is not a concern or striving for uprightness; it is the desire, fed by painful lack, [46] that God's will should be done, Mt. 6:10, 33 → II, 198, 29 ff. Because God's dominion comes in Jesus, the promised stilling of the hunger for righteousness is to be had in Him.

Lk. contrasts the hunger which means salvation with a hunger which is the expression of damnation: "Blessed are ye that hunger now: for ye shall be filled" (6:21); "Woe unto you that are full! for ye shall hunger" (6:25). Both are set forth in the parable of the rich man and Lazarus: the beggar longed for the crumbs which fell from the rich man's table but is now in Abraham's bosom and has no lack (cf. Lk. 13:28 f.); the rich man is tormented by an unquenchable desire for even the slightest relief (Lk. 16:19-31). Lk. is certainly not referring the beatitude to the hungry who desire what the rich have (Lk. 6:24; 12:15-21). [47] Lazarus does not want the satiety of the rich man; he desires only the crumbs which fall from his table, cf. Lk. 16:21 and 15:16; Mt. 7:28 and par. [48] If the self-sufficient satiety of the rich (Lk. 16:25, cf. 6:24) does not become a lack which can seek help only in God it will become the hunger for which there is no further promise and which means perdition, Lk. 6:25. By relating hunger to physical nourishment Lk. makes it

---

only a faint echo (→ n. 35 and Test. Iss. 7; G. 5:7; Jos. 17). Lk. 1:53, however, takes up again the OT praise of the God who simply for His mercy's sake fills with good things the hungry and lowly who fear Him (= Ps. 107:9), and sends the rich empty away. The Magnificat has pre-Chr. features, but on the basis of these one cannot assume, as H. Gunkel does ("Die Lieder in d. Kindheitsgeschichte Jesu bei Lukas," *Harnack-Festgabe* [1921], 43-60), that Lk. 1:46 f., 49-55 come from a pre-Chr. Jewish group. The Magnificat came into being along with the infancy stories, for it follows the pattern of such stories in the OT and borrows directly from 1 S. 2:1-10. It takes up the OT word of promise under the influence of God's new saving acts, and ultimately of the work of Jesus. Cf. G. Erdmann, "Die Vorgeschichte des Lk.- u. Mt.-Ev. u. Vergils 4. Ekloge," FRL, NF, 30 (1932), 31-33; H. Sahlin, *Der Messias und das Gottesvolk* (1945), 168-171, 312-322.

[44] Jesus' beatitude does not refer to the ʿammē ha-arez or to one of the existing groups of anawim among them, as assumed by, e.g., Dib. Jk., 39-44; W. Sattler, "Die Anawim im Zeitalter Jesu Christi," *Festgabe f. A. Jülicher* (1927), 1-15; Str.-B., I, 190; Hck. Lk. ad loc. and W. Grundmann, op. cit., 81; for the opp. view cf. R. Meyer, "Der Am ha-Ares," Judaica, 3 (1947), 196.

[45] To the beatitude corresponds the Woe on Pharisaism in Mt. 23 and the Woe on the full in Lk.

[46] The addition of thirst strengthens the element of desire.

[47] The Ebionite interpretation espoused by J. Weiss, *Die Ev. d. Mk. u. Lk.*⁹ (1901), 369 f., 371 would lead in this direction.

[48] This very pointed ref. in Lk. is not then, as Bultmann thinks we must assume (Trad., 221; *Jesus* [1929], 90 f.), the proclamation of a reversal of earthly relations; it is the word of penitence and promise which indicates the starting-point of grace, the nadir of self-glorying, cf. Lk. 18:10-14.

plain that the decision whether man will have God's gifts given to Him is decided at this point. He who is ready to live by God's grace receives everything essential to true life (Lk. 15:21-24; Mt. 6:33 par. Lk. 12:31; Lk. 22:35; Ac. 4:34). This satisfying of the hungry when the rich go empty away (Lk. 1:53) comes after the not irrelevant introduction to the parables of what is lost (Lk. 15:1 f.). Here the word of promise is renewed and God's help is sought in Jesus. The stronger emphasis on the physical side in the beatitude shows that the accent is on fulfilment, → IV, 1115, 24 ff.

b. The nature of this hunger which is shaped and satisfied by Jesus' saving work is brought out more clearly by the hunger which Jesus, like His disciples, undergoes for the sake of His calling. According to Mt. 4:1 f. (par. Lk. 4:1 f.) the first temptation of Jesus arises out of His hunger, → 34, 27 ff. [49] Jesus upholds the faith which Israel had to learn in the wilderness according to Dt. 8:3. [50] In Mt. 4:4 par. Dt. 8:3 He does not point away from physical to spiritual nourishment, [51] but from that which is only of earth to that which comes from God. He bears the hunger laid upon Him without creating for Himself the necessities of life. How, then, can He justify the fact that His disciples attempt to appease their hunger by plucking ears of corn, even though this involves breaking the Sabbath (Mt. 12:1-8 and par.)? In Mt. 12:3 and par. Jesus refers to what the Scriptures say about David (1 S. 21:2-7), who, when he was hungry, ate the shewbread which according to the Law only the priests are permitted to eat, Lv. 24:9. Does this mean, then, that hunger (Mt. 12:1, 3) excuses even the type of self-help which entails transgression of the ceremonial Law? [52] Jesus does not in fact say that the hungry have a right to help themselves. What He justifies is the readiness to receive, or freedom on the basis of discipleship. [53] What David received in the house of God only He in whom God's help and goodness are present in incomparably greater measure may truly grant to those who have left all for His sake (Mt. 19:27) and who may consequently be hungry even on the Sabbath. [54] The point made in Mt. (cf. 12:6 f.), and even more simply in Mk. (2:27 f.), is that everything is at the disposal of the man who stands at God's disposal (1 C. 3:22 f.), and especially of the Messiah and His disciples. There is fulfilled in them that which is prefigured in David and his men. [55] Like any other affliction which waits for God's salvation, the hunger behind which stands a believing and ministering waiting upon God's saving work is symbolically appeased even externally by the grace manifested in Jesus. He who provided His disciples with ears of corn on the Sabbath gives daily bread unasked to the thousands who have followed Him into the wilderness

---

[49] The first thing to oppose the realisation of God's rule on earth is acc. to the Lord's Prayer anxiety about one's daily bread, Mt. 6:11 par.

[50] Dt. 8:2 f. (LXX): μνησθήσῃ πᾶσαν τὴν ὁδόν, ἣν ἤγαγέν σε κύριος ὁ θεός σου ἐν τῇ ἐρήμῳ, ὅπως ἂν ... ἐκπειράσῃ σε ... καὶ ἐλιμαγχόνησέν σε.

[51] In this sense Philo puts the giving of the Law side by side with the provision of manna, Decal., 16 f., cf. Fug., 139.

[52] So Bultmann Trad., 14 : "Defence of desecration of the Sabbath through hunger by a verse from Scripture," cf. Kl. Mk. on 2:25 and W. G. Kümmel, "Jesus and der jüdische Traditionsgedanke," ZNW, 33 (1934), 121.

[53] For a different view cf. Bultmann Trad., 14 : "The primitive community puts the justification of its Sabbath practice on the lips of Jesus." But how could this situation be invented by the Palestinian community with its zeal for the Law (Ac. 21:20 f.)? A general freedom in Sabbath observance could hardly be deduced from the episode recounted in Qoh. r., 1, 8.

[54] Acc. to Pea, 8, 7 a meal should be ready even for the wayfarer on the Sabbath.

[55] J. Schniewind, Mk. (NT Deutsch), ad loc.

as a sign that those who come to Him will not lack anything essential to life.[56] Since Jesus, as He who brings in the kingdom, gives everything that is necessary to life as God understands this, earthly bread is put in its proper place (Mt. 6:33 par. Lk. 12:31) and hunger for the essentials of life acquires its true content.

c. Mt. 21:18 f. and 25:31-46. The cursing of the fig tree (Mt. 21:18 f. par. Mk. 11:12-14, 20 f.)[57] can be regarded either as a parabolic action or possibly as a parable — perhaps based on a withered fig tree in Jerusalem — which tradition changed into a story.[58] He who patiently waits for daily bread from God would hardly curse a tree because fruit is sought thereon in vain.[59] The pt. of the story, which Mk. perhaps indicates by interweaving it with the account of the cleansing of the temple, can only be as follows. Jesus proclaims judgment on Israel (or Jerusalem), which is like an unfruitful tree (cf. Mi. 7:1; Lk. 13:6-9), cf. Hos. 9:16; Mt. 3:10 par.; Mt. 21:41, 43. Jesus' hunger does not have to be the external occasion or framework for the parabolic action.[60] It may be an original feature in the parable. If so, it shows that Jesus, like those whom He calls blessed in Mt. 5:6, is hungry for the fruit of righteousness in Israel, and proclaims a curse on those who allow Him to hunger in vain for mercy, Mt. 9:13; 12:7; cf. Mt. 25:41 ff.

In Mt. 25:40 Jesus is speaking of the gracious reward given for mercy shown to the hungry. The basis of this is that the mercy is shown to Jesus Himself in His brethren. In keeping with the universal scope of the parable (Mt. 25:32: πάντα τὰ ἔθνη), He is not referring merely to disciples who specifically share His way to the cross (Mt. 10:40 ff.)[61] but to all His brethren who stand in need of mercy. Similarly the beatitude declared that all who suffer lack are fellow-heirs of the kingdom.[62] Because Jesus Himself, in the humiliation of hunger, willingly associated Himself with them (Mt. 4:1-4) and was merciful to them (Mt. 12:7), He can here give to the ancient command of mercy[63] the authority of the new command. Here, as in the beatitude, the brotherly relation in which Jesus stands to the hungry becomes for the first time real to them through this association with Him.

2. The Pauline Epistles.

In 1 C. 4:6-13 one may see how the calling of the hungry blessed works out in these days when we walk by faith and not by sight.[64] With bitter irony Paul describes the attitude of one part of the community as an inauthentic anticipation of the consummation arising out of a Gnostic misunderstanding of redemption.[65]

---

[56] This is proclaimed in the story of the feeding, which is told 6 times; cf. Schl. Mt., 466 f.

[57] Mk. 11:22-25 and par. are independent sayings, Bultmann Trad., 24.

[58] So Schniewind, op. cit. (→ n. 55), ad loc.; for the first view cf. esp. Zn. Mt., 625 f.; Schl. Mt., 618; Dausch Synpt.⁴, 281 f., for the second D. F. Strauss, Leben Jesu, II (1864) §281; Kl. Mk., ad loc. But cf. also Jülicher Gl. J., II, 444-447; Hck. Mk.; Loh. Mk., ad loc.

[59] As against Loh. Mk. on 11:12 f., who thinks the pt. is that Jesus as Lord of nature declares that which does not serve man to be unworthy to live.

[60] Cf. Zn. Mt., ad loc.

[61] Ibid., 415-417; Dausch Synpt.⁴, 179; Kl. Mt.; J. Schniewind, op. cit., ad loc.; H. v. Soden → I, 145. On the history of interpretation cf. W. Brandt, "Die geringsten Brüder," Jbch. d. Theol. Schule Bethel, 8 (1937), 1-28.

[62] This interpretation in the light of Mt. 5:3 ff. is considered by O. Michel → IV, 656 f. and esp. Schl. Mt., 133 f.

[63] → n. 31 and Bultmann Trad., 130 f.

[64] The Beatitudes are echoed so strongly that Pl. possibly had them in mind.

[65] In distinction from the satiety of the world or Pharisaism, that which is rejected here is based, not on one's own power, but on Gnostic redemption. This elevates above faith to a present enjoyment of the spiritualised consummation, and gives dominion over the physical

Over against this he sets the way to consummation which faith takes by way of the cross and which finds illustration in his own life, 1 C. 4:8, 11: "Now ye are full, now ye are rich, ye have attained to dominion without us." "Even unto this present hour we both hunger, and thirst, and are naked, and are buffeted, and have no certain dwellingplace, and labour." The hunger which Paul suffers in spite of all the provision made by the churches is for him a sign of the fact that he still awaits the consummation of salvation though already apprehended by Christ, the salvation of God. His life ἐν λιμῷ καὶ δίψει is a demonstration of the fact that he is a "minister" of Christ, 2 C. 11:27. [66] In R. 8:35, too, he lists λιμός and γυμνότης among the sufferings for Christ's sake which cannot separate from His love but are made supportable by it, and of which we may boast as a pledge of hope, R. 5:3 ff. Even the life consumed by lack of the basic essentials is an expression and fulfilment of dying with Christ. It is thus a pledge of participation in His resurrection which is already at work to give life, 2 C. 4:7-11, cf. 1:8 ff.; 12:9. Here hunger is no longer waiting for salvation as in the beatitude. It is the subsuming of the old under the new, which is apprehended in faith.

In contrast hunger is not a sign in the "philosophically" formulated passage Phil. 4:11-13. Paul describes it here as one possibility of life in alternation with fulness. He does not boast of inner independence of the alternation between being full and being in want. The Stoic claims to achieve this with his ἄσκησις and the Gnostic through redemption. [67] Paul, however, boasts of the power to accept and even to affirm both. [68] In the light of Christ's crucifixion and resurrection he accepts both poverty and abundance as related parts of the way of life which he pursues. Here too, then, πεινᾶν is not a chance of fate but an expression of the poverty [69] in which the beatitude is worked out in faith.

3. The Johannine Writings.

The content of the beatitude is presented in new words as a self-testimony of Jesus in Jn. 6:35: "I am the bread of life; he that cometh to me shall not hunger (any more); and he that believeth on me shall never thirst." There is experienced by the believer in Jesus that which was promised for the age of salvation: οὐ

---

and earthly things set under one's feet, 1 C. 4:10; 9:3-5; 2 C. 11:19 f. It is no accident that in the fellowship of the full some are hungry at the fellowship meal while others are drunk, 1 C. 11:21. Ign., too, charges the Gnostics with lack of mercy for the hungry, Sm., 6, 2. This fulness, too, is without mercy. Paul concedes that all may appease their hunger at home, 1 C. 11:34. He demands, not equality of concern for all, but that everything and esp. the community meal, should stand under love, which is greater than all knowledge (1 C. 13:2), and which accepts as a new commandment the obligation to feed a hungry enemy (R. 12:20 = Prv. 25:21).

[66] In the similar sounding passage in Act. Thom., 145 this is no longer the result but the fulfilment of service : "Behold, I have achieved thy work and fulfilled thy command and am poor, needy, alien, a slave, despised, imprisoned, hungry, thirsty, naked and weary ... may my steadfast prayers and fasting not be confounded !" Cf. 156 : "Poor one, who was needy and hungry for forty days, thou who dost satisfy thirsty souls with thy good things." Cf. also 149.

[67] αὐτάρκης reminds us esp. of the former (v. Loh. Phil. on 4:11 and Dib. Gefbr. Beilage z. Phil.), μεμύημαι perhaps of the latter, → IV, 828. But here both words are used to express new content.

[68] Not ἀπάθεια but ὑπομονή. Cf. Loh. Phil., ad loc.

[69] The ταπεινοῦσθαι (Phil. 4:12, cf. 3:21) goes with Christ's ἐταπείνωσεν ἑαυτόν in 2:8. Though both words come from a different background, they echo what Ps. says about the ταπεινοί (= עֲנָוִים) and hence put the par. πεινᾶν in the same light.

πεινάσουσιν οὐδὲ διψήσουσιν, Is. 49:10. [70] Even here, however, Jn. does not take over directly the terminology of the OT. The hunger whose relief is offered is not a state of hunger [71] (→ 16, 9 ff.) but the regularly recurring need for food in the underlying sense. [72] In those appointed to die there is set forth herein the demand for life. [73] No material gift, no earthly bread (Jn. 6:27), not even the miracle of manna (Jn. 6:31 f., 49), can appease this craving. There resides in it the desire which seeks to maintain itself against its fate and is prepared to use any gift to this end (Jn. 6:26, 30 f.). Hence it is referred to the Son of Man who really has life in Himself as He who comes from above and gives His σάρξ to death (Jn. 6:27, 51, 53 f., 62 f.; 5:21, 26 f.). Commitment to Him appeases the craving for bread inasmuch as it also directs it to its true goal. Not hungering any more means that the desire enclosed in the need of bread is both removed and satisfied. This approximation to the usage of Hellenistic Gnosticism does not mean that the promise of Jesus is dualistically evaporated. [74] What it does mean is that its spiritual core is brought out more strongly than in Mt. (→ 18, 10 ff.), and its comprehensive significance is presented in a new way. [75] In distinction from Gnostic analogies, [76] the offer of Jn. 6:35 includes rather than excludes the physical fulfilment promised in Rev. 7:16.

We have here a more OT form of the same formula which takes a more Hellenistic form in Jn. In the words of Is. 49:10 Rev. 7:16 f. promises the perfected who come out of tribulation, and are washed in the blood of the Lamb, redemption from all the affliction which they have suffered with and through the world, including hunger and thirst: "They shall hunger no more, neither thirst any more ... for the Lamb ... shall feed them." The promise of the beatitude and of the offer of the bread of life is experienced here in the tribulation only in the harsh dissonance to which Paul bears witness (→ 20, 30 ff.). Not until the new world (Rev. 21:4 ff.) is it experienced in physical totality.

Goppelt

---

[70] The fact that the satisfying of hunger and thirst is here presented as feeding with the bread of life is an indication that what is offered is the consummation as depicted esp. in the banquet of the day of salvation, Lk. 22:30, cf. Jn. 6:52 f.

[71] So H. Strathmann, *J.* (*NT Deutsch*) (1951), *ad loc.*: "to suffer hunger."

[72] Like the recurring need for water (Jn. 4:14 f.) in Jn. 4:10-14, this is the starting-pt. of the address, Jn. 6:26 f. The real goal of this demand is indicated.

[73] Cf. Bu. J., 136 f.

[74] πεινᾶν is not a figure for spiritual yearning as in Sir. 24:21 (→ 16, 21 ff.), or for the hunger of the soul as in Act. Thom., 133, cf. 156 (→ n. 66). It is related to the totality of existence by the association of the bread of heaven with the feeding, and its offer as the flesh and blood of the Son of Man. On the literary unity of Jn. 6 cf. J. Jeremias, "Joh. 6:51c — 58 — redaktionell," ZNW, 44 (1952/53), 256 f.

[75] The offer of the bread of life is to all, as the need of all, esp. for the dualist, is denoted by the recurrent demand for bread. The beatitude is addressed to the poor, but esp. in OT thought this obviously includes everybody. The historical connection between the two sayings is an open question.

[76] Act. Thom., 36, → n. 74.

---

† πεῖρα, † πειράω, † πειράζω, † πειρασμός, † ἀπείραστος, † ἐκπειράζω

Contents : A. The Meaning of the Terms in Secular Greek. B. The Old Testament and Later Judaism : 1. Man is Tempted ; 2. Man Tempts God. C. The New Testament : I. Secular Use of the Terms. II. Theological Use of the Terms : 1. Man is Tempted ; 2. Man Tempts God. III. The Temptations of Jesus.

A. The Meaning of the Terms in Secular Greek.

1. πειράω comes from the root περ- and is related to περάω, πέρας, Lat. *peritus, experiri* etc., Germ. (*er*)*fahren.*[1] It means 1. act. a. "to attempt," "to strive," "to make an effort," Hom. Il., 8, 8 : ... πειράτω διακέρσαι ἐμὸν ἔπος, Aristoph. Eq., 517: πολλῶν γὰρ δὴ πειρασάντων ..., b. "to put to the test," esp. in a hostile sense, with gen.,[2] Hdt., VI, 82: πειρᾶν τῆς πόλιος, "to test whether a city can be taken," c. "to lead into temptation" (post-Hom.) with acc., Plut. De Bruto, 10 (I, 988b): τοὺς φίλους ἐπὶ Καίσαρα πειρᾶν, "to stir up the mind of friends against Caesar." 2. It is used more commonly in the mid. and pass. a. in the same sense as the act. "to try someone," "to put to the test," almost always in expression of distrust, Hom. Il., 10, 444: ... πειρηθῆτον ἐμεῖο, Hdt., VI, 86: πειρηθῆναι τοῦ θεοῦ, "to put God to the test," b. with gen. of obj.: "to test a thing" in order to assess its value, Hom. Od., 21, 282 : χειρῶν καὶ σθένεος πειρήσομαι, c. often in the perf. mid. in the sense "to know by experience," Hdt., IV, 159: οὐ πεπειρημένοι πρότερον οἱ Αἰγύπτιοι Ἑλλήνων. Plat. Ep., VI, 323a : πεπειραμένος Ἐράστου πλέονα ἢ σύ. The word rarely has a religious sense, cf. Hdt., VI, 86 (→ line 16) and I, 46 f., where the ref. is to a tempting of God by testing the truth of the oracle, or of the god who gave it. The following derivates, too, are used only in a secular sense.

2. πειράζω[3] means "to make an attempt," "to test someone." The word occurs in Hom. Od., 9, 281: ὣς φάτο πειράζων, but then not until Apoll. Rhod., 1, 495: Ὀρφεὺς ... κίθαριν πείραζεν ἀοιδῆς. Cf. Epict., I, 9, 29: Ῥοῦφος πειράζων μ᾽ εἰώθει λέγειν ... The word is very seldom used in profane Gk.

πεῖρα κτλ. M. Kähler, Art. "Versuchung," RE[3], 20, 582-586; O. Piper, Art. "Versuchung," RGG[2], V, 1575 f.; Cr.-Kö., 913-918; Trench § 50; Bl.-Debr. § 101, *s.v.*; Lexicons, *s.v.* F. Köster, *Die bibl. Lehre von d. Versuchung* (1859); A. Sommer, *Der Begriff d. Versuchung im AT u. Judt.,* Diss. Breslau (1935). J. H. Korn, ΠΕΙΡΑΣΜΟΣ, "Die Versuchung des Gläubigen in d. gr. Bibel," BWANT, 4. F., 20. H. (1937). P. Vallotton, *Etude linguistique sur le concept de Tentation dans la Bible,* Diss. Strasbourg (1943); also *Essai d'une doctrine chrétienne de la Tentation* (1954). For bibl. on the 6th petition in the Lord's Prayer → n. 44 and on the temptations → n. 53.

[1] On the etym. and meaning *v.* E. Fraenkel, *Gesch. d. gr.* Nomina agentis auf -τηρ, -τωρ, -της, II (1912), 101 f. and → Korn, 18, n. 1.

[2] On the constr. with the gen. *v.* Schwyzer, II, 105.

[3] On the relation between πειράω and πειράζω *v.* P. Buttmann, *Ausführliche gr. Sprachlehre,* II (1827), 208, *s.v.* and Korn, 18, n. 1: "The intensive form πειράζω strengthens ... the special subjective voluntaristic meaning already present in the root ... Α πειράζω desires πειρᾶν, i.e., ... seeks to experience something." But the difference between the two is predominantly linguistic rather than a distinction of sense : -άω Attic and -άζω Ionic and *koine* [Debrunner]. On πειράζειν and δοκιμάζειν cf. Trench and Cr.-Kö. In most cases πειράζειν denotes hostile intent, but this element is not present in δοκιμάζειν. But the two words can be used interchangeably, Korn, 11, n.

3. ἐκπειράζω does not occur at all in secular Gk., where we find only the mid. ἐκπειράω with the aor. pass. ἐξεπειράθην "to try out," Eur. Suppl., 1089 : κἀξεπειράθην τέκνων, Aristoph. Eq., 1234: καί σου τοσοῦτο πρῶτον ἐκπειράσομαι, "to sound out someone on something."

4. πεῖρα, attested from Pind., means "test," "attempt," "experience," Soph. El., 470 f.: πικρὰν δοκῶ με πεῖραν τήνδε τολμήσειν ἔτι. In the NT only the common phrase πεῖράν τινος λαμβάνειν is important. In the act. it means "to make an attempt with something," Xenoph. Cyrop., VI, 1, 54: ἐλάμβανε τοῦ ἀγωγίου πεῖραν, or in the pass. "to get experience of something," Diod. S., 12, 24, 4: τὴν θυγατέρα ἀπέκτεινεν, ἵνα μὴ τῆς ὕβρεως λάβῃ πεῖραν. [4]

5. πειρασμός has been found so far only 3 times in profane Gk.: Diosc. Mat. Med. praef.: τοὺς ἐπὶ τῶν παθῶν πειρασμούς, "medical experiments"; Cyraniden : [5] κίνδυνοι καὶ πειρασμοὶ ἔν τε γῇ καὶ θαλάσσῃ, πειρασμός being synon. here to κίνδυνοι, → n. 35; Syntipas : [6] ὑπὸ πειρασμῶν τοῦ κόσμου στενοχωρούμενοι.

6. ἀπείραστος does not occur in secular Gk., though we sometimes find ἀπείρατος, "what is untried, unknown," i.e., "where no attempt or test has been made," Demosth. Or., 18, 249: οὐδὲν ἀπείρατον ἦν. Luc. Toxaris, 3: ὁ Πόντος ἀπείρατος ἔτι τοῖς Ἕλλησιν ὤν. [7]

B. The Old Testament and Later Judaism.

Like profane Gk., the LXX can use πειράομαι, πειράζω in a purely secular sense, [8] e.g., 1 Βασ. 17:39: David says to Saul : οὐ μὴ δύνωμαι πορευθῆναι ἐν τούτοις (weapons), ὅτι οὐ πεπείραμαι, "I have no experience," cf. also 3 Βασ. 10:1 (= 2 Ch. 9:1); Qoh. 7:23 and frequently in Macc., cf. 1 Macc. 12:10; 2 Macc. 10:12; 3 Macc. 1:25 etc.

Alongside the purely secular use, however, there is a distinctly religious understanding of the concept. The Hebrew term נסה pi, which the LXX renders by πειράζω, very frequently has a religious tinge, and it passes this on to the Greek equivalent. Hence πειράζω (also πειρασμός etc.) takes on a wider range of signification, and it is used much more often than in profane Greek, since the idea of testing is an essential one in the Bible. The God of the OT is in the first instance the God who makes demands, requiring man's fear, faith and confidence. But man, as may be seen from Gn. 3:1-19, is tempted to seek to be as God. In so doing he rebels against God's commandment, transgresses it, and thus becomes guilty. From the time of the fall his obedience to God is subject to constant threat through trial, whether it be that God tests and proves him or that the adversary (Satan) is at work. [9] On the other hand, πειράζων can also be used when man tempts God.

---

[4] For further examples cf. Pass. and Pr.-Bauer, s.v.

[5] Ed. F. de Mély and C.-E. Ruelle, Les Lapidaires de l'antiquité et du moyen âge, II : Les Lapidaires grecs (1898), 40, 24.

[6] Ed. V. Jernstedt and P. Nikitin, Mémoires de l'Académie Impériale des Sciences de St. Pétersbourg, 8me Série, Classe des Sciences historico-philologique, Tome XI, No. 1 (1912), p. 124, 18.

[7] On other possible meanings v. the lexicons.

[8] The act. πειρᾶν does not occur in the LXX or NT. Cf. Helbing Kasussyntax, 143. The LXX and NT both use πειράζειν more often than πειρᾶσθαι. ἀποπειρᾶσθαι is found in Prv. 16:29 "to seduce."

[9] Cf. E. Lohmeyer, "Kyrios Jesus," SAH, 1927/28, Abh., 4 (1928), 25 f.: "Thus the idea of testing is no more than a religious formula for the dialectical opposition between good and evil ... The result is that whenever the creation of the world is thought of as a moral act, the concept of testing has to be associated with it in some form." Cf. also Korn, passim.

1. Man is Tempted.

a. The best known example of man's being tested by God is in Gn. 22:1-19. The introductory words read: καὶ ἐγένετο μετὰ τὰ ῥήματα ταῦτα ὁ θεὸς ἐπείραζεν τὸν Αβρααμ, → I, 8 f. [10] God Himself comes into the life of Abraham and "tempts" him, i.e., puts his faith and obedience to the test. Abraham withstands the test by unresistingly obeying the command of God and taking Isaac to the altar of sacrifice. God then says to him: νῦν ... ἔγνων ὅτι φοβῇ τὸν θεὸν σύ, v. 12. In the older parts of the OT we often find the idea of God testing the people of Israel as a whole. The content of the trial is here again the same as with Abraham ; God is testing the people's obedience. In Ex. 20:20 the gift of the Law is called a test of this kind : ἕνεκεν γὰρ τοῦ πειράσαι ὑμᾶς παρεγενήθη ὁ θεὸς πρὸς ὑμᾶς, ὅπως ἂν γένηται ὁ φόβος αὐτοῦ ἐν ὑμῖν, ἵνα μὴ ἁμαρτάνητε, cf. 15:25 f. 16:4 speaks of a test of the people which will establish εἰ πορεύσονται τῷ νόμῳ μου ἢ οὔ. The character of this test is described thus in Dt. 8:2 : ὅπως ἂν ... διαγνωσθῇ τὰ ἐν τῇ καρδίᾳ σου, εἰ φυλάξῃ τὰς ἐντολὰς αὐτοῦ (sc. θεοῦ) ἢ οὔ. In the light of these passages the meaning of the trial of Abraham is plain : God is testing him to see whether he has a true fear of God and faith in Him. The same applies to the whole people. In Ju. 2:22 the failure to drive out of the land the heathen whom Joshua left there is explained in terms of the divine purpose τοῦ πειράσαι ἐν αὐτοῖς τὸν Ισραηλ εἰ φυλάσσονται τὴν ὁδὸν κυρίου πορεύεσθαι ἐν αὐτῇ ... ἢ οὔ. The theological concept clearly to be seen here is that God Himself constantly directs history and that all events are subordinate to His saving purpose for the people Israel. [11] The πειρασμός of His people is a means to fulfil this purpose.

b. The story of the fall in Gn. 3:1-19 occupies a special position. If the term נסה or πειράζω is not used, there is clear ref. to the testing or tempting of Eve by the serpent. [12] The essential difference from previous instances is that the test comes from the serpent rather than God. Even though the serpent is one of God's creatures, it here represents the adversary of God and its purpose is to separate men from God, → V, 573, 14-575, 17. [13] We thus have the new thought, elsewhere found in the later tradition, that through the adversary of God man is forced to decide for or against God. Neither this thought nor the figure of Satan may be found in the older tradition. There it is God who tests man and forces him to decide.

The figure of Satan appears in the introductory framework to Job (→ σατανᾶς). The tt. for "to test" do not occur in the Mas. text of Job, but in some vv. they have made their way into the LXX. [14] 7:1: πότερον οὐχὶ πειρατήριόν ἐστιν ὁ βίος ἀνθρώπου ἐπὶ τῆς γῆς; 10:17: ἐπήγαγες δὲ ἐπ' ἐμὲ πειρατήρια. Cf. 16:9; 19:12; 25:3. The dialogue deals with the whole problem of the testing of the righteous, and esp. with the central problem of innocent suffering. [15] The passing of the test is plainly indicated in the words of Job to God in 42:2 : οἶδα ὅτι πάντα δύνασαι, ἀδυνατεῖ δέ σοι οὐθέν. Complete submission to God's will even in incomprehensible suffering constitutes the essence of the obedience demanded. With this the test is passed. Fundamentally the idea is the same here as in the testing of Abraham or Israel by God. When a man is tested, it is his readiness to commit himself wholly to God which is on trial.

---

[10] Korn, 48-60, with further bibl. Cf. D. Lorch, Isaaks Opferung in chr. Deutung (1950).
[11] H. W. Hertzberg, Die Bücher Josua, Richter, Ruth (AT Deutsch) (1953), 160 f.
[12] This understanding is fully developed in Vit. Ad., cf. esp. v. 10, where Adam says to Eve : "How could you let yourself be led astray by our adversary !"
[13] Cf. also O. Procksch, Theol. d. AT (1950), 493 f.
[14] Korn, 4-18 : "Die Mächtigkeit der ΠΕΙΡΑΣΜΟΣ-Typologie im biblischen Sprachgebrauch." Cf. also 70-76. Cf. ψ 17(18):29, where the LXX has ἐν σοὶ ῥυσθήσομαι ἀπὸ πειρατηρίου for the not very clear HT כִּי־בְךָ אָרֻץ גְּדוּד. On the interpretation of the HT v. the comm.
[15] J. Fichtner, "Hiob in der Verkündigung unserer Zeit," Wort u. Dienst, Jbch. d. Theol. Schule Bethel (1950), 71-89; Procksch, op. cit., 372-383.

To be obedient and to come out of the trial successfully is thus to count on God. This is how the NT interprets the obedience of Abraham when Hb. 11:17-19 says of him in connection with the sacrifice of Isaac: λογισάμενος ὅτι καὶ ἐκ νεκρῶν ἐγείρειν δυνατὸς ὁ θεός, v. 19. To doubt God, not to count on him, means disobedience and failure.

c. In the Wisdom lit. of the OT there are many refs. to testing.[16] In Sir. 2:1 we find the admonition: τέκνον, εἰ προσέρχῃ δουλεύειν κυρίῳ, ἑτοίμασον τὴν ψυχήν σου εἰς πειρασμόν. Sir. 33:1 has the assurance: τῷ φοβουμένῳ κύριον οὐκ ἀπαντήσει κακόν, ἀλλ᾽ ἐν πειρασμῷ καὶ πάλιν ἐξελεῖται. These two examples show that there has been a sharp change in the understanding of the concept of testing. Though the sayings are so general that one cannot say for certain what is implied in πειρασμός, there can be no doubt that the term approximates closely to the predominantly Gk. concept of education, → V, 596-625:[17] God educates His elect, cf. Wis. 3:5 f.: (δίκαιοι) ... ὀλίγα παιδευθέντες μεγάλα εὐεργετηθήσονται, ὅτι ὁ θεὸς ἐπείρασεν αὐτοὺς καὶ εὗρεν αὐτοὺς ἀξίους ἑαυτοῦ· ὡς χρυσὸν ἐν χωνευτηρίῳ ἐδοκίμασεν αὐτούς. Cf. 11:9 and Sir. 34:9 f.[18] But the idea of testing is in this way robbed of the seriousness it has elsewhere in the OT, for there is no longer any real danger of failing the test and resisting God. Only in this light can one understand the petition in ψ 25:2:[19] δοκίμασόν με, κύριε, καὶ πείρασόν με, πύρωσον τοὺς νεφρούς μου. Finally, any misfortune or suffering which smites the righteous is in the Wisdom lit. regarded as educative. This may be seen in Wis. 3:5 and esp. in Sir. 4:17, where it is said (of σοφία): καὶ βασανίσει αὐτὸν ἐν παιδείᾳ αὐτῆς ... καὶ πειράσει αὐτὸν ἐν τοῖς δικαιώμασιν αὐτῆς, → I, 561-563. Thus the whole life of the righteous is a test, since God educates His own throughout their lives. The righteous Abraham is an example; it is said of him in Sir. 44:20: ἐν πειρασμῷ εὑρέθη πιστός, cf. 1 Macc. 2:52. He is again an example in Jdt. 8:25 f.: (κύριος) ... ὃς πειράζει ἡμᾶς καθὰ καὶ τοὺς πατέρας ἡμῶν. μνήσθητε ὅσα ἐποίησεν μετὰ Αβρααμ, καὶ ὅσα ἐπείρασεν τὸν Ισαακ ...[20] One should model oneself on Abraham and others in order to pass the test or overcome temptation.

d. Only in the last c. of Da. do we read of a πειράζεσθαι of believers in connection with the eschatological tribulation which will precede the judgment and the consummation, Zeph. 1:15; Hab. 3:16; → III, 140, 12-143, 13. In Da. 12:10 the prophecies are to be sealed ἕως ἂν πειρασθῶσι καὶ ἁγιασθῶσι πολλοί. The sufferings of the last time will be for them a final testing and hence a final sanctifying; ἁγιάζεσθαι is to be found along with πειράζεσθαι. Their redemption is the goal of this test and hence the explanation of their sufferings; cf. Eth. En. 94:5; 96:2 f.

e. Like the Wisdom lit., the Rabb. writings like to take Abraham as an example. His model constancy and exemplary steadfastness are continually emphasised, cf. Ab., 5, 3: "Through ten temptations our father Abraham was tempted, and he overcame them all in order to make known how great the love of our father Abraham (for God) was."[21] A favourite theme in this connection is that of the evil impulse which is rooted

---

[16] Sommer, 10-15, where in particular the connection between the later Jewish and older understanding is indicated.

[17] Cf. G. Bertram, "Der Begriff der Erziehung in d. gr. Bibel," Imago Dei, Festschrift G. Krüger (1932), 33-51.

[18] At Sir. 34:10 read ἐπειράσθη (א) for ἐπειράθη, Korn, 27 f.

[19] On the interpretation of the Ps. in the HT (Ps. 26) v. the comm. and R. Press, "Das Ordal im alten Israel, II," ZAW, NF, 10 (1933), 246-248.

[20] On the testing of Isaac, which is not mentioned in Gn., cf. Korn, 50 f. and Str.-B., IV, 108.

[21] Cf. the ed. of Ab. by K. Marti-G. Beer in the Giessen ed. of the Mishnah (1927), 119 f. Cf. also Abraham in Jub. 17 and Str.-B., III, 187, 197. Cf. Korn, 48-60. In Test. Jos. 2:7 we read: "He (God) found me proved in ten temptations." The Rabb. also bring out the positive aspect, v. Str.-B., I, 135. On the number ten cf. ibid., III, 411. W. Staerk, "Die sieben Säulen d. Welt u. d. Hauses der Weisheit," ZNW, 35 (1936), 232 f. adduces a Chr.

in every man. [22] In bBer., 60b we have a prayer : "Let me not come to destruction nor to temptation nor to shame, and bend my evil impulse to submit itself to thee ... Let me cleave fast to the good impulse ..." The Rabb. have a sense of the peril which testing implies for man. In bSanh., 107b we have the following saying : "Rab Jehuda (d. 299) has said, Rab (d. 247) has said : Let man never bring himself under the power of temptation." There follows a ref. to Ps. 26:2 and to David's fall ; he did not pass the test which he brought upon himself. Ex. r., 31 (91c) preserves the saying : "For there is no man whom God did not test."

f. Philo fully shares the view of testing found in the Wisdom lit. In him the idea of education is to the fore ; ἄσκησις ἀρετῆς, [23] education in virtue, in which he sees God's work and purpose, so dominates his thinking that he has no understanding of the thought of testing itself. [24] The word πειρασμός occurs neither in him nor in Josephus.

g. In Essene writings, and esp. in the Dead Sea Scrolls (Manual of Discipline), men are divided into the children of light and the children of darkness. The main thought here is that of a situation of conflict in which the believer finds himself. The spirits of evil continually tempt him to cross over to the side of darkness. His position is under constant assault. Since such thoughts are alien to the OT and later Judaism, their origin is to be sought in the concepts of later Parseeism. If the word "testing" does not occur in the Scrolls, the thing itself is undoubtedly present. [25]

2. Man Tempts God.

a. In the OT and later Judaism we repeatedly find the idea that man tests God. In Ex. 17:1-7 we are told that at Rephidim the people complained against Moses because there was no water. Moses answered : τί λοιδορεῖσθέ μοι, καὶ τί πειράζετε κύριον; v. 2, → I, 730, 37 ff. In memory of the incident the place was given the name מַסָּה = Πειρασμός, cf. Dt. 9:22. Nu. 14 contains God's penal judgment on the murmuring people. In v. 22 we read : ὅτι πάντες οἱ ἄνδρες οἱ ὁρῶντες τὴν δόξαν μου καὶ τὰ σημεῖα, ἃ ἐποίησα ἐν Αἰγύπτῳ καὶ ἐν τῇ ἐρήμῳ ταύτῃ, καὶ ἐπείρασάν με τοῦτο δέκατον καὶ οὐκ εἰσήκουσάν μου τῆς φωνῆς. [26] Cf. also ψ 77:17 f., 40 f.; 94:8 f.; 105:14. To test or tempt God is not to acknowledge His power, not to take seriously His will to save. This finds expression in complaint against His guidance, in the failure to see His glory or to note His signs and wonders. To test God is thus to challenge Him. It is an expression of unbelief, doubt and disobedience. [27] This is why Dt. 6, in its explanation of the first commandment, adds to the admonition to love God with all one's heart and soul and strength (v. 4 f.), the demand : οὐκ ἐκπειράσεις κύριον τὸν θεόν σου, ὃν τρόπον ἐξεπειράσασθε ἐν τῷ Πειρασμῷ. φυλάσσων φυλάξῃ τὰς ἐντολὰς κυρίου τοῦ θεοῦ σου, v. 16 f. If we love God and keep His commandments we cannot test Him or question His power by an attitude of doubt and unbelief. This helps us to understand the words of Ahaz in Is. 7:12. He is told to ask for a sign, but refuses to

series of 10 pairs from Adam to Christ who were ordained as a tentatio for the world, Ps.-Clem. Hom., 3, 61 (55).

[22] Str.-B., IV, 470-480.

[23] Cf. W. Völker, Fortschritt u. Vollendung bei Philo v. Alex., TU, 49, 1 (1938), 154-259.

[24] The idea of testing finds some echoes in Philo, e.g., Conf. Ling., 130, where there is ref. to the πειρατὴς τῆς ἀδικίας, and the name Gideon is interpreted in terms of πειρατήριον. πεῖρα and δοκιμασία are associated in Fug., 149 with a ref. to Gn. 38:20-23 [Bertram].

[25] Cf. K. G. Kuhn, "πειρασμός — ἁμαρτία — σάρξ im NT u. die damit zusammenhängenden Vorstellungen," ZThK, 49 (1952), 200-222.

[26] "Tenfold" here undoubtedly means "many times."

[27] Both Korn, 31-38 and Sommer, passim seek to establish a connection between the thought of man being tested by God and that of God being tested by man. Korn does it through the actual concept of testing, Sommer (cf. also Kähler) through that of challenge. The latter seems clearer, but it should not be forgotten that between the lines of thought there are really more differences than similarities.

do so on the ground that he does not want to test God. The fact that the words are hypocritical does not affect the meaning of נסה. On the contrary, it enables us to see for the first time how firmly anchored was the certainty that nothing is to be allowed which might border on doubt of God's power, i.e., on disobedience.

b. The same thought is to be found in Judaism. At the beginning of Wis. we find in 1:2 : (κύριος) εὐρίσκεται τοῖς μὴ πειράζουσιν αὐτόν, ἐμφανίζεται δὲ τοῖς μὴ ἀπιστοῦσιν αὐτῷ. Not to tempt God is to believe in Him, to trust Him, not to doubt His power. Cf. Sir. 18:23 : μὴ γίνου ὡς ἄνθρωπος πειράζων τὸν κύριον. In Ass. Mos. 9:4 the precursor of the end [28] says: "See and know that I was never a tempter of God nor my fathers nor their forefathers, that they should have transgressed His commandments." He is thus describing the exemplary attitude of the believer. Here is fresh confirmation that to test God is not to believe in but to doubt His power.

C. The New Testament.

The use of πεῖρα κτλ. in the NT is like that in profane Gk. πειράζω is more common than the Attic πειράομαι, [29] which occurs for certain only in Ac. 26:21; Paul is speaking : Ἰουδαῖοι ... ἐπειρῶντο διαχειρίσασθαί (με). The meaning corresponds to that familiar elsewhere. Another possible instance is at Hb. 4:15, where acc. to CKLP it is said of the Lord : πεπειραμένον δὲ κατὰ πάντα. [30] The more strongly attested reading, however, is undoubtedly πεπειρασμένον, so that this alone calls for consideration, → 33, 7 ff. Similarly ἐπείραζεν is to be preferred at Ac. 9:26. The noun πειρασμός, which only came into more common use in the LXX (some 15 times), occurs 21 times in the NT.

I. Secular Use of the Terms.

The noun πεῖρα occurs only twice, in Hb. 11:29, 36, where it is linked with the verb λαμβάνειν, though the sense is different in each verse : v. 29 "to make an attempt," v. 36 "to make acquaintance," "to experience." In neither case is there any echo of the idea of testing or tempting. The verb πειράζω, too, can sometimes be used in a profane sense, cf. Ac. 9:26; 16:7; 24:6; also Herm. s., 8, 2, 7; Ign. Mg., 7, 1. πειράζειν occurs twice in the NT in the sense "to examine," "to prove" = δοκιμάζειν, → n. 3 and II, 255, 14-260, 37. 2 C. 13:5 : ἑαυτοὺς πειράζετε εἰ ἐστὲ ἐν τῇ πίστει, ἑαυτοὺς δοκιμάζετε. Neither here nor in Rev. 2:2, where the church in Ephesus is praised for its investigation of the apostles who had come to it (cf. Did., 11, 7), do we find any transition to the special religious sense "to test." A further step is taken when we are often told in the Synoptics that opponents like the Pharisees and Sadducees put Jesus to the test in order to get material against Him. πειράζειν here means "to prove," though with an emphasis on the hostile element as compared with δοκιμάζειν; they act thus with the hostile intent of bringing about His downfall. Mk. 8:11 and par.: Φαρισαῖοι ... ζητοῦντες παρ' αὐτοῦ σημεῖον ἀπὸ τοῦ οὐρανοῦ, πειράζοντες αὐτόν (cf. Mk. 10:2 and 12:15 par.; Mt. 22:35; Lk. 10:25; [Jn. 8:6]). One should not overstress, however, the element of tempting in the true sense, → 35, 26 ff. In Jn. 6:6 πειράζειν is used of Jesus Himself in the same sense "to prove," "to put to the test."

II. Theological Use of the Terms.

1. Man is Tempted.

a. In 1 C. 10:13 Paul describes the difficulties into which a Christian can be brought by the πειρασμός to which all are exposed. In this connection he has to

---

[28] Cf. C. Clemen in Kautzsch Apkr. u. Pseudepigr., II, 326.
[29] Bl.-Debr. § 101, s.v.
[30] So Pr.-Bauer, s.v. πειράω 2.

point out to the Corinthians that they have not yet borne the full weight of temptation. Thus far they have been under only human temptation, i.e., that which the nature of man can bear, → I, 366, 28 ff. [31] The test can in fact be a much greater one. Paul adds, though it hardly fits the context, a word of consolation and promise: σὺν τῷ πειρασμῷ God will give a way of escape so that they may bear it. He is not here reflecting on the origin of temptation. One can hardly say that it is just a divine test of faith (→ 25, 2-23), nor that Satan is the author (as in 1 Th. 3:5 and 1 C. 7:5, → 32, 5-12). Elsewhere, too, Paul simply issues a general warning against temptation, e.g., in Gl. 6:1: σκοπῶν σεαυτόν, μὴ καὶ σὺ πειρασθῇς. When we admonish our neighbour, we must do so in humility; otherwise we who give the admonition may ourselves be tempted and fall. Hence it is not possible to say precisely who is the author of the human temptation in 1 C. 10:13. Paul is rather warning the over-strong and self-confident Corinthians against falling, a possibility which they obviously do not take seriously enough. He is also consoling the weak; they should not be too worried about their capacity. [32]

b. One passage in the NT expressly forbids us to call God the author of temptation. Jm. 1:13 is directed against Christians who are in danger of taking temptations too lightly, and who even seem to be disposed to make God responsible for their sins. [33] James opposes this view. In so doing he makes a statement about the nature of God which we do not find elsewhere in the Bible, namely, that He cannot be tempted to do evil [34] and that He Himself does not tempt anyone, i.e., lead anyone into sin. Jm. makes the point even more plainly in v. 14. The author of temptation, and hence also of sin, is one's own ἐπιθυμία, the evil impulse which is in every man, → III, 171, 22-24. Where this comes from, he does not, of course, say.

Jm. 1:2 f.: πᾶσαν χαρὰν ἡγήσασθε ..., ὅταν πειρασμοῖς περιπέσητε ποικίλοις ..., does not seem to fit in too well with this. Here we have a completely different use of the same word. A similar expression occurs in the materially related verse 1 Pt. 1:6: ἀγαλλιᾶσθε ... λυπηθέντες ἐν ποικίλοις πειρασμοῖς. Both passages leave us in no doubt but that sufferings for the sake of the faith are implied by πειρασμοί. [35] In Jm. as in 1 Pt. sufferings are a reason for joy

---

[31] Schl. K., 292 f. thinks differently, but he can hardly be right in view of v. 13b. Cf. also H. v. Soden, Sakrament u. Ethik bei Pls. = Marburger Theologische Studien, 1 (1931), 11 f.

[32] Kuhn's exposition of 1 C. 10:13 (217 f.) "... when Satan makes his constant assaults God provides the believer with the needed power of resistance," ignores the context of the verse; it is also open to question whether ἀνθρώπινος πειρασμός is to be taken in this way.

[33] Wnd. Kath. Br., ad loc. even suggests that the Christians whom Jm. was addressing might have appealed to the 6th petition of the Lord's Prayer in support of their thesis.

[34] ἀπείραστος can be construed here only as a pass. verbal adj., v. Bl.-Debr. § 182, 3, also Wnd. Kath. Br. and Dib. Jk., ad loc., with other instances. Cf. also Agr., 21: ἀνὴρ ἀδόκιμος ἀπείραστος. Korn, 32, n. 2 suggests that there has been some intrusion of Gk. thought into the saying of Jm.

[35] The only other instances of the plur. πειρασμοί in the NT are at Lk. 22:28 and Ac. 20:19, also 2 Pt. 2:9 as a vl. acc. to ℵ* 69 al syʰ. On Lk. 22:28 → 35, 20 ff. In Ac. 20:19 Paul refers to the πειρασμοί to which he was exposed in his missionary work. The meaning here is almost that of "danger," which seems natural for πειρασμοί in the plur. and for which we have other examples, → 24, 12 f. The element of temptation is not ruled out, but it should not be automatically included wherever the word occurs. Cf. in the OT Dt. 7:19 and 29:2, where we read of the πειρασμοί (plagues) which smote Pharaoh. At Ac. 15:26 DE we find the addition (ἀνθρώποις παραδεδωκόσι τὰς ψυχὰς αὐτῶν) εἰς πάντα πειρασμόν. Here πειρασμός even in the sing. can only mean "danger." God is perhaps regarded as the author of sufferings in Wis. 3:5 f. (→ 26, 13 ff.), which was perhaps known to James and Peter. The testing of the righteous is a proof of divine grace, Sommer, 13.

and serve to prove the steadfastness of faith, cf. R. 5:3 f. But neither author even suggests that God is the author of the sufferings, so that there is no reference whatever to their educative character. [36] They are tests whose aim and purpose is that of proving and demonstrating, → II, 258, 7-259, 14. [37] Jm. 1:12: μακάριος ἀνὴρ ὃς ὑπομένει πειρασμόν, ὅτι δόκιμος γενόμενος λήμψεται τὸν στέφανον τῆς ζωῆς, ὃν ἐπηγγείλατο τοῖς ἀγαπῶσιν αὐτόν. [38] We are reminded here of the Beatitudes; Jesus calls those who suffer and are persecuted blessed, Mt. 5:4, 10-12; Lk. 6:22 f. Jm. 1:12, however, seems to go much further than 1:2 f. (→ 29, 26 f.). The beatitude is more comprehensive. The crown of victory is promised to those who overcome every temptation and not just that which comes through suffering. In 1 Pt. 4:12, however, there is a stronger reference to temptation through suffering: μὴ ξενίζεσθε τῇ ἐν ὑμῖν πυρώσει πρὸς πειρασμὸν ὑμῖν γινομένῃ, ὡς ξένου ὑμῖν συμβαίνοντος. Yet here, too, the main concern is not with the question as to the nature of temptation but with the nature and source of suffering. The answer is controlled by the understanding of Christ's sufferings: καθὸ κοινωνεῖτε τοῖς τοῦ Χριστοῦ παθήμασιν χαίρετε, 4:13. For the Christian suffering is participation in the sufferings of Christ, and hence in the last analysis it means joy. This does not mean, of course, that the sufferings of Christians do not also have the character of temptation or trial. One may see this from 4:17, where sufferings are regarded as a judgment (→ lines 22 ff.) which begins in the house of God, → III, 806, 6-38.

c. The association of temptation and judgment occurs in other parts of the NT quite apart from 1 Pt. Thus in Mk. 13:22 and par. Jesus points out that in the last time, before God's judgment day, ψευδόχριστοι and ψευδοπροφῆται will arise πρὸς τὸ ἀποπλανᾶν, εἰ δυνατόν, τοὺς ἐκλεκτούς. In Mk. 13 and par. we read not only of seductive signs and wonders but also of the trial of sufferings in the last time. [39] Nevertheless, the word πειρασμός is rare in this connection. In the letter to Philadelphia we find in Rev. 3:10 the promise of deliverance ἐκ τῆς ὥρας τοῦ πειρασμοῦ τῆς μελλούσης ἔρχεσθαι ἐπὶ τῆς οἰκουμένης ὅλης, πειράσαι τοὺς κατοικοῦντας ἐπὶ τῆς γῆς. πειρασμός here is not so much the temptation of the individual; it is rather the total eschatological terror and tribulation of the last time. But it can also be the temptation of the individual, cf. the prophecy to the church at Smyrna in Rev. 2:10: ἰδοὺ μέλλει βάλλειν ὁ διάβολος ἐξ ὑμῶν εἰς φυλακὴν ἵνα πειρασθῆτε. [40] The aim of the διάβολος (→ II, 79-81) is to overthrow Christians. The more urgent, then, is the admonition to be faithful (Rev. 2:10b, cf. Jm. 1:12) and to rest in the assurance that the Lord will protect those who are His: οἶδεν κύριος εὐσεβεῖς ἐκ πειρασμοῦ ῥύεσθαι, 2 Pt. 2:9.

d. From early times the meaning of the 6th petition of the Lord's Prayer has been debated. Though Mt. 6:13 and Lk. 11:4 are the same in all the MSS: καὶ

---

[36] → παιδεύω, V, 596-625 passim, esp. under B. 3 and C. 3; cf. Korn, 13 n.

[37] In the NT 2 C. 13:5: ἑαυτοὺς πειράζετε ... ἑαυτοὺς δοκιμάζετε shows how readily δοκιμάζειν and πειράζειν may be interchanged, → 28, 28-31.

[38] The need for ὑπομονή in temptations is also mentioned in Hb., which in 2:18 calls all Christians πειραζόμενοι. In c. 11 Hb. then lists the righteous of the old covenant as examples of this ὑπομονή (and πίστις), and in 12:2 f. ref. is made to the exemplary patience of Jesus. In 10:36 an appeal is made to the readers: ὑπομονῆς γὰρ ἔχετε χρείαν, ἵνα ... κομίσησθε τὴν ἐπαγγελίαν, → IV, 588, 5 ff. On Hb. 11:17, 37 → n. 57.

[39] Cf. E. Stauffer, Theol. d. NT⁴ (1948) § 53: "The full revelation of antichrist."

[40] The continuation (καὶ ἕξετε θλῖψιν ἡμερῶν δέκα) shows that there is here an allusion to Da. 1:12, 14.

μὴ εἰσενέγκῃς ἡμᾶς εἰς πειρασμόν, Marcion already reads: καὶ μὴ ἀφῇς ἡμᾶς εἰσενεχθῆναι εἰς πειρασμόν. [41] He takes the petition to be a request for God's protection against temptation. [42] The petition is not related to Ps. 139:23, which asks God to try the heart. If it were, it would have to be the direct opposite: Lead us into temptation. [43] What is at issue here is in no sense a test. The Lord is rather teaching His disciples to ask God not to withdraw His hand from them, but to keep them against temptation by ungodly powers. On the other hand, it is a mistake to think that the petition is grounded only in Jesus' imminent expectation of the end or to regard it merely as a request for preservation in the great eschatological tribulation. [44] Though it undoubtedly refers to this, a more general application to all affliction yields a better sense. It should not be forgotten, of course, that every affliction, and therewith every πειρασμός, is an eschatological tribulation or temptation according to the total understanding of the preaching of Jesus, → III, 144, 32-146, 20. [45] Lk. 8:13 is to be taken in the same sense. In the exposition of the parable of the Sower Lk., as distinct from Mk. 4:17 and Mt. 13:21: γενομένης θλίψεως ἢ διωγμοῦ διὰ τὸν λόγον, has Jesus utter words of warning to those who πρὸς καιρὸν πιστεύουσιν καὶ ἐν καιρῷ πειρασμοῦ ἀφίστανται. This interpretation is perhaps secondary. [46] Nevertheless, Luke's substitution of πειρασμός for διωγμός or θλῖψις διὰ τὸν λόγον shows what he understands by the term. [47] For him πειρασμός consists in persecution and oppression for the faith. There can be little doubt that he took the 6th petition of the Lord's Prayer in the same way.

In Mk. 14:38 and par. (in Lk. cf. also 22:40) Jesus says to the three disciples in the Garden of Gethsemane: γρηγορεῖτε καὶ προσεύχεσθε, ἵνα μὴ ἔλθητε εἰς πειρασμόν· τὸ μὲν πνεῦμα πρόθυμον, ἡ δὲ σὰρξ ἀσθενής. [48] The verse is related to the numerous NT passages which exhort to watchfulness, → II, 338, 28-339, 2. Here, however, the reason offered is not the imminence of the last events (cf. Mk. 13:35-37 and par.; 1 Th. 5:6; Rev. 3:2 f.; 16:15) but the weakness and susceptibility of the flesh (→ σάρξ). In content the warning corresponds to that

---

[41] Cf. the critical apparatus in Nestle on Lk. 11:4.

[42] An understanding also found in Tertullian, De Oratione, 8 (ne nos inducas in temptationem, id est, ne nos patiaris induci ab eo utique qui temptat) and many others (Luther's Smaller Catechism: "That the devil, the world and our flesh may not deceive and seduce us").

[43] Cf. E. Lohmeyer, Das Vater-unser² (1947), 134-146.

[44] So esp. A. Schweitzer, Das Messianitäts- u. Leidensgeheimnis² (1929), 84-86, also R. Eisler, "Das letzte Abendmahl," ZNW, 24 (1925), 191. Nor can one construe πειρασμός here simply as "suffering," "affliction," so K. Knoke, "Der urspr. Sinn d. 6. Bitte," NKZ, 18 (1907), 200-220. A. Harnack, "Zwei Worte Jesu. 1. Zur 6. Bitte des Vaterunsers (Mt. 6:13 = Lk. 11:4)," SAB (1907), 942-947 tried to see in the 6th petition no more than a request for protection against an afflictio punitiva (penal suffering). The attempt of C. Jaeger, "A propos de deux passages du sermon sur la montagne," Revue d'histoire et de philosophie religieuse, 18 (1938), 415-418 to take Mt. 6:13 in the sense of "prevent us from doubting thy help and power" (as Satan tempts us to do) hardly corresponds to the wording of the petition. Cf. also Lohmeyer, loc. cit.; H. Greeven, Gebet u. Eschatologie im NT (1931), 93-95; D. Bonhoeffer, Versuchung (1953).

[45] Lohmeyer, op. cit., 144-146.

[46] Cf. J. Jeremias, Die Gleichnisse Jesu² (1952), 60 f.

[47] Comparison of the 3 Synoptic Gospels suggests that it is Lk. who makes the substitution.

[48] Cf. K. G. Kuhn, "Jesus in Gethsemane," Ev. Theol., 12 (1952/53), 260-285. Kuhn, who analyses the incident closely, refers in interpretation to analogous ideas in the Manual of Discipline.

of 1 Pt. 5:8: νήψατε, γρηγορήσατε· ὁ ἀντίδικος ὑμῶν διάβολος ὡς λέων ὠρυό-
μενος περιπατεῖ ζητῶν τινα καταπιεῖν· ᾧ ἀντίστητε στερεοὶ τῇ πίστει. There
is also a close connection with the 6th petition of the Lord's Prayer; watching
consists in prayer in view of our defencelessness in temptation.

e. The personification ὁ πειράζων is very rare in the NT. Outside the story
of the temptation in Mt. 4:1-11 (→ 34, 13 ff.) we find it only in 1 Th. 3:5, where
Paul asks concerning the faith of the Thessalonians μή πως ἐπείρασεν ὑμᾶς ὁ
πειράζων καὶ εἰς κενὸν γένηται ὁ κόπος ἡμῶν. ὁ πειράζων here means Satan,
whom Paul more commonly describes as σατανᾶς, and whose work according
to 1 C. 7:5 consists in the πειράζειν of believers. [49] This is how we are to understand the work of Satan in Paul even where he is not called the author of πειρασμός. Nevertheless, we must beware of schematisation. [50] Each passage has to
be taken in context. Perhaps the difficult saying in Gl. 4:14: καὶ τὸν πειρασμὸν
ὑμῶν ἐν τῇ σαρκί μου οὐκ ἐξουθενήσατε, means that Paul rejoices that the
Galatians did not fall victim to the tempter, who sought to exploit the apostle's
sickness. [51] But we do not have to take it thus, for the general interpretation:
"You did not succumb to the temptation to despise me because of the weakness
of my flesh," is an adequate rendering of the verse. [52] Rather weaker is 1 Tm. 6:9,
where those who would be rich are warned against the πειρασμός, παγίς and
ἐπιθυμίαι to which they can easily fall victim. Here, too, one may easily think
of Satan as the author of the snare and lusts as well as the temptation, → V,
595, 7-10. But there is no explicit reference.

2. Man Tempts God.

Like the OT (→ 27, 21), the NT recognises that man tempts God. Twice in
the NT the idea is taken from the OT. In 1 C. 10:9 Paul is alluding to ψ 77:18
when he says that the Israelites tempted God in the wilderness and God answered
by sending serpents among them (Nu. 21:5 f.); this illustration is designed to
warn the Corinthians against disobedience of the same kind. Perhaps the thought
is best brought out by the rendering "to challenge God." V. 13a fits in well with
this. The other passage is Hb. 3:8 f. = ψ 94:8 f. (cf. Ex. 17:1-7). This, too, contains a warning: "Be careful not to miss the σήμερον and therefore not to defy
God in disobedience instead of yielding to Him." Two further references occur
in Ac. 5:9 and 15:10, both on the lips of Peter. In the former he is speaking to
Sapphira, who with her husband has tempted the Spirit of the Lord by reporting
falsely on the proceeds of the sale. What is meant is that the couple, by their
conduct, have challenged the Spirit of the Lord, who searches all things (1 C. 2:10),
whether He would observe the deception. In 15:10 Peter warns the assembly
against imposing the Law on Gentile Christians. As he sees it, to do this would
be to challenge God, who by the revelation in the house of Cornelius, which was
known in Jerusalem, had shown the freedom of Gentile Christians from the Law
to be in accordance with His will.

---

[49] Cf. Bultmann Theol., 253 f.
[50] Kuhn, loc. cit., finds too strong a uniformity in the NT use of πειρασμός.
[51] On the text and exegesis v. the comm. and J. de Zwaan, "Gl. 4:14 aus dem Neu-
griechischen erklärt," ZNW, 10 (1909), 246-250.
[52] Cf. Ltzm. Gl., ad loc. The οὐδὲ ἐξεπτύσατε can serve only to explain the origin of
the sickness by demonic influences; it cannot be the basis for an interpretation of πειρασμός.
Cf. also → I, 492, 29-493, 14.

III. The Temptations of Jesus. [53]

1. Among the NT epistles Hb. emphasises with particular urgency the fact that Jesus was tempted during His life on earth. If it does so chiefly in passages designed to strengthen the readers in their temptations and conflicts, there is still no doubt that the life of Jesus is here understood as a life in temptation. 2:18: ἐν ᾧ γὰρ πέπονθεν αὐτὸς πειρασθείς, δύναται τοῖς πειραζομένοις βοηθῆσαι. 4:15: οὐ γὰρ ἔχομεν ἀρχιερέα μὴ δυνάμενον συμπαθῆσαι ταῖς ἀσθενείαις ἡμῶν, πεπειρασμένον δὲ κατὰ πάντα καθ᾽ ὁμοιότητα χωρὶς ἁμαρτίας. These sayings, especially the second, make it plain that the 1st century was already asking whether Jesus could be tempted, and that the author of Hb. was answering this question in the affirmative. Otherwise he certainly could not call the temptation a πειράζεσθαι καθ᾽ ὁμοιότητα, for his whole point was to emphasise that the temptation of Jesus is like ours. [54] In other words, it carried with it the possibility that He might fall, → V, 190, 1-3. Nevertheless, Hb. also recognises a distinction from us. Jesus remained χωρὶς ἁμαρτίας even in temptations. In this respect He was quite different from all other men. It is true that these two statements can hardly be brought into logical harmony. Two main points are made by them, first, that Jesus is in all ways like men who are tempted, and second, that He is completely unlike men who in temptations do not remain χωρὶς ἁμαρτίας. [55] If one asks what temptations Hb. has in view, 5:7-9 refers us first to the hour in the Garden of Gethsemane. In the conflict which preceded His true passion, Jesus was here confronted by the terror of death, and then — καίπερ ὢν υἱός — He learned obedience through suffering. Once again it may be seen that the content of temptation is the seduction into disobedience. That is to say, the temptation placed the Lord in a situation of open choice between surrender to God's will and revolt against it. [56] But the Lord came out of temptation victorious (τελειωθείς — χωρὶς ἁμαρτίας). Hb. 2:18 — πέπονθεν πειρασθείς — also has in view the temptations which came upon Jesus in His suffering, → V, 917, 10 ff. In 12:3 there is reference to the contradiction which He experienced at the hands of His

---

[53] Bibl.: H. Willrich, "Zur Versuchung Jesu," ZNW, 4 (1903), 349 f.; A. Harnack, *Sprüche u. Reden Jesu* (1907), 32-37; F. Spitta, *Zur Gesch. u. Lit. d. Urchr.*, III, 2 (1907), 1-108; A. Meyer, "Die evangelischen Berichte über d. Versuchung Jesu," *Festgabe H. Blümner* (1914), 434-468; D. Völter, "Die Versuchung Jesu," *Nieuw Theologisch Tijdschrift*, 6 (1917), 348-365; E. Böklen, "Zu d. Versuchung Jesu," ZNW, 18 (1917/18), 244-248; P. Ketter, "Die Versuchung Jesu," *Nt.liche Abh.*, VI, 3 (1918), with full bibl. pp. VII ff.; B. Violet, "Der Aufbau d. Versuchungsgeschichte," *Harnack-Ehrung* (1921), 14-21; M. Albertz, *Die synopt. Streitgespräche* (1921), 41-48, 165; N. Freese, *Die Versuchung Jesu nach d. Synpt.*, Diss. Halle (1922); "Die Versuchlichkeit Jesu," ThStKr, 96/97 (1925), 313-318; S. Eitrem-A. Fridrichsen, *Die Versuchung Christi* (1924); Clemen, 214-218; H. J. Vogels, "Die Versuchungen Jesu," BZ, 17 (1926), 238-255; S. Hirsch, *Taufe, Versuchung u. Verklärung Jesu* (1932); E. Lohmeyer, "Die Versuchung Jesu," ZSTh, 14 (1937), 619-650; E. Fascher, *Jesus u. d. Satan* (1949); R. Schnackenburg, "Der Sinn d. Versuchung Jesu bei d. Synpt.," *Theol. Quart.*, 132 (1952), 297-326. On the question whether Jesus can be tempted acc. to Hb. cf. K. Bornhäuser, "Die Versuchungen Jesu nach dem Hb.," *Theol. Studien f. M. Kähler* (1905), 69-86; Wnd. Hb. Exc. on 4:15; Mi. Hb.⁸ Exc. on 4:15.

[54] We can only regard as misjudged the attempt of Freese, ThStKr (→ n. 53) to show that Jesus was without ἐπιθυμία, v. Jn. 1:14.

[55] Cf. on this J. Schniewind, *Mt.* (*NT Deutsch*), on 4:1 ff.

[56] The suggestion of J. Jeremias, "Hb. 5:7-10," ZNW, 44 (1952/53), 107-111, that the content of the petition in Hb. 5:7 is deliverance from death which has already taken place rather than from the threat of death (the usual interpretation) can hardly be adopted in view of Hb. 4:15; the temptations of Jesus are temptation κατὰ πάντα καθ᾽ ὁμοιότητα with us.

opponents, and which did not wear Him down. The context compels us to see in this contradiction a temptation to grow weary, and consequently to fall; but He victoriously withstood it. [57] It is impossible to say whether Hb. has in mind the attacks and tempting questions recorded in the Synoptics. The author might well have been familiar with this tradition. The Synoptists commonly introduce such questions with the verb (ἐκ)πειράζειν, Mk. 8:11 and par.; 10:2 and par.; 12:15 and par.; Mt. 22:35; Lk. 10:25; 11:16 [Jn. 8:6]; cf. also the interpolation τί με πειράζετε in Lk. 20:23 AD. Nevertheless, Hb. does not speak of such temptations elsewhere; the temptation as Hb. sees it is always to avoid suffering. In the Synoptic passages we do not have temptation καθ᾽ ὁμοιότητα. It is also doubtful, then, whether the author of Hb. knew the temptation story (Mt. 4:1-11 and par.), to which he never alludes.

2. The Synoptic account of the temptation (Mt. 4:1-11 and par.), in which the πειράζων comes to Jesus in person, is placed immediately after the story of the baptism of Jesus and just before the commencement of His public ministry. This order already underscores its significance. The πειράζων (→ 32, 5-22) attempts to turn Jesus from the task which God has laid upon Him in His baptism, and therewith to render His mission impossible. He exerts himself in every possible way to deflect Jesus from obedience to God. [58] In this respect it makes no difference whether the temptations come at the end of the 40 days and nights (Mt. 4:2 f.) or whether they take place during this period (Mk. 1:13 and obviously also Lk. 4:2). Their essence remains the same, namely, that Jesus should be unfaithful to His Messianic task. The story presupposes, then, that Jesus is obedient. He is aware of His Messianic task, and the individual temptations are a threefold repetition of the fact that He remains obedient. [59] These ideas already underlie the brief mention in Mk. 1:12 f., where we read: ἦν ... πειραζόμενος ὑπὸ τοῦ σατανᾶ, → II, 79-81. They are worked out in Mk. 4:1-11 and Lk. 4:1-13. [60] The πειράζων (Mt. 4:3; Lk. has διάβολος) makes three attempts to reduce Jesus to disobedience. In the first he tests the power of Jesus, and tries to induce Him to use it for purposes which are not in keeping with His divine mission, → 19, 12 ff.

---

[57] In Hb. 11:37, acc. to אA and many other MSS, ἐπειράσθησαν is among the dangers which the great men of salvation history underwent. In the context this can only mean that they were tempted but did not fall. Contradiction and suffering did not wear them down. But ἐπειράσθησαν can hardly be original, cf. A. Debrunner, "Über einige Lesarten d. Chester Beatty Pap. d. NT," Coniectanea Neotestamentica, 11 (1947), 44 f. Hb. 11:17 adduces the example of steadfast Abraham (Gn. 22:1 ff.), → 26, 1-5.

[58] A review of the most diversified interpretations of the Synoptic temptation story, and esp. of attempts to eliminate the figure of the πειράζων, is given by Fascher, op. cit. (→ n. 53). The thesis of K. H. Rengstorf, Lk. (NT Deutsch), on 4:1 ff., that the temptation is simply a test which is ultimately conducted by God Himself, hardly does justice to the account or to the description of the personal intervention of Satan.

[59] The development of the Synpt. temptation story cannot be explained with certainty. Albertz (→ n. 53) regards it as a problem (44), but thinks it derives from Jesus Himself (48). Acc. to Bultmann Trad., 271-275 it reflects scribal Haggada and Rabb. disputation, cf. also Kuhn, 221 f. and → n. 68.

[60] On the literary problem cf. the bibl. in → n. 53. As regards order, most exegetes favour Mt. on account of the unmistakable crescendo, but Böklen and Violet, e.g., regard Lk. as original. Cf. also T. W. Manson, The Sayings of Jesus (1950), 43 f. On the question of pars. in religious history (the battle of the gods for world dominion, the temptation of Buddha etc.) cf. Clemen and esp. Eitrem, op. cit. None of these contributes to our understanding of the temptation of Jesus. Fridrichsen, op. cit.: "The religious pars ... are not of such a sort as to offer the key to an understanding of the story in Mt. 4:1-11 ..." (27).

Jesus rebuffs him with the text Dt. 8:3b. The point of the answer lies in the reference to the power of God, to which alone Jesus yields, not turning from obedience to God by independent use of the power with which God has endowed Him. On the second occasion the tempter tries to get Jesus to invoke God's help on His own behalf, and this time he, too, appeals to a text (ψ 90:11 f.). Jesus again replies from Scripture (Dt. 6:16): οὐκ ἐκπειράσεις κύριον τὸν θεόν σου. It would be tempting God, and therefore acting contrary to His word and commandment, to seek His help for selfish reasons which are not in harmony with God's will. The third temptation is the most comprehensive. The διάβολος (Mt. 4:8; Lk. 4:6) is quite plainly seeking to induce Jesus to give up His obedience to God and to follow himself, Satan. The third time, too, Jesus answers with a text (Dt. 6:13): κύριον τὸν θεόν σου προσκυνήσεις καὶ αὐτῷ μόνῳ λατρεύσεις, and He prefaces this refusal with the words ὕπαγε, σατανᾶ, Mt. 4:10. In each answer, then. Jesus confirms His allegiance to God. He remains in union with God, and does not abuse His divine Sonship, the authority of the Messiah. [61]

Further temptation is seen by the Synoptists only in Gethsemane. Nevertheless, one must ask whether Lk. at least, when he concludes the temptation story with the words καὶ συντελέσας πάντα πειρασμὸν ὁ διάβολος ἀπέστη ἀπ᾽ αὐτοῦ ἄχρι καιροῦ (4:13), does not hint at renewed temptation by the διάβολος in the life and work of Jesus. Lk. 22:28 especially seems to fit in with this. Here Jesus says to His disciples : ὑμεῖς δέ ἐστε οἱ διαμεμενηκότες μετ᾽ ἐμοῦ ἐν τοῖς πειρασμοῖς μου. [62] Here, however, it is more natural to take the plural πειρασμοί in the sense of "dangers," "afflictions," "troubles." [63] In the light of this passage one cannot suppose that in Lk. the life of Jesus is a long series of temptations. It is also not very clear how Jesus could say of His disciples that they stood by Him in temptations. [64] We have referred already to the tempting questions and challenges of the opponents of Jesus, → 28, 33-41. One can hardly regard these as temptations in the sense of Mt. 4:1-11 and par. This is also apparent from the fact that in the so-called question of the Pharisees (Mk. 12:13-17 and par.) the tempting purpose of the questioners is characterised as follows: Mk. 12:13: ἵνα αὐτὸν ἀγρεύσωσιν λόγῳ, "that they might trap him with an (incautious) word"; [65] Mt. 22:15: ὅπως αὐτὸν παγιδεύσωσιν ἐν λόγῳ "to entangle him with a (specific) expression"; [66] Lk. 20:20: ἵνα ἐπιλάβωνται αὐτοῦ λόγου. In Mk. 12:15 and Mt. 22:18 Jesus prefaces His answer by the counter-question τί με πειράζετε. There can be not the slightest doubt but that this πειράζειν is to be understood only along the lines of the corresponding words of introduction to which we have

---

[61] So Schniewind, ad loc., who rightly finds pars. in the temptation of the people of Israel in the desert. On Adam-Christ typology in the temptation story → I, 141, 14 ff.

[62] H. Conzelmann, "Zur Lukasanalyse," ZThK, 49 (1952), 29 thinks that Lk. 22:3 takes up 4:13 and thus introduces the account of the passion with the words : "Satan was present again." But this sheds no great light, nor can one say that "the characteristic term πειρασμός now appears with frequency." Apart from 22:28 we find it only in 22:40, 46, and here with ref. only to the disciples.

[63] → n. 35. Cf. also the great no. of related terms and concepts in the NT associated with → ἀγών, ἀγωνίζεσθαι, I, 136, 35-139, 22, → δόκιμος, II, 260, 1-26, → θλῖψις, III, 143, 15-148, 24; → ὑπομένειν, IV, 586, 15-588, 39, → πόνος.

[64] So Korn, 76-86. Fascher, 37 also reads too much out of Lk. 22:28. Cf. again G. Bertram, NT u. historische Methode (1928), 31-35; also Die Entwicklung zur sittlichen Persönlichkeit im Urchr. (1931), 6-9.

[65] So Pr.-Bauer, s.v. ἀγρεύω.

[66] Ibid., s.v. παγιδεύω; → V, 595, 40-596, 2.

referred. There can be no question of an attack of Satan in and with the words of the questioners. At most one might perceive a temptation in the words of Peter after the first intimation of the passion, since Jesus here rebuffs him with the same words as He used to Satan in the temptation story at Mt. 4:10: ὕπαγε ὀπίσω μου, σατανᾶ (Mk. 8:33 and par.). The continuation brings this out even more clearly: οὐ φρονεῖς τὰ τοῦ θεοῦ, ἀλλὰ τὰ τῶν ἀνθρώπων. The remark of Peter is thus characterised as an attempt to turn Jesus from obedience to God. Elsewhere in the Synoptic Gospels, however, there is no express account of a temptation of Jesus between the temptation story and the depiction of Jesus in Gethsemane.

That the prayer of Jesus in Gethsemane (Mk. 14:32-42 and par.) is regarded as a prayer in temptation may be seen from Hb. 5:7 → 33, 20 f. Nevertheless, the word πειρασμός is not used in the story with reference to Jesus Himself. Jesus Himself, however, says that the hour was one of explicit temptation for the disciples: γρηγορεῖτε καὶ προσεύχεσθε, ἵνα μὴ ἔλθητε εἰς πειρασμόν (Mk. 14:38 and par.), → 31, 23-29. The passion of Jesus and the cry ἐλωΐ ἐλωΐ λαμὰ σαβαχθάνι in Mk. 15:34 enable us to appreciate once again the terrible nature of the temptation. [67] But the term πειρασμός does not occur. As the Synoptists describe it, and in spite of Lk. 4:13, Jesus' battle with the tempter in the wilderness represents His definitive decision for subjection to the will of God ; every other decision for obedience flows from it. [68]

Jn. has no express account of any temptations of Jesus. Neither the temptation story nor the saying of Peter, neither Gethsemane nor the cry of dereliction, is to be found in his Gospel. He does, however, report sayings of Jesus which indicate that he was not wholly ignorant of the temptation tradition. Cf. Jn. 12:27: νῦν ἡ ψυχή μου τετάρακται, καὶ τί εἴπω; πάτερ, σῶσόν με ἐκ τῆς ὥρας ταύτης, 14:30 : ἔρχεται γὰρ ὁ τοῦ κόσμου ἄρχων· καὶ ἐν ἐμοὶ οὐκ ἔχει οὐδέν. The last word on the cross acc. to Jn. also pts. in the same direction, 19:30 : τετέλεσται. Jesus dies when He has victoriously finished His work. These are, however, only obscure hints.

Seesemann

πεισμονή → 9, 8 ff.
πέμπω → I, 398 ff.

---

[67] Cf. LXX 2 Ch. 32:31: "The Lord left him (Hezekiah), to try him, that he might know what was in his heart." But the par. is purely formal, since the temptation of Jesus was not a test of this kind. Korn, 67. Cf. W. Hasenzahl, "Die Gottverlassenheit des Christus," BFTh, 39, 1 (1937).

[68] In contrast to the view represented here Kuhn (→ n. 25) finds in the temptation story only a dialogue after the manner of a Rabb. disputation in which Jesus defeats the devil with the right verses from Scripture. For him, therefore, the idea of temptation is present in pure form only at Lk. 22:28, where the word πειρασμοί characterises the whole life of Jesus as one under assault.

| πένης, πενιχρός | → πτωχός. |

† πένης.

A. Secular Greek.

πένης, related to πένομαι "to work hard," πόνος, "hard work,"[1] denotes the one who, having few possessions, must support himself by his industry, Xenoph. Mem., IV, 2, 37; Plat. Resp., VIII, 553c; Aristot. Pol., VI, 1, p. 1317b, 40; Arrian Anabasis, II, 3, 2. Artisans and small builders working for themselves are to be numbered esp. among the πένητες, Ps.-Xenophon Resp. Ath., 1, 2 f.; Aristoph. Pl., 511, 532 ff. The limits between πενία and πλοῦτος naturally vary acc. to time, status and person, but there is a clear distinction between πένης and the beggar (→ πτωχός)[2] or the needy (ἐνδεής). The πένητες are not the poor in our sense ; they are not the objects of private or public benevolence (quite the reverse, ψ 111:9; cf. 2 K. 9:9). The πένης stands to the πλούσιος in only relative antithesis (less and greater wealth), the one great difference being that the rich man can live on his income without working, Aristoph. Pl., 528, 532 ff. The two groups are in fact close to one another and sometimes merge into one another. The πένης, too, can hold slaves, and in favourable circumstances the artisan may be said

---

π έ ν η ς. J. H. Schmidt, *Synonymik d. gr. Sprache*, II (1878), 611-625; IV (1886), 388-393; Trench, 120-122; Moult.-Mill., 502; A. Rahlfs, עָנִי u. עָנָו in d. *Ps.* (1892); W. Nowack, *Die sozialen Probleme in Israel u. deren Bedeutung f. d. religiöse Entwicklung dieses Volkes* (1892); A. C. Paterson, Art. "Poor," EB, III, 3808-3811; R. Kittel, Art. "Armengesetzgebung bei d. Hebräern," RE, 2, 60-63; E. Sellin, *Beiträge z. isr. u. jüd. Religionsgeschichte*, II (1897), 284-291; A. van Iterson, *Armenzorg bij de joden in Palestina (100 B.C.-200 A.D.)*, Diss. Leiden (1911); W. W. Baudissin, "Die at.liche Religion u. d. Armen," *Pr. Jahrb.*, 149 (1912), 193-231; S. Mowinckel, *Psalmenstudien*, I (1916), 113-117; II (1925), 58-65; F. Hauck, *Die Stellung d. Urchr. zu Arbeit u. Geld* (1921); E. Lohmeyer, *Soziale Fragen im Urchr.* (1921); M. Weber, *Gesammelte Aufsätze zur Religionssoziologie*, III : "Das antike Judentum" (1921); A. Causse, *Les "pauvres" d'Israël* (1922); H. Bruppacher, *Die Beurteilung d. Armut im AT* (1924); Str.-B., I, 818-826; II, 643-647; IV, Index, *s.v.* "Armut"; J. Lewkowitz, Art. "Armut," Jüd. Lex., I, 477 f.; J. Hemmelrijk, Πενία en Πλοῦτος, Diss. Utrecht (1925); R. Pöhlmann, *Gesch. d. sozialen Frage u.d. Sozialismus in d. antiken Welt*, I, II³ (1925); E. Sachsse, " 'Ānī als Ehrenbezeichnung in inschriftlicher Beleuchtung," *Festschr. E. Sellin* (1927), 105-111; M. Lurje, *Studien zur Gesch. der wirtschaftlichen u. sozialen Verhältnisse im isr.-jüd. Reich*, = ZAW Beih., 45 (1927); J. Jeremias, *Jerusalem z. Zt. Jesu*, II : "Die sozialen Verhältnisse. A. Reich u. arm" (1934); R. Kittel, *Die Ps.³* (1929), 284-288 (Exc. "Die Armen u. Elenden im Ps."); J. Heller, Art. "Armut in d. Bibel," Encyclopaedia Judaica, III (1929), 368-370; A. Marmorstein, Art. "Armut im Talmud," *ibid.*, 370-393, esp. 374; J. J. van Manen, Πενία en Πλοῦτος *in de periode na Alexander*, Diss. Utrecht (1931); H. Birkeland, 'Ani u. 'Anaw in den Ps. (1933); H. Greeven, *Die Hauptprobleme d. Sozialethik in d. neueren Stoa u. im Urchr.* (1935), 62-112; E. Kalt, Bibl. Reallex.² (1938), 133-137; H. Bolkestein, *Wohltätigkeit u. Armenpflege im vorchr. Altertum* (1939); H. Bolkestein and A. Kalsbach, Art. "Armut I (Beurteilung d. Armut)," RAC, I, 698-705; A. Bigelmair, Art. "Armut II (freiwillige)," *ibid.*, 705-710; W. Schwer, Art. "Armenpflege," *ibid.*, 689-698; P. Humbert, "Le mot biblique 'ebyōn,' " *Revue d'histoire et de philosophie religieuses*, 32 (1952), 1-6.

[1] Walde-Pok., II, 661; Boisacq⁴, 766 f.; Hesych., *s.v.*: πένης = αὐτοδιάκονος.
[2] Aristoph. Pl., 551-554 : Πενία sharply forbids its equation with the wretched life of the πτωχός. The πένης lives simply by hard work, and if he has nothing over he has no lack.

to be wealthy, Aristot. Pol., III, 3, p. 1278a, 24; Plat. Resp., V, 465c; Ps.-Xenoph. Resp.
Ath., 1, 19; 1, 10. [3] On the other hand, χαλεπὴ πενία may mean the same as poverty,
Theogn., 182; Ps.-Xenoph. Resp. Ath., 1, 13. Acc. to Solon's legislation the πένητες are
the prop of democracy. This is the rule of the πένητες, Plat. Resp., VIII, 557a. Aristot.
sees two or three classes, the few πλούσιοι, and the mass of artisans, the πένητες, the
δῆμος, with sometimes the μέσοι between them, Aristot. Pol., VI, 1, p. 1318a, 31; IV, 9,
p. 1295b, 1-3; 1296a, 25. Since the πένητες play quite an active political role in Greece,
they are never regarded as oppressed or judicially disadvantaged, as in the OT, → 39,
12 ff. The idea that they have a particular helper and protector in God (→ 39, 15 ff.)
is thus alien to the Gk. world. [4] The ancient nobility sees in wealth (ὄλβος) the basis
of happiness ; to be forced to work is a misfortune, Hom. Od., 11, 489; Theogn., 181 f.;
525 f.; Eur. Fr., 327 (TGF, 458) the antithesis ὄλβιοι — πένης. It links the noblest
qualities with the state of nobility, ἀγαθός, ἐσθλός, Theogn., 173-192; Hes. Op., 313.
In contrast, after the time of Socrates, who said of himself that he lived ἐν πενίᾳ μυρίᾳ
(Plat. Ap., 23c; Stob. Ecl., V, 782, 10), the judgment gains ground that one's economic
situation is morally and spiritually neutral. Indeed, πενία is sometimes more favourably
regarded than πλοῦτος, Plat. Leg., II, 660e. [5] It is even γυμνάσιον ἀρετῆς. [6] Value
attaches to virtue alone. This makes us independent of contingent economic circumstances. The political theorists Plato and Aristot. think it desirable that extremes of
wealth and poverty should be avoided so far as possible, Plat. Leg., V, 744d; XI, 919b;
Aristot. Pol., IV, 9, p. 1295b, 9 ff., 40; Ps.-Xenoph. Resp. Ath., 1, 13. [7] The Gk. world is
inclined to find in πενία (cf. the connection between πονηρός, πόνος and πένης,
→ 37, 4) the cause of wrong action, Lys., 7, 14; Plat. Leg., XI, 919b. The Cynics criticise
extreme wealth to the point of contempt. Only κακόν is worse. πενία does not belong
to this. It is an impulse and thus an aid to curiosity, Diogenes in Stob. Ecl., V, 783, 2;
782, 18; also Fr., 39 (v. Arnim, III, 218, 16). He who has no possessions is free of many
worries. One should seek sufficiency (αὐτάρκεια), Teles, p. 7, 1-8, 6; Epict. Diss.,
III, 17, 9. Stoicism reckons πενία and πλοῦτος among the adiaphora. Only virtue is
good in the full sense, Chrysipp. Fr., 117 (v. Arnim, III, 28, 8); Epict. Diss., IV, 6, 3 ff.
Under the influence of philosophy Dio Chrys. in the Euboean address makes an express
apology for πενία in the ideal picture of the hunter's family living in simplicity and constant toil, Or., 7, 10-64, 82 ff.; 7, 9 : ὡς ἔστι πενία χρῆμα τῷ ὄντι ἱερὸν καὶ ἄσυλον.
Acc. to Plut., who is also under philosophical influence, πενία is nothing to be ashamed
of, Plut. De Exilio, 17 (II, 607a); Tranq. An., 6 (II, 467e). It should not cause any loss of
self-confidence. The only attitude to be desired is that of self-sufficiency on the basis of
a knowledge of the only true good. This makes our life rich in poverty and gives true
freedom, Plut. De Vitando Aere Alieno, 3 (II, 828c d); 6 (II, 830a); De Virtute et Vitio,
4 (II, 101d).

B. The Old Testament, Septuagint and Philo.

In the LXX πένης is mostly used for אֶבְיוֹן (29 times), then עָנִי (12), דַּל (9) and
רָשׁ (6), also occasionally for other words. Comparison of synonyms shows that the
LXX prefers πένης for אֶבְיוֹן, → πτωχός for עָנִי and דַּל, → πραΰς for עָנָו and → ταπεινός for שָׁפָל. [8] עָנִי ("one who is bowed down, in the position of a servant"), אֶבְיוֹן
("needy"), דַּל ("weak," "poor," Ex. 23:3; Lv. 14:21 etc.) and רָשׁ ("needy," "poor,"

---

[3] Hemelrijk, 26, 52 f.
[4] Bolkestein, 177-181.
[5] Acc. to Xenoph. Sym., 4, 34 f. πλοῦτος and πενία do not dwell ἐν οἴκῳ but ἐν ταῖς
ψυχαῖς, cf. Cyrop., VIII, 3, 39 ff.
[6] Arkesilaos in Stob. Ecl., V, 784, 13-16, cf. c. 32 πενίας ἔπαινος (V, 780-788); Hdt.,
VII, 102; Aristoph. Pl., 468 f., 532-534, 558 f., 576. Acc. to Plat. Symp., 203bc Ἔρως is
the son of Πόρος and Πενία.
[7] Bolkestein, 186.
[8] The differences are explained in part by the different usage of the individual authors

2 S. 12:1-4) are at first social terms. They denote the economically weak as distinct from the wealthy. The עָנִי is in the first instance one who has no patrimony and who has thus to earn his livelihood by working for others, esp. the day-labourer, Dt. 24:14 f.; Lv. 19:9 f.; 23:22. As distinct from the עֶבֶד he is a personally free wage-earner (שָׂכִיר). The true opposite of עָשִׁיר ("rich") is not עָנִי — it is not used in this way[9] — but רָשׁ 2 S. 12:1-4. The distinctive pt. in LXX usage is that πένης or πτωχός is not used uniformly for any one of the Heb. terms, which for their part merge into one another. Hence the original senses of πένης and πτωχός are blurred in the LXX; the two tend to be used as equivalents.[10]

Since the question of poverty in the OT is to be dealt with under → πτωχός there is needed here only a brief review of the use of πένης. The OT Law (πένης: book of the covenant, Ex. 23:6 אֶבְיוֹן; Dt. 15:11; 24:14 f. עָנִי; law of cleanness, Lv. 14:21 דַּל) already takes the socially weak under its protection.[11] The prophets fight against the oppression of the weak (with πένης: Am. [אֶבְיוֹן] 2:6; 4:1; 5:12; 8:4; Is. [עָנִי] 10:2; Jer. [אֶבְיוֹן] 20:13; 22:16; Ez. [אֶבְיוֹן] 16:49; 18:12; 22:29). The special feature in Israel is that the social demands have a religious basis. Yahweh is the Lord of all Israel. The lowly are also under His protection (with 2 S. 12:1-4; Jer. 20:13; ψ 9:12, 37; 21:26; 68:34; Job 34:28 etc.). In the exilic and post-exilic periods "poor," "lowly," becomes a religious concept, עָנִי וְאֶבְיוֹן, → πτωχός καὶ πένης, used as a self-designation of the righteous, esp. in the Ps. (ψ 39:17; 69:5; 85:1; 108:22).[12] The two words, both in Heb. and Gk., are often used as synonyms in parallelism, Am. 8:4; Ez. 16:49; 18:12; 22:29; Prv. 31:20; esp. ψ 9:18; 11:5; 34:10; 36:14 etc. When the Saviour King, himself called עָנִי in Zech. 9:9 → πραΰς, sets up his kingdom, he will exalt the lowly, ψ 71:4, 12 f. There is in the OT no ideal of poverty in the material sense. Normally wealth and prosperity are a reward for piety.[13] The rich man gives evidence of his piety in generosity to the poor, Ps. 112:9; Job, → πτωχός. Proverbial wisdom often deals with the subject of rich and poor. Without extenuation poverty is regarded as an evil, Prv. 10:15; 31:7. Often, in distinction from the Law and prophets, this literature thinks it is merited and warns against it, Prv. 6:11; 13:18; 24:34; 28:19; 30:9. The distinction between πένης and πτωχός is often made. The wise man, who does not fail to see the darker side of riches, asks God neither for wealth nor for πενία — he cannot possibly pray for πτωχεία — but for what is necessary and sufficient, 30:8. The LXX bases its warning against oppressing the lowly (πένης, Prv. 22:22) upon his need of help (πτωχὸς γάρ ἐστιν, in both instances דַּל in the original). One may enrich oneself by wronging the πένης (Prv. 22:16), but to do so is to despise one's Creator (14:31). When Sir. 34:20 warns against the religious abuse of the socially superior bringing an offering ἐκ χρημάτων πενήτων, the latter

---

and translators: Job and Qoh. in the LXX only πένης. Prv. prefers, e.g., דַּל and רָשׁ, LXX in Prv. and Sir. → πτωχός, probably connected with the fact that in both books the antithesis of rich and poor is prominent. In some 30 of the 75 or so instances of πένης in the LXX it is used as a synon. alongside πτωχός. On אֶבְיוֹן as the man who prays for God's grace in affliction cf. Humbert, 6.

[9] Rahlfs, 74. That עָנִי does not originally mean "poor" is shown by the noun עֳנִי, which always has the sense of "oppression," "suffering," "misery." ענה, "to take a lowly place," pi "to humiliate," "treat badly"; Assyr. enu "to bend," "suppress"; Arab. anin "prisoner," "slave." Cf. Lewkowitz, 477; → Paterson, 3808-3811.

[10] Thus we read, e.g., in ψ 106:41: ἐβοήθησεν πένητι ἐκ πτωχείας, 'Α ὑπερεπαρεῖ πτωχὸν ἐκ πενίας.

[11] For the poor elsewhere in the ancient Orient cf. on Egypt Bolkestein, 5-8; J. Fichtner, Altorientalische Weisheit in ihrer isr.-jüd. Ausprägung, ZAW Beih., 62 (1933), 30 f.

[12] Rahlfs and Kittel.

[13] Cf. Abraham and Job. Poverty is not grounded in the will of God, so rightly Bruppacher, 29-32. Dt. 15:11 simply states how things are and on this ground appeals for brotherly love. There is no "must" (Luther) in the original of Prv. 22:2.

cannot be poor to the point of beggary. Qoh. [14] has a strong sense of the futility of riches (6:8). Wisdom (4:13 f.; 9:15 f.) and humility (5:7) give the πένης superiority over those who are higher placed.

Philo, who does not use πτωχός, has πένης even when the LXX uses the former (Lv. 19:10; 23:22; Virt., 90). After the persecution under Flaccus had robbed the Jews of their trading capital, they were πένητες, who lived in poverty and could hardly provide the essentials of life, Flacc., 143. [15]

C. The New Testament.

πένης occurs only once in the NT at 2 C. 9:9. The verse is a quotation from Ps. 112(111):9, which depicts the good fortune and conduct of those who fear God, and which in so doing emphasises mercy to the poor as a special proof of piety. Paul, too, speaks of this as one of πᾶν ἔργον ἀγαθόν (though → 38, 7 ff. and 39, 26 ff.). With the LXX, πένης here carries with it the sense of needing help (original (אֶבְיוֹנִים). Elsewhere the NT describes poverty in terms of πτωχός, once (Lk. 21:2) → πενιχρός, and once (Ac. 4:34) ἐνδεής.

† πενιχρός.

Of persons and things, "very poor," "needy," "wretched," Hom. Od., 3, 348 (with ἀνείμων, "without clothes"); Theogn., 165 f. (opp. ὄλβιος); Polyb., 6, 21, 7; Philo Som., I, 98 of the poor who must borrow money (Ex. 22:24), so that the lender by exacting interest πενιχρότερον ἀπεργαζόμενος τὸν πένητα, Spec. Leg., II, 75. Jos. Bell., 4, 207: The well-to-do hire πενιχροτέρους to guard duty in their place; women without dowry : Diod. S., 12, 18, 4 (ἄνευ προικός); 12, 24, 2; Plut. Apophth. Lac., 24 (II, 242b) (παρθένος); Amat., 9 (II, 754b) (so also with ἄμορφος); cf. BGU, IV, 1024, VIII, 12 (4th cent. B.C.): πενιχρὰ καὶ πρεσβύτης, ἥτις διὰ τὴν συνέχουσαν αὐτὴν πενίαν τὴν ἑαυτῆς [θυγ]ατέρα[ν] τῆς σωφροσύνης ἀπεστέρη[σεν]. Socrates in Stob. Ecl., III, 467, 11 antithetically : βίον ἔχοντα πενιχρὸν παρρησιάζεσθαι; Philodemus De Oeconomia col. XVI, 2 f.: πενιχρᾶι διαίτηι. Transf. Plat. Resp., IX, 578a (ψυχή); Philo Som., II, 213 (ἀπαιδευσία).

In the LXX only Ex. 22:24 (עָנִי): Prv. 29:7 (דַּל).

In the NT the only instance is at Lk. 21:2 for the "poor" widow (Mk. 12:42: πτωχή).

Hauck †

† πένθος, † πενθέω

A. The Greek Usage.

In Gk. πενθεῖν, used from the time of Hom., means abs. (intr.) "to mourn," "to grieve" (Hom. Od., 18, 174; Aesch. Pers., 545; Soph. Oed. Col., 1753) and also with acc. of obj. (trans.) "to bewail," → n. 4. The noun πένθος, also used from Hom., can mean

---

[14] Qoh. prefers מִסְכֵּן (4:13; 9:15 f.), LXX πένης.
[15] Manen, 15 f.

π ε ν ι χ ρ ό ς. J. H. Schmidt, *Synonymik d. gr. Sprache,* II (1878), 619 f.; J. J. van Manen, *op. cit.* (→ Bibl. πένης), 17 f.

both "sorrow," "grief," and also painful event or fact, e.g., Pind. Isthm., 7, 37; 8, 6; Hdt., III, 14; Soph. Ant., 1249. Originally πενθεῖν or πένθος denotes sorrow of heart, so that it is hard to differentiate from λυπεῖσθαι (→ IV, 313, 1 ff.). [1] Nevertheless, in most instances it is a sorrow which is outwardly expressed in some way, e.g. by tears or laments, or which is at least associated with such expressions. [2] In particular the phrase πένθος ποιεῖσθαι (Hdt., II, 1) or τιθέναι (Hdt., II, 46, cf. VI, 21) shows that πένθος can have the sense of public mourning. [3] The words are used esp. for mourning for the dead, [4] though also for other sufferings. [5]

Acc. to Stoic teaching πένθος is one of the πάθη, a sub-branch of λύπη (Chrysipp. Fr., 394, 413, 414 [v. Arnim, III, 96, 9; 100, 8, 27] → IV, 315, 21 ff.). The wise man must obviously steer clear of πένθος (ibid., 571 [v. Arnim, 151, 18 f.]; Epict. Diss., II, 13, 17; IV, 1, 52); for πενθεῖν rests on a false idea of real evil, Epict. Diss., III, 11, 2; cf. I, 11, 3; III, 3, 15; thus it is a punishment for the ἀπαίδευτος who does not obey the divine orders, Epict. Diss., IV, 4, 32. A common theme in popular philosophical literature is the senselessness of πένθος for the death of a relative, → V, 783, 15 ff. [6] Acc. to Plut. Cons. ad Apoll., 19 (II, 112a b) a philosopher tells Queen Arsinoe, who is mourning the death of her son, that Πένθος was not present when Zeus assigned the various honours of men to the gods, and that when all these had been allotted Zeus assigned to him lamentations for the dead. Πένθος, like the other gods, remains kindly disposed to those who honour him. How senseless it is then, to perpetuate sorrow by lamentation. [7] Acc. to Luc. Demon., 25 the Cynic Demonax promises Herod, when he is mourning the death of his son, that he will conjure up the shade of the deceased if Herod will tell him the names of three men who have never bewailed the dead. The impossibility of the condition is designed to show how foolish it is to take death so tragically.

B. πένθος and πενθέω in the LXX (and Judaism).

πένθος and πενθεῖν are frequently used in the LXX, mostly for derivates from the stem אבל. [8] Both noun and verb denote the sorrow expressed in tears, lamentations and

---

π έ ν θ ο ς. [1] [So Debrunner, who tries to show that this is always true]. In fact πενθεῖν means "to sorrow" even when there is no external expression, Plat. Phaedr., 258b (opp. γεγηθώς), so also πένθος Hom. Od., 18, 324; 24, 423; Aesch. Choeph., 83; Soph. Oed. Tyr., 94.

[2] For lamentation cf. Aesch. Pers., 545 : πενθοῦσι γόοις ἀκορεστοτάτοις (cf. Hom. Il., 17, 37, where γόος and πένθος are combined); Soph. Oed. Col., 1751 ff.: παύετε θρήνων ... πενθεῖν οὐ χρή. Tears are a sign of πενθεῖν: Hom. Od., 18, 173 f.; cf. Epict. Diss., I, 9, 20 and Aesch. Choeph., 334 : πολυδάκρυτα πένθη. As acc. to Plut. Cons. ad Apoll., 19 f. personified Πένθος is honoured with δάκρυα, λῦπαι and θρῆνοι, so πενθεῖν is often combined with or made a par. of λυπεῖσθαι (Epict. Diss., III, 11, 2; IV, 4, 32), also θρηνεῖν (ibid., III, 11, 2), στενάζειν or στένειν (ibid., I, 6, 29 and 38; II, 13, 17; IV, 4, 32), οἰμώζειν (ibid., IV, 4, 32; cf. I, 4, 23 : πένθη καὶ οἰμωγαί), and ὀδύρεσθαι (I, 6, 38).

[3] For rites accompanying or expressing πένθος cf. Hdt., VI, 21 and Eur. Alc., 425-431.

[4] Hom. Il., 19, 225; Aesch. Pers., 296, 579; Plut. Cons. ad Apoll., 19 f. (II, 111e-112b); Luc. Demon., 24 f.; in all these instances πενθεῖν with acc.; Epict. Diss., III, 3, 15 with ἐπί and dat. πένθος for mourning for the dead : Hom. Il., 17, 37; Hdt., II, 1, 46; VI, 21; Aesch. Pers., 322; Eur. Alc., 426; Plut. Cons. ad Apoll., 19 (II, 111 f-112b); Luc. Demon., 25. πένθος is defined by Stoicism as λύπη ἐπὶ θανάτῳ (or τελευτῇ) ἀώρῳ Chrysipp. Fr., 413, 414 (v. Arnim, III, 100, 8, 27). The Lat. equivalent is luctus (Fr., 415, v. Arnim, III, 101, 12).

[5] For πενθεῖν : Soph. Oed. Col., 739 (τὰ πήματα); Eur. Med., 268 (τύχας); for πένθος : Hom. Il., 11, 658; 16, 548; Aesch. Pers., 536; Soph. Oed. Tyr., 1225.

[6] The Academician Crantor (→ V, 783, 4), wrote a work περὶ πένθους, which was imitated by Cicero, Plut. and Sen., and which took issue with the Stoic view, v. W. v. Christ-W. Schmid, Gesch. d. gr. Lit., II, 1 = Hndbch. AW, VII, 2, 1⁶ (1920), 54 and 509. Theophrast. wrote a work Καλλισθένης ἢ περὶ πένθους, a sentence of which is quoted in Cic. Tusc., V, 25, v. Christ-Schmid, 61 f.; E. Rohde, Der gr. Roman³ (1914), 300, n. 3.

[7] A variant of the story appears as a fable of Aesop in Plut. Consolatio ad Uxorem, 6 (II, 609e).

[8] πενθεῖν occurs in the LXX both with acc. and with ἐπί and dat. or acc. At 1 Esr. 9:2 A ἐπί with gen. is an error for ὑπέρ B. Cf. Helbing Kasussyntax, 73 [Bertram].

rites, [9] esp. mourning for the dead, which does, of course, include individual sorrow of heart (Gn. 37:34 f.; 2 Βασ. 19:2; Da. 10:2; cf. Test. R. 1:10), but which takes place acc. to fixed custom, whether on the part of the individual (Gn. 23:2; Jer. 16:7; Sir. 38:17, cf. Jos. Bell., 2, 1) or in some instances on that of the whole people or a group (Dt. 34:8; 2 Βασ. 19:3; Jer. 6:26; 1 Macc. 12:52). [10] The blows of fate which in divine judgment smite the people, or Jerusalem, or the enemies of the people are also an occasion of general mourning, Am. 8:10 (opp. ἑορταί), Lam. 5:15 (opp. χορός); 1 Macc. 1:39 (opp. ἑορταί); 9:41 (opp. γάμος) etc. → infra.

πένθος plays a special role 1. in prophecies of disaster : sorrow will come on Israel or Jerusalem (Am. 5:16; 9:5; Mi. 1:8; Is. 3:26; Jer. 6:26) or its enemies (Is. 16:3; 17:14; 19:8; Bar. 4:34). Nature itself will share this sorrow (Hos. 4:3; Is. 16:8; 24:4, 7; Jer. 4:28 etc.). Sometimes we read of present joy being turned into mourning (Am. 8:10; Is. 24:7 ff.; Bar. 4:34). It is also common 2. in descriptions of the fate or divine judgment which has overtaken Israel (Jl. 1:9 f.; Jer. 14:2; Lam. 2:8; 1 Macc. 1:25, 27; 2:14, 39 etc.). [11] Here, too, nature shares in the grief (Jl. 1:10; Is. 33:9; Jer. 12:4; 23:10 etc.), and we again read of joy being turned into sorrow (Lam. 5:15; 1 Macc. 1:39 f.; 9:41). In some instances this sorrow includes sorrow for the sin of the people (1 Εσδρ. 8:69; 9:2; 2 Εσδρ. 10:6). [12] The word also plays a special role 3. in prophecies of salvation : mourning will end (Is. 60:20), it will be turned into joy (Is. 61:3 [cf. Sir. 48:24]; 66:10; Ιερ. 38[31]:13; Bar. 4:23; 5:1). [13] Apocalyptic describes the lamentation of Zion and its transformation into joy, 4 Esr. 9:38-10:50. [14]

C. πένθος and πενθέω in Primitive Christianity.

In the NT, too, πενθεῖν denotes the sorrow expressed in lamentation and tears. [15] It is often combined with κλαίειν. [16] The same is true of πένθος. [17] That πενθεῖν (πένθος) can have the specific sense of mourning for the dead may be seen from Mt. 9:15; Rev. 18:7 f. If in 1 C. 5:2 (καὶ οὐχὶ μᾶλλον ἐπενθήσατε;) πενθεῖν does not have to be open lamentation, neither is it quiet sorrow of heart. What is meant is passionate grief which leads to corresponding action (ἵνα ἀρθῇ κτλ.), cf. also 2 C. 12:21.

---

[9] Gn. 23:2 (κόψασθαι καὶ πενθῆσαι : the one ceremonial mourning); Dt. 34:8 (αἱ ἡμέραι πένθους κλαυθμοῦ Μωυσῆ); Jer. 6:26 (κοπετὸς οἰκτρός as epexegesis of πένθος); Sir. 38:17 (πένθος as distinct from λύπη consists of κλαυθμός and κοπετός). Cf. the combination or parallelism of πενθεῖν or πένθος with κλαίειν or κλαυθμός (2 Εσδρ. 18:9; Bar. 4:11, 23), with κραυγή (Jer. 14:2; Est. 4:3), with κοπετός (Am. 5:16; Mi. 1:8; Est. 4:3), with θρῆνος (1 Macc. 9:41). Mourning rites are mentioned in, e.g., Gn. 37:34; 2 Βασ. 14:2; Am. 8:10; Jer. 6:26; Da. 10:2 f.; Test. R. 1:10.

[10] Jos. Ant., 17, 206 : The Jews executed by Herod τῆς εἰς τὸ πενθεῖσθαι τιμῆς (!) ... ἀπεστέρηντο.

[11] For Rabb. writings cf. Str.-B., I, 195-197. Philo, too, has the theme, though he takes it dualistically in his explanation of the name Abel (אָבֶל): ὄνομα δέ ἐστι τὰ θνητὰ πενθοῦντος καὶ τὰ ἀθάνατα εὐδαιμονίζοντος, Migr. Abr., 74.

[12] Acc. to a poor reading Sir. 51:19 too. Cf. Eth. En. 95:1 ff. Cf. also → IV, 989, 35. Sorrow for individual sin Test. R. 1:10; S. 4:2; for the sin of another, Test. R. 3:15; Jos. 3:9.

[13] Materially, too, cf. Is. 35:10; 65:16-19; ψ 125:5 f.

[14] Cf. also Eth. En. 96:3. For Rabb. material v. Str.-B., I, 195-197; III, 253; Ex. r., 15 (77d).

[15] Trans. only at 2 C. 12:21.

[16] With κλαίειν Lk. 6:25; 23:28 D; Jm. 4:9; Rev. 18:11, 15, 19 (ἔκραζον κλαίοντες καὶ πενθοῦντες); Mk. 16:10; that a κλαίειν corresponds to the πενθεῖν of Mt. 5:4 at Lk. 6:21 too shows how close are the two verbs. If Mt. 9:15 has πενθεῖν (D pc it νηστεύειν) for the νηστεύειν of Mk. 2:19, the πενθεῖν may denote the demonstrative mourning associated with fasting.

[17] In Rev. 21:4 πένθος is associated with κραυγή and in Jm. 4:9 its opp. is γέλως, hence it means lamentation out loud.

One cannot say that πενθεῖν (πένθος) is a theologically significant concept in the NT. Naturally the NT does not speak of πένθος (as of λύπη) in Stoic fashion as an emotion which must be subdued, → IV, 320, 10 ff. Only two usages are of any special significance.

a. According to Rev. 18 lamentation is part of the divine judgment which will fall on sinful Babylon and by which the whole world, which shared Babylon's glory, will also be smitten, so that merchants (18:11, 15) and mariners (18:19), like Babylon itself (18:7), will raise a lament. [18] πένθος is also God's judgment in Jm. 4:9 in a threat to ἁμαρτωλοί: ὁ γέλως ὑμῶν εἰς πένθος μετατραπήτω καὶ ἡ χαρὰ εἰς κατήφειαν. Hence the preceding ταλαιπωρήσατε καὶ πενθήσατε καὶ κλαύσατε might be construed as a prophecy of judgment, which, in prophetic style, is clothed in an imperative. [19] But the context is against this. It compels us (cf. esp. v. 10) to view the πενθήσατε (v. 9), and then εἰς πένθος μετατραπήτω too, as an admonition which calls forth lamentation, and this in turn can only be an admonition to repentance. [20] The author is weaving a traditional threat into his context of admonition, and interpreting it accordingly. [21] In 1 C. 5:2 πενθεῖν is not a sorrowful expression of repentance. It denotes grief at the shame brought on the community by the case of incest, or sorrow over a church in which such a thing was possible. Paul uses πενθεῖν in much the same way at 2 C. 12:21, when he bewails the sin that stains the church, → 42, 16 f. In 1 Cl., 2, 6 πενθεῖν is grief at the sin of one's neighbour (in the congregation).

b. The blessing of the πενθοῦντες in Mt. 5:4 is to be taken eschatologically. It takes up the prophetic promises. [22] As παρακληθήσονται denotes eschatological consolation in the βασιλεία τῶν οὐρανῶν (→ V, 792, 21 ff.; 798, 18 ff.), so the mourning to which the promise refers is that of men who suffer under the present aeon, which is an aeon of suffering, → IV, 318, 31 f. λύπη. Again, as παρακληθήσονται stands in synonymous parallelism to the promises of the other beatitudes, so does πενθοῦντες to πτωχοί (τῷ πνεύματι), πραεῖς, and πεινῶντες καὶ διψῶντες (τὴν δικαιοσύνην). Hence the sorrow referred to here is not to be regarded too narrowly as penitent sorrow for sin. [23] On the other hand, it is evident that not all who mourn are called blessed. The reference is plainly to those who see this suffering aeon as it is and who are not led astray by its charms like the γελῶντες (Lk. 6:25). The πενθεῖν of these men is a sign of their demarcation from this aeon and of their expectation of the βασιλεία τῶν οὐρανῶν. Hence one cannot fail to include penitent sorrow for sin in this πενθεῖν.

Bultmann

[18] → 42, 9 f.; cf. esp. Is. 19:8.

[19] Cf. 5:1; Eth. En. 94 ff.; Dib. Jk., 209 f.

[20] It hardly seems possible to take the admonition as an expression of the "sorrow which the righteous man feels in face of the course of the world," Hck. Jk., ad loc. (203).

[21] Cf. Dib. Jk., 209 f.

[22] → 42, 18-20. Cf. esp. Is. 61:2 : παρακαλέσαι πάντας τοὺς πενθοῦντας. This saying is quoted in Barn., 14, 9; cf. also Rev. 7:17.

[23] Schl. Mt., 135.

πενιχρός → 40, 16 ff.

---

† πεντηκοστή

Contents : A. Profane Use. B. The Old Testament and Jewish Pentecost : I. The Feast of Weeks in the Old Testament; II. The Jewish Feast of Pentecost : 1. The Date of the Feast ; 2. Pentecost as a Harvest Festival ; 3. Pentecost as a Festival of the Giving of the Law at Sinai. C. πεντηκοστή in the New Testament. D. πεντηκοστή in the Early Church.

A. Profane Use.

The ordinal πεντηκοστός is found from the time of Plato (Theaet., 175b) and is variously used in the LXX : Lv. 25:10 f. to denote the year of jubilee, elsewhere chronologically, 4 Βασ. 15:23, 27; 1 Macc. 6:20; 7:1; 9:3, 54; 2 Macc. 14:4. The noun πεντηκοστή is from the 4th cent. B.C. a tt. in taxation : ἡ πεντηκοστή (sc. μερίς) denotes the 50th part, 2%, of value or goods which must be paid as an impost to the state. [1] In Athens this rate was levied on all goods brought to the Piraeus or exported from the city, Demosth. Or., 14, 27; 21, 166; 59, 27; Andoc., 1, 133; Hyperides Fr., 106. Hence those who collect the toll are called πεντηκοστολόγοι, Hyperides Fr., 106. In respect of other countries too, e.g., Egypt, we find πεντηκοστή used as a tt. in taxation on

---

π ε ν τ η κ ο σ τ ή. On A : Liddell-Scott, 1362; Preisigke Wört., III, 246; Pr.-Bauer², 1171; W. H. Roscher, "Die Zahl 50 in Mythus, Kultus, Epos u. Taktik d. Hellenen u. anderer Völker, bes. d. Semiten," ASG, 33, 5 (1917). On B : J. Hamburger, Realencyclopädie f. Bibel u. Talmud, I (1870), 1056-1058; F. Delitzsch, Art. "Pfingsten" in E. C. A. Riehm, Handwörterbuch d. Biblischen Altertums, II² (1894), 1202-1204; J. Wellhausen, Prolegomena z. Gesch. Israels⁴ (1895), 82-117; T. Schärf, "Das gottesdienstliche Jahr d. Juden," Schriften d. Institutum Judaicum Berlin, 30 (1902), 36 f.; K. v. Orelli, Art. "Pfingstfest," RE³, 15, 255-257; H. Grimme, "Das isr. Pfingstfest u.d. Plejadenkult," Studien z. Gesch. u. Kultur d. Altertums, I, 1 (1907); J. D. Eisenstein and J. L. Magnus, Art. "Pentecost," Jew. Enc., IX (1905), 592-595; Str.-B., II, 597-602; J. Benzinger, Hbr. Archäologie³ (1927), 385 f.; G. Dalman, Arbeit u. Sitte in Palästina, I, 2 (1928), 461-468; I. Elbogen, Die Feier d. drei Wallfahrtsfeste im zweiten Tempel (1929) (= 46. Bericht d. Hochschule f. d. Wissenschaft d. Judentums), 10 f.; E. Brögelmann, "Pfingsten in Altisrael," Monatsschrift f. Gottesdienst u. kirchliche Kunst, 44 (1939), 119-128; K. H. Rengstorf, "Christliches u. jüd. Pfingstfest," ibid., 45 (1940), 75-78. On C : E. v. Dobschütz, Ostern und Pfingsten (1903); K. L. Schmidt, "Die Pfingsterzählung u. d. Pfingstereignis," Arbeiten zur Religionsgeschichte d. Urchristentums, I, 2 (1919); W. Michaelis, Täufer, Jesus, Urgemeinde, Nt.liche Forschungen, II, 3 (1928), 124-129; C. R. Erdman, "The Meaning of Pentecost," Biblical Review, 15 (1930), 491-508; N. H. Snaith, "Pentecost, the Day of Power," Exp. T., 43 (1931/2), 379 f.; K. Lake, "The Gift of the Spirit on the Day of Pentecost," in Jackson-Lake, I, 5 (1933), 111-121; K. Bornhäuser, Studien z. Ag. (1934), 1-28; E. Stauffer, "Was sagt die Pfingstgeschichte?" Deutsches Pfarrerblatt, 39 (1935), 353 f.; N. Adler, "Das erste chr. Pfingstfest, Sinn u. Bedeutung d. Pfingstberichtes Ag. 2:1-13," Nt.liche Abhandlungen, 18, 1 (1938); L. Goppelt, "Typos — d. typologische Deutung d. AT im Neuen," BFTh, II, 43 (1939), 139-142; J. G. Davies, "Pentecost and Glossolalia," JThSt, NS, 3 (1952), 228-231; E. Lohse, "Die Bdtg. des Pfingstberichtes im Rahmen d. lukanischen Geschichtswerkes," Ev. Theol., 13 (1953), 422-436. Cf. also the comm. on Ac. 2 : H. J. Holtzmann, Die Ag. in Hand-Comm. z. NT, 16² (1892); Pr. Ag.; Wdt. Ag.; R. Knopf Ag. (Schriften d. NT)³ (1917); Zn. Ag.; Jackson-Lake, I, 4; Steinm. Ag.; Bau. Ag.; H. W. Beyer (NT Deutsch)⁴ (1947). On D : O. Casel, "Art u. Sinn d. ältesten chr. Osterfeier," Jbch. f. Liturgiewissenschaft, 14 (1938), 1-78.

[1] Roscher, 87 conjectures that the development of πεντηκοστή as a tt. must have begun in a period when the chief measure was the cow, which was usually driven in herds of 50 head. This led to assessment in groups of 50 for tax purposes, and later the same practice was observed in respect of all imports and exports. This conjecture is likely enough, but thus far the sources have not produced any solid evidence in its favour.

pap. and ostraka.[2] Imports and exports, and the termination of a business, which led to the transfer of articles from the owner to someone else, were often assessed at 2% of the value. As regards exports the tax had to be paid by the one who exported dutiable articles, while in the case of a sale the man who purchased dutiable objects had to pay. The imposition of these taxes is confirmed by a receipt (P. Oxy., XII, 1440) which runs as follows: προσβ(έβληκε) πεντηκο(σ)τ(ὴν) τοῦ ἐνεσ[τῶτος] πέμπτου ἔτους Ἀδριανοῦ [Καίσαρος], "he has paid the tax of 2% for the current year, the fifth year of the Emperor Hadrian."

B. The Old Testament and Jewish Pentecost.

In the literature of Hell. Judaism πεντηκοστή (sc. ἡμέρα) is very commonly used for the Feast of Pentecost : Tob. 2:1; 2 Macc. 12:32; Philo Decal., 160; Spec. Leg., II, 176; Jos. Ant., 3, 252; 13, 252; 14, 337; 17, 254; Bell., 1, 253; 2, 42; 6, 299. The OT does not use the term but speaks of the חַג שָׁבֻעֹת, Ex. 34:22; Dt. 16:10, 16; 2 Ch. 8:13 LXX = ἑορτὴ ἑβδομάδων, cf. Nu. 28:26.

I. The Feast of Weeks in the Old Testament.

In the context of the calendar of feasts Ex. 34:22 tells us only that the Feast of Weeks was a harvest festival celebrated on the bringing in of the first-fruits of the wheat harvest. Ex. 23:16 confirms this and calls the feast (חַג הַקָּצִיר) a feast of the first-fruits of the harvest of the sown grain. To calculate the date of the feast Dt. 16:9 lays down that it shall begin seven weeks after the first putting of the sickle to the grain.[3] Then the gifts are to be joyfully offered to Yahweh "in the place which Yahweh, thy God, hath chosen to place his name there" (v. 11). The sole interest of Dt. is in this statute which centralises the cultus in Jerusalem, so that we are told nothing further about the festival. The most that one can deduce from the ancient traditions is that early Israel probably took over this and other agricultural feasts from the Canaanites dwelling in the land. The offerings were to be made, however, to Yahweh, who had given the land to His people.[4] For further details on the Feast of Weeks we have to turn to the priestly legislation. Acc. to Lv. 23:15 seven full weeks are to be reckoned מִמָּחֳרַת הַשַּׁבָּת, i.e., from the day after the Sabbath. The original ref. thus seems to be to a week of Sabbaths. It is then added that seven full weeks are to be reckoned from the bringing of the wave offering (עֹמֶר הַתְּנוּפָה), and the feast is to be held on the 50th day.[5] Two wave loaves baked of 2/10 ephah of fine flour are then to be brought to Yahweh as first-fruits, Lv.

---

[2] Materially cf. Preisigke Wört., III, 246; Ostraka, I, 182, 276-279, 343; II, 43, 150, 801, 806, 1056, 1076, 1569; Mitteis-Wilcken, I, 1, 190 f.; I, 2, 343 f.; Roscher, 113.

[3] As the term חַג שָׁבֻעֹת shows, this ordinance is obviously old. Cf. Dalman, 462 : "The possibility cannot be ruled out that in the calculation of seven weeks the number 7 plays a role to the degree that the working week with its day of rest is multiplied sevenfold in connection with the fact that a period of some two months was needed for the harvest of barley and wheat, which is all that is at issue here." On fifty-day periods, which played only a small part in antiquity, cf. Roscher, 90-94, 100.

[4] In his brilliant study of Pentecost Grimme has tried to trace back the OT feast to much earlier times and to derive it from an ancient oriental feast of the Pleiades worshipped as gods. The festival was then supposedly given a monotheistic form in the legislation of Israel, so that it could take on the character of a harvest feast. To prove his thesis Grimme relies in the main on the late texts Lv. 23 and Nu. 28 and the interpretation of שבועות as Pleiades. He himself, however, has to grant (70-75) that this understanding is by no means certain at Dt. 16:9 (or Ex. 23:16; 34:22). But this means that the conclusive link with ancient Israel is missing. Hence we must follow the usual view which seeks the origin of Pentecost in a simple harvest festival.

[5] Materially cf. E. Kutsch's diss. on the Feast of Tabernacles. On the differences in calculating the date of Pentecost in later Judaism → 46, 12-25.

23:17. [6] The sacrifices consist of 7 lambs of the first year without blemish, one young bullock, two rams as burnt offerings, one kid of the goats as a sin offering, and two lambs of the first year as peace offerings (Lv. 23:18 f.). [7] All these gifts are an expression of thanks to Yahweh for causing the harvest to ripen. On the day of the feast all work ceases (Lv. 23:21; Nu. 28:26) and the whole people joins in merry harvest rejoicing. In importance the Feast of Weeks cannot be compared, of course, with either the Feast of Passover and Unleavened Bread or the Feast of Tabernacles. Outside the Law it is mentioned only once in the OT at 2 Ch. 8:13. One may conclude from this that it played a lesser role in the life of the people than did the other yearly feasts.

II. The Jewish Feast of Pentecost.

1. The Date of the Feast.

The date of the feast came to be firmly fixed only in later Judaism. It was now dated on the 50th day after the Passover. Opinions varied as to the significance of the "day after the Sabbath" mentioned in Lv. 23:15. The Boethuseans (Sadducees) took this literally and counted from the first regular Sabbath (Saturday) after the first day of the Passover, so that Pentecost would always fall on a Sunday. [8] The Pharisees, however, took the שַׁבָּת of Lv. 23:15 to mean the first day of the Passover, the 15th Nisan, [9] and thus counted seven full weeks from the 16th Nisan, so that Pentecost would fall exactly on the 50th day after the 16th Nisan. [10] Acc. to this reckoning the day of the week on which Pentecost came would depend on the day of week the Passover began. [11] Prior to 70 A.D. the Pharisaic view seems to have controlled the observance. Philo and Joseph. agree in stating that Pentecost was celebrated 50 days after the first day of the Passover. [12] Tg. O. on Lv. 23:15 f. adopts the Pharisaic view in its rendering of the OT text : "You shall count from the day after the first day of the feast (Passover) ... seven full weeks shall it be ; you shall count 50 days to the day after the 7th week." [13] Since the date was reckoned from the first day of the Passover, and Pentecost was thus related closely to the Feast of the Passover and Unleavened Bread, it was also given in later Judaism the name of עֲצֶרֶת or עצרת של פסח, and was herewith regarded as the

---

[6] In distinction from the Mazzahs the Pentecost loaves are to be of leavened bread. Whereas the former suggest nomadic life in the desert, the latter presuppose regular agriculture.

[7] Nu. 28:27 ff. divides the offerings rather differently : two young bullocks, one ram and seven lambs of the first year as burnt offerings, a kid of the goats to make atonement, and also the regular burnt offerings, meat offerings and drink offerings.

[8] Men., 10, 3 : "The Boethuseans say : The cutting of the sheaf does not take place at the end of the (first) day of the feast (Passover), but only at the end of the next regular Sabbath." Chag., 2, 4 : The Boethuseans say : "Pentecost always falls on the day after the Sabbath." Cf. also Men., 65a; examples in Str.-B., II, 598-600.

[9] S. Lv., 23, 15 (407a): R. Jose bJehuda (c. 180) decides that שַׁבָּת must mean the first day of the Passover. For acc. to Lv. 23:16 the reckoning has to include 50 full days. But if we start only from the day after the Sabbath (Sunday), the number will vary between 51 and 56 days as the first day of the Passover falls at the end or the beginning of the week. Acc. to Men., 65b R. Eli'ezer bHyrcanos (c. 90) advanced a similar explanation. Cf. also S. Dt. § 134 on 16:8 (101b); Mek. Ex., 12, 15 (11b); instances in Str.-B., II, 599 f.

[10] Hence Pentecost fell on the 5th, 6th or 7th Sivan as 29 or 30 days were allotted to Nisan, Iyyar and Sivan. Cf. RH, 6b; Str.-B., II, 600.

[11] Cf. Chag., 2, 4.

[12] Philo Spec. Leg., II, 162 : ἑορτὴ δέ ἐστιν ἐν ἑορτῇ ἡ μετὰ τὴν πρώτην εὐθὺς ἡμέραν (= 16th Nisan) ... 176 : ἀπὸ γὰρ ἐκείνης ἡμέρα πεντηκοστὴ καταριθμεῖται ἑπτὰ ἑβδομάσιν, Jos. Ant., 3, 250-252; Bell., 2, 42 f.

[13] Cf. also Tg. J. I on Lv. 23:11, 15; Str.-B., II, 600.

closing feast of the Passover. [14] Already in Joseph., [15] the Mishnah, [16] and Tosefta [17] this expression is used, and it then becomes the main term for Pentecost in Rabb. writings. Whereas Passover-Mazzoth and Succoth extended over several feast-days, there was only one day of Pentecost. Only in the dispersion, where there was uncertainty in the observance of the lunar periods and difficulty in always getting the calendar right, was a second day added to the first in order that on one day at least the festival might be observed in common by the Jewish world both in the land of Israel and also in the dispersion. [18]

2. Pentecost as a Harvest Festival.

As in the OT, so in Judaism, Pentecost was a harvest festival. The Book of Ruth, which has the harvest as its setting, was read at Pentecost. [19] In the village there assembled the train of pilgrims who were going to Jerusalem to present their harvest offerings there. [20] When the environs of the holy city were reached, the priests and Levites came to meet the crowds of pilgrims and conducted them into the temple. As religious songs were sung, they entered with baskets on their shoulders. The Levites struck up the song of praise and then the first-fruits were handed to the priests and a confession of thanksgiving was made to the God of Israel in the words of Dt. 26:3-10. The two loaves (Lv. 23:17), concerning which the Mishnah gives more precise instructions (Men., 11, 1-2, 4, 9), [21] were offered as the first-fruits of the new wheat harvest [22] "in thanksgiving for the past in which we did not have to suffer the torments of want and hunger but lived in plenty, and also for the future, because we are provided for in this with stocks and resources, and with the best hopes we keep house with God's gifts." [23] In later Judaism, too, Pentecost is less important than the other two pilgrimages, the Passover-Mazzoth and Succoth. Though a sizable number of Jews from Palestine [24] and the Diaspora [25] assembled for it, participation in this feast was smaller than in the others, which both stretched over a whole week. The names πεντηκοστή and עֲצֶרֶת show that Pentecost increasingly lost its independent meaning and became an appendage

---

[14] Midr. Cant. 7:2 (126a), Str.-B., II, 598. The term עֲצֶרֶת, which is used in the OT only for the 7th day of the Mazzoth feast (Dt. 16:8) and the 8th day of Tabernacles (Lv. 23:36; Nu. 29:35; 2 Ch. 7:9; Neh. 8:18), originally denotes the rest from work, then the day of the feast, then the concluding festival. Materially cf. E. Kutsch, "Die Wurzel עצר im Hebr.," Vetus Testamentum, 2 (1952), 57-69, esp. 65-67.

[15] Ant., 3, 252 : αἱ τῶν ἑβδομάδων ἡμέραι τεσσαράκοντα καὶ ἐννέα, [τῇ πεντηκοστῇ], ἣν Ἑβραῖοι ἀσαρθὰ καλοῦσιν.

[16] Chag., 2, 4.

[17] T. Ar., 1, 11 (543).

[18] Examples in Str.-B., II, 601.

[19] On the lections at Pentecost cf. I. Elbogen, *D. jüd. Gottesdienst in seiner geschichtlichen Entwicklung*[2] (1924), 138; cf. Rengstorf, 77. Dt. 16:9 ff. was the reading from the Torah (Meg., 3, 5), then from the 2nd cent. onwards Ex. 19:1 ff. as well (T. Meg., 4, 5 [225]; Meg., 31a; jMeg., 74b, 27). Acc. to bTalmud Ex. 19 was read on the first day of Pentecost and Dt. 16 on the second. Thus at a later time the story of the giving of the Law tended to supplant Dt. 16. For the prophetic reading we find Ez. 1 and Hab. 3. Materially cf. also H. St. J. Thackeray. *The Septuagint and Jewish Worship* (1921), 46-60 and A. Guilding, "Some Obscured Rubrics and Lectionary Allusions in the Ps.," JThSt, NS, 3 (1952), 41-55, esp. 48-55. Attempts to trace back Synagogue practice to pre-Chr. times are insecurely grounded and can only be hypothetical in character.

[20] Cf. the depiction in Bik., 3, 2-6.

[21] Cf. Str.-B., II, 601 f.

[22] Philo Decal., 160. Jos. Ant., 3, 252 f. says that at Pentecost bread baked from leavened wheat meal was offered to God, and he mentions as burnt offerings 3 calves, 2 rams and 14 lambs, also 2 goats as sin offerings. The numbers are obviously based on Lv. 23 and Nu. 28 → n. 7.

[23] Philo Spec. Leg., II, 187.

[24] Jos. Ant., 14, 337; 17, 254; Bell., 1, 253; 2, 42 f.

[25] Ac. 2:1 ff.

of the Passover. The 16th Nisan, the day of the Omer, when the first-fruits of the barley harvest were offered to God as the first offering of the new harvest,[26] introduced the period of barley harvest, and the festival period which thus commenced with the Passover ended on the Day of Pentecost.[27]

3. Pentecost as a Festival of the Giving of the Law at Sinai.

In distinction from the Passover-Mazzoth and Succoth, whose content the OT associated with the exodus and wilderness tradition, Pentecost remained a pure harvest festival. Only in the Chr. period do we find evidence that later Judaism linked this feast too with the events of the age of Moses, and particularly remembered the giving of the Law at Sinai on this day. The immediate occasion for thus changing the meaning of Pentecost was the destruction of Jerusalem in 70 A.D., which meant that the ancient pilgrimage could no longer be held nor the first-fruits and sacrifices offered in the temple. The new understanding, which is attested for certain only from the 2nd cent. A.D., was fostered in two ways.

a. The Book of Jub. gives us the early beginnings of an anchoring of Pentecost in the story of God's dealings with His people. On the new moon of the third month Noah went out of the ark and built an altar, 6:1. When God made a covenant with him, we then read (6:17): "For this reason it is ordained and written in the tablets of heaven that in this month they (the children of Noah) shall keep the feast of weeks once a year to renew the covenant each year." As the covenant was made with Noah in the 3rd month, so also with Abraham: "And Abraham renewed the feast and the statute for ever," 14:20. Noah and his children kept the feast just as conscientiously as Abraham, Isaac and Jacob and their children, 6:18 f.; 22:1 ff. But then the children of Israel forgot it until God renewed it on the mount, 6:19. Except for this allusion to Sinai, which contains the command to keep the feast, Pentecost is always depicted in Jub. as a feast of thanksgiving and harvest. For after the account of the way in which God set a bow in the cloud as a sign of the everlasting covenant which guarantees the law of seedtime and harvest (Gn. 8:22; 9:14), there follows the ordinance that the feast of weeks is to be kept every year in this month (6:16 f.). In c. 22 we then read how Isaac and Ishmael came to their aged father Abraham to keep the feast of weeks with him as a festival of the first-fruits of harvest, 22:1. They slew burnt offerings and peace offerings and prepared a feast, and Rebekah baked cakes of fresh grain, 22:4. But Abraham magnified the Most High God who made heaven and earth and gave men to eat and to drink. Though it was a time of dearth, Jacob, too, celebrated the feast of first-fruits in the middle of the 3rd month, 44:1-4. By thus anchoring the feast in the story of the patriarchs Jub. is obviously trying to enhance the significance of Pentecost.[28] For as the forefathers set an example of keeping the feast, so their children and descendants are under obligation to be faithful to it.[29] This tendency in Jub. to associate the feast with the history of Israel must have exerted a significant influence after 70 A.D.

---

[26] Jos. Ant., 3, 250 f.

[27] In keeping with the lesser importance of Pentecost as compared with Passover-Mazzoth and Succoth is the fact that the Mishnah does not devote a special tractate to it but gives directions concerning this feast only in brief notes in other tractates.

[28] Cf. Dalman, 467: "It was natural to elevate the festival to a higher rank after the model of the Passover and Tabernacles." This elevation was supported by ref. to the oath which God swore to the fathers (24:10 etc.) and the vow by which the fathers bound themselves to Him (6:10 f.). חַג שָׁבֻעוֹת (feast of weeks) was obviously taken to be חַג שְׁבֻעוֹת (feast of oaths) (6:21). Cf. Thackeray, op. cit., 57. On the historicising of OT feasts cf. M. Noth, "Die Vergegenwärtigung d. AT in der Verkündigung," Ev. Theol., 12 (1952/3), 6-17, esp. 10 f.

[29] As the origin of Pentecost is traced back to the time of Noah, so it is recounted that Noah received directions that his children should offer a daily sacrifice at the morning hour (6:14). Cf. also the express rules given for the Passover in c. 49. These are designed to enhance sharply the significance of the feast. On the feast of weeks acc. to Jub. cf. also

b. Association of Pentecost with the giving of the Law at Sinai was also fairly easy after 70 A.D. in view of the fact that prior to 70 A.D. Pentecost had already been regarded as עֲצֶרֶת, the concluding festival of the Passover. Since we read in Ex. 19:1 that in the 3rd month after the exodus the Israelites came into the wilderness of Sinai, it was possible to count 50 days from the Passover celebrating the exodus to the giving of the Law and thus to celebrate Pentecost as the day when the Law was given. The first sure witness to the fact that the Rabb. regarded the giving of the Law as having taken place on the Day of Pentecost is R. Jose bChalaphta (c. 150). He said "In the 3rd month (Sivan), on the 6th day of the month, the ten commandments were given to them (the Israelites), and it was a sabbath day." [30] From the 2nd cent. on the account of the giving of the Law at Sinai (Ex. 19) was read as the lesson from the Law at Pentecost. [31] This new interpretation of Pentecost gained ground in the period which followed, so that in the 3rd cent. R. El'azar bPedath (c. 270) expressed a common conviction of his age when he said : "Pentecost, that is the day when the Torah was given," Pes., 68b. To this day Jews have since celebrated Pentecost as the feast of the giving of the Law. Neither Philo nor Joseph., however, says anything about this understanding of the festival. One may thus conclude that it was unfamiliar to them. It was the disaster of 70 A.D. which first forced the Jewish world to give new content to Pentecost. One may suppose, however, that this change found a basis in earlier attempts to anchor Pentecost, like the other feasts, in the history of Israel (Jub.). On the other hand, all attempts to understand the Chr. Pentecost as a festival of the new revelation as distinct from the Jewish Pentecost as that of the giving of the Law must be regarded as mistaken. [32] The story of Pentecost in Ac. 2 bears no relation to the Sinai tradition, nor can the Chr. Pentecost be derived directly from the Jewish. [33]

C. Albeck, "Das Buch d. Jubiläen u. d. Halacha" (47. Bericht d. Hochschule f. d. Wissenschaft d. Judentums [1930]), esp. 15 ff. As we have shown above, of course, the view of Albeck that "the feast of weeks is presented as the feast of the giving of the covenant and the Law" (16) is not quite accurate. On the calendar of Jub., acc. to which the feast of weeks falls on the 15th day of the third month (44:1-5), cf. A. Jaubert, "Le Calendrier des Jubilés et de la secte de Qumran. Ses origines bibliques," Vetus Testamentum, 3 (1953), 250-264. Further research is needed on the relations between Jub. and the Dead Sea Scrolls.

[30] Seder 'Olam Rabba, 5. Str.-B., II, 601. The tradition may be accepted as reliable, since Seder 'Olam Rabba contains a good deal of ancient material from the 1st and 2nd centuries. Cf. Rengstorf, 77.

[31] For instances cf. Str.-B., II, 601, materially → n. 19.

[32] The opposite view of some scholars finds no support in the texts, so that we have only unproved conjectures, cf. Elbogen, 11: "In the days of Jesus the festival was undoubtedly regarded already as one of revelation too, and the outpouring of the Holy Spirit in the passage of Ac. to which we have referred is thus no more than a renewal of the ancient revelation in the new form shaped by faith in Jesus Christ." Against this Dalman rightly states : "Nevertheless in the Roman period no one dare change the content of the feast without direct support in the Law ... Only the separation from Palestine and its harvest led to the later spiritualising, so that this cannot be regarded as the basis of the narrative in Ac. 2."

[33] One can hardly accept as valid any attempt to establish a connection with the Sinai tradition on the basis of Ac. 2. Ref. has often been made to the elaboration of the Sinai story by Philo in Decal., 32-49. But this account does not mention Pentecost and is simply a development of the OT narrative. R. Jochanan (d. 279) is also frequently quoted : "Each word which proceeded from the mouth of the Almighty (at the giving of the Law) divided into 70 tongues (languages)," Shab., 88b; cf. also a Bar. of the school of R. Jishma'el, loc. cit.; also Ex. r., 5 (71a); Tanch. B שמות § 22 (7a); Midr. Ps. 92 § 3 (202a); Str.-B., II, 605. But these embellishments of the Sinai story neither go back to NT times nor constitute a genuine par. to Ac. 2. Cf. the verdict of Billerbeck, Str.-B., II, 604 on Ac. 2:6. Hence we must reject even such a cautiously phrased conjecture as that of Bau. Ag., 35 : "The setting in which a pre-Lucan Pentecost narrative was possible, and in which we have thus to seek it, is plainly indicated by the Sinai tradition." Apart from the fact that a pre-Lucan narrative can hardly be reconstructed, Ac. 2 says nothing about the Law or its

C. πεντηκοστή in the New Testament.

1. In 1 C. 16:8 Paul says that he will remain in Ephesus until Pentecost. Here, as in Ac. 20:16, the dating is by the Jewish calendar. [34] We cannot say for certain whether a Christian Pentecost was already being celebrated in Ephesus or Corinth. [35] It is quite possible, however, that the first community in Jerusalem took part at first in the Jewish Pentecost. For when Paul was in a hurry to be at Jerusalem for Pentecost (Ac. 20:16), the apostle must have expected to meet a larger number of brethren than usual in Jerusalem on the feast day.

2. Luke introduces his account of the first Christian Pentecost with what is almost a heading: καὶ ἐν τῷ συμπληροῦσθαι τὴν ἡμέραν τῆς πεντηκοστῆς, Ac. 2:1. This difficult expression [36] must be regarded as analogous to Lk. 9:51, where Luke says: ἐν τῷ συμπληροῦσθαι τὰς ἡμέρας τῆς ἀναλήμψεως αὐτοῦ, "when the time up to his (Jesus') exaltation had run its course," i.e., "when the promised day of his exaltation had dawned." [37] Ac. 2:1 is thus to be translated: "When the promised day of Pentecost had come." [38] The story of Pentecost is hereby related to salvation history, and it is in this light that we are to understand the theme which Luke set at the beginning of Acts (1:8): Here is the fulfilment of the promise which the ascending Jesus gave His disciples: λήμψεσθε δύναμιν ἐπελθόντος τοῦ ἁγίου πνεύματος ἐφ' ὑμᾶς, καὶ ἔσεσθέ μου μάρτυρες ἔν τε Ἰερουσαλὴμ καὶ ἐν πάσῃ τῇ Ἰουδαίᾳ καὶ Σαμαρείᾳ καὶ ἕως ἐσχάτου τῆς γῆς. [39] Two aspects are thus emphasised in the narrative which follows: a. The gift of the Holy Spirit (→ πνεῦμα) which was promised for the last days is given. [40] The miraculous events associated with Pentecost had been foretold by the prophets, [41] and the outpouring of the Spirit means that those thus endowed ἤρξαντο λαλεῖν ἑτέραις γλώσσαις (v. 4). [42] The Holy Spirit thus gives full power to praise (v. 11) and to proclaim (vv. 14 ff.). [43] b. This event is regarded by Luke as the birthday of the Church. For he undoubtedly means that a miracle of tongues takes place (→ II, 702, 40 ff.), and that this is witnessed by the assem-

---

transcending, and hence the Lucan account cannot be understood in the light of the Jewish feast. Rengstorf, 78; Lohse, 428-430.

[34] It should be noted that Jewish feasts are used for dating elsewhere in Ac., cf. 12:3 ἄζυμα; 20:6 ἄζυμα; 27:9 νηστεία (Day of Atonement).

[35] One cannot assume from 1 C. 5:6-8 that there was already at this time a Chr. Paschal feast, → V, 901, 9-16.

[36] The rendering : "When the day of Pentecost drew to a close," is refuted by the express statement in v. 15 that it was only the third hour. The reading τὰς ἡμέρας in some versions refers to the 7 weeks, and is undoubtedly an attempt to make the phrase easier to understand.

[37] For the thought of fulfilling a set period cf. also Lk. 1:23, 57; 2:6, 21, 22.

[38] Strictly one would have expected the perf. συμπεπληρῶσθαι in Lk. 9:51 and Ac. 2:1. The pres. συμπληροῦσθαι means "in process of fulfilment," the aor. συμπληρωθῆναι "to reach fulfilment" [Debrunner]. Cf. Schmidt, 8 f.

[39] Cf. also Lk. 24:47-49; Ac. 1:4.

[40] Luke shows how he understands the story when Jl. is quoted in Peter's address. The words ἐν ταῖς ἐσχάταις ἡμέραις added in v. 17 emphasise the eschatological character of the promise now fulfilled.

[41] In v. 19 Jl. 2:30 is related to the miraculous events of the Day of Pentecost.

[42] That glossolalia is a result of the outpouring of the Spirit may be seen also from Ac. 10:44 : ἐπέπεσεν τὸ πνεῦμα τὸ ἅγιον ἐπὶ πάντας τοὺς ἀκούοντας τὸν λόγον and v. 46 : ἤκουον γὰρ αὐτῶν λαλούντων γλώσσαις καὶ μεγαλυνόντων τὸν θεόν. Cf. also Ac. 19:6.

[43] The verb ἀποφθέγγεσθαι (for Spirit-endowed utterance) is used both for tongues in v. 4 and for the preaching of Peter in v. 14. Both are traced back to the πνεῦμα ἅγιον.

bled crowd of those who, as representatives of their nations, [44] have come to the holy city. [45] Intentionally, then, Luke causes the story of Pentecost to issue in a depiction of the life of the community, 2:42-47. The account in 2:1-13 is thus firmly embedded in the structure of Luke's work. Behind it is the promise (1:8) of which it is the fulfilment; ahead of it is the description of the community living by the power of the Spirit. [46]

In vv. 1-4 and 13 (cf. 1 C. 14:23) one catches glimpses of an older tradition of glossolalia, → I, 724, 40 ff. But literary criticism is unable to disentangle the written source or sources [47] which Luke might have had before him. [48] Both linguistically and stylistically the account is wholly Lucan, and the word γλῶσσα, which originally might have suggested speaking in tongues, is interpreted as διάλεκτος, "language." [49] The most that one can say is that very probably Luke utilised a tradition concerning the first outbreak of inspired mass ecstasy in Jerusalem, → I, 725, 17 ff. It is certainly quite possible that this event did in fact take place on the occasion of the first Pentecost after the crucifixion [50] when many pilgrims were in Jerusalem. [51] In the account which Luke gives, however,

---

[44] In vv. 9-11 Lk. used a traditional list of nations and wove it into the story. It does not concern him that the inhabitants of Judaea are also listed. (Materially cf. E. v. Dobschütz, "Zu d. Völkerliste Ac. 2:9-11," ZwTh, 45 [1902], 407-410.) He is simply using the list to bring out the universal character of the event. Hence it is pointless to try to adjust the list to the context by elimination. A. v. Harnack, *Beiträge z. Einl. in d. NT*, III : *Die Ag.* (1908), 65 f. excises Ἰουδαίαν in v. 9 and regards Κρῆτες καὶ Ἄραβες in v. 11 as a gloss. He thus finds 12 territories, one for each apostle. Holtzmann, 330 finds in the 16 names a recollection of the 16 descendants of Noah in Gn. 10:1, 2, 6, 21, 22. Lk. can hardly have intended such allusions ; "the list is in the main a rhetorical way of saying that every land and nation was represented," Jackson-Lake, I, 4, 19. Worth noting, however, is the conjecture of O. Eissfeldt, "Kreter u. Araber," ThLZ, 12 (1947), 207-212, that the appended names Κρῆτες καὶ Ἄραβες are meant to denote inhabitants of the islands and the deserts. For "this pair does not add any new groups to those mentioned in the preceding table, but divides them into two main categories, the isles and the desert, West and East."

[45] Luke also finds the universality of endowment with the Spirit foretold in Jl.: v. 17: ἐκχεῶ ἀπὸ τοῦ πνεύματός μου ἐπὶ πᾶσαν σάρκα (Jl. 2:28). It has been shown above (→ n. 33) that he did not take this feature from Judaism. Since the Rabb. embellishment of the Sinai story was later (→ 48, 8 ff.), one should desist from trying to expound Ac. 2:1-13 in the light of it. Cf. also Adler, 46-58.

[46] That in the primitive Church there were other versions and understandings of the outpouring of the Spirit as well as Luke's may be seen quite clearly from Jn. 20:19-23.

[47] Materially cf. also M. Dibelius, "Aufsätze z. Apostelgeschichte," FRL, NF, 42 (1951), 20; Lohse, 426 f.

[48] On the various attempts at source disentanglement cf. esp. Adler, 19-46. Historical and literary evaluations are interwoven in these attempts, cf. Schmidt, 23 f. In face of them Adler (32-35) has shown clearly that the whole story is linguistically Lucan. Nevertheless, there are still some exegetes who believe they can work back to an earlier form, cf. W. Grundmann, "Das Problem d. hell. Christentums innerhalb d. Jerusalemer Urgemeinde," ZNW, 38 (1939), 49, n. 10.

[49] To the 2 meanings of γλῶσσα (1. "tongue," 2. "language") v. 3a adds a third, "tongue of fire." Cf. → I, 721, 40 ff. and K. G. Kuhn, "Jesus in Gethsemane," *Ev. Theol.*, 12 (1952/3), 269.

[50] Acc. to the Synoptic dating of the crucifixion on Friday the 15th Nisan Pentecost would fall on a Saturday. If, however, Friday was the 14th Nisan (Jn.) it would be a Sunday. But this is unimportant in Lk. Later πεντηκοστή was always reckoned from Easter Day, so that the 50th day always fell on a Sunday.

[51] Cf. Schmidt, 27, 32. E. v. Dobschütz, 33-43 has tried to show that when more than 500 brethren saw Christ at once (1 C. 15:6) this was at Pentecost. K. Holl, "Der Kirchenbegriff d. Pls. in seinem Verhältnis zu dem d. Gemeinde," *Ges. Aufsätze*, II (1928), 47, n. 1 and W. Grundmann, op. cit., 49 agree. But Jackson-Lake, I, 5, 121 rightly states : "All such hypotheses have too little definite evidence in their support ever to become more than interesting possibilities."

the author is not telling us about the first instances of glossolalia but about the miracle of the coming of the Spirit and the birthday of the world Church. [52] This falls on the Day of Pentecost, so that the Jewish calendar of feasts could now be worked into the nexus of promise and fulfilment in salvation history. [53]

D. πεντηκοστή in the Early Church.

In the early Church — instances are found from the second half of the 2nd cent. — πεντηκοστή is used for the 50 days of rejoicing which begin with the eucharist celebrated on Easter Eve. Since Easter was always kept on a Sunday in the main body of the Church, the seven weeks always ended on a Sunday too. [54] In this period, which was regarded as one long feast, [55] Christians rejoiced because their Lord rose again and gave the gifts of the Spirit to His Church. This joy found expression in the fact that in these days, as on the Lord's Day, there was to be no fasting, and prayer was to be offered standing rather than kneeling. [56] During this period catechumens were baptised [57] and the glances of believers were directed to the future. It was still expected that the Lord, who had ascended into the heavens during the time of πεντηκοστή, would come again in the same season. [58] In πεντηκοστή, the seven weeks of peace and rest, Christians set their thoughts on the future resurrection. [59] Hence πεντηκοστή could sometimes be regarded as a sign prefiguring the heavenly kingdom, and the OT harvest festival was then understood typologically: Christ has ascended into heaven as the first-fruits, to offer men as a gift to God. [60]

---

[52] Cf. Dibelius, 94 : "The story of Pentecost in Ac. 2:1-41, which records the first occurrence of ecstatic speaking in tongues in the community, is made into a prototype of world mission by the enumerating of the peoples from which the hearers come. The way is prepared for this by a direction of the Risen Lord, and the result is shown in a first depiction of the life of the community."

[53] As regards the Christianising of the Jewish calendar by Luke note should be taken not only of Ac. 2 but also esp. of the account of the Last Supper. More strongly than either Mt. or Mk., Lk. brings out the Paschal character of the Lord's Supper and emphasises the fact that the OT festival here finds fulfilment in salvation history. As in Judaism the festival which begins with the Passover ends with Pentecost, so in Lk. the events which begin in Jerusalem at the Passover come to an end at Pentecost.

[54] We have no information whether or in what way the Quartodecimans and other schismatic groups kept πεντηκοστή. On the Epistula apostolorum → n. 58.

[55] Tert. Bapt., 19 ... Pentecostes, qui est proprie dies festus. Materially cf. Casel, 18 f. For Tert., too, Pentecost is not the day but the 50 day period of rejoicing which begins with Easter Day.

[56] Thus the Act. Pl. (end of the 2nd cent., ed. C. Schmidt [1936], 1, 30-32) tell us that the brethren did not mourn when Paul was bound and condemned to the arena. Because it was πεντηκοστή they did not bend the knee but prayed full of joy (standing). Cf. also Tert. De Corona, 3; De Oratione, 23; Iren. in Ps.-Just. Quaest. et Resp. ad Orth., 115; Ps.-Hipp. in psalmos fr., IX (Origen ?) (GCS, I, 2, 138, 9 ff.); Testamentum Domini nostri Jesu Christi (ed. J. E. Rahmani [1899]), II, 12; Epiph. De Fide, 22, 5; Euseb. De Solemnitate Paschali, 5 (MPG, 24, 700).

[57] Tert. Bapt., 19.

[58] Loc. cit., with a clear ref. to Ac. 1:10 ff. On expectation of the parousia between Easter and Pentecost cf. also Epistula apostolorum, 17 (ed. H. Duensing, Kl. T., 152 [1925], 14). When we read here that Christ will return between Pentecost and Easter, the text in this form makes no good sense. Cf. Casel, 5. The ref. is to the return in the time of πεντηκοστή, so that we must reverse the words: "Between Easter and Pentecost." The expectation of the Quartodecimans is probably connected with the Jewish hope that the Messiah would come on the night of the Passover. Cf. B. Lohse, "Das Passafest d. Quartadecimaner," BFTh, 2., 54 (1953), 78-84. The view of Tert. is a development of older expectation on the basis of the account in Ac.

[59] Bas. Spir. Sct., 66 (MPG, 32, 192).

[60] Hipp. fr., IV from On Elkanah and Hannah (GCS, I, 2, 122, 9 ff.).

The last day of πεντηκοστή, which even in early times was perhaps a prominent one as the end of a great festival, later took on increasingly an independent significance. [61] Thus πεντηκοστή came to be used, not for the 50 day feast, but for Pentecost, as in Judaism and the NT. This was detached from Easter, and as a festival in its own right it was devoted exclusively to commemoration of the outpouring of the Spirit. [62]

Lohse

πεποίθησις → 7, 31 ff.

περί

A. περί [1] with Gen.

1. From the spatial sense of "around," which was already rare in the class. period and occurred almost exclusively in poetry (though → 56, 2), there developed the transf. sense "about," "concerning."

    a. With verbs and verbal concepts : [2] (a) of speaking, teaching, writing, hearing, understanding, thinking : "about," Ac. 8:34; 1 Jn. 2:27; 2 C. 9:1; Lk. 9:9; Ac. 26:26; Mt. 22:42; Ac. 25:16; Lk. 4:37. (b) Of questioning, enquiring, complaining, judging, punishing, praising : "concerning," "on account of," Mt. 19:17; 2:8; Ac. 24:13; Jn. 8:26; 10:33; [3] Lk. 3:19; 19:37; Hb. 11:20; Ac. 18:15. The abbreviated expression in Ac. 15:2 : ἔταξαν ἀναβαίνειν Παῦλον καὶ Βαρναβᾶν ... πρὸς τοὺς ἀποστόλους καὶ πρεσβυτέρους εἰς Ἰερουσαλὴμ περὶ τοῦ ζητήματος τούτου, means "go up to seek a decision regarding the dispute," cf. also Ac. 25:15, 24. In this connection we should mention the use of περί with verbs of contention, which is common also in class. usage. In the NT we

---

[61] Cf. Eus. Vit. Const., IV, 64.

[62] This is plainly presupposed already in Const. Ap. Cf. VIII, 33, 5 : τὴν πεντηκοστὴν ἀργείτωσαν διὰ τὴν παρουσίαν τοῦ ἁγίου πνεύματος τὴν δωρηθεῖσαν τοῖς πιστεύσασιν εἰς Χριστόν. It may be assumed with confidence that the Synagogue influenced the development of Pentecost in the early Church, e.g., in the order of the pericopes. Materially cf. G. Kretschmar, *Himmelfahrt u. Pfingsten.*

π ε ρ ί. Bl.-Debr. [7, 8] § 228 f., *v.* also § 266, 1; A. T. Robertson, *A Grammar of the Gk. NT*[3] (1919), 616-620, 1379; P. F. Regard, *Contributions à l'étude des prépositions dans la langue du NT* (1918), 527-544; C. F. D. Moule, *An Idiom Book of NT Gk.* (1953), 62 f.; Johannessohn Präpos., 219-226; Mayser, II, 2, 445-456; P. T. Stevens, "Aristot. and the Koine (Notes on the Prepositions)," *Class. Quarterly,* 30 (1936), 204-217; Schwyzer, II, 499-505. → διά (II, 65 Bibl.) and → παρά (V, 727 Bibl.).

[1] Related to παρά (→ V, 727 n. 1), περί derives from the Indo-Europ. *per(i), which acc. to the most likely etym. suggests "going beyond," "penetrating," "superabounding." This meaning is retained in Gk., though here, as in Indo-Iranian, "around" became the chief sense, and from this developed the transf. meaning "about." The distinction from ἀμφί "on both sides" became blurred already in class. usage. In Hell. Gk. ὑπέρ tends noticeably to replace περί in the sense "concerning," and in modern Gk. the latter prep. has dropped out of living usage. Cf. on this Schwyzer, II, 499-500. With verbs, nouns and adj. περί in the NT means 1. "beyond," transf. to denote a high measure or superfluity, e.g., περιλείπω, περίλυπος, περιούσιος, cf. περισσός, 2. "around," e.g., περιβάλλω, περιίστημι. In Hell. usage περί is mostly found with the gen. The acc. is less common, the dat. has almost completely disappeared. We find the dat. 3 times in the LXX (Prv. 1:9; 3:22; 6:21, cf. Johannessohn Präp., 223 f.), but in the NT and post-apost. fathers it is as rare as in the pap. Cf. Radermacher, 140 f.

[2] The prep. is sometimes used here like the class. gen., Radermacher, 125. The distinction between περί τινος and περί τι is that the gen. is preferred with verbs of speech and thought, the acc. to denote the object of action, cf. Mayser, II, 2, 370, 456.

[3] Cf. διὰ ποῖον αὐτῶν ἔργον ἐμὲ λιθάζετε; Jn. 10:32.

find it in the phrase λάχωμεν περὶ αὐτοῦ at Jn. 19:24 (casting lots for the garment of Jesus), cf. also Ac. 18:15. (c) Of emotion : [4] "about," "on account of," e.g., with θαυμάζειν, Lk. 2:18; σπλαγχνίζεσθαι, Mt. 9:36; τάραχος ἐγένετο, Ac. 19:23. (d) Of care, "about," "for," e.g., Mt. 6:28; 22:16.

b. In loose dependence on a verb or noun : (a) with a secondary causal sense : "for," προσένεγκε περὶ τοῦ καθαρισμοῦ σου, "offer for cleansing," Mk. 1:44; Lk. 5:14. (b) "in respect of," τοῦ ποιῆσαι αὐτοὺς κατὰ τὸ εἰθισμένον τοῦ νόμου περὶ αὐτοῦ "to do what the law lays down in respect of the child," Lk. 2:27; [5] περὶ πάντων εὔχομαί σε εὐοδοῦσθαι καὶ ὑγιαίνειν, 3 Jn. 2, of prosperity in every respect. [6] ἐξουσία περὶ τοῦ ἰδίου θελήματος, 1 C. 7:37 (cf. Col. 4:10); πρόφασιν οὐκ ἔχουσιν περὶ τῆς ἁμαρτίας αὐτῶν, no excuse in respect of (for) their sin, Jn. 15:22.

c. At the beginning of a sentence to denote the object or person under discussion : "As concerns," 1 C. 7:1; 16:1, 12; cf. 8:1. [7]

d. τὰ περί τινος, "what concerns someone," e.g., Ac. 23:15; Phil. 2:19 f. [8] τὸ περὶ ἐμοῦ, my life, Lk. 22:37; τὰ περὶ ἑαυτοῦ, the OT prophecies of Jesus as Christ, Lk. 24:27. Hence for the message of Jesus in the Gospels, and for the content of apostolic proclamation in Ac. and the Epistles : τὸ περὶ τοῦ Ἰησοῦ, Mk. 5:27; cf. Lk. 24:19; Ac. 18:25; 23:11; 24:22; 28:31; cf. 1:3; 19:8 vl.

2. To some degree the distinction between περί and ὑπέρ fades in the Hell. period, and a result is that περί with the gen. can be used in the sense "on behalf of," "for." [9]

Cf. already ἀνὴρ οὖ θνήσκω πέρι, Eur. Alc., 178; περὶ τούτου παρεκάλεσα τὸν θεόν, Ditt. Syll.[3], 1170, 30; ὃ διέγραψε Προῖτος περί μου, P. Zenon (ed. C. Edgar, IV [1931]), 59790, 23; εὔχομαι τῷ κυρίῳ θεῷ περὶ τῆς ὁλοκληρίας σου, P. Oxy., X, 1298, 4; cf. VII, 1070, 8 f.; XII, 1494, 6; τοῖς ἐντυγχάνουσι περὶ Πτολεμαίου, P. Greci e Latini, IV, 340, 5. In the LXX προσεύξεται περὶ σοῦ, Gn. 20:7, cf. 1 Βασ. 7:5; 2 Macc. 1:6; 15:14; δεήθητι περὶ ἡμῶν, Jdt. 8:31, cf. Sir. 21:1. [10]

In the NT this use is found especially in intercession. A request is made (ἐρωτᾶν) to Jesus to heal Peter's mother-in-law, Lk. 4:38. Jesus Himself prays for His disciples, Lk. 22:32 δεῖσθαι; Jn. 16:26; 17:9, 20 ἐρωτᾶν. The disciples for their part are to pray for those who persecute them, Lk. 6:28 προσεύχεσθαι. The apostles request the gift of the Spirit for those baptised by them, Ac. 8:15. When Peter is put in prison, the Church meets to pray for him, Ac. 12:5 προσευχή. Paul intercedes for Onesimus, Phlm. 10 παρακαλεῖν. To the regular intercession of the apostle for his churches (Col. 1:3; 2 Th. 1:11 προσεύχεσθαι) corresponds their prayer for him (Col. 4:3; 2 Th. 3:1; Hb. 13:18 προσεύχεσθαι; Eph. 6:18 δέησις). [11] The object of brotherly intercession is the forgiveness of sins by God:

---

[4] Rare in class. usage, Bl.-Debr. § 229, 2.

[5] *Loc. cit.*

[6] Bl.-Debr. § 229, 2 (App.) and some older exegetes take περὶ πάντων here to mean πρὸ πάντων, "above all." The salutation πρὸ πάντων εὔχομαί σε ὑγιαίνειν (or something similar) is found in letters from the Hell. period, *v.* Deissmann LO, 147; Moult.-Mill., 647.

[7] Cf. the passages in Pr.-Bauer, *s.v.,* also P. Lond., I, 1912, 52 and 66.

[8] But cf. τὰ περὶ ἐμέ in Phil. 2:23.

[9] Sometimes the two are simply alternated. Thus in Eph. 6:18 f. the introduction of ὑπέρ for περί emphasises the last member, cf. H. Zerwick, Graecitas biblica[2] (1949), 23. Cf. also on this Mayser, II, 2, 450-454; Johannessohn Präpos., 217 and 222; Bl.-Debr. § 229, 1. Though περί is for a time more common, this does not prevent its eventual disappearance, Radermacher, 146.

[10] Johannessohn Präp., 221 f.

[11] → n. 9.

οὐ περὶ ἐκείνης (τῆς ἁμαρτίας) λέγω ἵνα ἐρωτήσῃ, 1 Jn. 5:16. [12] In respect of acts for others, too, we read: ἀγῶνα ἔχω περὶ ὑμῶν, Col. 2:1; [13] μὴ Παῦλος ἐσταυρώθη περὶ ὑμῶν, 1 C. 1:13; [14] τὸ αἷμα ... τὸ περὶ πολλῶν ἐκχυννόμενον, Mt. 26:28; [15] τοῦ ἀποθανόντος περὶ ἡμῶν, 1 Th. 5:10. Of self-defence: ἐπιτρέπεταί σοι περὶ σεαυτοῦ λέγειν, Ac. 26:1. [16]

3. Of special significance in the biblical writings is the phrase περὶ ἁμαρτίας, strictly "on account of," "for (the remission) of sin."

In the LXX this phrase is the equivalent of the Heb. הַחַטָּאת and חַטָּאת in the sense of "sin-offering": [17] οὗτος ὁ νόμος τῶν ὁλοκαυτωμάτων καὶ θυσίας καὶ περὶ ἁμαρτίας, Lv. 7:37, cf. ὁλοκαύτωμα καὶ περὶ ἁμαρτίας οὐκ ᾔτησας, ψ 39:6. Less common is an emphasising of the substantive form by a preceding art.: τὰ περὶ τῆς ἁμαρτίας, Lv. 6:23; τὸ περὶ τῆς ἁμαρτίας, 14:19. An important pt. is that the phrase occurs in the framework of the theology of atonement associated with the παῖς θεοῦ ('Ebed Yahweh): ἐὰν δῶτε περὶ ἁμαρτίας, Is. 53:10, cf. v. 12 : καὶ αὐτὸς ἁμαρτίας πολλῶν ἀνήνεγκεν καὶ διὰ τὰς ἁμαρτίας αὐτῶν παρεδόθη, → V, 710, 18 ff.

In the NT the sense of "sin-offering" suggests itself for περὶ ἁμαρτίας when the reference is to the sacrifice of Christ for the redemption of His people. [18] A sacrificial meaning is evident in the quotation from ψ 39:6 ὁλοκαυτώματα καὶ περὶ ἁμαρτίας οὐκ εὐδόκησας, at Hb. 10:6. [19] But in other passages, too, a formal cultic use seems to have controlled the expression. As is not surprising, this is especially so in Hb. Cf. Hb. 5:3: καθὼς περὶ τοῦ λαοῦ, οὕτως καὶ περὶ ἑαυτοῦ προσφέρειν περὶ ἁμαρτιῶν, where the double use of περί is quite unique unless περὶ ἁμαρτιῶν is to be taken as a fixed expression. [20] In Hb. 10:18 we find the fuller προσφορὰ περὶ ἁμαρτίας, similarly θυσία περὶ ἁμαρτιῶν in 10:26. [21] In a section which alludes directly to the Eucharist we find the shorter form: Hb. 13:11: ὧν γὰρ εἰσφέρεται ζῴων τὸ αἷμα περὶ ἁμαρτίας εἰς τὰ ἅγια (Lv. 16:27). In the light of this usage one has to ask whether the meaning is not "sin-offering" in other verses as well, or at least whether there is not a suggestion of this sense, specifically at R. 8:3: ὁ θεὸς τὸν ἑαυτοῦ υἱὸν πέμψας ἐν ὁμοιώματι σαρκὸς ἁμαρτίας καὶ περὶ ἁμαρτίας, and 1 Pt. 3:18: ὅτι καὶ Χριστὸς ἅπαξ περὶ ἁμαρτιῶν ἀπέθανεν. [22]

---

[12] Cf. περὶ τῶν ἁμαρτιῶν αὐτοῦ δεῖται, Sir. 28:4; v. also Da. 4:27 LXX.

[13] vl. ὑπὲρ ὑμῶν.

[14] vl. ὑπὲρ ὑμῶν.

[15] ὑπὲρ πολλῶν Mk. 14:24; ὑπὲρ ὑμῶν, Lk. 22:20; cf. 1 C. 11:24 f.

[16] So אAC with many MSS ; the rest, including BLP, read ὑπέρ.

[17] In the passages quoted the Heb. has no prep., LXX περὶ ἁμαρτίας. On the other hand περὶ ἁμαρτίας with a verb is used for לְחַטָּאת e.g., Nu. 8:8, cf. Lv. 16:3, 5. Cf. also Pr.-Bauer⁴, s.v. ἁμαρτία 4. → ἱλάσκομαι, III, 305-310. Cf. esp. B. Reicke, The Disobedient Spirits and Christian Baptism (1946), 215-217.

[18] Cf. N. H. Snaith, I Believe in ... (1949), 67-69, who at 2 C. 5:21: τὸν μὴ γνόντα ἁμαρτίαν ὑπὲρ ἡμῶν ἁμαρτίαν ἐποίησεν, is inclined to find the sense of "sin-offering" in ἁμαρτία alone, though cf. E. B. Allo, St. Paul. Seconde épître aux Corinthiens (1937), ad loc.

[19] ἠθέλησας v. 8; ψ 39:6 ᾔτησας.

[20] But cf. ὑπὲρ ἀνθρώπων and ὑπὲρ ἁμαρτιῶν in Hb. 5:1. The text vacillates in part between περὶ (τῶν) ἁμαρτιῶν and ὑπὲρ (τῶν) ἁμαρτιῶν, cf. Gl. 1:4; Hb. 5:3. In related verses we find sometimes the one prep. and sometimes the other, Gl. 1:4 and 1 C. 15:3; Hb. 10:12, 18.

[21] Cf. θυσία ὑπὲρ ἁμαρτιῶν, Hb. 5:1; 10:12.

[22] Reicke, op. cit., 216; Moule, 63.

B. περί with the Accusative.

1. Of place : a. gen. "around," e.g., ἕως ὅτου σκάψω περὶ αὐτήν (the fig-tree), Lk. 13:8; περὶ τὴν ὀσφύν, Mt. 3:4; Mk. 1:6; a millstone περίκειται περὶ τὸν τράχηλον, Mk. 9:42 and par.;[23] αἱ περὶ αὐτάς (Sodom and Gomorrha) πόλεις, Jd. 7 (cf. Mk. 3:8; Ac. 28:7); τοὺς περὶ αὐτὸν κύκλῳ καθημένους, Mk. 3:34, cf. 3:32.

b. With ref. to those around a person. In class. usage the person is mentioned :[24] οἱ περὶ τὸν Ἐπιτάδαν, Epitadas and his followers, Thuc., IV, 33, 1; οἱ περὶ Λύσανδρον τριάκοντα, the 30 tyrants with Lysandros in their midst, Xenoph. Hist. Graec., III, 4, 20. In popular Hell. usage one has to infer from the context what is meant : οἱ περὶ τὸν Ἑστιεῖον, "the colleagues of Hestieios," P. Tebt., I, 30, 27; αἱ περὶ Ἀπολλωνίαν, "Apollonia and her sisters," P. Grenf., I, 21, 16, cf. P. Fay., 34, 11. In the LXX οἱ περὶ τὸν Νεεμίαν, "Nehemiah and his followers," 2 Macc. 1:33, cf. 8:30; 4 Macc. 2:19.

In the NT ἠρώτων αὐτὸν οἱ περὶ αὐτόν, "his disciples asked him," Mk. 4:10, cf. also Lk. 22:49. On the other hand οἱ περὶ Παῦλον means "Paul and his pupils" at Ac. 13:13.[25]

2. Of time, to give an approximate time, "about," e.g., περὶ τρίτην ὥραν, Mt. 20:3, cf. 5, 6.[26]

3. From the spatial use the transf. sense a. to denote occupation with something : περιεσπᾶτο περὶ πολλὴν διακονίαν, "she was fully occupied with many tasks (related to serving)," Lk. 10:40, cf. 41; οἱ περὶ τὰ τοιαῦτα ἐργάται, "the workmen occupied therewith," Ac. 19:25.

b. More generally "in respect of,"[27] e.g., ἀστοχεῖν περὶ τὴν πίστιν (ἀλήθειαν), "to err in respect of the faith (the truth)," 1 Tm. 6:21; 2 Tm. 2:18; cf. 1 Tm. 1:19; 6:4.[28] τὰ περὶ ἐμέ, "my circumstances, situation," Phil. 2:23;[29] αἱ περὶ λοιπὰ ἐπιθυμίαι, "lusts from other quarters," Mk. 4:19.[30]

Riesenfeld

---

[23] Cf. the dat. constr. LXX Prv. 1:9; 3:22; 6:21 → n. 1.

[24] Kühner-Blass-Gerth, III, 269-271, 494; Mayser, II, 1, 18 f.; common in the same sense ἀμφί with acc., rarer μετά with gen.; cf. Stevens, 214 f. Cf. also οἱ παρά τινος, → παρά, V, 730, 16 f.

[25] Cf. Ign. Sm., 3, 2; Ev. Pt., XI, 45. In the variant at Jn. 11:19 (p45 A C² Γ Θ al), which can hardly be authentic, πρὸς τὰς περὶ Μάρθαν καὶ Μαριάμ (instead of the πρὸς τὴν Μάρθαν καὶ Μαριάμ of the best MSS) denotes only Martha and Mary with no ref. to those around ; for par. in Hell. usage cf. Plut. Tib. Gracch., 2 (I, 825a); Ep. Ar., 51 and the refs. in Pr.-Bauer⁴, s.v. 2. Cf. also Stevens, 215; Bl.-Debr. § 228 (App.); F. Krebs, *Die Präp. bei Polybius* (1882), 103 f.

[26] In this sense κατά with acc. is more common.

[27] Similar to περί with gen.

[28] This sense occurs 8 times in the Past., but only once in the other Pauline epistles (Phil. 2:23).

[29] Cf. τὸ περί τινος, → 54, 14 f. On this Stevens, 212 f. and Moult.-Mill., s.v.

[30] Cf. Aristot. Rhet., II, 2, p. 1389a, 4; Heliodor. Aeth., I, 23; cf. Winer, 181. The prepositional expression is barely distinguishable from a gen., v. on this Kühner-Blass-Gerth, III, 494; Mayser, II, 2, 344; Johannessohn Präp., 225 f.; H. Widmann, *Beiträge zur Syntax Epikurs* (1935), 208. Cf. also G. Rudberg, "Ad usum circumscribentem praepositionum Graecarum adnotationes," Eranos, 19 (1919), 178-180.

περιέρχομαι → II, 682 f.

περιζώννυμι → V, 302, 19 ff.

περικάθαρμα → III, 430, 22 ff.

περίκειμαι → III, 656, 10 ff.

περικεφαλαία → V, 314, 11 ff.

περιλάμπω → IV, 24, 35 ff.

περίλυπος → IV, 323, 15 ff.

περιμένω → IV, 578, 25 ff.

---

† περιούσιος

1. In non-biblical usage περιούσιος[1] means "having more than enough," "rich," "wealthy."[2] Acc. to Poimandres[3] he who correctly knows his origin has come εἰς τὸ περιούσιον ἀγαθόν, "into special felicity."[4] P. Gen., 11, 17 calls the married man ὁ περιούσιος, "the chosen one."[5]

2. In the LXX περιούσιος occurs 5 times at Ex. 19:5; 23:22; Dt. 7:6; 14:2; 26:18. λαὸς περιούσιος is used for Heb. סְגֻלָּה עַם[6] or סְגֻלָּה.[7] If one notes that the verb סָגַל means "to heap up,"[8] and that twice in the LXX סְגֻלָּה is rendered περιουσιασμός (ψ 134:4 and Qoh. 2:8),[9] one may assume that the basic sense of סְגֻלָּה is not just property in general but "rich possession." Cf. esp. Ex. 19:5, also Dt. 26:18. Hence λαὸς (→ IV, 35, 17 ff.) περιούσιος is "the people which constitutes the crown jewel of God."[10] Because Israel is the precious stone, the pearl in His possession, it has a duty to avoid idolatry (Dt. 14:2) and to keep the commandments and statutes of Yahweh (Ex. 19:5; 23:22; Dt. 7:6-11; 26:18).

περιούσιος. Note : After the death of H. Preisker, S. Schulz prepared the manuscript for press.

Pape, Pr.-Bauer⁴, Cr.-Kö., Liddell-Scott, s.v.; Bl.-Debr. § 113, 1.

[1] περιουσία is very plainly and commonly derived from περιεῖναι, cf. ἀπ-ουσία, ἐξ (→ II, 562, 1 ff.), ἐπ-, μετ-, παρ-, περι-, συν-, also the simple οὐσία. Adj. in -ουσιος are mostly artificial constructs of later philosophy from οὐσία in the sense of essentia, so ἀν-, μετ-, ὁμο(ι)-, παν-, πολυ-, προ-, ὑπερ-ούσιος. In a special class are ἐπιούσιος (→ II, 590-599) and περιούσιος. περιώσιος, "immense," is of obscure construction. P. Chantraine, La formation des noms en grec ancien (1933), 42, suggests that it developed from ἐτώσιος, "useless." Schwyzer, II, 500 classifies it with περι-γίγνεσθαι and περι-εῖναι [Debrunner].

[2] The profane περιούσιος "rich" derives from περιουσία, "superfluity," "affluence," and is common in secular lit.; in Diod. S., 8, 18, 3 περιουσιάζω means "to be distinguished, eminent."

[3] Reitzenstein Poim., 334 App. I § 19; C. H. Dodd, The Bible and the Greeks (1935), 167, n. 2.

[4] περιουσία, "surplus," is common in Philo, e.g., διὰ περιουσίαν ἀγαθῶν, Spec. Leg., II, 12; Praem. Poen., 118 etc. and περιουσιάζειν, Spec. Leg., I, 24; II, 108. Jos. Ant., 11, 56 refers to "transitory wealth" (περιουσίαν ἀφαιρετὴν ὑπὸ τύχης), Bell., 4, 584 to "superiority of power" (περιουσία δυνάμεως).

[5] So Pr.-Bauer ; Preisigke Wört., II, 296.

[6] Dt. 7:6; 14:2; 26:18.

[7] So Ex. 19:5, whereas in Ex. 23:22 the Mas. text differs from that of the LXX, and there is no Heb. equivalent.

[8] Koehler, 649; Cr.-Kö., 412.

[10] [Debrunner.]

3. In the NT λαὸς περιούσιος occurs only at Tt. 2:14 [11] as a quotation from the LXX (Ex. 19:5; Dt. 14:2; Ez. 37:23). By Jesus' work of redemption God has created for Himself a people which is for Him a costly possession, [12] a choice treasure. [13, 14] As in the OT, and in keeping with the outlook of the Pastorals, which lay special stress on the ethical practice of religion, [15] a life full of zeal and good works, or a sober, righteous and godly life (2:12), is demanded. The basis of the λαὸς περιούσιος, then, is the eschatological offering of the Deliverer Christ Jesus (2:14), and its orientation is to the final epiphany of God and Jesus Christ. Belonging to God, it already fashions its life here on earth in such a way that God's command and promise are actualised in the present age. [16]

Preisker †

περιπατέω → V, 940, 33 ff.

περιπίπτω → πίπτω.

περιποιέομαι → ποιέω.

περιποίησις → ποιέω.

| περισσεύω, ὑπερπερισσεύω, περισσός, ὑπερεκπερισσοῦ, |
| ὑπερεκπερισσῶς, περισσεία, περίσσευμα |

περισσεύω, † ὑπερπερισσεύω.

A. Outside the New Testament.

1. Intr. a. of things, "to be present overabundantly," [1] Xenoph. Sym., 4, 35 : τἀρκοῦντα ἔχει καὶ περιττεύοντα, Jos. Ant., 16, 19 : χρήματα (opp. μὴ μόνον ἐπαρκεῖν); Jos. Bell., 7, 331 (with τροφῆς ἀφθονίαν); Philo Jos., 243 (opp. ἐκλιπεῖν). Med. P. Lond., II, 418, 4; Flor., 242, 2; "to be left over," Aristot. Hist. An., I, 9, p. 619a, 20 : ἡ περιττεύουσα τροφή, 670b, 5; Jos. Ant., 13, 55; 3, 229; censoriously "to be superfluous," Soph. El., 1288 : τὰ μὲν περισσεύοντα τῶν λόγων; "to be present to excess," Philo Leg. All.; III, 200 : τῷ δ' ἄφρονι περιττεύει τὸ πάθος; Spec. Leg., I, 80. b. Of persons, "to have superabundance of something," Polyb., 18, 18, 5 (opp. ἐλλείπειν), Xenoph. An., IV, 8, 11, "to be superior in number"; Philo Rer. Div. Her., 191 (with ref. to the manna, Ex. 16:16-18; opp. ὑστερῆσαι); "to overflow," Jos. Ant., 19, 150 (εὐνοίας).

---

[11] On Tt. 2:11-14 cf. H. Windisch, "Zur Christologie der Past.," ZNW, 24 (1935), 223, 225, 229, who ascribes this v. to a later tradition in which the thought of the epiphany and the Soter is central ; cf. also Dib. Past., ad loc., who draws attention to the formal language of the section.

[12] The usual view which renders περιούσιος possession and λαὸς περιούσιος people of possession (Dib. Past. and comm., ad loc.) is thus to be regarded as too weak. It is supported by 1 Pt. 2:9, which uses the same quotation but has περιποίησις for περιούσιος; περιποίησις strictly means "acquiring," then "acquisition, possession." On this cf. Kn. Pt.; Wnd. Kath. Br.[3] and comm., ad loc.

[13] So also J. Jeremias, Die Briefe an Tm. u. Tt. (NT Deutsch), ad loc.: "That we might be his chosen people"; cf. Cr.-Kö., 412, whose discussion has unfortunately been very largely disregarded.

[14] Holtzmann NT, ad loc., translates "a rich people," but the context is against this.

[15] H. J. Holtzmann, Lehrbuch d. Nt.lichen Theol., II (1911), 306 f.

[16] Cf. also 1 Cl., 64. The expression again derives from Ex. 19:5 (Kn. Cl., ad loc.) and can thus be rendered as in Tt. 2:14.

π ε ρ ι σ σ ε ύ ω κτλ. [1] Etym. from περισσός; this from περί, "round," "beyond," Schwyzer, I, 472; II, 499 f., → 53, n. 1.

Trans. "to make over-rich," "to provide in superabundance," Athen., II, 42b τὰς ὥρας ("to lengthen").

2. In the LXX the stem περισσ- is almost always used for the Heb. root יתר in various forms. ² 23 of the 60 occurrences are in Qoh. (→ 63, 3 ff.), only 2 in Gn.-Dt., 7 in Βασ., 13 in the prophets. The verb περισσεύειν is used in the LXX only personally, "to have more than enough," e.g., Sir. 11:12 (πτωχείᾳ); 19:24 (περισσεύων ἐν φρονήσει, "better the godfearing man who has less understanding than the over-clever man who transgresses the law"), "to take precedence of" others, 1 Macc. 3:30, or "to have an advantage over" others (Qoh. 3:19 παρὰ τὸ κτῆνος). In 1 Βασ. 2:33 πᾶς περισσεύων οἴκου σου is used for the Heb. מַרְבִּית in the sense of suboles, "increase" of family, "progeny."

3. The idea that the time of salvation, as a counterpart of Paradise, will bring super-abundance in many different ways is already to be found in the OT, though περισσεύειν is not used for this in the LXX, cf. Am. 9:13; Is. 65:17-25; Ez. 47; Jl. 3:18 etc. For a basis in the Torah Rabb. exegesis turns esp. to Lv. 26:4 f. ³ The later Jewish writings offer rich materials. 4 Esr. 8:52 sums it up : praeparatum est futurum tempus, praeparata est habundantia. ⁴ In detail the superabundance is depicted as miraculous fruitfulness, wealth of children, affluence in money and goods, cf. Eth. En. 10:16-19; Apc. Bar. 29:4-8. ⁵ The giving of the manna will be repeated in enhanced form, M. Ex. on 16:25 (p. 38b) and on 16:33 (p. 59b, 60a). Spiritual goods and gifts are also awaited, fulness of joy (Sib., III, 702-730), righteousness and wisdom (4 Esr. 8:52; Eth. En. 48:1), endowment with the Spirit of God (Test. L. 18; Test. Jud. 24; Sib., IV, 46 and 187). The super-abundance of the age of salvation offsets the loss of powers and goods caused by the fall. ⁶

B. In the New Testament.

In the NT περισσεύειν is almost always used in contexts which speak of a fulness present and proclaimed in the age of salvation as compared with the old aeon, or of a new standard which is required in this age. To this extent περισσεύ-ειν is an eschatological catchword.

1. Synoptic Gospels and Acts. At Mk. 12:44 and par. and Lk. 12:15 περισσεύειν is used non-eschatologically of transitory earthly possessions. Lk. 15:17 is theologically significant, for here the superabundance of the hired servants of the father is a pointer to the God who is rich in grace. Mt. 13:12; 25:29 (cf. Mk. 4:25), perhaps originally a Jewish proverb, ⁷ refers on the lips of Jesus to the super-abundant generosity of God on which the disciple may count. The feeding of the multitude is an antitype of the feeding in the wilderness. Jesus is the second Moses (→ IV, 869, 8). But the Messianic feeding transcends in fulness the Mosaic feeding, which only provided sufficient for each, Ex. 16:18. The fragments which remained, emphasised in all the accounts, point to the fulness of the meal, Mt. 14:20; 15:37; Lk. 9:17; Jn. 6:12 f.). ⁸ There is an eschatological reference in Mt. 5:20

---

² The stem περισσ- is not used in the LXX for the stem שאר, and consequently it is never used for the holy remnant.

³ S. Lv. 26:4 (448a) in Str.-B., IV, 938 f., 948 f., 950.

⁴ περισσ- is probably the underlying Gk., though this is not certain, cf. B. Violet, "Die Apk. des Esra u. des Baruch," GCS, 32, 1 (1924), 119 f.

⁵ For further details cf. Volz Esch., 359 f.; Str.-B., IV, 836 f.; cf. Philo Praem. Poen., 98-107.

⁶ Gn. r., 12; Str.-B., IV, 949 co.

⁷ Bultmann Trad., 108; Dalman WJ, I, 204.

⁸ Mk. 8:8, → 63, 23 f.

too. The righteousness which is required for participation in the kingdom of God must far surpass [9] even the highest achievements of the past as demanded by those masters of piety, the Pharisees and the scribes. The story of the surprisingly rapid growth of the community (Ac. 2:41; 4:4; 6:7; 9:31), for which ἐπερίσσευον τῷ ἀριθμῷ καθ᾽ ἡμέραν is used in 16:5, is not merely a statistical record. It bears witness to the work of the exalted Christ (2:47) and His Spirit (9:31, → V, 795, 12 f.).

2. Paul especially uses περισσεύειν, which he even intensifies to ὑπερπερισσεύ-ειν (R. 5:20; 2 C. 7:4; cf. Eph. 3:20; 1 Th. 3:10; 5:13), [10] often in eschatological contexts. As Paul lives in utter joy at the time of salvation inaugurated with the exaltation of Christ, he continually points to the superabundance of this time as compared with the pre-Christian period. Fulness, which is an essential mark of God (cf. ὑπερεκπερισσοῦ Eph. 3:20 → πλοῦτος) is achieved in the age of salvation to an enhanced degree as compared with anything known hitherto. But this superabundance is manifested, not in superfluity of material goods, [11] but in the sphere of the πνεῦμα. It applies above all to the → χάρις, the gift of grace of the time of salvation. It is lavishly imparted to many in Christ, R. 5:15. Whereas in earlier times sin increased through the Law, grace is superabundantly greater in Christ (5:20: ὑπερεπερίσσευσεν, cf. 5:17: τὴν περισσείαν τῆς χάριτος). In keeping with this wealth of grace, a δόξα which is superabundant in comparison with the old covenant appertains to the ministry of NT δικαιοσύνη 2 C. 3:9, → II, 251, 4 ff. God causes rich grace in the form of every kind of wisdom and understanding to flow richly (περισσεύω trans.) on the apostles by declaring to them the secret of His saving counsel, Eph. 1:8. [12] Known grace lavishly increases thanksgiving and thus overflows to the magnifying of God, 2 C. 4:15. Even sufferings (→ V, 931, 20 ff.) cannot destroy this new wealth of the age of salvation. If the sufferings of Christ come in abundant measure on the community (2 C. 1:5), so, too, does the apostolic comfort effected by fellowship with Christ, loc. cit. According to R. 3:7 the truth of God (→ I, 242, 41 ff.), which in v. 4 (Ps. 116:11) calls all men liars, is enhanced by the full disclosure of the unfaithfulness of men, and thus abounds to God's glory. To the "strong" in Corinth, who seem to have regarded the eating of meat sacrificed to idols as a proof of their Christian wisdom and consequently as something of religious value, Paul has to say that they do not hereby gain any advantage before God (1 C. 8:8), since external things are of no consequence in the kingdom of God, R. 14:17.

It is a feature of the age of salvation that the community is superabundantly rich in gifts, powers and ministries. Paul experiences this, and expects it, in the matter of the collection. He praises the churches of Macedonia because their deep poverty superabounded in the richness of their generosity, 2 C. 8:2. He magnifies God who has richly poured out His own grace on the churches (2 C. 9:8 περισσεῦ-σαι trans.), so that they for their part — in their αὐτάρκεια (→ I, 467, 13 ff.) — have a superabundance (περισσεύητε intrans.) for every good work. As they

---

[9] περισσεύειν strengthened by πλεῖον, cf. Bl.-Debr. § 246.

[10] Cf. 4 Esr. 4:50 : superabundavit; the instance of ὑπερπερισσεύω from Moschio (Pr.-Bauer, s.v.) is mediaeval rather than ancient, Deissmann LO, 66, n. 6. Pl. displays here the Hell. love of such constructs, cf. A. Fridrichsen, "Observationen z. NT aus Ael. Var. Hist.," Symb. Osl., 5 (1927), 63; R. Steiger, Die Dialektik d. paul. Existenz (1931), 97 f., 176 pts. to the theological basis of this predilection (this all-surpassing element, far above all human power, derives from God).

[11] → lines 35 ff.

[12] Cf. Ew. Gefbr., ad loc.

were more than rich in faith, knowledge, zeal and love, they could be super-abundantly rich in this demonstration of grace (χάρις) as well, 2 C. 8:7. [13] The collection does not merely meet the financial needs (→ ὑστερήματα) of the recipients. It is a liturgy with religious content. [14] It is rich beyond measure in the fact that it brings forth many thanksgivings to God, 2 C. 9:12. [15] For Paul himself, who thankfully acknowledges that he is greatly blessed, material περισσεύειν and ὑστερεῖσθαι have become matters of indifference, Phil. 4:12. Through the riches which he has in Christ, the very modest improvement in his circumstances through the gift of the congregation is more than abundance, Phil. 4:18.

The spiritual growth of the churches, indeed, their περισσεύειν according to his own more strongly expressed desire, is always of serious missionary concern to the apostle. It is thus the content of his admonitions and prayers. Hence he desires that the Romans might abound in hope in the power of the Holy Spirit (R. 15:13), and he admonishes the Corinthians that they should strive to super-abound in gifts which serve to edify the congregation (1 C. 14:12), or that they should abound in the work of the Lord (15:58). His petition for the Philippians is that their love should become increasingly richer in knowledge (Phil. 1:9), and he hopes that through their progress their praiseworthy state may become even better (1:26 → III, 651, 35 ff.). His request of the Thessalonians is that they will grow and abound in mutual love (1 Th. 3:12; 4:10) and the Christian walk (4:1).

† περισσός, † ὑπερεκπερισσοῦ, † ὑπερεκπερισσῶς.

1. Of things : "extraordinary," "more than usual," δῶρα Hes. Theog., 399; Philo Jos., 4 (with ἐξαίρετος), b. "strange," Theogn., 769; Soph. Oed. Tyr., 481; Isoc. Or., 12, 77 (with τερατώδη); Antiphon, 3, 4, 5 : περισσοτέροις παθήμασι; Aristot. Eth. Nic., II, 6, p. 1141b, 6 (with θαυμαστά), c. "more than sufficient," "overflowing," Xenoph. Mem., III, 6, 6 (δαπάναι); Dio C., 38, 20, 2 : πᾶν τὸ ὑπὲρ τὴν χρείαν τινὶ ὂν περιττόν ἐστι, Jos. Ant., 4, 117: God has the power καὶ τὰ περιττὰ μειοῦν ... καὶ τὰ λείποντα διδόναι. τὸ περισσόν, "surplus numbers, power," Xenoph. Cyrop., VI, 3, 20; "additional" provisions in a will, BGU, 326, II, 9; ἐκ περιττοῦ, "to excess," "unnecessarily," P. Tebt., II, 488. d. Often censoriously, "superfluous," "useless," "exaggerated," Aesch. Prom., 383 (μόχθος); Soph. El., 1241 (ἄχθος); Plat. Resp., III, 407b (ἐπιμέλεια τοῦ σώματος); Philo Praem. Poen., 99 (with περίεργος); περισσὰ φρονεῖν, "to think arrogantly," "to be proud," Eur. Fr., 924, 2 (TGF, 659). e. τὸ περισσόν "remainder," Anth. Pal., XI, 239; τὸ περισσὸν τῆς ἡμέρας, Xenophon Ephesius (R. Hercher, Erotici Scriptores Graeci [1858]), I, 3; II, 14. f. "Odd number" (opp. ἄρτιος) Plat. Prot., 356e.

Of persons : [1] a. "unusual," "noteworthy," Eur. Hipp., 948; Aristot. Probl., II, 10, p. 953a, 10 (περισσοὶ κατὰ φιλοσοφίαν); Plut. Demetr., 2, 2 (I, 889) (κάλλει with θαυμαστός); Dio C., 46, 21, 2 (ὁ δεινός, ὁ περισσός); Ps. Sol. 4:2 : περισσὸς ἐν λόγοις ... ὑπὲρ πάντας. b. Censoriously Eur. Hipp., 445 (with μεγὰ φρονοῦντα); Polyb., 9, 1, 4 (with πολυπράγμων).

The adv. περισσῶς means "unusually," Hdt., II, 37 (θεοσεβέες περισσῶς ἐόντες); Polyb., 1, 29, 7. Comp. Hdt., II, 129; superlative, Dio C., 37, 17, 2; 62, 7, 3. The neuter, adv. and comp. περισσότερον and περισσοτέρως are often used in the koine for πλέον and μᾶλλον, [2] Jos. Ant., 6, 59.

---

[13] Cf. Heinr. 2 K., ad loc.; Wnd. 2 K., ad loc.
[14] Wnd. 2 K. on 9:12, though → IV, 227, 4-21.
[15] Heinr.; Wnd. 2 K., ad loc.

π ε ρ ι σ σ ό ς κ τ λ. [1] Eustath. Thessal., 484, 10-19.
[2] Radermacher, 69; Bl.-Debr. § 60, 3.

2. In the LXX περισσός is used for various forms of the root יתר: a. "what remains," "remnant," Ex. 10:5: πᾶν τὸ περισσὸν (יֶתֶר) τῆς γῆς τὸ καταλειφθέν (הַנִּשְׁאֶרֶת); 4 Βασ. 25:11: τὸ περισσὸν (יֶתֶר) τοῦ λαοῦ τὸ καταλειφθὲν (הַנִּשְׁאָרִים) ἐν τῇ πόλει; also personally Ju. 21:7 B; 1 Βασ. 30:9; 3 Βασ. 22:47 A. "The rest," "what is not mentioned," 3 Βασ. 14:19; Ez. 48:23; 1 Macc. 9:22. b. Censoriously "superfluous," "useless," Qoh. 2:15; Sir. 3:23 (μὴ περιεργάζου); 2 Macc. 12:44 (with ληρῶδες). c. "Extraordinary," "excellent," Da. 5:12 Θ πνεῦμα περισσόν of Daniel ; also 6:4; Da. 5:14 Θ (σοφία). d. "Profit," Prv. 14:23 (מוֹתָר, opp. מַחְסוֹר disadvantage, ἔνδεια); on Qoh. → 63, 3 ff. The adv. περισσῶς simply means "very," Da. 8:9 Θ; 7:7 Θ; 7:19 Θ; 2 Macc. 8:27; ψ 30:23 : τοῖς περισσῶς (עַל־יֶתֶר) ποιοῦσιν ὑπερηφανίαν.

3. The adjective occurs only 6 times in the NT. It denotes the superabundance of the blessing of salvation which Christ as distinct from false prophets will give believers ἵνα ζωὴν ἔχωσιν καὶ περισσὸν ἔχωσιν (Jn. 10:10); or additional assurances which go beyond the simple Yes and No, which bring a world of evil in their train, and which are unnecessary to the full truthfulness of the disciple (Mt. 5:37); [3] or the perfected love which, like the love of God, does not simply repay the kindness of friends (Mt. 5:47); or the advantage which the Jew has over others (R. 3:1). It can mean "superfluous" in 2 C. 9:1, while ἐκ περισσοῦ is used of extraordinary astonishment at the miraculous power of Jesus (Mk. 6:51). The adverb is used similarly to denote surprise at the loftiness of the Christian demand (Mk. 10:26). The reference may also be to the vehemence of the enemies of Jesus against Him, Mt. 27:23; Mk. 15:14; Ac. 26:11.

The comparative περισσότερος (16 times in the NT) is in OT Gk. a popular substitute for πλείων. In the comparisons which the NT makes by means of the word some important theological statements occur. John excels the OT prophets in dignity and he is thus of decisive importance, Mt. 11:9 and par. [4] Love is more important than all sacrifices, Mk. 12:33. God demands more from him to whom he has entrusted more, Lk. 12:48. The sham righteousness of the scribes will bring down on them the sharper judgment, Mk. 12:40 and par. On pastoral grounds Paul wants to spare the evildoer too great sorrow, 2 C. 2:7. God wanted to establish the immutability of His saving counsel to an even higher degree, Hb. 6:17. Cf. also Mk. 7:36 (μᾶλλον περισσότερον, also 2 C. 7:13); [5] Lk. 12:4; 1 C. 12:23 f.; Hb. 7:15.

Paul often uses περισσότερος in comparisons. It seems to be a stronger form for him than the common μᾶλλον. He far surpassed his contemporaries in his zeal for the traditions of the fathers, Gl. 1:14. He also surpassed all the other apostles in his labours, 1 C. 15:10. He surpassed his Judaising opponents in his sufferings, 2 C. 11:23. [6] He speaks of his pious walk before the world, and especially before the Corinthians, 2 C. 1:12. He refers to his special love for them, 2:4; 12:15. He mentions his particular zeal to see the church of Thessalonica again, 1 Th. 2:17. Cf. also 2 C. 7:13, 15; Phil. 1:14; Hb. 2:1; 13:19.

---

[3] Bl.-Debr. § 60, 3 → V, 181, 9-14 and n. 54.

[4] To take περισσότερον as a masc. (Erasmus, C. A. Fritzsche, Ev. Matthaei [1826], ad loc.) is against NT usage and the analogy of Mt. 12:6.

[5] Bl.-Debr. § 60, 3.

[6] Also alien to class. Gk. and the LXX are ἐκπερισσῶς, Mk. 14:31; ὑπερπερισσῶς, Mk. 7:37; ὑπερεκπερισσοῦ (Da. 3:22 vl.), Eph. 3:20; 1 Th. 3:10; 5:13 vl.; ὑπερεκπερισσῶς, Mk. 7:37 vl.; 1 Th. 5:13; on these constructs cf. Bl.-Debr. § 12 App.; 116, 3; 185, 1; 230.

† περισσεία.

περισσεία χρημάτων, "surplus," IG, V, 550 = CIG, I, 1378. [1]

In the LXX only Qoh. (13 times) in keeping with the pessimistic view of the author acc. to which all human effort is futile. At 6:8; 7:11 it is used for יֹתֵר, at 2:11 for רְעוּת, [2] elsewhere for יִתְרוֹן "profit," "advantage," 1:3; 3:9; 5:8, 15; 10:10, "priority" 2:13; 7:12.

It the NT it is used of the superabundant fulness of the time of salvation, whether it be that of God's grace and righteousness poured forth in Christ in contrast to the dominion of death in the old aeon (R. 5:17), or that of over-flowing Christian joy which is prepared to be generous in spite of poverty (2 C. 8:2). According to 2 C. 10:15 Paul hopes for new and unbounded missionary victories when the Corinthian church shows obedient submission. [3] In Jm. 1:21 περισσεία κακίας does not denote a remnant of wickedness. Along with πᾶσαν (ῥυπαρίαν) and in accordance with the basic sense of περισσεύειν the term describes the wickedness which is to be set aside as "exceedingly great." [4]

† περίσσευμα.

"Excess," "surplus," Oribasius, 22, 7, 1. The only instance in the LXX, namely, at Qoh. 2:15, is to be regarded as a Chr. interpolation (cf. the Mas.). [1]

In the NT the word is used at Mt. 12:34; Lk. 6:45 to denote that which, present in abundance in the heart, comes to expression for good or evil in the words of a man. In 2 C. 8:13 f., with reference to the collection, Paul admonishes the Corinthians: their surplus is to compensate for the corresponding lack of the original community, while the surplus of the original community in spiritual goods will compensate for their lack of these. The reference in Mk. 8:8 is to the surplus of fragments (→ 59, 35 ff.) which is also a testimony to the superabundance of the food provided.

Hauck †

---

† περιστερά, † τρυγών

Contents: A. The Dove in the Ancient World. B. The Dove in the Old Testament and Judaism. C. The Dove in the New Testament. D. The Dove in the Early Church.

περιστερά is etym. obscure. It is possible [1] that the secondary consonant dissimilation in modern Gk. (πελιστέρι) takes us back by accident to the original form, in which

---

π ε ρ ι σ σ ε ί α. Deissmann LO, 66.

[1] The Mandaean uthras derive, not from יותרא (Heb. יוֹתֵר) "superabundance," but from עותרא (Heb. עֹשֶׁר), "wealth," Lidz. Ginza, 6, n. 8.

[2] Cf. G. Bertram, "Hbr. u. gr. Qoh.," ZAW, NF, 23 (1952), 26-49.

[3] Heinr. 2 K., ad loc.; Wnd. 2 K., ad loc.

[4] Dib. Jk., ad loc.; Hck., ad loc.

π ε ρ ί σ σ ε υ μ α. [1] H. W. Hertzberg, Der Prediger. Komm. z. AT, 16, 4 (1932), 78 f.; P. Katz, Review in ThLZ, 63 (1938), 34; Str.-B., I, 639.

π ε ρ ι σ τ ε ρ ά, τ ρ υ γ ώ ν. Steier, Art. "Taube," Pauly-W., 2nd Ser., 8, 2479-2500; O. Keller, Die antike Tierwelt, II (1913), 122-131; B. Lorentz, "Die Taube im Altertume," Schulprogramm Wurzen (1886); G. Weicker, Der Seelenvogel in d. alten Lit. u. Kunst

case the derivation is from πελιός, "dark gray." In view of the religious connections, however, there is still merit in the older conjecture [2] — even if it cannot be preferred — that περιστερά is a loan word from the Semitic *perach-Istar,* "bird of Istar." τρυγών, like the Lat. *turtur* and the verb τρύζω, is onomatopoeic.

A. The Dove in the Ancient World.

Among the various terms for types of doves περιστερά cannot always be differentiated with precision. πέλεια, πελειάς, the only word for dove in Hom., [3] is the field or rock dove, φάψ [4] and the synon. φάττα/φάσσα [5] is the woodpigeon or ring-dove, οἰνάς [6] the hole-pigeon, and τρυγών [7] the turtle-pigeon. Almost always the περιστερά [8] denotes the house-pigeon, but it can also serve as a common word to denote all the different species. [9]

The training of pigeons, and hence the house-pigeon, played an important role in antiquity. The dove-cots (περιστερεῶνες) [10] of Upper Egypt and East Jordan bear witness to this. We also learn that the trained white dove came from the East to Greece when a Persian fleet was wrecked on Cape Athos, 492 B.C. [11] It is hard to explain the popularity of keeping pigeons on purely economic grounds. The only explanation is to be found in the special religious significance of the bird.

The dove was the bird of the gods even in ancient Greece. Legend tells of doves at the oracle of Zeus in Dodona, where the priestesses were called πελειάδες. Zeus is shown with a dove on coins from Phaistos in Crete. [12] Much more frequently we find female deities with doves. [13] Comparison of the many examples [14] shows that by way of the Atargatis-Dorketo of Hierapolis (Bambyke on the upper Euphrates) a line can be traced from the dove-goddess of Askalon to the story of Semiramis, who, exposed as an infant by her mother Derketo, was fed by doves, found and brought up by shepherds, chosen as his bride by King Ninus of Assyria, and after her death transformed into a dove. [15] Though there are no direct examples, the connection of the dove with Istar is as good as certain. [16] Elsewhere in the Mediterranean area one may find

---

(1902); H. Gressmann, "Die Sage von d. Taufe Jesu u. die vorderorientalische Taubengöttin," ARW, 20 (1920/21), 1-40, 323-359; E. A. Abbott, *From Letter to Spirit* (1903); S. Hirsch, *Taufe, Versuchung u. Verklärung Jesu* (1933); F. Sühling, "Die Taube als religiöses Symbol im chr. Altertum," *Römische Quartalschrift, Suppl.-Heft,* 24 (1930); K. Galling, Art. "Taube," RGG², V, 999 f.; Pr.-Bauer, *s.v.*

[1] Schwyzer, I, 258.
[2] E. Assmann, "περιστερά," *Philol.,* 66 (1907), 313 f., followed by Boisacq⁴, 773.
[3] Though Il., 15, 237 f.: ἵρηξ φασσοφόνος, shows that φάσσα was known to Hom. too.
[4] Attested from Aesch. Fr., 210, 257 (TGF, 71 and 82).
[5] From Aristoph. Ach., 1104; Av., 393; Pax, 1004.
[6] From Aristot. Hist. An., V, 13, p. 544b, 6; VIII, 13, p. 593a, 20 (a comparison of the different kinds of pigeons).
[7] From Aristoph. Av., 302, 979.
[8] From Soph. Fr., 782 (TGF, 314).
[9] Ael. Var. Hist., IX, 2 has περιστερά and πελειάς interchangeably.
[10] For details cf. Steier, 2491; ill. in Keller, 126.
[11] Athen., IX, 51 (394e); cf. Steier, 2490.
[12] Keller, 123. Lorentz does not seem to have this example, though his comprehensive collection and arrangement of the material has been of benefit to all later workers in the field.
[13] Acc. to E. Werth, "Der heilige Vogel d. grossen Göttin," *Sitzungsberichte d. Gesellschaft Naturforschender Freunde zu Berlin* (1935), 273-283, the modern territory of the wild rock-dove, the only wild species of house-dove acc. to Darwin, is bounded to the north by the Jan. isotherm $+ 3°$, while to the south it is exactly co-extensive with the white race (agriculture), to which the cult of the great goddess was almost everywhere native.
[14] Gressmann, 332-359; Steier, 2495-2500; O. Gruppe, *Gr. Mythologie u. Religionsgeschichte (Hndbch. AW,* V, 2), II (1906), 1343-1346.
[15] Ktesias in Diod. S., 2, 4.
[16] Cf. the etym. → 64, 1-3.

the dove-goddess, and this long before 492 B.C. (→ 64, 14 f.). The Cypriot Aphrodite — "the name runs counter to Gk. etymology"[17] — was a dove-goddess on many coins, Paphos being one of her earliest cultic centres.[18] Examples of the dove-goddess at Knossos in Crete and Mycenae take us back into the 2nd millennium ; they are rather later in Etruria, Sicily, Carthage and Phoenicia. Everything pts. to an oriental origin ; it was realised at a later time that the practice of regarding the dove as sacred was oriental.[19] In a Lydian inscr. dedicated to Zeus Sabazios and Meter Heipta (2nd cent. A.D.) a malefactor confesses : ἐπεὶ ἐπείασα περισταρὰς τῶν θεῶν ἐκολάσθην ἰς τοὺς ὀφθαλμοὺς καὶ ἐνέγραψα τὴν ἀρετήν (miracle of healing).[20] The dove is not completely inviolate as a divine bird. It often serves as a sacrifice, though it is not, of course, to be eaten.[21]

The dove, however, is not only a messenger, attribute and indeed incarnation of the — originally theriomorphic — goddess. In antiquity it is also the bird of the soul. There were probably many associations and reciprocal interactions between the two ideas. The common Indo-European and also Egyptian idea of a soul-bird — often with a human head — gave plastic expression to the mysterious and incomprehensible aspect of the phenomenon of the soul as that which comes from the unknown and returns thereto.[22] The bird of death is the epiphany of the soul parted from the body. Among the many forms of the bird of the soul — the soul of the dead Alexander appears as an eagle[23] — the dove, too, plays a part. This is proved by the great no. of dove-grottos in burial grounds and of dove-cots as monuments.[24]

The dove frequently occurs in poetry, proverb and metaphor as a model or example of human conduct. As a term of endearment φάττιον etc. bears allusion to its tender affectionateness.[25] The dove is generally regarded as chaste, and it remains faithful to the chosen partner for life.[26] It is thought of as timid and shy.[27] Its gentleness[28] and guilelessness[29] are proverbial. On the other hand a garrulous person can be called

---

[17] U. v. Wilamowitz-Moellendorff, Die Ilias u. Homer (1916), 286. That Φερσέ- (Φερρέ-) φαττα, an alternative for Persephone, was also connected with the dove in popular etym. is perhaps shown indirectly in Diosc. Mat. Med., IV, 59, where we find φερσεφόνιον and περιστερεών together as names for Verbena officinalis. There is direct attestation in Porphyr. Abst., IV, 16 : ἱερὸν γὰρ αὐτῆς (sc. Persephone) ἡ φάττα. But this may be linked with the idea of the dove as the bird of the soul. For a different view cf. Steier, 2496.

[18] Nemesianus De Aucupio, 22 (A. Baehrens, Poetae latini minores, III [1881], 204) can still call doves Paphiae aves in the 3rd cent. A.D.

[19] Tib., I, 7, 17 f.: quid referam, ut volitet crebras intacta per urbes alba Palaestino sancta columba Syro.

[20] W. H. Buckler, "Some Lydian Propitiatory Inscr.," The Annual of the British School at Athens, 21 (1914-1916), 169.

[21] Xenoph. An., I, 4, 9; Ps.-Luc. Syr. Dea, 14, 54.

[22] For literary and iconographic testimonies cf. Weicker ; also Sühling, 155 f., 289.

[23] Ps.-Callisth., III, 33, 26-27.

[24] Gressmann, 325-330.

[25] Aristoph. Pl., 1011; Plaut. Casina, 138; acc. to Artemid. Oneirocr., II, 20, 22 ff. φάσσα denotes the tender maiden, περιστερά the one who loves honourably.

[26] Aristot. Hist. An., IX, 6, p. 612b, 33 f.; Plin. Hist. Nat., 10, 104; Ael. Nat. An., III, 5, 44. In a magical enticement in the Apotelesmata Apollonii Tyanensis doves are invoked : ὄρνεα καθαρὰ τοῦ θεοῦ τοῦ καθαρίσαντος τὸ πλάσμα αὐτοῦ, Patrologia Syriaca, II, 1388 f. (ed. R. Graffin [1907]).

[27] Aesch. Sept. c. Theb., 277 (πάντρομος), Soph., Ovid., Verg.; cf. Steier, 2489.

[28] Diog. L., VII, 64. Until late in the M. Ages the error persisted that the dove has no gall (in fact it is only without a true gall-bladder). This ignorant opinion is derided already in Gal. De Atra Bile, 147, 20 ff. (CMG, V, 4, 1, 1).

[29] Steier, 2495 : "A simple person who could easily be outwitted was called ἡμένη πελειάς," cf. Hesych., Suid., s.v. ἡμένη πελειάς. The opp. is the bold raven. Juv. Satura, II, 63 : dat veniam corvis vexat censura columbas ; Prud. Dittochaeon, 192 : corvos mutare (change into) columbis ; Steier, 2494 f.

τρυγόνος λαλίστερος. [30] The turtle's cooing, however, is construed as a complaint, so that (κατά) τρυγόνα ψάλλειν means "to bewail one's misfortune." [31] Here we seem to have the very different idea that the dove is a bird of misfortune and death; this explains the link with Persephone. [32]

B. The Dove in the Old Testament and Judaism.

The dove of the flood story (Gn. 8:8, 12) finds a counterpart in the Gilgamesh epic, where Utnapishtim sends out one after the other a dove, a swallow and a raven. It is an open question whether the dove was originally thought of as a divine bird or messenger. Plutarch [33] expressly mentions the dove in the saga of Deucalion and Pyrrha, and we find doves above Noah's ark on coins from Apameia Kibotos in Phrygia (3rd cent. A.D.). [34] This shows that the dove had a firm place in the story. In the creation story, too, the brooding of the רוּחַ אֱלֹהִים over the water (Gn. 1:2) seems to contain a mythical reminiscence related on the one side to the myth of the divine egg and on the other to the later legend that an egg from heaven fell into the Euphrates, was brought by a fish to the bank, and was hatched out by doves, the Syrian Venus springing forth from it. [35] On the other hand, when Ben Zoma (c. 90 A.D.) compares the hovering of the Spirit over the water with that of the dove over its brood he is simply trying to define the manner; other birds can be mentioned equally well in par. traditions. [36] The connection between the Spirit of God and the dove is rather clearer when the בַּת קוֹל in the temple is like the cooing of doves [37] or when a late exposition refers קוֹל הַתּוֹר (Cant. 2:12) to the Holy Spirit. [38] For Philo the dove is an allegory of λόγος, νοῦς or σοφία — and not just man's, as in the exposition of the laws of sacrifice. [39] Rather τρυγών is related expressly to divine σοφία and περιστερά to human σοφία. [40] At this pt. Philo's Gk. inheritance probably had a hand.

If the thought of the dove as a divine bird was alien to the OT world, we find hints of the notion of a bird of the soul. But in ancient Israel these are only half-concealed traces. Thus when the dead or the spirits of the dead speak, the same word can sometimes be used for this as for the piping and twittering of birds. [41] On the other hand one might ask at least whether the ref. in Ps. 84:3 to the bird [42] which has found a nest for its young does not stand in parallelism with the yearning of the soul (v. 2) which is satisfied only in the temple. Against the background of the idea of the soul-bird, however, this line of thought would be quite pointless. The idea can be shown to have played a certain role in Judaism, as attested by the mural painting of the synagogue at

---

[30] The proverb is attested from Menand., Ael. Nat. An., XII, 10.

[31] Hesych., Suid., s.v. τρυγών. So already Plin. Hist. Nat., 18, 267: gemitus.

[32] Steier, 2495 f.; → n. 17.

[33] De Sollertia Animalium, 13 (II, 968 f.).

[34] A. Jeremias, Das AT im Lichte des Alten Orients⁴ (1930), 146-153 f. [Bertram].

[35] Hyginus fabulae, 197; Lorentz, 26.

[36] T. Chag., 2, 5 (234), Str.-B., I, 124.

[37] bBer., 3a; Str.-B., I, 124 f. Abbott, 139-181 on Bath Qol. Noteworthy, too, is the interpretation of the dove's cooing as κύριε κύριε, bChull., 139b; v. Dalman WJ, I, 268 f. Similar ideas possibly led to the LXX rendering of דְּרוֹר in Ps. 84:3 (swallow?) as τρυγών, though cf. Prv. 26:2.

[38] Str.-B., I, 125, → n. 43. In the Mand. lit. the dove is mentioned once as an embodiment of the Rūhā at the baptism in the Jordan, Lidz. Joh., 108, 1 f. This is probably under Chr. influence, for elsewhere Rūhā takes the form of Hawwā, Lidz. Ginza R., 116, 1 ff. On the blood of the dove in the sacrament of modern Mandaeans cf. M. N. Siouffi, Etudes sur la religion des Soubbas (1880), 119.

[39] E.g., Mut. Nom., 248.

[40] Rer. Div. Her., 126 f.

[41] צְפַצֵף cf. Is. 8:19; 29:4 with 10:14; 38:14; on this P. Torge, Seelenglaube u. Unsterblichkeitshoffnung im AT (1909), 70 f.

[42] → n. 37.

Dura-Europos, [43] where souls as winged creatures are hastening to the resurrected bodies. That the dove is esp. important in this connection is proved both by the dove-cots of Palestine (→ 64, 13 f.) and also by Jewish funerary inscr. [44, 45]

Acc. to Lv. 1:14 turtle-doves (תּוֹר) and young pigeons (יוֹנָה) are the only birds offered in sacrifice. [46] Since wild animals were not offered in the OT cultus — the sacrifice is a part of one's possessions — this provision presupposes the keeping of pigeons in Israel. [47] Pigeons were sacrificed when a more valuable animal was too expensive. [48]

Helpless in the hands of its enemies, the dove is a symbol of Moab, of Judah, and of the troubled worshipper. [49] Its cooing is understood as complaint, → 66, 1 ff. [50] Its meaningless fluttering to and fro is compared to the vacillation of Ephraim between Assyria and Egypt, Hos. 7:11. The turtle-dove as a migratory bird knows its season, but God's people refuses all knowledge of God's judgment, Jer. 8:7. Nevertheless, as a returning flight of pigeons Israel will come back to their houses from Assyria, Hos. 11:11. God will not surrender the life of his turtle to the beasts. [51] He has chosen for Himself the one vine from all the trees, the one lily from all the flowers, the one dove from all the birds, the one sheep from all the animals. [52] One can hardly separate from this imagery the endearment "my dove" which Canticles addresses to the beloved. [53] As a love-song Canticles simply uses the poetic vocabulary of love available at the time. Applied to Yahweh and His elect bride, however, the name "dove" takes on a significance which strengthens the connection with the rest of the Canon. [54]

C. The Dove in the New Testament.

1. After the baptism of Jesus the Evangelists [55] record that the Holy Spirit "like a dove" came down upon Him (Jn.: and abode upon Him) from the opened

---

[43] So R. Meyer, "Betrachtungen zu 3 Fresken der Synagoge von Dura-Europos," ThLZ, 74 (1949), 35-38 as against W. G. Kümmel, "Die älteste religiöse Kunst d. Juden," Judaica, 2 (1946), 52, who regards the 4 psyche-like figures as depictions of the Spirit of God (on the basis of the 4 winds of Ez. 37:9 ?).

[44] Cf. J. B. Frey, Corpus Inscr. Judaicarum, I (1936), 664, *s.v. colombes* ; V. Aptowitzer, "Die Seele als Vogel," MGWJ, 69 (1925), 167. Cf. *ibid.*, 163 : the raven is the evil impulse, the dove the good impulse ; → n. 29.

[45] It is very doubtful whether there are any religious implications when the Mishnah, with usurers and dicers, excludes מפריחי יונים "those who fly pigeons," from admission as judges or witnesses, RH, 1, 8; Sanh., 3, 3; cf. bEr., 82a; bSanh., 27b. The discussion in bSanh., 25ab mentions as reasons only the enticing of other pigeons (→ n. 26), a form of theft, or wagering on contests, which as a game of chance is like dicing. Cf. G. Hölscher, *Sanhedrin u. Makkot* (1910), 60, n. 6; S. Krauss, *Sanhedrin u. Makkot* (1933), 123 f.

[46] Cf. also Gn. 15:9; Lv. 12:6; 15:14, 29; Nu. 6:10; Philo Spec. Leg., I, 162 : διότι περιστερὰ μὲν τῶν φύσει τιθασῶν καὶ ἀγελαστικῶν ἡμερώτατον, τρυγὼν δὲ τῶν φύσει μονωτικῶν (loving solitude) τιθασώτατον.

[47] Cf. Is. 60:8; 2 K. 6:25 (?).

[48] Lv. 5:7, 11; 12:8; 14:22, 30.

[49] Jer. 48:28; Ez. 7:16; Ps. 55:6.

[50] Is. 38:14; 59:11; Na. 2:8. Or does Is. 38:14 allude already to the voice of a dead person, so that one might compare it with 8:19; 29:4 ? → n. 41.

[51] Ps. 74:19 : נֶפֶשׁ תּוֹרֶךָ. But LXX obviously read תּוֹרֶךָ = ψυχὴν ἐξομολογουμένην σοι. On the other hand M. Flashar, "Exegetische Studien zum Septuagintapsalter," ZAW, 32 (1912), 177 f. thinks the translator made an intentional guess ; not understanding the image, he substituted what was for him the important thought of a confession of praise [Katz].

[52] 4 Esr. 5:26; cf. 2 S. 12:3 ? The symbols of the lamb and the dove are also found together among the Mandaeans, namely, for Eve ; Lidz. Joh., 215, 7 [M. Dibelius].

[53] Cant. 2:14; 5:2; 6:9; of the eyes of the beloved 1:15; 4:1; of her cheeks 1:10 LXX.

[54] For the many Rabb. instances of dove for the people of Israel, esp. in Midr. Cant., cf. Str.-B., I, 123 f.

[55] Mk. 1:9-11; Mt. 3:13-17; Lk. 3:21-22; Jn. 1:32-34 (the Baptist's testimony).

heavens. [56] Mk. and Mt., though hardly in a restrictive sense, describe this as an experience of Jesus. [57] Jn., in keeping with his concept of testimony, describes it as an experience of the Baptist. Lk. simply narrates what happened. Neither from the εἶδεν of Mk. and Mt. nor from ὡς before περιστεράν, [58] however, may one conclude that this is not a material phenomenon in the true sense. [59] The extension σωματικῷ εἴδει in Lk. is not directed against a Docetic view, nor is the emphasis on εἴδει designed to counteract too corporeal an understanding. What is stressed is simply that the Holy Spirit here revealed Himself in a particular way, whereas later He was manifested as a flame of fire (Ac. 2) or, more commonly, in spiritual effects → πνεῦμα.

The question arises why the Spirit appears as a dove rather than an eagle or sparrow or some other being. Perhaps the narrative in Jn. 1:32 f. shows that this form of manifestation was particularly appropriate. Here the Baptist was told by God of the descent of the Spirit on Him who was to baptise in the Spirit. Without any further instruction, then, he could correctly associate with the Holy Spirit the appearance of a dove at the decisive moment. Those who heard the account would find in this form of the Spirit, not an astonishing oddity, but a confirmation of the real descent. This all makes sense when one takes into account the many associations which had linked the dove and deity both in the OT and generally in Asia Minor throughout the centuries. It is hardly necessary to show in detail that in Assyria the dove was regarded as the bird of royal choice, [60] though research into religious history has helped us to appreciate the manifold

---

[56] The union of the Holy Spirit with Jesus is variously expressed by the Evangelists. Mk. links καταβαῖνον directly with εἰς αὐτόν; Lk. puts ἐπ' αὐτόν first, as also Mt., who interpolates ἐρχόμενον; Jn. combines καταβαίνειν with ἐπ' αὐτόν but adds the emphatic μένειν ἐπ' αὐτόν. Mt., Lk. and Jn. could well have been influenced by the form in which the LXX expresses the coming of the Holy Spirit : we find the verbs γίνεσθαι (Ju. 11:29), ἐπέρχεσθαι (Is. 32:15 cf. Mt.), ἐπιτιθέναι (Is. 44:3), ἅλλεσθαι (Ju. 14:6, 19; 15:14 — so Cod. B; Cod. A κατευθύνειν —; 1 S. 10:10, ἐφ- 1 S. 10:6; 11:6), ἀναπαύεσθαι (Is. 11:2), but always with ἐπί and acc. It is hard to say whether there is in Jn.'s μένειν ἐπ' αὐτόν an allusion to the Shekinah (μένω = שָׁכַן), so Sahlin, op. cit., 99, 104; ἐπί with acc. answers the question "where?" as well as (class.) "whither?" Bl.-Debr. § 233. More likely Jn. has Is. 11:2 in mind and sees a fulfilment of this prophecy (Just. Dial., 87 explains Is. 11:2: ἐπαναπαύσεται ἐπ' αὐτὸν πνεῦμα θεοῦ κτλ., as follows : ταύτας τὰς ... τοῦ πνεύματος δυνάμεις ... ἐπεληλυθέναι ἐπ' αὐτόν, cf. Mt. 3:16). For Mk., too, εἰς αὐτόν can hardly mean more than "to him"; it says nothing about the nature of the union. For this we have to turn to Ev. Eb. Fr., 3 : ἐν εἴδει περιστερᾶς κατελθούσης καὶ εἰσελθούσης εἰς αὐτόν. The older accounts attempt no interpretation and in their indefinite statements reflect the mysterious and incomprehensible nature of the whole event. μένειν ἐπ' αὐτόν in Jn. 1:32 f. certainly does not mean that the dove remained hovering over Jesus as the winged Ahuramazda hovered over the heads of the Persian kings, Gressmann, 39. Cf. Od. Sol. 24:1 f.: "The dove flew on the head of our Lord Christ because he was its head. It sang over him and its voice was heard." Cf. also Heliand., 987-989 of the Holy Spirit : "... like a beautiful bird, a lovely dove. This flew on the Lord's shoulder and rested on the child of him who rules" (Bultmann Trad., 265, n. 1).

[57] On the other hand, one can explain the restriction to Jesus in Mk. by the desire of the Evangelist to have the true rank of Jesus concealed at first from those around Him, cf. 1:34, 44; 9:9 etc. (the Messianic secret); in keeping is the 2nd pers. sing. of the heavenly voice, replaced in Mk. 9:7, but already in Mt. 3:17, by the 3rd pers., → V, 353.

[58] As against Hck. Mk., ad loc. The fire of Ac. is also a material epiphany and not just an appearance. ὡς or ὡσεί is simply an indication that what is perceived is transparent.

[59] The fairly common suggestion that "like a dove" refers to the descent rather than the Spirit (e.g., B. Weiss, Das Matthäusev. [1910], ad loc.) is quite improbable. Both authors and readers knew enough of the general descent of the divine breath not to need an image for this. The ref. is obviously to the visible manifestation which has to be expressed.

[60] Gressmann, 40, 359 thinks this is at least highly probable, though still in the sphere of hypothesis.

significance of the dove. [61] The image is in any case so impregnated with symbolic power in proverb and saga, in cultic use and custom, in the sacred records of patriarchs and prophets, that in the hour when God acknowledged His Son the dove could be the recognisable and almost exclusively suitable phenomenal form of the Holy Spirit of God. The fact that in Judaism the dove could mediate the Bath Qol (→ 66, 17-20) makes all the more natural its appearance in connection with the heavenly voice (both dove and voice come from the heavens). [62] Possibly the idea of proselytes coming under the wings of the Shekinah [63] is linked with the figure of the dove, esp. in view of the fact that we find, though not in ancient witnesses, the equation שְׁכִינָה = שְׁכִיּוֹנָה = what is as a dove = ὡς περιστερά. [64] The baptismal records do not seem to contain any reminiscence of Noah's dove. [65]

2. The dove is mentioned as a sacrifice in the infancy stories in Lk. (2:24). As an offering in purification Mary brings two turtle doves or [66] two young pigeons. The fact that she brings two shows that she could not afford a lamb as a burnt offering, and thus offered the sacrifice of the poor, [67] → 67, 4 ff. By birth Jesus belongs to the poor and humble. The sellers of doves are also mentioned in the accounts of the cleansing of the temple, Mk. 11:15; Mt. 21:12; Jn. 2:14, 16. [68]

---

[61] For possible religious associations cf. Clemen, 124 f.

[62] To trace back the dove to an ancient scribal error (יוֹנָה for יָנוּחַ, cf. Is. 11:2) is hardly satisfying in view of the unanimity of the tradition. On the same ground we must reject the daring and complicated thesis of F. Spitta, "Beiträge z. Erklärung d. Synopt.," ZNW, 5 (1904), 316-323, namely, that in the light of Ev. Eb. (Jerome in Is. 11:2 [MPL, 24, 148 B]): *descendet omnis fons Spiritus sancti,* we may conjecture an original κολυμβήθρα τοῦ πνεύματος, and only through confusion (κολυμβήθρα > κόλυμβος > *columbus* [sic!]) did the idea of a dove arise. Even less convincing is the rationalistic exposition of F. v. Edelsheim, *Das Ev. nach Mk.* (1931), 35, who thinks the experience of Jesus was caused by the sun breaking through the clouds and the accidental hovering of a wild dove over Him. G. Runze, *Das Zeichen des Menschensohnes u. der Doppelsinn des Jona-Zeichens* (1897), 74-114 argues that the dove of the Jordan is identical with the sign of Jonah and the sign of the Son of Man; on the debate → III, 406, Bibl.; 408, n. 18.

[63] Nu. r., 8, 7; Rt. r. on 2:12; cf. Moore, I, 330; Hirsch, 53.

[64] Hirsch, 57. To see in the dove a picture of the people Israel (Sahlin, *Studien z. 3. Kp. d. Lk.* [1949], 101-105) is thus unnecessary and out of place, since the dove comes from heaven and the identity of Jesus with the redeemed people of the old covenant plays no part elsewhere except allegorically at Mt. 2:15. Cf. M. Dibelius, *Die Formgeschichte des Ev.*² (1933), 272, n. 1.

[65] Though cf. A. Adam, "Das Sintflutgebet in d. Taufliturgie," *Wort u. Dienst, Jhbch. d. Theol. Schule Bethel,* NF, 3 (1952), 21: "At the baptism of Jesus in the Jordan, however, the mention of the dove seems to carry an allusion to the dove of the flood, and implicitly the olive-branch on which it alighted is equated with the promised branch, Zech. 3:8 and 6:12." But though we soon find speculation about baptism and the flood (1 Pt. 3:19-22) there is no mention of the dove prior to Tert. (Bapt., 8 [CSEL, 20, 207 f.]). It was even later in the East before it found a place as the link between the flood and baptism, namely, in Cyr. Catechesis, XVII, 10 (MPG, 33, 982a-b). Neither Just. in Dial., 138 nor Origen links the dove of Noah with that of the Jordan. For iconography cf. Sühling, 222: "I know of no depictions of Noah in baptisteries." G. B. de Rossi, *La Roma Sotteranea Cristiana,* I (1864), 324 reproduced the oldest depiction of the baptism in the Jordan (in the hypogaeum at Lucina) in such a way as erroneously to draw the dove with an olive-branch in its beak. Rather oddly this largely discredited his intrinsically correct interpretation among archaeologists. Only J. Wilpert's correction (*Die Malereien d. Katakomben Roms* [1903]) brought it recognition, cf. Sühling, 11.

[66] One cannot gather from the story which of the alternatives of Lv. 12:6, 8 she actually brought.

[67] Lv. 12:8; Str.-B., II, 123 f.

[68] On rises in pigeon prices and measures against them cf. Keretot, 1, 7, Str.-B., I, 851.

It is impossible to say whether these are private vendors or official salesmen for the temple authorities. [69]

3. The dove is a symbol of simplicity (→ 65, 25 f. and → ἀκέραιος, I, 209 f.) in the mashal in Mt. 10:16, in which Jesus is probably applying an ancient proverb to His disciples: [70] γίνεσθε οὖν φρόνιμοι ὡς οἱ ὄφεις καὶ ἀκέραιοι ὡς αἱ περιστεραί. The point of comparison is hardly that the dove is adapted for sacrifice, [71] since this is shared in common with many other animals. The inner antithesis demands that the cunning of the serpent (Gn. 3:1 φρονιμώτατος πάντων τῶν θηρίων) be balanced by an opposing but no less obvious quality on the part of the dove. Since such qualities were commonly ascribed to the dove throughout antiquity these have to be considered first, namely, its harmlessness and simplicity, cf. the use of ἀκέραιος for persons. [72] The disciples are to meet the hostility of their foes with every cunning, but they still stand under the norm that the heart must be pure and the eye single. [73]

D. The Dove in the Early Church.

The conflation of biblical testimonies (Noah's dove → 66, 6-11, Israel as God's dove → 66, 8-20, the dove of the Jordan → 67, 22-69, 11) with the religious notions of antiquity (divine bird, divine messenger → 64, 18-65, 11, bird of the soul → 65, 13-22) and popular wisdom (the dove as the symbol of various qualities → 65, 23 ff. and the opp. of the serpent → lines 3-14) gave the dove almost inexhaustible symbolical power in the early Church. The bird was not holy as such nor did it enjoy special veneration, but it recurs constantly in literature and iconography.

1. The dove as a sign of the Holy Spirit is the centre and connecting pt. of all statements. [74] Since, however, the Spirit and the Logos were often identified [75] and the dove of the Jordan was thus an image of the Logos, the dove could also be a symbol of Christ in spite of, along with, and long after the development of trinitarian dogma. Origen relates the doves of Cant. 4:1 (plur.) to the Son and the Spirit. [76] Cyril of Alex. finds an allegorical prefiguring of the death of Christ in the offering of pigeons. [77] For various heresies the dove of the Jordan was a welcome proof that only at baptism did the Messiah come upon and unite Himself with the man Jesus, the son of Joseph and Mary. [78] The

---

[69] Str.-B., I, 850 f.

[70] At least this best explains its occurrence in R. Jehuda b. Simon (c. 320) in Midr. Cant., 2, 14 (101a) and perhaps already in R. Jochanan (d. 279) in Ex. r., 21 (83c); both in Str.-B., I, 574 f.; cf. Bultmann Trad., 107 and 112.

[71] So G. Kittel, → I, 210, 2 f.

[72] E.g., Eur. Or., 922 and → I, 209, 25-28.

[73] In Ign. Pol., 2, 2 the meaning is a little different, since the saying is taken as a rule for different situations, cf. also Midr. Cant., 2, 14 (101a), Str.-B., I, 574.

[74] Cf. on what follows the full collection of material in Sühling ; on the dove in exposition and depiction of the annunciation and Pentecost, also at the election of bishops etc., cf. ibid., 34-51.

[75] So Cl. Al. Paed., I, 6, 43, 3 etc., v. F. J. Dölger, ΙΧΘΥΣ, I (1910), 49, 82. On the dove in the epiclesis at baptism and the Lord's Supper, cf. Sühling, 80-86.

[76] Comm. in Cant., III (GCS, 33, 174, 14 ff.): ... duae columbae intelligantur esse filius Dei et Spiritus sanctus. Et ne mireris, si columbae simul dicantur, cum uterque similiter advocatus dicatur, sicut Johannes evangelista declarat ... (cf. Jn. 14:16 f. with 1 Jn. 2:1). That Orig. (ibid., 200, 22 ff.) expounded the call of the turtle (Cant. 2:12) as the voice of Christ is a misunderstanding on the part of Sühling, 58; for Orig. ibid., 226, 34 ff. turtur = ipsa sapientia Dei. There is an understanding in terms of the Baptist in Hipp. Comm. on Cant. 2:12 Fr. XIX (GCS, 1, 365, 34 ff.).

[77] De adoratione, XV f. (MPG, 68, 969, 972, 1001, 1009, 1020, 1048).

[78] So the Gnostic Cerinthus, also perhaps the Jewish Chr. Ebionites, Iren. Haer., I, 26, 1 f.; Hipp. Ref., VII, 33 f.; Epiph. Haer., 28, 1, 5 f.

equation Christ = dove was established with the help of gematria : Π (80) + Ε (5) + Ρ (100) + Ι (10) + Σ (200) + Τ (300) + Ε (5) + Ρ (100) + Α (1) = 801 = Α (1) + Ω (800) = Christ (Rev. 1:8). [79] In Pistis Sophia even God the Father appears in the form of a dove. [80]

2. That the symbolism of the dove could be worked out in many different ways is shown by the discussion of the well-known passage in Tert.: [81] *nostrae columbae domus.* Writing against the Valentinians the rhetorically minded jurist, appealing to Mt. 10:16, claims for himself and his companions too the gift of gnosis. If one could have only cleverness or simplicity, one should choose the latter, since it is nearer to God. It is the nature of the serpent (*solita est*) to tempt Christ, while that of the dove is to demonstrate Him (*demonstrare*). [82] The dove is the messenger of divine peace, the serpent the spoiler of the divine image. In a bold expression Tert. then sets the serpent in its corner in the underworld as a symbol of the Valentinians' love of mystery and of their secret discipline. He then continues : *Nostrae columbae etiam domus simplex, in editis semper et apertis et ad lucem. Amat figura spiritus sancti orientem, Christi figuram.* Is the ref. to God's house or to the dove-cot, which would fit the description very well ? If the former, might it be that there were eucharistic vessels in the form of doves ? [83] What is the bearing on the position of the cultic building ? [84] We best do justice to Tert. if we realise that his intention was to draw a metaphorical par. between the nature and housing of the dove and that of the Church ; hence everything is deliberately ambiguous. Only when he abandons fig. language (*amat ...*) can one expect more direct symbolism : the dove is *figura spiritus sancti*. Previously *nostrae columbae domus ...* simply means : "With us who keep to the dove (non-Gnostic Christians) even the house (of God) is simple" — and not just the heart and mind. Very broadly, then, the dove stands for authentic divine sonship.

3. It is not surprising, therefore, that believers themselves are called doves. Cl. Al. is the pioneer of this usage, and Orig. develops it. [85] In association with Mt. 10:16 the belief in the indwelling of the Holy Spirit in believers smoothed the way for the expression. Related are the accounts which tell of a dove flying out of martyrs after death ; the dove is here both a symbol of the Holy Spirit and also the bird of the soul. If the ref. to a dove in Mart. Pol., 16, 1 is hardly part of the original, [86] we find similar refs. quite frequently in stories of martyrdom from the time of Prudentius. [87]

---

[79] So the Valentinian Marcus acc. to Iren. Haer., I, 14, 6; Hipp. Ref., VI, 47, 2; 49, 5; Ps.-Tert., Adv. Omnes Haer., 5 (CSEL, 47, 22); H. Leisegang, *Die Gnosis* (1924), 40 f.; F. M. M. Sagnard, *La gnose valentinienne* (1947), 373 f.

[80] 1:1.

[81] Val., 3, cf. F. J. Dölger, "Unserer Taube Haus," *Antike u. Christentum,* II (1930), 41-56, with bibl. of the discussion.

[82] Some expositors take *demonstrare* to mean "signify," as though the dove were a symbol of Christ. In this case, however, the opp. would not be *temptare* but *diabolum demonstrare.* The ref. is surely to the dove of the Jordan, and the phrase *solita est* is to be ascribed to Tert.'s rhetorical style.

[83] So also H. Leclercq, *Dict. d'archéologie chrétienne et de liturgie,* 31 (1913), 2231. But such vessels are first mentioned only in the 5th art. of the Council of Constantinople in 536, v. J. Sauer, *Symbolik d. Kirchengebäudes ...* (1902), 193, or the Consuetudines of Cluny acc. to Dölger, *op. cit.,* 43.

[84] Acc. to Dölger, 55 f.: eastward entrance.

[85] Cl. Al. Paed., I, 5 (GCS, 12, 98, 10 f.); Orig. Comm. in Mt., 26, 21 f. (GCS, 40, 549, 13-550, 27; 552, 29-553, 2); cf. Sühling, 97-109.

[86] Due to their absence from Eus. Hist. Eccl., IV, 15, 39 the words περιστερὰ καί are under strong suspicion of having been added later ; they are not supported by a (misleading) par. in the martyrdom of St. Mamas (as against E. Nestle, "Ein Gegenstück zum Gewölbe u. zur Taube im Mart. Pol.," ZNW, 7 [1906], 359 f.). There is no need for a conjecture like περὶ στύρακα (Wordsworth); cf. also Sühling, 124-130.

[87] Peristephanon, III, 161-172 in the hymn on the martyrdom of Eulalia.

4. The dove of peace has an assured place in the lit. and art of the early Church. Antiquity regarded the olive-branch as a sign of peace [88] and the dove as timid and innocent, → 65, 25 f. But the dove became the dove of peace (with or without the olive-branch) only in the preaching of the early Church, [89] which proclaimed God's peace on earth and found in Noah's dove [90] a type of the end of wrath. [91]

5. Among the Manicheans, too, the dove plays an important role. [92] In the Psalm-Book it embodies the Holy Spirit esp. as the Spirit which indwells believers : "Beautiful is the dove which had found a sacred union : Jesus is ... in the heart of the believer in Him." [93] The serpent, on the other hand, represents the unclean spirit. [94] In particular the love of God is symbolised as a white dove : [95] "Make a place for the dove, the white-winged ; do not put the serpent with it lest it be frightened away from thee." [96] The Christian himself is addressed as the sacred white dove floating in the heavens with the three-branched anēš (branch of life ? wreath of flowers ?) in its mouth. [97] But the image of the dove also seems to be used of believers. [98] Acc. to Mani the Son of God was no more a real man than the dove of the Jordan was a real dove. [99]

Greeven

† περιτέμνω, † περιτομή, † ἀπερίτμητος → ἀκροβυστία, I, 225, 4 ff.

Contents : A. The Non-Biblical Use : 1. περιτέμνω, 2. περιτομή, 3. ἀπερίτμητος. B. Circumcision in the Old Testament : 1. Usage ; 2. Origin, Original Meaning and Distribution of the Rite ; 3. The OT Tradition. C. Circumcision in Judaism : 1. In the Hellenistic Roman Period ; 2. In the Period after the Destruction of the Temple. D. Circumcision in Primitive Christianity : 1. Usage ; 2. The Problem of Circumcision in the Apostolic Period.

---

[88] E.g., Verg. Aen., 7, 153-155; 8, 116.

[89] So Tert. Bapt., 8 : quemadmodum enim post aquas diluvii, quibus iniquitas antiqua purgata est, post baptismum, ut ita dixerim, mundi pacem caelestis irae praeco columba terris adnuntiavit dimissa ex arca et cum olea reversa, quod signum etiam apud natione paci praetenditur, eadem dispositione spiritalis effectus terrae id est carni nostrae emergenti de lavacro post vetera delicta columba sancti spiritus advolat pacem dei adferens, emissa de caelis, ubi ecclesia est arca figurata. Cf. Sühling, 217-222 et al.

[90] The Synagogue, on the other hand, wondered why the dove would bring anything so bitter as an olive in its beak, Str.-B., I, 123.

[91] The raven is its counterpart (→ n. 29, 44); with its liking for refuse and corpses it does not return to the ark, v. Sühling, s.v. "corax," "corvus," "Rabe."

[92] I am grateful to A. Adam for friendly hints and counsel in Coptic questions.

[93] Manichaean MSS in the Chester Beatty Collection, II : A Manichaean Psalm-Book, Part II (ed. C. R. C. Allberry [1938], 161, 7 f.).

[94] Ps.-Book, II, 156, 28.

[95] Ibid., 156, 25 f., 158, 8.

[96] Ibid., 167, 57-60; cf. 158, 11 f.; 182, 29-34.

[97] Ibid., 185, 11-13. 165, 2 f. also seems to refer to Christ : "Beautiful is a cooing dove whose young surround it ; beautiful is a shepherd who pastures his flock."

[98] Manichaean MSS, I : Manichaean Homilies (ed. H. J. Polotzky [1934], 12, 5-8 : "... she (?) killed the doves [...] who cooed over the mysteries of God [... she opened ?] their (earum) dove-cot and let them out. She dipped [her hands in the] blood of their (earum) young."

[99] At least acc. to Hegemonius (Acta Archelai, 59 [GCS, 16, 86 f.]).

π ε ρ ι τ έ μ ν ω κτλ. Liddell-Scott, Moult.-Mill., Pape, Pass., Pr.-Bauer⁴, Thes. Steph., s.v. On B : Steiner, Art. "Beschneidung" in Schenkel, I, 404-411; B. Stade, "Der Hügel d. Vorhäute," ZAW, 6 (1886), 132-143; I. H. Gray, G. Foucart, D. S. Margoliouth, G. A. Barton, Art. "Circumcision," ERE, III, 659-680; C. v. Orelli, Art. "Beschneidung," RE³, II, 343-346; H. Gressmann, Mose u. seine Zeit (1913), 56-61; A. Bertholet, Art. "Beschnei-

A. The Non-Biblical Use.

1. a. Attested from Hom. in Gk. lit., the verb περιτέμνω originally means "to cut round," Hes. Op., 570: οἴνας περιτάμνειν, "to prune vines," Hdt., IV, 71: περιτάμνεσθαι βραχίονας, "to make incisions round one's arms" as a sign of mourning, Dio C., 62, 7, 2 : τοὺς μαστοὺς περιτέμνειν, "to cut the breasts." b. περιτέμνω then means "to encircle with a view to taking away," "to rob," so, e.g., in the mid. in Hom. Od., 11, 402 : βοῦς περιταμνόμενον ἠδ' οἰῶν πώεα καλά, "driving away cattle or fine flocks of sheep" (cf. 24, 112); Hdt., IV, 159 : περιταμνόμενοι γῆν πολλήν, "since they were robbed of a considerable territory," Polyb., 23, 13, 2 : πανταχόθεν περιτέμνεσθαι αὐτοῦ ἡ ἀρχή, "that his dominion should everywhere be cut short," Diog. L., III, 63 : περιτάμνεσθαι πᾶσαν σοφίαν, "to be deprived of all wisdom." Militarily Xenoph. Cyrop., V, 4, 8 mentions the capture of chariots (ἅρματα) which were "encircled by the cavalry," περιτεμνόμενα ὑπὸ τῶν ἱππέων. c. περιτέμνω occurs as a ritual tt. from Hdt., II, 36, 104, where the mid. περιτάμνεσθαι τὰ αἰδοῖα means "to circumcise." At a later period ref. might be made to Diod. S., 1, 28, 3; 3, 32, 4 : περιτέμνειν τοὺς γεννωμένους παῖδας, "to circumcise newborn children," and among the many pap. refs. P. Tebt, II, 292, 20 (189-190 A.D.), where a *strategos* is asked for a missive on the basis of which two boys who were to enter the priesthood of Soknebtunis could be circumcised (περιτμηθῆναι). [1]

2. The noun περιτομή, "circumcision," is found in lit. from Agatharchides [2] and Artapanos (2nd cent. B.C.); for Artapanos cf. the quotation in Eus. Praep. Ev., IX, 27, 10 : ἡ περιτομὴ τῶν αἰδοίων. The plur. occurs in Strabo, 16, 2, 37, who refers to περιτομαί ("circumcisions") as a Jewish custom [3] derived from Egypt, → 75, n. 19. Cf. finally P. Tebt., II, 314, 3-6 (2nd cent. A.D.): πιστεύω σε μὴ ἀγνοεῖν ὅσον κάμ[α]τον ἤνεγκα ἕως τὴν [π]ερι[το]μὴν ἐκπλέξω, "I definitely believe you know what trouble I had to carry out the circumcision."

3. The adj. ἀπερίτμητος occurs in the sense "unmaimed" in Plut. De Amore Prolis, 3 (II, 495c) and in the sense "uncircumcised" in Preisigke Sammelbuch, 6790, 14 (257 B.C.).

B. Circumcision in the Old Testament.

1. Usage.

a. In the LXX the verb περιτέμνω occurs exclusively as a ritual tt., predominantly literal : Gn. 17:10-14, 23-27; Ex. 4:25; 12:44, 48; Lv. 12:3; Jos. 5:2-8; 21:42d; 24:31a; Est. 8:17; Jdt. 14:10; 1 Macc. 1:60 f.; 2:46; 2 Macc. 6:10; 4 Macc. 4:25, though also transf., e.g., Dt. 10:16 : καὶ περιτεμεῖσθε τὴν σκληροκαρδίαν ὑμῶν for וּמַלְתֶּם אֵת עָרְלַת לְבַבְכֶם; Ier. 4:4. [4] A notable aspect of LXX usage is that not merely the root מול and derivates

---

dung," RGG², I, 946 f.; R. Kittel, *Gesch. d. Volkes Israel,* I ⁵, ⁶ (1923), Index, *s.v.*; J. C. Matthes, "Bemerkungen u. Mitteilungen über die Beschneidung," ZAW, 29 (1924), 70-73; H. Ranke, A. Alt, E. Ebeling, K. Sudhoff, Art. "Beschneidung," RLV, 1 (1924), 445 f.; J. Benzinger, *Hbr. Archäologie³* (1927), 126-129. On C : Bousset-Gressm., Index, *s.v.*; S. Krauss, *Talmudische Archäol.,* II (1911), 11 f.; Moore, Index, *s.v.* "Circumcision"; Str.-B., IV, 23-40; L. Finkelstein, *The Pharisees* (1938), Index, *s.v.* "Circumcision"; H. Sahlin, "Die Beschneidung Christi," Symbolae Biblicae Upsalienses, 12 (1950); F. Sierksma, "Quelques remarques sur la circoncision en Israël," *Oudtestamentische Studiëen,* 9 (1951), 136-169, with additional bibl.

[1] Cf. also P. Lond., I, 24, 12 (163 B.C.): ὡς ἔθος ἐστὶ[ν] τοῖς Αἰγυπτίοις περι(τε)-τέμνεσθαι; v. Preisigke Wört., Liddell-Scott, Pr.-Bauer⁴, *s.v.*

[2] Geographi Graeci minores, I (ed. C. Müller), 154; cf. also Timagenes (1st cent. B.C.) Fr., 88 (FGH, II, n. 321) in Pr.-Bauer⁴, *s.v.*

[3] Strabo mentions in the same connection the circumcision of girls (plur. ἐκτομαί), cf. 17, 824 : τὰ γεννώμενα παιδία καὶ θήλεα ἐκτέμνειν, ὅπερ καὶ τοῖς Ἰουδαίοις νόμιμον, but this does not apply to Judaism.

[4] Ez. 44:7, 9 refers to men of foreign descent who are of uncircumcised heart and body : ἀπερίτμητοι καρδίᾳ καὶ ἀπερίτμητοι σαρκί.

are transl. περιτέμνω but all other Heb. terms for "to circumcise": e.g., Ex. 4:25 : περιέτεμεν τὴν ἀκροβυστίαν τοῦ υἱοῦ αὐτῆς for וַתִּכְרֹת אֶת־עָרְלַת בְּנָהּ; Jer. 4:4 : περιτέμεσθε τὴν σκληροκαρδίαν ὑμῶν, Heb. הָסִרוּ עָרְלוֹת לְבַבְכֶם. Even the stem הִתְיַהֵד, which occurs only once in later parts of the OT, in the sense "to come over to Judaism," is rendered in Est. 8:17 by the explanatory περιτέμνεσθαι καὶ ἰουδαΐζειν. This uniform usage is obviously explained by the fact that the vocabulary of the Egyptians, who were regarded as the classical exponents of circumcision in antiquity (→ 75, n. 19), had had a normative influence on the usage of the Jewish translators and effaced the distinctions in the Heb. terms. [5] There are deviations in the LXX only at Dt. 30:6 (περικαθαρίζειν for the Heb. root מול) [6] and Jos. 5:4 (περικαθαίρειν for the same original). [7] The Egyptian-influenced uniformity of the LXX [8] is broken only by Symmachus, a Jewish Christian of the end of the 2nd century, who sharply distinguishes between the tt. for true circumcision and the transf. use. For the latter, in analogy to Dt. 30:6 LXX, he uses καθαρίζειν, → 83, 36 ff.

b. The noun περιτομή is also used only in a ritual sense for "circumcision," e.g., Gn. 17:13 for the inf. abs. ni הִמּוֹל "to be circumcised," Ex. 4:26 for the plur. מוּלֹת "circumcisions," cf. also Ex. 4:25 : τὸ αἷμα τῆς περιτομῆς τοῦ παιδίου μου, "my son's blood of circumcision," → 74, 24 ff. Jer. 11:16 is obscure.

c. The adj. ἀπερίτμητος "uncircumcised," usually corresponds to עָרֵל. In the vast majority of instances it is used lit., cf. the ritual Gn. 17:14 : ἀπερίτμητος ἄρσην for Heb. עָרֵל זָכָר, or to denote non-Israelites, e.g., the Philistines in Ju. 14:3; 15:18. For the fig. use cf. esp. Jer. 9:25 : ὅτι πάντα τὰ ἔθνη ἀπερίτμητα σαρκί, καὶ πᾶς οἶκος Ἰσραηλ ἀπερίτμητοι καρδίας αὐτῶν.

d. It is to be noted that the LXX refers more often to circumcision and uncircumcision than does the original Heb. Apart from Est. 8:17 (→ line 4 f.) cf. Ex. 4:25, where there is no Heb. for τὸ αἷμα τῆς περιτομῆς (→ line 16 f.), also Jos. 5:4, 6, where the LXX deviates widely from the Heb. [9]

e. The usage of Philo and Joseph. does not differ from that of the LXX. [10]

2. Origin, Original Meaning and Distribution of the Rite.

a. Circumcision is usually practised on males (περιτομή), more rarely on females (ἐκτομή). [11] It is of magical or primitive religious derivation, [12] and has two functions,

---

[5] The aspect of preventive magic (→ 76, 7 ff.) is clearer in the Heb. כָּרַת than מול, which is an economic term originally meaning "to cut," e.g., grass, cf. Köhler-Baumg., s.v. The hiph'il of מול, "to ward off," which in ψ 117:10 ff. is transl. ἀμύνω (so also 'A in v. 10), while Σ reads מָלַל "to weaken" and renders διαθρύπτω, cf. ψ 57:6 θρύπτω [Bertram], is probably to be distinguished from I מול: cf. Köhler-Baumg., s.v.

[6] καὶ περικαθαριεῖ κύριος τὴν καρδίαν σου for וּמָל יְהוָה אֱלֹהֶיךָ אֶת־לְבָבְךָ.

[7] In Lv. 19:23 the singular verb עָרֵל, "to leave standing as foreskin" (→ 75, 3 ff.), is changed by the LXX into its opp. (περικαθαρίζω), cf. Tg. O. ad loc. and Vulgate. The verb περικαθαίρω, which, like περικαθαρίζω, is sacrificial, cf. Dt. 18:10; Is. 6:7 [Bertram], also occurs in 4 Macc. 1:29 in the sense "to cut" (of plants).

[8] Deissmann B, 151 has drawn attention to this.

[9] Cf. v. 4 : ὅσοι ποτὲ ἐγένοντο ἐν τῇ ὁδῷ καὶ ὅσοι ποτὲ ἀπερίτμητοι ἦσαν τῶν ἐξεληλυθότων ἐξ Αἰγύπτου, v. 6 : διὸ ἀπερίτμητοι ἦσαν οἱ πλεῖστοι αὐτῶν τῶν μαχίμων τῶν ἐξεληλυθότων ἐκ τῆς Αἰγύπτου.

[10] Cf., e.g., Philo Spec. Leg., I, 1-9 (→ 79, 6 ff.); Jos. Bell., 2, 454 (ἰουδαΐζειν μέχρι περιτομῆς); Ant., 1, 192 (plur. περιτομαί); Ap., II, 137, 141 ff.

[11] Circumcision is still practised among 200 million people to-day. It is not customary among Europeans or the non-Semitic peoples of Asia except in so far as they are Mohammedan or have accepted the Mosaic Law, like the Chazars (c. 740), cf. E. Waldschmidt-B. Spuler-H. O. H. Stange-O. Kressler, Gesch. Asiens (1950), 321-322. Among Christians Copts and Abyssinians practise it.

[12] Bertholet, RGG, 946 f.; G. v. d. Leeuw, Phänomenologie d. Religion (1933), 176, 452.

being on the one side a sacrifice of redemption and on the other a tribal or covenantal sign. Both play a role in the OT, though the covenantal aspect gradually comes to predominate. An analogy to the idea of redemption (→ 76, 3 ff.) may be found in the agricultural sphere in Lv. 19:23 f. (Holiness Code). This lays down that for the first three years the fruits of newly planted trees are to be regarded as a foreskin (עָרְלָה) and are not to be used for food. In the fourth year these fruits are to be dedicated to Yahweh as a thank-offering. We obviously have here the development or influence of an older practice whose original sense has been lost at the stage of the Holiness Code. Acc. to this practice the first fruits were to be devoted to the demons of fertility and spirits of the field to redeem later harvests and secure the protection of the numina. The vocabulary of the circumcision ritual in Lv. 19:23 f. is derived from sacrificial ceremonial. In contrast to the magico-religious understanding of the rite the hygienic aspect is of secondary derivation; the first to speak of this is Hdt., II, 37, → n. 44. Circumcision is partly a puberty rite and partly a marriage rite. But circumcision of the newly born is also widespread. All three forms occur in the OT, though, apart from converts, the circumcision of newly born boys gains the upper hand.

b. Whereas the Eastern Semites are apparently unfamiliar with circumcision, [13] the Israelites are not the only Western Semites to practise it. [14] Gn. 17:23 ff. (P) bears express witness to the circumcision of Ishmael, i.e., to circumcision among the Arab tribes; this is also attested in the Hell.-Roman period. That among the Western Semites there were also uncircumcised tribes and federations (cf. Gn. 34:15 ff.), [15] indeed, that the practice was not everywhere continuous, [16] is intrinsically very probable. [17] As far as Israel is concerned the origin of the rite is lost in the mists of pre-history. [18] Ancient West Semitic usage seems to suggest that the rite played a part in the marriage ceremonial of the West Semites. In possible agreement with this is the fact that the OT tradition does not support Israel's derivation of circumcision from Egypt. [19]

---

[13] B. Meissner, *Babylonien u. Assyrien,* I (1920), 349 f.; Ebeling, RLV, 446. This is certainly true in the historical period.

[14] Acc. to Hdt., II, 104 the Syrians and Phoenicians were circumcised; the Jews and Samaritans were probably included here as a comparatively less numerous part of the population of the hinterland.

[15] Cf. H. Gunkel, *Gn.* [5] (1922); O. Procksch, *Gn.* [2, 3] (1924), *ad loc.* One must, of course, reckon with the possibility that the rulers of Shechem, insofar as the story contains ancient tradition, might have been of non-Canaanite or non-Semitic descent.

[16] Cf. Hdt., II, 104: Φοινίκων ὁκόσοι τῇ Ἑλλάδι ἐπιμίσγονται, οὐκέτι Αἰγυπτίους μιμέονται κατὰ τὰ αἰδοῖα. Insofar as Hdt. is here speaking from his own experience, contact with non-Semites led to abandonment of the ancient national or tribal custom.

[17] There is excellent material for, e.g., Egypt. At an early time circumcision was generally a wedding rite, cf. Ranke, 445. Jos. 5:8 (though cf. W. Rudolph, *Jer.* [1947] on 9:25); Ez. 31:18; 32:19-32 presuppose the practice. Possibly in the Hell. period circumcision was given up as a general custom, for the pap. refer only to the circumcision of priests, which was dependent on official permission after Hadrian's prohibition, → 80, 9 ff. Cf. W. Otto, *Priester u. Tempel im hell. Ägypten,* I (1905), 213-216 (*ibid.,* 213, n. 2 for older bibl.); also A. Erman, *D. Religion d. Ägypter* (1934), 400; for a somewhat different view H. Kees, *Ägypten* (1933), 87.

[18] In the Ugaritic tablets (14th cent. B.C.) the root *ḥtn* = **ḥatana* "to marry" occurs with the related noun *ḥtn* = **ḥatanu,* "son-in-law" (Gordon, 232, 807), which corresponds to the Heb. חָתָן "bridegroom" and חֹתֵן "father-in-law." The same root means "to circumcise" in Arab., cf. J. Wellhausen, *Reste arab. Heidentums²* (1927), 174 f. and Köhler-Baumg., *s.v.* חָתַן. One has thus to presuppose as ancient West Semitic **ḥatana,* "to marry," "to circumcise," with a later secondary separation of the two meanings.

[19] Hdt., II, 104 says that the Colchians, Egyptians and Ethiopians were originally the only peoples to practise circumcision, and that the Syrians and Phoenicians took over the rite from the Egyptians. But Hdt. can hardly be accepted as an authority, cf. A. Alt, *Reallex.,* 445 f. Similarly, Jos. 5:9 does not support an Egypt. origin for circumcision in Israel.

3. The OT Tradition.

a. The oldest literary witness for circumcision in Israel is Ex. 4:24 ff., which gathers up various historically significant traditions. [20] The basis is a wilderness tradition rooted in the pre-Yahwistic belief in demons. Moses and Zipporah obviously want to get married at a holy place — בַּדֶּרֶךְ בַּמָּלוֹן. The numen of the place disputes with Moses for the *ius primae noctis* and seeks his life. Spirited Zipporah circumcises her husband with a stone knife, [21] and with the apotropaic cry חֲתַן דָּמִים אַתָּה לִי, "a bridegroom of blood art thou to me !" she puts the demon to shame, so that he leaves Moses. [22] The circumcision of Moses thus denotes his redemption, cf. the ancient West Semite root *ḥatana = "to marry," "to circumcise," → n. 18. The stage of the story offered by J presupposes a further development in the concept of God and the practice of circumcision. To all appearance it is now the newborn boy who is redeemed when his mother circumcises him with the apotropaic cry : "A bridegroom of blood art thou to me !" Yahweh it is who now demands this. A theologically significant pt. is that in Ex. 4:24 ff. circumcision is obviously a traditional and primitive rite, though it is very loosely connected with Israel's belief in Yahweh.

Jos. 5:2, 8 f. rests on an ancient popular tradition. At the undoubtedly pre-Israelite sanctuary of Gilgal, near Jericho, there was a hill of foreskins, גִּבְעַת הָעֲרָלוֹת, obviously an ancient place of circumcision for the circumcision of adults as a rite of puberty or redemption. This tradition, which belongs to the Benjamite cycle, is historicised in Jos. 5:2, 8 f., associated with the Ephraimite tribal hero Joshua and extended to all Israel. [23] It is worth noting that the ancient rite carried out with stone knives (→ n. 21) is traced back to a command of Yahweh but not associated with the intrinsically close concept of the covenant. For in the popular etym. of Gilgal it is simply said that through circumcision Yahweh rolled off [24] from Israel the shame of Egypt, i.e., Egypt's scorn for all who were uncircumcised. With the preceding tradition this supports our previous suggestion that in Israel circumcision is an older rite which reaches back into pre-history and which was variously explained and understood, as well as administered, in the individual tribes. The rite of circumcision is not essentially related to faith in Yahweh, and only gradually does it come to be embedded in Israel's life of faith. [25] We may assume that it was already well established in the 11th cent. B.C. [26] This is supported esp. by the fact that Israel could appeal to circumcision in proof of its tribal or national identity over against the Philistines. [27]

b. Gn. 17:1-27 (P) is an advance on Ex. 4:24 ff. and Jos. 5:2, 8 f. Here circumcision is integrated into the theological exposition of the priestly author. Administered on the

---

[20] Cf. G. Beer, *Ex., Hndbch. z. AT*, 3 (1939), *ad loc.*, with main bibl.

[21] צֹר, "flint," "stone knife," cf. Köhler-Baumg., *s.v.* Apart from Ex. 4:25 and Jos. 5:2 f. the LXX mentions the concealment of the stone knives with which Joshua circumcised the Israelites in the 2 additions Jos. 21:42d; 24:31a (μάχαιραι πέτριναι).

[22] Correctly noted for the first time by E. Meyer, *Die Israeliten u. ihre Nachbarstämme* (1905), 59.

[23] H. J. Kraus, "Gilgal, ein Beitrag zur Kultgeschichte Israels," *Vetus Testamentum*, 1 (1951), 181-199 attempts to deduce from Jos. 3-5 an ancient covenant tradition in Gilgal to which Jos. 5:2, 8 f. belongs in some way not specified by the author. This hypothesis tells us nothing about the nature of circumcision in the pre-exilic period.

[24] The etym. is obscure and allows of many different interpretations, cf. M. Noth, *Jos.*,[2] *Hndbch. zu AT*, 7 (1953), *ad loc.* with bibl.

[25] Cf. G. Hölscher, *Gesch. d. isr. u. jüd. Religion* (1922), Index, *s.v.* "Beschneidung." Eichr. Theol. AT, I³, 60 pts. out that the original home of the rite is not in the official cultus.

[26] This does not have to imply, of course, that at this stage the rite was carried out everywhere in the same way.

[27] Cf., e.g., Ju. 14:3; 15:18; 1 S. 14:6; 17:26.

8th day (v. 12; cf. Lv. 12:3), it is now a sign of the covenant [28] (v. 11: אוֹת בְּרִית) and applies not only to freeborn Israelites but also to slaves born in the house (יְלִיד בַּיִת), or alien slaves acquired by purchase (מִקְנַת כֶּסֶף מִכֹּל בֶּן־נֵכָר). [29] P undoubtedly adopts earlier traditions, and the polemical statements in Jer. 4:4; 6:10 (→ lines 18 ff.) possibly indicate that the Jews attached special significance to circumcision towards the end of the 7th cent. [30] The palpable nomism of Gn. 17, however, makes it probable that it marks a theological advance and that we have here an anchoring of basic Jewish laws in salvation history such as the Babylonian exiles undertook for reasons of religious self-preservation. P does not disguise the fact that other nations practised the same rite. Thus he refers to the circumcision of all Abraham's descendants, and tells us how the 13-year Ishmael, the representative of the Arabs, was circumcised at a time when the birth of the true seed of Abraham, namely, Isaac, was only promised, vv. 19-26. If all the descendants of Abraham are distinguished from those around them by circumcision, Israel is itself distinguished from kindred tribes by the fact that through circumcision its people are set in covenant with God in the true sense, so that the divine promises apply to them alone, vv. 4-7.

c. Long before P, namely, in the days of Josiah (639/8-609 B.C.), we find on the lips of Jeremiah the transf. use of the term circumcision: "Circumcise yourselves for me, [31] and take away the foreskins of your heart" (Jer. 4:4); "their ear is uncircumcised" (6:10; cf. also 9:25). In the prophecy of Jer., who like his great predecessors is in sharp conflict with the popular cultic religion of Israel, there is raised for the first time, so far as the sources tell us, the theological problem of a rite which ultimately belongs to the sphere of sacramental magic, and which can thus acquire a certain justification in Yahweh belief only if it is divested of its cruder side and referred to the inward man and his relationship with God. Along these lines Jer. initiates a theological understanding which gains in prominence during the succeeding centuries [32] and which finally reached its climax in Paul's assessment of circumcision, → 82, 26 ff.

C. Circumcision in Judaism.

1. In the Hellenistic Roman Period.

a. It is only in the age of the Seleucids that the sources begin to speak of circumcision as a sign of the covenant. The religious conflicts under Antiochus IV (176/5-163 B.C.), which were in the last resort caused by the attempts at reform made by certain circles in Jerusalem, [33] led to the prohibition of circumcision. Women who had their children circumcised were executed, and babies marked with the covenant sign were also put to death, cf. 1 Macc. 1:60 f. [34] Hence circumcision, as an essential expression of the national religion, came to be regarded as worth dying for. From another angle the same sign

---

[28] Eichr. Theol. AT, I, 60 rightly says that this is the oldest evidence in Israel's history for the adoption of circumcision into covenant theology. Not least of the reasons for this development might be that with the loss of national autonomy Israel laid increasing stress on the family and its place in the covenant relationship.

[29] Cf. the secondary P law of Ex. 12:43 ff. acc. to which no foreigner (בֶּן־נֵכָר), resident alien (תּוֹשָׁב) or day-labourer (שָׂכִיר) may take part in the Passover. The bought slave, however, may do so if circumcised. So too, acc. to v. 48 f., may the stranger (גֵּר) who has had the male members of his family circumcised, for he is reckoned as a native (אֶזְרַח הָאָרֶץ).

[30] It is possible that the 7th cent. Jews were led to overestimate the rite by foreign settlement in neighbouring Samaria and the resultant need for differentiation.

[31] So acc. to the textus emendatus (for יְהֹוָה); cf. W. Rudolph, Jer., Hndbch. z. AT, 12 (1947), ad loc.

[32] Cf. Dt. 10:16; 30:6 (→ n. 6); Ez. 44:7; O. Sol. 11:1 ff.; 15:4. Cf. further Ltzm. R. on 2:29.

[33] E. Bickermann, Der Gott d. Makkabäer (1937), 59-65.

[34] Cf. also 2 Macc. 6:10; 4 Macc. 4:25.

was a symbol of victory over subjugated peoples in times when political supremacy was enjoyed. [35] In romance form Est. 8:17 LXX (→ 74, 2 ff.) describes how many Gentiles, after the victory of the Jews in the party struggle at the Persian court, had themselves circumcised and became Jews for fear of the Jews. [36] The Hasmonaean John Hyrcanus I (c. 128 B.C.), in the course of his successful wars of expansion among the Idumaeans, put into effect a policy of mass circumcision and compulsory Judaising, cf. Jos. Ant., 13, 257: "He allowed them to stay in the land if they would be circumcised and keep the laws of the Jews." [37] This atavistic procedure, which goes far beyond Gn. 34 and finds an echo in Jub. 30:1-18, [38] was not just a secular operation. [39] Though we are without more detailed information on the inner motives for these compulsory measures, there would appear to stand behind them the idea of restoring the "Holy Land," in which no Gentiles may live. In fact the Idumaeans later regarded themselves as full Jews ; the fact that the Jerusalem aristocracy contemptuously described them as ἡμιου-δαῖοι did not alter this. [40] The subjection of the Ituraeans in Northern Palestine [41] by Aristobulus I (104-103 B.C.) followed a similar pattern, and though there is no direct attestation it seems highly probable that when Jewish law was imposed with the Jewish conquests of Alexander Jannaeus (103-76 B.C.) compulsory circumcision was included. [42] As a basic Jewish law, circumcision was in the Hell. Roman period one of the presuppositions without which intimate dealings with the Jews were not conceivable. This is plain from the attitude of the Herod family to their non-Jewish neighbours. For all that they participated in the life of Hell. Roman society, they would rather forego a politically advantageous marriage than allow an uncircumcised son-in-law into the family circle. [43]

b. Though circumcision was highly regarded, the Jews themselves were often aware of problems inherent in the traditional rite. For one thing, even apart from political conflicts and latent hostility to the Jews, the whole of Jewish religion was challenged by the Hell. world, which was no less predominant in Syria-Palestine than in the rest of the Mediterranean basin and contiguous territories. The barbaric rite of circumcision was particularly exposed to Hell. criticism. For both Gks. and Romans the rite was indecorous and even perverse. Hadrian compared it to *castratio* (→ 80, 9 ff.), [44] which

---

[35] For the compulsory circumcision of uncircumcised Jewish children in the first instance cf. 1 Macc. 2:46.

[36] Cf. M. Haller-K. Galling, *Die fünf Megilloth, Hndbch. z. AT*, 18 (1940), ad loc.

[37] The circumcision of Arabs and Edomites is reported in Gn. 17:18 ff. The Edomites/Idumaeans also occupied considerable tracts of the former kingdom of Judah including the royal city of Hebron. It is hardly likely that the resident population, which was partly ancient Jewish, was uncircumcised. More probably the impulse behind Ant., 13, 257 was to bring under subjection to a distinctively Jewish rite, though cf. W. Rudolph, who follows H. Cornill, *Jer.* (1905), on 9:25.

[38] Cf. Test. L. 6:1 ff. In the institution of the posterity of Levi as priests because of Levi's "justice, judgment and revenge" on Israel's enemies one may discern propaganda for the Hasmonaeans, cf. R. Meyer, "Levitische Emanzipationsbestrebungen in nachexilischer Zeit," OLZ, 41 (1938), 723-726. The midrash on circumcision in Jub. 15:23-34 (Gn. 17) is also best understood against the background of Hasmonaean politics.

[39] So Schürer[4], I, 264 f.

[40] Cf. Jos. Bell., 4, 270-282; Ant., 14, 403.

[41] Jos. Ant., 13, 319 with appeal to a quotation from Timagenes in Strabo : τὸ μέρος τοῦ τῶν Ἰτουραίων ἔθνους ᾠκειώσατο δεσμῷ συνάψας τῇ τῶν αἰδοίων περιτομῇ.

[42] Jos. Ant., 13, 395 ff.; cf. Schürer, I, 286.

[43] Acc. to Jos. Ant., 16, 220-225 the Arab Syllaeus unsuccessfully sought the hand of Salome, the daughter of Herod the Gt. In this connection circumcision is not expressly mentioned, though it was probably the chief obstacle in spite of the possibility that the Arab was circumcised in another way, → n. 37. It is expressly attested that the betrothal of Epiphanes of Commagene with Drusilla, the daughter of Herod Agrippa I, was broken off because circumcision was demanded, cf. Jos. Ant., 20, 139 f.

[44] Thus Hdt., II, 37 already says of the Egyptians that they are προτιμῶντες καθαροὶ εἶναι ἢ εὐπρεπέστεροι.

was punishable as murder. [45] Where a sense of inferiority brought complete openness to Hell. culture, as in reforming Judaism in Jerusalem at the beginning of the 2nd cent. B.C., [46] the ancient rite of circumcision had to go. Hence the scorn of others when circumcised Jews in Jerusalem took part in games often led to ἐπισπασμός, the restoration of the foreskin, cf. 1 Macc. 1:15 : καὶ ἐποίησαν ἑαυτοῖς ἀκροβυστίας.

Though this radical course had no serious consequences except in times of persecution (→ 80, n. 64), Jewish apologetic shows that Judaism was continually under pressure to reflect on the rite. One such defence, which in essence obviously follows the traditional line of Alexandrian apologetics, is offered by Philo, Spec. Leg., I, 1-11. In favour of the rite Philo argues that it is hygienically necessary, [47] that it befits a priestly people (as shown by the example of the Egyptians), [48] and that it makes the member that produces material life like the heart, which gives birth to higher thoughts and has a richer progeny. Philo also advances two allegorical considerations : on the one side circumcision combats sensuality, while on the other it resists the idea that the power of procreation confers divine likeness. [49] It would seem that this form of apologetic rather suspiciously omits the covenant aspect of circumcision. In fact, it is at this pt. that the whole ambivalence of the atavistic rite is disclosed. [50] Circumcision thus constitutes a main obstacle to apologetics in the Hell. Roman world. It also limits missionary activity and propaganda, for many φοβούμενοι or σεβόμενοι τὸν θεόν, who later abandoned their original home for the primitive Gentile Chr. Church, would not accept the obligation of circumcision.

c. In respect of groups within Judaism, circumcision is, of course, a self-evident presupposition, but it is less important than its figurative understanding. Thus the spiritualising of the ancient rite, which is found from the time of Jeremiah and is attested in Deuteronomistic circles (→ 77, 17 ff.), is mentioned in the Manual of Discipline, 5, 5 : "And men of truth are to circumcise in the community the foreskin of desire and obduracy," [51] cf. also 5, 28, where there is ref. to the uncircumcision of a heart (עורלת [לבבו]) which is hardened against a member of the community." [52] This example, which comes from Essene circles, [53] is of particular significance because, in addition to prior materials, it shows that in NT days the figurative and spiritualised view of circumcision was by no means unknown in Palestinian Judaism.

2. In the Period after the Destruction of the Temple.

a. With the fall of the hierocracy of Jerusalem under Vespasian, Pharisaic-Rabbinic nomism increasingly carried the day until finally it achieved complete ascendancy in the second half of the 2nd cent. A.D. [54] In this period the purely physical understanding of circumcision was exclusively asserted. This was strengthened by the fact that in the

---

[45] How close *circumcisio* and *castratio* are for Pl. may be seen from the polemical utterance in Gl. 5:12.

[46] Cf. esp. 1 Macc. 1:11. This concern to link up with the Hell. world by abandoning an ancient custom is by no means peculiar to Syria, cf. already Hdt., II, 104 and E. Bickermann, *loc. cit.*

[47] Cf. Hdt., II, 37 (→ n. 44).

[48] Jos. Ap., II, 140-143 appeals to the circumcision of the Egypt. priests.

[49] Philo mentions spiritual circumcision in Spec. Leg., I, 304-306. He also seems to know Jews who value this alone. On the other hand, in opposition to them he emphasises both spiritual and physical circumcision in Migr. Abr., 92 (cf. 89).

[50] Cf. Sib., IV, 164, where in a sermon on conversion only washing and not circumcision is demanded of Gentiles. The story of the conversion of Izates in Jos. Ant., 20, 38-48 also shows what a problem the rite constituted.

[51] ואנשי האמת=ואאם. On ואאם למול ביחד עורלת יצר ועורף קשה cf. Habakkuk Comm., 7, 10.

[52] H. Bardtke, *Die Handschriftenfunde am Toten Meer* (1952), 95, n. 3.

[53] Cf. L. Rost, "Der gegenwärtige Stand d. Erforschung der in Palästina neu gefundenen hbr. Hdschren.," ThLZ, 77 (1952), 277-280, 317-320.

[54] R. Meyer, "Die Bdtg. des Pharisäismus f. Gesch. u. Theol. d. Judt.," ThLZ, 77 (1952), 677-684.

years of crisis circumcision was also a sign of confession. [55] Thus along with R. Ishmael R. Akiba (d. 135 A.D.) in particular opposes any spiritualising of the term foreskin. In Gn. r., 46 § 5 on Gn. 17:1 he takes literally the biblically attested uncircumcision of heart, ear and mouth, [56] shows that these cannot be circumcised, and thus arrives at the normative place of circumcision, which he describes as the foreskin of the member עָרְלַת הגוף. Emphasis on the physical aspect rules out spiritualising on the basis of the refs. to heart, ear and mouth. [57] Hence the fig. understanding, which is attested from Jeremiah to NT days, is banished from official theology. [58]

b. Circumcision was prohibited by Hadrian (117-138), Egypt. pap. (→ 73, 15 ff.) show that this was a general ban throughout the empire, [59] and Spartianus is probably right when he suggests that it was the cause of the Bar-Cochba revolt : *moverunt ea tempestate et Iudaei bellum, quod vetabantur mutilare genitalia.* [60] Acc. to the lex Cornelia Hadrian ordered that *circumcisio* as well as *castratio* should be punished as murder. The prohibition was enforced after the suppression of the revolt, and was suspended only when Antoninus Pius issued an edict of toleration in 138. [61] Thus in contrast to the Egyptians, who in individual cases were able to secure official permission for the circumcision of new priests, Judaism only a few yrs. after the end of the Bar-Cochba revolt enjoyed again a general liberty to practise circumcision.

c. Following or developing ancient traditions, but enriched by experiences in the years of crisis, the Tannaites of the post-Hadrian period worked out the interpretation of the ritual which became normative in all its basic features. [62] On this view circum-**cision, now** called מִילָה, is unconditionally obligatory for every healthy Jewish boy. [63] It is to be administered on the 8th day after birth. If this falls on a Sabbath, the duty of circumcision takes precedence of the law of the Sabbath, b. Shab., 132a : "Circumcision, as all say, even supplants the Sabbath מילה גופה דברי הכל דוחה שבת). The administration comprises the following acts : the cutting of the foreskin (מִילָה), the baring of the glans penis (פְּרִיעָה), the removing of the remaining membranes (צִיצִים), the draining of the blood of circumcision with the mouth (מָצַץ) and finally the putting on of a plaster (אִסְפְּלָנִית) along with caraway (כַּמּוֹן). The detailed description shows that an attempt was made to rule out all possibility of ἐπισπασμός, which had often taken place in times of persecution and which had certainly been a problem in the age of Hadrian. [64] The ceremony was accompanied by benedictions and it concluded with a feast.

d. The theological significance of circumcision is that it is a precondition, sign and seal of participation in the covenant which God made with Abraham. He who invalidates

---

[55] Hence Rabbis in their judgments have to take ἐπισπασμός into account, and try to guard against it.

[56] With ref. to Jer. 6:10; Ex. 6:30; Jer. 9:25.

[57] So also H. J. Schoeps, *Theol. u. Gesch. des Judenchristentums* (1949), 139. On the other hand Wnd. Barn. on 9, 5, on the basis of an incorrect rendering of Gn. r., 46 § 5, finds here both spiritual and physical circumcision, cf. Philo, → n. 49.

[58] Cf. the anti-Jewish polemic in Just. Dial., 12, 3 : δευτέρας ἤδη χρεία περιτομῆς, καὶ ὑμεῖς ἐπὶ τῇ σαρκὶ μέγα φρονεῖτε.

[59] Schürer[4], I, 677-679; cf. also Schl. Gesch. Isr., 373 f.; M. Noth, *Geschichte Israels* (1950), 380 f.

[60] Vita Hadriani commentario illustrata (1869), 14. For a different view, which can hardly be correct even though based on A. Schlatter (→ n. 59) *et al.,* cf. H. Bietenhard, "Freiheitskriege d. Juden unter den Kaisern Trajan u. Hadrian u. d. messianische Tempelbau, II," Judaica, 4 (1948), 93 f.

[61] Modestinus, Digesta, 48, 8, 11: *circumcidere Iudaeis filios suos tantum rescripto divi Pii permittitur : in nos eiusdem religionis qui hoc fecerit, castrantis poena irrogatur ;* on this cf. Schürer[4], I, 677, n. 80.

[62] Krauss, 11 f.; J. Preuss, *Biblisch-Talmudische Medizin* (1911), 278-289.

[63] For examples of what follows cf. Str.-B., IV, 28-31.

[64] Cf. T. Shab., 15, 9 : "He who has drawn the foreskin forward must be circumcised afresh ... Many were circumcised (again) in the days of Ben Koseba," i.e., they had effected ἐπισπασμός. Cf. Str.-B., IV, 32-40.

this sign by ἐπισπασμός breaks the covenant and loses the salvation mediated thereby.[65] If he is to be accepted again, he must submit afresh to circumcision. Circumcision is also a confessional sign for whose sake Israel accepted bloody martyrdom.[66] The blessing which accrues to Israel therefrom is as follows : Because of it God undertook to protect His people and gave them the land of Israel. The lifegiving power of circumcision is everywhere at work in the universe and in history. In the coming aeon Israel will be redeemed from Gehinnom in virtue of it, and will participate in the joys of the Messianic age.[67]

D. Circumcision in Primitive Christianity.

1. Usage.

a. In the NT, as in the LXX, the verb περιτέμνω is a cultic tt.[68] In the lit. sense it occurs in the act. at Lk. 1:59; 2:21; Jn. 7:22; Ac. 7:8; 15:5; 16:3; 21:21 and Barn., 9, 8 with ref. to Gn. 17:23 ff. It is used in the mid.-pass. at Ac. 15:1; 1 C. 7:18; Gl. 2:3; 5:2 f.; 6:12 f. περιτέμνω has fig. significance in Col. 2:11 with ref. to baptism : περιετμήθητε περιτομῇ ἀχειροποιήτῳ, cf. also Barn., 9, 1-4; 10, 12.

b. The substantive περιτομή occurs as a verbal noun in the act. at Jn. 7:22; Ac. 7:8 διαθήκη περιτομῆς on the basis of Gn. 17:10; cf. also Gl. 5:11 εἰ περιτομὴν ἔτι κηρύσσω, Barn., 9, 7: πρῶτος περιτομὴν δούς, "who first circumcised." The mid.-pass. occurs in Jn. 7:23 : περιτομὴν λαμβάνειν, "to be, to have oneself, circumcised." Cf. also R. 2:25 ff.; 3:1: τίς ἡ ὠφέλεια τῆς περιτομῆς, 4:10 : ἐν περιτομῇ εἶναι, with which cf. Barn., 9, 6 and Ign. Phld., 6, 1; 4:11: περιτομῆς σφραγίς; 1 C. 7:19; Gl. 5:6; 6:15; Phil. 3:5 : περιτομῇ ὀκταήμερος (→ supra); also Barn., 9, 4; Dg., 4, 1. περιτομή is used in a transf. sense at R. 2:29 περιτομὴ καρδίας (→ 83, 1 ff.); Col. 2:11 (→ 83, 5 f.); Barn., 9, 4. It is also used abstractum pro concreto for "the circumcised," "Jews," in distinction from ἀκροβυστία, "Gentiles," R. 3:30; 4:9; Eph. 2:11; Col. 3:11; cf. also R. 4:12 οἱ ἐκ περιτομῆς; 15:8; Gl. 2:7 ff. At Ac. 10:45 περιτομή is a tt. for Jewish Christians in the expression οἱ ἐκ περιτομῆς πιστοί, though the simple οἱ ἐκ περιτομῆς is more common : Ac. 11:2; Gl. 2:12; Col. 4:11; Tt. 1:10. Only once is the word used fig. for Christians as the true Israel : ἡμεῖς γάρ ἐσμεν ἡ περιτομή, Phil. 3:3, → 83, 14 f.

c. The adj. ἀπερίτμητος does not occur in the canonical writings in the lit. sense, though cf. Barn., 9, 5 : πάντα τὰ ἔθνη ἀπερίτμητα ἀκροβυστίᾳ (Jer. 9:25). It is once used fig. of Jews in a mixed quotation from the LXX at Ac. 7:51: σκληροτράχηλοι καὶ ἀπερίτμητοι καρδίαις καὶ τοῖς ὠσίν, "stiffnecked and obstinate in hearts and ears."[69] Cf. also Barn., 9, 5b : ὁ δὲ λαὸς οὗτος ἀπερίτμητος καρδίᾳ with allusion to Jer. 9:25.[70]

2. The Problem of Circumcision in the Apostolic Period.

a. In the Synoptic tradition, which takes it for granted that Jesus and the earliest disciples belong to Palestinian Judaism, circumcision is no problem. It is true that, e.g., the preaching of the Baptist in Mt. 3:9; Lk. 3:8 (Q) radically challenges Abrahamic sonship,[71] and for Jewish ears this is also a challenge to the Abrahamic covenant, and herewith to circumcision as the means of incorporation into it. On the other hand, in contrast with the law of the Sabbath, circum-

---

[65] Str.-B., IV, 34.

[66] Ibid., 37 f.

[67] Ibid., 38 ff.

[68] It should be noted that in the NT, esp. in Pl., περιτέμνω and περιτομή are used much more often than in the OT.

[69] Cf. Lv. 26:41; Jer. 6:10; Ez. 44:7, 9 (Wdt. Ag. and Bau. Ag., ad loc.).

[70] On the nature of the quotation cf. Wnd. Barn., ad loc.

[71] The threatening speech of the Baptist may derive from a pre-Chr. tradition, though it has been worked over in its present form, cf. Kl. Mt., ad loc.; also R. Meyer, Der Prophet aus Galiläa (1940), 116 and 124 f.

cision plays no part in the Synoptic disputes, whether in the literal or the figurative sense. In the infancy stories in Lk. 1:59; 2:21 there is uninhibited reference to the circumcision of both the Baptist and Jesus. In both cases it is linked with the giving of the name, on which the main emphasis falls; [72] there is in contemporary Judaism no attestation for this practice. [73]

b. John's Gospel mentions circumcision in a disputation between Jesus and the Jews concerning the Feast of Tabernacles, 7:22. We read here that circumcision was given by Moses, which simply means that it is in the Mosaic Law. We are then told in parenthesis that circumcision derives from the fathers, and this is correct insofar as the law of circumcision to which allusion is made, namely, that circumcision takes precedence of keeping the Sabbath (→ 80, 23 ff.), is in fact part of the oral law. On the basis of the command to circumcise on the Sabbath a conclusion is drawn from the less to the greater: "If a man on the sabbath day receive circumcision, that the law of Moses should not be broken, are ye angry at me, because I have made a man every whit whole on the sabbath day?" [74]

The close relation between Rabb. statements and Jn. 7:23 suggests that Jn. was acquainted with Rabb. discussions, just as he shows elsewhere a good knowledge of contemporary Judaism. In the preceding discussion the Johannine Christ — though only theoretically, for in fact He is opposing Judaism — takes the Rabb. understanding of the Law as His platform. Against His opponents He uses a *reductio ad absurdum* by proving the legality of His action from their standpoint : "Judge not according to the appearance, but judge righteous judgment" (v. 24). Though it is quite probable that we have here a tradition which goes back to Jesus Himself, the historical position of the Gospel suggests that Jn. 7:23 f. reflects the dispute between early Christianity and Judaism in the period shortly after the destruction of the second temple.

c. Paul in his conflict with 'Ιουδαϊσμός [75] was compelled to devote a good deal of attention to the problem of circumcision. On the hypothetical assumption that the Law can be fulfilled (→ IV, 1072), he deals with the nature and value of circumcision in R. 2:28 f. [76] In so doing he emphasises the περιτομὴ καρδίας ἐν πνεύματι οὐ γράμματι. This brings him into decisive opposition to the Jewish view that only physical circumcision mediates salvation both in this world and the next — a view which was to achieve dominance in the Synagogue and Jewish Christianity after the victory of Pharisaic Rabbinism in the era after Hadrian, → 83, 34 ff. Paul himself continues a line which begins with Jeremiah (→ 77, 17-27) and which leads to the group, probably Essene, whose theology is partly known to us from the Dead Sea Scrolls → 79, 18 ff. Nevertheless, there is a decisive difference. For the Essenes, as for the first disciples, a self-evident presupposition is to be a Jew, and consequently to possess the covenant sign, even though its physical presence alone is not enough to protect one from falling under the sway of Belial. [77] Paul, on the other hand, transcends the limits of 'Ιουδαϊσμός in

---

[72] Kl. Lk., *ad loc.*

[73] PREl (8th cent. A.D.), 48 proves no more in this connection than Gn. 17:5; 21:3 f. For a discussion → n. 72.

[74] There is a par. deduction in bShab., 132b. R. Eleazar b. Azariah (c. 100 A.D.): "If even circumcision, which affects only one of man's members, supplants the Sabbath, how much more (is it so) of saving life, that it supplants the Sabbath." Cf. on this and other materials Bau. J. on Jn. 7:22; Bultmann J., 208, n. 3.

[75] Cf. for this tt. Gl. 1:13 f.; Ign. Mg., 8, 1; 10, 3; Ign. Phld., 6, 1.

[76] On what follows cf. Ltzm. R., *ad loc.*

[77] As do all Jews (acc. to the Manual of Discipline) who do not belong to the fellowship embodied in the legal demand, cf., e.g., 1, 1-11; 1, 24-2, 1a; 2, 1b-9 etc.

principle. For him the only true Jew is the one who is a Jew in secret, and the only true circumcision is that of the heart (περιτομή καρδίας), R. 2:28 f. This circumcision of the heart is, of course, the work of the Spirit, not of man, v. 29. This means that the circumcision of the heart is for Paul identical with redemption by Christ, and in Col. 2:11 f. he can even call baptism the περιτομή Χριστοῦ. [78] Inasmuch as εἶναι ἐν Χριστῷ means περιτομή καρδίας, he can go on to say that both ἀκροβυστία and περιτομή are done away. This helps us to understand, e.g., Gl. 5:6: ἐν γὰρ Χριστῷ 'Ιησοῦ οὔτε περιτομή τι ἰσχύει οὔτε ἀκροβυστία, ἀλλὰ πίστις δι' ἀγάπης ἐνεργουμένη. [79] If to be ἐν Χριστῷ means that one is neither Jew nor Greek, this implies that the physical sign of the covenant is quite unimportant. Paul thus argues that, as the onetime Gentile does not have to be circumcised, so the onetime Jew must not practise ἐπισπασμός, 1 C. 7:18 f. Materially this gives us the most important concept of the true Israel, so that in Phil. 3:3 Paul can say: ἡμεῖς γὰρ ἐσμεν ἡ περιτομή, a completely new content being hereby given to περιτομή as the true Israel. [80]

Decisive for the spread of the Gospel in the ancient world was the fact that Paul put into practice in a battle against 'Ιουδαϊσμός the insight of faith which he had gained from life in Christ. In Antioch the Jewish Christianity of Jerusalem had laid down that the salvation of uncircumcised Christians was dependent on their accepting the covenant sign. [81] This constituted a fundamental challenge to the theology and missionary practice of the apostle Paul. A meeting took place between Paul and the original apostles in Jerusalem, the so-called Apostolic Council. [82] Paul rejected the Jewish Christian demand, cf. Gl. 2:3: ἀλλ' οὐδὲ Τίτος ὁ σὺν ἐμοί, "Ελλην ὤν, ἠναγκάσθη περιτμηθῆναι, [83] and there was agreement to differ. Gl. 2:7 shows us, of course, that fundamentally freedom from 'Ιουδαϊσμός was simply noted in Jerusalem; in fact, for all the mutual loyalty, the two fronts remained. [84] Paul was now accepted as the preacher of the εὐαγγέλιον τῆς ἀκροβυστίας and Peter as the preacher of the εὐαγγέλιον τῆς περιτομῆς, with no clarification of the theological antithesis. Neither then nor later was any compromise reached which would have finally united the two parties, but compelled either the one or the other to revise basically its theological position.

d. We soon find literary attestation of the separation between Jewish and Gentile Christians. In Barn., 9, 1-9 physical circumcision has been abolished; the only valid περιτομή is the fig. circumcision of the heart. [85] Jewish Christianity, on the other hand, deliberately takes the path of nomism, [86] even though it is excommunicated by the Synagogue. [87] Thus the Jewish Christian Symmachus, in his Gk. rendering of the OT, eliminates περιτέμνω in the transf. sense, replacing it by καθαρίζειν, → 74, 11 ff. This means that along the lines of normal Jewish theology in the latter half of the 2nd cent.

---

[78] Cf. Dib. Gefbr. on Col. 2:11 f.
[79] Cf. also Gl. 6:15.
[80] Dib. Phil., ad loc.
[81] Ac. 15:1 f.; cf. Wdt. Ag. and Bau. Ag., ad loc.
[82] On the historical value of Ac. 15:3-21 v. M. Dibelius, Aufsätze zur Ag. (1951), 84-90. On the history of the problem cf. O. Cullmann, Petrus (1952), 39-52, with further bibl.
[83] On Gl. 2:1-10 v. Ltzm. Gl., ad loc.
[84] For a fine depiction of the Jewish Chr. view cf. Ac. 21:21.
[85] Cf. the explicit presentation in Wnd. Barn., ad loc.
[86] On what follows v. Schoeps, 137-139.
[87] Cf. the Cairo Rec. of the Birkat ha-Minim, which goes back to Samuel the Little (c. 90 A.D.); J. Elbogen, Der jüd. Gottesdienst in seiner geschichtlichen Entwicklung³ (1931), 36-40.

(→ 79, 32 ff.) he does not recognise a fig. view of circumcision. In this way he also demarcates himself from Gentile Christianity in the area of the biblical text.

Meyer

περιφρονέω → III, 633, 1 ff.

| † περίψημα | (→ περικάθαρμα, III, 430, 22 ff.).

Contents : A. The Meaning of the Word outside the New Testament : I. Derivation and Development of Meaning ; II. περίψημα as an Expiatory Sacrifice among the Greeks ; III. The Hellenistic (and Hellenistic-Jewish) Use of περίψημα. B. περίψημα in the New Testament. C. περίψημα in the Post-Apostolic Fathers.

A. The Meaning of the Word outside the New Testament.

I. Derivation and Development of Meaning.

περίψημα is one of the verbal nouns in -μα [1] which were common in Ionic and then even more so in the *koine*. It derives from περιψάω, [2] "to wipe round," "to rub," "to wipe off or clean out," e.g., the eyes, [3] the body, [4] but also objects. [5] Hence περίψημα can mean a. "what is wiped or rubbed off," [6] "something which arises only for what is thrown away," [7] "something which is treated as valueless," [8] hence "refuse," "scum,"

π ε ρ ί ψ η μ α. Thes. Steph., Pass., Liddell-Scott, Pr.-Bauer[4], *s.v.*; F. Zorell, Novi Testamenti Lex. Graecum[2] (1931), *s.v.*; Cr.-Kö., 548, *s.v.* περικάθαρμα. C. du Cange, Glossarium Mediae et Infimae Latinitatis, VI[2] (1886), 276 *s.v. peripsema, peripsima* ; V. Gebhard, Art. "Thargelia," Pauly-W., 5 A, 1296 f.; "Pharmakos," *ibid.*, 19, 1841 f.; H. Usener, "Der Stoff d. gr. Epos," SAW, 137 (1897), III, 62 = *Kleine Schriften,* IV (1913), 258; P. Stengel, *Gr. Kultusaltertumer*[3] (1920), 131, 162, 245 f.; F. Schwenn, "Die Menschenopfer bei d. Griechen u. Römern," RVV, 15, 3 (1915), 36-59; J. Leipoldt, *Der Tod bei Griechen u. Juden* (1942), 42; Joh. W. 1 K., 114 f.; Euthymius Zig. Komm. z. d. nt.lichen Briefen, 228 on 1 C. 4:13; H. Veil in E. Hennecke, *Hdb. z. d. nt.lichen Apkr.* (1904), 218; T. Zahn, *Ignatius v. Antiochien* (1873), 420-423; H. v. Campenhausen, *Die Idee d. Martyriums in d. alten Kirche* (1936), 67-78.

[1] Cf. Bl.-Debr., § 109, 2.

[2] On the etym. deriv. cf. Boisacq[4], 1076 (ψῆν); Pokorny, 145 f.; Hofmann, 428; Schwyzer, I, 328.

[3] E.g., Aristoph. Eq., 909; cf. Pl., 730.

[4] Cf. Euthymius Zig. on 1 C. 4:13 : περιψᾶν γὰρ τὸ ἀποκαθαίρειν τὸν ἱδρῶτα, also Ps.-Oecumenius Comm. in Ep. 1 ad Corinthios on 4:13 (MPG, 118, 692 D), → n. 12, 19.

[5] E.g., IG, XI, 2, 287, 84 (Delos): σπόγγοι περιψῆσαι τὰ ἀναθήματα. On the sponge as a means of περιψῆν (as of περικαθαίρειν) cf. also Theophylactus on 1 C. 4:13 (MPG, 126, 616 D): ὅταν γὰρ ῥυπαρόν τι ἀποσπογγίσῃ τις, περικάθαρμα λέγεται τὸ ἀποσπόγγισμα ἐκεῖνο. καὶ τὸ περίψημα δὲ τὸ αὐτὸ δηλοῖ. περιψᾶν γὰρ λέγεται τὸ περισπογγίζειν, Eustath. Thessal. Comm. in Od., 22, 799, 6 : ὥσπερ αὖ πάλιν τοῦ λύματος ἀφελέστερον τὸ περίψημα, σπόγγισμά τε ὂν αὐτὸ καὶ κατὰ τοῦτο ἐοικὸς τῷ λύματι (→ n. 59), cf. *ibid.*, Index, *s.v.* περίψημα : σπόγγισμα καὶ ἀπόνιμμα.

[6] So Hesych., *s.v.*: περίψημα = περικατάμαγμα (from [περι-]καταμάσσω, "to wipe off"); cf. also Theod. Mops. on 1 C. 4:13 : τὸ περίψημα ἐκ μεταφορᾶς εἴρηται τῶν τὰς τραπέζας μετὰ τὸν τοῦ φαγεῖν καιρὸν ἀποψώντων καὶ ἀπορριπτούντων ὡς περιττὰ ψήγματα.

[7] Cf. Theophylactus on the use of περίψημα in 1 C. 4:13 in the continuation of the passage mentioned in → n. 5 : φησὶν οὖν, ὅτι τοῦ ἀπορρίπτεσθαί ἐσμεν ἄξιοι, καὶ ὡς βδέλυγμα λογίζεσθαι, also the passage from Ps.-Ammon. Adfin. Vocab. Diff., *s.v.* κάθαρσια (→ n. 10); Euthymius Zig. (→ n. 11); Theod. Mops. (→ n. 6).

[8] Cf. Suid., *s.v.* περίψημα : καταπάτημα ὑπὸ τὰ ἴχνη, also Phot. Lex., *s.v.* and the later expansion of Hesych., *s.v.*; also Poll. Onom., V, 163 and other instances in Wettstein on 1 C. 4:13.

"trash," "rubbish," "filth," [9] all in the first instance lit., but then also trans. (→ 86, 17 ff.), as with the synon. κάθαρμα [10] and → περικάθαρμα; [11] b. the "means or instrument of rubbing or cleansing," esp. the "sweat-rag" or "bath-towel," [12] then fig. "the means of religious cleansing," "the means of expiation," "the expiatory offering," "the scapegoat." [13]

II. περίψημα as an Expiatory Sacrifice among the Greeks.

In the last sense περίψημα is first expressly attested in a late lexicographical note which is the same in Photius and Suidas, s.v.: οὕτως ἐπέλεγον τῷ κατ' ἐνιαυτὸν ἐμβαλλομένῳ τῇ θαλάσσῃ νεανίᾳ ἐπὶ ἀπαλλαγῇ τῶν συνεχοντων κακῶν· περίψημα ἡμῶν γένου, ἤτοι σωτηρία καὶ ἀπολύτρωσις· καὶ οὕτως ἐνέβαλλον τῇ θαλάσσῃ ὡσανεὶ τῷ Ποσειδῶνι θυσίαν ἀποτιννύντες. This note is of basic significance for a correct understanding of Paul's use of περίψημα. It shows that περίψημα is a tt. from the circle of ideas and customs relating to so-called φαρμακοί. φαρμακός, the masc. of φάρμακον, [14] is the "means of healing as a person," the "medicine-man." [15] Some men were appointed to secure healing for a city or country by their violent death. [16] These ideas and rites probably originate in the concept of the taboo which is transferred to these sacrifices and set aside in them. [17] We meet them historically in the Greek idea of catharsis. When disaster struck a city or land it was deduced that a μίασμα [18] or (religious) impurity was present. Like the taboo, this μίασμα was laid on a representative of the people, [19] who was then put to death. An accompanying and sometimes related idea is that of an enraged deity, esp. Artemis or Apollo, Poseidon or Athena, who must be placated by a human sacrifice, though originally these were not

---

[9] Cf. the meanings of peripsema in du Cange and the (late) example, ibid., s.v. peripsima.

[10] Cf. Ps.-Ammon. Adfin. Vocab. Diff., s.v. καθάρσια : καθάρματα = τὰ μετὰ τὸ καθαρθῆναι ἀπορριπτούμενα.

[11] Cf. Theophylactus, loc. cit.; Euthymius Zig. on 1 C. 4:13 also takes περίψημα to be identical with περικάθαρμα and understands this as ὁ ἀπορριπτόμενος τῶν σωμάτων ῥύπος.

[12] So Ps.-Oecumenius on 1 C. 4:13 (MPG, 118, 692 D): περίψημα δὲ λέγεται τὸ σάβανον, ὃ τοὺς ἰδρῶτας τοῦ κάμνοντος ἀποψήχει. Cf. also the explanation of περίψημα by the editor N. Calogeras on Euthymius Zig.: συνεκδοχικῶς ... πᾶν τὸ πρὸς καθαρισμὸν πράγματός τινος ῥυπαροῦ ἢ σκεύους ἢ δοχείου ἀκαθάρτου χρησιμεῦον.

[13] These meanings arise naturally from the sense "means of cleansing"; to explain the meaning "expiatory sacrifice" or "scapegoat" there is no need to follow Bchm. K., ad loc. and Cr.-Kö., s.v. περικάθαρμα in pointing to a transfer of dirt or (cultic) impurity to the agent of cleansing and expiation, correct though the thought is in itself, → n. 19.

[14] Acc. to A. Klotz, "φαρμᾰκός?" Glotta, 3 (1912), 236-241 the correctness of the long ᾱ is questionable (though cf. Gebhard, "Thargelia," 1290); hence there is nothing to prevent a close relation to φάρμᾰκον. Nevertheless, φαρμακός as "expiatory offering" is to be differentiated from φάρμακός, "mixer of poison," "magician," e.g., Rev. 21:8; 22:15; Athanasius Apologia ad Constantium, 7 (MPG, 25, 604 D); Ep. ad Serapionem, 22 (MPG, 26, 673 A); Liddell-Scott, s.v. Related to φαρμακός is καθαρμός along with κάθαρμα, Hdt., VII, 197; Plut. De Curiositate, 6 (II, 518b); cf. Schwenn, 39.

[15] F. Pfister, Art. "Kultus," Pauly-W., 22, 2163 takes φαρμακός to mean "medicineman" ("fetish-man," 2180).

[16] Cf. Harp., I, 298, 9 ff. (on this II, 446); Rohde, II, 78 f. with n. 2; Usener, 59-63 (255-259); Schwenn, 26-59; Gebhard, "Thargelia," 1290-1302; "Pharmakos." For examples from antiquity cf. Usener, 61, n. 1 (or n. 134); Schwenn, 36, n. 5; 37, n. 1.

[17] This deriv. is usually accepted by religious historians; cf. J. G. Frazer, The Golden Bough, VI : "The Scapegoat"³ (1913) [1951]), 1-71; Schwenn, 26-28 etc.

[18] E.g., Schol. in Aristoph. Eq., 1136.

[19] In the transfer wiping off (περιψᾶν) could sometimes play a part. Either those present rubbed their hands on the περίψημα to impart to him their own uncleanness (cf. N. Calogeras on Euthymius Zig.) or those who sought cleansing rubbed themselves with things which would absorb what was unclean (damp earth, clay, yolks of eggs, figs, the bodies of young dogs), and these were then washed off again and thus became περίψημα, cf. Rohde, II, 406 f.; Stengel, 162.

true sacrifices[20] but ritual slayings.[21] In addition to φαρμακός[22] there were many other terms for these "sacrifices," e.g., κάθαρμα, περικάθαρμα (→ III, 430, 23), καθάρσια,[23] καθαρτήριος,[24] κραδησίτης,[25] δημόσιος,[26] also περίψημα. The slaying of the φαρμακοί took place either every yr., esp. at the widespread feast of Thargelia[27] which is probably presupposed in the note on περίψημα (→ 85, 8 f.: κατ᾽ ἐνιαυτόν), or as needed, i.e., when some general affliction arose such as drought, famine,[28] plague[29] etc.

In addition to the regularity of the custom the note tells us something which is highly significant for a correct understanding of Paul's use, namely, that an individual[30] is vicariously put to death for the whole people (→ 90, 15 ff.); this would be a young man, since young men and even children were usually preferred for human sacrifices.[31] We are not told whether this individual was esp. valuable or worthless. Usually prominent men were offered as sacrifices, the king himself,[32] members of the leading families of a city,[33] pure virgins,[34] etc., but less estimable characters seem to have been chosen as φαρμακοί, e.g., criminals, who were condemned to die anyway,[35] ne'er-do-wells,[36] paupers,[37] who preferred a brief period of good nourishment at the end of life[38] to prolonged starvation, and also misshapen creatures.[39] This kind of φαρμακοί helps us to see why the word and its synonyms became terms of abuse, → 89, 3 ff. This was

---

[20] It is worth noting that the ancient sensed this distinction, cf. Suid., s.v.: ὡσανεὶ θυσίαν, J. Tzetzes, Historiarum Variarum Chiliades, V (1826), 726, 729 : ὡς πρὸς θυσίαν, though usually the rites fused, cf. Tzetzes; Schol. in Aristoph. Pl., 445 : καθάρματα ἐλέγοντο οἱ ἐπὶ καθάρσει λοιμοῦ ἤ τινος ἑτέρας νόσου θυόμενοι τοῖς θεοῖς.

[21] Cf. Schwenn, 19, 26 etc.

[22] E.g., Aristoph. Ra., 733.

[23] E.g., Harp., s.v.

[24] Hesych., s.v. φαρμακοί.

[25] Hesych., s.v.: on the fig-branches (κράδαι) with which the φαρμακοί were pelted or struck (Hipponax. Fr., 6, 7, 10, Diehl) cf. Frazer, op. cit., 255-273.

[26] E.g., Aristoph. Eq., 1136; Schol. on this : δημοσίους δέ, τοὺς λεγομένους φαρμακοὺς οἵπερ καθαίρουσι τὰς πόλεις τῷ ἑαυτῶν φόνῳ. ἢ τοὺς δημοσίᾳ καὶ ὑπὸ τῆς πόλεως τρεφομένους.

[27] Cf. Usener, 60 f. (257); Gebhard, "Thargelia," 1287-1290.

[28] E.g., Schol. in Aristoph. Ra., 730; Tzetzes, loc. cit.

[29] E.g., Servius, In Vergilii Carmina Comm., I (1881), 346 on Aen., 3, 57; cf. also N. Calogeras on Euthymius Zig.

[30] At an earlier stage two φαρμακοί were publicly put to death, one for the men and another for the women of a city or land, cf. Usener, 59, n. 2 (255, n. 128).

[31] Cf. e.g., Philo Byblius in Eus. Praep. Ev., IV, 16, 11: ἀντὶ τῆς πάντων φθορᾶς ... τὸ ἠγαπημένον τῶν τέκνων ... λύτρον τοῖς τιμωροῖς δαίμοσι ...

[32] Cf. the story of Codros, the last king of Athens, and on this Schwenn, 77.

[33] Cf. Schwenn, 43.

[34] E.g., Plut. Sept. Sap. Conv., 20 (II, 163b); Athen., XI, 15 (p. 466c); Antoninus Liberalis, Μεταμορφωσέων Συναγωγή, 25, 2 f. (in E. Martini Mythographi Graeci, II, 1 [1896]), 25, 2 f.; cf. Ju. 11:34-40 Jephthah.

[35] E.g., Strabo, 10, 2, 9 : τῶν ἐν αἰτίαις ὄντων, Eus. Praep. Ev., IV, 16, 1: ἕνα γὰρ τῶν ἐπὶ θανάτῳ δημοσίᾳ κατακριθέντων. Criminals because they possess a particularly strong mana or orenda (?), so Pfister, 2163.

[36] Cf. Schol. in Aristoph. Eq., 1136 ... λίαν ἀγεννεῖς καὶ ἀρχήστους. Worth noting is the malicious observation of Aristoph. (Ra., 731-733) that πονηροί who previously were not fit to be φαρμακοί are now entrusted with the most responsible tasks of state.

[37] Cf. ὠνητὸς ἄνθρωπος in Callimachus ΔΙΗΓΗΣΕΙΣ (ΔΙΗΓΗΣΕΙΣ Di poemi Di Callimaco, ed. M. Norsa and G. Vitelli [1934], 35); Servius, op. cit., 346 : unus ex pauperibus.

[38] So Hipponax. Fr., 9 Diehl; Servius; Schol. in Aristoph. Eq., 1136; also Callimachus (Gebhard, "Pharmakos," 1842).

[39] E.g., Tzetzes (→ n. 20): τῶν πάντων ἀμορφότερον, in this sense also Schol. in Aristoph. Ra., 730 (→ III, 430, n. 2): φαῦλοι καὶ παρὰ τῆς φύσεως ἐπιβουλευόμενοι, "men against whom nature has conspired." Usener, 62 f. (258 f.) regards the description of Thersites in Hom. Il., 2, 216-219 as the typical depiction of a φαρμακός.

apparently not because of the original meaning of περίψημα and περικάθαρμα as "scum," "refuse" (→ 84, 14 ff.) [40] but because men who were the scum of society (περίψημα in the first sense) were used as expiatory offerings (περίψημα in the second sense). In this contemptuous evaluation of φαρμακοί some part seems to have been played by the fact that these poor specimens volunteered for the fate of the φαρμακός. [41] For voluntariness enhanced (or even guaranteed) the expiatory value of the περίψημα, just as in other spheres voluntary self-offering was often demanded as a condition of success, [42] or the voluntariness of the sacrifice was emphasised. [43] The appointed περίψημα was drowned in the sea, not because the sea, [44] or god of the sea, [45] demanded its offerings, but rather because this manner of death [46] guaranteed a perfect removal of the one who bore the taboo or μίασμα, [47] and ruled out any fresh contact. [48] The same end is sought in other attested modes of death for φαρμακοί, [49] e.g., the combination of drowning [50] and throwing from a cliff, [51] stoning [52] outside the camp, or some other death outside the city. [53] When the victim was plunged under

---

[40] This is shown by the fact that the main word φαρμακός does not have negative connotations like περίψημα and περικάθαρμα and yet can be used equally as a term of abuse, → n. 59.

[41] This is patent in the use of the reflexive pronoun in Schol. in Aristoph. Eq., 1136 : οἵπερ καθαίρουσι τὰς πόλεις τῷ ἑαυτῶν φόνῳ.

[42] Antoninus Liberalis, op. cit. (→ n. 34), 25, 2 f.

[43] E.g., Eur. Heracl., 550 f.

[44] So L. Bürchner, Art. "Leukas," Pauly-W., 12, 2236.

[45] By adding ὡσανεί (→ n. 20), the author of the above note himself shows that this is not the meaning of περίψημα.

[46] Other instances are esp. the well-known fall from the Leucadian cliff (Strabo, 10, 2, 9; Servius, 390 f. on Aen., 3, 279; Ampelius Liber Memorialis, 8; Phot. Lex., s.v. Λευκάτης) and the statements in Plut. Sept. Sap. Conv., 20 (II, 163b); Athen., XI, 15 (p. 466c). An important pt. in support of the sea is that the water of the sea cannot be polluted so easily as that of lakes or rivers, cf. Stengel, 162.

[47] The model for the practices of Gk. catharsis in this respect is to be found in Hom. Il., 1, 313 f.: After the freeing of the Achaeans from the wrath and punishment of Apollo by the lustration of the whole army the καθάρσια ("means of purification," water of lustration etc.) are cast into the sea (καὶ εἰς ἅλα λύματ᾽ ἔβαλλον).

[48] What applies to that which is unclean applies also to that which is holy (cf. Wnd. Hb. on 13:12). Crucifixion outside the city, originally for reasons of taboo, is in Hb. based on Lv. 16:27 (not 24:14) and explained in terms of the discussion of the holy. Later both pts. were forgotten and in spite of the clear witness of the Gospels the crucifixion was located in Jerusalem, cf. W. Bauer, Das Leben Jesu im Zeitalter d. nt.lichen Apokryphen (1909), 210.

[49] Originally φαρμακοί always met with a violent death, but later deliverance or flight were often made possible, or banishment was imposed, cf. esp. the customs attested in Strabo (10, 2, 9) and Callimachus (Gebhard, "Pharmakos"); cf. Schwenn, 45, 47-51.

[50] For the combination cf. the plunge from the Leucadian cliff (→ n. 46). Whether Stengel (131) is right to identify this with the drowning of the περίψημα in Phot. and Suid. is doubtful, for there is no fall in these.

[51] E.g., Hdt., IV, 103; Pherecydes Fr., 85 (FHG, I, 92); Strabo, 14, 6, 3; Servius on Aen., 3, 57; also Ps.-Ammon. Adfin. Vocab. Diff., 142; cf., too, Plut. De Sera Numinis Vindicta, 12 (II, 557a) and Lk. 4:29 : What the people of Nazareth try to do is hard to explain from Jewish sources alone (Str.-B., II, 157 can shed no light); Rengstorf (Lk. [NT Deutsch], ad loc.) is not wholly convincing when he tries to show that Jesus was thought to have blasphemed, and that He was to be punished by stoning, which was preceded by the throwing of the condemned person from a height, Sanh., 6, 4 (Str.-B., II, 521, 685); bSanh., 45a Bar. (Str.-B., 686). It is possible that Galilee was influenced by pagan customs in dealing with religious or social outcasts after the manner of φαρμακοί, unless Lk. is responsible for this feature of the story, for which there is no par. in the other Synoptists.

[52] E.g., Istros Fr., 33 (FHG, I, 422); Ovid Ibis, 465 f.; Lactantius Placidus, Qui dicitur Commentarios in Statii Thebaida (ed. R. Jahnke [1898]), 10, 793; Callimachus (Gebhard "Pharmakos").

[53] Cf. on this Eus. Praep. Ev., IV, 16, 1: προαγαγόντες τὸν ἄνθρωπον ἔξω πυλῶν ... ἔσφαττον, also Ac. 7:58 (on the basis of Lv. 24:14 and later additions ; Str.-B., II, 684).

the waves a formula was pronounced which was designed to effect the transfer of the μίασμα or guilt to the "sacrifice" : περίψημα ἡμῶν γενοῦ (→ 90, 20 ff.). This formula is one of the so-called expiatory suffrages uttered either by the one about to die [54] or, as in this instance, by others. Comparable to the cry περίψημα ἡμῶν γενοῦ is the *devovere* of the annual expiation in Abdera (Ovid Ibis, 465), cf. also the *exsecrationes* in Massilia, whose pt. was to bring it about *ut in ipsum* (the one to be offered) *reciderent mala totius civitatis.* [55]

The aim of putting the περίψημα to death is the averting of grievous evil from the people, → 85, 8 f. Hence the περίψημα can be regarded as personified deliverance and redemption (cf. Ac. 13:47; 1 C. 1:30). The περίψημα is an expiation and ransom which saves from cultic impurity and guilt. The synon. words περίψημα and περικάθαρμα (in the LXX for כֹּפֶר) can thus be used also as synonyms of ἀντίλυτρον and ἀντίψυχον, [56] cf. the expiatory suffrages of the Jewish martyrs (→ n. 54) and the self-evaluation of Ign. of Antioch, → 92, 17 ff.

III. The Hellenistic (and Hellenistic-Jewish) Use of περίψημα.

The cultic ref. of περίψημα explains its use in Hellenism, including the transl. of the OT. Here the term occurs only twice all told, LXX Tob. 5:19; Σ Jer. 22:28. Two forms of use may be discerned.

1. The first expresses a weaker concept of expiation and substitution in which money takes the place of a man, as once in the LXX and once in a pap., though in both instances in such a way that the money is to save a forfeited or seriously threatened life : in Tob. 5:19 the mother of Tobit says of the money which her son is to bring from Media : ἀργύριον τῷ ἀργυρίῳ μὴ φθάσαι, ἀλλὰ περίψημα τοῦ παιδίου ἡμῶν γένοιτο, "may the money as far as I am concerned not be added to the other money (what is already in our possession) but may it serve as a ransom for our boy." In other words, she will gladly give a big sum as an offering for her son, which is also an offering to God. [57] Related is the thought of another son who has obviously murdered a relative of the one addressed, P. Michigan, VIII (ed. H. C. Youtie and J. G. Winter

---

[54] The aim here was partly the expiation of one's own sins — thus Jewish malefactors were to say before execution : My death be the expiation of all my sins, Sanh., 6, 2. But it was also in part the making of atonement for others, as in the suffrages of the Jewish martyrs, esp. 4 Macc. 6:29 : καθάρσιον αὐτῶν (sc. fellow-citizens and fellow-believers) ποίησον τὸ ἐμὸν αἷμα καὶ ἀντίψυχον αὐτῶν λαβὲ τὴν ἐμὴν ψυχήν, cf. 2 Macc. 7:37 f. Cf. Moore, I, 546-552, esp. 548. The best known and most important example here is R. 9:3, where Paul expresses his readiness, indeed, his passionate desire, to suffer death in the deepest NT sense of separation from Christ as an offering for his own countrymen. Perhaps this thought lies behind Lk. 23:34 and Ac. 7:60 too, → V, 715 and n. 475. There is a possible echo of these concepts in the Arab. formula of profound devotion : *Ju'iltu fadāka,* "may I be made a ransom for you," "may I be able to offer up myself for you" (*fada* = פָּדָה); cf. Wnd. Barn. on 4, 9.

[55] Prv. 21:18 is formally analogous : περικάθαρμα δὲ δικαίου ἄνομος, but quite different in sense, since it expresses the Jewish theology of retribution.

[56] So Hesych., *s.v.* On the whole idea of the atoning effect of death as such cf. K. G. Kuhn, "R. 6:7," ZNW, 30 (1931), 305-310.

[57] The mother either means that renouncing the money (which remains in the possession of the debtor) will count as a sacrifice before God, or she is proposing that the debtor should consecrate the money as an offering to God in the form of good works. With this sacrifice the parents hope to gain God's protection for the life of their son, which they do not wish to hazard. It is also possible, however, that the mother is ready to dedicate the money as an offering for the safe return of her son, cf. J. Jeremias, "Das Lösegeld f. Viele (Mk. 10:45)," Judaica, 3 (1947/48), 251. Worth noting once again (→ 87, 14 ff.; 90, 18 ff.; n. 64, 72) is the formula περίψημα γένοιτο, which in a context like this is meant in its original sense as a dedication formula to the powers of destiny (cf. the ring of Polycrates). For ransom by money cf. already Ex. 30:12-16; cf. also bBer., 62b with ref. to 2 S. 24:15 f., and on this J. Jeremias, *op. cit.*, 250 f.

[1951]), 473, 17 f.: ὡς ἔβλαβές με χιλίας διακοσίας δραχμάς περίψημά μου τοῦ υἱοῦ ἀπέλθωσιν, "since you caused me damage of 1200 drachmas, may this count as a satisfaction [58] for my son."

2. περίψημα is then used for an unworthy subject in the double form of a term of abuse and of self-abasement, which is common to it with many of the synonyms mentioned above (→ 86, 2 f.). [59] Equation with βδέλυγμα [60] and σκύβαλα [61] shows how contemptuous this use was. It is thus that Symmachus uses περίψημα at Jer. 22:28 : μὴ περίψημα [62] φαῦλον καὶ ἀπόβλητον ὁ ἄνθρωπος; "is this man (Jeconiah) a poor and contemptible subject?" [63] But περίψημα is esp. used to express strong self-abasement. In this form it occurs throughout the empire as a highly polite phrase. [64] We even find a transcription of it in Lat., [65] and through the mediation of the Vg

[58] Otherwise the legal statutes would provide for a confiscation of the property of the murderer ; cf. also P. Oxy., XVI, 1897.

[59] For φαρμακός cf. Aristoph. Eq., 1405; Demosth. Or., 25, 80; for κάθαρμα Poll. Onom., V, 162 in a list of contemptuous expressions for μηδενὸς ἄξια, cf. III, 66 in a list of terms for a-social men : τοὺς πολλοὺς καθάρματα καὶ πτωχοὺς ἀποκαλῶν, also Schol. in Aristoph. Pl., 454 : καθάρματα αὐτούς φησιν ἀντὶ τοῦ εὐτελεστάτους, "men who degrade themselves." Pharmacus is used in the same sense in Lat.: Petronius Saturae, 107, 15; cf. also the Lat. equivalent purgamentum : Curtius, Historiae Alexandri Magni (ed. E. Hedicke² [1931]), VIII, 5, 8 (of contemptible poets) urbium suarum purgamenta ; similarly as a term of opprobrium in Petronius, 74, 9; Curtius, VI, 11, 2; X, 2, 7; Colloquium Montepessulanum, 14 (Corp. Gloss. Lat., III, 657). Cf. the synon. λῦμα (Eur. Tro., 591), ἄλημα (Soph. Ai., 381, 390, from ἀλέω "to pound"), "smooth or arrant knave," περίτριμμα ἀγορᾶς (Demosth. Or., 18, 127), ἀποφιλοκάλημα (Ps.-Oecumenius on 1 C. 4:13 [MPG, 118, 692 D]; cf. Thes. Steph., s.v. περίψημα) et al. On this whole question cf. Usener, 61 f. (258) with 62, n. 1 (n. 137).

[60] So Euthymius Zig. → n. 11.

[61] Ps.-Oecumenius, → n. 12.

[62] עֶצֶב ("vessel," "creature"), here rendered περίψημα, has originally no contemptuous undertone ; this arises perhaps through the formal proximity of עָצָב ("idol") unless the attributes (נִבְזֶה‎, נָפוּץ) suggested a derogatory rendering for the noun too.

[63] This is obviously where N. Calogeras on Euthymius Zig. finds his interpretation of περίψημα : ἀπὸ μεταφορᾶς δὲ τὸ περίψημα ὑποδηλοῖ καὶ τὸν εὐτελῆ ἄνθρωπον καὶ φαῦλον καὶ ἀπόβλητον.

[64] Syria : Zorava in Trachonitis, Waddington, 1, 566 (No. 2493): Πάτρων περίψημά σου. Asia Minor : Smyrna in the Chr. inscr., CIG, IV, 9282 : ἐγὼ περίψημα πάντων. Egypt : Alexandria in Eus. Hist. Eccl., VII, 22, 7; here περίψημά σου (or ὑμῶν) is a common courtly flourish (τὸ δημῶδες ῥῆμα μόνης ἀεὶ δοκοῦν φιλοφροσύνης ἔχεσθαι). As this δημῶδες ῥῆμα, μόνης ἀεὶ δοκεῖν φιλοφροσύνης ἔχεσθαι is certainly not meant (most witnesses have δοκοῦν, not δοκεῖν), as A. W. van Buren suggests (Epigraphica, II : "A Greek Graffito of Ostia," in Classical Studies in Honor of J. C. Rolfe [1931], 319), but ἀπιόντες αὐτῶν (Cod A : + πάντων, assimilation to 1 C. 4:13) περίψημα. The striking combination with the verb ἄπειμι shows that this verb is probably part of a standing combination, → n. 72. Rufinus pushed the Christianising of the expression even further (beyond Cod A) with his transl.: et effecti sunt eorum, ut dicit apostoli sermo, περίψημα (GCS, 9, 2, 683). North Africa : Carthage, burial inscr. of the philosopher Flavius Maximus of Gortyn in Crete, CIL, VIII, 1, 12924 : εὐψύχει κύριέ μου Μάξιμε, ἐγὼ σου περίψημα τῆς καλῆς ψυχῆς. The widow here, like the widower in the inscr. of Zorava, uses a strong expression to show that she was not the better half, cf. T. Mommsen's note on CIL, VIII Suppl., I, 12924 and W. Thieling, Der Hell. in Kleinafrika (1911), 34. Italy : Ostia, in Monumenti Antichi, 26 (1920), 368 : η ματοων περιψημα σου (also van Buren, 318).

[65] So on the floor mosaic of a fountain in Brescia, CIL, V, 1, 4500 (Dessau Inscr. Lat. Select., II, 1 [1902], 5725): Bene lava. Salvu lotu. Peripsuma (sic !) su. These are just stereotyped expressions from current speech (for salvu lotu = salvum lutum, cf. Hermeneumata Montepessulana, 144r [Corp. Gloss. Lat., III, 287, 29]; Mart. Perpetuae, 21, 2; on this K. J. Neumann, Der röm. Staat u. d. allg. Kirche bis auf Diokletian I [1890], 175); the self-abasement in peripsema is hardly felt here any more than in the free and easy greeting servus with which this greeting and parting can best be compared. Haupt and Mommsen (CIL, V, 1, 4500) think the su should be sume, i.e., take the bath towel (→ n. 12); van

(1 C. 4:13) the loan word *peripsema* became a current formula of self-abasement. [66]

B. περίψημα in the New Testament.

In a somewhat loose construction περίψημα in 1 C. 4:13 is set alongside περι-καθάρματα τοῦ κόσμου as a second predicate noun with ἐγενήθημεν, and the sense shows that it is placed under the same ὡς. The two expressions, however, are not just parallel; they are almost synonymous. Nevertheless, both admit of a double meaning and translation. περίψημα can be an expression of supreme self-abasement (→ n. 54; 89, 9 ff.) or a word of contempt applied to oneself by others (→ 86, 17 ff.): "refuse," "scum," "trash," "rubbish," "filth," etc. [67] Here, however, it can also be one who dies vicariously, the "scapegoat" or "expiatory offering," with a strong undertone of contempt and self-degradation, → n. 64. [68] It is quite possible that Paul is alluding here to a reproach which he and other servants of the Gospel had to bear. These apostles were poor and useless people on whom everybody could vent scorn and contempt and who threw away their own lives — this is also implied — in a ridiculous way. By accepting the reproach, Paul agrees, but he reinterprets: [69] we do indeed throw away our lives, but it is for the world, and our apparently useless lives are for the good of all.

That this is not just conventional self-abasement (→ 89, 9 ff.) on a universal scale (πάντων περίψημα), but that the apostle has in view a picture of the contemptible περίψημα vicariously given up to death for all (→ 85, 6 ff.) is supported by the following considerations : 1. the association with πάντων, [70] for a feature of the practice

---

Buren, 319 supports this conjecture. Nevertheless, though it makes sense alongside *bene lava, salvum lutum,* the commonly attested conventional use of περίψημά σου and the equally commonly attested transcription of Gk. expressions on Lat. inscr. (cf., e.g., → V, 785, n. 84) favour the traditional text, i.e., the adoption of the Gk. flourish περίψημά σου into current Lat.

[66] For examples cf. du Cange, *s.v. peripsema.*

[67] Cf. K. Barth, *Die Auferstehung d. Toten* (1926), *ad loc.;* W. Bousset, *1 K.* in *Schr. NT,* II[3], *ad loc.;* K. Heim, *Die Gemeinde des Auferstandenen* (1949), *ad loc.;* J. C. K. Hofmann, *Die Heilige Schrift d. NT,* II (1864), *ad loc.;* Ltzm. K., *ad loc.;* H. D. Wendland, *Die Briefe an d. Korinther (NT Deutsch), ad loc.* Usener, 62 (258) renders περίψημα by "water for washing" and περικάθαρμα by "expiatory offering," but the two words must have much the same sense ; the one cannot express profound self-abasement and the other supreme self-exaltation ; two phrases would have to be used to express these two things in the one sentence. The observations in Str.-B., III, 338 f. show how one can often miss the true sense of a NT term or passage if one considers only one of the two surrounding spheres, in this case Judaism.

[68] Bengel takes the word in this double sense, *ad loc.: non solum abiectissimi, sed pia-culares;* Joh. W. 1 K., *ad loc.* and J. B. Lightfoot, *The Apostolic Fathers,* II, 2 (1889), 74; we also find an inclination this way in Bousset; Clemen, 319 : "... a pagan sacrificial practice which has this implication"; H. Schlier, *Religionsgeschichtliche Untersuchungen zu d. Ignatiusbr.* (1929), 63, n. 3. Lightfoot, 50 paraphrases Ign. Eph., 8, 1: "I am as the meanest among you," and transl. (p. 546): "I devote myself for you." He takes 18, 1 (p. 74) in the same way : "I am content ... to give up everything, and to become as nothing, for that Cross in which others find only a stumbling-block."

[69] Cf. the same thing with ἔκτρωμα (1 C. 15:8; → II, 466, 21 ff.), except that this reproach comes from the Jewish Christians of Jerusalem, while that of περίψημα is from Gks. Common to the background imagery of ἔκτρωμα and περίψημα is the character of the ἄμορφον, → II, 465, 21 f.; 466, 32; 467, 15 f. (cf. esp. Iren., I, 4, 7: ἄμορφος καὶ ἀνείδεος, also Tzetzes, V, 726 : τῶν πάντων ἀμορφότερον.

[70] Whether the gen. supports this (N. Calogeras on Euthymius Zig., cf. also Veil on Barn., 4, 9) on the ground that one would expect the dat. with the sense "scum" etc., seems to me to be very doubtful in view of the current expression περίψημά σου or ὑμῶν, cf. the understanding of πάντων περίψημα in Theophylactus (MPG, 124, 616 D, 617 A): ... ἄξιοι, καὶ ὡς βδέλυγμα λογίζεσθαι, οὐχ ὑμῖν μόνοις, ἀλλὰ παντὶ τῷ κόσμῳ καὶ πᾶσιν ἀνθρώποις.

denoted by περίψημα is that an individual or individuals must perish for a whole city or people (→ 86, 9 ff.); [71] 2. the association with ἐγενήθημεν, for by choosing the same verb γίνεσθαι Paul formally adopts the expiatory suffrage spoken over the victim : περίψημα ἡμῶν γενοῦ (→ 87, 14 ff.), thus showing that the apostles see this fulfilled in themselves : ἐγενήθημεν περίψημα; [72] 3. these last words take up again, in an easy change of image, the opening words of the section (v. 9 : ὁ θεὸς ἡμᾶς τοὺς ἀποστό-λους ἐσχάτους ἀπέδειξεν ὡς ἐπιθανατίους) which turn our thoughts to condemned criminals, [73] who are regarded as the very last of men (ἔσχατος, → II, 698, 16 ff.), i.e., the dregs of human society, [74] and whose human dignity is so completely lost that their execution is a public spectacle and entertainment; this image, after a realistic depiction of apostolic life (vv. 10-12), obviously suggested to the apostle the associated image of the one who is publicly slain for all, or, if the word περίψημα was suggested by the contempt of the world, he and his readers were led by the words περικάθαρμα and περίψημα from the image of the criminal in the arena to that of the despised malefactor dying as an expiatory offering; [75] 4. most significant of all, however, are the three antithetical pairs of verbs in v. 12b and 13a, for precisely what these are de-signed to convey, the blessing which comes through the accursed and the salvation which those who are regarded as lost bring, is also stated by the two tt. περικάθαρμα and περίψημα, namely, that the reviled and despised are blessing and expiation. Paul is thus confessing that he is a man who throws away himself and his life and that he thus looks like a useless scapegoat and despised sin-offering, but in so doing he also confesses that he is the bearer of reconciliation for the world and of salvation for all men.

The thought of 1 C. 4:13 is found in a series of passages, e.g., Gl. 6:17; 2 C. 4:10 f.; 6:9; 1 C. 15:31; Phil. 2:17; Col. 1:24 etc. The image of the despised offering for all, however, brings the apostle closer than any other expression to the cross of Christ, for it is τὸ σκάνδαλον τοῦ σταυροῦ that precisely the despised malefactor is the one who is destined to bring salvation. Paul is not suggesting, of course, that he himself plays the role of the crucified Lord; he makes this plain at the very beginning of the section by the use of ὡς. He himself is the messenger of salvation, not the ground. Like Jesus Himself, he and his life with its mark of the Crucified are despised by all, and yet, like Jesus, they are divinely ordained to salvation. [76]

---

[71] This is the idea underlying all human sacrifices, cf., e.g., Philo Byblius in Eus. Praep. Ev., IV, 16, 11 ἀντὶ τῆς πάντων φθορᾶς.

[72] Something analogous may be seen if we compare two other instances of περίψημα. In P. Michigan, VIII (1951), 473, 18 we have a secularised expiation formula : περίψημα μου τοῦ υἱοῦ ἀπέλθωσιν (sc. 1200 drachmas, → 89, 1 ff.). This formula (in the original sense), the Christians who sacrificed themselves for their pagan opponents in a time of epidemic put into effect ἀπιόντες αὐτῶν περίψημα (Dionysius of Alex. in Eus. Hist. Eccl., VII, 22, 7 → n. 64); cf. Zahn, 420, n. 4.

[73] ἐπιθανάτιος has thus far been found only twice in this sense outside the NT, Dion. Hal. Ant. Rom., VII, 35, 4 : ἔστι δὲ τὸ χωρίον κρημνὸς ἐξαίσιος (the rupes Tarpeia) ὅθεν αὐτοῖς ἔθος ἦν βάλλειν τοὺς ἐπιθανατίους, LXX Bel and the Dragon, 31: ἐχορη-γεῖτο αὐτοῖς (Daniel's lions) καθ’ ἑκάστην ἡμέραν τῶν ἐπιθανατίων σώματα δύο.

[74] Cf. Ltzm. K., ad loc.

[75] The association of images is all the closer in view of the fact that the modes of death were often the same, e.g., throwing from a cliff (→ n. 73 and → 87, 13 with n. 51). Even though the slaying of the περίψημα no longer took place in Paul's day, the formula to which he alludes, and which still lives on into our own time (→ n. 54), preserved recollection of the practice.

[76] Thus Jesus Himself could be called a περίψημα, as once by Orig. (Comm. in J., 28, 18 [161] on 11:50 [GCS, 10, 413]), cf. also ibid., 6, 55 (284) on 1:29 (GCS, 10, 163 f.), where he brings into parallelism the τεθνηκότες διὰ λοιμικὰ καταστήματα, i.e., the expiatory offerings called περίψημα — εἰ γὰρ τάδε μὲν ὑπὸ Ἑλλήνων οὐ μάτην ἱστόρηται, the sufferings of the witnesses of Christ and the sacrificial death of the Lamb of God. Cf. on this whole question W. Meyer, Der 1. Brief an d. Korinther (Prophezei, 1947), ad loc.

C. περίψημα in the Post-Apostolic Fathers.

The Pauline use of περίψημα influences Ign. (Eph., 8, 1; 18, 1) and Barn. (4, 9; 6, 5). In Ign., too, the renderings "scum," [77] "refuse" [78] etc., also "most humble servant," [79] do not quite get the point. For Ign., as for Pl., περίψημα is neither a common flourish of modesty nor an expression of particularly exalted self-abasement. It is based on his peculiar sense of martyrdom. Eph., 8, 1: περίψημα ὑμῶν καὶ ἁγνίζομαι ὑμῶν Ἐφεσίων. The direct relation to ἁγνίζομαι suggests the meaning "expiatory offering" here. Either we should supply the copula with περίψημα ὑμῶν (cf. R., 4, 3): "I am an offering for you and (as such) I consecrate myself for you Ephesians," or we should transl.: "As a sin-offering I consecrate myself also for you Ephesians." 18, 1: περίψημα τὸ ἐμὸν πνεῦμα τοῦ σταυροῦ ὅ ἐστιν σκάνδαλον τοῖς ἀπιστοῦσιν, ἡμῖν δὲ σωτηρία καὶ ζωὴ αἰώνιος, "my spirit [80] is a despised offering of the cross, i.e., I give myself to the scorn of the world for the cross of Christ." The relative clause which follows can either be taken with the whole saying or specifically with περίψημα; in this case Ign. uses the thought of 1 C. 1:23 f. to interpret the distinctive twofold sense of περίψημα. But we press Ignatius' self-evaluation as a martyr too far if we think that he is describing his sacrifice of life so generally as "salvation and eternal life." Ign. might well be expressing here a certainty stated elsewhere in his writings (Eph., 1, 2; 3, 1; R., 3, 2; 4, 2 etc.), namely, that only through his martyrdom will he become a disciple, a Christian, a believer, and thus be saved and attain to eternal life. It is simpler, however, to see here a looser constr. (cf., 17, 2) or an assimilation to σκάνδαλον. Like the Maccabean martyrs (cf. 4 Macc. 6:29, → n. 54; 17:21 f.) and to some degree under the influence of Paul (Phil. 2:17; 2 Tm. 2:10), Ign. sees in his death a ransom (ἀντίψυχον, Eph., 21, 1; Sm., 10, 2; Pol., 2, 3; 6, 1) for his fellow-believers, and he does so, indeed, in the sense that he goes to death vicariously for the many others who are spared in the persecution. Ign. certainly does not wish to deny the uniqueness of the atoning death of Jesus (cf. the significance of the πάθος of Christ, Eph. inscriptio; 7, 2; Mg., 11; Phld., 9, 2; Sm., 1, 2 etc.). [81] He seems to have been using the expression of 1 C. 4:13 in the same sense as Paul acc. to his own understanding. Nevertheless, one is forced to say that he emphasises the sacrificial and expiatory value of martyrdom in a way which differs markedly from the NT. His death is an offering for God (cf. R., 2, 2; 4, 2) and a saving death for the churches [82] which would rival Christ's passion if the thought were systematically developed. The use of περίψημα is a proof of this view of the martyr bishop which both goes beyond Paul and also deviates from him.

Much less important is the use of περίψημα in Barn., though this bears formal resemblance to that of Ign. Here, too, the word expresses self-abasement, [83] but it is re-

---

[77] G. Krüger, *Ign.* (Hennecke, 521, 523).

[78] F. Zeller, *Die Apost. Vät., Bibliothek d. Kirchenväter*, 35 (1918), 124 (Ign. Eph., 18, 1); Zeller correctly transl. "expiatory offering" at Eph., 8, 1 (120).

[79] Bau. Ign. on Eph., 8, 1; 18, 1. Only as a second possibility does Bau. consider "expiatory offering," "ransom."

[80] This understanding of τὸ ἐμὸν πνεῦμα is suggested among other things by comparison with Sm., 10, 2 and Pol., 2, 3, where ἐγὼ καὶ τὰ δεσμά μου and τὸ πνεῦμά μου καὶ τὰ δεσμά μου are called the ἀντίψυχον of those addressed, and esp. by Tr., 13, 3, which has the same thought and the same constr. of ἁγνίζομαι (with the simple gen.). Reitzenstein Hell. Myst., 394 f. and Schlier, *op. cit.* (→ n. 68) take πνεῦμα in the sense of πνοή ("breath," "savour," "proclamation") and περίψημα in the sense of "sacrifice." But the relevant "despised sin-offering" does not fit their interpretation ("my proclamation of the cross is a sacrifice"), as Schlier himself is aware. The only advantage of this understanding is that ὅ can relate directly to πνεῦμα and that the general sense corresponds to 1 C. 1:23 f. Zahn, 420 f. had already clearly perceived the true meaning of the passage.

[81] Cf. on this v. Campenhausen, 74 f.; J. Moffatt, "Ign. of Antioch," *The Journal of Religion*, 10 (1930), 177 f., 184; Zahn, 421 f.

[82] Cf. v. Campenhausen, 71-73, 76, 78; H. W. Bartsch, *Gnostisches Gut u. Gemeindetradition bei Ign. v. Antiochien* (1940), 84, denies — wrongly in my judgment — that the suffering of martyrs has objective value before God in the opinion of Ign.

[83] Cf. Veil, 218, *ad loc.*

lated in both instances to the nature of the writing. We obviously have here the meaning "expiatory offering" in a very diluted and generalised sense with no theological implications : "one who (in love) gives himself wholly for you" (6, 5 : περίψημα τῆς ἀγάπης ὑμῶν), "who would fully accommodate himself to you," "your most obedient servant" (as one might put it, → 92, 3 ff.). In this weakened sense the word lives on into the Middle Ages in both Lat. and Gk. [84]

Stählin

---

† περπερεύομαι

The etym. is debated ; one can hardly sustain a connection with the Lithuanian *puȓpti* "to boast" or *paȓpti* "to whine," [1] and borrowing from the Lat. *perperam* [2] is also uncertain. The word obviously belongs to the circle of verbs in -εύεσθαι which emphasise the possession of good or esp. bad (e.g., ἀκρατεύεσθαι, ἀλαζονεύεσθαι, ἀναιδεύεσθαι) qualities (→ lines 25-28). [3] The verb and the related noun πέρπερος are late [4] and rare. [5] Polyb. calls the grammarian Isocrates (32, 2 and 5) and Aulus Postomius (39, 1, 1-3) πέρπερος. What he has in mind is arrogance of speech. In both passages it is used with words like "loquacious," "talkative," "exaggerating," "asserting oneself, wounding, attacking with words." Epict.'s list of vices (Diss., III, 2, 14) mentions πέρπερος along with "cowardly," "irascible," "turbulent," esp. in connection with a variously expressed mania for criticism, and with emphasis on the real thing as compared with this mere show of culture. Finally, for Sext. Emp. (Math., I, 54) πέρπερος Γραμματική is characterised by the fact that it is not satisfied with mere tradition but goes into the details of phonetics (i.e., it is "too pedantic").

The compound ἐμπερπερεύεσθαι in Cic. Att., I, 14, 3 [6] denotes, not without some irony (*clamores*), the artificial, rhetorical construction of periods, while in Epict. Diss., II, 1, 34 it means literary superficiality. The simple περπερεύεσθαι, which to the best of my knowledge is used only once in Hell. lit. apart from 1 C. 13:4 [7] — is found in M. Ant., V, 5, 4 along with censoriousness, greed, flattery, self-exculpation, and restlessness (γογγύζειν καὶ γλισχρεύεσθαι καὶ κολακεύειν καὶ τὸ σωμάτιον καταιτιᾶσθαι καὶ ἀρεσκεύεσθαι καὶ περπερεύεσθαι καὶ τοσαῦτα ῥιπτάζεσθαι τῇ ψυχῇ). If πέρπερος/περπερεύεσθαι are to be translated "braggart," "bragging," the emphasis is thus on the rhetorical or literary form of boasting, on the element of exaggeration, obtrusiveness, offensiveness, unsettlement, or flattery, on the mere show as

---

[84] Cf. → n. 64-66.

π ε ρ π ε ρ ε ύ ο μ α ι. [1] Walde-Pok., II, 50; Boisacq⁴, 774.

[2] Prellwitz Etym. Wört., 363; Walde-Hofmann, 290 f.

[3] E. Fraenkel, *Gr. Denominativa* (1906), 198.

[4] Cf. the Schol. on Soph. Ant. (Schol. in Soph. Tragoedias vetera No. 324, ed. P. N. Papageorgius [1888], 234): κομψοὺς γὰρ ἔλεγον οὓς νῦν ἡμεῖς περπέρους καὶ πολυλάλους φαμέν.

[5] Preisigke Wört. does not list περπερεύεσθαι and derivates, nor do they occur in the LXX.

[6] ἐμπερπερεύεσθαι and rhetorical tt. appear in Gk. form in the Lat. text. As T. K. Abbott (review), Class. Rev., 1 (1887), 108b rightly emphasises against Wilke-Grimm.³ (353a), flattery is not the direct content of this ἐμπερπερεύεσθαι of Cic. before Pompey, though it is included, as the ensuing quotation from M. Ant. shows.

[7] Wettstein on 1 C. 13:4 adduces a περπερεύεται under the name of Libanius, Or., 46, 19 (Libanii opera, III, ed. R. Förster [1906], 388), but this is a corrupt reading, as the first editor of Libanius showed ; it ought to be πεπόρευτο on the basis of the Cod. Vindobonensis, 12th cent.

opposed to genuine culture. [8] Basilius, [9] Synesius, [10] Eustathius [11] and Zonaras [12] confirm this, without exegetical ref. to 1 C. 13:4.

In the NT περπερεύεσθαι is a hapax legomenon at 1 C. 13:4. The translators and lexicographers speak very generally of corrupt action [13] or emphasise in detail the bluster, superfluity, futility and presumption coupled with sloth. [14] The immediate context puts περπερεύεσθαι in the setting of defiant conduct through the proximity of ζηλοῦν, [15] and of unbounded arrogance, which naturally had to be reprimanded in this gnosis-happy congregation (1 C. 8:1), [16] through the proximity of φυσιοῦσθαι. The broader context at least hints at the rhetorical and aesthetic background of περπερεύεσθαι with the rejection of σοφία λόγου (1 C. 1:17; 2:1, 4, 13), which, though for the most part it indicates a content hardly compatible with the *kerygma,* [17] also contains certain formal elements (cf. 2 C. 10:10; 11:6). περπερεύεσθαι seems to be baseless chatter in the light of the contrast between λόγος and δύναμις (1 C. 4:19 f.; cf. Col. 2:18, → n. 16). The congregation is plainly threatened by it in view of the σχίσματα (1. C. 1:10 ff.), the Gnostic intoxication with freedom (1 C. 8) and the preferring of the conspicuous λαλεῖν γλώσσαις among the χαρίσματα (1 C. 12 and 14). What Hellenism repudiates in περπερεύεσθαι from Polybius to Marcus Aurelius Antoninus is in essentials opposed in the NT too, namely, the aesthetic, rhetorical form of boasting which wounds others, causes unrest and discord, and represents unfounded presumption.

And yet the subject ἡ ἀγάπη [18] sets οὐ περπερεύεται as thus expounded in a connection which is typically different from Hellenistic Stoicism. Natural inclination or disinclination [19] does not control the practice or renunciation of περπερεύεσθαι but ἀγάπη, in which is achieved the possibility of eschatological life disclosed in πίστις and ἐλπίς. [20] Because it is God who has opened up this

---

[8] J. A. H. Tittmann's def. (De synon. in Novo Test. [1829], 74) is thus off the mark: περπερεύεσθαι *dicitur, qui bona, quae ipsi vere insunt, nimia iactatione elevat et ostentat.*

[9] Basilius, Regulae Brevius Tractatae, 49 (MPG, 31, 1116 C): τί ἐστιν τὸ περπερεύεσθαι; πᾶν δ μὴ διὰ χρείαν, ἀλλὰ διὰ καλλωπισμὸν παραλαμβάνεται, περπερείας ἔχει κατηγορίαν.

[10] Synesius (c. 1000 A.D.), De Febribus, 136 (ed. J. S. Bernard [1749]) (in Wettstein on 1 C. 13:4): διὰ τὸ εἶναι τὴν χολὴν ὠμήν, πέρπερον καὶ ἄσωτον καὶ ἐλαφρόν.

[11] Eustath. Thessal. Comm. in Il., 145, 20: ἐκ τούτου δὲ καὶ ῥωποπερπερήθρα τις προσερρήθη ἐπὶ χυδαιότητι καὶ φλυαρίᾳ σκωπτόμενος.

[12] Zonaras, Ad Petri Alexandrini Canon X (MPG, 138, 500 C): περπερείαν δ' ἐνταῦθα τὴν οἴησιν καὶ τὴν ἀλαζονείαν καλεῖ.

[13] The Lat. MSS dem: *non est perpera* ; g.: *non perperat* ; t f Vg Orig, Cyprian, Ambrosiaster: *non perperam agit* or *non agit perperam.*

[14] Tert. De Patientia, 12 (CSEL, 47, 19, 17 f.): *nec protervum sapit.* Cl. Al. Paed., III, 1, 3, 1: περπερεία γὰρ ὁ καλλωπισμὸς περιττότητος καὶ ἀρχειότητος ἔχων ἔμφασιν. Hesych., *s.v.*: περπερεύεται· κατεπαίρεται. Suid., *s.v.*: ἡ ἀγάπη οὐ περπερεύεται, ὁ 'Απόστολος Παῦλός φησιν· τουτέστιν, οὐ προπετεῖ. Etym. M., 665, 37 f. (in Wettstein on 1 C. 13:4): περπερεύεται, ἀντὶ τοῦ ματαιοῦται, ἀτακτεῖ, κατεπαίρεται μετὰ βλακείας ἐπαιρόμενος.

[15] ζηλοῦν and ζῆλος, → II, 877-882 *voces mediae,* here naturally with a negative evaluation as in Gl. 4:17, though cf. Jm. 4:2; 1 C. 3:3; 2 C. 12:20; Gl. 5:20; Jm. 3:14, 16.

[16] Of the 7 instances of φυσιοῦσθαι in the NT (1 C. 4:6, 18, 19; 5:2; 8:1; 13:4; Col. 2:18), 6 are in 1 C. The baselessness (εἰκῆ, *sine causa*) of φυσιοῦσθαι is expressly stated in Col. 2:18, but since it is everywhere implied, there is nothing new in this.

[17] H. Braun, "Exegetische Randglossen zu 1 K.," Theologia Viatorum, 1 (1948/9), 26-29.

[18] It makes no difference to the sense whether one omits ἡ ἀγάπη with p46 B 33 al f vg fathers or relates it to οὐ ζηλοῖ with B. Weiss, *Das NT,* II², *ad loc.*

[19] M. Ant., V, 5, 1, 3, 4: οὐ γὰρ πέφυκα ... οὐδεμία ἀφυίας καὶ ἀνεπιτηδειότητος πρόφασις, ... διὰ τὸ ἀφυῶς κατεσκευάσθαι.

[20] → ἀγαπάω, I, 49-52; Bultmann Theol., 340.

possibility in the Christ event, the action of this ἀγάπη is spoken of in markedly suprapersonal terms. Not the loving Christian, but ἡ ἀγάπη οὐ περπερεύεται. In respect of οὐ περπερεύεται as well as the other functions of ἀγάπη only the setting (1 C. 12:31b; 14:1a) points to the adoption of this ἔτι καθ' ὑπερβολὴν ὁδός by the Christian. This is in sharp contrast to the Stoa, which issues direct imperatives concerning the setting aside of περπερεύεσθαι by practice, close attention, and the renunciation of sloth. [21]

Braun

πέτρα

Contents : A. Usage in Profane Greek and the Old Testament : 1. Profane Greek ; 2. The Old Testament. B. The Symbolic Meaning of Rock. C. πέτρα in the New Testament : 1. πέτρα in the Literal Sense ; 2. The Rock which Followed, 1 C. 10:4; 3. R. 9:33 and 1 Pt. 2:7 f.; 4. Mt. 16:18. D. The Post-Apostolic Fathers and Apologists.

A. Usage in Profane Greek and the Old Testament.

1. The fem. πέτρα is predominantly used in secular Gk. for a large and solid "rock." It may denote equally well the individual cliff or a stony and rocky mountain chain. [1] Thus it is often linked with ἠλίβατος in Hom. [2] Fig. πέτρα denotes firmness and immovability (Hom. Od., 17, 463), also hardness and lack of feeling (Aesch. Prom., 242). The etym. is obscure. [3] The masc. πέτρος is used more for isolated rocks or small stones, including flints and pebbles for slings. [4] Since there is such a great difference in content, the emphasis should be noted, though in practice one cannot differentiate too strictly between πέτρα and πέτρος; they are often used interchangeably. [5]

2. In the LXX πέτρα bears the following senses : a. "rock," "cliff" (Ex. 17:6; ψ 80:16); b. place-name or geographical note, Ju. 1:36; 1 Βασ. 23:28; 4 Βασ. 14:7; c. fig. (Is. 8:14), of an unbending character (Is. 50:7) or the hardened mind (Jer. 5:3); d. occasionally a name for God (2 Βασ. 22:2). πέτρος is very seldom used in the LXX. [6]

The main Heb. equivalents of πέτρα are צוּר and סֶלַע; אֶבֶן on the other hand is almost always rendered λίθος. [7] Along with the secular sense of "rock" צוּר is often a name for God, [8] though there is no simple equation of God and rock in the OT. [9] Since the

---

[21] Epict. Diss., II, 1, 36 : τἆλλα (ἐμπερπερεύεσθαι is included) δ' ἄλλοις ἄφες, μηδὲ φωνήν τις ἀκούσῃ σου περὶ αὐτῶν ποτε μηδ', ἂν ἐπαινέσῃ τις ἐπ' αὐτοῖς, ἀνέχου, δόξον δὲ μηδεὶς εἶναι καὶ εἰδέναι μηδέν. M. Ant., V, 5, 5 : ἀλλὰ τούτων (including περπερεύεσθαι) μὲν πάλαι ἀπηλλάχθαι ἐδύνασο ...· καὶ τοῦτο δὲ ἀσκητέον μὴ παρενθυμουμένῳ μηδὲ ἐμφιληδοῦντι τῇ νωθείᾳ.

π έ τ ρ α. [1] Pass., s.v.; e.g., Hom. Od., 3, 293; 4, 501.
[2] Hom. Il., 15, 273; Od., 9, 243; 10, 88; 13, 196; but also Xenoph. An., I, 4, 4.
[3] Hofmann, s.v.; but cf. Boisacq⁴, 776.
[4] Xenoph. An., VII, 7, 54; Plat. Leg., VIII, 843a; Hom. Il., 7, 270; Pind. Olymp., 10, 72; Soph. Phil., 296.
[5] Hom. Od., 9, 243; Hes. Theog., 675; Soph. Oed. Col., 1595 etc.
[6] 2 Macc. 1:16; 4:41; in Aquila Ex. 4:25.
[7] The borderline between צוּר and סֶלַע on the one side and אֶבֶן on the other is fluid.
[8] Dt. 32:4, 15, 18, 30, 31, 37; 1 S. 2:2; 2 S. 23:3; Is. 26:4; 30:29; 44:8; Hab. 1:12; in many Ps. and also in proper names ; cf. A. Wiegand, "Der Gottesname צוּר u. seine Deutung in dem Sinne Bildner oder Schöpfer in der alten jüd. Lit.," ZAW, 10 (1890), 85-96; A. Jirku, *Altorientalischer Komm. z. AT* (1923), 224. On צוּר as a theophorous element in personal names (e.g., Nu. 1:5), cf. H. Schmidt, *Der heilige Fels in Jerusalem* (1933), 87.
[9] The LXX does not usually have πέτρα for צוּר but relaces the fig. word by terms which give the meaning of the image, e.g., θεός Dt. 32:4, 30; ἀντιλήμπτωρ ψ 88:26.

Aram. כֵּפָא normally means a "weight" and corresponds to the Heb. שֶׁקֶל the Targumim use כֵּיפָא for סֶלַע. This is also equivalent to צוּר. On the other hand, the Aram. טוּרָא corresponds more to the Heb. הַר. [10] It is also true that כֵּיפָא is often used in the sense of λίθος. [11] From these two facts it follows that כֵּיפָא embraces both the originally more specific meanings of πέτρα and πέτρος (λίθος). [12] It is thus very unlikely that the simple meaning כֵּיפָא = λίθος underlies the play on πέτρα and Πέτρος in Mt. 16:18, which rests on a basic כֵּיפָא. [13]

B. The Symbolic Meaning of Rock.

The concept of the rock is part of the common mythical imagery of the ancient East. It also belongs to the ancient Israelitish view of the world. As a "hollow mountain" [14] the earth comes up out of the original flood which surrounds it on all sides. In keeping is the fact that in the chaotic sea of primeval time temples were built first, coming up out of the sea like islands. [15] Similar ideas are to be found in later Judaism : "The Holy One, blessed be He, threw a stone into the sea ; from this the world was founded ; for it is said : On what are its (the earth's) foundations sunk, and who has laid its foundation stone ? (Job 38:6)." [16] "What did the Holy One, blessed be He ? With his right foot he sank the stone to the depths of the primal flood, and made it the keystone of the world, like a man who sets a keystone in an arch. For this reason it is called אֶבֶן שְׁתִיָּה, for there is the navel of the earth, and from there the whole world was extended, and on it stands the temple." [17] The rock in the holy of holies [18] is thus the origin of the creation of the world and the supreme point of the earth. It is the gate of heaven [19] and belongs to the future Paradise. [20] As the stone which stops up the primal flood it is also the origin of the waters of earth [21] and the portal [22] to the realm of the dead. [23]

That in the broader sense this view stands behind Is. too may be seen from Is. 28 and 8. Acc. to the custom of his age the prophet gave an inscr. for the foundation stone of the temple : "He that believeth shall not be put to shame," 28:16. [24] But this is the inscr. of the cornerstone of the new temple which God will build, not of the old temple. [25] The old temple no longer offers any protection against the inrushing flood of the Assyrian hosts. It will be destroyed. Acc. to Rabb. legend David arrested the surging primeval flood with an inscr. of this kind. [26] The sacred stone which stops up the flood is also the gate to the underworld and the realm of the dead. It is no accident that alongside the image of the inrushing flood (the Assyrians) Is. sets the compact which apostate Israel has made with the underworld and death, Is. 8 and 28. The same concepts find an echo in Mt. 16:18 : καὶ πύλαι ᾅδου οὐ κατισχύσουσιν αὐτῆς (→ Πέτρος, 107, 24 ff.).

---

[10] Cf. Levy Wört., s.v.

[11] A. Dell, "Mt. 16:17-19," ZNW, 15 (1914), 19; cf. → IV, 268, n. 3.

[12] λίθος has more the sense of the individual stone (or rock) of varying sizes, whether dressed or not.

[13] As against Dell, 19. On the linguistic problem cf. H. Clavier, "Πέτρος καὶ πέτρα," Nt.liche Studien f. R. Bultmann, Beih. z. ZNW, 21 (1954), 101-107.

[14] J. Jeremias, Golgotha (1926), 66 f.

[15] H. Gressmann, Der Messias (1929), 110.

[16] R. Jichaq the Smith (c. 300) in Jeremias, op. cit., 54.

[17] Jalqut Gn., 120 on 28:22, Jeremias, 55.

[18] On the association of rock and altar of burnt offering cf. Schmidt, 3-6; Jeremias, 58-65.

[19] Jalqut Gn., 120 on 28:22, Jeremias, 53.

[20] Jeremias, 53 f.

[21] Ibid., 56-57.

[22] Ibid., 57 f. Against Jeremias' attempt to find traces of the symbolism of the sacred rock in the OT itself cf. H. W. Hertzberg, "Der heilige Fels u. d. AT," The Journal of the Palestine Oriental Society, 11 (1931), 32-42.

[23] This paragraph is by S. Schulz.

[24] Gressmann, 110.

[25] יסַד in the Mas. is a dogmatic emendation, → n. 36.

[26] Jeremias, 55.

C. πέτρα in the New Testament.

1. πέτρα in the Literal Sense.

Apart from 1 C. 10:4; R. 9:33; 1 Pt. 2:8 and Mt. 16:18 πέτρα is used literally. Thus Mk. 15:46; Mt. 27:60 refer to the sepulchre carved into the πέτρα. Rev. 6:15 f. speaks of attempts to find shelter in clefts of the rock and in the mountains. Mt. 27:51 tells us that the earthquake rent the rocks and opened the graves. In the parable of the Sower in Lk. 8:6 the ref. is not just to individual rocks but to a rocky sub-stratum. [27] In the parable in Mt. 7:24-27 and Lk. 6:47-49 the house built on the rock is contrasted with the house built on the sand. Here πέτρα serves as a basis for the foundation (θεμελιόω, → III, 64, 13 ff., οἰκοδομέω → V, 138, 29. The Word of Christ is the only foundation of the existence of the community, Mt. 7:24. Related to this building parable is the saying to Peter in Mt. 16:18, though here πέτρα has a transf. sense, → 99, 12 ff.

2. The Rock which Followed, 1 C. 10:4.

Underlying this passage is the miracle of water from the rock described in Ex. 17 and Nu. 20 and presented with many variations in the OT, [28] → ὕδωρ. Acc. to Ex. 17:6 the site of this miracle is the rock of Horeb (עַל־הַצּוּר בְּחֹרֵב).[29] Already in OT exposition [30] this miraculous rock, like the wilderness wandering, is given typical significance. It is viewed as a paradisial gift of salvation with a plain eschatological ref. In later Jewish speculation a combination of Ex. 17 and Nu. 20 give birth to the legend of a rocky fountain which followed the people in the time of Moses and supplied them with water : "Even so it was with the fountain which was with Israel in the wilderness ; it resembled a rock full of holes like a sieve, and the water trickled through and rose up as from the opening of a flask. It went up the mountains with them and descended with them to the valleys ..." [31] As compared with the OT statements rationalism has gained an entry here.

Paul makes use of this legend when he speaks of the rock which followed in 1 C. 10:4. He refers this to Christ: ἡ πέτρα δὲ ἦν ὁ Χριστός. Later Judaism does not interpret the rock of Ex. 17 and Nu. 20 Messianically, → IV, 273, 16 ff. Paul is perhaps dependent here on texts like Jn. 7:37 f., → IV, 277, 21 ff. [32] He is not equating the rock directly with Christ, as though the latter took the form of the rock, → n. 33. Christ is a spiritual (πνευματικός) reality. But He is not a reality of such a kind that one may allegorically abstract Him either from the concrete rock which followed in the past or from the concrete empirical gift of the Lord's Supper in the present. [33] The same Christ, acting in history, stands over both the old covenant and the new in His pre-existence and post-existence. The faithfulness of this Christ to His people both then and now is expressed by Paul in the ἀκολουθούσης (v. 4).

3. R. 9:33 and 1 Pt. 2:7 f. [34]

a. R. 9:33 (→ IV, 276, 29 ff.). Because Israel rejected the way to salvation by faith and expected everything from itself and its own righteousness, Christ has

---

[27] Mk. and Mt.: πετρώδης.
[28] Cf. Dt. 8:15; 32:13; Is. 48:21; Neh. 9:15; Job 29:6; Ps. 78:15-20; 81:16; 105:41; 114:8.
[29] This topographical note in Ex. 17:6 is in tension with that of 17:8 (Rephidim) as well as with the par. in Nu. 20.
[30] Cf. the passages mentioned in → n. 28, esp. Is. 48:21; Ps. 81:16; 114:8.
[31] Tractate Sukka, 3, 11 ff. in Str.-B., III, 406.
[32] Jeremias, 84.
[33] As is well known, the allegory is used in various ways in the history of exegesis. Already in later Judaism Philo refers the πέτρα to the λόγος and σοφία, Leg. All., II, 86.
[34] On the Messianic interpretation of the OT passages cf. λίθος → IV, 272, 22 ff.

become for it a stone of stumbling and rock of offence: ἰδοὺ τίθημι ἐν Σιὼν λίθον προσκόμματος καὶ πέτραν σκανδάλου, καὶ ὁ πιστεύων ἐπ' αὐτῷ οὐ καταισχυνθήσεται.

Paul has here conflated 2 OT verses : Is. 28:16 and 8:14. Textually neither corresponds to the LXX rendering ; they are both closer to the Heb. [35] The saying from Is. 28, however, shares with the LXX the ἐπ' αὐτῷ which bears witness to Messianic exposition. Is. 28:16, which forms the framework, speaks of the basic cornerstone of the temple which Yahweh will establish again on Zion. [36] הַמַּאֲמִין לֹא יָחִישׁ is the prophet's inscr. on the stone acc. to the custom of his day. [37] By rendering פִּנָּה as ἀκρογωνιαῖον the LXX prepares the way for the understanding of this cornerstone as the keystone above the gate, → IV, 274, 12 ff. Thus the stone of Is. 28:16 comes to be associated with the κεφαλὴ γωνίας of Ps. 118:22. Is. 8:14 makes Yahweh אֶבֶן נֶגֶף וּלְצוּר מִכְשׁוֹל. There is a powerful dynamic in this parallelism. Yahweh is identified with the אֶבֶן on the path and becomes the rock of falling, → σκάνδαλον.

The decisive words from Is. 8:14 are integrated by Paul into the framework of Is. 28:16 in such a way that quite paradoxically this stone of stumbling and rock of offence (Is. 8) takes the place of the tested, valuable and basic cornerstone of the word of salvation (Is. 28). Because the reference is to the fall of Israel, the combination of the two verses enables Paul to give a sudden and wholly new turn to the image of the precious cornerstone. The cornerstone of the temple shows itself to be a terrible and invincible thing in the face of unbelief. It becomes πέτρα τοῦ σκανδάλου. And yet on this very stone Paul leaves the inscription with its gracious invitation to Israel: καὶ ὁ πιστεύων ἐπ' αὐτῷ οὐ καταισχυνθήσεται. Behind the combination of the two OT verses stands the whole hope of Paul for his brethren κατὰ σάρκα, R. 9-11.

b. 1 Pt. 2:7 f. (λίθος → IV, 276, 37 ff.). The author of 1 Pt. follows R. 9:33 in combining two quotations from OT stone theology. [38] In this instance, however, Ps. 118:22 and Is. 8:14 are combined. The joyous word of Ps. 118:22 (LXX 117:22) refers to the crowning keystone above the gate, which is solemnly fitted in in the course of rebuilding the destroyed temple. As in R. 9:33, however, this adornment of the whole temple acquires under the influence of Is. 8:14 the aspect of a terrible and invincible rock of σκάνδαλον lying on the way. Strengthened by the introduction of the concept of predestination (v. 8b), this exposition of the glad saying Ps. 118:22 in malam partem is antithetically contrasted with the salvation saying Is. 28:16, which is applied only to believers (v. 6). One can no longer detect any hope for Israel κατὰ σάρκα — for here, too, the reference is to the Jews — such as that found in Paul's combination of quotations in R. 9:33.

4. Mt. 16:18 (→ 104, 23 ff.).

The obvious pun which has made its way into the Gk. text as well suggests a material identity between πέτρα and Πέτρος, the more so as it is impossible to differentiate strictly between the meanings of the two words. On the other hand, only the fairly assured Aramaic original of the saying enables us to assert with confidence the formal and material identity between πέτρα and Πέτρος: πέτρα = כֵּיפָא = Πέτρος. Elsewhere in the NT the individual Christian is never called πέτρα, though he is λίθος in the spiritual building, the body of Christ (1 Pt. 2:5,

---

35 Cf. 1 Pt. 2:8.
36 Read מוסד.
37 Cf. the discussion under Mt. 16:18.
38 G. Stählin, Skandalon (1930), 196.

→ IV, 276, 37 ff.). Rightly understood, Christ alone is πέτρα. If, then, Mt. 16:18 forces us to assume a formal and material identity between πέτρα and Πέτρος, this shows how fully the apostolate, and in it to a special degree the position of Peter, belongs to and is essentially enclosed within, the revelation of Christ. Πέτρος himself is this πέτρα, not just his faith or his confession, → 108, 9 ff. He is this, of course, only as the Simon whom Christ has taken in hand. But in this way, like the one who walked on the sea, he truly is this Πέτρος. If Christ is to build a spiritual house, the ἐκκλησία, on this πέτρα, Πέτρος is the foundation of this ἐκκλησία on the basis of the saying of Christ: "Thou art Peter." [39] This foundation, however, is a supremely historical entity — the uniqueness of the apostolate and of the place of Peter within it.

Since, however, כֵּיפָא carries with it the distinctive content of πέτρα, it is from the very first highly improbable that it is to be taken simply in the sense of λίθος. This possibility is indeed ruled out by a Rabb. analogon: "When God looked on Abraham, who was to arise, he said: Lo, I have found a rock on which I can build and found the world. For this reason he called Abraham a rock." [40] In a way which transcends the Rabb. view of Abraham, Peter is brought into this picture of Abraham as the cosmic rock. He takes the place of Abraham, but he does so as the foundation of Israel κατὰ πνεῦμα, the community of the new covenant which Christ builds on the rock Peter (οἰκοδομέω, → V, 139, 3 ff.; ἐκκλησία, → III, 518-526).

D. The Post-Apostolic Fathers and Apologists.

In Barn., 11, 5 (quoting Is. 33:16), πέτρα seems to be used of God, cf. also 11, 3; Is. 16:1. God or Christ, the Lord, who reveals Himself in the OT, is the rock which gives water. Barn., 5, 14; 6, 3 also seem to be allusions to Is. 50:7 (the face of Christ as a rock), cf. Just. Apol., 38, 3. πέτρα and λίθος are used interchangeably both here and elsewhere. Acc. to Herm. s., 9, 2-14 Christ is the rock on which the tower of the Church is built from stones, i.e., believers, so that they constitute a perfect unity. If these stones are of different significance and value, none of them has, like Christ, a unique position in relation to the rest. The foundation of the tower consists of 10 of the first generation of just men, then 25 of the second generation, then 35 prophets of God and their servants, and finally as a fourth course in the foundation 40 apostles and teachers of the message of God. A special position is assigned neither to the twelve apostles nor to Peter. The rock on which Polycarp builds is also Christ, Ign. Pol., 1, 1. Similarly, Just. says in Dial., 113, 6: λίθος καὶ πέτρα ἐν παραβολαῖς ὁ Χριστὸς διὰ τῶν προφητῶν ἐκηρύσσετο. This sets forth a fixed principle of exposition. Wherever rock and stone occur in the OT, the ref. is to Christ; He is the καλὴ πέτρα, Dial., 114, 4. His sayings, which accomplish the circumcision of the heart, are symbolised by the stone knives of Jos. 5:2, 3, Dial., 24, 2; 113, 6, 7; 114, 4. In Dial., 114, 4 Just. quotes Da. 2:34: ἐτμήθη λίθος ἐξ ὄρους ἄνευ χειρῶν. This, too, is referred to Christ. In Dial., 70, 1 he uses the same v. to show that the myth of the rock-birth of Mithras is a pagan imitation. [41]

Cullmann

---

[39] Cf. the parable in Mt. 7:24-27.
[40] Jalqut, 1 § 766 in Str.-B., I, 733.
[41] Section D. is by G. Bertram.

Πέτρος, Κηφᾶς

Contents : A. Philological Questions. B. The Person of the Disciple and His Position among the Twelve : 1. Biographical Note ; 2. The Special Position of Peter ; 3. His Name-giving. C. Peter the Rock on which the Church is Built : 1. The Question of the Apostolic Commission apart from Mt. 16:17-19; 2. The Logion Mt. 16:17-19 : a. The Setting of the Logion ; b. The Question of Authenticity ; c. The Meaning of the Saying. D. Peter's Leadership of the Primitive Community and His First Missionary Activity. E. Peter's Later Missionary Activity and Death.

A. Philological Questions.

Except at Jn. 1:42, where it is used to elucidate the Aram. κηφᾶς, πέτρος is used in the NT only as the nickname of Simon, one of the disciples of Jesus.

This disciple is also called Συμεών, Σίμων, Σίμων Πέτρος and Κηφᾶς. The thesis that the Cephas of Gl. 2:11 is not identical with the disciple and apostle, but belongs to the circle of the seventy, obviously owes its origin to apologetic reasons, and though it has constantly found supporters from the days of Cl. Al., [1] it is without foundation. The name of the disciple is Symeon (שִׁמְעוֹן), a Heb. name common among the Jews. We find this in Gk. only at Ac. 15:14 and in some MSS at 2 Pt. 1:1. [2] The Gospels, however, use Simon, a Gk. proper name attested already in Aristoph. Nu., 351. [3] The disciple later came to be known as Simon, since there is a similarity of sound between the Gk. and Heb. names, and Simon could easily replace the non-Gk. Symeon. It is possible, indeed, that from the very first Peter bore the Gk. as well as the Heb. name, esp. if, like Philip, he came from Bethsaida, which was under Gk. influence, Jn. 1:44. [4]

In the NT sources the disciple Symeon/Simon also bears the sobriquet Κηφᾶς, which is a Gk. transcription of the Aram. כֵּיפָא.

This is not, as one might suppose, [5] attested as a proper name in Aram., where it is a noun denoting an object and simply means "rock" or "stone." This Gk. transcription of the Aram. form of the nickname is found for the most part — the Πέτρος of Gl. 2:7 f. is an exception [6] — in Paul : Gl. 1:18; 2:9, 11, 14; 1 C. 1:12; 3:22; 9:5; 15:5. Here the

Πέτρος. On the whole question cf. O. Cullmann, *Petrus, Jünger — Apostel — Mär-tyrer. Das historische u. das theologische Petrusproblem* (1952), ET (1953); K. G. Goetz, *Petrus als Gründer u. Oberhaupt der Kirche u. Schauer von Gesichten nach den altchr. Be-richten u. Legenden* (1927); F. J. Foakes-Jackson, *Peter, Prince of Apostles. A Study in the History and Tradition of Christianity* (1927); F. Sieffert, Art. "Petrus," RE³, 15, 186-212; H. Koch, Art. "Petrus," Pauly-W., 19, 1335-1372; E. Stauffer, "Zur Vor- u. Frühgeschichte des Primatus Petri," ZKG, 62 (1943/44), 3-34; H. Strathmann, "Die Stellung d. Petrus in d. Urkirche. Zur Frühgeschichte des Wortes an Petrus Mt. 16:17-19," ZSTh, 20 (1943), 223-282. For further bibl. cf. Cullmann, *op. cit.*

[1] Eus. Hist. Eccl., I, 12, 2; also in apostolic lists, cf. T. Schermann, *Propheten- u. Apostel-legenden nebst Jüngerkatalogen* (1907), 302. More recently D. W. Riddle, "The Cephas-Peter Problem and a Possible Solution," JBL, 59 (1940), 169.

[2] The equation of the Symeon of Ac. 15:14 and Peter has been disputed from time to time.

[3] Bl.-Debr. § 53, 2; A. Fick-F. Bechtel, *Die gr. Personennamen²* (1894), 30, 251; A. Deiss-mann, *Bibelstudien* (1895), 184, n. 1.

[4] G. Dalman, *Orte u. Wege Jesu³* (1924), 177: "Anyone who grew up in Bethsaida would not only understand Gk. but would also have been polished by dealings with foreigners and would have become accustomed to Gk. culture."

[5] So Zn. Mt. on Mt. 16:18, though he gives no examples. M. J. Lagrange, *Év. selon St. Matthieu* (1923), *ad loc.*, thinks it possible, though he gives no reasons.

[6] He perhaps uses Πέτρος here because he is quoting an official document. Against all textual attestation A. Merx, *Die vier kanonischen Ev. nach ihrem ältesten bekannten Text,* II, 1 (1902), *ad loc.* regards this reading as a secondary one in place of an original Κηφᾶς.

Aram. word is given a Gk. ending in -ς: Κηφᾶς. We find the name transl. into Gk. as Πέτρος (Κηφᾶς, ὃ ἑρμηνεύεται Πέτρος, Jn. 1:42).[7] As a masc. noun this is preferred to the more literal πέτρα, which is attested as a transl. at LXX Jer. 4:29; Job 30:6, but which has the fem. ending in -α. The difference in meaning between the two Gk. words is not fixed, though in common Gk. usage ὁ πέτρος tends to denote the isolated rock and ἡ πέτρα the cliff, → 95, 15-22.

The Greek Πέτρος established itself in the NT.[8] The Evangelists sometimes use Simon, sometimes Peter, sometimes Simon Peter. The fact of translation supports the contention that Cephas was not a proper name, since one does not translate proper names. In order to bring out the power of the nickname as the authors and early readers of the NT felt it, we ought perhaps to follow the NT practice and reproduce the name as "Simon Rock."

B. The Person of the Disciple and His Position among the Twelve.

1. Biographical Note.

Simon is the son of Jona[9] and probably comes from Bethsaida, the "city of fishermen" (Jn. 1:44), a small Jewish town on the east bank of the Jordan which was under Greek influence.[10] He was an "uneducated" man who had studied neither acc. to Rabbinic nor Greek ideas, Ac. 4:13. He was a simple fisherman (Mk. 1:16 and par.; Lk. 5:2; Jn. 21:3) who worked in partnership (Lk. 5:10) with the two sons of Zebedee. Later he lived in Capernaum (Mk. 1:29 and par.). Here Jesus was a frequent visitor at his house and perhaps lived with him for a longer period (Mt. 8:14). Acc. to Mk. 1:29-31 and par. and 1 C. 9:5 Peter was married. The later accounts of his children and of the martyrdom of his wife are legendary. Before Simon joined Jesus, he seems to have belonged to the circle of John the Baptist along with his brother Andrew, cf. Jn. 1:35-42.

2. The Special Position of Peter.

According to the Synoptists Peter assumed a special position in the group around Jesus. With the sons of Zebedee and his brother Andrew he belonged to the innermost and most intimate circle of those associated with Jesus. Even in this inner circle (Mk. 9:2 and par.), however, he had an important position of precedence, so that the Synoptic Gospels always portray him as standing in the forefront, Mk. 9:5. Thus Jesus allows only Peter and the sons of Zebedee to go with Him into the house of the ruler of the synagogue, Mk. 5:37. Peter is also the leading character in the story of the miraculous catch, Lk. 5:1 ff. According to Mt. 14:28 it is also he who tries to imitate the Lord by walking on the lake. He is distinguished by excess of zeal and effort, though these also lead to his denial. He acts as spokesman for the twelve,[11] and he has to hear the harsh

---

[7] Petrus (short for Petronius) is hardly to be found in the pre-Christian period. A. Merx, op. cit., 160 appeals to Jos. Ant., 18, 6, but this is an error for πρῶτος. Cf. also A. Meyer, Jesu Muttersprache (1896), 51, but on the other hand A. Dell, "Mt. 16:17-19," ZNW, 15 (1914), 14-17.

[8] That there was in Aram. a proper name Petros (Str.-B., I, 530) which perhaps meant "firstborn" (Levy Wört., s.v. פֶּטֶר; Dalman Wört., s.v.) might have influenced the preference for Petros, but this is by no means certain.

[9] An alternative to the usual explanation of the Aram. bar Jona (Jona = John, Jn. 1:42; 21:15) is given by R. Eisler, Jesous basileus ou basileusas, II (1930), 68: "Extremist."

[10] → n. 4.

[11] It is also worth noting that in one Gospel only Peter speaks, whereas in the par. all the disciples ask, cf. Mk. 7:17 with Mt. 15:15; Mt. 21:20 with Mk. 11:21.

words: "Get thee behind me, Satan: for thou savourest not the things that be of God, but the things that be of men," Mk. 8:29-33 and par. What is said to him applies to all the disciples ("... and looked on his disciples ...," Mk. 8:33). In the name of his fellow-disciples he asks the casuistical question: "Lord, how oft shall my brother sin against me, and I forgive him? till seven times?" Mt. 18:21. With John he is given the task of preparing the passover, Lk. 22:8. In Gethsemane, he is, like the others, unable to meet the request to watch with the Lord for an hour; hence Jesus puts to him and to the sons of Zebedee the reproachful question of Mk. 14:37; Mt. 26:40. Even outsiders like the tax-collector (Mt. 17:24) turn to him as the most obvious representative of the circle around Jesus. The lists of disciples (Mk. 3:16; Mt. 10:2; Lk. 6:14; Ac. 1:13) confirm this position. There are differences between these, but they all put the name of Peter first (Mt. πρῶτος) and in so doing support the view of Peter's role found in the Gospel stories. Particularly worth noting is the expression "Peter and they that were with him" in Mk. 1:36 and Lk. 9:32 (8:45 acc. to some MSS), cf. also the saying of the angel in Mk. 16:7: "Tell his disciples and Peter."

There is no difference between the individual Synoptists in their treatment of Peter. The specific features mentioned above have not been preserved in the same way by all of them, but they are evenly distributed. Thus Mk. does not have the saying about the Church (Mt. 16:17-19), nor does he try to conceal the weaknesses of Peter, but his total presentation leaves no doubt as to the role which he ascribes to Peter. [12] Nor can one say that Mt. has a particular ecclesiastical interest [13] in Peter because he alone records the saying about the rock on which the *ecclesia* is to be built, whereas Lk. says nothing about Peter's significance as the foundation of the Church. The saying in Lk. 22:31 f.: "Simon, Simon, behold, Satan hath desired to have you, that he may sift you as wheat. But I have prayed for thee, that thy faith fail not : and when thou art converted, [14] strengthen thy brethren," offers a par. [15] to Mt. 16:17-19 (→ 105, 19 ff.), for it lays on Peter a special future task in relation to his brethren, though here, too, he is grouped with the other disciples and shares their weaknesses.

We find a rather different picture in John's Gospel. Here the Synoptic singling out of Peter, though not disputed, causes difficulty. The mysterious and anonymous disciple whom Jesus loved enters into some competition with Peter ; perhaps a contemporary interest of the author explains this. Nevertheless, the special position of Peter is not contested, Jn. 1:42; 6:68. It is simply subordinated to the author's interest in the relation of the beloved disciple to Jesus. This proves how firm was the tradition about the precedence of Peter among the disciples. While the other disciples retreat into the background, the rivalry between the beloved disciple and Peter is obvious in the story of the passion. At the Last Supper (13:24 ff.) the beloved disciple leans on Jesus' breast, and Peter has to turn to him to learn a secret of Jesus. Later the other disciple, who knew the high-priest, goes with Jesus into the palace, and has to come back for Peter (18:16), who then proceeds to deny Jesus. Only the mysterious disciple is present at the cross, 19:26. The incident at the tomb (20:1-10) is obviously the key to the author's treatment of the two rivals. Peter, the impulsive activist, goes into the tomb ; the beloved disciple,

---

[12] R. Bultmann, "Die Frage nach dem messianischen Bewusstsein Jesu u. das Petrus-Bekenntnis," ZNW, 19 (1919/20), 170 speaks of an "animosity" of Mk. against Peter. On the other hand M. Goguel, *L'Eglise primitive* (1947), 191 says : "il n'y a aucune trace d'antipétrinisme chez Marc."

[13] Strathmann, 223 f. assumes that the Gospels took different attitudes to Peter acc. to their postulated connections with various churches.

[14] Another reading is "convert." Stauffer, 20, n. 58 gives various reasons for preferring this reading.

[15] → 103, 34 ff.

who arrived first, follows him. But he was the first to believe when he saw. [16] This verse sheds light on Jn. 1:41, where the differences in the MSS (πρῶτος, πρῶτον) demonstrate an early recognition that the Fourth Evangelist was interested in the question of precedence. The supplementary chapter (21) also contrasts the primacy of Peter with the very different primacy of the beloved disciple. Indirectly, then, John's Gospel confirms the Synoptic testimony to Peter's special position by its very tendency to single out the disciple whom Jesus loved. The author gives Peter his name at the very beginning (1:42): "Thou shalt be called Cephas."

3. His Namegiving.

One cannot ascribe the namegiving to the other disciples or set it in the period after Easter on the ground that Peter was the first to see the Lord. [17] The fact that Jesus consistently calls him Simon is unquestionably a difficulty. Difficult, too, is the question when Jesus gave him his nickname. Was it on the occasion of his confession of Jesus as the Messiah at Caesarea Philippi, where Jesus also explained the name? Was it on the occasion of his call, Mk. 3:16? Was it on the even earlier occasion of the first encounter, Jn. 1:42? There can be no certainty in this matter, since recollection of the circumstances of the incident perished quite early. The Gospel tradition has simply preserved the fact that Jesus marked off Simon among the twelve by giving him the name "rock." According to OT models (Gn. 17:5, 15; 32:29; Is. 62:2; 65:15) and Rabbinic usage nicknames either refer to a particular situation as a promise or else they lay upon those who bear them a specific task (→ ὄνομα, V, 253, 44-254, 42). [18] This name cannot be explained exclusively in terms of Peter's character. [19] To be sure, Jesus knows his zeal, exuberance and energy as well as his lack of courage. When He gives Simon the name Peter, He knows the many-sided strength of his temperament. On the other hand, these qualities unfold only in the discharge of the task laid upon him.

If, then, all the Gospels recognise the representative role of Peter, he occupies this position only in relation to Jesus, not outside it, as in the apocryphal Petrine literature.

C. Peter the Rock on which the Church is Built.

1. The Question of the Apostolic Commission apart from Mt. 16:17-19.

The special position of Peter does not mean that he leads the other disciples during the lifetime of Jesus. For a while the guidance of the developing community does in fact fall on him after the death of Jesus, → 109, 1 ff. Is this position of Peter in the Jerusalem church based on his singling out by Jesus as expressed in the namegiving and in Lk. 22:31 f. (→ 102, 12 ff.), or is it based on a commission of the risen Lord analogous to the call of Paul? [20] As regards the Petrine apostolate great significance undoubtedly attaches to the commission of the risen Lord in Jn. 21:15 ff. as well as to the call of the incarnate Lord. 1 C. 15:5 and Lk. 24:34 mention an appearance of the Lord to Peter and thereby show that this important

---

[16] This is for the author of Jn. the sign of a true disciple, v. O. Cullmann, "Εἶδεν καὶ ἐπίστευσεν," Festschrift f. M. Goguel, Aux sources de la tradition chrétienne (1950), 56 f.

[17] So Goetz, 67 and E. Hirsch, Frühgesch. d. Ev., II (1941), 306.

[18] Cf. Boanerges in Mk. 3:17. On Rabbinic usage cf. P. Fiebig, Die Gleichnisreden Jesu im Lichte d. rabb. Gleichnisse des nt.lichen Zeitalters (1912), 53.

[19] Cf. esp. Sieffert, 53.

[20] On the question of the need for a special call to the apostolate by the risen Lord cf. A. Fridrichsen, The Apostle and His Message, Uppsala Universitets Årsskrift, 3 (1947), 3-23.

though not exclusive[21] precondition of apostolic calling applies to Peter in a special way. One cannot tell from 1 C. 15:5 or Lk. 24:34 whether the appearance of the risen Lord carried with it for Peter an express confirmation of his apostolic office, though Jn. 21:15 ff. associates with this appearance the special commission to feed the sheep. In any case it is of supreme importance that in 1 C. 15:5 Peter is the first eye-witness of the risen Lord. [22] In the brief note in Lk. 24:34, where the two who return from Emmaus tell the others: "The Lord is risen indeed, and hath appeared to Simon," indirect support is offered. It is strange, however, that the Evangelists do not specifically record this appearance.

> Acc. to Mk. 14:28 and Mk. 16:7 it is possible that the lost Marcan ending contained an account of this incident. [23] Such an account might well lie behind Jn. 21:15-23. [24] But there can be no certainty about this. [25] We find only traces of the event, and the question thus arises as to why it has almost completely disappeared from the Gospel records. The reason is probably to be sought in the attempts of Jewish Christians to disparage appearances as a basis of apostolate. This trend developed in opposition to Paul's basing of the apostolate on the appearances; Paul could appeal only to an appearance. In Ps.-Clem. Recg., II, 62 and Ps.-Clem. Hom., 17 we find express testimony to this. [26]

This silence, however, does not invalidate the fact that Peter, commissioned by the earthly Lord, received confirmation of this commission through the first appearance of the Lord after the resurrection, so that he was properly instituted the first leader of the Christian community.

2. The Logion Mt. 16:17-19.

a. The Setting of the Logion. The story in which the verse about Peter and the Church is embedded in Mt. may be found also in Mk. and Lk., though not as a setting for this saying of Jesus. In Mt. the saying about the rock is associated with Peter's confession of Jesus as the Messiah at Caesarea Philippi, while the other two Evangelists do not record it at all.

> Mark's is probably the original version of the story. This may be seen from the crisp and vivid presentation and esp. from the central position which Mk. gives the pericope in his Gospel as a whole. Thus far Jesus has not allowed any discussion of His Messiahship. But now He provokes it. Peter, in the name of the rest, says: "Thou art the Christ." Though Jesus forbids them to tell others of this, He expounds to them His

---

[21] Cf. esp. H. v. Campenhausen, "Der urchr. Apostelbegriff," Studia theologica, 1 (1948), 112 f.

[22] F. Kattenbusch, "Die Vorzugsstellung des Petrus u. der Charakter der Urgemeinde zu Jerusalem," Festgabe f. K. Müller (1922), 328; also "Der Spruch über Petrus u. die Kirche bei Mt.," ThStKr, 94 (1922), 130 wrongly denies this and tries to take the εἶτα chronologically. But the order is obviously important in 1 C. 15:5-8. A. Harnack, "Die Verklärungsgesch. Jesu," SAB (1922), 68; Goetz, 4 f.; Stauffer, 8-9 all pay due heed to the fact that Peter saw the risen Lord first.

[23] This might even be postulated from Mk. 14:28 and 16:7, cf. Stauffer, 11-12. Goetz, 73 also reckons with this possibility. On the other hand K. L. Schmidt, Kanonische u. apokryphe Evangelien u. Apostelgeschichten (1944), 27 and N. B. Stonehouse, The Witness of Matthew and Mark to Christ (1944), 86 believe that the words ἐφοβοῦντο γάρ are the real end of the Gospel.

[24] So already A. Meyer, Die Auferstehung Christi (1905), 168.

[25] Cullmann, 62 f.

[26] O. Cullmann, Le problème littéraire et historique du roman pseudo-clémentin (1930), 248 f.; C. Holsten, Die Messiasvision des Petrus und die Genesis des petrinischen Ev. (1867), 120. The non-canonical writings offer very rich material on Peter's vision, Goetz, 89-93.

view of the Messianic calling in contrast to the current view of the people and their tense expectations. This startles the disciples so much that Peter takes Jesus aside and protests vehemently against this completely new understanding of the Messiah. The disciples had had very different ideas in view when they followed Jesus. The sharp rebuke of Jesus: "Get thee behind me, Satan," closes the incident in Mk. [27]

In contrast, Mt. in his account weakens the distinctiveness of the incident by setting another confession by the disciples before it, Mt. 14:33. From the standpoint of narrative technique he does not have the same precision as Mk. [28] One may also ask whether he does not break the sequence of the story by the saying to Peter. It is quite possible to see in the confession an alien body in a story which is condemning Peter's view of the Messiah as satanic. For the point in Mk. is the correction of this view. In this context, then, it is hard to understand the dominical saying about Peter's revealed knowledge as this is recorded in Mt.

One may thus assume with some probability that Mt. was seeking a place for the orally transmitted saying of Jesus to Peter (→ III, 520, 3 ff.), and that under the influence of the parallelism between "Thou art the Christ" and "Thou art Peter" he believed he had found a suitable point at Peter's confession.

If we seek the original setting of Mt. 16:17-19, we are reminded of Jn. 21:15-23, which Mt. might have put back into the earthly life of Jesus. [29] Attractive though this suggestion is, however, it is unlikely that Jesus should not have given Simon his nickname during His lifetime. Hence there is more to be said for seeking the original setting in that of the saying in Lk. 22:31 f., which is an exact par. to Mt. 16:17-19. The conversation in Lk. 22:31-34 contains Peter's promise to go to prison with Jesus and Jesus' prediction of the denial and His command to strengthen the brethren. Jn. 21:15-23, which may be regarded as a direct par. to Mt. 16:17-19, presupposes an incident in the earthly life of Jesus such as Lk. 22:31-34 depicts; it is perhaps to be understood in the light of this passage. In place of the threefold denial we now have the threefold protestation: "Yea, Lord, thou knowest that I love thee." To Peter's promise corresponds the prediction of martyrdom. The command to strengthen the brethren is replaced by the charge to feed Christ's sheep. The link between the three passages is such, then, that Jn. 21:15-23 bears witness to acquaintance with a story from the passion. When Peter promises to go with the Lord even to death, his denial is predicted, but so, too, is his conversion, and the founding of the flock upon him as upon a rock. This combination is to be seen in Lk. 22:31-34. Mt. possibly used a special tradition which might well have been known to the author of Jn. 21:15-23, who presupposes this relationship. For the image of the sheep whom Peter is to feed implies that of the flock, and this concept is closely related to that of the Church in Mt. 16:18, → 107, 7 f.

Hence the saying in Mt. 16:17-19 might well be part of the passion story, related to the prophecy of Peter's denial after the Last Supper on the eve of the crucifixion. If this is probably the original setting, the question of the authenticity and meaning of the saying now arises.

b. The Question of Authenticity. The authenticity of the saying has been hotly contested since the 19th century. Discussion of the matter occupies a good deal of

---

[27] The protest of Peter is the point of the incident at Caesarea Philippi and not a new story, as suggested in Bultmann, op. cit., 169-173; Bultmann Trad., 277; K. L. Schmidt, Der Rahmen d. Geschichte Jesu (1919), 217-220; W. Michaelis, Das Ev. nach Mt. (Prophezei), II (1949), 339; Schl. Mt., ad loc. The relationship of the story to what precedes is demonstrated by the fact that the complete difference in the understanding of the Messiah has to be stressed in view of the Messianic confession. Even Peter, who makes the confession, represents the "diabolical" view.

[28] Thus Mt., anticipating the answer, writes: "Who do people say that the Son of Man is?" whereas Mk. has the undoubtedly more original: "Who do people say that I am?"

[29] So esp. Stauffer, 26.

space in exegesis. Scholars are by no means unanimous on the issue. [30] It is fairly generally recognised that the linguistic character of the saying is Semitic, [31] and this proves that it could not have arisen in the Greek *diaspora*. The pun can be fully appreciated only in Aram., which has the same word *kepha* both times, not πέτρος ... πέτρα as in Gk. [32] The denoting of Peter's father by Bar-Jona, the expression "flesh and blood" for men, [33] the strophic rhythm, and the image of the rock for foundation, for which there is an exact par. in Rabbinic literature (Abraham as the rock of the world, → 99, 13 ff.), [34] all bear witness to the Semitic character of the saying and consequently to its antiquity, [35] → III, 749, 25 ff.

But can Jesus Himself have spoken already of a Church which He would establish? This is the main objection which has always been brought against the saying's authenticity. The question is legitimate, but before returning a negative answer one should set aside later ideas of the Church and understand the *ecclesia* as the people of God acc. to its Jewish sense. [36] In particular one should recall that the word occurs more than 100 times in the LXX, cf. also Ac. 7:38. Establishment of God's people goes hand in hand with the Messianic claim. Jesus' view of the people of God, in distinction from general Jewish ideas, is, of course, strongly influenced by the concept of the remnant of Israel (→ III, 526, 15 ff.), the "lost sheep" (Mt. 10:6; 15:24), and esp. by the emphasis on the suffering of the Messiah. The new covenant which Jesus announced and instituted (→ II, 133, 12 ff.) at the Last Supper on the eve of His death had the Messianic reconstitution of the people of God as its goal. In this connection it is significant that the Qumran sect uses "covenant" among other terms with ref. to the community. If the promise of Jesus in Mt. 16:17-19 really has the Last Supper as its setting (→ 105, 38 ff.), the prediction of the building of the ἐκκλησία has special significance in this context. The words "to build," "to build up" (→ V, 138 ff.) show that elsewhere in Jesus, in truly Jewish fashion, the people of God is presented as the house of Israel.

But how can Jesus have believed that the building would take place in this aeon? In Jesus this question does not arise in the form of an alternative between the present and the future community. In His preaching the kingdom of God has still to come, and

---

[30] On the story of modern exegesis v. J. R. Geiselmann, "Der petrinische Primat (Mt. 16:17), seine neueste Bekämpfung u. Rechtfertigung," *Bibl. Zeitfragen,* 12, 7 (1927); K. L. Schmidt, → ἐκκλησία, III, 518 ff.; R. Bultmann, "Die Frage nach d. Echtheit von Mt. 16:17-19," ThBl, 20 (1941), 265-267; A. Oepke, "Der Herrenspruch über d. Kirche Mt. 16:17-19 in der neuesten Forschung," Studia Theologica, 2 (1950), 110-165; Cullmann, 181-190.

[31] A. Harnack, "Der Spruch über Petrus als den Felsen d. Kirche (Mt. 16:17 f.)," SAB (1918), 637; Bultmann Trad., 277.

[32] M. Goguel, *L'Eglise naissante* (1947), 189, n. 4 does not regard this argument as decisive since a pun does not demand exact correspondence.

[33] In the NT 1 C. 15:50; Gl. 1:16; Eph. 6:12; Hb. 2:14; not in the OT, but in Jewish lit. Sir. 14:18 and often as a fixed tt. in the Rabb. writings, Str.-B., I, 730 and K. G. Kuhn, "πειρασμός — ἁμαρτία — σάρξ im NT," ZThK, 49 (1952), 209.

[34] J. Jeremias, *Golgotha* (1926), 73; he rightly refers to Da. 2:34 f., 44 f.

[35] The fact that only Mt has the saying shows that the source of the tradition is Palestinian, W. Michaelis, *op. cit., ad loc.* The antiquity of the tradition is also supported by the consideration that it could hardly have arisen at a time when Peter was no longer head of the Jerusalem church and James was its leader. A Palestinian origin and antiquity do not prove authenticity but they are important presuppositions.

[36] → III, 524, 6 ff.; L. Rost, "Die Vorstufen v. Kirche u. Synagoge im AT," BWANT, IV, 24 (1938). It does not seem to me to be necessary to prefer כְּנִישְׁתָּא as the original; it is better to leave the choice of original open. Cf. M. J. Lagrange, *ad loc.* The question is of no decisive importance because all the equivalents (קָהָל, כְּנִישְׁתָּא, צִבּוּרָה, עֵדְתָא) belong to the circle of the concept of God's people. The material needs fresh examination in the light of the Qumran texts. The most common term for this community is יַחַד. We also find בְּרִית, עֵצָה, עֵדָה, סוֹד, but surprisingly קָהָל occurs only twice in the texts known to us thus far.

yet it has already come with His own presence, Mt. 12:28; 11:5. [37] The concept of the people of God relates to the present as well as the future actualisation. Jesus finds both aspects of the reality of the people of God united in Himself. He relates the founding of the community to His own person. Through Him the establishment of this true people of God takes place first in the circle of the twelve (→ II, 326, 18 ff.), to whom He gives the decisive task of going to the lost sheep of the house of Israel, Mt. 10:6. [38] In their work, as in His own, He sees the dawn of the age of salvation. [39] This concept of the *ecclesia* comes to expression in such NT words as sheep, flock, shepherd. [40] In the sect which is now better known to us, and whose writings find par. in the Damascus document and the "cave" texts, [41] the concept of the shepherd (→ ποιμήν) was common, and so, too, was the idea of the community. To the same context belongs the saying about building the temple, Mk. 14:57 f. and par.; cf. Mk. 13:2; Jn. 2:19 → IV, 883, 9 ff. It is an exact par. to Mt. 16:17-19. Acc. to the Synoptic tradition one may assume that Jesus proclaimed the building of a temple not made with human hands. The ref. could only be to the new people of God which He would establish. As in Mt. 16:17, we have the image of building, which makes the material parallelism between the sayings even clearer, → V, 139, 3 ff.

But how can Jesus say that He *will* build His *ecclesia*? Does not His death usher in the final age of salvation? [42] A whole series of dominical sayings confutes this idea. The age of Messianic preparation begins with the word and work of Jesus. Though it reaches a decisive climax with His death, it is not completed herewith. The tension between present and future continues after His death. [43] This is shown esp. by the missionary sayings and also the eucharistic sayings. Hence there is no need to contest the authenticity of the logion if it is put in its material theological context. Against God's people, the *ecclesia* which Jesus will build, the gates of hell shall not prevail, Mt. 16:18b → I, 149, 13 ff. The hitherto triumphant kingdom of the dead [44] has lost its power; its gates must open before the power of the *ecclesia*. The function of the *ecclesia* is thus to follow up the victory over hell which Jesus has won with His death and resurrection. The fellowship of the Church has an active share in the resurrection, and in an extension of the image Peter is said to have been given the keys (→ III, 749, 21 ff.) of the kingdom of heaven, the realm of resurrection and life.

Since Peter, the rock of the Church, is thus given by Christ Himself, the master of the house (Is. 22:22; Rev. 3:7), the keys of the kingdom of heaven, he is the human mediator of the resurrection, and he has the task of admitting the people of God into the kingdom of the resurrection. Jesus Himself has given him power

---

[37] W. G. Kümmel, *Verheissung u. Erfüllung*[2] (1953).

[38] Jesus is aware that the fulfilment is present in His person, whereas the primitive Church sees the fulfilment in the Church. But fulfilment in the person of Jesus leads directly to fulfilment in the community, and the latter pts. to the former. This must be stressed in answer to W. G. Kümmel, *Kirchenbegriff u. Geschichtsbewusstsein in d. Urgemeinde u. bei Jesus*, Symbolae Biblicae Upsalienses, 1 (1943), who finds here an impossible juxtaposition of two different forms of historical consciousness, and on this ground contests the authenticity of Mt. 16:17-19.

[39] Bultmann, 275, following A. Loisy, *Les Évangiles synopt.* (1908), 23, thinks that Jesus' associating of disciples with Himself has nothing whatever to do with the Church.

[40] Bultmann, 268 does not think there is any idea of a group in the Synoptic refs., and he finds a completely different meaning for the terms in Jn.

[41] L. Rost, "Die Damaskusschrift," Kl. T., 167 (1933); K. G. Kuhn, "Die in Palästina gefundenen hbr. Texte u. d. NT," ZThK, 47 (1950), 199.

[42] So A. Schweitzer, *Das Abendmahl im Zshg. mit dem Leben Jesu u. d. Gesch. des Urchr.* (1901), 61 f.

[43] W. Michaelis, *Der Herr verzieht nicht d. Verheissung* (1942); Kümmel, 38-40; O. Cullmann, *Christus u. d. Zeit* (1948), 131 f.

[44] This is the primary ref. of Hades rather than the kingdom of sin and perdition; so Kl., Schl. Mt., *ad loc.*

to open entry to the coming kingdom of God, or to close it, like the Pharisees, who with their mission close the door to the kingdom of heaven, Mt. 23:13. Hence what Peter does on earth will be valid in heaven, → III, 751, 11 ff. This power is expressed in the words "to bind" and "to loose," → II, 60, 16 ff. The best interpretation is that Peter has the power to forgive sins, though the idea of the laying down of precepts cannot be ruled out completely. [45] To the functions which were allotted to the disciples during the lifetime of Jesus, and which were the same as those discharged by Jesus Himself (Mt. 11:4 ff.; 10:7 f.), there is thus added the supreme office of the remission of sins which had hitherto been reserved for Christ alone but which He now transmits to Peter with a view to the constitution of the earthly people of God. Peter, of course, shares the power of binding and loosing with the other disciples (Mt. 18:18); this corresponds precisely to the situation in the apostolic band.

c. The Meaning of the Saying. But what does Jesus mean when He says: "On this rock [46] I will build my church"? The idea of the Reformers [47] that He is referring to the faith of Peter is quite inconceivable in view of the probably different setting of the story, → 105, 38 ff. For there is no reference here to the faith of Peter. Rather, the parallelism of "thou art Rock" and "on this rock I will build" shows that the second rock can only be the same as the first. It is thus evident that Jesus is referring to Peter, to whom He has given the name Rock. He appoints Peter, the impulsive, enthusiastic, but not persevering man in the circle, to be the foundation of His *ecclesia*. To this extent Roman Catholic exegesis is right and all Protestant attempts to evade this interpretation are to be rejected. A supposed reference to "disciple" does not improve matters, for there is no mention of "disciples" in the text. The meaning of the logion rests on the two words Peter and *ecclesia*. What is stated is that the Church which is to be built is founded on the one rock. This is the person of Peter, but it is limited to a specific lifetime. In other words, the task which Peter is given to fulfil is unique, and this makes possible the building of the Church. The work of building belongs to a future which is not limited in time by Mt. 16:17 f. The laying of the foundation, however, is connected with the person of Peter, whose ability to act is necessarily limited to the period of his own life, Jn. 21:18. If the power to bind and to loose is given to Peter, this power does not relate to an unlimited future but to the life of Peter after the death of Jesus.

In Peter, in the saying about the founding and the ensuing building of the Church, the NT view of the rootage of what continues in what is once-for-all finds almost classical expression. Hence the task of Peter can be understood only in terms of the high-priestly prayer, which says that the new generation will believe through the word of the apostles, Jn. 17:20. For the foundation of the Church is simply the attestation of the death and resurrection of Jesus Christ, and of the identity of the Christ who promises and the Christ who is exalted. The apostles are the one foundation on which the community is built, Eph. 2:20; Rev. 21:14. Among them Peter is the first and chief eye-witness of the life, death and resurrection of Jesus.

---

[45] The two verbs (אסר and שרא) allow both interpretations : a. "to forbid" and "to permit," i.e., "to lay down rules" (Dalman, WJ, I, 175 f.; Kl. Mt., *ad loc.*; Zn. Mt., *ad loc.*; W. Michaelis, *ad loc.*); b. "to excommunicate" and "to absolve" (Rabb. examples, Str.-B., I, 738).

[46] On the image of the rock *v.* Jeremias, *op. cit.*, esp. 73.

[47] Str.-B., I, 732 tries to support this explanation philologically by appeal to the Aram.

D. Peter's Leadership of the Primitive Community and His First Missionary Activity.

1. Acts tells us how Peter, after the death of Jesus, carries out the commission which he had received. The representative of a band of disciples gathered around their rabbi becomes their appointed leader. His position of leadership is, of course, limited in time. Nor should we think of it in terms of the monarchical episcopate of a later age. To depict the history of primitive Christianity in its relation to Peter is not our present task. [48] We must restrict ourselves to a few points which are important in discussion of the significance of Peter from the standpoint of salvation history.

His position of leadership may be seen in the election of the twelfth apostle (Ac. 1:15), the interpretation of the miracle of Pentecost (2:14), the healing of the lame man (3:1), [49] the defence of the Gospel against the authorities (4:8 and 5:29), the exercise of church discipline (5:1-11), the inspection of the mission in Samaria (8:14-17), and the missionary activity in Lydda, Joppa and Caesarea, along with the conversion of the Gentile Cornelius (9-10). [50]

> Since Paul's letters all belong to a later period than the events in Ac. 1-12, they do not mention this side of Peter's activity apart from a brief ref. in Gl. 1:18 to Paul's first visit to Jerusalem, where he wanted to see Cephas. It is true that this was the sole purpose of his journey. He obviously knew that this man was at the head of the community. Yet he spent some time with James too, who as the physical brother of Jesus already played a role alongside Peter.

2. After his imprisonment by Herod and his liberation from prison, Peter left the holy city (Ac. 12:17), where James took over the leadership of the church, and from now on he devoted himself to missionary activity. [51] Only once does he appear again in Ac., namely, at the so-called Apostolic Council (Ac. 15), which is identical with the meeting described by Paul in Gl. 2:1-10. [52] According to Acts, however, James rather than Peter presides over this council. Paul, too, puts James first when he mentions the "pillars," Gl. 2:9. [53] The agreement reached here,

---

[48] Cullmann, 30-169.

[49] It is noteworthy that John is mentioned along with Peter both here and later. The way in which he is introduced and the fact that his part is not much more than that of a supernumerary suggests that his name might have been added to that of Peter later. If the anonymous beloved disciple of John's Gospel had already been identified as John, one might ask whether the mention of John along with Peter does not bear witness to the same trend as that already noted in Jn., → 102, 30 ff.

[50] In Jerusalem Peter had held a middle position between the Judaisers and the Hellenisers, cf. W. Grundmann, "Das Problem des hell. Christentums innerhalb d. jerusalemer Urgemeinde," ZNW, 38 (1939), 54, who recognises a historical kernel in the account of the conversion of Cornelius through Peter ; cf. also his "Die Apostel zwischen Jerusalem u. Antiochia," ZNW, 39 (1940), 132-136; on the other hand M. Dibelius, "Das Apostelkonzil : Die Bekehrung d. Cornelius," Aufsätze zu Ag. (1951), 85, 96 f. thinks the story derives in the main from the tendentious interests of the author of Ac.

[51] The reason why Peter left Jerusalem, where James had become the leader after his imprisonment, is perhaps connected with the persecution, which affected only him and not James. Do we have here a repetition of what took place after the Stephen persecution ? Then only the Hellenists were affected and the twelve could stay in Jerusalem, Ac. 8:1. If so, this, too, shows that Peter was closer to Paul than the other members of the Jerusalem church.

[52] For a review of this question cf. W. G. Kümmel, "Das Urchristentum," ThR, 14 (1942), 82; 17 (1948/49), 3 f., 103 f.; 18 (1950), 1 f.

[53] The order can hardly be accidental in a text like this. The ancient scribes realised this ; hence the textual variations. MS D, which puts Peter before James, undoubtedly offers the easier reading.

namely, that Paul and his fellow-workers should go to the Gentiles and those of Jerusalem to the circumcision, brought Peter's missionary activity officially under the aegis of James, whereas Paul was bound to Jerusalem only by the bond of the common collection. Peter now becomes the leader of the Jewish Christian mission, which is directly superintended from Jerusalem.

It must be stressed that Peter was closer to Paul than the other members of the Jerusalem mission. [54] This may be seen quite clearly from the way in which Paul speaks of him at the very point where he has to censure him, Gl. 2:14. Paul's only reproach is that out of fear he concealed his true convictions, Gl. 2:11 f. This fits in very well with the psychological picture of the impulsive Peter which may be drawn from the Synoptic Gospels. On the other hand, it may be said in Peter's defence that as a missionary leader dependent on the Jerusalem church he was in a much more difficult position *vis-à-vis* the representatives of James than was the independent Paul. This conflict must have brought him into a particularly painful dilemma to which 1 Cl., 5 is possibly alluding when it refers to the many πόνοι which he had to bear through envy, → 112, 5 ff. The fact [55] that he had cause to "fear" the representatives of James shows plainly that there could be no question of a Petrine primacy at this period; if there was any primacy it was in the hands of James. [56]

3. The difficult position in which Peter found himself was directly connected with the fact that theologically he was closer to Paul than to those who had commissioned him in Jerusalem. It is true that we do not know a great deal about Peter's theology and have to rely on inference. Even if 1 Peter is regarded as authentic, it offers too slender a base for direct evaluation. Nevertheless, the Antioch conflict shows how close was the universalism of Peter to Paul's attitude to the Gentiles. From his relation to Jesus Peter had obviously learned that salvation is for all those who "shall come from the east and west, and shall sit down with Abraham, and Isaac, and Jacob, in the kingdom of God," Mt. 8:11. This universalism, however, seems to be even more deeply anchored in the understanding of Christ's death as an atonement which he gained after he had seen the risen Lord. It is quite wrong to view the theology of the cross as exclusively Pauline. It might well be that the apostle Peter is the author of the oldest Christology we have, namely, the interpretation of the person and work of Jesus along the lines of the figure of the suffering servant. Jesus is called παῖς αὐτοῦ or σου (sc. τοῦ θεοῦ) (→ V, 704, 4 ff.; 707, 15 ff.) four times in Ac. 3 and 4: 3:13 (with a ref. to Is. 52:13); 3:26, where we have a christological title; 4:27, 30, a liturgical passage in which παῖς almost tends to becomes a proper name. Of these 4 verses — the only ones in all the 28 chapters of Ac. — two are in addresses by Peter and two in prayers which he prays along with the congregation. Perhaps it is not too daring to say that the author of Ac. is reminding us that it was Peter who called Jesus the Ebed Yahweh. Quite conceivably the disciple who in the lifetime of Jesus protested against the path

[54] E. Hirsch, "Petrus u. Pls.," ZNW, 29 (1930), 64, rightly emphasises against H. Lietzmann, "Zwei Notizen z. Pls.," SAB (1930), 154, that it is incorrect to see in Peter a mere representative of the Jerusalem view.

[55] Cf. esp. F. Overbeck, *Über die Auffassung d. Streites d. Pls. mit Petrus in Antiochien bei d. Kirchenvätern* (1877); A. M. Voellmecke, "Ein neuer Beitrag zur alten Kephasfrage," *Jbch. v. St. Gabriel* (1925), 69-104.

[56] Roman Catholic critics of Cullmann, *Petrus,* rightly perceive that the decisive pt. in the question of primacy is the historical role allotted in this work to James. Their most important counterargument in trying to weaken James' leadership relates to the term φοβούμενος in Gl. 2:12. They give it the sense of "fear of difficulties," in this case with subordinates. But this is not in keeping with the use of the verb in other passages, where it always means fear of higher authority. Furthermore, the fact that Peter fears higher authority at the decisive moment agrees with the picture presented in the Gospels.

of suffering taken by his Lord later proclaimed the necessity of the death and passion of Christ in the light of the resurrection, which was attested to him first of all acc. to 1 C. 15:5.

E. Peter's Later Missionary Activity and Death.

1. Apart from the fact itself (1 C. 9:4 f.) we know virtually nothing about the second half of Peter's missionary work. The introduction to 1 Pt. (1:1) seems to presuppose that he worked in Asia Minor. His name is connected particularly with three centres : Antioch, Corinth, and Rome. The fairly early tradition that he founded the church at Antioch is hardly tenable historically, for acc. to Ac. 11:19 those dispersed during the persecution after Stephen's martyrdom came to Antioch, while the apostles (8:1) remained in Jerusalem. Peter was at Antioch later acc. to Gl. 2:11-14. The unverifiable tradition that he was founder and bishop of this church is important only from the standpoint of the exclusive claim made to Mt. 16:17-19 by the bishops of Rome. [57] We have no more certain data concerning a stay of Peter in Corinth. This is possible enough. But the later testimony of Dionysius of Corinth that Peter preached in the city [58] is weakened by the claim also made by Dionysius that Peter was a co-founder of the church. This is ruled out by 1 C. 3:6; 4:15. Even the existence of a Cephas party in Corinth (1 C. 1:12) is no actual proof that he must have paid a personal visit. [59]

2. More important is the much discussed question whether Peter came to Rome in the course of his missionary work, and suffered martyrdom there. Since this question is closely related to the Roman claim to primacy its discussion has often been influenced by confessional polemics. A true answer can be given only by historical research, and since, in addition to the NT sources, the literary testimonies of non-canonical and post-canonical early Chr. writings, later liturgical documents, and also excavations form the basis of a controversy which has continued for centuries right up to our own time, a detailed treatment is impossible in the present context. [60] We may simply point out that up to the 2nd half of the 2nd century we have no express ref. to Peter's residence and martyrdom in Rome. There is an ancient tradition concerning the martyrdom in Jn. 21:18 f. It also seems to be presupposed in 1 Pt. 5:1 and 2 Pt. 1:14. The silence of Ac. is not too significant as regards a stay in Rome, since Ac. says nothing about the end of Peter or indeed of Paul. The silence of the Epistle to the Romans is more important. This shows that a Roman ministry is to be ruled out, if not altogether, at least at the time when the letter was written. R. 15:20 f., however, provides indirect evidence. It traces the founding of the community, not to Peter, but very probably to Jewish Christians, cf. also Ac. 2:10. Acc. to the Jerusalem agreement, to which Paul seems to be referring, it is likely enough that Peter, as the responsible leader of the Jewish Christian mission, had visited the capital. There are also indications of tensions at some period between the Jewish and Gentile parts of the church, 1 Cl., 5, perhaps Phil. 1:15 ff., also the apparent presupposition of the whole contents of R. 1 Pt., whether authentic or not, bears witness in the greeting (5:13) to a Roman stay on the part of Peter ; when the church which sends greetings is

---

[57] Orig. Hom. in Lk. 6 (MPG, 12, 1815 A); Eus. Hist. Eccl., III, 36, 2 and 22; Chrys. Hom. in Ign. (MPG, 50, 591); Hier. Gl., 1, 2 (MPL, 26, 340 B); Hier. De Viris Illustribus, 1 (MPL, 23, 607 B-609 A).

[58] Eus. Hist. Eccl., II, 25, 8.

[59] Among those who champion a stay in Corinth cf. Meyer Ursprung, III, 441; Harnack Miss., 63, n. 2; H. Lietzmann, "Die Reisen des Petrus," SAB (1930), 153; among those who contest it, cf. W. Bauer, *Rechtgläubigkeit u. Ketzerei im ältesten Christentum* (1934), 117; M. Goguel, "L'apôtre Pierre a-t-il joué son rôle personnel dans les crises de Grèce et de Galatie ?" Rev. Th. Ph., 14 (1934), 461.

[60] For details on this question, and esp. on the ongoing controversy stirred up by H. Lietzmann when in his *Petrus u. Pls. in Rom*[2] (1927) he argued for a stay of Peter in Rome, and found his chief opponent in K. Heussi (cf. esp. *War Petrus in Rom?* [1936]), cf. Cullmann, 73-169, with bibl.

located in Babylon, the most probable hypothesis (→ I, 516, 23 ff.) is that Rome is meant. [61] More recently Rev. 11:3-12 has been brought under discussion as yet another NT text supporting a Roman martyrdom, for the two witnesses have been identified as Peter and Paul. [62]

The most important key to a solution of the problem is 1 Cl. Though c. 5 does not state explicitly that Peter was martyred in Rome, the larger section dealing with the results of envy speaks of the death of Peter (and Paul) in such a way that the detailed circumstances apply only in Rome. It is thus probable that Peter (and Paul) fell victim to the Neronic persecution in the context of internal conflicts in the congregation. Among other ancient witnesses Ign. R., 4, 3 also supports a Roman martyrdom, though not so securely.

No clue is given by early sources as to the work of Peter during his probably short [63] stay in Rome. Only in the 4th century is there ref. to an episcopal office. Nevertheless, the tradition about his stay and martyrdom in Rome begins to take on a more precise form in the 2nd half of the 2nd century. It is known to Irenaeus, Tertullian, Clement of Alex., Origen, and the Roman presbyter Gaius. The latter gives the tradition topographical support. [64] It has been claimed that recent excavations under St. Peter's confirm what he says about the *tropaion* on the Vatican, [65] though there is as yet no solid archaeological proof that the pillar which can now be reconstructed is this "trophy." These excavations certainly do not enable us to identify Peter's grave.

Cullmann

| † πηγή |

A. πηγή outside the New Testament.

1. πηγή "(water) source," from Hom. for the spring which is the source of brooks and rivers, κρήνη being used for the artificial fountain whose water does not flow into a brook (κρήνη, "source," "well," does not occur in the NT; the "draw-well" is φρέαρ). In antiquity springs, whether natural or in the form of κρῆναι (also φρέατα and conduits), were regarded as the property or dwelling of divine beings and played an important role in the cultus. [1] Quite early πηγή was used fig., e.g., of tears, πηγαὶ κλαυμάτων, Aesch. Ag., 887 f., πηγαὶ δακρύων, Soph. Ant., 803, of richly flowing fulness, e.g., πηγαὶ γάλακτος, Soph. El., 895 (Suid.: πηγὰς γάλακτος : πολὺ γάλα. ὡς πηγὰς δακρύων, πολλὰ δάκρυα), παγὰ ἐπέων, Pind. Pyth., IV, 299, πηγὴ ἀργύρου, Aesch. Pers., 238; then in the sense of "origin," "cause," e.g., αἱ τέχναι ἃς

---

[61] On the various explanations cf. Cullmann, 88-92.

[62] J. Munck, *Petrus u. Pls. in der Offenbarung Johannes* (1950).

[63] A short stay in Rome is attested by the statement of Macarius Magnes, III, 22, which goes back to the opponent of Christianity, Porphyry.

[64] Eus. Hist. Eccl., II, 25, 7.

[65] B. M. Apolloni-Ghetti, A. Ferrua, E. Kirschbaum, E. Josi, *Esplorazioni sotto la Confessione di S. Pietro in Vaticano* (1951).

π η γ ή. [1] For the Gk. and Roman field cf. H. Herter, Art. "Nymphai, 1" in Pauly-W., 17, 1527-1581, esp. 1535 f.; M. Ninck, "Die Bdtg. des Wassers im Kult u. Leben der Alten," *Philol. Suppl. Vol.*, 14, 2 (1921), *passim*. In general cf. J. Hempel, Art. "Quellen," RGG², IV, 1668 f. (Bibl.), → n. 24.

πηγάς φασι τῶν καλῶν εἶναι, Xenoph. Cyrop., VII, 2, 13 : πηγὴ καὶ ἀρχὴ κινήσεως, Plat. Phaedr., 245c; ἀρχὴν δὲ καὶ πηγὴν τῶν ἐπιφανεστάτων καὶ βασιλικωτάτων γενῶν, Plut. De Herodoti Malignitate, 11 (II, 856e); πηγὴ γὰρ καὶ ῥίζα καλοκἀγαθίας, τὸ νομίμου τυχεῖν παιδείας, Plut. Lib. Educ., 7 (II, 4c). [2] Individual "sources" are often mentioned in inscr., e.g., Ditt. Syll.[3], 546, A 11 and B 5 (3rd/2nd cent. B.C.); Ditt. Or., I, 269, 2 (241 B.C.); II, 634, 2 f. as the title of a Palmyrenian official : ἐπιμελητής ... Ἔφκας πηγῆς (161/2 A.D.; cf. the inscr. which deals with ἐπιμέλεια τῶν κρηνῶν in Ditt. Syll.[3], 281, 24 ff. [4th cent. B.C.] and the section περὶ τὰς κράνας in the inscr. of Andania, Ditt. Syll.[3], 736, 84 ff. [92 B.C.]). [3] The usage in the pap. agrees with what has been said thus far. [4]

2. The word πηγή occurs about 100 times in the LXX. Various Heb. terms are the originals : in some 30 instances עַיִן (always rendered πηγή in this sense); in 20 מַעְיָן (always πηγή); also מָקוֹר, מַבּוּעַ etc. κρήνη occurs as well as πηγή : Sir. 48:17 and 6 times in 2-4 Βασ., Heb. always בְּרֵכָה "(artificial) pool." φρέαρ, which occurs over 50 times, corresponds almost always to בְּאֵר, which for its part is exclusively transl. φρέαρ. Where these are not equivalents φρέαρ is used for בּוֹר or בְּאֵר, elsewhere rendered λάκκος, "cistern." [5] In such cases there is, under the influence of the readily interchangeable בְּאֵר and בּוֹר, no real difference between well and cistern. The two are alike inasmuch as the water collects in them subterraneously, though only the cistern serves also to collect and store rainwater. In this respect it differs both from the well and also esp. from the fountain or natural spring. When Gn. 26:19 speaks of a φρέαρ ὕδατος ζῶντος (cf. Cant. 4:15), it has in view this antithesis to the rainwater of the cistern and also to underground water, cf. also Jer. 2:13. The fountains mentioned in the OT are always artificial fountains or wells. This is why Gn. 16:7; 24:16 can first use עַיִן = πηγή and then 16:14; 24:20 can use בְּאֵר = φρέαρ for the same spring.

Quite early in Palestine fountains were made and attention was devoted to the conservation of the sources acquired by boring for underground water or springs. This was due to the aridity of the country. [6] The importance of springs may be seen from the great number mentioned either with or without names (many of them connected with important events in OT history, though OT fountains were not sacred sites in the non-biblical sense). The vital significance of springs may be seen also in the judgments of Hos. 13:15; Ιερ. 28(51):36, the promises of Is. 35:7; 41:18; 49:10; 58:11, and the eschatological image of Jl. 3:18 : πηγὴ ἐξ οἴκου κυρίου ἐξελεύσεται (cf. Ez. 47:1 f.; Zech. 14:8). It is also the basis of the rich transf. use of πηγή : in the expression πηγαὶ δακρύων, Jer. 8:23 (→ 112, 30. 32); in erotic lyrics (Cant. 4:12, 15); in wisdom sayings referring to sex

---

[2] Cf. Pass., Liddell-Scott, s.v.

[3] The importance of public waterworks may be seen from other sources. Cf. on the other hand the proud saying in Callim. Epigr. Fr., 28, 3 f. (II, 88): οὐδ' ἀπὸ κρήνης πίνω· σικχαίνω πάντα τὰ δημόσια.

[4] Preisigke Wört., II, 303; Moult.-Mill., 511, s.v. ὕδωρ ποτάμιον plays a greater role in the magic pap., but ὕδωρ πηγαῖον is also required, e.g., Preis. Zaub., IV, 2456.

[5] On Wis. 10:14 cf. J. Fichtner, *Weisheit Salomos = Handbuch z. AT*, II, 6 (1938), 38 and 41. λάκκος does not occur in the NT. Cf. 1 Cl., 45, 6 : λάκκος λεόντων (allusion to Da. 6, a cistern acc. to A. Bentzen, "Da. 6," *Festschr. A. Bertholet* [1950], 59 f.). The distinction between πηγή and λάκκος is important in Chr. symbolism. Thus Just., referring to Jer. 2:13, contrasts Chr. βάπτισμα as the ὕδωρ τῆς ζωῆς (Dial., 14, 1; cf. 114, 5; 140, 1 f.) with Jewish rites of purification as βάπτισμα ... ἀνωφελὲς τὸ τῶν λάκκων (Dial., 19, 2). Cf. also the Messianic interpretation of Is. 35:1-7 in Dial., 69, 5 f. On related statements in the LXX → διψάω, II, 227, 24 ff. [Bertram].

[6] Cf. H. Guthe, Art. "Palästina, V: Bewässerung u. Fruchtbarkeit," RE[3], 14, 591 f.; J. Benzinger, Art. "Wasserbauten," *ibid.*, 21, 10-12; P. Thomsen, Art. "Bewässerung u. Wasserversorgung," RLV, 2, 10-14; K. Galling, Art. "Wasserversorgung," *Biblisches Reallexikon* (1937), 534-536.

(Prv. 5:16, 18; 9:18c; cf. 4:21 [confusion of עַיִן "eye" and עַיִן "source"]), and esp. in the common phrase πηγή ζωῆς. In the Wisdom lit. this is often the goal of prudent action (often == good fortune, Prv. 10:11; 13:14; 14:27; 16:22; 18:4; Sir. 21:13). [7] Its true depths may be seen, however, when, outside the Wisdom lit., it is applied to God. In ψ 35:9 the righteous man confesses : παρὰ σοὶ πηγὴ ζωῆς, ἐν τῷ φωτί σου ὀψόμεθα φῶς; [8] in Jer. 2:13 God complains against the disobedient people : ἐμὲ ἐγκατέλιπον, πηγὴν ὕδατος ζωῆς, and in 17:13 : ἐγκατέλιπον πηγὴν ζωῆς τὸν κύριον (cf. the promise of the prophet : ἀντλήσετε ὕδωρ μετ᾽ εὐφροσύνης ἐκ τῶν πηγῶν τοῦ σωτηρίου, Is. 12:3). In πηγή ζωῆς there is approximation to the sense of "origin" (cf. πηγὴ τῆς σοφίας, Bar. 3:12), but with no sense of the abstract.

3. Philo uses πηγή 150 times, mostly in a transf. sense. Even when, on an OT basis, he refers to actual springs, he allegorises. Fig. πηγή (often with ἀρχή, → 113, 2) has in Philo the meaning "origin," "cause," e.g., ἐλπίς, ἡ πηγὴ τῶν βίων, Praem. Poen., 10; τὸ δ᾽ ἄνισον πηγὴ κακῶν, Spec. Leg., I, 121 (cf. ἀνισότητα, τὴν ἀδικίας ἀρχήν, ἐνηφάνισεν ἰσότητι, ἥτις ἐστὶ πηγὴ δικαιοσύνης, Leg. Gaj., 85); ἐπιθυμία ... ἁπάντων πηγὴ τῶν κακῶν, Spec. Leg., IV, 84; πηγὴ δὲ πάντων ἀδικημάτων ἀθεότης, Decal., 91. We read of the θεῖος λόγος (→ IV, 88, 29 ff.) in Fug., 97: σοφίας ἐστὶ πηγή, while in Som., II, 242 the θεῖος λόγος springs forth ἀπὸ πηγῆς τῆς σοφίας like a river ποταμοῦ τρόπον. In Sacr. AC, 64 God Himself is called ἡ πηγὴ τῆς σοφίας. In Fug., 197 f., after allusion to the πηγή verses in Gn. 24:16; 14:7 (195 f.), it is explained that the πατὴρ τῶν ὅλων spoke through the prophets (Jer. 2:13 is quoted) περὶ τῆς ἀνωτάτω καὶ ἀρίστης πηγῆς, i.e., about Himself : οὐκοῦν ὁ θεός ἐστιν ἡ πρεσβυτάτη <πηγή>, ... ὁ δὲ θεὸς πλέον τι ἢ ζωή, πηγὴ τοῦ ζῆν, ὡς αὐτὸς εἶπεν, ἀένναος. In Virt., 79 Philo calls the invincible sources of God's grace τὰς τῶν χαρίτων αὐτοῦ πηγὰς ἀενάους μὲν οὔσας, which are not, however, accessible to all, but only to the ἱκέται, namely, the καλοκἀγαθίας ἐρῶντες who may draw (ἀρύτεσθαι) ἀπὸ τῶν ἱερωτάτων πηγῶν when they thirst after σοφία.

4. In the usage of Joseph. (cf. also → n. 11, 15, 21) there are no peculiarities (e.g., Ant., 4, 81; Bell., 1, 406; 2, 168; 3, 45. 181. 519). In his use of OT sources Joseph. mostly follows the original in his employment of πηγή (e.g., Ant., 7, 347) or φρέαρ (e.g., Ant., 1, 212. 260. 262), and also in the synon. use of the two, Ant., 1, 246. 254, cf. Gn. 24:11, 42 f. Hence at one pt. he can put πηγή for the φρέαρ of Gn. 21:19 (Ant., 1, 219). On the other hand the two are clearly differentiated in Ant., 8, 154 (also πηγή and κρήνη in Ant., 8, 341). Ep. Ar., 89 extols Jerusalem for its wealth of water, which is guaranteed by a strong source flowing in naturally (φυσικῶς). [9] In later Judaism Rabb. refs. testify to the importance of springs in both town and country. [10] The Messianic Test. Jud. 24:4 : αὕτη ἡ πηγὴ εἰς ζωὴν πάσης σαρκός is a Chr. interpolation, perhaps under the influence of Jn. 4:14 (cf. also 24:5a, Charles). On Eth. En. → n. 25.

---

[7] For one who believes in the resurrection the LXX makes possible an eschatological or transcendental understanding of this and similar fig. sayings. Cf. G. Bertram, "Die religiöse Umdeutung altorientalischer Lebensweisheit in d. gr. Übers. d. AT," ZAW, NF, 13 (1936), 166. → II, 854, 1 ff., 14 ff. [Bertram].

[8] One may speak here of a kind of "life mysticism" (G. v. Rad, " 'Gerechtigkeit' u. 'Leben' in d. Kultsprache d. Ps.," Festschr. A. Bertholet [1950], 431), cf. also, apart from its constant confusion of the mystical and the mysteries, R. Kittel, "Die hell. Mysterienreligion u. d. AT," BWANT, NF, 7 (1924), 91 f. → V, 324, 32 ff.

[9] Cf. G. Dalman, Jerusalem u. sein Gelände (1930), 266-284.

[10] Cf. S. Krauss, Talmud. Archäologie, I (1910), 78-83, 212, 417-427, 669; II (1911), 164. 206. As the loan word פיגי, πηγή passed into the vocabulary of the Rabb., cf. S. Krauss, Gr. u. lat. Lehnwörter in Talmud, Midr. u. Tg., II (1899), 440.

B. πηγή in the New Testament.

1. In the NT a specific well is mentioned only once in a story. This is the πηγὴ τοῦ Ἰακώβ of Jn. 4:6a, called πηγή again in 6b [11] but φρέαρ in 4:11 f. This is certainly not a cistern according to the usage elsewhere, including the LXX. It is a draw-well, which could be called either πηγή or φρέαρ, → 113, 24 f. [12] Jm. 3:11, to show how unnatural it is that the same mouth utters both blessing and cursing (3:10), uses the illustration: μήτι ἡ πηγὴ ἐκ τῆς αὐτῆς ὀπῆς βρύει τὸ γλυκὺ καὶ τὸ πικρόν; [13] This is self-explanatory, for springs are either sweet or bitter and salty; a brackish spring cannot give sweet water, 3:12b. [14] Rev. 8:10 says that the great star Ἄψινθος fell on the ποταμοί and also on the πηγαὶ τῶν ὑδάτων; in 8:11 ὕδατα embraces both ποταμοί and πηγαί, and it is said that many people died ἐκ τῶν ὑδάτων, ὅτι ἐπικράνθησαν. The πηγαί can hardly be fountains whose drinking water is then contrasted with the water of rivers, which are not so drinkable. They are springs, and the point is that the rivers become bitter even at their sources. [15] In the same way Rev. 16:4, in an intensification of the plague of 8:10 f., mentions the πηγαὶ τῶν ὑδάτων as well as the ποταμοί. All these waters become blood (cf. Ex. 7:19, though this does not mention the springs). Rev. 14:7 speaks of God as τῷ ποιήσαντι τὸν οὐρανὸν καὶ τὴν γῆν καὶ τὴν θάλασσαν καὶ πηγὰς ὑδάτων. The springs here certainly do not give us a fourfold division of creation; they supplement τὴν θάλασσαν, [16] just as Rev. 8:10 and 16:4 refer to the springs of waters as well as the ποταμοί. [17]

---

[11] ἐπὶ τῇ πηγῇ in 4:6 can mean "by the well" (cf. Jos. Ant., 5, 58; Wettstein, II, 858 f.), but it might also be "on the well," i.e., "on the stone rim," Zn. J. [5], [6], 236. Cf. Jos. Ant., 2, 257: καθεσθεὶς ἐπί τινος φρέατος ἐκ τοῦ κόπου καὶ τῆς ταλαιπωρίας ἠρέμει μεσημβρίας οὔσης οὐ πόρρω τῆς πόλεως (Ex. 2:15; Schl. J., 117).

[12] In the light of this use it is a secondary question whether the well (as conjectured by Holtzmann NT, 977 on 4:11) might have contained a subterranean spring as well as ground water, which would be a special reason for calling it πηγή. The term could not, of course, denote ground water if the well contained "living water," → 116, 12 ff. It is certainly incorrect to say that "the well is called a 'spring' because it was filled with underground water as well as rainwater," Schl. J., 116, ad loc. (cf. also Bu. J., 129, n. 7). A well is not for catching rainwater, and a cistern, being walled, cannot receive underground water. Cisterns might be put in the fields (cf. Krauss, Archäologie, II, 546, n. 115), but Jacob's well was not a cistern, nor is it to-day (as against Holtzmann NT, 977, on 4:6). Since it is not mentioned in the OT, we know nothing about its origin, but it was obviously a well which was dug (on personal property, cf. Dalman, Orte u. Wege Jesu³ [1924], 228) in the search for a layer of water and which had come on a rich supply at a great depth. Archaeology pts. in this direction, and Jn. 4:12 can be taken thus inasmuch as ἔδωκεν presupposes that Jacob controlled this well and had thus dug it himself.

[13] One cannot assume too easily a parallelism between man and spring on the one side, στόμα (3:10) and ὀπή (3:11) on the other, Dib. Jk., 189. ὀπή, "opening" (in the NT also Hb. 11:38), is common in the LXX, but is not used for the mouth of a well. The στόμα πηγῆς of 2 Ἐσδρ. 12:13 is the gate (cf. πύλη τῆς πηγῆς, 13:15 vl.).

[14] The koine reading at 3:12b: οὕτως οὐδεμία πηγὴ ἁλυκὸν καὶ γλυκὺ ποιῆσαι ὕδωρ, which repeats and answers the question of 3:11, is secondary, though 3:12b is not itself a gloss, Hck. Jk., 174 f.

[15] We are not told that men died because they drank the water, nor can the meaning be that it fouled the air or affected the skin and thus led to illnesses of which men died (πικρός → 124, 18 ff.). πηγαὶ τῶν ὑδάτων, like πηγὴ (τοῦ) ὕδατος, is a common expression in the LXX. It usually refers to wells or artificial fountains (e.g., Ex. 15:27; Lv. 11:36), but it can also denote springs (e.g., ψ 17:16; 41:1; Prv. 8:24). Cf. also (with or without an OT basis) Jos. Ant., 2, 294; 8, 329; 9, 41 (cf. 9, 36).

[16] There is no art. before πηγὰς ὑδάτων as before θάλασσαν (cf. also 𝔓⁴⁷), → n. 17.

[17] Is the ref. to the springs of the sea? Cf. ἦλθες δὲ ἐπὶ πηγὴν θαλάσσης in Job 38:16 and the πηγαὶ τῆς ἀβύσσου or ἀβύσσων of Gn. 7:11; 8:2; Dt. 8:7; 33:13, → I, 9, 28 ff.

2. Inasmuch as there is no reference to water πηγή is used fig. in Mk. 5:29, which says of the healing of the woman who had an issue of blood: καὶ εὐθὺς ἐξηράνθη ἡ πηγὴ τοῦ αἵματος αὐτῆς. This is peculiar to Mk. What is meant is not that the source or origin of the flux was removed but that the flow of blood dried up like a spring, and no more blood came. [18] One might compare πηγή in 2 Pt. 2:17, where the false teachers, who at first kindle great expectations by their sudden appearance, but then cause disillusionment by their impiety, are aptly described as πηγαὶ ἄνυδροι. Since the author deviates here from Jd. 12, he is probably seeking an expression which is easier to understand, and springs rather than wells is the more likely reference. [19]

In Jn. 4:14b Jesus says to the woman of Samaria: τὸ ὕδωρ ὃ δώσω αὐτῷ γενήσεται ἐν αὐτῷ πηγὴ ὕδατος ἁλλομένου εἰς ζωὴν αἰώνιον. He is pointing out what distinguishes the water which He can give from the water of Jacob's well. [20] This water quenches thirst εἰς τὸν αἰῶνα, → II, 226, 20 ff. It will also become a πηγὴ ὕδατος [21] ἁλλομένου εἰς ζωὴν αἰώνιον. He does not mean that the man himself will now control this water that wells up inexhaustibly, but that possession of this πηγὴ ὕδατος is linked to abiding fellowship with Christ, cf. Jn. 15:4. The πηγὴ ὕδατος is not described directly as πηγὴ ζωῆς (or πηγὴ τοῦ ὕδατος τῆς ζωῆς, → 117, 5 f., [22] but the connection with eternal life is indicated by adding ἁλλομένου εἰς ζωὴν αἰώνιον to ὕδατος. The idea is that of the move-

---

But these verses are no reason for regarding πηγαὶ ὑδάτων in Rev. 14:7 as a term for the underworld. The φρέαρ τῆς ἀβύσσου of Rev. 9:1 f. is not a fountain from which water flows but the well-like shaft which is the entry to the ἄβυσσος, → I, 10, 2 ff.

[18] Cf. מְקוֹר דָּמֶיהָ (Lv. 12:7), rendered πηγὴ τοῦ αἵματος αὐτῆς in the LXX; also ῥύσις τοῦ αἵματος αὐτῆς (cf. Lk. 8:44 and Mk. 5:25 and par.) at Lv. 20:18 (just before in the same v. מְקוֹר = πηγή). The Heb. expression, however denotes not so much the flux as its place, the pudenda (cf. also the Rabb. use of מְקוֹר in Str.-B., II, 10). πηγὴ τοῦ αἵματος in Mk. 5:29 is not a medical tt. in this latter sense. We find ξηραίνω for the drying up of a πηγή in Ιερ. 28(51):36 and of a χειμάρρους in 3 Βασ. 17:7.

[19] Kn. Pt., 302, ad loc.: "In the hot season the underground watercourse runs dry and the thirsty traveller who knows the site of the spring stands disappointed at its dried up mouth."

[20] The Samaritan woman is not of the view that Jacob's well does not give living water, cf. Bu. J., 132, n. 5, who would cut out v. 11a as a poor gloss which does not agree with the controlling antithesis between well water and spring water in v. 12. These are not actually set in antithesis, since φρέαρ is here an enclosed πηγή, and a well of this kind also contains living water, Gn. 26:19 → 113, 21 ff.; Zn. J. [5, 6], 235, n. 7; → n. 12.

[21] πηγὴ (τοῦ) ὕδατος (cf. → n. 15) is common in the LXX, mostly for wells or fountains, e.g., Gn. 16:7; 24:13, 43; Jos. 15:9, though also for natural springs, e.g., Is. 35:7. Cf. Jos. Ant., 2, 294 : πηγὴν ἑτέραν ὑδάτων οὐκ ἔχουσιν.

[22] The obvious restraint of the author ought to warn us against extending the exegetical findings by assuming a twofold or multiple use, cf. O. Cullmann, "Der johann. Gebrauch doppeldeutiger Ausdrücke als Schlüssel zum Verständnis d. 4. Ev.," ThZ, 4 (1948), 367 f.; also Urchr. u. Gottesdienst², Abh. TANT, 3 (1950), 53. If there is a ref. to baptism in 4:10 ff. (for criticism cf. W. Michaelis, Die Sakramente im Joh.-Ev. [1946], 15-19), it does not lie in the word πηγή. Nor is the expression ὕδωρ ζῶν a sufficient ref. to baptism, though in the earliest days baptism was administered in flowing or living water, cf. T. Klauser, "Taufet in lebendigem Wasser!" Antike u. Christentum, Suppl., Vol. I : Pisciculi (1939), 157-164. A ref. to the Holy Spirit (Cullmann, ThZ, 4 [1948], 367 f.) is even further from the mark. On omnis fons spiritus sancti at the baptism of Jesus in Jerome in Is., IV, 11 on 11:2 (MPL, 24, 144d-146a) cf. W. Bauer, Das Leben Jesu im Zeitalter d. nt.lichen Apokryphen (1909), 119 f. Against further applications of this kind cf. Bultmann Trad., 266, n. 1 (he mentions here an association of Mary with the goddess of springs, Πηγή, from the Sassanid period ; on this cf. also R. Reitzenstein, Die Vorgeschichte d. chr. Taufe [1929], 35, 48, n. 2, 277, n. 1).

ment to eternal life into which man is brought by fellowship with Christ, and by this alone. [23] Hence we have here the more narrowly eschatological concept of eternal life found elsewhere in Jn. at, e.g., 5:29; 12:25. [24]

The common LXX (→ 114, 2 ff.) expression πηγὴ ζωῆς, which is not used directly in Jn. 4:14, occurs in Rev. at least in the form ἐκ τῆς πηγῆς τοῦ ὕδατος τῆς ζωῆς in 21:6 and ἐπὶ ζωῆς πηγὰς ὑδάτων in 7:17 (here again ζωῆς goes with ὑδάτων, cf. 22:1, 17). [25] The image of springs of the water of life is used for the consummation [26] which Christ will give at the Last Day. [27]

Michaelis

---

[23] Jn. 7:38 is related in many ways, but it is rather different inasmuch as the ref. is to the effects of fellowship with Christ on others, cf. H. Bornhäuser, *Sukka* (1935), 36 f.

[24] For a rather different view → II, 870, 31 ff. Historical material on ὕδωρ ζῶν and on the significance of water (and springs) may be found in Bu. J., 133-136; → ὕδωρ. Acc. to K. H. Rengstorf, "Die Anfänge der Auseinandersetzung zwischen Christusglaube u. Asklepiosfrömmigkeit," *Schriften d. Gesellschaft z. Förderung der Westfälischen Landesuniversität zu Münster, 30* (1953), 21 f. there is in Jn. 4:14 a deliberate polemic against the cult of Aesculapius. This is unlikely. The word πηγή alone does not prove this, for the situation in Jn. 4 is quite adequate to account for its use. The polemic of 4:14 also grows too naturally out of the story to have to be traced back to the world around the Gospel. It is obviously not directed against another source which (like the springs at shrines of Aesculapius) can give only "health, and consequently life as a continuation of life in spite of sickness and mortal peril," but not eternal life (*loc. cit.*). Nor does the ref. to 4:42 bear any weight, for though the description of Jesus as σωτὴρ τοῦ κόσμου comes in the same story, it bears no direct relation to Jn. 4:14, and in itself it can hardly be regarded as directed exclusively against Aesculapius (Rengstorf, 8-19, esp. 13 ff.).

[25] The OT par. (for 21:6 esp. Is. 55:1; for 7:17 esp. Is. 49:10; ψ 22:2) do not refer to springs. Eth. En. 96:6 speaks of the well of life, 22:2, 9 of a spring of water for the spirits of the just in the realm of the dead (cf. F. Cumont, *Die orientalischen Religionen im röm. Heidentum*[3] [1931], 250 f.), 48:1 of the fountain of righteousness in Paradise. Cf. → n. 15, 21, 24.

[26] Loh. Apk., 165 refers 21:6 esp. to martyrs (cf. 21:7), but this restriction is refuted by 21:8.

[27] Post-apost. fathers: the 8th mountain, which is rich in springs, in the vision of the rock and the hills in Herm. s., 9, 1, 8; 25, 1; ἀέναοι πηγαί in the description of the wonders of creation in 1 Cl., 20, 10; πηγὴ ζωῆς, Barn., 11, 2 (quoting Jer. 2:13); also 1, 3 (vl. ἀγάπης). In the Act. Joh., 108 Christ is addressed as ἡ ῥίζα τῆς ἀθανασίας καὶ ἡ πηγὴ τῆς ἀφθαρσίας. On the later use of πηγή for God, Christ, the Holy Spirit, Mary, baptism etc. cf. F. J. Dölger, ΙΧΘΥΣ, I (1910); II (1922), Index. Mandaean texts often speak of fountains (of life, of light; אינא and מאמבוהא or מאמבונא), but since the NT never speaks of fountains of light, and not directly of fountains of life, these passages bear no specific relation to NT use.

† πηλός

With πηλόω, which is not found in the NT (or LXX), and a series of compounds πηλός (from *palsós) is perhaps related etym. to the Lat. *palus* ("swamp") [1] and from the class period it means "morass," "mud," [2] "muck," [3] "dung," [4] also "loam," "clay." [5] It is thus a mixture of dust [6] or soil with a fluid, esp. water. It can denote on the one side that which rests in fluid on the bottom of e.g., a vessel, like the dregs of wine, [7] and on the other side dust which is mixed with water and which can thus be manipulated. [8] In acc. with common Gk. usage the LXX uses the term for "mud" (ψ 68:14 etc.), "filth" (2 Βασ. 22:43 etc.), "loam," "clay" (Wis. 15:7; Jer. 18:6 etc.). The use in Philo and Joseph. (Ant., 1, 244; 4, 275; Ap., II, 252) is the same, though the word is not common in these authors. [9]

In the expression ὁ κεραμεὺς τοῦ πηλοῦ at R. 9:21 Paul makes use of a common OT image [10] based on God's making of the first man out of dust [11] or loam, a concept also found in non-Jewish antiquity. [12] With a clear reference to Is. 29:16, this serves to bring out plainly the freedom and sovereignty of God in relation to men as His creatures and in relation to their desires and claims. Here then, as in the corresponding OT verses, πηλός means "loam" or "clay," though we are not to seek any deeper significance or intention in the use of the term.

In Jn. πηλός means the mixture which Jesus made out of spittle and earth to put on the eyes of the man born blind. The occurrence of the word here and in this sense along with spittle [13] (which is supposed to have healing power, cf. Mk. 8:22 ff.) and with such emphasis (five times in v. 6, 11, 14 f.) suggests that there is more behind it than a mere stress on the fact that Jesus was here again showing His freedom in respect of the law of the Sabbath, [14] though this has some

---

π η λ ό ς. [1] Hofmann, 267, though the etym. is not certain, cf. Boisacq[4], 779 and Walde-Hofmann[3], II, 243, *s.v. palus.*

[2] Hdt., IV, 28 : In the districts inhabited by the Scythians it is so unbearably cold for 8 months of the year that it can be said of them : ἐν τοῖσι ὕδωρ ἐκχέας πηλὸν οὐ ποιήσεις, πῦρ δὲ ἀνακαίων ποιήσεις πηλόν.

[3] πηλός with ῥύπος : Plat. Parm., 130c, with κονιορτός : Plut. De Communibus Notitiis, 2 (II, 1059 f.).

[4] Aristoph. Vesp., 257: τὸν πηλὸν ὥσπερ ἀτταγᾶς τυρβάσεις βαδίζων.

[5] Plat. Theaet., 147a : πηλὸς ὁ τῶν χυτρέων etc.

[6] Aesch. Ag., 494 f.: κάσις πηλοῦ ... κόνις.

[7] This is probably the meaning in Soph. Fr. (ed. A. C. Pearson [1917]), 783 : πολὺς δὲ πηλὸς ἐκ πίθων τυρβάζεται, though πηλός does not mean οἶνος, not even "thick or muddy wine" (Liddell-Scott, *s.v.*; cf. A. C. Pearson on Fr., 783). Nor is this use supported by the constantly repeated refs. Plut. De Cohibenda Ira, 15 (II, 463a) and Tryphiodorus (5th cent. A.D., probably Egypt), 349 (Tryphiodori et Collynthi Carmina, ed. W. Weinberger [1896]).

[8] Ael. Arist. Or., 48, 74 f.: Rubbing τῷ πηλῷ πρὸς τῷ φρέατι τῷ ἱερῷ — the ref. is to the sacred spring of Aesculapius at the shrine of the god in Pergamon — followed by washing αὐτόθεν. Acc. to the Apellas stele of Epidauros (c. 160 A.D.; Ditt. Syll.[3], 1170) the same god directed his patient among other things ἀφῇ (dust) πηλώσασθαι.

[9] This is also true of the other Gk. transl. of the OT so far as we can glean from the remnants known to us (Hatch-Redp., *s.v.*).

[10] Is. 45:9; Jer. 18:6.

[11] Gn. 2:7; 3:19; Job 4:19.

[12] E.g., Epict. Diss., IV, 11, 27: τὸ σωμάτιον δὲ φύσει πηλός ἐστι.

[13] The attention of expositors is mostly directed to this alone, cf. Bau. J., ad loc.

[14] So Schl. J., ad loc.

place too. [15] Nor does the occasional occurrence of πηλός in magical formulae [16] suffice to explain this passage; the same applies to the use of πηλός or πηλόω in medical prescriptions. [17] More helpful, perhaps, is the fact that both words are attested in the directions of the Σωτήρ Aesculapius to the sick who seek healing from him. They are here combined with washings at the sacred shrine, and both in time (1st half of the 2nd century) and place (Pergamon, → n. 8) these rules are not too far removed from the Fourth Gospel. Hence there might be a connection with the use of πηλός in Jn. 9:6 ff. The Evangelist is perhaps seeking hereby to differentiate the σωτήρ whom he proclaims, namely, Jesus, [18] from the saviour Aesculapius. [19] This unheard of miracle, the healing of a man born blind, shows the absolute superiority of Jesus. [20] This does not, of course, exhaust the deeper significance of the event for the author.

Rengstorf

| † πήρα |

→ βαλλάντιον, I, 525, 16 ff.

1. πήρα [1] is used by Hom. in Od., 13, 437; 17, 197, 357, 411, 466; 18, 108 for the "knapsack" which Odysseus carries on a strap (13, 438; 17, 198) over his shoulder (17, 197; 18, 108) when dressed as a wandering beggar. But πήρα does not have the specific sense of a beggar's sack; it may be used for any open sack made of leather and carried at the left hip by a strap over the right shoulder, cf. Suid., s.v.: ἡ θήκη τῶν ἄρτων; Thom. Mag. Ecloge, s.v. πεῖρα: δέρμα τι ἀρτοφόρον. [2] Peasants can use a sack of this kind to carry fowls or a small lamb to market; [3] hunters use a similar sack for their gear and shepherds and travellers for their provisions. [4] The Hell. wandering philosophers, esp. the Cynics, always carried a πήρα, more to show their freedom from want than for begging. [5] On the other hand the ref. is to begging sacks in the inscr. discovered at Kefr-Hauar in Syria, in which a δοῦλος of Dea Syria reports: ἀ(π)οφόρησε ἑκάστη ἀγωγή πήρας ο', "each journey has brought in 70 sacks." [6]

---

[15] The material in Str.-B., II, 530 offers no par. to πηλός in Jn. 9:1 ff. in the strict sense.
[16] Preis. Zaub., I, 28 f.: λαβὼν πηλὸν καθᾶρον τὰς φλιὰ[ς τοῦ κο]ιτῶνος ... καὶ οὕτω πηλώσας ἐπ[ί]γραφε τὰ γρα[φόμ]ενα ταῦτα χαλκῷ γραφείῳ εἰς τὴν δεξιὰν φλιάν ... (magical words and signs follow).
[17] Cf. Gal. De Theriaca, 19.
[18] Cf. the description of Jesus as σωτὴρ τοῦ κόσμου, Jn. 4:42; 1 Jn. 4:14.
[19] → n. 8 and the whole context of Ael. Arist. Or., 48, 74 ff.
[20] Cf. K. H. Rengstorf, *Die Anfänge der Auseinandersetzung zwischen Christusglaube u. Asklepiosfrömmigkeit* (1953), 17 f. with n. 56-62.

π ή ρ α. Deissmann LO, 86-88; F. Schulthess, "Zur Sprache d. Ev.," ZNW, 21 (1922), 234; S. Krauss, "Die Instruktion Jesu an d. Ap.," *Angelos*, 1 (1925), 96-102; K. H. Rengstorf, *Jebamoth* (1929), 214 f.; F. Wotke, Art. "Pera 2" in Pauly-W., 19, 563 f.
[1] Boisacq⁴, s.v.: "Etymologie inconnue."
[2] Wotke, 563.
[3] Cf. Ill. 5566 in G. Lafaye, Art. "Pera (Πήρα)," Daremberg-Saglio, IV, 1, 386.
[4] There are many examples cf. Wotke, cf. also Pass., Liddell-Scott, s.v.
[5] For examples cf. Wotke, 564; Wendland Hell. Kult., 84.
[6] C. Fossey, "Inscr. de Syrie," BCH, 21 (1897), 59 f. (the quotation is on p. 60d, lines 1 ff.; cf. also line 7 f.); Deissmann LO, 87 was the first to adduce it in exposition of Mt. 10:10 and par. On the customary begging expeditions of the cults of Asia Minor cf. F. Cumont,

2. πήρα occurs in the LXX only at Jdt. 10:5; 13:10, 15. On her way to the Assyrian camp, Judith has her slave carry (10:5) a skin of wine (ἀσκοπυτίνην οἴνου), a jug of oil (καψάκην ἐλαίου) and a πήρα with barley bread, fig-cakes and pure bread as food for several days, cf. 12:2, 9 f., 19. [7] In this fairly roomy πήρα the head of Holophernes is later hidden, cf. 13:15. [8]

3. For the κάδιον (ποιμενικόν) of 1 Βασ. 17:40, 49 (for [הָרֹעִים] כְּלִי). Joseph. in Ant., 6, 185, 189 has πήρα (ποιμενική). [9] It is open to question whether πήρα was adopted as a loan word by the Rabb. [10] The יַלְקוּט of 1 S. 17:40 (→ n. 8) is rendered תַּרְמִיל in the Tg. This is a common term in the Mishnah for a leather bag or sack in which provisions, esp. bread, were taken for a journey. [11]

4. In the NT πήρα is used in Mt. 10:10 (par. Mk. 6:8; Lk. 9:3) and also in Lk. 10:4; 22:35 f. In the charge in Mt. 10:10 and par. the disciples are forbidden to take a πήρα along with them. Quite apart from the question whether the different handling of the staff (→ ῥάβδος) in the Synoptists is due to the fact that the reference in one case is to a traveller's equipment and in the other to a beggar's, [12] the πήρα of Mt. 10:10 and par. is undoubtedly part of the equipment of the traveller. This may be seen from the fact that in Lk. 10:4 πήρα stands in immediate proximity to βαλλάντιον ("purse") and hence cannot be equivalent to this word in meaning, → I, 526, 10 ff.; Mk. and Mt. do not have βαλλάντιον. In any event πήρα does not originally or customarily mean the beggar's sack, → 119, 17 ff. [13] Furthermore, against the Jewish background of Jesus, whether תַּרְמִילָא or some other Aram. word was used, "pocket," "purse," or "satchel" would be primarily a container in which the traveller could take provisions, esp. bread,

---

Die orient. Religionen im röm. Heidentum[3] (1931), 255, n. 2. Cf. Preis. Zaub., IV, 2381, 2400 : Description of a wax figure which is designed to lead the one who made it to wealth, a miniature beggar with the right hand outstretched and in the left a πήρα (with a magic saying as an inscription) and a staff.

[7] For πήρα in the LXX Rengstorf, 215 refers to Krauss, 99, though there are some inaccuracies here. Thus acc. to Krauss (cf. also *Talmud. Archäologie,* II [1911], 265) one may assume from the ἀσκοπήρα of Jdt. 10:5 that a πήρα "was like a leather bottle." But the LXX does not have ἀσκοπήρα here (in any case it is very rare acc. to Liddell-Scott, *s.v.*). The Vg, which left πήρα untranslated, has for the LXX ἀσκοπυτίνη (ἀσκός א) ascopa (cf. Thes. Ling. Lat., II, 772 *s.v.*) or ascopera (this form only here). Also erroneous is Krauss' adducing of 4 Βασ. 4:42 as an instance of πήρα; the LXX did not transl. בְּצִקְלֹנוֹ (in Cod A the Θ transcription βακελλεθ), but Vg has pera (on πήρα as a loan word in Lat. cf. Wotke, 563).

[8] Σ also transl. יַלְקוּט at 1 Βασ. 17:40 by ἐν τῇ πήρᾳ, which is better than εἰς συλλογήν LXX (cf. BHK³) or ἐν τῷ ἀναλεκτηρίῳ 'Α.

[9] I have not found any other examples of πήρα in Joseph. Leisegang does not list it in Philo. It does not occur in Test. XII or Gr. En.

[10] Cf. S. Krauss, *Gr. u. Lat. Lehnwörter in Talmud, Midrasch u. Targum,* I (1898), 87 (cf. 248); II (1899), 433 on פורה, jBQ, 3a, 47. But cf. II, 614, where acc. to I. Löw one should read פורנה = φοῦρνα ("stove") here, cf. II, 434.

[11] On appearance and construction cf. G. Dalman, *Arbeit u. Sitte in Palästina,* III (1933), 304 f.; IV (1935), 109; II (1932), 152 f. (with a good deal of comparative material both ancient and modern). The Mandaean כנאף הייא "purse of life," Lidz. Liturg., 84, 5; Ginza, 452, 5; 587, 24 (combined Ginza p. VIII with צרור החיים, 1 S. 25:29) is the fold in a garment in which, as in a girdle, objects can be kept (→ I, 526, 18 f.); hence it bears no relation to πήρα.

[12] Cf. Schulthess, 234, but also Schl. Mk., 124; Zn. Mt.⁴, 399, n. 22; Zn. Lk. ³, ⁴, 367, n. 65.

[13] Jesus could hardly have met the type of wandering religious or philosophical teacher with a beggar's sack as found among the cults of Asia Minor or the Cynics, → n. 18.

→ I, 477, 16. [14] It is no tautology that the wallet for bread can be mentioned after bread. [15] ἄρτος and πήρα belong together as do χαλκός and ζώνη. That bread belongs εἰς τὴν πήραν may best be seen from the fact that Mt. thought he could leave out any special mention of bread along with πήρα, → n. 14. Hence the command not to take a πήρα is not a prohibition of begging. [16] What is meant is that the disciples should not take with them a (big) wallet with (considerable) provisions, like others journeying across the country. This rule, too, shows that they were to put their whole trust in God's generous help. [17] They experienced this according to Lk. 22:35. πήρα has the same sense in Lk. 9:3. [18] We are not to take it that either in Lk. 9:3 or 10:4 the prohibition of the πήρα is a special demarcation from specifically bourgeois customs (though this is possible in respect of βαλλάντιον, → I, 526, 20 ff.). [19] Lk. 22:35 f. refers back to 10:4 rather than 9:3, and points plainly to the changed situation of the disciples, → I, 526, 18 ff.

　　5. In the post-apost. fathers πήρα occurs only in Herm. It is here a typical part of the shepherd's gear: v., 5, 1 (cf. s., 9, 10, 5); s., 6, 2, 5. [20] The only instance in the Apologists is at Tat. Or. Graec., 25, 1; the πήρα is part of the equipment of the wandering philosopher of paganism. [21]

Michaelis

---

[14] When he put εἰς ὁδόν after πήραν Mt. was undoubtedly thinking of the travelling wallet which would contain what was needed *en route,* not of the beggar's sack which would be empty at the start and filled during the journey.

[15] As against Deissmann LO, 87: "One is reluctant to find a tautology in the crisp and gritty commands of Jesus." In Gk. there is no more tautology between ἄρτος and πήρα than between χαλκός and ζώνη.

[16] Rengstorf, 215; Krauss, 99 f.; as against E. C. Hoskyns and F. N. Davey, *The Riddle of the NT* (1938), 10.

[17] K. H. Rengstorf Lk. (*NT Deutsch,* 3), on 9:3.

[18] In the Synoptic conception of the πήρα there is no "conflict between Jewish and Hell. culture" (Schulthess, 234). Hck. Lk., 120 on 9:3 offers an interpretation which would apply only to Hell. readers when he says that the disciples were to be poorer than the wandering Cynics familiar to every Hellenist.

[19] On the relation between the two passages cf. Schl. Lk., 275 f.

[20] Pr.-Bauer rightly refers to the well-known statue of the Good Shepherd in the Lateran Museum (3rd cent.), which includes a shepherd's satchel. In the symbolical interpretation of the various parts of the shepherd's equipment (staff, flute, pail) the satchel apparently played no role. Cf. T. Kempf, *Christus d. Hirt* (1942), esp. 139-143, and W. Jost, ΠΟΙΜΗΝ, *Das Bild vom Hirten in d. bibl. Überlieferung u. seine christologische Bdtg.* (1939), 50-57. The satchel can no more symbolise the nature and power of Christ than the nature of God as Shepherd in Philo, cf. Agric., 50-54 on the basis of Ps. 23 [Bertram].

[21] On Const. Ap., III, 6, 4 cf. Deissmann LO, 87, n. 3; here, too, the transl. "(roomy) wallet or sack," which can carry many things, is quite adequate. On Prot. Ev. Jc., 21, 3 and the view of Epiph. De Fide, 8, 3 (GCS, 37, 504, 7 ff.) that τὰς πήρας was the original wording of Mt. 2:11 cf. Zn. Mt.⁴, 103, n. 93.

πικρός, πικρία, πικραίνω, παραπικραίνω, παραπικρασμός

---

† πικρός, † πικρία, † πικραίνω.

1. πικρός, originally "pointed," "sharp," e.g., of arrows (Hom. Il., 4, 118), of the κέντρον (Eur. Herc. Fur., 1288), then more generally of what is "sharp" or "penetrating" to the senses, a pervasive smell (Hom. Od., 4, 406), "shrill" of a noise (Soph. Phil., 189), "painful" to the feelings (Hom. Il., 11, 271), esp. "bitter," "sharp" to the taste (Hdt., IV, 52; VII, 35), opp. γλυκύς. The final sense, so also in derivates like πικρία, "bitterness," the bitter taste of plants (Theophr. Hist. Plant., VI, 10, 7), exerts the greatest influence ; it is behind the transf. use in the sphere of the soul, where the experience of what is unpleasant, unexpected, or undesired is predominant. Thus the adj. is used with λύπη because it is painful, with laughter when this is tormented (Anth. Pal., V, 180, 2), with tears (Hom. Od., 4, 153), not because they taste bitter, but because there is no desire to weep, because weeping brings no release. Men can be called πικροί when they are "strict" (of δικαστής, Polyb., 5, 41, 3), "severe," "hostile" (Aesch. Choeph., 234), "cruel" (Hdt., I, 123); the adv. πικρῶς makes, e.g., ἐξετάζειν into a stern and pitiless hearing (Demosth. Or., 2, 27); cf. πικρῶς διακεῖσθαι πρός τινα, "to be embittered against someone," Polyb., 4, 14, 1. Similarly πικρία has (from the Attic period) the transf. sense of "sternness," "severity" (Demosth. Or., 25, 84), "bitterness" (Polyb., 15, 4, 11); dep. πικραίνομαι "become angry, bitter," act. (late) πικραίνω "make angry," "provoke." [1]

2. The LXX has the adj. πικρός some 40 times, 12 in 2-4 Macc. In 17 instances the Heb. is מַר. The lit. use is rare (e.g., bitter water Ex. 15:23; as a comparison Jer. 23:15); mostly we have the transf. use, cf. the Heb. מַר. Men are πικροί when they are soured (Rt. 1:20) or cruel (Hab. 1:6; 4 Macc. 18:20); πικροί (vl. κατώδυνοι) ψυχῇ in Ju. 18:25 [2] means "of wild resolution." For the LXX reader Esau's φωνὴ μεγάλη καὶ πικρὰ σφόδρα (Gn. 27:34) suggests loud and shrill, whereas the Heb. means grievous lamenting (the HT is also the norm at Zeph. 1:14). In 1 Βασ. 15:32 death is πικρός (cf. πικρότερον ὑπὲρ θάνατον Qoh. 7:26). Acc. to Sir. 30:17 it is κρείσσων ... ὑπὲρ ζωὴν πικράν. When used of ἀνάγκη in 2 Macc. 6:7 and ἀπειλή in 3 Macc. 2:24 (cf. 5:18), βάσανος in 2 Macc. 9:5 and πόνος in 4 Macc. 15:16, the word means "painful," "terrible," "grievous." Adverbially ἀνεστέναξεν πικρά Sir. 25:18; cf. Ez. 27:30 : κεκράξονται πικρόν (vl. πικρῶς A; influence of Θ). The adv. πικρῶς (9 times) is twice

---

π ι κ ρ ό ς κ τ λ. [1] Hesych., s.v. πικρόν· χαλεπόν, ἀργαλέον and πικρῶς· κατακόρως, ἀκρατῶς. In Ditt. Syll.³ and Or. (Index) there are no instances of the group. Death as δαίμων ὁ πικρός IG, III, 1338 (burial inscr. 3rd cent. B.C.); Epigr. Graec., 640 (burial inscr. 2nd cent. B.C.): καὶ καλὸν τὸ τύχης καὶ πικρὸν οἶδα βίου. In the pap. πικρός (also transf.) is early (Preisigke Wört., II, 305; Moult.-Mill., 512 f.), but such typical expressions as πικρὰ ἀδικήματα "bitter wrong," ἀναλώματα πικρά "grievous expenses" are later. πικρῶς already in P. Petr., III, 42 H 8 (f), 8 (3rd cent. B.C.): πικρῶς σοι ἐχρήσατο, "he has treated you roughly"; comp. P. Par., 46, 20 (152 B.C.). πικραίνω is not attested in the pap., but we find προσπικραίνω (cf. Liddell-Scott, s.v.). Etym., since formations in -αίνω are very limited, the development is to be traced by analogy. One line is sure. The oldest examples are deponents and mean "to become angry," hence the group ἀφραίνω, μαργαίνω, ἀγριαίνω etc. (all intrans.) is the starting-point. Cf. A. Debrunner, "Zu den konsonantischen jo-Präsentien im Griech.," Indogerm. Forschungen, 21 (1907), 57 f. (on the transition from the intrans. act. to the deponent, cf. 60-62, on πικραίνω esp. 63). The factitive act. "make angry" is secondary (and later). A second line is more dubious: trans. πικραίνω like γλυκαίνω (whose own formation, however, is by no means certain, ibid., 32 f., 44). Cf. also Debr. Griech. Wortb. § 222 [Debrunner].

[2] Cf. κατάπικροι τῇ ψυχῇ in 2 Βασ. 17:8. Acc. to Liddell-Scott, s.v. κατάπικρος occurs only in one pap. (4th cent. A.D.) apart from Job 6:3 Σ.

linked with κλαίειν (→ n. 12): πικρῶς κλαύσομαι ═ אֲמָרֵר בַּבֶּכִי Is. 22:4 (of disconsolate crying); ἄγγελοι γὰρ ἀποσταλήσονται ἀξιοῦντες εἰρήνην πικρῶς κλαίοντες παρακαλοῦντες εἰρήνην ═ מַלְאֲבֵי שָׁלוֹם מַר יִבְכָּיוּן, 33:7. Whereas in the HT the bitter crying expresses the boundless disillusionment of the deceived intermediaries, the LXX refers to the unrestrained but possibly simulated sobbing which accompanies their request for peace.

The verb πικραίνω (some 12 times) occurs only fig. Act. trans.: τὴν ψυχήν, Job 27:2 (vl. πικρόω Α [3]); κλαυθμόν, Sir. 38:17; opp. εὐφραίνω, 1 Macc. 3:7; [4] only Ιερ. 39(32):32 of God's chiding, elsewhere παραπικραίνω (→ 125, 27 ff.). More common (apart from the singular constr. ἐπικράνθη μοι ὑπὲρ ὑμᾶς in Rt. 1:13 and the etym. note in 1:20) is the dep. pass. "to be enraged, angry, incensed," Ex. 16:20; 1 Εσδρ. 4:31; Ιερ. 44(37):15 etc. (never of God).

The noun πικρία occurs about 30 times. The place-name מָרָה in Ex. 15:23 was first transcribed as Μερρα, then transl. Πικρία (Nu. 33:8 f. plur. Πικρίαι); → 127, 1 f. The combination πικρία and χολή in Dt. 29:17 (in the phrase ἐν χολῇ καὶ πικρίᾳ, → 124, 31 f.) occurs again in Dt. 32:32; Lam. 3:15, 19; cf. πικρότερον χολῆς, Prv. 5:4. χολή here corresponds to רֹאשׁ II (as elsewhere) or to לַעֲנָה in Lam. 3:15; Prv. 5:4, while πικρία in Dt. 29:17; Lam. 3:19 (also Am. 6:12) is equivalent to לַעֲנָה (→ n. 7 f.), but in Dt. 32:32; Lam. 3:15 to מְרֹרֹת or מְרוֹרִים. The words are thus felt to be related. The rendering of סִלּוֹן מַמְאִיר by σκόλοψ πικρίας in Ex. 28:24 rests on a false derivation from מר or מרר instead of מאר. πικρία ψυχῆς in Job 7:11; 10:1; 21:25 (cf. 3:20 A; here and elsewhere combined with ὀδύνη); Sir. 7:11 "oppression of soul," "grief," though in 4:6 more the "bitterness" of the repulsed needy which causes them to curse the heartless. In ψ 9:28 (10:7) proximity to ἀρά and δόλος yields the sense of "bitterness full of hate," [5] while combination with θυμός in Is. 28:21; [6] 37:29 gives the sense of "angry bitterness." In Is. 28:21 and 28:28 (par. ὀργίζεσθαι), with no HT support, the ref. is to God's πικρία, which is ἀλλοτρία acc. to 28:21 and does not endure acc. to 28:28. In Jer. 15:17 the pass. πικρίας ἐνεπλήσθην obscures the ref. to God's wrathful judgment (וַזַּעַם), cf. Job 9:18. The noun πικρασμός, which is not attested prior to the LXX, occurs in Εσθ. 4:17 o; Ez. 27:31. [7]

3. Philo, who also uses πικρός lit. when he speaks of the bitter water in Rer. Div. Her., 208 and of bitter πηγαί in Vit. Mos., I, 182 (expounding Ex. 15:22 ff., cf. also Poster. C., 154-156), is familiar with the transf. use. Acc. to Virt., 130 hunger and thirst are πικραὶ δέσποιναι, cf. πικροὶ τύραννοι in Omn. Prob. Lib., 106, πικρὸς συκοφάντης in Leg. Gaj., 355. δουλεία is bitter in Vit. Mos., I, 247, πόνος ibid., II, 183, ἀλγηδών Spec. Leg., I, 292; Exsecr. 145, ὠδῖνες Conf. Ling., 26. The noun πικρία (10 times) introduces in Ebr., 223 a list of vices πονηρία, πανουργία, ὀργή, θυμός etc. In Migr. Abr., 36 Philo speaks in the plur. of τῆς ψυχῆς πικρίας; cf. in the interpretation of the bitter water of Ex. 15:25 the πικρίας γέμοντα νοῦν which is changed

---

[3] Lucianic, and taken from 'A, which likes new factitive constructs in -όω [P. Katz]. Liddell-Scott, s.v. has only the pass. (1 instance, 3rd cent. A.D.).

[4] Are we to conjecture a Heb. מרה (instead of מרר, → 126, n. 3) and to transl. "and he rose up against many kings" [P. Katz]? The antithesis καὶ εὔφρανεν τὸν Ιακωβ would suggest a trans. verb (ἐπίκρανεν ═ παρώργισεν) but cf. → 126, n. 6.

[5] HT has מִרְמָה "deception," "falsehood" (often transl. δόλος in the Ps. though this ═ תֹּךְ here). Did the translator take the nominal prefix מ as the first radical of מַר [P. Katz]? → 127, n. 11. On ψ 13:3 → n. 14.

[6] On the vl. σαπρία cf. C. Lindhagen, "ΕΡΓΑΖΕΣΘΑΙ. Die Wurzel ΣΑΠ im NT u. AT," Uppsala Universitets Årsskrift (1950), 47-53.

[7] 'ΑΘΣ have πικρός at Nu. 5:23; Is. 38:17, πικρία at Jer. 9:14 (לַעֲנָה → line 18). πικρασμός, which is rare in LXX, is common in 'ΑΘΣ. πικραμμοί in Job 3:5 'A is also a slip for πικρασμοί (Schleusner, IV, 325), though cf. the Attic ὕφαμμα from ὑφαίνω etc. in Schwyzer, I, 524, n. 2 and App. Middle and modern Gk. πικραμός [Georgakas].

into sweetness only by the perfect good. πικραίνομαι (5 times) denotes "vexation," "indignation," e.g., Congr., 164; Vit. Mos., I, 302. Neither πικρία nor πικραίνεσθαι is used of God. Joseph., who describes the Dead Sea as πικρά καὶ ἄγονος in Bell., 4, 476 (cf. Ant., 3, 2 f.), often uses the adj. πικρός (the noun πικρία is very rare in him) fig., with θάνατος in Ant., 6, 155; 10, 122, ὀδύνη 2, 294; 7, 325, δουλεία 11, 263, βάσανος 12, 255, ἔρευνα 15, 290, λοιδορία Bell., 1, 642, δεσπότης, Ap., 1, 210, 2, 277, νίκη (victory which is no cause for rejoicing), Bell., 1, 540. Cf. also Ant., 7, 177 and 264; 14, 367; Bell., 1, 473. πικρῶς is common, of great agitation, Ant., 3, 13, of strong reproaches, Vit., 339, of strict enquiry, Bell., 2, 41; cf. Ant., 9, 118; 12, 4 and πικρῶς ἔχειν "to be angry," 8, 220; 12, 122. Test. XII : πικρός lit. G. 5:1 and transf. D. 4:2; Jos. 1:7; πικρία transf. N. 2:8 (par. θυμός), also L. 11:7 in interpretation of the name מְרָרִי (which the OT does not interpret, Gn. 46:11 etc.) as πικρία μου (the reading πικριασμός [Charles] can hardly be original). Test. Sol.: πικρῶς with στενάζειν, V, 12 H; D. I, 11 and θρηνεῖν D. I, 6; cf. also V, 13; XX, 2 (θάνατος πικρός); XXVI, 5 Q.

4. In the NT πικρός is used lit. at Jm. 3:11: μήτι ἡ πηγὴ ἐκ τῆς αὐτῆς ὀπῆς βρύει τὸ γλυκὺ καὶ τὸ πικρόν; (→ 115, 6 ff.) of spring water which is bitter or brackish to the taste, cf. 3:12b. πικραίνεσθαι is similarly used in Rev. 8:11 of the waters of rivers and fountains which were made bitter by the great star Ἄψινθος and which brought death as a result: πολλοὶ τῶν ἀνθρώπων ἀπέθανον ἐκ τῶν ὑδάτων ὅτι ἐπικράνθησαν. [8] In Rev. 10:9 f. bitter [9] taste is a figure of speech; the divine finds the message or the task of proclaiming it (unlike Ez. 3:1 ff.) grievous and painful. [10] The adv. πικρῶς is used for Peter's weeping in Mt. 26:75 par. Lk. 22:62 [11] (→ III, 722, 12 f.). What is meant is that the weeping was violent and uncontrolled, expressing utter despair at the denial. [12] The transf. use of the adj., which is so common elsewhere and which normally has a pessimistic or complaining note (πικρὸς θάνατος, πικρὰ ὀδύνη etc.), may be found in the NT only at Jm. 3:14, where ζῆλος (→ II, 881, 35 ff.) is called πικρός. In Hb. 12:15: μή τις ῥίζα πικρίας ἄνω φύουσα ἐνοχλῇ, a warning against the harm which even the sin of an individual can do to the whole community, is obviously influenced by Dt. 29:17: μή τίς ἐστιν ἐν ὑμῖν ῥίζα ἄνω φύουσα ἐν χολῇ καὶ πικρίᾳ, though in a corrupt form. [13] On the other hand, behind Peter's declaration

---

[8] → 115, 9 ff. and esp. n. 15. In spite of the plur. ἐπικράνθησαν must be related to ὕδατα. In the OT "wormwood" לַעֲנָה (in 'A Prv. 5:4; Jer. 23:15 transl. ἀψίνθιον, which is used for רֹאשׁ II at Jer. 9:14) is regarded as esp. bitter, → 123, 18, though it is not poisonous, Zn. Apk., 391, n. 4; Had. Apk., 102, ad loc. Does Rev. 8:11 imply that the bitter waters of the earlier period (Ex. 15:23 f.) find a counterpart in the last time, J. Behm Apk. (NT Deutsch, 1), ad loc. ? 4 Esr. 5:9 (cf. Paral. Jerem. 9:16) does not support this view, since it is too general.

[9] 10:9 act. πικραίνω in the sense "lend a bitter taste," which occurs only here in the LXX and NT.

[10] Behm, op. cit., ad loc.: "Because the last and hardest battle comes before victory." The ref. is not the effect on the hearers (any more than in Ez. 3:1 ff.). → III, 787, n. 6; IV, 553, 12 ff.

[11] Lk. 22:62 is perhaps based on Mt. 26:75, cf. Hck.; Kl. Lk., ad loc.

[12] More important than non-bibl. par. (→ 122, 12 ff.; 124, 13 f.; Wettstein, I, 528 on Mt. 26:75; Rabb. par. in Schl. Mt., 765) are those from the OT : Is. 22:4; 33:7 (→ 123, 1 ff.). πικρῶς strengthens (cf. Hesych., → n. 1) but does not interpret ἔκλαυσεν. Repentance or remorse is not elsewhere called bitter. The placing of πικρῶς at the end of the sentence serves to give it the force expressed by the rendering "bitterly."

[13] On the textual question cf. Rgg. Hb. [2], [3], 403 f., n. 80; P. Katz (review), ThLZ, 76 (1951), 537. It is clear that the LXX MSS of Dt. 29:17 which put a πικρίας after ῥίζα as a doublet, and have ἐνοχλῇ for ἐν χολῇ, are already influenced by Hb. 12:15. On the

of the corruption of Simon Magus in Ac. 8:23: εἰς γὰρ χολὴν πικρίας ... ὁρῶ σε ὄντα, we do not have a particular text like Dt. 29:17 but the whole OT association of χολή and πικρία, → 123, 15 ff. R. 3:14 quotes ψ 9:28 (→ 123, 24 f.) with slight alterations. [14] In Eph. 4:31 πικρία stands at the head of a short list of vices. [15] It is followed immediately by θυμός and ὀργή. Hence it does not mean the "embitterment" which involves withdrawal and isolation (the word is not attested elsewhere in this sense) but "bitterness," "resentment," "an incensed and angry attitude of mind" to one's neighbour. Not to let oneself be mastered by such πικρία is the point of πικραίνεσθαι in the admonition to husbands in Col. 3:19: μὴ πικραίνεσθε πρὸς αὐτάς, "do not become angry, incensed against your wives" either in thought or more particularly in word and deed. [16]

5. In the post-apost. fathers, apart from the admonition in Did., 4, 10 par. Barn., 19, 7 not to issue orders to slaves ἐν πικρίᾳ, in "an incensed mood," the group is used only in Herm., where it is common. πικραίνω pass. lit. m., 5, 1, 5; dep. πικραίνομαι transf. (cf. also ἐν πικρίᾳ γενέσθαι, m., 5, 2, 2) m., 10, 2, 3 as a consequence of ὀξυχολία, "sudden anger." In m., 5, 2, 4 and 8; 6, 2, 5 πικρία is combined with ὀξυχολία (which for its part is called bitter in m., 5, 1, 6). It here means "ill-humour" which also finds expression in word or deed. Adj. transf. also in m., 5, 2, 3 of the oppressive commands of the devil, m., 12, 4, 6 of terrible angels, m., 6, 2, 4; s., 6, 3, 2; also 6, 2, 5 the (rare and late) adj. περίπικρος of an angry glance.

† παραπικραίνω, † παραπικρασμός.

1. These words are not found prior to the LXX. They are late and rare and are always influenced by their bibl. use. The verb παραπικραίνω occurs over 40 times in the LXX : 12 in Ps., 21 in Ez. (here alone we find οἶκος παραπικραίνων 14 times), always act. except for the pass. at Lam. 1:20 vl. → n. 1, whereas the simple form is rare as act., → 123, 7 ff. It is probably (though → n. 4) coined by the LXX; the choice of παρα- might reflect the influence of παροργίζω (cf. also παροξύνω). When it is used for כָּעַס hi, the meaning is obviously "to provoke," "to enrage," [1] so with God as obj. (→ 123, 8 f.), Ιερ. 39(32):29, 32 vl.; 51(44):3, 8. [2] In the Gk. related passages are

---

other hand the author of Hb., esp. in putting ἐνοχλῇ for ἐν χολῇ, can hardly have changed the LXX original independently. There must have been a text which had the secondary ἐνοχλῇ as a mistake for the similar ἐν χολῇ. This error possibly led even before Hb. to the changing of καὶ πικρία, which no longer fitted the sentence construction, into (ῥίζα) πικρίας. One can hardly agree with Mi. Hb.[8], 308, n. 5 that "the original of the Hb. text is Semitic and is closer to the basic text than the LXX." πικρίας is a Semiticising gen. qual. and is meant lit. as in Dt. 29:17, though the whole is a metaphor : a root or shoot from which bitter fruits come forth. πικρία cannot mean poison, cf. → n. 8, also Hom. Il., 11, 846 : a ῥίζα πικρή related to the assuaging of pain and blood.

[14] With R. 3:13-18, 3:14 also has made its way secondarily into the LXX text of ψ 13:3.

[15] As in Philo Ebr., 223 (→ 123, 36 f.), though ὀργή and θυμός follow later there. Cf. A. Vögtle, "Die Tugend- u. Lasterkataloge im NT," Nt.liche Abh., XVI, 4/5 (1936), 218, n. 83.

[16] The constr. with πρός (not attested in LXX or Philo ; cf. Helbing Kasussyntax, 212) perhaps suggests that what is also, or esp., in view is the πικρία vented on the wife though not caused by her.

π α ρ α π ι κ ρ α ί ν ω κ τ λ. In this art. we are indebted to P. Katz for numerous observations.

[1] In this sense synon to παροργίζω, which is usually the equivalent of כָּעַס hi (cf. also Hesych.: παραπικραίνων· παροργίζων). Cf. Philo : παραπικραίνειν καὶ παροργίζειν (θεόν), Som., II, 177; ὀργίζονται καὶ παραπικραίνονται, Leg. All., III, 114 (dep. pass. elsewhere only in Herm. s., 7, 2 f. → line 25).

[2] Also as vl. at Dt. 32:16 for ἐκπικραίνω, which is also rare (e.g., Jos. Ant., 5, 234) and occurs only here in the LXX.

ψ 5:10; 77:17, 40, in which God is obj.; with some modification of sense one might also list verses in which the obj. is God's ῥῆμα (3 Βασ. 13:21, 26), λόγοι (ψ 104:28) or λόγια (ψ 106:11), στόμα (Lam. 1:18) or πνεῦμα (ψ 105:33), though in these and other passages the original is מרה q or hi ("to be rebellious") or in Ez. the noun מְרִי. The suggestion that there has merely been confusion between מרה and מרר ("to be bitter") is hardly adequate to explain this remarkable rendering. For one thing the great number of relevant verses (about 30 in all) shows that we have more than the incidental slip which is involved in confusing מרה and מרר and which might be expected once or twice. Again, the translators cannot have used παραπικραίνω only in the sense "to provoke"; the word must have had also the sense "to be recalcitrant," for סרר too is transl. παραπικραίνω in ψ 65:7; 67:6, and מרר in Ez. 2:3 (twice). Though both these terms could also have been confused with מרר (on the combination of סרר and מרה in ψ 77:8 → IV, 840, 3 ff.), the data as a whole force us to the conclusion mentioned above. [3] While one must assume system rather than accident in the use of παραπικραίνω for מרה, it may be accepted that an oversight possibly formed the starting-point and then set a fashion. [4] Furthermore, ref. should be made to a practice of the translators which is not to be observed only in 'A. This is the habit of seeing as one homonymous or similar Heb. roots and rendering them uniformly in Gk. even though this involves a violent extension of the meaning of the words chosen. In the case of מרה and מרר this might well have led to an expansion of the range of παραπικραίνω under the influence of מרה. [5] The translators could well have associated the meaning "to be recalcitrant," "to oppose," with παραπικραίνω. [6] This is important in respect of παραπικρασμός too.

The noun παραπικρασμός, derived from παραπικραίνω as πικρασμός (→ 123, 29 f.) is from πικραίνω, is used only once in the LXX, [7] but this single instance exerted an influence on the NT. In ψ 94:8 the name of the well מְרִיבָה, which in Ex. 17:7 (in connection with the use of λοιδορεῖσθαι in 17:2) is rendered λοιδόρησις (→ IV, 293, 9 ff.), in Nu. 20:24 λοιδορία, in Nu. 20:13; 27:14; Dt. 32:51; 33:8; ψ 80:7; 105:32 ἀντιλογία (and transcribed only at Ez. 47:19; 48:28), is transl. by παραπικρασμός. Since the place-name מַסָּה is already transl. πειρασμός in Ex. 17:7, then in Dt. 6:16; 9:22; ψ 94:8 (πεῖρα in Dt. 33:8), the attentive reader of the LXX will catch a clear ref. to Ex. 17:7 in ψ 94 (cf. the contents of v. 9 f.). But why was the singular rendering παρα-

---

[3] 1 Εσδρ. 6:14 does not really support the sense "to be recalcitrant," "to rebel," for, though παραπικραίνω is used in the abs., it corresponds to the trans. παροργίζω in the par. 2 Εσδρ. 5:12 and is a rendering of רגז hi. Nor is any certain proof offered by 1 Macc. 3:7 → 123, n. 4.

[4] Thus M. Flashar, "Exegetische Studien zum Septuagintapsalter," ZAW, 32 (1912), 185-188, regards Dt. 31:27 as the prototype of the stereotyped rendering of מרה by παραπικραίνω in 10 passages in the Ps. Helbing Kasussyntax, 101 f. wrongly thinks that in the Ps. "we simply have a consistent confusion of מָרָה and מָרַר" (102). Flashar (186) pertinently observes that if we have in Dt. 31:27 a single and probably accidental misunderstanding of the original, the word παραπικραίνω would hardly have been invented specifically for this one verse, but must have been in popular use (Helbing Kasussyntax, 103: "undoubtedly popular") in the sense "to provoke," as in Dt. 32:16.

[5] P. Katz, Philo's Bible (1950), 64, n. 2 etc.; → V, 584, n. 13.

[6] The element of bitterness simply serves to bring the hostility into relief [P. Katz]. The trans. use of παραπικραίνω for "to oppose" could have been facilitated by the construing of מרה etc. with אֶת.

[7] The other translations, which also have πικρασμός more frequently than LXX → 123, n. 7, use παραπικρασμός likewise: 'A in 1 Βασ. 15:23 (HT מְרִי, LXX ὀδύνη, Σ προσερίζειν), Σ in Job 7:11 (HT מַד, LXX πικρία), Θ in Prv. 17:11 (HT מְרִי, LXX ἀντιλογία, Σ ἐρεθισμός). Cf. Field, ad loc. and Schleusner, IV, 215. παραπικραίνω, too, is used by 'A and esp. Θ and Σ (LXX mostly ἀπειθέω).

πικρασμός selected, and in what sense ? There can hardly be confusion with the well-name מָרָה in Ex. 15:23, [8] quite apart from the fact that this is rendered Πικρία or Πικρίαι (→ 123, 13 f.). מָרָה is too rare and is never connected with מַסָּה, whereas מַסָּה and מְרִיבָה are closely related not only in Ex. 17:7 and ψ 94:8 but also in Dt. 33:8. [9] That LXX should have read or misread מְרֵרָה for מְרִיבָה in Ps. 95 [10] is highly improbable in spite of the rendering of מְרֹרֹת and מְרוֹרִים by πικρία (→ 123, 18). מְרֵרָה itself is very rare (only Job 20:14, 25) and it is also not a place-name. As regards the use of παραπικραίνω one should rather consider whether the prefix מ in מְרִיבָה is not taken as the first radical of מַר, "bitter" ? [11] One might also think quite naturally of a combination with מְרִי (מרה), esp. as this is transl. παραπικρασμός by 'A and Θ, → n. 7. It is even simpler, however, to take מְרִיבָה in the sense "strife," "dispute" (Gn. 13:8; LXX μάχη), and in so doing to remember how extensively παραπικραίνω had come to be used for "to be obdurate," "to rebel." This easily gives to παραπικρασμός the meaning "opposition," "rebellion," which is not far removed from the rendering of מְרִיבָה by ἀντιλογία etc., → 126, 27 f. It should also be considered that a noun derived from a verb presupposes the meaning of the verb. Nor does it seem impossible that the juxtaposition of παραπικραίνω and (ἐκ)πειράζω in ψ 77 (→ n. 9) influenced the transl. in ψ 94. At any rate, the use of παραπικραίνω shows that the etym. concept of bitterness did not dominate παραπικρασμός but that the word was also taken in the sense of "rebellion." The sum total of the renderings of מְרִיבָה and מַסָּה also shows that there is still allusion to place-names in the LXX ; this applies to ψ 94 too. [12]

2. Hb. 3:8, 15 quotes ψ 94:8, and thus repeats ἐν τῷ παραπικρασμῷ. Then the verb is used in 3:16: τίνες γὰρ ἀκούσαντες παρεπίκραναν; By using the verb in the abs. the author shows that he cannot have taken it in the sense "to provoke." He uses it rather in the common LXX sense "to be recalcitrant," "to rebel" (→ 126, 3 f.), just as he faithfully followed the LXX (→ line 13 f.), his OT Bible, in construing παραπικρασμός as "obduracy," "rebellion." Hence Gk. etymology cannot be our starting-point if we are to understand his use of the terms. [13] On the contrary, we have to take into account the change of meaning which they underwent in the LXX. One may also suspect that (like the LXX) he caught the echo of a place-name in παραπικρασμός, also in πειρασμός (3:8). [14]

Michaelis

---

[8] So E. Nestle, "Hb. 3:8, 15," Exp. T., 21 (1909/1910), 94.

[9] Cf. also the combining of παραπικραίνω and (ἐκ)πειράζω in ψ 77:17b, 18a, 56 [P. Katz].

[10] So G. Harder, "Die Septuagintazitate d. Hb.," Theologia Viatorum (1937), 35; cf. Mi. Hb.[8], 101, n. 5.

[11] The transl. of מְרִמָה by πικρία in ψ 9:28 is analogous (→ 123, n. 5). The rendering παρεπίκρανάν in Ps. 5:11 may be based on מְרִיבֶיךָ (part. hi) for מְרוּ בָךְ, cf. the analogous treatment of ריב [P. Katz].

[12] Except here and in Ex. 17:7 it is always מֵי מְרִיבָה or ὕδωρ ἀντιλογίας or λοιδορίας. The art. before παραπικρασμός and πειρασμός in ψ 94:8 may be regarded as an anaphoric ref. back to the places mentioned in Ex., cf. Bl.-Debr. § 260 f. [P. Katz].

[13] To be rejected, then, are the interpretations "bitterness which was called forth in God" (Wnd. Hb., 31) and "embitterment at what is required of man" (Mi. Hb.[8], 104). We have here a psychologising which LXX usage does not justify.

[14] Suid., s.v.: παραπικρασμός· ἡ ἐν ἐρήμῳ πολλάκις γενομένη ἀντιλογία τῶν Ἰσραηλιτῶν takes up ψ 94:8; Hb. 3:8, 15, refers to the predominant LXX rendering of מְרִיבָה by ἀντιλογία (→ 126, 27 f.), and indirectly bears witness to the rarity of the word outside the Bible. On Herm. s., 7, 2 f. → n. 1.

πίμπλημι, ἐμπίμπλημι, πλησμονή   → πληρόω.

† πίμπλημι, † ἐμπίμπλημι.

A. The Word Group outside the New Testament.

1. Both words occur in Hom., though they are rare in many authors and the pap. [1] The stem is the same as in → πλήρης etc. The words agree in the main senses : "to fill," hence "to satisfy" (constr. → 128, 25 ff.).

πίμπλημι "to fill" (mid. "oneself"), e.g., the eyes with tears (for joy, Soph. El., 906); λέκτρα ... δακρύμασιν, Aesch. Pers., 134; in conception, Aristot. Hist. An., VI, 22, p. 576b, 29; 29, p. 578b, 32. Transf. the soul λήθης τε καὶ κακίας πλησθεῖσα falls to the earth, Plat. Phaedr., 248c; ἀφροσύνης καὶ θράσεος πίμπλανται, Democr. B, 254; "to satisfy (perfectly, richly)," ἢ σίτων ἢ μέθης πλησθέν, Plat. Resp., IX, 571c (→ 131, 12 ff. πλησμονή); αἱμάτων, Soph. Ant., 121; ἡδονῶν, Plat. Resp., IV, 442a; also pass. "to be satiated," Soph. Phil., 520.

ἐμπίμπλημι a. lit.: κοφίνους Aristoph. Av., 1310; often an emphasis on "filling up," a vessel Aristot. Hist. An., V, 18, p. 550a, 2; with the matter from a wound 66 great dishes (tubs ; a miraculous healing at Epidauros) are filled, Ditt. Syll.[3], 1169, 57. b. Fig., common in Plato, e.g., ψυχὴν ἔρωτος, Phaedr., 255d; the man who is filled with hideous lust is incapable of *gnosis,* Corp. Herm., 7, 3. c. The dead have completed and fulfilled their destiny (περαίνοντα καὶ ἐμπιμπλάντα τὴν αὐτοῦ μοῖραν), Plat. Leg., XII, 959c. d. "To fulfil wishes" (ἁπάντων τὴν γνώμην), Xenoph. An., I, 7, 8. e. "To satisfy (fully)," mid. lit., e.g., Plat. Gorg., 505a; transf. φρονήσεως (in distinction from γεύεσθαι), Philo Som., I, 48; the soul by the contemplation of imperishable goods, Deus Imm., 151.

2. In the LXX the simple form is somewhat rarer than the compound. It is used 77 times for forms of מלא and 25 for forms of שׂבע (ψ 64:12 for רעף "to drop"). a. The main use is lit. "to fill," what is filled in the acc., content in the gen. (as usually in class. Gk.), occasionally dat. [2] (cf. already Hom. Il., 16, 373 f.), ἀπό in Sir. 36:13b for מן (with ἐμπίμπλημι, Sir. 1:17; 24:19); on the double acc. → *infra* ; 129, 10 and 14. Example: ταμίεια Prv. 3:10; cf. Ez. 28:16, the rooms of the forecourt with unlawful things (= ἀνομίας, → lines 32-35); Sir. 37:24 εὐλογίας (blessings). b. Fig.: κακῶν (with evil, distress), Prv. 12:21; θυμοῦ Da. LXX Θ 3:19; ἀρεταλογίας (the ref. is to deeds which evoke praise) Sir. 36:13; ἀδικίας (the earth with wicked acts) Gn. 6:11, 13; Da. LXX 12:4; Ιερ. 28(51):5; cf. ἀνομίας (violence) Ez. 8:17, (licentiousness) Lv. 19:29, (unlawful acts) Sir. 23:11a; it should be noted here that the noun (in the sing.) denotes acts (in the plur.). δόξης κυρίου (ἡ σκηνή), Ex. 40:34 f., cf. 2 Ch. 7:1 f.; 3 Βασ. 8:10 f.; Ez. 10:3 f. (νεφέλη), → *infra* ἐμπίμπλημι. c. Of time : pass. "to run out," "to end" (ταπείνωσις), Is. 40:2. d. → πληρόω for the sense "to fulfil" a promise of God. e. "To satisfy": οἴνου, Wis. 2:7; transf. κακῶν ἡ ψυχή μου, ψ 87:3; also "to satiate," pass. "to acquire too much," Prv. 30:9, 22, perhaps also 1:31 ἀσεβείας (the results of ungodly conduct ; → lines 32-35).

The compound occurs 59 times for forms of מלא and 60 for forms of שׂבע. Close to the original, though with more or less pronounced shifts of accent and sometimes with alteration of sense and sentence construction, are passages where ἐμπίμπλημι is used

---

π ί μ π λ η μ ι, ἐ μ π ί μ π λ η μ ι. [1] Diels[6], Index : simple form 3 times ; Aristot. Index : twice each ; neither in Epict.; Preisigke Wört. once each ; Ditt. Syll.[3] Index : compound twice, simple not at all. Philo does not have the latter, Dio C. only twice, though both make common use of the compound ; this is a tendency of the *koine.*

[2] Also the instrumental dat. for that with which one fills (Heb. ב), 4 Βασ. 9:24. For details *v.* Helbing Kasussyntax, 144-150 [Bertram].

for קבל "to receive" (Sir. 31:3 "to satiate oneself"); פוק hi "to obtain" (Sir. 32:15 the Law, LXX "to be filled or satisfied" with it); צוף hi "to flow over" (Sir. 47:14 "to be filled to overflowing"); גיל "to rejoice" (Is. 29:19 "to be filled" with joy); דשן pu "to be made fat" (Is. 34:7 "to be satiated," alongside μεθυσθήσεται); נוח hi "to give rest" (Ez. 24:13 "to satisfy," τὸν θυμόν μου). The content of statements is altered in the LXX at Sir. 4:12 (פוק hi); Sir. 47:15 (קבל "to receive"); Is. 11:3 (רוח inf. hi "to take pleasure"); Job 40:13 (חבש "to bind," a difficult v. in Heb.). The simple and compound alternate some 20 times in different MSS. a. ἐμπιμπλάναι τί τινος "to fill" something with something (less commonly τινι). b. Fig. esp. in the vivid language of Job : στόμα γέλωτος, 8:21; στόμα ἐλέγχων (with proofs), 23:4; the bones with youthful vigour, 20:11; με πικρίας, 9:18 (cf. Jer. 15:17). Also to be emphasised are ἐμπίμπλημι εὐφρο-σύνης in Sir. 4:12; Is. 29:19; νόμου, Sir. 2:16 (→ line 1, Sir. 32:15); συνέσεως, Sir. 47:14; πνεύματος αἰσθήσεως, Ex. 28:3; πνεύματος συνέσεως (by laying on of hands), Dt. 34:9; πνεύματι συνέσεως, Sir. 39:6; πνεῦμα φόβου θεοῦ, Is. 11:3; πνεῦμα θεῖον σοφίας κτλ. (double acc.), Ex. 31:3; 35:31; πνεύματος αὐτοῦ (Elijah's), Sir. 48:12. Particularly ambiguous are statements in which the verbs are used with ref. to the δόξα κυρίου. Spatial and material ideas are evoked when one reads of the temple being filled with the cloud of the glory of the Lord (2 Ch. 5:13), so that it is impossible for men to tarry in it (v. 14, cf. πίμπλημι → 128, 35 f.). These statements about God's presence stress on the one side the gracious coming of the transcendent God to the place of revelation and on the other side God's holiness, which is intolerable for man. [3] Nu. 14:21 at least must be taken fig.: ἐμπλήσει ἡ δόξα κυρίου πᾶσαν τὴν γῆν (acc. to the context through the acts of God towards His people). The prophecy of Is. 11:9 is fig.: ἐνεπλήσθη ἡ σύμπασα (sc. γῆ) τοῦ γνῶναι τὸν κύριον. c. Temporal fulfil-ment only Is. 65:20 : ἐμπλήσει τὸν χρόνον αὐτοῦ, he will "reach" normal age, → 130, 25 ff. d. Fulfilment of a divine promise is denoted by → πληρόω. e. Not infrequent is the meaning "to satisfy" (e.g., ἄρτον οὐρανοῦ ψ 104:40, double acc.; also transf. κάλλους Sus. Θ 32); the ref. to ἐμπλησθῆναι of the ψυχή is often to be taken in the sense of bodily satisfaction, e.g., Prv. 6:30; 13:25; even of an animal, Job 38:39. There is a singular mixture of the lit. and transf. use in Dt. 33:23 : ἐμπλησθήτω εὐλογίαν παρὰ κυρίου, acc. of content ; ψ 102:5. Plainly the salvation of God is here sought and found in the first instance in external goods, though these also kindle joy in God's favour. The latter is emphasised in ψ 62:5. The ref. in Ez. 16:28 f. is to sexual satisfaction (fig.). In a strongly transf. sense Ez. 24:13 (τὸν θυμόν). οὐκ ἐμπλησθήσεται ὀφθαλ-μὸς τοῦ ὁρᾶν, Qoh. 1:8, cf. 4:8. God satisfies with His grace, ψ 89:14 (though here there is some relation to the passages from the Ps. already mentioned ; cf. ψ 90:16 with long life. Death is insatiable, Hab. 2:5 : θάνατος οὐκ ἐμπιπλάμενος, Prv. 27:20 : ᾅδης καὶ ἀπώλεια οὐκ ἐμπίμπλανται, cf. 30:15 f.

B. The Word Group in the New Testament.

Rather strangely, the two main senses "to fill" and "to satisfy" are in the NT cleanly divided between the simple and compound forms. The content is always in the gen.

1. πίμπλημι is used a. spatially in Lk. 5:7; Mt. 22:10; 27:48 (the only two instances of the simple form outside the Lucan writings; Jn. 19:29 ℵ is obviously not original).

b. It is also used of intellectual and spiritual processes. Reactions to the words and works of Jesus are at issue in Lk.: ἐπλήσθησαν θυμοῦ (anger 4:28, cf. Da. 3:19) or ἀνοίας (6:11) is said of His opponents, φόβου (5:26) of the masses who see God's work in Him. These expressions make it quite plain that unconditional

---

[3] → II, 240 f., also 245, 4-7; cf. Eichr. Theol. AT, II⁴, 9 f.

decisions are taken in relation to Jesus. We note similar responses to the preaching of the apostles in Ac.: ἐπλήσθησαν θάμβους καὶ ἐκστάσεως is said of the sympathetic crowd (3:10), ζήλου of the fanatical leaders of Judaism in Jerusalem (5:17) or of the synagogue at Pisidian Antioch (13:45), τῆς συγχύσεως of confused and excited Ephesus (19:29). Even more striking is the restriction of the word to Luke in respect of the Holy Spirit. It occurs in Lk. only in the infancy stories, and here only in statements whose view of the Holy Spirit continues a specific OT trend (Nu. 11:25-29; Is. 59:21; 61:1). [4] The Spirit of prophecy causes Elisabeth (1:41) and Zacharias (1:67) to magnify the fulfilment of God's promise of salvation in the sons of Mary and Elisabeth. The same Spirit is promised to the Baptist from his mother's womb, 1:15. In Ac. πλησθῆναι describes the work of the Holy Spirit in Christians. The primary reference here is not to the receiving of the Spirit of prophecy but to the fact that filling with the Spirit conveys the power of preaching, e.g., to Peter before his address in Ac. 4:8, to all believers prior to their witness at the prayer meeting in 4:31 (with accompanying external phenomena), to Paul before his sermon in 13:9. In 2:4 the receiving of the Spirit brings the gift of tongues. At 9:17 several interpretations are possible: the receiving of the Spirit in connection with becoming a Christian; the receiving of special powers (cf. Paul as a prophet in 13:1), the receiving of particularly efficacious gifts as teachers (cf. 13:1) or apostles (→ πνεῦμα). In harmony with other statements in Ac., the usage includes rather than excludes the fact that the author is acquainted with a normal Christian endowment with the Spirit which is to be differentiated from His intensive and concentrated work in, e.g., preaching, tongues, or the apostolate. [5] Cf. also → πλήρης.

c. Only in Lk. again is πλησθῆναι used for the ending of regular periods, and in this case the usage is restricted to the infancy stories. Thus the priest's course comes to an end in Lk. 1:23, the period for circumcision in 2:21 and for the καθαρισμός (Lv. 12) in 2:22; the period of pregnancy in 1:57; 2:6. The expression is influenced by the Semitic style of the source used in the infancy stories, → 129, 24 f.

d. Only in Lk. does πλησθῆναι express the thought that OT prophecies [6] "come to fulfilment" (21:22: in the destruction of Jerusalem, cf. esp. Hos. 9:7; → 128, 36 f.; elsewhere → πληρόω is used instead).

2. ἐμπίμπλημι is reserved exclusively for "to satisfy" in the NT. It is predominantly pass.: "to be satisfied." The satisfaction is physical in Jn. 6:12. It is used with the gen. of that which brings satisfaction in Ac. 14:17. God is He who satisfies the heart with nourishment and hence with εὐφροσύνη; the expression is to be understood in the light of LXX usage. [7] Lk. 1:53 is somewhat ambiguous (→ 129, 29-33): πεινῶντας ἐνέπλησεν ἀγαθῶν. This is based on ψ 106:9, which undoubtedly has a bodily reference. The saying in Lk. relates to the Messianic kingdom whose dawn is seen. If the canticle has its source in Jewish piety, what was originally meant might have been, in the first instance, the removal of external want. There is a plain transition to transf. usage in Lk. 6:25. The satisfied

---

[4] But v. Eichr. Theol. AT, II⁴, 24 f.

[5] Cf. H. v. Baer, *Der Heilige Geist in den Lukasschriften* (1926); F. Büchsel, *Der Geist Gottes im NT* (1926), 228-266; esp. R. Asting, "Die Heiligkeit im Urchr.," FRL, 46 (NF, 29) (1930), 95, 118, 125-127.

[6] Cf. F. Baumgärtel, *Verheissung* (1952), 16-27.

[7] → 129, 28 f. on Prv. 6:30; → II, 774 f.; M. Dibelius, *Aufsätze z. Ag.* (1951), 65 f., n. 3.

are those who have enough to eat and drink well. What excludes them from participation in the rule of God is the fact that they are inwardly satisfied with external goods. Purely fig. is the use in R. 15:24. Paul wants to "satisfy himself" with the faith and fellowship of the Roman church when he stays in the city. The idea of joy and strength is contained in the word "to satisfy" here.

† πλησμονή.

A. The Usage outside the Greek Bible.

I. General Usage.

1. In the forms of use treated below πλησμονή [1] can denote both the condition of fulness and also the act of filling or process of becoming full ; one cannot always make a precise distinction between them. a. First fulness (or filling, opp. κένωσις, Plat. Symp., 186c), (a) lit. esp. as a result of satisfying nourishment, "satisfaction," Poll. Onom., V, 151: ἐν πλησμονῇ εἰμι, with many other expressions denoting satisfaction ; Xenoph. Mem., III, 11, 14 : τῆς πλησμονῆς παυσάμενοι when they no longer have the "feeling of satisfaction"; Eur. Fr., 892, 4 (TGF, 646): to sate oneself with bread and water is not enough ; Plat. Phaedr., 233e : do not invite friends to a meal, but those who need to be satisfied (the hungry). Then for the stilling of sexual desire, → 132, 1-5. (b) Also transf.: satisfying of the soul, Philo Cher., 75 : κένωσιν ἀντὶ πλησμονῆς ... ψυχῇ δεξάμενος, → 132, 11-13. The use in 1. a. is common from the oldest examples in Eur., by way of the frequent use in the LXX, to patristic exegesis of Col. 2:23. b. Then "over-fulness" (opp. ἔνδεια "lack," Plat. Resp., IX, 571e), esp. the result (or act) of immoderate eating, "satiety," Xenoph. Resp. Lac., 2, 5 : so much bread ὡς ὑπὸ πλησμονῆς ... μήποτε βαρύνεσθαι, or "lack of moderation," "gluttony," Xenoph. Cyrop., IV, 2, 40; also with μέθη, Philedem. Philos. De Musica, 62, 1. So in the literary (first popular ?) expression παραμύθια πλησμονῆς (obj. gen.): that which tells the one who is already fully satisfied (abstractum pro concreto) to take even more (dessert Plat. Critias, 115b; Dio C., 65, 4, 3; emetics etc. Plut. De Tuenda Sanitate Praecepta, 22 [II, 134a]); cf. the proverb ἐν πλησμονῇ Κύπρις : Only he who is sated falls victim to erotic desire, [2] Antiph., 242, 3; Aristot. Probl., IX, 47, p. 896a, 24. Also transf. Aristoph. Pl., 189-192 : One has enough and more than enough of everything, of the enjoyment of art, of honour, of influence, but not of wealth, → 128, 38 f. πίμπλημι.

2. a. Occasionally πλησμονή can be "that which fills," Ps.-Xenoph. Cyn., 7, 4 : βαρεῖαι πλησμοναί "heavy food" (opp. milk). Hence — the transition is clear in Philo Rer. Div. Her., 297: ἁμαρτημάτων πλησμονῆς — b. the meaning "great number," "host" Geoponica, I, 10, 8 : πληγῶν πλησμονάς, "profusion of blows."

II. The Use in Philosophy.

The philosophical use does not differ fundamentally from that already outlined ; it is clear that here, too, the word does not necessarily imply an adverse judgment, → 131,

---

π λ η σ μ ο ν ή. T. K. Abbott, A Critical and Exegetical Commentary on the Epistles to the Ephesians and to the Colossians, ICC on Col. 2:23 (1922); G. Bornkamm, "Die Häresie d. Kolosserbriefes," ThLZ, 73 (1948), 11-20; also "Das Ende des Gesetzes" (1952), 139-156; Dib. Gefbr.[3]; Ew. Gefbr.; Haupt Gefbr.; P. L. Hedley, Ad Colossenses 2:20-3:4," ZNW, 27 (1928), 211-216; J. B. Lightfoot, St. Paul's Epistles to the Colossians and to Philemon (1904), ad loc.; Loh. Kol., ad loc.; E. Percy, Die Probleme d. Kolosser- u. Epheserbriefe. Skrifter utgivna av Kungliga Humanistiska Vetensskapssamfundet Lund, 39 (1946), 79, 138; B. Weiss, Das NT (Handausgabe), II² (1902), ad loc.
[1] Formation : -μονή fem. abstract formation from -μων (Schwyzer I, 524, d 2; Bl.-Debr. § 109, 6) [Debrunner].
[2] Plut. De Tuenda Sanitate Praecepta, 8 (II, 126c) inveighs against this : οὐ γὰρ ἐν πλησμοναῖς Κύπρις, ἀλλὰ μᾶλλον ἐν εὐδίᾳ σαρκός (!) καὶ γαλήνη καὶ Κύπρις εἰς ἡδονὴν τελευτᾷ καὶ βρῶσις καὶ πόσις. Here πλησμονή is obviously given the adverse sense of excess.

12-20. This is formally true even in a series of censorious statements, cf. the rejection of paederasty in Plat. Phaedr., 241c : These lovers love "for the sake of satisfaction, as wolves love lambs"; Leg., VIII, 837c : He who loves with the soul the soul of another regards as a vice τὴν περὶ τὸ σῶμα τοῦ σώματος πλησμονήν. There is no obvious censure in the humorous speech of Aristoph. in Symp., 191c, or in the description of the one who like an animal seeks satisfaction in food, drink, and physical love, Leg., VIII, 831e, or in the picture of the one who simply "pursues the satisfaction of ambition, the desire for victory, and passion," Resp., IX, 586d, or in the saying that there is no limit in the satisfying of hubris and wickedness, Phileb., 26b. "Filling" with food and drink certainly leads to illness if done unreasonably, Gorg., 518d. The wise man avoids both lack and satiety in physical things, Resp., IX, 571e. Yet there can be the latter in intellectual and spiritual relations too. Hence it is not desirable that the younger generation, when married, should live with their parents, Leg., VI, 776a. More basic is a thought of Diogenes of Apollonia (5th cent.), which is handed down by Theophr. De Sensu et Sensibilibus, 44 and which belongs to the context of speculation about the elements in natural philosophy. This is that moisture hampers the (aethereal) νοῦς; hence φρονεῖν (insight, reflection) is diminished in sleep or during orgies of eating and drinking (μέθαις ... πλησμοναῖς).

In Philo (apart from Cher., 75; Rer. Div. Her., 297) the word has a part in the attack on overestimation of physical needs. The lust of the flesh already brought destruction to the wilderness generation (Nu. 11:4 ff.) (ὑπὸ τῆς πλησμονῆς ἀπόλλυσθαι, Spec. Leg., IV, 129). Animals were roasted or cooked εἰς πλησμονὴν ἄδικον of the wretched belly, Vit. Mos., II, 156. Its (ἄμετρος) πλησμονή causes not only illnesses (Sobr., 2) but also the stimulation of sexual desire (cf. the proverb → 131, 27 f.; Agr., 38; Vit. Mos., II, 24; also Som., I, 122), and not least of all ὑπεροψία (arrogance, Virt., 163). It clouds the eye of λογισμός (reason, Leg. Gaj., 2). It is thus emphasised that the Therapeutae shun πλησμονή as the enemy of body and soul (they eat and drink so as not to hunger or thirst, Vit. Cont., 37) and that the Jews fast on the Day of Atonement so that they will not be hampered by physical desires (→ line 23 f.) when they seek to reconcile the Father of all things by prayer, Vit. Mos., II, 24. In this connection πλησμονή usually means "gluttony."

B. Greek Old Testament.

πλησμονή occurs 28 times in the LXX. It is mostly used for words of the stem שׂבע Exceptions are Is. 30:23 for דָּשֵׁן "fat"; Is. 1:14 טֹרַח "burden"; Jer. 14:22 רְבִבִים.[3] 1. a. The usual sense is "satisfaction" by nourishment, Ex. 16:3, 8; Lv. 25:19; 26:5; ψ 77:25; Hag. 1:6 (Prv. 27:7: ἐν πλησμονῇ οὖσα); Sir. 45:20; cf. Is. 56:11; the "quenching" of thirst, Jdt. 7:21; generally "satisfaction" with the gifts of God, Dt. 33:23 (par. εὐλογίαν). The process of "becoming full," Jdt. 8:31 (another reading is πλήρωσιν). b. Censoriously "satiety," Ez. 39:19 (with μέθη); "satiety" which leads to sin (apostasy from Yahweh), Hos. 13:6 (ἐνεπλήσθησαν εἰς πλησμονήν), partly in comparison and then basically transf., so also Is. 65:15; drunkenness, Hab. 2:16 (ἀτιμίας); plainly transf. Is. 1:14 : "excess." There are several possibilities at Lam. 5:6. 2. a. "That which satisfies," Is. 30:23 (or b ?); both lit. and fig. Is. 55:2. b. "Fulness," Sir. 18:25; Prv. 3:10; "profusion" Jer. 14:22 (rain as a blessing); Gn. 41:30 (par. to εὐθηνία, "superfluity" in v. 29, both for שָׂבָע); "excess," Ez. 16:49; transf. "fulness" (supreme measure) σοφίας, Sir. 1:16.

In 'ΑΣΘ πλησμονή is a regular equivalent of (ה)שׂבע; it is plainly affirmative in ψ 15:11 'ΑΣ ("fulness" of joys given by God); Gn. 26:33 'ΑΣ ("well of fulness"); Is. 55:2 Σ (like the LXX : "that which does not satisfy") and 23:18 'ΑΣ (eating for

---

[3] At ψ 105:15 LXX reads a form of רוה "to sate oneself with drink," hence πλησμονή = "excess." At Prv. 26:16 (also Gn. 26:33 'ΑΣ) שִׁבְעָה "seven" is confused with שׂבע (ἐν πλησμονῇ, "to excess" or "with satisfaction"). At Is. 65:15 שְׁבֻעָה "curse" is read as שׂבע "to satisfy" (πλησμονή = "excess") [Bertram].

satisfaction), but negative in Qoh. 5:11 Σ (satiety does not allow the rich to sleep). πλησμονάς in Jer. 5:24 'ΑΘ is the mechanical rendering of an obviously dittographical שׁבֻעוֹת (sense affirmative acc. to the context). At Hos. 7:14 Ε' reads πλησμονῆς (σίτου) with no original (acc. to the context censorious).

C. The New Testament.

1. In Col. 2:23 the fathers almost unanimously equate σάρξ with σῶμα and thus take it positively, so that πλησμονή is the "satisfaction of natural (not sinful) desire." [4] They obviously regard the whole expression οὐκ ἐν ... πρός ... as an elucidation of ἀφειδίᾳ σώματος. That the false teachers do not indulge the body means that they do not give it the respect accorded to it by God (ὁ δὲ θεὸς τὴν σάρκα ἐτίμησεν). They deprive it rather than satisfying it. [5] Or else it means that they do not regard as worthy of honour τὸ διὰ πάντων πληροῦν τὴν σάρκα [6] ⸗ nihil honoris dignum existiment, ut ex omnibus repleant corpus. [7] Vg obviously separates ἀφειδίᾳ completely from the preceding ἐν : [8] non (!) ad parcendum corpori, non in honore aliquo ad saturitatem carnis; the dat. is thus understood as ὥστε ἀφειδεῖν (the negation is inferred from what follows). There is no distinction in the worthiness of the foods by which the flesh is satisfied, says Aug. Ep., 149, 30 (CSEL, 44, 376); it should be nourished only by the food which is conducive to health. A distinctive position is that of Paulinus of Nola. He first conjectures that there is an antithesis between non parcendum and ad saturitatem, Ep., 50 (CSEL, 29, 416 f.). This seems to incline to a positive interpretation of πλησμονή τῆς σαρκός, but he goes on to interpret non parcere corpori in the light of 1 C. 9:27. As a second possibility he considers an equation of cura saturandae carnis and non parcere corpori; not to indulge the flesh is not to violate it (non honorifice possidere acc. to 1 Th. 4:4, which he relates to one's own body). What is meant is obviously that to fill the body is to ravage it (quia distentio corporis animae sobrietatem necat et inimica est castitati). Even this ascetic interpretation maintains the equation of σῶμα and σάρξ. Another line is taken in an interpretation in Ambrosiaster (MPL, 17, 457). The author takes σάρξ to be the carnal mind : sagina (πλησμονή) carnalis sensus traditio humana est "which says that that suffices which care for the flesh has taught." He relates the conclusion of Col. 2:23 to λόγον ... σοφίας when he continues : rationem enim videtur habere sapientiae, iuxta carnem.

2. Modern interpretations cannot be discussed in detail. One can only try to present a line of understanding on the basis of certain common conclusions in the comm. [9] a. πρός denotes effect. [10] In this use of πρός in Paul the final and consecutive senses are not always plainly differentiated, cf. 2 C. 4:6; the former is common when the prepos. is combined with a noun. [11] b. σάρξ, as in v. 18, is to be taken in malam partem : [12] it denotes "the whole sinful nature," "the old man," [13] esp. the "pride and self-satisfaction of the natural man" [14] "in his selfishness." [15] c. πλησμονή is the "satisfying," [16] "full

---

[4] Cf. H. Delafosse, Les écrits de St. Paul, 3 (1927), 208 : "ils ne tiennent pas compte de ce dont la chair a besoin pour se soutenir" (transl.).

[5] Cramer Cat., VI, 327, ad loc. (traced back to Severian).

[6] Theod. Mops., cf. Cramer Cat., VI, 327.

[7] Theod. Mops. In Epistolas B. Pauli Commentarii, ed. H. B. Swete, I (1880), 297.

[8] The elimination of καί before ἀφειδίᾳ in B etc. follows this line.

[9] Generally rejected is the suggestion of Lightfoot (204-206) that πρὸς κτλ. means "to remedy indulgence of the flesh" cf. Haupt Gefbr., 117; Hedley, 215, and esp. Abbott, 276 f.

[10] Cf. Hedley, 215 : "to produce"; Bornkamm, 18, n. 2 "serves (only) to ...; Weiss, "to cause"; Haupt Gefbr., 118 : "issues ... in"; cf. Loh. Kol., 130, n. 4 : "seems to be modelled on the fairly constant εἰς πλησμονήν of the LXX" (εἰς πλησμονήν 14 times).

[11] Cf. esp. Bl.-Debr. § 239, 7.

[12] Dib. Gefbr.³, ad loc.; Pr.-Bauer⁴, 1225; Hedley, 215; "a bad sense," Lightfoot, 205b.

[13] Haupt Gefbr., 118.

[14] Percy, 139, also Weiss.

[15] Percy, 79. If there is contrast between πλησμονὴ σαρκός and ἀφειδία σώματος (Weiss), then σάρξ, too, stands in antithesis to σῶμα.

[16] Weiss ; Loh. Kol. (transl.).

satisfaction," [17] but it takes on a negative sense, [18] naturally only in combination [19] with σάρξ. d. More debatable is the syntactical integration of πρὸς κτλ. into the sentence as a whole. There seems to be textual corruption, but none of the conjectures offered is satisfactory. [20] Most probable is a loose relation of πρὸς κτλ. to ἅτινά ἐστιν; [21] λόγον ... σώματος is then a parenthesis. [22] If οὐκ ἐν τιμῇ τινι is taken as an independent statement and λόγον ... σώματος is detached as a subsidiary clause ("although ..." [23]), [24] the result is at least a possible syntactical order. To be sure, "the absence of any adversative particle is ... surprising"; [25] nevertheless, the antithesis between ἔχοντα and οὐκ ... or πρὸς ... is adequately indicated by ἐστίν and μέν. [26] Elsewhere in Paul it is not always possible to establish a precise syntactical construction. [27]

3. The context of Col. 2:23 shows that the form of piety combatted parades an earthly-cosmic glory (3:4) as distinct from the life of Christians which is now "hid with Christ in God" (3:3). The line κόσμος (2:20) — ἀνθρώπων (2:22) — σάρξ (2:23) — τὰ ἐπὶ τῆς γῆς (3:2) is contrasted with the line ἀπεθάνετε (2:20) — συνηγέρθητε (3:1) — τὰ ἄνω (3:1 f.). Precepts which forbid the use of certain earthly gifts confer on these undue significance, take on for themselves an importance which is quite unfitting, [28] and serve the "satisfaction" [29] of the selfish desire which conceals itself in the garb of religion (autonomous religion simply promotes man's self-exaltation). [30] Such precepts have the name of wisdom — in self-ordained piety and humility and non-indulgence of the body — but they have no (true) validity and simply serve to satisfy (pious) self-seeking.

Delling

---

[17] Haupt Gefbr., 118; similarly Weiss; cf. Percy, 139; Dib. Gefbr.³, *ad loc.*; Abbott, 278 "full satisfaction."

[18] Bengel: *fere excessum notat;* Haupt Gefbr., 116: "... morally at least a very dubious concept."

[19] This must be said as against Haupt Gefbr., 116; Abbott, 276; Lightfoot, 205, → 131, 12 ff. for the use outside the NT.

[20] Haupt Gefbr., 118, n. 1 considers whether ἐν τιμῇ τινι might not be a gloss on ἀφειδίᾳ (before σώματος); Hedley, 215 takes the opp. view that some lines might have dropped out; cf. also the textual apparatus in Nestle. B. G. Hall, "Colossians 2:23," Exp. T., 36 (1924/25), 285 suggests an original ἐπιλησμονήν (adducing Aristoph. Nub., where ἐπιλήσμων occurs 3 times, 129, 485, 629; cf. also Lys., 1288): asceticism "is of no value to the *forgetting* of the flesh."

[21] Cf. Bengel; Ew. Gefbr., 406 f.

[22] Dib. Gefbr.³, however, proposes a link with v. 22a, but cf. Hedley, 215.

[23] On this cf. Ew. Gefbr., 407 f., though he relates ἐν τιμῇ τινι (τινί = to anyone!) to the other prepos. statements.

[24] Weiss puts a comma after ἐστίν as well as τινί.

[25] Bornkamm, 18, n. 2; *loc. cit.*: "The antithesis is already stated, however, in the οὐκ ἐν τιμῇ τινι."

[26] Cf. Lightfoot, 203 (who pts. to the use of μέν without δέ in class. Gk.; *v.* Bl.-Debr. § 447, 3 f.); Bengel: *Vis particulae* δέ ... *latet in verbo finito* ἔστι, cf. Ew. Gefbr., 406; Weiss.

[27] Loh. Kol., 131, n. 1: Col. 2:23 heaps up opposing slogans, so that one "should not ask concerning the syntactical relationship between these final terms."

[28] ἐν τιμῇ εἶναι denotes the value or regard accorded to someone, Xenoph. An., II, 5, 38; Hom. Il., 9, 319; one should probably compare 1 Th. 4:4; → τιμή.

[29] Bornkamm, 18, n. 2 presupposes the sense "filling" ("to stuff the flesh"), which is occasionally found outside the NT but makes no sense in the context; most natural is a use in the sense amply attested → 131 f. The choice of πλησμονή is probably no accident, but it is hardly an antithetical allusion to the πληροῦσθαι of the opponents, Col. 1:9; 2:10.

[30] Cf. Weiss; Haupt Gefbr., 118.

πίνω, πόμα, πόσις, ποτόν, πότος, ποτήριον, καταπίνω, ποτίζω

πίνω.

Contents : A. πίνω in the World Around the New Testament : πίνω in the Literal Sense :
1. In the Secular Sphere ; 2. In the Cultus : a. Abstinence from Drinks ; b. Drinking as a
Means of Salvation. II. πίνω in the Transferred Sense : 1. General ; 2. In the OT ; 3. In
Judaism and Gnosticism. B. πίνω in the New Testament : 1. Eating and Drinking as an
Expression of the Subjection of the World ; 2. The Eating and Drinking of Jesus and
His Disciples as an Expression of their Freedom in Relation to the World ; 3. The Eating
and Drinking of Jesus with His Disciples in its Significance from the Standpoint of the
History of Salvation ; 4. The Figurative Use of the Concept : a. The Drinking of the Cup
of Wrath and Suffering ; b. The Drinking of the Water of Life.

A. πίνω in the World Around the New Testament.

I. πίνω in the Literal Sense.

Drinks to quench thirst are, esp. in the Orient, even more necessary to life than food,
→ II, 689, 10 ff. ἐσθίω. As an intoxicant, drink invades the personal life even more
deeply than food. Hence drinking both during and between meals has a stronger religious
impact, and becomes to a highly developed degree a cultic instrument.

1. In the Secular Sphere.

In ancient Palestine [1] water, [2] milk [3] and wine (→ V, 162, 11 ff.) [4] served as drinks.
πίνω is common in the LXX [5] in the phrase "eat and drink," which is widespread from

π ί ν ω κ τ λ. On B. 3 : Bibl. on the Lord's Supper up to 1937 → III, 726, thereafter
E. Lohmeyer, "Vom urchr. Abendmahl," ThR, NF, 9 (1937), 168-227, 273-312; NF, 10
(1938), 81-99; also "Das Abendmahl in d. Urgemeinde," JBL, 56 (1937), 217-252; E. Käsemann, "Das Abendmahl im NT," Abendmahlsgemeinschaft (1937), 60-93; also "Anliegen
u. Eigenart d. paul. Abendmahlslehre," Ev. Theol., 7 (1947/48), 263-283; W. v. Loewenich,
Vom Abendmahl Christi (1938); A. Arnold, Der Ursprung des chr. Abendmahls im Lichte
d. neuesten liturgiegeschichtlichen Forschung² (1939); H. Sasse, "Das Abendmahl im NT,"
Vom Sakrament des Altars (1941), 26-78; E. Gaugler, Das Abendmahl im NT (1943) =
Internationale Kirchliche Zschr., 33 (1942), 97-164; N. Johansson, Det urkristna nattvards-
firandet (1944); M. Barth, Das Abendmahl, Passamahl, Bundesmahl u. Messiasmahl (1945);
W. Michaelis, Die Sakramente im J. (1946); M. Goguel, L'Église primitive (1947), 343-391;
Stauffer Theol.⁴, 141-144; F. J. Leenhardt, Le sacrement de la Sainte Cène (1948); P. Alt-
haus, Die chr. Wahrheit, II (1948), 362-379; J. Jeremias, Die Abendmahlsworte Jesu² (1949),
bibl. 5-9; W. Marxsen, Die Einsetzungsberichte z. Abendmahl (Diss. Kiel, 1949); C. Maurer,
Ign. v. Ant. u. das J. (1949), 77-99; O. Cullmann, Urchr. u. Gottesdienst² (1950); G. Walther,
Jesus, Das Passalamm d. Neuen Bundes, Der Zentralgedanke des Herrenmahles (1950);
K. G. Kuhn, "Über den urspr. Sinn des Abendmahls u. sein Verhältnis z. den Gemeinschaftsmahlen der Sektenschrift," Ev. Theol., 10 (1950/51), 508-527; J. Schniewind and E. Sommerlath, Abendmahlsgespräch (1951); B. Reicke, Diakonie, Festfreude u. Zelos in Verbindung
mit der altchr. Agapenfeier (1951); A. J. B. Higgins, The Lord's Supper in the NT (1952);
Bultmann Theol., 41, 59 f., 143-151, 309 f.; P. Brunner, Grundlegung des Abendmahlsge-
sprächs (1954); E. Schweizer, "Das Herrenmahl im NT," ThLZ, 79 (1954), 577-592.
[1] Sir. 39:26; Is. 55:1; cf. G. Dalman, Arbeit u. Sitte in Palästina, VI (1939), 119-129.
[2] With bread this is the most vital necessity : 1 K. 18:4; 19:6, 8; Ez. 4:16; 12:18 f.; Sir.
39:26 → ὕδωρ.
[3] Gn. 18:8; Ju. 5:25 → I, 645 ff.
[4] This figures chiefly in festal meals (Gn. 49:12; Qoh. 9:7; Mt. 11:19 par. Lk. 7:34; Jn.
2:1 ff.; cf. Jeremias, op. cit., 27 f.), esp. the joyous feast of the last time (Is. 25:6; cf. 65:13;
Str.-B., I, 992; Schl. Mt. on 26:29; Jeremias, 113; → II, 691, 29 ff.
[5] It is almost a full equivalent of the Heb. רָוָה. שָׁתָה, "to drink one's fill," is usually
rendered → μεθύσκομαι or →μεθύω, so that the distinction from שָׁכַר "to get drunk,"
virtually disappears in Gk., which uses the same verbs for this. Both languages have special
verbs for "to give to drink," → 159, 19 ff. ποτίζω.

the time of Hom., → II, 688 f.[6] By withholding or providing these elemental necessities,[7] fundamentally in the miracles of the desert period,[8] the God of Israel, in opposition to all self-glorifying on man's part (Is. 22:13), shows Himself to be the Lord of life. Hence "profane" eating and drinking take on a religious significance which is more important than all the eating and drinking in direct religious practice. In Judaism this finds particular expression at every meal in the grace and in table fellowship.[9]

2. In the Cultus.

a. Abstinence from Drinks.

In the OT and Jewish sphere drinking is a subject of cultic legislation primarily from the standpoint of abstinence. Fasting includes abstinence from drink, Ex. 34:28; Dt. 9:9, 18, cf. Philo Vit. Mos., II, 24; Str.-B., IV, 77 f. → II, 693, 33 ff. Only over a longer period are there relaxations.[10] A special form of abstinence is the renunciation of wine and intoxicating drink, which in the Nazirite vow is at first for life (Ju. 13:13 f.; Am. 2:12; cf. 1 S. 1:11), then for a fixed period (Nu. 6:2 ff.).[11] Drinks as distinct from foods are Levitically unclean only on the basis of pollution by contact (Lv. 11:34, cf. Str.-B., I, 934 ff.). For Jews living in Gentile surroundings Daniel's refusal of wine was an example; this might well have been wine offered in libation.[12]

In the Hellenistic world, too, fasting, e.g., in preparation for initiation to the mysteries, often included abstention from drinks, → IV, 926, 10 ff. A constant refusal of wine such as we often find in Judaism in the NT period (→ n. 11 f.) was first practised by the Neo-Pythagoreans (for ascetic reasons).[13]

b. Drinking as a Means of Salvation.

In OT and Jewish religion drinking is a cultic means of effecting fellowship with God, not independently, but only as a (subordinate) part of the ancient Israelite covenantal or sacrificial meal[14] and of Jewish practices at meals.[15]

In the pagan world around, the cultic meals which were supposed to unite men and gods in table fellowship included a good deal of unmixed wine and a richly furnished

---

[6] Tippling apart from eating is viewed unfavourably, Is. 5:11 f., 22; Am. 4:1; Prv. 20:1; 21:17; Sir. 19:1 ff.

[7] Am. 4:6-12; 5:11; 9:14; Mi. 6:13-16; Zeph. 1:13; Ez. 4:9-17; 12:17-20; Hag. 1:6-11; Qoh. 2:24 ff. (3:13; 5:7 ff.; 9:7).

[8] Ex. 17:6; Nu. 20:5, 11; 1 K. 19:6, 8; Dt. 29:5 f.; Is. 43:20; 48:21; 49:10; Ps. 78:15; cf. Philo Spec. Leg., II, 197-199, 203.

[9] → τράπεζα, cf. Jeremias, 112. There is no direct witness to grace in the OT (cf. Dt. 8:10), but it is a general practice in the NT period, Str.-B., I, 685-687; IV, 621-623, 627-634. The pagan world dedicates food and drink in various ways through sacrificial ceremonies and prayers to the gods, Quintilianus, Declamationes, 301; Chant. de la Saussaye⁴, II, 322; Ltzm. 1 K. on 10:20; → 157 f., n. 88 f.

[10] Da. 10:2 f. R. Ṣadoq (c. 70 A.D.) is reputed to have satisfied himself by sucking dried figs during his 40 yr. fast, Str.-B., IV, 95, 98 f.

[11] Cf. E. Sellin, Gesch. d. isr.-jüd. Volkes, I² (1935), 128 f.; Eichr. Theol. AT, I³, 150 f.; Philo Vit. Cont., 37; Str.-B., II, 80-89, esp. 84-89, 747-751; Lk. 1:15; Ac. 18:18; 21:23 ff.; Eus. Hist. Eccl., II, 23, 4. The Rechabites, too, refrained from the use of wine, Jer. 35; cf. 2 K. 10:15 f.

[12] Da. 1:5, 8, 12; cf. Str.-B., IV, 366 f.; G. Dalman, Arbeit u. Sitte in Palästina, IV (1935), 392 → 157, n. 89. Acc. to the Law only ministering priests had to refrain from wine, Lv. 10:9; Ez. 44:21; Jos. Bell., 5, 229.

[13] H. Strathmann, Gesch. d. frühchr. Askese (1914), 307. Elsewhere abstinence from alcoholic beverages is sometimes demanded in preparation for cultic acts, ibid., 216, 218 f.

[14] Ex. 24:11; Test. Jud. 21; cf. 1 K. 10:18, v. Eichr. Theol. AT, I³, 72-74; → II, 690, 32 ff.; → III, 801 f.

[15] Jeremias, 112, cf. 23-26. Among these the meals of the Essenes and similar groups occupy a special place, Jos. Bell., 2, 129-133, cf. 138 f., 143; Manual of Disc., VI, 1-6; cf. Bousset-Gressm., 460 f.; Kuhn, 509-512.

board. [16] Even apart from the cultic meal drinking had here a varied religious significance. [17] This influences at many pts. both the practice [18] and the fig. religious speech [19] of the OT and Judaism. In pagan religion we find all kinds of drinks which magically impart a share in various kinds of potency. [20] Drinks plays a role in caring for the dead [21] or mediating the power of immortality [22] for the soul in the hereafter. Drinks induce ecstatic inspiration by the spirit of prophesying deities. [23] In all these rites drinking is a mythical, magical, or pneumatic instrument, but it is not sacramental. The term sacrament, if already used in a general religio-historical sense, is limited to the "sublimation of a very simple and elemental vital activity" for the establishment of redemptive communion with a redeemer-god. [24] Eating and drinking have something like sacramental significance in this sense at sacrificial meals when the deity maintains aloofness from direct table fellowship and eating and drinking give only indirect participation in it, or in its redemptive operation. [25]

Acc. to the early Church, the closest pars. to the Chr. sacraments in the Hell. sphere were to be found in the mysteries, → 157, n. 86. Here drinking, esp. the drinking of intoxicants, was often a more or less important part of the rite whose general aim was to effect sacramental communion with the redeemer god and its destiny. At most one can speak of theophagy here only in relation to the Dionysus cult. [26] Nevertheless, the readily explicable consuming of the bull which represents the deity is one of the primitive features of the cult, and it is connected with the primitive piety [27] which alone refers to direct appropriation of a deity by partaking of the substance which represents it. [28] To show the significance of drinking in rites of initiation one might mention the following

---

[16] Philo Vit. Mos., II, 23 f.; Tert. Apol., 39, 14-16; Aug. Ep., 29, 9; cf. Ltzm. 1 K. on 10:20; T. Klauser, Art. "Becher," RAC, II, 41 and 43; → III, 799 f.

[17] → II, 690, 36 ff., cf. also Mithr. Liturg., 170-173; G. van d. Leeuw, *Phänomenologie der Religion* (1933), 342 f.

[18] Cf. the drinking of the water of cursing in God's judgment, Nu. 5:11-28 (Philo Spec. Leg., III, 61).

[19] Cf. the image of the poisoned water which developed out of the water of cursing, Jer. 8:14; 9:14; 23:15 → 150, n. 20. → n. 22 f.

[20] A magical book in Preis. Zaub., I, 20 f. directs : καὶ λαβὼν τὸ γάλα σὺν τῷ μέλιτι ἀπόπιε πρὶν ἀνατολῆς ἡλίου, καὶ ἔσται τι ἔνθεον ἐν τῇ σῇ καρδίᾳ. Cf. Chant. de la Saussaye⁴, I, 489; II, 292; van d. Leeuw, *op. cit.*, 339; T. Klauser, RAC, II, 45 f.

[21] Chant. de la Saussaye⁴, I, 586 f.; II, 297 f. Libations are part of the cult of the dead, Rohde, I ⁹,¹⁰, 241 f. In the Hell. world drinking vessels are often buried with the dead, Klauser, RAC, II, 43 f.

[22] In ancient Iran this effect was ascribed amongst other things to a drink brewed from the haoma plant, F. Bammel, *Das heilige Mahl im Glauben d. Völker* (1950), 54, 131; Chant. de la Saussaye⁴, II, 248. In Hell. funerary inscr. we often find the formula : δοίη σοι ὁ Ὄσιρις τὸ ψυχρὸν ὕδωρ, Rohde, II ⁹,¹⁰, 390 f.; cf. Eth. En. 22:9.

[23] Cf. the Pythia of the Delphic oracle (drinking from a spring, Luc. Hermot., 60) and the priests of Apollo Deiradiotes in Argos (drinking the blood of a lamb of sacrifice, Paus., II, 24, 1). Cf. Tat. Or. Graec., 19, 3. For primitive religions v. J. G. Frazer, *The Golden Bough,* I, 1 (1911), 382 f. Possibly this widespread notion exerted some influence when the apocalyptist in 4 Esr. 14:38-41 depicted the receiving of revelation as the visionary drinking of a cup : "Then a full cup was handed to me, which was filled with water, but its colour was like fire ... And when I had drunk, my heart brimmed over with understanding, ... my spirit held recollection, and my mouth opened." Since drinking here symbolises an intellectual process, the passage is close to Gnostic usage, → 138, 19 ff.

[24] Van d. Leeuw, 341 f.; cf. Bultmann Theol., 133 f.

[25] Van d. Leeuw, 336; Chant. de la Saussaye⁴, II, 293; E. Reuterskiöld, *Die Entstehung der Speisesakramente* (1912), 3-10. Eichr. Theol. AT, I³, 72-74 calls the sacrifice of fellowship the OT sacrament. In Judaism the fellowship meals of sects influenced by syncretism have a sacramental character, → n. 15.

[26] So van d. Leeuw, 342 f., but cf. Ltzm. 1 K. on 10:21 and Bau. J. on 6:59, though neither makes sufficient differentiation, → 157, n. 87.

[27] So Reuterskiöld, 126-133; K. Prümm, *Der chr. Glaube u. d. altheidnische Welt,* II (1935), 390-395.

[28] Reuterskiöld, 92-102; Bammel, 65-69.

examples. In the Hell. Dionysiac mysteries the initiate who dances in the open by night is helped by wine to ἐνθουσιασμός, to union with the god. [29] In the Eleusinian mysteries initiation is introduced by fasting followed by the drinking of κυκεών, the ancient Gk. intoxicant. [30] Inscr. in Lower Italy mention among dedicatory rites the drinking of milk, and of the water of recollection. [31] In the mysteries of Attis [32] and Mithras [33] symbolical eating and drinking are associated with the rites of dedication. In all these mysteries physical drinking is a more or less emphasised part of a ritual action which as such releases redemptive power and is thus a sacramental event.

On the other hand, in Gnosticism physical drinking is a dualistic counterpart of true drinking, of appropriation of the true life-giving gift of the upper world [34] by the soul. [35] This usage [36] is formally fig. (→ 138, 33 ff.), but it is meant literally. Real satisfaction is contrasted with the meeting of vital needs by drinking. [37] Moralistically watered down, Gnostic usage occurs in this form in Philo. Earthly food and drink are corruptible nourishment for the corruptible body (Op. Mund., 119; Leg. All., III, 161; Det. Pot. Ins., 112-118, 156-158); but the "heavenly soul," "which is filled by contemplation of true and imperishable values" and "has loosed itself from the inauthentic and temporal values" (Deus Imm., 151), seeks the drink of immortality which is virtue (Spec. Leg., I, 304). "Thus he cannot drink from a well to whom God gives pure intoxicants" (Deus Imm., 158, cf. 155, → 151, n. 26). This Gnostic view may be seen also in Eth. En. 48:1: "In that place (heaven) I saw a well of righteousness which was inexhaustible. Round about it were many springs of wisdom; all the thirsty drank therefrom and were filled with wisdom ..." (cf. 96:6; 4 Esr. 14:38-40 → 137, n. 23). To the degree that the dualistic antithesis to earthly and physical drinking fades into the background, Gnostic usage becomes figurative, → 139, 22 ff.

II. πίνω in the Transferred Sense.

1. General. With ref. to the partaking of fluids by non-animal subjects πίνω means "to suck in," "to absorb." Plants (Xenoph. Sym., 2, 25; Ez. 31:14, 16) or the earth (Hdt., III, 117; IV, 198; Dt. 11:11; Hb. 6:7), "to drink" water or rain. The earth drinks blood (Aesch. Sept. c. Theb., 736, 821; Eum., 979; Soph. Oed. Tyr., 1401). Fixed phrases containing πίνω denote fig. an accompanying circumstance of drinking: Hom. Il., 2, 825: πίνοντες ὕδωρ ... Αἰσήποιο = "those who live by the Aesepus," cf. Jer. 2:18. "To drink blood" is a fig. for killing (Is. 49:26; cf. Rev. 16:6; 17:6) taken from the beast of prey (Nu. 23:24; Ez. 39:17 ff.). Purely fig. πίνω expresses the processes contained in the biological act of drinking: "to take" something important which is desired or something bitter which is forced on one; "to accept," "to appease desire." The latter may be used for the enjoyment of love (Sir. 26:12; Prv. 5:15; Cant. 5:1); the former occurs in Luc.

---

[29] J. Leipoldt, *Dionysos* (1931), 38.

[30] Cl. Al. Prot., 2, 21, 2; cf. Mithr. Liturg., 124-126.

[31] Mithr. Liturg., 172, 199.

[32] Firm. Mat. Err. Prof. Rel., 18, 1; Cl. Al. Prot., 2, 15; cf. Nilsson, II, 620 f.

[33] Just. Apol., 66, 4: ἄρτος καὶ ποτήριον ὕδατος τίθεται ἐν ταῖς τοῦ μυουμένου τελεταῖς μετ' ἐπιλόγων τινῶν. Cf. Nilsson, II, 663.

[34] For a historical analysis of the idea cf. H. Lewy, "Sobria Ebrietas" ZNW, *Beih.* 9 (1929), 90-103.

[35] E.g., Act. Thom., 36: "We speak about the upper world, about God and angels, about ambrosial (incorruptible) food and the drink of the true vine," cf. c. 25. Also c. 7: "They were enlightened in contemplation of their Lord whose divine food they received, which dwelt in them undiminished; and they also drank his wine, which stirred up in them neither thirst nor desire." Though there are differences, the partaking of the sacrament is basically the symbolical counterpart of a spiritual receiving which takes place along with rather than through the physical reception, cf. Act. Thom., 133, 158.

[36] Adopting this pre-Chr. idea, Chr. *gnosis* refers Jn. 4 to the drinking of heavenly water (Hipp. Ref., V, 9 of the Naassenes, V, 19 of the Sethians, V, 27 of Justin the Gnostic).

[37] Addiction to the improper food of the lower world causes forgetfulness of the true home, Act. Thom., 109: "I ate of their foods, then I no longer knew that I was the son of a king." → n. 46.

Dial. Deorum, 4, 5 : πιόντα τῆς ἀθανασίας or in the LXX of Job : πίνων ἀδικίας ἴσα ποτῷ (Job 15:16) and πίνων μυκτηρισμὸν ὥσπερ ὕδωρ (34:7 Θ).

2. In the OT. Two thoughts in the fig. use of the OT are theologically significant. a. The drinking of Yahweh's cup (→ 149, 21 ff.) [38] is the suffering of His judgment, → V, 399, 36 ff. The image of drinking expresses the fact that those smitten by it execute the judgment on themselves by their own bemused acts. The compulsion (Jer. 25:28 f.; 49:12; Ps. 75:8) reminds us of the drinking of the condemned (→ 150, n. 20), the urge to drink at the table of the exalted (cf. Hab. 2:15 f.) and the irresistible self-destroying craving for intoxicating drink (cf. Rev. 18:3). b. The second idea occurs in Is. 55:1: οἱ διψῶντες, πορεύεσθε ἐφ' ὕδωρ, καὶ ὅσοι μὴ ἔχετε ἀργύριον, βαδίσαντες ἀγοράσατε καὶ πίετε ἄνευ ἀργυρίου καὶ τιμῆς οἴνου καὶ στέαρ. Here to drink is to take the salvation offered by grace alone, and to live thereby. The suggested antithesis is not the taking of material nourishment but the vain attempt to provide oneself with the necessities of life, cf. Jer. 2:13.

3. In Judaism. In Judaism πίνω is used fig. for to take intellectually and spiritually that which promises life. In Prv. 9:5 wisdom issues the invitation : ἔλθατε φάγετε τῶν ἐμῶν ἄρτων καὶ πίετε οἶνον, ὃν ἐκέρασα ὑμῖν, and in 9:18c (LXX) the warning is given : ἀπὸ πηγῆς ἀλλοτρίας μὴ πίῃς Sir. 24:21 (LXX): οἱ πίνοντές με (wisdom) ἔτι διψήσουσιν, cf. 15:3. Where the OT spoke of drinking water the Rabb. interpreted it allegorically of receiving the Spirit (Str.-B., II, 433 f.), and often of studying the Torah ; [39] the phrase "to drink of the water of a scholar" is a common one for the student relationship. [40] In the Gnostic O. Sol. gnosis is compared to a river which overflows the whole earth to supply the thirsty, [41] or to a paradisial spring from which the redeemed have drunk immortality (O. Sol. 11:6-8, cf. Ps. 36:9), or to a well of life which pours forth as a word of knowledge from the lips of the Lord, O. Sol. 30. This fig. use merges into the specifically Gnostic ref. to true drinking (→ 138, 9 ff.); the borderline is fluid.

B. πίνω in the New Testament.

In the NT πίνω occurs some 70 times, 30 in the form ἐσθίειν (τρώγειν) καὶ πίνειν, 10 along with ἐσθίω, 30 independently. To a large degree, then, one need only amplify what has been said already under ἐσθίω (→ II, 689 ff.).

1. Eating and Drinking as an Expression of the Subjection of the World.

Eating and drinking as the appeasing of hunger and thirst are vital functions of human life. [42] They are also basic occasions of sin. Because the contemporaries of Jesus were content with this satisfying of the most primitive vital needs, like the men before the flood and the men of Sodom they missed the signs of the eschaton which discloses the true meaning and basis of life, Mt. 24:38 par. Lk. 17:27; Lk. 17:28 cf. also Lk. 14:18-20; 16:19-31. [43] Eating and drinking are for most of this generation the goal of human striving (Mt. 6:32 f. par. Lk. 12:30 f.) and the object of their anxiety (Mt. 6:31 par. Lk. 12:29). The satisfaction of this need, or sure provision for it, is also the basis of self-satisfied and self-secure pleasure. [44]

---

[38] Jer. 25:16, 27 f.; 49:12; 51:7; Hab. 2:16; Ez. 23:32 ff.; Is. 51:17, 22; Ps. 75:8; cf. the drinking of the drink of wrath, Ob. 16; Ps. 60:3 Mas.; Job 21:20 Mas.

[39] Str.-B., II, 434 ff., 483, 485, 492; cf. H. Odeberg, The Fourth Gospel (1929), 157-160. Cf. Hod., IV, 19 f. and without the term for drinking Damasc. 3:13-17; 6:1-11; 19:33 f.

[40] Str.-B., II, 436; Schl. J. on 7:38; Ab., 1, 4 : "Drink their words with thirst."

[41] O. Sol. 6:11 ff.: "All the thirsty drank therefrom," cf. Ez. 47:1-12.

[42] Ign. Tr., 9, 1, cf. Philo Leg. All., III, 147.

[43] This rather than table fellowship (so Hck. Lk., ad loc.) is the point at issue in Lk. 13:26.

[44] Cf. the verbs which are found in association with the formula : Lk. 12:19 : ἀναπαύου ... εὐφραίνου, Mt. 24:49 (par. Lk. 12:45): ἄρξηται τύπτειν τοὺς συνδούλους ... μετὰ τῶν μεθυόντων (Lk.: καὶ μεθύσκεσθαι), 1 C. 10:7: ἐκάθισεν ... καὶ ἀνέστησαν παίζειν.

Security and the fulfilling of life are sought therein, Mt. 6:25 par. Lk. 12:22; Lk. 12:15, 19. Awareness of inevitable death simply confirms this attitude, 1 C. 15:32 (= Is. 22:13): "Let us eat and drink, for tomorrow we die." In Paul this fundamental principle of this-worldliness [45] is the logical conclusion of a dualistic Gnostic philosophy which gives free rein to a condemned and lightly esteemed corporeality, 1 C. 6:13 f. This attitude to eating and drinking is an elementary expression of paganism (Mt. 6:32 par. Lk. 12:30; 1 C. 10:7), of the folly [46] and drunkenness [47] of this world. Nevertheless, as the result of ἐπιθυμεῖν (1 C. 10:6) it is a constant temptation to believers against which they are expressly warned, Mt. 24:49 par. Lk. 12:45; 1 C. 10:7. The frontier between the quenching of thirst and drunkenness (cf. Lk. 12:45), which is fluid elsewhere, is plainly demarcated at the community meal, 1 C. 11:21; cf. Eph. 5:18 f.; → IV, 547, 42 ff. This is an unmistakable sign against the deification of eating and drinking as an end in itself.

2. The Eating and Drinking of Jesus and His Disciples as an Expression of their Freedom in Relation to the World.

By eating and drinking with grateful joy Jesus and His disciples bear witness to the freedom of the children of God both in relation to the world's subjection to the satisfaction of natural needs and also in relation to any attitude of protest against this subjection. [48]

The formula "not eating and drinking" is used for the fast which Paul penitently observed for three days in Damascus (Ac. 9:9), [49] for that which the 40 "zealots" undertook as a vow of abstinence (Ac. 23:12, 14), [50] and for that which John the Baptist kept throughout his ministry to give symbolical force to his call for conversion (Mt. 11:18: "neither eating nor drinking," cf. the par. Lk. 7:33, which offers a correct elucidation by adding "bread" and "wine" acc. to Mt. 3:4 par. Mk. 1:6). [51]

In contrast it is said of Jesus (Mt. 11:19 par. Lk. 7:34) and His disciples (Lk. 5:33, cf. Mt. 9:14 par. Mk. 2:18) that "they ate and drank," i.e., they abstained neither as a whole nor in part from common food and drink. Thus, whereas John seemed "unnatural" to his contemporaries, Jesus appeared to be "worldly." Fasting, as Jesus explains, is suitable for the one who awaits God's rule, not for the one who brings it, Mk. 2:19 par. → IV, 931 f. As concerns life in the world, this means that the man who is wholly God's is a "free lord of all things," Mk. 2:28 and par.; 1 C. 3:21-23; 1 Tm. 4:4; Tt. 1:15. [52] To those who seek God's kingdom in Jesus,

---

[45] Cf. Wettstein, ad loc. and Ltzm. 1 K. on 15:32.

[46] Lk. 12:20 cf. Mt. 24:45 par. Lk. 12:42 (φρόνιμος); 1 C. 15:34 ἀγνωσία τοῦ θεοῦ, cf. the par. in Reitzenstein Hell. Myst.³, 292, in which we find ἀγνωσία with drunkenness: Corp. Herm., I, 27: ὦ λαοὶ ... οἱ μέθῃ καὶ ὕπνῳ ἑαυτοὺς ἐκδεδωκότες καὶ τῇ ἀγνωσίᾳ τοῦ θεοῦ, νήψατε. Ibid., VII, 1 ποῖ φέρεσθε, ὦ ἄνθρωποι, μεθύοντες, τὸν τῆς ἀγνωσίας ἄκρατον (λόγον) ἐκπιόντες ... στῆτε νήψαντες.

[47] Mt. 24:49: μετὰ τῶν μεθυόντων, cf. 1 Cor. 15:34: νήψατε δικαίως, → n. 46.

[48] Cf. Philo on the ideal of moderation in Leg. All., II, 29: ἐὰν δὲ ὁ λόγος ἰσχύσῃ ἀνακαθᾶραι τὸ πάθος, οὔτε πίνοντες μεθυσκόμεθα οὔτε ἐσθίοντες ἐξυβρίζομεν διὰ κόρον.

[49] This is in no way related to the later practice of fasting before baptism, Did., 7, 4: Just. Apol., 61.

[50] To spur them on and as a sacrifice to secure God's assistance (1 S. 14:24; Jer. 14:12; Ps. 132:3 f.).

[51] Lk. 1:15 regards the Baptist as dedicated to God in the ancient sense, → 136, 12 ff.

[52] The post-canonical v. Mk. 16:18 carries this to the pt. of asserting that no creature can harm Jesus' disciples acc. to the prophecy of Paradise renewed (cf. Is. 11:8): ὄφεις ἀροῦσιν κἂν θανάσιμόν τι πίωσιν οὐ μὴ αὐτοὺς βλάψῃ. For examples of this in Chr. legend v. Kl. Mk., ad loc.

what is necessary for life in this world is "added" (Mt. 6:31 ff. par. Lk. 12:29 ff.), though this does not invalidate the interrelationship of labour and self-support (Lk. 10:7 cf. Mt. 10:10; 1 C. 9:4). Like all things else, eating and drinking, being provided for by God's grace, takes place to His honour and in love for one's neighbour (1 C. 10:31 ff.; R. 14:21, cf. Mt. 10:42 par. Mk. 9:41). In Mt. 23:25 f. par. Lk. 11:39 and Mt. 15:11 par. Mk. 7:15 Jesus also releases His disciples from the laws governing the Levitical impurity of drinks, → 149, n. 14. Paul admonishes the "strong" in Rome that as free men and for love's sake they should refrain from drinking wine since this causes offence to the "weak" by reason of their bondage to Jewish practice (→ 136, 16 f.), R. 14:21 → II, 694, 14 ff. Drinking from the cup from which a libation has been poured out to the gods (→ 157, 10 ff.) he forbids for the Lord's sake (1 C. 10:21 f.), for this drinking is no longer an intrinsically indifferent satisfying of vital needs (1 C. 6:13; Mt. 15:17 par. Mk. 7:18) but a cultic act.

3. The Eating and Drinking of Jesus with His Disciples in its Significance from the Standpoint of the History of Salvation.

The eating and drinking of Jesus with His companions also has significance from the standpoint of salvation history. The enjoyment of food and drink, especially wine, is a sign of the coming of the age of salvation (Mk. 2:18 f. par.; Mt. 11:19 par. Lk. 7:34). Table fellowship with Jesus gives a share in the eschatological salvation of God now present in Him [53] and guarantees a place at the banquet of consummation. [54] On the other hand, the eating and drinking to which Jesus summoned His disciples with the words of institution at the supper on the night before His death [55] does not grant a portion in Him simply as table fellowship. This is an independent action separated from the rest of the supper. [56] Jesus does not pronounce the blessing and then drink from the same cup as His disciples. [57] With the words of institution He hands them the cup. According to these words the redemptive dying of the Redeemer is represented by the drink. [58] Physical drinking is thus sublimated (→ 137, 7 ff.) for receiving the event of redemption. This drinking, as the accounts of the institution portray it, is sacramental. [59]

---

[53] Mk. 2:15 ff. par.; Mt. 11:19 par. Lk. 7:34; Lk. 15:1 f.; cf. Jeremias, 100, 112, → n. 4.
[54] Mk. 14:25 par.; Lk. 22:29 f.; cf. Mt. 8:11 f. par. Lk.; → n. 66 and 146, n. 9.
[55] Mk. 14:22-24 par. Mt. 26:26-28; 1 C. 11:23-25; Lk. 22:19 f. With Jeremias, 67-79 and Bultmann Theol., 144 we are to regard the longer Lucan text as original and historical, while Mk. and 1 C. are secondary. (For a review of the history of the text cf. A. Merx, *Die vier kanonischen Evangelien nach ihrem ältesten bekannten Text,* II, 2 : "Mk. u. Lk." [1905], 432-449; H. Schürmann, *Der Paschamahlbericht, Lk. 22:7-18* [1953].) The text in Mk. is probably more original than 1 C. (so Jeremias, 96; Bultmann Theol., 144, though cf. W. Marxsen, "Der Ursprung des Abendmahls," *Ev. Theol.,* 12 [1952/53], 293-303 and E. Schweizer, "Das joh. Zeugnis vom Herrenmahl," *Ev. Theol.,* 12 [1952/53], 341 f.). In literary form the accounts of institution reflect the liturgical tradition of the community.
[56] The independence of the two acts is not diminished even if Jesus had in view the flesh and blood of the paschal lamb, as conjectured by Jeremias, 105 f. and Walther, 47 f. → 156, n. 75.
[57] This is the more noteworthy in that it is contrary to Jewish practice, Str.-B., IV, 631; Jeremias, 83, 118 f.
[58] Acc. to a widely accepted line of exposition (→ I, 174, 24 ff.; Jeremias, 83 f., 91, 107-111) the gift of Jesus mentioned in the cup-saying is the death of Jesus in its significance from the standpoint of salvation history. Already during His ministry, however, He did not give any saving gift which could be detached from fellowship with His person. Paul and John both understood the words of institution along these lines, → n. 70 → 143 f.
[59] Bultmann Theol., 59, 144-147 rightly perceives that the wording of the texts implies sacramental eating and drinking but wrongly interprets them by analogy with the Hell.

Its nature is to be read in the first instance from its setting in salvation history : the earthly work of Jesus which in all historical probability concluded with the Supper, and the salvation event in the community, which was observed from the very first. [60] The earthly ministry was orientated, not to the *parousia* immediately after His violent death, but to an age of the Church. [61] At the supper characterised by the eschatological saying (→ 154, 5 ff.) Jesus, by handing out bread and wine along with the words of institution, promises that the table fellowship which during His earthly ministry had been the bodily symbol of the appropriation of salvation, would continue after His death until consummated in the eschatological banquet. [62] As the One who died for them, Jesus will so give Himself to His disciples when they partake of the bread and wine that He comes into them. [63] On the basis of the OT promise of the Spirit such a promise is quite possible on the lips of Jesus, Mk. 1:10 and par.; Mt. 10:20 par. Lk. 12:11 f.; cf. 2 K. 2:9 f. It became intelligible to the disciples through its fulfilment, namely, the coming of the exalted Lord in the Spirit, to which the events of Easter led up, Jn. 20:22. [64] The sacral meal of the primitive community (Ac. 2:42, 46) was never simply a continuation of the table fellowship of the incarnate ministry at which the risen Lord was now thought to be invisibly present. This idea [65] is a romantic fantasy which does not take note of the situation of the community from the standpoint of salvation history. The table fellowship of the days of incarnation is renewed only when the risen Lord eats and drinks with the disciples at the resurrection appearances, Ac. 10:41; cf. Lk. 24:30 f., 35, 43; Jn. 21:13. [66] These appearances however, are restricted to the first witnesses. The Lord is present to the community of Pentecost in such a way that He works in them as the Spirit. [67] As a physical concretion of fellowship with the Lord the sacrament corresponds to this age of the Church.

---

mysteries (cf. Theol., 293). Jeremias (88-99) and Kuhn (513-515, 521 f.) show in opposition to this view that philologically and historically the texts belong to Palestinian Judaism, and very probably go back to Jesus Himself. Nevertheless, on the basis of a principle of religio-historical analogy, they incorrectly conclude from the setting that the sayings have to be understood acc. to the thought-forms of Palestinian Judaism, so that they cannot be sacramental : Eating and drinking gives a share (Jeremias, 106, 112, 124) or symbolically ensures participation (Kuhn, 521, 523-527) in the atoning power of Jesus' death, of which the elements are an explanatory likeness. The setting in salvation history rather than the non-Chr. world discloses the true meaning of the sayings.

[60] The Supper has been related in various ways to OT salvation history (L. Goppelt, *Typos* [1939], 131-137, 173-176): The Synoptists relate it to the Passover, the feast of the first redemption within which it is set historically (→ 154, n. 49), and also to the blood of the covenant at Sinai. Paul relates it also to the miracles of bread and water in the wilderness, → 143, 2 ff. The NT regards these OT par., not as historical analogies, but as biblical types. Their contribution to an understanding of the Lord's Supper derives, then, from the work of Christ in the context of salvation history, → 146, 24 f.

[61] L. Goppelt, *Christentum u. Judt. im ersten u. zweiten Jhdt.* (1954), 67.

[62] In Jn. the parting discourses, which embody this promise, are appropriately put in place of the institution (Jn. 13-17). The Palestinian tradition of the establishment of a sacramental community meal by Jesus (1 C. 11:23-25), which Paul inherited hardly more than 10 yrs. after Jesus' death, finds an obvious starting-point in the earthly ministry ; there is none such in the situation of the primitive community.

[63] This appropriation was valid from the institution and came into effect with the death and resurrection (though cf. Stauffer Theol.³, 141-143).

[64] Cullmann, 18-23 over-emphasises the influence of the breaking of bread at the Easter appearances on the development of the liturgical meal of the primitive community.

[65] So H. Lietzmann, *Messe u. Herrenmahl* (1926), 250-255; Bultmann Theol., 59; Kuhn, 520. In contrast cf. Gaugler, 34 f. For a review of the question cf. E. Schweizer, "Das Abendmahl eine Vergegenwärtigung des Todes Jesu oder ein eschatologisches Freudenmahl?" ThZ, 2 (1946), 81-101.

[66] This is not yet, as M. Barth, 44 ff. would have it, the "new" drinking (Mk. 14:25 par. Mt. 26:29); the eschatological saying refers to the visible coming of the kingdom (→ n. 54), while the resurrection appearances are the last part of the *kenosis*, → 146, n. 9.

[67] Mt. 18:20; 28:20 is fulfilled along the lines of Ac. 4:31; Jn. 14:23.

The nature of the eating and drinking at the Lord's Supper is more specifically set forth by Paul and John. Acc. to Pl. this eating and drinking may be compared with the saving gifts of manna and water from the rock in the age of Moses (1 C. 10:3 f. → 146, 18 ff.) and also with partaking of sacrificial flesh or the cup of libation at the cultic meal (1 C. 10:18-21). [68] Only the first par. is used to interpret the Lord's Supper. Pl. refers to the second merely to forbid participation in the cultic meals of paganism, since this rules out participation in the Lord's Supper, → 157, 10 ff. The OT type makes it impossible to expound the Lord's Supper acc. to the notions of Hellen. religion. [69] The sacrament does not confer a share in salvation *ex opere operato,* 1 C. 10:5-13. It is an encounter with the saving work of God symbolically experienced by the people in the wilderness. If, however, partaking of the elements is neither magic nor mystery, it is also not the symbol of an event which takes place along with it. Simply by physical participation, the man who eats the broken bread and drinks the consecrated cup inescapably encounters the self-proffering of the risen Lord as the One who died for him. [70] Hence eating and drinking which is no more than a physical function turns the saving work of God encountered here into a judgment. [71] What is demanded, then, is an eating and drinking which differs from the usual, since in it man by faith [72] physically opens himself to the act of God which encounters him physically, 1 C. 11:27-32.

John in Jn. 6 speaks of a twofold eating and drinking of the life-giving gift of Jesus, which in both instances consists in Him, 6:35, 48, 57. In Jn. 6:26-51ab there is a formal borrowing from the vocabulary of Gnosticism; eating and drinking is the spiritual receiving of the self-offering of Jesus by faith, 6:35. In 6:51c-58 the language is that of the mysteries, and eating and drinking is a receiving through partaking of the eucharistic elements, → τρώγω. [73] As regards the material definition of the gift, however, this section is a development of the preceding section rather than an alternative. [74] It adds

---

[68] On discussion of 1 C. 10 cf. H. v. Soden, "Sakrament u. Ethik bei Pls.," *Urchr. u. Geschichte,* I (1951), 239-275; Lohmeyer, ThR (1937), 286-290; Ltzm. K.⁴, 181 ff.

[69] Hence one should not expound Pl.'s statements acc. to Hell. ideas, as has often been attempted since W. Heitmüller's *Taufe u. Abendmahl im Urchr.* (1911), 69-75.

[70] The αἷμα τοῦ Χριστοῦ in which this drinking grants participation (1 C. 10:16) is not the substance but the death of Jesus as a saving event, → I, 174, 21 ff. Participation is possible only through God's appointment and the self-proffering of the exalted Lord (hence 1 C. 12:13 : ἓν πνεῦμα ἐποτίσθημεν). The gift, then, is neither "the atoning power of the death of Jesus" (Jeremias, 124, cf. 115) nor "the crucified body of Christ, which as such (by virtue of the resurrection) is also the efficacious body of δόξα" (Bultmann Theol., 145). The former is an OT-Jewish notion, the latter is Hell. (→ 147, n. 22) and it cannot be reconciled with the strictly par. sayings about the αἷμα (Ign. was the first to abandon this parallelism, → 147, n. 22) → 147, n. 17.

[71] At 1 C. 11:29 A. Ehrhardt, "Sakrament u. Leiden," Ev. Theol., 7 (1947/48), 100 proposes the transl.: "He who eats and drinks, eats and drinks to himself condemnation if he does not make an exception for his person." But the progressive changes of meaning in formulae from the stem κρίνω in the context (Käsemann, *Anliegen,* 276 f.) and the material train of thought favour the traditional rendering : "He who eats and drinks, eats and drinks to himself condemnation if he does not distinguish the body (of the Lord) (from ordinary food)." On this view the physical penalties for unworthy eating (1 C. 11:27) mentioned in 1 C. 11:30 spring from the κρίμα, the divine sentence, not from the fact that an object which has divine power becomes the φάρμακον θανάτου to him who does not use it aright (the magical interpretation of Joh. W.; Ltzm. 1 K., *ad loc.*). The κρίμα, however, is not a subsequent penalty for unworthy eating (Lohmeyer, ThR [1937], 291); it is effected through the eating. He who eats unworthily, though he does not eat κρίμα instead of the body and blood (Schl. K., *ad loc.*), "brings about the κρίμα by his eating" (Bchm. K., I, *ad loc.* : κρίμα is an inner acc. of obj.). κρίμα is an effect of the self-offering of the crucified Lord when received, but not in faith ; it is its negative side (R. 8:3; 2 C. 5:14). Cf. materially Jn. 3:18 f.; Hb. 10:29.

[72] δοκιμαζέτω in 1 C. 11:28, as in 2 C. 13:5, finally involves the question of faith. This alone makes one "worthy" at the community meal, 1 C. 11:18 ff.; R. 14:23.

[73] Cf. Bultmann J., 166, n. 1.

[74] On the literary unity of Jn. 6 cf. J. Jeremias, "J. 6:51c-58 — redaktionell ?" ZNW, 44 (1952/53), 256 f.

that this life-giving gift is not just He who is incarnate (6:33, 41, 50) but He who died for the world (Jn. 6:51c, 53), whose reception gives life, and is possible, only because His dying is an ascent to the Father through which the Spirit comes into play (Jn. 6:60-63). [75] Similarly it is said of appropriation that reception of Jesus through faith must be a reception through taking the elements (Jn. 6:53). This is just as necessary to salvation as the unabridged incarnation of the Word (cf. 1 Jn. 5:6). Reception of Jesus takes place, not along with reception of the elements, but through it ; Jn. 6 speaks directly of an eating and drinking of the gift of flesh and blood mediated through the elements. Jn. here is not thinking ontically of the substances united with the elements. [76] He has in view the death of Jesus (Jn. 6:51c) which is proffered with the self-offering of Him who died for the world (Jn. 6:57), → 147, 16 ff.

According to the plain statements of the NT, then, eating and drinking in the Lord's Supper are a physical encounter with the physical self-offering of the exalted Lord, as the One who died for all, in the consecrated and proffered elements. This eating and drinking are to salvation if they express the physical openness of the whole man to the physical work of salvation which here encounters him in faith.

4. The Figurative Use of the Concept [77] (→ 139, 3 ff.).

a. The Drinking of the Cup of Wrath and Suffering. The man who undergoes God's judgment of wrath drinks the cup or wine of wrath (→ 149, 21 ff.). This may mean either that he is led astray by the power of the world (Rev. 18:3 → 151, 12 ff.) or that he suffers eternal torment (Rev. 14:10). Drinking the cup of suffering (→ 152, 6 ff.) is a metaphor for experiencing and taking to oneself the suffering sent by God (Mk. 10:38 f. par. Mt.; Mt. 26:42; Jn. 18:11). The expressions become so stereotyped that one may doubt whether there is in individual verses any great sense of the conceptual background (→ 139, 5 ff.).

b. The Drinking of the Water of Life (Jn. 4:13 f.; 7:37; cf. 6:35 → ὕδωρ). This is par. to the eating of the bread of life (Jn. 6:35, 50 f.; cf. 4:32). It signifies receiving the means of salvation offered by Jesus, and finally receiving Jesus Himself (→ n. 81), through faith. [78] Here the OT promise of the quenching of thirst in the age of salvation (→ 16, 11 ff.), to which Jn. 7:38b refers explicitly, is formally changed into the Gnostic idea of true drinking to quench the thirst for life (→ 138, 9 ff.). This is shown by the antithesis to natural drinking (Jn. 4:13; cf. 7:37a) [79] and to drinking in the past age of salvation (Jn. 4:12 f.; cf. 6:32 → 147, 15 ff.). This figurative ref. to drinking expresses certain essential aspects of faith. [80] Faith receives to itself that which truly gives life. [81] This reception is

---

[75] For this reason the sayings about the flesh are "spirit" (Jn. 6:63). The verse is not saying that in the last resort only the word brings life, as taught by E. Schweizer, op. cit., 362; against this cf. Schl. J., ad loc.

[76] As against Bultmann J., 162, 175; Theol., 145 f.

[77] Lk. 5:39 does not come under this head, since drinking here is used lit. in a parable.

[78] Mediation of this receiving through the sacrament (cf. Just. Dial., 14, 1; 114, 4) is expounded by Jn. differently. Drinking the water cannot be linked conceptually with baptism, not even after the manner of Cullmann (82-86), who refers to the occasional Gnostic practice of drinking the baptismal water (W. Bousset, Hauptprobleme d. Gnosis [1907], 293 and L. Fendt, Gnostische Mysterien [1922], 36).

[79] The situation sets the call of Jesus in antithesis to the dispensing of water at the Feast of Tabernacles, which was linked with prayer for rain, Str.-B., II, 799-805; J. Jeremias, Golgotha (1926), 60-64, 80-84.

[80] Cf. also the sayings about the "coming" of Jesus (v. Schl. on 5:40 and Bultmann J., 168, n. 4); Bultmann Theol., 416 f. over-schematises the expressions.

[81] Faith lets the word of Jesus (Jn. 8:37; 15:7), His Spirit (7:39; 14:17), Jesus Himself (6:56; 14:20; 15:4 f.), and therewith life (6:53), dwell within it.

possible only after the lifting up of Jesus (Jn. 7:39). It leads to a corresponding giving forth (Jn. 7:38). [82]

† πόμα, † πόσις, † ποτόν, † πότος.

1. The Usage.

τὸ πόμα (Pind. Nem., 3, 79 and later poets, also Ionic and later prose, Hdt., III, 23, also LXX for ancient Attic πῶμα): "drink," "beverage," in the NT 1 C. 10:4; 12:13 (vl.); Hb. 9:10; cf. Ign. R., 7, 3.

ἡ πόσις (from Hom. often with → βρῶσις, e.g., Hom. Od., 10, 176, so the only OT instance Da. Θ 1:10 and always in the NT): a. "the act of drinking," "drinking," R. 14:17; Col. 2:16; b. "what one drinks," "drink," Jn. 6:55.

τὸ ποτόν, which is common from Hom., also LXX, means "what is drinkable," "drink." In primitive Chr. literature it occurs only in the post-apost. fathers, Did., 10, 3; Ign. Tr., 2, 3. ὁ πότος (Xenoph., Plat. etc., LXX) means "drinking-bout," "carouse." 1 Pt. 4:3.

2. The Material Use of the Terms in the NT.

a. In the Attitude to Legal-Ritual and Ascetic-Dualistic Questions.

Acc. to Hb. 9:10 the sacrificial laws of the OT, [1] like the statutes concerning βρώματα (→ I, 643, 6 ff.) and πόματα, [2] are only δικαιώματα σαρκός, "carnal ordinances" (→ II, 221, 27 f.). That is, they are laws which relate only to man's physical, earthly existence, which is delivered up to temptation and death. They cannot reach beyond this existence. Hence they are only "imposed until the time of a better order" (Hb. 9:10b). Along with the whole of the old covenant, the rules of food and drink are set aside by the new covenant for all those for whom it is present (→ 141, 5 ff.). [3] Along these lines the NT generally teaches that, although all means of nourishment are pure in themselves, since they are God's creation, [4] they are so only for him who has the pure heart which brings the new covenant. [5] On the basis of the fact that a new world has dawned in Christ's resurrection Col. 2:16 can thus give the admonition : "Let no one judge you in respect of eating and drinking" (ἐν βρώσει καὶ ἐν πόσει). A Gnostic, Judaistic

---

[82] ὁ πιστεύων as an abs. nominative belongs to the next sentence ; αὐτοῦ probably relates to the one who drinks rather than the one who dispenses.

π ό μ α, π ό σ ι ς. Bibl. → πίνω bibl.

[1] ἐπί is cumulative, Rgg. Hb. and H. Strathmann Hb. (NT Deutsch), ad loc. μόνον ... ἐπικείμενα in v. 10 is best understood in apposition to δῶρα καὶ θυσίαι in v. 9, Rgg. and Strathmann, ad loc.

[2] The ref. is to the laws of Levitically unclean drinks, Lv. 11:33 f., 36; Hag. 2:12 f. It can hardly be to the rules of priestly abstinence in Lv. 10:9 (Strathmann Hb., ad loc.). In the rational explanations of the laws of purity in Ep. Ar. "drink" simply occurs formally with "food," and no specific examples are given (Ep. Ar., 128, 142, 162). A similar explanation is given of the laws of sacrifice (170).

[3] Unlike Hell. Judaism (Ep. Ar., 128-171) and early Catholicism (Goppelt, op. cit. [→ 142, n. 61], 294-296, 304 f.), Hb. does not distinguish the cultic and ceremonial laws of sacrifice and cleanness from the abiding moral commandments. It characterises the central OT order of expiation as inadequate and provisional, putting it on the same level as the peripheral ceremonial statutes.

[4] R. 14:14; 1 C. 10:26; 1 Tm. 4:4.

[5] This christological argument is also used in Paul (→ 145, 27 ff.), Past. (1 Tm. 4:4; Tt. 1:15) and Ac. (10:15; 15:9).

error, [6] obviously with an ascetic-dualistic intention (Col. 2:23 : ἀφειδίᾳ σώμα-τος), and with a ref. to cosmic powers (Col. 2:20), demands times of fasting or probably permanent abstention from certain foods and drinks. [7] Similarly the injunction to the "strong" in Rome (R. 14:21 → 141, 7 ff.) not to give offence to the "weak" (→ I, 492, 3 ff.) is finally based on the statement in R. 14:17: οὐ γάρ ἐστιν ἡ βασιλεία τοῦ θεοῦ βρῶσις καὶ πόσις (→ I, 642, 28 ff.). [8] Since eating and drinking serve to preserve the physical, earthly body by nourishment, they have no more to do with the dominion of God than earthly food itself (R. 14:15; 1 C. 8:8). For the rule of God brings the union of the heart with God and, as the instruments of new action, a new corporeality and a new world (1 C. 6:13; 15:50; cf. Mk. 12:25 and par.). [9] Nevertheless, Christ does not bring redemption from the body; He brings the redemption of the body. Hence eating and drinking express physical action, and to this extent they are not indifferent matters, as in Gnosticism (1 C. 15:32 → 139, 41 ff.). They are simply free from attachment to the form of this world, so that they are practised, not self-assertively in the world, but in obedience, R. 14:21; 1 C. 10:31-33.

b. In Statements about the Lord's Supper.

Acc. to 1 C. 10:3 f. (→ 143, 2 ff.) the people of the old covenant, having been baptised in the Red Sea (1 C. 10:2), constantly received πνευματικὸν βρῶμα (→ I, 643, 19 ff.) and πνευματικὸν πόμα during the wilderness wandering to the promised land. [10] In the Pauline congregations, esp. at Corinth, [11] "spiritual food" and "spiritual drink" were probably current expressions for the distributed eucharistic elements [12] (Did., 10, 3 : πνευματικὴν τροφὴν καὶ ποτόν).

What happened to Israel prefigures typologically that which is given in the last time (1 C. 10:11). [13] In both the OT and the NT community spiritual food and spiritual drink are not that which is proffered along with the elements; they are the elements themselves in their efficacy. → πνευματικός does not mean here improperly [14] or supraterrestri-ally, [15] but according to the manner of the Spirit of God. [16] Manna and water in the

---

[6] Cf. G. Bornkamm, "Die Häresie d. Kol.," ThLZ, 73 (1948), 11-20, esp. 16.

[7] Col. 2:21: μὴ ἅψῃ μηδὲ γεύσῃ μηδὲ θίγῃς; cf. E. Percy, Die Probleme d. Kolosser-u. Epheserbr. (1946), 140-142. A similar demand is raised by the related error combatted in the Past. (1 Tm. 4:3; Tt. 1:14 f.), cf. 1 Tm. 5:23, with its probable tilt at the sectaries : μηκέτι ὑδροπότει, ἀλλὰ οἴνῳ ὀλίγῳ χρῶ.

[8] The apparent par. in bBer., 17a: "In the future world there is no eating and drinking, no begetting and propagation . . .," refers to the heavenly world of souls, not to the kingdom of the consummation (acc. to Str.-B., I, 890).

[9] The eating and drinking of the risen Lord with His disciples (→ 142, 18 ff.) is designed originally to denote the resuming of fellowship with them rather than to demonstrate a corporeality which no longer needs this food. At the final banquet the drinking will be new (→ III, 449, 9 f.) (Mk. 14:25 par. Mt. 26:29). Its nature is hidden like that of the new corporeality (1 C. 15:35-44).

[10] Ex. 17:6; Nu. 20:7-11; → 97, 13 ff. πέτρα, cf. J. Jeremias, Golgotha (1926), esp. 84.

[11] → πνευματικός 25 times in the NT, 14 in 1 C.

[12] So acc. to F. Dibelius, Das Abendmahl (1911), 110 and Joh. W. 1 K., ad loc.; E. Käse-mann, "Das Abendmahl im NT," Abendmahlsgemeinschaft (1937), 74.

[13] The events of the wilderness period are not just models of those of the last time (→ 142, n. 60), nor are they identical with them (so E. Käsemann, "Anliegen u. Eigenart d. paul. Abendmahlslehre," Ev. Theol., 7 [1947/48], 268). The common feature is their correspondence from the standpoint of salvation history.

[14] Sickb. K., ad loc.

[15] Ltzm. K. and Joh. W., 1 K., ad loc., → I, 643, 20-24.

[16] Schl. K. and Bchm. K., ad loc. The interpretation of the rock (1 C. 10:4) forces us to take the term in this christological sense.

desert, or bread and wine acc. to the interpretative sayings (→ 157, 1 ff.), are the gift and (thereby at least) the vehicle of the saving work of God mediated through Christ. [17] As such they offer the possibility of living by God's work in faith and obedience, whether historically on the one side or eschatologically on the other. [18] They are not, as the Corinthians believed, a magical means of bringing immortality to the soul, so that physical obedience is not required (→ 143, 7 ff.). After reception of the Eucharist the Did. first gives thanks for the γνῶσις καὶ πίστις καὶ ἀθανασία mediated through Christ (10, 2), then for πνευματικὴ τροφὴ καὶ ποτὸν καὶ ζωὴ αἰώνιος. [19] The combination of the two formulae excludes a magical misunderstanding and includes faith.

Did., 10, 3 f. extols the eucharistic gift as the fulfilment of the gifts of creation which confer temporal life. Jn. 6:55 depicts it as the ἀληθής [20] (true, genuine, → I, 248, 23 ff.) βρῶσις or πόσις. It thus sets it in antithesis to all that which serves to maintain earthly life, including manna, Jn. 6:31 f. [21]

Materially, however, this is not the Gnostic antithesis to creation and OT salvation history. It is the ancient biblical antithesis to the attempt to live solely in terms of the natural environment, → I, 644, 8 ff.; → 139, 12 f. The distributed elements are not here the true food or drink which gives life (→ 138, 9 ff.). This role is filled directly by that which acc. to the words of institution they impart, namely, flesh or blood. Here too, however, that which is associated with the elements is not a substance but an event, which takes place when they are distributed and taken. Even more plainly than σῶμα the term → σάρξ, [22] with the par. αἷμα (→ 143, n. 70), points to the crucifixion, which in the way intimated in Jn. 6:62 f. (→ 144, 1 ff.) becomes the true bread of life through the self-impartation of Him who is lifted up, yet also through real (→ n. 20) eating and drinking.

A misunderstanding of the eucharistic gifts along the lines of a materialisation of the divine, as in magic or the mysteries, is first found in the post-canonical writings, be-

---

[17] Käsemann, 267: "βρῶμα and πόμα πνευματικόν are ... food and drink which transfer the Spirit ..." This view over-hellenises the apostle's concept of the πνεῦμα (cf. Käsemann, op. cit. [→ n. 12], 76 : "The elements ... are bearers of the heavenly pneuma-substance") and contradicts his view of the position of the OT community in salvation history (2 C. 3:7-18, cf. Jn. 7:39); 1 C. 12:13 : πνεῦμα ἐποτίσθημεν applies primarily to the eschatological fulfilment, not the type. Cf. the later (demythologising) interpretation of Käsemann, ibid., 271: "The sacramental gift of the pneuma is not for the apostle ... a kind of heavenly force ... The gift gives its Giver ; it is the mode of appearing of the exalted Lord, who is manifest in it." Here, however, the cross is so strongly pushed into the background that the author can no longer do justice to 1 C. 10:16a (ibid., 264 f.) → 143, n. 70; 157, 3 ff.

[18] In this sense 1 C. 12:13b can say of the Lord's Supper : πνεῦμα ἐποτίσθημεν, → n. 17.

[19] In both instances the last word is a hendiadys alongside the first two.

[20] So 𝔖 pm Cl; ἀληθῶς in ℵ*D al lat sy. This reading can give a sense also suggested by ἀληθής, namely, that Jesus' flesh is real food, His blood real drink. But this is emphasised already by → τρώγω. Jn's general approach suggests the meaning given above.

[21] Cf. the similar antithesis in Ign. R., 7, 3 : "I have no joy in corruptible food and the joys of this life, I desire God's bread ... and His blood as drink (πόμα)." The renunciation of living by what this world has to offer, and the desire for true food such as is offered in the Lord's Supper, is here a metaphor for the desire for martyrdom. In martyrdom that which the Supper offers to faith becomes sight ; by sharing in Christ's death there is sharing in His immortality. This shows that the vivid image of φάρμακον ἀθανασίας (Ign. Eph., 20, 2) is not to be taken so magically as it often is. Ign. Tr., 2, 3 : "Not for foods and drinks (ποτῶν) are they deacons, but servants of the Church of God." Even if there is here a ref. to the deacons distributing the elements, an antithesis is at least not pronounced.

[22] Ign., on the basis of his definitely changed anthropology, is the first to describe the eucharistic gift (Sm., 7, 1) as (τὴν) σάρκα ... Ἰησοῦ Χριστοῦ, τὴν ὑπὲρ τῶν ἁμαρτιῶν ἡμῶν παθοῦσαν, ἣν ... ὁ πατὴρ ἤγειρεν. The idea of resurrection is incompatible with the Johannine and NT concept of σάρξ (Lk. 24:39 is the only exception in the NT); it is the earthly existence which is condemned to die (cf. Jn. 3:5 f.) and which Jesus has given up to death (6:51b). → 143, n. 70.

ginning with Ign. (→ n. 22), though the polemic of 1 C. 10 shows that it had been present long before. Justin presupposes as an established ecclesiastical teaching : οὐ γὰρ ὡς κοινὸν ἄρτον οὐδὲ κοινὸν πόμα ταῦτα λαμβάνομεν· ἀλλ᾽ ὃν τρόπον διὰ λόγου θεοῦ σαρκοποιηθεὶς ᾽Ιησοῦς Χριστὸς ὁ σωτὴρ ἡμῶν καὶ σάρκα καὶ αἷμα ὑπὲρ σωτηρίας ἡμῶν ἔσχεν, οὕτως καὶ τὴν δι᾽ εὐχῆς λόγου τοῦ παρ᾽ αὐτοῦ εὐχαριστηθεῖσαν τροφήν, ἐξ ἧς αἷμα καὶ σάρκες κατὰ μεταβολὴν τρέφονται ἡμῶν, ἐκείνου τοῦ σαρκοποιηθέντος ᾽Ιησοῦ καὶ σάρκα καὶ αἷμα ἐδιδάχθημεν εἶναι (Apol., I, 66). There is, of course, no discussion of the manner of this ontically intended equation. Irenaeus bases his rejection of Docetic Christology on this doctrine of the Lord's Supper (Iren. Haer., IV, 18, 5; V, 2, 2 f.).

† ποτήριον.

Contents : 1. The Usage. 2. The Cup in the Literal Sense (Mt. 23:25 f. par. Lk. 11:39 f.). 3. The Figurative Use : a. The Cup of Wrath ; b. The Cup of Suffering. 4. The Cup at the Lord's Supper : a. The Cup in the Eschatological Saying Lk. 22:17 f.; b. The Cup of the Interpretative Saying ; c. The Cup of the Lord and the Cup of Demons (1 C. 10).

1. The Usage.

τὸ ποτήριον (from Alcaeus, 34 [Diehl]; Sappho Suppl., 55a, 10 [Diehl], Hdt., II, 37; III, 148): "drinking-vessel," "goblet," "cup." In the LXX the word is essentially equivalent to כּוֹס, [1] in most instances fig. (→ 149, 20 ff.). The word is rare in non-bibl. Gk. [2] It has analogies and roots in the ancient Orient, → 150, 8 ff.

In the Palestinian home [3] the drinking-vessel (כּוֹס, generally כְּלִי מַשְׁקֶה 1 K. 10:21) was the pitcher (צַפַּחַת or כַּד) which stood filled on the table ; it was usually an earthen bowl (also סֵפֶל = λεκάνη), [4] though vessels of stone and metal are found from ancient times, [5] and of glass from the Hell. period. [6] Coins of the time of Simon Maccabaeus depict a true cup with stem. [7] Except in Ps. 116:13 ποτήριον = כּוֹס is not mentioned among the many vessels used in the temple ministry. [8] In non-bibl. Gk., however, the word is common in lists of temple furnishings. [9]

ποτήριον. T. Klauser and S. Grün, Art. "Becher," RAC, II, 37-62; on 3. a : H. Gressmann, *Der Ursprung d. isr.-jüd. Eschatologie* (1905), 129-136; also "Der Festbecher," *Sellin-Festschr.* (1927), 55-62; W. Lotz, "Das Sinnbild des Bechers," NKZ, 28 (1917), 396-407; J. G. Davies, "The Cup of Wrath and the Cup of Blessing," *Theology*, 51 (1948), 178-180; on 5 → πίνω Bibl., also E. Huber, *Das Trankopfer im Kulte der Völker* (1929); F. J. Dölger, "Der Kelch der Dämonen," *Ant. Christ.*, IV, 266-270.

[1] Once (Is. 51:17) for קֻבַּעַת, for which the largely synon. τὸ κόνδυ is used in Is. 51:22 ("goblet"); this occurs for גְּבִיעַ at Gn. 44:2, 12, 16 f.; the two Heb. words denote a larger cup. In Gk. as in Hb. there is a large no. of words for drinking-vessels ; so far not all of these can be identified with the various kinds of vessels discovered (for the Gk. cf. T. Klauser, RAC, II, 37-39, for the Heb. → n. 8).

[2] For instances of the fig. use in the Gk.-Rom. world, Klauser, RAC, II, 46 f.

[3] For Hell. and oriental archaeological material, Klauser, 37-39, 47.

[4] G. Dalman, *Arbeit u. Sitte in Palästina*, IV (1935), 390; VII (1942), 227-229.

[5] Golden cups are mentioned in 1 K. 10:21; 2 Ch. 9:20; Jer. 51:7; Rev. 17:4.

[6] Dalman, VII, 229.

[7] *Ibid.*, IV, 391.

[8] The LXX mentions the following cup-like vessels in the temple : τὸ σπονδεῖον, "vessel," "bowl" for cultic alms (קְשָׂוָה, "can"); ἡ φιάλη "bowl" (→ n. 89), almost always מִזְרָק, "sacrificial vessel or bowl," only Prv. 23:31 (Heb. כּוֹס) and Cant. 5:13; 6:2 (poetic) not of cultic vessels, in the Rabb. a loan-word פֵּילָא; ἡ θυΐσκη "censer" (almost always כַּף, "bowl"); ὁ κύαθος, "scoop" (always for מְנַקִּית, drink-offering "bowl"). There are no LXX renderings of כְּפוֹר ("bowl") and סַף ("basin") in the LXX. For ill. cf. C. Watzinger, *Denkmäler Palästinas,* I (1933), esp. ill. 42.

[9] Ditt. Syll., I, 144, 10; 495, 10; III, 1099, 10; Ditt. Or., I, 214, 10.

2. The Cup in the Literal Sense (Mt. 23:25 f. par. Lk. 11:39 f.).

The NT refers to the cup of everyday use in Mk. 9:41 par. Mt. 10:42 and Mk. 7:4. In addition, this occurs in the saying of Jesus to Pharisaism preserved in two versions at Mt. 23:25 f. and Lk. 11:39-41. According to OT Law impurities were to be wiped from the inside of vessels. [10] The Pharisee goes beyond this and makes a difficult attempt to keep clean τὸ ἔξωθεν τοῦ ποτηρίου (Mt. 23:25; Lk. 11:39, τὸ ἐκτὸς αὐτοῦ in Mt. 23:26). [11] But this is blind hypocrisy, for he overlooks the fact that the inside — the inside of the cup in Mt. [12] — is unclean, even though he himself naturally regards it as more important. For Jesus the inside of the cup is clean, and hence the whole vessel, if its contents are not the proceeds of robbery, i.e., greed and avarice (cf. Mk. 12:40 par. Lk. 20:47; Lk. 16:14) and are not regarded with pleasure-seeking desire, [13] i.e., if they are in the hands of a man who is pure of heart, Mt. 7:20 par. Mt. 15:18. [14] The demand for purity of heart follows from the demand for cleansing of the cup, but is not the figurative meaning of this, as in the interpretation introduced already by Lk. (11:39 : τὸ ἔσωθεν ὑμῶν). [15] Jesus shows the Pharisee the way of conversion, not by a metaphor, but more profoundly by an illustration from everyday life, the cup on his table.

3. The Figurative Use.

a. The Cup of Wrath.

The metaphor of the cup of wrath, which is found in Rev., derives directly from the OT. In half of the 28 instances of כוֹס or ποτήριον in the OT, we find the image of the cup in or from the hand of Yahweh (Ps. 75:8; Is. 51:17; Jer. 25:15; Hab. 2:16). It is a leading theme in the judgments on the nations in Jer. 25:15-38; 46-51, [16] which it introduces : "Thus saith Yahweh ... Take this cup (the wine is wrath) out of my hand, and cause all the nations, to whom I send thee, to drink it. And they shall drink, and be moved, and be mad, because of the sword that I shall send among them," Jer. 25:15 f., cf. 25:17, 27 f.; 49:12; 51:7. The same thought is present in Hab. 2:16 and Lam. 4:21, also Ez. 23:31-34; Dt. Is. 51:17-23; Ps. 75:8. The contents of the cup, as rightly indicated in the gloss on Jer. 25:15, are the judicial wrath of God. Like an intoxicating drink, [17] this robs the one who must drink it (→ 139, 3 ff.) of his senses, and causes him to stagger and fall, so that he cannot stand up again. [18] Hence in Ez. and Dt. Is. the cup is expressly called the cup of astonishment and stupefaction (Ez. 23:33), or the cup of staggering (τὸ ποτήριον τῆς πτώσεως) or cup of fury (τὸ ποτήριον or τὸ κόνδυ τοῦ θυμοῦ), Is. 51:17, 22. Handing the cup means bringing under wrathful judgment,

---

[10] Lv. 11:33; 15:12, cf. Str.-B., I, 934 f.; Dalman, IV, 391.

[11] He does not merely dip it in water when unclean (Mk. 7:4; Str.-B., I, 935 f.) but is anxiously concerned to keep the outside from being bespattered (Schl. Mt. and J. Schniewind Mt. [NT Deutsch], ad loc.).

[12] Mt. 23:25 : ἔσωθεν, 23:26 : τὸ ἐντός, which is in the first instance the inside.

[13] Acc. to Kl. Mt., ad loc.

[14] With this view of purity Jesus does not merely set aside legalistic casuistry and the hypocrisy of Pharisaism which uses it ; He also sets aside the OT law of purity which is the basis of both.

[15] Dalman WJ, I, 50, 372 rightly rejects the suggestion (J. Wellhausen, Einl. in die drei ersten Evangelien² [1911], 27) that Luke gives a more correct rendering of an Aram. original. The adding of ὑμῶν confuses the sense of the whole saying, as vacillation in the exposition of Lk. 11:40 f. shows.

[16] Even if in whole or in part this was not written by Jer., it is close to his time.

[17] It contains wine (Jer. 25:15; 51:7; Ps. 75:8), and yet not wine (Is. 51:21).

[18] Is. 51:17, 20; Jer. 25:15 f., 27.

and passing it on the movement of judgment from one nation to another, Is. 51:22; Jer. 49:12; Ez. 23:31; Hab. 2:16. The comparison of wrath with an intoxicating drink, and of judgment with drunkenness, developed independently of the image of the cup. [19] The cup, however, is not here, as in other cup-images (→ n. 39), the mere bearer of the contents. It has its own symbolical significance. Handing the cup is not the proffering of a host ; it is the majestic act of a mighty one. In Hab. 2:15 f. it stands in juxtaposition to forced drinking at the table of the great. But the image contains more than the transferred use of table customs. [20] The cup in Yahweh's hand reminds us of the cup which is found in the hands of deities in illustrations from Babylonia, probably as a sign of their control of destiny. [21] This is perhaps the ultimate basis of the idea. [22] In the hand of the holy and righteous God of the covenant the cup of destiny becomes the cup of judgment. [23] The cup of Yahweh represents God's judicial sway in history, His power to judge. Ps. 75:7 f. "For God is the judge : he putteth down one, and setteth up another. For in the hand of the Lord there is a cup ... even the dregs thereof ... all the wicked of the earth shall drink them." Hence the cup can be directly equated with the cosmic power which as God's judicial power executes His judgment ; Jer. 51:7: "Babylon is a golden cup in Yahweh's hand, making all the earth drunken ..." [24]

The metaphor still occurs in later Judaism. Hab. 2:16 is expounded thus in Hab. Midr., XI, 14 f.: "The cup of God's wrath will destroy him ('the ungodly priest') by increasing ... and sufferings ..." (text corrupt). Ps. Sol. 8:14 f.: "Wherefore (God) gave them a cup of unmixed wine to intoxicate them. He brought on ... ordained war on Jerusalem ..." Rabb. exegesis harmonised the most diverse OT statements. The cup symbolises the judicial distributions of God which bring punishments on the nations but temporal punishment and then gracious consolations on Israel. This idea is also associated with the Paschal cup, jPes., 10, 37c, 5; [25] the four Passover cups "correspond to the four cups of punishment which God will some day cause the nations of the world to drink, Jer. 25:15; 51:7; Ps. 75:8; 11:6 ... and corresponding to them God will some day cause

---

[19] Jer. 13:13; 51:39; Ob. 16; Na. 3:11; Ps. 11:6; 60:3.

[20] Nowadays attempts are made to derive the metaphor, not from observation of the effects of intoxicating drink (Lotz, 404 f.), nor from the changing of a banquet of salvation into one of wrath (Gressmann, *Eschatologie,* 135), but from the mantic cup (Gn. 44:5), which is originally a means of prophesying and then becomes a symbol of destiny (P. Volz, *Der Prophet Jer.*² [1928], 393), or from the cup of poison which the condemned must drink (cf. R. Kittel, *Die Ps.* ⁵,⁶ [1929] on Ps. 75:8), though this was not customary in oriental jurisprudence (Gressmann, *Sellin-Festschr.,* 60), or from the cup of poison which in God's judgment (cf. Nu. 5:11 ff.) brings death to the guilty and acquittal to the innocent (H. Schmidt, *Die Ps.* [1935] on Ps. 75:8).

[21] AOB, No. 45, cf. 42; M. Jastrow, *Bildermappe z. Religion Babyloniens u. Assyriens* (1912), Ill. 86 and 97; B. Meissner, *Babylonien u. Assyrien* (1920), Plate 17. Acc. to the usual view the water of life is proffered in the vessels depicted ; they express the loftiness of destiny (Gressmann, *Sellin-Festschr.,* 61).

[22] Gressmann, *op. cit.,* 61, also H. Gunkel, *Die Ps.* (1929) and R. Kittel, *op. cit.* on Ps. 75:8.

[23] In the OT, then, the cup is not, as often maintained (e.g., Pr.-Bauer, *s.v.*; Str.-B., I, 836), a symbol of destiny in the good sense as well as the bad. There is approximation to this in the weak expressions in Ps. 11:6 and 16:5 Each has "his portion of the cup," or perhaps "his cup" in Ps. 16:5, LXX ἡ μερὶς ... τοῦ ποτηρίου μου. His lot is distributed to him by God as by a father. This use is close to the symbolical significance variously ascribed to a cup. Ps. 23:5 : "My cup is fulness"; the full cup always allotted to the righteous (at the sacrificial meal) signifies the grace of God granted to him. Ps. 116:13 (115:4): "The cup of deliverances" (ποτήριον σωτηρίου); this is the cup which is lifted up as a thank-offering for deliverance (Kittel, *ad loc.*), or the cup which has brought saving acquittal in God's judgment (Nu. 5:11 ff., Schmidt, *ad loc.*). At a mourning feast in Israel the cup of consolation (ποτήριον εἰς παράκλησιν, Jer. 16:7) was handed to the mourners as well as the bread of consolation, cf. Ez. 24:17.

[24] Cf. Zech. 12:2 → n. 33.

[25] Str.-B., I, 836 f., cf. J. Jeremias, *Die Abendmahlsworte Jesu*² (1949), 32.

Israel to drink four cups of consolations," Ps. 16:5; 23:5; 116:13 (plur. 2). S. Dt., 324 (138b) on 32:34 (Str.-B., I, 837): "... (Ps. 75:8) ... From that drop the generation of the flood, ... Pharaoh, Nebuchadnezzar ... have drunk, and from that drop all that come into the world will one day drink ... Thus it says (Jer. 51:7): 'Babylon was a golden cup ...' As it is of the nature of gold to be capable of restoration when broken, so punishment, when it has turned away from the nations, will one day return to them ... As it is of the nature of an earthen vessel to be incapable of restoration when broken, so punishment, when it has turned aside from Israel, will no more return to them." [26]

Here, too, Rev. makes independent use of the OT. The harlot Babylon has in her hand a golden cup "full of abominations and filthiness of her fornication" (17:4, cf. Jer. 51:7). The cup signifies the influence of this world capital on the nations. Its contents, proffered in the magnificent vessel (χρυσοῦν?) of power and beneficence (17:18; 18:3), are the abomination of idolatry and the corresponding moral declension. These contents are elsewhere called ὁ οἶνος τοῦ θυμοῦ τῆς πορνείας αὐτῆς (Rev. 14:8; 18:3, cf. 17:2, based on Ιερ. 28:7 [51:7b], cf. Hab. 2:15), "the wine of wrath of her fornication" [27] (→ III, 167, 24 ff.). This drink is the wine of wrath, not merely because wrath smites those who drink it (Rev. 14:9 f.), [28] but primarily because God's wrath hands them the drink. [29] The cup in Babylon's hand is thus the symbol of her divinely given power (13:5, cf. Jn. 19:11) not merely to subjugate the nations by force and propaganda (Rev. 13) but also to subject them inwardly to her self-deification. The eschatological power of God's wrath comes to light in this power of Babylon. It gives up to the sphere of Antichrist all those whose names are not in the book of life (13:8, cf. R. 1:24). At the appointed hour this divinely given power passes to others and turns against those who previously possessed it. In 18:6 there is a summons to the nations who in the service of Antichrist, but really in that of God (17:15-18), trample down Babylon: "Reward ... unto her double according to her works; in the cup which she hath filled fill to her double." He who is charged to hand this cup to others becomes for them the agent of God's wrath. The summons is a fulfilment of the resolve of Rev. 16:19: "And great Babylon came in remembrance before God, to give unto her the cup of the wine of the fierceness of his wrath." As Babylon falls victim to the power of judgment conferred on historical powers, all the individuals who succumbed to the cult of world power will fall victim to the power of God's wrath in its pure and definitive form when the Last Judgment draws the concluding line under history: "They shall drink of the wine of the wrath of God, which is poured out without mixture (→ V, 165, 17 ff.) into the cup of his indignation," Rev. 14:10. According to v. 10b this means eternal damnation. Thus the wine and the cup refer to many different events in Rev., but ultimately they denote one and the same reality (→ V, 165, 14 ff.). The wine is a picture

---

[26] In Philo ποτήριον occurs only in Som., II, 200 and 203, but he uses synonyms to describe the cup as the vessel in which the soul receives the divine gift (Som., II, 246 ff.) or in which it or the *logos* proffers itself (Som., II, 183, cf. Ebr., 152) → 138, 12 ff. Cf. 4 Esr. 14:38 ff., → 137, n. 23. Cf. Pist. Soph., 147 (I, 252): "As man rises up out of hyle, a helper brings him a cup filled with thoughts and wisdom, and soberness is found in it, and he hands it to the soul."

[27] "The wine of her passionate licentiousness" is a possible rendering, but it is not the sense here.

[28] J. Behm, *Die Offenbarung d. Joh.* (*NT Deutsch*) on 14:9 and Loh. Apk. on 14:8.

[29] Bss. Apk. and Had. Apk. on 14:8 (→ III, 168, 6 ff.; V, 437, 12 ff.). In 14:10 and 16:19, too, the wine of wrath is not a wine which brings on wrath but a wine which consists of wrath.

of God's active wrath, not only in 14:10; 16:19; 19:15, but also in 14:8 [30] (17:2) [31] and 18:3. Similarly, the cup is a picture of the power of God's wrathful judgment [32] not merely when it is in God's hand (14:10; 16:19) but also when it is temporarily and partially lent to historical powers in various manifestations (17:4; 18:6), even though it has the form of temptation to idolatry (17:4). [33]

b. The Cup of Suffering.

In the cup-saying addressed to the sons of Zebedee (Mk. 10:38 f. par. Mt. 20:22 f.) and again in the cup-saying in Gethsemane (Mk. 14:36 par. Mt. 26:39; Lk. 22:42; cf. Jn. 18:11), Jesus refers to "this cup" (Mk. 14:36 and par.) and characterises it as "the cup that I drink of" (Mk. 10:38 par. Mt. 20:22), i.e., the cup which is laid on Him, the cup of His death and passion. When the sons of Zebedee ask for a special share in His kingly rule, [34] the reply of Jesus is an intimation not merely of the bearing of the cross [35] which applies to all disciples but of martyrdom. [36, 37] The question : "Can ye drink of the cup that I drink of ?" has in view, not resolution for the act but acceptance of that which God has ordained → 144, 22 ff. The significance and force of what Jesus intimates to the brothers may be perceived only when Jesus Himself, trembling and hesitant, asks that "this cup" may pass from Him (Mt. 26:39, cf. 42) or be taken from Him (Mk. 14:36; Lk. 22:42). Only through wrestling in prayer does He attain to the readiness expressed in Jn. 18:11: "The cup which my Father hath given me, shall I not drink it ?" The more precise definition of the term by the use of the demonstrative pronoun or relative clause suggests that "cup" here simply means destiny or fate (esp. in the evil sense). In this use the OT image of the cup is on the margin [38] of primitive Christianity and belongs to its environment. [39] Materially,

---

[30] The forced ποτίζειν (14:8) finds a par. in the forced passing on of the cup (18:6), → 151, 29 ff.

[31] Wrath can seduce into idolatry as well as smite the idolater, → V, 166, 1 ff. This is confirmed by the adding of θυμός to πορνεία in 14:8; 18:3.

[32] The cup as such stands for the power which shapes history, but this is judicial power, and consequently wrath. In Rev. all judgment (κρίνειν, κρίσις, κρίμα) is wrath (ὀργή, θυμός, cf. Rev. 19:11, 15); the hour of judgment (14:7; 20:12 f.) is the day of wrath (6:16 f.; 14:10, 19); all wrath is also judgment (cf. 16:1 and 5:7 etc.). But the imagery (cup, vial, wine, winepress) is always related to wrath, not judgment.

[33] The vial of wrath (15:7; 16:1: φιάλη τοῦ θυμοῦ) denotes the accumulation of wrath (cf. R. 2:5). Acc. to Zech. 12:2 Jerusalem in the last days will be a vial of staggering (סַף־רַעַל) for the nations which come up against it. As a cup, it is not, like Babylon (Jer. 51:7), an active historical power, but the inviolable sanctuary of God, the stone of stumbling. The transition from cup to vial is fluid ; Tg. Is. 51:17 reads פַּיְילֵי כָסָא דִּלְוָטָא "the vial of the cup of his curse," → n. 8.

[34] At the side of His royal throne (Schl. Mt., ad loc. cf. Mt. 19:28; Lk. 22:29 f.) or of His seat of honour at the Messianic banquet (Jeremias, op. cit., 100).

[35] Mk. 8:34 par.; Mt. 10:38 f. par. Lk. 14:27; 17:33; Mt. 5:11 par. Lk. 6:22.

[36] In Mk. there is a par. to the drinking of the cup in the baptism of death, the overflowing which extinguishes earthly life (→ I, 538, 28 ff., V, 436, 19 ff.). It is an open question whether Mk. saw in the formal harmony a ref. to the two Chr. sacraments.

[37] For bibl. on the discussion of the meaning of this prophecy, which in ancient tradition was fulfilled only in James, not John, cf. Pr.-Bauer, s.v. ποτήριον 2.

[38] Ps. 11:6; 16:5 → n. 23. Many comm. (e.g., Kl. Mk. on 10:38) also refer to Is. 51:17, 22, Ez. 23:32 f. because they wrongly take the cup there to be a symbol of destiny, → n. 23.

[39] The Rabb. harmonising of the cup-images of the OT is close to this interpretation, → 150, 22 ff. It is introduced in Midr. Ps. 75 § 4 (170a) with the words : "Thou findest that there are 4 cups for good and 4 cups for evil" (Str.-B., I, 837). S. Dt., 349 (144b) on 33:8 : "Simeon and Levi (have) drunk from the same cup, v. Gn. 49:7," i.e., they suffered the same punishment (rather than the same fate, so Str.-B., I, 838, ad loc.). But along these lines a usage is possible similar to that attested in Lat., cf. Plaut. Casina, 933 : ... ut senex (hoc)

however, Jesus sees Himself confronted, not by a cruel destiny, but by the judgment of God. [40] The ineffable sorrow and anguish (Mk. 14:33 f. par. Mt. 26:37 f. cf. Lk. 22:44) which gives rise to the request that what is approaching might pass from Him is not fear of a dark fate, nor cringing before physical suffering and death, but the horror of One who lives by God at being cast from Him, [41] at the judgment which delivers up the Holy One to the power of sin (Mk. 14:41 par. Mt. 26:45, cf. Lk. 22:53). Hence one may suppose that there is an actual connection with the dominant concept in the OT metaphor of the cup. According to this the cup-sayings express for Jesus [42] more than for the Evangelists the fact that the approaching passion is not fate but judgment — for the disciples too in the sense of 1 Pt. 4:12. [43]

On the basis of the cup-sayings of Jesus the cup becomes a symbol of martyrdom in early Chr. writings. The dying Polycarp prays in Mart. Pol., 14, 2 : "I bless thee in that thou hast deemed me worthy ... that I might take a portion among the martyrs in the cup of thy Christ." [44] In accordance with the NT sayings the cup of suffering is defined decisively by the fact that Jesus Himself drank it.

4. The Cup at the Lord's Supper.

a. The Cup in the Eschatological Saying Lk. 22:17 f.

Lk. 22:17 f. associates the eschatological saying of Mk. 14:25 and par. with a cup. To-day it is generally recognised in textual and historical analysis of the accounts of the institution (→ 141, n. 55), that the eschatological saying and the interpretative saying belong to two independent traditions. [45] That the eschatological saying comes from Jesus can hardly be contested. That it was originally connected with the blessing of a cup (Lk. 22:17a) is suggested by the use of the phrase "fruit of the vine" (Mk. 14:25 and par.), for the blessing reads : "Blessed be thou, Lord our God, King of the world, who hast created the fruit of the vine." [46] The head of the house gave thanks thus at every meal when wine was drunk. It came after the breaking of bread, and he prayed the

---

eodem poc(u)lo, quo ego (bibi), biberet, that he comes to detect the same evil (cf. Plaut. Aulularia, 279; Rudens, 884). If it were not a Chr. interpolation, Mart. Is. 5:13 would be a direct par.: Is. sends his companions away prior to martyrdom, "for God has mixed the cup for me alone." We are not to regard as closer analogies the fig. expressions in which the cup is the bearer of a fate denoted by an attributive gen.: the cup of bitterness (G. Dalman, Jesus-Jeschua [1922], 145, n. 4), the cup of tears (Ps.-Philo, 50, 6, Riessler, 839, cf. Ps. 80:5), the (bitter) cup of death (Test. Abr. 16; Gn. Tg. Fr., 40, 23 in Schl. Mt. on 20:22).

[40] Cf. Schl. Lk. on 12:50 : "He is given up to those who crucify Him by God's judicial sentence," → V, 436, 25 ff. The Jewish martyrs discerned God's judgment in their execution, S. Dt., 307 on 32:4; cf. E. Lohse, Märtyrer u. Gottesknecht (1955), 73 f.

[41] The final prayer of the psalmists is not to be kept from death but to abide with God, Ps. 73:25-28. This prayer is fulfilled in the cry of Mk. 15:34 par. Mt. 27:46, which seeks God out of dereliction.

[42] The cup-saying is attested by the whole Gospel tradition. Who would have dared put it on the lips of Jesus ? For the historicity of the saying to the sons of Zebedee cf. J. Schniewind Mk. (NT Deutsch) on 10:39, though cf. also → I, 538, 28 ff.

[43] Acc. to Jn. 18:11 the cup, which is Yahweh's cup in the OT, is handed to Him directly by God. If it is then passed to the disciples there is a direct analogy in Ez. 23:32 f. etc. → 150, 1 f. The material objection that it is the cup of suffering (Schl. J. on 18:11) or death (→ V, 437, n. 386), not judgment, is not convincing → n. 40.

[44] Further instances of this comparatively uncommon formula may be found in Mart. Is. 5:13 → n. 39 and materially Ign. R., 7, 3 → 147, n. 21.

[45] For an analysis cf. Jeremias, op. cit. (→ n. 25), 55-57, 77 f., which is notably supplemented by K. G. Kuhn, "Über d. urspr. Sinn des Abendmahls u. sein Verhältnis z. d. Gemeinschaftsmahlen der Sektenschrift," Ev. Theol., 10 (1950/51), 512-523.

[46] Ber., 6, 1; bPes., 103a, 106a, cf. Str.-B., IV, 62; Dalman, op. cit. (→ n. 3), 137; Jeremias, op. cit., 93; → III, 732, 25 ff.

prayer for all over his own cup. [47] At the Passover it came before the breaking of bread,
and he prayed it over the first of the 4 cups along with the festal dedication, the
kiddush. [48] Acc. to the account in Lk. the eschatological saying is related to the first
Passover cup. This might very well be its historical place. In all probability the Last
Supper was the Passover. [49] The eschatological saying is not just an announcement ;
it is an oath-like declaration. It confirms the fact that this is the last meal which Jesus
will take with His disciples prior to the meal of consummation. [50] The interpretative
words can be understood only against the background of this declaration, → 142, 3 ff.
Hence everything points to the authenticity of the Lucan order. [51] The position of the
eschatological saying in Mk. corresponds to its place in the liturgy of the community. [52]

Jesus handles this cup in the same way as the cup of the interpretative saying,
→ lines 26 ff. Though, contrary to custom, He does not drink of it Himself, [53] He
circulates it among the disciples : λάβετε τοῦτο καὶ διαμερίσατε εἰς ἑαυτούς.
They are all to drink of this cup, [54] or, less probably, to fill their own cups from
it. [55] The common drinking unites the disciples in table fellowship under the saying
uttered with this cup. [56] This fellowship is different both from that of an ordinary
Passover and also from that of previous meals. [57] This meal leaves behind the
table fellowship of earthly days and look forward to the meal of consummation.
The interpretative sayings show what lies between.

b. The Cup of the Interpretative Saying.

The Jewish cup of blessing (כּוֹס שֶׁל בְּרָכָה) corresponds to the cup of the interpretative
saying (Mk. 14:23 par. Mt. 26:27; 1 C. 11:25; Lk. 22:20). At every meal when wine was
drunk the prayer of thanksgiving was said over this cup after the main meal. [58] At the
Passover this was the third cup. [59] The relationship to this cup finds direct expression
when the tradition calls the cup which Jesus proffered μετὰ τὸ δειπνῆσαι (1 C. 11:25;
Lk. 22:20) [60] τὸ ποτήριον τῆς εὐλογίας (1 C. 10:16 → 156, 21 ff.). The introduction

---

[47] Str.-B., IV, 621, cf. Man. of Disc. VI, 4 f.
[48] Str.-B., IV, 61 ff.; Dalman, 138; Jeremias, 23-25, 47 f. For another possibility → n. 73.
[49] Jeremias, 10-49 has shown this in answer to the objections of H. Lietzmann, *Messe u.
Herrenmahl* (1926), 211-213, → III, 734. For the order of the Passover cf. Str.-B., IV, 56-74;
→ III, 732 f.
[50] So Dalman, 141 f. Jeremias, 118-123 takes it too narrowly as a strict oath of renunciation ; he deduces therefrom that it was linked with the third Passover cup which concluded
the meal, → 120, n. 7.
[51] So Str.-B., IV, 75; Jeremias, *op. cit.* (→ n. 25) [1](1935), 62 f.; W. Marxsen, *Die Einsetzungsberichte zum Abendmahl,* Diss. Kiel (1949), 9 f.
[52] Here the eschatological saying had to come at the end (cf. Did., 10, 6) and its connection with the cup was lost. In the Lord's Supper the community moves on from the cross
and resurrection to the meal of consummation (1 C. 11:23, 26). Blessing of the cup merges
with thanksgiving over it to become a consecration of the cup which the Lord proffers,
Did., 9, 2 → n. 72 f., → 156, 21 ff. Perhaps the cup was blessed first on the basis of the
original supper, but then consumed after the bread, 1 C. 10:16 → n. 85; Did., 9, 2-5; 10, 3.
That the Lord's Supper was celebrated by the primitive community only in the setting of
the Passover (Zn. Ag. on 2:42-47a; → III, 731, 2 ff.; 738, 12 ff., cf. B. Lohse, *Das Passafest
der Quartadecimaner* [1953], 101-112) is an untenable conjecture.
[53] → 141, n. 57.
[54] Dalman, 140; Jeremias, 39 f.
[55] Str.-B., IV, 58, 75.
[56] Jeremias, 112.
[57] Cf. Loh. Mk., 309 f. This setting in salvation history explains the distinctiveness of this
meal as compared with the Passover, → n. 75.
[58] bBer., 51a, cf. Str.-B., IV, 630 f.; Dalman, 138-141; → n. 73.
[59] Pes., 10, 7, cf. Str.-B., IV, 72, 627 f.
[60] The absence of any such indication in Mk. shows that the sacramental eating and
drinking had since come to be separated from the general meal and brought together,
Jeremias, 98 f.

to the interpretative saying (Mk. 14:23 par. Mt. 26:27) follows exactly the customary rite. [61] He who gives thanks for all, after the required blessing, lifts the cup of blessing a hand's breadth above the table (λαβών), and with His eyes fixed on the cup [62] says on behalf of all the prayer of thanksgiving (εὐχαριστήσας). Then Jesus, though contrary to custom He Himself does not drink, [63] circulates the cup among His disciples and speaks the words of interpretation.

It is indisputable, then, that the circle from which the cup and saying in the accounts of the institution come is the Palestinian Church [64]. There can also be little doubt that both cup and saying derive from Jesus Himself. That there was originally no such cup in the meal of the primitive community [65] is proved neither by the short Lucan text (→ 141, n. 55), nor by the description of the meal as the breaking of bread. It certainly gains no support from the important reference of this cup to the death of Jesus. [66] Possibly shortage of wine caused the cup to be left out at times in the primitive community. [67] Up to the 3rd century water was used by the Church instead of wine in some areas. [68] Among some heretical Jewish Christians and Gnostics the Eucharist was sometimes celebrated without the cup on principle. [69] These facts have no bearing, however, on the question of its historical authenticity.

Whether the interpretation begins with τοῦτο τὸ ποτήριον (Paul, Lk.) or with τοῦτο alone (Mk., Mt.), it refers, not to the cup, but to its contents, [70] (red) wine. [71] Nevertheless, the second element in the Lord's Supper is almost always called the cup rather than the wine in the NT. [72] Along with the figure of the red "blood of grapes" (→ n. 71), the prominent position of the cup of blessing in Jewish table practice [73] provided an occasion for the sublimation of the cup in the interpretative saying. The cup of blessing concluded the meal, as the breaking of bread opened it. The eucharistic elements are the two basic elements in a Jewish

---

[61] Cf. Str.-B., IV, 630; Schl. Mt. on 26:27.

[62] In Mk. 6:41 and par., however, Jesus, contrary to custom, lifted up His eyes to heaven when breaking the bread (Str.-B., II, 246). He was free in this respect too.

[63] bPes., 105b → 141, n. 57.

[64] For detailed proof, Jeremias, 90-94.

[65] So W. Heitmüller, Taufe u. Abendmahl im Urchr. (1911), 52; Lietzmann, op. cit. (→ n. 49), 239-255; Bultmann Theol., 41, 59 f., 149.

[66] Eschatological joy at the feast of the primitive community (Ac. 2:46) does not rule out the fact that the same feast shows forth the Lord's death (1 C. 11:26), for the Pauline Lord's Supper was not just a memorial of the death of Christ (Lietzmann, op. cit., 251).

[67] This is how Schl. (Lk. and K, ad loc.) explains the qualifying note in the command relating to the cup in 1 C. 11:25 (ὁσάκις ἐὰν πίνητε) and the absence of the command in Lk. 22:20. Mt. 26:27: "Drink ye all of this" can hardly be a polemic against communio sub una.

[68] Harnack Dg., I⁵, 234 → III, 738, n. 69.

[69] Lietzmann, 239-249; J. Betz, "Der Abendmahlskelch im Judenchristentum," Abhandlungen über Theol. u. Kirche. Festschr. f. Karl Adam (1952), 109-137.

[70] "In Lk. 22:20b; 1 C. 11:25b the cup is used metonym. for what it contains," Pr.-Bauer, s.v., also Kl. Mk. on 14:23; Loh. Mk., 305; Jeremias, 84, 104 f., but not M. Barth, Das Abendmahl, Passamahl, Bundesmahl u. Messiasmahl (1945), 18-22.

[71] Wine is already the "blood of grapes" in Gn. 49:11. Red wine was normally used, though this was not a rule in the time of Jesus, Dalman, 145, n. 3; Str.-B., IV, 61; Kuhn, 516 f.

[72] Adapting the Jewish blessing of the wine (→ 153, 25 ff.), the blessing of the cup in Did., 9, 2 gives thanks ὑπὲρ τῆς ἁγίας ἀμπέλου Δαυίδ, → n. 52. The usual ref. after 1 C. 10:4 is to πόμα (Just. Apol., I, 66, cf. Ign. R., 7, 3), or ποτόν (Did., 10, 3), though cf. πόσις in Jn. 6:55. The elements are described as εὐχαριστία after Did., 9, 5; Ign. Phld., 4; Just. Apol., I, 65 f.

[73] Cf. Dalman, 138 : "If there was only one cup of wine, it was recommended that this be left to the end of the meal, and that the blessing of wine, offering and food be said over it."

meal, [74] as eating and drinking are in every meal. [75] The distributing of the bread and cup with the interpretative sayings is not just a symbolic action; [76] it is a real distributing of the necessities of life. [77] The varied significance of the cup in Scripture formed a second point of connection for the interpretative saying. Though the meaning of the cup is no more intrinsic to the Passover rite than its emphasising, both are suggested in a particular way by this rite. [78] The comprehensive interpretation of the 4 Passover cups to which we referred above (→ 150, 22 ff.), which is based on OT statements about the cup of judgment and salvation, and which sees in them the cups of punishment and consolation in the last days, belongs to a later period. Nevertheless, this way of viewing them cannot have been unknown to Jesus or to Christianity as an offshoot of Judaism. The cup from the hand of Jesus, which He sends round without drinking of it Himself, at least reminds all who know the Scriptures of the cup from the hand of Yahweh, τὸ ποτήριον ἐκ χειρὸς κυρίου (cf. Ιερ. 32[25]:15; 28[51]:7; ψ 74[75]:8; Is. 51:7). He who proffers the cup is the Mediator of God's work; he who receives it is the one in whom God is at work in the grace which saves through judgment. The NT community saw a connection with the cup of blessing, and materially at least a reference to the cup of Yahweh stands behind the idea of the cup of the Lord. [79]

c. The Cup of the Lord and the Cup of Demons (1 C. 10).

The eucharistic formula [80] handed down in the community (1 C. 10:16), from which Paul draws conclusions about participation in pagan feasts (vv. 17-22), takes over from Jewish table practice the term τὸ ποτήριον τῆς εὐλογίας (→ 154, 20 ff.) and calls the eucharistic cup the cup of blessing. The by no means "pleonastic" [81] addition ὃ εὐλογοῦμεν differentiates the Christian cup of blessing from that of the Jews. In it the subject is stressed as well as the object. The reference is to the cup which we bless. We do not thank Him for other things, but for that which is handed to us in this cup. [82] The eucharistic prayers in Did.

---

[74] Cf. also Jer. 16:7 → n. 23.

[75] With historical truth (→ n. 49), the Synoptists put the institution in the framework of a Passover meal, but, as Kuhn has pointed out (op. cit., 516-519), they do not link the interpretative sayings directly with any specific Passover practice (e.g., ἄρτος, not ἄζυμον). This is underlined in the rest of the NT. Though Pl. and Jn. stress that Jesus died as the true Passover lamb (1 C. 5:6-8; Jn. 18:28; 19:31, 36 → I, 339, 9 ff.), they relate the eucharistic elements, not to those of the Passover, but to the basic elements in every meal, food and drink (1 C. 10; Jn. 6). The Passover setting does not constitute the meaning of the meal; it simply underlines it. The relation to the sacrificial meal in 1 C. 10:18 simply emphasises a detailed feature for polemical reasons.

[76] E. Lohmeyer, "Vom urchr. Abendmahl," ThR, NF, 9 (1937), 210-213 rightly emphasises this.

[77] This idea (→ n. 75), found in 1 C. 10 and even more plainly in Jn. 6, is related to the concept of drinking not merely in Gnosticism and Hellenism (→ 138, 9 ff.) but also in Palestinian Judaism (→ 139, 15 ff.).

[78] The figurative interpretation of features in the Passover meal is not a material analogy to the interpretation of the eucharistic elements, as correctly perceived by Kuhn, op. cit., 517 f.

[79] Dalman, 145 f. refers to a connection between the cup which is a figure of the death of Jesus and the cup in which He proffers His death, but this is just as dubious as that between the saying about the baptism of death and the sacrament of baptism, → n. 36.

[80] E. Käsemann, "Anliegen u. Eigenart der paul. Abendmahlslehre," Ev. Theol., 7 (1947/48), 263 f., cf. Ign. Phld., 4.

[81] Ltzm. K. on 10:16.

[82] Acc. to Schl. Lk., ad loc.; → II, 763, 2 ff.

(9, 2 f.) offer an example of this εὐλογία. Through the thanksgiving the cup is attested and acknowledged to be that which is received from the hand of the Lord with the interpretative word; it is thus taken out of profane use.[83] The cup received from the Lord with praise is the κοινωνία[84] τοῦ αἵματος τοῦ Χριστοῦ, participation in Christ's death, i.e., committal to Him who died for us, → 143, n. 70. The cup of blessing is τὸ ποτήριον (τοῦ) κυρίου (1 C. 10:21; 11:27), the cup of the Lord, because it is received with praise from His hand, and because it objectively (→ 143, n. 71) subjects the one who drinks it to the efficacious power of the Lord who was crucified for him.

It is thus impossible to drink both the cup of the Lord and the cup of demons, 1 C. 10:21.[85] The cup of demons is not just any cup containing wine which has in some way come in contact with sacrificial ceremonies; Paul no more shares the general rejection of such wine by the Jews (→ 136, 16 f.) than he does the corresponding rejection of sacrificed meat (1 C. 10:25 f.; R. 14:14, → 141, 7 ff.). Nor does Paul, like the later Apologists,[86] differentiate the Eucharist here from the apparently related meals of the mysteries. On the basis of the Lord's Supper he is forbidding participation in the customary cultic meals (1 C. 10:21b, → τρά-πεζα, → 143, n. 68) .The reference to the cup of demons is his main argument for this prohibition. He is arguing here, not from pagan notions (→ 136, 26 ff.),[87] but from the OT principle that every sacrifice which is not offered to the living God is dedicated to demons.[88] The cup of demons is the cup from which a drink-offering is made to the deity at public (1 C. 8:10) or private (1 C. 10:27 ff.) meals or on other occasions.[89] For this cup thanks were given by pouring out a drink-

---

[83] Cf. 1 C. 10:30; 1 Tm. 4:4; → II, 760, 21 ff. Like all that the community does in the Lord's Supper, the blessing takes place εἰς τὴν ἐμὴν ἀνάμνησιν (1 C. 11:24 f. → I, 348 f.). There is no trace here of primitive ideas of magically efficacious blessings (→ II, 755, 23 ff.), though perhaps we catch an echo of them when many MSS add an acc. obj. to εὐλογήσας at Mk. 8:7 (→ II, 762, 36 ff.).

[84] → III, 804-806; Lohmeyer, 287; Loh. Phil., 17; Käsemann, op. cit. (→ n. 80), 275 : "Subjection to a sphere of power."

[85] In the context of this antithesis Paul welcomes the fact that the cup comes first (1 C. 10:16), as demanded by liturgical practice (→ n. 52). The bread suggests the inner unity of the community (v. 17), the cup its separation from every other cultus (vv. 18-22). The latter can be illustrated only by the cup, not by the breaking of bread, which was unknown in the cultic meals of paganism.

[86] Just. Apol., I, 66; Tert. Praescr. Haer., 40 (Mithras mysteries); Firm. Mat. Err. Prof. Rel., 18, 2 (Attis mysteries).

[87] This is the interpretation of, e.g., Ltzm. 1 K. on 10:21: At the Lord's Supper Christ comes into you, at the idol feast the demon, → III, 799 f. In criticism of the presupposed concept of pagan religion cf. Clemen, 183-190; Lohmeyer, 204-207; A. Arnold, Der Ursprung d. chr. Abendmahls im Lichte der neuesten liturgie-geschichtlichen Forschung² (1939), 113-174: also Ltzm. K.⁴, 183. In any case, pagan ideas are rejected as unreal by those addressed, 1 C. 8:4.

[88] 1 C. 10:20, cf. Dt. 32:17, 37 f. → II, 11, 14 ff.; 12, 3 ff.; 17, 11 ff. The expression is not to be derived, then, from the use of μετάνιπτρον Ἀγαθοῦ Δαίμονος for the cup from which the Greek, after eating, caused a few drops to fall to the ground in honour of the good spirit, and then drank a sip (Athen., XI, 486 f.; XV, 692 f., cf. Hanell, Art. "Trank-opfer," Pauly-W., VI, A. 2 [1937], 2135 and Deissmann LO, 299, n. 4).

[89] So Dölger, 268-270. This is how Basilius Magnus (Comm. in Jesaiam Prophetam, 10; MPG, 30, 533 f. in Dölger, 270), with the outlook of antiquity, expounds the saying : "He who drinks from the cup from which the offering is poured out drinks the cup of demons." On the varied drink-offerings cf. → Huber, also K. Kircher, Die sakrale Bedeutung des Weines im Altertum (1910), 5-73; Hanell, Art. "Trankopfer," Pauly-W., VI, A. 2 (1937), 2131-2138. At sacrifices the libation was mostly from a φιάλη (H. Luschey, Art. "φιάλη," Pauly-W., Suppl. VII [1940], 1026-1030), at table from a ποτήριον. In ancient times the

offering, not to God, but to the gods. Hence he who drinks it, and thereby denies God, falls victim to the rule of demons. This cup, then, is the antithesis to the cup of the Lord. The cups are mutually exclusive, not because their contents are engaged in physico-magical conflict, [90] but because those who drink them belong to two mutually exclusive dominions, cf. Mt. 6:24 par. Lk. 16:13; 12:28 ff. par. Lk. 11:20. The cup of the Lord or of demons, like the cup of Yahweh (→ 150, 12 ff.; 156, 11 ff.), expresses the power to which he who drinks is subject. Thus the history of the term comes to fulfilment in the fact that light is shed on the final cup of the Lord by the OT cup of Yahweh and the Jewish cup of blessing.

† καταπίνω.

καταπίνω, "to drink down," occurs already in pre-class. Gk., to a large extent apart from the idea of drinking, usually in the more general sense "to gulp down," "to swallow." 1. Lit. a. of living beings as subj. τοὺς (παῖδας) κατέπινε Κρόνος, Hes. Theog., 459, cf. 467: προσέρχεται ... ὡς δὴ καταπινόμενός με, Aristoph. Eq., 691, cf. Eur. Cyc., 219; b. Of material subjects : the earth τὸ καταποθὲν ... ὕδωρ, Plat. Crit., 111d; (πόλεως) ὑπὸ τῆς θαλάσσης καταποθείσης, Polyb., 2, 41, 7; of rivers which disappear under the earth, Aristot. Meteor., I, 13, p. 351a, 1. 2. Transf., common in many senses : a. positively, "to assimilate" καταπιὼν Εὐριπίδην, Aristoph. Ach., 484; Luc. Jup. Trag., 1, or a craft Antidotus Fr., 2, line 4; b. negatively, "to overwhelm" καταπιοῦνται ὑμᾶς Ἀθηναῖοι, Plut. Alcibiades, 15 (I, 198d); τὸν ἡμίοπον (little flute) ... ὁ μέγας (αὐλὸς) καταπίνει, Aesch. Eleg. Fr., 91 (TGF, 30); c. "to consume," "use up," e.g., the revenues of a state, Aristoph. Ra., 1466.

In the same sense, but with some transposition into the negative, καταπίνω occurs in the LXX almost always for בָּלַע "to swallow up," "to destroy." [1] The obj. is usually man ; he is swallowed by wild beasts (Jon. 2:1; Tob. 6:2), by the earth which opens up (Ex. 15:12; Nu. 16:30, 32, 34; 26:10; Ps. 106:17, cf. Prv. 1:12), by the depths, i.e., misfortune (Ps. 69:15), esp. by other men (the people by the enemy, Hos. 8:8; Ιερ. 28[51]:34; Lam. 2:16; Is. 49:19; Ps. 124:3, the righteous by sinners, Ps. 35:25; Prv. 1:12; Hab. 1:13), by God, who tears out the ungodly like a plant (Job 8:18). Abs. for the extinguishing of human wisdom, Ps. 107:27. Philo uses the word fig. for psychic processes. Thus the soul of the foolish is swallowed up by the body as by a river (Gig., 13 par. καταποντόω in Gig., 15). Balaam is engulfed by the river of folly, Deus. Imm., 181. Thoughts are swallowed up by delusion as by a flame, Leg. All., III, 230.

The NT use of καταπίνω is along the same lines as that of the OT, which it follows in different ways, 1 C. 15:54 → n. 6; Hb. 11:29; Rev. 12:16 → n. 5. With no sense of drinking, the word means "to swallow," "to gulp down." The lit. and fig. meanings merge into one another. In line with its root it denotes swallowing whole (e.g., Jon. 2:1) rather than grinding and consuming (Gl. 5:15; Rev. 11:5).

Gk. meal began with a sacrifice and usually ended with a libation (K. Schneider, Art. "Mahlzeiten," Pauly-W., XIV, 1 [1930], 525; Hanell, Art. "Trankopfer," VI A. 2 [1937], 2135) → n. 88. So also the Roman ; Valerius Maximus, Factorum et dictorum memorabilium, VIII, 15, 7 (→ Dölger, 268 f.): When the news of victory came, "there was none who had not poured out a drink-offering to him as to the immortal gods in the religious ceremonial of his table." → σπένδω. In the Decian persecution drinking from libation-cups was an accepted sign of apostasy : "And the fatal cup of death was offered from mouth to mouth," Cyprian, De Lapsis, 9. Thus the certificates constantly declare : "I have sacrificed and poured out a libation and partaken of the offerings," Dölger, 268.

[90] So Cyprian, De Lapsis, 25 : An infant who was made to drink of the wine of libation during persecution vomits out the contents of the eucharistic cup which are later poured into him in spite of violent struggles. Cf. ibid., 26.

κ α τ α π ί ν ω. [1] Conversely בָּלַע corresponds to καταπίνω in 19 of some 47 instances.

It is thus a total and definitive process, in the negative sense of hostile destruction. Except in the proverbial saying at Mt. 23:24, ² it thus describes the (eschatological) action of suprahuman subjects. This may be the overpowering of man by the forces of darkness, or the devil (1 Pt. 5:8), ³ or the despair of hopeless remorse (2 C. 2:7) ⁴ in which is no place for repentance and remission (2 C. 7:9 f.; Hb. 12:17). Or it may be the extirpation of that which is hostile to God by God's work of judgment and salvation (Hb. 11:29; Rev. 12:6; 2 C. 5:4; 1 C. 15:54).

Whereas God's people in faith passes through the Red Sea dryshod, its persecutors, venturing to follow without faith, are swallowed up by the flood, Hb. 11:29. The river spewed out by the dragon against the Church is swallowed up by the earth, Rev. 12:16; ⁵ the reference here is perhaps to the attack of the nations on the community (Rev. 17:1, 15; cf. 16:13 f.; 17:13 f.; 20:8), which the earth sucks into the realm of the dead (cf. Gn. 3:19), while the community remains (Mt. 16:18). When we are clothed upon (→ II, 320 f.), death will be swallowed up by life (2 C. 5:4), the body of death being changed into that of glory (1 C. 15:52 ff.). According to 1 C. 15:54 ⁶ death, which reigned over the body that had fallen subject to it (1 C. 15:44-49; R. 5:12 ff.; 7:24), will perish in the victory of life won through Christ (1 C. 15:57, 26); it is no more (Rev. 21:4).

† ποτίζω.

ποτίζω 1. of men and animals, "to cause or give to drink," Hippocr. Aphorismi, 7, 46; 2. of plants, "to water," Xenoph. Sym., 2, 25. In the LXX it is used almost always for the hi of הקש, which for its part is mostly rendered ποτίζω. ποτίζω is the causative of πίνω; giving to drink makes drinking possible. Hence it belongs to the same circle of ideas as πίνω and goes through much the same shifts of meaning.

Thus in the OT God's ποτίζειν is a proof of His continuing glory as Creator ¹ and also of the working of His salvation ² and wrath ³ up to the end. Here, too, the boundary between the lit. and fig. use is fluid.

In the NT the ancient demand that the thirsty should be given to drink is renewed on a christological basis, Mk. 9:41 par. Mt. 10:42; Mt. 25:35, 37, 42; R. 12:20 = Prv. 25:21. ⁴ Various motives are seen for giving Jesus to drink on the

---

² The Pharisee filters his drinks through a cloth so that no dead insect will touch his lips (Str.-B., I, 933 f. and Schl. Mt., ad loc.), but he swallows camels, which are big, unclean (Lv. 11:4) beasts. He struggles against transgression of the smallest statutes but accepts non-observance of the great unattainable commandments, Mt. 23:23 par. Lk. 11:42.
³ The devil seeks to gain power over members of the community by inducing them to apostatise, esp. through persecution.
⁴ Cf. Ps. 69:15.
⁵ The passage is formally based on the account of the destruction of the company of Korah, Nu. 16:30, cf. 32. For the conceptual background cf. J. Jeremias, Golgotha (1926), 57 f., 85 f.
⁶ Formulated acc. to Is. 25:8; cf. A. Rahlfs, "Über Theodotion-Lesarten im NT u. Aquila-Lesarten bei Justin," ZNW, 20 (1921), 183 f.
π ο τ ί ζ ω. ¹ Ps. 104:11, 13.
² Ps. 78:15 : the miracle of water in the wilderness (→ 136, n. 8); transf. Ps. 36:8 : the stream of God's joy; cf. Sir. 15:3 : with the water of wisdom, → 139, 15 ff.
³ Ps. 80:5 : with tears : Ps. 60:3 : the wine of astonishment (→ 150, 2 ff.); Is. 29:10 LXX : the spirit of stupefaction ; Jer. 8:14; 9:14; 23:15 : Mas. poisoned water, LXX bitter water, → 137, n. 19.
⁴ In the Sabbath conflict it is said in Lk. 13:15 that one is permitted to water cattle on the Sabbath, cf. Str.-B., II, 199.

cross, Mk. 15:36 par. Mt. 27:48; cf. Lk. 23:36; Jn. 19:29 quoting Ps. 69:21.⁵ The use in 1 C. 3:2, 6-8 is metaphorical. The basic instruction and confirmation of the community by the Word is the feeding of a child with milk (→ I, 645, 37 ff.) or the watering of a plant. In Rev. 14:8 the term occurs in the metaphor of the wine of wrath, → 152, n. 30. The ref. of ποτίζειν with the → πνεῦμα in 1 C. 12:13 is to the Lord's Supper, → 147, n. 18.

Goppelt

---

† πιπράσκω

πιπράσκω ¹ means "to sell," Hom. Il., 21, 102 etc.; Od., 15, 453 etc.; Hdt., II, 54, 56; Aesch. Choeph., 915; Ag., 1041; Soph. Trach., 252; Plat. Leg., 850a; BGU, I, 13, 11; P. Oxy., XII, 1494, 4 (private sale); P. Eleph., 27, 7 (public offers); "to sell for a bribe," Demosth. Or., 10, 63; τοὺς πεπρακότας αὐτοὺς ἐκείνῳ, cf. 17, 13; τὰ δ' ὅλα ... πεπρακέναι, 18, 28; τὴν πατρῷαν γῆν πεπρακέναι, Dinarch., 1, 71; "to lease," P. Lond., III, 842, 9. Finally πιπράσκω can be used fig.: "betrayed," "sold out," "led astray," "ruined," so πέπραμαι κἀπόλωλα, Soph. Phil., 978; εὐμορφίᾳ πραθεῖσα, Eur. Tro., 936. The ref. may be to persons or things; the price is in the gen., Xenoph. An., VII, 7, 26.

In the LXX, usually for מָכַר, πιπράσκω may refer to the sale of men, Gn. 31:15; Ex. 22:2; Lv. 25:39, 42, 47 f.; Dt. 15:12 etc.; Est. 7:4; Is. 52:3; ψ 104:17; 2 Macc. 5:14; 8:74; 10:21;² Wis. 10:13; of cattle, Lv. 27:27; of things, Lv. 25:23, 34 (land); Ez. 48:14 (landed property); 2 Macc. 4:32 (the vessels of the temple). Where God is dealing with individuals (1 Βασ. 23:7) or the people (Is. 50:1; 48:10;³ Jdt. 7:25) πιπράσκω means "to deliver up." In 3 Βασ. 20:20, 25; 4 Βασ. 17:17; 1 Macc. 1:15 men sell themselves to wrong (ποιῆσαι τὸ πονηρόν). Here πιπράσκω means "self-abandonment to sinful impulse." Philo does not use the word. It is rare in Joseph., e.g., Ant., 2, 42; 3, 283. He usually has πωλέω with the gen. of price (e.g., Bell., 5, 421) or ἀποδίδομαι.

In the NT πιπράσκω is used in the lit. sense ⁴ "to sell" of things and persons, with the acc. of thing (Mt. 13:46; Ac. 2:45; 4:34; 5:4) or person (Mt. 18:25, cf. Herm. v., 1, 1, 1) and gen. of price (Mt. 26:9; Mk. 14:5; Jn. 12:5). The word is also used fig. in R. 7:14 of the man who is sold under sin as his mistress, → I, 296, 17 ff. Man as σάρξ ⁵ has lost his independence. He has become subject to ἁμαρτία like a bondslave, and is now a mere object. He is delivered up to the most terrible lord whose wages are death. Thus πεπραμένος ὑπὸ τὴν ἁμαρτίαν describes the desperate situation of man from which only God can rescue him. ⁶

Preisker †

---

⁵ → V, 288 f., cf. also Hod., IV, 19 f.
π ι π ρ ά σ κ ω. Pape, Liddell-Scott, *s.v.*; Bl.-Debr.⁹ § 101.
¹ Etym.: root *perä-prä "to sell," identical with *perä-* "to transfer" (cf. περάω), Walde-Pok., II, 40; Boisacq⁴, 774; P. Chantraine, "Conjugaison et histoire des verbes signifiant vendre (πέρνημι, πωλέω, ἀποδίδομαι, ἐμπολῶ)," *Revue de Philologie,* 14 (1940), 11-24; Hofmann, 265, *s.v.* πέρνημι [Debrunner].
² On the selling of the debtor cf. Jos. Ant., 9, 47.
³ LXX : ἰδοὺ πέπρακά σε οὐχ ἕνεκεν ἀργυρίου, the Mas. is different. Cf. also Bar. 4:6
⁴ On the connection with πωλέω and ἀποδίδομαι cf. Bl.-Debr.⁹ § 101.
⁵ Cf. Bultmann Theol., 240 f.
⁶ On the use of πεπραμένος in R. 7:14 cf. Dt. 32:30; 1 K. 21:20, 25; 1 Macc. 1:15 (Str.-B., III, 238).

πίπτω, πτῶμα, πτῶσις, ἐκπίπτω, καταπίπτω,
παραπίπτω, παράπτωμα, περιπίπτω

---

† πίπτω.

Contents : A. Outside the NT. B. In the NT : I. In the Literal Sense : 1. General ; 2. πίπτω and προσκυνέω ; II. In the Figurative Sense : 1. General ; 2. Falling as Becoming Guilty.

A. Outside the NT.

1. From the basic meaning "to fall," "to fall down," "to plunge down" (Hom. Il., 6, 307-11, 425; Hes. Op., 620) there developed several different possibilities of use ; cf. the great no. of compounds. In so far as the ref. is to inanimate objects or animals, a swift and irresistible movement is denoted with a push from outside (πίπτω can often = a pass. of βάλλω). When the ref. is to men the fall may often be intentional, i.e., "to throw oneself," Hom. Il., 13, 742, "to cast oneself down," Eur. Hec., 787. Already in Hom. πίπτω can mean "to be slain" in battle, e.g., Il., 8, 67; οἱ πεπτωκότες, "the fallen," Xenoph. Cyrop., I, 4, 24. In a transf. sense πίπτω has the following meanings : "to go down," "to perish," Aesch. Choeph., 263; Hdt., VIII, 16; "to be lost," Hom. Il., 23, 595, "to pass away," Aesch. Sept. c. Theb., 794. In expressions like πίπτω εἰς ὀργήν (Eur. Or., 696), εἰς κακότητα (Theogn., 42), αἰσχύνῃ (Soph. Trach., 597), the verb as such does not contain any moral judgment ; in such contexts it simply describes the fact. In particular there is no instance of the abs. use of πίπτω for a guilty fall in the sense of moral delinquency, though there is a tendency in this direction in Plat. Phaed., 100e : τούτου ἐχόμενος ἡγοῦμαι οὐκ ἄν ποτε πεσεῖν, ἀλλ' ἀσφαλὲς εἶναι. In inscr., in which πίπτω is mostly used lit. (e.g., of the collapse of buildings, Ditt. Syll.³, II, 852, 46 f.; III, 963, 17; 1116, 5 f.), the word also has the weaker sense "to fall under," "to be counted under," e.g., ὑπὸ τὴν ἀρχήν, II, 714, 6 (2nd cent. B.C.); it is also a tt. in finance, e.g., II, 495, 172 f. (230 B.C.). In the pap. the technical legal and financial sense is even more strongly present. [1]

2. In the LXX πίπτω occurs over 400 times. When there is an original, it corresponds almost exclusively to נפל q, and it is the preferred transl. of this. The range of meaning shows the same breadth and manifoldness as outside the Bible (→ 162, 27 ff.; 164, 3 ff.), esp. in view of the use of נפל. On the other hand, πίπτω is not an administrative or commercial tt. in the LXX, → 161, 25 ff. The non-biblically attested sense "to go under," "to perish" (→ 161, 16 f.) could have acquired in the LXX the more radical meaning "to lose salvation," "to be lost" (in a soteriological and eschatological sense), but one may at most detect something of this only in Prv. 11:28; Σιρ. 1:30; 2:7, and even here the sense of suffering loss as a punishment is the same as the experiencing of (un-deserved) misfortune in ψ 36:24; Prv. 24:16 f.; Qoh. 4:10. The meaning "to sin" (→ lines 21 ff.) is also alien to the LXX (though cf. παραπίπτω → 170, 20 ff.). [2]

π ί π τ ω. [1] Cf. Preisigke Wört., II, 360 f. and Moult.-Mill., 514, *s.v.*; Mayser, II, 3 (1934), 5, 199 f.

[2] Apart from compounds and derivates treated in this art. we find in the LXX (according to frequency of use) : ἐπι- (also ᾽ΑΘΣ), ἐμ- (also ᾽ΑΘΣ), προσ- (also Σ), δια- (also Σ), συμ- (also ᾽ΑΣ), κατα-, ἀπο- (also ᾽ΑΘΣ), προ- (also Σ), ἀνα- (also ᾽ΑΣ), μετα-πίπτω, σύμπτωμα (also ᾽Α), ὑπο-, ἀντιπίπτω, ἀπόπτωμα (also ᾽ΑΣ), διά- (also Αλλ.), πρόπτωσις, παρεμπίπτω, and in Αλλ. ἀνάπτωσις and σύμπτωσις.

3. In Philo, on the other hand, we find πίπτω used for the sin of the νοῦς or ψυχή, but the concrete side of the metaphor is still so strong that the meaning "to sin" is not attained here either, cf. Virt., 7; Abr., 269 (with ὑποσκελίζομαι, "to be brought down"); Mut. Nom., 54-56, 154 f., 175 (exposition of Gn. 17:3, 17). Agric., 74 f. has the picture of the chariot of the soul (the reins fall, the rider drops off and the horses stumble), but in 94 f., 122, and even more strongly Leg. All., II, 99-101 (in exposition of Gn. 49:16-18), the falling of the rider is his salvation : the rider (νοῦς or ψυχή) is freed, while the horse (passion, πάθος) goes rushing on alone. Joseph. uses πίπτω and compounds [3] very frequently. The verb is almost always lit.: buildings "collapse" (e.g., Ant., 15, 122; 16, 18; 18, 280; Bell., 3, 254; Ap., I, 192); animals "fall to the ground" (Ant., 4, 275; 19, 87); men "fall" (5, 206; Bell., 1, 593) or "cast themselves down" (before the king, Ant., 6, 285; Bell., 1, 621; in prayer, Ant., 3, 310, with προσκυνέω, 7, 95; 9, 11). Very common is "to fall in battle," "to be slain," Ant., 6, 345, 369, 374; 7, 2, 9, 13; Vit., 24; Bell., 1, 102, 172; Ap., II, 212 etc. Ant., 13, 208 speaks of the snow which falls, Bell., 1, 444 of wrath (θυμός) which fades or disappears. It is said of the φρένες in Ant., 16, 380 that by reason of unaccountability πεπτώκασιν ἐκ τῆς ψυχῆς. In Ep. Ar. [4] and Gr. En. πίπτω does not occur. In Test. XII we often find the phrase ἐπὶ πρόσωπον πίπτειν, Zeb. 2:1; 3:7; Jos. 6:8. The meaning "to be slain" is found in Jud. 9:3. The reading ἔπαισεν for ἔπεσεν is secondary here, though in Test. G. 4:3 πέσῃ is secondary to πταίσῃ (otherwise we should have here an example of πίπτω in the sense "to transgress," "to sin").

B. In the NT.

I. In the Literal Sense.

1. General.

πίπτω is common in the NT. [5] In most instances it is used lit. and denotes an unintentional fall.

a. Of buildings which "collapse" through earthquakes or structural defects ; of walls, Hb. 11:30 (cf. Jos. 6:5, 20, also 3 Βασ. 21:30; Is. 24:23 etc.); a πύργος Lk. 13:4 (Is. 30:25, perhaps fig. of the fall of world powers depicted as πύργοι); houses, Mt. 7:25, 27 (cf. Ez. 13:11 f., 14 f.); Lk. 11:17; [6] Ac. 15:16 (= Am. 9:11, cf. Ju. 7:13); [7] whole sections of a city, Rev. 11:13; cities, 16:19, cf. the fall of Babylon (Rev. 14:8; 18:2, cf. Is. 21:9; Ιερ. 28:8) as a figure of judgment, with an ensuing depiction of the ruins (Is. 13:21 etc.).
b. Of the "fall" of a stone which crushes a strong man, Lk. 20:18b (cf. Mt. 21:44b vl.), of the "falling" or "overturning" of hills, mountains and cliffs, Lk. 23:30; Rev. 6:16 (cf. Hos. 10:8), also the "falling" of crumbs from a (low) table, Mt. 15:27; [8] Lk. 16:21, and

---

[3] Apart from those treated in the art. the most common are ἐμ-, ἐπι-, προσ- and συμπίπτω, also ἀνα-, Ant., 6, 329; 8, 256 and 282; Bell., 4, 50, ἀπο-, 1, 527, δια-, Ant., 15, 264; Bell., 2, 347, εἰσ-, Ant., 14, 410; Bell., 4, 292 etc., μετα-, Ant., 2, 287; 12, 2 etc., προ-, 4, 195; Bell., 2, 37 etc., ὑποπίπτω, Ant., 15, 251; Vit., 381; Bell., 5, 329, 382; 7, 371, cf. also διεκ-, Ant., 14, 334; 19, 118 and 136, ἐπεισ-, Bell., 6, 431, ἐπισυμ-, Ant., 15, 359, συνεκ-, Ap., I, 300, συνεισπίπτω, Ant., 15, 154; Bell., 1, 337 etc., also σύμπτωμα, Ant., 3, 267; 15, 144: Bell., 4, 287 and ἔκπτωσις, Ap., I, 247 and 266.
[4] Apart from → ἐκ- and καταπίπτω : δια- (29, 189), προσ- (180) and ὑποπίπτω (214), cf. also ἀνάπτωσις (187, 203) and σύμπτωμα (316).
[5] Apart from the compounds discussed we also find ἀνα-, ἀπο-, ἀντι-, ἐμ-, ἐπι-, προσ- and συμπίπτω.
[6] Hck. Lk., 155 ad loc.; Zn. Lk., 459, n. 39 → n. 21.
[7] The σκηνὴ Δαυιδ which is called πεπτωκυῖα is not a palace which is in ruins but an audience-tent which has collapsed. Cf. W. Michaelis, "Zelt u. Hütte im bibl. Denken," Ev. Theol., 14 (1954), 38.
[8] In comparison with Mk. 7:28 Mt. shows that in the answer of the woman (which caps 15:26 par. Mk. 7:27, where βάλλω is used) he sees a ref. to crumbs which have been inadvertently dropped by those who eat at table.

the "falling" of the seed, Mt. 13:4-8 and par.; Jn. 12:24; [9] also Ac. 27:34 vl.; (cf. 1 Βασ. 14:45; 2 Βασ. 14:11). c. Of the "falling" of stars (eschatologically), Mt. 24:29 par. Mk. 13:25; Rev. 6:13 (cf. Is. 34:4; Test. Sol. 20:16 and Test. Sol. D 4:14 → I, 504, 9 f.), also Rev. 8:10; 9:1 (→ I, 504, 12 f.; IV, 26, 40 ff.), [10] as a comparison Lk. 10:18 : ἐθεώρουν τὸν σατανᾶν ... ἐκ τοῦ οὐρανοῦ πεσόντα. [11] d. Of animals which "fall" (Mt. 10:29; Lk. 14:5), also of men who "fall" unintentionally and without being able to stop themselves, Ac. 20:9; Mt. 15:14; 17:15; Mk. 9:20; Jn. 18:6; Ac. 9:4; 22:7 (on Lk. 20:18a → 164, 17 ff.). Of the collapse of someone suddenly stricken by death, Ac. 5:5, 10; cf. Rev. 1:17. [12] On the borders of a lit. use is the sense (also common in the LXX) "to fall" = "to be slain," "to die" : στόματι μαχαίρης, Lk. 21:24, abs.; 1 C. 10:8; Hb. 3:17; Rev. 17:10 (here perhaps "to perish").

2. πίπτω and προσκυνέω.

In most of the instances in which men are said to fall in a literal sense, the reference is to casting themselves down, or intentional falling. In various combinations [13] πίπτω is commonly used here with → προσκυνέω. The required obeisance of slaves before their lord or king occurs in Mt. 18:26, though this is obviously not indicated in v. 29. [14] In all other instances the reference is to the worship which should be rendered to deity, Mt. 4:9; Ac. 10:25; 1 C. 14:25; Rev. 4:10; 5:14; 7:11; 11:16; 19:4, 10; 22:8 (in Rev., except at 5:8, πίπτω means "to cast oneself down" only along with προσκυνέω), also Mt. 2:11. πίπτω alone without προσκυνέω does not mean "to worship." Falling down before Jesus is meant to emphasise a petition in Mk. 5:22 (par. Lk. 8:41); Lk. 5:12, and gratitude in Lk. 17:16. It is a greeting of respect in Jn. 11:32, and Jesus Himself adopts this attitude in prayer acc. to Mt. 26:39 par. Mk. 14:35. [15]

---

[9] The seed "falls" because it is "cast" (cf. Mk. 4:26; βάλλω can even be used for the embedding of the seed in the earth, Lk. 13:19). But when it is cast it falls into the earth of itself. Nevertheless, one is not to allegorise πεσών in Jn. 12:24 (Jesus is led into death by God, or goes into death) (→ III, 811, 14 and n. 4; Zn. J., 514 f.).

[10] The πέση of Rev. 7:16 should perhaps be παίση (Is. 49:10 πατάξει). The Gnostic idea of the falling of particles of light on earth (cf. H. Jonas, Gnosis u. spätantiker Geist, I² = FRL, NF, 33 [1954], 105) did not influence the NT.

[11] As referred to Satan, πεσόντα might be understood as βληθέντα (cf. ἐκβληθήσεται in Jn. 12:31). This does not have to be a Semitism, so K. G. Kuhn, "πειρασμός — ἁμαρτία — σάρξ im NT," ZThK, 49 (1952), 220, n. 2 with a ref. to Rev. 12:9, 12. The meaning can hardly be that Satan left heaven of his own accord, → I, 505, n. 3; Test. Sol. D. 4:14 → V, 533, 13 f., 20 ff. Perhaps ἐκ τοῦ οὐρανοῦ is to be related to ὡς ἀστραπήν (Jn. 12:31 refers to the removal of Satan from the κόσμος, not heaven); if so, πίπτω might have the fig. sense "to be overthrown" = "to lose power," and the comparison with lightning simply illustrates the swiftness with which it happened.

[12] Either "I collapsed and was as dead" (so K. G. Kuhn, with a ref. to Eth. En. 14:13 f., 24 f.), or : "I collapsed like one who is stricken by death as he stands or walks," cf. Schl. J., 51.

[13] The words are always co-ordinated in Rev. (cf. 2 Ch. 29:30); only in 19:10; 22:8 is προσκυνῆσαι dependent on πίπτω as an inf. of purpose (Bl.-Debr.⁹ § 390, 1) (cf. Sir. 50:17). In the rest of the NT πίπτω is used in the aor. part. with προσκυνέω as a finite verb, cf. Jdt. 6:18; Job 1:20; Da. LXX 3:5 f., 10 f., 15; Θ 3:5 f., 11, 15.

[14] J. Horst, "Proskynein," Nt.liche Forschungen, III, 2 (1932), 226. Cf. ibid., 175 for προσπίπτω in a sense close to that of proskunesis. In Mk. 3:11 par. Lk. 8:28 προσπίπτω originally expresses a hostile attitude. πίπτω itself is not used in the NT for "to fall on someone" (with hostile intent).

[15] We usually find explanatory additions : ἐπὶ (τὸ) πρόσωπον, Mt. 17:6; 26:39; Lk. 5:12; 17:16; 1 C. 14:25; Rev. 7:11; 11:16 (cf. Gn. 17:3, 17; Nu. 16:4, 22; 1 Βασ. 5:3 f. etc.), ἐπὶ τοὺς πόδας, Ac. 10:25 (cf. 1 Βασ. 25:24 etc.), παρὰ τοὺς πόδας τινός, Lk. 8:41; 17:16 (cf. also Ac. 5:10 vl.), πρὸς τοὺς πόδας τινός, Mk. 5:22; Jn. 11:32 (cf. εἰς τοὺς πόδας, Mt. 18:29 vl.), ἔμπροσθεν τῶν ποδῶν, Rev. 19:10; 22:8, ἐνώπιον, Rev. 4:10; 5:8; 7:11 (cf. Ju. 20:32, 39). πίπτω is not combined with ἐπὶ τὰ γόνατα (cf. 2 Ch. 6:13) in the NT, → I, 738, 15 ff.

II. In the Figurative Sense.

1. General.

The expression "the lot falls on someone" (cf. 1 Ch. 26:14; Est. 3:7; Ez. 24:6; Jon. 1:7; also ψ 15:6 vl.) arose because originally the lot was in a container and fell out when this was shaken. [16] The phrase is already a stereotyped one in Ac. 1:26. The use is fig. when we read that darkness (Ac. 13:11) or fear (Rev. 11:11 vl., cf. 1 Βασ. 26:12; 2 Εσδρ. 16:16; Jdt. 2:28; 15:2) falls on someone. The word expresses the sudden and irresistible nature of what happens. [17] The meaning in Lk. 16:17 is "to become invalid or null," "to be deprived of force," cf. Jos. 23:14 vl.; Rt. 3:18; 1 Βασ. 3:19; 4 Βασ. 10:10; also ἐκπίπτω, → 169, 1 ff.

2. Falling as Becoming Guilty.

Though this use is not yet found in the LXX, πίπτω is brought into the ethico-soteriological sphere in the NT. Even here πίπτω does not have the meaning "to fall" = "to commit a specific gross sin," and the concept is certainly not restricted to the sexual sphere. Nevertheless, there can be no mistaking the fact that being a sinner is taken much more radically in the use of πίπτω too. This is obviously connected with the general NT deepening of the idea of sin, → I, 302 ff. This may be seen already in the wholly fig. saying about falling on the stone in Lk. 20:18a (cf. Mt. 21:44a vl.; → 163, 7 f.). This warning is addressed not merely to the Jewish leaders who encompass the death of Jesus but to the whole attitude of rejection which takes offence at the person and claim of Jesus. [18] No less strongly fig. is R. 11:11: μὴ ἔπταισαν ἵνα πέσωσιν; Israel's guilt is denoted not just by falling but already by stumbling (→ πταίω). Falling does not mean becoming guilty; it refers to the possibility that Israel will persist in its guilt, or rather that it will be abandoned by God in its guilt, that it will be excluded from salvation. [19] The image of falling suggests lying after a fall rather than the fall itself. On the other hand, falling clearly denotes the guilt of Israel in R. 11:22, where Paul without qualification calls the unbelieving Jews πεσόντες. [20]

πίπτω is also a figure of speech for loss of faith and separation from grace in 1 C. 10:12 : ὁ δοκῶν ἑστάναι βλεπέτω μὴ πέσῃ. This falling is not to be related to the committing of specific sins. It is true that the reference in 1 C. 10:5 ff. is to particular sins on the part of Israel, but these are simply illustrations of Israel's basic apostasy from God. [21] Apostasy from God and from Christ is the issue in

---

[16] נפל is also used in Damasc. 20:4; Man. of Disc. 4:26, while in Damasc. 13:4; Man. of Disc. 6:16, 18, 22 the process is the same : the lot comes forth (יצא) [K. G. Kuhn].

[17] Even when it is said in Ac. 10:44 that the Holy Ghost has fallen on someone (ἐπιπίπτω, which is a vl. in all the verses mentioned on → line 6 f., cf. 1 Βασ. 18:10; Ez. 11:5), it is certainly presupposed that the Spirit comes from above, but comparison with other statements about the gift of the Spirit shows that the ref. is esp. to the swiftness of the movement. Cf. W. Michaelis, Reich Gottes und Geist Gottes nach dem NT (1931), 38, n. 22.

[18] On the OT par. and the question of πίπτειν ἐπί in Lk. 20:18a (and 20:18b) cf. → IV, 275, 33 ff., 281, 10 ff., and esp. 281, n. 9; also → 170, n. 3.

[19] Zn. R., 505 relates πίπτω to the condition of the unbelieving Jews which is described in 11:7 f. and which is a consequence of the rejection of Jesus. He sees here the question whether this state is the final goal of God in the direction of the history of Israel. But πίπτω is not exclusively orientated to the eschatological situation.

[20] The use of πίπτω in 11:22 is independent of the context (and controlled by reminiscence of 11:11). The meaning is not that the branches which have broken off acc. to 11:17 ff. have fallen or have been thrown down (cf. the figure of falling φύλλα in Prv. 11:14; Is. 34:4; Test. Sol. D. 4:16; cf. 20:16 [ἐκπίπτω]).

[21] The choice of πίπτω in 10:12 is not influenced by ἔπεσαν in 10:8 (→ 163, 10 f.). The orientation of πίπτω is to ἕστηκα, cf. also the common use of ἕστηκα or στήκω in Pl.

1 C. 10:12 too. The man who is proud of his ἑστάναι because he ascribes it to his own Christianity is particularly exposed to this danger. Though the warning of 10:12 derives eschatological point from v. 11 and v. 13 (→ 28, 44 ff.), the fall is not the eschatological loss of salvation. It is a failure which makes the one who is so sure of himself an ἀδόκιμος, 1 C. 9:27. Paul also uses the antithesis of standing and falling²² in R. 14:4 : τῷ ἰδίῳ κυρίῳ στήκει ἢ πίπτει. Though the Christian who sits in judgment on his brother (14:1 ff.) argues that the latter has sinned, standing and falling are not just the same as not sinning and sinning. The metaphor is orientated to the fact that each must answer to his Lord as his Judge. ²³

The use is also abs. in Hb. 4:11: ἵνα μὴ ἐν τῷ αὐτῷ τις ὑποδείγματι πέσῃ τῆς ἀπειθείας. ²⁴ Here again the ref. is not to a specific sin. πίπτω = ἀπείθεια, ²⁵ and is elucidated by ἀποστῆναι ἀπὸ θεοῦ ζῶντος in 3:12. ²⁶ The admonition in Rev. 2:5 : μνημόνευε οὖν πόθεν πέπτωκας is distinguished from 1 C. 10:12 (→ 164, 29 ff.); Hb. 4:11 by the fact that falling does not imply complete apostasy from God and Christ but leaving of the first love, Rev. 2:4. πόθεν recalls the earlier high standing of the community. It marks the depth of the fall, while πίπτω denotes the rapidity of the downward movement of which the community is guilty.

The statement in 1 C. 13:8 : ἡ ἀγάπη οὐδέποτε πίπτει, is usually related to what follows. In this case πίπτει is equivalent to a καταργηθήσεται or παύσεται; it thus means "to perish," "to come to an end," "to cease" (→ I, 52, 4 ff.); ²⁷ the μένει of v. 13 is its opposite.

Suspicion is aroused, however, by the fact that πίπτει is pres. while the fut. is used in what follows. ²⁸ Furthermore, οὐδέποτε is not used anywhere else in the NT in the sense of οὐκ εἰς τὸν αἰῶνα, cf. 1 C. 8:13 → I, 199, 4 f. Formally and materially the statement also resembles the short sayings in 13:4-7 in which ἀγάπη is again the subj.

---

for "to stand fast." Cf. W. Straub, Die Bildersprache d. Ap. Pls. (1937), 23. A shift of meaning is involved when οὐ σταθήσεται in Mt. 12:25 par. Mk. 3:25 is changed to πίπτει in Lk. 11:17, → n. 6.

²² There is no instance in the LXX, though the antithesis to fall / to rise up is common, Am. 5:2; 8:14; Mi. 7:8; Is. 24:20 etc., cf. also Prv. 24:16; Qoh. 4:10.

²³ He "stands" originally means that he may stand before the judge, that he need not humble himself, that he is not set aside, that he may live before him. Cf. the σταθήσεται which follows and the usage in ψ 129:3 and Rev. 6:17. He "falls" (= "he cannot stand") possibly means that he must confess his guilt, but more probably that he is condemned (pass. made to fall). On the other hand πίπτω does not seem to be a legal tt. for "to be condemned" (a judgment may also fall). In the phrase ἵνα μὴ ὑπὸ κρίσιν (vl. εἰς ὑπό-κρισιν) πέσητε in Jm. 5:12 πίπτω, as in the constr. with εἰς (→ 161, 17 ff.), means "to fall under" (i.e., judgment, which perhaps rests on the malefactor like a crushing burden). Schl. Jk., 279, n. 1 observes that Jos. has ὑποπίπτω for this. πίπτω ὑπό is also very rare in the LXX, cf. 2 Macc. 7:36; lit. 2 Βασ. 22:39.

²⁴ πίπτω does not here take an ἐν, cf. Mi. Hb.⁸, 113, ad loc.

²⁵ Cr.-Kö., 920 f. takes πίπτω to be more than a consequence of ἀπείθεια.

²⁶ The many warnings against falling in Sir. (1:30; 2:7; 22:27; 28:26; cf. also 28:18) are no par. to this NT use, → 161, 35.

²⁷ This meaning is obviously presupposed by the textual witnesses which have strength-ened it by the reading ἐκπίπτει, though πίπτει is the original (as against Bchm. 1 K., 400, n. 1). There is no relation to Ab., 5:16 : "Love, which does not cleave to a thing (a sensual object), never ceases (אֵינָהּ בְּטֵלָה לְעוֹלָם)," → I, 51, n. 146. Nor is anything decisive to be gleaned from 1 Εσδρ. 4:38, cf. H. Sahlin, "I Esdras et 1 Cor. 13," Coni. Neot., 5 (1941), 29. Only observance of the eschatological orientation of 1 C. 13:8 can protect the transl. "love never faileth" from slipping into moral and devotional sentimentality.

²⁸ W. Theiler raises the question (in a written communication) whether πίπτω is not given a subsidiary fut. sense by the accompanying οὐδέποτε.

One may thus ask whether this is not the conclusion of the section 13:4-7.[29] If so, the fourhold πάντα of 13:7 (= in all circumstances) is contrasted with the οὐδέποτε of 13:8 (= in no circumstances).

πίπτω means here "to be defeated," "to be brought to the ground,"[30] "not to stand." To be sure, it cannot mean "to sin,"[31] since there is no clear instance of this in the NT. Nevertheless, one may ask whether it does not have the same sense as in R. 11:22 (→ 164, 27 ff.); 1 C. 10:12 (→ 164, 29 ff.) etc.; whether it does not denote an attitude of disobedience which resists God's claim. How this attitude may work out in detail may be seen if the negatives of 13:4 ff. are turned into positives and the positives into negatives. With its many examples the section is in this case the most comprehensive statement of what the NT means by falling, namely, the non-observance of the divine command to love, whose fulfilment is possible only in the power of fellowship with God and Christ.[32]

† πτῶμα.

πτῶμα means "fall," "plunge," "collapse," Aesch. Suppl., 797, transf. "evil," "defeat," Aesch. Choeph., 13; Eur. Herc. Fur., 1228, then "what has fallen." In relation to buildings "ruins," Polyb., 16, 31, 8, in relation to living creatures "corpse" (from Aesch.), with gen., e.g., πτώματα νεκρῶν, Eur. Phoen., 1482, later (Polyb., etc.) without gen. (incorrect Suid., s.v. πτῶμα· σῶμα, ἄνευ τῆς κεφαλῆς). In the pap. only in the sense of "fall," "collapse," P. Oxy., I, 52, 12 (4th cent. A.D.), "windfall," P. Fay., 102, 20 (2nd cent. A.D.; cf. Suid., s.v.), also a financial tt., P. Lond., I, 3, 37 (2nd cent. B.C.).[1]

In the LXX 23 times, 8 in Job (only 11 also in Heb., almost as many Heb. equivalents): Is. 30:13 f. of the collapse of a wall, 2 Macc. 9:7 of the overturning of a chariot, Jdt. 8:19 of death in battle, predominantly for "overthrow," "disaster," "destruction" (as a punishment), with πρόσκομμα in Is. 8:14 (also ΘΣ); Σιρ. 34:16 vl., with σύντριμμα Is. 51:19; 30:14, with συντριβή Prv. 16:18, with ἀπώλεια Σιρ. 31:6. The meaning "corpse" occurs only in Ju. 14:8 (carcass of a lion), perhaps also ψ 109:6 (this use gains ground somewhat in ᾿ΑΘΣ).

Philo mostly uses πτῶμα for "fall," "tumble" (e.g., Deus Imm., 130; Agric., 110, 171); often πτῶμα πίπτειν: Mut. Nom., 55, 57; Migr. Abr., 80. We also find in Philo the sense of "corpse," Jos., 17 (vl. σῶμα); Leg. Gaj., 308. This can even be predominant in Joseph., cf. Ant., 7, 16; Bell., 5, 34, 440, 570; 6, 2, 405 as compared with 1, 594; 6, 30 and 217.[2]

The only meaning in the NT is "corpse," the carcass of an animal in Mt. 24:28 (vl. σῶμα ℵ; influence of Lk. 17:37), otherwise a human corpse: Mt. 14:12 (vl. σῶμα ℵ) par. Mk. 6:29 of the body of John the Baptist, Rev. 11:8 f. of the bodies

---

[29] Cf. E. Lehmann and A. Fridrichsen, "1 K. 13. Eine chr.-stoische Diatribe," ThStKr, 94 (1922), 89 f.; W. Michaelis, "Ἡ ἀγάπη οὐδέποτε πίπτει," Pls.-Hellas-Oikumene (1951), 135-140. Worth noting is the objection that in this case there is no true explanation of the δέ in εἴτε δὲ προφητεῖαι (13:8).

[30] Cf. the transl. of A. Deissmann, Pls.² (1925), 163 : "Love never goes to pieces."

[31] Only with this proviso is 1 C. 13:8 a par. to R. 14:23b. Cf. Michaelis, op. cit. (→ n. 29), 140 : "What is not of love and what is not of faith is sin."

[32] The usage of the post-apost. fathers is similar to that of the NT. Pr.-Bauer⁴, 1201, s.v. 2αβ finds the idea of a moral slip in 1 Cl., 59, 4, but acc. to the context πεπτωκότας is related to the preceding τοὺς ἐν θλίψει, cf. Kn. Cl., ad loc.

π τ ῶ μ α. [1] Cf. Preisigke Wört., II, 434, s.v.; Mayser I (1906), 435; Moult.-Mill., 558, s.v.

[2] In Test. Sol. D 1:7 πτῶμα corresponds to the ἁμάρτημα of 1:6, but since διόρθωσις in 1:7 is the opp. of πτῶμα, we do not have the direct sense of "moral slip."

of the two witnesses (11:8, 9a collective sing., 9b plur.). The body of Jesus is called πτῶμα only in Mk. 15:45 א BD. [3]

† πτῶσις.

πτῶσις, less common than πτῶμα (though in compounds -πτωσις is more common than -πτῶμα), has the sense of "fall," Plat. Resp., 604c (it is also a tt. in grammar for case, Aristot. Poet., 20, p. 1457a, 18). [1]

In the LXX it is more common than πτῶμα, and occurs 38 times (12 in Sir., 7 in Ez.); there are several equivalents in the Mas. (18 times). Only seldom does it mean "fall" in the lit. sense, Jdt. 10:2 (falling down to pray); Ez. 31:13, 16 (fall of a tree as a sign of the fall of the king of Egypt; in 31:13 the Mas. refers to the fallen trunk, and one would expect πτῶμα, since πτῶσις does not have elsewhere the sense of "what has fallen"); Ιερ. 30:15 (Mas. 49:21: figure for the punishment of Edom, but depiction of a real fall which causes the earth to tremble); Ju. 20:39 B in the phrase πτώσει πίπτειν, "to be struck dead" (cf. Nah. 3:3, where the Mas. refers to the many fallen warriors, but βαρεῖα πτῶσις can only mean their falling in battle, not those who have fallen). [2] In all the other verses the meaning is "disaster," "misfortune," "destruction" (as a punishment).

In Philo πτῶσις is a grammatical tt. at Deus Imm., 141. In Joseph. the ref. in Ant., 17, 71 is to a fall from a roof. Gr. En. 100:6 refers to the collapse of ἀδικία.

In the NT the ref. in Mt. 7:27 is to the collapse of a house (par. ῥῆγμα in Lk. 6:49). The meaning in Lk. 2:34 is the figurative one of "downfall," "destruction"; the term is used here for the fate of those to whom Christ is an offence: οὗτος κεῖται εἰς πτῶσιν καὶ ἀνάστασιν πολλῶν (cf. → I, 372, 3 ff.). [3]

† ἐκπίπτω.

ἐκπίπτω (from Hom.) "to fall out of or down from," lit. in Hom. Il., 5, 585; 11, 179, also "to burst forth," "to make a sortie," "to flee," Hdt., IX, 74; of the lot which falls from an urn, Xenoph. Sym., 5, 10 and the oracle which "goes forth" (from the sanctuary), Luc. Alex., 43. Cf. also "to swerve from something," "to deviate from the way," Xenoph. An., V, 2, 31, or "to digress" in speaking, Aeschin. Ep., 2, 34, "to give up hope," Thuc., VIII, 81. Pass. "to be cast ashore (from the sea)," Hom. Od., 7, 283; "to be driven forth, banished, expelled," Hdt., I, 150; with gen., ἐκ or ἀπό: "to be deprived of or to lose something," Hdt., III, 14. [1] In the pap. "to fail," "to be omitted," "to be lost," P. Tebt., I, 27, 26 (113 B.C.); "to stretch," e.g., BGU, II, 603, 9 (2nd cent. A.D.); also with gen. "to let slip" something, P. Tebt., I, 50, 14 (112 B.C.). [2]

---

[3] AC and most texts have σῶμα, which is also found in Mk. 15:43 and par. πτῶμα is not vulgar (as against Hck. Mk. on 6:29; 15:45). Perhaps the sense of "what has fallen" (= the dead body lying on the ground, Rev. 11:8 f.) is still too strong to permit a body hanging on a cross to be called a πτῶμα.

π τ ῶ σ ι ς. [1] The indexes to Ditt. Syll.³ and Or., Preisigke Wört., s.v. and Moult.-Mill., s.v. do not have any instances.

[2] At 3 Macc. 6:31 πτῶσις is used with τάφος, but the meaning is "destruction" rather than "death" (par. ὄλεθρος, 6:30). At Job 21:20 Σ has πτῶσις (LXX σφαγή); cf. Hab. 3:5 Αλλ.

[3] It is an open question whether the fall is due to stumbling on a stone, as the par. adduced in → I, 372, 4 f. suggest. Certainly the ref. is not to falling over a stone when the LXX uses the metaphor of falling and rising again (only with the verbs → 165, n. 22).

ἐ κ π ί π τ ω. [1] For details cf. Pass. and Liddell-Scott, s.v.

[2] Cf. Preisigke Wört., I, 452 f.; Mayser², I, 3 (1935), 218; II, 1 (1926), 209, 308; II, 2 (1934), 237 f., 248. The noun ἔκπτωμα can also mean "collapse" (2nd cent. B.C.).

ἐκπίπτω occurs 15 times in the LXX, with different equivalents in the Mas. (13 times). It is almost always used lit.: of the σιδήριον of an axe which flies from the haft (Dt. 19:5), or the woodchopper which slips from the hand, 4 Βασ. 6:5 (cf. Qoh. 10:10), of the morning star which falls from heaven, Is. 14:12, of a tree which falls ἐκ or ἀπό τῆς θήκης, 6:13 (cf. vl. ἐκσπασθῇ A), of the horns which fall, Da. 7:20, often of the flower (ἄνθος) which fades, as a figure of transience and rapid change, Job 14:2; 15:30, 33; Is. 28:1, 4; 40:7; fig. of a ψήφισμα, a command, which goes forth, 2 Macc. 6:8. In Σιρ. 34:7 it is said of those who set their hopes in dreams: ἐξέπεσον, "they went forth empty," they were deceived. ἐκπεπτωκότα δὲ ἐταπείνωσαν in Job 24:9 means that they have not yet fully abased one who was already rejected. [3]

Joseph. mostly uses ἐκπίπτω for "to be driven forth," e.g., Ant., 8, 271; 10, 59 and 183; 15, 180; Ap., I, 228; II, 35, also "to lose (power)," Ant., 15, 191 and 323, "to escape," Vit., 162; Bell., 3, 414, and lit. "to fall out of," Ant., 10, 274; Bell., 7, 453; also of news which goes forth, Ant., 16, 207. The meaning "to be expelled" occurs in Ep. Ar., 249. ἐκπεσεῖν κυρίου is used in an addition to Test. Jud. 21:4; it means "to separate oneself from, to fall away from."

In the NT, though ἐκπίπτω occurs only 10 times (on 1 C. 13:8 vl. → 165, n. 27), the range of meaning is greater than in the LXX. ἐκπίπτω is used lit. in the saying from Is. 40:7 which is quoted in 1 Pt. 1:24 and which is also the basis of Jm. 1:11: τὸ ἄνθος (αὐτοῦ) ἐξέπεσεν. Another instance of the lit. sense is in the freeing of Peter from prison in Acts 12:7: καὶ ἐξέπεσαν αὐτοῦ αἱ ἁλύσεις ἐκ τῶν χειρῶν, "the chains fell off from his hands." [4] Cf. also Ac. 27:32 : εἴασαν αὐτὴν (sc. τὴν σκάφην) ἐκπεσεῖν, where the meaning might be that when the soldiers had cut the ropes off the boat, it fell on to the water. This seems to be ruled out however, by the fact that the boat had already been lowered into the sea according to v. 30. [5] Hence one has to consider [6] whether we do not have here a meaning already found in Acts (27:17, vl. ἐκπλέσωσιν א*; 27:26, 29, vl. ἐμπέσωμεν א), namely, that of "moving" in the sea or "being driven" by it. The sense "to lose," [7] which is found outside the Bible (ἐκπίπτω with gen.), occurs in 2 Pt. 3:17: ἵνα μὴ ... ἐκπέσητε τοῦ ἰδίου στηριγμοῦ, Gl. 5:4 : τῆς χάριτος ἐξεπέσατε. In 2 Pt. 3:17 the συναπαχθέντες which comes immediately before ἐκπέσητε might suggest movement in ἐκπέσητε too, and hence the rendering "to fall from"; [8] this is hardly possible, however, in Gl. 5:4. [9]

---

[3] The vl. ἐξεπίπτουν with acc. in 2 Macc. 10:30 A (for ἐξερρίπτουν) is obviously a slip. For ἐκπίπτω in the other transl. cf. Job 13:25 Σ; Is. 40:7 ΘΣ (cf. LXX).

[4] αὐτοῦ corresponds here to the non-emphatic dat. sympatheticus in which ref. is made to the person from whom something slips, cf. already Hom. Il., 15, 465 : τόξον δέ οἱ ἔκπεσε χειρός. This is why αὐτοῦ comes first, cf. Bl.-Debr.[9] § 284, 1; 473, 1; Schwyzer, II, 147 f.; O. Merlier, "Le remplacement du datif par le génitif en grec moderne," BCH, 56 (1931), 216-219; D etc. put the pronoun at the end as though it belonged to χειρῶν.

[5] Another objection is that in this case ἐάω with inf. would be almost a substitute for a factitive verb — a use not found elsewhere in the NT, even at Ac. 23:32.

[6] Cf. Pr.-Bauer[4], 441, s.v.

[7] → 167, 31 f. The LXX does not have this constr. Sir. 14:2 : οὐκ ἔπεσεν ἀπό τῆς ἐλπίδος αὐτοῦ. But cf. Jos. Ant., 7, 203 : ὡς ἄν βασιλείας ἐκπεσών, "as though he had already lost the kingdom."

[8] στηριγμός ("steadfastness") is in this case a sphere.

[9] The preceding par. κατηργήθητε ἀπό Χριστοῦ certainly contains the thought of moving away from or being taken out of a sphere of power (→ I, 454, 7 ff.), but to regard grace as a sphere from which one may fall is to suppose that elsewhere it is presented as a sphere in which one can stand. But "to stand in grace" has no basis in Paul or the NT. Hence one must translate : You have lost grace, grace has left you.

In R. 9:6 : οὐχ οἷον δὲ ὅτι ἐκπέπτωκεν ὁ λόγος τοῦ θεοῦ, ἐκπίπτω in the abs. has the sense "to be in vain," "to lose force and validity," "to be lost." This meaning, which is attested outside the Bible, [10] is not found in the LXX (though cf. Σιρ. 34:7 → 168, 7 ff.). In the LXX, however, πίπτω (→ 164, 8) and διαπίπτω (Jos. 21:45) are used with reference to the non-fulfilment of the divine words of promise (which is always contested, of course, in the OT). [11] The statement of Paul is certainly more comprehensive inasmuch as he has in view the whole promise concerning Israel, → IV, 112, 19 f.

† καταπίπτω.

Lit. "to fall down," e.g., πρηνὴς ἐπὶ γαίη κάππεσε, Hom. Il., 16, 311 and 414; 12, 386 : ἀφ' ὑψηλοῦ πύργου, Xenoph. Oec., 1, 8 : ἀφ' ἵππου. In the inscr. and pap. "to collapse," of buildings, Ditt. Syll.[3], II, 852, 31 f. (149 A.D.); BGU, I, 282, 7 (2nd cent. A.D.) etc. Infrequently as a pass. related to καταβάλλω, Aesch. Ag., 1553. Transf. of the fall of courage, Hom. Il., 15, 280 : παραὶ ποσὶ κάππεσε θυμός, in the sense "to fall into" always in malam partem, e.g., εἰς ἀπιστίαν, "to become untrustworthy," Plat. Phaed., 88d. Common as a perf. part. in the sense "lowly," "contemptible" : γένος ἄτιμον καὶ καταπεπτωκός, Plut. Phoc., 4 (I, 743c).

In the LXX καταπίπτω occurs 8 times, and at Is. 49:19 א we find καταπεπτωκότα as a vl. for πεπτωκότα (assimilation to vl. κατεφθαρμένα or a mistake arising out of καὶ τά). Only twice do we have the Mas. At 2 Εσδρ. 18:11 this is צצע ni, rendered διαπίπτω in 18:10 (λυπέομαι would be good, e.g., Gn. 45:5). At ψ 144:14 we find נפל; the meaning here and in 3 Macc. 2:20 is transf. "to succumb" (par. "to be subdued, oppressed"). [1] We also have "to fall down" at Wis. 13:16, "to crash" at Wis. 7:3; 4 Macc. 4:11 (ἡμιθανής), transf. "to sink down" (in fear) at Wis. 17:15 (also the addition to Job 15:23 in A). [2]

Philo uses καταπίπτω in Agric., 83 for "to fall" (the νοῦς as charioteer, → 162, 4 ff.), Jos., 144 transf. for "to sink" (of courage). The main sense in Joseph. is "to fall down," "to sink to the ground" in battle, Ant., 5, 147; 6, 223; 7, 142; 10, 7; 13, 61; Bell., 2, 544; 5, 513; 6, 64 (ἐπ' αὐτήν sc. πέτραν), also "to plunge down," 3, 232; "to collapse" (of walls), Ant., 5, 27; 9, 237, also "to throw oneself on the ground," Bell., 2, 171. Transf. εἰς νόσον καταπίπτειν, Ant., 13, 304 and 398, εἰς ὕπνον Ant., 7, 48; also "to fall to pieces," "to lose heart," Ant., 2, 336; 6, 329 vl.; Bell., 7, 87. In Ep. Ar., 144 a λόγος (view) is called καταπεπτωκώς, "void," "untenable."

In the NT καταπίπτω is used only by Lk. in the lit. sense "to fall," Ac. 26:14 of crashing down εἰς τὴν γῆν (cf. πίπτειν εἰς τὴν γῆν in 9:4 → 163, 7), also καταπίπτειν νεκρόν "to fall down dead," "to fall down and be dead," Ac. 28:6 (cf. 4 Macc. 4:11 → line 23 f., also Rev. 1:17 → 163, n. 12. In the parable of the

---

[10] Cf. esp. Plut. Lib. Educ., 13 (II, 9b): Many parents over-exert their children through too lofty demands : πόνους αὐτοῖς ὑπερμέτρους ἐπιβάλλουσιν οἷς ἀπαυδῶντες ἐκπίπτουσιν. But one might almost refer to the meaning "to lose," → 167, 31 f. There is no direct model in the sense "to be unsuccessful" (orators and poets in selection), cf. Ltzm. R., ad loc.

[11] Of man's word, Jdt. 6:9; cf. 6:4.

κ α τ α π ί π τ ω. [1] H. G. Meecham, The Letter of Aristeas (1935), 252 (wrongly) contests a fig. use of καταπίπτω in the LXX (even in 3 Macc. 2:20 he will accept only "a semi-metaphorical use").

[2] Cf. κατάπτωμα in ψ 143:14 (Mas. פֶּרֶץ, also κατάπτωσις in 3 Macc. 2:14; Σιρ. 35(32):15 vl.

sower Lk. 8:6 has κατέπεσεν (ἐπὶ τὴν πέτραν) for the ἔπεσεν of Mk. 4:5 par. Mt. 13:5 (ἔπεσεν in Lk. 8:5, 7 f.; cf. 8:14). [3]

† παραπίπτω, † παράπτωμα.

A. The Word Group outside the New Testament.

1. The verb παραπίπτω means "to fall beside or aside," Aristot. Gen. An., I, 7, p. 718a, 1, also "to stumble on something by chance," e.g., ὁ παραπίπτων, "the first comer," Plut. Galb., 8 (I, 1056d), "to be led somewhere or other," Polyb., 4, 80, 9. The sense "to be led past," "to go astray," "to be mistaken," also occurs in Polyb., with the gen. τῆς ὁδοῦ in 3, 54, 5, fig. τῆς ἀληθείας, 12, 12, 2, τοῦ καθήκοντος, 8, 11, 8, also abs. "to make a mistake," 18, 19, 6 (though the neighbouring ἀγνοέω shows that this is an accidental and pardonable mistake); cf. Xenoph. Hist. Graec., I, 6, 4.

Hence the noun παράπτωμα (from Polyb.) has the meaning "slip," "error" (with ἄγνοια, Polyb., 15, 23, 5; 16, 20, 5); cf. παράπτωσις (Polyb., 16, 20, 5), which also bears other senses of the verb as noun. [1]

2. The verb παραπίπτω occurs 8 times in the LXX (παραπεσεῖν in 2 Macc. 10:4 A is a slip for περιπεσεῖν). Est. 6:10 : μὴ παραπεσάτω σου λόγος (Mas. נפל), uses it in the sense "to be in vain" ("not to be carried out"). It is abs. in Wis. 6:9; 12:2. In the admonition to τύραννοι in 6:9 : ἵνα μάθητε σοφίαν καὶ μὴ παραπέσητε, the meaning is perhaps "to commit an error" which could be avoided by σοφία, but the context supports a more serious understanding. In 12:2 : τοὺς παραπίπτοντας κατ᾽ ὀλίγον ἐλέγχεις, the meaning "to sin" is proved by the ensuing καὶ ἐν οἷς ἁμαρτάνουσιν ὑπομιμνῄσκων νουθετεῖς. This is also the meaning in the other refs., which are all in Ez.: παράπτωμα with acc. 14:13; παραπτώματι with dat. 15:8; 18:24; with ἐν 20:27 (παραπτώμασιν) 22:4 (αἵμασιν); Mas. אשם at 22:4, מעל elsewhere, → n. 7. In all the Ez. refs. the context shows that what is at issue is a culpable mistake, or sin.

The same applies to the noun παράπτωμα, which is used 19 times in the LXX; where there is a Mas. equivalent it is usually מַעַל, פֶּשַׁע or עָוֹן. [2] The only weaker use is in Da. Θ 6:5, the one passage where the ref. is not to a fault in relation to God; the mistake here is in official matters. The fact that παράπτωμα refers to a single fault is plain not merely in passages which have the plur. (ψ 18:13; Job 36:9; Ez. 14:11 etc.). In the LXX use of παράπτωμα there is no par. theological development to that of ἁμαρτία (→ I, 289, 10 ff.) whereby sin comes to be understood as basic attitude and total conduct. Nevertheless, παράπτωμα is by no means a mild term for the individual sin. Its place in the review in → I, 268, 10 ff. would be small, but not unimportant.

---

[3] The choice of καταπίπτω is hardly connected with the substitution of πέτρα (or another view of what happens) for the πετρῶδες of Mk. and Mt. Zn. Lk., 343, n. 16 can hardly be right when he suggests an original ἔπεσεν (κατέπεσεν is simply "a mechanical repetition of the κατ- in κατεπατήθη and κατέφαγεν, v. 5"). Jos. Bell., 6, 64 is no true par. (→ 169, 28 f.) since the ref. there it is to slipping, stumbling (πταίω) against a πέτρα, and falling on this πρηνής; the par. here is rather to Lk. 20:18a (→ 164, n. 18).

παραπίπτω, παράπτωμα. [1] In inscr. the word group is evidently rare (there are no examples in the indexes to Ditt. Syll.³ and Or.). The main sense of παραπίπτω in the pap. (from the 2nd cent. B.C.) is "to be lost" (cf. Preisigke Wört., II, 254; Moult.-Mill., 488 f., s.v.), though we also find "to fall to," "to present itself" (cf. Mayser³, I, 3 [1935], 227). παράπτωμα occurs in P. Tebt., I, 5, 91 (118 B.C.); Preisigke Wört., II, 255 transl. "vain request," Moult.-Mill., 489 and Mayser, I³ (1935), 57 "mistake"; in this sense cf. also H. I. Bell, *Jews and Christians in Egypt* (1924), 82, No. 1917, 14 (4th cent. A.D.).

[2] Da. Θ 4:27 is a very free rendering of the Mas. (4:24). παράπτωμα corresponds here to the Aram. שְׁלֵוָא "rest," though the Heb. שַׁלְוָה (Jer. 22:21) is also transl. παράπτωσις (in the LXX only here).

The group plays no great role in Philo.[3] In Migr. Abr., 170 : μεγάλα δὲ τὰ ἐξ ἀνεπιστημοσύνης καὶ πολλοῦ θράσους παραπτώματα, the force is very weak, cf. also the philologically inadequate and theologically superficial def. of παράπτωμα in a Fr. of Philo :[4] if someone who is generally accepted to be blamelessly religious ἐκπέσῃ εἰς ἁμαρτίαν, τοῦτό ἐστι παράπτωμα· ἀνῆλθεν γὰρ εἰς τὸ ὕψος τοῦ οὐρανοῦ καὶ πέπτωκεν εἰς τὸν πυθμένα τοῦ ᾅδου.[5] The word παράπτωμα does not occur in Joseph.,[6] but we find παραπίπτω in Ant., 13, 362; 16, 200 in the sense "to befall." Cf. also παράπτωμα in Ps. Sol. 3:7; 13:5, 10.

B. The Word Group in the New Testament.

1. The verb παραπίπτω occurs only in Hb. 6:6 : (6:4) ἀδύνατον γὰρ τοὺς ἅπαξ φωτισθέντας ... (6:6) καὶ παραπεσόντας πάλιν ἀνακαινίζειν εἰς μετάνοιαν. Although the sense seems to be "fallen away" along the lines of ἀποστῆναι ἀπὸ θεοῦ ζῶντος in 3:12, παραπίπτω does not mean "to fall away," but "to offend," "to fall," "to sin," as in the LXX.[7] In elucidation one may adduce ἑκουσίως ἁμαρτάνειν in the related Hb. 10:26, especially as the reference in both cases is not to specific offences as such, but to these as the expression of a total attitude.[8]

2. The noun παράπτωμα occurs frequently in Paul, but elsewhere only in Mt. 6:14 f.; Mk. 11:25. Mt. 6:14 : ἐὰν γὰρ ἀφῆτε τοῖς ἀνθρώποις τὰ παραπτώματα αὐτῶν, is the only passage in which the word is used of faults against men.[9] This is also true in Da. Θ 6:5 (→ 170, 27 ff.), but in a very different sense. The τὰ παραπτώματα ὑμῶν of Mt. 6:15 (cf. Mk. 11:25 and the secondary Mk. 11:26) are offences against God. If παραπτώματα is used for both, this does not mean that παραπτώματα against God are reduced to the level of those against men. On the contrary, the severity of offences against men is emphasised by the use of παραπτώματα for them too. It may be added that in neither 6:14 nor 6:15 is an "against you" or "against him" put in to show against whom the παραπτώματα are committed, as in the rather different formulation in Mk. 11:25. In both instances the reference is simply to παραπτώματα. There are no παραπτώματα against one's neighbour which do not affect one's relation to God, and vice versa.[10]

---

[3] It is not listed in Leisegang.

[4] Ed. T. Mangey, Philonis Iudaei Opera, II (1742), 648.

[5] This passage is over-rated in Cr.-Kö., 922 and Trench, 159.

[6] Cf. Schl. Mt., 217 on 6:14; Schl. Theol. d. Judt., 137.

[7] Cf. Mi. Hb.[8], 149, n. 1. In view of the familiarity of the author of Hb. with LXX usage it is not intrinsically impossible that he is aware of the correspondence between מעל ("to be unfaithful," "to fall away") and παραπίπτω, → line 170, 24.

[8] 1 Cl., 51, 1: ὅσα οὖν παρεπέσαμεν, refers to a plurality of individual offences (the Gk. Bible does not construe with the acc.). On παρέμπτωσις, loc. cit. cf. Pr.-Bauer[4], 1139, s.v.; Kn. Cl., 128, ad loc.

[9] In the corresponding conditional clause in 6:15 ἀφίημι is used abs. acc. to א D etc. (as in the main clause, 6:14), whereas τὰ παραπτώματα αὐτῶν is inserted here in B et al. (cf. also 18:35 vl.). The replacing of the τὰς ἁμαρτίας of Jm. 5:16 by τὰ παραπτώματα in א is perhaps connected with the fact that ἀλλήλοις (incorrectly) suggested offences against one another and τὰ παραπτώματα was thus felt to be more appropriate in view of Mt. 6:14.

[10] Schl. Mt., 217 explains the choice of παράπτωμα as follows : This word shows "that Jesus demands from the disciple forbearance and helpful love not only for frailty and need but expressly for the reprehensible conduct which falls under moral condemnation."

Paul in R. 5:15a b, 17 f. describes the sin of Adam (παράβασις in 5:14) as παράπτωμα (a term already used for it in Wis. 10:1). The sing. is justified, since Paul undoubtedly has in view the one actual sin of Gn. 3. παράπτωμα is thus equivalent to ἁμάρτημα, which is rare in Paul (cf. the secondary reading at R. 5:16). On the other hand R. 5:20 : ἵνα πλεονάσῃ τὸ παράπτωμα, shows that the apostle — going beyond LXX usage (→ 170, 31 ff.) — can use παράπτωμα for the totality, since the ensuing οὗ δὲ ἐπλεόνασεν ἡ ἁμαρτία makes it apparent that παράπτωμα and ἁμαρτία are synonyms. [11] As ἁμαρτία was in the world before the Law according to 5:13, so was the synonymous παράπτωμα according to 5:20. The Law simply caused it to increase. Hereby the distinction between παράπτωμα = ἁμάρτημα and παράβασις is established. παράβασις is orientated to the presence of the Law (cf. 5:13 f.; Gl. 3:19); it implies transgression of a commandment (→ V, 739, 37 ff.). παράπτωμα, however, goes further ; it refers directly to the disruption of man's relation to God through his fault. [12] The plur. παραπτώματα in R. 5:16 is plainly the same as παράπτωμα = ἁμάρτημα, cf. also 4:25 (ἁμαρτίαι in Is. 53:12); 2 C. 5:19, cf. Col. 2:13b; Eph. 1:7 (ἁμαρτίαι, Col. 1:14); 2:1 (with ἁμαρτίαι); 2:5, cf. Col. 2:13a. The sing. bears the same sense in Gl. 6:1: ἐὰν καὶ προλημφθῇ ἄνθρωπος ἔν τινι παραπτώματι κτλ. In view of the use of παράπτωμα elsewhere it is hardly likely that the apostle would select it as a mild term for sin as distinct from ἁμαρτία, [13] especially as ἁμαρτία does not occur elsewhere in the exhortatory part of Gl. (only at 1:4; 2:17; 3:22). Hence προλημφθῇ, too, is not an exculpation but presupposes that the one concerned is caught in the actual commission of a παράπτωμα. [14] At R. 11:11 f. Paul speaks of the παράπτωμα of Israel which consists in its rejection of the Gospel, → 164, 21 ff. [15]

C. The Word Group in the Post-Apostolic Fathers.

The usage of the post-apost. fathers follows the same lines as that of the NT. παραπίπτω occurs only in 1 Cl., 51, 1 (→ n. 8). 1 Cl., 56, 1: ἐντύχωμεν περὶ τῶν ἔν τινι παραπτώματι ὑπαρχόντων, reminds us of Gl. 6:1; cf. Barn., 19, 4 par. Did., 4, 3. [16]

---

[11] Pr.-Bauer⁴, 1132, s.v. calls this use of παράπτωμα in R. 5:20 collective, cf. also the plur. τῶν παραβάσεων χάριν in the related Gl. 3:19. A collective παράπτωμα and ἁμαρτία are not, of course, full synonyms ; otherwise Pl. would not have used different words. παράπτωμα certainly does not share in the personal use of ἁμαρτία if there is this in R. 5:21 (→ I, 296, 22, 27 ff.).

[12] Cr.-Kö., 922, however, thinks that παράβασις denotes sin obj. as an act, while παράπτωμα emphasises more strongly its guilt as the subj. side of the event and its consequences.

[13] Oe. Gl., 111, ad loc.: "The mildest word for sin." The transl. "slip" (ibid., 110; Pr.-Bauer⁴, 1132, s.v.) is not as such a softening. More clearly than "transgression" it brings out the fact that the original sense is that of aberration (→ 170, 5 ff.) rather than going too far and crossing a boundary, cf. K. Barth, K.D., IV, 1 (1953), 551 (C.D., IV, 1 [1956] 495): "where he has no business to be." Cf. παραβαίνω in relation to ὑπερβαίνω.

[14] But cf. → IV, 14, 41 ff.; Trench, 158.

[15] παράπτωμα is undoubtedly connected with the use of πίπτω in 11, 11 and 22. There seems to be no good reason to adopt the sense of "defeat" proposed by Cr.-Kö., 923; this is in any case very rare outside the Bible, cf. Pass., s.v.

[16] For details cf. Pr.-Bauer⁴, 1132, s.v. παράπτωμα. παράπτωσις is used at 1 Cl., 59, 1. → 170, 12 f.

† περιπίπτω.

The main sense of περιπίπτω is "to come on something accidentally," Hdt., VI, 105, "to be innocently involved in something," commonly with mishaps etc., Eur. Or., 367, also "to be overturned," "to sink," Plut. Anton., 67 (I, 947b). [1] The noun περίπτωμα means "mishap." περίπτωσις, "accident," is more common, Sext. Emp. Math., 1, 25. There are 9 instances in LXX, 5 of them in Macc.; 2 Macc. 9:7 "to suffer a severe fall," Rt. 2:3 and 2 Βασ. 1:6 in a fig. etym. with περιπτώματι (noun only here) in the sense of "lighting on a place by chance," cf. also Prv. 11:5; Da. 2:9; 2 Macc. 6:13; 9:21; 10:4 (vl. παραπίπτω) in the sense of falling into an awkward situation or under punishment, in part innocently, e.g., ἀσθενείᾳ (2 Macc. 9:21), in part culpably, e.g., ἐπιτίμοις (2 Macc. 6:13). At 4 Macc. 1:24 the text is probably corrupt, [2] but περιπίπτω is here combined with the dat of the person who is confronted by something which causes pain or pleasure. Philo uses περιπίπτω abs. in Deus Imm., 73 in the sense of falling through one's own fault (transf.). Elsewhere he uses it with the dat. in the sense "to fall into": ἡ ψυχὴ περιπίπτει τοῖς ὄφεσιν, Leg. All., II, 84, cf. 86; ἡδοναῖς, 77; Spec. Leg., I, 224. Joseph. uses περιπίπτω with dat. for "to meet," "to overtake," Ant., 4, 252; 19, 123 and 125; Bell., 3, 499; "to fall on" one's sword etc., Ant., 15, 152; 19, 273; "to fall into the hands," 19, 153 (cf. 1, 59; 3, 96 f.), mostly in the sense "to be involved in," e.g., sickness, 10, 25; 15, 244; Ap., I, 305 and 313; imprisonment, Ant., 8, 229; misfortune, 1, 42 and 110; 5, 264; 10, 39; Bell., 7, 219; danger, Ant., 4, 293; 20, 48; Vit., 83. This is also the sense in Test. XII : D. 4:5; Jos. 10:3.

At Lk. 10:30 : λῃσταῖς περιέπεσεν, the meaning is not "to encounter" i.e., "to come on the robbers unawares," but the far more common "to come into" an awkward situation, or here, with the dative of person, "to fall into the hands of someone," "to become the victim of someone by whom one is surprised." [3] The unusual construction with εἰς in Ac. 27:41: περιπεσόντες δὲ εἰς τόπον διθάλασσον, is to be explained by the fact that a place is mentioned in this instance. [4] περιπίπτω here means "to be unexpectedly brought somewhere," unless the thought is that the course set in v. 40 could not be held. In Jm. 1:2, where we have the fig. ὅταν πειρασμοῖς περιπέσητε ποικίλοις, the emphasis is again on the swift and unexpected way in which man can be involved in temptations. [5]

In the post-apost. fathers 1 Cl., 51, 2 reads : αἰκίαις περιπίπτειν, "they were subjected to torments"; περιπτώσεις (with συμφοραί) in 1 Cl., 1, 1 means "misfortunes."

Michaelis

περιπίπτω. [1] Also in inscr., e.g., Ditt. Syll.³, I, 495, 56 (230 B.C.); 667, 9 (161/0 B.C.). In the pap. mostly "to be involved in something," though also "to encounter someone," P. Tebt., I, 230 (2nd cent. B.C.); P. Oxy., XIV, 1639, 20 (1st cent. B.C.), "to fall on something," P. Greci e Latini, III, 172, 13 f. (2nd cent. A.D.). Cf. Preisigke Wört., II, 297; Moult.-Mill., 507; Mayser, II, 2 (1934), 249. Constr. always with dat.

[2] Cf. A. Deissmann in Kautzsch Apkr. u. Pseudepigr., II, 153, *ad loc.*

[3] Cf. Diog. L., 4, 50 : πλέων ... λῃσταῖς περιέπεσε; Artemid. Oneirocr., 3, 65 : χειμῶνι μεγάλῳ ἢ λῃστηρίῳ περιπεσεῖται, cf. 1, 5; 2, 22.

[4] Cf. Bl.-Debr.⁹ § 202.

[5] The idea behind the ἐμπίπτουσιν εἰς πειρασμόν of 1 Tm. 6:9 is more that of the ineluctability of the temptation which wealth brings with it.

πιστεύω, πίστις, πιστός, † πιστόω,
ἄπιστος, † ἀπιστέω, ἀπιστία,
ὀλιγόπιστος, ὀλιγοπιστία

Contents : A. Greek Usage : I. Classical Usage : 1. πιστός; 2. ἄπιστος; 3. πίστις :
a. Confidence, Trust; b. Trustworthiness, Reliability; c. Assurance; 4. πιστεύω; 5. ἀπιστέω;
6. ἀπιστία; 7. πιστόω; 8. The Question of Religious Terminology. II. Hellenistic Usage :
1. The Development of a Religious Usage in Philosophical Discussion ; 2. The Usage of
Religious Propaganda ; 3. Stoic Usage. B. The Old Testament Concept : I. General Remarks ;
II. The Stem אמן and Related Expressions 1. Qal ; 2. Niphal ; 3. אָמֵן; 4. Hiphil ; 5. אמן
and Derivates ; 6. The Religious Dynamic. III. The Stem בטח: 1. State of Security ;
2. Feeling of Assurance ; 3. Comparison with אמן. IV. The Stem חסה; 1. Seeking Refuge ;
2. Relation to Yahweh. V. The Stems קוה, יחל, חכה: 1. Basic Meaning ; 2. Religious Use ;
3. Isaiah ; 4. Later References. VI. Summary. C. Faith in Judaism : I. The Old Testament

πίστις κτλ. In general, apart from OT and NT Theologies, M. Flacius, De voce et
re fidei (1549); H. Hoelemann, Bibelstudien, I "Die bibl. Grundbegriffe der Wahrheit"
(1859), 1-53; H. H. Wendt, "Der Gebrauch d. Wörter ἀλήθεια, ἀληθής u. ἀληθινός im
NT auf Grund d. at.lichen Sprachgebrauches," ThStKr, 56 (1883), 511-547; A. Pott, Das
Hoffen im NT in seiner Beziehung zum Glauben (1915); A. Nairne, The Faith of the NT
(1920); R. Gyllenberg, Pistis, I and II (Swedish) (1922); A. Schlatter, Der Glaube im NT⁴
(1927); B. B. Warfield, Biblical Doctrines (1929), 465-508; W. G. Kümmel, "Der Glaube im
NT," ThBl, 16 (1938), 209-221; J. Dupont, Gnosis (1949), 250-252, 260 f., 398-409 and
passim ; V. Warnach, Agape (1951), 581-585 and passim. On A. II : Reitzenstein Hell.
Myst., 234-236; R. Walzer, Galen on Jews and Christians (1949), 48-56. On B : L. Bach,
"Der Glaube nach d. Anschauung d. AT," BFTh, 4 (1900), 1-96; J. Pedersen, Israel, Its
Life and Culture, I (1926), 336-348; K. H. Fahlgren, Sedaka nahestehende u. entgegen-
gesetzte Begriffe im AT (1932); K. J. Cremer, "Oudtestamentische semasiologie," Gerefor-
meerd Theologisch Tijdschrift, 48 (1948), 193-200; 49 (1949), 1-15, 79-99; S. Virgulin, "La
fede nel profeta Isaia," Biblica, 31 (1950), 346-364, 483-503; J. C. C.van Drossen, De deri-
vata van den stam אמן in het Hebreeuwsch van het OT (1951); G. J. Botterweck, " 'Gott
erkennen' im Sprachgebrauch des AT," Bonner Bibl. Beiträge, II (1951). On C : Bousset-
Gressm., 193-196 and passim ; Moore, passim ; Str.-B., III, 187-201; Volz Esch., 80 f. On
C. III : H. Windisch, Die Frömmigkeit Philos (1909), 23-29; W. Bousset, Kyrios Christos²
(1921), 145-147; Bousset-Gressm., 447 f.; M. Peisker, Der Glaubensbegriff bei Philon, Diss.
Breslau (1936); E. Käsemann, Das wandernde Gottesvolk (1939), 48-52. On D. II : M.
Dibelius, Jesus² (1949), 106 f.; E. Käsemann, Das wandernde Gottesvolk (1939), 19-27. On
D. III : W. H. P. Hatch, The Pauline Idea of Faith in its Relation to Jewish and Hellenistic
Religion (1917); W. Bousset, Kyrios Christos² (1921), 145-154; E. Wissmann, Das Ver-
hältnis v. πίστις u. Christusfrömmigkeit bei Pls. (1926); W. Michaelis, "Rechtfertigung aus
Glauben bei Pls.," Festgabe f. A. Deissmann (1927); E. Lohmeyer, Grundlagen paul. Theol.
(1929); K. Mittring, Heilswirklichkeit bei Pls. (1929); M. Dibelius, "Glaube u. Mystik bei
Pls.," N. Jbch. Wiss. u. Jugendbildung, 7 (1931), 683-699; W. Mundle, Der Glaubensbegriff
d. Pls. (1932); R. Gyllenberg, "Glaube bei Pls.," ZSTh, 13 (1937), 612-630; M. Hansen, Om
Trosbegrebet hos Pls. (1937); R. Schnackenburg, Das Heilsgeschehen bei der Taufe nach
dem Ap. Pls. (1950), 115, 188 f. and passim. On D. IV: J. O. Buswell, "The Ethics of 'Believe'
in the Fourth Gospel," Bibliotheca Sacra, 80 (1923), 28-37; W. H. P. Hatch, The Idea of
Faith in Chr. Literature from the Death of St. Paul to the Close of the Second Century
(1926); J. Huby, "De la connaissance de foi dans Saint Jean," Recherches de Science religieuse, 21 (1931), 385-421; R. Schnackenburg, Der Glaube im 4. Ev., Diss. Breslau (1937);
W. F. Howard, Christianity acc. to St. John³ (1947), 151-165.

Legacy. II. The Concept of Faith in Judaism : 1. Old Testament Motifs ; 2. The Difference from the Old Testament. III. Philo's Concept of Faith. D. The πίστις Group in the New Testament : I. Formal Considerations : 1. πιστεύω; 2. πίστις; 3. πιστός; 4. πιστόω; 5. ἄπιστος; 6. ἀπιστέω; 7. ἀπιστία; 8. ὀλιγόπιστος. II. General Christian Usage : 1. The Continuation of the Old Testament and Jewish Tradition : a. πιστεύω as to Believe ; b. as to Obey ; c. as to Trust ; d. as to Hope ; e. as Faithfulness ; 2. Specifically Christian Usage : a. πίστις as Acceptance of the Kerygma ; b. The Content of Faith ; c. Faith as a Personal Relation to Christ ; d. Believing ; e. πίστις as *fides quae creditur* ; f. Development of the Use of πιστεύω ; 3. The Relation of Christian Faith to That of the Old Testament. III. πίστις and πιστεύω in Paul : 1. Paul and the Common Christian Concept of Faith : a. Acceptance of the Kerygma, ὁμολογία and ὑπακοή; b. Ways of Believing ; 2. The Pauline Concept of Faith in Contrast to That of Judaism : a. πίστις and ἔργα νόμου; b. The Eschatological Character of πίστις; 3. The Pauline Concept of Faith in Contrast to Gnosticism : a. Faith as Orientation to the Future (ἐλπίς); b. πίστις and φόβος; c. πίστις and Historical Existence. IV. πιστεύω in John : 1. πιστεύω as Acceptance of the Message ; 2. πιστεύω εἰς and πιστεύω with the Dative ; 3. Faith and Salvation ; 4. Faith as Renunciation of the World ; 5. The Relation between the Johannine Concept of Faith and the Pauline Concept; 6. The Anti-Gnostic Character of the Johannine Concept of Faith ; 7. Faith and Knowledge ; 8. Faith and Love.

A. Greek Usage.

I. Classical Usage. [1]

First attested of the words with πισ-τ- [2] is the (verbal) adj. πιστός, with the privative ἄπιστος. It has the act. and pass. senses of "trusting" and "worthy of trust" ("reliable"). [3] It bears only the latter sense in Hom., but, since ἄπιστος is used by him for "distrustful" (e.g., Od., 14, 150), it is evident that both meanings are original ; they recur in the noun πίστις.

1. πιστός. In lit. this first means a. "trusting" in Theogn., 283 : ἀστῶν μηδενὶ πιστὸς ἐὼν πόδα τῶνδε πρόβαινε. [4] In Aesch. Prom., 915-917; Pers., 52-55 it is used poetically of confidence in weapons or skill in weapons ; [5] of trust in men, Theogn. and also Soph. Oed. Col., 1031; Dio C., 37, 12, 1. Inasmuch as trust may be a duty, πιστός can come to have the nuance "obedient." [6] b. πιστός in the sense "trustworthy" is a word first used in the sphere of sacral law ; ὅρκια are called πιστά (Hom. Il., 2, 124 etc.), also τεκμήρια (Aesch. Suppl., 53 etc.). The expression πιστὰ διδόναι καὶ λαμβάνειν denotes the conclusion of a treaty. [7] τὰ πιστά is the reliability of those bound by the treaty, Aesch. Ag., 651; Xenoph. An., II, 4, 7, i.e., "fidelity"; cf. τὸ πιστόν in Thuc., I, 68, 1. Similarly πιστός ("trustworthy," "faithful") is used of those who stand in a contractual relation : [8]

---

[1] A. deals only with the main uses of πίστις etc. in the Gk. world which are of importance in the history of the bibl. concept or in comparison with this.

[2] Constructs in πιστ- derive from the dep. πείθομαι (→ 1, 1 ff.). Cf. Walde-Pok., II, 139; S. Schulz, *Die Wurzel* ΠΕΙΘ (ΠΙΘ) *im älteren Gr.*, Diss. Bern (1952), 50-58; J. Holt, *Les noms d'action en -σις (-τις). Etudes de linguistique grecque* (1940), 36 f., 41, 57, 63 f.

[3] Schwyzer, I, 501.

[4] Cf. Theogn., 284 : the synon. πίσυνος from the stem πειθ-. This is used in the same sense in Aesch. Pers., 112.

[5] Cf. Plat. Leg., VII, 824.

[6] Xenoph. Hist. Graec., II, 4, 30 : τὴν τῶν Ἀθηναίων χώραν οἰκείαν καὶ πιστὴν ποιήσασθαι. Cf. Hesych.: πιστός = εὐπειθής and → n. 32 and 46.

[7] Xenoph. An., III, 2, 5; IV, 8, 7 etc. Cf. P. Petr., II, 19, 1, 4 (3rd cent. B.C.): τὰ πιστὰ διδόναι, "to give firm assurance."

[8] Cf. Xenoph. Hist. Graec., II, 3, 29 : τοσούτῳ δ' ἔχθιον (is treason as open opposition : προδοσία πολέμου) ὅσῳ πολεμίοις μὲν ἄνθρωποι καὶ σπένδονται καὶ αὖθις πιστοὶ γίγνονται, ὃν δ' ἂν προδιδόντα λαμβάνωσι, τούτῳ οὔτε ἐσπείσατο πώποτε οὐδεὶς οὔτ' ἐπίστευσε τοῦ λοιποῦ. On a Syr. inscr. πιστός is even a title for a "confidant." *v.* Ltzm. K. on 1 C. 7:25.

the ἑταῖρος, φίλος, husband, [9] μάρτυς, also the ἄγγελος, φύλαξ, δοῦλος etc., are all called πιστός, and the wife πιστή. But the meaning broadens out, so that (τὸ) πιστόν can denote "reliability" or "certainty" in general, [10] and πιστός can be used for the quality of "fidelity." [11] In the lit. sense πιστός is not used of things; it is used only of men and of matters constituted or pursued by them. The constancy of things is denoted by βέβαιος, which, since it can also be used of persons and personal conduct (→ I, 600, 17 ff.), is partially synon. with πιστός. [12] In particular a word (ἔπος, ῥῆμα, or λόγος) can be called πιστός, [13] also the γλῶσσα, [14] so that in philosophy the λόγος (Plat. Tim., 49b), the ὑπόθεσις (Plat. Phaed., 107b), or the ἀπόδειξις (Plat. Phaedr., 245c) is πιστός or πιστή, and πιστός can be combined with ἀποδεικτικός (Aristot. Rhet., II, 1, p. 1377b, 23).

2. ἄπιστος. The same pattern is to be found in the use of ἄπιστος : a. "distrustful," so in Hom. Od., 14, 150 etc. and frequently later, [15] b. "unfaithful," "unreliable." The unreliability of relations as well as persons can be denoted by ἄπιστος, Thuc., I, 120, 4, esp. that of word or speech, Hdt., III, 80; Plat. Phaedr., 245c. Thus ἄπιστος can mean "untrustworthy." [16]

3. πίστις. Along the lines of the use of πιστός, πίστις means a. (abstr.) "confidence," "trust," [17] with a ref. in this sense to persons, relations (Thuc., I, 120, 5) and also things. [18] In so far as it contains an element of uncertainty, trust can be contrasted with knowledge, Soph. Trach., 588-593 and expressly in Plat. [19] Nevertheless, it can also mean

---

[9] Eur. Med., 511, cf. J. B. Bury, "Euripides, Medea," Class. Rev., 3 (1889), 220b. For φίλος πιστός = φίλος σαφής in Plat. cf. A. S. Ferguson, "Plato's Simile of Light," The Classical Quarterly, 15 (1921), 144.

[10] Thuc., I, 141, 5 (par. τὸ βέβαιον); II, 40, 5; Eur. Hec., 956. Cf. τὸ πιστὸν τῆς ἀληθείας, Soph. Trach., 398, or τῆς ἐπιστήμης, Thuc., VI, 72, 4; Plat. Crat., 437b: καὶ τὸ πιστὸν ἱστὰν παντάπασι σημαίνει. Occasionally πιστός can also mean "genuine."

[11] Hom. Od., 11, 456; Soph. Trach., 541; Pind. Nem., 10, 78 etc. Cf. also Paus., I, 11, 3 : πιστῶς ἔχειν, "to remain faithful."

[12] Plat. Tim., 49b: πιστῷ καὶ βεβαίῳ χρήσασθαι λόγῳ.

[13] Hdt., VIII, 83; Soph. Oed. Col., 625 f.; Polyb., 15, 7, 1. Cf. γράμματα πιστά in the Aberkios inscr., 6, T. Klauser, Art. "Aberkios," RAC, I, 13.

[14] Eur. Iph. Taur., 1064; cf. Eur. Hipp., 395.

[15] Thuc., I, 68, 1; IV, 17, 5; Epic. in Diog. L., X, 11; Ditt. Syll.[3], III, 1168, 30 ff. (inscr. of the temple of Aesculapius), where ἄπιστος occurs in the two correlative senses : ὅτι τοίνυν ἔμπροσθεν ἀπιστεῖς (sc. τοῖς ἐπιγράμμασιν) οὐκ ἐοῦσιν ἀπίστοις (which are not unworthy of credence") τὸ λοιπὸν ἔστω τοι, φαμέν, Ἄπιστος (the unbeliever) ὄνομα. Subst. τὸ ἄπιστον, "distrust," Thuc., VIII, 66, 4.

[16] Eur. Hec., 689; Aristoph. Pax, 131; Corp. Herm., 9, 10.

[17] Hes. Op., 372 : πίστιες ἄρ τοι ὁμῶς καὶ ἀπιστίαι ὤλεσαν ἄνδρας, Theogn., 831: πίστει χρήματ' ὄλεσσα, ἀπιστίῃ δ' ἐσάωσα, Soph. Oed. Col., 950. Nouns in -τις (-σις) are originally only abstr.; specific concrete meanings have to be derived. Cf. W. Porzig, Die Namen f. Satzinhalte im Griech. u. Indogermanischen (1942), 115-117, esp. 115 on combinations with διδόναι ... For good examples of the movement from the abstr. to the concrete cf. Xenoph. Hist. Graec., VII, 1, 44 : ἐγὼ ὑμῖν ταύτην πίστιν ἐμαυτοῦ δώσω, "I will therewith give you assurance for my person" (confidence in me), i.e., "for my fidelity"; Hom. Il., 14, 198 : δὸς νῦν μοι φιλότητα καὶ ἵμερον, "give me love potions" (lit. the charm of love, Hera to Aphrodite). Cf. also the Lat. fides : 1. "trust"; 2. fidem dare (et accipere), "to give (and receive) a guarantee, one's word" [Debrunner]. On fides cf. R. Heinze, "Fides," Herm., 64 (1929), 140-166.

[18] Plat. Phaedr., 275a : διὰ πίστιν γραφῆς.

[19] Cf. esp. Resp., VI, 511d-e, where νόησις ("insight"), διάνοια ("understanding"), πίστις ("belief") and εἰκασία ("probability") are listed in their graded relation to ἀλήθεια. In Resp., VII, 533e-534a the sequence is ἐπιστήμη, διάνοια, πίστις, εἰκασία, and the last two are summed up as δόξα, the first two as νόησις; the relation of νόησις to δόξα is that of ἐπιστήμη to πίστις. Cf. also Plat. Tim., 29c : ὅ τί περ πρὸς γένεσιν οὐσία, τοῦτο πρὸς πίστιν ἀλήθεια. On the Platonic concept of πίστις cf. J. Stenzel, Plato als Erzieher (1928), 333, Index, s.v. πίστις.

"conviction" and (subj.) "certainty," for δόξῃ μὲν ἕπεται πίστις, Aristot. An., III, 3, p. 428a, 18-20. Parmen. contrasts πίστις ἀληθής (Fr., 1, 30 [Diels⁷, I, 230, 12] "dependable truth" or "trust in what is real") with βροτῶν δόξαι. [20] In Resp., VI, 505 e Plato speaks of πίστις μόνιμος ("firm belief"), and in Tim., 37bc he refers to δόξαι and πίστεις, which are βέβαιοι and ἀληθεῖς though they have to be differentiated, of course, from νοῦς and ἐπιστήμη. Similarly, Plato contrasts πίστις ὀρθή and ἐπιστήμη in Resp., X, 601e. In many cases, however, πίστις is "firm conviction" without such distinctions. [21] b. In acc. with the Gk. feel for language πίστις can denote not only the confidence one has but also the confidence one enjoys (cf. → II, 233, 39 ff. δόξα), i.e., "trustworthiness." This is related to "reliability" (→ 175, 34; 176, 3), though there is a distinction. It is the same as the pass. πιστεύεσθαι. Plut. Pericl., 33, 2 (I, 170a) etc., v. also → n. 25. Stress is often laid on the fact that this πίστις is a higher endowment than wealth. [22] In this sense πίστις is related to παραδοχή (Polyb., 1, 5, 5) and ἀποδοχή (Polyb., 1, 43, 4). c. Concretely πίστις means the "guarantee" which creates the possibility of trust, that which may be relied on, or the assurance of reliability, "assurance." The first use here is in the sphere of sacral law; πίστις is often combined with ὅρκος, Hdt., IX, 92; Plat. Leg., III, 701c etc., and we find πίστεις (πίστιν) διδόναι and λαμβάνειν or δέχεσθαι. [23] πίστις is the "oath of fidelity," "the pledge of faithfulness," "security." [24] This leads on the one side to the sense of "certainty," "trustworthiness," [25] on the other to that of "means of proof," "proof." [26] In particular πίστις denotes the reliability of persons, "faithfulness." [27] It belongs esp. to friendship (φιλία). [28]

4. πιστεύω. πιστεύω (only from the 7th cent.), derived from πιστός, means "to trust," "to rely on." [29] Objects are contracts and oaths, Xenoph. An., III, 1, 29; V, 2, 9, also laws, Aeschin. Oratio in Ctesiphont., 1, then means of power, e.g., arms, Polyb.,

---

[20] Cf. Parm. Fr., 8, 27 f. (Diels⁷, I, 237, 8): πίστις ἀληθής (Diels: "true conviction," i.e., conviction about what is true).

[21] Muson., 35, 9 ff.: πῶς δ᾽ ἂν ἄλλως μᾶλλον ἀνθρώπῳ ὑπάρξειεν (sc. ἡ ἀνδρεία) ἢ εἴ τις περὶ θανάτου καὶ πόνου λάβοι πίστιν ἰσχυρὰν ὡς οὐ κακοῖν ὄντοιν αὐτοῖν; (πίστις ἰσχυρά also Plut. Sertorius, 8, 5 I, 572b); Plot. Enn., I, 3, 3, p. 59, 27 ff.: τὰ μὲν δὴ μαθήματα δοτέον πρὸς συνεθισμὸν κατανοήσεως καὶ πίστεως ἀσωμάτου.

[22] Gorgias Fr., 11a, 21 (Diels⁷, II, 299, 14-19); Demosth. Or., 20, 25; 36, 57.

[23] Hdt., III, 7; Plat. Phaedr., 255d; Xenoph. Hist. Graec., VII, 1, 44 etc. Acc. to Plut. Numa, 16, 1 (I, 70 f.) Numa was the first to build a temple to Πίστις and Terminus and τὴν μὲν Πίστιν ὅρκον ἀποδεῖξαι Ῥωμαίοις μέγιστον. On depictions of Πίστις cf. Roscher, III, 2512, and of Fides (an ancient goddess), I, 1481-1483. Cf. also Theogn., 1135-1138: Ἐλπὶς ἐν ἀνθρώποισι μόνη θεὸς ἐσθλὴ ἔνεστιν, ἄλλοι δ᾽ Οὔλυμπόνδ᾽ ἐκπρολιπόντες ἔβαν. ᾤχετο μὲν Πίστις, μεγάλη θεός, ᾤχετο δ᾽ ἀνδρῶν Σωφροσύνη, ... For personification of πίστις cf. the (badly attested) verse Hes. Op., 372 (→ n. 17) and Soph. Oed. Col., 611: θνήσκει δὲ πίστις, βλαστάνει δ᾽ ἀπιστία. Πίστις is invoked with Δίκη in Orph. Hymn. prooem, 25. On Πίστις in the Aberkios inscr. (→ n. 13) v. F. J. Dölger, Ichthys, II (1922), 482 f.

[24] Soph. Oed. Col., 1632: δός μοι χερὸς σῆς πίστιν ἀρχαίαν τέκνοις, also Trach., 1182 f.

[25] Aristot. Eth. Nic., X, 9, p. 1179a, 17 f.; Polyb., 4, 33, 1; Plut. Demosth., 2, 1 (I, 846d). So also Thuc., VI, 53, 2: διὰ πονηρῶν ἀνθρώπων πίστιν? Plat. Phaedr., 275a: διὰ πίστιν γραφῆς (or is "trust" the meaning here? → n. 18).

[26] Democr. Fr., 125 (Diels⁷, II, 168, 8); Eur. Hipp., 1321; Plat. Phaed., 70b; Aristot. Rhet., III, 13, p. 1414a, 34 ff.: τούτων δὲ τὸ μὲν πρόθεσίς ἐστι, τὸ δὲ πίστις, ὥσπερ εἴ τις διέλοι ὅτι τὸ μὲν πρόβλημα, τὸ δὲ ἀπόδειξις.

[27] Aesch. Pers., 443; Theogn., 1137 (→ n. 23); Xenoph. Hier., 4, 1: πίστεως ὅστις ἐλάχιστον μετέχει, πῶς οὐχὶ μεγάλου ἀγαθοῦ μειονεκτεῖ; ποία μὲν γὰρ ξυνουσία ἡδεῖα ἄνευ πίστεως τῆς πρὸς ἀλλήλους, ποία δ᾽ ἀνδρὶ καὶ γυναικὶ τερπνὴ ἄνευ πίστεως ὁμιλία, ποῖος δὲ θεράπων ἡδὺς ἀπιστούμενος; Cf. Plut. Lib. Educ., 14 (II, 10 f.).

[28] Xenoph. An., I, 6, 3; Hist. Graec., II, 3, 28; Aristot. Eth. M., II, 11, p. 1208b, 24; Eth. Eud., VII, 2, p. 1237b, 12: οὐκ ἔσται ἄνευ πίστεως φιλία βέβαιος.

[29] Cf. E. Fraenkel, Gr. Denominativa (1906), 179.

5, 62, 6, or abstr. facts [30] or probability, Plat. Resp., X, 603b, finally persons, [31] in which case πιστεύειν can acquire the nuance "to obey." [32] The pass. πιστεύεσθαι means "to enjoy confidence." [33] Since words can be the obj. of πιστεύειν, [34] it can also mean "to believe," and in this sense it can have a personal obj. (dat.) [35] or a material obj. (acc.). [36] It can also be construed with περί, [37] with acc. and inf., [38] or with a ὅτι clause, Plat. Gorg., 512e. It can also be abs., yet in such a way that an obj. is to be supplied. [39] In the sense "to believe" πιστεύειν can also be used in the pass., Plat. Leg., I, 636d; Aristot. An., III, 3, p. 428b, 4. The personal obj. in the dat. can be the subj. in the pass. [40] Later πιστεύειν often means "to confide in" [41] (rare in Attic), [42] so commonly in the pass. [43]

5. ἀπιστέω. The private ἀπιστέω (from ἄπιστος) is not clearly attested in the sense "to be untrustworthy," "unreliable"; it means "to be distrustful," "unbelieving." [44] Its special ref. in this sense is to words, [45] and it can mean "not to believe," Epict. Diss., II, 22, 23; Plot. Enn., V, 8, 11, p. 246, 2 ff. The pass. can also be used thus, Xenoph. Hier., 4, 1 (→ n. 27). From this developed the sense "not to obey," [46] esp. with laws as obj., Soph. Ant., 219, 381 f., 655 f.

6. ἀπιστία. This related noun means a. "unreliability," "unfaithfulness," Soph. Oed. Col., 611; Xenoph. An., II, 5, 21; III, 2, 4, hence also "untrustworthiness," Hdt., I, 193; Plat. Phaed., 88d; b. "distrust," "doubt." [47]

7. πιστόω. Of other words in πιστ- only πιστόω need be mentioned with ref. to the NT. [48] It means "to make someone a πιστός," namely, a. one who is bound by an oath, contract, pledge, etc., and who may thus be relied on, Soph. Oed. Col., 650; Thuc., IV, 88; also pass. in this sense, Hom. Od., 15, 436; Eur. Iph. Aul., 66; in the mid. "to give

---

[30] Demosth. Or., 44, 3 : ἡμεῖς μὲν γὰρ ταῖς ἀληθείαις πιστεύοντες.
[31] Thuc., III, 83, 2; VII, 85, 1; VIII, 81, 3 (twice); Xenoph. An., I, 9, 8; Eur. Or. 1103; also ἑαυτῷ, Thuc., III, 5, 2; Xenoph. Vect., 2, 4.
[32] Soph. Oed. Tyr., 625; Oed. Col., 174 f.; Trach., 1228 f.: πείθου τὸ γάρ τοι μεγάλα πιστεύσαντ' ἐμοὶ σμικροῖς ἀπιστεῖν τὴν πάρος συγχεῖ χάριν, cf. 1251. Cf. J. S. Phillimore, "Notes on Sophocles Oedipus Tyrannus," Class. Rev., 16 (1902), 338b (→ n. 6, 46).
[33] Xenoph. An., VII, 6, 33; Cyrop., VI, 1, 39; Aristot. Pol., V, 5, p. 1305a, 21 f.; Plut. Praec. Coniug., 36 (II, 143c).
[34] Hdt., II, 118; Soph. El., 883-886; Eur. Hel., 710; Plat. Phaed., 88d; Phileb., 13a.
[35] Hdt., II, 120; Aristot. Rhet., II, 14, p. 1390a, 32 f.: οὔτε πᾶσι πιστεύοντες οὔτε πᾶσιν ἀπιστοῦντες.
[36] Aristot. An. Pri., II, 23, p. 68b, 13 : ἅπαντα γὰρ πιστεύομεν ἢ διὰ συλλογισμοῦ ἢ ἐξ ἐπαγωγῆς.
[37] Hdt., IV, 96; Aristot. Eth. Nic., VIII, 4, p. 1157a, 21.
[38] Hdt., VI, 105; Plat. Gorg., 524a: ἃ ἐγὼ ἀκηκοὼς πιστεύω ἀληθῆ εἶναι. Luc. Philops., 32; Plot. Enn., IV, 7, 10, p. 138, 7 f.; V, 8, 11, p. 246, 4 f.
[39] Soph. Oed. Tyr., 625; Corp. Herm., 9, 10.
[40] Xenoph. An., VII, 7, 25 : πιστευθεὶς ἀληθεύσειν ἃ λέγεις.
[41] Plut. Apophth.: Agis junior, 2 (II, 191e): οὐκ ... πιστεύειν τοὺς ἀλλοτρίους τῷ προδόντι τοὺς ἰδίους. In pap., v. Preisigke Wört., s.v.
[42] Thuc., II, 35, 1 (?); Xenoph. Mem., IV, 4, 17: τίνι δ' ἄν τις μᾶλλον πιστεύσειε παρακαταθέσθαι ἢ χρήματα ἢ υἱοὺς ἢ θυγατέρας; cf. (sc. παρακατατίθεσθαι) Xenoph. Sym., 8, 36.
[43] Polyb., 8, 17, 4; Preis. Zaub., II, 13, 140 f. (and 445 f.): ὁ ὑπό σου ταχθεὶς καὶ πάντα πιστευθεὶς τὰ αὐθεντικά, Ἥλιος ...
[44] Hom. Od., 13, 339; Eur. Alc., 1130; Aristoph. Eccl., 775. Cf. the maxims of Epicharmus Fr., 13 (Diels⁷, I, 201, 2): νᾶφε καὶ μέμνασ' ἀπιστεῖν· ἄρθρα ταῦτα τᾶν φρενῶν.
[45] Eur. Med., 927.
[46] Hdt., VI, 108 (οὐκ ἠπίστησαν = ἐπίστευσαν); Aesch. Prom., 640; Soph. Trach., 1224; 1229 (here opp. πιστεύειν; → n. 6, 32), 1240; Xenoph. An., II, 6, 19 (not "to be unfaithful," as in Pr.-Bauer⁴, s.v.); VI, 6, 13.
[47] Theogn., 83; (→ n. 17); Hes. Op., 372 (→ n. 17); Aesch. Ag., 268; Eur. Hel., 1617.
[48] Cf. E. Fraenkel, op. cit., 150.

reciprocal guarantees," Hom. Il., 6, 233; 21, 286; Polyb., 1, 43, 5; 18, 22, 6, or b. "to make him one who trusts," "to engage confidence," Hom. Od., 21, 217 f.; Soph. Oed. Col., 1039.

8. The Question of Religious Terminology. The words in πιστ- did not become religious terms in classical Greek. It is true that faithfulness to a compact is a religious duty, [49] and fidelity and piety are closely related. [50] πίσυνος, which means the same as πιστός in the sense "trusting," can have the deity as object, Aesch. Sept. c. Theb., 211 f.; ἄπιστος = "unbelieving" can also carry a reference to deity. [51] But in no sense is πιστός used for the true religious relationship to God or for the basic religious attitude of man. Nor did πίστις become a religious term. At most one can only say that the possibility of its so doing is intimated by the fact that it can refer to reliance on a god, [52] and that in the sense of "conviction" it can take the existence of the deity as its object. [53] Again, there are only the first beginnings of religious use in respect of πιστεύειν, ἀπιστεῖν and ἀπιστία. In the sense of "to trust" πιστεύειν can refer to τύχη [54] and also to deity. [55] When it means "to put faith" the object can be, not only human words, but also divine sayings [56] and even deity itself. [57] The same applies to ἀπιστεῖν and ἀπιστία. [58]

II. Hellenistic Usage.

1. The Development of a Religious Usage in Philosophical Discussion.

Whereas in the older Gk. world the idea that there are gods used to be expressed by νομίζειν, [59] πιστεύειν can be used instead in a later period. In keeping is the fact that πιστεύειν can take on the sense "to believe" (→ 178, 3 ff.).

---

[49] Xenoph. Ag., 3, 5 : μέγα καὶ καλὸν κτῆμα ... ἀνδρὶ δὴ στρατηγῷ τὸ ὅσιόν τε καὶ πιστὸν εἶναί τε καὶ ὄντα ἐγνῶσθαι.

[50] Eur. Hec., 1234 f.: οὔτ' εὐσεβῆ γὰρ οὔτε πιστὸν οἷς ἐχρῆν, οὐχ ὅσιον, οὐ δίκαιον εὖ δράσεις ξένον.

[51] Eur. Iph. Taur., 1475 f.: ἄνασσ' Ἀθάνα, τοῖσι τῶν θεῶν λόγοις ὅστις κλύων ἄπιστος, οὐκ ὀρθῶς φρονεῖ.

[52] Soph. Oed. Tyr., 1445 : καὶ γὰρ σὺ νῦν τἂν τῷ θεῷ πίστιν φέροις = "now you may put faith in the god," i.e., the saying of Apollo. In Emped. Fr., 71, 1; 114, 3 (Diels[7], I, 338, 1; 356, 2) πίστις can hardly mean "belief" (in the divine revelation), so W. Nestle, Vom Mythos zum Logos (1940), 113; it rather means "conviction," → 177, 1.

[53] Plat. Leg., XII, 966d : ἆρα οὖν ἴσμεν ὅτι δύ' ἐστὸν τὼ περὶ θεῶν ἄγοντε εἰς πίστιν, ὅσα διήλθομεν ἐν τοῖς πρόσθεν (namely, the nature of the soul and the order of the cosmos). This πίστις is the presupposition for being a θεοσεβής, 967d; the ἄθεος does not have it, 966e; 967a c.

[54] Thuc., V, 104; 112, 2; Aristot. Rhet., II, 17, p. 1391b, 1 ff.; Plut. Apophth. Lac.: Leotychides, 2 (II, 224d).

[55] Aristoph. Nu., 437; Thuc., IV, 92, 7; Aeschin. Oratio in Ctesiphont., 1; Ps.-Plat. Epin., 980c. For πίσυνος (→ n. 4) cf. Hdt., VII, 153; VIII, 143. Cf. Vergil. Aen., 2, 402 : Heu nihil invitis fas quemquam fidere divis.

[56] Aesch. Pers., 800 f.; Xenoph. Ap., 15; Luc. Alex., 11.

[57] Soph. Phil., 1374 : θεοῖς τε πιστεύσαντα τοῖς τ' ἐμοῖς λόγοις.

[58] Hdt., I, 158 (τῷ χρησμῷ); Eur. Ion, 557: τῷ θεῷ γοῦν οὐκ ἀπιστεῖν εἰκός, 1606; Plat. Tim., 40d-e.

[59] Aesch. Pers., 497 f.; Aristoph. Nu., 819; Plat. Ap., 24b (complaint against Socrates); Xenoph. Mem., I, 1, 1; Plut. Pericl., 32 (I, 169d) (motion of Diopeithes under Pericles): εἰσαγγέλλεσθαι τοὺς τὰ θεῖα μὴ νομίζοντας, Luc. Jup. Trag., 42. Cf. Ps.-Luc. Syr. Dea, 2 : θεῶν ἔννοιην λαβεῖν, → IV, 1024, 6. Cf. also K. Latte, Review in Gnomon, 7 (1931), 120; J. Tate, "Greek for 'Atheism,'" Class. Rev., 50 (1936), 3-5; also "More Greek for 'Atheism,'" Class. Rev., 51 (1937), 3; K. Kerényi, Die Antike Religion (1940), 77-79; B. Snell, Die Entdeckung des Geistes (1946), 41 f.

This use develops in the debate with scepticism and atheism. Thus Plut. (Superst., 11 [II, 170 f.]) says : οὐκ οἴεται θεοὺς εἶναι ὁ ἄθεος, ὁ δὲ δεισιδαίμων οὐ βούλεται, πιστεύει δ' ἄκων· φοβεῖται γὰρ ἀπιστεῖν. [60] The belief that there are gods has its own certainty, but it is not self-evident ; it presupposes the overcoming of objections. [61] The fact that the divine direction of the world is invisible is no reason for not believing in it. [62] Thus acc. to Plot. (→ n. 21) man ought to be led by knowledge to belief in the incorporeal, for the subj. of faith cannot be αἴσθησις, which is oriented to the corporeal, but only νοῦς. [63] Acc. to Vett. Val. the deity itself also brings the unbeliever to faith. [34] This makes it evident that πίστις is not just theoretical conviction but piety (εὐσέβεια) as well. Faith in God is also faith in the divine providence, [65] and the piety of such faith is emphasised by Plut. [66] How this faith determines conduct is described by Porphyr. [67]

---

[60] Luc. Pseudolog., 10 : σύ μοι δοκεῖς ... τὰ τοιαῦτα λέγων οὐδὲ θεοὺς εἶναι πιστεύειν.

[61] Corp. Herm., 4, 9 : τὰ μὲν γὰρ φαινόμενα τέρπει, τὰ δὲ ἀφανῆ δυσπιστεῖν ποιεῖ.

[62] Ps.-Aristot. Mund., 6, p. 399b, 12 f.: the invisibility of the divine direction of the world οὐδαμῶς ἐστιν ἐμπόδιον οὔτε ἐκείνῃ πρὸς τὸ δρᾶν, οὔτε ἡμῖν πρὸς τὸ πιστεῦσαι. But cf. already Heracl. Fr., 86 (Diels⁷, I, 170, 5 f.): ἀλλὰ τῶν μὲν θείων τὰ πολλά, καθ' Ἡράκλειτον, ἀπιστίῃ διαφυγγάνει μὴ γιγνώσκεσθαι = "in large measure knowledge of the divine escapes the understanding because there is no belief therein" (so Diels², I, 74, 34 ff.); cf. Plut. De Coriolano, 38 (I, 232c), who refers to this statement when he speaks of the wonderful nature of the δύναμις of God.

[63] Plot. Enn., V, 8, 11, p. 246, 2 ff.: τὸ οὖν ἀπιστοῦν ἡ αἴσθησίς ἐστιν, ὁ δὲ ἄλλος (the νοῦς) ἐστὶν ὁ ἰδών· ἤ, εἰ ἀπιστοῖ κἀκεῖνος, οὐδ' ἂν αὐτὸν πιστεύσειεν εἶναι.

[64] Vett. Val., IX, 1, p. 331, 12 ff.: (He who has perceived the law in the alternation of life, to him comes life, deity ; he who has not perceived it, to him they are denied) ὅπως διὰ τούτων οἱ ἀμαθεῖς καὶ θεομάχοι πίστιν ἐνεγκάμενοι καὶ ἑταῖροί γε τῆς ἀληθείας γενόμενοι ὑπαρκτὴν καὶ σεβάσμιον τὴν ἐπιστήμην καταλάβωσιν.

[65] Plut. Ser. Num. Pun., 3 (II, 549b): ὅτι τὴν πίστιν ἡ βραδύτης ἀφαιρεῖται τῆς προνοίας. For ἀπιστέω and ἄπιστος in relation to the miraculous power of deity → n. 15.

[66] Plut. Pyth. Or., 18 (II, 402e): δεῖ γὰρ μὴ μάχεσθαι πρὸς τὸν θεὸν μηδ' ἀναιρεῖν μετὰ τῆς μαντικῆς ἅμα τὴν πρόνοιαν καὶ τὸ θεῖον, ἀλλὰ τῶν ὑπεναντιοῦσθαι δοκούντων λύσεις ἐπιζητεῖν, τὴν δ' εὐσεβῆ καὶ πάτριον μὴ προΐεσθαι πίστιν. Amat., 13 (II, 756a b): μεγάλου μοι δοκεῖς ἅπτεσθαι ... καὶ παραβόλου πράγματος ... μᾶλλον δὲ ὅλως τὸ ἀκίνητα κινεῖν τῆς περὶ θεῶν δόξης ἣν ἔχομεν, περὶ ἑκάστου λόγον ἀπαιτῶν καὶ ἀπόδειξιν· ἀρκεῖ γὰρ ἡ πάτριος καὶ παλαιὰ πίστις ... ἀλλ' ἕδρα τις αὕτη καὶ βάσις ὑφεστῶσα κοινὴ πρὸς εὐσέβειαν, ἐὰν ἐφ' ἑνὸς ταράττηται καὶ σαλεύηται τὸ βέβαιον αὐτῆς καὶ νενομισμένον ἐπισφαλὲς γίνεται πᾶσι καὶ ὕποπτος. Is. et Os., 23 (II, 359 f.): the euhemeristic explanation of myths should ἐξ οὐρανοῦ μεταφέρειν ἐπὶ γῆν ὀνόματα τηλικαῦτα καὶ τιμὴν καὶ πίστιν ὀλίγου δεῖν ἅπασιν ἐκ πρώτης γενέσεως ἐνδεδυκυῖαν ἐξιστάναι καὶ ἀναλύειν → n. 77.

[67] Porphyr. Marc., 21 ff.: ... θεὸν οἱ μὲν εἶναι νομίζοντες καὶ διοικεῖν ἅπαντα τοῦτο γέρας ἐκτήσαντο διὰ τῆς γνώσεως καὶ τῆς βεβαίας πίστεως, τὸ μεμαθηκέναι ὅτι ὑπὸ θεοῦ προνοεῖται πάντα καὶ εἰσὶν ἄγγελοι θεῖοί τε καὶ ἀγαθοὶ δαίμονες ἐπόπται τῶν πραττομένων, οὓς καὶ λαθεῖν ἀμήχανον. καὶ δὴ τοῦτο οὕτως ἔχειν πεπεισμένοι φυλάττονται μὲν μὴ διαπίπτειν τοῖς κατὰ τὸν βίον, πρὸ ὄψεως ἔχοντες τὴν τῶν θεῶν ἀναπόδραστον ἐφόρασιν· εὐγνώμονα δὲ βίον κτησάμενοι μανθάνουσι θεοὺς γινώσκονταί τε γινωσκομένοις θεοῖς. (22) οἱ δὲ μήτε εἶναι θεοὺς πιστεύσαντες μήτε προνοίᾳ θεοῦ διοικεῖσθαι τὰ ὅλα, δίκης κόλασιν πεπόνθασι τὸ μήτε ἑαυτοῖς πιστεύειν μήθ' ἑτέροις ὅτι θεοί εἰσι καὶ οὐκ ἀλόγῳ φορᾷ διοικεῖται τὰ πάντα ... They act lawlessly, ἀναιρεῖν πειρώμενοι τὴν περὶ θεοὺς ὑπόληψιν. καὶ δὴ τούτους μὲν ἀγνοίας ἕνεκα καὶ ἀπιστίας θεοὶ διαφεύγουσιν ... (23) κἂν θεοὺς τιμᾶν οἴωνται καὶ πεπεῖσθαι εἶναι θεούς, ἀρετῆς δὲ ἀμελῶσι καὶ σοφίας, ἤρηνται θεοὺς καὶ ἀτιμάζουσιν. οὔτε γὰρ ἄλογος πίστις δίχα τοῦ ὀρθῶς <ζῆν> ἐπιτυχὴς θεοῦ, οὔτε μὴν τὸ τιμᾶν θεοσεβὲς ἄνευ τοῦ μεμαθηκέναι ὅτῳ τρόπῳ χαίρει τὸ θεῖον τιμώμενον ... (24) ... τέσσαρα στοιχεῖα μάλιστα κεκρατύνθω περὶ θεοῦ· πίστις, ἀλήθεια, ἔρως, ἐλπίς. πιστεῦσαι γὰρ δεῖ ὅτι μόνη σωτηρία ἡ πρὸς τὸν θεὸν ἐπιστροφή, καὶ πιστεύσαντα ὡς ἔνι μάλιστα σπουδάσαι τἀληθῆ γνῶναι περὶ αὐτοῦ, καὶ γνόντα ἐρασθῆναι τοῦ γνωσθέντος, ἐρασθέντα δὲ ἐλπίσιν ἀγαθαῖς τρέφειν τὴν ψυχὴν διὰ τοῦ βίου.

Part of faith in the invisible is faith in the immortality of the soul, [68] in one's own membership in the divine world, [69] and in judgment after death. [70] One may thus understand why Porphyr. Marc., 24 regards πίστις as one of the four στοιχεῖα, → n. 67. [71]

2. The Usage of Religious Propaganda. [72]

The use of πίστις as a religious term is also promoted by the fact that πίστις became a catchword in those religions which engaged in propaganda. This did not apply to Christianity alone. All missionary preaching demanded faith in the deity proclaimed by it.

Thus Celsus (Orig. Cels., VI, 11 [GCS, 80, 33 ff.]) says that some (Christians) proclaim one saviour and others another, but they all say : πίστευσον, εἰ σωθῆναι θέλεις, ἢ ἄπιθι. The Herm. writings reflect this vocabulary. [73] Following the word of preaching, the νοῦς rises to truth and attains to faith, καὶ τῇ καλῇ πίστει ἐπανεπαύσατο. [74] Lucius, initiated into the Isis mysteries, confesses : plena iam fiducia germanae religionis obsequium divinum frequentabam, Apul. Met., XI, 28. The same terminology is presupposed in the Isis litany in P. Oxy., XI, 1380, 152 : ὁρῶσί σε οἱ κατὰ τὸ πιστὸν ἐπικαλούμενοι, which may mean either : "Those who call upon thee as is in keeping with the relation of faith (between God and man)," or : ... "in the manner of believers." [75] We find the same usage in the Od. Sol. "Grace is revealed to your redemption. Believe, and you shall live and be redeemed." [76] In the sphere of belief in miracles and dogmas πιστεύειν etc. occur in the Pythagorean legend. [77] Finally, the vocabulary made its way into the magical world. [78] There can be no certainty whether

---

[68] Plot. Enn., IV, 7, 10, p. 138, 6 ff.: (if each man had a divine soul) οὐδεὶς οὕτως <ἂν> ἦν ἄπιστος ὡς μὴ πιστεύειν τὸ τῆς ψυχῆς αὐτοῖς πάντη ἀθάνατον εἶναι. Cf. Scott, I, 370, 9 ff.: (Whoever lets himself be illuminated by God and is liberated from his mortal nature) immortalitatis futurae concipit fiduciam.

[69] Plot. Enn., IV, 8, 1, p. 142, 10 ff.: πολλάκις ἐγειρόμενος εἰς ἐμαυτὸν ... θαυμαστὸν ἡλίκον ὁρῶν κάλλος καὶ τῆς κρείττονος μοίρας πιστεύσας τότε μάλιστα εἶναι.

[70] Scott, I, 366, 6 ff.: incredibilitas humana despises the belief in judgment after death, but the incredibiles ... post delicta cogentur credere, non verbis, sed exemplis, nec minis, sed ipsa passione poenarum, Scott, I, 366, 20 f.

[71] πίστις is also a τριάς with ἀλήθεια and ἔρως in Orac. Chald. (W. Kroll, "De oraculis Chaldaicis," Breslauer Philologische Abh., VII, 1 [1894], 26).

[72] Cf. Reitzenstein Hell. Myst., 234-236; O. Kitzig, Die Bekehrung d. Pls. (1932), 176-180.

[73] Corp. Herm., 4, 4 : (man's heart is addressed) βάπτισον σεαυτὴν ἡ δυναμένη εἰς τοῦτον τὸν κρατῆρα (whom God has sent down), ἡ πιστεύουσα ὅτι ἀνελεύσῃ πρὸς τὸν καταπέμψαντα τὸν κρατῆρα. In Corp. Herm., 1, 2 the believer confesses : διὸ πιστεύω καὶ μαρτυρῶ· εἰς ζωὴν καὶ φῶς χωρῶ.

[74] Corp. Herm., 9, 10; the text is unfortunately not quite certain ; cf. Scott, I, 185, 25-186, 4 and Reitzenstein Hell. Myst., 235.

[75] Cf. R. Reitzenstein, "Die Formel Glaube, Liebe, Hoffnung bei Pls.," NGG, Philologisch-hist. Klasse (1917), 132.

[76] Od. Sol. 34:6; cf. also 4:5; 8:11; 28:3; 29:6; 35:5, 13, and the believers in 4:3; 15:10; 22:7. How far what is said about faith in the Mandaean and Manichean lit. derives from the general religious history of Hell., and how far it is influenced by Chr. usage, it is, of course, impossible to say. Cf. H. Jonas, Gnosis u. spätantiker Geist, I² (1954), 137 and the material assembled in Wissmann, 44 f.

[77] Iambl. Vit. Pyth., 138, p. 78, 17 ff. of the Pythagoreans : πᾶσι γὰρ πιστεύουσι τοῖς τοιούτοις (namely, μυθολογούμενα concerning θεῖοι ἄνθρωποι) ... ὡς οὐδὲν ἀπιστοῦντες ὅ τι ἂν εἰς τὸ θεῖον ἀνάγηται. 148, p. 83, 18 ff. of Pythagoras : ὑπῆρχε δὲ αὐτῷ ἀπὸ τῆς εὐσεβείας καὶ ἡ περὶ θεῶν πίστις (→ n. 66). παρήγγελλε γὰρ ἀεὶ περὶ θεῶν μηδὲν θαυμαστὸν ἀπιστεῖν μηδὲ περὶ θείων δογμάτων, ὡς πάντα τῶν θεῶν δυναμένων. καὶ τὰ θεῖα δὲ δόγματα λέγειν (οἷς χρὴ πιστεύειν) ἃ Πυθαγόρας παρέδωκεν. οὕτως γοῦν ἐπίστευον καὶ παρειλήφεσαν περὶ ὧν δογματίζουσιν ὅτι οὐκ ἐψευδοδόξηται.

[78] In Preis. Zaub., I, 4, 1012 ff. the deity is invoked : ὁ ἐπὶ τῆς τοῦ κόσμου κεφαλῆς καθήμενος καὶ κρίνων τὰ πάντα, περιβεβλημένος τῷ τῆς ἀληθείας καὶ πίστεως

the "virgin of faith" whom king Bel married (Aram. inscr. from Cappadocia) is to be understood along these lines. The "virgin of faith" seems to be a personification of mazdayasnian religion. [79] The title of the Gnostic work Pistis Sophia bears witness to the mythological personification of Πίστις, but this may have its origin in Chr. usage. [80]

3. Stoic Usage.

In the older Stoa the attitude of πίστις (= "trust") befits the σοφός as a κατάληψις ἰσχυρά, βεβαιοῦσα τὸ ὑπολαμβανόμενον, Chrysipp. Fr., 548 (v. Arnim, III, 147, 9-11). πίστις acquires special significance in the sense of "reliability," "faithfulness," in the later Stoics Epict. and M. Ant., cf. Epict. Diss., II, 4, 1: ὁ ἄνθρωπος πρὸς πίστιν γέγονεν καὶ τοῦτο ὁ ἀνατρέπων ἀνατρέπει τὸ ἴδιον τοῦ ἀνθρώπου. The background of this estimation is the Stoic distinction of things into those which are ἐφ᾽ ἡμῖν and those which are not. Man must fashion his προαίρεσις so that it is directed only to τὰ ἐφ᾽ ἡμῖν and is thus σύμφωνος τῇ φύσει. It is then πιστή, the man who directs his striving only to the ἐφ᾽ ἡμῖν is a πιστός, a man who is "unalterably reliable" (Epict. Diss., I, 4, 18 f.), and his ἡγεμονικόν is πιστόν (II, 22, 25). πίστις is thus solidity of character, and it is typical that πιστός and πίστις are used abs.; no obj. needs to be supplied. πιστός is only the reverse side of ἐλεύθερος, with which it is not infrequently combined. [81] As God is πιστός and ἐλεύθερος, so should man be, Epict. Diss., II, 14, 13. The nature of πιστός is further characterised by the fact that πιστός is often associated with αἰδήμων [82] and πίστις with αἰδώς, → I, 170, 3 ff. [83] Primarily, then, πίστις is an attitude of man to himself, not to others. As man's faithfulness to himself, however, πίστις makes possible a right relation to others. He who is πιστός = "faithful to himself" can also be πιστός = "faithful" to others ; he alone is capable of genuine friendship. [84]

In Stoicism, then, πίστις has no religious significance in the sense of denoting man's relation to deity or of having deity and its sway as objects. The attitude of πίστις is, however, a religious attitude to the degree that in it man, as πιστός, ἐλεύθερος and αἰδήμων, actualises his relationship to God.

Bultmann

B. The Old Testament Concept.

I. General Remarks.

If very generally faith is regarded as man's relation and attitude to God, the OT statements regarding it are not of primary importance. For the most part anthropological interest is here secondary to a theocentric view. As the OT understands it, faith is always man's reaction to God's primary action. Related hereto is the fact that older OT religion was collective in structure, [85] and it was difficult to give expression to the inner life of the community. Thus a wealth of usage

---

κύκλῳ. The conjuration in XII, 228 f. reads : ἐγὼ ἡ Πίστις εἰς ἀνθρώπους εὑρεθεῖσα καὶ προφήτης τῶν ἁγίων ὀνομάτων εἰμί.

[79] M. Lidzbarski, *Ephemeris,* I (1900), 69; Reitzenstein Hell. Myst., 235; H. Gressmann, "Das religionsgeschichtliche Problem des Ursprungs der hell. Erlösungsreligion," ZKG, NF, 3 (1922), 186.

[80] C. Schmidt, Pistis Sophia (1925), XXI; cf. the personification of Πίστις in the Aberkios inscr. → n. 23; Ign. Sm., 10, 2, where Jesus Christ Himself is described as ἡ τελεία πίστις (vl. ἐλπίς).

[81] Epict. Diss., I, 4, 18 f.; II, 14, 13; 22, 27; IV, 3, 7.

[82] *Ibid.,* II, 2, 4; 4, 2; III, 28, 18 etc.

[83] *Ibid.,* I, 3, 4; III, 14, 13; M. Ant., 3, 7; 5, 33; 10, 13 etc.

[84] In Epict. Diss., IV, 1, 126 πιστός and φιλάλληλος are combined. Cf. also II, 4, 1-3 and II, 22 : περὶ φιλίας : only the πιστός is capable of friendship.

[85] Cf. F. Baumgärtel, *Die Eigenart der at.lichen Frömmigkeit* (1932), 20-25, 49-63, 95-103.

begins to appear only when the individual breaks free from the collective bond, and on the basis of his own experience devotes special attention to the attitude of man to God. The prophets, by a deepening of content, gave a new creative impulse to the vocabulary and imagery of faith. The greatest extension of range and colour in the language of faith takes place in the Psalms, where the piety of the individual is most clearly expressed.

A consideration of faith in the OT cannot overlook the astonishing fact that two basically different and even contradictory groups of meaning are used for man's relation to God, namely, fear on the one side and trust on the other. These were felt to be contradictory right up to the later period, and yet they were close, and even shaded into one another, so that the fear of God could often be quite simply an expression for faith. [86] In the contradictory nature of the usage there is expressed the living tension and polar dynamic of the OT relationship to God. This is of fundamental significance for the OT attitude of faith. [87]

Statistical analysis of the use of the individual groups yields the following results. Fear and trust are used more or less equally for the relationship to God (about 150 times each). Of verbal stems in the second group בטח comes first in quantitative use : 57 times in a religious sense (37 times in the Ps., 3 with ref. to idols), and 60 times in a secular sense. Next comes חסה; 34 times in a religious sense (24 in the Ps.), 5 in a secular sense. There then follow the verbs of hope : קוה 32 times with ref. to God (12 in Ps.), 11 with a secular ref.; יחל 15 times with ref. to God, 14 with a secular ref.; חכה 6 times with ref. to God and 8 with a secular ref.; the hi of אמן, for which alone the LXX uses the stem πίστις and derivates, and which is directly related to God only 15 times, while in 10 instances it is either used abs. or related to God's word, commandment, or act, and in 23 instances it bears a secular ref. The ni, which occurs 45 times, is used of God Himself 12 times, but is used of man's relation to God in only 3 instances.

The question arises whether the statistics relating to the use of the individual verbal stems, in which אמן = πιστεύειν comes only fourth, really give a true picture of the qualitative importance of these stems in the OT, as though the use of πιστεύειν in the LXX and NT were the arbitrary selection of a less important OT stem. Or could it be that the NT adopted a form which was essential and basic in relation to the OT view of faith, giving a high place on its escutcheon to a term in which the profundity of the OT concept of faith was really brought to full and comprehensive expression? None of the stems mentioned is specifically religious in origin. In each the religious use seems to have secular roots. In establishing the special significance of the individual stems, therefore, the profane use and meaning must be considered first. An attempt must then be made to depict the historical change in meaning and significance.

II. The Stem אמן and Related Expressions (→ I, 232-238).

1. Qal. The qal, found only in the part., has a narrowly circumscribed range of meaning ; it is used of the mother, nurse, or attendant of a child (2 S. 4:4; Rt. 4:16; Nu. 11:12) and is a term for the guardian or foster-father (2 K. 10:1, 5; Est. 2:7; [Is. 49:23]). The pass. part. in Lam. 4:5 denotes the child "wrapped" in purple, the ni in Is. 60:4 the child which is "carried" at the mother's side. In an abstr. fem. construct

---

[86] E.g., Gn. 20:11; 22:12; Is. 8:13; 11:2; Prv. 1:7; Ps. 19:9; 111:10 etc.
[87] J. Hempel, "Gott u. Mensch im AT²," BWANT (1936), 4-33, 233-249. I am intentionally avoiding Hempel's expressions "feeling of distance and relationship" because fear in the OT is more than this, being an awareness of the menacing and destruction of one's own existence, while trust includes a special mode of being beyond that of relationship.

the noun אָמְנָה is used in Est. 2:20 for "education," "upbringing." Whether the usual transl. "to carry," "to hold," or the close connection between mother, nurse, attendant, guardian and child, comes closest to the original sense can no more be decided with certainty than the question whether or what connection there is between this use of the word and the religious use, → 185, 15 ff.; 187, 9 ff. and n. 111. [88]

2. Niphal. The range of the ni is essentially broader. The usual transl. "firm," "secure," "reliable" is only an approximation and does not really get down to the basic and final meaning. [89] This may best be seen when in secular use the word is connected with an object. Thus, e.g., it is used with a place in Is. 22:23 to show its suitability for a specific purpose : "I will fasten him as a tent-peg in a מָקוֹם נֶאֱמָן." Again it is used of the dynasty (posterity) to indicate that it will not die out, 1 S. 2:35; 25:28; 2 S. 7:16; 1 K. 11:38. [90] In Dt. 28:59 the part. is used for "great blows and severe sicknesses," and refers not merely to their long duration but also to their devastating effect. That the usual transl. is not ultimately adequate is shown by the LXX, which is forced to paraphrase with θαυμαστός. In Is. 33:16 the part. means that the waters will not give out. In Jer. 15:18, on the other hand, the ni, par. to the "deceptive brook," is used for water which does not "contain what it promises." [91] Finally, the ni is used for the word which shows itself to be right by its correspondence with the real facts, Gn. 42:20. [92] These examples make it clear that a consistent rendering with one word is quite impossible. [93] נֶאֱמָן does not express a quality which belongs to the subj. at issue and which might apply equally to something else. אמן is shown to be a formal concept whose content is in each case determined by the specific subj. It states that the qualities which belong to the subj. concerned are really present. It thus has something of the meaning of the term "specific," indicating the relation of the reality to that which is characteristic of the particular subj. In keeping with the total thinking of the OT the ref. is not simply to one feature but to the totality of all the features belonging to this subj. The nature of the Hebr. mind also demands that this relation between concept and reality be seen not in the abstraction of logical thought but always in the living proximity of practical experience, so that the formal concept is always thought, felt and experienced along with the corresponding content, and in this way the logical connection is always a living one as well. The given content can always be deepened and extended according to the loftiness of claim and the sharpness of perception. [94]

---

[88] On the meaning of אָמְנֹת in 2 K. 18:16 ("doorposts") and the connection with אמן ("to carry" ?) it is impossible to be certain.

[89] The LXX transl. 29 times πιστός, 9 times πιστοῦν and once each ἀξιόπιστος, ἐμπιστεύειν, πίστιν ἔχειν and θαυμαστός.

[90] In the same sense שָׁלוֹם וֶאֱמֶת at 2 K. 20:19 "lasting peace which never ends."

[91] Cf. Ex. 17:12 : "His hands (Moses') were אֱמוּנָה == they did not fall," and Jer. 2:21, where זֶרַע אֱמֶת means "plant of pure strain" as opp. to נָכְרִיָּה "strange bastard plant."

[92] Cf. the pass. part. haphal מְהֵימַן of the interpretation of dreams, Da. 2:45.

[93] The resultant difficulties in transl. may be perceived already in the LXX, which follows different methods in the various strata. The oldest layer — the Pent. and the early transl. influenced by it, esp. Is. — unconcernedly presents the equivalent in sense. The later stratum — in a development which culminated in Aquila — prefers a fixed rendering for each term in the original so as to reflect it as exactly (and mechanically) as possible, interpretation being left to those who were called thereto (P. Katz, Philo's Bible [1950], esp. 34 f., 42 f., 64-67, 83 ff., 149). Understandably, then, the LXX has ἐστηριγμέναι for יָדָיו אֱמוּנָה at Ex. 17:12, substituting the thing for the figure, as in the Targums. Aquila, however, uses πίστις, which is not a literal transl., but simply the fixed term for אֱמוּנָה, whatever the meaning in the context. Another example of the mechanical method of the later translators is to be found in the rendering of אֱמוּנָה ("official duty") in 1 Ch. 9. בֶּאֱמוּנָה is transl. τῇ πίστει αὐτῶν in v. 22, ἐν [+ τῇ] πίστει in v. 26, and ἐν τῇ πίστει in v. 31 [Katz].

[94] One may think of the different elements which make up the concept of a plant of pure strain.

The use of the ni in respect of men is to be assessed in the light of these findings. It is applied to the servant (1 S. 22:14; Nu. 12:7 Moses); the witness (Is. 8:2; Jer. 42:5), where it embraces not merely the truthfulness of the statements but also the power of perception, the retentiveness of memory, recollection, understanding and the ability to portray;[95] the messenger (Prv. 25:13);[96] the prophet (1 S. 3:20, where Samuel, the ideal of what a prophet should be, is described as נֶאֱמָן); also the priest (1 S. 2:35); the city in the metaphor of the bride, Is. 1:21, 26;[97] the supervisor in Neh. 13:13.[98] The results mentioned above can easily be correlated with these examples. Though formally the same, the word refers in content to very different qualities. The enduring point of similarity consists in the relation, according to the sense, between the qualities required of the subj. and those actually present. This, and the difference in content, may be seen clearly in Prv. 11:13, where, in contrast with the calumniator who betrays secrets, the נֶאֱמַן רוּחַ is the one who in his conduct corresponds to the point of secrets, i.e., keeps them secret.[99]

This sheds light on the religious use of the stem. When the reference of the word is to God, its formal character makes it possible for a rich plenitude of different aspects of the divine life to be comprised under the one term אמן. Thus in Dt. 7:9 the "faithful" God is the One who keeps covenant and חֶסֶד with those that love Him and keep His commandments, who observes the oath which He swore to the fathers. In Is. 49:7 the word is used with reference to the election in the sense of executing the promise in the servant. The actualising and coming into force of God's Word is denoted by the niphal of אמן whether in terms of promise (1 K. 8:26; 1 Ch. 17:23 f.; 2 Ch. 1:9; 6:17; Is. 55:3; Ps. 89:28) or in terms of threat (Hos. 5:9).[100] Self-fulfilment is of the nature of the promise (or threat). Similarly, the word is used of the commandments (Ps. 111:7) and the Law (Ps. 19:7) where par. expressions like "established for ever, made in אֱמֶת and יָשָׁר", "the works of his hands are אֱמֶת and מִשְׁפָּט," or, in Ps. 19, תָּמִים, יָשָׁר, בַּר, טָהוֹר, אֱמֶת, make it plain that the concept of אמן embraces the totality of the characteristics demanded of the Law if it is to achieve its purpose as an expression of the divine will for the structure of life. Similarly, the OT speaks of God's אֱמֶת and אֱמוּנָה (→ I, 232 ff.). Here, too, the fundamental meaning is "that which is essential," i.e., "that which makes God God." The closer material definition, which is always present, is, however, dependent in each instance on the current view of God or the aspect of God which is to the fore in this instance. Thus in what is almost a fixed liturgical expression like חֶסֶד וָאֱמֶת[101] or חֶסֶד וָאֱמוּנָה the word חֶסֶד (love, grace) provides the material definition, while אֱמֶת (אֱמוּנָה) (the steadfast faithfulness of love and its expression) represents the more formal element.

The ni is used for man's relation to God[102] in Neh. 9:8 (alluding to the הֶאֱמִין of Gn. 15:16): "And foundest his heart (Abraham's) נֶאֱמָן before thee, and madest a covenant

---

[95] Cf. אֱמוּן Prv. 14:5.

[96] Cf. אֱמוּן Prv. 13:17; of the friend, Prv. 20:6.

[97] Cf. Zech. 8:3 : "city of אֱמֶת."

[98] Cf. the pass. part. haphal, Da. 6:5.

[99] In Job 12:20 נֶאֱמָן abs. denotes the tried, experienced, just man (par. to the aged and noble).

[100] In Ps. 93:5 the testimonies are promises and threats.

[101] Cf. A. Weiser, Die Ps.⁴ (AT Deutsch [1955]), 28. On אֱמֶת cf. the similar subst. אֹמֶן in Is. 25:1, probably also 65:16.

[102] Hos. 12:1 is uncertain.

with him"; Ps. 78:37: (of the children of Israel in the days of Moses) לֹא נֶאֶמְנוּ בִּבְרִיתוֹ,
par. to "their heart was not right with him" (נָכוֹן עִמּוֹ), with a ref. to the covenant relation ; Ps. 78:8 : לֹא נֶאֶמְנָה אֶת־אֵל רוּחוֹ, with ref. to disobedience to the commandments.
Here the term express the attitude of man to God which corresponds to the specific claim
of God. It denotes not merely the correctness of the external relation but also that of
the disposition (רוּחַ, לֵב). It is not limited to the single act but refers to the totality of
man's relation to God.

3. אָמֵן. The use of the verbal adj. אָמֵן points in the same direction, → I, 335, 14 ff. [103]
The ref. in 1 K. 1:36 is to confirmation of a royal command, in Nu. 5:22; Dt. 27:15-26;
Jer. 11:5; Neh. 5:13 to acknowledgment of the (divine) curse, and in Jer. 28:6, after a
promise of salvation, to the desire that it be fulfilled. In Neh. 8:6; Ps. 41:13; 72:19; 89:52;
106:48; 1 Ch. 16:36 it is the concluding liturgical formula after a doxology. In 1 K. 1:36
Benaiah answers אָמֵן when ordered by the king to anoint Solomon as king. This means
that he has understood the command, that he accepts it and that he cherishes the desire
that Yahweh may fulfil the king's word. It also carries with it, however, his own commitment to contribute, as much as in him lies, to the execution of the order. Hence in אָמֵן,
too, we find the concept of relationship between the claim of the word and the reality
— a concept which expresses the fact that the totality of the elements in the command
(curse, doxology) is to be fulfilled. This aspect is again plainly reflected in the LXX,
which in 14 instances transl. אָמֵן by γένοιτο and in only 3 instances transcribes it as
ἀμήν, → I, 336, 21 ff. [104] Alongside the objective relation between concept and reality
one should not miss, of course, the subjective relation of him who says אָמֵן to the thing
which he enforces with his Amen. This contains subjective (theoretical) recognition
and acknowledgment, but it also contains the practical subjection of the total person,
in knowledge, will and conduct, to the claims of the relevant command (curse, doxology).
In this use, then, the concept of אָמֵן embraces a twofold relation : recognition and
acknowledgment of the relation of claim and reality, and the relation of the validity of
this claim for him who says Amen to all its practical consequences.

4. Hiphil. This leads us to the simplest definition of the hi הֶאֱמִין ("to believe"), [105]
which the LXX renders 45 times by πιστεύειν, 5 by ἐμπιστεύειν, and once each by
καταπιστεύειν and πείθεσθαι (→ 197, 1 ff.). It means "to say Amen with all the
consequences for both obj. and subj." It expresses both recognition of the objective
relation of object to reality and also recognition of the subjective relation of the believing subj. to the obj. The combination with לְ or כִּי (also לְ with inf.) [106] sets the act
to the forefront, while that with בְּ gives emphasis to the total attitude. [107] Thus in
secular usage "to believe" a word, account, or report is first to take cognisance of the
matter and to accept that it is true. It also implies, however, a corresponding relation to
the matter (Gn. 45:26; Ex. 4:1, 8 f.; [108] 1 K. 10:7 = 2 Ch. 9:6; Jer. 40:14; Is. 53:1; Hab. 1:5
[Prv. 14:15]; 2 Ch. 32:15). While in these instances the emphasis is on the single act,

---

[103] Cf. the adv. אָמְנָם "surely," 2 K. 19:17; Is. 37:18; Job 9:2; 12:2; 19:4 f.; 34:12; 36:4;
Rt. 3:12 and אָמְנָם in questions, "truly ?", Gn. 18:13; Nu. 22:37; 1 K. 8:27; 2 Ch. 6:18; Ps. 58:1,
and אָמְנָה, Gn. 20:12; Jos. 7:20.

[104] The LXX reads ἀληθῶς at Ιερ. 35(28):6. In Nu. 5:22 and Dt. 27:15-26 Symmachus
and Theodotion have the transcription ἀμήν, which was commended by liturgical use, while
Aquila prefers πεπιστωμένως, but πιστωθήτω at Ιερ. 35(28):6 in the second of his two
editions [Katz].

[105] Da. 6:24 haphal הֵימִן.

[106] The combination with אֶת־ (not acc. but = "with") in Ju. 11:20 is to be rendered "to
agree with ..." = "to concede." Perhaps a לְ has dropped out through haplography in
the construct inf. which follows.

[107] This distinction no longer seems to be made in Ps. 106:24, cf. v. 12 (also 78:32).
[108] Here the secular usage merges into the religious.

the use of הֶאֱמִין toward men gives prominence to the total basic attitude along the lines of "to trust." Confidence in the vassal (1 S. 27:12), the friend (Mi. 7:5; Jer. 12:6), the flatterer (Prv. 26:25), the servant (Job 4:18), the saints (Job 15:15) implies on the one side a recognition of the claim inherent in such terms as "friend," "servant" etc. and on the other the validity of this claim for the one who trusts. Inherent in הֶאֱמִין, then, is not a single relation but the reciprocal relation which makes trust what it is. A further pt. is that the OT uses הֶאֱמִין only for the personal relation, for behind the word which is believed is the man whom one trusts. [109]

The hiphil finds an analogous use as an expression for man's relation to God. Here, too, it has declarative [110] rather than causative significance. It means "to declare God נֶאֱמָן," "to say Amen to God." But this does not embrace the whole meaning. In this sphere of usage הֶאֱמִין is first found as a formal concept in the sense of recognising and acknowledging the relation into which God enters with man, i.e., setting oneself in this relation, so that here, too, the mutual relation between God and man is of the very essence of faith, [111] and is so in such a way that, even where faith is a human activity for which man may be held responsible (the requirement of faith), man is never the one who initially establishes this relation. Even in passages where there is no express mention of this the presupposition of faith is always the fact that God is the true author of the relation between God and man. [112] In content the orientation of this use is in detail to the particular aspect which is set in the foreground in this mutual relation. If the reference is to God's requirement, order, or command (Dt. 9:23; Ps. 119:66 [2 K. 17:14 [113]]), then faith implies acknowledgment of the requirement and man's obedience. If the divine promise occupies the stage (Gn. 15:6 [Ps. 106:12]), then האמין expresses acknowledgment of the promise and of God's power to fulfil it, and it also denotes the implied worship of God as the almighty Lord (Nu. 20:12). [114] The two motifs of requirement and promise are both comprised in האמין in Ex. 4:1, 8 f.; Ps. 106:24.

This does not exhaust, however, the range of meaning; in virtue of its formal character האמין can undergo further deepening and extension. In particular, it can come to embrace the total relation between God and man, Ex. 14:31; 19:9; Nu. 14:11; Dt. 1:32; Ps. 78:22, perhaps already Gn. 15:6. [115] On God's side this carries a reference to all the elements whereby God is God and seeks to establish a

---

[109] There are two exceptions: Job 39:12: "dost thou trust the wild ox that he will return?"; the expression "trust one's life" in Dt. 28:66; Job 24:22. Of these the first is a metaphorical transferring of the human relation, while in the second the negative bearing : "A man cannot trust his life," denotes the impossibility of a personal relation to life ; perhaps there is also an approximation of הֶאֱמִין to the original distinct sense of בטח, "to be sure," → 191 f.

[110] Ges. K. § 53d.

[111] In view of this one may ask whether this religious use does not have its root in the concrete relation indicated by the q, namely, that between mother, nurse etc. and child, → 183, 40 ff.

[112] It seems to me that the fact that אמן embraces the reciprocal relation is also expressed in the transl. of Ps. 31:23 : אֱמוּנִים נֹצֵר יְהֹוָה, where there may be vacillation between "Yahweh keeps faithfulness" (LXX, F. Hitzig, Die Ps. [1863], ad loc.; E. König, Die Ps. [1927], ad loc.), and "Yahweh keeps the faithful" (B. Duhm, Die Ps. in Kurzer Hand-Komm. z. AT, 14³ [1922], ad loc.; R. Kittel, Die Ps. in Komm. z. AT, 13 ¹,² [1914], ad loc.; Kautzsch, ad loc.; H. Gunkel, Die Ps. in Göttinger Hand.-Komm. z. AT [1926], ad loc.) according to emphasis on the divine aspect on the one side or the human aspect on the other.

[113] Hab. Midr., II, 14 f.

[114] Cf. the nuance of faith in God's wondrous acts, Ps. 78:32.

[115] In Jon. 3:5, too, the ref. of Gentiles' faith in God (Yahweh) is to religion in totality, cf. faith in the divine covenant, Hab. Midr., II, 4.

relation to man, namely, His might, His miraculous power, His electing will, His
love, the steadfastness and faithfulness of His conduct, the actualising of His word
and plan, His demand, His righteousness, just as especially מִשְׁפָּט, חֶסֶד and צְדָקָה
can commonly be used in the OT to define the divine אֱמֶת (אֱמוּנָה) more closely. Thus
the religious use of האמין in the OT inclines in the direction of "taking God as God
with unremitting seriousness," and it herewith contains as an essential element the
exclusiveness of the relation to God. This may also be seen from the fact that
in the OT "not to believe" is often equivalent to פשׁע "to commit apostasy." [116]
Since the concept of apostasy is rooted in the ideology of the covenant, and makes
sense only in this context, it is plain that the setting and origin of the religious
use of the stem אמן in the OT tradition is to be sought in the sacral covenant
with Yahweh. To the extensive exclusiveness corresponds an intensive exclusiveness in the sense that the concept of אמן brings into the relation with God the
totality of the expressions of human life. Hence האמין is used in different nuances.
In Is. 43:10, par. to ידע and בין; "that ye may believe that . . . before me there was
no God formed, and that there will be none apart from me," the emphasis in the
relation to God is on the aspect of knowledge. In the threefold חֶסֶד, אֱמֶת, דַּעַת אֱלֹהִים
of Hos. 4:1, however, a stronger impulse of feeling is discernible. The element of
will is to the fore in those passages in which faith is to be understood as obedience.
The concept of faith carries with it an element of fear in Ex. 14:31; Jos. 24:14;
2 Ch. 19:9; Ps. 86:11. [117] We are pointed in the same direction of the exclusiveness
of the divine relation in disposition and conduct by the expression which characterises the opposite attitude in Hos. 10:2 : חָלַק לֵב ("to be of divided heart"). On the
other hand, the phrase "with all one's heart, with all one's soul," which is particularly favoured by Dt. (6:5 etc.), leaves us in no doubt whatever as to the way
in which the OT itself would have the attitude of faith understood. Extensive
and intensive exclusiveness as the basic feature of the OT relation of faith may
also be perceived in verses where שָׁלֵם ("committing oneself undividedly and
totally") is used to define the relation, [118] or where the "unremitting loyalty of
faith" finds expression in מָלֵא אַחֲרֵי יְהוָה [119] or תָּמִים עִם יְהוָה. [120] In all these passages
one may see a genuine understanding of what is meant by faith in the OT. In all
of them the orientation of the use of הֶאֱמִין is clearly visible. It denotes a relation
to God which embraces the whole man in the totality of his external conduct and
inner life. Hence הֶאֱמִין is never used for the relation to other gods, whereas בטח
and חסה, e.g., can be uninhibitedly applied to idols. This is understandable, for only
in a form of religion which, like the OT concept of the covenant with Yahweh,
is oriented to monotheism, can the thought of the exclusiveness of the reciprocal
relation between God and man be developed with the comprehensiveness and
depth which are to be found in the use of הֶאֱמִין.

---

[116] Cf. Dt. 32:20 : "children in whom there is no אֱמֻן," which is par. to idolatry.

[117] Is. 8:13 : "Yahweh Sabaoth, regard him as lofty (תַּקְדִּישׁוּ), he alone be your fear and
your dread," might be mentioned in this connection along with the demand of the prophet
for faith, cf. Ps. 78:22 with v. 32 ff.

[118] שָׁלֵם עִם יְהוָה 1 K. 8:61; 11:4; 15:3, 14; 2 Ch. 16:9 (with אֶל); cf. בְּלֵבָב שָׁלֵם 2 K. 20:3;
Is. 38:3; 2 Ch. 19:9, both times par. to אֱמֶת, אֱמוּנָה; 1 C. 28:9; 29:9 (19); 2 Ch. (15:17) 25:2;
commonly in opposition to idolatry.

[119] Nu. 14:24; 32:11; Dt. 1:36; 1 K. 11:6.

[120] Dt. 18:13; Ps. 18:23 = 2 S. 22:24 (here with לְ); as noun par. to אֱמֶת Jos. 24:14, cf.
1 K. 9:4 בְּתָם־לֵבָב.

The most significant extension and deepening are to be found in the absolute use of הֶאֱמִין, particularly in the form which goes back to Isaiah. [121] For Isaiah the problem of the possibility of existence, the question of faith and being, is of central interest. The thought of the remnant, the hope of Zion, the establishing of a fellowship of faith in his band of disciples, are all to be understood in this light, and are very closely related to the prophet's general view of faith, which for its part goes back to the prophet's personal encounter with God in the framework of the cultic tradition, 6:1 ff. The differentiation of faith from political considerations (7:1 ff.), [122] from security in face of perils (28:14 ff.), and from trust in human might (30:15 ff.), shows, along with the absolute use of הֶאֱמִין, that faith is for Isaiah a particular form of existence of those who are bound to God alone — a form which works itself out as heroic strength (גְּבוּרָה, 30:15) and which is the divinely established basis of the community of God (28:16). [123] Faith and being are identical for Isaiah, for in the well-known saying Is. 7:9 : אִם לֹא תַאֲמִינוּ כִּי לֹא תֵאָמֵנוּ "to be established," which refers to the totality of human existence (→ 184, 25 f.), is not a reward for faith, as though faith were the presupposition of existence. The כִּי is to be taken as a demonstrative explicative, so that the identity of faith and being established (= existence) is implied. The positive meaning of the saying, then, is that the particular mode of life and the permanence of the people of God are to be found in faith itself. [124] This goes hand in hand with the rejection of all fear of human might (7:1 ff.) or trust in it (30:15 f.), since human might is transitory. It also carries with it an incorporation of fear of God alone into the relation of faith (8:13). From this one may see that faith is for Isaiah the only possible mode of existence ; it radically excludes any autonomy of man or any commitment to other gods. In Isaiah Yahweh alone, His plan and will, and the corresponding attitude of man, are the only things which count in respect of all occurrence or understanding. This brings the exclusiveness of the relation of faith to fulfilment on the extensive side, while the intensive form of the exclusive relation is brought to fulfilment by the close connection between

---

[121] Ps. 116:10 is possibly related to Isaiah's view of faith, but the same cannot be said of the profane use in Job 29:24. The contesting of an abs. use of הֶאֱמִין in Is. by J. Boehmer, "Der Glaube u. Js.," ZAW, 41 (1923), 84-93 has rightly found no support.

[122] This is not the place to enter into the much debated question of the prophet and politics, cf. the comm. (esp. O. Procksch, *Js.* I, *Komm. AT*, 9 [1930], 10-17; V. Herntrich, *Der Prophet Js., AT Deutsch*, 17² [1954], 11 f., 118-122), also J. Hempel, "Chronik," ZAW, 49 (1931), 152 f.; F. Weinrich, *Der religiös utopische Charakter d. prophetischen Politik* = *Aus der Welt d. Religion, Bibl. Reihe, Heft* 7 (1932); K. Elliger, "Prophet u. Politik," ZAW, 53 (1935), 3-22; J. Hempel, *Gott u. Mensch im AT²* (1936), 321 f.; K. Elliger, "Nochmals 'Prophet u. Politik,'" ZAW, 55 (1937), 291-296, with an epilogue by J. Hempel ; H. J. Kraus, "Prophetie u. Politik," *Theol. Existenz heute*, NF, 36 (1952); E. Würthwein, "Js. 7:1-9. Ein Beitrag z. dem Thema 'Prophetie u. Politik,'" *Festschr. f. K. Heim* (1954), 47-63. The attempt of G. v. Rad, *Der heilige Krieg im alten Israel* (1952), 56-61, to interpret Is. 7:1 ff.; 30:15 ff.; 31:1 ff. as a fulfilment of ancient sacral ordinances relating to holy war, and to see in these the origin and setting of OT faith (cf. p. 31), hardly does justice to the breadth of the concept in the OT, cf. A. Weiser's review, *Für Arbeit u. Besinnung*, 7 (1953), 158-160.

[123] The later Jewish ref. of the foundation stone to the Messiah (→ IV, 272, 16 ff.), which is found in Tg. Jonathan and Rashi, and which is adopted by A. Delitzsch, *Komm. über das Buch Js.⁴* (1889), 316 and O. Procksch, *Js.* I, *Komm. AT*, 9 (1930), 358 etc., cannot be derived directly from the text. In 1 Pt. 2:6 f. Is. 28:16 and Ps. 118:22 are quoted to show that Christ is the foundation of the primitive Chr. community, → 98, 23 ff.

[124] This is not wholly clear in O. Procksch, *Theol. d. AT* (1950), 181, where faith is defined as the "condition of existence."

faith and being. Hence there can be no further deepening of the usage in this direction. From the standpoint of usage, too, Isaiah deserves to be called the prophet of faith. He played a decisive part both in the final deepening of the linguistic content and also in the influencing of further linguistic development by the content.

5. אמן and Derivates. This will be shown by a brief glance at the development of the religious use of אמן and derivates. The emphasis which Isaiah placed on the word and concept was never lost again in the further history of the usage. From this period there dates in essentials the strongly qualitative influence of the meaning of הֶאֱמִין on the other stems which religious speech used for the attitude of man to God. In spite of the purely statistical insignificance of the use of אמן, the meaning of the stems חכה, יחל, קוה, חסה, בטח, which originally was very limited, expanded along the lines of הֶאֱמִין in expression of the exclusive personal relation between man and God, → 191 ff. Where the word הֶאֱמִין itself is used, one can hardly fail to note its tendency to extend into the most comprehensive possible sphere of application, just as אֱמוּנָה too embraces the whole attitude of a life lived in faith, Hab. 2:4; [125] 2 Ch. 19:9; Jer. 7:28 (5:3). [126] Finally אֱמֶת, in correspondence with אֱלֹהֵי אֱמֶת = "the true God" (2 Ch. 15:3), becomes a general term for true religion (Da. 8:12; 9:13; 10:21), [127] so that with final logic the thought of exclusiveness becomes a claim to absoluteness.

6. The Religious Dynamic. We have still to ask what is the source of the strong religious dynamic which with the stem אמן brought to expression the particularity of OT religion in its various stages. From the very first it seems to be very closely related to the unique religious structure and thought of the Yahweh religion of Israel. In the story of the succession to David's throne, recounted by a contemporary, there is handed down in 2 S. 20:18 f. the ancient proverb: [128] "Let it be asked in Abel and Dan whether there will be discontinued that which the אֱמוּנֵי יִשְׂרָאֵל have ordained." The accusation was also brought against Joab that in besieging Abel he was trying to destroy the "inheritance of Yahweh." The fact that the term "the faithful things of Yahweh" is used here in a proverb, and that it is brought into close material connection with the religio-dogmatic concept of the "inheritance of Yahweh," strongly suggests that the origin of this ancient use of אמן is to be sought in the fellowship of the covenant of Yahweh and in its sacral tradition, so that the uniqueness of the development of Yahweh religion in Israel seems to have shaped from the very first the religious meaning of אמן in the OT. It is true that in the actual usage the more general בְּרִית established itself as the term for the special relation between Yahweh and Israel, → II, 120 ff. It is also true that אֲמָנָה is used for the first time only in Neh. 10:1 to denote documented

---

[125] In the original prophecy of Hab. 2:4 (v. BH) the "righteous" are the national community. During the OT period itself however, the prophecy changed into a wisdom saying. Only with this change did it come to be applied to the righteous individual. This is what underlies Paul's use of it in R. 1:17 (→ II, 206, 3 ff.); Gl. 3:11 (→ II, 191, 5 ff.; 216, 14 ff.). The LXX ὁ δὲ δίκαιος ἐκ πίστεώς μου ζήσεται presupposes בֶּאֱמוּנָתִי = God's covenant faithfulness, and gives the word a different sense by this switch to a theocentric perspective.

[126] On אֱמוּן in this sense cf. Dt. 32:20.

[127] Cf. also perhaps Ps. 25:5; 26:3; 86:11.

[128] Acc. to the LXX, which has preserved the better text here.

committal to renewal of the covenant in the religious reformation of Nehemiah. [129] Nevertheless, the fact that most of the instances of הֶאֱמִין refer to the relationship with God in the days of Moses (Ex. 4:8 f.; 14:31; 19:9; Nu. 14:11; 20:12; Dt. 1:32; 9:23; 2 K. 17:14; Ps. 78:22, 32; 106:12, 24) shows plainly enough the close connection between the special use of אמן and the sacral tradition from the very beginnings of Yahweh religion in Israel. In the relation denoted by הֶאֱמִין the OT saw the special religious attitude of the people of God to Yahweh. [130] This is the more significant in that it provided an example for the continual regeneration and reconstruction of OT religion.

III. The Stem בטח.

1. State of Security. As compared with הֶאֱמִין, the situation is very different in respect of בטח, which is for the most part rendered πεποιθέναι or ἐλπίζειν in the LXX (→ II, 118 ff.; VI, 4 f.). The word "trust" implies more than the original meaning of the stem. The basic meaning is still clearly discernible in the abs. use, esp. in the older passage Ju. 18:7, 27, where בֹּטֵחַ is elucidated by שֹׁקֵט and in v. 7 by יוֹשֶׁבֶת לָבֶטַח (LXX ἡσυχά- ζειν). בטח here means "to be in a state of security" (בֶּטַח). In Ju. 18; Prv. 11:25 (LXX ἀσφάλεια) (Job 40:23) the obj. state is emphasised, while in Is. 32:9-11; 12:2; Jer. 12:5; Ps. 27:3; Prv. 14:16; 28:1; Job 6:20; 11:18 the stress is on the subj. feeling as opp. to fear. [131] Even where בְּ, עַל or אֶל is added to denote the author or means of security, בטח in distinction from הֶאֱמִין expresses the state rather than the relation, so that the transl. "to feel secure on the basis of ..." ("to ground one's security on ...") is nearest the mark. This may be seen from verses which speak of confidence in one's own power (Ps. 49:6; Prv. 28:26), work (Hab. 2:18; Jer. 48:7) or righteousness (Ez. 33:13), or which refer to things like ambushes (Ju. 20:36), chariots (Hos. 10:13 [LXX A]; Is. 31:1), cities (Am. 6:1; Jer. 5:17), walls (Dt. 28:52), bows (Ps. 44:6), riches (Jer. 49:4; Ps. 52:7; Prv. 11:28), beauty (Ez. 16:15), oppression (Is. 30:12; Ps. 62:10), or wickedness (Is. 47:10), and where there can be no question of alternation with אמן. Even where the word relates to persons, in some older passages, esp. with עַל (2 K. 18:20, 24) or the dat. ethicus (2 K. 18:21, 24 [Jer. 7:4, 8]), one may see that the self-relation of the subjective feeling of security is to be distinguished from the concepts of relationship denoted by אמן. Even the pass. part. בָּטֻחַ בַּיהוָה "to be made secure by Yahweh" (Ps. 112:7; Is. 26:3) and the hi: "Do not let Hezekiah comfort (assure) you by Yahweh," 2 K. 18:30, [132] point to the same root meaning. One may also refer to the strong negative use in the prophets, which expresses and combats human (self-) security (of 30 instances in which the ref. is to things 20 occur in the prophetic writings, 11 in Jer., and only 1 positively, 39:18). The fact that אמן can never be used of trust in idols but בטח can be used thus without a qualm (Is. 42:17; Jer. 46:25) helps to make plain the distinction in meaning and usage between בטח and אמן in the sense mentioned. [133]

---

[129] Cf. the use of אֱמוּנָה for the official duty of the various ministers in the temple cultus, 1 Ch. 9:22, 26, 31.

[130] This is not refuted by the use of הֶאֱמִין in Gn. 15:6, since the author is projecting into the ideal figure of Abraham his own post-Mosaic concept of faith.

[131] Similarly מִבְטָח is the "ground or author of security" (LXX 9 times ἐλπίς, 3 πεποι- θέναι), esp. in Is. 32:18; Prv. 14:26; כֶּסֶל Ps. 49:13 (LXX σκάνδαλον); Job 31:24; 8:14 (כִּסְלָה, Job 4:6; LXX ἀφροσύνη), though in the vocabulary of ritual this still kept the original sense of "loins," Lv. 3:4, 10, 15 etc.

[132] Cf. Ps. 22:9 : מַבְטִיחִי עַל־שְׁדֵי אִמִּי.

[133] Par. is "to rest on" סמך in the pass. part. q Is. 26:3; Ps. 112:8, ni Ps. 71:6 (Is. 48:2); the ni of שען Is. 30:12; 31:1; Job 8:15 in secular usage and Is. 50:10 (2 Ch. 13:18; 14:10; 16:7 f.; Mi. 3:11) in religious usage.

2. Feeling of Assurance. Nevertheless, alongside the religious use of בטח for a sense of security, there is also an extension of the sphere of meaning in the direction of assimilation to הֶאֱמִין, Jer. 39:18; Zeph. 3:2 (Mi. 7:5). This is particularly true in Dt., where distinction is no longer made between בטח and הֶאֱמִין. Even in later additions to the prophetic literature בטח has taken on the significance of a term of relationship, though sometimes one catches a weak echo of the original sense of a feeling of security, Is. 50:10; Jer. 46:25. [134] This process goes so far that, esp. in the Wisdom lit. and Ps., בטח in the sense of האמין almost completely crowds out the latter. Thus Prv. 3:5 speaks of trusting in Yahweh with one's whole heart in the same way as believing in Him. Again, in Ps. 78:22; 37:3 בטח and הֶאֱמִין (אֱמוּנָה) are in synon. parallelism. Again, in Ps. 40:3; 56:3; 26:1, 3 fear is included in the total relation to God. Even where there is no direct par. to האמין, בטח is used very generally of the righteous, Prv. 16:20; 28:25; 29:25; Ps. 32:10; 125:1; Jer. 17:7. In a weakened sense it can often be used for the attitude of prayer in liturgical introductions and conclusions, Ps. 91:2; 84:12; 25:2; 31:6 etc. The development of usage is par. here to that of אמן.

3. Comparison with אמן. The meaning of אמן develops without any shift in basic sense. In comparison the change in the meaning of בטח demands explanation. Very generally the forces which brought about this linguistic reorientation were 1. the development in the tradition of the Yahweh cultus of an ever more clearly asserted monotheistic faith in Yahweh in the conflict with alien religions, 2. the influence of the prophets and the pressure of history, 3. the religious situation of the exile and political impotence in the post-exilic period, 4. the growing feeling of being cast back upon God (cf. Ps. 22:10), which seeks and finds security in God alone, 5. the emergence of religious individualism, in association with which the nation turns into a community of faith and the lay piety awakened by prophetism continually gains ground. One decisive climax in the use of בטח for the whole attitude of faith may be fixed with even greater precision. This is to be found in the influence of Isaiah on religious usage, as, for example, in the important v. Is. 30:15. Is. is obviously acquainted with the employment of בטח in the sense of the human security (30:12; 31:1; 32:9 ff.) which he combats. In 30:15, however, he uses the stem in a positive sense : "With conversion (שׁוּבָה) and rest (נַחַת) are you helped, in stillness (הַשְׁקֵט) and confidence (בְּטְחָה) lies your strength (גְּבוּרָה)." The fact that Is. does not select a form of בטח, but breaks new ground with בְּטְחָה and שׁוּבָה, [135] is perhaps because he is intentionally dissociating the word from the sense of בטח rejected elsewhere. In any case the wrestling for linguistic expression is obviously the struggle for a content which is new in relation to the previous sense of בטח. To be sure, one still catches here an echo of the older idea of a sense of security, but both שׁוּבָה and גְּבוּרַתְכֶם show that the concept of faith in Is. 7:9; 28:16 lies behind it, and what follows : "But you would not, and said, No, we will flee upon horses," shows that גְּבוּרַתְכֶם does not signify man's own strength here, but the strength which flows from his relation to God (בְּטְחָה). This is the point where the change in meaning is palpable. Isaiah filled the stem with the content of his own concept of faith, and here too, as with אמן, he exerted a new and creative influence on the development of the usage.

IV. The Stem חסה.

1. Seeking Refuge. חסה "to seek (find) refuge," "to shelter" [136] (Akkadian ḫisu in the same sense ; LXX 20 times ἐλπίζειν, 9 πεποιθέναι, 3 εὐλαβεῖσθαι, 2 σκεπάζειν, once

---

[134] Here for the first time is the rendering "to trust" appropriate in a strict sense, cf. כֶּסֶל in Ps. 78:7.

[135] This is the only OT occurrence of either construct.

[136] Cf. "refuge" חָסוּת Is. 30:3; מַחֲסֶה Ps. 104:18; Job 24:8; Is. 28:15 profane (LXX καταφυγή, σκέπη, ἐλπίς); Ps. 46:1; 61:3; 91:9 etc. of Yahweh (LXX καταφυγή, ἐλπίς).

each σῴζειν and ἀντέχειν) undergoes a development similar to that of בטח. More lofty speech provides the original sphere of use, and this is more restricted as compared with בטח. Whereas בטח can denote security in one's own strength (→ 191, 22 f.), חסה presupposes the seeking of protection and the need of help. The poetic root may still be seen in the use of the term in the metaphor of the tree under whose shade shelter is sought (Ju. 9:15; Is. 30:2), in the expression "to seek refuge under the shadow of Egypt," and in the comparison of the outstretched pinions of a bird under whose shadow protection is found (Rt. 2:12; Ps. 36:8; 57:1; 61:4; 91:4). The latter comparison is used only with reference to Yahweh. Here again the primary meaning is not that of a reciprocal relation between the one who seeks protection and the one who offers it, but the fact of being protected or the act of seeking this state. This may be seen from the combination with תַּחַת (Rt. 2:12; Ps. 91:4) and also from the expression "to seek refuge in one's own perfection," Prv. 14:32. [137] Like בטח (→ 191, 36), חסה can be used with ref. to idols, Dt. 32:37.

2. Relation to Yahweh. Even when used for the relation to Yahweh, חסה often retains something of the original sense, esp. in the Ps., where the petitioner seeks God in time of temptation and danger, Ps. 57:1; 91:4; 25:20; 61:4 etc. But often — there is obvious similarity to בטח in this — the term bears a weaker sense in liturgical introductions and conclusions, and the meaning is extended to cover the total relation to God, Ps. 7:1; 16:1; 18:2; 25:20; 31:1; 2:12; 5:12; 34:23. It stands in synon. parallelism to בטח Ps. 118:8 f. (cf. 25:2 and 20), and is par. to "to fear God," Ps. 31:20. The final stage in this linguistic development seems to be the abs. use of the part. qal חֹסִים in the sense "the righteous," Ps. 17:7. [138] The extension of מַחֲסֶה follows a similar course. Originally it denotes "shelter" or the "place" or "giver of refuge." In Ps. 62:7; 94:22; 73:28 : "I have put my trust in Yahweh," in parallelism with "fellowship with God" (קִרְבַת אֱלֹהִים), it is used for the actual relation to God ; in depth of content it does not here fall short of the concept of faith to be found in an Isaiah, → 194, 37 ff. [139]

V. The Stems חכה, יחל, קוה.

An essential element in OT faith, its look to the future, would not be brought out if we were not to consider the stems of words of hope. These also belong to the sphere of enquiry into faith because later in the OT they were used in the same sense as terms for faith. Though the individual stems differ in basic sense, a common treatment of the group is justified by the fact that they all underwent the same development in meaning, and also by the fact that the 3 verbal stems are often used as equivalents, cf. the translations "to hope," "to wait on."

1. Basic Meaning. On the LXX transl. → II, 521, 20 ff. The basic meaning of these words is the concrete state of tenseness. קוה, whose stem bears the same sense in Akkad., Arab. and Syr., means first "to be taut"; this sense is most clearly preserved in קַו "measuring line" and תִּקְוָה (Jos. 2:18, 21) "cord." יחל seems to be related to חִיל "to be in

---

[137] Read בְּתֻמּוֹ for בְּמוֹתוֹ with LXX, Syr.

[138] LXX, however, adds ἐπί σέ.

[139] In some sense comparable is the development of דָרַשׁ and בְּקֵשׁ, which in a religious sense were originally restricted to consulting the divine oracle, Gn. 25:22; 1 S. 9:9; 1 K. 22:8; 2 K. 22:13, 18 (of Baal 2 K. 1:2 f., 6, 16, of the soothsayer, 1 S. 28:7; of the dead, Is. 8:19; Dt. 18:11) or the seeking of the face of God in the cultus, 2 S. 21:1; Ps. 24:6; 27:8; 105:4; Hos. 5: (6:)15 (2 S. 12:16; Zeph. 1:6), but which can finally express the whole inner relation to God, e.g., Am. 5:4; Dt. 4:29 ("to seek with all one's heart and soul"), cf. Jer. 29:13, or in the part. the "righteous," e.g., Ps. 9:10; 40:16; 69:6 etc. The rejection of cultic externalisation by the prophets, and their inwardising and deepening of the relation to God, seems to have been the decisive factor in this change of meaning.

labour," "to bear." [140] This probably explains the stronger emotional dynamic of the word even in its later use. The basic meaning is a "state of painful expectation." חכה is used in 2 K. 9:3 in the sense "to hold back," "to hesitate." The basic meaning is most purely preserved in Hos. 6:9 where it is used for "lying in wait" (in a hostile sense). Sometimes the original meaning may still be seen in the secular use, so קוה in Job 7:2 of the labourer who waits for his reward, or Ps. 56:6; 119:95 of those who lie in wait to kill. The painful undertone may be caught in יחל at 1 S. 13:8, where it is said that for seven days Saul waited in vain for Samuel, or at Job 14:14, where Job says that he wanted to endure the days of his conflict. Everywhere here the subjective state of waiting is to the forefront. These two words undergo an extension of the original sense esp. in Prv. and Job, where they are commonly used for living hope (or energy). This use obviously betrays the influence of reflection, קוה Job 3:9; 30:26; [141] יחל Job 6:11; 13:15; 30:26. [142]

2. Religious Use. In religious usage these verbs of hope are first found as an expression of tense waiting for a concrete goal. In collective piety this is usually the hope of salvation, or metaphorically hoping for light : קוה Jer. 8:15; 13:16; Is. 59:9, 11; 64:2; Jer. 14:19 par.; יחל Ez. 13:6; חכה Zeph. 3:8; Ps. 106:13. In individual piety it is hope for divine help in some affliction, or in prayers it is the expectation of being heard, so esp. Ps. 119:81 hope of God's salvation, v. 74, 114, 147 of God's Word, v. 43 of God's judgments, or Ps. 33:18 of God's grace. In the case of קוה, though Yahweh Himself is always called the object of hope, there sometimes stands quite plainly behind hope in Yahweh a very concrete expectation, as in Prv. 20:22 : hope of help, Ps. 40:1: that prayer will be heard, cf. also Ps. 130:5 par. to יחל, and Ps. 33:20 ff., where the three stems חכה, בטח and יחל are all used in much the same sense. [143] The last mentioned passages point to a form of usage which cannot simply be regarded as a direct transfer of the basic meaning to the religious field : waiting upon God Himself. The root of this linguistic form, which is most common in the Ps., is perhaps to be found in the expectation of theophany, whether in the cultus or in world events which are esp. proclaimed by the prophets. From here the development of the usage probably went by way of Dt. Is. [144] to the eschatological use which is found in later Judaism and in Da. 12:12 : "Blessed is he that endureth ... to the end of the days" (חכה Θ ὑπομένειν cf. Mt. 10:22; 24:13; Mk. 13:13). In all the verses in which hope in God includes a concrete goal, the strongly this-worldly character of OT piety follows the lines of theophany, with esp. tense interest in the visible manifestation of the divine governance.

3. Isaiah. Along with this, however, there is another development which made "hope in God" into a specific expression of faith as a total relation to God. Here again, as in the case of אמן (→ 189, 1 ff.) and בטח (→ 192, 26 ff.), it is in Isaiah that one discerns in the OT the decisive reorientation of verbs of hope in the form of a final deepening. Is. 8:17 presents the prophet in an attitude of faith

---

[140] Grammatically we have here a tendency which is found in the imp. and inf. of the verbs פ"י, namely, to make two-radical stems into three-radical. On this cf. G. Beer, Hbr. Grammatik, II (1921), 42.

[141] Cf. the fem. תִּקְוָה in the same sense, Prv. 23:18; 24:14; 26:12; 29:20; Job 5:16; 8:13; 11:18, 20; 14:7; 17:15; 19:10; 27:8; מִקְוֶה, 1 Ch. 29:15.

[142] Cf. תּוֹחֶלֶת par. to תִּקְוָה Prv. 10:28; 11:7.

[143] Cf. also the verb שֹׁבֶר (q = "to investigate thoroughly," Neh. 2:13, 15), which in the pi is used for "to hope," Ps. 104:27; 145:15, in the sense of waiting upon God as the giver of nourishment; Ps. 119:166, for hope of help; Is. 38:18 of God's אֱמֶת, cf. the noun שֶׁבֶר = "hope" in God's help, Ps. 146:5.

[144] Is. 51:5 : "The isles wait on me" (קוה) (60:9); 42:4 (יחל) seem to be meant in the sense of waiting for God's revelation.

in the hidden God: "I wait (חִכִּיתִי) upon Yahweh who hideth his face from the house of Jacob, and I hope (קִוֵּיתִי) in him." The change present here is quite palpable when one compares the antithetical par. in 2 K. 6:33. There the king (Joram?), confronted by the famine in Samaria, says to Elisha: "This comes from Yahweh, what should I wait (יחל) for Yahweh any longer?" The distinction is clear. The moment the king of Israel gives up hope in Yahweh is the moment Isaiah first dares to "hope." For him the judgment and wrath of God have not broken the prior relation to God. Isaiah's faith goes on, though now — this is the new element in his knowledge of faith, wherein the original sense of קוה and חכה is still re-flected — it consists in a tension, a supreme tautness of the energy of faith, behind which one may discern the tension between fear and hope. This waiting or hope is faith which does not yet see, but still believes. The tension within the prophet, which is expressed in the original meaning of the words קוה and חכה, has its source in awareness of the monstrous venture of this faith in face of the desperate ex-ternal situation of the prophet. Enclosed in this tension of faith is not resignation with the weak and flickering hope of a Perhaps, but the enhanced energy of a Nevertheless which arises out of a final wrestling assurance.

No one had a better understanding of these final depths of the wrestling of an Isaiah for faith than Dt. Is., to whom we owe the classical formulation of OT hope in 40:31. His view grew out of a similar inner situation and it points in the same direction. With him, too, it is a question of the hidden God. Under the impress of the collapse the people in exile believes that it is forsaken by God, 40:27: "My way is hid from Yahweh, and my right passes God by." Dt. Is. — and here we see the same Nevertheless as in Is. — plucks back these weary souls from the edge of despair by referring them precisely to this hidden God, to His unsearchable wisdom, to His unwearying power, which He gives to those who are without strength, v. 28 f. In this connection he coins the saying: קוֵי יְהוָה יַחֲלִיפוּ כֹחַ "those who wait on Yahweh change [145] strength," v. 31. Here hoping in Yahweh is seen to be a new form of existence and a new vital energy. It is a superhuman, miraculous power which makes the impossible possible. Youths may grow weary and exhausted, and young men may break down (v. 30; note the stylistic adynaton), but he who waits on Yahweh can run without tiring. The difference between physical strength and the living energy of faith as strength of quite another (spiritual) kind, which confesses God at all times, and which in this relation to God overcomes all temptation and weakness, is clearly expressed here. Dt. Is. is also aware — and in this respect he is very close to the concept of faith in Is. (cf. 28:16) — that God Himself is the One who gives this power of faith to man, 40:29. The whole prophecy of Dt. Is., including the song in c. 53, is living proof of the victorious might of this energy of faith, which is inwardly master over even the most serious afflictions in this life, including death itself, because its roots are in another, transcendent world.

4. Later References. An extension and deepening of verbs of hope such as we find in their use in Dt. Is. may also be discerned in later passages, especially in the Ps. Along with the use already mentioned, namely, for hope that help will be given or prayer heard, and with a strong emotional element of yearning, the word "to hope" is particularly used in the Ps. for the total relation of man to God,

---

[145] חלף pi and hi = "to put in the place of," "to change" (of clothes), Gn. 41:14; 2 S. 12:20.

e.g., in Ps. 42:5, 11; 43:5 : "Wait (יחל) on God ; for I shall yet praise him, who is
the help of my countenance (v. BH), and my God," cf. Ps. 130:5 f. In the course
of this development the stems of hope become synonyms of בטח (Ps. 25:3, 5; cf.
v. 2; 33:21 f.), [146] of חסה (Ps. 25:21, cf. v. 20), and of ירא (cf. v. 14; 33:22, cf.
v. 8), with no palpable distinction in meaning. The almost playful interchanging of
the most varied terms for the relation to God in Ps. 119 [147] is the clearest proof
of the fact that in the OT the most varied tributaries flow into one stream. What
has been noted already in respect of the other stems is true also of the verbs
of hope, namely, that finally in a fixed usage they describe the attitude of the
righteous man of prayer, especially in liturgical formulae, e.g., Is. 33:2 : קוה; Ps.
33:22; 119:147: יחל; Is. 30:18; Ps. 33:20 חכה, or else denote the righteous in contrast
to the ungodly, Ps. 37:9.

VI. Summary.

If on this basis we consider the whole development of OT usage, the following
answer is the only one which can be given to the question with which we began.
The LXX and NT were right when they related their term for faith (πιστεύειν)
to the OT stem אמן, for in this word is expressed the most distinctive and profound
thing which the OT has to say about faith. From a purely quantitative view the
use of הֶאֱמִין may well be secondary to that of other terms, but its qualitative pre-
eminence is undoubtedly to be seen in the fact that assimilation to the content of
אמן, combined with a more or less strong shift of meaning, must be described as
one of the most essential marks of the linguistic development of all the other
stems. The reasons for this highly remarkable process are to be sought 1. (linguistically) in the formal character of the stem אמן, which shows itself thereby
to be the broadest and in content the most fluid term, capable of absorbing new
elements without losing its basic sense, so that in the form of the hiphil it embraces the comprehensive, exclusive and personal relation between God and man ;
2. (historically) in the fact that the concept אמן in this sense was closest to the
unique relation between Yahweh and Israel and very quickly came to express
the specifically OT divine relationship preserved in the covenant tradition ; and
3. (theologically) in the fact that the prophets, especially Isaiah, being led by
their own experience and thought to the ultimate depths of the divine relation
and to an understanding of its nature, gave the usage a creative profundity and,
from the OT standpoint, completion, which, adopted by individual piety, promoted
inner triumph over the catastrophes of history and the afflictions of individual
life. [148] The significance of the OT view of faith may be seen in the fact that,
as an expression of the particular being and life of the people of God which
stands both individually and collectively in the dimension of a vital divine relationship, it embraces the whole span of this form of life, even to the final depths
which are disclosed only when, under the threat to human existence, certainty in
God releases new energies of faith and life.   *Weiser*

---

[146] Cf. the description of Yahweh as the hope of the petitioner in Ps. 71:5 תִּקְוָתִי par.
to מִבְטַחִי.

[147] Cf. esp. "to wait" in v. 43, 49, 74, 147.

[148] From the very first the stems חכה, יחל, קוה, חסה, בטח are more strongly plastic than
the formal הֶאֱמִין. This is perhaps a reason why these stems, when they had assimilated the
content of אמן, far surpassed it in use.

C. Faith in Judaism.

I. The Old Testament Legacy.

The הֶאֱמִין of the OT (→ 186, 29 ff.), which is almost always rendered πιστεύειν in the LXX,[149] does in fact correspond to the Gk. πιστεύειν to the degree that both can mean "to trust" (persons, 1 S. 27:12; Mi. 7:5 etc.), "to believe" (words, Gn. 45:26; 1 K. 10:7; Prv. 14:15 etc.) (→ 177, 23 and 178, 3 f.). Even the fact that trust can be put in God (Gn. 15:6; Dt. 1:32 etc.) and that God's words can be believed (Ps. 106:12, 24) corresponds to the Gk. use of πιστεύειν, → 179, 5 f. and 179, 15 ff. The phenomenon denoted by הֶאֱמִין, and herewith the OT concept of faith, is richer, however, than the phenomenon denoted by πιστεύειν, and the Greek concept of faith. If the Gk. πιστεύειν can have the nuance "to obey" (→ n. 6, 32, 46), this element is very much stronger in the "belief" of the OT, and is often predominant. In relation to God הֶאֱמִין can often mean "to acknowledge" (Ex. 14:31 par. ירא; Nu. 20:12 par. הקדיש; Is. 43:10) or "to obey" (Dt. 9:23 par. שמע; Nu. 14:11 opp. נאץ; 2 K. 17:14 par. שמע; also with ref. to Moses as God's representative, Ex. 4:1, 8 f. par. שמע); hence God's commandments can also be objects of הֶאֱמִין → 187, 22.

---

[149] 45 times; ἐμπιστεύειν 5 times, and once each καταπιστεύειν and πεισθῆναι → 3, 25 ff., also θέλειν in variants. Similarly πιστεύειν is used almost exclusively for הֶאֱמִין, once for the ni and aphel of אמן, once for שמע (Jer. 25:8, though obviously only for the sake of variety; in v. 7 שמע is rendered ἀκούειν). The other constructs of πιστ- are almost without exception used for constructs of the stem אמן. It may be noted that πιστός is almost always (29 times) used for the ni of אמן, and that πίστις is used 6 times for אמת, 20 for אמונה, but that ἀλήθεια is used 87 times for אמת and 22 (esp. Ps.) for אמונה; אמת is also transl. ἀληθινός 12 times, and for אמת we find δικαιοσύνη 6 times and δίκαιος 4 times. Worth noting is the fact that πιστεύειν is never used for בטח, → II, 521, 21 ff. It is remarkable that πιστεύειν and πεποιθέναι are never used for the same Heb. original. On the one side אמן ni hi is with philological exactitude transl. πιστεύειν. Even the derivates of this root, though sometimes they have or receive in the LXX a different meaning, are rendered by πιστεύειν, never πεποιθέναι. Only once at Prv. 26:25 do we find πεισθῆναι in the sense of being deceived. On the other hand πέποιθα is used for several Heb. words apart from בטח, and these are transl. in many different ways in the LXX (אמן with its uniform rendering in Gk. is in this respect an exception). For none of these originals, however, is πιστεύειν a possible transl. This is no accident. Trust and faith are not coextensive in the LXX. πέποιθα (= בטח) is already a religious term. As such it is used independently in the LXX, and gains ground in the later translations. In contrast πιστεύειν (= אמן) was not felt to be a religious term. This is true in the later transl. as well as the LXX. There is a shift only in so far as 'A and Σ of the Hexapla transl. prefer πίστις for אמונה. Other specific renderings are also dropped. But there are philological reasons for this. Even in the Hexapla transl. ἀλήθεια, however, is still used for אמת [Bertram]. In the LXX πιστεύειν and compounds always take the dat. of person, also Joseph. (cf. Schl. Jos., 28) and Philo, or the dat. of material obj. (e.g., λόγῳ, ἀκοῇ etc., also σημείοις, Ex. 4:9). We also find constr. with ἐν 1 Βασ. 27:12; Mi. 7:5; Jer. 12:6; ψ 77:22; 105:12; 2 Ch. 20:20 (Θ Da. 6:24), with ἐπί c. dat., Is. 28:16 (the authentic text); with ἐπί c. acc., Wis. 12:2; with κατά c. gen., Job 4:18; 15:15; 24:22. Naturally πιστεύειν can also govern a ὅτι clause, e.g., Ex. 4:5; Job 9:16; Lam. 4:12; Philo Migr. Abr., 18; Rer. Div. Her., 101, or an acc. c. inf., Jos. Ap., II, 160. The noun πίστις is construed with the gen.: Jos. Ap., II, 218, or with πρός, 4 Macc. 15:24; 16:22; Philo Rer. Div. Her., 94; Som., I, 68; Abr., 268, 270 f., 273; Praem. Poen., 27; or with περί, Jos. Ap., II, 169.

In the OT to believe in God is to acknowledge Him as such, → 187, 9 ff. This includes trust (→ 191, 10 ff.) and hope (→ 194, 14 ff.), fear (→ 188, 20 f.) and obedience (→ 187, 22 f.). But these are a unity, since trust is taken radically (→ 189, 1 ff.) and thus includes the overcoming of both anxiety and self-confidence. [150] Faith is a daring decision for God in man's turning aside both from the menacing world and also from his own strength, → 189, 20 ff. As is sometimes stressed (e.g., Gn. 15:6), it is thus faith in spite of appearances. "As a confident decision for God it contains within itself suppressed temptation." [151] This faith in God is not just general trust. It is grounded in what God has done in the past. [152] Hence it has its own firm relation to the past; it is also faithfulness, → 188, 29. The trusting man (מַאֲמִין = πιστεύων) is also the faithful man (נֶאֱמָן = πιστός). Similarly, faith has a firm relation to the future, → 187, 23 ff. It is the assurance that God will do what He has promised. Its opposite is murmuring and doubt (→ I, 729, 28 ff. γογγύζω, → II, 97, 46 ff. διαλογισμός), whereby God is tempted. It is expectant hope (→ II, 522, 22 ff., → 194, 35 f.) and stillness. Again, it has a firm relation to the present as obedience to God's commands (→ 187, 21 ff.), in the fulfilment of which the covenant faithfulness of the people must be demonstrated.

In the OT, however, this faith is essentially related to the history of the people, whose existence is grounded in God's act and whose obedience God demands. Thus the individual is essentially the subj. of faith in so far as he is a member of the people; his faith is orientated to the future of the people. [153] Now it is self-evident that faith in God, corresponding to God's total claim on the people, will shape the whole life of the people, and is not just demanded occasionally in specific situations. But according to the NT it is also clear that the OT does not see in faith the attitude which dominates the life of man absolutely. This is apparent from the fact that, e.g., the question of death is not set under the concept of faith. In the Ps., when trust in God is expressed with ref. to the destiny of the individual (→ 195, 42 ff.), this faith is one-sidedly understood as trust in God's help esp. in affliction. This is apparent already in the fact that in these instances the term used is not האמין, which binds faith to history, but בטח, קוה, or the like. [154] Thus the human situation is not radically understood as the situation of uncertainty before God, nor is it recognised that in good no less than evil man can stand before God only in faith as a radical looking away from self, nor that all his work can be accepted by God only as it springs from faith, R. 14:23. Frequently, indeed, this trust appeals to man's own piety. [155] Piety, then, is not radically understood as faith.

Finally, the divine action to which man knows that he is bound in loyalty, and which he may confidently hope for in the future, is regarded in the OT merely as action in this world. It is fulfilled in the history of the people or the destiny of the individual. Faith, though it is a surrender of anxiety and self-confidence, and thus means a turning aside from the world, is not a radical attitude of desecularisation like NT πίστις, for which εἰρήνη πρὸς τὸν θεόν (R. 5:1) is independent of the history of the nation or the destiny of the individual in this present world.

---

[150] Naturally the radical understanding is not developed with equal clarity in every instance, cf. esp. Is. 7:4-9; 8:5-15; 28:15 f.; 30:15-17 and the Ps.

[151] Cf. Schlatter, Glaube, 10 f.

[152] Faith, then, is not an attribute, like the πίστις of Stoicism.

[153] Even the faith of Abraham in Gn. 15:6 relates to the future of the people whose ancestor he is rather than to his personal destiny. His faith is prototypical.

[154] It should also be noted that in the case of האמין there is no noun corresponding to מבטח or תקוה, though אמת in the sense of faithfulness might be regarded as to some extent a substitute. Aram. first forms the noun הימנותא "faithfulness," "faith"; cf. Schlatter, Glaube, 559 f.

[155] E.g., Ps. 16; 37; 52; 71.

II. The Concept of Faith in Judaism. [156]

The OT legacy was shared by both Palestinian and Hellenistic Judaism. It is thus hard to distinguish at this pt. between the two trends. One can only emphasise the distinctive features of each within the common whole. Philo also merits special treatment.

1. Old Testament Motifs.

The structure of the Jewish concept of faith, which must be presented here only acc. to religious and not secular usage, displays all the motifs found in the OT. Faith is both trust (→ 191, 10 ff.) and giving credence. It includes faithfulness (→ 188, 29) and obedience (→ 187, 21 ff.) as well as hope and expectation (→ 194, 14 ff.). In view of the inner connection between the elements it is often hard to say where the accent lies. It is worth noting, however, that in Rabb. writings faith is understood one-sidedly as obedience to the Law, whereas in the apcr. and pseudepigr. the other elements in the structure are more prominent. [157]

The element of faithfulness is often to the fore. [158] Its ref. is to God's "covenants" (4 Esr. 3:32); it must be kept in persecution. [159] Faith will triumph, [160] "for in truth he who is believing attains life therefrom," S. Bar. 54:16. "Great is fidelity of faith before God." [161] Fidelity of faith is also meant when works and faith are connected in 4 Esr. 9:7; 13:22. Abraham and the patriarchs are examples of this. [162] As in the case of Abraham, faithfulness must be maintained esp. in temptation. [163] Faithfulness is also obedience. Hence the Law and commandments are among the objects of faith. [164] In the Rabb. writings to believe in God and to obey God are equivalent in meaning. [165] Hand in hand with obedience goes trust. To keep the Law (נצר, LXX πιστεύειν) is par. to trusting God (בטח, LXX πεποιθέναι). [166] Naturally there are many statements in which faith is extolled as trust in God. [167] We also find admonitions to trust in God in affliction or times of testing. [168] A specifically Hell. expression for trust in God is belief in the divine providence, Jos. Ant., 4, 60; Ap., 2, 170. The opp. of faith, whether as faithfulness or trust, is the doubt which tempts God, [169] or distrust. [170] On the other hand, a mark of faith is simplicity, [171] singleness of heart. This is demanded in Test. XII as distinct from

---

[156] Cf. Schlatter, Glaube, 9-42; Bousset-Gressm., 190-201; Moore, 237 f.; Wissmann, 50-54; A. Meyer, Das Rätsel d. Jacobusbr. (1930), 123-141.

[157] Str.-B., III, 188.

[158] Cf. Schlatter, Glaube, 15 f. So in the Qumran texts : Manual 8:3; 10:26; Hab. Midr. 8:3. Here אֱמוּנָה is always used ; אֱמֶת seems to be truth (even in the expression עָשָׂה אֱמֶת, 1:5; 8:2 ?).

[159] 4 Macc. 15:24; 16:22; 17:2; Slav. En. 62:1; 66:6; Ex. r., 15, 7 (Schlatter, 17); Tg. J. I on Is. 28:16 (Meyer, op. cit. [→ n. 156], 130), cf. Schlatter, 17 f.; Str.-B., III, 192 f.

[160] 4 Esr. 7:34. Cf. Str.-B., III, 193.

[161] M. Ex. on Ex. 14:31 and 15:1 (Meyer, 130).

[162] Sir. 44:20; Jub. 19:9; 1 Macc. 2:52; 4 Macc. 16:22; cf. Str.-B., III, 199 ff.; Moore, II, 237 f.

[163] Sir. 2:1 ff.; Jdt. 8:25 ff.; Ps. Sol. 16:14 f.; cf. A. Sommer, Der Begriff der Versuchung im AT u. Judt., Diss. Breslau (1935), 12-15.

[164] S. Bar. 54:5; 4 Esr. 7:24; cf. Schlatter, 19 f.

[165] Str.-B., III, 191.

[166] Sir. 32:24; cf. 11:21; S. Bar. 48:22; in the Gk. text of Sir. 33:3 the Law takes the place of God : ἄνθρωπος συνετὸς ἐμπιστεύσει νόμῳ, καὶ ὁ νόμος αὐτῷ πιστὸς ὡς ἐρώτημα δήλων (vl. δικαίων).

[167] 1 Macc. 2:59; Jos. Ant., 3, 309; 20, 48; cf. Moore, I, 136 f.

[168] Sir. 2:1 ff.; Jos. Ant., 2, 333; cf. Meyer, op. cit., 131; Str.-B., III, 191 f.

[169] Jdt. 8:12 ff.; Wis. 1:2; cf. Sommer, op. cit., 11 f.

[170] Wis. 1:2 : ἀπιστεῖν.

[171] Wis. 1:1: ἁπλότης.

doublemindedness, [172] which is also combatted in the Rabb. writings. [173] The concept of the man of little faith arises in this connection. [174] So, too, does that of the hypocrite. [175] To the degree that trust in God is faith in His promise, it is also hope. [176] But to the degree that it looks to the future generally it is also belief in retribution in a more general sense. [177] To the degree that retribution is expected in the world to come, this belief becomes a party affair, → I, 370, 5 ff.

Regarding something as true is inherent in faith. The original objects are God's Word and promises. [178] This aspect takes on special significance in the conflict with alien religions and in propaganda. Faith in God becomes a monotheistic confession. [179] Naturally this meaning of faith is developed esp. in Hell. Judaism, Sib., III, 584 ff. We also find in Philo statements which seem to borrow from confessional formulations, Philo Op. Mund., 170-172; Virt., 216; → 201, 38 ff. The first mandate of Herm. may also be traced back to the same tradition. [180]

Since faith expresses in such broad compass the relation of man to God and His Law, and consequently the attitude of the righteous, it is understandable that the words which denote this faith could also be used abs. In the main, of course, faith is defined by adding the obj. (God, God's witnesses and the like). [181] But the abs. use is also found. As the righteous can simply be called the faithful, [182] so they can be called believers, 4 Esr. 7:131. This usage is obviously developed 1. in antithesis to the ungodly among the people, [183] and 2. in antithesis to the heathen. [184] There is a corresponding use of faith in the abs. [185]

In sum it may be stated that in Judaism the concept of faith contains the same structural elements as in the OT, but that there is nevertheless a great difference. [186]

---

[172] Bousset-Gressm., 418 f.

[173] Schlatter, 18 f.; Str.-B., III, 751 on Jm. 1:8; Hck. Jk., 49, n. 47.

[174] קְטַנֵּי אֲמָנָה Str.-B., I, 438 f., cf. esp. Sota, 48b: "He who has bread in his basket and says : 'What shall I eat tomorrow ?' is a man of little faith."

[175] Schlatter, 19.

[176] S. Bar. 42; 57:2; 59:2, 10; 4 Esr. 6:5; cf. the combination of believing and hoping in 1 Macc. 2:59, 61; Sir. 2:6, 8 f.

[177] Str.-B., III, 190 f.

[178] Tob. 14:4; Wis. 18:6; Tg. J. I on Is. 7:9 (the words of the prophets).

[179] Jdt. 14:10; Eth. En. 43:4; 46:7 f. etc.; cf. Str.-B., III, 189 f.

[180] Herm. m., 1, 1: πρῶτον πάντων πίστευσον ὅτι εἷς ἐστίν ὁ θεός κτλ. Cf. Dib. Herm., ad loc.; Wnd. Jk. on Jm. 2:19; Wissmann, 49 f.

[181] Cf. Schlatter, 20, n. 1: "It is instructive that the Targum can no longer adopt the abs. use of Is. but provides an obj. for faith in the words of the prophets."

[182] נאמן Schlatter, 15 f.; Str.-B., III, 189; πιστός 1 Macc. 2:52, perhaps also Wis. 3:9 → n. 183.

[183] Wis. 3:9 (unless πιστοί means the righteous); 4 Esr. 7:131; S. Bar. 42:2; 54:16, 21; Slav. En. 51:2; Rabb. in Str.-B., III, 189.

[184] Eth. En. 46:8; Sib., III, 69 (πιστούς τ' ἐκλεκτούς θ' κτλ.), 724 (πιστοὶ ἄνθρωποι); V, 161, 426; cf. πιστεύσαντες 1 Macc. 2:59; ἀπιστοῦντες Wis. 18:13; cf. Str.-B., III, 189.

[185] Wis. 3:14 f.; M. Ex., 16, 19, 49b (cf. Schlatter, 21); Tg. J. I on Is. 28:16 (Meyer, 130); Ass. Mos. 4:8; 4 Esr. 6:27; 7:34; 9:7; Eth. En. 58:5; 61:4, 11; Slav. En. 62:1; 66:6; S. Bar. 59:10; Sib., III, 585; Test. L. 8:2 (τὸ πέταλον τῆς πίστεως). Inscr. of the Jewish catacomb at Monteverde, 145 : quae vera fides (N. Müller, Die Inschr. d. jüd. Katakombe am Monteverde zu Rom [1919], 134; J. B. Frey, Corpus Inscr. Judaicarum, I [1936], No. 476, cf. ibid., No. 72 and 641). We also find the phrase "men of faith," אַנְשֵׁי אֲמָנָה or בַּעֲלֵי אֲמָנָה (Str.-B., III, 189). In Heb. En. these אנשי אמונות seem to be a circle in which secret apocalyptic traditions were handed down. So, too, in the Qumran texts ? Cf. H. Bardtke, Die Handschriftenfunde am Toten Meer (1952), 93, n. 4; also Wissmann, 40-43.

[186] Schlatter, 12 : "For the inner form of faith depends on what is presented to us as the divine deed and gift in history. The divine gifts which Judaism was conscious of possessing

2. The Difference from the Old Testament.

As a result of the canonisation of the tradition in Scripture obedient faithfulness acquires the character of obedience to the Law. That is to say, it is no longer in the strict sense faithfulness to the experienced acts of God in history, with trust in His future acts therein.

History is arrested, and there is no true relation to it. The significance of past history is restricted to the fact that it gives the Jew the sense of being a member of the chosen people. The present can no longer continue history and its tradition in a living way. It simply mediates canonised tradition. The codex of Scripture, now given as a timeless present, is annexed and interpreted by theological-juridical study. Faith loses the character of present decision in the historical situation, and "thus represents itself as something static and enduring, as the form of consciousness which results from the entrance of scriptural doctrine therein." [187] The concept of inspiration limits the work of the Spirit to the past [188] and restricts God's dealings to past history. The result is a despising of the natural conditions of life. [189] Faith, in so far as it hopes for God's acts, is one-sidedly orientated to miracles. [190] Hence trust is no longer related to the historical destiny in which the people and individuals have a part through their own deeds. It is essentially a surrender to suffering. [191] It is either a general belief in providence or the expectation of miracles. Hope looks beyond history to supernatural eschatological events, and God's judgment is no longer thought of as taking place in this life, but as the eschatological forensic act. Thus the earlier Messianic figure is transformed under the influence of the figure of the Son of Man, or else replaced by it. Salvation is no longer for the future generation of the people, but for the faithful, the righteous. Judgment becomes world judgment, and the belief in the future is essentially the belief in individual retribution, which as such loses assurance. [192]

Belief in retribution is also belief in merits. Believing obedience to the Law leads to obedience to the letter and to the reckoning of fulfilled commands as merits. This presupposes a freedom of man which is the opposite of true faith. [193] Man is not wholly thrown back on God's grace, and God's grace and judgment are sundered. [194] Grace is understood simply as the leniency which overlooks individual faults. The righteous man does not need grace. Only the converted man receives it. [195] The righteous man stands on his own merits. As faith is set alongside works, it is certainly perceived that there is an obedience of faith which is not replaced by the righteousness of works but which involves submission to the divine will as a whole. This insight is robbed of its value, however, by the understanding of faith itself as a merit. [196]

III. Philo's Concept of Faith.

Philo's description of faith groups him with Hell. Judaism to the degree that for him faith is primarily belief in the one God and trust in His providence. These two thoughts

---

in the NT period were the Bible and the temple. From this arose the distinctions between the attitude of faith of the Judaism contemporary with the NT and that of pre-exilic Judaism."

[187] Schlatter, 20.

[188] Ibid., 14 f.

[189] Ibid., 22 f. The question whether use of a doctor is consonant with faith is symptomatic.

[190] Ibid., 25.

[191] This may be seen particularly impressively in Akiba, ibid., 45-48.

[192] Ibid., 32-35.

[193] Ibid., 26 : "Man establishes God's act by his own act."

[194] Ibid., 40 : "Divine forgiveness ... is ... not a total thing embracing the unity of the person and all its history, and uniting them to God."

[195] Ibid., 38 f.

[196] On the idea of the merit of faith (זְכוּת אֱמָנָה) ibid., 29-32; Meyer, 132; Str.-B., III, 199-201.

are combined in Virt., 2, 16 : διὸ καὶ πιστεῦσαι λέγεται τῷ θεῷ πρῶτος (Abraham acc. to Gn. 15:6) ἐπειδὴ καὶ πρῶτος ἀκλινῆ καὶ βεβαίαν ἔσχεν ὑπόληψιν, ὡς ἔστιν ἓν αἴτιον τὸ ἀνωτάτω καὶ προνοεῖ τοῦ τε κόσμου καὶ τῶν ἐν αὐτῷ. Cf. Op. Mund., 170-172. After the same manner as Judaism generally Philo speaks of trust in God's help [197] and in His promises. [198, 199] For him, however, the real point of faith is that it is the turning from the world of becoming and perishing and the turning to the eternal God, whereby man finds the certainty which he continually seeks. Philo thus understood man's relation to God along the lines of the Gk.-Platonic tradition. In so doing he held fast to "trust" as the basic meaning of πίστις. Thus he says : [200] ἀληθὲς μέν ἐστι δόγμα τὸ πιστεύειν θεῷ, ψεῦδος δὲ τὸ πιστεύειν τοῖς κενοῖς λογισμοῖς, or : [201] ὁ μὲν τοίνυν ἀψευδῶς πιστεύσας θεῷ τὴν ἐν τοῖς ἄλλοις ὅσα γενητὰ καὶ φθαρτὰ κατείληφεν ἀπιστίαν, or : ὅτῳ δ' ἐξεγένετο πάντα μὲν σώματα πάντα δ' ἀσώματα ὑπεριδεῖν καὶ ὑπερκύψαι, μόνῳ δ' ἐπερείσασθαι καὶ στηρίσασθαι θεῷ μετ' ἰσχυρογνώμονος λογισμοῦ καὶ ἀκλινοῦς καὶ βεβαιοτάτης πίστεως, εὐδαίμων καὶ τρισμακάριος οὗτος ὡς ἀληθῶς (Praem. Poen., 30). Turning to God is not a response to His Word or to His acts in history. It rests on contemplation of the world [202] and is a disposition of the soul (διάθεσις, Conf. Ling., 31), an ἀρετή, indeed, the τελειοτάτη ἀρετῶν (Rer. Div. Her., 91), the βεβαιοτάτη τῶν ἀρετῶν (Virt., 216), the βασιλὶς τῶν ἀρετῶν (Abr., 270). To attain to it is no easy matter ; it is μεγάλης καὶ ὀλυμπίου ἔργον διανοίας ; [203] it is the ἆθλον which Abraham won. [204] It is very closely related to the ἀρετή of εὐσέβεια. [205] It is the ἄμωμον καὶ κάλλιστον ἱερεῖον for God, Cher., 85. Hence it is also the μόνον ἀψευδὲς καὶ βέβαιον ἀγαθόν.

At root, then, πίστις is man's firmness, or impregnability, on the basis of committal to the only solid thing, to the one thing that is. In so far as πίστις means turning from the corruptible and turning to the eternal Philo follows the Platonic tradition. But in so far as it is described as this disposition of soul he follows the later Stoa. He seems to part company with the Stoa when he adds to the concept of πίστις as "faithfulness to self" (→ 182, 20 f.) or "imperturbability" the OT and Jewish sense of faith as trust, which was easy enough in view of the inner unity of faith and faithfulness in the OT and Judaism. In place of the ἐφ' ἡμῖν to which man's intention should be oriented acc. to Stoicism Philo sets God, who is always the obj. of faith. But since the connection of the individual with the people and with history is snapped, and since God is not seen in His historical action, that to which faith is oriented is pure being, which essentially can only be characterised in negative terms as non-world. Faith is desecularisation in a purely negative sense ; the positive content of the non-world which is entered in πίστις is not accessible to faith but only to ecstasy. In πίστις man does not stand before God to be accepted by Him. Faith is the goal of the piety which man develops in his own strength. [206] In truth it is not his relation to God ; as in the Stoa, it is a relation to himself.

---

[197] Sacr. AC, 70; Vit. Mos., I, 225; II, 259.
[198] Leg. All., III, 308; Mut. Nom., 166; Abr., 275.
[199] Philo also uses πίστις abs., Poster. C., 13; Conf. Ling., 31; Migr. Abr., 43 f.; Mut. Nom., 182 etc.
[200] Leg. All., III, 229 and generally 222 ff.
[201] Praem. Poen., 28. Cf. Rer. Div. Her., 93; Ebr., 40; Mut. Nom., 201; Abr., 269; Virt., 218; → Peisker, 5, 9.
[202] Leg. All., II, 89 : πῶς ἄν τις πιστεύσαι θεῷ; ἐὰν μάθῃ ὅτι πάντα τὰ ἄλλα τρέπεται, μόνος δὲ αὐτὸς ἄτρεπτός ἐστι.
[203] Rer. Div. Her., 93; cf. Abr., 262; Peisker, 13.
[204] Migr. Abr., 44; Praem. Poen., 27.
[205] Migr. Abr., 132 : ἁρμόζουσι γὰρ καὶ ἑνοῦσι αἱ ἀρεταὶ (namely, εὐσέβεια and πίστις) ἀφθάρτῳ φύσει διάνοιαν.
[206] Schlatter, 61: "Here, too, the gaze of the believer is on his past attitude of faith, and it makes this a support on which his portion in God is to rest."

D. The πίστις Group in the New Testament.

I. Formal Considerations.

1. πιστεύω. From a purely formal standpoint there is nothing very distinctive in the usage of the NT and early Chr. writings as compared with Gk. usage. As in Gk. (→ 177, 22 ff.) πιστεύειν means "to rely on," "to trust," [207] "to believe." [208] It is construed with the dat. of person [209] or thing, [210] or acc. of thing. [211] The Gk. πιστεύειν περί occurs only once at Jn. 9:18. [212] We naturally find the abs. use. [213] A ὅτι clause can depend on πιστεύειν, [214] or the inf. or acc. c. inf. [215] The pass. ("to be believed") also occurs. [216] Under the influence of Semitic usage (→ n. 149) πιστεύειν can be used with ἐπί c. acc. [217] or dat., [218] or with ἐν. [219] Particularly distinctive is the common πιστεύειν εἰς (→ II, 432, 31 ff.) in the sense "to believe in," which is neither Gk. nor LXX. [220] This can hardly be regarded as a development of πιστεύειν c. dat. ⊨ "to trust." On the contrary, πιστεύειν c. dat. is used more after the analogy of πιστεύειν εἰς for "to believe in." [221] The fact that πιστεύειν εἰς is equivalent to πιστεύειν ὅτι shows rather that πιστεύειν εἰς arises out of the use of πιστεύειν for "to regard as credible, as true." [222] πιστεύειν εἰς Χριστὸν Ἰησοῦν (Gl. 2:16), εἰς αὐτόν and εἰς ἐμέ (often in Jn.) etc. simply means πιστεύειν ὅτι Ἰησοῦς ἀπέθανεν καὶ ἀνέστη ... (1 Th. 4:14; cf. R. 10:9) or ὅτι Ἰησοῦς ἐστιν ὁ χριστός (Jn. 20:31) etc. In Jn. esp. πιστεύειν εἰς and πιστεύειν ὅτι are constantly used interchangeably in the same sense. [223] This is proved also by the pass. expression ἐπιστεύθη (sc. Ἰησοῦς Χριστός, 1 Tm. 3:16) and the fact that πίστις εἰς is equivalent, not to πίστις c. dat., but to πίστις c. gen. obj., → 204, 15 f. πιστεύειν εἰς is thus to be regarded as an ab-

---

[207] In a word, Jn. 4:50; in God, Ac. 27:25; Barn., 16, 7; Herm. v., 4, 2, 6; m., 12, 6, 2 etc.; πνεύματι, Herm. m., 11, 17 and 21.

[208] A word or the speaker, Mk. 13:21; Jn. 4:21.

[209] Jn. 4:21; Ac. 27:25; Ign. R., 8, 2; Herm. m., 1, 2 etc. So also R. 4:17, where the gen. is by attraction. To be distinguished is πιστεύειν c. dat. in the sense "to believe in," → n. 221.

[210] Jn. 4:50 (λόγῳ); Ac. 24:14 (τοῖς ... γεγραμμένοις); 2 Cl. 11:1 (τῇ ἐπαγγελίᾳ); Herm. m., 2, 2 (τῇ καταλαλιᾷ).

[211] Jn. 11:26 (τοῦτο); 1 C. 13:7 (πάντα); Pol., 8, 2 (τοῦτο).

[212] In Pol., 6, 1 we find πιστεύειν κατά "to believe (something) against (someone)."

[213] Mk. 13:21; Lk. 22:67; 1 C. 11:18. To be distinguished is the religious use of πιστεύειν in the abs. → 210, 11 ff.

[214] Lk. 1:45; Ac. 9:26; 27:25; Jn. 6:69; Barn., 7, 2; Herm. v., 3, 8, 4; 4, 2, 4 etc. In such instances πιστεύειν often has the nuance "to regard as possible," v. J. Jeremias, "Beobachtungen zu nt.lichen St. an Hand des neugefundenen gr. Hen. Textes," ZNW, 38 (1939), 120.

[215] Ac. [8:37]; 15:11; Ign. R., 10, 2; cf. also Ign. Sm., 3, 1: ἐν σαρκὶ αὐτὸν οἶδα καὶ πιστεύω ὄντα. On R. 14:2 → 218, 40 f.

[216] 2 Th. 1:10; 1 Tm. 3:16; Herm. m., 3, 3; Dg., 11, 3; 12, 8.

[217] R. 4:5, 24; Mt. 27:42; Ac. 9:42; 11:17; 16:31; 22:19.

[218] 1 Tm. 1:16; on the basis of Is. 28:16 vl. at R. 9:33; 1 Pt. 2:6.

[219] Mk. 1:15.

[220] Apart from Sir. 38:31 (εἰς χεῖρας αὐτῶν ἐνεπίστευσαν), which is a mistransl., cf. v. 31b and R. Smend, Die Weisheit des Sir. (1906), 351; also Helbing Kasussyntax, 201.

[221] Ac. 16:34 (τῷ θεῷ, D: ἐπὶ τὸν θεόν); 18:8 (τῷ κυρίῳ, D: εἰς τὸν κύριον); Tt. 3:8 (θεῷ). In Jn., too, πιστεύειν εἰς alternates with πιστεύειν c. dat., yet in such a way that the latter has its original sense: "to believe someone" (with ref. to what he says); so 5:38, 46 f.; 8:45 f.; 10:37 f.; 14:11. Hence the alternation (e.g., in 6:29 f.) does not rest on a change in the use of πιστεύειν c. dat. (this may be assumed only in Jn. 8:31; 1 Jn. 3:23). It rests on the fact that "to believe the words of Jesus" is materially the same as "to believe in Jesus," → 210, 25 ff.

[222] The Jewish formula הֶאֱמִין לְשֵׁם (Schl. J. on 1:12) is thus hardly a par.

[223] Cf. also Ac. 8:37 E, where πιστεύειν in the abs., elsewhere interchangeable with πιστεύειν εἰς, is an alternative for πιστεύειν c. acc. c. inf.

breviation which was formulated in the language of mission [224] and which is the more understandable in that the word πίστις played a role in both pagan and Hell.-Jewish propaganda, → 181, 4 ff.; 200, 7 ff. In so far as πιστεύειν εἰς (esp. in the aor.) means "to be converted from (Jewish or) pagan belief to Chr. faith" (→ 208, 26 ff.) πιστεύειν εἰς is to be construed on the analogy of ἐπιστρέφειν ἐπί or πρός c. acc. This may be seen from the juxtaposition of 1 Th. 1:8 (ἡ πίστις ὑμῶν ἡ πρὸς τὸν θεόν) and 1:9 (πῶς ἐπεστρέψατε πρὸς τὸν θεόν). πιστεύειν abs. is often interchangeable with πιστεύειν εἰς, and is thus to be taken in the same sense. [225]

πιστεύειν is also fairly common in the sense "to entrust or commit oneself" (Lk. 16:11; Jn. 2:24); the pass. is also used thus. [226] This is not a specifically Chr. use even when it is to Christ that one commits oneself, Ign. Phld., 9, 1.

2. πίστις. As in Gk. (→ 176, 17 ff.) this can mean both "faithfulness" and "trust," though it is seldom used in the former sense. [227] As "trust" or "faith" it occurs only in religious usage. Here it is mostly abs., though it can be construed with εἰς, [228] with ἐπί c. acc. (Hb. 6:1), with πρός c. acc. (1 Th. 1:8; Phlm. 5). With ἐν too [229] (→ II, 434, 10 f.) it has the same meaning, and an obj. gen. can be used instead of prepositions. [230]

3. πιστός. This, too, has the two Gk. meanings (→ 175, 27 ff.) of "faithful" and "trusting." In a secular sense it is common for "faithful." [231] There is no specifically religious sense when the ref. is to the service of God (1 C. 4:2, 17; 7:25), but we find this when it refers to the loyalty of faith (Rev. 2:10; 17:14?) or when the μάρτυς (→ IV, 495, 14 ff.) is described as πιστός (Rev. 2:13). Nevertheless, the usage is not religious when the word of Chr. preaching is called "reliable" (πιστός) as in the formula πιστὸς ὁ λόγος (καὶ πάσης ἀποδοχῆς ἄξιος, → II, 55, 39 ff.) [232] or when we read of Chr. prophecy: οἱ λόγοι πιστοὶ καὶ ἀληθινοί εἰσιν (Rev. 21:5; 22:6). Even less does πιστός have a religious sense when God Himself, or Christ, is called πιστός. [233] In the sense of "trusting" πιστός is not used in a profane sense but only in a religious or Chr. sense, so that the meaning is "believing," → 214, 21 ff.

4. πιστόω. This word occurs in the NT only in the pass. at 2 Tm. 3:14 in the sense "to be made believing (certain)"; cf. 1 Cl., 42, 3. In 1 Cl., 15:4 (ψ 77:37), however, the sense is "to remain faithful to ..."

5. ἄπιστος. Of the privative forms ἄπιστος could means "faithless" at Lk. 12:46 (opp. of "faithful" in v. 42), but Lk. more probably uses it in the sense of "unbelieving,"

---

[224] Mg., 10, 3 is quite clear (πιστεῦσαι = "to come to believe") εἰς Ἰουδαϊσμόν ... εἰς Χριστιανισμόν.

[225] In contrast cf. the abs. πιστεύειν for "to believe" in the sense "to trust," "to have confidence," Mk. 5:36; 9:23 f.; 11:23 f.; cf. also ψ 115:1, to which Pl. alludes in 2 C. 4:13, though here he reinterprets ἐπίστευσα in the sense of the Chr. term.

[226] R. 3:2; 1 C. 9:17; Gl. 2:7; 1 Th. 2:4; 1 Tm. 1:11; Tt. 1:3.

[227] Of God's faithfulness, R. 3:3; faithfulness in human dealings, Mt. 23:23; Gl. 5:22; Tt. 2:10. To Christ, 1 Tm. 5:12 (here πίστις almost means "oath," v. Pr.-Bauer); also in the tradition used in Lk. 22:32 (v. Bultmann Trad., 288), though the Evangelist finds the sense of "faith." In Ac. 17:31 πίστιν παρέχειν has the Gk. sense "to give a pledge," "to offer proof," M. Dibelius, Aufsätze z. Ag. (1951), 54.

[228] Ac. 20:21; 24:24; 26:18; Col. 2:5; 1 Pt. 1:21 (?).

[229] Gl. 3:26 (?); Col. 1:4; Eph. 1:15; 1 Tm. 3:13; 2 Tm. 3:15; not R. 3:25 (→ III, 321, 25).

[230] Mk. 11:22; Ac. 3:16; 19:20 D; R. 3:22, 26; Gl. 2:16; 3:22; Phil. 1:27; 3:9; Col. 2:12; Eph. 3:12; 2 Th. 2:13; Rev. 14:12; 1 Cl., 3, 4; 27, 3; Ign. Eph., 16, 2; 20, 1; Barn., 6, 17; Herm. m., 11, 9. There is no reason to excise the gen. Ἰησοῦ Χριστοῦ or Ἰησοῦ from R. 3:22, 26; Gl. 2:16; 3:22, as proposed by G. Schläger, "Bemerkungen z. πίστις Ἰησοῦ Χριστοῦ," ZNW, 7 (1906), 356-358.

[231] Mt. 24:45; 25:21, 23; Lk. 16:10 f.; 1 Tm. 3:11; 2 Tm. 2:2; cf. 3 Jn. 5 : πιστὸν ποιεῖν, "to act faithfully."

[232] 1 Tm. 1:15; 3:1; 4:9; 2 Tm. 2:11; Tt. 3:8; cf. Tt. 1:9; v. Dib. Past. on 1 Tm. 1:15.

[233] 1 C. 10:13; 2 C. 1:18; 1 Cl., 27, 1; 60, 1; 2 Cl., 11, 6; Ign. Tr., 13, 3 etc. of God ; 2 Tm. 2:13; Hb. 2:17; 3:2 of Christ.

"non-Christian."[234] It is common in this sense, → 215, 3 f. In the more general sense of "unbelieving" it appears in Mk. 9:19 and par. ("without trust or confidence") and Jn. 20:27 (in respect of the story of the resurrection, cf. v. 25). At Ac. 26:8 the meaning of ἄπιστος is "unworthy of credence."

6. ἀπιστέω. This means "to be unfaithful" in R. 3:3; 2 Tm. 2:13, "not to believe" (words) in Lk. 24:11, 41; Ac. 28:24 (opp. πείθεσθαι); the non-authentic Marcan ending, Mk. 16:11, and more technically "to refuse to believe" the Chr. kerygma, Mk. 16:16.

7. ἀπιστία. This means "unfaithfulness" in R. 3:3; Hb. 3:12. How closely related hereto is "disobedience" may be seen in Hb. 3:19 (cf. ἀπειθεῖν, v. 18). It is used more generally for "unbelief" as lack of belief or trust in Mk. 6:6 and par.; 9:24; Mt. 17:20 vl.; R. 4:20. In Mk. 16:14 it denotes lack of belief in words, and in R. 11:20, 23; 1 Tm. 1:13 unbelief vis-à-vis the Chr. kerygma.

8. ὀλιγόπιστος. This word, which does not occur in Gk. and derives from Judaism (→ n. 174), is found only in the Synoptists : Mt. 6:30 and par.; 8:26; 14:31; 16:8. The noun ὀλιγοπιστία is used in Mt. 17:20 א B.

II. General Christian Usage.

1. The Continuation of the Old Testament and Jewish Tradition.

In primitive Christianity πίστις became the leading term for the relation of man to God. This rests in part on the fact that already in the OT and Judaism "faith" had become an important term for the religious relationship, → 187, 9 ff.; 200, 14 ff. It is also due to the fact that primitive Christianity, like Judaism, was a missionary religion. To turn to the God revealed in its proclamation is "faith." In common Christian usage, then, the OT and Jewish heritage may be discerned in what is signified by πίστις (πιστεύειν, πιστός).

a. πιστεύω as to Believe. πιστεύω often means to believe God's words. Belief is thus put in Scripture (Jn. 2:22), in what is written in the Law and the prophets (Ac. 24:14), in what the prophets have said (Lk. 24:25), or simply in the prophets (Ac. 26:27), in Moses or his writings (Jn. 5:46 f.), also in what God is saying at the moment, e.g., through an angel (Lk. 1:20, 45; Ac. 27:25). In this sense John the Baptist can also be mentioned as one whom people should believe (Mk. 11:31; Mt. 21:32). In this sense, too, John's Gospel (and this alone) says that people believe, or should believe, Jesus or His Word.[235] He is sent by God (5:38) and speaks the words of God (3:34 etc.). What Jn. means by this is materially none other than believing in Jesus, → 210, 25 ff. and → n. 221. It is characteristic of Jn., however, that the two converge.[236]

b. As to Obey. The fact that "to believe" is "to obey," as in the OT (→ 199, 19 ff.), is particularly emphasised in Hb. 11. Here the πιστεύειν of OT characters has in some instances the more or less explicit sense of obedience.[237] How naturally πιστεύειν includes obeying may be seen from the use of πείθεσθαι rather than πιστεύειν for receiving the Christian message, → 4, 18 ff. Unbelief can be

---

[234] The v. comes from the source whose text Mt. 24:51 has perhaps retained with its μετὰ τῶν ὑποκριτῶν, while Lk. changed it to μετὰ τῶν ἀπίστων.

[235] Jn. 2:22; 5:46 f.; 8:45 f. etc.

[236] The attitude of unbelief vis-à-vis (decisive) words can be expressed by ἀπιστεῖν (Lk. 24:11, 41; Ac. 28:24 [opp. πείθεσθαι]; Mk. 16:11) or ἀπιστία (Mk. 16:14).

[237] E.g., Hb. 11:4-6, 8, also 27 f., 30 f., 33. Similarly ἀπιστία means "disobedience" in Hb. 3:19 (cf. ἀπειθεῖν, v. 18).

denoted not merely by ἀπιστεῖν but also by ἀπειθεῖν, → 11, 16 ff. Paul in particular stresses the element of obedience in faith. For him πίστις is indeed ὑπακοή, as comparison of R. 1:8; 1 Th. 1:8 with R. 15:18; 16:19, or 2 C. 10:5 f. with 10:15, shows. Faith is for Paul ὑπακούειν τῷ εὐαγγελίῳ, R. 10:16. To refuse to believe is not to obey the righteousness which the Gospel offers for faith, R. 10:3. Paul can call believing confession of the Gospel the ὑποταγὴ τῆς ὁμολογίας εἰς τὸ εὐαγγέλιον τοῦ Χριστοῦ, 2 C. 9:13. He coins the combination ὑπακοὴ πίστεως, R. 1:5. [238] On the theological interpretation of faith contained herein → 217, 35 ff.

c. As to Trust. In the OT and Judaism (→ 199, 21 ff.) the sense of "trust" is combined with faith. The same is true in the NT as well. This sense is especially prominent where the influence of the OT and Jewish tradition is strong. Reference to trust in God is comparatively rare, → 6, 24 ff. It is natural, however, that the πίστις of the OT characters in Hb. 11 should be trust as well as obedience. This may be seen from v. 11: (Sara) πιστὸν ("faithful") ἡγήσατο τὸν ἐπαγγειλά-μενον. The πίστις of v. 11 f. is on the one side trust that God will fulfil His promise (→ 200, 3) [239] and on the other side trust in His miraculous power, as in vv. 17-19 and v. 29 f. In this sense the Synoptists speak of faith in the miraculous power of Jesus. [240] In the Christian mission this is replaced by faith in the wonder-working ὄνομα (→ V, 277, 14 ff.) of Jesus (Ac. 3:16) or in the power of the apostles to work miracles, Ac. 14:9. More generally faith signifies in the Synoptists confidence in God's miraculous help [241] or even in one's own miraculous power; [242] so also in Paul, 1 C. 12:9; 13:2. That this πίστις is fundamentally the faith of prayer is intimated already in Mk. 11:22 by the fact that it is called πίστις θεοῦ, [243] and it is made quite explicit by the saying which Mk. adds in 11:24 with its reference to believing prayer. In other verses, too, πίστις means the confident belief of prayer which does not doubt. [244] The sense of "trust" is in general less prominent in Paul (→ 204, 13 ff.) but we find it when Paul describes Abraham's faith as confidence in God's miraculous power, R. 4:17-20. It is probable that εἰς τὸ εἶναι κτλ. in R. 4:11 is not meant consecutively but denotes the content of Abraham's πίστις; if so, πίστις is confidence in the fulfilment of the divine promise ; so possibly also the εἰς τὸ γενέσθαι κτλ. of R. 4:18. πιστεύειν might also mean "to trust" in R. 9:33; 10:11, where Paul speaks of πιστεύειν ἐπ' αὐτῷ (sc. God) on the basis of Is. 28:16. [245] ἀπιστία is used similarly in a few cases.

---

[238] The εἰς ὑπακοὴν πίστεως of R. 16:26 and ὑπηκούσατε δὲ κτλ. of R. 6:17 correspond to Pauline usage even though they may not come from Paul himself, cf. R. Bultmann, "Glossen in R.," ThLZ, 72 (1947), 202.

[239] So also Hb. 11:7, 8 ff., 13, 17 etc.; also 2 Cl., 11, 1; Herm. s., 1, 7; m., 12, 6, 2; cf. faith in God's future reward, Herm. s., 2, 5; cf. v., 3, 8, 4; 6, 5.

[240] πιστεύειν Mk. 5:36; Mt. 8:13; 9:28; πίστις Mk. 2:5; 5:34; 10:52; Mt. 8:10 and par.; 9:29; 15:28; in a formula, Lk. 17:19.

[241] Mk. 4:40; 9:23 f. (πάντα δυνατὰ τῷ πιστεύοντι κτλ.).

[242] Mk. 11:22 f. and par.; Mt. 17:20; Lk. 17:6.

[243] The ἔχετε πίστιν θεοῦ is an introductory addition by Mk. (v. Bultmann Trad., 95) which is not found in the source-variants at Mt. 17:20 and Lk. 17:6 and which is also avoided in the par. to Mk. at Mt. 21:21. πίστις θεοῦ is used only here in this sense (R. 3:3 God's faithfulness). It does not correspond to OT or Jewish usage but to missionary terminology (the θεοῦ is missing in some MSS ; cf. Loh. Mk., ad loc.).

[244] Jm. 1:6; 5:15; Herm. m., 9, 6-12 (opp. διψυχία); cf. v., 4, 2, 6.

[245] Cf. the even weaker expressions δουλεύειν ἐν πεποιθήσει πίστεως ἀγαθῆς as a description of piety in 1 Cl., 26, 1 (→ 8, 27); Herm. m., 1, 2 : πίστευσον οὖν αὐτῷ (sc.

It means lack of faith in God's miraculous power in R. 4:20; lack of faith in Jesus in Mk. 6:6; 9:24; lack of confidence in one's own miraculous power in Mt. 17:20 D latt syrˢ. ἄπιστος is used in the same sense in Mk. 9:19. So, too, is ὀλιγόπιστος, which was taken over from Judaism, → n. 174. [246] In the general sense of lack of belief or confidence ἀπιστία is combined with διψυχία in 2 Cl., 19, 2.

d. As to Hope. Trust in God is very closely related to hope (→ 200, 3 and → II, 531, 18 ff.). This relationship is emphasised by the ὃς παρ' ἐλπίδα ἐπ' ἐλπίδι ἐπίστευσεν of R. 4:18 and it is also clear in the description of πίστις in Hb. 11: faith in God's promise is also hope. This is indeed the predominant sense in Hb. 11. [247] Is explains why the heroes of the OT can be examples for Christians, whose faith is also directed to the future which God has promised, and who also know that they are "strangers and pilgrims on the earth," v. 13. This is the more apposite in that the future promised to the saints of the OT is the same as that promised to Christians, [248] and the men of the OT have not yet experienced its fulfilment. [249] The paradox of hoping confidence is strongly emphasised in R. 4:19 as well as Hb. 11 (→ III, 617, 20 ff.). It is directed to that which is invisible (v. 7) or to Him who is invisible (v. 27). For the sake of this paradox Hb. 11 adopted the Hellenistic (Philonic) idea that πίστις is directed to the invisible to the degree that this is not only the promised future but also the heavenly reality which cannot be perceived by the senses but can only be believed in faith: πίστει νοοῦμεν κατηρτίσθαι τοὺς αἰῶνας ῥήματι θεοῦ, εἰς τὸ μὴ ἐκ φαινομένων τὸ βλεπόμενον γεγονέναι (v. 3 → IV, 951, 22 ff.). The prior definition in v. 1 embraces both aspects: ἔστιν δὲ πίστις ἐλπιζομένων ὑπόστασις ("assurance," → II, 531, 3 ff.), πραγμάτων ἔλεγχος οὐ βλεπομένων (→ II, 476, 8 ff.). [250] One consequence of this view of faith is that Hb. 11 can also understand faith in the OT sense along the lines of the vocabulary of mission: πιστεῦσαι γὰρ δεῖ τὸν προσερχόμενον θεῷ, ὅτι ἔστιν καὶ τοῖς ἐκζητοῦσιν αὐτὸν μισθαποδότης γίνεται, v. 6; cf. 6:1. Another consequence is that in faith special emphasis can be laid on turning from the earthly world and turning to the heavenly world, v. 7, 15 f., 24-26; cf. 12:2. [251] Even where, according to specific Christian usage (→ 208, 34 ff.), πίστις is faith in Christ, the character of faith as hope is maintained, though in such a way that hope is mentioned with πίστις and explicitly distinguished from it. The less Christian πίστις εἰς ... is as such hope, the more ἐλπίς (especially in Paul) contains within it the element of believing confidence derived from the OT (→ II, 531, 1 ff.) πίστις and ἐλπίς occur together (and with ἀγάπη) in 1 Th. 1:3; 1 C. 13:13. They are also found in other combinations. [252] Their basic

---

θεῷ) καὶ φοβήθητι αὐτόν, cf. Dg., 10, 1. As πίστις ἐν πεποιθήσει is one of the blessings of salvation in 1 Cl., 35, 2 (→ 8, 28 f.), so πίστις is a virtue along with φόβος and ἐγκράτεια in Herm. m., 6, 1, 1-2, 10. In what follows πίστις is described as faith in the δίκαιον or the angel of δικαιοσύνη. In Herm. s., 9, 15, 2 f. Πίστις is the first of the virgin virtues as opp. to Ἀπιστία, the first of the vices.

[246] In Mt. 6:30 and par. the ref. is to the weakness of trust in God, in Mt. 8:26; 14:31; 16:8 to the lack of trust in the miraculous power of Jesus. At Mt. 17:20 א B read ὀλιγοπιστία to denote the weakness of the faith of the disciples in their own power to work miracles.

[247] Cf. Käsemann, 19-27.

[248] v. 7, 10, 14-16, 26.

[249] v. 13, 39 f.

[250] πίστις can also have this nuance in Paul, 2 C. 5:7.

[251] Cf. the similar deduction in Paul, 2 C. 5:6 ff.

[252] Col. 1:4 f., 23; Hb. 6:11 vl.; cf. Barn., 4, 8: ἐν ἐλπίδι τῆς πίστεως αὐτοῦ.

relationship is stressed in 1 Pt. 1:21, where we read : ὥστε τὴν πίστιν ὑμῶν καὶ ἐλπίδα εἶναι εἰς θεόν, "that your faith is also hope in God," → II, 531, n. 105.

e. As Faithfulness. In πίστις there is also an echo of the OT sense of "faithfulness," → 199, 4 ff. This may be seen in the deduction which Hb. 12:1 draws from recollection of the witnesses of faith : δι' ὑπομονῆς τρέχωμεν τὸν προκείμενον ἡμῖν ἀγῶνα, corresponding to the introduction to c. 11: ... ὑπομονῆς γὰρ ἔχετε χρείαν (10:36). ἐλπίς and ὑπομονή are closely related, → II, 531, 1 ff. So also are πίστις and ὑπομονή, 2 Th. 1:4. [253] So are πίστις and μακροθυμία, Hb. 6:12. So are ἀγάπη, πίστις, διακονία and ὑπομονή, Rev. 2:19. The πίστις of the ἡγούμενοι which Hb. 13:7 summons us to follow is also to be understood essentially as faithfulness, and this is also the meaning when 2 Tm. 4:7 says : τὴν πίστιν τετήρηκα, [254] or when the church in Pergamon is praised in Rev. 2:13 : κρατεῖς τὸ ὄνομά μου καὶ οὐκ ἠρνήσω τὴν πίστιν μου. Conversely ἀπιστία in Hb. 3:12 and ἀπιστεῖν in 2 Tm. 2:13 denote the "unfaithfulness" of Christians. Hb. 11:17 tells us that πίστις proves itself as faithfulness in temptation, and Jm. 1:2 f. says that it becomes ὑπομονή. In 1 Pt., too, πίστις is seen to be the faithfulness which must be demonstrated when tested. [255] When Paul thinks of the faith of Israel, the element of faithfulness in πίστις is not without its influence. Thus in R. 3:3 he speaks of the ἀπιστεῖν and ἀπιστία ("unfaithfulness") of Israel. On the other hand, when he exhorts to faithfulness in believing, he has in view στήκειν ἐν τῇ πίστει (1 C. 16:13), [256] so that πίστις itself is not faithfulness ; it is the faith to which one should be faithful.

2. Specifically Christian Usage.

a. πίστις as Acceptance of the Kerygma. To be distinguished from all the senses under 1. is the specifically Christian use of πίστις which is to be seen most clearly in the formula πίστις εἰς, → 203, 10 ff.; 204, 14. πίστις is understood here as acceptance of the Christian kerygma. It is thus the saving faith which recognises and appropriates God's saving work in Christ. Here too, of course, πίστις contains the element of believing. Obedience, trust, hope and faithfulness are also implied. Conversely, if any one of these elements is primary, faith in Christ can be included. [257] Nevertheless, the primary sense of πιστεύειν in specifically Christian usage is acceptance of the kerygma about Christ. [258] This usage is to be explained by the fact that we are here in the sphere of the vocabulary of mission (→ 200, 7 ff.; → 203, 21 f.). Faith in Christ is used first in the same sense as faith in God, in contrast to those who do not yet know the one God, who do not yet believe in Him, who have first to "believe" in Him in the sense of acknowledging His existence if they are to be able to "believe" in Him in the OT sense of the word.

---

[253] Also Rev. 13:10 (cf. 14:12).

[254] On τὴν πίστιν τηρεῖν = "to keep faith," v. Pr.-Bauer⁴, s.v.

[255] 1 Pt. 1:7; cf. 1:5, 9; 5:9.

[256] Cf. στήκειν ἐν κυρίῳ, Phil. 4:1; 1 Th. 3:8.

[257] This is clearest in, e.g., Rev. 14:12, where there is added to πίστις ("faithfulness") the obj. gen. Ἰησοῦ, which strictly denotes the theme of the kerygma.

[258] πίστις is expressly characterised as reception of the kerygma in R. 10:14-17. κήρυγμα is the obj. of faith in 1 C. 1:21; 2:4 f.; 15:11, 14; Herm. s., 8, 3, 2; εὐαγγέλιον in 1 C. 15:2; Phil. 1:27 (?); Eph. 1:13; Ac. 8:12; 15:7; Mk. 1:15; cf. Dg., 11, 6; μαρτύριον in 2 Th. 1:10; 1 Jn. 5:10; cf. Jn. 1:7; ἀκοή in R. 10:16; Jn. 12:38; cf. Herm. s., 9, 17, 4; λόγος in Ac. 4:4; 13:48; Eph. 1:13; Barn., 9, 3; cf. 11, 11 and Barn., 16, 9 : ὁ λόγος αὐτοῦ τῆς πίστεως.

Hb. 11:6 explicitly uses πιστεύειν in the first sense : πιστεῦσαι γὰρ δεῖ τὸν προσερχόμενον θεῷ, ὅτι ἔστιν κτλ., → 207, 26 f. In fact the primitive missionary community proclaims faith in Christ along with faith in the one God to whom the heathen, turning from idols, must be converted. Hence the conversion of the Thessalonians is described in 1 Th. 1:8 as their πίστις πρὸς τὸν θεόν, and this expression is elucidated in v. 9 : πῶς ἐπεστρέψατε κτλ., → 204, 7 f. According to Hb. 6:1 one of the first principles of Christianity, along with μετάνοια ἀπὸ νεκρῶν ἔργων, is πίστις ἐπὶ θεόν. [259] Whereas in the OT and Judaism (except in propaganda) faith is required as the appropriate attitude to the God who has long since made Himself known and whose existence cannot be doubted, the primitive Christian kerygma brings the message that there is one God, and with this it also brings the message about Jesus Christ His Son, and about what God has done and will do through Him. Acceptance of this kerygma is πιστεύειν. It is thus clear that the element of confident hope is less prominent in the specifically Christian concept of πίστις. πίστις εἰς ... looks primarily to what God has done, not to what He will do. [260]

b. The Content of Faith. Paul in R. 10:9 (→ 203, 17) states the content of Christian faith in a sentence in which he does not simply give his own view but is saying what is obviously self-evident to every Christian preacher : ὅτι ἐὰν ὁμολογήσῃς ἐν τῷ στόματί σου κύριον Ἰησοῦν, καὶ πιστεύσῃς ἐν τῇ καρδίᾳ σου ὅτι ὁ θεὸς αὐτὸν ἤγειρεν ἐκ νεκρῶν, σωθήσῃ. Since ὁμολογεῖν and πιστεύειν are obvious equivalents in the synonymous parallelism (→ V, 209, 15 ff.), it is apparent that acknowledgment of Jesus as Lord is intrinsic to Christian faith along with acknowledgment of the miracle of His resurrection, i.e., acceptance of this miracle as true. The two statements constitute an inner unity. The resurrection is not just a remarkable event. It is the soteriological fact in virtue of which Jesus became the κύριος. This is self-evident, and other statements confirm it. Naturally, in view of the inner unity, either one of the statements can be made alone, or the event of salvation can be described differently or more explicitly. The totality is always in view. In 1 C. 15:11 Paul says : οὕτως κηρύσσομεν καὶ οὕτως ἐπιστεύσατε with reference to the εὐαγγέλιον (v. 1) which includes ἐν πρώτοις (v. 3) the fact that Christ died for our sins, that He was buried, that on the third day He was raised again, and that He bore witness to Himself as the risen Lord. According to R. 4:24 Christians believe ἐπὶ τὸν ἐγείραντα Ἰησοῦν τὸν κύριον ἡμῶν ἐκ νεκρῶν (cf. Col. 2:12), and according to 1 Th. 4:14 : ὅτι Ἰησοῦς ἀπέθανεν καὶ ἀνέστη. [261] If the sketch of the humiliation and exaltation of Christ in Phil. 2:6-11 is not expressly described as the object of πίστις, it is certainly to be understood in this way. The ἐξομολογεῖσθαι ὅτι κύριος Ἰησοῦς Χριστός, in so far as it is made by the ἐπίγειοι, is simply the confession of πίστις (cf. R. 10:9). The kerygmatic sections of the sermons in Acts [262] describe the content of πίστις even when this is not expressly stated (as in 13:39). Kerygma and faith always go together (→ n. 258; cf. 1 Tm. 3:16). It makes no difference if instead of kurios other titles denoting the dignity of Christ refer to Him as the object of

---

[259] Cf. the relation between theological and christological preaching in Ac. 17:22-31. Cf. also Herm. m., 1, 1: πρῶτον πάντων πίστευσον ὅτι εἷς ἐστιν ὁ θεός (→ n. 180).

[260] Cf. J. Weiss, Das Urchristentum (1917), 323; Wissmann, 71 f.; Mundle, 73-114.

[261] Cf. 1 Pt. 1:21; Pol., 2, 1.

[262] Ac. 2:22-24; 3:13-15; 10:37-41; 13:26-37.

πιστεύειν, cf. Jn. 20:31: ἵνα πιστεύητε ὅτι 'Ιησοῦς ἐστιν ὁ χριστὸς ὁ υἱὸς τοῦ
θεοῦ, [263] or whether the work of salvation is described in some other way in a
ὅτι clause, e.g., ὅτι ἐγὼ παρὰ τοῦ θεοῦ ἐξῆλθον (Jn. 16:27, 30), ὅτι σύ με
ἀπέστειλας (Jn. 11:42; 17:8, 21), or according to the specific usage of John : ὅτι
ἐγὼ ἐν τῷ πατρὶ κτλ. (Jn. 14:10), or in a simple ὅτι ἐγώ εἰμι (Jn. 8:24; 13:19). [264]
The work of salvation accomplished by God in Christ can be described even more
generally as the object of faith, as the ἀγάπη, ἣν ἔχει ὁ θεὸς ἐν ἡμῖν (1 Jn. 4:16),
or in terms of its significance : εἰ δὲ ἀπεθάνομεν σὺν Χριστῷ, πιστεύομεν ὅτι
καὶ συζήσομεν αὐτῷ (R. 6:8). [265] An abbreviated expression for this saving faith
is the formula πιστεύειν (πίστις) εἰς . . .; [266] with πίστις an obj. gen. can take the
place of the prepositional phrase. [267] In this sense πίστις and πιστεύειν can be used
in the abs. This usage is so common in the Pauline corpus, Acts, John and elsewhere
that there is no need to give examples. It has also influenced Mk. and Lk. [268]

c. Faith as a Personal Relation to Christ. The question arises whether the
abbreviated expression πίστις (πιστεύειν) εἰς . . ., which is in the first instance
a linguistic phenomenon, can also take on a special sense, i.e., denote a personal
relation to Christ, so that — since πιστεύειν εἰς Χριστὸν 'Ιησοῦν is the way to
salvation — faith in Christ has the same material significance as the relation to
God.

Now it is worth noting that in the NT the relation to God is practically never indicated by πιστεύειν εἰς. [269] Conversely, the LXX formulae for the relation to God,
i.e., πιστεύειν c. dat. and πιστεύειν ἐπί c. dat. (→ 203, 9 f.), are practically never used
for the relation to Christ. It is true that πιστεύειν c. dat., which in R. 4:3 (17); Gl. 3:6;
Tt. 3:8; Ac. 16:34 (D : ἐπὶ τὸν θεόν) is used for the relation to God, [270] does occur
commonly in Jn. for the relation to Christ, but it means here, not "to believe in" Jesus,

---

[263] Cf. also Jn. 11:27: ὅτι σὺ εἶ ὁ χριστὸς κτλ.; 6:69 : ὅτι σὺ εἶ ὁ ἅγιος τοῦ θεοῦ,
also 1 Jn. 5:1, 5; Ac. 8:37 E al.
[264] In the period which followed the formulations are often motivated by opposition to
error, as, e.g., in Ign. Sm., 3, 1: ἐγὼ γὰρ καὶ μετὰ τὴν ἀνάστασιν ἐν σαρκὶ αὐτὸν
οἶδα καὶ πιστεύω ὄντα.
[265] The πίστις θείου πνεύματος of Herm. m., 11, 9 is the faith that there is the divine
Spirit, or that He is given in the community.
[266] πιστεύειν εἰς : εἰς τὸν 'Ιησοῦν, Ac. 19:4; Jn. 12:11; εἰς Χριστὸν 'Ιησοῦν, Gl. 2:16;
cf. 1 Pt. 1:8; εἰς τὸν κύριον, Ac. 14:23; Herm. m., 4, 3, 3; cf. R. 10:14; εἰς τὸν υἱόν, Jn. 3:36;
cf. 3:16, 18; εἰς τὸν υἱὸν τοῦ θεοῦ, 1 Jn. 5:10; εἰς τὸν υἱὸν τοῦ ἀνθρώπου, Jn. 9:35; εἰς
αὐτόν, Ac. 10:43; Jn. 2:11; 4:39; 7:31; 8:30 etc.; εἰς ἐμέ, Jn. 6:35; 14:1; 16:9; 17:20; Mt.
18:6; εἰς τὸ φῶς, Jn. 12:36; εἰς τὸ ὄνομα, Jn. 1:12; 2:23 (αὐτοῦ); Jn. 3:18 (τοῦ μονογενοῦς υἱοῦ τοῦ θεοῦ); 1 Jn. 5:13 (τοῦ υἱοῦ τοῦ θεοῦ); εἰς ὃν ἀπέστειλεν ἐκεῖνος,
Jn. 6:29. πίστις εἰς : εἰς τὸν κύριον ἡμῶν 'Ιησοῦν, Ac. 20:21; εἰς Χριστὸν 'Ιησοῦν,
Ac. 24:24; εἰς Χριστόν, Col. 2:5; πρὸς τὸν κύριον 'Ιησοῦν, Phlm. 5; εἰς ἐμέ, Ac. 26:18.
[267] πίστις with obj. gen.: 'Ιησοῦ Χριστοῦ, R. 3:22; Gl. 2:16; 3:22; 'Ιησοῦ, R. 3:26;
Rev. 14:12; Χριστοῦ, Phil. 3:9; τοῦ κυρίου ἡμῶν 'Ιησοῦ Χριστοῦ, Jm. 2:1; cf. Eph. 3:12;
τοῦ κυρίου, Herm. v., 4, 1, 8; s., 6, 1, 2; 3, 6; τοῦ υἱοῦ τοῦ θεοῦ, Gl. 2:20; Herm. s., 9, 16, 5;
τοῦ ὀνόματος αὐτοῦ, Ac. 3:16; μου, Rev. 2:13.
[268] πίστις, Lk. 18:8; πιστεύειν, Mk. 9:42; Lk. 8:12 f.; also the inauthentic Marcan ending
16:16 f.
[269] There are only 2 possible instances : a. 1 Pt. 1:21 → 208, 1 ff.: if the meaning is "so
that your faith and hope might be in God," the εἰς is governed by ἐλπίς rather than πίστις
(similarly 1 Cl., 12, 7), in acc. with usage attested from the time of the LXX (v. 2 C. 1:10;
Ac. 24:15; Jn. 5:45 → II, 523, n. 34); b. Jn. 14:1: πιστεύετε εἰς τὸν θεόν, καὶ εἰς ἐμὲ
πιστεύετε, an isolated case, since the formulation is selected to express the unity of Jesus
with God.
[270] Cf. Ac. 16:15 D : πιστὸς τῷ θεῷ, also Jn. 5:24; 1 Jn. 5:10 πιστεύειν c. dat., though
here in a special sense : "to believe" (God).

but "to believe" Jesus or His words. For Jn. this is, of course, materially identical with πιστεύειν εἰς (αὐτόν), but linguistically it is not interchangeable with it, → 203, 10 ff. For the rest, πιστεύειν c. dat. is rare with ref. to Jesus, and only once in the NT is a personal relation to Christ expressed thereby : 2 Tm. 1:12 : οἶδα γὰρ ᾧ πεπίστευκα, where the sense of "believing in" contains also that of "trusting," so also Ign. Tr., 9, 2. On the other hand, in Mt. 27:42 D; Ac. 18:8 (cf. 16:15); 1 Jn. 3:23, as this verse esp. shows, πιστεύειν c. dat. is to be construed after the analogy of πιστεύειν εἰς → 203, 13 f. πιστεύειν ἐπί c. dat. denotes the relation to God in R. 9:33; 10:11; 1 Pt. 2:6; 1 Cl., 34, 4 (Is. 28:16); the only instance of the relation to Jesus is in 1 Tm. 1:16, where the addition of εἰς ζωὴν αἰώνιον shows that the predominant sense is that of expectant confidence. [271] Equation of the relations to God and to Christ may be seen in πιστεύειν ἐπί c. acc., which is fairly rare in the LXX but occurs a few times in the NT. [272] This is undoubtedly not an abbreviating formula but denotes turning to the person of the Lord, just as πίστις ἐπὶ θεόν (Hb. 6:1; cf. Ac. 16:34 D) and πίστις πρὸς τὸν θεόν (1 Th. 1:8 → 204, 14 f.) denote turning to God from paganism. [273] Similarly the τὴν πίστιν ἣν ἔχεις πρὸς τὸν κύριον Ἰησοῦν of Phlm. 5 shows that πιστεύειν can be used for a personal relation to Christ.

The decisive point, however, is this. Faith in Christ as acceptance of the kerygma about Him does not indicate only the presence of a previously unknown divine person, a strange deity, Ac. 17:18. For the figure of Jesus Christ cannot be detached from its "myth," i.e., the history enacted in His life, death and resurrection. This history, however, is salvation history. That is, the man who accepts the kerygma in faith recognises therewith that this history took place for him. [274] Since Jesus Christ was made the *Kurios* by His history, [275] acceptance of the kerygma also includes acknowledgment of Jesus Christ as the *Kurios*. This is expressed in the formula πίστις εἰς τὸν κύριον ἡμῶν Ἰησοῦν or the like. Hence πιστεύειν εἰς Χριστὸν Ἰησοῦν does in fact entail a personal relation to Christ analogous to the relation to God, though different from it. If the OT relation to God is described as faith in God, this faith in God is distinguished already from πίστις εἰς Χριστὸν Ἰησοῦν by the fact that OT faith — as obedience and faithfulness — is directed to the God whose existence is always presupposed. In its original and true sense, however, faith in Jesus Christ is not obedience to a Lord who is known already. Only in faith itself is the existence of this Lord recognised and acknowledged. Faith embraces the conviction that there is this Lord, Jesus Christ, for it. For only in faith does this Lord meet it. It believes on the basis of the kerygma. It can always believe only on the basis of this message. The message is never a mere orientation which can be dispensed with once it is known. It is always the foundation of faith. God has instituted the λόγος τῆς καταλλαγῆς with the Christ event, 2 C. 5:18 f. For this reason faith in the kerygma is in-

---

[271] The occasional πιστεύειν ἐν (Mk. 1:15; Jn. 3:15 [?]) or πίστις ἐν (Gl. 3:26 [?]; Col. 1:4 [?]; Eph. 1:15; 1 Tm. 3:13; 2 Tm. 3:15; 1 Cl., 22, 1) is not to be regarded as an adoption of the LXX expression but as a linguistic variant on πιστεύειν (πίστις) εἰς.

[272] Ac. 9:42; 11:17; 16:31; 22:19; Mt. 27:42 (D αὐτῷ, א ἐπ᾽ αὐτῷ).

[273] Though not R. 4:24 (cf. Col. 2:12; 1 Pt. 1:21), where τοῖς πιστεύουσιν ἐπὶ τὸν ἐγείραντα Ἰησοῦν κτλ. is obviously constructed after the analogy of ἐλπίζειν ἐπί (cf. Barn., 11, 8 : ἐπὶ τὸν σταυρὸν ἐλπίσαντες). Similarly R. 4:5 (cf. 4:18).

[274] What is stated in the NT by formulae with ὑπέρ, περί etc. is later expressed in phrases like πιστεύειν εἰς τὸν θάνατον αὐτοῦ, Ign. Tr., 2, 1; εἰς τὸ αἷμα Χριστοῦ, Ign. Sm., 6, 1; cf. Barn., 7, 2 : πιστεύσωμεν ὅτι ὁ υἱὸς τοῦ θεοῦ οὐκ ἠδύνατο παθεῖν εἰ μὴ δι᾽ ἡμᾶς. Barn., 11, 8 → n. 273.

[275] Phil. 2:9-11; Ac. 2:36; cf. Ac. 5:31: σωτήρ.

separable from faith in the person mediated thereby. In the sense that it believes on the basis of the kerygma, faith is always a "venture."

Certain verses show that a personal relation can really be expressed by the initially formal phrase πιστεύειν εἰς Χριστὸν 'Ιησοῦν. One may refer first to R. 10:9, which proves clearly that to believe in Jesus Christ is to acknowledge Him as Lord. Again, in R. 10:14 the πιστεύειν εἰς αὐτόν leads to calling upon Him, so that πιστεύειν, being followed by baptism, brings into a personal relation to Christ. R. 6:8; Gl. 2:20 also show that faith brings into fellowship with Him. In its own way so, too, does Phil. 1:29 : ὅτι ὑμῖν ἐχαρίσθη τὸ ὑπὲρ Χριστοῦ, οὐ μόνον τὸ εἰς αὐτὸν πιστεύειν ἀλλὰ καὶ τὸ ὑπὲρ αὐτοῦ πάσχειν, or 1 Pt. 1:8 (ἐν τῇ ἀποκαλύψει 'Ιησοῦ Χριστοῦ) ὃν οὐκ ἰδόντες ἀγαπᾶτε, εἰς ὃν ἄρτι μὴ ὁρῶντες πιστεύοντες δὲ ἀγαλλιᾶσθε ..., or Ac. 14:23 : παρέθεντο αὐτοὺς τῷ κυρίῳ εἰς ὃν πεπιστεύκεισαν. One may also add the instances in which the relation to Christ is expressed by πιστεύειν c. dat. in the sense "to trust" (→ 211, 3 ff.), [276] by πιστεύειν ἐπί (→ 211, 8), or by πίστις πρός (Phlm. 5). [277]

d. Believing. The saving faith denoted by πίστις and πιστεύειν, whether in the abs. or with some qualification, can be considered either in respect of its origin or in respect of its continuation. When μετάνοια and πίστις are preached (Ac. 20:21; cf. Hb. 6:1), the hearers are summoned to repent and believe. πίστις is to be understood as acceptance of the Christian message in, e.g., R. 1:5; 3:25; 10:17; 1 C. 15:14, 17, also 1 Th. 1:8 ("that ye believed"); R. 1:8; 11:20 ("thou hast attained thy status by believing"), and wherever Paul speaks of δικαιοῦσθαι or of δικαιοσύνη ἐκ πίστεως as in R. 3:28; 5:1; Gl. 3:24; Phil. 3:9 etc. Similar examples may naturally be found elsewhere. [278] Along the same lines ἀπιστία is rejection of the Christian kerygma, R. 11:20, 23.

On the other hand, πίστις also means "to be believing," "standing in faith." This is particularly clear when there is reference to the χρόνος τῆς πίστεως, [279] but also in 1 C. 2:5; 2 C. 1:24; 13:5; Gl. 2:20; 1 Th. 3:2, 5 ff.; Eph. 6:16; 1 Tm. 3:13; Jm. 2:1, 5 etc. [280] Often the question arises whether confidence is not a better rendering, for πίστις can frequently denote the living and dynamic aspect of faith rather than the mere fact. This applies when there is ref. to the μέτρον πίστεως (R. 12:3, → I, 347, 21 ff.), to the weakness of faith (R. 14:1), [281] to its strength, [282] to its growth (2 C. 10:15), [283] to enduring in

---

[276] Later cf. πιστεύειν τῇ χάριτι 'Ιησοῦ Χριστοῦ, Ign. Phld., 8, 1 (cf. Pol., 7, 3); τῇ χρηστότητι αὐτοῦ, Dg., 9, 6.

[277] It might be that Phlm. 5 even speaks of ἀγάπη for the κύριος 'Ιησοῦς, though this is probably an inversion (Lohmeyer Phlm., ad loc.), so that the ref. is to πίστις in Christ and ἀγάπη for the ἅγιοι.

[278] Col. 1:4; Eph. 1:15; 2 Th. 3:2; Ac. 13:8; 14:27; 20:21; 26:18; Hb. 4:2; Herm. v., 1, 3, 4.

[279] Did., 16, 2; Barn., 4, 9; cf. Herm. v., 3, 5, 4 : νέοι ... ἐν τῇ πίστει.

[280] ἀπιστία is used in a corresponding sense in 1 Tm. 1:13, so also Ign. Eph., 8, 2, unless this is a reduced use in which πίστις simply means Christianity and ἀπιστία paganism.

[281] Cf. Herm. s., 9, 26, 8 : κολοβοὶ ... ἀπὸ τῆς πίστεως αὐτῶν, though cf. Herm. m., 5, 2, 3 : τὴν πίστιν ἔχειν ὁλόκληρον.

[282] Col. 2:7: βεβαιούμενοι τῇ πίστει, Herm. v., 3, 5, 5 : ἰσχυροὶ ἐν τῇ πίστει, m., 12, 6, 1: ἰσχυροποιῆσαι αὐτοὺς ἐν τῇ πίστει, v., 3, 12, 3 : ἐνδυναμοῦσθαι ἐν τῇ πίστει, 1 Cl., 1, 2 : τὴν ... βεβαίαν ὑμῶν πίστιν, Ac. 16:5 : στερεοῦσθαι τῇ πίστει, Col. 2:5 : βλέπων ὑμῶν τὴν τάξιν καὶ τὸ στερέωμα τῆς εἰς Χριστὸν πίστεως ὑμῶν, Ign. Eph., 10, 2 : ἑδραῖοι τῇ πίστει, → n. 284.

[283] Phil. 1:25 : εἰς τὴν ὑμῶν προκοπὴν καὶ χαρὰν τῆς πίστεως, cf. Pol., 3, 2 : οἰκοδομεῖσθαι εἰς τὴν δοθεῖσαν ὑμῖν πίστιν.

faith, [284] to its fulness, [285] to its superabundance (2 C. 8:7), to its practice (1 Th. 1:3 : μνημονεύοντες ὑμῶν τοῦ ἔργου τῆς πίστεως cf. Phlm. 6), or to its unity, [286] and also in all the verses where πίστις and ἀγάπη [287] are combined. [288]

e. πίστις as fides quae creditur. In all these instances πίστις, though naturally related to its object, is fides qua creditur. The usage develops, however, in such a way that πίστις can also mean fides quae creditur. Thus if Paul can call the message which demands faith (fides qua creditur) the ῥῆμα τῆς πίστεως (R. 10:8), or if he can describe it as the ἀκοὴ πίστεως, "the preaching which demands faith or ... opens up the possibility of faith" (Gl. 3:2, 5), it is obvious that he can also abbreviate and say εὐαγγελίζεσθαι τὴν πίστιν (Gl. 1:23). The message itself, then, can be called πίστις. It thus follows that, since πίστις is the divinely demanded relation of man to God, and is as such the divinely opened way of salvation, Paul can use the word in the sense of a norm or principle, e.g., when he contrasts νόμος and πίστις as the two ways of salvation (R. 3:31; 4:14), or when he speaks of the coming (→ II, 674, 35 ff.) of πίστις as an independent entity (Gl. 3:23, 25). He can thus form the combination νόμος πίστεως, R. 3:27 → IV, 1071, 9 ff. πίστις is also regarded as a principle in R. 4:16; Gl. 3:12; 1 C. 13:13. For this reason Paul can already use πίστις in the sense of Christianity, which may be further differentiated into being a Christian and the Christian message, teaching, or principle. This is the usage when he speaks of οἰκεῖοι τῆς πίστεως = "fellow-Christians" (Gl. 6:10), or when he employs πίστις as the object of εὐαγγελίζεσθαι or πορθεῖν (Gl. 1:23), or perhaps when he has the formula : εἴτε προφητείαν, κατὰ τὴν ἀναλογίαν τῆς πίστεως, R. 12:6.

πίστις is also found for the preaching of faith at Ac. 6:7: ὑπήκουον τῇ πίστει, and it is a principle in Eph. 4:5 : εἷς κύριος, μία πίστις, ἓν βάπτισμα. [289] πίστις as fides quae creditur is also in view when there is reference to the μυστήριον τῆς πίστεως (1 Tm. 3:9; we are told what this is in 3:16). πίστις and καλὴ διδασκαλία can thus be linked in 1 Tm. 4:6. To fall victim to error is ἀφίστασθαι τῆς πίστεως (1 Tm. 4:1) or ναυαγεῖν or ἀστοχεῖν περὶ τὴν πίστιν (1 Tm. 1:19; 6:21). [290] The orthodox doctrine handed down by the Church is also πίστις in Jd. 3, 20; 2 Pt. 1:1. In correspondence with the use of πίστις for Christianity we also find formal expressions in place of the as yet unused adjective "Christian": κατὰ κοινὴν πίστιν (Tt. 1:4), κατὰ πίστιν ἐκλεκτῶν (Tt. 1:1), ἐν πίστει (1 Tm.

---

[284] Col. 1:23 : εἴ γε ἐπιμένετε τῇ πίστει τεθεμελιωμένοι καὶ ἑδραῖοι (→ n. 282); ἐμμένειν τῇ πίστει, Ac. 14:22; Herm. s., 8, 9, 1; ὑπομένειν ἐν τῇ πίστει, Did., 16, 5; cf. Ign. Sm., 1, 1: κατηρτισμένους ἐν ἀκινήτῳ πίστει.

[285] πλήρης πίστεως Ac. 6:5; 11:24; πλήρης ἐν τῇ πίστει, Herm. m., 5, 2, 1; 12, 5, 4; πεπληρωμένος ἐν πίστει καὶ ἀγάπῃ, Ign. Sm. introitus.

[286] Eph. 4:13 : μέχρι καταντήσωμεν οἱ πάντες εἰς τὴν ἑνότητα τῆς πίστεως καὶ τῆς ἐπιγνώσεως ...; Ign. Eph., 13, 1: ὁμόνοια τῆς πίστεως; 20, 2 : συνέρχεσθαι ἐν μιᾷ πίστει καὶ ἐν Ἰησοῦ Χριστῷ; Herm. s., 9, 17, 4 : μία πίστις αὐτῶν ἐγένετο καὶ μία ἀγάπη, similarly 9, 18, 4.

[287] 2 Th. 1:3; Eph. 3:17; 6:23; 1 Tm. 1:14; 2:15; 4:12; Ign. Sm. introitus, → n. 285; Herm. s., 9, 17, 4; 18, 4 → n. 286.

[288] Cf. also R. 1:12; 14:22 f.; 2 C. 4:13. The ἐκ πίστεως εἰς πίστιν of R. 1:17 (→ II, 251, 27 f.) can hardly be taken in the sense "from first faith to confidence."

[289] Cf. also 1 Cl., 58, 2 : ζῇ γὰρ ὁ θεὸς ... ἥ τε πίστις καὶ ἡ ἐλπὶς τῶν ἐκλεκτῶν. Ign. Sm., 10, 2 : οὐδὲ ὑμᾶς ἐπαισχυνθήσεται ἡ τελεία πίστις (vgl. ἐλπίς), Ἰησοῦς Χριστός.

[290] Cf. 1 Tm. 1:6 and 2 Tm. 2:18 : ἀστοχεῖν περὶ τὴν ἀλήθειαν.

1:2, 4; Tt. 3:5), or ἐν πίστει καὶ ἀληθείᾳ (1 Tm. 2:7), ἐν πίστει Ἰησοῦ Χριστοῦ (Ign. Mg., 1, 1).

f. Development of the Use of πιστεύω. The meaning of πιστεύειν followed a similar course of development and differentiation. In most cases it means "to receive the message,"[291] esp. when used in the aor.,[292] though also in the perf.[293] The same sense is borne by the aor. part.[294] and perf. part.,[295] and naturally by the imp. too.[296] Again, this is often the meaning in ἵνα clauses.[297] The ind. pres. can have as one of its meanings "to come to believe," "to be ready to believe."[298] The occasional combination with μετανοεῖν[299] and βαπτισθῆναι[300] also shows that πιστεύειν can denote the basic Christian act of believing.[301] Less commonly πιστεύειν means "to be believing," "to have faith," though the pres. is often to be construed thus.[302] We are pointed in rather a different direction, however, by the timeless present in a statement like R. 10:10 : καρδίᾳ γὰρ πιστεύεται εἰς δικαιοσύνην, where πιστεύειν can mean both "to come to believe" and "to be believing." The common use of the pres. part. in Pl. and Jn. is to be taken in the same way.[303] The meaning is whittled down, as may be seen particularly in the use of the part. It is true that the pres. part. can often be a true part. ("those who are believing in me"), e.g., when some definition is given (εἰς ..., ἐπί ...),[304] or when the meaning is "we (you) the believing (i.e., believers)."[305] On the other hand, οἱ πιστεύοντες is simply a phrase for "Christians";[306] the aor.[307] and perf.[308] parts. can be used in the same way.

Thus the meaning of the parts. of πιστεύειν merges with that of πιστός. πιστός, too, can sometimes be qualified by an obj. so that it has the verbal force of "believing."[309]

---

[291] Cf. δέχεσθαι (ἀποδέχεσθαι) τὸν λόγον and πιστεύειν as synon. in 1 Th. 1:6; Ac. 8:13 f.; 17:11 f.; Lk. 8:13. Similarly ἀπιστεῖν is rejection of the kerygma, Mk. 16:16; Ign. Eph., 18, 1.

[292] R. 10:14, 16; 13:11; 1 C. 3:5; 15:2, 11; 2 C. 4:13; Gl. 2:16; Ac. 4:4; 8:13; 9:42; 18:8 etc.; Jn. 4:39, 41; 7:31, 48; 17:8 etc.; Herm. v., 3, 6, 1; s., 9, 22, 3; 2 Cl., 15, 3; Pol., 8, 2; aor. inf.: Barn., 16, 7.

[293] Ac. 14:23; 2 Tm. 1:12; Jn. 3:18; 6:69; 11:27; 1 Jn. 4:16; 5:10.

[294] Eph. 1:13; Ac. 11:17, 21; 19:2; Hb. 4:3; Jn. 7:39; Mk. 16:16; Herm. m., 4, 3, 3; s., 8, 3, 2; 9, 13, 5 etc.; Ign. Phld., 5, 2; 2 Cl., 2, 3.

[295] Tt. 3:8; Ac. 16:34; 18:27; 19:18; 21:20, 25; Herm. v., 3, 6, 4; 7, 1.

[296] Mk. 1:15; Ac. 16:31; Jn. 10:37 f.; 12:36; 14:1, 11. Fut. Barn., 3, 6.

[297] Jn. 1:7; 9:36; 11:42; 17:21; 19:35; 20:31; 1 Jn. 3:23.

[298] Jn. 1:50; 3:12; 4:42; 6:64 (?); 10:26; 14:10; 16:30 f., though cf. R. 10:9; 1 Tm. 1:16; Ac. 15:7; Jn. 3:12; 5:44.

[299] Mk. 1:15; Kg. Pt. (Kl. T., 3, 15); Herm. s., 9, 22, 3.

[300] Ac. 8:12; 16:31-33; 18:8 (cf. 2:41; 11:18; Hb. 6:1 f.); Mk. 16:16.

[301] Cf. also οἱ μέλλοντες πιστεύειν, 1 Cl., 42, 4; Herm. m., 4, 3, 3; s., 9, 30, 3.

[302] R. 6:8; 1 Th. 4:14; Ac. 15:11; Lk. 8:13; Jn. 16:9; Ign. Mg., 9, 1 (2); 2 Cl., 17, 3; 20, 2.

[303] R. 4:24; 1 C. 1:21; Gl. 3:22; Jn. 1:12; 3:18, 36; 6:35, 47; 7:38; 11:25 etc.; 1 Jn. 5:5, 13 (vl.). Also 1 Pt. 2:6 (Is. 28:16); Herm. s., 8, 3, 3. Often with πᾶς : R. 1:16; 3:22; 10:4; Jn. 3:15 f.; 1 Jn. 5:1; Ac. 10:43; 13:39.

[304] Ac. 22:19; Mt. 18:6; Jn. 1:12.

[305] Eph. 1:19; 1 Pt. 1:8; 2:7; 1:21 ℵ Cℜ. Also Ac. 5:14.

[306] Ac. 19:18 D; 2 Th. 1:10 vl.; Mk. 9:42.

[307] Ac. 2:44 (?); 4:32 (?); 2 Th. 1:10; Herm. s., 9, 27, 1 etc. Worth noting is the phrase in Ign. Mg., 10, 3 : εἰς ὃν (sc. Χριστιανισμὸν) πᾶσα γλῶσσα πιστεύσασα ...

[308] Ac. 21:10, 25.

[309] Ac. 16:15 : τῷ κυρίῳ (D θεῷ); 1 Pt. 1:21 (vl. πιστεύοντες) εἰς θεόν. On the other hand ἐν Χριστῷ (Ἰησοῦ) with πιστός (Col. 1:2; Eph. 1:1) is obviously not meant as the obj. but refers to "those in Christ (Jesus)," πιστός being used in the abs.

If it still has this in the μὴ γίνου ἄπιστος ἀλλὰ πιστός of Jn. 20:27, [310] it has lost it for the most part. The adj. πιστός simply means "Christian," [311] the noun "the Christian." [312] In keeping is the use of ἀπιστία (→ 204, 31 ff.), which has verbal force in Jn. 20:27, but is normally used in the technical sense of "non-christian." [313]

3. The Relation of Christian Faith to That of the Old Testament.

The common Christian understanding of faith in the NT and primitive Christianity may be summed up as follows. Faith is used partly in the sense of the OT and Jewish tradition (→ 205, 17 ff.) and partly in a wholly new sense (→ 208, 23 ff.), though the two meanings are not mutually exclusive (→ 208, 28 ff.). Their interrelation, however, will be greatly clarified by a consideration of the relation between the specifically Christian concept of faith and the concept of the OT. In so far as πίστις (πιστεύειν) is in the NT belief in God's Word (→ 205, 25 ff.), there is formally no difference from the OT and Judaism (→ 200, 7 f.), and the specifically Christian πιστεύειν εἰς ... (→ 203, 10 ff.) also includes this belief, since it is always belief in the proclamation which encounters us as God's Word. The Word of God, however, has taken on a different character, → 209, 7 ff. It is no longer related to God's work in the sense that on the basis of this work it demands faithfulness and obedience, or promises God's work in the future. It is now related to God's deed in the sense that this deed is disclosed only in the Word.

In the OT the righteous (in faithfulness and obedience) believe in God on the basis of His acts. They do not need to believe the acts themselves, since these are plain to see in the history of the people. [314] In the NT, however, it is precisely God's act which has to be believed. For what is plain to see is the life of Jesus which He lived on earth in servant-form, and which ended on the σταυρός. It is not evident that the folly of the cross is the divine wisdom, that the crucified Jesus is the risen and ascended Lord, that what happened in Him is the divine act of salvation. This has to be brought to light in the Word of proclamation. Hence one may even say that God's act is His Word, so that John — making this deduction — can describe Jesus as the Logos, the Word. On this basis πιστεύειν τῷ λόγῳ τοῦ θεοῦ becomes πιστεύειν εἰς Χριστόν.

To say this is to say already that in the NT summons to faith there is no returning to the situation of the prophets (and Psalms) of the OT. Faith is not

---

[310] Perhaps also 1 Tm. 4:3; in Rev. 17:14, however, πιστός means "faithful." πιστός seems to have verbal force in the list of Chr. virtues in 1 Cl., 48, 5 and in the combination πιστοὶ καὶ ἀγαθοί, Herm. s., 8, 7, 4; 10, 1. Cf. ἐὰν γὰρ ᾖ τις πιστότατος ἀνήρ ... Herm. m., 6, 2, 7, καί γε λίαν πιστοὺς καὶ ἰσχυρούς, Herm. m., 9, 9.

[311] 1 C. 7:14 vl.; 1 Tm. 6:2; Tt. 1:6; Ac. 16:1; Ign. R., 3, 2; Mg., 5, 2; Herm. s., 8, 9, 1. Cf. πιστὸς ἐν κυρίῳ = "Christian" in Herm. m., 4, 1, 4.

[312] 2 C. 6:15; 1 Tm. 4:10, 12; 5:16; Ac. 10:45. Cf. Ign. Sm., 1, 2 : οἱ ἅγιοι καὶ πιστοὶ αὐτοῦ. On πιστός in inscr. and pap. cf. E. Peterson, Εἷς Θεός (1926), 32-34, 309. Cf. Tertullian De cultu feminarum, II, 4 and 5 (CSEL, 69, 78 f.): fidelis = Christianus.

[313] 1 C. 6:6; 7:12-15; 10:27; 14:22-24; 2 C. 4:4; 6:14 f.; 1 Tm. 5:8; Tt. 1:15; Rev. 21:8; Ign. Mg., 5, 2; 2 Cl., 17, 5; Mart. Pol., 16, 1; Dg., 11, 2. In Ign. Tr., 10, 1; Sm., 2, 1; 5, 3 the word seems to be used more specifically for false teachers.

[314] Even in Ps. 78:32, where God's נִפְלָאוֹת (LXX θαυμάσια) are the obj. of הֶאֱמִין, the ref. is not to belief in the divine acts but to faithfulness to God on the basis of His miracles. Cf. Ex. 4:8 f., where there is ref. to הֶאֱמִין "in the voice of the sign" and then more briefly "in the signs," on the basis of which the people is to believe Moses.

confidence in the covenant faithfulness of God which has been and will be demonstrated in the history of the people. For the work of God in which πίστις trusts is not set forth in the destiny of the national community or of the individual connected with it. It is set forth in God's eschatological action — for such is the act done in Christ — which brings all history to an end. [315] To the degree that πίστις means "trust" in this sphere (→ 206, 10 ff.), it is trust in the miraculous power of God which can raise up life from death and which, as it has raised up Christ, can also raise up us. [316] Again, to the degree that it is hope (→ 207, 6 ff.), it is orientated to the consummation of the work of salvation begun in Christ, whose outcome is not the fulfilment of the history of a people but the perfecting of the ἐκκλησία. Inasmuch as there may be a more general confidence of hope on the basis of Christian πίστις — confidence in Christ as well as God — this is the confidence that in the situation created by Christ, the interval between the No longer and the Not yet, the Lord, or God, will not suffer those who trust in Him to be confounded. [317] It is the belief that if we are dead with Christ we shall also live with Him (R. 6:8), that God will keep believers to "that day" (2 Tm. 1:12), to eternal life (1 Tm. 1:16). It is the confidence of hope expressed in statements which begin: πιστὸς ("faithful") ὁ θεός [318] or ὁ κύριος (2 Th. 3:3; 2 Tm. 2:13) and which all tell us that God or the Lord will not let believers fall, cf. Phil. 1:6; 2:13. In so far as faith itself is faithfulness (→ 208, 3 ff.), it is faithfulness, not to God's manifestations of grace in the history of the people, but to the saving act in Christ, to the one name in which is salvation (Ac. 4:12). Faithfulness, steadfastness in faith, [319] must be displayed in all temptations, and especially in persecution. The obedience of πίστις (→ 205, 36 ff.) is not obedience to God's commandments with their demand for right and righteousness in the life of the people; it is the obedience of faith to the way of salvation opened up in Christ. Since salvation includes the forgiveness of sins, it is also, of course, a turning aside from sin. [320]

In all these areas faith is the act in virtue of which a man, responding to God's eschatological deed in Christ, comes out of the world and makes a radical reorientation to God. It is the act in which the new eschatological existence of Christians is established, the attitude which is proper to this existence. [321] As this attitude which constitutes existence, πίστις governs the whole of life. This is why the absolute use of πίστις and πιστεύειν, which is alien to the OT (apart from Is. 7:9 [?]; 28:16) and which only begins to be fashioned in Judaism (→ 200, 14 ff.), is so predominant. Now for the first time faith is religion and believers are Christians. If this decisive act and attitude of faith are orientated to Christ, it might

---

[315] This is shown by the fact that the blessings of salvation appropriated in faith are eschatological gifts: ἄφεσις ἁμαρτιῶν (Col. 1:14; Eph. 1:7; Lk. 24:47; Ac. 2:38; 5:31; 10:43; 13:38; 26:18 etc.); δικαιοσύνη (R. 1:17; 10:10; Phil. 3:9; Ac. 13:39; 1 Cl., 32, 4 etc.), σωτηρία in an eschatological sense (R. 1:16; 10:10; 1 C. 1:21; 2 Tm. 3:15; Lk. 8:12; Ac. 15:11; 16:31 etc.), ζωή sc. αἰώνιος (R. 1:17; Gl. 3:11; Jn. 20:31; Barn., 1, 6; 11, 11 etc.), πνεῦμα (Gl. 3:14; 5:5 etc.).

[316] R. 6:8; 8:11; 1 C. 6:14; 2 C. 4:14.

[317] R. 9:33; 10:11; 1 Pt. 2:6.

[318] 1 C. 1:9; 10:13; 1 Th. 5:24; Hb. 10:23.

[319] 1 C. 16:13; 2 C. 13:5; cf. Gl. 5:1; Col. 4:12; Eph. 6:11 ff.

[320] Cf. the combination of πίστις and μετάνοια, → n. 299.

[321] Cf. the combination of πιστεύειν and βαπτισθῆναι, → n. 300.

seem as though Christian faith were pushing the relation to God into the background. Nevertheless, the faith which is orientated to Christ believes precisely in God's act in Christ. Moreover, the very fact that the NT does not speak in the same way of πιστεύειν εἰς τὸν θεόν and πιστεύειν εἰς Χριστόν (→ 210, 20 ff.) shows that God and Christ are not set before the believer as two different objects of faith which are either co-ordinated or subordinated. On the contrary, God Himself meets us in Christ. But He meets us only in Christ. In Christ dwells all the fulness of the Godhead (Col. 1:19; 2:9). In other words, Christ is God's eschatological act alongside which there is no place for other acts which demand or establish faith. If the righteous of the OT, on the basis of experienced acts of God, waited for His further act, the righteous of the NT simply wait for the full manifestation of the salvation which God has already wrought. Christ is God's final act which also embraces the future. [322]

III. πίστις and πιστεύω in Paul. [323]

1. Paul and the Common Christian Concept of Faith.

a. Acceptance of the Kerygma, ὁμολογία and ὑπακοή. Basic to Paul's usage is the common Christian usage which we have described already with the help of Pauline references, → 205, 16-215, 4. Paul put the concept of πίστις at the very centre of theology. For him, too, πίστις is no mere disposition of the human soul. Primarily, it is acceptance of the kerygma, [324] i.e., subjection to the way of salvation ordained by God and opened up in Christ. For Paul, too, πίστις is always "faith in ..." [325] This is why πίστις and ὁμολογία belong together, as expressly stated in R. 10:9 (→ 209, 17 ff.). In ὁμολογία the believer turns away from himself and confesses Jesus Christ as his Lord, which also means confession that all he is and has he is and has through what God has done in Christ. For this reason Paul, like the NT generally, does not describe the growth of faith in terms of its psychological development. [326] What is outlined, e.g., in Gl. 3:23-26, is the history of salvation and not (in Philonic fashion) the genesis of individual faith. Paul shows faith to be a historical rather than a psychological possibility. According to Paul, the event of salvation history is actualised for the individual, not in pious experience, but in his baptism (Gl. 3:27-29). Faith makes it his. Hence faith is not at the end of the way to God, as in Philo (→ 202, 15 ff.). It is at the beginning. If faith is believing acceptance of that which the kerygma proclaims, it is not thereby reduced to a *fides historica*, for, as confession of God's act, it recognises the validity of this act for me. Faith is ὑπακοή (→ 205, 36 ff.) as well as ὁμολογία. That is to say, it is acknowledgment of the day of grace and salvation which God has ordained. Acceptance of the divine grace is ὑπακοή because this grace encounters man in the paradoxical form of the cross of Christ, i.e.,

---

[322] Awareness of this is clearly expressed in, e.g., Hb. 1:1 f.

[323] For bibl. cf. → Bibl. under D. III, also the rich Pauline literature. Cf., e.g., Michaelis, 116-138; Lohmeyer, 62-156; Mittring, 146.

[324] R. 10:17: ἄρα ἡ πίστις ἐξ ἀκοῆς etc. → n. 258.

[325] On πίστις with obj. gen. → 204, 16. In interpretation of Paul cf. A. Deissmann, *Pls.*² (1925), 126 f.; O. Schmitz, *Die Christusgemeinschaft des Pls. im Lichte seines Genitivgebrauchs* (1924); A. Wikenhauser, *Die Christusmystik d. hl. Pls.* (1928), *passim*; Wissmann, 68-75; Mundle, 75-94; πιστεύειν with εἰς → 203, 10 ff., with ὅτι clause → 203, 7 ff.

[326] Schlatter, *Glaube*, 260.

because the divine act of grace is also the judgment executed at the cross on man, on his sins, and also on his striving for righteousness or wisdom. Faith is thus obedient acceptance of the divine judgment on man's previous self-understanding.

The knowledge imparted in the kerygma and appropriated in faith embraces not only knowledge of God's act in Christ but also a new self-understanding on man's part. πίστις is the distinctive way of understanding the divine χάρις and hence also of understanding oneself under χάρις. Paul, then, speaks of the knowledge of the believer in a twofold sense. On the one side it is knowledge of the event of salvation mediated through the kerygma. [327] On the other it is the knowledge which discloses itself to faith as a new self-understanding. [328] The element of trust is enclosed within this self-understanding under God's act of salvation. In Paul, of course, it is only seldom that πίστις has the direct sense of trust (→ 206, 10 ff.), since πίστις is primarily ὁμολογία and ὑπακοή. But trust, like hope (→ 207, 6 ff.), is part of faith. This is shown by the use of πεποιθέναι (→ 6, 17 ff.). The concept of παρρησία (→ V, 882, 49 ff.) brings this element of πίστις into relief.

b. Ways of Believing. If πίστις is both ὁμολογία and ὑπακοή, one may understand why the state of believing as well as the act of coming to believe is denoted by πίστις (πιστεύειν) (→ 212, 26 ff.). For this, Paul can fashion expressions like πίστιν ἔχειν (R. 14:22; Phlm. 5), εἶναι ἐν τῇ πίστει (2 C. 13:5), ἑστάναι ἐν τῇ πίστει (1 C. 16:13; 2 C. 1:24). The meaning of the last of these is elucidated by the parallel expressions ἑστάναι ἐν κυρίῳ (1 Th. 3:8), in χάρις (R. 5:2), [329] in the εὐαγγέλιον (1 C. 15:1). To be a believer is to belong to the Lord and to the grace manifested by Him and proclaimed in the Gospel.

The context in which εἶναι and ἑστάναι ἐν τῇ πίστει occur also makes it clear that being a believer is not a static affair. It takes place in the flux of individual life. It has to be maintained constantly in face of the danger of πίπτειν (→ 164, 29 ff.). [330] Faith, then, is not exhausted by acceptance of the kerygma as though this were a mere declaration on joining a new religion. It has to establish itself continually against assaults as an attitude which controls all life. This may be seen, e.g., in R. 11:20: σὺ δὲ τῇ πίστει ἕστηκας. This does not mean: "Thou standest in faith," but: "Thou hast attained thy standing through faith," and, as the context shows, only through faith, not in virtue of merits. This is a plain indication of the fact that being a Christian is a constant self-relating to God's act of salvation. For this reason, in apparent antithesis to the understanding of faith as a single, definitive turning to God's grace, reference is also made to grades and individual possibilities of πίστις. We read of ὑστερήματα τῆς πίστεως (1 Th. 3:10); of growth in faith (2 C. 10:15); of fulness of faith; [331] of weakness of faith (R. 14:1). If the ἀσθενεῖν τῇ πίστει of R. 14:1 f. corresponds to ἀσθενεῖν in respect of συνείδησις in 1 C. 8:7-12, then it is clear that in the Christian πιστεύειν works itself out in knowledge of what he has to do in a given situation. This explains the distinctive formulation: ὃς μὲν πιστεύει φαγεῖν πάντα (R. 14:2), and especially the principle: πᾶν δὲ ὃ οὐκ ἐκ πίστεως ἁμαρτία ἐστίν (R. 14:23).

---

[327] R. 6:8 f.; 2 C. 4:13 f.; cf. R. 10:14-17.

[328] R. 5:3; 14:14; 2 C. 1:7; 5:6; Phil. 1:19.

[329] Cf. Gl. 5:4: τῆς χάριτος ἐξεπέσατε.

[330] 1 C. 10:12; R. 14:4; Gl. 5:4.

[331] For this Pl. uses πληροφορηθῆναι (R. 4:21; 14:5) or πληροφορία (1 Th. 1:5). He has in view the full conviction and assurance proper to πίστις.

Though all believers stand in the one πίστις, judgment may differ as to what they should do or not do, since πιστεύειν has to be worked out in individual life. The rule is : ἕκαστος ἐν τῷ ἰδίῳ νοΐ πληροφορείσθω (R. 14:5), for the relation to God in faith is always that of the individual life: σὺ πίστιν ἣν ἔχεις κατὰ σεαυτὸν ἔχε ἐνώπιον τοῦ θεοῦ (R. 14:22). φρονεῖν is to be guided : ἑκάστῳ ὡς ὁ θεὸς ἐμέρισεν μέτρον πίστεως (R. 12:3). The reference is not merely to stages or grades of πίστις, but to differences conditioned by individual gifts and situations, as may be seen from the relation of 12:6 (ἔχοντες δὲ χαρίσματα κατὰ τὴν χάριν τὴν δοθεῖσαν ἡμῖν διάφορα) to 12:3 (→ line 5 f.). Hence Paul can speak of an ἔργον πίστεως (1 Th. 1:3), and he uses the phrase πίστις δι' ἀγάπης ἐνεργουμένη (Gl. 5:6) for the whole sphere of that wherein πίστις must work itself out in individual life. [332]

In statements of this kind Paul is already developing more richly and clearly the basic significance of Christian πίστις. In particular, however, he brings out the full sense when he sets πίστις in antithesis to the ἔργα νόμου and radically develops its character as ὑπακοή.

2. The Pauline Concept of Faith in Contrast to That of Judaism.

a. πίστις and ἔργα νόμου. To express the newness and complete otherness of the relation to God which is implied by πίστις as a turning and constant reference to God's saving act, Paul connects the blessing of salvation strictly, consistently and exclusively to πίστις. Like Judaism, he describes this blessing as δικαιοσύνη. But this leads Paul to make a statement which is paradoxical for Judaism, namely, that δικαιοσύνη is given to πίστις, that it is not, therefore, ascribed to man on the basis of his works (→ II, 206 f.). Man can stand before God only in virtue of his πίστις and not in virtue of his works. [333] The whole of Galatians combats the possible misunderstanding that πίστις has to be supplemented by the accomplishment of certain works of the Law. It is thus made perfectly plain that πίστις is man's absolute committal to God, a committal in which man cannot make any resolutions of his own — which would be to remain in the sphere of ἔργα — but which can only be committal to God's grace, an answer to God's act (→ 216, 29 ff.). Equally plain, however, is the fact that this committal is a movement of the will ; it is indeed the radical decision of the will in which man delivers himself up. It is the act in which men really *is,* whereas in ἔργα he always stands alongside that which he accomplishes. In Paul the character of πίστις as act is expressed on the one side by the fact that he understands πίστις as ὑπακοή (→ 217, 35 f.) and on the other quite unintentionally by the fact that, unlike Augustine, [334] he never describes faith as inspired. Though the Spirit is given to the believer, πίστις is not a gift of the Spirit. [335] Faith is the manner of life of the man who is crucified with Christ, who can no longer live as an I, who lives

---

[332] Cf. the combination of πίστις with ἀγάπη in 1 C. 13:13; 1 Th. 1:3; 3:6; 5:8; Phlm. 5, and with ὑπομονή in 1 Th. 1:3. In the list of virtues in Gl. 5:22 πίστις is not, of course, Chr. faith but faithfulness in human relations.

[333] R. 3:20-22, 25, 28; 4:2, 5 f.; 9:30-32; 10:4-6; Gl. 2:16; 3:6 ff.; Phil. 3:9 etc.

[334] Cf. H. Jonas, *Augustin u. das paul. Freiheitsproblem* (1930), 54-62.

[335] The matter is rather different when πίστις is mentioned in thanksgivings at the beginning of epistles, R. 1:8; 1 Th. 1:3; Phlm. 5; so also Col. 1:4. Paul can certainly regard it as a gift (of God) that a congregation has come to believe, Phil. 1:29. In contrast, πίστις is typically not mentioned among the gifts granted to the community, 1 C. 1:4-7.

in Christ (Gl. 2:19 f.). If one does not understand the paradox that πίστις as a movement of the will is the negation of the will itself, the antithesis of πίστις and ἔργα νόμου will easily be misunderstood, as though πίστις were another work or achievement (→ II, 651, 24 ff.). On this view the Pauline rejection of works would be taken to apply only to the works of the Mosaic Law, while faith as an act of obedience would always entail a certain measure of activity on man's part. [336] In truth, however, more than a measure of activity is presupposed in faith. Faith is act in the supreme sense. As such it is the opposite of every work or achievement, since the act of faith consists in the negation of all the work which establishes man's existence. That Paul rejects ἔργα, not in a limited, but in a fundamental sense, is shown by the fact that the antithesis of πίστις and ἔργα is accompanied by the antithesis of χάρις and ἔργα. [337] Paul deliberately opposes χάρις to an ἐργάζεσθαι which can claim a μισθός. He also fashions the antithesis κατὰ χάριν — κατὰ ὀφείλημα (R. 4:4 f.). Moreover, it is clear that when Paul demands of the believer a fulfilling of the Law in a new sense, namely, in ἀγάπη (R. 13:8-10; Gl. 5:14), he rejects the ἔργα νόμου, not in respect of their content (as the Law of Moses), but in respect of the manner of their fulfilment. Finally, Paul makes it quite clear why he rejects works. The way of ἔργα νόμου is a false way of salvation because man seeks to base upon it his καύχημα, his claim before God. [338] Since the Jewish righteousness of works and pagan wisdom are both affected by the bringing to nothing of human boasting, it is evident that in rejecting ἔργα Paul is rejecting a specific and indeed a characteristic attitude — the attitude of human self-assurance before God, or the attempt to attain it. Thus πίστις as genuine ὑπακοή, as the basic attitude made possible by God's gracious act in Christ, stands opposed not only to the specifically Jewish attitude but also to the specifically pagan attitude of man, i.e., to the attitude of natural man generally, who fancies that he can stand before God in his own strength.

b. The Eschatological Character of πίστις. It is clear that as this attitude πίστις is not something which man can accomplish incidentally or along with other things. It is the basic attitude of life which determines all detailed conduct (→ 218, 24 ff.). Also clear is the fact that to come to believe and to be a believer are very closely related (→ 218, 16 ff.), since the abandonment of human certainty in the act of believing must be continued in the form of a steady overpowering of the natural man. To the degree that πίστις as genuine ὑπακοή is the surrender of the natural man, it is the eschatological attitude of man which is made possible by God's eschatological act. It is the attitude of the new man. This eschatological character of πίστις is marked by the fact that ἐν πίστει is parallel to ἐν κυρίῳ and ἐν χάριτι (→ 218, 18 ff.). These expressions denote eschatological existence. He who is ἐν Χριστῷ is a new creature (2 C. 5:17). The period of χάρις has brought to an end the age of the νόμος (R. 6:14 etc.). The "coming" of πίστις is the eschatological time (Gl. 3:23 ff.).

3. The Pauline Concept of Faith in Contrast to Gnosticism.

a. Faith as Orientation to the Future (ἐλπίς). Paul did not develop the meaning of πίστις in such express antithesis to the Gnostic concept as he did to the Jewish.

---

[336] Mundle, 101.
[337] R. 4:16; 6:14; 11:5 f.; Gl. 2:21.
[338] R. 3:27; 4:1 f.; → III, 648, 20 ff.

Nevertheless, his statements are plain enough. As an eschatological attitude, πίστις is not to be misunderstood as though it were itself eschatological fulfilment. It is not, as in Philo, a διάθεσις of the soul. It is not the ἆθλον, the reward of conflict (→ 202, 16 and 19). The man who is justified in faith (Phil. 3:9) is constantly engaged in the struggle for perfection, in pursuit of the βραβεῖον (Phil. 3:12-14). There is not actualised in πίστις, as in the γνῶσις of the Gnostics, the definitiveness of eschatological being. Faith does not escape the provisional nature of historical being. It actualises eschatological being in temporality. [339] For, as it is always referred back to what God has done in Christ (R. 10:9), it is also orientated to the future, to what God will do (R. 6:8 : πιστεύομεν ὅτι καὶ συζήσομεν αὐτῷ). The relation to past and future forms a unity (1 Th. 4:14), for God's act in the past is an eschatological act which controls the whole future. Related to the future is the awareness of a new existence which is given along with faith (2 C. 4:13 f.; R. 6:8 f. → 218, 8 ff.). Thus ἐλπίς stands alongside πίστις (→ 207, 6 ff.). And though πίστις as the reference to God's grace can never be exhausted even in the eschatological consummation, though it will "abide" (1 C. 13:13), nevertheless the present life in πίστις is a provisional one inasmuch as it does not include sight : διὰ πίστεως γὰρ περιπατοῦμεν, οὐ διὰ εἴδους (2 C. 5:7). Our σωτηρία is not made a disposable possession by πίστις. It has become a sure hope (R. 8:24 f.; Gl. 5:5; → II, 531, 9 ff.).

b. πίστις and φόβος. In keeping is the fact that πίστις is man's self-understanding under divine χάρις (→ 218, 6 f.). For this χάρις is not a divine δύναμις in the Gnostic sense. It is not poured into man ; it does not change him in substance, destroying his historical being. It is understood strictly as the grace of God, who is the Judge. It always encounters man, therefore, as the grace of forgiveness, which embraces the condemnation of sin and man's commitment under the requirement of the divine will, which ordains that good be done. Hence it never allows man to escape from the concrete situation of his historical life. This is why → φόβος as well as ἐλπίς belongs constitutively to πίστις. πίστις is not, of course, the anxiety which lies behind all the efforts of the natural man to win salvation in his own strength. The believer has not received a πνεῦμα δουλείας πάλιν εἰς φόβον, but a πνεῦμα υἱοθεσίας (R. 8:15). Nevertheless, the divine imperative is not set aside. The appropriate φόβος is simply awareness that man does not stand on his own feet. It is the concern not to fall from χάρις, whether in frivolity or the pride of supposed security. Hence the admonition : μετὰ φόβου καὶ τρόμου τὴν ἑαυτῶν σωτηρίαν κατεργάζεσθε, is given the paradoxical motivation : θεὸς γάρ ἐστιν ὁ ἐνεργῶν ἐν ὑμῖν καὶ τὸ θέλειν καὶ τὸ ἐνεργεῖν (Phil. 2:12), cf. the admonition to Gentile Christians : τῇ ἀπιστίᾳ ἐξεκλάσθησαν (the Jews), σὺ δὲ τῇ πίστει ἕστηκας. μὴ ὑψηλὰ φρόνει, ἀλλὰ φοβοῦ (R. 11:20). The way in which this φόβος is linked to the πεποίθησις and παρρησία of faith may be seen from 2 C. 5:11: The εἰδότες οὖν τὸν φόβον τοῦ κυρίου corresponds to ἔχοντες οὖν τοιαύτην ἐλπίδα πολλῇ παρρησίᾳ χρώμεθα in 3:12 and πεποίθησιν δὲ τοιαύτην ἔχομεν in 3:4. φόβος means that the believer realises that he is κατέναντι θεοῦ (2:17) or ἐνώπιον τοῦ θεοῦ (4:2). For this reason there is admonition to stand in faith ; [340] the believer is exposed to temptation [341] and has constantly to prove himself. [342]

---

[339] H. Jonas, Der Begriff d. Gnosis, Diss. (1930), 43 f.
[340] 1 C. 16:13; cf. 1 C. 10:12; Gl. 5:1; Phil. 1:27; 4:1.
[341] 1 C. 7:5; Gl. 6:1; 1 Th. 3:5.
[342] 1 C. 11:28; 2 C. 13:5; Gl. 6:3 f.

c. πίστις and Historical Existence. If πίστις as the constitution of Christian life means No longer in relation to Judaism, it means Not yet in relation to Gnosticism. Christian being in πίστις is thus a paradoxical eschatological being in historical existence. It is a being in both the No longer and the Not yet. This is most clearly depicted in Phil. 3:12-14. No longer, for the resolve of faith has abandoned the past of self-confidence and self-boasting (Phil. 3:4-8). But this resolve, since it leads under God's χάρις and not out of historical existence, must be sustained by constant renewal. The forgotten past is always present in the sense of being overcome. To that degree recollection (not remorse) is part of faith, whose forgetting is not a putting out of mind but a no longer being entangled. Not yet, to the degree that the surrender of the old being is a surrender of the self-assurance which thinks it can control its own existence, to the degree, then, that this surrender rules out any receiving in exchange of a disposable new possession. There is no new disposable possession in place of an old one. The change from Then to Now implies the renunciation of all desire to possess and a radical committal to the grace of God. Not yet in relation to the man concerning whom no κατειληφέναι can be asserted in his historical existence, but Already to the degree that καταλημφθῆναι ὑπὸ Χριστοῦ Ἰησοῦ applies to him.

IV. πιστεύω in John.

1. πιστεύω as Acceptance of the Message.

Apart from 1 Jn. 5:4, where ἡ πίστις ἡμῶν is called the power which overcomes the κόσμος (→ III, 895, 14 f.), the noun πίστις does not occur in the Gospel or Epistles of Jn. The verb πιστεύειν, however, is very common, being used in the general Chr. sense for acceptance of the message about Jesus. The content of the message can be denoted in various ways by ὅτι clauses (→ 203, 7 f.), or instead abbreviated expressions with πιστεύειν εἰς can occur in many variations (→ n. 266). πιστεύειν is also commonly used in the abs. in the same sense. [343]

2. πιστεύω εἰς and πιστεύω with the Dative.

Specifically Johannine is the fact that πιστεύειν with the dat. can be used for πιστεύειν εἰς (→ n. 221); the linguistic variation contains no material distinction. Thus in Jn. "to believe Jesus when He preaches (or tells the truth, 8:40, 45), or to believe His Word (2:22) or words" (5:47), is equivalent to "believing in the Jesus who is proclaimed." [344] This corresponds to the fact that Jn. achieves a unity of Proclaimer and Proclaimed not yet attained in the Synoptic presentation. In this respect Jn. is not correcting the Synoptic depiction. One might rather say that he is correcting the kerygma. He wants to make it plain that it is the One proclaimed who Himself meets and speaks with us in the kerygma. What the kerygma proclaims as an event, God's act, has itself the character of word. For this reason Jn. can call Jesus Himself the Logos (1:1). In this way he radically develops the thought that God's word and act are a unity. In the word we meet God's act, and in God's act is His word, → 215, 29. ἀκούειν can be equivalent

---

[343] Thus πιστεύειν εἰς αὐτόν, the abs. πιστεύειν, and πιστεύειν εἰς τὸ ὄνομα ... in 3:18 are interchangeable, cf. also πιστεύειν εἰς and the abs. πιστεύειν in 4:39, 41, the abs. πιστεύειν and πιστεύειν ὅτι in 11:40, 42; 16:30 f., πιστεύειν εἰς and πιστεύειν ὅτι in 11:25-27.

[344] Cf. the alternation between πιστεύειν εἰς αὐτόν and πιστεύειν αὐτῷ in 8:30 f. Similarly we find λαμβάνειν τὰ ῥήματα (12:48; 17:8) as well as λαμβάνειν αὐτόν (1:12; 5:43).

in meaning to πιστεύειν. [345] "To believe in Him" is "to come to Him," [346] "to receive Him" (1:12; 5:43), "to love Him." [347]

3. Faith and Salvation.

Faith directed to the word which is proclaimed by Jesus, and which proclaims Him, brings salvation. This is expressed in constantly repeated and varied sayings to the effect that the believer has (everlasting) life [348] (→ II, 870, 23 ff.), that he has passed from death to life (5:24, cf. 8:24), that he will not be judged (3:18) and so forth. [349] Self-evidently the thought is that only this faith brings salvation. Unlike Paul, John did not, of course, state this in the antithesis of πίστις and ἔργα (→ 219, 18 ff.), for "the Jews" whom Jesus combatted in John's Gospel (→ III, 377, 3 ff.) are quite different from the Jews (and Judaisers) whom Paul was opposing (→ III, 380, 31 ff.). The occasion of John's statements about πίστις is not, as in Paul, the question of the way of salvation. John is contending for a right view of salvation itself. His characteristic term for this is not δικαιοσύνη, as in Paul, but always ζωή. Now in this respect there seems to be agreement between Christian proclamation and the world to which it is directed, for the whole world was seeking life as salvation. But the very point of John's proclamation is to show that this agreement is only apparent. What the world calls life is not life ; it is a mere appearance of life. The world is in falsehood rather than error (8:44, 55), and just because Jesus tells the truth it does not believe Him (8:46). Unlike the Jews of Paul, the world does not dispute the demand for faith as such. It would be ready enough to believe that Jesus is the Son of God if only He would demonstrate His credibility, [350] if only He whose speech it does not understand (8:43) would say what He has to say in a way it does understand (10:24), i.e., if only He would accept its own standard of what is true. But what He says is for it a παροιμία, a riddle (10:6; 16:25, 29); it is a clear saying [351] only for him who believes (16:25, 29). He cannot put it in a way they would understand, for if He did it would be something different.

4. Faith as Renunciation of the World.

Herein it is apparent the fact that the world does not know what salvation or life really is. Thus the Jews search the Scriptures thinking they will find life there (5:39), [352] and they will not come to Jesus that they might have life. They need to turn from falsehood to the truth. They need to set aside all their previous standards and judgments. This renunciation of the world, this turning of man from himself, is the primary meaning of faith. Its is man's self-surrender, his turning to the invisible (20:29) and sovereign.

The opposite make this quite clear. Men cannot believe because "they receive honour one of another" (5:44), i.e., because they seek security in mutual acceptance, because

---

[345] Jn. 5:25; 6:60; 8:43, 47; 18:37.
[346] 5:40; 6:35, 37, 44 f., 65; 7:37.
[347] 8:42; 14:15, 21, 23 f., 28; 16:27.
[348] 3:15 f., 36; 6:40, 47; 20:31; 1 Jn. 5:13.
[349] 6:35; 11:25 f.; 12:36, 46; 1 Jn. 5:1, 5.
[350] 6:30; cf. the demand of 2:18.
[351] As παρρησία: 10:24.
[352] ἐρευνᾶτε ind., not imp.

they fortify their world and seal it off from God, because they do not seek honour from God. Thus c. 6 makes it plain that the multitude cannot believe in Jesus as the bread of life because they seek a bread which will assure them of bodily life on earth. Again, 5:1-16; 9:1-34 show that the "Jews" will not tolerate any disruption of a form of life guaranteed by legal correctness. 5:17 ff. and c. 11 demand that a man abandon his present ideas of life and death in order to be open to the life which Jesus gives and which appears where the world sees only death. It is required that the world give up the notion of a "son of man," a bringer of salvation, who will abide for ever when he comes (12:34), which means, of course, that it must give up the idea that the time of salvation ushered in by God will be a permanent state on earth.

The fact that faith is a radical renunciation of the world is also brought out in a series of sayings to the effect that the act of faith itself is not a worldly action but an event which has its roots in the other world, an act or gift of God Himself. [353] A man must be "of God," "of the truth," to be able to hear God's voice (8:47; 18:37). He must be one of His to be able to believe (10:26). Dogmatically construed these statements would simply be saying that only he may believe who is ordained thereto — though this harmonises ill with the universal call for the decision of faith and the charge of an evil will (→ 223, 19 ff.). Factually, the statements mean that the process of faith is to be understood, not as a worldly event, but only as a miracle. They thus characterise faith itself as an act of desecularisation. Jesus has chosen His own out of the world, so that they are no more ἐκ τοῦ κόσμου, i.e., they no longer belong to the world (15:19; 17:14 → III, 895, 3 ff.).

This aspect of faith is also brought out by the fact that its object is shown to be unworthy of credence from the standpoint of worldly understanding. Between Jesus and the world there is agreement that God or the divine world is the object of faith. But the offence which causes the world either to go astray or to decide definitively for darkness is that the Son of God appears as man: ὁ λόγος σάρξ ἐγένετο, 1:14. [354] For now, of course, faith is not a dualistic view of things in which man, less sure of himself, turns from this world to soar up to the world to come in speculative or pious thought and feeling. The desecularisation achieved in faith is not an act which man may freely accomplish for himself, as though the Word of Jesus were simply the occasion for it. Such an act would carry with it the presupposition that the divine world may be grasped by man. The presupposition itself would thus destroy what it is supposed to underlie, i.e., desecularisation. Man acting freely would still be world. A radical view of desecularisation is presented, however, because it is God who is thought of the One who acts in His freedom. Desecularisation is a possibility for man only through God's revelation. This revelation is the eschatological event which makes an end of the world because it means judgment for it, [355] so that the verdict of life or death is according to man's faith. Only now, when light has come into the world (3:19), is there the possibility of faith or unbelief in a decisive sense. [356] Now for the first time, then, desecularisation has been made possible by the coming of the Revealer. But the revelation is the offence. The invisible becomes visible, visible in a way it neither could nor should be acc. to worldly standards. God's Son has come in the flesh, [357] as a man whose parents and background

[353] 6:37, 44, 65; cf. Bultmann J. on 6:45.

[354] It is characteristic that in Jn., as distinct from Pl., the cross of Jesus is not the real offence, i.e., the fact which throws doubt on His claim. The offence is His humanity as such, i.e., the fact that His divine quality is not demonstrable. In Jn. the cross is more the end of His humanity, His δοξασθῆναι.

[355] 3:16-21 (cf. on this Bultmann J., 111 f.); 5:21-27; 9:39; 12:31.

[356] Cf. R. Bultmann, Glauben u. Verstehen, I² (1954), 134-152.

[357] 1:14, and in plain opposition to Gnosticism 1 Jn. 4:2; 2 Jn. 7.

are known (6:42; 7:27, 41), who does not correspond at all to what Messianic dogma or worldly ideas of God's revelation require (7:27, 41 f.), who breaks the Law, who claims to be equal to God (5:17-19). He will build a new temple in three days (2:20), He claims to be greater than Abraham (8:58), His Word is to preserve from death — whom does He make Himself? (8:53). He refuses to give any proof, or does so only in a paradoxical sense (2:19; 8:28). In fact, the truth of the Word can be known only in faith itself. [358] Even the σημεῖα are not an unequivocal proof which meets the demand of the world; they are misunderstood (6:26), and in the main they only cause offence and finally bring Him to the cross. [359]

All this shows that desecularisation is not to be regarded as a flight from the world but as the reversing and destroying of worldly norms and values. Similarly, it would be a misunderstanding to think that the believer is to be taken out of the world (17:15). His turning from the world is a turning from evil (17:15). "World" for John is not a natural entity. It is not, as in Gnosticism, a sphere which encloses man with the compulsion of fate, and which is alien to him by nature. It is a historical entity and power constituted by the men who turn from the light, from God, and who through their own conduct all share in its force and power. [360] For this world, revelation is an offence because it calls this world in question; it is the judgment of the world (3:19; 12:31). Faith is an act of desecularisation in the sense that it overcomes the offence and banishes all the autonomous power of man. Positively it is a grasping of the revelation which comes in the Word.

5. The Relation between the Johannine Concept of Faith and the Pauline Concept.

The inner unity with Paul is plain. For Paul, too, faith is a surrender of one's own power, of the righteousness achieved in one's own strength, of καυχᾶσθαι (→ 220, 18 ff.). For both John and Paul faith is not a good work, nor is unbelief a bad work. Faith, like unbelief, is, of course, a decision. It is thus an act in the true sense. [361] There is unity between John and Paul in the fact that for both faith has the character of obedience. The possibility of using τηρεῖν τὸν λόγον or τὰς ἐντολάς as alternatives for πιστεύειν makes this apparent. These expressions, which denote obedience to a command, [362] are used by Jn. in different ways, partly for obedient acceptance of the Word, [363] partly for the fidelity of this obedience. [364]

6. The Anti-Gnostic Character of the Johannine Concept of Faith.

It is equally plain, however, that John is attacking, not the specifically Jewish striving for ἰδία δικαιοσύνη, but the world in general, of which the Jews are only a single instance. What prevents the Jews from believing is not their insistence on the Law of Moses or their works, but the fact that they are ἐκ τοῦ κόσμου. [365] The Jews are thus representatives of the world as a whole. This is plainly shown by the transition from an

---

[358] 3:33; cf. on this Bultmann J., ad loc. and also on 5:31-37.
[359] Bultmann J., 152 f., 161 and on 6:30.
[360] Ibid., 33 f.
[361] Ibid., 112-115 and on 6:28 f.
[362] So 1 Βασ. 15:11; Sir. 29:1; Jos. Ant., 8, 120; Mt. 19:17; cf. 1 K. 7:19.
[363] 15:20 and also 8:51 f.; 17:6. Here always τηρεῖν τὸν λόγον.
[364] So τηρεῖν τὸν λόγον or τοὺς λόγους, 14:23 f., τὰς ἐντολάς, 14:15, 21 (cf. Rev. 12:17; 14:12). Also φυλάττειν sc. τὰ ῥήματα, 12:47. For Jesus' obedience to His calling τηρεῖν τὸν λόγον αὐτοῦ (sc. God's), 8:55. On the further significance of these expressions → 227, 35 ff.
[365] 8:23; 15:19; 17:14, 16; 18:36; cf. 8:44, 47.

attack on the Jews to an attack on the world in c. 3. [366] In so far as John tackles a particular form of worldliness, it is the form which sought to establish itself in Christianity, namely, Gnosticism.

If πιστεύειν is viewed as an act of radical desecularisation (→ 224, 11 ff.), πιστεύειν as such can be construed as being taken out of the world in a false sense. If it is negatively a turning from the world, it must also be positively a grasping of the world above. In fact we are told again and again that faith has life (3:15 f. etc.), that the believer has already passed from death to life (5:24; 1 Jn. 3:14), that he will not die eternally (11:26). In faith, then, the eschaton is attained already. Hence every worldly or temporal future is transcended. The eschaton has become the present.

Such formulations are also familiar to Gnosticism, whose vocabulary has exerted considerable influence on that of John. But it would not merely be false to interpret the formulations in a Gnostic sense. In fact, they serve as a demarcation against Gnosticism, whose problem the Evangelist takes up only to set it under the light of the revelation in Jesus. In truth the concept of faith in John is directed against Gnosticism, since it brings out clearly the relation of the Already of faith to its Not yet. The Already or No longer enclosed in faith is evident inasmuch as faith is a radical turning from the world and inasmuch as it already has life. The believer has life "only" in faith; he does not have it as a possession, as a natural attribute. He is not deified, as he would have to be according to the Gnostic view. John shows no acquaintance with the Gnostic phenomenon of culmination, with ecstasy, in which the non-worldly (in a strange contradiction) is reduced to worldly reality. [367] Seeing the δόξα of the Son is granted only to those who look on the incarnate Lord (1:14). The reality of the incarnation is emphasised in opposition to Gnosticism (1 Jn. 4:2; 2 Jn. 7). Direct vision of the δόξα is reserved for a future existence outside the world (17:24). So long as believers are in the world, they are not to imagine that they are taken out of worldly existence, 17:15. They are exposed to the constant assault of the world as Jesus Himself was in His bodily life, 15:18 ff. This means, however, that faith cannot break free from its relation to the Word. What it has "already," it has "only" as faith in the Word. Precisely thus is it desecularisation in a radical sense. For "only" as the Word which challenges the world is God's revelation present in the world. Faith, then, has a provisional character. This may be seen in the fact that knowledge is ascribed to the Revealer Himself, but not faith, → 227, 23 ff.

7. Faith and Knowledge (→ I, 712, 30 ff.).

The act of faith, then, does not set us in a desecularised state. It is the act of desecularisation which has to be constantly performed afresh, so that the whole of life is dominated by it. The admonitions to "abide" make this plain (→ IV, 576, 22 ff.). Faith must become an abiding in His Word (8:31). Belonging to Him, abiding in Him, is dependent on the abiding of His words in them. [368] To abiding, knowledge of the truth is promised (8:32), just as the movement of πιστεύειν

---

[366] Cf. Bultmann J., 103 f.

[367] Cf. H. Jonas, op. cit. (→ n. 339), 21; H. Jonas, Gnosis und spätantiker Geist, I² (1954), 199-203.

[368] 15:4-7. The steadfastness of faith can also be denoted by τηρεῖν τὸν λόγον or τὰς ἐντολάς, → n. 364.

generally is elucidated by its relation to γινώσκειν. John cannot set πιστεύειν in antithesis to γινώσκειν as Paul sets πίστις in antithesis to ἔργα νόμου, → 219, 18 ff. For γινώσκειν is not a way of salvation in the sense that ἔργα are ; hence it is no rival of πιστεύειν. [369] Its relation to πιστεύειν is complicated. In respect of their objects, there is no difference between πιστεύειν and γινώσκειν. Both faith and knowledge are concerned with the fact that the Father has sent Jesus. [370] Both faith (16:27-30) and knowledge (7:17) realise that He or His teaching is from the Father. If knowledge relates to ἀλήθεια (8:32), faith relates no less to Him who is the ἀλήθεια (14:1, 6). The fact that He is the Christ is an object of faith (11:27; 20:31), but it is also an object of both πιστεύειν and γινώσκειν together (6:69). Since faith is not infrequently used for the act of the first turning to Jesus, [371] in verses where we find both verbs in the order πιστεύειν-γινώσκειν we are to regard πιστεύειν as this first turning and γινώσκειν as the ensuing knowledge to which faith presses on. [372] But the reverse order is also possible (16:30; 17:8; 1 Jn. 4:16). Here πιστεύειν seems to be the attitude which grows out of γινώσκειν. The fact that either is possible shows that πιστεύειν and γινώσκειν are not simply to be differentiated as initial and final stages, and it certainly rules out any distinction into two kinds of Christians, the pistics and the gnostics, as in Christian Gnosticism. In antithesis to Gnosticism it is apparent that knowledge can never take us beyond faith or leave faith behind. As all knowledge begins with faith, so it abides in faith. Similarly, all faith is to become knowledge. If all knowledge can only be a knowledge of faith, faith comes to itself in knowledge. Knowledge is thus a constitutive element in genuine faith. If one also realises that the relation of the Son to the Father is never described as a relation of faith, but only of knowledge, it is evident that this interconnection of faith and knowledge describes human faith, which must come to knowledge but which cannot attain to a definitive state of pure gnosis. Only when human existence ceases to be earthly and human will vision take the place of knowing faith or believing knowledge — the vision which no longer refers to the δόξα of the Son concealed by the σάρξ, but which has this δόξα as its immediate object, 17:24.

8. Faith and Love.

The believer cannot actualise the possibility of his desecularisation in such a way as to make it a state. Precisely and only in faith is he one who overcomes the world, 1 Jn. 5:4. He does have, however, the possibility of demonstrating his desecularisation, namely, in conduct. This is generally described as a τηρεῖν of the ἐντολαί given by Jesus or of His λόγος, [373] → II, 553, 30 ff. As these expressions can denote the obedience and steadfastness of faith (→ 225, 29), so they can also be used for the conduct which follows after faith (15:10; 1 Jn. 2:3 f.; 3:22; 5:2). The fact that the expressions have this twofold meaning brings out the inner unity between faith and action, just as the content of the ἐντολή of God in 1 Jn. 3:23 f. is the twofold one of faith and love. The content of the command-

---

[369] In both the Gospel and the Ep. Jn. deliberately avoids the noun γνῶσις.

[370] Faith : 11:42; 17:8, 21; knowledge : 17:3.

[371] → 214, 4 f. and cf. the admonitions to abide, → 226, 39 ff.

[372] 6:69; 8:31 f.; cf. 10:38. Thus the ἐν αὐτῷ μένειν of 1 Jn. 2:6 can take up again the γινώσκειν αὐτόν of v. 4.

[373] The meaning is the same, as shown esp. by the alternation in 1 Jn. 2:3-5.

ments corresponds to the unity of faith and love in so far as the action demanded therein is simply that of love, 13:34; 15:12; 1 Jn. 2:7 f.; 4:21, → I, 53, 12 ff. Faith sees in Jesus the Revealer of the divine love (3:16). Hence it is itself the reception of this love, and from the reception of this love there springs forth love in believers. In the love which Jesus showed for His own, their own ἀλλήλους ἀγαπᾶν is grounded. [374] ἀλλήλους ἀγαπᾶν (15:11-17) corresponds to abiding in Him or in His love (15:1-10). Similarly, 1 Jn. develops in various ways the principle that reception of the love of God which is given us in the sending of His Son engages us to brotherly love. [375] This ἀγαπᾶν, however, has the character of a demonstration, for : ἐν τούτῳ γνώσονται πάντες ὅτι ἐμοὶ μαθηταί ἐστε, ἐὰν ἀγάπην ἔχητε ἐν ἀλλήλοις (13:35).

Bultmann

| † πλανάω, † πλανάομαι, † ἀποπλανάω, † ἀποπλα- νάομαι, † πλάνη, † πλάνος, † πλανήτης, † πλάνης | → ἀπατάω, I, 384 f. → γινώσκω, I, 689- 719. → ὁδός, V, 42-96. |

Contents : A. The Classical and Hellenistic Use of the Word Group : I. Literal Usage , II. Transferred Usage : 1. The Verb in Epistemological and Ethical Statements ; 2. Religious and Metaphysical Error ; 3. The Nouns and Adjectives of the Group. B. The Word Group in the LXX : I. Literal Usage ; II. Transferred Usage. C. Apocalyptic and Hellenistic-Mystical Literature : I. Philo ; II. The Dualistic-Eschatological Use of the Word Group : 1. Seduction by Powers ; 2. The Dualistic Background ; 3. The Eschatological Use. III. The Word Group in the New Testament : I. Non-Transferred or Semi-Transferred ; II. Transferred : 1. The OT and Later Jewish Use ; 2. The Stoic Use of μὴ πλανᾶσθε ; 3. The Dualistic Use ; 4. The Eschatological Use ; 5. The Rationalising and Moralising Use ; 6. The Apostles and Christ as "Deceivers"; 7. Summary. E. The Usage in the Early Church : 1. In the Post-Apostolic Fathers ; 2. In the Later Period.

A. The Classical and Hellenistic Use of the Word Group.

πλανάομαι is found from Hom., act. πλανάω only from Aesch. and Hdt., and obviously rarer than the mid.-pass.; πλάνη from Soph. and Hdt., πλάνος from Soph.,

---

[374] 13:34; as often in Jn., καθώς means "on the basis of the fact that."
[375] 1 Jn. 2:5, 9-11; 3:10 f., 13-17, 23 f.; esp. 4:7-21; 5:1-3.

π λ α ν ά ω κ τ λ. Walde-Pok., II, 62; Hofmann, 273; Liddell-Scott, Preisigke Wört., Wilke-Grimm, Pr.-Bauer, Hatch-Redpath, *s.v.*; E. Fraenkel, *Gesch. d. gr.* Nomina agentis auf -τήρ, -τωρ, -της (-τ-), I (1910), II (1912); K. Kerényi, *Die Griech.-Orientalische Romanliteratur* (1927), *passim* (*v.* Index, 272 *s.v.* πλάνη); O. Becker, *Das Bild des Weges* (1937), *passim* (Index, 216 *s.v.* πλανᾶσθαι); W. and H. Gundel, "Planeten bei Griechen u. Römern," Pauly-W., 20 (1950), 2017-2185; E. Mäder, "Die abendländische Aufgabe des Lehrers der alten Sprachen," *Gymnasium*, 61 (1954), 40 f.; G. v. Rad, "Die falschen Propheten," ZAW, 51 (1933), 109-120; G. Quell, *Wahre u. falsche Propheten* (1952), 85-104; W. Bauer, *Rechtgläubigkeit u. Ketzerei* (1934), 198-242.

πλάνης [1] from Hipponax (6th cent.), πλανήτης from Soph. The group πλαν- reminds us of the Norwegian *flana* (French *flâner* from the Germanic), [2] and like πλάζω, ἔπλαγξα pass. (common in Hom.), which has much the same meaning ("to make to wander"), it comes from the Indo-European root *pela-* ("to spread"). There is debate as to the relations between the words of the family which have been mentioned, [3] and other etym. links are most uncertain. [4]

I. Literal Usage.

πλανάω means "to lead astray," πλανάομαι "to go astray," πλάνη and πλάνος "going astray," πλανήτης and πλάνης "one who leads astray," all at first in a topographical sense, which persists into the Hell. period. a. πλανάω : Argos causes Io to wander, Aesch. Prom., 573. b. πλανάομαι, ἀποπλανάομαι : Men wander about, Thuc., V, 4, 3; Plat. Ep., XI, 358e; Eur. Hel., 598; Lys., XII, 97; Plut. Lucull., 34 (I, 515b); Epict. Diss., II, 12, 3; Luc. Pergr. Mort., 16; Luc. Verae Historiae, II, 27; BGU, II, 372 II 20; cf. also members of the body, Emped. Fr., 57 (Diels[7], I, 333, 11 and 14); [5] Democr. Fr., 152 (Diels[7], II, 125, 34), physical powers, Plat. Tim., 86e; 88e; 91c, the body, Plat. Tim., 43b, body-bound souls after death, Plat. Phaed., 81d; 108c, animals (πλανάομαι of horses which wander off the race-course, Hom. Il., 23, 321, the earliest instance of the group, ἀποπλανάομαι of wild bees and wasps which have neither leader nor goal, Aristot. Hist. An., V, 23, p. 554b, 23), rumours, Soph. Oed. Col., 304, trouble, Aesch. Prom., 275, dreams and apparitions, Hdt., VII, 16, the αἰτία at the origin of the world, Plat. Tim., 48a. Sometimes places are noted, sometimes the use is abs. The use of πλανᾶσθαι for wandering stars is debated in Plat. Leg., VII, 821c; 822a on account of the implied lack of plan or rule, but the word is common in Aristot. (Meteor., I, 8, p. 346a, 2). c. πλάνη, "going astray," threatens the embryo, Democr. Fr., 148 (Diels[7], II, 171, 25). The journeys of men represent a wandering (cf. Hdt., II, 103), e.g., of Paris-Alexander (Hdt., II, 116), of Plato (Plat. Ep., VII, 350d), also Demeter (Orpheus Fr., 15 [Diels[7], I, 13, 15]). d. The oldest instance of πλάνης is in Hipponax Fr., 65 (Diehl[3], III, 98). The context is uncertain, but the word is beyond question. The term occurs as a noun (plur.) for the maenads spurred on by Bacchus (Eur. Ba., 148 vl.). As an adj. it is used of a wretched life of wandering (Eur. Heracl., 878) and from Democr. Fr., 86 (Diels[7], II, 105, 7) [6] it is used of the planets. [7] e. πλάνος, too, is used adj. of the planets, Manetho Astrologus, IV, 3.

Sometimes the special sense of going astray is not so prominent. Thus πλανάομαι, ἀποπλανάομαι : the adherents of the crypteia, inuring themselves to fatigue, "wander" day and night through the whole land (Plat. Leg., 633c); blood and breath "pulse" through all parts of the body (Hippocr. περὶ τροφῆς, 31). πλάνη : The account tells of the wisdom of Solon and of his journey, Hdt., I, 30; the wandering stars accomplish temporally measured, numerous and wonderfully intricate journeys, Plat. Tim., 39d; 40b. πλανήτης : Merchants are defined as those "who journey to cities" (πλανῆται ἐπὶ τὰς πόλεις, Plat. Resp., II, 371d; cf. also Ps.-Xenophon Cyn., V, 17).

Of special significance is the use of the group for certain figures in class. tragedy who wander about. The Io of Aesch., frightened away by Argos at the behest of Hera,

---

[1] Acc. to Fraenkel (II, 200 f.) πλάνής (related to πλανήτης as γυμνής to γυμνήτης etc.) is to be emphasised in spite of Herodian.

[2] Walde-Pok., II, 62.

[3] J. Wackernagel, "Miscellen zur gr. Grammatik," *ZvglSpr.*, 30 (1890), 300 thinks πλάνη comes from πλανάομαι, while Fraenkel (I, 27) sees a normal derivation of πλανάομαι from πλάνη.

[4] [Debrunner]; cf. Hofmann, 273.

[5] Becker, 147.

[6] On this terminology cf. Gundel, 2021 f.

[7] → ἀστήρ, I, 503 ff. Xenoph. Mem., IV, 7, 5; Aristot. Meteor., I, 6, 342b, 28 and 31; Plut. De Exilio, 11 (II, 604a); Luc. De Astrologia, 4, 362; Salt., 7, 271.

wanders off (πλανάομαι, Aesch. Prom., 565); her wanderings (πλάνη and πλάναι, 576, 585, 622, 784) lead her through Greece, Macedonia, and Asia Minor to Egypt. The blinded Oedipus is also a wanderer (πλανήτης, Soph. Oed. Col., 3, 124); he wanders about, guided by Antigone (πλανάομαι, 347); his wandering (πλάνος, 1114) only ends in Colonus.[8] The group is not used in this sense in Hom., nor is it found for the wanderings of Demeter in the two Homeric hymns of the same name.[9] Esp. in the figure of Io — this is what makes her, and in some sense Oedipus, typical of the race — two things are clear: the lack of goal affects man inwardly too, for geographical wandering is combined with spiritual aberration; then this wandering is not ultimately without goal, for it seeks a goal in accordance with divine fiat, cf. πλάναι θεήλατοι in Plut. Def. Or., 16 (II, 418e) → 231, 20-232, 31.

II. Transferred Usage.

In the non-geographical sense the word group denotes vacillation and then absence of goal in the field of knowledge, speech and action. Often this absence is affirmed even though no reasons are given. When reasons are mentioned they are in the main either naive or more sophisticated epistemological reasons; only rarely are they metaphysical or religious. Even in this case the deity can sometimes be regarded as the original author, though hardly as the authority before whom there is responsibility for the deficiency.

1. The Verb in Epistemological and Ethical Statements.

a. πλανάω, ἀποπλανάω takes on the sense "to lead astray," "to deceive." This is brought about by men through conduct (Menand. Peric., 79; Theognet., 2, 2 [CAF, III, 365]; P. Oxy., I, 119, 12), through speech or writing, often in the critical sense of "leading from the matter by digression": πλανάω Demosth. Or., 19, 335; ἀποπλανάω, Hippocr. περὶ ἄρθρων ἐμβολῆς, 34; Aeschin. Oratio in Ctesiphontem, 176, 190; Luc. Anacharsis, 21 (act. form in mid. sense). Eros (Moschus Reliquiae, I, 25), external things like the labyrinth (Apollodorus Bibliotheca, III, 11),[10] sensual character (Plat. Prot., 356d), or obscurity of reality and concepts (Plat. Leg., 655cd; Aristot. Meteor., I, 12, p. 347b, 35; Rhet., III, 14, p. 1415a, 14; διαπλανάω Epict. Diss., I, 20, 10) bring about the deception. Ref. might also be made to the Stoic and Neo-Platonic proverb about the deceived deceiver.[11] This deceiving and leading astray misleads in a geographical sense (e.g., the labyrinth) but esp. in theoretical or practical and ethical perception and judgment. In Plato theoretical and ethical failure in judgment and action go hand in hand. For the most part this aberration is not religious.

b. πλανάομαι, ἀποπλανάομαι, "to vacillate," "to be mistaken," denotes vacillation of action (Hdt., VI, 52)[12] and irregularity in state or conduct (Hippocr. Progn., 24; Plat. Menex., 248a; Resp., VI, 484b; IG², IV, 1, 81, 13). As regards speech the ref. may be critical ("to talk at random," "not to tell the truth," Hdt., II, 115),[13] factual ("to digress," with no censure, Plat. Polit., 263a; ἀποπλανάομαι, Isoc., 7, 77; "to make contradictory statements," Ps.-Plat. Alc., I, 112d; 117ab), or even laudatory ("to adapt one's speech to the situation," Hermogenes περὶ στάσεων, 3, 24). In most instances the aber-

---

[8] Becker, 210-212; H. Braun, "Der Fahrende," ZThK, 48 (1951), 32-38.

[9] Cf. Hymni Homer., ed. A. Baumeister (1915), 5 and 13. For Odysseus, who does not wander around but is driven, cf. πλάγχθη Hom. Od., 1, 2.

[10] Moschus Reliquiae in Bucolici Graeci, ed. O. Koenicke (1914); Apollodorus Bibliotheca in Mythographi Graeci, I, ed. R. Wagner (1894), 109.

[11] P. Wendland, "Betrogene Betrüger," Rhein. Mus., 49 (1894), 309 f.

[12] Becker, 124 f.

[13] Ibid., 116.

ration is in judgment (ἀποπλανάομαι, "to be turned aside," without blame, Ps.-Plat. Ax., 369d). It implies doubt, Hdt., VI, 37; Soph. Oed. Col., 316 (act. in mid. sense); Isoc., 15, 52, par. ἀπορεῖν, opp. εἰδέναι, Plat. Hi., I, 304c; II, 372d and 376c; Phaedr., 263b; Soph., 230b; Ps.-Plat. Alc., I, 117, b-d. Expression of this vacillating judgment is sometimes intended. There can also be vacillation in fixing a goal, opp. εἰς ἓν βλέπειν, Plat. Leg., XII, 962d. Vacillation leads to aberration. This error, where it is not left unspecified (like ἀποπλανάομαι, Chrysipp. Fr., 137 v. Arnim, III, 33), is in relation to the right moment (Pind. Nem., 8, 4; P. Flor., I, 61, 1, 16), in too luxurious a life (Xenoph. Cyrop., I, 3, 4), but esp. again in judgment [14] and discussion (Plat. Lys., 213e).

If aimless conduct can produce error (Isoc., 6, 10), in relation to vacillation and error, as in large measure to ἁμαρτάνω (→ I, 293, 9-18), there is no note of censure in the classical and Hellenistic testimonies, whether the field be epistemological or practical and ethical (as expressly in Epict. Diss., I, 18, 3 and 6; 28, 9 f.). There is a summons to correct knowledge and right action, but πλανᾶσθαι does not involve guilt. The μὴ πλανᾶσθε of the Stoic κηρύσσων (Epict. Diss., IV, 6, 23) demands recognition of the frugality of the sage. This non-metaphysical outlook is not abandoned even in Philodem. (περὶ σημείων καὶ σημειώσεων, [15] 7, 11 f.; 36, 24 f.).

2. Religious and Metaphysical Error. [16]

a. A series of characters in class. tragedy are led into error which is both innocent and guilty, i.e., tragic. Thus the group is used for madness in the tragedians. On Oedipus, who begins to create suspicion against himself, there comes ψυχῆς πλάνημα κἀνακίνησις φρενῶν (Soph. Oed. Tyr., 727 → 230, 2-5). [17] The song of the Furies is "mindconfusing madness" (παραφορὰ φρενοπλανής, [18] Aesch. Eum., 330, 342). Similarly the πλανᾶσθαι of Prometheus, who is at his wit's end in his terrible suffering, borders on frenzy, Aesch. Prom., 473. [19] Diogenes Oenoandensis (Fr., 27) [20] also speaks of the gt. danger of πλανώμενα πάθη, cf. also πλάνη in Fr., 33.

This type of aberration is sent by the gods and leads through the delusion to a divinely appointed end. The Io of Aesch. finds the redemptive end of πλανᾶσθαι in Egypt, while Oed. finds it in Colonus, → 229, 41 ff.

b. Plato (Phaed., 79c) speaks of a vacillation of the soul (synon. ταράττεσθαι and μεθύειν) which comes about as a result of man being drawn into what is changing through the senses [21] of the body. All their lives (Plat. Resp., IX, 586a) such materialists, without φρόνησις and ἀρετή, wander in the middle and lower regions, without relation

---

[14] Parmen. Fr., 8 (Diels⁷, I, 239, 10); Isoc., 15, 265; 6, 10; Dion. Hal. De Demosthene, 9, 981 (in Opuscula, ed. H. Usener and L. Radermacher, I [1899], 148, 12 f.); general in Epict. (Diss. I, 7, 31; 20, 10; II, 7, 7; III, 1, 31; 21, 23; IV, 6, 23) or with specific ref. to the question of good and evil (Diss., I, 18, 3. 6; 28, 9. 10; III, 22, 23); Alexander Aphrodisiensis, Commentaria in Aristotelem Graeca, I, 139, 12.

[15] Herkulanische Studien, ed. T. Gomperz (1865).

[16] In what follows I am indebted to H. Kleinknecht for a list of refs. which both clarify and develop the matter.

[17] Becker, 201, 203.

[18] Acc. to the conjecture of H. Weil, Aesch. Tragoediae (1921).

[19] Becker, 157, 160.

[20] Ed. J. William (1912).

[21] αἴσθησις, cf. the seductive power of the φαινόμενον and the ensuing μεταμέλειν, Plat. Prot., 356d → 230, 27 f.

πρὸς τὸ ἀληθῶς ἄνω. On the other hand true οὐσία (ibid., VI, 485b), as ἀεὶ οὖσα, is not shaken by γένεσις and φθορά. Hence jumbled (τεταραγμέναι), vacillating thoughts should be orientated to the ἀτάρακτοι and ἀπλανεῖς περίοδοι of the stars, Plat. Tim., 47c.

The metaphysically dualistic outlook of later Gnosticism is intimated here both materially and linguistically. πλανᾶσθαι now becomes "entanglement." The wise man is saved from this error (→ 233, 9-13, 19 f.) by turning aside from the world of the senses and turning to the world of ideas. Here, too, πλάνη as a detour to the goal of true knowledge acquires the character of indispensability when Socrates calls the afflictions (πάσχειν, πόνοι, Plat. Apol., 22a) of his search for knowledge his πλάνη (loc. cit.) to which his σοφία (ibid., 20e) corresponds — both taken ironically and dialectically in distinction to the σοφιστῶν γένος ... πλανητὸν ὂν κατὰ πόλεις (Plat. Tim., 19e), but in independent analogy to the πλάναι of the mysteries.

c. Plut. (Is. et Os., 27 [II, 361d-e]) tells us that in imitation of her painful search for her husband and brother Isis cultically instituted the instructive and consoling δρώμενα. Her seeking involves ἆθλοι, ἀγῶνες, πλάναι, [22] πολλὰ ἔργα σοφίας and ἀνδρείας, παθήματα. The link with the wandering of Io and Oedipus (→ 229, 41 ff.) and the entanglement of the Platonic man of the sense world [23] is the more patent in that Plato in this connection refers expressly to initiates (κατὰ τῶν μεμυημένων, Phaed., 81a), so that the δρώμενα of the Hell. Isis mysteries are closely related to the Eleusinian Demeter mysteries. [24] Worth noting, too, is the correspondence between πλάνη and σοφία in Plato (→ supra) and also in Solon (Hdt., I, 30 → 229, 36 f.).

The reference in this πλανᾶσθαι, then, is to the destiny of a god which is cultically imitated by the initiate. We thus have a way of salvation which is customary and even indispensable in certain mysteries (→ 231, 28 ff.; 232, 8 ff.) and at the end of which, after πλάναι, περιδρομαὶ κοπώδεις, διὰ σκότους τινὲς ὕποπτοι πορεῖαι καὶ ἀτέλεστοι and the like, there stand φῶς τι θαυμάσιον and τόποι καθαροί (Themistios). [25] In this sense πλάνη becomes a topos in the novel of antiquity. [26] Tragedy rather than guilt is the metaphysical characteristic of all this πλανᾶσθαι.

3. The Nouns and Adjectives of the Group.

a. πλάνη, "vacillation," "error." The noun has the same range of meanings as the verb. The life of men who strive after various things (Critias Fr., 15 [Diels⁷, II, 381, 20]), indeed, the action of many men (Philodem. Philos. Volumina Rhetorica, [27] VIII, 33, before παραλογισμός) can be called an "error." Aristot. uses πλάναι (An., I, 1, p. 402a, 21) for mistakes in investigation and πλάνη (Eth. Nic., I, 1, p. 1094b, 16) for the incalculable effect of καλά and δίκαια. The act sense "deceit" is late and rare (Diod. S., II, 18, perhaps P. Lond., II, 483, 19). The pass. "illusion" in seeing (Plat. Resp., X, 602c) and sense perception generally (Epic. De rerum natura, [28] 28, Fr. 7), the vacillation of knowledge (Plat. Soph., 245e) found even in the wise man (Plat. Hi.,

---

[22] In Def. Orac., 15 (II, 417e) Plut. does not ascribe πλάναι to the gods, but to demons.
[23] → 231, 31-232, 14; 233, 7-13; 233, 19 f.
[24] Cf. Cl. Al. Prot., 12, 2 : καὶ τὴν πλάνην καὶ τὴν ἁρπαγὴν καὶ τὸ πένθος αὐταῖν Ἐλευσὶς δᾳδουχεῖ.
[25] Mithr. Liturg., 163 f.
[26] Kerényi, 88, 92, 188 f.
[27] Ed. S. Sudhaus, I (1892), 30.
[28] Cf. Liddell-Scott, s.v.

II, 376e), the error which is to be explained by overestimation of ἡδονή (Plat. Resp., VI, 505c) — all these things can be denoted by πλάνη or πλάναι. There is never any censorious or underlying metaphysical note, cf. the def. of ἀπάτη in Moeris, 65 (→ I, 385, 11 f.), where πλάνη and τέρψις are equated. πλάνη can even be the tt. for the "excursus" which in reflection back and forth (Plat. Parm., 135e; 136e) and in varied presentation (Plat. Leg., III, 683a) is indispensable for the discovery of truth and helps to promote it, → 230, 39-41. Nevertheless, we find the same shift to the censorious and metaphysically negative aspect as in the case of the verb (→ 231, 20 ff.). This is clearly present when (Plat. Resp., IV, 444b) "confusion" of the parts of the soul (with ταραχή) forms the basis of ἀδικία and every κακία, or when (Plat. Phaed., 81a) "error" (with ἄνοια, φόβοι, ἄγριοι, ἔρωτες, ἄλλα κακά) characterises this life, from which the soul of the dead philosopher is liberated, cf. also Plut. (→ 232, 17 f.). b. πλανήτης "unstable," of the unhappy life of the atheist, Porphyr. Ad Marc., 22. c. πλάνος adj.: to the original pass. sense of "unstable" (with ποικίλος, Menand. Cith., 8; Mosch. Reliquiae, V, 10 → n. 10) there is added later (cf. the act. sense of πλάνη → 232, 38 f.) the act. meaning "luring," "seducing" (the decoy in Theocr., 21, 43; the weapons of Eros, Mosch. Reliquiae, I, 29 → n. 10). d. πλάνος as noun is used in a transf. sense for things — poetic "digression" (Plat. Ep., VII, 344d), the "vacillation" which the soul leaves behind when it renounces sense perception (Plat. Phaed., 79d), "confusion" in comedy (Aristoph. Vesp., 873). It is then applied to persons, the "conjurer" (Nicostratus, 24 [CAF, II, 226]; Dionysius, 4 [CAF, II, 426]). πλάνος becomes a term of opprobrium, Diod. S. (ed. L. Dindorf, V [1868], 90), Fr. 2, 14; Vett. Val., II, 16, p. 74, 16-20 between μάγος and θύτης.

B. The Word Group in the Septuagint. [29]

The translators of the LXX took over this developed usage. The changes connected with its adoption are theologically instructive. The literal sense is maintained intact, but when we come to the transferred sense of leading astray or making a mistake the non-censorious and non-religious meaning is rare, and the purely theoretical orientation to knowledge is not found at all. Instead the group is used generally for transgression of the revealed will of God and more specifically for instigation to idolatry. There is responsibility to God for this transgression. It is culpable, and brings down punishment. God is not, as in the Greek world, eternal being. He works, demands, commands (→ I, 697, 22-698, 13). Transgression is brought about, not by ungodly metaphysical forces like the devil, but by man, or even God Himself.

The verb occurs 121 times in the LXX. In 42 instances it is used for a q, hi or ni form of תעה. [30] Sometimes there is no Heb. equivalent (as in Wis.); of the many other Heb. originals none is sufficiently common to call for notice. The same is true of the equivalents of πλάνη and πλάνος. In 9 instances the verbal forms of the LXX are an expansion of the Mas. [31] and in 21 instances the LXX with the verb paraphrases the Mas. [32]

---

[29] We are indebted to G. Bertram for notes on πλανάω in the LXX, and also to J. Fichtner. On this whole question cf. Hatch-Redp.

[30] Like πλανάομαι, תעה denotes lit. wandering in the first instance. Cf. the same change of meaning in שׁוּב.

[31] πλανάω is added at Qoh. 7:26 vl.; Is. 30:21; Δα. 6:23, πλανάομαι at Job 2:9d vl.; 19:4a; Prv. 9:12b; 13:9a; Is. 13:14; 21:15.

[32] πλανάω is a paraphrase at 2 Esr. 9:11 א*; Job 12:23; Hos. 8:6; Is. 9:15; 30:20 (twice); 41:29; Ez. 8:17 B, and πλανάομαι at Job 12:25; Is. 16:8; 17:11; 22:5; 35:8; 41:10; 44:8 vl., 20; 46:5, 8; 64:4; Ez. 33:12; 44:13.

I. Literal Usage.

a. πλανάω "to lead astray," "to confuse," "to cause to stagger." The ref. is lit. in the command not to lead the blind astray, Dt. 27:18. Staggering as the result of drinking wine (1 Εσδρ. 3:18; Is. 19:13 f.) is in the first instance lit., though with transition to spiritual vacillation, cf. later in Damasc., 1, 15, where being carried off into the trackless wilderness (תעה) by the mocker becomes seduction from the truth. b. πλανάομαι "to wander or stagger about" : men wander on journeys, in flight, in judgment. [33] In the eschatological time of salvation there will be no more "wandering from the way" (Is. 35:8, not the Mas.). Men "stagger" as a result of wine (Job 12:25; Is. 19:14; 21:4; 28:7; 45:15), they "wander about" in affliction (Sir. 29:18; 36:25), they "rush about" (Prv. 9:12b; 29:15; Sir. 9:7). Animals "wander about" : the ox (Ex. 23:4; Dt. 22:1), the sheep (Dt. 22:1; Is. 13:14; Ιερ. 27[50]:17), young ravens (Job 38:41). c. πλανήτης : God's punishment makes the Israelites into "restless wanderers" (Hos. 9:17) among the Gentiles. d. πλανῆτις : Job's wife as a wanderer and day-labourer (Job 2:9d). e. ἀποπλανάω, ἀποπλανάομαι, πλάνη and πλάνος are used only in a transf. sense.

II. Transferred Usage.

a. πλανάω is seldom used for profane deceiving. In the few instances the ref. is always practical rather than epistemological, Ju. 16:10, 13, 15 B; 4 Βασ. 4:28; Tob. 10:7; Sir. 34:7.

Religious seduction leads to the worship of idols and false gods. It is the work of false prophets and unfaithful rulers (Dt. 13:6; 2 K. 21:9; 2 Ch. 33:9; Is. 30:20 twice, 21; 41:29; Jer. 23:13, 32) or of the false gods themselves (Hos. 8:6; Am. 2:4; Tob. 14:6 א) and plastic art (Wis. 15:4).

The obj. of seduction is almost always Israel, the means are ἐνύπνιον (Dt. 13:2; Jer. 23:32), σημεῖον and τέρας (Dt. 13:2 f.). The familiarity of the theme may be seen from the fact that in the prophets the LXX often expands or paraphrases the Mas. with the help of forms of πλανάω (→ n. 31, 32). The seducing of Israel by lying prophets is also accomplished by prophecies which are not commanded by Yahweh and which are sometimes made for bribes (Is. 3:12; 9:15 twice ; Mi. 3:5; Ez. 13:10). In the Wisdom literature esp. there is ref. to temptation to modes of conduct which are against the good-pleasure of Yahweh and later the Torah. [34] This temptation is usually the work of the ungodly (Qoh. 7:26 vl.; Prv. 1:10; 12:26; 28:10; Sir. 3:24; Δα. 6:23).

A special group is constituted by passages which speak of Yahweh leading astray. The reference may be to the Gentiles (Job 12:23), the mighty (Job 12:24; ψ 106:40), lying prophets (Ez. 14:9), or the whole people (Is. 63:17). Identical are ἀπολλύειν (Job 12:23) and σκληρύνειν τὰς καρδίας (Is. 63:17). As in the case of ἀπατᾶν (→ I, 384, 12 f.) idolatry is never expressly mentioned as the content of this leading astray by Yahweh. Elements of the demonic and the *tremendum* seem to be present in Yahweh in this respect. [35] A later period could no longer tolerate this strong God (Sir. 15:12), though the predestinating God of the Damascus Document can still lead astray those whom He hates (2:13). No

---

[33] Gn. 21:14; 37:15; Ex. 14:3; Job 2:9d vl.; ψ 106:4; Sir. 34:9, 10; 51:13; Is. 16:8; 21:15; 22:5.
[34] J. Fichtner, "Die altorientalische Weisheit," Beih. ZAW, 62 (1933), 79-97.
[35] Cf. Quell, *op. cit.*, 85-104.

πλανᾶν is ascribed to Satan in the LXX, though he exercises ἐπισείειν in 1 Ch. 21:1 (Yahweh in 2 S. 24:1). [36]

b. Similar senses occur in relation to the mid.-pass. πλανάομαι. Sympathetically rather than censoriously (synon. are, e.g., ἀπολωλέναι, συντετρῖφθαι, μὴ πλανῶ with μὴ φοβοῦ) Israel is said to have erred and gone astray ; with an express metaphor (ψ 118:176; Is. 53:6), a loose metaphor (Ez. 34:4, 16) or no metaphor at all (Job 19:4a; Prv. 16:10) the word is also used of the πρόβατον. If there is already a note of blame in the ref. to "error in speech" (Job 19:4a; Prv. 16:10), in most of the verses there is denoted an "aberration" or "apostasy" or "seduction" which is completely condemned from a religious standpt. The ref. is esp. to Israel, or, in the later period of religious individualism, to its ungodly members. The use is either abs. with no more precise explanation, [37] or what is meant is apostasy (Hos. 4:12; Dt. 4:19; 11:28; 30:17; Ez. 44:10, 13, 15 [quoted Damasc. 4:11]; 48:11), wandering away from Yahweh and the way of righteousness (Ez. 14:11; Bar. 4:28; Prv. 21:16; Wis. 5:6), or an individual transgression against the will of Yahweh or the Torah (ψ 118:110; Job 6:24; 19:4; Prv. 7:25 vl.; 13:19a; Sir. 9:8). Though obscure in detail, Is. 17:11; 44:8 vl. may also be cited in this connection. Only later verses speak of the spiritual aberration of the Gentiles too, with respect to idolatry in Is. 46:5, 8; Wis. 11:15; 12:24; 13:6; 14:22; [38] Bel. 7 Θ; 3 Macc. 4:16, and individual errors in Wis. 17:1; 2 Macc. 7:18.

The sing. imp. μὴ πλανῶ encourages against fear (Is. 41:10) and warns against gadding about (Sir. 9:7), illusion (Bel. 7 Θ) and error (2 Macc. 7:18). The plur. imp. μὴ πλανᾶσθε, which occurs once at Is. 44:8 vl., warns against being led into idolatry.

In the LXX the word group is used in rejection of the false prophecy which, rooted in the cultus and intercession, infringes on the transcendence and creatorhood of Yahweh with its prophecies of salvation (3 Βασ. 22:2-28). [39] It also serves to strengthen monolatry (→ III, 79-89). The usage in individual authors is instructive. Only Yahweh is the subject of πλανάω in Job. The common literal use of πλανάομαι is noteworthy in Is., Job and Sir. The group bears no reference to idolatry in Job, Prv., or Sir. Job likes to use the group for the Heb. stem שגה, "to sin in error and weakness" (6:24; 29:4 twice). Prv. often has the word for acting contrary to the good-pleasure of Yahweh.

c. ἀποπλανάω : the transf. use denotes secular "deceiving" (Sir. 13:6) and leading astray into idolatry (Ιερ. 27[50]:6; 2 Ch. 21:11) or offending against the will of Yahweh (Prv. 7:21). ἀποπλανάομαι, with no religious censure, means "to be taken advantage of" in Sir. 13:8, and with censure, "to let oneself be led," "to fall" into idolatry (2 Macc. 2:2) or into sin against Yahweh's good-pleasure (Sir. 4:19). πλάνη as "error," "seduction," is used generally for Israel's disobedience (Ez. 33:10 before ἀνομίαι), or specifically for its idolatry (Jer. 23:17; Tob. 5:14 vl.), or for that of the Gentiles (Wis. 12:24), or for individual transgressions (Prv. 14:8; Sir. 11:16 vl.), so that life can be regarded as πλάνη (Wis. 1:12). [40] In spite of the protest against any idea that Yahweh practises

---

[36] The transl. of Hos. uses πλανάω once (2:16) for Yahweh's friendly wooing of Israel. On the positive sense → 230, 38 ff.; 233, 3-7. Cf. ἀπατάω in the LXX.

[37] Is. 29:24; 64:4; Ιερ. 38(31):9; Ez. 14:9; 33:12; ψ 57:3; 94:10; Job 5:2; Prv. 10:17; 14:22; Sir. 16:23; Wis. 2:21; Tob. 5:14; 2 Macc. 6:25.

[38] The Wis. verses give evidence of rationalistic Stoic influence, → I, 117, 29 ff.

[39] v. Rad, 110-120.

[40] This formulation pts. already in the direction of the dualistic view which will be treated later, → 236, 18-22.

πλανᾶν (Sir. 15:12, → 234, 39 f.), πλάνη was created along with sinners acc. to at least the secondary version in Sir. 11:16 vl. The sense "deceiving," which is rare in the Gk. world (→ 232, 38 f.), does not occur in the LXX. πλάνος, which is always used of things, never of persons (→ 233, 17-23), denotes "religious error" with a ref. to idolatry (Jer. 23:32 alongside ψεῦδος) or the sin of weakness (Job 19:4).

d. Finally, it is of theological significance in relation to LXX usage that the negative judgment expressed in the word group applies predominantly to Israel and only in later texts to the Gentiles as well. The background of going astray is not metaphysical dualism. Man does not err simply because he is. He errs inasmuch as he does not hear and obey God's will, [41] but leaves God's way and follows an evil path. [42] For this reason he must be warned of judgment and summoned to ἐπιστρέφειν (Is. 46:8; Bar. 4:28; Ez. 33:11 f.; 34:4, 16) and μετανοεῖν (Is. 46:8). Typical of the non-metaphysical character is the fact that there is no connection between the group and the διάβολος even in later texts where the devil is mentioned (Wis. 2:24; → 234, 41 f.). The group is not used to describe the fall in Gn. 3. [43] Eschatologically the first use of the group is in relation to freedom from πλανᾶσθαι in the age of salvation, Is. 35:8; 30:20; Ιερ. 38(31):9. [44]

The first beginnings of dualism may be seen in the juxtaposition of πλάνη and σκότος in the secondary Sir. 11:16 vl. Elsewhere πλάνη corresponds to not hearing rather than not seeing (→ lines 8-10). The use of πλανᾶσθαι and ἀποτυφλοῦν together in Wis. 2:21 pts. in a similar direction. In the LXX these are rare and late combinations which are already linked with a different total view. [45]

C. Apocalyptic and Hellenistic-Mystical Literature.

In a considerable number of instances NT use of the word group follows directly neither classical and Hellenistic usage on the one side nor that of the LXX on the other. For three features of NT usage are not to be found generally in the passages mentioned thus far : metaphysical powers as the instigators of human error ; the embedding of the error in a dualistic outlook ; the connection of the group with eschatology. These features occur, though infrequently, in a series of passages from later Jewish apocalyptic, Hellenistic and Gnosticising Judaism, and Hellenistic-oriental mysticism. Platonic-Neo-platonic and Iranian-Babylonian influences are unmistakable. [46] In the framework of this ultimately Gnostic understanding of being there is a leading astray by powers. This takes place in the field of light and darkness or truth and error, and there is a connection with the eschata.

---

[41] Hos. 9:17; Dt. 11:28; 30:17; Is. 29:24; 44:8 vl.; ψ 57:4 f.; 94:7, 8, 10; in Wis. 13:6 f. the relative exculpation of the divinisation of the creature by the strong emphasis on creation is Greek.

[42] Is. 3:12; 35:8; Ιερ. 38(31):9; Dt. 11:28; 13:6; Is. 63:17; ψ 94:10; 106:40; Job 12:24; Prv. 12:26; 21:16; 28:10; Wis. 5:6; 12:24.

[43] → ἀπατάω, I, 384, 29.

[44] Typically there are deviations from the Mas., → n. 32.

[45] On Wis. as an apocalyptic book of wisdom, J. Fichtner, "Die Stellung d. Sap. in der Lit.- u. Geistesgesch. ihrer Zeit," ZNW, 36 (1937), 124-132.

[46] On the religio-historical question cf. Bousset-Gressm., 469-524.

I. Philo.

The usage of Philo occupies a special place. [47] a. The act. πλανάω is not used. b. πλανάομαι means lit. "wandering about," cf. Joseph (Det. Pot. Ins., 10, 17, 22), the stars (Cher., 21; Mut. Nom., 67; Rer. Div. Her., 208; Congr., 104, Decal., 104), the κόσμος-σῶμα (Plant., 5). Transf. πλανᾶσθαι expresses "imprecision" of speech (Det. Pot. Ins., 131), "groundlessness of opinion" resting on visibility (Praem. Poen., 29), the "aberration of sensory perception" with its distorted evaluation of φύσις and chance (Leg. Gaj., 2), the "errant vacillation" of the νοῦς which, without σοφία, operates in ὕλη (Plant., 97), ἡδονή and ἐπιθυμία (Praem. Poen., 117), the "errant vacillation" of the ψυχή (Rer. Div. Her., 82) which finds itself in danger (Fug., 119), without freedom (Congr., 108), in careful seeking (Fug., 131), the allegorical spiritualised "wandering" of individuals to whose lit. wanderings the OT refers, e.g., Joseph (Det. Pot. Ins., 17, 22) and Rachel (Leg. All., III, 180), the content of this aberration, which is deviation from the straight and middle way (Migr. Abr., 133), being orientation to the external (Det. Pot. Ins., 28; without διάνοια, Rer. Div. Her., 12), overestimation of the cultus (Det. Pot. Ins., 21), contempt for allegorising (ibid., 22) or ἄσκησις (ibid., 10), and the polytheistic worship of the stars (Spec. Leg., I, 15, 16). The imp. μὴ πλανῶ and μὴ πλανᾶσθε do not occur. c. πλάνη. In Philo, as in the LXX, this is less common, and it is used only in a transf. sense for the moral "aberration" of man (Decal., 104) or the ψυχή (Det. Pot. Ins., 24), for the opp. of Joseph's ἐγκράτεια (Det. Pot. Ins., 19), or for the polytheism of the apostate Jews (Exsecr., 163). There is no instance of the act. sense "deceiving." d. The customary word in Philo is πλάνος. Lit. this means "going astray," Spec. Leg., IV, 158. Transf. it means "aberration" in consequence of ungrounded opinions (Ebr., 38; Spec. Leg., I, 60 adj.), along with the loss of freedom (Congr., 108), esp. in views about God (Leg. All., III, 180; Decal., 52) as a result of sensory perceptions (Cher., 66), particularly through idolatry or worship of creatures (Vit. Mos., II [III], 272; Spec. Leg., I, 15, 16; Virt., 65, 178). The ref. of πλάνος is never to a person. e. πλάνητες in Philo is almost always a tt. for the planets as distinct from fixed stars (ἀπλανεῖς).

Though the intellectual world is sometimes said to be in error, the main concern in Philo is aberration in the knowledge of God. Almost always, then, blame attaches. The true way (Det. Pot. Ins., 19) or the truth (Ebr., 38) has been missed. The αἰσθήσεις rule and make error unavoidable (Cher., 66; Vit. Mos., II [III], 272; Decal., 52). Moral defects and idolatry are not so prominent (except in the case of πλάνος). The seeing of the eyes, which is never ruled out in the LXX, is now rejected in principle as a way of knowing God, since it constitutes the false path of sensuality (Fug., 131; Spec. Leg., I, 16; Leg. Gaj., 2). But hearing is also inadequate (Rer. Div. Her., 12). The true way is again a seeing (→ V, 334, 25 ff.; Det. Pot. Ins., 22). As in the LXX, the group is still linked with ὁδός (→ 236, 11; Det. Pot. Ins., 10, 21 and 22; Migr. Abr., 133; Plant., 97; Fug., 131; Praem. Poen., 117; Det. Pot. Ins., 19; Spec. Leg., I, 60). But the absence of ἐπιστρέφειν and μετανοεῖν for the return from error, and the replacement of these LXX terms (→ 236, 11 ff.) by ἐμβαίνειν εἰς τὴν φρονήσεως ὁδόν (Plant., 98), μεθορμίζεσθαι (Congr., 108), μεταβάλλειν (Exsecr., 163), μεταδιδάσκειν, ἀποστῆναι, ἀκολουθεῖν (Ebr., 38), and esp. ἐπανιέναι (Congr., 108) and ἀνάγεσθαι (Praem. Poen., 117 vl.), make it quite clear that error is not so much disobedience — idolatry is less to the fore — but a fate to be borne, the fate of being tied to the senses (τὸν ἀκούσιον πλάνον εἰσάπαν ἐκδῦναι χαλεπόν, Cher., 66). There is at any rate no temptation by mythological powers. Eschatology is also out of the picture. On the other hand, the group is not linked with μέθη as in Corp. Herm. (→ 239, 36), though Philo does use this term quite often.

---

[47] Cf. Leisegang's Index.

II. The Dualistic-Eschatological Use of the Word Group.

Naturally the apocalyptic and Hell.-mystical writings sometimes use the group in a way which is not different from that of class. and Hell. usage : πλανάω as profane "deceiving" (Test. Iss. 1:13), or as religious "seduction" by men (Test. L. 10:2; R. 5:3) and wine (Test. Jud. 14:1, 5, 8); πλανάομαι (Corp. Herm., 2, 6b; 10, 7; 16, 17), πλάνος (Stob. Excerpt., 6, 4 [Scott, I, 412]) and πλανήτης (ibid., 6, 2 [Scott, I, 410]) of stars, πλάνος (of things, not persons, in Herm.) epistemologically (ibid., 2 A, 3 [Scott, I, 382]), πλάνη and πλανάομαι of a concrete "erroneous opinion" (Corp. Herm., 2, 10; 10, 20; 12, 16). In general, however, the world of Gnostic thought is unmistakable.

1. Seduction by Powers.

In Eth. En. not only sinners (94:5) but the angels of Gn. 6:2 ff. or Azazel tempt men to licentiousness and idolatry (Gr. En. 8:2; 19:1). In the visions the hosts of Azazel also tempt the dwellers on earth or the world (Eth. En. 54:6; 64:2; 67:6 f.; 69:4, 27), esp. Eve (69:6), to sin.

In Test. XII a decisive part is played by τὸ πνεῦμα or τὰ πνεύματα τῆς πλάνης, [48] the δαίμονες τῆς πλάνης (Jud. 23:1), the ἄρχων τῆς πλάνης (S. 2:7; Jud. 19:4), and even Βελίαρ himself (L. 3:3; Jud. 25:3 vl.; Zeb. 9:8 vl.; B. 6:1 vl.). They, not God, practise πλανᾶν, mostly on Israel, very rarely on the Gentiles (N. 3:3). Beliar is called πλάνος (B. 6:1 vl.), cf. the Jewish name for Jesus in the Chr. gloss (L. 16:3). In Test. XII πλάνος is used only as a personal designation. The πλάνη (or πλανάω, πλανάομαι) to which the spirits tempt, and which has to be guarded against (μὴ πλανᾶσθε, G. 3:1), is the opp. of the νόμος and the ἐντολαὶ κυρίου (A. 5:4; 6:2 f.; Jos. 1:3). It consists but rarely in idolatry (R. 4:6; L. 16:1; Zeb. 9:7; Jud. 19:1; 23:1; N. 3:3) and mostly in concrete failings (drunkenness, Jud. 14:1, 8; μῖσος, G. 3:1; θυμός, D. 2:4; ζῆλος, S. 2:7; φθόνος, S. 3:1; πλεονεξία, Jud. 19:4; ὕπνος, φαντασία, R. 3:7), among which πορνεία is given the strongest emphasis (R. 4:6; 5:3; Jud. 14:1, 8; 17:1; Iss. 4:4; D. 5:5; Jos. 3:9; B. 6:3). In keeping with this the 8 πνεύματα τῆς πλάνης are specified as the 8 vices whose names they bear, R. 3:2-7.

In Sib. too (III, 63-69) Beliar is the name of the tempter who through nature miracles practises eschatological πλάνη on Hebrew believers and the elect. The Chr. part of Asc. Is., which works over Jewish traditions, speaks of the power of the miracles of Beliar, 4:10, 2-6.

Similarly in Jub. seduction is practised by unclean demons and evil spirits, the spirits of Mastema (10:1, 2; 11:4; 19:28). This applies to the descendants of Noah (10:1, 2; 11:4), and it is not completely ended by the penal decimation of demons (10:8). God gave the spirits power over all nations and people (15:31) apart from Abraham and his seed (19:28). This seduction consists in leading away from God (15:31; 19:28) and into idolatry (11:4) and vice (50:5).

The dualism of the Qumran texts is palpable. Error (תָּעוּת) comes on all the sons of righteousness through the angel of darkness (Manual [49] 3:21 f.). On תָּעָה cf. also Manual 5:4 and 11; 11:1. Beliyaal (1:18, 24; 2:5, 19; 10:21) or Mastema (3:23) is the supreme opponent. God has appointed two kinds of spirits for men (3:18). In the Psalms [50] lying prophets practise seduction ; this consists in weaning away from a strict observance of the Law.

---

[48] R. 2:1; 3:2, 7; S. 3:1; 6:6; L. 3:3; Jud. 14:8; 20:1; 25:3; Iss. 4:4; Zeb. 9:7 vl., 8 vl.; D. 2:4; 5:5 vl.; N. 3:3; A. 6:2 vl.; B. 6:1 vl.

[49] I owe the examples of תָּעָה to K. G. Kuhn. On the Manual cf. L. Rost, "Der gegenwärtige Stand d. Erforschung d. in Palästina neu gefundenen hbr. Handschriften," ThLZ, 75 (1950), 341-344.

[50] E. L. Sukenik, אוצר המגילות הגנוזות (1954), 38 IV 16 and 20.

In Damasc. "seduction" (תעה, 5:20) consists in transgression of the Torah and esp. in polygamy and incest (3:1, 4, 14; 12:3). It is practised by those who erase the boundaries (5:20), resisting the intensification of the Torah by the sect, [51] but esp. by Beliyaal (4:13-18; 5:18; 12:2) and the angel of Mastema (16:5). [52]

In spite of the dogmatic definition : "Satan comes down and seduces" (BB, 16a Bar., Str.-B., I, 139), the Rabb. seldom speak of this. When they do, the ref. is usually (Str.-B., I, 140 f.) to temptation by Satan (→ 26, 6 ff.), though this is materially equivalent to seduction when it is wholly or partially successful, cf. the people at Sinai, or David, or Abraham. Sometimes the portrayal of Satan as the seducer verges on the grotesque, as in Pelimo (Qid., 81a, Str.-B., I, 140).

Theophil. (Ad Autol., II, 15), obviously borrowing Jewish material, describes the πλανῆται as τύπος τῶν ἀφισταμένων ἀνθρώπων ἀπὸ τοῦ θεοῦ. In apocalyptic the fallen angels of Gn. 6 are compared to the 7 stars which have left their courses, Eth. En. 18-21; 90:21-24. [53] In the Kyriakos Prayer, 8, [54] which uses later Jewish Gnostic material, the δράκων seduces the angels, the first Adam, Jeroboam and Solomon (πλανάω, πλάνη).

The Mandaean texts speak of seduction by the 7 planets (Lidz. Ginza, 46, 29; 52, 7 and 15; 131, 25), by the 12 apostles, who are equated with the spirits of the zodiac (51, 27), by Christ (47, 16; 52, 6 f., 28 ff.), by Ruha (134, 26; Lidz. Joh., 199, 19) and by the Dewes of Samis (Ginza, 28, 25; 46, 36 f.). These powers seduce through miracles (Ginza, 47, 17 ff.; 49, 8 ff.), through gold, silver and plenty (28, 31 f.; 52, 26), through a charming appearance and magic (52, 33). They lead the children of men (28, 33; 46, 37) into the dreams and illusions of the seducers (52, 24 f.), i.e., into worship of the stars (28, 33 f.; 46, 30), lying, pride, boasting and gluttony (46, 36-38; 52, 34-53, 9; 134, 26 etc.). Teaching counteracts this seduction (41, 5). The polemic against Chr. asceticism, which belongs to a later stratum of the text, gives this Mandaean rejection of seduction a special character.

In the O. Sol. seduction is embodied in the pair of ungodly aeons (38:9 f.) which, par. to Christ and the Church, robs the world of wisdom and understanding, and plunges it into confusion and destruction, 38:11-14.

In the Hermetic writings the πλανᾶν and πλανᾶσθαι of ἔρως, whose opponent is τὸ λογικὸν μέρος τῆς ψυχῆς, denotes spiritual and corporal subjection to demons, Corp. Herm., 16, 16. The astrological bondage [55] of man to the circle of the zodiac promotes his seduction, his πλάνη, his surrender to the τιμωρίαι τοῦ σκότους, 13, 11c. and 12. Though there is no express mythological nomenclature, the fact that πλάνη is practised by the powers is plain from the synonyms μέθη, ὕπνος (ἄλογος), ἀγνωσία τοῦ θεοῦ, θάνατος, ἄγνοια, σκότος, φθορά, 1, 27 f.

The soul which wanders in the labyrinth of the world, far from the heavenly breath (Naassene Hymn, Hipp. Ref., V, 10), is hopelessly entangled in bitter chaos. Though no mythological forces are mentioned, its πλανᾶσθαι represents a cosmic fate.

2. The Dualistic Background.

Basically all these features point already to the second essential characteristic of the Gnostic use of the word group. This aberration takes place against the background and in the context of a metaphysical dualism which even in texts of

---

[51] H. Braun, "Beobachtungen zur Tora-Verschärfung im häretischen Spätjudt.," ThLZ, 79 (1954), 347-352.

[52] But cf. → 234, 39-41.

[53] Cf. Bousset-Gressm., 252, 323.

[54] H. Gressmann, "Das Gebet des Kyriakos," ZNW, 20 (1921), 25 f.

[55] Gundel, 2119-2122.

diverse origins is expressed by a terminology that is uniform, though employed with varying degrees of intensity.

The combination of πλάνη and σκότος, and the opposing of πλανᾶσθαι to ἀλήθεια and φῶς (→ 236, 18-22), which are both very rare in the LXX, do not occur in apocalyptic (En.; 4 Esr.). [56]

On the other hand the Test. XII, in spite of strong reminiscences of the OT (cf. the importance of hearing and obeying, S. 3:1; N. 3:3; G. 3:1), dogmatically proclaim the distinction between ἀλήθεια and πλάνη and between the two corresponding πνεύματα (Jud. 20:1, 3 vl.; cf. also A. 5:4; Jos. 1:3). The ἄρχων τῆς πλάνης brings about τυφλοῦν (Jud. 19:4) and thus hinders sight. The κόσμος, then, is characterised by its subjection to the πλάνη of transgressions of the commandment (Iss. 4:6). Important in this connection is the strong predominance of πλάνη over πλανᾶσθαι (25:8) in Test. XII; the relation is the direct opposite in LXX.

In the Manual the seduction of men by Beliyaal (→ 238, 39-44) takes place against the background of the difference between the sons of light (1:9; 2:16; 3:13 and 25) and the sons of darkness (1, 10). Everything is dominated by the antithesis between light (3:3, 7, 19, 20, 25; 4:8; 10:1; 11:3, 5) and darkness (2:7; 3:3, 19, 21, 25; 4:11, 13; 10:2; 11:10), with such synonyms as certainty-obduracy, 3:19. [57]

In the Mandaean texts the error and confusion of this world are mentioned along with Satan, idols and images (Lidz. Ginza R., 16, 28 f.), Tibil (the world), and the works of seducers (280, 26 f.). This helps to brings out the central significance [58] of light, life, kusta (truth) and their antitheses.

Similarly truth and seduction are personified opponents in O. Sol. (38:4-7, 15). The way of error is the sphere of corruptibility and mortality (15:6), of folly, ignorance and vanity (11:10), in which God has no part (3:10; 18:10) and from which man is snatched in the ascent of the soul (15:6; 38:1).

The most explicit development of this dualism is in the Hermetic writings. The θεῖα cannot and will not πλανᾶσθαι (= ἁμαρτάνειν, Scott, I, 420), like men who are constituted of κακὴ ὕλη. The man who dashes aside his immortality and loves his body in πλάνη remains with his πλανᾶσθαι ἐν τῷ σκότει, in the world of the senses (cf. ἡ τοῦ κόσμου ἀπάτη, Corp. Herm., 13, 1), in the sphere of death (1, 19). The συνοδεύσαντες τῇ πλάνῃ καὶ συγκοινωνήσαντες τῇ ἀγνοίᾳ are summoned by the deified mystagogue (though we do not find the imp. μὴ πλανῶ, μὴ πλανᾶσθε): ἀπαλλάγητε τοῦ σκοτεινοῦ φωτός, μεταλάβετε τῆς ἀθανασίας, καταλείψαντες τὴν φθοράν (1, 28). Hostility against the σῶμα and its αἰσθήσεις (1, 24) is typical. The ὕλη character of the σῶμα conceals from man insight into his fallen being. This failure to see his situation is the true evil in the πλάνη of man, 6, 3b. [59] Because this πλάνη is τόλμα in the strict sense, par. to ἀνάγκη, εἱμαρμένη and ἄγνοια, it must be distinguished from ἀσέβεια; it involves no responsibility and will not be punished by the gods, 16, 11. Later Jewish (Test. XII) and Mandaean texts, even where they opened the door to dualism, did not draw this conclusion; at the most we find only occasional cautious hints, → 236, n. 41.

Finally, the soul of the Naassene Hymn, which wanders hopelessly in the labyrinth of the world, is plainly entangled in the antitheses of νοῦς and χάος, of φῶς and ἐλεεινά;

---

[56] Cf. Bousset-Gressm., 253 and the absence of dualism in 4 Esr. and S. Bar.; the Rabb., too, do not speak dualistically.

[57] On dualism in the other Qumran texts cf. K. G. Kuhn, "Die in Pal. gefundenen hbr. Texte," ZThK, 47 (1950), 197-199. As compared with the Scrolls dualism is far less prominent in Damasc. (→ 239, 1-4). There is no antithesis of light and darkness at all.

[58] Cf. the index to Lidz. Ginza.

[59] With Scott (II, 177) I regard ἡ γαστριμαργία as an ascetic gloss.

the fact that its wandering is a cosmic destiny is indicated by the comparison with the hind, Hipp. Ref., V, 10.

3. The Eschatological Use.

a. The *eschata* cause confusion both for the stars (Eth. En. 80:6; 4 Esr. 5:5) and for men. These are led into the error of idolatry (Eth. En. 80:7), into spiritual confusion and terror (S. Bar. 70:2). Reports, rumours and fantasies are spread abroad (S. Bar. 48:34). Peoples and their leaders are brought into confusion (4 Esr. 5:5; 9:3). There will be ἐπὶ τῇ συντελείᾳ τῶν αἰώνων πλανῶντες τὸν 'Ισραήλ (Test. L. 10:2), who acc. to the Chr. glossator refer to the Jewish rejection of Christ. This πλανᾶσθαι lasts 70 weeks (Test. L. 16:1). In the last time, which is now present, lying prophets see and babble abroad error (Hod.). [60] In Damasc., too, the last time in which the community lives (1:12) brings seduction and visitation (5:20; 7:21; 19:10), though the teacher of righteousness also comes at the end of the days (6:11). Deceivers come when the times move on to the end (Ass. Mos. 7:4, 1). The eschatological πλανᾶν practised by Beliar in Sib., III, 68 seems to be a Chr. addition [61] and not pre-Christian, [62] but it is an established eschatological theme. The seduction is by mythically conceived metaphysical powers (→ 238, 10 ff.), but these can be depicted as antichrist coming in human form. [63] The ψευδοπροφήτης (also plur.) is a similar eschatological figure. We do not yet find the false prophet in LXX (Zech. 13:2; Jer. 6:13) or Philo (Spec. Leg., IV, 51); ψεῦδος is simply combined with πλανᾶν (→ 234, 20 f.). On the other hand the Qumran texts combine the נביאי כזב, the אנשי מרמה, the מליצי רמיה (Hod., IV, 16. 20. 7) [64] and the מטיף הכזב (Hab. Midr., X, 9) [65] with תעות. Joseph. is obviously familiar with the theme. He practically never uses the group however (apart from Bell., 2, 259 : πλάνοι γὰρ ἄνθρωποι καὶ ἀπατεῶνες) but employs ἀπατᾶν and εἰς ἀπόστασιν ἀπάγειν when he describes the instigation to political revolt by Judas the Galilean (Ant., 18, 4 ff.; Bell., 2, 118), or Theudas (Ant., 20, 97) or the Egyptian (Ant., 20, 167-172; Bell., 2, 261), or to persist in the last battle for Jerusalem by the ψευδοπροφήτης and other προφῆται (Bell., 6, 285). The means by which the pseudo-prophets practise their politically and theocratically coloured seduction in Joseph. are winning speech (Ant., 18, 4 ff.; Bell., 2, 118; Ant., 10, 111) and the promise of saving miracles (Ant., 20, 97 and 170; Bell., 2, 261), which are called σημεῖα (Bell., 6, 285) or τέρατα καὶ σημεῖα (Ant., 20, 168). Seducing miracles (cf. Dt. 13:2 f. → 234, 24 f.) are part of the apocalyptic theme (cf. Sib., Asc. Is., Mandaean writings → 238, 29-32; 239, 17 ff.). In the Rabb. there is only a weak continuation of this line of eschatologically caused confusion. [66]

b. The *eschata* bring error to an end. The LXX (→ 236, 16 f.) had already introduced this theme. The fallen angels, Azazel and his hosts who seduce men (Eth. En. 19:1; 54:6; 64:2; 69:27), the πνεύματα τῆς πλάνης καὶ τοῦ Βελίαρ (Test. S. 6:6; L. 3:3; Zeb. 9:8 vl.), the *homines dolosi* (Ass. Mos. 7:4), Zabulus (Ass. Mos. 10:1) will be eschatologically punished and eliminated. In the *eschaton* the Gentiles will see and admit that their idolatry is transgression : ἡμεῖς δ' ἀθανάτοιο τρίβου πεπλανημένοι εἰμέν (Sib., III, 721). καὶ οὐκ ἔσται ἐκεῖ πνεῦμα πλάνης τοῦ Βελίαρ (Test. Jud. 25:3 vl.; cf. Jub. 50:5; 23:29). There is only a weak echo of these ideas in the Rabb. [67] Only very

---

[60] Cf. → n. 50 and Kuhn, *op. cit.* (→ n. 57), 208 f.

[61] Cf. Kautzsch Apokr. u. Pseudepigr., II, 182; Hennecke, 402; J. Geffcken, *ad loc.* in *Handbuch z. den nt.lichen Apkr.*, ed. E. Hennecke (1904); W. Schmid-O. Stählin, *Gesch. d. Griech. Lit.*, II, 1[6] (1920), 613 f.

[62] Schürer, III, 440 f. maintains that it is.

[63] Bousset-Gressm., 254-256; Dib. Th., 47-51.

[64] Sukenik, *op. cit.*

[65] I owe the last two refs. to K. G. Kuhn.

[66] Str.-B., IV, 981-986.

[67] *Ibid.*, 914 f.

formally may this eschatological elimination of πλάνη be compared with that in the Hermetica (Ascl., III, 26a [Scott, I, 344]), with the Stoically influenced abolition of ἀταξία, πλάνη and κακία by the δημιουργός, and with the associated restoration of the original world.

D. The Word Group in the New Testament.

The use of the group in the NT is characterised first by a confluence of classical-Hellenistic and LXX usage with that of the dualistic apocalyptic texts. The predominance of one or several types in this mixture varies in each individual instance. The decisive point, however, is that the terminology with its different emphases is always more or less controlled by the core of the NT, the Christ event.

I. Non-Transferred or Semi-Transferred.

1. In the lit. sense the NT uses only the mid-pass. πλανάομαι at Hb. 11:38. This usage corresponds to secular (→ 229, 11-14) and LXX usage (→ 234, 6 ff.). The content denoted by the verb, the loss of a permanent dwelling for God's sake, is familiar in the OT and Jewish tradition, though the word group is not used for it there. [68, 69] As the whole of c. 11 is based on this tradition, so also 11:38 carries an allusion to it : "They wandered in deserts, and in mountains, and in dens and caves of the earth." [70] Through their πλανᾶσθαι these πρεσβύτεροι make it plain what πίστις is : ἐλπιζομένων ὑπόστασις and πραγμάτων ἔλεγχος οὐ βλεπομένων, Hb. 11:1 f.

2. Borrowing from the LXX (→ 235, 3 ff.) Mt. 18:12 f. speaks of the πλανᾶσθαι of the sheep. Lk.'s depiction is similar, except that he speaks of the losing of the sheep, or of its being lost, [71] rather than of its πλανᾶσθαι. The expression in Mt. disengages πλανᾶσθαι from a purely literal sense. The reference of the straying of the sheep is originally to the backsliding of the hearers or the unrighteous, though later it applies to members of the community too. This wandering is culpable (the Lucan par. rightly has ἁμαρτωλός, 15:7), and it is brought to an end by the act of Jesus or by the proclamation of the community in the name of the exalted Lord.

3. The same LXX metaphor (→ 235, 3 ff.) of the straying sheep occurs in 1 Pt. 2:25. The first person plur. of the aor. of Is. 53:6 is replaced in this para-

---

[68] Ps. Sol. 17:17 is an exception.

[69] Cf. for David 1 Βασ. 24:1 f.; Jos. Ant., 6, 247; for the prophets in the time of Ahab, 3 Βασ. 18:4, 13; 19:4, 8; for the righteous in the days of the Maccabees, 1 Macc. 2:29 ff.; 2 Macc. 5:27; 6:11; 10:6; Jos. Ant., 12, 271 f.

[70] Wnd. Hb., ad loc.; E. Käsemann, Das wandernde Gottesvolk (1939), 117 f.: One might well think in terms of a fixed Jewish tradition, since the author does not give a concluding Chr. example.

[71] Hence the form of the parable in Mt. is probably older than that of Lk. On the other hand, the expression in Mt. 18:10, 14, which relates the parable to the μικροί of the community who are not to be despised, seems to be quite clearly the work of the community ; the original ref. to the ἁμαρτωλοί who need to be converted is better preserved in Lk., Bultmann Trad., 184 f. In view of the later Jewish mode of speech (for 1:100 cf. Str.-B., I, 784 f.) and the high evaluation of the penitent sinner as compared with later Judaism, which was not uniform on this pt. (Str.-B., II, 210-212), it is probable that an original saying of Jesus underlies the text. There is no means of determining whether this original form of the parable was aimed polemically at the religious assurance of later Judaism or directed to sinners as an invitation, Bultmann Trad., 216.

phrase by the part. πλανώμενοι with a preceding ἦτε, [72] whereby the state is underlined as well as the fact that it is past. To be a Christian is to have left behind the time of straying (→ IV, 1117, n. 67) and to have returned to the Shepherd and Overseer (→ I, 686, 8 ff.; II, 615, 18 ff.) of souls ; there is also an allusion here to the metaphor of the sheep without a shepherd. [73] The masc. form [74] makes it plain that the reference is to the straying of men in the pre-Christian period, not to the wandering of sheep. More strongly than in the LXX version (→ 235, 3 ff.), the straying is culpable here. It is no longer a pitiable state. Straying and returning are parallel to ἁμαρτίαι and δικαιοσύνη in 1 Pt. 2:24.

II. Transferred.

The transf. use in the NT does not denote purely epistemological straying or being led astray ; there is only an occasional (→ 250, 23 ff.) echo of this. In the main the categories are religious.

1. The OT and Later Jewish Use.

In R. 1:27 the Gentile fall from God is equated with the deifying of the creature and with idolatry; the content of the πλάνη of 1:27 is described in 1:21-23. The later LXX view is very obviously the background here, → 235, 32 ff. It is already erased, however, when the previous wandering in paganism (ἦμεν) no longer refers specifically to idolatry but is set it in the framework of a list of vices (Tt. 3:3), or when πλάνη in the absolute denotes Gentile immorality (as in 2 Pt. 2:18); dualistic influences, mediated through Hellenistic Judaism, may be discerned here. [75] A familiar primitive Christian theme is expressed in this whole characterisation of earlier paganism as apostasy. [76]

More along the lines of the OT understanding of the group are those expressions which have in view, not pagans, but the backsliding of Christians (→ 235, 10 ff.; 235, 17 f.). In Hb. 3:10 these are warned in an almost literal quotation from ψ 94:7-11 not to be guilty of ἀεὶ πλανᾶσθαι τῇ καρδίᾳ, which in wholly OT terms (→ 235, 9 f.) is interpreted in 3:12 as ἀποστῆναι ἀπὸ θεοῦ ζῶντος. Christians are expressly included (Hb. 4:15; 2:17) when in 5:2 men are called πλανώμενοι, and the parallel term ἀγνοοῦντες makes it clear that the reference is to the familiar OT (→ 235, 27 f.) sins of weakness and ignorance for which atonement may be made, though rational-Stoic terminology also plays some part, → n. 38. In the present Christian version of Jm. a Christian brother who falls into πλανᾶσθαι and the πλάνη ὁδοῦ αὐτοῦ can be called a ἁμαρτωλός, 5:19 f. The combination with ὁδός and ἐπιστρέφειν (→ V, 86, 2 ff.; → 236, 9-12) points to the OT background, while the combination with ἀλήθεια [77] indicates the later Jewish background → I, 244, 7 ff. There is as yet no specifically Christian form of straying.

Nor does πλανᾶσθαι go beyond the later Jewish framework in relation to the question of the Sadducees in Mk. 12:24, 27 and Mt. 22:29. Lk. again leaves the

---

[72] Cf. R. 6:17; v. Bl.-Debr. § 327.

[73] Cf. Ez. 34:5 etc.

[74] The attributive form πλανώμενα is a koine assimilation.

[75] Cf. the content of πλάνη in Test. XII → 238, 20-28.

[76] Cf. Dib. Past. on Tt. 3:3.

[77] The vl. ἀπὸ τῆς ὁδοῦ τῆς ἀληθείας combines both ideas (Jm. 5:19).

word out, → 242, 23 f. Since the διὰ τοῦτο of Mk. might refer either to what precedes [78] or to what follows, [79] it is uncertain whether ignorance of the Scriptures and the power of God describes or underlies the πλανᾶσθαι. On the other hand, the content of what is rejected with πλανᾶσθαι is unambiguous. It is the understanding of the resurrection as a continuation of the mode of life on earth, or, as Lk. formulates it, a failure to differentiate between the two aeons. [80]

> In this connection it is important to realise that the antithesis between a spiritual understanding of the resurrection and the materialistic belief propounded in the story of the Sadducees is found in precisely this form on the soil of later Judaism. [81] The argument of Jesus for the fact of the resurrection corresponds to, rather than christologically precedes, Rabbinic exegesis. [82] As in the LXX the error of πλανᾶσθαι [83] is understood critically in a non-intellectual, religious sense. As regards the content of belief in the resurrection, it certainly goes beyond the LXX, but not beyond what is found in apocalyptic and Rabb. texts.

2. The Stoic Use of μὴ πλανᾶσθε.

Though addressed to Christians as a warning, the μὴ πλανᾶσθε of the NT (1 C. 6:9; Gl. 6:7; Jm. 1:16; 1 C. 15:33) does not contain any specifically Christian content. Its formal roots are to be found, not in the LXX, which does not use the plural imperative in the sense "do not err" (→ 235, 21 f.), but in the Stoic diatribe. [84] It has almost the value of an interjection, [85] and can serve as a transition, as in Jm. 1:16. [86] It always precedes that to which it refers. In the vocabulary of later Judaism, [87] Christians are warned against the dangerous error of not recognising the penal severity of God. In 1 C. 6:9 the expression introduces a list of vices, [88] which comes from the tradition of Hellenistic Judaism. The μὴ πλανᾶσθε [89] of Gl. 6:7, possibly quoting a proverbial saying, [90] warns against the idea that God can be mocked. The μὴ πλανᾶσθε of Jm. 1:16, in what is probably another quotation, [91] contests, according to the literal wording of the hexameter,

---

[78] Wellh. Mk. and Kl. Mk., ad loc.; probably also syr sin in A. Merx, "Die Ev. des Mk. u. Lk.," Die vier Ev. nach ihrem ältesten bekannten Texte, II, 2 (1905), ad loc.

[79] The usual view.

[80] Whether a traditional saying of the earthly Jesus underlies the incident (Loh. Mk., ad loc.) or whether there is a reflection here of the debates between primitive Christianity and Judaism (Bultmann Trad., 25), it is impossible to say for certain (Bultmann Trad., 51 f.), nor is it of any great significance.

[81] Str.-B., I, 888-891; III, 473 f.; IV, 890 f.; 1132 f.; Bousset-Gressm., 274-277; → I, 369, 35-370, 20.

[82] Str.-B., I, 893-895.

[83] There is no Heb. or Aram. equivalent in the relevant Rabb. disputes. Cf. Gn. r., 14 (10c) (Str.-B., III, 473); Ab. R. Nat., 5 (Str.-B., IV, 343); Sanh., 90b (Str.-B., I, 893); Tanch., 3a (Str.-B., I, 885).

[84] → 231, 15 f.; cf. Ltzm. K. on 1 C. 6:9.

[85] Ltzm. Gl. on Gl. 6:7.

[86] Dib. Jk., 95; A. Meyer, Das Rätsel des Jk. (1930), 175.

[87] Cf. only 2 Macc. 7:18.

[88] Only here, not in the lists in Gl. 5:19; Col. 3:5; Eph. 5:5; hence the term is not an integral part of the list itself.

[89] The changing of the warning into a statement by the omission of μή in one part of the vetus latina and in Marcion is undoubtedly an emendation in view of the stereotyped character of the expression.

[90] Ltzm. Gl. on 6:7.

[91] Dib., Wnd. Jk., ad loc.

the view that any good gifts might not come from God, though according to the context, in partial dissent from the OT [92] but in harmony with Hellenistic Judaism, [93] it rejects as pernicious the idea that God might send a bad thing like temptation, → 29, 16 ff. An open question at 1 C. 15:33 is whether the expression should be rendered in the usual sense "do not err." The quotation which is again annexed hereto is a formal argument in favour of this (→ V, 855, 30 f.), and the warning expressed against contesting the resurrection or not perceiving retribution offers material support. If, on the other hand, we adopt the passive "be not deceived," [94] then here, as in Test. G. 3:1 (→ 238, 21 f.), the reference to the repudiation of idolatry in the one OT instance of μὴ πλανᾶσθε (→ 235, 21 f.) is replaced by a dualistic-Gnostic background (ἐκνήφειν, ἀγνωσία θεοῦ, → I, 118, 19 ff.). He who falls victim to seduction is betrayed into ἁμαρτάνειν and therewith into a situation which does not befit a Christian, 1 C. 15:34. The difference between the two renderings is not of fundamental significance, for the translation "do not err" is also a warning, not against theoretical self-deception, but against guilt.

3. The Dualistic Use.

When in the NT the word group is linked centrally with a Christian content, the usage displays the three characteristics already mentioned above (→ 236, 24-35): dualism, ungodly powers which lead astray, and eschatology. Hardly any one of these is found alone ; they are mostly combined. In particular, eschatology controls the statements.

a. In Eph. 4:14 πλάνη is related in a new way to the Christ event. Its opposite is growth into Christ as the κεφαλή of the σῶμα, [95] or the growth of the whole body into Him. [96] This comes about through the pursuit of truth (i.e., true faith) [97] in love. Error, on the other hand, is marked by craftiness (μεθοδεία, Eph. 4:14 → V, 102 f.), at which (πρός, Eph. 4:14) men insidiously (κυβεία, πανουργία, Eph. 4:14) aim, and by fickleness (κλυδωνιζόμενοι καὶ περιφερόμενοι παντὶ ἀνέμῳ τῆς διδασκαλίας), against which Christians (ὦμεν, Eph. 4:14) must be urgently warned. The dualism [98] of πλάνη and ἀλήθεια, [99] to which attention has been drawn already (→ 239, 41-241, 2), is quite plain here ; at the same time, the use of κυβεία [100] and μεθοδεία [101] indicates the share of ungodly powers in this πλάνη.

b. It is not surprising to find a dualistic background [102] for the use of the word group in 1 John. πλανᾶν and πλάνη are not of the ἀλήθεια (1:8; 4:6). They take place in the sphere of ἀλήθεια and ψεῦδος (2:21 f., 27), of φῶς and σκοτία

---

92 → πειράζω and → 234, 33 ff.
93 Wnd. Jk., ad loc.; to the instances from Philo add Leg. All., III, 180.
94 Vg nolite seduci ; so also Joh. W. 1 K., ad loc. and Pr.-Bauer, s.v.
95 αὐξάνειν thus in Dib. Gefbr.³, ad loc. and Pr.-Bauer, s.v.
96 So H. Schlier, Christus u. d. Kirche im Eph. (1930), 70-72.
97 Dib. Gefbr.³, ad loc. and → I, 251, 6 f.
98 So also 1 C. 15:33; → lines 8-13.
99 Dib. Gefbr.³, ad loc.
100 For the demonological background cf. loc. cit.
101 Cf. Eph. 6:11 and the addition of Cod. A in Eph. 4:14.
102 In interpretation → I, 245, 1-247, 29.

(1:5-7; 2:11), of θάνατος and ζωή (3:14), and do not belong intrinsically to the community (2:19). Error is the opposite of ἀλήθεια, the divine reality. The πλανῶντες or false teachers (2:26; 3:7) and the Christians who echo their words (1:8) either dispute the presence of sin in the Christian and the need for a life in forgiveness (1:8 f.) or in antinomian fashion they make light of the significance of the ποιεῖν of δικαιοσύνη and ἁμαρτία for the Christian (3:7). This practical reference is not abandoned even when the group is centrally linked to Christology, i.e., when the false teachers deny that Jesus is the Christ (2:22, 26) or when the spirit of error or the seducers (πλάνοι, 2 Jn. 7) oppose docetically the confession of the incarnation of Jesus Christ, the confession of Jesus (4:2, 3, 6; 2 Jn. 7). [103] The test proposed for these false teachers, listening to the preaching of the community (4:6) and the abiding of the traditional proclamation in Christians (2:24), brings out in both instances the ultimately practical character of the error, → I, 247, 13-16. This πλανᾶν is practised by men (2:26; 3:7); indeed, it may be directed by Christians against themselves (1:8). But these false teachers [104] are metaphysical figures (ἀντίχριστοι, 2:18; ὁ πλάνος, ὁ ἀντίχριστος 2 Jn. 7). The demonic power of the κόσμος (4:4), the διάβολος (3:8), the πνεῦμα τῆς πλάνης (4:6), to which the πνεῦμα τῆς ἀληθείας is opposed, work in them. The seducing powers known to us from Gnostic usage (→ 238, 11 ff.) are here mentioned explicitly by name. This error constitutes a danger for Christians against which they must be warned, 3:7; 1:8. In the last resort, however, they are proof against it, since they are of God (4:4), have the Spirit, and know the truth (2:20 f., 27). The πλανῶντες of 2:26 are thus to be understood as those who wish to deceive. These seducing powers are apocalyptic figures (→ 241, 13-34). The false teachers rise up in the ἐσχάτη ὥρα (2:18) and bear the name of the great apocalyptic adversary [105] (2:18; 2 Jn. 7). The plural in 2:18, however, shows that these figures which are apocalyptic by derivation have taken historical form, and have thus become false teachers, → 249, 12 ff.

4. The Eschatological Use.

a. As in general, so for the word group the background of the Synoptic Apocalypse is unequivocally that of later Jewish apocalyptic. πλανᾶν is practised by a τις (Mk. 13:5; Mt. 24:4), the πολλοί (Mk. 13:6; Mt. 24:5), the ψευδόχριστοι [106] and ψευδοπροφῆται (Mk. 13:22; [107] Mt. 24:11, 24; in Mt. 24:24 there is textual vacillation between the act. and pass.); these represent, not two categories, but one and the same category of men. [108] ψευδοπροφήτης has been found in apocalyptic-dualistic texts, and ψευδόχριστος may be conjectured. [109] Here again Lk. (→ 242, 23 f.; 243, 40 f.) avoids the group except that in 21:8 he has the pass. for the act. of Mk. and Mt.

---

[103] On the text of 4:3, the nature of the false teachers and the eschatological or non-eschatological meaning of ἐρχόμενον (2 Jn. 7) v. Wnd. J., ad loc. and H. Braun, "Literaranalyse u. theol. Schichtung im 1 J," ZThK, 48 (1951), 287-292; on πλάνος as noun → 233, 17-23.

[104] Wnd. Kath. Br.³ on 1 Jn. 4:3 and app.

[105] The use of capitals, which is considered by Wnd. (Kath. Br. on 2 Jn. 7), would emphasise the fact that a name is used.

[106] The absence of this from the Western text of Mk. 13:22 is probably secondary.

[107] In Mk. 13:22 the compound ἀποπλανάω, → 230, 21 ff. and 235, 32 ff.

[108] Kl. Mk., ad loc.

[109] → 241, 14-34. Lohmeyer's conjecture (Mk. on 13:23) that ψευδόχριστος is an analogous Chr. construct is not very likely.

The means of seduction used by these apoc. figures are also traditional. [110] The false prophets proclaim that they are eschatological deliverers (Mk. 13:6; Mt. 24:5; [111] the claim is implied by the ψευδόχριστοι of Mk. 13:22; Mt. 24:24); they do signs and wonders (Mk. 13:22; Mt. 24:24, borrowing from Da. 13:2, [112] refers to the giving of signs, and also calls them "great").

The objects of seduction are the πολλοί (Mk. 13:6; Mt. 24:5, 11). Those addressed, however, are also to take care lest they be led astray (Mk. 13:5; Mt. 24:4; Lk. 21:8). This is a possibility even for the ἐκλεκτοί (Mk. 13:22 speaks of this more weakly than Mt. 24:24 → III, 824, 6). The seducing of the Gentile world (cf. simply the refs. from the visionary discourses of Eth. En. → 238, 12-14), the term ἐκλεκτοί (→ IV, 183, 45 ff.), and the fact that the ἐκλεκτοί can be led astray [113] are all part of the later Jewish apoc. framework.

As concerns the πλανάω words the apoc. tradition is christianised by the fact that they are used after the introductory observation by Jesus (Mk. 13:5 and par.) and that the deceivers appeal to Christ (Mk. 13:6). The very expression ἐπὶ τῷ ὀνόματί μου (Mk. 13:6) shows, however, that disparate elements have been brought together here. The pseudo-christs of later Jewish tradition say ἐγώ εἰμι without any appeal to Jesus, while Chr. pseudo-prophets appeal to the sayings of Jesus without raising any claim to be the Christ. [114] Later Jewish apoc. materials, with small additions, have thus been made into sayings of Jesus. That the earthly Jesus Himself did this is hardly likely, and it is not essential. [115] The literary process is simply to be noted, though there is debate [116] as to the degree of fixity in the Jewish tradition and the boundary between this and the refashioning which took place when it was put into Chr. service or when the Evangelists finally edited it. In Mt. 24:11 — 24:10-12 is an interpolation of Mt. who distributes the materials differently [117] — it is hard to say whether we have genuine Jewish tradition or Jewish tradition which has been subjected to Chr. revision. When Christianity took over the apoc. tradition, an obvious shift in sense took place. The false prophets now lead away from Jesus, the false christs stand opposed to the Messiah Jesus, and the ὑμεῖς who are addressed are members of the community.

b. The same later Jewish apocalyptic background as in Mk. 13 and par. lies behind the πλανάω passages in Rev. (mostly active, only once passive). The only difference here is that there are now two distinctive features. The first is that the seducing powers are presented in strongly mythical garb, the second that except in 2:20 they always seek to seduce the world rather than Christians.

Seduction is an attribute of the great dragon, the ancient serpent, who is called the devil and Satan (Rev. 12:9). His name, his work as the seducer, his mythical destiny, his fall from heaven (12:9), his provisional chaining (20:3), his new release (20:8) and his final destruction (20:10) are all taken from the world of apocalyptic myth. [118] So,

---

[110] → 241, 28-34. On the Gnostic version of seduction by imitation c. O. Sol. 38:9 f. → 238, 28-31.

[111] Mt. correctly interprets the ἐγώ εἰμι of Mk. as ἐγώ εἰμι ὁ Χριστός.

[112] For the change of content in the error cf. → 234, 20-23 with 241, 24-30.

[113] Cf. Sib., III, 68 → 238, 29 f., cf. the need for warning in face of the cunning of the homines dolosi in Ass. Mos. → 241, 13 f., 38 f.; also the urgency of exhortation even to elect members of the community of the new covenant, → 239, 1 ff.; 241, 11 f.

[114] Cf. Wellh., Kl., Loh. Mk. on Mk. 13:6.

[115] J. Schniewind, Das Ev. nach Mk. (NT Deutsch, I) on Mk. 13.

[116] Apart from the comm. cf. Bultmann Trad., 129, 133; E. Hirsch, Frühgeschichte des Ev., I (1941), 140.

[117] V. the Synopsis.

[118] → 238, 11 ff. and 241, 3 ff., esp. 239, 14-16; → II, 75-81; 281-283; Bousset-Gressm., 251-256, 286-289; Loh. Apk. on 12:3, 9; Dib. Th., 47-51.

too, is his equation with the serpent of the fall [119] (12:9), whereby πλανᾶν is at least indirectly substituted for the customary ἀπατᾶν of the fall story, → I, 384, 29. There seems to be no significance in the fact that in apoc. texts which, like Rev. 20:8 f., speak of the final attack of the heathen on Jerusalem, [120] πλανᾶν is not used. [121]

The second beast (→ III, 135), a mythical entity, [122] which the divine interprets in terms of the apoc. theme (→ 241, 13-34) of the false prophet (16:3; 19:20; 20:10), practises seduction (13:14). This seducing prophet accompanies antichrist, the first beast, or the beast, and with him he comes to a suitable apoc. end (→ 241, 35 ff.) in battle against the Rider on the white horse and His army (19:20). Here the Chr. content controls the existing apoc. form. The divine takes the keenest interest in the destruction of this seducing opponent. [123]

Among the seducing powers in Rev. there is thirdly Babylon the Great (18:23, here pass.). This secret name for Rome, found also in Sib. and the Rabb., has an apoc. impress, [124] but this is the only instance in which πλανᾶν is used of Babylon (18:23). [125]

In Rev., as in one part of apocalyptic, [126] the seduction of these powers is directed exclusively against the Gentiles : [127] οἰκουμένη ὅλη 12:9; οἱ κατοικοῦντες ἐπὶ τῆς γῆς, 13:14; οἱ λαβόντες τὸ χάραγμα τοῦ θηρίου καὶ οἱ προσκυνοῦντες τῇ εἰκόνι αὐτοῦ, 19:20; πάντα τὰ ἔθνη, 18:23; τὰ ἔθνη, 20:3, 8 = αὐτοί 20:10. The community is not affected by this πλανᾶν. The persecution of the community by the dragon (12:17), by the beast and the false prophet (13:15-17), and by Babylon (17:6; 18:24; 19:2) is not regarded as πλανᾶν. The goal of the seduction is not specified in the case of the dragon ; this accords with the stereotyped character of the idea (12:9; 20:3, 8, 10). In the case of Babylon it is πορνεία (18:3) and in that of the beast and his pseudo-prophet it is the setting up of an εἰκών for the beast and the προσκυνεῖν of this εἰκών (13:14 f.). These are all OT (→ 234, 20 ff.) and later Jewish apoc. (→ 238, 11 ff.) motifs, which here again do not denote the cult of Baal or pagan idolatry in general but the religious and cultic worship of antichrist whose refusal means boycotting and death, 13:15-17. The monstrous and world-wide character of the antichristianity to which the seduction leads arouses the wrath and abhorrence of the seer, and hence the heaping up of synonyms in 12:9. [128]

The means of seduction are the traditional ones when they are not omitted as self-evident (12:9; 20:3, 10). The dragon incites the Gentiles (Gog and Magog, → I, 789-791) to a final assault on Jerusalem (20:8 f. → lines 2-4). The false prophets performs miracles as in apoc. (→ 241, 28-34), cf. 13:13 f.: the miracle of Elijah ; 19:20; he does them ἐνώπιον τοῦ θηρίου (13:14; 19:20), thus pointing esp. to antichrist as the counterpart to Christ (→ III, 134, 23 ff.; → n. 110). The sorcery wherewith Babylon led astray (18:23) also derives from the OT [129] and already perhaps it had become a fixed element

---

[119] For seduction by powers at the fall cf. Eth. En. 69:6; Kyriakos Prayer, → 239, 14-16.
[120] Ez. 38 f.; Eth. En. 56:5-8; 4 Esr. 13.
[121] But v. Est. 1:1d-1k.
[122] Cf. Loh. Apk. on 13:11.
[123] Ibid., on 20:1-3.
[124] → I, 514-517; Str.-B., III, 816.
[125] Rightly, then, Babylon is not included in the historical review of seducing powers → 238, 11 ff. and 241, 4 ff.
[126] Eth. En., Jub. and 4 Esr. → 238, 11-14; 238, 33-36; 241, 4-7.
[127] Cf. the πολλοί of the little Syn. apocalypse, → 241, 5-10.
[128] Cf. Loh. Apk. on 12:9.
[129] Is. 47:12 Babylon, Nah. 3:4 Nineveh, in neither case πλανάω.

in apoc. [130] All these weapons were used in the eschatological war which antichrist waged against Christ for the world.

c. The expression "power of error" in 2 Th. 2:11 unites all the motifs which we have come to recognise as traditional apoc. themes. [131] All the phenomena mentioned in 2 Th. 2:3-10 [132] constitute the suprahuman efficacy (ἐνέργεια) of eschatological error. At two pts., however, the situation has changed in comparison with the Chr. apoc. considered thus far. The whole tradition of eschatological πλάνη, and hence esp. the section on κατέχων (→ II, 829, 38 ff.), is introduced in order to contest the immediate proximity of the *parousia* (2:2). So, then, God sends this πλάνη to unbelievers as a punishment for disobedience (2:10-12). In its effect apocalyptic is here used for the purpose of de-eschatologising and moralising. [133]

5. The Rationalising and Moralising Use.

a. In 2 Th. 2:11 πλάνη still has an eschatological content even though it is used in the interests of de-eschatologising. This passage is a connecting link in the development of the history of the term. The delusions and seducers of the last time now become the false teachers — mainly Gnostic — who threaten the Church of the present. In a process of rationalising and moralising eschatological apostasy from the faith becomes backsliding into error.

b. The Pastoral Epistles formulate in 1 Tm. 4:1 a reconstructed doctrine which is presented as Christian prophecy and which, without the πλανάω group, may be applied generally (2 Tm. 3:1; 4:3; 2 Pt. 2:1; 3:3; Jd. 18) to the apostates of future and final [134] ages who follow seducing spirits (πλάνος as an adj. is here used in an act. sense, → 233, 12 ff.) and doctrines of devils. These false teachers (no longer false prophets), who are typically [135] called "deceived deceivers" in 2 Tm. 3:13 in adoption of a contemporary proverb, [136] πλανῶντες καὶ πλανώμενοι, along with other moral aspersions (hypocrisy in 1 Tm. 4:2; sorcery, 2 Tm. 3:13), commend to the community (no longer the world or pagans, → 247, 30 ff.) an ascetic-Gnostic spiritualism [137] (no longer a pseudo- or anti-messiah, → 246, 30 f.) which is at odds with rational teaching [138] (1 Tm. 4:3-6; 2 Tm. 4:3). Immorality in general, e.g., avarice, [139] is apostasy from the faith (ἀποπλανᾶσθαι ἀπὸ τῆς πίστεως, [140] 1 Tm. 6:10). Apostasy here is no longer from God as in the OT

---

[130] Sib., V, 165; the proximity of πλάνος and μάγος in Vett. Val., → 233, 22 f.

[131] Proof of the historical derivation of individual traits is not repeated here ; it may be gathered from what was said earlier, esp. in our analysis of the word group in the little apoc. of the Synoptists and in Rev., → 246, 30 ff.

[132] For details cf. Dib. Th., *ad loc.*

[133] This is used as an argument against Pauline authorship, cf. H. Braun, "Zur nachpaul. Herkunft d. 2 Th.," ZNW, 44 (1952/53), 152-156.

[134] The choice of words pts. to the fictional nature of the eschatological terminology, cf. Dib. Past., *ad loc.*; Pr.-Bauer, *s.v.* ὕστερος.

[135] Dib. Past. Exc. on 1 Tm. 2:2 and 3:1.

[136] → 230, 30 f.; cf. Dib. Past., *ad loc.*

[137] Dib. Past. Exc. on 1 Tm. 4:5.

[138] *Ibid.* Exc. on 1 Tm. 1:10.

[139] Also a rational theme deriving from the diatribe and Hell. Jew. exhortation, *v.* Dib. Past., *ad loc.*

[140] On ἀπό cf. Jm. 5:19 (→ 235, 12 f.) and → 243, 33 ff.

(→ 235, 12 f.) and Hb. 3:10. Nor is it dualistically from the ἀλήθεια, → 239, 41 ff. [141] Its reference is now to πίστις rationally viewed as a new norm. [142]

c. In the use of the word group for false teachers and false teaching, OT and apocalyptic features are used in the description. At first these had a genuine eschatological reference, → 248, 25-28. Jezebel, who calls herself a prophetess (→ III, 217 f.), [143] leads astray (πλανᾷ, Rev. 2:20) by teaching the Christians in Thyatira a false doctrine which is elsewhere connected with the Nicolaitans (2:6, 14, 15). She seduces them into fornication [144] and participation in the cultic feast of paganism. [145] When we come, however, to the Gnostic and libertinistic false teachers who threaten the community in Jd. and 2 Pt., [146] use is made of the OT and later Jewish-Rabbinic (→ I, 524 f.) theme of the reward of Balaam to emphasise their avarice. [147] Jd. 11 refers to the "illusion" (πλάνη) of the reward of Balaam, [148] 2 Pt. 2:15 to the "going astray" (πλανᾶσθαι) of those who follow the way of Balaam. [149] On the other hand, the description of the same teachers in Jd. 13 as ἀστέρες πλανῆται [150] harks back to a later Jewish mythical motif (→ 239, 11-14) which is connected with Gn. 6:2 ff. The equation with the planets [151] (not comets) brings out the demonic quality of the false teachers. The community must be warned against the deception of the libertinists (ἡ τῶν ἀθέσμων πλάνη, 2 Pt. 3:17). It carries those who are threatened along with it, as the false teachers are carried away by deception in Jd. 11. It robs them of assurance, and will be overcome, as in Eph. 4:15 (→ 245, 23-26), by spiritual growth.

6. The Apostles and Christ as "Deceivers."

In 1 Th. 2:3, in the context of an apology, Paul declares that he does not preach as one who has fallen victim to "deception." [152] To the superficial view of adversaries that the apostles are "deceivers" (πλάνοι, 2 C. 6:8) [153] there is thus opposed the true if hidden fact of the reliability (ἀληθεῖς) of the apostles. They are not sorcerers like the false teachers (2 Tm. 3:13 → 249, 23-29). If the assertion

---

[141] As compared with dualistic terminology, the ref. to πίστις gives the mode of expression an independent Chr. flavour, even though the content of πίστις is already rationalised.

[142] Dib. Past. Exc. on 1 Tm. 1:5 and 2:2.

[143] Not even in the form ψευδοπροφῆτις is the title obj. conceded to her.

[144] Whether lit. in the sense of libertinism (→ I, 525, n. 11) or with a fig. ref. (cf. the OT) to pagan syncretistic trends; cf. Loh. Apk.², 29; H. Kraft, Gnostisches Gemeinschaftsleben, Diss. (1950); cf. the brief summary of the contents of this diss. in ThLZ, 75 (1950), 628.

[145] The word group πλανάω is never used of Jezebel in the LXX.

[146] For these false teachers cf. Wnd. Kath. Br.³ on 2 Pt. 2:22.

[147] The Gk. instances of the Balaam theme (Philo Vit. Mos., I, 265-300; Migr. Abr., 113-115; Jos. Ant., 4, 118-125) do not use the πλανάω group; the Rabb. do (Sanh., 106b, Str.-B., I, 1025).

[148] Unless μισθοῦ is a gen. pretii (so Pr.-Bauer, s.v. μισθός): "They have yielded to the deception of Balaam for reward."

[149] On the link with ὁδός v. Jm. 5:20 (→ 243, 33 ff.).

[150] On the term → 229, 27-32; the vl. (plur. of πλάνης) does not affect the sense.

[151] So Wnd. Kath. Br., ad loc.; cf. the figure seven (the planets) in Eth. En. (→ 239, 11-14) for the angels interpreted as stars.

[152] πλάνη here hardly in the rare act. sense (→ 232, 38 f.), v. the comm., ad loc.

[153] πλάνος in an act. sense, → 233, 13 ff.

of the resurrection of Jesus is called "the latter deception" (ἐσχάτη πλάνη, Mt. 27:64), [154] the life and teaching of Jesus, and especially His Messiahship, are indirectly called the πρώτη πλάνη, just as Jesus Himself is called a "deceiver" (πλάνος) in Mt. 27:63, and just as reference is made to His deceiving of the people in Jn. 7:12 and to the deception of the officers in Jn. 7:47. The accusation reflected in these expressions [155] applies to Jesus the later Jewish idea (→ 241, 4 ff.) of the false Messiah.

7. Summary.

The possibility which we have just mentioned, namely, that opponents might speak of the error of the apostles and Jesus, shows that the group did not become genuinely Christian even when employed in the NT. It did not penetrate to the heart of the message. The trivialising and externalising of the Torah were not πλάνη and πλανᾶσθαι for the Synoptists, nor was the rejection of the δικαιο-σύνη θεοῦ and πίστις for Paul, nor the missing of ἀλήθεια and ζωή in Jesus for the Fourth Gospel. Neither behind the temptation of Jesus nor behind His passion was there a πλανᾶν on the part of the devil or the Jews. [156] 1 Jn. is an exception, → 245, 34 ff. There is echoed here something of the necessity of error, → 231, 28 ff. The later Jewish and apocalyptic content of the word group is at first preserved in the NT. Only gradually is it combined with the Christ event, and then moralised and rationalised. In spite of an interwoven dualism, the NT, like the LXX, everywhere emphasises the culpability of error ; the tragic view (→ 232, 30 ff.) finds no place at all. The overcoming of this culpable straying, whether it be thought of as the pre-Christian state or as seduction and error which threaten the community, is provided by the eschatological work which has taken place in Jesus. Exhortation more or less explicitly appeals to this in its promises and warnings.

E. The Usage in the Early Church.

1. In the Post-Apostolic Fathers.

In the post-apostolic fathers, except in so far as the earlier texts are con-temporary with or intersect the later texts of the NT, the development of the usage continues in characteristic fashion. Individual branches of meaning (e.g., LXX, dualistic, eschatological), which are still clearly differentiated in the NT, lose their individuality to a great extent, and the use of the group extends both in subject-matter and with respect to synonyms. This extension [157] takes the form of new material and linguistic combinations.

a. New Material Combinations.

Secular deceiving (Ign. Mg., 3, 2; Phld., 7, 1; Herm. v., 2, 4, 1) goes back beyond the NT to general usage (→ 230, 20 ff.; 234, 16 ff.). Many subjects already mentioned in

---

[154] The story of the guards is told in Mt. 27:62-66; 28:12-15 to refute this ; cf. H. v. Campenhausen, "Der Ablauf d. Osterereignisse," SAH, 1952, App. 4 (1952), 26 f., 30-33.

[155] Str.-B., I, 1023; cf. → 238, 19 f.

[156] Cf. Test. L. 10:2, → 241, 7-10.

[157] No attempt is made here to study the usage of the post-apost. fathers in so far as it conforms to the NT.

the NT are now combined with the group. The refuted Gnostics are said to be seduced by the serpent (Dg., 12, 6), whereas the group is not used in, e.g., 1 C. 8:1-3. As in dualism (→ 238, 11 ff.), demons practise seduction (Test. Sol. 8:9; 15:10; [158] Just. Dial., 7, 30, 39, 70, 88), while in the NT the primitive demonology of the Synoptists does not use the group, and the group is combined with demonology only where the spirits have become the historical persons of the false teachers, and are no longer understood in primitive fashion, 1 Jn. → 245, 34 ff. For Barn. the Jews are fundamentally in error (2, 9; 12, 10; 16, 1); [159] in contrast, the NT does not use the group with ref. to the Jews. [160]

The group is also used, however, to denote a new situation which is characteristically different from that found in the NT. More basically than in the first beginnings in the NT, [161] and in contrast to false teaching in the Past. (→ 249, 19 ff.), the straying of the soul can now be a rejection of asceticism, 2 Cl., 15, 1. Error may also be opposition to reason and philosophy, Just. Dial., 3, 3. The persecution of confessors, in a way which differs from that of Rev. (→ 248, 19-21), is now caused by the seducing serpent, Just. Dial., 39, 6. Those who go astray in the community are a subject of intercession, 1 Cl., 59, 4, and they are esp. commended to the care of the presbyters, Pol., 6, 1, [162] whereas in the NT [163] they were not yet the objects of any structured or official pastoral concern. The warnings attached to μὴ πλανᾶσθε, in contrast to those of the NT (→ 244, 15 ff.), are now warnings to cling fast to the community and the bishop (Ign. Eph., 5, 2) and to avoid the heretic (Ign. Phld., 3, 3). The group is under the influence of a growing asceticism, the situation of persecution, and the consolidation of the community and its ministry. The usage in some of the texts mentioned is typical, e.g., the ref. to the Jews being in error (Barn.), the mention of seducing spirits (Test. Sol. and Just.), and the anti-heretical summons to the bishop and the community : "Be not deceived" (Ign.).

b. New Linguistic Combinations.

πλανᾶν occurs in Ign. Phld., 7, 1 in the same sense as ψεύδεσθαι in Ac. 5:4, cf. also μυκτηρίζεσθαι in Gl. 6:7. πλάνη is used for the seduction of our first parents by the serpent in Dg., 12, 3, whereas Pl. in 2 C. 11:3, like Gn. 3:13 (→ 236, 13 ff.), used ἐξαπατᾶν. [164] The apostasy denoted by σκανδαλίζεσθαι in Mk. 4:17; Mt. 13:21, by ἀφίστασθαι in Lk. 8:13 and by μὴ μένειν in Jn. 15:6 is ἀποπλανᾶσθαι ἀπὸ τῆς διανοίας in Herm. m., 10, 1, 5. The synon. of πλάνη in 2 Cl., 13, 3 is μῦθος, which is not linked with the group in the Past. Though the simple πλάνος is not combined with μάγος in the NT (→ 250, 23 ff.), in Just. Dial., 69, 7 [165] (cf. Vett. Val. → 233, 22 f.), we find λαοπλάνος with μάγος. [166] The NT opp. of ἑδραῖοι, i.e., μετακινεῖσθαι (Col. 1:23; 1 C. 15:58), is replaced in Ign. Eph., 10, 2 [167] by πλάνη.

2. In the Later Period.

a. The apocryph. Acts naturally know and adopt the Chr. usage of the first 2 centuries. The decisive development here is twofold. First, the word group is set in a more

---

[158] Test. Sol. has at least undergone Chr. revision, cf. Introduction, 51-111.

[159] Cf. in the NT Mk. 12:24, 27, → 243, 39 ff.

[160] Cf. 1 Th. 2:15, the Ἰουδαῖοι in Jn., and esp. the question about the son of David, Mk. 12:35-37 par. In Barn., 12, 10 the last passage is linked with the πλάνη of the Jews.

[161] Cf. Rev. 2:20 (→ 250, 5-9), also 1 C. 6:9 (→ 244, 23 f.).

[162] Cf. Hennecke and Kn. Cl., ad loc.; cf. also Mark Liturg., I, 131; Const. Ap., VIII, 10, 17.

[163] In the NT those who go astray are corrected by Jesus (Mt. 18:12 f. → 242, 22 ff.; Hb. 5:2 → 243, 29-33; 1 Pt. 2:25 → 242, 31 ff.) and by the brethren (Jm. 5:19 → 243, 33 ff.).

[164] Rev. 12:9 (→ 248, 1-2) already uses πλανάω for apocal. seduction by the mythical dragon.

[165] Just. Dial., 108, 2; Test. L. 16:3 (→ 238, 19 f.) and the later Rabb. witnesses, Sanh., 43a, Str.-B., I, 1023.

[166] Cf. already Rev. 18:23 (→ 248, 37 f.).

[167] As in 1 Tm. 6:10 πίστις is the opp. of the group.

consistently cosmological-ascetical and hence heretical dualism ; secondly, Jesus is dogmatically viewed as the liberator from error. The soul has come into nature by aberration [168] (πλανᾶσθαι, πλάνη, Act. Andr., 15). It still has pledges of this. It must learn to perceive the mysteries of its own nature. Error (πλάνη, Act. Andr. et Matth., 2) is mediated by magic and is magical in nature. Thus the birth of the serpent is derived from the world as the storehouse of that which has gone astray (ἀποθήκη τοῦ πλανηθέντος, Act. Phil., 131). In consequence the norm is strongly ascetical. The apostles are charged with seduction (πλάνος, πλανᾶν, Act. Thom., 96; Act. Phil., 121) because they urgently preach against marriage, esp. to young men. In doctrinaire fashion, and with great emphasis, it is constantly underlined that Jesus is the liberator from this entanglement. He liberates (Act. Thom., 38, 67), saves (Act. Thom., 98) and redeems (Act. Thom., 67) from error (πλάνη), which is slavery (Act. Thom., 67) and darkness (Act. Thom., 80). He is the destroyer of error (τῆς πλάνης ἐξαλειπτής, Act. Thom., 80). He is this as companion (ibid., 37) and leader (ibid., 156) in the land of error (πλάνη). In analogy to the antithesis ascribed to the apostles (2 C. 6:8 → 250, 25-27) Jesus is addressed as "Thou who art called deceiver (πλάνος) and yet who redeemest thine own from deception" (ibid., 48). It is worth noting that the eschatological sense of the group does not occur at all in the apocr. Acts. The group is completely captured by a consistent ascetical dualism.

b. The group may enter into other typical new material relations. Notable is the usage of Pistis Sophia. [169] Jesus turns the archons, their aeons, their heimarmene and their spheres into the reverse direction, so that they are deceived (πλανᾶσθαι, Pist. Soph., 32, 38) or are under a delusion (πλάνη, 31, 32, 38), and as a result of this change of course, to man's salvation, they can no longer exert their planetary influences. The Gnostic theologoumenon of the deceiving of the powers by the Jesus event, of which there is a hint in the NT (1 C. 2:8), is now understood materially as a cosmological process, and is thus brought into connection with the word group.

c. Finally one may refer to the meaning of the group in the history of the Canon. Athanasius in the 39th Festal Letter, quoting Mt. 22:29 and 2 C. 11:3, [170] speaks of self-deception, deception, and deceiving [171] with ref. to the true scope of the Canon. [172] Though this is not the original meaning of the two verses, [173] they are thus used, along with the group, as a warning against heterodoxy concerning the sources of salvation, i.e., the scope of the Canon.

Braun

---

[168] Cf. the Naassene Hymn, → 240, 43 ff.
[169] The ref. is to conjectured Gk. equivalents (Intr. XIX-XXIII) and the Copt. text.
[170] πλανηθῶσιν for φθαρῇ, cf. Dg., 12, 3, → 252, 26-28 and → n. 119.
[171] E. Preuschen, *Analecta* (1893), 146, 15 and 144, 5 πλανᾶσθαι, 145, 8, 9 πλανᾶν.
[172] The word group does not occur in Eus. Hist. Eccl., III, 3; 25; 31, 6, where he deals with the Canon.
[173] On the original meaning of Mt. 22:29 → 243, 39 ff.; in 2 C. 11:3 Paul is warning against super-apostles.

πλάσσω, πλάσμα, πλαστός

→ δημιουργός, II, 62, 29 ff.   → κατεργάζομαι, III, 634,
→ ἑτοιμάζω, II, 704, 17 ff.   19 ff.
→ θεός, III, 65, 1 ff.   → κτίζω, III, 1000, 20 ff.
                                    → ποιέω.

† πλάσσω, † πλάσμα.

πλάσσω (from πλαθιω, phonetically pres. from guttural stems) is post-Homeric. Presumably from the standp. of the ancient technique of the potter, it denotes the shallow clapping which accompanies spreading on interwoven forms. It means "to form or fashion out of a soft mass," Plat. Leg., V, 746a. It is impossible to establish any sure connection with other languages.[1] In the Gk. world and Philo, though hardly in the LXX and not at all in the NT, there is a series of fig. meanings in addition to the original one : "to fashion by education and training" (Plat. Resp., II, 377c), "to invent," "devise" (Plat. Phaedr., 246c), "to invent in opp. to the truth" (Hdt., VIII, 80).

A. The Greek World.

1. The Verb.

πλάσσω and πλάσσομαι originally denote the art or craft of "fashioning" ἐκ πηλοῦ ... ἤ τινος ἄλλης ὑγρᾶς συστάσεως, Aristot. Part. An., II, 9, p. 654, 29 f.; Φειδίας πλάττων, Plut. Ad principem ineruditum, 3 (II, 780e). In the Gk. world the words are used only sparingly of the fashioning activity of a divine being, cf. the ancient myth of the forming of Pandora[2] by Hephaistos, which predates Hesiod, though it is he who first gives it palpable expression :

αὐτίκα δ᾽ ἐκ γαίης πλάσσεν κλυτὸς Ἀμφιγυήεις
παρθένῳ αἰδοίῃ ἴκελον Κρονίδεω διὰ βουλάς

(Hes. Op., 70 f.; cf. Theog., 571). In the course of time Prometheus came to replace Hephaistos in the πλάσσειν of human and living creatures, especially women ;[3] the misogynistic impulse in the tradition,[4] however, goes back to Lucian.[5] The subjects as well as the objects of this divine πλάσσειν are of double rank. The chief deity, who does not create out of nothing (→ III, 73 f.) but fashions what is present πᾶν παραλαβών (Plat. Tim., 30a), is called θεός (Tim., 30a), δημιουργός (28a; 29a; 41a), πατήρ (41a), ὁ ποιητὴς καὶ πατὴρ τοῦδε τοῦ παντός (28c), and ὁ γεννήσας πατήρ (37c). This chief deity, however, does

---

π λ ά σ σ ω, π λ ά σ μ α. Thes. Steph., VI, 1155-1157; Wilke-Grimm, s.v.; Pr.-Bauer⁴, s.v.; Liddell-Scott, s.v.

[1] Walde-Pok., II, 63; Boisacq, 791; Hofmann, 273.

[2] On the complex data relating to the Pandora tradition v. W. A. Oldfather, "Pandora," Pauly-W., 18, 2 (1949), 529-548.

[3] Philemo Comicus Fr., 89 (CAF, II, 504); Apollodorus Bibliotheca, I, 45 in Mythographi Graeci, I, 19 (ed. R. Wagner [1894]); Luc. Prometheus sive Caucasus, 3, 13; Prometheus es in verbis, 3; Amor, 43; Plot. Enn., IV, 3, 14 (p. 27, 5 f.).

[4] Hes. Theog., 585 : woman as the καλὸν κακόν.

[5] Quotation from Menander in Luc. Amor, 43 : women as ἔθνος μιαρόν.

not concern itself with πλάσσειν. The giving of soul to the world, which is the work of the Father and is linked to endowment with reason, is described as ξυνιστάναι (Tim., 30b c d; 31b; 32c), (ξυν)τεκταίνεσθαι (30b; 33b), ποιεῖν (31b; 37d; 38c), ξυγκεράννυσθαι (35a), ἀπεργάζεσθαι (39e; 40a), γεννᾶν (41a), γεννᾶσθαι (34b) and σπείρειν (41c). After the soul is given to the world by the Father of all, the new and visible gods are given the task of applying themselves to the δημιουργία τῶν ζῴων (41c). Here again, however, it is God Himself who creates individual souls and co-ordinates them with the individual stars. The ἀπεργάζεσθαι (41d; 43a), γεννᾶν (41d) and αὐξάνειν (41d) of the new gods is directed to the fashioning of bodies, and only now do we find πλάσσειν : τοῖς νέοις παρέδωκε θεοῖς σώματα πλάττειν θνητά (42d). The lower rank of πλάσσειν is typical of the Gk. understanding of man. Man receives his immortal soul directly from God, but he does not receive the body and its mortality from the Godhead ; he receives this from created gods, and here the indirect πλάσσειν is the right word.

Theocrit. (Idyll., 7, 44) can certainly speak of the πεπλασμένον[6] ἐκ Διὸς ἔρνος. In Aristot., however, it is φύσις which, like an artisan, practises πλάσσειν.[7] The gods of Plut. refrain from τὸ σῶμα πλάττειν or influencing men from without, Plut. De Coriolano, 32 (I, 229d). Epictet. uses πλάσσειν only for care of the hair[8] or the body,[9] just as the Gk. world can use πλάσσειν generally to denote the training of the body[10] or the soul[11] or self-cultivation (Plat. Resp., VI, 500d) and the παιδεύειν of others, → V, 596-603. An echo of the Platonic idea of the πλάσσειν of deity may be heard in the Hermetic Κόρη κόσμου : God as τεχνίτης begets souls, the admixture established by Him, πρὸς ὃ θέλει πλάσσων, Stob. Excerpt., 23, 15 (Scott, I, 464, 32);[12] Hermes practises the πλάσσειν of the bodies into which souls enter, ibid., 23, 30 (Scott, I, 474, 8).

2. The Noun.

τὸ πλάσμα means "figure," "forgery," "pretence," distinctive "style" in writing, speech or music, Dion. Hal. Ep. ad Pompeium, 4. The third sense does not occur at all in the bibl. writings, the second occurs in Philo (→ 259, 29-38), but our main interest is in the first.

πλάσμα is commonly used for the product of the artisan or artist (Plat. Soph., 239e; Hi., I, 298a; Luc. Philops., 18), or the construct of the imagination (e.g., in the epistemological passages in Plat. Theaet., 197d; 200c). But the description of men as πλάσματα πηλοῦ (Aristoph. Av., 686) is rare. πλάσμα occurs in the Hell. period for body in dualistic antithesis to ψυχή (Stob. Exc., 23, 39 [Scott, I, 478, 19]; Exc., 24, 9 [I, 500, 8]; Exc., 25, 5 [I, 508, 31]; Exc., 26, 4 [I, 516, 18]) and πνεῦμα (Exc., 23, 67 [I, 492, 24]), or without this (Ascl. Epilogus, 41b [I, 376]); Preis. Zaub., I, 4, 212). In the magic pap. πλάσμα is the figure which is made of the one on whom magical influence is to be exerted : τὸ πλάσμα ἀγομένης (the beloved to be influenced, Preis. Zaub., I, 4, 304),

---

[6] The text is, however, uncertain.
[7] Cf. the index to the Academy ed., V, 597b; also Plut. Cons. ad Apoll., 10 (II, 106e).
[8] Diss., II, 24, 24; III, 1, 26, 42; 22, 10; IV, 11, 25.
[9] Diss., II, 24, 28; IV, 9, 7.
[10] Plat. Tim., 88c; Plut. Lib. Educ., 5 (II, 3e).
[11] Plat. Resp., II, 377c and commonly in Plut. πλάττειν τὸ ἦθος or τὴν ψυχήν, cf. Thes. Steph., VI, 1159.
[12] Here the use of πλάσσειν in relation to souls goes beyond Plato.

ὅλον τὸ φύραμα καὶ πλάσμα 'Ερμοῦ (Hermes, who is to be constrained by the granting of the oracle, Preis. Zaub., Ι, 5, 378). In all these passages πλάσμα as a body is not an idol. Only by way of exception is a deity mentioned as the one who fashions the body qua πλάσμα: ἡ 'Αθηνᾶ ἐμπνέουσα τὸν πηλὸν καὶ ἔμψυχα ποιοῦσα εἶναι τὰ πλάσματα (sc. those made by Prometheus, → 254, 22-25; Luc. Prometheus es in verbis, 3). The a-religious and in part dualistically negative tenor of πλάσμα is plain.

B. Judaism.

I. The Septuagint. [13]

1. The Verb.

Of the 50 instances of the act. πλάσσω in the LXX, 7 [14] are in works for which we have no Heb. original, 2 [15] are extensions and 4 [16] paraphrases of the Heb. In 29 or 30 of the remaining 37 instances the Heb. equivalent is יצר [17] (never in Job); in 3 or 2 instances [18] we find צור, once עצב pi, once נצר (read as יצר by the transl. at Prv. 24:12), 3 times or once עשׂה and once or twice [19] כון pi. Thus in the Heb., too, expressions denoting the products of the potter (יצר, צור, עצב pi) are predominant. In the one mid. πλάσασθαι in the LXX (3 Βασ. 12:33) the Heb. original is ברא. Of the 7 pass. forms one [20] has no original, 2 [21] are extensions and one [22] is a paraphrase of the Heb. text. For the other three we find once each חיל pilel יצר q and pu.

a. The act. πλάσσειν is used 36 times of God, 14 of men. Yahweh as Creator [23] is the One who gives shape and form, the πλάσας (ψ 32[33]:15; 93[94]:9; Prv. 24:12; Is. 27:11; 43:1; 44:2; 49:5; Ιερ. 10:16; 28[51]:19; 2 Macc. 7:23) or the πλάσσων (Zech. 12:1; Is. 44:24; Ιερ. 40[33]:2). He formed the first man out of the earth (Gn. 2:7, 8, 15). He also formed the animals (Gn. 2:19) and especially Leviathan (ψ 103[104]:26). The righteous man confesses that He formed me (Job 10:9; ψ 138[139]:5; Hab. 1:12), that he fashioned man out of clay as a living, speaking being (Job 38:14), the origin of man (2 Macc. 7:23), even the Samaritans (Is. 27:11?) and the maker of idols (Wis. 15:11). More specifically Yahweh formed the eyes (ψ 93[94]:9), the breath (Prv. 24:12), the spirit of man (Zech. 12:1), and the heart (ψ 32[33]:15). He also formed the earth (Is. 45:18 vl.; Ιερ. 40[33]:2), all things (Ιερ. 10:16 = 28[51]:19), summer and spring (ψ 73 [74]:17 vl.). The anthropomorphic idea of fashioning like a craftsman or artist is not avoided, for Yahweh's hand fashioned me (Job 10:8; ψ 118[119]:73) and the solid earth (ψ 94[95]:5).

Yahweh also shapes and fashions in the election, guidance and liberation of His people. His πλάσσειν applies to Israel and Jacob (Dt. 32:6 editio Sixtina; Is.

---

[13] Cf. Hatch-Redp. and Helbing Kasussyntax, 56.

[14] Wis. 15:7, 8, 9, 11, 16 (twice); 2 Macc. 7:23.

[15] Gn. 2:15; Is. 45:10 vl.

[16] Job 38:14; Hab. 1:12 (cf. G. Bertram, "Der Begriff der Erziehung in der gr. Bibel," Imago Dei, Festschr. f. G. Krüger [1932], 49); Is. 29:16; 53:11.

[17] For other Gk. renderings of יצר → III, 1007, n. 57.

[18] This depends on whether one counts the Qᵉre or the Kᵉtib at Jer. 1:5.

[19] This depends on whether one follows the א or the א² A reading at ψ 118(119):73.

[20] 4 Macc. 13:20.

[21] Job 34:15; Prv. 8:25 א.

[22] Εσθ. 1:6 א*.

[23] On the terminology → III, 1007-1009.

43:1, 7; 44:2, 21, 24), to the daughter of Zion (2 K. 19:25), and also to individual agents of salvation, Jeremiah (Jer. 1:5), the δοῦλος (Is. 49:5, 8 vl.), the παῖς (Is. 53:11). The ἐκ κοιλίας (Is. 44:2, 24; 49:5) or ἐν κοιλίᾳ (Jer. 1:5) used in this connection denotes the all-embracing character of the divine fashioning. Here the anthropomorphic idea of the work of the craftsman is clearly refined. The πλάσσειν τῇ συνέσει of Is. 53:11 (in contrast to the Heb. בְּדַעְתּוֹ יַשְׂבִּ֑יעַ) is even Gk. in concept, → 255, 20-22. Distinctive, too, is the preparing of evil by Yahweh in Jer. 18:11. [24]

> A glance at the synon. will be instructive. For Yahweh's creative πλάσσειν cf. the synon. ποιεῖν (Job 10:8; ψ 94[95]:5; Is. 27:11; 29:16; 45:18; Ιερ. 40[33]:2), φυτεύειν (ψ 93[94]:9), ἑτοιμάζειν (ψ 118[119]:73 vl.), ἐκτείνειν οὐρανόν, θεμελιοῦν γῆν (Zech. 12:1), γένεσιν ἐξευρίσκειν (2 Macc. 7:23). With the creative πλασθῆναι we also find ἐν τῇ μητρῴᾳ γαστρὶ κατοικεῖν, αὐξηθῆναι, τελεσφορηθῆναι, ἀποτεχθῆναι (4 Macc. 13:20). Along with Yahweh's historical πλάσσειν are found such terms as πατήρ (Dt. 32:6), ἄγειν vl. συνάγειν (2 K. 19:25), ποιεῖν (Dt. 32:6; Is. 43:1, 7; 44:2), λυτροῦσθαι (Is. 44:24), κατασκευάζειν (Is. 43:7) and διδόναι (Is. 49:8). πλάσσειν is used with λογίζεσθαι for the preparing of evil by Yahweh (Jer. 18:11). Finally ποιεῖν is a synon. for the human πλάσσειν of idols (Is. 44:9); so, too, is γλύφειν (Is. 44:9, 10).

In the use of the verb πλάσας may be seen the absolute sovereignty of Yahweh (Job 10:8, 9; 34:15; 38:14; ψ 94[95]:5; 138[139]:5, 16; Ιερ. 28[51]:19) in which He might equally well call the prophet (Jer. 1:5) or play with Leviathan (ψ 103[104]: 26). This sovereignty is displayed in the help (ψ 73[74]:17; 89[90]:2; Zech. 12:1) and salvation which Yahweh alone (Is. 45:18) brings (Is. 43:1; 44:2, 24; 45:10 vl.; 49:5, 8 vl.; Ιερ. 10:16; 40[33]:2), in the imparting of chastisement (Hab. 1:12 → n. 16), in retribution (Is. 29:16 twice; Prv. 24:12) and in the denying of mercy (Is. 27:11). Yahweh as πλάσας understands man (ψ 32[33]:15). He perceives (ψ 93[94]:9), and in the resurrection restores breath and life to martyrs, as is emphasised in later Judaism (2 Macc. 7:23). Hence He must teach man (ψ 118 [119]:73), and man must not forget the things concerning Him (Is. 44:21). Fashioned by Yahweh, brotherly love arises (4 Macc. 13:20).

There is an obvious difference from the Greek world in usage. The texts, apart from the creation account in P, nowhere suggest an anthropomorphic ascribing of πλάσσειν to God. The πλάσσειν of Yahweh does not denote merely the natural side of creating. It also includes historical processes which are interpreted as decisive saving acts. Finally, man is not regarded as living on two levels, that of body and that of soul. Yahweh formed eyes and breath on the one side, heart and spirit on the other (though ψυχή is not the object of πλάσσειν). The inward aspect is not of higher worth, nor is the body regarded negatively. Man is a totality.

> b. The LXX never speaks neutrally of the πλάσσειν of man, e.g., the work of the potter. The image of the potter, which expresses the potter's sovereignty over his work, is used for Yahweh (Is. 29:16 twice; 45:10 vl.). Or else the sight of the potter (Wis. 15:7) leads to an attack on the fashioning of images, on which the artist lavishes inordinate concern (Wis. 15:8, 9, 16 twice), cf. Aaron and the golden calf (Ex. 32:4). The trouble here is that the artist trusts in his work (Hab. 2:18 twice), and is confounded (Is. 44:9, 10). In one instance πλάσσειν can be used for the doing of harm by the unjust judge, ψ 93[94]:20.

---

[24] Cf. Is. 45:7: Yahweh as עֹשֶׂה שָׁלוֹם וּבוֹרֵא רָע, ὁ ποιῶν εἰρήνην καὶ κτίζων κακά.

The mid. πλάσασθαι, which occurs only once, denotes the arbitrary rearrangement of the feasts by Jeroboam in 3 Βασ. 12:33. The pass. "to be formed" is used of man (Job 34:15), of his days (ψ 138[139]:16 in a distortion of the Heb.), of the 7 martyred brothers (4 Macc. 13:20), of the circle of the earth (ψ 89[90]:2; Prv. 8:25 א), and of handiwork (Εσθ. 1:6 א*; Jer. 19:1). In the first refs. God stands behind πλασθῆναι as the One who fashions (cf. the explicit θεία πρόνοια in 4 Macc. 13:20).

2. The Noun.

Of the 6 πλάσμα refs. in the LXX one (Jdt. 8:29) has no Heb. original, one (Is. 45:10 vl.) is an extension of the Heb. text; of the remaining 4, 3 are a rendering of יֵצֶר and 1 of דְּרָכִים. Though יֵצֶר is 3 times transl. πλάσμα (ψ 102[103]:14; Hab. 2:18; Is. 29:16), יֵצֶר רַע. which is already known to Sir., is never rendered πλάσμα, but ἐννόημα (Sir. 21:11), πονηρὸν ἐνθύμημα (Sir. 37:3) and διαβούλιον (Sir. 15:14; 17:6). [25]

Man is a figure made from the earth (ψ 102[103]:14); his heart can be an ἀγαθὸν πλάσμα (Jdt. 8:29). Animals (Heb. the hippopotamus) are the first-fruits of Yahweh's creative sovereignty (πλάσματος) (Job 40:19). πλάσμα is also used for the product of the potter (Is. 29:16; 45:10 vl.) and esp. for the idol (Hab. 2:18). In the LXX use of πλάσμα the main theological insights are the superiority of the Creator (Job 40:19; Is. 29:16; 45:10 vl.; Hab. 2:18) and His pity for men who are made of dust (ψ 102 [103]:14).

II. Philo.

1. πλάσσω.

πλάσσειν is used exclusively of God in Philo. [26] He has it first in quotations from Gn. 2:7 (Op. Mund., 134; Leg. All., I, 31; in both instances he adds λαβών after χοῦν and before ἀπὸ τῆς γῆς), Gn. 2:8 (Leg. All., I, 43, 47) and Gn. 2:19 (Leg. All., II, 9). In Gn. 2:18, 22 he has a text with πλάσσειν βοηθόν and γυναῖκα instead of the ποιεῖν and οἰκοδομεῖν of the LXX (Leg. All., II, 5, 9; II, 14, 24). On the other hand, in Gn. 2:15 he seems to read ποιεῖν instead of the LXX πλάσσειν (Leg. All., I, 88). God it is who fashions the mortal species (Leg. All., I, 16) and the human form (Op. Mund., 137). Distinction is to be made, however, between the man ὃν ἔπλασεν and the man ὃν ἐποίησε (Leg. All., I, 53), between the earthly man and the man who is like God, the νοῦς (→ 259, 4-8); the different verbs cover an allegorising distinction. God "fashions" the πάθη, the allegorised θηρία according to genus and individual species, as may be seen from the twofoldness of Gn. 1:24 and 2:19 with the ἔτι (Leg. All., II, 5, 9-12); He "fashions" αἴσθησις, the allegorised γυνή of Gn. 2:21 f. (Leg. All., II, 14, 24). πάθη and αἴσθησις are denoted by the βοηθός whom God "fashions" in Gn. 2:18 (Leg. All., II, 5). Philo does not expressly repudiate an anthropomorphic understanding of God's πλάσσειν, but his rejection of a literal understanding of the divine γεωπονεῖν and φυτεύειν (Leg. All., I, 43) and his spiritualised concept of God leave us in no doubt on this pt. In the distinction between πλάττειν and ποιεῖν, πλάττειν stands on the negative side by reason of its material background. This open distinction is alien to the LXX except in the usage of P, → 257, 31 f. At the heart of Philo's depiction of creation stands δημιουργεῖν, which is only on the margin of the LXX in Wis. and 2 and 4 Macc. (→ II, 62, 30 ff.). πλάσσειν is not used with ref. to Israel and salvation history. Nor does Philo speak of the πλάσσειν of the potter or the maker of idols.

---

[25] Bousset-Gressm., 403.
[26] ζωοπλαστεῖν is used of φύσις, Op. Mund., 67.

The mid. πλάσασθαι is used to indicate man's inventions in the religious (Op. Mund., 2; Vit. Mos., II, 281; Spec. Leg., I, 315) or legal field (Spec. Leg., III, 82). In the pass., unlike the act., there is no possibility of quoting from the LXX Torah, and it is here that Philo's true intention regarding the group comes to light. Here esp. one may perceive the dualistic distinction already noted between ὁ νῦν πλασθεὶς ἄνθρωπος and ὁ κατὰ τὴν εἰκόνα θεοῦ γεγονώς (Op. Mund., 134; Leg. All., I, 53; II, 4 and 15), between πεπλάσθαι on the one side and τετυπῶσθαι (Leg. All., I, 31; Plant., 44), γίνεσθαι (Leg. All., I, 32) and ποιεῖσθαι (Leg. All., I, 88) on the other. The meaning is dualistically negative when man is described as πεπλασμένος χοῦς moistened with blood (Rer. Div. Her., 58), when there is ref. to his πεπλασμένη διάθεσις (Plant., 44), when the body is regarded as πεπλασμένος ἀνδριάς, ἄχθος τοσοῦτον (Agric., 25). Naturally the animals (Leg. All., II, 11) and woman (Op. Mund., 151; Leg. All., III, 185), who are to be understood allegorically, are "fashioned," but not, as in the LXX (→ 256, 29), the earth. The same dualism obtains in the allegorising of Ex. 31:2 ff.; the πλάσσειν which goes back to Moses is derived directly from the ἀρχέτυπα, that traced back to Bezaleel only indirectly (Leg. All., III, 102 ff.). Here πλάσσεσθαι is synon. with γίνεσθαι and τορεύεσθαι; thus the synonyms (→ lines 4-8) alternate in Philo according to the demands of allegory. Op. Mund., 141 and Migr. Abr., 167 refer neutrally to artistic πλάσσεσθαι. These refs. do not serve, as in the LXX, to emphasise the superiority of the Creator. Finally, the pass. πλάσσεσθαι, as in the Gk. world but not the LXX, can denote the "pretence" or "falsity" of word (Exsecr., 162; Aet. Mund., 142; Flacc., 108) or attitude (Virt., 39; Leg. Gaj., 59).

2. πλάσμα.

The noun has the same nuances as the pass. of the verb. As γήϊνον πλάσμα τοῦ τεχνίτου man, the second man (→ lines 4-8), stands in dualistic antithesis to the γέννημα, the οὐράνιος ἄνθρωπος (Leg. All., I, 31). Isaac is not γενέσεως πλάσμα but ἔργον τοῦ ἀγενήτου (Det. Pot. Ins., 124); σάρξ- and πνεῦμα- men stand opposed to one another as πλάσμα γῆς and θείας εἰκόνος ἐκμαγεῖον (Rer. Div. Her., 57). πλάσματα is used in Decal., 70 for cultic objects fashioned by the craftsman. As in the Gk. world (→ 255, 28), but not the LXX, πλάσμα in the overwhelming majority of instances denotes an "invention" or "fabrication." Thus πλάσμα is combined with μῦθος and μυθικός, [27] with ὑπόκρισις (Rer. Div. Her., 43; Leg. Gaj., 22) and τῦφος (Cher., 91; Ebr., 36; Spec. Leg., I, 309; Virt., 178). In the world of myth πλάσμα is esp. used for the Stoic world conflagration (Aet. Mund., 90), the Egyptian worship of the bull (Vit. Mos., II, 161) and the mysteries (μυστικὰ πλάσματα, Spec. Leg., I, 319). πλάσματα can derive from an individual like Sejanus (Leg. Gaj., 160), or from a soul which produces unreal imaginations (Flacc., 164). These stand on the side of τέχνη in antithesis to φύσις (Leg. All., III, 64).

When one moves on from the LXX to Philo, in spite of the many refs. in Philo and the new use for "to fabricate," "fabrication," there is a narrowing of meaning as compared with the multiplicity of the LXX. Philo borrows from the LXX, but only in part and even here allegorically. The other source of his usage is the Gk. world as influenced esp. by Plato. The dualistic disparagement of πλάσσειν (→ 254, 26 ff.) has its roots here. Philo's unequivocal OT monotheism prevents this disparagement from exerting any metaphysical influence. Thus πλάσσειν cannot be ascribed to a lesser deity, as in Plato. Nevertheless, this Platonic dualism established itself in the field of anthropology; it affected Philo's understanding of man, → 255, 11 ff. [28]

---

[27] Op. Mund., 1. 157. 170; Cher., 91; Det. Pot. Ins., 125; Congr., 61 f.; Fug., 42; Abr., 243; Vit. Mos., II, 271; Decal., 55. 76. 156; Spec. Leg., I, 51; Virt., 102. 178; Praem. Poen., 8; Vit. Cont., 63; Aet. Mund., 58; Leg. Gaj., 13. 237.

[28] On the dualism of the Naassene Sermon, v. Nilsson, II, 580.

III. The Development of the Word Group in Hellenistic and Rabbinic Judaism.

In the Jud. Sib. God is ὁ πλάσας (III, 24 → 256, 19 ff.), Adam is πρῶτος πλασθείς (III, 25; πρῶτος goes beyond the LXX), and men are θεόπλαστον ἔχοντες ἐν εἰκόνι μορφήν (III, 8).[29] In Jos. God accomplishes the πλάσσειν of man (Ant., 1, 32 and 34).[30] The inability of the fashioned clay to reply or to understand a resolve displays the sovereignty of God over pre-determined man (Manual, 11, 22).

Rabb. exegesis is interesting. R. Gamaliel II (c. 90) contests the polytheistic deduction which might be drawn from the two verbs in Gn. 1:27 and 2:7 (Sanh., 39a; Str.-B., IV, 411). From "fashioning" or the double י in the וייצר of Gn. 2:7 follows the resurrection (Gn. r., 14 [10c], cf. Str.-B., I, 895 f.; III, 473; cf. 2 Macc. 7:23). The earth from which man was formed was taken from the place where the altar of the burnt offering later stood in the temple (R. Shemuel b. Nachman, Gn. r., 14 [10c], cf. Str.-B., III, 478 f.), or from the 4 corners of the world (Tg. J. I, Gn. 2:7, cf. Str.-B., III, 479; cf. Sib., III, 25 and 26). Rabb. of the 2nd and 3rd cent. relate the יצר of Ps. 103:14 and the וייצר of Gn. 2:7 to the evil impulse;[31] others (c. 300) deduce from Gn. 2:7 the creation of both impulses by God (Tg. J. I, Gn. 2:7, cf. Str.-B., III, 479; Ber., 61a, cf. Str.-B., IV, 467). In analogy to the dualism of Philo there is also in the Rabb. a tendency to suppose that Yahweh formed man out of the noble part of the human sperm, Nidda, 31a; Lv. r., 14 § 6.[32]

C. The New Testament.

1. Paul, quoting from the LXX, uses the image of the potter in R. 9:20 to show how impossible it is to speak back to God, who can have mercy or harden according to His discretion. The vessel does not say to the one who made it : "Why hast thou made me thus ?"

The first half of the quotation, the introduction in the form of a rhetorical question : μὴ ἐρεῖ τὸ πλάσμα τῷ πλάσαντι, comes almost word for word from Is. 29:16. The question of the vessel in Paul is not a literal quotation. One is reminded of the τί ποιεῖς of Is. 45:9 (the vessel to the potter) or the τί ἐποίησας of Job 9:12; Wis. 12:12 (though here the image of the vessel and the potter does not occur). In none of the 3 passages does one find the με or the οὕτως of Pl. ἔπλασας for ἐποίησας in D Theophyl mg is almost certainly a later assimilation.

Like κεραμεύς and πηλός (→ 118, 12 ff.) in R. 9:21, and as in the LXX quotations (Is. 29:16; 45:9), πλάσας and πλάσμα denote in the first instance the potter and his product; the parallelism of πλάσσειν and ποιεῖν is familiar from the LXX (→ 257, 9-18). But as already in the OT (→ 257, 41 f.), the true reference is to God. Typically OT is the underscoring of God's sovereignty by the figure of the potter who shapes the vessel (→ 257, 19-26, 41 f.; cf. the pars. in Jer. 18:6; Is. 64:7; Sir. 33:13, though the group is not used in these verses). In Is. 45:9, 10, as in most of the similar passages, this sovereignty is orientated to the bringing of salvation (→ 257, 21-24). Here, however, man is set before the

---

[29] In tendency, if not in terminology, this is OT and non-Philonic.

[30] In 1, 34 λαβών is added to the text of Gn. 2:7, as in Philo (→ 258, 25 f.); Ant., 1, 35 describes the πλάσσειν of the woman, cf. Philo (→ 259, 12 f.).

[31] Gn. r., 34 (21a), cf. Str.-B., IV, 469; Ab. R. N., 16 (6a), ibid., 474; Erub., 18a, ibid., III, 240.

[32] R. Meyer, Hellenistisches in der rabb. Anthropologie (1937), 33-43; K. H. Rengstorf, Mann u. Frau im Urchr. (1954), 40, n. 83.

tremendum of a demonstration of judgment by the God [33] who exercises both mercy and hardening. Man, as God's product and creature, is absolutely dependent on the deity. He is thus delivered up to God's judgment and referred to His mercy.

This view is obviously the one developed by Luther in his De servo arbitrio. It is quite different from the Gk. understanding of God and man expressed in the use of the same image by Plut. [34] (→ 255, n. 7). Here the artist's shaping and kneading together of the same mass is a consoling ref. to nature, which fashions and then destroys man in the flux of becoming and perishing.

2. In 1 Tm. 2:13 the command that women should not teach or rule men, and that they should keep silence, is based on the fact that Adam was formed first, then Eve (→ I, 141, 4 ff.). The LXX does not speak, as this v. does, of the πλάσσειν or πλασθῆναι of the woman (→ 256, 19-33); we find this first in Philo (→ 259, 11 f.), then Josephus (→ n. 30). In this matter the author is simply following an existing Jewish-Hellenistic tradition. The order of creation — first the man, then the woman — follows the account in J, also in the dependent literature and in the myth of Pandora (→ 254, 18-22). Elsewhere the order is not particularly emphasised. Even the πρῶτος of Sib., III, 25 (→ 260, 2 f.) has all Adam's descendants in view rather than Eve in particular. The only similar line of thought is in 1 C. 11:8. The secondariness of woman, which is taken for granted in Hellenism and later Judaism (→ I, 776-784) but which is abandoned in practice in the NT (→ I, 784-788), is here and in 1 C. 11:8 derived from the well-known [35] OT and later Jewish norm that the older ranks first.

3. The NT, unlike the LXX (→ 256, 34 ff.), does not use the word group to denote God's saving acts in history nor to express the new spiritual creation of the individual by God, as in the case of κτίζω (Eph. 2:10, 15; 4:24), κτίσις (2 C. 5:17; Gl. 6:15), κτίσμα (Jm. 1:18), ποίημα (Eph. 2:10) → III, 1033, 43 ff. On the other hand, there is no dualistically negative use, as in Philo (→ 258, 30-33; 259, 4-16). NT usage corresponds in essentials to that of the LXX → 256 f.

D. Later Christian Usage.

1. The Verb.

The use of the LXX by the community [36] influences the usage of the post-apost. fathers more than the two NT passages. God as the πλάσας of man [37] or the πεπλακώς of the human καρδία, [38] God's πλάσσειν of man on the basis of the εἰκών of God, [39] man as χοϊκὸς πλασθείς (Sib., VIII, 445), the χεῖρες of God as the organs of πλάσσειν, [40] the literal quotation of Is. 53:11 in 1 Cl., 16, 12, the πλάσσειν of the

---

[33] Cf. Ltzm. R. on 9:22.

[34] H. Almquist, *Plut. und das NT* (1946), 87 f.

[35] Cf. Str.-B., III, 256-258, 645 f.

[36] It is almost ironical that 4 of the refs. in the post-apost. fathers are in Barn.

[37] Barn., 19, 2, in the catechism of the 2 ways; 1 Cl., 38, 3: the ref. of τάφος and σκότος is to the earth, not the womb.

[38] Barn., 2, 10 quoting ψ 50(51):17, but not literally acc. to the LXX; on the composition and history of the quotation cf. Wnd. Barn., *ad loc.*

[39] Dg., 10, 2; 1 Cl., 33, 4; on the constr. cf. Kn. 1 Cl., *ad loc.*; Sib., I, 22 f.: the ref. is thus to Adam.

[40] 1 Cl., 33, 4; the attributes ἱεραί and ἄμωμοι are Hellenistic.

craftsman in the making of images (Dg., 2, 3) — all these correspond to the LXX
→ 256, 19 ff. The severity of God's absolute sovereignty over man, which Paul took from
the LXX (→ 260, 32 ff.), is no longer found in this epoch with its exposure to the rational.
Leading features of the word group in the post-apost. fathers are praise of the Maker
(Barn., 2, 10; 1 Cl., 38, 3), recognition of His benefits (Dg., 10, 2), fear before Him
(Barn., 19, 2), and the taking of the divine work of creation as a model for the doing of
works of righteousness (1 Cl., 33, 8).

2. The Noun.

The noun πλάσμα is now given a place in central Chr. statements. The creation of
man in Gn. 1:27 pts. to the spiritual renewal of Christians by the remission of sins. The
Lord saw τὸ καλὸν πλάσμα ἡμῶν, "us, his beautiful handiwork" (Barn., 6, 12). [41] The
φθορεῖς πλάσματος θεοῦ of Did., 5, 2; Barn., 20, 2, which is obviously taken from a
later Jewish-Hell. catechism, does not refer [42] to destroyers of spiritually renewed
Christians but to those who destroy the developing fruit of the body ; [43] this is shown
by its established and consequently traditional position after φονεῖς τέκνων.

† πλαστός.

The literal meaning of this verbal adj. ("formed" or "formable") is interesting. Though
not found in the LXX, it has in dualistic writings the sense of "merely physical." The
second, earthly man, who is not in the image of God, is described by Philo (→ 258, 32-34;
259, 2-8) as πλαστός (Leg. All., I, 54. 55. 90; II, 4). With the bodily eye as τῷ πλαστῷ
τούτῳ στοιχείῳ one cannot perceive the nature of regeneration (Corp. Herm., 13, 3).
Transf. πλαστός means "forged," "fabricated," "invented." A person may be "false"
in respect of supposed descent (Soph. Oed. Tyr., 780), love (Xenoph. Ag., 1, 38)   and
passions (Luc. Amor, 49). Religious inspirations (πλασταῖσι βακχείαισιν with ref. to
the νεωστὶ δαίμων Διόνυσος, Eur. Ba., 218 f.) and a mythical story (λόγος πλαστός,
Hdt., I, 68) can also be regarded as fabricated. Light is shed on the content by the
attributive position of πλαστός alongside φέναξ ("deceitful") with τῦφος ("hallucina-
tion," "imagination"), Philo Som., II, 140.

In 2 Pt. 2:3 [1] the πλαστοὶ λόγοι (on the connection with λόγος → IV, 789, 14 f.)
are the teachings and claims with which the false teachers, in their greed, seek
to win over the members of the community. In so far as the reference is to an
imaginary metaphysics (angels), one is reminded of the σεσοφισμένοι μῦθοι of
2 Pt. 1:16 (cf. Philo's use of πλάσμα as "fabrication" with μῦθος, → 259, 29 f.).
In so far as the libertinistic ethics combatted by 2 Pt. are in view, slogans like
πάντα μοι ἔξεστιν (1 C. 6:12), ἑστάναι (1 C. 10:12) and γινώσκειν τὰ βαθέα
τοῦ σατανᾶ (Rev. 2:24) suggest the content of the λόγοι. The use of πλαστοί
stamps the mythologoumena as "inventions," not in the modern rationalistic sense
but in respect of their lack of seriousness. It also criticises the slogans for reflecting an ethically spurious attitude, a Gnostic-enthusiastic (ἐνυπνιαζόμενοι,
Jd. 8) hubris.

Braun

---

[41] Cf. the pre-existent Christ as the πλάστης μερόπων κτίστης τε βίοιο, in Sib.,
VIII, 440.
[42] As Wnd. Barn. argues, *ad loc.*
[43] So Kn. Did., *ad loc.*

π λ α σ τ ό ς. Thes. Steph., VI, 1161; Wilke-Grimm, Pr.-Bauer⁴, Liddell-Scott, *s.v.*
[1] Cf. Wnd.-Preisker Kath. Br., *ad loc.*

† πλεονάζω, † ὑπερπλεονάζω	→ περισσεύω, 58-61.

A. Outside the New Testament.

1. From the very first, in literature at least, the πλέον in πλεονάζω [1] has the sense of "too much" [2] (→ lines 10 f. Thuc., esp. Aristot.). From the time of Thuc. it contains a note of censure in ethical contexts. Only gradually do we find instances of the sense of "much." It is not always easy to decide between "too much" and "much." Found from Thuc., the word does not occur in, e.g., Plato, Xenoph. or Epict.

Intr. "to be too much," parts of the body (Aristot. Gen. An., IV, 4, p. 770b, 32; p. 773a, 11; παρὰ φύσιν, ibid., p. 772b, 13; "to be too big," the ἴσον (→ 267, 18 f., 48 f.; 268, 18) is that which μήτε πλεονάζει μήτε ἐλλείπει, Aristot. Eth. Nic., II, 5, p. 1106a, 31 f.; hence "to go too far" with ἐπαίρεσθαι, Thuc., I, 120, 4; πέρα τοῦ μετρίου, Demosth. Or., 9, 24; τοὺς πάνυ δεινούς ..., ὅταν πλεονάζωσ', ἐπίστασθ' ὑμεῖς κοσμίους ποιεῖν (→ 267, 15, 18 πλεονέκτης), Demosth. Or., 39, 14; "to become too big," "arrogant" τὸ εὐτυχῆσαν ὕβρει πλεονάζει (the ref. in 1. is to the κύκλος ... τῶν κακῶν of retaliation), Dio C., 44, 29, 2; "to be excessive," of money τὰ πλεονάζοντα ἱερὰ ἔστω τῶν θεῶν, Ditt. Syll.[3], II, 736, 39 (92 B.C., common in the pap., from the 3rd cent. B.C.); "to overflow," of the sea, Aristot. Meteor., I, 14, p. 351b, 6, a river, Dio C., 54, 25, 2; 57, 14, 8 (opp. ἐλλείπειν); "to become overrich" synon. ὑπερβάλλειν τῷ πλήθει, Aristot. Gen. An., I, 18, p. 725b, 10; "to have a superfluity" (opp. ἐνδεᾶ εἶναι) c. gen. Aristot. Pol., I, 9, p. 1257a, 33; "to have more," the fem. mixture "has more" of what is moist and cold (with dat.) Stob. Ecl., I, 410, 11; "to be more," "to preponderate," in the male "the dry and warm πλεονάζει, hence souls are hard and more active in such bodies," loc. cit.; "to become (too) numerous" (of the Jews in Rome), Dio C., 60, 6, 6; "to increase" synon. συναυξάνεσθαι (πληθύνεσθε in LXX Gn. 1:22), Jos. Ant., 1, 32; "to be present in fulness," fulness of ἡδοναί is no criterion for a happy life, Teles, 49, 3; "to be multiple," Aristot. Eth. Eud., II, 8, p. 1224a, 24 (opp. ἁπλῆ); "to be common," of particular notes, Aristides Quintilianus De Musica, II, 14; "to be rich in," Aristot. Metaph., I, 2, p. 994b, 18. Trans.: [3] "to make (too) abundant," τὰ σελάχια ... πλεοναζόμενα (sharks enjoyed too lavishly), Athen., 8, 53 (356d); "to increase" (to estimate a greater number, πλεονάζει αὐτά ⸗ miles), Strabo, VI, 3, 10.

ὑπερπλεονάζω is rare and does not occur in the LXX or, thus far, the pap.; it is a fundamentally unnecessary intensification of the simple form, which already carries the nuance of "too much." There are no instances prior to the 1st cent. B.C. It means "to be over-abundant" of air, Hero Alexandrinus Pneumatica, I, 10; [4] "to be excessive" of gains, opp. ἐνδεής, Vett. Val., II, 21, p. 85, 17.

2. The usage in Thuc., Demosth., Aristot. shows already that the simple form is significant in the ethical vocabulary of the Gk. world. Like πλεονεκτεῖν (→ 267, 15 and 18) it is here a counterpart to the golden mean, the ἴσον, the κόσμιον, and it

---

πλεονάζω κτλ. [1] Intrans. constr. from πλέον with -άζειν, Debr. Griech. Wortb. § 240 [Debrunner].

[2] Obviously in distinction from περισσεύειν, which sometimes seems to be a formal par. → 58, 20 ff.

[3] Helbing Kasussyntax, 79 [Debrunner]. On the factitive use of intrans. verbs in Hell. Gk. cf. Bl.-Debr. § 148.

[4] Ed. W. Schmidt, Heronis Alexandrini Opera, I (1899), 76, 14.

denotes what is παρὰ φύσιν. This content of the term is still influential in a specific way in the Stoic definition which is often quoted in philosophical literature: ἔστι δὲ αὐτὸ τὸ πάθος κατὰ Ζήνωνα ἡ ἄλογος καὶ παρὰ φύσιν ψυχῆς κίνησις, ἢ ὁρμὴ πλεονάζουσα. Acc. to Zeno passion is "the irrational and unnatural movement of the soul, or an impulse which leads to excess," Diog. Laert., VII, 110 (v. Arnim, I, 50, 22 f., cf. III, 95, 15; 113, 15). Cic. Tusc., IV, 11 renders Zeno as follows: *perturbatio* (πάθος) = *aversa a recta ratione contra naturam animi commotio*, or more briefly: *perturbationem esse appetitum vehementiorem* (the comp. aspect of πλεονάζω may be seen here); *ibid.*, 47: *vehementior* = *qui procul absit a naturae constantia*. In Cl. Al. Strom., II, 59, 6 (GCS, 15, 145, 4 ff.) πλεονάζουσα is interpreted as ὑπερτείνουσα τὰ κατὰ τὸν λόγον μέτρα, as ἀπειθὴς λόγῳ. Chrysipp. Fr., 479 (v. Arnim, III, 130, 8-15) takes the formula to mean that excess, enormity, is the opp. of λόγος, reason, nature (in the sense of what is originally healthy). Cf., *ibid.*, 462 (v. Arnim, III, 114, 1-17): πλεονασμὸς τῆς ὁρμῆς is transgression (ὑπερβαίνειν) of the natural and rational συμμετρία of the impulses etc. Here it is plain that πλεονάζω means crossing the limit which is set for the impulsive will, which is not reprehensible as such (→ V, 467 f.). On the far side of this limit impulse becomes passion, → V, 926 f.

Philo often uses the Stoic formula; its influence is esp. clear in Spec. Leg., IV, 79 (which is important because the discussion of οὐκ ἐπιθυμήσεις begins here, cf. R. 7:7). Every πάθος is culpable since καὶ πᾶσα ἄμετρος (→ line 9 f., 14) καὶ πλεονάζουσα ὁρμή and the irrational (ἄλογος) and unnatural (παρὰ φύσιν) movement of the soul is to be condemned; a mean is to be set for the impulses, and they must be held in rein like horses. From πλεονάζουσα ὁρμή grow ἄλογοι ἐπιθυμίαι, Rer. Div. Her., 245. In Som., II, 276 ἡδονή and ἐπιθυμία as πλεονάζουσα ὁρμή are par. to ἄλογον πάθος. Agric., 94 says that the wildness of passion which gains the upper hand must be checked by reining in the irrational powers. Cf. Conf. Ling., 90: τὰς ἀλόγους καὶ πλεοναζούσας τῶν παθῶν ὁρμᾶς (→ V, 468, n. 5).

3. In the LXX [5] (all the refs. are given) the intr. sense is "to be over" (Ex. 16:23), "to remain over" (Ex. 26:12), [6] "to be more" (Nu. 3:46, 48 f., twice here, for עדף q), 51, "to have to excess" (Ex. 16:18 for עדף hi), "to do too much" (λόγῳ Sir. 20:8), "to do more or much" (τοῦ with inf. 2 Βασ. 18:8 for רבה hi; Ez. 23:32 for מִרְבֶּה), "to become much" (2 Ch. 24:11 HT רב; 1 Esr. 8:72 ἁμαρτίαι), "to become great" (ἐν πλεοναζούσῃ δικαιοσύνῃ ἰσχὺς πολλή, quite different from the HT, Prv. 15:6), "to increase" (1 Ch. 4:27 for רבה hi; Sir. 23:3 ἁμαρτίαι). Trans. it means "to make great" (Nu. 26:54, inheritance; 2 Ch. 31:5 ἀπαρχήν; ψ 70:21, the greatness of God [HT 71:21 of man]; in all these 3 refs. Heb. רבה hi); τὸ στόμα σου ἐπλεόνασεν κακίαν "has spoken much evil" (ψ 49:19); opp. ἐπιτεμεῖν "to shorten" (2 Macc. 2:32 the introduction to the book); ארך hi, "to lengthen" (Nu. 9:22); for רבה hi, opp. ἐλαττοῦσθαι (Ιερ. 37[30]:19); "to multiply" (Sir. 35:1, "he who keeps the law brings many offerings"), pass. "to become many" (1 Ch. 5:23 for רבה q); πλεοναστόν, "filled up" (1 Macc. 4:35).

B. In the New Testament.

1. The words occur only in the Epistles, and only in Paul apart from 2 Pt. 1:8. They are most common in the better attested writings. Except for 1 Th. 3:12 (and 2 C. 4:15 ?) they are used only intr., and apart from 1 Th. 3:12; Phil. 4:17; 2 C. 8:15 they always have abstr. subjects. The meaning is "to increase," "to prevail," "to superabound" etc., often in a superlative sense. Formally πλεονάζω is par. to περισσεύω in the NT; it is used with this or a compound in R. 5:20; 2 C. 4:15; 1 Th. 3:12, cf. also R. 5:20 with

---

[5] πλεονάζειν does not occur in the other Gk. transl. of the Hexapla [Bertram].
[6] Negatively ("still lacking") in 1 Macc. 10:41.

6:1 etc. περισσεύω is three times as common as πλεονάζω. πλεονάζω has an eschatological ref. (→ 59 f.) only in the light of the contexts in which it occurs. Fulness is a mark of the saving work of God. πληρόω (→ 290 ff.) rather than πλεονάζω, however, has the specific sense of eschatological fulfilment.

2. In one instance πλεονάζω can even denote the effect of an event which took place long before the eschatological present (R. 5:20). The Law intervened (→ II, 682, 31 ff.; V, 620, 15 ff.) — the justified man alone can see this — in order that transgression might superabound, being displayed in all its ungodly reality (cf. R. 5:13; 3:20; 4:15) and waxing great (R. 5:21a; 7:8, 13 → IV, 1073 f.).

The train of thought in R. 5:20 is very different from that of the Stoic πλεονάζουσα ὁρμή (→ 264, 1-17, 20-27). The ref. in the latter is not to man before God, but to man in himself. It is not to an absolute event — sin revealed in its essence as revolt against God's declared will — but to a relative intensification of human impulses which are not to be repudiated as such. In the Stoic statement the appeal is to reason, and man is implicitly summoned to develop his natural resources; in the saying of Paul, however, the full hopelessness of man's ethical situation is grounded in his religious predicament.

This effect of the Torah, however, aims finally (cf. the ἵνα in v. 21; → III, 328, 23) at the supreme deployment of the saving grace of God; the greater sin is, the greater is the act of God which removes it. To avoid an ethical deduction from the misunderstanding of this principle (R. 6:1) Paul appeals to the full efficacy of the saving event which has taken place in baptism. The goal of Paul's work as a preacher (2 C. 4:13, ἵνα v. 15, → III, 333, 5 ff.) is that in the coming to faith of as many as possible [7] (there is a play on πλεονάσασα and πλειόνων) [8] grace "should attain to its greatest fulness," "should be mighty in supreme fulness," or "should make abundant" the thanksgiving offered by as many as possible (→ 60, 23 f.). The grace "of our Lord" has been rich "beyond every measure" of comprehension in the mercy shown to Paul the persecutor, 1 Tm. 1:13 f.; ὑπερεπλεόνασεν emphasises the paradoxical nature of the event of Gl. 1:15 (cf. v. 13 f.; on ὑπερ- cf. R. 5:20, → 60, 8).

3. Where the word has a materially superlative sense in statements about χάρις, when used of love it bears the comparative sense of "increasing." Paul can give thanks for this growing love in 2 Th. 1:3 (with ὑπεραυξάνει). His prayer in 1 Th. 3:12 is that Christ may make his readers rich in love. Here, too, the thought of fulness is clearly implied. 2 Pt. 1:8 is more restrained. If the 8 religious and ethical abilities mentioned in vv. 5-7 are present, and if they increase, they can make Christians active and fruitful (→ III, 446, 11 ff.) "in the knowledge (→ I, 707, 12 ff.) of our Lord Jesus Christ" (obj. gen. as elsewhere). [9] From the Philippians Paul does not seek [10] a present as such (Phil. 4:17). In their free

---

[7] Or "should receive increasing fulness" in the coming to faith of an increasing multitude. The use of πλείονες, however, is surely the same as in 1 C. 9:19; Paul does not use the superlative πλεῖστος.

[8] Grammatically the διὰ τῶν πλειόνων of 2 C. 4:15 belongs to what follows. The sequence of thought is thus restricted (as not infrequently in Paul); the ref. is to πλεονάσασα ἐν τοῖς πλείοσι who then give thanks. For the relation of εὐχαριστίαν to περισσεύσῃ cf. also Ltzm. K., ad loc.

[9] Cf. 1:2 f.; 2:20; esp. 3:18. Cf. Wnd. Kath. Br., ad loc., though also → I, 452, 21-24; III, 616, 8 ff.

[10] The ἐπιζητῶ may also carry with it a demand (→ II, 895, 34 ff.); Paul's readers might think that he is expecting remuneration for his preaching, cf. v. 15; 1 C. 9:11.

generosity he seeks fruit (the fruit of their believing, faith and love) which "will abound" to their account (→ IV, 104, 1 ff.). That is to say, in the gifts of the Philippians Paul sees the increasing outworking of their Christian life whose results he enters up with joy (v. 10).[11]

4. The principle of ἰσότης (→ 263, 9 f.) was adopted by Christianity in the sense of financial equality through voluntary and relative liberality, → III, 348 f. In 2 C. 8:15 Paul bases this on an explicit quotation (γέγραπται) from Ex. 16:18. In the time of the desert wandering (cf. 1 C. 10:1-11, v. 11 → τυπικῶς) the divine order saw to it that in the gifts of God to His people equality was naturally achieved. The same equality is now to be established voluntarily in the Christian world. He who in the first instance has received (relatively) much, is not finally to "have more" than others.

Delling

---

† πλεονέκτης, † πλεονεκτέω, † πλεονεξία

A. The Non-Jewish and Non-Christian Greek Sphere.

The word group means first a. "having more" (πλεονέκτης is formed from πλέον ἔχειν with the suffix -της[1,2]), then b. "receiving more," and finally c. "wanting more." From the first literary examples on it is not restricted to material possession. In Hdt. πλεονεξία is "hunger for power" (VII, 149, 3 of the Spartans), πλεονεκτεῖν "striving for power" (VIII, 112, 1, Themistocles for Athens), πλεονέκτης "presumptuous" (VII, 158, 1). The fact that the group plays a political role here is obviously due to the nature of the material in Hdt., but even after Hdt. the group is important in national and international life. In Thuc. πλεονεκτεῖν is "to take the greater share" (VI, 39, 2, the aristocrats), "to increase one's possessions" (IV, 62, 3 with πλέον ἔχειν), "to seek aggrandisement" (IV, 61, 5), "to take advantage of" (I, 77, 3), "to seek political gain" (IV, 86, 6). πλεονέκτης is the "robber" (I, 40, 1 with βίαιος), πλεονεξία "the will to press one's advantage" (III, 45, 4, deriving from the ὕβρις of power). In III, 82, 8 πλεονεξία, with φιλοτιμία, means "selfishness."

The two last refs. prepare the way for the importance of the group in ethical discussions relating to society and moral conduct generally. In Xenoph. and Plato there is also an extension of usage for which we do not always know how far the way had been prepared before them: "to outdo someone (gen.) in something" (dat.), Xenoph. Cyrop., IV, 3, 21; "to be in force," ibid., VIII, 4, 4, for someone παρά τινι, Xenoph. Hist. Graec., VII, 1, 34; "to be superior" in number and weapons, Cyrop., VII, 1, 33; "to take precedence" in power, Hist. Graec., II, 3, 16; "to forge ahead" at the expense of others, ibid., VI, 3, 9, cf. 3, 11; "to treat someone arrogantly," Pass. Mem., III, 5, 2;

---

[11] In the main the same view is taken by Dib. Th., Haupt Gefbr. and Ewald Phil., ad loc., but → III, 615, 28-30.

πλεονέκτης κτλ. A. Vögtle, "Die Tugend- u. Lasterkataloge im NT," NTAbh., 16, 4 f. (1936), Index, s.v.

[1] E. Fraenkel, Geschichte d. gr. Nomina agentis, I (1910), 166 [Debrunner].

[2] On πλεονέκτης κτλ. cf. εὐεργέτης — εὐεργετεῖν — εὐεργεσία, → IV, 1089, 25; 1090, 1. Debr. Griech. Wortb. § 72, 101, 103, 146 [Debrunner].

πλεονέκτης in a list : πῶς γὰρ ἂν ἢ ἀχάριστοι ἢ ἀμελεῖς ἢ πλεονέκται ἢ ἄπιστοι ἢ ἀκρατεῖς ἄνθρωποι δύναιντο φίλοι γενέσθαι; Mem., II, 6, 19. What was said above (→ 266, 30-32) applies esp. to the fig. use of the group in Plat. πλεονεκτεῖν means a. "to be superior" in battle, La., 182b, 183a; "to surpass" in numbers, Parm., 149b; "to be ahead of someone" in goods, right conduct, Resp., I, 349bc, here with πλέον ἔχειν, cf. 350a; "to excel in something," of opposite kinds of music, Leg., VII, 802d; b. "to receive more" in material distribution, Gorg., 490c-491a; "to be at an advantage" in dealings with the gods, Euthyphr., 15a; "to gain" fig., Leg., III, 683a; c. "to gain advantages," Gorg., 483c; "to take advantage of someone," Resp., II, 362b; 365d; also fig. when truth is exchanged for δόξα, Symp., 218c; "to seize the goods of others," Leg., X, 906c; "to seek something by force," Resp., I, 344a; fig. "to do violence to," laws, Leg., III, 691a. The use of πλεονεξία is more restricted. Formally it is "excess," Tim., 82a (opp. ἔνδεια), but the meaning is usually adverse : "greed", Critias, 121b; "insatiability" in respect of food and pleasures, Resp., IX, 586b; "immoderation" with ἀκοσμία περὶ ἄλληλα, Symp., 188b; "desire," erotically Symp., 182d; finally the act of "encroaching on what belongs to others," a ἁμάρτημα in Leg., X, 906c; plur. Leg., III, 677b; [3] then esp. the desire for power etc., and esp. the "urge to assert oneself," Resp., II, 359c. In Gorg., 508a the opp. of πλεονεξία is ἰσότης γεωμετρική → III, 345 f., the κοινωνία, κοσμιότης, σωφροσύνη, δικαιότης which hold together heaven and earth, the gods and men. πλεονεξία goes with ἀκοσμία and ἀκολασία. It disrupts the cosmos, the harmony of the universe and of the world of gods and men. In this connection Plato's Socrates takes issue with the morality of the Sophists who say that striving for more is wrong only νόμῳ, not → φύσει (→ IV, 1028 f.) and that only the weaker declare πλεονεκτεῖν (= πλέον τῶν ἄλλων ζητεῖν ἔχειν) to be αἰσχρὸν καὶ ἄδικον, Gorg., 483a-c. This struggle against the ethics of the master race continued through the centuries which followed ; one is not to think that τὸ κράτος τὸ ἐπὶ τῇ πλεονεξίᾳ is ἀρετή and obedience to the laws is cowardice ; this view is the source of all evil, anon. Iambl., 6, 1 (Diels[7], II, 402). Men cannot live without laws and δίκη, ibid., 7, 13 (Diels[7], II, 404). Kingship and tyranny proceed from ἀνομία and πλεονεξία, cf. Plat. Leg., III, 691a : The kings of the past violated (πλεονεκτεῖν) the laws.

In Aristot. the word group occurs mainly in Eth. Nic. and Pol. a. πλεονεκτεῖν is "to have more," Pol., V, 2, p. 1302a, 26 (= πλέον ἔχειν, 28), b, 1; πλεονεξία is "the greater number," Pol., III, 12; p. 1282b, 32. b. πλεονεκτεῖν also means "to receive (get) more," Pol., IV, 6, p. 1293a, 23; V, 1, p. 1301a, 35; ἢ χρημάτων ἢ τιμῆς, Pol., II, 7, p. 1266b, 37; ἀγαθοῦ ... ἐπλεονέκτει, οἷον δόξης ἢ τοῦ ἁπλοῦ καλοῦ, Eth. Nic., V, 12, p. 1136b, 21 f.; χάριτος ἢ τιμωρίας, ibid., 1137a, 1. c. πλεονεξία means "covetousness," Pol., V, 3, p. 1302b, 9; πλεονεκτεῖν with ὑβρίζειν, ibid., 1302b, 6 f.; V, 7, p. 1307a, 20. The πλεονέκτης (with παράνομος and ἄνισος) is ἄδικος, Eth. Nic., V, 2, p. 1129a, 32 f., b, 1 f.; the adulterer as ἀκόλαστος is expressly distinguished from the πλεονέκτης (covetous man) as an ἄδικος, V, 4, p. 1130a, 24-27; πλεονέκτης in IX, 8, p. 1168b, 1-19 relates to money, fame and physical desires.

In the battle against πλεονεξία various motifs from social and personal ethics combine. Thus antiquity always has the ideal of a relative equality among men, → III, 345-348. As regards possessions this is demanded only within limits in ideal political projections. In particular, slaves are originally excluded from it, Aristoph. Eccl., 651 f.; Plat. Leg., VI, 777b; on Aristot. → II, 263. A rational mean helps to set up a balance between rich and poor. πλεονεξία is excluded by this and ἰσότης established (so the politician and philosopher Archytas Fr., 3 [Diels[7], I, 437, 7-12], cf. also → III, 346, 20), and for further details → III, 791-796. Again, behind the fight against πλεονεξία there stands the ideal of moderation, σωφροσύνη. πλεο-

---

[3] Acc. to a Romantic view πλεονεξίαι are a phenomenon of city life ; men did not know them after the great flood, cf. → 269, 16-23.

νεξία does not simply seek the goods of others. It is not just a social evil. "It is the greatest evil for a man himself" (Dio Chrys. Or., 67, 7); "one must also think of God, who punishes the πλεονεκτοῦντας" (ibid., 16). These two motifs are finally brought together in the idea of a just order of human society. σωφροσύνη and δικαιότης are inseparable. The inner harmony of the individual and that of human society are interdependent; "hence they (the wise) name this totality κόσμος," Plat. Gorg., 508a. The fusion of motifs may be seen in, e.g., Eur. Phoen., 531-567. On the one side ἔλασσον is constantly opposed to πλέον (539 f.), and tyranny arises thence (the ἀδικία εὐδαίμων, 549). On the other: "But what is πλέον? It has only the name; for what is adequate is enough for the thoughtful (σώφροσι, 553 f.). Money is not for mortals (555). The primary target in the words of Iocaste to the one of the two sons is φιλοτιμία, but this very fact makes it plain that πλέον is not just greater property but increase in authority, power, pleasure etc., and πλεονεξία is "grasping beyond what is ordained for man."

Not without material justification Dio Chrys., 67, 9 reads πλεονεξία for the φιλοτιμία of Eur. Phoen., 532. Dio Chrys. combines several considerations in the speech περὶ πλεονεξίας, Or., 67. "No one takes pity on the πλεονέκτης, no one honours him, all despise him and regard him as their enemy," 67, 7. The ἴσον makes mutual peace for all, 67, 10. In the divine spheres there is no πλεονεξία; they are incorruptible because each keeps the proper order, night and day and the hours, 67, 11; → 267, 19 f. Plat. Gorg., 508a. Balanced moderation is good in all things, Dio Chrys. Or., 67, 18 f. πλεονεξία appears as ὑπερβῆναι τὸ δίκαιον, 67, 12. The ideal of being without needs (→ I, 464, 35; 466, 27 ff.) plays a part in the repudiation of πλεονεξία when it is understood primarily as seeking possessions; cf. Dio C., IX, 40, 38: πλεονεξία as the opp. of ἀρκεῖσθαι in present possessions; Apollonius in Philostr. is the ideal of the one who is content, [4] and the Stoic-Cynic diatribe generally emphasises the freedom of the wise from all desire, Epict. Diss., IV, 4, 33; cf. Ench., 1, 4: possessions deprive of freedom. But the range of meanings persists. πλεονεξία is "superiority" (before the judgment), Philodem. Rhet., V, Fr. β 29. [5] πλεονεκτεῖν is fig. "to arrogate something," Epict. Diss., III, 4, 11; "taking advantage" (here an ethical gain), II, 10, 9; πλεονεκτεῖν, "to have an advantage" (at the start), Plut. Apophth. Lac., Λέων ὁ Εὐρυκρατίδα, 2 (II, 224 f.), πλεονεξία "fulness" of endowment, opp. ἔλλειψις, Lib. Educ., 13 (11, 9e) etc. In Dio C. πλεονεκτεῖν often means "to be superior," "to gain the upper hand," cf. also τὸ θρασυνόμενον as compared with ἐπιεικές, 41, 29, 2; with ὑβρίζειν, opp. κόσμιος, εὐβίοτος, εἰρηναῖος, 52, 39, 3; with συκοφαντεῖσθαι, 52, 37, 6; πλεονεξία then means "infringement," with ἀσέλγεια, 45, 26, 1; with κιναιδία (licentiousness), 45, 26, 3.

In Muson., too, πλεονεξία plays no mean role. Debauchery gives rise to ἀδικία and πλεονεξία, 113, 10. God cannot be overcome by ἡδονή and πλεονεξία. He is stronger than desire, envy and jealousy, 90, 10. Philosophy teaches man to stand above ἡδονή and πλεονεξία, 34, 20 f. Hence women, too, must be taught philosophy in order to be cleansed from greed and covetousness, 11, 4. As it is better to suffer injustice than to do it, so it is better to be wronged than to take advantage, 11, 8. Plut. (Ser. Num. Pun., 26 [II, 565c]) has particular colours for particular evils; ἀνελευθερία (→ 269, 7) and πλεονεξία are dark and dirty. Corp. Herm., 13, 7 mentions twelve "punishments" which result from being bound to matter and from which man must cleanse himself: ἄγνοια, λύπη, ἀκρασία, ἐπιθυμία, ἀδικία, πλεονεξία, ἀπάτη, φθόνος, δόλος, ὀργή, προπέτεια, κακία; their opponent is κοινωνία, 13, 9.

Along with the emphasis on πλεονεξία the ref. to φιλαργυρία in the lists of vices in Gk. literature shows how important the treatment of avarice was in the ethics of anti-

---

[4] Cf. H. Strathmann, Gesch. der frühchristlichen Askese, I (1914), 308.
[5] Ed. S. Sudhaus, II (1896), 164, 21.

quity. Ceb., 19, 5 has the following list : ἐπιθυμία, ἀκρασία, θυμός, φιλαργυρία; in 24, 2 ἀκρασία, ἀλαζονεία, φιλαργυρία, κενοδοξία are given prominence among the κακά; 34, 3 mentions μέθυσος, ἀκρατής, φιλάργυρος, ἄδικος, προδότης; in 23, 2; 26, 2 φιλαργυρία and ἀκρασία are set alongside sorrow and lamentation. In Theophr. Char. four satirical depictions are devoted to the various forms of avarice : in 30 the αἰσχροκερδής is described with concrete instances of his conduct ; in 10 we have the μικρολόγος (skinflint); 22 presents the ἀνελεύθερος (niggard); the ἀναίσχυντος (in 9) is simply another variation on the miser.

Finally avaritia plays a part in the ethical discussions of popular Latin philosophy. In a fundamental treatment of the aegrotationes animi Cic. deals with greed, ambition and loose-living, Tusc., IV, 24 f., 26 (other vices are also added); he singles out the spiritual sickness of covetousness and gloriae cupiditas, ibid., 79. In Nat. Deor., III, 71 libido, avaritia and facinus are associated, and in Fin., II, 27 we find avarus, adulter and luxuriosus (all under the master-concept of cupiditas). In Fin., III, 75 it is said of Sulla : trium pestiferorum vitiorum, luxuriae, avaritiae, crudelitatis magister fuit ; cf. De Legibus, I, 51: quid enim foedius avaritia, quid immanius libidine . . .? Acc. to Sen. ad Lucilium Epistularum Moralium, 90, 3 [6] philosophy teaches that there was originally a common ownership of all goods among men until avaritia disrupted society. The invention of locks and bolts gave avarice a signum, 90, 8. Only avaritia or luxuria (cf. πλεονεξία and ἀσέλγεια) dissociavere mortales, so that they leave society for robbery, 90, 36. Avaritia wanted something as its own. It thus made everything else alien, and lost everything in seeking much, 90, 38. This led to the loss of the original happy state in which everything belonged to everybody (90, 39) and each shared with the rest (90, 40).

B. Jewish Literature in Greek.

1. In the LXX the word group is used only for בצע and בּצַע,[7] which originally denote "unlawful gain" (lit. "to cut off"). Only occasionally is the sense neutr., i.e., "gain," so πλεονεξία in Hab. 2:9 (where κακήν has been added); Ju. 5:19 A (B δῶρον). Striving for unlawful wealth leads to violence and murder, Jer. 22:17, cf. Ez. 22.27. Esp. in view is the unrestricted longing for possessions which sets aside the rights of others ; this is the attitude of the powerful, loc. cit. (οἱ ἄρχοντες), cf. 2 Macc. 4:50 (τῶν κρατούντων). As opposed to the greed of the violent, wisdom helps those who follow it to riches, Wis. 10:11. πλεονεξία is also "dishonest gain" in ψ 118:36 (opp. God's testimonies). In fact πλεονεξία is never used where the ref. is to the honest gaining of a possession. The use of πλεονέκτης (only Sir. 14:9 : the covetous man) is similar, and so, too, is that of πλεονεκτεῖν (only Ju. 4:11 B; Hab. 2:9; Ez. 22:27).

2. In the Hexapla the group is fairly common as compared with the LXX. Where there is a Heb. original the LXX uses the group 10 times, Σ 16 times and Θ and ᾽Α 12 times each. In ᾽ΑΣΘ it is used only in a negative sense, and apart from the 2 passages about to be mentioned and 3 at the end the ref. is always to material advantage. We have mistransl. at Ju. 4:11 Θ, where a place-name is rendered πλεονεκτούντων as in LXX B (the only agreement of ᾽ΑΣΘ with LXX in the use of the group), and also in Job 27:8 ᾽ΑΣΘ, where בצע = "to cut off" is wrongly transl. as "to desire," "to carry off" ? or "to do violence" ? At ψ 9:24 (10:3) πλεονέκτης is the "usurer"; πλεονεκτεῖν means "to take advantage of" (τοὺς πλησίον σου) in Ez. 22:12 ΣΘ; "to seek advantage" in Jer. 6:13 ᾽Α; with πλεονεξίαν "to aim at (dishonest) gain" in Prv. 1:19

---

[6] Cf. H. v. Schubert, "Der Kommunismus der Wiedertäufer u. seine Quellen," SAH, 10, 11 (1919), 31 f. Cf. in general Vögtle, 25 : "Every reader of esp. the Roman classics knows that avaritia, cupido divitiarum etc. was almost a normative principle in private and public life" (with a ref. to Wettstein, II on R. 1:29).

[7] Apart from Sir. 14:9 (where the equivalent word is corrupt), Ju. 4:11 B (where a proper name is misunderstood) and Is. 28:8 (where the LXX deviates completely from the Heb.).

'ΑΣΘ 15:27 Σ; Jer. 8:10 Θ. πλεονεξία is "unlawful gain" in Is. 33:15 'ΑΣΘ (of bribes, LXX ἀνομία); 56:11 'ΑΣΘ; 57:17 'ΑΣΘ; Jer. 6:13 Σ; 51(28):13 'Α (usurer); Ez. 33:31 ΣΘ (opp. obedience to God's Word); 1 Βασ. 8:3 'ΑΣΘ (LXX συντέλεια with bribery), "bribery" in Ex. 18:21 'ΑΣΘ (LXX ὑπερηφανίαν). In the verses mentioned the Heb. is always יֶצַע or יֶצַע; only in Σ Ez. 7:11 (LXX ὕβρις, [8] 'Α ἀδικία); Hab. 1:9; 2:17 (LXX ἀσέβεια, 'Α αἷμα) is πλεονεξία used for חָמָס "deed of violence."

3. In Test. XII, [9] too, the word group denotes "covetousness," "taking advantage of". πλεονεξία destroys the relation to one's neighbour and incenses God (A. 2:6); it is also associated with presumption (ὑψούμενοι Jud. 21:8) and ὕβρις (G. 5:1).

4. The 3 words have only a negative sense in Philo. a. πλεονεξία is the "superiority" of the ἄνισον as opp. to equality, Spec. Leg., II, 190. b. It is "privilege" as opp. to ἴσον, ibid., IV, 54. c. πλεονεκτεῖν is "wanting more" at a distribution, Vit. Mos., I, 324 opp. ἰσότιμοι "having equal right"; also "to exercise force" of bodily functions, Poster. C., 162; πλεονέκτης Sacr. AC, 32 in a list of vices with far more than 100 adj.: ἄδικος, ἄνισος, ἀκοινώνητος, ἀσύμβατος, ἄσπονδος, πλεονέκτης, κακονομώτατος, ἄφιλος, ἄοικος, ἄπολις, hence one who sets himself outside the orders of society by virtue of his conduct; so also "violent" (in self-interest), Vit. Mos., I, 56. πλεονεξία (over 40 times) commonly means "covetousness," "the malignant passion which is hard to cure," Spec. Leg., IV, 5, "the source of an unhappy life," Vit. Mos., II, 186, "unlawful enrichment" (he who makes an offering of ill-gotten gains makes God a participant in his πλεονεξία), Spec. Leg., I, 278, and its acts, "seizing the property of others," Agric., 83. Yet we also find the transf. sense: "desires" of the ψυχή (beget evil), Spec. Leg., II, 52; "immoderation" (of the dominion of bodily πάθη), Praem. Poen., 121. Philo, too, frequently contrasts πλεονεξία with the natural equality of men, Omn. Prob. Lib., 79, cf. Mut. Nom., 103; Vit. Cont., 70 (the original evil of ἀνισότης). In a series of ethical antitheses πλεονεξία stands opposed to δικαιοσύνη, Omn. Prob. Lib., 159, to "discretion and righteousness and other virtues," Praem. Poen., 15, to ἐγκράτεια and freedom from need, Spec. Leg., I, 173. πλεονεξία is related to ἀταξία, Decal., 155 (they are the causes of oligarchy and ochlocracy), also to ἀδικία (Praem. Poen., 15), to ἀκολασία ("licentiousness," Spec. Leg., I, 173), to ἀντεπιθέσεις (acts of hostility) in contrast to ἱλαρὰ εὐθυμία (Spec. Leg., II, 43); in a list we also find ἡδοναὶ καὶ ἐπιθυμίαι καὶ λῦπαι καὶ φόβοι πλεονεξίαι τε καὶ ἀφροσύναι καὶ ἀδικίαι, Vit. Cont., 2. These combinations and the contexts show that often πλεονεξία is for Philo, not just coveting or grasping at the goods of others, but "man's snatching beyond the measure ordained for him" or the "violation of the orders in which men are set together." πλεονεξία disrupts the cosmos, the harmonious order in man, or in his life with others, or in both.

5. Ps.-Phocylides [10] gives quite a number of admonitions which bear on the question of ownership. The group is first paraphrased: μὴ πλουτεῖν ἀδίκως, 5; ἀρκεῖσθαι παρεοῦσι καὶ ἀλλοτρίων ἀπέχεσθαι, 6. "Keep away from thy neighbour's field, μὴ ... ὑπερβῆις, 35. Love of money is the mother of all evil 42. To this is appended in 43-47 a complaint about the disruption of human orders by gold. Hubris esp. is an evil result of wealth 62. Do not cling to money, you cannot take it with you to Hades 109 f. To each his own — ἰσότης δ᾽ ἐν πᾶσιν ἄριστον, 137 (→ 267, 19, 47 f.). In 14 f. there is an attack on deceitful conduct, e.g., on the scales. Oppression of the poor is censured in 10, 19. There is a warning against receiving stolen property in 135 f., and against the indolence which leads to theft or sponging in 153-157, cf. Luc. De Paras.

---

[8] At Ez. 7:11 πλεονεξία obviously carries with it the concept of immoderation in the sense of the Jewish Hell. view of sin [Bertram].

[9] If Test. XII be viewed as wholly Chr. (M. de Jonge, The Testaments of the Twelve Patriarchs [1953], cf. the review by O. Eissfeldt in ThLZ, 79 [1954], 478 f.) this section should be under D.

[10] Diehl³, II, 91-108.

C. The New Testament.

The word group occurs chiefly in the Pauline writings (15 out of 19 instances). The sense "striving for material possessions" is possible in every case apart from 2 C. 2:11. Where this is the meaning, taking advantage of one's neighbour is obviously the main thought. It is an open question whether there is a continuation of the full range of the Greek and Hellenistic understanding sketched above.

1. In ethical exhortations the material peculiar to Luke (Lk. 12:15) contains a fundamental warning against all active striving for the increase of material possessions as a means of security. [11] The brother is in view in the admonition in 1 Th. 4:6, which is based on the thought of judgment, → II, 444 f. → 268, 1 f.

→ πρᾶγμα (1 Th. 4:6) does not mean the matter alluded to in v. 4, nor does it mean business. [12] It means "dispute"; [13] ὑπερβαίνειν καὶ πλεονεκτεῖν is materially a double expression, → V, 744, 16 ff. [14] The view of some fathers that the ref. is to interference in the marriage of a brother [15] finds no adequate basis in non-christian usage. [16] Furthermore ἀκαθαρσία (used comprehensively in v. 7) does not have to denote sexual immorality in particular, → III, 428, 20-429, 2; cf. also Eph. 4:19. In Eph. 4:19 the possibility has to be considered whether ἐν πλεονεξίᾳ is not used modally (in dependence on ἐργασίαν): on the basis of unlawful enrichment they do all conceivable uncleanness (ἀσέλγεια does not just refer to sexual impurity, → I, 490, 6-9). If not, ἐν πλεονεξίᾳ is to be taken with ἀκαθαρσίας as a loosely appended attribute which did not take into account the preceding construction (one should consider how slow a business letter-writing was in antiquity).

In the NT, as in the literature of antiquity (→ 267, 39 f.; 269, 11. 13), we obviously find quite often a common discussion of filthiness in both sex and business life. In Eph. 5:3 this group of sins is (purely formally) distinguished from certain sins of the tongue, → I, 191, 1 ff.; IV, 844 f.; V, 282, 12 ff.), and it alone is emphasised in v. 5. Here the πλεονέκτης is called an idolater, cf. Col. 3:5 (→ V, 928, 8 ff.). This surprising statement (→ II, 380, 8 ff.), which is impressively underlined in Pol., 11, 2, is best explained by acquaintance with the saying of Jesus about Mammon (on Mt. 6:24 → IV, 389 f.), but the fact that the thought was taken up (or newly coined) shows how important was the battle against sins of possession in the primitive Christian community. [17] Along with sensual desire, which includes immoderation in food and intoxicating drink (→ IV, 547 f.), material covetousness is a special threat to the new life of the Christian. It brings him under an ungodly and demonic spell which completely separates him from God through serving an alien power. In 1 C. 5:10 f. Paul demands avoidance of any intercourse with a πλεονέκτης in the community. In v. 10 the πλεονέκτης is grouped with the fornicator and the idolater; the list is extended in v. 11.

---

[11] Cf. Schl. Lk., 310; also 464: The evangelist used by Luke in his special material attacks "the culture which finds the meaning of life in the acquisition of money."

[12] So Dob. Th., ad loc., 167: This understanding is suggested in Gk. texts, e.g., Plut. Adulat., 14 (II, 57c): πλεονέκταις ... καὶ πλουτοῦσιν ἀπὸ πραγμάτων αἰσχρῶν καὶ πονηρῶν.

[13] So Dib. Th., ad loc.; cf. 1 C. 6:1.

[14] Formally ὑπερβαίνειν can be used in the abs. ("to transgress") as well as with the acc. of person; it is mostly used with acc. of object, → 268, 21 Dio C.; abs. and with acc. of obj. in Ps.-Phocylides, 35 → 270, 39 f. For details on this verb cf. Dob. Th., 168.

[15] Cf. Dib. Th., ad loc.

[16] E. Klaar, πλεονεξία, -έκτης, -εκτεῖν, ThZ, 10 (1954), 395-397, esp. 397, no examples.

[17] Cf. 1 Tm. 6:10, where φιλαργυρία is the root of all evil, in repetition of a pre-Chr. saying, → 270, 40; 2 Tm. 3:2; Hb. 13:5 → D.

In 1 C. 5:11; 6:10 there is also express mention of the ἅρπαξ.[18] The meaning of this group naturally overlaps that of πλεονέκτης etc. Probably it contains more of a suggestion of violent seizure of the property of others,[19] whereas the present group carries with it the thought of cunning except where it has the specific sense of covetousness. Thieves are also mentioned in 1 C. 6:10. It is hardly possible to establish a systematic order here (v. 9 f.), but obviously sexual offences are mentioned first in v. 9 (interrupted by the ref. to idolatry), and the rapacious are mentioned only after thieves (→ III, 755). In the light of these and other passages (cf. also Eph. 4:28; R. 2:21; Mk. 7:21 f.) it is highly unlikely that in other less unambiguous verses the word group is to be construed in a sexual sense, → n. 16. In the light of what is said elsewhere in the NT the frequency of the warning against covetousness or against seizing the property of others is no more surprising than its emphatic condemnation.[20] The sayings discussed under 2. and 3. also show what importance primitive Christianity attached to sins relating to possessions.

In R. 1:29 πλεονεξία is for Paul one of the basic facts in which the total abandonment of the human race by God works itself out. It occurs in a group of four nouns which comprehensively describe the power of sin in the ravaging of human relationships,[21] → III, 484, 7 ff.; cf. → I, 155, 29 ff. Here it is possible that πλεονεξία signifies man's "snatching beyond the sphere ordained for him in society" with its expression in acts of violence (fig. as well as literal) towards his neighbour, → 266-268. If not, the introduction of πλεονεξία shows how very serious an offence is covetous grasping at the property of others.

In lists of vices in the Gospels the word is found only at Mk. 7:22 (in a group of 12 nouns, v. 21 f.; the par. Mt. 15:19 has 6). Here again there is no systematic order,[22] but twice a sexual offence is grouped with one relating to property, so obviously there is some arrangement here. πλεονεξία denotes (cf. v. 21) the inner impulse which leads to an evil deed. As distinct from κλοπαί it points to "covetous desires" which "lead to cheating one's neighbour."

2. For Christian ministers in particular there is the danger that they will abuse their office to satisfy their greed or that they will usurp an office for this purpose. 2 Pt. 2:3 refers to lying teachers whose preaching is governed by their covetousness.

There is apparently a pun here: "In greed they shall ... sell you" (cf. v. 1: "who bought them"; those who were freed by Christ in His unselfish love will now be brought by covetous false teachers into dependence on lying powers). Intrinsically it is also possible that πλεονεξία is used here in a broader sense: in their striving for authority or power (→ 266-268), but the context seems to favour the meaning: to make you inclined to support them, they attract you to them by false (and esp. libertinistic, v. 2)

---

[18] Str.-B., III, 362 (on 1 C. 5:11) refers to a later Rabb. discussion which calls all those who get rich dishonestly robbers, Sanh., 26b.

[19] Cf. rapina, rapere, diripere, rapax, raptor; also ἁρπάζειν in the NT.

[20] S. Laukamm, "Das Sittenbild des Artemidor von Ephesus," Angelos, 3 (1930), 32-71, shows how much "the question of money dominates life" here (56); cf. 40 f. on the poor. W. B. Sedgwick, "Covetousness and the Sensual Sins in the NT," ET, 36 (1924/25), 478 f. refers in explanation to the economic difficulties and social tensions of the Mediterranean world for some centuries before the time of the NT. Cf. on this F. Heichelheim, Wirtschaftliche Schwankungen der Zeit von Alexander bis Augustus (1930), 45-47, 97-106; cf. also his Wirtschaftsgeschichte des Altertums, I (1938), 640-646 (slaves and proletariat); on Augustus' attempts at stabilisation cf. 677-682.

[21] The group in v. 29a is obviously detached from the series in 29b-31, where individual vices are listed.

[22] There is, however, a formal arrangement, for the 6 plurals are in 2 groups of 3 each.

teachings. The ἑαυτοὺς ποιμαίνοντες of Jd. 12 corresponds to v. 3a. [23] The charge is taken up again and pressed in v. 14. The false teachers are practised in covetousness. It is a routine for them. Their acts are essentially (καρδίαν) and totally (γεγυμνασμένην) controlled by it. Materially one may recall the conditions presupposed in Did., 11, 9 (the prophet shares the meal which he orders for the poor) [24] and Herm. m., 11, 12 (prophecy against remuneration).

The charge of πλεονεξία against Christian ministers obviously goes back (at least) [25] to the beginnings of the European mission. Paul affirms by oath ($\rightarrow$ IV, 491, 1 ff.) in 1 Th. 2:5 that his missionary work (v. 1) in Thessalonica and his preaching generally (v. 3) were free not only from self-seeking motives (v. 4 $\rightarrow$ I, 455, 26 ff.; v. 5 $\rightarrow$ III, 818, 11 ff.) which might have been concealed behind his unselfish activity (δόλῳ v. 3) but also from covetousness ; when he preached he had no ulterior purpose of enriching himself. [26] Obviously πλεονεξία is here subordinate to the master concept of ἀκαθαρσία (v. 3). In 2 C. 7:2 πλεονεκτεῖν is used with ἀδικεῖν ($\rightarrow$ 267, 19, 40; 268, 3, 38; 269, 3; $\rightarrow$ I, 161, 5 ff.) and φθείρειν : Paul has neither harmed nor taken advantage of anyone in Corinth. The two other verbs might suggest a figurative interpretation, namely, an accusation that Paul had kept back something from the Corinthians spiritually. It is more likely, however, that Paul is alluding to the charges referred to in 12:17 f. [27] Here the context shows that financial matters are at issue (v. 14 f. $\rightarrow$ III, 138, 31 f.; $\rightarrow$ I, 561, 14 ff.). Even through those whom he commissioned Paul did not exploit the Corinthians. 2 C. 8:20 suggests that the Corinthians made this accusation with special reference to the collection for Jerusalem, cf. 8:22 f.

3. The choice of words in 2 C. 9:5 is possibly influenced too by the suspicions of the Corinthians. At any rate, the passage maintains that the gift of the Corinthians should be the imparting of a blessing ($\rightarrow$ II, 763, 28 ff.) and not something calculated by covetousness. Love blesses, whereas covetousness takes advantage of the brother by a close scrutiny of the gift, which becomes thereby a gift of covetousness.

4. It is worth noting that in the same epistle the word group occurs already at 2 C. 2:11. Here one may translate either "overpower" or "take advantage of." Satan does this if forgiveness is denied. [28] Or — and this is the main emphasis in the epistle at large — the community and the apostle will experience this in the disruption of the relationship between them unless they agree in their attitude to the offender, whom Paul is ready to pardon.

D. The Post-Apostolic Fathers.

Here the two nouns occur only in ethical connections. They denote quite unambiguously the coveting of the possessions of others, Barn., 10, 4; 19, 6; Did., 2, 6 (with "robber"; sexual offences are dealt with in 2, 2). Elsewhere they occur in lists of vices. There is obviously a specific order in Herm. s., 6, 5, 5 : adulterer, drunkard, calumniator, liar, covetous man, robber. In m., 6, 2, 5 various kinds of intemperance are followed by "lusts

---

[23] As v. 2a corresponds to the saying about love feasts in Jd. 12 if we are to read ἀγάπαις.

[24] Cf. Kn. Did., ad loc.

[25] Cf. Dib. Th. transl. of 2 Th. 2:5.

[26] Cf. generally Mk. 12:40 par.; Mt. 10:8 f.; Ac. 8:18-20.

[27] Cf. Ltzm. K. on 2 C. 12:16.

[28] Schl. K., 492.

for women and riches (gen.), ... arrogance and talebearing." Pol., 2, 2 enumerates "all unrighteousness, (namely) covetousness, avarice, calumniation, false witness," cf. 1 Cl., 35, 5 : "All unrighteousness and wickedness, (namely) covetousness, strifes, maliciousness etc." In the remaining passages there is no precise order (Did., 5, 1; Herm. m., 8, 5; Barn., 20, 1). Nowhere is there any example of the specialised sense of coveting the wives of others. It may be noted that πλεονεξία comes first in Pol., 2, 2; 1 Cl., 35, 5. Pol. fights strongly against avarice in his refs. to φιλαργυρία in 2, 2 (with πλεονεξία); 4, 1 (echoing 1 Tm. 6:10); 4, 3; 6, 1; cf. 2 Cl., 6, 4 (property sins along with those of sex); Did., 3, 5 (with κενόδοξος → 269, 2).

Delling

πλῆθος, πληθύνω

→ 128-131 πίμπλημι, 263-266 πλεονάζω, 286-298 πληρόω.

† πλῆθος.

A. Non-Biblical Use.

1. General Usage.

πλῆθος, etym. "fulness,"[1] means "crowd" in Hom., at first with no stress on greatness of numbers (Il., 17, 330), then the "many" as opp. to individuals (Il., 23, 639), like the Ionic πληθύς which is more common in Hom. (Od., 11, 514 par. ὅμιλος; Il., 15, 295 and 305 opp. ἄριστοι). πλῆθος then became a general term of measurement denoting *tantum,* "how much," first in number independently of size, e.g., Anaxag. Fr., 3 and 6 (Diels[7], II, 33, 17 and 35, 19), cf. the def. in Aristot. Metaph., IV, 13, p. 1020a, 8 f.: πλῆθος is "how many" when this can be counted, but also in size (quantitatively), Fr., 2 (Diels[7], II, 33, 3): τό γε περιέχον ἄπειρόν ἐστι τὸ πλῆθος, cf. Philo Spec. Leg., IV, 234 : πλῆθος is a kind of quantity (τοῦ ποσοῦ).

Platonic usage shows the breadth of the term. πλῆθος is the relative greatness of a "number," Gorg., 451c; Leg., V, 737c = *numerus,* Resp., V, 460a, cf. Xenoph. Mem., II, 4, 4 : small no. of friends ; with μέγεθος Resp., X, 614a; Critias, 118b; then *quantum,* χρυσοῦ, Phaedr., 279c; "amount," "sum of money," Resp., VIII, 551b; also of time, "length," "duration," Leg., III, 676b. In this use the superl. has to be denoted by addition of an adj., ἀμήχανον, Tim., 39d, ἄφθονον (water), Critias, 117a, πάμπολυ (land), Leg., III, 677e, ἄπειρον πλήθει, Parm., 144a; Soph., 256e; Phileb., 17b, so occasionally also in the plur., Critias, 115b. Or πλῆθος as such means "many" : small is the mean between one and many, Polit., 303a, opp. εἷς, Leg., VII, 800c; Polit., 300c; Soph., 239b; "great amount" of fluidity, Resp., IV, 437e, income, Resp., IX, 591e (opp. ὀλιγότης); adj. "much," μετὰ πλήθους ἱδρῶτος, with a strong outbreak of sweating, Tim., 84e; πλῆθος χρόνου "long period of time," Theaet., 158d; Polit., 269b; compar. or superlat. "the (great) majority" or "most" τῶν σοφιστῶν, Prot., 314d, ἐπὶ τὸ πλῆθος "most" Resp., II, 364e, "to a supreme degree," Phaedr., 275b. Sometimes Plato puns on πλοῦτος

π λ ῆ θ ο ς. Jackson-Lake, 4 (1933), 47 f.; 5 (1933), 376 f., 389; Schl. Lk., 696, *s.v.* and the passages adduced there.

[1] From the root *plē-* "to fill" (in πίμ-πλη-μι, πλή-ρης, Lat. *plē-nus* etc.), extended by -θ-, πλῆθος, cf. πλήθω, "to be full" (from Hom.) and Lat. *plēbēs* (*plēbs*), "crowd." Walde-Pok., II, 63 f.; Boisacq, 783 f.; Walde-Hofmann, II, 320 f. [Debrunner].

and πλῆθος; an artisan rises through wealth or expansion (πλήθει) of his trade, Resp., IV, 434b, numbers and wealth yield to virtue, Menex., 240d. In Plato, however, the usual ref. of the word is to men, → 274, 15-18. It is often a political and sociological term. The specific content varies. Mostly the transl. "crowd" is not incorrect, but πλῆθος often means "people" (as in many translations), for it seems to be synon. with δῆμος as a word for "the greater part of the populace," Leg., III, 689b. Hence πλῆθος is used for δῆμος where the sense is positive or at least neutral, Leg., VI, 768a : it is right to give the "totality" a share in certain political decisions; Menex., 238d : The Athenian form of state is an aristocracy with the consent of the crowd; Resp., VIII, 563b: the freedom of all (τοῦ πλήθους); Menex., 238d : the people has power over most things in the state because it disposes of the offices; Polit., 291d : Democracy is the rule of the crowd. Here πλῆθος is mostly the antonym of the one or few, cf. Xenoph. Mem., I, 2, 42 f.: πλῆθος, ὀλίγοι, τύραννος as law-givers. The sense is patently neutr. when πλῆθος suggests the "assembled crowd," as in Plat. Ap., 31c : τὸ πλῆθος τὸ ὑμέτερον, Leg., III, 700d : τῶν πολιτῶν τὸ πλῆθος, and where the name of the citizenry is added, Men., 90b : Ἀθηναίων τῷ πλήθει, cf. Ep., III, 315e : Συρακουσίων. [2] In both cases the word implies the "totality." πλῆθος is chiefly negative in sentences which speak of the intellectual, artistic or esp. ethical judgment of the "majority." [3] "Most men" cannot be philosophers, Resp., VI, 494a; cf. Leg., II, 670e; Polit., 304d (synon. ὄχλος). To be successful, acc. to the Sophists, the orator must says what pleases the "crowd," Phaedr., 260a; cf. Leg., II, 659b and III, 700c; Resp., VIII, 554a; most people extol a pederastic relation as virtuous, Phaedr., 256e. Sometimes the sense is pleonastically strengthened in a plur. use. The great mass of men want to become rich, Leg., XI, 918d; to persuade the masses, Gorg., 452e etc.

In Aristot. πλῆθος plays a special role in the Pol. Here it seems to be synon. with δῆμος, V, 10, p. 1310b, 13 or οἱ πολλοί, III, 8, p. 1279a, 26 f.; opp. οἱ πλούσιοι, III, 10, p. 1281a, 12; οἱ εὔποροι, the "well-to-do," V, 9, p. 1309b, 39; οἱ ὀλίγοι, III, 13, p. 1283b, 24 and 33. τὸ πλῆθος can obviously mean "the majority" [4] in Pol., synon. with τὸ πλέον μέρος, IV, 4, p. 1290a, 31 f. etc. A part. question in such contexts is whether the "majority" or the "mob" will rule (κύριον εἶναι). Sometimes πλῆθος can also be used for the "whole group," V, 8, p. 1308b, 29 f. [5] πλῆθος πολιτικόν means πλῆθος πολιτῶν, III, 13, p. 1283b, 2 f.

2. The One and the Many in Greek Philosophy.

Implied in the word from Hom. on is the opp. of the one or the few; "the many" or "many" is a term already important in Eleatic philosophy. Parm. Fr., 8 (Diels[7], I, 235-237) emphasises that being πᾶν, ἕν, συνεχές (v. 5 f.), ξυνεχὲς πᾶν ἐστιν (v. 25), οὐλομελές (v. 4), "not divisible" (v. 22; cf. Plat. Parm., 128a ἓν ... εἶναι τὸ πᾶν). Herewith, acc. to his pupil Zeno, the existence of the πλῆθος is denied ; [6] if there were plurality, it would consist of many ones, but there cannot be several ones (ἑνάδες). There is only one ἕν, cf. Plat. Parm., 127e, where Zeno's view is presented thus : "If being is plural (πολλά), ... then it must be both homogeneous and heterogeneous,

---

[2] For examples of this use on inscr. cf. Deissmann NB, 59; Pr.-Bauer[4], 1217. πλῆθος is an exact equivalent of δῆμος (the people) as the totality of those who have a political voice [Debrunner].

[3] Cf. the hexameter of Cleanthes Fr., 559 (v. Arnim, I, 128, 1 f.): οὐ γὰρ πλῆθος ἔχει συνετὴν κρίσιν, οὔτε δικαίαν οὔτε καλήν, ὀλίγοις δὲ παρ᾽ ἀνδράσι τοῦτό κεν εὕροις.

[4] For the political use on inscr. cf. Kn. Cl. on I, 54, 2.

[5] In this usage πλῆθος does not imply primarily the organisation of a group but simply "a great number." This applies also to the instances of the sense "corporation" etc. given in Preisigke Wört., s.v. Ditt. Or., I, 56, 24 (3rd cent. B.C.) speaks, e.g., of various φυλαὶ τοῦ πλήθους τῶν ἱερέων = the "whole" priesthood; cf. Porphyr. Abst., IV, 8 (p. 241, 3) τὸ ... λοιπὸν τῶν ἱερέων ... πλῆθος "all" other priests ... In Ditt. Or., II, 669, 11 (1st cent. A.D.) κατ᾽ ὀλίγους καὶ κατὰ πλήθη refers to individuals or more.

[6] Joannes Philoponus, In Aristot. Physicorum Libros Tres Priores Commentaria, ed. H. Vitelli, Comment. in Aristot. Graeca, 16 (1887), 42, 9 ff.

but this is impossible." Cf. also the dialogue between Parmenides and Aristotle, *ibid.*, 137c ff. [7]

Plat. frequently opposes this view either directly or indirectly. His most explicit polemic is in Parm., [8] cf. more briefly Phileb., 14c-18b, 25a-26d, [9] also Soph. [10] To some degree (at least formally) he adopts a Pythagorean theory which mentions ἕν καὶ πλῆθος among the 10 ἀρχαί (→ I, 480, 1 ff.), the 10 pairs of opposites which determine being and occurrence (Aristot. Metaph., I, 5, p. 986a, 22-24). At any rate the young Socrates of Plato maintains against the Eleatics that εἶδος (the idea) is contained in the plurality of many individual things (Parm., 131a : ὅλον τὸ εἶδος ἐν ἑκάστῳ εἶναι τῶν πολλῶν ἕν ὄν; cf. b); the ideas are paradigms (παραδείγματα) in the sphere of the existent (ἐν τῇ φύσει); things have a share in them because they copy them, 132d. In Phileb. we find μονάδες (15b) rather than εἴδη in the discussion of the ἕν and the πολλά (15b); these are identical (ταὐτόν, 15d, [11] cf. 16c d, where μία ἰδέα is used). Unity does not exclude plurality. Plurality is included in it, 17d-18a. On the relation of the one good to the many in ethics cf. Resp., VII, 507b, 509b, 508e, 534bc; Phileb., 65a. On Aristot. → I, 11, 28-41. On this whole question → 297 πλήρωμα.

B. The Meaning in the Septuagint.

1. In the LXX πλῆθος [12] is mostly used for derivates of רבב; about 100 times for רֹב (or רוֹב): "plurality," "crowd," "totality," "quantity." As a rendering of רֹב, and like the Heb. and the non-biblical πλῆθος, it is often used adjectivally with the subj. gen.: "much," "great," "powerful," cf. Prv. 5:23; Qoh. 1:18 (LXX read ναβ דַּעַת); 5:2, 6; 11:1; Na. 3:4; Lam. 1:3; Ez. 28:16. The prepos. phrases in which רֹב is found in the Heb. are fairly uniformly rendered by phrases with πλῆθος in the LXX. [13] The expression εἰς πλῆθος (without dependent gen.), which also occurs in non-bibl. Gk., is a transl. from the Heb. in the LXX. The formula κατὰ τὸ πλῆθος ... refers esp. to the grace and mercy of God to His people (ψ 105:45) or to righteous individuals (cf. ψ 50:1; 68:17; Neh. 13:22; Lam. 3:22), or else it refers to His righteousness (Is. 63:7 HT grace); for the former we also find ἐν πλήθει ... Ps. 5:7; ψ 68:14. Elsewhere the emphasis is on the "fulness" or "greatness" of God's majesty (δόξης, Ex. 15:7, μεγαλωσύνης, Ps. 150:2) or kindness (ψ 144:7). In contrast, man has no reason to rely on the greatness of his strength (ψ 32:16) nor the people to rely on the host of its warriors (Hos. 10:13) or the plenitude of its offerings (Is. 1:11; naively extolled, 2 Ch. 5:6). Indeed, the multitude

---

[7] Cf. also K. Riezler, *Parmenides, Frankfurter Studien zur Religion u. Kultur der Antike,* 5 (1934), on Parm., esp. 53-57, 71 f., 75, 79, 84, 87; on Zeno, 85 f.; on Plat. Parm., 81, 85, 90-92; on Aristot., 80 f.

[8] Cf. on this C. Ritter, *Platon,* II (1923), 63-96.

[9] *Ibid.*, 177, 179.

[10] *Ibid.*, 123 f., 179.

[11] Cf. also Resp., VII, 525a : We see the same (the real) as one and as infinite plurality (ἄπειρα τὸ πλῆθος).

[12] πληθύς only at 3 Macc. 4:17.

[13] So מִן (mostly "in consequence or on account of") by ἀπό (cf. Johannessohn Präpos., 281) Gn. 16:10; 2 Ch. 5:6; Job 35:9; Na. 3:4; Lam. 1:3; Ez. 27:12; by ἐκ 1 Βασ. 1:16; 3 Βασ. 7:32; Ez. 27:18; by διά and acc. Ez. 28:18; לְ by εἰς Gn. 30:30; 48:16 (רֹב πλῆθος πολύ); Ju. 6:5; 7:12; 2 Βασ. 17:11; 3 Βασ. 1:19, 25; 10:10, 27; 1 Ch. 4:38; 22:3, 4, 8; 29:21 etc.; by a simple dat. Dt. 1:10; 10:22; 28:62; Jos. 11:4 (the obvious meaning of the LXX here is "in number"; without dependent gen.); by a simple acc. 2 Ch. 11:23 (רֹב πλῆθος πολύ); בְּ by ἐν Ps. 5:8; ψ 68:14; 32:16, 17; 65:3; Qoh. 1:18; 5:2, 6; 11:1; Hos. 10:13; by κατά and acc. (cf. Johannessohn, 256) Ps. 5:11; 150:2; by ἐκ Prv. 5:23; by ἀπό Ez. 28:16; by a simple dat. Ex. 15:7; עַל by ἐπί and dat. ψ 36:11; and acc. Lam. 1:5; by ὑπό Hos. 9:7; כְּ ("according to" cf. Johannessohn, 255, "corresponding") is rendered by κατά and acc. Neh. 13:22; ψ 50:3; 68:17; 105:45; Is. 63:7; Lam. 3:32.

of its sins is often stressed, Ps. 5:10; Hos. 9:7; Lam. 1:5; Ez. 28:18. The fulness of salvation promised to the πραεῖς in ψ 36:11 is the gift of God. Thus the πλῆθος sayings serve to underline the OT view of God and man. To make more vivid the fact that the descendants promised to the patriarchs (Gn. 32:13) and Hagar (Gn. 16:10), or the people of Israel (Dt. 1:10; 10:22; 28:62), are without number, comparisons with the sand of the sea (Gn. 32:13) and the stars of heaven (Dt. 1:10; 10:22; 28:62) are chosen; these carry an implication of infinity. [14] The same applies to the comparison of the enemies of Israel with the sand of the sea (Jos. 11:4) and swarms of locusts (Ju. 6:5 and 7:12).

2. πλῆθος is used some 13 times for רַב; it is also quite common in the LXX for the adj. (→ 274, 33-36) in the sense "numerous" Ex. 1:9 (with μέγα); Ez. 31:6; "many" Ex. 19:21; [15] Nu. 32:1a; 2 Ch. 30:17; Qoh. 6:3; Ez. 47:10 (πλῆθος πολύ); "the crowd" Job 31:34 (A λαοῦ); "great" πολὺ τὸ πλῆθος τῆς χρηστότητός σου, ψ 30:20 (cf. 144:7); "fulness" θησαυρῶν Ιερ. 28:13, ὕδατος Ez. 31:15; the use of πλῆθος is mechanical at Is. 51:10 : ὕδωρ ἀβύσσου πλῆθος. πλῆθος occurs 7 times for verbal forms of רבה: q Qoh. 5:10 : of the increasing of worldly goods; pi ψ 43:13 "gain" in selling; hi Ex. 36:5 : "more" … than ; 2 Ch. 11:12; 16:8 : εἰς πλῆθος σφόδρα "very much"; Ιερ. 26:16 of the military power of Egypt; 2 Εσδρ. 15:18 : "in fulness," text corrupt. πλῆθος is used once each for רִבּוֹ (elsewhere "ten thousand") Hos. 8:12, מַרְבִּית "multitude" 2 Ch. 9:6, תַּרְבִּית "advance," "usurer" Lv. 25:36 (with τόκος) = πλεονασμός v. 37.

3. Some 30 times πλῆθος is the transl. of הָמוֹן, which lit. means "murmuring," "roaring," "noise," then the "roaring crowd," finally transf. the "multitude." Naturally πλῆθος was not adapted to render the original sense of הָמוֹן; where this is determinative in the HT the LXX more or less alters the sense by using πλῆθος, cf. Jer. 10:13; Ez. 26:13; Is. 17:12; 60:5 א*, where the Heb. has a sonorous depiction of roaring or murmuring. Even when the HT refers to the "tumult" of men (2 Βασ. 18:29; πλῆθος Αἰγυπτίων Ez. 30:10; πλῆθος Μέμφεως Ez. 30:15) or armies (2 Ch. 20:2, 12, 24; 14:10), the primary thought is that of the noise, though this is not always evident (Ju. 4:7; 4 Βασ. 7:13; Ez. 39:11); this aspect is completely lost in the LXX. Sometimes, of course, הָמוֹן simply means "crowd" or "great number" in the HT, cf. πατὴρ πλήθους ἐθνῶν Gn. 17:4 and Sir. 44:19, γυναικῶν 2 Ch. 11:23, "mass" or "swarm" Is. 29:5 B etc., of flocks Ιερ. 30:27, then "host" 2 Ch. 13:8 (elucidated by רַב or πολύ). Finally, הָמוֹן = πλῆθος can be used of inanimate objects : 1 Ch. 29:16; Ez. 29:19; 30:4 (both A etc.): riches ; 2 Ch. 31:10 : tithes. הָמוֹן is obviously misunderstood at Is. 63:15 (as at Jer. 10:13 etc. → lines 25-27), where the ref. of the HT is to the inner movement of Yahweh, but the LXX has τὸ πλῆθος τοῦ ἐλέους σου. The LXX apparently took הָמוֹן to mean "great number," "crowd," and thus transl. it πλῆθος when the original sense was implicit or even dominant. The latter is esp. probable in a few refs in Ez. : 31:2, 18; 32:32, where there is judgment on the tumult of Pharaoh, on his vainglorious power (the LXX seems to have seen a ref. to his army, cf. 7:12-14 A).

4. In the LXX πλῆθος is also used for the following equivalents : עֵדָה Sir. 7:7, 14; 42:11c (there is an obvious ref. here to those assembled); קָהָל Ex. 12:6; 2 Ch. 31:18 (apparently in the sense of the group); עָצוּם "numerous" Nu. 32:1b (of the cattle); Dt. 26:5 (= πλῆθος πολύ); עָצַם Is. 31:1 (πλῆθος); עַם "host" 2 Ch. 12:3; מְלֹא Gn. 48:19;

---

[14] ἄπειρος and cognates occur in the LXX, not in the sense of "infinite," but in that of "unfathomed," Nu. 14:23; Wis. 13:18; Zech. 11:15 (here for אֱוִלִי "foolish"), probably also Jer. 2:6 ἐν γῇ ἀπείρῳ (for עֲרָבָה) in the sense of ἀνέργαστος Schleusner, s.v.

[15] Here too ἐκ is used for מִן (Johannessohn, 17), though the LXX could have read רֹב here.

כְּבֵד "in large quantity" Ex. 8:20; שִׁפְעָה "host" of war-horses Ez. 26:10; מְתִים "people" Sir. 7:16; מִסְפָּר "number" ψ 146:4 (only God counts πλήθη [16] ἄστρων); כַּבִּיר "in bulk" Is. 28:2 (ὕδατος πολύ πλῆθος). Sometimes the choice of πλῆθος may rest on a misunderstanding, so obviously Da. 10:1, where צָבָא means "affliction" but the LXX sees a ref. to "army." [17] In ψ 9:25 אַף is construed as "wrath" (ὀργῆς) rather than lit. "nose," and hence גֹּבַהּ means "gain," חַיִל ("height") is rendered πλῆθος. At Mi. 4:13 חַיִל = "gain" but LXX has ἰσχύς ("host") and thus takes בֶּצַע (gain from usury) to mean "fulness" = "host of men" dedicated to God in the ban (or ἰσχύς = πλῆθος = riches). Possibly רֶגֶשׁ "roaring mob" is at the back of the rendering of רִגְשָׁה by πλῆθος in ψ 63:3. The LXX follows another reading when it has πλῆθος at, e.g., Zech. 9:10; Ez. 32:6; Ex. 23:2; Na. 2:14.

5. The normal use of πλῆθος is found in LXX writings for which there is no Heb. original (→ 274, 14; 275, 2-22). Sometimes a distinction is here made between individuals (leaders) and the mob. [18] So Wis. 6:2 : οἱ κρατοῦντες πλήθους 8:15 : ἐν πλήθει (Solomon); 1 Εσδρ. 9:12 : οἱ προηγούμενοι τοῦ πλήθους (cf. Ep. Ar., 310 : οἵ τε ἡγούμενοι τοῦ πλήθους, along with the elders of the πολίτευμα), 3 Macc. 7:13 : the priests and πᾶν τὸ πλῆθος, also 2 Macc. 4:5 : Onias considers what is profitable παντὶ τῷ πλήθει. If there is a hint of the "whole body" here, and also at 1 Εσδρ. 9:4 : the whole body of the exiles τῆς αἰχμαλωσίας from which those who live in mixed marriages are to be excluded, so the evident sense of πλῆθος elsewhere is the "whole people," so esp. in diplomatic usage, cf. 1 Macc. 8:20 : speech of the envoys of the Maccabeans and the πλῆθος τῶν Ἰουδαίων in Rome ; [19] 2 Macc. 11:16 : letter of the imperial minister Lysias to the Jews, τῷ πλήθει τῶν Ἰουδαίων; cf. Ep. Ar., 308 (→ 275, 15 f.). When 2 and 3 Macc. want to lay emphasis on the crowd, they often choose the plur.: "masses," 2 Macc. 5:26; 3 Macc. 5:24, 46, cf. Ep. Ar., 15 and 21; "hosts," 2 Macc. 13:1; 14:20, 41; 15:21, cf. Ep. Ar., 118. In 1 Εσδρ. 9 πλῆθος often means the "assembled multitude," cf. v. 45, 48, 49 in the abs.; sometimes with πᾶν cf. Ep. Ar., 42 and 45; cf. עֵדָה in Sir. (→ 277, 42 f.); also Sir. 6:34 : πλῆθος πρεσβυτέρων.

C. The Word in the New Testament.

In the NT, too, πλῆθος has the sense of "crowd" with a wide range of meanings. Which of these predominates one cannot always say for certain. In the NT there is never an abstract reference, as in the LXX. Of the 30 instances 7 are in Lk. (1 par. with Mk., 4 in the material peculiar to Lk.: 1:10; 2:13; 5:6; 23:27). There are 17 instances in Ac., and of the other 7 we find 2 each in Mk. and Jn. and 1 each in Hb., Jm. and 1 Pt. The Synoptists and Pl. sometimes use οἱ → πολλοί (→ 279, 1) in the sense of πλῆθος, so Mk. 6:2 : the "crowd gathered" in the synagogue, 9:26 : the "multitude" present, Mt. 24:12 : the "majority"; so also 2 C. 2:17; οἱ πολλοί also has much of the sense of the "whole body" in 1 C. 10:33, and cf. also — πολλοί without art. — Mk. 10:45 and par. [20] πλῆθος in the specific Lucan sense is sometimes replaced by this.

---

[16] The plur. is probably based on the par. ὀνόματα שֵׁמוֹת [Katz].

[17] The military use is common in Xenoph., cf. already Hom. and even more plainly Eur. Phoen., 715 : "Small is the host of this land."

[18] Cf. 2 Ch. 30:5 : the "great part" of the people ; Job 35:9 : calumniated by the "crowd."

[19] The expression reminds us of inscr. on Hasmonean coins which mention the high-priest and the חֶבֶר of the Jews together, cf. G. F. Hill, Catalogue of the Gk. Coins of Palestine (1914), pp. 192-207, No. 11-60 for Alexander Jannaeus, pp. 212-214 for Antigonus Mattathias.

[20] On the Semitic → πολλοί = רַבִּים "all" cf. J. Jeremias, Die Abendmahlsworte Jesu[2] (1949), 92 f., with art. 91 f.

In some Lucan passages the "crowd" (→ 278, 12 ff.) is clearly distinguished from a smaller select group, [21] Ac. 6:2, 5 the "multitude" of disciples (opp. the twelve), cf. 15:30 : the "host of Christians" at Antioch to which a commission is sent from Jerusalem with specific authority; cf. also Lk. 1:10 : the whole "multitude" of the people was praying outside (opp. the priest in the temple). [22] Related hereto is the usage in which πλῆθος denotes the whole of a greater number, Ac. 15:12 : the apostles, elders and community (? v. 22) at Jerusalem; 4:32 : the "whole body" of believers was of one heart and soul; 14:4 : the "whole population" of a city, the "multitude," [23] 23:7: the "totality" of all the members of the council present (in both cases ἐσχίσθη). One may then add the use in which the majority is emphasised, and probably also the unanimity of the group denoted, Lk. 19:37: the followers of Jesus, 23:1: the whole council, Ac. 25:24 : all the Jews; in these three verses ἅπαν is added to give emphasis to πλῆθος. In Ac. 21:36 the word is not meant contemptuously; πλῆθος is hardly ever used disparagingly in the NT. At most one might refer to Ac. 25:24 (on pagan lips) and less strongly Ac. 2:6; cf. 19:9 (the audience).

πλῆθος is then more generally "crowd" or "great number," strengthened by πολύ at Lk. 5:6; 23:27; Mk. 3:7, 8; Ac. 14:1; 17:4; πλῆθος πολύ par. ὄχλος πολύς, the one of the people, the other of the disciples of Jesus, Lk. 6:17; the heavenly host, Lk. 2:13 (cf. 1 Cl., 34, 5), the sick, Jn. 5:3, the fishes, 21:6, in both instances with obvious ref. also to the greatness of the number as at Jm. 5:20; 1 Pt. 4:8 (on these 2 passages → III, 558, 4-20), then "population," Lk. 8:37; Ac. 5:16 (→ line 7 f., Ac. 14:4; in Ac. δῆμος is also used for this → 275, 55 f.; 275, 26; → II, 63, 14 ff.). Without art. πλῆθος can sometimes be equivalent to πολλοί; it is thus used adjectivally (→ 277, 10 ff.; so Jn. 5:3; Jm. 5:20; 1 Pt. 4:8; Lk. 2:13 etc.); it is occasionally strengthened by πολύ; in the plural, Ac. 5:14; with article in the singular "all" at Ac. 4:32 (cf. Test. Jud. 14:5, synon. πάντες). Finally, it can simply mean "number," probably Hb. 11:12, certainly Ac. 28:3 (with τι "a handful").

† πληθύνω.

1. Originally πληθύνω [1] is the trans. "to fill" of the intr. πληθύω, "to become or be full" etc.; [2] the latter is used, e.g., in Soph. for "to be abundant," Oed. Col., 377: subj. a "report"; 930, ὁ πληθύων χρόνος, fulness of years; Hdt., IV, 181, 3 : ἀγορᾶς πληθυούσης, "at the time when the market fills," a fixed expression, cf. Suid., s.v. πλήθουσα ἀγορά: the third hour; Hdt., II, 19, 1; 20, 2 : πληθύειν, "to rise" of the Nile, but also II, 24, 1: πληθύεσθαι, Plat. πληθυόντων τῶν ἀνθρώπων, Leg., III, 682c,

---

[21] Cf. 1 Cl., 53, 5 : Moses — the people; 54, 2 : the majority of the congregation; Ign. Mg., 6, 1: few members of the congregation — τὸ πᾶν πλῆθος; Sm., 8, 2 : the bishop — τὸ πλῆθος, the whole of the Christian group led by him, cf. Tr., 1, 1; the use in Ign. almost yields the sense of "community," Tr., 8, 2 : τὸ ἐν θεῷ πλῆθος the multitude united to God. On lines 1 ff. cf. ὄχλος → V, 582, 25 ff. On Ac. → V, 587, 30 ff. Cf. ἐκκλησία in Ac. → III, 504 f.

[22] The thought of being assembled may also be important in this and the next use, cf. Herm. m., 11, 9 : λαλεῖ εἰς τὸ πλῆθος (of just men).

[23] Cf. Mart. Pol., 12, 2 πᾶν τὸ πλῆθος of the Gk. and Jewish inhabitants of Smyrna.

π λ η θ ύ ν ω. [1] From πληθύς → 274, 17, A. Debrunner, "Zu den konsonantischen io-Präsentien im Griech.," Indog. Forsch., 21 (1907), 78 [Debrunner], corresponding to trans. verbs in -ύνω formed from adj. in -υς, Schwyzer, I, 728, 1 (cf. 733ε).

[2] Like other verbs in -ύνω the word has a factitive, causative sense, cf. the examples in Debr. Gr. Wortb. § 224-226, though the extent of such formations "remained within narrow limits," § 223.

cf. 678b; ἀκολασίας ... καὶ νόσων πληθυουσῶν, Resp., III, 405a; "to replenish itself," of blood, Tim., 83e. But we already find both in Aesch., πληθύω intr. "to increase," Choeph., 1057, "to become full of" (νεκρῶν), Pers., 421, pass. Ag., 1370 : πληθύνομαι, "I incline most to ..." (or : "I am led by the majority to ..."), Suppl., 604 : χεὶρ πληθύνεται, "most of the voices are to the effect that ..." (in Aesch., then, a tt. in voting); [3] Ag., 869 (842) may be either trans. or intr., hence the text vacillates between the 2 verbs (this is also true in other passages and authors, → line 12 f.; n. 4). Aristot. is obviously already using πληθύνω intr., (θάλαττα) τοῖς ῥεύμασι πληθύνουσα (→ 263, 17 f. πλεονάζω), Meteor., I, 14, p. 351b, 7; trans. ταῖς γυναιξὶ τὸ γάλα πληθύνεται, Hist. An., VII, 11, p. 587b, 20. πληθύνω probably took over the intr. function of πληθύω; hence its pass. also has a mid. sense : "to increase" (no aor. or fut. mid.). Plut. Quaest. Plat., VII, 8, 4 (II, 1005 f.) has πληθύνοντες along with the better attested οἱ ποταμοὶ πληθύοντες; Def. Orac., 8 (II, 414b): τὸ χωρίον ἀνθρώποις ἐπλήθυνε "filled ..."; Joseph. [4] has πληθύειν intr. "to be full" ἀνδρῶν, Bell., 3, 50, "to flow abundantly," springs of water, Bell., 5, 410, "to increase," the number of casualties, Bell., 5, 80, with πληθύνειν intr.: "to become numerous," ibid., 338 (subj. Ἰουδαῖοι) and trans., Ap., II, 139 (true pass.) the world "became filled" (ἐπληθύνθη) with wild beasts. Dio C. uses πληθύω intr. "to rise" of the Tiber, 78, 25, 5; "to become numerous," 56, 7, 6, and πληθύνομαι "to become numerous," 7, 1, 6 (so Zonaras); "to fill" (become full) of vessels, 75, 13, 4 in the same sense. πληθύνω intr.: greed "increased" in someone, Herodian, III, 8, 8 (3rd cent. A.D.), but trans. in Gk. En. 16:3 : "to increase, augment" (πληθύνουσιν ... τὰ κακά). Neither verb occurs in Xenoph., Philo, or, thus far, the pap.

2. In the LXX [5] we find [6] πληθύνω [7] mostly for forms of רבה, [8] esp. hi (some 78 times), and usually with a trans. sense. Exceptions : act. intr. 1 Βασ. 1:12; "to be much occupied," Sir. 11:10; τοῦ with inf. or part. (→ line 33 f.); mid. pass. for hi at Prv. 13:11; Ez. 21:20; 22:25 "to be or become abundant or numerous." It is often used for "to increase" (posterity, people), common in Gn., Lv. 26:9; Dt. passim ; Jos. 24:3 etc. πληθυνῶ τὰ σημεῖά μου Ex. 7:3; "to multiply" θυσιαστήρια, Hos. 8:11; 10:1; "to extend" borders, 1 Ch. 4:10; "to exalt," God of man, 2 Βασ. 22:36; [9] "to heap up," κενὰ καὶ μάταια ἐπλήθυνεν, Hos. 12:2; τὴν δέησιν, Is. 1:15; δόξαν (glory), Da. 11:39; offences, 2 Ch. 33:23, ἀνομίας ... ὑπὲρ αὐτάς "more" ... than ..., Ez. 16:51; τοῦ with inf. 4 Βασ. 21:6; 2 Ch. 33:6 (ποιῆσαι τὸ πονηρόν); 36:14; 2 Εσδρ. 10:13; ψ 77:38; Am. 4:4; with part. ἐπλήθυνε προσευχομένη 1 Βασ. 1:12. On the other hand the mid. pass. [10] is mostly used for q (act. for q only Ex. 1:20; 1 Βασ. 7:2, both intr. "to multiply," and Ex. 11:9 trans.). The word is used for q some 38 times all told, often for the command of God to His creatures to "multiply" (frequently with αὐξάνεσθε), Gn. 1:22, 28; [11] 8:17; 9:1, 7; 35:11; αἱ ἡμέραι "increase," Gn. 38:12; ἔτη, Prv. 4:10; δίκαιοι, 28:28; "increase," ἐπληθύνθη Σαλωμων ... ὑπὲρ τὴν φρόνησιν πάντων ..., 3 Βασ. 5:10. The LXX has πληθύνω for the pi of רבה at Ju. 9:29 ("increase" thine

---

[3] Thackeray, 282 : "receive the support of the πλῆθος."

[4] The text varies however, cf. L. Dindorf, "Über Joseph. u. dessen Sprache," Jbch. f. Phil., 99 (1869), 843 f.

[5] Cf. Thackeray, 282.

[6] Of the verbs of filling πληθύνω is the most common in the LXX, → 287 f. πληροῦν, → 128 f. πιμπλάναι, → 289, 19 f. γέμειν, γεμίζειν, μεστοῦν [Bertram], though cf. → 128, 24 and 41.

[7] πληθύω occurs only in 3 Macc. 5:41 "to be rich in or full of" (dat.).

[8] At Ez. 16:7 the LXX read רְבִי = πληθύνου for HT רְבָבָה.

[9] There is a similar unusual expression in early Chr. literature, Herm. s., 9, 24, 3 ἐπλήθυνεν αὐτοὺς ἐν τοῖς κόποις τῶν χειρῶν αὐτῶν, "the Lord increased believers (gave them success) in the work of their hands" (as a reward for their surrender, v. 2).

[10] Aor. and fut. pass., no aor. or fut. mid.

[11] Gn. 1:28 plays a role in Corp. Herm., 1, 18; 3, 3b, no doubt under Jewish influence ; cf. C. H. Dodd, The Bible and the Gks. (1935), 163-165.

army); Lam. 2:22; Ez. 19:2, always trans. The LXX has the mid. pass. for רָבַב q : "to be or become numerous," Gn. 6:5; 1 Βασ. 25:10; Ps. 3:1; ψ 24:19; 37:20; 68:5; Qoh. 5:10 ("to be satiated" ? Ps. 4:7 misunderstanding the HT); act. trans. Jer. 5:6; intr. Ιερ. 26:23; for pu act. intr. ψ 143:13. For רַב we find the act. intr. at 1 Βασ. 14:19; the act. trans. at ψ 17:15; Ez. 27:15; the act. with τοῦ and inf. ψ 64:10; the mid. pass. "to be or become numerous," Hos. 9:7; Jl. 3:13; Is. 6:12; Lam. 1:1.

Apart from derivates of the stem רבב the words for which the LXX uses πληθύνω normally have a sense in the HT corresponding to that of the Gk. term. So עָצַם "to be numerous," act. intr. Ιερ. 37:14, mid. pass. v. 16 (in both instances αἱ ἁμαρτίαι σου); Jer. 15:8; ψ 39:6, 13 (ἀνομίαι); פָּרָה act. intr. "to increase," Sir. 16:2. Frequently also in the mid. pass. for פָּרַץ, "to increase" (lit. "to burst forth") 1 Ch. 4:38; ψ 105:29; for שָׁרַץ "to teem," Ex. 1:7; דָּגָה "to multiply" like fishes, Gn. 48:16; the special imagery of these Heb. words is not reproduced, of course, in the LXX. Quantitatively the mid. pass. is used for נוב "to be fruitful," ψ 91:15, for שָׂגָה "to grow," ψ 91:13, for שׂגא "to grow (up)," 2 Εσδρ. 4:22, for גָּדַל "to be great," Sir. 47:24; the act. trans. for יתר hi, "to cause to abound," "to make plenteous," Dt. 28:11, for מלא ni (grammatical alteration of the sentence by the LXX), Ex. 1:7, for עָטַף ψ 64:14 (a free and arid rendering of the fine image : in the HT the valleys are wrapped in grain, in the LXX they bring forth abundantly), for ארך hi "to lengthen," 3 Βασ. 3:14 LXX "to multiply" τὰς ἡμέρας σου, [12] for פלה hi (lit. "separate") Sir. 48:16 simply ἐπλήθυναν ἁμαρτίας; act. intr. for חלף hi (lit. "renew") Sir. 43:30 πληθύνατε ἐν ἰσχύι.

3. In the NT the act. trans. occurs at Hb. 6:14 : "to give numerous descendants" (→ 280, 28 f.), a quotation from Gn. 22:17. [13] For the author the patient waiting of Abraham for the fulfilment of the promise is decisive (→ II, 584 f.). Hence he does not say what he took the πληθύνων πληθυνῶ σε to mean. [14] In 2 C. 9:10 the sense is "to multiply" : God will cause a rich harvest to grow or to abound from your gift ; [15] He will deal lavishly with you. Act. intr. "to increase," Ac. 6:1. In Ac. the verb occurs as a mid. pass. up to 7:17 (LXX) only in missionary records, and not in this sense elsewhere in the NT. In 7:17 the mid. pass. "to multiply" refers to the people of Israel in Egypt, with allusion to Ex. 1:7 (cf. the combination of αὐξάνειν and πληθύνεσθαι, also the ref. to Ex. 1:8 in v. 18). Stephen's speech has in view the promise to Abraham in Gn. 17:2; 22:17, and hence a specific period in the history of Israel, namely, its commencement, → line 22 ff. Ac. 6:7: ὁ ἀριθμὸς τῶν μαθητῶν in Jerusalem, 9:31: ἡ ... ἐκκλησία throughout Palestine, 12:24 : ὁ λόγος τοῦ κυρίου. The probable reference in 12:24 is to increase in the number of Christians (cf. 6:7: ὁ λόγος τοῦ θεοῦ ηὔξανεν καὶ ἐπληθύνετο ὁ ἀριθμός ...), [16] through the propagation of the Word Christians "multiply." The theological background of this kind of statement may be found in 9:31 → V, 795, 12 f.

Elsewhere Ac. uses αὐξάνειν for the increase of the Word in the growth of the community, 6:7; 12:24; 19:20. This word perhaps echoes the thought of a power at work

---

[12] πληθύνειν ἡμέρας is a late slavish transl. The good early renderings paraphrase, using various constructions with πολυ-, μακροημερ-, v. P. Katz, Philo's Bible (1950), 61 f. [Katz].

[13] Cf. Hb. 11:12; Pl. quotes other verses from Gn. with a similar sense, R. 4:17 f.

[14] The promise is related to the growth of ancient Israel in Ac. 7:17; the par. possibly indicates that the thought-complex played a role in various circles of primitive Christianity, possibly in different senses, → 282, 5-19.

[15] Schl. K., 608. This understanding relates πληθυνεῖ to χορηγήσει, while the other makes it par. to αὐξήσει.

[16] Cf. 16:5 ἐπερίσσευον τῷ ἀριθμῷ.

in the Word [17] (19:20 : ηὔξανεν καὶ ἴσχυεν; [18] cf. Mk. 4:8 : αὐξανόμενα καὶ ἔφερεν εἰς ..., Col. 1:6); in the last analysis, however, it differs only slightly from πληθύνομαι in Ac. [19] The author probably took both words from the LXX (→ 280, 36 f.) and transferred them from the OT people to the NT people.

Early Chr. literature can first repeat quite simply the LXX statement of Gn. 1:22, 28 (→ n. 11) in its original sense, cf. 1 Cl., 33, 6 in a depiction of God's pleasure in His good work. In the epiclesis in 59, 3 God is addressed as the One who multiplies the peoples on earth (τὸν πληθύνοντα ἔθνη) and who — this is the point of His action — has elected His own from among them. This thought is also included in Herm. v., 1, 1, 6 : God has created and increased all things (πληθύνας καὶ αὐξήσας) for the sake of His holy Church. The work of the Creator and Sustainer is at any rate subordinate to the work of redemption. Barn., 6, 12 and 18 seems to take Gn. 1:28 rather differently, for v. 11 shows that 12a refers to the new creation, and one may thus assume that the same applies to 12b, esp. as there is again a ref. to the new creation in 13. God speaks Gn. 1:28 to the Son (v. 12) because He is making ready the new creation (the new people of Barn., 5, 7) which is also to multiply. The increase of Christianity (v. 18a, leading to its eschatological rule in v. 18b-19) takes place as men are made alive by the Word (v. 17b). Thus Barn. pursues allegorically a line which is perhaps sketched typologically in Ac.

The use in Mt. 24:12 stands in contrast to the employment of the word as a tt. of missionary history in Acts. Stylistically it seems one should regard πλανήσουσιν πολλούς (→ 246 f.) and πληθυνθῆναι [20] τὴν ἀνομίαν (→ IV, 1086, 10 ff.) as parallel. Because resistance against God becomes open and "gains the upper hand," [21] love for God [22] grows cold even among the righteous, cf. also v. 24 and par.

In three NT epistles the verb is used in the salutation. [23]

1 Pt. 1:2 :	χάρις	ὑμῖν	καὶ	εἰρήνη		πληθυνθείη
2 Pt. 1:2 :	„	„	„	„		„
Jdt. 2 :	ἔλεος	„	„	„	καὶ ἀγάπη	„

2 Pt. is shown to be an imitation by the addition ἐν ἐπιγνώσει κτλ., which does not fit the style. The form of greeting adopted (from 1 Pt.) is not natural to the author. He extends it devotionally. On the other hand, the salutations in 1 Pt. and Jd. are obviously independent of one another. 1 Pt. perhaps follows the Pauline greeting in the choice of nouns; instead of χάρις Jd. has ἔλεος (→ II, 484, n. 100 f.) and he adds ἀγάπη.

The introduction to 1 Cl.: χάρις ὑμῖν καὶ εἰρήνη ἀπὸ παντοκράτορος θεοῦ διὰ Ἰησοῦ Χριστοῦ πληθυνθείη (cf. Pol. Pr.: ἔλεος ὑμῖν καὶ εἰρήνη παρὰ θεοῦ παντοκράτορος καὶ Ἰησοῦ Χριστοῦ τοῦ σωτῆρος ἡμῶν πληθυνθείη, Mart. Pol. Pr.: ἔλεος καὶ εἰρήνη καὶ ἀγάπη θεοῦ πατρὸς καὶ τοῦ κυρίου ἡμῶν Ἰησοῦ Χριστοῦ πληθυνθείη, cf. Jd. 2) [24] might well be dependent on a NT epistle, or a non-Pauline epistle

---

[17] Cf. also Boisacq, s.v.; Prellwitz Etym. Wört. s.v.; G. Curtius, Grundzüge d. gr. Etymologie[5] (1879), 383.

[18] Schematically altered in D ; here a redactor has also emended the intr. act. to a mid. pass.

[19] Haupt Gefbr. on Col. 1:6 (αὐξανόμενον) refers to Theodoret, ad loc. (MPG, 82, 596 A): αὔξησιν δὲ (the author calls) τῶν πιστευόντων τὸ πλῆθος.

[20] D reads intr. act. Did., 16, 4 has αὐξανούσης τῆς ἀνομίας, 16:3 πληθυνθήσονται οἱ ψευδοπροφῆται for Mt. 24:11: πολλοὶ ψευδοπροφῆται ἐγερθήσονται.

[21] Schl. Mt., ad loc. has Mt. refer rather "to the numerous actions in which ... every moral norm is transgressed."

[22] → I, 45, 20-30, but cf. Schl. Mt., ad loc.: neighbourly or brotherly love, as already in Did., 16, 3 f.

[23] Cf. O. Roller, Das Formular der paul. Briefe (1933), on these epistles 134-138.

[24] There is a later echo in Mart. Sabae, P. Halloix, Illustrium ecclesiae orientalis scriptorum ... vitae ..., I (1633), 594 : misericordia pax et caritas dei patris et domini nostri Jesu Christi impleatur, a transl. of the salutatio in Mart. Pol.

unknown to us, in its choice of greeting, since the use of πληθυνθείη pts. to the Orient. So bSanh., 11b: שְׁלָמְכוֹן יִשְׂגֵּא [25] (official letter of Jews to Jews); earlier εἰρήνη ὑμῖν πληθυνθείη, Δα. 6:26 Θ; 4:1; εἰρήνη ὑμῖν πληθυνθείη ἐν παντὶ καιρῷ, Δα. 4:37c (LXX).

Whether the formula arose in the Jewish world or was borrowed by it, one can hardly say. [26] It certainly came into the NT by way of Judaism. Whether one should translate "grow" or "share richly" cannot be decided on formal grounds. [27] The wish is at all events that the fulness of the divine gifts of salvation may be at work in the churches. The meaning of πληθυνθῆναι here is not just the same as that of περισσεύειν (→ 60) and πλεονάζειν (→ 265, 21 ff.) in the Pauline verses in which χάρις is the subject (though cf. 2 C. 4:15). The ref. in 1 Pt. 1:2 is especially to outworkings in the life of the congregation, [28] cf. Jd. 2 ἀγάπη. [29]

Delling

πλήρης, πληρόω, πλήρωμα, ἀναπληρόω, ἀνταναπληρόω, ἐκπληρόω, ἐκπλήρωσις, συμπληρόω, πληροφορέω, πληροφορία

† πλήρης. [1]

1. From Aesch. (πλήρης δακρύων, Prom., 146). a. "Full," "filled," baskets full of sand, Hdt., VIII, 71, ἐπεὰν πλήρης γένηται of the Nile, II, 92, of ships: "manned," Thuc., I, 29, 1; "completely full," the face of the moon, Hdt., VI, 106. Also transf. "full of" the sickness of μὴ φρονεῖν, Soph. Ant., 1052, of empty delusions (δοξασμάτων), Eur. El., 384, ἀρετῆς, Plat. Leg., X, 897c, (the soul) αἰδοῦς, Polit., 310d, ὀδυνῶν, Resp., IX, 579e, ἡδονῶν ... ἀκολάστων, Iambl. Myst., 3, 31, p. 177, 3. Time is "overfull" of the eternally flowing stream, Critias Fr., 18 (Diels⁷, II, 384, 15). Of enthusiastic divine possession, πλήρης θεοῦ, Poll. Onom., I, 15; in the philosophical interpretation of the world: Θαλῆς ᾠήθη πάντα πλήρη θεῶν εἶναι, Aristot. An., I, 5, p. 411a, 8. Since the stars are directed by (souls or) a world soul, everything is full of gods, Plat. Leg., X, 899b; everything is full of God (here: He is everywhere), Diog. L., 6, 37.

---

[25] On the original meaning of שָׁלוֹם in Rabb. usage (prosperity) → II, 409, 1 ff., on its meaning in the NT greetings, *ibid.*, 412 f.

[26] J. A. Montgomery, *A Critical and Exegetical Comm. on the Book of Daniel*, ICC (1927), 224 refers to Tob. 5:10 א χαίρειν σοι πολλὰ γένοιτο etc. The same author in his "Adverbial kúlla in Bibl. Aram. and Hebrew," *Journal of the American Oriental Society*, 43 (1923), 392 doubts whether Ezr. 5:7 is to be transl. "all salvation" though this is the sense of εἰρήνη πᾶσα in 2 Εσδρ. 5:7.

[27] The translations of Da. and Talmud vary.

[28] Dg., 11, 5 has in view the increase of knowledge in the ἐκκλησία when it refers to the expanding grace "increased" ("given in fulness") by the Son among the saints: δι' οὗ ... χάρις ἁπλουμένη ἐν ἁγίοις πληθύνεται (naturally ἐν ἁγίοις can also go with ἁπλουμένη).

[29] One might also compare Phil. 1:9; 2 Th. 1:3, and materially 1 Th. 3:12. 2 C. 9:8 corresponds to these verses (→ 60, 38 f.). Cf. the περισσεύω sayings in which believers are the subj., e.g., 1 C. 14:12; 15:58; 2 C. 8:7.

π λ ή ρ η ς. C. H. Turner, "On ΠΛΗΡΗΣ in St. Jn. 1:14," JThSt 1 (1900), 120-125, 561 f.; G. P. Wetter, *Charis* (1913), *v.* Index; J. Dupont, Gnosis. *La connaissance religieuse dans les épîtres de S. Paul,* Universitas Cathol. Lovaniensis, Diss. ad gradum magistri in facultate theologica, II, 40 (1949), 457-465.

[1] Root πλη- → πίμπλημι, r-suffix, cf. Lat. *plērus, pleri-que* [Debrunner].

"Satisfied," "stilled," fig. of the soul, par. ἀνενδεής, M. Ant., X, 1, 2 : πλήρη τὴν ἐπιθυμίαν, Aristot. Eth. Eud., I, 5, p. 1215b, 18; πλήρη δ' ἔχοντι θυμὸν ὧν χρήζοις, Soph. Oed. Col., 778; θεεύμενοι πλήρεες, "satisfied" with seeing, Hdt., VII, 146. b. "Wholly covered," altars with the food of dogs and birds, Soph. Ant., 1017, with fertile soil, Plat. Critias, 111c. c. "Wholly filled," hence "perfect," "complete," τὸ δὲ πλῆρες τέλειόν ἐστι, τὸ δὲ στέφειν πληρωσίν τινα σημαίνει, Aristot. Fr., 108, p. 1495b, 8 f., "in full number," the δῆμος in the popular assembly, Aristoph. Eccl., 95, four "full" years, Hdt., VII, 20, "at an end," πλήρης ἤδη σοι ἡ ἱστορία τοῦ βίου, M. Ant., V, 31, 3, "complete" synon. ἀπροσδεές, XI, 1, 2. Later πλήρης is popularly used indecl., in non-christian writings for "fully paid" : P. Leid., I C, p. 118, II 14 for πλῆρες (160 B.C.); P. Oxy., II, 237, IV 14 (2nd cent. A.D.); BGU, III, 707, 15 (2nd cent. A.D.) etc.[2] d. "Fully pressed," "thick" (→ 283, 18 Aesch.). For the founders of atomistic philosophy, Leucipp. and Democrit., πλῆρες and κενόν as being and non-being are, acc. to Aristot. Metaph., I, 4, p. 985b, 4-9; Diog. L., 9, 31; Cl. Al. Prot., 66, 1; Hipp. Ref., I, 12, 1; 13, 2, the στοιχεῖα or ἀρχαί (→ I, 479 f.) of the origin of the world, the causes of all things, through the movement between them. πλῆρες is here synon. with ναστόν, "dense," or στερεόν, "solid" (κενόν with μανόν, "thin").

2. In the LXX[3] the Heb. equivalents bring out well the specific content of πλήρης. It is used mainly (47 times) for the adj. מָלֵא, then 19 times for verbal forms of מלא (16 q), 8 times for מְלוֹא, 7 for שָׂבֵעַ "satisfied," 4 for שׂבע "to be or become satisfied" (→ lines 33-36). שָׁלֵם "intact," "whole," is 7 times transl. πλήρης (→ line 37 f.); עֹבֵר "overflowing," "flowing abundantly," is rendered thus in Cant. 5:5, 13; כָּבֵד in Is. 1:4; בֹּל (עֹל) in Sir. 42:16 (here the HT is misconstrued). The use corresponds in general to the senses listed supra (→ 283, 18 ff.). Cf. esp. a. "full" of δόλου, Sir. 1:30, εὐσεβείας 1 Εσδρ. 1:21, ὀργῆς Job 14:1; the saying of God (His lips in the HT) is full of anger, Is. 30:27; ἡ ἐλπὶς αὐτῶν ἀθανασίας πλήρης (certainty of the resurrection; cf. → πληροφορ-), Wis. 3:4; with ref. to God, τοῦ ἐλέους κυρίου πλήρης ἡ γῆ, the earth is full of proofs of God's mercy, ψ 32:5, cf. 118:64; δικαιοσύνης πλήρης ἡ δεξιά σου, ψ 47:11; τῆς δόξης κυρίου etc. (→ 128, 35 f.; 129, 16 ff.), Ez. 43:5; 44:4; Is. 6:1, 3; Sir. 42:16. Again λαὸς πλήρης ἁμαρτιῶν, Is. 1:4; πόλις πλήρης ἀνομίας, Ez. 7:23. Also of time, πλήρης ὁ χρόνος σου, Δα. 4:27; number of months, Job 39:2. Abs. "full" (I went out "rich"), Rt. 1:21; of the moon, Sir. 50:6; of a city ἡ πλήρης ἠρήμωται, Ez. 26:2. "Satisfied," 1 Βασ. 2:5; πλήρης ἡμερῶν, Gn. 25:8 (no "with days" in the HT); 35:29; 1 Ch. 23:1; 29:28; 2 Ch. 24:15; Job 42:17; "sated" ἀτιμίας, Job 10:15, ὀργῆς 14:1; πλήρη γίνεσθαι, "to sate oneself" (ὀδυνῶν), Job 7:4; to be "sated" with sacrifices, Is. 1:11. b. "Wholly covered," with blood, Is. 1:15, eyes, Ez. 1:18; 10:12, barley, 1 Ch. 11:13 etc. (→ n. 4). c. "Complete," a reward, Rt. 2:12; ἐν καρδίᾳ πλήρει, "with un-divided heart," 4 Βασ. 20:3; 1 Ch. 29:9; 2 Ch. 16:9; 19:9; 25:2, cf. 15:17: καρδία ... πλήρης (no HT 1 Macc. 8:25). In the LXX MSS πλήρης is sometimes treated as indecl.;[4] this happens in the most varied connections (the meaning "fully paid" → line 10 f. is not attested).

3. Philo[5] uses πλήρης in various ways in religious, philosophical and ethical state-ments. God is full of perfect goods, Spec. Leg., II, 53. He is full of Himself αὐτὸς ἑαυτοῦ πλήρης and sufficient to Himself, Leg. All., I, 44; the same is said of being

---

[2] Cf. Mayser[2], I, 2 (1938), 58.
[3] [I owe some of these refs. to Bertram.]
[4] Of the 24 instances adduced by Turner, 121 and Thackeray, 177, Rahlfs thinks πλήρης is in app. only in Job 21:24; Sir. 19:26; 42:16 (Is. 63:3 is to be taken as a nom. sing.: I am "wholly covered" with (the blood of) the trampled). B obviously loves the indecl. use (of 11 instances 5 are indecl. only in B), then א (8, 4 only in א and 2 only in א c a), cf. also Helbing, 52.
[5] Cf. also J. Grill, Untersuchungen über die Entstehung des vierten Ev., I (1902), 365-368; Dupont, 466, n. 1 f.

(ὄν), Mut. Nom., 27; similarly of the divine *logos,* Rer. Div. Her., 188. In particular πλήρης defines God as the perfect One; He is the μόνος πλήρης; hence the singular is His εἰκών, Rer. Div. Her., 187. As the πλήρης θεός He has need of nothing, Det. Pot. Ins., 54. He remains totally the same, Sacr. AC, 9. Of faith, Philo says with ref. to Gn. 15:6 that it is περὶ πάντα πλήρης, Mut. Nom., 182. He also speaks of the truly perfect good, the πλήρες ὄντως ἀγαθόν, Det. Pot. Ins., 7; he says of the higher nature which permeates all things, the μείζων φύσις : πλήρης ὅλη δι᾽ ὅλων ἐστίν, Rer. Div. Her., 217; of every virtue : ἀνελλιπής (completely) ἐστι καὶ πλήρης, τὸ ἐντελὲς (its fulfilment) ἔχουσα ἐξ αὑτῆς, Spec. Leg., IV, 144; of the ideal nature (φύσις) of a man that it is πλήρης καὶ πάντα τελειοτάτη, Ebr., 135. Elsewhere, too, πλήρης is synon. with τέλειος or very close to it, "complete," of creation : τέλεια μὲν καὶ πλήρη πάντα διὰ πάντων, Plant., 128; in the superlative of the cosmos, Abr., 2; cf. Spec. Leg., II, 203; Agric., 53.

4. In a transf. sense the word is used especially in the NT to denote "rich fulness." In Jn. there is a specific use in 1:14. [6] The glory of the incarnate Logos (→ IV, 130, 134), which is manifest to believers (→ II, 249, 12 ff.), has as its content the → χάρις and ἀλήθεια (→ I, 246) [7] of God, which have been enacted by Him (v. 17 ἐγένετο). This is not abstractly His own glory. It is a glory in which God's χάρις and ἀλήθεια are actively declared. The glory of the Son consists in the fact that it is the sheer event of the divine χάρις and ἀλήθεια (→ 284, 27 f. ψ). Conversely, it is a demonstration of the divine χάρις and ἀλήθεια because it is the glory of the only-begotten Son (→ IV, 740 f.).

πλήρης is not to be related to πατρός, but neither is it to be related to λόγος; it is thus used indecl. [8] The central concept in v. 14b is δόξα; this is developed in twofold apposition : δόξαν ὡς ... and πλήρης ... Hence πλήρης is to be linked formally with δόξαν (→ II, 249, so very largely the Gk. Church, [9] also the D reading etc.; → I, 246, 30 ff., [10] though cf. → IV, 134 and n. 244). The first apposition elucidates δόξαν in respect of the person of the Revealer, the second in respect of the event of revelation.

The usage of Lk. differs from that of Jn. 1:14. This is especially so in Ac., and notably in the formally similar statement in Ac. 6:8 : Stephen is πλήρης χάριτος καὶ δυνάμεως. The obvious meaning here is that he possesses in abundant measure a special χάρις [11] from God which is shown particularly in acts of power. Elsewhere Ac. has πνεῦμα (ἅγιον) for χάρις. A condition in the election of the seven is the rich indwelling of God's Spirit in spiritual wisdom, 6:3. Similarly, 6:5 says that Stephen was "wholly filled" or "rich" in πίστις and in the Holy Ghost. [12] These sayings clearly refer to enduring possession. On the other hand, the probable reference in 7:55 is to a special endowment with the Holy Spirit which is granted to the martyr Stephen in the hour of death, so that he sees the glory of God. The saying in Lk. 4:1, which is formally similar, means simply that the moving of Jesus to Galilee (v. 14) was "fully" under the direction of the Holy Spirit. [13]

---

[6] → 284, 27 f. ψ 32:5.

[7] The two terms are neither identical nor to be added together ; interpretation of the one has to be "fulfilled" by interpretation of the other.

[8] Only weakly attested elsewhere in the NT (Bl.-Debr. § 137, 1); acc. to Turner, 121 Ac. 6:5, 3; 19:28; Mk. 8:19; 2 Jn. 8. In contrast, the indecl. use is preferred in Gr. En. 21:7; 28:1; 31:2.

[9] Turner, 123-125.

[10] Though cf. Bu. J., 49, n. 2.

[11] Ac. does not use the word χάρισμα.

[12] So also 11:24 of Barnabas ; here again the two dependent nouns are essentially connected, → n. 7.

[13] v. 14 underlines the fact that the ensuing work of Jesus is in the power of the *pneuma.*

The series of statements emphasises the fact that supernatural powers are granted to those named "in extraordinary measure." On this whole subject → 129 f.; also on Ac. 13:10; 19:28.

Ac. 13:10 stands in impressive contrast to v. 9. The power of the Spirit comes on Paul to endow him with authority, whereas the magician is filled with satanic powers. πλήρης can hardly be used in a fig. sense in Ac. 9:36. Tabitha does not have a store of good works; she is "constantly occupied with" them. [14]

In the external spatial sense πλήρης is used in sense a. "full" (→ 283, 18 ff.) only in Mt. (14:20; 15:37) and Mk. (8:19), and in sense b. "wholly covered" (→ 284, 4 f., 36 f.) only in Lk. (5:12 → IV, 233 f.). It is found in sense c. "complete" (→ 284, 5 f.) only in Mk. 4:28 and 2 Jn. 8 (→ IV, 700 and n. 23; 724), then a few times in the post-apost. fathers, e.g., Herm. s., 5, 1, 3: "complete fasting," 1 Cl., 2, 2: "a complete" outpouring of the Holy Ghost, 2 Cl., 16, 4: He is blessed who is found ἐν τούτοις (prayer, fasting almsgiving) πλήρης (perfect). On gnosis cf. Hipp. Ref., V, 16, 7: No one can save those who go forth from Egypt (this world) but ὁ τέλειος, ὁ πλήρης τῶν πληρῶν ὄφις (Nu. 21:6 ff.).

† πληρόω.

A. Non-Biblical Usage.

The verb is found from Aesch.; [1] it is mostly trans., predominantly construed with the gen. Lit. it means "to fill," e.g., a bottle with water, Philo Poster. C., 130 (specially "to man" ships, Hdt., VII, 168 etc.); pass. "to fill" (become full), the place of assembly with men, Aesch. Eum., 570, abs. of a river, Ep. Ar., 116, with air, πνεύμασιν Aesch. Sept. c. Theb., 464, πνεύματος, Eum., 568. Fig. "to fill" 1. a. with a disposition, Eros fills with familiarity (opp. ἀλλοτριότητος κενοῖ), Plat. Symp., 197d; with an emotion, εὐελπιστίας, Philo Jos., 255; χαρᾶς, Abr., 108; Vit. Mos., I, 177; ὀργῆς δικαίας, ibid., 302; intellectually, with the knowledge of true reality, Plat. Resp., IX, 586a; the soul is full τῶν χαρίτων (gifts of grace) τοῦ θεοῦ, Philo Ebr., 149. b. In religious speech: Almighty Sarapis rules the life of men, and gives them as ταμίας (steward) that which makes life worth living; hence he is called Zeus (acc. Δία) Sarapis, because he διὰ πάντων ἥκει καὶ τὸ πᾶν πεπλήρωκε, Ael. Arist. Or., 45, 21. ἐπλήρωσας

---

[14] The ref. of ἔργων ἀγαθῶν is to works of love, not to meritorious works along the lines of Judaism. Cf. on Jewish usage Str.-B., IV, 536 f.

π λ η ρ ό ω. S. Aalen, "Begrepet πλήρωμα i Kol.-og Efeserbrevet," Tidsskrift for Teologi og Kirke, 23 (1952), 49-67; F. Baumgärtel, Verheissung (1954); R. Bultmann, "Weissagung u. Erfüllung," ZThK, 47 (1950), 360-366; G. Dalman, Jesus-Jeschua (1922), 52-58; J. Dupont, Gnosis, La connaissance religieuse dans les épîtres de S. Paul, Univ. Cath. Lovaniensis, Diss. ad gradum magistri in facultate theol., II, 40 (1949), s.v.; A. Fridrichsen, " 'Accomplir toute justice,' " Annales d'histoire du christianisme, I (1928), 167-177, esp. 172-176; J. Gewiess, "Die Begriffe πληροῦν u. πλήρωμα im Kol.- u. Eph.-Br.," Vom Wort des Lebens, Festschr. M. Meinertz = NT Abh., Suppl. Vol. I (1951), 128-141; W. H. P. Hatch, "Jesus' Summary of the Law and the Achievement of the Moral Ideal acc. to St. Paul," Anglican Theol. Review, 18 (1936) 129-140; W. G. Kümmel, Verheissung u. Erfüllung² (1953); H. Ljungman, "Das Gesetz erfüllen," Lunds Univ. Årsskrift, NF, I, 30, 6 (1954); C. F. D. Moule, " 'Fulness' and 'fill' in the NT," Scottish Journal of Theology, 4 (1951), 79-86; F. R. Montgomery Hitchcock, "The Pleroma of Christ," Church Quarterly Review, 125 (1937/38), 1-18; E. Percy, Die Probleme d. Kol.- u. Eph.br., Skrifter utgivna av Kungl. Humanistiska Vetenskapssamfundet i Lund, 39 (1946), 384-386; also "Der Leib Christi (Σῶμα Χριστοῦ) in d. paul. Homologumena u. Antilegomena," Lunds Univ. Årsskrift, NF, I, 38, 1 (1942); H. Schlier, "Christus u. d. Kirche im Eph.," Beiträge zur historischen Theol., 6 (1930); for further bibl. → I, 742, bibl. n.; II, 665, n. 12.

[1] πληρόω to πλήρης probably like the synon. μεστόω and (or) the anton. κενόω etc., E. Fraenkel, Griech. Denominativa (1906), 89; examples, 150 [Debrunner].

ἡμᾶς, ὦ πάτερ, τῆς ἀγαθῆς καὶ καλλίστης θέας, Corp. Herm., 10, 4b. πληρωθῆναι θεοῦ = ἐνθουσιάσαι etc., Poll. Onom., I, 16; "to be fructified" (by God), Plot. Enn., VI, 9, 9, cf. τῶν ἀρετῆς σπερμάτων, Philo Deus Imm., 137; the Pythia gives the oracle πληρωθεῖσα with the πνεῦμα of God, Orig. Cels., VII, 3. 2. a. Intellectually "to satisfy," "to appease," θυμόν, Soph. Phil., 324; pass. φρονήσεως, Philo Poster. C., 136; "to satisfy" a demand, ἐπιθυμίας, Plat. Gorg., 494c. b. Of Augustus : οὗ ἡ πρόνοια τὰς πάντων εὐχὰς ... ἐπλήρωσε, Ancient Gk. Inscr. in the British Museum, IV, 1 (ed. G. Hirschfeld [1893]), 894, 12. c. In Philo also of ethical directions, "to fulfil" them, τοὺς λόγους ἔργοις ἐπαινετοῖς, Praem. Poen., 83. 3. "To bring to the right measure," a. "to balance," χρείαν (fig.), Thuc., I, 70, 7; b. "to make complete," "to round off" a sum, Hdt., VII, 29; pass. Ep. Ar., 10; "to pay in full," a recompense, θανὼν τροφεῖα (allowance) πληρώσει χθονί (home), Aesch. Sept. c. Theb., 477, common in pap. both for "to satisfy" someone financially and "to pay off" the remainder, P. Tebt., 36, 6 (2nd cent. B.C.); [2] of a span of time, act. "to complete," pass. "to run its course," μέχρι τοῦ τὸν χρόνον πληρωθῆναι, P. Oxy., II, 275, 24 (66 A.D.), also of fixtures, Ael. Arist. Or., 22, 9 : festivals fall due every 5 and 3 yrs., πανηγύρεις ... πληροῦνται, esp. Jos. Ant., 6, 49 of the date of an event which God has entrusted to the prophets (κατὰ τήνδε τὴν ὥραν): Samuel, sitting on the roof of his house, ἐξεδέχετο τὸν καιρὸν γενέσθαι, πληρωθέντος δ' αὐτοῦ καταβάς. 4. "To fulfil" promises ὑποσχέσεις, Herodian, II, 7, 6; ἐπαγγελίαν ἀνθρώπου or φιλοσόφου, Epict. Diss., II, 9, 1; 3; 22 (cf. III, 23, 10); pass. "to come to fulfilment," of an oracular saying τοῦ λογίου πεπληρωμένου, Polyaen. Strat., I, 18. 5. "To fulfil" duties, P. Oxy., X, 1252, Recto 9 (3rd cent. B.C.) πλήρωσον τὸ κεκελευσμένον etc.

B. The Lexical Data in the LXX.

πληρόω is used about 70 times for forms of מָלֵא (→ 128, 24 ff.). The other equivalents strengthen the sense of "to fill up the measure," so תָּמַם in Lv. 25:29 (of time); Da. 8:23 → line 48; כָּלָה "to fill up to the top," 2 Ch. 24:10; "to fulfil" a word of Yahweh, 36:22; שָׂבַע "to fill completely" ψ 15:11; שְׁלַם haphel "to complete" (a span of time), Da. 5:26 Θ, with ἐμέτρησεν; this is true even where the Heb. expressions are transf. only acc. to sense, מְקָם ὅταν πληρωθῇ, "after the lapse of ..." Ιερ. 41:14; "to fill out completely" (for נָשָׂא ni), Is. 40:4; "to fill" (the earth), for שָׁרַץ "to swarm" → 281, 12 πληθύνω, Gn. 9:7.

Lit. "to make (completely) full," γαστέρα Job 20:23, men with intoxicating drink, Jer. 13:13; "to fill" with men, Ιερ. 28:14, with the creatures of God, ψ 103:24; "to populate," Gn. 1:22, 28; 9:1, 7; the hand, ψ 128:7, mostly (also plur.) specific, with offerings, to fill one's hand with one's offering = to offer sacrifices, 1 Ch. 29:5; 2 Ch. 29:31, as priests with the offerings of others = to receive sacrifices for presentation, 2 Ch. 13:9; hence (cf. Lv. 8:33 HT) [3] the special sense of appointing someone as a priest (lit. "to fill his hands with offerings"), Ju. 17:5 B, 12 B; 3 Βασ. 13:33; Sir. 45:15. Pass. "to be (completely) filled," a vessel, 4 Βασ. 4:4, a skin with wine, Jer. 13:12, a river with water, ψ 64:10 (sometimes also act. intr. "to be full," Jos. 3:15; 1 Ch. 12:16); abs. "to be satisfied," Job 20:22, ψυχή Qoh. 6:7, "to become full," of the moon and transf. with wisdom, Sir. 39:12.

Fig. "to fill," 1. a. someone with something, τὰ πρόσωπα ἀτιμίας, ψ 82:17, someone with confusion, 3 Macc. 6:19; pass. "to be filled," with artistic understanding, 3 Βασ. 7:2, joy, 3 Macc. 4:16, a noble mind, 2 Macc. 7:21, arrogance, 9:7, καρδία ... πονηροῦ Qoh. 9:3. b. "To fill up (completely)," → 288, 23-37 on Wis. 1:7; Jer. 23:24; of the almighty command of God which brings about the death of the first-born in Egypt : στὰς ἐπλήρωσεν τὰ πάντα θανάτου, καὶ οὐρανοῦ μὲν ἥπτετο, βεβήκει δ' ἐπὶ γῆς, Wis. 18:16. 2. "To satisfy," "fulfill" the will or desires of a man, ψ 19:5 f., one's

---

[2] Preisigke Wört., II, 321 f.; Mayser, II, 2 (1934), 206.
[3] So E. Riggenbach, "Der Begriff τελείωσις im Hb.," NKZ, 34 (1923), 186, but cf. R. Kittel in Kautzsch on Ju. 17:5 : "to fill the hand with money" = "to appoint," "engage."

own human plan, ταῖς χερσὶν ὑμῶν, Ιερ. 51:25; the divine commission, ᾿Ιησοῦς ἐν τῷ πληρῶσαι λόγον ἐγένετο κριτῆς ἐν ᾿Ισραήλ, 1 Macc. 2:55; cf. Is. 13:3, the wrath of God (not the HT). 3. "To make full," pass. "to become full," of a specific measure, [4] a. a measure of sins appointed by God as the extreme limit, Da. 8:23 (cf. 4:34 LXX). b. a set span of time, καιροὶ τοῦ αἰῶνος, Tob. 14:5 BA or χρόνος τῶν καιρῶν (א), the divinely ordained times of the world up to the redemption of Israel; times in God's history with His people, the 70 yrs. of Babylonian dominion, Ιερ. 36:10; in legal statutes ἔτη Ιερ. 41:14, ἐνιαυτός Lv. 25:29 f., chiefly in expressions with ἡμέραι (→ II, 947, 24 ff.), of the fixed term of Jacob's service, Gn. 29:21, the time of the Nazirite's separation, Nu. 6:5 (act. Nu. 6:13; 1 Macc. 3:49), of the wedding festivities, Tob. 8:20 BA, of a stretch of time appointed in God's plan for history, Jer. 25:12; the measure of your time (and that of the patience of God with you) is full, and the time of divine judgment has come, Ιερ. 32:34; plainly then of the coming of a specific time, until the appointed day has come, Lv. 8:33 LXX : ἕως ἡμέρα πληρωθῇ (a misunderstanding of the HT), Gn. 25:24 : the time of bearing, 1 Βασ. 18:27 vl.: the time of the wedding. More generally ἔτη αὐτοῦ the yrs. of life given to him, Sir. 26:2; of Enoch χρόνους μακρούς, Wis. 4:13 (both act.). 4. "To fulfil," of divine promises which God has spoken ἐν τῷ στόματι αὐτοῦ and "fulfilled" or "fully executed" [5] ἐν ταῖς χερσὶν αὐτοῦ, "with his own hand," 3 Βασ. 8:15, 24; 2 Ch. 6:4, 15; inf. πληρωθῆναι λόγον (ῥῆμα) κυρίου διὰ στόματος ᾿Ιερεμίου, 2 Ch. 36:21 f., cf. 3 Βασ. 2:27. 5. There is a hint of the sense "to complete" at 4 Macc. 12:14 : to achieve the supreme measure of εὐσέβειαν (by martyrdom).

C. God as the One who Fills the World in the Old Testament and Judaism.

1. That there are no limits to God's knowledge Jer. 23:24 bases on the fact that He is omnipresent. Fig. one might say that His eye reaches to every corner. But the anthropomorphic expression (→ V, 376, 13 ff.) is avoided by means of the expression : "Do not I fill heaven and earth ?" LXX μὴ οὐχὶ τὸν οὐρανὸν καὶ τὴν γῆν ἐγὼ πληρῶ; λέγει κύριος. The personal conception of God is not, of course, abandoned herewith. There is a related saying in Wis. 1:7. God hears all things (v. 6) ὅτι πνεῦμα (the power of perception) κυρίου πεπλήρωκεν τὴν οἰκουμένην, καὶ τὸ συνέχον τὰ πάντα γνῶσιν ἔχει φωνῆς. Though the description of God in v. 7b is philosophically tinged, the context makes it plain that a simple biblical thought is stated here. Nothing spoken on earth is hidden from God, since his hearing רוּחַ reaches everywhere, cf. ψ 138:7; → V, 549, 3-6. The ref. is not to the filling of the universe by the → πνεῦμα in the Stoic sense of an impersonal material power. God fills the world, and He also sustains it. These two thoughts are complementary in Wis. 1:7 along the lines of the Jewish view of God as the One who upholds the whole world and watches over all human actions as Creator and Lord. They are both found already in Ep. Ar., 132 : Moses first showed ὅτι μόνος ὁ θεός ἐστι καὶ διὰ πάντων ἡ δύναμις αὐτοῦ φανερὰ γίνεται πεπληρωμένου παντὸς τόπου τῆς δυναστείας, καὶ οὐθὲν αὐτὸν λανθάνει ...

2. Philo in the first instance continues the biblical usage. This is evident in spite of philosophical influences on many of his statements. It is quite obvious in places where, like the OT, he bases his ethics on the concept of God as the One who fills all things. Thus there is kinship to biblical statements in Gig., 47: πάντα ... πεπληρωκὼς ... ἐγγύς ἐστιν, so that we keep ourselves from wrongdoing in order that the divine spirit of wisdom may not depart from us ; the combination of πεπληρωκὼς and ἐγγύς (also πλησίον ὄντος) shows that when he uses πεπληρωκὼς Philo is not calling God the world soul. His supraterrestrial concept of God prevents him from doing this : [6] "The

---

[4] Measure of time in the LXX → ἀναπληρόω, συμπληρόω; measure of sins → 293, 12 f.

[5] The transl. of Ljungman, 27.

[6] Undoubtedly there are many par. and intersecting lines in Philo's understanding of God ; our present task is simply to indicate those which are important in relation to πληρόω. Philo is close to the Stoic view in a very different way when he says of the *logos* that it is the πάντα τῆς οὐσίας ἐκπεπληρωκώς, Rer. Div. Her., 188.

whole cosmos ... would not be a place worthy of God, since God is His own place (τόπος) and is Himself full ...; He fills (πληρῶν) and embraces all else, that which is deficient (ἐπιδεᾶ) and waste and empty, but He is embraced by nothing," Leg. All., I, 44. In full self-sufficiency God is distinct from the world. This is very clear in Poster. C., 14. God is "above space and time," ἐπιβέβηκε δὲ πᾶσιν; "existing outside what is created He has nevertheless filled the world with Himself." Safeguarding against an anthropomorphic misunderstanding of Gn. 11:5,[7] he offers a sharply paradoxical statement in Conf. Ling., 136: ὑπὸ ... τοῦ θεοῦ πεπλήρωται τὰ πάντα ... ᾧ πανταχοῦ τε καὶ οὐδαμοῦ συμβέβηκεν εἶναι μόνῳ, nowhere, because one cannot say that the Creator is embraced by what has come into being, "but everywhere because, deploying His powers through earth and water, air and heaven, He has not left any part of the universe empty." At root, then, the concept of creation renders the idea of the world soul impossible for Philo. When he speaks of God as the πεπληρωκώς he is describing God as the One who was at work in the creation of the world and who is still at work in its preservation. He makes fruitful use of this thought as the basis of ethics (Leg. All., III, 4): πάντα ... πεπλήρωκεν ὁ θεὸς καὶ διὰ πάντων διελήλυθεν, how, then, can a man hide from God (Gn. 3:8)? "For God is before everything that has come into being;[8] (6): "the wicked man is under the illusion that God is enclosed in a place rather than enclosing it; he thus thinks that he can hide."[9] Now it is quite apparent that the thought of the demanding God, the personal God, the God of the Bible, is combined with what is said about the πεπληρωκώς. The word denotes the omnipresence of God on the basis of His almightiness and His judicial office. Philo also combines herewith the concept of revelation (Vit. Mos., II, 238 in a saying of God: He is also declared herein as ὁ πάντα διὰ πάντων πεπληρωκὼς τῆς εὐεργέτιδος ἑαυτοῦ δυνάμεως) and that of God's immutability (Som., II, 221 paraphrasing Ex. 17:6: οὗτος ἐγὼ ὁ ἐμφανὴς καὶ ἐνταῦθα ὢν ἐκεῖ τέ εἰμι καὶ πανταχοῦ, πεπληρωκὼς τὰ πάντα, ἑστὼς ἐν ὁμοίῳ καὶ μένων, ἄτρεπτος ὤν).[10] As He who has filled all things He is constant, abiding and unchanging,[11] cf. Poster. C., 29 f.: Peculiar to God are rest and stability, not movement. Gn. 46:4 does not mean that God changes places; He is, however, the One who has filled all things with Himself. This emphasis on the immutability of God also includes the fact that He is outside the world.

It would seem that the statements of Philo about God as the One who fills all things are not always differentiated from the idea of a substantial filling. This differentiation is emphatic, however, when he speaks more precisely and biblically. The term τὰ πάντα (or τὸ πᾶν, Det. Pot. Ins., 153) is philosophical, but in this context it means God's creation. The formula πάντα διὰ πάντων lays emphasis here on God's working through the powers which emanate from Him; He fills through all that He does in creation (Sacr. AC, 67; Vit. Mos., II, 238); this is plain in the explanation of the formula in Leg. All., III, 4 (→ line 16 f.). Naturally in many statements God is formally the content of the filling. But a formally spatial understanding[12] of πεπληρωκώς is patently inadequate materially. As He who sustains the world and reveals Himself God works in the world, and fills it with His operations. Passages in which this filling is contrasted with the need and emptiness of the world (Leg. All., I, 44), or which speak of leaving nothing empty (Leg. All., III, 4; Det. Pot. Ins., 153; Conf. Ling., 136; Sacr. AC, 67), obviously have this in view. This interpretation is also supported by the use of περιέχων

---

[7] Cf. Deus Imm., 57: If God had feet, where could He go, He "who has filled all things"?

[8] Sacr. AC, 67 similarly differentiates the thought of the omnipresence of the active God (πεπληρωκὼς πάντα διὰ πάντων) from the interfusion of God and nature by the fact that He precedes all that has come into being.

[9] There is a similar train of thought in Det. Pot. Ins., 153 on Gn. 4:14.

[10] On the texts cf. P. Katz, Philo's Bible (1950), 75-78 [Katz].

[11] On this cf. Deus Imm., 20-85 (on Gn. 6:5-7).

[12] On this question cf. Leisegang, Raumtheorie im späteren Platonismus, Diss. Strasbourg (1911), 29-38. The formal pars. in the non. Jewish world are discussed in M. Zepf, "Der Gott Αἰών in d. hell. Theologie," ARW, 25 (1927), 227-232.

οὐ περιεχόμενος with πληρῶν (Leg. All., I, 44; Conf. Ling., 136; cf. Poster. C., 14): God is not enclosed in the world; the combination of formally contradictory sayings shows that Philo is not thinking of purely spatial permeation. Even the statement that God fills the world with Himself (Poster. C., 14, 30) does not rule out a specific ref. to His work; like other statements (Deus. Imm., 57) it is designed to keep at bay a mythical (μυθοποιΐα, Leg. All., I, 43) or anthropomorphic (Conf. Ling., 134 f.) localising of God. Thus Philo's statements about the God who fills all things have in view His omnipresence as the almighty, all-ruling and all-seeing God, but not as universal nature.

3. Similar thoughts are sometimes found in the Rabb. Here Jer. 23:24 plays a certain role, [13] but elsewhere, too, the OT provides occasion for utterances on the relation between God and the world from the standpt. of space, 1 K. 8:27; 2 Ch. 2:5; Is. 6:3 f. [14] God is above all heavens and He upholds the world; they cannot embrace Him. It is His grace, His good-pleasure, to let His shekinah dwell among men. [15] It pleases God to fill heaven and earth; it pleases Him to speak with Moses from out of the ark. [16] The shekinah shines like the sun over the whole world, Sanh., 39a. God is in the supreme heaven, Eth. En. 1:3; Test. L. 3:4 etc. The shekinah "filled the sanctuary." [17] These three statements do not merely stand alongside one another; they complement one another. [18] Nor should it be overlooked that in the expression the "shekinah of Yahweh" [19] the shekinah, originally a term for the presence of God among His people, can be a name for God Himself. [20] Obviously at issue in this series of statements is the question of the relation between God's transcendence and His immanence in the world, as in Philo, though essentially the statements of Philo go further than those of the Rabbis.

D. The Content of the Word in the New Testament.

The use of πληρόω in the NT does not stand out sharply from the par. [21] γέμω (NT 11 times, LXX 8 times) or γεμίζω (9 and 3) and μεστόω (1 and 2) merely by reason of its frequency. In the NT γεμίζω and μεστόω are used only in an externally spatial sense, though they are also fig. in the LXX, and γεμίζω can also have the common non-biblical sense "to load" (Gn. 45:17; γέμω "to be laden," Gn. 37:25; 2 Ch. 9:21). Even where these verbs are used fig. however (γεμίζω in 3 Macc. 5:47, γέμω in ψ 9:28; 13:3; μεστόομαι in 3 Macc. 5:1), the spatial implication is maintained. This is also true in the NT. R. 3:14 is an OT quotation; Lk. 11:39 is a transposition of the lit. Mt. 23:25. Even when one takes into account the numerical relation, it is evident that γεμ(ιζ)ω and μεστόω start from the spatial concept. This also attaches to πληρόω (→ 291, 3-9, 10 ff.), [22] but the particular content of this word in the NT is determined by 2.-5. (→ 291-298): "to fulfil a norm, a measure, a promise," "to complete or achieve" something, [23] and in 1. the idea of "totality" or "fulness" is decisive. Senses 2.-5. are prepared, or at least intimated, in non-biblical Gk. (→ 287, 4-23) and further developed

---

[13] Aalen, 54; Moore, I, 371 f.; Str.-B., III, 598 f., cf. II, 680.
[14] Cf. on this W. Müller, *Js. 6 in den alten Übers. u. im NT*, Diss. Greifswald (1954).
[15] Targ. on 2 Ch. 2:5; 1 K. 8:27; Ps. 68:16, Aalen, 57 f.
[16] R. Meir on Jer. 23:24, → Aalen, 58.
[17] On the basis of Ex. 40:35; Bacher Pal. Am., II, 427; Moore, I, 370.
[18] Aalen, 60 f.
[19] So often in the Targumim, J. Bonsirven, *Le judaïsme palestinien au temps de Jésus-Christ,* I (1934), 130.
[20] Str.-B., II, 314.
[21] Also from πίμπλημι (except for the inexact use in Lk. 21:22 → 130, 31-33), → 128, 37 f.; 129, 26 f.
[22] Paul sometimes uses πεπληρωμένος synon. with μεστός, R. 1:29; 15:13 f., but here the perf. pass. part. approximates to the adj. rather than *vice versa,* and the image of space is plain in the transf. use of μεστός.
[23] In this last sense πληρόω is closer to → τελειόω, but is distinguished clearly therefrom by the characteristic idea of filling up a measure.

in the LXX (→ 288, 1-21). The multiplicity of nuances does not always permit us to integrate individual passages into a firm lexical schema.

Lit. the term means "to fill something completely," a place, Ac. 2:2 (pass. Jn. 12:3; Mt. 13:48; Lk. 3:5), a material lack, Phil. 4:19; in a transf. sense Ac. 5:28 : "You have filled all Jerusalem ..."

1. Non-lit. it means "to fill with a content." Pass. "to be filled with" something ; [24] the content may not be specified, the subj. itself is the content, "to fill completely" : a. act. abstract subj. λύπη Jn. 16:6 (→ IV, 320, 5 f.). b. Act. subj. ὁ σατανᾶς Ac. 5:3; Satan finds a place in the heart of the deceiver, so that he dominates it (→ 286, 5 f.). c. Act. God as subj., Ac. 2:28 (→ II, 775): in a petition, [25] R. 15:13; the gift is through πιστεύειν, → II, 538, 29 ff.

d. In pass. sayings God is in part to be inferred as the One who fulfils richly, esp. in the prayers at Phil. 1:11 and Col. 1:9. He it is who gives spiritual gifts, and He gives them with fulness, → 60. Paul prays for those to whom he writes that the full knowledge of God's will may be in them and that they may stand before the coming Christ with the fulness of the fruit of righteousness brought forth in them, Col. 1:9, cf. Phil. 1:9 ff., → II, 210, 15-18. [26] Fulness of insight into the will of God (→ I, 704 f.) makes mutual correction possible for the community, R. 15:14, → IV, 1021 f. In distinction from the → πλήρης sayings adduced → 285, 30-37, Ac. 13:52 describes the particular experience which, when the missionaries are persecuted, a whole community undergoes in a rich spiritual movement characterised by the word → χαρά. In these sayings πληρόω also implies that a man is completely controlled and stamped by the powers which fill him, → also 292, 13-22. There is in the term a strong element of exclusiveness or totality. The joy, knowledge etc. which fill the Christian shape his whole existence and imperiously claim his whole being.

Lk. 2:40 (→ σοφία, cf. Ac. 6:3, → 285, 35 f.) is illustrated by v. 47 or v. 47 prepared by v. 40. In Eph. 5:18 there is perhaps a play on "to be drunk with"; the licentious life (→ I, 506 f.) of the drunkard is contrasted with the disciplined life of the man who, wholly filled by [27] the Holy Spirit and His gifts, worships and praises God. In the context of Eph. there is no ref. to the danger of slipping into orgiastic celebrations. In 2 C. 7:4 (→ V, 797) the meaning is : "I am wholly comforted," with a transition to "satisfied" with comfort ; this aspect is less prominent in 2 Tm. 1:4. R. 1:29 : The human race, given up by God to self-will, is full of all the conceivable effects of ἀδικία ..., knows and accomplishes nothing but ..., → I, 155, 29 ff.; III, 484, 7 ff. (though cf. Phil. 1:11, → lines 13 ff.).

Of the four disputed verses in Eph. and Col., Eph. 1:23; 4:10 at any rate bear the sense "to fulfil." In Eph. 4:7-11 Christ is described as the One who dispenses in fulness the gifts of grace. He is this because (διό v. 8) He has achieved dominion over all powers, both the lowest and the highest (v. 8 f.). V. 10 shows wherein the unlimited power of Christ has its basis in His all-comprehensive descent and ascent (→ III, 641 f.), which took place ἵνα πληρώσῃ τὰ πάντα.

---

[24] The content is mostly in the gen., dat. only R. 1:29; 2 C. 7:4, acc. with pass. Phil. 1:11 and Col. 1:9, cf. Bl.-Debr. § 159, 1 and App.

[25] In 2 Th. 1:11 the sense : May God fill you (ἵνα ὑμᾶς ...) with all good will, is less likely (on the double acc. with the act. cf. Helbing, Kasussyntax, 147 f.), cf. → n. 24.

[26] καρπὸς δικαιοσύνης, Prv. 11:30, plur. 3:9; 13:2, Loh. Phil., 34, n. 1.

[27] πληρόω ἐν = "with" (cf. Bl.-Debr. § 172 with App.) is also attested in the vl. of the Imperial Text at Col. 4:12. It is not to be translated by "with" at Col. 2:10, → 292, 20 f. and n. 37. πληρόω ἐν = "by," R. 8:4.

The context suggests that πληρώσῃ is to be taken here along the lines sketched under C. (→ 288-290). [28] The statement is transferred from God to Christ. [29] Christ can give rich gifts to His community because He is absolute Lord, because He "fulfils" or reaches [30] all things with His powerful presence. Like similar sayings in Judaism, [31] the statement thus goes with that about His exaltation above all heavens (v. 10, cf. Eph. 1:23 and 1:20, "at the right hand of God"). There is no reference to the spatial extension of the "aeon" Christ. Eph. 1:23 is to much the same effect. τὰ πάντα is not used for the all-embracing cosmos on its natural side. It denotes the totality of cosmic beings endowed with will and capable of decision, not men alone, hence the neuter plural; [32] it covers both v. 22a and b. ἐν πᾶσιν [33] corresponds either to the use of the singular expression "in every respect" which occurs elsewhere in Paul (10 times in 2 C.), or to the Philonic διὰ πάντων with πάντα. With all the powers which go forth from Him Christ rules over and among [34] all the forces which have become subject to Him (v. 22a), giving life to the whole Church (v. 22b). The personal nature of Christ is in no way diminished in these sayings. In Eph. 3:19 the verb is used in the abs., nor is this merely because the content of πληρωθῆτε has been sketched previously. The prayer is to the effect that those addressed may be filled absolutely with the boundless gifts of God, → 302, 30. In Col. 2:10 there is a play on πλήρωμα. [35] The abs. use permits two possible renderings, either: You are brought to fulness [36] in His sphere of life or through Him, or more probably: You are filled absolutely by Him as the Giver, [37] cf. on Eph. 3:19.

2. "To fulfil a demand or claim," always in the NT with reference to the will of God, never to a human demand, cf. → 287, 6 f., 50.

a. In Paul always of the total legal demand (R. 8:4; → II, 221, 24 f.) of the νόμος (R. 13:8; Gl. 5:14) which the Christian "fulfils completely." [38] He can do this only because sin has no more hold over him. Definitive judgment has been passed on sin itself in its original sphere of dominion (→ σάρξ) by the act of God in Christ, who creates a new life in the believer through His Spirit, R. 8:4, 9 f.

---

[28] Cf. perhaps Ael. Arist. Or., 45, 21 and context, e.g., 24 → 286, 27-30.

[29] Gewiess, 132; Percy, Probleme, 312 f.

[30] Gewiess, 131 f.

[31] → 288-290; Aalen, 55.

[32] In Gl. 3:22 τὰ πάντα means in the first instance humanity; (τὰ) πάντα ἐν πᾶσιν is not a general formula, cf. the specific statements in 1 C. 12:6; 15:28. Cf. Schlier, 55, n. 1: "Who fulfils the 'all' in all (creatures)."

[33] On τὰ πάντα ἐν πᾶσιν v. C. F. D. Moule, An Idiom Book of the NT Greek (1953), 160.

[34] The mid. is also used elsewhere, e.g., Plat. Gorg., 493e (casks), often "to man" ships, Xenoph., Demosth.; v. Montgomery, 13. The idea in Eph. and Col. is not one of spatial penetration, as in Wis. 7:22, 24 of the πνεῦμα of wisdom, or in 8:1 of wisdom itself, on the basis of Stoic notions of the higher πνεῦμα as an infinitely rarified material.

[35] There is no connection with the πλήρωμα of v. 9, as against Dib. Gefbr.³ ad loc.: πεπληρωμένος "one who has attained to fellowship with the pleroma"; Dupont, 422: "c'est en lui que vous avez part au pleroma." H. Schlier (-V. Warnach), Die Kirche im Eph. (1949), 110, n. 15 turns things upside down in Eph. and Col.: "πληροῦν is ... to make into the pleroma, to fill with the pleroma, πληροῦσθαι is to be taken or made into the pleroma."

[36] Cf. Haupt Gefbr. on Col. 2:10.

[37] On the instrumental ἐν in the phrase ἐν Χριστῷ → II, 542, 15 ff., 23 ff., 541, 38 ff.; F. Büchsel, " 'In Christus' bei Pls.," ZNW, 42 (1949), 141-158, esp. 142-149.

[38] Cf. E. Sommerlath, Der Ursprung des neuen Lebens nach Pls.² (1927), 38. In Eph. 6:6 Christians are ποιοῦντες τὸ θέλημα τοῦ θεοῦ.

The claim of the νόμος is completely fulfilled by love for one's neighbour, R. 13:8; [39] Gl. 5:14. [40]

The will of God is not regarded as a mere vessel or form which is given its content by ἀγάπη; this idea would be commensurate neither with the Jewish understanding of the Law nor Paul's view of the νόμος. Hence we are forced to a different interpretation, esp. in R. 8:4, namely, "to correspond to a requirement," "to fulfil a norm." This use of the word expresses the unconditional nature of the claim. This is indeed the only thing it has in common with the Heb. הֵקִים Aram. קַיֵּם. "To establish or confirm by obedience" and "to complete a measure" are two different ideas. Hence in the LXX the verb קוּם is never rendered by πληρόω in any of its forms. The equivalents of הֵקִים in the sense "to confirm," "to execute," are mainly used as follows : [41] ἵστημι : Yahweh (through His act) maintains His oath, Gn. 26:3; Jer. 11:5 (man in 2 Εσδρ. 15:13), verifies His Word, 3 Βασ. 2:4; 6:12; 12:15; 2 Εσδρ. 19:8; Da. 9:12; ψ 118:38, that of a prophet, Is. 44:26; Ιερ. 35:6; man does not keep the διαθήκη of Yahweh, Ιερ. 41:18, fulfils God's injunctions, 1 Βασ. 15:13 (also those of men, Ιερ. 42:14 ho, 16); Josiah puts into effect the words of the newly found Law, 4 Βασ. 23:24 (v. 3 ἀνίστημι); 2 Ch. 35:19a; the husband validates a vow of his wife, Nu. 30:14 f. ἀνίστημι : Yahweh puts His Word into effect, 3 Βασ. 8:20; 2 Ch. 6:10; 10:15, His resolve, Jer. 23:20; similarly καθίστημι in Ιερ. 37:24, ἐφίστημι in Ιερ. 36:10, πιστόω in 2 Βασ. 7:25. ἐμμένω : Yahweh keeps to His Word, Nu. 23:19, man stays within the commands of the Torah (by his acts), Dt. 27:26. τηρέω : man keeps God's injunctions, 1 Βασ. 15:11 (A ἔστησεν). Distinction between ἵστημι and πληρόω is legitimate in the NT, since the NT plainly uses the former in the special sense just illustrated : "to declare the Law to be valid," R. 3:31, opp. καταργεῖν (→ I, 452 f.), cf. Mk. 7:9 vl.: the tradition ; "to bring into force" God's order of salvation, Hb. 10:9 (cf. Ιερ. 41:18), opp. ἀναιρεῖν. It thus sees a possibility of differentiating between the two verbs. This is not without ultimate significance for an understanding of the v. in Mt. [42]

b. The meaning of πληρόω in Mt. 5:17 cannot be determined simply by the contrast with καταλῦσαι (→ IV, 336, 11-16) in the sense of בַּטֵּל "to do away," "to set aside." In v. 19 λύω stands in antithesis to ποιεῖν as well as διδάσκειν. [43] The one who put Mt. 5:17 in Gk. found in πληρῶσαι, not στῆσαι, the right term for what was meant. [44] If an equivalent is sought for the πληρόω of Mt. 5:17, in accordance with the predominant use of πληρόω elsewhere in the NT this can only be מלא. The meaning of πληρόω cannot be deduced in the first instance from a supposed Aram. original ; [45]

---

[39] → II, 704, 11 f. as against → IV, 1076, 35 f.; Zn. R., ad loc.; W. Marxsen, "Der ἕτερος νόμος R. 13:8," ThZ, 11 (1955), 237 sees here the Mosaic Law too. Ljungman, 122 ad loc.: So that "there remains no portion of the Law which is not fulfilled." Zn. R., ad loc.: The ἀγαπῶν "has fulfilled the Law so that it has no further demands to make of him" (perf. also Gl. 5:14). Hence the perf. is not gnomic, as suggested by Hatch, 138 f., n. 22 f.

[40] The context emphasises practice of the law of love, so that in spite of the formal par. to R. 13:9 (→ 305, 1 ff.) the v. is not to be understood principially : "to be brought to its supreme norm." λόγος is obviously the saying from the Torah quoted in v. 14b, → IV, 112, 12 f. (cf. Schlier Gl., ad loc.).

[41] The hi statements are the most numerous and decisive.

[42] Ljungman, 26-33 emphatically rejects the equation of πληρόω and קַיֵּם or הֵקִים at Mt. 5:17; he also rejects the senses = ποιεῖν "to execute" (19 f.; → IV, 1062) and "to complete," "to conclude" (21-23).

[43] בַּטֵּל is also used in the sense "not to fulfil" in Ab., 4, 9, cf. Ljungman, 51 on Mt. 5:19 : "removed," "unloosed," "separated."

[44] The use of יסף in Shab., 116b : I [the Evangelium] have not come to take from the Law of Moses but to add to it, is based on Dt. 4:2 acc. to Dalman, 53; cf. on Shab., 116b B. H. Branscomb, Jesus and the Law of Moses (1930), 229 f., n. 23; on Mt. 5:17, 226-229.

[45] In particular it is impossible to transfer an equivalent which is alien to the fig. character of πληρόω to the other senses of πληρόω in virtue of a certain analogy to one specific meaning.

it must be based on the context. This then raises the question of Semitic equivalents, which may contribute in turn to an understanding of the Gk. word.

The goal of the mission of Jesus is fulfilment (Mt. 5:17b); according to Mt. 5:17a this is primarily fulfilment of the Law and the prophets, [46] i.e., of the whole of the OT (→ IV, 1058, 15) as a declaration of the will of God. Jesus does not merely affirm that He will maintain them. As He sees it, His task is to actualise the will of God made known in the OT (→ IV, 1062, 32). He has come in order that God's Word may be completely fulfilled, in order that the full measure appointed by God Himself may be reached in Him. His work is an act of obedience also and specifically in the fact that He fulfils God's promise, cf. Mt. 3:15. He actualises the divine will stated in the OT from the standpoint of both promise and demand. How this is done is illustrated in vv. 21-48 (→ 292, 25 ff.; R. 13:8; Gl. 5:14). [47] With no express reference to the OT (though cf. v. 17: Is. 42:1), Mt. 3:15 stresses the fact that by having Himself baptised by John Jesus fulfils a requirement of the divine will manifest to Him, → II, 198, 26 ff.; I, 538, 19-23. [48]

3. "To fill up completely a specific measure" : [49] a. the present generation of Jews will [50] fill up [51] the measure of guilt of the Jewish people [52] by crucifying Jesus, so that this people is rejected, Mt. 23:32. b. Rev. 6:11: "to complete the number" of the martyrs foreordained by God. [53] c. Esp. temporally, only pass.: "to come to an end" (preterite "be at an end"), only Ac.: 7, 23, 30, in a schematic division of the life of Moses (Dt. 34:7); [54] also 9:23; 24:27. Then in a richer sense of divinely appointed stretches or points of time : An end of the time of the dominion of the Gentiles has been fixed by God, Lk. 21:24 → V, 430, 35 ff. On Jn. 7:8 → III, 459 ff. Mk. 1:15 : Of the καιρός which, awaited by God's people on the basis of the promise, has come with the appearance of Jesus.

The thought of fulfilled καιρός shows no trace of the idea of a chronological schema fixed by God (Jewish apocalyptic); that the time of an event has been fulfilled can neither be calculated nor read off from external signs ; [55] it may be known only in the moment of fulfilment by God's sovereign decision. [56] This view of fulfilment differs also from the Gk. concept. The Gk. view certainly speaks of a necessity (χρεών) of occurrence κατὰ τὴν τοῦ χρόνου τάξιν, Anaximand. Fr., 1 (Diels[7], I, 89, 15). Heraclit. acc. to Simplicius (Diels[7], I, 145, 15 f.) taught : χρόνον ὡρισμένον τῆς τοῦ κόσμου μετα-

---

[46] The prophets are not mentioned merely because they speak of God's ethical will. One might also ask whether the promises of the Torah are not in view as well.

[47] Cf. Ljungman, 35 : "The reference is to both action and teaching," cf. 75 f.

[48] Cf. O. Cullmann, Die Tauflehre d. NT (1948), 15 f.; Schl. Mt., 89 f. → V, 701. F. D. Coggan, "Note on St. Matthew 3:15," ET, 60 (1948/49), 258 sees in δικαιοσύνη the "saving activity" of God which is to be fully effected.

[49] Cf. the profane use in Phil. 4:18 : "I have enough."

[50] → IV, 632, 34 f. fut. with B et al.

[51] → 288, 4 f.; → 306, 35 ff.; → 308, 13 ff.

[52] → V, 31; πατέρες → V, 975 f., n. 174.

[53] Cf. 4 Esr. 4:36 : "When the number of those like you shall be full," of the righteous.

[54] E. Preuschen, "Die Apostelgeschichte," Hndbch. NT (1912) on 7:23, cf. Str.-B., II, 679 f.

[55] For Judaism cf. Volz Esch., 138 : "Everything has its time and everything has its measure"; in eschatology this is true even down to details "whose measure must be filled up until salvation can come" (139); this applies even to sin (examples loc. cit.); the periods can be calculated etc. (141-145). Cf. Str.-B., III, 570.

[56] Cf. Luther's Erste Vorlesung über Gl. (1516/17), on 4:4 (Weimar ed. 57, 30, 15 f.): Non ... tempus fecit filium mitti, sed econtra missio filii fecit tempus plenitudinis.

βολῆς κατά τινα εἱμαρμένην ἀνάγκην (cf. Plat. Prot., 320d: χρόνος εἱμαρμένος). [57] But the Greek, when he uses such expressions, has in mind foreordination by an impersonal power in which compulsion rules, not the personal and consequently free decision of the living God, whose mercy brings about the fulfilment which kindles the rejoicing of human thanksgiving acc. to Mk. 1:15; εὐδόκησεν is the word which gives us the clue to the meaning of πεπλήρωται.

4. "To complete," "to fulfil" prophetic sayings which were spoken with divine authority and which can thus be called directly the words of God. In biblical thinking it is quite incompatible with the concept of God that the event should lag behind God's Word, that the full measure should not be reached. [58] God fulfils His Word by fully actualising it. [59] To be sure, this is stated with express use of the word "God" only in Ac. 3:18. Nevertheless, when it is said in a synagogue sermon in Ac. 13:27 that the Jews of Jerusalem fulfilled the OT by condemning Jesus, what is meant is the same as in Ac. 3:18, which is parallel in content, namely, that in this way, which does, of course, defy human comprehension, God has filled up the measure of His Word, and the Jews as His instrument have necessarily helped to bring about the fulfilment of prophecy in salvation history, 13:27, cf. → 288, 17 f.

In the NT proof from Scripture the following formulae are used, → 288, 18 f. In the material peculiar to Mt., and here alone, we constantly find : ἵνα (ὅπως) πληρωθῇ τὸ ῥηθὲν διὰ τοῦ προφήτου, 1:22; 2:15; 13:35; 21:4; plur. 2:23; with the name of the prophet Jeremiah 2:17; 27:9; with that of Isaiah 4:14; 8:17; 12:17; with ὑπὸ κυρίου in 1:22; 2:15. Elsewhere we find ἵνα or πῶς πληρωθῶσιν αἱ γραφαί, Mt. 26:54, 56; Mk. 14:49; ἔδει πληρωθῆναι τὴν γραφήν, Ac. 1:16; πεπλήρωται ἡ γραφή, Lk. 4:21; δεῖ πληρωθῆναι πάντα τὰ γεγραμμένα, Lk. 24:44; ἐπληρώθη ἡ γραφή, Jm. 2:23; ἵνα ἡ γραφὴ πληρωθῇ, Jn. 13:18; 17:12; 19:24, 36. Limited to Jn. are the formulae ἵνα ὁ λόγος Ἠσαΐου ... πληρωθῇ in 12:38 and ἵνα πληρωθῇ ὁ λόγος ὁ ἐν τῷ νόμῳ αὐτῶν γεγραμμένος in 15:25. Finally Ac. has two special expressions : ἃ προκατήγγειλεν διὰ ..., 3:18; τὰς φωνὰς τῶν προφητῶν ... ἐπλήρωσαν, 13:27. On the Semitic equivalents → 287, 25, 27 f.; 293, 9 f. There is some restriction in the NT use of the proof with such formulae (on the lips of Jesus only at Mt. 26:54 ⊨ Mk. 14:49, apparently an ancient tradition ; Jn. 13:18; 15:25; 17:12). It is by far the most common in Mt. (12 times). [60] Here it is used in the infancy stories (1:22; 2:15, 17), the story of the passion (26:54, 56 [the par. to v. 56 in Mk. 14:49 is the only instance in Mk.]; 27:9), the story of the entry (21:4), the explanation of teaching the people by parables (13:35; → V, 554 f., 757 f.), the demonstration that eschatological expectation is fulfilled in the healing work of Jesus (8:17; 12:17), and finally the reference to Jesus' move to Capernaum (4:14). In the infancy and passion stories Mt. shows an inclination to extend the proof by the ὅλον formula, 1:22; 26:56, though cf. the general observations on the work of Jesus in 8:17; 12:17; 13:35. God's promise is absolutely fulfilled in the person and work of Jesus. In Jn. the proof from Scripture is related to details of the passion (19:24, 36; → τελειόω is chosen in 19:28 for the passion as a whole); the main concern here, however, is with the figure of Judas (13:18; 17:12; cf. Ac. 1:16) and the rejection of Jesus by the Jews (12:38; 15:25). πληρόω is used in Lk. only in two important verses

---

[57] W. Theiler, *Zur Geschichte der teleologischen Naturbetrachtung bis auf Aristot* (1925), 81.
[58] For the difference from מָלֵא, perceived in Schl. Mt. on 1:22, cf. → 293, 7-26.
[59] Cf. Ljungman, 59 and 63.
[60] Except in proof from Scripture πληρόω occurs in Mt. only at 3:15; 5:17; 13:48; 23:32; in Mt. it always has a specific sense and the closeness to מלא is particularly evident.

which are part of the special Lucan material. [61] While Mk. 1:15 sums up the message of Jesus in the saying : the καιρός is fulfilled, Lk. 4:21 says that the promise of the messenger of joy is fulfilled with the → σήμερον of His preaching. In 24:44 the risen Lord Himself pts. out that the divine δεῖ [62] of the cross and resurrection is based on the whole of the OT, v. 27. Lk. formulates particularly clearly the enigma of the suffering Messiah which primitive Christianity answered from the OT, Lk. 24:46, cf. v. 26; Ac. 3:18 αὐτοῦ. Primitive Christianity found the absolute answer in the fact that the death of Jesus fulfilled Is. 53, → V, 709 f. Dt. Is. was thus important for the proof of fulfilment offered in the Gospels (for πληρόομαι cf. Mt. 8:17; 12:17; Jn. 12:38; Tt. Is. Lk. 4:21). [63]

The point of the Scripture proofs to which we have referred is brought out by the fact that Jn. always uses a ἵνα (also Mk.) and that Mt. mostly has a ἵνα or ὅπως (exceptions 2:17; 26:54; 27:9). This ἵνα is in fact final (→ III, 323). The reference to fulfilment is an answer to certain questions of faith raised by primitive Christianity. Mt. grounds the events of the life of Jesus in the will of God. This will may be known from God's Word. For those who handed down the material the features to which they ascribed the character of fulfilment were never secondary (cf. the review → 295, 32 ff.). Even details in the life of Jesus were significant for them in virtue of the relation to the will of God.

The characteristic feature of the NT concept of the fulfilment of God's Word is the eschatological content. This distinguishes it normatively from the Rabbinic proof from Scripture. Fulfilment means that in the to-day of the NT God's saving will achieves its full measure in the Christ event. The NT concept of fulfilment is summed up in the person of Jesus.

The πληρόω formulae referring to the OT are restricted statistically to the Gospels and Acts, and materially to the Jesus event, [64] with the sole exception of Jm. 2:23. Paul does not use them even when he calls the Christ event a fulfilment of Scripture. Paul puts his theological proof from Scripture in simpler expressions which he has in common with other NT writings, including the Gospels, → I, 746-749. In Lk. 1:20 the certainty of the fulfilment of a divine Word spoken by an angel is expressed in a πληρόω formula. God's Word is not closed and complete, as in Rabb. Judaism. God speaks in the to-day of the NT, which also belongs to salvation history. In Jn. 18:9, 32 ἵνα ... πληρωθῇ is used of words of Jesus [65] which are fulfilled in the passion. Obviously the same claim to validity is raised for them as for God's words in the OT.

According to Lk. 22:16 the passover will be "fulfilled" in the future consummation of fellowship with God. In what way is not stated, so that various interpretations are possible.

The passover is a reminder of deliverance from Egypt ; [66] along these lines the OT and the eschatological events are perhaps contrasted as type and antitype. [67] Judaism

---

[61] Lk., then, adopts neither the many proofs of Mt. nor the one in Mk. He is also independent of Mt. and Mk. in his use of → τελέω for the fulfilment of Scripture : 18:31; 22:37; cf. Ac. 13:29.

[62] → II, 23 f.; δεῖ alone can also be a veiled ref. to the biblically grounded divine necessity of an event, as in the almost stereotyped sayings in Mk. 8:31 par.; 13:7 par., cf. Lk. 24:26; cf. esp. Mt. 26:54.

[63] On the question whether Jesus Himself already saw in His work a fulfilment of the OT cf. → V, 715 f. on the concept of the Servant of the Lord.

[64] The same is true of → τελέω and τελειόω.

[65] The analogy of OT proofs supports the obvious final sense for these sayings too.

[66] Zn., Schl. Lk., ad loc.; B. Weiss, Das NT, I² (1905), ad loc.

[67] Cf. Pr.-Bauer⁴, 1223 with bibl.

also links the expectation of coming redemption with the passover; [68] in these terms Lk. 22:16 is merely a continuation of the Jewish view. Above all, the Gospels use the image of a banquet for the eschatological consummation; [69] on this view Lk. 22:16 is simply referring to the given situation, and this is not unlikely if one compares Mk. 14:25 and par. [70]

5. "To complete" : a. πληρόω has a purely temporal sense in statements which refer expressly to a span of time ; in the following passages, according to context, it means "to finish" (Lk. 7:1, with some solemnity in this reference to the sermon on the plain); [71] Ac. 13:25 : of the Baptist (→ τρέχω) with the implication of according to God's will ; 19:21: pass. in comprehensive description of the varied events in Ephesus. b. "To execute" of a commanded action ; decisively it is almost always God's commission which is to be fulfilled, with particular reference to the ministry of the individual or total community : the thought of a full measure is apparent in the admonition in Col. 4:17; "to execute fully" (perf.) in R. 15:19 with reference to Paul's total activity in the Eastern Mediterranean (→ II, 729, 27); of preaching again in Col. 1:25; of a piece of missionary work in Ac. 14:26; of a mission of assistance in 12:25; of the way of Jesus to the cross in Lk. 9:31 (chosen intentionally here). c. "To bring to full or supreme measure, to completion," always with an impersonal object (on Col. 2:10 → 292, 19-22). Active : Paul prays for the Thessalonians that God may mightily (→ II, 315) bring to completion in them His gracious counsel (→ II, 746), which aims at their doing of good [72] and the work of πίστις (→ II, 649, 36-39), 2 Th. 1:11. Paul asks the Philippians to make the joy which he already has in them (4:1) full by their unanimity, Phil. 2:2. Pass.: Paul in 2 C. 10:6 counts on it that the obedience of the Corinthians will "become complete" (its first beginnings are already there); to whom it should be rendered is not stated : obedience to God [73] will also mean obedience to the apostle.

In the Johannine writings πληροῦσθαι is distinctively related to the → χαρά directly brought by the actuality of eschatological salvation ; this is "perfected," "brought to its full measure." The joy of the Baptist, which is compared to that of the best man when the bridegroom is united with the bride (→ IV, 1101, 8-10), has reached its fulness with the coming of Christ, Jn. 3:29. The other sayings are all in ἵνα clauses. In them (apart from Jn. 16:24) the goal of the revealing Word of Jesus (15:11; 17:13, first in the Parting Discourses) and the preached word of His messengers (2 Jn. 12; [74] 1 Jn. 1:4) is that the joy of the recipients of revelation "may be perfected." In this connection the Johannine writings never use → τελειοῦν etc. πληροῦσθαι, then, does not signify the reaching of a goal ; here again it implies a full measure. By revelation "everything" is received, the "complete ful-

---

[68] J. Jeremias, *Die Abendmahlsworte Jesu*² (1949), 32, 101, with bibl. n. 3.

[69] → II, 34 f.; Hauck Lk. on 22:16.

[70] Cf. H. Schürmann, "Der Paschamahlbericht Lk. 22: (7-14) 15-18, I," NTAbh., 19, 5 (1953), 21 f.; M. Black, "The 'Fulfilment' in the Kingdom of God," ET, 57 (1945), 25 f. Mk. 14:25 acc. to Jeremias, *op. cit.*, 93 *ipsissima vox.*

[71] Ljungman, 57 f. thinks he can see a "natural relation between 'to fill' and 'all' " in the NT.

[72] ἀγαθωσύνη is used in LXX etc. both of the good which men do to others (Ju. 8:35 A, B ἀγαθά; 2 Ch. 24:16) and of good moral actions in general, ψ 51:5; εὐδοκία can also denote the disposition, → II, 746. Another possibility, then, is "that God may perfect in you every will to do what is good."

[73] → I, 224, 23; Schl. K., 617 f. on 10:5 : Christ.

[74] This v. is to be taken with the other Johannine refs ; it does not refer to joy at being together.

ness" [75] of the actuality of salvation itself. Joy is perfected because it is given by the fulness of salvation which is granted with the exaltation of Jesus. Jn. 16:24 does not deviate from this specific line of usage, for here there is granted to the man who prays for the salvation given in fellowship with Christ (cf. v. 22 f.) the promise that he will receive the gift of perfect joy (in this fellowship). [76]

† πλήρωμα.

A. The Word Outside the New Testament.

I. The Lexical Aspect.

Already outside the NT the word can denote a "fulness" of "contents," so that in different passages several meanings or their totality may be implied. This makes translation difficult and explains the tendency to use the general term "fulness" or to leave the term untranslated. With πλήρης (→ 283, 17 ff.) and πληρόω (→ 290, 36 f.) it esp. carries with it in its specific usage the thought of full measure. It thus denotes in particular completeness, the absence of any lacunae.

1. First "that which fills," [1] "full contents," e.g., of a basket, Eur. Ion, 1412, common of ships (Poll. Onom., I, 121 groups it under τά ... τῆς ναυμαχίας), [2] "freight," esp. in connection with the full contents of the ark, Philo Vit. Mos., II, 62, in Omn. Prob. Lib., 41 (καλοκαγαθίας) and 128 synon. with ἕρμα "cargo," or the complement (obviously only in this sense in Plut., 8 times in Vitae, also plur.), Hdt., VIII, 45; Lys., 21, 10 etc.; then "crew of workers," P. Petr., II, 15, 3, 2 (3rd cent. B.C.), → I, 728, 10 f.; "total

---

[75] Schl. J. on 3:29 adduces Rabb. sayings with שָׁלֵם, "complete," → 284, 21 f., 37 f.

[76] Acc. to E. Gulin, "Die Freude im NT," Annales Academiae Scientiarum Fennicae, B. 37, 3 (1936), 67-71 πληροῦσθαι here means that the object of joy is realised. In criticism cf. Bu. J., 387 f., n. 2.

π λ ή ρ ω μ α. Apart from bibl. under → πληρόω, 286 : Bau. Ign., 192; F. C. Baur, Die chr. Gnosis (1835), 129 f., 141 f., 156 f., 166 f.; Bu. J., 51 f., n. 7; L. Cerfaux, "La théologie de l'église suivant S. Paul," Unam Sanctam, 10 (1948), Index s.v. "plérôme"; Dib. Gefbr.[3] on Col. 1:19; J. Dupont, "Gnosis, La connaissance religieuse dans les épîtres de S. Paul," Universitas Catholica Lovaniensis, Diss. ad gradum magistri in facultate theologica, II, 40 (1949), esp. 419-427; 453-476; E. de Faye, Gnostiques et gnosticisme[2] (1925); C. F. A. Fritzsche, Pauli ad Romanos epistula, II (1839), 469-473; J. Grill, Untersuchungen über die Entstehung des vierten Ev., I (1902), 364-372; S. Hanson, "The Unity of the Church in the NT," Acta Seminarii Neotestamentici Upsaliensis, 14 (1946), 155-161; H. J. Holtzmann, Lehrbuch d. nt.lichen Theol.[2] (1911), I, 556-558; II, 276-280; H. Jonas, Gnosis u. spätantiker Geist, I[2] (1954), esp. 362-373; W. L. Knox, St. Paul and the Church of the Gentiles (1939), 163-166, 193 f.; J. B. Lightfoot, St. Paul's Ep. to the Colossians and to Philemon (1904), 255-271; W. Lock, "Pleroma," DB, IV, 1 f.; C. L. Mitton, The Epistle to the Eph. (1951), 94-97; F. R. Montgomery Hitchcock, "The Pleroma as the Medium of the Self-realisation of Christ," Exp., VIII, 24 (1922), 135-150; K. Müller, "Beiträge zum Verständnis d. valentinianischen Gnosis," NGG, Philosophisch-historische Klasse (1920), 179-242; Reitzenstein Poim., 25 f., n. 1; J. A. Robinson, "The Church as the Fulfilment of the Christ," Exp., V, 7 (1898), 241-259; also St. Paul's Ep. to the Eph.[2] (1907; = 1943), 42-44, 87-89, 110 f., esp. 255-259; J. Schmid, "Der Eph. d. Apostels Pls.," BSt, 22, 3-4 (1928), 182-193, 420 f.; T. Schmidt, Der Leib Christi (1919), 180-191; A. F. Simpson, "Pleroma," ERE, X, 62-66; G. C. Storr, Opuscula, I (1796), 144-187; A. Wikenhauser, Die Kirche als der mystische Leib Christi[2] (1940), 187-191.

[1] Acc. to the usual meaning of -μα (Debr. Griech. Wortb. § 311; cf. Schwyzer, I[2], 522c : Later fundamentally nomina rei actae), "that which is caused by filling," "hence full contents" [Debrunner].

[2] Even here there may be several possibilities at the same passage ; ἐμ πληρώμασι τρισί in Ditt. Syll.[3], II, 709, 40 (c. 107 B.C.) might refer to the "cargo" (Moult.-Mill., s.v.), the "ship," or even the "crew."

population" [3] of a city, Ael. Arist. Or., 22, 9, with an original implication of completeness ; all callings constitute the πλήρωμα of the *polis,* Aristot. Pol., IV, 4, p. 1291a, 17.

2. With sense 1. there is easily combined the idea of "entirety," then of the "great mass," hence the "whole sum," ὥστε καὶ ἐς χιλίους τὸ πλήρωμα τῆς γερουσίας αὐξηθῆναι, Dio C., 52, 42, 1; "totality," τῶν φίλων πλήρωμ' ἀθροίσας, Eur. Ion, 663 f.; "the whole," πλήρωμα ... πολυανθρώπου συγγενείας, μηδενὸς ἐλλειφθέντος ἢ μέρους ..., "full measure" of a numerous kindred in which no part (no degree of relationship) is missing, [4] Philo Praem. Poen., 109; to offer oneself to God as πλήρωμα καλοκαγαθίας is the best sacrifice, Spec. Leg., I, 272; "full number" of the yrs. of life, Hdt., III, 22. Generally "crowd," of men, Eur. Or., 1642; πλήρωμά τινος εὐτυχίας, Philo Leg. Gaj., 11. Finally, the word approximates (→ 284, 5-9) to the sense of "consummation," Philo Spec. Leg., II, 213 : Tabernacles is the climax of the festivals (with συμπέρασμα, conclusion), *ibid.,* 200 : πλήρωμα ... τελειότατον (of the number ten) the most perfect synopsis.

3. Outside the Bible the meaning "what is filled" is found for certain only of a fully manned ship, Luc. Verae Historiae, II, 37, πέντε ... πληρώματα, 38 and Hesych., *s.v.;* it is debatable elsewhere : the soul is a πλήρωμα ἀρετῶν, "wholly filled" with [5] virtues by disposition, learning and practice οὐδὲν ἐν ἑαυτῇ καταλιποῦσα κενόν, Philo Praem. Poen., 65.

4. "The act of filling," probably [6] at Eur. Tro., 823 f.: Ζηνὸς ἔχεις κυλίκων πλήρωμα, καλλίσταν λατρείαν (of the office of Ganymede), also Soph. Trach., 1213 : πυρᾶς πλήρωμα, the piling up of the funeral pyre (for Heracles); [7] in my judgment also Philo Abr., 268 : faith in God is παρηγόρημα βίου, πλήρωμα χρηστῶν ἐλπίδων, ἀφορία μὲν κακῶν, ἀγαθῶν δὲ φορά (etc.); acc. to the context πλήρωμα is par. to παρηγόρημα βίου (encouragement to live) and hence a "filling" with good hopes (choice of the word because of the ending, cf. R. 11:12).

II. The Use in Specific Literary Groups.

1. In the LXX the word is used only spatially, mostly "content" (Qoh. 4:6), esp. "fulness" or "totality," e.g., inhabitants and riches of the sea (3 times) and the earth (8, e.g., ψ 23:1); cf. also Cant. 5:12 : πληρώματα ὑδάτων, "ample waters" (v. b : πλήρωμα "fulness") or simply "waters" (v. a : πλήρωμα, "what is filled"). Of the other transl. ᾽ΑΣΘ have πλήρωμα at Ex. 28:17 for מִלֻּאָה ("border") [8] and ψ 95:11 (also LXX) for מְלֹא, also mechanically in ᾽Α 2 Βασ. 5:9 for the name מִלּוֹא (lit. "filling"). The LXX agrees with ᾽Α at Ez. 12:19, with Σ at ψ 97:7; Qoh. 4:6 (all for מְלֹא.) Σ has the word at Is. 31:4 for מְלֹא (not the LXX). Comparison of πλήρωμα and πλήρωσις (→ n. 8) is instructive in the LXX ; they are used *promiscue* for מְלֹא [9] (πλήρωσις the

---

[3] There is no real instance of the sense "supplement"; Plat. Resp., II, 371e is often quoted, but πλήρωμα here means formally "content" (πλήρωμα ... πόλεώς εἰσιν ... καὶ μισθωταί) and acc. to the sense the (necessary) "population," → lines 1-2. Cf. E. Percy, "Der Leib Christi (Σῶμα Χριστοῦ) in d. paul. Homologumena u. Antilegomena," Lunds Universitets Årrskrift, NF, I, 38, 1 (1942), 51, n. 93.

[4] Cf. J. Gewiess, "Die Begriffe πληροῦν u. πλήρωμα im Kol.- u. Eph.-Brief," *Vom Wort des Lebens, Festschr. M. Meinertz, NT Abh., Suppl.* I (1951), 135.

[5] To be taken thus in view of the anton. κενόν [P. Katz], though others render "full sum."

[6] Or "thou dost hold the full measure of the cup of Zeus in thine hand ═ thou dost hand the full cup to Zeus" ? cf. Eur. Ion, 1051: κρατήρων πληρώματα [Debrunner].

[7] The two passages are interrelated in Liddell-Scott, *s.v.;* Thes. Steph., *s.v.* on Eur.: *ubi* πλήρωσις *dici poterat.*

[8] But cf. for מִלֻּאִים "border," πλήρωσις in Ex. 25:7; 35:9 ᾽ΑΣΘ; for the same Heb. word in the sense of taking up office (Lv. 7:37) or initiatory sacrifice (Lv. 8:33) the same Gk. word is used in other Gk. transl. (LXX τελείωσις).

[9] For מְלֹא we also find πλήρης (4 Βασ. 4:39; Lv. 2:2; 16:12; 5:12; Ju. 6:38; Nu. 22:18;

"fulness" of the earth, Dt. 33:16, the land, Ez. 32:15); the "act of filling" is in view in Jdt. 8:31 (cisterns) and perhaps Ex. 35:27; 1 Ch. 29:2 (putting on adornment, cf. ʾΑΣΘ *supra*); of time, times are fulfilled, limits reached, Jer. 5:24; Ez. 5:2 (Da. Θ 10:3); adj. "powerful" of the wind, Jer. 4:12. This covers all the NT refs. Here πλήρωσις more clearly suggests the action, whereas only πλήρωμα is used for this, too, in the NT.

2. Ign. uses the term in the sense of πληροφορία, sense a. (→ 310, 28; 311, 1 ff.). In Ign. Tr. introitus ἐν τῷ πληρώματι is to be related to ἀσπάζομαι, which immediately precedes : the "fulness" of wishes contained in a NT epistle is enclosed in the greeting of Ign. [10] Eph. introitus refers to the "fulness" with which God has blessed the church addressed. [11] Justin (cf. 1 Cl., 54, 3, quotation from ψ 23:1) uses the term only of earth and the sea (→ 299, 29), Dial., 22, 9; 36, 3; 73, 4; Cl. Al., except in accounts of Gnosticism outside the Church, uses it only with respect to means of sustenance, Paed., I, 96, 3; II, 103, 2.

3. In Corp. Herm. πλήρωμα is not used as in Chr. Gnosticism ; it can mean the same as πληρέστατος ("completely full") in Lact. Inst., IV, 6, 4 (Scott, 298): The cosmos (the second god) is πληρέστατος πάντων τῶν ἀγαθῶν, cf. Corp. Herm., 12, 15: The cosmos πλήρωμά ἐστι τῆς ζωῆς, though in content cf. 6, 4: ὁ γὰρ κόσμος πλήρωμά ἐστι τῆς κακίας, [12] ὁ δὲ θεὸς τοῦ ἀγαθοῦ, "sheer" evil or good. 16, 3 says of God the Lord and Creator of the universe (τῶν ὅλων) that He is all and one, "for the 'fulness' [13] (πλήρωμα) of all is one and in one"; the all is not a second thing alongside the one ; they cannot be distinguished ; the term πάντα does not mean ἐπὶ πλήθους (in summation) but ἐπὶ πληρώματος (in totality). Here the word is clearly meant to define a concept of God in which God and the world merge into one another. The use is again purely formal.

4. In Chr. Gnosticism, [14] esp. Valentinians, [15] πλήρωμα is a tt. particularly for the totality of the thirty aeons, Epiph. Haer., 31, 10, 13, cf. τὸ πᾶν πλήρωμα τῶν αἰώνων, 31, 13, 6. Obviously God, the Father of the all, does not Himself belong to the pleroma ; He has brought forth the highest aeons from Himself, Hipp. Ref., VI, 29, 6, cf. Iren. Haer., I, 1, 1. The pleroma is in its way closest to God, but it is His product, so that God stands over it as μόνος ἀγέννητος, οὐ τόπον ἔχων, οὐ χρόνον, . . . ἀναπαυόμενος αὐτὸς ἐν ἑαυτῷ μόνος, Hipp. Ref., VI, 29, 5. [16] The specific use of the term probably derives from the sense of "totality." It also includes an evaluation : πλήρωμα obviously means "fulness of being," of what is in the true sense of the word. [17] This may be seen particularly clearly in the fact that κένωμα can be its opp., for this signifies emptiness of everything divine, Epiph. Haer., 31, 16, 1: To be ἐν σκιᾶς καὶ

24:13; Ex. 16:33; 9:8; Is. 6:3), πλῆθος (Gn. 48:19), πάντες (Mi. 1:2), οἱ κατοικοῦντες (Am. 6:8 etc.).

[10] Cf. also Bau. Ign., *ad loc.*; F. X. Funk, Patres Apostolici, I² (1901), *ad loc.*

[11] H. W. Bartsch, *Gnostisches Gut u. Gemeindetradition bei Ign. v. Antiochien* (1940), 32 makes a connection here with Valentinian Gnosticism.

[12] Scott, 169, 17: "one mass of evil"; comm., *ad loc.*: completely filled so that there is no room for anything good, Jonas, 149 : "fulness of evil." C. H. Dodd, *The Bible and the Greeks* (1935), 127: "totality" (cf. 134).

[13] "Totality" [Katz]. On Corp. Herm. cf. Dupont, 451-461; 459 : in Corp. Herm. πλήρωμα is to be taken Stoically ; the cosmos is both unity and plurality, the totality of things, permeated by a divine principle.

[14] Whether the Gnostic tt. lies behind the Syr. text of O. Sol. (Bu. J., 51 f., n. 7) is debatable. W. Frankenberg, *Das Verständnis d. O. Sal.* (1911) suggests words of the τελειο- group in the refs. adduced by Bultmann.

[15] On its use elsewhere cf. Lightfoot, 269-271.

[16] de Faye, 119 : "Le plérome, c'est . . . la divinité sans Dieu lui-même"; 458 : "Dieu . . . est une pure abstraction . . . il est au-dessus des idées et du monde intelligible."

[17] In keeping is the fact that the "all" in Valentinian Gnosticism can in effect be the same as the pleroma, Müller, 179 f. (with some exaggeration in my view). The material world does not belong to the all.

κενώματος τόποις is to be ἔξω ... φωτός ... καὶ πληρώματος. [18] In Cl. Al. Exc. Theod., 35, 1 Phil. 2:7 is referred to the leaving of the pleroma by Jesus. [19] Since, however, the two spheres are strictly separated spatially as well as essentially, formally πλήρωμα is mostly a spatial term. [20] In this sense it simply denotes the supreme spiritual world (τὸ ἀόρατον καὶ πνευματικὸν ... πλήρωμα, Epiph. Haer., 31, 10, 13) in its total distinctness. [21] It is divided by Ὅρος from the lower world, the cosmos, which is made after its image, [22] Cl. Al. Exc. Theod., 22, 4; 42, 1. [23] Jesus brought the angels with Him from the pleroma, [24] and they may not return thither without the gnostics, Exc. Theod., 35, 1 and 4. The whole pleroma is the bridal chamber (νυμφών) into which there enter the pneumatics who have put off their souls, found their angel bridegrooms, and become pure spirits (αἰῶνες νοεροί), Exc. Theod., 64. Acc. to a recurrent formula (Hipp. Ref., VI, 32, 1, 2, 4, 9; 34, 3; 36, 4), the Redeemer Jesus [25] is the "common fruit of the pleroma," brought forth by all the aeons, and hence a particularly great aeon, *ibid.*, 32, 6. "The whole pleroma of the aeons ... has brought forth the most perfect beauty and the star of the pleroma, the perfect fruit Jesus, who is also called Saviour and Christ," Iren. Haer., I, 2, 6. Absolutely everything which is of spiritual origin may be found again in the pleroma. This obviously means that the sense of perfection is also implied in the use of πλήρωμα in Chr. Gnosis, cf. also Hipp. Ref., VI, 34, 2 : ἵν' ᾖ τὸ πλήρωμα ἐν ἀριθμῷ τελείῳ συνηθροισμένον. This may be seen also in the plur. use. The aeons, the transcendent powers, which proceed hierarchically from the chief aeons by syzygy (Iren. Haer., I, 1, 1 f.), can also be called πληρώματα : ὅσα ἐκ συζυγίας προέρχεται, πληρώματά ἐστιν (Cl. Al. Strom., IV, 90, 2; Exc. Theod., 32, 1, cf. 33, 1; Iren. Haer., I, 14, 2; 14, 5 = Hipp. Ref., VI, 43, 1; 46, 3). Finally, in a logical combination of the other two senses, πλήρωμα can be used in a third way for the angelic partner of the Gnostic, → line 8. The husband of the Samaritan woman (Jn. 4:17) is τὸ πλήρωμα αὐτῆς with whom she must be united to achieve salvation. [26] Here the thought of the Saviour from the upper world is individualised ; each who is capable of redemption has his own personal saviour, who bears up him and him alone to the upper world, his own heavenly perfection. Here again it is the value concept which is finally decisive.

5. In Iambl. Myst. πλήρωμα means "content" : when the soul unites itself with the gods it receives τὰ ἀληθέστατα ... πληρώματα τῶν νοήσεων (III, 3, p. 107, 7); τὰ δ' ἐπὶ γῆς ἐν τοῖς πληρώμασι τῶν θεῶν ἔχοντα τὸ εἶναι (I, 8, p. 28, 18) through that which the gods pour in ... In Procl. in Tim. the usage is obviously developed in

---

[18] The opp. can go back formally to the vocabulary of pre-Socratic philosophy, which contrasts, as στοιχεῖα, τὸ πλῆρες as τὸ ὄν and τὸ κενόν as τὸ μὴ ὄν (→ 284, 15 ff. πλήρης). ὑστέρημα is also used for κένωμα, i.e., lack of true being, Hipp. Ref., VI, 31, 6, cf. Lightfoot, 267, n. 1 for further examples.

[19] In the Chr. expositors the Gnostic distinction between the earthly Jesus and the heavenly Christ is not always made clearly (it is clear in Hipp. Ref., VI, 36, 3, cf. 35, 4-6; Iren. Haer., II, 16, 1); similarly the statements handed down to us are to a large degree inconsistent and unsystematic.

[20] The pleroma lies to the East (the direction of the divine world acc. to the ancient view, F. J. Dölger, Sol salutis,² *Liturgiegeschichtliche Forschungen,* 4/5 [1925], Index, *s.v.* "Osten u. Osthimmel") and above the cosmos, G. Hoffmann, "Zwei Hymnen der Thomasakten," ZNW, 4 (1903), 289 f., 292.

[21] This does not imply, of course, the impregnability of this world, Hipp. Ref., VI, 31, 1 θόρυβος ἐγένετο ἐν τῷ πληρώματι.

[22] Iren. Haer., II, praef. 1: *conditionem secundum imaginem invisibilis ... Pleromatis factam dicunt.*

[23] Obviously also from God, hence originally two *horoi* in Valentinus himself, Iren. Haer., I, 11, 1, Jonas, 367.

[24] → n. 19.

[25] The name, Hipp. Ref., VI, 32, 2; the second Christ acc. to 36, 4.

[26] Heracleon in Orig. Comm. in Joh., 13, 11 on 4:17; he is her σύζυγος ἀπὸ πληρώματος, her spouse from the pleroma, with whom there must be syzygy, Lock, 2.

a more specific way: the plur. (15 times) denotes "contents," the idea of perfection is expressed by the adding of πάντα (II, 67e) [27] or ὅλα (III, 160b). [28] The sing., found 8 times, embraces the meanings "vessel" (also πλήρωμα εἶναί τινων, "to be full" of something; the soul, which is itself εἶδος [idea], πλήρωμά ἐστιν εἰδῶν, III, 208b) [29] and "totality," "sum"; so τὸ μὲν αὐτοζῷον πλήρωμά ἐστι τοῦ πλήθους τῶν νοητῶν ζῴων (IV, 240e); [30] of the world soul: πλήρωμα γάρ ἐστι τῶν ὅλων, εἰκόνας ἔχουσα τῶν πάντων (III, 228 f.). [31] The technical meaning of Chr. Gnosticism is not present here either. The same is true of the last Neo-platonist, Damascius. In his De Principiis, 46 πλήρωμα denotes the unsundered (→ V, 455, 39, 37) "totality" of being (ἐν τῷ ἀδιορίστῳ πληρώματι τῶν ὄντων). [32] It particular, it is the "sum" of qualities which constitute the nature of a thing (also plur.), ibid., 14 (28, 4); 56 (117, 22). It is a formal term for totality or unity as distinct from multiplicity or individuality, cf. Corp. Herm. etc.

B. The Word in the New Testament.

It should be noted that πλήρωμα is already used in different senses in Romans. Because of its wealth of meaning Paul is relatively fond of the term.

1. "That which fills," "content," Mk. 6:43; 8:20; in an OT quotation 1 C. 10:26 (→ 299, 28 f.); "patch," Mk. 2:21 = Mt. 9:16 → V, 717 f.

2. a. In measurement, "full measure," R. 11:25 numerically "the whole," for πάντα τὰ ... (cf. 1:5), with πᾶς Ἰσραήλ, v. 26 intentionally chosen as a fuller expression, → II, 370. In Eph. 4:13 it is used along with an image from personal life: the ἀνὴρ τέλειος is the adult; ἡλικία corresponds to this, denoting maturity (→ II, 941 f.) in contrast to the νήπιοι of v. 14; Christ is the example (v. 13). Hence πλήρωμα can hardly be rendered "vessel" [33] nor taken in a Gnostic sense (→ II, 942 f.); it can only mean "full measure." [34] The members of the community (→ III, 624) which has attained the measure of adulthood, the full measure of Christ, are no longer children who can be easily influenced (v. 14). b. "Fulness," "wealth," R. 15:29 vl. πληροφορία, → 311, 1 ff. The use here is almost adjectival: with the "full" blessing. The noun, however, underlines the overflowing wealth (Vg abundantia) of the blessing with which Christ accompanies His apostle. The ἵνα clause in Eph. 3:19 gathers together the petitions of vv. 16-19a: that you may be completely filled, that the whole fulness which God gives may be yours, especially in the knowledge of the love of Christ, v. 18 f. (→ I, 49). [35] In Jn. 1:16 πλήρωμα takes up the πλήρης (→ 285, 15 ff.) of v. 14. [36] The reference in the context is to the incarnate Word. In Him the whole fulness of divine grace has

---

[27] Ed. E. Diehl, I (1903), 220, 4.
[28] Ed. Diehl, II (1904), 68, 15.
[29] Ibid., 222, 2.
[30] Ed. Diehl, III (1906), 8, 18 f.; cf. Dupont, 467: "sum."
[31] Ed. Diehl, II (1904), 286, 17 f.
[32] Ed. C. E. Ruelle, I (1889), 92, 6.
[33] "To the measure of the stature of the Chr. community fulfilled by Christ."
[34] The cumulative tautology with μέτρον (ἡλικίας) is not surprising in Eph., cf. also → n. 44.
[35] On the final εἰς cf. 2 C. 8:2 → II, 429, 36 f.; it is certainly intended thus, Dib. Gefbr.[3], ad loc.; Pr.-Bauer[4], s.v. πληρόω 1b; E. Percy, Die Probleme der Kol.- u. Eph.-Br., Skrifter utgivna av Kungl. Humanistiska Vetenskapssamfundet i Lund, 39 (1946), 301, 385, n. 34, also the possibility discussed → 304, 28 f.
[36] Cf. also the correspondence between the end of v. 14 and v. 17b. V. 17b ⁓ ὅτι v. 17a ⁓ provides a basis for what is said in v. 16.

become actively present. [37] For this reason the relation of the believer to Him can be described as a continual receiving from the superabundance in whose historical manifestation God has more than fully made Himself known as the Saviour. [38]

In Col. 1:19 πλήρωμα is used directly in the abs., but here precisely in the context of a developed terminology, cf. already ψ 67:17: εὐδόκησεν ὁ θεὸς κατοικεῖν ἐν αὐτῷ (Mt. Zion). There are similar formulations in the Rabb. writings. Here however, because of the emphasis on God's transcendence, the concept of the *shekinah* is introduced, → 290, 14 ff. Cf. esp. Tg. on 1 K. 8:27: "Has it really pleased the Lord [39] to cause his *shekinah* to dwell among men who live on the earth ?" [40] In Col. Christ replaces the Jewish temple. [41] But both formally and materially the statements in Col. go much further than the Jewish statements (cf. Mt. 12:6), [42] including those on the eschatological Jewish expectation that God will dwell among His people (Test. L. 5:2), which means, acc. to Jub. 1:17, in His sanctuary "in their midst." [43] The word πλήρωμα emphasises the fact that the divine fulness of love and power acts and rules in all its perfection through Christ. The choice of the word is thus easy to understand. It is selected because it suggests completeness [44] (cf. the πληρ- group in Paul generally, also → 59-61). For this reason it is not enough to say that in πλήρωμα the author is simply catching up a slogan of the false teachers at Colossae, [45] quite apart from the liturgical character of the two sayings (1:12-20, a prayer of thanksgiving), → V, 154, 20.

Col. 1:19 : It has pleased God [46] that the whole fulness of essence should take up dwelling (aor.) in Christ. According to the context, in a combination of thoughts from 2 C. 5:19 and 8:9 etc., [47] the reference is to the historical Jesus (v. 20 : διὰ τοῦ αἵματος τοῦ σταυροῦ αὐτοῦ), and hence to the fulness of the essence of the God of love. In Col. 2:9 [48] the whole fulness of Godhead, understood from the

---

[37] πλήρωμα αὐτοῦ, "the fulness manifest in him"; → 285, 20 on 1:14. Neither Gnostic nor cosmological, Dupont, 469.

[38] Obj. of ἐλάβομεν is ἐκ τοῦ (Bl.-Debr., 169, 2), the ensuing καί epexegetical (*ibid.*, 442, 9); cf. Bu. J., 51, n. 6.

[39] אתרעי יי; the stem רעא corresponding to Heb. רצה, → II, 745, 18.

[40] S. Aalen, "Begrepet πλήρωμα i Kol.-og Efeserbrevet," *Tidsskrift for Teologi og Kirke,* 23 (1952), 57 f.

[41] Aalen, 60. G. C. A. Harless, *Commentar über den Brief Pauli an d. Eph.* (1834), 125 on 1:23 already suggested that Paul "used πλήρωμα for what the Jews generally understood by שכינה," cf. L. Baeck, "Zwei Beispiele midraschischer Predigt," MGWJ, 69 = NF, 33 (1925), 258-271, esp. 268 (n. 2; "analogous concepts"). Similarly, Aalen does not equate the two terms but thinks they are formally and materially par. for Col. 1:19; 2:9 (60 f.); he also includes כָּבוֹד (on Jn. 1:14), wisdom (63 f. cf. Knox, 164, but not Dupont, 470 f.) and המקום (65). Yet the distinctiveness of πλήρωμα is to be maintained. The Rabb. statements are only the intellectual background against which the sayings in Col. are set.

[42] Schl. Mt., *ad loc.:* "In Jesus God is present in a higher way than in the temple."

[43] Test. D. 5:1 is to be taken thus ; cf. Loh. Kol., 65, n. 1 for the refs.

[44] One may also refer to מְלֵאָה "completeness," Gn. r., 14, 7 on 2:7: "The world (mankind) was created with Adam's 'fulness' (i.e., he did not have to develop), Adam was 20 yrs. old when created" (cf. Eph. 4:13). [The interpretation is acc. to Rengstorf].

[45] Percy, *op. cit.,* 77: "Highly improbable" in view of the importance of that which is denoted for Pl.; cf. Haupt Gefbr., 39, n. 1.

[46] → II, 741, 31 f., 746, 22-24; Loh. Kol., 65, n. 4. The πλήρωμα is not God Himself, nor is it said that Christ is the πλήρωμα (→ II, 739, n. 16 : God is no It for Pl.). The conjecture κατοικίσαι, which on behalf of this interpretation avoids a change of acc. and inf. in v. 19 to simple inf. in v. 20, is unnecessary.

[47] There is obviously a material connection between the πλήρωμα statements and what is said about pre-existence and the Son.

[48] Possibly polemical in content, → στοιχεῖα.

standpoint of power, [49] is ascribed (pres.) to the exalted Lord ; this belongs wholly and undividedly to Christ. πλήρωμα τῆς θεότητος is a higher form of πλήρης θεότης [50] (→ σωματικῶς). The πλήρωμα statements in Col. present the full unity of the work of God and Christ in such a way that the distinctness of person is preserved and yet monotheism is not imperilled. God works through Christ in His whole fulness (1:19), in His full deity (2:9).

In should be noted that the use of πλήρωμα in Eph. and Col. is consistent neither formally nor in content. [51] The use in Col. follows a single line materially, but this differs from the three lines which are unquestionably to be found in Eph. both formally and in part materially. The varied use makes it difficult to explain the word as a tt. at least in Eph. Nor should it be overlooked that in both Col. and Eph. the expression with πλήρωμα can often be replaced by a construction with the adj. πλήρης or the verb πληρόω (though there are good material reasons for the choice of πλήρωμα when it is used); this would be impossible if the use of πλήρωμα were technical in the Gnostic sense.

The πλήρωμα sayings occur in part in passages which speak of Christ as Head of the ἐκκλησία. The connections are as follows. In Col. 1:18 ff. Christ, the historical bearer of the divine fulness in whom God has reconciled His enemies, has become the Head of the Church. From the head vital powers flow into the body. It can thus be said that Christ has actively fulfilled this (Eph. 1:22 f.). As He in whom the fulness of Godhead dwells with power, Christ is also in Col. 2:9 f. the Head of the powers which are to some degree drawn into the reconciliation acc. to 1:18 ff. The idea of a gigantic aeonic body cannot be deduced from these statements. [52]

3. In Eph. 1:23 the πλήρωμα saying is elucidated and expanded by the genitive which follows (→ 292, 7 ff.). πλήρωμα denotes the σῶμα as that which is wholly filled by the mighty working of Christ. [53] Here, then, is an obvious development of the thought of the body in 1 C. 12 (cf. Eph. 4:16 etc.). [54]

Eph. 3:19 could be taken in the same way : So that you may be that which is wholly filled by the manifold work of God (on εἰς cf. 2:22); nevertheless, the similarity between the two passages (1:23; 3:19), which form a general frame for the basic part of the epistle, should not cause us to attempt an analogous interpretation in detail.

---

[49] → III, 119, 27 f.; Aalen, op. cit., 56. V. 10, elucidated by v. 15, explains v. 9.

[50] The NT seems to avoid the abs. use of πλήρης in strict theological statements (→ 285 f.); furthermore, greater fulness is attained by the use of the noun, esp. if πᾶν is added.

[51] This is effaced in the thesis of Schlier (→ 292, n. 35), for whom Eph. 1:10 is obviously the only exception : "Pleroma is ... in Eph. and Col. the divinely filled reality which in its fulness fills again. Three formal senses are combined in the term pleroma : that which is filled, that which fills, and fulness in the sense of superabundance" etc. The richness of the word does not absolve us from the duty of trying to fix the meaning with the greatest possible precision in each reference.

[52] Cf. generally Hanson, 114-116, 129 f., 159 f.

[53] Cf. Mitton, 96, but for a different view C. F. D. Moule, " 'Fulness' and 'fill' in the NT," Scottish Journal of Theology, 4 (1951), 81: Christ is the πλήρωμα of God ; cf. also Moule, "A note on Eph. 1:22, 23," Exp. T., 60 (1948/49), 53; E. J. Goodspeed, "Theory regarding the Origin of Eph.," ibid., 224 f., but in opposition Percy, 51, n. 93.

[54] On the other hand, the Jewish idea of the presence of God in the temple is not transferred to the work of the exalted Lord in the community. In the NT the temple idea is related to God's presence in the community through the Holy Spirit (cf. → IV, 885 f.). If prayer is made in Const. Ap., VIII, 13, 4 ὑπὲρ ... παντὸς τοῦ πληρώματος τῆς ἐκκλησίας, this is preceded by intercession for the ecclesiastical offices ; the meaning is the profane one of the "totality" (cf. the distinction between πλήρωμα and ἱερεῖς in Chrys. Hom. in Ac. 21:5, MPG, 60, 170).

4. The "act of filling"; a. active : as ἀγάπη is not an ethical disposition, so πλήρωμα in R. 13:10 is not a formal ethical concept ("sum"). Both words refer to the act. Loving conduct (cf. vv. 8-10a) is a "complete and entire fulfilment" of what God demands in the Law.

An act. meaning is suggested for R. 13:10 by v. 8b (→ 292 f.). We have a compact train of thought in vv. 8b-10b. The statement in 8b is proved in 9-10a (v. 9 γάρ) and then recapitulated in 10b when proof has been given (οὖν). The argument would be poorly handled, however, if πλήρωμα had the same meaning as ἀνακεφαλαιοῦται, which is part of the actual proof. [55] πλήρωμα, then, does not mean "sum"; it is the "complete fulfilment" of the Law in deed, and in this sense it is the opp. of the formal ἀνακεφαλαιοῦται.

b. Passive : In R. 11:12 the verbal sense is suggested by the play (→ 299, 23 ff.) on ἥττημα; πλήρωμα is an antonym and thus means πληρωθῆναι, [56] "to come to full strength." Only when the number of the redeemed of Israel is complete (opp. "remnant"; → IV, 211 f.) can the Gentile world receive the riches of eschatological consummation. πλήρωμα is clearly used in a pass. temporal sense in statements about the divine plan of salvation. Gl. 4:4 would seem to run more simply as follows : ὅτε δὲ ἐπληρώθη ὁ χρόνος. [57] But the fuller expression is not accidental. ἦλθεν (par. 3:23) is a specific word for the eschatological event (→ II, 674, 24 ff.). Gl. 4:4 is not just saying that a divinely determined span of time has run its course or that a divinely ordained point has been reached. [58] Gl. 4:4 carries the concept of the fulfilment of time decisively beyond the Jewish view (→ 294, 25 ff.). [59] With the sending of the Son time (cf. Eph. 1:10) is fulfilled absolutely; it attains to its full measure in content as well as extent. The saying does not refer to the abolition of time but to the fact that God's saving work has come directly into history; [60] in the historical event of the earthly Jesus (γενόμενον ἐκ γυναικός) God accomplishes His eschatological act. This understanding of the πλήρωμα statements is confirmed and elucidated by Eph. 1:10a. The pretemporal resolve of God leads to the saving dispensation (→ V, 151 f.) of the fulfilment of the times, in which the times are to be and have been fulfilled. [61] The original decree of God had this fulfilment of the times (αἰῶνες, 1 C. 10:11, → τέλος; cf. χρόνος Gl. 4:4) in view. It is grounded solely in God's free will (v. 9 heaps up terms to this effect : θέλημα [→ III, 57, 1 ff.], εὐδοκία [→ II, 747, 1]).

† ἀναπληρόω.

1. "To fill completely," [1] mid. one's house with possessions, Eur. Hel., 907, "to fill up" a gap in the verse, Luc. Tim., 1, an empty space τὸ κενωθὲν πάλιν ἀνεπλήρωσεν, Plat. Tim., 81b, τὴν ἕδραν, 79b, transf. μέρος, "to take over the part in place of

---

[55] The two words, of which one is very rare (→ III, 681), are also found together in Eph. 1:10.

[56] As ἥττημα = ἡττᾶσθαι "to give place to" (the Gentiles); so ἡττάομαι, e.g., Xenoph. Cyrop., V, 3, 33; 4, 32; An., II, 3, 23; 6, 17.

[57] Ltzm. Gl., ad loc.

[58] So the Jewish understanding, Str.-B., III, 570, 580.

[59] It has certainly nothing whatever to do with evolutionary ideas. If Zn. Gl., 200, ad loc. says "that the length of the period and the attainment of its end depend on the inner development which Israel had to undergo," he does not say how Israel was ripe for the coming of Christ. Cf. C. Schneider, Einführung in die nt.liche Zeitgeschichte (1934), 1.

[60] History as the setting of human life rather than that which man controls.

[61] Less probably : the plan of salvation whose goal is the fulfilling of the times.

ἀ ν α π λ η ρ ό ω. [1] "Up to," cf. Schwyzer, II, 440 [Debrunner].

someone who is absent, Plat. Tim., 17a; [2] "to complete," a number Demosth. Or., 14, 16; 27, 13 (mid.); ἀνεπλήρουν τὸ τῆς καλλονῆς ἐναργές, Ep. Ar., 75; "to fill up," God promises Gideon, who draws attention to his youth and the small number of his kindred, αὐτὸς ἀναπληρώσειν τὸ λεῖπον, Jos. Ant., 5, 214; courage ἀνεπλήρου τὰ λείποντα (in weapons and the number of soldiers), Jos. Bell., 4, 198; "to add to," εἴ τι ἐξέλιπον, σὸν ἔργον (so it is your work) ... ἀναπληρῶσαι, Plat. Symp., 188e; "to supplement and complete," Leg., XII, 957a; σὺ δέ μου καὶ τὰ ὑστερήματα ἀναπλήρωσον (in gnosis), Corp. Herm., 13, 1; "to settle" τὴν ἔκδειαν (arrears), Demosth. Ep., 1, 15. "To do completely," "to pay in full" (pap.), "to complete a work," Jos. Ant., 8, 58, "wholly to fulfil a duty," that befitting children, P. Oxy., XI, 1121, 11 f. (295 A.D.). "To terminate" a prayer of thanksgiving, Corp. Herm., 1, 29. "To sate," "appease" ὀργήν, Demosth. Ep., 1, 10.

2. In the LXX 13 times, 6 for forms of מלא (always with ref. to stretches of time). Act. "to insert" into a gap Gn. 2:21 (for סגר "to close"; ἀντί "in place of"), "to bring to full measure," the number of the days of life, Ex. 23:26; "to complete a customary period," the marriage week Gn. 29:28 (συντέλεσον in v. 27, both for מלא), a period of preparation Est. 2:12 מקה); intr. "to be wholly full of" etc., σύνεσιν (subj. the Torah), Sir. 24:26. Pass. "to become full," of the measure of sins, Gn. 15:16 (for שלם "complete"), of a span of time, Ex. 7:25; Est. 1:5, "to come to an end" acc. to God's will, Is. 60:20; of a regular period of time, Est. 2:12, 15; cf. Lv. 12:6.

3. In the NT "to fill a want," "to make up for," τὸ ὑμέτερον ὑστέρημα [3] = what is missing in your action, what you still owe me, 1 C. 16:17, the settling of tensions between me and you (cf. v. 18), Phil. 2:30 personal ministrations (→ line 10 f., though → IV, 227, 13 f.); in both instances the account is balanced representatively by members of the community which is in arrears. 1 Th. 2:16 : "to fill up the measure of sins" (as in Gn. 15:16 → line 18 f.), though the reference here is not to the extreme limit of God's patience after the attainment of which His wrathful judgment will break on pious Judaism, [4] but to the constant (πάντοτε) augmentation of sin by Judaism in its conflict with the free Gentile mission. In 1 C. 14:16 "to occupy" the position of the ἰδιώτης (→ III, 316 f.), to play the role of the ἰδιώτης in God's service (→ n. 2). [5] According to Gl. 6:2 (cf. R. 13:8-10, → 292, 25 ff.; 305, 5 ff.) the Christian completely fulfils the law of Christ through burden-bearing love (→ I, 555 f., IV, 1076, 36-39); materially the phrase "law of Christ" is based on Mt. 22:39 and par.; Jn. 13:34. The pass. occurs in Mt. 13:14 : The prophetic saying [6] about Israel being closed to the word and deed of God is "fully [7] actualised" in the rejection of Christ's message and work.

---

[2] Cf. ἀποπληρόω, which very largely corresponds to ἀναπληρόω : στρατιώτου τάξιν, to take the place of a common soldier (Titus), Jos. Bell., 5, 88; χώραν ἀποπληρῶσαι ἀνθρωπικήν, to fill the place of a man, i.e., to play the role of a true man, to be a genuine man in one's conduct, Epict. Diss., II, 4, 5. ἀποπληρόω does not occur in the LXX or NT.

[3] Pl. also has προσαναπληροῦν τὸ ὑστέρημα μου in 2 C. 11:9, τὰ ὑστερήματα τῶν ἁγίων in 2 C. 9:12; both refer to material needs — the verb does not occur elsewhere in the NT — in the sense "to supply," "to make good"; the προσ- is added intentionally as in Wis. 19:4; Plat. Men., 84d mid. "to supplement." Str.-B., III, 485 f. relates 1 C. 16:17 to the Jewish word of comfort in bereavement : "May God make good your loss" (e.g., Ber., 16b, also plur.), but Paul does not refer to compensation by God.

[4] As against Dib. Th., ad loc. Cf. → 288, 4 f.; 294, 17-19; 308, 12-14.

[5] The ref. in n. 2 undermines the interpretation of G. H. Whitaker, "1 Cor. XIV, 16," JThSt, 22 (1921), 268 : to fill the part of the layman without which the worship of God is incomplete.

[6] Formally cf. 1 Εσδρ. 1:54 εἰς ἀναπλήρωσιν τοῦ ῥήματος τοῦ κυρίου ἐν στόματι Ἱερεμίου.

[7] Cf. Zn. Mt., 478.

† ἀνταναπληρόω.

In this rare compound, [1] not found in the LXX, the ἀντ- denotes mutual, representative or repeated "supplementing" or "replacing," with some overlapping of the specific nuances. Demosth. Or., 14, 17: To add the most needy to the most wealthy; Dio C., 44, 48, 2 pass.: to be filled up mutually by the perfecting which comes from others; Apollon. Dyscol. Synt., I, 19: "to supplement" = to define more closely, II, 44: pronouns vicariously fulfil what is impossible for the noun (αἱ ἀντωνυμίαι τὸ ἀδύνατον τοῦ ὀνόματος ἀνταναπληροῦσαι), III, 111: pass. "to be mutually augmented," IV, 64: "to add to"; cf. Epic. in Diog. L., X, 48: ἀνταναπλήρωσις, the (constant) "reaugmentation."

The only NT instance is at Col. 1:24. Predominant here is the thought of vicarious filling up with reference to the measure [2] of eschatological affliction laid on the community in the non-mystical but soberly realistic fellowship of its destiny with Christ (τῶν θλίψεων [3] τοῦ Χριστοῦ, → III, 143 f.) on the basis of its dying with Him (→ III, 19, n. 79, cf. esp. Phil. 3:10, → III, 806 f. → συμμορφίζω), though → V, 932 f., [4] where other references are given.

† ἐκπληρόω.

1. ἐκ- denotes more strongly the intention or goal behind the act stated in the verb. [1] The word is found from Soph. El., 708 (chariots, → line 20). a. "To fill," e.g., ships "to man," Aristot. Pol., VII, 6, p. 1327b, 14; of God with ref. to the cosmos, πάντα διὰ πάντων ἐκπεπληρωκότος, Philo Post. C., 6; of the divine logos, πάντα τῆς οὐσίας ἐκπεπληρωκώς, Philo Rer. Div. Her., 188; "to make up" a certain number, Hdt., VII, 186 (pass. "to reach," VIII, 82); "to fill up," the coffers of state, Xenoph. Mem., III, 6, 5; "to furnish" a household, ibid., III, 6, 14; τὸ ἐλλεῖπον ἐκπληρώσατε ("to complete"), Xenoph. Cyrop., V, 5, 39. "To bring to full measure," ἡ χάρις (favour) ἐκπεπλήρωται (in deeds), Hdt., VIII, 144; by endowment with mental organs God brings the soul to totality, Philo Cher., 60. b. "To fulfil" a duty, "fully to pay" χρέος (a debt), Plat. Leg., XII, 958b, φόρον, 2 Macc. 8:10 (cf. pap.; "to satisfy" someone financially); πάτριον ἔθος, Philo Spec. Leg., II, 148; the city φαίνηται πᾶσαν τειμὴν καὶ εὐσέβειαν ἐκπεπληρωκυῖα to the imperial house (Nero), Ditt. Syll.³, II, 814, 54 f.; promises, τὰ τῆς ὑποσχέσεως, P. Tebt., I, 10, 7 (119 B.C.), τὰς ἐλπίδας καὶ τὰς ἐπαγγελίας, Polyb., I, 67, 1, curses (ἀράς), Aelian. Var. Hist., III, 29; pass. "to come to fulfilment," of a voice in a dream, Ael. Arist. Or., 51, 46. c. "To fulfil," "to carry out," a proposal, a plan, 3 Macc. 1:2, 22; a sacrifice, Joseph. Ant., 19, 293. d. "To appease," ἐπιθυμίας, Epic. Adlocutio, 21. [2] The word occurs in the LXX only in the vv. mentioned → line 28, 34.

2. The only NT instance is in Ac. 13:33 (ἐπαγγελίαν, → line 31 f.; → II, 582); here the content of the good news to the Jews is that God has "definitively

---

ἀνταναπληρόω → V, 933, n. 20. A. Steubing, Der paul. Begriff "Christusleiden," Diss. Heidelberg (1905), 4-17; A. Wikenhauser, Die Kirche als der mystische Leib Christi² (1940), 192-197.
[1] From class. times ἀντι- is increasingly put before compounds, Schwyzer, II, 442.
[2] → ὑστέρημα; Loh. Kol., 78 refers to the background of apocalyptic ideas in Judaism and the NT, cf. Str.-B., IV, 977-985.
[3] θλῖψις is never used in the NT for Jesus' own sufferings; it always refers to afflictions which result from union with Him.
[4] Exegesis has to explain why ὑστερήματα and ἀνταναπληρόω are used; G. Kittel fails to do this too in "Kol. 1:24," ZSTh, 18 (1941), 186-191, esp. 190 f.

ἐκπληρόω. [1] Schwyzer, II, 462 [Debrunner].
[2] ed. K. Wotke, "Epikurische Spruchsammlung," Wiener Studien, 10 (1888), 193.

(→ 307, 18) fulfilled" the promise to the forefathers[3] in the resurrection of Jesus (v. 34; → I, 370 f.) as the goal of the promise ; in support reference is made to Ps. 2:7 (→ I, 670 f.) in v. 34 and to Is. 55:3; ψ 15:10 (→ V, 492, 5-10) in v. 34 f. 1 C. 15:4 also emphasises the fact that the act of salvation promised in the OT has been accomplished in the resurrection of Jesus (cf., too, the eschatological δεῖ of Lk. 24:7).

† ἐκπλήρωσις.

1. Rare; "filling," γαστρός, Phil. Leg. All., III, 145; temporally "completion" τοῦ ὅλου ἐνιαυτοῦ (365 days do not make up a whole year), Strabo, 17, 1, 46; making up the number ten, Philo Congr., 91; "completion" of the cosmos (κόσμος), Phil. Cher., 110; "perfecting," Philo Op. Mund., 146; "satisfaction," τοῦ ἀκρατοῦς, Philo Somn., II, 201, ἐπιθυμίας, Philo Fug. Inv., 144, ἐπιθυμιῶν, Dion. Hal. Ant. Rom., VI, 86, "fulfilment," ἐπιθυμουμένων, Epict. Diss., IV, 1, 175. In the LXX only at 2 Macc. 6:14, ἁμαρτιῶν : God allows the measure of the sins of the Gentiles to be filled completely only to punish them no less completely.

2. In the NT the only instance is at Ac. 21:26 : Paul announces in the temple (→ I, 68, 22) that the period (cf. v. 27: seven days) for the purifying (→ I, 124) of the four Nazirites (v. 23) has "come to an end."[1]

† συμπληρόω.

1. "To fill with," "to fill completely," a threshing-flood with corn, P. Petr., II, 38a, 22 (3rd cent. B.C.), "up to the pillars," Ditt. Syll.[3], III, 969, 71, σαρξίν, Plat. Tim., 75a; συμπληρωθείς, "completely filled," of the cosmos, Plat. Tim., 92c → III, 871; an outline, sketch, Plat. Leg., VI, 770b; "to man" ships, Hdt., VIII, 1, 1 (along with others, supporting them), Thuc., VI, 50, 2; VII, 60, 4, often in Xenoph. Hist. Graec., e.g., IV, 8, 7; of a period of time, pass. "to be completed," BGU, IV, 1122, 22 (14/13 B.C.), "to come to an end," Jos. Ant., 4, 176. "To make complete," συνεπλήρωσε τὸ ὅλον ὁ θεός, ἐντελεχῆ ποιήσας τὴν γένεσιν, Aristot. Gen. Corr., II, 10, p. 336b, 31, perception with the senses (interpreting Gn. 2:21 ἀνεπλήρου [sic] ... σάρκα), Philo Leg. All., 38; pass. "to become complete," ἐξ ἁπάντων ... συμπληρουμένης τῆς εὐδαιμονίας, Diod. S., I, 2, 1; in number, Philo Op. Mund., 101, "to be constituted (of)," ibid., 13, constellations (of 7 stars), ibid., 115; Leg. All., I, 8. In the LXX only Jer. 25:12 AQ (BS πληρωθῆναι) pass. "to be fulfilled," of a divinely appointed period of time (70 yrs.); cf. συμπλήρωσις, the "completion" of the time of the desolation of Jerusalem (70 yrs.), 2 Ch. 36:21; 1 Εσδρ. 1:55; Da. Θ 9:2.

2. Only the pass. occurs in the NT; spatially Lk. 8:23 : "completely filled" (supply "with water").[1] Transf. in two par. expressions of a span of time, ἡμέρας (Lk. 9:51), or a point of time ἡμέραν (Ac. 2:1), which is fulfilled according to God's plan. The constr. with pres. infin. expresses the fact that it is coming (→ 50, n. 38). The verb itself points to the fulfilment of God's saving will in the event which takes place. The reference in Lk. 9:51 is the specific period of time which leads to the death of Jesus. Jesus says that it is approaching and

---

[3] → V, 975 f., n. 174, patriarchs, n. 178.

ἐ κ π λ ή ρ ω σ ι ς.   [1] Cf. Str.-B., II, 758.

σ υ μ π λ η ρ ό ω.   J. H. Ropes, "Three Papers on the Text of Acts," II, HThR, 16 (1923), 168-175; E. Lohse, "Lukas als Theologe der Heilsgeschichte," Ev. Theol., 14 (1954), 256-275, esp. 262 f.

[1] The logical subj. is naturally the ship, but in a popular expression the harassed occupants are mentioned instead.

sets His face steadfastly towards Jerusalem, cf. 9:31. The emphasis is on His readiness for death (→ IV, 8, 34-9, 3); on the ultimate twofold sense of ἀνάλημψις → ὑψοῦν. On Ac. 2:1 → 50, 9 ff. [2] The expression underscores the significance of the fact of salvation history proclaimed. It stresses the fact that this happens in time. The occurrence is thus given the character of a genuine event, → IV, 786, 4.

Whereas in statements about time the words for "to fill" originally denote the completion of a period up to an event, here one of the verbs is transferred to the point in time or to the time of the event itself. [3] There are formal pars. to this in non-biblical usage (cf. the quite close one in Ael. Arist. Or., 22, 9 → 287, 15 f.) and esp. in the LXX (→ 288, 13-16); on the NT → 130, 23-30. Nevertheless, the word has here a peculiar theological signification which links it with πληρόω (→ 294, 25 ff.), as the compound shows. The Semitic background may be seen clearly in the special phrase in Lk. 9:51; Ac. 2:1.

† πληροφορέω.

1. Late compound, lit. "to bring to fulness," [1] "to full measure," [2] in part just a strengthening of πληρόω, [3] in part with its own sense (→ lines 23 ff.). a. "To fulfil completely" (pass. "wholly filled," with love, 1 Cl., 54, 1): προαίρεσιν (design), Vett. Val., V, 9, p. 226, 20; σχῆμα, pass. ibid., I, 22, p. 43, 18; a request, Herm. m., 9, 2; an existing obligation, οὐ πρηροφοροῦσα τὸ πατρῷον συνάλλαγμνα, P. Hawara, 69, verso 5; [4] "to complete," also abs. "to do one's utmost, or everything conceivable or humanly possible," P. Amh., 66 II, 42 (124 A.D.). From the first sense b. "to satisfy someone completely," erotically (magic), Preis. Zaub., 7, 910 (= P. Lond., I, 121; 3rd cent. A.D.), financially in the pap., pass. P. Oxy., III, 509, 10 (2nd cent. A.D.). c. Act. "to convince," so probably Ctesias Fr., 29, 39 : [5] πολλοῖς ... ὅρκοις καὶ λόγοις πληροφορήσαντες, and plainly so in the pass. "to be fully convinced" of something, [6] "to come to full certainty," 1 Cl., 42, 3; Ign. Mg., 11, 1; Sm., 1, 1.

2. The only instance in the LXX is at Qoh. 8:11: Because the refutation of evil-doers (by their punishment) does not take place quickly, "the heart of men is full (מָלֵא), to do evil," LXX ἐπληροφορήθη καρδία ... τοῦ ποιῆσαι τὸ πονηρόν. The choice of the word here is based on the sense "to become sure," "to be confirmed," "to be strengthened." [7] The same is possibly true in Test. G. 2:4 : [8] τῇ πλενοεξίᾳ ἐπληροφορήθημεν τῆς ἀναιρέσεως αὐτοῦ, "in consequence of greed we were strengthened in the purpose

---

[2] Including Debrunner's correction → 50, n. 38.
[3] Cf. Zn. Lk., 396, n. 27; Zn. J., 220 f., n. 12; Zn. Ag., 70 f.

π λ η ρ ο φ ο ρ έ ω. M. J. Lagrange, "Le sens de Luc 1:1 d'après les papyrus," *Bulletin d'ancienne littérature et d'archéologie chrétienne*, 2 (1912), 96-100; O. A. Piper, "The Purpose of Luke," *Union Seminary Review*, 57 (1945), 15-25; Deissmann LO, 67 f., with further bibl.

[1] Zn. Lk., 46, n. 11 refers to τελεσφορέω "to bring or come to maturity" (cf. the examples in Pr.-Bauer, s.v.); on words with -φορέω cf. P. Kretschmer-E. Locker, *Rückläufiges Wörterbuch d. griech. Sprache* (1944), 586 f.
[2] From a non-attested πληροφόρος "bringing full measure," Debrunner Gr. Wortb. § 38 [Debrunner]. Cf. also Bl.-Debr. § 119, 1.
[3] On the later period → III, 457, 32 f., 462, 16 ff.
[4] APF, 5 (1913), 383.
[5] Lat. *fidem faciendam*. So in C. Müller and W. Dindorf, *Herodoti Historiarum libri, IX et Ctesiae Cnidii et Chronographorum Castoris, Eratosthenis etc. fragmenta* (1887); Zn. Lk., 47, n. 14.
[6] Lagrange, *op. cit.*, 98 would deduce this sense from b.
[7] Est. 7:5 has the same expression with ἐτόλμησεν, Zn. Lk., 47, n. 14.
[8] Cf. R. H. Charles, *The Gk. Versions of the Test. XII* (1908), ad loc.

to remove him," otherwise : "We were filled with greed, so that we thought of removing him,"[9] though in this case the dat. would be irregular.

3. The NT uses the word act.[10] at 2 Tm. 4:5 (→ 297, 12 ff.): "to fulfil." Pass. 2 Tm. 4:17 is along the same lines (→ III, 717, 3 ff.). The word means "to achieve," "to bring forth" in Lk. 1:1. It has here, however, a richer content, for it is used with reference to divine acts[11] in a historical sphere into which the author is directly drawn (ἐν ἡμῖν).[12] The statement that these acts were "brought to fulness"[13] obviously underlines their significance as divine acts which bring salvation. The meaning "to achieve complete certainty" (→ 309, 23 ff.) is undoubtedly attested in Romans, cf. 4:21: Abraham's faith is completely certain of the full agreement between God's promise and His power, which can call into being things which are not,[14] awaken what is dead to life, and give Abraham a posterity. Because the faith of Abraham in R. 4 is a model for the faith of Christians, justifying faith, based on confidence in God's promise and creative power, is a faith which is "fully certain" of God's act, a faith in the new life which is given to the Christian in justification (→ III, 449, 14-18). In R. 14:5 Paul does not lay down any specific rules on the question of eating flesh (→ IV, 66 f.) or the observance of set days.[15] He simply asks that each should "achieve full certainty" in his own judgment, so that his conduct may build on this without wavering[16] (on the origin of this certainty, cf. v. 22 f., → 219, 33 ff.). In Col. 4:12[17] πεπληρο-φορημένοι is used in the abs. Formally possible is an interpretation along the lines of R. 14:5 : "filled with certainty,"[18] though the general drift of Col. would suggest "brought to full measure."[19] The latter rendering is favoured by the combination with τέλειοι (→ 285, 10-13): As those who are mature and have come to full stature (the stature of Christ) in Christ, Christians stand firm (R. 14:4b) ἐν παντὶ θελήματι τοῦ θεοῦ (→ III, 59, 6 f.).

† πληροφορία.

Lit. a. "supreme fulness," though in non-christian literature we find only b. "certainty," Rhet. Graec.,[1] VII, 108, 3 : ἐπίρρημα βεβαιώσεως ὃν μετὰ πληροφορίας τὸ πάγιον ἐμφαίνει τῆς καταλήψεως, cf. Hesych., s.v.: βεβαιότης. The word possibly bears the same sense in P. Giess., 87, 25 (2nd cent. A.D.). It does not occur in the LXX.

---

[9] Cf. the transl. of F. Schnapp, Kautzsch Apokr. u. Pseudepigr., II.

[10] "To fill someone completely with something," R. 15:13 BFG (→ 291, 10 f.).

[11] E. Lohse, "Lk. als Theologe der Heilsgeschichte," Ev. Theol., 14 (1954), 261, n. 21: "Pass. for the divine name." The author certainly thinks of the πράγματα as coming from God.

[12] This is not refuted by the fact that he knows of the historical acts only through the "tradition" of "eye-witnesses" (→ V, 347 f., 373), v. 2. The author is obviously thinking primarily of the story of Jesus, cf. already in v. 1 πολλοί.

[13] The interpretation of Schl. Lk., 20 ("to come to certainty") is found already in the fathers (from Orig.), cf. Zn. Lk., 46, n. 13 and his criticism, 47.

[14] Cf. Ltzm. R.; C. H. Dodd, The Epistle of Paul to the Romans (1947), The Moffatt NT Commentary; Mi. R.; Schl. R. on 4:17.

[15] Which ? Mi. R., ad loc. considers various possibilities.

[16] Schl. R., 171; cf. Zn. Lk., 47, n. 14.

[17] The Imperial Text substitutes a more common term for this little known word (→ 292, 20 on Col. 2:10).

[18] Cf. the transl. of Dib. Gefbr.³ on Col. 4:12.

[19] Haupt Gefbr. on Col. 4:12.

πληροφορία. ¹ Ed. C. Walz (1833).

In the NT it is used only of spiritual goods. In 1 Th. 1:5 the antithesis of πληροφορία πολλῇ (ἐν λόγῳ μόνον) should be noted as well as the par. ἐν δυνάμει and ἐν πνεύματι ἁγίῳ. As in 1 C. 2:4, these three concepts are brought into juxtaposition in characterisation of Paul's first preaching (→ IV, 102; II, 309 f.). πληροφορία is to be construed along the same lines as δύναμις and πνεῦμα ἅγιον in 1 Th. 1:5. The declaration[2] of the glad tidings by the apostle took place, not in mere word, but in great "fulness of divine working" (→ 310, 7 f.). The word is thus one of the terms which Paul uses to try to define linguistically the great richness of the divine work in the present life of Christianity, cf. the compounds with ὑπερ- and also → 60 f. Similarly in Col. 2:2, tautologously with πλοῦτος, the term denotes the superabundance of a knowledge of God which is not just formally linked with ἀγάπη, of the Christian understanding of God and life which is epitomised in Christ as the One through whom God actively reveals Himself. According to Hb. 6:11 the readers do not lack the zeal[3] which leads to "full preservation"[4] of the final hope in patient faith, v. 12. On the other hand, the obvious reference in Hb. 10:22 is to the "full assurance"[5] of the faith which rests on appropriation of the atoning work of Jesus the High-priest. Purified thereby, the Christian can stand with "full confidence" before God. Here πληροφορία approximates theologically to παρρησία (→ V, 884, esp. lines 9 ff.). Formally, of course, the thought of a full measure is still present in sense b.

Delling

| † πλησίον | (→ ἀγαπάω, I, 21, 23 ff.; ἀδελφός, I, 144 ff.; ἕτερος, II, 702, 1 ff. |

A. πλησίον in the Greek World.

Adv. acc. of πλησίος (from Hom.) "near," "close by,"[1] also from Theognis found as a noun like πέλας (e.g., Eur. Med., 86 : ὡς πᾶς τις αὐτὸν τοῦ πέλας μᾶλλον φιλεῖ): ὁ πλησίον "the neighbour" (in space), "the person next to one" (in school,

---

[2] → II, 729, 27 and esp. E. Molland, "Das Paulinische Euangelion," *Avhandlinger utgitt av Det Norske Videnskaps-Akademi i Oslo,* 2, *Hist-Filos. Klasse Heft* 3 (1934), 49.

[3] Here, too, with ἀγάπη, v. 10 (Wnd. Hb.; Mi. Hb., *ad loc.*), though αὐτήν refers to the degree of zeal, not the content.

[4] Wnd. Hb. renders "full development," cf. also Mi. Hb.

[5] This interpretation is suggested also by the expression μετὰ ἀληθινῆς καρδίας; on this → I, 249, 5.

π λ η σ ί ο ν. I. Abrahams, *Studies in Pharisaism and the Gospels,* I (1917), 18-29; II (1924), 33-40, 206 f.; K. Barth K.D.³, I, 2 (1945), 460-462 (C.D., I, 2 [1956], 417-419); R. Bultmann, *Aimer son prochain, commandement de Dieu* (1930), German *Glauben u. Verstehen* (1933), 229-244; H. Cohen, "Der Nächste," *Jüd. Schriften,* I (1924), 182-195; Cr.-Kö., 931 f.; G. Eichholz, *Jesus Christus u. d. Nächste* (1952); J. Fichtner, "Der Begriff des 'Nächsten' im AT," *Wort und Dienst, Jbch. d. Theol. Schule Bethel,* NF, 4 (1955), 23-52; E. Fuchs, "Was heisst : 'Du sollst deinen Nächsten lieben wie dich selbst'?" ThBl, 11 (1932), 129-140; S. Hochfeld, "Nächstenliebe," *Die Lehren des Judts. nach den Quellen³,* I (1928), 328-389; J. Lewkowitz, Art. "Nächstenliebe," Jüd. Lex., IX, 374 f.; H. Kosmala, "Gedanken zur Kontroverse Farbstein-Hoch," Judaica, 4 (1948), 241-258; F. J. Leenhardt, "La parabole du Samaritain," *Aux sources de la tradition chrétienne, Mélanges offerts à M. Goguel* (1950), 132-138; O. Michel, "Das Gebot der Nächstenliebe in d. Verkündigung Jesu," *Zur sozialen Entscheidung* (1947), 53-101; Moore, II, 85-88; A. T. Nikolainen, "Der

Plat. Charm., 155c; in the army, Jos. Bell., 5, 295) then "fellow-man" generally, so in the expression ἐπὶ λύμῃ τῶν πλησίον ζῆν in Philo Spec. Leg., III, 11; IV, 21, though sometimes Philo, too, has the more pregnant sense "neighbour," e.g., Vit. Mos., I, 137. It is also used in this sense in ethical discourses, e.g., Aeschin. Or. in Ctesiphontem, 174 : τὰ τῶν πλησίον αἰσχρά. The idea of proximity may be vividly brought out in this use, e.g., Plat. Ap., 25d : ὅτι οἱ μὲν κακοὶ κακόν τι ἐργάζονται ἀεὶ τοὺς μάλιστα πλησίον ἑαυτῶν. It is also ethically important in the doctrine of concentric circles in the midst of which stands the human ego,[2] as portrayed by the Stoic Hierocles.[3] Muson., 65, 6 ff. mentions another and different duty along with love of one's neighbour, i.e., that of not sinning against oneself.

Greeven

B. πλησίον in the LXX and the Neighbour in the OT.

1. πλησίον occurs some 225 times in the LXX, 50 times in works with no Heb. original. Of the other instances 15 have no Heb. original or this is uncertain, so that comparison is possible in about 155 refs. In 12 of these πλησίον is used prepos.[4] in a spatial sense for Heb. equivalents like מוּל, עַל־יַד, אֶל, מִצַּד, cf. Ex. 34:3; Nu. 33:38 vl. A; Jos. 12:9. In the other 140 instances it is a noun and is used 125 times for רֵעַ (112 times) or related derivates.[5] Elsewhere we have synon. of רֵעַ, 11 times עָמִית, 5 times אָח and once קָרוֹב אֶל־הַבַּיִת. Hence רֵעַ is the chief equivalent.[6] This occurs almost 190 times, and in the LXX and other Gk. renderings many other words as well as πλησίον are used for it, the most common being φίλος and ἀλλήλ ...[7] The concept of the neighbour is thus expressed in the OT predominantly by רֵעַ and other derivates of the stem, and by synonyms of רֵעַ.

2. The word רֵעַ and related derivates come from רָעָה II. This verb is comparatively rare in the OT. It is attested in the sense "to have dealings with someone" (Prv. 13:20; 28:7; 29:3 q; Prv. 22:24 hitp),[8] "to associate oneself," or specifically "to serve as best man," Ju. 14:20. The basic meaning is "to have dealings with someone," "to associate."[9] The noun רֵעַ and most of the other derivates reflect the basic meaning in various nuances which portray dealings between men. The narrowness or breadth of the relation may be very different. The extreme limit is to be seen on the one side in verses in which רֵעַ

Nächste als religiöse Frage im NT," *Akademische Abh. Helsinki* (1937); Pr.-Bauer[4], 1224 f.; H. Preisker, *Das Ethos des Urchr.* (1949), 68-81; M. Rade, "Der Nächste," *Festgabe f. A. Jülicher* (1927), 70-79; C. H. Ratschow, "Agape, Nächstenliebe u. Bruderliebe," ZSTh, 21 (1950/52), 160-182; F. Rosenzweig, *Stern der Erlösung,*[3] II (1954), 168.

[1] Etym. root *pela-, plā-* (πέλας, πελάζω etc., Doric πλᾶτίον = πλησίον) "to draw near to." Walde-Pok., II, 57 f.; Boisacq, 760 f. [Debrunner].

[2] Cf. → I, 46, 10 ff.

[3] *Ethische Elementarlehre,* ed. H. v. Arnim (1906), 61, 10 ff.

[4] As an improper prep. with gen. (Pr.-Bauer, *s.v.*).

[5] 9 times רֵעָה with suffix 1st sing. (transl. ἡ πλησίον μου) only in Cant., 3 times רְעוּת (2 of these ἡ πλησίον), and once רֵעָה plur. with suffix (αἱ πλησίον αὐτῆς) ψ 44:15; the other derivates (רֵעֶה and מֵרֵעַ) are not transl. πλησίον in the LXX.

[6] πλησίον is even less common in the plur. in the LXX than the HT; ψ 27:3; 37:12; 121:8; Zech. 3:8; 1 Βασ. 30:26.

[7] Only about one third of the 180 instances of φίλος have Mas. equivalents, and in half of these the word is רֵעַ (19 times in Prv., 8 in Job); in some 30 instances the Gk. is ἀλλήλ ... and other renderings of רֵעַ are e.g., ἕτερος (6 times), ἑταῖρος and πολίτης (5 each), συνεταιρίς (3 times) and ἀδελφός (only 1-2 times).

[8] Elsewhere the text is disputed or derivation is probably from רעה I.

[9] L. Köhler's rendering (Köhler-Baumg., *s.v.*) "to have to do with" seems to me not quite to catch the dynamic and initiatory aspect.

(and even more so רֵעֶה) is used for the dignitary or official, the "friend of the king," [10] and on the other in the stereotyped use with the suffix with reference back to אִישׁ, אִשָּׁה or the like, and in the sense "one another." [11] Between these poles lies a whole list of nuances of רֵעַ [12] which cannot always be differentiated sharply : "friend" [13] (Dt. 13:7; 2 S. 13:3; Mi. 7:5; Ps. 35:14; Prv. 14:20; 18:24; Job 2:11; 16:20 etc.); "lover," "paramour" (Jer. 3:1, 20; Hos. 3:1, also רַעְיָה Cant. 1:9, 15 etc.); "companion," "comrade" (Job 30:29; Prv. 17:17; רֵעוּת for the youthful playmates of the queen [Ps. 45:14] and the companions of the daughter of Jephthah [Ju. 11:38]); "neighbour" (Prv. 3:29; 25:17; Ex. 11:2 רְעוּת par. רֵעַ); [14] often more generally "fellow-man," the person encountered in daily life (Prv. 6:1, 3; 18:17; 25:8; 26:19); [15] hence "another" (1 S. 28:17; cf. 2 S. 12:11 and רְעוּת Jer. 9:19; Est. 1:19).

3. Always there is denoted an encounter which is not expressly referred to relationship within the covenant of Yahweh but which in the OT is actually with men who are members of the covenant, who worship the one God, and who stand under His command. More clearly than in the רֵעַ ref. so far given this connection comes out in one part of the usage of רֵעַ in the legal texts, which we have not considered thus far. רֵעַ is not as common here as one might expect. It occurs 4 times each in the 2 versions of the Decalogue in Ex. 20 and Dt. 5, [16] 10 times in the Book of the Covenant, [17] 14 times in the Deuteronomic Law, [18] and only 4 times in the Holiness Code. [19] The laws are given to the people of Israel; Israel, or the individual Israelite ("thou shalt"), is thus addressed therein. [20] This fact, though unquestionable, obviously finds varying degrees of expression in the individual collections. The individual recipient of the individual laws of the Book of the Covenant is usually denoted very generally by אִישׁ, אִשָּׁה or a part. which describes a fault (מַכֶּה Ex. 21:15, גֹּנֵב 21:16 etc.). The one in relation to whom he must ask is either named specifically (father, mother, daughter, servant, maid) or indicated more generally (a man, Ex. 21:12, 16), רֵעַ (→ n. 17) being used in a few instances. Furthermore, there are even here no parallels to the very common "man"

---

[10] 1 Ch. 27:33; 3 Βασ. 4:5. Cf. W. Rudolph, *Chronikbücher, Hndbch. AT,* I, 21 (1955), *ad loc.* and Fichtner, 29.

[11] In expressions like אִישׁ אֶת־רֵעֵהוּ אֶל (עַל, מֵאֵת) רֵעֵהוּ even of inorganic things Gn. 15:10, cf. רְעוּת of animals, Is. 34:16. This use of רֵעַ is very common in the OT, and is not infrequently par. to similar formulae, cf. Ex. 32:37 אִישׁ אֶת־אָחִיו וְאִישׁ אֶת־רֵעֵהוּ וְאִישׁ אֶת־קְרֹבוֹ. Rather oddly קָרֹב is only once rendered ὁ πλησίον in the LXX (Ex. 12:4).

[12] Only occasional ref. can be made to the derivates; attention is focused in the main on רֵעַ. For details cf. Fichtner, 33-35.

[13] מֵרֵעַ also has the special sense of "companion," "friend of the bridegroom" (Ju. 14:20, cf. 15:2, 6). Job is God's "friend" (רֵעַ, 16:21), cf. J. Fichtner, "Hiob in der Verkündigung unserer Zeit," *Wort u. Dienst, Jbch. d. Theol. Schule Bethel,* NF, 2 (1950), 81.

[14] On Ex. 11:2 : אִשָּׁה מֵאֵת רְעוּתָהּ, cf. 3:22 : אִשָּׁה מִשְּׁכֶנְתָּהּ וּמִגָּרַת בֵּיתָהּ.

[15] This sense of רֵעַ, which often has to be assumed, forms in some sense the bridge to the formal use with suffix in the sense "one another," and in many refs. cannot be distinguished from this with any precision.

[16] Once in the prohibition of false witness (Ex. 20:16; Dt. 5:20) and three times in the command against covetousness (Ex. 20:17; Dt. 5:21).

[17] Ex. 21:14, 18, 35; 22:6, 7, 8, 9, 10, 13 with suffix 3rd masc. sing. (mostly casuistical statutes), 22:25 with 2nd sing.

[18] With suffix 2nd sing. only Dt. 19:14; 23:25 f. (3 times); 24:10. With suffix 3rd masc. sing. Dt. 15:2 (twice); 19:4, 5 (twice), 11; 22:24, 26; Dt. 13:7 in the sense "friend."

[19] With suffix 2nd sing. Lv. 19:13, 16, 18, with suff. 3rd sing. 20:10.

[20] Cf. M. Noth, "Die Gesetze im Pent.," *Schriften d. Königsberger Gelehrten Gesellschaft,* 17, 2 (1940), 63-70 (the community addressed in the OT); G. v. Rad rightly says of Dt.: "The 'Thou' of Dt. on the lips of Moses always has a collective ring with ref. to the people," "Das Gottesvolk im Dt.," BWANT, III, 11 (1929), 17.

and "his רֵעַ", which characterised these as members of the covenant people. [21] In form, then, most of the laws of the Book of the Covenant have a relatively general character corresponding to their close kinship to the world of ancient oriental legislation, [22] and linguistically at least רֵעַ does not mean only a fellow-member of the covenant. It should not be overlooked, however, that the Book of the Covenant did not simply take over ancient oriental law without scrutiny. By selection, reconstruction and supplementation, esp. through apodictic clauses, this law becomes Israel's own law, [23] the law of the Book of the Covenant, so that the אִישׁ (and his רֵעַ) who appears in it is in fact the אִישׁ יִשְׂרָאֵל. [24] Nevertheless the broad and general character of the formulation is worth noting. In form at least the statements are of general validity. This is even more true of the Ten Commandments, three of which are formulated with no mention of a personal object : לֹא תִּנְאָף, לֹא תִּרְצָח and לֹא תִּגְנֹב, while the prohibition of false witness and of covetousness refers to the רֵעַ. [25] It is true that in the introduction to the Decalogue the recipient of the commandments is quite unequivocally the people which Yahweh has liberated from bondage in Egypt and now claims for His service. On the other hand, the individual commandments have such breadth and general validity that one cannot without qualification restrict the רֵעַ in them to members of the covenant, with respect to whom it is in fact used in the first instance. In the Deuteronomic Law and the Holiness Code the legal statutes are more expressly related to the fact of Israel's election as the people of God, [26] so that more specific terms are used for the recipients of the commands and those in relation to whom they must act. In close proximity to רֵעַ Dt. often has אָח, [27] while in the Holiness Code we find אִישׁ מִבֵּית־יִשְׂרָאֵל at Lv. 17:3 (בְּנֵי־יִשְׂרָאֵל at 17:14), [28] and he is summoned to act vis-à-vis his עָמִית (9 times) or the בְּנֵי־עַמֶּךָ. Particularly significant is the juxtaposition of such terms precisely in those vv. of the Code which contain the commandment of love, Lv. 19:16-18 :

v. 16   לֹא־תֵלֵךְ רָכִיל בְּעַמֶּיךָ

לֹא תַעֲמֹד עַל־דַּם רֵעֶךָ אֲנִי יְהוָה׃

v. 17   לֹא־תִשְׂנָא אֶת־אָחִיךָ בִּלְבָבֶךָ

הוֹכֵחַ תּוֹכִיחַ אֶת־עֲמִיתֶךָ

וְלֹא־תִשָּׂא עָלָיו חֵטְא׃

v. 18   לֹא־תִקֹּם, וְלֹא־תִטֹּר אֶת־בְּנֵי עַמֶּךָ

וְאָהַבְתָּ לְרֵעֲךָ כָּמוֹךָ אֲנִי יְהוָה׃

There can be no doubt that the terms used here, including רֵעַ, denote fellow-members of the covenant or the community who share in the election and the

---

[21] "The Book of the Covenant makes its demands on the much naiver assumption of their validity," v. Rad, op. cit. (→ n. 20), 13. Only rarely is the relation to the people expressly mentioned (e.g., Ex. 22:24; 23:11), and the name of Yahweh occurs in the mishpatim only at Ex. 22:10.

[22] Cf. the relevant labours of A. Alt, "Die Ursprünge d. isr. Rechts," *Kleine Schriften zur Geschichte des Volkes Israel,* I (1953), 278-332; A. Jirku, *Das weltliche Recht im AT* (1927); v. Rad ; Noth.

[23] Cf. esp. Alt, 33-71, also A. Jepsen, "Untersuchungen zum Bundesbuch," BWANT, III, 5 (1927), 82-86.

[24] Cf. v. Rad's observation on Ex. 21:16 and Dt. 24:7: "The אִישׁ of the Book of the Covenant has become (in Dt.) a בֶּן־יִשְׂרָאֵל," op. cit., 12.

[25] Cf. on the 9th (8th) commandment H. J. Stoebe, "Das achte Gebot," *Wort u. Dienst, Jbch. d. Theol. Schule Bethel,* NF, 3 (1952), 108-126.

[26] v. Rad, 9, 11-19; Noth, 63-70.

[27] v. Rad, 9 : "By the addition of this word all Israelites from the king to the slave or debtor are brought under a single term."

[28] Cf. the observation of L. Rost on the alternation of עֵדָה and בְּנֵי־יִשְׂרָאֵל in P, "Die Vorstufen von Kirche u. Synagoge im AT," BWANT, IV, 24 (1938), 78.

covenant and the implied duties and rights. According to Lv. 19:18 the command to love one's neighbour applies unequivocally towards members of the covenant of Yahweh and not self-evidently towards all men. It is true — and this confirms the narrower understanding of רֵעַ here — that Lv. 19:34 also imposes an obligation towards the גֵּר who dwells in the land (cf. Dt. 10:19), and the same words are used in this connection as Lv. 19:18 uses with reference to Israelites, cf. → V, 10, 10 ff.; 843, 17 ff. The commandment is thus given a decisive extension. From this, however, one may deduce an implied limitation. The stranger who simply travels through the land without dwelling in it is not included. In the existing situation the law applies to specific "legal persons." In a legal statement of this kind extension beyond this circle is not to be expected in advance. The right and duty of hospitality applies to the נָכְרִי (→ V, 19, 3 ff.), and the confines of this are, of course, very broad. [29]

The use of רֵעַ in the commandment of love thus makes possible both restriction on the one side and extension on the other. Later Jewish exposition presupposed an express limitation. Here the commandment applies only in relation to Israelites and full proselytes (גֵּר הַצֶּדֶק). Samaritans, foreigners (נָכְרִי) and resident aliens (גֵּר תּוֹשָׁב) who do not join the community of Israel within 12 months are excluded. [30]

4. Along with this restriction, which obviously lies behind the question of the νομικός in Lk. 20:29 (→ 316, 25 ff.), voices were heard even in pre-Christian Judaism which favoured an extension of the commandment to all men. [31] One sign of this is the rendering of רֵעַ by πλησίον in the LXX. This equivalent, which is the most common in the LXX (→ 312, 13 ff.), is found in all the רֵעַ passages in the legal collections mentioned above. [32] Not by accident did the Greek translation tradition choose a term which is so broad and general, and which is not in any way to be restricted to the fellow-member of the covenant. [33]

In this respect the Hell. Jewish tradition joins forces with one stream of Palestinian Judaism which on the basis of the belief in the divine likeness of all men demanded respect and consideration for all [34] and thus helped to prepare the way for the unrestricted validity of the OT commandment of love. [35]

Fichtner

---

[29] Gn. 18:1 ff.; cf. 19:1-8; Ju. 19:11 ff. Cf. A. Bertholet, *Die Stellung d. Israeliten u. der Juden zu den Fremden* (1896), 21-27 etc.

[30] Mekiltha Ex. 21:35. There is as yet no distinction between גֵּר הַצֶּדֶק and גֵּר תּוֹשָׁב in the OT. Abraham calls himself גֵּר־וְתוֹשָׁב in relation to the Hittites, Gn. 23:3 f. In the Manual, where רֵעַ occurs some 20 times, apart from general use in, e.g., 5:23; 8:20, probably 5:21, it is employed in the narrowest sense and denotes members of the sect, Fichtner, 42-44.

[31] The great Jewish scholar L. Baeck, in his work *Das Wesen des Judts.*⁴ (1926), 213, writes: "To be a man is for each to be a fellow-man," and similar statements are often made in the dialogue between Israel and the Church. Cf. also the Jewish works in the bibl. and individual observations in the NT section of this art.

[32] The Decalogue, Book of the Covenant, Deuteronomic Law and Holiness Code (on Dt. 13:7 → n. 18).

[33] Various individual observations confirm the fact that the thought of neighbourly love presses in and finds expression here, as also in other connections; we read in Sir. 13:15: ἀγαπᾷ ... πᾶς ἄνθρωπος τὸν πλησίον αὐτοῦ (in the Heb. original part. of דמה). Cf. also ψ 14:4 [G. Bertram].

[34] Already in Prv. belief in creation is a motive for right conduct: He who oppresses the lowly blasphemes his Creator, i.e., the Creator of the lowly, Prv. 14:31; cf. 17:5; Job 31:15.

[35] Michel, 63 is of the opinion that a dominical saying like Mt. 7:12 is only possible "if the OT commandment of love in an unrestricted sense is presupposed." Later Rabb.

C. πλησίον in the New Testament.

1. Except at Jn. 4:5 (πόλιν ... πλησίον τοῦ χωρίου) only the noun form occurs in the NT.[36] It is used in the sense of "neighbour." The close material link with the OT may be seen in the fact that in 12 NT instances of ὁ πλησίον there is allusion to Lv. 19:18, and that once each there is quotation from Zech. 8:16 (Eph. 4:25) and allusion to Ex. 2:13 (Ac. 7:27), while only twice is the word used independently (R. 15:2; Jm. 4:12).

From the very first the word has an established place in debates on the commandment of love. First there is the question of the sum of the Law, in answer to which Jesus refers (Mk. 12:28-31; Mt. 22:34-40), or evokes the reference (Lk. 10:25-28),[37] to the twofold commandment to love God (Dt. 6:5) and to love one's neighbour (Lv. 19:18). Though it is possible that similar answers were current in the Judaism of the day,[38] the strong emphasis on the unity of the two commandments seems to be particularly significant in Jesus; there cannot be the one without the other.[39] In Paul the commandment to love one's neighbour as oneself is the fulfilment of the whole Law (Gl. 5:14) or the sum (ἀνακεφαλαιοῦται) of all the commandments (R. 13:8-10, ὁ πλησίον in alternation with ὁ ἕτερος [→ II, 704, 6 ff.]). Jm. 2:8 describes the same commandment as the royal law. The fact that love for God is not mentioned here (cf. R. Aqiba → n. 38) is adequately explained by the purpose of the passages and does not justify an assumption that the Synoptic logion was not known. The adding of καὶ ἀγαπήσεις τὸν πλησίον σου ὡς σεαυτόν to the commandments specified for the rich young ruler (Mt. 19:19) is obviously meant as a *consummatio,* and there is no specific mention here of love for God.

2. More important as regards ὁ πλησίον, however, is the debate as to the definition of "neighbour," which was in full swing in the days of Jesus.[40] In His criticism (Mt. 5:43-48) of what seems to have been the usual exposition of the commandment: "Thou shalt love thy compatriot but needst not love thy (personal) enemy,"[41] Jesus demands love of enemies. This alone is a περισσόν (v. 47) which is promised a reward (v. 46). What seems to be formally a universalising of the concept of neighbour and a transcending of the commandment of love is at root a reversal of the question. If a man wants to know precisely whom he is to love and not love, he is asked concerning this supposed love which

discussion shows that the narrower and broader interpretations were present together as a subject of debate, *ibid.,* 56-65.

[36] The predicative use in Lk. 10:29, 36 presupposes the substantive.

[37] On the authenticity of the Lucan form cf. Kl. Mk. on 12:28-34.

[38] Cf. Lk. 10:26 f. and the well-known saying of R. Aqiba in S. Lv., 19, 18 (Str.-B., I, 357 f.): "'Thou shalt love thy neighbour as thyself.' Aqiba (d. c. 135) said: This is a great and comprehensive principle in the Torah." Cf. also the material from Test. XII in Preisker, 72 f. In bShab., 31a Bar. a non-Jew who comes to Hillel and wants to learn the whole Torah while standing on one foot receives the answer: "What you would not have done to you, do not do to your neighbour (חבר). This is the whole Torah. All the rest is exposition. Go and learn." Cf. on this Bacher Tannaiten, I², 4 f. On the Jewish debate on the sum of the Law cf. the material in Str.-B., I, 900-908, on the Golden Rule *ibid.,* 459 f.

[39] The parable of the wicked servant in Mt. 18:23-34 is an illustration. On the inner structure of the twofold commandment cf. Fuchs, 134-137; Gutbrod, → IV, 1063, 39-1064, 5.

[40] Str.-B., I, 353 f.

[41] So with J. Jeremias, *Die Gleichnisse Jesu*³ (1954), 144. To be compared is the command to hate the "children of darkness" which occurs repeatedly in the Manual, 1:10; 9:21 f. (the אנשי שחת, "men of the pit"), though here there is to be no vengeance against personal enemies, 10:17 f., cf. 19-21.

he wants to dole out so economically when it should burst forth with irresistible force and go to work. By nature love is not primarily act but being : being a son of God, being perfect as the Father in heaven is perfect (v. 45, 48). The love which springs forth from being loved is quite incapable of asking about any limits.

3. The classical witness to the way in which Jesus spoke of the "neighbour" is the parable of the Good Samaritan. [42] By putting it in the context of the debate on the greatest commandment, Luke find the right place for it materially. Even if it had previously been independent, what other theme could it have than "Who then is my neighbour ?" With jabbing clarity this is linked to it by the very circumstance that the man in need of help is a Jew and the man who shows mercy is a Samaritan. [43] Here one may see explicitly the reversal [44] of the question as to the neighbour which is implicit already in Mt. 5:43-48.

Modern man, esp. since the Enlightenment, is mostly inclined to think that the neighbour is simply one's fellow-man. But this is not in accord with ὁ πλησίον, which has a particular rather than a general reference. There has thus been a tendency to translate ὁ πλησίον by "friend." [45] But this word has by nature more emotional content than ὁ πλησίον. "Fellow-countryman" would be the best rendering in the debate with the νομικός except that it misses the aspect of fellowship in cultus and promise which is implied in רֵעַ and it has a more political and national tang. There is also another reason for keeping the true sense of the older translation instead of seeking a new one. "Neighbour," originally a spatial term, carries with it the element of encounter. Hence it expresses vividly "the actuality of the evangelical demand." [46]

The story of the Good Samaritan shows that one cannot say in advance who the neighbour is but that the course of life will make this plain enough. Indeed, the questioner, who at the end is told to do as the Samaritan did, is the one to whom the parable comes home directly : One cannot define one's neighbour ; one can only be a neighbour. [47]

4. If the other πλησίον passages in the NT (R. 15:2; Eph. 4:25; Jm. 4:12) are compared with the use of ἀδελφός, it is hard to see any true distinction. ὁ πλησίον can be used for the brother Christian (R. 15:2) just as ἀδελφός can have a wider range of meaning (e.g., Mt. 5:22-24). On the whole ἀδελφός is preferred, probably because it corresponds more directly to the sense of divine sonship.

5. Nevertheless, ὁ πλησίον does not fade from view. In the post-apost. fathers it is much more common outside quotations than in the NT. Striking are ἀγαπήσεις τὸν

---

[42] For Rade, 72 the combining of the story with the question as to the neighbour is an "inherited complication" which we owe to Lk. If, like Rade, one insists on a definition of the neighbour and overlooks Jesus' attack on this starting-point, even at the most general one can only end with the man whom Jesus put in the place of the compatriot for His followers.

[43] There is agreement that v. 35 cannot be the end of an independent story. Suggested alternatives, e.g., Jülicher Gl. J., II, 597: "an ending like 18:14," or : "Which of the three seems to have been worthy of attaining to eternal life ... or near to the kingdom of God ?"; Rade, 79 : Lk. 10:37b, or 10:28, or esp. 17:16b; Bultmann Trad., 192 : a question (τίς τούτων τῶν τριῶν ... the rest open) and answer (v. 37a), all sound insipid on the lips of Jesus or else materially they simply show what it really means to be a neighbour.

[44] Fuchs, 137 speaks similarly of transposition.

[45] Jeremias, op. cit., 143.

[46] So M. Dibelius, "Das soziale Motiv im NT," Botschaft u. Geschichte, Gesammelte Aufsätze, I (1953), 197.

[47] Cf. Leenhardt, 136.

πλησίον σου ὑπὲρ τὴν ψυχήν σου, Barn., 19, 5 and ... τῆς ἀγάπης, τῆς εἰς θεὸν καὶ Χριστὸν καὶ εἰς τὸν πλησίον, Pol. Phil., 3, 3. πλησίον does not occur at all in Herm.

Greeven

| † πλοῦτος, † πλούσιος | → θησαυρός, III, 136-138; μαμωνᾶς, IV, 388 ff.; |
| † πλουτέω, † πλουτίζω | πένης, VI, 37-40; πλεονεξία, 266-274; πτωχός. |

Contents : A. Non-Biblical Use : 1. General : a. Linguistic ; b. Lexical ; 2. Riches and the Rich in Greek and Hellenistic Thought : a. The Early Period ; b. From the Pre-Socratics to Aristotle ; c. The Cynics and Stoics. B. Riches and the Rich in the Old Testament : 1. Linguistic ; 2. The Evaluation of Riches : a. The Early Period ; b. The Prophetic Criticism of Wealth ; c. The Later OT Tradition. C. Riches and the Rich in Judaism : 1. The Non-Philonic Tradition ; 2. Philo. D. Riches and the Rich in the New Testament : 1. The Attitude of Jesus to Wealth in Mark and Matthew ; 2. In Luke ; 3. The Word Group in Pauline Usage ; 4. The Other NT Writings. E. Riches and the Rich in the Post-Apostolic Period up to Clement of Alexandria and Cyprian : 1. The Post-Apostolic Fathers ; 2. Clement and Cyprian.

π λ ο ῦ τ ο ς κ τ λ. In general : W. Bienert, *Die Arbeit nach der Lehre der Bibel* (1954); H. Bolkestein, *Wohltätigkeit u. Armenpflege im vorchr. Altertum* (1939); F. Heichelheim, *Wirtschaftsgeschichte d. Altertums,* I and II (1938); H. Meyer, Art. "Eigentum," *Evangelisches Soziallex.,* ed. F. Karrenberg (1954), 275-280; R. v. Pöhlmann, *Gesch. d. sozialen Frage u. des Sozialismus in d. antiken Welt,* I and II³ (1925); M. Rostovtzeff, *Social and Economic History of the Hellenistic World,* I-III (1941); also *Geschichte d. alten Welt,* transl. H. H. Schaeder, I and II (1941 f.); also *Gesellschaft u. Wirtschaft im röm. Kaiserreich,* transl. L. Wickert, I and II (no date); C. Schneider, *Geistesgeschichte des antiken Christentums,* II (1954), 37, 517-519; E. Troeltsch, *Die Soziallehren d. chr. Kirchen u. Gruppen* (1912); G. Wünsch, *Religion und Wirtschaft* (1925); Art. "Eigentum," RGG², II, 57-66; J. Zwicker, Art. "Plutos," Pauly-W., XXI (1951), 1027-1052. On A. 1: Boisacq, 797; Pokorny, 798-800, 835; H. Schmidt, *Synonymik d. gr. Sprache,* IV (1886), 376-387; Walde-Pok., II, 63-65. On A. 2 : J. Hasebroek, *Gr. Wirtschafts- u. Gesellschaftsgeschichte bis zur Perserzeit* (1931); J. Hemelrijk, Πενία *en* Πλοῦτος, Diss. Utrecht (1925); S. Laukamm, "Das Sittenbild des Artemidor v. Ephesus," *Angelos,* 3 (1928), 32-71; J. J. van Manen, Πενία *en* Πλοῦτος *in de Periode na Alexander,* Diss. Utrecht (1931); M. Pohlenz, *Der hellenische Mensch* (1948), 31-57; S. Schilling, *Das Ethos der Mesotes* (1930). On B.: F. Horst, "Das Eigentum nach dem AT," *Kirche im Volk,* 2 (1949); H. J. Kraus, "Die Bdtg. des Eigentums im Deuteronomium," *ibid.,* 2 (1949); A. Kuschke, "Arm u. Reich im AT mit besonderer Berücksichtigung der nachexilischen Zeit," ZAW, NF, 16 (1939), 31-57; M. Lurje, "Studien zur Geschichte der wirtschaftlichen u. sozialen Verhältnisse im isr.-jüd. Reich," Beih. 45, ZAW (1927); P. A. Munch, "Das Problem des Reichtums in den Ps. 37, 49, 73," ZAW, NF, 14 (1937), 33-46. On C.: F. Geiger, *Philon v. Alex. als sozialer Denker, Tübinger Beiträge zur Altertumswissenschaft,* 14 (1932); M. Weber, "Das antike Judt.," *Gesammelte Aufsätze zur Religionssoziologie,* III (1921). On D.: K. Bornhäuser, "Der Christ u. seine Habe nach dem NT," BFTh, 38, 3 (1936); A. Feuillet, "Les riches intendants du Christ," *Recherches de science religieuse,* 34 (1947), 30-54; H. Greeven, *Das Hauptproblem der Sozialethik in d. neueren Stoa u. im Urchr.* (1935); F. Hauck, "Die Stellung d. Urchr. zu Arbeit u. Geld," BFTh, II, 3 (1921); J. Jeremias, *Jerusalem zur Zeit Jesu,* II (1928); E. Lohmeyer, "Soziale Fragen im Urchr.," *Wissenschaft u. Bildung,* 172 (1921); E. Percy, "Die Botschaft Jesu," *Lunds Universitets Årsskrift,* NF, I, 49, 5 (1953), 45-106; H. Preisker, *Das Ethos d. Urchr.* (1949), 94-105; H. J. Schoeps, *Theol. u. Gesch. d. Judenchristentums* (1949), 196-202; H. E. Weber, "Das Eigentum nach d. NT," *Kirche im Volk,* 2 (1949). On E.: W. Haller, "Das Eigentum im Glauben u. Leben d. nachapostolischen Kirche," ThStKr, 64 (1891), 478-563; O. Schilling, *Reichtum u. Eigentum in d. altkirchlichen Lit.* (1908), with bibl. pp. IX-XII.

Note : After the death of F. Hauck, W. Kasch prepared this art. on the basis of the MS left by him.

A. Non-Biblical Use.

1. General. a. Linguistic. The etym. has a strong bearing on the meaning of the word. The group is connected with the Indo-Europ. root *pel-* "to flow," which originally seems to mean the same as *pel-* "to fill," "full." From this are derived the Gk. stems πλε(ϝ)ω (πλοῦτος, πλούσιος, πλουτέω, πλουτίζω), πλη- (πίμπλημι, πλῆθος, πλήρης) and *pelu* (πολύς), so that all the words go back to a common root meaning "to fill," "to be filled." [1] In the πλοῦτος group the content of the root narrows down to the basic sense of "fulness of goods." πλοῦτος expresses and denotes the benefit of a happy life which is lived within the given order and which thus stands under the blessing of the gods. [2] From the time of the pre-Socratics there is a characteristic shift of meaning on both economic and religious grounds. πλοῦτος means on the one side material wealth (esp. money) irrespective of person or status, while on the other, usually with a gen., and often in polemic against material riches, it is used for true and genuine wealth as the basis of real security. Hence it is materially a mistake to regard combinations like "wealth of wisdom" or "wealth of grace" as transferred usage. It is better to distinguish between the specific use for material riches and a general use.

b. Lexical. πλοῦτος: lexicography clearly reflects the position outlined above. Hom. Il., 1, 171 with ἄφενος; 16, 596; 24, 536 with ὄλβος; 24, 546: πλούτῳ τε καὶ υἱάσι κεκάσθαι "to be distinguished by power and sons"; Od., 24, 486 on the lips of Zeus: πλοῦτος δὲ καὶ εἰρήνη ἅλις ἔστω as the mark of an eschatological state after the conclusion of peace between Odysseus and his opponents. As material prosperity ὑπέρ τε εἰρήνης καὶ πλούτου καὶ σίτου φορᾶς in a prayer, Ditt. Syll.[3], II, 589, 30; φυσικὸς πλοῦτος ... ἐπειδὴ μακάριον κτῆμα νενόμισται πλοῦτος, Philo Som., II, 35; plur. πλοῦτοι, Philo Jos., 131; with gen. ἀργύριου, Hdt., II, 121, 1; χρημάτων, Antiphon Fr., 54 (Diels[7], II, 362, 15), in a pun as the opp. of ἀρετή: οὔτε πενίας ὑπερορῶν, οὔτε πλοῦτον ἀρετῆς ἀλλ' ἀρετὴν πλούτου προτιμῶν, Gorgias Fr., 11a (Diels[7], II, 302, 12). Generally: πραπίδων πλοῦτος, Emped. Fr., 129 (Diels[7], I, 364, 2); σοφίας, Plat. Euthyphr., 12a; ἐν τῇ ἐμῇ ψυχῇ, Xen. Symp., IV, 4, cf. IV, 34; ὁ σοφίας θεοῦ πλοῦτος, Philo Poster. C., 151. ὁ ἀληθινὸς πλοῦτος ἐν οὐρανῷ, Praem. Poen., 104; in Hell. Gk. also neuter, P. Flor., III, 367, 11.

πλούσιος, adj. "well-to-do," "rich," from Hesiod. Materially of persons, Hes. Op., 22; Theogn., 621; P. Oxy., III, 471, 79 (2nd cent. B.C.); Philo Plant., 69; of things, Soph. El., 361: τράπεζα, with gen. Plat. Resp., VII, 521a; dat. Plut. Cato Maior, 18 (I, 347a): τοῖς ἀχρήστοις καὶ περιττοῖς. Generally: Antiph. Fr., 327 (CAF, II, 134): ψυχὴν ἔχειν δεῖ πλουσίαν. Ep. Ar., 15: πλείᾳ καὶ πλουσίᾳ ψυχῇ. As a noun and without art. either materially or in general: "rich or wealthy man." Anon. Iamblichi Fr., 3 (Diels[7], II, 401, 27); Aristoph. Pl., 346; Plat. Resp., VII, 521a. Adv. πλουσίως, "richly," Hdt., II, 44, 3; Ditt. Or., II, 767, 18 (1st/2nd cent. B.C.). Compar.: Ditt. Syll.[3], II, 888, 144; Philo Leg. Gaj., 203. Superlat.: Philo Virt., 174.

πλουτέω, "to be rich," aor. "to become rich," from Hesiod. Hes. Op. 313; Theogn., 663; Prodikos Fr., 8 (Diels[7], II, 318, 8); Isoc., 3, 50; P. Giess., I, 13, 19; with gen. Xen. An., VII, 7, 42: φίλων, with dat. Xen. Ath., 2, 11: σιδήρῳ, with acc. Luc. Tim., 48: ὑπερμεγέθη τινὰ πλοῦτον.

πλουτίζω, "to make rich," Aesch. Ag., 586, 1268; Xen. Cyrop., VIII, 2, 22.

2. Riches and the Rich in Greek and Hellenistic Thought.

a. The Early Period. In Hom. nobility and wealth are identical. To be noble means πλούτῳ τε καὶ υἱάσι κεκάσθαι, Il., 24, 546. The noble and rich — πλούσιος is not used — are the ἀφνειοί (Il., 9, 483; 24, 398) and ὄλβιοι, who have everything in

---

[1] Walde-Pok., II, 63-65; Pokorny, 798-800.

[2] Cf. E. Schwartz, *Charakterköpfe aus d. Antike*, ed. J. Stroux[3] (1950), 23 on πλοῦτος: "a reviving breath of blessing which heaven and earth grant to the human power of action, of the blessing which the ancient Hellene describes by the single untranslatable word πλοῦτος."

abundance (Hom. Hymn., 30, 8-12). The gain or loss of wealth, and hence of nobility, is in the hands of the gods (Il., 24, 525-533), for misfortune and guilt can no more be separated than fortune and virtue. Since wealth can here consist of happy circumstances, it does not have to be financial wealth. Originally rich possession of herds, [3] in Homer's day it is made up of extensive landed property together with the products, i.e., crops, cattle, oil and wine, also precious stones, artistic and other furnishings, and slaves (Il., 23, 549 f.). [4]

If the Homeric poems are written from the standpoint of the aristocracy, peasant relationships lie behind the portrayal in Hesiod. This does not alter the meaning of πλοῦτος, but it does alter the presuppositions under which it is attained and the dimensions to which it attains. If for the wealthy of Hom. πλοῦτος signifies a state of life in which no work is required (→ 38, 7 ff.), in Hesiod we find the principle that wealth is through work, [5] and that work is honourable, not shameful, [6] → II, 635, 32 ff. Nevertheless, it is still true that only riches bring virtue and blessing, and that poverty is θυμοφθόρος and frays the nerve of life, Op., 717. In the criticism of the arrogance of the rich noble who despoils the labouring peasant, [7] wealth and work, or individual conduct, are interwoven, so that we have here the first step in the later development to a position where social status and worth are no longer coincident.

b. From the Pre-Socratics to Aristotle. The Greek of the class. period, for whom the *polis* was at the centre of thought and action, judges riches from the standpoint of social rather than individual ethics, i.e., with ref. to its consequences for the *polis* and the position of man in society. This political ref. maintains the older view that wealth is the self-evident and comprehensive expression of a self-evident social order as an order of existence. On the other hand, the period from the 6th to the 4th cent. is distinguished from the earlier period by the fact that there is now no unquestionable social order nor any permanent criterion for such an order. Only against this background can one understand the political ethics of Plato and Aristot. with their classifying of riches and the rich. This whole process, however, begins in the lyric and in the pre-Socratics. In economic and political upheavals it is noted that wealth and all it carries with it is exposed to sudden forfeiture, and can give true security only conditionally. [8] Only he who has insight into the march of events can estimate the worth of goods and handle them in such a way that they endure. [9] There is thus a juxtaposition of the social order and culture, the individual and society. Experience teaches that there are poor who are cultured and uncultured who are rich. [10] If, however, man is no longer conscious of being protected by the old orders, he himself is the measure of all things, and he can say: πενίη πλοῦτος ὀνόματα ἐνδείης καὶ κόρου. οὔτε οὖν πλούσιος ὁ ἐνδέων οὔτε πένης ὁ μὴ ἐνδέων. [11] The position of a man is no longer orientated

---

[3] Cf. Hasebroek, 2.

[4] *Ibid.*, 10-33.

[5] Hes. Op., 308 : ἐξ ἔργων δ' ἄνδρες πολύμηλοί τ' ἀφνειοί τε.

[6] *Ibid.*, 311 ff.: ἔργον δ' οὐδὲν ὄνειδος, ἀεργίη δέ τ' ὄνειδος, εἰ δέ κε ἐργάζῃ, τάχα σε ζηλώσει ἀεργὸς πλουτεῦντα· πλούτῳ δ' ἀρετὴ καὶ κῦδος ὀπηδεῖ.

[7] Significant and comprehensive in this regard is the fable of the nightingale and the hawk in Hes. Op., 202-212.

[8] Cf. Democr. Fr., 302 (Diels[7], II, 223, 6 f.): μηδέποτε μακαρίσῃς ἄνθρωπον ἐπὶ πλούτωι καὶ δόξηι· πάντα γὰρ τὰ τοιαῦτα τῶν ἀγαθῶν ἐλάττονι πίστει τῶν ἀνέμων δέδεται, cf. Theogn., 659-666 (Diehl[3], II, 42).

[9] Democr. Fr., 77 (Diels[7], II, 160, 1 f.): δόξα καὶ πλοῦτος ἄνευ ξυνέσιος οὐκ ἀσφαλέα κτήματα, cf. also Fr., 288 (Diels[7], II, 205, 14).

[10] Democr. Fr., 185 (Diels[7], II, 183, 3 f.): κρέσσονές εἰσιν αἱ τῶν πεπαιδευμένων ἐλπίδες ἢ ὁ τῶν ἀμαθῶν πλοῦτος, Solon Fr., 4, 9 (Diehl[3], I, 31): πολλοὶ γὰρ πλουτοῦσι κακοί, ἀγαθοὶ δὲ πένονται, cf. Theogn., 683-686, 1052-1062, 1109-1114 (Diehl[3], II, 43, 63, 66).

[11] Democr. Fr., 283 (Diels[7], II, 204, 12 ff.); cf. also Fr., 284 (II, 204, 15 ff.): ἢν μὴ πολλῶν ἐπιθυμέῃς, τὰ ὀλίγα τοι πολλὰ δόξει· σμικρὰ γὰρ ὄρεξις πενίην ἰσοσθενέα πλούτωι ποιέει.

to riches ; [12] what is wealth or poverty is orientated to his judgment and attitude. Hence to be rich can be either good or bad according to an individual's use of his riches. [13] Now for the first time there can also be the building up of material technical wealth, χρημάτων πλοῦτος. [14] The individual can decide materialistically for technical riches as the best means of security. [15] But he can also regard the striving for wealth as a mistake, [16] and oppose to external riches the true wealth of virtue [17] or wisdom. [18] Now that riches are regarded as a means of life rather than its expression, there can also be discussion of the point whether wealth, poverty, or moderate possessions offer the best security in life. [19] These ideas of the pre-Socratics on the theme of wealth are by no means fixed. Nor are there any definitive conclusions in comedy or tragedy. [20] We find these for the first time in the great ethical systems of Plato and Aristot. Both take seriously the functional character of material wealth discovered by the pre-Socratics. They regard it as a means [21] whose value is judged by its significance for virtue. [22] Since trade and commerce can lead to riches, [23] it follows that the political significance of wealth can be only indirect. Not wealth, but the attitude towards it, must decide concerning membership of the *polis*. Wealth should be a way to culture, since it liberates from the necessity of manual labour. [24] As hereditary wealth and nobility it should promote the purity of individual striving after justice, [25] since it makes possible a dedication to virtue rather than to gain. [26] In content these statements are a warning

---

[12] Bias Fr., 13 (Diels⁷, I, 65, 8 f.): ἀνάξιον ἄνδρα μὴ ἐπαίνει διὰ πλοῦτον.

[13] Ps.-Plat. Eryx., 397e : Prodikos was asked : πῶς οἴεται κακὸν εἶναι τὸ πλουτεῖν καὶ ὅπως ἀγαθόν· ὁ δὲ ἔφη τοῖς μὲν καλοῖς κἀγαθοῖς τῶν ἀνθρώπων ἀγαθὸν καὶ τοῖς ἐπισταμένοις, ὅπου δεῖ χρῆσθαι τοῖς χρήμασι, τούτοις μὲν ἀγαθόν, τοῖς δὲ μοχθηροῖς καὶ ἀνεπιστήμοσιν κακόν. ἔχει δ᾽, ἔφη, καὶ τἆλλα πράγματα οὕτω πάντα· ὁποῖοι γὰρ ἄν τινες ὦσιν οἱ χρώμενοι, τοιαῦτα καὶ τὰ πράγματα αὐτοῖς ἀνάγκη εἶναι.

[14] Cf. Antiphon. Fr., 54 (Diels⁷, II, 362, 15).

[15] Critias Fr., 29 (Diels⁷, II, 390, 2 f.): σοφῆς δὲ πενίας σκαιότητα πλουσίαν κρεῖσσον σύνοικόν ἐστιν ἐν δόμοις ἔχειν, cf. Theogn., 699-718 (Diehl³, II, 44 f.).

[16] Thales (Diels⁷, I, 71, 26): μὴ πλούτει κακῶς, Anon. Iambl. Fr., 4, 4 (Diels⁷, II, 402, 12 f.): ὅστις δέ ἐστιν ἀνὴρ ἀληθῶς ἀγαθός, οὗτος οὐκ ἀλλοτρίωι κόσμωι περικειμένωι τὴν δόξαν θηρᾶται, ἀλλὰ τῆι αὐτοῦ ἀρετῆι.

[17] Gorg. Fr., 1a, 32 (Diels⁷, II, 302, 11 f.): οὔτε πενίας ὑπερορῶν, οὔτε πλοῦτον ἀρετῆς ἀλλ᾽ ἀρετὴν πλούτου προτιμῶν.

[18] Democr. Fr., 303 (Diels⁷, II, 223, 19 f.).

[19] → n. 13; Democr. Fr., 78 (Diels⁷, II, 160, 3 f.); Anon. Iambl. Fr., 3, 4 (II, 401, 23 ff.); cf. → n. 17, also Theogn., 1067 f., 1153 f. (Diehl³, II, 64 and 68).

[20] Thus in Aristoph. Pl., 489-612 the goddess Πενία tries to make clear to Chremylos in a contest that art and knowledge, trade and commerce have their lasting origin in πενία, in unfulfilled striving for the development and shaping of life, cf. also Pl., 510 ff.: εἰ γὰρ ὁ Πλοῦτος βλέψειε πάλιν διανείμειέν τ᾽ ἴσον αὐτόν, οὔτε τέχνην ἂν τῶν ἀνθρώπων οὔτ᾽ ἂν σοφίαν μελετῴη οὐδείς. 553 f.: τοῦ δὲ πένητος (sc. βίος ἐστί) ζῆν φειδόμενον καὶ τοῖς ἔργοις προσέχοντα. Cf. also 593 f.: πάντ᾽ ἔστ᾽ ἀγάθ᾽ ὑμῖν διὰ τὴν Πενίαν. Though these arguments cannot be refuted by Chremylos (cf. Pl., 571), he, and with him the poet, decide for Plutus, who is made to see ; they thus decide for a restoration of the ancient ideal of an aristocratic order in which wealth and morality are identical.

[21] Cf. Plat. Resp., I, 331 a b; Aristot. Pol., I, 8, p. 1256b, 35 f.: οὐδὲν γὰρ ὄργανον ἄπειρον οὐδεμιᾶς ἐστὶ τέχνης οὔτε πλήθει οὔτε μεγέθει, ὁ δὲ πλοῦτος ὀργάνων πλῆθός ἐστιν οἰκονομικῶν καὶ πολιτικῶν, Eth. Nic., I, 3, p. 1096a, 6 : ὁ πλοῦτος δῆλον ὅτι οὐ τὸ ζητούμενον ἀγαθόν· χρήσιμον γὰρ καὶ ἄλλου χάριν.

[22] Cf. Plat. Resp., VII, 521a; Aristot. Eth. Nic., I, 2, p. 1095a, 23; Pol., II, 7, p. 1266b, 1-40.

[23] Cf. Plat. Resp., IV, 434b; Aristot. Pol., III, 5, 1278a, 24.

[24] Aristot. Pol., VII, 15, p. 1334a, 32-34 : μάλιστα γὰρ οὗτοι δεήσονται φιλοσοφίας καὶ σωφροσύνης καὶ δικαιοσύνης, ὅσῳ μᾶλλον σχολάζουσιν ἐν ἀφθονίᾳ τῶν τοιούτων ἀγαθῶν, cf. II, 9, p. 1269a, 34 f.

[25] Plat. Resp., I, 329e-331; For the connection between wealth and aristocracy cf. Aristot. Pol., V, 1, p. 1301b, 3 f.: εὐγενεῖς γὰρ εἶναι δοκοῦσιν οἷς ὑπάρχει προγόνων ἀρετὴ καὶ πλοῦτος. Cf. Plat. Resp., VI, 494c: πλούσιος καὶ γενναῖος.

[26] Cf. Plat. Resp., VIII, 547b; → n. 28, 29.

against too great wealth[27] and the temptations and dangers it brings.[28] Moderate wealth is better.[29] It is easier to handle, and thus allows time for virtue and culture, which qualify for a proper life in the *polis*.[30] Surveying the whole field, we find here two forms of wealth which are distinguished with full clarity by Aristot.: a functional wealth which serves, and an uncontrolled and unrestricted wealth which seeks security at all costs and which finds salvation in the accumulation of material goods, → 266 ff.[31] The latter is objectionable from the standpt. of social ethics, for it leads to political ruin and renders the individual a-social. The former is desirable, since the freedom of the free man would be impossible without it.[32] At this pt. there is also a difference in terms between Plato and Aristot. In the vocabulary of Aristot. wealth is always material, and it is thus a means which one can use wrongly or rightly. Plato, however, keeps to the idea of spiritual as well as material wealth, distinguishing between material riches and the true riches which consist in wisdom, virtue and culture.[33]

c. The Cynics and Stoics. Both radicalise previous thought by making the individual and his fate the pt. of reference rather than the *polis*.[34] Their concern is not merely with the inner attitude to goods.[35] They reject riches because the pursuit thereof makes man dependent on things and relations, so that he does not rest on the only sure support, namely, himself.[36]

The Cynics esp. champion this rigorous view. Acc. to Diogenes the εὐγενέστατοι are those who despises riches, honour, joy, life (πλοῦτος, δόξα, ἡδονή, ζωή).[37] One might call this attitude the embodiment of the reversal of the Gk. ideal of nobility. In clear antithesis to previous ideas, the Cynic says that πενία is an aid to wisdom[38] because it frees from the cares which absorb time.[39] Epigrammatically it is maintained that true παιδεία is possible only for the poor,[40] and that wealth and virtue are mutually exclusive.[41]

In contrast a new horizon appears in Stoic statements on the question of riches. The older, middle and younger Stoa agrees that wealth is an adiaphoron.[42] Since all men

---

[27] *Ibid.*, VI, 491c; VIII, 550e; Aristot. Eth. Nic., X, 14, p. 1178b, 33 ff.; Pol., IV, 11, p. 1295b, 5 f.

[28] Plat. Resp., IV, 421d; 422a; Leg., 744d; Aristot. Pol., IV, 11, p. 1295b, 15-21.

[29] Plat. Euthyd., 281b c; Aristot. Pol., IV, 11, p. 1295b, 40; p. 1296a, 1; p. 1295b, 4 f.: φανερὸν ὅτι καὶ τῶν εὐτυχημάτων ἡ κτῆσις ἡ μέση βελτίστη πάντων.

[30] Cf. Aristot. Eth. Nic., IV, 1, p. 1120a, 5 and 6; Pol., VII, 9, p. 1328b, 33 ff.; Xen. Cyrop., VIII, 3, 40 f.

[31] Cf. Aristot. Pol., I, 9, p. 1256b-1258a, 8.

[32] Aristot. Pol., II, 9, p. 1269a, 34 f.: ὅτι μὲν οὖν δεῖ τῇ μελλούσῃ καλῶς πολιτεύεσθαι τὴν τῶν ἀναγκαίων ὑπάρχειν σχολήν, ὁμολογούμενόν ἐστιν.

[33] Plat. Resp., VII, 521a (in the ideal constitution): ἐν μόνῃ γὰρ αὐτῇ ἄρξουσιν οἱ τῷ ὄντι πλούσιοι, οὐ χρυσίου ἀλλ' οὗ δεῖ τὸν εὐδαίμονα πλουτεῖν, ζωῆς ἀγαθῆς τε καὶ ἔμφρονος. Cf. VIII, 547b; Phaedr., 279c.

[34] Cf. E. Meyer, *Gesch. des Altertums*, IV[2] (1901), 111; J. Kaerst, *Gesch. d. Hellenismus*, I[3] (1927), 57; P. Barth-Goedeckemeyer, *Die Stoa*[6] (1946), 2 ff.

[35] Cf. K. Reinhardt, *Poseidonios* (1921), 336-342, esp. 339.

[36] Cf. Eur. in Stob. Ecl., V, 782, 1: πλουτεῖς· τὰ δ' ἄλλα μὴ δόκει ξυνιέναι· ἐν τῷ γὰρ ὄλβῳ φαυλότης ἔνεστί τις. πενία δὲ σοφίαν ἔλαχε διὰ τὸ δυστυχές. Cf. also Crates Fr., 10, 16 (Diehl[3], I, 123 and 125).

[37] Diogenes of Sinope, ed. G. A. Mullach, Fragmenta Philosophorum Graecorum, II (1867), 305; cf. Stob. Ecl., V, 807, 4.

[38] Stob. Ecl., V, 782, 18.

[39] Xen. Cyrop., VIII, 3, 40 f.; cf. Crates Fr., 7 (Diehl[3], I, 122 f.).

[40] Stob. Ecl., V, 785, 15 ff.

[41] *Ibid.*, 766, 12, cf. 806, 17 ff.

[42] Cf. v. Arnim, III, 28-39; Zeno Fr., 190 (v. Arnim, I, 47, 25); Aristo Chius Fr., 359 (I, 81, 33); Epict. Diss., II, 19, 13 : ἀγαθὰ μὲν οὖν αἱ ἀρεταὶ καὶ τὰ μετέχοντα αὐτῶν, κακὰ δὲ κακίαι καὶ τὰ μετέχοντα κακίας, ἀδιάφορα δὲ τὰ μεταξὺ τούτων, πλοῦτος, ὑγίεια, ζωή. θάνατος, ἡδονή, πόνος.

are by nature equal, it is not of the essence of a man. It is a loan, [43] and can thus exert no direct influence on his essential nature. Numerous statements make it plain that neither wealth nor poverty as such can determine human destiny. Thus one reads in Aristo of Chios : ὁ μὲν πεπαιδευμένος καὶ ἐν πλούτῳ καὶ ἐν πενίᾳ οὐ ταράττεται, ὁ δὲ ἀπαίδευτος ἐν ἀμφοῖν. [44] If wealth is one of the adiaphora like health, honour, or fame, it is by nature neither good nor bad. [45] Hence practical advantages and disadvantages have to be weighed against one another. One of the former is that it makes life easier if handled sensibly, i.e., by a wise man. [46] It offers greater opportunities for spiritual development. [47] It makes possible the difficult art of giving. [48] It is significant in relation to the order and social well-being of the state. [49] A disadvantage, however, is that the unwise use it amiss. [50] It is a temptation even for the wise, [51] since it threatens to lead to the pt. where trust is placed in it even though it is uncertain and transient. [52] When the advantages and disadvantages are weighed, one will conclude that wealth has a certain value for the living of life according to nature. [53] One good alone, of course, is true wealth. This consists in wisdom, in harmony with the cosmic order. This alone makes the σπουδαῖος truly rich. [54]

B. Riches and the Rich in the Old Testament.

1. Linguistic.

The word group πλοῦτος occurs about 180 times in the LXX. In 76 instances it is used for the Heb. root עָשַׁר, in 14 for חַיִל, in 7 for הָמוֹן, in 6 for הוֹן, in 4 there is no equivalent (1 S. 2:10; Is. 24:8; Jer. 24:1; Prv. 11:16), while in 13 it is used for words with a different meaning (גְּדוּלָה Est. 1:4; 10:2; אֱמוּנָה ψ 36:3; שַׁאֲנָן Is. 32:18), or freely (Is. 5:14; 29:2; Prv. 31:28), or in emendation (Is. 60:16; Prv. 13:23). The other examples are in writings with no Heb. original. The distribution is worth noting : 6 times in the Pentateuch, 9 in the Historical Books Joshua to Samuel, 23 in the later Historical Books, 34 in the Prophets (17 in Is.), 16 in the Psalter, and 93 times in the Wisdom literature, including Sir.

2. The Evaluation of Riches.

a. The Early Period. Statistics show already that the question of riches was not prominent in the early period. This is confirmed by a comparison with the frequency of the use of the groups πένης (→ 39, 9 ff.) and → πτωχός, which both together are found only 15 times in the Pentateuch, Judges and 1 and 2 S., and mostly in the later sections. There are famines in ancient Israel as in Homer (Gn. 41 ff.), but no social question. Where the group is used (πλούσιος Gn. 13:2; 2 S. 12:1, 2, 4; πλουτεῖν Gn. 30:43; πλουτίζειν Gn. 14:23; πλοῦτος Gn. 31:16), it denotes wealth in flocks,

---

[43] Epict. Diss., IV, 5, 15 : τούτων γὰρ οὐδὲν ἴδιον τῷ ἀνθρώπῳ ἐστίν, ἀλλὰ πάντα ἀλλότρια, δοῦλα, ὑπεύθυνα. Cf. Sen. Ad Lucilium epistularum moralium, 41, 5 ff.

[44] Aristo Chius Fr., 396 (v. Arnim, I, 89, 20 f.).

[45] Ibid., 359 (I, 81, 21); Chrysippus Fr., 117 (III, 28, 13).

[46] Cf. Fronto Fr., 196 (v. Arnim, III, 47, 4); Stob. Fr., 615 (III, 158, 24 ff.); Chrysippus Fr., 698 (III, 175, 6-10); Diog. L., VII, 122; Cic. Off., II, 86; what is meant by a sensible use is finely brought out in Seneca De vita beata, 22, 5: aput me divitiae aliquem locum habent, aput te summum. Ad postremum divitiae meae sunt, tu divitiarum es.

[47] Sen. De vita beata, 22, 1.

[48] Ibid., 24.

[49] Barth-Goedeckemeyer, op. cit., 139.

[50] Plut. Fr., 123 (v. Arnim, III, 29, 43); Alex. Aphr. Fr., 152 (III, 36, 28).

[51] Sen. Ad Lucilium epistularum moralium, 20, 10.

[52] Sen. Marc., 9, 2 and 4; 10, 1; cf. also Epict. Diss., I, 29, 14 on that wherein ten are stronger than one, so that the one will have to expect defeat.

[53] Diog. L., VII, 105.

[54] Stob. Fr., 593 (v. Arnim, III, 155, 13; cf. 153-157).

servants and precious stones ; this is pointless without progeny (Gn. 15:2 f.). Gn. 14:11-23; 29:14 — 31:16 give a clear picture of the origin and increase of such riches. They arise by means of warlike booty, dowries, and successful breeding. They are judged favourably. Acc. to the OT view, as distinct from the Gk. (→ 319, 46 ff.), wealth is the gift of God and an expression of His personal blessing (Dt. 28:1-14).

b. The Prophetic Criticism of Wealth. The prophetic criticism of wealth presupposes sociological and social relations very different from those of the earlier period. Jerusalem and Samaria were now royal cities, and alongside a great host of poor and deprived there had arisen a relatively small stratum of plutocrats and aristocrats, cf. Is. 3:2 f.; 10:1 ff.; Jer. 5:4 f., 25-31; Ez. 22:25-29; Am. 2:6 ff.; 3:10; 5:7-12; Mi. 2:1 ff.; 3:9 ff. [55] The core of the criticism is the theologically based repudiation of this process (cf. Ju. 8:22, 23; 1 S. 10:18 f.) because of such social consequences as forced labour (Am. 5:7-12), the enslaving of fellow-countrymen (Jer. 34:8-11), and the depriving of widows, orphans and the poor of their rights (Is. 5:8-24 etc.). Behind this repudiation is the conviction that the existence of a rich [56] upper stratum runs contrary to God's will, since it destroys the people which God has created in salvation history, cf. Jer. 2:6 f.; 31:31 f.; Ez. 20:5-26; Da. 9:15; Am. 2:10; Mi. 6:3 ff. In Jer. 5:26 f. members of the upper class are called ἀσεβεῖς who have grown great and rich because they have amassed wealth by cunning and transgressed the right. In Mi. 6:11 f. they are charged with graft, falsehood and violence. In Is. 53:9 the ungodly and the rich are identical. But these charges constantly made by the prophets against the upper class (Jer. 5:26-31; Ez. 22:6-13; Am. 3:10; 5:7-12) are stereotyped. They are directed against the class as such rather than individuals. The prophecies of disaster are also addressed against the whole group rather than individuals (cf. Is. 3:1 ff.; 3:16-4:1; Jer. 5:26-31; Ez. 22:24-31; Am. 5:7-12; Mi. 2:1-11). The rich are expressly mentioned. With the pomp and glory of Jerusalem they will go down into the underworld, Is. 5:14. Their wealth will be scattered like chaff, Is. 29:5. The rich city will stand waste and empty, Is. 32:12 ff. The wives of the nobility will be deprived of their social standing, Is. 32:9-14.

c. The Later OT Tradition. Most of the OT statements about wealth occur in the Wisdom literature. That the poor man is unacceptable to his neighbour, but the rich has many friends (Prv. 14:20), is an established principle in the world, as is also the fact that the great and rich are allowed scope while the little man is not, cf. Sir. 13:3, 22 f. What the Wisdom literature has to say about the question of riches is mostly drawn from practical experience. A man becomes rich if he is economical (Prv. 24:4), industrious (Sir. 31:3) and strong (Prv. 10:4; 11:16) and refrains from wickedness (Sir. 19:1 ff.). The fruits of wealth are security (Prv. 10:15), friends (14:20), honour (Sir. 10:30), peace (44:6), a full and happy life (cf. 1 Ch. 29:28; Sir. 44:1-8) and the chance to give alms (Sir. 31:8; Tob. 12:8). Though riches are valued and approved, their dangers are not missed. Wealth leads to self-importance (Prv. 28:11) and to the pride which goes before a fall (18:10 ff.; 11:28). It also leads to trust in riches (Sir. 11:19; ψ 48:7; 51:9), even though one cannot take them into the grave (Sir. 11:17-19; Qoh. 5:12-19). There is gt. danger of entering a crooked path in the pursuit thereof (Prv. 28:6; Sir. 31:5, 7 f.). Wealth is only a relative good inferior to many others (health, Sir. 30:14 ff.; a good name, Prv. 22:1, wisdom, Wis. 7:8). It also carries with it disadvantages (sleeplessness and care) unknown to the poor (Sir. 31:1 f.; Qoh. 5:11).

In comparison with later Gk. thought (→ 322, 14 ff.), the later thinking of the OT seems to give less restricted approval to wealth. [57] There are also three other differences.

---

[55] Cf. A. Alt, "Das Königtum in den Reichen Israel u. Juda," *Kleine Schriften zur Gesch. des Volkes Israel*, II (1953), 116-134; also M. Noth, *Gesch. Israels*[3] (1956), 152 f., 194-198.

[56] Cf. Is. 5:14 HT with LXX (שְׁאוֹל = πλούσιοι); Jer. 24:1; Is. 53:9 (on the textual question cf. K. F. Euler, "Die Verkündigung vom leidenden Gottesknecht aus Js. 53 in d. griech. Bibel," BWANT, IV, 14 (1934), 73-75; H. W. Wolff, *Js. 53 im Urchr.*[3] (1952), 41, 77.

[57] Some sceptical statements in Qoh. (cf. 2:11; 4:8; 6:2; 10:6; 5:14) are the only exception.

This thinking is existential; it arises out of life and is not just theoretical. It is also marked by an unbroken belief in retribution which associates quite naturally wealth and piety on the one side, poverty and ungodliness on the other (cf. Prv. 10:15; Sir. 13:24; 44:6; Prv. 3:16; 22:4). Finally, it is characterised by a faith in God which regards riches as God's gift to the righteous, i.e., as a blessing (Prv. 10:22; cf. Sir. 11:15 f., 23; Prv. 15:16).

The understanding of wealth as a blessing, however, raises the difficult problem of theodicy. This is posed by the fact that many of the ungodly seem to be rich and fortunate, while many of the righteous seem to be unlucky and poor (cf. Job 21:7; ψ 36; 48; 72). In the Wisdom books, and within the doctrine of retribution, the constant answer is that God will soon establish a just order of things (ψ 36; Job 20 etc.). ψ 48:17 f. goes deeper: "Do not fret when one is made rich, when the δόξα of his house increases, for he cannot carry all this with him in death." There is a ref. here to the impermanent and relative nature of earthly wealth and fortune. ψ 33:11, however, is closest to the NT message, and to a basic answer to the problem: "Even the rich become poor and suffer lack, but they that seek the Lord shall not want any good thing." Here faith in God, which is stronger than the experience of reality, leads to a solution nowhere surpassed in the OT, cf. ψ 72:23-26.

C. Riches and the Rich in Judaism.

1. The Non-Philonic Tradition.

At the end of OT history and in the Judaism of the time of Jesus the eschatological movement [58] offers a new answer to the problem of theodicy. Wealth, then, has also to be discussed in terms of eschatology. Where there is refusal to do this, e.g., among the Sadducean hierarchy, [59] riches are still regarded as an expression and indeed a constitutent part of salvation, as in the OT. [60] Where, as among the Essenes, [61] a radical determinism rules, [62] and the present age is strictly contrasted with the age to come, [63] earthly wealth and possession [64] is rejected as the most visible sign of captivity to this passing world. [65] What is now evil and painful will then be good; what is now good will then be much worse than the evil of this world. [66] Where, finally, the eschatological hope is earthly national expectation, fulness and wealth are part of it as a sign and gift. [67] These motifs interfuse and combine in Pharisaism. Since salvation is finally in the hereafter, earthly wealth cannot be an ultimate blessing of salvation. [68] It is an

---

[58] Cf. Volz Esch., 63-134; O. Procksch, *Theol. d. AT* (1950), 407-419; Eichr. Theol. AT³, 247-250.

[59] Cf. Jos. Ant., 13, 173, 297-299; on their teachings cf. Ant., 13, 173; 18, 16 f.; Bell., 2, 164 ff.; cf. Schl. Gesch. Isr., 165-170; Schürer, II, 263.

[60] Schl. Gesch. Isr., 167; on the luxury and wealth of the priestly houses cf. S. Dt., 303 on 31:14; jKet., 5, 13 (30b, 65 ff.); cf. Jeremias, II, 95, n. 5.

[61] Cf. the accounts of the Essenes and their teachings in Jos. Bell., 2, 119-161; Ant., 18, 18-22; 13, 173; Schl. Gesch. Isr., 173-178.

[62] Cf. Jos. Ant., 18, 18; materially cf. also Ps. Sol. 5:4; on determinism Volz Esch., 299 f.

[63] On the formulae of the antithesis of the two periods cf. Volz Esch., 65.

[64] Jos. Bell., 2, 122 on the Essenes: καταφρονηταὶ δὲ πλούτου, καὶ θαυμάσιον αὐτοῖς τὸ κοινωνικόν, οὐδὲ ἔστιν εὑρεῖν κτήσει τινὰ παρ᾽ αὐτοῖς ὑπερέχοντα, cf. 1 QS 3:2; 6:2, 20, 25; 7:25; 8:23 etc.

[65] Cf. S. Bar. 15:8; 50-52; Eth. En. 94:8.

[66] Cf. S. Bar. 29:6; 51:12-52; 83; 4 Esr. 7; Eth. En. 96:4; 100:6; 103:4 f.

[67] Cf. the data in Volz Esch., 359-408.

[68] jPea, 4 (18ᵃ, 60) on 1 Ch. 22:14 (Str.-B., I, 826): "R. Abin has said: What does 'in my poverty' mean? That there is no wealth before him who spake, and the world came into being," cf. also Ps. Sol. 1:3.

actual presupposition for almsgiving, [69] for a life in which the Law is observed. [70] But knowledge of the Torah and good works accompany a man from this world to the next, not riches. [71] Thus the high evaluation of riches, [72] which Judaism shares with the OT, finds a limit here. There are also those who point out the perils of wealth. [73] Emphasis on eschatological judgment brings a transvaluation of values, so that the question arises whether wealth, instead of expressing divine blessing and good-pleasure, may not be an indication of God's future wrath and destruction in the judgment. [74] Finally, then, both riches and poverty are instruments of divine testing : God sees whether the rich will open his hand to the poor and whether the poor will accept his suffering without complaint. [75] According to the motif of reward the whole of the salvation at man's disposal is also a quantitatively fixed thing, so that those who have received more goods here will have correspondingly fewer in the hereafter. [76]

In connection with the question of salvation, then, later Judaism develops a plenitude of thoughts. Though these are varied and even self-contradictory in detail, they may all be brought under the common denominator that in Judaism, as in the OT (→ 324, 4 f.; 325, 4 ff.), God is the only Giver of riches and salvation. [77] Wealth also sets under an obligation towards one's neighbour which it is sin to evade. [78] Finally, the concept of retribution carries with it the dubious teaching that wealth, like salvation, is a reward for the fulfilling of the divine commandments.

2. Philo.

Philo's views on riches are strongly influenced by Platonic and Stoic strands of thought. This Gk. influence singles him out from other Jews of his day. External goods, wealth, fame and offices are adiaphora, Vit. Mos., II, 53; Decal., 71; Det. Pot. Ins., 122. Disparagingly Philo calls earthly wealth νόθος, τυφλός (Jos., 258), αἰσθητός (Migr. Abr., 95), since it is uncertain (Jos., 131), has no true value (Migr. Abr., 95), and its acquisition involves dangers to the soul (Vit. Cont., 17). Riches are not, of course, rejected by him. As a Stoic he can distinguish between things indifferent. Poverty and low esteem are hard to bear (Virt., 5). A man of understanding will not be radical in despising external goods (Fug., 25). But he will not set his heart on them, nor, like the gt. majority, imagine that εὐδαιμονία can be won on the basis of earthly goods (Spec. Leg., I, 23 f.). In the last resort it is the OT belief in God which prevents Philo from completely rejecting the goods of creation. He is aware that God has created them for man to salvation. In wealth, then, the pt. is to fulfil the duties which God has given

---

[69] The poor man who has nothing can, of course, exercise benevolence with a good word, Str.-B., IV, 543 x and y. But these sayings show that there is a problem here as to the religious significance of alms.

[70] This may be seen indirectly from the Rabb. estimation of poverty. "There is nothing harder in the world than poverty ; it is the most grievous of all sufferings in the world," Str.-B., I, 818 (with other refs.). Cf. also Ps. Sol. 16:13 : "If God does not give strength, who can stand being punished by poverty ?"

[71] Cf. Ab., 6, 9 (Str.-B., III, 655).

[72] "R. Eleazar has said: From this (Ex. 2:3) it follows that the righteous value their money more than their body," Sota, 12a (Str.-B., I, 827). Cf. the other instances and the overestimation of riches in Jos. Ant., 7, 391.

[73] Cf. the collection of refs. in Str.-B., I, 827 f.

[74] Cf. Eth. En. 96:4 : "Woe to you sinners that your riches mark you as righteous but your hearts convict you as sinners," cf. also Beth ha-Midr., 3, 22, 34 : "He who is poor in this world will be rich in the future world, like the Israelites, because they devote themselves to keeping the commandments," Str.-B., III, 656 f.

[75] Ex. r., 31 (91c), cf. Str.-B., I, 822.

[76] Cf. Str.-B., IV, 490-500.

[77] "God says (to the rich man who shows mercy): Know that I am he who has made that man poor and you rich ; I can also make you poor again in a moment" (Tanch. B § 8 [43ª]; Str.-B., I, 820; cf. the other examples here).

[78] Cf. Str.-B., IV, 536-610, exc. on private benevolence and works of love in ancient Judaism.

therewith, and to use riches with understanding (Fug., 28). For riches, like all possessions, belong to God [79] who has all things and needs nothing (Leg. All., III, 78; Vit. Mos., I, 157), who gives them to man as a loan (Cher., 109), and who demands an account from him (Cher., 118). Finer and more important than the possibility of helping through riches (Jos., 144), however, is the participation of the wise as God's servants (Cher., 107, cf. Spec. Leg., I, 311) in the riches of God who is rich in fulness, Leg. All., I, 34. Through God's rich manifestations of grace (Op. Mund., 23; Leg. All., III, 163), which the φιλό-δωρος θεός gives, this is true life fulfilment. Thus Moses confesses that God has given him country, kin, home, citizenship and freedom, and that He is the great wealth which is to be lauded and which cannot be snatched away, Rer. Div. Her. 27. At this pt., with the help of Gk. modes of thought, Philo has in fact broken free from Jewish narrowness in this matter, and on the soil of the OT revelation of God he has been able to give a new definition of wealth. But in spite of its inner strength this is carried out anthropo-centrically, individualistically, and in terms of the concept of reward, though in a spiritualised form. This differentiates it from the NT.

D. Riches and the Rich in the New Testament.

1. The Attitude of Jesus to Wealth in Mark and Matthew.

In Matthew and Mark the whole traditional complex, with its various answers (→ 323 ff.), is completely set aside in favour of a new and radically eschatological view.

a. In the interpretation of the parable of the Sower [80] in Mt. the ἀπάτη τοῦ πλούτου as well as anxiety chokes the word (13:22; cf. Mk. 4:19; Lk. 8:14). But nothing distinctive is said here about riches, for the human body can act in the same way, cf. Mt. 5:29 f. (→ IV, 559, 32 ff.); 18:8 f. (→ IV, 532, 26 f.). Again, it is said of the rich man that he would not follow Jesus : ἦν γὰρ ἔχων κτήματα πολλά (19:22), and that Jesus then referred to the fact that it is easier for a camel to go through the eye of a needle than for a rich man to get into heaven (v. 24). The reaction of the disciples however: τίς ἄρα δύναται σωθῆναι; (v. 25), show that the πλούσιος here is in practice everyman. He is man according to the structure of this world (cf. 13:22), who gains nothing even if he wins the whole world, since in so doing he destroys his soul, cf. 16:26. What is meant is made clear in the passage on anxiety in the Sermon on the Mount, → IV, 592, 22 ff. Anxiety is the sign which characterises pagan life, 6:25-32. In contrast is seeking the kingdom and its righteousness, which characterises the life of the disciple, 6:33 f., cf. 16:24 ff. This eschatological and theocentric rather than ethical way of viewing riches is confirmed in Mt. 27:57 and 26:11. It is simply noted, without judgment, that Joseph of Arimathea was a rich man, [81] and in the story of the anointing at Bethany the context of Mt. permits us to assume (cf. also 5:3 f.) that poverty has no particular religious significance.

b. As compared with the total incorporation of the question of riches in the desecularising eschatological proclamation of Jesus in Mt., the problem of wealth seems to have greater independence in Mk. Its formulation in the explanation of the parable of the Sower (4:19 : καὶ αἱ μέριμναι τοῦ αἰῶνος καὶ ἡ ἀπάτη τοῦ πλούτου καὶ αἱ περὶ τὰ λοιπὰ ἐπιθυμίαι εἰσπορευόμεναι συμπνίγουσιν τὸν λόγον) is closer to the Lucan version than to the Matthean, and casts a

---

[79] Cher., 113-117; Leg. All., III, 33, 195; Plant., 54.
[80] On the question of the authenticity of the interpretation cf. Jeremias, 49-51.
[81] Cf. Wolff, op. cit., 41, 77.

critical light on wealth, which stands alongside μέριμναι and ἐπιθυμίαι, → II, 925, n. 96. Furthermore Mk. has the story of the widow's mite (12:41-44, cf. Lk. 21:1-4), which does not occur in Mt., though there is here, of course, no direct attack on the wealthy (cf. καὶ πολλοὶ πλούσιοι ἔβαλλον πολλά, Mk. 12:41b). On the whole one may say that for Mark riches are one of the obstacles to true hearing of the message of the βασιλεία τοῦ θεοῦ.

2. In Luke.

The question of the rich occupies more space in Lk. than in Mt. and Mk. In this regard it is worth noting that the term πλοῦτος occurs only in the Synoptic saying in Lk. 8:14. The special Lucan material deals with the rich (18:25 and par.; 21:1 = Mk. 12:41; Lk. 6:24; 12:16; 14:12; 16:1, 21, 22; 18:23; 19:2) and being rich (πλουτεῖν, 1:53; 12:21), but not with riches. This distinction between being rich and riches raises the question whether the πλούσιοι are not more than mere possessors of material goods. In fact such a conclusion is supported by the version and setting of the story of the rich man (18:18-27), who was a rich ἄρχων in Lk. For this is preceded by the parable of the Pharisee and the publican, vv. 9-14. That this combination is no accident is shown by the pericope of the poor widow (21:1-4), which is preceded by the debate with the Jewish leaders (20:1), and the parable of Dives and Lazarus (16:19-31), which is preceded by criticism of the righteousness of the Pharisees (vv. 14-18), while the story of Zacchaeus, the chief publican (19:1-10), is followed by the parable of the pounds (19:12 ff.), and the section 14:12 ff. by the parable of the great supper (vv. 15-24). The context shows that the rich in these passages are the Jewish opponents of Jesus. If materially Luke is here adopting the collectivist concept of the rich fashioned by the prophetic criticism (→ 324, 20 ff.), in keeping is the total, non-individual negation of the existence of the rich (18:25, cf. 16:25; 6:24 f.; 12:21) and the total reversal of order: those invited first to the feast do not partake of it (14:24), the hungry are filled with good things and the rich sent empty away (1:53), the lost are saved (cf. 19:10), those who abase themselves will be exalted (14:11, cf. 18:29 f.).

But there is more to the Lucan understanding of riches than this. The situation of the Jewish leaders, who regard themselves as rich in virtue of their inheritance and who consequently despise Jesus, is a paradigm of the situation of the rich man who relies on his possessions (12:19). Being rich is a hindrance to discipleship (18:22 f., cf. 12:21). Wealth is a negative good (8:14). Hence ethical directions are given to the community. The conduct of Zacchaeus, who gave half his goods to the poor and restored fourfold what he had exacted wrongfully, is held up as an example (19:8; cf. 16:9; also 14:12-14: the duty of inviting without hope of return). Corresponding to these instructions is the promise that separation from riches in discipleship is the very thing which will result in manifold gain in this time and eternal life in the world to come.

3. The Word Group in Pauline Usage.

In Paul, too, there is no discussion of the question of wealth from the traditional standpoint. A distinctive feature of his usage is the applying of the term to God, Christ and the community. This is a material continuation and fulfilment of the Synoptic sayings about riches. In the Synoptists the vanity of earthly wealth is laid bare by the eschatological message of Jesus. Paul, however, redefines wealth. It is incorrect to speak of transferred usage in relation to him. Paul goes back to the original sense of "fulness of goods," → 319, 8. Riches is for him a term to denote the being of Christ, the work of God in Christ, and the eschatological situation of Christ's community. Christ is the πλούσιος (2 C. 8:9) who is πλουτῶν εἰς πάντας τοὺς ἐπικαλουμένους αὐτόν (R. 10:12). In R. 2:4 Paul speaks of the πλοῦτος τῆς χρηστότητος of God, in 9:23 of the πλοῦτος τῆς δόξης αὐτοῦ, in 11:33 of the βάθος πλούτου καὶ σοφίας καὶ γνώσεως θεοῦ. [82] The Word of Christ dwells πλουσίως in the community (Col. 3:16), which is rich through the poverty of Christ (πλουτεῖν, 2 C. 8:9), which is made rich in every respect in Christ (pass. πλουτίζειν, 1 C. 1:5, cf. 2 C. 9:11), to which God has declared the riches of the glory of the mystery (Col. 1:27, cf. 2:2).

The same usage is to be found in Eph. God is πλούσιος ἐν ἐλέει (2:4). In Him the community has the forgiveness of transgressions κατὰ τὸ πλοῦτος τῆς χάριτος αὐτοῦ (1:7, cf. 2:7). It knows through the Spirit what are the riches of the glory of its inheritance (1:18, cf. 3:16). The apostle's task is to proclaim τὸ ἀνεξιχνίαστον πλοῦτος of Christ (3:8).

This eschatological filling out of the concept of riches, which sees in riches a mark of the future world present in Christ, can be properly understood only if one realises that by nature this wealth is poverty and folly to the world (cf. 1 C. 1:23; 3:18), since the world in its σοφία does not see the true nature of things (cf. 1 C. 1:20 f.). The way of these riches is that of Christ, who, though He was rich, became poor in order to make the world rich through His poverty (2 C. 8:9, cf. Phil. 2:7 f.). But this is an offence to natural thought, which, a prisoner to anxiety, trusts in self or possessions, but not in God. The μορφὴ δούλου corresponds to the μορφὴ κυρίου (2 C. 6:4-10, cf. 11:23-31). Hence it is true of the apostle also that, being poor, he makes many rich (2 C. 6:10). Indeed, the figure of Christ seems to him to show that it is a law of salvation history that renunciation of one's own rights makes others rich. Only thus can he understand the destiny of his people, which rejected with Christ the wealth that now accrues to the Gentile world through the preaching of Christ (cf. R. 11:12-15). Here, then, is the solution to the problem of wealth which neither Greek philosophy nor OT and Jewish thought could solve. True riches consist in the love which expresses itself in self-sacrifice in following Jesus, which does not seek its own (1 C. 13:4-13), which shows itself to be genuine by not bragging about the riches it has received, as the Corinthians did according to Paul (1 C. 4:7 f.), by its consequent freedom from the demonism of the world and of things, by its confidence that God will supply every need according to His riches in glory (Phil. 4:19), [83] and therefore by having an open hand for the brethren (2 C. 8:1-10, cf. 9:6-14). Of every possession or earthly holding one must say that it is not wealth or security but simply an instrument in the ministry of love, with no dignity of its own. This is the substance of Paul's admonition to the Corinthians (→ III, 893, 37 ff.): καὶ οἱ χρώμενοι τὸν κόσμον ὡς μὴ καταχρώμενοι (1 C. 7:31).

4. The Other NT Writings.

After what has been said the other NT writings need no extended treatment. Some references, indeed, are without theological significance: πλουσίως, "richly," Tt. 3:6; 2 Pt. 1:11; in Rev. 6:15 (cf. Is. 2:19, 21); 13:16 the rich are one group of men among others. For the rest, two strands [84] may be distinguished. The one is that of hortatory warning against the danger of coveting riches: οἱ βουλόμενοι

---

[82] On the text cf. Ltzm. R.⁴, ad loc.
[83] On the eschatological character of the saying cf. Loh. Phil., ad loc.
[84] Cf. Schneider, 517-519.

πλουτεῖν ἐμπίπτουσιν εἰς πειρασμὸν καὶ παγίδα καὶ ἐπιθυμίας πολλὰς ἀνοήτους καὶ βλαβεράς, αἵτινες βυθίζουσιν τοὺς ἀνθρώπους εἰς ὄλεθρον καὶ ἀπώλειαν (1 Tm. 6:9). The rich as such are not condemned ; according to the tradition they are admonished to be humble, to trust in God rather than uncertain riches, and to do good works, 1 Tm. 6:17 ff. The second, which is found especially in James, involves a radical condemnation of wealth and the wealthy.[85] In Jm. 1:10 f. the rich are told to boast of their low estate, since the rich will fade away in their ways ; Jm. 2:1-9 contains a warning against regard for wealth and status in the community ; this is sin, and leads to a singling out of the rich over the poor (v. 5 f.), though the poor are elected by God, while the rich treat the community with violence, hale its members to judgment, and blaspheme the name of Christ (v. 6 f.). In Jm. 5:1-6 the rich are accused of slaying the righteous (v. 6), of living voluptuously and sumptuously (v. 5), and of withholding wages from the reapers (v. 4). Their gold and silver will rise up in witness against them at the last judgment and will consume them like fire (v. 3).[86]

The usage of Rev. is essentially the same as that of Paul. The Lamb is worthy to receive τὴν δύναμιν καὶ πλοῦτον καὶ σοφίαν καὶ ἰσχὺν καὶ τιμὴν καὶ δόξαν καὶ εὐλογίαν (5:12). In the letter to the church at Smyrna we read : οἶδά σου τὴν θλῖψιν καὶ τὴν πτωχείαν, ἀλλὰ πλούσιος εἶ (2:9), while against the church of Laodicea the accusation is made that it thinks it is rich (cf. 1 C. 4:8), but in reality it is poor, blind and naked, and should thus repent in order that it may receive what is necessary to its spiritual life, Rev. 3:17 f. This is also Pauline. In Rev. 18:3, 15, 17, 19 a description is given of the way in which the merchants who have become rich through the violence and luxury of great Babylon will be involved, with their riches, in the overthrow of the city.

Mention should also be made of Hb. 11:25 f.,[87] where it is said that Moses was willing to suffer affliction with the people of God rather than enjoy the pleasures of sin for a season, esteeming the reproach of Christ (→ IV, 702, 1 ff.; 871, 28 ff.) greater riches than the treasures of Egypt. This, too, is Pauline.

E. Riches and the Rich in the Post-Apostolic Period up to Clement of Alexandria and Cyprian.

1. The Post-Apostolic Fathers.

The NT line of approach is found also in the post-apostolic fathers. Barn., 1, 2 speaks of the rich and lofty declarations of God[88] to the community, in which the grace of the gift of the Spirit has been planted, which derives from the rich source of the Lord (1, 3).[89] In addition, however, the young community, set in the pagan world,[90] is faced by the question how it is to treat riches and the rich in the community itself. Hermas emphasises that wealth is useless as such, cf. s., 2, 8. One should not strive for it nor

---

[85] Cf. the exc. on "rich" and "poor" in Dib. Jk., 37-44.

[86] On the various attempts at historical integration cf. the brief review in H. Rendtorff, "Hörer und Täter. Eine Einführung in den Jk.," Die urchr. Botschaft, 19 (1953), 10 f.

[87] Cf. Mi. Hb., ad loc.; L. Goppelt, "Typos, die typologische Deutung d. AT im NT," BFTh, 43 (1939), 210 f.

[88] μεγάλων μὲν ὄντων καὶ πλουσίων τῶν τοῦ θεοῦ δικαιωμάτων εἰς ὑμᾶς. On the meaning of δικαίωμα v. Wnd. Barn., ad loc.

[89] On the text (and its meaning) cf. Wnd. Barn., ad loc.; cf. also the (inauthentic) ending Dg., 11, 5 : Christ ... δι' οὗ πλουτίζεται ἡ ἐκκλησία ...; cf. Herm. s., 1, 9; on the group cf. also Barn., 9, 7; 1, 7; 19, 2.

[90] On the attitude of the pagan world to riches cf. Schneider, 517; Laukamm, 40.

desire it, s., 1, 1-8, cf. 1 Tm. 6:9.[91] Pol., 4, 1 quotes 1 Tm. 6:10 : ἀρχὴ δὲ πάντων χαλεπῶν φιλαργυρία, cf. 2, 2; 4, 3; 6, 1; Did., 3, 5.[92] The luxury to which wealth leads is condemned, Herm. m., 8, 3; 12, 2, 1; cf. R. 13:14; Bas. Sermo, VI, 2 and 4. Apart from these general lines there are also two sets of statements which cannot be reduced to a single common denominator. The one (→ 330, 5 ff.) involves a radical rejection of riches. It points to the insuperable dangers and the technical demands of wealth which keep a man from faith and prayer, cf. esp. Herm. s., 9, 20, 1 and 2; v., 3, 6, 5-7; m., 10, 1, 4. Nevertheless, in the same works one also finds a conditional acceptance of riches. Wealth and possession are God's gift, Herm. s., 1, 8; cf. 2, 10 : μακάριοι οἱ ἔχοντες καὶ συνιέντες, ὅτι παρὰ τοῦ κυρίου πλουτίζονται. They should serve to help the brethren who are in want, s., 1, 8; cf. v., 3, 6; Did., 4, 8; 1 Cl., 38, 2; Dg., 10, 5 f. If they are used thus they cannot harm the rich. This view is found most clearly in the distinctive section Herm. s., 2, 4-10, which is influenced by the Jewish concept of reward and retribution.[93] This section may be regarded as an attempt to combine the two divergent estimations of wealth. By the figure of the fruitless elm with which the vine associates itself and from which it draws moisture in time of drought, the author tries to show that the poor man who has time for prayer and whose prayer is rich and acceptable to God intercedes spiritually for the rich man, who sustains him in earthly life by gifts from his store. This is undoubtedly a first stage in the interrelation of church and world which underlay monasticism. It rests on a concept of spiritual, good and meritorious works which is in opposition to the Pauline doctrine of justification.[94] Nevertheless, one should not overlook the fact that the motive is that of the evangelical commandment of love which, regarding every possession as God's gift, finds in it a task and duty, and in so doing confers upon the Chr. community a new social order in a perishing world.

2. Clement of Alexandria and Cyprian.

In the extended discussion of the ancient Church concerning riches[95] Clement of Alex., Cyprian and Basil play a special part, for they bring the ideas of the post-apostolic age on the question to a conclusion which has considerable influence on later Chr. thinking about wealth and poverty. It is the merit of Clement to have defined afresh the legitimacy and limits of earthly wealth in a Chr. spirit. Above all in his work Quis Div. Salv., taking up on Chr. soil the thought of Gk. philosophy (→ 320, 33 ff.; 322, 26 ff.),[96] he teaches the ethical and religious indifference of wealth or poverty. Both rich and poor can be filled by harmful desires, Quis Div. Salv., 18. Hence the presence of earthly wealth or poverty cannot possibly fix the true and eternal destiny of a man. The man who is truly rich is he who is rich, not after the flesh, but in virtues (ἀρετῶν) which he can use in a holy and believing way in any situation. The same applies to the poor, cf. 19. To this thought, which is very close to Gk. philosophy (→ 320, 33 ff.), there is added, however, the decisive Chr. concept of God. God gives man possessions and goods for his use, 14. Man is to control them, and to do so aright, 31, cf. Bas. Sermo, VI, 3. Their worth is thus decided by the use to which they are put, and this depends again on the attitude or virtue of the one who uses them. "He who had gold, silver and houses as God's gifts, and therewith served the God who gave them, by (using) them for the salvation of men . . ., would not need to detach himself from them" (16), is Clement's judgment in interpretation of the story of the rich young

---

[91] On the text cf. Dib. Herm., ad loc.

[92] Cf. 1 Tm. 6:5 f.

[93] Cf. Dib. Herm. Exc. on rich and poor, 555 f.

[94] The par. to 1 C. 9:11 (Dib., op. cit. [→ n. 93]) is only formal. For a material par. cf. Cl. Al. Quis Div. Salv., 32.

[95] Cf. Schilling ; Haller.

[96] Here one is to think esp. of the Stoic discussion whether or how far wealth is a good (Paed., III, 85, 4 ff.), also of the definition of neighbour (Quis Div. Salv., 28), the relation of the evaluation of wealth to use (16), and the Aristotelian concept of the μέση κατάστασις (Paed., II, 16, 4). There is a ref. to Plat. in Paed., II, 35, 2 cf. Strom., II, 22, 1.

ruler, cf. 14. The true and virtuous use, however, is that which is in keeping with Christ's will (cf. 13 f.), namely, service of one's neighbour, or every man acc. to Cl. (28, cf. Paed., 3, 7), by benevolence and generosity, Quis Div. Salv., 33. In this way Cl. arrives at a consistent social classifying of wealth, its legitimacy and limits, which corresponds to the basic orientation of Chr. faith. Cyprian and Basil are in fundamental agreement with this view, [97] though they give more prominence to the ethical admonition to practise freedom from wealth in active love, and to avoid bondage to it and consequent seduction from Christ. [98] The whole difficulty of the Chr. attitude to riches is in fact set forth in the tension between these two attitudes, which corresponds to the Christian's being in the world and yet not of the world.

† *Hauck/Kasch*

πνεῦμα, πνευματικός, πνέω, ἐμπνέω,
πνοή, ἐκπνέω, θεόπνευστος

πνεῦμα, πνευματικός.

Contents : πνεῦμα in the Greek World : I. The Meaning of the Term : 1. Wind ; 2. Breath ; 3. Life ; 4. Soul ; 5. Transferred Meaning : Spirit ; 6. πνεῦμα and νοῦς ; 7. μαντικὸν πνεῦμα; 8. θεῖον πνεῦμα; 9. θεὸς πνεῦμα; 10. Ungreek Development of the Meaning. II. πνεῦμα in Mythology and Religion : 1. Life-creating πνεῦμα; 2. πνεῦμα and In-

---

[97] Cf. Cyprian, De opere et eleemosynis, 9; De habitu virginum, 7-10; cf. Bas. Sermo, VI, 3.
[98] Cf. Bas. Sermo, V, VI; Cyprian, De habitu virginum, 7-10; De opere et eleem., 10.
πνεῦμα, πνευματικός. In general : a. On usage : Pass., Liddell-Scott (not without deficiencies in spite of addenda et corrigenda); Pr.-Bauer, *s.v.*; b. on the history of the word : A. Bertholet and L. Baeck, Art. "Geist u. Geistesgaben im AT u. Judt.," RGG², II, 940-943; F. Büchsel, *Der Geist Gottes im NT* (1926); E. de W. Burton, *Spirit, Soul and Flesh ... in Greek Writings and Translated Works from the Earliest Period to 180 A.D. ... and in Hebrew OT* (1918); Cr.-Kö., *s.v.*; H. Cremer, Art. "Hl. Geist," RE³, 6, 444-450; also "Geist des Menschen im bibl. Sinn," *ibid.*, 450-457; C. H. Dodd, *The Interpretation of the Fourth Gospel* (1953), 213-227; A. J. Festugière, *L'idéal religieux des Grecs et l'évangile²* (1932), 196-220; H. Gunkel, *Die Wirkungen des hl. Geistes³* (1909); K. Kerényi, "Der Geist," Albae Vigiliae, NF, 3 (1945), 29-41; H. Leisegang, *Der Hl. Geist*, I, 1 (1919); also "Pneuma Hagion," *Veröffentlichungen des Forschungsinstituts f. vergleichende Religionsgeschichte an d. Universität Leipzig*, 4 (1922); K. Prümm, *Religionsgeschichtliches Handbuch f. d. Raum d. altchr. Umwelt* (1954), 199-201, 427-434; Reitzenstein Hell. Myst., 70-73, 308-393; F. Rüsche, *Blut, Leben u. Seele. Ihr Verhältnis nach Auffassung d. griech. u. hell. Antike, d. Bibel u. d. alten Alexandrinischen Theologen, Studien z. Gesch. u. Kultur des Altertums*, Suppl. Vol. 5 (1930); also "Pneuma, Seele u. Geist," *Theol. u. Glaube*, 23 (1932), 606-625; also *Das Seelenpneuma. Seine Entwicklung v. d. Hauchseele zur Geistseele, Studien z. Gesch. u. Kultur d. Altertums*, 18, 3 (1933); E. Schweizer, "Gegenwart d. Geistes u. eschatologische Hoffnung bei Zarathustra, spätjüd. Gruppen, Gnostikern u. den Zeugen d. NT," *The Background of the NT and Its Eschatology, Studies in Honour of C. H. Dodd* (1956), 482-508; G. Verbeke, *L'évolution de la doctrine du pneuma du stoicisme à S. Augustin. Étude philosophique* (1945), with all relevant passages and bibl.; P. Volz, *Der Geist Gottes u. d. verwandten Erscheinungen im AT u. im anschliessenden Judt.* (1910); H. H. Wendt, *Die Begriffe Fleisch u. Geist im bibl. Sprachgebrauch* (1878). On A. II : P. Amandry, *La mantique Apollinienne à Delphes* (1950), 215-224; in criticism G. Klaffenbach, "Das delphische Orakel," *Wissenschaftliche Annalen*, 3 (1954), 519-526; H. Bacht, "Religionsgeschichtliches zum Inspirationsproblem," *Scholastik*, 17 (1942), 50-69; E. Fehrle, "Die kultische Keuschheit im Altertum," RVV, 6 (1910), 7-9, 79-89; E. Norden, *Die Geburt des Kindes* (1924), 76-92. On A. III : W. Jaeger, "Das Pneuma im Lykeion," Herm., 48 (1913), 29-74; also *Diokles v. Karystos* (1938), Index, *s.v.*; M. Pohlenz, *Die Stoa*, I (1948), Index II, *s.v.*; H. Siebeck, "Die Entwicklung d. Lehre v. Geist (Pneuma) in d. Wissen-

spiration : a. In Poetry ; b. in Manticism. III. πνεῦμα in Natural Science and Philosophy. IV. The Greek Concept of Pneuma and the NT. B. Spirit in the OT : I. Review of the Term : 1. רוּחַ in the OT : a. רוּחַ as Breath, Wind : (a) Breath of the Mouth ; (b) Breath of Air, Wind ; b. רוּחַ in Man : (a) The Principle which Gives Life to the Body ; (b) The Seat of Emotions, Intellectual Functions and Attitude of Will ; (c) Divinely Effected רוּחַ; c. The רוּחַ of God : (a) Effective Divine Power ; (b) Specifically God's Creative Power ; (c) The Inner Nature of God ; (d) רוּחַ as Personal Being ; 2. נְשָׁמָה in the OT : a. נְשָׁמָה as Breath ; b. נְשָׁמָה in Man ; c. The נְשָׁמָה of God : (a) The Principle which Gives Physical Life ; (b) That which Gives Man Insight ; 3. אוֹב in the OT : a. Spirit of the Dead ; b. Conjurer up of Spirits of the Dead. II. The Spirit of God. C. Spirit in Judaism : I. πνεῦμα

schaft d. Altertums," Zschr. f. Völkerpsychologie u. Sprachwissenschaft, 12 (1880), 361-407; also "Neue Beiträge z. Entwicklungsgeschichte d. Geist-Begriffs," Archiv f. Gesch. d. Philosophie, NF, 20 (1914), 1-16; M. Wellmann, "Die pneumatische Schule," PhU, 14 (1895), esp. 137-143. On B.: Eichr. Theol. AT[3, 4], II, 18-31; J. Hehn, "Zum Problem d. Geistes im alten Orient u. im AT," ZAW, NF, 2 (1925), 210-225; P. van Imschoot, "L'action de l'esprit de Jahvé dans l'Ancien Test.," Revue de Sciences Philosoph. et Théologiques, 23 (1934), 553-587; also "L'esprit de Jahvé, source de vie, dans l'Ancien Test.," Rev. Bibl., NS, 44 (1935), 481-501; also "L'esprit de Jahvé et l'alliance nouvelle dans l'Ancien Test.," Ephemerides Theol. Lovanienses, 22 (1936), 201-226; A. Jepsen, Nabi (1934), 12-42; A. C. Knudson, The Religious Teaching of the OT (1918), 93-114; R. Koch, Geist u. Messias, Beitrag z. bibl. Theologie d. AT (1950); also "Der Gottesgeist u. d. Messias," Biblica, 27 (1946), 241-268; J. Köberle, Natur u. Geist nach d. Auffassung d. AT (1901); L. Köhler, Theol. d. AT[3] (1953), 96-105; E. König, Theol. d. AT[3, 4] (1923), 183-186; also Der Offenbarungsbegriff d. AT (1882), 104-210; S. Linder, Studier till Gamla Testamentets föreställingar om anden (1926); J. Pedersen, Israel, I/II (1926), 102-106; O. Procksch, Theol. d. AT (1950), 459-468; P. Torge, Seelenglaube u. Unsterblichkeitshoffnung im AT (1909), 1-28; T. C. Vriezen, An Outline of OT Theology (1958), 248-251; A. Westphal, Chair et Esprit (1885); W. G. Williams, "The Ras Shamra Inscr. and Their Significance for the History of Hebrew Religion," American Journ. of Semitic Languages and Literatures, 51 (1935), 233-246. On C.: J. Abelson, The Immanence of God in Rabb. Literature (1912), 174-277; W. Bacher, Die älteste Terminologie d. jüd. Schriftauslegung (1899), 180-182; L. Blau, Art. "Holy Spirit," Jew. Enc., VI, 447-450; J. Bonsirven, Le judaisme palestinien au temps de Jésus-Christ, I (1934), 210-246, 323-326, 497 f., 536; II, 4-8; Bousset-Gressm., 269-286, 394-409; L. Broydé and L. Blau, Art. "Soul," Jew. Enc., XI, 472-474; Dalman WJ, I, 166 f.; N. Johansson, Parakletoi (1940), 84-95, 157-161; R. Meyer, "Hellenistisches in d. rabb. Anthropologie," BWANT, 4 F. 22 (1937); Moore, I, 237, 247, 371 f., 401-413, 421 f., 445-459, 485-489; II, 287-322, 353, 384, 389 f.; also "Intermediaries in Jewish Theology," HThR, 15 (1922), 41-85, esp. 58 f.; S. Mowinckel, "Die Vorstellungen d. Spätjudt. vom Hl. Geist als Fürsprecher u. der johann. Paraklet," ZNW, 32 (1933), 97-130; W. O. E. Oesterley, "The Belief in Angels and Demons," Judaism and Christianity, I (1937), 191-209 ; H. Parzen, "The Ruach hakodesh in Tannaitic Lit.," JQR, 20 (1929/30), 51-76; B. Reicke, "The Disobedient Spirits and Christian Baptism," Acta Seminarii Neotestamentici Upsaliensis, 13 (1946), 52-91; H. Ringgren, Word and Wisdom (1947), 165-171; B. Stade and A. Bertholet, Bibl. Theol. d. AT, II (1911), 374-393, 407-414, 450-453; Str.-B., II, 126-138, 341-346, 615-617; IV, 443-446 and passim (v. Index, IV, 1229 f.), 501-535, 1016-1198; Volz Esch. 59, 117-119, 221 f., 229-272, 392; Weber, 80 f., 166-177, 190-195, 205, 210-212, 225-231, 251-259, 336-347. On E. : E. W. Bullinger, The Giver and His Gifts (1953); Bultmann Theol., 151-162, 199-207, 330-332 (§ 14, 18, 38); E. de W. Burton, A Critical and Exegetical Comm. on the Ep. to the Galatians, ICC (1921), 486-492; M. Goguel, "Pneumatisme et Eschatologie dans le Christianisme primitif," RHR, 132 (1946), 124-169; 133 (1947/48), 103-161; Jackson-Lake, I, 1, 322-327; A. J. MacDonald, The Interpreter Spirit and Human Life (1944); R. Prenter, Le St.-Esprit et le renouveau de l'Eglise (1949); K. L. Schmidt, "Das Pneuma Hagion als Pers. u. als Charisma," Eranos-Jbch., 13 (1945), 187-235; E. Schweizer, "Geist u. Gemeinde im NT u. heute," Theol. Ex., NF, 32 (1952); also "The Spirit of Power," Interpretation, 6 (1952), 259-278; E. F. Scott, The Spirit in the NT (1923); Stauffer Theol., 144-145; H. B. Swete, The Holy Spirit in the NT (1912); V. Taylor, "The Spirit in the NT," The Doctrine of the Holy Spirit (1937). On E. I : C. K. Barrett, The Holy Spirit and the Gospel Tradition (1947); J. W. Batdorf, The Spirit of God in the Synoptic Gospels, Diss. Princeton (1950); D. A. Frövig, Das Sen-

in the LXX : 1. The Translation of the Hebrew Terms in the LXX ; 2. πνεῦμα as Wind ;
3. πνεῦμα as the Breath of Life ; 4. πνεῦμα as the Superhuman Power of Blessing and
Punishment ; 5. πνεῦμα as Spiritual Ability, Resolve of the Will, Constitution of Soul ;
6. πνεῦμα as Eschatological Gift ; 7. πνεῦμα in Qoheleth ; 8. πνεῦμα in Wisdom.
II. πνεῦμα in Hellenistic Judaism : 1. Philo ; 2. Josephus. III. רוּחַ in Palestinian Judaism :
1. Wind, Quarter of the World, Direction ; 2. Angels and Evil Spirits ; 3. The Deceased
in the Grave ; 4. The Spirit of Man : a. Terminology ; b. Legacy of the OT ; c. Spirit
and Body in Rabbinic Anthropology ; d. Age of the Idea of the Pre-existence and Immortality
of the Soul ; e. The Historical Problem ; 5. The Spirit of God : a. Terminology ; b. The
Works of the Spirit ; c. The Spirit and the OT ; d. The Spirit and Righteousness ; e. Endowment with the Spirit in Past, Future and Present ; f. The Cosmic Function of the Spirit ;
g. The Autonomy of the Spirit ; h. The Spirit as Advocate. D. Development to the Pneumatic Self in Gnosticism : I. The Dead Sea Scrolls and Their Influence ; II. Gnosticism :
1. The Problem : The Spirit as Creator of Matter ; 2. The Redemption of the πνεῦμα from
Matter ; 3. Trichotomy. E. The New Testament : I. Mark and Matthew : 1. The Demonic
and the Anthropological Spirit ; 2. The Spirit as the Power of God ; 3. General Endowment
with the Spirit ; 4. Jesus' Endowment with the Spirit at Baptism ; 5. Verses Peculiar to
Matthew ; 6. Jesus' Supernatural Conception by the Spirit ; 7. Summary. II. Luke and
Acts : 1. The Relation of the Spirit to Jesus ; 2. The Abiding of the Spirit with the Com-
munity ; 3. The Outward Manifestations of the Spirit ; 4. The Works of the Spirit ; 5. The
Spirit as a Feature of the Age of the Church ; 6. The Reception of the Spirit ; 7. Different
Meanings of πνεῦμα. III. Paul : 1. The OT and Hellenistic Strands : a. The Problem ;
b. Adoption of Hellenistic Ideas in Paul ; c. Correction in the Light of Primitive Christian
Eschatology ; d. πνεῦμα as a Sign of What is to Come ; 2. Paul's Own Interpretation :
a. The Problem ; b. πνεῦμα as the Power of πίστις ; c. πνεῦμα as Renunciation of the
σάρξ ; d. πνεῦμα as Openness for God and One's Neighbour ; 3. The Relation of the
Spirit to Christ ; 4. The Anthropological πνεῦμα ; 5. πνευματικός. IV. John : 1. The
Significance of Eschatology ; 2. πνεῦμα as a Sphere in Antithesis to σάρξ ; 3. πνεῦμα
as a Life-Giving Power in Antithesis to σάρξ ; 4. The Paraclete. V. The Rest of the New
Testament : 1. The Pauline Circle : a. Ephesians ; b. The Pastorals ; 2. Hebrews ; 3. The
Catholic Epistles : a. James ; b. 1 Peter ; c. 2 Peter ; d. 1 John ; 4. Revelation. F. The Post-
Apostolic Fathers : 1. The Gnostic-Substantial Line ; 2. The Ecstatic Line ; 3. The Official
Line.

A. πνεῦμα in the Greek World.

I. The Meaning of the Term.

Derived from *πνέϝω, the verbal noun πνεῦμα means the elemental natural and
vital force which, matter and process in one, acts as a stream of air in the blowing of

dungsbewusstsein Jesu u. d. Geist (1924); W. Michaelis, Reich Gottes u. Geist Gottes nach
d. NT (1931); H. Windisch, "Jesus u. d. Geist nach synpt. Überlieferung," Studies in Early
Christianity, ed. S. J. Case (1928), 209-236. On E. II (cf. E. I): H. v. Baer, Der hl. Geist in
d. Lukasschriften (1926); H. E. Dana, The Holy Spirit in Acts (1943); G. W. H. Lampe,
"The Holy Spirit in the Writings of St. Luke," Studies in the Gospel, ed. D. E. Nineham
(1955), 159-200. On E. III : E. B. Allo, "Sagesse et Pneuma dans la première épître aux
Corinthiens," Rev. Bibl., 43 (1934), 321-346; H. Bertrams, Das Wesen des Geistes nach d.
Anschauung d. Apostels Pls. (1913); E. Fuchs, Christus u. d. Geist bei Pls. (1932); P.
Gächter, "Zum Pneumabegriff d. hl. Pls.," Zschr. f. kathol. Theol., 53 (1929), 345-408;
W. Gutbrod, "D. paul. Anthropologie," BWANT, IV, 15 (1934); Ltzm. R. Exc. on 8:11;
H. D. Wendland, "Das Wirken d. hl. Geistes in d. Gläubigen nach Pls.," ThLZ, 77 (1952),
457-470. On E. IV: C. K. Barrett, "The Holy Spirit in the Fourth Gospel," JThSt, NS, 1
(1950), 1-15; M. Goguel, La notion johannique de l'esprit et ses antécédents historiques
(1902); W. F. Howard, Christianity acc. to St. John (1943); H. Windisch, "Jesus u. d. Geist
im Joh.-Ev.," Amicitiae Corolla, Festschr. J. R. Harris (1933), 303-318. On F. : T. Rüsch,
D. Entstehung d. Lehre vom Hl. Geist bei Ign., Theophil. u. Iren., Diss. Zürich (1952);
H. Weinel, Die Wirkungen d. Geistes u. d. Geister im nachapostolischen Zeitalter bis auf
Iren. (1899).

the wind and the inhaling and exhaling of breath, and hence transf. as the breath of the spirit which, in a way which may be detected both outwardly and inwardly, fills with inspiration and grips with enthusiasm. [1] Whether visibly or not there resides in the word an effective and directed power which it owes, not so much to the -μα, but rather to the basic idea of energy contained in the root *πνεϝ-. This finds cosmologically representative expression in Plat. Phaed., 112b when in the myth about the constitution of the earth the movement of the wind and the process of breathing are compared : ὥσπερ τῶν ἀναπνεόντων ἀεὶ ἐκπνεῖ τε καὶ ἀναπνεῖ ῥέον τὸ πνεῦμα, οὕτω καὶ ἐκεῖ ξυναιωρούμενον τῷ ὑγρῷ τὸ πνεῦμα δεινούς τινας ἀνέμους καὶ ἀμηχάνους παρέχεται καὶ εἰσιὸν καὶ ἐξιόν. [2] From this there are logically developed and expanded the various occasional uses and nuances, both lit. and fig., acc. to the sphere or context of reality. Within these the force of πνεῦμα may be seen in its varied nature and strength.

1. Wind. In place of the Homeric πνο(ι)ή, and occurring in both poetry and prose from Aesch. and Hdt. (on Anaxim. → 353, n. 81), πνεῦμα is used in the macrocosm physically for the breath of wind in its movement as a blowing force and also acc. to its distinctive invisibly rarefied materiality as an element, so that one may equally well speak both of ἀνέμων πνεύματα (Aesch. Prom., 1086; Hdt., VII, 16α) and of the ἄημα πνευμάτων (Soph. Ai., 674). As the most comprehensive term for any type of "wind," which increasingly assimilates the qualities of the synonyms πνοή, ἄημα, ἀήτη (Plat. Crat., 410b), ἄνεμος and αὔρα (Poll. Onom., I, 15), πνεῦμα may be the "storm" which blows powerfully, the "fair wind" which rises quickly and unexpectedly and which may be favourable or unfavourable, the "breeze" (Xenoph. Hist. Graec., VI, 2, 27; Aristoph. Ra., 1002 f., not without a subsidiary fig. meaning), the light "breath of wind" (from heaven) which is divinely soft and pure and which quietly invigorates (Eur. Hel., 867; Tro., 758; Plat. Phaedr., 229b), or the "exhalation," the "vapour" (= ἀτμός, ἀναθυμίασις) which, rising up at certain points from the interior of the earth, contains or releases mantic powers, and can be fatal. [3] For some πνεῦμα as the agent of natural meteorological processes influences climate, health and even human character, Hippocr. De Aere Aquis Locis 3-6 (CMG, I, 1, 57-60). For some it pours forth as a fluid with the divine scent of the epiphany of Artemis, Eur. Hipp., 1391. Always, however, there is force in πνεῦμα. Power flows from it, is mediated by it, and disappears with it, Cic. Divin., I, 19, 37. What is true without is no less true within. As a part of nature, πνεῦμα is like nature both external and internal at the same time. It is both material and spiritual, both natural and divine.

2. Breath. Thus in the microcosm of organic life, and esp. in men and animals, πνεῦμα is physiologically the "breath" which, again both process and matter, is either inhaled and exhaled in breathing (πνεῦμ' ἀνεὶς ἐκ πνευμόνων, Eur. Or., 277; cf. Phoen., 851; Thuc., II, 49, 2; Plat. Tim., 66e, 91c), or medically, in distinction from ἀήρ as outside air, the "gas" or "flatulence" which circulates inside the organism τῇ μὲν ὄψει ἀφανής, τῷ δὲ λογισμῷ φανερός, Hippocr. De Flatibus, 3 (CMG, I, 1, 93, 5): πνεῦμα δὲ τὸ

---

[1] So W. Porzig, "Bedeutungsgeschichtliche Studien," *Idg. Forschungen*, 42 (1924), 226 f., 244 f.; also *Die Namen f. Satzinhalte im Griech. u. Idg.* (1942), 267 f.; cf. Schwyzer, I, 522, n. 13; Verbeke, 1 f., n. 1.

[2] Gk. philosophy has only the general use in mind when from Emped. (Fr., 100, 21 and 24 [Diels⁷, I, 347 ff.]) to Philo (Gig., 22) it defines πνεῦμα fairly consistently as κίνησις or ῥύσις ἀέρος (Ps.-Plat. Def., 414c; Aristot. Probl., 26, 2, p. 940b, 7) or as κινούμενος ἀήρ (Chrysipp. Fr., 471 [v. Arnim, II, 152, 31-35]) etc. (cf. Leisegang, *Hl. Geist*, 34 f.). It likes to combine with this the idea of a force or power which sweeps away by natural impulse : ὑπὸ βίας τοῦ πνεύματος, Aristoph. Nu., 164; cf. Hippocr. De Flatibus, 3 (CMG, I, 1, 92 f.); Polyb., 1, 44, 4. Philo Leg. All., I, 42 links herewith the distinction which he makes between πνεῦμα and πνοή in his exposition of Gn. 2:7, and which brings out a characteristic of πνεῦμα in the correlates ἰσχύς, εὐτονία and δύναμις.

[3] Auct. Sublim., 13, 2; Plut. Def. Or., 48 (II, 436 f.); Iambl. Myst., III, 11 (p. 126, 4); Ps.-Aristot. Mund., 4, p. 395b, 26 ff.; Valerius Maximus, I, 8, 10.

μὲν ἐν τοῖσι σώμασι φῦσα καλέεται, τὸ δὲ ἔξω τῶν σωμάτων ἀήρ, *ibid.*, 3 (Ι, 1, 92, 20 f.); cf. Plut. Quaest. Rom., 95 (II, 286e). The nuances vary from the strong "snorting" of an animal (Aesch. Sept. c. Theb., 464; Philo Aet. Mund., 128) to the light and quickly vanishing "breath" which fades away like a shadow or smoke, and which expresses the vanity of everything human : ἄνθρωπός ἐστι πνεῦμα καὶ σκιὰ μόνον, εἴδωλον ἄλλως. [4] When used with poetic pregnancy of inanimate objects, πνεῦμα denotes the living musical "voice" which human "breath" (cf. Aesch. Eum., 568) confers by blowing upon such instruments as the flute and trumpet : ἀδυβόα Φρυγίων αὐλῶν πνεύματι, Eur. Ba., 128. This technical musical function of πνεῦμα gives point and relevance to Paul's comparison between spiritually effected "tongues" and the blowing of a flute or trumpet (1 C. 14:7 f.), for in tongues, as in blowing, a φωνή is called forth by πνεῦμα.

3. Life. Breath may be discerned only in movement, and it is also a sign, condition and agent of life, which seems to be esp. tied up with breathing. Hence it is natural that *via* the sense "breath of life" (πνεῦμα βίου, Aesch. Pers., 507) πνεῦμα itself should take on the direct sense of "life" or "living creature," as in the fictitious funerary inscr. of Ninos : ἐγὼ Νίνος πάλαι ποτ' ἐγενόμην πνεῦμα, νῦν δ' οὐκ ἔτ' οὐδέν, ἀλλὰ γῆ πεποίημαι in Phoenix of Colophon Fr., 3, 16 f. (Diehl[3], III, 129), cf. IG, 14, 769. "To owe life to someone" is τὸ πνεῦμα ἔχειν διά τινα, Polyb., 31, 10, 4. Conversely dying is "to yield up the spirit of life" : ἀφῆκε πνεῦμα θανασίμῳ σφαγῇ, Eur. Hec., 571, expounded by the schol., *ad loc.* as follows : ἐξέπνευσε τὴν ψυχήν.

4. Soul. Next πνεῦμα takes on the meaning and function of → ψυχή, "soul." By virtue of its related character as the breath or principle of life, πνεῦμα is largely coterminous with ψυχή, and hence can easily be used in place of it,[5] so that Suid., *s.v.* finally gives the brief definition : πνεῦμα ἡ ψυχὴ τοῦ ἀνθρώπου. [6]

On the one side, then, πνεῦμα is an element (along with earth, water and fire) from which the human body is made, Epict. Diss., III, 13, 14 f. On the other, like ψυχή, it stands in contrast to the σῶμα with which it is bound in life. At death it is separated from this, [7] for, breath-like, it escapes with the last breath, returning to fulfil its higher destiny in the element from which it came or in the upper region to which it is by nature related, in the atmosphere of heaven or the aether (which later in Stoic teaching was equated with πνεῦμα as a kind of *quinta essentia*): ὅθεν δ' ἕκαστον ἐς τὸ φῶς ἀφίκετο, ἐνταῦθ' ἀπελθεῖν, πνεῦμα μὲν πρὸς αἰθέρα, τὸ σῶμα δ' ἐς γῆν, Eur. Suppl., 532 ff.; cf. Eur. Fr., 971 (TGF, 674), ἄνω τὸ πνεῦμα διαμενεῖ κατ' οὐρανόν, Epicharm. Fr., 22 (Diels[7], I, 202, 5); cf. Epigr. Graec., 250, 6; 613, 6.

5. Transferred Meaning : Spirit. In the metaphorical speech of poetry in particular, concrete natural processes such as the blowing of the wind or breathing express corresponding experiences of mental or spiritual reality. πνεῦμα is more or less strongly spiritualised and takes on the transferred sense of any kind of breath or spirit which blows in interpersonal relations or from the invisible world of the divine. On the basis of the concrete sense of a favourable or unfavourable wind for sailing, Eur. Herc. Fur., 216 speaks fig. of the θεοῦ πνεῦμα which exalts a man but which can also change into a πνεῦμα συμφορᾶς, such as Thoas sees at work in the flight of Iphigeneia, Eur. Iph. Taur., 1317. Another *wind* blows in the affairs of men or the state, the same *spirit* is not present as it once was between citizens and states, when πίστις dies and

---

[4] Soph. Fr., 12 (TGF, 133); cf. Nicarch. Anth. Pal., XI, 110, 4; Xenophanes Fr., 1 (Diels[7], I, 113, 28); Plat. Phaed., 70a, 77d-e; M. Ant., 2, 2.

[5] Xenophanes Fr., 1 (Diels[7], I, 113, 28); Zeno Fr., 136 (v. Arnim, I, 38, 6-9), 140 (I, 38, 30-33), 715 (II, 205, 10-15), 774 (II, 217, 13-17), 798 (II, 221, 3-5); Epict. Diss., III, 3, 22.

[6] It is worth noting that the development of the Gk. view of the soul was in terms of → ψυχή rather than πνεῦμα, cf. W. Jaeger, *D. Theol. d. frühen griech. Denker* (1953), esp. 88-106, 241 f., n. 63.

[7] Demosth. Or., 60, 24 : τά τε τούτων πνεύματ' ἀπηλλάγη τῶν οἰκείων σωμάτων, Epict. Diss., II, 1, 17: θάνατος τί ἐστι; ... τὸ σωμάτιον δεῖ χωρισθῆναι τοῦ πνευματίου, ὡς πρότερον ἐκεχώριστο.

ἀπιστία reigns, Soph. Oed. Col., 611 ff. How the concrete and spiritual meanings inter-fuse may be seen in a passage like Aesch. Suppl., 29 f.: When the fleeing Hiketides ask that their homeland Argos may receive them with the merciful breath of the land (αἰδοίῳ πνεύματι χώρας), it is almost impossible to say whether the basis of the poetic image of the spirit or atmosphere of religious uprightness and awe is the physical phenomenon and actuality of the wind of the country or the physiological breath of its inhabitants. By way of analogy the lit. and transf. usage constantly interfuses, so that even in the most developed spiritual sense one can better understand the fig. use of πνεῦμα the more closely one takes into account the concrete reference. [8] As πνεῦμα is palpable in the case of the snorting animal, so in men and gods, as the breath which is exhaled by them and imparted to another, it is a visible image and sign of the in-visible force or influence which for good or ill one has to receive from them : ὁ ῎Ερως ... οὐδὲ ἑνὶ πνεύματι τὰς ἡμετέρας ψυχὰς ἐρεθίζων ... δισσὰ γὰρ ὄντως κατὰ τὸν τραγικὸν (fr. adespotum, 187 [TGF, 878]) πνεύματα πνεῖ ὁ ῎Ερως (Ps.-Luc. Amores, 37). In accordance with its etym. πνεῦμα is often used of abstract concepts, esp. those which express excitement of spirit, of λύσσης πνεῦμα μάργον in which a man, no longer master of his tongue (γλώσσης ἀκρατής), utters confused speeches (θολεροὶ λόγοι) in a kind of glossolalia (with ref. to Io, Aesch. Prom., 883 ff.), of θυμοῦ καὶ ὀργῆς πνεύματα (Themist. Orationes, I, 7a), of the ἄγρια ... χαλεπῆς πνεύματα θευφορίης of a raving priest of Cybele whom an αὔρη δαίμονος saves from certain death, Dioscorides Anth. Pal., VI, 220. [9]

6. πνεῦμα and νοῦς. It is justifiable and meaningful to transl. by "spirit" in contexts such as this. For the word "spirit" (cf. Germ. *Geist*) originally means "wind" or "breath," and under the influence of the same experience has gone through a par. development to πνεῦμα (Lat. *spiritus*). [10] In the transf. employment of πνεῦμα for mental and spiritual realities profane Gk. firmly maintains the basic etym. idea of a powerful, material, moving breath with its many functions in man and the cosmos. [11] On the other hand, it makes it clear that in distinction from theoretical νοῦς (→ IV, 954 f.), which in its contemplation of things does not essentially do more than "touch" (θιγγάνει, Aristot. Metaph., XI, 7, p. 1072b, 21), the characteristic feature of the Gk. concept of spirit, as

---

[8] In the light of this Kerényi, 33-40 compares the discussion with Nicodemus (Jn. 3:1-8) and the story of Pentecost (Ac. 2:1-4) with the revelation of Apollo imparted to the sibyl of Cumae in Verg. Aen., 6, 42-53, 74 ff., and he is thus able to find in the concept and ex-perience of spirit, as represented by πνεῦμα, a pt. in which Christianity and antiquity are in agreement from the standpt. of religious phenomenology. The specific quality of spirit is, of course, just as different as the nature of the deity from which it comes, whether this be the θεὸς τοῦ κυρίου ἡμῶν ᾿Ιησοῦ Χριστοῦ (Eph. 1:17), Apollo of Delphi, or the storm-breathing God of Goethe's *Wanderers Sturmlied*. Cf. O. Becker, "Das Bild des Weges u. verwandte Vorstellungen im frühgr. Denken," *Herm. Einzelschrift*, 4 (1937), Index s.v. πνέω, πνεῦμα.

[9] To be distinguished from this is a usage which is not secular Gk. but strongly influenced by Heb. even to the pt. sometimes of personification. This makes the most varied abstract concepts dependent on πνεῦμα by a gen. of quality.

[10] For the German *Geist* cf. R. Hildebrand, Art. "Geist," *Deutsches Wörterb. v. J. u. W. Grimm*, IV, 1, 2 (1897), esp. 2623-2626.

[11] The transf. use of the group πνέω (πνεῦμα), ἐπίπνοια for the spiritual is notably limited in class. Gk. to the emotional and affective aspects of spiritual life ; the noetic aspects are distinguished from these. Nevertheless a certain original ref. to the noetic side has been sought in the etym. relationship of *πνέϝω/πνεῦμα to the Homeric πεπνυμένος in the sense "intelligent" (lit. "inbreathed"). This argument cannot be accepted, however, since nowadays πεπνυμένος is no longer related to the root πνεϝ- but to a special basic root for "intelligent" : πινυτός = ἔμφρων, σώφρων, cf. H. Frisk, "Gr. Wortprobleme," *Eranos*, 43 (1945), 223-225; A. Nehring, "Homer's Descriptions of Syncopes," *Class. Phi-lology*, 42 (1947), 111 [A. Debrunner]. Apart from this, the noetic element had completely disappeared in the period after Homer. Noetic functions in the sense of Ps.-Plat. Ax., 370c were indirectly ascribed to πνεῦμα only later in Stoic and Neo-Pythagorean epistemology, → 355, 15 ff.

represented by πνεῦμα, is that of something which is elementally dynamic, which fills vitally, which snatches away in enthusiasm. [12] Two basically different forms of the being and action of the spirit are expressed by the two words πνεῦμα and νοῦς. They are as different as the unmoving and calm medium of light, which for the pure and remote contemplation of the eye presents things statically as they are in truth, differs from the much more material and powerful movement of air, which by nature fills, permeates, seizes and embraces either beholder or object with elemental force, catching him up into tension or movement either ὡς ἀνέμου ῥιπὴ ἢ λεπτή τις αὔρα νοηθῆναι δυναμένη or οἱονεὶ μύρου τις ὀσμὴ ἢ θυμιάματος ἐκ συνθέσεως κατεσκευασμένου λεπτὴ διοδεύουσα δύναμις ἀνεπινοήτῳ τινὶ καὶ κρείττονι ἢ λόγῳ ἐστὶν ἐξειπεῖν εὐωδίᾳ, Hipp. Ref., V, 19, 3. The vocabulary which Hipp. uses here to describe the Gnostic and philosophical view of the spirit held by the Sethians shows that the anti-noetic concept behind the secular Gk. use of πνεῦμα was still in full force in this later period.

7. μαντικὸν πνεῦμα. On this basis, and along the lines of ἐπίπνοια (→ 343, 32 ff.), which is related both in stem and sense, πνεῦμα later acquires in manticism, and in poetry interpreted acc. to this model, the special meaning of a breath which inspires, stirs, enthuses and fills. As ἱερόν or δαιμόνιον (Democr. Fr., 18 [Diels[7], II, 146, 15]; Plut. De Exilio, 13 [II, 605a]; Dio C., 63, 14, 2), μαντικόν (Plut. Def. Orac., 40; 42 [II, 432d f; 433d]), ἐνθουσιαστικὸν πνεῦμα (Strabo, 9, 3, 5), [13] it is experienced by the select souls of poets, [14] priests and prophets, esp. the Pythia at Delphi, in specific physical and spiritual operations, Auct. Sublim., 8, 4; 13, 2; Dion. Hal. Ant. Rom., I, 31. For the range of meaning and content of μαντικὸν πνεῦμα cf. Poll. Onom., I, 15: εἴποις ἂν καὶ ἀτμὸν μαντικόν, καὶ ἆσθμα δαιμόνιον, καὶ θείαν αὔραν, καὶ ἄνεμον μαντικόν, καὶ φωνὴν προαγορευτικήν.

Finally, πνεῦμα is used more generally as a tt. for lofty speech in ancient rhetoric and literary aesthetics. It denotes here, not so much the inspiration, but rather the expressive and captivating flow of the orator or poet from whom the onrushing "breath" of poetry or address comes forth neither physically, spiritually, nor technically, Auct. Sublim., 9, 13; 33, 5; Dion. Hal. De Demosthene, 20, 22 (I, 170, 13; 177, 22 Radermacher); Luc. Encomium Demosthenis, 14; Horat. Sat., I, 4, 46 f. [15]

8. θεῖον πνεῦμα. In virtue of its uncontrollable elemental nature and its direct efficacy, πνεῦμα is often felt to be something divine, and in other spheres too it is thus predicated directly as θεῖον or θεῶν or θεοῦ πνεῦμα. The material content varies in detail. Sometimes the divine breath is an element in music (Eur. Fr., 192; TGF, 417), sometimes, as distinct from νοῦς, it is the essence of the almighty Hell. tyche (Menand. Fr., 482 [CAF, III, 139; cf. Polyb., 11, 19, 5]), a θεῖον ὄντως ἐν(ὸν) πνεῦμα τῇ ψυχῇ which makes possible knowledge of the processes of the universe (Ps.-Plat. Ax., 370c), the καθαρὸν δίκαιον ... πνεῦμα θεοῦ σωτῆρος (Collection of Ancient Gk. Inscr. in the Brit. Museum, IV, 2 [1916], 1062), or a πνεῦμα θεοῦ which may even conceive in a human woman, Plut. Numa, 4, 6 (I, 62c).

On the other hand, there is as yet no instance of the concept of a πνεῦμα ἅγιον in secular Gk. Here biblical Gk. has coined a new and distinctive expression for the very different, suprasensual, supraterrestrial and in part personal character and content which πνεῦμα has in Judaism and Christianity. An expression of this kind was bound to remain alien to the immanentist thinking of the Greek world. [16]

---

[12] Kerényi, 41; cf. J. Stenzel, "Zur Entwicklung d. Geistbegriffes in d. gr. Philosophie," Antike, 1 (1925), 244-272; also Platon der Erzieher (1928), 197-199.

[13] The special concept of Philo here finds linguistic expression when he speaks of the θεῖον καὶ προφητικὸν πνεῦμα, Fug., 186, cf. Verbeke, 250 ff.

[14] Cf. Lat. spiritus in Horat. Carm., IV, 6, 29; II, 16, 38. On Democr. Fr., 18 → 344, n. 42.

[15] Cf. F. Wehrli, "Der erhabene u. d. schlichte Stil in d. poetisch-rhetorischen Theorie d. Antike," Phyllobolia (1946), 11 f.

[16] Cf. E. Williger, "Hagios, Untersuchungen zur Terminologie d. Heiligen in d. hellenisch-hellenistischen Religionen," RVV, 19, 1 (1922), 96 f. The lexical question is not at all

The usage of the NT was felt to be equally distinctive in Latin. Here πνεῦμα ἅγιον was not translated by the current and in part Stoically loaded terms *sacer* or *divinus spiritus* or *afflatus,* which were equivalents for the Gk. θεῖον or ἱερὸν πνεῦμα in the religious and philosophical tradition, [17] but by the special and no less original expression *spiritus sanctus.*

9. θεὸς πνεῦμα. As with so many other basic cosmological concepts (→ λόγος, → νόμος, → νοῦς), the development in profane Gk. reaches a climax when in the religious philosophy of Stoicism πνεῦμα as a cosmic and universal power or substance, as ἡ ... ἐν φυτοῖς καὶ ζῴοις καὶ διὰ πάντων διήκουσα ἔμψυχός τε καὶ γόνιμος οὐσία acc. to the definition of Ps.-Aristot. Mund., IV, 10, p. 394b, 8 ff., is used linguistically for the being and manifestation of deity itself : ὁρίζονται δὲ τὴν τοῦ θεοῦ οὐσίαν οἱ Στωϊκοὶ οὕτως· πνεῦμα νοερὸν καὶ πυρῶδες (Aetius Placita, I, 6 [v. Arnim, II, 1009]); θεὸν ἀποφαίνονται ... καὶ πνεῦμα μὲν διῆκον δι' ὅλου τοῦ κόσμου (*ibid.,* I, 7, 33 [v. Arnim, II, 1027]; cf. Sext. Emp. Pyrrh. Hyp., III, 218 [v. Arnim, II, 1037]; Tert. Apol., 21, 10; Orig. Cels., 6, 71).

10. Ungreek Development of the Meaning. From the time of Wis. (cf. 7:22) and Philo (→ 372 ff.), under Jewish and Chr. influence, there is a final non-Greek development in two different but complementary directions. In the first, as in the NT and the Herm. writings, πνεῦμα is cut off from its basic relation to nature, transcendentally spiritualised, and hypostatised and personified as an independent, personally living and active cosmological and soteriological Spirit or God *sui generis,* whether of supreme or lower rank. Hence in the Κόρη κόσμου Minos is described as ἰσχυρότατον ... πνεῦμα, ἀκατάληπτον μὲν περιοχῇ σώματος, δυνάμει δὲ φρονήσεως ὑπάρχον ... τὸ σῶμα μὲν κατὰ τύπον ἀνδρὸς περικείμενον καὶ καλὸν καὶ σεμνοπρεπὲς ὄν (Stob. Ecl., I, 399, 10 ff.; cf. I, 389, 6 ff.). As a Gk. philosopher Celsus pours scorn on unknown wandering prophets of Phoenicia and Palestine who say about themselves : ἐγὼ ὁ θεός εἰμι ἢ θεοῦ παῖς ἢ πνεῦμα θεῖον. ἥκω δέ· ... ἐγὼ δὲ σῶσαι θέλω, Orig. Cels., 7, 9, cf. Preis. Zaub., II, 69, 174 f.: ὅ[τι] με ἔ[λυσε]ν τὸ ἅγιον πνεῦμα, τὸ μονογενές, τὸ ζῶν. In the second non-Gk. direction, esp. in the non-literary and strongly syncretistic usage of the Gk. magic pap., πνεῦμα is materialised downwards into the magical and demonic sphere to denote supernatural spirits or intermediaries, whether good or evil : δαίμονες καὶ πνεύματα, IG, XIV, 872, 3. As αὐτοφανῆ (Iambl. Myst., II, 3 [p. 73, 13 ff.]; II, 10 [p. 93, 9 ff.]) and ἀέρια πνεύματα (opp. καταχθόνιοι δαίμονες, Ps.-Callisth., 1, 1) which inhabit the air they do good or harm by means of the demonic magical power which emanates from them (δαιμόνιον πνεῦμα, Preis. Zaub., I, 170; II, 69 etc.), and with which the magician or prophet must fill himself or his object (*ibid.,* II, 25; 101) if he is to be able to carry out his practices, whose supreme goal is the deifying and immortality of the initiate ἀθανάτῳ πνεύματι, *ibid.,* I, 90 and 94. [18]

II. πνεῦμα in Mythology and Religion.

1. Life-creating πνεῦμα.

The concept of πνεῦμα in the Gk. and Hell. world develops on the basis laid down in specific modalities of general usage and in the earliest notions of popular religious belief concerning the direct and comprehensive connection of being and operation be-

---

irrelevant, as Büchsel thinks (52); the new and non-Gk. extension of πνεῦμα from the time of Philo is nowhere so evident as in the corresponding usage which goes beyond adjectives like ἅγιον or → προφητικόν and in expressions like εἶναι ἐν πνεύματι (R. 8:9), γίνεσθαι εἰς πνεῦμα (1 C. 15:45) etc., invades even the syntax, cf. Verbeke, 147, 393-396.

[17] Cic. Pro Archia, 8, 17; Nat. Deor., II, 7, 19; Divin., I, 6, 18; Valerius Maximus, I, 8, 10; Ps.-Quint. Declamationes, 4, 3; Sen. Epist. Morales, 41, 2; 66, 12; Dialogi, XII, 8, 3.

[18] Good material in Reitzenstein Hell. Myst., 159; Verbeke, esp. 323, n. 290; Festugière, 297 f., n. 4 f.

tween wind, breath, soul, and the power of generation, life and spirit. [19] In the first instance these ideas are in part expressed by older or contemporary synonyms related in stem or sense, e.g., πνοιή, ἐπίπνοια, ἐπίπνους, εἰσ-, ἐμ-, ἐπιπνέω, ἄνεμος, ἀήρ, ψυχή, which are later systematised under the single term πνεῦμα. In more than one respect wind is offered by nature itself as a category of being and a form for that which is without beginning before all beginning. The concept of the generative and life-creating cosmogonic power of wind is thus widespread in primitive mythology. [20] "Fructified by the wind" is a principle in the most ancient Orphic cosmogony of the cosmic egg, Orph. Fr., 1 (Kern). As a first-begotten the god Eros or Phanes, who brings all things to the light, proceeds from this προνοίαι τοῦ ἐνόντος ἐν αὐτῶι θείου πνεύματος, 56 (Kern). In the prose theogony of Pherekydes of Syros (6th cent. B.C.) πνεῦμα, with fire, water, earth and a Ταρταρίη μοῖρα, is one of the 5 original, spatial, cosmic regions of matter which Chronos brought forth from himself, A 8 (Diels[7], I, 46, 10). Here a concept of Ionic natural science, which was originally cosmological and physical, is artificially mythologised in ancient style. There thus begins the tradition of a φυσικὴ θεολογία such as is found later, not without the influence of Stoicism and Gn. 1:2, in Hell. and imperial cosmogonies, cf. the Egyptian cosmogony of Hermopolis (Eus. Praep. Ev., III, 2, 6 f.; Diod. S., I, 12, 1 f.) or the Phoenician cosmogony of Philo of Byblos-Sanchunjaton (c. 100 A.D.) (Diod. S., I, 10, 1-2). [21] Here πνεῦμα has an established and even a privileged place.

The ancient popular belief in conception by the wind (esp. in the animal kingdom), though changed into mythological speculation on the cosmos in Orphism, continues in the poetic sphere, cf. in Hom. Il., 20, 223 f. the myth of the fructifying of the mares of Dardanos by the wind-god Boreas in the form of a stallion, or in Vergil the miraculous story of the Thracian mares. [22] From poetry the mythologoumenon passed into Gk. natural science [23] and then finally into the Stoic theory of pneuma. The cosmic wind

---

[19] This sphere has hardly yet been considered as a whole, not even in R. Muth, *Träger der Lebenskraft, Ausscheidungen d. Organismus im Volksglauben d. Antike* (1954). Yet breath in comparison with seed, blood, tears, sweat, spittle, urine and excrement is the physically most refined and least material secretion of the organism which is thus particularly well adapted to represent spiritual powers not merely substantially but also in terms of their impartation and operation. Of basic importance in this connection is Plut. Quaest. Conv., V, 7, 2 (II, 680 f-681a). Cf. also Fehrle, 85-89; S. Eitrem, *Opferritus u. Voropfer d. Griechen u. Römer* (1914), Index, *s.v.* "Hauch"; Leisegang, *Hl. Geist*, 50-54; W. Aly, Art. "blasen," *Handwörterbuch d. deutschen Aberglaubens*, 1 (1927), 1354-1360; F. X. Lukmann, "Das Anblasen des Teufels beim Taufgelöbnis," *Festschr. f. Rudolf Egger*, I (1952), 343-346.

[20] Cf. E. Riess, Art. "Aberglaube," Pauly-W., 1 (1894), 42; Leisegang, *Pneuma Hagion*, 71; W. Schmid, *Gesch. d. gr. Lit., Hndbch. kl. AW*, VII, 1, 2 (1934), 440, n. 7 (with refs. and bibl. for Soph. Fr., 477, ed. A. C. Pearson[2] [1917], 130 f.); V. Lundström, "Mons Tagrus," *Eranos*, 37 (1939), 84; Nilsson, I (1941), 655, n. 1; S. Morenz, "Ägypten u. d. altorphische Kosmogonie," *Aus Antike u. Orient* (1950), 71-103. On the historical position of Orphism as a new and speculative stage of the religious thought of Greece reached in conflict with contemporary, rational, Ionic science, cf. the basic work of Jaeger (→ n. 6), 69-87.

[21] Phoenician cosmogony, which presupposes the cosmological thought and speculation of the Gks., corresponds in principle and structure to what we know of the cosmogonic lit. of the so-called Orphic circle in the Hell. and Neo-Platonic period. As these tractates rest on the ancient name and venerable authority of Orpheus, so Philo of Byblos, to guarantee the cogency of his presentation and esp. its antiquity, appeals to a supposed underlying Phoenician work of Sanchunjaton (2nd half of the 2nd millennium B.C.) which he has translated. The question of the historicity and value of this older Phoenician original has been comprehensively discussed by O. Eissfeldt, "Taautos u. Sanchunjaton," SAB (1952), No. 1, esp. 25-70; also "Sanchunjaton v. Berut u. Ilumilku v. Ugarit," *Beiträge z. Religionsgesch. d. Altertums*, 5 (1952). Referring to recent finds in Ras Shamra and Boghazköy, Eissfeldt definitely favours its historicity.

[22] Georg., III, 274 f.; cf. Varro, De Re Rustica, II, 1, 19; Plin. Nat. Hist., 10, 166.

[23] Cf. Aristot. Hist. An., VI, 2, p. 560a, 7 f.: φαίνονται δεχόμεναι τὰ πνεύματα αἱ ὄρνιθες. Schol. Nicand. Alexipharm., 560 : αἱ ὀρειναὶ χελῶναι ὑπ' ἀνέμων πληροῦνται

is a generative potency : *ille generabilis rerum naturae spiritus huc illuc tamquam in utero vagus*, Plin. Nat. Hist., 2, 116. In the later mythologoumenon of the creator of man, Prometheus, Zeus has the winds blow life into his creatures, Etym. M., 471, 1, *s.v.* Ἰκόνιον, cf. Gn. 2:7.[24] Acc. to Lucian, Toxaris, 38 the Scythians swear by the god Ἄνεμος, who is for them ζωῆς αἴτιος. Anthropogony by wind is parodied in Luc. Vera Historia, I, 22, which tells how moon-men, who were first brought out dead (νεκρά) from the tibia of men, were brought to life when exposed with their mouths open to the wind : ἐκθέντες δὲ αὐτὰ πρὸς τὸν ἄνεμον κεχηνότα ζῳοποιοῦσιν.[25] The first development of the idea of the wind as genitor of life is found in Egypt. In the cosmogony of Hermopolis the breath of wind is linked with the god Amun and concentrated into mythical and even theological form.[26] Interpretatio Graeca equated the god of moving air in his life-creating omnipotence with Zeus and πνεῦμα : τὸ μὲν οὖν πνεῦμα Δία προσαγορεῦσαι μεθερμηνευομένης τῆς λέξεως, ὃν αἴτιον ὄντα τοῦ ψυχικοῦ τοῖς ζῴοις ἐνόμισαν (sc. οἱ Αἰγύπτιοι) ὑπάρχειν πάντων οἰονεί τινα πατέρα, Diod. S., I, 12, 1 f.; Plut. Is. et Os., 36 (II, 365d).

The earliest Greek witness to the Egyptian theologoumenon is Aeschylus, who in Suppl. is not only familiar with the Amun-Re of the Egyptians as "life-begetting Zeus" (584 f., cf. 212 f.), but who also offers the only Greek instance of a god begetting a divine son in a mortal woman by his breath. This is the myth of the miraculous generation of Epaphos, i.e., of the Egyptian Apis-bull, "by the touch and breath of Zeus" (ἐξ ἐπαφῆς κἀξ ἐπιπνοίας Διός, Suppl., 18 f.). The "venerable mother" (141), daughter of a king, the Argive Io, a kind of Isis, bears Epaphos, the steer of Zeus, in the land of Zeus, Egypt (5). He is "a fruit of a touch from the breath of Zeus" (44 ff.). Under the powerful hand and breath of the god, according to the law ὁ τρώσας ἰάσεται, the violation, straying and affliction of Io find their beginning in the conception and their gracious redemptive end in the birth : βίᾳ δ' ἀπημάντῳ σθένει καὶ θείαις ἐπιπνοίαις παύεται, 575 ff. In the style of pious legend the divine child is hailed as "the blameless son who is always blessed through a long life," and the whole land rejoices at his birth with the cry : "This is indeed the son of life-begetting Zeus," 581-585.[27] In ἐπαφή

ὥσπερ αἱ ὄρτυγες. Geoponica (ed. H. Beckh [1895]), 9, 3 : οἱ ἄνεμοι οὐ τὰ φυτὰ μόνον, ἀλλὰ καὶ πάντα ζῳογονοῦσιν.

[24] S. Eitrem, "Die vier Elemente in d. Mysterienweihe," Symb. Osl., 4 (1926), 57 refers to the Capitoline replica of the Prometheus sarcophogus, where Prom. stands before his model of a man and a wind god blows into a shell trumpet as a sign of the ἐμπνευμάτωσις and endowment with a voice which is taking place here. ἐμψύχωσις by Athena, on the other hand, is indicated by the butterfly which the goddess holds over the head of the newly created man.

[25] For all the differences R. 8:11 is at least comparable in formal structure. Here from within, not from without, νεκρά or θνητὰ σώματα are made alive by ἄνεμος or πνεῦμα in the framework of a cosmogony which in this "pneumatic" way first makes of man a real υἱός and τέκνον (R. 8:14-16). The exaggerated physiological background of the concept in Luc. is the very thing which brings out the more vividly the complete spiritualisation in Pl., though → n. 591.

[26] On the Egyptian aspect cf. esp. Morenz (particularly 89-103), who claims an Egypt. origin for the heart of ancient Orphic cosmogony, the cosmic egg fructified by the wind (71-73). Jaeger, appealing to the zoomorphic feeling of the Gks. for nature, independently pronounces against an oriental derivation, 80.

[27] Cf. Hdt., III, 27: ἐφάνη Αἰγυπτίοισι ὁ Ἆπις, τὸν Ἕλληνες Ἔπαφον καλέουσι· ἐπιφανέος δὲ τούτου γενομένου αὐτίκα οἱ Αἰγύπτιοι ... ἦσαν ἐν θαλίῃσι ... τότε πάντες Αἰγύπτιοι κεχαρηκότες ὁρτάζοιεν.

and ἐπίπνοια the two different modes of genesis [28] are remarkably associated, [29] though this is only the one divine act. Theology, confronted by religious tradition [30] and seeking, if possible, to preserve it, has a liking for this type of fusion of miracles. ἐπίπνοια, since it is not, like ἐπαφή, constructed by the poet himself out of name-etymology, is the older and original miracle. It reflects the Egyptian view in Greek form. The idea of the conception and birth of a son of god by divine breath, which has passed into Aeschylus' belief in Zeus, is the more significant historically and theologically in that it does not occur later even in the Hellenistic sphere. This differentiates it from all other forms of miraculous conception and rules out automatically any possibility of a direct connection with Christ's birth of the Spirit, → E, I, 6. [31]

On the other hand, there are in Greece, as in Egypt, many instances of a decorous, sublimated and spiritualised understanding of conception which is not so completely removed from the world of sense as to be Docetic. Herodot., III, 28 shows acquaintance with the Egyptian tradition according to which the holy bull of Apis was born of a virgin cow, which was fructified by a beam of light from heaven (or the moon). Plut. Quaest. Conv., VIII, 1, 2 f. (II, 717d-718a) appeals to this in his discussion of the theologoumenon of Plato's sexual begetting as a παῖς θεοῖο (Hom. Il., 24, 259) by Apollo. God does not beget as man does διὰ σπέρματος but by another kind of power (ἄλλη δὲ δυνάμει). [32] As in the process of creating the world, he activates a generative principle in matter and thus brings to birth. [33] God does not have intercourse with man as husband with wife. "In other ways, through other forms of handling and touching, he gives the mortal another direction and fills it with more divine seed." The Egyptian μῦθος of the birth of Apis ἐπαφῇ τῆς σελήνης is adduced in proof. [34] The difference in mode of begetting is due to the difference in the essence and substantiality of the gods, who are here, among other things, expressly set ἐν πνεύμασι. The differences in the divine mode of operation according to πνεῦμα, ἐπίπνοια, ἐπαφή, σέλας or φῶς decrease in importance, however, when in later Greek these terms are commonly used as correlates, synonyms or equivalents, → 351, 13 ff. The more unequivocally is the parallel critical, philosophical discussion of Egyptian speculation about the ἱερὸς γάμος set under the concept πνεῦμα θεοῦ in Plut. Numa, 4, 4 ff.

---

[28] Aesch. Prom., 849 ff. speaks of Διὸς γεννήματα in a similar connection, cf. Plat. Soph., 266d.

[29] Touch and breath are also associated elsewhere: How could God have known the ψυχή if he had not breathed into it (His) πνεῦμα and touched it (εἰ μὴ ἐνέπνευσε καὶ ἥψατο αὐτῆς), asks Philo in Leg. All., I, 38 in a passage which is important for the πνεῦμα concept. Spiritualised, the impartation of the Spirit is linked with the laying on of hands in Ac. 8:17 ff.

[30] Cf. Aesch. Suppl., 291-299; Schol., 580.

[31] On the notion of pneuma in the story of Epaphos cf. S. Eitrem, Art. "Io," Pauly-W., 9 (1916), 1734; Weinreich, AH, 19-21, 23-25; J. Vürtheim, Aischylos' Schutzflehende (1928), 30-48; esp. W. Kranz, Stasimon (1933), 102-106, 295; F. Zucker, "Athen u. Ägypten bis auf den Beginn d. hell. Zeit," Aus Antike u. Orient (1950), 150.

[32] Just. Apol., I, 33, 6 makes the same distinction in relation to Lk. 1:35 : οὐ διὰ συνουσίας, ἀλλὰ δυνάμεως.

[33] τοῦ θεοῦ τῇ ὕλῃ γόνιμον ἀρχήν, ὑφ' ἧς ἔπαθεν καὶ μετέβαλεν, ἐντεκόντος· "λήθουσι γάρ τοι κἀνέμων διέξοδοι θήλειαν ὄρνιν, πλὴν ὅτ xν παρῇ τόκος" (= Soph. Fr., 436 [TGF, 236]; → 340, n. 20).

[34] Cf. Plut. Is. et Os., 43 (II, 368c): τὸν δὲ Ἆπιν εἰκόνα μὲν Ὀσίριδος ἔμψυχον εἶναι, γίνεσθαι δὲ ὅταν φῶς ἐρείσῃ γόνιμον ἀπὸ τῆς σελήνης καὶ καθάψηται βοὸς ὀργώσης. On the spiritual character of the moon in Stoicism cf. Pohlenz, Die Stoa, I, 223.

(I, 62b/c). With regard to the question how far not merely φιλία but even corporal fellowship between a god and a man is conceivable, Plut. does not find incredible the distinction whereby the πνεῦμα of a god may draw near to an earthly woman and propagate in her certain seeds for the rise of life. For a man, physical intercourse with a god (or goddess) [35] is in his eyes quite impossible, Numa, 4, 6 (I, 62c). [36]

What has become, more weakly, the theme of theological speculation in Plut. is in Aesch. a pious myth expressing his faith in Zeus, Suppl. 532 ff. The style and ethos of Aesch. show no trace of "unrestricted delight in the erotic situation." [37] His basic interest is in the miraculous nature of the birth of a son of god by the pneuma. This son, as his mother foretells, is not just one of the many children whom Zeus sires in myth. He is the forefather of the race from which there will spring, after 13 generations, the hero and saviour Heracles. Through him Zeus will bring to an end the sufferings of Prometheus, the representative of mankind, Aesch. Prom., 771 ff.; Schol., 774. His virgin mother, [38] as a kind of *mater dolorosa,* is depicted as a gracious example of the εὐμενὴς βία, Suppl., 1069. In the spiritual-sensory form of ἐπίπνοια and ἐπαφή Zeus had caused this to rule in her, 574 ff.

2. πνεῦμα and Inspiration.

The "breath" of wind or of breathing is a form of being and mode of presentation in which esp. higher divine powers of the most varied kinds, which man cannot control, impart something of the vital essence and power which they are to man or nature, whether it be for good or evil. Here again the originally sensory element of blowing upon or breathing in is never wholly eliminated. Thus by breathing the πνοιή Βορέαο the mortally wounded Sarpedon, whose ψυχή and θυμός have already departed, awakens yet again to a final gasp, Hom. Il., 5, 696 ff. Athena breathes μένος into Diomedes and Apollo into Aeneas, 10, 482; 20, 110. A god breathes ἀρετή into the Eleans in the battle, Xenoph. Hist. Graec., VII, 4, 32. A δαίμων breathes cunning into Penelope (ἐνέπνευσε, Hom. Od., 19, 138). The sweet breath of Demeter causes the little Demophoon to flourish like a god, Hom. Hymn. Cer., 238. Polyb. speaks of the ἐπιπνεῖν of *tyche,* or generally of a θεία τις ἐπίπνοια which fills those who make history in the eyes of the πολλοί, 11, 19, 5; 10, 2, 12; 10, 5, 7. [39]

Plato still uses the older term ἐπίπνοια for divine inspiration; πνεῦμα is for him a word used only in natural science. Thus certain regions, as domains of specific deities, stand under a θεία τις ἐπίπνοια Leg., V, 747d-e. The authority of ancient oracles such as those of Delphi or Dodona is linked up with the co-operation of a divinely derived ἐπίπνοια, Leg., V, 738c. To the participants the poetic discussions of the Leges seem to be guided οὐκ ἄνευ τινὸς ἐπιπνοίας θεῶν, Leg., VII, 811c. According to the basic principle of Resp. (VI, 499b) the true love of the kings of this world is impelled to true philosophy ἔκ τινος θείας ἐπιπνοίας. In Phaedr., 265b Plato systematised and defined the notions of the Gk. world concerning the operation of divine inspiration. Four forms of ἐπίπνοια are distinguished and allotted to Apollo, Dionysus, the Muses, and Aphrodite

---

[35] Plut. Quaest. Conv., VIII, 1, 3 (II, 718b).

[36] Cf. Reitzenstein Hell. Myst., 245 f.; Norden, 73-82; Büchsel, 191-201; → παρθένος, V, 830, 8 ff.

[37] Büchsel, 192 f. thinks pagan conception-myths, even though they did not know the story of Epaphos, were all more or less influenced by it.

[38] Aesch. Prom., 704-898; Nonnus Dionys., 3, 284 ff.

[39] Cf. the same view in the Lat. use of *afflare* and *afflatus* (*divinus*). Venus confers on Aeneas a fiery glance (*laetos oculis adflarat honores,* Verg. Aen., I, 590 f.), while in 7, 350 f. the serpent sent by the fury Allecto to the Laurentian queen Amata *attactu nullo vipeream inspirans animam* thereby drives her mad. Again, in Ovid Metam., 8, 819 f. the goddess Fames takes possession of Erysichthon when she *se ... viro inspirat faucesque et pectus et ora afflat.*

with Eros. Similarly, manticism, mysticism,[40] poetry and eroticism[41] are the four cultural spheres of Gk. life. For Plato these are linked by the fact that all are dependent on the work of the divine pneuma.

a. In Poetry.

Already when Hes. was called to be a poet the Muses breathed a divine voice into him (ἐνέπνευσαν δέ μοι αὐδὴν θείην) in order that he might proclaim the future as well as the past, Theog., 31 f., → 340 f., n. 24; 345, 31 ff. In Plat. Phaedr., 262d Socrates ironically makes the gods of the place or the singing cicadas responsible as οἱ τῶν Μουσῶν προφῆται for the divine gift of poetic and enthusiastic speech with which he is inspired. Eur. and Democr. seem to have brought the content of poetic inspiration under the rubric of πνεῦμα. The one refers to the θεῶν πνεῦμα which the poet needs, Fr., 192 (TGF, 417). The other speaks of the ἐνθουσιασμός and ἱερὸν πνεῦμα which alone makes all poetry what it is: ποιητὴς δὲ ἄσσα μὲν ἂν γράφηι μετ' ἐνθουσιασμοῦ καὶ ἱεροῦ πνεύματος, καλὰ κάρτα ἐστίν, Fr., 18 (Diels[7], II, 146, 14 f.).[42] From now on πνεῦμα is the fixed term for the divine power (Plat. Ion, 533d, 534c) of enthusiastic inspiration which in a θεία ἐξαλλαγή lifts the poet above the orders that normally apply (Plat. Phaedr., 265a),[43] carrying him along with it in the way known to the Pythia when she stands under the divine breath (κατ' ἐπίπνοιαν): πολλοὶ (sc. poets) γὰρ ἀλλοτρίῳ θεοφοροῦνται πνεύματι τὸν αὐτὸν τρόπον ὃν καὶ τὴν

---

[40] The divine breath plays a part in the Gk. mysteries when the Bacchantes are filled with μανία by the θεοῦ (Dionysus) πνοιαῖσιν, Eur. Ba., 1094, or when Dionysus and his slave Xanthias, on their journey into the underworld, receive a foretaste of the supreme degree of initiation as over them from flutes and torches αὔρα τις εἰσέπνευσε μυστικωτάτη, Aristoph. Ra., 313 f.; cf. 337 f. On the ἄγρια ... χαλεπῆς πνεύματα θευφορίης in the cult of Cybele → 337, 20 f. In the account of cultic marvels in Ael. Nat. An., 11, 16 a singular πνεῦμα θεῖον leads the virgins who offer sacrifices to the sacred snake in the grove of Juno of Lanuvium.

[41] The oldest belief in the generative power of breath, which, to speak in later terms, is σπέρμα as well as πνεῦμα (Diog. of Apoll. Fr., 6 [Diels[7], II, 62, 12]; Zeno Fr., 128 [v. Arnim, I, 36, 2 f.]; Chrysipp. Fr., 836 [v. Arnim, II, 227, 34 f.]), is still preserved in the periphrastic expressions εἰσπνήλας, εἴσπνηλος, εἰσπνεῖν, ἐμπνεῖσθαι which the Spartans used in connection with pederasty, Callim. Fr., 68; Schol. Theocr. Idyll. (ed. K. Wendel [1914]), 12, 13; Ael. Var. Hist., 3, 12; Plut. De Cleomene, 3 (I, 805). In this usage, however, there is already a first beginning of spiritualisation such as is found in the Platonic view of love. Acc. to this ἀρετή and a spiritual nature are breathed by the older into the younger in an act of spiritual generation, Xenoph. Symp., 4, 14; cf. R. Pfeiffer, Callimachus, I (1949), 74, Adnotatio ad loc.; also E. Bethe, "Die dorische Knabenliebe," Rhein. Mus., 62 (1907), 459-461; T. Hopfner, Art. "Mysterien," Pauly-W., 16, 2 (1935), 1327-1329; J. Stenzel, Platon d. Erzieher (1928), 201. Poetically humanised, πνοή and (ἐπι)πνέω are a mode of divine rule in love, whether it be that the πνοαὶ Ἀφροδίτης impel Helen (Eur. Iph. Aul., 69; cf. Theocr. Idyll., 17, 51 f.), Apollo πνέων χάριν strives for the love of the prophetess Cassandra (Aesch. Ag., 1206), or that prayer is made to the Loves to breathe equally upon two lovers, Theocr. Idyll., 12, 10; → 337, 12 f. Cf. the Lat. Venus adflat amores (Tib., II, 4, 57); adflat or aspirabat Amor (Tib., II, 1, 80; 3, 71).

[42] If the wording of the Fr. is authentic and the ἱερὸν πνεῦμα, which is almost tautological with ἐνθουσιασμός, does not bear the Christianising mark of Cl. Al. as compared with the formulation of the same thing in Dio Chrys. Or., 36, 1 ⟵ Democr. Fr., 21 (Diels[7], II, 147, 4 ff.). For ἱερὸν πνεῦμα in the sense of Platonic θεία ἐπίπνοια and in combination with the act of γράφειν is an expression and concept which, as a rendering of ἐνθουσιασμός, seems to be just as remote from the secular Gk. of the 4th cent. B.C. as from the Christian Cl. Al.

[43] This power which takes possession of man, which is ecstatic and temporarily supplants the νοῦς, and which is proper to the ἐπίπνοια ποιητικὴ Μουσῶν in Plat. (Phaedr., 265b), is ascribed by Philo to the θεῖον πνεῦμα: ἐξοικίζεται μὲν γὰρ ἐν ἡμῖν ὁ νοῦς κατὰ τὴν τοῦ θείου πνεύματος ἄφιξιν, κατὰ δὲ τὴν μετανάστασιν αὐτοῦ πάλιν εἰσοικίζεται, θέμις γὰρ οὐκ ἔστι θνητὸν ἀθανάτῳ συνοικῆσαι· διὰ τοῦτο ἡ δύσις τοῦ λογισμοῦ καὶ τὸ περὶ αὐτὸν σκότος ἔκστασιν καὶ θεοφόρητον μανίαν ἐγέννησε, Rer. Div. Her., 265; cf. Spec. Leg., IV, 49. On Plato's criticism → 347, 31 ff.

Πυθίαν λόγος ἔχει τρίποδι πλησιάζουσαν, Auct. Sublim., 13, 2; cf. 8, 4. [44] Poetry is regarded as ἐκβολή τοῦ δαιμονίου πνεύματος, ἥν ὑπὸ νόμον τάξαι δύσκολον, 33, 5. Manticism offers a prototype for this view of poetry. [45]

b. In Manticism.

The religious view of the pneuma takes on special significance at the pt. where it is most ancient, namely, in Apollonian inspiration-manticism. As a typical form of θεία μανία it was part of the pre-Gk. cult of the god in Asia Minor and came with him to Delphi. [46] In a kind of ἱερὸς γάμος Apollo fills a woman (his beloved in the myth, the priestess in the cultus) with his divine breath. Once again the matter is expressed first in a verb : ὅταν θεοῦ μαντόσυνοι πνεύσωσ᾽ ἀνάγκαι (Eur. Iph. Aul., 760 f.). Only much later, from the 1st cent. B.C. and not without Stoic influence, is the noun πνεῦμα used in learned discussion of the nature of divination and inspiration. πνεῦμα is here a tt. for the material force whose breath sets the Pythia in an ecstatic or rapturous state of prophetic infilling with deity. Because of this effect it is called ἐνθουσιαστικόν (Strabo, 9, 3, 5), ἱερόν (Dio C., 63, 14, 2), δαιμόνιον (Dion. Hal. Ant. Rom., 1, 31; Max. Tyr., 8, 1b), or simply μαντικὸν πνεῦμα (Poll. Onom., I, 15; Iambl. Myst., III, 11; Themist. Or., 4 [53a]). [47] It evokes physical effects as the wind may also do : streaming hair, panting breath, violent filling or seizing or snatching away in a Bacchantic frenzy of ἔκστασις or μανία : τοῦτο γὰρ μάντεως ἴδιον, τὸ ἐξεστηκέναι, τὸ ἀνάγκην ὑπομένειν, τὸ ὠθεῖσθαι, τὸ ἕλκεσθαι, τὸ σύρεσθαι ὥσπερ μαινόμενον, Chrys. in Epistulam I ad Corinth. Hom., 29 [MPG, 61, 241]). The associated complex of ideas is comprehensively elucidated in the list of synons. which Pol. Onom., I, 15 gives for being filled with πνεῦμα μαντικόν : ἔνθεος καὶ ἐπίπνους καὶ κάτοχος καὶ ἐπιτεθειασμένος καὶ κατειλημμένος ἐκ θεοῦ ... καὶ ἐνθουσιῶν καὶ κεκινημένος ἐκ τοῦ θεοῦ καὶ ἀναβεβακχευμένος καὶ πλήρης θεοῦ καὶ παραλλάττων ἐκ θεοῦ. The longest list of traditional effects of the spirit, which includes fiery phenomena, is to be found in Lucan De Bello Civili, V, 169-174, 190-193, 211-218. The supreme and (historically) most important result of the spirit's working is the giving of oracles : τὴν Πυθίαν ... δεχομένην τὸ πνεῦμα ἀποθεσπίζειν ἔμμετρά τε καὶ ἄμετρα, Strabo, 9, 3, 5; cf. Auct. Sublim., 13, 2; Orig. Cels., VII, 3. [48]

Theologically significant is the idea that πνεῦμα is the cause and source of ecstatic speech [49] in which the priestess becomes so directly the "divine voice" (→ 344, 5 ff.) that the Delphic πνεῦμα can be called the voice (ὀμφή) which blows forth from the στόμιον (ἀναπνεῖ, Ps.-Luc. Nero, 10; Dio C., 63, 14, 2).

---

[44] Again there are Lat. par.: Cic. Divin., I, 38, 80 : negat enim sine furore Democritus quemquam poetam magnum esse posse, quod idem dicit Plato ; De Orat., II, 46, 194 : saepe enim audivi poetam bonum neminem, id quod a Democrito et Platone in scriptis relictum esse dicunt, sine inflammatione animorum existere posse et sine quodam adflatu quasi furoris ; Pro Archia, 8, 17: poetam ... quasi divino quodam spiritu inflari. Horat. Carm., IV, 6, 29 : spiritum Phoebus mihi, Phoebus artem carminis nomenque dedit poetae ; cf. Reitzenstein Hell. Myst., 321; Leisegang, Hl. Geist, 132-134; Verbeke, 271 f., 283-285; O. Falter, Der Dichter u. sein Gott bei d. Griechen u. Römern (1934), 88-90.

[45] Cf. Pos. in Strabo, 10, 3, 9 : ὅ τε ἐνθουσιασμὸς ἐπίπνευσίν τινα θείαν ἔχειν δοκεῖ καὶ τῷ μαντικῷ γένει πλησιάζειν. On the other hand Suid., s.v. ἐπίπνοια has the direct rendering ἐνθουσιασμός.

[46] Cf. K. Latte, Art. "Orakel," Pauly-W., 18, 1 (1939), 839 f.; also "The Coming of the Pythia," HThR, 33 (1940), 9-18.

[47] In contrast Philo describes as a προφητικὸν πνεῦμα the comparable gift of divination given to Moses or some other chosen προφήτης, Fug., 186. He thus coins a linguistic expression for his very different view of pneuma, cf. Verbeke, 250-257.

[48] For details on the actual giving of the oracle cf. Amandry, 81-168.

[49] It is worth noting that secular antiquity does not speak of inspired writing, θεόπνευστος γραφή (2 Tm. 3:16; cf. Orig. Cels., 5, 60 : τὰ μὲν βιβλία θείῳ γεγράφθαι πνεύματι ὁμολογοῦμεν) → 454, 14 ff.

Lucan (De Bello Civili, V, 83) speaks of the *venti loquaces* of the site of the oracle. The coming and going of the πνεῦμα are characteristically linked with φωνή-effects, e.g., the sound of a wind-instrument (Vergil. Aen., 6, 82 ff.) or of the πρωκτός (Aristoph. Nu., 164), the ecstatic speech of the sibyl (Vergil. Aen., 6, 82 ff.) and Delphic prophecy (Diod. S., 16, 26), or the κραυγὴ ἰσχυρά of a Pythia into which an ἄλαλον καὶ κακὸν πνεῦμα came (Plut. Def. Orac., 51 [II, 438b]). From the standpoint of religious phenomenology the NT bears witness to the same original combination when it constantly links πνεῦμα and προφητεύειν (Lk. 1:67; 2 Pt. 1:21 etc.), or when it refers to speaking with tongues as a gift of the Spirit (a reflection of Pythian prophesying in Corinth, 1 C. 12-14),[50] or when it speaks of the crying out either of the unclean spirit which departs from a man or of the Holy Spirit which fills him.[51]

> Acc. to the traditional view the process of inspiration is as follows. The Pythia, sitting on a tripod, receives the mantic πνεῦμα as it rises up from a cleft in the earth below her: φασὶ δ᾽ εἶναι τὸ μαντεῖον ἄντρον κοῖλον κατὰ βάθους οὐ μάλα εὐρύστομον, ἀναφέρεσθαι δ᾽ ἐξ αὐτοῦ πνεῦμα ἐνθουσιαστικόν, ὑπερκεῖσθαι δὲ τοῦ στομίου τρίποδα ὑψηλόν, ἐφ᾽ ὃν τὴν Πυθίαν ἀναβαίνουσαν δεχομένην τὸ πνεῦμα ἀποθεσπίζειν, Strabo, 9, 3, 5. The reception is concretely depicted as an act of marriage. With splayed out thighs the Pythia receives the generative πνεῦμα in her womb[52] διὰ τῶν γεννητικῶν μορίων, and becomes pregnant by it: τὴν Πυθίαν λόγος ἔχει τρίποδι πλησιάζουσαν, ἔνθα ῥῆγμά ἐστι γῆς ἀναπνέον, ὥς φασιν, ἀτμὸν ἔνθεον αὐτόθεν ἐγκύμονα τῆς δαιμονίου καθισταμένην δυνάμεως παραυτίκα χρησμῳδεῖν κατ᾽ ἐπίπνοιαν, Auct. Sublim., 13, 2. Even to a relatively late period the idea enshrined the most ancient religious belief. The very age of the profane Gk. witnesses is against the judgment that this representation is simply a tendentious travesty on the part of the Church fathers.
>
> As a religious phenomenon the process of inspiration and experience of the divine spirit is most purely preserved in the poets. Verg. Aen., 6, 42-54, 77-82 describes the revelation of Apollo imparted to the sibyl Deiphobe in the cave of Cumae: *deus, ecce deus!* is her first word as she *adflata est numine ... iam propiore dei ... dehiscent attonitae magna ora domus ... at Phoebi nondum patiens immanis in antro bacchatur vates, magnum si pectore possit excussisse deum: tanto magis ille fatigat os rabidum fera corda domans, fingitque premendo. ostia iamque domus patuere ingentia centum sponte sua vatisque ferunt responsa per auras ...*, cf. Lucan De Bello Civile, V, 97 ff., 161-169.

The characteristics of experience of the divine spirit here are formally no different from those found in the NT in the story of Pentecost (Ac. 2:1-4), the conversation with Nicodemus (Jn. 3:1-8), or the outbreak of tongues in the church at Corinth (1 C. 12-14).[53] As something "other" (Auct. Sublim., 13, 2), which comes from without, πνεῦμα fills the interior of the house where those who seek the oracle are located either with a sound as of thunder or with a costly divine aroma;[54] it fills everything around, both men and beasts who draw near

---

[50] Cf. S. Eitrem, "Orakel u. Mysterien am Ausgang d. Antike," Albae Vigiliae, NF, 5 (1947), 42. G. Delling, however, links glossalalia with Dionysiac enthusiasm such as that in Eur. Ba., *Der Gottesdienst im NT* (1952), 39-47.

[51] → κράζω, III, 899-903.

[52] Schol. Aristoph. Plut., 39; Orig. Cels., III, 25; VII, 3; Chrys. in Epistulam I ad Corinth. Hom., 29 (MPG, 61, 242).

[53] Cf. Kerényi, 33-39.

[54] Plut. Def. Orac., 50 (II, 437c): ὁ γὰρ οἶκος, ἐν ᾧ τοὺς χρωμένους τῷ θεῷ καθίζουσιν ... εὐωδίας ἀναπίμπλαται καὶ πνεύματος, οἵας ἂν τὰ ἥδιστα καὶ πολυτελέστατα τῶν μύρων ἀποφορὰς ὥσπερ ἐκ πηγῆς τοῦ ἀδύτου προσβάλλοντος.

(Diod. S., 16, 26), but especially the inner being (ψυχή, *mens, pectus, corda*) of the sibyl or Pythia. Inasmuch as the latter becomes pregnant herewith, the bridegroom-spirit (cf. Rev. 22:17) is shown to be a male overcoming female resistance. It powerfully takes possession of the whole man and carries him off like a stormy wind, cf. 2 Pt. 1:21. It makes of him a winged and light being (κοῦφον ... καὶ πτηνὸν καὶ ἱερόν, Plat. Ion, 534b), as the poet is under the θεία ἐπίπνοια of the Muses. It catches him up out of the usual orders of life into the extraordinary state of ἔκστασις and μανία, chasing the understanding out of his head and taking its place, → lines 32 ff. Hand in hand herewith πνεῦμα has a liberating effect. It discloses and reveals [55] what was hidden, unknown, at most only suspected, and it thus establishes a relation to the truth of things, Cic. Divin., I, 19, 37; Plat. Tim., 71e. Coming spasmodically without mediation, though basically not unexpected, πνεῦμα is something which man does not control as a possession of spirit; on the contrary, he himself is passively possessed by it. For the theme and content as well as the source of the experience of the spirit, which is not granted to everyone but only to chosen and pre-disposed souls, is always something divine or a god, especially the most "spiritual" of the gods, Apollo.

A final poetic witness to Apollonian inspiration manticism is the Didyma inscr. of 263 A.D. [56] which extols the new form of the ancient oracular source of Apollo: its θεῖον πνεῦμα προφήταις ἄρδεται etc. through nymphs, to whom manticism is dear. Here πνεῦμα θεῖον might well be an apologetic concept of the movement of pagan restoration in opposition to the spiritual utterances of Christianity. In a late magic pap. which has rules for giving oracles the ἅγιον πνεῦμα which makes magic possible by causing ecstasy is called syncretistically the "messenger of Apollo": πρὸς ἐπιταγὴν ἁγίου πνεύματος, ἀγ[γέλ]ου Φοίβο[υ], Preis. Zaub., III, 289.

In what we read elsewhere of the inspiration of pneuma at Delphi and other places the original cultic-mythological understanding of the religion of Apollo has been widely permeated partly by scientific and partly by speculative theories which Platonism, Stoicism and Neo-Platonism developed in explanation and evaluation of the phenomenon of manticism and its decline.

Mantic ἐπίπνοια is already assessed as a religious phenomenon, critically of course, by Plato. It certainly makes a man "full of God" (ἐπίπνους ὄντας καὶ κατεχομένους ἐκ τοῦ θεοῦ, Men., 99d), but it also robs him of understanding, so that he ἔνθεός τε γένηται καὶ ἔκφρων καὶ ὁ νοῦς μηκέτι ἐν αὐτῷ ἐνῇ, Ion, 534b. In this state he can prophesy, and thus do much good (Phaedr., 244a), but he does not know what he is saying (ἴσασι δὲ οὐδὲν ὧν λέγουσιν, Men., 99c-d; Ap., 22c). His utterances do not come forth from himself as a man. The god is the one who through him as a "ministering organ" speaks to us and makes himself known: τούτοις χρῆται ὑπηρέταις ... ἀλλ' ὁ θεὸς αὐτός ἐστιν ὁ λέγων, διὰ τούτων δὲ φθέγγεται πρὸς ἡμᾶς, Ion, 534c-d. Plato establishes herewith the view of inspiration in profane Greek. Philo (→ 374, 29 ff.), Plutarch and even the early Christian Apologists follow him unreflectingly in this. The ἱερὸν πνεῦμα or the soul of the Pythia is an ὄργανον θεοῦ (Plut. Pyth. Or., 21 [II, 404b]) which

---

[55] *Magnam cui* (sc. the sibyl) *mentem animumque Delius inspirat vates aperitque futura,* Verg. Aen., 6, 12, cf. on this E. Norden, *Vergils Aen. Buch VI*² (1916), 144-149. The ancient belief in the revealing power of the θεῖον πνεῦμα found cultic expression in the miracle of opening doors, cf. O. Weinreich, "Gebet u. Wunder," *Tübinger Beiträge z. Altertumswissenschaft,* 5 (1929), Index *s.v.* πνεῦμα.

[56] Inscr. of Didyma, ed. A. Rehm (1956), 207-209, No. 159 [R. Harder].

is blown as a flute is blown by the flute-player (Athenag. Suppl., 9) [57] or sounded as the zither is sounded by the πνεῦμα as by a πλῆκτρον. [58]

For Plato a second and no less important factor must be added to the enthusiastic-ecstatic utterances of θεία ἐπίπνοια, i.e., their correct appraisal, the πάντα λογισμῷ διελέσθαι, ὅπη τι σημαίνει καὶ ὅτῳ μέλλοντος ἢ παρελθόντος ἢ παρόντος κακοῦ ἢ ἀγαθοῦ, Tim., 72a. Plato is alluding to the historically developed cultic usage as a result of which the words of the Pythia, burbled out in ecstasy, are normally taken up, supplemented, clarified and made into valid oracles only by the Delphic priests or prophets. He appeals expressly to tradition when he demands that the μάντις, as the ἔκφρων and μανείς he already is (etymologically), must be prepared to have someone else, a σώφρων προφήτης μαντευομένων, as a κριτής who fulfils the Platonic requirement of πράττειν καὶ γνῶναι τά τε ἑαυτοῦ καὶ ἑαυτόν. The man who stands directly under the captivating power of a θεία ἐπίπνοια which rules out all understanding, is incapable of this, Tim., 71e-72b. The man for the job is the philosopher. [59]

The criticism [60] to which Plato here subjects the manifestations of μαντική ἔνθεος καὶ ἀληθής (Tim., 71e) is basically akin to the διακρίσεις πνευμάτων of 1 C. 12:10, the δια-, ἀνα- and συγκρίνειν of 1 C. 2:13-15; 14:29, and the δοκιμάζειν of 1 Th. 5:19-22, whereby Paul steers into the right channels the ecstatic glossolalia of the church in Corinth ταῖς φρεσί (1 C. 14:20) and can thus distinguish the καλὸν πνεῦμα from the πονηρὸν πνεῦμα. Not differing formally from the ῥήματα τῆς μαντείας ἢ μᾶλλον μανίας of the Pythia (Schol. Aristoph. Pl., 39), the γλῶσσαι of the Christian ecstatic also need ἑρμηνεία (→ II, 665, 9 ff.) if they are not to be for unbelievers mere μαίνεσθαι (1 C. 14:23) but if διὰ τῆς γλώσσης there is to be for them an εὔσημος λόγος (v. 9), for the "laity" profit and for the community edification (vv. 3 ff., 27 f.). There is need to understand τὴν δύναμιν τῆς φωνῆς (v. 11). The νοῦς (→ IV, 959, 7 ff.) must have a part in ecstatic spiritual utterance in tongues (vv. 14-16). For this reason, on an OT basis, Paul himself prefers the προφητεύων (vv. 1-5). In this, linguistically at least, he is at one with Plato, who in principle differentiates the προφήτης, a special and higher type, from the ecstatic μάντεις along exactly the same lines

---

[57] κατ' ἔκστασιν τῶν ἐν αὐτοῖς λογισμῶν κινήσαντος αὐτοὺς (sc. Moses and the OT prophets) τοῦ θείου πνεύματος, ἃ ἐνηργοῦντο ἐξεφώνησαν, συγχρησαμένου τοῦ πνεύματος, ὡς εἰ καὶ αὐλητὴς αὐλὸν ἐμπνεῦσαι.

[58] → n. 69.

[59] Here is a basic theme which extends beyond the question of manticism to the whole of Plato's philosophy. In face of all human products, discoveries and achievements, there must always be someone who can test aright (βασανίζειν) and finally judge (κρίνειν Theaet., 150b-c) that which is physically born, technically produced or spiritually conceived and inspired by others in the light of its true reality and worth. Of the invention of writing Plato says in Phaedr., 274e: ἄλλος μὲν τεκεῖν δυνατὸς τὰ τῆς τέχνης, ἄλλος δὲ κρῖναι, τίν' ἔχει μοῖραν βλάβης τε καὶ ὠφελίας τοῖς μέλλουσι χρῆσθαι. The Socratic calling of maieutics, for which in this masculine instance (in analogy to Artemis as the female goddess of birth) Apollo is just as appropriate as he is traditionally for manticism, has as its supreme function (κάλλιστον ἔργον) the κρίνειν τὸ ἀληθές τε καὶ μή, Theaet., 150b ff. Mathematicians, geometricians and astronomers must also submit their findings to the dialectician, who alone can assess and apply them correctly, Plat. Euthyd., 289d ff.; cf. Crat., 388b, 390c. As concerns the famous Delphic oracle imparted to Socrates by Chairephon, acc. to Ap., 21a ff. Socrates himself became its critic and thus made it "true." It is in express accordance with this Platonic principle that Celsus, the opponent of Christianity, deals with the religious δόγματα advanced by barbarians, Orig. Cels., I, 2.

[60] Cf. E. Fascher, ΠΡΟΦΗΤΗΣ. Eine sprach- u. religionsgeschichtliche Untersuchung (1927), 20.

(Tim., 72a-b; Charm., 173c) as Paul distinguishes him from the more general category of the spiritual ecstatic (1 C. 14:37). A difference is that for Paul the speaker in tongues and the interpreter can and should be one and the same person (1 C. 14:13), the more so as προφητεία and διάκρισις πνευμάτων, γένη and ἑρμηνεία γλωσσῶν are only different gifts of one and the self-same Spirit of the one God who works all in all (1 C. 12:4-11). The result is that the evaluation of spiritual utterances is not here, as in Plato, performed by νοῦς, φρόνησις and dialectic. It is by the gift of the Spirit of God Himself : πνευματικοῖς (or πνευματικῶς) πνευματικά ἀνα- (or συγ-)κρίνεται (1 C. 2:13 f.); ὁ δὲ πνευματικὸς ἀνακρίνει μὲν πάντα, αὐτὸς δὲ ὑπ' οὐδενὸς ἀνακρίνεται (1 C. 2:15, cf. 14:32). The true Pauline πνευματικός herewith takes the place of the Platonic φιλόσοφος.

Delphic inspiration-manticism is for Plato the formal element and prototype by which he explains the musical inspiration of the poet and by which he also fashions the aspect of enthusiasm or eros in his own philosophy in discussion with rhetoric, poetry and politics.[61] An idea which is originally cultic and religious, thus systematised and apprehended critically, becomes in this way a general intellectual phenomenon which is not limited to manticism but appears also in other spheres of actuality. The artist ὥσπερ ἔκ τινος ἐπιπνοίας κινηθείς receives inspiration also for his creative work θειοτέρων πνευμάτων ἐράνοις (Callistratus Descriptiones, Philostr., ed. C. L. Kayser, 2 [1871], 422, 23-29). Nemo vir magnus sine aliquo adflatu divino umquam fuit, says Cic. Nat. Deor., II, 66 (167). Acc. to Ps.-Plat. Virt., 379c-d good men, as οἱ θεῖοι τῶν μάντεων καὶ οἱ χρησμολόγοι, are and become what they are, οὔτε φύσει ... οὔτε τέχνῃ, ἀλλ' ἐπιπνοίᾳ (i.e., πνεύματος πληρωθέντες, Plut. Amat., 16 [II, 758e]) ἐκ τῶν θεῶν, cf. Aristoxenus in Stob. Ecl., I, 89, 11 f.; M. Ant., I, 17, 11. With ref. to the decline of the oracle the concept of inspiration is discussed by philosophy under the influence of Stoic teachings, and it is revived and re-established as a speculative theologoumenon in a notable material form in Plut. and a dematerialised form in Iambl. The term πνεῦμα takes on special significance in this connection.

Plut. first adopts expressly the Platonic systematising of θεία ἐπίπνοια, Plat. Phaedr., 244a ff., 265a ff. Prophecy is the form of ἐνθουσιασμός which derives from an ἐπίπνοια καὶ κατοχή of Apollo, Plut. Amat., 16 (II, 758d, 759a ff.). Direct inspiration, as though the god himself entered the prophet's body and spoke from him like a ventriloquist, is rejected as incompatible with the dignity of godhead, Def. Orac., 9 (II, 414e). Nevertheless, the Platonic idea of ἐπίπνοια is materialised, for a material μαντικὸν ῥεῦμα καὶ πνεῦμα (Def. Orac., 40 [II, 432d-e]), also called directly μαντικὴ ἀναθυμίασις (ibid., 41 [II, 433a]), functions as the source, agent and medium of inspiration and prophecy, and through this the divinatory power awakens and is set to work in the soul of the Pythia. As a materially conceived breath or mist (ἀτμός, Paus., X, 5, 7; ἀναθυμίασις, Plut. Def. Orac., 46 [II, 435a]), which arises under the effect of warmth or some other influence (Def. Orac., 50 [II, 437c]) and which is directly carried up by air or water out of a cleft[62] or arises out of a well (Themist. Or., 4 [53a]; Orig. Cels., VII, 3), the Delphic πνεῦμα is one of the many natural forces of the earth (vis terrae, quae mentem Pythiae divino adflatu concitabat, Cic. Divin., I, 19) which acc. to the Stoic view manifest themselves in various places and have extraordinary effects, mostly beneficial but sometimes harmful : τῶν πνευμάτων πολλὰ πολλαχοῦ γῆς στόμια ἀνέῳκται, ὧν τὰ μὲν ἐνθουσιᾶν ποιεῖ τοὺς ἐμπελάζοντας, τὰ δ' ἀτροφεῖν, τὰ δὲ χρησμῳδεῖν, ὥσπερ τὰ ἐν Δελφοῖς καὶ Λεβαδείᾳ, τὰ δὲ καὶ παντάπασιν ἀναιρεῖ, καθάπερ τὸ ἐν Φρυγίᾳ, Ps.-Aristot. Mund., 4, p. 395b, 26 ff.; cf. Verg. Aen., 6, 236-241; Plut. Def. Orac., 40 (II, 432d-e). As a telluric cosmic phenomenon, like everything between earth and moon subject to natural change and corruption, πνεῦμα

---

[61] Cf. H. Gundert, "Enthusiasmos u. Logos bei Plato," Lexis, 2 (1949), 37-46.

[62] Strabo, 9, 3, 5; Auct. Sublim., 13, 2; Dio C., 63, 14, 2; Iambl. Myst., III, 11. Anhelitus terrae, adflatus e terra, we read in Cic. Divin., II, 57, obviously on the basis of Chrysipp. or Poseidonios.

appears more strongly or more weakly at irregular intervals; it will even dry up completely in the course of time: ἔστι δὲ (sc. ἡ τοῦ πνεύματος δύναμις) θεία μὲν ὄντως καὶ δαιμόνιος, οὐ μὴν ἀνέκλειπτος οὐδ' ἄφθαρτος οὐδ' ἀγήρως καὶ διαρκὴς εἰς τὸν ἄπειρον χρόνον, ὑφ' οὗ πάντα κάμνει τὰ μεταξὺ γῆς καὶ σελήνης, Plut. Def. Orac., 51 (II, 438c-d); cf. 50 (II, 437c); Pyth. Or., 17 (II, 402b). If it is also divine and sacred (θειότατόν ἐστι καὶ ὁσιώτατον, Def. Or., 40 [II, 432d]), this is not in a supernatural sense but in the same way that illnesses which have their origin in atmospheric processes that man cannot control are called divine (θεῖα), Hippocr. Morb. Sacr., 18 (Littré, VI, 394 f.). In keeping is the fact that for Plut. the earth and esp. the Apollo-like sun, which bring forth πνεῦμα, are divine essences. Furthermore daemons supervise and regulate the process of inspiration in detail, Plut. Def. Orac., 48 (II, 436 f.-437a). Here Plut. is meeting what was felt to be the dangerous objection that a physical and scientific understanding of the nature and operation of πνεῦμα leads away from the gods into irreligion (ἄθεον, Def. Orac., 48 [II, 436e]): ἀπάγουσι τὴν δόξαν ἀπὸ τῶν θεῶν (ibid., 46 [II, 435a]).

The πνεῦμα fills the oracle-chamber of the Adyton (οἶκος) "as from a spring" with a costly scent (→ εὐωδία, II, 809, 5 f.) such as that sent forth by the presence of the divine, and it "draws near"[63] to the Pythia, Def. Orac., 50 (II, 437c-d).[64] As a warm principle, which permeates the body and enters into union with the ψυχή, here thought of as breath or spirit, πνεῦμα works like wine[65] inflaming the soul; it opens up corridors for the entry of ideas of the future and discloses what is hidden; ἔνθερμος ... γενομένη καὶ πυρώδης the soul divests itself of earthly rationality (θνητὴ φρόνησις), which so often puts out the fire of enthusiasm, Def. Orac., 40 (II, 432e-f). Warmth, however, may make the pneuma of the soul "dry" in the sense of Heracl. (Fr., 118 [Diels⁷, I, 177, 4 f.]), i.e., ethereal, a pure mirror of the divine, unclouded by any humidity. πνεῦμα can also have a cooling and toughening effect on the soul, as iron is hardened when plunged into cold water, Def. Orac., 41 (II, 432f-433a). Most commonly, however, the soul is joined to πνεῦμα as the eye to light, which is related by nature. As the eye becomes light, and sees only through the light of the sun,[66] so μαντικὸν πνεῦμα is the related divine force which, like medicine (ὥσπερ φάρμακον, Def. Orac., 47 [II, 436d])[67] awakens and increases the sleeping power of divination in the soul (ibid., 42 [II, 433d-e]): ἡ τοῦ πνεύματος δύναμις ... ὑπέκκαυμα παρέχει καὶ ἀρχήν (45 [II, 438c]). Only a harmonious relation of spirit and right constitution of soul gives rise to prophetic enthusiasm. This may be seen from the contemporary account (Def. Orac., 51 [II, 438a-c]) of a Pythia which in giving oracles had to become the victim of an ἄλαλον (cf. Mk. 9:17 f.) καὶ κακὸν πνεῦμα. The soul of man or the Pythia is also the material instrument[68] which the god causes to sound with the πλῆκτρον of the ἐνθουσιαστικὸν πνεῦμα and the (μαντικὴ) ἀναθυμίασις, Def. Orac., 50 (II, 437d). For Plut. this image[69] offers an interpretation of the process of

[63] In πλησιάζειν, which is, of course, used fig. here with ref. to the ψυχή, but which elsewhere (Plut. Quaest. Conv., VIII, 1, 3 [II, 718a] and Numa, 4, 6 [I, 62b]) is used in a special sense as a decorous tt. for sexual intercourse between a divine pneuma and an earthly woman, the original generative concept of inspiration may still be discerned.

[64] Cf. E. Will, "Sur la nature du pneuma delphique," BCH, 66/67 (1942/43), 161-175.

[65] Based on the same experience as that which causes unbelievers (cf. 1 C. 14:23) to scoff at those who had been filled with the Spirit at Pentecost as full of new wine, Ac. 2:13.

[66] The sun (helios) is again via analogiae like Plut.'s chief and favourite god Apollo in nature and operation, Def. Orac., 42 (II, 433e); of him we read in Pyth. Or., 7 (II, 397c): φῶς ἐν τῇ ψυχῇ ποιεῖ πρὸς τὸ μέλλον· ὁ γὰρ ἐνθουσιασμὸς τοιοῦτόν ἐστι.

[67] In principle the interpretation of the religious process of inspiration does not differ from the contemporary medical theory of πνεῦμα in terms of which Plut. explains the health and sickness of body and soul, Verbeke, 265 f.

[68] ψυχὴ δ' ὄργανον θεοῦ γέγονεν, Plut. Pyth. Or., 21 (II, 404b); cf. Philo Rer. Div. Her., 259.

[69] When they adopted the πλῆκτρον motif (Ps.-Just. Cohortatio ad Graec., 8 [MPG, 6, 256]; Athenag. Suppl., 7 and 9; cf. Epiph. Haer., 48, 4) the Apologists were primarily

inspiration which excludes neither deity nor reason : οὐ γὰρ ἄθεον ποιοῦμεν οὐδ' ἄλογον τὴν μαντικήν, *ibid.*, 48 (II, 436 f). Now excavation at Delphi has brought to light neither a cleft under the Adyton nor a natural, nor even, as suggested, an artificial, material pneuma. [70] It thus follows that what we have here is not a physical reality but a phenomenon of faith [71] or a theology which uses the philosophical and scientific resources of the period to try to save mantic inspiration as a traditional part of Delphic religion.

The same is true of Iamblichus. [72] In his theory and phenomenology of manticism θεία (or θεοῦ or even θεῶν) ἐπίπνοια and πνεῦμα, as the principle, form and medium of supernatural inspiration which comes down as a pure gift from the gods quite apart from any cosmico-physical, spiritual or corporeal factors, [73] are given a place alongside one another. [74] πνεῦμα, which as in current magic is almost synon. with φῶς, πῦρ or αὐγή, [75] becomes more and more a phenomenon of light rather than the original one of breath, while ἐπίπνοια is spiritualised as an act of illumination from above in the sense of a filling with radiance, [76] which acc. to the will of the gods evokes divine visions and revelations in our imagination, Myst., III, 14 (p. 132, 11 ff.): ἐλλάμπουσαν ἔχει τὴν τοῦ θεοῦ ἐπίπνοιαν, is said of the προφήτης, III, 11 (p. 126, 1). As the principle of the genesis of θεία μανία, θεοφορία and ἐνθουσιασμός there are mentioned together almost as a hendiadys τὰ καθήκοντα ἀπὸ τῶν θεῶν φῶτα καὶ τὰ ἐνδιδόμενα πνεύματα [77] ἀπ' αὐτῶν, which embrace and control everything in us, excluding our own intellectual response and causing us to utter words which even as the speakers we do not understand but simply cry out with raving mouths, like the sibyl in Heracl. Fr., 92 (Diels⁷, I, 172, 3), Myst., III, 8 (p. 117, 1-12); cf. III, 11 (p. 123, 3 ff.). In surrender to the θεῖον, which in Delphi rises up like an ethereal fiery breath out of a cleft and in Didyma steams up like vapour from a spring, the προφῆτις or γυνὴ χρησμῳδός is lit up by the radiance of the divine fire, filled by the divine beam of light, and taken over entirely by the god: ἀπὸ πνεύματος λεπτοῦ καὶ πυρώδους ἀναφερομένου ποθὲν ἀπὸ στομίου θεμιστεύει ... δίδωσιν ἑαυτὴν τῷ θείῳ πνεύ-

---

seeking to follow Pl., who in the figure of such instruments as the αὐλός, κιθάρα and σάλπιγξ (1 C. 14:7 f.), which derives in part from the living original concept of πνεῦμα, was trying to bring out the difference between empty and edifying operations of the Spirit. On the other hand they were also drawing a par. between bibl. revelation on the lips of the prophets and the pagan (Cumaean) sibyl tradition, which was certainly known to Ps.-Just. In distinction from Pl., whose imagery is concerned with the rational and practical content of inspiration, the pagan feature in the Apologists lies in the specific interest which this image shows them to have in the form and manner of the process of inspiration. Nevertheless, behind the formal similarity there is a basic distinction in the view of πνεῦμα. In Plut. this is a vapour arising out of the earth, while in Ps.-Just. it is pure spirit coming down from heaven. For the distinction between the pagan mantic view of inspiration and the OT and Chr. view cf. Fascher, 70-75; Bacht, 62-69, esp. 59 f., n. 45; Prümm, 432; Art. "Inspiration" in *Dict. de la Bible*, Suppl., 20 (1947), 503-505; H. Sasse, "Sacra Scriptura, Bemerkungen zur Inspirationslehre Augustins," *Festschr. F. Dornseiff*, ed. H. Kusch (1953), 262-265.

[70] Amandry, 215-230, esp. 224, goes too far when on this ground he denies all inspiration manticism at Delphi and will accept only the giving of oracles by lots; in criticism cf. Klaffenbach, 519, 523-525.

[71] To doubt oracles or the native divinatory power of the soul is to betray weakness of faith (ἀσθένειαν ἀπιστίας) in divine works of power, Plut. Def. Orac., 45 (II, 434d); 39 (II, 432a).

[72] Cf. Verbeke, 374-385, esp. 379-381.

[73] Iambl. Myst., III, 10 (p. 120, 16 f.; 121, 1-8, 12); III, 1 (p. 100, 17 ff.); III, 27 (p. 164, 5 f.).

[74] *Ibid.*, III, 6 (p. 113, 2-6); III, 5 (p. 111, 4 ff., 16); III, 11 (p. 124, 16-125, 3; 127, 16 ff.).

[75] Cf. R. Bultmann, "Zur Gesch. d. Lichtsymbolik im Altertum," *Philol.*, 97 (1948), 25 f.

[76] What was only a comparison in Plut. Def. Orac., 42 (II, 433d) has become a definition of the nature of πνεῦμα in Iambl.

[77] Both elements are already singled out in Philo's doctrine of creation, Op. Mund., 29-30.

ματι, ἀπό τε τῆς τοῦ θείου πυρὸς ἀκτῖνος καταυγάζεται ... πληροῦται ἀπ' αὐτοῦ θείας αὐγῆς ... ὅλη γίγνεται τοῦ θεοῦ, Myst., III, 11 (p. 126, 4-16). Nevertheless, the πνεῦμα is not the god himself. In his illuminating *parousia* the god remains distinct. He is different from the fire and πνεῦμα, and more worthy of reverence : πάρεστιν ... χωριστῶς ὁ θεὸς ἐπιλάμπων, ἕτερος ὢν καὶ τοῦ πυρὸς καὶ τοῦ πνεύματος, Myst., III, 11 (p. 126, 16 ff.; 127, 18; 128, 1 ff.). Again, the oracular water of Colophon is not permeated directly or in immanent fashion by the πνεῦμα μαντικόν, as πνεῦμα extends into all parts of the cosmos acc. to the Stoic view. The θεῖον, non-material and hence non-distributable, sheds from without its light on the spring whose waters are thus filled with mantic power, Myst., III, 11 (p. 124, 16 ff.; 127, 1-8). Similarly, in the inspiration of men the μαντικὸν πνεῦμα comes from without on the αἰθερῶδες καὶ αὐγοειδὲς πνεῦμα (or ὄχημα) which surrounds our ψυχή, V, 26 (p. 239, 7 f.); III, 14 (p. 132, 10 ff.). Incorporeal, so that, though perceived, it cannot be seen, it comes with rustlings, infusing itself around us without touching us, freeing soul and body from the πάθη (III, 2, p. 103, 13 ff.; 104, 1 ff.) and thus bringing about the preparation and purification which is necessary to receive the god : τοῦγε θεοῦ ... ἡ ἐπίπνοια ... ἐπιτηδειότητα μόνον καὶ ἀποκάθαρσιν ... ἐμποιεῖ, δι' ἣν δυνατοὶ γιγνόμεθα χωρεῖν τὸν θεόν, III, 11, p. 125, 3-6. When the πνεῦμα comes down on and enters into the theurge, who at the summit of manticism is capable of ἀγωγὴ τῶν πνευμάτων (or φωτός, Myst., III, 14, p. 132, 9 f.), it enables him to see its nature and extent and to be guided and directed by it in a mysterious way : τὸ δὲ μέγιστον ὁρᾶται τῷ θεαγωγοῦντι τὸ κατιὸν πνεῦμα καὶ εἰσκρινόμενον, ὅσον τέ ἐστι καὶ ὁποῖον. μυστικῶς τε πείθεται καὶ διακυβερνᾶται, Myst., III, 6, p. 112, 10 ff.; cf. 113, 2, 6. Not all men are equally adapted for operations of pneuma ; the simpler and younger are more receptive, III, 24, p. 157, 14-17. For the rest, the intensity and the forms of manifestation and operation, which can develop from mere μετουσία *via* κοινωνία to ἕνωσις with the inspiring deity, are, like the signs τῶν ἐπιπνεομένων, as different as the gods (or demons and angels) are different, ἀφ' ὧν ἐπιπνεόμεθα, III, 5, p. 111, 3-17; III, 10, p. 121, 12 f. [78]

III. πνεῦμα in Natural Science and Philosophy.

The physical theories of the Gks. about the significance of air (as breath or wind) for the life of the cosmos and its members find linguistic expression and speculative development in Orphism, [79] though in Anaximenes and Diogenes of Apollonia we do not at first find the later term πνεῦμα but the older, more noetic and ἀρχή-like words ἀήρ and → ψυχή, which are, of course, very largely par. to πνεῦμα in their basic sensory meaning. The pre-Socratics, at least, offer no certain original example of the use of πνεῦμα, which appears only in doxographical refs. [80] In view of its predominance from the days of Stoicism, one is tempted to suppose that later narrators retrospectively used the current term for similar phenomena earlier. This applies esp. to the earliest use of πνεῦμα (if authentic) in Anaxim. Fr., 2 (Diels[7], I, 95, 17 ff.): οἷον ἡ ψυχὴ ἡ ἡμετέρα ἀὴρ οὖσα συγκρατεῖ ἡμᾶς, καὶ ὅλον τὸν κόσμον πνεῦμα καὶ ἀὴρ περιέχει (λέγεται δὲ συνωνύμως ἀὴρ καὶ πνεῦμα). This is also the first instance of the concept of the cosmos, which, understood in Stoic fashion after the analogy of the human organism, has ψυχή = ἀήρ = πνεῦμα, i.e., soul = air = breath,

---

[78] Evil πνεύματα of evil demons can disturb the divination, but they must yield as darkness does to light once the τῶν θεῶν δύναμις which fills all things with good shines forth : τῆς πάντα ἀγαθῶν πληρούσης τῶν θεῶν δυνάμεως πολλαχόθεν ἐπιλαμπούσης οὐκ ἔχει χώραν ἡ τῶν κακῶν ταραχὴ πνευμάτων, Iambl. Myst., III, 13, p. 130, 12 ff.

[79] Acc. to Orphic teaching, which as Jaeger has shown (69-87), presupposes the findings of Ionic natural philosophy, the soul, as breath, is carried by the winds from the universe into the body : φησὶ γὰρ (sc. ὁ ἐν τοῖς Ὀρφικοῖς ἔπεσι καλουμένοις λόγος) τὴν ψυχὴν ἐκ τοῦ ὅλου εἰσιέναι ἀναπνεόντων φερομένην ὑπὸ τῶν ἀνέμων, Orph. Fr., 27 (Kern).

[80] Emped. Fr., 100, 15-21 (Diels[7], I, 348, 7 ff.) does not offer a precise use; on Democr. Fr., 18 (Diels[7], II, 146, 13 ff.) → n. 42.

as the comprehensive life-principle (ἀρχή) which integrates and overrules all things. [81] Also under suspicion of Stoic formulation is the doxographical account of Sext. Emp. Math., IX, 127, acc. to which, in the school of Pythagoras [82] as well as Empedocles, the bond which unites men not only among themselves and upward to the gods but also downward to the animals is based on ἕν ... πνεῦμα τὸ διὰ παντὸς τοῦ κόσμου διῆκον ψυχῆς τρόπον τὸ καὶ ἑνοῦν ἡμᾶς πρὸς ἐκεῖνα, Emped. Fr., 136 (Diels⁷, I, 367, 1-5). If acc. to Diog. L., 9, 19 Xenophanes (A 1 [Diels⁷, I, 113, 27 f.]) was the first to address the ψυχή as πνεῦμα, in the context in which it took place, ὅτι πᾶν τὸ γινόμενον φθαρτόν ἐστι, the ref. is simply to the "perishable breath" which is often regarded as the essence of the soul, → 336, 22 ff. On the other hand πνεῦμα is an important term in Gk. medicine from Hippocr. [83] It is developed esp. in Morb. Sacr., 4, 7 (Littré, VI, 368, 372, 374) and De Flatibus, 3-4, 7 (CMG, I, 1, p. 92 f., 95) and is expressly ascribed to Hippocr. by doxography, which goes back to imperial and peripatetic research, unless influenced at this pt. by the Stoic doctrine of pneuma. [84] In this connection pneuma is the vital and decisive element (τὸ γ[ὰρ] πνεῦμ[α] ἀναγκαιότατον καὶ κυριώτατον ... τ[ῶν] ἐν ἡμῖν) on whose true measure and circulation in the body health depends. [85] As a meteorological phenomenon πνεύματα influence both the physical constitution and the character of men, Hippocr. De Aere Aquis Locis, 3-6 (CMG, I, 1, p. 57-60). πνεῦμα here is a term for the air which is taken in not merely by breathing but also with foods and drinks which contain it (μετὰ δὲ πολλῶν σιτίων ἀνάγκη καὶ πολὺ πνεῦμα ἐσιέναι, De Flatibus, 7 [CMG, I, 1, p. 95, 6 ff.]), which is changed within into the psychical πνεῦμα, which then flows, first into the brain, then into the whole organism, and which not only keeps it in life and movement but also endows it with consciousness: τὴν φρόνησιν καὶ τὴν κίνησιν τοῖς μέλεσι παρέχει (sc. τὸ πνεῦμα), Hippocr. Morb. Sacr., 7 (Littré, VI, 372 f.). Filling everything between earth and heaven, πνεῦμα is a mighty force in the life of all nature, both organic and inorganic: τὸ πνεῦμα καὶ ἐν τοῖς ἄλλοις πρήγμασι δυναστεῦον καὶ ἐν τοῖσι σώμασι τῶν ζῴων. [86]

The Hippocratic doctrine of pneuma, which still influences Plato's Tim. (84d) in the 4th cent., was probably altered by the older "Sicilian" medical school, which possibly followed Emped. This distinguishes between the cold air of the atmosphere, which is breathed in, and the inner, native and warm ψυχικὸν πνεῦμα which, constantly vaporising under the influence of bodily warmth from the blood, circulates through the veins, and has its seat in the heart, being regarded as the true vital force. [87] Aristot. took over

---

[81] K. Reinhardt, Kosmos u. Sympathie (1926), 209-213 has challenged the authenticity of the Anaximenes Fr. on good grounds. He has shown that the formulation is Stoic-Poseidonian. This view is supported by U. v. Wilamowitz-Moellendorff, Der Glaube d. Hellenen, 1 (1931), 374, n. 3. We find the same specifically Stoic use in a later pneumatic like Ps.-Gal., Definitiones Medicae, 96 (Kühn, 19, 372): ἕξις ἐστὶ πνεῦμα συνέχον καὶ συγκρατοῦν τὰ μέρη. But cf. W. Kranz, "Kosmos als philosophischer Begriff frühgr. Zeit," Philol., 93 (1939), 436; Jaeger, 48, 240 f., n. 62.

[82] Acc. to Aristot. Phys., IV, 6, p. 213b, 22 ff. the older Pythagoreans thought of the universe as surrounded by infinite πνεῦμα (or πνοή, Stob. Ecl., I, 18, 1ᶜ) which the cosmos in some sense breathes in from without: ἐπεισιέναι αὐτὸ τῷ οὐρανῷ ἐκ τοῦ ἀπείρου πνεύματος ὡς ἀναπνέοντι (cf. Aristoph. Nu., 627) Xenophanes A 1 (Diels⁷, I, 113, 26 f.) and Plato take issue, cf. Tim., 33c: πνεῦμά τε οὐκ ἦν περιεστὸς δεόμενον ἀναπνοῆς.

[83] Acc. to K. Deichgräber, "Die Epidemien u. das Corpus Hippocraticum," AAB (1933), 162; M. Pohlenz, Hippokr. u. d. Begründung d. wissenschaftlichen Medizin (1938), 66-68, 84 f., 92-94.

[84] So L. Edelstein, "Περὶ ἀέρων u. d. Sammlung d. hippokratischen Schriften," Problemata, 4 (1931), 142, n. 1.

[85] Anonymus Londinensis, 6, 13-31; 7, 15 f. (= Suppl. Aristotelicum, III, 1 [1893], 9 ff.); cf. Hippocr. De Natura Hominis, 9 (Littré, VI, 52, 11).

[86] Hippocr. De Flatibus, 3 (CMG, I, 1, p. 92, 20 ff.; 93, 6 ff.); 4 (I, 1, p. 93, 19 ff.); 15 (I, 1, p. 101, 19 f.).

[87] Cf. Rüsche, Blut, Leben u. Seele, 78, 147, 159; Pohlenz, 93-95; M. Wellmann, "Die Fr.

this distinction from the natural science of his day and made it a central part of his physiology of the organism. [88] πνεῦμα is the breath of life which gives soul to various degrees and which in some way characterises all living creatures as distinct from dead matter, Mot. An., 10, p. 703a, 9 f. As σύμφυτον πνεῦμα (Gen. An., II, 6, p. 744a, 2 ff.) it is the inner formal principle which develops and morphologically differentiates fixed tendencies and organs in the embryo, Gen. An., II, 6, p. 741b, 37. At the higher stage of the development of animal life the greater quantity of πνεῦμα necessary for existence is added from without as ἐπείσακτον (Part. An., II, 16, p. 659b, 17 ff.) to the inner organic πνεῦμα to support it and regulate its warmth, so that the functions are divided between the two forms of πνεῦμα. In the developed creature πνεῦμα as *spiritus rector* is the organ through which φαντασία in animals and διάνοια in men bring the body where they would have it, Mot. An., 10, p. 703a, 4 ff. Working like the systole and diastole of the heart πνεῦμα is in the body both that which moves and that which is moved, Mot. An., 10, p. 703a, 11 ff. It is also the bearer of warmth. Ministering as a corporeal-material instrument (ὄργανον) by means of which the ψυχή directs and sustains the body in its movements and experiences, πνεῦμα as πρῶτον ὑπὸ τὴν ψυχήν (Ps.-Aristot. De Spiritu, 5, p. 483a, 26) is even more plainly distinguished from ψυχή than from ἔμφυτος θερμότης, whereas Stoicism materialistically equates πνεῦμα (ἔν-θερμον, διάπυρον, συμφυὲς ἡμῖν) and ψυχή, Zeno Fr., 135 (v. Arnim, I, 38, 3 ff.), 127 (35, 33 f.). [89] Through the medical writer Diocles of Carystos [90] the pneumatology of Aristot. was not without influence on the rise of the doctrine of πνεῦμα which stood at the heart of Stoic philosophy.

What was in Aristot. and Diocles physiology or psychology or even pathology of the animal world, and hence a part of scientific biology or medicine, becomes in the Stoa a universal speculative theory which acc. to the model of the medical ψυχικὸν πνεῦμα (Diocles Fr., 44, 59) [91] in its relation to the human body offers an explanation of the whole world, both organic and inorganic, in its constitution and unity, its tension and vitality, its being as a whole and the individual qualitative nature of each individual creature within it. Assimilating both natural science and the popular belief in the divine, life-giving power of breath, the doctrine of pneuma found here in philosophy its most consistent and historically most influential systematic development.

Along with the elementary physical aspect the Stoic concept of πνεῦμα has a psychological-anthropological, a cosmological, and a metaphysical-theological aspect. [92] Only rarely equated with air as one of the four elements, [93] πνεῦμα is mostly regarded as a substance of its own (σῶμα, οὐσία) which unites πῦρ and ἀήρ in itself. [94] As the source and divine principle of the four elements, it surpasses and permeates these by its greater rarity, activity and vitality, [95] and like the Aristotelian αἰθήρ it is a kind of quintessence. [96] Invisibly fine corporeality, [97] air-like form, the bearing of warmth or fire, [98] spontaneous movement [99] and tension [100] make πνεῦμα the mighty substance which permeates, integrates, moves, vivifies and gives soul to all reality in all its forms

---

d. sikelischen Ärzte Akron, Philistion u. des Diokles v. Karystos," *Fragmentsammlung d. gr. Ärzte,* I (1901), 79.

[88] Acc. to Jaeger, *Das Pneuma,* 43-55.

[89] Cf. Verbeke, 20-24, n. 46; 47.

[90] Jaeger, *Diokles,* 228 saw in him a peripatetic and a contemporary of the founder of Stoicism.

[91] Wellmann, 137, 142.

[92] Cf. Verbeke, 11-174; Pohlenz, Index, *s.v.* "pneuma."

[93] Chrysipp. Fr., 440 (v. Arnim, II, 145, 1 ff.); Epict. Diss., III, 13, 15.

[94] *Ibid.,* 310 (II, 112, 33 ff.); 442 (II, 145, 41 ff.); 786 (II, 218, 34 f.).

[95] ἐκ τῶν τεσσάρων διήκοντος δι᾽ αὐτῶν τοῦ θεοῦ, *ibid.,* 414 (II, 137, 16).

[96] *Ibid.,* 310 (II, 112, 36); 416 (II, 137, 29 ff.).

[97] Cleanthes Fr., 484 (v. Arnim, I, 108, 28 f.); Chrysipp. Fr., 897 (II, 246, 15).

[98] Zeno Fr., 127 (v. Arnim, I, 35, 33 f.); Chrysipp. Fr., 1009 (II, 299, 11 f.).

[99] Chrysipp. Fr., 442 (II, 147, 28 f.); 471 (II, 152, 32 f.).

[100] ὁ τόνος τοῦ πνεύματος, Chrysipp. Fr., 441 (II, 145, 24 f.); 447 (II, 147, 28 f.).

in a κρᾶσις δι' ὅλου (Chrysipp. Fr., 479 [v. Arnim, II, 157, 36 f.]), thus fashioning
it into a single sympathetic organism : ἡνῶσθαι μὲν ὑποτίθεται τὴν σύμπασαν οὐσίαν, πνεύματός τινος διὰ πάσης αὐτῆς διήκοντος, ὑφ' οὗ συνέχεταί τε καὶ
συμμένει καὶ συμπαθές ἐστιν αὐτῷ τὸ πᾶν. [101] πνεῦμα, however, is also the basis
of the individuality of things in detail : τὰς δὲ ποιότητας πνεύματα οὔσας καὶ τόνους
ἀερώδεις, οἷς ἂν ἐγγένωνται μέρεσι τῆς ὕλης, εἰδοποιεῖν ἕκαστα καὶ σχηματί-
ζειν. [102] In ascending degree of purity, strength and tension, πνεῦμα as ἑκτικὸν
πνεῦμα gives individual unity to lifeless things like stone or wood in the inorganic
world : ἔστι δὲ ἕξις πνεῦμα σώματος συνεκτικόν (Chrysipp. Fr., 368 [v. Arnim,
II, 124, 20]); as φυσικὸν πνεῦμα it gives growth to plants and as ψυχικὸν πνεῦμα it
gives soul to animals (Fr., 715-716 [II, 205, 11-23]); in man this consists of a specially
light and fine πνεῦμα (Fr., 897 [II, 246, 16 f.]) which is native to man, [103] which
carries warmth and which glows with fire. [104] From its seat in the heart, the centre of
the soul's life, [105] it circulates in special channels through the organism (Fr., 826 [II,
226, 8 f.]), making possible not only the vital functions but also those of mind and soul,
esp. the activity of the five senses, also conceiving, [106] speaking and thinking (Fr., 827-
830 [II, 226, 14-31]). But even in the centre and chief organ of the soul (Cleanthes
Fr., 484 [I, 108, 28 f.]) πνεῦμα is less a principle than a material basis and sub-stratum
of the ἡγεμονικόν, which, by nature pure reason (λόγος or in Pos. νοῦς), is not in
antithesis to πνεῦμα, because in its pure form this is rational pneuma (ἔννουν τὸ
πνεῦμα καὶ πῦρ νοερόν). [107] This is a portion, inserted into the human body, of the
most rarefied cosmic divine πνεῦμα, ex illo caelesti spiritu (Sen. Dialogi, XII, 6, 7),
which has its seat in the region of ether as the ἡγεμονικόν of the world : ratio autem
nihil aliud est quam in corpus humanum pars divini spiritus mersa (Sen. Epist. Morales,
66, 12). [108] As spiritus sacer, which intra nos sedet, malorum bonorumque nostrorum
observator et custos (Sen. Epist. Morales, 41, 2), it embodies God in the inner being of
man : est deus in nobis et sunt commercia coeli, sedibus aethereis spiritus ille venit, says
Ovid Ars Amatoria, III, 549 f. of the poet. Stoic πνεῦμα has absorbed ψυχή and also
Aristotelian νοῦς into its functions.

M. Ant. [109] deviates from the classical Stoic doctrine. For him πνεῦμα, often in the
disparaging diminutive form πνευμάτιον with its suggestion of the unstable and transient
(II, 2; V, 33, 6; XII, 14, 5), [110] is equated with ψυχή as the agent of its animal functions
of impulse and imagination, V, 33, 4. In the triple structure of the human organism it is
expressly put in second place as compared with νοῦς, which as the ἡγεμονικόν of the
soul and that which has mental permanence constitutes the true essence of man : τρία
ἐστίν, ἐξ ὧν συνέστηκας· σωμάτιον, πνευμάτιον, νοῦς, XII, 3, 1. No longer the
spiritus, as in Sen., but ὁ ἑκάστου νοῦς θεὸς καὶ ἐκεῖθεν ἐρρύηκεν, XII, 26. [111]

Both matter and also an instrument of the purposeful creative artist nature, πνεῦμα
is in the cosmos not merely the vital force and substance which, giving birth, life and

---

[101] Ibid., 473 (II, 154, 7 ff.); cf. 416 (II, 137, 30 ff.); 441 (II, 145, 16 ff., 24 ff., 31 ff.); 447
(II, 147, 28 f.).
[102] Ibid., 449 (II, 147, 45-148, 2); cf. 389 (II, 128, 20 f.).
[103] Ibid., 774 (II, 217, 15 f.); 885 (II, 238, 32 f.).
[104] Ibid., 773 (II, 217, 8 f.); cf. Zeno Fr., 135 (v. Arnim, I, 38, 3 ff.).
[105] Chrysipp. Fr., 897 (v. Arnim, II, 246, 13 f.); Diogenes Babylonius Fr., 30 (v. Arnim,
III, 216, 15 ff.).
[106] → 344, n. 41.
[107] Cf. Chrysipp. Fr., 443 (v. Arnim, II, 146, 17 f.); cf. 779 (II, 217, 31).
[108] Verbeke, 144-147.
[109] Cf. Verbeke, 166-171; Pohlenz, 342-344.
[110] In Epict. Diss., III, 13, 15; II, 1, 17 πνευμάτιον is one of the four material elements
whose separation from the σωμάτιον means death.
[111] Pohlenz, 343, 381, 420 finds similar tendencies to depreciate πνεῦμα, the seat and
agent of emotions, as compared with the νοῦς and ἡγεμονικόν of man in the Gnostics
Basileides and Isidorus (Cl. Al. Strom., II, 112, 1 ff.) and also in Cl. Al. (Strom., VI, 134-
136), who sharply distinguishes the σαρκικὸν πνεῦμα (135, 1 ff.) as pure ζωτικὴ δύναμις
from τὸ ἁγίου πνεύματος χαρακτηριστικὸν ἰδίωμα, 134, 2.

subsistence, permeates the world from within even to its most contemptible materials, [112] and has its true shaping factor in the πῦρ τεχνικὸν ὁδῷ βαδίζον ἐπὶ γένεσιν κόσμου, Chrysipp. Fr., 1027 (v. Arnim, II, 306, 19 ff.). It is also the rational soul, whose functions of guidance and order are carried out by the πνεῦμα : spiritum ... motivum illum fore non naturam, sed animam et quidem rationabilem, quae vivificans sensilem mundum exornaverit eum ad hanc, qua nunc inlustratur, venustatem, quem quidem beatum animal et deum adpellant, Zeno Fr., 88 (v. Arnim, I, 25, 20 ff.).

εἱμαρμένη, which rules all things through τάξις, is thus regarded as a δύναμις πνευματική (Chrysipp. Fr., 913 [v. Arnim, II, 264, 14 f.]), just as the λόγος τοῦ θεοῦ, ὁ μέχρι ἀνθρώπων καὶ τῶν ἐλαχίστων καταβαίνων is no other than a πνεῦμα σωματικόν, Fr. 1051 (II, 310, 24 f.). In the indissoluble unity of matter, power, life, form and spirit πνεῦμα, as πρῶτον αἴτιον (Fr., 338; 340 [II, 119, 12 f.; 18 f.]) that all being as a whole and individually is wholly what it is, is finally itself God : [113] θεὸς ... σῶμα, πνεῦμα ὢν νοερὸν καὶ ἀΐδιον, Fr., 310 (II, 112, 31 f.). Cleanthes seems to have been the first to define deity as πνεῦμα. [114] The def., which goes back to Poseidonios, runs as follows : God is by nature πνεῦμα νοερὸν καὶ πυρῶδες, οὐκ ἔχον μὲν μορφήν, μεταβάλλον δ᾽ εἰς ὃ βούλεται καὶ συνεξομοιούμενον πᾶσιν, Fr., 1009 (II, 299, 11 ff.).

In religion, myth and poetry Zeus esp. is the name for the cosmic πνεῦμα made up of air and fire. The Orphic hymn to Zeus (Orph. Fr., 21a [Kern], from Ps.-Aristot. Mund., 7, p. 401a, 27 ff.) calls God πνοιὴ πάντων and ἀκαμάτου πυρὸς ὁρμή, cf. → 341, 11 ff. But the various manifestations and operations of πνεῦμα are also equated with the other traditional deities of popular Gk. religion. [115]

In a reduced form the Stoic doctrine of pneuma still exerts an influence in the so-called pneumatic medical school of the 1st/2nd cent. A.D. [116] The concept pneuma is again a central dogma here, but it is again restricted almost exclusively to the medical aspect. This school traces back physiological and esp. pathological processes to the state and circulation of the πνεῦμα, which is a basic element in the constitution of the human organism : συνέστηκεν ἡμῶν τὰ σώματα ἐκ στερεῶν, ὑγρῶν καὶ πνευμάτων, Ps.-Gal. Definitiones Medicae, 33 (Kühn, 19, 356). To the inner organic warm σύμφυτον πνεῦμα καὶ ζωτικόν (Gal. De Dignoscendis Pulsibus, 4, 2 [8, 936]), which produces inner warmth through friction and movement [117] and which has its central seat in the heart (Ps.-Gal. Def. Med., 33 [19, 357]), there is added the earthly πνεῦμα (air) of the atmosphere, which is breathed in through the mouth and nose and also through the veins and pores, which gives nourishment and helps to regulate the temperature, and which is exhaled again after use, Ps.-Gal. Def. Med., 74, 110 (19, 366, 376). After the manner of Stoicism these doctors also distinguish from the ἑκτικόν and φυσικόν the ψυχικὸν πνεῦμα, δι᾽ οὗ ζῶμεν καὶ λογιζόμεθα καὶ ταῖς λοιπαῖς αἰσθήσεσιν

---

[112] ἡ ἐν φυτοῖς καὶ ζῴοις καὶ διὰ πάντων — καὶ διὰ τῶν εἰδεχθῶν, Chrysipp. Fr., 1037-1039 (v. Arnim, II, 307, 21-28) — διήκουσα ἔμψυχός τε καὶ γόνιμος οὐσία, Ps.-Aristot. Mund., 4, p. 394b, 9 f.

[113] The Stoic theory of πνεῦμα as the bearer of life and spirit, even to its predication as divine, is prefigured pt. by pt. in the ἀήρ-theology of Diog. of Apollonia, esp. Fr., 4 (Diels⁷, II, 60, 19 ff.); 5 (II, 61, 4-62, 10); 7 (II, 65, 15-66, 2); 8 (II, 66, 3 ff.). Cf. Leisegang, Hl. Geist, 47 f.; Jaeger, 188 f.

[114] Fr., 533 (v. Arnim, I, 121, 6 f.); Zeno Fr., 160 (v. Arnim, I, 42, 23-30).

[115] Chrysipp. Fr., 1093 (v. Arnim, II, 319, 29 ff.); Cornut. Theol. Graec., 31.

[116] Cf. Gal. Introductio, 9 (Kühn, 14, 699): οἱ δὲ περὶ Ἀθηναῖον καὶ Ἀρχιγένην μόνῳ τῷ διήκοντι δι᾽ αὐτῶν πνεύματι καὶ τὰ φυσικὰ συνεστάναι τε καὶ διοικεῖσθαι καὶ τὰ νοσήματα πάντα, τούτου πρωτοπαθοῦντος γίνεσθαι ἀπεφήναντο, ὅθεν καὶ πνευματικοὶ χρηματίζουσιν. Cf. Wellmann, esp. 137-143; Rüsche, Blut, Leben u. Seele, 275-277; Verbeke, 191-206.

[117] Cf. Antyll. in Oribasius Collectiones Medicae, VI, 10, 19 (CMG, VI, 1, 1, p. 163).

ἐνεργοῦμεν, *ibid.*, 29 (19, 355). But these higher functions of the ψυχή are expounded in purely physiological terms.

In Plotin. [118] πνεῦμα plays only a negative role in criticism of the Stoic view, Enn., IV, 7, 4 = Chrysipp. Fr., 443 (v. Arnim, II, 146, 17 ff.); IV, 7, 7 f. Because of its corporeality through extension and divisibility πνεῦμα does not do any of the things that ψυχή does in Plotin. [119] Hence it can as little constitute the essence of ζωή and ψυχή as αἷμα. ψυχή is the higher principle as compared with it : καὶ μὴν οὔτε πνεῦμα διὰ πάντων οὔτε αἷμα, ψυχὴ δέ, Enn., IV, 7, 8. Only once is there cautious ref. to the πνεῦμα which "encircles" the soul, Enn., II, 2, 2.

Beyond Plotin. this thought is systematically developed in Porphyrius [120] and Corp. Herm. (Fr., 26, 13 [Nock-Fest., IV, 85, 3 ff.]) into the doctrine of the αἰθερῶδες καὶ αὐγοειδὲς πνεῦμα (or σῶμα) which derives from the ethereal spheres, which has the form of light, which is immaterial, and yet which is also changeable and transitory. As that which encloses not only the world but also analogically man, it forms the bridge, as πνευματικόν or ψυχῆς ὄχημα (Ps.-Plut. Vit. Poes. Hom., 122 [II, 1157c]), between the completely distinct essences of body and soul, matter and spirit. By means of it there takes place both the descent of the soul into the bodily world and also its reascent therefrom. On its purity depends not only the power of divination but also the whole fate of the soul on earth and even after death, Iambl. Myst., III, 11 (p. 124, 16 f.); IV, 13 (p. 198, 11 ff.). The bodies of heroes and daemons are of the same spiritual nature as the husk of the ψυχή, II, 3 (p. 73, 13). These are good or evil in so far as their ψυχαί either rule the πνεῦμα on which they rest or are ruled and affected by it, Porphyr. Abst., II, 38. Thus in spite of a certain spiritualisation which the concept has undergone as compared with Stoicism, πνεῦμα is still regarded predominantly as matter and ὄργανον (→ 354, 33 ff.) and this makes of it a phenomenon of the second rank in the constitution of the world and man.

IV. The Greek Concept of Pneuma and the NT. [121]

In spite of Stoicism, πνεῦμα has only slight and secondary significance in Greek thought as a whole. This is in contrast to its leading role in the NT. There is a certain parallelism in formal understanding. Thus, in both, πνεῦμα as a δύναμις fills, generates, catches away, inspires and discloses. It gives the power to say and do extraordinary things. It sets in relation to the truth. Nevertheless, this parallelism counts for little in comparison with that which divides the πνεῦμα of the NT from that of secular Greek thought, namely, the difference in origin and the corresponding difference in the content of essence and truth.

1. The constitutive factor of πνεῦμα in the Greek world is always its subtle and powerful corporeality. Because of its material character it is never spiritual in the strict sense, as in the NT. It is never wholly outside the realm of sense.

---

[118] Cf. Verbeke, 351-358.

[119] τίς γὰρ τάξις ἐν πνεύματι — σκεδαστοτάτῳ — δεομένῳ παρὰ ψυχῆς τάξεως, ἢ λόγος ἢ νοῦς; Enn., IV, 7, 3.

[120] Sententiae, 29 (ed. B. Mommert [1907]); Procl. in Rem. Publ., II, 196, 24 ff.; in Tim., 311a; Iambl. Myst., V, 26 (p. 239, 7); III, 14 (p. 132, 11 f.); De Anima in Stob. Ecl., I, 49, 43; Hierocl. Carm. Aur., 26.

[121] Cf. A. Bonhoeffer, "Epiktet u. d. NT," RVV, 10 (1911), 67, 160-164; Prümm, 199-201, 427-434; Verbeke, 511-544; Pohlenz, *Die Stoa*, I, 409 f., 420-422, 425 and n. To gauge the abs. difference in use cf. πνευματικόν in Plut. Quaest. Rom., 95 (II, 28b-e) (of legumes which are cultically unclean because they cause flatulence and incite to fornication) and in 1 C. 10:3 (of manna as heavenly food).

Whether in terms of Aristotelian noeticism, modern idealism or the NT under-standing, it is never set in antithesis to matter as the supernatural, wonder-working spiritual gift or manifestation of a transcendent personal God. Where all have πνεῦμα, it is a vital natural force, immanent and impersonal. As a mode or action of the air, it constantly indwells the organism of the cosmos in all its parts. Both essence and instrument, in its purest and most rarefied form as a substance of the soul it can be the seat and agent of the higher intellectual and spiritual functions. But unlike ψυχή, φρόνησις, λόγος or νοῦς, it cannot be the true subject of these. The noetic concept of spirit and the epistemology of the Greeks (except in Ps.-Plat. Ax., 370c) are orientated to and developed around, not the pragmatic ex-perience of πνεῦμα, but that of the light of day which rises upon the world. [122] Only Stoic monism consistently predicates as πνεῦμα the essence and efficacious power of deity inasmuch as this permeates the universe, giving it life and unity : θεὸς ... σῶμα, πνεῦμα ὢν νοερόν τε καὶ ἀίδιον, Chrysipp. Fr., 310 (v. Arnim, II, 112, 31 f.). Though the dominical saying : πνεῦμα ὁ θεός (Jn. 4:24), offers a formal parallel, the doxographical Stoic statement differs radically from this since it also predicates σῶμα of God. The criticism of the Apologists (Tat. Or. Graec., 2; Theophil. Autol., I, 4; II, 4) and the fathers starts at this offensive point. Though not uninfluenced by Stoic pneumatology, they contrast the divine pneuma of the NT with that of Stoicism. In the Christian Platonism of Clement of Alexan-dria (Strom., V, 89, 2), God, standing beyond the intelligible, cannot be material πνεῦμα. In its true sense πνεῦμα is explained to be οὐσία ἀσώματος καὶ ἀπερί-γραπτος, Fr., 39 (CGS, 17, 220, 6 f.), and only once (Prot., III, 43, 2) is the term used of Christ. Expounding πνεῦμα in the Stoic sense, the Platonist Celsus saw a contradiction between the character of the Christian God as πνεῦμα and His immortality; Origen's rejoinder (Cels., VI, 70 f.) is that the description of God as πνεῦμα is only a figurative attempt to explain the nature of spiritual essence with words taken from the sphere of sense : ἐὰν λέγηται 'πνεῦμα' ὁ θεός, οὐ σῶμα αὐτὸν λέγομεν εἶναι. πρὸς γὰρ ἀντιδιαστολὴν τῶν αἰσθητῶν ἔθος τῇ γραφῇ τὰ νοητὰ ὀνομάζειν πνεύματα καὶ πνευματικά, cf. Orig. Comm. in Joh., 13, 21-25.

2. If along the lines of scientific and philosophical development πνεῦμα as a physical or physiological term thus remains essentially materialistic and vitalistic, in its poetic, mythico-religious development, in which again, especially in manticism, it is never wholly freed from matter, it is an exceptional phenomenon imparted only in special circumstances to the elect, and it thus bears a very definite enthu-siastic and ecstatic character. Herewith an essentially alien Hellenistic feature was introduced already into the Jewish theology of Philo, → 374, 29 ff. The NT, though not unacquainted with enthusiastic spiritual phenomena, judges these and all kinds of μανία critically by consciously avoiding the religious vocabulary which profane Gk. customarily uses in general synonymity with πνεῦμα (cf. Poll. Onom., I, 15 : ἔνθεος, ἐνθουσιασμός, ἐπίπνους, ἐπίπνοια, ἔμπνευσις, ἐμπνεῖσθαι, κάτο-

---

[122] On the distinction between the Gk. νοῦς and the Chr. πνεῦμα, Festugière, 50, n. 3 refers to Cl. Al. Strom., V, 87, 4-88, 3 : πολλοῦ γε δεῖ ἄμοιρον εἶναι θείας ἐννοίας τὸν ἄνθρωπον, ὅ γε καὶ τοῦ ἐμφυσήματος ἐν τῇ γενέσει μεταλαβεῖν ἀναγέγραπται καθαρωτέρας οὐσίας παρὰ τὰ ἄλλα ζῷα μετασχών. ἐντεῦθεν οἱ ἀμφὶ Πυθαγόραν θείᾳ μοίρᾳ τὸν νοῦν εἰς ἀνθρώπους ἥκειν φασί, καθάπερ Πλάτων καὶ Ἀριστοτέλης ὁμολογοῦσιν. ἀλλ' ἡμεῖς μὲν τῷ πεπιστευκότι προσεπιπνεῖσθαι τὸ ἅγιον πνεῦμά φαμεν, οἱ δὲ ἀμφὶ τὸν Πλάτωνα νοῦν μὲν ἐν ψυχῇ θείας μοίρας ἀπόρροιαν ὑπάρ-χοντα, ψυχὴν δὲ ἐν σώματι κατοικίζουσιν ... ἀλλ' οὐχ ὡς μέρος θεοῦ ἐν ἑκάστῳ ἡμῶν τὸ πνεῦμα.

χος, κατέχεσθαι). Instead, it coins the new and distinctive term λαλεῖν γλώσσαις
(→ I, 722, 8). Only in the apologetic and post-apologetic writings are the Greek
expressions again used in Christian statements about the Spirit: Δανίηλος γέγονε
κάτοχος τῷ θείῳ πνεύματι, Ps. Ign. Mg., 3.

3. Along both lines the Greek mind is distinguished from that of the NT by
a theoretical and aetiological interest in the process and manner of the pneuma's
operation. No such interest is to be found at all in the NT, which is orientated
to the transcendent and divinely effected content of πνεῦμα.

4. In medicine, philosophy and religion πνεῦμα plays a specific mediatorial
role. As in the microcosm and the macrocosm it constantly mediates mechanically
between the outer and the inner, warmth and cold, centre and periphery, the
physical and the psychical, matter and spirit, so it is in religion, manticism and
magic the impersonal medium which, whether generatively, enthusiastically, magico-
theurgically or cosmogonically, achieves sporadic communication between the
divine and the human, the upper world and the nether world : τὸ δὲ πνεῦμα τὸ
τεταγμένον ἐν μέσῳ τοῦ σκότους, ὅπερ ἐστὶ κάτω, καὶ τοῦ φωτός, ὅπερ ἐστὶν
ἄνω (Sethians in Hipp. Ref., V, 19). The character of religious mediation, which
finally sets πνεῦμα on the frontier between the material and the immaterial (τὸ
δὲ μεταξὺ τοῦ κόσμου καὶ τῶν ὑπερκοσμίων μεθόριον πνεῦμα (Basileides in
Hipp. Ref., VII, 23), as ὄχημα τῆς ψυχῆς or as δαίμων establishing in the world
of later antiquity a contact between the otherwise completely separate essences of
body and soul, has been maintained as such in Christian pneumatology, though
with completely different theological presuppositions. Profane Greek knows no
hypostatic person of the Spirit understood as an independent divine entity. In the
Greek world πνεῦμα is always regarded as a thing, never as a person.

5. The Greek understanding of πνεῦμα stops at the point where the term,
even if only figuratively, breaks loose from its etymology and origin and is no
longer tied to the natural sense-phenomenon of wind or breath. For the Greeks
this cannot be separated from the nature of "spirit" in so far as it is represented
by πνεῦμα. In the NT, however, the sensory mediation of spirit no longer has
anything to do with the nature of the Spirit as the Spirit of truth who can react
to sin and give birth to faith in Christ (cf. Büchsel, 497). The secular Greek concept of πνεῦμα, whether understood physiologico-cosmologically, mantico-enthu-
siastically or in the last resort spiritually, is distinguished from the NT concept
by the fact that the God who stands behind it is quite different.

Kleinknecht

B. Spirit in the OT.

This art. deals with the linguistic foundations and hermeneutical presuppositions of
an understanding of the word πνεῦμα. The theological concept, along with related
leading concepts in biblical anthropology (ψυχή, νοῦς, καρδία etc.), is dealt with in
the art. ψυχή. No more is offered here than a development of the idea of the Spirit of
God, → 365, 6 ff.

I. Review of the Term.

The Heb. equivalents of the Gk. πνεῦμα are רוּחַ (in the LXX 264 times) and נְשָׁמָה
(3 times). [123] In the light of Lk. 24:37, 39 etc. אוֹב should also be mentioned. In Sir. 38:23
πνεῦμα stands for the Heb. נֶפֶשׁ.

---

[123] Excluding Da. Θ and Sir.

1. רוּחַ [124] in the OT.

Etym. רוּחַ (in Heb. only hi = "to smell") Arab. *rāḥā* "to blow." In Arab. there is a difference between *rīḥ* ("wind") and *rūḥ* ("spirit").

a. רוּחַ as Breath, Wind.

(a) Breath of the Mouth. רוּחַ פִּיו Ps. 33:6; רוּחַ שְׂפָתָיו Is. 11:4; אֵין־יֶשׁ־רוּחַ בְּפִיהֶם (of idols) Ps. 135:17; breath Job 19:17; to draw breath הָשִׁיב רוּחַ Job 9:18; to gasp for breath שָׁאַף רוּחַ Jer. 2:24; 14:6; breath of life Jer. 10:14; 51:17; in man and beast Qoh. 3:19, 21. Heavy breathing, snorting, rage Job 15:13; רוּחַ עָרִיצִים Is. 25:4; the snorting fury of the nations Is. 33:11; [125] a man without self-control אִישׁ אֲשֶׁר אֵין מַעְצָר לְרוּחוֹ Prv. 25:28; God's wrath רוּחַ אַפֶּיךָ Ex. 15:8; נִשְׁמַת רוּחַ אַפּוֹ par. 2 S. 22:16; גַּעֲרַת יְהוָה רוּחַ אַפּוֹ par. נִשְׁמַת אֱלוֹהַּ Job 4:9; Is. 30:28; cf. also Jer. 22:22.

(b) Breath of Air, Wind. Soft breeze Job 4:15; 41:8; par. רוּחַ הוֹלֵךְ וְלֹא יָשׁוּב הֶבֶל Is. 57:13; Ps. 78:39. Wind *passim* (also Job 15:30, reading פָּרְחוֹ for פִּיו with LXX; Job 26:13 uncertain); [126] daily wind from the west רוּחַ הַיּוֹם Gn. 3:8. Strong wind, storm par. זֶרֶם Is. 32:2; par. סוּפָה Is. 17:13; Job 21:18; par. סְעָרָה Is. 41:16; par. תְּשׁוּאָה (read תְּשֻׁאָה) Job 30:22; with צרר (perhaps "to seize") Hos. 4:19; רוּחַ גְּדוֹלָה Job 1:19; Jon. 1:4; רוּחַ חָזָק Ex. 10:19; 1 K. 19:11; רוּחַ גְּדוֹלָה וְחָזָק Ex. 14:21; רוּחַ קָדִים עַזָּה Ex. 14:21; רוּחַ קָשָׁה Is. 27:8; [127] רוּחַ כַּבִּיר Job 8:2; רוּחַ סֹעָה tearing wind par. סַעַר Ps. 55:8; (= רוּחַ צַח) רוּחַ מָלֵא hot wind, v. 11) Jer. 4:12; רוּחַ סְעָרוֹת Ez. 1:4 etc. רוּחַ סְעָרוֹת par. גֶּשֶׁם שֹׁטֵף Ez. 13:11, 13; burning wind רוּחַ זִלְעָפוֹת Ps. 11:6; רוּחַ יְהוָה for the demonic force of the storm Is. 59:19, cf. Ex. 15:8, 10. A specific wind רוּחַ (הַ)קָּדִים Ex. 14:21; 10:13 etc.; רוּחַ מִדְבָּר Jer. 13:24; רוּחַ יָם Ex. 10:19; רוּחַ צָפוֹן Prv. 25:23; Sir. 43:20. For the four corners of heaven or four regions of the world (Assyr. *erbitti šârê*) (הַשָּׁמַיִם) אַרְבַּע רוּחוֹת Zech. 6:5; Da. 7:2; 8:8 etc.; אַרְבַּע רוּחוֹת מֵאַרְבַּע קְצוֹת הַשָּׁמַיִם Jer. 49:36; לְכָל־רוּחַ (רוּחוֹת) זָרָה (פָּרַשׂ) Jer. 49:32; Ez. 17:21 etc.; east etc. side of an area (הַיָּם, הַדָּרוֹם, הַצָּפוֹן) רוּחַ הַקָּדִים Ez. 42:16 ff. Wind in a transf. sense "vanity," "futility," "deception" Job 6:26; 7:7 par. תֹּהוּ, אֶפֶס, אָוֶן Is. 41:29; par. שֶׁקֶר Mi. 2:11; par. הֶבֶל Qoh. 1:14, 17 etc.; windy knowledge דַּעַת רוּחַ Job 15:2; windy speech דִּבְרֵי־רוּחַ Job 16:3; to be air הָיָה לְרוּחַ Jer. 5:13; רְעֶה רוּחַ Hos. 12:2; זְרַע רוּחַ Hos. 8:7; יֶלֶד רוּחַ Is. 26:18; נָחַל רוּחַ Prv. 11:29; עָמָל לְרוּחַ Qoh. 5:15; רְעוּת רוּחַ Qoh. 1:14 etc. "vain striving" רַעְיוֹן רוּחַ Qoh. 1:17; 4:16. God sends the wind, Jer. 4:12 (יָבוֹא לִי); Ez. 13:13 (pi בקע); Am. 4:13 (ברא); Ex. 10:19 (הפך); Jon. 1:4 (hi טול); Ps. 135:7; Jer. 10:13; 51:16 (hi יצא); Jon. 4:8 (pi מנה); Ex. 10:13 (pi נהג); Nu. 11:31 (נסע מֵאֵת יְהוָה); Ps. 147:18 (hi נשב); Gn. 8:1 (hi עבר); Ps. 107:25 (hi עמד); Ex. 14:21; Ps. 48:7; the wind is יְהוָה רוּחַ Is. 40:7; 59:19; Hos. 13:15; it is His רוּחַ Ex. 15:10 (נשף בְּ); Ps. 147:18; Is. 27:8. [127]

b. רוּחַ in Man.

(a) The Principle which Gives Life to the Body, → 368, 23 ff.

רוּחַ חַיִּים is also said of the beast, Gn. 6:17; 7:15. [128] A sign of the רוּחַ indwelling and giving life to the body is נְשָׁמָה, the breath of life, בְּאַפָּיו (cf. Gn. 7:22, [129] and

---

[124] On the gender cf. K. Albrecht, "Das Geschlecht d. hbr. Hauptwörter," ZAW, 16 (1896), 42-44; on the usage cf. Cremer.

[125] Though possibly we should read רוּחִי כְמוֹ with Targ. or רוּחַ כְּמוֹ with O. Procksch, *Jesaia* I, *Komm. AT*, 9, 1 (1930), ad loc.

[126] The meaning of שִׁפְרָה is not clear.

[127] Unless we are to read כְּרוּחַ חַקַּשׁ with Procksch, *op. cit.*, ad loc.

[128] Cf. → n. 129.

[129] Gn. 7:22 perhaps נִשְׁמַת חַיִּים with the LXX.

רוּחַ אַפֵּנוּ as a term for the king in Lam. 4:20, [130] also Job 27:3); רוּחַ par. נְשָׁמָה Is. 42:5; [131] idols have no life, Hab. 2:19. The entry of רוּחַ gives life : וְנָתַתִּי בָכֶם רוּחַ וִחְיִיתֶם Ez. 37:5 f.; if God (אֱלֹהֵי הָרוּחֹת לְכָל־בָּשָׂר) Nu. 16:22; 27:16) takes away רוּחַ (אסף) Ps. 104:29) or it returns to God (שׁוּב Qoh. 12:7) they die ; the spirit of life or life-force [132] is sustained (שׁמר) Job 10:12, revives (חיה) Gn. 45:27; (שׁוּב) 1 S. 30:12; Ju. 15:19, vanishes (יצא) Ps. 146:4, fades away (כלה) Ps. 143:7, languishes par. נְשָׁמָה (עטף) Is. 57:16; dies out (רוּחִי חֲבָלָה) Job 17:1; [133] loss of vital force שֶׁבֶר בְּרוּחַ Prv. 15:4; it became powerless (through astonishment) וְלֹא־הָיָה בָהּ עוֹד רוּחַ 1 K. 10:5. Then "life" Ps. 31:5; par. נֶפֶשׁ Job 12:10; Mal. 2:15 f. (on נִשְׁמַר בְּרוּחַ "to take care one does not lose one's life" cf. נִשְׁמָר בְּנֶפֶשׁ Jer. 17:21; נִשְׁמַר לְנֶפֶשׁ Dt. 4:15; Jos. 23:11); חַיֵּי רוּחִי (though text uncertain) Is. 38:16.

(b) The Seat of the Emotions, Intellectual Functions and Attitude of Will, → 369, 17 ff.

The seat of emotions : inner disquiet 2 K. 19:7; [134] Gn. 41:8; Da. 2:3 (to be un-settled ni פעם); Da. 2:1 (hitp פעם); Da. 7:15 (to be confused ithpeal כרא); oppression, harassment מֹרַת רוּחַ Gn. 26:35; an unhappy woman אִשָּׁה קְשַׁת־רוּחַ 1 S. 1:15; [135] עֲצוּבַת רוּחַ Is. 54:6; a spirit which is cast down רוּחַ נְכֵאָה Prv. 15:13 etc.; despondency רוּחַ כֵּהָה Is. 61:3; par. לֵב Ez. 21:12 (extinguish pi כהה); lack of spirit קְצֶר רוּחַ Ex. 6:9; impatience Job 21:4 and Prv. 14:29 (קצר); bad temper Ju. 8:3; Prv. 1:23; 18:14; [136] 29:11; Qoh. 10:4; Sir. 4:9 (קוץ); בַּחֲמַת רוּחַ Ez. 3:14; [137] one who can control his wrath מֹשֵׁל בְּרוּחוֹ Prv. 16:32; bitterness רוּחַ סָרָה 1 K. 21:5; irritation par. כַּעַס Qoh. 7:9; I am vexed תִּתְעַטֵּף רוּחִי par. מַר רוּחַ Job 7:11; יִשְׁתּוֹמֵם לְבִּי Ps. 77:3; 143:4 (cf. 142:4); despair בְּצַר רוּחַ par. בְּמַר נַפְשִׁי Job 7:11; Sir. 7:11; שֶׁבֶר רוּחַ par. כְּאֵב לֵב Is. 65:14; terror Job 6:4; arrogance Ps. 76:12; (par. לֵבַב) Da. 5:20; jealousy רוּחַ קִנְאָה Nu. 5:14, 30; religious emotion רוּחַ חֵן Zech. 12:10.

Seat of the intellectual functions, of rational and religious perception : reason Job 32:8; [138] a residue of reason שְׁאָר רוּחַ Mal. 2:15; [139] רוּחַ חָכְמָה Dt. 34:9; extraordinary cleverness רוּחַ יַתִּירָא Da. 6:4 (par. מַנְדַּע and שָׂכְלְתָנוּ) Da. 5:12; insight into divine mysteries רוּחַ אֱלָהִין קַדִּישִׁין בֵּהּ Da. 4:5; 5:11 etc.; artistic sense Ex. 28:3; fulness of thoughts Job 32:18; planning 1 Ch. 28:12; a spirit which knows more than I רוּחַ מִבִּינָתִי [140] Job 20:3; inability to perceive and act aright (spirit of confusion) רוּחַ עִוְעִים Is. 19:14; the erroneous thoughts of the nebiim Ez. 13:3; lack of religious and moral insight תֹּעֵי־רוּחַ Is. 29:24; רוּחַ תַּרְדֵּמָה Is. 29:10; seat of religious reflection par. לֵבָב Ps. 77:6 (the רוּחַ searches pi חפש), of prophetic vision Sir. 48:24.

Seat of the disposition, attitude of will, character ; will and character generally. Active readiness for something נָדְבָה רוּחוֹ par. impulse of the heart נְשָׂאוֹ לִבּוֹ Ex. 35:21; resolve

---

[130] Also šari balâtiia = "breath of my life," to the king in the Amarna letters (J. A. Knudtzon, Die el-Amarna-Tafeln [1915], No. 141, 2; 143, 1; 144, 2; cf. šariia "my breath," 281, 3.

[131] רוּחַ אָדָם Zech. 12:1, based on Is. 42:5, is not relevant here.

[132] Possibly חַיֵּי רוּחִי Is. 38:16 (cf. v. 16b וְהַחֲיֵנִי), though the text is uncertain.

[133] The par. יָמַי (time of life) demands this interpretation, hence not "my spirit is con-fused."

[134] The meaning is not wholly clear, cf. Volz, Geist, 13.

[135] Unless we are to read קְשַׁת יוֹם with the LXX.

[136] Read מְחַלֵּהוּ with LXX.

[137] Though cf. J. Herrmann, Ez., Komm. AT, 11 (1924), ad loc.: "רוּחַ is not the spirit of the prophet, but the Spirit which has come into him."

[138] But cf. → 363, 19.

[139] The meaning, however, is uncertain.

[140] So correctly G. Beer, Der Text d. Buches Hi. (1895), ad loc. (unless the text is corrupt); acc. to others "spirit of my understanding"; hardly "wind without understanding" (reading מִבִּינָה with LXX).

of the will הֵעִיר אֶת־רוּחַ Jer. 51:1; Hag. 1:14; Ezr. 1:1; 1 Ch. 5:26 etc.; considered will par. עֵצָה Is. 19:3; thoughts which arise מַעֲלוֹת רוּחֲכֶם Ez. 11:5 (related to עֵצַת־רָע in v. 2); what comes into the mind הָעֹלָה עַל רוּחַ Ez. 20:32; another (better) attitude of will רוּחַ אַחֶרֶת Nu. 14:24; courage par. לֵב Jos. 2:11; 5:1; Sir. 48:12; of a cool spirit קַר רוּחַ Prv. 17:27; reliability נֶאֱמַן רוּחַ Prv. 11:13; forbearance אֶרֶךְ־רוּחַ Qoh. 7:8; Sir. 5:11; humility שְׁפַל־רוּחַ Prv. 16:19; 29:23; pride גֹּבַהּ רוּחַ Prv. 16:18 (cf. Qoh. 7:8); total personal attitude Prv. 16:2. Religious and moral attitude of will. Active freedom רוּחַ נְדִיבָה Ps. 51:12; longing for God par. נֶפֶשׁ Is. 26:9 (pi שׁחר); readiness to repent רוּחַ נִשְׁבָּרָה par. לֵב Ps. 51:17; דַּכָּאֵי־רוּחַ par. נִשְׁבְּרֵי לֵב Ps. 34:18; שְׁפַל־רוּחַ and רוּחַ שְׁפָלִים par. לֵב נִדְכָּאִים Is. 57:15; [141] נְכֵה־רוּחַ Is. 66:2; he does not seek to hide his sin אֵין בְּרוּחוֹ רְמִיָּה Ps. 32:2; renewal of will רוּחַ חֲדָשָׁה par. לֵב חָדָשׁ [142] Ez. 11:19; 18:31; 36:26; "firmness" רוּחַ נָכוֹן par. לֵב טָהוֹר Ps. 51:10; obduracy par. אִמֵּץ אֶת־לְבָבוֹ Dt. 2:30 (hi קשׁה); ungodly attitude: unfaithfulness רוּחַ הַטֻּמְאָה Zech. 13:2. רוּחַ זְנוּנִים Hos. 4:12; 5:4; לֹא נֶאֶמְנָה רוּחוֹ [143] par. לֹא הֵכִין לִבּוֹ Ps. 78:8; Zech. 13:2.

(c) Divinely Effected רוּחַ.

God is אֱלֹהֵי הָרוּחוֹת לְכָל־בָּשָׂר Nu. 16:22; 27:16; God gives vital force, the spirit of life Is. 42:5; Ez. 37:6 (נתן); Ez. 37:5 (hi בוא); Zech. 12:1 (יצר); He upholds it Job 10:12 (שמר); it returns to Him Qoh. 12:7 (שוב); God takes away the spirit of life, which is רוּחַ of His רוּחַ (cf. v. 30) Ps. 104:29 (אסף); life is in the power of God Job 12:10. God causes disquiet 2 K. 19:7 (נתן), religious fervour Zech. 12:10 (שפך). He gives reason Job 32:8 (the par. נִשְׁמַת שַׁדַּי shows that it is God's work); [144] the divine רוּחַ is imparted by laying on of hands with the רוּחַ חָכְמָה Dt. 34:9; God gives an artistic sense Ex. 28:3 (pi מלא). Incapacity for true perception Is. 19:14 (מסך) and Is. 29:10 (נסך); insight into divine mysteries is given by the gods (a Gentile statement) Da. 4:5; 5:11 etc.; God is behind planning Jer. 51:1, 11; Hag. 1:14; Ezr. 1:1, 5; 1 Ch. 5:26; 2 Ch. 21:16; 36:22 (in each case hi עור); He destroys it Is. 19:3 (ni בקק); [145] He gives the will moral power Ez. 11:19 (נתן) and also hardens it Dt. 2:30 (hi קשׁה).

c. The רוּחַ of God.

(a) Effective Divine Power.

The divine agent in general: God's רוּחַ is the force behind the cherubim Ez. 1:12, 20, Samson Ju. 13:25 (פעם); gives unusual bodily powers Ju. 14:6, 19; 15:14 (צלח על); sets the prophet on his feet Ez. 2:2; 3:24 (בוא ב).

The רוּחַ of God induces ecstasy Nu. 11:25, 29 (נתן על); Nu. 11:17 (שׂים על); Nu. 11:25 f.; 2 K. 2:15 (נוח על); 1 S. 10:6, 10 (צלח על); 1 S. 19:20, 23 (היה על); 2 K. 2:9 (היה אל); lifts up 1 K. 18:12; 2 K. 2:16; Ez. 3:12, 14; 8:3; 11:1, 24; 43:5 (נשׂא); snatches away Ez. 3:14 (לקח); sets in another place 2 K. 2:16 (hi שׁלך); Ez. 8:3; 11:1, 24; 43:5 (hi בוא); Ez. 37:1 (hi יצא); the ecstatic is אִישׁ הָרוּחַ par. הַנָּבִיא Hos. 9:7.

The רוּחַ is responsible for prophetic or ecstatic speech: רוּחַ אֱלֹהִים בּוֹ (cf. הוֹדִיעַ אֱלֹהִים v. 39) Gn. 41:38; רוּחַ יְהוָֹה דִּבֶּר בִּי 2 S. 23:2; 1 K. 22:24 par. 2 Ch. 18:23 (דבר pi אֵת); Nu. 24:2 (היה על); Is. 61:1 (רוּחַ עָלַי); Ez. 11:5 (נפל על); Jl. 2:28 f. (שפך על); 2 Ch. 24:20 (לבשׁ); God gives the prophetic message through the רוּחַ [146] Zech. 7:12. Of inspired

---

[141] Cf. P. Volz, *Jesaia II, Komm. AT*, 9, 2 (1932), *ad loc.*

[142] So also Ez. 11:19 as against Mas. (אֶחָד) and LXX (אַחֵר); cf. H. Cornill, *Das Buch d. Propheten Ez.* (1886), *ad loc.*

[143] Excise אֶת־אֵל. cf. H. Gunkel, *Die Ps., Handkomm. AT*, II, 2⁴ (1926), *ad loc.*

[144] Unless the text is corrupt and originally רוּחַ אֵל (Symmachos), in which case → 363, 9 f.

[145] God is subj., cf. the par. אֲבַלַּע.

[146] Unless בְּרוּחוֹ is an addition.

speech generally 1 Ch. 12:19 (לבש); 2 Ch. 15:1; 20:14 (על היה). Visions as works of the רוּחַ Ez. 8:3 (בְּרוּחַ אֱלֹהִים); 11:24 (בַּמַּרְאֶה בְּרוּחַ אֱלֹהִים). [147]

The רוּחַ gives the charisma of leadership Ju. 3:10; 11:29 (על היה); 6:34 (לבש); 1 S. 11:6; 16:13 (צלח; opp. סור 16:14). The charismatic leader אִישׁ אֲשֶׁר־רוּחַ בּוֹ Nu. 27:18.

The רוּחַ is behind the demonic (רוּחַ רָעָה) in man Ju. 9:23 (שלח subj. God); 1 S. 16:14 f. (the רוּחַ overtakes suddenly בעת), 16 (אל היה); 23; 1 S. 19:9 (על היה); 1 S. 18:10 (צלח).

In the ref. under (a) the verbal predicates show that what it at issue is the mysterious aspect of the work of God's Spirit rather than the creative power of God through the gift of the Spirit, as under (b).

(b) Specifically God's Creative Power.

The divine power which creates physical life : God is this power Ez. 37:9, 10 (cf. v. 14); He injects it into His people Ez. 37:14 (נתן ב), par. בְּרָכָה [148] Is. 44:3 (יצק); He sends it to man Ps. 104:30 (שלח); it is בָּאָדָם Gn. 6:3; it is identical with His נִשְׁמָה Job 27:3; God withdraws it par. נִשְׁמָה Job 34:14 (אסף); it creates the cosmos Gn. 1:2 [149] and life within it רוּחַ פִּיו Ps. 33:5 (עשה); par. נִשְׁמָה Job 33:4 (עשה); Is. 32:15 (ni ערה).

The divine power which gives mental abilities : God fills (pi מלא) with חָכְמָה (cf. Dt. 34:9), insight (תְּבוּנָה), artistic sense (דַּעַת), skill (מְלָאכָה) Ex. 31:3; 35:31, enlightenment (נָהִירוּ), perspicacity (שָׂכְלְתָנוּ), wisdom (חָכְמָה) Da. 5:14; perhaps one may also refer in this connection to Job 32:8 (read רוּחַ יְהוָה for רוּחַ הִיא, cf. par. נִשְׁמַת שַׁדַּי.

The charisma of the prophet : מָלֵאתִי כֹּחַ אֶת־רוּחַ יְהוָה וּמִשְׁפָּט וּגְבוּרָה Mi. 3:8; [150] Neh. 9:30 (בְּרוּחֲךָ) identical with (בְּיַד נְבִיאֶיךָ); the prophet as a man inspired by God [151] Is. 48:16. [152]

Equipment to be a perfect ruler : [153] the רוּחַ יְהוָה (נוח על) fashions wisdom (חָכְמָה), understanding (בִּינָה), true kingly action (עֵצָה), constancy (גְּבוּרָה), piety (דַּעַת וְיִרְאַת יְהוָה) Is. 11:2; cf. Is. 42:1 (נתן על).

God's Spirit fashions moral powers : the רוּחַ gives מִשְׁפָּט and צְדָקָה Is. 32:15 (ni ערה על), in the judge מִשְׁפָּט and in the soldier גְּבוּרָה Is. 28:6 confident will Hag. 2:5; Zech. 4:6 (opp. חַיִל and כֹּחַ); 6:8, [154] sanctification (רוּחַ קָדְשֶׁךָ) Ps. 51:11, sanctification of the people Is. 59:21; [155] Ez. 36:27 (נתן); 39:29 (שפך על).

God's judging and saving power : Through the רוּחַ God effects judgment (רוּחַ מִשְׁפָּט, רוּחַ בָּעֵר Is. 4:4; 30:28, רוּחַ אַפּוֹ par. נִשְׁמַת אֱלוֹהַּ Job 4:9; the Spirit brings paradisial fulness, material fortune, social peace, security Is. 32:15 (ni ערה על) as רוּחַ טוֹבָה it gives aid Ps. 143:10 (hi נחה) and shows what is right Neh. 9:20 (נתן subj. God); God puts His Holy Spirit in the hearts of His people (רוּחַ קָדְשׁוֹ) Is. 63:11; His רוּחַ brings it rest Is. 63:14 (הֵנִיחַ). [156]

---

[147] Though perhaps בְּרוּחַ is a gloss.

[148] Cf. Mal. 3:10.

[149] רוּחַ אֱלֹהִים: the sense "God's storm" (cf. G. v. Rad, *Das erste Buch Mose, AT Deutsch,* 2² [1950], 37 and K. Galling, "Der Charakter d. Chaosschilderung in Gn. 1:2," ZThK, 47 [1950], 153-156, with bibl) is questionable, for רוּחַ is adequately attested elsewhere as creative principle, and this fits in well here.

[150] Unless אֶת־רוּחַ יהוה is a gloss.

[151] A. Dillmann, *Der Prophet Jesaia⁵, Kurzgefasstes exeget. Handbuch z. AT* (1890), ad loc.

[152] רוּחוֹ is obj., though perhaps the text is not original, cf. the proposals in Volz, ad loc.; J. A. Bewer, "Textkrit. Bemerkungen z. AT," *Festschr. f. A. Bertholet* (1950), 66.

[153] Cf. Dillmann, *op. cit.* on Is. 11:2.

[154] The meaning of רוּחַ in Zech. 6:8 is contested (spirit of wrath?); I am construing it in the sense of a promise, cf. E. Sellin, *Das Zwölfprophetenbuch, Komm. AT,* 12 (1922), ad loc.; F. Horst, *Die zwölf Kleinen Propheten, Hndbch. AT,* I, 14 (1954), ad loc.

[155] Is. 59:21 is, however, very hard to understand, cf. Volz, ad loc.

[156] One should keep to the Mas. here as against the versions, cf. Volz, ad loc.

(c) The Inner Nature of God.

רוּחַ denotes God's incorruptibility and sustaining power (opp. בָּשָׂר) Is. 31:3, His omnipresence par. פְּנֵי יְהוָֹה Ps. 139:7, His unfathomable power and wisdom as Creator Is. 40:13, the fact that He is commanding will Is. 34:16, holy, demanding will : refractoriness against Him (רוּחַ קָדְשׁוֹ) Is. 63:10 (pi עצב); Ps. 106:33 (hi מרה); His overlooking (לֹא רוּחִי) Is. 30:1; His patience הֲקָצַר רוּחַ יְהוָֹה Mi. 2:7.

(d) רוּחַ as Personal Being.

In 1 K. 22:21 par. 2 Ch. 18:20 (וַיֵּצֵא הָרוּחַ וַיַּעֲמֹד לִפְנֵי יְהוָֹה) the רוּחַ releases demonic powers (שֶׁקֶר), → 363, 5; in Ez. 37:9 the רוּחַ is distinguished from God. Whether Is. 48:16 should be mentioned in this connection is doubtful → n. 152. [157]

2. נְשָׁמָה or נִשְׁמָא in the OT.

Etym. נָשַׁם = Arab. *nasama* "to blow" (in Heb. only q "to breathe heavily" Is. 42:14).

a. נְשָׁמָה as Breath.

נְשָׁמָה בְּאַפּוֹ Is. 2:22 strong breathing, snorting, of God's wrathful breath Is. 30:33, in this sense par. רוּחַ Job 4:9 (→ 360, 10), par. גַּעֲרַת יְהוָֹה 2 S. 22:16 (→ 360, 10).

b. נְשָׁמָה in Man.

The principle which gives life to the body : the breath of life Gn. 7:22 [158] (→ 360, 38) par. רוּחַ אֱלוֹהַּ בְּאַפִּי Job 27:3; נִשְׁמַת חַיִּים (God blows it in וַיִּפַּח בְּאַפָּיו) Gn. 2:7; the vital force which God gives Is. 42:5 (נתן); par. כֹּחַ Da. 10:17; 1 K. 17:17; נְשָׁמוֹת par. רוּחַ fail Is. 57:16; everything living כָּל־(ה)נְשָׁמָה Dt. 20:16; Jos. 10:40; 11:11, 14; 1 K. 15:29; Ps. 150:6; life par. אָרְחָתְךָ (destiny) Da. 5:23; with לקח Sir. 9:13. Seat of understanding or inspiration Job 26:4.

c. The נְשָׁמָה of God.

(a) The Principle which Gives Physical Life : נִשְׁמַת שַׁדַּי תְּחַיֵּנִי par. רוּחַ Job 33:4; God withdraws His spirit of life par. רוּחַ Job 34:14 (אסף); as the creative power in nature נִשְׁמַתְאָ ל [159] Job 37:10 (נתן); cf. also Gn. 2:7 (→ line 17 f.).

(b) That which Gives Man Insight : intellectual par. perhaps רוּחַ־יְהוָֹה for רוּחַ הִיא Job 32:8, moral נֵר יְהוָֹה נִשְׁמַת אָדָם [160] (נִשְׁמַת אָדָם) here equals נִשְׁמַת שַׁדַּי in Job 32:8) Prv. 20:27.

3. אוֹב in the OT.

Etym. unknown (perhaps from אוֹב = Arab. *'âba* "to return" or connected with אוֹב in Job 32:19 a "water-skin which gives off a dull sound").

a. Spirit of the Dead, → 376, 23 ff. [161] (often with יִדְּעֹנִי spirit of soothsaying)

---

[157] The meaning of רוּחַ is uncertain in the following passages : Is. 11:15 : here בְּעָיָם is inexplicable, and the versions are no help ; storm seems to be suggested by the context, cf. LXX πνεύματι βιαίῳ; Jer. 52:23 : רוּחָה makes no sense, the text is uncertain, LXX obviously took it to mean "direction" (ἕν μέρος), cf. μέρος for רוּחַ LXX Ez. 42:20; Ez. 1:20, 21; 10:17: רוּחַ הַחַיָּה "spirit of the living creature," more likely acc. to the context LXX "spirit of life" (πνεῦμα ζωῆς), but this is impossible on philological grounds, cf. H. Cornill, *Das Buch d. Propheten Ez.* (1886), on 1:20; in the usual emendations (רוּחַ חַיָּית or רוּחַ אַחַת) is the striving will, unless the ref. is to the miracle of harmony of movement, cf. Volz, *Geist*, 44.

[158] → n. 129.

[159] "Storm" is also a possible meaning in view of v. 9 and Sir. 43:20.

[160] If the text is in order. Perhaps one should read נֹצֵר for נֵר, cf. BHK³ and B. Gemser, *Sprüche Salomos, Hndbch. AT*, I, 16 (1937), *ad loc.*

[161] Other meanings, e.g., object with the help of which one conjures up the dead, A. Jirku,

Lv. 19:31; 20:6; Dt. 18:11; 1 S. 28:8; Is. 8:19; 19:3; 29:4; 1 Ch. 10:13; the spirit can be in (בְ) man Lv. 20:27; a woman who has power over the spirits of the dead בַּעֲלַת אוֹב 1 S. 28:7.

b. Conjurer up of spirits of the dead (always with יִדְּעֹנִי) 1 S. 28:3, 9; 2 K. 21:6; 23:24; 2 Ch. 33:6.

II. The Spirit of God.

1. "The Egyptians are אָדָם and not אֵל, and their horses are בָּשָׂר and not רוּחַ," says Is. 31:3. בָּשָׂר is earthly frailty and impotence and its bearer is אָדָם, while רוּחַ is absolute power and majesty and its bearer is אֵל. The dynamic enclosed in the רוּחַ יְהוָה is expressed hereby. This dynamic may be discerned in the works of the רוּחַ. The Spirit of God changes the desert into paradise, and through the Spirit the wilderness becomes the abode of מִשְׁפָּט and צְדָקָה, Is. 32:15 ff. There is in this dynamism an ethical element, cf. Is. 30:1, where plans are followed which are outside the רוּחַ יְהוָה, and sin is thus added to sin. The רוּחַ יְהוָה has the power to refashion creatively, cf. Ps. 51:10 f. The creation of a religious and moral sphere is the goal. In this sense the רוּחַ יְהוָה rests on the Messiah as רוּחַ עֵצָה וּגְבוּרָה and as רוּחַ דַּעַת וְיִרְאַת יְהוָה, Is. 11:2. In the same sense the Spirit works through the servant of the Lord, Is. 42:1 ff. The perfecting of Israel is through God's Spirit, through whom a heart of stone is changed into a heart of flesh and the people is transformed thereby into a community fixed on God, Ez. 36:26 f. [162] It would be mistaken to think, however, that according to the prophets the Spirit of God deploys His life-giving power only in the new aeon. [163] The transformation of the people into a true people of God is indeed by way of judgment upon it. Prophecy sees this judgment already at work (imminent expectation). In Is. 31:3 (also 30:1 ff.) promise and judgment go together. For the prophets both are in the same way a present work of God's Spirit.

In principle, then, it is plain, especially in classical prophecy, that the רוּחַ יְהוָה is power, morally defined power. This power is effective i.e., it is the working out of God's personal will directed to a religious and moral end. It is also a historical power worked out upon Israel. The transformation of Israel into a new condition, the creation of the רוּחַ חֲדָשָׁה (Ez. 11:19; 18:31; 36:26; cf. Ps. 51:10), takes place through the divine judgment in historical events. This transformation means both the end and also the consummation of the history of Israel. Divine power filling the world in a polytheistic sense is thus negated. Such power is recognised to be a flight from the personal work of the will of God, from His unconditional majesty. It is thus characterised as revolt against God, as sin. Also negated herewith is the idea that divine powers may be habitually present in man. At this point there is antithesis to Egyptian and Babylonian religion, in which the king is the incarnation of divine power. Man is not deified in Israel. Man is subject to this power; he is not himself the power. He is בָּשָׂר not רוּחַ. Furthermore, the רוּחַ יְהוָה, though experienced as the work of God's will, is inscrutable. No one knows when or how it will work. The dates and contents of prophecy are imprecise. No attempt at harmonising can remove the distinctions and even the contradictions. Though the dynamic of the רוּחַ יְהוָה may be detected, the logic

---

Die Dämonen u. ihre Abwehr im AT (1912), 10, or humming wood, H. Schmidt, "אוֹב," Festschr. f. K. Marti (1925), 253-261, are open to question.

[162] Cf. also Is. 4:2 ff.; 44:3; Zech. 12:10.
[163] Eichr. Theol., II² (1948), 26 f.

defies analysis. The רוּחַ is the free incalculable working of the divine will. As regards God's plan the when and the how are unknown. The fact of the power of the divine will is, however, beyond dispute.

2. The second characteristic of the רוּחַ יְהוָה is best brought out by the saying in P: "The Spirit of God moved upon the face of the waters," Gn. 1:2. Here, too, the רוּחַ יְהוָה is viewed as a dynamic creative principle. The reference is not just to the work of God's will in the creation of the cosmos (cf. Ps. 33:5). Everything living, all physical life, derives from this dynamism. The רוּחַ יְהוָה, coming from God, is the active principle which gives physical life, Gn. 2:7. [164] Closeness to דְּבַר יְהוָה "and God spake" is implicit in רוּחַ יְהוָה: God creates בְּרוּחַ פִּיו (Ps. 33:5 par. בִּדְבַר יְהוָה). With His רוּחַ, however, God is also at work as Sustainer of His creation. If God withdraws His רוּחַ, His נְשָׁמָה, all flesh must die, Job 34:14; cf. Ps. 104:29 f. "The רוּחַ אֵל hath made me, and the נִשְׁמַת שַׁדַּי hath given me life," Job 33:4.

In this connection, too, the רוּחַ יְהוָה is the personal, creative power of God. Excluded, therefore, is any belief in divine powers along the lines of a pantheistic-mythical-mystical understanding of the cosmos and natural events. There are no immanent divine forces in nature. In contrast to the religious beliefs of the world around, nature is stripped of power and de-deified. Once again the creative power of God is a power which gives freely. But again it is also unfathomable and even mysterious. The gift of the רוּחַ is limited, Gn. 6:3. When God will withdraw His "breath" cannot be known. The divine dynamism may be discerned and experienced, but it is unsearchable. These are the basic points.

3. Israel, however, experiences the historically active רוּחַ יְהוָה in yet another way in which we miss the religious and ethical element so strongly emphasised hitherto. [165] Through His רוּחַ God equips for national political action by raising up charismatic leaders for the people in the period when there was as yet no hereditary monarchy, e.g., Othniel (Ju. 3:10), Gideon (6:34), Jephthah (11:29), Saul (1 S. 11:6). On David, too, the רוּחַ יְהוָה descends when he is anointed by Samuel, 1 S. 16:13. Here again the Spirit is unfathomable and incalculable, distributing where and to whom He will. Men hitherto disregarded suddenly emerge as leaders under the work of the רוּחַ.

The sudden and mysterious aspect of the work of the רוּחַ is particularly stressed when the reference is to states of ecstasy. The ecstatic is called אִישׁ הָרוּחַ, Hos. 9:7. The רוּחַ יְהוָה leaps on Saul (צָלַח עַל) so that he is set in an ecstatic state, 1 S. 10:6, 10. Samson's sudden strength comes on him when he is ecstatically stimulated by the רוּחַ יְהוָה Ju. 14:6, 19; 15:14 (צלח על here too). In Nu. 11:24 ff. there is reflection on the work of the Spirit (E). God takes of the Spirit that is in Him and imparts it to the seventy elders, who are set in a state of ecstasy which then spreads to others. We are also referred to the ecstatic sphere by passages in which the רוּחַ יְהוָה produces prophetic utterance or rapture, → 362, 32 ff. Here, too, the רוּחַ יְהוָה is an unpredictable but irresistible power of God, often demonic in nature. The dynamism of the רוּחַ יְהוָה is certainly experienced, but neither its logical basis nor its timing and duration can be discerned.

---

[164] Cf. Gn. 2:7 נִשְׁמַת חַיִּים with Gn. 6:17 רוּחַ חַיִּים.

[165] This is, of course, self-evident for Israel, since holy war is a sacral institution, cf. G. v. Rad, Der heilige Krieg im alten Israel (1951), 29-33.

4. The final observations have already brought us to the sphere of comparative religious phenomenology, for similar works of divine power are familiar in the religions around Israel. Ecstasy can hardly have had its root in Israel, nor in other Semitic religions. It points rather in the direction of the Indo-European religions. It is no accident that the same Hebrew word רוּחַ is used for both "spirit" and "wind," → 360, 2 ff. The wind is powerful ; it is indeed irresistible in its force. It is also mysterious : "The wind bloweth where it listeth, and thou hearest the sound thereof, but canst not tell whence it cometh, and whither it goeth," Jn. 3:8. Mysterious and unfathomable forces are at one in this with the wind. These divine forces are a breathing, a רוּחַ, of God. Hence in other religions, too, they are known as divine powers which bring either deliverance or destruction. In terms of its belief in רוּחַ Israel is embedded in its environment.

Classical prophecy took the thought of the רוּחַ from the surrounding world, lifted the divine רוּחַ out of religious and ethical neutrality, and understood it as the teleological will and work of personal divine power. רוּחַ יְהוָה is a term for the historical creative action of the one God which, though it defies logical analysis, is always God's action. Hence רוּחַ יְהוָה can be an expression for God's inner nature and presence. [166]

הֲקָצֵר רוּחַ יְהוָה was once the answer of opponents to Micah and his threats, Mi. 2:7. When judgment was executed on the people, the belief persisted that God's רוּחַ is not "too short," that in spite of all appearances God is present in His רוּחַ as Lord of history. God keeps the promise in terms of which His רוּחַ has fashioned history and will lead it to its goal. The רוּחַ יְהוָה as God's powerful and irresistible saving action becomes helping power : "My spirit is among you ; fear ye not" (Hag. 2:5); "not by might, nor by power, but by my spirit" (Zech. 4:6). The Spirit of God assembles the whole people of God, Zech. 6:1 ff. The רוּחַ יְהוָה seals the faithfulness of God to His covenant, Is. 59:21.

5. Attention may be drawn to yet another aspect of the understanding of the רוּחַ יְהוָה in Israel. Depriving cosmic and earthly forces of their strength, the OT anchors the demonic in the only power there is, i.e., the רוּחַ יְהוָה. The רוּחַ יְהוָה can work as רוּחַ רָעָה, Ju. 9:23; 1 S. 16:14 ff.; 18:10. This רוּחַ יְהוָה may then be hypostatically differentiated from God. Thus in 1 K. 22:19 ff. the "spirit" comes forward from among those who are about God and offers to become a lying spirit on the lips of the prophets. In a very similar situation Job 1:6 ff. uses Satan for the embodiment of this evil spirit of God, and it is under this name that this aspect of the idea of the spirit in Israel has to be treated, → διάβολος II, 74, 16 ff.

C. Spirit in Judaism.

I. πνεῦμα in the LXX.

1. The Translation of the Hebrew Terms in the LXX.

a. The usual transl. of רוּחַ is πνεῦμα (277 times), [167] or ἄνεμος (52 times), [168] cf. also θυμός (6 times) and πνοή (4). Other LXX words are ἀνεμόφθορος at Hos.

---

[166] Cf. Ps. 139:7, where רוּחַ יְהוָה is par. to פְּנֵי יְהוָה.

[167] Including Da. Θ and Sir., though not Sir. 39:28, where the original is probably רוּחוֹת, cf. R. Smend, *Die Weisheit d. Jesus Sirach* (1906), *ad loc.*

[168] Including Da. Θ and Sir.

8:7, ἀνήρ Prv. 17:22; 18:14, αἷμα Job 6:4, ψυχή Gn. 41:8; Ex. 35:21; Sir. 7:11, νοῦς Is. 40:13, φρόνησις Jos. 5:1. ἄνθρωπος ὁ πνευματοφόρος is used for אִישׁ הָרוּחַ Hos. 9:7, πνευματοφορεῖσθαι for שָׂאַף רוּחַ Jer. 2:24, θυμοῦν for קָצְרֵי רוּחִי Job 21:4, μακρό-θυμος for אֶרֶךְ רוּחַ Qoh. 7:8 and for קַר־רוּחַ Prv. 17:27, μακροθυμία for אֶרֶךְ רוּחַ Sir. 5:11, πραΰθυμος for שְׁפַל־רוּחַ Prv. 16:19, ἀναπνεῖν for הֵשִׁיב רוּחַ Job 9:18, ὀλιγο-ψυχεῖν for קְצַר רוּחַ Sir. 4:9, ὀλιγοψυχία for קְצַר רוּחַ Ex. 6:9, ὀλιγόψυχος for עֲצוּבַת רוּחַ Is. 54:6, for וּשְׁפַל רוּחַ וְדַכָּא Is. 57:15, for קְצַר רוּחַ Prv. 14:29 and for נְכֵאָה רוּחַ Prv. 18:14, ταπεινόφρων for שְׁפַל רוּחַ Prv. 29:23, κακοφροσύνη for גְּבַהּ רוּחַ Prv. 16:18, ἡσύχιος for נְכֵה־רוּחַ Is. 66:2, σκυθρωπάζειν for רוּחַ נְכֵאָה Prv. 15:13, ἐρίζειν for מָרַת רוּחַ Gn. 26:35, σκληρὰ ἡμέρα for קְשַׁת רוּחַ 1 S. 1:15, τὸ δειλινόν for רוּחַ הַיּוֹם Gn. 3:8, ἀνα-τολή for רוּחַ הַקָּדִים Ez. 42:16, and μέρος for רוּחַ Jer. 52:23; Ez. 42:20.

b. The normal rendering of נְשָׁמָה or נִשְׁמָא is πνοή (14 times). The LXX also has πνοή for נִשְׁמַת רוּחַ at Gn. 7:22. Other words for נְשָׁמָה are ἔμπνεον at Dt. 20:16; Jos. 10:40; 11:11, 14, ἔμπνευσις at Ps. 18:15, πνεῦμα at 1 K. 17:17; Da. 5:23 LXX; Da. 10:17 LXX Θ; Job 13:14 (for רוּחַ alongside נְשָׁמָה), and θυμός Sir. 9:13.

c. ἐγγαστρίμυθος (14 times) is the usual transl. of אוֹב. Also found are οἱ ἐκ τῆς γῆς φωνοῦντες at Is. 19:3; 29:4, θελητής at 2 K. 21:6 LXX A; 23:24, and ἔλλην at 2 K. 21:6 LXX B.

Baumgärtel

2. πνεῦμα as Wind.

On this sense → 335, 14 ff.; 360, 12 ff. Among individual passages we may simply mention Jon. 4:8 [169] and Jer. 4:11. [170]

3. πνεῦμα as the Breath of Life, [171] → 360, 36 ff.; 364, 17 ff.

a. This breath is not from man (2 Macc. 7:22), but from God (Job 27:3). God sends it, controls it (Da. 5:4 LXX), and withdraws it (ἀναλαβεῖν Tob. 3:6) [172] so that man dies (Bar. 2:17; Sir. 38:23). Man can take the breath of life from others (3 Macc. 6:24) and yield up his own spirit (ἀπέδωκε 4 Macc. 12:19), but he cannot fetch it back (ἀναστρέφει, Wis. 16:14). Some think the breath of life rises up (Eccl. 3:21), others that it vanishes (Wis. 2:3). King Zedekiah is called "the breath of our life, the anointed of Yahweh" (πνεῦμα προσώπου ἡμῶν χριστὸς κυρίου, Lam. 4:20). [173] b. Temporarily the vital force can withdraw (Da. 10:17 LXX; Jdt. 14:6) and then return (Ju. 15:19), kindle itself again (1 Macc. 13:7), or be restored (1 Βασ. 30:12). c. As cosmic spirit the πνεῦμα constructs and fills the world and holds it together (Jdt. 16:14; Wis. 1:7). The use of θεὸς θεὸς τῶν πνευμάτων καὶ πάσης σαρκός for אֵל אֱלֹהֵי הָרוּחֹת לְכָל־בָּשָׂר at Nu. 16:22 (cf. 27:16) shows how a term for the Creator which is understandable in

---

[169] Since the hot wind is *ipso facto* from the east, קָדִים is not transl. in the LXX.

[170] πνεῦμα πλανήσεως Heb. רוּחַ צַח ("hot wind"). Σ has πνεῦμα καύσωνος and 'Α πνεῦμα λαμπηδόνος. The translator of Jer. often uses the root πλαν- for rare words, cf. 23:32; 23:17; the "spirit of seduction" is already familiar to the translator. Cf. also 1 Jn. 4:6; Hos. 4:12 : πνεύματι πορνείας ἐπλανήθησαν, cf. Hos. 5:4.

[171] On the Egypt. origin of the notion cf. the description of the Egypt. king as "air pour tout nez par lequel on respire," Imschoot, *L'esprit de Jahvé source de vie*, 493.

[172] At Job 7:15 the LXX does not give a lit. transl. of the Heb.: ἀπαλλάξεις ἀπὸ πνεύματός μου τὴν ψυχήν μου, dying is a freeing of the soul from the spirit of life (Hell.).

[173] Orig. and Thdrt. presuppose Χριστὸς Κύριος in their comm., cf. I. L. Seeligmann, "The Septuagint Version of Is.," *Mededeelingen en Verhandelingen,* 9 (1948), 25; Imschoot, *op. cit.* → n. 171, 495. On κύριος, nominative from the abbrev. ΚΥ, cf. A. Rahlfs, *Genesis* (1926), 21. 'Α has πνεῦμα μυκτήρων ἡμῶν, Σ πνοὴ μυκτήρων ἡμῶν. The formulations are to be taken Messianically, M. Haller, *Die fünf Megilloth, Hndbch. AT,* I, 8 (1940), *ad loc.*

the light of the creation story can change into a formulation in which the earthly material world is contrasted with the heavenly world of spirits, though there is still a link through faith in the one God. Cf. Is. 31:3, where the LXX avoids dualism by putting βοήθεια for רוּחַ ('ΑΣΘ lit. πνεῦμα). 2 Macc. 3:24 offers a transcendent designation of God which ignores matter : ὁ τῶν πνευμάτων καὶ πάσης ἐξουσίας δυνάστης. The transl. of Job 12:10 אֲשֶׁר בְּיָדוֹ נֶפֶשׁ כָּל־חָי וְרוּחַ כָּל־בְּשַׂר־אִישׁ by ἐν χειρὶ αὐτοῦ ψυχὴ πάντων τῶν ζώντων καὶ πνεῦμα παντὸς ἀνθρώπου restricts the belief in a universal Creator which associates man and animal to an anthropological relating of God to the vital, intellectual and moral power of human life. d. In the last time God will give the πνεῦμα as resurrection power to bring the people of Israel to life again, Ez. 37:6, 14. [174] Belief in individual resurrection is plain in 2 Macc. 7:23; 14:46.

4. πνεῦμα as the Superhuman Power of Blessing and Punishment.

The teacher of wisdom is inspired by πνεῦμα, Sir. 39:6. In Is. 11:4 πνεῦμα and λόγος are par.; this has been regarded as a Stoic, pre-Gnostic interpretation of the HT. [175] Cf. Prv. 1:23. God gives to drink of the spirit of stupefaction (πνεῦμα κατανύξεως, Is. 29:10). [176] Tob. 6:8 refers to the evil spirit.

5. πνεῦμα as Spiritual Ability, Resolve of the Will, Constitution of the Soul, → 361, 12 ff.; 363, 16 ff., 25 ff.

God fills with artistic sense (Ex. 28:3) and gives understanding (Job 32:8). [177] He stirs up the will of the Jews to build, 1 Εσδρ. 2:5. [178] πνεῦμα is the seat of all the functions of the soul, Wis. 5:3; Da. 3:39, 86; Tob. 4:3. The fulness of thoughts (τὸ πνεῦμα τῆς γαστρός, Job 32:18) constricts man. The spirit of man can be without understanding (Job 20:3), [179] or this may be given to it, Sus. 45 LXX. Through the spirit of reason (τῷ πνεύματι τοῦ λογισμοῦ 4 Macc. 7:14 A) man may make himself young again. [180] Courage (Jdt. 7:19; Bar. 3:1) ebbs (ἀπὸ συντριβῆς πνεύματος,

---

174 Cf. A. Bertholet, *Hesekiel, Hndbch. AT*, I, 13 (1936), *ad loc.* The LXX is not thinking of God creating through His Spirit ; πνεῦμα is an independent divine creative force which is given to all men as a "hereditary possession" (Barrett, *Gospel Tradition*, 19) as long as they live.

175 Cf. Seeligmann, 119.

176 The rendering of תַּרְדֵּמָה by κατανύξεως is influenced by the expression οἶνος κατανύξεως in ψ 59:5, *v.* Seeligmann, 53. Cf. G. Bertram, " 'Religion' in d. Bibel," *Kirche im Angriff,* 12 (1936), 100 f.

177 The πνοὴ διδάσκουσα is par. to πνεῦμα, cf. 2 Εσδρ. 19 (πνεῦμα + ἐπιμαρτύρεσθαι) and 1 Jn. 2:27. In Prv. 15:4 the LXX, independently of the Mas., has : ἴασις γλώσσης ... ὁ δὲ συντηρῶν αὐτὴν πλησθήσεται πνεύματος. Elsewhere in Prv. πνοή is used for רוּחַ, cf. πιστὸς δὲ πνοῇ ('ΑΣ πνεύματι) Prv. 11:13, ἀνδρὸς δὲ λυπηροῦ ('Α πνεῦμα πεπληγμένον, Σ τεταπεινωμένον, Θ κατανενυγμένον) 17:22, θυμός, ὀλιγόψυχος 18:14. At Job 32:8 the LXX has ἀλλὰ πνεῦμά ἐστιν ἐν βροτοῖς, Σ πνεῦμα θεοῦ. At Job 33:4 LXX has πνεῦμα θεῖον, Σ πνεῦμα θεοῦ for רוּחַ־אֵל. In Is. 57:16 HT רוּחַ seems to be the principle of life which fades away, but the LXX associates πνεῦμα as spiritual endowment and πνοή in the biological sense : πνεῦμα γὰρ παρ' ἐμοῦ ἐξελεύσεται καὶ πνοὴν πᾶσαν ἐγὼ ἐποίησα. Cf. also in ψ 102:16 the reconstruction of a biological saying about wind and flowers into an anthropological statement that the spirit only passes through man and does not abide in him.

178 The idea of πνεῦμα is taken up again in the νοῦς of v. 6.

179 Translations of the HT vary : "Wind without understanding dost thou answer me," C. Steuernagel in Kautzsch ; "Yet spirit from mine understanding gives me information," G. Hölscher, *Das Buch Hiob, Hndbch. AT*, I, 17² (1952), *ad loc.* Similarly the ἐκ in ἐκ τῆς συνέσεως can be construed either as "from" or "without." Cf. Job 16:3 : speech full of wind or of the spirit ? LXX : μὴ τάξις ἐστὶν ῥήμασιν πνεύματος ; in 20:3 the Gk. transl. (Θ) seems to mean that I shall hear chiding to my shame, and a spirit without understanding answers me, παιδείαν ἐντροπῆς μου ἀκούσομαι, καὶ πνεῦμα ἐκ τῆς συνέσεως ἀποκρίνεταί μοι.

180 The LXX συνέσεως πνεύματος at Job 15:2 seems also to have reason in view, rendered πνεῦμα (unlike the HT).

Is. 65:14) [181] and flows back in again (1 Macc. 13:7). Man is constricted in spirit (τὸ πνεῦμα στενοχωρούμενος, 4 Macc. 11:11). He is given up to his greed, Sir. 9:9. [182]

6. πνεῦμα as Eschatological Gift, → 384, 11 ff.

God will act ἐν πνεύματι κρίσεως καὶ πνεύματι καύσεως, Is. 4:4. He will slay the wicked ἐν πνεύματι διὰ χειλέων, Is. 11:4. He can destroy men by a breath (ἐνὶ πνεύματι) and crush them by His mighty breath (ὑπὸ πνεύματος δυνάμεώς σου, Wis. 11:20). The breath of the Lord of judgment is like water rushing through a ravine, Is. 30:28. It will put to flight the unclean spirit (ἐξαρῶ Zech. 13:2). In the future age of salvation the Spirit will bring animals together, Is. 34:16. [183] God will lay His new Spirit on the whole of the elect people, πνεῦμα καινόν Is. 44:3; Ez. 11:19; 36:26. He will pour out His Spirit (ἐκχεῶ Jl. 2:28) and give the spirit of grace and pity (πνεῦμα χάριτος καὶ οἰκτιρμοῦ, Zech. 12:10). The eschatological Spirit will come down from on high as a possession of the community. (Is. 32:15) and like a personified power [184] stand (ἐφέστηκεν) in the midst of the renewed temple community, Hag. 2:5. The elect servant will be a bearer of the πνεῦμα (Is. 42:1) and the Spirit will rest on the prophet (Is. 61:1).

Thus the man who cannot escape God's Spirit (ψ 138:7), who gives up his own πνεῦμα into the hand of God (ψ 30:6), longs for Messianic salvation (πνεῦμα σωτηρίας Is. 26:18).

7. πνεῦμα in Qoheleth.

The difficult expression רְעוּת רוּחַ (1:14; 2:11, 17, 26; 4:4, 6; 6:9) is rendered in the Hexapla transl. by νομὴ (βόσκησις) ἀνέμου and in the LXX by προαίρεσις πνεύματος. πνεῦμα is always an anthropologico-psychological expression in Qoh. LXX. ἄνεμος is expressly used twice at 5:15 and 11:4. Thus προαίρεσις πνεύματος or καρδίας in 2:22 is self-selected and hence erroneous and deceptive musing and aspiring, the arbitrariness of the human spirit. [185]

8. πνεῦμα in Wisdom.

a. As the principle of life in man. The author, who was probably active in Alexandria in the 1st cent. B.C., took over the concept of πνεῦμα from the Alexandrian teacher Erasistratos, [186] though Gn. 2:7 (πνοὴν ζωῆς) might well have had some influence too. This principle of life belongs to God, who inbreathes it (15:11) or loans it (15:16). That which lives in all living creatures from the beginning of life is not a breath that perishes (2:3), [187] nor, in spite of the pantheistic ring of ἀπόρροια in 7:25, some part of a universal pneuma into which the breath of each living creature retreats. It is the incorruptibility of God giving Himself to the individual entity (ἄφθαρτόν σου πνεῦμα, 12:1). At death man loses the breath of life (16:14) but he gains a portion in ἀφθαρσία (5:15; 2:23). If ψυχή seems to be the equivalent of πνεῦμα in 15:11 and 16:14, one

---

[181] On Is. 65:14 cf. 66:2 'A πεπληγότα τὸ πνεῦμα, Θ τυπτόμενον καρδίᾳ, LXX ἡσύχιον; Prv. 17:22; 18:14, → n. 177.

[182] For τῷ πνεύματί σου Cl. Al. and the Latins read αἵματι, which Burton, Spirit, 144 n. 1 regards as original, cf. I. Lévi, "La sagesse de Jésus, fils Sirach," Rev. d. Etudes Juives, 35 (1897), 48-64. R. Smend, D. Weisheit d. Sir. (1906), 86 reads דמים at Sir. 9:9, cf. Job 6:4 : ὁ θυμὸς αὐτῶν ἐκπίνει μου τὸ αἷμα (Gk. corruption for πνεῦμα). 'A has πνεῦμα, Σ ἀναπνοή.

[183] Procksch, op. cit. → n. 125, ad loc. relates αὐτάς to prophecies which are being fulfilled, not to the beasts of the wilderness, but cf. Imschoot, op. cit. → n. 171, 499 : "et son souffle les a rassemblés."

[184] 3 Βασ. 22:21 and perhaps Job 4:15 refers to the personified πνεῦμα which goes forth from and stands before the Lord.

[185] Cf. G. Bertram, "Hbr. u. griech. Qohelet. Ein Beitrag z. Theol. d. hell. Bibel," ZAW, NF, 23 (1952), 26-49.

[186] Verbeke, 223-236.

[187] As the ungodly say, possibly the Epicureans.

has to ask whether the author is not seeking to distinguish the divine principle of life from actual life, though man has no control over either.

b. To be differentiated from πνεῦμα as the principle of life in man is the πνεῦμα which is identical with → σοφία. [188] This does not come to man with the beginning of life ; it is imparted in answer to prayer, 7:7; 9:17. Acc. to 7:22 f. [189] this πνεῦμα is the intellectual (νοερόν) power which can see clearly (σαφές) and sharply (ὀξύ) and which, not limited to time or space (εὐκίνητον), can with universal efficacy (πολυ-μερές) permeate (τρανόν) objects in virtue of its fineness (λεπτόν) without being affected by them (ἀπήμαντον). As this intellectual power πνεῦμα is orientated to the good (φιλάγαθον) and is free from any stain (ἀμόλυντον). In and with this orientation to the good it addresses itself beneficently (εὐεργετικόν) to men (φιλάνθρωπον cf. 1:6). In distinction from the breath of life it is not in all things. It permeates thinking men who are morally pure and who open themselves to it in prayer. [190] By reason of their suitability for the πνεῦμα these men are called πνεύματα, 7:23. The capacity for thought and power of moral resolve (νοερῶν καθαρῶν) present in the πνεύματα is already an outworking of the permeating πνεῦμα which enables them to see the concrete will of God which is to be done, 9:17. In the fact that the πνεῦμα permeates (χωρεῖ) the πνεύματα its superiority over all things human is displayed : it is free from care (ἀμέριμνον) and from all human uncertainty and failure (βέβαιον, ἀσφα-λές). It is unlimited in its possibilities (παντοδύναμον). It sees (πανεπίσκοπον) and hears all things, 1:7. This intellectually and ethically suprahuman power stands in a unique relation to God (μονογενές) to whom it properly belongs (ἅγιον). Solomon is regarded as the wise man who sought the πνεῦμα σοφίας (7:7) and thus himself became πνεῦμα. He also knows the mighty powers of spirits (πνευμάτων βίας, 7:20) [191] for ethically he lives free from reproach. [192] As the spirit of discipline (πνεῦμα παιδείας, 1:5) [193] the πνεῦμα has no fellowship with evil. The divine πνεῦμα and the pure πνεῦμα of man are thus inter-related.

Since the πνεῦμα in its cosmic function (→ 354, 32 ff.) represents the divine activity in the world, it is forced into a certain hypostatic independence. But the author does not try to round off his statements systematically. Hence, even though the πνεῦμα is virtually independent, he can locate it in God and make it subject to God's free will to send, 9:17. The πνεῦμα δυνάμεως (5:23) is not the natural force of a strong wind, [194] but the judicial spirit of God. [195]

In Wis. the πνεῦμα is a reality which is dependent on God and yet in some sense elevated to independence. No answer is given to the question whether it is more a

---

[188] πνεῦμα σοφίας 7:7, φιλάνθρωπον γὰρ πνεῦμα σοφία, 1:6a. ἔστιν (sc. ἡ σοφία) γὰρ ἐν αὐτῇ πνεῦμα in 7:22 can be taken reflexively : wisdom is in itself πνεῦμα. P. Heinisch, *D. Buch d. Weisheit, Exegetisches Hndbch. z. AT*, 24 (1912), ad loc., P. v. Imschoot, "Sagesse et Esprit dans l'AT," *Rev. Bibl.*, NS, 47 (1938), 39, n. 1. In Sir. 24:3 wisdom comes forth from the mouth of the Most High and covers the earth ὡς ὁμίχλη : the πνεῦμα which comes out of the mouth of Yahweh as a breath crystallises into a dark cloud lying over the earth.

[189] 21 (3 times 7) attributes are ascribed to πνεῦμα, cf. G. Kuhn, "Exegetische u. text-kritische Anmerkungen z. Buche d. Weisheit," ThStKr, 103 (1931), 448.

[190] λεπτοτάτων does not refer merely to the immateriality of the spirit but also to the access it finds in those who pray.

[191] Solomon is the chief of magicians, cf. G. Salzberger, *Die Salomosage in d. semitischen Lit.*, Diss. (1907), 92-129.

[192] "Before Solomon had sinned, he ruled over male and female demons," Salzberger, *op. cit.*, 93.

[193] Imschoot, *op. cit.* → n. 188, 44, reads at 1:5 : ἅγιον γὰρ πνεῦμα παιδείας ... ἐλεγχθήσεται (*sera repoussé*), K. Siegfried in Kautzsch Apkr. u. Pseudepigr., *ad loc.*: "... will be filled by the spirit of censure." On Wis. 1:5 and its relation to 7:7; 9:17 cf. Is. 63:10 and J. Fichtner, *Weisheit Salomos, Hndbch. AT*, II, 6 (1938), *ad loc.*

[194] So Burton, *Spirit*, 141.

[195] Fichtner, *op. cit.* → n. 193, *ad loc.* sees in δύναμις a term for God and refers to Mt. 26:64, cf. also Is. 4:4; 11:4.

material or an immaterial reality. [196] For when the author, who stands in the Jewish tradition, wants to speak of the work of the πνεῦμα, he has to bear witness to the immaterial God on the one side and yet also declare on the other that this God has acted and still acts concretely in matter. The πνεῦμα shares both God's transcendence over the world and also His participation in the events of this world ; hence it can be called both νοερόν and also λεπτόν. In vocabulary the author is very dependent on Stoicism, but he differs in his emphasis on God's superiority to the spirit ; God creates all individual beings and imparts His transcendence over the world to the πνεῦμα. With no attempt at harmonisation the spirit which is identical with the ψυχή is set alongside the πνεῦμα which is identical with σοφία. In this distinction between two divinely given πνεύματα the author was probably influenced by Erasistratos (who differentiates the πνεῦμα ζωτικόν from the πνεῦμα ψυχικόν), though Jewish tradition (the πνεῦμα as the spirit of life) and his pedagogic goal (wisdom as teacher) also lead him to discern a distinct twofold activity of the cosmic pneuma in the world — an activity which is to the advantage of mankind as a whole as well as the circle of the elect.

II. πνεῦμα in Hellenistic Judaism.

1. Philo.

a. πνεῦμα is a term for the higher [197] element of the air (Ebr., 106), which remains God's property [198] even though man uses it (Sacr. AC, 97), [199] for the wind (→ 335, 16; 360, 12) with its good mixture (Op. Mund., 41; Abr., 92) and moralistically applicable instability and force (Leg. All., III, 53; Som., II, 85, 166), and also for human or animal breath (Spec. Leg., I, 338). [200]

b. Philo, influenced by Stoicism, maintains that that which holds wood and stone together, giving them ἕξις, is πνεῦμα as the substance of air, as συμφυέστατος δεσμός, Rer. Div. Her., 242. This moves from the middle to the end and back again from the end to the middle, Deus Imm., 35. [201] The earth at large also consists primarily through the power of this binding substance (πνεύματος ἐνωτικοῦ δυνάμει, Op. Mund., 131). [202] All matter is permeated by πνεῦμα. It is dependent on νοῦς as the ἡγεμονικόν of the soul, Fug., 182.

c. In psychology πνεῦμα plays a role in the question as to the essence of the soul. Philo describes both blood and πνεῦμα as the soul's essence, Det. Pot. Ins., 80, 84. He distinguishes the non-rational soul, which man has in common with the beasts, from the ψυχὴ ψυχῆς (Rer. Div. Her., 55), which differentiates man from the beasts. The non-rational soul has its essence in blood, while the rational soul as the soul of man is equated with πνεῦμα, Det. Pot. Ins., 80-84. If the Stoics define the soul as πνεῦμα ἔνθερμον, Philo adopts this definition but understands by ἔνθερμον καὶ πεπυρωμένον πνεῦμα, not the material substance, [203] but the impress of divine power, Det. Pot. Ins., 83

---

[196] Verbeke, 232.

[197] Philo distinguishes between higher and lower elements. He is dependent here on Chrysipp., who introduces the distinction between στοιχεῖα δραστικά and παθητικά into the Aristotelian dualism of matter and form, cf. Verbeke, 238.

[198] Philo never equates πνεῦμα with God ; he maintains the divine transcendence.

[199] The element of air is to be distinguished as such from the idea of air which is called πνεῦμα ζωτικώτατον in Op. Mund., 29 f.

[200] To be distinguished from human breath is the sound which in analogy to the human voice was fashioned in the air for the purpose of revelation and which καθάπερ πνεῦμα διὰ σάλπιγγος can come to men both near and distant, Decal., 33.

[201] "Qui se retourne sur soi-même par un mouvement de tension, de concentration," Festugière, 212.

[202] Burton, Spirit, 142 renders πνεῦμα by "wind (air ?)." One may ask, however, whether the ref. here, too, is not to the substance of air which gives solidity to bodies and then also to earthly bodies.

[203] Burton, Spirit, 158.

(τύπον τινὰ καὶ χαρακτῆρα θείας δυνάμεως), since man is still a θεοειδὲς δημιούργημα and φυτὸν οὐράνιον, *ibid.,* 84. This πνεῦμα stands in analogy to God the Creator, for as λογικὸν πνεῦμα (Spec. Leg., I, 171) it begets thoughts and thus functionally it stands alongside the organ of generation at a higher level, Spec. Leg., I, 6 : ... πρὸς ... γένεσιν ... παρεσκεύασται ἐγκάρδιον πνεῦμα νοημάτων.

d. To be distinguished from πνεῦμα as the impress of divine power is the divine Spirit, the πνεῦμα θεῖον, which man acquired by inbreathing (Op. Mund., 135 ὃ γὰρ ἐνεφύσησεν, οὐδὲν ἦν ἕτερον ἢ πνεῦμα θεῖον), which flowed into him (*ibid.,* 144 πολλοῦ ῥυέντος εἰς αὐτὸν τοῦ θείου πνεύματος). As man as a rational being is πνεῦμα, he is also the recipient of a divine πνεῦμα which is breathed into him. Philo here follows the traditional dichotomy : man is a being composed of γεώδης οὐσία and πνεῦμα θεῖον. Man has received his total psychical life as a divine gift.

The heavenly man (Leg. All., I, 42) [204] as well as the earthly man (I, 31) receives the πνεῦμα. The refined purity of the heavenly νοῦς (Som., I, 146) rests on the fact that it has become a partaker of the πνεῦμα (Leg. All., I, 42). Philo in Leg. All., I, 42 distinguishes πνεῦμα from πνοή, ascribing the former to the heavenly man and the latter to the earthly man. This distinction, which is based on Gn. 1:2 and 2:7, enables Philo to explain the quantitatively different endowments of the heavenly and the earthly man with the divine spirit. By defining πνοή as ἀποφορά he makes it clear that for all the distinction between πνεῦμα and πνοή he is not setting the two in antithesis, for ἐνέπνευσεν is used (Leg. All., I, 36) in interpretation of the ἐνεφύσησεν of Gn. 2:7.

If Philo can both make the πνεῦμα θεῖον the obj. of divine action (Op. Mund., 135) and also view it as an entity which flows in as it were autonomously (*ibid.,* 144), his theistic view is influenced here by Jewish wisdom speculations. The symbolical interpretation of the raining down of manna as nourishment with wisdom provides the basis for regarding the πνεῦμα, thus equated with wisdom, as a river. [205] This *influx spiritualis,* however, is of ethical rather than physico-magical relevance. If God gives His πνεῦμα, this gift is one of the ἀγαθά which God wishes to be of benefit to all men. His purpose herewith is to give men a share in virtue (Leg. All., I, 34) [206] and also to produce zealous striving for it and to reveal the fulness of divine riches in the introduction into this ethical sphere. The man who strives thus knows God through the πνεῦμα which is given him, Leg. All., I, 38. But he knows Him in His unknowability ; [207] that is, the knowledge of God extends to the fact of God, Som., I, 231 → I, 702, 22 f.

When Philo tries to describe the πνεῦμα θεῖον, he is guided on the one hand by an attempt to say something authoritative about it. On the other hand, however, he is chained to a philosophically and esp. a Stoically determined vocabulary. In Gig., 22 he cites two attempts at a definition of the πνεῦμα θεῖον. Acc. to the one it is the third element, acc. to the other it is the ἐπιστήμη which the wise man shares. Philo himself does not decide between them ; he simply explains that he has learned the nature of the πνεῦμα θεῖον from Ex. 31:2 f. In the LXX the words σοφία, σύνεσις and ἐπιστήμη are used here. Philo obviously has in view the equation of σοφία and πνεῦμα already mentioned → line 27. For in Gig., 27 he calls the πνεῦμα τὸ σοφόν, τὸ θεῖον, τὸ

---

[204] As opposed to J. Dupont, *Gnosis. La connaissance religieuse dans les Epîtres de S. Paul,* Universitas cathol. Lovaniensis. Diss. ad grad. magistri in fac. theol., II, 40 (1949), 173 f., we must insist that the heavenly man is regarded as a recipient of the πνεῦμα in Leg. All., I, 42.

[205] Cf., e.g., Sir. 39:6; "behind the comparison of the substance of wisdom with a stream lies ... the idea of a divine pneuma of wisdom which is poured out upon and which inspires favoured mortals," H. Lewy, "Sobria Ebrietas, Untersuchungen z. Gesch. d. antiken Mystik," Beih. z. ZNW (1929), 56.

[206] μετουσία does not mean "possession" as Heinemann renders it (L. Cohn-I. Heinemann, *Philos Werke,* III [1919], 27).

[207] H. A. Wolfson, *Philo* (1947), II, 110-126.

ἄτμητον, τὸ ἀδιαίρετον, τὸ ἀστεῖον, τὸ πάντη δι' ὅλων ἐκπεπληρωμένον. In Stoic terms Philo is here presenting the by no means pantheistic view that God contributes (προστεθέν) the πνεῦμα to the νοῦς of man, that man comes to have a share (μετα-δοθέν) in the indivisible πνεῦμα. As an omnipotent power (Plant., 24) the πνεῦμα θεῖον is one of the divine ἀγαθά. It is for Philo a "heavenly breath and even something better than a heavenly breath," Spec. Leg., IV, 123. There is a demarcation here. To the question where is the homeland of the soul the Stoics reply that the soul is dissolved in the element of ether. [208] If the πνεῦμα θεῖον is something better than a heavenly breath, then by nature it is remote from the Stoic sphere of redemption and close to the side of God.

But there is yet another strand in Philo. Here the πνεῦμα θεῖον is close to the side of man. In Philo the chief part of the soul, the νοῦς, can be called πνεῦμα θεῖον, Rer. Div. Her., 55 (τὴν οὐσίαν ... τοῦ δ' ἡγεμονικωτάτου πνεῦμα θεῖον). It can be called this, however, only if the one who bears the spirit, man, has made ethically good decisions and shown that he belongs to the class of those "who truly live through the divine breath, reason," Rer. Div. Her., 57. The fact that he holds aloof from those who vegetate "through blood and in the lust of the flesh" makes it apparent that his πνεῦμα, which is identical with νοῦς, is πνεῦμα θεῖον. Hence the divinity of reason is ethically grounded, though reason is also divine by origin, since it is a "genuine impress of the divine, invisible πνεῦμα," Plant., 18 → II, 389, 8 ff.

In spite of the similarity in terms, however, Philo is not a pantheist. He sets the πνεῦμα θεῖον at the side of God and equates it with the divine λόγος, which in distinction from the immanent λόγος [209] is defined as ἀΐδιος. In sum, then, the πνεῦμα which represents the rational soul is an impress of the divine power but the πνεῦμα which man receives as a morally striving rational being is also an emanation of the divine nature. Wherein lies the difference between the two πνεύματα if they both come from God? Does this distinction pt. to a cleft in Philo which can only be brought to light but not explained?

e. Philo speaks of the prophetic spirit, → 362, 37 ff.; 366, 24 ff. He is dependent here on Plato's criticism of Apollonian inspiration manticism, and sets the prophetic spirit in antithesis to the νοῦς, Rer. Div. Her., 265. [210] As Plato selected the philosopher to be the interpreter of the ecstatic (→ 348, 3 ff.), so Philo thinks that he himself, as an allegorical expositor, is gifted with the spirit of inspiration (Som., II, 252) which has its prototype in Moses (Vit. Mos., II, 251 f., 259, 263-265, 268, 272, 280, 288, 291: note the periodicity of inspiration).

f. The divine πνεῦμα κατ' ἐξοχήν which is received by the man who is esp. called thereto is the πνεῦμα προφητικόν. If prophecy is for Philo the highest form of knowledge, [211] there is between the higher and lower forms of knowledge the decisive distinction that on the one side the νοῦς has this knowledge in virtue of the gift of the πνεῦμα θεῖον but on the other the same νοῦς cannot have this knowledge and it has thus to be replaced by the πνεῦμα προφητικόν. In Philo two worlds clash at a time of transition. In the one the man endowed by God meets God in and with his reason, while in the other the man inspired by God is lifted up into a world inaccessible to the rational man. Philo did not try to integrate the two worlds systematically; the prophetic πνεῦμα stands alongside the cosmic πνεῦμα. The two worlds of cosmic enlightenment and divine prophecy meet in the wise man. If they cannot be brought under a single denominator, they can be understood in their origin only in terms of the transcendent God. If linguistically Philo is close to pantheistic Stoicism on the one side and to dualistic Gnosticism on the other, in content he is neither a pantheist nor a dualist. As a Jew,

---

[208] Wolfson, op. cit., I, 400.
[209] Ibid., 325-332.
[210] On the disjunction of the rational and the pneumatic cf. G. Quispel, "Philo u. d. altchristliche Häresie," ThZ, 5 (1949), 429-436.
[211] Wolfson, op. cit., II, 21.

he is an ethical theist in Gk. garb, who sees that pneumatically permeated rationalism reaches its limit in prophetic ecstasy. The new thing which man as a rational creature receives with the divine πνεῦμα adumbrates the pneumatic reality which pts. to the world of revelation of a transcendent God. If man as a rational creature receives the divine πνεῦμα, the recipient of this divine gift lives in the forecourt of a divinely pneumatic reality which in prophetic ecstasy is imparted to the man esp. chosen therefor.

2. Josephus.

The usage of Jos. is related to that of the LXX and Philo. ψυχή as well as πνεῦμα is contained in αἷμα (→ 372, 32), Ant., 3, 260. πνεῦμα is the constitution of the soul of Esther (Ant., 11, 240, → 369, 17 ff.), or the seat of warlike passion (ἀρήϊον πνεῦμα, Bell., 3, 92). In Jos., as in the LXX (1 S. 16:23), Saul is possessed by a πονηρὸν πνεῦμα. But this is either par. to the δαιμόνια (Ant., 6, 211) or as δαιμόνιον πνεῦμα it is much more plainly regarded as an intermediate being than in the LXX (ibid., 214). The δαιμόνια are equated with the πνεύματα of the wicked dead, Bell., 7, 185 (→ II, 10, 19 f.). On the other hand, the ἄγγελος θεῖος is equated with the πνεῦμα θεῖον, Ant., 4, 108. [212] Jos. practically never uses πνεῦμα (τοῦ) θεοῦ for the spirit of inspiration and when he does the ref. is always to the biblical prophets of the past, Ant., 4, 119. If he has instead πνεῦμα θεῖον, he is emphasising that the prophetic norm has vanished from the present circle of vision. The Zealots and the Essenes may prophesy (→ προφήτης), but they have nothing whatever to do with the Spirit of God. [213] If πνεύματος ἐπιθέοντος in Gn. 1:2 (Ant., 1, 27) refers to the breath, the Lat. transl. spiritus dei seems to be suggesting that the ref. is to the cosmic Creator-Spirit.

Bieder

III. רוּחַ in Palestinian Judaism.

1. Wind, Quarter of the World, Direction.

As in the OT (→ 359 f.), so in later Heb. and Aram. רוּחַ is the usual word for "wind." In post-bibl. Judaism we also find a common use of "the four winds" for "the four quarters of the world." רוּחַ can then denote quite simply the "direction" or "side" of an object or place, e.g., Kil., 3, 1.

2. Angels and Evil Spirits.

Beings belonging to the heavenly world, i.e., angels and other servants of God, can be called "spirits." This term is common in the apocal. lit. [214] The angels are immortal spirits which have their dwelling in heaven, Eth. En. 15:4, 6 f.; 61:12; 106:17. The elemental spirits of wind, rain, snow etc. are a special class of angels; these reign over the various events of nature acc. to the will of God, Jub. 2:2; Eth. En. 60:14-21; 69:22; 75:5; 4 Esr. 6:41. The fallen angels have left their heavenly habitation and in spite of their immortal nature they have commingled with the flesh of women and thus begotten the evil spirits or demons which live on earth. [215] The contrast between the higher nature of spiritual beings and the lower but not sinful nature of the carnal dwellers on earth is presupposed in this notion. Belief in evil spirits who dwell in the world and threaten men with all kinds of perils is esp. strong in post-bibl. Judaism. [216] It is everywhere presupposed in apocal. writings as well as the Rabb. works. Both these make it clear

---

[212] Unless the πνεῦμα θεῖον is that which seeks to make itself understood by means of the angel.

[213] Schl. Theol. d. Judt., 58.

[214] Jub 1:25; 2:2; 15:31 f.; Eth. En. 15: 4, 6 ff.; 60:14-21; 61:12; 69:22; 75:5; 106:17; Slav. En. 12:1 f.; 16:7; Test. L. 4:1; 4 Esr. 6:41. The divine name "Lord of spirits" in the similitudes of Eth. En. (cf. also 2 Macc. 3:24; LXX Nu. 16:22; 27:16) is to be understood in this light. Again, in the song of praise to the Lord of spirits who fills the earth with spirits (Eth. En. 39:12) the spirits are these spiritual beings, not the spirits of men.

[215] Eth. En. 15:4, 6-10; 106:13 f., 17. The Gk. text here must also ref. to the fall of angels. They are the anonymous subj. of παρέβησαν, v. 13.

[216] Cf. Str.-B., IV, 501-535; Bousset-Gressm., 336-341; Bonsirven, I, 239-246.

that belief in demons was not merely widespread among the common people but was also shared by the religious leaders and even the scribes. In post-bibl. Judaism it was linked to the religiously far more central belief in Satan and the spirits subject to him. Satan and the evil spirits are the cosmic adversaries of God and the foes of men. Their goal is esp. to seduce men into sin and to ruin them thereby. This idea plays a considerable role in the apocal. lit. [217] In Rabb. writings, however, the demons are only seldom tempters. Their activity is directed almost exclusively to damaging man in life and limb, → II, 13, 17 ff. They are not closely related to Satan in these works, → II, 13, 34 ff. There is a prince of evil spirits, but he is not identical with Satan. [218] Nevertheless, Gn. r., 20 on 3:30 shows that the idea of tempter-demons was not alien to the Rabb. Here a house-spirit can be regarded as an evil spirit because it knows the evil impulse in man and as a result can easily lead him into sin. [219] Again, the fact that a spirit can enter a man and confuse his mind, so that he may unintentionally transgress a divine commandment, means that the spirit can lead men into sin. [220]

It is distinctive of Judaism that the origin of powers which are hostile to God is always sought in a distortion of the original creation of God. Judaism has no place for an evil power standing in eternal confrontation with God. Its dualism is relative, not absolute. Hence the activity of Satan and evil spirits can even be integrated into the divine government of the world. They are allowed by God to perform in this world the task of tempting and perverting men because of their wickedness. [221] Only in the last time will they all be bound and punished. [222]

3. The Deceased in the Grave, → 364, 33 ff.

The deceased who dwells in the grave, and who perhaps comes out at night to roam the earth, or is perhaps a guest in heaven to overhear divine secrets behind the heavenly curtain, is called a spirit (רוּחַ). [223] In this connection the spirit is simply the dead man who lives in the burying-ground and who can sometimes wander about. There is no connection between this idea and the concept of demons, → II, 15, 39 ff.

4. The Spirit of Man (→ ψυχή).

Later Jewish anthropology strongly underlined the idea of the spirit of man and went far beyond what is found in the OT in this respect.

a. Vocabulary.

It is hard to find in Judaism any clear distinction between the terms used for the human soul. In the earlier period the identity of רוּחַ and נֶפֶשׁ is esp. clearly attested in Sir. 16:17: (כָּל בְּנֵי אָדָם) וּמָה נַפְשִׁי, בְּקִצוֹת רוּחוֹת "and what is my soul among the totality of the spirits (of all men)?" [224] In keeping is the fact that the souls of the dead can be called πνεύματα as well as ψυχαί. [225] In the Rabb. נֶפֶשׁ, רוּחַ and נְשָׁמָה are common

[217] It is esp. plain in Jub., Eth. En., Test. XII, → II, 15, 6 ff.

[218] In Lv. r., 5, 1 on 4:3 a demon which wants to kill a newborn child is called שָׁרִיהוֹן דְּרוּחָתָא; in jSheq., 5, 6 (496, 3) R. Chanina b. Papa is threatened at night by the prince of evil spirits, רַבְּיהוֹן דְּרוּחַיָּא.

[219] Ed. J. Theodor (1903), 196 (Str.-B., IV, 516), cf. bSota, 3a (Str.-B., IV, 504).

[220] Erub., 4, 1; cf. bErub., 41b (Str.-B., IV, 503).

[221] Jub. 10:7-11: At the request of Mastema a tenth of the evil spirits will be released by God for this task, cf. Jub. 15:31. With God's authority the evil spirits bring misfortune on men as a punishment for their sins, Str.-B., IV, 521 f.; → 390, 16 ff.

[222] Str.-B., IV, 527, 914; Volz Esch., 309-313.

[223] bBer., 18b; cf. Meyer, 3-8.

[224] Cf. also the parallelism in Wis. 15:11; 16:14.

[225] Cf. the sections of Eth. En. preserved in Gk.: πνεύματα 22:3, 6, 7, 9, 11, 12, 13; (98:3, 10); 103:4; ψυχαί 9:3, 10 (cf. the textual variants τὰ πνεύματα καὶ αἱ ψυχαί or τὰ πνεύματα τῶν ψυχῶν τῶν ἀνθρώπων — hendiadys; also 22:3: τὰ πνεύματα τῶν ψυχῶν τῶν νεκρῶν); 102:4 f., 11; 103:3, 7 f. On this whole question Abelson, 43; H. Odeberg, 3 Enoch (1928), I, 174-180; Bousset-Gressm., 400.

terms for the human soul. It is expressly stated in Gn. r., 14, 9 f. on 2:7 [226] that what is meant is the one soul, not three different souls or three different parts of the soul. Where all three words, or two of them, occur together, so that they seem to be speaking of different things, this is really to be explained on stylistic grounds. There is in the Rabb. no strict threefold division of the human soul as in later Jewish mysticism. [227] One may note, however, certain gradations as one or other term is chosen in particular contexts. Thus נֶפֶשׁ and רוּחַ are used esp. for the animal and psychical functions of the soul, [228] while נְשָׁמָה is the usual term for the soul as coming from heaven. But the latter word is equally common for the soul as vital force, e.g., bNas, 21b; bKeth, 46a, and the other two can be used for the heavenly soul, though נְשָׁמָה is more common. Hence there is no distinction between spirit and soul in the Rabb. They can speak quite freely of man's נְשָׁמָה when expounding OT passages which refer to the נֶפֶשׁ or רוּחַ.

b. Legacy of the OT.

In Sir., Tob., Jdt., Bar. and 1 Macc. the OT view of man is unchanged. There is no concept of a resurrection and of real life after death. The Sadducees kept to this view, Jos. Ant., 18, 16 f.; Bell., 2, 164 f. But even when there was advance on OT anthropology, ideas about the spirit as the vital force and the seat of spiritual functions remained the same. In the Rabb. expression is often given to the understanding of the spirit as the vital force. When men make an image, they cannot introduce a spirit into it. Hence it neither moves nor lives. God, however, blows the spirit into man and he lives. [229] Every living creature has in it a רוּחַ חַיִּים. [230]

In the idea that the spirit is the seat of the functions of the soul a prominent place is occupied by the emotional and volitional element in both the OT and Rabb. writings, → 361 f. The proud man has a רוּחַ גְּבוֹהָה, the rapacious a נֶפֶשׁ רְחָבָה, the humble a רוּחַ נְמִכָה, the modest a נֶפֶשׁ שְׁפֵלָה. [231] The spirit may be refreshed (קוֹרַת רוּחַ) when one experiences a great joy like that of the coming age, Ab., 4, 17. It may also be given rest when something pleases one, Sheb., 10, 9; BB, 8, 5. Such expressions are used with ref. to God too, though this has nothing to do with any special idea of the Spirit of God. R. Chanina b. Dosa has said: "In whom the spirit of man finds pleasure, in him the spirit of God finds pleasure, and in whom the spirit of man finds no pleasure, in him the spirit of God finds no pleasure." [232]

c. Spirit and Body in Rabbinic Anthropology.

Judaism did not keep to OT views about the spirit of man. In particular, it developed the distinction between spirit and body, so that there arose what is in some sense a dualistic anthropology with a belief in the pre-existence and immortality of the soul, → 379, 12 ff. These ideas are already full-fledged in Rabbinism. Man consists of body and spirit. The body is of earthly derivation, the spirit of heavenly derivation.

This consistent Rabb. view is plainly expressed in the saying of R. Simai: "All creatures created from heaven, their soul (נֶפֶשׁ) and their body derive from heaven, and all creatures created from earth, their soul and their body derive from earth. Man is the only exception; for his soul (נֶפֶשׁ) derives from heaven, and his body from

---

[226] Ed. J. Theodor (1903), 132 f.

[227] Cf. J. Abelson, *Jewish Mysticism* (1913), 160 f.

[228] Bonsirven, II, 6, n. 1.

[229] bBer., 10a. Cf. Mek. R. Shimon b. Jochai Ex. 15:11 (ed. D. Hoffmann [1905], 67) f.; Midr. Shemuel, V, 6 (10a). Cf. further Meyer, 120 f.

[230] Erub, 1, 7; Git., 2, 3; BQ, 1, 1; 7, 1; Men., 9, 9; Ohaloth, 6, 1; 15, 9.

[231] Ab., 5, 19; cf. Ab., 4, 7 גַּס רוּחַ "proud"; 4, 4.10 שְׁפַל רוּחַ "humble."

[232] כֹּל שֶׁרוּחַ הַבְּרִיּוֹת נוֹחָה מִמֶּנּוּ רוּחַ הַמָּקוֹם נוֹחָה מִמֶּנּוּ וְכֹל שֶׁאֵין רוּחַ הַבְּרִיּוֹת נוֹחָה מִימֶּנּוּ אֵין רוּחַ הַמָּקוֹם נוֹחָה מִמֶּנּוּ Ab., 3, 10. Cf. Eth. En. 68:2 on angels.

earth." [233] Acc. to the view of ancient Israel the spirit as the vital force is from God, → 362, 14 ff. In the Rabb. this developed into the idea of the pre-existence of individual souls, → 379, 12 ff. Before or at the creation of the world God created the souls of all men. The number of men to be born in the whole course of the world was thus fixed in advance. Pre-existent souls were kept in the 7th heaven (bChag., 12b), in the hand of God, [234] or in a special store-room (גוּף), [235] up to the time when God commanded that a soul should enter the body constructed for it, and the man was fashioned. In virtue of its origin the soul which comes from heaven is pure, holy and righteous, bBer., 60b. Man has the task of returning the soul to God in purity as he received it in purity, bShab., 152b. Coming from heaven, the spirit is the higher part of man. When the Gentile Antoninos asked concerning the destiny of the body after death, Rabbi answered: "Instead of asking me about the body which is unclean, ask me about the spirit (נְשָׁמָה) which is clean," M. Ex., 15, 1 (Horovitz [→ n. 269], 125). Since, acc. to Gn. 2:7, the spirit is given by God, it can also be called the "spirit of God" or the "holy spirit of God." God has put His holy spirit in man, Tg. J. I Gn. 6, 3. [236] The spirit of life in man is the spirit of God. At the resurrection, then, God will give man a new life by putting His spirit in him, → 379, 8 ff. Nevertheless, the spirit is not a divine element in man in the sense of purely Hell. anthropology. Even the pre-existent soul is the soul of man and a creature of God. The distinction between God and man is upheld. If man does the will of God, then in virtue of the soul which comes from heaven he becomes as one of the heavenly creatures, i.e., the angels, not as God. [237] Nor is there any trace of the thought that the union of the soul with the body is a fall from its divinely willed heavenly existence. On the contrary, this union takes place through a divine act of creation. It is at God's behest. Again, there is no suggestion that the soul is led into sin because it is burdened with an earthly body, or that sin is caused by the material body.

Because the spirit in man is something different from the body, in some circumstances it can also act independently after its union with the body. This happens during sleep. Then the spirit (רוּחַ) roams through the whole world and foretells future events in dreams, [238] or the soul (נְשָׁמָה) mounts up to heaven and fetches new life for man. [239] When the gt. mystics rise up to heaven, however, no distinction is usually made between the spirit and the body. Ref. is simply made to their entry into heaven ("I rose up," "they entered in"), Heb. En. 1:1; bChag., 14b; 15b. Cf. the ambivalent account of the rapture of Enoch in Eth. En. 71: his spirit was caught up to heaven (71:1), but he was in heaven with both spirit and body (71:3, 11).

After death the spirit lives on in a place appointed for it. More distinctive in the Rabb. than the idea of the deceased living in burying-grounds (→ 376, 22 ff.) is the concept that after death the spirit is led to a hidden place in heaven or in the realm of the dead where it will await the hour of reunion with the body at the resurrection for the Last Judgment. Acc. to this view the souls of the righteous are sundered from those of the wicked immediately after death, → I, 147, 7 ff.; V, 768, 2 ff. The soul (נֶפֶשׁ) of the

---

[233] S. Dt., 306 on 32:2 (ed. M. Friedmann [1864], 132a); cf. Str.-B., II, 430.
[234] Lv. r., 4, 1 on 4:2, cf. Meyer, 65.
[235] R. Jose said: The son of David will not come before the souls (נְשָׁמוֹת) in the guph are at an end, for it is written: " 'The spirit (רוּחַ) is covered by me, and I have created the souls (נְשָׁמוֹת) (Is. 57:16),' " bAZ, 5a; bNidda, 13b; bJeb., 62a.
[236] Cf. Heb. Test. N. 10:9: "Blessed is the man who does not soil the holy spirit of God which God has placed and breathed into his inward parts." Cf. also Damasc. 5:11 (7:12); 7:4 (8:20). But cf. also Sus. Θ: ἐξήγειρεν ὁ θεὸς τὸ πνεῦμα τὸ ἅγιον παιδαρίου νεωτέρου ᾧ ὄνομα Δανιήλ, where the spirit of Daniel is called holy because he is pious and just; cf. also Jub. 1:21; Test. B. 4:5.
[237] Cf. the continuation of the saying of R. Simai in S. Dt., 306 on 32:2 (Friedmann [→ n. 233], 132a).
[238] Pirqe R. Eliezer, 24, cf. Meyer, 51, n. 1.
[239] Gn. r., 14, 9 on 2:7 (Theodor → n. 226, 133 f.) R. Meir → n. 249.

righteous is kept by God in the hour of death, but not that of the transgressor, S. Nu., 40 on 6:24 (ed. H. S. Horovitz [1917], 44). The souls of the righteous will be kept in the 7th heaven (bChag., 12b), in the heavenly store-chamber, [240] under the throne of God (bShab., 152b [R. Eliezer]), or in Paradise. [241] The souls of sinners, on the other hand, are tossed out by God and have to wander about without rest (Qoh. r., 3, 21; bShab., 152b), or they are banished at once to Gehenna. [242] At the resurrection, body and soul will be reunited. The spirit of man will be brought back into its sheath, i.e., the body. Because the spirit is the divinely derived vital force of man, it can be said (on the basis of Ez. 36:26 f. and 37:14) that at the resurrection God again sets His spirit in man. The Rabb. vacillate between the two views 1. that the life of the resurrected is from the returning spirit of man and 2. that it is from God's spirit. [243]

d. Age of the Idea of the Pre-existence and Immortality of the Soul, → 378, 2 ff.

These ideas are found quite early in Hell. Judaism, → 368, 23 ff.; 370, 28 ff.; 373 ff. On Palestinian soil the idea of the life of the spirit after death is first attested in Jub. and Eth. En. Acc. to Jub 23:26-31 the spirit of the righteous dead experiences the joy of the redemption of Israel in the last time, while their bones rest at peace in the earth. The ref. here, then, is not to the resurrection of the body of the righteous, but only to the joy of their spirit, which still lives on. These thoughts are further developed in Eth. En. where there is not only a continued existence of the soul immediately after death but also a future resurrection of man at the Last Judgment. Souls await the resurrection at the place assigned to them, → I, 147, 5-11. [244]

The thought of a store-chamber where the souls of the righteous are kept between death and the resurrection, while those of sinners are tossed hither and thither (→ lines 2 ff.), is worked out in 4 Esr. (7:75-101) and S. Bar. (21:23; 23:5; 30:2). At the Last Judgment the earth will yield up the bodies which sleep in it and the store-chamber will return the souls which are kept therein, 4 Esr. 4:35; 7:32; S. Bar. 42:7. It is perfectly plain, therefore, that Judaism (apart from the Sadducees) had in the time of Christ a belief both in the resurrection of man and also in the continued existence of the soul in the intermediate state after death. When Joseph. says (Ant., 18, 14) that the Pharisees ascribed to the soul an immortal power, this is not just a Hellenising interpretation. The Pharisees believed both in the immortality of the soul and also in the resurrection. The two ideas were understood in such a way as not to be mutually exclusive. The link between them is the idea of the intermediate state of the soul after death and before the resurrection.

More difficult is the question of the age of belief in the pre-existence of souls. In Hell. Judaism the matter is clear enough, → 368, 23 ff.; 370, 28 ff.; 373 f. On the other hand, there can be no certainty when the idea of the pre-existence of the soul arose in Palestinian Judaism. [245] In fact there are in the apocr. and pseudepigr. works of Palestine

---

[240] S. Dt., 344 on 33:3 (Friedmann, 143b); Qoh. r., 3, 21.

[241] Str.-B., IV, 1130 ff.

[242] *Ibid.,* 1032 ff.

[243] Gn. r., 26, 6 on 6:3 (Theodor → n. 226, 249 f.): "And JHWH said: 'My spirit shall not rule in man'; R. Jishmael bJose said: I will not bring my spirit (רוחי) into them when I give the righteous (in the future world) the gift of their reward ... R. Huna said in the name of R. Acha: When I bring back the spirit into its sheath, I will not bring back their spirits (רוחן) into their sheaths. R. Chiyya bAbba said: I will not fill my spirit into them when I fill my spirit into men; for in this age the spirit embraces (only) one member, but in the age to come it will embrace the whole body; this is as it is written: 'And I will bring my spirit into them' (Ez. 36:27)." Cf. also, e.g., jKeth., 12, 3 (35b, 5) with par. (Str.-B., III, 828 f.).

[244] Eth. En. 22; 39:4 ff.; 91:10; 92:3; 98:3, 10; 103:3 f., 7 f.

[245] Acc. to Str.-B., II, 341 f. it is not found until the middle of the 3rd cent. A.D. Meyer, 49-61 finds it already in R. Meir, 4 Esr. and even Hillel. Other scholars discern the idea of pre-existence in the apocr. and pseudepigr. writings, esp. 4 Esr., cf. H. Gunkel, Kautzsch Apkr. u. Pseudepigr., II, 356, 358; G. H. Box, *The Ezra-Apocalypse* (1912), 26.

no unambiguous instances of the idea. 4 Esr. and S. Bar. are familiar with the thought that God ordained from the very first the number of men to be born (4 Esr. 4:36; S. Bar. 23:3 ff.), but they do not speak of heavenly store-chambers where souls not yet born are kept (→ 378, 5 ff.), so that the thought of pre-existence does not occur in this connection. In 4 Esr. 7:78 ff. the death of man is described as follows: "So soon as the judgment of the Most High has gone forth that a man shall die, when the soul [246] escapes from the body to be sent back to him who gave it, it worships first the glory of the Most High." Here one might infer that the soul which returns to heaven had had a heavenly existence before its life on earth. It is probable, however, that the passage is simply developing the ancient idea that the spirit of life in man comes from God. Acc. to the later Jewish view of the spirit of man, this thought is carried over to the spirit which exists independently after life on earth. It is this spirit which comes from heaven. This does not carry with it, however, the pre-existence of this spirit. Hence it is probable that the idea in 4 Esr. 7:78 ff. is simply that the soul of man is from heaven with no speculation as to its pre-existence. [247]

This seems to have been the general understanding in Pal. Judaism in the 1st cent. A.D. [248] The story about Hillel (Lv. r., 34, 3 on 25:25) which tells us that he called the soul a guest in the body is to be interpreted along these lines. The oldest instance of belief in the pre-existence of the soul is probably the account of the contents of the 7th heaven in bChag., 12b, → 378, 5 ff. [249] With some probability, then, one may conclude that the belief in the pre-existence of souls was adopted in Rabb. Judaism in the 2nd cent. A.D. There is certainly no justification for assuming that it was present already in the 1st cent.

e. The Historical Problem.

That the anthropology of Hell. Judaism (→ 368, 23 ff.; 370, 28 ff.; 373 ff.) developed under the influence of Hell. ideas is self-evident. But Palestinian Judaism and the anthropology which was fully worked out in Rabbinism undoubtedly stood under a similar influence. [250] Palestine was not an isolated territory in the Hell. world. It was influenced by the Hell. culture around it. On the other hand, one should not overlook the fact that the new anthropological ideas could attach themselves to ancient Hebrew and Jewish concepts, especially the view that the spirit which comes from God is the vital force in man. With the development of the idea of a resurrection and a real human life after death, it was natural that the thought of a divine element of life in man should be worked out further. At this point specifically Jewish and Hellenistic ideas were interwoven. But the Jewish

---

[246] The Heb. word is probably נְשָׁמָה, cf. B. Violet, "Die Apk. d. Esr. u. Bar. in deutscher Gestalt," GCS, 32 (1924), 89. Acc. to later Jewish usage spirit or soul is the right transl.; breath would be quite wrong, as against Violet.

[247] H. Gunkel, op. cit., II, 358 wrongly finds the thought of pre-existence in 4 Esr. 4:41 as well. In fact this v. is speaking of the souls of the righteous deceased in just the same way as 4 Esr. 4:35 f. For a correct understanding cf. Str.-B., II, 341; Box, op. cit., 37 f. Nor is the thought of pre-existence present in 4 Esr. 4:12, cf. Violet, II, 13 as against Gunkel, 356 and Box, 26.

[248] So also J. Jeremias, review of R. Meyer, "Hellenistisches in d. rabb. Anthropologie," ThLZ, 65 (1940), 240.

[249] Here souls not yet born are found in the 7th heaven. This inventory is handed down as a statement of Resh Laqish, an Amoraean of the 2nd generation, but in its main essentials at least it probably comes from the Tannaitic period, as discussion of some of the details shows, cf. bChag., 12b; bMen., 110a. Acc. to Meyer, 51-54 the list comes from R. Meir. But this view is based on the unnecessary textual emendation proposed in Bacher Tannaiten, II, 65, n. 3. Meyer also finds the idea of pre-existence in a saying of R. Meir handed down in Gn. r., 14, 9 on 2:7 (Theodor, 133 f.): "In the hour when man sleeps the soul mounts up on high and creates for him new life from above." Cf. the same concept of the soul coming from above in Jos. Bell., 7, 349, c. Meyer, 50 f.

[250] Cf. Meyer.

legacy prevented a complete Hellenising of anthropology, particularly through the exclusion of the Hellenistic view of the body as the seat of evil, → σῶμα.

5. The Spirit of God.

a. Terminology.

In the apocr.-pseudepigr. writings, as in the OT (→ 362 ff.), we find the titles "the Spirit" or "God's (His, Thy) Spirit."[251] Occasionally "the Holy Spirit" also occurs.[252] In the Rabb. רוּחַ הַקּוֹדֶשׁ became the standing term. It is quite plain that the transl. "the Holy Spirit" is the only right one here, and that הַקּוֹדֶשׁ is not to be taken as a periphrasis for God's name.[253] Since the spirit of man comes from God, it, too, can be called the spirit of God or His holy spirit, → 378, 13 ff. But the Spirit of God in the true sense is an entity which stands outside man, and which comes to him from God in special situations and under special circumstances.

b. The Works of the Spirit.

(a) That the spirit of man can be influenced by forces outside him may be seen in passages which, like some OT verses (→ 362, 18 ff.), speak of a specific spirit controlling him. There may come on him a spirit of understanding, wisdom, folly, unrest etc., → 389, 30 ff.[254] The ref. here is not to good or evil demons by which man is possessed or influenced; only in Test. XII is there development in this direction.[255] What is meant is a moulding of the human spirit which does not have its source in man but is accomplished from without. With increasing force, however, such influences come to be regarded in Judaism as works of the Spirit of God.[256] He who possesses the Spirit of God receives thereby a spirit of understanding, power, wisdom etc.

In Judaism the Spirit of God is esp. the spirit of prophecy, → 382, 4 ff. Through the Spirit one sees hidden things and things to come, Sir. 48:12 f., 24; Eth. En. 91:1; Test. L. 2:3. Through the Spirit one can determine and foresee in benediction the fate of one's descendants, Jub. 25:14; 31:12. A moral life acc. to the divine commandments is also the work of the Spirit; this is esp. plain in Test. XII, where the righteousness or the sin of man is inspired by the spirit of truth or falsehood or the many spirits of evil.[257] Because God's Spirit knows all the deeds of a man, He can also come forth as the Accuser in the divine judgment: "The Spirit of truth bears witness to all and accuses all," Test. Jud. 20:5.[258]

(b) Acc. to the Rabb. view the presence of the Spirit may manifest itself in external phenomena such as lights and a loud noise. When Phinehas possessed the Spirit, his face shone like flame.[259] When the Holy Ghost alighted on Samson his hairs became

---

[251] E.g., Eth. En. 91:1; S. Bar. 21:4; Test. Jud. 24:2; Jdt. 16:14; Jub. 40:5; S. Bar. 23:5; Test. S. 4:4; Test. B. 8:2. In Wis. 11:20 πνεῦμα has the older sense of "breath."

[252] 4 Esr. 14:22; Asc. Is. 5:14; cf. Sir. 48:12 LXX Cod A; Da. 5:12 LXX; 6:4 LXX; Ps. Sol. 17:37; Wis. (1:5) 9:17. On Sus. 45 Θ and Jub. 1:21 → n. 236.

[253] Cf. Bacher, 180; Dalman WJ, I, 166 (Bonsirven, I, 210, n. 2 is mistaken).

[254] Sus. 45 LXX, 63 LXX; Sir. 39:6; Eth. En. 56:5; 99:14 Gr.; Ps. Sol. 8:14.

[255] Cf. R. Eppel, Le piétisme juif dans les Testaments des douze Patriarches (1930), 83-87, 128 f. In the Test. XII there is also vacillation between a psychological and a concretely mythological view, v. Eppel, 85 f.; Moore, I, 191; Bonsirven, I, 243, n. 3, → 391, 10 ff.

[256] Sir. 39:6 speaks generally of the πνεῦμα συνέσεως with which the wise man is filled, but Wis. 9:17 of the Holy Spirit of God who gives wisdom, cf. Wis. 1:4 f.; 7:7 f. Cf. also Test. L. 2:3 (πνεῦμα συνέσεως κυρίου); Jub. 25:14; 31:12; 4 Esr. 5:22. Acc. to Test. L. 18:7 the Messiah will possess the spirit of understanding and sanctification; this is simply the Spirit of God, as may be seen from Test. Jud. 24:2 and already Is. 11:2.

[257] Test. Jud. 20; the Spirit of God Test. S. 4:4; L. 18:11 (cf. 18:7); Jud. 24:3; B. 8:2; evil spirits Test. R. 2:1 f.; 3:3-6; L. 3:3; 18:12 etc. Cf. the Dead Sea Scrolls → 389, 29 ff.

[258] For the Spirit as Advocate → 388, 29 ff.

[259] Lv. r., 1, 1 on 1:1 (Str.-B., II, 131), cf. Pesikt., 178a. Cf. also the fig. expressions "the Spirit shines forth" (הוֹפִיע), "the Spirit lights up" (נָצֵץ); bMak., 23b; Gn. r., 85, 9 on 38:18 (Theodor, 1042); 91, 7 on 42:11 (1127). The divine presence is often related to phenomena of fire and light, cf. Str.-B., II, 603 f.

firm and struck together like a bell, so that the sound was heard from Zorah to Eshtaol, Lv. r., 8, 2 on 6:13, R. Nachman. On the other hand, in the Rabb. the Holy Spirit never appears in the form of a dove, → 66, 15 ff. [260]

For the Rabb., too, the Holy Spirit is in the first instance the prophetic spirit (→ 381, 23 ff.) and the instrument of divine revelation. In the Targums the Spirit of the OT text is often called expressly רוּחַ נְבוּאָה, "the spirit of prophecy." [261] In other instances, where the emphasis is on the mighty acts of those inspired by the Spirit, רוּחַ גְּבוּרָה, ("the spirit of power") is used. [262] In the Talmud and Midrash the fact that the patriarchs and other righteous men of the OT possessed the Spirit is illustrated by their ability to foretell hidden things and things still to come. [263] "All that the righteous do, they do in the Holy Spirit," says Gn. r., 97 on 49:27 (Theodor, 1224), and the context shows that the ref. is not to the Holy Spirit as the power of their righteous life but to the fact that their acts contain a prophecy which is fulfilled later. Where there are no prophets there is obviously no Holy Spirit. [264]

c. The Spirit and the OT.

In particular the Spirit is, acc. to the Rabb. view, the prophetic Spirit who speaks in the OT, → 362, 37 ff. Each OT work is inspired by the Holy Spirit. [265] The question of canonicity is identical with the question whether a book is written in the Holy Spirit. [266] Hence an OT saying may be adduced either as a word of the Torah or as a word of the Holy Spirit. [267] The fact that Holy Scripture as a whole is inspired by the Holy Spirit does not mean that specific passages cannot be ascribed to various speakers, among whom the Holy Spirit is one. Thus one saying may be regarded as uttered by Israel or other persons, while another is called a saying of the Holy Ghost. For example, in Dt. 21:7-8 v. 7 is said to have been spoken by the elders of the city concerned, v. 8a by the priests, and v. 8b by the Holy Ghost. In Ju. 5:28-31 Sisera's mother utters v. 28b, his wife and daughters-in-law v. 29, and the Spirit v. 31a. [268] Two different passages can also be brought together in which the one is presented as a statement of Israel and the other as the reply of the Holy Spirit. These are texts in which God is exalted on the one side and Israel on the other. Hence Israel confesses YHWH as the one God in the shᵉma (Dt. 6:4), and the Holy Spirit replies in 2 S. 7:23 by calling Israel the only people on the earth. [269] In statements of this kind the Holy Ghost represents God and expresses His reaction to what has been said or done, though there is no direct equation. A passage of Scripture can also be expounded in such a way

---

[260] Str.-B., I, 123 ff. Billerbeck, however, is too cautious. For this fact is not altered by the legend that R. Jose b. Chalaphta once heard in the ruins of Jerusalem a bath-qol which cooed like a dove, bBer., 3a (Str.-B., I, 124). The cooing of the bath-qol is due to the fact that God sorrowed over the destruction of the temple and the dispersion of Israel which are here at issue. For cooing as an expression of sorrow cf. Is. 38:14; 59:11; Na. 2:8. Nor does it make any difference that the Targum refers "the voice of the turtle-dove" (Cant. 2:12) to the voice of the Holy Spirit proclaiming redemption from Egypt, Str.-B., I, 125. This is allegorical exegesis after the common Rabb. pattern and no special relation between the Holy Spirit and the dove need be assumed. (On T. Chag., 2, 5 (234) → 66, 15 ff.)

[261] Cf. Volz, Geist, 78, n. 1; Str.-B., II, 129.

[262] Volz, Geist, 78, n. 1; Str.-B., II, 129. Cf. רוּחַ גְּבוּרָה in Sir. 48:24 and "the spirit of prophecy" in Jub. 31:12.

[263] Examples in → n. 284.

[264] jSanh., 10, 2 (28b, 59); R. Chunya (Str.-B., II, 129).

[265] Cant. r., 1, 1 § 5-10; Lv. r., 15, 2 on 13:2 (Str.-B., II, 134 f.; IV, 444). Cf. 4 Esr. 14:21; Jos. Ap., 1, 41.

[266] T. Jad., 2, 14 (Str.-B., II, 135); bMeg., 7a.

[267] One cannot conclude from this that the Torah and the Holy Spirit are equated, as Abelson does (225).

[268] T. Sota, 9, 2 f., 9; jSota, 9, 7 (23d/24a); cf. Bacher, 129 f., 146, 163, 180 f.; Parzen, 56-60.

[269] M. Ex., 15, 2 (ed. H. S. Horovitz and J. A. Rabin [1931], 126); S. Dt., 335 on 33:26 (Friedmann [→ n. 233], 148a); cf. Str.-B., II, 136; Bacher, 181.

that some words in it are said by the Holy Spirit to God Himself. This takes place, e.g., in the very few instances in the Rabb. in which the Holy Spirit appears before God as an Advocate, → 388, 29 ff.

d. The Spirit and Righteousness.

In the Rabb. there is also a sense of the link between the Holy Spirit and a life which is obedient to God. Here the gift of the Spirit is esp. viewed as a reward for a righteous life. Possession of the Spirit is in the first instance the result of a righteous life, not the basis of such a life. Naturally the Spirit also inspires men who have this gift to continue in holiness. Where the Holy Spirit is, there are righteous and religious men, and where there are righteous and religious men, there the Holy Spirit is given. Because the Israelites believed at the Red Sea, the Holy Spirit rested upon them. R. Nechemiah derives from this the general conclusion: "He who undertakes a commandment in faith, is worthy that the Holy Spirit rest on Him." [270] "He who studies (the Torah) with the intention of doing it, deserves the gift of the Holy Spirit," says R. Acha in Lv. r., 35, 7 on 26:3. [271] "He who sacrifices himself for Israel will receive the wages of honour, greatness, and the Holy Spirit." [272]

When the righteous man sins, the Holy Ghost turns from him, [273] as also when he draws near to a place where sin reigns. [274] The Spirit cannot work in unclean localities. Acc. to a common view He is thus bound to the land of Israel; outside Palestine there is no divine inspiration. [275] At the beginning, however, the Gentiles too could receive the Holy Spirit, and there could thus be prophets among them. [276] But after Balaam misused his prophetic gift, the Holy Spirit was taken from the Gentiles and reserved for Israel. [277] Health and strength of body and soul are also conditions for possession of the Spirit. "The Holy Spirit rests only on a merry heart." [278] When Jacob gave way to grief on hearing of the death of Joseph, the Holy Spirit departed from him. [279] The saying that particularly joy in a divine commandment is favourable to the attainment of the Holy Spirit [280] brings us back to the religious and moral understanding.

e. Endowment with the Spirit in Past, Future and Present.

(a) Acc. to the Jewish view the gt. figures of the OT past were inspired by the Holy Ghost. Naturally this applies in the first instance to the prophets, Sir. 48:12, 24. But others spoke, too, by prophetic inspiration. Rebekah blessed Jacob "when the spirit of truth had come down into her mouth," Jub. 25:14. Through the Spirit of prophecy Jacob blessed Levi and Judah, Jub. 31:12. Joseph had the Spirit of God within him as the power

---

[270] M. Ex., 15, 1 (Horovitz, 114); cf. Str.-B., II, 135.

[271] Str.-B., II, 134.

[272] Nu. r., 15, 20 on 11:16 (Str.-B., II, 133 f.). The so-called chain-saying of R. Pinchas bYair corresponds to the general view: "Zeal (in obedience to the Law) leads to physical purity, this leads to cultic purity, this to abstemiousness, this to holiness, this to humility, this to abhorrence of sin, this to piety, this to the Holy Spirit, this to the resurrection, and this comes through the prophet Elijah of blessed memory"; Sota, 9, 15; bAZ, 20b (Str.-B., I, 194). Cf. A. Büchler, Types of Jewish Palestinian Piety (1922), 42-67.

[273] Gn. r., 60, 3 on 22:14 (Theodor, 644).

[274] E.g., Esther when she drew near to the palace of the Gentile king, Jalqut Shimeoni Est. 5:2; cf. Abelson, 270. Cf. also Gn. r., 65 on 26:34 (Theodor, 715). R. Jehoshua bLevi: The Holy Spirit left Isaac because of Esau.

[275] M. Ex., 12, 1 (Horovitz, 3); cf. Str.-B., I, 643; Parzen, 53.

[276] Str.-B., II, 130.

[277] Tanch. בלק, 231a; Nu. r., 20, 1 on 22:2 (Str.-B., II, 130). Acc. to other sayings it took place when Israel had received the Torah, Seder Olam Rabba, 21 (Str.-B., II, 130) or after the completion of the tabernacle, Cant. r., 2:3 R. Jishaq.

[278] jSukka, 5, 1 (55a, 63), cf. Str.-B., I, 643.

[279] Gn. r., 91, 6 on 42:1 (Theodor, 1121); Tg. J. I, Gn. 45:27. In Jacob's last days his prophetic gife diminished through age and physical weakness, Gn. r., 97 on 48:10 (Theodor, 1243).

[280] bPes., 117a (Str.-B., III, 312).

for a moral life : "merciful and sympathetic, he never paid back evil," Test. S. 4:4. In Rabbinism this concept of the fathers was further developed. Acc. to the Rabb. view all the righteous of the OT spoke and acted under the influence of the Holy Spirit. All the pious and righteous of former generations were initiated into God's secrets through their endowment with the Spirit. [281] Naturally, however, the gt. personages in salvation history possessed the Spirit in special measure. The OT bears witness that Moses was a prophet. David and Solomon must have had the Spirit as authors of OT writings. [282] Only if a priest had the Holy Spirit could he successfully give oracles through the Urim and Thummim. [283] The patriarchs were naturally bearers of the Spirit, but their wives, too, saw and spoke through the Holy Spirit. [284]

(b) In the last time (→ 370, 3 ff.), as the OT testifies (Is. 11:2), the Messiah will possess the Spirit of God. This idea lives on in Judaism. This is shown both by the apocr. and pseudepigr. writings and also by the Rabbinic literature. ὁ θεὸς κατειργάσατο αὐτὸν δυνατὸν ἐν πνεύματι ἁγίῳ, says Ps. Sol. 17:37 of the Messianic king, cf. Ps. Sol. 18:7. On the elect, the Son of Man, rests "the spirit of wisdom, and the spirit who gives understanding, and the spirit of counsel and power, and the spirit of those who have fallen asleep in righteousness," says Eth. En. 49:3 (on the basis of Is. 11:2). "The spirit of righteousness has been poured out upon him," says Eth. En. 62:2. Test. L. 18:7 and Test. Jud. 24:2 speak similarly of the Messiah. Tg. Is. 42:1-4 refers the 'ebed to the Messiah and has God say of Him : "I will cause my holy spirit to rest on him," cf. also Tg. Is. 11:2. The Targum reflects the Rabb. view which has its basis in Is. 11:2. On the other hand, the Messiah Himself is not equated with the Spirit of God, not even in the saying of R. Shimeon bLaqish in Gn. r., 2, 4 on 1:2 (Theodor, 16 f.), where in the words which describe primeval chaos he finds an allusion to the four Gentile kingdoms of the world, and in the saying about the spirit which broods over the waters he sees a reference to the Spirit of the Messiah. The Messiah is no more equated here with the Spirit of God than are the Gentile kingdoms with primeval chaos. [285]

In the last time the redeemed righteous will also receive the Spirit of God. Moral renewal is expected through an alteration of the spirit and heart of man. According to some sayings this will be brought about by God Himself (e.g., Jub. 1:23; 4 Esr. 6:26), while according to others it will be effected by the Spirit poured out upon the righteous. The "spirit of sanctification" or "spirit of grace" will be given them by God Himself (Test. Jud. 24:3) or by His Messiah (Test. L. 18:11). In the apocr. and pseudepigr. writings there are only a few instances of

---

281 Gn. r., 97 on 49:27 (Theodor, 1224); Tanch. ויהי, 58a (ed. S. Buber [1885], § 13, 110a); cf. Str.-B., II, 131 f.

282 Str.-B., II, 132.

283 bYoma, 73b; Str.-B., II, 132.

284 Gn. r., 75, 8 on 32:4 (Theodor, 886) Isaac ; 84, 19 on 37:33 (Theodor, 1024) Jacob ; 98, 7 on 42:11 (1127) Jacob; 93, 12 on 45:14 (1170) Joseph ; 45, 2 on 16:2 (449) Sarah ; 72, 6 on 30, 31 (845): "The mothers of the race were prophetesses, and Rachel belonged to them." Cf. also bMeg., 14a: Sarah had the power of vision through the Holy Spirit ; she was one of the seven prophetesses in Israel : Sarah, Miriam, Deborah, Hannah, Abigail (cf. Qoh. r., 3, 21), Huldah and Esther. Tamar (Gen. r., 85, 9 on 38:18, Theodor, 1042) and Rahab (S. Dt., 22 on 1:24, Friedmann, → n. 233, 69b) also saw and prophesied in the Spirit.

285 In this interpretation the rabbi is not seeking to describe the events at the creation of the world but acc. to the customary Rabb. method of exegesis he is trying to get at the deeper sense of the saying which is present along with the lit. sense. This passage, too, has something to say about the enemies of Israel and about the Messiah who will come to redeem Israel when it turns to God (this is the meaning of the brooding over the waters, which contains a ref. to conversion acc. to Lam. 2:19). Cf. Str.-B., II, 350. One should not speak, however, about allegorical exposition among the Rabb.; as they saw it, this was a true interpretation of the saying and not just a capricious flight of fancy.

the link between eschatological renewal and endowment with the Spirit. [286] All the clearer, then, are the Rabbinic sources. Here Ez. 36:26 f. and 37:14 are central passages for expectations of the future. On the basis of them resurrection by the Spirit of God is awaited, → 379, 8 ff. [287] Ez. 36:26 f. is also the basis of the hope that God will destroy the evil impulse in the coming age. He will take away the heart of stone and set His Spirit within the people of Israel. [288] If here the Spirit is taken to be the power which inspires man morally and changes his will, in other places the power of prophetic inspiration is to the forefront : in the last time all Israelites will be prophets. Jl. 2:28 f. is the decisive passage in this connection. [289]

(c) In the apocr. and pseudepigr. writings it is believed quite freely on the one hand that the Spirit can still be given to man to-day, and yet there is awareness on the other hand that the great epoch of prophetic inspiration is over. He who obeys the Law can receive the Spirit, Wis. 9:17; cf. 7:7; Sir. 39:6. The Spirit of God seeks to inspire men to obey God, as the spirit of Beliar seeks to lead them into sin. [290] The apocalyptists speak and write through the Holy Spirit, but only in the name of personages in the sacred history who have been long since dead. [291] Prophecy is defunct. [292] Acc. to a widespread theological conviction, prophetic inspiration departed from Israel with the closing of the canon by the last prophets. Nevertheless, there are prophetic experiences (→ προφήτης) even in this period. John Hyrcanus uttered a prophecy acc. to Joseph., and Joseph. tells of others who came forth as prophets. If he mentions spiritual experiences esp. among the Essenes, this agrees with the fact that members of the sect of the new covenant in Qumran regarded themselves as possessors of the Holy Spirit. Through the Spirit they had insight into the divine mysteries, were cleansed from sin, and were enabled to live a new life acc. to God's will (1 QH 4:31; 7:6 f.; 12:11 f. etc.). [293]

In the Rabb. it is expressly stated that the Holy Spirit departed from Israel after the last prophets Haggai, Zechariah and Malachi. [294] It was even accepted that the Spirit was no longer present in the second temple. [295] There was no longer any inspired revelation comparable with the OT. This was not just a theological speculation but played a role in practical life, as may be seen esp. in statements that this or that rabbi had become worthy to possess the Holy Spirit but had not received Him because the present genera-

---

[286] There are only the passages adduced here. 2 Macc. 7:23; 14:46; Sib., IV, 46, 189 — God will give "spirit and life" again to the righteous — do not refer to the Holy Spirit but to the restored vital force in man.

[287] For the same idea of the Holy Spirit as the power behind resurrection cf. the chain-saying of R. Pinchas bJair, Sota, 9, 15; bAZ, 20b (→ n. 272).

[288] Pesikt., 165a; Tanch. קדושים, 170b; שלח לך 216a (Str.-B., III, 240).

[289] Str.-B., II, 134, 615 f.; IV, 915; cf. Sib., III, 582.

[290] Test. B. 8:2 : The righteous has no stain in his heart because the Spirit rests on him. Cf. Test. Jud. 20:1 and the Dead Sea Scrolls, → 389, 29 ff.

[291] Eth. En. 91:1 (but not 71:5 where acc. to the better text Michael snatches away the "spirit of Enoch"); 4 Esr. 5:22; 14:22, 37 ff.

[292] 1 Macc. 4:46; 9:27; 14:41; S. Bar. 85:1-3. In spite of the historical garb the last of these refs. undoubtedly echoes its own age. On the other hand Da. 3:38 LXX is depicting the situation after the destruction of Solomon's temple.

[293] Ant., 13, 282 f., 299 f.; 17, 42 f.; Bell., 1, 68 f.; 6, 300 ff., 285 ff. Cf. R. Meyer, *Der Prophet aus Galiläa* (1940), 41-70. On 1 Q H cf. E. Sjöberg, "Neuschöpfung in den Toten-Meer-Rollen," Studia Theologica, 9 (1955), 135.

[294] "Since the last prophets Haggai, Zechariah and Malachi died, the Holy Spirit has ceased in Israel," T. Sota, 13, 2, par. in Str.-B., I, 127.

[295] bYoma, 21b; jTaan., 2, 1 (65a, 59), par. Str.-B., II, 133. Cf. Qoh. r., 12, 7: after the destruction of the temple the Holy Spirit departed from Israel, Str.-B., II, 133.

tion is not worthy of Him. [296] R. Akiba laments that the Spirit is no longer given, though men do what should properly lead to the gift of the Spirit. [297]

Nevertheless, the Rabbis did not keep strictly to the idea that the Spirit is no longer to be had. Sometimes there is unqualified ref. to the fact that a life pleasing to God leads to the gift of the Spirit, → 383, 5 ff. Acc. to a saying of Hillel all Israelites possessed the Holy Spirit. [298] It is told of individual rabbis of the Tannaitic period that they had visions through the Holy Spirit. On a chance encounter with a Gentile R. Gamaliel acted and spoke through the Holy Spirit, as may be seen from the fact that he knew the name of this Gentile who was a complete stranger to him. Valid legal regulations could thus be established from his conduct. [299] Similarly R. Shimeon bJochai saw hidden things through the Holy Spirit. [300] The same is said of R. Akiba and R. Meir. [301] On the other hand it is unlikely that the laying on of hands at Rabbinic ordination was commonly associated with impartation of the Spirit. [302] If so, the categorical sayings about the cessation of the Spirit with the last prophets would be inexplicable, as would also be the sayings mentioned above about rabbis who were worthy of the Spirit but did not receive Him. If later, with the consent of contemporary and later rabbis, R. Abdimi bChaipha maintains that the prophetic gift was taken from the prophets but not from the wise men, i.e., the scribes, [303] this is a correction of the ancient view, and it is quite understandable in a situation in which people had long since been accustomed to see in the rabbis the uncontested and wholly adequate spiritual leaders of Judaism.

f. The Cosmic Function of the Spirit.

The idea that the Spirit is the instrument of the divine creation lives on in the apocr. and pseudepigr., Jdt. 16:14; Wis. 1:7; 12:1; S. Bar. 21:4. [304] This belief that the Spirit was God's tool at creation must have been common in Palestinian Judaism and could appeal to the OT (→ 363, 14 f., 36 f.; 366, 4 ff.), but examples are few, and this function of the Spirit was definitely secondary as compared with the understanding of the Spirit as the agent of prophetic revelation and a gift to the righteous. The cosmic function of the Spirit does not seem to be mentioned at all in the older Rabb. literature. [305] The רוּחַ of Gn. 1:2 is commonly transl. "wind." [306] On the basis of Ps. 139:5 R. Shimeon bLaqish

---

[296] This is said of Hillel and Shemuel the Less, T. Sota, 13, 3 f. par. Str.-B., I, 129. Acc. to T. Sota 13, 4 Shemuel the Less actually prophesied in the hour of death and thus received some inspiration through the Holy Spirit, Str.-B., II, 133.

[297] bSanh., 65b. In S. Dt., 173 on 18:11 (Friedmann, 107b) this is a saying of R. Eleazar bAzaria, Str.-B., II, 133.

[298] T. Pes., 4, 2, also without mention of the Holy Spirit in jShab., 19, 1 (17a, 4); bPes., 66a, Str.-B., II, 627.

[299] T. Pes., 1, 27 (Str.-B., I, 528). Here we find legal definitions on the basis of prophetic inspiration. But cf. bBB, 12a, R. Jose : What cannot be supported from Scripture is rejected as "prophecy," as subjective thinking. The ensuing discussion of the saying (quoted below) of R. Abdimi bChaipha maintains, however, that correct interpretation of Scripture presupposes a kind of prophetic gift, as may be seen from the fact that two rabbis can independently come to the same result and even find a halacha given to Moses on Sinai.

[300] jSheb., 9, 1 (38d, 37), cf. Str.-B., I, 557.

[301] Lv. r., 21, 8 on 16:3 (Str.-B., II, 133); jSota, 1, 4 (16d, 44), cf. Str.-B., I, 216.

[302] As Weber, 126 f., Volz, Geist, 115, n. 2; Str.-B., II, 654 and Bousset-Gressm., 169 believe, cf. E. Lohse, Die Ordination im Spätjudt. u. im NT (1951), 53-55.

[303] bBB, 12a, Str.-B., I, 670.

[304] In S. Bar. 21:4, on the basis of Ps. 33:5, it is said that God established the firmament by His Word and the heights of heaven by His Spirit. Similarly we find the Spirit as the instrument of creation in S. Bar. 23:5, here on the basis of Ps. 104:30 and with particular ref. to men, probably in the last time, not the first : "My spirit creates the living," coming into man and giving him life → 379, 8 ff.

[305] Str.-B., I, 48 f.

[306] Tg. O. Gn. 1:2; bChag. 12a: R. Jehuda bJechezqel ; Gn. r., 1, 9 on 1:1 (Theodor, 8): R. Gamaliel ; Gn. r., 2, 3 on 1:2 (16): R. Jehuda b R. Simon; Gn. r., 2, 4 on 1:2 (17): R. Chaggai in the name of R. Pedath, cf. Str.-B., I, 48 f.

referred it to the spirit of Adam, which was the first work of creation while his body acc. to Gn. 1:26 was the last. [307] In Tg. J. I and II Gn. 1:2, however, the Spirit of God is the "spirit of the mercy of YHWH," and there is seen here the thought that God created the world with mercy. [308]

g. The Autonomy of the Spirit.

The autonomy of the Spirit in Judaism is surprising. In Rabbinic writings the Spirit is often spoken of in personal categories. There are many instances of the Spirit speaking, crying, admonishing, sorrowing, weeping, rejoicing, comforting etc. [309] Indeed, the Spirit can even be said to speak to God, → 388, 37 ff. For this reason it has often been thought that the Spirit is regarded in Judaism as a hypostasis, as a personal angelic being. [310] But this is to introduce ideas which are not in keeping with the Jewish view. The Spirit is no angelic or heavenly being. [311] In Jewish writings He is never present in the heavenly assembly before the throne of God. [312] One might call Him a hypostasis if one intends to express His independent action thereby. But even this view, which is taken from a non-Jewish circle of concepts, can easily give rise to false notions. The personal categories used to describe the activity of the Spirit are not designed to present Him as a special heavenly being but rather to bring out the fact that He is an objective divine reality which encounters and claims man. His presence can also be described in non-personal categories — He rests on man (שָׁרָה), fills him (מָלֵא), shines in him (נִצְנֵץ), appears at a place (הוֹפִיעַ) — with no different concept of the Spirit from that which lies behind the personal expressions. The decisive thing is that man

---

[307] Tanch. תזריע, 153a (Buber [→ n. 281] § 2, 16b); Midr. Ps. 139:5 (ed. S. Buber [1891], 265a). "The spirit of the Messiah" instead of "the spirit of Adam" in the same context Gn. r., 8, 1 on 1:26 (Theodor, 56 emends the text) and Lv. r., 14, 1 on 12:2 is, as Billerbeck has shown without raising any objections (Str.-B., II, 351), a secondary revision under the influence of another interpretation of the same rabbi, acc. to which Gn. 1:2 is to be referred to the four kingdoms of the world and the spirit of man, → 384, 22 ff. At issue here is a collection of Rabb. interpretations of Ps. 139:5 which all relate the v. to Adam. Among them is the view of R. Shimeon bLaqish, who interprets the v. of the creation of the spirit and body of Adam. This view is supported and elucidated by a ref. to his interpretation of Gn. 1:2, where acc. to R. Shimeon the creation of Adam's soul before all other creatures is taught. A saying about the spirit of the Messiah would make sense in this context only if the spirit of the Messiah were equated with that of Adam. But for all the par. between Adam and the Messiah (cf. B. Murmelstein, "Adam, ein Beitrag zur Messiaslehre," WZKM, 35 [1928], 242-275; 36 [1929], 51-86; → I, 141 f.) this assumption is not to be found in the Rabb., as against W. Staerk, Die Erlösererwartung in d. östlichen Religionen (1938), 25 and H. Odeberg, The Fourth Gospel (1929), 54, n. 2.

[308] Str.-B., I, 48 f. Acc. to the common Rabb. view the world was made with righteousness as well as mercy, Moore, I, 389; Bonsirven, I, 171; E. Sjöberg, "Gott u. d. Sünder im paläst. Judt.," BWANT, IV, 27 (1939), 4, n. 1.

[309] Cf. Abelson, 224-237; Str.-B., II, 134-138.

[310] Volz, Geist, 145-194; Linder, 132-134; Bousset-Gressm., 347-349; V. Hamp, Der Begriff "Wort" in d. aram. Bibelübersetzungen (1938), 116-120; Ringgren, 165, though cf. Str.-B., II, 134 f.; Moore, I, 415-437; Moore, Intermediaries, 55; Bonsirven, I, 212-216; Abelson, 224-237.

[311] Mowinckel, 116 refers to the designation "angel of the Holy Spirit," but this occurs only in the Chr. sections of Asc. Is. 3:16; 4:21; 9:39 f.; 10:4; 11:4; Herm. m., 11, 9. In the saying of R. Pinchas bChama in Ex. r., 32, 1 on 23:20 (Str.-B., II, 132) the Holy Spirit is not the highest of the angels but is differentiated from the angels: "Aforetime you (Israel) rejoiced in guidance by the Holy Spirit, but now (after the sin of the golden calf) you must be content with guidance by an angel." The Holy Spirit represents God's presence in a way very different from that of angels, as against Mowinckel, loc. cit.

[312] Cf. H. Bietenhard, Die himmlische Welt im Urchr. u. Spätjudt. (1951), 61.

stands here before a reality which comes from God, which in some sense represents the presence of God, and yet which is not identical with God.

In assessing the Rabb. depictions of the work of the Spirit two further pts. must be kept in mind. First, it is typical of the style of the Rabb. to personify and dramatise. Hence the two chief qualities of God, His mercy and righteousness, מִדַּת רַחֲמִים and מִדַּת הַדִּין, are said to speak before Him, though they are not depicted as hypostases or even as personal beings. Secondly, the personal reaction of the Spirit is always associated with the words of Holy Scripture. The Holy Spirit speaks, cries, admonishes etc. in biblical words. [313] When it is said that He weeps, Lam. 1:16 is adduced: "The Holy Spirit cries and weeps: 'For these things I weep.'" [314] This is meant to express a true divine reaction represented by the Spirit. As regards the question of the personifying of the Spirit, however, it is important that in such sayings the ref. is always to the Spirit who speaks in Scripture. There is never a heavenly scene in which the Spirit comes before the throne of God. The Spirit who speaks in Scripture causes the saying of Scripture to be addressed to God Himself. [315]

For all the autonomy of the Spirit it is still perceived that the Spirit finally proceeds from God Himself. The Spirit is God's Spirit and is sent by God. This is very plain in the apocr. and pseudepigr. lit., [316] nor are matters different in the Rabb. writings. Possession of the Spirit is a sign of divine grace and implies contact with the divine world, relationship to God. The Spirit is not regarded as a substitute for God's presence, as has been thought on the basis of the idea that God is only the remote God in later Judaism. The divine presence in man can be expressed by saying either that the Holy Spirit rests on him or that the *shekinah* rests on him. [317] Nevertheless, the Holy Spirit is not identical with the *shekinah*. While the *shekinah* is simply God in His presence, [318] the Holy Spirit is a special divine entity which is sent by God and which acts independently within the limits set by the divine will. But because He comes from God and represents Him, His possession means a connection with the divine world, and in the last analysis with God.

h. The Spirit as Advocate.

The concept of the Spirit as advocate is only weakly attested in Judaism. This is undoubtedly connected with the fact that the Spirit is not a special heavenly being. That Michael and other angels are advocates for Israel and for individuals before God is a common notion in Judaism, → V, 810, 13 ff., 811, 12 ff. But the Spirit is not an angel and is not equated with the interceding angel. [319] Only occasionally can He be depicted in a similar role. In Test. Jud. 20:5 the Spirit is a witness against men, → 381, 28 ff.; → V, 810, 13 ff.; 811, 12 ff. The negative aspect is emphasised here; the Spirit comes forward as an accuser of sinners. [320] In two partly par. passages in the Rabb. the Spirit

---

[313] Sota, 9, 6 is no exception. Though it is not a literal quotation of the relevant text in Dt. 21:8, the saying of the Spirit elucidates the v., which is regarded as a statement of the Spirit, as against Str.-B., II, 136.

[314] Lam. r. on 1:16 § 45, Str.-B., II, 135.

[315] Cf., apart from the v. adduced → lines 37 ff., Lam. r. on 3:59 (Str.-B., II, 135): When Hadrian massacred the Jews with gt. brutality, the Holy Spirit cried out in the words of Lam. 3:59 f. and said: "Thou dost see, YHWH, my oppression ..., thou dost see all their revenge." Cf. also jSota, 9, 7 (24a, 8); Cant. r., 8, 14 : R. Levi.

[316] Jdt. 16:14 also rests on this assumption, and cf. Wis. 1:6 f.; 9:17; 12:1.

[317] Cf. Abelson, 377 ff.; Moore, I, 437; Moore, *Intermediaries*, 58.

[318] It used to be thought that the *shekinah* was a special being alongside God. That this is not so may be seen from, e.g., the saying of R. Jose ha-Gelili in bSota, 30b: When the Israelites saw the *shekinah* at the Red Sea, all of them, even the little children, said : "This is my God, I will praise him," Ex. 15:2. If the *shekinah* had been something other than God in His presence, this view would have been the worst of all heresies, i.e., the idea that there are two divine powers. Par. in Meyer, 84, n. 1.

[319] As might be concluded from Mowinckel's presentation, 109-116.

[320] Cf. Wis. 1:7 f.

is expressly presented as an advocate, Lv. r., 6, 1 on 5:1 and Dt. r., 3, 11 on 9:1. Both are expounding Prv. 24:28 f., which is interpreted in both as a saying of the Holy Spirit to Israel and to God, → V, 811, 15 ff.

In the light of Rabb. presuppositions there is nothing surprising about this interpretation ; it is in keeping with a customary mode of Rabb. exposition, → 382, 19 ff.; 388, 7 ff. Hence one may not conclude therefrom that the idea of the Spirit as advocate and witness had become so common in Judaism that mention of witness before God immediately carried with it the thought of the Holy Spirit as advocate. On the contrary, there is no more here than an occasional introduction of the concept of advocacy within the context of biblical exposition. Apart from the two passages mentioned there is only one place in the Rabb. where one might see traces of the idea of the Holy Spirit as advocate, namely, Cant. r., 8, 11 on 8:10, where the bath-qol, which is a substitute for the Holy Spirit, is called an advocate (סָנֵיגוֹר), → V, 811, 23 ff.

Sjöberg

D. Development to the Pneumatic Self in Gnosticism. [321]

Judaism is inescapably confronted by the OT message that God and His Spirit stand over against man, → 365, 36 ff. To be grasped by God is grace, not nature, → 366, 16 ff. This is the point of the saying that the soul of man derives from God's Spirit. But from this develops the problem that occupies the generations. Once the soul was no longer the mere vital force, but the genuinely responsible ego which survives after death (→ 379, 13 ff.), the following questions became urgent : If the soul is a part of God's Spirit, will it not be saved automatically ? Or is there to be differentiated from the soul a human ego which can receive or repulse, keep pure or sully, this part of God's Spirit ? Or is one to understand this portion of God's Spirit as the possibility of free decision ? How is the actual work of the Spirit of God to be distinguished from this ? What is the nature of ongoing life after death ? Judaism, the NT and Gnosticism all wrestled with these questions.

I. The Dead Sea Scrolls and their Influence.

1. Already in the later parts of the OT increasing importance is assumed by the idea that Yahweh's Spirit is not just the power of the extraordinary but also the power of the ethically good, → 363, 25 ff.; 365, 12 ff.; 367, 13 ff. The further we penetrate into Judaism, the more significant becomes the ethical decision of the individual, his choice between good and evil. In the 200 yrs. which Israel spent under Persian rule, [322] it found in the Persian concept of two opposing spirits [323] which determine man and between which he has to choose [324] an ideal form for this thought. [325] The Spirit is de-

---

[321] For details cf. Schweizer, *Gegenwart*, 485-501; cf. also F. Nötscher, *Zur theol. Terminologie d. Qumran-Texte* (1956), Index, s.v. "Geist u. Geister."

[322] Naturally one has to take mixed forms into account too. Mesopotamia or Syria (W. Baumgartner, "Die Bdtg. d. Höhlenfunde aus Palästina f. die Theol.," *Schweizer theol. Umschau*, 24 [1954], 62) might have been a link.

[323] Cf. E. Schweizer, "Die sieben Geister in d. Apk.," *Ev. Theol.*, 11 (1951/52), 506, n. 23; A. Dupont-Sommer, "L'instruction sur les deux Esprits dans le Manuel de Discipline," RHR, 142 (1952), 16 f.; K. G. Kuhn, "Die Sektenschr. u. d. iranische Religion," ZThK, 49 (1952), 296-298.

[324] "And in the beginning were these two spirits, the twins, ... good and evil. Between them those who act rightly have chosen well, not those who act amiss. And when these two spirits first came together, they determined life and death," Yasna, 30, 3 f.; cf. 45, 2 etc. Both are surrounded by a host of associated spirits. On the transl. cf. F. C. Andreas, "Die dritte Ghātā des Zaratušthro," NGG (1909), 42-49; J. C. Tavadia, "Zur Interpretation der Gata des Zarathustra," ZDMG, 100 (1950), 232-237.

[325] Asc. Is. 3:26, 28 perhaps marks the starting-pt. in Judaism, cf. Nötscher, 79-92.

picted as something which is always present to man and which determines him in his whole existence, → 381, 14 ff. He is the good for which man has to decide already in a life before this world, and for which he decides continually. He is not regarded as a mere idea but as the power of God which claims and supports him. [326] Unlike that of Hellenism, this dualism is felt to run right through the physical and spiritual world. Thus 1 QS is dominated by the idea of the two spirits "of truth" and "of wickedness" which wrestle for man, 3:18 f.; 4:23 ff. [327] They are also called the "spirit of light," "angel of truth," "prince of lights" (also Damasc., 5:18 [7:19]), "spirit of knowledge" and "spirit (or angel) of darkness" (3:20-25; 4:4). [328] This concept is first used quite simply to show the nature of human life as decision, cf. the OT choice between Yahweh and Baal or the Rabb. choice between good and evil. [329] Thus in 1 QS 3:20 f. walking in them (the two spirits) is no other than "walking in the ways of light or darkness." The "counsels" of the good spirit command a whole list of virtues, while a list of vices enumerates that which "belongs to the spirit of wickedness." More strongly than in the Rabb., and with closer approximation to the OT, it is emphasised here that man does not live by his own spirit. He lives by the power of God [330] or else falls victim to evil. A difference from Persian thought is the insistence that both the spirits or angels [331] are created by God, 1 QS 3:25. Experience of the overwhelming power of evil is expressed by the concept of a majority of evil spirits, 1 QH 3:18; 1 QS 3:14; 1 Q 36:2, 5. [332] Here the sense of being determined from without is so strong that many statements verge on a doctrine of predestination. [333]

There is, however, another usage. [334] Spirit can also mean the spirit of man [335] (1 QS 4:3 ?; 8:3; 11:1; 1 QH 1:8 f., 15, 32; 2:15) and can be identical with the ego (1 QH 4:36; 7:29). On the one side the understanding is meant (1 QS 5:23 f., 6:14,

---

[326] The "holy Spirit" is sometimes one side of the being of Ahura Mazda, the side which is most characteristic, his true being, and sometimes it is an independent being alongside him, E. Abegg, "Das Problem des Bösen im Glauben Zarathustras," Neue Zürcher Zeitung, 11. 1. 1955, p. 6.

[327] Cf. the fight between angels and Azazel in Apc. Abr. 13 f.; Philo Abr., 13 f.; Plant., 23 f., or between the angel of God and the devil in Just. Dial., 116, 1.

[328] 1 QM 13:10 f. (H. Bardtke, "Die Kriegsrolle von Qumrān übersetzt," ThLZ, 80 [1955], 401-420) contrasts the prince of light and the angel of hostility.

[329] B. Otzen, "Die neugefundenen hbr. Hdschr. u. d. Testamente d. 12 Patriarchen," Studia Theol., 7 (1954), 139 : Mythologising of the yezer-concept. But perhaps the idea of the two spirits is the origin on the one side, that of the evil impulse the origin on the other, cf. Schweizer, Gegenwart, 490, n. 4. Cf. an expression like "spirit of ambition" in 1 Q 29:14. "The spirit of the counsel of the truth of God" is materially identical with the Law, Nötscher, 60. Cf. the "spirit of integrity, fornication" etc. in 1 QS 3:8; 4:10.

[330] 1 QH 4:31: "The walk of man is not constant except in the spirit God has created in him."

[331] Spirits and angels are also synon. in 1 QM 13:10 f. Cf. Test. XII (though this is less sectarian, Otzen, op. cit., 136 f., 140-142) and Herm. → 391, 11 f., 20 f.; also Jub. 1:25; 15:31 f.; Eth. En. 15:4-6; Sl. En. 16:7. On the further history of the idea of two spirits cf. Ps.-Clem. Hom., 2, 16, 4; 3, 12-16 (H. J. Schoeps, Theol. u. Gesch. d. Judenchristentums [1949], 165, n. 1).

[332] There is a majority of good angels in 1 QM 12:9; 13:10; 19:1 (evil in 13:2, 11 f.; 14:10; 15:13); cf. חי אמת(רוח?) 1 QH 2:4; "spirits of knowledge" 3:22; "holy spirits" 8:12; "thy spirits" 1 Q 36:17 (with ref. to God).

[333] 1 QS 4:24 f.; 1 QH 3:22 f.; cf. 1 QS 3:13 f., 24; 3:26-4:1 refer to the two spirits, cf. Nötscher, op. cit., 179 f.

[334] 1 QH 1:10 : "winds," 1:11: "eternal spirits in their dominion," par. to "messengers of God," "bearers of light" and "stars"; 1 QS 9:3; 1 QH 12:12; 16:12 : "holy spirit"; 1:28 breath (?).

[335] But not enclosed in the body, as Dupont-Sommer, op. cit., 32 interpreted 1 QS 4:20 f. Cf. 1 QM (→ n. 328) 7:5 : "Perfect in spirit and flesh ורוח ובשר)"; 1 QH 9:16 where man is both spirit and flesh. Cf. J. P. Hyatt, "The View of Man in the Qumran 'Hodayot'," NTSt, 2 (1955/56), 276-284.

17),[336] on the other it embraces both understanding and acts (5:21; cf. 2:20; 4:26; 9:14; Damasc. 20:24 [B 9:48]). It is the spirit of a man who falls away from God and is cleansed by Him again (1 QS 7:18, 23; 8:12; cf. 1 QH 1:22 f.; 3:21; 7:5; 13:15). The word is thus on the pt. of becoming a term for the human life which is lived specifically before God, of being used to describe the self which is above both body and soul. It is possible that the Persian idea of *daēna,* of spiritual religious individuality which is also regarded as distinct from its bearer, of the power or part of the soul which comes into effect in religious vision, of the organ of immortality in the broadest sense,[337] also had some influence at this pt.[338]

2. A direct continuation of this line of thought is to be found in the Jewish Test. XII[339] and the Chr. Herm. In Test. XII, too, there are two spirits or angels (Jud. 20:1; L. 5:6; D. 6:1 f.; B. 6:1), the evil one being also referred to in the plur. (Iss. 7:7; D. 1:6 f.; 5:5 f.; 6:1; cf. R. 2 f.;[340] Damasc. 12:2 [14:5]). These evil spirits are plainly traced back to Beliar (Iss. 7:7; D. 1:7; B. 3:3 f.; cf. Damasc. 5:18 [7:19]) or Satan (G. 4:7), while the good spirit is God's Holy Spirit (Jud. 24, cf. 1 QS 4:21). The evil spirit seduces, the good intercedes (L. 5:6; D. 4:5; 6:2; B. 6:1). Decision lies with man (S. 3:1), with his "middle spirit of insight and understanding, in which direction he will incline" (Jud. 20:1; cf. Sir. 15:14). Hence man can also be viewed as a vessel indwelt by the devil (N. 8:6). In Herm.,[341] too, two spirits strive for man (m., 5, 1, 4; 2, 5 etc.), the "spirit of truth" (m., 3, 4) or "angel of righteousness" and the "angel of wickedness" (m., 6, 2, 1 f. 8 f.). Here again man is a vessel indwelt by one spirit or the other.[342] The evil spirit, however, is no other than a bad conscience (m., 3, 4), while the good spirit is the Holy Spirit of God (m., 5, 2, 5. 7) who "dwells in thee," who is "set in this thy flesh" (m., 3, 1; 5, 1, 2; 10, 2, 5 f.). The moral element is esp. clear at this pt. Once again the evil spirit develops into a plurality of spirits which are equated with individual vices (e.g., m., 5, 2; 10, 1, 2), while the holy spirits are equated with the virgins who themselves represent the different virtues (viewed as powers of God), s., 9, 13, 2. 7; 15, 1 f.[343] There is still found the ancient sense of the inescapable pull of these spirits (m., 6, 2, 7 f.), but all that matters for the author is the moral summons (v. 9).[344]

How obscure these ideas are may be seen from the fact what is originally a very different conception has been assimilated to them. Already in later Judaism the divinely

---

[336] Cf. 1 QH 1:28 f.; 10:8 ("Lord of each spirit or angel? and master of each work") and Yasna, 31, 21: "In the spirit and in works" the believer is the friend of Ahura Mazda.

[337] E. Abegg, *Der Messiasglaube in Indien u. Iran* (1928), 204, n. 3; H. S. Nyberg, *Die Religionen d. alten Iran* (1938), 115 f.

[338] The exposition of Nyberg (118-129) is most instructive but it is still much contested → σῶμα Χριστοῦ.

[339] Cf. P. A. Munch, "The Spirits in the Testaments of the Twelve Patriarchs," Acta Orientalia, 13 (1935), 257-263. I myself, however, regard the demonology as primary and the psychologising (Test. D. 2-4: "spirit of wrath" = "wrath") as secondary. For a Jewish Chr. origin of the Test. XII cf. M. de Jonge, *The Test. of the Twelve Patriarchs* (1953); J. T. Milik, "Le Test. de Lévi en Araméen," *Rev. Bibl.,* 62 (1955), 406; against it Albright, *op. cit.* (→ n. 382), 166; G. Molin, *Die Söhne des Lichtes* (1954), 162; also "Qumran-Apokalyptik-Essenismus," Saeculum, 6 (1955), 252-254, emphasises the relation to the Qumran Scrolls. Cf. M. Burrows, *The Dead Sea Scrolls* (1955), 221 and → 381, 18 ff.

[340] The seven neutral spirits between the hosts of good and evil spirits are a secondary interpolation, Test. XII, ed. R. H. Charles, ad loc.; B. Noack, *Satanas u. Soteria* (1948), 45.

[341] Cf. J. P. Audet, "Affinités littéraires et doctrinales du 'Manuel de Discipline'," *Rev. Bibl.,* 59 (1952), 219-238.

[342] If both dwell within at the same time, the evil spirit drives out the good, m., 5, 1, 2-4; 2, 5-7; 10, 1, 2; 2, 1-6 (though cf. 6, 2, 2). Cf. non-mythologically 3, 4; 10, 2, 2. 4; 3, 2 : The good spirit is "grieved" (Is. 63:10; Eph. 4:30).

[343] Against Dib. Herm., 518 it must be asserted that this equation is not the source of the idea of a conflict of spirits.

[344] m., 10, 2, 5 also regards as a responsible act of man that which is elsewhere traced back to the spirits; s., 9, 15, 6 solves the question by supposing that man can just as well withdraw from the spirits as the reverse, cf. also 24, 2.

given soul had become a term for responsible existence before God, and as such it was called spirit. But this raised the problem of human decision. A first solution was to distinguish the human ego as that which could either preserve or destroy the spirit, Damasc. 5:11 (7:12); 7:3 f. (8:20), [345] which can obviously be distinguished from the biological vital force, Test. N. Heb. 10:9. Along these lines the spirit is given by God and ultimately belongs to Him, yet it is not now the spirit which actively produces ethical decision but that which is passively determined thereby. Thus in Herm. it is the παρακαταθήκη of God which can be given back to Him "false," "unserviceable" or "intact," "renewed," m., 3, 2; s., 9, 14, 3; 32, 2-4. [346] The problem has arisen. One particular aspect is developed in Gnosticism. It is to be seen everywhere in the NT → 396, 24 ff.; 401, 11 ff.; n. 466; 412, 30 ff.; 444, 15 ff.; 449, 3 ff. It finds in Paul esp. a radical solution, → 436, 8 ff.

II. Gnosticism.

1. The Problem : The Spirit as Creator of Matter.

The Hellenist thinks of power in the form of substance. [347] When Judaism took up the original Gk. question of the ἀρχή, which did not merely seek scientifically the first cause of cosmogony but also explored the nature of the cosmos (of God also for the Gks.), it naturally had to give the answer : Yahweh. If it wanted to put this in contemporary scientific terms, it had to say : His Spirit. [348] This word was particularly suitable because it corresponded to the OT message, contained for the Gks. the concept of vital substance (→ 336, 13 ff.), and in Egypt, the centre of Hell. Judaism, evoked the ancient idea of the breath of God which gives life when it enters into matter, → 341, 8 ff. [349] Thus the creative role of the Spirit in Gn. 1:2 takes on unsuspected significance, → 386, 23 ff. [350] The new thing here is that spirit always has now a stronger sense than substance, though for the most part there is, of course, no awareness how much the individual fills out the concept from the OT or Hell. thought. When the Jew spoke anthropologically of the holy "spirit" to denote the divinely given spiritual existence of man, which is for him so important, the Hellenist naturally found here the idea of a soul which has come down from the divine sphere, is imprisoned in the body (→ 355, 21 ff.; 357, 10 ff.), and will mount up again to the divine sphere after death. The unity of God and world is increasingly broken in the Hell. period. The antithesis between the heavenly region of light and the world of matter is ever more clearly felt. More and more the soul is felt to be alien, though of the same substance as God, → 338, 31 ff.; 356, 8 ff. [351]

From this feeling about the world there developed the longing for the golden age which once was and will come again. The story of Paradise took on increasing significance in Judaism. Adam played a more important role as the first divine man, → I, 141.

---

[345] Here = "your souls," Lv. 20:25. Rabb.: Str.-B., I, 205 f. → 377, 32 ff.

[346] The soul, a portion of God dwelling in the alien body, is a παρακαταθήκη of God in Jos. Bell., III, 372, 378. The motif is presented wholly in the categories of substance in Ps.-Clem. Hom., 20, 2, 3 f.: Man consists of 2 substances, σῶμα and πνεῦμα, and as αὐτεξούσιος he can choose between the 2 ways open to him.

[347] Nemesius, De natura hominis, 30 and 40 (MPG, 40, 540b, 561a): "Power (δύναμις) is matter (ὕλη τις)," "power consists of matter," "partakes of it," "so matter is power"; Diog. L., VII, 56 : πᾶν τὸ ποιοῦν σῶμά ἐστιν, esp. on πνεῦμα cf. Nilsson, II, 254, 672; also Schweizer, Gegenwart, 497, n. 1. On the OT → n. 545.

[348] On the almost identical (MacDonald, 33) alternative → σοφία.

[349] Eichr. Theol. AT³, II, 19 (§ 13a); Verbeke, 335-337; examples in E. Norden, Die Geburt des Kindes (1924), 77, n. 7; Staerk, op. cit., 308-316, cf. 325-329.

[350] Herm. s., 5, 6, 5; Corp. Herm., 1, 5; 3, 1 (C. H. Dodd, The Bible and the Greeks [1935], 101-134, 217-231; Verbeke, 318 f.); also Ascl., 14; Gnosticism : Iren. Haer., I, 30, 1; Hipp. Ref., V, 19, 13-19; cf. 10, 2; Epiph. Haer., 25, 5, 1; Ps.-Clem. Hom., XI, 22-24; cf. Recg., VI, 7 f.; Hegemonius, Acta Archelai, 8 (GCS, 16 [1906]).

[351] Examples : E. Schweizer, Erniedrigung u. Erhöhung bei Jesus u. seinen Nachfolgern (1955), 118 f., 124 f.

Widespread in Judaism, then, was the idea on the one side of a fallen divine being in the first time, and on the other side the idea of a coming man in the last time. The fact that the ancient Gk. divinities had already been changed into symbols of the *logos,* which constituted this divine part of man (→ IV, 87, 6-29), probably helped to promote the combination of the Gk. myth of the soul with the myth of the first divine man who had fallen. Myths of the gods were interpreted as a depiction of the destiny of the soul, and this was depicted mythically. If the community of Jesus proclaimed that the man of the last time had already come, the Hellenist naturally found here the return of the fallen first man, the second Adam. The idea, borrowed from the mysteries, that the believer undergoes the fate of the god, may have made some contribution towards seeing the destiny of the soul in the story of his descent and ascent. [352]

If, however, from the time of Is. 31:3 the divine world was characterised by πνεῦμα, the human world by σάρξ, [353] in the Hell. world around this was bound to be understood in terms of substance. In the Son of Man, then, the original heavenly substance found its way back into matter to liberate the related substance of the human soul for ascent into its original heavenly home. But how can God and His Spirit be the Creator of (intrinsically evil) matter ? [354] How can the divine πνεῦμα reside therein in man ?

2. The Redemption of the πνεῦμα from Matter.

With great variety [355] Gnosticism attempts an answer at this pt. [356] God is spiritual by nature. [357] In some way [358] spiritual substance [359] was at creation bound to matter. It cries out for liberation from this. [360] Sometimes it can be called ψυχή [361] or λογική ψυχή, [362] though in the main πνεῦμα as the divine self is expressly differentiated from

---

[352] For details Schweizer, 154-162.

[353] Cf. Nu. 16:22; 27:16, where the LXX distinguishes the kingdom of spirits from the flesh by transl., not "God of the spirits of all flesh," but "God of spirits and of all flesh" (cf. 1 Cl., 59, 3; 64; Ditt. Syll.³, III, 1181, 2 f.), and E. Schweizer, "Der vorpaulinische Gegensatz v. Fleisch u. Geist in R. 1:3 f.," *Ev. Theol.,* 14 (1955), 563-571 → n. 335.

[354] This is radically denied in Cerinthus (Iren. Haer., I, 26, 1), the Manichees (Acta Archelai [→ n. 350], 7). Iren. Haer., II, 3, 2 wrestles against the blasphemy that the world is a product of the fall and ignorance. On Marcion cf. Tert. Marc., I, 15 and the material in A. v. Harnack, *Marcion* (1924), 97-106. Similar ideas can fashion the myth that matter became such only as the πνεῦμα (or λόγος) departed therefrom before creation, Corp. Herm., 1, 10; Iren. Haer., I, 11, 1; cf. G. Quispel, "La conception de l'homme dans la gnose valentinienne," *Eranos Jbch.,* 15 (1947), 281 f.

[355] We are simply giving a broad sketch. It is quite impossible to go into differences in detail. For the Valentinians cf. the model collection of texts in F. Sagnard, *La gnose valent. et le témoignage de St. Irenée* (1946).

[356] It is too simple to regard the Gnostic self as a development of the Pauline statements (Sagnard, *op. cit.,* 607).

[357] Heracleon Fr., 24 (Orig. Comm. in Joh. 13:25); cf. Corp. Herm., 18, 3 (and the lexicographical collection under πνεῦμα in Gächter, 362 f.). The Egypt. Amon is equated with the πνεῦμα in Plut. Is. et Os., 36 (II, 365d); Diod. S., I, 12, 2; Preis. Zaub., I, 168. In Stoic terms Plut. also tells us in Quaest. Conv., VIII, 1 (II, 718a b) about the Egypt. belief in the warm, moist, air-like οὐσία of the gods, cf. Verbeke, 292.

[358] Basilides even seeks to introduce the thought of *creatio ex nihilo* into Gnostic thought, G. Quispel, "L'homme gnostique [La doctrine de Basilide]," *Eranos Jbch.,* 16 (1948), 120 f.

[359] πνευματικὴ οὐσία Iren. Haer., I, 2, 4; for Valentinus cf. Sagnard, *op. cit.,* 398-415.

[360] Cl. Al. Strom., IV, 26, 3 f.: ὑπερκόσμιος φύσει ... φύσει τοῦ κόσμου ξένος, Heracleon Fr., 23 (Orig. Comm. in Joh. 13:20): the spirit has lost itself in the βαθεῖα ὕλη τῆς πλάνης, Hipp. Ref., V, 10, 2; 19, 16; 26:17; Acta Archelai, 8; for the Mandaeans cf. H. Jonas, *Gnosis u. spätantiker Geist,* I² (1954), 96-120.

[361] E.g., Hipp. Ref., V, 10, 2; Pist. Soph., 111 and 132 (GCS, 13, 182, 21-185, 20, 222, 7-226, 22); Acta Archelai, 8.

[362] Cl. Al. Strom., II, 20, 112 : Here the πνεύματα with which the soul clothes itself are the evil element, cf. the ἀντίμιμον πνεῦμα in Pist. Soph. Finally in the Mandaeans *rūha* is the evil principle while the soul takes over the role of the Gnostic πνεῦμα. On the idea of the two souls cf. Iambl. Myst., VIII, 6.

the earthly ψυχή. [363] It is of the same nature as God or Christ. [364] This is particularly vividly put in Valentinus, in whom the σπέρμα τῆς ἄνωθεν οὐσίας, the κύημα or σπέρμα πνευματικόν, created after the manner of angels, is put into the ψυχή by the Redeemer without the demiurge being aware of it. [365] But this σπέρμα is put to death by living in the world. Only its alter ego is alive, the "angel," [366] which is present only from the time of Christ, since it is simply Christ entering into the individual. [367] The whole concern of this mythology is to separate the spirit, as a substance which is given by grace and which cannot be lost, from the soul and the body. [368] In Gnostic thought redemption is thus no other than a reassembling of all the sparks of πνεῦμα. It takes place when the Redeemer, Himself spiritual by nature, [369] comes down into matter, [370] gathers together the remnants of spirit there, [371] and with them [372] re-ascends. [373] His ascent is the beginning of separation, [374] for He commits His somatic and psychic elements to chaos but commits the spiritual element to God. [375] Like Him, the redeemed become pure πνεύματα by liberation from all the fetters of body and

---

[363] Iren. Haer., I, 21, 4; cf. Hipp. Ref., V, 26, 8. 25; VI, 34, 1; VII, 27, 6. The πνευματικός ἄνθρωπος is equated with Philo's first man (→ 373, 13 ff.), Iren. Haer., I, 18, 2, cf. Hipp. Ref., V, 26, 36; on this v. E. Haenchen, "Das Buch Baruch," ZThK, 50 (1953), 123-158. This inner self is a "revolutionary concept," Jonas, op. cit., 238, and strictly it can be described only negatively (R. Bultmann, Das Urchr. [1949], 186). On the Mand. cf. Jonas, 183, on Orig., ibid., 187 f.

[364] Heracl. Fr., 24 (Orig. Comm. in Joh. 13:25); O. Sol. 26:6 f.; Iren. Haer., I, 5, 6 : ὁμοούσιον τῇ μητρί (Σοφία).

[365] Iren. Haer., I, 4, 5; 5, 6; II, 19, 1. 3; Cl. Al. Strom., II, 36, 2 f.; IV, 90, 3 f.; Exc. Theod., 2; 53, 2-5.

[366] Cl. Al. Exc. Theod., 22, 2; each angel is sent to "his soul," Heracl. Fr., 35 (Orig. Comm. in Joh. 13:49).

[367] Cl. Al. Exc. Theod., 36, 1 f.: angels are εἷς ὄντες ὡς ἀπὸ ἑνὸς προελθόντες = the Christ "separated" in baptism for "the separated," cf. Quispel (→ n. 354), 264, 276.

[368] "The spiritual element is not nature but grace," Tert. Val., 29; cf. Quispel, 262-267, 274 f.

[369] Iren., I, 26, 1; Epiph. Haer., 30, 3, 4; cf. the ζῶν πνεῦμα of the Manichees, though this is only a first redeemer who creates the world (Acta Archelai, 7 f.); cf. also the numerical equating of Christ with the dove of the Holy Spirit (Hipp. Ref., VI, 49, 5) and the equation of Simon with the Holy Spirit (Iren. Haer., I, 23, 1).

[370] He passes through the spheres and everywhere invests Himself with the appropriate figure (on the origin of this notion v. Schweizer, op. cit. [→ n. 351], 124 f.). In the main this is taken to be a garb which will mislead the demons, Asc. Is. 10:8-30; Pist. Soph., 7 (GCS, 45, 7, 26-30); Epiph. Haer., 21, 2; Iren. Haer., I, 23, 3 (where it is emphasised that this is only an appearance and not a real incarnation); 30, 11 f.; cf. 24, 6; on a stronger soteriological basis 6, 1 (the Valentinians, though they teach that Christ came down only at baptism and ascended before the cross, and that even the psychic Christ passed through Mary only as water through a pipe, 7, 2). Cf. the classical formulation of Docetism in Epiph. Haer., 26, 10, 5.

[371] Hence the Gnostic can "assemble himself," Epiph. Haer., 26, 3, 1; 10, 9; 13, 2; cf. Porphyr. Marc., 10.

[372] He takes them with Him as His booty : Eus. Hist. Eccl., I, 13, 20; carries them on His shoulder into the pleroma : Cl. Al. Exc. Theod., 42, 2; propels them upwards with the well-wheel of the zodiac, Acta Archelai, 8 (cf. H. Schlier, "Religionsgeschichtliche Untersuchungen z. d. Ignatiusbriefen," Beih. ZNW, 8 [1929], 115-123); His power or gnosis or magic formula saves the believer on his own ascent through the spheres, Act. Thom., 148; Act. Phil., 144; Act. Joh., 114; Epiph. Haer., 16, 10. 7; 13, 2; for the Mandaeans cf. Jonas, op. cit., 120-140.

[373] Ascent through all the spheres in glory, Asc. Is. 11:23-32; Pist. Soph., 11-14 (GCS, 45, 12, 26-15, 2); Schweizer, op. cit., 125-127.

[374] "Their whole doctrine (that of the disciples of Basilides) is the mixing ... and separating and bringing back of the mixed to their original place," Hipp. Ref., VII, 27, 11.

[375] Hipp. Ref., V, 26, 31 f.; VII, 27, 10-12; the πνεῦμα which Jesus commits to the Father is identical with the host of the elect, Cl. Al. Exc. Theod., 1, 1 f.

soul. [376] When they are all reassembled into the gt. spiritual body, [377] redemption is achieved. In spite of the mythological ideas, the descent and ascent of the Redeemer are in the last resort only a duplicate of the destiny of the πνεῦμα which is imprisoned in man. Whether it is a real event or not [378] is immaterial. [379] For in some way the spiritual man is simply reminded thereby [380] of the indestructible substance which lives in him, the φύσει σῳζόμενος. [381] In the last analysis the Redeemer is no other than the spiritual man himself, [382] → I, 692-696.

3. Trichotomy.

The separation here made between πνεῦμα and ψυχή implies an express threefold division of man into body, soul, and an additional divinely given πνεῦμα. [383],[384] In the Gk. world we find the threefold division of the soul in Plato [385] and the later triad of νοῦς-ψυχή-σῶμα. [386] But this is not a true trichotomy. [387] The νοῦς is not differentiated from the soul. [388] In the daemons of Xenocrates the θεῖον is added to the ψυχή and σῶμα. [389] The magic texts in which πνεῦμα comes first in this triad [390] are very

---

[376] Iren. Haer., I, 7, 1 (cf. 21, 5); Cl. Al. Exc. Theod., 64.

[377] Act. Joh., 100; → σῶμα Χριστοῦ. Examples in Bu. J., 285, n. 1.

[378] Cf. Quispel, op. cit. (→ n. 354), 249 f.

[379] It is an open question whether the Gnostic Redeemer is pre-Christian, Schweizer, op. cit., 161 f.

[380] Act. Thom., 110; Cl. Al. Paed., I, 32, 1; cf. Iren. Haer., I, 4, 1; 8, 2.

[381] Iren. Haer., I, 6, 2; Cl. Al. Strom., II, 10, 2; IV, 89; 4; V, 3, 3; Exc. Theod., 56, 3; cf. Strom., II, 155, 1; V, 3, 2; Corp. Herm., 13, 14; in Stoicism theology is part of physics (Jonas, op. cit., 175). Immorality is advocated because it is the best demonstration that the spiritual substance cannot be lost, Iren. Haer., I, 6, 2. Gnosticism certainly tries to think of πνεῦμα in strictly transcendental terms (Cl. Al. Exc. Theod., 81, 3 differentiates the ἄνωθεν δοθὲν ἡμῖν πνεῦμα ἀσώματον from the σωματικὸν πνεῦμα which becomes smoke in fire), but this is doomed to failure so long as the whole Gnostic understanding rests on the natural distinction between πνεῦμα and ὕλη.

[382] "Le point de départ est toujours l'homme," Sagnard, 568. Hipp. Ref., V, 8, 10 : κατὰ πάνθ᾽ ὁμοούσιος. It is no accident that the supreme god is called Ἄνθρωπος, Iren. Haer., I, 30, 6. In the Valentinians the angel (the Christ who comes to the individual) is the other half of the spiritual seed in man. He leads the individual to salvation and prays for him, but cannot be saved without him, Cl. Al. Exc. Theod., 35. In this way the absolutely gracious character of salvation can be emphasised. It is equally true that man is no other than the Redeemer, cf. also Quispel, op. cit. (→ n. 354), 277-280. On Gnosticism cf. R.P. Casey, "Gnosis, Gnosticism and the NT," The Background of the NT and Its Eschatology (1956), 52-80; W. F. Albright, "Discoveries in Palestine and the Gospel of St. John," ibid., 162 f.; H. J. Schoeps, "Zur Standortbestimmung d. Gnosis," ThLZ, 81 (1956), 413-421.

[383] → n. 363; cf. Jonas, op. cit., 212-214, and the refs. → n. 398.

[384] Iren. Haer., I, 5, 6; 6, 1; there are also 3 classes of men, 7, 5 (for further ref. Sagnard, 172-198); cf. Cl. Al. Strom., II, 10, 2; Exc. Theod., 54-56; Heracl. Fr., 15 (Orig. Comm. in Joh. 10:37); Iren. Haer., I, 24, 4.

[385] → IV, 954, 20 ff.; adopted in, e.g., Philo Leg. All., I, 22 f.; Cl. Al. Strom., III, 68, 5; 93; Paed., III, 1, 2; cf. Quispel, op. cit. (→ n. 354), 272 f.

[386] On Aristot., Plut. cf. Allo, 335; cf. also M. Ant., XII, 3, 1 (cf. 14, 5); V, 33, 6; VIII, 56, 1 f.; II, 2, 1 (σαρκία, πνευμάτιον, ἡγεμονικόν). Often νοῦς replaces πνεῦμα in Gnosticism, e.g., Hipp. Ref., V, 10, 2; 19, 14 f.; in Corp. Herm. νοῦς merges into πνευματικὸς λόγος (which is ὁμοούσιος), 1, 5, 10; Dodd, op. cit., 125. In Heb. En. we find the Neo-platonic νοῦς, but not as yet the trichotomy of later Jewish mysticism, Odeberg, op. cit. (→ n. 225), I, 174 and n. 1.

[387] Dob. Th. Exc. on 1 Th. 5:23 with patristic ref.; in the review in Burton, Spirit, 205-207 there are no Gk. par. for putting πνεῦμα above ψυχή apart from those influenced by Judaism or Chr.

[388] Jonas, 180.

[389] Plut. Is. et Os., 25 (II, 360e); Def. Orac., 13 (II, 416d); E. Schweizer, "Zur Trichotomie v. 1 Th. 5:23 und d. Unterscheidung d. πνευματικόν vom ψυχικόν in 1 Kor. 2:14; 15:44; Jak. 3:15; Jud. 19," ThZ, 9 (1953), 76 f.

[390] Reitzenstein Hell. Myst., 308-314; Verbeke, 322-332.

late and much influenced by Stoicism, Judaism, and Christianity. [391] In the Corp. Herm. πνεῦμα is subordinate to ψυχή, [392] as also in many Gnostic circles. [393] In Judaism the idea of the Spirit of God over against the body and soul of man is a central thought which is transferred to the spirit that dwells in man. The transition is particularly plain in Iren., where the Spirit of God is viewed as resurrecting power for body and soul, [394] but where it is also maintained that man is perfect only when spirit is added to body and soul. [395] The Jew remembers that in the OT the soul belong to the flesh, [396] so that when he wants to define man as a conscious being which thinks and decides, he can equally well use either σωματικός [397] or ψυχικός as the antithesis of πνευματικός, → 435, 12 ff. Since the antithesis has been found thus far only in Jewish and Chr. works, or those influenced thereby, the Jewish conception of the πνεῦμα which is transcendent to man and abides in him seems to have been the decisive one, [398] → 391, 2 ff.

E. The New Testament.

Long before the Spirit was a theme of doctrine, He was a fact in the experience of the community. This is the basis of the marked variety and unity of the NT statements.

I. Mark and Matthew.

1. The Demonic and the Anthropological Spirit.

Of 23 πνεῦμα sayings in Mk., 14 contain the expression πνεῦμα ἀκάθαρτον (or the like) = δαίμων or δαιμόνιον. [399] This concept is found in Judaism. [400] Mt. usually avoids it, though without addition he has τὰ πνεύματα in 8:16 for the δαιμόνια of Mk. 1:34, → n. 460; 443, 22 f. πνεῦμα is used purely anthropologically in Mk. 2:8 (cf. 5:30); 8:12, where it is the seat of perceptions and feelings, also in Mt. 27:50, where it is the vital force, → 451, 12 ff. There is a special nuance in Mk. 14:38, where πνεῦμα πρόθυμον is set in antithesis to σὰρξ ἀσθενής. Behind this is the experience of man at odds with himself. This is found already in the Dead Sea Scrolls, and does not have the same sense as in Hellenistic psycho-

---

[391] Allo, 328-332; Verbeke, 326, 333-337; Dupont, op. cit. (→ n. 204), 166-168.

[392] Corp. Herm., 10, 13. 16 f.; the idea that the πνεῦμα is the outer husk of the ψυχή finds exact Gk. par.; πνεῦμα is here regarded medically as the nervous system, Scott, II, 253, 256, 262; also Cl. Al. Strom., VI, 136, 1.

[393] Cl. Al. Strom., VI, 135, 3-5 puts the λογιστικὸν καὶ ἡγεμονικὸν πνεῦμα above the πνεῦμα σαρκικόν (cf. Tert. De Anima, 14). The Ophites put an intermediate psychophysical kingdom between the kingdom of God and the cosmos (H. Leisegang, Die Gnosis⁴ [1955], 169 f.); the body of the risen Lord belonged to this sphere (Iren. Haer., I, 30, 13). In the Sethians (under the influence of Gn. 1:2 and Stoic thought [?], cf. Verbeke, 294-297) πνεῦμα is a buffer kingdom between light and darkness, Hipp. Ref., V, 19, 4, cf. Basilides in VII, 23, 1 (on this Quispel, op. cit. [→ n. 358], 102 f.); cf. VI, 36, 7. This middle πνεῦμα corresponds to the ψυχή in normal Gnostic usage, Leisegang, 219. → n. 806.

[394] Epid., 42; cf. Mart. Pol., 14, 2 (Eus. Hist. Eccl., IV, 15, 34).

[395] Iren. Haer., V, 6, 1; cf. Cl. Al. Strom., V, 87, 4-88, 4; Tat. Or. Graec., 15, 2.

[396] Eth. En. 16:1: "soul of flesh"; J. A. T. Robinson, The Body (1952), 23, n. 2. This usage cannot derive from Gn. 2:7 alone, R. Bultmann, "Gnosis," JThSt, NS, 3 (1952), 14-16.

[397] E.g., Epiph. Haer., 33, 5, 13 or σαρκικός Ign. Eph., 7, 2; 10, 3; Sm., 12, 2; 13, 2; Mg., 13, 2; Pol., 1, 2; 2, 2.

[398] Allo, 336-341; Dupont, op. cit. (→ n. 204), 155-180; Verbeke, 538-543.

[399] So in the par. to Mk. 5:13. Cf. E. Langton, Essentials of Demonology (1949), 147-171; S. Eitrem, "Some Notes on Demonology in the NT," Symb. Osl., 27 (1950); V. McCasland, By the Finger of God (1951).

[400] → 375, 34 ff.; II, 10-16; as against → III, 427, 27 ff. but → 389, 35 ff.; 391, 11 ff. and Noack, op. cit. (→ n. 340), 51: Is ἀκάθαρτον meant to be an ethical antithesis to ἅγιον?

logy; [401] what stands opposed to (sinful) flesh is not a better part of man but the divine election. Once it is seen that the expression "willing spirit" comes from the Heb. of Ps. 51:12, [402] that it is identical there with God's Holy Spirit, and that it is here used in a prayer for endurance in temptation, it is plain that what is meant is the Spirit of God which is given to man and which strives against human weakness.

2. The Spirit as the Power of God.

In essentials, however, πνεῦμα is used in Mk. and Mt. in the thoroughly OT sense (→ 362, 28 ff.) of God's power to perform special acts. According to Mk. 3:28-30 blasphemy against the Holy Ghost is committed by those who find in the exorcisms of Jesus, not the power of God, but the power of the devil expressing itself in a way which is formally the same. [403, 404]

The development of the logion is hard to assess. The Mk. form contrasts blasphemy against the Spirit with all other sins and blasphemies, while the Q form contrasts it with blasphemy against the Son of Man. Mt. puts the two together (→ 407, 13 ff.), while Lk. follows Q alone. One has to consider whether a pre-Marcan form did not contain τῷ υἱῷ τοῦ ἀνθρώπου, [405] which would lead on the one side to an attempt to rule out all misunderstanding by using τοῖς υἱοῖς τῶν ἀνθρώπων in Mk., but which also led Q on the other side to take the Son of Man to refer to Jesus alone. [406] Another possibility is that the saying was a missionary rule which was designed to set before the Jews the gravity of decision. [407] It corresponds materially to Ac. 3:17. The community realises that the time of ignorance has ended with awareness of possession of the Spirit, 1 Th. 1:6 etc. In this case the title "Son of Man" indicates the earthly Lord who has not yet been instituted Son of God κατὰ πνεῦμα, → 417, 10 ff.

The logion undoubtedly proclaims the unqualified certainty of the community that it is in possession of the Spirit. It may be noted that in Mk. 3:28; Mt. 12:32a [408] primary emphasis falls on the inconceivable greatness of forgiveness. Only in contrast thereto can one understand the severity with which resistance to the Spirit's testimony is punished. If the community believes in the reality of the Spirit acting in it, it can regard such resistance only as conscious defiance of the over-

---

[401] E. Käsemann, Leib u. Leib Christi (1933), 96 takes it thus, but Büchsel, 180-183 understands it strictly as God's Spirit. There is a ref. to 1 QS in K. G. Kuhn, "πειρασμός — ἁμαρτία — σάρξ im NT," ZThK, 49 (1952), 209-211. (Cf. G. Schrenk, Studien zu Pls. [1954], 34 for Hillel.)

[402] Loh. Mk., ad loc.; K. G. Kuhn, "Jesus in Gethsemane," Ev. Theol., 12 (1952/53), 277. It is the LXX which makes of this the πνεῦμα ἡγεμονικόν of the Stoa. Cf. Ps. 51:17 in 1 QS 8:3 and Kuhn, op. cit., 274-285.

[403] Gunkel, 34-38. Hence both can be called πνεῦμα, but this is always strictly avoided. Nor is the πνευματικός (only the Epistles) set in analogy and contrast with the δαιμονιζόμενος (only the Synoptics), Jackson-Lake, I, 5, 102 f.

[404] There are many examples from a later period in W. Bauer, Das Leben Jesu im Zeitalter d. nt.lichen Apkr. (1909), 465 f.

[405] The title Son of Man is hardly ever used again in Mk. prior to the confession of Peter, T. W. Manson, The Teaching of Jesus (1931), 214; cf. also Jackson-Lake, I, 380 f.

[406] Well. Mt., ad loc.; A. Loisy, Les évangiles synoptiques (1907), ad loc. Materially cf. Did., 11, 7; 2 K. 7:2, 17 and Volz, Geist, 142.

[407] A. Fridrichsen, "Le péché contre le St.-Esprit," RevHPhR, 3 (1923), 369; cf. Windisch, Synpt. Überlieferung, 220 with a ref. to Lk. 23:34. There is doubt as to derivation from Jesus Himself, Michaelis, 16, as against R. N. Flew, Jesus and His Church² (1943), 49. → n. 408.

[408] Mt. 12:32a strongly recalls the situation after Pentecost (→ I, 104, 8 ff. → Batdorf, 497 f.), while Mk. relates it to an event prior to Pentecost, v. 30.

whelming power of the Spirit, → I, 304, 24 ff. There can be no forgiveness for this defiance because it does not want it. [409]

Mt. 12:28 may also be quoted in this connection. Possibly the community, having experienced the works of the Spirit within it, substituted πνεύματι for an original δακτύλῳ, Lk. 11:20 → II, 20, 20 ff. The fact that the Spirit of God is not mentioned by the Rabbis as one of the many means of driving out demons [410] shows how different was their approach, → 382, 4 ff.; → I, 528, 1 ff. The distinctiveness of the saying lies in the fact that the presence of the Spirit (of exorcism) is interpreted as the presence of the βασιλεία, → I, 584, 5 ff. [411] Similarly, the promise that God will lay His Spirit on the Servant is seen to be fulfilled in the healings of Jesus according to Mt. 12:18. This is in keeping with the view of the community, which perceives the dawn of the last time in the coming of the miracle-working Spirit. Mk. 1:12 is to the same effect. Here the OT colouring (→ 362, 33 ff.) is so vivid that Mt. tones it down. The Spirit is here understood, not as help in temptation, but as the irresistible power of God which leads off those who are seized by it, → 408, 18 ff.

3. General Endowment with the Spirit.

An essential point is that the Rabbinic equation of the Holy Spirit and Scripture (→ 382, 16 ff.) occurs only in Mk. 12:36. [412] The community realises that the prophetic Spirit is given to it not merely in the blessed past at the time of the biblical prophets but also in the present, Mk. 13:11 par. [413] The OT view is that the Spirit mediates God's Word (2 S. 23:2). This is now reinterpreted, however, for the speaking of the Spirit is a sign of God's help in eschatological tribulation. [414]

A general endowment with the Spirit is mentioned, of course, only in Mk. 1:8. Mk. undoubtedly found the fulfilment of this saying in the outpouring of the Spirit on the community. [415] Ac. 1:5; 11:16 interpreted it in the same way.

> There can be little doubt but the Q version is the more original. Omission of the difficult καὶ πυρί is readily understandable, but not its addition, for there was never any baptism with fire. Lk. himself did not see any such in Ac. 2:3, since he quotes the saying only in the Marcan form in 1:5. Hence it must go back to the Baptist (or Jesus), [416] and it belongs to a group of tense eschatological expectations. Fire is a widespread symbol of judgment. [417] It is so esp. in the verses directly encircling the

---

[409] The saying cannot be directed, then, against those who are afraid of being seized by the Spirit.

[410] Str.-B., IV, 532-535 (cf. the dramatic exorcism before Vespasian).

[411] The saying may well go back to Jesus (materially E. Käsemann, "Das Problem d. historischen Jesus," ZThK, 51 [1954], 148), cf. E. Percy, Die Botschaft Jesu (1953), 179, but not Goguel, Pneumatisme, 148 f.

[412] → 453, 9 ff.

[413] The Q form is probably original, Loh. Mk., 273; Dupont, op. cit. (→ n. 204), 226, n. 1.

[414] The saying, which restricts endowment with the Spirit to special emergencies (Loh. Mk., ad loc.; Howard, 78), is dominical. Lk. 21:15 replaces the Spirit by the risen Lord and makes the promise more general ; it is thus secondary.

[415] Did. Mk. 16:9 ff. originally tell of this (Barrett, Gospel Tradition, 125)?

[416] Frövig, 202. Nor can the depreciation of water baptism be ascribed to the community.

[417] Is. 66:15 f. (cf. 1:31; 30:30, 33; 31:9; 34:9 f.); Am. 1:4; 7:4; Mal. 3:2 (the day of his coming ... like a refiner's fire); Ps. Sol. 15:4; 4 Esr. 13:4, 10 (appearing of the Messiah); S. Bar. 48:39; Test. Abr. 14 (ed. M. R. James [1895], 94, 18); Mk. 9:43-49; 1 C. 3:13; 2 Th. 1:8; 2 Pt. 3:7; Rev. 20:9; 1 QH 3:28-31; 6:18; 1 QS 2:8, 15; 4:13 (on the ultimate connection of the Baptist with the sect and Persian par. cf. W. H. Brownlee, "Jn. the Baptist in the New Light of Ancient Scrolls," Interpretation, 9 [1955], 71-90, esp. 90 f.) etc.; for further details → V, 399, 15 ff., 436, 2 ff.; v. Baer, 159-161.

logion, Mt. 3:10, 12 = Lk. 3:9, 17 = Q. In the oldest form of the saying available to us baptism with fire is thus to be interpreted as eschatological judgment. [418] If so, the coming one is certainly not Elijah ; he is the Messianic Judge. [419] In this light one may ask whether the promise of baptism with the Spirit makes much sense or whether it is simply a Chr. addition. [420]

The imparting of the Spirit, often under the figure of purifying water, [421] corresponds, like the judgment of fire, to eschatological expectation, [422] and is to be found also in 1 QS 4:13, 21. The Messiah has thus a twofold task, to destroy the ungodly and to sanctify the righteous. [423] The two ideas are not linked directly, however, and the Messiah is rarely viewed as a dispenser of the Spirit, → 384, 11 ff. It is also difficult, within the imagery of judgment, to present the πνεῦμα as a gift of grace and πῦρ as judgment without bringing to light the cleavage. Perhaps πνεῦμα originally meant "wind" here, → 360, 12 f. [424] Stormy wind and fire often go together, e.g., in the depiction of the Son of Man who comes down to judgment with the clouds of heaven. [425] Both are certainly presupposed in the verse which follows in Mt. 3:12 : Winnowing takes place in the stormy wind (Is. 41:16; cf. 27:12; Jer. 4:11; Am. 9:9), and the chaff will be burned in the fire. [426] If John's baptism was originally understood as the rite of a host of penitents who hoped thereby to escape threatening judgment (→ I, 537, 31-36), [427] a decisive step was taken in the understanding of the Synoptists, where participation

---

[418] The saying is formed by analogy to John's baptism with water, C. H. Kraeling, *John the Baptist* (1951), 114-118; βαπτισθῆναι is also used transf. in Mk. 10:38 f.; Lk. 12:50. The idea of a river or lake of fire is a common one, Da. 7:10; 4 Esr. 13:10; Sib., 3, 54; Rev. 19:20; 20:10, 14; Str.-B., III, 773c; cf. R. Eisler, ΙΗΣΟΥΣ ΒΑΣΙΛΕΥΣ ΟΥ ΒΑΣΙΛΕΥΣΑΣ, II (1929), 106, n. 8; → I, 530, 1 ff., 538, 36 ff.; V, 436, 11 ff. Str.-B., I, 121 f. shows at least that the combining of baptism in water and in fire was not unnatural in the light of Nu. 31:23 (cf. the purifying of the mediators in Heb. En. 44:5).

[419] Frövig, 202 as against A. Schweitzer, *Gesch. d. Leben-Jesu-Forschung*⁴ (1926), 418 f.; at most a Messianic Elijah, Brownlee, *op. cit.*, 86 f.

[420] Cf. V. Taylor, *The Gospel acc. to St. Mark* (1953), ad loc. (though → n. 424). → πῦρ is certainly not just a form in which the Spirit is manifested (Leisegang *Pneuma*, 72-80). Worthy of consideration is the influence of the Iranian idea of judgment by spirit and fire (Yasna, 31, 3; 36, 1. 3; 47, 6), where both have a judicial and also a saving function. But without intermediate links this is a mere theory (1 QS 4:13, 21 is no help). Cf. W. Michaelis, "Zum jüd. Hintergrund d. Johannestaufe," Judaica, 7 (1951), 81-120; on the further history C. M. Edsman, *Le baptême de feu* (1940), 182-190; J. Kosnetter, "Die Taufe Jesu," *Theol. Stud. d. österreichischen Leo-Gesellschaft*, 35 (1935), 223 f.; E. Stauffer, "Probleme d. Priestertradition," ThLZ, 81 (1956), 144 f.

[421] T. F. Torrance, "Proselyte Baptism," NTSt, 1 (1954/55), 152 f.; Schl. J. on 3:5; → n. 736, 750.

[422] Frövig, 203; Jl. 2:28 ff. Cf. → n. 417.

[423] Frövig, 203; Zn. Mt.⁴, 140; E. Lohmeyer, *Das Urchr.*, I (1932), 84-86; F. Lang, *Das Feuer im Sprachgebrauch d. Bibel*, Diss. Tübingen (1950), 139-142; Mal. 3:17-20.

[424] Eisler, *op. cit.*, 104-114; Barrett, *Gospel Trad.*, 126; Kraeling, *op. cit.*, 63; Taylor, *op. cit., ad loc.* as a possibility.

[425] 4 Esr. 13:10, 27 (*spiritus, ignis, tempestas*); cf. Is. 29:6; 30:27 f. (judgment); Ez. 1:4 (theophany). Stormy wind alone Is. 4:4 (cf. v. 5); 40:24; 57:13; Jer. 23:19; 30:23; Ez. 13:11, 13. In Ps. 1:1-5 we find together the images of the fruitful tree (Mt. 3:10) and the storm which scatters the chaff (Mt. 3:11 f.). Gn. r., 83 esp. (G. Klein, "Predigt d. Joh.," ZNW, 2 [1901], 343 f.) compares the judgment of the Gentiles with winnowing, which involves both fire (Mal. 3:19) and wind (Is. 41:16). Cf. 1 QSb 5:24 f., where the Messiah slays the wicked with the breath of His mouth and uses the spirit of counsel (?) and the spirit of knowledge.

[426] M. Goguel, "Note sur Apc. 14:14," RevHPhR, 5 (1925), 68 finds the influence of this saying in Rev. 14:14-20 (v. 18 πυρός).

[427] Kraeling, 118-122; Barrett, *Gospel Trad.*, 31-34.

in the Spirit in the community of Jesus is already an advance deliverance from eschatological judgment. Baptism πνεύματι καὶ πυρί is the fulfilment of John's saving baptism. It, too, is thus regarded as a sifting and purifying judgment. No longer, however, is this merely expected in the future. It is already experienced in the present, and it is experienced as deliverance for those who are ready to undergo it. [428]

4. Jesus' Endowment with the Spirit at Baptism.

The story of the baptism of Jesus has been preserved only in the form found in Mk. 1:9 ff. [429, 430] It is meant to be something more than the account of a prophetic call. For a positive interpretation → 67, 22 ff. From every standpoint it seems to lead on to the story of the endowment of the Messiah with the Spirit. The OT had already promised that the Messiah would be the bearer of the Spirit, and this was repeated in Judaism, → 384, 11 ff. [431] The fact that something takes place here which does happen in the case of the prophets [432] is not expressed by a new understanding of the Spirit [433] but by the visible appearance of the dove, the audible accreditation by God, and esp. the fact that this endowment of the Spirit takes place at the end of the times when the Spirit had long since been silenced, → 385, 10 ff. [434] This event is stamped hereby as the beginning of the new age of God, → I, 103, 38 ff. It is also completely distinguished in this way from Hellenistic accounts of ecstatic experiences. [435] Originally the gift of the Spirit at baptism is regarded as the beginning of the Messiahship of Jesus. But this was not, as in later adoptionism, a developed theory which excluded other approaches. Hence no difficulty was experienced in placing this story alongside the account of the miraculous conception of Jesus by the Spirit. [436] There was no thought of trying to explain the origin of this wonderful man in the categories of

---

[428] Cf. 4 Esr. 13:37 f., where v. 10 is reinterpreted, Lang, op. cit., 78.

[429] Mt. 4:3a 6a certainly favours the view that Q was also acquainted with a prior proclamation of the Son of God, Frövig, 195 f.

[430] The idea of a cultic legend (A. Loisy, L'évang. selon Luc [1924], ad loc.) runs into the difficulty that baptism is not instituted (cf. Mt. 28:19), while the receding of the Baptist and the voice from heaven destroy the theory of a Baptist legend which attests the subordination of Jesus (cf. M. Goguel, "Le 'Jésus' de M. Ch. Guignebert," RevHPhR, 13 [1933], 424, n. 13). As against Bultmann's scepticism (Trad., 263-267) cf. Schweizer, op. cit. (→ n. 351), n. 203. The abs. use of πνεῦμα is not necessarily Hell., 1 QS 4:6; 1 QM 7:6 ? Institution as Son = King is most definitely not.

[431] Cf. Barrett, Gospel Trad., 42-44; bibl. in H. Riesenfeld, Jésus transfiguré (1947), 76, n. 69. Cf. esp. M. A. Chevallier, Le don de l'Esprit-Saint au Messie-Jésus, Diss. Strasbourg, 1956.

[432] Loh. Mk., ad loc.

[433] Other works of the Spirit apart from those in the refs. already given are not presupposed.

[434] Where individuals are bearers of the Spirit in Judaism (→ προφήτης), signs of the last time may be seen in them too. The Synoptists do not wish to suggest a strengthening of Jesus, but neither was this a mere demonstration for the Baptist, Kosnetter, op. cit. (→ n. 420), 137-139.

[435] Batdorf, 360. These are self-evoked and remain in the self-contained experience of the individual, which is not the sign of a new work of God. εἰς αὐτόν simply means ἐπ' αὐτόν (Bl.-Debr. § 207, Mk. 3:13, not Ev. Eb. 4). Later we read of cosmic effects, O. Sol. 24; cf. J. H. Bernard, "The Odes of Solomon," JThSt, 12 (1911), 21-24; H. Braun, "Entscheidende Motive in den Berichten über d. Taufe Jesu von Mk. bis Justin," ZThK, 50 (1953), 39-43. The story was only regarded secondarily as a model for Chr. baptism, W. F. Flemington, The NT Doctrine of Baptism (1948), 29; Windisch, Synpt. Überlieferung, 215; Loisy, op. cit., 142.

[436] Though cf. Just. Dial., 87 f.

substance. Both stories proclaim the already believed uniqueness of Jesus. Both present God's direct work upon Him at decisive points, and in so doing they show that God Himself is at work in Him.

5. Verses Peculiar to Matthew.

Of verses peculiar to Mt. the first to claim our attention is 5:3. οἱ πτωχοὶ τῷ πνεύματι cannot mean those who are poor in the Holy Spirit. [437] Nor can one take πνεύματι as an instrumental dative. Parallel to καθαροὶ τῇ καρδίᾳ and the Rabbinic שְׁפַל רוּחַ (Prv. 29:23; Is. 57:15), it is a dative of relation. [438] πνεῦμα thus refers to the human spirit. The new thing as compared with Jewish parallels, [439] however, is that there is no summons to this attitude as to a virtue which man may achieve. Those to whom it is given are called blessed. If in Judaism רוּחַ had already taken on more and more of the nuance of man's religious individuality (→ 391, 4 ff., 31 ff.), Mt. 5:3 blesses the poor 'am hā'ārez whose sole help is God, not in contrast to those who are rich materially (Lk. 6:20, 24) or intellectually, but in contrast to those who are rich in religious knowledge and religious achievement.

A special place is occupied by the baptismal command in Mt. 28:19. [440] The surprising thing here is not the reference to the Holy Ghost in baptism (→ 413, 7 ff.), but the mention of the ὄνομα τοῦ πνεύματος along with the other two ὀνόματα (→ V, 274, 28 ff.). This means that we have a very different understanding of the Spirit from that found elsewhere in Mt. Mt. must have been acquainted with the formula as a baptismal formula (perhaps of a very limited circle), → III, 108, 10 and V, 989, n. 279). Once the κύριος was associated with God, it was easy for the πνεῦμα to be added too. This does not entail speculation as to their mutual relations. It bears testimony to the fact that God cannot be inferred logically as the climax of a monotheistic system but is encountered only where He Himself confronts the community, i.e., in the Son, or, for the individual, in the Spirit, in whom this encounter with the Son takes place. [441]

---

[437] As the Hellenist would take it, Leisegang *Pneuma*, 134 f.

[438] Bl.-Debr. § 197; cf. ψ 33:19. Against Schl. Mt., *ad loc.* (the Spirit makes them poor), with P. Fiebig, *Jesu Bergpredigt* (1924), 2 (2 Rabb. appeal hereto c. 100 A.D.) → 338, 2 f. Esp. instructive is 1 QM 11:9-13, where the crushed or poor in spirit are those who fight on God's side, cf. 13:14; 14:7; other ref. in A. Dupont-Sommer, "La guerre des fils de lumière," RHR, 148 (1955), 160, n. 4.

[439] Str.-B., *ad loc.*

[440] It has to be considered whether the three-membered formula is not an ancient interpolation, Barrett, *Gospel Trad.*, 102 f. In 21 of 25 instances Euseb. quotes without this, and it is three-membered only after Nicaea, but this may be an abbreviation of his own. Acc. to Just. Ap., I, 61 baptism in the triune name is based on Is. 1:16 ff. and the apostolic tradition, with no ref. to Mt. 28:19. Did., 7, 1 is the first instance in the practice of the community, but Did., 9, 5 shows that a single-membered formula was also in use. Since there was no developed doctrine of the Trinity behind it, the three-membered form could be used occasionally without incurring suspicion of novelty, just as Paul sometimes uses triadic formulae ; hence it is by no means impossible in the time of Mt., cf. A. H. McNeile, *The Gospel acc. to St. Matthew* (1952), *ad loc.* Against a derivation from Jesus Himself the main arguments are its absence in Lk., Jn., Pl. and even Mk. 16:15, and the fact that the early community seems to be acquainted neither with the three-membered baptismal formula nor the great commission, cf. Flemington, *op. cit.*, 108. → n. 842.

[441] To be sure, one cannot make a sharp distinction between liturgical formulae and confessions of faith (Batdorf, 401-411 against O. Cullmann, "Die ersten Chr. Glaubensbekenntnisse," *Theol. Studien*, 11 [1943], 31, n. 62 E.T. [1949], 36, n. 1). This does not mean, however, that such formulae were possible only in a period which gives evidence of the literary influence of three-membered confessions.

6. Jesus' Supernatural Conception by the Spirit.

Finally, reference must be made to Jesus' supernatural conception by the Spirit in Mt. 1:18, 20.

This tradition is secondary as compared with that in Lk., for it presupposes opposition. The event is not narrated; we are simply told that an angel dispels suspicion. Analysis of Lk. seems to show 1. that the stories about the Baptist are originally independent and do not refer to Jesus, and 2. that 1:26-38 does not presuppose the Christmas story. [442] The stories about the Baptist and Jesus are so interwoven that the latter run parallel to the former but also transcend them, most clearly in 1:26-38. [443] The most probable conclusions seem to be a. that 1:26-38 and 2:1-20 were originally independent stories, b. that Lk. or his predecessor uses them as a parallel which goes even further than the current tradition about the Baptist, and c. that this motif determines the tradition in 1:26-38 from the very outset, so that the parallels are plainer here than in 2:1-20.

In Mt. 1:18, 20, as in Lk. 1:35, πνεῦμα is the creative power of God (→ V, 835, 25-31) which fashions the life of this unique child — a view which, though it does not occur in Rabbinic Judaism, [444] is to be found in popular writings, → 386, 23 ff. and n. 304.

If there was already faith in the creative intervention of God in conception, it was only a step to Lk. 1:35 and Mt. 1:20. The way had also been prepared from another angle. In Hell. Judaism Is. 7:14 had been taken to refer to the miracle of a birth without any father. Again, the idea of a begetting by the πνεῦμα of God had already been developed in Egypt, → 342, 12 ff. Finally, a vast no. of religious par. [445] shows that conception by a God was accepted widely, and esp. in current Hellenism, as an absolutely necessary feature of the one who should bring salvation, → V, 830, 1 ff. [446]

Thus the belief here in God's unique creative intervention is linked with the concept of the creative power of the divine Spirit to which the OT already bears witness (→ 363, 11 ff.), [447] and which, in the light of Greek and Egyptian parallels, was transferred to the process of conception as well in Hellenistic Judaism.

7. Summary.

This review shows that there are surprisingly few statements about the Spirit in Mt. and Mk. With certainty only one of these (Mk. 13:11 and par.) may be traced back in substance to Jesus Himself. This reveals first the astonishing fidelity of the tradition. Experiences of the Spirit in the community were not

---

[442] M. Dibelius, "Jungfrauensohn u. Krippenkind," SAH, 22 (1932), 24-26, 4 f., 11 f.

[443] G. Erdmann, Die Vorgeschichten des Lk. u. Mt.-evangeliums u. Vergils vierte Ekloge (1932), 9-11. The miraculous conception must have been present, then, at least from the time of the fusion with the Baptist stories, S. Hirsch, Die Vorstellung von einem weiblichen πνεῦμα ἅγιον, Diss. Berlin (1926), 4 f. As against Bultmann Trad., 321 f. one must agree with Dibelius, op. cit., 12-14 that if there is an alien element it is Joseph in v. 27 not the miracle in v. 34 f. (Hirsch, 7 distinguishes two traditions, v. 28 f., 31-33, 38 and 30, 35, 34, 36 f.).

[444] The story is emulating the account of God's direct intervention in the birth of John (v. Baer, 48), cf. also Str.-B., I, 49 f.

[445] O. Rühle, Art. "Jungfrauengeburt," RGG², III, 569 f.; Meyer Ursprung, I, 54-57; for Orpheus cf. W. Wili, "Orphische Mysterien," Eranos Jbch., 11 (1944), 67.

[446] In the par. in Philo (Cher., 40-52; Fug., 108 f.; Ebr., 30; Leg. All., 2, 49-51; cf. Barrett, Gospel Trad., 9 f.) one may still see the mythical background of Egypt. thought, though the happening is purely spiritual in Philo himself (in opposition to other explanations cf. Barrett, op. cit., 10-15).

[447] Cf. Barrett, Gospel Trad., 17-24; Frövig, 117.

imported back into the depiction of the life of Jesus. [448] There also seems to be here, however, an essential theological concern.

The temptation to portray Jesus as a pneumatic must have been considerable. Even if Jesus did not manifest many of the traits of ecstatic piety, [449] there is even in the critically expurgated tradition a good deal of the pneumatic about Him as compared with the Rabb. Thus the mention of His ἐξουσία and δύναμις is strictly only a variation on ref. to the Spirit in the popular and OT sense. [450] To point to Is. and Jer. [451] does not explain the failure to mention the Spirit, since they were reacting against the abuses of the nebiim. Jesus, however, was not opposing any similar figures, though they might have appeared occasionally in Judaism, → προφήτης. It seems highly unlikely that Jesus was first portrayed as a pneumatic and that these traits were later suppressed in the interests of a developed Christology. [452] Since Judaism expected the Messiah to be a bearer of the Spirit (→ 384, 11 ff.), one might expect the importing of clear Messianic features but not the elimination of the pneumatic traits. The idea that the Spirit as an intermediary authority sets God at a distance, while Jesus proclaims the direct proximity of the Father, [453] does not square with the facts, since the community experienced in the Spirit Himself the presence of God. Nor is it any explanation so say that the presence of the Spirit was so incontestable that there was no need to mention Him, for the Gospels seek to tell and proclaim, not just to clear up doubtful points, [454] and Ac. and Paul often speak of the Spirit.

It is no doubt a historical fact that Jesus Himself seldom referred to the Spirit. [455] This may be because He regarded Himself only as the Messiah *designatus,* or because the understanding of His disciples was open to such teaching only after the conclusion of His work, [456] or because He did not expect an outpouring of the Spirit. [457] This means, however, that there is truth in John's view (→ 443, 11 ff.) that full knowledge of Jesus is to be found, not in His words, but in the proclamation of the community after Easter. This community experienced the gift of the Spirit as the sign of God which stamped it as the people of the last time. It realised that this rested solely on the coming of Jesus and faith in Him. For a long time, however, it was unable to formulate this belief clearly, → 415, 26 ff. On the other hand, by avoiding so consistently the solution of simply portraying Jesus as the first pneumatic, it displayed with astonishing clarity an awareness that Jesus was not making it the people of the last time either as a pneumatic Example or as a Teacher. The one essential point is that in Him God Himself encountered His people. All the Spirit-statements concerning Jesus simply under-

---

[448] Flew, *op. cit.,* 49; Barrett, *Fourth Gospel,* 1. Flemington, *op. cit.,* 95 emphasises this also in respect of baptism.

[449] C. H. Dodd, "Jesus as Teacher and Prophet," *Mysterium Christi* (1931), 76. Goguel, *Pneumatisme,* 132, 141-157 would eliminate these completely.

[450] Windisch, *Synpt. Überlieferung,* 225-230, cf. the relatively large no. of prophecies ascribed to Jesus, Dodd, *op. cit.* (→ n. 449), 76 f.

[451] Dodd, *op. cit.,* 76; Frövig, 114; J. E. Fison, *The Blessing of the Holy Spirit* (1950), V; Barrett, *Gospel Trad.,* 152 is right here.

[452] Windisch, *op. cit.,* 230-234.

[453] Scott, 79.

[454] Barrett, *Gospel Trad.,* 141 f., though cf. Taylor, 53 f.

[455] Michaelis, 9, but not W. F. Lofthouse, "The Holy Spirit in the Acts and in the Fourth Gospel," Exp. T., 52 (1940/41), 334-336.

[456] Flew, *op. cit.,* 51.

[457] So C. K. Barrett, "The Holy Spirit and the Gospel Tradition," Exp. T., 67 (1955/56), 142-145. The following writers place experience of the Spirit in the Hell. community alone : Leisegang, *Pneuma,* 140-143; Bultmann Theol., 41; M. Goguel, *La naissance du christianisme* (1946), 112-115; also *Le premier temps de l'église* (1949), 53, though → n. 462.

line His uniqueness, His eschatological position, the fact that in Him God Himself is really present as He is not present anywhere else. [458] This is the point of the few passages which depict Jesus as the bearer of spiritual power (Mt. 12:18, 28, Mk. 3:29 f.), and even more so of those which, on the basis of the Spirit's work in Him, exalt Him absolutely above all others (Mt. 1:20; Mk. 1:10) or portray Him as the One who gives eschatological baptism with the Spirit (Mk. 1:8; cf. 13:11).

In Mark and Matthew, then, the Holy Spirit is viewed in the same way as in the OT. He is the power of God which makes possible speech and action of which human resources are not capable. Only in the idea of conception by the Spirit is there a par. to the later thinking of Hellenistic Judaism. Completely new, however, is the strict subordination of phenomena of the Spirit to the realisation that the Messianic end-time has dawned. [459] Thus all the pneumatological statements have a purely Christological reference.

II. Luke and Acts.

The new estimation of the Spirit in this circle may be seen already in the fact that as a term for the divine Spirit πνεῦμα is used three times as often in Lk. as in Mk. [460] In particular Ac. 1-12 has comparatively the greatest number of occurrences in the NT with 37 instances. [461] Materially, too, Lk. will be seen to have a new understanding of the Spirit. This is mostly ascribed to influences from Asia Minor and Greece, [462] but it will become clear that the development is strongly affected by Judaism. In method we shall always begin with Lk., since the progress in understanding as compared with Mk. is patent here. We shall then conclude each sub-section with a review of Acts.

1. The Relation of the Spirit to Jesus.

Mk. 1:12 reads : τὸ πνεῦμα αὐτὸν ἐκβάλλει εἰς τὴν ἔρημον. For this Lk. 4:1 has : Ἰησοῦς δὲ πλήρης πνεύματος ἁγίου ὑπέστρεψεν ... καὶ ἤγετο ἐν τῷ πνεύματι ἐν τῇ ἐρήμῳ. Luke, then, avoids the idea that the Spirit stands over Jesus. The OT view of the power of God coming upon men (→ 366, 24 ff.) does

---

[458] The situation is the reverse of what we find in Judaism, where the blessings of the last time are to the fore and the Messiah plays a subsidiary role as the One who mediates them (Bousset-Gressm., 222 f.); the statement concerning the community's possession of the Spirit is much less firmly embedded in the early *kerygma* than that concerning the Messiah, C. H. Dodd, *The Apostolic Preaching and its Developments* (1936), 133-135 ≡ (1944), 57 f.

[459] Barrett, *Gospel Trad.*, 153.

[460] πνεῦμα ἀκάθαρτον and the like 12 times ; anthropologically, → 415, 13 ff.

[461] Ac. 13-28 contains only 18 instances, though it is a third longer than 1-12, Gächter, 374 f.

[462] Volz, *Geist*, 198, cf. → I, 104, 38 ff. It is not easy, however, to argue that the Palestinian community was non-pneumatic, → n. 457; cf. the bibl. in W. Kümmel, "Das Urchr.," ThR, 17 (1948/49), 26 f.; 18 (1950), 6, n. 1; E. F. Scott, *The Varieties of NT Religion* (1943), 32 f.; C. C. Torrey, "The Aramaic Period of the Nascent Chr. Church," ZNW, 44 (1952/53), 207 f.; Schweizer, *op. cit.* (→ n. 351), 77 f. Ac. mentions only Jewish prophets (even in the we-passages, 21:4, 9 f.), though it presupposes that there will be prophets on the mission field, 20:23. The upbuilding of the eschatological community (with migration to Jerusalem), the taking up of proclamation and the movement into the Gentile world are inconceivable without strong spiritual experiences. It may even be asked whether the Palestinian community was not marked by a pronounced pneumatic life which emphasis on the tradition in no way rules out, H. v. Campenhausen, "Tradition u. Geist im Urchr.," Studium Generale, 4 (1951), 351-357. Cf. E. Käsemann, „Sätze heiligen Rechtes im NT," NTSt, 1 (1954/55), 257 f.

not satisfy him. Jesus becomes the subject of an action in the Holy Spirit. [463] He is not a pneumatic, but the Lord of the πνεῦμα. Luke adds another πνεῦμα in 4:14, and sets the portrayal of Jesus as a possessor of spiritual power above all that follows. [464] 4:18 (which is peculiar to Lk.) also emphasises the abiding of the Spirit on Jesus. The reinterpretation in 12:10 is worth noting. Lk. here removes the saying about the sin against the Holy Ghost (→ 397, 9 ff.) from its Marcan context [465] because he cannot possibly see the decisive manifestation of the Spirit in the exorcisms of the pneumatic Jesus. 2:40 is a perfect par. to 1:80, but Jesus is not said to grow in spirit as the Baptist is. [466] On the other hand, Luke can give the story of the conception of Jesus by the Spirit, 1:35 (→ 402, 14 ff.). Even more strongly than in Mt. (→ 402, 1 ff.) the πνεῦμα here is the life-giving creative power of God, [467] but only the result is important, not the nature of the act. [468] As One who is born of the Spirit, Jesus is from the very first a possessor of the Spirit and not just the Spirit's object, like the pneumatic. The fact that Luke adopts the tradition concerning endowment with the Spirit at baptism (3:22) [469] is no argument to the contrary, nor is the filling of Jesus with the Spirit before an inspired saying (10:21), [470] nor His definitive receiving of the Spirit at His exaltation (Ac. 2:33). What is described here is not a gradual growth of participation in the Spirit. On the contrary, there lies behind these statements the biblical recollection (→ 365, 36 ff.) that the Spirit, even though given to man, always remains the Spirit of God, so that each actualisation is ultimately a new divine act, → n. 476. The fact that the baptism in the Jordan and the story of Pentecost were in no way assimilated to one another is a possible indication that for Luke the endowment of Jesus with the Spirit lay on a different plane from that of the community.

As He who from the very first possessed the Spirit in fulness, Jesus is after the resurrection [471] the One who dispenses the Spirit to the community, Lk. 24:49; Ac. 2:33. [472] Necessarily connected herewith is the thought that the Risen Lord

---

[463] Jesus is led "in (not by) the Spirit"; πλήρης (→ 283, 18 ff.) denotes abiding fulness as distinct from πλησθείς (→ 130, 11 ff.). Only here, then, does the Spirit become the power to fight Satan, Batdorf, 368.

[464] Lampe, 170 f. Lk. 4:14b, 15 describe this possession. The meaning is not : in virtue of spiritual impulse.

[465] This can hardly go back to Q, since Mt. does not have the combination and Lk. 12:10a can hardly be original alongside v. 9 (though the formulation is assimilated to the asymmetrical πᾶς ὅς ..., ὁ δέ ..., or τῷ δέ ...). At any rate Lk. avoids the interpretation he found in Mk. 3:30 → 407, 13 ff.

[466] v. Baer, 49; Lampe, 168. The adding of τὸ πνεῦμά μου to the OT text (1:47) shows that πνεῦμα is par. to ψυχή but also that Luke wants to stress the fact that we have here, not human ability, but the I which is given to man and which cannot in the last analysis be differentiated from God's πνεῦμα, → 392, 9 f.; 396, 9 ff. The same applies to 1:80; 2:40.

[467] Naturally we hardly yet have the schema of creation and new creation, as against C. F. Burney, *The Aramaic Origin of the Fourth Gospel* (1922), 44, 47, who refers to 1:78 f.; 2:32; 3:38 : Christ as the new Adam.

[468] There is no reflection here on the nature of the conception, → II, 300, 20-37; the event is not sexual, v. Baer, 112-131 as against Leisegang, *Pneuma*, 28 f. רוּחַ is fem., πνεῦμα neut., par. here to δύναμις, Hirsch, *op. cit.*, 3 f.

[469] He stresses this even more strongly than Mk. and Mt., v. Baer, 59 f.

[470] πνεῦμα ἅγιον in Lk. 10:21, not πνεῦμα αὐτοῦ as in Mk. 2:8 (8:12).

[471] As an earthly being Jesus is the only bearer of the Spirit, H. Conzelmann, *Die Mitte d. Zeit* (1954), 155 f.

[472] The underlying tradition, unlike Lk., supposes that the risen Lord has received the Spirit, cf. Jn. 20:22 (v. 17); Eph. 4:7-12 and the fixing of the Feast of the Ascension on the 50th day in the ancient Eastern Church, G. Kretschmar, "Himmelfahrt u. Pfingsten," ZKG, 66 (1954/55), 209-221.

Himself encounters His people in this gift of His. Thus the Spirit becomes parallel to the Risen Lord, Lk. 12:12/21:15; Ac. 10:14/19; 16:7; cf. → n. 534.

Luke, then, has made a clear-cut theological decision. Mark and Matthew could still naïvely depict Jesus as a pneumatic even though they were already making it plain that in so doing they wanted to describe Him as the unique eschatological Deliverer. Luke clarified this insight. Jesus is not a pneumatic like the pneumatics in the community. He is not an object of the Spirit who is at work in the community. The Spirit of God reveals Himself for the first time in Him. Through Him He comes to the community.

2. The Abiding of the Spirit with the Community.

In analogy thereto it may be said that even when he thinks of the community Luke seeks to overcome the concept of the Spirit as a power which leaps on man and then leaves him again. [473] A sign of this is the fact that alongside the originally animistic view whereby the Spirit is an independent entity which comes on man and stands outside him we now find the originally dynamic view according to which the Spirit is a fluid which fills man. [474] This view is better adapted to define the Spirit as that which moulds the whole existence of man. Yet the Gnostic danger is avoided; the Spirit is not just a natural possession of the believer. Animistic terminology is retained, for it emphasises the fact that the Spirit is fundamentally the Spirit of God, alien to man. Even in dynamic formulations, the expression πλήρης πνεύματος, which stresses the lasting union with the Spirit (Ac. 6:3; 11:24; cf. 7:55; Lk. 4:1), [475] is accompanied by πλησθῆναι πνεύματι, which maintains that each actualisation of the Spirit is the act of God and comes from Him. [476] The believer has the Spirit only as, through Jesus Christ, he "has" the faithful God, on whose new action He may continually depend.

3. The Outward Manifestations of the Spirit.

In the story of the baptism of Jesus Luke adds that the Spirit came down σωματικῷ εἴδει, nor does he depict this merely as the content of what Jesus saw. [477] His concern is for the objectivity of the descent of the Spirit. The same is true when he reports the visible phenomena at Pentecost [478] or finds in an earthquake witness to the reality of an event, Ac. 2:3-6; 4:31. The fact that προφητεύειν finds expression at high points in glossolalia, which is stated to be an astonishing phenomenon even by those who do not share in it (→ n. 488), is of the same order.

---

[473] Cf. already Gn. 41:38; Nu. 11:17; 27:18; Is. 42:1; 61:1; Zeph. 3:4 LXX ; Hos. 9:7 (cf. Gunkel, 30, not A. H. McNeile, NT Teaching in the Light of St. Paul's [1923], 130). We do not finding the Spirit speaking in the disciple in Lk. 12:12; 21:15, Conzelmann, op. cit., 198, n. 2.

[474] The former esp. in the OT, the latter in Hellenism. For instances of both cf. Bultmann Theol., 154 f. Cf. J. E. L. Oulton, Holy Communion and Holy Spirit (1951), 42-48.

[475] It is also presupposed in Ac. 2:38; 19:2; Lk. 2:25; cf. also the impf. ἐπληροῦντο in Ac. 13:52. On Ac. 5:3, 9; 15:28 → 408, 18 ff. ἐπληθύνετο (→ 281, 28 ff.) in Ac. 9:31, acc. to 6:1, 7; 7:17; 12:24; 19:20 D, is to be transl. "grew," as against Dupont, op. cit., 239, n. 1; hence it does not belong here.

[476] In the individual Ac. 4:8; 13:9, in the community, 4:31. This passage is too meagre to be an ancient variant of the story of Pentecost, and 4:8 would be impossible on this view (v. Baer, 97). Cf. also Lk. 1:41, 67 and 1:15; Ac. 2:4; 9:17, where it is regarded as the beginning of a lasting possession.

[477] Mt. avoided this already with ref. to the opening of heaven.

[478] It is not quite certain whether the flames were perceptible to all, but the noise was. The Spirit, however, is not equated with the dove, the fire, or the wind (ὡς, ὥσπερ, ὡσεί).

Luke is a Hellenist. This means that he can portray power only in the form of substance, → n. 347. Nevertheless, this is not his real concern. [479] He never depicts the manner of the interpenetration of man by the Spirit, as Hellenism does (→ n. 468). Thus the substantial character of πνεῦμα is an independent category of thought which Luke brings with him, but his real interest is not in this; it is in the fact that the πνεῦμα manifests Himself visibly and demonstrably. Precisely these manifestations are more important for him than for the other NT witnesses. [480] The Spirit gives plain directions from God which there is no gainsaying. [481] Though many statements here need to be checked by other NT sayings, the essential thought is that the Spirit seeks to subordinate man's physical nature also to God, and that His work extends to this area too.

4. The Works of the Spirit.

According to Lk. 12:10 (→ 405, 5 ff.) the Spirit, against whom it is unpardonable to blaspheme, is no longer the power of God manifested in exorcisms [482] but quite definitely (v. 12) the power of God manifested in the inspired utterance of the witnesses of Jesus. [483] Luke adopts the typically Jewish idea that the Spirit is the Spirit of prophecy (→ 381, 23 ff.; 382, 4 ff.). This may be seen in Lk. 4:23-27, where the miraculous signs mentioned in the quotation in v. 18 are specifically rejected as manifestations of the Spirit and only authoritative preaching is regarded as a fulfilment of the prophecy. [484] Though the miracles are important for Luke, they are never ascribed to the Spirit. Healing power is associated with the name of Jesus, with faith in Jesus, with Jesus Himself, with prayer, with bodily contact through the disciple, his shadow or his handkerchief, [485] or more simply with the δύναμις of Jesus. [486] Though Luke can use δύναμις and πνεῦμα almost as synonyms, [487] the distinction between them is clear at this point. This does not

---

[479] → 406, 17 ff. Is the concept of δύναμις, which is so closely related to πνεῦμα, really developed so strongly in terms of substance (→ II, 300, 33; 310, n. 86; the passage mentioned 301, 17 f. is from Mk.!)? It is true that Lk. can incorporate stories which ascribe the healing power of the apostles to their shadow or handkerchief (Ac. 5:15; 19:12), but he avoids the physical contacts of the Synoptic tradition (Barrett, *Gospel Trad.*, 83 f.) and 2 K. 13:21 shows that such ideas were to be found everywhere in primitive thinking.

[480] Ac. 10:47; 11:17; 15:8. He does not forget, however, that they are never incontestable proof for unbelievers, Ac. 2:13.

[481] It is true that strictly 21:4 tells us that the Spirit can also give wrong direction. Hence the responsible decision of man is not unnecessary. Nevertheless, Lk. is merely trying to emphasise that the prophecy of the Spirit is correct but it is associated with advice which, though understandable from a human standpoint, is wrong.

[482] These are much less prominent in Ac., Jackson-Lake, I, 5, 108.

[483] So also Lampe, *op. cit.*, 190 f. There is doubt as to whether the disciples are being comforted — in this case the persecutors are the blasphemers — or warned — in this case they are the blasphemers if they do not obey the voice of the Spirit and refuse to make confession. Since the similar saying in v. 8 f. is undoubtedly addressed to the disciples, and the βλασφημεῖν of Ac. 26:11 in a similar context also refers to them, the second alternative is to be preferred. The view of Fridrichsen, *op. cit.* (→ n. 407), 370 is highly improbable.

[484] But cf. Mt. 11:5 = Lk. 7:22 (though there is no mention of the πνεῦμα here).

[485] Ac. 3:6, 16; 4:30 (the distinction is esp. plain in v. 31b as against W. Knox, *The Acts of the Apostles* [1948], 88); 5:15; 9:34, 40; 16:18; 19:13; 20:10; 28:8.

[486] Lk. 5:17; 6:19 (added to the original); only acc. to Ac. 10:38 is the anointing of Jesus manifested with πνεῦμα and δύναμις in the miracles (→ II, 300 f.), but a formula is used here. The distinction between πνεῦμα and δύναμις is also observed quite plainly in Ac. 6:8, 10 (as against → II, 311, 12 f.).

[487] Lk. 24:49; Ac. 1:5, 8; Lk. 1:17; 4:14; already associated with Mi. 3:8, H. A. Guy, *NT Prophecy* (1947), 90, n. b.

mean that Luke did not regard the witness effected by the Spirit as miraculous. This is certainly true when it takes the form of speaking in tongues. [488] It is equally true when a sudden inspiration makes possible the vision of things to come. [489] To the same category of prophetic vision belongs the ability of the disciples, under the influence of the Spirit, to discern thoughts which are hidden from the natural man, and to proclaim to this man what is in his inmost heart. [490] Especially strongly emphasised as the work of the Spirit is insight into the will of God which is otherwise concealed, the more so when this yields immediate directions for concrete action. [491] In particular, however, the preaching of the disciples is ascribed to the Spirit. This is a divine miracle, though it is preaching to a hostile world which persecutes the preachers. [492] προφητεύειν is for Luke quite central as *the* work of the Spirit. This may be seen from the addition of the word to the long quotation from Joel, otherwise left almost completely unaltered, about the eschatological outpouring of the Spirit. [493] The eschatological community is for Luke the community of the prophets. Only on the margin do we find formulae in which the Spirit is generally understood as dwelling continually in the individual or the community. [494]

Hard to assess is Ac. 5:3, 9. It is highly unlikely that Luke is here depicting the sin against the Holy Ghost of Mk. 3:28 f., → 407, 13 ff. [495] On the other hand, one can hardly think that the disciples as such are supposed to be in possession of the Spirit. The idea seems to be that of 13:9, → n. 490. One might ask whether there is not to be seen in

[488] Ac. 2:4 (→ 410, 21 ff.); 10:46; 19:6; probably also 8:18.

[489] Lk. 1:41, 67; Ac. 11:28 (σημαίνειν here does not mean what Heracl. said of the Delphic oracle : οὔτε λέγει οὔτε κρύπτει ἀλλὰ σημαίνει [Bau. J. on 12:33]); 20:23; 21:4, 11; cf. 1:16; 4:25 (gloss ? E. Haenchen, "Schriftzitate u. Textüberlieferung in d. Ag.," ZThK, 51 [1954], 157); 28:25. If in Lk. 1:41, 67 there is a more general depiction of the disposition of the speaker as one which is shaped by the Spirit, the ref. in the verses in Ac. is to the actual speech : prophecy is διὰ τοῦ πνεύματος or even by the πνεῦμα Himself. Lk. 10:21 is to be attributed to Luke, → n. 470. As the other refs. show the ἀγαλλίασις itself is not the work of the Spirit but the ἀγαλλίασις expressed in prophetic witness, cf. Dodd, *op. cit.*, 75.

[490] Ac. 13:9 (on 5:3, 9 → lines 18 ff.). Hell. par. Bu. J., 71, n. 4. The πνεῦμα here causes neither intense stimulation (Zn. Ag., *ad loc.*) nor the evil eye (Jackson-Lake, I, 1, 4, *ad loc.*), which brings about 99 out of 100 deaths, Str.-B., II, 713-715.

[491] Ac. 8:29; 10:19; 11:12; 13:2, 4; 16:6 f.; 20:22 is also to be taken thus (ἅγιον is often left out even in the case of the divine πνεῦμα); the ref., then, is to the direction of the Spirit given to Paul himself, while v. 23 mentions directions given to other members of the community ("from city to city") (with Zn. Ag.; Haench Ag., *ad loc.*, against Jackson-Lake, I, 1, 4, *ad loc.*). It might be that this is also the pt. in 7:51, but not in 7:55, where the Spirit gives a vision of the heavenly world in the hour of death, though this also leads to μαρτυρεῖν in word and deed.

[492] Lk. 12:12 is taken from the tradition, but strongly underlined by association with v. 10 (→ 407, 13 ff.); cf. also Ac. 1:8 (as v. 8 shows, not miraculous power, against Jackson-Lake, I, 1, 4; Pr. Ag., *ad loc.*); 4:8, 31; 6:10. 5:32 is also to be understood thus ; the Spirit's witness does not consist in the visible event (2:33) of Pentecost but in the preaching of the apostles and all the "obedient." The parataxis is to be resolved hypotactically, not related to the witness of the Spirit in other preachers after the possible execution of the apostles (as against Bau. Ag., *ad loc.*). 18:25 (→ 413, 30 ff.) is (like 5:32; 6:10) a ref. to the enduring capacity for witness. The spiritual power mentioned in Lk. 1:17 (→ II, 300, 3); 4:14 also seems to express itself esp. in preaching.

[493] Ac. 2:18. D it emend acc. to the OT. Cf. Lk. 2:26.

[494] Par. to σοφία (Ac. 6:3), πίστις (6:5; 11:24), φόβος τοῦ κυρίου (9:31), χαρά (13:52).

[495] With v. Baer, 145 against W. Fritschy, *Notes sur le péché contre le St. Esprit*, Diss. Neuchâtel (1942), 35 f. At most this is conceivable only at a preliminary stage of the pericope, since the Q form of the saying in Lk. 12:10 allows of the possibility of its being made into a disciplinary rule fixing various grades of transgression, cf. Fridrichsen, 370.

15:28 (and perhaps 20:28) the view of a later period acc. to which the direction of a church court is *eo ipso* that of the Holy Spirit. [496] Nevertheless, though πνεῦμα and ἡμεῖς occur together, there is no ref. to the πνεῦμα ἐν ἡμῖν, and this suggests strongly that here as elsewhere Luke has in view the prophetic Spirit which the ἡμεῖς follow, cf. 5:32 → n. 492. 20:28 is also to be read in the light of 13:1-3, though it should be noted that Luke presupposes the work of the Spirit in all instances and not just in unusual circumstances. This carries with it the possibility of a later misunderstanding which links the Spirit automatically to a correctly discharged ecclesiastical vocation, → 451, 17 ff.

A verse apart is Ac. 8:39, which attributes the snatching away of Philip to the Spirit. One cannot avoid the miracle by adopting the (uncertain) reading ἀπ' αὐτοῦ, Zn. Ag., *ad loc.* There are many par. to miraculous rapture, 1 K. 18:12; 2 K. 2:16; Ez. 3:14; 8:3; Ev. Hebr. (Orig. Comm. in Joh., II, 12); Bel et Draco, 36; Herm. v., 1, 1, 3; 2, 1, 1; Philostr. Vit. Ap., VIII, 10 (mid-day in Rome, evening in Puteoli). It is possible, however, that the text of MS A is original, in which case the act is ascribed to the angel. The singularity of the view of the Spirit in the usual text and the regularity with which the outpouring of the Spirit is narrated or promised elsewhere up to c. 10 are arguments for the accepted reading. Elimination of the term might have come about through mechanical deviation from πνεῦμα to κυρίου or on dogmatic grounds, since no apostle is mentioned here as the bearer of the Spirit. [497] Another possibility is that it is the remnant of a pre-Lucan tradition.

Luke thus shares with Judaism the view that the Spirit is essentially the Spirit of prophecy. [498] This does not prevent him from directly attributing to the πνεῦμα both the χαρίσματα ἰαμάτων [499] on the one side and strongly ethical effects like the common life of the primitive community on the other. [500] Luke is relatively close to a line of thought which measures the work of the Spirit by its peculiarity. His interest, however, is not in the peculiarity as such; it is in the fact that God gives to His community visible signs of His work and clear directions. Spirit-given preaching is always regarded as a divine miracle but not usually as a peculiarity. [501] Yet it is here primarily that the work of the Spirit is granted to the community. Hence, even though the Hellenist Luke is strongly interested in the visibility of the Spirit's works, the limitation of these works to prophetic proclamation is completely Jewish. [502]

5. The Spirit as a Feature of the Age of the Church.

Lk. 11:13 promises the πνεῦμα ἅγιον to those who ask God therefor. Originally just ἀγαθά were promised, Mt. 7:11. [503] The emendation is natural in Lk. since

---

[496] Cf. Gunkel, 27.

[497] Pr. Ag. and Zn. Ag., *ad loc.*

[498] Guy, *op. cit.*, 93, n. a; Lampe, 193.

[499] 1 K. 12:28; in the OT, too, miracles were not directly attributed to the רוח but simply ascribed in many instances to bearers of the Spirit, Eichr. Theol. AT³, II, 21, n. 9 = § 13, n. II.

[500] L. S. Thornton, *The Common Life in the Body of Christ* (1942), 6, 74 f.; Dodd, *op. cit.* (→ n. 458), 137 overlook the fact that there is no express attributing to the Spirit. Mission rather than moral renewal is the gift of the Spirit acc. to Lk., cf. v. Baer, 108.

[501] In the second half of Ac., where fewer sources are used, the miraculous in the sense of the strange is less prominent and the express direction of the Spirit replaces that through angels in the first half, Knox, *op. cit.*, 91 f. (Ac. 27:23 is a vision). Even in 4:31 the community prays for παρρησία, not tongues. This is in 9:27 f. *the* proof of the genuineness of conversion, and Ac. closes with a ref. thereto, 28:31 (v. Baer, 102).

[502] A pt. of difference from the Hell. view of the πνεῦμα μαντικόν is that he has no interest in the process of the penetration of the pneumatic substance into man, cf. Verbeke, 396 f. Only with this modification does Acts "depict historically the power of the Spirit of Jesus in the apostles," A. v. Harnack, *Die Ag.* (1908), 4.

[503] Πνεῦμα ἅγιον is a Lucan phrase often found elsewhere.

ἀγαθά might well be suspect for him as merely earthly goods, 12:18 f. It shows, however, that for him the Spirit is the absolute gift which accrues to the believer in the community of Jesus. This would be even more strongly emphasised if the petition : "May thy Holy Spirit come upon us and cleanse us," were the older reading in Lk. 11:2. [504] For Mark and Matthew the Spirit was an eschatological event. But the link with the OT view which regards the coming of the Spirit as something extraordinary was still so strong that apart from the saying of the Baptist only one logion promises the community the special help of the Spirit in times of particular need. Luke realises that the OT prophecies which promised the Spirit to the people of the last time (Nu. 11:29, → 384, 29 ff.) have been fulfilled. This means that the Spirit is given, and permanently given, to all members of the community. [505]

That each of the baptised possesses the Spirit, and does so in a way which is visible and perceptible, is presupposed in Ac. 19:2, also in 2:38 f., where the promise of the Spirit is to all, 15:8 f., where the Gentiles are specifically included, and 8:16-18 (39 → 409, 10 ff.); 9:17; 10:44; 11:16 f.; 19:6, which regard endowment with the Spirit as a natural consequence of coming to faith. [506]

A first inclination is to regard the outpouring of the Spirit as the true eschatological event in Luke. The quotation from Joel (Ac. 2:17-21) depicts it as such, [507] and there are eschatological touches in the description of the event of Pentecost itself, → I, 724 f. The one language is a phenomenon of the last time : Test. Jud. 25:3; Plut. Is. et Os., 47 (II, 370b); cf. Is. 66:18 f. [508] In spite of the ἤκουον of v. 6 and the ἀκούομεν of v. 8 the author does not have in mind a mere miracle of hearing (cf. v. 4). [509] Analysis of the pericope is extremely difficult, → 50 ff. Historically there must have been a decisive experience of the outpouring of the Spirit in the primitive community. Possibly glossolalia occurred for the first time on this occasion. [510] The problem, however, is how this came to be understood as a miracle of speech. The story cannot possibly be explained in terms of the Gk. habit of calling on the deity πάσῃ φωνῇ καὶ πάσῃ διαλέκτῳ. [511] The suggestion that Luke simply misunderstood γλῶσσα because he had no acquaintance with glossolalia is untenable in the light of 10:46; 19:6. Nevertheless, the arrangement of the story might well be due to Luke. He regards the first endowment with the Spirit as something *sui generis* and could put such an event at the beginning of Ac. as Lk. 4:16-30 stands at the beginning of the Gospel. [512] It is far more probable, however, that

---

[504] Kl. Lk., *ad loc.*; Lampe, 184; R. Leaney, "The Lucan Text of the Lord's Prayer," Nov. Test., 1 (1956), 103-111; but this was probably a pre-Marcionite baptismal petition (though Marcion's text is not absolutely certain), cf. Act. Thom., 27; E. Lohmeyer, *Das Vaterunser* (1946), 185-192; Zn. Lk., Exc. IX.

[505] Prenter, 30 f. sees in this the main difference between the OT and the NT.

[506] From 11:19 on there are no ref. to an outpouring of the Spirit except in 19:6. This is only to say, however, that Luke takes over from the tradition accounts of objective endowments with the Spirit and sees in them a special demonstration of God at decisive turning-points.

[507] The addition of ἐν ταῖς ἐσχάταις ἡμέραις in v. 17 characterises the outpouring of the Spirit as an eschatological event, but it is perhaps a later emendation, E. Haenchen, *op. cit.* (→ n. 489), 162.

[508] Pl. also connects Is. 28:11 with glossolalia, thus marking it as an eschatological phenomenon (1 C. 14:21).

[509] So K. L. Schmidt, *Die Pfingsterzählung u. d. Pfingstereignis* (1919), 20-22, with ref. to a corresponding Buddha legend.

[510] Only v. 13 fits in with this, but the idea of a misunderstanding which the apostolic address answers is a Lucan schema, 3:11 f.; 14:11-15; cf. 4:9 f.; 6:13 f.; 17:22 f. Glossolalia also occurs at decisive stages in Ac.

[511] Leisegang, *Pneuma*, 131 f.

[512] v. Baer, 91; Lampe, 159.

already in the pre-Lucan period [513] the concept of the new covenant, of the renewal of the giving of the Law for world-wide Judaism, [514] strongly influenced the account of the first coming of the Spirit. Undoubtedly pre-Chr. are Jub. 6:17, 19 (→ 48, 18-23, though cf. also Jub. 1:1; 15:1; 44:4 f.) and Philo's account of the divine voice at Sinai which evokes a special sound in each individual soul, turns into flame, and passes like a πνεῦμα through a trumpet, so that it is heard by those both near and afar off, and the sound goes forth even to the ends of the earth, Decal., 33, 35; Spec. Leg., II, 189. [515] If even before 70 Pentecost was regarded as the end of the passover which celebrates the exodus from Egypt (→ 49, 3), and if already in Dt. 4:10; 9:10; 18:16 LXX the day of the giving of the Law is called ἡ ἡμέρα τῆς ἐκκλησίας, such an interpretation is natural. In the (non-orthodox) circles of Jub. and sectarian groups Pentecost was probably celebrated as an oath-festival when the covenant was renewed and the spiritual year began. [516] The saying of the Baptist about those who are baptised with storm and fire (→ 399, 13 ff.) might have been historicised and thus helped to shape the formulation of v. 2 f. Luke takes this up. For him ref. to the new Law was not essential (as it was for Mt.), [517] but he sees here the beginning of the age of the Church and also a symbol of the progress of the Gospel through the nations. He is perhaps thinking of the speech of the Spirit as a new miraculous speech which all understand. [518] Perhaps some influence was also exerted by the antitype to Gn. 11:1-9. [519]

But this event is not eschatological for Luke. It ushers in a new age, but not *the* new age. Surrounded by the salvation history of the OT and the history of mission, the Christ event is for him the centre of time. [520] Hence the outpouring of the Spirit can be repeated wherever men come to faith. It takes new forms where a new step is made into the world of the nations, Ac. 8:17 f.; 10:44 f. If acc. to Lk. 1 f. some men were already filled by the Spirit prior to the coming of Jesus, Lk. takes this from the tradition [521] and sees in it a sign of what is to come. On the other hand, he sometimes avoids saying

[513] W. Grundmann, "Das Problem d. hell. Christentums innerhalb d. Jerusalemer Urgemeinde," ZNW, 38 (1939), 49, n. 10 likewise thinks two traditions have been redacted here.

[514] Knox, 80-82; on the list of peoples (apart from → 51, n. 44) ibid., 84, n. 1; H. Fuchs, "Zum Pfingstwunder Act. 2:9-11," ThZ, 5 (1949), 233 f. The hope of a reuniting of all the dispersed is to be seen here. The question is discussed (with good bibl.) in U. Holzmeister, "Quaestiones pentecostales," Verbum Domini, 20 (1940), 131-134. A par. between Sinai and Pentecost is also seen by L. Cerfaux, "Le symbolisme attaché au miracle des langues," Ephemerides Theol. Lovanienses, 13 (1936), 258 f. The echoing of Dt. 32:8 in v. 3 (ibid., 257) is accidental.

[515] Law and fire are also combined in the Rabb., Str.-B., II, 603 f.

[516] Jub. 6:21 (Kretschmar, op. cit. [→ n. 472], 227 f. and n. 84; Molin, op. cit. [→ n. 339], 96). For further arguments in favour of a pre-Chr. celebration of Pentecost as a commemoration of the giving of the Law cf. Kretschmar, 223-234. Unlike Kretschmar (236, 243) I believe that ecstasy, if not perhaps speaking in tongues, is historical (cf. Nu. 11:16 f.; Eph. 4:7-11 is no argument to the contrary, though the ecstatic was then less prominent). I also believe that the miracle of speech was older than the concept of mission.

[517] It is correct that Lk., unlike Mt., does not make the Sermon on the Mount a par. of Sinai, Knox, op. cit. (→ n. 485), 81 f. But this is not because Pentecost replaces it.

[518] H. H. Wendt, Die Ag. (1899), 86 f.; cf. A. Wikenhauser, Die Ag. (1951), 84 f., ad loc. Acc. to 10:47; 11:15, 17 Lk. sees in 10:46 (and 19:6) a basically similar event, so that 2:6 records glossolalia understood by men of various tongues.

[519] J. G. Davies, "Pentecost and Glossolalia," JThSt, NS, 3 (1952), 228 f. → γλῶσσα, φωνή, συνεχύθη.

[520] Conzelmann, op. cit. (→ n. 471); cf. P. Vielhauer, "Zum 'Paulinismus' d. Ag.," Ev. Theol., 10 (1950/51), 12 f.; G. Vos, "The Eschatological Aspect of the Pauline Conception of the Spirit," Bibl. and Theol. Studies Princeton (1912), 223 f. But one should not overemphasise the distinctions from Paul in the light of R. 9-11. For Luke, too, the salvation enacted in Christ is not surpassed in history ; history is the history of faith in this salvation, i.e., missionary history.

[521] Goguel, Notion, 45, n. 1, though cf. Lampe, 167. A further pt. here is that all those

that an OT writer spoke in the Spirit, Mk. 12:36 = Lk. 20:42, though cf. Ac. 1:16; 28:25. The same applies to the par. δύναμις at the *parousia,* Mk. 9:1.

Luke took an important step beyond Mark and Matthew. He did not think it enough to present Jesus as a bearer of the Spirit by pointing to individual pneumatic features or to the birth and baptism stories. His special concern was with the time of the Church. Here the promises are fulfilled by the people of God, to whom the Spirit is given in totality. The prophets are no longer isolated individuals. All the members of the eschatological community are prophets.

At this point one may sees the limits of his outlook and his adherence to the Jewish tradition. Fundamentally he does not cease to regard the Spirit merely as the extraordinary power which makes possible unusual acts of power. It is true that this conception has been corrected, partly by the Jewish tradition, which found in the Spirit almost exclusively the One who empowers for prophetic utterance (→ 381, 23 ff.), then by the statement of the community that all members of the new community possess the Spirit. The Spirit is not limited, then, to momentary manifestations which go beyond what is usual. All the same, Luke stands by the ancient tradition. It is true that the manner of the Spirit's manifestation does not have to be externally strange ; it can consist in παρρησία, → n. 501; V, 882. The Spirit, however, does not totally shape the existence of the believer as a completely new, eschatological existence. The Spirit gives the believer a special gift which makes him capable of certain additional expressions of his faith which are essential to, and alone make possible, the ongoing and as yet incomplete history of mission.

This may be seen negatively in the fact that even when Luke wants to emphasise that πιστεῦσαι is not a natural event but one which is miraculously granted by God, he never attributes faith to the Spirit. [522] Similarly the ideal state of the community can be depicted without mention of the Spirit. [523] Salvation, too, is never ascribed to the Spirit. [524] According to Ac. 2:38 the Spirit is imparted to those who are already converted and baptised. Obedience must also precede the reception of the Spirit according to 5:32. Days, and in exceptional cases even weeks and years may pass before endowment with the Spirit follows faith, but this does not make believers into unbelievers again, 9:17; 8:16; 19:2. Prayer, too, is never regarded as an act of the Spirit ; it is preparation for receiving the Spirit, → n. 532. No doubt it would be wrong to ascribe only extraordinary religious effects to the Spirit. [525] Nevertheless, according to Luke the Spirit gives only the power which enables the believer to discharge a special task, to express his faith in concrete action. The distinction between this view of the Spirit and the OT understanding, then, is simply that in the new age of salvation all members of the community rather than special individuals are bearers of the Spirit, and that along the lines of the subsequent development of the understanding of the Spirit in Judaism the action of the Spirit is almost exclusively taken to be prophetic action.

---

endowed with the Spirit (apart from Mary) are connected with the temple cultus. It is thus highly unlikely that Luke shaped the introductory material along the lines of Jl. 2:28 f., Guy, *op. cit.* (→ n. 487), 28 f.

[522] Ac. 16:14 : ὁ κύριος διήνοιξεν τὴν καρδίαν, 3:16 : ἡ πίστις ἡ δι' αὐτοῦ (= Jesus).

[523] E.g., Ac. 2:42-47 (cf. Gunkel, 6).

[524] This is thoroughly Jewish. In Hellenism deification and regeneration bring salvation, Jackson-Lake, I, 1, 326.

[525] Gunkel, 8. On the one side παρρησία is attributed to the Spirit even where its expression is not unusual, while on the other side miracles of healing are not attributed to the Spirit.

The distinctiveness of the Lucan witness consists, then, in the fact that a community without the specific power to execute concretely its missionary task is shown to be a community without the Spirit. By not attributing the mere existence of the community to the Spirit, Luke reminds it of the necessity of this activity which is granted by the Spirit.

6. The Reception of the Spirit.

As a rule baptism in the name of Jesus confers the Spirit. The disciples of Ac. 19:2 who had not received this baptism were necessarily without the Spirit. The endowment with the Spirit promised in 9:17 seems quite obviously to have been fulfilled by the baptism of v. 18. In 2:38 the gift of the Spirit at least follows baptism. On the other hand, 10:44-48 shows that baptism may follow the outpouring of the Spirit, but is not rendered superfluous thereby.

It may be asked how far historically reliable reminiscences are enshrined in these verses. Baptism is not mentioned at all in 11:15-17; κωλῦσαι τὸν θεόν replaces κωλῦσαι τὸ ὕδωρ (10:47). The quotation in 11:16b is to the pt. only if no baptism follows, or if baptism is at least non-essential. Acc. to 11:3 Peter is accused only of having table fellowship, not of giving baptism. Yet one cannot deduce from this that the baptism of 10:44-48 is a secondary addition. If so, why was it not also added in 11:3, 17? On the contrary, one may conclude that Luke took the ref. to baptism in 10:47 f. from the tradition, though without attaching any special significance to it. [526] For 11:16, as 1:5 shows, is a Lucan addition, and it proves that for him baptism was at most an "accident" of the thing that really counts, namely, the outpouring of the Spirit.

2:38, then, is simply saying that baptism is a natural part of the much more important conversion. [527] Hence he need not be concerned that the Spirit was poured out on the 120 (1:15) without baptism. This is confirmation that for him baptism is not an essential means of obtaining the Spirit. The same applies in 19:1-7, esp. if 18:25 is also taken into account. In 19:1-7 Luke is telling about Christians who have not experienced the outpouring of the Spirit. The historical probability is that twelve disciples of John were converted by Paul, so that in the original story the baptism of John, which did not impart the Spirit, was distinguished from that of Jesus, which did. [528] Similarly Apollos is already a Christian for Luke, though it is more likely historically that he was a Jewish missionary first converted in Ephesus. [529] In the one case baptism was given, in the other it was not. In the depiction in Ac. there is no place either for a Jewish missionary working in the Spirit or for a group still loyal to the Baptist. For Luke both stories serve to illustrate the movement of salvation from the OT via the Baptist to the Church. A time in which the baptism of the Spirit rendered that of water superfluous certainly cannot be deduced therefrom. [530] It is most unlikely that baptism and the outpouring of the

---

[526] 10:9-16 may also be ascribed to Luke, M. Dibelius, "Die Reden d. Ag. u. d. antike Geschichtsschreibung," SAH, 35 (1949), 31 = Aufsätze zur Ag. (1951), 140 E.T. [1956], 111.

[527] In 1 QS 3:4-12; 5:13 baptism is the outward sign of an accomplished conversion which alone cleanses. M. Barth, Die Taufe — ein Sakrament? (1951) lays gt. stress on this aspect of baptism (on Ac. cf. 134-154).

[528] The passage does not prove, of course, that the Baptist said nothing about the Spirit, only that these disciples had not experienced the actual outpouring, Gunkel, 51; E. Lohmeyer, op. cit. (→ n. 423), 26 as against Leisegang, Pneuma, 72 f.; v. Baer, 162 f.; B. W. Bacon, "The 'Coming One' of John the Baptist," Exp., VI, 10 (1904), 14; Windisch, Synpt. Überlieferung, 214.

[529] E. Käsemann, "Die Johannesjünger in Ephesus," ZThK, 49 (1952), 144-154; E. Schweizer, "Die Bekehrung d. Apollos," Ev. Theol., 15 (1955), 247-254. W. Michaelis, "Die sog. Johannesjünger in Ephesus," NkZ, 38 (1927), 727-735 thinks the men were Christians who had not experienced Pentecost, possibly Galileans (E. Lohmeyer, Galiläa u. Jerusalem [1936], 75 f., 78); there is, however, no historical basis for this hypothesis.

[530] Flemington, op. cit., 44, n. 1; 45, as against Jackson-Lake, I, 1, 337-343; J. Weiss, Das Urchr. (1917), 36. On the historical question of the origin of baptism cf. Kraeling, op. cit. (→ n. 418), 171-175.

Spirit were not yet associated in the primitive community because baptism was viewed only negatively as a rite of purification.[531] Baptism was at least a pre-condition for reception of the Spirit.

Luke takes over the association of baptism and impartation of the Spirit from the tradition. He regards baptism as a self-evident expression of conversion, though without laying any undue stress upon it. As a preparation for reception of the Spirit prayer is far more important than baptism in Luke's eyes.[532] πιστεῦσαι is always mentioned as a presupposition, 2:38; 8:12; 9:1-19 etc. Faith, not baptism, purifies for reception of the Spirit acc. to 15:8 f. Nevertheless, Luke does not regard water baptism as an unnecessary external rite. He is not a "spiritualiser" who recognises only the baptism of the Spirit.[533] A far more significant point is that precisely in Acts the freedom of the Spirit is strongly emphasised. The Spirit is not tied to baptism. Once He comes on men before baptism (10:44), once without it (2:1-4), once on a disciple who knew only John's baptism (18:25), which according to 19:3 f. could not impart the Spirit to others.[534]

But does not 8:14-17 bear witness to the fact that endowment with the Spirit[535] is associated with the apostolic laying on of hands? Do we not have here at least an incipient Catholicism in which the Spirit is tied to office and ritual rather than vice versa?[536] This passage, however, stands alone. There is no laying on of hands in 2:38 or 10:48.[537] An ordinary member of the community acts in 9:12. Laying on of hands is mentioned there, but only with a view to healing.[538] Above all, Luke is interested in the free operation of the Spirit even in passages where ecclesiastical considerations play a decisive role. He is acquainted with the collection for Jerusalem (Ac. 24:17) which even Paul regarded as a proof of loyalty to Jerusalem after the manner of the Jewish temple tax (Gl. 2:10; R. 15:27).[539] He does not depict it, however, as in any sense an expression of uniformity in organisation but prefers an account which attributes the collection to free prophetic inspiration, 11:28. Similarly, in 8:14-17 neither the rite of laying on hands nor the

---

[531] W. G. Kümmel, "Das Urchr.," ThR, 22 (1954), 143 as against Bultmann Theol., 138.

[532] Lk. 3:21; Ac. 9:9, 11 at the first reception of the Spirit, 4:31; 13, 1-3 at a repetition; the apostles pray for the Spirit in 8:15 and a magical view is sharply rejected in 8:18-20, cf. E. v.d. Goltz, Das Gebet in d. ältesten Christenheit (1901), 3.

[533] Otherwise he could neither write 2:38 nor incorporate 10:47 f.; 19:5. Luke is neither one-sidedly static nor one-sidedly dynamic, Bau. Ag. on 10:44-48.

[534] On the freedom of the Spirit cf. also 10:20 (with an emphatic ἐγώ); 13:1-4; 16:6 f.; 20:22 f.; 21:4, 11.

[535] For a distinction between the Spirit of the charismata and the general Spirit already given before cf. Wikenhauser, 81-83; also J. E. L. Oulton, "The Holy Spirit, Baptism, and Laying on of Hands in Acts," Exp. T., 66 (1954/55), 238; N. Adler, Taufe u. Handauflegung (1951), 81-91 perceives here the Spirit of Pentecost mediated through the apostolic laying on of hands, which perfects the baptismal gifts of the Spirit by giving them in fulness (106). The passage is thus the oldest instance of confirmation (111). G. B. Caird, The Apostolic Age (1955), 71 finds here a special divine sign which indicates to the apostles that they have taken the right way beyond Judaism.

[536] For details cf. Schweizer, op. cit. (→ n. 529), 249.

[537] If it is taken for granted (Flemington, 44, n. 1; but it is not mentioned by Paul at all), it is at least not important for Lk. The same applies in 19:6, where the whole story shows that what matters is the baptism of Jesus, not the laying on of the apostles' hands.

[538] Not because only an apostle can mediate the Spirit, for in 9:17 the Spirit is expected through the mediation of Ananias. Again it is not the apostles who lay on hands in 13:3, J. Brosch, Charismen u. Ämter in d. Urkirche (1951), 163: a rite in prayer. Cf. also 8:39 (MS A).

[539] Or as a fulfilment of Is. 2:2 f.; 60:5-16, J. Munck, Pls. und die Heilsgeschichte (1954), 298 E.T. [1959], 303 f. ?

office of the apostles seems to be decisive, only the connection with Jerusalem. As there is a link with pious Judaism in Lk. 1 f., so Ac. 8:14-17 bears witness to the fact that the Spirit does not conduct the community at a bound into new regions, but acts in evident association with the history already enacted. For this reason it is just as essential that prophets speaking by momentary inspiration of the Spirit should come from Jerusalem (11:27) as it is that the apostles should come from thence (8:14). This is why Paul's journey to Jerusalem is as strongly emphasised as that of Jesus in the Gospel. God's history goes forth from Jerusalem and continually leads back thither. From this there developed later a kind of Jerusalem caliphate. Luke's concern, however, is simply to set forth the way of God in salvation history.

7. Different Meanings of πνεῦμα.

πνεῦμα is used anthropologically in Lk. 1:47, 80, though in both verses there is also a strong suggestion of the divine power which strictly stands over against man and is simply given to him, → 405, 8 f. and n. 466. Par. to Lk. 1:47 is Ac. 17:16, whereas in Ac. 19:21, as in Lk. 2:27, the Spirit of God is meant, cf. also Ac. 18:25; 20:22, → 413, 30 ff. and n. 491. πνεῦμα is the part of man which survives death (→ 379, 13 ff.) in Lk. 8:55 (new as compared with Mk.), cf. also the quotation in 23:46 and the dependent Ac. 7:59. Whether one may conclude from Lk. 23:43; Ac. 2:24, 31 f. that Luke had in mind an existence of Jesus as πνεῦμα apart from the (incorruptible) σάρξ in the *triduum mortis* [540] is, however, very doubtful. In a manner quite different from that of Hellenism πνεῦμα in Lk. 24:37, 39; Ac. 23:8 f. certainly denotes a shadowy, non-corporeal existence which does not constitute the ἐγὼ αὐτός (Lk. 24:39).

III. Paul.

1. The OT and Hellenistic Strands. [541]

a. The Problem.

All that has been examined thus far has been basically shaped by the OT. As in the OT and Judaism as a whole, the Spirit is not necessary to salvation but is a power for additional deeds. Understood thus, the Spirit naturally becomes a sign of something still to come, of the real thing. Thus in the quotation from Joel in Ac. 2:19-21 the outpouring of the Spirit is clearly depicted as the beginning of the eschatological catastrophe, and in Hb. 6:4 f. the wonder-working πνεῦμα (2:4) is a foretaste of the good things of the world to come. This means, however, that the Spirit is only a singular prelude to the *parousia*, a welcome but basically unnecessary sign of the real thing which is yet to come. For salvation is not to be discerned in the mere presence of all kinds of miraculous powers.

Luke tried to get away from this, for he lived at a period when there was no longer so tense an expectation of the *parousia*. But it is here precisely that the difficulty arises. The history of mission replaces the *parousia*. This means, however, that the Spirit is no longer a blessing of eschatological salvation but historical power for the intervening period. No matter what the interpretation, however, the real problem is that of the relation between the message of the Spirit and that of the crucified, risen and coming κύριος. [542]

---

[540] W. Bieder, *Die Vorstellung von d. Höllenfahrt Jesu Christi* (1949), 69, n. 234. Cf. the disembodied blessed of Hellenism, Luc. Vera Historia, II, 12.

[541] On the one side Hell. and Palestinian society exerted a strong reciprocal influence in Judaism and esp. in nascent Christianity; on the other gnosis seems to be very largely heterodox Judaism influenced by Iranian and Hell. dualism, Schweizer (→ n. 351), 154-162. The two strands are hard to disentangle even in Paul.

[542] This is the decisive question for primitive Christianity, O. Michel, *Das Zeugnis des NT von d. Gemeinde* (1941), 65.

So soon as the witness to Christ reached men who were strongly influenced by Gk. thought, it was planted in a society to which the idea of a history which develops and moves towards a goal was alien. [543] This society does not think in terms of detached aeons. Being generally dualistic, it thinks in terms of superimposed spheres. [544] Here, then, the πνεῦμα cannot be regarded as the mere sign of what is to come. As a part of the heavenly world πνεῦμα is the thing itself. Since the Hellenist always thinks of power in terms of substance (→ n. 347), [545] the coming of the Spirit is for him the breaking in of heavenly substance. If Jesus was the bringer of the Spirit, then He was the bearer of heavenly substance with which He endowed believers and united them with the heavenly world. A radical solution thus became possible for the first time. The point of the mission of Jesus was to bring the heavenly substance πνεῦμα into the world. Attachment to Jesus is attachment to this substance of power, to the heavenly world. It is thus salvation itself.

The Gnosticism of the 2nd cent. (→ 393, 18 ff.), which resolutely works out this possibility, shows us how the interpretation must have appeared in its early stages. Here the purpose of the mission of Jesus was actually to impart the Spirit. Here the Spirit was actually salvation itself ; He was the φύσις which delivered the pneumatic, → n. 381.

Logically the latter thought meant that the spiritual nature of man was regarded as already pre-existent. The redemptive event did not create this nature for man ; it simply instructed him concerning it. [546] But in this case, was not the myth enough to mediate the insight (→ 395, 2 ff.)? Was it not a matter of indifference whether anything really happened or not ? It is no accident that the cross has no place in this conception, or that the whole incarnation can be understood merely as a deception of hostile powers. [547]

b. Adoption of Hellenistic Ideas in Paul.

In Paul the decision is taken in eschatology. More than all who preceded him, Paul regards the cross and resurrection as the great turning-point (→ I, 207, 25 ff.), not merely as the overture to the *parousia*. Hence he is forced to view life in the Spirit as the life of the new κτίσις. [548] This means that he can take over in part the Hellenistic interpretation of the Christ event. The presence of the Spirit is unequivocally related to the descent and ascent of the Redeemer ; it is also the new existence of the community itself, not merely an additional phenomenon.

R. 1:3 f. shows that even before Paul πνεῦμα denotes the heavenly sphere or its substance, and that Paul for his part adopts this understanding. [549]

The related formula in 1 Tm. 3:16 is constructed with strict chiastically arranged parallelism : a-b/b-a/a-b. [550] There is correspondence between σάρξ, ἔθνη, κόσμος

---

[543] O. Cullmann, *Christus u. d. Zeit* (1946), 44-50 (E.T. 51-58); Schweizer, 118-120. Gnosticism is a "révolte contre le temps," Quispel, *op. cit.*, 122, n. 23.

[544] On Gnosticism → 392, 28 ff.; on the avoidance of both approaches in later Judaism cf. Schweizer, 130-132.

[545] For רוּחַ as substance in the OT cf. Gunkel, 44-47; Volz, *Geist*, 23, though cf. N. H. Snaith, *The Distinctive Ideas of the OT* (1944), 156. What W. D. Davies, *Paul and Rabbinic Judaism* (1948), 184 has to say about Rabbinism does not go beyond what is said → 381, 32 ff., namely, that the substance idea of Hellenism links up with primitive notions everywhere present in the OT, but only in Hellenism does this concept become constitutive for the understanding of the Spirit.

[546] The knowledge of the Gnostic is at all events self-knowledge (Bu. J., 210), but does not this show that it is only that, that here man encounters only himself, → n. 382 ?

[547] Ltzm. K. Exc. on 1 C. 2:6, → n. 370.

[548] It is the lasting merit of A. Schweitzer, *Die Mystik d. Ap. Pls.* (1930), 159-174, to have drawn attention to this. His mistake was to confuse the adopted vocabulary with Paul's own concern.

[549] For proof of this cf. Schweizer, *op. cit.* (→ n. 353), 563, 568 f., also Schweizer, *op. cit.* (→ n. 351), 55 f.

[550] For an analysis cf. Schweizer (→ n. 351), 63-66.

and πνεῦμα, ἄγγελοι, δόξα.[551] In antithesis to ἐν σαρκί, ἐν πνεύματι is thus to be transl. "in the sphere of the Spirit" (→ II, 215, 5 f.). Salvation consists in the rediscovered unity of the two spheres.[552] πνεῦμα does not simply describe a local sphere ; it defines this as the sphere of heavenly substance. How self-evident here is the originally spiritual nature of the Redeemer may be seen in the fact that the μυστήριον sets in with the φανερωθῆναι ἐν σαρκί.[553] The formulation in 1 Pt. 3:18b is to be assessed similarly. It might seem natural to take πνεύματι as an instrumental dat.,[554] but this is ruled out in the case of σαρκί, so that here, as in 1 Tm. 3:16, one must translate : in the carnal sphere, in the spiritual sphere.[555]

Again in R. 1:3 f. it is said that Jesus Christ is the Son of David in His carnal existence and the Son of God in His spiritual existence, → II, 304, 35 ff.; V, 453, 10 ff.[556] The formula originally contains a Christology according to which Jesus is instituted the Son of God only by exaltation, Ac. 13:33; 2:36; cf. materially Mk. 9:3, 7. The community combined the insight in the schema κατὰ σάρκα/κατὰ πνεῦμα with the official view, taken over from Judaism, that Jesus is the earthly Son of David. Paul corrects this by putting υἱοῦ αὐτοῦ before the whole formula.

Even before Paul, then, πνεῦμα denotes the sphere of divine glory (→ I, 114, 27 ff.) into which the Redeemer enters on His exaltation.[557] The OT antithesis between the Holy Spirit of God and the weak and sinful flesh (Is. 31:3) is here in the process of adopting Hell. features prepared already in the distinction made by Apocalyptic and Rabbinism between the lower and the upper worlds. If the Jew thinks this world is stamped by its rebellion against God or at least by its corruptibility, for the Hellenist its substance is alien to God.[558] Man's existence here is controlled by the sphere, the field of force, in which it is set.[559] But if the sphere really controls existence, entry into the pneumatic sphere also means entry into pneumatic existence. Hence Christ, having entered into this, must Himself be called πνεῦμα, and, though this is formally a statement about His substance, materially it is a statement about His power, i.e., His significance for the community.

---

[551] δόξα (→ II, 244, 28 ff. 246, 2 ff., 247 f., 252 f.), like πνεῦμα (→ n. 357, 369; cf. 1 C. 15:43 f.: δόξα = δύναμις = πνευματικόν Reitzenstein Hell. Myst., 358-361), denotes the nature of God, but also of the angels (→ II, 251, 34 ff.). On ὤφθη ἀγγέλοις → n. 372 f., on δικαιωθῆναι → II, 214, 25 ff. and Schweizer (→ n. 351), 64 f.

[552] Dib. Past.³, ad loc.

[553] For details cf. H. Windisch, "Zur Christologie d. Past.," ZNW, 34 (1935), 222 f. If the formulation goes back to the enthronement ceremonial in ancient Egypt (J. Jeremias, Die Briefe an Tm. u. Tt., NT Deutsch, 9⁵ [1949], ad loc.) it is even clearer 1. that the language is Egypt. Hell., 2. that the theme is exaltation and endowment with divine quality, presentation to the heavenly and earthly world, and enthronement.

[554] So already Calvin, In NT Comm., ed. A. Tholuck (1838), ad loc.; cf. materially 1 C. 15:42; 2 C. 3:6; R. 8:11?; Ez. 37.

[555] Schweizer (→ n. 353), 569. In no sense "is the person of Jesus split into flesh and spirit" (Wnd. Kath. Br., ad loc.; cf. also Bieder, op. cit. [→ n. 540], 103-105); for if πνεῦμα is taken as = ψυχή (E. Kühl, Die Briefe Petri u. Judae, Krit.-exegetischer Komm. über d. NT by H. A. Meyer⁶ [1897], ad loc.) or = the eternal divine πνεῦμα (Wbg. Pt., ad loc.), the ζωοποιηθείς is unintelligible. For detailed par. in the confessions in 1 Tm. 3:16 and 1 Pt. 3:18-22 cf. E. G. Selwyn, The First Epistle of St. Peter (1947), 325.

[556] Cf. P. Althaus, Der Brief an d. Römer, NT Deutsch, 6⁸ (1954), ad loc., and the influence on the Christology of Ignatius (Sm., 1, 1 f.; R., 7, 3; Eph., 18, 2) and Irenaeus (Epid., 30). On patristic exposition of R. 1:3 f. cf. K. H. Schelkle, Pls., Lehrer d. Väter (1956), 21-26.

[557] Cf. Phil. 2:9-11; Rev. 5; E. Käsemann, "Das wandernde Gottesvolk," FRL, NF, 37 (1939), 58-74 for Hb. and Gnosticism.

[558] 1 Tm. 3:16 is probably close to this, while R. 1:3 f. is still strongly Jewish.

[559] E. Käsemann, "Krit. Analyse v. Phil. 2:5-11," ZThK, 47 (1950), 331. Hence knowledge of the whence and whither controls man (Bu. J., 210, n. 6). For a modern formulation cf. C. Michalson, "The Holy Spirit and the Church," Theology Today, 8 (1951/52), 43 f.

Paul shares the idea of a spiritual body of the exalted κύριος which embraces all the members, → n. 377. This may be seen already in the natural way in which he speaks about the → σῶμα Χριστοῦ. He is obviously presupposing this, not introducing it. [560] It may also be seen in the phrase ἐν Χριστῷ. [561] The idea is also present in 1 C. 12:13. The obvious identification of the ἕν σῶμα with ὁ Χριστός in v. 12 shows that this does not merely denote the goal reached with the coming together of the members; on the contrary, it denotes the existing body into which believers are baptised. [562] The ideas are thus consistent. The body is the pneumatic element into which believers are integrated and with which they are all made to drink, v. 13b. [563] It is probable that the ἐν πνεύματι of v. 13a is to be taken instrumentally as in 1 C. 6:11. [564] The force which effects the incorporation, however, is again understood substantially as an element, par. to the common ἐν ὕδατι. [565]

If here the relation between πνεῦμα and σῶμα Χριστοῦ is not entirely clear, the κύριος is identified with the πνεῦμα in 2 C. 3:17.

This exegesis is, of course, contested. [566] The saying is regarded as a note in interpretation of the quotation, so that it is to the effect that the κύριος mentioned in the quotation means the Spirit (which would require τὸ δὲ κύριος acc. to Gl. 4:25). [567] Hence turning to the Spirit signifies removing of the veil, and in v. 17b the Spirit is more precisely defined as the Spirit of Jesus. The arguments in favour of this view are not entirely cogent. The saying is in no sense a casual and dispensable christological note. In v. 6 and v. 8 the new ministry is depicted as that which is controlled by the πνεῦμα, not the γράμμα. It is then shown that the unbelieving Jew still lives under the veil which is done away only ἐν Χριστῷ (v. 14). Turning to the κύριος (= Χριστός in v. 14 as always, → III, 1087, 5 ff.) takes the veil away. The statement that this κύριος is the Spirit connects the two trains of thought. The exalted κύριος to whom Israel must turn instead of to Moses (cf. R. 10:4 f.; 1 C. 10:2) is identified with the πνεῦμα. This shows that turning to Him means turning to the new διακονία in the πνεῦμα. It is not wholly true that, while Paul ascribes the same functions to Christ and the Spirit, [568] he does not elsewhere equate them, → lines 419, 7 ff.; 16 ff. Nor can appeal be made to R. 1:4 in favour of a different view, → 417, 10 ff.

---

[560] Schweizer, op. cit. (→ n. 351), 156-160. This does not rule out the influence of OT ideas or of the thought of the body given for us on the cross, cf. E. Schweizer, Lordship and Discipleship, c. 4.

[561] → II, 541, 48 ff.; Käsemann, op. cit. (→ n. 401), 168.

[562] Ltzm. K.⁴ (with Kümmel against Ltzm.), ad loc. Barth, op. cit. (→ n. 527), 332-337 interprets : baptised into the body of Christ.

[563] Pr.-Bauer, s.v. On the image of the pouring out of the Spirit cf. Bu. J., 133, n. 5; Thornton, op. cit., 89-91. Drinking gives inspiration, Tat. Or. Graec., 19, 3. In view of the aor. v. 13b probably refers also to baptism rather than the Lord's Supper (with Kümmel [Ltzm. K.⁴, ad loc.]; G. Friedrich, "Geist u. Amt," Wort u. Dienst, 3 [1952], 65, n. 17 against E. Käsemann, "Anliegen u. Eigenart d. paul. Abendmahlslehre," Ev. Theol., 7 [1947/48], 267). If so, this is the only v. in which Paul expressly attributes possession of the Spirit to baptism, cf. Büchsel, 427.

[564] Thornton, op. cit., 89.

[565] Hence πνεῦμα can be either the causative power of baptism (13a) or the new "element" mediated thereby (13b); cf. Flemington, op. cit., 69. Why do Lk. 3:16; Ac. 1:5; 11:16 always have ὕδατι but ἐν πνεύματι (ibid., 39, n. 2)?

[566] Cf. K. Prümm, "Die katholische Auslegung von 2 K. 3:17a in den letzten vier Jahrzehnten," Biblica, 31 (1950), 316-345; 32 (1951), 1-24; B. Schneider, Dominus autem Spiritus est (1951); in English Davies, op. cit. (→ n. 545), 196, n. 1; C. H. Dodd, History and the Gospel (1938), 55-57; for patristic exegesis cf. J. Lebreton, Les origines du dogme de la Trinité (1910), 492.

[567] Kümmel (Ltzm. K.⁴, ad loc.), with bibl.; E. Fuchs, "Warum fordert der Glaube von uns ein Selbstverständnis?" ZThK, 48 (1951), 357; Wendland, 459.

[568] 1 Th. 1:5; 2 K. 12:9; Phil. 4:13; cf. C. A. A. Scott, Christianity acc. to St. Paul (1927), 260; cf. also 2 C. 4:10 f. and Col. 3:4; Gl. 5:25 and 2 C. 3:6; Friedrich, op. cit., 63 f.

It is thus maintained that the exalted Christ is the πνεῦμα and that turning to Him entails entry into the sphere of the πνεῦμα. Whosoever comes to Him comes into this sphere. [569] If κύριος and πνεῦμα are distinguished in v. 17b, this simply makes it plain that v. 17a is not asserting the identity of two personal entities. πνεῦμα is defined as the mode of existence of the κύριος. Where there is reference to the πνεῦμα κυρίου, His mode of existence is depicted, and this means the power in which He encounters His community. [570] In so far as Christ is regarded in His significance for the community, in His powerful action upon it, He can be identified with the πνεῦμα. In so far as He is also Lord over His power, He can be differentiated from it, just as the I can be distinguished from the power which goes out from it. The same idea is stated even more precisely in 1 C. 6:17, for here there is a reference to the spiritual body of the exalted Lord which includes believers within it. This union of believers to Christ is regarded as fully analogous to sexual union with a harlot. This is given added emphasis inasmuch as licentiousness is viewed as the worst sin because it takes place in the body and thus affects the union with Christ with particular force. [571] It is declared expressly in 1 C. 15:45 that Christ became a πνεῦμα ζωοποιοῦν in the resurrection. [572] The endowing of believers with a → σῶμα πνευματικόν [573] is connected herewith. The whole argument rests on the assumption that Christ, like Adam, encloses a whole humanity within Himself. With this understanding, which is influenced by the OT idea of the fathers as well as by Hellenism, [574] Paul is contending that the resurrection

---

[569] It is not correct, however, that acc. to 1 C. 9:1 the freedom of a "lonely soul" chained to no tradition is based on vision of the pneumatic Christ, Reitzenstein Hell. Myst., 379 f.; → n. 615.

[570] The expression "spirit of Christ" is very rare in Pl. (cf. R. 8:9; Phil. 1:19; Gl. 4:6; Friedrich, op. cit., 62 f.). On v. 18 → II, 696 f.; IV, 758, 17 ff. (but cf. Dupont, op. cit. [→ n. 204], 126 f., who interprets "to reflect"). The πνεῦμα grants miraculous vision and transformation into the δόξα of what is seen, → II, 396, 32 ff.; 251, 12 ff. E. Fuchs (in a letter) sees the reflection fulfilled in mutual encounter within the community. Whether in κύριος πνεύματος this is a gen. qual. (like κύριος τῆς δόξης), i.e., "the Lord who is Spirit," is open to question, cf. Ltzm. K.⁴, ad loc.; if not, it is to be taken in the light of v. 17b.

[571] This is traditional (Prv. 6:23-35; Muson. Dissertationes, 12 [p. 65, 8] in Ltzm. K.⁴, ad loc.). The ἓν πνεῦμα is not emphasising the different nature of the union (ibid. with Kümmel against Ltzm.); Pl. has also put σῶμα for the σάρξ of the quotation. The three terms are thus interchangeable, E. Percy, Der Leib Christi (1942), 14 f. In the πνεῦμα Christ is the world-embracing σῶμα, Käsemann, op. cit. (→ n. 563), 282 f. Paul simply varies them as one or the other aspect is more strongly to the fore.

[572] There can be no thought of the creation of the pre-existent Lord before the world, Joh. W. 1 K., ad loc.; M. Werner, Die Entstehung d. chr. Dogmas (1941), 305. The twofold creation in Philo (Leg. All., I, 31) whereby the heavenly man was created first and then the earthly man (πνεῦμα and ψυχή for the Gnostic, Ltzm. K., ad loc.) is not in view, for vv. 20 ff., 46 show that the ref. is to the resurrection, just as ζωοποιεῖν is used only soteriologically and not cosmologically in the NT, → II, 874, 32 ff. The par. with Adam is not under Philo's influence; it derives from the concept of the primal man presupposed already in v. 21 f. and R. 5:12-21, → I, 142 f.; 366, 8 ff. but not → II, 396, 2 ff.; cf. Nyberg, op. cit. (→ n. 337), 311. This enables Pl. to add the decisive terms πρῶτος and 'Αδάμ in v. 45 and to draw the conclusion in v. 45. W. Michaelis, Zur Engelchristologie im Urchr. (1942), n. 71, but not Burney, op. cit. (→ n. 467), 45-47, who traces back the quotation and exposition to a Rabb. collection. Cf. Käsemann, op. cit. (→ n. 401), 166, and on speculations about Adam Staerk, op. cit. (→ n. 307), 7-61.

[573] The idea of a body of the human πνεῦμα which can live apart from earthly bodies (Burton, Galatians, 489; Selwyn, op. cit. [→ n. 555], 282 f.) is quite impossible.

[574] Cf. Schweizer, op. cit. (→ n. 351), 156-160.

(or exaltation) sets Christ in the sphere of the Spirit, and that union with Him ensures believers of spiritual life, which is life in the community. [575]

c. Correction in the Light of Primitive Christian Eschatology.

In 1 C. 15 the event of the resurrection is Paul's starting-point. Hence he differs from the Gnostic, for whom myth simply renders the service of kindling recollection of a reality already alive within him. The resurrection has completely altered the situation. Hence it is no accident that Paul, unlike the Gnostic, never speaks of the spiritual substance of the pre-existent Lord. This means, however, that the thought of the spiritual body of the exalted Lord is for him merely an aid to clarifying for the community the meaning of the event of the resurrection of Jesus for their own resurrection. In 1 C. 15:35-50 Paul undoubtedly begins with the ideas of the Corinthians. But he refutes them by understanding the σῶμα πνευματικόν, not as something which is already given to the believer, and which simply outlasts death, but as something which is yet to be given by God in the resurrection. Hence he does not speak of the πνεῦμα ζῶν whose vitality is contagious, but of the πνεῦμα ζωοποιοῦν, i.e., of the creative act of the Risen Lord. [576]

> There is no thought whatever of a pneumatic body concealed under the earthly body. [577] Indeed, Pl. is expressly rejecting this view acc. to v. 46. Since v. 45 is simply documenting the thesis of v. 44b, v. 46 refers to this rather than to v. 45, [578] so that σῶμα must be supplied, → I, 143, 12 ff. Pl. is not refuting an idea which would replace the eschatological coming of the Redeemer by a doctrine of a pre-existent primal man (→ n. 572). He is contending against a belief which regards the pneumatic σῶμα as original, as proper to man as such, so that it does not have to be given to him for the first time in the resurrection. It is true that v. 44b seems to presuppose that his opponents know nothing of this. Nevertheless, v. 29 makes it clear that they still reckon with a life after death. [579] They know a pneumatic body, not in Paul's sense, but in the Gnostic sense, acc. to which it is hidden under the psychic body and will survive after death. [580] Hence Paul uses φορέσομεν in v. 49, → II, 396, n. 100. If Christ, like Adam, shapes the humanity belonging to him, then it is natural for the Corinthians to conclude that all who belong to Him are already ἐπουράνιοι. For Paul, however, they "are"

---

[575] The reality of this statement is the correct pt. in the interpretation in W. Bousset, *Kyrios Christos*² (1921), 120-145. Cf. Joh. W. 1 K. on 15:44a. More cautious and pertinent are the remarks of J. Knox, *Chapters in a Life of Pl.* (1950), 128-140; K. H. Rengstorf, *Die Auferstehung Jesu* (1952), 64-67 about the new creation which is achieved in the resurrection of Jesus and into which the believer is assumed. Cf. C. H. Dodd, *The Epistle of Pl. to the Romans, Moffatt NT Comm.* (1932), on R. 6:6; J. Moffatt, *The First Epistle of Pl. to the Cor., ibid.* (1945), on 1 Cor. 15:44.

[576] There is an even sharper distinction in F. W. Grosheide, *Comm. on the First Epistle to the Cor.* (1953), 387 on 1 C. 15:45ab, who thinks Christ is made a πνεῦμα ζωοποιοῦν by His whole work as Mediator and not specifically by the resurrection.

[577] O. Cullmann, "La délivrance anticipée du corps humain d'après le NT," *Hommage et Reconnaissance à K. Barth* (1946), 31; Bertrams, 130-132 against Schweitzer, *op. cit.* (→ n. 548), 99 f.; Ltzm. K., *ad loc.* and 2 C. 5:5. Cf. also 2 C. 4:11, where the new life is made manifest in (not under) our mortal flesh and Kümmel (Ltzm. K.⁴, *ad loc.*). The traditional image from the plant world (Str.-B., II, 551; III, 475; Kn. Cl., 87; Nyberg, *op. cit.* [→ n. 337], 311) is naturally not to be understood in terms of evolution.

[578] As against Michaelis, *op. cit.* (→ n. 572), n. 76; W. Schmithals, *Die Gnosis in Korinth* (1956), 136 f.

[579] The exposition "with ref. to deceased Chr. relatives" (M. Raeder, "Vikariatstaufe in 1 C. 15:29 ?" ZNW, 46 [1955], 258-260) seems to me to be too artificial.

[580] On 2 C. 5:1-10 cf. R. Bultmann, "Exegetische Probleme d. 2 K.," Symbolae Biblicae Upsalienses, 9 (1947), 3-12; though cf. also Kümmel (Ltzm. K.⁴, *ad loc.*); Schmithals, *op. cit.*, 223-236; Bertrams, 138-142 and → 422, 24 f.

this only in faith in the One who will one day make them this, not by their physical distinction from non-pneumatics.[581]

But the idea that σῶμα as a form represents the continuum which simply exchanges the carnal substance for the spiritual substance[582] is also quite untenable. The true concern of Paul may be seen in the fact that ψυχικός (v. 44) on the one side is interpreted by φθορά (v. 42, 50), ἀσθένεια and ἀτιμία (v. 43; cf. Phil. 3:21 ταπείνωσις), and πνευματικός on the other side is interpreted by ἀφθαρσία (v. 42, 50), δύναμις and δόξα (v. 43; Phil. 3:21). Behind the form of thinking in terms of substance there thus lies the OT distinction between weakness and power.[583] Man is referred to the creative power of his Lord, who will raise him up.[584] Continuity between the earthly and the heavenly body rests on a miracle.[585] The same is to be seen in v. 47, where the first clause with γῆ denotes the stuff from which the first man is made, while the second clause characterises the second man, not by the substance of which he consists[586] but by his origin.[587] Thus the σῶμα πνευματικόν of either Redeemer or believer is to be understood, not as one which consists of πνεῦμα, but as one which is controlled by the πνεῦμα.[588] It must be realised, however, that this applies only to the concern of Paul. It is obvious in his terminology that like any Hellenist he thinks of power in terms of substance, → n. 347. Hence the matter in Paul is Jewish, his vocabulary Hellenistic.

Similarly in 1 C. 6:14 the starting-point is the resurrection of Jesus and the stress is on the futurity[589] of the resurrection of the body for believers. It is again clear that the idea of the consubstantiality of the believer with Christ, which the par. with bodily union in the sexual act seems to express (→ 419, 11 ff.), does not control the statements; it simply illustrates the interrelationship between the two creative acts of God, the resurrection of Jesus and that of all believers. Here again, therefore, → σῶμα is not just a physical substance. It is differentiated from the κοιλία (→ III, 788, 5 ff.), to which the promise of resurrection does not apply, v. 13. That it can be absorbed by ἡμεῖς shows that for Pl. the sexual act is controlled esp. by the personal relation. Thus the union of the believer with Christ, though bodily, is thought of in personal rather than physical terms.

---

[581] As against Reitzenstein Hell. Myst., 348.

[582] Ltzm. K., ad loc.; but the σώματα change acc. to v. 37 f., and in vv. 39 ff. σάρξ, σῶμα, δόξα are par., Kümmel, ibid.[4]

[583] Cf. R. 6:19; 8:26 (Dupont, op. cit. [→ n. 204], 273); that δόξα is not a material ray of light may be seen from 2 C. 3:8-4:6 (in spite of 3:7, cf. Bertrams, 115-118).

[584] In this sense the pneumatic belongs to the ἐπίγειοι (v. 48 f., 40; cf. Allo, 342; the aor. ἐφορέσαμεν is to be construed in the light of the fut. φορέσομεν).

[585] Käsemann, op. cit. (→ n. 401), 134. When Bertrams, 94 f. defines πνεῦμα as the power which increasingly permeates man until he becomes wholly πνεῦμα he overlooks the significance of the miracle of creation in the resurrection. On the other hand, 1 C. 15:45 cannot be reduced to the thought that the Risen Lord simply takes on the function of the Creator πνεῦμα of Gn. 1:2 (Scott, op. cit. [→ n. 568], 259), though the concern of Paul is along these lines. The ἐγένετο εἰς shows that the ideas mentioned → 419, 16 ff. are in the background.

[586] Bertrams, 136.

[587] But cf. Rengstorf, op. cit. (→ n. 575), 91, n. 9. To be sure, this is not instruction about the incarnation or the parousia, but a qualification of Christ (Michaelis, op. cit., 42 and n. 86). Nevertheless, Christ is qualified, not by the matter of which He consists (there is no ref. to the pneumatic nature of the pre-existent Lord), but by the fact that God has sent Him. The externally complete par. masks the fact that Paul is emphasising materiality ἐκ γῆς and mission ἐξ οὐρανοῦ.

[588] Bchm. K.[3] on 1 C. 15:44a/b; Kümmel (Ltzm. K.[4], ad loc.).

[589] With Kümmel (Ltzm. K.[4], ad loc.). That believers are already raised is taught for the first time only in Col. 2:12; 3:1, and even there we have the qualifying διὰ πίστεως (2:12), cf. 3:3 f.

R. 8:11 (→ I, 313, 35 ff.; II, 361, 13 ff.; 867, 7 ff.) also starts with the event of the resurrection and presupposes the futurity of the raising up of believers [590] "on account of" the Spirit who dwells in them. [591] Here, however, there is no idea of a guaranteeing substance. [592] Two thoughts are brought together : 1. the God who has raised up Jesus is already at work in them by the πνεῦμα and will also continue to work after death ; [593] the natural man, as a sinner, has fallen victim to death (v. 10), but the one who is righteous in virtue of the work of the πνεῦμα (→ 427, 5 ff.) will rise again (v. 11).

The fact that substantial thinking is not finally predominant in 2 C. 3:17 either may be seen both from the afore-mentioned change to πνεῦμα κυρίου in v. 17b and also from the use of the definite article with πνεῦμα. Paul starts with the developed concept of πνεῦμα, which is in no sense a miraculous substance (→ 428, 34 ff.), and then explains that the κύριος is this πνεῦμα. This means that he adopts the prevailing view of the spiritual body of the exalted Lord and uses it to express something which lies quite outside the category of the substantial. [594]

d. πνεῦμα as a Sign of What is to Come.

If the resurrection on the one side, the *parousia* with the resurrection of believers on the other, is the decisive event, then the Spirit, as in the primitive community, must be understood as a sign of that which is yet to come. Since the event of the resurrection of Jesus the resurrection at the end of the ages is no longer an indefinite hope ; the present reality of the Spirit is a pledge of the reality of what is to come. Thus Paul can describe the πνεῦμα as ἀπαρχή for the awaited redemption of the body (R. 8:23) or as ἀρραβών for the new "house" which awaits us (2 C. 5:5; 1:22). [595] He can also adopt the view that extraordinary and miraculous acts are to be ascribed to the Spirit, → II, 311, 14 ff. [596] In 1 Th. 5:19 πνεῦμα is par. to προφητεῖαι and denotes a power which manifests itself in an extraordinary way. [597] The only question is whether there is a specific ref. here

---

[590] A non-eschatological ref. to awakening to righteousness (Ltzm. R., *ad loc.*) is most improbable, for νεκρόν (v. 10) is replaced by θνητά.

[591] The acc., found three times in Orig. and unequivocal in Tert., is to be preferred as the *lectio difficilior* (G. Volkmar, *Paulus' Römerbrief* [1875], 93), for πνεῦμα is never creative power in Pl. except in an allusion in 1 C. 15:45.

[592] As against Mithr. Liturg., 176 f. ("abs. non-Jewish"), cf. also Bu. J., 175, n. 12, where comparison is made with Jn. 6:53, and Robinson, *op. cit.* (→ n. 396), 72.

[593] → 422, 20 ff.; cf. E. Gaugler, *Der Brief an d. Römer* (1945), *ad loc.*

[594] Scott, *op. cit.* (→ n. 568), 259 f., has the following interpretation : the κύριος (Christ) represents (signifies for believers) the πνεῦμα.

[595] Τοῦ πνεύματος is in all 3 instances gen. appos. (so already in Eph. 1:14 even if ὅς is original, cf. Ew. Gefbr., *ad loc.*), not gen. part. as in the LXX (→ I, 475, 12; Bl.-Debr. § 167; E. Fuchs, *Die Freiheit des Glaubens* [1949], *ad loc.*; as against → I, 486, 12; Pr.-Bauer,⁴ on ἀπαρχή; P. Menoud, *Le Sort des Trépassés* [1945], 34). Otherwise the full outpouring of the Spirit would have to be either one which embraces all creation (H. A. W. Meyer, *Der Brief d. Pls. an d. Römer*⁴ [1865]; Ltzm. R., *ad loc.*) or an endowment with the spiritual body of the resurrection (Michaelis, n. 59; cf. Ltzm. K. on 2 C. 5:5 [p. 117]), and neither of these is conceivable. On ἀρραβών as a term in commercial law cf. → I, 475, 4 ff.; Pr.-Bauer,⁴ *s.v.*; on the whole problem Cullmann, *op. cit.* (→ n. 577), 31-42.

[596] The Gnostic, too, might say this. For him, however, the miracles are a demonstration of the new pneumatic substance, while for the primitive community and primarily for Pl. as well they are a prelude to God's eschatological intervention.

[597] The triadic formula in vv. 16-18a is typically rounded off in v. 18b. v. 23 is the concluding wish. Hence the section between is to be taken as a unity. As the δέ shows, after the negatives of v. 19 f. the positive formulation is introduced in v. 21a and then

to glossolalia, → I, 724, 6 ff. 2 Th. 2:2, however, is certainly not to be construed thus, for the πνεῦμα makes a definite utterance there. Eph. 5:18 seems to have an ecstatic event in view, but acc. to v. 17 this can hardly be glossolalia.[598] In 1 C. 14:37 (→ I, 724, 11 ff.), as in v. 1, πνευματικός is to be regarded as a master concept, under which προφήτης is a special type. This is also the sense in 1 Th. 5:19.[599] In antithesis to νοῦς, πνεῦμα is in 1 C. 14:14-16 the miraculous power which confers the gift of tongues, but the emphasis there is simply on the non-participation of νοῦς, and it may be that v. 15 is not describing two different possibilities but the union of πνεῦμα and νοῦς which is needed in gatherings of the community. In 1 C. 2:4 f. the ἀπόδειξις πνεύματος καὶ δυνάμεως is differentiated from the σοφίας λόγοι and σοφία ἀνθρώπων, and indeed from the λόγος generally in 1 Th. 1:5, cf. → II, 312, 12 f. In R. 15:19 δύναμις πνεύματος is par. to δύναμις σημείων καὶ τεράτων,[600] and πνεῦμα to δυνάμεις in Gl. 3:5. The πνεῦμα is thus everywhere understood as something whose reception may be verified.[601] Paul, e.g., can list glossolalia, gifts of healing and miraculous powers among the works of the Spirit, 1 C. 12:9 f., 28-30; 14:18-26; → II, 315, 15 ff.[602] The formal similarity of the manifestations to the ecstatic phenomena of paganism is so broad that Paul gives the Corinthians a criterion by which they can distinguish the expressions of the Spirit from those of other derivation, namely, confession of Christ as Kurios, 1 C. 12:2 f.[603]

> The same problem is to be found everywhere in the early Church. 1 Jn. 4:2 gives precision to the dogmatic formula. Mt. 7:16; Did., 11, 7-12 find the criterion in the ethical conduct of the prophet, while his positive relation to the community is also taken into account in Herm. m., 11, 7-16. In the last two passages the sudden and sporadic manifestation of the Spirit is also a positive criterion. In Ps.-C. 3 ff.[604] the authority of the apostle is invoked. Ps.-Clem. Hom., 2, 6-11 regards the fulfilment of predictions as a proof of authenticity, cf. Recg., 4, 21.

The fact that Paul presupposes such phenomena in Thessalonica as well as Galatia, in the church of Rome, which he did not found, as well as that of Corinth, seems to show that this is not just the accompanying remnant of a primitive concept. In some sense Paul is even more naïve than Luke in regarding all miraculous

---

divided into 2 possibilities in 21b and 22, → II, 375, 15 ff.; J. Jeremias, *Unbekannte Jesusworte* (1948), 76-78; there is no hint of a ref. to the eucharist (H. Schlier, "Die Verkündigung im Gottesdienst d. Kirche," *Die Zeit d. Kirche* [1956], 255 f.).

[598] Dib. Gefbr.³, *ad loc.*

[599] As against Gunkel, 19; → Bertrams, 37; cf. on the whole subject Dob. Th. on 1 Th. 5:19 and 2 Th. 2:2; Verbeke, 402.

[600] It is possible that the λόγῳ is meant to be caught up again in a chiastic sequence, but this is not likely in the light of 1 C. 2:4 f.; 4:20; 1 Th. 1:5 (cf. 2 C. 12:12).

[601] Gl. 3:2; Dodd, *op. cit.* (→ n. 458), 51 f.; L. Cerfaux, *La théologie de l'Eglise suivant St. Paul* (1948), 129 f.

[602] Cf. further Bultmann Theol., 152 f.

[603] A ref. to court testimony is impossible in the context. 1 C. as a whole does not speak of persecution, and 11-14 deal only with divine worship (with Kümmel, Ltzm. K.⁴, *ad loc.* as opposed to the scholars cited there). V. 2 undoubtedly refers to ecstatic phenomena: Liv., 39, 13, 11-13; Hdt., IV, 79; Tert. Nat., II, 7 (though cf. Dg., 9, 1; Dupont, *op. cit.*, 149, n. 2). On the whole problem cf. also → n. 689; Schmithals, *op. cit.*, 45-52. For the history of exegesis cf. G. de Broglie, "Le texte fondamental de St. Paul contre la foi naturelle," *Recherches de science religieuse*, 39 (1951/52), 253-266, who understands ἀνάθεμα ᾽Ιησοῦς simply as a counterpart to κύριος ᾽Ιησοῦς along the lines of Holtzmann: "Just as (self-evidently) no one curses Jesus in the Spirit of God, so . . ." The pt. of the saying, then, is that no one can believe or confess except in the power of the Spirit.

[604] Ed. P. Vetter, *Der apokr. dritte Korintherbrief* (1894), 52 f., 58.

phenomena as manifestations of the Spirit, for he does not accept the later Jewish Rabbinic restriction to the πνεῦμα προφητείας. The provisional character of the Spirit as ἀρραβών of that which is to come is also more clearly evident in Paul than it is in Luke.

We have pointed out that the Hellenistic view of the spiritual body (→ 418, 21 ff.), which emphasised the presence of the Spirit now, underwent a notable correction whereby the Spirit became the pledge of that which is not yet. We now find something of the same in the reverse sense. Not only does Paul, like Luke (→ 410, 11 ff.), insist that all members of the community are bearers of the Spirit, [605] R. 8:9. Above all, and unlike Luke, he deduces therefrom that the manifestations of the Spirit do not have to be extraordinary. Thus, in distinction from the Corinthians, he reckons among such manifestations ἀντιλήμψεις and κυβερνήσεις, [606] or διακονία and ἐλεεῖν, μεταδιδόναι and προῖστασθαι, R. 12:7 f. [607] An even more vital point is that Paul obviously plays down speaking with tongues, which was for the Corinthians the most striking and hence the most important of the gifts of the Spirit. [608] This shows that the criterion of the extraordinary was fundamentally irrelevant. [609] Pagan religions could meet this test, 1 C. 12:2. The criterion by which the worth or worthlessness of the gifts of the Spirit is to be measured is confession of the κύριος Ἰησοῦς, and therewith the οἰκοδομή, the συμφέρον of the community. [610] But this implies a completely new understanding, → 432, 12 ff.

2. Paul's Own Interpretation.

a. The Problem.

A distinctive dialectic has come to light. Paul adopted the Hell. line because here for the first time there was presented with impressive consistency an opportunity to interpret πνεῦμα as the new existence, and this new existence as relationship to the Redeemer. But Paul corrected all the naturalistic statements and also adopted the line controlled by the OT. This clearly expressed the fact that salvation is not a possession at man's disposal. But here, too, Paul had to make a correction. If the new creation was already present, the Spirit could not be merely a preliminary sign of what was still to come, a mere exception. The Spirit had to represent the new existence as such.

The new understanding of the Spirit which unites both concerns is essentially controlled also by the fact the event which had been the decisive stumbling-block for Paul could now be regarded as the decisive event of salvation. This was the cross.

---

[605] In some passages πνευματικός seems to refer to a narrower group (Gunkel, 19 : pre-Pauline ; Bultmann Theol., 156 f.: Gnostic). But 1 C. 14:37 → 423, 3 ff. and Gl. 6:1 cannot be taken thus. 1 C. 2:13-3:3 does not describe a group of ecstatics as πνευματικοί, but those who understand the message of the cross → 425, 2 ff. and 437, 3 ff., so that what is stated in 3:1-3 is simply that believers are constantly exposed to the temptation to become unbelievers, cf. Scott, op. cit. (→ n. 568), 147 f.; Fuchs, 50. Nevertheless, the idea of the extraordinary nature of the πνεῦμα still had such an influence that οἱ πνευματικοί was never used for the community like οἱ ἄγιοι, οἱ ἐν Χριστῷ, Cerfaux, op. cit. (→ n. 601), 161.

[606] 1 C. 12:28; that they are not mentioned in v. 29 f. shows that these were not gifts sought in Corinth.

[607] Hence the Spirit is not distinguished by His sudden and sporadic coming (1 C. 14:30), but esp. by His abiding indwelling, Bertrams, 92-94, though → 423, 24 f.

[608] 1 C. 14. He values it, however, for private edification.

[609] For this reason he can as little whittle down God's present work in the Spirit to ἐκστῆναι of the ψυχή as he can whittle down the resurrection of the dead by God's creative power to Hell. ἐκδημῆσαι in death (on Hellenism cf. Reitzenstein Hell. Myst., 372).

[610] → V, 140 f.; 1 C. 14:3-5, 12, 26; 12:7; cf. Schrenk, op. cit. (→ n. 401), 124-127.

b. πνεῦμα as the Power of πίστις.

1. C. 2:6-16 is based on Paul's claim that he has nothing to preach but Christ crucified, v. 2. In this section Paul defines the πνεῦμα as the miraculous power which mediates supernatural knowledge, σοφία ἐν μυστηρίῳ ἀποκεκρυμμένη (v. 7), in distinction from ἀνθρωπίνη σοφία (v. 13). In so doing, he is formally adopting the same understanding as that which was widespread in the community as influenced both by the OT and also by Hellenism. The miraculous power πνεῦμα determines both the content and form of preaching, and it is thus perceptible only to the spiritual. [611] But what is the content of this spiritual instruction? Paul's answer is formally Gnostic : τὰ βάθη τοῦ θεοῦ (v. 10 → I, 517, 23 ff.; cf. → II, 656, 42 ff. and 657, n. 8). In content, however, it is not at all Gnostic : God's saving work at the cross. According to v. 12b the content is τὰ ὑπὸ τοῦ θεοῦ χαρισθέντα ἡμῖν. According to 1:24 the σοφία θεοῦ, which is revealed by the πνεῦμα in 2:7-10, is simply Χριστὸς ἐσταυρωμένος (1:23; 2:2); this is confirmed in 2:8. [612] According to 2:14 it is μωρία for the non-spiritual, cf. 1:23. [613] The Christian Gnostic could regard the cross only as a stratagem to deceive demons lest they should hamper the saving event of exaltation, → n. 370. A decisive step is taken here. The cross is seen to be the already accomplished crisis which divides the new creation from the old. With the Hellenists, then, Paul regards the Spirit as the power which takes man out of this aeon and sets him in that aeon, v. 6. But he also carries out a decisive correction. The union of the believer with the κύριος is not granted in pneumatic materiality. It is granted with the knowledge which the πνεῦμα gives of the One who was crucified for him. [614]

It is thus plain how Paul can take up the idea of the spiritual body of the κύριος. Once the substantial is regarded as only a form of thought for the power which alone is vital to the Israelite, it simply expresses the insight that the believer lives only by indissoluble union with the κύριος in whom God's saving action has been accomplished for him. In fact, then, entry into the field of force of the πνεῦμα body simply implies entry into the field of force of the saving events, i.e., into the community which lives by the cross and resurrection. But this also does justice to the OT concern that he who bears the Spirit is always referred wholly and utterly to God's work. He does not live by his new substance but by God's action at the cross. There is thus created the possibility of an understanding of the Spirit in which the πνεῦμα establishes the existence of the believer and is no longer regarded as a purely supplementary miraculous power, though without becoming the substantial possession of the φύσει σῳζόμενος. In this light it is easy to see why the extraordinary nature of the manifestations can no longer be a decisive criterion. The fact that the knowledge is supernatural no longer rests on the

---

[611] → III, 953, 23 ff., though cf. Kümmel (Ltzm. K.⁴, ad loc.). Par. showing that ὅμοιον is known ὁμοίῳ are Emped. Fr., 109 (Diels⁷, I, 351, 20 ff.); Orph. Fr., 345 (Kern); in Gnosticism Ltzm. K., ad loc.; magic texts Reitzenstein Hell. Myst., 310 f.; Mithr. Liturg., 4, 10 f. Demons of air and fire can usually be seen only by pneumatics, Tat. Or. Graec., 15, 3.

[612] Jewish authorities (J. Schniewind, "Die Archonten dieses Äons," Nachgelassene Reden u. Aufsätze [1952], 104-109) are out of the question (at most as the tool of demons, G. H. C. MacGregor, "Principalities and Powers," NT St., 1 [1954/55], 22 f.; cf. O. Cullmann, "Zur neuesten Diskussion über die ἐξουσίαι in R. 13:1," ThZ, 10 [1954], 330 f.).

[613] → I, 709, 17 ff.; IV, 819, 20 f.; cf. Thornton, op. cit. (→ n. 500), 108 f.

[614] Dodd, op. cit. (→ n. 458), 146 f. rightly emphasises that participation in the Spirit is participation in Christ and not merely in a gift dispensed by Him, though neither R. 1:4 nor 2 C. 3:17 adequately supports this, since both could be taken in a purely naturalistic sense.

fact that it is received or taught ecstatically [615] and built up logically or non-logically. The miracle is that a man may believe that God is for him in Jesus Christ. [616] The content of this supernatural knowledge is not disclosure of mysteries of the heavenly world [617] but the divine act of love effected at the cross, or the divine sonship granted to the believer thereby. [618]

Thus the πνεῦμα can be called specifically the πνεῦμα τῆς πίστεως, 2 C. 4:13. To possess the ἀρραβὼν τοῦ πνεύματος is διὰ πίστεως περιπατεῖν, 2 C. 5:5, 7. In 1 C. 12:3, in distinction from all subsidiary characteristics, knowledge and confession of Jesus as the κύριος is the gift which gives evidence of the πνεῦμα as such. Only in appearance is this contradicted in the statement in Gl. 3:14 (and 5:5?) according to which the Spirit is received διά or ἐκ πίστεως. [619] In its permanent antithesis to ἐξ ἔργων νόμου this statement is simply to the effect that no human merit has secured the Spirit. [620] According to Gl. 5:5 the content of what is received is expectation of the ἐλπὶς δικαιοσύνης, which in deed and truth is nothing other than the πίστις which understands itself in the light of the δικαιοσύνη achieved in Christ. This shows that πνεῦμα is not just an initial event. [621] The whole tradition also helps us to understand why Paul finds the work of the πνεῦμα more strongly in ongoing and outwardly oriented πιστεύειν than in the first event of πιστεῦσαι. [622] For this reason Paul in Gl.4:6, unlike R. 8:16, [623] can trace back to the Spirit the concrete life in sonship, and not just the knowledge of sonship. [624] He is simply insisting in this that the πνεῦμα is not merely a mysterious force which appears prior to πίστις and explains its genesis,

---

[615] As against Schweitzer, op. cit. (→ n. 548), 172 (cf. → n. 569), 1 C. 15:3, e.g., shows that the spiritual revelation of 1 C. 2:6-16 does not stand in necessary antithesis to traditional formulations, → II, 172, 26 ff.

[616] Cf. Fuchs, 37 f., 119 f. The dynamic aspect, then, is not the really vital thing in Paul's concept of the Spirit, as against R. Schnackenburg, Die Johannesbriefe (1953), 209.

[617] ἡμεῖς (v. 12) can only apply to all believers, so also in v. 10 (cf. Eph. 3:18, where βάθος is also used). The βάθη τοῦ θεοῦ are the τὰ τοῦ θεοῦ of v. 11 and the τὰ ... χαρισθέντα ἡμῖν (aor.) of v. 12, so that the ref. is to the gracious action which God has already accomplished, not to something special or future. λόγοις (v. 13) can be understood only if the discussion of 2:1-5 is continued here, and 3:11, 18-23 shows that the train of thought is unbroken from 1:18 onwards. Thus 3:1-3 (with 1:7; 3:16) is to be understood in terms of the inconsistency with which the existing believer does not live by what he believes (cf. 8:7 and 8:1; R. 8:12-14 and 8:9). If we are probably to read μυστήριον at 2:1, this can only be that mentioned in 2:7. Cf. → 436, 31 ff. and E. Sjöberg, Der verborgene Menschensohn in den Evangelien (1955), 22-24.

[618] R. 5:5 (interpreted by v. 8; on 15:30 → n. 656); 8:16. In a secondary way Paul can attribute knowledge even in a concrete topical question (1 C. 7:40) or in a question of conscience (R. 9:1) to the πνεῦμα.

[619] The gen. of Gl. 3:14 is appos., Ltzm. Gl., ad loc.

[620] Perhaps Gl. 3:2, 5 uses the odd ἀκοὴ πίστεως (not ἀκοῆς πίστις) instead of πίστις because strictly this is already the work of the πνεῦμα.

[621] The first endowment with the Spirit can be in the aor, His ongoing work only in the perf., Thornton, op. cit., 82 on R. 5:5; cf. ἐκ πίστεως εἰς πίστιν, R. 1:17.

[622] For this reason it is not said that the Spirit gives faith, even verbaliter.

[623] H. Braun, Gerichtsgedanke u. Rechtfertigungslehre bei Pls., Diss. Halle (1930), 83.

[624] One can avoid this by transl. with Ltzm. Gl., ad loc.: "That you are sons (you know by the fact that) ..." Pl., however, has in view the objective υἱοθεσία which is based on the cross and which carries with it the mission of the Spirit as the power of life in this knowledge, as in R. 8:3 f., cf. Mi. R., 159. Par. to v. 4 ἐξαπέστειλεν corresponds to the first and basic sending (Pentecost), while κρᾶζον, par. to v. 5b, describes the work in the believer, as against Flemington, op. cit. (→ n. 435), 58 f.; Thornton, op. cit., 114-126; Oe. Gl., ad loc., who refer to baptism. 3:14 simply shows that Pl. is thinking of a Pentecost of Gentile Christianity, the basic outpouring of the Spirit on the Gentiles.

but that it is the force which constantly manifests itself in πίστις, [625] → 219, 34 ff.

Incorporation into the σῶμα Χριστοῦ, the saturation of the believer with the πνεῦμα (1 C. 12:13), is thus in the last analysis exactly the same as what is proclaimed in 1 C. 2:12 and R. 8:16, namely, the event that reveals and assigns to man God's saving act in Jesus Christ which makes him a son, so that he now lives hereby. [626] Because integration into the σῶμα Χριστοῦ and integration into the saving events of the cross and resurrection (= δικαιωθῆναι) are ultimately one and the same, this, too, can be ascribed to the πνεῦμα (1 C. 6:11). The ὄνομα τοῦ κυρίου is the objective cause and πνεῦμα the subjective cause of δικαιωθῆναι. Accordingly εἶναι ἐν πνεύματι is synonymous with ἐν Χριστῷ. Both denote the existence of the believer. If he lives in the sphere of the work of Christ as the One who was crucified and raised again for him, he also lives in the sphere of the work of the Spirit, who reveals Christ and imparts salvation to him. [627] On the basis of the OT, however, the orientation of the believer is still to the future gracious action of the Lord. Thus ἐλπίδα δικαιοσύνης ἀπεκδέχεσθαι (Gl. 5:5), walking in faith and not in sight (2 C. 5:7), faith in the future resurrection (2 C. 4:13 f.), [628] awareness of the coming redemption of the σῶμα (R. 8:23), ζωὴ αἰώνιος (Gl. 6:8), is presented as the gift of the πνεῦμα. [629]

If it is seriously believed, however, that the Spirit is a divine power which is not characterised by the extraordinariness of its operation, but by the fact that it makes men believers and lets them live as such, then this power can no longer be regarded as a magical force into whose hand man is hopelessly delivered up. [630] It must be regarded as the miraculous power of God which gives the man completely separated from God the possibility of consciously and affirmatively living by this power which is not his own. [631] Denoted herewith, however, is the development in which the πνεῦμα, as the power with creates faith, is also the norm by which faith lives, though a strict distinction need not always be made between them. In so far as Paul wants to stress that πνεῦμα is wholly God's gift and not man's own possibility, he regards the Spirit as power; in so far as he seeks to emphasise

---

[625] The fact that πίστις is dominant in R. 1-5, πνεῦμα in 6-8 (e.g., Braun, op. cit. [→ n. 623], 82) shows that the one, as the antithesis to works of the Law, is the precondition of the new life, whereas the other is its possibility.

[626] "Baptism with the Spirit," then, is not initiation to a higher knowledge or enabling for special acts of power, Flemington, op. cit., 56 f. As subjection to God's saving act in Christ it is the basis of all the gifts of the Spirit (1 C. 12:4-11), and it thus coincides with water baptism. Paul is indeed contending against spiritualisers, W. Bieder, "Um d. Ursprung d. chr. Taufe im NT," ThZ, 9 (1953), 165 as against Barth, op. cit. (→ n. 527), 325 f.; cf. G. W. H. Lampe, The Seal of the Spirit (1951), 56 f., cf. 60.

[627] R. 8:1, 9; cf. Bultmann Theol., 331 f. E. Lohmeyer, Grundlagen d. paul. Theol. (1929), 140 f. is right to contest the customary idea of Christ mysticism, though one should not on this account devaluate statements which also speak of a being in Christ or the Spirit. On the pt. that this always includes a being in the community → 432, 12 ff.

[628] Cf. Ltzm. K., ad loc.

[629] → II, 867, 5 ff. Cf. Schl. Theol. d. Ap., 355-360.

[630] 1 C. 14:32 (cf. 1 Th. 5:19) ascribes control of the πνεῦμα to the believer. In 1 C. 14:1, 39 he is exhorted to ζηλοῦν and warned against κωλύειν. R. 12:6 binds the prophet to the faith proclaimed by the apostle, H. v. Campenhausen, Kirchliches Amt u. geistliche Vollmacht in den ersten drei Jahrhunderten (1953), 67; cf. 60 : "The sphere of Christ and the sphere of the Holy Spirit are ... conjointly regarded as the sphere of personal decision." In 1 C. 7:40 the Spirit does not rule out rational deliberation, nor the ego in R. 8:15 f. (cf. W. Bieder, "Gebetswirklichkeit u. Gebetsmöglichkeit bei Pls.," ThZ, 4 [1948], 39 f.), nor the natural function of → συνείδησις in R. 9:1, Schweitzer, op. cit. (→ n. 548), 168-170; Gutbrod, 241. The νοῦς plays a positive role acc. to 1 C. 14:14.

[631] In Pauline terms to cease from καύχημα, → III, 648 ff., cf. → II, 866 f.

that the Spirit is the power which summons to faith and not a substance which automatically deifies, the πνεῦμα is the norm by which the believer is summoned to live. This twofoldness is most sharply expressed in the saying in Gl. 5:25 : εἰ ζῶμεν πνεύματι, πνεύματι καὶ στοιχῶμεν. The first clause maintains that the power πνεῦμα which is above man sustains his life, while in the second clause man is summoned consciously to acknowledge this fact and to let his conduct be wholly shaped thereby. [632] Negatively, then, to live in the πνεῦμα is to renounce the σάρξ; positively it is to stand in openness for God and one's neighbour.

c. πνεῦμα as Renunciation of the σάρξ.

As in the OT (→ 365, 7 ff.) the antithesis of πνεῦμα and → σάρξ is originally the antithesis between the power which is different from man and the weakness of man. [633] For this reason God, or the κύριος, or His grace or promise, can also be the counterpart to σάρξ, and in Gl. 3:2, 5 πνεῦμα is undoubtedly understood in the first instance as miraculous power (→ 423, 13 ff.). If v. 3 says that the Galatians had begun πνεύματι but wanted to finish σαρκί, this means in the first instance that they wanted to carry on in human strength. Though this is true, however, it is not wholly adequate, for σαρκί is parallel to ἐξ ἔργων νόμου and πνεύματι to ἐξ ἀκοῆς πίστεως, v. 2, 5. If the antithesis is viewed as one of principle, with no limitation merely to moments of ecstasy or miracle, πνεῦμα must be at all events the power which shapes the whole existence of the believer as one who lives by the event of salvation. In the indicative, then, πνεύματι ἐνάρχεσθαι implies that man lives, not in his own strength, but by another power, while in the imperative it carries with it a summons to fashion his life in reliance on this power rather than his own, i.e., to accept also as a norm the power which in fact shapes his life. This is clear in Phil. 3:3. πνεύματι θεοῦ λατρεύειν means οὐκ ἐν σαρκὶ πεποιθέναι; in vv. 4-6 σάρξ is defined as the totality of the qualities or deeds of which man might boast as his own, i.e., as one's own righteousness by the Law, v. 9. πνεῦμα, on the other hand, is the power of God, and hence the power of Christ. To live by this power is thus to live by this norm, and hence καυχᾶσθαι ἐν Χριστῷ Ἰησοῦ, v. 3. It is the paradoxical boasting which in faith in Christ builds solely on the δικαιοσύνη ἐκ θεοῦ which is given in Christ, and thus regards all one's own excellencies as dung, v. 8 → III, 649, 8 ff. Similarly it is plain already in 1 C. 2:6-16 (→ 425, 2 ff.) that the πνεῦμα as the miraculous power which gives man knowledge of the saving work which God has accomplished for him demands of him the renunciation of his own σοφία (vv. 1-5) and indeed any verification by human standards, v. 14 f. Again, in 2 C. 3:6 πνεῦμα is the miraculous power to which, as in the future in 1 C. 15:45, so now in the present, [634] ζωοποιεῖν is ascribed. But v. 9 shows that it is the power which reveals to man God's saving act on his behalf, enables him to live thereby, and thus gives him the chance to let go his own righteousness, → 440, 2 ff. In R. 2:29, too, the περιτομὴ καρδίας ἐν πνεύματι οὐ γράμματι includes within it a renunciation of submission to human criteria. [635] R. 7:5 f. is to be understood in a way which is

---

[632] Cf. the ind. and imp. in Phil. 3:16; Col. 3:1 etc.; Bultmann Theol., 332-335; Gutbrod, 220-223.

[633] On this whole subject cf. Schweizer, op. cit. (→ n. 353), 563-571. The antithesis can also be that of πνεῦμα and ἄνθρωπος, 1 C. 3:1-4; Ign. Eph., 5, 1 (Bultmann Theol., 152).

[634] If the one stresses that the newness of life is not a possession of man but the sovereign gift of God, the other shows that the decisive change has already taken place. This is proleptic rather than realised eschatology, H. V. Martin, "Proleptic Eschatology," Exp. T., 51 (1939/40), 88-90.

[635] For details cf. Schweizer, op. cit. (→ n. 353), 564-567, on γράμμα → I, 765 ff.

materially the same when the νόμος does not merely uncover and judge sin, but also incites thereto, whereas the πνεῦμα gives the new δουλεύειν. The only point is — and R. 8:13 makes this even clearer — that the aspect of faith which expresses itself in concrete actions is emphasised here, → 430, 27 ff. In Gl. 4:23, 29 ὁ κατὰ σάρκα γεννηθείς and ὁ κατὰ πνεῦμα are contrasted. Since γεννηθείς is not used in the second instance, and κατὰ πνεῦμα is replaced by δι(ὰ τῆς) ἐπαγγελίας in v. 23, πνεῦμα is not thought of as a seed-like generative substance (→ 340, 25 ff.), and there is certainly no suggestion of a feminine πνεῦμα which bears children as a divine mother. [636] δι(ὰ τῆς) ἐπαγγελίας is undoubtedly to be construed instrumentally. Since ἐπαγγελία in 3:18 is a direct antithesis to νόμος (→ II, 582, 22 ff.), [637] and according to 4:29 ὁ κατὰ σάρκα γεννηθείς is the one who stands under the νόμος, the concern is not to depict a marvellous birth [638] but to show that the one son lives by human possibilities, the other by God's promise of grace. Cause and norm are united again in the application. πνεῦμα defines God's promise of grace fulfilled in Jesus Christ as the cause of the new life and also as the norm by which man lives this life. If πνεῦμα was in the first instance the miraculous power which reveals God's saving action, here as a parallel to ἐπαγγελία it is even more directly the objective power of the divine promise of grace which creates this life, → 439, 24 ff. [639] In Gl. 5:17 man seems to the neutral battleground of σάρξ and πνεῦμα. But v. 16, 18 show that here, too, there is no thought of irresistible compulsion. [640] In particular, the ἵνα of v. 17 is to be taken quite seriously. [641] The purpose of both is in view. This means that even as a believer man stands both under the promise of grace and also under the threat of apostasy. It does not mean that both are at work in him at the same time, and that he is delivered up to both with no will or choice of his own. He has the chance with an already crucified σάρξ πνεύματι στοιχεῖν, v. 24 f. → 431, 5 ff. → σάρξ here is not just a force which is alien to man but his own will; the insight expressed here is that this can seize control and threaten him.

πνεῦμα clearly denotes the norm of one kind of life in Gl. 6:8. A man's life is decided by whether he sows to the πνεῦμα or to his σάρξ. Similarly in R. 8:4 f. the formula κατὰ σάρκα or κατὰ πνεῦμα περιπατεῖν is taken up again in τὰ τῆς σαρκός or τὰ τοῦ πνεύματος φρονεῖν. Here, of course, one may see again the paradox that the liberating norm of the πνεῦμα is simply the fact that God has acted and done what the νόμος could not do. [642] A point worth noting in

---

[636] As against Hirsch, op. cit. (→ n. 443), 25 f.

[637] Cf. R. 9:8, where ἐπαγγελία is the opp. of σάρξ as πνεῦμα is elsewhere.

[638] As against Dibelius, op. cit. (→ n. 442), 29 f.

[639] Cf. ζωοποιεῖ in 2 C. 3:6; but Pl. thinks more strongly in legal categories (πνεῦμα = ἀρραβών, ἀπαρχή, His activity = μαρτυρεῖν, δικαιοῦν) than in biological categories (cf. T. Preiss, "Das innere Zeugnis d. hl. Geistes," Theol. Studien, 21 [1947], 20, 23, n. 4). For this reason the πνεῦμα υἱοθεσίας is defined in R. 8:15 as the πνεῦμα which bears witness rather than gives rise to sonship.

[640] Bertrams, 71, n. 2 as against Gunkel, 73.

[641] A consecutive view in a strictly factual sequence is hardly conceivable, Bl.-Debr. § 391, 5, cf. ibid., suppl. as against Oe. Gl., ad loc.

[642] There is here no anthropological dualism whereby man is divided into two parts (so R. Leivestad, Christ the Conqueror [1954], 117 n.). The passage would have a rather different sense if the νόμος τοῦ πνεύματος were the Mosaic Law understood acc. to R. 13:8-10, Fuchs, op. cit. (→ n. 595), ad loc. In 7:23, however, νόμος must be construed as the norm, and 8:4 f. and 3:27 are to be taken similarly, Dodd, op. cit. (→ n. 350), 37. The fact that in v. 3 νόμος in the abs. again means the Law of Moses is made easier by Paul's use of this for the norm of the natural man which is determined by sin and death, v. 2.

Gl. 6:8 is that the ἑαυτοῦ used with σάρξ is not used with πνεῦμα. [643] This shows that the norm of the Spirit by which a man directs his life is not his own possibility but an alien possibility granted to him. [644] Hence the two are not on the same plane. κατὰ πνεῦμα περιπατεῖν signifies man's acceptance of the power of God which is not under his own control and which is now to shape his life instead of his own power. It is thus no accident that in R. 8:13 there is contrasted with κατὰ σάρκα, which expresses the norm, a πνεύματι, which denotes the power of the new life, → III, 453, 24 ff. Phil. 3:3 speaks even more clearly of πνεύματι θεοῦ λατρεύειν (→ IV, 64, 42 ff.) in contrast to πεποιθέναι ἐν σαρκί. [645] To live κατὰ πνεῦμα and to be free from the σάρξ is thus again quite simply to live in the field of force of God's saving work except that the emphasis here is more strongly on the decision of the believer than on what is done in him. [646] This decision of faith, however, is also interpreted as the gift of God, not as man's own act. The norm by which he decides is still in fact the power of his decision. This may be seen in the noteworthy saying in R. 8:4 that on the basis of the event of salvation the righteous demand of the Law is fulfilled in (not by) those who walk after the Spirit and not after the flesh. [647] This is even plainer in 2 C. 1:12, where the χάρις θεοῦ is the opposite of carnal activity, cf. R. 5:2.

We are thus in a completely different world from that of the Gnostics. The same antithesis was known there, but as a cosmological factor. In Paul, it is brought into being by God's act in Christ which man either accepts or rejects. [648]

d. πνεῦμα as Openness for God and One's Neighbour.

According to R. 8:15, 26 f.; Gl. 4:6 the proper act of πνεῦμα is prayer. [649] This is particularly stressed in R. 8:27, where the πνεῦμα intercedes before God for man, who does not even know what he should pray for. [650] The ethical function of the πνεῦμα is thus the same as the soteriological. The πνεῦμα bears witness to man of the sonship which has been established by God in Christ, and enables him to live therein. Freedom from the παλαιότης γράμματος, however, is δουλεύειν ἐν καινότητι πνεύματος. The παθήματα τῶν ἁμαρτιῶν to which the

---

[643] Braun, op. cit. (→ n. 623), 65.

[644] Cf. also Schlier Gl. on 5:16; Dodd, op. cit. (→ n. 575), 136 f. on R. 8:28 ff.

[645] It is clear enough (→ I, 767, 25 ff.) that πνεῦμα even in antithesis to γράμμα naturally does not denote the inner being of man in distinction from everything external (J. Goettsberger, "Die Hülle des Mose nach Ex. 34 u. 2 K. 3," BZ, 16 [1924], 10). Again, the Gk. antithesis ῥητὸν καὶ διάνοια (B. Cohen, "Note on Letter and Spirit in the NT," Harvard Theol. Review, 47 [1954], 197-203) can hardly have had any influence.

[646] Gutbrod, 220 : Life κατὰ πνεῦμα is possible only ἐν πνεύματι, i.e., as πνεῦμα has been given. It is thus wholly a gift and yet also affirmative rather than necessary obedience. Cf. Gl. 5:16, 18, for this is not a dat. of norm, with Schlier Gl., ad loc. against F. Sieffert, Der Brief an d. Gl., Kritisch exegetischer Komm. über d. NT v. H. A. W. Meyer⁹ (1899), ad loc.

[647] As the ref. here is clearly to the concrete action of the believer, no less clearly this is grounded in the power of God, cf. Gutbrod, 149 and terms like "push," "bear witness," "impel," which in what follows are interpreted by "dwell," Mi. R., 167, n. 3.

[648] As against W. L. Knox, St. Paul and the Church of the Gentiles (1939), 99, 109, 127. 1 C. 14:14 shatters the view that πνεῦμα strengthens the νοῦς (ibid., 99; cf. P. Althaus, Paulus u. Luther über den Menschen² [1938], 58 and in opposition G. Bornkamm, „Der Mensch im Leibe des Todes," Wort u. Dienst, NF, 2, [1950], 42).

[649] Never in the Rabb. (Str.-B., III, 243). → V, 1006, 13 ff., cf. Stauffer Theol., 145; Bieder, op. cit. (→ n. 630), 22-40.

[650] This is not the Gnostic πνεῦμα which sighs in matter (→ n. 360) and which is the innermost self of the pneumatic, cf. Fuchs, op. cit. (→ n. 595), ad loc. Similarly in Phil. 1:19 one should transl. "support by the Spirit," Dib. Ph., ad loc. Also relevant here is the fact that χαρά is the gift of the πνεῦμα acc. to R. 14:17.

Law gave rise are no longer to be fulfilled, R. 7:5 f. The righteous demand of the Law will be met in those who no longer live κατὰ σάρκα but κατὰ πνεῦμα, R. 8:4. The φρόνημα τῆς σαρκός could not subject itself to the Law of God, R. 8:7. In virtue of the πνεῦμα, however, believers mortify the deeds of the → σῶμα, R. 8:13. Life in sonship is thus a believing which is also concrete.

This is most clearly stated in Gl. 5:13-25, where it is plain (v. 13, 16) that πνεύματι περιπατεῖν = ἐπιθυμίαν σαρκὸς μὴ τελέσαι means διὰ τῆς ἀγάπης δουλεύειν ἀλλήλοις and therewith to fulfil the whole νόμος, v. 14. [651] In fact, then, ἀγάπη is simply life in the Spirit which is freed from trust in the σάρξ. But it is this in outward orientation. It is faith at work (Gl. 5:6), → II, 654, 1 ff. In faith there is a concrete fulfilment of the Law precisely because all striving for self-righteousness is lifted from man, vv. 14-18. [652]

To live by the power and according to the norm of the Spirit is thus to live in freedom from the νόμος and wholly by Χριστός, χάρις, the σταυρός. It is thus to be free for ἀγάπη. This stands out particularly sharply in Gl. 5:19-23. While the work of the σάρξ finds outward attestation in ἔργα, one can speak only of καρπός [653] in relation to the πνεῦμα. This does not mean in the least that everything here is inward and invisible. 5:25-6:10 and even 5:21b show that Paul has concrete acts in view. [654] But these are pure acts which cannot be displayed or enumerated as acts of the Spirit. [655] In 1 C. 13:1-3 as well neither the extraordinariness of miracle not the superhuman greatness of sacrifice is an unambiguous sign of ἀγάπη or the πνεῦμα expressed therein. Nevertheless, it is maintained that the Spirit does find expression, e.g., in worship (1 C. 12-14), in concrete acts of love. In Gl. 5:22 ἀγάπη is the first gift of the πνεῦμα, → I, 50, 32 ff. R. 15:30, [656] Col. 1:8, and especially 1 C. 13 show that it includes all the other gifts within itself. [657] Nevertheless, it is still insisted that ἀγάπη can be understood only as πίστις and in orientation to the other gifts. Similarly, when πνεῦμα is the power of sanctification (R. 15:16; 1 C. 6:11; also 2 Th. 2:13), one cannot say whether Paul's emphasis is that the Spirit sets us in God's saving action and justifies us, or that He enables us to live thereby in concrete obedience. [658] The two are one and the same. [659]

---

[651] ἀγάπη rather than πνεῦμα is the opp. of σάρξ, Oe. Gl. on 5:16.

[652] σάρξ (v. 13, 16 f.), νόμος (v. 2-4, 18), περιτομή (v. 6, 11), and δουλεία (v. 1) interpret one another on the one side, and πνεῦμα (v. 5, 16-18), Χριστός (vv. 2-4), χάρις (v. 4), σταυρός (v. 11), ἀγάπη (v. 6, 13) and ἐλευθερία (v. 1, 13) on the other. Cf. Schlier Gl., on 5:18. One's own existence is silenced, Fuchs, 54. Hence νόμος can again be the antithesis of πνεῦμα in v. 18. On the other hand, the work of the σάρξ means the oppressing and destroying of others, v. 15.

[653] R. 6:21, where καρπός is used in malam partem, also denotes the result which has not been earned but which has accrued.

[654] Fuchs, 53.

[655] Hence φανερά is not used as the plur. The φανέρωσις τοῦ πνεύματος (1 C. 12:7) is His work in the community, but this is not measurable objectively (e.g., by its unusual nature), → 424, 8 ff. Cf. Schlier Gl. on 5:22.

[656] If the par. Phlm. 9 is really to be expounded in terms of Gl. 5:22 and not R. 5:5 → n. 618 (so Ltzm. R., ad loc.).

[657] As Christ's body does the members, G. Bornkamm, "Der köstlichere Weg," Das Ende des Gesetzes (1952), 110.

[658] The former is stressed in 1 C. 6:11, the latter in 1 C. 6:19; 2 C. 6:6; 1 Th. 4:7 f. (cf. R. 14:17). It makes no material difference that there are cultic echoes in the terms used.

[659] C. T. Craig, "Paradox of Holiness," Interpretation, 8 (1952), 147-161. There is no neutral zone between flesh and Spirit; hence freedom from sin is necessarily obedience, Gutbrod, 228 f.

The difference from the Gnostic understanding is particularly plain at this pt. On the Gnostic view possession of the πνεῦμα destroys the individuality of the ecstatic — only the divine substance within him is important [660] — and separates him from others who as non-pneumatics are completely alien or as pneumatics simply lead him to find himself (i.e., the same pneumatic substance) in them. [661] Here γνῶσις, i.e., awareness of the divine substance within, is necessarily the supreme thing. This seals off a man from others, 1 C. 8:1-3. In Paul, however, γνῶσις is subordinate to ἀγάπη, → I, 710, 4 ff. If the knowledge given by the Spirit is knowledge of God's saving work, it liberates man from himself and opens him to others. It also restores his individuality, not in such a way that he can only contemplate it, but in order that he may stand before God and others therewith, and live for others therein.

Thus the true regulative concept is that of the community. When Paul speaks of incorporation into the body of Christ, apparently adopting a Hell. phrase, he is emphasising thereby the unity of the body which binds together the various members. [662] The value of spiritual gifts is not that those who enjoy them are shown to be pneumatics thereby, but that they edify the community, 1 C. 14. It is certainly edified by pneumatics. But all are pneumatics; each has his → χάρισμα. [663] Where individuals separate themselves, they simply show that they are non-pneumatics, σαρκικοί. [664]

πνεῦμα, of course, is still the miraculous power of God which is not under man's control but comes down wholly and altogether from God. Paul, however, thinks out this thought to its radical conclusion. As God's power, πνεῦμα is not to be found in unusual phenomena, so that man might still appeal to his wonderful religious potentialities. The Spirit is fundamentally the power which sets a man in God's saving work in Christ, thus taking him out of his own control, making impossible any trust in his own σάρξ, and yet also opening him for a life in ἀγάπη. All that Paul has done here is to think out consistently interpretations of the cross already found in the Synoptists, namely, as a ransom for many (Mk. 14:24 → 425, 1 ff.), as a call to repentance which shatters all false religious security (Mk. 12:1-12 → 428, 7 ff.), as the event which makes possible discipleship in διακονία (Mk. 10:42-45 → 430, 21 ff.

The difference from the view of the Spirit is Ac. is not, then, the adoption of the category of the ethical. [665] It is not that the inner life of the individual rather than the outer history of the community is now guided by God, nor that possession of the Spirit is now an object of faith rather than something which can be controlled, nor that a being in Christ is now emphasised in distinction from the dynamic concept of the Spirit. [666] All these are at most only symptoms of the deeper distinction that πνεῦμα is now the power of God which brings a man to faith in the cross and resurrection of Jesus. This power can be presented dynamically as an unusual miraculous force if there is a desire to emphasise its otherworldliness. But it can also be the basis of a lasting being in Christ. It can direct both the external destiny of the community and also the inner life of the individual. It can work visibly or invisibly, spasmodically or continuously. Either way, it is no longer a supplementary phenomenon as in Ac. but the power which determines the new life of faith as such.

---

[660] Schrenk, op. cit. (→ n. 401), 110 f.; Plato and Philo, ibid. and → 374, 29 ff. Observation of singular states of soul (ibid., 116) leads to loss of fellowship.

[661] For this reason the Gnostic pneumatic can at most found θίασοι, not lasting ἐκκλησίαι, Reitzenstein Hell. Myst., 392. Cf. H. Kraft, Gnostisches Gemeinschaftsleben, Diss. Heidelberg (1950), ThLZ, 75 (1950), 628.

[662] R. 12:4 f.; 1 C. 12:13-27; 10:17; Gl. 3:28. To be integrated into the saving act of God means death for all that man boasts of or that separates him from others, R. 6:3 par. Gl. 3:27 f.

[663] Käsemann, op. cit. (→ n. 401), 170; the community (1 C. 3:16) and not just the individual (6:19) is God's temple.

[664] 1 C. 3:3 f., Bertrams, 69. For this reason the community is not subject to individual pneumatics but has judgment over them, Schrenk, op. cit., 124 f.

[665] Gunkel, 71, though cf. Weinel, 150, n. 1.

[666] All in Gächter, 376.

3. The Relation of the Spirit to Christ, → 418, 13 ff.

In R. 8:1-11 πνεῦμα θεοῦ ἐν ὑμῖν (v. 9) alternates with Χριστὸς ἐν ὑμῖν (v. 10), ὑμεῖς ἐν πνεύματι (v. 9) with τοῖς ἐν Χριστῷ (v. 1). No material distinction can be discerned here. [667] One may explain the alternation linguistically in terms of the Hellenistic view that the exalted Christ is substantially a spirit (→ 416, 24 ff.), so that abiding in Christ, understood locally, is also abiding in the Spirit, [668] or the abiding of Christ in us is also the abiding of the Spirit. If in many cases the ἐν πνεύματι is to be taken instrumentally, [669] this can be adduced as a counter-argument only so long as it is not perceived that the idea of the substantial sphere into which the believer enters is for Paul only the form in which he conceives of the idea of power. To say this, however, is also to say that the idea can only explain the choice of words and not the matter expressed thereby. In the context the περιπατεῖν κατὰ πνεῦμα or φρονεῖν τὰ τοῦ πνεύματος is traced back to εἶναι κατὰ πνεῦμα (v. 4 f. or ἐν πνεύματι v. 9), and this in turn to the οἰκεῖν of the πνεῦμα ἐν ὑμῖν (v. 9). [670] Here again it is evident (→ 425, 25 ff.) that Paul is trying to state precisely what the idea of the sphere in which the believer lives means for him. It is the idea of a power into whose sphere man has come and which thus shapes his φρονεῖν, his περιπατεῖν, his ὑποτάσσεσθαι τῷ νόμῳ τοῦ θεοῦ. [671]

This power is not anonymous or unknown. It is identical with the exalted Lord once this Lord is considered, not in Himself, but in His work towards the community. [672] The metaphysical question of the relation between God, Christ and the Spirit is hardly alluded to by Paul at all. [673] For this reason it would be a mistake to think that Paul finds in "the third person of the Trinity" the original meaning of πνεῦμα. [674] Often πνεῦμα is clearly impersonal (1 C. 12:13; 1 Th. 5:19), and it can alternate with σοφία or δύναμις (1 C. 2:4 f., 13). The spirit given to man can be called "his" πνεῦμα or the πνεῦμα υἱοθεσίας. If the πνεῦμα is said to teach, think etc., the same is true of σοφία or σάρξ. [675] It could well be that the question of the personality of the πνεῦμα is wrongly put, [676] since neither Hebrew

---

[667] For further par. Davies, op. cit. (→ n. 545), 178.

[668] So already A. Deissmann, Die nt.liche Formel "in Christo Jesu" (1892), 97 f. on the basis of R. 8:9-11; cf. also Käsemann, op. cit. (→ n. 401), 168.

[669] R. 15:13; 1 Th. 1:5; alternation between ἐν ... and dat.: 1 C. 12:3/14:2 (cf. Eph. 1:13/4:30; 5:18); dat. for local ἐν: Gl. 3:3; 5:5, 16, 25, Bertrams, 97, n. 1.

[670] This is even less to be expected on an OT basis than the former, for which there is at least a starting-pt. in the idea that the Spirit clothes a man, Köhler, n. 102; cf. p. 125: Nu. 27:18.

[671] The basis is "the Spirit in us." If we live by this, then "we in the Spirit" is true, Fuchs, 55; cf. Käsemann, op. cit. (→ n. 563), 268. One can render ἐν Χριστῷ by in regno Christi (Büchsel, 293), but this differs from the Hell. concept of the spiritual element in which the believer lives only to the degree that the substantial form in which the Hell. necessarily thinks is avoided. Similarly, the fact that the new power is not thought of as working magically, but as a norm to be accepted by man, is developed in the twofold meaning of regnum, which denotes the sphere in which the ruler both exercises his power and also seeks its acknowledgment.

[672] This is not new in Paul (as against Scott, op. cit. [→ n. 568], 141-145), for in Ac., too, the Spirit is not merely the τοῦτο 2:33) in distinction from the Pauline or Johannine ἐκεῖνος (Jn. 14:26). κύριος and πνεῦμα can also alternate there, → 406, 1 f.

[673] Goguel, Notion, 62.

[674] As against Gächter, 407 f.

[675] Similarly death, sin and Law are personified (Bertrams, 149, 153-155).

[676] Cf. C. Welch, "The Holy Spirit and the Trinity," Theology Today, 8 (1951/52), 33.

nor Greek has this word. Paul shares with Judaism (→ 370, 3 ff.; 384, 11 ff.) and the primitive Christian community (→ 404, 8 ff.; 412, 1 ff.; 415, 29 ff.) the view that the πνεῦμα is a gift and power of the last time. He has no desire to set aside "power" in favour of "person," but it is a concern of his that this power is not an obscure something, but the manner in which the κύριος is present to the community. This explains the equation with and subordination to the κύριος, 2 C. 3:17 f. → 419, 1 ff. [677] Sometimes Paul can use θεός, κύριος and πνεῦμα together (→ III, 108, 10 ff.) because their encounter with the believer is one and the same event. [678] This is plainest in 1 C. 12:4-6, not merely because the three terms are fully parallel here, but also because the πνεῦμα, as manifested in the life of the community, is now distinguished with linguistic precision as φανέρωσις τοῦ πνεύματος (v. 7) from the source of this work. 2 C. 13:13 is more difficult.

Is κοινωνία τοῦ ἁγίου πνεύματος to be taken as a subj. or obj. gen. ? The par. in 1 C. 1:9 and Phil. 3:10 favour the latter. [679] But the arguments for this interpretation are not at all convincing. [680] The closest par. in Phil. 2:1 is at least not to be construed as fellowship in the Holy Spirit of God (→ III, 807, 8 ff.); κυρίου and θεοῦ are undoubtedly subj. gen. Hence one may ask whether the par. rendering "fellowship given by the Spirit" is not the true one. On this view it is still an open question whether the thought is that of mutual brotherly fellowship or of fellowship with the Spirit. In view of χάρις and ἀγάπη the second is to be preferred, and in this case κοινωνία is to be construed actively as the Spirit's giving of a share (in Himself) (→ III, 808, 22 ff.), which may well include brotherly fellowship too. Materially this amounts to the same thing as the exposition in terms of an obj. gen. Nevertheless, κοινωνία τοῦ ἁγίου πνεύματος is better construed as a subj. gen. if the complexity of the concept is perceived. For materially the object in which the fellowship consists determines it no less than the subject which grants it. [681]

The three terms occur together, though not as parallels, in R. 5:1-5; also Gl. 4:4-6. [682] They show that the work of God in the Son or the Spirit is always to be understood as genuinely God's own work, but the question of the way in which God, Lord and Spirit are related is not felt to be a problem.

4. The Anthropological πνεῦμα.

The anthropological terms of Paul are neither consistent nor original. The Holy Spirit affects the whole man and cannot be explained psychologically. [683] This enables Paul to adopt popular ideas quite freely. The thesis that there is no

---

[677] Similarly it can be almost synon with θεός (1 C. 3:16; cf. 14:25; 2 C. 6:16), though also distinct therefrom (1 C. 2:10; R. 8:26 f.).

[678] A liking for triadic formulae (H. Usener, "Dreiheit," Rhein. Mus., 58 [1903], 1-47, 161-208, 320-362; Kn. Pt. on 1 Pt. 1:2) may have played some part but certainly not the idea of a divine family, since Father, Son and Spirit do not occur together, Büchsel, 411. Triadic formulae (→ V, 1011, n. 395) also occur in Mt. 28:19; 1 Pt. 1:2; Rev. 1:4 f., which are hardly Hell. (Büchsel, 414). Cf. K. L. Schmidt, "Le Dieu trinitaire," RevHPhR, 18 (1938), 126-144. E. Lewis, "The Biblical Doctrine of the Holy Spirit," Interpretation, 7 (1953), 281-298 shows how in the OT and NT God, the Lord etc. are often used for the Spirit with no difference of sense.

[679] Cf. Kümmel (Ltzm. K.⁴, ad loc.): "To have a share in ..."; Trinitarian-personal, Sickb. K., ad loc.: "Fellowship with the ..." Cf. also Oulton, op. cit. (→ n. 474), 62-64.

[680] As against Seesemann (→ III, 807, n. 63), cf. G. J. Jourdan, "ΚΟΙΝΩΝΙΑ in 1 C. 10:16," JBL, 67 (1948), 116-118.

[681] Jourdan, 119, 123 f.; cf. Thornton, op. cit. (→ n. 500), 74 f.

[682] There are almost 50 further passages in Gächter, 388-401.

[683] Preiss, op. cit. (→ n. 639), 30 f.

anthropological πνεῦμα in Paul [684] can hardly be sustained. Along with σῶμα and σάρξ, πνεῦμα is used almost exclusively for the psychical functions of man, 1 C. 7:34; 2 C. 7:1; Col. 2:5 ? It can be a par. to ψυχή (Phil. 1:27 → 446, 4 ff.) or, par. to σάρξ, it can denote man as a whole, with a stronger emphasis on his psychical than on his physical nature, 2 C. 2:13; 7:5; cf. 7:13; 1 C. 16:18, all with personal pronouns. In concluding salutations (Gl. 6:18; Phil. 4:23; Phlm. 25) πνεῦμα ὑμῶν means exactly the same as ὑμεῖς (1 Th. 5:28). Thus in 1 C. 2:11 πνεῦμα as man's self-awareness is distinguished from the par. πνεῦμα of God ; the par. controls the usage. In the well-known verse 1 Th. 5:23 πνεῦμα, alongside ψυχή and σῶμα, is to be regarded along the lines of popular anthropology [685] as a constituent part of man. [686]

Paul can thus uncritically adopt the Jewish use of πνεῦμα as a psychological term, → 376, 28 ff. Even so, however, πνεῦμα is still for him the God-given πνεῦμα, in the last resort alien to man. [687] He does not have to stress this, and in one instance can leave it out of account altogether. [688] But it is quite evident at times. In 1 C. 14:14 the πνεῦμα given to the pneumatic, which is plainly differentiated from his νοῦς (→ IV, 959, 7 ff.), can still be called "his" πνεῦμα. [689] R. 1:9 (→ IV, 64, 26 ff.; cf. 509, 32 ff.) also refers to the Spirit of God individually imparted to the apostle. [690]

1 C. 5:3-5 (→ V, 169, 10 ff.) is not wholly clear. The πνεῦμα of the sinner which is to be delivered is the I given to him by God, a portion of God's Spirit, though the whole of the new man of the believer is represented therein. [691] But this is not an indelible character, for Paul reckons with the possibility of perdition if judgment is not exercised on the σάρξ (sickness, death ? 11:30, cf. Ac. 5:1-11). It is the new I of man which perishes if he ceases altogether to be a Christian.

---

[684] C. Clemen, Pls. II (1904), 69 f.; on the whole question cf. W. Kümmel, "Römer 7 u. die Bekehrung d. Pls.," UNT, 17 (1929), 30-34; Bertrams, 5-28.

[685] → 395, 8 ff. The wish is traditional, perhaps liturgical, and thus tells us little about the Pauline understanding of man, Dib. Th.³, ad loc. The combination may be accidental as in Dt. 6:5, W. Robinson in Robinson, op. cit. (→ n. 396), 27, n. 2.

[686] It seems to me to be impossible to take πνεῦμα as a term for the whole man, who is then split up into ψυχή and σῶμα, C. Masson, "Sur 1 Th. 5:23," Rev. Th. Ph., NS, 33 (1945), 100 f. πνεῦμα is also not God's Spirit in contrast to soul and body, Dob. Th., ad loc.

[687] Even the fact that the πνεῦμα can be kept pure or sullied (1 C. 7:34; 2 C. 7:1; Kümmel, op. cit. [→ n. 684], 31) is no argument to the contrary, → 391, 2 ff. and 31 ff.

[688] Dob. Th. on 1 Th. 5:23 and 2 Th. 2:13 does not take sufficient note of this, though he rightly sees that πνεῦμα is fundamentally the new thing which, though part of the Christian's nature, is set in him by God.

[689] Cf. also R. 8:15 f. and the πνεύματα προφητῶν of 1 C. 14:32. There is no more to the plur. than this. It is not an accommodation to primitive Chr. usage, Ltzm. R., Exc. on 8:11. True, the πνεύματα can also speak falsely, so that the animistic view is in the background. It cannot simply mean "works of the Spirit" (M. Dibelius, Die Geisterwelt im Glauben d. Pls. [1909], 74), nor can it mean "Holy Spirit and demons" (as against A. L. Humphries, The Holy Spirit in Faith and Experience [1917], 210), for there is no thought of demons in 1 Cor. 14:32. Fundamentally there is for Paul only the one Spirit of God imparted severally to individuals, 2 C. 11:4. He can summarily bring under the same master concept the formally similar phenomena attributed to Satan (→ n. 702), but it is worth noting that he avoids the phrase πνεῦμα εἰδώλων in 1 C. 12:3.

[690] Kümmel, op. cit. (→ n. 684), 33; cf. also R. 12:11. The derivation from God is heavily stressed in R. 8:10 f. (as against Bertrams, 7-9).

[691] Certainly it is not just the human soul, for Paul never reckons with the salvation of a mere soul, Gutbrod, 82 f. It is he himself in the existence given to him by Christ, not in his natural abilities and powers, cf. 3:15 αὐτός. The interpretation of G. Bornkamm (in v. Campenhausen, op. cit. [→ n. 630], 147, n. 1) whereby God's πνεῦμα may no longer be left with the sinner is impossible in the light of 1 Pt. 4:6 and the ref. to the day of judgment.

Purifying judgment is to be exercised on the σάρξ in order that this final, dreadful, marginal possibility might be averted. [692] Here and in Col. 2:5 the πνεῦμα of the apostle is to be regarded as the gift of the Spirit of God which has been given to him, which denotes his authority, and which also exerts an influence beyond his physical presence. [693] On πνεῦμα πραΰτητος (1 C. 4:21; Gl. 6:1) → n. 329 and 381, 14 ff.; an original animistic concept seems already to have become quite stereotyped here. [694]

A vital point is that this πνεῦμα which abides in man is not described as more than something which, related to God, is set in him. It is not the soul perfected by God's πνεῦμα. [695] If Paul uses πνεῦμα non-technically almost in the sense of ψυχή, this is the current usage of Judaism (→ 376, 28 ff.) which he naturally brings with him and has to employ. [696] Paul never says that the ψυχή finds its fulfilment in the πνεῦμα. In a single reference to the idea of a vehicle for the Spirit of God he calls this, too, a πνεῦμα, and says expressly that it is not man's own, but is given him by God, R. 8:15 f.; 1 C. 2:11. [697] When Paul makes a considered statement, like the Gnostics he sets this individual πνεῦμα, which is transcendent to man and proper to God, in antithesis to both ψυχή and σῶμα. [698] This may be seen not only positively in the strict differentiation from the human νοῦς (1 C. 14:14) but also negatively in the fact that he avoids πνεῦμα when he wants to describe the innermost I of the pre-Christian man. [699]

The data may seem confusing at first (→ 391, 30 ff.), but they become quite clear when one realises that Paul thinks wholly in terms of the work of the Spirit of God and perceives that the whole existence of the believer is determined thereby. For Paul the Spirit of God is not an odd power which works magically; the Spirit reveals to the believer God's saving work in Christ and makes possible his understanding and responsible acceptance thereof (→ 424, 22 ff., esp. 427, 18 ff.). For this reason the πνεῦμα, though always God's Spirit and never evaporating into the πνεῦμα given individually to man, [700] is also the innermost ego of the one who no longer lives by his own being but by God's being for him.

5. πνευματικός.

Paul's usage is specific when he contrasts the πνευματικοί and the ψυχικοί. In 1 C. 2:13-15 the πνευματικός is the man who knows God's saving work by virtue of the Spirit of God (→ 425, 22 ff.), while the ψυχικός is blind thereto. [701]

---

[692] The σάρξ which is destroyed is not sin, so Grosheide, op. cit. (→ n. 576), 123, ad loc. Cf. 1 Pt. 4:1, 6, 17 → 447, 11 ff., 448, 9 ff.

[693] As against Joh. W. 1 K., ad loc. It is no more meant than the natural soul. For the distinction from the δύναμις Ἰησοῦ cf. R. 8:15 f., → 436, 12 ff.

[694] Bultmann Theol., 204; cf. 2 C. 12:18.

[695] Cf. Festugière, 219 f.

[696] The spirit of man is not understood in Stoic fashion as the root of the divine Spirit, though Gn. 2:7 might suggest this, Büchsel, 417.

[697] Cf. Od. Sol. 6:7. Brosch, op. cit. (→ n. 538), 64 finds in R. 8:16 the πνεῦμα immanent to man, though cf. 65 f., 68 f., 81.

[698] Cf. → 436, 31 ff.; Snaith, op. cit. (→ n. 545), 184-186; F. C. Synge, "The Holy Spirit and the Sacraments," Scottish Journal of Theology, 6 (1953), 68 f. The dualism of immanence and transcendence is shattered by the πνεῦμα as that which comprehends both, cf. Wendland, 468-470.

[699] For this ἐγώ or νοῦς is used, R. 7:17-23.

[700] R. 8:16. → IV, 509, 36 f. as against the exposition referred to ibid., 37-41, which might seem to set the personal experience of faith alongside the Spirit of God rather along the lines of Wesley, cf. Preiss, op. cit. (→ n. 639), 24; Bultmann Theol., 203.

[701] Cf. also Jd. 19 → 448, 13 f. Cf. → n. 384.

The contrast is especially sharp because Paul recognises no neutral ground between them. Not to have the πνεῦμα of God is to be controlled by the πνεῦμα τοῦ κόσμου. [702, 703] No less specifically the σῶμα πνευματικόν is distinguished from the σῶμα ψυχικόν in 1 C. 15:44-46, → 408, 1 ff. This shows that the terms had already been developed and circulated prior to Paul, → 395, 9 ff. and n. 396. In keeping with what has been said πνευματικά can denote the content of the knowledge given by God's πνεῦμα, i.e., the heavenly things inaccessible to the νοῦς, or, materially, the message of Christ, 1 C. 2:13; [704] 9:11; R. 15:27. In the last two references earthly things are σαρκικά, though without taking on the character of what is evil. These are simply the things which promote natural life, but do not unite with God. Thus the spiritual food and drink which comes directly from God's sphere and gives divine power (1 C. 10:3 f., → 146, 17 ff.) is distinguished from ordinary food and drink. The idea that the elements are bearers of the πνεῦμα [705] is not present here; this is shown by parallels to the usage [706] and also by v. 4b. [707] πνευματικά is used for the totality of the gifts of the Spirit in 1 C. 14:1. [708] When the νόμος is called πνευματικός in R. 7:14, it is characterised thereby as the νόμος θεοῦ (v. 22, 25) which comes from the world of God and not from that of man. [709]

IV. John.

1. The Significance of Eschatology.

While the saying transmitted in Jn. 21:22 still takes the view of Mk. 9:1; 1 Th. 4:17 that some will experience the *parousia*, while mockers are already scoffing (2 Pt. 3:4; 1 Cl., 23, 2 f.; 2 Cl., 11) and their opponents are postponing the *parousia* (2 Pt. 3:8-10; 1 Cl., 23, 4 f.; Barn., 21, 3), [710] John, though insisting that the consummation has still to come, [711] proclaims even more definitely than Paul the presence even now of the salvation which will one day be consummated. The primary distinction from the Synoptists and Paul, then, is that the older ideas are more consistently eliminated.

---

[702] Presented mythologically as in Eph. 2:2, cf. Bertrams, 19 f.

[703] On 2:16 → IV, 959, 21 ff.; on 3:1-3 and 1 C. 14:37; Gl. 6:1 → n. 605.

[704] On πνευματικοῖς → III, 954, 2 ff., though the neutral understanding (par. ἐν διδακτοῖς πνεύματος = πνευματικῶς B) is to be considered seriously, since ἄνθρωπος is added to ψυχικός to emphasise that it is to be taken personally. Materially cf. Dibelius, *op. cit.* (→ n. 689), 91, n. 4, though he with some difficulty supplies λόγοις. The knowledge which is not natural but comes from God is also called πνευματική in Col. 1:9.

[705] As against H. Lietzmann, *Messe u. Herrenmahl* (1926), 252 cf. already Schweitzer, *op. cit.* (→ n. 548), 263. The interpretation "conveying the Spirit" (E. Käsemann, *op. cit.* [→ n. 563], 267, cf. Schlier, *op. cit.* [→ n. 597], 24) is too narrow, nor is "consisting of πνεῦμα" suitable (Gunkel, 45), → n. 706. On the idea that the glory of the shekinah is nourishment for the believer cf. Heb. En. 5:4 (Odeberg, *op. cit.* [→ n. 225], II, 15).

[706] 1 Pt. 2:5 and cf. Barn., 16, 10 (spiritual temple as distinct from the perishable temple made with hands, v. 7, 9); Did., 10, 3 (spiritual food and drink as distinct from ordinary food and drink); Ptolem. ad Floram in Epiph. → n. 397 (spiritual fasts); Ign. Eph., 5, 1 (spiritual relation to the bishop); cf. 11, 2; Mg., 13, 1. Cf. C. F. D. Moule, "Sanctuary and Sacrifice in the Church of the NT," JThSt, NS, 1 (1950), 34 f. (spiritual = rejection of the external cultus).

[707] The spiritual rock is a miraculous, non-earthly rock which comes from God's world, → 96, 20 ff.; 97, 26 ff.

[708] Also 12:1; cf. R. 1:11.

[709] Cf. also Eph. 1:3; on Col. 3:16 = Eph. 5:19 → 423, 2 f.; on the whole subject cf. Selwyn, *op. cit.* (→ n. 555), 281-285.

[710] Barrett, *Fourth Gospel,* 2 f.; also *The Gospel acc. to St. John* (1955), *ad loc.*

[711] 6:27; 12:25; 14:2 f.; 17:24. Even if 11:24 is not enough, it has not been contested. For details E. Schweizer, "Das joh. Zeugnis vom Herrenmahl," *Ev. Theol.,* 12 (1952/53), 353-355; also "The Reinterpretation of the Gospel by the Fourth Evangelist," *Interpretation,* 8 (1954), 387-396. On the whole question cf. Howard, 106-128.

In John there is no thought of the sporadic coming of the Spirit, the extra-ordinary nature of His manifestations, ecstatic phenomena, or miraculous acts. [712] Jesus is not presented as a pneumatic. [713] His inspired speech and His miracles are nowhere attributed to the Spirit. [714] The path taken by Luke does not satisfy John. He completely abandons the idea of inspiration because this emphasises the distinction between God and Jesus — a distinction which can be overcome only by a third, namely, the Spirit. If the Christ event is really to be understood as the turning-point of the aeons, then everything depends on the fact that the Father Himself, not just a gift of the Father, is genuinely encountered therein. [715] There is thus no reference to the conception of Christ by the Spirit or to His endowment with the Spirit in baptism.

The former was introduced early into 1:13, [716] but the verse shows that while there is for Jn. a spiritual birth of believers, there is no such birth for the Son. The descent of the Spirit on Jesus in 1:33 is simply a proof, not the cause, of the divine sonship of Jesus. [717]

2. πνεῦμα as a Sphere in Antithesis to σάρξ.

Other differences from Paul are not fundamental. They result from the fact that Jn. thinks more in the categories of a heterodox Judaism than in those of Rabbinism. Among them one may mention the pre-Pauline usage (→ 416, 32 ff.) in which πνεῦμα and σάρξ represent the sphere of God on the one side and that of the world on the other, 3:6; 6:63. [718] If 3:6 speaks of γεννηθῆναι ἐκ τοῦ πνεύματος, 3:3 and 1:13 speak of γεννηθῆναι ἄνωθεν or ἐκ θεοῦ. εἶναι ἐκ τοῦ θεοῦ is contrasted with εἶναι ἐκ τῶν κάτω, ἐκ τοῦ διαβόλου, ἐκ τοῦ κόσμου, [719] and similarly γεγεννημένον ἐκ τοῦ πνεύματος is the opposite of γεγεννημένον ἐκ τῆς σαρκός, 3:6. πνεῦμα, ἄνω, θεός are thus equivalent on the one side, σάρξ, κάτω, διάβολος, κόσμος on the other.

4:24 makes the equation: πνεῦμα ὁ θεός. [720] Here Jn. proclaims that the

---

[712] Frövig, 81. Pentecost takes place without fiery tongues or stormy wind, 20:22 f. (Barrett, Fourth Gospel, 3 f.). Nor is 16:13 a relic of the ancient view that the prophetic πνεῦμα gives esp. a vision of things to come, Bu. J., ad loc. and Barrett, op. cit. (→ n. 710), ad loc. as against Goguel, Notion, 141; H. Windisch, "Die fünf joh. Parakletsprüche," Festgabe f. A. Jülicher (1927), 121; cf. 118; Weinel, 52 f. The witness of the Spirit never takes the form of miracles (as in Mk. 16:17 f.).

[713] On the contrary, He is "the Godhead who imparts the Spirit," Volz, Geist, 196, n. 1.

[714] E.g., 7:28, 37; 12:44; 5:8; 6:11; 9:6 f.; 11:43. Nor is there any ref. to the shaking of the pneumatic in 11:33; 13:21; the πνεῦμα is to be taken anthropologically = ἑαυτόν, 11:33, cf. 12:27 (Barrett, Fourth Gospel, 3 as against Windisch, Joh. Ev., 315). It denotes the physical life-force in 19:30, → 451, 12 ff.

[715] One might say epigrammatically that in the Synoptists the unity of God and Spirit is presupposed and is extended to Jesus in His endowment with the Spirit, while in Jn. the unity of Father and Son is presupposed and leads to the outpouring of the Spirit by both, cf. Windisch, Joh.-Ev., 315.

[716] Howard, 66-68; W. v. Loewenich, Das Johannesverständnis im 2. Jhdt. (1932), 81 f.

[717] Goguel, Notion, 99. It might be that for Jn. Jesus was not baptised at all (M. Goguel, Jean-Baptiste [1928], 160 f., though cf. Bu. J., 65, n. 3); at any rate the baptism had no significance for Jesus Himself, not even as a sign of His "hour" (as against Büchsel, 492). At most the μένειν might indicate (Windisch, Synpt. Überlieferung, 232, n. 1) that there is still to be found here a relic of the Lucan attempt (→ 406, 10 ff.) to make the endowment of the Spirit into a lasting one, Barrett, op. cit. (→ n. 710), 74.

[718] Not adopted by Paul, Bultmann Theol., 354. → n. 735. Cf. Käsemann, op. cit. (→ n. 401), 96 and Schweizer, op. cit. (→ n. 353), 563-569.

[719] 8:23, 42-47; 15:19; 17:14, 16; for Gnostic material cf. G. P. Wetter, "Eine gnostische Formel im 4. Ev.," ZNW, 18 (1917/18), 56-58; Schlier, op. cit. (→ n. 372), 141 f.

[720] Formally cf. → 356, 14 ff. and Bu. J., 141, n. 2. Jn., however, avoids the term νοῦς and gives the word πνεῦμα a completely new sense through the abs. antithesis to σάρξ.

eschatological hour of the meeting of above and below, spirit and flesh, God and the world, has already come, even though it has still to be consummated. [721] In complete antithesis to Greek and Gnostic thinking he declares that the meeting is not between the substance of God and the originally similar substance which has been entombed in man, → 393, 18 ff. On the contrary, God summons man to faith, and seeks to encounter him, in the historical man Jesus of Nazareth. To worship God in πνεῦμα and ἀλήθεια is thus no longer (→ I, 246, 33 ff.) to worship with an awareness of one's own spiritual substance, and certainly not to worship in one's own spirituality as distinct from everything external. It is to worship in the sphere of God and no longer in that of the κόσμος, in reality and no longer in the realm of mere appearance. This is possible, however, only where God Himself enters the world in Him who is ὁ ἀληθινὸς θεός, 1 Jn. 5:20. [722] There had been many repudiations of cultic worship. [723] One might say epigrammatically that the true worship of Jn. 4:24 is orientated to the flesh and blood of Jesus. [724] πνεῦμα, then, does not mean man's soul or understanding, that which is most like God in him, his immaterial or purely inward part. [725] Like ἀλήθεια, [726] it denotes the reality of God. Formally it is a substantial term, as in Hellenism. Materially, however, it is wholly sustained by the recognition that this reality is to be found only in Jesus. To know ἀλήθεια is to know τὸν ἀληθινὸν θεόν in Jesus, 8:32; 17:3. [727] Hence ἐν πνεύματι corresponds materially to the Pauline ἐν Χριστῷ. [728] God's sovereign act of revelation in Jesus has marked out the sphere in which there is true worship. Hence any cultus, however spiritual, is judged as not in the πνεῦμα if it is not based on this divine act. [729]

3. πνεῦμα as a Life-Giving Power in Antithesis to σάρξ.

As in Jn. 4:23 f. (→ 438, 27 ff.), so also in 3:3-5 πνεῦμα is the world of God which remains inaccessible to man so long as he does not live ἐν πνεύματι. [730] Here, however, this life is traced back to a birth of the πνεῦμα. [731]

This radical distinctness of God from everything human is OT and Jewish rather than Gk.

[721] Cf. Barrett, Fourth Gospel, 6; also op. cit. (→ n. 710), ad loc., thinks that πνεῦμα here is the life-giving power of God, while ἀλήθεια emphasises the relation to the historic Jesus. One should say rather more precisely: the power which links to God's world (and thus gives life).

[722] Cf. 1:9; 6:32-35; 10:11; 15:1; 10:30; 14:9 f. This is quite different from what is found in Plato, → 341, 37 ff. The key to understanding is in fact in 14:26 (not as in D); 16:12 f.: The Spirit is simply the interpretation of the incarnate Word, O. Cullmann, Urchr. u. Gottesdienst² (1950), 48 f.

[723] 1 K. 8:27; Jewish and Gk.: Bu. J., 140, n. 3; Bau. J., ad loc.; cf. also Sen. Epistulae, 41, 1 f. (cf. 66, 12): "Hands are not to be lifted up to heaven ... God is near thee, with thee, in thee ... a holy spirit dwells in us." Only Zn. and Bau. J., ad loc. take Jn. 4:23 f. thus.

[724] E. C. Hoskyns, The Fourth Gospel (1947), ad loc.

[725] As against Verbeke, 392; Howard, 61; G. H. C. McGregor, The Gospel of John, Moffatt NT Commentary (1949), ad loc.; Bau. J., ad loc.

[726] → I, 240, 29 ff.; 245-247; Bultmann Theol., 365 f.

[727] Odeberg, op. cit. (→ n. 307), 170.

[728] As against → II, 543, 10 f. with J. Horst, Proskynein (1932), 306.

[729] Bu. J., 140 f. The distinction between the spirit of truth, knowledge, and light and the spirit of error, wickedness, and darkness has its roots in pre-Gnostic Judaism, → 390 f. and Test. Jud. 20:1; Damasc. 2:13 (2:10). Hence πνεῦμα ἀληθείας is not to be construed along OT lines as the spirit of faith, → I, 247, 6 f. (as against Snaith, op. cit. [→ n. 545], 181).

[730] Odeberg, op. cit., 169.

[731] The Spirit is the begetter, not the mother, 1:13; 1 Jn. 3:9. In the first instance this corresponds to Aristotle's principle that each nature begets its own substance, Eth. M.,

The decisive question of Jn. is how a man may attain ζωή (→ II, 870, 5 ff.). [732] Paul could ask the same question, and he could answer like Jn. that only the πνεῦμα exercises ζωοποιεῖν, Jn. 6:63; 2 C. 3:6. But Paul thinks in the Rabb. category of δικαιοσύνη, and he thus defines ζωή as δικαιοσύνη (→ II, 209, 25 ff.) in distinction from κατάκρισις (→ 428, 34 ff.). For Jn., however, ζωή consists in the γινώσκειν of God, [733] 17:3. Hence he does not go all the way with Paul in asserting that the Spirit gives life because He mediates knowledge of God's atoning act at the cross (→ 425, 35 ff.), and therefore freedom from καύχημα (→ 428, 7 ff.), and openness for one's neighbour (→ 430, 21 ff.), in short, δικαιοσύνη in its full compass. Without basically saying anything different from Paul, he can thus take up more directly than Paul an idea which was originally developed along very different lines, namely, that of the life-giving πνεῦμα. In Jn., too, the original substantial concept is completely transcended. The distinction from Pl. is simply that union with the Redeemer as such means abolition of the separation between God and the world, [734] so that the πνεῦμα, more strongly than in Pl., [735] denotes the world of God in antithesis to the σάρξ as the sphere by which man is controlled in his new life. With less difficulty than Pl. Jn. can thus ascribe γεννᾶν to this world of God. [736], [737] He does not have in view an alteration of the substance of the soul [738] but the gift of a realisation that in Jesus God Himself has come to the κόσμος — a gift which becomes a reality in the event of believing. Thus 3:3-5 tells us that this realisation can only be the gift of God. It does not lie in any sense within man's own capabilies. Hence Nicodemus is summoned to renounce his own possibilities and to open himself up wholly and utterly to the gift of God, i.e., to believe. [739]

In v. 8a πνεῦμα means "wind." [740] The wind in its incomprehensibility and uncontrollability is like the Spirit of God, → 452, 7 ff. The important point, however, is that the pneumatic, not the Spirit, is described thus. The "otherness" of the one who is begotten by the Spirit is particularly heavily underlined herewith. The believer, concerning whose whence and whither the κόσμος knows

---

I, 10, p. 1187a, 31. It is not a mere development of R. 6:3 f.; 1 C. 15:45 nor a mere transfer of Ps. 2:7 from Jesus to the believer (as against Burney, op. cit. [→ n. 467], 45; Wnd. J., Exc. on 1 Jn. 3:9; Howard, 198). On regeneration → I, 673, 686 ff.; Wnd. J., loc. cit.; Dib. Past.³ on Tt. 3:5; Dib. Jk. on 1:18; Dodd, 303 f. The understanding of πνεῦμα as the substance of life (→ 340, 25 ff.) hardly contributed to the usage since it is only in Jn. 3:5 (and there less precisely than in Tt. 3:5) that πνεῦμα is associated with regeneration.

[732] Goguel, Notion, 145.

[733] γνῶσις is not used at all, perhaps in opposition to a Gnostic use ; the verb is common.

[734] Hence the cross is regarded primarily, not as an atonement, but as the completion of the incarnation, in which God takes His step of love towards the κόσμος, cf. Dodd, 441 f. etc.

[735] Jn., however, does not radicalise the antithesis ; he simply corrects it less clearly than Pl., as against Goguel, Notion, 158 → n. 718.

[736] Behind → ὕδωρ, which is probably original, there might well stand cosmological speculations about the upper waters, Eth. En. 54:8; Ps.-Clem. Hom., 11, 24; Hipp. Ref., V, 27, 3, cf. Haenchen, op. cit. (→ n. 363), 130 and 155, n. 1. For others who construe ὕδωρ as (natural or spiritual) seed cf. Barrett, op. cit. (→ n. 710), ad loc. John and his readers, however, were assuredly thinking of baptism.

[737] This is the truth in the statement of Schweitzer, op. cit. (→ n. 548), 341, though cf. W. Michaelis, "Das Joh.-Ev. u. d. Hellenisierung d. Christentums," Kirchenblatt f. d. reformierte Schweiz, 86 (1930), 260; → n. 739.

[738] Humphries, op. cit. (→ n. 689), 235 f.

[739] Paul has the same pt. in view when he regards δικαιοσύνη as the gift which, grounded in God's atoning act, makes all καύχημα impossible and thus makes possible a life in πίστις. On the other hand, the relation of the believer to Christ can hardly be regarded as a par. to that of Christ to the Father, as in Jn., so long as one thinks in the Pauline category of δικαιωθῆναι (not 1 Tm. 3:16), cf. W. v. Loewenich, "Joh. Denken," ThBl, 15 (1936), 270 f.

[740] Note πνεῖ, φωνή → 368, 20 f.; 375, 25 ff., though cf. T. M. Donn, "The Voice of the Spirit (Jn. 3:8)," Exp. T., 66 (1954/55), 32.

nothing, [741] is also beyond the reach of human perception. Though this faith will find active expression in ἀγάπη, birth of the Spirit does not as such signify moral renewal. [742] It cannot be demonstrated, whether in its outworking or in its manifestation, e.g., in its suddenness, in the preceding penitential conflict, or in the feeling of liberation. It is the event which the world can no longer measure or evaluate.

In 6:63 (cf. 15:3) the σάρξ profits nothing but to the πνεῦμα there is ascribed a γεννᾶν which takes place in the Word of Jesus as Son of God.

Acc. to vv. 51-58 σάρξ can only be the σάρξ of the incarnate Lord which in a way that causes supreme offence is visible in the eucharist in its saving necessity for man. Nothing is said about any identity between the σάρξ of Jesus and the eucharistic element. It is simply emphasised that in the eucharist the individual must concretely accept the ministry of Jesus proclaimed in His address on the bread. For Jn. the function of baptism and the Lord's Supper is to bear witness to the incarnation. [743] The pt. of 6:63, however, is that this σάρξ helps only when the πνεῦμα grants the realisation that ζωή is to be found in it, → 443, 11 ff. [744] It is thus to be expounded in terms of 8:15. If a man considers only the σάρξ of Jesus, His incarnation, as it is proclaimed and proffered to him in the eucharist as his salvation, then οὐκ ὠφελεῖ οὐδέν, → 143, 19 ff. Only when the words of Jesus in which the πνεῦμα is at work show him in this σάρξ the δόξα of the Father, ζωοποιεῖ, cf. 13:10; 15:3. This is true of the intensification of the σκάνδαλον in the ἀναβαίνειν of Jesus on the cross [745] as in each eucharist, where man naturally reacts as Peter did in 13:6. The meaning is not that we are not to stop at the external element but to take it spiritually, for this would be an evasion of the offence. On the other hand, life is not to be sought in the element. The real point is that, faced with the scandalously concrete σάρξ, one can discern δόξα and consequently ζωή therein only in the power of the πνεῦμα. This emphasising of the Word, and of the summons to faith in it, shows that the tying of ζωή to (sacramental) substance is overcome here even more thoroughly than in Pl. The meaning of the sacraments in Jn. has been sought [746] in the union of spirit and matter. As water is first concentrated in a canal and then spread over the land in a network of channels, so the Spirit is first concentrated in Jesus and then flows into the sacraments. The elements of water and blood, which still remain of the matter of His body, are the fruit of the death of Jesus and they are able to unite with the Spirit, 19:34 f. This view founders, however, on the fact that → σάρξ does not mean matter in Jn., [747] that the eucharist here is regarded as a heightening of the σκάνδαλον, i.e., a summons to faith, that in 6:63; 15:3 ζωή is ascribed to the Word alone (cf. 5:24; 6:68; 8:51; 12:47), that ὕδωρ is not taken up

---

[741] Cf. 7:27 f.; 8:14; 9:29; 15:19. For Gnostic material → n. 719.

[742] As against H. Strathmann, Das Ev. nach Joh., NT Deutsch, 4 (1955), 18, who sees in this the decisive mark from the very first.

[743] For detailed arguments cf. Schweizer, op. cit. (→ n. 711), 353-362, also Art. "Abendmahl," RGG³, I, 12. It is true, of course, that this offence is changed into grace and help for the believer, cf. Barrett, op. cit. (→ n. 710), ad loc.

[744] As against MacGregor, op. cit. (→ n. 725), 161 f., who sees material communion in vv. 51c-58 and spiritual communion in v. 63. Dodd, 342, n. 5 finds the solution in the unity of act and word. H. van den Bussche, "L'attente de la grande Révélation dans le quatrième évangile," Nouvelle Revue Théol., 75 (1953), 1016 f. takes σάρξ in its OT sense = man in his limitation.

[745] So with H. A. W. Meyer, Das Ev. d. Joh., Krit.-exegetischer Komm. über d. NT² (1852); Bu. J., ad loc.; E. Ruckstuhl, Die literarische Einheit d. Joh.-Ev. (1951), 257 as against Bau. J., Schl. J., MacGregor, op. cit., ad loc.; the ascension is not recorded in Jn., so that the world sees only execution in the ἀναβαίνειν, 8:22; 12:32 f. Again in 3:12-14 the ἀναβαίνειν (= lifting up on the cross) seems to be one of the ἐπουράνια which are much more offensive than anything thus far.

[746] Schweizer, op. cit. (→ n. 548), 343 f., 348 with ref. to Just. Apol., I, 66, 2; Ign. Mg., 13, 2; R., 7, 3; cf. also Cullmann, op. cit. (→ n. 722), e.g., 77.

[747] Michaelis, op. cit. (→ n. 737), 263.

again in 3:6-8, and that in 4:23 f.; 20:22 f. (in distinction from Mt. 28:19) the sacrament is not mentioned at all, so that, while it is accepted by Jn., it is certainly not central. [748]

The teaching is the same in 7:38 f., [749] where in substantial, but not sacramental, form the material point is simply that the Spirit as the water of life will flow into the community in the proclamation which takes place in word and act. [750] The new statement here, however, is that the Spirit will come only after the death of Jesus. In the first instance this simply corresponds to the historical facts. It acquires for John, however, a special significance, as the sayings about the Paraclete will show. [751]

The imparting of the Spirit is recounted in 20:22 (→ II, 536, 23 ff.). [752] Here the eleven are representatives of believers generally. [753] The incident can be regarded as a rather meagre fulfilment of the Paraclete sayings, or a solution to the difficulty that Pentecost is not recorded in any of the Gospels, [754] only if it is not perceived that for John ζωή lies in the knowledge of the ἀληθινὸς θεός in Jesus, so that the πνεῦμα is simply the power of proclamation which leads to this knowledge. Hence everything depends on the authority of the proclamation.

4. The Paraclete, → 388, 29 ff.

When the Paraclete (→ V, 803, 27 ff.) is called the πνεῦμα τῆς ἀληθείας (→ I, 247, 2 ff.) in 14:17; 15:26; 16:13, He is presented as the representative of the world of reality in contrast to mere appearance. [755] In Him God's world is present as it was present in Jesus and will continue to be present in His Word, 17:13-17. [756] As it was said of Jesus (14:20), so it is said of Him that He is in the disciples, 14:17. These, but not the κόσμος, know both Him (14:17) and Jesus (16:3). Both He and Jesus are sent by the Father (14:24, 26). Both go forth from

---

[748] Cf. Howard, 147; Bultmann Theol., 405. Barrett, op. cit. (→ n. 710), 75 emphasises that the sacrament does not mediate the Spirit but that the Spirit is the power which alone confers the blessing.

[749] If the vv. are originally related. Acc. to Bu. J., ad loc. v. 38 is a gloss, while v. 39 is a gloss acc. to Windisch, Joh.-Ev., 309 f.; J. M. Thompson, "Some Editorial Elements in the Fourth Gospel," Exp. VIII, 14 (1917), 221 f.

[750] This should be traced back to the ideas → 399, 6, cf. → n. 736 (also Damasc. 3:16 [5:3]), not to the dispensing of water at the Succoth feast (Bu. J. as against J. Jeremias, Golgotha [1926], 81-83 and Jesus als Weltvollender [1930] 46-52; punctuation after ἐμέ [v. 38] rather than πινέτω is difficult and hardly tenable in the light of 4:14). For in this case πινέτω would no longer be directly related to διψᾷ, Barrett, op. cit. (→ n. 710), ad loc. The ongoing of proclamation is always important in Jn., 1:40-46; 4:28 f.; 20:21-23.

[751] The thought in Ac. 2:33 (based on Rabb. speculation?) may be the source of this saying, Knox, op. cit. (→ n. 485), 85 f., but it is no longer vital for Jn.

[752] Mt. 28:19 f. (Windisch, Joh.-Ev., 312) and Ac. 2:1-13 (J. Kaftan, Nt.liche Theol. [1927], 199) merge into one another. Barrett, op. cit., (→ n. 710), emphasises the echoing of Gn. 2:7; Ez. 37:9; Wis. 15:11: it is a new, life-giving creation. On the original sensory and magical idea of breathing cf. Staerk, op. cit. (→ n. 307), 316, n. 1; on the difference from the Johannine understanding elsewhere cf. Dodd, 430.

[753] Cf. 6:63; 7:38. If they are to be regarded only as office-bearers (Schweitzer, op. cit. [→ n. 548], 350 f.; J. H. Bernard, A Critical and Exegetical Comm. on St. Jn., ICC [1928], 672, 676; cf. 575 on 17:18; L. S. Thornton, "The Body of Christ" in The Apostolic Ministry, ed. K. E. Kirk [1946], 108 f.), then the Parting Discourses (including, e.g., the commandment of love) must be completely restricted to them. For a correct understanding cf. Flew, op. cit. (→ n. 407), 173 f.

[754] Bau. J., ad loc.; Michaelis, 47, n. 80.

[755] As ἄρτος τῆς ζωῆς in 6:35 (cf. 33, 50 f.) = the one who gives ἀλήθεια (→ I, 245, 8 ff.) and is ἀλήθεια (→ 439, 16 ff.). For the Paraclete promises in general cf. W. M. Firor, "Fulfillment of Promise," Interpretation, 7 (1953), 299-314.

[756] Howard, 74.

the Father (16:27; 15:26), teach (7:14; 14:26), witness (8:14; 15:26), convince the κόσμος of sin (3:18-20; 16:8-11), yet do not speak of themselves (14:10; 16:13). [757] Thus the Spirit is only the ἄλλος παράκλητος alongside Jesus (14:16 → V, 800, n. 1), and one might be tempted to say that strictly John has no place for the Spirit. [758] Jesus Himself comes in the Paraclete (14:18), [759] and yet He is not identical with Jesus. [760] He comes only after Jesus has gone (7:39; 16:7), [761] and while Jesus is present with His own only for a period and will one day be with them again (13:33; 14:3; 16:4; 17:24), the Spirit will be with them for ever (14:16). One can see Jesus and yet not see Him, hear Him and yet not hear Him (6:36; 5:37 f.), if one remains closed to Him in unbelief. Indeed, in a certain sense this also applies to His own so long as He is with them (14:5-11). Only the πνεῦμα which comes to the community in the Word gives life; the historical Jesus as such is the σάρξ which profits nothing, 6:63 → 441, 14 ff. Only the Christ of preaching is the Redeemer. [762] Hence it is only the πνεῦμα τῆς ἀληθείας who genuinely discloses Jesus to the disciples (14:26; 16:13), who glorifies Him (16:14). Though His words are not different from those of the historical Jesus (6:63; 14:26; 16:14 → n. 722), it is only in them that the latter take on real force (16:8-11). Hence it is only here that we find the idea of an advocate or supporter — an idea which plainly goes beyond that of the revealer, → V, 813, n. 98. But these words of the Spirit are no different from those spoken in the authoritative proclamation of His community, 20:22 f.; 15:26 f. [763]

On the derivation → V, 813, 14-18. [764] To the best of my knowledge the phrase "spirit of truth" occurs in the surrounding world only in Test. Jud. 20:5, where the Spirit is He who "bears witness to all things and accuses all" (cf. already Wis. 1:5 f. of the Spirit), then in Herm. m., 3, 4 and finally in 1 Q S (→ 390, 6 f.). In all three passages the same ideas of the Spirit prevail; in all three the "spirit of truth" is also thought of as an independent angelic figure. [765] He is also the "spirit of knowledge" → 340, 12 (cf. Test. R. 2:1; 3:1 f.; S. 3:1). In Test. D. 6:2 he is fused with the intercessory angel, the "mediator between God and man for the peace of Israel." In all three passages this

---

[757] Cf. the association of sayings about the Paraclete and sayings about Jesus in 14:15 ff. and 18 ff.; 14:25 f. and 21-24; 16:12-15 and 16-24 (Bu. J., 451 on 16:24). On the exegesis of 16:9 cf. Barrett, op. cit. (→ n. 710), ad loc.

[758] E. F. Scott in J. G. Simpson, "The Holy Spirit in the Fourth Gospel," Exp., IX, 4 (1925), 293.

[759] Not at all a secondary combination as Windisch thinks, op. cit. (→ n. 712), 111. In opposition cf. Barrett, op. cit. (→ n. 710), 75 f. and on 15:26.

[760] Goguel, Notion, 136, as against R. H. Strachan, The Fourth Gospel (1941), 288 f., who presupposes 2 C. 3:17 in Jn. He is not just the λόγος released from earthly manifestation, Michaelis, op. cit. (→ n. 737), 260 f. as against Schweitzer, op. cit. (→ n. 548), 344. Nothing is said about the work of the Paraclete or Spirit prior to Jesus, though Judaism sees the Spirit almost exclusively in the OT, Goguel, Notion, 91-93.

[761] Michaelis, 29 f.; F. Büchsel, Das Ev. nach Joh., NT Deutsch on 7:39 is wrong here.

[762] For this reason Jn. does not put it: "I come to you in the Spirit." Cf. Simpson, op. cit. (→ n. 758), 294-297. There is no speculation on an intra-Trinitarian relation, Bu. J., 426.

[763] Naturally two different witnesses are not mentioned; the sense is the same as in 8:18; 3 Jn. 12 (Bu. J.; Hoskyns, op. cit. [→ n. 724], ad loc.); ἐστέ (instead of ἦτε) shows that the ref. is to witnesses in all ages. Materially cf. K. Barth, K.D., IV, 1 (1953), 723 f. (C.D., IV, 1 [1956], 647 f.).

[764] "Comforter" is again supported by J. G. Davies, "The Primary Meaning of παράκλητος," JThSt, NS, 4 (1953), 35-38, but even in the cautious form in Barrett, Fourth Gospel, 14 this is hardly possible, → V, 800-803.

[765] There is thus no difficulty in equating the personal Paraclete (Barrett, op. cit. [→ n. 710], 77) with the Spirit (even in 20:22 f.), as against Windisch, op. cit. (→ n. 712), 130, 133.

figure stands in a system which expresses Johannine dualism in almost the same terms. [766] In the circles of heterodox Judaism most closely related to Jn. we thus find the concept of an angel-like holy spirit who as the "spirit of truth" bears witness and accuses, who as the "spirit of knowledge" promotes the spiritual life of his people, and who thus stands in absolute contrast to the spirit of the world. Jn. gave this concept a Chr. form as Test. Jud. 20 gave it a Jewish form. [767]

Once again, therefore, it is clear that for Jn. πνεῦμα is simply the power of the preaching of Jesus as Redeemer in which the divine world encounters man. [768] True ζωή is to be found only in God, in the sphere of the πνεῦμα, as a community which stood under Hellenistic influence had long since stated. God is πνεῦμα, not σάρξ. Only he who himself stands in the πνεῦμα comes to God. But what is this πνεῦμα? In the circles of heterodox Judaism two very different answers were given: a heavenly substance in which matter is included, or an angel who works in the good. For Jn, as for the whole community, πνεῦμα could be only the power which causes man to know Jesus as the Redeemer in whom God encounters him. Thus in John, as in Paul, the answer of Judaism is taken up in a new form. πνεῦμα is πνεῦμα προφητείας, not as a phenomenon of the remote past, but as the power of God which is present in the proclamation of the community, which shapes the life of the eschatological people of God, [769] and which in so doing summons and judges the world.

V. The Rest of the New Testament.

1. The Pauline Circle.

a. Ephesians. The Pauline usage is somewhat watered down in Eph. πνεῦμα is generally the power of the community's growth (3:16), specifically that of prayer (6:18), but especially, as in Paul (→ 425, 1 ff.), the power of revelation, 1:17; 3:5. The primitive Christian view exerts an influence here to the degree that the reference is to special revelation as imparted to apostles and prophets or continually sought for the community, not to the basic knowledge of the Christ event. In a traditional formulation 6:17 says that the Spirit works especially in Scripture. 5:18, on the other hand, stresses the ecstatic aspect, → 423, 2 f. 4:4 is probably

---

[766] Cf. K. G. Kuhn, "Die in Palästina gefundenen hbr. Texte u. d. NT," ZThK, 47 (1950), 197-211. Barrett, Fourth Gospel, 12, also op. cit. (→ n. 710) on 14:17 rejects the ref. to Test. Jud. 20 on the ground that this is speaking of the good yezer, not the Spirit of God. Bu. J., 433, n. 1 also rejects it because the process is individual, not cosmic. All this may be true of the Judaised form here, but not of the more mythological par. → 389, 35 ff.

[767] On the merging of Jesus and the Spirit → n. 830. Behind the Paraclete sayings there may be reminiscence of the words of Jesus (definitely acc. to W. F. Lofthouse, "The Holy Spirit in the Acts and the Fourth Gospel," Exp. T., 52 [1941], 335; cf. also Strachan, op. cit. [→ n. 760], 287 f.), but they are certainly not an exposition of Mk. 13:11 or Lk. 12:12 (Howard, 77-80; Fridrichsen, op. cit. [→ n. 407], 370, n. 1; cf. Windisch, Joh.-Ev., 312 f.) or of Mt. 10:17-22 (so for Jn. 15:18-16:2 B. W. Bacon, Introduction to the NT [1900], 259). The vital thought there is that of help in persecution by the authorities, but this is absent from Jn., Barrett, Fourth Gospel, 9.

[768] Cf. Barrett, op. cit. (→ n. 710), 76 f. The Paraclete is the preached Gospel acc. to A. Ström, "Vetecornet," Acta Seminarii Neotestamentici Upsaliensis, 11 (1944), 439. There is naturally no thought whatever of the human spirit awakened to self-awareness, Bu. J., 432 against Hegel.

[769] For definition of the Church as the visible sign of the Spirit cf. H. Stirnimann, "Die Kirche u. d. Geist Christi," Divus Thomas, 31 (1953), 3-17. Y. M. J. Congar deals with the unity and differences in the mission of the apostles and the Spirit in "Le St. Esprit et le corps apostolique réalisateurs de l'oeuvre du Christ," Revue des Sciences philosophiques et théologiques, 36 (1952), 613-625; 37 (1953), 24-48.

applying the anthropological truth ἓν σῶμα, ἓν πνεῦμα to the → σῶμα Χριστοῦ which includes all the members. Hence the πνεῦμα at work in all is necessarily one, that of the κύριος. 2:18; 4:3 are to be interpreted thus and not according to Phil. 1:27. Thus Eph. approximates more strongly to Gnostic ideas, though also to the concepts of pre-Gnostic Judaism, → 389, 29 ff. 2:2 refers to the evil πνεῦμα (→ 396, 19 ff.) [770] which is at work in the lost, cf. also the πνευματικὰ τῆς πονηρίας that rule in the air according to 6:12. In 4:30 we find the typical concept of grieving the Holy Spirit of God (→ n. 342) given to man. The Pauline view that the Spirit is an ἀρραβών of the coming κληρονομία is given even more pointed form in the concept of the seal (guarantee?) in 1:13 f.; [771] 4:30; cf. 2 C. 1:22; [772] the reference, however, is not to a substance which cannot be lost, → 446, 22 ff. On 2:22 → n. 706; 4:23 is uncertain. [773]

b. The Pastorals. In a way which is quite un-Pauline πνεῦμα occurs in the Past. only 6 times, also once in the sense of "seducing spirit" (1 Tm. 4:1). [774] Of these 1 Tm. 3:16 (→ 416, 34 ff.) and 2 Tm. 4:22 (→ 435, 6 f.) [775] are formulae. 1 Tm. 4:1 is a traditional reference to the prophetic spirit (→ 381, 23 ff.). 2 Tm. 1:7 is close to 1 C. 4:21, → 436, 5 ff. Did the Pauline insight that the extraordinary is not constitutive for the Spirit (→ 424, 5 ff.) lead to the substitution of Hellenistic lists of virtues for the works of the Spirit? It is more likely that in opposition to enthusiasts who saw only the unusual nature of their own spiritual gifts the author is insisting that demonstration of the Spirit is to be found in everyday things. On 2 Th. 1:12, 14 → n. 346. A new thought appears in Tt. 3:5, → n. 731. [776] In good Pauline fashion (→ 426, 12 ff.) the works of the Spirit in these formulae are not to be found in miraculous powers but in the new birth which sets us in justification and hope. [777] The author himself, however, seems to have understood this ethically, vv. 1-3. [778]

2. Hebrews.
Here the usage is fairly complex and strongly influenced by Judaism. The πνεύματα of 12:23 are the departed, → 378, 35 ff. [779] 12:9 shows that the dualism of a carnal and spiritual world lies behind this. The idea that the divinely created nature is the basis of divine sonship is quite remote. All that is said is that God

---

[770] Cf. Noack, op. cit. (→ n. 340), 52 f.

[771] τῆς ἐπαγγελίας empasises the eschatological aspect, cf. Gl. 3:14.

[772] Cf. Ez. 9:4; Lampe, op. cit. (→ n. 626), 3-18; R. Schnackenburg, Das Heilsgeschehen bei d. Taufe nach dem Ap. Pls. (1950), 81-83. Jewish par. E. Dinkler, "Zur Geschichte des Kreuzsymbols," ZThK, 48 (1951), 163-168; though cf. W. Michaelis, "Zeichen, Siegel, Kreuz," ThZ, 12 (1956), 505-525.

[773] More probably an instr. dat. in which νοῦς simply indicates where God's Spirit works (Gutbrod, 235 f.) than a dat. of relation ("in your ..."; cf. R. 12:2), in which case νοῦς would show the πνεῦμα to be the human πνεῦμα, Bertrams, 15 f.

[774] The δαιμόνια which lie behind the false teachers.

[775] Not denoting the grace of calling, Dib. Past.³, ad loc.

[776] It makes no material difference whether πνεῦμα is made to depend on both expressions, or only on the second, or on λουτροῦ. The most probable ref. is to the "bath of a regeneration and renewal effected by the Holy Spirit," → III, 453, 26 ff.; at any rate ἀνακαινώσεως must be taken as a par. to παλιγγενεσίας (→ I, 688, 30 ff.), not λουτροῦ.

[777] This is also a rejection of all Hell. ideas of deification, Dib. Past.³, ad loc.; for the difference from Paul cf. esp. B. S. Easton, The Pastoral Epistles (1947), Note ad loc.; Scott, 176 f.; Flemington, op. cit. (→ n. 435), 103 f. On 2 Tm. 1:6 → 451, 20 f.

[778] Flemington, op. cit., 101.

[779] Eth. En. 22:9; 41:8; 103:3 (Wis. 3:1; 4:14 : ψυχαί); C. Spicq, L'épître aux Hébreux, II (1953), ad loc. The emendation D*d is under Trinitarian influence, Wnd. Hb., ad loc. It is doubtful whether the passage is as consistently eschatological as Bieder thinks, op. cit. (→ n. 540), 148.

is not just the Father of the corruptible flesh but also of the innermost I which will one day have to answer before Him. [780] In 1:14 the angels are called πνεύματα. [781] In the traditional manner (→ 382, 15 ff.) the Spirit who speaks in Scripture is referred to in 3:7; 9:8; 10:15. There is a purely anthropological distinction between πνεῦμα and ψυχή in 4:12; these are two particularly closely related parts, and the distinction is simply the current one. [782] Along the lines of primitive Christianity (→ 415, 27 ff.) the works of the Spirit are found especially in miracles in 2:4; 6:4 f. The predominant thought in 2:4 is that the Spirit of God can be apportioned and distributed in various ways to the individual. [783] He is viewed particularly as a foretaste of the coming aeon in 6:4 f. (→ 415, 32 f.). [784] In spite of the parallel to αἷμα τῆς διαθήκης, πνεῦμα τῆς χάριτος (= Zech. 12:10 LXX) in 10:29 is not to be construed as the cause of salvation; the Spirit here is a sign of the eschatological grace of God. [785] 9:14 is difficult (→ III, 280, 29 ff.; IV, 339, 15 ff.): "Christ offered himself without spot to God διὰ πνεύματος αἰωνίου." Here too, as in 12:9, the antithesis to σάρξ seems to be predominant (v. 13). In the old covenant purely earthly and corruptible things were offered in the sphere of σάρξ; here, however, there offers Himself One who comes from the sphere of πνεῦμα and possesses the πνεῦμα, [786] so that He brings a salvation which lasts beyond the σάρξ; [787] διά refers to the nature and manner of this sacrifice. [788]

3. The Catholic Epistles.

a. James. In James, apart from the purely anthropological use in 2:26, the only reference to the πνεῦμα is in 4:5, where it would seem to be the spirit which God

---

[780] → 392, 10 ff. (against Wnd. Hb., ad loc.).

[781] Here we are again on orthodox Jewish ground as compared with Paul's view of angels as subjected hostile powers, Wnd. Hb. Exc. on 2:14.

[782] Spicq, op. cit. I (1952), 52 f.: as in Philo ψυχή is the vital force, while πνεῦμα is the divine power added thereto. Spicq, "Alexandrinismes dans l'épître aux Hébreux," Rev. Bibl., 58 (1951), 483, n. 6, refers on the other hand to Gk. physicians who locate the πνεῦμα ζωτικόν and the ψυχικόν in different parts of the body.

[783] Πνεύματος is an obj. gen., since αὐτοῦ is to be related to ὁ θεός, J. Moffatt, A Critical and Exeg. Comm. on the Ep. to the Hebrews, ICC (1924), ad loc. The idea is to be found already in the OT, Gunkel, 30 f.

[784] Wnd. Hb., ad loc. The structure is in doubt; it is easiest to set δωρεά ἐπουράνιος and πνεῦμα ἅγιον in synon. parallelism, with a further development in ῥῆμα and δυνάμεις. Mi. Hb., ad loc. gives precedence to δωρεά as "salvation," while Moffatt, op. cit., ad loc. treats all the members as par. descriptions of φωτισθέντας.

[785] Or simply "the spirit who offers himself in free grace" (Mi. Hb., ad loc.)? There can hardly be an allusion to Mk. 3:29.

[786] It is impossible to decide here whether, acc. to the view of the author, this Spirit is granted to Jesus in adoptionist fashion (Wnd. Hb., ad loc.), or whether He was already proper to the pre-existent Lord (Goguel, Notion, 66). Is the Spirit, in analogy to the anthropological spirit (4:12), regarded as a part of Jesus, His spiritual being (Weinel, 31), His divine nature (Spicq, op. cit. [→ n. 779], ad loc.), or His immortal soul (Büchsel, 469), and not rather as the sphere in which the sacrifice is offered? Cf. Käsemann, op. cit. (→ n. 557), 99-102; R. Bultmann, "Ursprung u. Sinn der Typologie als hermeneutischer Methode," ThLZ, 75 (1950), 210 f.

[787] On the idea of a continuing sacrifice of Christ in heaven cf. Käsemann, op. cit., 137-139. Moffatt, op. cit., ad loc. compares 7:16 and esp. Midr. Ps. 31 (Str.-B., III, 741): "Because ... your redemption took place through flesh and blood, ... therefore your redemption was a redemption for a casual sin; but in the future I myself will redeem you; for I live and abide; then will your redemption be a redemption which lasts for ever." The idea that Jesus in virtue of the eternal Spirit enters into life again and can continue to work as High-priest in heaven (Rgg. Hb., ad loc.) is hardly present here.

[788] Bl.-Debr. § 223, 3. To be preferred to Mi. Hb., ad loc.: "In the Holy Spirit priest and victim become one."

has set in man and which will be demanded back from him pure, [789] → 392, 1 ff. Materially → σοφία is identical with the πνεῦμα in 3:17, → II, 590, 13 ff. [790]

b. 1 Peter. There is more to be gleaned from 1 Pt. The traditional prophetic Spirit of 1:11 f. (→ 381, 23 ff.) is restricted to the OT prophets and the apostles, [791] to whom He was sent from heaven. [792] But the difference between the time of the writing prophets and the post-Easter period is smoothed over; even in the earlier epoch the πνεῦμα was the πνεῦμα Χριστοῦ. [793] Very generally the Spirit is the power of sanctification in 1:2. [794] 4:14 is in keeping with Jewish thought and limits the gift of the Spirit to martyrs, → 398, 19 ff. [795] ἡσύχιον πνεῦμα in 3:4 (cf. 1 C. 4:21 → 436, 5 ff.) is very weak. On 2:5 → n. 706. [796] Difficulties arise in 3:18 f. (→ I, 104, 2 ff.; IV, 386, n. 111) and 4:6. In 4:6, as in 3:18 (→ 417, 6 ff.), there is a reference to the two spheres in which judgment and deliverance are enacted and which are, of course, characterised by the substance of the body and that of the spirit which transcends it. [797]

Four questions remain. 1. Is ἐν ᾧ in 3:19 to be related to πνεύματι? Certainly not in the sense that Christ in the Spirit already preached in the time of Noah to those who are now in prison, cf. Ign. Mg., 9, 2. A possible thought is that after the crucifixion Christ as a disembodied spirit went to spirits, but it is fairly certain that as in 1:6; 4:4 ἐν ᾧ simply means "wherein." [798] Nor is the resurrection to be differentiated from ζωοποιηθῆναι as a second event; the event of the resurrection is unfolded in the descent to Hades and the ascent to heaven. The only remaining question is whether this is not one journey, so that the φυλακή is to be thought of as "on the way" in the air. [799] If we have here the reconstruction of an ancient formula, [800] this was the original idea. In the present context the two are separated.

2. Are the πνεύματα demons [801] or the departed (→ III, 707, 15 ff.)? Since 4:6 cannot be separated from this passage, the second view is the right one. It is possible, however,

[789] The conjecture πρὸς τὸν θεόν (= Ps. 42:1) is improbable; πρὸς φθόνον with λέγει yields no sense. Since God is the subj. in v. 6a, πνεῦμα must be taken as an acc. and πρὸς φθόνον is then to be construed adverbially: "God zealously desires the spirit whom he has caused to dwell in us," i.e., He zealously sees to it that the πνεῦμα is kept unsullied, → 392, 7 f. (cf. Preisker [Wnd. Kath. Br.³, ad loc.]; Weinel, 159). H. Greeven in Dib. Jk.⁸ (1956), ad loc. quotes bShab., 152b: "Yield him up (the spirit) in purity, as he hath given him to thee in purity."
[790] W. Bieder, "Chr. Existenz nach d. Zeugnis d. Jk.," ThZ, 5 (1949), 111 f. Büchsel, 463.
[791] This is overlooked by H. A. Guy, The NT Doctrine of the Last Things (1948), 95 when he suggests that here, as in Ac., the Spirit is a breaking in of the eschaton.
[792] At their calling (Pentecost) rather than in miracles (as against Preisker [Wnd. Kath. Br.³, ad loc.]).
[793] Goguel, Notion, 66 f. B (without Χριστοῦ) is a secondary softening. There are material parallels in Barn., 5, 6; Ign. Mg., 9, 2; Just. Apol., 62, 3 f.
[794] = 2 Th. 2:13; 1 Th. 4:7 → 431, 26 f. Par. to θεοῦ πατρός and Ἰησοῦ Χριστοῦ, πνεύματος in 1 Pt. 1:2 can only be taken as a subj. gen. The triadic formulation is already well advanced, but the Spirit comes before Christ, → n. 842.
[795] Wnd. Kath. Br., ad loc.
[796] Selwyn, op. cit. (→ n. 555), following E. Lohmeyer, "Vom urchr. Abendmahl," ThR, 9 (1937), 296, thinks the ref. of the spiritual sacrifices is to the eucharist, but cf. F. W. Beare, The First Epistle of Peter (1947), ad loc. Cf. also Flew, op. cit. (→ n. 407), 160.
[797] Hell. influence can hardly be denied in view of 2:11, as against Preisker (Wnd. Kath. Br.³), ad loc.
[798] With Bieder, op. cit. (→ n. 540), 106 against Wnd. Kath. Br., ad loc.
[799] Schlier, op. cit. (→ n. 372), 19-23; R. Reitzenstein, "D. mandäische Buch d. Herrn d. Grösse," SAH, 12 (1919), 30.
[800] R. Bultmann, "Bekenntnis u. Liedfragment in 1 Pt.," Coniectanea Neotestamentica, 11 (1947), 1-14, though cf. J. Jeremias, "Zwischen Karfreitag u. Ostern," ZNW, 42 (1949), 194-196, who discerns older formulae behind v. 18 and v. 22.
[801] Cf. Bieder, op. cit. (→ n. 540), 112.

that in some obscure fashion the demons (at work in persecutors?) are included. [802] But would they be localised in Hades?

3. Who are the νεκροί of 4:6? Even if in Herm. s., 9, 16, 3-6 the real and the spiritual meanings of "living" and "dead" merge into one another, ref. to the spiritually dead who are still alive on earth [803] is very difficult, the more so as the phrase in 4:5 can hardly be taken thus. It is also highly unlikely that dead Christians who heard the Gospel in their lifetime are in view here. [804] Alongside 3:19 one has to think of the πνεύματα mentioned there. [805]

4. But what is σάρξ here? If one compares 4:6 with 3:18 and 1 C. 5:5 (→ 435, 20 ff.), one can speak only of a judgment in the earthly sphere, i.e., death. κριθῶσιν (4:6) is thus to be regarded as a pluperfect. [806]

c. 2 Peter. Here the Spirit is still simply the power which inspires what was already regarded as canonical Scripture (1:21), [807] whereas in Jude the πνεῦμα is in Gnostic fashion a sign of the non-psychic, expressed especially in prayer. [808]

d. 1 John. In 1 Jn. πνεῦμα is first used along primitive Christian lines for the distinguishing mark of the great turning-point. The new thing made known thereby, however, is no longer just the eschaton which has now come; it is the abiding of Christ in believers, 3:24; 4:13. [809] The unusual nature of the gifts of the Spirit is not emphasised. To be sure, πνεῦμα is regarded strictly as a gift from without and not as native in any sense to man, 4:13. [810] As in Jn. however (→ 441, 14 ff.) the Spirit bears testimony here (5:6-8), and does so first and comprehensively in "water" and "blood" (v. 6), then more narrowly along with these (v. 7 f.) as the power of the proclamation of the Word, which is to a special degree the work of the πνεῦμα, [811] alongside the sacraments. [812] The same concept of the prophetic Spirit bearing witness may be seen in 4:1-6, though here the Johannine view (→ 444, 7 ff.) combines with ideas of two warring spirits — ideas which agree

---

[802] Wnd. Kath. Br., ad loc.; Reicke, 115-118; Bieder, op. cit. (→ n. 540), 112 f.; cf. Test. N. 3:5; S. Bar. 56:13-15.

[803] Bieder, op. cit., 125 f., 154.

[804] Beare, op. cit., ad loc. as against Selwyn, op. cit., 338 f.

[805] Ev. Pt. 41 already suggests those who have fallen asleep.

[806] For reasons cf. E. Schweizer, "1 Pt. 4:6," ThZ, 8 (1952), 152-154. There is no hint of the punishment of the resurrected σάρξ (→ n. 692). C. Schmidt, "Gespräche Jesu mit seinen Jüngern nach der Auferstehung," TU, 43 (1919), 76, n. 1, shows that 2nd cent. Christians divided man into body, soul and spirit. It is highly debatable whether there is any thought of a separate treatment of flesh and spirit in the hereafter.

[807] Cf. E. Käsemann, "Begründet der nt.liche Kanon die Einheit d. Kirche?" Ev. Theol., 11 (1951/52), 19; → 382, 16 ff.; 398, 18 ff.

[808] On v. 19 f. → n. 384 and → 436, 31 ff. In 20 f. we have the πνεῦμα ἅγιον along with θεός and κύριος ἡμῶν ᾽Ιησοῦς Χριστός, → n. 842.

[809] Naturally this is the eschatological fulfilment, but the view taken of it is very different from that of the primitive community, cf. Guy, op. cit. (→ n. 791), 171.

[810] The Spirit is still transcendent and comprehensive (ἐκ).

[811] The sacraments do not convey the Spirit here. They are important because the prophetic πνεῦμα preaches the real life and death of Jesus through them too. The Gnostic opponent could accept the fact that the baptism in the Jordan was the true redemptive event while the death of Jesus had only the function of liberating the Spirit therein received for transmission to believers, Flemington, op. cit. (→ n. 435), 89-91. But the author has more than this in view, as 1:7 shows.

[812] Cf. Jn. 19:34. αἷμα is debated; acc. to 4:2 the antagonists are docetic Gnostics. 5:6a then tells us that Jesus passed through baptism and death, Flemington, op. cit., 88. The opponents in Iren. Haer., I, 26, 1 maintain the direct opposite : Christ came down in baptism but ascended before death. There is some ambivalence, however, in 6b. The ref. in v. 8 is to the sacraments as testimonies to His baptism and death, Howard, 47 f.; Schweizer, op. cit. (→ n. 711), 344-348.

with 1 Jn. 4:6 even in detailed formulation. [813] The naming of the opposing power as ἀντίχριστος (v. 3) is Christian, and so especially is the confession of the incarnate Lord as the criterion of utterances of the Spirit, → 423, 19 ff. On the plural πνεύματα → n. 689. Animistic ideas exert an even stronger influence here. Nowhere else in the NT is there so strong an emphasis as here on trust in the πνεῦμα who works in the community, who needs no official authorisation, who bears witness, not by bringing new and unheard of revelations, but by bringing the old message. [814]

4. Revelation.

In its understanding of the Spirit this book occupies a place of its own which obviously suggests circles in pre-Gnostic Judaism. As in popular Judaism (→ 375, 30 ff.) [815] unclean demonic spirits are called πνεύματα here (16:13 f.; 18:2), and the vital force is the πνεῦμα given by God or a demon (11:11; 13:15). Dominant, however, is the idea of the πνεῦμα τῆς προφητείας (19:10 → IV, 501, 7 ff.). [816] The reference here is obviously to an extraordinary event : the state ἐν πνεύματι is differentiated from the usual state, 1:10; 4:2; → V, 352, 19 ff. The πνεῦμα is the power which gives visions the ordinary man cannot have. [817] The πνεῦμα can lead a man off (17:3; 21:10) into wonderful regions which the natural man does not perceive. [818] Hence πνευματικῶς in 11:8 means in prophetic rather than ordinary speech. [819] But the Spirit did not speak only in the past ; He speaks to-day. Not only does He recall the promises of Scripture ; He formulates them afresh (14:13). In this respect the deity of the Spirit, far transcending everything human, is felt so strongly that the human speaker can fade from the scene altogether. [820] In Rev. the Spirit is related to the community rather than the individual inasmuch as He always speaks to the community, and the one through whom He speaks is immaterial. [821] But this Spirit — and this is the decisive point — is no other than the exalted Lord Himself, 2:1 = 7, 8 = 11 etc. He is the exalted Lord as the One who speaks to the community. Only as πνεῦμα is He with His own.

---

[813] Test. Jud. 20:1: τὸ τῆς ἀληθείας καὶ τὸ τῆς πλάνης (πνεῦμα) → 391, 11 f. Cf. Schnackenburg, op. cit. (→ n. 616), 187-191.

[814] → χρῖσμα (2:20, 27); Schweizer, Geist, 31 f.; Bu. J., 484, n. 8; E. Käsemann, "Ketzer u. Zeuge," ZThK, 48 (1951), 292-311.

[815] Scott, 212 : Without Rev. we would not know how primitive were the ideas of the Spirit among Christians. But is not the absence of a doctrine of the Spirit here due to the fact that in this book, as in primitive Christianity, the whole emphasis lies on the future, not on the presence of the Spirit ?

[816] It seems to me, however, that acc. to 19:10 all members of the community (at least potentially, Loh. Apk. on 19:10) are prophets (→ IV, 501, 19 ff.; cf. Rev. 10:7; 11:18; 22:6 with 1:1; 2:20; 7:3; 19:2, 5). In Luke, too, πνεῦμα is fundamentally an extraordinary prophetic gift which can find ecstatic expression and yet which is conferred on all members of the community, → 409, 22 ff.

[817] Man's "self-conscious inwardness" (Cr.-Kö., 885 : πνεῦμα, II, 1b) is quite impossible. In Ac. 12:11 ἐν ἑαυτῷ γενόμενος is the opp. of being ἐν ἐκστάσει, 11:5; 22:17 (Had. Apk., on 1:10).

[818] But cf. the ἐν (in distinction from Mk. 1:12, where the reality of the change of place is unmistakable).

[819] Reitzenstein Hell. Myst., 319. One cannot properly transl. "allegorically." A text relating to Sodom and Egypt is not applied to Jerusalem, nor is Jerusalem given an allegorically concealing name ; Jerusalem is seen with prophetic eyes and identified with the biblical Sodom and Egypt. Cf. M. Rissi, Zeit u. Geschichte in der Offenbarung d. Joh. (1952), 72 : "corresponding to the measure of God."

[820] 2:17; 14:13; 22:17 (Gunkel, 49).

[821] Loh. Apk. on 2:28.

This is never said of the κύριος as such; the κύριος is wholly in heaven. [822] Hence 22:17 can tell us that the πνεῦμα and the νύμφη say: "Come." When the community calls for its Lord in the power of the Spirit, [823] it is not ultimately its own power or religiosity which calls, but the Lord Himself. At the same time, however, the πνεῦμα can be differentiated from the Lord as the power which goes forth from Him, → 392, 7 ff.; 419, 7 ff.

This tension is again sharply emphasised in the singular idea of the seven spirits. From a religio-historical standpoint these are simply the seven archangels. [824] In Rev. they stand between God and Christ; grace and peace go forth from them, 1:4. [825] Like the angels, they stand before the throne of God as lights, 4:5. [826] They are sent over the whole earth as messengers of God and Christ, 5:6. With the angels of the communities (1:20) they are in the hand of Christ, 3:1. They thus represent the Spirit of God in His fulness and completeness. [827] But they also represent the throne angels, [828] and in addition they are parallel to the angels of the churches.

This is understandable only in the light of pre-Gnostic Jewish thinking. The same idea may be found in a developed Gnostic sense in Valentinus, where the angels are simply Christ Himself, but the individualised Christ who comes to the individual and who is also the *alter ego* of the human πνεῦμα. [829] The only essential distinction is that Rev. is a church book and relates the Spirit to the community, not to the individual, → n. 821. [830] The individualising of God's Spirit as the Spirit imparted to the individual as his πνεῦμα has taken place long since, and the unity of this πνεῦμα which comes forth from God with the new and given I of man is everywhere maintained, → 392, 8 ff. Rev., however, thinks in terms of the community rather than the individual. Hence the seven spirits correspond to the seven churches, and they are thought of as the new and favoured I of the community as well as the work of the Spirit which comes from God and is directed to the community, and which in their totality are simply the one Spirit of God.

[822] Loh. Apk., 186. Cf. the Johannine Paraclete (*ibid.* on 2:7).

[823] On the parataxis cf. Ac. 5:32; Jn. 15:26 f. → n. 492, 763.

[824] Tob. 12:15; cf. Bss. Apk. on 1:4; 8:2; though cf. G. H. Dix, "The Seven Archangels and the Seven Spirits," JThSt, 28 (1927), 233-250, who thinks the seven-branched candelabra may have had some influence, 4:5. On the number seven cf. Zech. 4:2, 10 (Rev. 5:6); Philo Op. Mund., 99-128; Zn. Apk., 169 f.; on the seven Persian archangels (Bertholet-Leh., II, 206) Yast, 13, 83.

[825] The passage is certainly not interpolated, as against Loh. Apk.; R. H. Charles, *The Revelation of St. John*, ICC (1920), ad loc.

[826] 8:2; cf. S. Bar. 21:6; Ps.-Clem. Hom., 8, 13, though cf. Str.-B., III, 788; W. Bietenhard, *Die himmlische Welt im Urchr. u. Spätjudt.* (1951), 60 f. They are also called servants of God in 1:4, P. Joüon, "Apocalypse, I, 4," *Recherches de science religieuse*, 21 (1931), 487.

[827] They were viewed as *spiritus septiformis* (Is. 11:2; the Heb. has only 6 gifts of the Spirit but in different ways the LXX and Syr. arrive at 7; Eth. 61:11 etc. in Charles, op. cit. on 1:4; cf. R. Koch, "Der Gottesgeist u. d. Messias," Biblica, 27 [1946], 247-249) and as the third person of the Trinity in all the older expositors, Bss. Apk., ad loc.; cf. also Zahn in Zn. Apk. on 1:4b.

[828] Joüon, op. cit., 486 f. stresses this, cf. also Bss. and Loh. Apk. on 4:5.

[829] → 394, 1 ff.; cf. Quispel, op. cit. (→ n. 354), 264: "L'ange est le Christ rapporté à l'existence individuelle de l'homme spirituel"; cf. also Cl. Al. Exc. Theod., 12, 2 (angels = πνεύματα νοερά).

[830] That the Spirit is here more plainly differentiated from Christ is simply the pre-Gnostic Jewish stage of the concept of Valentinus. That the Holy Spirit and Christ (pre- or post-existent) soon merge may be seen already in Herm. s., 5, 6, 7 (and Dib. Herm., ad loc.); 5, 2. Though 1 QH strongly emphasises the community, the Spirit is given to the individual, A. Dietzel, "Beten im Geist," ThZ, 13 (1957), 22-24, cf. 1 QH 17:17: "The spirits which thou hast set in me" (ibid., 25).

The fact that the spirits are regarded as angels is no longer a difficulty. The two terms are often interchangeable. [831] In heterodox Judaism angels often stand almost on equality with God [832] or the Messiah. [833] The angel is a mediator between God and men who intercedes for men [834] and presents their prayers to God. [835] Hence the triad God-Christ-angel is a current one, and occurs in Rev. itself. [836] As everywhere in Rev. God's work is depicted in concrete and active figures. Yet it remains His own work, as here in the seven spirits, who are simply God's own action. [837]

F. The Post-Apostolic Fathers.

In the period directly following three dangers characterise the development.

1. The Gnostic-Substantial Strand (→ 393, 18 ff.). The fact that Christ is made of spiritual substance becomes increasingly important. It applies already to the pre-existent Lord (→ 420, 7 ff.) in 2 Cl., 9, 5; 14, 2; Herm. s., 9, 1, 1. [838] Though Ign. upholds the Jewish doctrine of the resurrection against Gnosticism, his own thinking follows Gnostic lines. The union of the substances of spirit and flesh in Christ makes the resurrection of the flesh of the believer possible, Eph., 7, 2; Mg., 1, 2; Sm., 3, 2 f.; 12, 2. [839] Cf. further → 391, 19 ff., esp. n. 346.

2. The Ecstatic Strand. The Spirit is confused with unusual psychic phenomena [840] (→ 423, 21 ff.; Herm. v., 1, 1, 3; 2, 1, 1). This quickly paves the way for the idea that these phenomena are a reward for special faith, cf. 1 Cl., 2, 2.

3. The Official Strand. No longer is the one whom God appoints by endowment with the Spirit ordained to the ministry; the one who is rightly instituted into office is now guaranteed the Spirit of God. 2 Tm. 1:6 is supported by 1 Tm. 4:14; 1:18. More questionable are Ign. Phld., 7, 1 f.; Mg., 13, 1; 1 Cl., 41 f. (though cf. 42, 4) and esp. Iren.: *qui cum episcopatus successione charisma veritatis certum ... acceperunt,* Haer., IV, 26, 2. [841] Nevertheless, the NT *kerygma* retains its force and will constantly break through in the centuries which follow. [842]

---

[831] → n. 331; also Herm. m., 11, 9; Rev. 17:3; 21:10.

[832] 4 Esr. 5:43 is spoken to the angel (v. 31).

[833] Eth. En. 39:5-7.

[834] Test. L. 5:6 f.; D. 6:2 and the many par. in R. H. Charles, *Apocrypha and Pseudepigr. of the OT,* II (1913), 307, 335.

[835] Tob. 12:15 (the seven archangels).

[836] Lk. 9:26; 1 Tm. 5:21; Rev. 3:5. Just. Apol., I, 6, 2 conceptually distinguishes the πνεῦμα προφητικόν as the fourth member from the angelic host (which is identical therewith in Rev.).

[837] Cf. also M. Kiddle, "The Revelation of St. John," MNTC (1940) on Rev. 4:6. On the whole subject cf. Schweizer, *op. cit.* (→ n. 323), 502-512.

[838] Cf. esp. Dib. Herm. Exc. on s., 5, 6, 7.

[839] Schweitzer, *op. cit.* (→ n. 548), 332-338 (open to question in detail [Rüsch, 52-54], but clear later in Iren., V, 1, 3); cf. Herm. s., 5, 6, 5-7.

[840] On this cf. esp. Weinel.

[841] The traditional teaching is, of course, intended (v. Campenhausen, *op. cit.* [→ n. 630] 188), but cf. Ac. 6:3; 13:2 and also 1 C. 16:15-18; 1 Th. 5:12 f. for a very different view; cf. E. Schweizer, *Das Leben des Herrn in der Gemeinde u. ihren Diensten* (1946), 130-132; for the NT *ibid.,* 97 f. and 114, n. 33; also *Geist,* 14-16; W. D. Davies, "Light on the Ministry from the NT," *Religion in Life,* 21 (1952), 267 f. On the further development → 455, 1 ff.

[842] On the question of Trinitarian formulae → 401, 16 ff.; 434, 12 ff. and n. 440, 794, 808, also Ign. Mg., 13, 1 f.; in the repeated ἐν in 1 and the formulae of 1 Cl., 46, 6; 58, 2 there may be seen a slight hesitation to make the Spirit fully par. to God and Christ. Cf. Welch, *op. cit.* (→ n. 676), 29-40.

† πνέω, † ἐμπνέω.

1. From Hom. πνέω denotes a. the "blowing of the wind" (Od., 4, 361; also pap.: Preisigke Wört., s.v.) → 334, 36 ff.; b. "breathing" (Il., 17, 447) or "snorting" (13, 385); also the "blowing" of a flutist or flute (Poll. Onom., IV, 72, 81) → 335, 36 ff.; c. the "wafting forth of a scent" (Hom. Od., 4, 446; of the sweet savour of the god) → 346, n. 54 and 350, 17 ff.; d. transf. "being full of ...," "panting for ..." (Hom. Il., 3, 8 : courage; Eur. Iph. Taur., 288 : fire and slaughter; Aesch. Ag., 1206 : grace; Eur. Andr., 189 : μεγάλα = arrogance) → 336, 36 ff.; cf. Herond. Mim., VIII, 58 : τὰ δεινὰ πνεῦσαι → 337, n. 11 and 344, n. 41.

2. In the LXX the word means a. the "blowing of the wind" (Ep. Jer., 60) behind which stands Yahweh, ψ 147:7; Sir. 43:(16), 20 = נשׁב; b. the "snorting" of Yahweh which is like a stormy wind (Is. 40:24 = נשׁף), or of the ungodly (2 Macc. 9:7); in Philo breathing or snorting (esp. with μέγα, μεγάλα of arrogance or rage : Vit. Mos., I, 155; II, 240; Mut. Nom., 215; Som., I, 107; with λαμπρός [-όν] of courage, the soul, a kingdom : Jos., 21; Congr., 108; Deus Imm., 174).

ἐμπνέω occurs in Dt. 20:16; Jos. 10:28-40; 11:11, 14 in the form πᾶν ἐμπνέον = נשׁמה, נפשׁ cf. also Wis. 15:11 and Philo Leg. All., I, 33 and 36 (here elucidated by ἐνεφύσησεν) of the inbreathing of the soul, Gn. 2:7; breathing in Som., II, 94; in Joseph. "blowing" in Bell., 7, 317, "breathing" in Ant., 12, 256.

3. In the NT πνέω is used only of the "blowing" of a dangerous stormy wind or of the south wind which brings heat (Mt. 7:25, 27; Jn. 6:18; Lk. 12:55), or of the destructive winds in Rev. 7:1, cf. Da. 7:2; Sib., 8, 204. [1] The noun ἡ πνέουσα (αὔρα) occurs in Ac. 27:40. In Jn. 3:8 the "blowing" of the wind illustrates the work of the Spirit. What was plain already in the LXX (→ lines 9 ff.) may be seen again here. The action of the Spirit is not understood in natural terms (→ 359, 26 ff.), but neither has it become abstract in the sense of something purely spiritual. [2] The work of Yahweh or His Spirit is a stormy wind. Only once in the NT (Ac. 9:1) does ἐμπνέω mean "to breathe out," "to snort." [3]

4. The meaning "to be fragrant" occurs in Mart. Pol., 15, 2, where the scent of the dying martyr is compared to that of incense, and Ign. Eph., 17, 1, acc. to which the anointed Jesus wafts incorruption upon the Church. The last passage is not to be derived merely from the Gk. usage mentioned above; it is also influenced by the idea of the divine fragrance, → II, 810, n. 16; V, 495, n. 14.

† ἐκπνέω.

ἐκπνέω, "to breathe out," "to snort," "to blow out ... from," "to flag," occurs with βίον or ψυχήν ("to expire") from Aesch.; also abs. in this sense in Soph. (Ai., 1026), Eur. (Herc. Fur., 886; Hyps. Fr., 34[60], 38), Plut. (Gen. Socr., 32 [II, 597 f.]), M. Ant. (IV, 33, 2), Jos. (Ant., 12, 357).

In the NT the word occurs only in Mk. 15:37 (= Lk. 23:46), 39 (not MS D). Behind it stands the primitive idea that at death the vital force leaves the body in the breath, → 336, 20 f. But the parallels Mt. 27:50 (→ 396, 24); Jn. 19:30

πνέω κτλ. [1] It is a Jewish idea that the elemental angels which restrain the winds are different from the natural forces controlled by them, which are not themselves divine or demonic powers, Loh. Apk., ad loc.; par. in Bss. Apk., ad loc.

[2] "Only a language which has become hoplessly abstract differentiates between spirit and wind," E. Gaugler, Der Brief an d. Römer, I (1945), 253.

[3] For the constr. with the gen. cf. Anth. Pal., 2, 233 and 415; 5, 258; 7, 25; 9, 159; Aristaenetus, I, 5 (ed. R. Hercher, Epistolographi Graeci [1873]); Dion. Hal. Ant. Rom., 7, 51, 3.

(→ 438, n. 714) and esp. Lk. 23:46 (→ 415, 17 ff.) show that there may easily be connected with this the idea that the true self survives death, → 378, 35 ff. This is to be found explicitly in Ev. Pt. 19 and the Syr. translation of Mt. 27:50 (ἀνέβη τὸ πνεῦμα).

ἐκπνέω does not occur at all in the LXX, Moult.-Mill. and Preisigke Wört.; in Philo Poster. C., 113 it denotes the "fading" of inscr., in Leg. Gaj., 125 "expiring." The usage is thus typically Gk.

† πνοή.

1. πνοή is used from Hom. for the "blowing" of the wind (Il., 11, 622; Bacchyl., 5, 28 f.; Preisigke Sammelbuch, 358, 13) or of fire (Eur. Tr., 815), "breathing" and "snorting" (Eur. Herc. Fur., 1092) of anger (Phoen., 454), also "afflation" (→ 343, 19 ff.), e.g., of the god of inspiration (Eur. Ba., 1094 → 344, n. 40), Aphrodite and Eros (Iph. Aul., 69 → 344, n. 41), or the "sound" of flutes (Pind. Nem., 3, 79).

2. In the LXX πνοή is used for נֶפֶשׁ or נְשָׁמָה. The original meaning is very plain in 2 S. 22:16; Job 37:10, where the stormy wind is the snorting of Yahweh, cf. Ez. 13:13 = רוּחַ; also the concrete idea of inbreathing in Gn. 2:7; 7:22, and cf. Job 27:3; 32:8; 33:4, where the human πνεῦμα (or its πνοή) is simply God's πνοή (or πνεῦμα). Even where the meaning is simply the "breath of life" (Wis. 2:2; Sir. 33:21; 2 Macc. 3:31; 7:9 with emphasis on mortality) it is the breath given by Yahweh (Is. 42:5 and 57:16 par. πνεῦμα; Da. 5:23 and 10:17 vl. with πνεῦμα). πᾶσα πνοή in 3 Βασ. 15:29 corresponds exactly to πᾶν ἐμπνέον, → 452, 15 f. In Prv. 1:23; 11:13; 20:27; 24:12 it means the spirit of man or of wisdom.

3. Philo in Leg. All., I, 33 obviously sees a difficulty in the fact that Gn. 2:7 uses πνοή rather than the tt. for the Stoic world soul, i.e., πνεῦμα. He replies in I, 42 that the light breathing (πνεῦμα) is for the man formed of matter, but the strong and mighty πνοή is for the spirit created in the divine image, → 373, 15 ff. πνοὴ ζωῆς (cf. Gn. 2:7) and πνεῦμα θεῖον are par. in Spec. Leg., IV, 123.

4. In Ac. 2:2 the coming of the Spirit is announced by the noise of a mighty wind (πνοή). This shows with what concrete realism it is understood.[1] In Ac. 17:25, as often in the LXX (→ lines 18 ff.), πνοή is the "breath of life" which the Creator gives to all.[2]

† θεόπνευστος.

This word refers very generally to all wisdom as coming from God (Ps.-Phocylides, 122 [Diehl³, II, 101]), then more specifically to dreams given by God as distinct from natural dreams (Herophilus in Plut. Plac. Phil., V, 2 [II, 904 f.]), the θεῖον δημιουρ-

---

π ν ο ή. [1] Eur. Tro., 815 shows that the idea of fire can easily be associated with it; from the standpt. of usage there is no reason why v. 3a should be regarded as a gloss (so K. G. Kuhn, "Jesus in Gethsemane," Ev. Theol., 12 [1952/53], 269 f., but cf. E. Lohse, "Die Bdtg. des Pfingstberichtes im Rahmen des lk. Geschichtswerkes," Ev. Theol., 13 [1953], 424, n. 5).

[2] For bibl. cf. W. Nauck, "Die Tradition u. Komposition der Areopagrede," ZThK, 53 (1956), 11-52; H. Hommel, "Neue Forschungen zur Areopagrede," ZNW, 46 (1955), 145-178; also E. Schweizer, "Zu den Reden d. Ag.," ThZ, 13 (1957), 1-11; for the present v. cf. esp. the occurrences of πνοὴ ζωῆς; 1 QH 1:8 f., 15 f. (also 1 QM 10:13); 2 Macc. 7:23 (τὸ πνεῦμα καὶ τὴν ζωήν) of the Creator of the cosmos and man [H. Conzelmann]; Sib. Fr., 1, 5 (GCS, 6, 227).

θ ε ό π ν ε υ σ τ ο ς. [1] It is not quite certain whether the ref. is to Campanian or Aeolian Kyme, Λ. Rzach, Art. "Sibyllen," Pauly-W., 2 A (1923), 2091-2095.

γημα in us (Vett. Val., IX, 1 [p. 330, 19]), substantially the sources of Kyme which serve the sibyl, Sib., 5, 308; cf. 5, 406.[1] In Chr. works it is used of the Scriptures (Maxim. Conf. Scholia in librum de Coelesti Hierarchia, 3 [MPG, 4, 52A]), of an archbishop (Epigr. Graec., 1062), par. to χριστοφόρος as a term for the anchorites (Cyril of Scythopolis, Vitae Sabae, 16);[2] cf. also → I, 758, 18-20. θεόπνοος is used of water in Porphyr. Antr. Nymph., 10; of the face of the sphinx in Epigr. Graec., 1016; of the ecstatic in Corp. Herm., 1, 30; of the superiority of the νοῦς in Georgius Pisida, Hexaemeron, 1489 (MPG, 92, 1547).

In the NT θεόπνευστος occurs only in 2 Tm. 3:16 (→ III, 121, 31 ff.). The word here is used attributively to describe γραφή (→ I, 754, 1 ff.) more closely as "holy." The emphasis, however, is on ὠφέλιμος ... It is thus evident that the author is differentiating the writings ordained by God's authority from other, secular works.

The usage is Hell. Hence Hell. inspiration manticism lies behind it, → 345, 4 ff.[3] But only in a limited way does the Greek speak of inspired writings, → 345, n. 49. Democr., 18 maintains that the poet writes with enthusiasm and the holy spirit, and the same applies materially wherever what is uttered by inspired men is written down or the work of the poet is regarded as inspiration. But discussion of the relation of the original prophecy to the (poor) record of it (Plut. Pyth. Or., 4-24 [II, 396-406]; Ps.-Just. Cohortatio ad Graecos, 37)[4] shows how strongly the record was taken to be something secondary, a step removed from inspiration. Sacred scriptures are found, however, in Egypt (Strabo, 17, 1, 5; P. Oxy., XI, 1381, 121, 162, 186 f., 195 f.)[5] and esp. in Judaism. The commandments are dictated by God (Ex. 34:27 f.) or inscribed by Him on the tablets (24:12; 31:18; 32:16). Jub. refers to heavenly tablets on which not only the Law (4:5, 32) but the history, too, is already inscribed (23:32; 31:32; 32:28; cf. Test. L. 5:3 f.; A. 7:5).[6] The work of God in the prophets is specifically called inspiration (Nu. 24:2-4; Hos. 9:7). This doctrine of inspiration guarantees the authority of the Prophets and Writings in the older Synagogue, though this authority is less than that of the Law, which is given by God. While the Law was pre-existent, was taught to Moses by God, and was literally dictated or even written down by God Himself, the Prophets and Writings were inspired by God, or, acc. to a later view, they were revealed to Moses and passed on by him, or disclosed by him to the pre-existent souls of their authors at Sinai, Str.-B., IV, 435-451. On the other hand, Hell. Judaism understands the authority of Scripture primarily in the category of inspiration. Acc. to Philo all the OT writers are prophets, Rer. Div. Her., 259-266; Vit. Mos., II, 188, 246-292; Decal., 175; cf. Jos. Ap., 37 and 40, → 374, 29 ff. That similar ideas made their way into Palestinian Judaism, too, may be seen from 4 Esr. 14:22, where the author asks God for the gift of the Holy Spirit that he may be able to write down again just as it was everything that was in the destroyed Law and everything that took place from the beginning of the world.

On the other hand, it may be asserted that 2 Tm. 3:16 is not using a specific term from the world of enthusiasm (→ 358, 38 ff.) nor referring to any particular theory thereanent. As in the NT as a whole, there is also no mention of the sacredness of Scripture, → I, 751 f.[7]

---

[2] Ed. E. Schwartz, "Kyrillos v. Skythopolis," TU, 49, 2 (1939), 100, 3.

[3] Cf. esp. J. Leipoldt, "Die Frühgeschichte d. Lehre von der göttlichen Eingebung," ZNW, 44 (1952/53), 118-145. On the religio-historical phenomenon cf. J. Leipoldt and S. Morenz, H. Schriften. Betrachtungen z. Religionsgesch. d. antiken Mittelmeerwelt (1953), 24-36.

[4] Cf. Leipoldt, op. cit. (→ n. 3), 126 f.; for sacred books in the mystery religions cf. W. Bauer, Der Wortgottesdienst der ältesten Christen (1930), 40-42.

[5] Cf. also Leipoldt, op. cit., 118 f.

[6] For further instances cf. Bousset-Gressm., 149; cf. esp. Jub. 32:25 f.

[7] How far Paul is from an authenticating theory of inspiration may be seen from 1 C. 7:10, 40; cf. 14:37. On Mk. 23:36 → 382, 16 ff.; 398, 18 ff.

Only later do we find a theory of mechanical inspiration supported by the agreement of the many witnesses, [8] the age of the work, and the fulfilment of prophecies contained therein. [9] The divine spirit is then viewed as a flow of air which causes the flute to sound, or as the instrument which strikes the cither or lyre, → 347, 42 ff.; 350, 37 f. Finally, the same guarantee is ascribed to translations, as had been done already in Judaism. [10] Only in reaction to Montanism does a counter-movement appear. [11]

Schweizer

---

† πνίγω, † ἀποπνίγω,
† συμπνίγω, † πνικτός

---

1. The word group [1] occurs in Gk. from the tragedians. In secular Gk. the compounds are more common than the simple form and have the same meaning. The sense is a. "to stifle," e.g., of plants τί γάρ, ἔφη, ἣν ὕλη πνίγῃ συνεξορμῶσα τῷ σίτῳ καὶ διαρπάζουσα τοῦ σίτου τὴν τροφήν ..., Xenoph. Oec., 17, 14; ἐπεὶ ... ἀπόλλυται τὰ δένδρα ... συμπνιγόμενα καὶ οὐδεμίαν ἔχοντα δίοδον τῷ πνεύματι, Theophr. de causis plantarum, VI, 11, 6. The Indians offer up animals by strangling: οὐδὲ σφάτ-τουσι τὸ ἱερεῖον ἀλλὰ πνίγουσιν, ἵνα μὴ λελωβημένον ἀλλ᾽ ὁλόκληρον διδῶται τῷ θεῷ, Strabo, 15, 1, 54. The prophet Jer. was to have been put to death by suffoca-tion: οἱ δὲ παραλαβόντες αὐτὸν (sc. Jeremiah) εἴς τινα λάκκον βορβόρου πλήρη καθίμησαν ὅπως ... πνιγεὶς ἀποθάνῃ, Jos. Ant., 10, 121; cf. Jer. 38:6; he was to be choked by the gases in the miry pit. [2] b. "to choke": ὅταν τὸ ὕδωρ πνίγῃ, τί δεῖ ἐπιπίνειν; (Aristot. Eth. Nic., VII, 3, p. 1146a, 35). Before a children's court a physician was condemned who τοὺς νεωτάτους ὑμῶν διαφθείρει τέμνων ... καὶ πνίγων

---

[8] Ps.-Just. Cohort. ad Graecos, 8; Iren. Haer., II, 28, 3.
[9] Theoph. Autol., II, 9; Tert. Apologeticum, 19 f.
[10] Iren. Haer., III, 21, 4; Philo Vit. Mos., II, 37.
[11] Eus. Hist. Eccl., V, 17, 1-3; cf. Leipoldt, *op. cit.*, 136.

πνίγω κτλ. Pr.-Bauer⁴; Pass.; Liddell-Scott; H. Coppieters, "Le décret des Apôtres," *Rev. Bibl.*, NS, IV, 4 (1907), 34-58; F. Dibelius, "Die doppelte Überlieferung des Apostel-dekretes," ThStKr, 87 (1914), 618-625; H. Diehl, "Das sogenannte Aposteldekret. Ein Bei-trag zur Kritik von Harnacks 'Apostelgeschichte,'" ZNW, 10 (1909), 277-296; A. Harnack, "Das Aposteldekret (Ac. 15:29) u. d. Blass'sche Hypothese," SAB (1899), 170-176; also *Die Ag.* (1908), 188-198; also *Neue Untersuchungen zur Ag.* (1911), 22-24; R. Herzog, "Aus dem Asklepieion v. Kos," ARW, 10 (1907), 402, 409; J. Klausner, *Von Jesus zu Paulus* (1950), 345 f.; 373; W. G. Kümmel, "Das Urchr.," ThR, 17 (1948), 32 f.; also "Das Urchr.," ThR, 18 (1950), 26-29; B. Lauff, *Schechitah u. Bedikah*, Diss. Tierärztl. Hoch-schule Berlin (1922); K. Meuli, "Gr. Opferbräuche," *Phyllobolia f. Peter von d. Mühll zum 60. Geburtstage*, by O. Gigon, K. Meuli, W. Theiler, F. Wehrli and B. Wyss (1945), 255, 259, 286; E. Nestle, "Zum Erstickten im Aposteldekret," ZNW, 7 (1906), 254-256; H. van Oort, "Het Besluit der Apostelsynode v. Hand. 15," ThT, 40 (1906), 97-112; E. Preuschen, "Untersuchungen zur Ag.," ZNW, 14 (1913, 1-20; G. Resch, "Das Apostel-dekret," TU, NF, 13 (1905); W. Robertson Smith, *The Religion of the Semites*, 213 ff.; 312 ff.; J. H. Ropes, "The Text of Acts" (1926), 265-269, in Jackson-Lake, I, 3; P. W. Schmidt, *De Wette-Overbecks Werk z. Ag.*, Festschr. d. Universität Basel (1910), 18-25; W. Schulze, "Beiträge zur Wort- u. Sittengeschichte," SAB (1918), 320-332; A. Seeberg, *Die beiden Wege u. d. Aposteldekret* (1912); K. Six, *Das Aposteldekret* (1912); G. Strothotte, *Das Aposteldekret im Lichte d. jüdischen Rechtsgeschichte*, Diss. Erlangen (1955); H. Waitz, "Das Problem d. sogenannten Aposteldekrets," ZKG, 55 (1936), 227-263; J. Wellhausen, "Noten zur Ag.," NGG (1907), 19-21; T. Zahn, "Die Urausgabe d. Ag. des Lucas," *Forschungen zur Geschichte d. nt.lichen Kanons u. d. altkirchlichen Lit.*, IX (1916), 154-160, 358-366.
[1] The etym. is uncertain; there is perhaps a connection with πνέω [Debrunner].
[2] Schulze, 321.

456

πνίγω κτλ. 1, 2, 3

ἀπορεῖν ποιεῖ, πικρότατα πόματα διδούς ..., Plat. Gorg., 521e f; the meaning of πνίγω here is "to cause to choke." c. "To strangle," "to throttle." Rebellious Babylonians each choose a woman τὰς δὲ λοιπὰς ἀπέπνιξαν, Hdt., III, 150; cf. the similar instances in II, 92 : πνίξαντες, II, 169 : ἀπέπνιξαν, IV, 72 : ἀποπνίξωσι. Herod πέμψας δὲ καὶ τοὺς υἱεῖς εἰς Σεβαστὴν ... προσέταξεν ἀποπνῖξαι, Jos. Bell., 1, 551. Jos. Ant., 6, 166 refers to πνιγμός as the work of δαιμόνια. d. Metaphorically "to afflict," "to alarm" : ἔν με πνίγει μάλιστα ... δι' ὅπερ ἐπόθουν ... ἐς τὸ φῶς ἀνακύψαι πάλιν, Luc. Tyr., 12. ὃ δὲ μάλιστά με ἀποπνίγει, τοῦτ' ἔστιν ὅτι μεμφόμενοι τὴν ἀνθρωποποιίαν καὶ ... τὰς γυναῖκας ὅμως ἐρᾶτε αὐτῶν, Luc. Prometheus, 17. In the pass. (ἀπο-, συμ-) πνίγεσθαι means esp. "to drown" :[3] ... φεύγει καὶ ἐκδιωκόμενος ῥίπτει αὐτὸν εἰς τὴν θάλατταν, διαμαρτὼν δὲ τοῦ λέμβου ... ἀπεπνίγη, Demosth. Or., 32, 6. If the ship sinks : τοῦτο μόνον ποιῶ· μὴ φοβούμενος ἀποπνίγομαι ..., Epict. Diss., II, 5, 12. ὥσπερ ὁ πῆχυν ἀπέχων ἐν θαλάττῃ ... οὐδὲν ἧττον πνίγεται τοῦ καταδεδυκότος ὀργυιὰς πεντακοσίας, Chrysipp. Fr., 539 (v. Arnim, III, 143, 40).

The verbal adj. πνικτός "strangled," "throttled," occurs outside the NT only in the special sense "suffocated." Antiph. Fr., 1 (CAF, II, 13): ἔπειτα πνικτὰ τακερὰ μηκάδων μέλη (αἴρω). As a prohibition of food the word has come down — though only supplied — in an inscr. from the island of Cos[4] dating from the 3rd cent. B.C.: μηδὲ τῶν θνα[σιδίων μηδὲ τῶν κενεβρείων μηδὲ τῶν πνι]κτῶν ... ἔσθεν. It does not occur in Jos.[5]

2. The group is rare in the LXX ; πνικτός does not occur at all, and πνίγω only in 1 Βασ. 16:14, 15 for the Heb. בעת pi : an evil spirit torments (πνίγει) king Saul. ἀποπνίγω is used for חנק pi in Na. 2:13 : The lion strangled (ἀπέπνιξεν) for his lionesses. Cf. 2 Βασ. 17:23, where the Heb. וַיֵּחָנַק is rendered by ἀπήγξατο. Job 7:15 Heb. runs : "And my soul chooseth strangling (מַחֲנָק)," which the LXX translates not inaccurately, but poetically : ἀπαλλάξεις ἀπὸ πνεύματός μου τὴν ψυχήν μου, ἀπὸ δὲ θανάτου τὰ ὀστᾶ μου. There is no Heb. original in Tob. 3:8, where the word has the general sense "to kill" : οὐ συνίεις ἀποπνίγουσά σου τοὺς ἄνδρας;

3. In the NT the word occurs first in the story of the demoniac(s) of Gerasa (Mk. 5:1-20 and par.). The herd of swine into which the demons go plunges over a cliff καὶ ἐπνίγοντο (drowned) ἐν τῇ θαλάσσῃ, v. 13; Lk. 8:33: ἡ ἀγέλη ... ἀπεπνίγη (Mt. 8:32 ἀπέθανον). The verb — with both compounds — also occurs in the parable in Mk. 4:3-9 and par., where Jesus tells how some of the seed fell among thorns[6] καὶ ἀνέβησαν αἱ ἄκανθαι καὶ συνέπνιξαν (Mt. 13:7; Lk. 8:7: ἀπέπνιξαν) αὐτό (Mk. 4:7). As in the parable, the verb συμπνίγω also occurs in the interpretation in Mk. 4:13-20 and par.[7] Here the thorns are related allegorically to temptation by the riches and cares of the world (Mt. 13:22), also by other desires (Mk. 4:19) and the pleasures of life (Lk. 8:14), which choke the seed of the word. In the parable of the wicked servant in Mt. 18:23-35 the evil nature of the servant is depicted in his conduct towards his fellow-servant, which includes : καὶ κρατήσας αὐτὸν ἔπνιγεν λέγων ..., v. 28. In the story of the raising of Jairus' daughter (Mk. 5:21-43 and par.) Mark and Luke tell how Jesus was surrounded by a great press of people which thronged Him. In so doing Lk. has the plerophoric expression (8:42): ἐν δὲ τῷ ὑπάγειν αὐτὸν οἱ ὄχλοι συνέπνιγον αὐτόν, "the crowd almost suffocated him."

---

[3] *Ibid.*, 321-323.
[4] Herzog, 402, 409.
[5] Liddell-Scott gives examples of ἡμίπνικτος ("half-choked") from secular Gk.
[6] J. Jeremias, *Die Gleichnisse Jesu*[4] (1956), 6, 130 f.
[7] For the authenticity of the interpretation cf. W. Michaelis, "Die Gleichnisse Jesu," *Die urchr. Botschaft*, 32 (1956), 17-35; for the opp. view, Jeremias, *op. cit.*, 65-67.

The use of πνικτόν in Ac. 15:20, 29; 21:25 raises many problems which in part affect the so-called apostolic decree as a whole and in part concern only the occurrence and meaning of this particular word, → II, 441, n. 37.

In the main passage (Ac. 15:20, 29) the first difficulties are critical,[8] since πνικτόν is missing from most witnesses of the so-called Western text.[9] In this regard the situation is more favourable in Ac. 21:25, though there, too, πνικτόν is not undisputed on textual grounds. The alternation of number : πνικτοῦ in Ac. 15:20; πνικτῶν in 15:29; πνικτόν in 21:25, is without significance. The textual question cannot be decided here;[10] what we have to ask is what πνικτόν means in these verses.

According to the context the point at issue is a prohibition of meats which Jewish Christians are imposing on Gentile Christians. The command not to eat of πνικτόν is clearly par. to the command not to eat of αἷμα, → I, 173, 13 ff.[11]

The regulations in Lv. 17:13 f. and Dt. 12:16, 23 lay down that an animal should be slaughtered in such a way that all the blood drains from the carcase. If it is put to death in any other way, it "chokes," since the life seated in the blood remains in the body. If the animal dies it is נְבֵלָה (LXX θνησιμαῖον). If it is torn to pieces by a wild beast it is טְרֵפָה (LXX θηριάλωτον). OT statutes do not allow the flesh of such animals to be eaten, cf. Ex. 22:30; Lv. 17:15; Dt. 14:21 (though here the גֵּר is allowed to eat). The Rabbis extended and sharpened the biblical rules. Every animal is נְבֵלָה which is not put to death by ritual slaughter, for which there are detailed regulations. Every animal is טְרֵפָה which has a lethal blemish or dies of such.[12]

The debatable issue[13] is whether πνικτόν in the apostolic decree simply forbids the eating of what is forbidden in the OT[14] or whether the extended regulations of the Rabbis are included as well.[15] It is noteworthy that Ac. does not use the LXX words θνησιμαῖον and θηριάλωτον but chooses πνικτόν, which does not occur in the OT. That there is a connection between טְרֵפָה and πνίγω is suggested by Na. 2:13. The Rabbinate certainly did not call such killing "strangling" or such meat "strangled."[16] Perhaps the LXX terms were too general and did not cover what the authors had in view. In this case πνικτόν simply denotes the meat which is provided by the strangling of an animal.[17]

Of later Jewish witnesses[18] against the eating of things strangled only Philo Spec. Leg., IV, 122 f. need be cited : ἔνιοι δὲ ... καινὰς ἐπινοοῦντες ἡδονάς, ἄθυτα

---

[8] Cf. the comprehensive review in Resch, 7-17; Six, 11, 17 f.; Ropes, 265-268.
[9] Ropes, 269 and Strothotte, 129-132 do not accept the authenticity of πνικτοῦ.
[10] Cf. Bau. Ag., 195 f.; Kümmel, ThR, 17 (1948), 32 f.
[11] But is not necessarily included in this, as against Wellhausen, 21.
[12] Str.-B., II, 730-734.
[13] Schl. Jk., 59, n. 1: "I am not certain what is meant by the prohibition of πνικτὸν καὶ αἷμα."
[14] So Str.-B., II, 733.
[15] So Bau. Ag., 196, as against Strothotte, 129.
[16] Though cf. Chul., 1, 2 : "All may slaughter at all times and with all instruments except scythe, saw, teeth and finger-nails, because these merely throttle (חונקין)."
[17] In Gn. r. on 34:14 we find the חונק "the one who chokes or strangles" along with the שׁופך דם האדם "the one who sheds human blood." In the case of the חנוק "the one who is strangled" (the word does not occur, but the idea is present) the blood remains in the body. חנוק is to be found in bSot., 45b; jSot., 9, 2 (23c 38) alongside תלוי באילן, "he who hangs on a tree" (the suicide), cf. also TSot., 9, 1 .
[18] Nestle, 254 f. appeals to Ps. Clem. Hom., 7, 3 in support of a Jewish derivation of the prohibition of πνικτόν. Seeberg, 42 f., 46, 55 refers to Ps. Clem. Hom., 7, 8; 8, 19; Ps. Clem. Recg., 4, 36 in support of derivation from the Jewish "two ways."

παρασκευάζουσιν ἄγχοντες καὶ ἀποπνίγοντες καὶ τὴν οὐσίαν τῆς ψυχῆς, ἣν ἐλεύθερον καὶ ἄφετον ἐχρῆν ἐᾶν, τυμβεύοντες τῷ σώματι τὸ αἷμα. The ref. proves the aversion of the Jews to such pagan customs, though these did not arise out of the desire for enjoyment but were part of the sacrificial cultus. [19] For the Jews of Alexandria the Gentile practice of eating the flesh of choked or strangled animals naturally fell under the prohibition of Lv. 3:17; 17:11, 14.

It appears that the four-membered formula of the apostolic decree first arose in Alexandria and then came to be regarded as a Christian measure taken against the above-mentioned pagan practices. [20] Hence the πνικτόν of the decree might well be a secondary addition of the popular text.

Bietenhard

ποιέω, ποίημα,
ποίησις, ποιητής

Contents: A. God's Action as Creator and in Dealings with Man: I. In the Greek World and Stoicism; II. In the Septuagint; III. In Rabbinic Judaism; IV. In Josephus, Philo and the Hermetic Writings; V. In the New Testament and Early Christianity. B. Man in His Work before God: I. In the Greek World and Stoicism: 1. Man's Work and Salvation; 2. Details of Usage; II. In the Septuagint: 1. Non-Commanded Secular ποιεῖν; 2. Non-Commanded Secular ποιεῖν in Parables; 3. Commanded Secular ποιεῖν; 4. Commanded ποιεῖν towards one's Neighbour; 5. Commanded ποιεῖν towards the Law, the Will of God and Individual Commands: a. Terminology; b. Man's Work and Salvation; 6. The Doing of Miracles; 7. ποιεῖν as Bringing Forth; 8. ποίημα, ποίησις, and ποιητής; III. In Rabbinic and Apocalyptic Judaism; IV. In Philo and the Hermetic Writings: 1. Usage; 2. Man's Work and Salvation; 3. The Performance of Magic; V. In the New Testament: 1. The Work of Jesus; 2. Non-Commanded Secular ποιεῖν; 3. Non-Commanded Secular ποιεῖν in Parables; 4. Commanded Secular ποιεῖν; 5. Commanded or Forbidden ποιεῖν towards one's Neighbour: a. Doing Good; b. Doing Harm; 6. Commanded ποιεῖν towards Jesus; 7. Commanded ποιεῖν towards the Law, the Will of God and the Proclamation of Jesus: a. Terminology; b. Man's Work and Salvation: (a) in the Synoptic Jesus; (b) in Paul; (c) in the Johannine Writings; (d) in the Post-Apostolic Age; c. Cultic Action; 8. The Doing of Miracles; 9. ποιεῖν as Bringing Forth; VI. Early Catholic Usage.

By way of ποι-Ϝό-ς the word group stands in a multiple etym. relation. [1] The two main branches of meaning, "to make" or "to do" on the one side, "to act" or "to behave" on the other, include a plenitude of nuances which we do not propose to enumerate nor to illustrate individually in this article.

A. God's Action as Creator and in Dealings with Man.

I. In the Greek World and Stoicism.

1. In the more or less rational renderings of aetiological myths ποιέω means the creative activity of deity: χρύσεον μὲν πρώτιστα γένος μερόπων ἀνθρώπων ἀθάνατοι ποίησαν, Hes. Op., 109 f. The gods, themselves originated, make the gold and

---

[19] Resch, 153; cf. Strabo (→ 455, 17 f.); Strabo, 15, 3, 15 telis us that in Macedonia sacrifice was not by the knife but by stumps and clubs. For Semitic sacrifices in which the blood was eaten (cf. Is. 65:4; 66:3, 17) cf. Robertson Smith, 213 ff.; 312 ff.; 417, n. 5. For other historical instances of the strangling of sacrificial beasts cf. Meuli, 255, 259, 286.

[20] Cf. Cl. Al. Strom., 4, 15, 99; Strothotte, 128.

π ο ι έ ω. Pr.-Bauer⁴, Liddell-Scott, Preisigke Wört., *s.v.*; Bl.-Debr.⁷, Index *s.v.*; Radermacher², 121 f.; Ditt. Syll.³, Index *s.v.*; Epict. Diss., Index *s.v.*; v. Arnim, Index *s.v.*; Witkowski, Index *s.v.*; Leisegang, Index *s.v.*; Hatch-Redp., *s.v.*; Kassovksy, *s.v.* ברא and עשׂה.

[1] Walde-Pok., I, 509 f.; Boisacq⁴, 799 f.; Hofmann, 278. Compounds with -ποιός are found at least from the 5th cent., cf. Schwyzer, I, 450, n. 4.

silver, i.e., first and second generations of men, 109 f., 128. Zeus makes the second and third ages, the bronze age and the age of heroes, 144, 158. Acc. to Ael. Arist. Or., 43, 7 Zeus creates τὰ πάντα, heaven and earth with their individual contents, gods and men ; in Ael. the goat is a ποίημα Προμηθέως, Nat. An., 1, 53. Plato uses the verb in various ways. The "creating" of the chief deity — along with a series of synonyms, → 254, 29 ff. — has reference to the body of the universe (Tim., 31b), to time (37d) and to the 7 planets (38c). The establishment of individual souls by the chief deity and that of bodies by the newer gods is not ποιεῖν (41d to 42e). This fashioning by the δημιουργός is not creation out of nothing ; it is the making of the original matter of chaos into the cosmos on the basis of the gods' being as ἀγαθός (29e, 30a). [2] The related mythical concept of the γεννᾶν of the πατήρ is strongly to the fore (34b, 37c, 41a). The dualism which allots the formation of human bodies to the newer gods and not the chief god (→ 255, 9 ff.) is unmistakable. God is ὁ ποιῶν (31b, 76c : here there is a distinction from the myth, for God, not the newer gods, creates the human body), ὁ ποιητὴς καὶ πατὴρ τοῦδε τοῦ παντός (28c); the object and its reflection are works of divine activity (θείας ἔργα ποιήσεως, Soph., 266c).

2. Ref. has often been made to the high significance of the cosmological and teleo-logical proofs of God in Stoicism of every period. [3] In view of this it is remarkable how seldom words in ποιε- are used to denote the Stoic deity. It is true that Zeno, Cleanthes and later Stoics define ὕλη as τὸ πάσχον and the λόγος ὁ θεός which dwells in ὕλη as τὸ ποιοῦν. [4] But elsewhere the group is absent not only from Cleanthes' hymn to Zeus [5] but also from most of the theological explanations of Stoicism. [6] One may refer only to the *opera* (Nat. Deor., II, 97) and *effector* (Tusc., I, 70) of Cicero's theology. The real exception to this silence of the Stoa is Epictetus, for whom God or Zeus as τὸ ποιοῦν (Diss., I, 6, 11), as φύσις (IV, 11, 9), has made all things in the world and the world (τὸν κόσμον) itself (IV, 7, 6), sun, fruits, seasons, cohesion (IV, 1, 102; I, 14, 10), colours, sight, light (I, 6, 3-6), hands and nose (IV, 11, 9), thee (II, 8, 19; IV, 1, 107). This personal understanding of God in Epict. — God as ποιητής, πατήρ and κηδεμών (I, 9, 7) — also makes it clear why Stoicism can so largely refrain from using the group : the deity dwells pantheistically in the world ; [7] the Stoic's interest is claimed, not by a past act of creation, but by the present beauty and harmony of the world in its permeation by deity. [8]

II. In the Septuagint.

A considerable no. of the more than 3200 ποιέω ref. in the LXX relate to God's action. ποιεῖν denotes the activity of Yahweh in the creation of the world. It often stands for עָשָׂה, more rarely for בָּרָא, [9] which occurs only later and which in the Mas., unlike ποιέω, is used only for God's work (on the terminology → κτίζω, III, 1007 ff.; → πλάσσω, 257, 9 ff.).

1. Yahweh created heaven and earth, the individual parts of creation and man (Gn. 1:1-2:3). He created man κατ᾽ εἰκόνα θεοῦ, ἄρσεν καὶ θῆλυ (Gn. 1:27, [10]

---

[2] Nilsson, I, 31-34; W. Theiler, Art. "Demiurgos," RAC, III, 694-711; → θεός, III, 73 ff.; → κτίζω, III, 1001 ff.; → πατήρ, V, 954, 15 ff.

[3] M. Pohlenz, *Die Stoa*, I (1948), 93-98; II (1949), 53-55; Ltzm. R. on 1:20; H. Almquist, *Plut. u. d. NT* (1946), 83 f.; H. Hommel, "Pantokrator," Theologia viatorum, 5 (1953/54), 322-378.

[4] Zeno Fr., 85 (v. Arnim, I, 24, 5 ff.); Fr., 98 (I, 27, 9 ff.); Cleanthes Fr., 493 (v. Arnim, I, 110, 25 ff.); cf. ibid., Index s.v. τὸ ποιοῦν.

[5] Fr., 537 (v. Arnim, I, 121 ff.).

[6] Chrysipp. Fr., 1009 (v. Arnim, II, 299 f.); Fr., 1011-1020 (II, 301-305); cf. also Pohlenz, op. cit., II, 55-57.

[7] Chrysipp. Fr., 1015 (v. Arnim, II, 303, 23 ff.).

[8] Cf. v. Arnim, Index s.v. διακόσμησις and διοίκησις with the relevant verbs.

[9] Cf. P. Humbert, "Emploi et portée du verbe *bārā* (créer) dans l'AT," ThZ, 3 (1947), 401-422.

[10] On Gn. 1:27 cf. P. Katz, *Philo's Bible* (1950), 110.

→ εἰκών, II, 390 ff.). This theologoumenon, which is essentially post-exilic (→ κτίζω, III, 1005, 7 ff.), occurs frequently, e.g., Ex. 20:11 etc. Thus God is ὁ ποιήσας, Prv. 14:31. Only later (Wis. 9:9) is τὸν κόσμον used instead of individual objects. God did not create death, Wis. 1:13. Nevertheless, dualistic tendencies, acc. to which material things would not be created by Yahweh (as in Plato → 459, 4 ff.; 257, 35 ff.), are remote from the OT. Original suggestions that Yahweh shaped matter are caught up into the later idea of Yahweh's sovereign creation by the Word[11] (explicitly in Wis. 9:1). If use is made of the mythical idea of Yahweh's creative action at the beginning, this leads up to the insight that Yahweh is the Creator of the chosen people (ὁ ποιήσας σε, Is. 43:1; 44:2 etc.). ποίησις can be used act. for the work of God's hand in creating (ψ 18:2), pass. for the fact that God's works are created (Sir. 16:26), and finally for that which is made by God, the creature (Da. Θ 9:14). ποιητής is not used for "creator" in the LXX, → 471, 34 ff.

2. The LXX very often speaks of God's dealings in history. These dealings are usually with Israel as a whole or, from the time of the prophets, with the Gentiles, and only occasionally with leading individuals (Yahweh as ὁ ποιήσας τὸν Μωυσῆν καὶ τὸν Ἀαρών, 1 Βασ. 12:6). In this work God does τὸ ἀγαθὸν ἐνώπιον αὐτοῦ, e.g., 1 Βασ. 3:18. He acts κατὰ τὸ θέλημα αὐτοῦ, Da. Θ 4:35. ἐθέλειν and ποιεῖν (Job 23:13; ψ 113:11), λαλεῖν and ποιεῖν (Ez. 12:28), correspond to one another. Yahweh executes His λόγος (4 Βασ. 20:9), His ῥῆμα (Is. 38:7). The ποιήματα (more rarely sing. = מַעֲשֶׂה) denote His action (Qoh. 1:14) or works, mostly in express connection with God (Qoh. 3:11; 7:13; 8:17; 11:5). Human destinies, whose guidance by Yahweh is expressed in this form, are meaningless and empty acc. to the well-known formula of Qoh.

Yahweh's action brings judgment and punishment (personal obj. in the dat. Nu. 14:35 or acc. Dt. 20:15). Hence Yahweh executes ἐπισκοπή (mid. Prv. 29:13), κρίσις (Gn. 18:25; Is. 1:24), κρίμα (Ez. 5:8 etc.), κρίματα (Ez. 5:10, 15), ἐκδίκησις (Ex. 12:12; Mi. 5:14); He ushers in the eschatological ἡμέρα (Mal. 3:21). Man's questioning of God's action (Job 11:10) is human criticism of His judgment.

Yahweh's dealings also bring help and salvation to His people. The classic texts for this are the Exodus tradition (e.g., Ex. 13:8), Dt. Is. and Da. Thus Yahweh shows σωτηρία (Ex. 14:13 etc.), ἔλεος (Ex. 20:6; particularly to the anointed, ψ 17:51), ἐλεημοσύναι (ψ 102:6), δικαιοσύνη (Dt. 33:21), μεγαλωσύνη (2 Βασ. 7:23), γνῶσις (1 Ch. 4:10), ἀλήθεια (2 Εσδρ. 19:33), μεγαλεῖα (ψ 70:19) and δύναμις (ψ 117:15). He carries out His plans (Is. 46:10) and the wish of Moses (Ex. 33:17). His ζῆλος acts (4 Βασ. 19:31). He establishes διαθήκη (Ιερ. 38:32 Q), εἰρήνη (2 Macc. 1:4), and μνεία (mid. ψ 110:4); He executes saving remembrance (μνείαν μου mid. Job 14:13) and provision (πρόνοιαν αὐτοῦ mid. Da. LXX 6:19). He brings about helpful judgment (τὸ κρίμα μου, Mi. 7:9; μοι κρίσιν, ψ 118:84; κρίματα, ψ 9:17; τὸ δικαίωμα αὐτοῖς, 3 Βασ. 8:45); He does well (εὖ ἐποίησεν ὑμᾶς, Jos. 24:20). God's ποιήματα (ψ 63:10 and ψ 142:5 alongside ἔργα) or ποίημα (ψ 91:5) are His aid expressed in vengeance on ungodly opponents.

Various objects of ποιεῖν express God's miraculous action: τέρατα Ex. 15:11; σημεῖα and τέρατα Dt. 11:3; ἔνδοξα Ex. 34:10; θαυμαστά Jos. 3:5; θαυμάσια ψ 76:15; ἐπιφάνειαν μεγάλην 2 Macc. 3:24; no special obj. Ex. 8:9.

3. By way of appendix ref. may be made to the work of superhuman beings: angels made the hippopotamus (Job 40:19); angels, powers and elements execute God's Word (ψ 102:20); the mythical horn wages war with the saints (Da. Θ 7:21).

III. In Rabbinic Judaism.

When creation, even though a secret doctrine, is under discussion with all its details and with the Torah as mediator,[12] the Rabbis express God's creative activity by עשׂה

---

[11] G. Hölscher, Isr. u. jüd. Religion (1922), 41 f., 185 → III, 1009 ff.
[12] Str.-B., s.v. "Schöpfung," "Schöpfungsgeschichte," "Schöpfungslehre"; → III, 1015 ff.

(Ber., 9, 2) and ברא (Ab., 4, 22) [13] (the latter being more customary in this sense). There is frequent ref. to creation in prayer, → III, 1019, 3 ff. Thus God is addressed in prayer as the עֹשֶׂה בְרֵאשִׁית, Ber., 9, 2; עָשָׂה בְרָא אֲשֶׁר בִּרְיוֹתָיו לְכָל-בְּרִיוֹתָיו מֵכִין מָזוֹן is found in the first of the three thanksgivings after a meal which are in use up to our own day. [14] In the dualism of the sect the ref. to the creation (ברא) of man and the two kinds of spirits by God (1 QS 3:17, 25) naturally has enhanced significance since it limits the radicalness of the dualism, cf. also the eschatological new creation עָשָׂה 4:25. In Damasc. 4:21 (7:2) the ref. to God's creation of man and woman (Gn. 1:27) is an argument against polygamy. In the Rabb. עָשָׂה is also used for the miracles performed by God (Ab., 5, 4) and for God's saving action towards man in circumcision, Gn. r., 39 (24a). [15]

IV. In Josephus, Philo and the Hermetic Writings.

1. Joseph. and Sib. modify only slightly LXX usage regarding God's work. Joseph. has the common OT objects (Ap., II, 121) but avoids the repeated use of ποιεῖν in his rendering of the LXX creation story, Ant., 1, 27-36. [16] Sib. is archaic in its reformulation of the obj. commonly found in the LXX, Fr., 3, 3.

2. Philo, in comparison with the LXX, is far more Platonic and Stoic, → V, 956, 26 ff. It is true that God's ποιεῖν relates to heaven and earth and the other LXX objects (Op. Mund., 36 ff.), also to man (65). In this sense there is ref. to God's works (ποιήματα Det. Pot. Ins., 125) or to the creature (τὰ ποιητά Ebr., 61). In Philo, however, we also find objects which are absent from or rare in the LXX (→ 459, 39 ff.), namely, τόδε τὸ πᾶν (Vit. Mos., II, 99) and τὸν κόσμον (Op. Mund., 172). Furthermore, the significance of the common LXX objects is curtailed by dualistic interpretation. God's ποιεῖν of θεῖα is to be distinguished from His πλάσσειν of θνητά, Leg. All., I, 16. His ποιεῖν relates only to the ἰδέα of νοῦς and αἴσθησις, Leg. All., I, 21. Matter (οὐσία) as μηδὲν ἔχουσα καλόν is affixed by God to the good (Op. Mund., 21 f.), but it does not derive from Him. Only the good and not the bad impulses and deeds of men are ascribed to God, who cannot be the author of a κακόν; this emerges from the plur. ποιήσωμεν in Gn. 1:26, which restricts the sole authorship of God, Op. Mund., 75. Hence a distinction must be made between man as fashioned (πλάσσω) and man as made (ποιέω), Leg. All., I, 55 → πλάσσω, 258, 32 ff.; 259, 7 ff. [17] It is also part of the philosophical tradition that Philo ascribes ποιεῖν to God but denies Him πάσχειν as a not γενητόν (Cher., 77; → 459, 19 f.), or that he emphasises the unceasing nature of God's action (Leg. All., I, 5 f.) and its foundation in His goodness (Leg. All., III, 73; → 459, 8 ff.), or that he compares God's creating with the father's begetting (Plant., 9; 459, 10 f. → πατήρ V, 957, 1 ff.), or that he calls the deity in the pres. abs. ποιῶν [18] or ποιητής [19] or neut. abs. τὸ ποιοῦν (Poster. C., 19) or abs. τὸ πεποιηκός [20] or τὸ πεποιηκὸς αἴτιον (Rer. Div. Her., 289), or that he says nothing about the miraculous work of God, [21] or that finally, with Plato (Tim., 31a b) and the LXX but against Stoicism, he insists on the singleness of the cosmos (Op. Mund., 172). On the other hand, in Philo as in the LXX, we find the designation of God abs. as the πεποιηκώς, [22]

---

[13] On the terminology → III, 1015, 23 ff.; Kassovsky s.v. ברא and עֹשֶׂה.

[14] Ber. ed. O. Holtzmann (1912), 78.

[15] Str.-B., II, 421. → III, 1023, 25 ff.

[16] A. Schlatter, "Wie sprach Josephus von Gott?", BFTh, 14 (1910), 43-49.

[17] Only πλάσσεσθαι is ascribed to animals and women (Leg. All., II, 5, 14); Philo stresses this by quoting the LXX text of Gn. 2:18, 22 (ποιήσωμεν and ᾠκοδόμησεν) but paraphrasing it with forms of πλάσσω (as against → 261, 5 f.; acc. to a written communication from P. Katz).

[18] E.g., Op. Mund., 13 etc.; cf. also Leisegang, s.v.

[19] Very common, cf. Leisegang, s.v.

[20] Op. Mund., 171 etc.; cf. Leisegang, s.v.

[21] Leisegang does not list τέρατα and σημεῖα; for the LXX → 460, 43 ff.

[22] E.g., Som., I, 243; cf. Leisegang, s.v. Cf. the LXX ὁ ποιήσας.

the unity of God's λέγειν and ποιεῖν (Sacr. AC, 65; → 460, 19), and an emphasis on ποιεῖν out of nothing (Mut. Nom., 46; → III, 1011, 36 ff.; → 460, 6 ff.), which is in tension with the dualistic view noted above. God's εὖ ποιεῖν (without obj.) can denote either the Creator's endowment of unqualified nature with the good (Op. Mund., 23) or God's rewarding of those who do good (Plant., 87). For Philo it is self-evident that God may be known from creation. [23]

3. The way in which the Herm. writings speak of God's ποιεῖν is even further from the LXX, → V, 958, 5 ff. ποιεῖν is the affair of the πατήρ, Corp. Herm., 2, 17. Thus we find the titles θεός, ποιητής, πατήρ together, 14, 4; 16, 3. ποιητής can be used, however, without πατήρ, 5, 4. More rarely God is abs. ὁ ποιῶν or τὸ ποιοῦν (14, 5-7; with obj. πάντα in Stob. Ecl., III, 440, 12) as distinct from γενόμενον, or, as in the LXX (→ 460, 2 f.) and Philo (→ 461, 40 f.), ὁ ποιήσας (4, 1 but not abs. here). Generation is par. to ποιεῖν (as in Plato → 459, 10 f. and Philo → 461, 33 f.), for πατήρ is meant physiologically (2, 17 → V, 958, 14 ff.). One may also think of the μέγιστος θεός of Mithras, the γεννήσας and ποιήσας of Helios (Preis. Zaub., I, 4, 644), the πάντων ποιητὴς καὶ πατήρ. [24] δημιουργεῖν is also a synonym in the Hermetica, Corp. Herm., 4, 1. God creates all things; πάντα, mostly without art., is by far the most common and hence the typical obj. of ποιεῖν, e.g., 2, 17 etc. Much more rarely individual objects are enumerated, 4, 8; ὁ κόσμος is not among them (there is a difference here from Hellenism → 459, 24 ff.; 460, 3 f.) because ποιεῖν is also ascribed to the κόσμος itself as a secondary deity, [25] 10, 2 and 3; → lines 31 ff. Thus ποιεῖν is found in the cosmological proof of God (11, 11) which aims to set forth the existence of one Creator (11, 9); doing is God's δόξα and σῶμα (14, 7); God cannot be without doing the ἀγαθόν (11, 17). In such contexts ποίησις means both the act of creating (11, 9) and what is created (14, 3). This proof of God includes rather than excludes pantheism in the Hermetica : not merely that God ἀεὶ ποιεῖ (14, 3; cf. Philo → 461, 33) but ὁ ποιῶν ἐν πᾶσίν ἐστιν (11, 6), πάντα ποιῶν ἑαυτὸν ποιεῖ (16, 19). If this pantheism destroys a strict concept of creation, this monistic strand, which reminds us of Stoicism, is crossed by an express dualism which brings clearly to light the syncretistic character of the Hermetica. In δημιουργεῖν God makes all things like Himself ; πάντα derive from Him only in so far as they are ἀγαθά, 9, 5. There thus arises a distinction between θεός and ποιεῖν. Only πάντα θέλειν εἶναι is true of God, not πάντα ποιεῖν, for the latter presupposes a certain need which cannot be ascribed to God, 10, 3. The δημιουργός of the ἀΐδια σώματα, who only once created something, is to be distinguished from the δημιουργός of the σώματα διαλυτὰ καὶ θνητά, who creates and always will create, Stob. Ecl., I, 291, 5. The primal man in Poimandres is certainly begotten of the supreme God, the Νοῦς ὁ θεός, Corp. Herm., 1, 12. But between Himself and the earthly elements the supreme God interposes the Νοῦς δημιουργός which He has begotten and also the διοικηταί created thereby, 1, 9. In this way He replaces His own creating by strict transcendence. We have here the same separation between God and creation as in heretical Chr. Gnosticism : [26] *secundum autem eos, qui sunt a Valentino, (sc. mundus) iterum non per eum (sc. Deum) factus est, sed per Demiurgum*, Iren. Haer., III, 11, 2. It is outside the framework of the two tendencies, the pantheistic and the dualistic, that in a naïve metaphysics εὖ ποιεῖν is ascribed to the θεοί, εὐσεβεῖν to men, and ἐπαμύνειν to demons, Corp. Herm., 16, 11.

V. In the New Testament and Early Christianity.

1. The NT takes it for granted that God is Creator. Only rarely, however, does it uses words in ποιε- for this. As in the LXX (→ 460, 1 f.) God is ὁ ποιήσας; [27] the author of Ac. especially, quoting Ex. 20:11, speaks of God in OT fashion as

---

[23] G. Kuhlmann, Theologia naturalis *bei Philon u. Pls.* (1930), 9-37.

[24] Mithr. Liturg., 68, n. 1.

[25] Cf. Scott, Index *s.v.* κόσμος.

[26] Bultmann Theol., 108 f., 169.

[27] Mt. 19:4 אCאD lat sy ; the syn. in BΘ is κτίσας.

the One who made heaven and earth and all that therein is, Ac. 4:24; 14:15; Rev. 14:7. The OT background is plain to see in other verses too. To show the indissolubility of marriage in contrast to the practice of bills of divorce in the Torah, God in the beginning made man male and female, Gn. 1:27 in Mk. 10:6 and par. [28]

Is. 66:2 is quoted in Ac. 7:50, Is. 42:5 in Ac. 17:24, ψ 103:4 in Hb. 1:7. God is the ποιήσας of Jesus, Hb. 3:2. The critical question concerning God's work in R. 9:20 (except D) also echoes the LXX, → 460, 27 f.; → 260, 21 ff. On the other hand when God is called the ποιήσας of the κόσμος (Ac. 17:24 in combination with Is. 42:5; → 460, 2 f.) and the "aeons" (αἰῶνες [29] Hb. 1:2), this is more Hellenistic. The train of thought is expressly Stoic [30] when in Ac. all peoples have a single and common origin and God has set for each the temporal and spatial boundaries of its political existence in order that they make seek God (Ac. 17:26; ἐποίησεν thus means "appointed" rather than "made"). [31] The NT even goes beyond the OT (→ 460, 3 ff.) in a dualistic direction when it describes what is shaken as made (πεποιημένα negatively as "merely made" in contrast to the βασιλεία ἀσάλευτος, Hb. 12:27). Elsewhere, however, the central significance of the saving Christ event in the NT and the description of man's lostness in dualistic categories does not mean that God's being as Creator is called in question, as in Philo and to an even greater degree in the Hermetica and heretical Gnosticism.

It is easy to discern the main elements in the NT use of the group for the creative activity of God. The almost complete absence of the group in that part of the preaching of Jesus which is closely related to Judaism (e.g., Mt. 6:25-34) is probably accidental. The paraenetic tendency of the quotation of Gn. 1:27 by Jesus (Mk. 10:6 par.) corresponds to what we find in the school of Shammai. [32] For Pl. the works of creation (ποιήματα R. 1:20) certainly guarantee God's basic knowability along the lines of Stoicism (→ 459, 17 ff.); de facto, however, ungrateful man refuses this knowledge, so that in very unstoic fashion he has been thrust into vices by reason of his culpable idolatry. [33] In so far as R. 1 f. reflects Paul's missionary preaching, the fact that God is Creator is part of this preaching in the sense depicted. The overcoming of criticism of God (R. 9:20) by assertion of the sovereignty of God is OT as well as Pauline (→ 260, 21 ff.). The post-Pauline period adopts the extended LXX usage (cf. the above quotations from Ac. and Hb.) to express creatorhood. For the author of Ac., in distinction from Pl., God may be known almost completely from creation, so that the heathen have only to slough off their comparatively guilty ignorance and orientate themselves to the world judgment exercised by Jesus, Ac. 17:22-31. The Stoic proof of God, stripped of its pantheism and combined with the theism of OT quotations, is on the way to becoming the natural basis of theological reflection on which the storey of supernatural grace rises. [34] There is a definite Christianising when, on the basis of trains of thought in Philo and Wisdom writings, [35] the υἱός is regarded as the One δι' οὗ ἐποίησεν (sc. ὁ θεός) τοὺς αἰῶνας, Hb., 1:2 → line 10. In the Fourth Gospel, on the other hand,

---

[28] Cf. a similar proof in Damasc., → 461, 7 ff.

[29] Cf. Pr.-Bauer, s.v. αἰών, → I, 203, 31 ff.

[30] M. Dibelius, "Pls. auf dem Areopag," Aufsätze zur Ag.² (1953), 30-38; M. Pohlenz, "Pls. u. d. Stoa," ZNW, 42 (1949), 83-95. Stoic, also Philonic and Hermetic (→ 459, 30 ff.; 461, 34 ff.; 462, 23 ff.), is the interest in the present tense of God's creating in Ac. 17:28 (not found elsewhere in the NT). Nowhere in the NT do we find the Gk. and Philonic (→ 459, 19 f.; 461, 30 f.) antithesis between ποιεῖν and πάσχειν.

[31] Pohlenz, op. cit., 83-85 as against Dibelius, op. cit., 36 f.

[32] Str.-B., I, 312-320; in Jesus only the juxtaposition of individual quotations from Scripture is non-Jewish.

[33] G. Bornkamm, "Die Offenbarung d. Zornes Gottes," Das Ende d. Gesetzes (1952), 12-26.

[34] → n. 30; P. Vielhauer, "Zum Paulinismus d. Ag.," Ev. Theol., 10 (1950/51), 2-5: Hommel, op. cit., 322-378.

[35] Cf. the material in Bultmann J., 8.

the word group is used neither to describe the mediatorial role of Jesus in creation nor to emphasise against the Gnostics the fact that God is Creator. Neither ποιητής nor ποίησις is used in the NT to describe God's creative work.

Non-canonical writings continue the speculative Christological line. If 1 Cl. quotes Gn. 1:26 literally (33, 5), in Barn. (5, 5) ποιήσωμεν is addressed by God to the κύριος or Son (v. Philo → 461, 26 ff.) and in 2 Cl. ἄρσεν and θῆλυ from Gn. 1:27 are fully accepted as terms for Christ and the Church. Herm. speaks of ποιήσας ἐκ τοῦ μὴ ὄντος εἰς τὸ εἶναι τὰ πάντα, m., 1, 1. In Just. God is the ποιητὴς πάντων, e.g., Apol., I, 20, 2. The Eastern symbols later refer to the ποιητὴς τῶν πάντων. [36]

2. With regard to God's ποιεῖν apart from the work of creation it is characteristic that the word is less often used for God's judicial punishment and more often used with reference to His helping and redeeming activity. The κράτος ποιεῖν of Lk. 1:51 speaks of God's immanent judgment and ἐκδίκησιν in Lk. 18:7 f., κρίσιν ποιεῖν in Jd. 15, and ποιεῖν in the sense of "behave" in Mt. 18:35 all refer to eschatological judgment. ποιεῖν denotes God's saving work in combination with the appropriate objects: λύτρωσις in Lk. 1:68, ἔλεος in Lk. 1:72, τὸ εὐάρεστον ἐνώπιον αὐτοῦ in Hb. 13:21. God makes the διαθήκη for the patriarchs (Hb. 8:9). He makes the Gospel known to the Gentiles (Ac. 15:17). He acts through Paul and Barnabas (Ac. 14:27; 15:4; 21:19). He puts an end to temptation in 1 C. 10:13, and His work surpasses all that we can ask or think in Eph. 3:20. It concerns individuals, Elisabeth in Lk. 1:25, Mary in 1:49, the demoniac in Mk. 5:19 and par. Finally God will make all things new, Rev. 21:5. Hence Christians, as those who are raised up with Christ and set in the heavenly world, are God's ποίημα Eph. 2:10. God performs what He has promised, R. 4:21; 9:28. He completes what He has begun as He who calls, 1 Th. 5:24. As in the LXX (→ 460, 43 ff.) He does σημεῖα, τέρατα (Ac. 15:12) and δυνάμεις (Ac. 19:11) through the apostles, or τέρατα καὶ σημεῖα through Jesus (Ac. 2:22). He has actualised His purpose in Christ Jesus, Eph. 3:11. He acted towards Jesus by bringing the sinless One to the cross and treating Him judicially as a sinner, 2 C. 5:21 → I, 312, 3 ff., but also by instituting Him as Kurios and Messiah through the resurrection, Ac. 2:36. The acting Father controls the work of the Son who is dependent on Him in love (Jn. 5:19, 20) in such a way that it may now be said that the Father dwelling in the Son does His works in the words of the Son, Jn. 14:10.

This NT material on God's work apart from creation is interesting by reason of the usage of the individual authors and also by reason of the derivation. A first pt. to catch attention is the liking of the author of Lk. and Ac. for the verb. In Pl. (R. 4:21; 1 Th. 5:24; 1 C. 10:13; cf. also Eph. 3:20) the verb expresses the faithfulness and reliability of the God who acts in the Christ event. The strictly Christological limitation of the usage is typical in Jn. Direct quotations from the LXX occur in Lk. 1:68 ＝ ψ 110:9; Ac. 15:17 ＝ Am. 9:12; Hb. 8:9 ＝ Ιερ. 38:32; Rev. 21:5 ＝ Is. 43:19; R. 9:28 ＝ Is. 10:23; Jd. 15 ＝ Gr. En. 1:9. No less numerous are phrases taken from the LXX: God's ποιεῖν ἐκδίκησιν in Lk. 18:7, 8, κράτος in Lk. 1:51 (＝ δύναμιν), ἔλεος in Lk. 1:72, διαθήκην in Hb. 8:9, μεγάλα in Lk. 1:49, τέρατα καὶ σημεῖα in Ac. 2:22; 15:12, God's ποιεῖν λόγον in R. 9:28 cf. R. 4:21. The fact that the authors mentioned derive their vocabulary from the LXX may be seen from this usage. By contrast, the Johannine use of the group for God's Christological action derives from a Gnosticism whose ideas Jn. historicises in order to express the fact that God does a work of revelation in the words and deeds of the man Jesus. [37] The two strands are both to be seen again in the post-canonical writings. On the one hand, in general OT terms, God is able ποιῆσαι

---

[36] H. Lietzmann, "Symbolstudien, I," ZNW, 21 (1922), 6-8; Hommel, op. cit., 363-368.
[37] Bultmann J., 186-189.

ταῦτα (1 Cl., 61, 3, cf. also 59, 3, both liturgical). On the other, in a more specific Gnostic sense, the work of the Kurios is performed in unity with the Father, Ign. Mg., 7, 1.

3. By way of appendix one may also refer to the work of supernatural beings in the NT. In contrast to the LXX (→ 460, 46 ff.), the NT speaks only of a negative work in this connection, and this is to be found only in Rev., which mentions the work of the beast (11:7 etc.), the dragon (12:15), the second beast (13:12), or the three unclean spirits (16:14). ποιεῖν here is esp. the instigation of war (Rev. 11:7; 12:17; 13:7; 19:19), the performance of miracles (13:13a b, 14a; 16:14; 19:20), efficiency (13:5) and the exercise of full power (13:12a) whereby the Church is persecuted (12:15) and the inhabitants of the earth are seduced into recognising false prophecy (Rev. 13:12b, 16; → πλανάω, 247, 35 ff.). Da. 7:21 Θ is quoted in Rev. 11:7 and 13:7 and the doing of miracles also comes from the LXX, → 460, 43 ff.

B. Man in His Work before God.

I. In the Greek World and Stoicism.

This section will simply deal thematically with the question how far man's work is a problem for him in the sight of God. Since the Gk. world speaks of man's activity in so many different ways, it must suffice simply to mention those meanings which are significant for LXX and NT usage, → 466, 19 ff.

1. Man's Work and Salvation.

a. The Platonic use of the Orphic myths of judgment (Gorg., 523a-527a; Phaed., 111c-114c) has an important bearing on the question in two different ways. First, not ποιεῖν, but βιοῦν, βίος (e.g., Gorg., 523a c) and the δικ- stems (e.g., Gorg., 522d e), also ἐργάζεσθαι (Gorg., 522d; cf. Phaed., 113e) and πράξεις (Gorg., 525a), ὁσίως (Gorg., 523a and 526c), ὑγιής (Gorg., 526d), ἀνιάτως and ἰάσιμα (Phaed., 113e; Gorg., 526b) are the terms used when the matter to be expressed is what will be determined about the soul in the judgment of the underworld and therefore what the soul has to strive for prior to death, namely, a healthy and even state which is not influenced either way by individual πράξεις. The emphasis, however, is not on the individual mode of conduct but on the required basic apprehension of the idea of the good, on the distinction between δίκαιον δοκεῖν and δίκαιον εἶναι, Resp., II, 361d-362a. [38] Here then, in distinction from the OT (→ 469, 50 ff.), later Judaism (→ 472, 1 ff.) and the NT (→ 481, 19 ff.), πᾶν ποιεῖν takes on the sense of "to make all efforts" (Phaed., 114c). It thus follows — and this is the second point — that this conduct which is shaped by the idea of the good (which is God, even though the judges of the underworld are only heroes, → θεός, III, 67, 1 ff.) is by nature commensurate with man and hence attainable. [39] Doing is no problem. Where tragedy deals with the ambivalence of conduct, e.g., in the Antigone of Sophocles, what is in question is not the ποιῶν but the νόμος, reality, and therewith deity, → νόμος, IV, 1027, 9 ff.

b. For the Stoic too, in spite of the rigour of the distinction between the wise and the fool, action is no basic difficulty. The idea of judgment is now rejected. Deity, understood in terms of immanence, coincides with the κοινὸς νόμος to which man is directed and to follow which constitutes the essence of the sage. [40] The aim of the

---

[38] H. Hommel, "Die Satorformel," Theologia viatorum, 4 (1952), 124-133.
[39] H. Braun, Gerichtsgedanke u. Rechtfertigungslehre bei Pls. (1930), 3, n. 5, 6.
[40] Pohlenz, op. cit., I, 153-158.

ethical appeal is orientation to this conduct which is truly appropriate to man, and this orientation, as that which is in keeping with φύσις, is what man may do in contrast to the many external and physical modes of conduct which are not in his power. In particular an analysis of the use of ποιεῖν in Epict. makes this clear. The main pt. is, μηδὲν ἀνάξιον ποιεῖν τοῦ κατασκευάσαντος μηδὲ σεαυτοῦ (Diss., II, 8, 18 → 459, 27 f.), not to do everything to-day as earlier from moment to moment (III, 9, 8), not ποιεῖν πᾶν τὸ ἐπελθόν (IV, 12, 6), not to do the ἴδιον πρόσταγμα but that of ἀνάγκη (II, 6, 15 f.); it is thus precisely that a man does τὸ ἴδιον ἔργον (III, 18, 9). A man can be censured only on account of the things which are subordinate to his ποιεῖν (III, 26, 9). If a man ceases to consider what is outward he attains to right ποιεῖν αὐτοῦ ἕνεκα (I, 19, 11 and 14), to right ποιεῖν πάντα ὡς θέλει (IV, 1, 46), which includes εὖ ποιεῖν towards one's fellows as conformable to φύσις (IV, 1, 122). Even though a man does not neglect the required vigilance, even though he does not practise ποιεῖν πᾶν τὸ ἐπελθόν (IV, 12, 6), he may not be ἀναμάρτητος. But in πρὸς τὸ μὴ ἁμαρτάνειν τετάσθαι διηνεκῶς he can be free from some faults and one may be satisfied herewith (IV, 12, 19); there is no real problem for the ποιῶν on this level. In Epict. πάντα ποιεῖν also denotes full involvement, e.g., in the successful politician (IV, 6, 27).

2. Details of Usage.

Of the various nuances which are of interest with ref. to the LXX and NT, [41] and which have man's ποιεῖν as their content, the following may be noted. From the time of Hom. ποιεῖν denotes the making of, e.g., a house (Hom. Il., 1, 608), a grave (Il., 7, 435), a temple (Xenoph. An., V, 3, 9); the material is denoted by ἀπό (Xenoph. An., V, 3, 9), ἐκ (IV, 5, 14) or the gen. (Hdt., V, 62). In Plato ποιεῖν is the humbler work of the artisan as compared with ἐργάζεσθαι and → πράττειν, Charm., 163b c. But ποιεῖν and πράσσειν are often used as synonyms, Demosth. Or., 4, 5. ποιεῖν is often contrasted with πάσχειν, Hdt., V, 11; [42] → 459, 20 f. Material objects of ποιεῖν are κακά, ἀγαθά (Hdt., III, 75), κακόν (Ditt. Syll.[3], III, 1175, 20), τὰ δίκαια (Demosth. Or., 20, 12), ἔπος and ἔργον (Hdt., III, 134; for ποιεῖν and λέγειν cf. Plat. Ap., 39a), and τὸ προσταχθέν (Soph. Phil., 1010). We also find εὖ (Xenoph. Mem., II, 3, 8) and κακῶς (Demosth. Or., 1, 18) ποιεῖν, usually with acc. of person, cf. also κακά and ἀγαθά ποιεῖν. Also attested are ποιεῖν πόλεμον (Isaeus, 11, 48), εἰρήνην (Aristoph. Pax, 1199, "to bring peace to someone," while εἰρήνην ποιεῖσθαι in Andoc., III, 11 means "to conclude peace for oneself"), διαθήκην, [43] ἱκανόν, [44] ποιεῖσθαι [45] ὁδόν (Hdt., VII, 42), μνείαν, [46] πρόνοιαν, σπουδήν. [47] ποιεῖν can denote the celebrating of feasts and sacrifices: ἱρά (Hdt., IX, 19), τὴν θυσίαν (Xenoph. Hist. Graec., IV, 5, 1), ἑορτήν (Thuc., II, 15). [48] ποιεῖν also occurs with adj. or predicative noun from the time of Hom.: σὲ βασιλῆα (Od., 1, 387), [49] cf. also the mid.: φίλον ποιεῖσθαί τινα (Xenoph. An., V, 5, 12). [50] ποιεῖν can be used for the bringing forth of fruit by the earth (γαῖα ποιήσασα γένος πολιοῦ ἀδάμαντος, Hes. Theog., 161) or the procuring of money (λόγος ... ἀργύριον τῷ λέγοντι ποιήσων, Ps.-Demosth. Or., 10, 76). Special stress must be laid on ποιεῖν for "to suppose" (Plat. Theaet., 197d) and "to spend the time" (with χρόνον or another acc. of time, Demosth. Or., 19, 163), [51] ἔξω

---

[41] It is esp. plain in Liddell-Scott how much richer these are than in the NT.

[42] Cf. W. Aly, Volksmärchen (1921), 168.

[43] Preisigke Wört., II, 329.

[44] Ibid., I, 693.

[45] The mid. for a simple verbal concept, cf. Liddell-Scott, s.v. ποιέω A, II, 5.

[46] Witkowski, 35, 6 and Pr.-Bauer[4], s.v. μνεία, 2.

[47] For both Preisigke Wört., II, 331; Pr.-Bauer[4], s.v. ποιεῖν II, 1; cf. also ibid., s.v. ποιεῖσθαι πορείαν and συνωμοσίαν.

[48] For details Liddell-Scott, s.v. ποιέω A, II, 3.

[49] Ibid., A, III.

[50] On ποιέω with acc. inf., ὅκως and ὡς in the sense "to cause that," ibid., A, II, 1b.

[51] Preisigke Wört., s.v. ποιέω 1d; Liddell-Scott, s.v. ποιέω A, VII; hence not merely from the time of the LXX, as against W. Schulze, Graeca-Latina (1901), 23 f.

ποιεῖν "to bring out" (Xenoph. Cyrop., IV, 1, 3) and ποιεῖσθαι mid. "to value" (from Hdt.).[52] When ποιεῖν has the sense "to act" we often find εὖ or καλῶς with the part. in the sense of "to see to it well that."[53] ποιεῖν in the abs. can mean "to work" (Xenoph. An., I, 5, 8). The human ποιητής[54] is the "maker"; the ποιητής νόμων (Ps.-Plat. Def., 415b) is not the one who keeps the laws (as in Jewish and Chr. usage → 471, 34 ff.), but the one who issues them. In the special sense of "poet" ποιητής is found from Hesiod and Pindar.[55] Human ποίημα is what is produced by man whether in external workmanship or in the intellectual sphere.[56] It is also "action" (Plat. Charm., 163c), so that a man's ποιήματα are his deeds.[57] Human ποίησις is constructive activity both manual and intellectual; the devaluation of ποίησις as compared with πρᾶξις and ἐργασία (Plat. Charm., 163b)[58] is not without significance for LXX and NT usage. In a specialised sense ἡ ποίησις is "poetry" or "poem."[59]

II. In the Septuagint.

The LXX speaks very often and in many different ways (→ 459, 34) of man's ποιεῖν. There can be no question of even approximating to a full list of all the relevant passages. All that we can do, as later in the case of the NT, is to give an orderly presentation of the essential aspects. If in this arrangement, which seems to us to be imperative, things which belong together grammatically are sundered, and may occur at different pts. or more than once, allowance must be made for this.

1. Non-Commanded Secular ποιεῖν.

A considerable number of sayings refer to man's secular action for which there is no basis in a command or prohibition of God. Thus man prepares cakes (Gn. 18:6), traverses a road (ὁδόν act. Ju. 17:8; τὴν πορείαν mid. 2 Macc. 12:10), makes feasts (δοχήν Gn. 21:8; γάμον Gn. 29:22), makes war (πόλεμον Gn. 14:2) and also peace (εἰρήνην 1 Macc. 6:58),[60] appoints overseers (ἐπισκόπους 1 Macc. 1:51; the destructive activity of Antiochus Epiphanes described here prevents us from seeing in this any analogy to the creative work of God); as a seaman he throws things overboard (ποιεῖσθαι ἐκβολήν mid. Jon. 1:5; as in secular Gk. to describe a simple verbal concept → 466, 34 f.); he holds a count (ἀπογραφήν mid. 3 Macc. 4:17), passes a specific time (ἔτη πολλά Prv. 13:23). Thus occurrence in the worldly sphere is τὸ πεποιημένον Qoh. 1:9. ποιεῖν can be secular conduct (Ju. 14:10), ultimately in an appreciative sense (καλῶς ποιήσετε γράφοντες, 1 Macc. 12:22), and also the work of man (2 Ch. 2:13). The close dependence of the usage of the LXX on the general Gk. employment of ποιεῖν (→ 466, 19 ff.) is already evident here. In the passages listed, and in many similar verses, ποιεῖν has no gt. theological significance.

2. Non-Commanded Secular ποιεῖν in Parables.

As compared with the NT (→ 475, 35 ff.) it is notable how rarely the LXX makes use of human ποιεῖν in parables to illustrate the divine dealings and man's reaction thereto. God's sovereignty is reflected in the potter, who after the failure of a vessel he was making πάλιν αὐτὸς ἐποίησεν αὐτὸ ἀγγεῖον ἕτερον, Jer. 18:4. How unjustified are human objections to this sovereignty is plain once it is realised that no vessel says to the ποιήσας or potter: οὐ συνετῶς με ἐποίησας (Is. 29:16), or: τί ποιεῖς (Is. 45:9). In both ref. πλάσσειν is synon. with ποιεῖν → 257, 40 ff.; 257, 9 ff.

---

[52] Cf. Liddell-Scott, s.v. ποιέω A, V.
[53] Ibid., B, I, 3.
[54] For the full range of the Gk. use of ποιητής, ποίημα and ποίησις, which is not relevant here, cf. Liddell-Scott.
[55] Liddell-Scott, s.v. ποιητής II; Boisacq⁴, 799 f.; Preisigke Wört., s.v. ποιητής.
[56] Liddell-Scott, s.v. ποίημα I; Boisacq⁴, 799.
[57] Liddell-Scott, s.v. ποίημα II.
[58] Ibid., I, 1; Preisigke Wört., II, 332.
[59] Liddell-Scott, s.v. ποίησις I, 2 a b.
[60] So often act. in contrast to the customary mid. use in secular Gk., → 466, 32 ff.

3. Commanded Secular ποιεῖν.

The normal position in the OT is that man's action is subject to what is commanded or forbidden by Yahweh. This is esp. plain when, from the standpoint of content, the action is wholly secular and this-worldly. Yahweh asks concerning the concrete ποιεῖν of Eve and Cain, Gn. 3:13; 4:10. All the conduct of an individual king (πάντα ὅσα ἐποίησε 3 Βασ. 11:41; very often of Solomon in 3 and 4 Βασ.) is under the well-known theological judgment of the Deuteronomist. The successful wooing of a bride by Abraham's servant (πάντα τὰ ῥήματα ἃ ἐποίησεν Gn. 24:66), the method of payment which Jacob expects from Laban (ἐὰν ποιήσῃς μοι τὸ ῥῆμα τοῦτο Gn. 30:31), these and many other kinds of earthly activity are the subject of narration because the writer believes they correspond to the will of God. At home, i.e., not at feasts, one should carry out one's ideas (ποίει τὰ ἐνθυμήματά σου, Σιρ. 32:12), and one thus enjoys the good-pleasure of Yahweh. Here, as everywhere in the Wisdom literature, this is not the only sense underlying the detailed direction. The very common question of one man to another: τί τοῦτο ἐποίησας (Gn. 12:18 etc.) censures a concrete attitude as impermissible. Yahweh commanded the making of an ark (ποίησον, Gn. 6:14-16). The commanded making of cultic objects is particularly important: an altar of earth (Ex. 20:24), and the sanctuary (Ex. 25:8) with its many contents (Ex. 25-30) are to be made acc. to the model shown to Moses (ποιήσεις κατὰ τὸν τύπον τὸν δεδειγμένον, Ex. 25:40). The cultic parts of the temple (3 Βασ. 7) and the taber-nacles (2 Εσδρ. 18:16) are to be made similarly. Yahweh gives the skill for this (ποιεῖν ἐν παντὶ ἔργῳ σοφίας, Ex. 35:33). The oil and incense used in the cultus are not to be taken from secular use, οὐ ποιήσετε ὑμῖν αὐτοῖς, Ex. 30:37, 32. The attempt of Heliodorus to bring about the delivering up of the temple money (ποιήσασθαι, 2 Macc. 3:7) is a sin. Moses is to set up the sacred serpent, Nu. 21:8. In addition to the temple objects mentioned there is another group of cultic objects whose fashioning is emphatically forbidden. The prohibition of images (οὐ ποιήσεις σεαυτῷ εἴδωλον οὐδὲ παντὸς ὁμοίωμα, Ex. 20:4) demands that Yahweh be worshipped without representation (→ εἰκών, II, 381, 7 ff.) and rejects the making of θεοὶ ἀργυροῖ (Ex. 20:23) and βδελύγματα (Dt. 20:18), of a γλυπτὸν ὁμοίωμα (Dt. 4:16). Wherever there is the fashioning of θεοί (Ex. 32:1), βδελύγματα (3 Βασ. 14:24; Ez. 33:26 A) and ὑψηλά (2 Ch. 21:11) or an εἰκών (2 Ch. 33:7), a passionate protest is made which was softened only in the Diaspora (→ 236, n. 41; → II, 384, 3 ff.). Not just cultic action, but right conduct is directed by what Yahweh commands or forbids: in the law of inheritance (Ex. 21:9), in the treatment of a dangerous ox (Ex. 21:31 AB), one must ποιεῖν κατὰ τὸ δικαίωμα. The vengeance which David commanded Solomon to take on Joab is a ποιεῖν κατὰ τὴν σοφίαν σου, 3 Βασ. 2:6.

4. Commanded ποιεῖν towards one's Neighbour.

ποιεῖν towards one's neighbour (→ 312 ff.) is esp. subject to the commands and prohibitions of Yahweh. Only gradually do we have a coalescence of social and religious approaches, of conduct on the basis of custom and practice [61] and express obligation to Yahweh's commands concerning the neighbour. This process, which goes on over the years, is clearly reflected in the relevant usage of the LXX. For action towards one's neighbour, whether good or bad, is in the first instance highly concrete; it is done by one man to another, or is prevented or forbidden by men. The view of the OT is naturally that Yahweh wills or does not will this concrete doing of good or ill to one's neighbour, and that He reacts thereto accordingly. But only later do we find explicit and basic formulations which describes the right treatment of one's neighbour as the command of Yahweh.

Sarah is to do ταύτην τὴν δικαιοσύνην to Abraham (Gn. 20:13) and Abraham to Abimelech (Gn. 21:23). The scouts are to do ἔλεος to Rahab (Jos. 2:12) and the spies to the inhabitants of Bethel (Ju. 1:24; ἔλεος ποιεῖν is esp. common in Jos. and Ju.).

---

[61] Hölscher, op. cit., 51 f.

Joseph is to do ἐλεημοσύνην καὶ ἀλήθειαν to Jacob (Gn. 47:29). Where there is commandment from Yahweh not to show mercy because of the threat of alien cults (e.g., οὐκ ἐπιποθήσεις Dt. 13:9), the demand is not stated in a negative form of ἔλεος ποιεῖν. Equally concrete at first are the ref. to the doing of what is negative towards one's neighbour. ἐποίησα τοῦτο (Gn. 20:5) is used for the fetching of Sarah which Abimelech did not realise was a sin, and μηδὲ ποίησῃς αὐτῷ μηδέν (Gn. 22:12) for the command to Abraham to spare Isaac. The warlike expeditions of the Ammonites against Jephthah and of Samson against the Philistines are a ποιεῖν πονηρίαν (Ju. 11:27). Isaac is to do no hurt to Abimelech nor Joab to Absalom (κακὸν ποιεῖν Gn. 26:29 ; ἄδικον ποιεῖν 2 Βασ. 18:13). The original basis of such conduct in custom is particularly clear in sexual ethics : ἔργον δ οὐδεὶς ποιήσει πεποίηκάς μοι (Gn. 20:9; cf. 2 Βασ. 13:12) applies to the yielding of Sarah to Abimelech by Abraham. The objects of ποιεῖν, ἄσχημον in Gn. 34:7 and ἀφροσύνην in Dt. 22:21; Ju. 19:23, point in the same direction. That such ποιεῖν involves something which is ἀγαθόν or κακία in the eyes of the doer expresses concrete action acc. to an inverted norm, like the licentiousness of the Gibeonites (Ju. 19:24) or the expected peaceableness of David (1 Βασ. 29:7): it also expresses the recognised sovereignty of the king, 2 Βασ. 19:27. The concrete ποιεῖν of Ju. 13:8 is neutral. On the other hand, fundamental stress is laid on the doing of ἀγαθόν by David in 2 Βασ. 2:6, on merciful action (ἐλεημοσύνη Tob. 1:3; ἔλεος Zech. 7:9; εδ ποιεῖν Prv. 3:27), and on the exercising of just judgment (δικαίωμα, κρίμα, δικαιοσύνη 3 Βασ. 3:28; 10:9; 2 Ch. 9:8; for legal ref. → 468, 33 ff.), in brief, on the doing of what is right, which is expressly demanded by God (κρίμα ποιεῖν Mi. 6:8) or radically forbidden by Him (οὐ ποιήσεις φόνον Dt. 22:8). In this later ποιεῖν of principle there are at least the beginnings of a fundamental questioning of ποιεῖν, → 465, 22 ff. For when, in the context of Yahweh's judicial punishment, it is asked : τί ἐλεημοσύνη ποιεῖ (Tob. 14:11: what does benevolence bring with it ?), the answer does not have to be always optimistic as it was in the Wisdom literature.

In conclusion it may be pointed out that, as distinct from Gk. (→ 466, 31), the LXX puts the personal objects towards whom man's action is directed very rarely in the acc. (e.g., Prv. 3:27), often in the dat. (e.g., Sir. 12:2) and also in the combination μετά τινος, e.g., Gn. 21:23. [62]

5. Commanded ποιεῖν towards the Law, the Will of God and Individual Commands.

In spite of the exceptions mentioned above (→ 467, 20 ff.), the whole of life was very strongly encompassed by the commands and prohibitions of Yahweh. This may be seen from the very common passages in which what is done is related to the Torah, to the will of God, to individual commands, to sin and transgression.

a. Terminology.

φυλάττεσθαι is a synonym here, Dt. 4:6. In the case of ποιεῖν = "to do" the objects are the neuter of the rel. pronoun, e.g., ἅ Ex. 4:15, a relative clause, e.g., ἃ ἐγώ σοι ἐντέλλομαι, Prv. 6:3, often τὰ ἔργα, e.g., Ex. 18:20, ἀγαθόν ψ 36:27 and καλόν Is. 1:17. The obj. are even more numerous when ποιεῖν means "to execute" : δικαιοσύνην and κρίσιν Gn. 18:19, κρίμα καὶ δικαιοσύνην ψ 118:121, τὰ κρίματα Lv. 18:4, 5 : statutes whose observance gives life, cf. Ez. 20:13, δικαιοσύνη, e.g., ψ 105:3, δικαιοσύνας Ez. 3:20, κρίσιν Is. 5:7, δικαιώματα Ez. 5:7, τὸ θέλημα ψ 39:9, τὸν νόμον, e.g., Jos. 22:5, τὰ προστάγματα Lv. 26:14, τὴν εὐχήν Ju. 11:39, ἀγαθωσύνην 2 Ch. 24:16, χρηστότητα ψ 13:1, σύνεσιν ἀγαθήν Prv. 1:7 and ἀλήθειαν Is. 26:10. ποιεῖν = "to act," when combined with καθά, e.g., Ex. 12:28, 50, with καθώς 2 Βασ. 5:25, with κατὰ τὸν νόμον Sus. Θ 62, with ὃν τρόπον εὔξω Dt. 23:24, with καλῶς Lv. 5:4, expresses the conformity of an act with the Torah. The importance of keeping each statute, and hence the character of action as obedience, is expressed by the linking of

---

[62] Bl.-Debr. § 151, 1; 227, 3. In spite of Liddell-Scott, s.v. B I, 2 this construction seems to be not quite unattested even on Gk. soil, BGU, III, 798, 7; 948, 8 in Pr.-Bauer⁴, s.v. I, 1d β.

many of the objects of ποιεῖν with plur. forms of πᾶς : [63] πάντα ὅσα, e.g., Ex. 19:8, πάντας τοὺς λόγους, e.g., Ex. 24:3, πάντα τὰ ῥήματα Dt. 29:28, πάντα τὰ δικαιώματα Lv. 25:18, πάσας τὰς ἐντολάς, e.g., Lv. 26:15, πάντα τὰ θελήματα Is. 44:28 and πάντα τὰ γεγραμμένα Jos. 1:8. Yahweh's ruling sovereignty may be seen in the fact that human action must orientate itself to τὸ ἀρεστὸν καὶ τὸ καλὸν ἐναντίον κυρίου, Dt. 6:18; cf. also the doing of transgression → lines 26 ff. Esp. in the sphere of ritual and the cultus the expressions τὸ καλὸν καὶ τὸ ἀρεστὸν ἐναντίον κυρίου (Dt. 12:25) or τὸ εὐθὲς ἐνώπιον ἐμοῦ (3 Βασ. 11:33, 38) denote that Yahweh demands a specific action. ποιεῖν is the word for cultic acts generally, τὴν λατρείαν ταύτην, Ex. 13:5; τὰ ἔργα λειτουργίας, 1 Ch. 23:24; λειτουργεῖν καὶ ποιεῖν ἐν τῇ σκηνῇ, Nu. 4:35, 39; cf. also the special phrase for the required observance of feasts, e.g., very often τὰ σάββατα Ex. 31:16, τὸ πάσχα, Ex. 12:48, τὴν ἡμέραν ταύτην, Ex. 12:17; in this connection cf. μνείαν ποιεῖσθαι (Is. 32:10), which was taken over from secular Gk. (→ 466, 35 ff.) and for the prescribed offering of a sacrifice τὸ μοσχάριον τῆς ἁμαρτίας (Ex. 29:36), ὁλοκαυτώματα καὶ θυσίας (Ex. 10:25), τὸν ἀμνόν (Nu. 28:4, 8), for profane usage → 466, 35 ff. ἔργα ποιεῖν is forbidden on the Sabbath (Ex. 20:9, 10) and the Passover (Ex. 12:16). ποιεῖν is used in just as many ways for transgressions of the Law as for observances. ποιεῖν = "to do" has as obj. πονηρά (2 Βασ. 3:39), (τὸ) πονηρόν (2 Ch. 12:14; 1 Macc. 1:15), (τὰ) κακά (2 Βασ. 12:18) and ἔργα ἄδικα (Prv. 11:18). With ποιεῖν = "to carry out," "to commit" one finds ἁμαρτίαν (Nu. 5:7), ἁμαρτίας (Ez. 33:16 A), ἁμαρτήματα (Ez. 18:10 AQ), ἀνόμημα (Jos. 7:15), (τὰ) ἄνομα (Job 34:8), ἀνομίαν (Is. 5:7), τὰς ἀνομίας (Ez. 8:17), ὑπερηφανίαν (ψ 100:7), ἀδικίαν (Zeph. 3:13), παράπτωμα (Ez. 3:20) and ἀνόσια (Ez. 22:9). Forms of πᾶσ- are used for comprehensive sinning as also for perfect keeping of the commandments (→ 469, 50 ff.): ποιεῖν πάσας τὰς κακίας (Dt. 31:18), πᾶσαν τὴν κακίαν (3 Βασ. 16:7), πᾶσαν πονηρίαν ταύτην (2 Εσδρ. 23:27). Yahweh's sovereignty and the nature of sin as disobedience are reflected in the formulation of objects of ποιεῖν (→ lines 4 ff.): ποιεῖν τὸ πονηρὸν ἐναντίον κυρίου (e.g., Dt. 31:29; very common in the Deuteronomic view of history); similarly, sin is a doing of that which seems right to man : ποιεῖν τὸ εὐθὲς ἐν ὀφθαλμοῖς αὐτοῦ (Ju. 17:6), ποιεῖν τὰ θελήματα of man (Is. 58:13). ποιεῖν = "to achieve" is used for the heaven-storming thirst for renown of those who built the Tower of Babel (ποιήσωμεν ἑαυτοῖς ὄνομα, Gn. 11:4), of leading into sin by the Canaanites (ἁμαρτεῖν ποιεῖν, Ex. 23:33), and of the setting up of soothsayers by Manasseh (ἐποίησεν [→ 467, 25 ff.] ἐγγαστριμύθους καὶ ἐπαοιδούς, 2 Ch. 33:6).

b. Man's Work and Salvation.

In the LXX what man does before God is not regarded as a radical problem. It is true that for Jer. the eschatological new covenant is the basis of true obedience, Ιερ. 38(31):31-34; → 460, 36. It is also true that in connection with Yahweh's eschatological act of salvation invisible powers are summoned ποιεῖν εὐθείας τὰς τρίβους τοῦ θεοῦ, Is. 40:3. Normally however, in spite of all the prophetic preaching of judgment, the ability of the Israelites and the Jews to do what they are commanded to do is, at least in the Torah and the Wisdom literature, the basis of the covenant. Upon right doing of the Torah depends life, i.e., in most of the OT temporal salvation, Lv. 18:4, 5 → 469, 43 f. ὀρθὰς τροχιὰς ποίει σοῖς ποσίν is the confident admonition of Prv. 4:26. [64] The warning against ritual pollution also presupposes the possibility of observance (εὐλαβεῖς ποιήσετε, Lv. 15:31). The general reference is to detailed ethical commandments or ritual statutes which may be kept. Even renewal (ποιήσατε ἑαυτοῖς καρδίαν καινὴν καὶ πνεῦμα καινόν, Ez. 18:31), i.e., the alteration of one's basic attitude, is no problem

---

for Ezekiel. How much observance is taken for granted may be seen from the distinction between the sin of ignorance (ποιεῖν ἀκουσίως, Nu. 15:29), which may be expiated cultically, and wilful sin (ποιεῖν ἐν χειρὶ ὑπερηφανίας, Nu. 15:30; cf. Dt. 17:12), which is punished with death. At least in part there is a strong sense of the dependence of sinful man on God, [65] but the incipient challenge to pious action is averted and turned into its opposite by an intensification of the cultic and moral means of atonement [66] and by a special concentration on divine retribution on the Gentiles (cf. Ob. 15 : ὃν τρόπον ἐποίησας, οὕτως ἔσται σοι), so that in the OT the religious significance of works is in general as little affected as the thesis that the righteous prosper, which is only occasionally shaken.

6. The Doing of Miracles.

As in connection with Yahweh Himself (→ 460, 43 ff.), so also in connection with righteous individuals like Moses, Aaron and Elijah, also the Egyptian magicians, ποιεῖν, in analogy with a widespread use in Hell. (→ 473, 21 ff.), is a term for the performing of miracles with the obj. σημεῖα (Ex. 4:17, 30), τέρατα (Ex. 4:21), πάντα τὰ μεγάλα (4 Βασ. 8:4), δύναμιν (= act of military power ψ 107:14) or with the adv. οὕτως, ὡσαύτως (e.g., Ex. 7:6), in which case ποιεῖν means the carrying out of what is commanded. In the Rabb., too, עָשָׂה מַעֲשֶׂה is used for magical acts, Sanh., 7, 11.

7. ποιεῖν as Bringing Forth.

As in profane Gk. (→ 466, 39 f.) ποιεῖν denotes the bringing forth of fruits by the γῆ (δράγματα, Gn. 41:47; τὰ γενήματα αὐτῆς, Lv. 25:21), the ξύλον (καρπόν, Gn. 1:11) and the ἀμπελών (σταφυλήν, Is. 5:2, 4).

8. ποίημα, ποίησις, ποιητής.

a. ποίημα, used of man, means, as in secular Gk. (→ 467, 7 ff.), what is produced by the artisan (3 Βασ. 7:17 A; Is. 29:16 → 467, 40 ff.), work and works (Qoh. 2:4), action (e.g., Qoh. 3:17) and deeds (e.g., Ju. 13:12), all in a neutral, negative, or positive sense. In Qoh., the main source for the word, it bears a well-known semi-sceptical nuance.

b. Human ποίησις can be act. "performance," "doing" (Sir. 51:19) and "keeping" (ποίησις νόμου, Sir. 19:20; typically Jewish and non-Gk. → 467, 3 ff.), pass. (→ 460, 10 ff.) "being made" (Ez. 43:18; Ex. 28:8). The absence of the sense "poetry" (→ 467, 12), like the meaning "to observe," is characteristic of the attitude of the OT and LXX, which is orientated, not to art and theory, but solely to practical obedience to God.

c. The same is true of the human ποιητής. The only instance in the LXX (1 Macc. 2:67) refers in non-Gk. fashion, not to the maker, but to the doer of the Law ; the sense "poet" is not to be found in the LXX, → 467, 6 f.

III. In Rabbinic and Apocalyptic Judaism.

Though there is hardly any problem of works in the LXX (→ 470, 36 ff.), there are more or less clear intimations of the difficulty in later Judaism. [67] Akiba's saying that the multitude of acts is at issue in the judgment (לְפִי רֹב הַמַּעֲשֶׂה, Ab., 3, 15) is symptomatic of the general situation. The naivety of action has given place to calculating reflection. On the soil of apocalyptic this reflection expresses itself in an extremely negative estimation of the actual position of pious Jews before the judgment : *O tu quid fecisti, Adam! ... nos vero mortalia opera egimus* (4 Esr.

---

[65] Hölscher, op. cit., 150, n. 6; Braun, 7, n. 2. → ἔλεος, II, 479 ff.
[66] Hölscher, 144-147, 148-151; Eichr. Theol. AT, III, 118-136.
[67] A few typical examples must suffice.

7:118 f.). . . . *iniquitatem faciebamus* (4 Esr. 7:126). Again, the sects of the Dead Sea Scrolls and the Damascus Document, who are close to the Essenes, proclaim a rigorism which lays enhanced emphasis on the totality and minuteness of observance of the Torah. [68] This problem of conduct does not become really acute. The righteous man who becomes uncertain in his works [69] withdraws into an intensified legalism [70] and avails himself of the many means of expiation. [71] This movement of escape naturally has many nuances. The Rabb., to achieve right conduct, stress the ineluctability of judgment (Ab., 1, 7; 2, 1; 3, 1. 15. 16; 4, 22) and the consequent need for an increasingly casuistical caution (Ab., 1, 9) in individual pious acts. The apocalyptist is consoled by the fact that the very humility of his confession of sin will help him before God. [72] For the Scrolls right conduct is possible only after entry into the sect, or conversion. [73] In the Damascus Document right action becomes explicitly ritual correctitude. [74] Later Judaism avoids the incisive questioning of works with the help of legalism.

IV. In Philo and the Hermetic Writings.

1. Usage.

On the basis of his link with Stoicism (→ 459, 19 f.; 466, 26 f.), Philo is interested in the connections between ποιεῖν and πάσχειν from the philosophical (Decal., 30 f.) and psychological (e.g., Cher., 79) angles. Like secular Gk. (→ 466, 28 f.), he sees a relation between λέγειν and ποιεῖν (Som., II, 83), and like the LXX (→ 468, 14 f.), he has the censorious question with τί and an act. form of ποιεῖν, Det. Pot. Ins., 74. He uses (→ 467, 3. 32) ποιεῖν in the sense "to work" (Plant., 27); in distinction from profane Gk. (→ 466, 25 f.), synonyms are δρᾶν (Det. Pot. Ins., 57) and ἐνεργεῖν (Leg. All., I, 6). Philo realises that εὖ or κακῶς ποιεῖν to others is in reality ascribed to the doer himself, Det. Pot. Ins., 57. For him ποιήματα, [75] ποίησις (Plant. 154) and ποιητής [76] are poetic terms whereby Philo, unlike the LXX (→ 471, 31 ff.), shows himself to be a Hellenist sympathetic to culture (→ 467, 3 ff.). The ποιητής does not seem to be for him, as for the LXX (→ 471, 34), a doer of the commandments.

2. Man's Work and Salvation.

What is the position regarding the problem of human action in Philo? The λογισμός undoubtedly has knowledge of things ὧν δεῖ ποιεῖν καὶ ὧν μή (Leg. All., I, 70; he is speaking to man generally), but it is for God, not the νοῦς in its action, to implant ἀρεταί, Leg. All., I, 49. This divine activity, however, involves no crisis for pious human works. The φρονεῖν, λέγειν and ποιεῖν of that wherewith man pleases God is close to man by nature (συμπέφυκε). [77] God's implanting of ἀρεταί and man's

---

[68] H. Braun, "Beobachtungen zur Toraverschärfung im häretischen Spätjudt.," ThLZ, 79 (1954), 347-352.

[69] Bousset-Gressm., 387-394; Braun, *op. cit.* (→ n. 39), 71.

[70] For examples in Ps. Sol. cf. H. Braun, "Vom Erbarmen Gottes über den Gerechten," ZNW, 43 (1950/51), 15-43.

[71] E. Lohse, *Märtyrer u. Gottesknecht* (1955), 18-37.

[72] *Sed et in hoc mirabilis eris coram Altissimo, quoniam humiliasti te, sicut decet te, et non iudicasti te inter iustos, ut plurimum glorificeris,* 4 Esr., 8:48 f.

[73] H. Braun, "Umkehr in spätjüd.-häret. u. in frühchr. Sicht," ZThK, 50 (1953), 243-258; also *Spätjüd.-häret. u. frühchr. Radikalismus,* I (1957), 10-14, 41-47, 63-66, 85-89, 133-138.

[74] Braun, *op. cit.* (→ n. 68), 350-352.

[75] In praise, Plant., 131; in censure, Vit. Mos., I, 3; along with the negative sense of "invented lies" in Congr., 62 etc.

[76] Common, *v.* Leisegang, *s.v.*

[77] Som., II, 180; like Pl. in R. 10:6-8 Philo quotes Dt. 30:12-14, but with ref. to the natural situation of man's διάνοια, not (as in Pl.) with ref. to the man addressed by the kerygma. Cf. Kuhlmann, *op. cit.* (→ n. 23), 23, 36.

activity coincide in such a way that πίστις, which is for Philo essentially de-sensualising (cf. → 461, 22 ff.), may be understood as a state of the soul and as ἀρετή, so that, in contrast to the view of Paul (→ 480, 23 ff.), it does not have to be set in antithesis to human works of piety. [78] Thus the ἀρεταί are only the lower level, while on the highest level, that of ecstasy, the νοῦς and with it all activity are left behind when man is caught up in the vision of God. [79] On the lower level ποιεῖν is no problem, and on the higher level of the ecstatic way it drops away as pointless.

When in the Hermetic writings Poimandres summons the initiate to ποιεῖν τὰ καλά immediately after deification (Corp. Herm., 13, 14 f.), this seems at root to reflect an awareness that the unregenerate are unable to do what is right. But regeneration is through a regrasping of the natural divine element in man. Since this partakes of the divine essence, the regenerate is no longer identical with himself acc. to his empirical existence. To be sure, he is above εἱμαρμένη and can ποιεῖν ὅπερ βούλεται (Corp. Herm., 12, 8), in spite of Corp. Herm., 12, 5, acc. to which the ποιήσας τὸ καλόν [80] also stands under the authority. But for him as the regenerate his own corporeality, concrete ethics and regard for others are no longer of any importance. His actual conduct is a matter of indifference. [81] The essential content of the appeal intentionally looks away from the plane of action [82] when it summons to the leaving of death, ignorance and error (→ 240, 28 ff.), Corp. Herm., 1, 27 f. Even more radically than in Philo, the problem of human works is in some sense passed over in the Hermetic literature.

3. The Performance of Magic.

Still to be mentioned is the use of the word group for the performing of miracles and magic, → 460, 43 ff.; 471, 11 ff. Alongside the general ποιεῖν θεσπέσια (Luc. Philops, 12) we find ποιεῖν used as a tt. for the carrying out of a magical practice against whose common repetition or careless execution there are warnings (Preis. Zaub., I, 4, 2569) and for the fulfilment of which an astrologically defined term is commanded (I, 5, 42). The magician performs it in the power of a specific deity (II, 13, 281); it consists in the pronouncing of an incantation (I, 4, 635). Similarly, ποίησις denotes the performance (I, 2, 20. 65). πράσσειν (I, 4, 2467) and πρᾶξις (I, 1, 276) are synonyms.

V. In the New Testament.

1. The Work of Jesus.

We may refer first to the ποιεῖν of Jesus. Only rarely is the reference to what the exalted Lord purposes (μονὴν ποιησόμεθα, Jn. 14:23 → IV, 580, 11 ff.; on the mid. → 466, 34), what He will bring about (Rev. 3:9), or what He makes or will make of believers (Rev. 1:6; 3:12; 5:10). In the main the ποιεῖν is that of the earthly Jesus.

In this ποιεῖν secular contents (πορείαν ποιεῖσθαι Lk. 13:22; → 466, 34; φραγέλλιον ποιεῖν Jn. 2:5) play a very minor part; the same is true of the cultic acts of Jesus (only τὸ πάσχα ποιεῖν Mt. 26:18 → 466, 34 ff.; 470, 9 ff.). On the other hand, the Evangelists show a definite interest in the doing of miracles by Jesus. [83] The objects in the Synoptists are mostly pronouns, only seldom δυνάμεις (Mk. 6:5 and par.) and

---

[78] Bultmann Theol., 312; Kuhlmann, op. cit., 24-29; W. Völker, Fortschritt u. Vollendung bei Philo (1938), 248.

[79] Bousset-Gressm., 448-452; H. Jonas, Gnosis u. spätantiker Geist, II, 1 (1954), 91 f.

[80] δρᾶν is a synon. of ποιέω, as in Philo (→ 472, 23 f.); on the text cf. the apparatus in Nock-Fest., ad loc.

[81] R. Bultmann, "Das Problem d. Ethik bei Pls.," ZNW, 23 (1924), 131-133; H. Braun, "Literaranalyse u. theol. Schichtung im ersten Johannesbrief," ZThK, 48 (1951), 280 f.

[82] In regeneration κτίζειν, νομοθετεῖν and ποιεῖν μυστήριον are more appropriate to the deity, Preis. Zaub., I, 4, 723 = Mithr. Liturg., 14: ἐποίησας μυστήριον.

[83] Mk. 3:8; 5:20 and par.; 6:5 and par.; 7:37; 10:51 and par.; Mt. 9:28; 21:15; Lk. 4:23; 9:43; Jn. 2:11, 23; 3:2; 4:45, 46, 54; 5:11, 15, 16; 6:2, 6, 14, 30; 7:3, 23, 31; 9:26, 33; 11:37, 45, 46, 47; 12:18, 37; 20:30.

θαυμάσια (Mt. 21:15), though σημεῖα is common in Jn.; the choice of obj. derives from the LXX → 460, 43 ff.; 471, 11 ff. The tendency towards a legendary expansion of miraculous materials in the tradition may be seen in the remarkable increase in the use of ποιέω in Jn. (26 times) as compared with the Synoptists (10 times). [84] On one occasion the use of ποιέω rests on that found in secular magic (→ 473, 21 ff.); this is when the ref. is to a miraculous practice [85] (ἐποίησεν πηλὸν ἐκ τοῦ πτύσματος, Jn. 9:6, 11, 14).

ποιεῖν is used generally for the appointment of the disciples by Jesus (ποιήσω ὑμᾶς γενέσθαι ἁλεεῖς ἀνθρώπων, Mk. 1:17 and par.; ἐποίησεν δώδεκα, Mk. 3:14, not in the sense of an authoritative act of creation, → 467, 25 ff.; cf. Jn. 4:1) and also for that which Jesus shows (the foot-washing [86] in Jn. 13:7, 12, 15) or will show to them, Mk. 10:35 f. When Jesus is asked concerning the basis or justification of His ποιεῖν (Mk. 11:28, 29, 33 and par.; 15:14 and par.; Lk. 2:48; Jn. 2:18; 18:35), this is an expression of the objection, made explicit only in Jn., that Jesus unjustifiably makes Himself God, Jn. 5:18; 8:53; 10:33; 19:7. Of particular importance is the ποιεῖν of the Johannine Jesus, who does the will or commandments or works [87] of the Father, or what He has seen with the Father. [88] This vocabulary, which is taken from Gnostic myth, [89] is not used to express the subordination of Jesus to the Father nor His humility before God. Along with the statements of majesty in Jn. (e.g., the κρίσιν ποιεῖν of the Son of Man, Jn. 5:27), it is designed to bring out the fact that God is He who in the words and works of this Man sets those addressed in decision. [90] The author of Ephesians expresses the acts of Jesus in the same Gnostic terms when he speaks of the cross as the act of union and peace-making (→ 466, 32 ff.) between above and below, between Jew and Gentile, Eph. 2:14 f. [91] In Hb. the work of Jesus consists in the unique self-offering according to the will of God which puts an end to the sacrificial cultus, Hb. 1:3; 7:27; 10:7, 9 (→ ψ 39:9). The acts of the earthly Jesus are viewed retrospectively in Ac. (1:1, ποιεῖν along with διδάσκειν [→ 466, 29 f.; 472, 19 f.]; 10:39) and 1 Pt. ([ἁμαρτίαν] οὐκ ἐποίησεν, 2:22, a quotation from Is. 53:9). In conclusion one may say that a noteworthy feature of the acts of the earthly Jesus is that the number and Christological significance of the references grows only with the developing tradition, especially in Jn. The fact that Jesus taught is in the tradition increasingly fenced off from rationalistic misunderstanding by an emphasis on what He did. This carries with it a strengthening of the accent on His person. The very accentuating of the revealing work of Jesus in His unmistakable action is also a safeguard against the dissolution of the historical singularity of the coming of Jesus in a metaphysics of Christological ontology.

[84] Here and later synpt. par. are treated as one ref.; on the other hand, if ποιέω occurs more than once in the same v., all the ref. are counted.

[85] The working of the miracle is described elsewhere only in Mk., not Mt. or Lk., but ποιέω is not used in this connection in Mk.

[86] G. Bertram, Die Leidensgeschichte Jesu u. der Christuskult (1922), 41; H. v. Campenhausen, "Zur Auslegung v. Jn. 13:6-10," ZNW, 33 (1934), 258-271; E. Lohmeyer, "Die Fusswaschung," ZNW, 38 (1939), 74-94; A. Fridrichsen, "Bemerkungen zur Fusswaschung," ZNW, 38 (1939), 94-96; Bau. J.³ and Bultmann J., ad loc.

[87] To the ἔργα of the Johannine Jesus the σημεῖα also belong.

[88] Jn. 4:34 (synon. τελειοῦν τὸ ἔργον αὐτοῦ); 5:19, 30, 36; 6:38; 8:29, 38 sy^s; 10:25, 37, 38; 14:12, 31; 17:4.

[89] R. Bultmann, "Die Bdtg. der neuerschlossenen mandäischen u. manichäischen Quellen," ZNW, 24 (1925), 114 f.

[90] Bultmann Theol., 398 f.; Bultmann J., 295-298; → 464, 46 ff.

[91] H. Schlier, Christus u. d. Kirche im Eph. (1930), 18-48.

2. Non-Commanded Secular ποιεῖν.

As compared with secular Gk. texts and even the LXX (→ 467, 20 ff.), the work of man which is referred to no command or prohibition of God plays a very small part in the NT.

Such ποιεῖν is ascribed to personages in political history (Mk. 6:20 D𝔄, 21), esp. the opponents of Jesus and of Christians, [92] but also subsidiary characters (Ac. 27:18) and even disciples and Christians. [93] The ref. is often to the observance of an existing custom or rule or common mode of action (Mk. 15:8; Jn. 7:4; 19:12; Jm. 4:13, 15). But even where God's will is not explicitly mentioned as the norm and basis of the ποιεῖν, it is sometimes implied, as is highly probable when a proof from prophecy is given in the context of Jn. 19:23 or when the author of Ac. expresses his basic belief that missionary activity is guided by the Holy Spirit, Ac. 15:33; 18:23; 20:3. In the passages mentioned ποιεῖν has the sense "to make," "to do," with all the different nuances up to "to act," but it is hardly necessary to discuss the detailed grammatical ramifications in the present context. A common use is that of mid. forms with noun for a verbal concept (→ 466, 34); also common is the sense "to spend" with an acc. of time, → 466, 42 f.

The sparse number of instances of non-commanded ποιεῖν in the NT as compared with the LXX is not due to the fact that the web of statutes is narrower and more detailed in the NT than in the OT and later Judaism. The point is that the Christ event — with no casuistry — embraces firmly the whole ποιεῖν of those addressed, 1 C. 10:31. Furthermore, there are in the NT, as compared with the LXX, far fewer historical narratives in which such action might be particularly in place. For in the life of Jesus (→ 473, 37 f.), as in the mission of the Church, God's authority is so predominant that any non-commanded neutral acts on the part of man more or less vanish from the NT as irrelevant. It is true that the NT, unlike the LXX (→ 471, 34 ff.), can use ποιητής in the general Greek sense (→ 467, 16 f.) of "poet," but this occurs only once and characteristically in the author of Ac., who is longer eschatologically oriented and who is much more open to culture (17:28): the ποιηταί, though not standing under God's command in the strict sense of later Judaism, confirm the truth of the Christian message and thus show that in the last resort they have been sent by God. ποίημα (→ 463, 25 ff.; 464, 22 ff.) and ποίησις (→ 479, 32 f.), however, have in the NT, as in the LXX (→ 471, 23 ff.), nothing whatever to do with poetry, so that the usage is quite different from that of ordinary Greek (→ 467, 7 ff.).

3. Non-Commanded Secular ποιεῖν in Parables.

Far more broadly than the LXX (→ 467, 36 ff.) the NT mentions the non-commanded secular action of man in parables. Such parables [94] — all in the Synoptic Gospels — exhort to right conduct and warn against wrong conduct by means of the secular example.

The unjust steward is an example in his conduct (Lk. 16:3, 4 : "do"; Lk. 16:8 : "act" φρονίμως). So, too, is the industrious slave who puts to use the talents entrusted to him (ἐποίησεν ἄλλα πέντε τάλαντα, Mt. 25:16 𝔄*𝔄 : "to gain" → 466, 39 ff.; ἐκέρδησεν is a synon. in other parts of the textual tradition). So, too, is the watchful slave (οὕτως ποιοῦντα Mt. 24:46 and par.: "to act"). So, too, is the man who cannot alter the colour of his hair (λευκὴν ποιῆσαι ἢ μέλαιναν Mt. 5:36; on the double acc. → 466, 36 ff.).

---

[92] Mk. 15:15; Mt. 28:14, 15; Jn. 18:18; 19:24; Ac. 23:12, 13; 25:3, 17.

[93] Mk. 2:23 𝔄; Lk. 5:29; 14:12, 13; Ac. 8:2; 15:33; 18:23; 20:3.

[94] We cannot distinguish here between figurative sayings, similitudes, parables and allegories.

The rich fool who provided for his security is a warning (Lk. 12:17, 18). So, too, is the slave who wittingly or unwittingly (→ 470, 49 ff.) does not act acc. to his master's will (ποιήσας Lk. 12:47; the context has ἑτοιμάσας as a synonym), or does things worthy of punishment (ποιήσας 12:48). So, too, are the vinedressers who slay and stone the messengers of the owner (ἐποίησαν αὐτοῖς ὡσαύτως Mt. 21:36 : "treat"). [95]

Particularly directed against the Pharisees, and hence touching on the problem of works, are the parable of the two sons, one of whom at first refuses but then obeys and does his father's will (Mt. 21:31), and also the parable of the slave who receives no thanks for doing his master's will (Lk. 17:9). Here action is viewed very radically as obedience, as in the OT (→ 469, 32 ff.), but the parable is mainly aimed against the claim of the righteous before God, which in practice at least is hardly separable from later Jewish legalism, → 471, 37 ff. In the parables, again almost exclusively in the Synoptists, the secular ποιεῖν of man reflects the dealings of God or Jesus with men. This reflection is seldom direct, as in the allegory (→ n. 95) of the wicked husbandmen, where the penal ποιεῖν of the owner of the vineyard (Mk. 12:9 "do"; Mt. 21:40 and Lk. 20:15 "render") depicts the judgment of God on the Jews. In the main, however, the parables cannot be interpreted allegorically, and hence the ποιεῖν of the characters does not represent directly the dealings of God or Jesus. ποιεῖν in later Jewish proverbs (→ V, 38, 8 ff.) [96] depicts God's punishment of Jerusalem (Lk. 23:31), while the holding (Mt. 22:2; Lk. 14:16 : ποιεῖν, → 466, 35 ff.; 467, 23 f.) of a wedding or supper denotes invitation into the kingdom of God which is about to come. The parable of the equal reward with its varied ποιεῖν (Mt. 20:5 : "act"; 20:12a : "work" [→ 467, 3, 32]; 20:12b : double acc. [→ 466, 36 ff.]; 20:15 : "do") is an anti-Jewish polemic against the equation of reward and merit ; [97] touching on the ambivalence of ποιεῖν, it establishes the sovereign generosity of God. God gives like the father who does far more than the prodigal son dare ask him to do, Lk. 15:19. Jesus' power to heal is represented by the obedient action of the centurion's servant, Mt. 8:9 and par. The slave who does not know what his master is doing is the very opposite of the disciples of Jesus who know the Father and who are called friends, Jn. 15:15. The action of the enemy who sows the tares creates the presupposition for the growing together of tares and wheat as demanded in the parable, Mt. 13:28. Even when the parables refer to God's work, in instances where the divine conduct set forth is in antithesis to Jewish standards, as in Mt. 20:1-15, there stands in the background the relation of Jesus to the 'am ha-arez, which was offensive to the Jews. It was on this basis perhaps that the later community, allegorising and theologising (→ 474, 30 ff.), depicted the mission of the Son as the action of the lord of the vineyard, Lk. 20:13.

4. Commanded Secular ποιεῖν.

Like non-commanded secular ποιεῖν, that which is commanded (or forbidden) is rare in the NT.

In connection with the cultus ποιεῖν as "to make" (prohibition) occurs in Mk. 9:5 and par.; Ac. 7:40, 43; 19:24; Rev. 13:14, and also (command on an OT basis) in Ac. 7:44 and Hb. 8:5, both with ref. to Ex. 25:40. Non-cultically ποιεῖν "to make" occurs only in Ac. 9:39. Those around censure the action of the disciples when at the command of Jesus they fetch the ass (Mk. 11:3, 5), and the act of Paul is also censured

---

[95] This allegory is perhaps the work of the community *ex eventu*.
[96] Str.-B., II, 263 and Kl. Lk., *ad loc.*
[97] Str.-B., IV, 492 f., 498 f. G. Bornkamm, *Der Lohngedanke im NT* (1947), 15-22; H. Braun, *Spätjüdisch-här. u. frühchr. Radikalismus,* II (1957), 41, n. 1.

when he is accused of plotting a revolt (Ac. 24:12). Similar very concrete acts of obedience entailing specific external conduct are the ποιεῖν (either "to do," "to bring about" or "to act") of Joseph in Mt. 1:24, the disciples in Mt. 21:6; 26:19; Lk. 5:6; 9:15; Jn. 6:10, Peter in Ac. 10:33 (on καλῶς ποιεῖν → 467, 2 ff.), the Christians in Colossae in Col. 4:16, and the ten kings in Rev. 17:16. In these passages the difficulty of the commanded action arises only in Ac. 10:33 and context, where even before Paul the author finds a radical transition made by Peter from a ritually narrow Judaism to a ritually broad Gentile Christianity. [98]

If, compared with the LXX (→ 468, 1 ff.), the NT speaks very little of commanded secular ποιεῖν, this is because of the unimportance of the cultus and the less prominent role of descriptive historical records in the NT, → 475, 21 ff.

5. Commanded or Forbidden ποιεῖν towards one's Neighbour.

In the NT, as in the LXX (→ 468, 38 ff.), there is a great abundance of material relating to commanded or forbidden acts towards one's neighbour. It is thus impossible in this context to consider the various lexicographical meanings, which range from "to do," by way of "to bring about," "to execute," "to practise," on to "to act" or "to deal." In general it will also be impossible to examine the special content of the individual references. We can only group them according to the leading material aspects.

a. Doing Good (→ 316, 8 ff.). ποιεῖν is used generally for doing good to one's neighbour in Mk. 3:4 אD and par.; [99] Mt. 5:46, 47 and par.; 7:12 and par.; 23:23; Lk. 6:27. ποιεῖν is used for showing love (ἀγαπᾶν) in Mt. 5:46 f., 1 Th. 4:10 and Jm. 2:8. Rendering material aid is expressed by ποιεῖν in Mk. 14:7; [100] Mt. 25:40; Lk. 3:11; 10:37 (on ἔλεος ποιεῖν → 468, 51 f.); R. 12:20 (quoting Prv. 25:22); Gl. 6:9; Phil. 4:14 (καλῶς ποιεῖν → 467, 2 ff.). ποιεῖν is used specifically for almsgiving in Mt. 6:2, 3; Ac. 9:36; 10:2 and for the collection in Ac. 11:30; 24:17; R. 15:26; 1 C. 16:1; 2 C. 8:10, 11; Gl. 2:10. ποιεῖν serves to denote a function of promoting or guiding the community in 1 C. 9:23; 1 Th. 5:11; 1 Tm. 5:21; Hb. 6:3; 13:17; 3 Jn. 5, 6. It can also be used for preaching without remuneration in 2 C. 11:7, 12 and for intercession. [101] The establishment of joy and peace (Ac. 15:3; Jm. 3:18; → 466, 32 f.) and the demonstration of friendliness (Eph. 6:9; Phlm. 21, with juxtaposition of ποιεῖν and λέγειν → 466, 29 f.) are expressed by ποιεῖν. It is also used for the making of Jews (προσήλυτον ποιεῖν Mt. 23:15) and Christians (Χριστιανὸν ποιεῖν Ac. 26:28) by missionary endeavour. It can denote asceticism in sexual ethics, 1 C. 7:36-38.

b. Doing Harm. ποιεῖν seldom has a neutral sense, as in Ac. 5:34 (on ἔξω ποιεῖν → 466, 43 f.); 1 C. 15:29; Phlm. 14. Where the ref. is not to doing good to one's neighbour, doing harm is mostly censured or forbidden. The general ref. is to wrong treatment of the neighbour by the disciples or Christians (Mt. 25:45; Jm. 2:13), and specifically to sexual offences (Mt. 5:32). The culpable action may also be on the part of Jews (Mk. 7:12; Mt. 6:2; 23:15b; Lk. 5:34; 6:26; Ac. 7:24) or Gentiles (Ac. 14:15; 22:26), and it may be particularly the harm which persecutors of the Gospel do to believers. [102] As in the LXX (→ 469, 28 ff.), but not secular Gk. (→ 466, 31 f.), the person towards whom the action, whether positive or negative, is committed, is mostly in the dat., not the acc. [103] A difference from the LXX (→ 312 ff.) is that the neighbour to whom good

---

[98] Dibelius, op. cit. (→ n. 30), 103-107.
[99] In the par. to Mk. 3:4 in Mt. 12:12 καλῶς ποιεῖν naturally means "to do good" (→ 466, 30 ff.), not "to do right."
[100] For εὖ ποιεῖν → n. 99.
[101] μνείαν ποιεῖσθαι R. 1:9; Eph. 1:16; 1 Th. 1:2; Phlm. 4; → 466, 35; δέησιν [δεήσεις] ποιεῖσθαι Phil. 1:4; 1 Tm. 2:1; cf. Hb. 13:19.
[102] Mk. 9:13 and par.; Lk. 6:23; 12:4; Jn. 15:21; 16:2, 3; Ac. 4:16; 7:19; 9:13; 23:12, 13 (συνωμοσίαν ποιεῖσθαι → 466, 35); 25:3; Hb. 13:6; 3 Jn. 10.
[103] Bl.-Debr.[7] § 151, 1; for the acc. of person Pr.-Bauer[4], s.v. I, 1, dα.

is to be done is man generally and not just the fellow-member of the Jewish cultus or people, → 315, 19 ff. The questioning of human action, to which attention has been drawn already (→ 476, 6 ff.), occurs here in consequence of the subordination of cultic and ritual commandments (Mk. 3:4; Mt. 12:12) to radical obedience and the unrestricted character of the commandment of love. In the Synoptic tradition the sayings which demand such radicalised action [104] are very probably authentic, whereas agreement with later Judaism might seem to indicate an origin in the primitive community. As concerns the contents of admonitions the hortatory traditions of Jewish Hellenism and the Cynic-Stoic diatribe take on increasing significance. The texts which speak of the hostile action of persecutors become notably more numerous with the progressive development of the community.

6. Commanded ποιεῖν towards Jesus.

Most instructive are the NT verses which speak of the action of men towards the person of Jesus. The reference is almost always to the person of the earthly Jesus whom His fellow-men meet in all kinds of different ways: with cultic correctitude (Lk. 2:27), seeking healing (Mk. 5:32), showing friendliness and reverence (Mk. 14:8, 9 and par.), but also with a complete lack of understanding (Jn. 6:15) so that the keeping of the Messianic secret must be enjoined (Mk. 3:12 and par.), and even with full enmity prior to the passion (e.g., Mk. 3:6 א C D Θ ℜ; Lk. 6:11; 19:48; Jn. 8:40; 11:47a), and then in the passion, whether on the part of members of the Sanhedrin, the procurator, or Judas (Mk. 15:1 [B ℜ D Θ συμ-βούλιον ποιεῖν, א C συμβούλιον ἑτοιμάζειν]; 15:12 and par.; Lk. 23:34 א C ℜ; Ac. 4:28; Jn. 13:27). Only occasionally is it in relation to the exalted Lord that men act in acceptance (Mt. 25:40) or rejection (Mt. 25:45; Ac. 26:10). The Messianic secret (Mk. 3:12 and par.), the supplementary character of Mk. 14:8, 9 in comparison with the original compass of the story, [105] the textually and materially doubtful authenticity of Lk. 23:34, [106] the prophetic nature of Jn. 12:16 and Ac. 4:28 and the initiative of Jesus in the "Satanic sacrament" in Jn. 13:27 [107] make it plain that only in the light of the Easter faith is right conduct towards the person of Jesus also emphasised as important in the story, and even this group of statements is by no means exhaustive. For in the case of later generations, who are no longer contemporaries of the earthly Jesus, action towards the exalted Lord is indirectly by way of needy brethren or the community, Mt. 25:40, 45; Ac. 26:10.

7. Commanded ποιεῖν towards the Law, the Will of God and the Proclamation of Jesus.

The great majority of NT ποιεῖν passages refer to obedient or disobedient action in relation to the Law, the will of God and the proclamation of Jesus, whether in principle or in respect of individual commandments. [108] Right action is demanded. Once again we must desist from pursuing the lexical distinctions between "to do," "to bring about," "to execute," "to render," "to act," and "to deal," in favour of the theological aspects. The contexts yield as synonyms τηρεῖν (Mt. 23:3; 1 Jn. 5:2), πράσσειν (R. 1:32; 2:3; 7:15, 19; 13:4; Jn. 5:29), ἐργάζεσθαι (Col. 3:23) and κατεργάζεσθαι (R. 7:15).

---

[104] In this context it is, of course, impossible to discuss the individual commands.
[105] Bultmann Trad., 283.
[106] The v. is not found in B or most of the Western witnesses. Bertram, op. cit. (→ n. 86), 87 f.
[107] Bultmann J., 368.
[108] The acts towards one's neighbour treated → 477, 13 ff. are not included here.

a. Terminology.

The idea that man should do what is commanded and not do what is forbidden, and that it is God who commands and forbids, and who demands an account from man, derives from the OT and is upheld in the NT. The objects of commanded or forbidden action are largely formulated as in the LXX (→ 469, 39 ff.); this may be seen from Jn. 9:31 and the quotation in Ac. 13:22. They are, e.g., the will of God or the will of the Father. This object makes it plain that personal proximity to the man Jesus, which may well be combined with ecstasy and miraculous gifts, cannot replace obedience (Mk. 3:35 and par.; Mt. 7:21), and that faith is for the Fourth Evangelist in particular a matter of existential involvement, Jn. 7:17.

To be done are the will of God (Eph. 6:6; Hb. 10:36; 13:21; 1 Jn. 2:17; cf. Rev. 17:17), τὰ ἀγαθά or τὸ ἀγαθόν (Jn. 5:29; R. 13:3; Eph. 6:8; 1 Pt. 3:11), τὸ καλόν (2 C. 13:7; Jm. 4:17; cf. Mt. 12:33, where ποιεῖν means "suppose"), ἡ ἀλήθεια (Jn. 3:21; 1 Jn. 1:6), δικαιοσύνη (Rev. 22:11), ἔργον and ἔργα (2 Tm. 4:5; Rev. 2:5). Fruits are to be brought forth (Mt. 3:8 and par.; 21:43) and ἔθη fulfilled by the Gentiles (Ac. 16:21). But sin is not to be committed (various terms, Mt. 13:41; R. 3:12; 13:4; 16:17; 1 C. 6:18; 2 C. 13:7; Eph. 2:3; Jm. 5:15; 1 Pt. 3:12; Rev. 21:27; 22:15). What is commanded or forbidden is put in a pronoun or relative clause [109] with ποιεῖσθαι for a simple verbal concept (R. 13:14; 2 Pt. 1:10, 15; Jd. 3), in a constr. with the double acc. and ποιεῖν (Mk. 1:3 and par.; Ac. 20:24 apart from D; 1 Jn. 1:10; 5:10), ποιεῖν having various senses, e.g., "to do well" Jm. 2:19; "to provide" Lk. 12:33; "to spend" 2 C. 11:25; "to suppose" Mt. 12:33, "to compose" a writing, "to make" a speech, Ac. 1:1a; 11:2 D (on the whole section → 466, 19 ff.).

Individually these passages do not go beyond the OT and later Jewish understanding of ποιεῖν (cf. the obj. in the LXX → 469, 39 ff.), and the LXX is expressly quoted in some of them. Lk. 10:28, where the attainment of life is linked to the doing of the commandments (cf. Rev. 22:14 ℵ), is OT and later Jewish in orientation (→ 470, 41 ff.), nor do we go much beyond this in essentials when there is emphasis on the necessary and generally accepted (→ 466, 29 f.) agreement between saying and doing (Mt. 7:21; 21:31; 23:3; Jm. 2:12) or between hearing and doing (Lk. 6:47, 49 and par.) or between the hearer and the ποιητής (R. 2:13; Jm. 1:22, 23, 25 [→ 471, 34 ff.]), and therewith on the importance of practical observance (Jm. 1:25, the only NT instance of ποίησις, → 471, 29 ff.), or indeed when the content of what is commanded is summed up in popular terms with an echo of Stoicism, R. 1:28; 2:14. [110]

b. Man's Work and Salvation.

The questioning of human action is carried through far more radically in the NT than in later Judaism, where this movement only begins (→ 470, 37 ff.; 471, 37 ff.). For in the NT the pious work of man experiences both judgment and also establishment on a new level.

(a) The movement of conversion centred on the earthly Jesus sharpens the question of what man is commanded to do (Mk. 10:17 and par.; Lk. 10:25) to attain salvation, and this anxious question seems to persist through all stages of the tradition (Jn. 6:28; Ac. 2:37; for the circle about the Baptist Lk. 3:10, 12, 14). [111] Jesus seems to answer such questions on His own authority not merely in later texts (Jn. 13:17; 15:14; cf. the ποιεῖν of Christians in face of the commands of

---

[109] 1 C. 10:31; Phil. 2:14; Col. 3:17, 23; 1 Tm. 4:16; 2 Pt. 1:10; Mk. 7:13; Lk. 3:19; Jm. 4:29, 39; 7:51; Ac. 16:18; 21:33; R. 1:32; 2:3.

[110] Pohlenz, op. cit. (→ n. 30), 73; → n. 40.

[111] The movement of the Baptist, and cf. the Essene-like Qumran sect (→ 471, 37 ff.), was agitated by such questions, though it has been conjectured that the preaching of the Baptist to various classes is a Chr. redaction of older material, cf. Bultmann Trad., 155, 158 f.

the apostles in 2 Th. 3:4) but also in sayings which belong to the oldest stratum (Lk. 6:46; Mt. 7:24, 26 and par.). For according to the texts Jesus does not merely command action from men when He heals or helps them (Lk. 6:10; Jn. 2:5). He also preaches. And though his preaching relates to the OT and specifically to the demands of the Torah (Lk. 10:28 → 479, 27 ff.), it is nevertheless plain that Jesus was sturdily independent of the Torah. For although He accused His opponents of desecrating the temple (Mk. 11:17 and par.; Jn. 2:16), cultic matters and ritual demands are less prominent, → 478, 2 ff. The ποιεῖν of fasting (Lk. 5:33) and cultic purity (Mk. 7:8 ℵ) is depreciated, and the non-observance of the Sabbath is advocated. [112] The concrete act of love to the neighbour is the important thing ; God's demands are also intensified in motivation as well as concreteness. The claims of man on God are radically negated (Lk. 17:10; → 476, 6 ff.). The attack not only criticises materially the requirements of the Pharisees and the Torah, Mt. 6:1; 23:3, [113] 5, cf. the Sermon on the Mount *passim*. Even the man who has done all that is commanded is also set without any claim at all before God. He is directed as a poor wretch into the circle of the 'am ha-arez and is thus made dependent only on the undeserved goodness of the God of sovereign giving. The work which Jesus requires of man is thus made possible only in the sense that it is confronted equally by an unparalleled sharpening of the demand and a divine Yes to man which excludes all merit and is uttered without any presuppositions. In this teaching, as distinct from that of later Judaism, the problem of human action is pressed, to the advantage of right conduct. [114]

(b) The earthly Jesus does not with full explicitness call human ποιεῖν in question. Paul however, without dependence on Jesus, develops the challenge in theological terms. If observance of the commandments (Lv. 18:5) is not expressly contested as a path to life in broad areas of primitive Christianity, or even in the earthly Jesus Himself (→ 479, 27 ff.), Paul, using the same text Lv. 18:5, expressly contrasts ποιεῖν of δικαιοσύνη ἡ ἐκ νόμου as a way of salvation which does not lead to its goal with ἐκ πίστεως δικαιοσύνη (→ II, 206, 3 ff.) as the true way of salvation, R. 10:5, 6; Gl. 3:10, 12. The way of the Law cannot lead to life because man does not in fact keep the commandments. There are no true ποιηταὶ νόμου, R. 2:13. Indeed, it is out of the question that the way of the Law should lead to salvation, since this would render the Christ event pointless and would give the last word to man's spiritual boasting. Among the arguments which Paul uses against the ancient way of salvation we find one which is known to us already from Qumran (→ 472, 1 ff.), i.e., that in the sphere of Law observance must be consistent, unwearied, unbroken and total (Gl. 3:10 πᾶσιν; 5:3 ὅλον). Rejection of the saving significance of the ποιεῖν of δικαιοσύνη ἐκ νόμου does not affect the content of the Torah as the demand of God ; Paul still lays emphasis on judgment according to works, [115] he uses the contents of the Torah in exhortation, and he has no misgivings about promoting the ποιεῖν of what is right. [116]

---

[112] Even if these are sayings from discussions in the primitive community (Bultmann Trad., 48-50), the free attitude revealed therein is undoubtedly to be traced back to Jesus Himself, since there was a retrogressive movement back to observance of the Torah in the further development of the Church, → 482, 29 ff.

[113] This unqualified acceptance of the Pharisaic interpretation by Jesus may perhaps be ascribed to the community as part of the retrogressive movement mentioned → n. 112.

[114] R. Bultmann, "Die Bedeutung des geschichtlichen Jesus f. d. Theologie des Pls.," *Glauben u. Verstehen,* I² (1954), 191-199; Braun, *op. cit.* (→ n. 97), 34-53.

[115] Braun, *op. cit., passim.*

[116] Cf. the Pauline ref. → 477, 22 ff.; 479, 12 ff.

The new way of salvation does not entail the exclusion of righteous ποιεῖν along the lines of quietism; faith itself is indeed the obedience which renounces all boasting about what it does. [117] What Paul means by faith, then, is not the rejection of works but a very special way of understanding works, → 219, 33 ff. It rests on a misunderstanding that his opponents ascribe to him the lax saying : ποιήσωμεν τὰ κακὰ ἵνα ἔλθῃ τὰ ἀγαθά, R. 3:8. But this misunderstanding shows how much the Jew and indeed every man felt himself to be called in question by this contesting of legal observance. This righteousness of faith sets existence under the Law [118] in a new light. Legal existence is now shown to be, not a contradiction between purpose and performance, [119] but the contradiction which the legalist cannot perceive (R. 7:15), namely, that between impotent intention (θέλειν) and what is actually done, [120] R. 7:19. The Law is thus shown to be good (R. 7:16), but the human ego is overpowered by sin and subject to evil, [121] R. 7:20, 21. Whether the objects of θέλειν and ποιεῖν are life and death [122] or good and evil is less essential than the recognition that what we have here is not the description of a psychological state which the legalist may already be aware of [123] but the disclosure, possible only by faith, of the actual situation of the legalist. The ποιεῖν which is commanded for the believer who sees that legalism does not lead to its goal is described with its antithesis in Gl. 5:17. Here the indicative of present salvation and the received πνεῦμα are the basis of the walk to which the exhortation summons. In this, πάντα ποιεῖν (1 C. 10:31; Phil. 2:14; Col. 3:17) does not denote the observing of all statutes without exception (→ 465, 35 f.) but the Christian walk which embraces all the commands of love. In the conflict between spirit and flesh one must place oneself on the side of spirit, of the gracious Yes of God which is the foundation of the life of the Christian, in order that the personal will of the man who walks according to the spirit may be fulfilled. [124] On the basis of the message of salvation right conduct is possible for man as a miracle, a paradox.

(c) The problem of human action is also dealt with in the Fourth Gospel. Only by way of exception, of course, does John illustrate it by the Law which the Jews have failed to keep (7:19). [125] Human action is called in question because it arises necessarily from the whence of man. What a man does is according to which father he has, whose child he is, what he has heard from his father (Jn. 8:38, 39, 41, 44), so that ἁμαρτίαν ποιεῖν is a proof of his corrupt origin, of his slavery (Jn. 8:34), as may be seen in the derivation of the Jews, not from Abraham or God, but from the devil (8:41, 44), and in their corresponding works. Man can attain to the works which are essential before God only if, accepting existentially (→ 479, 7 ff.) the paradoxical revelation of God which has appeared in Jesus Christ, he allows his standards concerning God and man to be shattered and is

[117] Bultmann Theol., 310-313.
[118] This relation may be accepted in view of W. G. Kümmel, R. 7 u. d. Bekehrung d. Pls. (1929), notwithstanding A. Nygren, Der Römerbrief (1951), 208-222.
[119] This traditional interpretation is criticised by G. Bornkamm, "Sünde, Gesetz u. Tod," Das Ende des Gesetzes (1952), 62.
[120] R. Bultmann, "R. 7 u. d. Anthropologie des Pls.," Imago Dei, Beitr. z. theol. Anthropologie (1932), 53-62. For further bibl. cf. Bornkamm, op. cit. (→ n. 119), 62-67.
[121] R. Bultmann, "Christus des Gesetzes Ende," Glauben u. Verstehen, II (1952), 45.
[122] So Bultmann, op. cit. (→ n. 120), and more carefully Bultmann Theol., 244.
[123] As ποιεῖν and θέλειν are meant psychologically in 2 C. 8:10 f.
[124] P. Althaus, ". . . das ihr nicht tut, was ihr wollt," ThLZ, 76 (1951), 15-18.
[125] It makes no difference whether the transgression of the Law by the Jews is seen in their purpose to kill (Bau. J.³, ad loc.) or is viewed more generally (Bultmann J. ad loc.).

creatively attached again to the divine essence as a shoot is to the tree of life or the vine: χωρὶς ἐμοῦ οὐ δύνασθε ποιεῖν οὐδέν (15:5, here in the sense "to bring forth," → 469, 25 f.). Jesus does not merely give an example of the action which is possible for the man who abides in Him; man's action rests on the fact that Jesus has first shown him the kind of action required, 13:15. [126] Indeed, the ultimate indirectness of the revelation through Jesus' going to the Father makes the believer so much a participant in the existence of Jesus that he does the same and even greater works than Jesus (14:12): greater not in the sense of supplementing or surpassing quantitatively but because the temporally restricted life of the Revealer in the world finds its fulfilment (just as indirect as in the case of the Revealer Himself) only in the host of believers in whom the event of revelation is constantly present afresh. [127] Probably in conflict with false teachers [128] — one is reminded of the setting aside of concrete ethics in the Hermetica (→ 473, 8 ff.) — there is constant and deliberate emphasis in 1 Jn. on the indispensability of ποιεῖν δικαιοσύνην, the impossibility of ποιεῖν ἁμαρτίαν for the one who is born of God, and hence the ethically actual character of the life which is from God, 1 Jn. 2:29; 3:7-10. We cannot be quite certain what is at issue in the battle against a contesting of the equation of ἁμαρτίαν and ἀνομίαν ποιεῖν (1 Jn. 3:4 → I, 306, 18 ff.), [129] but there can be no doubt that a trivialising of the actual committal of sin is resisted. The demanded ποιεῖν no longer stands in tension with the event of salvation. [130] It is organically integrated into it. The doing of the ἐντολαί (including faith) is a test by which true brotherly love may be known, 1 Jn. 5:2. [131] Hence the commanded ποιεῖν of δικαιοσύνη may be found in paradoxical unity with the confession of sin and the renouncing of any assertion of sinlessness, [132] 1 Jn. 1:8-10. Nevertheless, this paradox is no longer so sharp that it leaves no place for the early catholic hope, which derives from the later Jewish idea of merit (→ 471, 37 ff.), that ποιεῖν τὰ ἀρεστὰ ἐνώπιον αὐτοῦ (on the expression → 470, 44 f.) ensures the hearing of prayer, 1 Jn. 3:22. [133]

(d) We are thus brought to the group of NT passages in which pious human action is no longer challenged and hence a paradoxical overcoming of the problem by the saving act of God is no longer felt to be necessary. If the Pauline questioning of pious action is still echoed in Tt. 3:5, elsewhere there are plain signs of a retrogressive movement (→ n. 122). Thus Jesus is regarded as a teacher who demands fulfilment of the Law and the teaching of extreme legal correctitude, Mt. 5:19. It also seems unthinkable that Paul should not have observed the precepts of the fathers, Ac. 28:17. The saving action of God loses its paradoxical character if the sinner to whom it is directed can at least claim in excuse ἀγνοῶν ποιεῖν after the manner of the OT and later Judaism, [134] 1 Tm. 1:13. Christianity becomes a more or less undented moral action. [135]

---

[126] Bultmann J., ad loc.; 474, 10 f.

[127] Bultmann J., ad loc.

[128] Braun, op. cit. (→ n. 81), 291.

[129] R. Bultmann, "Analyse des ersten Johannesbriefes," Festgabe f. A. Jülicher (1927), 147.

[130] Legalism is no longer a problem for John as it was for Paul.

[131] Braun, op. cit., 275 f.

[132] ποιεῖν is not used in 1 Jn. 1:8-10. On the paradoxical unity of 1 Jn. 1:8-10 and 3:6-10 v. Braun, op. cit., 276 f., and on the fact that this is the first conscious and explicit paradox in the NT v. R. Bultmann, "Die kirchliche Redaktion des ersten Johannesbriefes," In memoriam Ernst Lohmeyer (1951), 193.

[133] Braun, op. cit. (→ n. 81), 277.

[134] Braun, op. cit. (→ n. 70), 24, n. 266; → 471, 1 ff.

[135] Bultmann Theol., 544-557.

c. Cultic Action.

Commanded cultic action occupies an astonishingly small place in the NT. Where we do not simply have LXX exegesis (as in Hb. 11:28) or a continuation of OT and later Jewish feasts (Ac. 18:21 ℜ : τὴν ἑορτὴν ποιῆσαι → 470, 9 ff.) in the developing Church, cultic action, perhaps in some relation to magical practice [136] (→ 473, 21 ff.), occurs only in the formula of anamnesis (1 C. 11:24, 25; Lk. 22:19 non-western text) which derives from probably ancient texts relative to meals for the dead. [137] The vow which the Lord's brother suggested to Paul in Ac. (τοῦτο οὖν ποίησον, 21:23) and which Paul undertook could be part of the retrogressive movement mentioned above (→ 482, 29 ff.) [138] if a later age was no longer aware of the tension between the real Paul and legal piety.

8. The Doing of Miracles.

The NT speaks broadly of the working of miracles by Christians. The objects are the usual ones found in the LXX (→ 471, 11 ff.): δυνάμεις (Mk. 9:39; Mt. 7:22), σημεῖα (Jn. 3:2; 9:16; 10:41; Ac. 6:8; 7:36; 8:6), τέρατα (Ac. 6:8; 7:36), ἔργα (Jn. 15:24), or a pronoun (Mk. 6:30 and par.; Ac. 4:7; 14:11; 19:14). The workers of miracles are the disciples or Christians generally (Mk. 6:30 and par.; 9:39; Mt. 7:22; 21:21), or individuals mentioned by name like Peter and John (Ac. 3:12), Stephen (Ac. 6:8), Philip (Ac. 8:6) and Paul (Ac. 14:11), [139] also Moses (Ac. 7:36), though not the Baptist (Jn. 10:41). Naturally this miraculous action is in the name of Jesus, though He is expressly mentioned only in Mk. 9:39; Mt. 7:22 and Ac. 3:12. Most of the passages which record miracles are summaries; only the healing of the lame man in Ac. 3 f. has concrete features. Two intersecting views may be discerned throughout the material. On the one hand, the miraculous action of Jesus is continued in that of His disciples. On the other, Jesus is absolutely transcendent in His doing of miracles. The first view leads in Acts to stories which go far beyond anything found in the Synoptics. The second or apologetic view (John did no miracles, Jn. 10:41) is strongly emphasised in Jn. (3:2; 9:16; 15:24), though the Johannine σημεῖα are more than just magical acts of power, → 474, 1 ff. If non-christian miracles are adduced for the sake of unfavourable comparison (Jn. 3:2; 9:16; 15:24) or rejected as demonic (Ac. 19:14), it is at least made clear that for the NT the working of miracles is not exclusive to Christianity, and the historical materials relating to ποιέω (→ 473, 21 ff.) confirm this. Mt. 7:22 can even express plainly the danger which a merely magical working of miracles presents to true obedience, → 479, 7 ff.

9. ποιεῖν as Bringing Forth.

At the end of this survey of the NT material brief ref. may be made to ποιεῖν with material objects. Rarely it can mean "to do" (Mt. 6:3) or "to bring about" (Mt. 26:73). Usually, however, it means "to bring forth" either of vegetation (the tree in Mt. 3:10 and par.; 7:17 and par., 19; the fig-tree in Lk. 13:9; Jm. 3:12; the tree of life in Rev. 22:2; the vine in Jm. 3:12; the blade in Mt. 13:26, the seed in Lk. 8:8; Mt. 13:23, the grain of mustard seed in Mk. 4:32, the salt water in Jm. 3:12), or in the sense of capital yielding interest (Lk. 19:18). Either way the usage corresponds to secular usage and to that of

---

[136] Ltzm. K. on 11:24.
[137] Ltzm. K. on 11:24.
[138] Vielhauer, op. cit. (→ n. 34), 5-10.
[139] Paul himself in R. 15:18 f. and 2 C. 12:12 does not use ποιεῖν for the signs and wonders which he wrought; Ac. 15:12 and 19:11 speak of God's miraculous work through Paul and Barnabas, → 464, 18 f.

the LXX (→ 466, 39 ff.; 471, 19 ff.). Almost always — Mt. 26:73 and Rev. 13:15 are the exceptions — ποιεῖν is fig. in such instances. In metaphors (Mk. 4:32; Mt. 13:26; Rev. 22:2) it needs no interpretation, but it usually represents the action of the man addressed, who is to bring forth fruits (e.g., Mt. 3:10 and par.), or the growth of the Church (Eph. 4:16).

VI. Early Catholic Usage.

Because the materials are so abundant only a sketch can be given of early catholic usage outside the NT. ποιητής is still used for "poet" (→ 475, 25 ff.) only with reservations. The Phoenix myth in 1 Cl. (25) manages without the word, and so in many cases do the Apologists (thus Just. Apol., 18, 5 does not refer to Hom. as a ποιητής, and the same applies in the many quotations from Hom. in Tat. and Athenag.), [140] even though they were obviously open to culture in other matters. Indeed, even Iren. [141] is sparing in his use of ποιητής. Developing sacramentalism refers to ποιεῖν τὸν ἄρτον (Just. Dial., 41, 1; 70, 4) and ποιεῖν τὸ ποτήριον (ibid., 70, 4 → 483, 5 ff.). The proponent of a broadening asceticism can be regarded as ποιῶν εἰς μυστήριον κοσμικὸν ἐκκλησίας, Did., 11, 11 → IV, 824, 40 f.; → 464, 6 f. Above all, the retrogressive attitude as regards human action which had begun in the NT (→ 482, 29 ff.) now gathers considerable momentum. In 1 Cl. (in spite of 32, 4) there is no longer any awareness of Paul's questioning of legal observance and his resolving of the question by faith; Abraham is regarded as δικαιοσύνην καὶ ἀλήθειαν διὰ πίστεως ποιήσας, 1 Cl., 31, 2. It is esp. noteworthy that the same quotation which Paul used with ref. to the believing elect (1 C. 2:9) now serves to illustrate the statement : ἐὰν οὖν ποιήσωμεν τὴν δικαιοσύνην ἐναντίον τοῦ θεοῦ, εἰσήξομεν εἰς τὴν βασιλείαν αὐτοῦ καὶ ληψόμεθα τὰς ἐπαγγελίας, 2 Cl., 11, 7. Since the presence of salvation (→ 481, 18 ff.) is restricted to the sacramental sphere and no longer shapes the conduct of the Christian, the OT and later Jewish strand which is already to be found in the NT (→ 479, 1 ff.) now acquires greater emphasis and sharpness. It is typical that the positive final clause in Mt. 7:21 is now quoted in the form ἀλλ' ὁ ποιῶν τὴν δικαιοσύνην, 2 Cl., 4, 2. Nor is it any accident that pious action is now back in the vicinity of later Jewish casuistry and mediocrity (→ 471, 37 ff.): ὃ δύνῃ τοῦτο ποίει (Did., 6, 2); ἐγὼ μὲν οὖν τὸ ἴδιον ἐποίουν (Ign. Phld., 8, 1). The legalistic understanding of ποιεῖν has re-asserted itself. [142]

Braun

---

† ποικίλος, † πολυποίκιλος

† ποικίλος.

1. The word can have very different meanings : [1] "many-coloured," "gay," so from Hom., cf. Il., 10, 30; 14, 215 etc. Also LXX, which in Gn. 37:3 has χιτὼν ποικίλος ("coat of many colours") for the difficult כְּתֹנֶת פַּסִּים, which probably denotes a sleeved garment, cf. Gn. 37:23, 32. In early Chr. literature this sense occurs only in Herm. s., 9, 4, 5 : λίθοι ποικίλοι, "many-coloured" stones. The main use of the word, however, is for "various," "manifold," so from Pind. Olymp., 1, 29; 6, 87; Eur. Med., 300; cf. 2 Macc. 15, 21; Mart. Pol., 2, 4.

---

[140] Cf. the index in E. J. Goodspeed, Die älteren Apologeten (1914), 379 f. Just. Apol., II, 10, 6, e.g., mentions the ποιηταί.

[141] Cf. the index in A. Stieren, Irenaeus, I (1853), 1052.

[142] As regards individual passages this process is traced in detail in Bultmann Theol., 499-570.

ποικίλος. [1] Cf. Pass. and Liddell-Scott, s.v.

2. Of the distinct meanings of this much employed word, only the second occurs in the NT, namely, "various," "of many kinds," Mk. 1:34 (par. Mt. 4:24; Lk. 4:40): ποικίλαις νόσοις, Hb. 2:4 : ποικίλαις δυνάμεσιν, 13:9 : διδαχαῖς ποικίλαις, 2 Tm. 3:6 : ἐπιθυμίαις ποικίλαις, Tt. 3:3 : ἡδοναῖς ποικίλαις, Jm. 1:2 : πειρασμοῖς ποικίλοις (cf. 1 Pt. 1:6). Only 1 Pt. 4:10 (→ II, 86, 19 ff.) is of theological importance : διακονοῦντες ὡς καλοὶ οἰκονόμοι ποικίλης χάριτος θεοῦ, "minister as good stewards of the manifold grace of God, i.e., of the varied grace of God which manifests itself in many different ways." Peter has in mind (cf. v. 11) the charismata of primitive Christianity to which Paul especially refers, cf. R. 12:6-8; 1 C. 12:4-11.

† πολυποίκιλος.

A strengthened form of ποικίλος, "most varied," Orph., 6, 11; 61, 4 : πολυποίκιλος λόγος, Sib., 8, 120 : πολυποίκιλος ὀργή.

The only NT occurrence is at Eph. 3:10 : ἵνα γνωρισθῇ ... ἡ πολυποίκιλος σοφία τοῦ θεοῦ. The liking of Eph. for plerophory in expression is apparent here. The wisdom of God (→ σοφία) has shown itself in Christ to be varied beyond measure and in a way which surpasses all previous knowledge thereof.

Seesemann

> ποιμήν, ἀρχιποίμην,
> ποιμαίνω, ποίμνη,
> ποίμνιον

† ποιμήν, † ἀρχιποίμην, ποιμαίνω. [1]

Contents : A. The Palestinian Shepherd. B. Transferred Usage : I. In the Ancient Orient ; II. In the OT. C. The Shepherd in Later Judaism : I. In Palestinian Judaism ; II. In Philo. D. The Shepherd in the NT : I. Jesus and Shepherds ; II. The Shepherds in the Nativity Story (Lk. 2:8-20); III. The Shepherd as a Picture of God ; IV. Jesus as the Good Shepherd : 1. According to His Own Sayings in the Synoptic Gospels ; 2. In the Christological Statements of the Primitive Church ; 3. John 10:1-30; 4. In Post-Canonical Writings and Early

---

ποιμήν κτλ. On A : G. Dalman, "Arbeit u. Sitte in Palästina, VI," BFTh, II, 41 (1939), 146-287. On B : L. Dürr, *Ursprung u. Ausbau d. isr.-jüd. Heilandserwartung* (1925), 116-124; V. Hamp, "Das Hirtenmotiv im AT," *Festschr. f. Kardinal Faulhaber* (1949), 7-20. On C. I : J. Jeremias, *Jerusalem z. Zt. Jesu,* II, B (1937), 174-184. On D. II : A. M. Schneider, Art. "Bethlehem," RAC, II, 224-228. On D. III : J. Jeremias, *Die Gleichnisse Jesu*[4] (1956), 28-30, 116-118. On D. IV: H. Leclercq, Art. "Pasteur (Bon)," *Dict. d'Archéologie Chrétienne et de Liturgie,* 13, 2 (1938), 2272-2390; W. Jost, ΠΟΙΜΗΝ, *Das Bild vom Hirten in d. bibl. Überlieferung u. seine christologische Bedeutung* (1939); T. K. Kempf, *Christus der Hirt. Ursprung u. Deutung einer altchr. Symbolgestalt* (1942), and on this cf. the review by G. Bertram in ThLZ, 69 (1944), 275-277; J. Jeremias, *Jesu Verheissung f. d. Völker* (1956), 54 f. On E : Reitzenstein Poim., 13, 31 f., 115 f.; M. Dibelius, "Der Offenbarungsträger im 'Hirten' d. Hermas," *Harnack-Ehrung* (1921), 105-118; Dib. Herm., 494-496; K. Latte, "Die Religion d. Römer u. d. Synkretismus d. Kaiserzeit," *Religionsgeschichtliches Lesebuch,* ed. A. Bertholet, 5² (1927), 71-74.
[1] On the etym.: ποιμήν is an ancient Indo-European word = Lithuanian piemuõ (formerly written pēmũ), gen. piemeñs (Pokorny, 839) [Debrunner].

Christian Art; V. Shepherds as a Term for Congregational Leaders. E. The Shepherd of Hermas.

A. The Palestinian Shepherd.

Throughout the biblical period tending flocks, with agriculture, was in Palestine the basis of the economy. [2] The dryness of the ground made it necessary for the flocks of sheep and cattle to move about during the rainless summer and to stay for months at a time in isolated areas far from the dwelling of the owner. [3] Hence the herding of sheep etc. — and this is the only ref. in the NT — was an independent and responsible job; indeed, in view of the threat of wild beasts (→ IV, 308, 1 ff. λύκος) and robbers it could even be dangerous. [4] Sometimes the owner himself (Lk. 15:6; Jn. 10:12) or his sons did the job, but usually it was done by hired shepherds [5] who only too often did not justify the confidence reposed in them (Jn. 10:12 f.).

B. Transferred Usage.

I. In the Ancient Orient.

Already on Sumerian royal inscr. the king (from Lugal-zaggisi) is described as the shepherd appointed by deity. [6] In Babylonian and Assyrian rê'û ("shepherd") is a common epithet for rulers and the verb re'û ("to pasture") is a common figure of speech for "to rule." [7] Courtly style honours the king with this title, which is combined with a whole number of recurrent attributes; on inscr. the king also uses it of himself as the one divinely chosen to bring salvation. Gathering the dispersed, righteous government and care for the weak are marks of the shepherd function of the ruler. Gods, too, bear the title of shepherd. [8] In Egypt [9] the image of the ruler of the world to come (usually Osiris or the dead king as Osiris), who, as a herd tends his flock, protects his subjects (as stars), is already common in the royal funerary (or pyramid) texts of the ancient kingdom, e.g., "thou hast taken them up in thine arms as a herd his calves," [10] or the god of the underworld is said to be "thy herd who is behind thy calves." [11] From the early Middle Kingdom (in the first interim period) the image of the king as the shepherd of his subjects is then a favourite one in literature; he is, e.g., a "herd for all the people" or the "herd who watches over his subjects." [12] The same metaphor is used for the gods; thus Amun is "the strong drover who guards his cattle" (hymn of the 18th dynasty). [13] Similarly, it is said of men as subjects: "Men are well cared for, the cattle

---

[2] In 1920 the following figures were given for cattle in Palestine west of the Jordan: 325,512 goats, 205,967 sheep, 108,500 oxen, 32,689 donkeys, 8,846 camels, 6,548 horses, 3,934 mules and 615 buffaloes, Dalman, 146.

[3] "Pasture cattle (as distinct from stall cattle) are driven out at passover time, graze on rough ground and return with the first autumn rain (the beginning of November)," bBeza, 40a, Bar. The pattern is much the same to-day west of the Jordan, Dalman, 207.

[4] Cf. David's description of his fights against wild beasts as a shepherd boy, 1 S. 17:34-37.

[5] Dalman, 213-218, 231-236.

[6] C. J. Gadd, Ideas of Divine Rule in the Ancient East (1948), 38.

[7] F. Thureau-Dangin, Die sumerischen u. akkadischen Königsinschr. (1907), passim; S. H. Langdon, Die neubabyl. Königsinschr. (1912), passim; Dürr, 117-120. There is a comprehensive collection of passages in A. Schott, "Die Vergleiche in d. akkad. Königsinschr." Mitteilungen d. Vorderasiatisch-Aegyptischen Gesellschaft, 30 (1926), 70-72 [W. v. Soden].

[8] Dürr, 121 f.; A. Jeremias, Hdbch. d. altorient. Geisteskultur[2] (1929), Index, s.v. "Hirte."

[9] H. Kees kindly placed the section on Egypt (lines 22 ff.) at my disposal.

[10] K. Sethe, Die altaegypt. Pyramidentexte, II (1910), Text 1533b.

[11] Ibid., I (1908), Text 771b.

[12] For this reason, e.g., J. A. Wilson, The Burden of Egypt (1951), 125 entitles the chapter on the 11th and 12th dynasties "The King as the Good Shepherd."

[13] H. Grapow, Die bildlichen Ausdrücke des Ägyptischen (1924), 156.

of God," [14] or : "Let us crown a king, for we are a herd of oxen without a herd." [15] Thus far there is no attestation of the transf. use of the title in Canaan. [16]

II. In the OT.

1. In the OT the description of Yahweh as the Shepherd of Israel is ancient usage, [17] but the surprising paucity of references in which the title is used of Yahweh [18] shows that this is not just a formal oriental divine predication. The application of the shepherd image to Yahweh is embedded in the living piety of Israel. This may be seen from the great number of passages which use the rich shepherd vocabulary for Yahweh and depict God in new and vivid developments of the metaphor as the Shepherd who goes before His flock, [19] who guides it, [20] who leads it to pastures [21] and to places where it may rest by the waters, [22],[23] who protects it with His staff, [24] who whistles [25] to the dispersed and gathers them, [26] who carries the lambs in His bosom and leads the mother-sheep (Is. 40:11). It is to be noted that the references are not spread evenly over the whole of the OT. It is true that in Exodus-Deuteronomy shepherd terms are used in the Exodus stories ("to lead," "to guide," "to go before"), but in general it is hard to determine whether there is any conscious feeling for the shepherd metaphor. More commonly, and with details which show how vital the concept is, the figure of speech is found in the Psalter [27] and in the consoling prophecy of the Exile. [28] The content of the metaphor is more clearly developed in the latter than in any other place apart from Ps. 23. More than almost any other expression it is well fitted to bring out the fact that Israel is sheltered in God.

2. In view of the fact that in, e.g., the threats of Jeremiah "shepherds" is also a common term for political and military leaders, [29] it is surprising that there is

---

[14] H. Kees, *Aegypten, Religionsgeschichtliches Lesebuch*, ed. A. Bertholet, 10² (1928), 44 (doctrine of kingship for Merikarê ; first interim period c. 2050 B.C.).

[15] H. Schäfer, *Urkunden d. älteren Äthiopenkönige* (1905), III, 87.

[16] The designation of the ruler or God as shepherd is constantly found in antiquity outside Mesopotamia and Egypt. There is a good introductory survey in Bau. J., Exc. after 10:21. In Greece as early as Hom. the ruler is ποιμὴν λαῶν. In Plat. Resp., IV, 440d the rulers are called shepherds of the πόλις; they must see to the well-being of their subjects as shepherds do to that of their animals, I, 343b-345e; III, 416a b; Leg., V, 735b-e. The human shepherd is a σχῆμα τοῦ θείου νομέως (Polit., 275c) because in the primitive age men were fed by a god, Polit., 271e (there are examples of νομεύς alternating with ποιμήν in Plat., cf. F. Ast, Lexicon Platonicum, II [1836], s.v.). Cf. K. Stegmann v. Pritzwald, "Zur Gesch. d. Herrscherbezeichnungen v. Hom. bis Plat.," *Forschungen zur Völkerpsychologie u. Soziologie,* VII (1930), 15-21. The pastoral terminology of the Hell. world strongly influenced Chr. thought and art, though only in the post-canonical period (→ 497, 8 ff.; 498, 22 ff.), hardly as early as NT times (→ 497, 3 ff.; 501, 29 ff.).

[17] Gn. 49:24 (textus crrp, J); 48:15 (E).

[18] Apart from Gn. 48:15; 49:24 only Ps. 23:1; 80:1.

[19] יָצָא לִפְנֵי Ps. 68:7.

[20] נְהָה Ps. 23:3 etc.

[21] נָוֶה Jer. 50:19 etc.

[22] מֵי מְנֻחוֹת Ps. 23:2.

[23] נהל pi Is. 40:11; Ps. 23:2 etc.; נָהַג Ps. 80:1; Is. 49:10 (pi) etc.

[24] מִשְׁעֶנֶת, שֵׁבֶט Ps. 23:4.

[25] שָׁרַק Zech. 10:8; שְׁרִקָה Ju. 5:16.

[26] קבץ pi Is. 56:8.

[27] Ps. 23:1-4; 28:9; 68:7; 74:1; 77:20; 78:52 f.; 79:13; 80:1; 95:7; 100:3; 121:4.

[28] Jer. 23:3; 31:10; 50:19; Ez. 34:11-22; Is. 40:10 f.; 49:9 f.; Mi. 4:6-8; 7:14.

[29] 1 S. 21:8; 2 S. 7:7 par. 1 Ch. 17:6; Jer. 2:8; 3:15; 10:21; 22:22; 23:1-4; 25:34-36; 50:6;

no single instance in the OT of "shepherd" ever being used in Israel as a title for the ruling king. [30] The distinction from the courtly style of the ancient Orient is even more palpable if we add that in the time of impending disaster "shepherd" still occurs as a title for the ruler, but only for the future Messianic son of David. Because the shepherds have refused and become unfaithful, Yahweh will visit them; [31] He Himself will take over the office of shepherd and gather and feed the scattered flock; [32] He will appoint better shepherds (Jer. 3:15; 23:4) and proclaim: "I will set up one shepherd over them, and he shall feed them, even my servant David; he shall feed them, and he shall be their shepherd. And I Yahweh will be their God, and my servant David prince among them; I, Yahweh, promise it," Ez. 34:23 f. [33] Israel and Judah will become one people (37:22) under one shepherd (37:24). With the title "shepherd" Ez. seeks to guard against a one-sidedly political understanding of the figure of the future ruler, and also to leave the manner of the fulfilment of the promise to God. [34]

Shepherd as a title for the Messiah undergoes a unique and, from the NT standpoint, final development in Deutero-Zechariah. [35] After the return from exile bad shepherds ruled who provoked the wrath of Yahweh, Zech. 10:3; 11:4-17. He summons the sword: "Awake, O sword, against my shepherd, and against my fellow ... Smite the shepherd, so that the sheep scatter," Zech. 13:7. This divine judgment is the beginning of the purification from which the people of God moves on as a remnant into the time of salvation, v. 8 f. The shepherd whom the sword smites was originally the worthless shepherd of 11:15 ff.; [36] in the present context, however, he can only be the one "whom they pierced" (12:10) and whose death ushered in the time of salvation (13:1-6). [37] Thus at the end of the OT shepherd sayings there stands an intimation of the shepherd who suffers death according to God's will and who thereby brings about the decisive turn, → 492, 24 ff.

C. The Shepherd in Later Judaism.

I. In Palestinian Judaism.

a. In a Rabb. list of thieving and cheating occupations we find that of the shepherd. [38] This classification of herds as notorious robbers and cheats means that like the publicans and tax-gatherers they were deprived of civil rights, i.e., they could not fulfil a judicial

---

Ez. 34:2-10; Is. 56:11; Mi. 5:4; Zech. 10:3; 11:5 f., 16 f. Foreign rulers are also called "shepherds" in Jer. 25:34-36; Na. 3:18; Is. 44:28 HT (Yahweh calls Cyrus "my shepherd"; the LXX avoids this expression).

[30] It is quite early said of David that he "tends" Israel (2 S. 5:2 par. 1 Ch. 11:2; Ps. 78:71 f.) and the people is called by him a flock (2 S. 24:17 par. 1 Ch. 21:17), but the royal title "shepherd" does not occur.

[31] Jer. 2:8; 23:2; Ez. 34:1-10 etc.

[32] Jer. 23:3; 31:10; Ez. 34:11-22; cf. Mi. 4:6 f.

[33] Cf. Mi. 5:3 (the ruler of Israel from Bethlehem, the town of David, will feed the people in the power of the Lord); 4:8 (the dominion returns to the tower of the flock).

[34] [K. Galling].

[35] Cf. K. Elliger, Das Buch d. zwölf Kleinen Propheten, II AT Deutsch, 25³ (1956) on Zech. 13:7.

[36] So many commentators since H. Ewald, Die Propheten d. Alten Bundes, I² (1867), 266-271.

[37] 13:7 is expounded thus by E. Sellin, Das Zwölfprophetenbuch ², ³, Komm. AT, XII (1930), 567 f.; A. Jeremias, Die ausserbibl. Erlösererwartung, II (1931), 253; O. Procksch, Theol. d. AT (1950), 413; K. Elliger, op. cit. (→ n. 35), ad loc.

[38] Qid., 4, 14 and bSanh., 25b. For a table of the 4 Rabb. lists of despised occupations cf. Jeremias, Jerusalem, 175.

office or be admitted in court as witnesses.[39] This discrimination against shepherds on the part of Pharisaic Rabbinism is best understood if one realises that the independence of the shepherd, who during the summer was on the move with the flock for months at a time with no supervision (→ 486, 5 ff.), constituted a serious temptation to steal some of the increase of the flock. It is worth noting that to buy wool, milk, or a kid from a shepherd was forbidden on the assumption that it would be stolen property.[40] The Rabb. ask with amazement how, in view of the despicable nature of shepherds,[41] one is to explain the fact that God is called "my shepherd" in Ps. 23:1.[42]

b. Though shepherds were despised in everyday life, nevertheless even in later Judaism, on the basis of the statements of the OT, God was described as the Shepherd of Israel who led His flock out of Egypt (Eth. En. 89:22, 24, 28), guides them in the present,[43] will one day gather again the scattered flock, and will feed them on the holy mountain.[44] Moreover the leaders and teachers of Israel are also called shepherds;[45] in particular Moses[46] and David[47] are extolled as faithful shepherds. In the vision of the shepherds in Eth. En. 85-90, however, the term shepherds is restricted to 70 Gentile rulers (or the angel princes of the peoples) which have dominion over Israel up to the establishment of the Messianic kingdom, Eth. En. 89:59; 90:22.

In relation to the NT two passages are of particular importance. In Damasc. 13:9 f. (16:2 f.) it is said of the *mebaqqer*[48] of the community that he "should pity the members of the community as a father does his children and (there is here a short gap in the text) ... their offences; 'as a shepherd his flock' (cf. Is. 40:11; Ez. 34:12) he should loose all the bands with which they are tied." This comparison of the leader of the community with the shepherd is the closest analogy to the similar statements in the NT, → 498, 16 ff. Then in Ps. Sol. 17:40 it is said of the Messiah: ἰσχυρὸς ἐν ἔργοις αὐτοῦ καὶ κραταιὸς ἐν φόβῳ θεοῦ ποιμαίνων τὸ ποίμνιον κυρίου ἐν πίστει καὶ δικαιοσύνῃ. This passage shows that the comparison of the Messiah with a shepherd was known to pre-Christian Judaism. If apart from one passage[49] this comparison does not occur in any of the Rabb. writings, this is due to conscious avoidance[50] of a terminology which had been commandered by Christians, → V, 697, 19 f.

---

[39] bSanh., 25b; Jeremias, *op. cit.*, 183 f.

[40] BQ, 10, 9; T BQ, 11, 9. Shepherds were also accused of pasturing their flocks on the lands of others, Str.-B., II, 114; III, 108.

[41] "No position in the world is so despised as that of the shepherd," Midr. Ps. 23 § 2, ed. S. Buber (1891).

[42] *Loc. cit.* The author is R. Jose bChanina (c. 270). Kindly sayings about shepherds are hardly found except in relation to biblical texts, e.g., Ex. r., 2 on 3:1: Moses as a faithful shepherd.

[43] Str.-B., I, 574; II, 536 etc.

[44] Ps.-Ez. Fr., 1, verso lines 12 ff., ed. C. Bonner, *Studies and Documents,* XII (1940), 186.

[45] Str.-B., II, 537; S. Bar. 77:13-16; 4 Esr. 5:18; S. Nu., 139 on 27:17.

[46] Str.-B., I, 755, 972; II, 209, 536, 538 etc.

[47] *Ibid.,* I, 972; II, 537.

[48] → II, 618, 26 ff. The discovery in cave 1 at Qumran (1947) has initiated a new stage in the discussion of a possible connection between the Essene *mebaqqer* and the Chr. ἐπίσκοπος. Since the sect did not have a monarchical *mebaqqer* (Damasc. 14:8 f. [17:6]) but several *mebaqqerim* with different functions, the matter has not been settled, but a vital objection against the possibility of a connection has been removed.

[49] Midr. Ps. 29 § 1: "What will I (God) then do to them? My servant David shall feed them. For it is said: 'And I will set a shepherd over them' (Ez. 34:23)."

[50] It is worth noting that Tg. Ez. 34:23; 37:24 has פַּרְנָס (provider) and פַּרְנֵס (provide) for "shepherd" and "feed."

II. In Philo. [51]

In Philo the shepherd stories of the OT and the shepherd figures of Jacob, Laban, Joseph, Moses etc. (cf. Gn. 31:11-13; Ex. 3:1; Nu. 27:16, 17 etc.) are often the starting-points for a shepherd typology. First νοῦς (→ IV, 955 f.; also ὀρθὸς λόγος) is expounded as the shepherd (also ἐπιτετραμμένος, ἡνίοχος or κυβερνήτης) of the irrational powers of the soul, Sacr. AC, 45; Som., II, 152-154; Sobr., 14. He who exercises himself in knowledge also pastures these irrational powers and admonishes them to act sensibly, Det. Pot. Ins., 3. Again, Philo can compare the leading of a nation by the ruler to the watching of a shepherd over his flock (Leg. Gaj., 44); he can also describe sheep-herding as a good preparation for rule (Vit. Mos., I, 60 ff.; Jos., 2). On the whole, however, he is sparing in his use of shepherd for the ruler; he is usually content to refer to poetic usage. Like the OT (→ 487, 23 ff.), he never has the title for the kings of Israel and Judah. All the nuances of Philonic usage are to be found in the connected passage Agric., 26-66. As the flock of men, driven by irrational impulse of soul, can stand for the isolated powers of soul, so the image of the supreme power of soul as a shepherd can be transferred to the work of the king protecting the irrational flock, Agric., 41. On the other hand, God is also brought into connection with the image. God is Shepherd and King, and He feeds the world and all that therein is representatively through His λόγος, Agric., 50-52.

D. The Shepherd in the NT.

I. Jesus and Shepherds.

The shepherd is never judged adversely in the NT. In the Gospels his sacrificial loyalty to his calling is depicted with loving sympathy in true-to-life pictures. He knows each of his animals, calls them by name (Jn. 10:3, 14, 27), [52] seeks the lost sheep, is happy when he finds it (Lk. 15:4-6), and is prepared to hazard his life to protect the sheep from the wolf (Jn. 10:11-13). Jesus does not hesitate to use the shepherd as a figure for God in His parables, Lk. 15:4-7 par. Mt. 18:12-14 → 491, 24 ff. The high estimation of the shepherd in all this stands in such striking contrast to the contempt of the Rabbis (→ 488, 29 ff.) that one is forced to conclude that it mirrors directly the actuality of the life of Jesus, who had fellowship with the despised and with sinners, and who shared sympathetically in their life.

II. The Shepherds in the Nativity Story (Lk. 2:8-20).

Setting aside parables and figurative sayings, we find real shepherds in the NT only in the Lucan story of the nativity, Lk. 2:8-20. There has been much discussion of the way in which these come to have a place in the Christmas story. This is an important issue, since the answer helps to determine our assessment of the story as literature and history.

Of the many solutions the most important are the following. a. This is the story of a founding like the child Osiris, whom Kronos put in charge of a drawer of water (Plut. Is. et Os., 12); the shepherds are primary in the Christmas story, the parents secondary. [53] This fantastic theory is shattered by the fact that the ref. in Plut. Is. et Os., 12 is not to a foundling. b. In Hell. bucolic literature the life of the shepherd is glorified as the ideal existence; hence the shepherds are representatives of the paradisial world. [54] Against this derivation of the mention of the shepherds from Hell. ideas the

---

[51] For this section I am indebted to G. Bertram and C. Colpe.
[52] The Palestinian shepherd chooses the name acc. to the shape, colour and attributes of the animal, and the name which it received as a lamb or kid, and with which it was thus familiar from the first, was always retained, Dalman, 250 f.
[53] H. Gressmann, Das Weihnachts-Ev. auf Ursprung u. Gesch. untersucht (1914), 16-28.
[54] Bultmann Trad., 325, cf. M. Dibelius, "Jungfrauensohn u. Krippenkind," SAH (1932), **74 f.**

Hebraic language of the section is a telling argument. c. The shepherds who were regarded as thieves in Palestine (→ 488, 29 ff.) are paradoxically the first recipients of the Christmas message ;[55] there is, however, no suggestion of any such paradox. d. We have an allusion to David, who pastured his flock in the fields of Bethlehem,[56] or to the expectation that the Messiah would appear in a shepherd tower, Tg. J. I on Gn. 35:21;[57] once again, however, there is no hint of this. e. The idea that the shepherds received the angelic message because they were the only ones awake that night is also unsatisfying.[58]

The point at which to begin is the tradition that, because the village inn was full (Lk. 2:7), the birth of Jesus took place in a stall. The birth in a stall is supported twice indirectly. First Luke's mention of a manger (2:7, 12, 16) suggests a stall. Then local tradition in Bethlehem points to a cave as the place of birth ;[59] in Palestine caves outside villages regularly served as stalls.[60] Since the local tradition is not dependent on Luke,[61] it is an independent witness for the birth in a stall and must be older than its fairly early [62] attestation. The shepherds in the nativity story are part of this tradition of the birth of Jesus in a stall. They are obviously the owners of the stall ; this is also why they can be told without further elaboration that the manger is the site of the sign from God, 2:12. In other words, the shepherds of the Christmas story,[63] like the manger and the cave, are a solid part of the local tradition in Bethlehem that a stall was the birthplace of Jesus.[64]

III. The Shepherd as a Picture of God.

God is never called a shepherd in the NT, nor is this surprising in view of the OT data, → 487, 3 ff. In the light of the OT, however, it is astonishing that comparison of God with a shepherd, which is so common in the OT (→ 487, 8 ff.), is restricted in the NT to the parables of Jesus, and does not occur again later until Ign. (R., 9, 1, → n. 123). The paucity of ref. to God in the pastoral usage of the NT may be explained by the great prominence given here to the Christological application of the shepherd figure, → 493, 30 ff.

---

[55] Considered but rightly rejected by Dibelius, op. cit., 66 f.

[56] 1 S. 16:11; Ps. 78:70.

[57] E. Nestle, "Die Hirten v. Bethlehem," ZNW, 7 (1906), 257-259; H. Sahlin, Der Messias u. das Gottesvolk (1945), 210 f.

[58] Schl. Lk., 187.

[59] The following are the oldest testimonies. 1. The excavations of 1933-34 have confirmed that the cave under the Church of the Nativity in Bethlehem was the sanctissimum of the Church built by the emperor's mother Helena, shortly before 330, Schneider, 226. 2. The desecration of the cave by the cult of Adonis (Hier. Ep. ad Paulinum, 58, 3 [CSEL, 54, 532]; Paulinus of Nola Ep. ad Severum, 31, 3 [CSEL, 29, 270]), which probably took place under Hadrian, possibly under Decius, proves that the cave was honoured by Christians in the 2nd (or 3rd) century ; 3. The fact that the cave tradition is independently attested by the oldest Arm. Gospel MS (A.D. 887 on Mt. 2:9), Origen (Cels., 1, 51 [GCS, 2, 102]), Prot. Ev. Jc. (18:1; 19:1-3; 20:4; 21:3), Justin (Dial., 78, 5, cf. 70, 2) and Barn. (11, 5) enables us to trace it back to the early 2nd cent. A.D., cf. J. Jeremias, "Golgotha," Angelos Beih., 1 (1926), 14-16; E. Benz, "Die heilige Höhle in der alten Christenheit u. in der östlich-orthodoxen Kirche," Eranos-Jbch., 22 (1953), 365-432.

[60] G. Dalman, "Orte u. Wege Jesu,"[3] BFTh, II, 1 (1924), 48.

[61] Lk. says nothing about a cave.

[62] → n. 59.

[63] Acc. to Arkulf (c. 670, cf. Adamnanus, De locis sanctis libri tres, II, 6 [Itinera Hierosolymitana, ed. P. Geyer, CSEL, 39, 258]) there were three shepherds. Even if the number is legendary it is obviously based on knowledge of shepherd life → 499, 14 ff.

[64] Evaluation of this local tradition depends on whether one puts the birth of Jesus in Bethlehem or (as against Mt. and Lk.) in Nazareth.

In the parable of the lost sheep (Lk. 15:4-7 par. Mt. 18:12-14) [65] Jesus tells of the joy of the shepherd when he finds his sheep after a difficult search. This is a picture of the joy of God when in the last judgment (Lk. 15:7 ἔσται) He can proclaim remission to a penitent sinner. It is greater than His joy over the 99 who stayed on the right path. The parallel in Mt. (18:14) agrees in content with Lk. 15:7: In the light of the Aramaic original this should be translated : "So your heavenly father is well pleased if one of even the least escapes destruction." [66] With "the soteriological joy of God" [67] Jesus justifies His love for sinners against the criticisms of opponents. Because God, like the rejoicing shepherd of the parable, is filled with such boundless joy at the bringing back of the lost, the fetching of sinners home is the saving office of Jesus. [68] The fact that Jesus uses the image of the despised shepherd to illustrate God's love for sinners reflects particularly vividly His antithesis to the Pharisaic despising of sinners, → 489, 7 ff.

IV. Jesus the Good Shepherd.

1. According to His Own Sayings in the Synoptic Gospels.

Not merely in Jn. 10, but in the Synoptic Gospels too, Jesus referred to Himself as the Messianic Shepherd promised in the OT, → 488, 2 ff. He used the figure of speech in three ways.

a. To describe His mission He uses an ancient motif of world renewal, [69] namely, that of gathering again the dispersed flock which is abandoned to destruction, Mt. 15:24; 10:6 : τὰ πρόβατα τὰ ἀπολωλότα οἴκου 'Ισραήλ; [70] the allusion to Ez. 34 is particularly plain in Lk. 19:10. [71, 72] As the scattering is an image of disaster, so the gathering is an image of the coming of the age of salvation.

b. In Mk. 14:27 f. (par. Mt. 26:31 f.) Jesus uses the figure of speech to intimate to the disciples His death and return : πάντες σκανδαλισθήσεσθε, ὅτι γέγραπται· πατάξω τὸν ποιμένα, καὶ τὰ πρόβατα διασκορπισθήσονται (= Zech. 13:7b). (v. 28) ἀλλὰ μετὰ τὸ ἐγερθῆναί με προάξω ὑμᾶς εἰς τὴν Γαλιλαίαν.

This is an ancient tradition. For Zech. 13:7 is quoted acc. to the HT (הַ֤ךְ אֶת־הָֽרֹעֶה֙ וּתְפוּצֶ֣יןָ הַצֹּ֔אן). Only the introductory imp. has been changed (into the fut. 1st pers. sing.

---

[65] For detailed exegesis cf. Jeremias, Gleichnisse, 116-118. In connection with v. 5 it should be noted that carrying on the shoulder does not prove any influence of depictions of Hermes Kriophoros on Lk., since it was an everyday occurrence in Palestine, Dalman, Ill. 35.

[66] In Mt. (18:12-14) the accent has been somewhat shifted secondarily by integration οὐρανοῖς ἵνα ἀπόληται ἓν τῶν μικρῶν τούτων) it should be noted linguistically that θέλημα = רְעוָא has here the sense of good-pleasure, that the negation belongs materially to the 2nd half of the v. and that τούτων is redundant, as the demonstrative often is in Aram., Jeremias, Gleichnisse, 28-30.

[67] E. G. Gulin, Die Freude im NT, I (1932), 99.

[68] In Mt. (18:12-14) the accent has been somewhat shifted secondarily by integration into directions to leaders of the community (c. 18). It thus lies, not on the joy of the shepherd, but on the example of his seeking, → 498, 12.

[69] → 486, 18 ff. A. Jeremias, Das AT im Lichte d. Alten Orients⁴ (1930), 183; also Hndbch. der altorientalischen Geisteskultur² (1929), 108.

[70] An ancient Aram. tradition underlies both verses, Jeremias, Verheissung, 16 f., 22 f. Also ancient is the restriction of Jesus' mission to Israel, 22-33. This may be explained by the fact that Jesus expected the integration of the Gentiles into the people of God in the form of the eschatological pilgrimage of the nations to the Mount of God, 47-62.

[71] ζητῆσαι τὸ ἀπολωλός cf. Ez. 34:16 : אֶת־הָאֹבֶדֶת אֲבַקֵּשׁ.

[72] The image of the shepherd underlies not only Lk. 19:10 but also Mt. 12:30 par. Lk. 11:23 (συνάγειν/σκορπίζειν are tt. among shepherds, cf. Jn. 11:51 f.).

πατάξω, → n. 78), and there is no trace at all of the divergent LXX text. [73] Also ancient is the mention of the flight of the disciples (cf. Mk. 14:50; Jn. 16:32), for this feature was soon smoothed over. [74] Finally v. 28 is ancient. [75] The word προάγειν (→ n. 80) hardly corresponds to the course of events at Easter and therefore it has not been formulated *ex eventu*. v. 28 is repeated in Mk. 16:7 with the addition ἐκεῖ αὐτὸν ὄψεσθε, which probably refers to the *parousia*. [76] If this is correct, and προάγειν (14:28; 16:7) implies an immediate rising for the *parousia*, it is obvious that this must be a pre-Easter tradition. Jesus is the promised Good Shepherd, the "fellow" of God (Zech. 13:7 → 488, 18 f.), whom God smites (this is how the πατάξω of Mk. 14:27 must be transl.), [77] i.e., upon whom He causes judgment to fall. [78] The fate of the shepherd involves the scattering of the flock: *qualis rex, talis grex*. In Zech., however, the whole emphasis is upon the cleansing and receiving of the remnant of the flock (13:8 f.), and so, too, in Mk. it rests on the promise in v. 28. [79] The fact that the promise of v. 28 is correlative to the prophecy of the passion in v. 27 is perfectly clear once it is realised that the προάγειν of v. 28 is a shepherd term [80] and that v. 28 thus continues the shepherd metaphor of v. 27. In other words, v. 28 quotes Zech. 13:7b literally, while v. 28 is a free rendering of the contents of Zech. 13:8 f. The death of Jesus thus initiates the eschatological tribulation, the scattering (13:7) and decimation (13:8) of the flock and the testing of the remnant which is left in the furnace (13:9a). But the crisis, the scandal (Mk. 14:27), is the turning-point, for it is followed by the gathering of the purified flock as the people of God (Zech. 13:9b) under the leadership of the Good Shepherd (Mk. 14:28).

c. Finally in Mt. 25:32 Jesus uses the image of the shepherd and the flock to illustrate the execution of eschatological judgment. Like a scattered flock the nations are assembled around the glorious throne of the Son of Man (v. 31 f.) [81] and here there takes place the process of judgment, which is compared to the separation of the (white) sheep from the (black) goats, v. 32 → 499, n. 3. The judgment is followed by God's gracious rule over His small flock, Lk. 12:32 → 501, 10 ff.

2. In the Christological Statements of the Primitive Church.

Though the shepherd title and metaphor are not used of Christ in the Pauline Epistles, both are common elsewhere in the NT. We find the following predicates

---

[73] Acc. to the oldest tradition (J. Ziegler, Duodecim prophetae, Septuaginta. Vetus Testamentum Graecum auctoritate Societatis Litterarum Gottingensis editum, XIII [1943], 322) Zech. 13:7 LXX runs: πατάξατε (plur.; HT sing.) τοὺς ποιμένας (plur.; HT sing.) καὶ ἐκσπάσατε ("drive forth"; HT "will be scattered") τὰ πρόβατα. None of the LXX deviations from the LXX is to be found in Mk.

[74] There is nothing corresponding to Mk. 14:50 in Lk.

[75] V. 28 does not occur in one pap. (3rd cent.) of the collection of Duke Rainer in Vienna erroneously called the Fr. Fayyumense (definitive ed. by the finder C. Wessely, "Les plus anciens monuments du Christianisme écrits sur papyrus," Patrologia orientalis, 4 [1908], 173-177), but this is not, as often assumed, an original shorter text; it is an abbreviated summary of Mk. 14:26-30 which leaves out v. 28, *ibid.*, 177.

[76] Cf. ὄψεσθε in Mk. 14:62 and par., and on this E. Lohmeyer, "Galiläa u. Jerusalem," FRL, 52 (1936), 11-14.

[77] הִכָּה = πατάσσειν, used of the sword, means "to smite."

[78] The fact that Mk. 14:27 changes the Heb. imp. of Zech. 13:7 ("smite") into a fut. 1st pers. sing. (πατάξω, "I (God) will smite") is to be explained by Is. 53:6b, Jost, 25. The smitten Shepherd is the Servant of the Lord. God vicariously lays on him the judgment which should have smitten the whole flock.

[79] In the Joh. par. 16:32 f. the emphasis is all on the promise in v. 33.

[80] Cf. Jn. 10:4 (of the shepherd): ἔμπροσθεν αὐτῶν πορεύεται. Materially cf. Dalman, 249 f., 253-255: the shepherd usually goes in front; only on the way home does he follow behind to protect the flock and round up strays.

[81] συνάγειν is a tt. among shepherds, → n. 72.

of Christ : ὁ ποιμὴν καὶ → ἐπίσκοπος τῶν ψυχῶν (1 Pt. 2:25), ὁ ποιμὴν τῶν προβάτων ὁ μέγας (Hb. 13:20 : liturgical formula) and ὁ ἀρχιποίμην (1 Pt. 5:4). [82] The description of Christ as Shepherd of souls in 1 Pt. 2:25 characterises Him (cf. the synonym ἐπίσκοπος) as the One who provides for and watches over His people (→ II, 615, 29 f.). The predicate "chief shepherd" in Hb. 13:20 is used to denote the uniqueness of Christ who surpasses all previous examples, especially Moses, [83] while in 1 Pt. 5:4 it expresses the majesty of the Lord, who demands a reckoning from His shepherd, → 497, 30 ff. The metaphor describes Christ as the ruler of Israel (Mt. 2:6) promised in Mi. 5:3. [84] As the earthly Lord He is the merciful One who has pity on the leaderless flock, Mk. 6:34; Mt. 9:36. As the exalted Lord, He is the Lamb [85] who watches over the innumerable multitude of those who come out of great tribulation and leads them to the springs of living water, Rev. 7:17, cf. 14:4b. [86] As the returning Lord He is the apocalyptic Ruler who feeds the Gentiles with a rod of iron, Rev. 12:5; 19:15, cf. 2:27 → 501, 3 ff. [87]

3. John 10:1-30.

a. In recent decades numerous efforts have been made to make a critical literary analysis of the shepherd address in Jn. 10:1-30 which will differentiate various sources and their redaction, → III, 178, 36 ff. [88] In opposition to such attempts, however, there have always been good and cogent reasons for supporting the unity of John's Gospel. [89] At most the possibility of a confusion of pages in c. 10 deserves serious consideration. There are two points in favour of this. First, after the address on the shepherd there is a ref. in 10:19-21 to the healing of the blind man (9:1-41), and these verses are perhaps the conclusion of that story. Secondly, 10:22-24 introduces an address of Jesus about the flock of Jesus (vv. 26-29) and this is related in content to 10:1-18. If we assume that 10:1-18 and 10:19-29 have been misplaced (correct order 9:1-41; 10:19-29, 1-18, 30-39) [90] a smooth sequence is achieved : 10:19-21 is the end of the story of the man born blind, 10:22-24 sets the stage for the shepherd address, and 10:25-29, 1-18 and 30 contain the

---

[82] For profane instances of this word, which occurs only here in the NT, cf. Jost, 47 f. and Pr.-Bauer⁵, s.v.

[83] This interpretation is based on the allusion to Is. 63:11 LXX (ὁ ἀναβιβάσας [= God] ἐκ τῆς γῆς τὸν ποιμένα τῶν προβάτων [= Moses]).

[84] Mt. 2:6 : ὅστις ποιμανεῖ τὸν λαόν μου τὸν Ἰσραήλ, quotes Mi. 5:3 (καὶ ποιμανεῖ τὸ ποίμνιον αὐτοῦ), though 2 Βασ. 5:2 (σὺ ποιμανεῖς τὸν λαόν μου τὸν Ἰσραήλ) has influenced the wording. Nevertheless ποιμαίνειν = "to rule" is so firmly embedded in OT usage that it is doubtful whether Mt. was even aware of the metaphor.

[85] ἀρνίον is so accepted a predicate in Rev. that there was no sense of incongruity in calling the Lamb the Shepherd.

[86] In the present context Rev. 7:9-17 describes the present time, not the future consummation, for the opening of the seventh and last seal comes only in 8:1.

[87] This difficult image arises out of a mistake in the LXX. The HT of Ps. 2:9 runs : תְּרֹעֵם בְּשֵׁבֶט בַּרְזֶל, "thou wilt break them (רָעַע) with a rod of iron" (correctly rendered in Ps. Sol. 17:24 : ἐν ῥάβδῳ σιδηρᾷ συντρῖψαι) but the LXX erroneously read רָעָה תְּרֹעֵם "to feed") and transl. ποιμανεῖς αὐτοὺς ἐν ῥάβδῳ σιδηρᾷ, "thou wilt feed them with a rod of iron." Rev. relates this intrinsically contradictory expression to the terrible judgment on the heathen which Christ executes at the parousia (19:15, hence also 12:5) and in which those who overcome will take part (2:27a cf. b). How far there was any sense of the shepherd metaphor it is impossible to say.

[88] Cf. Bultmann J., 272-274. For a survey E. Fascher, "Zur Auslegung v. Joh. 10:17-18," DTh, 8 (1941), 47-55.

[89] E. Ruckstuhl, "Die literarische Einheit d. Joh.-Ev.," Studia Friburgensia, NF, 3 (1951).

[90] So, following J. Moffatt and J. H. Bernard, E. Schweizer, "Ego Eimi . . .," FRL, 56 (1939), 141 f.; J. Jeremias, "Joh. Literarkritik," ThBl, 20 (1941), 33-46.

address itself. Technically confusion of pages, of which there are many firm examples, [91] is quite conceivable. 10:19-29 contains 777 letters, 10:1-18 contains 1488 (twice 744). [92] The original thus had pages of about 750 letters each, and the page with 10:19-29 was put after instead of before the two pages containing 10:1-18. Nevertheless, there are many serious difficulties in the way of this conjecture. In the early codices the number and length of lines vary quite considerably, so that too much weight should not be attached to the similarity in the no. of letters. [93] The hypothesis of a confusion of pages also demands an assumption that Jn. was originally written on individual sheets which were then glued together to form a roll or sewn together in a codex. But this is against all probability. It is true that the technique of first writing on individual pages was prescribed for the Jewish Scriptures, [94] but it was not the common practice. [95] Above all, the fact that all three of the sheets supposedly confused must have begun with new sentences (Jn. 10:19, 1, 30) makes the whole hypothesis, if not totally impossible, at least extremely difficult, for normally a new page will begin in the middle of a sentence or even in the middle of a word. [96] It is thus as well to take the text as it stands without any critical manipulations. [97]

b. Basic for an understanding of this Johannine chapter on the shepherd is our assessment of the train of thought in 10:1-18. In vv. 1-5 we have a simple parable contrasting the shepherd with a thief on the one side, a stranger on the other. [98] In distinction from the thief or robber he comes through the door (vv. 1-2); in distinction from the stranger he is the keeper of the door and is known to the sheep, who follow him with "instinctive assurance," [99] whereas they will flee from a stranger, 3-5. The parable has its origin in ancient Palestinian tradition. [100] What follows is simply an allegorising, paraphrasing interpretation controlled by the eastern love of colourful depiction. Two concepts in the parable are now referred to Christ, namely, the door (vv. 7-10) and the shepherd of the sheep (vv. 11-18). [101] The two interpretative sections are both constructed in the same way. First, in line with the technique used in Mt. 13:37-39, an interpretative saying is put at the head (v. 7, 11a). To give emphasis there then follows a contrast in each case (v. 8, 11b-13), as in the parable itself. The interpretative saying is then repeated (v. 9, 14a), for its truth has finally to be demonstrated (v. 9b f.; 14b-18). The repetition of both ἐγώ εἰμι ἡ θύρα (v. 7, 9) and ἐγώ εἰμι ὁ ποιμὴν ὁ καλός (v. 11, 14) is to be explained in this simple way. If this is correct, then ἐγώ εἰμι κτλ. ("I am the door" [v. 7, 9], "I am the good shepherd" [v. 11, 14]) is not a formula of

---

[91] Thus in the LXX Sir. 33:16b-36:10a (acc. to Rahlfs, previously thought to be 33:13b-36:16b) has been displaced from its original position between 30:24, 25 through confusion; again in Eth. En. the proper sequence in the Ten Week Apocalypse is 93 (1st-7th weeks); 91:12-17 (8th-10th weeks).

[92] Cf. Schweizer, op. cit. (→ n. 90), 110 f. (bibl.) with slight variations.

[93] Cf. the abrupt judgment of a leading expert, C. H. Roberts, "The Christian Book and the Greek Papyri," JThSt, 50 (1949), 163: "No such calculations can be seriously regarded."

[94] Str.-B., IV, 126 f.

[95] Roberts, op. cit., 163; O. Roller, "Das Formular d. paul. Briefe," BWANT, IV, 6 (1933), 272, n. 48. The examples in → n. 91 (LXX, Eth. En.) may be explained by the technique laid down for the Jewish Scriptures but have little bearing on John's Gospel.

[96] In the case of Eth. En. (→ n. 91) each of the sheets does in fact seem to have begun with a new sentence (93:1; 91:12; 94:1) but this could be due to later adjustment. One would have to assume a similar adjustment in Jn. 10.

[97] Observations on the Johannine technique of composition seem to support this, cf. J. Schneider, "Zur Komposition v. Joh. 10," Coni. Neot., 11 (1947), 220-225.

[98] There are Synoptic par. for the general nature of the depiction, Mk. 4:4-8, 26-29 and par.; Mt. 13:31-33 and par.

[99] Bultmann J., 283.

[100] Cf. on Jn. 10:3 (τὰ ἴδια πρόβατα φωνεῖ κατ' ὄνομα) → n. 52. Another sign of antiquity is that in v. 6 Jesus seems to have been speaking the parable to opponents. Jeremias, Gleichnisse, 23-31; J. A. T. Robinson, "The Parable of Jn. 10:1-5," ZNW, 46 (1955), 234 f.

[101] Cf. Fascher, op. cit. (→ n. 88), 52; Schneider, op. cit. (→ n. 97), 220-225.

revelation derived from the sacral speech of the Orient [102] but simply an interpretative formula. [103]

The second interpretative section is introduced by the saying: "I am the good shepherd" (v. 11a). Here Jesus relates the shepherd of the parable to Himself (vv. 1-5), → III, 548, 15 ff. He goes on at once to mention the decisive mark of the true shepherd, namely, a readiness to give his life for the flock (v. 11b). [104] In accordance with the technique used in the parable (v. 1, 5) and also in the first interpretative section (v. 8, 10), this statement is elucidated by a contrast, in this instance the contrast with the hireling (→ IV, 701, 11 f.) who bears no relation to a shepherd, [105] as is proved by his cowardly flight in time of danger (v. 12 f.). In v. 14 f., as in v. 9, the interpretative saying is repeated, and by means of the marks mentioned in vv. 3-5 and 11b-13 it is shown that the reference truly is to Jesus; he is the *pastor bonus,* as is proved both by the inward fellowship which unites Him to His own (vv. 14b-15a) [106] and also by the laying down of His life (→ n. 104) for the flock (v. 15b, 17 f.). The address reaches its climax in v. 16. Jesus' office as Shepherd is not restricted to Israel; it is universal, → II, 440, 11 ff. [107] When He brings the other sheep, the promise will be fulfilled: μία ποίμνη (cf. Mi. 2:12), εἷς ποίμην (Ez. 37:24; 34:23 → 488, 4 ff.). The conclusion (v. 17 f.) looks on from the sacrifice of life (→ IV, 342, 17 ff.) to the receiving of life. On 10:25 ff. → 501, 29 ff.

c. As regards the origin of the imagery of Jn. 10, the Palestinian materials, [108] the many Semitisms [109] and the numerous echoes of the OT (esp. Ez. 34) [110] all point to an OT and Palestinian background. [111] The essential features of the interpretative section 10:11-18 — Jesus the Shepherd, the lack of prominence given to the ruler motif in the metaphor, the disciples as the flock, the shepherd going first, the death of the shepherd, the gathering of the flock of nations — are also in agreement with the statements of Jesus Himself in the Synoptic Gospels, → 492, 15 ff. The new aspect as compared with the shepherd sayings of the OT and the Synoptics is the thought that the death of the shepherd is a voluntary and

---

[102] Bultmann J., 167, n. 2.

[103] L. Cerfaux, "Le thème littéraire parabolique dans l'évangile de saint Jean," Coni. Neot., 11 (1947), 15-25.

[104] The Semitism τιθέναι τὴν ψυχήν (→ V, 710, 22 ff.) can mean 1. "to hazard his life" or 2. "to give his life." In the general statement in 10:11b, in which the art. is generic, we have sense 1. ("the good shepherd risks his life for the sheep"). But when the ref. is to Jesus (v. 15, 17 f.) we have sense 2. ("I give my life for the sheep").

[105] v. 12 καὶ οὐκ ὢν ποιμήν: the οὐ, which is not normally used with the part. in the *koine,* and only here in Jn., expresses emphatic negation, Bl.-Debr. § 430, 1.

[106] In v. 14 f. (mutual recognition) we have a Semitism rather than a formula of Hell. mysticism (Bultmann J., *ad loc.*). Heb. and Aram. do not have a reciprocal pron. and they are thus forced to express a mutual relation in this way, cf. Mt. 11:27. The Semitic colouring of γινώσκειν in v. 14 f. supports this, cf. W. L. Knox, *Some Hellenistic Elements in Primitive Christianity* (1944), 7.

[107] There is no linguistic or stylistic argument to justify our regarding v. 16 as unjohannine and hence as an addition. On the universalism of v. 16 → 502, 13 ff.

[108] Dalman, 229-231, 234 f., 248, 255, 284 f. Also Palestinian is ὁ ποιμὴν ὁ καλός = רוֹעֶה טוֹב (Str.-B., II, 537), רוֹעֶה יָפֶה (*loc. cit.*), cf. רוֹעֶה נֶאֱמָן (M. Ex., 14, 31 and on this P. Fiebig, "Die Mekhilta u. d. Joh.-Ev.," *Angelos,* 1 [1925], 57-59; 1 Q, 34 Fr., 3, II, 8).

[109] Schl. J., 233-239.

[110] E. C. Hoskyns-F. N. Davey, *The Fourth Gospel*² (1947), 366-368; C. H. Dodd, *The Interpretation of the Fourth Gospel* (1953), 358-361.

[111] On the other hand, Rabb. influence cannot be proved.

vicarious death for the flock; here the Lord's predictions of the passion and the historical event of the crucifixion brought about a development of the impulse already present in Mk. 14:27 f. There are no shepherd sayings from the world of syncretism or Gnosticism which could have influenced Jn. 10. The only possible passages are three late ones from the Mandaean writings, [112] which include two elaborate shepherd allegories in the Book of John, but these are obviously based on free reminiscences of Jn. 10. [113]

4. In Post-Canonical Writings and Early Christian Art.

In Christological shepherd predication from the early 2nd century the didactic element constantly gains in strength alongside the soteriological. [114] The Aberkios inscr. may be quoted as an example (lines 3-6): "I am called Aberkios, I am a pupil of the pure shepherd who feeds flocks of sheep on mountains and plains, who has great eyes, seeing in all places. He taught me ...[115] reliable knowledge." [116] That the shepherd Christ becomes the teacher of true knowledge of God is an example which shows how strongly Hell. ideas were now influencing Christology. Philo had depicted the *logos* as the shepherd of mankind. [117] The development of Logos Christology through Gnosticism and in conflict with it led to the increasing endowment of Christ with the features and symbols of the Logos Shepherd. [118] Nevertheless, one should not overlook the gt. difference that, while the task of the Logos Shepherd of Philo is to free men from the dominion of the senses and sensuality, the Λόγος-Ποιμήν Christ leads the senses to eternal salvation by the transmission of divine truth. [119] From the 3rd cent. onwards (not earlier) there may be found in the catacombs numerous depictions of Christ as the Good Shepherd. He is presented as a radiantly youthful figure, either with a sheep on His shoulders or with the flock. Once it was customary to interpret this figure one-sidedly as the guide of souls in terms of funeral symbolism. [120] But this has now yielded to the insight that the symbolism is to be taken more comprehensively. He is the Bringer of salvation, the Redeemer and Teacher (→ line 13 f.) in one. [121] Normative for this new interpretation is the correct recognition that early Chr. art is to be understood in terms of early Chr. literature.

V. Shepherds as a Term for Congregational Leaders.

Only once in the NT are congregational leaders called shepherds, namely, in the list of offices in Eph. 4:11 (→ II, 158, 23 ff.). The absence of art. before the διδασκάλους which follows (τοὺς δὲ ποιμένας καὶ διδασκάλους) shows that the pastors and teachers form a single group, obviously because they both minister to the individual congregation. The term "shepherd," however, is not yet an

---

[112] Lidz. Ginza, 181, 18 ff.; Lidz. Joh., 44, 25-51, 4; 51, 5-54, 5.

[113] Though cf. Schweizer, *op. cit.* (→ n. 90), 64-66; Bultmann J., 279-281.

[114] For materials on the shepherd and the flock in early Chr. literature up to Cl. Al. cf. Kempf, 42-65.

[115] A lacuna in the text.

[116] Ed. T. Klauser, Art. "Aberkios," RAC, I, 13. The Chr. origin of this funerary inscr., which was discovered in 1883 and is to be dated c. 200 A.D., is rightly recognised by almost all scholars to-day, cf. H. Strathmann, Art. "Aberkios," RAC, I, 16.

[117] → 490, 12 ff.; J. Quasten, "Der Gute Hirte in hell. u. frühchr. Logostheologie," *Hl. Überlieferung, Festschr. f. I. Herwegen,* ed. O. Casel (1938), 51-58.

[118] Kempf, 150-195.

[119] Quasten, *op. cit.,* 55 f.

[120] V. Schultze, *Archäologische Studien über altchr. Monumente* (1880), 69; W. Neuss, *Die Kunst der alten Christen* (1926), 35; J. Sauer, Art. "Hirt," Lex. Th. K., 5 (1933), 78; H. Lietzmann, *Gesch. d. alten Kirche,* II (1936), 138; F. Gerke, "Die chr. Sarkophage der vorkonstantinischen Zeit," *Studien zur spätantiken Kunstgeschichte,* 11 (1940), 317.

[121] Kempf, 150-195; Bertram, 276 f.; J. Kollwitz, "Das Christusbild des 3. Jhdts.," Orbis Antiquus, 9 (1953), 6-22.

established title in Eph. 4:11; [122] this is obvious once the usage of Eph. 4:11 is set in a broader framework. Thus examples from the following period [123] give evidence that there is always a sense of the metaphor when congregational leaders are called shepherds; the same is true of passages in which the verb ποιμαίνειν is used for the work of such leaders (1 Pt. 5:2; Ac. 20:28; Jn. 21:16) or the noun ποίμνιον is used for the congregation, → 501, 23 ff. These shepherds are the leaders of the local church (πρεσβύτεροι in 1 Pt. 5:1; Ac. 20:17; ἐπίσκοποι in Ac. 20:28), or the bishop in Ign. (Phld., 2, 1; R., 9, 1); only in Jn. 21:15-17, which describes the appointment of Peter as a shepherd by the Risen Lord, does the whole church seem to have been in view as the sphere of activity. The pastor's task is to care for the congregation (Ac. 20:28; 1 Pt. 5:2-4; Ign. Phld., 2, 1; R., 9, 1), [124] to seek the lost (Mt. 18:12-14; [125] cf. 12:30 par. Lk. 11:23), and to combat heresy (Ac. 20:29 f.). The fulfilment of this task by the pastor is to be an example for the flock, 1 Pt. 5:3. The chief Shepherd (→ 494, 5 ff.) will recognise the ministry of the pastors on His appearing, v. 4.

The closest analogy to the comparison of congregational leaders with shepherds is not in the Hell. sphere [126] but in Damascus 13:9 f. (16:2 f.) → 489, 18 ff. The task of the *mebaqqer* here is to show fatherly mercy to those entrusted to him, to liberate them from guilt, to loose their bands as a shepherd does. This corresponds materially to the task of the primitive Chr. ποιμήν. At other pts., too, Eph. in particular gives evidence of many contacts with the Essene group of writings, → V, 300, 23 ff.

E. The Shepherd of Hermas.

In the Apc. of Hermas, which was written before the middle of the 2nd cent. in Rome, an angel of repentance appears in shepherd garb as the mediator of revelations. [127] After this angel-shepherd the work even in the 2nd cent. came to be called the Pastor (Hermae), i.e., "The Shepherd (who appeared to Hermas)." [128] Sent by the Most Holy Shepherd (Christ) (v. 5, 2, cf. s., 10, 1, 1), the shepherd is the teacher, instructor, guardian angel and companion of Hermas, whose task is to proclaim the summons to repentance revealed to him.

There is no root in the NT sphere for the idea of the shepherd as a mediator of revelation. The only analogy is in the Hermetica. In the first tractate of the Corp. Herm., which has the title Poimandres, revelation is mediated through a "being of gigantic size" (1, 1) which presents itself as "Poimandres, the Nous of the supreme power" (Ποιμάνδρης, ὁ τῆς αὐθεντίας Νοῦς, 1, 2). Though it is debatable whether the name Ποιμάνδρης is originally related to ποιμαίνειν, [129] by popular etym. it was taken

---

[122] P. H. Menoud, "L'Eglise et les ministères selon le NT," *Cahiers théologiques de l'actualité protestante*, 22 (1949), 44, who mistakenly regards the pastors and teachers of Eph. 4:11 as identical.

[123] Ign. Phld., 2, 1: ὅπου δὲ ὁ ποιμήν ἐστιν, ἐκεῖ ὡς πρόβατα ἀκολουθεῖτε, cf. R., 9, 1: μνημονεύετε ἐν τῇ προσευχῇ ὑμῶν τῆς ἐν Συρίᾳ ἐκκλησίας, ἥτις ἀντὶ ἐμοῦ ποιμένι τῷ θεῷ χρῆται, Herm. s., 9, 31, 4-6.

[124] Acc. to 1 Pt. 5:3 and Asc. Is. 3:23-25 looking after the finances seems to have been included.

[125] Mt. 18 can hardly be called a church order, as is customary; it rather contains directions for the leaders of the churches, → III, 752, 9 ff.

[126] It is frequently pointed out that the term shepherds is attested for the sacral founders and leaders of Gk. societies, cf. E. Maass, *Orpheus* (1895), 180 f.

[127] From Herm. v., 5 to s., 9 the angel-shepherd is the mediator of the revelation; only in v., 1-4 (the oldest part of the work, Dib. Herm., 421) does an old lady have this function.

[128] The oldest instance is Canon Muratori, lines 73 ff. (KIT, 1 [1902]): pastorem uero nuperrime temporibus nostris in urbe roma herma conscripsit.

[129] C. H. Dodd, *The Bible and the Greeks* (1935), 99, n. 1 follows F. Griffith (in W. Scott, Hermetica, II [1925], 16 f.) in deriving the word from the Coptic π-ειμε-ν-ρη = "the knowledge of the Sun-God."

to mean "the shepherd of men." [130] The author of Herm. perhaps took the idea of an angel-shepherd as the mediator of revelation from this world of thought. [131]

† ποίμνη, † ποίμνιον.

A. The Palestinian Flock.

Ποίμνη, ποίμνιον ("herd") is always used in the NT for the herd of small cattle, the flock. The size of a Palestinian flock varies to-day from 20 to over 500 head. Among the Bedouin a small flock (cf. Lk. 12:32) would be one of 20-30 animals. [1] The 100 of Lk. 15:4 is a round figure, and 300 is used for a large no. in TBQ, 6, 20. [2]

A mixed herd is in view in Mt. 25:32. Mixed herds of sheep and goats were common in Palestine in antiquity. This may be seen from the comprehensive term צאן for both in the OT. The sheep and goats would feed together during the day, but the shepherd would separate them at night (Mt. 25:32) [3] because goats are more susceptible to cold and have to be kept warmer than sheep, which like fresh air at night. [4] To keep night by watch over pasturing flocks in summer (→ 486, n. 3) several shepherds would usually come together with their flocks, as they still do to-day; [5] this is presupposed in both Lk. 2:8 (plur. ποιμένες) and Jn. 10:4 (τὰ ἴδια). The difference between the two passages is that Lk. is referring to a night spent in open pasture, when the presence of several shepherds would largely dispense with the need for special measures of protection, [6] whereas in Jn. 10 the flocks are kept overnight in a walled court which belonged to the village and the door of which could be closed (v. 1, 16 : αὐλή). [7] Along with thieves (Jn. 10:1, 8, 10), wild beasts, esp. wolves (→ IV, 308, 1 ff.), constituted the danger against which the shepherds, who were always armed, had to protect the flock, Mt. 10:16; Lk. 10:3; Jn. 10:12; Ac. 20:29.

B. Flock as a Term for the Community in the OT and Pre-Christian Judaism.

Israel shared the common ancient oriental description of the people as a flock. [8] In Israel, however, the secular use of the image was completely replaced by the religious use. Israel is the flock of God ; this is implicit already in the description of Yahweh as the Shepherd of Israel (→ 487, 4 ff.) and it is made explicit for

---

[130] Corp. Herm., 13, 19: λόγον γὰρ τὸν σὸν (God's) ποιμαίνει ὁ Νοῦς (= Poimandres). The alchemistic tractate of Zosimos offers another example in the name Ποιμενάνηρ, "shepherd-man," cf. C. F. G. Heinrici, *Die Hermes-Mystik u. d. NT* (1918), 15 f.

[131] This is supported by the similarity between the opening visions of Herm. v., 5, 1-4 and Corp. Herm., 1, 1-4. In both instances the apparition is asked who it is ; it replies that it is ὁ ποιμήν or ὁ Ποιμάνδρης, and is then transformed. Nevertheless, literary dependence of Herm. on Corp. Herm., 1 is ruled out, since the latter represents a later form of Gnosticism, cf. E. Haenchen, "Aufbau u. Theologie des 'Poimandres,' " ZThK, 53 (1956), 191.

π ο ί μ ν η, π ο ί μ ν ι ο ν. G. Dalman, "Arbeit u. Sitte in Palästina, VI," BFTh, II, 41 (1939), 146-213, 246-287.

[1] Dalman, 246.

[2] Not a normal no., as Dalman assumes (248).

[3] Mt. 25:32 (ὥσπερ ὁ ποιμὴν ἀφορίζει τὰ πρόβατα ἀπὸ τῶν ἐρίφων) is not speaking of the separation between male and female (rams and sheep) but of the separation between (white) sheep and (black) goats.

[4] Dalman, 276.

[5] Ibid., 276 f.

[6] G. Dalman, "Orte u. Wege Jesu³," BFTh, II, 1 (1924), 51-53.

[7] Dalman, *op. cit.* (→ Bibl.), 284 f.

[8] Ps. 23:1-4; 28:9; 68:7; 74:1; 77:20; 78:52 f.; 79:13; 80:1; 95:7; 100:3; 121:4. Cf. 1 K. 22:17. Gentile peoples, too, are compared to flocks, Is. 13:14; Jer. 25:34-36.

the first time in Hos. 4:16 ("Will Yahweh now feed them as a lamb ...? cf. 13:6). From the days of Jer. (13:17; 23:1 f.; cf. 50:6) it is an established feature in prophecy and prayer (the Psalter). In a variety of expressions Israel is "Yahweh's flock," [9] "the flock of his pasture," [10] "the sheep of his pasture," [11] "the sheep of his hand," [12] "the sheep of thy (God's) possession," [13] "my (God's) sheep." [14] The implication of the metaphor is that Israel is God's possession and that it can yield itself with full confidence to the guidance, provision and help of its Shepherd.

There is a universal extension of the image of God as Shepherd in Sir. 18:13. In distinction from men, God's mercy extends "to all flesh ; he sets up, instructs, teaches, leads back to the right path ὡς ποιμὴν τὸ ποίμνιον αὐτοῦ." This universalism, now limited to the state of consummation, may be found again at the end of the gt. shepherd vision in Eth. En. 85-90, which broadly depicts the history of Israel under the image of a flock. Here, after the last judgment (90:31), "all beasts of the field and all fowls of heaven" are gathered in a new house (v. 33), pray at all times to the white bullock, the Messiah (v. 37), and are changed into white bullocks, while the Messiah becomes a buffalo (v. 38). In Ps. Sol. 17:40 the ποίμνιον κυρίου which the Messiah feeds (→ 489, 26) is restricted to Israel (v. 42), but the dominion of the Messiah extends also over the Gentile nations, v. 30-32, 34. [15]

C. The Community as a Flock in the NT.

1. OT usage, according to which Israel is the flock of God (→ 499, 28 ff.), lives on in the Synoptic Gospels. It is plainly present in the saying of Jesus that He is sent by God and that He sends His disciples to τὰ πρόβατα τὰ ἀπολωλότα οἴκου Ἰσραήλ (Mt. 15:24; 10:6). [16] Since the genitive οἴκου Ἰσραήλ is to be taken epexegetically, [17] the saying is to the effect that all Israel, including the pious, are in the eyes of Jesus like a flock which is abandoned and without protection. Building on Ez. 34:16 (→ 492, n. 71), the variation in Lk. 19:10 adds that it is the task of Jesus to go after (ζητῆσαι) the dispersed of the flock and to save them (σῶσαι). [18] Mk., quoting Nu. 27:17, notes that Jesus bewailed the

---

[9] Jer. 13:17: עֵדֶר יְהֹוָה. Is. 40:11; Zech. 10:3 : עֶדְרוֹ.

[10] Ps. 95:7: עַם מַרְעִיתוֹ.

[11] Ps. 100:3 : צֹאן מַרְעִיתוֹ, cf. 74:1; 79:13; Jer. 23:1; Ez. 34:31.

[12] Ps. 95:7: צֹאן יָדוֹ.

[13] Mi. 7:14 : צֹאן נַחֲלָתֶךָ.

[14] Jer. 23:2 f.; Ez. 34:6, 8 etc.: צֹאנִי; cf. Is. 63:11.

[15] In Philo (as distinct from Aristot., e.g., Pol., I, 2, p. 1253a, 3-8) the comparison of men with a flock is sometimes derogatory, Congr., 174; none of the flocks of men (τῶν ἀγελαίων) will have a share in the true life, Mut. Nom., 213. (This does not mean, however, that the social union of men is in general a contemptible herd existence, Decal., 132.) The irrational powers of the soul, which are gendered by man and which need a shepherd, are often called a flock, e.g., Poster. C., 66 f., also Agric., 26-66 → 490, 12 ff.

[16] On the antiquity of the saying → 492, n. 70.

[17] The gen. in the phrase εἰς (πρὸς) τὰ πρόβατα τὰ ἀπολωλότα οἴκου Ἰσραήλ (Mt. 15:24; 10:6) is ambiguous. It may be a partitive gen. ("to the lost sheep of the house of Israel"), in which case the mission of Jesus is restricted to a portion of Israel, or it may be an epexegetical gen. ("to the lost sheep, namely, the house of Israel"), in which case Jesus calls the whole house of Israel a lost flock. OT usage (Jer. 50:6; Ez. 34:5 ff.; Is. 53:6) supports the second interpretation, as do the antitheses in the context of Mt. 15:24 (Israel/Gentiles) and 10:6 (Israel/Gentiles/Samaritans).

[18] On the gathering of the scattered flock as a sign of the dawn of the age of salvation → 492, n. 69. The metaphor of the lost sheep which was found again also underlies Lk. 15:24 (ἦν ἀπολωλὼς καὶ εὑρέθη), 32.

absence of a shepherd (6:34). Mt. gives as a further reason for the compassion of Jesus the despair of the completely exhausted and weakened flock, 9:36.

The OT idea that Israel is God's flock is echoed again in the saying in Rev. (quoting ψ 2:9) that the returning Christ (Rev. 12:5; 19:15) or those who overcome (2:27) will feed the (flock of the) heathen with an iron rod (→ 494, n. 87), i.e., destroy them (cf. 2:27b; 19:15).

2. For the most part, however, Jesus uses the image of God's flock for His band of disciples as the eschatological people of God, Mk. 14:27 f. par. Mt. 26:31 f.; Mt. 10:16 par. Lk. 10:3; Lk. 12:32; Jn. 10:1-29 cf. 16:32. This usage, too, is based on that of the OT, → 488, 4 ff. In the originally isolated [19] saying in Lk. 12:32, which goes back to Aramaic tradition, [20] Jesus addresses His own as a "little flock." He combines the image of God's flock with the motif of the eschatological reversal of relations when, on the basis of Da. 7:27 (→ n. 20), He tells His disciples that in spite of their fewness in number they may contemplate threatened persecution without fear because a kingdom, dominion and power over all kingdoms is promised to them as the people of the saints of the Most High, Da. 7:27. God's eschatological flock is not merely threatened from without by wolves to which it is defencelessly given up, Mt. 10:16 par. Lk. 10:3. It is also threatened from within by wolves in sheep's clothing, Mt. 7:15. In the last tribulation, which robs it of the shepherd, it will be scattered to the four winds, but after the time of sifting its shepherd will again go before it, Mk. 14:27 f. par. Mt. 26:31 f. → 493, 11 ff. Then the righteous from among the peoples will also belong to it, Mt. 25:32. [21]

In the primitive Church the comparison of the new people of God with a flock is still a common figure of speech. [22] Thus in John's Gospel the "flock" is one of the substitutes for the missing term ἐκκλησία, and in 1 Clement "flock of Christ" (→ n. 22) is used for the community. A mark of the members of the flock is that they know the Good Shepherd (Jn. 10:4 f., 14), believe in Him (v. 26), hear His voice and follow Him (v. 27).

For the Johannine view of the flock of Jesus Jn. 10:26 is important: ἀλλὰ ὑμεῖς οὐ πιστεύετε, ὅτι οὐκ ἐστὲ ἐκ τῶν προβάτων τῶν ἐμῶν. This might be understood in predestinarian terms; "You cannot believe because you do not belong to my flock (by God's foreordination)." If so, the flock is not the Church but the whole number of the predestinate, [23] which includes the children of God who do not yet belong to the Church and who are dispersed in the world, Jn. 11:52. In the background would be the Gnostic myth of the body of the primal man who was torn apart by demonic forces and who

---

[19] Lk. 12:32 is peculiar to Lk. and has been added to the traditional context of Lk. 12:22-31 par. Mt. 6:25-33 with the help of the catchword τὴν βασιλείαν (v. 31/32).

[20] The rendering of the vocative by nominative with art. (τὸ μικρὸν ποίμνιον) is Semitic, Bl.-Debr. § 147, 3. The words ποίμνιον/εὐδόκησεν are linked by a pun in Aram. (mar'ita/ra'e) (M. Black, An Aramaic Approach to the Gospels and Acts² [1954], 126). The expression δοῦναι τὴν βασιλείαν (without addition to βασιλεία) = "to transfer (a share in) the royal dominion" is based on Da. 7:27 מַלְכוּתָה....יְהִיבַת. The latter expression does not mean that every member of the flock becomes a king but that the totality of the flock constitutes the βασιλεία, J. W. Doeve, Jewish Hermeneutics in the Synoptic Gospels and Acts (1954), 145.

[21] J. Jeremias, Jesu Verheissung f. d. Völker (1956), 54 f.

[22] Ac. 20:28 f.; 1 Pt. 5:3 : τὸ ποίμνιον, 1 Pt. 5:2 : τὸ ποίμνιον τοῦ θεοῦ (cf. LXX Jer. 13:17: τὸ ποίμνιον κυρίου), 1 Cl., 44, 3; 54, 2 cf. 16, 1: τὸ ποίμνιον τοῦ Χριστοῦ, also Jn. 10:26 f.: τὰ πρόβατα τὰ ἐμά (Jesus'), 21:16 f.: τὰ προβάτιά μου, v. 15 : τὰ ἀρνία μου. The metaphor of the flock also stands behind 1 Pt. 5:8.

[23] Bultmann J., 276, cf. 284 f. finds the distinctive Johannine concept of predestination in Jn. 10:26.

will be brought together again by the Redeemer (through the gathering of the pre-existent souls scattered in the world like sparks). [24] But the context of Jn. 10:26 does not suggest in any way that Jn. was using this Gnostic myth, → 497, 3 ff. Jesus, when asked to give an unmistakable Messianic self-witness (v. 24), answers that He has long since given such witness by word and deed, but without finding faith in His partners in debate (v. 25), because they do not belong to His own (v. 26). As in Mk. 4:11 f. He is thus stating the fact that this witness which finds a hearing and obedience in His own (v. 27) remains unintelligible to those who are without and finds no faith in them. If this is correct, then in v. 26, as elsewhere in the primitive Church, the flock of Jesus means His community. In the lifetime of Jesus this is called forth from the αὐλή of the Jewish people (v. 3 f.), and after the resurrection the Good Shepherd will associate with it the children of God from among the Gentiles (v. 16).

The limitation to Israel was definitively abandoned in the primitive Church. After the death and resurrection of Jesus the sheep which were going astray (1 Pt. 2:25) and which did not belong to the fold (Jn. 10:16), the scattered children of God (11:52), were gathered from among the Gentiles into the eschatological flock of God. [25] The context of all three passages agrees that only the atoning death of Christ mediates to them membership of the flock which is the community of salvation.

J. Jeremias

---

† πόλεμος, † πολεμέω

Contents : A. The Religious Understanding of War in the Greek World and Hellenism : 1. The Problem : a. The Starting-Point : Homer and Hesiod ; b. Religious Practice ; c. Critical Reflection ; 2. The Basic General Attitude to the Political Reality of War ; 3. The Expectation of a State of Peace in the First Imperial Period. B. The Religious Understanding of War in the OT and Later Judaism : 1. Reconstructed Tradition : a. The

---

[24] Bultmann J., 285.

[25] For the first beginnings of this universalism in later Judaism → 500, 9 ff.

π ό λ ε μ ο ς, π ο λ ε μ έ ω. E. Auerbach, J. Gutmann, Art. "Kriegswesen," EJ, X, 422-434; K. Barth, K.D., III, 4 (1951), 515-538 (C.D., III, 4 [1961], 450-470); F. Beckmann, *Der Friede des Augustus* (1951); A. Bertholet, O. Procksch, P. Althaus, Art. "Krieg," RGG², III, 1303-1312; W. Bienert, *Krieg, Kriegsdienst u. Kriegsdienstverweigerung* (1952), cf. bibl. 118-122; H. v. Campenhausen, "Der Kriegsdienst der Christen in d. Kirche des Altertums," *Offener Horizont, Festschr. f. K. Jaspers* (1953), 255-264; W. Caspari, "Was stand im Buch der Kriege Jahwes ?" ZwTh, 54 (1912), 110-158; O. Eissfeldt, "Krieg u. Bibel," *Religionsgeschichtliche Volksbücher*, V, 15-16 (1915); A. Fridrichsen, "Krig och Fred i NT," *Uppsala Universitets Årsskrift*, 3 (1940); H. Fuchs, *Antike Gedanken über Krieg u. Frieden* (1946); A. v. Harnack, *Militia Christi* (1905); A. Heuss, "Die archaische Zeit Griechenlands als geschichtliche Epoche," *Antike u. Abendland*, 2 (1946), 26-62; O. Kern, "Krieg u. Kult bei den Hellenen," *Rektoratsrede Halle* (1915); S. Krauss, Art. "Heerwesen der Juden," Jüd. Lex., II, 1498-1501; W. Künneth, *Politik zwischen Dämon u. Gott* (1954), 317-347; J. Lasserre, *Der Krieg u. d. Ev.* (1956); D. Loenen, "Polemos, Een studie over oorlog in de Griekse oudheid," *Mededelingen der Koninklijke Nederlandse Akademie van Wetenschappen, Afd. Letterkunde*, NR, 16, 3 (1953); G. H. C. Macgregor, *The NT Basis of Pacifism* (1953); E. Müller, *Friedens- u. Wehrbereitschaft der Christen* (1956); G. Naumann, Art. "Krieg," RGG¹, III, 1770-1780; W. Nestle, "Der Friedensgedanke in d. antiken Welt," *Philol. Suppl.-Bd.*, 31, 1 (1938); W. F. Otto, *Die Götter Griechenlands³* (1947), 222-256; G. v. Rad, *Der hl. Krieg im alten Israel* (1951); F. Schwally, *Semitische Kriegsaltertümer*, 1. "Der hl. Krieg im Alten Israel" (1901); E. Seckel, *Über Krieg u. Recht in Rom* (1915); W. Theimer, *Gesch. der politischen Ideen* (1955), esp. 359-381; H. Trümpy, *Kriegerische Fachausdrücke im griech. Epos*, Diss. Basel (1950); H. Windisch, *Der messianische Krieg u. das Urchr.* (1909). Cf. also → II, 400 f. εἰρήνη.

Holy War; b. The War of Yahweh against Israel; c. Divine and Human Initiatives; 2. The Problem; 3. The Basic General Attitude to the Political Reality of War; 4. The Expectation of a State of Peace; 5. Later Judaism. C. πόλεμος/πολεμέω in the NT: 1. War in the Events of the Last Time; 2. Other References to War.

The noun (also the verb πολεμίζω) is found from Hom., the verb πολεμέω from Hdt. In Hom. and Hes. the noun is often synon. with μάχη- (→ IV, 527 f.), though the two words occur together in Hom. (Il., 16, 251; 20, 18 etc.), so that a difference in sense was felt between them. [1] Since in both cases the etym. is uncertain, the mutual relation is hard to determine. [2] The predominant sense by far is "war," "state of war," "prosecution of war" (opp. → εἰρήνη, Plat. Resp., VIII, 543a) either lit. or occasionally in a transf. sense. In the LXX πόλεμος is mostly the rendering of מִלְחָמָה and πολεμέω of לחם ni. The only significant exception is the late text B in Ju., which uses παράταξις or παρατάσσω.

A. The Religious Understanding of War in the Greek World and Hellenism.

1. The Problem.

Undoubtedly pre-Homeric in origin is the sense that the divine good-pleasure rests from the very first on holy wars [3] and that the gods invoked in the oath are displeased at wars which begin with the breach of a sworn treaty. [4] The early period which produced Homer and Hesiod [5] had already laid down the main criteria in discussion of the problems which arose between these two extremes.

a. The Starting-Point: Homer and Hesiod. In Homeric epic war is closely bound up with the rule of the gods. Whether one can speak of gods of war in the strict sense may be left an open question. [6] The warlike scene depicted on the shield of Achilles can be regarded as a distinctive symbol of the view of the Homeric period. Here Ares and Pallas Athene go before the host (Hom. Il., 18, 516), a pair which is united (only) through specially active participation in war, though dissimilar and even alien in other respects. Ares, adopted from the age before Homer, is the ideal of the hero impelled by wild martial courage, ἆτος πολέμοιο (Il., 5, 388) and ἄφρων ὃς οὔ τινα οἶδε θέμιστα, "without reflection and without asking which side is right" (Il., 5, 761). Athene, on the other hand, promotes and rewards through her active power, which is by no means restricted to the sphere of war, not random striking, but reflection on the part of heroes and in the conduct of war. [7] She vividly demonstrates (Hom. Il., 5, 851 ff.; 21, 385 ff.) her superiority over the merely bloodthirsty Ares, who is in bad odour even on Olympus itself (Il., 5, 890; Od., 8, 267 ff.).

---

[1] In πολεμ- the noun is original, the verb derived, in μαχ- vice versa, so that πολεμ- primarily denotes a process or state, thus "tumult of battle" in Hom. as distinct from ἀγορή and βουλή "council," Il., 1, 490 f.; 2, 273; often πολέμοιο γέφυραι for security against πόλεμος. μάχεσθαι, on the other hand, denotes an activity. Hence later πολεμ- for state of war, μαχ- for an individual battle [Debrunner].

[2] Cf. Trümpy, 122-136. On the etym. (stem pelem == "to set in motion," "to shake") cf. Walde-Pok., II, 52 f.; Bienert, 20, n. 15; Trümpy, 130-133.

[3] All sense of the breadth of this concept must have been lost quite early, as is shown by the attempts to understand its use in Aristoph. Av., 556, cf. J. W. White, The Scholia in the Aves of Aristophanes (1914), 116 f.

[4] It is worth noting that Xenoph. An., II, 5, 7 uses the same word for human hostilities and for the action taken by the gods against human hostilities which involve the breaking of oaths (θεῶν πόλεμος → 509, 25 f.; 513, 11).

[5] How strongly the contrast between the poems from the standpt. of the problem of war affected later centuries may be seen from the history and dissemination of the work Certamen Homeri et Hesiodi, cf. E. Bethe, Art. "Ἀγὼν Ὁμήρου καὶ Ἡσιόδου," Pauly-W., 1 (1894), 867-869; text in Homeri Opera, ed. D. B. Monro and T. W. Allen, V (1911), 225-238.

[6] Otto, 244.

[7] Ibid., 44 f., 234 f., 249.

Hesiod does not contest the divine origin and quality of destructive Ares (Theog., 922), and he reports of the goddess Athene, without comparing her to Ares, that she rejoices in war and battle (926). On the whole, however, he has a different view of the relation of the divine world to war. It is true that for Hesiod, too, the counsel of the immortals stands behind the war of mortals. Nevertheless, war is caused [8] by Ἔρις, not the honourable Ἔρις of the stirring and noble contest, who is still close to her origin (Op., 17-24), but the very different σχετλίη Ἔρις who arose only later. War was still unknown in the first two cosmic epochs; only the third began traffic in this sorry trade of Ares (145 f.). It is the lofty task of Hes. to pay to the gods and heroes the honour due to them, but it is not his task to continue with the same fervour : "War also has its glory." The honour shown to σχετλίη Ἔρις and her fruits is rather a forced (ὑπ' ἀνάγκης) honour. [9] War was not originally a natural divinely ordained sphere of activity and self-proving for the true man.

In the more warlike of the two θειότατοι ποιηταί, [10] then, the martial direction of Athene has a considerable advantage over that of Ares. One might almost say that Ares is something which has to be vanquished. The second poet does not pursue this theme of the rivalry between the two gods ; he sets a greater distance generally between the gods and war.

b. Religious Practice. If Ares, who is strictly a god of earlier periods, was never elevated to the full dignity of an Olympian deity, [11] his ancient power was constantly felt. The troops of whom Xenoph. (An., I, 8, 18; V, 2, 14; Cyrop., VII, 1, 26) tells us went into battle with the name Ἐνυάλιος [12] on their lips, and young Athenians who swore their readiness for war in the ephebe-oath named among the ἴστορες of their oath, not Athene, but the names Ἐνυάλιος and Ἄρης, Poll. Onom., VIII, 106. The development which may be traced in Hom. (→ line 15 f.) did not carry with it a complete emancipation from the less worthy partner of Athene.

c. Critical Reflection. Critical reflection worked out in different ways the themes raised by the juxtaposition of the gods Ares and Athene and the poets Homer and Hesiod. In what follows an attempt will be made to group schematically the various possibilities presented. Irrational joy in conflict could have an organic place in a view of the world based on exact observation and rational reflection. A way had thus to be paved for a positive estimation of the gods of war, esp. Ares. Heracl. seems to have moved in this direction. At any rate, he objected to the cursing of Ἔρις by Achilles (→ n. 9). [13] Fr., 53 (Diels⁷, I, 162, 7 ff.) is well-known : πόλεμος πάντων μὲν πατήρ ἐστι, πάντων δὲ βασιλεύς, καὶ τοὺς μὲν θεοὺς ἔδειξε τοὺς δὲ ἀνθρώπους, τοὺς μὲν δούλους ἐποίησε τοὺς δὲ ἐλευθέρους, πόλεμος has the very qualities of Zeus himself. War is a generally valid principle of life. Observation and reflection can lead, of course, to the diametrically opposite conclusion that the organised πόλεμος of men is without parallel and transgresses the law of nature observed by the beasts. [14]

In opposition to admiration for the achievements of a well-considered waging of war it might be argued that the true goal of responsible reflection is the prevention of war

---

[8] ὀφέλλει Hes. Op., 14, cf. Nestle, 6, but cf. also Pass., Pape, Liddell-Scott, s.v.

[9] Lines 14-16 of the poem, which undoubtedly state the personal conviction of the author (Nestle, 6), run : ἢ μὲν γὰρ πόλεμόν τε κακὸν καὶ δῆριν ὀφέλλει, σχετλίη· οὔ τις τήν γε φιλεῖ βροτός, ἀλλ' ὑπ' ἀνάγκης ἀθανάτων βουλῆσιν Ἔριν τιμῶσι βαρεῖαν. Already in Hom. (Il., 18, 107) Ἔρις is cursed by Achilles, though only in a momentary transport.

[10] Certamen Homeri et Hesiodi (→ n. 5), 225.

[11] Otto, 244.

[12] "The warlike one" is a nickname for Ares here.

[13] Aristot. Eth. Eud., 8, p. 1235a, 25-27. Heracl. repudiated both Hom. and Hes.; that Hom. was materially closer to him may be seen from the fact that he spoke of him with vexation (Fr., 42 [Diels⁷, I, 160, 9 f.]) but of Hes. with contempt (Fr., 40 [I, 160, 3 ff.]; 57 [I, 163, 7]). On this and Fr., 53 below cf. also Fr., 67 (I, 165, 8 f.).

[14] Cf. Ps.-Heracl. ep., 7 (R. Hercher, Epistolographi Graeci [1873], 283 f.), Zeno's image of the herd, Fr., 262 (v. Arnim, I, 60, 38 ff.) and Dio Chrys. Or., 38 (cf. Nestle, 49).

rather than its prosecution. Acc. to the view represented in Eur. Suppl., 734-749 by Adrastos it is in the power of states to avert κάμψαι κακά, the evils (of war); λόγος (negotiation) is at their command as a means thereto.[15] Along the same lines it is maintained by Eteocles in Eur. Phoen., 516 f. that war (φόνος) has no advantage — not even a political advantage — over λόγος, for "what the sword of enemies can achieve may all be attained by negotiation."[16] If nevertheless states prefer φόνος to λόγος, if responsible deliberation is not successful in warding off the threat of war, then it must be concluded that what it achieves in the waging of the war which breaks out can no longer be regarded as a direct outworking of heavenly power. Any idea of gods of war, including Athene as well as Ares, would thus have to be evaluated negatively and even regarded as impious. This is the judgment of the pseudonymous 7th epistle of Heracl.: "You do violence to deity when you call Athene the goddess of war and Ares the god of battles."[17]

Whether the positive evaluation went beyond that of Hom. or the reservations went beyond those of Hesiod, philosophy did not try any more than religious practice to separate altogether the two deities which had been linked in antithetical unity by Homeric epic. Here and there, perhaps, there were dreams of a political state in which wars would be waged only because the two sides, entangled in a dispute which could not be settled by political means, submitted to a higher arbitrament in war. In such cases rejection of λόγος in favour of φόνος was at root a humble and pious submission to the wisdom of Athene, who, when human counsel failed, stepped in to settle things as the executrix of the divine will. To espouse such ideas with any confidence, however, was contrary to the Gk. sense of reality. For there was only too clear a realisation of the fact that those who include in their planning the hope of a supernatural direction of battles never pay homage simply to the wise Athene but always do so as well to the insatiably warlike Ares (→ 503, 28), who does not ask which side is right.

But once the doubt sets in that political calculation on military successes rests, not on the divine gift of wisdom, but on a god-forsaken shortsightedness and perhaps on the all too human interests of unscrupulous individuals (Aristoph. Pax, esp. 1210 ff.), then, quite apart from the tension between Ares and Athene, the radical question arises whether war can be recognised as imposed in any way at all by a superior force which calls for respect. Even on the above assumption, this could still be accepted. If war naturally accompanied higher stages of culture (Porphyr. Abst., IV, 2), or if it was the only possible defence against the danger of overpopulation,[18] then there was an ultimate reason for what at first seemed to be without reason. But in this case it made no gt. difference whether a higher decree was thus sturdily defended or whether a complete antithesis was affirmed between the warlike action of men and the divine will : "Zeus wills that men should be friends the one to the other and that none should be the enemy of another," Dio Chrys. Or., 1, 40 (cf. also 41 ff.). What is made out to be a more or less direct divine dispensation is in truth the result of human wickedness.[19] For there is no historical situation in which war is the only possible way apart from human guilt ; there is always injustice on one side at least. On this view the question of the relation of deity to war is subsumed under the comprehensive question of the relation of deity to evil.[20] War is integrated into the divine rule only in the sense that evil is. In practice this means that he who seriously seeks to avert and fight war must also be led by a serious desire to fight evil, whose root lies within man. The inward war is the most

---

[15] πόλεις τ', ἔχουσαι διὰ λόγου κάμψαι κακά, φόνῳ καθαιρεῖσθ', οὐ λόγῳ, τὰ πράγματα (748 f.), "states which have (the possibility) of averting the evil (of war) by λόγος, you force by bloodshed, not by λόγος, the πράγματα."

[16] πᾶν γὰρ ἐξαιρεῖ λόγος ὃ καὶ σίδηρος πολεμίων δράσειεν ἄν, cf. Nestle, 21.

[17] ὑβρίζεται δι' ὑμῶν θεός, 'Αθηνᾶ πολεμίστρια καὶ "Αρης ἐνυάλιος καλούμενος, Heracl. Epistulae, VII, 6 (Hercher, 285).

[18] Chrysipp. Fr., 1177 (v. Arnim, II, 338, 10-18), appealing to Eur.

[19] Plut. Stoic. Rep., 32 (II, 1049b); Chrysipp.'s apologetic (→ n. 18) is expressly rejected here.

[20] Cf. the Cleanthes Hymn to Zeus, Fr., 537 (v. Arnim, I, 121 ff.).

difficult, and the outward war, whether in the individual, the home, or the πόλις, grows out of it. [21] From the very outset efforts to avert war which rest on an ethically neutral understanding and do not tackle the inner problem can only be incomplete.

2. The Basic General Attitude to the Political Reality of War.

The critical struggle against the legacy of the heroic age (→ 504, 27 ff.) was sufficiently impressive to irritate practical politicians on occasion. [22] The thing which hampered the struggle was, however, the simple question : How can the individual man, and, so long as the hoped for single world state (→ πολίτευμα) is not yet a reality, how can the individual state actualise the peaceful impulses which have been attained if wicked neighbours will not let them do so ? The radical restriction to an intellectual fighting of war with a renunciation of all external protection against aggression [23] was in the eyes of many leaders [24] an evasion of the question rather than an answer to it. If war was an evil, it was an unavoidable evil (Plat. Phaed., 66c), and the best one could hope for was that the single world state would put an end to it. For a long period, then, the general attitude to the political reality of war remained unchanged in the last analysis. In practice, as in the Homeric and pre-Homeric age, the guiding principle was that every peace (→ II, 400, 19 f.) was painfully won from the general state of war, and was like an island continually threatened by its floods. The treaties by which attempts were made to secure peace were for the most part, in view of the constant shifting of the political situation, concluded only for limited periods, and because of the inconstancy of man they had to be sworn by higher powers which, though enigmatic, could at least be expected to deny their favour to aggressors who broke the oaths, and even to proceed against them with their πόλεμος, → n. 4. [25]

3. The Expectation of a State of Peace in the First Imperial Period.

The generation of the first imperial period believed it was close to a dissolving of the tense relation hitherto presupposed as normal, → n. 25. The state of peace prevailing throughout the empire (→ II, 402, 3 ff.) promised to last. The construction of the single world state which would obviate wars had taken a big step forward even if it had not yet been completed. It is true that wrestling with the religious and philosophical problems

---

[21] This order from within outwards is also found in connection with peace ; inner peace is the presupposition of outer peace. Nevertheless, the connection with the motif of war is probably older, cf. H. Leisegang's review of H. Fuchs, *Augustin u. der antike Friedensgedanke* in *Philol. Wochenschr.*, 47 (1927), 1178 f. (→ 512, 26; → II, 411, 5 ff.).

[22] Thuc., II, 40, 2; 63, 2; Polyb., 12, 26, 9, cf. Nestle, 18 f., 22, 32.

[23] Nestle, 33-36; cf. the saying of the cynic Theodorus recorded in Diog. L., II, 98 : (ἔλεγεν δὲ καὶ) εὔλογον εἶναι τὸν σπουδαῖον μὴ ἐξαγαγεῖν ὑπὲρ τῆς πατρίδος αὑτόν.

[24] On Plato and Aristot. cf. Nestle, 28-31.

[25] This is how we are to understand the saying : "The international law of antiquity differs from that of our own time in that acc. to the modern view peace is the normal relation whereas acc. to the ancient view war was the normal relation between states," K. J. Neumann, Art. "Foedus," Pauly-W., 6 (1909), 2818, cf. on this Heuss, 56, n. 18. "Normal" does not mean "desirable." Nestle, 2 rightly emphasises that in antiquity there established itself a mode of thought which was oriented to peace as the normal and desirable state of the world. This is, however, supplementary to the statement quoted above rather than a contradiction of it. Those who accept's Nestle's evaluation of ancient efforts to avert war (as in substance Bienert, 18, n. 7 does) should not underestimate the connection, however indirect, between these efforts and modern non-christian pacifism. It is open to serious doubt whether "the rise of a humanistic, a-christian pacifism alongside Christianity" may in some sense be regarded by the churches "as the bad conscience of humanity on the basis of remnants of Christianity," Bienert, 65 f. This pacifism is certainly an "admonition" to the churches, but would it cease to be this if its true roots lay in antiquity rather than remnants of Christianity ? The questions concerning "wars between the times" (Bienert, 46) were in fact treated much more precisely by the authors of antiquity than by those of the Bible, → 510, 18 f.; 514, 38 ff. Chr. theology should take note of these problems even though it seeks the answers which are to be found directly in the Bible, → n. 95.

of war had not led to any true solutions, and hope of the final extinction of the outer state of war could hardly be based on the assumption that the inward war ($\rightarrow$ 506, 1 f.) had already been ended. But if outward peace did not come from within, it might come from above. The state of peace already attained supported the conclusion that in the march of world epochs under the regulation of an unbreakable order [26] the turning-point had been reached when a golden age would inevitably return [27] in which there would be no inner war or bad neighbours, Horat. Carm., IV, 15. The personage who on the basis of higher necessity had brought in the new age and "put an end to war" [28] was Caesar Augustus. It was not surprising, then, that the experience of peace was accompanied everywhere by a powerful resurgence of the worship of the divine ruler which was by no means alien to Hellenism, $\rightarrow$ I, 565, 16 ff.; III, 1048, 28 ff. There could be confident belief in the divine mission of the emperor. The concentric operation of political experience, cyclic thought and the nimbus of the emperor strengthened the hope of peace to such an unheard of degree that there already seemed to be assurance against any refutation by facts. Wars which still broke out — even if they assumed Homeric proportions — could only be the last gasps of yesterday with no gt. influence on tomorrow, Vergil Ecl., 4, 35 f. In the treaties which were still made to keep the peace confirmation by oath was finally dispensed with as no longer necessary; [29] this is an oblique but fairly certain sign that the general attitude to the problem of war [30] was no longer the same as it had been in the pre-imperial period.

In the long run, however, the facts did not bear out the altered attitude. The bad neighbour had only apparently lost his actuality, and the way in which he challenged the supposedly assured *pax Romana* hardly differed at all from the way in which this had been established. An epochal change in Vergil's sense had not been written in the book of fate, and the glow of faith in the divine mission of the ruler sank to the moderate temperature of a westernised cult of the divine king. The hope of a peace coming directly from above was disappointed; after this disappointment could peace be expected from within, and indirectly from above? Imperial philosophers like Marcus Aurel. and Julian, who wanted nothing to do with the steel bath of war, hoped so, but they still had to spend considerable stretches of their lives on campaigns. The fact that the emperor Probus fell a victim to his own mutinous soldiers was connected with his protest against the majesty of war. [31] Whether such a protest could still be made on a different basis it was left to the heirs of antiquity to say.

B. The Religious Understanding of War in the OT and Later Judaism.

1. Reconstructed Tradition.

a. The Holy War.

If Greek literature shows acquaintance with the holy war only by name and no longer in fact ($\rightarrow$ n. 3), even the name is absent from the OT. But neither the

---

[26] Nestle, 59; $\rightarrow$ χρόνος.

[27] Vergil Ecl., 4, 9 ff., cf. A. Kurfess, "Vergil u. d. Sibyllinen," *Zschr. f. Religions- u. Geistesgeschichte*, 3 (1951), 253-257; G. Jachmann, "Die vierte Ekl. Vergils," *Arbeitsgemeinschaft f. Forschung des Landes Nordrhein-Westfalen, Geisteswissenschaften*, 2 (1953), 37-62.

[28] Ditt. Or., II, 458, 36 f.: τὸν παύσαντα μὲν πόλεμον; cf. Sib., III, 652 f., 753.

[29] Cf. G. Quabbe, *Die völkerrechtliche Garantie*, Diss. Breslau (1910), 8, n. 1.

[30] Undoubtedly there was more than one reason for giving up the ratification by oath. Nevertheless, apart from a real change of attitude there could hardly have been a break with well-established tradition in this field. One should not miss the fact, of course, that this was only a secularising change of no gt. religious profundity. It was a surge of self-confidence. If the oath had been dropped because of pious respect for it, or because of confidence that the gods would exercise their favour even without the oath, the domestic oath of loyalty would have had to be dropped too.

[31] E. Dannhäuser, *Untersuchungen zur Gesch. des Kaisers Probus*, Diss. Jena (1909), 83-85.

terminology (→ I, 92, 26 ff.) nor the historical data leave us in any doubt as to the fact that considerable significance is attached to the holy war in the OT. [32] The tribes of Israel never forgot that help had been given them in early times against hostile threats to their existence. Through charismatically gifted personages [33] Yahweh had called them to defensive war, [34] and by this means, often fighting for them Himself, [35] He had given the enemy into the hands [36] of His warriors. These warriors, made willing by Yahweh, had assembled voluntarily [37] from the different tribal territories [38] and made up a single army. Yet all the obligations of the soldier rested on them. [39] Indeed, their response was so powerful that it could even be said of them that they came to the help of Yahweh, Ju. 5:23. Nevertheless, neither their equipment [40] nor their numbers [41] turned the scale. It was Yahweh who went before them, [42] gave them courage, [43] and took it from their foes. [44] To Him and Him alone belonged the praise [45] and the spoil, → I, 354, 15 ff. These were holy wars, holy even down to the details of rites and customs. [46]

If with the establishment of a solidly organised kingdom more careful planning of war became customary, [47] and if there was no longer any experience of the holy war in the ancient and true sense, [48] the dynamic of holy war was not extinguished. [49] It lived on as an ideal in the politics of Josiah [50] and even in later times ; [51] the prophetic movement especially regarded itself as the "guardian of the patriarchal order of the holy war." [52] The fact that there could be discerned in the charismatic endowment of the prophets the invisible forces on which alone the safety of Israel finally depended [53] explains the cry recorded in the Elijah-Elisha cycle אָבִי אָבִי רֶכֶב יִשְׂרָאֵל וּפָרָשָׁיו (2 K. 2:12; 13:14); cf. the many allusions thereto in Isaiah. [54] Even though there are no more references to the rites and

---

[32] Cf. on what follows v. Rad, with detailed ref. in the notes → infra.

[33] Cf. esp. Ju. 4:14-16; 5:11 f.; v. Rad, 20, 23, 27, n. 44.

[34] Caspari, 132; v. Rad, 26, 32, though cf. Procksch, RGG², III, 1305.

[35] Ex. 14:14; Dt. 1:30; Jos. 10:14, 42; 23:10.

[36] Jos. 2:24; 6:2, 16; Ju. 3:28; 1 S. 23:4; 1 K. 20:28 etc.; cf. v. Rad, 7 f.

[37] Ju. 5:2, 9, cf. v. Rad, 6, 37.

[38] Nu. 26:2-51; v. Rad, 26.

[39] Thus by a solemn oath they had to pledge themselves under Yahweh's banner for continual war against Amalek, Ex. 17:16, cf. Eissfeldt, 27; v. Rad, 26; A. Weiser, Review of G. v. Rad, Der hl. Krieg im alten Israel in Für Arbeit u. Besinnung, 7 (1953), 159.

[40] Ju. 7:2 ff.; 1 S. 14:6; 17:45, 47.

[41] 2 S. 24:1 ff.; Ex. 30:12; v. Rad, 9, 37.

[42] Ju. 4:14; Dt. 20:4; 2 S. 5:24; on the sacred ark cf. v. Rad, 28, n. 45.

[43] 1 S. 30:6; cf. v. Rad, 10.

[44] Ex. 15:14-16; 23:27 f. (v. Rad, 10); by miracles, Jos. 10:11; 24:7; Ju. 5:20; by terror, 1 S. 14:15 (v. Rad, 12).

[45] Ex. 14:4, 18; Zech. 4:6 f.

[46] v. Rad, 29, 49.

[47] Ibid., 21, 33, 45.

[48] Ibid., 38.

[49] Ibid., 29.

[50] Ibid., 76-78.

[51] Cf. → 511, 34 ff. (→ n. 84).

[52] v. Rad, 53.

[53] Ibid., 55 f.

[54] Cf. esp. Is. 5:12; 7:4, 9; 22:8-11; 30:15; 31:1, 3, 4. Acc. to v. Rad it was on the basis of the tradition of the holy war that Is. rejected "armaments and alliances" and commended "looking to Yahweh and standing still" (61). Prophecy with its function led "to the very place where in early times the institution of the holy war stood" (56). But for reservations cf. A. Weiser, op. cit. (→ n. 39), 158-160, also → 189, n. 122.

customs of the holy war, and even though the holy war is no longer accepted as the only way in which Yahweh rendered help to Israel,[55] nevertheless, reading between the lines in the prophetic writings, one may see that fundamentally no type of war corresponded to the nature of Israel in the same way as did the holy war commanded and waged by Yahweh Himself.

When the prophets looked into the distant future, they could have the vision of a last and general attack[56] on Israel and its definitive repelling by a final holy war.[57] Things were the same when the prophets looked back into the past. Indeed, the idea of a holy war could influence the historical picture in a way which modern historical criticism finds it hard to accept. Thus in Dt. and the narratives which underwent Deuteronomic redaction the holy war has coloured the traditional picture of the conquest.[58] Here then, at a stage subsequent to that of actual experience, even aggressive wars could be regarded as holy wars to the degree that they ensured to the people, united in obedience to the one God, a place among the other nations, which were far superior to them in power and which did not confess this one God.[59] If, however, the political goal of the holy war became more comprehensive in retrospect, it always had its origin in a higher goal, namely, that of subjection to the one God in defiance of all idols.

b. The War of Yahweh against Israel.

This higher goal necessarily gave the prophetic movement an unflinching eye for the possibility that it might be violated by Israel itself. If Israel was the people of Yahweh in distinction from all other peoples, this did not give it any claim to extenuating circumstances, Am. 3:2. If the war of Yahweh could be against the arrogance of foreign nations (→ II, 944 f.; III, 928, 40 ff.),[60] it could also be directed against Israel itself, and foreign nations could be the instruments of this war. Am. 2:14-16 almost sounds as though such a war of Yahweh against Israel might be described paradoxically as a holy war too.[61] At any rate, the invisible forces which guarantee victory in a holy war are now at work against Israel. The fact that the God who not without reason is called יְהֹוָה צְבָאוֹת[62] could prove Himself in the fullest sense to be אִישׁ מִלְחָמָה might be experienced with the joy of victory as a surpassing of even the greatest expectations, Ex. 15:3.[63] Nevertheless, the prophets were well aware that the worst fears of Israel might also be surpassed by Yahweh's warlike intervention.

If Israel was called to a way of unique majesty, the danger that it might be betrayed into hopeless war against the overwhelming strength of God was also singularly acute. The classical period of gloomy prophecies of divine war against Israel is separated by centuries from the classical period of holy wars. But as the period of holy wars still exerted an influence, so the prophetic threat of Yahweh's war against Israel had a long preparatory history. Reverses in holy wars, for example, seem to have been interpreted

---

[55] v. Rad, 67.

[56] Mi. 4:11; Is. 8:9 f.; 17:12 f.; 29:7 f.; Ez. 38 f.; Jl. 3.

[57] Mi. 4:12; cf. v. Rad, 64. It is natural that ideas of national vengeance could be combined with the thought of the victory of the power of Yahweh, cf. Is. 59:15b-20; 63:1-5 (→ II, 945, 1 ff.).

[58] Dt. 6:18 f.; 7:1 f.; 11:23 ff.; 12:29; 19:1; 20:16 f.; cf. v. Rad, 68-76.

[59] Dt. 20:18 (cf. v. Rad, 70). In Ju. 3:1 f. we seem to have a view which goes even beyond Dt. (if in the LXX [except B] 'Ιησοῦς is the subj. here rather than κύριος, this is the result of mechanical assimilation to 2:21 rather than theological reflection).

[60] Cf. esp. Is. 10:5 ff.; Jer. 46, 51, cf. Eichr. Theol. AT³, I (1948), 233; O. Procksch, Theol. d. AT (1950), 579.

[61] Cf. v. Rad, 63.

[62] Cf. esp. H. Frederikson, Jahwe als Krieger (1945), 50-55, 109.

[63] Caspari, 129; v. Rad, 32.

along these lines from the very first; [64] "Yahweh had withdrawn His help from His people, or even assisted the enemies of His people." [65]

c. Divine and Human Initiatives.

In the OT war is as a whole more closely related to the rule of the God of Israel than it is to that of the gods of Greece in Homer. It is unlikely that a book of the wars of Athene or Ares could ever have been written; in contrast, a book of the wars of Yahweh was actually written, Nu. 21:14. The fact that Yahweh decides the conflict is not merely known to individual personages at the heart of the struggle; the whole host believes it from the outset [66] and consciously experiences it. When the armies of Egypt are destroyed (Ex. 15), and when the walls of Jericho fall down (Jos. 6), Yahweh does it all by miracle, and all that is asked of men is that they should engage in certain preparations whose purpose is hard to fathom. Even if in these instances the picture of "autarchic miracles" is a later one which does not wholly correspond to the impression of those who lived through the events, it is a sign that the military initiative of man is less important [67] than in Homer.

2. The Problem.

There is in the OT no basic discussion of the religious understanding of the phenomenon of war, [68] though among the wars which affected Israel there were naturally some which could be understood neither as holy wars nor as wars of God against Israel, [69] cf. David's action in 1 S. 21:6, the conquest of Laish (Ju. 17 f.), and the wars between Israel and Judah or between individual tribes. Events like the questioning of Yahweh in Ju. 18:5 [70] or the many cultic acts which acc. to later tradition (Ju. 19-21) followed the transgression of Gibeah (Hos. 9:9; 10:9) rested on a "primitive pansacralism" [71] and do not justify us in speaking of holy wars in the true sense, important though Ju. 19-21 may be for an understanding of the sacral tribal league. [72]

If the lines indicated in the OT are followed up, then as a counterpart to the considerations advanced above (→ 503, 15 ff.) we may conclude that it is beyond question that the reason for the wars of Yahweh against Israel is always to be sought in human transgression. If one asks concerning the reason for holy wars, one is again directed to human arrogance or human guilt, for the holy war always presupposes an attack or at least a real threat of war. [73] If the same question is raised in respect of other wars, it is natural that they should be judged similarly as evils brought on by human sin and mysteriously interwoven into the plan of Yahweh. [74] The main themes in the problem of religious war had already been laid down at an early period in the world of the OT as in the Greek world. [75]

---

[64] Lv. 26:36; Jos. 7:5; 1 S. 17:11; 28:5; 1 K. 19:15-18.

[65] Eissfeldt, 32 cf. 45 and v. Rad, 11.

[66] Only afterwards in Ex. 14:30 f.; cf. on this v. Rad, 47.

[67] Cf. Caspari, 110 f.

[68] Cf. Eissfeldt, 41.

[69] v. Rad, 24, 29, n. 47.

[70] Ibid., 25, n. 35.

[71] M. Buber, Mose (1948), 176.

[72] Cf. v. Rad, 24, 29, n. 47, but also M. Weber, Gesammelte Aufsätze zur Religionssoziologie, 3 (1923), 52, 99 and Weiser, op. cit., 158-160.

[73] Or in Dt. the existence of abominable pagan idolatry in the land destined to be the dwelling-place of those who confess the one God, Dt. 7:4, 16, 25 f.; 20:18.

[74] Cf. Eissfeldt, 38 f.: "It is no strange idea in ancient Israel ... that war and fighting ... have arisen contrary to the will of God through human wickedness and sin ... Thus it (war) is nevertheless a weapon in God's hand."

[75] Ibid., 58: "The exilic and post-exilic period of the religious history of the OT ... produced no new ideas in the religious and moral evaluation of war."

3. The Basic General Attitude to the Political Reality of War.

At this pt. there is no essential difference from the non-biblical world. In the sense mentioned above (→ n. 25) war is the normal if often undesired relation between nations. This was even more strongly felt, however, in view of the religious antithesis between Israel and all other peoples.

4. The Expectation of a State of Peace.

The question of a state of peace could be for Israel a matter of political accommodation, but in the main it boiled down to the religious question whether war had to be waged by higher counsel against hostile Gentile peoples or against the people of Israel itself when it fell into disobedience. How little human initiative could accomplish in this sphere had been taught by the fratricidal wars between tribes who in the last resort, in subjection to Yahweh, were one. If there was still hope of a warless future, it could grow only out of the paradoxical confidence that Yahweh, even though He summoned to war and threatened with war, would Himself usher in a state in which this rod of discipline would no longer be needed. [76] The fact that such confidence was possible was grounded in the nature of Yahweh; the Man of War is also the One who puts a stop to wars (מַשְׁבִּית מִלְחָמוֹת) even to the border of the earth. [77] The promise of Is. 2:4 (Mi. 4:3) presupposes that the final war will also come to an end.

5. Later Judaism.

a. No new guidelines on war are to be found in later Judaism, though the concept of final wars or the final war takes on enhanced significance and is depicted in many different colours in apocalyptic and Messianism. [78] It is not surprising that these overlap and interfuse with no clear-cut distinctions. Thus the war of extirpation against ungodly might (Test. D. 5:10 f.; Test. A. 7:3) and against sin (Eth. En. 94) sometimes seems to be identical with the final day of judgment, [79] or at least to be so closely related to it that one cannot differentiate between the situation of war and the act of judgment. [80] For this reason the conduct of believers in the period just before the end may be seen in different ways. It is a firm presupposition that all who were caught up in a final war and hoped to emerge with honour would have to be a match for the requirement of readiness for suffering and sacrifice which this war imposes, esp. this war which surpasses all others in its afflictions, Da. 12:1; Ass. Mos. 16. In practice, however, it makes a gt. difference whether one takes to arms in the rank and file as in all other wars [81] or whether it is expected that God [82] or the Messiah [83] will wage the war so directly that there is no place at all for the idea of human participation. Where there was the conviction that already one was actively engaged in the prelude to the eschatological conflict or at least caught up in a holy war (→ II, 886 ff.), naturally only the former of the two possibilities mentioned could be considered, as, e.g., in the period of the

---

[76] Is. 2:2 ff.; 11:1 ff.; Hos. 2:20 ff.; Zech. 9:9 f., → II, 405 f.

[77] Ps. 46:9; cf. Jdt. 9:7; 16:2. The LXX has συντρίβων πολέμους for אִישׁ מִלְחָמָה at Ex. 15:3 and συντρίψει πόλεμον at Is. 42:13. No matter how the substitution took place, it is in some sense an indication that a synthesis was seen between Yahweh's present readiness for war and His ultimate goal of peace.

[78] Cf. Volz Esch., 157, 213.

[79] Volz Esch., 94 can even say on the basis of Ass. Mos. 10: "This leads to the second innovation. A judicial process takes the place of war and victory; judgment becomes a forensic act." It should not be forgotten, however, that the victories of Israel are already called צִדְקוֹת יְהוָה in the OT (Ju. 5:11; 1 S. 12:7; Mi. 6:5), so that from ancient times Yahweh is for Israel the Lord of war because He is primarily the Guardian of right, → III, 925, 39 ff.

[80] Eth. En. 94:7, 9; esp. 100, 1-5; cf. 46, 51, 53 with 55 f., 62.

[81] Eth. En. 90:19; 95:3; Jub. 23:30; Apc. Abr. 29; Test. S. 5:5; 1 QSa I, 21:26. Angels can take part in the fighting, 1 QSa II, 8 f.; 1 QM 12:1. Visible and invisible wars are mentioned alongside one another in Test. R. 6:12.

[82] Eth. En. 94:10; Ass. Mos. 10:7-10; Test. A. 7:3.

[83] Ps. Sol. 17:21 ff.; 4 Esr. 12:33; S. Bar. 40:2 f.; Damasc. 7:20 f. (9:9 f.); 1 QH 6:28 ff.; 1 QSb 5:25.

Maccabees [84] or the rebellions of 66-70 and 132-135 A.D. [85] The war scroll (1 QM) also presupposes that a decision along these lines has already been made. It paints a picture of the decisive 40 year campaign against the sons of darkness which is in every detail a holy war (1 QM 9:5), so holy that the sabbatical years which occur in the course of it (→ σάββατον) may be kept strictly and there need be no fear of military reverses, although this sanctity goes hand in hand with military realism. [86] Development from this military path to the other possibility is plainly indicated in the fact that the Manual later found a place in the same sacred collection of writings of which the war scroll is an older [87] part. This scroll can speak of the weapon of the curse (1 QS 2:5), of hatred and enmity (1:4 and 10; 4, 17; 9:21 ff.; 10:19 ff.) and it refers to capital punishment for offenders in the sect's own ranks (6:27[?]), but the active role of the sons of light in the coming time of testing (1:17) seems to be limited in the main to the doing of good works (1:5) and the preserving of the unrelenting steadfastness of which Jos. speaks in Bell., 2, 152 ff., i.e., in passive resistance. The only problem is that the military order in 1 QS 2:21 f.; 10:14 and the ref. to the day of vengeance in 9:23; 10:19 leave us in doubt as to whether the possibility of using deadly weapons against the sons of darkness is entirely ruled out. One may probably add that acc. to the mind of the Manual there may be resort to active resistance only in response to a higher direction which may not be anticipated. To give such direction is the privilege of the authorised persons expected in 9:10 f. And since this is a political decision, the ref. here is esp. to the political leader, the Messiah of Israel, [88] who is mentioned after the priestly Messiah of Aaron. Whether a holy war after the ancient pattern is to be expected, or whether this will be a war of God or the Messiah without military action on the part of believers, is a question which is bound up indissolubly with the further question as to the person of the Messiah of Israel.

b. Philo's attitude to war corresponds to his attitude to peace, → n. 21; → II, 410 f. Acc. to Conf. Ling., 41-59 the presupposition of true συμφωνία is consideration of the fact that all derive from the one common Father (41) along with listening to God and the doing of His will (58). Men who obey more gods than one (τῷ πολυθέῳ ... κακῷ προσνείμαντες ἑαυτούς) bear within them the seeds of inward conflict and hence also of outward political war (42 f., cf. Som., II, 14). Everything that makes war so terrible is set in train in a state which is from the political standpt. "peace" (46 ff.;

---

[84] Cf. 1 Macc. 3:18 ff.; 4:8 ff.; 2 Macc. 8:23; 11:13; 12:15; 13:15. In 1 Macc. 11:51 the glory is not ascribed to Yahweh alone, as in a holy war, cf. v. Rad, 83 f.

[85] Cf. H. Bardtke, "Bemerkungen zu den beiden Texten aus dem Bar Kochba-Aufstand," ThLZ, 79 (1954), 295-304.

[86] Cf. Y. Yadin, The Scroll of the War (1962), pp. 141 ff. The fact that enemy defeats are mentioned (1:10 and 13) but one's own are at most suggested (16:11, cf. H. Bardtke, "Die Kriegsrolle v. Qumran übersetzt," ThLZ, 80 [1955], 416, n. 218) is in keeping with military reporting found in every age and not just with a purely "utopian theory" (as against L. Rost, "Zum 'Buch des Krieges d. Söhne des Lichts gegen die Söhne der Finsternis,'" ThLZ, 80 [1955], 208). A very natural question here is how far the political goal of destroying enemies (→ n. 57) was subordinate to a higher goal, e.g., how far the biblical view of the one God had, in spite of a basic monotheism, been obscured by the shadows of pre-Israelite and non-Israelite gods of war (→ ψευδόχριστος). Joseph. thinks a decisive cause of the war against Rome (τοῦτο δὲ ἦν τοῦ πρὸς Ῥωμαίους πολέμου καταβολή, Bell., 2, 409) was the impious (τοῦτο μὲν γὰρ ἀσεβέστατον, Bell., 2, 413) and inhuman (ἀπανθρωπία, 2, 415) suppression of the offering for non-Jews in Jerusalem. This national particularism stands opposed to the nature of the one God who is the Lord of all mankind, cf. A. Schlatter, "Die Theol. d. Judt. nach dem Bericht d. Jos.," BFTh, II, 26 (1932), 24-45, esp. 29 f. On wars in which Yahweh was in truth both Leader and Victor cf. Bell., 5, 376 ff., 390, → 509, 2 ff.

[87] Cf. L. Rost, op. cit. (→ n. 86), 206, though cf. also J. Carmignac, "L'utilité ou l'inutilité des sacrifices sanglants dans la 'Règle de la communauté' de Qumran," Rev. Bibl., 63 (1956), 524-532, esp. 525, n. 1, 2; but cf. also Yadin, op. cit. (→ n. 86), 141.

[88] Cf. K. G. Kuhn, "Die beiden Messias Aarons u. Israels," NT Studies, 1 (1954/55), 168-179; E. Stauffer, "Probleme der Priestertradition," ThLZ, 81 (1956), 135-150.

Fug., 174). Strict war must be declared on this latent state of war (49, 57). God Himself ordains war (πόλεμος θεήλατος, → n. 4) where nature is set in στάσις with itself. [89] As may be seen from Praem. Poen., 85-97, Philo is well aware that the presupposition of a true state of peace is a gt. structural change in creation. Only God can bring about this change (87), but man must not expect his own role to be limited to that of a spectator. As a start, the wild beasts in the human ψυχή must be tamed (88). Then one may hope (οὐκ ἀπελπιστέον, 88) that Is. 11:6 ff. will be fulfilled, that the "older war" in the animal kingdom will come to an end (88-91). If there should still be men who cannot break free from their joy in battle (τῇ τοῦ πολεμεῖν ἐπιθυμίᾳ, 94), then there will have to be a trial of strength (χειρῶν ἄμιλλα, 94) between them and the ὅσιοι (96), in which the ὅσιοι will come out the victors without shedding of blood (ἀναιμωτί, 97).

C. πόλεμος/πολεμέω in the NT.

The NT is familiar with the Davidic descent and the royal (→ II, 568 f.; I, 577 ff.) dignity of the Messiah. It would thus be surprising if nothing were said about a campaign of this King and the resultant demands made upon His followers. Obviously, however, it never entered the heads of NT Christians, as distinct from the political activists of Judah (→ 511, 34 ff.), that an open summons to war in the service of the Messiah was one of these demands. [90] If, on the other hand, they also did not in some sense leave open the possibility of such a summons in the last time, this is connected with the fact that the person, teaching (→ II, 153 ff.) and prophecy [91] (→ προφήτης) of the Messiah were already known to them, as they were not known to believers of the sect. Acquaintance with His person influenced and limited the expectation of future warlike activity. This comes out in the apocalyptic texts, which are the only ones in the NT to offer true pictures of war.

1. War in the Events of the Last Time.

How war will be overcome by war (→ line 1 f.), and how closely the concluding war is related to the last judgment (→ III, 936 ff.), is shown in Rev. by the events between the end of the millennial reign (20:4-6) and the appearing of the new heaven and the new earth (21:1 ff.). The eschatological disturber of the peace, who had been foreseen already in Ez. (38:2 f.), comes forth with an army (Rev. 20:8) which seems to be invincible. Nevertheless, he cannot execute the final stroke which he had planned; instead, the final blow is launched against him and against war generally from above. Directly linked herewith are the definitive overthrow of Satanic power and the Last Judgment (20:10 ff.). The reader of the book has already been told in 19:11 that the basic theme in both the war and the judgment is the same: ἐν δικαιοσύνῃ κρίνει καὶ πολεμεῖ, "in righteousness he judges and makes war." The decision taken at the end of the millennial reign is the necessary consummation of a decision which has already been taken in heaven.

---

[89] Spec. Leg., II, 190. On the attitude of Philo to war generally cf. J. Heinemann, *Philons gr. u. jüd. Bildung* (1932), 408-413; Windisch, 15 f.

[90] Nor is it to be assumed that such a call could have been heard in the pre-NT period of primitive Christianity (as against R. Eisler, 'Ιησοῦς βασιλεὺς οὐ βασιλεύσας [1928 ff.]; S. G. F. Brandon, *The Fall of Jerusalem and the Christian Church* [1951]).

[91] That near and distant wars would accompany the beginning of the end acc. to divine fiat is in the tradition an intimation of Jesus (in wording similar to 4 Esr. 13:30 f.), cf. Mk. 13:7; Mt. 24:6; Lk. 21:9. But this does not mean that Christians were to play an active part in these wars or that war in general was regarded as a "divinely instituted emergency measure," Künneth, 330-335.

As the final war here precedes the fall of Satan into hell (20:10), so the heavenly prelude to the final war preceded the fall of Satan from heaven to earth (12:7): καὶ ἐγένετο πόλεμος ἐν τῷ οὐρανῷ, ὁ Μιχαὴλ καὶ οἱ ἄγγελοι αὐτοῦ τοῦ πολεμῆσαι μετὰ τοῦ δράκοντος. [92]

Not only is this heavenly event, with its ineluctable consequences for the earth, concealed from the unenlightened eye ; there is also the danger that men will disregard the higher logic of the overcoming of war by God's righteous war. Even the Christian church at Pergamos, though remote from any active military engagement, needs to be warned that the war from above is nearer than it imagines — the war of the One who can use His sharp two-edged sword if necessary against His own people (→ 509, 19 ff.), cf. Rev. 2:16. It is completely hidden from the well-armed kings of the world, who are swayed by demonic power, where their military way will lead. That is to say, they do not realise that the attack which they make in concert will bring about the opposite result from that intended, namely, the war of the great day (→ II, 952, 4 f.) of God, Rev. 16:14. Indeed, the idea that such a war against the power authorised by the δράκων (→ II, 283, 2 ff.) is even possible seems to be beyond the capabilities of the "whole earth," Rev. 13:3 f. The stronger, then, is the readiness to be seduced into participating in the war of this power (20:8), which is directed against the prophetic witnesses (11:7), against the community (12:17; 13:7), against the beloved city (20:8 f.), and finally against the Lamb (17:14), against the Rider on the white horse (19:19). This war is personified in the figure of the second horseman of the Apocalypse (6:3 f.); his terrors (9:5 f.) and symbols (9:7, 9) accompany the events of the fifth trumpet and in latent fashion survive the thousand years of peace (20:1 ff.). According to Rev. there can arise doubt as to the majesty of this war which is waged with the biggest battalions (→ 507, 30 ff.), or rather there can be a persistence of such doubt, only where there is faith in the righteousness of the King of kings and Lord of lords (19:11, 16).

2. Other References to War.

No one in NT times doubted that the divine goal (→ n. 86) was also normative for the events of the past which, according to the OT presentation, God Himself had ordained. This fact, however, is stated only once, and even there only indirectly and incidentally (Hb. 11:34). The incidental nature of this reference, and the consistent silence about war elsewhere, can only be taken to mean that the idea of a resurrection of the holy war, and the justification of the waging of new holy wars by those who share in the new covenant, is quite alien to the whole of the NT including Rev.

The NT authors never thought of engaging in basic discussion of the wars which would still take place during the period between the divinely commanded wars of the past and a final war which would bring on the judgment, nor of examining the justification which there might be for such wars, [93] → 510, 18 ff. There is no evidence, nor

---

[92] It is by no means obvious that the campaigns of the rider on the white horse (Rev. 19:11) and of Michael (12:7) were "imported from without into the sphere of the life of faith" (Bienert, 21), nor is it in keeping with the evidence that in the NT the subject of war or wars is always Satan-Diabolos or his servants (loc. cit.); thus the subj. of πολεμέω in the NT is Satanic power only in Rev. 12:7b; 17:14 and not in the other 5 instances of the verb, Jm. 4:2; Rev. 2:16; 12:7a; 13:4; 19:11.

[93] The parable in Lk. 14:31 does not raise the issue of a deeper material justification for military calculation, though it is plain that the king who thus calculates is neither one of the disturbers of the peace in the last time (→ 513, 31) nor under obligation to wage a holy war. Neither here nor in 1 C. 14:8 is any attitude expressed towards the problem of war ; the military element is simply metaphorical, as against Bienert, 90-94.

does it anywhere appear, that a baptised Christian was prepared for military participation in a war or for military service generally. [94] The situation was different when a man who was already a serving soldier (→ στρατιώτης) became a Christian. No one suggested to him that he should try to leave the service, just as no one suggested that a Christian slave should seek freedom from his pagan master, 1 C. 7:17 ff., though → II, 272, n. 86. To the profession of arms there thus attached no more special stigma than to slavery, → II, 271, 3 ff. Terms from slavery and soldiering were indeed favoured to illustrate the Christian life and later the conduct of the martyr. If honour was thus paid to the soldier, to the legionary who was either a pagan or who had become a Christian, for his constantly observed excellence of achievement in courage, in sacrificial loyalty and simple matter-of-factness, this did not mean, any more than in Hesiod (→ 504, 10 f.), that similar honour was being paid to the institution of war as such. It is worth noting, and is certainly no accident, that in spite of the positive use of images from the soldier's life the words πόλεμος and πολεμέω or μάχη and μάχομαι (→ IV, 528, 2 ff.) are never used either literally or fig. to describe what the Christian should do; acc. to Jm. 4:2 warrings and fightings are not compatible with the Christian. [95]

Bauernfeind

---

[94] v. Harnack, 51: "Hence it is not surprising that up to the time of Antoninus or Marcus Aurelius the question of soldiers did not arise in the churches; a Christian did not become a soldier ..." The fact that a baptised Christian obviously did not become a soldier in this period forms a significant supplement to the clearly irrefutable statement of Bienert (33) that "in the NT soldiering was not then a profession which had to be adopted or abandoned for reasons of faith."

[95] The question whether a Christian should undertake or refuse military service is not put in the NT (→ 514, 38 ff.; cf. v. Campenhausen, 257, esp. n. 10; Lasserre, 254), nor can it be directly answered from the NT, certainly not on the basis of the πόλεμος sayings, though it must be admitted that the NT should not be ignored in any answer given. There is no uniform judgment on what the guidelines indirectly contained in the NT demand in practice, cf. Theimer, 379 f. The most important of the positions which have been advanced may be briefly noted. For those who on the basis of exact calculation of the end are convinced that any present war is the war against Christ (→ 514, 21), refusal of military service is self-evident (cf. K. Hutten, "Die Zeugen Jehovas," *Materialdienst*, 15 [1952], 175-231). The same applies to those who regard the deliberate use of deadly weapons as incompatible with the NT, Lasserre, 209-229, esp. 221, 228. On the other hand, those who start with the fact that Christians are commanded to help their neighbours (→ 316 ff.), and who regard the help given by means of deadly weapons as emergency help in the NT sense, believe that defensive wars are justified and that they are summoned on occasion to take part in them. They usually assume that a meaningful distinction can be made between unlawful aggression and lawful defence, cf. esp. Acta apostolicae sedis, 37, Ser. 2, Vol. 12 (1945), 18; M. Luther, *Ob Kriegsleute im seligen Stand sein können* (1526), WA, 19 (1897), 656 f.; Müller, 15 f. The possibility of such distinction is, however, contested, Theimer, 379; W. Picht, *Vom Wesen des Krieges* (1952), 11. If this objection is sound, the question remains whether the Christian cannot still obediently accept war as an emergency measure once instituted by God and nowhere abrogated in the NT (→ n. 91), and whether he has not confidently to leave the responsibility for military action in the hands of the state, which "upholds his existence" (Künneth, 343). Might it not be argued that the opportunity which human societies have to renounce the use of weapons by treaty (→ 505, 1 ff.) is also a divine institution which in a NT sense is at least equal in rank to war (with reservations Künneth, 452) and which also demands sacrificial obedience? Furthermore, a renunciation of one's own δοκιμάζειν (→ II, 260) in favour of the state entails at some stage a renunciation of the guidelines of the NT, cf. Barth, 537 (E.T. 469). It may also be asked whether the NT is not ignored from the very outset in the taking of the modern military oath, which is often regarded as the axis of the soldier's existence (H. G. Backhaus, *Wehrkraft im Zwiespalt* [1952], 28 f.). Do not the holy wars of an earlier period thus find an illegitimate (→ 514, 29 ff.) continuation (cf. O. Bauernfeind, *Eid. u. Frieden* [1956])? Finally, it is by no means in place to direct only to Judaism the question of a continuing (if sometimes reconstructed) tribute to the gods of war, → n. 57, 86. H. Thielicke, *Theol. Ethik*, II, 1 (1955), 314-316 has rightly emphasised that this must also be put to consciously

---

πόλις, † πολίτης, † πολιτεύομαι,
† πολιτεία, † πολίτευμα

→ Σιών, 'Ιερουσαλήμ.

Contents : A. πόλις κτλ. in Non-Biblical Greek : I. Lexicography ; II. Ideal Content.
B. πόλις κτλ. in the Septuagint and Later Judaism : I. πόλις : 1. Hebrew Originals ;
2. Description of Cities ; 3. Importance of Cities ; 4. Jerusalem ; 5. Jerusalem in the Hope
of Later Judaism ; II. πολίτης, πολιτεία, πολιτεύομαι, πολίτευμα in the OT ; III. Josephus and Philo. C. πόλις κτλ. in the NT : I. πόλις ; 1. Distribution and Secular Use ;
2. Jerusalem the Holy City ; 3. The Heavenly Jerusalem ; 4. The Translation of πόλις as
Civitas in the Vulgate ; II. πολίτης, πολιτεύομαι, πολιτεία, πολίτευμα. D. The Post-
Apostolic Fathers.

A. πόλις κτλ. in Non-Biblical Greek.

I. Lexicography.

1. πόλις, poetically used subsidiary dialect form of πτόλις (Aeolic, Cyprian, Cretan),
is an ancient word. The etym. is unexplained. "The original meaning of πόλις is close
to that of town, the oldest term for a fortified settlement or a larger settlement in
general." [1] A relic of this most ancient sense is to be found in the fact that even in the
days of Thuc. the Acropolis in Athens was simply called πόλις. [2] It should be noted,
however, that in its further development the term inclined to the political side, so that
the idea of fortification was no longer essential. Thuc. speaks of πόλεις ἀτείχιστοι

---

believing Christians. In a century in which rhetorical confession of σχετλίη "Ερις (→ 504, 7;
504, 33 f.) is possible (Kern, 17), there might even be sincere confession too. Where, however, the false gods of war take over, discussion of the ethical problems of war is a mere
sham, for in truth Ares does not ask which side is right, → 503, 28 f.

π ό λ ι ς   κ τ λ. For bibl. cf. Pohlenz, Keil ; from the abundant lit. only a few of the
more significant titles will be mentioned here. On A. : H. Bengtson, *Gr. Gesch. Hndbch.
AW*, III, 4 (1950); R. Bultmann, "Polis u. Hades in d. Antigone des Soph.," *Glauben u.
Verstehen*, II (1952), 20-31; J. Burckhardt, *Gr. Kulturgeschichte*, I (1898); G. Busolt, *Gr.
Staatskunde*, I, *Hndbch. AW*, IV, 1, 1[3] (1920); C. N. Cochrane, *Christianity and Classical
Culture*[2] (1944); F. de Coulanges, *La cité antique* (1864); V. Ehrenberg, "Vom Sinn d. gr.
Geschichte," *Historische Zschr.*, 127 (1923), 377-392; also "Der gr. u. hell. Staat," in
A. Gercke and E. Norden, *Einl. in d. Altertumswissenschaft*[3], III, 3 (1932); E. Fabricius,
Art. "Städtebau der Griechen," Pauly-W., 3 A (1929), 1982-2016; G. Glotz, *La cité grecque,
Nouvelle édition augmentée d'une bibliographie complémentaire et d'un appendice par
P. Cloché* (1953); A. H. M. Jones, *Cities of the Eastern Roman Provinces* (1937), also *The
Greek City from Alexander to Justinian* (1940); J. Kaerst, *Gesch. d. Hell.*, I (1917); B. Keil,
"Gr. Staatsaltertümer," in A. Gercke and E. Norden, *Einl. in d. Altertumswissenschaft*[2],
III, 3 (1914), 353-434; M. Pohlenz, *Staatsgedanke u. Staatslehre d. Griechen* (1923); also
Die Stoa, I (1948), Index *s.v.* "Staat"; W. W. Tarn, *Alexander the Great*, II (1948), 199-
259 (Appendix 7: "Alexander and the Greek Cities of Asia Minor"; App. 8 : "Alexander's
Foundations"); U. v. Wilamowitz-Moellendorff, *Platon*, I (1919), 399-444; also "Staat u.
Gesellschaft d. Griechen," *Kultur der Gegenwart*, II, 4, 1[2] (1923), 1-214; On C. : W. Bieder,
Ekklesia u. Polis im NT u. in d. Alten Kirche (1941); R. Bultmann, "Das Verständnis v.
Welt u. Mensch im NT u. im Griechentum," *Glauben u. Verstehen*, II (1952), 59-78;
T. Maertens, *Jerusalem cité de Dieu* (1954); K. L. Schmidt, "Das Gegenüber von Kirche u.
Staat in d. Gemeinde d. NT," *ThBl*, 16 (1937), 1-16; also "Polis in Kirche u. Welt," *Basler
Rektoratsprogramm* (1939).
[1] Busolt, 153 and n. 2; cf. also C. Schuchhardt, "Hof, Burg u. Stadt bei Germanen u.
Griechen," N. Jbch. Kl. Alt., 11 (1908), 308 f. and O. Schrader-A. Nehring, Art. "Stadt,"
Reallex. d. indogermanischen Altertumskunde[2], II (1929), 433 f.
[2] Thuc., II, 15, 1-4 explains this on the ground that later Athens was founded by a
ξυνοικισμός of the other towns of Attica enforced by Theseus ; the Acropolis was, however, the oldest and at first the only part of the city.

(I, 5, 1). Sparta was not a city, but a complex of four or five open villages, never fortified. [3] A ξυνοικισμός, [4] which was often the beginning of the πόλεις of Greece, was unknown there. Life was lived in the old Hellenic fashion κατὰ κώμας (Thuc., I, 10, 2). Nevertheless, Sparta was a πόλις. "Unfortified towns and even open territories like Laconia are called πόλις as well as fortified cities." [5]

The distinctive element in the word is plain once one notes the distinction from ἄστυ. [6] In the class. period the state is called πόλις rather than ἄστυ because πόλις contained a political sense from the very first while ἄστυ did not. ἄστυ is the town as a spatially defined place of habitation made up of houses, walls and streets. The opposite is the surrounding countryside with κῶμαι or δῆμοι "as they are called with ref. to their inhabitants." [7] πόλις, on the other hand, is the ruling political centre of a given district, or the territory ruled therefrom. [8] The towns subordinate to this are not πόλεις. As a result of geographical relations and historical development the Gk. states are city states, often very small in size. Hence the πόλις is in the first instance the city. When the state becomes more extensive, the πόλις embraces a wider area. The Acropolis in Athens is part of the ἄστυ. But the ἄστυ of the Athenians is also a part of the πόλις. [9] Worth noting is Thuc., VI, 44, 2 : παρεκομίζοντο τὴν 'Ιταλίαν, τῶν μὲν πόλεων οὐ δεχομένων αὐτοὺς ἀγορᾷ οὐδὲ ἄστει. This linguistic distinction is already plain in Hom. (II., 6, 287 ff.; 17, 144; Od., 6, 177 f.), though he not infrequently uses the terms indiscriminately. [10] "The political connection of πόλις is already to some degree the core of Homeric usage." [11]

2. Similarly, the πολίτης is one who shares with others in the πόλις as such, in the πόλις in its political quality, Plat. Prot., 339e; Apol., 37c; Eur. Fr., 360 (TGF, 467, 11 ff.). He is thus a "citizen" (of the town or state) with all the active and passive privileges appertaining thereto and in distinction from resident aliens and slaves, Aristot. Pol., III, 1, p. 1275a, 7 and 22. Thus even apart from women and children the citizens are only one part [12] of the total population.

3. πολιτεύω and the more common mid. come from πολίτης as ἱκετεύω does from ἱκέτης. [13] The word does not occur in Hdt. and is found for the first time only in Thuc. Along the lines of verbs in -εύω, esp. the mid., it means "to be a citizen," "to live as such," "to act as such (by taking part in political life)," "to share in state government," "to rule the state," "to prosecute its business." [14] a. Of life as a citizen, Demosth.,

---

[3] Cf. E. Meyer, Gesch. des Altertums, III (1937), 271 f.

[4] Thuc., II, 15, 2 offers a definition of this word : Theseus καταλύσας τῶν ἄλλων πόλεων τά τε βουλευτήρια καὶ τὰς ἀρχὰς ἐς τὴν νῦν πόλιν οὖσαν, ἓν βουλευτήριον ἀποδείξας καὶ πρυτανεῖον, ξυνῴκισε πάντας. Cf. on this R. Pöhlmann, Gr. Gesch., Hndbch. AW, III, 4⁵ (1914), 59 f.; Busolt, 154-160; Meyer, op. cit., 271, 303.

[5] J. H. H. Schmidt, Synonymik d. gr. Sprache, II (1878), 496. Cf. also E. Kornemann, "Polis und Urbs," Klio, 5 (1905), 77 f.

[6] Fabricius, 1983.

[7] Meyer, op. cit., 271.

[8] This is not to dispute the fact that πόλις was originally the fortified refuge near a manor to which the residents and the population connected therewith would flee in times of danger, cf. esp. Schuchhardt, op. cit. For this stronghold associated with the manor was a given political centre. Linguistically, however, the political element became more and more prominent as compared with the original sense.

[9] Schmidt, op. cit., 500.

[10] For examples cf. Busolt, 154, n. 7.

[11] Schmidt, 498. This is not clear in the older lex. Cf. Etym. Gud., s.v.: πόλις καὶ ἄστυ διαφέρει. πόλις μὲν λέγεται τὸ οἰκοδόμημα, ἄστυ δὲ ἡ κατασκευὴ τῆς πόλεως. πόλις λέγεται τὸ πολίτευμα, ἄστυ δὲ τὸ τεῖχος. — πόλις καὶ ἄστυ διαφέρει, πόλις μὲν ὁ τόπος καὶ οἱ κατοικοῦντες, ἤγουν τῶν συναμφοτέρων· ἄστυ δὲ μόνον ὁ τόπος. Etym. M., s.v.: πόλις σημαίνει δύο· τὰ κτίσματα ... καὶ τὸ πλῆθος καὶ τὸν λαόν.

[12] On the numerical proportions cf. Busolt, 165-169.

[13] Cf. Debr. Gr. Wortb., 106 f.; E. Fraenkel, Gr. Denominativa (1906), 183, 197.

[14] Strictly speaking the act., as in other cases and esp. with words in -εύω, denotes a state in which a man finds himself whereas the mid. denotes the related action or conduct.

18, 184; Xenoph. Hist. Graec., II, 4, 22; Andoc. orat., II, 10. b. Of life in a specific political order, Xenoph. Cyrop., I, 1, 1; Plat. Resp., VIII, 568b; Demosth., 10, 4 : ἐν ἐλευθερίᾳ καὶ νόμοις ἐξ ἴσου πολιτεύεσθαι as compared with ἄρχειν βίᾳ καὶ δουλεύειν
ἑτέρῳ, Aeschin. Tim., 5. c. Of political action, Aristot. Pol., VIII, p. 1324a, 41, where
ἰδιῶται are compared with τοῖς τὰ κοινὰ πράττουσι καὶ πολιτευομένοις, cf. Aeschin.
Tim., 195 ἰδιωτεύοντες and πολιτευόμενοι, Thuc., II, 46, 1: ἄνδρες ἄριστοι πολι-
τεύουσι; Epicurus, on the other hand, thought οὐδὲ πολιτεύσεσθαι τὸν νοῦν ἔχοντα,
he should not be bothered with politics, men mattered to him as little as flies, Epict.
Diss., I, 23, 6. d. Of the direction of politics, the control and use of political power,
Aristot. Pol., IV, 11, p. 1295b, 40; IV, 6, p. 1292b, 26 f.; III, 6, p. 1279a, 37. In the days
of Theseus it could be said of individual places in Attica ἕκαστοι ἐπολίτευον καὶ
ἐβουλεύοντο, they pursued their own politics, Thuc., II, 15, 1: The Lacedaemonians
were concerned σφίσιν αὐτοῖς μόνον ἐπιτηδείως ὅπως πολιτεύσωσι θεραπεύοντες
instead of considering the welfare of allies, Thuc., I, 19; [15] Ditt. Syll.[3], II, 612, 10. e. In
the sense "to rule" : πολιτείαν πολιτεύεσθαι, "to discharge an office," Epict. Diss.,
III, 22, 85; also without πολιτείαν, as often in the pap., where we also find πολιτεύεσθαι πόλεως, e.g., Ἀλεξανδρείας or Ἑρμοῦ πόλεως, "to rule a city." [16] The
word always has, then, a constitutional sense.

In Hesych., s.v. we find πράττει, ἀναστρέφεται. For this diluted sense, which is
known in the NT (e.g., Ac. 23:1) and is common in the fathers, the Platonist Proclus
offers an example in the 5th cent. A.D. [17] The meaning "to walk" occurs also in Macc.
(→ 526, 34 ff.), Jos. (→ n. 66) and Ep. Ar. (→ n. 65). From the pre-Christian era
outside this sphere, however, only one instance of this usage is known : ἐγὼ γὰρ
πιστεύσας σοί τε καὶ τοῖς θεοῖς, πρὸς οὓς ὁσίως καὶ δικαίως πολιτευσάμενος
ἐμαυτὸν ἀμεμψιμοίρητον παρέσχημαι. [18] Here, of course, the ὁσίως καὶ δικαίως
πρὸς τοὺς θεοὺς πολιτεύεσθαι of the writer of the letter stands in antithesis to the
breach of contract (παραβαίνειν τὰ κατὰ τὰς συνθήκας) by the recipient, who is
accused of acting contrary to εὐσέβεια, whereas the writer was directed by religious
reverence in his civic conduct. If we accept the general sense of "walk" here, this isolated
example is rather surprising. [19] Epict. does not use the term in this weak sense, cf.
Diss., I, 23, 6; II, 20, 27; III, 9, 9; 22, 83 and 85. Nor do Plut., Polyb. [20] or other pap. [21]
Here the word can sometimes crop up in commercial dealings ; in such instances πολιτεύεσθαι can mean "to have commercial or business dealings." [22]

πολιτεύω "I am a citizen," πολιτεύομαι "I live and act as a citizen," cf. Kühner-Blass-
Gerth, II, 1, 112; Schwyzer, II, 239.

[15] Cf. also Wilcken Ptol., I, 482, No. 110, 77 f.

[16] For examples cf. Preisigke Wört., III, 141 f.

[17] Cf. R. Hercher, Epistolographi Graeci (1873), 13 : οἶδα μὲν ὡς εὐσεβῶς ζῇς καὶ
σεμνῶς πολιτεύῃ καὶ τῇ τῆς ἀνεπιλήπτου τε καὶ ἁγνῆς πολιτείας ἀρετῇ τὸ περι-
βόητον αὐτὸ τῆς φιλοσοφίας κοσμεῖς ὄνομα.

[18] Cf. Wilcken Ptol., I, 625, No. 144, 12 ff. (2nd cent. B.C.); "πολιτεύεσθαι here refers,
not to civic conduct, but to the walk before the deity," ibid., 627, ad loc.

[19] Wilcken Ptol., I, 627 can give only late instances which were under biblical influence,
from the NT, Ep. Ar., 31 and the fathers.

[20] Cf. J. Schweighaeuser, Polybii Historiae, VIII, 2 Lexicon Polybianum (1795), s.v.

[21] There are no examples to prove that in the koine πολιτεύεσθαι was often a whittled
down expression for private conduct (Loh. Phil., 74; also Mich. Ph. on 1:27; more cautiously
Dib. Ph. on 1:27). The note in Schmidt, Polis, 5, n. 5 that Wettstein on Phil. 1:27 gives
many instances (from Xenoph., Jewish-Hell. authors etc.) of πολιτεύεσθαι in the sense
"to live," "to walk," is misleading. All the examples adduced by Wettstein are from the
Hell.-Jewish or Chr. sphere. In the only exception (Xenoph. Cyrop., I, 1, 1) the word does
not mean "to walk." Nor does it mean this in P. Hibeh, I, 63, 11, where the ref. of πολιτεύεσθαι ἀλλήλοις is to commercial dealings (→ n. 22). Again in the inscr. in Ditt. Syll.[3],
II, 708, 24 f. (end of the 2nd cent. B.C.) εὐσεβέστατα καὶ κάλλιστα πολιτεύεσθαι
refers, not to general conduct, but to public work for the welfare of the city Istropolis.
There remains only the ref. given in → n. 18, cf. Deissmann B, 211. But here the proof of
a pious walk is found primarily in loyalty to an agreement.

[22] Cf. Preisigke Wört. on πολιτεύεσθαι.

4. Plut. De unius in republica dominatione, 2 (II, 826c ff.) gives the following meanings for πολιτεία. 1. μετάληψις τῶν ἐν πόλει δικαίων, 2. βίος ἀνδρὸς πολιτικοῦ καὶ τὰ κοινὰ πράττοντος, 3. μία πρᾶξις εὔστοχος εἰς τὰ κοινά, 4. τάξις καὶ κατάστασις πόλεως διοικοῦσα τὰς πράξεις. The word thus denotes a. the specific quality of the πολίτης, i.e., "citizenship," Hdt., IX, 34 (the only example); cf. Thuc., VI, 104, 2; Ditt. Or., I, 9, 34 of the conferring of citizenship ; 9, 6 of conferred titles of citizenship. b. πολιτεία is also the life of the citizen, life in civil order, esp. participation in state life, political activity in all its forms and stages, Andoc., II, 10; Xenoph. Mem., III, 9, 15; Ditt. Syll.³, I, 495, 173. c. The state order in which the citizen lives, i.e., the constitution : Plat. Resp., VII, 536b; Plat. Tim., 23c; Aristot. Pol., I, 13, p. 1260b, 24; αἱ μεταβολαὶ τῶν πολιτειῶν, IV, 11, p. 1296a, 6. ²³ ὀρθαὶ πολιτεῖαι, namely, βασιλεία, ἀριστοκρατία and πολιτεία in the narrower sense as distinct from παρεκβάσεις, namely, tyranny, oligarchy and democracy, III, 7, p. 1279a, 30 ff. On the concept of πολιτεία in the narrower sense cf. III, 6, p. 1279a, 37: ὅταν τὸ πλῆθος πρὸς τὸ κοινὸν πολιτεύηται συμφέρον, καλεῖται τὸ κοινὸν ὄνομα πασῶν τῶν πολιτειῶν. d. The state as such : Aristot. Pol., I, 13, p. 1260b, 19; IV, 6, p. 1293a, 9; Thuc., I, 127, 3; Plat. Resp., VIII, 68b. The individual city can also be called πολιτεία even though it no longer has any political independence, or has so only in a limited sense, Ditt. Or., II, 441, 103 (imperial period). e. Walk, conduct, Hesych., s.v.: πολιτεία· ἡ πόλις ἢ βίος καὶ ἡ ἀναστροφή· καὶ ἡ πρᾶξις. Cf. Athen., I, 19a; Stob. Ecl., I, 395, 22. ²⁴ But examples of this use are late and few ; it first occurs in the Gk. of Hell. Judaism and then in Chr. writings. Epict. does not have it, nor do Plut., Polyb. or the pap.

5. The word πολίτευμα has many different senses. ²⁵ Nouns in -μα usually denote the result of an action. ²⁶ a. πολίτευμα, found from the 5th cent., is first the result of πολιτεύεσθαι and thus denotes individual "political acts," "dealings," or "machinations," Aeschin. Tim., 86. ²⁷ b. πολίτευμα is then used esp. for acts and departments of the government, Demosth., 18, 109; Plat. Leg., XII, 945d. c. Aristot. likes to use πολίτευμα for the "government" or for those who hold power or have a share in it. These are οἱ ἐν τῷ πολιτεύματι, Pol., V, 1, p. 1301b, 6 ff. ἔστι δὲ πολιτεία (constitution) πόλεως τάξις, τῶν τε ἄλλων ἀρχῶν (authorities, councils) καὶ μάλιστα τῆς κυρίας πάντων. κύριον μὲν γὰρ πανταχοῦ τὸ πολίτευμα (the government) τῆς πόλεως, πολίτευμα δὲ ἐστιν ἡ πολιτεία, Aristot. Pol., III, 6, p. 1278b, 9; cf. III, 7, p. 1279a, 25; III, 13, p. 1283b, 30. d. The latter ref. show the transition to the sense of "constitution," "state," "commonwealth." πόλις, πολιτεία and πολίτευμα thus merge into one another. Instances may be found esp. in Plut. and Polyb. ²⁸ e. "Citizenship" can also be denoted by πολίτευμα. ²⁹ f. A distinctive development in the Hell. period is the use of the term

---

²³ Cf. H. Ryffel, Μεταβολὴ τῶν πολιτειῶν. Der Wandel der Staatsverfassungen. Untersuchungen zu einem Problem der gr. Staatstheorie, Diss. Bern (1949).

²⁴ The ref. adduced by Pr.-Bauer⁴ on πολιτεία: ἕως ἀγανακτήσαντα τὰ στοιχεῖα τῷ μονάρχῳ θεῷ ἐντυχεῖν ἐδοκίμαζον ὑπὲρ τῆς τῶν ἀνθρώπων ἀγρίου πολιτείας (Stob. Ecl., I, 403, 9 ff.), is not pertinent here. It refers to wars, murders, suppression, so that πολιτεία means "political action" rather than "walk," "manner of life."

²⁵ Cf. Fraenkel, op. cit., 228; W. Ruppel, "Politeuma. Bedeutungsgeschichte eines staatsrechtlichen Terminus," Philol., 82 (1927), 268-312, 433-454, where the literary and epigraphical material is assembled and discussed. Cf. also L. Fuchs, Die Juden Aegyptens in ptolemäischer u. römischer Zeit (1924), 79, 86. M. Engers, "Πολίτευμα," Mnemosyne, 54 (1926), 154-161 is important for the use in the pap.

²⁶ Cf. Kühner-Blass-Gerth, I, 2, 272; Debr. Gr. Wortb., 157; Schwyzer, I, 522 : "Later fundamentally nomina rei actae (in contrast to -μός and -σις), they (neuters in -μα) are already used earlier to denote things as well."

²⁷ Further examples in Ruppel, op. cit., 289 f., esp. from Plut.

²⁸ Cf. Ruppel, 275-279, 291. Cf. also Ditt. Or., I, 332 (2nd cent. B.C.), 229, 60 and 72 (3rd cent. B.C.).

²⁹ Examples from the lit. and inscr. in Ruppel, 290, 297 f. Cf. also Engers, op. cit., 154, n. 3. The main instance is Ditt. Syll.³, I, 543, 6 and 32 : ἕως ἂν οὖν καὶ ἑτέρους ἐπινοήσωμεν ἀξίους τοῦ παρ' ὑμῖν πολιτεύματος and Ῥωμαῖοι ... τοὺς οἰκέτας ... προσδεχόμενοι εἰς τὸ πολίτευμα (3rd cent. B.C.).

for "foreign colonies." Thus the Jews in Alexandria were a πολίτευμα, Jos. Ant., 12, 108; Ep. Ar., 310; [30] cf. also the Jews in Berenice/Cyrenaica. [31] We also hear of a πολίτευμα of Cretans in the district of Arsinoe, of Idumaeans in Memphis, and of Caunians in Sidon. [32] These πολιτεύματα are not private associations but publicly recognised national bodies, foreign colonies with specific political rights. This legal form apparently developed esp. under the Ptolemies in consequence of the policy of national intermingling pursued by Alexander and the Diadochi.

II. Ideal Content. [33]

The πόλις, or small Gk. state, has been described as "the most typical phenomenon in ancient Hellenic culture." [34] The significance of the term, however, rested on its ideal content. There was awareness of this. In Prot., Plat. has the well-known Sophist describe "in mythical form" how through the establishment of the πόλις man emerges from a state of cultural uncertainty and treads the path of higher development. [35] This takes place through free union, but is possible only because, apart from the ἔντεχνος σοφία of Hephaestus and Athene which Prometheus gives to men, Zeus through Hermes adds reverence and righteousness αἰδῶ τε καὶ δίκην, ἵν᾽ εἶεν πόλεων κόσμοι τε καὶ δεσμοὶ φιλίας συναγωγοί. These gifts are for all. He who does not have them is to be eliminated as νόσος πόλεως, Prot., 322. The funeral oration of Pericles in honour of the first Athenian victims of the Peloponnesian War (Thuc., II, 35-46), the speech in which "the distinctive national and cultural sense of the Athenians found full literary expression," [36] is sustained by the conviction that the πόλις which is free, but which stands under the authority of the law voluntarily recognised by all its citizens, is the presupposition for the development of all spiritual values, of all cultural achievements, and of all well-being. The national sense lives on in the free subjection of the citizens to the laws which protect the common welfare, each citizen having the task of furthering the whole to the best of his ability, He who stands aside, him οὐκ ἀπράγμονα ἀλλ᾽ ἀχρεῖον νομίζομεν, II, 40, 2. By reason of this national sense, the corresponding order of state, the related conduct, and the resultant development, Athens feels that it is the intellectual leader of Hellas. The life of the πόλις finds its consummation in freedom. All the citizens support it. There is a constant sense of opposition to the tyranny of barbarian peoples, who, being mere objects of the state, obey an alien will, whereas it is of the very essence of the citizen μετέχειν κρίσεως καὶ ἀρχῆς, Aristot. Pol., III, 1, p. 1275a, 22. [37] In this common national life man genuinely comes to himself, to the unfolding of his nature; in the well-known phrase of Aristot. he is a ζῷον φύσει πολιτικόν, Pol., I, 2, p. 1253a, 3; III, 6, p. 1278b, 19. But the life of the πόλις is also consummated in subjection to law, whose authority is encircled by religious awe and cannot be destroyed with impunity. The order of state has a religious sanction. The πόλις is a religious society. Its νόμος "unites church and state." It cannot be imagined without religion and the cultus. It is a "sacral organisation." [38] Its origin is with the supreme God, who not for nothing is called, like Athene, πολιοῦχος, the protector of the state, whose spouse is Themis and whose daughter is Dike. These are the poles around which the concept of the πόλις revolves. Hence Aesch. warns that one should not overturn the δόμος δίκας, the seat of right, but cherish it with the pious awe without which

[30] Cf. on this Fuchs, op. cit., 79 and 86.

[31] CIG, III, 5361, 21 f.; cf. Schürer, III⁴, 79 f.

[32] Cf. Ditt. Or., II, 592, 1; 658, 3; 737, 3 and 19. There has been much discussion of the character of these πολιτεύματα, cf. Engers, 155 and Ruppel, 299-306, with bibl.

[33] W. Otto, Kulturgeschichte des Altertums (1925), 90.

[34] F. Baumgarten, F. Poland, R. Wagner, Die hell.-röm. Kultur (1913), 13 f.

[35] Plato in Resp., II, 369/370 shows how the state grew out of a ξυνοικία which was based on the need and possibility of mutual help, and how increasing cultural development was the result.

[36] Kaerst, 37.

[37] Thus for Aristot. the kingdom of Philip was no more a state than that of Darius, Wilamowitz-Moellendorff, Staat, 25.

[38] Pohlenz, Staatsgedanke, 10; J. Heinemann, Philons gr. u. jüd. Bildung (1932), 431, n. 2.

neither the society of the πόλις nor the individual ἔτ' ἂν σέβοι δίκαν, has regard to the right, Eum., 516 ff. The full ideal is described in Eum., 695-699 :

> Let no man live
> Uncurbed by law nor curbed by tyranny,
> Nor banish ye the monarchy of awe
> Beyond the walls ; untouched by fear divine
> No man doth justice in the world of men. [39]

The fact that the political reality did not correspond to the ideal content of Gk. thinking on the state, that rational criticism, such as that of the Sophists, overthrew the religious foundations of this thinking, that egoistic individualism, the democratic surrender of the state to the masses and their instincts, the war of parties as the champions of business interests all conspired to destroy the state, since the ruling clique identified itself with the state, and furthermore that this concept of the state, even in Plat. and Aristot., remained confined within the cantonal limits of the city state, this was the tragedy of Gk. history. [40]

The cantonal limits of this thinking — and beyond these the national limits — were transcended, not by the theoreticians, but by the march of events, by the gt. historical figures, by Alexander and Rome. Stoicism, and indeed its founder Zeno, who was born about the year when Alexander came to the throne, provided the theory for this in his πολιτεία. This interrelation found acceptance already in antiquity. Plut. says that the much admired πολιτεία of Zeno was designed to overcome national particularism, ἵνα ... πάντας ἀνθρώπους ἡγώμεθα δημότας καὶ πολίτας, εἷς δὲ βίος ᾖ καὶ κόσμος, ὥσπερ ἀγέλης συννόμου νόμῳ κοινῷ συντρεφομένης. τοῦτο Ζήνων μὲν ἔγραψεν ὥσπερ ὄναρ ἢ εἴδωλον εὐνομίας φιλοσόφου καὶ πολιτείας ἀνατυπωσά-μενος. Ἀλέξανδρος δὲ τῷ λόγῳ τὸ ἔργον παρέσχεν, Alex. Fort. Virt., I, 6 (II, 329b). Aristot. advised Alexander to act ἡγεμονικῶς with the Hellenes and δεσποτικῶς with the barbarians. But Alexander would not do this. He preferred κοινὸς ἥκειν θεόθεν ἁρμοστὴς καὶ διαλλακτὴς τῶν ὅλων νομίζων, ... ὥσπερ ἐν κρατῆρι φιλοτησίῳ ... to mix τοὺς βίους καὶ τὰ ἤθη. πατρίδα μὲν τὴν οἰκουμένην προσέ-ταξεν ἡγεῖσθαι πάντας, ἀκρόπολιν δὲ καὶ φρουρὰν τὸ στρατόπεδον, συγγενεῖς δὲ τοὺς ἀγαθούς, ἀλλοφύλους δὲ τοὺς πονηρούς· τὸ δ' Ἑλληνικὸν καὶ βαρβαρι-κὸν μὴ χλαμύδι μηδὲ πέλτῃ ... διορίζειν, ἀλλὰ τὸ μὲν Ἑλληνικὸν ἀρετῇ, τὸ δὲ βαρβαρικὸν κακίᾳ τεκμαίρεσθαι (loc. cit.). This is the consistent theory of the ideal world kingdom which transcends all historical and natural limitations. The ideas of Zeno were in keeping herewith, but in such a way that they left all reality behind and described the state as the fellowship of the wise which is so ordered by the universal reason which governs all things that it does not need the usual legal and social in-stitutions — "a pure phantasmagoria." [41] In the unrealistic abstraction of its thought Stoicism hits upon the most eccentric ideas, and its followers naturally found it difficult to apply them to the concrete work of politics, Plut. Stoic. Rep., 2 (II, 1033b ff.) even when they did not argue for political withdrawal in the fatal manner of Chrysipp.: διότι εἰ μὲν πονηρὰ πολιτεύεται, τοῖς θεοῖς ἀπαρέσει· εἰ δὲ χρηστά, τοῖς πολί-ταις, Fr., 699 (v. Arnim, III, 174, 26 ff.). There is a complete loss of any relation to the actualities of politics when cosmopolitanism in the strict sense is advocated by the Stoics. One cannot speak of this in relation to the thinking mentioned above, which simply extends the limits of the state until a universal state is reached. But it is present when Stoicism parts company with all empirical politics but still uses the concept πόλις

---

[39] J. G. Droysen and W. Nestle, *Aischylos. Die Tragödien u. Fr.* (1944), 327. Further examples from the poets and philosophers cannot be given here. The strong moral content of the Gk. view of the state has been impressively described by Kaerst, 1-52. Cf. also Bultmann, *Verständnis.*

[40] Cf. R. Pöhlmann, *Gesch. d. antiken Kommunismus u. Sozialismus,* I (1893), 269-476; A. Dyroff, *Ethik der alten Stoa* (1897), 215.

[41] Pöhlmann, *op. cit.* (→ n. 40), 617; E. Zeller, *Philosophie d. Griechen,* III, 1⁴ (1909), 302; Dyroff, *op. cit.,* 213-216.

to clarify the interrelationship of the cosmos as a totality which is governed by a single divine law, and to clarify also its own position within this totality.[42]

History had left the ancient Gk. πόλις behind. When the thing itself vanished, the concept lost its vividness and vitality. It became bloodless, and fell victim to philosophical spiritualising. The very thought itself dissolved in cosmopolitanism.

B. πόλις κτλ. in the Septuagint and Later Judaism.

With the move from non-biblical to biblical Gk. there is a pronounced change of climate. This is reflected in the statistics. πόλις is still found at every turn. But πολιτεία, πολίτευμα, πολιτεύομαι are found only a few times in 2-4 Macc., πολίτευμα only once, πολιτεύεσθαι once also in Est. 8:12 p. Except in 2 and 3 Macc. even πολίτης occurs only half-a-dozen times in various books of the Palestinian Canon, where it is an inexact term for Heb. words denoting the neighbour or fellow-countryman. The many derivates and compounds in the Gk. lex.[43] do not occur at all apart from πολιορκεῖν and πολιορκία. In respect of πόλις the theoretical content is unmistakably quite different from what is found in the non-biblical world.

I. πόλις.

1. Hebrew Originals. In the LXX πόλις is usually the transl. of עִיר. With few exceptions this is always rendered πόλις. ἄστυ does not occur in the LXX (or the NT). There is no need to differentiate between πόλις and ἄστυ. In Is. 22:9 עִיר־דָּוִד is transl. ἡ ἄκρα Δαυιδ; this is correct, but unusual as compared with the customary ἡ πόλις Δαυιδ. Occasionally LXX has κώμη, Jos. 10:39; 1 Ch. 27:25; 2 Ch. 14:13; Is. 42:11. The translators seem to be indicating that the ref. here is not to towns, though they do not take this into account in every instance where called for. In Jer. 19:15 עִיר is not transl. κώμη,[44] but the LXX found a ref. to villages as well as towns in its copy; עִיר is rendered πόλις. עִיר הַמַּמְלָכָה in Jos. 10:2 is (not very accurately) transl. μητρόπολις. There is no Heb. original for the μητρόπολις of Est. 9:19. In over 100 of its full 1500 occurrences πόλις is used for other terms than עִיר, esp. קִרְיָה and שְׁעָרִים, cf. Dt. 14:21. As concerns the use of πόλις in the LXX, however, these and other secondary features are of no significance. The use is controlled by that of עִיר.

This is much more comprehensive than the word "town" and embraces any fortified place. The Israelites set up high places for sacrifice בְּכָל־עָרֵיהֶם מִמִּגְדַּל נוֹצְרִים עַד־עִיר מִבְצָר, 2 K. 17:9. The watch-tower is also a עִיר. Hence the fortress of Zion מְצֻדַת צִיּוֹן can be described as עִיר דָּוִד (ἡ πόλις Δαυιδ 2 S. 5:7, 9). Such a fortress is also in view in the עִיר עֲמָלֵק of 1 S. 15:5, though the LXX has the plur. πόλεις Αμαληκ. In Nu. 13:19 מִבְצָרִים πόλεις τειχήρεις LXX (fortified places) and מַחֲנִים πόλεις ἀτείχιστοι LXX (camps) seem to be included in the concept עָרִים πόλεις. In 1 Ch. 4:32 certain חֲצֵרִים ἐπαύλεις (villages or farmsteads) are later called עָרִים πόλεις. In 2 S. 12:27 a part of Rabbah is called עִיר הַמָּיִם ἡ πόλις τῶν ὑδάτων ("city of waters"). Acc. to what became customary usage, however, עִיר is a walled town. In contrast the country is שָׂדֶה ἀγρός in Dt. 28:3, 16, while the pasture belonging to the town is מִגְרָשׁ τὰ ἀφωρισμένα in Jos. 21:21 ff. or τὰ περισπόρια in Jos. 21:36; the surrounding villages are חֲצֵרִים κῶμαι or ἐπαύλεις in Jos. 15:32, 54, those related to the μητρόπολις being called "daughters" in Nu. 21:25, 32; 32:42; 2 S. 20:19; Neh. 11:25;[45] cf. also עִיר מִבְצָר

---

[42] Cf. Clem. Al. Strom., IV, 172, 2; Plut. Comm. Not., 34 (II, 1076 f.); Epict. Diss., II, 5, 26; 10, 3; Sen. De otio, 4, 1; Dio Chrys. Or., 36, 22 f.; M. Ant., VI, 44. Chrysipp. in H. Diels, Doxographi Graeci (1929), 465, 14; on this Dyroff, 215 and n. 2.

[43] For a list cf. Schmidt, Polis, 1-11.

[44] So Hatch-Redp., s.v. κώμη and s.v. עִיר (Suppl., 254d).

[45] Cf. P. Volz, Bibl. Altertümer (1914), 446-449; R. Kittel, Gesch. d. Volkes Israel, II⁶ (1925), 44-48, 170-178.

πόλις ἐστερεωμένη as compared with כְּפַר הַפְּרָזִי in 1 S. 6:18 and עָרִים בְּצֻרוֹת πόλεις ὀχυραί as compared with עָרֵי הַפְּרָזִי in Dt. 3:5, though in both verses the LXX misread the latter phrase as a proper name and imported the Perizzites into the text (κώμη τοῦ Φερεζαίου or πόλεις τῶν Φερεζαίων). The text, however, has in view unprotected country places, villages. In 1 S. 27:5 Gath as עִיר הַמַּמְלָכָה (πόλις βασιλευομένη LXX = residence) is contrasted with עָרֵי הַשָּׂדֶה (πόλεις κατ' ἀγρόν LXX = country towns).

2. Description of Cities. Cities are described not only by their names but also acc. to the locality or district in which they lie (e.g., Gn. 13:12; Nu. 32:26), acc. to the peoples to whose territory they belong (e.g., Nu. 21:25; 31:10; 2 Ch. 17:7), acc. to individuals who reside there (e.g., Gn. 23:10; 1 S. 8:22; cf. 2 Εσδρ. 2:1, 70), acc. to the clan which has its seat there (1 S. 20:6), or acc. to special features (Dt. 34:3; 1 S. 22:19; Nu. 35:28 or 35:6; 2 Ch. 8:6), but never acc. to the form of constitution. [46]

3. Importance of Cities. Acc. to the judgment of the Israelites cities were not significant as cultural centres, nor for the advanced forms of civic government and law developed there, nor because the city is the basic form of the state. Whereas in Gk. literature the senses "city" and "state" continually intertwine — the unavoidable result of the political history of Hellas — the question never arises in the OT whether πόλις should be rendered "state." For Oriental states are kingdoms, and hence the Jewish word for state is מַמְלָכָה.[47] There is in the OT no trace whatever of the world of ideas which the Gks. associated with πόλις. Paradoxical though it may sound, πόλις is "de-politicised" in the LXX. Its specific content has been lost, for the thing which the Gk. had in view when he spoke of the πόλις is no longer present. As one may see from the list of the 31 conquered kings of West Jordan in Jos. 12:7 ff. and from Ju. 9:2 ff., the cities of the Canaanites were political miniatures dynastically governed. In the cities of Israel power was in the hands of an aristocratic class, the elders (Ju. 9:2; 8:14; 1 S. 11:3; 16:4; the "lords of the city" בְּעָלִים [LXX inaccurately ἄνδρες] Ju. 9:2, 18, 23 f.; 1 S. 23:11, headed sometimes by a שַׂר הָעִיר ἄρχων τῆς πόλεως Ju. 9:30). The importance of cities lay in the resistance they could offer to aggressors because of their fortifications, in the protection they could give to their inhabitants. The terrifying effect of the heaven-high walls of the Canaanite cities on the nomadic tribes of Israel is plainly to be discerned in Nu. 13:19; Dt. 1:28; 9:1; Jos. 14:12.[48] The conquest of strongholds like Jericho seemed like a miracle to men of a later time (Jos. 6). The fact that in the conquest the πόλεις ὀχυραί, τείχη ὑψηλά, πύλαι καὶ μοχλοί (Dt. 3:5) could not withstand the Israelites was constantly emphasised with grateful pride, cf. Nu. 21:25; 31:10; Jos. 11:12; 2 K. 3:19. Steps were soon taken to restore the shattered cities or to found them afresh, e.g., Nu. 32:16, 24, 34, 38, 42; Ju. 1:26. Even Jericho rose again, 1 K. 16:34. Once settled in the land, Israel could not do without the protection of cities and placed its confidence in them, Dt. 28:52. Both concepts, the battlemented fortress which is hard to take and the fortress under whose protection one may feel secure, live on in proverbial expressions. "To walk on the battlements of the city" in Sir. 9:13 is a figure of speech for the insecurity of an adopted position; he who controls his anger is stronger than he who takes a city, Prv. 16:32; a wise man scales πόλεις ὀχυράς, Prv. 21:22, cf. Qoh. 9:13 f. Again, a man who does not act μετὰ βουλῆς is like a πόλις ἀτείχιστος, Prv. 25:28; the rich man feels safe in his posessions as under the protection of a strong city, Prv. 10:15. In contrast, Job 6:20 LXX insists that οἱ ἐπὶ πόλεσιν καὶ χρήμασιν πεποιθότες will be confounded. In the great prophetic admonition of Dt. 28 it is declared to disobedient Israel that even the high and strong walls of its cities, ἐφ' οἷς σὺ πέποιθας ἐπ' αὐτοῖς, will not protect it against judgment, v. 52. Gn. 11 speaks of the building of the city in the

---

[46] The words ἀριστοκρατία, δημοκρατία, ὀχλοκρατία do not occur in the LXX. Τυραννίς occurs in the Gk. apocr. a few times, but not in combination with πόλις.

[47] Cf. Heinemann, op. cit., 185.

[48] Cf. A. Bertholet, Kulturgeschichte Israels (1919), 34 f.

land of Shinar, and of its tower, as a sign of the ungodly arrogance of man. The righteous man knows, however, that all the attempts of self-reliant man to find security are in vain: ἐὰν μὴ κύριος φυλάξῃ πόλιν, εἰς μάτην ἠγρύπνησεν ὁ φυλάσσων, ψ 126:1.

4. Jerusalem. The city in view in such ref. is always Jerusalem. This has unique significance among all the cities of Israel. [49] It is *the* city, Ez. 7:23. It is true that acc. to the saying of Joab, David's captain, all the cities of Israel are πόλεις τοῦ θεοῦ ἡμῶν, 2 Βασ. 10:12. Nevertheless, Jerusalem is this in a special sense, for this is the place which God has chosen to cause His name to dwell there (Dt. 12:5, 11; 14:24), to be the site of worship and sacrifice. As the LXX puts it, deviating from the Mas. in all 3 passages, God has chosen the place ἐκεῖ ἐπικληθῆναι τὸ ὄνομα αὐτοῦ, → V, 256, 17 ff., 263, 22 ff. [50] As 2 Ch. 6:38 succinctly says, Jerusalem is "the city which thou hast chosen." Hence it is towards this city ὁδὸν τῆς πόλεως ἧς ἐξελέξω ἐν αὐτῇ that the army of Israel prays when it has gone out to battle, 3 Βασ. 8:44. Jerusalem is called the city of God (Ps. 46:4; 48:1, 8; 87:3; Da. 3:28; 9:16), or the city of the gt. king (Ps. 48:2) or of the κύριος or κύριος τῶν δυνάμεων (Is. 60:14; ψ 47:9; 100:8) or of the Holy One (Tob. 13:9). It is often described, then, as the holy city, Is. 48:2; 52:1; 66:20; Neh. 11:1; Da. 9:24 Θ; 1 Macc. 2:7; 2 Macc. 1:12; 3:1; 9:14; Jos. Ant., 4, 70; 20, 118; Ap., 1, 282; Philo Som., II, 246. How well-established this became may be seen from the inscriptions on coins. [51] In Sir. 49:6 cf. 36:12 ἐκλεκτὴ πόλις ἁγιάσματος is used for Jerusalem. For the righteous of the OT this Jerusalem became more and more the symbol both of religious faith and also of national independence and greatness, and they set their whole affection on it: πόλις κυρίου Σιων ἁγίου Ισραηλ, Is. 60:14.

Naturally the conduct of the citizens in no way corresponded to the ideal character of the city. As the cisterns hold its water fresh, so does Jerusalem its wickedness, Jer. 6:7. Thus there are constant prophetic declarations of judgment on this city of blood-guiltiness and idolatry, Ez. 22:2-4. Its devastation is imminent. In all the seriousness of judgment, however, there still echoes the confident expectation of a new and better Jerusalem. [52] God established this city εἰς τὸν αἰῶνα, ψ 47:9 and He loves this foundation of His more than all the dwellings of Jacob, Ps. 87:1 f. Though it be destroyed, the time will come καὶ οἰκοδομηθήσεται πόλις τῷ κυρίῳ, Ιερ. 38(31):38. One day Jerusalem will be called πόλις δικαιοσύνης, μητρόπολις πιστὴ Σιων, Is. 1:26 (Zion in v. 27 Mas.). My people will dwell ἐν πόλει εἰρήνης, Is. 32:18. It will be called πόλις κυρίου Σιων ἁγίου Ισραηλ, Is. 60:14. καὶ ἔσται Ιερουσαλημ πόλις ἁγία, καὶ ἀλλογενεῖς οὐ διελεύσονται δι' αὐτῆς οὐκέτι, Jl. 3:17. The Lord whose glory has left Jerusalem acc. to Ez. 11:23 will come back again and set up His tent in the midst thereof, and Jerusalem will be called πόλις ἡ ἀληθινή, Zech. 8:3. Only because of the sins of the inhabitants has God been angry with this city for a brief time, 2 Macc. 5:17. In this concept of a restored Jerusalem are concentrated all the hopes of salvation, religious,

---

[49] On Jerusalem cf. G. Dalman, "Jerusalem u. sein Gelände," BFTh, 2, 19 (1930), 284, 285; J. Simons, *Jerusalem in the OT* (1952). For the way in which, in defiance of its geographical situation, Jerusalem acquired this (primarily political) importance through an act of David based on political considerations, cf. A. Alt, "Jerusalems Aufstieg," ZDMG, 79 (1925), 1-19.

[50] With no mention of causing His name to dwell there. But cf. 3 Βασ. 9:3: The Lord has sanctified the temple, τοῦ θέσθαι τὸ ὄνομά μου ἐκεῖ εἰς τὸν αἰῶνα, and 11:36 ἐν Ιερουσαλημ τῇ πόλει, ἣν ἐξελεξάμην ἐμαυτῷ τοῦ θέσθαι ὄνομά μου ἐκεῖ, and 4 Βασ. 21:4 ἐν Ιερουσαλημ θήσω τὸ ὄνομά μου. Yet we find the same deviation from the Mas. in 2 Ch. 12:13.

[51] Str.-B., I, 150; Schürer, I, 762. Worth noting is that Jos. and Philo have ἱερὰ πόλις rather than the ἁγία πόλις of the bibl. authors. The adj. ἱερός is almost never used in the LXX; it comes in only in the Hell. works 1 Εσδρ. and Macc. Obviously the LXX translators regarded ἱερός as too freighted with pagan cultic ideas to be a possible rendering of קֹדֶשׁ, → ἱερός, III, 226-229. The usage of Jos. and Philo is to be seen as a Hell. concession.

[52] Cf. also on what follows A. Causse, "Le mythe de la nouvelle Jérusalem du Dt.-Esaie à la IIIe Sibylle," RevHPhR, 18 (1938), 377-414.

but also national and political, as may be seen from Jl. 3:17; Is. 60; Zech. 2:9 ff.; Hag. 2:7 ff. If the OT idea of the πόλις does not have the distinctively Gk. political content, in its focus on the future Jerusalem it combines with eschatological expectations for which there are no par. in Gk. thought. Gk. thought is bound to immanence in a way which is not true of the prophetic thought of the OT. The latter can reach beyond history to a final change which is brought about by the miracle of God. It has a hope, even though this is not yet the hope of the NT.

5. Jerusalem in the Hope of Later Judaism. In later Judaism [53] these OT ideas continue to flourish. The future hope of a restored Jerusalem is sustained by the fourteenth petition of the daily Prayer of Eighteen Benedictions, which in the Pal. version begins : "In thy great mercy, O Lord our God, have mercy on thy people Israel and on thy city Jerusalem, on Zion the dwelling-place of thy glory, on thy temple and on thy dwelling." [54] This petition is regarded as so important that the short prayer of Haᵇhinenu, which served as a substitute for the long Eighteen Benedictions, refers in both its Pal. and Bab. versions to "all who trust in thee and rejoice in the building of thy city and the restoration of the house of thy sanctuary." [55] There are similar statements in contemporary sources. Worth noting is the fact that the restoration of the city is always linked with that of the temple and its worship. Sir. prays : "Have mercy on the city of thy sanctuary οἰκτίρησον πόλιν ἁγιάσματός σου, Ιερουσαλημ τόπον καταπαύματός σου, πλῆσον Σιων ἀρεταλογίας σου καὶ ἀπὸ τῆς δόξης σου τὸν ναόν σου, 36:12 f. [56]

The more hopeless the present situation seems, the loftier is the expectation. The future Jerusalem is not built with earthly implements. It comes down from heaven. It is already prepared there from the very beginning and will be kept in heaven to be manifested already from time to time to selected righteous individuals during the course of earthly history.

Similarly, in the visions of 4 Esr. Zion is a city of glory which is as yet invisible to the human eye but which is already built and which will appear and be manifest to all, 7:26; 8:52; 10:27, 54-59; 13:36. The Lord will "purify in sanctification" (καθαριεῖ ἐν ἁγιασμῷ) this future Jerusalem, as at the first, Ps. Sol. 17:30, 27; Jub. 50:5. This does not mean only that no one who knows wickedness will dwell therein but that no ἀπερίτμητος or ἀκάθαρτος will enter the holy city, cf. already Is. 52:1. Ps. Sol. also has in view that πάροικος καὶ ἀλλογενὴς οὐ παροικήσει αὐτοῖς ἔτι (17:28b) — an expectation of complete exclusiveness which is hardly compatible with the hope of a conversion of the Gentiles to the God of Israel. In face of this hope, however, the nationalistic wing had the upper hand. [57] In this Jerusalem the Creator will dwell (Sib., III, 787), and the Rabb. also proclaim that the shᵉkhina will find its eternal resting-place in the new Jerusalem, and that all Israelites will see it. [58] This does not mean, however, that there will not be a temple with its worship in this new Jerusalem of the time of salvation. The only pt. is that this temple will be infinitely more glorious than was the temple in the historical Jerusalem. [59]

II. πολίτης, πολιτεία, πολιτεύομαι, πολίτευμα in the OT.

With the exception of πολίτης these words do not occur at all in the OT writings except in 2-4 Macc. and πολιτεύομαι once in the LXX additions to Est. Here, in the edict of Artaxerxes in favour of the Jews appended after 8:12 LXX, we read that the Jews are not malefactors but δικαιοτάτοις πολιτευόμενοι νόμοις, v. 12 p.

---

[53] Cf. Bousset-Gressm., 242-286; Volz Esch., 371-376; Weber, 390-400.

[54] W. Staerk, "Altjüd. liturgische Gebete," KlT, 58 (1910), 13. The form of the text does not force us to assume that it was composed only after the destruction of Jerusalem by Titus. Cf. on this Bousset-Gressm., 177.

[55] Staerk, op. cit., 20.

[56] We are to read ναόν with the Syr. (rather than λαόν with the Gk.), cf. V. Ryssel, ad loc. (Kautzsch Apkr. u. Pseudepigr.), who also refers to 49:12 and 50:5.

[57] Examples in Str.-B., III, 144 f., 153-155 on R. 3:9.

[58] Examples ibid., IV, 923-925.

[59] Examples ibid., IV, 884 f., 929-937. For further bibl. on the "heavenly Jerusalem" cf. Ltzm. Gl. on 4:25 and Rgg. Hb. on 11:10 and 356, n. 17.

1. The word πολίτης occurs 9 times in 2 Macc., once in 3 Macc., and only 7 times in the rest of the OT. [60] It is normally used there for רֵעַ, the "neighbour" (→ πλησίον 311-318) of one's own people (Jer. 29:23; 31:34; Prv. 11:9, 12; 24:28), and once each for עָמִית and בְּנֵי עַמִּי, again in the sense of compatriot or co-religionist, → 313, 12 ff. [61] πολίτης is never a true equivalent of the Heb. original. It has a political and legal colouring, whereas the Heb. word belongs to the sphere of social ethics and religion. Neither term can reproduce the specific element in the other. This is naturally no accident. It is based on the fact already mentioned that the Gk. world of ideas at the heart of which the Gk. words are used is alien to the OT. In Macc. πολίτης corresponds to the רֵעַ of the 7 OT passages mentioned. It means "fellow-citizen" or, better, "compatriot" rather than citizen, cf. 2 Macc. 4:5, 50; 14:8; 15:30; with particular clarity 2 Macc. 5:6, where Jason instigates a slaughter τῶν πολιτῶν τῶν ἰδίων, for which συγγενεῖς and ὁμοεθνεῖς are also used. Only in 2 Macc. 9:19 and 3 Macc. 1:22 does it have the meaning "citizen," as ἰσοπολίτης means equality of civil rights in 3 Macc. 2:30. Apart from a few passages the Gk. terms are thus thoroughly Hebraised in these writings. They also lose their political flavour.

2. Similarly, πολιτεία does not mean civil rights, constitution, or state. The προγονικὴ πολιτεία of 2 Macc. 8:17 is rather the pious order of life which, ordained by the Law of Moses, is inherited from the fathers, and which Judas Maccabaeus fights to preserve. Antiochus Epiphanes, on the other hand, wanted τὴν Ἑβραίων πολιτείαν καταλῦσαι, 4 Macc. 17:9. When it is said of the high-priest Jason (2 Macc. 4:11) that he τὰς ... νομίμους καταλύων πολιτείας παρανόμους ἐθισμοὺς ἐκαίνιζεν, newly introduced customs which were against the Law, the meaning is not that "he abolished legal institutions," [62] e.g., the constitution and civil rights, but that he undermined the legal orders of practical piety by promoting Hellenisation. Cf. also 4 Macc. 8:7: The Jews should hold leading positions in the state ἀρνησάμενοι τὸν πάτριον ὑμῶν τῆς πολιτείας θεσμόν, and 4:19: the high-priest Jason ἐξεδιῄτησεν τὸ ἔθνος καὶ ἐξεπολίτευσεν ἐπὶ πᾶσαν παρανομίαν, i.e., he brought it about that the people abandoned the previous way of legal piety. In all cases πολιτεία here is a religious and moral concept rather than a political concept ; it denotes the "walk" determined by the Mosaic Law. Only in 3 Macc. 3:21, 23 is πολιτεία used in the sense of civil rights, ἡ πολιτεία Ἀλεξανδρέων, ἡ ἀτίμητος πολιτεία. The πολιτεία of 2 Macc. is ἐμβίωσις in 3 Macc. 3:23.

3. Furthermore in these works πολιτεύομαι always means "to walk" rather than "to be a citizen," "to rule the state," cf. τοῖς τοῦ θεοῦ νόμοις πολιτεύεσθαι, 2 Macc. 6:1; 3 Macc. 3:4; πολιτεύεσθαι κατὰ τὰ ἐπὶ τῶν προγόνων αὐτῶν ἔθη, 2 Macc. 11:25; τῷ νόμῳ or κατὰ νόμον πολιτεύεσθαι, 4 Macc. 2:8, 23. Eleazar seeks θείῳ νόμῳ πολιτεύεσθαι, part of which is not to eat swine's flesh, 4 Macc. 5:16. Est. 8:12 (→ 525, 43 f.) is also to be construed thus. The ref. is always, not to political rights, to their distribution and exercise in the state, but to religion. This religion, however, is a law which by its many precepts regulates both the life of society and also the conduct of the individual ; as a religious order of life it confers a specific character on the whole "walk." One may thus understand why the terms πολιτεία and πολιτεύεσθαι lose their flavour at the pt. where Hellenism and Judaism meet. This is because the society to which the Jew belongs, in consequence of the totalitarian religious claim, bears a different character from that of the society in which these words have their true home. Since membership of this society finds expression in the whole of conduct, the words take on the sense of "walk." This is a specific feature of Hell. Jewish usage which is also attested in Aristeas and Jos. and even on inscr. (→ n. 65).

---

[60] In Nu. 4:18 πολιτῶν Β* is a slip for Λευιτῶν.

[61] It may be expressly noted that the familiar ψ 38:13 ("I am a stranger with thee, and a sojourner, as all my fathers were") has the more accurate Gk. transl. : πάροικος (גֵּר) ἐγώ εἰμι παρὰ σοὶ καὶ παρεπίδημος (תּוֹשָׁב).

[62] So A. Kamphausen in Kautzsch Apkr. u. Pseudepigr., transl. ad loc.

4. πολίτευμα occurs only in 2 Macc. 12:7, where it has the sense of "commonwealth." Judas Macc. seeks τῶν 'Ιοππιτῶν ἐκριζῶσαι πολίτευμα.

III. Josephus and Philo.

1. A first difference between Jos. [63] and LXX is to be found in the rich use which Jos. makes of the terms πολιτεία, πολίτευμα, πολιτεύομαι with ref. to the interrelations and history of Israel. God ordained for the people through Moses διάταξιν πολιτείας or πολιτείας κόσμον, Ant., 4, 45; 3, 84. He gave it a political order, a constitution. πολιτεία also means civil rights. The Alexandrian Jews have ἴσην πολιτείαν like other residents (Ant., 19, 281); those living in Antioch are called 'Αντιοχεῖς because Seleucus τὴν πολιτείαν αὐτοῖς ἔδωκεν, Ap., 2, 39; cf. Ant., 12, 119. Jos. is fond of πολίτευμα as well as πολιτεία. He seeks to depict ἅπασαν τὴν παρ' ἡμῖν ἀρχαιολογίαν καὶ διάταξιν τοῦ πολιτεύματος, Ant., 1, 5. What he has in mind is the order of the commonwealth and also life in this commonwealth as controlled by the basic νομοθεσία, cf. Ap., 2, 145. The Jews thanked Ezra for the setting aside τῶν περὶ τὸ πολίτευμα παρανομηθέντων, of all the things in the social order which contradicted the Law, Ant., 11, 157. πολιτευμάτων μεταβολαί are revolutions, Ant., 1, 13. The Jews living in a particular place, e.g., Alexandria, are also a πολίτευμα, Ant., 12, 108. πολιτεύομαι means "to take part in public life." Jos. began πολιτεύεσθαι, τῇ Φαρισαίων αἱρέσει κατακολουθῶν, [64] Vit., 12, cf. Vit., 262 : περὶ τῶν ἐμοὶ πεπολιτευμένων, Ant., 12, 38 : the Gk. historians do not take note τῶν κατ' αὐτὴν (τὴν τοῦ Μωϋσέως νομοθεσίαν) πολιτευσαμένων ἀνδρῶν, cf. also Ant., 15, 263; 17, 16. πολιτεύεσθαι can also mean "to direct the state," as, e.g., Moses did, Ant., 4, 46. But sometimes the word can lose its political sense and mean "to conduct oneself," "to walk." Though the ref. in Vit., 12 are not examples of this, one may refer to the expression πολιτεύεσθαι κατὰ τοὺς πατρίους νόμους in Ant., 12, 142. For this has in view only a mode of life controlled by religious statutes. [65]

Jos. is a political Hellenist. Expressions taken from the political sphere will, he hopes, help his Graeco-Roman public to penetrate the alien world of Israel and Judah. He has a clear sense, however, that the distinctive elements cannot be properly known in this way. This is shown by the observation in Ap., 2, 164 f.: ἐξουσία τῶν πολιτευμάτων, power over political societies, is in different hands among the different peoples ; "our lawgiver" however, to use a bold expression, established the state as a theocracy ὁ δ' ἡμέτερος νομοθέτης, ... ὡς δ' ἄν τις εἴποι βιασάμενος τὸν λόγον, θεοκρατίαν ἀπέδειξε τὸ πολίτευμα, θεῷ τὴν ἀρχὴν καὶ τὸ κράτος ἀναθείς. Among the Jews everything is orientated to εὐσέβεια, ὥσπερ ... τελετῆς τινος τῆς ὅλης πολιτείας οἰκονομουμένης, Ap., 2, 188. The use of terms taken from the political sphere is calculated to conceal the religious orientation of the political thought of Israel. Connected herewith is the material deviation of Jos. from the spirit of the OT, which consists in the fact that he suppresses the whole group of ideas revolving around the hope of a new and better Jerusalem as the mid-point of a religio-political age of salvation. Jos. sacrificed the Messianic hope for the sake of peace with Rome. He applies to Vespasian the χρησμὸς ἀμφίβολος, the ambiguous oracle about a future world ruler (Da. 2), which played a fateful role on the outbreak of the Vespasian war, since it had been interpreted of an Israelite, cf. Bell., 6, 312 f.; Ant., 10, 210 and 280. Messianic eschatology was thus transferred to the political present, i.e., it was surrendered. The vision of the new Jerusalem faded.

---

[63] Cf. Schl. Theol. d. Judt., 89 f., 252-263; G. Hölscher, Art. "Jos." in Pauly-W., 9 (1916), 1934-2000.

[64] In Pr.-Bauer⁴ s.v. πολιτεύομαι this passage is erroneously adduced as an example of "to lead his life," "to behave," "to walk."

[65] On the usage cf. Ep. Ar., 31 and the foundation inscr. of the synagogue in Stobi, where it is said of the founder that he is πολιτευσάμενος πᾶσαν πολιτείαν κατὰ τὸν 'Ιουδαϊσμόν. Cf. H. Lietzmann, "Die Synagogeninschr. in Stobi," ZNW, 32 (1933), 93-95, who dates it in the 2nd or 3rd cent. A.D.; also E. Sukenik, Ancient Synagogues in Palestine and Greece (1934), 79 f., 81, n. 1: "This expression seems ... to have been favoured among Jewish writers for designating Jewish life according to the Jewish Law."

2. In a different way the same thing happens in the case of the philosophical Hellenist Philo. [66] Though he, too, is no stranger to the use of the words in the ordinary political sense, this is not the distinctive aspect in Philo. The distinctive aspect is the philosophical, spiritualising transposition. A passage which is particularly characteristic of his mode of thought is Op. Mund., 142-144 : Adam is not just the first man but also μόνος κοσμοπολίτης. For the κόσμος was for him οἶκος καὶ πόλις. Hence he abode καθάπερ ἐν πατρίδι μετὰ πάσης ἀσφαλείας ... φόβου μὲν ἐκτὸς ὤν ..., ἐν εὐπαθείαις δὲ ταῖς ἐν εἰρήνῃ ἀπολέμῳ ζῶν ἀνεπιλήπτως. Every well-ordered state (πόλις εὔνομος) has, however, a constitution (πολιτείαν). Hence the cosmopolitan lives acc. to the same constitution (πολιτείᾳ) ᾗ καὶ σύμπας ὁ κόσμος. This is, however, ὁ τῆς φύσεως ὀρθὸς λόγος, better θεσμός, νόμος θεῖος ὤν, καθ' ὃν τὰ προσήκοντα καὶ ἐπιβάλλοντα ἑκάστοις ἀπενεμήθη. This πόλις and πολιτεία has, however, τινὰς πρὸ ἀνθρώπου πολίτας, οἳ λέγοιντ' ἂν ἐνδίκως μεγαλοπολῖται τὸν μέγιστον περίβολον οἰκεῖν λαχόντες καὶ τῷ μεγίστῳ καὶ τελειοτάτῳ πολιτεύματι ἐγγραφέντες (they are enrolled in this state as citizens). These are the λογικαὶ καὶ θεῖαι φύσεις, αἱ μὲν ἀσώματοι καὶ νοηταί, αἱ δὲ οὐκ ἄνευ σωμάτων, ὁποίους συμβέβηκεν εἶναι τοὺς ἀστέρας. He who has dealings with these εἰκότως ἐν ἀκράτῳ διέτριβεν εὐδαιμονίᾳ. The κόσμος νοητός is the true μητρόπολις of the sage, who has his part in the νοητὴ πόλις, Conf. Ling., 77 ff.; Som., I, 46. Moving along Stoic lines and building a Platonic superstructure Philo puts the words πόλις, πολίτης, πολιτεία and πολίτευμα in the service of his spiritual cosmopolitanism. Adam is a cosmopolitan. On the other hand this is also true of the ἀσκηταί or ὁμιληταὶ σοφίας who devote themselves to the θεωρία φύσεως, i.e., esp. the contemplation of the starry heaven, who certainly stand here below with their bodies but who float in the aether with their souls (αἰθεροβατοῦντες, Spec. Leg., II, 45). Typical representatives of this attitude are the Therapeutae, Vit. Cont., 90. Also a cosmopolitan is the representative of the ἀστεῖος τρόπος Moses, ὁ τὸν κόσμον ὡς ἄστυ καὶ πατρίδα οἰκήσας (Conf. Ling., 106), or the νόμιμος ἀνήρ who shapes his conduct acc. to the βούλημα τῆς φύσεως, καθ' ἣν καὶ ὁ σύμπας κόσμος διοικεῖται (Op. Mund., 3), or the σπουδαῖος ἄνθρωπος who thus οὐδεμιᾷ τῶν κατὰ τὴν οἰκουμένην πόλεων ἐνεγράφη (as a citizen, Vit. Mos., I, 157). To this world citizen the individual state with its constitution (ἡ κατὰ δήμους πολιτεία) seems to be of lesser worth both theoretically and practically : theoretically because it is only an addition (προσθήκη) to φύσις, Jos., 28, 31; practically because political life is the theatre of the basest passions and the most degrading dependence, as depicted with gt. perspicacity in the tractate on Joseph, the πολιτευόμενος or πολιτικός (Migr. Abr., 159), the type of the politician with his gay coat of many colours (cf. Plat. Resp., VIII, 561d), cf. also Som., I. 219-224. [67] For this reason the ἀσκηταὶ σοφίας avoid τὰς τῶν φιλοπραγμόνων ὁμιλίας ... δικαστήρια καὶ βουλευτήρια καὶ ἀγορὰς καὶ ἐκκλησίας, Spec. Leg., II, 44; Sacr. AC, 50. This is why the Essenes will not live in cities. They want nothing to do with the usual ἀνομίαι τῶν πολιτευομένων, Omn. Prob. Lib., 76. This did not prevent Philo himself from living in the gt. city of Alexandria, nor from taking part in the Legatio ad Gaium (even if only with gt. displeasure, Spec. Leg., III, 3), nor from concerning himself, at least theoretically, with the question of the best constitution. He naturally thinks this is democracy (cf. e.g., Agric., 45; Abr., 242; Conf. Ling., 108), whose basic principle he finds controlling world history, since Tyche sees to the constant shifting of all property relationships, Deus Imm., 176. Oligarchy and mob rule are corrupt forms of government ἐπίβουλοι πολιτεῖαι (Decal., 155), κακοπολιτεῖαι (Agric., 45). Philo thus follows the main route of Gk. philosophy in its political deliberations. But he also agrees with the principle of Plato (Resp., V, 473c-d) that it is best if

---

[66] There are rich materials in Bieder, 70-78; E. Goodenough, The Politics of Philo Judaeus. Practice and Theory (1938), and on this G. Bertram, "Philo als politisch-theol. Propagandist des spätantiken Judt.," ThLZ, 64 (1939), 193-199; cf. also H. Leisegang, "Der Ursprung der Lehre Augustins von der civitas dei," Archiv f. Kulturgeschichte, 16 (1925), 127-158.
[67] Cf. H. Strathmann, Gesch. der frühchr. Askese, I (1914), 141.

either the rulers are philosophers or philosophers the rulers, Vit. Mos., II, 2. But these are only theoretical considerations. Philo has no understanding of the moral dignity of the state or political action as such, though the rule of Augustus offered an instructive example. He himself is an αἰθεροβατῶν, and hence he cannot appreciate the significance of actual history. For this reason he has also no understanding of the eschatological hope which in OT prophecy and later Judaism is linked with the name Jerusalem. He naturally calls Jerusalem the holy city, Som., II, 246. He quotes Ps. 46:4. But in one instance he has the cosmos in view, in another the soul of the wise in whom God moves about ὡς ἐν πόλει, Som., II, 248. The name Jerusalem means ὅρασις εἰρήνης. Hence one should seek τὴν τοῦ ὄντος πόλιν, not ἐν κλίμασι γῆς, ἀλλ' ἐν ψυχῇ ἀπολέμῳ, in the peaceful soul which has chosen the βίος θεωρητικὸς καὶ εἰρηναῖος, 250. Cosmopolitanism, psychology and ethics have dismissed and dissolved history and eschatology.

C. πόλις κτλ. in the NT.

NT usage builds on that of the OT, but gives it a new and spiritual focus in terms of hope.

I. πόλις.

1. Distribution and Secular Use.

In the NT as in the OT (→ 522, 6 ff.) there is no trace at all of the aura which attended πόλις and the whole group for the Greeks.

The word πόλις occurs about 160 times, most commonly in the Lucan writings (half of the instances), about equally in Mt. (26 times) and Rev. (27), only 4 times each in Paul and Hb., 3 times in the Catholic Epistles, the rest divided almost equally between Mk. and Jn. The word is thus most common where concrete relations are depicted, in historical presentations, and in the eschatological images of Rev. On the other hand, it occurs only occasionally in works of pastoral or dogmatic content.

This is connected with the fact that πόλις never means "state." In no passage in the NT can this translation even be considered.

When the NT wants to speak of the state, it refers to the emperor (Mt. 22:17) or king (1 Pt. 2:13, 17; 1 Tm. 2:2) or authorites (R. 13:1) or rulers (Mt. 20:25), but never the πόλις. When the ref. is to cities, there is no suggestion that they are political organisms. The trinity of ἄρχοντες, βουλή and δῆμος, which characterises the Gk. city, does not occur in the NT. The βουλή is never mentioned at all. δῆμος is found in Ac. 12:22; 17:5; 19:30, 33. In all four instances, however, the ref. is to a tumultuous mob rather than a regularly called popular assembly. ἄρχοντες for city officials occurs only in Ac. 16:19 as a loose expression for what are called in v. 20, 22, 35, 36, 38 the praetors (στρατηγοί) of the colony of Philippi, cf. the πολιτάρχαι of Thessalonica in Ac. 17:6, 8. [68] Elsewhere ἄρχων is used for Jews in leading positions of various kinds (e.g., the leader of the synagogue, Lk. 8:41, the member of the Sanhedrin, Lk. 23:13; Jn. 3:1, the judge, Lk. 12:58, the high-priest, Ac. 23:5 ἄρχων τοῦ λαοῦ), for various rulers, esp. pagan (Mt. 20:25; Ac. 4:26; R. 13:3), for Christ (Rev. 1:5 ὁ ἄρχων τῶν

---

[68] On the position of ἄρχοντες or στρατηγοί cf. J. Weiss, Art. "Macedonien," RE³, 12 (1903), 39. On πολιτάρχης cf. Jackson-Lake, I, 4 on Ac. 17:6 : "πολιτάρχης is mainly if not exclusively a Macedonian title for the non-Roman magistrates of a city." On inscr. the title occurs almost exclusively in Macedonia and neighbouring territories, cf. the collection of materials in E. D. Burton, "The Politarchs," American Journal of Theology, 2 (1898), 598-632. The number of politarchs varied from 2 to 6 in individual cities of Macedonia.

βασιλέων τῆς γῆς), also for Satan and demonic powers (e.g., Jn. 12:31; Mk. 3:22; 1 C. 2:6-8). Nowhere, however, is there any interest at all in constitutional questions.

The use of πόλις in the NT is thus completely non-political. [69] πόλις simply means an "enclosed place of human habitation" as distinct from uninhabited areas, pastures, villages and single houses. Sometimes it can also mean the "population" of the city, Mt. 8:34: ἡ πόλις ἐξῆλθεν, 21:10 ἐσείσθη πᾶσα ἡ πόλις, Mk.1:33 ἡ πόλις ἐπισυνηγμένη. There is no sharp distinction between πόλις and κώμη.

This may be seen most clearly from the mixed κωμόπολις of Mk. 1:38, though this is replaced by πόλις in Lk. 4:43. The word denotes a town-like place without municipal standing. Nazareth is a πόλις Mt. 2:23; Lk. 1:26; 2:4, 39. Bethany (Jn. 11:1, 30 cf. Lk. 10:38) and Emmaus (Lk. 24:13, 28) are κῶμαι. Bethsaida, however, is κώμη in Mk. 8:23, 26 and πόλις in Mt. 11:20. Bethlehem, too, is κώμη in Jn. 7:42 and πόλις in Lk. 2:4, 11. The περιῆγεν τὰς κώμας κύκλῳ of Mk. 6:6 is taken by Mt. to include πόλεις among the κῶμαι, cf. Mt. 9:35. In general walled towns are πόλεις while open places of habitation are κῶμαι. The κῶμαι mentioned in the Gospels — the only other occurrence of the term is in Ac. 8:25 — are to be regarded as in some way subordinate to the cities; in districts the whole area is inter-related with the towns. But the only v. where this official relationship is evident is Mk. 8:27: κῶμαι Καισαρείας. [70]

Sometimes the context makes it evident which city is in view (cf. Mt. 8:33: city of the Gadarenes; 21:17; 26:18; 28:11: Jerusalem; Ac. 8:5 ἡ πόλις τῆς Σαμαρείας the capital of Samaria). If not, the name is used (either in the gen. Ac. 16:14; 2 Pt. 2:6 or the same case as πόλις, e.g., Ac. 11:5; 27:8), or various additions are made to set it in a specific locality (e.g., Lk. 4:31; cf. Jn. 4:5; Ac. 8:5; 14:6; 16:12), or to relate it to the nation (e.g., Mt. 10:5, 23; Lk. 23:51), the inhabitants (cf. Ac. 19:35; 2 C. 11:32) or individuals (cf. Lk. 2:4, 11; 2:3; Mt. 9:1; Jn. 1:44). All this is within the sphere of everyday usage.

2. Jerusalem the Holy City.

As in the OT (→ 524, 5 ff.), so also in the NT special significance attaches to passages which speak of Jerusalem as the holy city or the beloved city (Mt. 4:5; 27:53; Rev. 11:2; 20:9), [71] and also to passages which use the expression "holy city" for the heavenly Jerusalem, or which refer to this generally (Gl. 4:25 f.; Hb. 11:10, 16; 12:22; 13:14; Rev. 3:12; 21:9-23; 22:14, 19). In Mt. 4:5; 27:53; Rev. 11:2 Jerusalem is simply called the holy city without any name; this corresponds to the widespread practice of later Judaism and of a tradition which reaches well back into OT history, → 524, 17 ff. The "beloved city" is also a term for the historical Jerusalem, Rev. 20:9. This does not actually occur in the OT, but it is based on the OT idea of the election of Jerusalem by Yahweh (→ 524, 8 ff.) and on passages which speak of Yahweh's love for Jerusalem or Zion, cf. Jer. 11:15; Ps. 78:68; 87:2. The fact that these reminiscences of Israelite and Jewish modes of thought and expression are to be found in Mt. and Rev. is one of the indications how strongly these books are rooted in Jewish tradition. For the oldest Christian community, however, these predicates are not just a recollection of the traditions

---

[69] Antonyms of πόλις are ἐρημία in 2 C. 11:26; ἔρημος τόπος κατ' ἰδίαν in Mt. 14:13; κῶμαι καὶ ἀγροί in Mk. 6:56; κῶμαι in Mt. 9:35; 10:11; Lk. 8:1; 13:22; τόπος in the sense of "inhabited place" (εἰς πᾶσαν πόλιν καὶ τόπον οὗ ἤμελλεν ... ἔρχεσθαι, Lk. 10:1); οἰκία in Mt. 10:14; 12:25 cf. Ac. 12:10.

[70] Cf. Schürer, II⁴, 95, 227-229; also K. Galling, Art. "Stadtanlagen," Bibl. Reallexikon (1937), 496.

[71] It need hardly be shown that the ref. in Rev. 11:2 is to the Palestinian Jerusalem.

of Israel and Judah. They are a sign of the particular significance which Jerusalem still had for the faith of this community.

In Paul's day Jerusalem was the recognised headquarters for all Christianity. The community there controlled and judged whatever took place in Samaria, Caesarea, and Antioch, and gave directions on matters of conduct. This can hardly be explained merely by the fact that through its national, political and religious importance Jerusalem naturally attracted to itself any greater movement in the country and that all important decisions on matters of faith in Israel had ultimately to be made here. The real religious concern is reflected in the retaining of the designation of Jerusalem as the holy city in the Chr. circles to which Mt. and Rev. belong. The seer of Rev. uses this description in 11:2 even though in the same c. Jerusalem is the gt. city ἥτις καλεῖται πνευματικῶς Σόδομα καὶ Αἴγυπτος, ὅπου καὶ ὁ κύριος αὐτῶν ἐσταυρώθη, v. 8.

It is thus unmistakable that the name Jerusalem has a religious interest for the Chr. community, even though this be only traditional. The same pt. comes out in the fact that in Rev. 20:7-10 the beloved city is the site of the battle which destroys the power of Satan at the end of the millennial reign, and that in Rev. 11 the two martyrs to whom ref. is here made do their work and are put to death and are then raised again in no other place than Jerusalem.

3. The Heavenly Jerusalem.

The inner bond between the Christian community and Jerusalem has, however, nothing whatever to do with romantic feelings for the historical city. The destruction of this city is certain, Mk. 13:2; Mt. 24:15 f. Hence expectation is focused on a new Jerusalem which is not a Jerusalem freed from defects (Rev. 21:2) but which will descend to earth, to a new earth, at the time of the consummation of salvation, Rev. 21:10. This idea is found in Paul at Gl. 4:25 f., where ἡ ἄνω Ἰερουσαλήμ is contrasted with τῇ νῦν Ἰερουσαλήμ. If the latter corresponds to Hagar, then the former must correspond to the free Sarah, which means that law-free Christianity and the Jerusalem which is above, our "mother," belong together. The notable thing here is the natural way in which the expected consummation of salvation is incidentally expressed in the concept of the Jerusalem which is above ; the thought obviously must have been a very familiar one for the apostle.

Hb. takes us a step further. According to 11:10, 16 the patriarchs already knew of the heavenly Jerusalem. In obedience to God's command Abraham could leave his home and live as an alien in the land of promise because he "looked for a city which hath foundations, whose builder and maker is God," v. 10. This alone would endure. Even the most firmly established of earthly cities are only encampments. The death of the fathers was a death in faith, for it took place in the certainty of a heavenly city which was glimpsed only from afar but which was steadfastly longed for, v. 14, 16. On account of it they regarded themselves during their lifetime as pilgrims and strangers τῆς γῆς, which according to v. 14 means "on earth" rather than "in the land." God, however, had fashioned a city for them, namely, a city in heaven, v. 16. This is the same city as that which in 12:22-24 is called Mount Zion, the city of the living God, the heavenly Jerusalem, and which is now described more fully, though again in contrast to Mount Sinai and its terrors, as in Gl. 4:25. This is the future city to which Christians look forward, having here no abiding city (13:14); as the Shepherd of Hermas later puts it (s., 1, 1): They dwell here as in an alien city living under other laws in contrast to their own city, to which they will return if they do not deny its law, → V, 30, 20 ff. This city of Hb., however, is not just future ; already it is a heavenly reality in relation to which the earthly phenomenon is at best, i.e., in the OT cultus, only a reflection (8:5), a shadow (8:5; 10:1) and a likeness (9:9). [72]

> The continual recurrence of the thought in Hb., and the lofty and solemn, though also loving and grateful dwelling of the author on the idea of this heavenly Jerusalem, show how important the circle of ideas was for him. Nevertheless, he had not just taken it from the apocalyptic tradition of the OT and Judaism. It has been thoroughly Christianised. All national, political and external elements have disappeared without a trace. The fellowship of all believers of all ages with God, with the pledge of the new covenant, and with the angelic world — this alone is what fills the wholly purified thought and longing of the author of this strange and powerful letter, who has completely outgrown and outstripped the Jewish community.

The picture of the Jerusalem which will one day come down from heaven is painted in rich and vivid colours in Rev. 21. This new Jerusalem which comes down from heaven is "prepared as a bride adorned for her husband," 21:2. Indeed, it is "the bride, the Lamb's wife," 21:9. It is the perfected community which includes all who have come out of the afflictions of persecution as victors and upon whom there is thus written "the name of the city of my God, which is new Jerusalem, which cometh down out of heaven from my God," 3:12, i.e., who have the privileges of citizenship in it. The image of the heavenly city is used to depict the blessedness of this perfected community.

> Neither from a literary nor a material standpt. does the image constitute a unity. The repetitions in c. 22 as compared with c. 21 (cf. esp. 22:5 with 21:23-25; 22:3 with 21:27; 22:3 with 21:3) show that it is not a literary unity. The paradise motif of 22:1 f., which is difficult to harmonise with the tower-like city of heaven, shows that it is not a material unity. When the nations and kings of the earth go through the gates of the new Jerusalem (21:24), the ref. is obviously no longer to the Jerusalem which is in heaven. Motifs of the most varied derivation combine in the image. The whole c. is shot through by OT reminiscences, esp. of Jer. and Ez. (in particular Ez. 48:30-35) and also Gn. 2. The most important contribution is made, however, by the ancient mythology of heaven. The signs of the Zodiac and the related division of heaven may be seen in the 12 gates [73] with their angelic guards, and also in the 12 foundation stones. The street of pure gold is the milky way, as is also the pure river, clear as crystal. The adornment of precious stones is the glittering starry heaven, and the comparatively low wall [74] of many-coloured jasper is the corona of the night horizon. That the city is foursquare can hardly be based on the town plan of Babylon [75] or other cities; it is to be explained by the ref. in the astronomy of antiquity to the four corners on which the vault of heaven rested. The cubic shape of the city is quite understandable in this light. [76]

---

[72] This antithesis, however, bears no relation whatever to the pseudo-idealism of Philo. For it is not cosmologically speculative, as in Philo's doctrine of the *logos*. It is eschatological, and oriented to salvation history. The idea that Hb. uses the image of the heavenly Jerusalem unrestrictedly for the *civitas dei* in Philo's sense (Leisegang, *op. cit.* [→ n. 66], 158) rests on a misunderstanding.

[73] The figure 12 is schematic so that one need not ask who the twelfth is.

[74] The ἐνδώμησις is the material; one need not think in terms of the substructure, Pr.-Bauer⁴, *s.v.* The θεμέλιοι are the foundation.

[75] Cf. D. H. McQueen, "The New Jerusalem and Town Planning," Exp., IX, 2 (1924), 220-226.

[76] On this cf. esp. F. Boll, *Aus d. Offenbarung d. Joh., Hell. Studien zum Weltbild d. Apk.* (1914), 39 f.; Bss. Apk. on 21:9 ff.; Had. Apk. on 21:9 ff. These ref. are not discussed in Zn. Apk. Cf. also R. Knopf, "Die Himmelsstadt," *Nt.liche Studien, Festschr. f. G. Heinrici* (1914), 213-219; F. Dijkema, "Het hemelsch Jeruzalem," *Niew Theol. Tijdschrift*, 15 (1926), 25-43, which adds support to the thesis of H. Gunkel that Christianity was a syncretistic religion.

The important pt., however, is that in Rev. all these adopted ideas and motifs are only metaphors in an attempt to depict the blessedness of the perfected community. In spite of promising beginnings, even the prophecy of Israel, let alone Jewish apocalyptic, could never wholly free itself from specific Israelitish features. For Ez. a new temple belongs esp. to the new Jerusalem. In the expectation of Rev., however, nothing is more distinctive than that there is no temple in the new Jerusalem, 21:22. There is no further need of temple, cult, or offering. "The Lord God Almighty and the Lamb are the temple of it." The dwelling of God is not with Israel alone (Zech. 2:14; Ez. 37:27) but "with men," who will be His → λαός [77] (21:3). This refers, of course, only to those who have washed their clothes (22:14), who have a share in the redeeming work of Christ. The heavenly city is thus an image of the perfected divine fellowship of the redeemed community which cannot be disrupted. That the Chr. hope of the future takes this form is a legacy of the tradition of Israel and Judah. But as the Chr. community, the true Israel, is to be differentiated from "Israel after the flesh," so the hope has become essentially different in spite of all the OT reminiscences. This faith is in fact no longer interested in the replacing of the earthly Jerusalem by a better one. Jerusalem is simply an inherited traditional name with no concrete spatial reference. Here, too, the principle applies : Lo, I make all things new.

All attempts to establish a relation between the eschatological language of the apocalyptist, which transcends history when he speaks of the heavenly city, and the cosmopolitan ideas of the Stoic philosophy of immanence, even in the Platonising form represented by Philo, are wide of the mark. [78] There yawns here the abyss which separates history from nature.

4. The Translation of πόλις as *Civitas* in the Vulgate.

In the Vg NT is always rendered *civitas* except in Ac. 16:12, 39, where Philippi, previously called *civitas*, is referred to as *urbs*. [79] Thus we find *civitas, cuius artifex et conditor Deus* in Hb. 11:10; *civitas Dei viventis, Ierusalem caelestis* in Hb. 12:22; *civitas futura* in Hb. 13:14; *nomen civitatis Dei mei novae Ierusalem* in Rev. 3:12; *sancta civitas Ierusalem nova* in Rev. 21:2. *Civitas Dei* or *Dei nostri* also occurs in Ps. 46:4; 48:1, 8; 87:3 as a rendering of πόλις θεοῦ (ἡμῶν), *civitas Domini* in Ps. 101:8 for πόλις κυρίου. This rendering of πόλις involves quite a shift of meaning as compared with the NT, because it gives πόλις a political nuance. This shift of sense is important because Augustine acc. to his own testimony gave to his masterpiece the title Civitas Dei on the basis of these biblical ref., cf. Civ. D., 5, 19; 11, 1; 14, 1. [80] Almost the only thing that Aug. Civ. D. links with the ref. is the word. The passages in the Ps. speak of Jerusalem ; Aug. disregards the historical ref. The NT passages speak of the community of the eschatological consummation ; Aug. retains this ref. in Civ. D., but the concept is used in varying senses, so that he can also equate the *civitas Dei* with the community of the just or the historical form of the organised Church. The opposite is not earthly Jerusalem but the *civitas terrena*, which is sometimes the society of the ungodly and reprobate, sometimes the secular state. [81] The term has thus lost its eschatological and figurative character and become a concept of ecclesiastical and philosophical thought. This development was made possible only by the inexact rendering of πόλις as *civitas*.

---

[77] To be read rather than λαοί.

[78] Leisegang's view (→ n. 72) overlooks the eschatological character of the NT statements.

[79] *Civitas* is the ordinary word for town in popular Latin, Thes. Ling. Lat., III, 1232-1234.

[80] Cf. on this Leisegang, *op. cit.* (→ n. 66), 127-158. Acc. to him Aug. is here dependent on philosophical influences mediated through Ambrose. W. Kamlah, *Christentum u. Geschichtlichkeit. Untersuchungen zur Entstehung d. Christentums u. zu Augustins "Bürgerschaft Gottes"* (1951), 155-174.

[81] Cf. F. Loofs, *Leitfaden zum Studium der Dogmengeschichte*⁵ (1950), 330-334; R. Seeberg, *Lehrbuch d. Dogmengesch.*, II³ (1923), 472-482.

II. πολίτης, πολιτεύομαι, πολιτεία, πολίτευμα.

1. There is nothing distinctively theological about πολίτης in the four instances in which it occurs in the NT. In Hb. 8:11, in a quotation from Jer. 31:31 ff., it means "fellow-citizen," "compatriot," "neighbour," so that πλησίον can be used instead in one part of the textual tradition, → 311 ff. συμπολίτης, which is used figuratively in Eph. 2:19, might also have been used. In Ac. 21:39 Paul says that he is Ταρσεύς, τῆς Κιλικίας οὐκ ἀσήμου πόλεως πολίτης, that he has citizenship in Tarsus. In the other Lucan ref. the sense is much weaker. It is said of the prodigal son in Lk. 15:15 : ἐκολλήθη ἑνὶ τῶν πολιτῶν τῆς χώρας ἐκείνης. πολίτης here means an "independent inhabitant" with his own property. Similarly, in the parable of the pounds in Lk. 19:12 ff. the πολῖται as distinct from the δοῦλοι are economically and personally "independent inhabitants." In relation to the ἄνθρωπος εὐγενής they are in a sense fellow-citizens. But they are not citizens in the Greek sense, since, being under a king, they do not have any share in κρίσις and ἀρχή, → n. 37. The use of the term thus remains within the confines of the everyday.

2. The verb πολιτεύομαι occurs only in Ac. 23:1 and Phil. 1:27. In the former Paul declares to the assembled Sanhedrin in Jerusalem : ἐγὼ πάσῃ συνειδήσει ἀγαθῇ πεπολίτευμαι τῷ θεῷ ἄχρι ταύτης τῆς ἡμέρας. In the latter he admonishes the Philippians : ἀξίως τοῦ εὐαγγελίου τοῦ Χριστοῦ πολιτεύεσθε. Neither here nor in Ac. 23:1 does the word contain any reference to life in society as such. In both cases it is used with no political implications of the "walk," of a walk which is shaped by religion. The usage of Hellenistic Judaism, which is first attested in Maccabees, is thus adopted, → 526, 34 ff. In this way it came to have an established place in Christian literature. [82]

3. πολιτεία, too, occurs only twice in the NT. Characteristically it is not used in an abstract sense of the state or constitution, for the NT has no interest in theories, [83] but only in the concrete sense of "civil rights," whether meant literally or figuratively. It is used for Roman citizenship in Ac. 22:28. Paul appeals to the fact that he is an ἄνθρωπος Ῥωμαῖος (a Roman citizen) in order to avoid the threatened examination by scourging. His statement is the more impressive because he did not buy citizenship like the tribune of the Antonia guard but inherited it from his father. [84] πολιτεία is also used in Eph. 2:12, which says of the readers that during their pagan period they had been ἀπηλλοτριωμένοι τῆς πολιτείας τοῦ Ἰσραὴλ καὶ ξένοι τῶν διαθηκῶν τῆς ἐπαγγελίας, ἐλπίδα μὴ ἔχοντες καὶ ἄθεοι ἐν τῷ κόσμῳ. Here the expression πολιτεία τοῦ Ἰσραὴλ does not refer to the state of Israel, which had not existed for a long time and membership of which the Greeks of Asia can hardly have thought worth seeking. Nor can it refer to citizenship in the literal sense, since Christian status would

---

[82] Cf. Jackson-Lake, I, 4 on 23:1. That this usage occurs in the koine as well as Hell. Judaism is often asserted, but thus far no examples have been adduced.

[83] "The NT manifests no ideal of a πολιτεία such as that projected by Gk. philosophy and Stoicism," Bultmann, Verständnis, 69. It is thus more interested in the state as a concrete phenomenon ; one need only refer to R. 13:1-7 and similar passages in proof of this. Since πόλις is not used for state, however, this aspect need not be discussed here.

[84] On the protection of Roman citizens against degrading punishments in Roman penal law cf. O. Holtzmann, Nt.liche Zeitgeschichte² (1906), 90 f.; also T. Mommsen, Röm. Strafrecht (1899), 31, n. 3, 47; Jackson-Lake, I, 4 on Ac. 22:15 ff.; Liv., 3, 56; 10, 9 (with ref. to the Leges Porciae et Valeriae); Cic. Verr., II, 5, 62 f., 66. Here we find the frequently quoted saying : Facinus est vincire civem Romanum, scelus verberare, prope parricidium necare.

be no true counterpart to this. It is rather used in the figurative sense of the privileged religious position of Israel as the recipient of the promise. Once excluded from the promise, the readers also now have access to the Father through Christ. [85] They are now no longer ξένοι and πάροικοι but συμπολῖται τῶν ἁγίων. They share the spiritual citizenship which belongs to the ἅγιοι, the believers of Israel. They have access to God. They have becomes members of God's household and partake of salvation, 2:19.

4. Finally πολίτευμα occurs in the NT only in Phil. 3:20. The readers are admonished to take Paul as an example in their walk. The walk of the τὰ ἐπίγεια φρονοῦντες is the opposite. ἡμῶν γὰρ τὸ πολίτευμα ἐν οὐρανοῖς ὑπάρχει, ἐξ οὗ καὶ σωτῆρα ἀπεκδεχόμεθα κύριον Ἰησοῦν Χριστόν : The commonwealth to which Christians belong, their "homeland," is in heaven. Hence τὰ ἐπίγεια are neither normative nor attractive for them. Here, as 1 Pt. 2:11 says on the basis of ψ 38:13, they are only πάροικοι καὶ παρεπίδημοι, with no rights of domicile. They are not citizens rooted here in nature, thought and interests. Exposition, then, is not to be based on the usage which employed πολιτεύματα for foreign colonies outside the mother country with certain specified rights. If so, the Christian community would be a heavenly πολίτευμα in the world. What we have here is rather a figurative use of the term in the sense of state or commonwealth and with a view to describing the fact that Christians are inwardly foreigners, not specifically in relation to the earthly state, which is not mentioned at all in the context, but very generally in relation to the earthly sphere. More positively, the word is used to describe their membership of the heavenly kingdom of Christ, to which they belong as it were by constitutional right. The βασιλεία τῶν οὐρανῶν is the πολίτευμα of Christians. [86]

D. The Post-Apostolic Fathers.

The usage of the post-apostolic fathers follows closely that of the NT. None of the words in question gives evidence of any political interest. πόλις is simply a town. Sometimes the word is used in the sense of Phil. 3:20 for the heavenly world, and as the ἰδία πόλις of the Christian it is contrasted with the temporal world, Herm. s., 1, 1, 1-6. πολῖται are the inhabitants, sometimes natives as distinct from ξένοι, Dg., 5, 5. πολιτεία means "conduct," "walk," e.g., ἀνεπίληπτος πολιτεία, Mart. Pol., 17, 1. πολιτεύομαι can sometimes mean "to be a citizen," "to be a national" (Christians dwell on earth but ἐν οὐρανῷ πολιτεύονται, Dg., 5, 9), but in the main it simply means "to walk." There is an echo of the original constitutional sense when it is said fig. that God ἐν οὐρανοῖς πολιτεύεται ("rules in heaven") while the Christian is still a pilgrim on earth, Dg., 10, 7. The phrase in 1 Cl., 54, 4 : πολιτεύεσθαι τὴν ἀμεταμέλητον πολιτείαν τοῦ θεοῦ, is best transl.: "to conduct oneself in one's walk as a citizen of God, which will never give occasion for remorse."

Strathmann

---

[85] Cf. Haupt Gefbr., *ad loc.*

[86] The Lutheran transl. "our walk is in heaven," like the Vg (*nostra autem conversatio in caelis est,* cf. A.V.) on which it is based, is philologically unsound. Hence the revisions of 1938 and 1956 rightly replace it by "our homeland is in heaven" (cf. R.S.V., N.E.B.).

πολλοί

Contents : A. Inclusive Meaning of הָ(רַבִּים) / סַגִּיאִין / (οἱ) πολλοί in Judaism : I. In the OT : 1. As Noun : a. With Article ; b. Without Article ; 2. As Adjective ; 3. Is. 52:13-53:12. II. In Post-Biblical Judaism : 1. As Noun : a. With Article ; b. Without Article ; 2. As Adjective ; 3. Is. 52:13-53:12 in Later Jewish Writings. B. Inclusive Meaning of (οἱ) πολλοί in the NT : I. In Passages not Relating to Is. 53 : 1. As Noun : a. With Article ; b. Without Article ; 2. As Adjective. II. (οἱ) πολλοί in Statements concerning the Saving Work of Jesus : 1. οἱ πολλοί ; 2. πολλοί without Article : a. NT Interpretations of πολλοί ; b. The Original Sense : (a) The Age of the Tradition ; (b) The Reference of All Four Passages to Is. 53.

Of the many NT instances of πολύς [1] theological significance in the narrower sense attaches only to those which use the plur. πολλοί to describe the circle of men to whom the saving work of Jesus applies. In what follows, then, our main concern will be with the significance of the saying that Jesus dies for many. Basic to this enquiry is the examination of a distinctive Semitic usage, namely, the inclusive use of "many."

A. Inclusive Meaning of סַגִּיאִין / (הָ)רַבִּים [2] / (οἱ) πολλοί in Judaism.

In Greek πολλοί is differentiated from πάντες (ὅλοι) by the fact that it is the antonym of a minority. It is thus used exclusively for many (but not all). In contrast, the Heb. (הָ)רַבִּים / Aram. סַגִּיאִין can have an inclusive sense : "the many who cannot be counted," "the great multitude," "all." [3] The same is true of (οἱ) πολλοί in Jewish Greek writings. This inclusive use is due to the fact that Heb. and Aram. have no word for "all." [4]

I. In the OT.

1. As Noun.

   a. With Article. The inclusive sense of the noun is quite clear in the OT when it is used with the art. Thus, when Elijah says to the prophets of Baal : אַתֶּם הָרַבִּים

π ο λ λ ο ί. Bibl. on the inclusive use of (οἱ) πολλοί, P. Joüon, "L'Évangile de Notre-Seigneur Jésus-Christ," Verbum salutis, V (1930), 125 ; J. Jeremias, "Das Lösegeld f. Viele (Mk. 10:45)," Judaica, 3 (1948), 249-264, esp. 263 f.; also Die Abendmahlsworte Jesu² (1949), 91-93, 108-111 ; O. Cullmann, "Nt.liche Wortforschung. ὙΠΕΡ (ʼΑΝΤΙ) ΠΟΛ-ΛΩΝ," ThZ, 4 (1948), 471-473 ; H. Hegermann, "Js. 53 in Hexapla, Tg. u. Peschitta," BFTh, II, 56 (1954), 68 f., 91-93, 96 f.

[1] On πολλὰ παθεῖν → V, 913, 23 ff.

[2] The st. emphaticus *סַגִּיאַיָּא is not attested in the Aram. of Pal. Judaism ; סַגִּיאִין covers both the definite and the indefinite sense.

[3] How (ה)רבים contains the inclusive sense may be seen in 1 Εσδρ. 4:14 : οὐ ... πολλοί οἱ ἄνθρωποι ; "Are not the men many ?" "Does not mankind consist of many ?" Cf. also 1 QH 4:27 → 539, 10 ff. The idea of totality is reached by way of the consideration that it consists of many individuals.

[4] Heb. כֹּל / Aram. כֹּלָּא certainly means the totality, but it does not correspond to our "all" inasmuch as כל/כלא is not a plur.; the totality is in view from the very first, whereas "all" expresses the sum as well as the totality. The Heb. and Aram. can express at one and the same time only one of these concepts, either totality (by means of כל/כלא) or sum (by means of רבים[ה]/סגיאין), Joüon, 125.

(1 K. 18:25), this means : "You are the great host" (i.e., you are in the majority). The inclusive sense is even clearer in the other instances (Is. 53:11c, 12a; Est. 4:3; Da. 9:27; 11:33; 12:3), where הָרַבִּים means "the multitude." [5]

b. Without Article. Even more significant is the fact that even without the art. the noun can often be used inclusively, Ps. 109:30 : בְּתוֹךְ רַבִּים אֲהַלְלֶנּוּ ("the [whole] congregation," cf. 22:22 : בְּתוֹךְ קָהָל אֲהַלְלֶךָ; 22:25; 35:18; 40:10 : קָהָל רָב; 26:12 : מַקְהֵלִים; 107:32 : קְהַל־עָם), [6] cf. also Ps. 71:7: כְּמוֹפֵת הָיִיתִי לְרַבִּים (by adding the art. [7] the LXX shows that it takes this inclusively). Similarly Ex. 23:2 : לֹא־תִהְיֶה אַחֲרֵי־רַבִּים, "thou shalt not follow the multitude," and Neh. 7:2 : מֵרַבִּים, "above all others."

2. As Adjective.

Adjectivally the inclusive sense of (הָ)רַבִּים occurs in the OT only in the expression עַמִּים (גּוֹיִם, אִיִּים) רַבִּים = "the (whole) host of the peoples." The oldest instance is in Is. 2:2-4 (par. Mi. 4:1-3) : וְהָלְכוּ עַמִּים רַבִּים (v. 3) וְנָהֲרוּ אֵלָיו כָּל־הַגּוֹיִם "and all peoples shall go up thither, nations in great number shall set forth"; 2:4: וְשָׁפַט בֵּין הַגּוֹיִם וְהוֹכִיחַ לְעַמִּים רַבִּים, "and he will judge between the peoples, give direction to the nations in great number." The expression thus alternates with כָּל־הַגּוֹיִם (v. 2) or הַגּוֹיִם (v. 4); in the par. Mi. 4:1-3 [8] כָּל־הָעַמִּים is also used in v. 5 with the same meaning. Other examples are in Is. 52:15 (cf. 42:1: לַגּוֹיִם; 49:6); Ez. 3:6 f.: עַמִּים רַבִּים / בֵּית יִשְׂרָאֵל : 27:33 : עַמִּים רַבִּים; 31:6 : מַלְכֵי־אֶרֶץ; 38:23 : I (God) will make myself known לְעֵינֵי גּוֹיִם רַבִּים with כֹּל גּוֹיִם רַבִּים : 39:27 with art. before גּוֹיִם: I will manifest myself to them as the Holy One לְעֵינֵי הַגּוֹיִם רַבִּים; Mi. 4:11, 13 (cf. Jl. 3:2 : אֶת־כָּל־הַגּוֹיִם); 5:7 (par. with art. בַּגּוֹיִם); Zech. 8:22 : עַמִּים רַבִּים וּבָאוּ (on the basis of Mi. 4:3 [→ n. 8] and with the same universalist content ; on עֲצוּמִים → n. 9); Ps. 89:50 : כָּל־רַבִּים עַמִּים (corrupt, cf. Ez. 31:6 → line 18 f.); 97:1: אִיִּים רַבִּים/הָאָרֶץ. With art. Neh. 13:26 : וּבַגּוֹיִם הָרַבִּים לֹא־הָיָה מֶלֶךְ כָּמֹהוּ, "and among all nations there was no king like him (Solomon)."

3. Is. 52:13-53:12.

Already a special word must be said about Is. 53 because the striking five-fold repetition of (הָ)רַבִּים in Is. 52:13-53:12 makes the word a distinctive feature of the c. Of the five instances the word is used in four as a noun (53:11c, 12a with art., 52:14; 53:12e without) and in one as an adjective (52:15). If the concrete reference and scope of the word (הָ)רַבִּים is obscure and ambivalent in the first four of these passages, so that we do not know who are the many who are

---

[5] The noun with art. is rare in the OT. All the ref. are given here, and their number might be reduced in view of the fact that only in 1 K. 18:25 and Da. 12:3 are there sure indications in the unpointed text that an art. was intended. Da. 12:3 and R. 5:19 show, however, that Is. 53:11 was read with art., and Da. 12:3 also shows that this was so in the case of Da. 9:27; 11:33. The Mas. pointing was thus right in this respect. An approximation to this usage in Gk. is the employment of οἱ πολλοί for "the crowd," "the multitude," "the people," "the public," often with a note of contempt : "the common people," "the mob" (examples in W. Bauer, *Rechtgläubigkeit u. Ketzerei im ältesten Christentum* [1934], 77, n. 3; Pr.-Bauer⁴, 1253). Nevertheless, the derogatory nuance shows that the word was not used inclusively in the strict sense ; the speaker is differentiating himself and his kind from the πολλοί.

[6] E. Sahlin, "Der Messias u. das Gottesvolk," Acta Seminarii Neotestamentici Upsaliensis, 12 (1945), 76, n. 1.

[7] ψ 70:7: τοῖς πολλοῖς.

[8] Here the corresponding par. are גּוֹיִם רַבִּים (v. 2) /עַמִּים (v. 1) and גּוֹיִם עֲצֻמִים (v. 3b) /עַמִּים רַבִּים (v. 3a).

astonished at the servant (52:14), whom he vindicates (53:11), among whom a portion is assigned him (53:12) and whose sins he bore (v. 12), the meaning is certainly not exclusive but inclusive. This is vouched for by the fifth instance, which has the inclusive expression גּוֹיִם רַבִּים (52:15) to which reference has already been made (→ 537, 11 ff.), and also by the use of the article in v. 11c and 12a, the parallel עֲצוּמִים "the many, innumerable" (v. 12a),[9] and finally the interpretation of the four verses in the following period, → 540, 12 ff.

II. In Post-Biblical Judaism.

1. As Noun.

a. With Article. That the noun with article always has inclusive signification is confirmed by investigation of later Jewish writings, in which there is great increase of examples as compared with the OT.

הרבים is very common in 1 QS and fairly common in Damasc. as a fixed tt. "The many" exercise jurisdiction (1 QS 6:1) and decide to accept (6:15 f., 18, 21) or to exclude (7:23 f.). 6:8-13 regulates the order of seating and business in the session of the many (מושב הרבים, 6:8 and 11), in which the priests, the elders and the rest of the people take part (6:8 f.). The האיש המבקר על הרבים presides (6:11 f.).[10] A resolve of the many (עצת הרבים, 6:16) decides as to the acceptance of new members when the candidate has been tested by האיש הפקיד ברואש הרבים (6:14).[11] But during his first year the novice must not injure the purity of the many (טהרת הרבים, 6:16 f.; 7:16 and 19; without art. 6:25; 7:3) nor enjoy the goods of the many (הון הרבים, 6:17). In the second year he is excluded only from the drink of the many (משקה הרבים, 6:20); the reward of his work is in this year to be given to האיש המבקר על מלאכת הרבים (6:19 f.) but is not to be used for the account of the many (על הרבים, 6:20). Only after the two-year probationary period can he be enrolled as a full member (6:21-23). These examples show that in 1 QS and Damasc.[12] "the many" denotes the panel of members with full privileges.[13] There is an analogous use of הרבים as a tt. in the vocabulary of the Pharisees, who sometimes describe their society (chabura) as הרבים.[14] In the Rabb.

---

[9] E. Sellin, "Die Lösung des deuterojesajanischen Gottesknechtsrätsels," ZAW, 55 (1937), 210. The strongly advocated rendering of the parallelism בָּרַבִּים/אֶת־עֲצוּמִים by "among the great / with the strong" is debatable, since הָרַבִּים as noun is nowhere else in the OT used in the sense "the great."

[10] Cf. Damasc. 15:8 (19:8) המבקר אשר לרבים.

[11] In Damasc. 14:6 f. (17:5) there corresponds to this הכהן אשר יפקד אשר הרבים (a word, perhaps על or בראש, needs to be supplied after the second אשר).

[12] On Damasc. cf. → n. 10 f.; cf. also Damasc. 13:7 (16:1); 14:12 (18:1).

[13] H. Bardtke, Die Handschriftenfunde am Toten Meer² (1953), 117-120; J. Hempel, "Die Wurzeln des Missionswillens im Glauben des AT," ZAW, 66 (1954), 250; R. Marcus, "Mebaqqer and Rabbim in the Manual of Discipline VI, 11-13," JBL, 75 (1956), 299.

[14] jDemai, 2, 2 (22d, 44): "In (the eyes of) the many (נרבים) he is not regarded as reliable until before the many (נרבים) he has accepted (the obligation to keep the rules of purity and tithing). R. Ammi (c. 300) in the name of R. Jannai (c. 240): 'I myself would not be regarded as reliable until before the many (נרבים) I had taken on myself (read עליי for עליו) (the obligation)'." Who the "many" are may be seen from T. Demai, 2, 14, where it is said that the obligation is accepted בפני חבורה. Cf. S. Lieberman, "The Discipline in the So-Called Dead Sea Manual of Discipline," JBL, 71 (1952), 200 f.

writings הרבים is always used for "public enterprise,"[15] "multitude,"[16] "congregation,"[17] "assembly."[18] The sphere of the many is even broader in 4 Esr. 5:28 Syr., where it is said with ref. to the servitude of Israel : "And now, Lord, why hast thou delivered up the one to the many, despised the one root more than the many, and scattered thine only one among the many?" i.e., among the Gentiles (Arm. *inter ethnicos*, Georg. *apud omnes*); 7:20 Syr. "May the many who have come perish," i.e., all the living.[19]

b. Without Article. In later Judaism, as in the OT (→ 537, 4 ff.), the noun without article can also be used sometimes in an inclusive sense.

In Bar. 4:12 Jerusalem describes itself as a widow "which is forsaken by all" (καταλειφθεῖσα ὑπὸ πολλῶν). The parallelism in 1 QH 4:27[20] is instructive : בי האירותה פני רבים ותגבר עד לאין מספר, "Through me thou hast lit up the face of many and wilt cause to become great beyond computation." When we read in 4 Esr. 8:3 : *Multi quidem creati sunt, pauci autem salvabuntur*, there is no doubt an antithesis between the many and the few, but materially *multi creati* means the totality of created things, or all mankind.[21] *Multi* has the same comprehensive sense in the preceding antithesis in 8:1: *Hoc saeculum fecit Altissimus propter multos, futurum autem propter paucos*. Ref. might also be made to 4:34 : *Non festinas tu* ("thou wilt no longer press") *super Altissimum? Tu enim festinas propter temet ipsum nam excelsus pro multis*, where the Arab. version[22] is materially right when it renders *pro multis* by "for the sake of the general public."[23] Finally, in the Mishnah של רבים is a common phrase for "public."[24]

2. As Adjective.

Adjectivally the inclusive use of "many" found in the OT in the expression גּוֹיִם רַבִּים "the (whole) multitude of the peoples" (→ 537, 11 ff.), still occurs in post-biblical Judaism.

In the LXX addition to Est. 3:13b ἔθνη πολλά is par. to πᾶσα οἰκουμένη and in Tob. 13:13 א it is par. to κάτοικοι πάντων τῶν ἐσχάτων τῆς γῆς. The promise to Abraham that he will be אַב־הֲמוֹן גּוֹיִם, "the father of a host of peoples" (Gn. 17:5) is rendered as follows in the LXX : πατέρα πολλῶν ἐθνῶν τέθεικά σε; Rabb. exegesis of the v. shows that this means "the whole world of the nations."[25] מִים רבים is taken

---

[15] רשות הרבים "public sphere" (opp. רשות היחיד "private sphere") is itself found 97 times in the Mishnah.

[16] המזכה את־הרבים "he who leads the multitude to righteousness" (opp. המחטיא את־הרבים, "he who leads the multitude into sin"), Ab., 5, 18. Note the ref. to Da. 12:3 מַצְדִּיקֵי הָרַבִּים.

[17] E.g., תפלת הרבים "the prayer of the congregation" (opp. תפלת יחיד "the prayer of an individual") S. Dt., 27 on 3:24.

[18] MQ 3:7: הָרַבִּים "the assembly of mourning."

[19] In Jewish Hell. works οἱ πολλοί often has the inclusive sense "the multitude" (ψ 70:7; LXX Da. 12:4; En. 104:10 Gk.; Jos. Bell., 2, 599; 5, 422; Ant., 3, 212; 20, 153; cf. Schl. Mt., 701); it can also mean "laymen" (as distinct from priests, Ant., 8, 95), though there may be Gk. influence here (→ n. 5), as there certainly is in 2 Macc. 1:36; 2:27.

[20] Ed. E. L. Sukenik, אוצר המגילות הגנוזות (1954).

[21] In the lost Gk. original the word behind *multi* was obviously πολλοί without art., and this is itself based on רבים without art.

[22] Ed. J. Gildemeister, Esdrae liber quartus arabice e cod. Vat. (1877).

[23] Cf. the negative in 4 Esr. 5:7: *non multi* (Lat.), not many (Syr.), "none of all the peoples" (Arab.; cf. H. Ewald, "Das vierte Ezrabuch," AGG, 11 [1863], 25, 17) knows him whose voice sounds forth nightly.

[24] Bik. 1, 1 (public place); Er., 5, 6; Meg., 3, 1 (public property); Parah 12, 4 (public recess).

[25] jBik., 1, 4 (64a, 16): אב לכל הגוים; bBer., 13a : אב לכל העולם; bShab., 105a אב לאומות; T. Ber., 1, 13 : אב לכל באי העולם.

just as universally as גוים רבים. The expression וְזַרְעוֹ בְּמַיִם רַבִּים in the prophecy of Balaam (Nu. 24:7) is transl. in the LXX : καὶ κυριεύσει ἐθνῶν πολλῶν, in Tg. J. I : ישלטון בעממין סגיאין, in Tg. J. II ישלטון באומין, in Tg. O. וישלוט בעממין סגיאין, in Midr. Agada : [26] שישלוט...בכל העמים, and paraphrased in Leqach tob (= Pesikta zutarta): [27] מלכותן...ככל (read בכל) מלכי האדמה; how firmly established was this interpretation of מַיִם רַבִּים may be seen in Tg. Cant., 8, 7, where it is paraphrased : "all nations כל עממיא, which are like the waters of the sea, that are many." Finally, in the Mishnah we find the formula of benediction בורא נפשות רבות וחסרונן (Ber., 6, 8): "He who makes living creatures, as many as there are, and what they need." [28] In general it may be said that the sphere of the adjectival use of the inclusive "many" is still restricted here as it was earlier.

3. Is. 52:13-53:12 in Later Jewish Writings.

In relation to the question how the "many" of the suffering servant passage was understood by Judaism in the NT period, one may ignore the few post-Christian expositions, [29] especially that of the Targum, [30] since anti-Christian polemic from the 2nd century A.D. onwards led increasingly to reinterpretations of Is. 53. [31] It should be noted, however, that Tg. Is. 53:12a has עֲמְמִין סַגִּיאִין for הָרַבִּים. As regards pre-Christian expositions of the five verses (52:14, 15; 53:11c, 12a e), the following are the available data. In En. 62:3, 5 the שָׁמְמוּ עָלֶיךָ רַבִּים of Is. 52:14 is rendered : "All kings, mighty men, lofty ones and those who possess the earth, shall be ... terrified"; in Wis. this astonishment (5:2 ἐκστήσονται = LXX Is. 52:14) is very generally ascribed to the ungodly and unrighteous (4:16) who oppress the righteous (5:1). In agreement with this interpretation of the "many" in Wis. is the statement in Test. B. 3:8 ("the innocent one will be polluted for the lawless and the sinless one will die for the ungodly"), if the "many" for whom the innocent one suffers and dies are the lawless and the ungodly. If in Wis. and Test. B. it is an open question whether the lawless and ungodly are Jews, Gentiles, or both, Peshitta Is. 52:15 is of help at this point. It renders the יַזֶּה גוֹיִם רַבִּים of Is. 52:15 by "he will purify many peoples" (מדכא עממא סגיאא). Thus the statement of the Heb. text that the atoning work of the servant of the Lord was for the nations still lived on in the 1st century A.D. [32]

B. Inclusive Meaning of (οἱ) πολλοί in the NT.

I. In Passages not Relating to Is. 53.

1. As Noun.

a. With Article. As a noun with the art. πολλοί has the exclusive sense of "most" in the NT only at Mt. 24:12 and 2 C. 2:17 (vl. οἱ λοιποί).

Elsewhere οἱ πολλοί is always used inclusively. The classical example is R. 5:15b : οἱ πολλοὶ ἀπέθανον (= πάντες ἄνθρωποι v. 12 = πάντες 1 C. 15:22)

---

[26] Ed. S. Buber (1894), II, 142, line 3 from the bottom.

[27] Ed. S. Buber (1894), III, 129a, line 27 f.

[28] With Men., 11, 8 this ref. is the only place in the Mishnah where the plur. רבים is used adjectivally.

[29] For material cf. Jeremias Abendmahlsworte², 108 f.

[30] Hegermann, 68 f., 90-93.

[31] → V, 691, 27 ff., 695, 7 ff., 697, 19 ff.; Hegermann, 69 f., 91 f.

[32] Hegermann, 96 f. P. Kahle, The Cairo Geniza (1947), 184, 186 and Hegermann, 22-27 have shown that the Peshitta on the OT is probably pre-Chr. in origin.

"all (descended from Adam) had to die"; here both meaning and context agree in supporting an inclusive understanding of οἱ πολλοί. As far as the other Pauline references are concerned this understanding is established by the alternatives: R. 5:15c : ἡ χάρις τοῦ θεοῦ ... εἰς τοὺς πολλοὺς ἐπερίσσευσεν (= εἰς πάντας ἀνθρώπους, v. 18b); v. 19a : ἁμαρτωλοὶ κατεστάθησαν οἱ πολλοί ... 19b : δίκαιοι κατασταθήσονται οἱ πολλοί (= πάντες ἄνθρωποι v. 18a b = οἱ πάντες 11:32a b; on 5:19b cf. also → 543, 1 ff.); 12:5 : οἱ πολλοὶ ἓν σῶμά ἐσμεν ἐν Χριστῷ (= ἡμεῖς πάντες 1 C. 12:13); 1 C. 10:17a : ἓν σῶμα οἱ πολλοί ἐσμεν (= οἱ πάντες v. 17b); v. 33b : μὴ ζητῶν τὸ ἐμαυτοῦ σύμφορον ἀλλὰ τὸ τῶν πολλῶν (= πάντες v. 33a). The multiplication of the inclusive οἱ πολλοί in R. 5:12-21 (four of the seven Pauline instances) is to be explained by the reference to Is. 53 apparent in R. 5:16, 19b (→ 543, 1 ff.). οἱ πολλοί as noun is also to be found in Mk. 6:2 (Lk. 4:22 πάντες); 9:26 "all present"; Hb. 12:15 "the whole community" (→ 278, 34-39). In all three instances it is inclusive.

b. Without Article. Without article, too, πολλοί as noun is often used inclusively in the NT. This fact has enhanced significance in the light of the passages discussed under II, 2 (→ 543, 9 ff.).

In place of πολλοί without art. we find ὁ ὄχλος (Mk. 10:48/Mt. 20:31); οἱ ὄχλοι (Mk. 6:33/Mt. 14:13 par. Lk. 9:11); πᾶς ὁ λαός (Lk. 1:14/2:10); εἷς ἕκαστος (Mk. 1:34/Lk. 4:40); πάντες (Mk. 1:34/Mt. 8:16b; Mk. 3:10/Mt. 12:15b and Lk. 6:19; Mk. 6:2 vl./Lk. 4:22); conversely πολλοί can be used in place of πάντες (Mk. 1:32/Mt. 8:16a). Hence Mk. 1:34 (ἐθεράπευσεν πολλούς) is not taken exclusively by Mt. and Lk. (as though Jesus healed only some of the sick who lay round about Him); it is taken inclusively, and Mk. unquestionably meant it thus ("great was the number of those healed").

That Mt. 8:11 (πολλοὶ ἀπὸ ἀνατολῶν καὶ δυσμῶν ἥξουσιν) is in no sense exclusive may be seen from the reference to the OT idea of the eschatological pilgrimage of all peoples to Mt. Zion, [33] so that one should translate : "great hosts shall come from the east and west." The πολλοί in Lk. 1:14 (πολλοὶ ἐπὶ τῇ γενέσει αὐτοῦ χαρήσονται) does not refer to the restricted circle of friends and neighbours but to the people of salvation, as may be seen from 2:10 (χαρὰν ... παντὶ τῷ λαῷ). [34] The sense is also comprehensive in Lk. 2:34 f. (v. 34 : οὗτος κεῖται εἰς πτῶσιν καὶ ἀνάστασιν πολλῶν ἐν τῷ Ἰσραήλ ... v. 35 ... ὅπως ἂν ἀποκαλυφθῶσιν ἐκ πολλῶν καρδιῶν διαλογισμοί). πολλῶν ἐν τῷ Ἰσραήλ (v. 34) belongs no less to εἰς πτῶσιν than to (εἰς) ἀνάστασιν; hence the meaning of the phrase, which echoes Is. 8:14 f., is not that many will at first stumble on the rock Christ (→ IV, 271) and then rise up again, but that there will be division in Israel regarding Christ, some falling and others being raised up. After this comparison of the two groups into which Israel will divide according to v. 34, the πολλῶν of v. 35, which is to be taken as a noun, covers both groups : "so that the thoughts (coming) from the hearts of many may be revealed." Materially, then, the πολλοί of v. 35 denotes the whole people. In Jn. 5:28 the πολλοὶ τῶν καθευδόντων of Da. 12:2 LXX Θ is expounded inclusively by οἱ ἐν τοῖς μνημείοις. [35] In 2 C. 1:11 πολλοί is used first as adjective and then as noun, in both cases inclusively : ἵνα ἐκ πολλῶν προσώπων (→ 542, 27 ff.) τὸ εἰς ἡμᾶς χάρισμα

---

[33] → 537, 13 ff. J. Jeremias, Jesu Verheissung f. die Völker (1956), 47-62.
[34] Sahlin, op. cit. (→ n. 6), 75 : "the whole community"; Hck. Lk., ad loc.: "the whole people."
[35] Cf. 1 C. 15:22 : πάντες ζωοποιηθήσονται.

διὰ πολλῶν ("by many" = "by the whole community") εὐχαριστηθῇ ὑπὲρ
ἡμῶν. In Hb. 12:15 (→ 541, 13 f.) the reading πολλοί (without art.) is well
attested. Sometimes the most ancient expositors vary. Thus Mk. 10:31 par. Mt.
19:30 (πολλοὶ δὲ ἔσονται πρῶτοι ἔσχατοι) is taken inclusively in Mt. 20:16b
(ἔσονται . . . οἱ πρῶτοι ἔσχατοι, generally valid rule) but exclusively in Lk. 13:30b
(εἰσὶν πρῶτοι οἳ ἔσονται ἔσχατοι, the rule does not always apply).

The fact that "many" can be used inclusively in Semitic is the solution to the
crux interpretum in Mt. 22:14 : πολλοὶ γάρ εἰσιν κλητοί, ὀλίγοι δὲ ἐκλεκτοί
→ III, 494, 25; IV, 186, 26 ff. The first clause is indeed difficult if πολλοί is taken
exclusively (many but not all), for then there is a selection in both clauses. In
reality the situation is exactly the same as in 4 Esr. 8:3 : *Multi quidem creati sunt,
pauci autem salvabuntur* → 539, 12 ff. Formally there is an antithesis between a
great and small number, but materially the many represent the totality. If 4 Esr. 8:3
contrasts the totality of those created with the small number of the saved, Mt. 22:14
contrasts the totality of those invited with the small number of the chosen. God's
invitation, like His creation, embraces all without restriction, but the number of
those who will stand in the last judgment is only small. This is how Mt. (or his
source) took it when the originally isolated logion [36] 22:14 was appended as a
generalising interpretation [37] to the parable of the wedding-feast (22:1-13). For in
the present context πολλοὶ κλητοί embraces both those who were invited first
and also those who were invited last, i.e., Jews and Gentiles as Mt. understands it.

2. As Adjective.

In R. 4:17 f. Paul quotes Gn. 17:5 LXX : πατέρα πολλῶν ἐθνῶν τέθεικά σε
(Abraham). That in so doing he adopted the universalist understanding (→ V,
1005, 9 ff.) which later Judaism found here (→ n. 25) is shown with a high degree
of probability by R. 4:11: εἰς τὸ εἶναι αὐτὸν πατέρα πάντων τῶν πιστευόντων
δι' ἀκροβυστίας, cf. v. 16 : ὅς ἐστιν πατὴρ πάντων ἡμῶν. πολλοί as adjective
is also inclusive in 2 C. 1:11: ἐκ πολλῶν προσώπων ("by many persons, i.e., from
the lips of all"); Hb. 2:10 : πολλοὺς υἱοὺς εἰς δόξαν ἀγαγόντα, to bring "many
sons" (i.e., the great host of sons) to glory ; [38] with article Lk. 7:47: ἀφέωνται
αἱ ἁμαρτίαι αὐτῆς αἱ πολλαί, "as many as there are."

The breadth of the inclusive use of (οἱ) πολλοί in the NT, especially as noun
but also as adjective, illustrates the strength of Semitic influence on NT Greek.

II. (οἱ) πολλοί in Statements concerning the Saving Work of Jesus.

1. οἱ πολλοί (with Article).

οἱ πολλοί occurs twice in connection with statements concerning the saving
work of Jesus. R. 5:15c : ἡ χάρις τοῦ θεοῦ καὶ ἡ δωρεὰ ἐν χάριτι τῇ τοῦ ἑνὸς
ἀνθρώπου Ἰησοῦ Χριστοῦ εἰς τοὺς πολλοὺς ἐπερίσσευσεν· v. 19b : διὰ τῆς
ὑπακοῆς τοῦ ἑνὸς δίκαιοι κατασταθήσονται οἱ πολλοί. Paul himself interprets
these two sayings when he uses οἱ πολλοί interchangeably with πάντες ἄνθρωποι,
v. 18b. He thus ascribes the greatest conceivable breadth to οἱ πολλοί; Christ's
obedience affects mankind in the same way as does Adam's disobedience.

---

[36] J. Jeremias, *Die Gleichnisse Jesu*⁴ (1956), 89.
[37] *Ibid.*, 94.
[38] Cf. also Mt. 10:31 par. Lk. 12:7: πολλῶν στρουθίων διαφέρετε with Mt. 6:26 par.
Lk. 12:24, where (without the addition of πολλῶν) we have the unrestricted διαφέρετε
αὐτῶν (Lk. τῶν πετεινῶν).

R. 5:19b (δίκαιοι κατασταθήσονται οἱ πολλοί) is a rendering of Is. 53:11c acc. to the Heb. (לְרַבִּים...יַצְדִּיק). Paul thus takes the הָרַבִּים of Is. 53:11c inclusively: the "many" are all men. R. 5:16 takes the רַבִּים of Is. 53:12e (without art.) no less inclusively (→ 544, 24 ff.); in this respect he agrees with Jn., who in 1:29 has ὁ αἴρων τὴν ἁμαρτίαν τοῦ κόσμου for the חֵטְא־רַבִּים נָשָׂא of Is. 53:12e. [39] In his reading of Is. 53 Paul thus applied both הָרַבִּים and רַבִּים without distinction to all mankind (πάντες ἄνθρωποι → 542, 39 ff.).

2. πολλοί without Article.

All that has been said thus far is only a preparation for the real problem posed by the four passages in the NT in which πολλοί without article is used in connection with the saving work of Jesus: Mk. 10:45 (= Mt. 20:28): ὁ υἱὸς τοῦ ἀνθρώπου ... ἦλθεν ... δοῦναι τὴν ψυχὴν αὐτοῦ λύτρον ἀντὶ πολλῶν· Mk. 14:24 (par. Mt. 26:28): τοῦτό ἐστιν τὸ αἷμά μου τῆς διαθήκης τὸ ἐκχυννόμενον ὑπὲρ πολλῶν· R. 5:16: ... τὸ δὲ χάρισμα ἐκ πολλῶν παραπτωμάτων εἰς δικαίωμα [40] Hb. 9:28: εἰς τὸ πολλῶν ἀνενεγκεῖν ἁμαρτίας. The question raised by these verses is whether πολλοί is understood exclusively in Greek fashion (many, but not all) or inclusively in the sense that "many" can have in Semitic (the totality which embraces many individuals). In other words, does the vicarious work of Jesus avail only for the redeemed community or does He die for all without limitation?

a. NT Interpretations of πολλοί.

1 Tm. 2:6 has πάντων for the πολλῶν of Mk. 10:45 (→ 544, 9 f.). The πάντες of R. 5:12 also elucidates the πολλῶν of v. 16. ὑπὲρ παντός in Hb. 2:9 sheds light on the πολλῶν of 9:28. Thus in all three instances πολλοί is understood inclusively. Only in the case of Mk. 14:24 does the NT offer us two varying equivalents for πολλοί, namely, ὑμεῖς in 1 C. 11:24; Lk. 22:19 f. and ὁ κόσμος in Jn. 6:51c (the Johannine version of the explanatory saying about the bread). [41] It seems that here, then, we have both a restrictive and a comprehensive understanding of πολλοί. But it can be shown that this conclusion is not appropriate in the case of Paul. Paul says unequivocally that Christ died ὑπὲρ πάντων (2 C. 5:14 f.) and that God reconciled the world to Himself through Him (v. 19). It would thus seem that the substitution of ὑμεῖς for πολλοί in 1 C. 11:24; Lk. 22:19 f. is the result of liturgical practice rather than theological reflection; the use of the eucharistic sayings as formulae of distribution entails a change to the second person. This means that the NT, following Semitic usage, took the πολλοί in statements concerning the atoning work of Jesus in a comprehensive sense. Jesus died for all, for the reconciliation of the world. [42]

b. The Original Sense.

This conclusion, however, still does not answer a final question. This is the question whether the broad interpretation of πολλοί corresponds to the original

---

[39] It is very probable that there is a ref. to Is. 53:12e in Jn. 1:29b because, although the OT commonly speaks of (עון) נשא חטא, only Is. 53:12e (רבים) provides occasion for the closer definition τοῦ κόσμου in Jn. 1:29.

[40] In R. 5:16 πολλῶν might be taken either as adj. ("of many sins") or as noun ("of the sins of many"). The parallelism suggests that it is intended as a noun (ἐξ ἑνός / ἐκ πολλῶν), and the ref. to Is. 53:12e (→ 544, 24 ff.) confirms this.

[41] Cf. also Jn. 1:29; 11:51 f.

[42] The passion with which Tg. Is. 53 avoids this concept by violent wresting of the text of Is. 53 confirms the fact that the Chr. community held it, Hegermann, 91-93, 116-122.

sense of Mk. 10:45; 14:24 or whether we have here a secondary and more comprehensive understanding designed to avoid the offence of a restriction of the scope of the atoning work of Jesus to "many." Two considerations will help us to answer this question.

(a) The Age of the Tradition.

As regards the age of the tradition it may first be said that both Mk. 10:45 and 14:24 derive from pre-Hellenistic tradition. They give evidence of a Semitic character linguistically. In respect of 10:45 this is apparent when the saying is compared with 1 Tm. 2:5 f. Mk. 10:45 : ὁ υἱὸς τοῦ ἀνθρώπου ... ἦλθεν δοῦναι τὴν ψυχὴν αὐτοῦ λύτρον ἀντὶ πολλῶν, 1 Tm. 2:5 f.: ἄνθρωπος Χριστὸς Ἰησοῦς, ὁ δοὺς ἑαυτὸν ἀντίλυτρον ὑπὲρ πάντων. It is true of all five variations that the Marcan version agrees with Semitic usage whereas the version in 1 Tm. is more Greek. [43] The Palestinian origin of Mk. 10:45 and 14:24 is also supported by the fact that for both sayings there are other translations which point to a common Semitic original. [44] It may also be added that both verses use the HT of Is. 53. [45] Paul also builds on an older tradition in R. 5:16. This may be seen from the fact that he follows the HT of Is. 53 (→ n. 49) whereas elsewhere he normally uses the LXX. [46] Finally, Hb. 9:28 not only uses ἀναφέρειν / αἴρειν ἁμαρτίας as formulae (→ V, 710, 32 ff. and n. 440) but the whole context of 9:27 f. uses "older catechetical material." [47] These considerations support the conclusion that in fixing the original sense of πολλοί Semitic usage, or more precisely Is. 53, must be our starting-point.

(b) The Reference of All Four Passages to Is. 53.

Mk. 10:45 is based on Is. 53:10-12 HT (→ V, 712, 24 ff.), Mk. 14:24 on Is. 53:12 HT (→ V, 713, 1 ff.). Hb. 9:28 follows Is. 53:12e LXX. As concerns R. 5:16 we now know from new textual discoveries that v. 16 (ἐκ πολλῶν παραπτωμάτων) agrees with Is. 53:12e חטאי רבים,[48] and the context supports our assuming a ref. We have seen already (→ 543, 1 f.) that R. 5:19 (δίκαιοι κατασταθήσονται οἱ πολλοί) is a rendering of Is. 53:11c יַצְדִּיק...לָֽרַבִּים. Above all, however, the conjecture that R. 5:16 refers to Is. 53:12e is confirmed by the striking alternation of the form without art. (R. 5:16 πολλοί) and the form with art. (v. 19 οἱ πολλοί); this alternation is dictated by the HT of Is. 53 (v. 12e without art., v. 11c with art.). We can also see from this how thoroughly Pl. knew the HT of Is. 53. In all the ref. apart from Hb. 9:28 the HT of Is. 53 is used; LXX influence may be ruled out in view of the deviations of the LXX from the HT. [49]

---

[43] For detailed proof cf. Jeremias Lösegeld, 260 f. For further observations on the Semitic character of Mk. 10:45 ibid., 249-258, 261. On the Semitisms of Mk. 14:22-25 cf. Jeremias Abendmahlsworte, 88-94.

[44] Mk. 10:45 : 1 Tm. 2:5 f.; Mk. 14:24 (τὸ ἐκχυννόμενον ὑπὲρ πολλῶν): Mt. 26:28 (τὸ περὶ πολλῶν ἐκχυννόμενον.

[45] As concerns Mk. 10:45 LXX influence may be discounted since the LXX splits the expression שִׂים נַפְשׁוֹ (Is. 53:10) by division into two clauses. As concerns Mk. 14:24 ὑπέρ does not occur in LXX Is. 53.

[46] O. Michel, "Pls. und seine Bibel," BFTh, II, 18 (1929), 55-68.

[47] Mi. Hb. on 9:28.

[48] The Mas. text has the sing. חֶטְא־רַבִּים, but 1 QIsᵃ and 1 QIsᵇ both have the plur. חטאי רבים, which is also shown to be the older text by LXX, Tg, Peshitta, Θ, Σ (on ʾA → Hegermann, 44 and n. 1), cf. J. Jeremias, "Ein Anhalt für d. Datierung der masoret. Redaktion?" ZAW, 67 (1955), 289 f. On the basis of Is. 53:12e HT it may also be stated that in R. 5:16 πολλῶν is to be construed as a noun, not an adj. → n. 40.

[49] On Mk. 10:45 and 14:24 → n. 45. Nor can there be any question of LXX influence (Is. 53:12e ἁμαρτίας πολλῶν) on R. 5:16 (πολλῶν παραπτωμάτων).

As we have seen, however, רַבִּים in Is. 53 is interpreted inclusively not only by later Judaism (→ 540, 12 ff.) but also by Paul (→ 543, 1 ff.) and John (→ 543, 4 f.). It is taken to refer to the whole community, comprised of many members, which has fallen under the judgment of God. There is no support for the idea that Jesus interpreted Is. 53 any differently.

J. Jeremias

---

† πολυλογία

1. In correspondence with the verb πολυλογέω "to speak a lot," Democr. Fr., 44 (Diels⁷, II, 190, 12 f.) and the adj. πολύλογος "loquacious," Xenoph. Cyrop., I, 4, 3, πολυλογία[1] means "loquacity," "volubility," "talkativeness," Xenoph. Cyrop., I, 4, 3; Crete prefers πολύνοια to πολυλογία, Plat. Leg., I, 641e; Plut. De curiositate, 9 (II, 519c); Aristot. Pol., IV, 10, p. 1295a, 2. The word always has a negative ring.

2. The only instance in the LXX is at Prv. 10:19 : in much talking there will be sin. Both literally and in sense πολυλογία is here a transl. of רֹב דְּבָרִים. There are material par. in Sir. 32:4, 9; Qoh. 6:11. Volubility in prayer is suggested in Is. 1:15 and warned against in Sir. 7:14. The majesty of God is an argument in favour of the warning against it, Qoh. 5:1 f. Acc. to the OT view 1 K. 18:26 ff. depicts pagan πολυλογία in prayer which is designed to draw God's attention and to make it impossible for Him to overlook one's need.

3. In later Judaism, too, warnings against much speaking are found along with the magnifying of silence.[2] In prayer there is tension between crisp and sober calling on God and great loquacity. A famous anecdote in Tanch. B מקץ § 11 (986)[3] yields both an admonition against wearisome crying on God and also a basis for the fixed hour of prayer of the Rabbis. On the other hand, there are many passages which, quite apart from the praise of God in hymns, prefer the long prayer.[4]

4. In the NT and early Christian writings[5] the word occurs only in Mt. 6:7 in the sense of "verbosity."

In the composition of Mt. the logion in v. 7-8 is based on the standardised sayings about almsgiving, public or private prayer and fasting, but it is not so strictly constructed.[6] As distinct from the other sayings it is directed against pagan rather than Jewish piety.[7] The "much speaking" of the Gentiles refers either to the enumeration of

---

πολυλογία. Cf. Pass., Liddell-Scott; Moult.-Mill.; Pr.-Bauer⁴.

[1] On the composition of the word either πολυ-λόγος "speaking much" (Bl.-Debr. § 119, 1; Debr. Griech. Wortb. § 97) or better πολύ-λογος, "rich in words" (Bl.-Debr. § 120, 1; Debr. Griech. Wortb. § 90); they amount to the same thing; πολυλογία Bl.-Debr. § 110, 2; Debr. Griech. Wortb. § 38, 287 [Debrunner].

[2] Str.-B., III, 753 on Jm. 1:19 A; in Damasc. 10:17 f. (13:2) there is a prohibition of meaningless prattle on the Sabbath.

[3] Str.-B., I, 1036.

[4] Ibid., I, 403-406.

[5] πολύλαλος also occurs, though only in Herm. m., 11, 12. Cf. also ματαιαλογία (→ IV, 524, 3 ff.) and μωρολογία etc. (→ IV, 844, 13).

[6] Cf. Bultmann Trad., 140 f.

[7] In Lk. 11:2 the gloss (D) based on Mt. speaks only very generally of the πολυλογία "of some."

all the deities to be invoked, of which not one must be left out, or to the long list of epithets ascribed to the individual deity, or more likely to the attempt, satirised even by pagan authors, [8] to wear down the gods by endless prayers and promises. Materially there is probably a side-glance at Judaism too. [9] For in Judaism the question of shorter or longer prayer gives evidence of a shift of emphasis from the personal relation with God to the number of words uttered, which is an approximation to the Gentiles. πολυ-λογία is closely related to βατταλογέω, → I, 597. Quantity to the point of verbosity corresponds to an absence of quality; the petitioner attempts hereby to get through to God. The ἐν expresses the basis of the hope that the prayer will be heard: *longae orationis causa*. [10]

Jesus bases the assurance of being heard, not on the petitioner or his mechanical words, but on the readiness of the Father to hear. The Father takes seriously even the brusquest cry, vv. 8 ff. This is also apparent in the Lord's Prayer, which teaches us to pray great things in few words.

Maurer

πολυποίκιλος → 484, 34 ff. ποικίλος.   **πολύσπλαγχνος** → σπλαγχνίζομαι.
πολύς → 536, 1 ff. πολλοί.   **πόμα** → 145, 4 ff. πίνω.

πονηρός, πονηρία

---

† πονηρός.

Contents: A. πονηρός in the Greek World: I. The Classical Period; II. The Hellenistic Period. B. The Old Testament and Later Judaism: I. The LXX and Other Greek Translations; II. Later Judaism: 1. The Dead Sea Scrolls; 2. The Rabbis; 3. Hellenistic Judaism: a. The Pseudepigrapha; b. Philo and Josephus. C. πονηρός in the New Testament: I. In the Sense of Bad, Harmful, Unserviceable, Useless; II. In the Moral Sense: 1. Adjectival Use: a. In Connection with Persons; b. In Connection with Things and Concepts; 2. Use as Noun: a. The Bad Man; b. The Devil; c. Evil.

A. πονηρός in the Greek World.

I.   The Classical Period.

πονηρός belongs to the group of ρο- forms or r-suffixes and in a way analogous to βλαβερός and νοσηρός it is derived from the verb πονέω or πονέομαι. [1] The original verb is πένομαι from which come πενία "poverty" and πένης, πενιχρός "poor,"

---

[8] Sen. Epistulae, 31, 5; Mart., VII, 60, 3.
[9] Schl. Mt., *ad loc.* Cf. vl. ὑποκριταί B sy[c].
[10] H. Grotius, Annotationes in Novum Testamentum, I (1641), *ad loc.*; Bl.-Debr. § 219, 2.

π ο ν η ρ ό ς. J. B. Bauer, "Libera nos a malo," Verbum Domini, 34 (1956), 12-15; H. Braun, "Beobachtungen zur Tora-Verschärfung im häretischen Spätjudt.," ThLZ, 79 (1954), 347-352; J. H. Case, *The Lord's Prayer in the Early Church, Texts and Studies,* I, 3 (1891). Dalman WJ, I, 283-365; P. Fiebig, *Das Vaterunser* (1927), 91-93; H. Greeven, *Gebet u. Eschatologie im NT* (1931), 95 f. K. G. Kuhn, *Achtzehngebet u. Vaterunser u. der Reim* (1950); E. Lohmeyer, *Das Vaterunser*[3] (1952), 147-162 with further bibl.; R. Schwarz, "Der Böse oder das Böse," Chr. W., 47 (1933), 6-16, 50-56; on this F. Ménégoz, "Zum Thema: Das Böse oder der Böse," Chr. W., 47 (1933), 112-118; H. J. Stoebe, "Gut u. Böse in der jahwistischen Quelle des Pent.," ZAW, 65 (1953), 188-204.
[1] Hofmann, 262; Boisacq, 766 f.; Debr. Griech. Wortb., 169; Schwyzer, I, 482.

"needy" (→ 37, 4 f.). The late development of the term is shown by the fact that it does not appear in Hom., though we find it in Hesiod (Fr., 138, 139).

Related to πόνος, it has throughout class. Gk. the original sense 1. "laden with care," "sorrowful," "unhappy." πονηρότατος (Hes. Fr., 138) is equivalent to ἐπίπονος καὶ δυστυχής (Comm. in Aristot. Eth. Nic., III, 7, p. 1113b, 14). The πονηρός is ἄταν ἔχων (Epicharmus Fr., 7 [Diels⁷, I, 199, 16]). πονωπόνηρε (Aristoph. Vesp., 466, cf. Lys., 350) acc. to the commentator (Schol. on Vesp., 466) ² means ἀσκήσει καὶ μελέτῃ πεπονημένε τῆς τυραννίδος "laden with the exercise and care of rule." To distinguish this sense from πονηρός in the moral sense Attic used a different accent as proparoxytonon : πόνηρος. ³ 2. Then πονηρός can denote "that which causes trouble and brings sorrow." φήμη πονηρά, "speech which brings disaster," ⁴ φορτίον πονηρόν, "trouble which brings evil," Aristoph. Pl., 352. 3. πονηρός can thus take on the sense of "pitiable," "incompetent," "wretched," "poor." ⁵ It can also mean "badly contrived," "in poor shape," "unattractive," "unfit," "unserviceable," "pernicious," Plat. Theaet., 167b; Xenoph. Cyrop., I, 4, 19; also "prejudicial," Plat. Leg., V, 735c; Gorg., 464d; "unfavourably disposed," Xenoph. An., VII, 4, 12; III, 4, 34; and in the following combinations : "fatal" prophetesses, Epicharmus, 9 (CGF, I, 92), "bad" counsels, Aristoph. Lys., 517, "unfavourable" beginning of education, Aeschin. Tim., 11, "unlucky" voyage, Plat. Resp., VIII, 551c, "poor" workmanship, "poor" functioning of the instruments of sense, Plat. Hi., II, 374d; Resp., IV, 421d, "bad" dog, Plat. Euthyd., 298d, "harmful" or "noxious" smoke of coal, Aristot. Mirabiles Auscultationes, 115, p. 841a, 33. 4. This leads on quite naturally to the sense of "unsuccessful" in political or military affairs, often with πράγματα. ⁶ 5. A new aspect appears in the social realm, where πονηρός is the opp. of the Gk. ideal of the καλὸς κἀγαθός. The πονηροί are contrasted with the καλῶς γεγονότες, τεθραμμένοι καὶ πεπαιδευμένοι, i.e., aristocrats of good origin, education and appearance, Isoc., 8, 122. They are the plebeians, rude and insolent in manner, using the jargon of the market-place, in poor circumstances. ⁷ The πονηρὸς ἀνήρ is the one who was previously nothing (οὐδὲν ὢν τὸ πρίν) and has now come to esteem (ἀξίωμα), Eur. Suppl., 424. 6. The political sense derives from the social. The πονηρός is the "politically useless," the "parasite on the commonwealth," even the "enemy of state." Not quite in this category is the expression πονηρῶς φερόμενος which is used of Alcibiades : one who is poorly esteemed in the army because of stinginess in pay, Xenoph. Hist. Graec., I, 5, 17. On the other hand ἀπὸ συκοφαντίας ζῶντες (Xenoph. Hist. Graec., II, 3. 13. 14) certainly belongs here with its ref. to those who during the age of democracy calumniated the aristocrats. Aristoph. (Pl., 31) lists πονηροί with temple-

---

² Ed. F. Dübner (1855), 146.

³ On Eupolis Fr., 321 (CAF, I, 344): καὶ μὴ πονηρούς, ὦ πονήρα, προξένει, "do not promote evil, O unfortunate," we find the grammatical note ὁ κατὰ ψυχὴν ὀξυτόνως — ὁ δὲ κατὰ σῶμα προπαροξυτόνως, cf. also Etym. M., 682, 25; similarly Herodianus Technicus, περὶ καθολικῆς προσῳδίας, 8 (ed. A. Beetz, I [1867], 197, 19 ff.); Arcadius De Accentibus, 8 (ed. C. H. Barker [1820], 71, 16); Schwyzer, I, 380 and 383.

⁴ μηδ᾽ ἐπιζευχθῇς στόμα φήμῃ πονηρᾷ μηδ᾽ ἐπιγλωσσῶ κακά, "take no words of evil omen on thy lips and utter no words of objurgation" is the warning of the chorus to Orestes (Aesch. Choeph., 1044 f.); φήμη πονηρά is here elucidated by the par. κακά.

⁵ Abs. (Aristoph. Vesp., 977; Isoc., 19, 12, 24; Demosth. Or., 59, 57; Xenoph. Cyrop., VII, 5, 75); of σῶμα, Plat. Prot., 313a, ἕξις τοῦ σώματος, Tim., 86e, βίος, Aesch. Fr., 90 (TGF, 31), σύμμαχοι, Aristoph. Nu., 102; Pl., 220, χρῆμα, Xenoph. Cyrop., V, 2, 34.

⁶ Isoc., 8, 115; Lys., 14, 35; Thuc., VIII, 97, 2; Aristot. Rhet., III, 14, p. 1415b, 22. The Schol. on Thuc., VII, 48, 1 (ed. J. Bekker [1821]) expounds it as οὐκ ἀσφαλῆ, ἀσθενῆ, ἐπικίνδυνα, "uncertain," "unstable," "dangerous."

⁷ Aristoph. Eq., 336 f.: πονηρὸς ... κἀκ πονηρῶν. 181: πονηρὸς κἀξ ἀγορᾶς εἶ καὶ θρασύς. The opp. may be seen in the question of Demos to the sausage-seller, 185 : μῶν ἐκ καλῶν εἶ κἀγαθῶν; he answers, 186 : μὰ τοὺς θεούς, εἰ μὴ 'κ πονηρῶν γ᾽. With biting irony the aristocrat Aristoph. has Demos reply : ὦ μακάριε τῆς τύχης, ὅσον πέπονθας ἀγαθὸν εἰς τὰ πράγματα, Lucky man, how useful this will prove to you in politics ! cf. also Isoc., 15, 316 : πονηρῶν ἀνθρώπων καὶ μεστῶν θρασύτητος, and the ref. to the φαυλότης τῶν ἐξ ἀρχῆς αὐτοῖς ὑπαρχόντων. Cf. also 15, 100.

robbers, orators and sycophants. The antithesis now is not πονηρός — καλός κἀγαθός but πονηρός — χρηστός, the worthless as distinct from the worthy citizen. [8] Aeschin. emphasises expressly the relation between public and private conduct. The man who is politically bad cannot be good in private life and *vice versa*, Aeschin. Tim., 30; In Ctesiphontem, 78. War snatches away the worthy citizen and soldier, not the bad, Soph. Phil., 437. Thus political failings affect the concept of πονηρός, e.g., bad leaders and orators, Aeschin. In Ctesiphontem, 78 and 134; Aristot. Pol., V, 9, p. 1304b, 26. The neut. form πονηρά also comes to mean that which is politically "disadvantageous" for the commonwealth, Plat. Theaet., 167c. 7. The final stage is the moral concept of πονηρός which arises by abstraction from social and political life. In this sense πονηρός means "morally reprehensible" in conduct towards the gods and men, "willingly and knowingly bad." [9] In this use, too, πονηρός is the anton. of χρηστός, but now in a moral sense, Plat. Symp., 183d, also of ἐσθλός, Eur. Hec., 596 f. It is thus synon. with ἄχρηστος (Plat. Leg., XII, 950b), also ἄδικος, ἀσεβής (Isoc., 8, 120; Aristot. Eth. Nic., IV, 3, p. 1122a, 6) and κακός (Philemon Fr., 114 [CAF, II, 514]). With gt. thoroughness Xenoph. defines πονηροί as ἀχάριστοι, ἀμελεῖς, πλεονέκται, ἄπιστοι, ἀκρατεῖς, Mem., II, 6, 19 f. Aristoph. has παράβολος and πονηρός together, Vesp., 192. In Aristot. πονηροί are ἄδικοι who do harm of evil intent in contrast to those who act out of θυμός and πάθη, while the ἄκρατος is not ἄδικος and only ἡμιπόνηρος, Eth. Nic., V, 10, p. 1135b, 24; VIII, 11, p. 1152a, 16. 20-24. μοχθηρός is also used with πονηρός, but πονηρός is the more emphatic term, Poet., 13, p. 1453a, 1; p. 1452b, 34 and 36. Thus there is general ref. to ἄνδρες πονηροί or simply πονηροί, [10] or to a πονηρά whom it is foolish to marry simply because she is rich and of noble family (Eur. El., 1098), or to those who are "bad" to their friends (Xenoph. Cyrop., VIII, 4, 33). Actions and conduct may also be morally bad : ἦθος (Democr. Fr., 192 [Diels⁷, II, 185, 11]), δίαιτα which a man will not give up out of ἀκολασία, "licentiousness" (Plat. Resp., IV, 425e), ἔργα (Demosth. Or., 19, 33; Hom. Epigrammata, 14, 20), [11] κέρδη (Eur. Cyc., 312), τελεταί (Eur. Ba., 260), πράγματα (Isoc., 5, 77), σκώμματα "railleries" (Aristoph. Nu., 542), αἰτία (Aeschin. Tim., 48) τρόπος "character" or "mode of life" (Aeschin. In Ctesiphontem, 173), λόγος (Antiphon. Or. Tetralogia, II, 3, 3), finally πονηρά in general alongside ἄδικα (Eur. Hec., 1190). By nature the moral man cannot do πονηρόν (Aristot. Rhet., 5, p. 1426b, 35; Menand. Fr., 530 [Körte, 176]). Even in misfortune he remains a χρηστός (Eur. Hec., 596).

II. The Hellenistic Period.

In the Hell. period the general use of πονηρός does not change much. Here, too, it means "full of trouble," "unfortunate" (with πράττειν), [12] also "useless," "false," "wrong," "harmful," "unfavourable," "offensive," thus "deceptive" hope (Herodian., II, 1, 7), "contrary" winds (Dion. Hal. Ant. Rom., 1, 52), of the root of a family (Plut. Ser. Num. Pun., 7 [II, 553c]), of water, of wild beasts, [13] of magic (Ditt. Syll.³, I, 985), of the word (*ibid.,* III, 1175). A new concept under religious influence is that of the πονηρός δαίμων [14] who unsettles marriage or snatches away the blushing maiden,

---

[8] Cf. Xenoph. Resp. Ath., I, 1; Aeschin. Tim., 11; In Ctesiphontem, 177; Antiph. Fr., 205 (CAF, II, 99).

[9] For definitions → πονηρία.

[10] Eur. Cyc., 645; Eupolis Fr., 321 (CAF, I, 344); Antiph. Fr., 233 (CAF, I, 113 f.); Menand. Fr., 7 (Körte, II, 17).

[11] Ed. E. Abel (1886).

[12] Diod. S., 79; Synesius Epistulae, 43 (MPG, 66, 1365); E. L. v. Leutsch and F. G. Scheidewin, Paroemiographi Graeci, I (1839), 446 : Appendix Proverbiorum, 4, 59.

[13] Of water Plut. De capienda, 2 (II, 86e); so also later in the Byzantine hymn : To the Holy Fathers, 2, 3 (P. Maas, *Frühbyzantinische Kirchenpoesie*, KlT, 52/53 [1910], 25); of animals, *ibid.,* 10, 6 (29).

[14] P. Lond., V, 1713, 20; Porphyr. De philosophia ex oraculis haurienda, II, 164b (ed. G. Wolff [1856], 147) writes of πονηροί δαίμονες. Rom. inscr. from the 2nd cent. Epigr. Graec., 566, 4.

and also that of the πονηρὸν πνεῦμα which, so far as one can see, is taken from the usage of the LXX.[15] πονηρός is also used politically.[16] From Latin law comes an expression constantly found in contracts and wills, namely, δόλος πονηρός[17] or μετὰ δόλου πονηροῦ (= dolo malo).[18]

Naturally there is a general use of πονηρός in the moral sense for "morally reprehensible," "useless," "bad," "evil." The πονηροί are contrasted with the καλοὶ κἀγαθοί or ethically with the ἀγαθοί and μεγαλωφελεῖς, Plut. Aud. Poet., 21 (II, 21e); Ser. Num. Pun., 7 (II, 553c), also the χρηστοί, P. Flor., II, 120, 1, 6. We find the same sense in neuter combinations, e.g., Plut. Tranq. An., 19 (II, 477a): πραγμάτων καὶ βουλευμάτων πονηρῶν. In a list of vices the πονηρός occurs with the πάροινος and βάναυσος, and again in contrast with the καλὸς κἀγαθός, P. Hibeh, I, 1, 3. The πονηρός is defined as συκοφάντης or θρασύς or πρόφασιν ζητῶν,[19] a πονηρὸς βίος as ληστρικός, BGU, II, 372, 2, 1; P. Masp., I, 4, 8; 9 verso 2. πονηρός is also found without closer definition for the morally reprehensible,[20] and it can thus be used in the abs. too.[21] When ὁ πονηρός is used for the devil, it is based on NT usage,[22] → 558, 27 ff.

B. The Old Testament and Later Judaism.

I. The LXX and Other Greek Translations.

The use of πονηρός for רַע and derivates of רָעַע] remains within the sphere of the Heb. original. a. "Bad" in nature or condition, "of little worth," "useless," of "cultically useless animals" (Lv. 27:10, 12, 14, 33), of fruits and foods (2 K. 2:19; Jer. 24:2, 3, 8), of land (Nu. 13:19; 20:5), of men (1 S. 25:3; Sir. 42:5). b. "Ill-natured," "dangerous," "harmful," of animals (Gn. 37:20, 33; Lv. 26:6; Is. 35:9; Ez. 5:17; 14:15; 34:25). c. "Unfavourable" of a man's reputation (Dt. 22:14, 19; Neh. 6:13), of censure (ψόγος Gn. 37:2; μῶμος Dt. 15:21; Sir. 5:14; 20:24), what is "prejudicial" to the soul (Sir. 37:27), of the πονηρὸν πνεῦμα, "the spirit which brings ruin" (Ju. 9:23; 1 S. 16:14-16, 23; 18:10; 19:9; Tob. 3:8, 17), "human conduct which brings ruin."[23] In this connection ref. should be

---

[15] P. Masp., II, 188, 3; B. P. Grenfell and A. S. Hunt, New Class. Fragments and Other Greek and Latin Pap. (1897), 76, 3; P. Masp., I, 121, 9; P. Flor., I, 93, 13; P. Lond., V, 1713, 20; P. Lips., I, 34, 8; 35, 11; Preisigke Sammelbuch, I, 4426, 6.

[16] Diphilus Fr., 66, 2 (CAF, II, 562): ἰχθυοπώλας ... πονηροὺς τοὺς 'Αθήνησιν "hostile"; P. Masp., III, 354, II, 15 of the tyrant : "wicked."

[17] First in the treaty of the Romans with the Methymnaeans, 129 B.C., Ditt. Syll.³, II, 693, 6. They pledged themselves μήτε ὅπλοις μήτε χρήμασι ... βοηθείτωσαν δημοσίαι βουλῇ δόλωι πονηρῶι. The constantly recurring formula runs δόλος φθόνος πονηρὸς ἀπίτω ἀπέστω or ταύτῃ τῇ διαθήκῃ δόλος πονηρὸς ἀπέστω, P. Lond., I, 77, 65 c. 600 A.D. Cf. also P. Hamb., I, 73, 12; P. Oxy., XVI, 1901, 54 f.; Ditt. Or., II, 629, 112 (age of Hadrian); χωρὶς δόλου πονηροῦ Ditt. Syll.³, I, 319, 2. The Lat. formula runs : h(uic) t(estamento) d(olus) m(alus) abesto, thus in a Lat. will ed. P. M. Meyer, "Römischrechtliche Papyrusurkunden d. Hamburg. Stadtbibliothek," Zeitschr. f. vergleichende Rechtswissenschaft, 35 (1918), 82 f.; for the testamentary clause, ibid., 88; cf. also C. G. Bruns, Fontes iuris Romani antiqui⁷ (1909), No. 136, 26; 137, 19; 139, 18; 140, 2, 11; 141, 4, 6.

[18] In the afore-mentioned treaty of the Romans with the Methymnaeans, Ditt. Syll.³, II, 693, 9.

[19] P. Masp., I, 3, 23; P. Oxy., VI, 885, 17; Preisigke Sammelbuch, III, 6751, 9.

[20] P. Oxy., III, 409, 26; 410, 93; Papyrologica Lugduno-Batavia, VI : "A Family-Archive from Tebtunis," ed. B. A. van Groningen (1950), 15, 63.

[21] Dion. Hal. Ant. Rom., 11, 2.

[22] Mt. 13:19; Jn. 17:15; Eph. 6:16; 1 Jn. 2:13; Byzant. Evening Hymns, 1, 9 (Maas, op. cit. [→ n. 13], 4); P. Lond., III, 1029, 10, where there is ref. to the πλάνη or πλανήστρης τοῦ πονηροῦ.

[23] The περιφέρεια of the ἄφρων in Qoh. 10:13 is a transl. of הוֹלֵלוּת. The LXX perhaps read this as חוֹלֵלוּת and related it to חוּל, "to move around in a circle." הוֹלֵלוּת occurs only in Qoh.; at 9:3 it is transl. πλάνη by 'A; at 2:12 (B) the LXX has παραφορά "madness";

made to the expression טוֹב וָרָע in so far as this denotes what is advantageous or hurtful, what promotes life or injures it (2 S. 13:22 : לְמֵרָע וְעַד טוֹב neither in good nor in bad ; probably also Gn. 2:17; 3:22 : Man himself can decide concerning what helps or hurts him).[24] d. "To look bad, ugly, sorrowful," of the face, Neh. 2:2. e. "Unhappy," "troubled," of the age[25] or day, Ps. 49:5. The "evil" or "hurtful" in gen.,[26] the "futile," "meaningless," in the acts of man, "the misfortune" against which God can preserve us but which He precisely brings on transgressors (Qoh. 11:2; Is. 3:11; 'Ιερ. 51[44]:29), the "bad," "sorrowful" life (Sir. 29:24), "plagues" (Bar. 2:25), "sickness" (Dt. 7:15; 28:35, 59; Job 2:7; Qoh. 5:15; 6:2), angels which "bring destruction" (ψ 77:49), "stinginess" (Sir. 31[34]:24), "laborious" work (Qoh. 1:13), poverty (Sir. 13:24), manner of death (ψ 33:22; 143:10; Sir. 28:21), punishment and retribution (Ez. 14:21; Jdt. 7:15), in short, the works of God which point in this direction, His *opera aliena* (Sir. 39:34). To this corresponds the "bad" hope which is set on such events (Is. 28:19), the "evil" report ('Ιερ. 30:49 [49:23]). f. The expression ῥῆμα πονηρόν can be used in various senses, e.g., for the threat whose theme is "evil,"[27] the speech which is "detrimental" to someone (Jdt. 8:8), the "evil" word directed against a person (Jdt. 8:9), and finally the reported event, a "bad" experience.[28]

g. Like רַע πονηρός is used in the moral sense. The impulse is "evil" (a thought particularly developed in post-biblical Judaism, → 552, 13), cf. Gn. 6:5; 8:21. So, too, is the heart (Bar. 1:22; 2:8), or the eye, especially the covetous eye (Sir. 14:10; 31[34]:13). It is typical of biblical thinking that acts are evil or false, not only before men (Neh. 2:10; 13:8; 1 S. 8:6; 18:8; 2 S. 11:25; Gn. 44:5), but also and especially before God (Gn. 38:7; 1 K. 11:6 [LXX]; 14:22; 2 S. 11:27 cf. 1 Ch. 21:7). God decides what is good and evil, Is. 5:20; Am. 5:14, 15; Mi. 3:2; Mal. 2:17.[29] As מְרֵעִים can mean "evil-doers," so רַע or ὁ πονηρός can be used abs. for "the wicked man,"[30] sometimes with ἄδικος, sometimes with σκληρός, sometimes with ἁμαρτωλός and ἄνομος (1 S. 25:3; 1 Esr. 4:39; ψ 9:36; 1 Macc. 14:14), sometimes in antithesis to ἀγαθός or δίκαιος (Sir. 14:5). The wicked man is the transgressor of the Law who is to be rooted out, Dt. 17:7, 12; 19:19; 21:21; 22:21, 22, 24; 24:7. He is characterised by ὕβρις (Job 35:12) and ὑπερηφανία (Prv. 8:13). In the OT, however, הָרָע or ὁ πονηρός is not yet used for Satan, → 549, 15. In contrast to the wicked are those who seek Yahweh, Prv. 28:5b. The wicked, then, are those who do not seek Yahweh or His commands, who will not be guided by Him, Ez. 11:2. Who is wicked is thus measured by God, by His commands, and by

---

at 7:25 it uses περιφορά "confusion." The parallelism in 9:3 virtually identifies περιφέρεια with πονηρόν, cf. G. Bertram, "Hbr. u. gr. Qoh.," ZAW, NF, 23 (1952), 33. The παιδεία πονηρά of Sir. 9:1 is also to be understood thus as a "teaching which is injurious to thee" rather than morally reprehensible : Thy jealousy might teach thy wife to do what thou believest of her, so that thy conduct would turn against thyself (עָלֶיךָ). The Heb. has only רָעָה whereas the LXX perhaps read דַּעַת רָעָה, cf. Prv. 1:29, where the LXX (cod A) has παιδία for דַּעַת. It is also possible that למד pi is rendered by διδάσκειν παιδείαν, G. Bertram, "Der Begriff der Erziehung in d. gr. Bibel," Imago Dei (1932), 45 f.

[24] Stoebe, 201.

[25] Gn. 47:9; ψ 36:19; 40:2; 48:6; Jer. 17:17, 18; Am. 5:13; Qoh. 9:12; Sir. 51:11.

[26] Gn. 44:4; 50:17; Nu. 14:37; 1 S. 25:21; ψ 34:12; Qoh. 9:3; 11:2; Is. 3:11.

[27] "Bad, hard" words, Ex. 33:4; "evil" thing, 4 Βασ. 4:41; the opp. is ῥήματα καλά, "words of promise," Nu. 24:13; Jos. 23:15.

[28] Qoh. 8:5; like the Heb. original ῥῆμα can mean both word and reported event. Perhaps by using ἐν λόγῳ πονηρῷ at Qoh. 8:3 the LXX wants to suggest that it understands דְּבַר רַע differently here from v. 5.

[29] Acc. to a later understanding, if not perhaps the J source, Gn. 2:17 as well.

[30] Dt. 13:6; 22:22; 24:7; Is. 9:16; Jer. 15:21; Ez. 7:24 A; Sir. 17:31; 4 Macc. 12:11.

obedience to them. God determines what is evil, and in this sense evil is to be understood simply as that which is contrary to God.

Hence רַע or πονηρός is used gen. of men in the sense of "morally bad," "culpable," ψ 139:2; Is. 25:4; 31:2. It is used of men (Gn. 13:13; 1 S. 30:22), women (Sir. 25:16, 23; 42:6) and children (Wis. 3:12), of neighbours (Jer. 12:14), calumniators (1 Macc. 1:36), and of a society, a city or an assembly (1 Esr. 2:14; Nu. 14:27), also of individuals (Gn. 38:7; 1 Ch. 2:3; Est. 7:6). The inner part of man is evil, the will which has turned aside from God : βουλή (Is. 3:9; Ez. 11:2), λογισμός (Jer. 11:19; Ez. 38:10; 1 Macc. 11:8), ἐνθύμημα (Sir. 37:3), καρδία (Jer. 3:17), ὑπόνοια (Sir. 3:24), ψυχή (Sir. 6:4). The organs at the disposal of the evil will and thoughts are also morally evil, ὀφθαλμός (Sir. 31[34]:13), χείρ (Jer. 23:14). The genesis of man is evil too (γένεσις, Wis. 12:10). The ὁδός is evil and culpable (Jer. 18:11; Ez. 13:22; Jon. 3:8; Zech. 1:4; 1 S. 3:21; 2 K. 17:13; ψ 118:101), and so is the δρόμος (Jer. 23:10), ἐπιτήδευμα (Dt. 28:20 for רֹעַ מַעֲלָלֶיךָ; Neh. 9:35; Jer. 23:2), λόγος (ψ 140:4 vl.), ἔργον (1 Esr. 8:83), ποίημα (2 Esr. 9:13), βδελύγματα (2 K. 21:11), ἀνομία (Ez. 8:9 vl.), ἁμάρτημα (1 K. 5:18 vl.), πρᾶγμα (Dt. 17:5 vl.), ῥῆμα "deed" (Gn. 38:10 vl.; Dt. 23:10; 1 S. 8:6; 2 S. 11:27).

πονηρόν is "evil" in the abs. as distinct from the ἀγαθόν, 2 S. 13:22; 14:17; Qoh. 12:14, or καλόν (Gn. 2:9, 17; 3:5, 22; Is. 5:20; Am. 5:14); πονηρόν or τὸ πονηρόν stands alone in Neh. 9:28; Sir. 17:31 AB². In the plur. we find τὰ πονηρά or πονηρά alone as the object of will and speech, Gn. 8:21 cf. 6:5; Mi. 3:2; Nu. 11:1; ψ 108:20; Na. 1:11.

There are numerous references to "evil" before God or according to His judgment (τὰ πονηρὰ ἔναντι κυρίου, Nu. 32:13; Dt. 4:25 et al.; ἐνθυμεῖσθαι κατὰ τοῦ κυρίου Wis. 3:14), and even where it is not expressly stated evil is characterised by its antithesis to God and His will. A review of all the instances[31] in the Septuagint shows that in most of them (220 of 360) πονηρός is used in a moral sense. No social evaluation is connected therewith, → 547, 23 ff.

II. Later Judaism.

1. The Dead Sea Scrolls.

Here, too, רַע means "bad," "harmful," "disadvantageous." To the desire to be kept from all evil corresponds the desire for blessing with all good, 1 QS 2:3; 1 QpHab 9:13. It is characteristic of all the texts that they link a כֹּל with טוֹב or רַע as a form of intensifying and completion. In the moral sense of רַע one also finds כֹּל רַע in the combination of being kept from all evil and cleaving to all good, 1 QS 1:4, cf. 10:17; 5:1. Expressed here is a radicalising of the demand of the Torah in an extensive sense.[32] The positive side may also be described as keeping to what God has commanded, 1 QS 5:1. God's commands, His מִצְוֹת, define what is good. On the other side are those who do all evil, 1 QS 1:7. What is evil may be seen plainly from the enumeration in the Manual, which is almost a list of vices.[33] It is surprising how little concrete this enumeration is. Abominable deeds in the spirit of whoredom or apostasy are all that are mentioned, along with a lack of desire to do what is good. What is in view here is the disposition and inner attitude towards the command of God.

---

[31] Sometimes the transl. have πονηρός where LXX reads the text differently or does not give any transl.: Prv. 20:14 Θ; Ez. 5:16 Θ; Jer. 21:14 ᾽ΑΘ; 5:28 ΣΘ; 11:8 ΣΘ. Θ adds a strengthening πονηρός at Jer. 13:10.

[32] Braun, 350, cf. also his Spätjüd.-häretischer u. frühchr. Radikalismus, I (1957), esp. 15-47.

[33] 1 QS 4:9-11: "Spirit of corruption, covetousness of soul, slothful hands in the service of righteousness, infamy, falsehood, arrogance and pride of heart, deceit and deception, terrible and full of hypocrisy, quick to wrath, zeal in presumption, abominable acts in the spirit of whoredom and ways of impurity in impure service."

2. The Rabbis.

Apart from the characteristic radicalising formula the meaning of רַע is the same in the Rabb.: "bad," "harmful," "disadvantageous." Prayer is made for deliverance from harmful events, grievous sufferings and bad dreams, bBer., 16b; 17a; 60b, cf. 1 QpHab 9:2. There are many ref. to the "bad" repute into which someone falls. [34]

רַע is also common in the moral sense. It is the evil in the abs. which a man has in his mind. [35] What is good and bad is expressed esp. in the picture of the two ways, Ab., 2, 9. To the bad way belongs a bad (covetous) eye or heart or a bad companion, all of which may lead on to this evil way. [36] God determines what is good and bad, and all bad conduct is against both God and man (bSanh., 27a), against heaven and creation (cf. Lk. 15:18). The tongue of the calumniator is evil, so that the tongue of evil means calumniation in bSota, 35a; bAr., 15a. The contrast between good and evil is found esp. in relation to the impulse. [37] The evil impulse is the mind or sensual desire which is directed to what is ungodly, earthly, corruptible and esp. contrary to the Law. [38] In the Talmud in a saying of R. Shimeon bLaqish (3rd cent.) the evil impulse is brought into relation to Satan and the angel of death, [39] but Satan is not called the evil one. Nevertheless, the saying of Job (9:24) that the earth is in the hand of רָשָׁע is referred to Satan by the Tannaite R. Jehoshua bChananiah (90-130 A.D.). [40]

3. Hellenistic Judaism.

a. The Pseudepigrapha.

In the pseudepigr., esp. Test. XII, πονηρός is seldom used for "worthless," "bad," "hurtful." In one passage there is a ref. to the threat of "evil" death, Test. R. 6:6. The moral sense is, however, predominant. It is used of persons who do not please God, [41] of sexual desire (Test. R. 4:9; Test. Jos. 3:10; 7:8), of the evil eye (Test. Iss. 4:6), of an act, [42] of advice (Test. Iss. 6:2), and of moral conduct in general. [43] τὸ πονηρόν is often used for that which is displeasing to God. [44]

---

[34] הוֹצִיא שֵׁם רַע עַל "to bring a bad name on someone" (Dt. 22:14, 19 → 549, 23 f.), esp. a woman, cf. Ar., 3, 5; v. also Sota, 3, 50. The Aram. equivalent is שׁוּם בִּישׁ Dalman, 351.

[35] E.g., bBer., 17a; cf. jPea, I, 1 (16b, 8), where רָעָה is abstract, as in Ps. 140:3. The Aram. equivalent is בִּישָׁא Tg. O. and Tg. J. I on Gn. 48:16; 26:29; Ex. 10:10; Tg. Ps. 121:7. רַע is used in connection with both persons and things, 1 QpHab 9:1 f., 12; cf. Tg. O. on Gn. 6:3.

[36] There is a similar list in bBer., 60b in a prayer to be kept, and further features of the evil way may be found in bBer., 17a.

[37] Cf. on this Str.-B., IV, 466-483 Exc. 19 : "The good and evil impulse."

[38] Ibid., 466. Cf. Ab., 2, 11: "The evil impulse, the evil eye and human hatred bring man out of the world," Str.-B., IV, 468.

[39] bBB, 16a (Str.-B., IV, 468).

[40] bBB, 16a : לֹא דָּבַר אִיוֹב אֶלָּא כְּנֶגֶד הַשָּׂטָן. The same saying is handed down by Abaye (d. 338/9 A.D.). Dalman, 352 f. pts. out that Sammael as the chief under Satan is called הָרָשָׁע and that in Tg. on Is. 11:4 Armilos, the opponent of the Messiah, is called רַשִּׁיעָא. But this is not used as a name.

[41] Test. Jud. 10:2; Χαναναῖοι, 11:1; ἄνθρωποι Test. Iss. 7:7; Test. B. 5:1; gen. οἱ πονηροί Test. G. 4:2.

[42] πονηρὸν ἔργον Test. L. 13:8; Test. D. 6:8; like θυμός and ψεῦδος (in antithesis to ἀλήθεια and μακροθυμία). These are called πονηρός in Test. D. 1:3; 3:1. πρᾶγμα, again combined with ἐνώπιον κυρίου in Test. S. 2:14, πρᾶξις in Test. Zeb. 9:7; Test. Jos. 5:2; Test. G. 3:1; Test. A. 6:5.

[43] τὸ ὅλον πονηρόν, also with partly good, partly bad conduct Test. A. 2:2, 5, 17. In keeping is the fact that good men are called μονοπρόσωποι in 4:1.

[44] Again in combination : πονηρὸν ἐνώπιον κυρίου Test. R. 1:8 (whoredom); Test. Jud. 13:2 (self-glory); τὸ πονηρὸν ἐν Ἰσραήλ in the style of the giving of the Law in the OT Test. Zeb. 4:12 (murder), also Test. S. 5:1; Test. L. 13:6; Test. A. 1:8; Test. B. 3:6.

It is striking how strong is the idea of evil spirits as compared with what we find in the OT, → 549, 26. These are restless spirits, they suffer hunger and thirst, they assault men, they snatch them away, they wrestle with them and they bring about their overthrow, Eth. En. 5:11. Along with the mythical and eschatological understanding of evil spirits there is also a moralising interpretation. In wine dwell 4 evil spirits : desire, excitement, extravagance and filthy avarice, Test. Jud. 16:1; the ref. is to the moral dangers and immoral effects of alcohol. Similarly, covetousness is said to work like an evil spirit and to confuse the soul by evil spirits, Test. S. 4:4.

b. Philo and Josephus.

Philo and Joseph., too, use πονηρός in the customary way. The older meanings recur, "full of trouble or sorrow," [45] and there is even a ref. to the Attic accentuation (→ n. 3) πόνηρος. [46] We also find "detrimental" (Philo Poster. C., 71) and "valueless." [47] In Joseph. one may still see the older social significance of πονηρός, → n. 7. [48]

More widespread in both is the use of πονηρός in the moral sense. In Joseph. the word often has the secondary sense of what is politically reprehensible, → n. 8. [49] It is worth noting that in Philo the evaluation of the σῶμα as πονηρὸν καὶ δυσμενές or as φίλον καὶ συγγενὲς καὶ ἀδελφόν is made dependent on whether one is concerned with investigating the supraterrestrial. The more this is true, the more evil and contemptible the body appears. Thus it is not God's judgment, but thinking focused on the hereafter and the divine mysteries, which sets the body in an unfavourable light. The judgment of the righteous man replaces the divine judgment in the Law. [50] For Philo, then, the χρηστόν arises out of a ἥμερος γνώμη, the πονηρόν out of a διάνοια κακοήθης, Vit. Mos., I, 244. What Philo says elsewhere about the antithesis of the καλόν and the πονηρόν is based on the text of Gn. 3, Leg. All., I, 60 and 101; Plant., 36. The πονηροί are contrasted with the ἀγαθοί (Virt., 189, 194, 227; Praem. Poen., 67) or σοφοί (Abr., 37). They know nothing of virtues and seek only pleasures. [51] In content, then, bad and good are defined Hellenistically. In contrast to the social use (→ 547, 23), it is said of the πονηροί in Stoic fashion that they are not εὐγενεῖς, that the σώφρονες and δίκαιοι are this even though they are slaves and are thus πονηροί in the social sense, Virt., 191. Virtues cannot be inherited. The ἀρεταὶ πατέρων are of no avail for the one who becomes bad ; the κακία of his own soul is to his hurt, Virt., 211. Stoic individualism makes its influence felt at this pt. Finally, πονηρότατοι are "offenders" (Jos., 80; alongside ἐναγεῖς, μάγοι, φαρμακευταί, Spec. Leg., III, 93;

---

[45] Philo Praem. Poen., 2 : βίοι σπουδαῖοι καὶ πονηροί. In Poster. C., 95 he expounds the quotation from Lv. 27:32, 33 οὐκ ἀλλάξεις καλὸν πονηρῷ (lit. the worthless offering) by ἐπίπονον ἀλλ' οὐ φαῦλον.

[46] In Poster. C., 94 he expounds πονηρά by καματηρά καὶ ἐπίπονα, ἅπερ Ἀττικοὶ τὴν πρώτην ὀξυτονοῦντες συλλαβὴν καλοῦσι πόνηρα.

[47] Leg. Gaj., 166 : πονηρὰ σπέρματα, though this might mean an "evil brood."

[48] Jos. Vit., 29 : πονηροί as the opp. of κράτιστοι, Vit., 151 as the opp. of μεγιστᾶνες, Bell., 1, 212 : οἱ πονηροὶ παρώξυνον τὸν Ὑρκανόν, gen. ἀγαθὸς-πονηρός, Ant., 8, 314 (reading along with μοχθηρούς); 6, 307.

[49] Vit., 102 : of John of Gischala, who is also called ἐπίορκος. Vit., 134 : of Jesus son of Sapphias : πονηρὸς ἄνθρωπος. Bell., 4, 238 : οἱ πονηροί of the radicals who call in the help of the Idumeans ; cf. 4, 389. Vit., 133 : πονηρὸς προδότης, Bell., 4, 179 : πονηροὶ οἰκεῖοι, Ant., 2, 56 : δοῦλος πονηρός, Bell., 1, 545 : the πονηρότατοι in contrast to the φίλτατοι, Bell., 7, 34 : πονηροί gen. the "bad," Bell., 7, 185 : δαιμόνια expounded as πονηρῶν ἀνθρώπων πνεύματα, Ant., 6, 211 : πονηρὸν πνεῦμα.

[50] Leg. All., III, 71 : ὅταν γὰρ ὁ νοῦς μετεωροπολῇ καὶ τὰ τοῦ κυρίου μυστήρια μυῆται, πονηρὸν καὶ δυσμενές κρίνει τὸ σῶμα· ὅταν δὲ ἀποστῇ τῆς τῶν θείων ἐρεύνης, φίλον αὐτῷ καὶ συγγενὲς καὶ ἀδελφὸν ἡγεῖται. Thus it is explained why Er is called πονηρός in Gn. 38:7, χωρὶς αἰτίας, as is said expressly in Leg. All., III, 69. But Er is interpreted as δερμάτινος. The σῶμα, however, is the δερμάτινος ὄγκος ἡμῶν, πονηρός καὶ ἐπίβουλος τῆς ψυχῆς. In this its true character, however, the σῶμα is known only by the initiate, the sage.

[51] αἴσθησις is deceived by the false comeliness, the νόθος εὐμορφία of the ἡδοναί, in contrast to διάνοια, which perceives the γνήσιον κάλλος of virtues, Gig., 17.

κακούργων πονηρότατοι, Flacc., 75). Along with persons, material things like βου-
λεύματα (Jos., 266), ἐπιτηδεύματα (Abr., 40; Exsecr., 142; Leg. Gaj., 91), ἔργα
(Exsecr., 142) and ἤθη (Virt., 196) are called πονηρός in the sense of morally bad.

C. πονηρός in the New Testament.

I. In the Sense of Bad, Harmful, Unserviceable, Useless.

1. In the NT, too, πονηρός has the sense of "bad" or "harmful," → 547, 12 ff.;
550, 4 ff. In Rev. 16:2 πονηρός denotes the grievousness of the sores, that which
constitutes the burden, while κακός suggests their dangerous and abominable
character. [52] The days are evil in Eph. 5:16 because they are part of the last time,
threatened by the approaching last judgment and darkened by the woes of the
end time. If a moral sense is seen, then one has to find the evil nature of the
days in the fact that moral corruption is the vogue in them, [53] or that all our
efforts and resources are needed, the exploiting of every moment, to set forward
in them anything that is good. [54] Similarly the ἡμέρα πονηρά of Eph. 6:13 is the
"evil," "dangerous," "critical" day, the day of distress, [55] no matter whether it
be regarded as a day in the present life, the day of death, the day of judgment,
a day of conflict and peril, or the day when the devil has special power. In any
case it is not a morally evil day. In Gl. 1:4 Paul calls the present aeon "evil" [56]
because it is filled with the sufferings and temptations of the last time.

2. As in the OT (→ 549, 20 f.), πονηρός is used in Mt. 7:18 to denote "unserviceable" or "useless" fruits as distinct from the καρποὶ καλοί of the good
tree. The address δοῦλε πονηρέ (Mt. 18:32; 25:26; Lk. 19:22) also denotes the
"unprofitable" servant according to the OT model. [57]

II. In the Moral Sense.

1. Adjectival Use.

a. In Connection with Persons.

In contrast to God, who alone is good (Mk. 10:18), men generally are called
πονηροί (Mt. 7:11; Lk. 11:13). [58] πονηρός bears a stronger sense in Mt. 12:34.

---

[52] Acc. to the correct distinction in Had. Apk., *ad loc.,* cf. Ex. 9:10 f.; Dt. 28:35 LXX.
[53] So, e.g., W. Schmidt, *Der Brief an d. Eph., Kritisch-exegetischer Komm. über d. NT*[6]
(1886), *ad loc.*
[54] So, e.g., Ew. Gefbr., *ad loc.* Greeven (Dib. Gefbr., *ad loc.*) rightly pts. out that the
days are πονηραί as days of the old aeon.
[55] Str.-B., III, 617, *ad loc.* refers to Rabb. par.: Satan accuses in the hour of danger,
bAZ, 18a.
[56] Ltzm. R. on 12:2 rightly pts. to 4 Esr. 7:12 f.: "The ways in this aeon have become
narrow and sorrowful and difficult, wretched and bad, full of dangers and near to great
afflictions." Zn. Gl., *ad loc.* would take πονηρός morally here: The αἰών is πονηρός in
so far as a will which is against God is done in this age. Cf. also F. Sieffert, *Der Brief an
d. Galat., Kritisch-exeg. Komm. über d. NT*[6] (1886), *ad loc.*: "with reference to the sinful
effects of the powers which control the aeon," and Schlier Gl., *ad loc.*: "The aeon is evil
when it shows itself to be the power of evil possessed by evil." Not until Herm. do we find
an anthropological ref.; in Herm. m., 5, 1, 4 it is ἀσύμφορον and πονηρόν for man when
a holy and an evil spirit dwells within him.
[57] Str.-B., I, 800 refers to the Aram. expression עבדא בישא. In Mt. 25:26 the word stands
close to ὀκνηρός "lazy." In this connection the meaning naturally leads into the moral
sphere in the sense of "morally bad." On the other hand, πονηρός here does not mean
"wicked."
[58] Chrys. Hom. in Mt. 23:4 (MPG, 57, 313) goes too far: πρὸς ἀντιδιαστολὴν τῆς
ἀγαθότητος τῆς αὐτοῦ (God's), τὴν φιλοστοργίαν τὴν πατρικὴν πονηρίαν καλῶν·

It denotes obstinacy in face of God's offer of salvation. Decision against God and those whom He has sent makes the Pharisees πονηροί. They bring forth their evil words from the evil store within, Mt. 12:35. [59] Because of this decision against Jesus and His message hardened Israel is called a γενεὰ πονηρά which asks for Messianic signs. Their goodness or badness is decided by the Word of God which encounters them in living force, Mt. 12:39; Lk. 11:29; Mt. 16:4. As γενεὰ πονηρὰ καὶ μοιχαλίς they are threatened by eschatological disaster and judgment like the generation of the flood.

In contrast to πονηροὶ ἄνθρωποι and πλανῶντες καὶ πλανώμενοι (2 Tm. 3:13) are those who under persecution hold fast to apostolic doctrine. Here too, then, πονηρός acquires its content from the decision made in relation, not now to Jesus and His message, but to the message of the apostles. Similarly, 2 Th. 3:2 summons the readers to prayer that the writers may be delivered or preserved from ἄτοποι καὶ πονηροὶ ἄνθρωποι. These are men who have no part in faith but decide against the Church's norm of faith and deviate from it. In Ac. 17:5 πονηρός is used of the rabble, and there is thus approximation to a derogatory social use, → n. 48.

b. In Connection with Things and Concepts.

The name of the disciples is despised and rejected as a "bad" or "morally reprehensible" name, nor is it of any moment whether the reference is to the name of each individual disciple, which is perhaps struck off the Jewish register of names, or to the name of Christ as in Jm. 2:7: βλασφημοῦσιν τὸ καλὸν ὄνομα τὸ ἐπικληθὲν ἐφ' ὑμᾶς. It is also possible [60] that the expression in Lk. 6:22 is a poor translation of הוֹצִיא שֵׁם רַע → n. 34. ὀφθαλμὸς πονηρός reminds us directly of the common expression in later Judaism (→ 552, 8 f., 24). It denotes the covetous eye filled with envy, Mk. 7:22; Mt. 20:15. It might also mean a wicked look, but this is not the reference in either of these two verses, → n. 60.

There is debate whether πονηρός means "wicked" or "sick" in Mt. 6:23; Lk. 11:34, → V, 377, 22 ff.

The following are the main arguments in favour of referring ἁπλοῦς-πονηρός to physical conditions : 1. the σῶμα is mentioned in each instance ; 2. the concluding clause in Mt. 6:23 and the verse Lk. 11:35, in a deduction a minore ad maius, apply the preceding parable to the inner light in contrast to the external or physical ; 3. a saying in Philo shows that this contrasting of the outer and the inner eye was familiar, [61] cf. also an expression like ὀφθαλμὸς τῆς καρδίας in Eph. 1:18; 4. Plato Hi., II, 374d. writes of a πονηρία ὀφθαλμῶν in the sense of an eye-affliction, so that ὀφθαλμὸς πονηρός may mean an afflicted eye (cf. ἁπλότης τῆς διαίτης for a healthy way of life in Jos. Ap., 2, 190); 5. the extension in Lk. may then be explained as follows. Through the addition in v. 36, the parable in Q, whose interpretative saying does not belong to the original material, as shown by the differences in Mt. and Lk., [62] is divested of its

τοσαύτη αὐτοῦ τῆς φιλανθρωπίας ἡ ὑπερβολή : Not the love of parents for their children is bad, but in spite of their badness men who are wholly bad show love for their children.

[59] The par. in Lk. 6:45 refers only to the θησαυρὸς τῆς καρδίας. Mt. goes a step further by supposing that in an ἄνθρωπος πονηρός there is only a θησαυρὸς πονηρός. One may refer to Test. A. 2:2, 5, 17 (→ n. 43).

[60] Wellh. Lk. on 6:22.

[61] Op. Mund., 53.

[62] Bultmann Trad., 91.

true character as a parable. It is taken as a mere statement about the condition of man within the body, about the inward man, and the explanation is given that the body can be wholly bright only when the inward spiritual life which dwells within it is bright and truly shines. Not a few commentators, then, have decided for a physical interpretation of ἀπλοῦς-πονηρός here, and therewith also for the related understanding of the Q core as a parable. [63]

The decision to construe πονηρός as "evil" in spite of the five arguments adduced above depends on whether ἀπλοῦς (→ I, 386, 1 ff.) can mean "healthy," "intact" in a physical sense. Not a single instance has thus far been found in support of this. [64] On the other hand, it is evident that the OT and later Judaism as well as the NT assume a close relation between the heart and the eye, that in the last two centuries B.C. ἀπλοῦς and ἀπλότης were commonly used as renderings of םֹח and that the statement in Test. Iss. 4 concerning the ἀπλοῦς, πορευόμενος ἐν ἀπλότητι ὀφθαλμῶν must have had some influence on the passage. In Test. XII the term ἀπλότης bears witness to the "struggle for the unity of ethical reflection." [65] It may also be remembered that ὀφθαλμὸς πονηρός and its Heb. equivalent mean the "wicked," "envious," "covetous," "greedy," "avaricious eye," → 551, 10 f.; 552, 8 f. If one cannot rule out the possibility that the Aram. original of the saying was a similitude, the traditional Gk. forms seems to have used ἀπλοῦς and πονηρός already in a moral sense. This would mean that the translation into Gk. is already a stage on the way from the parable to anthropological explication, i.e., on the way whose final stage is the Lucan expansion in 11:36 and the general understanding of the logion which was shaped thereby. The position of the saying in Mt. shows further that he understood by the ὀφθαλμὸς πονηρός a "covetous, avaricious eye." [66]

From within man come διαλογισμοὶ πονηροί (Mt. 15:19), called διαλογισμοὶ κακοί in the par. Mk. 7:21. Not quite clear is the expression in Jm. 2:4: ἐγένεσθε κριταὶ διαλογισμῶν πονηρῶν, → II, 98, 12 ff.; III, 943, n. 3. As in Lk. 18:6: κριτὴς ἀδικίας, the genitive here has adjectival significance: judges with bad motives, who are swayed by base considerations, [67] namely, love of money and renown. [68] Close to διαλογισμοί are ὑπόνοιαι πονηραί (1 Tm. 6:4), evil reservations or insinuations which are listed along with φθόνος, ἔρις, βλασφημίαι. [69] Individual inner impulses can be called evil, but so, too, can the whole inner man, Hb. 3:12: [βλέπετε, ἀδελφοί], μήποτε ἔσται ἔν τινι ὑμῶν καρδία πονηρὰ ἀπιστίας ἐν τῷ ἀποστῆναι ἀπὸ θεοῦ ζῶντος. The genitive denotes the quality of the evil heart. [70] Its wickedness consists in apostasy from faith, in self-will and turning from God, the same, then, as that which characterises the πονηρὸς ἄνθρωπος. [71] Hb. can also use συνείδησις πονηρά for this, 10:22. The συνείδησις

---

[63] E.g., Zn. Mt.; Kl. Mt. Schl. Mt., ad loc. also regards this as a possibility.

[64] C. Edlund, Das Auge der Einfalt. Mt. 6:22-23 und Lk. 11:34-35 (1952), 17; cf. also W. Brandt, "Der Spruch vom lumen internum," ZAW, 14 (1913), 191.

[65] Cf. Edlund, op. cit., 79; cf. also Test. B. 6:6 of the righteous man: οὐκ ἔχει ὅρασιν οὔτε ἀκοὴν διπλῆν. Test. Iss. 4:6 deals with the ὀφθαλμὸς πονηρός in its depiction of the ἀπλοῦς. Cf. Prv. 23:6 Αλλ: πονηρόφθαλμος instead of LXX βάσκανος for עַיִן רָע.

[66] Jülicher Gl. J., 98-108 gives exhaustive reasons for taking ἀπλοῦς and πονηρός in the moral sense.

[67] Dib. Jk., ad loc. rightly rejects construing the gen. as an obj. gen.

[68] So Schl. Jk., ad loc.

[69] B. Weiss, Die Briefe Pauli an Timotheus u. Titus, Kritisch-exeget. Komm. über d. NT⁵ (1886), ad loc. rightly rejects the view of J. C. K. v. Hofmann, Die hl. Schrift. Neuen Testamentes, 6 (1874), 185 that πονηραί cannot be appended to ὑπόνοιαι.

[70] Cf. καρδία ἀνομίας ψ 57:3, καρδία εὐτονίας Qoh. 7:7.

[71] καρδία πονηρά 1 Cl., 3, 4.

is called πονηρά because its content is πονηρόν. Α συνείδησις πονηρά separates from God and keeps apart from Him. [72]

The words and deeds of man are wicked as well as his inner being, e.g., his καύχησις (Jm. 4:16), his confident speech which does not take God into account but acts as if man alone were in control of himself and his future. In such talk the non-recognition of God's sovereignty is the wicked element.

The ἔργα done in pre-Christian days are πονηρά in Col. 1:21. Because men were enemies of God and estranged from Him, [73] their ἔργα are called πονηρά. [74] The ἔργον πονηρόν is also that which is done against the messenger and servant of God and hence against His will and plan. This is how we are to take the expression in 2 Tm. 4:18: ῥύσεταί με ὁ κύριος ἀπὸ παντὸς ἔργου πονηροῦ. This is the wicked blow which threatens the apostle, perhaps prison, torture, or even execution. [75]

In the expression ἦν γὰρ αὐτῶν πονηρὰ τὰ ἔργα (Jn. 3:19) the content of πονηρός is determined by the Johannine antithesis between light and darkness. Decision for darkness and against light causes men to do wicked works. In the parallel verses 20 and 21 there is a contrast between φαῦλα πράσσειν and ἀλήθειαν ποιεῖν. πονηρός is that which is opposed to the revealed ἀλήθεια practised in deeds, → I, 245, 1 ff. There is a similar use in Jn. 7:7: τὰ ἔργα αὐτοῦ (τοῦ κόσμου) πονηρά ἐστιν. The works of the world are evil because they are not worked by God. The reference is not to immoral acts in the narrower sense. [76] What is against the Gospel is wicked. This includes error, its propagation, the whole nature bound up with it (2 Jn. 11) and the λόγοι of the adversary who is being fought (3 Jn. 10). Here again, if in typical Johannine transformation, what is good and evil is decided by the Word of God and one's attitude thereto. Wicked works result from a primal decision which is brought about by Satan as redemption and salvation are brought about by God. For this reason Cain's works are evil, 1 Jn. 3:12. [77]

---

[72] Cf. συνείδησις πονηρά Barn., 19, 12; Did., 4, 14; Herm. m., 3, 4. A bad conscience is one which is burdened with unforgiven sins and which is thus injurious to sincerity in prayer and the spirit of truth.

[73] Not enemies of the mind (i.e., of God), as the reading αὐτοῦ (God's) with διάνοια obviously understands the dat., nor enemies acc. to their mind; ἐν τοῖς ἔργοις is not a more precise definition of διάνοια, but expresses the outworking of an enmity to God which is grounded in the mind, cf. Test. G. 3:1; Test. A. 6:5; cf. Test. Zeb. 9:7: πλανῶνται ἐν ταῖς πονηραῖς αὐτῶν πράξεσιν.

[74] ἔργον πονηρόν is more common in the post-apost. fathers as the opp. of ἔργον καλόν. Herm. m., 6, 2, 4: works of the ἄγγελος τῆς πονηρίας, which correspond to his nature, characterised here as ὀξύχολος, πικρός, ἄφρων, cf. also Herm. v., 3, 7, 6; 8, 4.

[75] Cf. esp. Weiss, op. cit., ad loc., though also Schl. Past. and Wbg. Past., ad loc.

[76] Bu. J., ad loc. rightly says that the acts are not wicked as immoral acts but as worldly action in which no decision is made.

[77] The circle of things called πονηρός is broader in the post-apost. fathers. The influence of Hell. Judaism may be seen here. βουλή (→ I, 633) Barn., 19, 3; Did., 2, 6; Herm. v., 1, 2, 4; ἐπιθυμία (→ III, 168) 2 Cl., 16, 2 (ἐπιθυμίαι πονηραί of the ψυχή); Herm. v., 1, 1, 8; 2, 4; s., 6, 2, 1; they are traced back here to the influence of the ἄγγελος τρυφῆς καὶ ἀπάτης; this is in keeping with the distinctive view of Herm. that virtues and vices derive from godly and ungodly spirits or angels; ὁδός Did., 5, 1 cf. the list of vices which follows; ἔργα τῆς πονηρᾶς ὁδοῦ Barn., 4, 10; πρᾶγμα Herm. v., 1, 1, 8; ῥῆμα with ἐπιθυμία, Herm. s., 5, 3, 6; καταλαλιά "calumny," Herm. m., 2, 3; ψεῦσμα "lying," Herm. m., 3, 5. The διδαχή of the ἄγγελος πονηρίας is called πονηρά in Herm. m., 6, 2, 7 in keeping with its effect on man.

In Acts 18:14 we find a comparatively secular use of πονηρός in the expression put on the lips of Gallio : εἰ μὲν ἦν ἀδίκημά τι ἢ ῥᾳδιούργημα πονηρόν, wrong-doing or villainy, [78] i.e., something punishable by law as distinct from purely religious behaviour. The concept of πονηρὰ πνεύματα (→ 553, 1 ff.), which derives from the OT and which had become part of the world-picture of later Judaism, [79] has also left its mark in the NT. Degrees of wicked and more wicked spirits are differentiated, Mt. 12:45; Lk. 11:26. Both Jesus (Lk. 7:21; 8:2) and the apostles (Ac. 19:12, 13, 15, 16) grant healing from evil spirits. [80]

2. Use as Noun.

a. The Bad Man.

Along with the adjectival use, many NT verses have the noun οἱ πονηροί ("the wicked") as distinct from the ἀγαθοί (Mt. 22:10) or the δίκαιοι (Mt. 13:49). [81] In Mt. 22:10 it is possible that the distinction between πονηρός and ἀγαθός is to be taken in the social sense. Since the parable in the Matthean version is so strongly allegorised that the figurative part is no longer presented clearly, there are good grounds for construing it thus. Mt. probably wants the antithesis to be understood with reference to the appended parable of the unworthy guest, vv. 11-14. [82] With the πονηροὺς καὶ ἀγαθούς of Mt. 5:45 one may compare the κακούς τε καὶ ἀγαθούς of Prv. 15:3. Lk. 6:35 contrasts ἀχαρίστους καὶ πονηρούς, to both of whom God shows Himself to be kind, χρηστός. The wickedness of the wicked is thus that they ungratefully harden themselves against God's goodness. When the angels at the last judgment separate the wicked from the righteous (Mt. 13:49), the antithesis shows that the πονηροί are those who do not meet God's righteous demand. Finally, in 1 C. 5:13, under the direct influence of the OT model (→ 550, 24 ff.), Paul uses πονηρός in the singular for the evil-doer who offends against the Law of God.

b. The Devil.

We have seen that on the basis of OT usage (→ 550, 18 ff.) the content of πονηρός in the moral sense is determined by the antithesis to God's word and will (→ 551, 22 ff.), to the Law (→ 550, 34 ff.), to the preaching of Jesus (→ 555, 3 ff.) and to the message of the apostles (→ 555, 9 ff.). In the singular, then, it can also be used for the one who is in absolute antithesis to God, i.e., the devil. This is a distinctive NT usage for which no models have been found in the world into which primitive Christianity came (→ 549, 15 f.; 550, 30) apart from the interpretation of צרע already mentioned → 552, 16 ff. Quite indisputably ὁ πονηρός is the devil in Mt. 13:19. The par. Mk. 4:15 has ἔρχεται ὁ σατανᾶς, while Lk. 8:12 has ἔρχεται ὁ διάβολος.

Did this use of πονηρός arise perhaps in replacement of references to the devil by name? For even though σατανᾶς was not originally a name, it had become this in Gospels written in Gk. Was there a wish to avoid the name of the devil as there was

---

[78] Cf. Bau. Ag., ad loc.

[79] On this whole theme cf. Bousset-Gressm., 331-342; in Herm. m., 5, 1, 2 the πονηρὸν πνεῦμα is one which resists the ἅγιον πνεῦμα → n. 80.

[80] Anthropologically and ethically the πονηρὸν πνεῦμα of Herm. m., 5, 1, 2 is the opp. of the ἅγιον πνεῦμα; both may dwell in man (on the concept v. Dib. Herm. on m., 5, 2, 7); Barn., 9, 4 : ἄγγελος πονηρός, which deludes the Jews ; 4, 13 πονηρὸς ἄρχων (the devil).

[81] Cf. also Barn., 4, 2 : πονηροί alongside ἁμαρτωλοί.

[82] So esp. Kl. Mt., ad loc.

to avoid the name of God ? Is this related to a mode of thought such as finds an echo in the proverb : Speak of the devil ? If the development of this way of referring to the devil is to be explained thus, then one has to ask, of course, why it does not occur in Mt. 4:10; 12:26 as well. [83] It may also be noted that ὁ πονηρός is used again for Satan in Eph. 6:16; expositors are generally agreed on this.

This term for the devil is esp. common in 1 Jn. : 2:13, 14 : νενικήκατε τὸν πονηρόν, 5:18 : καὶ ὁ πονηρὸς οὐχ ἅπτεται αὐτοῦ, namely, as a consequence of the fact that Christ, ὁ γεννηθεὶς ἐκ τοῦ θεοῦ, preserves him. This contrast alone shows that ὁ πονηρός here is Satan, while man is the battleground between Satan and Christ. [84] Not quite so clear is the expression ἐκ τοῦ πονηροῦ εἶναι in 1 Jn. 3:12. Since Jn. 18:37 reads : ὁ ὢν ἐκ τῆς ἀληθείας, it might be that here the typically Johannine formula of origin, which expresses the essential, true and original allegiance, is connected with the abstract τὸ πονηρόν. A masculine understanding is supported by the fact that the same phrase incontestably contains a personal name in Jn. 8:44, ὑμεῖς ἐκ τοῦ πατρὸς τοῦ διαβόλου ἐστέ. The opposite in Jn. 8:47a is ὁ ὢν ἐκ τοῦ θεοῦ. [85] The masculine is again none too sure in 1 Jn. 5:19 : ὁ κόσμος ὅλος ἐν τῷ πονηρῷ κεῖται. [86] Here it is supported by the antithetical ἐκ τοῦ θεοῦ ἐσμεν in the same verse. Since πονηρός is undoubtedly the devil in the preceding verse (→ III, 654, n. 3; 894, 38 ff.), it is highly probable that ἐν τῷ πονηρῷ refers also to the devil, who is called ἄρχων τοῦ κόσμου in Jn. 12:31; 14:30; 16:11.

c. Evil.

Another debatable passage is Mt. 13:38, which contrasts οἱ υἱοὶ τοῦ πονηροῦ and the υἱοὶ τῆς βασιλείας.

In v. 39 the ἐχθρός of the parable is expressly called the διάβολος. From this two contradictory exegetical conclusions have been drawn. 1. Since the devil is mentioned here, he is also referred to in πονηρός, as in the address in Ac. 13:10 υἱὲ διαβόλου. [87] 2. Because the enemy is expressly declared to be the διάβολος, πονηροῦ cannot relate to Satan. [88] This conclusion is strengthened by the consideration that the opp. is not υἱοὶ τοῦ θεοῦ but τῆς βασιλείας. The first thesis is supported by a ref. to Jn. 8:41, 44; 1 Jn. 3:8, 10, but this does not help much, since Johannine dualism cannot simply be transferred to Mt. What we have here is the familiar Semitic idiom of making classifications by the use of "son" with an abstract word (→ υἱός). If υἱοὶ τοῦ πονηροῦ is employed rather than the simple πονηροί, this is because the opp. is υἱοὶ τῆς βασιλείας

---

[83] In the OT χρηστός, the opp. of πονηρός, is used almost exclusively of God. It was read as χριστός and referred to Christ (cf. 1 Pt. 2:3; Lk. 6:35 vl. This probably contributed to the development of πονηρός as the opp. of χρηστός-χριστός.

[84] The post-apost. fathers continue this line of thought. The evil one is the opponent of the race of the righteous, Mart. Pol., 17, 1. He seeks to seduce them and rob them of salvation. But the day of judgment is his end, Barn., 2, 10; 21, 3.

[85] The mythologoumenon of R. Eleazar quoted Zohar on Gn. 4:4 (ספר הזוהר לרבי שמעון בן יוחאי [1926]), namely, that Cain was conceived of the devil in Eve, has no particular cogency, but it pts. in the right direction.

[86] Ref. is made to the Gk. expression κεῖσθαι, "to be dependent" (Polyb., 6, 15, 6; Soph. Oed. Col., 247), but this does not establish a masculine understanding any more than Corp. Herm., 6, 4 : ὁ γὰρ κόσμος πλήρωμά ἐστι τῆς κακίας, ὁ δὲ θεὸς τοῦ ἀγαθοῦ, cf. Wnd. Kath. Br., ad loc.

[87] So, e.g., B. Weiss, Das Ev. nach Mt., Kritisch-exeg. Komm. über das NT⁸ (1890), ad loc.

[88] So, e.g., Zn. Mt. and Kl. Mt., ad loc.

(cf. Mt. 8:12), of which υἱὸς γεέννης is the true antithesis, Mt. 23:15. A neuter sense of πονηροῦ is thus more probable.

In accordance with Johannine usage (→ 559, 13 ff.) a masculine is to be preferred at Jn. 17:5 : τηρήσῃς αὐτοὺς ἐκ τοῦ πονηροῦ.

In the phrase ῥύσασθαι αὐτὴν (scil. τὴν ἐκκλησίαν) ἀπὸ παντὸς πονηροῦ in Did., 10, 5 it is clear that πονηροῦ is to be taken neutrally. The τηρεῖν ἐκ in Jn. corresponds to an expression which is common in the Rabb. and which is linked to ὥρα τοῦ πειρασμοῦ in Rev. 3:10, which in turn reminds us of the seventh petition of the Lord's Prayer. Hence it is clear that this is to be understood in the same way as Mt. 6:13. Materially it makes no essential difference whether πονηροῦ is interpreted as masculine or neuter. [89] It may be pointed out that in John's Gospel — not the epistles, → 559, 6 ff. — this is the only v. in which the devil is spoken of as πονηρός, though there are comparatively quite a large number of ref. to the devil in this Gospel.

The most important of the disputed verses is undoubtedly Mt. 6:13 : ῥῦσαι ἡμᾶς ἀπὸ τοῦ πονηροῦ.

The difference in interpretation is even a confessional one in this instance. The Easterns [90] construe τοῦ πονηροῦ as a masculine, while the Westerns, apart from Tertullian, regard it as a neutral in the sense of "evil." The older Latins translate the petition : *libera nos a malo*. Luther follows this tradition when in the *Greater Catechism* he shows that he includes the devil, the "wicked, malicious arch-enemy," in this evil. [91] Calvin in his exposition of Mt. 6:13 leaves the question open whether πονηροῦ is masculine or neuter, but if it is neuter he relates it to sin. [92]

An argument in favour of the masc. interpretation is that in Mt. 13:19 and elsewhere in the NT (→ 558, 27 ff.) ὁ πονηρός means devil. Prior to and outside the NT there is only a slender base for this equation. Strictly one may refer only to the designation of the devil as רְשַׁע or Aram. רְשִׁיעָא, "the godless one." [93] The identification of the evil one with the angel of death [94] can hardly be adduced here, since the prayer of Mt. 6:13 is not for deliverance from death. Aram. usage offers no sure support for a masc. understanding. In the expression בִּישָׁא, מִן בִּישָׁא can mean either the evil one or evil. Nor is it any sure proof of an original מִן שָׂטָנָא that שָׂטָנָא would "rhyme" with חַיָּבִינָא and נִסְיוֹנָא at the end of the preceding petitions. [95] The strongest argument for a masc. is that in repetition of the sixth petition the prayer is one for deliverance from the eschatological tribulation. [96] The content of the last time is the assault and fall of the devil. In the OT and later Judaism there are many requests for deliverance from affliction, oppression and sin, from all evil, [97] if not from the power of the devil. Since, however, it is part of the outlook of the OT and later Judaism that the devil is the true author of this whole tribulation, the prayer for ultimate deliverance may well refer to him.

Nevertheless, the case as a whole is weak. There are countless ref. to τὸ πονηρόν as evil. [98] Precisely as an eschatological petition the prayer may be for deliverance from

---

[89] So rightly Bu. J., *ad loc.*

[90] E.g., Chrys. Hom. in Mt. 19:6 (MPG, 57, 282): πονηρὸν δὲ ἐνταῦθα τὸν διάβολον καλεῖ.

[91] Weimar Ed. 30, 1, 210.

[92] Calvin, In NT Commentarii, I, 1 (1891), *ad loc.*

[93] Dalman, 352 f. Tg. Is. 11:4, *v.* also → n. 40. Nowhere is הָרָע or בִּישָׁא the evil one in the absolute, Str.-B., I, 422.

[94] Cf. also Midr. Ps. 21:3 : At the breath of his (the Messiah's) lips, the wicked one slays. Here, as the angel of death, he is in the service of the judicial power of the Messiah and is not his opponent, as he undoubtedly would be in Mt. 6:13.

[95] Kuhn, 37 f., cf. the review of this by E. L. Dietrich, ThLZ, 76 (1951), 291-293.

[96] Lohmeyer, 159-161.

[97] Ps. 25:22; 26:11; 69:18; Dalman, 352.

[98] → n. 32, 35, 44; → 550, 5.

all evil. A prayer from the Geniza fragments [99] reads : "Deliver me from every evil thing." The morning prayer quoted in bBer., 60b corresponds in structure to the 6th and 7th petitions, [100] so that one may assume that the addition of the 7th petition, which does not occur in Lk., [101] is based on Jewish practice. In such petitions prayer is made for deliverance from temptation, shame, evil impulse, evil events and sickness, evil thoughts and dreams, and consequently from πονηρόν in the sense of the evil and the bad, → 552, 3 ff. The ref. here, of course, is to daily rather than ultimate deliverance from these. [102] A further pt. is that ῥύεσθαι ἀπό or ἐκ does not refer to the devil in the NT but to men (R. 15:31; 2 Th. 3:2; 2 Pt. 2:7) and powers (2 C. 1:10 θάνατος; 2 Tm. 3:11 διωγμοί; 2 Tm. 4:17 στόμα λέοντος; 2 Tm. 4:18 πᾶν ἔργον πονηρόν; 2 Pt. 2:9 πειρασμός), or to the eschatological deliverance which has already taken place (Col. 1:13 ἐξουσία τοῦ σκότους) or which is expected (Lk. 1:74 ἐχθροί; R. 7:24 σῶμα τοῦ θανάτου; 1 Th. 1:10 ὀργὴ ἐρχομένη).

τοῦ πονηροῦ is thus to be taken neutrally as mostly in Mt. It is evil in the sense of the Jewish prayers, especially the eschatological tribulation. It is also the bad which one might do or plan to do against someone. The eschatological character of the prayer does not allow us to take τὸ πονηρόν merely in the sense of temporal evil. The prayer is for definitive, eschatological deliverance.

Along the lines of Did., 10, 5 and Mt. 6:13 πονηροῦ is also to be regarded as a neuter in the expression κύριος, ὃς ... φυλάξει ἀπὸ τοῦ πονηροῦ, 2 Th. 3:3. It is naturally possible to construe it as a masculine too. [103] The early Church already related Mt. 5:37: τὸ δὲ περισσὸν τούτων ἐκ τοῦ πονηροῦ ἐστιν, to the devil, and right up to our own time there have been expositors who have taken the same line. [104] But this expression is to be understood as a neuter. [105] It would be more plausible in the case of lying than of mere asseveration to trace it back directly to the devil. [106] "Of evil," however, is what restricts the command against lying by the use of asseverations. In Mt. 5:39 : μὴ ἀντιστῆναι τῷ πονηρῷ, the reference on a masculine interpretation may be to the devil or to the wicked man. But the former is ruled out by the fact that the Christian must resist the devil, as we read expressly in Jm. 4:7 in a saying related to Q, and also in 1 Pt. 5:9; Eph. 6:14-17. This leaves open the possibility of the wicked man, [107] cf. 1 C. 5:13. Elsewhere ἀνήρ (Ac. 17:5), ἄνθρωπος (Mt. 12:35; Lk. 6:45; 2 Th. 3:2; 2 Tm. 3:13) or δοῦλος (Mt. 18:32; 25:26; Lk. 19:22) is added. In favour of a masculine interpretation is the fact that the saying continues : ὅστις σε ῥαπίζει, and thus refers

---

[99] Dalman, 353.

[100] Dalman, 358 ff.; Fiebig, 49-55.

[101] At Lk. 11:4 the petition is found in A C D W Θ φ 𝔎 it syr^c. It was probably added on the basis of Mt. and as a sign that this text had established itself.

[102] For further examples cf. Str.-B., I, 422 f. Of interest is the Chr. amulet of the 6th cent. found in BGU, II, 954, 24 (v. Mitteis-Wilcken, I, 431), which suggests exposition along these lines : ῥῦ(σαι ἡ)μᾶς ἀπὸ τῆς πο(ν)ηρ(ίας).

[103] Cf. M. Dibelius, Die Geisterwelt im Glauben des Pls. (1909), 57. Wbg. Th., ad loc. bases this on the antithesis to the invoked κύριος and on 1 Th. 2:18 : ἐνέκοψεν ἡμᾶς ὁ σατανᾶς. But ὁ πονηρός is not used for the devil in the Pauline Epistles.

[104] E.g., Chrys. Hom. in Mt. 17:6 (MPG, 57, 262); Wettstein, ad loc.; as early as Cl. Al. Paed., II, 103, 2 (GCS, 12, 219) on Lk. 12:28 with ref. to Mt. 5:37.

[105] Cf. ἐκ τοῦ ἐμφανοῦς and ἐκ τοῦ εὐπρεποῦς.

[106] Zn. Mt., ad loc. pts this out. Schl. Mt. favours the masc. and emphasises that Jesus sees Satan at work where others do not. He links God with the truth and sets lying in opposition to God's will. But one may again ask whether an asseveration is necessarily a lie or abets lying.

[107] So also Weiss, op. cit. (→ n. 87), ad loc.: homine maligno.

to a man who does evil. [108] On the other hand, πονηρῷ might just as well be the wicked act which men do to someone. [109] In 1 Th. 5:22 : ἀπὸ παντὸς εἴδους πονηροῦ, we are not to take the word as an adjective, "evil appearance," specie mala (Vg.). πονηροῦ is the genitive of πονηρόν even though it has no article, and the expression is to be rendered : "from every kind of evil." [110]

Mt. 5:11: εἴπωσιν πᾶν πονηρὸν καθ᾽ ὑμῶν, is perhaps another version of the original which Lk. translates by ἐκβάλωσιν τὸ ὄνομα ὑμῶν ὡς πονηρόν. What is meant is the evil which foes ascribe to the disciples. Equally clear is Mt. 12:35; Lk. 6:45 : ὁ πονηρὸς ἄνθρωπος ... ἐκβάλλει πονηρά. The ἐκ τοῦ πονηροῦ in Lk. is to be construed as adjective rather than noun and refers to the preceding ἐκ τοῦ θησαυροῦ. The "evil" in Mt. 9:4 refers to the thoughts of the scribes, while the πάντα ταῦτα τὰ πονηρά of Mk. 7:23 summarises the preceding list of vices. At Ac. 5:4 the Western text has τὸ πονηρὸν τοῦτο rather than τὸ πρᾶγμα for the act of Ananias. πονηρόν in Ac. 28:21 means the evil Paul might have done. The plural πονηρά is used very generally in Lk. 3:19. πονηρά has the same sense in Ac. 25:18. The singular in R. 12:9 : ἀποστυγοῦντες τὸ πονηρόν, κολλώμενοι τῷ ἀγαθῷ is to be taken as a neuter and refers very generally to what is morally bad. In the new ethics good and bad are known in terms of the total work of the community as this is accomplished by God's Spirit, but stylistically the expression is based on the Testaments of the Patriarchs. [111]

† πονηρία.

Contents : A. πονηρία in Classical and Hellenistic Greek. B. The Old Testament and Later Judaism. C. Hellenistic Judaism : 1. The Septuagint ; 2. The Pseudepigrapha ; 3. Philo and Josephus. D. πονηρία in the New Testament. E. πονηρία in the Post-Apostolic Fathers.

πονηρία, abstract of πονηρός, shares essentially the same nuances.

A. πονηρία in Classical and Hellenistic Greek.

πονηρία means "defectiveness," also "physical sickness," in both animals and men, πονηρία ποδῶν and πονηρία ὀφθαλμῶν, Plat. Hi., II, 374c. Plat. can call sickness a πονηρία σώματος as opp. to ἀδικία as a πονηρία ψυχῆς, Resp., X, 609c. The material "imperfection" of a skill can also be called πονηρία. [1] πονηρία also means "lack" of rain and air, Ael. Nat. An., 17, 40; deficient state of virtues, Xenoph. Cyrop., VII, 5, 75, also "offensiveness," Plut. Quaest. Conv., IV (II, 671a).

---

[108] This is pted. out by, e.g., Kl. Mt., ad loc. Schl. Mt., ad loc. also sees a masc. "adversary" and refers to Jos. Ant., 6, 284 : εἰ πονηρὸς οὗτος εἰς ἡμᾶς, ἀλλ᾽ οὐκ ἐμὲ δεῖ τοιοῦτον εἶναι πρὸς αὐτόν.

[109] So P. Fiebig, "Jesu Worte über die Feindesliebe," ThStKr, 91 (1918), 49 f. with ref. to Rabb. par.; v. also G. Hönnicke, "Neuere Forschungen zum Vaterunser bei Mt. und Lk.," NkZ, 17 (1906), 178-180.

[110] So Dib. Th., ad loc., who refers to Did., 3, 1: ἀπὸ παντὸς πονηροῦ καὶ ἀπὸ παντὸς ὁμοίου αὐτοῦ. Ps. Clem. Hom., 11, 27, 3 (GCS, 42, 168) adds to a list of vices the observation : τούτων δὲ εἴδη πολλά, and Jos. Ant., 10, 37 writes of πᾶν εἶδος πονηρίας. Dob. Th., ad loc. thinks the absence of the art. is so decisive that he transl.: "of every wicked kind" (scil. of the supposed work of the Spirit).

[111] Test. B. 8:1; D. 6:10; G. 5:2. Ref. may be made to the neuter use in the post-apost. fathers with no perceptible shift of meaning. It is the obj. of μισεῖν in Barn., 19, 11, ποιεῖν in Herm. m., 4, 2, 2, πράττειν in 2 Cl., 8, 2, ἀγρυπνεῖν in Barn., 20, 2 and Did., 5, 2.

πονηρία. [1] Plat. Resp., I, 342b alongside ἁμαρτία "failing"; Aristoph. Thes., 868 : Mnesilochos owes it to the incompetence of the ravens that he is still alive.

A broad span is covered by the political sense (→ 547, 29 ff.) of πονηρία, the πονηρία τῶν δημηγορούντων, Isoc., 8, 108, τῶν ῥητόρων who enrich themselves ;[2] πονηρία is "baseness," "depravity," "spite," Lys., 14, 9 and 35; Demosth. Or., 21, 19; Xenoph. Mem., III, 5, 18; Ditt. Or., 519, 11 (Emperor Marcus Julius Philippus): πάντων ἤρεμον καὶ γαληνὸν βίον διαγόντων πονηρίας καὶ διασεισμῶν πε(π)αυμένων.

πονηρία is the "intentionally practised evil will," ἐκ προαιρέσεως in contrast to conduct ἐκ θυμοῦ.[3] πονηρία συνεχής "unceasing baseness" is μοχθηρία, moral uselessness, Aristot. Eth. Nic., VII, 9, p. 1150b, 35. Similarly πονηρία is to be distinguished from ἄγνοια and ἀβελτερία "stupidity." πονηρία affects others, ἀβελτερία only the one who acts. The original social signification of the term (→ 547, 23 ff.) may be discerned here.[4] Its essential feature acc. to Demetrius Fr., 4 (CAF, I, 796) is that it is always out for gain — something which may still be seen in the NT use. In the Hell. period πονηρία is increasingly used in a gen. sense without specialisation,[5] though it should be remembered that Plat. and others also use it thus in antithesis to ἀρετή, Plat. Theaet., 176b; Aeschin. In Ctesiphontem, 172; Aristot. Rhet., II, 12, p. 1389a, 18.

B. The Old Testament and Later Judaism.

1. In essentials רָעָה and רֹע, and sometimes רַע. correspond to πονηρία in the OT. Like πονηρία they denote the "poor and useless state" or "badness" of fruits (Jer. 24:2, 3, 8), the "ugliness" and "unprepossessing nature" of animals (Gn. 41:19 : רַע, αἰσχρός), "bad mood" and "sorrowful mien" (Neh. 2:2 : רֹעַ לֵב; Qoh. 7:3 : רֹעַ פָּנִים, κακία); "displeasure" that is felt (Neh. 2:10 πονηρόν); "misfortune," "evil," esp. that brought on man by God (אֲלֵיהֶם רָעָה תָּבוֹא Jer. 2:3; 26:3 [= LXX 33:3]; Gn. 19:19 κακά; Am. 3:6 κακία; Ex. 32:12; יְמֵי הָרָעָה "days of disaster," Qoh. 12:1 κακία); "bad, troubled situation" (Neh. 1:3), "evil" men do to one another, hence in the sense of "injury" and also expression of an "evil disposition" (Gn. 26:29; 44:4; 1 K. 2:44; Neh. 13:27; 6:2; Ju. 11:27; 15:3); "evil plan" or "purpose," "maliciousness," "evil" gen. (Hos. 10:15 κακίαι; Job 20:12 κακία); individual "wicked acts" (Is. 1:16; Jer. 4:4; 21:12 no equivalent in the LXX; 23:2; 26 [LXX 33:3] πονηρός); "wickedness of the wicked," of the ungodly, of the bad (Ps. 7:9; 73:8 רַע, where it is interpreted as haughtiness, violence, hardness of heart).

2. The usage in later Judaism shows no variation.[6] The Talmud often uses רְעוּת, a late construction not found in the Mishnah, for "imperfection" and "defectiveness."[7] In the Qumran scrolls, too, רָעָה occurs for "evil" and "badness," 1 QS 2:16; 4:13; 5:14. Wherein the badness or wickedness consists may be seen from lists of vices, e.g., 1 QS 4:9-11 (→ 551, n. 33).

---

[2] Isoc., 8, 124; cf. Xenoph. Cyrop., II, 2, 95 : πολλάκις γὰρ δύνανται τὴν πονηρίαν πλεονεκτοῦσαν ἀποδεικνύναι. It should be noted that this combination of πονηρία and πλεονεκτεῖν occurs more than once in the NT too (NT πλεονεξία).

[3] Hence it is the opp. of εὔνοια in Menand. Fr., 98 (Körte, II, 46), cf. also Aristot. Eth. Nic., V, 10, p. 1135b, 24 ff.

[4] In Plat. Soph., 228d πονηρία is badness as distinct from ἄγνοια as νόσος τῆς ψυχῆς. Aristot. Rhet., V, 5, p. 1426b, 30 and 32 : πονηρία consists in πράξεις ἄδικοι, παράνομοι τῷ πλήθει τῶν πολιτῶν ἀσύμφοροι. Ἀβελτερία consists in πράξεις ἀσύμφοροι, αἰσχραί, ἀηδεῖς, ἀδύνατοι, but all this only for the one who acts.

[5] Plut. De invidia et odio, 6 (II, 537 f.): αἱ μὲν ἄκρατοι πονηρίαι συνεπιτείνουσι τὸ μῖσος, "unbridled wickednesses increase hate." P. Oxy., XIII, 1603, 18 f. from an Encratite sermon : κάκιστον γυνὴ πονηρά (π)ἀν(τ)ων, ἐὰν δὲ καὶ πλοῦτον ἔξῃ τῇ πον[ηρίᾳ αὐτῆς συ]νεργοῦντα. P. Oxy., III, 413, 46 from a play of the Hell. period : πῶς γὰρ ὑπακούουσι (the gods) ταῖς εὐχαῖς πονηρία τὸν ἔλεον μέλλοντες παρ[έχε]σθαι.

[6] bBer., 17a : כָּל רָעוֹת הַמִּתְרַגְּשׁוֹת לָבוֹא בָּעוֹלָם, which can mean all iniquities as well as all terrors "which rise up raging to come into the world."

[7] bNidda, 2b; bChul., 9a; bBeça, 34a.

C. Hellenistic Judaism.

1. Septuagint.

Here πονηρία is the equivalent of רָעָה and רֵעַ. Elsewhere these words are transl. κακία in the LXX (→ III, 476, 32 ff.). The translators of the various books show preferences for the one term or the other but no fundamental distinction is made between πονηρία and κακία. There is a tendency in this direction only in the Gk. text of Qoh. Here κακία is used for רַע and רָעָה in the sense of "misfortune," "injury," "dark mien" Qoh. 5:12; 7:3, and only once for רָעָה in the sense of "wickedness," 7:15. For this πονηρία is used 2:21 (par. ματαιότης); πονηρία also means "what is evil, wrong" under the sun in 6:1; 11:10. The situation is much the same in Ex. [8] In the other books the distribution is as follows : Gn., Dt., 1 and 2 S., 1 and 2 K., Job, Prv., Minor Prophets, Ez. and in the main Macc. use κακία, while Ju., Neh. and Is. prefer πονηρία. Ju. is unique, for here there has been revision. A has κακία, which in the LXX, as in Philo, is more common than πονηρία, while B prefers πονηρία. [9] Both words are used without essential distinction in Ps., Wis. and Sir. Sometimes in the LXX πονηρία is used for other originals like תּוֹעֵבָה, [10] אָוֶן, [11] יֵצֶר, [12] and עָמָל, [13] πονηρία is also used adjectivally in the LXX as a gen. qual., λόγοι or γογγυσμός πονηρίας ψ 140(141):4; Sir. 46:7. In a few verses 'Α and Σ use πονηρία in the moral sense where LXX has κακία, Qoh. 7:15 'Α; 1 Βασ. 25:28 Σ.

2. Pseudepigrapha.

Here, too, πονηρία occurs in the sense of "plague," "affliction," "misfortune," but only twice (Test. D. 5:8 and Test. B. 3:3). The word is used predominantly in a moral sense, its meaning being elucidated by combination with κάκωσις and διαφθορά in Test. G. 8:2 or with ὑπερηφανία. The latter, the term for sin בְּיָד־רָמָה, characterises πονηρία as "wilful, ungodly" action, Test. D. 5:5, 6. Evil is here traced back to Beliar or evil spirits. For the man who is ruled by Beliar the good is changed into badness Test. A. 1:8; Test. D. 5:5, 6. It is worth noting that πορνεία is often a vl. for πονηρία as later in the NT; this is not surprising in view of the Encratite character of Test. XII, cf. Test. Jud. 17:2; Test. D. 5:5, 6.

3. Philo and Josephus.

Philo and Joseph. use πονηρία mostly in the moral sense, Philo Ebr., 223 (alongside ὀργή, πανουργία, θυμός); Jos. Bell., 7, 34; Vit., 298. Worth noting in Philo is the sparseness of usage as compared with the very common occurrence of κακία, → III, 483, 22 ff. The situation is the same in the Hermetic writings, which use κακία rather than πονηρία or πονηρός. Joseph. has πονηρία in the sense of political wrong in e.g., Vit., 339.

---

[8] Ex. 32:12 : πονηρία "evil intention"; 32:12, 14 κακία "evil." κακία can also mean "iniquity," 23:12.

[9] Ju. 9:56, 57; 20:3, 12, 13, 41; 15:3; A, too, has ποιεῖν πονηρίαν μετά τινος at 11:27, since πονηρίαν means the "injury" done to someone.

[10] Prv. 26:25; elsewhere mostly βδέλυγμα, and in Ez. more commonly ἀνομία. In Prv. תּוֹעֵבָה is transl. βδέλυγμα when it means "horror" at someone ; it is abs. in 26:25 : "abomination" in the heart. Here, then, the LXX takes it in the moral sense, cf. ἀκάθαρτος and ἀκαθαρσία for תּוֹעֵבָה in Prv.

[11] Is. 10:1; in Ps. often rendered ἀνομία, ἀδικία, or πόνος, in the prophets κόπος.

[12] Dt. 31:21. יֵצֶר is thus understood as bad impulse or aspiration. διανοεῖσθαι is the rendering at Gn. 6:5, διάνοια and ἐνθύμημα in Ch.

[13] Is. 10:1, elsewhere usually κόπος, μόχθος or πόνος, probably here in the sense of "what is injurious."

D. πονηρία in the New Testament.

In the NT πονηρία occurs only in a moral sense, especially in a very generalised way, as in lists of vices, e.g., R. 1:29. [14] Here, alongside πλεονεξία (→ 272, 15), it denotes moral worthlessness as a result of avarice, Vg. *nequitia*, "uselessness." [15] Neither here nor in 1 C. 5:8 can any sharp distinction be made between πονηρία and κακία. [16] In the list of vices in Mk. 7:22 πονηρία occurs alongside κακία. Here again, especially in the plural, πλεονεξία and πονηρία are closely related, probably because both occur in formulae of a catechetical type. [17] In Ac. 3:26 πονηρία is used in the plural for various kinds of "iniquity," cf. the plural use in the post-apostolic fathers, → 566, 18 ff.

The situation is similar in the list in Lk. 11:39. Here again it occurs in the vicinity of wickedness based on covetousness, ἁρπαγή. [18] In Mt. 22:18, however, πονηρία is the concealed wicked purpose of the Pharisees to bring about the undoing of Jesus. [19] In Herm. s., 9, 19, 2 διδάσκαλοι πονηρίας are called ὑποκριταί. The same genitive of quality is used in Eph. 6:12, πνευματικὰ τῆς πονηρίας. It is a characterising genitive [20] to which the collective term πνευματικά (the world of spirits) is added. [21] This world is here depicted in its badness,

---

[14] The sequence as found in א ἀδικία, πονηρία, πλεονεξία, κακία, has undergone manifold alteration in the readings. The advancing of κακία is due to the fact that alongside ἀδικία, wrong conduct towards God, it is understood as a bad moral disposition, of which the other vices are outworkings.

[15] The change here is due to a desire to differentiate between κακία and πονηρία, a concern shared by expositors in all ages, e.g., H. A. W. Meyer, *Der Brief an d. Röm., Kritisch-exeg. Komm. über d. NT*⁴ (1865), ad loc.: πονηρία malice, *malitia*, κακία villainy; J. C. K. Hofmann, *Die Hl. Schrift. Neuen Testamentes*, III (1868), ad loc.: πονηρία with a focus on causing pain, κακία satisfaction in wrong-doing ; W. M. L. de Wette, *Kurze Erklärung des Briefes an d. Röm., Kurzgefasstes exegetisches Handbuch zum NT*, II, 1² (1838), ad loc. : πονηρία wicked disposition and conduct generally, κακία malice ; F. Godet, *Romans*, ad loc.: πονηρία evil inclination of the heart, κακία calculated wickedness issuing in injury to others. On the other hand, B. Weiss, *Der Brief an d. Röm., Kritisch-exeg. Komm. über d. NT*⁹ (1899), ad loc. is right when he says that at least in the best textual tradition no sure distinction is possible, esp. if regard is had to the LXX use of κακία and πονηρία.

[16] Joh. W. and Bchm. 1 K., ad loc. Bachmann 1 K., ad loc., however, suggests that κακία may be wickedness towards others while πονηρία is to be taken as that which is intrinsically bad. But this distinction is not adequately supported. The substitution of πορνεία for πονηρία in the Western text, which produced a combination of the two in even later texts, is partly due to the difficulty caused by the juxtaposition of πονηρία and κακία. Perhaps there were also theological reasons, e.g., Marcionite. It is notable that we find the same alteration in 1 C. 5:8 G, perhaps under the influence of v. 1: ὅλως ἀκούεται ἐν ὑμῖν πορνεία. An accidental slip may be ruled out both here and in R. 1:29.

[17] Loh. Mk., ad loc.

[18] Whether the ὑμῶν is taken with ἔσωθεν, e.g., B. Weiss, *Handbuch über das Ev. des Mk. u. Lk., Kritisch-exeg. Komm. über d. NT*⁶ (1878), ad loc., or with ἁρπαγὴ καὶ πονηρία e.g., J. C. K. Hofmann, *Die Hl. Schrift. Neuen Testamentes*, VIII, 1 (1878), ad loc.; Str.-B., II, 188, depends on one's understanding of the saying as a whole. Ref. to Mt. 23 is hardly an adequate proof of the second view. It is always possible that Lk. has given Q a freer form. Mt. took the saying to be a parable on the whole conduct of the Pharisees. There can be no question of truly loathsome contents in the vessels. As in the saying about the eye in Mt. 6:22 f. (→ 556, 16 ff.) Lk. abandons the parable and offers a simple exposition of the moral and psychical point. In this case ὑμῶν goes with ἔσωθεν.

[19] To what degree πονηρία was taken in this sense may be seen from the combination with ὑπόκρισις in Herm. s., 8, 6, 2, which speaks of those whose μετάνοια is not genuine and to whom genuine μετάνοια is not given because they are μέλλοντες ἐν ὑποκρίσει μετανοεῖν. Here ὑπόκρισις stands alongside δολιότης.

[20] Ew. Gefbr., ad loc.

[21] W. Schmidt, *Der Brief an d. Eph., Kritisch-exeg. Komm. über d. NT*⁶ (1886), ad loc., with ref. to πολιτικόν, ἱππικόν and τὰ ληστρικά.

malice and ungodliness. Its day is thus the ἡμέρα πονηρά (→ 554, 14) in which it must be resisted.[22] The genitive is in no case to be regarded as subjective as though one had to contend with the spiritual realm produced by or belonging to wickedness, i.e., the spiritual side of wickedness.[23] Perhaps this error lies behind the omission of ἐν τοῖς ἐπουρανίοις in p46. This topographical note shows that the reference is to the current demonological idea of a world of ungodly spirits in the middle layer of heaven.

E. πονηρία in the Post-Apostolic Fathers.

πονηρία is used in the moral sense in the post-apost. fathers. It has the general sense of "wickedness," "wicked conduct" in general, Herm. v., 3, 5, 4. Herm. s., 9, 18, 1 speaks of κόλασις τῆς πονηρίας, Barn., 4, 12 of μισθὸς τῆς πονηρίας, and Herm. v., 2, 2, 2 of blasphemy ἐν πονηρίᾳ μεγάλῃ. Herm. v., 3, 6, 1 calls the worthless and rejected the υἱοὶ τῆς ἀνομίας on account of their πονηρία. Herm. m., 2, 1 refers to πονηρίαν τὴν ἀπολλύουσαν τὴν ζωὴν τῶν ἀνθρώπων, the "baseness" which children do not yet know. But πονηρία can also be the "individual wicked act" or a single vice. Thus in Herm. s., 9, 15, 3 it is personified along with other vices, λύπη, ἀσέλγεια, δευχολία, ψεῦδος, ἀφροσύνη, καταλαλιά and μῖσος.

The list of πονηρίαι in Herm. m., 8, 3 is an illustration of the plural mentioned → 565, 7 ff.: μοιχεία, πορνεία, μέθυσμα ἀνομίας κτλ., a whole list of vices. Each vice, then is a πονηρία. This is how we are to understand the plur. elsewhere, or expressions like πᾶσα πονηρία in Herm. v., 3, 6, 1 or ποικίλαις πονηρίαις in Herm. s., 9, 18, 3, while the plur. in Herm. v., 3, 6, 3 is used because the ref. is to several persons in whose hearts πονηρίαι ἐμμένουσιν. Perhaps 2 Cl., 13, 1: μεστοὶ ... πολλῆς ἀνοίας καὶ πονηρίας has in view a fulness of πονηρίαι, cf. also Herm. v., 3, 7, 2, if the ref. is to ἐπιθυμία τῶν πονηριῶν (obj. gen.). On the one side πονηρία can be a collective term, on the other it denotes specific behaviour or a wicked disposition expressed therein. Thus Herm. s., 9, 18, 2 refers to πλείονα πονηρίαν ποιεῖν. In this sense, as one of many vices, πονηρία is personified along with others in Herm. s., 9, 15, 3.

Harder

πορεύομαι, εἰσπορεύομαι, ἐκπορεύομαι

πορεύομαι.

Contents: A. Non-Biblical Usage: 1. Meaning of the Word in Greek; 2. Journeys in the Hereafter. B. Septuagint and Later Judaism: 1. Literal Sense; 2. The Meaning "to Pass Away"; 3. Transferred Sense; 4. Theological Sense; 5. Imperative Use; 6. Going to

---

[22] Cf. the same gen. in Herm. v., 2, 2, 2: συμφυρμοὶ πονηρίας "evil licentiousness"; s., 9, 19, 2: διδάσκαλοι πονηρίας; m., 6, 2, 1. 4. 7: ἄγγελος πονηρίας (as distinct from the ἄγγελος δικαιοσύνης) whose works are harmful or evil. Also to be taken thus is ἐπιθυμία τῆς πονηρίας in v., 1, 1, 8; m., 11, 2.

[23] *Spiritualis versutia* acc. to Erasmus, Paraphrasis in NT (1768), *ad loc., et al.*

π ο ρ ε ύ ο μ α ι. Note: This art. was originally undertaken by F. Hauck, and sections A and B, apart from necessary abbreviations and minor additions, are by him. Section C has been recast by S. Schulz, though material gathered by F. Hauck is used.

Bibl.: W. Bousset, "Die Himmelsreise der Seele," ARW, 4 (1901), 136-169, 229-273; Clemen, 130-135; F. Cumont, Lux Perpetua (1949), 189-274; H. Diels, "Himmel- u. Höllenfahrten von Homer bis Dante," *NJbch. kl. Alt.*, 49 (1922), 239-253; T. R. Ganschinietz, Art. "Katabasis," Pauly-W., 10 (1919), 2359-2449; C. Hönn, *Studien zur Gesch. d. Himmelfahrt im klass. Altertum* (1910); R. Holland, "Zur Typik der Himmelfahrt," ARW, 23 (1925), 207-220; J. Kroll, "Beiträge zum Descensus ad inferos," *Verzeichnis der Vorlesungen*

Death, Journeys in the Hereafter ; 7. Philo and Josephus. C. New Testament : 1. Literal Sense ; 2. Going to Death; 3. Imperative Use; 4. The Mission of Jesus; 5. The Apostles ; 6. Transferred Moral and Religious Use ; 7. Parting Discourses ; 8. The Ascension of Jesus ; 9. Jesus' Descent into Hades.

A. Non-Biblical Usage.

1. Meaning[1] of the Word in Greek. [2]

The act. πορεύω, rare in prose, means "to set in motion," "to bring on the way," "to convey," "to lead," "to take over," στρατιὰν μέλλων πεζῇ πορεύσειν ὡς (to) Βρασίδαν, Thuc., IV, 132, 2, "to cause to stumble against someone"; ποῖ με τὰν μελέαν πορεύσεις, Eur. Hec., 447; τοὺς ἐνθένδε ἐκεῖσε πορεῦσαι, "to lead thence," Plat. Phaed., 107; "to bring" ἄνακτα, Soph. Oed. Col., 1476; "to send" ἐπιστολάς, ibid., 1602. In the mid. "to go," "to travel," "to journey," of the army "to march" μακροτέραν (ὁδόν), Xenoph. An., II, 2, 11; εἰς ἀγρόν, Plat. Resp., VIII, 563d; ἐπὶ τοὺς πόνους, "to go to work," Leg., II, 666a; ἐπ' ἔργον, Eur. Or., 1068; of stars δι' οὐρανοῦ πορεύομαι, Plat. Tim., 39d.

Only seldom and in few expressions transf. of traversing the way of life πῇ <ἂν> πορευθεὶς τὸν βίον ὡς ἄριστα διέλθοι; Plat. Resp., II, 365b (cf. Pind. Isthm., 8, 15 βίου πόρος); πορεύομαι διὰ τῶν κατὰ φύσιν, μέχρι πεσὼν ἀναπαύσωμαι, M. Ant., V, 4; εἴ τις ὑπέροπτα χερσὶν ἢ λόγῳ πορεύεται, "wickedly to follow a path," Soph. Oed. Tyr., 883; πονηρία διὰ τῶν ... ἡδονῶν πορευομένη, "who indulges in pleasures," Xenoph. Cyrop., II, 2, 24; of the course of discussion, Plat. Soph., 222a; Phileb., 31b; Xenoph. Mem., IV, 6, 15; cf. P. Tor., I, 1, 6, 13 (116 B.C.): εἴπερ γε δὴ ἐνόμιζεν ἐκ τῆς ἀληθείας κατὰ νόμους ὁδῶς πορευόμενος τὸν ἐξ εὐθυδικίας λόγον συνίστασθαι. On the figure of the two ways → V, 43, 35 ff.

2. Journeys in the Hereafter.

In connection with ideas of death in the religions of antiquity many myths refer to journeys in the hereafter. In mythical projection the setting of the sun or the arresting of vegetation becomes the entry of the gods of light or vegetation into the underworld, → I, 522 f. καταβαίνω. Acc. to Babylonian myth [3] the realm of the dead, the "land of no return," lies in the furthest west (sunset). The dead person wanders thither through a vast waste and must cross a fiery stream until finally he reaches the palace of the gods of the underworld. Privileged dead are snatched away to the fields of the blessed. Nature

---

an d. Akademie zu Braunsberg (1922), 3-56; also "Die Himmelfahrt der Seele in d. Antike," Kölner Universitätsreden, 27 (1931); also "Gott u. Hölle, der Mythus vom Deszensuskampfe," Studien der Bibliothek Warburg, 20 (1932); G. van der Leeuw, Art. "Geister, Dämonen, Engel," RGG², II, 962-967; F. Loofs, Art. "Descent to Hades," ERE, IV (1911), 648-663; H. Mende, De animarum in poesi epica et dramatica ascensu, Diss. Breslau (1913); K. Meuli, "Scythica," Hermes, 70 (1935), 121-176; H. Oepke, "Unser Glaube an d. Himmelfahrt Christi," Luthertum, 49 (1938), 161-186; F. Pfister, "Der Reliquienkult im Altertum," I, RVV, 5, 1 (1909); II, RVV, 5, 2 (1912), 480-489; K. Prümm, Der chr. Glaube u. d. altheidnische Welt, II (1935), 17-51, 53-85; L. Radermacher, Das Jenseits im Mythus der Hellenen (1903); also "Zu den Himmelfahrtslegenden," Wochenschr. f. klass. Philologie, 28 (1911), 81-86; Reitzenstein Ir. Erl., 2-92; Rohde Index, s.v.; H. Schlier, Religionsgeschichtliche Untersuchungen zu den Ignatiusbriefen, Beih. z. ZNW, 8 (1929), 5-32; F. Wehrli, "Die Mysterien von Eleusis," ARW, 31 (1934), 95-100.

[1] Etym. πορεύω from πόρος "way," "passage," as πορθμεύω from πορθμός "(place of) crossing" or ὀχετεύω from ὀχετός "canal," cf. E. Fraenkel, Gr. Denominativa, 188; Walde-Pok., II, 39 [Debrunner].

[2] On specific aspects of πορεύεσθαι as distinct from similar terms cf. O. Becker, "Das Bild des Weges u. verwandte Vorstellungen im frühgr. Denken," Hermes, 4 (1937), 207 f. [Kleinknecht].

[3] Texts in AOT, 168-186, cf. also E. Ebeling, Art. "Babylonien," RGG², I, 709-713; Kroll, Gott u. Hölle, 205-261; on Egyptian myth, Kroll, op. cit., 183-204.

mythology lies behind the journey of Ishtar into hell to liberate Tammuz. The Gilgamesh epic tells how the hero journeys into the underworld to ask his primeval ancestor Utnapištim about life and death.

The Gk. world speaks of the dead journeying in Hades. [4] They are called οἱ κάτω πορευόμενοι, [5] and Socrates waits for τὴν εἰς "Αιδου πορείαν ὡς πορευσόμενος ὅταν ἡ εἱμαρμένη καλῇ. [6] The Gks. also speak of the isles of the blessed in the west to which favorites of the gods are snatched away, Hom. Od., 4, 563-568; Hes. Op., 167-173. The νῆσοι μακάρων merge into the land of the future, 'Ηλύσιον πεδίον, which is described similarly. [7] Acc. to the Eleusinian mysteries this is the privileged place of devotees and acc. to Pindar it is open only to those who three times have pursued the difficult way of a righteous life to the very end, Ol., 2, 68 ff.; Fr., 129 ff. In poetry the dead are sometimes fetched back through journeys into Hades (Orpheus-Eurydice etc.), or information is gleaned about the hereafter (Hom. Od., 11 etc.). When the concept of the soul was further developed in the Gk. world, [8] a sharp distinction was made between the mortal body and the immortal soul which originates in the divine world. Only the latter journeys in the world to come ; the idea of a journey of the soul now makes its appearance in Gk. literature. [9] Acc. to the Orphic writings (6th/5th cent.), which introduce the idea, the goal of souls is to return to their heavenly home after long travels. [10] Hades now becomes the place of punishment, hell. Plato introduced into Gk. philosophy the belief in the immortality of the soul and its many incarnations up to the goal of final purification. Acc. to the myth in Resp., X, 614 ff. [11] the soul goes to the place of judgment after leaving the body. There the judges order the righteous πορεύεσθαι τὴν εἰς δεξιὰν (614c) and to ascend to heaven, while they put the unrighteous on the left hand and consign them to the place of punishment. New ones keep coming ὡς ἐκ πολλῆς πορείας, 614e. They gather in a meadow and tell one another what they have suffered and seen in their thousand-year journey on earth, while those who come from heaven describe their felicity there. Lachesis assigns individuals their further destiny and another thousand-year journey begins, 617d-621a. Plato draws a conclusion which shows that the myth is both the basis and goal of ethical action, namely, that it is necessary to keep the soul from impurity and to persist on the upward way in order that things may go well with us on the thousand-year journey described here. The ideas of Plato, which seem to be dependent on Iranian thought, [12] influence Plut. and the Stoa. [13] From Hell. days (under the influence of star worship and the planetary spheres) the idea gradually changes from a descent of the soul into the underworld to an ascent of the soul into heaven. The descent becomes an ascent. [14]

---

[4] → I, 146 ff. with bibl.

[5] Etym. M., s.v. οἶκτος; Apul. Met., IX, 31 ad inferos demeare ; Soph. Ai., 690 ἐγὼ γὰρ εἶμ᾽ ἐκεῖσ᾽ ὅποι πορευτέον.

[6] Plat. Phaed., 115a; cf. 113d πορευθέντες ἐπὶ τὸν 'Αχέροντα.

[7] Perhaps from the Egypt. elu field, Ganschinietz, 2376; Nilsson, I², 324 f.; Kroll Himmelfahrt, 7; J. Kroll, "Elysium," Arbeitsgemeinschaft f. Forschung des Landes Nordrhein-Westfalen, Geisteswissenschaft, 2 (1953).

[8] Nilsson, I², 192-197.

[9] Kroll Himmelfahrt, 9.

[10] Acc. to T. Gomperz, Griech. Denker, I (1896), 103 this belief is dependent on the Indian Samsara doctrine by way of the Persians ; Nilsson, however, finds its origin in primitive Gk. thought, I², 691-696. The "passes" given to the dead describe the way beyond, cf. A. Olivieri, "Lamellae aureae orphicae," KlT, 133 (1915), 12-21.

[11] Cf. Plat. Phaed., 80b ff., 110 ff.; Gorg., 522e ff.; Phaedr., 248c-249d (μετεωροπορεῖ, 246c).

[12] A possible hint of this is to be seen in his note that he took the myth from the Armenian Er, whom the Epicurean Colotes equates with Zoroaster, Procl. in Rem. Publ., II, 109, 4 ff., cf. Bousset, 257 f.

[13] Plut. Gen. Socr., 22 (II, 590b-592e); Ser. Num. Pun., 22 ff. (II, 563-568). M. Pohlenz, Die Stoa, I (1948), 226-233, 274.

[14] Examples in Rohde, II, 213, n. 2 : The milky way is ὁδὸς ψυχῶν τῶν ἅδην τὸν ἐν οὐρανῷ διαπορευομένων, Sen. ad Marciam, 17 f.; Kroll Himmelfahrt, 3-29.

The origin of the soul in heaven and its return thither are the theme of the Iranian myth [15] which in different forms passes into Mithraism, Mandaean thought, Judaism (Eth. En.) and Christianity (Asc. Is.). [16] The ascent of the soul is the centre of the Mithras mysteries ; the so-called Mithras liturgy [17] shows how to anticipate the ascent in ecstasy. [18] Similarly, acc. to the Mandaean writings souls are sparks from the divine realm of light (Lidz. Liturg., 128) which are now enclosed in bodies. Redemption consists in return to this realm and it is made possible by the heavenly redeemer Manda d'Hajje, *ibid.*, 196, 199. Baptism and the last rites are designed to help the soul so that on its ascent it may pass safely through the planetary spheres (guard-houses), [19] 106, 139.

There is a psychological as well as an eschatological form of the journey in the hereafter. The soul leaves the body and travels abroad in dreams ; esp. in ecstasy [20] (prophets, mystics, poets) the soul mounts up into the divine world. Thus Parm. in the introduction to his didactic poem (Fr., 1 [Diels[7], I, 228 ff.]) describes how he ascended to the house of deity in a chariot, cf. → V, 47, 3 ff. [21]

Alongside the ascent of the soul we find the independent idea of the ascent of the whole man to heaven. [22] Examples are the Babylonian Etana, the Gk. Heracles, [23] the Roman Romulus, [24] and the Hell. [25] and esp. the Rom. apotheoses of rulers, in which those celebrated rise up to heaven from their funeral pyres. [26] The honour of ascension is also paid to philosophers. [27]

Rapture [28] is understood as a divine act by which men are set in the supraterrestrial sphere without suffering death (Ganymede etc.). It is thus a form of journey in the hereafter, but in view of its passive character it does not fall under the concept of πορεύομαι (→ IV, 7 f. ἀναλαμβάνω; → I, 472 f. ἁρπάζω).

---

[15] Reitzenstein Ir. Erl.; Bousset, 155-169; Kroll Gott u. Hölle, 262-270.

[16] For the effect on Syrian Christianity cf. Schlier, 8-12.

[17] Mithr. Liturg., 2-15; F. Cumont, *Die Mysterien d. Mithra*[3] (1923), 95-135.

[18] Cf. the Isis mysteries acc. to Apul. Met., XI, 23, 14 ff.: *accessi confinium mortis ... et per omnia vectus elementa remeavi.* The flight through the elements is the same as the ascent to heaven, cf. Reitzenstein Hell. Myst., 21, 220 f.

[19] Further examples in R. Bultmann, "Die Bdtg. der neuerschlossenen mand. u. manich. Quellen für das Verständnis des Joh.-Ev.," ZNW, 24 (1925), 104-113, esp. 126, 132-138; Kroll Gott u. Hölle, 271-299.

[20] → ἔκστασις II, 449 ff., esp. 453, 17 ff.; T. K. Oesterreich, Art. "Ekstase," RGG[2], II, 95-97; Bousset, 253 f.; Rohde, II, 92-102 and Index.

[21] Cf. H. Fränkel, *Wege u. Formen frühgr. Denkens* (1955), 158-162.

[22] Hönn, 11-32.

[23] Seneca Hercules Oetaeus (ed. R. Peiper and G. Richter [1902]), 1977: *cessit, ex oculis, in astra fertur* ; 1988 : *iter ad supera* ; Apollodor., Bibliotheca (ed. R. Wagner, 1894), II, 160 : with thunder a cloud raises him up to heaven ; Pfister, II, 480-489. Among the Stoics and Cynics Heracles is a type of the sage who, journeying through the world in a life full of trouble (Dio C., 8, 26-36; Epict. Diss., II, 16, 44), merited heaven by many proofs of virtue and finally went thither ; cf. O. Edert, *Über Senecas Herakles u. d. Herakles auf dem Oeta*, Diss. Kiel (1909), 33-59. But Pfister goes too far when he tries to show that the first Gospels were influenced by this late picture of Heracles ("Herakles u. Christus," ARW, 34 [1937], 42-60). In opposition cf. Kroll Gott u. Hölle, 445 and for a moderate view O. Kern, *Die Religion d. Griechen*, III (1938), 249.

[24] Liv., I, 7, 16; Plut. Romulus, 27, 3 ff. (I, 34b-f); 28, 1 ff. (I, 35a-f).

[25] Esp. Alexander (Ps.-Callisth. Historia Alex. Magni, 33, 27: ἀνῆλθεν εἰς τὸν οὐρανὸν καὶ ὁ ἀετὸς σὺν αὐτῷ.

[26] Suet. Caes., I, 100, 4 : *nec defuit vir praetorius, qui se effigiem cremati euntem in caelum vidisse iuraret.* E. Bickermann, "Die röm. Kaiserapotheose," ARW, 27 (1929), 1-34, esp. 13-15.

[27] Apollonius of Tyana (Philostr. Vit. Ap., VIII, 30; Luc. Pergr. Mort., 360 f.).

[28] Cf. Oesterreich, *op. cit.*, 95 f., 107 f.; Rohde Index, *s.v.*; M. Goguel, *La foi à la résurrection de Jésus dans le christianisme primitif* (1933), 217 f.

B. Septuagint, Later Judaism.

In the LXX πορεύομαι is used a few times for בוא (Gn. 37:30; Nu. 32:6; 1 S. 17:45 etc.), יצא (1 S. 20:11; 2 Ch. 35:20), עבר (Jos. 3:4; 15:4; Rt. 2:8 etc.), עלה (Jos. 19:48 etc.), and once for ירד (Gn. 43:5), נגש (Jos. 8:11), שוב (1 S. 1:19), also very occasionally for other Heb. or Aram. originals. But in the main it is used for הלך. It takes on the rich significance of this word and thus acquires a broader sense than in profane Gk., in which the transf. use is hardly ever found.

1. Literal Sense. Lit. it means "to go," "to travel," "to journey," [29] Gn. 11:31; 28:20; ὁδὸν τριῶν ἡμερῶν, Ex. 3:18; of Abraham in his journeys, Gn. 12:4, 5, of the people of Israel journeying to the land of promise, Dt. 1:19, 33; ἐν τῇ ἐρήμῳ, Ju. 11:16; on the public highway Nu. 20:17 (ὁδῷ βασιλικῇ), "to wander about," 1 S. 23:13 (hitp), to go into captivity, Am. 1:15; Jer. 20:6; Lam. 1:18, of the creeping of the serpent, Gn. 3:14, the flowing of rivers, Ez. 32:14; Qoh. 1:7, the tossing of the sea, Jon. 1:11, 13, spreading branches, Hos. 14:7, the blowing of the wind, Zech. 6:7 and the movement of the chariot-throne of God, Ez. 1:9 ff. The parting greeting in the OT is usually πορεύου εἰς εἰρήνην, Ju. 18:6; 1 S. 1:17; 29:7 etc.; ἐν εἰρήνῃ, 2 S. 3:21. Common grammatical constructions in Heb. are variously rendered by πορεύεσθαι, e.g., וַיָּקָם וַיֵּלֶךְ ἀναστὰς ἐπορεύθη, Gn. 24:10; 2 S. 15:9; הֲלַכְתֶּם וַעֲבַדְתֶּם πορευθέντες λατρεύσητε, Jos. 23:16 cf. Gn. 12:9, esp. imp. 27:13 (πορευθεὶς ἔνεγκε); 37:14 (πορευθεὶς ἰδέ), Nu. 13:26 etc.; also the part. הֹלֵךְ with finite verb, e.g., הֹלֵךְ וְגָדֵל ἐπορεύετο καὶ ἐμεγαλύνετο, "constantly became bigger," 1 S. 2:26; הֹלֵךְ וְחָזֵק ἐπορεύετο καὶ ἐκραταιοῦτο, "constantly became stronger," 2 S. 3:1; Ju. 4:24; 2 S. 5:10; also the combination of inf. abs. with a verb, e.g., הָלוֹךְ וְרָחַצְתָּ πορευθεὶς λοῦσαι, 2 K. 5:10.

2. The Meaning "to Pass Away." The sense "to pass away," [30] which is inherent in הלך is transferred to πορεύομαι: δρόσος ὀρθρινὴ πορευομένη, Hos. 13:3; man is a breath which passes away, πνεῦμα πορευόμενον, ψ 77:39; ὁ ὑετὸς ἀπῆλθεν, ἐπορεύθη ἑαυτῷ, Cant. 2:11; ἐπορεύθησαν (זובֿ) ἐκκεκεντημένοι, "they pined away," Lam. 4:9.

3. Transferred Sense. Whereas in secular Gk. πορεύομαι is seldom used in a transf. sense (→ 567, 16 ff.), this common use of הלך is often found in the LXX and later Judaism. As all human life is a journeying in the OT (→ V, 50, 14 ff.), so conduct is a walking, e.g., ὡς ἐπορεύθη Δαυιδ ὁ πατήρ σου, 1 K. 3:14; 2 Ch. 7:17; 2 K. 13:6 (in sins). The metaphor is often completed by the use of "way" or "ways," e.g., 2 Ch. 11:17 (ἐν ταῖς ὁδοῖς Δαυιδ); 17:3 (ἐν ὁδοῖς τοῦ πατρός); 1 S. 8:3; 1 K. 15:26; Moses desires to teach the people the way that it should go, Ex. 18:20; often the ways are characterised, e.g., Prv. 2:13 (ἐν ὁδοῖς σκότους); Ju. 5:6 (ὁδοὺς διεστραμμένας); ψ 100:6 (ἐν ὁδῷ ἀμώμῳ); Is. 65:2 (ὁδῷ ἀληθινῇ).

The most important OT definition, which is again alien to the Greek world, is that which speaks of the ways of God on which man should go. God is the Law-giver who gives orders to man. The ways of Yahweh are not a mode of life which leads to God; they are a mode of life which God has ordained for His people as distinct from others (→ V, 56, 14 ff.) on the basis of the covenant, Ju. 2:22; cf. v. 20: τὴν διαθήκην μου, ἣν ἐνετειλάμην τοῖς πατράσιν αὐτῶν. To walk in the ways of Yahweh, i.e., to follow His commandments, is fundamental

---

[29] C. A. Kuschke, "Die Menschenwege u. der Weg Gottes," Studia Theologica, 5 (1951), 106-118.

[30] Cf. the same sense in Σ Gn. 15:2 for הלך, LXX ἀπολύομαι, Is. 51:20: οἱ υἱοί σου ἐπορεύθησαν ἀγόμενοι, LXX οἱ ἀπορούμενοι οἱ καθεύδοντες, Ἀ ἐριπτάσθησαν for בָּנַיִךְ עֻלְּפוּ שָׁכְבוּ. One may see from this that in bibl. Gk. πορεύεσθαι may be used for "to pass away" apart from הלך [Bertram].

for the faith of Israel, cf. Dt. 8:6; 10:12; 11:22. [31] In place of ἐν ὁδῷ, again in keeping with the use of הלך, many other definitions of the manner of true or false walking are added to πορεύεσθαι.

For Heb. בֿ הלך we find πορεύεσθαι ἐν, e.g., ἐν δικαιοσύνῃ, Is. 33:15, cf. Jub. 7:26; ἐν ἀληθείᾳ, Prv. 28:6; ἐν αἰσχύνῃ, Is. 45:16; ἐν ψεύδεσι, Jer. 23:14; ἐν ἀκακίᾳ, ψ 25:1; 83:12; Test. Iss. 5:1; ἐν κακίᾳ, Test. D. 5:5; ἐν ὑπερηφανίᾳ, Da. 4:37 Θ. The Test. XII have some expressions not found in the LXX, so ἐν ἁγιασμῷ, B. 10:11, ἐν ἀγνοίᾳ νεότητος, R. 1:6; ἐν εὐθύτητι καρδίας, Iss. 3:1; ζωῆς, Iss. 4:6; very often ἐν ἁπλότητι καρδίας, R. 4:1; Iss. 4:1, ψυχῆς, S. 4:5, ὀφθαλμῶν, Iss. 3:2, 4; more rarely in LXX with dat. alone, e.g., σοφίᾳ, Prv. 28:26; δόλῳ, Lv. 19:16; τοῖς θελήμασιν αὐτῶν ... πλάνῃ καρδίας, Jer. 23:17; commonly πορεύεσθαι with adv., e.g., ὀρθῶς, Prv. 14:2; δικαίως, Prv. 28:18; σκολιῶς, Jer. 6:28; ὁσίως, 1 K. 8:61.

In many cases the closer definition by ἐν or dat. is not controlled by man and his subjective mode of action but by God and His Law and commandments. This is expressed in the fact that God has charge of the life of covenant members. The νόμος and its statutes are thus presented as the way (→ V, 51, 23 ff.) which the righteous must keep to without qualification, e.g., ἐν νόμῳ κυρίου, ψ 118:1; Test. Jos. 4:5; 18:1; ἐν τοῖς προστάγμασί σου, Ιερ. 39(32):23, cf. 1 K. 8:61; Test. Jud. 24:3; ἐν ταῖς ἐντολαῖς αὐτοῦ, Test. Jud. 23:5; ἐν τῇ ἀληθείᾳ σου, ψ 85:11; or with the dat. τῷ νόμῳ, Ex. 16:4; τοῖς κρίμασί μου, ψ 88:31. On the other hand, a Gentile way of life is called a forbidden way which Israel must not tread ἐν τοῖς νομίμοις αὐτῶν, Lv. 18:3; 20:23. In contrast to the one νόμος of Yahweh are τὰ νόμιμα, the customs, of the Gentiles : τοῖς δικαιώμασιν ἐθνῶν, 2 K. 17:8; βουλῇ ἀσεβῶν, ψ 1:1. Another metaphor is that which depicts God or His countenance as the light which lights up the way of the righteous : τῷ φωτί σου, Is. 60:3; ἐν τῷ φωτὶ τοῦ προσώπου σου, ψ 88:16. To express the obedience of the Israelite who does not seek to evade the testing glance of God the Heb. phrase לְפְנֵי (q or hitp) הלך is used, and in Gk. this is rendered πορεύεσθαι ἐνώπιον, e.g., τῷ πορευομένῳ ἐνώπιόν σου ἐν ὅλῃ τῇ καρδίᾳ αὐτοῦ, 1 K. 8:23; ἐνώπιόν μου ἐν ἀληθείᾳ, 1 K. 2:4; ἐνώπιόν σου Is. 38:3. [32] Opposing God, sinners walk ἐναντίον μου πλάγιοι, Lv. 26:40.

4. Theological Sense. The Heb. אַחֲרֵי הלך, transl. πορεύεσθαι ὀπίσω τινός, means first "to go behind someone," Ju. 13:11, then transf. "to follow someone," "to be subject to him and to obey him," so esp. of the obedient following of God ὀπίσω μου, 1 K. 14:8, and esp. in the call of the lawgiver or the prophet for decision εἰ ἔστιν κύριος ὁ θεός, πορεύεσθε ὀπίσω αὐτοῦ (Dt. 13:5; 1 K. 18:21). Apostasy to other gods is a wicked following and going after ὀπίσω θεῶν ἑτέρων, Dt. 6:14; Ju. 2:12, 19; 1 K. 11:10, or ἀλλοτρίων, Jer. 7:9, 6; 25:6; specifically τῆς Βάαλ, Jer. 2:23, 'Αστάρτης, 1 K. 11:5; paraphrased ἀνωφελοῦς, Jer. 2:8; transf. to material or mental objects ὀπίσω τῶν ματαίων, Jer. 2:5; Hos. 5:11; ὀπίσω τῶν ἀρεστῶν τῆς καρδίας ὑμῶν, Jer. 16:12; χρυσίου Sir. 31:8; ἁμαρτιῶν Ιεροβοαμ, 2 K. 13:2; ὀπίσω ἐπιθυμιῶν, Test. Jud. 13:2.

5. Imperative Use. A counterpart to the bibl. and esp. the OT concept of sending (→ I, 398 ff. ἀποστέλλω) is the fact that in many passages πορεύομαι is used in the imp. as the divine command to discharge a divine task. Here the Gk. πορεύου (πορεύθητι) corresponds in the main to the crisp monosyllabic לֵך of the God who commands unconditionally. In itself πορεύεσθαι has no theological content here ; it acquires it only from the immediate context. This divine imp. of sending is found esp. in important sendings in the history between God and His people, and it constitutes men the bearers of divine commissions, e.g., Abraham in Gn. 22:2, Nathan in 2 S. 7:5, Elijah in 1 K. 19:15, Isaiah in Is. 6:8 f.; 38:5, Jeremiah in Ιερ. 3:12; 42(35):13, Ezekiel in Ez. 3:1, Hosea in Hos. 3:1.

---

[31] Cf. also Dt. 19:9; 26:17; 30:16; 1 K. 2:3; 8:58; ψ 118:3; 127:1; Is. 42:24.
[32] The translator of Gn. has the apposite rendering εὐαρεστεῖν ἐναντίον at Gn. 17:1; 24:40; 48:15; cf. also Gn. 5:22, 24; 6:9.

6. Going to Death, Journeys in the Hereafter. Human life is a journey which, like everything earthly, ends in death. David on dying says πορεύομαι ἐν ὁδῷ πάσης τῆς γῆς, 1 K. 2:2; cf. Test. R. 1:3. The original OT idea is that after death a man is gathered to his fathers in the family grave, [33] or that he goes to members of the family who died before him. Then *sheol* takes the place of the family grave ; as the general realm of shades it receives all the dead. [34] Since it lies in the depths of the earth καταβαίνειν (→ I, 522, f.) is the proper term, Is. 14:11, 15. It is the land of no return. Hence David complains that he can go to his dead child but it cannot come to him, 2 S. 12:23; cf. Job 10:21; 16:22. The preacher also confesses that in Hades ὅπου σὺ πορεύῃ ἐκεῖ, all human work and knowledge comes to an end, Qoh. 9:10. It is man's eternal home from which there is no return ἐπορεύθη ὁ ἄνθρωπος εἰς οἶκον αἰῶνος αὐτοῦ, Qoh. 12:5; cf. Jub. 36:1; Eth. En. 17:6. With the rise of the doctrine of retribution and the infiltration of the Gk. belief in immortality *sheol* becomes the place where souls stay between death and the resurrection. [35] For the righteous it is a place of rest, Rev. 6:11; 14:13; [36] thus Moses says in Ass. Mos. 1:15 : I go hence to the rest of my fathers. For sinners, on the other hand, *sheol* is the provisional place of punishment prior to the last judgment. [37] In acc. with Bab. ideas the underworld is located in the planetary sphere. Thus Enoch in his wanderings in the hereafter finds the place of punishment of fallen angels in the 2nd heaven, Slav. En. 7, and hell in the northern heaven, *ibid.* 10 (the 3rd heaven, Gr. Bar. 4 ff.).

There is no journey of Yahweh into Hades in the OT. [38] Such journeys are recounted in the Apocalypses. As for journeys to the hereafter, the OT [39] has the rapture of Enoch in Gn. 5:24 (לָקַח אֹתוֹ אֱלֹהִים, LXX μετέθηκεν αὐτὸν ὁ θεός) and the ascension of Elijah in 2 K. 2:11 (וַיַּעַל LXX ἀνελήμφθη). [40] In later Judaism journeys to the hereafter or to heaven are a favourite theme with reference to the great heroes of faith of the past, e.g., Enoch (→ Ἐνώχ II, 556 ff.), [41] Abraham (Apc. Abr. 15 ff.), Ezra (4 Esr. 14:9, 49) and Baruch (S. Bar. 48:30). For ascents into heaven during life cf. also Test. L. 2-5; Asc. Is. 6-11; Gr. Bar. 2 ff., and into Paradise, Vit. Ad. 25 ff. [42] Descriptions of such journeys are also found at a later period, as may be seen from 3 En., [43] not to speak of mystical and cabbalistic writings. The heavenly journeys of later Judaism are designed partly to disclose the secrets of the world to come (its lay-out and nature) and partly to admonish concerning future retribution. Ecstatic states are often described. The seer has experience of the soul leaving the body and ascending into the world to come. [44] The concrete descriptions show that ecstatic experiences were not unknown among the righteous in later Judaism. [45]

---

[33] Gn. 15:15; 49:29, 33; 25:8; Nu. 27:13 etc.

[34] Cf. Eichr. Theol. AT, II³, 112-116; G. Beer, *Der bibl. Hades* (1902), 7-19; A. Bertholet, *Die isr. Vorstellungen vom Zustand nach dem Tode*² (1914), 40-49; Str.-B., IV, 1016-1165; F. Schwally, *Das Leben nach dem Tode nach den Vorstellungen der alten Israeliten und des Judts.* (1892).

[35] Cf. Volz Esch., 256-267; → I, 147 ῞Αιδης; Str.-B., IV, 1016-1022; Bousset-Gressm., 269-274; 285-289.

[36] Volz Esch., 257; → I, 350 ἀναπαύω.

[37] For the relation of Hades and the realm of the dead cf. Volz Esch., 331 f.; Bousset-Gressm., 282-286; Schwally, *op. cit.*, 136-147.

[38] Kroll Gott u. Hölle, 316-362; acc. to Midr. Jonah (A. Wünsche, *Aus Israels Lehr-hallen*, II [1908], 42 f.) Jonah journeys to Hades when swallowed up with the whale by Leviathan-Hades.

[39] Cf. also Ps. 49(48):15; 73(72):24; Is. 53:8 etc.

[40] Cf. L. Ginsberg, Art. "Ascension," Jew. Enc., II, 164 f.

[41] Eth. En. 12-36, 70-81; Slav. En. 3 ff. has a later form.

[42] Cf. 2 C. 12:4 and Wnd. 2 K., *ad loc.*; in Ass. Mos. 10:12 this motif is only added later, cf. Kautzsch Apkr. u. Pseudepigr., II, 312.

[43] H. Odeberg, *The Fourth Gospel* (1929) on Jn. 3:13; also Str.-B., III, 531-533.

[44] Cf. esp. Asc. Is. 6:10 ff.

[45] For further later Jewish examples cf. Wünsche, *op. cit.* (→ n. 38), III, 94-96, 184-192; Sukka, 45b.

7. Philo and Josephus. Philo uses πορεύομαι in the lit. sense very seldom, and though he often has ὁδός in its fig. sense in different combinations (→ ὁδός V, 60, 4 ff.), the transf. sense of πορεύεσθαι is also uncommon in his works. We find it occasionally in the metaphors of the way of life (Migr. Abr., 133) or the two ways (→ V, 61, 19 f.; Migr. Abr., 204, cf. Decal., 50). A notable omission in Philo is the common LXX concept of walking under the claim of God, → 570, 37 ff. This does occur in Spec. Leg., IV, 183 (μὴ πορεύεσθαι δόλῳ), but it is perhaps to be regarded here as an allusion to Lv. 19:16. Typically Philo gives πορεύεσθαι a moral flavour. Thus the king's highway (Nu. 20:17-20 ὁδὸς βασιλική) is for him the royal way of virtue which Israel treads in its knowledge of God, Deus Imm., 144 f. [46] Borrowing the ethical principle of Aristot. (Eth. Nic., II, 6, p. 1107a, 2 f.), he calls it the true middle way. When it is said of the serpent in Gn. 3:14 LXX that it is to creep on its breast and belly (ἐπὶ τῷ στήθει σου καὶ τῇ κοιλίᾳ πορεύσῃ), Philo interprets the former as θυμός and the latter as ἐπιθυμία, and he applies this to the ἄφρων who δι' ἀμφοτέρων πορεύεται, Migr. Abr., 67. Zilpah, whose name means πορευόμενον στόμα acc. to the Jewish allegorising of names, is to go with Leah as an "accompanying mouth," and to keep her to virtue at all times by what she says, Congr., 30. [47]

The usage of Joseph. follows the lines described earlier (→ 570, 8 ff.) and contains no peculiarities, cf. Vit., 129, 228; Ant., 1, 282; Bell., 2, 309.

C. New Testament.

1. Literal Sense. πορεύομαι occurs in the NT only in the mid. and pass., often in the lit. sense [48] "to go," "to travel," "to journey" with no narrower definition, Lk. 13:33; 19:36; Ac. 9:3; 10:20; 24:25; 1 C. 16:4, 6. The OT parting (→ 570, 15) is also found in the NT πορεύου εἰς εἰρήνην, Lk. 7:50; 8:48 or ἐν Ac. 16:36. Sometimes the sense is "to go away," Jn. 7:35 (εἰς τὴν διασποράν); Mt. 11:7; 2:9; Lk. 4:42; Ac. 24:25; Jn. 8:59 vl. [49] Elsewhere it means "to go to" a task or goal, Jn. 11:11; 20:17 (πρὸς τοὺς ἀδελφούς μου); Lk. 22:8; Mt. 8:9; 22:9; 1 C. 10:27 (by invitation). Often there are narrower details, e.g., concerning the starting-point Lk. 13:31 (ἐντεῦθεν); Mt. 19:15 (ἐκεῖθεν), or the territory traversed (διὰ τῶν σπορίμων); Mk. 9:30 vl. (διὰ τῆς Γαλιλαίας). In many cases prepositions fulfil this role : ἔμπροσθεν speaks of the Good Shepherd going before His flock, Jn. 10:4; ὀπίσω refers to following after demagogues in the last times, Lk. 21:8; εἰς indicates the goal, Mt. 2:20 γῆν Ἰσραήλ; 17:27 θάλασσαν; Lk. 1:39 ὀρεινήν; 4:42 : ἔρημον τόπον; Ac. 18:6 : ἔθνη; R. 15:24 : Σπανίαν; 15:25 : Ἱερουσαλήμ; Jm. 4:13 : πόλιν (here of human plans which God does not ratify).

Heb. expressions may often be discerned. These Hebraisms are distributed equally in Mt. and Lk., e.g., Mt. 2:8 : πορευθέντες ἐξετάσατε; 9:13 : πορευθέντες δὲ μάθετε; 10:7 : πορευόμενοι κηρύσσετε. [50] A preceding ἀναστάς corresponds to the Heb. וַיָּקָם וַיֵּלֶךְ in Ac. 8:27; 22:10; cf. Lk. 15:18, ἐξελθών to the expression וַיֵּצֵא וַיֵּלֶךְ in Ac. 12:17; 21:5, and πορευομένη ... ἐπληθύνετο to a prefixed הָלֹךְ in the sense of "evermore."

2. Going to Death. As in the LXX (→ 572, 1 ff.) πορεύομαι has in the NT the sense of "going to death," "passing away." Nevertheless, the NT does not share the OT view of this as expressed in resignation and lamentation. Jesus as

---

[46] J. Pascher, Η ΒΑΣΙΛΙΚΗ ΟΔΟΣ. Der königliche Weg zu Wiedergeburt u. Vergottung bei Philon v. Alex., Studien zur Geschichte u. Kultur des Altertums, 34 (1931), 10-36.
[47] F. Wutz, Onomastica sacra, TU, 41 (1914/15), 238.
[48] As regards the use of πορεύομαι, it should be noted that in the weaker sense "to go" (which is favoured by LXX), it serves as a substitute for the awkward irregular εἶμι, Bl.-Debr. § 101; 126, 1b γ [Debrunner].
[49] It alternates with ὑπάγειν cf. Lk. 22:22 with Mk. 14:21; Mt. 26:24, also with ἀπέρχομαι cf. Jn. 16:7a with 7b.
[50] Further examples are Mt. 11:4; 17:27; 21:6; 22:15; 25:16; 26:14; 27:66; 28:7, 19; Lk. 9:12, 13, 52; 10:37; 14:10; 15:15; 17:14; 22:8.

the earthly Son of Man regards His going to death as the way which God has divinely appointed for Him for the saving of man (κατὰ τὸ ὡρισμένον πορεύεται, Lk. 22:22). Peter, though he does not perceive what his resolve would entail, declares that he is ready to accept imprisonment and even death with Jesus (Lk. 22:33 : εἰς θάνατον πορεύεσθαι). In the last judgment those who withhold ministering love from their neighbours are directed by the Judge of the world to depart from Him and to go into eternal fire, Mt. 25:41. The reference is to Gehennah when it is said of the betrayer in Ac. 1:25 that he went to his own place (πορευθῆναι εἰς τὸν τόπον τὸν ἴδιον). [51]

3. Imperative Use. As in the OT (→ 571, 41 ff.) the curt imperative πορεύου (πορεύθητι) is often theologically significant. It may express God's sovereign command as plainly declared in the direction to Joseph in Mt. 2:20 : ἐγερθεὶς παράλαβε τὸ παιδίον . . . καὶ πορεύου εἰς γῆν 'Ισραήλ. This mighty πορεύου is also used quite frequently in the Synoptic miracle tradition which tells about Jesus as the One sent down from heaven who is the Lord of sickness, demons and death, cf. the story of the sick man in Lk. 5:24 or of the suppliant father who is to go home certain that his request is granted even though he has not seen it, Jn. 4:50. The Gentile centurion also finds in the powerful πορεύου an analogy to the orders which he issues to those under him, Mt. 8:9; Lk. 7:8. We are pointed in a different direction by the commands of Jesus which have to do with mission ; in the NT apostolic sending corresponds to the sending of the prophets in the OT. As the Saviour who goes to His people Jesus sends His disciples with the message of salvation to the lost sheep of the house of Israel, Mt. 10:6 f.: πορεύεσθε . . . πορευόμενοι δὲ κηρύσσετε. Often this imperative is followed by the indicative of the obedient man, Mt. 2:21; Lk. 5:25; Jn. 20:18; cf. Jn. 4:50 : ἐπίστευσεν . . . καὶ ἐπορεύετο, Ac. 8:27: καὶ ἀναστὰς ἐπορεύθη, Ac. 9:17: ἀπῆλθεν . . . καὶ εἰσῆλθεν.

4. The Mission of Jesus. πορεύομαι also emphasises with theological pregnancy the mission of Jesus. John the Baptist establishes himself at the Jordan and declares to those who go there (Mt. 3:5) the message of threatening eschatological judgment. The work of Jesus consists from the very outset in a movement to His people. If, then, πορεύομαι is often used in relation to His travels, this is no mere description. The word expresses His mission. πορεύομαι is used when He looks for a solitary place (Lk. 4:42 : ἐπορεύθη εἰς ἔρημον τόπον). It is also used when He wants to tear Himself away from the multitude which throngs Him (Lk. 4:42 : τοῦ μὴ πορεύεσθαι ἀπ' αὐτῶν). It is used when He goes on (Mt. 19:15) and especially when He is rejected (Lk. 4:30; 9:56). In a word, the wandering life of Jesus is a renunciation (Lk. 13:33; 9:57). It stands under the divine δεῖ (Lk. 13:33; 9:51). It is a model for His followers (Lk. 9:58), and in a special way for the disciples (Mt. 10:6 : πορεύεσθε κτλ.). In the metaphor of the shepherd He illustrates the fact that He both goes out and searches (Mt. 18:12 : πορευθεὶς ζητεῖ) and also goes before the flock to provide for and to protect it, Jn. 10:4.

5. The Apostles. Wandering from place to place, Jesus the Son of Man is an example for the wandering apostles, [52] who as travelling preachers commissioned by Him carry the message first to the lost sheep of Israel, Mt. 10:6. But it is the

---

[51] Str.-B., II, 595 f.; Wdt. Ag., 77; cf. 1 Cl., 5, 4 of Peter : ἐπορεύθη εἰς τὸν ὀφειλόμενον τόπον τῆς δόξης. On the durative significance of the imp. cf. Bl.-Debr. § 336, 1 [Schneemelcher].

[52] Pfister, I, 259-278 compares them to heroes of journeys like Aeneas, Odysseus and Heracles, and to gods of travel like Dionysus.

Risen Lord who first sends out with power. In this connection πορεύομαι can become a tt. in the missionary command. Mary Magdalene goes with the message of the resurrection to the disciples, Jn. 20:17. The disciples then go with the preaching of judgment and salvation to the whole world, Mt. 28:19. Following the favourite literary device of syncrisis [53] Luke deliberately draws a parallel between Jesus and His disciples. Philip receives a command to travel a lonely road, Ac. 8:26. Ananias is to go to the persecutor, 9:15. Peter is ordered to visit the Gentile house, 10:20, cf. also 12:17. Acts, supplemented by the Pauline Epistles, depicts Paul especially as the indefatigable wandering preacher (Ac. 9:3; 19:21; 22:5, 10, 21) whose appeal to Caesar finally brings him to the capital, 25:12. [54] This theme of worldwide wandering is later depicted as *the* apostolic calling in the apocryphal Acts.

6. Transferred Moral and Religious Use. In a transferred sense the NT, unlike the LXX (→ 570, 28 ff.), uses πορεύομαι surprisingly infrequently for the moral and religious "walk." This use does not occur at all in the Synoptists apart from one verse in the infancy stories in Lk. (1:6), which are strongly influenced by the style of the LXX. Nor does it occur in John's Gospel or especially Paul, who has περιπατεῖν (→ V, 944, 13 ff.) instead. [55] On the outer edge of transferred usage is Ac. 14:16, which says that God let the Gentiles go their own ways. The only references to a pious walk are in Lk. 1:6, which echoes OT formulations : ἐν πάσαις ταῖς ἐντολαῖς καὶ δικαιώμασιν τοῦ κυρίου (cf. 1 K. 8:61), and Ac. 9:31, which speaks of walking in the fear of God (יִרְאַת יְהוָה). The remaining references in the epistles (1 and 2 Peter and Jude) are to an ungodly walk : 1 Pt. 4:3 : ἐν ἀσελγείαις, ἐπιθυμίαις etc.; Jd. 16 : κατὰ τὰς ἐπιθυμίας αὐτῶν; 18 : κατὰ τὰς ἑαυτῶν ἐπιθυμίας; 2 Pt. 3:3 : κατὰ τὰς ἰδίας ἐπιθυμίας αὐτῶν (Jd. 11 : τῇ ὁδῷ τοῦ Κάϊν, seems to be dependent on this). [56]

7. Parting Discourses. In the Parting Discourses in Jn. Jesus speaks several times of going to the Father, 14:2, 3, 12, 28; 16:7, 28. In this respect it should not be overlooked that πορεύομαι alternates with ὑπάγω, which is used even more frequently by the Evangelist. [57] In the main πορεύομαι occurs in sayings about the returning Lord and the Paraclete (→ V, 813, 1 ff.) [58] which form a more or less clear-cut complex of tradition within the corpus of the Parting Discourses. [59] Fear of loneliness threatens the disciples as a result of the departure of Jesus (14:1). Jesus meets this with the comforting assurance that He Himself will go on ahead to prepare a place (14:2) and that at His coming again He will take them up again into abiding fellowship with Himself (14:3). The departure of Jesus, however, is also of significance for those who remain in the world inasmuch as it will enable His disciples to do greater works on the basis of fellowship with the Father (14:12). Thus the going away of Jesus conquers both the uncertain

---

[53] F. Focke, "Synkrisis," Hermes, 58 (1923), 327-368; Hck. Lk., 8.

[54] Cf. Ac. 16:16; 17:14; 18:6; 19:1 vl.; 20:1; 21:5 for further examples.

[55] R. 6:4; 8:4; 13:13 etc.; common too in 1 and 2 Jn.; περιπατεῖν in the LXX (→ V, 942, 28 ff.) in the sense of "to walk in" only at 2 K. 20:3; Prv. 8:20.

[56] On the other hand this sense is very common in the post-apost. fathers : Herm. m., 3, 4; v., 2, 3, 2; m., 4, 4, 4; 8, 11 (almost abs. use); 1 Cl., 1, 3; 60, 2 etc. (cf. Pr.-Bauer⁴, ad loc.).

[57] Of 28 instances of ὑπάγω in Jn., 14 refer to going into the hereafter, cf. E. A. Abbott, Johannine Vocabulary (1905), 142-151; Schlier, 76, 180 pts. out that Ign. uses the "substantial" χωρεῖν rather than the personal πορεύεσθαι.

[58] Cf. K. Kundsin, "Die Wiederkunft Jesu in den Abschiedsreden d. J.," ZNW, 33 (1934), 210-215; H. Windisch, "Die fünf joh. Parakletsprüche," Festgabe f. Adolf Jülicher (1927), 110-137.

[59] Cf. the more recent comm., ad loc.

future (14:28a) and also the hostile and lonely present, since His going to the Father, who is the greater, implies exaltation for the Revealer (14:28). If in c. 14 the going to the Father is related to the coming again to the disciples, who are left in the world like orphans (14:18), in c. 16 the same going to the Father is the *conditio sine qua non* of the coming of the Paraclete (16:7 → V, 813, 18 ff.), [60] for only through His going can He be the Revealer who remains in the Spirit (16:7) and who thus overcomes all the sorrow of the disciples (17:6). Finally, the going to the Father is for the One who was sent from heaven and came forth from the Father the completion of His redemptive work on earth (16:28). [61]

8. The Ascension of Jesus. In the NT πορεύομαι [62] is also used for the ascension of Jesus (Ac. 1:10, 11; 1 Pt. 3:22), which is not found in the original Synoptic tradition. [63, 64]

The most ancient Easter statements refer simply to an ἐγερθῆναι (→ II, 335, 7 ff.) of Jesus as a divine act, Mk. 16:6; Mt. 28:6, 7. [65] The ascension belongs to the genre of rapture stories. [66] But whereas rapture involves separation from the body, ascension presupposes transit through death. In distinction from the heavenly journey of the soul, which is mostly after death and more rarely during life (ecstasy), it applies to the whole man. The ascension is not an independent event of salvation, since exaltation is part of the resurrection. It properly depicts the final epiphany of the Risen Lord in the form of a parting scene. [67, 68] In the framework of the world view of antiquity and under various religio-historical influences (e.g., analogous stories of Graeco-Roman heroes, emperors etc.), [69] this final manifestation is depicted as an ascension. [70] It is possible that this was suggested to the community by the expectation of the *parousia* from heaven. [71]

Ac. 1:9 f. (→ II, 424, 1 ff.; IV, 8, 12 ff.; V, 524, 17 ff.) describes the ascension as a happening which the disciples could see (v. 9 βλεπόντων αὐτῶν, v. 10 ἀτενίζοντες, v. 11 ἐθεάσασθε). Any further depiction, however, is prevented by the cloud which

---

[60] Bultmann J., 430 : "The historical Jesus must depart in order that His purpose to be the Revealer may be purely grasped."

[61] On the religio-historical background cf. Bau. J. and Bultmann J., ad loc.

[62] The real word for the ascension is → ἀναβαίνω, I, 520 f., which takes the place of the absent ἀναπορεύομαι, cf. also → ἀναλαμβάνω, IV, 7 f.

[63] Cf. Lk. 24:51, though W. Michaelis, "Zur Überlieferung der Himmelfahrtsgeschichte," ThBl, 4 (1925), 103 argues that the shorter text is the original ; if so, Ac. 1 is without par. in the Gospels ; cf. also → νεφέλη IV, 909, n. 42.

[64] On the ascension in early Chr. literature cf. L. Hahn, *Bibliothek der Symbole u. Glaubensregeln d. Alten Kirche*³ (1897), 382-386; W. Bauer, *Das Leben Jesu im Zeitalter d. nt.lichen Apkr.* (1909), 275-279; Michaelis, *op. cit.*, 101-109; G. Bertram, "Die Himmelfahrt Jesu vom Kreuz aus," *Festgabe f. A. Deissmann* (1927), 187-217; U. Holzmeister, "Der Tag der Himmelfahrt des Herrn," *Zschr. f. katholische Theologie*, 55 (1931), 44-82; Goguel, *op. cit.* (→ n. 28), 347-356; Stauffer Theol., 117-120; cf. also H. Schrade, *Zur Ikonographie der Himmelfahrt Christi, Vorträge der Bibliothek Warburg* (1928/9), 66-190; G. Kretschmar, "Himmelfahrt u. Pfingsten," ZKG, 66 (1954/55), 209-253; B. Reicke, "Glaube u. Leben d. Urgemeinde," Abh. ThANT, 32 (1957), 18-20; for further bibl. cf. bibl. note.

[64] Goguel, *op. cit.*, 107.

[66] → 569, 20 ff.

[67] Michaelis, *op. cit.*, 105.

[68] On the relation between the resurrection appearances and the taking or exalting of Jesus from the cross cf. E. Bickermann, "Das leere Grab," ZNW, 23 (1924), 281-292; Bertram, *op. cit.* (→ n. 64), 215-217. Instead of ἀφῆκεν τὸ πνεῦμα Mt. 27:50 syˢ has : "and his spirit ascended."

[69] Clemen, 259; R. Reitzenstein, *Hell. Wundererzählungen* (1906), 49-59.

[70] "The Lucan depiction of the ascension differs from similar pagan and Jewish depictions by reason of the fact that no earthly element (a wind or the cloud itself) bears up the exalted Lord," Haench Ag., ad loc.

[71] Cf. Michaelis, 108 f.; Bickermann, *op. cit.* (→ n. 68), 284-292 refers to the correlation between disappearance and rapture in the examples of antiquity ; Pfister, II, 480-489; Goguel, 217-233.

conceals the ascending Lord. [72] In 1 Pt. 3:22 the ascension leads to the enthronement of Jesus, [73] i.e., His session at the right hand of God (→ II, 39 f. δεξιός), and His dominion over all. The ascension is also the presupposition of His return in glory (Ac. 1:11) and the establishment of the kingdom of God (3:21). [74]

9. Jesus' Descent into Hades. πορεύομαι is also used in 1 Pt. 3:19 for the so-called descent of Christ into hell, [75] → I, 149, 20 ff.; IV, 386, n. 111. The proper term here is καταβαίνω, → I, 522 f. cf. Mt. 11:23. [76] As such πορεύομαι in 1 Pt. 3:19 means only "to go hence," [77] but a general examination of this difficult passage (cf. also Eth. En. 12-16) justifies our referring it to the descent of Christ. [78]

The location of the → φυλακή [79] and the timing of the descent [80] are debated. What is clear is that the event recorded in 3:19 took place in the transcendent sphere of spirits during the crucifixion and resurrection of Jesus. [81] The specific focus of this event is on the κηρύσσειν (→ III, 707 f.) of Jesus, and this preserves the relation to En. 12 ff. [82] If in the latter God's judgment is proclaimed to the fallen angels, [83] here Jesus preaches the Gospel to seducing powers [84] and also to the seduced souls of men, [85] though nothing

---

[72] → νεφέλη IV, 909, 6 ff.

[73] Cf. the enthronement of Yahweh, Eichr. Theol. AT, I⁵, 71-75; Ps. 68:33; 110:1; 2:7.

[74] Cf. the description of the ascension in Ep. Apostolorum, 51 (62), ed. H. Duensing KIT, 152 (1925), 42; there are further post-NT instances in, e.g., Barn., 15, 9, cf. Bauer, op. cit. (→ n. 64), 275-279; Goguel, op. cit. (→ n. 28), 352-356.

[75] Cf. inter al.: J. Spitta, Christi Predigt an die Geister (1890); Clemen, 91, 94-96; also Niedergefahren zu den Toten (1900); J. Turmel, La descente du Christe aux enfers (1905); W. Bousset, Hauptprobleme der Gnosis (1907), 255-260; H. Holtzmann, "Höllenfahrt im NT," ARW, 11 (1908), 285-297; Bauer, op. cit. (→ n. 64), 246-251; K. Gschwind, "Die Niederfahrt Christi in die Unterwelt," NT Abh., II, 3/5 (1911); C. Schmidt, "Gespräche Jesu mit seinen Jüngern nach d. Auferstehung," TU, 43 (1919), 315-319, esp. 453-576; R. Reitzenstein, Das mandäische Buch des Herrn der Grösse (1919), 25-34; W. Bousset, Kyrios Christos³ (1919/20), 50-66; B. Reicke, The Disobedient Spirits and Christian Baptism (1946); W. Bieder, Die Vorstellung von der Höllenfahrt Jesu Christi (1949); E. G. Selwyn, The First Ep. of St. Peter (1949) on 3:19 and 4:6; Loofs; G. Bertram, Art. "Höllenfahrt," RGG², II, 1968-1970; Wnd. Kath. Br., Exc. on 1 Pt. 3:19; W. Elert, Der christliche Glaube³ (1956), 320-322; P. Althaus, Die chr. Wahrheit, II (1949)², 261-268; further bibl. → 447, 11 ff.

[76] A verb καταπορεύομαι is rare and means only "to return."

[77] This is stressed by, e.g., Gschwind, op. cit., 40, 88 f., 111, who does not find the descent into hell here, but relates πορευθείς to the ascension as in 3:22.

[78] On other debatable verses like Mt. 27:52; Rev. 1:18; Mt. 12:40 cf. Clemen, 89 f., also op. cit. (→ n. 75), 176-180; on Eph. 4:9 f. → III, 641 ff. κατώτερος, Schlier, 19, n. 1; 23, n. 1; → I, 522 καταβαίνω; on post-NT ref. cf. Bauer, op. cit. (→ n. 64), 275-279. Ev. Pt., 41 f.: On Easter night the guards at the tomb hear a voice from heaven ἐκήρυξας τοῖς κοιμωμένοις and the answer Ναί from the cross, presumably a combination of Mt. 27:52 and 1 Pt. 3:19. Ep. Apostolorum 27 (38) (→ n. 74) "descended to the place of Lazarus." Ev. Nicod. 17 ff. (ed. K. Tischendorf, Evangelia apocrypha² [1876], 323-332); Sib., 8, 310-312; O. Sol. 42:15 ff.; 22:3 ff.; 17:8 ff.; cf. Kroll Gott u. Hölle, 34 ff.; Gschwind, op. cit., 228-234.

[79] Cf. Bieder, op. cit. (→ n. 75), 108-110; Selwyn, op. cit., ad loc.

[80] Selwyn, ad loc.; Bieder, 102-107.

[81] Cf. → 447, 15 ff.

[82] → Ἐνώχ II, 556 ff.; R. Harris, "An Unobserved Quotation from the Book of Enoch," Exp. VI, 4 (1901), 194-199, 346-349; also "On a Recent Emendation in the Text of St. Peter," Exp. VI, 5 (1902), 317-320 suggests the subject Ἐνώχ has dropped out after ἐν ᾧ.

[83] Eth. En. 12-16; cf. also Noah as preacher, 2 Pt. 2:5 (Str.-B., III, 769); Sib., 1, 127; 1 Cl., 7, 6; cf. further Gschwind, 115, n. 2.

[84] πνεῦμα (→ 447, 25), which is rare for this, means spiritual being, whether angel or demon (Mt. 12:43; Eph. 2:2; Hb. 12:9; 1:14; cf. Pr.-Bauer⁴, s.v.; Eth. En. 15:6, 8, 10; 19:1; 60:10 ff.) and is thus to be referred here to the fallen angels of Gn. who, disobedient (cf. ἀπειθήσασίν ποτε) to the divine order, left their heavenly places and intermingled with the daughters of men. Acc. to later Jewish legend they were kept in chains in darkness under

is said about the results of this preaching. The descent of Jesus [86] is thus a mighty proclamation of the victory which has been achieved over all forces and powers. [87] This whole complex of ideas clustered around πορεύομαι stands in critical relation to OT and later Jewish views of death and to the apocalyptic traditions of later Judaism, which for their part are dependent on oriental accounts of katabasis.

εἰσπορεύομαι.

1. "To go in," "to enter," Xenoph. Cyrop., II, 3, 21; of cultic entry into the sanctuary, εἰς τὸ ἄδυτον, Ditt. Or., I, 56, 4 (3rd cent. B.C.); 90, 6; of the "entry" of the demon into a man, Preis. Zaub., I, 4, 3206.

2. In the LXX almost always for בוא, "to go in," "march in," into a land, Ex. 1:1; Nu. 34:2; a house, Lv. 14:46; often cultically of entry into the sanctuary, Ex. 28:30, 43; 34:34; Nu. 4:3 (ὁ εἰσπορευόμενος λειτουργεῖν); ψ 95:8 (εἰς τὰς αὐλὰς αὐτοῦ); Ez. 44:17, 21; often in the expression "to go out and in," Dt. 28:19; 1 S. 18:13 etc.; transf. sexually Gn. 6:4 (πρὸς τὰς θυγατέρας τῶν ἀνθρώπων); Am. 2:7 (πρὸς ... παιδίσκην); so also Eth. En. 7:1.

3. The literal use occurs in the NT at Mk. 1:21 (εἰς Καφαρναούμ), especially for entering into a house : 5:40; Lk. 8:16; 11:33 (οἱ εἰσπορευόμενοι, "those who enter" sc. into the house); 22:10; Ac. 3:2 (εἰς τὸ ἱερόν); 9:28 ("to go in and out"). In a fig. sense εἰσπορεύομαι is used of the outward entry of food into the bodily organs (Mk. 7:15, 18; Mt. 15:17) which cannot make unclean (Mk. 7:19), or of the entry of desires etc. into the heart [1] (Mk. 4:19), [2] or of entry into the kingdom of God, which is depicted as a house or palace (Lk. 18:24). In both the LXX and the NT εἰσέρχομαι is by far the more common term in this kind of usage, → II, 676 ff.

ἐκπορεύομαι.

1. "To go out," "to march out," Xenoph. An., V, 1, 8; Polyb., 11, 9, 4 (εἰς στρατιάν); 11, 9, 8 (εἰς βουλευτήριον); 6, 58, 4 (ἐκ τοῦ χάρακος), "to go forth from," "to flow out," Eth. En. 14:19 (streams of fire); 31:1 (nectar from trees); Preis. Zaub., II, 12, 218 (from the womb); Gr. En. 16:1 (πνεύματα ἐκπορευόμενα ἐκ τῆς ψυχῆς τῆς σαρκὸς αὐτῶν); [1] Preis. Zaub., II, 13, 327 (κύριος τῆς οἰκουμένης ἐκπορεύεται ...).

2. It in the LXX it is almost always used for יצא, lit. of going out to war, 1 S. 11:7; Nu. 1:40, 42 etc., of the exodus from Egypt, Ex. 13:8; 14:8; Dt. 11:10; 23:5; in the phrase

---

the earth (Jd. 6; 2 Pt. 2:4; Eth. En. 106:13 f.; Jub. 5:13; Str.-B., III, 783-785); there seems to be allusion to this in ἐν φυλακῇ.

[85] Str.-B., I, 961-966; Jub. 5:10; Eth. En. 65:11; Bieder, 110-113; on ψυχαί as deceased persons cf. Ac. 2:27; Rev. 6:9; 20:4; 4 Esr. 4:35, 41; 7:32; esp. Apc. Pt. 25 : αἱ ψυχαὶ τῶν πεφονευμένων; Gr. En. also has ψυχαί generally at 9:3, 10; 22:3; 102:5 etc. and describes the departed as spiritual beings by nature, cf. also Eth. En. 22:3, 5, 9.

[86] Cf. also Ign. Mg., 9, 2 : Jesus raises the prophets by His journey into Hades (Bau. Ign., ad loc., with ref. to later material); related hereto is Herm. s., 9, 16, 5-7: the apostles and teachers as "ordained agents of the church" preached and baptised in Hades after death, Dib. Herm., ad loc. [Schneemelcher].

[87] Cf. also 1 Pt. 4:6, where there is further allusion to the descent into Hades ; on this Bieder, 122-128; Selwyn, ad loc.

εἰσπορεύομαι. G. D. Kilpatrick, "πορεύεσθαι and Its Compounds," JThSt, 48 (1947), 61-63.
[1] Cf. Herm. m., 10, 2, 2 f.; of the entry of the demon into a man 12, 5, 4.
[2] Lk. 8:14 revises the phrase.

ἐκπορεύομαι. [1] From the body of giants, the bastards of the fallen angels, Kautzsch Apkr. u. Pseudepigr., II, 247.

"to go out and in," Dt. 28:19; 31:2 etc.; of the mysterious bursting forth[2] of springs from the depths, Dt. 8:7; of hyssop from the cliff, 1 K. 4:33 (3 Βασ. 5:13); cultically of coming out of the tent of revelation, Ex. 34:34; of the breaking forth of water out of the sanctuary, Ez. 47:12, under the altar, 47:1, 8; of the going forth of the word from the mouth, Dt. 23:24; ψ 88:35; Sir. 28:12; Nu. 32:24, also the Word of God, Dt. 8:3 (ῥῆμα); Ez. 33:30; of the emergence of a child from the womb, Nu. 12:12; Job 3:16; 38:8 (metaph. of the sea); of the breaking out of wrath, Jer. 23:19; of phenomena which the prophet sees come forth, Zech. 5:5, 6; 6:1, 5 f. etc.

3. In the NT the word is used literally for "to go forth" in Mt. 20:29; Mk. 10:17, 46; 11:19, "to go out" in Ac. 25:4. It is narrated of the people that they "went out" to John in the desert, Mt. 3:5 and par. By the withdrawal of the apostles unbelievers are left to their own devices, Mk. 6:11. In the last hour the dead will emerge from the tombs, Jn. 5:29.

ἐκπορεύομαι is used for the going of demons out of a man, Ac. 19:12; Mt. 17:21.[3] Figuratively it denotes spiritual going forth (Lk. 4:37 ἦχος), especially that of the word through (διά) the lips, Mt. 4:4 cf. Dt. 8:3. The ῥῆμα of God is the creative word on the basis of which (ἐπί) man will live. From the lips of Jesus proceed words (τῆς χάριτος) about the dawn of the time of grace, Lk. 4:22. On the other hand, words which come forth from the lips of a man make him unclean because his heart is wicked, Mt. 15:11, 18. For this reason no evil or vile (σαπρός) word should proceed from the mouth of a Christian, Eph. 4:29.

Because He proceeds from the Father (Jn. 15:26) the Paraclete is described as the Helper of the disciples who is equal to Jesus and who can thus take His place with full adequacy, → I, 435, 9 ff.; V, 813, 6 ff.

In Rev. the divine sees things and processes which "go forth" or "break forth" with power : lightnings from God's throne (4:5). The Word of might and judgment which issues from the mouth of the Kurios Jesus is seen as a sharp sword[4] which smites the enemies of God (1:16; 19:15). Consuming fire goes forth from the mouth of the witnesses of Christ (11:5). Fire and brimstone proceed from the jaws of the supraterrestrial horses (9:17 f.), and three unclean spirits proceed from the mouth of the dragon, the beast and the false prophet (16:14).[5] In contrast, a river of living water flows out from the throne of God and the Lamb (22:1).

Here, too, ἐκπορεύομαι is a more popular term as compared with the more common ἐξέρχομαι.

Hauck/Schulz

> † πόρνη, † πόρνος, † πορνεία, † πορνεύω, † ἐκπορνεύω

Contents : A. The Non-Jewish World : I. Usage ; II. Extra-Marital Intercourse in the Non-Biblical World : 1. Cultic Prostitution ; 2. Secular Intercourse outside Marriage ; 3. The Sex Ethics of Stoicism. B. The Old Testament : I. Usage ; II. Fornication in National

---

[2] This is connected with demons, A. Jirku, *Die Dämonen u. ihre Abwehr im AT* (1912), 78.
[3] Elsewhere ἐξέρχομαι is used for this in the Synoptists, → II, 678, 42 ff.
[4] Cf. Bss. Apk., 196; Hb. 4:12; Is. 11:4; Wis. Sol. 18:15; Ps. Sol. 17:24 f.
[5] Cf. Herm. v., 4, 1, 6.

πόρνη κτλ. Note : F. Hauck prepared the basic text for this art., and this has been partly shortened and partly expanded by S. Schulz. The section on Josephus (→ 588, 47-589, 25) is by K. H. Rengstorf. Bibl.: A. Allgeier, "Die *crux interpretum* im nt.lichen Ehe-

Life in the OT; III. Cultic Prostitution in the OT; IV. Israel's Unfaithfulness to Yahweh
as πορνεία. C. Later Judaism (Apocrypha, Pseudepigrapha, Dead Sea Scrolls, Philo,
Josephus, Rabbis). D. The New Testament : I. The Proclamation of Jesus ; II. Acts ;
III. Paul, Hebrews and James ; IV. Revelation. E. The Post-Apostolic Fathers.

A. The Non-Jewish World.

I. Usage.

1. πόρνη, from πέρνημι, "to sell," esp. of slaves, means lit. "harlot for hire,"
"prostitute"; Gk. harlots were usually bought slaves, Aristoph. Ach., 527; ἐφασθέντα
πόρνης δημοσίας, BGU, IV, 1024, p. 6, 4 ff. (4-5th cent. A.D.); ὁ Κόλοβος δὲ
πόρνην με πεπύηκεν, P. Oxy., III, 528, 18; πόρνη γυνή, Archiloch. Fr., 142;[1] πόρνη

---

scheidungsverbot, Philologische Untersuchung zu Mt. 5:32 u. 19:9," *Angelicum*, 20 (1943),
128-142; J. Bachofen, *Mutterrecht*, ed. K. Meuli (1948), Index *s.v.* "Hetärismus"; F. Bernhöft,
"Zur Geschichte des europäischen Familienrechts," *Zschr. f. vergleichende Rechtswissenschaft*, 8 (1889), 1-27; E. Bethe, "Die dorische Knabenliebe, ihre Ethik u. ihre Idee,"
Rheinisches Museum, NF 62 (1907), 438-475; S. Biablocki, Art. "Ehebruch," *EJ*, 6 (1930),
253-259; also Art. "Ehescheidung," *ibid.*, 259-271; L. Blau, *Die jüd. Ehescheidung und der
jüd. Scheidebrief*, I and II (1911 f.); J. Bloch, *Die Prostitution*, I (1912); J. Bonsirven, *Le
divorce dans le NT* (1948); L. Brun, "Egteskap, skilsmisse, fraskilter vielse in lys fra det
NT," *For Kirke og Kultur*, 23 (1916), 65-86; R. H. Charles, *The Teaching of the NT on
Divorce* (1921); F. L. Cirlot, *Christ and Divorce* (1945); Darembg.-Saglio, III, 1, 171-174;
2, 1823-1839; G. Delling, "Pls. Stellung zu Frau u. Ehe," BWANT, 56 (1931), 14-38; 57-
160; G. Delling, "Das Logion Mark X 11 (und seine Abwandlungen) im NT," Nov. Test., 1
(1956), 263-274; M. Denner, *Die Auslegung der nt.lichen Schrifttexte über die Ehescheidung
bei den Vätern*, Diss. Würzburg (1910); P. Dufour, *Gesch. der Prostitution bei allen
Völkern*, I: *Die vorschr. Zeit*[5] (1908); A. Eberharter, "Das Ehe- u. Familienrecht der
Hebräer," *At.liche Abh.*, V, 1 and 2 (1914), 12-196; T. Engert, "Ehe- u. Familienrecht der
Hebräer," *Studien zu at.lichen Einleitung u. Gesch.*, 3 (1905), 8-90; G. Falck-Hansen, *Skilsmisse* (1932); A. Fridrichsen, "Excepta fornicationis causa," *Svensk Exegetisk Årsbok*, 9
(1944), 54-58; also "Scholia in NT," *ibid.*, 12 (1947), 140-147; H. Greeven, "Zu den Aus-
sagen d. NT über die Ehe," *Zschr. f. evangel. Ethik*, 1 (1957), 109-125; W. Gabriel, "Was
ist 'Porneia' im Sprachgebrauch Jesu ?" *Ethik*, 7 (1931), 106-109, 363-369; H. Haag, *Bibel-
Lexikon* (1951), *s.v.* "Dirne" ; A. Hermann and H. Herter, Art. "Dirne" in RAC, III, 1149-
1213; U. Holzmeister, "Die Streitfrage über die Ehescheidungstexte bei Mt. 5:32 u. 19:9,"
Biblica, 26 (1945), 133-146; T. Hopfner, *Das Sexualleben d. Griechen u. Römer*, II (1938);
A. Juncker, *Die Ethik d. Ap. Pls.*, II : *Die konkrete Ethik* (1919), 181-216; E. Kornemann,
"Die Stellung d. Frau in der vorgriechischen Mittelmeerkultur," *Orient u. Antike*, 4 (1927);
W. Kroll, Art. "Knabenliebe," Pauly-W., 11 (1922), 897-906; J. Leipoldt, *Jesus u. die
Frauen* (1921), 3-80; also *Die Frau in d. antiken Welt u. im Urchristentum* (1954), 10-145;
H. Licht, *Sittengeschichte Griechenlands*, I-III (1926-1928); A. Müller, Art. "Prostitution,"
RGG², IV, 1576-1580; J. J. B. Müller, Quaestiones nonnullae ad Atheniensium matrimonia
vitamque coniugalem pertinentes, Diss. Utrecht (1920); A. Ott, *Die Auslegung der nt.lichen
Texte über die Ehescheidung* (1911); H. Preisker, *Christentum u. Ehe in den ersten drei
Jahrhunderten* (1927), 13-177; Pr.-Bauer⁴, *s.v.*; J. Preuss, "Prostitution u. sexuelle Perversi-
täten nach Bibel u. Talmud," *Monatsschr. f. praktische Dermatologie*, 43 (1906), 271-279,
342-345, 376-381, 470-477, 549-555; H. Schmidt, *Synonymik d. gr. Sprache*, II (1878), 412-
421; R. Schnackenburg, "Die sittliche Botschaft d. NT," *Handbuch d. Moraltheologie* (1954),
170-176; K. Schneider, Art. "Hetairai," Pauly-W., 8 (1913), 1333-1372; P. T. Schwegler,
"De clausulis divortii (Mt. 5:32 und 19:9)," Verbum Dei, 26 (1948), 214-217; J. Sickenberger, "Die Unzuchtsklausel im Mt.," *Theol. Quart.*, 123 (1942), 189-201; also "Zwei neue
Äusserungen zur Ehebruchklausel bei Mt.," ZNW, 42 (1949), 202-209; K. Staab, "Die
Unauflöslichkeit d. Ehe u. d. sog. 'Ehebruchsklauseln' bei Mt. 5:32 u. 19:9," *Festschr. f.
E. Eichmann* (1940), 435-452; also "Zur Frage d. Ehescheidungstexte im Mt.," *Zschr. f.
katholische Theol.*, 67 (1943), 36-44; Str.-B., I, 315 f.; III, 64-74, 106 f., 342-358, 368; A. Tafi,
"Excepta fornicationis causa," Verbum Dei, 26 (1948), 18-26; A. Vaccari, "De Matrimonio
et divortio apud Matthaeum," *Biblica*, 36 (1955), 149-151; L. Wahrmund, *Das Institut d.
Ehe im Altertum* (1933), 1-125.

[1] ed. T. Bergk, Poetae lyrici Graeci⁴, II (1882), 427.

ἄνθρωπος, Lys. Or., 4, 9; πόρνην καὶ δούλην ἄνθρωπον, *ibid.*, 4, 19. 2. πόρνος (from Aristoph. Plut., 155), "whoremonger" who has intercourse with prostitutes, then specifically one who lets himself be abused for money, "male prostitute": τὴν ... ὥραν ἐὰν μέν τις ἀργυρίου πωλῇ τῷ βουλομένῳ, πόρνον αὐτὸν ἀποκαλοῦσιν (opp. φίλον, σώφρονα), Xenoph. Mem., I, 6, 13; παῖδες πόρνοι, Aristoph. Plut., 155; πόρνον μὲν ἐν παισί, Phalaris Ep., 4;[2] Demosth. Ep., 4, 11; Philo Leg. All., 8. 3. πορνεία, rare in class Gk., "fornication," "licentiousness." μοιχεύω is narrower than πορνεία (→ IV, 729 ff.) and refers solely to adultery. After her marriage the ἐραστής of the hetaira Neaira is a μοιχός, Demosth. Or., 59, 41; [ἡ δὲ Ἀφροδίτ]η παρατυγχάνουσα τῷ τοῦ ["Αρεως πορ]νίας < καὶ > μοιχείας κατίσ[τ]ησιν, Venus in conjunction with Mars causes fornication and adultery, P. Tebt., II, 276, 15 f. (1/2nd cent. B.C.); P. Lond., V, 1711, 30 (6th cent. A.D.); Σινώπης τῆς Θρᾴττης τῆς ἐξ Αἰγίνης Ἀθήναζε μετενεγκαμένης τὴν πορνείαν, Athen., 13, 595a; of homosexuality, Demosth. Or., 19, 200. 4. πορνεύω a. trans. "to prostitute," Harp., *s.v.* πωλῶσι, commonly[3] pass. of a woman "to prostitute oneself," "to become a harlot," Hdt., I, 93; Lys. Fr., 59; of a man, Aeschin. Tim., 52, 119; Demosth. Or., 19, 233; ἢ πεπορνευμένος ... ἢ ἡταιρηκώς. τὸν γὰρ τὸ σῶμα τὸ ἑαυτοῦ ἐφ' ὕβρει πεπρακότα, Aeschin. Tim., 29. b. intr. act. ═ pass. "to commit fornication," Luc. Alex., 5; πεπορνευκὼς ἄνθρωπος, Phalaris Ep., 121, 1.[4] 5. ἐκπορνεύω,[5] stronger form of πορνεύω, "to live very licentiously," pass. in the same sense, Poll. Onom., VI, 126; with acc. "to prostitute," Lv. 19:29; Test. D. 5:5.

II. Extra-Marital Intercourse in the Non-Biblical World.

A distinction must first be made between cultic and secular prostitution. The ultimate roots are in the pre-historical period of matriarchy and dawning self-awareness, though this period is for the most part wrapped in obscurity. It is at least clear that there are differences between oriental and especially Semitic culture on the one side and Greek culture on the other.

1. Cultic Prostitution.

In cultic prostitution[6] a further distinction must be made between the single act and the permanent state. The former was a national custom in Persia which even daughters of prominent families followed and to which no shame attached.[7] The latter was practised by the class of hierodules whose payment accrued to the goddess. This type of prostitution was widespread in Asia Minor in cults[8] of mother deities;[9] it is also found, how-

[2] ed. R. Hercher, Epistolographi Graeci (1873), 409 f.

[3] The starting-pt. is the deponent (not pass.) πορνεύεσθαι, cf. E. Fraenkel, *Gr. Denominativa* (1906), 181, 197, 272; the act. derives from the deponent (understood as pass.), *ibid.*, 200; → 1, n. 2; Debr. Gr. Wortb. § 215; cf. also Fraenkel, *op. cit.*, 200 : ἑταιρεύεσθαι [Debrunner].

[4] Hercher, *op. cit.* (→ n. 2), 444.

[5] Helbing Kasussyntax, 78.

[6] Cf. G. van der Leeuw, *Phänomenologie d. Religion*² (1956), 254-262; Nilsson, I², 120-122; A. Klinz, Ἱερὸς γάμος, Diss. Halle (1933); E. Fehrle, "Die kultische Keuschheit im Altertum," RVV, 6 (1910), 40 f. Bachofen, I, 128 finds in cultic prostitution a middle step between the older capricious sexual intercourse acc. to the unregulated natural principle of *jus naturale* and the sex life regulated in later marriage by the *jus civile*. Cf. Bernhöft, 22-25; Kornemann, 8 f.; Wahrmund, 1-32.

[7] Strabo, 16, 745; on Babylon, cf. Hdt., I, 199; Test. Jud. 12.

[8] Hdt., I, 199 : The fertility goddess Mylitta (from stem ילד, she who makes to bear).

[9] A. Jeremias, *Handbch. d. altorientalischen Geisteskultur*² (1929), 476-478; B. Meissner, *Babylonien u. Assyrien*, II (1925), 26, 68-71, the work of the hierodules (═ kadištu ═ Heb. קְדֵשָׁה) was not regarded as degrading. Cf. Ep. Jer. 42 f. ═ Bar. 6:42 f. For Lydia Hdt., I, 93; Athen., 12, 515d-516b; for Comana (Pontus) Strabo, 12, 558 and 559 (over 6000 hierodules); Abydos Athen., 13, 572 f.; Cataonian Comana Strabo, 12, 535 (over 6000, ἄνδρες ὁμοῦ γυναιξί); Armenia Strabo, 11, 532; in Ephesus there was a temple of Ἀφροδίτη ἑταίρα, Athen., 573a; the renowned Artemisium there also had many hierodules, Roscher, I, 591.

ever, in Syria [10] and Egypt. [11] Through the Canaanite cults (Baal, Astarte) it penetrated
into the religion of Israel. On Gk. soil sacral prostitution was generally rejected. It
found an entry only in Corinth and Athens, probably through the trading connections of
these cities with the Orient. In Corinth esp. the temple of Aphrodite with its 1000 hierodules was famous, and an inscr. recalls that the goddess answered their prayers for the
threatened fatherland in a critical hour. [12]

2. Secular Intercourse Outside Marriage.

The Gk. attitude to extra-marital intercourse is to be understood in relation to varying
historical and social circumstances. [13] Prostitutes and brothels are unknown in the
Homeric age. Masters may keep a concubine (παλλακή, פִּילֶגֶשׁ) or have casual intercourse
with female slaves, who are mostly carried off in war, Hom. Il., 1, 111; 8, 284. Prostitution
arises with increasing prosperity and commerce. Solon (c. 594) in his laws tries to
protect marriage and to prevent sexual excess. He forbids the giving up of daughters
or sisters to prostitution if they have not already fallen into it. [14] Among state revenues
was the πορνικὸν τέλος which was collected by πορνοτελῶναι. [15] In antiquity a
constant source of prostitution was slavery, which made people mere chattels. Female
slaves were at the mercy of their masters' lusts. Of gt. significance for the development
of prostitution was the Athenian law of purification in 451, which made a sharp distinction between natives and foreigners and denied civil rights to the children of mixed
marriages (Plut. Pericl., 37 [I, 172b-f]). As a result of their changed legal status a gt.
number of alien women had to become self-supporting. From this time on the professional
"friend" became a common figure in Gk. society. A crisis developed in marriage. Even
as early as Hdt. ἑταίρα is the euphemism for a woman who grants casual sexual intercourse for money. [16]

The main cause of prostitution is the Greek view of life which regards sexual
intercourse as just as natural, necessary and justifiable as eating and drinking [17]
Only civil marriage was protected by law and custom, → μοιχεύω, IV, 732 f. Even
the married man was permitted extra-marital intercourse as he pleased so long as

---

[10] For Byblos Luc. Syr. Dea, 6; Aphaca ibid., 9; Eus. Vit. Const., III, 55; Hierapolis
Luc. Syr. Dea, 43.

[11] Hdt., II, 113; Strabo, 7, 816; for further material on the practice cf. W. Otto, "Beiträge
zur Hierodulie im hellenischen Ägypten," A. A. Münch., NF, 29 (1950).

[12] Strabo, 8, 378; cf. 559; Athen., 13, 573; cf. H. Hepding, Art. "Hieroduloi," Pauly-W., 8
(1913), 1465; F. Dümmler, Art. "Aphrodite," ibid., 1 (1894), 2740 f.; Paus., I, 14, 6; on
cultic prostitution in Rome Liv., 39, 15; on this cf. van der Leeuw, op. cit., 256 f.

[13] A primary source for prostitution in antiquity, and esp. Greece, is Athen., 13, which
contains quotations from writings partially lost; cf. also Luc. Dialogi Meretricii.

[14] Plut. Solon, 23 (I, 90 f.); connected herewith is the report, incredible in this form, that
Solon set up a brothel from the proceeds of which the temple of Ἀφροδίτη πάνδημος was
built, Athen., 13, 569d; cf. W. Aly, Art. "Solon," Pauly-W., 3a (1929), 967, 11-19; also
Dümmler, op. cit. (→ n. 12), 2734.

[15] Aeschin. Tim., 119 ff.; Poll. Onom., VII, 202; the πορνοτελῶναι thus had lists of
licensed harlots.

[16] Hdt., II, 134; καλοῦσι δὲ καὶ τὰς μισθαρνούσας ἑταίρας καὶ τὸ ἐπὶ συνουσίαις
μισθαρνεῖν ἑταιρεῖν, οὐκ ἔτι πρὸς τὸ ἔτυμον ἀναφέροντες, ἀλλὰ πρὸς τὸ εὐσχημο-
νέστερον, Athen., 13, 571d. Sappho (Athen., 13, 571d) uses ἑταίρα with no implication of
censure, cf. also Plut. Solon, 15 (I, 86b ff.): The Athenians are wont to embellish unpleasant and painful things with mild terms, τὰς μὲν πόρνας ἑταίρας, τοὺς δὲ φόρους
συντάξεις ... καλοῦντες. The harsh term πόρνη was softened to πορνίδιον; for a long
list of similar terms cf. Poll. Onom., VII, 201.

[17] Plut. Solon, 31 (I, 96, b-e), Gal., Hippocr. and Rufus of Ephesus in Oribasius Collectionum medicarum reliquiae, 6, 37. 38 (CMG, VI, 1, 1 [1928], 187-192). Sexual abstinence was
regarded as more harmful than moderate free intercourse. Eur. Fr., 431 (TGF, 493) calls it
hubris to try to resist love. For further examples cf. J. Bloch, Ursprung der Syphilis (1901/
1911), 624 f.; Bernhöft, 172 f.

he did not violate a civil marriage. On the other hand, all extra-marital intercourse was forbidden to the wife. Towards the practical exercise of free sex relations the judgment of the Greeks was very tolerant (Athen., 13, 590d-e), especially in the case of intercourse between young men — the age of marriage was between 30 and 35 — and harlots. Only excess and overindulgence were censured, e.g., Alcibiades. On the other hand, visiting brothels was also regarded as scandalous. This ambivalence of outlook is characteristic of antiquity. Plato tries to solve the problem by compromise. Intercourse with harlots is permissible so long as it takes place in secret and causes no offence, Leg., VIII, 841a-c. With complete injustice to the wife, who was kept at home, a man sought with the hetaira what he could not find in his wife. [18] But the circle of eminent hetairae was probably small. [19] Most of them were sought only for reasons of sensual desire. Aristot. rightly wanted to improve the education of Greek women as a means to restrain hetairism, Polit., I, 13, p. 1260b, 15; II, 9, p. 1269b, 17.

Sparta and the Doric branch maintained sexual discipline more strongly than Athens, Corinth [20] and the Ionic sphere. It was here, however, that homosexuality developed and this then spread over the whole of Greece and was practised rather than censured even by notable figures. [21] Lesbianism was much less common. In a fateful way both opened the door to unnatural perversion.

Various groups of harlots may be distinguished. The lowest comprises those in brothels, [22] who were mostly female slaves, so that the owner had full power over them, Aristoph. Eccl., 721 f.; Demosth. Or., 59, 30. [23] A somewhat higher group was that of girls with various artistic skills such as music, singing and dancing, Plat. Prot., 347d; Luc. Dial. Meretricii, 15, 2; Xenoph. Sym., 2, 1 ff.; Plat. Symp., 176e. Higher than the harlots of brothels were those who plied their trade independently and who could sometimes ask higher and even very high prices (μεγαλόμισθοι). [24]

3. The Sex Ethics of Stoicism.

In this very period philosophy manifests a concern to reform sexual morality. Stoicism does not reject sexual enjoyment as such (Muson., p. 71, 11) but does seek to free men from passion, [25] Epict. Diss., IV, 1, 21. It uniformly condemns adultery (Zeno Fr., 244 [v. Arnim, I, 58, 14 ff.]; Epict. Diss., II, 4) and extra-marital intercourse on the part of married persons. With these principles it struggles resolutely against the sexual decay of the age, Muson., p. 67, 6 ff. Muson. is the strictest. He regards all sexual intercourse outside marriage as unlawful (παράνομος) and infamous (αἰσχρός, p. 64, 1. 5. 9). He rejects even that between master and female slave, p. 66, 2 ff. The man who has intercourse with hetairae sins against himself, p. 65, 4 ff. By all unclean acts a man defiles the god in his own breast, Epict. Diss., II, 8, 13. Ocellus [26] thinks chastity is best,

---

[18] The well-known saying in Demosth. Or., 59, 122 (→ IV, 732, n. 10) represents the Gk. point of view, cf. Athen., 13, 559a b.

[19] Cf. Aspasia, loved and honoured by Pericles ; orators, artists and poets had their hetairae, cf. Schneider, 1355 f.; Athen., 13, 589d e.

[20] Cf. κορινθιάζεσθαι, a proverbial term for a dissolute mode of life.

[21] Bethe, 438-475; Kroll, 897-906; also Art. "Kinaidos," Pauly-W., 11 (1922), 459-462; P. Brandt, "Homoerotik in d. griech. Lit. (Lucian von Samosata)," Abh. aus dem Gebiet d. Sexualforschung, 3, 3 (1920/21).

[22] Cf. the many derogatory terms for them in Schmidt, 420 f.

[23] πορνεῖον = οἴκημα Poll. Onom., VII, 201; ἐργαστήριον Demosth. Or., 59, 67; παιδισκεῖον Athen., 10, 437 f.; of brothel harlots κοινὰς ἅπασι, Athen., 13, 569e.

[24] Hermann and Herter, 1159 f.

[25] Gk. morality fights against base emotions, so that ἀκολασία rather than πορνεία occurs in the list of vices, Muson., p. 113, 9 ff.; Dio Chrys. Or., 8, 8 etc. as the opp. of the virtue of ἐγκράτεια, Vögtle, 199, 212.

[26] Ocellus Lucanus, De Universi Natura, ed. R. Harder in Neue philologische Untersuchungen, 1 (1926).

45 f. The man who is not capable of this should at least avoid the delights of love until he is 20, and even after this confine himself to the minimum, 54 f. [27]

B. The Old Testament.

I. Usage.

1. In the LXX the group πορνεύω is normally used for the root זנה,[28] while with equal consistency μοιχεύω is used for נאף (→ IV, 729, 14 ff.). a. The verb πορνεύω is predominantly the rendering of זָנָה, once of קָדֵשׁ, Dt. 23:18. After the analogy of Arabic this seems to have referred originally to sexual satisfaction on the part of the woman.[29] In the early period, esp. in nomadic life, it was customary for a young girl to be married in her own tribe. Sometimes young men might break the custom and marry girls from a neighbouring tribe. זֹנָה is used for the woman whose husband does not belong to her tribe.[30] Ju. 11:1 is probably to be understood in this sense, and perhaps also 16:1. b. Then זנה, which in the OT, with the uniform sway of patriarchate (Nu. 25:1 is an exception), is used only of the woman, develops into the proper term for "to have intercourse with another," "to be unfaithful," "to play the harlot" (LXX πορνεύω 16 times and the stronger ἐκπορνεύω 36 times). It is sometimes abs., Hos. 3:3; Jer. 3:6, 8; Ez. 23:19; Ps. 106:39 etc., sometimes used with a prep., most commonly אַחֲרֵי, ὀπίσω and the man with whom there is intercourse (Ex. 34:15, 16; Lv. 17:7; 20:6; Nu. 15:39; 1 Ch. 5:25 etc.), also with εἰς (Lv. 20:5), or the acc. or אֶל (Jer. 3:1; Ez. 16:28), then מִתַּחַת, מֵעַל, מִן, ἀπό and the man in question (Hos. 4:12; 9:1; Ps. 73:27). אִשָּׁה זֹנָה is the occasional or professional harlot (Lv. 21:7; Jos. 2:1 [γυνὴ πόρνη]; Ju. 11:1; 16:1; 1 K. 3:16 etc.), or simply זוֹנָה (fem. part.; Gn. 34:31; 38:15; Jos. 6:17 etc.). It is worth noting that LXX always has the sharply censorious and disparaging πόρνη; only in Ju. 11:2 and twice in the Wisdom literature (never in the NT) is ἑταίρα used in the sense of "harlot."[31] Examples show that זנה can be used of the married woman who is unfaithful to her husband, (Hos. 1, 2; Ez. 16, 23) or of the betrothed who by law already belongs to her husband, Gn. 38:24. In content πορνεύω here is equivalent to μοιχεύω. In the hi זנה means "to seduce into whoredom," Ex. 34:16; Lv. 19:29; 2 Ch. 21:11, 13; always ἐκπορνεύω in the LXX. It also has the strengthened sense of q, Hos. 4:10, 18; 5:3. c. In distinction from secular usage the OT employs πορνεύειν, like זנה, in the transf. sense (→ 587, 1 ff.).

2. πορνεία, "whoredom," is used for זְנוּנִים (Gn. 38:24; 4 Βασ. 9:22; Ez. 23:11, 29; Na. 3:4; Hos. 1:2 etc.), זְנוּת, which is lit. only in Hos. 4:11; Sir. 41:17, elsewhere fig. for "unfaithfulness to God" (→ 587, 1 ff.), and in the latter sense for תַּזְנוּת, which occurs only in Ez. 16 and 23 (22 times all told). Here, too, fornication may in some circumstances involve adultery, Sir. 23:23 → 587, 1 ff. 3. πόρνη → 585, 5 ff. 4. πόρνος, first found only in the Apocr., 3 times in Sir. 23:17, 18 vl. (no Heb. original). 5. ἐκ-

---

[27] Cf. Preisker, esp. 13-37; Delling, esp. 14-38. The mystery groups also fought against toleration of licentiousness, cf. J. Dölger, "Die Ächtung des Ehebruchs in der Kultsatzung," *Ant. Christ.*, III (1932), 132-148.

[28] קָדֵשׁ only at Dt. 23:18, → 584, 7.

[29] Cf. J. Wellhausen, "Die Ehe bei den Arabern," NGG (1893), 472.

[30] Cf. H. Winckler, *Gesch. Israels*, II (1900), 271 with ref. to 3 Βασ. 12:24b (HT 1 K. 11:26 אַלְמָנָה) and Ju. 8:31; 16:1; Köhler-Baumg., *s.v.* On various loose marriage-like relations in the Orient cf. Wellhausen, *op. cit.*, esp. 464 f. the so-called Mut'a, temporary marriage or marriage of use, which is sometimes close to an illicit union. Cf. W. Heffening, Art. "Mut'a," *Enzykl. des Islam*, III (1936), 835-838; on "visiting marriage" (*beena* marriage) cf. W. R. Smith, *Kinship and Marriage*² (1907), 87-93; F. A. Jaussen, "Coutumes des Arabes," *Rev. Bibl.*, NS, 7 (1910), 237-249.

[31] Prv. 19:13 (אִשָּׁה), Sir. 41:22 for אִשָּׁה זָרָה, cf. γυνὴ ἑταιριζομένη Sir. 9:3 (אִשָּׁה זָרָה).

πορνεύω, like πορνεύω, means a. "to fornicate," Gn. 38:24; with acc. "to prostitute," Lv. 19:19; b. "to lead into fornication" (like the Heb. hi), Ex. 34:16; 2 Ch. 21:11; c. transf. "to whore after other gods" (Ex. 34:15), "to turn aside from God," Hos. 1:2; 4:12.

II. Fornication in National Life in the OT.

The older historical books show that the harlot was a familiar figure in national life. Veiled like a harlot, Tamar sits by the wayside and thus achieves her goal of intercourse with Judah, Gn. 38:15. [32] The spies make their way to what seems to be the well-known house of the harlot Rahab, Jos. 2:1. [33] Jephthah is υἱὸς γυναικὸς πόρνης, Ju. 11:1. [34] Samson is acquainted with a harlot when he visits Gaza, Ju. 16:1. [35] 1 K. 3:16 depicts a quarrel in a brothel. Severe social problems might also drive women to earn their living in this way, Am. 7:17. Custom naturally scorned the πόρνη who distributed her favours thus. In the story of the raping of Dinah the family or brother undertook to protect and avenge the violated sister. An honourable παρθένος was not to be treated like a πόρνη, Gn. 34:31. [36] It should not be overlooked, however, that זנה refers only to the woman. Extra-marital intercourse on the part of a man did not come under this concept and was not forbidden so long as he did not take the wife of a fellow-countryman. This significant distinction is probably grounded in the unequivocal patriarchalism of the OT and it is a result of the unambiguously patriarchal stamp on the view of revelation and religion in Israel. The influence of the matriarchal nature religion of Canaan with its religious interpretation of unrestricted sex shattered the strict custom of Israel. On the high places secular and sacral prostitution went hand in hand, Jer. 3:2. On the basis of their understanding of God and man the prophets combatted both as strenuously as they could, Am. 2:7; Jer. 5:7 etc. From that time onwards any religious justification of extra-marital intercourse became impossible. The later provisions of the Law developed in part out of this prophetic attack, cf. also 1 K. 14:24. Acc. to Dt. 22:21 the licentiousness of a betrothed woman [37] is to be punished by stoning on the ground that she thereby commits a serious offence which threatens the whole people and that she has made her father's house into a house of whoredom. The social and religious ostracising of the πόρνη is expressed in the law that the holy priest of Yahweh may not take such a woman to wife (cf. the Holiness Code Lv. 21:7, 14) and also in the law that if the daughter of a priest is guilty of licentiousness she is to be burned alive because she has desecrated the sacred person of her father, Lv. 21:9. No child of fornication is to be accepted as a member of the holy community of God, Dt. 23:3. [38] Passages which originally prohibited cultic prostitution through the sacred Law of God became in the

---

[32] In v. 21, however, the friend avoids the coarse word זֹנָה and asks for the קְדֵשָׁה; with no attempt at glossing over, the story accepts the existence of such in Israel. The border between cultic and secular prostitution is also fluid in antiquity. Bodily dedication to something religious is combined with an offering to the fertility goddess. It is unlikely, however, that the kid of v. 17 is an offering of this type.

[33] In Jos. Ant., 5, 7, who elsewhere too avoids the word πόρνη, her house is called an inn on the city wall, καταγώγιον τοῦ τείχους, i.e., a brothel.

[34] His relatives in 11:2 use the milder υἱὸς γυναικὸς ἑταίρας for אִשָּׁה אַחֶרֶת; → n. 31.

[35] But v. → n. 32.

[36] For legal statutes cf. Ex. 22:15; Dt. 22:23 ff. The harsh punishment of Tamar (Gn. 38:24, an older custom) is due to the fact that she is the betrothed (νύμφη) of Shelah (Gn. 38:11). J. Benzinger, Hbr. Archäologie³ (1927), 272, 287 thinks she was to suffer a fiery death as a "sister of the god," as in the Codex Hammurabi § 110, AOT, 391.

[37] Engert, 24 thinks that betrothal, which ruled out all others, promoted modesty, and was a potent moral and legal factor in the fostering of a high estimation of virginity.

[38] The term מַמְזֵר, transl. ἐκ πόρνης in the LXX, was later defined in various ways, cf. S. Mowinckel, "Zu Dt. 23:2-9," Acta Orientalia, 1 (1922), 81-104; J. Jeremias, Jerusalem z. Zeit Jesu, II B (1937), 211-224; K. H. Rengstorf, Jebamot (1929), 64-69; Str.-B., IV, 379 and 383; J. Hamburger, Art. "Mamser," Realenzykl. d. Judentums, II (1896), 716-720; V. Aptowitzer, "Spuren des Matriarchats im jüd. Schrifttum," Hebrew Union Coll. Annual, 5 (1928), 267-277.

later tradition general prohibitions of fornication in Israel. Acc. to Lv. 19:29 the toleration or even the promoting of fornication, e.g., on the part of a daughter of Israel,
defiles the whole land and brings it under the threat of God's judgment.[39] In Dt. 23:18 f.
the repudiation of cultic prostitution in the original is in the LXX a general and unconditional divine prohibition of all πορνεία in the holy people. Prv. 5 warns against
the πόρνη, Prv. 6:24-35 admonishes the married man not to have intercourse with a
harlot, and c. 7 counsels the young man not to let himself be captivated by the charms
of the prostitute. Instead he should pay heed to the true wisdom which is grounded
in obedience to God, c. 8. From the repeated designation of the harlot as זָרָה it has been
deduced that in c. 1-9 the warning is against surrender to the alien secular wisdom of
Greece.[40] Such allegorising is not supported by the very concrete depictions of the
situation. On the other hand, the warnings do not seem to refer only to licentiousness.
Certainly the frequently used זָרָה does not refer only to the wife of another, nor does it
imply that harlots are mostly foreigners.[41] The ref. is to native women, strangers to
the locality, who constitute a dangerous temptation to the men of Israel.[42]

III. Cultic Prostitution in the OT.[43]

In the OT, too, a distinction must be made between secular and cultic prostitution.
Acc. to the original text of the OT prostitution deriving from various Canaanite cults
spread into Israel. Gn. 38:21 f. gives evidence of the "devoted to God" (קְדֵשָׁה) in Israel,
→ 585, 32 ff. Acc. to 1 K. 14:24 worship at the high places flourished under Rehoboam
and the kedeshim are specifically mentioned. Asa ended the former and chased the latter
out of the land, 1 K. 15:12. Jehoshaphat drove out those who still remained, 1 K. 22:47.
A hundred yrs. later Hosea (→ 587, 2 ff.) is angered that they are still shamelessly
abroad in Israel, 4:14. The Deuteronomic Law unconditionally forbids cultic prostitution.
No girl is to be a temple devotee, no man a קָדֵשׁ, 23:17. Profits derived herefrom are
not to be used on behalf of the temple. Josiah's sharp attack, under which the houses
of the kedeshim in the temple were destroyed, shows that the evil had made its way
even into the temple cultus in Jerusalem, 2 K. 23:7. It is true that the Chronicler, who has a
strong religious interest, makes no ref. to it in the par. passages, but his work is fairly
obviously a later priestly revision which suppresses or reinterprets the testimonies to a
syncretistic defilement of the worship of Yahweh, Lv. 19:29.

The way in which the LXX handles the unambiguous statements of the original about
cultic prostitution in Israel points in the same apologetic direction. Understandably the
translators avoid the loaded term ἱερόδουλοι for קְדֵשָׁה (קָדֵשׁ), but they do not coin their
own term instead, cf. Paul's εἰδωλόθυτα. At Dt. 23:18 f., also Gn. 38:21, they use the
secular πόρνη, which stands under strong religious condemnation and which transforms
the prohibition of cultic prostitution into a prohibition of licentiousness in general,
→ line 3 f. In 3 Βασ. 15:12 it is said of Asa : ἀφεῖλεν τὰς τελετὰς (festal rites)
ἀπὸ τῆς γῆς, and cf. μετὰ τῶν τετελεσμένων in Hos. 4:14, this being the usual
expression for devotees in the mystery cults. There is no LXX text for 1 K. 22:47,[44]
and the Heb. is left untranslated at 4 Βασ. 23:7 (τὸν οἶκον τῶν καδησιμ) even though,
without explanation, this makes no sense for the Gk. reader. ἄγγελοι is used for קְדֵשִׁים
at Job 36:14. Thus the reader of the LXX finds no express mention at all of cultic
prostitution in Israel.

---

[39] Cf. Kautzsch, ad loc.; R. Kittel, Gesch. Israels, I⁴ (1921), 290, n. 2.
[40] E.g., the exegetical tradition of the Rabb. acc. to M. Friedländer, Griech. Philosophie
im AT (1904), 68-76; E. Sellin, Die Spuren d. gr. Philosophie im AT (1905), 7, 18. Cf.
also G. Boström, "Proverbiastudien. Die Weisheit u. das fremde Weib in Spr. 1-9," Lunds
Universitets Årsskrift, NF Avd., 1, Vol. 30, 3 (1935), 14-32.
[41] Egypt. Wisdom lit. warns against wandering women from other places [Böhlig].
[42] Cf. B. Gemser, Sprüche Salomos, Hndbch. AT, I, 16 (1937), 5.
[43] Cf. B. Stade, Bibl. Theol. d. AT, I (1905), 133 f.; Benzinger, op. cit. (→ n. 36), 356-358.
[44] 3 Βασ. 14:24 : σύνδεσμος is based on קָשַׁר instead of קָדֵשׁ.

IV. Israel's Unfaithfulness to Yahweh as πορνεία.

The prophet Hosea (1-3) develops the metaphor of the marriage between God and His people. The conduct of his wife is a portrayal of the infidelity of Israel to its God, who chose it and declared it to be His own people. The unfaithfulness of Israel is thus set forth in an unequivocal image of great emotional force which brings it under the sternest condemnation and renders impossible any attempt to put it in a better light or to trivialise it. This forceful metaphor is found again and again in the prophetic writings which follow. [45] It is open to question whether Mi. 1:7 is to be understood in the sense of Hos. 2:7, 14, but this is obviously true in Is. 1:21, where the city of Jerusalem, once faithful and the refuge of the righteous, has now become a harlot. In 3:1-4:4 Jer. accuses Israel and Judah of playing the harlot with many lovers (3:2), of committing adultery with wood and stone (πορνεία alongside μοιχεύειν in 3:9), and of defiling the land by their πορνεῖαι (μιαίνω, 3:2). In Jer. as in Hos. the charge of infidelity goes hand in hand with an uncompromising rejection of the practice of sacral prostitution as this was found in the Canaanite cult, Jer. 2:20; 3:6; cf. Hos. 4:12-14. Shortly after the fall of Jerusalem the possibly pre-exilic author of Is. 57:7-13 adopts the metaphor of Hos. and accuses the city of being an unfaithful wife. In extended allegories Ez. develops the image (16 and 23), which also occurs once in the Ps. (73:27). In the legal books the metaphor occurs only at Ex. 34:16; Lv. 17:7; 20:5; Nu. 14:33; Dt. 31:16, and in the historical books only at Ju. 2:17; 8:27; 2 K. 9:22; 1 Ch. 5:25; 2 Ch. 21:11, 13.

In a few instances זנה is used fig. in a different sense for the commerce which woos other peoples and the political devices which ensnare them. Thus Is. 23:15-18 refers to Tyre and includes (v. 16) a song in mockery of the "forgotten harlot," while Na. 3:1-7 speaks of the whore Nineveh who "enmeshed the peoples with her harlotry and the nations with her magical arts," v. 4. The underlying view here is that a trading city which enters into relations with all nations is not pursuing an honest calling, cf. Ez. 16:26. [46]

C. Later Judaism (Apocrypha, Pseudepigrapha, Dead Sea Scrolls, Philo, Josephus, the Rabbis).

1. Later Judaism shows us how the use of πορνεία etc. gradually broadened as compared with the original usage. In the first instance πορνεία is mostly "harlotry," "extra-marital intercourse," Ab., 2, 8, often with adultery, Gr. Bar. 4:17; 8:5; 13:4; Asc. Is. 2:5; Treasure Cave, 12 (Riessler, 956 f.). Materially, however, it often means "adultery," cf. ἐν πορνείᾳ ἐμοιχεύθη, Sir. 23:23. In Test. Jos. 3:8 Potiphar's wife says of Joseph εἰς πορνείαν με ἐφελκύσατο; the "incest" of Reuben is also πορνεία ἐν ᾗ ἐμίανα κοίτην τοῦ πατρός μου in Test. R. 1:6, cf. 4:8; Test. Jud. 13:3. πορνεία can also be "unnatural vice," Sib., III, 764; IV, 33-36, e.g., sodomy, Test. B. 9:1: πορνεύσετε πορνείαν Σοδόμων, cf. Jub. 16:5; 20:5; "unlawful marriages" contradict Rabb. principles. Treasure Cave, 37, 6 (Riessler, 985). πορνεία can then comes to mean "sexual intercourse" in gen. without more precise definition, cf. Asc. Is. 2:5: ἐπλήθυνεν <ἡ> φαρμακεία καὶ ἡ μαγεία καὶ ἡ μαντεία ... καὶ ἡ πορνεία.

---

[45] The wife of Yahweh is in the first instance the land (1:2 אֶרֶץ fem.); the inhabitants are the children of the land who are themselves to judge their mother (2:2, 4 f.). But acc. to the sense the metaphor then applies to the people too (1:2; 4:18 f.; 5:3 f.).

[46] O. Procksch, Jesaia I, Komm. AT, 9, 1 (1930), 302. In Is. 47:10, however, the LXX adds the term to give us the image of the whore Babylon (Rev. 17:1 ff.), not in the cultic sense, but in the mercantile sense already found in the HT of Na. 3:4 with ref. to Nineveh. Rightly the LXX also found a ref. to commerce in Is. 23:17 when it transl. זנה by ἐμπόριον εἶναι. In other places, too, the LXX could add the already developed concept of harlotry, e.g., Ju. 2:15 A. Whereas HT and LXX B see here a ref. to the wars of Israel to which Yahweh denies success, A, in acc. with the context, makes the ἐκπορεύεσθαι into πορνεύειν and thus provides the reason why Yahweh is against them. Cf. also Prv. 26:7 S [Bertram].

2. In a series of warnings against sins of lust Sir. (23:16-27) portrays the whoring husband (ἄνθρωπος πόρνος, v. 17) and the unfaithful wife. Here again πορνεύω is materially μοιχεύω. The fornicator who is sexually so insatiable (23:17) that "all bread tastes good" (v. 17) and who commits whoredom on his own flesh (v. 17) [47] thinks that he can sin unpunished under the cover of darkness, vv. 18-21. In his warning against pleasures (18:30-19:3) Sir. includes wine and women; these can lead to apostasy (ἀποστήσουσιν). In his teaching about shame (41:16-42:1) he also warns against the shamelessness of זְנוּת (41:17; cf. also 26:9-12). Wis. Sol. in its battle against pagan idolatry has the comprehensive judgment that the beginning of πορνεία (in the context apostasy from God) is the devising of idols (14:12), and Wis. sees in sexual licentiousness (14:24-26) a consequence of the abnegation of the true God, 14:27 f. The positing of this causal connection is a basic element in Jewish apologetics and polemics, cf. R. 1:18-32.

3. The Test. XII, esp. Test. R., S., L. and Jud., contain numerous admonitions to flee πορνεία (R. 5:5) or to keep oneself from it (6:1; L. 9:9; Jud. 18:2). Among the 7 evil spirits in Test. R. (2:1) the first (3:3) is πορνεία, to whom women, being intrinsically bad (5:1), are more subject than men (5:3). In a ruinous way this spirit drives the soul away from God and leads it to idols or Beliar, 4:6; 5:3. πορνεία, which rests on nature and sense perceptions (αἰσθήσεις) acc. to 3:3, is one of the mortal sins (Test. Iss. 7:2) and is the mother of all evil (Test. S. 5:3).

Acc. to Jub. the testament of Abraham contains a warning against whoredom, 20:3. No man should commit whoredom with the wife of another, 39:6. Joseph proves his piety by recollecting the testament of his forefather in the hour of temptation and by maintaining his purity, 20:3. Fornication involves esp. the sin of paganism, 25:1. Hence all marriage ties with Gentiles are impurity and desecration of the sanctuary, 30:10. Whoredom is uncleanness and it defiles not merely the individual (30:2, 6) but the family (30:7) and the land and people of Israel (30:15); for this mortal sin there is no forgiveness, 33:13, 18.

In the Damascus Document the members of the community are warned against the licentious princes of Judah who have gone the way of whoredom and thus fallen victim to God's judgment, 7:1 f. (8:18 f.). Guilt-infected impulse and eyes full of wicked lust have already become a snare for the watchers of heaven, 4:17 (6:11). Bigamy is also branded as fornication, 4:20 (7:1). Above all licentiousness is one of the three nets of Belial, 4:15 ff. (6:10 f.) and with many other vices it belongs to the spirit of iniquity. In the Dead Sea Scrolls fornication is thus a mark of metaphysical dualism (1 QS 4:10) and it belongs to the children of darkness, from whom the children of light must separate themselves as sharply as possible.

4. Philo, too, rejects all πορνεία, which fills souls with ἀκολασία and prefers physical to spiritual beauty, Spec. Leg., III, 51. For him the πόρνη is a disgrace, a scandal and a blot on all mankind. Whereas in other nations there is freedom for intercourse with prostitutes, acc. to the special laws of Israel the ἑταίρα is subject to a capital penalty (Jos., 43), and there is a similar punishment for homosexuality (Spec. Leg., III, 37 f.). Philo also allegorises the concept. πόρνοι stand for polytheists (Leg. All., III, 8), who are for him the sons of harlots (Dt. 23:1 f.; Migr. Abr., 69; Mut. Nom., 205). The honourable woman (Dt. 21:15-17) is for him ἀρετή, which in gen. is not loved by men, while the dishonourable woman is ἡδονή, Sacr. AC, 20 f.

Joseph. [48] uses neither πορνεύω nor πόρνη. But his use of πορνεῖον, "brothel," [49] shows his familiarity with the group. [50] If he does not use it in the same way as the

[47] V. Ryssel in Kautzsch Apkr. u. Pseudepigr., ad loc. suggests self-pollution, while R. Smend, Die Weisheit d. Jesus Sir. (1906), ad loc. sees a ref. to marriage with relatives and conjectures an original בִּבְשַׂר שְׁאֵרוֹ Lv. 18:6; 25:49.

[48] This paragraph is by K. H. Rengstorf.

[49] Ant., 19, 357: τὰ πορνεῖα of Caesarea; Bell., 4, 562: Jerusalem takes on the shameful appearance of a πορνεῖον under the rule of the Zealots.

[50] It is not impossible that the use of πορνεῖον in Bell., 4, 562 is influenced by Ez. 16:25 ff.

LXX when describing certain events in the history of his people, there must be special reasons for this. What these were may be seen with some certainty from a comparison of some of his narrations with those of the OT. Thus the πόρνη Rahab becomes the owner of a καταγώγιον "inn" (Ant., 5, 7 ff.) and there is no suggestion that she might have plied a dubious trade as well (cf. Ant., 5, 13 f., 30); indeed, between the lines she is very much the hostess (7); there is here a verbal link at least with Tg. Jos. 2:1 (cf. Ant., 3, 276). Again, Ant., 5, 257 describes Jephthah, the son of a πόρνη (אִשָּׁה זוֹנָה), as an ἀνὴρ διὰ τὴν πατρῴαν ἀρετὴν δυνατὸς καὶ δι᾽ οἰκείαν αὐτοῦ στρατιὰν ἣν ἔτρεφεν αὐτὸς μισθοφόρων. It is expressly stated that, though he was not the son of the woman who was the mother of his brothers, he was the fruit of his father's body by another woman in a fully legitimate way, 259. Similarly, the δύο γυναῖκες πόρναι who appealed to Solomon in his wisdom to judge between them (3 Βασ. 3:16) have now become δύο γυναῖκες ἑταῖραι τὸν βίον, Ant., 8, 27. Further-more, in 3 Βασ. 22:38 the πόρναι who washed themselves in Ahab's blood have not only become αἱ ἑταιριζόμεναι, but the story is divested of its immediate horror by the addition of a note explaining that hetairae were accustomed to bathe in the stream from the time that its waters mingled with the blood of the fallen king, Ant., 8, 417.[51] Quite obviously the concern of Joseph. here is to show how exemplary was the moral life of his people. This is proved not least by the way in which he comprehensively describes the divine order for marriage and sex, Ant., 3, 247 ff., cf. Lv. 20:10 ff. He writes here as an apologist for Judaism. The same is true of the similar description in Ap., 2, 199 ff.,[52] 215. Nothing speaks more eloquently in this regard, however, than the avoidance of the group πορνεύω in passages referring to his own people. The same may also be said of the way in which he alters or softens the OT narrative when he does not avoid altogether or in part the thing to which πορνεύω refers.[53]

5. In later Rabb. usage זְנוּת applies not merely to all extra-marital intercourse but also to intercourse in marriages which run contrary to Rabb. decisions.[54] It is forbidden for a Jew to marry a proselyte prior to conversion, a freedwoman, or a woman guilty of cohabitation outside marriage or illegitimately.[55] For a priest the sphere of permissible marriage is even smaller.[56] If the illegitimacy comes to light only in the course of the marriage relationship, all previous intercourse is regarded as πορνεία. Unnatural forms of intercourse are also viewed as licentious.[57] Since there is no bibl. prohibition of un-natural intercourse with one's own wife, the later Rabbinate decided that it had no power to protect wives who might be troubled in this way. Later interpretation, however, expressly repudiated the view that this absence of a bibl. statement gave the husband the right to abuse his wife. The whole discussion shows how unsure the Rabbis were in their judgment.[58] One is certainly not to conclude that the Jewish husband could do as he liked with his wife as though she were merely a possession.[59]

(LXX), where the word occurs 3 times, v. 25, 31, 39. If there is a connection, the passage testifies to the presence of an apocalyptic tradition in Joseph. In relation to what follows it should be noted that for Joseph. the πορνεῖον belongs to the non-Jewish world in distinc-tion from the Jewish and bibl.

[51] Cf. also the Hbr. transl. of Ant. by Abraham Schalit קדמוניות היהודים II² (1955), 310.

[52] Jos. Ap., 2, 291 states succinctly that the Jewish νόμοι taught εὐσέβεια ἀληθεστάτη.

[53] On the apologetic attitude of Joseph. in gen. cf. P. Krüger, Philo u. Jos. als Apologeten des Judt. (1906).

[54] Cf. Str.-B., II, 729 f.; Sanh., 7, 4.

[55] Jeb., 6, 5 (61b); Str.-B., III, 342 f.

[56] Str.-B., II, 376.

[57] Ibid., III, 64-74 on R. 1:26 f.; Preuss, 549-555; cf. also Test. L. 17:11; Test. N. 4; Test. B. 9:1; Sanh., 7, 4.

[58] Lines 29-37 are by K. H. Rengstorf.

[59] Ned., 20b; Str.-B., III, 68. All the ref. in Str.-B. are late, and unnatural treatment even of one's own wife is always viewed as exceptional in the tradition, Str.-B., III, 69 under d. This seems to have been Billerbeck's own understanding. Obviously the whole discussion hinges on the lack of any clear ref. in the Torah and the impossibility of solving

Early marriage is advocated as a safeguard against fornication. [60] Since all Gentiles were suspected of this, various protective measures were taken to prevent entanglement with them. [61] As regards the moral responsibility of the Gentiles, the written Torah offered no guidance but later Judaism worked out an understanding on the basis of the Noachic commands. To prevent man from losing all knowledge of God after the fall, God gave Adam six basic commandments concerning idolatry, blasphemy, judging, murder, fornication and theft. [62] Hence Gentiles are responsible in relation to sins of fornication. The introduction of what are called chief commandments, e.g., those concerning idolatry, fornication and murder, represents an attempt at hierarchical distinction. [63] The irrevocability of the chief commandments may be seen from a resolution during the persecution under Hadrian which allowed Jews under threat of death to break all the commandments except these three. Not without some influence on the part of the moral preaching of Hell. philosophy the so-called list of vices developed in the Judaism of the Hell. *diaspora*. [64] If the list is always a variable one, there is still a traditional core which includes adultery and fornication along with idolatry, witchcraft, murder and the like.

D. The New Testament.

The NT is characterised by an unconditional repudiation of all extra-marital and unnatural intercourse. In this respect it follows to a large degree the judgment of OT and Israelite preaching and transcends the legalistic practice of later Judaism, which is shown to be inadequate by the Word of Jesus. Jesus can and does effect this radicalising because the Gospel as saving forgiveness manifests the divine dynamic in this age. A further result of this is a basically new attitude to woman. She is no longer man's chattel (→ 589, 26 ff.) but a partner of equal dignity before both man and God.

I. The Proclamation of Jesus.

The Gospels presuppose that there were harlots in Palestine and that their profession was in direct opposition to the righteousness required for the kingdom of God, Mt. 21:31 f.; Lk. 15:30. The Gospels also tell us, however, that the Baptist's message of repentance and Jesus' invitation into the kingdom of God awakened penitence for their way of life in many harlots (Lk. 7:50), and indeed brought them much more powerfully to repentance than it did the morally correct Pharisees (Mt. 21:31 f.). The forgiveness of Jesus was enjoyed precisely by these women

---

the matter acc. to the rules of exegesis. Children of forbidden unions are regarded as ממזר (bastard) in Jeb., 4, 13 and cf. K. H. Rengstorf, *Jebamot* (1929), 64 f. (which includes Rabb. material on the status of Jesus). Light is cast on the matter in T. Jeb., 6, 9, which rules that he who brings home his yebama for beauty or money (and thus satisfies the commandment of the Torah) is guilty of a בעילת זנות and any child of the union is קרוב להיות ממזר. בעילת זנות is also rape, cf. very clearly T. Jeb., 8, 2 [Rengstorf].

[60] Str.-B., II, 373; Qid., 29b.

[61] Str.-B., IV, 353-414 Exc. 15. For the attitude of the ancient synagogue to the non-Jewish world cf. esp. 356-383 (not to be alone with Gentiles, precautions in teaching, lodging, keeping cattle, *connubium* etc.).

[62] Str.-B., III, 36 f.; Noah is also given the 7th commandment not to eat blood; on the Noachic commandments cf. Str.-B., III, 37 f., 41 f.; also → 592, 26 ff.

[63] Str.-B., I, 255 and 278 and Index, s.v. "Kardinalsünde"; bSanh., 74a : חוק מעבודה זרה וגילוי עריות ושפיכות דמים. With regard to this it should be noted that the ref. of גילוי עריות is to the special sin of incest, bYoma, 9a and cf. the whole passage 9a/b. Non-observance of the laws of incest is for the Rabb. a specific mark of the Gentile world, whose genealogies etc. are not recognised on this account [Rengstorf].

[64] A. Vögtle, *Die Tugend- u. Lasterkataloge im NT* (1956), 98-120; K. Weidinger, "Die Haustafeln," *Untersuchungen z. NT*, 14 (1928), 23-27.

whom the self-righteousness of the Pharisees and the Rabbis had abandoned, Lk. 7:47. To the hard-hearted and exclusive separation of the Pharisees Jesus opposes His message of unconditional forgiveness which is for all who turn from their previous way. Not the physical act is sin; the thoughts of sexual licentiousness which dwell in the heart and rise up thence are the things which defile a man (κοινοῖ Mt. 15:18 f.), and these are a strict proof of unbelief in God.

Hotly debated is the interpretation of the two passages which deal with divorce, Mt. 5:32 and 19:9. [65]

In Mk. 10 (→ I, 649, 22 ff.) the tempting question of the Pharisees deals with divorce generally whereas Mt. by adding κατὰ πᾶσαν αἰτίαν (19:3) refers to the dispute between the schools of Shammai and Hillel regarding the grounds of divorce. [66] The clauses παρεκτὸς λόγου πορνείας in Mt. 5:32 and μὴ ἐπὶ πορνείᾳ in 19:9 occur neither in Mk. nor in Lk. It is mostly assumed that the simple form represents the older tradition and that in both passages the clauses may be traced back to the author of Mt. [67] On the other hand, it might be objected that Mt. usually tends to a stronger view of the Torah, whereas this is a notable divergence. The later radicalising which may be observed in some verses of the special Lucan material (cf. Lk. 6:20 f.; 12:33; 14:33 etc.), and the stricter practice of the Church (cf. Herm. m., 4, 1, 4-8) at a later time, are also arguments against a late date for these clauses. Hence one has to reckon with at least the possibility that the Matthean text is original; [68] it is certain not open to challenge on textual grounds. [69]

According to the version in Mk. and Lk. Jesus states in clear-cut fashion that the indissolubility of marriage is the unconditional will of God, cf. Mk. 10:9; Mt. 19:6. According to the testimony of Paul too (1 C. 7:10) Jesus demanded that marriage be indissoluble. [70]

In so doing He expressly sets aside the Jewish practice (→ 589, 26 ff.) which ascribes to the husband the one-sided and arbitrary right to divorce [71] and which simply requires that he give his wife a bill of divorce which will enable her to marry again if she so chooses. The biblical ref. on which all the scribal discussions are based is Dt. 24:1, which names עֶרְוַת דָּבָר (LXX ἄσχημον πρᾶγμα) as a ground of divorce. λόγος πορνείας in Mt. 5:32 is perhaps modelled linguistically on the Heb. formula, → IV, 105, 9 ff. Shammai and his school laid stress on עֶרְוָה and saw therein a ref. to what is morally objectionable. Hillel laid the accent on דָּבָר and took this to mean "any cause" (of offence), e.g., letting food burn. [72] It is worth noting that the contested additions

[65] Bultmann Trad., 25 f., 140, 159; Sickenberger Unzuchtsklausel; B. H. Streeter, *The Four Gospels* (1924), 259-261 suggests that, since Mt.'s formulation (κατὰ πᾶσαν αἰτίαν) corresponds better than Mk.'s to the Jewish dispute, he was following a par. tradition; cf. Hck. Mt., 118; Bultmann Trad., 26 takes the opposite view that Mt. is making a formal correction in the light of scribal learning.
[66] Cf. Str.-B., I, 312-320, 804 f.
[67] Cf. Wellh. Mt., 21; Wellh. Mk., 84; Kl. Mt., ad loc.; H. Wendt, *Die Lehre Jesu*[2] (1901), 403 f.; M. Albertz, *Die synpt. Streitgespräche* (1921), 39-41. Cf. E. v. Dobschütz, "Mt. als Rabbi u. Katechet," ZNW, 27 (1928), 344; Loh. Mt., ad loc.; Delling, 267-270; Greeven, 110-115. On the possibility of taking עֶרְוַת דָּבָר in the sense of דְּבַר עֶרְוָה v. A. Schulz. "Die Umkehrung des St. c.," BZ, 21 (1933), 150-152 and B. Zimolung, *Die Umkehrung beim St. c. im Hebräischen* (1939), 12-14.
[68] On this cf. Schl. Mt., ad loc. and J. Schniewind, *Das Ev. nach Mt.*, NT Deutsch, 2[4] (1950), ad loc.
[69] On the variant in Syr[sin] cf. A. Merx, *Das Ev. d. Mt.*, II, 1 (1902), 94-98.
[70] E. Hirsch, "Randglossen z. 1 K. 7," ZSTh, 3 (1926), 50-62.
[71] The addition of κατὰ πᾶσαν αἰτίαν in Mt. (19:3) is a hit at the lax view of the school of Hillel.
[72] Str.-B., I, 313-315. Acc. to Blau, I, 17-20 שנא is a tt. for a man taking a sexual dislike to his wife and thus being unwilling to continue living with her, Dt. 22:13; 21:15; Gn. 29:31;

to the saying of Jesus are found only in Mt. They are probably to be interpreted in the light of their material context. Whereas in the days of the prophets a husband might pardon his wife in the case of infidelity (cf. Hos. 3:1 ff.), in the time of Jesus the Law was stricter and an adulterous wife was forbidden to have any further intercourse with her husband or the adulterer; her husband had to divorce her. [73]

By means of the exception in 5:32 Mt. is telling his Jewish Christian readers that if a man puts away his life except for her infidelity, in which case he is compelled to do so by existing statutes, he is driving her into an adulterous relation should she remarry. In another version the point is the same in Mt. 19:9. In both verses πορνεία refers to extra-marital intercourse on the part of the wife, which in practice is adultery, cf. Sir. 23:23 : ἐν πορνείᾳ ἐμοιχεύθη. [74] The drift of the clauses, then, is not that the Christian husband, should his wife be unfaithful, is permitted to divorce her, but that if he is legally forced to do this he should not be open to criticism if by her conduct his wife has made the continuation of the marriage quite impossible. [75]

In Jn. πορνεία occurs only once at 8:41. Here Jesus says that the dissimilarity between the Jews and Abraham makes them bastards. Hence their claim to be the children of Abraham is only a nominal one. Their true father is the devil, 8:44.

II. Acts.

The only word of the group used in Ac. is πορνεία, and this occurs only 3 times in verses recording the prohibitions of the apostolic decree, [76] 15:20, 29 and 21:25. In content the decree is a concession to Gentile Christians. There is no insistence on the Jewish Law, only on the observance of minimal requirements for the interrelationships of Jewish and Gentile Christians, 15:28. Among these is the prohibition of fornication.

As is well-known, some important witnesses to the Western Text reduce the prohibitions to three by omitting πνικτῶν (→ 457, 1 ff.) and add the so-called Golden Rule,

---

Jub. 41:2 etc. In Dt. 24:3 it may be compared with לֹא תִמְצָא־חֵן in v. 1. The subsidiary clause כִּי מָצָא בָהּ עֶרְוַת דָּבָר is not specifying the legal ground adequate for divorce, i.e., that the woman is her husband's purchased possession, but simply noting an actual cause, namely, that the husband is disappointed after marriage because of sexual antipathy to his wife.

[73] Sota, 5, 1: As she (the adulteress) is forbidden (אֲסוּרָה) to her husband, she is also forbidden to the adulterer. Test. R. 3:15; Blau, I, 37 f.

[74] This is an answer also to Fridrichsen, 55 f., who emphasises that πορνεία within marriage ought to be called μοιχεία and who thus thinks the ref. is to pre-marital intercourse such as that which Joseph suspected in the case of Mary and which is brought to light only after marriage. In this case the Christian husband should be allowed to divorce his wife. K. Bornhäuser, Die Bergpredigt (1923), 82 arbitrarily restricts πορνεία to "wild and perhaps perverted sexuality" in married life. παρεκτός (5:32), like μή (19:9), indicates the one exception to the given rule, cf. Ac. 26:29.

[75] The Matthean additions naturally cause gt. difficulties for Roman Catholic exegetes, who must harmonise them with the principle that divorce is absolutely impossible. On Roman Catholic and Protestant exposition in detail cf. Ott. Ott himself thinks λόγος πορνείας is a transl. of עֶרְוַת דָּבָר and believes (292) παρεκτός is to be taken inclusively (which is linguistically impossible): "whosoever divorces his wife even in case of עֶרְוַת דָּבָר"; equally artificially he thinks μὴ ἐπὶ πορνείᾳ in Mt. 19:9 is a parenthesis (299): "... it is also not allowed on the ground of fornication ..." Cf. also Staab, Die Unauflöslichkeit and "Das Ev. nach Mt.," Echter Bibel (1951), on 5:32 and 19:9; H. Ljungman, Das Gesetz erfüllen (1954), 81 f. and A. Allgeier, "Alttestamentliche Beiträge z. nt.lichen Ehescheidungsverbot," Theol. Quart., 126 (1946), 290-299. On the formulation cf. Sanh., 74a (→ n. 63); Pr.-Bauer⁴, s.v. παρεκτός.

[76] On this whole subject cf. Haench. Ag., ad loc.

Mt. 7:12. [77] The whole decree is thus presented, not as a ritual order, but as a short moral catechism which mentions negatively the three chief sins (idolatry, murder and fornication, → 590, 1 ff.) and positively the basic ethical rule. [78] In all probability however, this is a secondary simplification. The surprising combination of πορνεία with dietary regulations is due to the fact that the four prohibitions are based on Lv. 17 and 18. πορνεία here is marrying within the prohibited degrees, which acc. to the Rabbis was forbidden "on account of fornication," Lv. 18:6-18. [79]

III. Paul, Hebrews and James.

Whereas the question of πορνεία is seldom dealt with in the preaching of Jesus and the primitive community, it arises more frequently in Paul. As compared with the different judgment of the Greek world and ancient syncretism, the concrete directions of Paul bring to the attention of Gentile Christians the incompatibility of πορνεία and the kingdom of God. [80] No πόρνος has any part in this kingdom, 1 C. 6:9; Eph. 5:5. In 1 C. 6:9 the sexual vices (πόρνοι, μοιχοί, μαλακοί, ἀρσενοκοῖται) are put next to the chief sin of idolatry. [81] The judgment which smote the Israelites, the fore-fathers of Christians (1 C. 10:1), in the wilderness when they fell victim to idolatry and lust, and thus tempted God, took place as an example (τυπικῶς), 10:8, 11. The situation of Christians is indeed much more serious, since they are at the end of the age, 10:11. In the shameful vices of unnatural sex relations, which spread like a plague in the Graeco-Roman world of his day, Paul sees the outworking of a severe judgment of God, R. 1:18 ff. → 582, 7 ff.

As individuals are to steer clear of πορνεία, so it is the apostle's supreme concern to keep the communities free from such sins, since toleration of the offender makes the whole church guilty and constitutes an eschatological threat, 1 C. 5:1 ff.; cf. Hb. 12:14-16. Thus Paul demands that the congregation expel the impenitent wrong-doer (1 C. 5:13) and break off all fellowship with those who live licentious lives (5:9). [82] 2 C. 12:19-21 expresses a concern lest the impenitence of those who have committed fornication should make necessary his intervention in the affairs of the community. The πορνεία of individual members makes the whole church unclean and threatens the whole work of the apostle, which is to present pure communities to Christ, 2 C. 11:2. In contrast to the different views of the matter in the Greek world and especially in Gnosticism, Paul warns against making light of the holy commandment of God in this field. God's mighty will for the salvation of men is ἁγιασμός, 1 Th. 4:3; cf. also Eph. 5:3-5. This includes sanctification of the body too and thus excludes any acceptance of fornication, 1 Th. 4:1-5. The Christian is a temple of the Holy Spirit, 1 C. 6:19. Hence he cannot do as he likes with himself. He may not give to a harlot the members

---

[77] On the textual problem cf. T. Zahn, *Einl. in d. NT*[3], II (1907), 358-365; Bau. Ag., 194-201, Exc. 8.

[78] On this cf. Haench Ag., 395, n. 5.

[79] Haench Ag., *ad loc.*

[80] In the lists of vices in Pl. (R. 1:24-32; 13:13; 1 C. 5:10 f.; 6:9 f.; 2 C. 12:20 f.; Gl. 5:19-21; Col. 3:5, 8 f.; cf. also Eph. 4:25-31; 5:3 f.; 1 Tm. 1:9 f.; 2 Tm. 3:2-5) πορνεία occurs 8 times, ἀκαθαρσία 4 times, while in 5 instances he begins with πορνεία or sexual sins, cf. Juncker, 113-117 and Exc. "Lasterkataloge" in Ltzm. R. on 1:31.

[81] In this respect he follows Jewish exhortation in the Hell. age, → 588, 37 ff.; Wis. 14:12 ff.; Vögtle, *op. cit.* (→ n. 64), 98-100, 223.

[82] Pl. is alluding to a — possibly very sharply worded — letter preceding 1 C. and in 5:10 (οὐ πάντως [not gen.] τοῖς πόρνοις τοῦ κόσμου τούτου) he tries to protect it against misunderstanding or misrepresentation on the part of the Corinthians.

which belong to Christ, 6:15 f. A man shames his own body by fornication, 6:18. [83]
He also brings shame on the body of Christ. Licentiousness is one of the expressions of the σάρξ, Gl. 5:19. It is totally opposed to the work of the Holy Spirit, Gl. 5:22. It belongs to what is earthly (Col. 3:5), whereas Christians should seek what is above (Col. 3:1-3). Paul again and again mentions πορνεία alongside (→ n. 80) ἀκαθαρσία, 2 C. 12:21; Gl. 5:19; Col. 3:5; cf. also Eph. 5:3, 5. [84] He realises that not every one has the gift of continence, 1 C. 7:7. As a protection against the evil of fornication the man who does not have it should take the divinely prescribed way of a lawful marriage, 1 C. 7:2. Severe though Paul's condemnation of fornication may be, there is no doubt that for him it is forgiven through Christ like all other sins (καὶ ταῦτά τινες ἦτε· ἀλλά ... κτλ. 1 C. 6:11). Along the same lines as Paul Hb. ascribes the salvation of Rahab the harlot to her faith (11:31), though Jm. (2:25) takes another view and thinks she is justified by her works.

IV. Revelation.

Among the seven letters of Rev. that to Pergamon accuses the Nicolaitans of leading the congregation astray by compromising with the cultural life of the surrounding world in the eating of meat sacrificed to idols and the practising of free sexual intercourse (πορνεία), 2:14. For the author the OT model for this is the doctrine of Balaam who led Israel astray in the same fashion, Nu. 25:1 ff.; 31:16. Along the same lines the church of Thyatira is charged with tolerating a prophetess who teaches the same practices 2:20 f.; the name of Jezebel is the OT reference in this instance, 2 K. 9:7, 22. Since there is mention of teaching in both instances, we are to think in terms of parties with the same basic principles, namely, libertine Gnostics [85] who not only permit the eating of idol meats and free sex but who boast of this freedom as a particular proof (cf. the "strong" of 1 C. 8:10) of Christian superiority.

Among the leading pagan sins to which men will cling in the last days despite all the divine judgments, Rev. 9:21 mentions idolatry, murder, witchcraft, and theft, and along with these unrestricted sexual indulgence.

In the description of the world power and metropolis of Rome, the counterpart of ungodly Babylon (c. 17-19), πόρνη and πορνεύω are used as comprehensive terms for its utter degeneracy. Like the city harlots of the day it bears its name on a golden head-band, and this name declares its nature: Βαβυλὼν ἡ μεγάλη, ἡ μήτηρ τῶν πορνῶν καὶ τῶν βδελυγμάτων τῆς γῆς, 17:5. It is the leading harlot of the world, the great seducer of the nations and their kings. The whoring of these with it (18:3, 9) is to be construed in the first instance along the lines of Is. 23:17; Na. 3:4. They seek its favours politically and economically. But the word embraces more than this. [86] The nations ape the customs of the metropolis even to whoredom in the literal sense. Above all, the capital is called πόρνη as the centre of paganism with its harlot-like apostasy from the true God. The great temptress offers her intoxicating drink to kings and merchants in a golden cup, 14:8; 17:2, 4. The cup (→ 144, 19 ff.), which is filled with the abominations

---

[83] Cf. H. Jacoby, Nt.liche Ethik (1899), 349; on the Stoic idea that a man dishonours himself by adultery and ἀκολασία cf. Muson., p. 65, 2 ff.; Joh. W. 1 K., ad loc.; → 583, 27 ff.

[84] This, too, is a Jewish view (→ 585, 28 ff.) but it was a completely new way of looking at things for Greeks.

[85] Cf. Loh. Apk., Exc. after 2:29; R. Knopf, Das nachapostolische Zeitalter (1905), 290-293.

[86] Cf. Had. Apk., 169.

associated with fornication (17:4), promises pleasure, but from God's standpoint it is a cup of God's wrath, 14:8; 16:19 → V, 434, 5 ff. [87] The great whore (19:2), the epitome of apostasy from the one true God and of the unavoidably related syncretistic intercourse with other gods, is contrasted with the pure community of God, the bride of the Messiah (21:9; 22:17), to which the unclean man has no access (21:27) because only the Lamb and God Himself is worshipped in it and by it. Among the manifest sinners whom the second death awaits πόρνοι are again mentioned along with idolaters, murderers and others, 21:8; 22:15.

E. The Post-Apostolic Fathers.

Herm. m., 4, 1, 1 warns against πορνεία which is the result of carnal desire, cf. also Did., 3, 3. Though πορνεία (or πορνεύω) is distinguished materially from μοιχεύω on the one side (Herm. m., 8, 3; Did., 5, 1; 2, 2; Barn., 19, 4), on the other μοιχεύω is πορνεύω (Herm. m., 4, 1, 5). [88] A noteworthy fact is that there is no transf. use of πόρνη κτλ. in the post-apost. fathers. This is esp. connected with the abandonment of the terminology of the OT prophets.

Hauck/Schulz

πόσις → 145, 3 ff.

```
ποταμός, ποταμοφόρητος,
       Ἰορδάνης
```

† ποταμός.

Contents : A. Greek Usage outside the New Testament : 1. Profane Greek ; 2. The LXX ; 3. Philo ; 4. Josephus. B. The River (or Stream) in the Old Testament and Later Judaism : 1. The OT; 2. The Rabbis. C. ποταμός in the New Testament : 1. Ordinary Use ; 2. ποταμός in the Apocalypse ; 3. The Saying of Jesus in Jn. 7:37 f.

A. Greek Usage outside the New Testament.

1. Profane Greek. Etym. related to πέτομαι "to move on with tearing speed," ποταμός has the primary sense of "(water) which rushes quickly by." The word is common in Hom. for "flowing water," esp. "stream" or "river." [2] What it denotes is plainly different from the sea into which ποταμοί flow, Plat. Tim., 22d : τῶν ποταμοῖς καὶ θαλάττῃ προσοικούντων, [3] and also from the sources from which they spring, e.g., Eur. Herc. Fur., 1297: πηγαὶ ποταμῶν. Oceanus, which encircles and streams around the disk of the earth, can be called ποταμός, Hom. Il., 14, 245 f.: ποταμοῖο ῥέεθρα Ὠκεανοῦ; all the water in the sea, in rivers, springs and wells, finally derives from it, Hom. Il., 21, 195 ff. In Egypt the word with art. denotes the Nile as the river

---

[87] The picture of God's cup of wrath derives from the OT, Is. 51:17; Jer. 51:7; sufferings and visitations are the drink which God hands men, Jer. 25:15 ff.; Ps. 60:3; 75:8. Cf. Loh. Apk. on 14:8; → θυμός III, 167 f. On πορνεία = ἀσέβεια (so Loh.) cf. Test. R. 4:3.

[88] Cf. Preisker, 144-147.

π ο τ α μ ό ς. [1] Boisacq⁴, s.v.; cf. also M. Runes, "Ποταμός," *Idg. Forschungen,* 50 (1932), 265 (as opp. to J. Wackernagel, *Vorlesungen über Syntax,* II, 2 [1924], 30 f. and after him Schwyzer, I, 493, n. 1, who espouse a derivation from πετάννυμι and give ποταμός the basis sense of "spreading").

[2] Examples in the dict.

[3] A Gk. proverb compares unequal combats with a fight between river and sea : ποταμὸς θαλάττῃ ἐρίζεις, Suid., IV, 181, No. 2124.

of the land,[4] a designation adopted in the OT, which often describes the Nile simply as the river of Egypt, Am. 8:8; 9:5; cf. also Gn. 41:1 ff. etc. (→ lines 22 ff.). As in the sea, so in the ποταμός there is violent power in the κύματα, which can seriously endanger and even destroy the one who enters them, Hom. Il., 21, 268-271, 281 ff. This is why a ποταμός can sometimes be called ὑβριστής like a violent man, Aesch. Prom., 717 f.: ἥξεις δ' ὑβριστὴν ποταμὸν οὐ ψευδώνυμον ὂν μὴ περάσῃς.[5]

It is perhaps connected with observation of the nature of ποταμοί that they were very early personified. At any rate river gods[6] hold a very prominent place in Gk. religion among personifications and local deities. The thought and the corresponding cult are already fully developed in Hom.[7] It is significant that Hesiod abstains from urinating in ποταμοί and springs.[8] River gods are often personified as bulls,[9] possibly because the noise of rushing masses of water and the way in which rivers toss to and fro whatever falls into them remind of the behaviour of bulls when they put forth their strength.[10] The Jordan in Palestine was also personified, though the only instance, non-Jewish and pre-Christian, is on a depiction of Titus' victory arch in Rome, → 613, 3 ff.[11]

ποταμός is already used in a transf. as well as the lit. sense in the classical period and its writings. Thus we read in Aesch. Prom., 367 f.: ἔνθεν ἐκφραγήσονταί ποτε ποταμοὶ πυρὸς δάπτοντες ἀγρίαις ... γνάθοις, "streams of fire which rend with vicious jaws." Once started, this use was an obvious one when it was desired to give a vivid picture of violent forces which carry things off with them. Nevertheless, it seems to be comparatively rare in the pre-Chr. era.

2. The LXX. In the LXX ποταμός is first used for יְאֹר, יְאוֹר, which seems to come from the Egyptian and in the sing. almost always[12] denotes the Nile (Gn. 41:1 ff.; Ex. 1:22 etc.) and its canals (Ez. 29:3 ff.), so that in this case ποταμός, like the original, naturally takes the art. → line 1. The other basic term is usually נָהָר, which is accompanied by the name of the relevant river, esp. the Euphrates (Jer. 13:7 etc.),[13] but also the Chebar (Χοβαρ Ez. 1:1 ff.), or the Bab. Σουδ (Bar. 1:4). In all these instances the context shows that the idea of flowing water goes hand in hand with that of a lasting flow, cf. also 2 K. 5:12: ποταμοὶ Δαμασκοῦ. This latter pt. should not be overlooked when ποταμός is used for the river of Paradise and the primary streams into which it divides (רָאשִׁים, ἀρχαί) (Gn. 2:10 ff.) or for the eschatological river of the prophet Ez. (47:1 ff.; cf. also Jl. 3:18) which flows out of the temple and whose rate of flow is the same both summer and winter, cf. Zech. 14:8.

From the sense one would expect that ποταμός would be well adapted to denote the wadi with its wild and dangerous torrents in times of rain. The Heb. נַחַל (wadi), however, means the stream-bed, which is dry except in the rainy season, rather than the stream itself, so that it is only seldom transl. ποταμός. Apart from Ez. 47:1 ff., where the translator changes the HT wadi into a permanent river, which is thus called a ποταμός (→ 596, 31 f.), and the two verses 2 Ch. 20:16; 32:4, which are both hard to

---

[4] Examples in Preisigke Wört. In the pap. ποταμός can also be used for the man-made arm of the Nile or Nile canal. The precise sense is often hard to fix here.

[5] It is a matter of debate whether we are to read Ὑβρίστην or Ὑβριστήν (so ed. P. Mazon, I [1920]; G. Italie, Index Aesch. [1955], 308a), i.e., a proper name or, as above, an adj. (cf. the editions and comm., ad loc.).

[6] O. Waser, Art. "Flussgötter," Pauly-W., 16, 2 (1909), 2774-2815 (older bibl.); Nilsson, I², 236-240.

[7] Nilsson, 236 f.

[8] Op., 757 f.; cf. Plut. Stoic. Rep., 22 (II, 1045a-b).

[9] Cf. Waser, op. cit. (→ n. 6), 2780-2782.

[10] Cf. the depiction of the raging Scamandros in Hom. Il., 21, 234 ff.

[11] O. Waser, "Vom Flussgott Jordan u. andern Personifikationen," Festgabe A. Kaegi (1919), 191-217.

[12] Only in Da. 12:5 ff. 4 times of the Tigris.

[13] The simple ὁ ποταμός for the Euphrates corresponds to a הַנָּהָר in the HT, Gn. 31:21 etc.

expound, the only instance is 1 K. 8:65 with its mention of the ποταμός Αἰγύπτου (נַחַל מִצְרַיִם), the wadi which in Solomon's time formed the frontier with Egypt (to-day the Wadi el-Arish). Here, however, it seems from Gn. 15:18 [14] and esp. Jdt. 1:9 [15] that a fixed formula is used for the southern boundary irrespective of the specific sense of ποταμός. [16]

The fig. use in the LXX is controlled by the idea of lasting fulness, here combined with ποταμός. In Is. 48:18 the prophet compares to a ποταμός the fulness of εἰρήνη (שָׁלוֹם) allotted to the people of God. Passages like Am. 8:8; 9:5 suggest that the origin of the comparison lies in the fulness of the waters of the Nile which controlled the life and prosperity of the Egyptians. [17] In the apocalyptic visions of Da. there is mention of a ποταμός πυρός proceeding from the divine throne, which for its part can be compared only with a flame of fire, 7:10 LXX; Θ for נְהַר דִּי־נוּר. It can hardly be that this is simply a reminiscence of the fact that God dwells in light, Da. 2:22. Other apocal. passages show that the "stream of fire" is a feature of divine epiphany, 4 Esr. 13:10 : fluctus ignis proceeding from the mouth of the Son of Man ; Gr. En. 14:19 : ποταμοὶ πυρός come forth from beneath the divine throne ; cf. Eth. En. 71:2, 9. [18] In Jesus Sirach ποταμός is very definitely an image of fulness, and indeed in such a way that certain specific rivers, esp. the Nile, fill out the concept, 47:14; [19] cf. 24:25 ff.; 39:22 (here God's εὐλογία ὡς ποταμός).

3. Philo. In Philo the ordinary use, in which the Nile naturally plays an important role, [20] is accompanied by a developed transf. use. Thus Philo speaks of the χειμάρρους ποταμὸς τοῦ βίου, Fug., 49. [21] The Euphrates, perhaps because of the similarity of its name to εὐφραίνω, [22] becomes the symbol of God's wisdom as τὸν μέγαν ὡς ἀληθῶς ποταμόν, χαρᾶς καὶ εὐφροσύνης καὶ τῶν ἄλλων πλημμυροῦντα ἀγαθῶν, Rer. Div. Her., 315. It can be said of the νοῦς that it διαβαίνει τὸν τῶν αἰσθητῶν ποταμὸν τὸν ἐπικλύζοντα καὶ βαπτίζοντα τῇ φορᾷ τῶν παθῶν τὴν ψυχήν, Leg. All., III, 18; cf. Det. Pot. Ins., 100. Speech (λόγος) is compared to a ποταμός, Som., II, 238, 240, 259 f., and so, too, is the divine logos, 243, 245. It should be noted, of course, that this fig. use is normally in the context of allegories, and that allegories play a gt. role in it, but this in no way limits the significance of the fact as such.

4. Josephus. In contrast Joseph. has the word only in a literal sense. As in the LXX, the river of Paradise is for him ποταμός, Ant., 1, 38. For him, too, ποταμοί are rivers with a steady flow of water, esp. the Jordan (Ant., 5, 16 ff.; 20, 97, commonly with the name), but also the Euphrates (18, 312 etc.), the Nile (2, 249 alongside 244, ποταμός without name for the Nile in 2, 81), the Arnon (4, 85 and 95) etc. That Joseph. appreciates the strict meaning may be seen from the fact that he calls the Jabbok, which

---

[14] For מִנְהַר מִצְרַיִם read perhaps with BHK מִנַּחַל מִצְרַיִם.

[15] This is esp. true of the א reading τοὺς χιμάρρους for τοῦ ποταμοῦ. χειμάρρους, χείμαρρος is the usual and accurate LXX transl. of נַחַל "winter brook," "winter river," "wadi." א thus seems to be deliberately correcting an error.

[16] On the question whether incorrect ideas about the specified wadi lie behind the term cf. F. Delitzsch, Neuer Comm. über die Genesis (1887), 279. If the ref. in v. 18b comes from a glossator (so H. Gunkel, Genesis, Göttinger Handkommentar z. AT³ [1910], ad loc.) and he really has the Nile in view, this is not to be assumed in the case of the translator.

[17] Cf. also Is. 66:12, where there is some divergence between Mas. and LXX so far as the metaphor is concerned.

[18] Streams of fire in the place of punishment, En. 67:7.

[19] HT has כַּיְאֹר instead of ὡς ποταμός, and is thus referring to the Nile as in 24:27 and 39:22.

[20] Cf. the ref. in Leisegang Index, 674.

[21] The context is an allegorical interpretation of the name Mesopotamia.

[22] Cf. Leg. All., I, 72 and on this E. Stein, "Die allegorische Exegese d. Philo aus Alex.," Beih. ZAW, 51 (1929), 60.

flows into the Jordan, a ποταμός (4, 95 and 97), [23] but quite correctly describes the Kedron or the valley of the Kedron as a χείμαρρους or wadi (8, 17), cf. also Jn. 18:1, which is equally well-informed on the pt.

B. The River (or Stream) in the Old Testament and Later Judaism.

1. The OT. For the righteous of the OT God is the Creator of all things. He is thus the Lord of watercourses too. [24] If He wills, He can dry up even rivers which are not dependent on the winter rains, Is. 44:27; 50:2; Ps. 74:15. Even the mighty Nile is no exception, Is. 19:5; cf. 2 K. 19:24. He can also change the water of rivers into blood, Ex. 7:14 ff.; Ps. 78:44; cf. Ps. 105:29; Wis. 11:6. Similarly, He determines where rivers flow (Hab. 3:9), and He can cause waters to break forth and become rivers in the arid steppes, Ps. 105:41; cf. Is. 43:19. For this reason rivers are among the works of God which praise Him by their very being, Ps. 98:8. In the Song of the Three Children they can thus be summoned to participate with all creation in the praise of God, Δα. 3:78. The fact of their being and the nature of their being are both of God. No more, then, than any other part of creation do they have independent significance alongside Him.

In the light of this it is self-evident that there is no place for a cult of river gods in the sphere of OT belief. Thus far we have no evidence that the God of Israel had to contend with such deities when He came into the land. The command not to worship images of what is in the water under the earth (Ex. 20:4; cf. Dt. 5:8) relates to fish rather than water deities according to the Deuteronomic interpretation (4:18). No Palestinian model has thus far been discovered for the divine representation of the Jordan on the arch of Titus in Rome, → ᾿Ιορδάνης, 613, 4 ff. It should not be overlooked, however, that there is a ruling in the Mishnah dealing with sacrifices לְשֵׁם נְהָרוֹת and forbidding the eating of the flesh, Chul., 2, 8. [25] There is also a Tannaitic statute which forbids any form of immolating into seas (יַמִּים) or rivers (נְהָרוֹת) (Chul., 2, 9) in order to avoid even the appearance of offering to an idol, cf. T. Chul., 2, 19. [26] It has thus to be accepted that river gods were at least worshipped by pagans in the land at the beginning of our era, so that the Rabbis thought it necessary to issue directions against such worship.

All else is hypothesis. Thus an amulet in the form of a fish dating from the Canaanite period has been found in Gezer. [27] This has been made by some [28] into the starting-point for the thesis that the amulets found on fallen soldiers of Judas Maccabeus in 2 Macc. 12:40, and regarded as a reason for their death in battle by the pious narrator, were fish amulets after the pattern of the idols of Jabneh [29] near Gezer (ἱερώματα τῶν

[23] In Ant., 1, 331 the Jabbok is called a χείμαρρους, but there is something wrong with the Gk. form of the name here (cf. the text; A. Schlatter, "Die hbr. Namen bei Jos.," BFTh, 17, 3 [1913], 53), so that any deductions must be made with caution.

[24] Cf. Ps. 24:1 f. with its threefold picture of the world: the earth, the surrounding sea, and the waters which are beneath the earth and which break forth from it; cf. also Ex. 20:4 and esp. Ps. 93:1-3 and on this G. Widengren, Sakrales Königtum im AT u. im Judt. (1955), 62 f. For ancient motifs in Chr. dress cf. Od. Sol. 39. One may also refer to the Qumran texts, where it is said of God in 1 QM 10:12 f.: הבורא מקוי .... נהרות.

[25] Cf. also bChul., 40a-41b. Obviously there is no direct observation on the part of the Amoreans, but this supports the age of the regulations.

[26] Cf. also S. Lieberman, Hellenism in Jewish Palestine (1950), 134-136, who pts. out that pagan sacrificial terminology is used in Chul., 2, 9.

[27] Ill. in E. R. Goodenough, Jewish Symbols in the Greco-Roman Period (1953 ff.), III, No. 380.

[28] F. J. Dölger, ΙΧΘΥΣ, II (1922), 205; Goodenough, op. cit., V, 17.

[29] On Jamnia/Jabneh cf. S. Klein, "Jabne," EJ, 8, 724-726.

ἀπὸ 'Ιαμνείας εἰδώλων), and that they bear witness to an influence of the cult of Atargatis [30] on the Jews of the Maccabean period. But even if this identification of the amulets were sufficiently convincing, in the context it would still be possible to see them primarily as symbols of immortality which only later, if at all, came to be connected with the cult of Atargatis. [31] Certainly they provide no evidence for the cult of a river god. Nor should it be overlooked that neither later Judaism nor the OT had any doubts about the eating of fish, for the water animals forbidden in Lv. 11:9 ff. are not fish at all. The NT also takes fishing and the eating of fish for granted. A Rabb. ruling even allows quite explicitly the eating of imported fish under certain conditions, Maksh., 6, 3. This seems to be strong evidence that no idolatrous notions were connected with fish as such.

2. The Rabbis. Apart from proverbs and similar sayings (e.g., that every river [נהרא] has its own course, bChul., 18b; 57a), the main concern of the Rabbinate with rivers is religious and legal.

a. Rivers plays an important role in casuistry. They are among the natural forces to which man and his possessions are often subject. They thus serve as very good examples when it is a matter of laying down rules for proper conduct in cases of "higher power." [32] Thus the case is discussed of a נָהָר carrying away the asses of two different owners and one owner can save only the ass of the other while his own beast is lost, BQ, 10, 4. Salvation from death through the overflowing of a river is a reason for granting relaxation of certain commands and prohibitions, Pes., 3, 7; BQ, 10, 2; RH, 2, 5; Taan., 3, 7; Ned., 3, 1. The damage which swollen rivers do also plays a role, bBQ, 117b/118a. The force of the water can be so great that a tree can be torn up with all its root structure and can then begin to grow again elsewhere, Orla, 1, 3.

b. For the Rabbis *the* river is not the Jordan but the Euphrates, Challa, 4, 8; cf. Gn. r., 16, 3 on 2:14. OT usage exerts an influence here, Gn. 31:21 etc. In particular there is expressed the conviction, based on the OT (the promise to Abraham in Gn. 15:18), [33] that the Euphrates is the eastern boundary of the promised land. [34]

Possibly related to this estimation of the Euphrates is the fact that the statement in Ber., 9, 2 that the sight of mountains, hills, seas, rivers and plains leads to benediction of the Creator, is later referred esp. to the Euphrates so far as the rivers are concerned. [35] The Palestinian Amorean Jochanan, who acc. to tradition died in 279 and whose school produced j Talmud, extolled the Euphrates for the fact that washing in its waters accounted for there being no lepers in Babylon, bKet., 77b. It is not impossible, however, that he owed this saying to his teacher Chanina (bChama), who came from Babylon. [36, 37]

---

[30] On Atargatis cf. F. Cumont, *Die orient. Religionen im röm. Heidentum*[3] (1931), 94-97.

[31] Cf. Goodenough, V, 14 with Ill. 11, also 16. The early widespread view that the Syrian Dagon was a fish-god may now be regarded as outdated, *ibid.*, 16.

[32] The concept is Rabb.; cf. the expression נִדְרֵי אֲנָסִים for "vows (whose fulfilment is impossible because) of unavoidable circumstances," Ned., 3, 3 etc. There are many examples of unavoidable situations which have or might have legal consequences (אוֹנֶס) in BM, 8, 9-10; T BM, 8, 15-16. The opp. of באונס is ברצון. On אונס cf.תלמודית אנציקלופדיה, I (1947), 168 ff.

[33] Cf. also Dt. 1:7; 11:24; Jos. 1:4; Mi. 7:12; Is. 27:12; Zech. 9:10 etc.

[34] This is plain in the pt. of the anecdote in Gn. r., 16, 3 on 2:14, namely, that the land of Israel begins immediately west of the river. Cf. also J. Obermeyer, *Die Landschaft Babylonien im Zeitalter des Talmuds u. des Gaonats* (1929), 96.

[35] bBer., 59b; cf. also Obermeyer, *op. cit.*, 52-61 on the place of the benediction.

[36] Bacher Pal. Am., I, 1 f.

[37] A related saying of his is found in the immediate context and is perhaps a prescription well-known in Babylonia, cf. bSanh., 64a.

c. Rivers and their waters are also important, of course, in the highly developed Rabbinic system of purification. Without water it is not possible either to be clean or to cleanse oneself. Now in antiquity the rivers of Palestine played only a modest role in providing water. This is true even of the Jordan, especially as its valley is poor in tributaries south of Gennesaret, → 610, 22 ff. Nevertheless, it is astonishing to what extent river waters seem to cause problems in the rules of purity rather than promoting cleanness.

This is due to the fact that rivers often contain particles of dirt which call in question the results of ritual bathing, cf. Miq., 9, 1 ff.; bShab., 65a-b. There is occasional ref. to ritual bathing in the Euphrates. A teacher arranges this for his daughter with certain precautions. He puts her on a bathing stand [38] so that she may not be defiled by the mud of the river-bed, bShab., 65a. On another occasion it is told that R. Jehuda bElai with exaggerated conscientiousness and to give visual instruction to his pupils took a ritual bath in the Jordan before their eyes, bBer., 22a. This is quite possible, since river water was equivalent to spring water, Miq., 5, 5. On the other hand, the bath of R. Jochanan in the Jordan of which we read in bBM, 84a seems not to have been an obligatory bath but simply for refreshment, as was often the case. [39] Passages like Maksh., 5, 1; T. Maksh., 2, 12 probably refer to ordinary bathing rather than to ritual baths in rivers. Of bathing in rivers for purposes of healing, as prescribed by Gk. doctors e.g., in the temples of Aesculapius in Epidauros and Pergamon, [40] the Rabb. have nothing explicit to say. The total impression is that the difficulty of being sure of the purity of river-water was strongly felt and was taken into account in practice also. The relation of the Qumran Community to all this is not yet apparent on the basis of the material thus far available. In 1 QS 3:4 f. ritual washings in seas and rivers seem to be an accepted custom, but this might well be only a rhetorical expression.

d. Perhaps connected with this fundamentally cautious use of rivers for ritual cleansing is the fact that, while brooks and rivers could in principle be the site of proselyte baptism, they obviously did not play any part as such.

Fundamentally any water that meets the requirements of the ritual bath may be used in proselyte baptism. [41] This includes river-water (Miq., 5, 5) apart from certain specific exceptions, ibid., 1, 8. But there is no record of such baptism in rivers. Quite apart from the disputed question of the age of proselyte baptism, [42] later Rabb. practice assumes that it will take place in a "bath-house" [43] which is used gen. for ritual cleansing [44] and is naturally to be distinguished carefully from ordinary baths. [45] In the Hell. propaganda of Judaism one occasionally finds the requirement that non-Jews, when converted to the true God, should wash the whole body in continuous flowing water. [46] It is natural

---

[38] On such stands, which were used in ritual washings and sprinklings in Egypt, cf. J. Leipoldt, Die urchr. Taufe im Lichte d. Religionsgeschichte (1928), 50 (bibl.).

[39] For material cf. S. Krauss, Talmudische Archäologie, I (1910), 212 f.

[40] R. Herzog, Die Wunderheilungen v. Epidauros (1931), 94 f., 104.

[41] bJeb., 47a/b Bar.; cf. Str.-B., I, 109.

[42] Cf. J. Jeremias, "Der Ursprung der Johannestaufe," ZNW, 28 (1929), 312-320, J. Thomas, Le mouvement baptiste en Palestine et Syrie 150 avant J. Chr.-300 après J. Chr. (1935); Bultmann Theol., 41. Cf. also H. H. Rowley, "Jewish Proselyte Baptism and the Baptism of John," Hebrew Union College Annual, 15 (1940), 313-334.

[43] Gerim., 1, 3 : "When he [the proselyte has solemnly declared that he wants to live in all circumstances as a Jew and] has taken upon himself [to keep] the Law, they then lead him into the bath-house ..." There was a house of this kind in the temple (Yoma, 3, 2; Sheq., 8, 2; Mid., 1, 9 etc.) and another on the Mt. of Olives (Para, 3, 7), but they would naturally be found wherever needed, and they were needed everywhere.

[44] Cf. bJeb., 47a/b and on this Str.-B., I, 109; VI on spring water.

[45] So esp. clearly in bYoma, 11a/b.

[46] Sib., 4, 165 : ἐν ποταμοῖς λούσασθε ὅλον δέμας ἀενάοισιν.

enough to refer this to proselyte baptism, and on this view it provides an instance of such baptism in ποταμοί. Nevertheless, it is odd that there is in the context no ref. to circumcision, which, as we know,[47] took precedence of baptism.[48] Spring or well water is used in the "bath-house."

C. ποταμός in the New Testament.

The literal and figurative uses of ποταμός may be found alongside one another in primitive Christian usage too. The word is rare. Nevertheless, it is possible to distinguish the following senses.

1. Ordinary Use.

a. In much the same terms Mt. (3:6) and Mk. (1:5) tell how the masses who were ready to repent streamed out to John the Baptist in the ἔρημος and were baptised by him in the river Jordan (ἐν τῷ ᾿Ιορδάνῃ ποταμῷ), confessing their sins. The formulation, especially in Mt., suggests that the linking of ποταμός with the name of the river had some significance for the authors. Purely linguistically they were, of course, following the usage of antiquity and of some pre-Christian biblical works at this point. Nevertheless, comparison with this usage shows that for the Evangelists or their source it is important that Jordan is a "river" both in connection with John's baptism and also in terms of historical reference.

In 3:5 etc. Mt. mentions the περίχωρος τοῦ ᾿Ιορδάνου as the home of those who come to John. The question arises whether it was really necessary in this connection to emphasise that Jordan was a ποταμός and thereby to emphasise also that as such it was the place of baptism. One should remember that the phrase ὁ ᾿Ιορδάνης ποταμός is seldom used in the LXX. In the three passages in which it occurs (Nu. 13:29; Jos. 4:7; 5:1), or at least in the last two, it also serves to interpret the HT. In both these instances the original מֵי־הַיַּרְדֵּן ("the waters of Jordan") becomes in transl. "the river Jordan." Hence even the formulation enables us to understand plainly and vividly what happened when the ark caused the Jordan to stay (Jos. 3:16); at this moment the Jordan cease to be a ποταμός, i.e., "water which rushes quickly by" → 590, 27 f. This LXX usage alone cannot explain the expression "the river Jordan" in Mt. and Mk.[49]

But if this is so, it is not enough simply to refer to secular usage as a par.? Jos. seems to adopt this when he twice speaks emphatically of the ᾿Ιορδάνης ποταμός (Ant., 20, 97; Vit., 399),[50] whereas elsewhere he either just mentions the name or refers to the Jordan without further definition as ὁ ποταμός. Analysis of the passages which have both shows that his interest there is in the Jordan as a river and not as the Jordan. Even these ref., then, are no true par. to the expression in Mt. 3:6 and Mk. 1:5.[51]

The textual tradition in both verses probably pts. in the right direction. In each case

---

[47] For materials cf. Str.-B., I, 103 ff. Cf. also G. Polster, "Der kleine Talmudtraktat über die Proselyten," *Angelos*, 2 (1926), 1-38.

[48] Cf. also Jos. Ant., 20, 34 ff.: The conversion of king Izates of Adiabene was in the reign of the emperor Claudius (41-54 A.D.) and here circumcision is emphatically enforced on the Jewish side. Since Sib., 4 arose in the last quarter of the 1st cent. A.D., it is accepted to-day that there is at this pt. a strong tension between the view of Sib. and the story of Jos.

[49] Worth noting among other things is that, on the basis of the original, the ποταμός character of the Jordan is preserved in the Gk. version of the story of Naaman by means of expressions par. to those in the accounts of the Baptist in Mt. and Mk. (4 Βασ. 5:10 : λοῦσαι ἑπτάκις ἐν τῷ ᾿Ιορδάνῃ, 5:14 : ἐβαπτίσατο ἐν τῷ ᾿Ιορδάνῃ ἑπτάκι).

[50] On the usage of Jos. → 597, 31 ff.

[51] In spite of Schl. Mt., 64.

one group of witnesses has left out the epithet, [52] and in each textual evidence forces us to accept its authenticity. There seem to be two main reasons for the omission of ποταμῷ. Either it is regarded as superfluous (on stylistic grounds) or it seems to be undesirable (on dogmatic grounds). Consideration of the Lucan par. and of traditions about John the Baptist and baptism (→ 616, 13 ff.) compels us to suppose that the elimination of the word rested on a tendency to evade the exegetical and historical basis for linking baptism with running water. It is a familiar fact that the practice of the early Church vacillated for a long time in this respect until finally baptisms took place in the baptistery. [53] The Did. (7, 1 ff.) would allow other than "living water," i.e., that of a fountain or river, only by way of exception, and many records from the early Church bear witness to a similar practice or even ground it in apostolic custom and tradition. [54] In contrast, Just. (Apol., I, 61, 3) simply mentions a place where there is water (ἔνθα ὕδωρ ἐστί) and thus follows a practice which one has to assume in many of the NT accounts of baptisms, Ac. 2:41; 8:12 f., 16, 36 ff. etc.

It is difficult and to some extent impossible to decide this problem with any finality. One can only say that the textual witnesses which reject ποταμῷ in Mt. 3:6; Mk. 1:5 must be seen and judged against the background of the disagreement on the kind of water to be used in baptism. On the other hand caution must be observed in relation to attempts to link Mt. and Mk. themselves with the original reading and to deduce their own attitude therefrom.

It is most natural to suppose that the uncommon expression used here in Mt. and Mk. does not express any dogmatic concern but is simply a historical reminiscence. This is of basic significance to the degree that it introduces into the historical picture of the Baptist a feature which sharply differentiates his baptism from the washings and baptisms practised by the pious Judaism of the period. The "bath-house" which he used was the Jordan. When he issued his baptismal summons in the ἔρημος, only the Jordan was adequate to make baptism possible for the crowds who came.

b. In the We-narratives of Ac. we read in 16:13 that after their arrival in Philippi Paul and his companions went τῇ ἡμέρᾳ τῶν σαββάτων ... ἔξω τῆς πύλης παρὰ ποταμὸν οὗ ἐνομίζομεν προσευχὴν [55] εἶναι, sat down, and spoke to the women who had gathered there. Here ποταμός without article denotes a constant stream close to the town which emptied its waters into the Strymon. Close to this the travellers found, as expected, a place where those in the town who worshipped the one God were accustomed to meet for divine service. The situation of the place, probably a house, was determined by proximity to water, which would make possible the observance of the rules of purity that were so important esp. for women, → II, 808, 12 ff.

The question discussed in many earlier comm. whether the situation in proximity to a ποταμός corresponded to a definite Jewish practice [56] may now be answered in the negative, since there is no evidence of any such custom in Rabb. sources. [57] Furthermore well water was more correct and important for the observance of the required washings than river water, [58] and this might be expected in proximity to a ποταμός.

---

[52] Mt. 3:6 : ℵ D lat ; Mk. 1:6 : D Θ it.

[53] Cf. T. Klauser, "Taufet in lebendigem Wasser ! Zum religions- u. kulturgeschichtlichen Verständnis von Did., 7, 1-3," *Pisciculi, Festschr. f. F. J. Dölger* (1939), 157-164.

[54] Cf. Klauser, *op. cit.,* 158-161.

[55] Acc. to the best attested reading.

[56] Cf. Jackson-Lake, I, 4, 190 f.

[57] Cf. Str.-B., II, 742 and the most recent comm. on Ac.

[58] Cf. Miq., 1, 1. 6. 7.

Thus the recently excavated synagogue at Caesarea, which is just by the Sea of Galilee, has a room which was probably a bath-house. Finally, it should not be overlooked in this respect that acc. to tradition [59] the ritual bath supplants the Sabbath, i.e., it is permissible on the Sabbath.

c. According to 2 C. 11:26 Paul had ample experience of the way in which rivers could be dangerous, especially when swollen by the autumn and winter rains. The same fact lies behind the concluding parable in the Sermon on the Mount, Mt. 7:24-27; Lk. 6:47-49. At the beginning of the rainy season rivers are incalculable as well as dangerous. Luke especially with his ποταμός suggests that the house was newly built by the side of a river which overflowed its banks, whereas Mt. with his ποταμοί is not depicting the storms and torrential rains of autumn [60] but the total mass of water which in the rainy season pours down all the gullies and will sweep away a house which is not well built.

The fig. content of the double parable agrees with what the Rabb. have to say about the force of the ποταμοί of the country, → 599, 14 ff. Acc. to its purpose this is to be defined as an eschatological parable. [61] It is easy to understand as such. In this light there is no reason to seek or to conjecture behind the ποταμοί a ref. to Noah's flood [62] or to the flood of eschatological tribulation. [63] Anyone who has heard about or experienced a winter storm in Jerusalem, which changes every open street, path, terrace and stairway into a raging stream, [64] finds in the ποταμοί of the parable [65] a reminder of the sober actuality of the land and its climate, [66] esp. when it is also taken into account that there are winter springs and winter ποταμοί nourished by them.

2. ποταμός in the Apocalypse.

a. Twice in the visionary course of eschatological events as disclosed to the divine severe harm is done to ποταμοί and πηγαί τῶν ὑδάτων. After the opening of the seventh seal and with the sounding of the third trumpet one third [67] of the ὕδατα becomes wormwood [68] (8:10 f.), while in the vision of the vials the contents of the third vial turn the ὕδατα completely into blood, 16:4. In both visions the ποταμοί are ruined as one part of a human world which in biblical fashion is depicted as threefold, being divided into the earth (γῆ), the sea, and the water under the earth (8:7 ff.; 16:1 ff.). [69] For the seer, then, the form and

---

[59] For a summary cf. S. Ganzfried, Kizzur Schulchan Aruch (no date), c. 86, 3; 162, 7.
[60] So J. Jeremias, Die Gleichnisse Jesu⁴ (1956), 164. There is no instance of ποταμός being used in this way. On the meaning of ποταμός in this parable cf. also Pr.-Bauer⁴, s.v.
[61] Jeremias, op. cit., 164; cf. also Jülicher Gl. J., II, 266.
[62] Schn. Mt., ad loc.; Jeremias, loc. cit., also 41, n. 3; 142, n. 1.
[63] Jeremias, op. cit., 148.
[64] Cf. the descriptions in G. Dalman, Arbeit u. Sitte in Palästina, II, 1 (1928), 203-210.
[65] Ab., 3, 8 is not strictly a par. to Mt. 7:24 ff.; Lk. 6:47 ff. (cf. Bultmann Trad., 218 f.).
[66] Cf. on this Heracl. Hom. All., 38 (p. 55, 8-10): ὑφ' ὑετοῦ δαψιλοῦς γενομένου καὶ τῶν ἀπ' Ἴδης ποταμῶν πλημμυράντων συνέβη καταρριφῆναι. On the basis of Is. 57:20 1 QH 8:14 f. refers to "raging streams (נהרות שוטפים)" and describes them as "casting their mud at me." On winter springs cf. Dalman, op. cit., 204 f.
[67] This apocal. measure seems to be related to the "round" nature of the number three and is used popularly. Two Chr. funerary inscr. from Fēnān in the Eastern Negeb contain the concluding formula: καὶ ἀπέθανεν τὸ τρίτον τοῦ κόσμου, A. Alt, "Aus der 'Araba, III: Inschr. u. Felszeichnungen," ZDPV, 58 (1935), 67-72; also "Bemerkungen zu der neuesten Sammlung gr. Inschr. aus Palästina," ZDPV, 62 (1939), 162. Cf. also Rev. 9:15, 18; 12:4.
[68] On the name of the star cf. F. Boll, Aus der Offenbarung Johannis (1914), 41 f. The idea of an eschatological corrupting of water occurs also in 4 Esr. 5:9.
[69] → n. 24 and also Ps. 95:4 f.; 104; Prv. 8:27 ff., also Gn. 1:6 ff.; Phil. 2:10b.

constitution of creation, including man, cannot be separated from the existence and non-pollution of ποταμοί; without them life is not possible.

The question of the origin of the mythological material can be set aside except in so far as it has been touched on already, → n. 68. Nor need we concern ourselves with typological features taken from the story of the exodus. [70]

b. The two passages which refer to the Euphrates as ὁ ποταμὸς ὁ μέγας Εὐφράτης (9:14; 16:12) both adopt an OT designation (Gn. 15:18; Dt. 1:7; Jos. 1:4) and also take up the idea that this river is the eastern boundary of the divinely chosen land, → 599, 25 ff. This explains why the kings who oppose almighty God come from beyond the Euphrates to fight against Him, 16:12-14; cf. Ps. 2:2. This is also why the river's protective function is shown to be ended when God causes it to dry up. The point of the figurative expression is that God will withdraw His protection from men who think they are safe against the attack of hostile powers. The ineluctable consequence is that the divinely chosen land will become the theatre of the final battle. [71]

"Great Euphrates" also plays a role in the Mandaean writings, [72] but it is not a boundary here, nor is it regarded as that which separates the world of men from the world of spirits. [73] In view of its great size its drying up is for the Mandaeans, too, the figure of a gigantic disaster. [74] As regards its function as a frontier, one should not forget that it served as the eastern boundary of the empire in the Roman period. In both passages the expression and outlook suggest that the author or the tradition used by him belonged to Palestine. Difficulties arise in connection with the name Ἁρμαγεδών as the place of the final battle (Rev. 16:16), for thus far it is has not been possible to find any convincing site for this in Palestine. [75]

c. In Rev. 12:15 we read that the dragon poured forth ὕδωρ ὡς ποταμόν after the woman it drove out. For all its mythical roots [76] the concept remains within the sphere of an OT and Jewish fig. use of נָהָר/ ποταμός, which serves to emphasise existing and unlimited fulness. [77]

d. The river of the water of life (ποταμὸς ὕδατος ζωῆς) which according to Rev. 22:1 issues from the throne of God and of the Lamb and flows through the new Jerusalem (22:2), combines in some sense the primal river of Paradise (Gn. 2:10 ff.) and the eschatological temple river of Ezekiel (47:1 ff. → 596, 29 ff.). Here, too, there is undoubtedly combined with the term ποταμός the thought of fulness (→ line 28), of the fulness of the life which God will give His people. There is a reminiscence of the tree of life (v. 2; cf. Gn. 2:9) and of the fruits of this tree to which access was barred after the fall of the first man, Gn. 3:22, 24. The consummation of God's dealings with creation and man thus takes up and transcends what was given in Paradise, cf. Gn. 3:22 with 2:9, 17. Similarly, what Rev. has to say about the river of the water of life shows that the end will not

---

[70] On the question whether there is in 8:7 f. a ref. to the eruption of Vesuvius in 79 A.D. cf. Had. Apk., ad loc.

[71] Cf. Schl. Erl., ad loc.

[72] Lidz. Ginza, 61, 24 f.; 414, 7 etc.

[73] Loh. Apk., 135.

[74] Lidz. Ginza, 524, 35, and cf. as a special Jewish par. 4 Esr. 13:43 ff.

[75] → I, 468 (J. Jeremias).

[76] Cf. the comm., ad loc.

[77] → 597, 6 ff.

merely be a restoration of the beginning in Paradise but will be something new in which God consummates with unrestricted fulness the works and ways begun at creation.

It should not be overlooked that the river of the water of life is mentioned only here and in Jn. 7:38, → lines 28 ff. There are no exact par. in religious history. The material par. [78] available, including those in the Dead Sea Scrolls, speak of the source of life or the water of life, but not, like Rev. and Jn., of the river of the water of life. [79] Of no relevance here is the ref. in Od. Sol. 6 where the river carries away everything with it (→ n. 66) and hence has nothing to do with the river of life in Paradise, [80] vv. 8 ff. This river is obviously describing the triumphant progress of Christianity [81] or a (Christian) Gnosticism [82] which sweeps everything before it. If older motifs are adopted, these again are unrelated to the water of life. In the total context of Johannine theology one has thus to integrate the image of the river of the water of life into the Johannine concept of completely consummated fulness as this is most plainly expressed in what is said about perfect joy in the Gospel of John (3:29; 15:11; 16:24; 17:13) and the Epistles of John (1 Jn. 1:4; 2 Jn. 12). [83] In relation to Rev. 22:1 f. it should be noted, of course, that there is no mention of this fulness of joy, though eschatological joy is by no means alien to Rev. (19:7; cf. 21:3 f.), and the same is true of the concept of fulness (3:2; 6:11).

For the fact that the river of the water of life issues forth from the throne of God and of the Lamb there is a par. statement in the Ginza of the Mandaeans. [84] It should also be noted that in the sanctuaries of Aesculapius, who was for a time the most serious rival of Christianity, [85] the associated sacred spring used to flow forth from under the sanctuary, the throne, and the feet of the god. [86] A final religio-historical pt. to consider is that the river of the water of life in Rev. 22:1 does not divide like the river of Paradise ; for this reason alone it is not to be regarded as a repetition except in some sense at a higher level. Indeed, one has to take into account the possibility of ´ non-biblical influences on the metaphor.

3. The Saying of Jesus in Jn. 7:37 f. (→ III, 788, 27 ff.; 991, 10 ff.).

On the last day of the Feast of Tabernacles, with its particularly solemn dispensing of water, [87] Jesus, according to Jn. 7:37 f., cried with a loud voice : ἐάν τις διψᾷ, ἐρχέσθω πρός με καὶ πινέτω. ὁ πιστεύων εἰς ἐμέ, καθὼς εἶπεν ἡ γραφή, ποταμοὶ ἐκ τῆς κοιλίας αὐτοῦ ῥεύσουσιν ὕδατος ζῶντος. The Evangelist adds (v. 39) [88] that the reference of Jesus here was to the Spirit whom those who came to faith in Him should later receive. He does not give the reasons, however, for this interpretation, and the whole passage is difficult and almost impossible to expound.

---

[78] Cf. the comm., ad loc.

[79] Stressed by Loh. Apk., ad loc.

[80] As against Loh. Apk., ad loc.

[81] So H. Gunkel, Art. "Salomo-Oden," RGG², V, 88.

[82] So H. Gressmann in Hennecke, 441.

[83] → 297, 28 ff. (G. Delling).

[84] Lidz. Ginza, 281, 21 f. (Loh. Apk., ad loc.).

[85] F. J. Dölger, "Der Heiland," Ant. Christ., VI (1950), 241-272; K. H. Rengstorf, *Die Anfänge der Auseinandersetzung zwischen Christusglaube u. Asklepiosfrömmigkeit* (1953).

[86] For materials cf. Rengstorf, *op. cit.*, 41, n. 81.

[87] Cf. the comm., ad loc.

[88] So also Bultmann J., 229.

Even the division of the verse is not immediately clear. In addition to the traditional punctuation given in Nestle there is another [89] which relates ὁ πιστεύων εἰς ἐμέ to what precedes and which makes the break only before καθώς. This is found in the older fathers before Origen. It rests not merely on the rhythm of the saying but also on its avoidance of the grotesquely comic notion that streams of water will flow forth from the body of the one who drinks to quench his thirst. [90] On this view "he" is naturally the One who gives the water and the person who drinks merely receives it. Jesus Himself, of course, is the He. In v. 38, then, a statement of Jesus about Himself (cf. 6:35; 8:12) is simply embedded in a quotation from Scripture (→ lines 21 ff.; 607, 25 ff.), and materially the saying stands related to 4:10. On the other hand, the concept herewith rejected is not so unusual as might at first appear. Jochanan b. Zakkai, the contemporary of the apostle, said of one of his pupils that he was a spring which gushes forth with ever increasing strength. [91] There are higher forms of praise than this, esp. those which regard it as the chief task of the pupil to guard what has been transmitted to him by his teacher. [92] Yet this does not alter the fact that the image which modern scholars find grotesque [93] would not have made this impression on the contemporaries of Jesus. Arguments of this kind are thus without cogency. [94]

The question whether the saying is now placed at the right point is still unsettled. There is no need to pursue this topic here, however, since the logion will have to be regarded as an isolated one in any case.

The use of the formula ἡ γραφή raises difficulties of its own. One solution is that the whole of v. 38 is the addition of an ecclesiastical redactor. [95] Thus far it has not been possible to say what the (apocr.?) Scripture is (→ I, 753, n. 13; III, 991, 10 ff., 27 ff.). There is always the possibility that the expression is to be understood collectively. A more recent [96] proposal is that we are to think in terms of a kind of florilegium which seems to have been esp. important for the libation at Tabernacles, Is. 12:3; Ez. 47:1 ff.; Zech. 14:8. [97] But the use of ἡ γραφή (הַכָּתוּב) seems to be against this — at least until the contrary can be proved.

In view of all these difficulties, and also of the fact that the context does not in any case help us to any particular decision, it is perhaps best to refer to what has been said already about the word ποταμός in Jn. A survey shows that Jn. 7:37 f. is close to Rev. 22:1. Here the river of the water of life is associated with the Lamb as well as God. It is not said, however, that the Lamb is also in some sense the source of the river. The divine is more interested in the nature of the river than its source. It should not be forgotten that in Jn. 4:10, too, Jesus is not called the source of the water of life; He is the One who controls and dispenses this water. The same applies in Jn. 7:37 f.

---

[89] C. H. Dodd, *The Interpretation of the Fourth Gospel* (1953), 349; Bultmann J., 228; on the Roman Cath. side E. Schick, *Das Ev. nach Johannes, Echter-Bibel* (1956), 79. For the history of exposition of Jn. 7:37 f. cf. H. Rahner, "*Flumina de ventre Christi*. Die patristische Auslegung von Jn. 7:37 f.," *Biblica*, 22 (1941), 269-302, 367-403.

[90] Bultmann J., 228, n. 6.

[91] Ab., 2, 8.

[92] Cf. A. Schlatter, "Jochanan Ben Zakkai," BFTh, 3, 4 (1899), 16.

[93] For religio-historical par. cf. Bauer J., 113 f.

[94] On earlier attempts to remove the difficulty by conjectures cf. Bultmann J., *ad loc.* The effort of L. Koehler to master the difficulties and also to locate the hitherto unlocated γραφή of Jn. 7:38 by ref. to Is. 58:11 f. (*Kleine Lichter* [1945], 39-41) must be regarded as outdated, esp. now that it is not confirmed by the Is. text in the Dead Sea Scrolls.

[95] Bultmann J., 216 relates vv. 37-44 to v. 30.

[96] On older proposals cf. Bultmann J., 229, n. 2.

[97] Dodd, *op. cit.* (→ n. 89), 399, n. 2.

But first another point must be made. There is something to be said for the traditional punctuation. In particular one may refer to the ancient invitation with which the Feast of the Passover opens even up to our own times : "Every one who is hungry, let him come and be satisfied! every one who is in need, let him come and keep the Passover!" [98] This applies not least of all to the poor who have no Passover table of their own. It is hardly necessary to be specific here. The par. to Jn. 7:37 f. is obvious except that the believer has to be mentioned explicitly because faith is not self-evident.

The Evangelist's interpretation is also essential. It looks ahead to a time when Jesus Himself will no longer be there. It expresses certainty that His work will continue. The means by which this is to happen, or has already happened in the Evangelist's experience, is the Spirit. The Spirit makes possible the continuation of the work of Jesus. He continues it in and through the disciples. Naturally the mark of Jesus' work is fulness. This again does not come to an end. It remains in the Spirit and is present in His work after the "transfiguration" of Jesus. In the image of the ποταμός this means that Jesus equips His disciples in such a way that the forces and fulness of life remain unrestrictedly at work, since the streams of living water flow *via* them into the world and are available for the thirsty so long as they believe. Integrated and understood thus, the logion Jn. 7:37 f. is a disciples-logion which bears witness to the apostolic function of the disciples after Jesus' "transfiguration" and which uses for this purpose figurative material employed elsewhere to denote the eschatological function of Jesus Himself. If the faith of the disciples is a presupposition for the fulfilment of their representative ministry, this shows how clearly the Fourth Evangelist distinguished the apostles of Jesus from Jesus Himself for all the authority prescribed to them.

The question of the γραφή (→ 606, 25 ff.) must remain an open one. This is esp. true in attempts to explain Jn. 7:37 f. Hence there will always be to this extent a strong element of uncertainty in any attempt at interpretation.

† ποταμοφόρητος.

For a long time unattested outside the NT, this word [1] is now shown [2] by some pap. texts to have been familiar in Egypt, though so far only in passages dealing with damage done by the Nile and in the sense "washed away by the Nile" (P. Amh., II, 85, 16 [78 A.D.]): ἐὰν δέ τι ἄβροχος ἢ καὶ ποταμοφόρητος ἢ ὕφαμμος ἢ κατεξυσμένη παραγένηται ...; P. Tebt., II, 610 (2nd cent. A.D. frequently); P. Ryl., II, 378, 2; P. Oxy., XVI, 1911, 98 etc. The word is thus Egyptian and is closely related to the use of the word ποταμός for the Nile, → 596, 22 ff.

Though we do not find a corresponding word, that which it expresses occurs in many of the oldest Rabb. texts dealing with floods and their effects. Thus Orla, 1, 3 speaks of a tree which a river has carried away (אילן שטפו נהר). BQ, 10, 5 of part of a field which was similarly washed away (שדה שטפה נהר). The נָהָר mentioned here corresponds to the Gk. ποταμός, → 595, 26 ff. These and similar ref. occur in a legal context. If

---

[98] At the very beginning of the feast after the introductory benedictions and the saying explaining the mazza : כָּל דִּכְפִין יֵיתֵי וְיֵכָל. כָּל דִּצְרִיךְ יֵיתֵי וְיִפְסַח (cf. E. D. Goldschmidt, *Die Pessach-Haggada* [1937], 2).

π ο τ α μ ο φ ό ρ η τ ο ς. [1] On the formation *v.* Bl.-Debr. § 117, 2; L. R. Palmer, *A Grammar of the Post-Ptolemaic Pap.,* I, 1 (1946), 44.

[2] For the first ref. cf. A. Wikenhauser, "ποταμοφόρητος Apk. 12:15 ua," BZ, 6 (1908), 171, and "Ein weiterer Beleg f. ποταμοφόρητος Apk. 12:15," BZ, 7 (1909), 48.

expressions of this kind in the Mishnah were to be put into Gk., ποταμοφόρητος would be the right word. For the rest, the damage is usually permanent in both cases.

The only NT instance in Rev. 12:15 refers neither to the Nile nor to any other river nor indeed to damage with legal consequences. We read here that the dragon who drove out the woman sent forth after her ὕδωρ ὡς ποταμόν, ἵνα αὐτὴν ποταμοφόρητον ποιήσῃ. The meaning is simply that it was the dragon's purpose to bring her into a situation where she had lost control of her own destiny, like someone who is swept away by the fulness and overwhelming strength (→ 596, 3 ff.) of an onrushing river.

† 'Ιορδάνης.

Contents : 1. The name and Its Meaning : a. The Course of the River ; b. The Form of Its name ; c. The Meaning of the Name Jordan ; 2. Estimation of the Jordan in the OT and Later Judaism : a. The Geographical Position of the Jordan ; b. Evaluation of the Water of Jordan ; 3. The River God Jordan ; 4. The Jordan in the NT and Primitive Christianity ; a. General Review of the Usage ; b. John the Baptist and the Jordan ; c. Jesus and the Jordan ; d. Primitive Christianity and the Jordan ; e. The Water of Baptism and the Water of Jordan in the Early Church.

1. The Name and Its Meaning.

a. The Course of the River. From Hermon to the Dead Sea the Jordan flows through a portion of the Great Rift Valley which runs in a north-south direction from North Syria between Lebanon and Anti-Lebanon by way of the Sea of Galilee to the Dead Sea, the Araba, the Gulf of Akaba and the Red Sea to the great lakes of Africa. The sources of the river are on Mt. Hermon. It empties into the Dead Sea about 400 m. below the level of the Mediterranean. Even in the southern portion between the Sea of Galilee and the Dead Sea the Jordan is not navigable. [1] It contains fish up to the point where its waters begin to intermingle with those of the Dead Sea. [2]

'Ι ο ρ δ ά ν η ς. G. Beer, Art. "Jordanes," Pauly-W., 9 (1916), 1903-1907; A. Y. Braver in הָאֶנְצִיקְלוֹפֶּדִיָּה הָעִבְרִית 6 : אֶרֶץ יִשְׂרָאֵל (1957), 81-98; H. Conzelmann, Die geographischen Vorstellungen im Lk.-Ev., Diss. Tübingen (1951) = Conzelmann I ; also Die Mitte der Zeit (1954) = Conzelmann II ; G. Dalman, Orte u. Wege Jesu³ (1924), 90-107, 249-256; F. J. Dölger, "Der Durchzug durch den Jordan als Sinnbild d. chr. Taufe," Ant. Christ., II (1930), 70-79; O. Eissfeldt, Art. "Jordan," RGG², III, 372; N. Glueck, The River Jordan (1946); H. Guthe, Art. "Palästina," RE³, 14, 573-578; 24, 304 f.; T. Klauser, "Taufet in lebendigem Wasser !" Pisciculi, Festschr. ƒ. F. J. Dölger (1939), 157-164; S. Klein, Art. "Jordan," EJ, 9, 293-297; L. Koehler, "Lexikologisch-Geographisches. 1. Der Jordan," ZDPV, 62 (1939), 115-120; Lidz. Joh., II, p. XVIII-XX; Lidz. Liturg., Index, s.v.; Lidz. Ginza, Index, s.v.; H. Lietzmann, "Ein Beitrag zur Mandäerfrage," SAB (1930), 596-608; P. Lundberg, "La typologie baptismale dans l'ancienne église," Acta Seminarii Neotestamentici Upsaliensis, 10 (1942), 146-166; A. Neubauer, La géographie du Talmud (1868), 29-31; M. Noth, "Der Jordan in d. alten Geschichte Palästinas," ZDPV, 72 (1956), 123-148; S. Rappaport, Agada u. Exegese bei Flavius Josephus (1930); S. Reinach, "L'arc de Titus," REJ, 20 (1890), LXV-XCI; R. Reitzenstein, Die Vorgeschichte d. chr. Taufe (1929), and on this H. H. Schaeder, Gnomon, 5 (1929), 353-370; A. Schwarzenbach, Die geogr. Terminologie im Hbr. d. AT (1954), 64, 202; E. Schweizer, EGO EIMI ... (1939), 49 f., 54 f.; W. v. Soden, "Zur Herkunft des Flussnamens Jordan," ZAW, 57 (1939), 153 f.; O. Waser, "Vom Flussgott Jordan u. andern Personifikationen," Festg. A. Kaegi (1919), 191-217.

[1] The ships of Jordan mentioned in bJeb., 116b are only small craft like those on the Madaba chart.

[2] G. Dalman, Arbeit u. Sitte in Palästina, VI (1939), 343 with n. 2. So correctly Paus., V, 7, 5 and the Madaba chart. For fishing cf. T. Jeb., 14, 6.

b. The Form of Its Name. The Gk. name (Heb. יַרְדֵּן, in narrative texts with art., not in poetic texts like Ps. 42:6) is usually 'Ιορδάνης. [3] 'Ιόρδανος however, is also found (Jos. 4:9 A; Sib., 7, 67; Paus., V, 7, 4). Jos. almost always has 'Ιόρδανος in Ant., 1-9 (exceptions 1, 170; 4, 168, 176; 8, 36 as variant 'Ιαρδάνου), but always 'Ιορδάνης in 13-20 and Bell. (the Jordan does not occur in Ant., 2, 10-11. 16. 19). Philo, too, uses 'Ιορδάνης. While the use of the art. is not uniform in these two authors, ὁ 'Ιορδάνης is the regular name in the NT. [4]

c. The Meaning of the Name Jordan. Various explanations were offered in antiquity. Philo has the explanation : 'Ιορδάνης δὲ κατάβασις ἑρμηνεύεται (Leg. All., II, 89), thus linking the name with the Heb. יָרַד καταβαίνειν. [5] This derivation, which he probably adopted in view of his own deficiency in Heb., [6] helps Philo to see in the crossing of the Jordan by Jacob (Gn. 32:11) a type of the conquest of low spiritual periods by the patriarchs. Jos. seems to derive the name from Dan, for in his account of Abraham's journey to Dan to free Lot from imprisonment there (Gn. 14:14) he adds the note : ... περὶ Δάνον, οὕτως γὰρ ἡ ἑτέρα τοῦ 'Ιορδάνου προσαγορεύεται πηγή, Ant., 1, 177, and the only natural meaning of this is that the source called Dan gave its name to the whole of the river fed therefrom. It may be [7] that Jos. is here adopting an explanation which is also preserved in the Talmud (bBech., 55a) [8] and which acc. to those who pass on the tradition [9] is Palestinian in origin : לָמָּה נִקְרָא שְׁמוֹ יַרְדֵּן: שֶׁיּוֹרֵד מִדָּן "why is it called Jordan ? Because it comes down from Dan." This is connected with Philo's explanation but not identical, since Philo does not refer to Dan. The crown of such attempts at etymology [10] is in Jerome when in his work on the sites and names of Hebrew localities [11] he appends to his derivation of Jordan from Dan (here expressly described as viculus) that ior, the first syllable of the name, means river in Heb., so that the name Jordan is made up of the two Heb. words יְאוֹר and דָּן, and means the river of Dan. [12]

Any modern explanation [13] must bear in mind that Jordan is not a unique name. Hom. mentions a Jardanos in Crete (Od., 3, 292) and another in Elis (Il., 7, 135). There are other examples of the same or closely related names in Asia Minor, Europe and elsewhere. [14] Since the name of the Palestinian Jordan is attested already in the 13th cent. B.C. on Egypt. records of Ramses II in the form jrdn, i.e., much earlier than there were Iranians in Asia Minor, [15] the suggestion that the name derives from the Iranian and

---

[3] So also Strabo, 16, 2, 16. The o in the first syllable might come from the Aram. of the country (יורדנא) e.g., jShebi. 35c, 19).

[4] Bl.-Debr. § 261, 8.

[5] The influence of Philo may be seen in the Onomasticum Coislinianum (P. de Lagarde, Onomastica sacra² [1887], 169, 81): κατάβασις, κατακυλιστός in Onomastica Vaticana (Lagarde, 176, 45): κατάβασις αὐτῶν, cf. 183, 21 f. in the Glossae Colbertinae (Lagarde, 203, 98 f.): κατάβασις ἀλαζονείας and in Hier. Liber interpretationis hebraicorum nominum (Lagarde, 7, 20; 64, 27): descensio eorum.

[6] I. Heinemann, Philons gr. u. jüd. Bildung (1932), 524 f.

[7] Cf. Rappaport, 103.

[8] It was not used later, for neither Gn. r. on 14:14 nor Rashi in his comm. ad loc. quotes it. Cf. also Neubauer, 30.

[9] R. Chiyya bar Abba in the name of Jonathan (Sepphoris ; 1st half of the 3rd cent.).

[10] These still influence Euseb.: Δάν ... ἔνθεν καὶ ὁ 'Ιορδάνης ἔξεισιν, Onomastikon, 25 (ed. E. Klostermann, CGS, 11, 1 [1904], 76, 6 ff.).

[11] De situ et nominibus locorum hebraicorum (Lagarde, op. cit. [n. 5], 117-190).

[12] Ibid., 114, 26 ff.: Dan viculus ..., de quo et Jordanis flumen erumpens a loco sortitus est nomen. ior quippe ῥεῖθρον (id est fluvium sive rivum) Hebraei vocant.

[13] Cf. the survey in Koehler, 116-118; Schwarzenbach, 202.

[14] For instances cf. J. R. Harris, "Crete, the Jordan, and the Rhône," Exp. T., 21 (1909/10), 303-306 Koehler, 118 f. From the 16th cent. the name jerdaň = Rhone is also found in White Russia, M. Vasmer, Russisches etym. Wörterbuch, I (1953), 401.

[15] Cf. v. Soden, 154.

means "the river which flows all the year" [16] is no longer tenable. [17] In the present state of scholarship the most one can say is that the name Jordan is probably a designation from the ancient Mediterranean period [18] which lingers on and which then becomes an appellative, as the regular Heb. use with the art. shows, → 609, 1 f. The rest — even though it be only a general definition like "the river" — is mere conjecture. This is the more true of the Palestinian Jordan in that it never came to be regarded as *the* river of the country. [19]

2. Estimation of the Jordan in the OT and Later Judaism.

a. The Geographical Position of the Jordan.

In Nu. 34:10 ff. the Jordan is fixed as the eastern frontier of the territory of Israel even though the tribes of Reuben and Gad and the half-tribe of Manasseh were located in the southern part of East Jordan, cf. also Jos. 13:15 ff. Historically, [20] this reflects the division of the land at the conquest acc. to the actual position in the days of the monarchy, though perhaps the presentation received its definitive form only after the destruction of Jerusalem. Certainly in the ancient narrative in Jos. 3 ff. the conquest by these tribes from the desert begins only with the crossing of the Jordan and the taking of Jericho. This account shows vividly that Jordan had the character of a natural boundary. [21] In this respect there has been remarkably little change even up to our own day. [22] This applies to the role of the Jordan at the beginning of our era. In the Gospels the territory of the rulers in Jerusalem ended at the Jordan. [23] The testimony of Joseph. is to the same effect. [24] The customs post at Jericho enhanced the significance of the river as a boundary [25] at this time. [26] Furthermore, there were on the banks no places which might have served as a natural bridge between West and East. This is also true right up to our own day.

Alongside the purely geographical and political evaluation of the Jordan [27] there is another which is controlled by the concept of the land of Israel as depicted in the divine promise to the patriarch Abraham. [28] Here in the framework of a theological eschatological view the Jordan is part of the land and not its frontier. The eastern frontier is the Euphrates [29] and the river of Egypt borders it to the South. [30] As one would expect, this way of looking at things is found esp. in scribal circles and comes to expression in religio-legal judgments, esp. those which group the territory on the far side of Jordan with Judaea and Galilee.

---

[16] Koehler, 120.

[17] v. Soden, 154.

[18] *Loc. cit.;* J. Hempel, "Westliche Kultureinflüsse auf das älteste Palästina," PJB, 23 (1927), 64 considers the possibility of a loan word from ancient Asia Minor.

[19] Koehler, 117.

[20] Cf. M. Noth, *Geschichte Israels*[3] (1956), 54-82, also the works of A. Alt quoted by him.

[21] To cross without friction was possible only as a miracle.

[22] Cf. the fact that the Jordan still divides more than unites, Dalman, 93-95; Glueck, 61-82; Noth, 126 f.

[23] This is a main reason why John the Baptist began his work east of Jordan.

[24] Cf. Bell., 4, 455 ff.

[25] So, e.g., bNed., 22a/b.

[26] Cf. Lk. 19:1 f. This Zacchaeus, a Jew (19:9), was probably in charge of Roman customs in Jericho, cf. Schürer, I, 474-479; Str.-B., II, 249.

[27] Cf. also Ep. Ar., 116 and Hier. De situ et nominibus locorum hebraicorum (Lagarde, *op. cit.* [→ n. 5], 131, 25): *Iordanis fluvius dividens Iudaeum, Arabiam et Aulonem ...*

[28] Cf. esp. Gn. 15:18, but also Ex. 23:31; Dt. 1:7; 11:24; Jos. 1:4; Is. 27:12; Mi. 7:12; Zech. 9:10; Ps. 72:8.

[29] → ποταμός 599, 24 ff.

[30] → ποταμός 597, 1 ff.

Nevertheless, caution is needed in respect of some Haggadic material. Thus it is told of the Palestinian Amoraean R. Zeïra (first decade of the 4th cent. in Tiberias) [31] that when, as a native Babylonian, he came to the Jordan on a journey to Israel his adopted country, finding no ferry there, he crossed the river in his clothes. This is taken to mean that he wanted to honour Jordan as part of Israel. [32] It is more correct, however, to conclude with the version of the anecdote in bTalmud [33] that he could not and would not curb his impatience to lay foot on the land. Could he know, if he did not hurry, that there would really be granted to him what was withheld from Moses and Aaron, namely, to enter the land of promise? [34] What we have here is thus joy at reaching the goal and leaving the border behind. There are other stories which express this joy in different but par. ways. [35]

The Jordan, for its part, is a unique river. It is sometimes said of it [36] that its waters do not intermingle with those of the Sea of Tiberias through which it flows. It borders but does not separate. What lies beyond Jordan is not a part of the land of Israel. But it is possible in many statements to group this territory with Galilee and Judah in such a way that there do not have to be any clear-cut distinctions. [37]

b. Evaluation of the Water of Jordan.

In the OT the water of Jordan cures Naaman, the Syrian general, of his leprosy. Following the instructions of Elisha the prophet he dips 7 times in the Jordan and is made whole, 2 K. 5. In an appendix to the story we are then told that the sons of the prophets in Gilgal set out to build houses for themselves by the Jordan and asked Elisha to accompany them ; when he did, Elisha worked another miracle, 2 K. 6:1 ff. In neither story is there any high regard for the water of Jordan as such. Elisha is the focus of interest, not the Jordan. The Jordan is mentioned because it played a role in the life of Elisha, not for its own sake. Neither here nor elsewhere is there even a hint of any peculiar dignity being ascribed to the water of Jordan. With the other Elisha stories the two narratives constitute a self-contained complex. [38] There is no par. to them in the rest of the OT. Jewish tradition says that the Euphrates rather than the Jordan protects against leprosy, → ποταμός, 599, 32 ff. [39]

Later Judaism, like the OT. ascribes no peculiar dignity to the water of Jordan. It has no developed Jordan myth. Vit. Ad., 6 ff. tells how Adam, after being expelled from Paradise, resolved to spend 40 days standing and fasting in the Jordan in order to do penance for the fall and perhaps to bring it about that God would be merciful and open Paradise again, and that he directed Eve to mortify herself in the same way for 37 days in the Tigris ; he himself carried out his resolve but Eve was seduced by Satan into breaking off her penance before the time, and she thereby rendered the penance of Adam valueless. In this form the story is probably the Chr. redaction of a Jewish original. [40],[41]

---

31 jShebi., 35c, 19.
32 Dalman, 94.
33 bKet., 112a.
34 Cf. also Bacher Pal. Am., III, 6.
35 Similarly a teacher returning from Babylon, when he arrived in the land, rolled in the dust on the basis of Ps. 102:14, bKet., 112b. Another, R. Jose bChanina, kissed at Akko the bank which was then regarded as the frontier and said : The land of Israel extends to this point, jShebi., 4, 8 (35c, 17 f.); cf. also bKet., 112a and the discussion in bBech., 55a.
36 Gn. r., 4, 5 on 1:6. The idea is obviously present already in Jos. Bell., 3, 509 : (ἡ λίμνη Γεννησάρ . . .) μέση ὑπὸ τοῦ 'Ιορδάνου τέμνεται.
37 Shebi., 9, 2 f.; Ket., 13, 10; T. Sanh., 2, 3 etc.
38 On the Elisha cycle cf. H. Gunkel, Meisterwerke hbr. Erzählungskunst, I, Elisa (1922).
39 On Elisha in the Haggada cf. H. Guttmann, Art. "Elischa," EJ, 6, 526-528; M. J. bin Gorion, Die Sagen der Juden, V (1927), 233-243.
40 Cf. the stone on which Adam and Eve place themselves so as not to touch the river-bed, cf. bShab., 65a and → 600, 8 ff.
41 O. Eissfeldt, Einleitung in d. AT² (1956), 786 f.

The more noteworthy it is, then, that although the Haggada speaks of a fast of Adam (probably even originally for 40 days) [42] in which he stood up to his neck in water, it does not say that he stood in the Jordan but in the upper Gihon. [43, 44] The substitution of the Jordan for this in the version of the story in Vit. Ad. is thus in all probability the work of a Chr. redactor and is not original.

In the Dead Sea Scrolls thus for published there is nothing to suggest any special relation to the Jordan. In Cave I fragments of a work called the Dires de Moïse were found and this twice refers to the crossing of the Jordan before entering the promised land, 1 Q 22 : I, 10; II, 2. But this is all. In the Damascus Document, so far as we have it, there is no mention of the Jordan.

The Rabbis assessed the water of Jordan carefully and critically in relation to their views and doctrines of the clean and unclean. They roundly denied the suitability of this water for some cultic acts. Nor can one speak of any special connection of the Jordan with the rites of purification and baptism in later Judaism.

From Bek., 55a one may infer that there was even discussion among the Rabbis as to what was the Jordan in the true sense. In T. Bek., 7, 4 it seems to be generally recognised that only from Jericho on [45] was the river regarded halachically as the Jordan, [46] namely, as a frontier which divides. [47] This has, of course, nothing to do with the dignity of the water ; it shows, however, that the Rabb. experienced no difficulties in this respect when they had to make decisions respecting the Jordan.

The Mishnah (Para, 8, 10) mentions the Jordan among rivers whose waters are unsuitable for cleansing when there is defilement with the dead (מֵי חַטָּאת; Nu. 19). The reason is that its water is mixed ; it is a mixture of suitable and unsuitable water. This is the more surprising in that the water of the source of the Jordan at Paneas is explicitly called suitable, Parah, 8, 11; cf. Miq., 1, 8. As concerns the cultic use of its water, then, the Jordan has to be examined by the Rabb. like any other river or water. Water which cannot be used for cleansing is also unsuitable for the washing of the leper (after healing) or of the man defiled by a discharge, Miq., 1, 8. It may be used, however, for normal washings, → ποταμός 600, 1 ff.; for these, then, the Jordan is theoretically possible. [48] Theoretically proselyte baptism may thus be given in the Jordan. In fact, however, there is no record of such baptism in rivers or specifically in the Jordan. In so far as accounts are available, there is only one example of the ritual bath of a teacher in the Jordan, → ποταμός 600, 8 ff. Such baths in the Jordan seem to have been an exception, then, and they would be taken only on special occasions or for special reasons. It should not be overlooked that south of its outlet from the Sea of Galilee the river is hard of access and also that the road from Jerusalem to Jericho was dangerous, Lk. 10:30.

---

[42] L. Ginzberg, "Die Haggada bei den Kirchenvätern u. in d. apokryphen Lit.," MGWJ, 43 (1899), 217 f.

[43] The ref. is certainly not to the river of Paradise (Gn. 2:13), esp. as this was identified with the Nile (Gn. r., 16, 3, ad loc.), but to the spring of Shiloah on the east slope of the temple hill (cf. 2 Ch. 32:30 [bPes., 56a, Bar.]), whence derives the Heb. expression גִּיחוֹן הָעֶלְיוֹן.

[44] PRE1, 20.

[45] S. Klein, Art. "Beth Jareach bzw. Beth Jerach," EJ, 4, 405, would read בית ירח for בית יריחו in T. Bek., 7, 4 and refer it to the ancient place of this name at the outlet of the Jordan from the Sea of Galilee (now excavated), esp. as the old name was never completely lost.

[46] Text T. Bek., 7, 4 : אֵיזֶהוּ יַרְדֵּן מִבֵּית יְרִיחוֹ וּלְמַטָּה.

[47] The question is raised in Bek., 9, 2 whether a herd of ten head which pastures half on the east and half on the west of the river is all subject to the tithe. It would not be if the Jordan "separated."

[48] Esp. stressed by I. Abrahams, Studies in Pharisaism and the Gospels, I (1917), 33.

At any rate, neither before nor after the destruction of the temple did the Jordan play for certain any notable part in the ritual washings of Judaism.

3. The River God Jordan. [49]

In the triumph of Titus depicted on the architrave of the Titus arch facing the Colosseum three Romans bear the Jordan on a bier in the form of an old man who, sitting to the left, supports himself on an urn. The depiction corresponds fully to the way in which elsewhere rivers as the personifications of conquered provinces were represented in the procession of the victor. Thus far it is also the only known instance of a depiction of the Jordan as a river god on ancient monuments. [50] On coins, too, there are no examples of the Jordan being represented thus. [51] Judaism was either unacquainted with this myth, or, more likely, ignored it.

There are isolated ref. in the Rabb. writings which can be understood only as deliberate rejection of water deities, Chul., 2, 8 f.; T. Chul., 2, 19; bChul., 40a-41a; → ποταμός 598, 26 ff. The name Jordan is never mentioned in this connection. This may be an accident, esp. as the depiction of the river on the Titus arch, which naturally suggests a comparison with the Rhine, the Rhone and the Nile, [52] is an unusual exaggeration. But it may be intentional. Do we have here one of the reasons why the Rabbinate showed such unmistakable restraint in relation to the Jordan (→ 612, 11 ff.)?

On the other hand, the personification of the Jordan as found on the arch of Titus was adopted by the Church. It was adopted thus in three connections, first in relation to the baptism of Jesus, secondly in relation to the rapture of Elijah, and finally in relation to the story of Joshua. The dominant role is played by the baptism of Jesus. This applies both to its artistic depiction [53] and also to the legendary embellishment of the Gospel story of the baptism which Jesus received from John the Baptist. [54]

The number of pictures of baptism in which the Jordan is a person is considerable. [55] The oldest seems to be the mosaic on the cupola of San Giovanni in Fonte at Ravenna (c. 450). [56] Close to it in Ravenna there is another in Santa Maria in Cosmedin (before 526). [57] It is not without interest that the older mosaic is in the baptistery of the orthodox, the later in that of the Arians. Obviously, then, the motif was generally known and loved. On these depictions, of course, the Jordan is not a god but simply a personification of the river of baptism designed to express in some way participation in the baptism of Jesus. [58] There is no historical link with the depiction on the arch of Titus. Again, one can only conjecture why the motif became popular. Perhaps it seemed to offer the possibility of bringing out the fact that the water of baptism is the water of Jordan, or takes its place. The fact that the motif appears first in baptisteries seems to point in this direction, → 623, 17 ff.

---

[49] On what follows cf. Reinach and Waser.
[50] Waser, 192.
[51] *Loc. cit.*
[52] Reinach, LXXX.
[53] Waser, 193-209.
[54] Cf. A. Jacoby, *Ein bisher unbeachteter apokrypher Bericht über die Taufe Jesu* (1902), and the texts assembled there.
[55] The iconography in Waser, 193-209 contains 50 examples.
[56] Cf. O. Waser, "Altchristliches," ARW, 17 (1914), 661 and n. 1.
[57] Cf. J. Kurth, *Die Wandmosaiken von Ravenna*² (1912), 73 f., 195 f.
[58] For details. which need not be pursued here, cf. Waser, 193-210.

4. The Jordan in the NT and Primitive Christianity.

a. General Review of the Usage.

Ἰορδάνης occurs 15 times in the NT (always with art. → 609, 6 f.). These instances are all in the Gospels. 6 are in Mt., 4 in Mk., 2 in Lk. and 3 in Jn. They occur in sayings about the location of the work of the Baptist, which is sometimes called ἡ περίχωρος τοῦ Ἰορδάνου (Mt. 3:5; Lk. 3:3) and sometimes simply πέραν τοῦ Ἰορδάνου (Jn. 1:28; 3:26; 10:40), or about the place where he baptised (Mt. 3:6; Mk. 1:5) and where Jesus received baptism (Mt. 3:13; Mk. 1:9; Lk. 4:1), or about the work of Jesus πέραν τοῦ Ἰορδάνου (Mt. 19:1; Mk. 10:1; Mt. 4:15, a proof from Scripture), or finally about the fact that many from the territory πέραν τοῦ Ἰορδάνου came to Jesus (Mt. 4:25/Mk. 3:8).

There are only two ref. in extant remnants of the apocryph. Gospels. The one is in Ev. Eb., 1 (Epiph. Haer., 30, 13; cf. 14) in the story of the baptism of John in a form which associates this use with that in the Synoptics. On the other hand P. Egerton 2 (*Unknown Gospel*), 65-67 contains the fragment of a hardly decipherable and otherwise unknown account of a miracle of Jesus (reminiscent of magic ?) [επι του] χειλους του Ιο[ρδα]νου, possibly with the intention of demonstrating His omnipotence. [59] Only by way of appendix to these two passages may one refer to the Ps.-Matthaei Ev. [60] with its two legends, the one (c. 35) about Jesus as a boy eight years old going down from Jerusalem to Jericho and near the river meeting lions who terrorised other travellers, the other (c. 36) about the river parting before the boy when He wants to go across with the lions. [61]

It should be remembered, however, that the post-apost. fathers do not mention the Jordan at all. In this respect they follow the example of the NT writings apart from the Gospels. Only with the Apologists does the Jordan begin to appear again, though only in Just., → 619, 29 ff.

Instructive in this respect is not merely what we learn about the word in the earliest Christian writings but also the obvious and characteristic restraint in usage. Naturally it may be an accident that neither Ac. (10:37; 13:24; 18:25; 19:3 f.) nor Ignatius (Sm., 1, 1) mentions the Jordan in connection with John's baptising or the baptism of Jesus. But the reason may be that the works have no basic interest in the Jordan.

b. John the Baptist and the Jordan.

In the light of the common OT and later Jewish attitude to the Jordan, baptism in the Jordan can be regarded only as the direct and personal work of John the Baptist. To be sure, the emphatic view has been espoused that the Jordan, "if it was not wholly kosher for the Rabbis, was probably ... venerated and used cultically in circles outside orthodox Judaism." [62] But this thesis rests on a *petitio principii*. Thus far no convincing evidence has been found to support it. Nor is such evidence to be expected in view of the inaccessibility and inhospitability of the Jordan valley. It must be accepted, then, that the popular movement initiated

---

[59] Cf. G. Mayeda, *Das Leben-Jesu-Fragment Pap. Egerton 2 u. seine Stellung in d. urchr. Literaturgeschichte* (1946), esp. 51-57.

[60] Evangelia apocrypha, ed. C. de Tischendorf² (1876), 54-57.

[61] Here a typical Elisha miracle (2 K. 2:8, 14) which proves the prophet to be such (cf. Jos. Ant., 20, 97: Theudas) is transferred to the boy Jesus.

[62] M. Lidzbarski, "Mandäische Fragen," ZNW, 26 (1927), 70-75, esp. 72. H. Sahlin, "Studien zum dritten Kapitel des Lk.-Ev.," *Uppsala Universitets Årsskrift*, 1949 : 2 (1949), 12 f. thinks the connection of the Jordan with the Baptist is secondary and attributes it to "the great significance of the Jordan in religious history."

by the Baptist probably had at least one of its roots in the novel practice of baptising in the Jordan. If John was predominantly regarded as the Baptist by his contemporaries, this is because Josephus (Ant., 18, 116) as well as the Synoptists (→ I, 545, 36 ff.) presented him to his readers under what was obviously a popular title (→ I, 546, 1 ff.), ὁ βαπτιστής.

In so far as the Gospel accounts make possible at all any geographical reconstruction of the Baptist's ministry, the data are so imprecise as to leave the picture very general if not totally obscure. An analysis of the individual statements does at least enable us to affirm that the Baptist often shifted his location in the course of his ministry, working sometimes to the east of the Jordan and sometimes to the west. In all parts of the tradition the Jordan is at any rate the centre of the Baptist's work. As concerns the practice of baptising in the Jordan, both Luke and especially John manifest an unmistakable reserve about this which is obviously less for historical reasons than for reasons of principle.

In Mt. the Baptist appears with his message in the ἔρημος τῆς 'Ιουδαίας (3:1), while his baptism takes place ἐν τῷ 'Ιορδάνῃ ποταμῷ (3:6). Mk. says the same when on the basis of Is. 40:3 he refers very generally only to the ἔρημος (1:4 f.). Lk. sets the call of John in the ἔρημος but then has him come εἰς πᾶσαν τὴν περίχωρον τοῦ 'Ιορδάνου with his summons to repentance and his baptism, 3:2 f. In connection with this he does not say expressly that the Jordan was either generally or predominantly the place where he administered baptism. Jn. on three occasions (1:28; 3:26; 10:40) uses πέραν τοῦ 'Ιουδάνου for the area where John baptised. This corresponds to the OT עֵבֶר הַיַּרְדֵּן, and like it signifies East Jordan, esp. the southern part. In 1:28 and 3:23 Jn. also mentions two places which it is no longer possible to locate, [63] though acc. to the Evangelist the first must be on the far side of the Jordan (1:28) and the other on the west bank (3:26).

Hence only Mt. and Mk. tell us precisely that John's baptism was administered in the Jordan. Nevertheless, this seems to be presupposed, if not mentioned, in Lk., for acc. to the source which he used Jesus returned from the Jordan after His baptism, Lk. 4:1; on Ac. → 618, 23 ff. Jn., on the other hand, does not make even an indirect ref. Indeed, not only does he not mention the Jordan but in relation to the second site he stresses the fact that ὕδατα πολλὰ ἦν ἐκεῖ, 3:23. If one may infer that the ref. is to the springs and brooks of ed-dēr, [64] Jn. mentions expressly only one place of baptism, and this is not the Jordan. If one asks why, it should be noted that Jn. is not polemicising against the Jordan. As compared with Mt. and Mk., and also to some extent Lk., he is simply shifting the emphasis from the baptising of John the Baptist in the Jordan to his baptising as such. In the first instance, however, historical reasons can hardly have caused him to do this. With his ref. to the actual places Jn. is making as specific as possible what is generally described in Lk. as πᾶσα ἡ περίχωρος τοῦ 'Ιορδάνου, 3:3. Certainly there can be no question of any contradiction between Jn. on the one side and Mt. and Mk. on the other [65] if the latter (esp. Mk. 1:1) have in view only the beginning of the Baptist's work whereas Lk. and Jn. consider it in its total compass. [66] In the light of such considerations caution is recommended in relation to attempts to explain Jn. 3:23

---

[63] On 1:28 cf. Dalman, 95-99; Bultmann J., 64, n. 5; on 3:23 Dalman, 250 f.; Bultmann J., 124, n. 5.

[64] G. Dalman, "Jahresbericht des Instituts," PJB, 8 (1913), 34 f. Cf. on this question C. K. Barrett, The Gospel acc. to St. John (1955), ad loc.

[65] Cf. also J. Schniewind, Die Parallelperikopen bei Lk. u. Joh. (1914), 11.

[66] Lk. ends his account of the Baptist before narrating the baptism of Jesus (3:19 f.); Jn. has only a brief ref. (3:24) and has no more about the death of John than does Lk., who takes it for granted later (9:9 ff.).

in terms of Church development. [67] It is more advisable to accept the insight that in speaking of ὕδωρ rather than the Jordan Jn. is simply following a line already laid down by the Baptist himself in the saying with which he explains his baptism. This saying, recorded in all the Gospels, shows that baptism with water rather than baptism in the Jordan is the true mark of the Baptist, Mt. 3:11; Mk. 1:8; Lk. 3:16; Jn. 1:26. The emphatic statement regarding the Baptist that he baptises with water pts. in the same direction, Jn. 1:31, 33. [68] In Jn. the obvious interest with respect to the nature of John's baptism is in water, not in the Jordan, though he has no thought of excluding the Jordan from John's ministry and of thus correcting the historical picture. This means, however, that if the approach is not accidental — and it cannot be this — then its only possible basis is in principle. That this is actually so may be seen already to some degree from the accounts which the Gospels give of Jesus' own relation to the Jordan.

c. Jesus and the Jordan.

Mt. (3:13), Mk. (1:9) and Lk. (4:1) all agree that Jesus was among those baptised by John the Baptist in the Jordan. There is no good reason why doubt should be cast on the correctness of this record or on the connection with the Jordan. Jn. indeed shows (1:29 ff.) that it was possible to speak quite intelligibly of the baptism of Jesus without express mention of the Jordan. [69] One may assume, then, that when Jesus was baptised He received baptism in the Jordan as the older Evangelists record or presuppose.

The Lucan account has two peculiar features as compared with Mt. and Mk. On the one side Lk. very emphatically integrates Jesus' baptism into the movement initiated by the Baptist; on the other he stresses Jesus' own share in the act by a ref. to His praying, which expresses His obedient waiting for the call from above to take up His ministry, 3:21 f. Both features are closely related to the picture of Christ in the 3rd Gospel. [70] The Johannine account (1:32 f.) obviously presupposes the Synoptic record, and there also seems to be a special connection with Lk. 3:2. Here again Jesus stands at the heart of the baptismal movement (1:26), and here again the event cannot be separated from the mission and call of Jesus (1:29). The way in which these features are emphasised is rooted again in the kerygmatic concern of the Evangelist. If the two accounts are set side by side, it is plain that in both the whole focus is on the person of Jesus and that what takes place in His baptism is wholly subordinated to Him. [71] In particular, neither account is interested in the place of baptism, the Jordan.

In view of the fact that Jesus was baptised by John in the Jordan, extra attention should be paid to the fact that this river plays no further part in His life or work as depicted by the tradition. No saying of Jesus referring to the Jordan has been

---

[67] K. Kundsin, *Topologische Überlieferungsstoffe im Joh.-Ev.* (1925), 26: "Aenon near Salim is to be regarded as a centre if not *the* centre of the baptismal movement in Palestine in the time of the Evangelist ..."; Bultmann J., 124, n. 5 is rightly less dogmatic at this pt.

[68] Bultmann J., 63, n. 1 regards the words ἐγὼ βαπτίζω ἐν ὕδατι (1:26) and ἐν (τῷ) ὕδατι of 1:31, 33 as additions of the redactor for the purpose of assimilation to the Synoptic tradition. Yet the attitude of the Evangelist to the Jordan suggests that he himself penned the words.

[69] The question whether the Synoptic account of the baptism of Jesus was once an independent part of the tradition (K. L. Schmidt, *Der Rahmen d. Geschichte Jesu* [1919], 29) is hardly at issue here. On the question of the historicity of Jesus' baptism cf. Bultmann Trad., 263.

[70] One can hardly say that the Lucan account gives evidence of the author's embarrassment in relation to the tradition about the baptism of Jesus (Schmidt, *op. cit.,* 30).

[71] From the very beginning the account of the baptism of Jesus was obviously passed on as testimony to the divine authorisation of His Messianic office. The unanimity of the tradition on the pt. supports this.

preserved. It is occasionally mentioned in the narratives, but never in such a way that some special significance of the river stands in the background. Indeed, there are some passages in which one might reasonably expect the Jordan to be mentioned but it is not.

Mt. (4:25) and Mk. (3:8), when speaking of the multitudes who came to Jesus, refer to the region πέραν τοῦ 'Ιορδάνου as the home of these people who thronged to Him. Later (Mt. 19:1; Mk. 10:1) they both tell us that Jesus came and worked in this region on His way to Jerusalem (Mt. ἐθεράπευσεν, Mk. ἐδίδασκεν). But this is all they have to say about the connection of Jesus with the Jordan.

Only at a first glance does the situation seem to be different in Jn. In the Fourth Gospel Jesus Himself after His baptism does His first work in the region of Jordan, and indeed in such a way that an impression of rivalry is left among the adherents of the Baptist, 3:22 ff. There is a ref. later to another period spent in East Jordan, 10:40. Much in these accounts is historically and geographically obscure, [72] but one may certainly gather from them that the Jordan as such played no significant role in the life and work of Jesus after His baptism. Nowhere does Jesus Himself seem to be personally linked to the river; nowhere is there any indissoluble connection with it. Not even in passages in which the Fourth Gospel speaks of Jesus' own ministry of baptism, or that of His disciples (3:22 ff.; 4:1 f.), does the ref. take such a form as to leave the reader with the impression that Jesus was in any way personally linked to the Jordan. What may be inferred from this Gospel regarding the relation between the Baptist and the Jordan is duplicated in the case of Jesus' relation to the Jordan. If one may speak of a relation at all, it is not one of principle but a purely practical relation which arises only because water is needed for baptism. In particular, there is in the relation of Jesus to the Jordan here no suggestion that Jesus might have ascribed a special dignity to its water and thus taken up a corresponding attitude to it.

The picture is the same in Lk. too. Indeed, the situation is esp. clear in his Gospel. One may refer in particular to the Zacchaeus incident in 19:1 ff., for Jesus does not Himself baptise this penitent customs-farmer of Jericho (→ n. 26) in the nearby Jordan, nor does He instruct him to take a bath of purification in it. [73] The Jordan is not even mentioned at any pt. in the passage. Nor does it occur anywhere in the Lucan journey, 9:51-19:27. This is certainly not because the Jordan, like the mountain, lake, plain or desert, was "in a way peculiar to Luke" merely a " 'typical' locality," [74] which as such enabled him to make a clear distinction between the Baptist's sphere of activity and that of Jesus, [75] so that they could be mentioned alongside one another without fear of confusion. If in Lk. the Jordan were not actually [76] mentioned in connection with the ministry of Jesus because this river, with other geographical concepts, had for the author only the significance of a principle of arrangement within a conception in terms of salvation history, [77] then one would expect Lk. to introduce it quite unambiguously under ποταμός as a geographical type. In so doing he might have followed the use in Mk. 1:5 (cf. Mt. 3:6) and not just gone back to contemporary usage. But he did not do this. In both instances in which the Jordan is mentioned (3:3; 4:1) Lk. does not call it ποταμός. On the other hand, there is in the Gospel no solid evidence that Jesus avoided the Jordan as the river of the Baptist. [78] If, however, the absence of any close relation between Jesus and the Jordan in Lk. is due neither to the Jordan's "typical" nature as

---

[72] On detailed questions, including that of Jesus' own baptismal work, cf. the comm.

[73] This does not mean that Lk. did not realise how near Jericho is to the Jordan, so Conzelmann II, 11.

[74] Conzelmann II, 58.

[75] Conzelmann, I, 49; II, 11, cf. 18.

[76] Rightly noted in Conzelmann II, 11 etc.

[77] Conzelmann II, passim, esp. 10-12.

[78] Conzelmann I, 49; Conzelmann II, 11.

a river nor to its association with the Baptist, if, then, it is not due to any historical circumstance, the only remaining possibility is that it is a matter of principle. Unfortunately Lk. himself does not tell us what the reason is any more than Jn. does. In Lk., however, it is at least clear that the reason cannot be stated, for there is no sign of it whatever. [79]

This review of the material confirms our earlier conjecture that the reserve of the NT in respect of the Jordan is obviously a matter of principle. But it is also enables us to arrive at a broader conclusion, namely, that this reserve in respect of the Jordan characterises the whole of the Gospel tradition and is closely related to the person of Jesus. This suggests that the principle at issue derives from a specific understanding of what is "Christian." Whether this thesis is possible or correct, however, can be proved only by a survey of the relationship of primitive Christianity to the Jordan in so far as the sources allow of such an investigation.

d. Primitive Christianity and the Jordan.

Naturally primitive Chr. convictions underlie the passages discussed → 616, 14 ff. But Chr. practice must also be taken into account. We must ask how this relates to the principial reserve in respect of the Jordan in order to find out what is the ultimate reason for this. Since the Jordan is the classical place of the baptism of repentance both in the tradition concerning the Baptist and also in the picture of Jesus in the Gospels, the question posed thereby lays upon us the task of considering primitive Chr. baptismal practice in relation to the Jordan.

Acts gives evidence of no relations at all between primitive baptismal practice and the Jordan. This is true quite irrespective of the question as to the extent of baptism in the very earliest community. That Christian baptism was very early, and took place even in the first community, can hardly be contested. [80] If one or another account may raise general or detailed questions, [81] the Jordan is certainly never mentioned. This is notably true even where it is difficult to say where the baptisms took place.

The account of the mass conversion and baptism on the Day of Pentecost (Ac. 2:37 ff.) raises many questions. [82] But no matters what answers are given, [83] there can hardly be any possibility of a baptism in the Jordan either then or later. The same applies to the conversion and baptism of the Samaritans in Ac. 8:9 ff. The situation is clear as regards the baptism of the eunuch in Ac. 8:26 ff.; when they reached "water" (ἐπί τι ὕδωρ) the eunuch who had become a believer was baptised. [84] Again in the Cornelius story there is ref. only to water (ὕδωρ) in connection with baptism, Ac. 10:47 f. In this connection there is no need to go into the accounts which Ac. gives of baptisms in Gk. missions, which took place far away from the Jordan, 16:14 f.; 16:33; 18:8; 19:5.

---

[79] Only in consequence of a typological exposition of Jos. 3:1 ff. does the Jordan take on here the character of a border river in the higher, spiritual sense. Cf. Lundberg, 146-166.

[80] So E. Barnikol, "Das Fehlen der Taufe in den Quellenschriften der Ag. u. in d. Urgemeinden der Hebräer u. Hellenisten," *Wissenschaftliche Zschr. der Martin-Luther-Universität Halle-Wittenberg, Gesellschafts- u. sprachwissenschaftliche Reihe,* VI (1956/57), 593-610.

[81] Barnikol, *op. cit.,* does not allow for any but official accounts in Ac.

[82] E.g., as to the place of baptism ; cf. → 600, 31 ff. and 623, n. 109.

[83] Cf. Haench. Ag., 156.

[84] M. Dibelius, "Stilkritisches zur Ag.," *Aufsätze zur Ag.*[2] (1953), 20 f. thinks v. 36 and v. 38 are part of the original, unlike Barnikol, *op. cit.,* 599 f.

In this light it is instructive to consider the portrayal of John the Baptist in the few references to him in Ac. In reminiscences of his baptism either no details are given (1:22; 10:37; 18:25), or it is called a baptism of repentance (13:24 f.; 19:3 f.), or there is reference to the fact that John baptised with water (ὕδατι, 1:5; 11:16 [quotation]). The Jordan is certainly never mentioned in connection with John's baptism in Ac.

The NT epistles and Rev. contain no clear references to the baptism of John at all. Even when they mention Christian baptism they do not speak of the Jordan. This obviously does not mean that the authors knew nothing about it. On the contrary, they would fairly certainly know the tradition that Jesus was baptised in the Jordan. Their silence thus indicates the more plainly that an immediate interest in the Jordan was not bound up with recollection of the historical event. Naturally water is needed when baptism is administered, whether in Palestine or on the Hellenistic mission field. This is so self-evident that Paul does not find it even necessary to mention water explicitly in R. 6:3 f.; 1 C. 1:13 ff.; 12:13; 15:29; Gl. 3:27 (though cf. 1 C. 10:1 f.). The only point is that this does not have to be any particular water, not even that of Jordan. [85]

> The freedom expressed here in relation to the ritual also includes the place of baptism in the primitive Church. Nowhere is baptism tied to a specific locality. The only prerequisite in a place is that there be water there, Ac. 8:36. This is also the situation in Ign. (Eph., 18, 2), [86] Herm. (v., 3, 2, 4 ff.; 7, 3; m., 4, 3, 1; s., 9, 16, 2 ff.) and Barn. (11, 1ff.). In all these authors ὕδωρ is the important word and immersion is presupposed as the form of baptism. Once this is asserted there is no need to discuss here what specific ideas were combined with this way of speaking of the baptismal water. The significant pt. is that the water of Jordan is not described as the basic type of the water of baptism nor is it renewed in some sense in this water. No such thoughts are expressed in the post-apost. period.

e. The Water of Baptism and the Water of Jordan in the Early Church.

> The Jordan recurs in Justin. Among the Apologists he is alone in this. It may also be noted that the ref. is restricted to the Dial. c. Tryph. To explain this is by no means easy. The Dial. was written in Rome in the sixties of the 2nd cent. Thus it is possible that specifically Roman ideas underlie the re-emergence of the Jordan. In Dial. it is again said quite naturally that John the Baptist worked by the Jordan (49, 3; 51, 2; 88, 3. 7; cf. the quotation of Is. 35:1 ff. in 69, 5). Jesus thus comes to the Jordan to be baptised (88, 8) and His baptism involves immersion in the Jordan (88, 3; 103, 6). This is all recounted in such a way as to bring out quite unmistakably the fact that God's holy history is here enacted. To this belongs everything that happens when Jesus is baptised in the Jordan, cf. also 88, 3. 6. The more significant, then, is the fact that the Jordan is subordinate to the concept of water. This may be seen from the way in which Elisha's miraculous recovery of the axe-head which fell into the Jordan (2 K. 6:1 ff.) becomes a type of water baptism, 86, 6. Here, then, is no Jordan myth. In particular baptismal water is not the water of Jordan in a higher sense. We simply have a reassertion of the temporarily disregarded Synoptic tradition linking both John the Baptist and the

---

[85] Strongly emphasised by H. G. Marsh, *The Origin and Significance of New Testament Baptism* (1941), 168.

[86] Acc. to this passage Christ was baptised in order that He τῷ πάθει τὸ ὕδωρ καθαρίσῃ. In Ign. πάθος always refers to Christ's passion. The dignity of the water of baptism is thus based on the baptism of the crucified Redeemer. On the spread of this concept cf. Bau. Ign., *ad loc.*, and on the concept itself (the purification of the water [of rivers] from the unclean demons resident in them) cf. H. Schlier, *Religionsgeschichtliche Untersuchungen zu den Ignatiusbr.* (1929), 44-48.

baptism of Jesus with the Jordan. Fresh contact is thus made with the Gospel narrative. In Just. Jesus' baptism in the Jordan is also combined with the idea of a general consecration of water by the Lord's immersion. In many Manichean liturgies and sermons [87] this is plainer than in Just. [88] There is thus a greater emphasis on the water as such. As concerns Just. this may be inferred from another passage which is not constructive but refers to Chr. baptism and which says that after suitable preparation the candidates ἄγονται ὑφ' ἡμῶν ἔνθα ὕδωρ ἐστί ..., Apol., I, 61, 3. Just., then, says nothing more specific about the nature of the baptismal water, but when he calls the act a λουτρόν (→ IV, 306, 35 f.) this shows that Chr. baptism was for him an immersion with real effects, Apol., I, 63, 10 ff.; 62, 1. This presupposes the presence of a sizable quantity of water. On the other hand, it does not say whether any water can be used or only flowing water.

Probably the very silence of Just. on this pt. reflects his position. The matter had certainly been debated. Did. will permit other than "living" or flowing water only when this is not available, 7, 1 f.; [89] only in case of necessity may threefold aspersion be substituted for the usual immersion, 7, 3. The so-called Church Order of Hippolytus also prescribes flowing water and allows any other only in case of necessity. [90] Ps.-Clem. Hom., 9, 19 [91] in a statement which reminds us of Sib., 4, 165, [92] i.e., an utterance of Jewish propaganda, [93] calls for the water of a constantly flowing river, or a spring, or the sea. [94] Hom., 11, 26 bases the requirement of ὕδωρ ζῶν on a version of Jn. 3:5 which has been tendentiously altered as compared with the original: ἀμὴν ὑμῖν λέγω, ἐὰν μὴ ἀναγεννηθῆτε ὕδατι ζῶντι ... οὐ μὴ εἰσέλθητε εἰς τὴν βασιλείαν τῶν οὐρανῶν. Hence Peter in Hom., 11, 36 baptises in Syr. Antioch in the springs close to the sea there. Similar baptismal anecdotes may be found, esp. in the apocryphal Acta. [95] They all show that there were for a long time in the Church groups which either regarded flowing water as the only correct baptismal water or were inclined at least to exalt it above all other water.

The total picture is thus as follows. As regards the question of the baptismal water two opposing schools developed at a comparatively early period in the Church. The one regarded flowing water as indispensable or at least more correct and significant. The other made no distinction between one kind of water and another but put all the emphasis upon the administration of baptism as Christian baptism. Those who advocate flowing water make it apparent that they are following the baptismal tradition of Judaism. [96] They also seem to be bound in a legal way to John the Baptist and his baptism in the Jordan according to the Synoptic tradition as found in Mt. and Mk. Not least of all they think that Jesus' own baptism in the Jordan lays on them an obligation to administer Christian baptism in running water. So far as the sources enable us to tell, these circles

---

[87] For examples cf. Schlier, op. cit., 47 f. (cf. Jacoby, op. cit., 44 f.). Cf. also Tert. Bapt., 4; Adv. Jud., 8.

[88] Possibly Sib., 7, 83 (cf. 6, 4 f.; 7, 66 f.) should also be cited in this connection.

[89] ... ἐν ὕδατι ζῶντι. ἐὰν δὲ μὴ ἔχης ὕδωρ ζῶν, εἰς ἄλλο ὕδωρ βάπτισον.

[90] Cf. also W. Till and J. Leipoldt, Der kpt. Text der Kirchenordnung Hippolyts (1954), 16-25.

[91] ... ἀενάῳ ποταμῷ ἢ πηγῇ ἐπεί γε κἂν θαλάσση ἀπολουσάμενοι ... λούεσθαι is also used for the bath in P. Oxy., V, 840, 14. 19. 24 f., 32 (cf. J. Jeremias, "Der Zusammenstoss Jesu mit dem pharisäischen Oberpriester auf dem Tempelplatz. Zu Pap. Ox., V, 840," Festschr. A. Fridrichsen, Coni. Neot., 11 [1947], 102.

[92] ἐν ποταμοῖς λούσασθε ὅλον δέμας ἀενάοισιν.

[93] → ποταμός 600, 34 ff. and cf. J. Geffcken, "Komposition u. Entstehungszeit der Or. Sib.," TU, 23, 1 (1902), 18-21.

[94] Cf. also Ps.-Clem. Recg., 4, 32.

[95] For further examples cf. Klauser, 100 f.

[96] Cf. on this → 600, 31 ff.

are either on the margin of the main body or outside it. The water of Jordan with its special qualities as river-water is apparently the shibboleth of certain legalistic Judaising groups in the early Church.

Tert. confirms this judgment. In his work on baptism, in which he also takes issue with heretical views, he is expressly referring to John's baptism in the Jordan when he argues that the kind of water is of no significance in baptism : *Ideoque nulla distinctio est, mari quis an stagno, flumine an fonte, lacu an alveo diluatur, nec quicquam refert inter eos, quos Ioannes in Iordane et quos Petrus in Tiberi tinxit. Nisi et ille spado* (eunuch), *quem Philippus inter vias fortuita aqua tinxit, plus salutis aut minus retulit,* Bapt., 4. In support of his view Tert. appeals to the fact that through Jesus' baptism in the Jordan all water is endowed with the capacity of serving as baptismal water. This must have been denied, however, by the groups which he had in mind. They thought that flowing or "living" water was alone adapted and suitable for baptism. As they saw it, their view of the origin of Chr. baptism forced them to this conclusion ; it rested on the fact that John the Baptist baptised in the Jordan. [97]

So far as the sources enable us to say (→ 619, 29 ff.), the proponents of these views seem to have had their centre in the Near East. [98] There are certainly no convincing references to show that they for their part are connected with a pre-Christian baptismal movement or sect focused on the Jordan. The reticence concerning the Jordan in the traditions concerning the Baptist, the accounts of the baptism of Jesus in the later canonical Gospels and the stories of primitive Christian baptism, leads rather to a different explanation. If this reticence is based on a conscious decision, then the conviction which it opposes, namely, that baptism must be in "living" water after the pattern of the Jordan, arose within the Christian community and in the primitive Christian period. To say more than this is no more possible than to fix the exact place in the Church except for the formal legal character of the conviction with its unmistakable tendency towards separation.

Another pointer to the East is the fact that the Mandaeans allow only running water for baptism, and actually mention the Jordan. [99] Quite apart from the question what traditions influenced them and helped to shape their religion, [100] they are dependent at this pt. on the Nestorian Syrians in whose liturgical language the baptismal spring with its water and also the baptismal basin are called Jordan. [101] Whether and how far such influences affected the Greek Orthodox Churches, in which all consecrated water, esp. that blessed on Jan. 6, is called Jordan, and the Jordan itself plays an important part in the baptismal liturgy, [102] is a question which need not be discussed in this context. At any rate the description of the baptismal water as Jordan seems to be ancient and

---

[97] Klauser, 101.

[98] This is perhaps true of the Didache, cf. A. Adam, "Erwägungen zur Herkunft der Did.," ZKG, 68 (1957), 1-47.

[99] Furthermore all running water has this name among them, Lidz. Joh., II, Intr. XIX; also op. cit. (→ n. 62), 71. In this practice oriental (Indo-Aryan ?) influences may be seen ; thus in Hinduism the name Ganges is used generally for rivers and ponds sacred to Śiva, v. H. W. Schomerus, *Śivaitische Heiligenlegenden* (1925), 9, 288, n. 21, also 214 (under 47).

[100] V. S. Pedersen, *Bidrag til analyse af de mandaeiske skrifter* (1940); W. Baumgartner, "Zur Mandäerfrage," *Hebrew Union College Annual*, 28, 1 (1950/51), 41-71; also "Der heutige Stand der Mandäerfrage," ThZ, 6 (1950), 401-410.

[101] Lietzmann, 601 f.; cf. the review by R. Bultmann, ThLZ, 56 (1931), 577 f.

[102] A. v. Maltzew, *Die Sacramente der Orthodox-kathol. Kirche des Morgenlandes* (1898), passim ; on the Jordan festival on Jan. 6 cf. F. Meyer v. Waldeck, *Russland*, II (1886), 130-134.

it also seems not to have been unfamiliar in Egypt. [103] Ref. may be made as well to the undoubtedly obscure Naassene Sermon which equates Oceanos with ὁ μέγας 'Ιορδάνης. [104] All these instances lead to groups on the margin of or even outside orthodoxy and hence to groups similar to those which are concerned about baptism being administered only in flowing water, → 620, 14 ff.

It should be noted that the NT offers no support for the view that the germs of this development are to be sought in Jewish Christian circles in Jerusalem. The attitude of the NT is also so uniform that it cannot be explained as a later correction of the picture of Peter in Ac. Thus, even if running water, symbolised by the Jordan, came to be venerated in Christianity as the proper baptismal water, one must accept the fact that non-Christian and pre-Christian motifs probably had a hand in the rise of this view. In the present state of research it is not possible to decide the question whether these motifs were linked primarily with the running water or the Jordan. The total picture suggests the former. Thus the possibility has to be taken into account that in liturgical texts which refer to it the Jordan is secondary as compared with flowing water. Among other things this would correspond to the fact that the John tradition is secondary in the Mandaean texts. [105]

The Jordan problem in the early Church, and probably in the Christianity of the time when the canonical Gospels were written, is thus very largely, if not wholly, a problem of Christian baptism as such, though less from the standpoint of its interpretation than that of its historical basis. [106] Does the Church baptise in continuation of the baptism of John, which Jesus also received, or does it baptise because Jesus was baptised, and because He took up His office and began His work in direct connection with His baptism, all under the direction of the Spirit? Once the question was put in this precise form — and it could hardly be evaded seeing that others also baptised and received baptism — the answer was by no means self-evident. Later development shows this. Where running water was particularly esteemed, John the Baptist unmistakably stood at the beginning of Christian baptism too; with him, unavoidably on the basis of the tradition (Mt./Mk.), the Jordan also demanded notice and respect. R. 6:3 ff. is probably a milestone in the clarification of the question by the bearers of the apostolic tradition, for here there is reference not only to the death of Jesus but also to His baptism. Also significant is the way in which Ac. especially relates baptism

---

[103] The Eth. version of the Egypt. Church Order has a prayer for the holy water of the Jordan, which is mixed with incense (H. Duensing, "Der aeth. Text der Kirchenordnung des Hippolyt," AGG, III, 32 [1946], 90 f.) before the priest immerses the candidate into the water of Jordan, 94 f. Cf. also Dölger, 74 (Alexandria).

[104] Cf. R. Reitzenstein-H. H. Schaeder, *Studien zum antiken Synkretismus aus Iran u. Griechenland* (1926), 166. Reitzenstein thinks the ref. is a Chr. interpolation, but this is questionable in view of ὁ μέγας 'Ιορδάνης (μέγας suggests Gnosticism; v. also Dölger, 73).

[105] Lietzmann, 596-601; Bultmann, *op. cit.* (→ n. 101), 577 f.

[106] Cf. Stauffer Theol., 139: "The development of this (sc. established) Chr. practice is a puzzle ..." It is then suggested that the puzzle will be solved "if we finally decide to take the traditions of the missionary command of the risen Lord with historical seriousness," but this is too simple a solution, since Mt. 28:19 does not in any case describe the mode of baptism. As the monuments also suggest, it is more correct to consider the relation of Chr. baptism to Jesus' own baptism, or to find in the latter the basis of the Chr. rite, cf. Bultmann Trad., 269 f. But this still leaves many questions unanswered. Above all it shows that the concentration of research on the problem of infant baptism in the last decades has hardly helped to throw light on the historical problem which Chr. baptism itself poses.

and the receiving of the Spirit. The receiving of the Spirit is the decisive thing, not baptism, or at least not a baptism which is tied to the matter and understood *ex opere operato*, Ac. 10:44 ff. Paul (R. 8:15; Gl. 4:6) and John (Jn. 3:5 f.) takes the same view. Alongside them, however, are others, unknown to us, who think and act differently.

In view of their fundamental importance these differences go far beyond baptism itself. Behind them is the question of the self-understanding of the community of Jesus and its related Christology. To that degree the problem of the Jordan in the early Church, which was a problem of the second generation if not already of the first, implies the whole problem of the Christian community as such. Is it only something different or is it something completely new? It would seem that the separation of baptism from the Jordan [107] is congruent to the corresponding separation of the Lord's Supper from the Passover in the sense that both sacraments come to be consistently regarded as autonomously Christian. Hence the problem of the Jordan may well shed light on central theological questions with which it has at a first glance little or nothing to do.

It is instructive to consider how things worked out in practice. Thus Hier. still found many being baptised in the Jordan c. 400. [108] Yet then and later there were baptisteries in Jerusalem [109] and esp. in the country; esp. worth nothing is a cave baptistery connected with a monastic institution. [110] In this context ref. may again be made to baptisteries decorated with pictures of the baptism of Jesus, → 613, 26 ff. These pictures are meant to be more than mere decoration. In them the baptising community confesses that there takes place here the same as that which took place in the baptism of Jesus, so that for all the differences the true Jordan is present in the baptismal water here and not where stress is laid on external correspondence in the kind of water, i.e., on running water. [111]

Rengstorf

πότηριον → 148, 11 ff.
ποτίζω → 159, 19 ff.
πότος → 145, 3 ff.

---

[107] Cf. Tert. Bapt., 10 f. and on this W. Bauer, *Das Leben Jesu im Zeitalter d. nt.lichen Apkr.* (1909), 104 f.

[108] De situ et nominibus locorum hebraicorum (Lagarde, *op. cit.* [→ n. 5]), *s.v.* "Bethabara." Cf. also Dölger, 74.

[109] A cistern with a Gk. inscr. referring to the baptismal liturgy in the north-west corner of the Church of the Holy Sepulchre probably was once part of a baptistery, G. Dalman, "Die Grabeskirche in Jerusalem," PJB, 3 (1907), 36 f.; P. Thomsen, "Die lat. u. gr. Inschr. der Stadt Jerusalem," ZDPV, 44 (1921), 8; J. Jeremias, "Das neugefundene Höhlen-Baptisterium bei Jerusalem," *Von der Antike zum Christentum, Festg. f. V. Schultze* (1931), 118.

[110] Jeremias, *op. cit.* (→ n. 109), 109-122.

[111] Cf. also Dölger, 75-77, who refers to Ambr. Sermo, 38, 2 : *Ubique enim nunc Christus, ubique Jordan est,* cf. also Klauser, 161 f.

πούς

Contents : A. Use of the Word in Profane Greek. B. Comparative Religion ; C. The Old Testament and Judaism : 1. The Use in the LXX ; 2. The Transferred Use ; 3. The Symbolical Use ; 4. Uncovering of the Foot ; 5. The Foot of Deity. D. The Situation in the New Testament : 1. Use for the Whole Person ; 2. Transferred Use ; 3. As a Symbol of Power ; 4. To Express Subordination ; 5. To Express Veneration of Jesus ; 6. The Foot-Washing ; 7. The Cultic Uncovering of the Foot.

A. Use of the Word in Profane Greek.

πούς (ancient Indo-Eur. word : Lat. *pes, ped-is,* Sanskr. *pad-,* Germanic *fōt*) [1] is found from Hom. for "foot" (of man or beast) in the lit. sense (also "claw," "talon") and also for the lower extremity as a whole. The feet of artefacts of all kinds are also πόδες. [2] But πούς has also the more general sense of the "lower end" and it can be used thus even where there is no foot-like shape. [3] Gk. shares with many other languages the use of the word and thing as a measure of length. [4] The poetic use [5] does not derive from the member but from its action, striding. The same is true of the metaphor χρόνου πούς. [6]

More important is another extension of use, namely, with ref. to the whole person. Esp. in view is the acting and of course in the first instance the moving person. [7] This understanding is also present in the phrase πόδα ἔχειν ἔν τινι, "to be involved in a matter." [8] The same is true of most of the adverbial expressions connected with πούς. The proximity or distance, height or depth etc. relates to the whole person, not just to the foot. [9] The thing related to the person can be evaluated thereby, [10] and the person, too, can be qualified by phrases like ἀφ' ἡσύχου ποδός, Eur. Med., 217. [11] A simple ref. to the feet can denote power available to the person. [12] The common equation of → χείρ and δύναμις (→ II, 291, 28 ff. and n. 34) applies also to πούς and δύναμις. [13]

π ο ύ ς. Pass., Liddell-Scott, Moult.-Mill., Pr.-Bauer⁴, Preisigke Wört., *s.v.*; J. C. Suicerus, Thesaurus ecclesiasticus e patribus graecis³ (1746), II, 814-816; G. Büchner, *Bibl. Real- u. Verbal-Hand-Concordanz*¹⁵, ed. H. L. Heubner (1877), *s.v.* "Bein," "Fuss."

[1] Walde-Pok., II, 23 f.

[2] Transference of meaning from parts of the body to objects is quite common, cf. H. Paul, *Prinzipien der Sprachgeschichte*⁵ (1937), 95 f.

[3] Hom. Il., 2, 824; 20, 59 : Foot of Mt. Ida. As nautical tt. for the bottom of the sail Hom. Od., 5, 260, also the whole of the lower part of the ship, Pind. Nem., 6, 55 : τὸ δὲ πὰρ ποδὶ ναὸς ἑλισσόμενον αἰεὶ κυμάτων.

[4] Cf. W. Becher, Art. "Pes," Pauly-W., 19 (1938), 1085 f.

[5] Aristoph. Ra., 1323. Also for a whole verse Luc. Pro Imaginibus, 18 : ταῦτά σοι ἔκμετρα ἔδοξε καὶ ὑπὲρ τὸν πόδα. For a sentence pronounced in one breath Luc. Demon., 65 : εἰπὼν πρὸς τοὺς παρόντας τὸν ἐναγώνιον τῶν κηρύκων πόδα.

[6] Eur. Alexandros Fr., 42 (TGF, 374): καὶ χρόνου προύβαινε πούς and Ba., 889 : δαρὸν χρόνου πόδα.

[7] Eur. Or., 1217: παρθένου δέχου πόδα, "await the coming of the maiden"; Eur. Hipp., 661: σὺν πατρὸς μολὼν ποδί.

[8] Pind. Olymp., 6, 8 : ἐν τούτῳ πεδίλῳ δαιμόνιον πόδ' ἔχων.

[9] ἀνὰ πόδα (cf. ἐπὶ πόδα) "backwards"; ἐκ ποδός (cf. κατὰ πόδας) "following on foot" (but ἐκποδών "afar," "out of the way"); ἐν ποσί, ἐμποδών (cf. παρὰ ποδός, πρὸ ποδός) "near."

[10] παρὰ ποδός "lightly," περὶ πόδα "aptly," ὑπὸ πόδα, "humbly," always with ref. to the person, not the foot.

[11] Cf. also Pind. Nem., 3, 41 ff.: ψεφεννὸς ἀνὴρ ἄλλοτ' ἄλλα πνέων οὔ ποτ' ἀτρεκεῖ κατέβα ποδί.

[12] Aristoph. Av., 35 : ἀμφοῖν τοῖν ποδοῖν, "with all power"; Aeschin. Fals. Leg., 115 : τιμωρήσειν καὶ χειρὶ καὶ ποδὶ καὶ φωνῇ καὶ πάσῃ δυνάμει.

[13] Weinreich AH, 71, n. 4.

In expressions denoting honouring or subjection the inferior or subordinate addresses himself to the feet of the mighty or the superior. [14]

Personified virtues or vices are characterised by the temperament and symbolical use of their feet. [15]

B. Comparative Religion.

Related to the general use of foot as a symbol of power is the idea that the foot or footprint of deity, of divinely honoured men and of certain other persons can bring about miraculous cures. Plut. [16] tells of such in relation to Pyrrhus, Tac. (Hist., IV, 81), Suet. (Caes., 7, 2) in relation to Vespasian or Sarapis. [17] Worship of the foot of Sarapis is attested by the bust of Sarapis set on a colossal foot [18] and that of his footprint by a Syr. monument with an eagle over the foot of Sarapis and the inscr. ἴχνος ἔχων, πόδ' ἀν' ἴχνος ἔχων, ἀνέθηκα Σεράπει. [19] To these Hell. examples may be added others from all peoples in all ages. [20]

The appearances of the gods may be symbolised by ref. to their feet or the impressions left by them. [21] Some depictions of ascensions simply show the feet of the deified figure protruding from a cloud. [22]

In all cults and superstitious practices the demand to bare one's feet in approaching the deity plays an important role. This applies esp. to priests in the discharge of their office but also to all who have a part in cultic actions or who visit holy places. [23] Closely related is the similarly widespread custom that those who mourn or do penance should go barefoot. [24] In all religions it is the practice to go barefoot in litanies or processions of all kinds. [25] Here again the foot represents the whole person, → 624, 17 ff. The naked

---

[14] As a sign of conferring life Caligula gives his left foot to a condemned man to kiss, Sen. Ben., II, 12. On the Pergamon frieze Aphrodite puts her foot on the face of her dispatched opponent; on the (originally magical) meaning of the gesture cf. A. Gotsmich, "Die 'grausame' Aphrodite am Gigantenfries des Pergamener Altars," *Archäologischer Anzeiger*, 56 (1941), 844-879 [Kleinknecht]. P. Oxy., I, 128, 9 ff. (to a high official): κατα-ξιώσῃ ἡ ὑμετέρα ἐνδοξότης ... ἐπιτρέψαι αὐτῷ ἀνελθεῖν εἰς τοὺς ἐνδόξους αὐτῆς πόδας, cf. 128, 8; Preisigke Sammelbuch, 4323, 5 (a son to his father): καταφιλῆσαι τοὺς τιμίους αὐτοῦ πόδας cf. also Preisigke Wört., *s.v.* πούς : Byzantine expressions of subjection.

[15] Soph. Oed. Tyr., 878 f.: ὕβρις ... οὐ ποδὶ χρησίμῳ χρῆται. Eur. Fr., 979 (TGF, 676): Δίκη ... βραδεῖ ποδὶ στείχουσα.

[16] Vita Pyrrhi, 3 (I, 384); *v.* Weinreich AH, 67.

[17] Cf. S. Morenz, "Vespasian, Heiland d. Kranken," *Würzburger Jahrbuch*, 4 (1949/50), 373 f.

[18] Cf. Haas, 9/11 Leipoldt (1926), V and Ill. 15.

[19] Cf. O. Weinreich, "Ein Spurzauber," ARW, 28 (1930), 184.

[20] Cf. G. Wilke, "Weitere Beiträge zur Heilkunde in d. indoeurop. Vorzeit," Mannus, 7 (1915), 1-9; E. Stemplinger, Art. "Fussspur," *Handwörterbuch d. deutschen Aberglaubens*, III (1930/31), 240-243; O. Eissfeldt, "Der Gott Karmel," SAB, 1953, 1 (1953), Plates IV-VI; K. Galling, "Der Gott Karmel u. d. Ächtung der fremden Götter," *Gesch. u. AT, Festschr. A. Alt* (1953), 110-121.

[21] Prehistorical depictions of the soles of feet on dolmens, rock-paintings and gravestones are rightly regarded as symbols of theophanies, cf. F. A. v. Scheltema, Art. "Fusssohlendarstellung," RLV, 4, 1 (1926), 162 f. For the Chr. sphere cf. H. Leclercq, Art. "Pied," *Dict. d'archéologie chrétienne et de liturgie*, 14, 1 (1939), 818 f.

[22] E.g., the ascension in Dürer's Little Passion. Cf. S. H. Gutberlet, *Die Himmelfahrt Christi in der bildenden Kunst* (1934), 247-250 and Plates XXIX and XXX.

[23] Cf. C. Weinhold, "Zur Gesch. d. heidnischen Ritus," AAB (1896), 4 f.; J. Heckenbach, "De nuditate sacra," RVV, 9, 3 (1911), 23-29; T. Wächter, "Reinheitsvorschriften im griech. Kult," RVV, 9, 1 (1910), 23 f., 57.

[24] Heckenbach, *op. cit.*, 31; E. Samter, "Zu röm. Bestattungsbräuchen," *Festschr. f. O. Hirschfeld* (1903), 253 f.

[25] E. Marbach, Art. "Nudipedalia," Pauly-W., 17 (1936), 1240 f.; Weinhold, 18-26; Heckenbach, 29 f., 67 f.

foot is a later substitute for complete nakedness. [26] The reason may be sought in rules of cultic purity, the putting off of defiled garments, [27] esp. those made of skins and furs, [28] in the magical idea of a direct influence of deity on the naked body, [29] or in the desire to avoid magical hindrances caused by the knots and ties of clothing. [30]

C. The Old Testament and Judaism.

1. The Use in the LXX. The LXX uses πούς for a whole series of Heb. words. The strict word for "foot" is רֶגֶל, "sole" כַּף־רֶגֶל. But other words are עָקֵב "heel," "hoof" (Gn. 48:19) and פַּרְסָה "hoof" (Is. 5:28). כְּרָעַיִם is also transl. πούς == "shin-bone" in Ex. 12:9; 29:17; Lv. 1:9, 13; 8:21; 9:14. πούς can also be the equivalent of פַּעַם "step," plur. "feet of artefacts," Ju. 5:28; 4 Βασ. 19:24; ψ 56:7; Prv. 29:5. Finally, it is used for מַרְגְּלוֹת, "that which lies at the feet," also "feet" themselves, Rt. 3:4, 7, 8, 14. Apart from the technical senses, the LXX thus employs the term in the wide range found in the later Gk. tradition.

2. The Transferred Use. This also applies to the transf. sense. As used thus πούς is common in the image of the walk, the walk of life, or the way gen. → V, 49 ff. [31] The true ref. here is to the person who treads the way; thus what is said about the πόδες ἀφρόνων in Wis. 14:11 and the πούς μωροῦ in Sir. 21:22 really applies to the fools themselves. When πόδες is par. to ψυχή in ψ 56:7 and 65:9 the ref. is obviously not to the physical march of the feet but to man's way or way of life. [32]

3. The Symbolical Use. The OT has some striking examples of the symbolical use of the foot as a sign of the power (→ n. 12) exercised by a person. The captains of Joshua put their feet on the necks of the five defeated kings of the Amorites, Jos. 10:24. Moses swears that "the land whereon thy feet have trodden shall be thine inheritance, and thy children's for ever," Jos. 14:9; cf. Dt. 11:24; Jos. 1:3; 2 K. 21:8. [33] David praises God because his enemies have fallen under his feet, 2 S. 22:39 == Ps. 18:38; cf. 1 K. 5:17;

---

[26] Cf. W. A. Müller, *Nacktheit u. Entblössung in d. altorient. u. älteren griech. Kunst*, Diss. Leipzig (1906), 42; Heckenbach, 14-21, 34; F. Dümmler, "Der Ursprung d. Elegie," *Philol.*, 53 (1894), 212. For the Arabs, J. Wellhausen, *Skizzen u. Vorarbeiten*, III (1887), 106 f.

[27] Weinhold, 5; the Arabs change clothes and shoes, Wellhausen, 106.

[28] Wächter, *op. cit.* (→ n. 23), 57, 61; Heckenbach, 24 f.

[29] Weinhold, 5. This may be the reason why the *nabi* takes off his clothes in a state of ecstasy, 1 S. 19:24. Cf. also F. Dümmler, "Sittengeschichtliche Parallelen," *Philol.*, 56 (1897), 6 f. on Is. 20:2; Weinhold, 6; Heckenbach, 21-23. Where magical powers are ascribed to the earth the naked bodies of newborn babies and the dead are laid on it and the magician goes to work with naked feet, Heckenbach, 46-49, cf. also Haas, 9/11 Leipoldt, Ill. 190; 13/14 Rumpf, Ill. 148.

[30] Wächter, 24. Heckenbach, 23, who adduces a schol. on Verg. Aen., IV, 518: *in sacris nihil solet esse religatum*. On this whole complex cf. F. Eckstein, Art. "Barfuss," *Handwörterbuch d. deutschen Aberglaubens*, I (1928), 912-922.

[31] E.g., Gn. 30:30; 1 S. 2:9; Job 23:11; ψ 118:105; Dt. 32:35: ὅταν σφαλῇ ὁ πούς αὐτῶν.

[32] When Zedekiah took the wrong course in his policies it was said that his feet sank in the mire, Jer. 38:22.

[33] Here perhaps we also have an explanation of the custom of taking off the shoe for renouncing an inheritance (Rt. 4:7; Dt. 25:9) if the shoe represents the foot. Cf. G. Jungbauer, Art. "Schuh," 1a; 18a b in *Handwörterbuch d. deutschen Aberglaubens*, VII (1935), 1292, 1346 f.; P. Sartori, "Der Schuh im Volksglauben," *Zschr. des Vereins f. Volkskunde*, 4 (1894), 179 f.; L. Levy, "Die Schuhsymbolik im jüd. Ritus,' MGWJ, NF, 26 (1918), 179 f. R. Forrer, Art. "Fussanhänger," *Reallex. der praehistorischen, klass. u. frühchr. Altertümer* (1907), 257 f. uses Dt. 11:24 as a legal principle to explain the use of a Roman (?) seal in the form of a foot which is designed to seal ownership.

Ps. 47:3. Acc. to Ps. 58:10 the righteous shall wash their feet by walking (פְּעָמָיו) in the blood of the ungodly, [34] cf. Mal. 3:21.

In strong antithesis is the low estimation of the foot when רֶגֶל/πούς is used euphemistically for the *pudenda*. [35]

4. Uncovering of the Foot. In the OT and Judaism, as in other religions, the foot is uncovered for religious reasons, → 625, 17 ff. One may think esp. of the significant incidents in Ex. 3:5 and Jos. 5:13-15 in which Moses and Joshua are told to take off their shoes because of the holiness of the place where God or His messenger appears. Again, it is everywhere assumed in the OT that the priests discharge their ministry barefoot. [36] The OT rules are listed in the Talmud and extended to all who set foot on the temple hill or the holy places. [37] How far the reasons given above for cultic nakedness (→ 626, 1 f.) exerted an influence need not be discussed here. [38] The true reason for putting off one's shoes in the religion of the OT and Judaism is respect and abasement before God. [39] The Jew who goes barefoot on days of fasting and atonement comes before God like a slave before his master. The priest and the righteous man do the same when they put off their shoes on treading holy ground. [40]

5. The Foot of Deity. The foot of deity plays a role in the OT in the description of theophanies. In the OT God does, of course, appear in various forms ranging from natural phenomena by way of human shape to spiritual manifestation. [41] But when appearances such as that in Ex. 33:20-23 are found in conjunction with the principle : "My face shall not be seen" (v. 23) or : "There shall no man see me, and live" (v. 20), it is natural that the description of the appearance of God should be not only in terms of His back (אָחוֹר, v. 23) but also of His feet, or what is under His feet, or His footprints, cf. Ex. 24:10, which does not describe God's person but refers to a costly and radiant foot-stool under His feet. Ps. 18:9 = 2 S. 22:10 says of the appearance of God only that darkness was under His feet. In 1 Ch. 28:2 David calls the ark a resting-place for God's foot-stool, cf. Ez. 43:7; Ps. 99:5; 132:7; Lam. 2:1. [42] Ps. 77:19 speaks of the way or path or step of God rather than God Himself, Nah. 1:3 of the dust of His feet,

---

[34] When the LXX has χεῖρες for πόδες here (ψ 57:11) it is esp. plain that the ref. is not to the member as such but to the power of the person which is represented either by hand or foot, → n. 19, 21.

[35] So 2 K. 18:27 Q: מֵי רַגְלֵיהֶם "urine" and Ju. 3:24 : ἀποκενοῦν τοὺς πόδας. Whether the Heb. הֵסֵךְ רַגְלָיִם (Ju. 3:24; 1 S. 24:4) is also a euphemism is doubtful, cf. Ges.-Buhl and Köhler-Baumg., *s.v.* סכך hi and Suicerus, *s.v.* I, 3. רֶגֶל may also be taken either lit. or euphemistically in Is. 6:2. The command that Uriah should go into David's house and wash his feet (2 S. 11:8) could mean (cf. vv. 11 ff.) that he should have intercourse with his wife, cf. the phrase *tollere pedem* (*pedes*) (*sc. ad concubitum*) in Cic. Att., II, 1, 5 and Mart., X, 81, 4; XI, 71, 8.

[36] In the rules about washing hands and feet before entering on priestly ministry (Ex. 30:19) and the sprinkling of blood on the right big toe (Ex. 29:20; Lv. 8:23 f.). In the detailed description of the priestly vestments in Lv. 8 shoes are not mentioned.

[37] Cf. S. Krauss, *Talmudische Archäol.*, I (1910), 183 f. The naked foot must itself be washed on feast-days, jJoma, 8, 1 (44d, 29 f.).

[38] Is. 32:11 and Mi. 1:8 seem to refer to complete nakedness as an expression of mourning. Cf. F. Schwally, *Das Leben nach dem Tode* (1892), 13.

[39] Cf. Jungbauer, *op. cit.* (→ n. 33), 1349 f.; Müller, *op. cit.* (→ n. 26), 5. The putting on of *sak* is linked with going barefoot — an unmistakable sign of abasement, Müller, 41; 1 K. 20:31; 21:27. If women had nothing over the *sak* their breasts would be bare, Is. 3:24; 32:11; cf. I. Benzinger, *Hbr. Archäologie*³ (1927), 75.

[40] Since God is present in the Law, Rabbah bR. Hona demanded that those who came to him for judgment should put of their shoes, bShebu., 31a. Acc. to Jos. Ant., 14, 172 the accused were expected to appear in court in the garb of penitents. Penitence and sorrow humble men and thus demand that they go barefoot, cf. Levy, *op. cit.* (→ n. 33), 181 f.

[41] Cf. Eichr. Theol. AT, II, 1-18 (§ 12); → μορφή IV, 749, 1 ff.

[42] It is not always possible to say whether the ref. is to the ark or the temple generally.

Hab. 3:5 of the treading of His feet. With ref. to the coming of Yahweh on the last day Zech. 14:4 says that His feet shall stand on the Mt. of Olives.

D. The Situation in the New Testament.

The NT uses words for the lower extremities very infrequently. Along with πούς and γόνυ, πτέρνα (LXX πτερνισμός) is used only in Jn. 13:18 (quoting ψ 40:10) and σκέλος only 4 times in the special section on the taking down from the cross in Jn. 19:31-37. Hence one has to take into account the fact that in the NT as in the LXX (→ 626, 6 ff.) πούς denotes not merely the foot but also the leg and its individual parts. [43] Since expressions like πίπτειν παρὰ τοὺς πόδας 'Ιησοῦ in Lk. 8:41; 17:16 and προσπίπτειν τοῖς γόνασιν 'Ιησοῦ in Lk. 5:8 are full material parallels, γόνυ, too, must be considered in relation to the signification of πούς (Cod. D has ποσίν instead of γόνασιν at Lk. 5:8).

The passages in which πούς simply refers to the part of the body or means of locomotion with no deeper content, or in which the word is added to verbs of standing, going etc. simply as a strengthening (e.g., Rev. 11:11; Ac. 26:16), need no further elucidation. πούς is a measure in Ac. 7:5 : βῆμα ποδός. [44] Calling for consideration are the verses in which other ideas are bound up with the mention of the member.

1. Use for the Whole Person. The NT, too, uses πούς or πόδες to denote the whole person (standing or walking), → 624, 17 ff. Thus the statement in Ac. 5:9 : ἰδοὺ οἱ πόδες τῶν θαψάντων τὸν ἄνδρα σου ἐπὶ τῇ θύρᾳ καὶ ἐξοίσουσίν σε, naturally means that the men are at the door. When in Mt. 4:6 and par. the devil, challenging Jesus to throw Himself from the pinnacle of the temple, quotes ψ 90:11a, 12 : ... μήποτε προσκόψῃς πρὸς λίθον τὸν πόδα σου, the omission of v. 11b removes the vivid idea of walking on a hard and stony path on which the foot stumbles and adapts the quotation to the situation with its threat, not to the foot alone, but to the whole person.

2. Transferred Use. On an OT basis (→ 626, 14 ff.) and in connection with the figurative use of ὁδός (→ V, 84, 18 ff.) for walk, preparation, girding (→ V, 307, 20 ff.), πούς has the transferred sense of the person who is ready or active, cf. Lk. 1:79 (Is. 59:8): τοῦ κατευθῦναι τοὺς πόδας ἡμῶν εἰς ὁδὸν εἰρήνης and Hb. 12:13 (Prv. 4:26): τροχιὰς ὀρθὰς ποιεῖτε τοῖς ποσὶν ὑμῶν. The words in R. 10:15 (Is. 52:7): ὡς ὡραῖοι οἱ πόδες τῶν εὐαγγελιζομένων ἀγαθά, are praising, not the feet, but the preachers of salvation and their work, though they do, of course, refer to their journeying through the world, so that the metaphor is closely related to that which it depicts. The same applies in Eph. 6:15, → V, 312, 4 ff. What Jesus says about the σκάνδαλον caused by the foot (Mk. 9:45) is also to be taken half-literally and half-figuratively. The σκάνδαλον is naturally caused by the corrupt way of life or by the man who acts scandalously ; the feet are only the instruments used to carry out his wicked designs.

3. As a Symbol of Power. The NT also employs the foot as a symbol of power. At this point, however, one may see a change in the relation of God's community to the world and its members as compared with the religion of the OT. This is caused by the NT message. In the OT the foot is often used as a symbol of power to depict the suppression, subjection and enslavement of one

---

[43] This is undoubtedly true in Rev. 1:15; 2:18; 10:1 f.; 13:2 and probably in Jn. 11:44 and 1 C. 12:15, possibly also in Mk. 9:45 and par.; Mt. 28:9; Ac. 14:8, 10; 16:24. For German usage cf. Trübner's Germ. dict., ed. A. Götze, I (1939), 269 and P. Kretschmer, *Wortgeographie der hochdeutschen Umgangssprache* (1918), 110 f. [Debrunner].

[44] Cf. also Herm. s., 4, 1, 6 and 4, 2, 1.

man by another, of other nations by the chosen people, or of the land by mighty conquerors, → 626, 21 ff. In the NT writings such ideas are found only in Rev., and even here only in the quotation from Is. 49:23 in Rev. 3:9. Elsewhere man is no longer a powerful figure represented by the foot, and the promise given to the community of God in R. 16:20 is that God Himself will crush Satan under their feet. The reason for this is obviously to be sought in the integrally eschatological character of NT proclamation. We are no longer caught in the shifting interplay of history in which power falls now to the one and now to the other. History ends with the final conflict between God and the prince of this world and his satellites. The promises of ψ 8:7: πάντα ὑπέταξας ὑποκάτω τῶν ποδῶν αὐτοῦ (1 C. 15:27; Eph. 1:22; Hb. 2:8) and ψ 109:1: ... ἕως ἂν θῶ τοὺς ἐχθρούς σου ὑποπόδιον τῶν ποδῶν σου (Mk. 12:36 and par.; Ac. 2:35; 1 C. 15:25; Hb. 1:13; 10:13; Barn., 12, 10) are genuinely fulfilled in the powerful eschatological figure of Jesus. In the case of other apocalyptic figures the depiction of their person and power is restricted to the head or to the feet and legs portrayed in strength or in an attitude of rule. Thus the angel of proclamation in Rev. 10:1 has legs which stand like fiery pillars over land and sea and which thus rule the whole world. Again, the resting of the feet of the woman of Rev. 12:1 on the sickle of the moon gives her the character of a figure of cosmic might. The same applies to the beast from the sea with his bear's feet, Rev. 13:2.

4. To Express Subordination. Sitting or falling at the feet of a man as a sign of subordination is found in the NT only when the man is characterised by a special relation to the power and majesty of God. [45] In Ac. 22:3 with reference to Paul one finds the expression : ἀνατεθραμμένος ... παρὰ τοὺς πόδας Γαμαλιήλ. There is here a reflection of the external situation of the pupil sitting at the feet of his teacher, but also expressed is the fact that respect for the Torah compels the student to adopt this position, → n. 40; IV, 434, 34 f. [46] The apostles at whose feet the prices for the sale of property were laid as an offering (Ac. 4:35, 37; 5:2) represent the Lord and God, since Sapphira is tempting the Holy Spirit when she practises a deception in this respect, 5:9. When she then falls down dead at Peter's feet (v. 10), it is because the judicial and penal might of God is at work through the apostle.

The shaking off of dust from the feet (Mk. 6:11 and par.; Ac. 13:51) should also be mentioned in this connection. [47] This is obviously a judicial and penal gesture. As the expressions εἰς μαρτύριον αὐτοῖς (Mk. 6:11) and ἐπ' αὐτούς (Lk. 9:5) show (→ IV, 502, 38 ff.), the shaking off of dust is a court accusation. [48] Here, then, we have an act of apostolic power on the authority of God and of Christ. But the powers of the apostles are limited. When Cornelius does obeisance at the feet of Peter (Ac. 10:25), Peter lifts him up and observes that he is only a man. In Rev. 19:10; 22:8 f. even the angel does not allow the divine to fall down at his feet in worship : ὅρα μή ... τῷ θεῷ προσκύνησον.

5. To Express Veneration of Jesus. On the other hand, expressions of subordination, subjection and worship are unrestrained and uncontested at the feet of Jesus. The Baptist confesses (Mk. 1:7, cf. Ac. 13:25) that he is not worthy to

---

[45] Cf. J. Horst, Proskynein (1932), 51-67, 115 f.; → προσκυνεῖν; → γόνυ I, 738 ff.

[46] Cf. Str.-B., II, 764 (e).

[47] Schlatter's view (Schl. Mt., 334) that this is dust which is churned up by the feet and then shaken out of the clothes is refuted by the wording of Mk. 6:11 and Lk. 9:5.

[48] This is esp. plain when one compares Mk. 6:11 with Mt. 10:14 f. and Lk. 10:11 f., also the gesture of Paul in Ac. 18:6 (cf. Ez. 3:18 f.; 33:1-9).

bend even to unloose the latchets of Jesus' shoes, → III, 294, 12 ff. The divine in Rev. 1:17, overwhelmed by the divinity of the appearance of Jesus, falls down like a dead man at His feet. The question arises whether the plain effect of divinity in such instances is also meant when the NT speaks elsewhere of sitting, falling or being laid at the feet of Jesus, or of grasping His feet. This question is one of the problems posed by the title Kurios, → III, 1092, 49 ff. [49] In most cases sitting or falling at the feet of Jesus may be explained quite naturally in terms of the given situation, or as the expression of a respect which would be paid to a rabbi (courtesy), or which would be due to the Messiah whom men thought to see in Jesus (protocol). In the main, however, the view of the narrator, even when it is not explicitly stated, is correctly judged if the gesture is seen to be one of worship. This is certainly true in Mk. 5:22 = Lk. 8:41 (Jairus); Mk. 7:25 (the Syrophoenician woman); Mt. 15:30 (the sick man at Jesus' feet); Jn. 11:32 (Mary in Bethany), where divine veneration is bound up with the request for help. The gesture of the Samaritan — he throws himself on his face at the feet of Jesus [50] — shows that the majesty of Jesus is seen and He is thus worshipped as God on His throne is worshipped by the angels and elders and beasts in Rev. 7:11 and 11:16, cf. Mt. 17:6; 1 C. 14:25. When Luke says that the cured demoniac of Gerasa (8:35) and also Mary (10:39) sat at the feet of Jesus, one can hardly say whether this attitude expresses more than grateful discipleship and a zealous readiness to learn. [51] On the other hand, grasping the feet of the risen Lord and the obeisance of Mt. 28:9 are obviously meant to denote divine veneration. [52]

All this is brought out most impressively in the story of the woman who sinned much, Lk. 7:36-50. It is not just that all the gestures of devotion with reference to the feet are found together in this story: washing and drying the feet, anointing, and kissing. Nor is it merely that a peculiar mode is used, tears being substituted for water, hair for a linen towel, oil for precious ointment, a kiss on the feet for a kiss on the head (v. 45 f.). When one also compares the relation of the host to Jesus — the Pharisee treats Him as a scribe, calling Him διδάσκαλε, v. 40 — with the relation between the woman and Jesus, the significance of washing, anointing and kissing the feet becomes clear. Understood as the One who according to His divine character forgives sins, Jesus in the totality of His person is already far above sinful man. As in theophanies (→ 627, 17 ff.), [53] only His feet still stretch into the sinful world, and therefore it is to His feet that honour and worship must be paid and a sacrificial offering made. This understanding of the Lucan story is effectively supported by a comparison with the accounts of the anointing in Bethany [54] as given by Mt. and Mk. on the one side and the Fourth Gospel on the other. Whereas the head is anointed in Mk. and Mt., the feet are

---

[49] E. v. Dobschütz, "Κύριος 'Ιησοῦς," ZNW, 30 (1931), 97-123.

[50] On falling on the face cf. Horst, op. cit., 53-55; Str.-B., II, 260 f.; S. Krauss, Synagogale Altertümer (1922), 348 f.

[51] Horst, 243 regards sitting at Jesus' feet as a religious concept of the community expressing the eager desire for salvation which underlies acceptance of the missionary message.

[52] The conclusion of Horst, 234 that this grasping is for the purpose of kissing seems to me to be inadmissible.

[53] The OT idea that the earth is God's foot-stool is taken up in Mt. 5:35; Ac. 7:49; Barn., 16, 2 in the words of Is. 66:1.

[54] It makes no difference whether this is the same incident or the account of the same incident as in Lk. In my essay "Der westliche Text Lk. 7:46 u. sein Wert," ZNW, 46 (1955), 241-245 I have tried to show that the anointing of the feet etc. in Lk. 7 is a later interpolation from Jn. 12.

anointed in Jn. 11:2 and 12:3. The reason for this change in the Fourth Gospel is again quite plain ; with such acts of devotion one can approach only the feet of the Christ of glory depicted by this Evangelist.

6. The Foot-Washing. Finally, this helps us to understand the act of foot-washing (→ III, 426, 25 ff.; IV, 947, 13 ff.) which Jesus performed for His disciples. In the light of all that has been said, this act seems at a first glance to be quite inexplicable. It is a paradox that the Lord of glory should stoop to the feet of men. The point of the story, however, is precisely in the paradox. Its goal is not to establish a fixed rite of washing of which this is the aetiological foundation, nor is it to provide a safeguard against erroneus rites. [55] The act offers an interpretation of the saving work of Jesus. He humbles Himself to the menial task of foot-washing, i.e., He lays aside His divine glory and by so doing accomplishes salvation for the man on whose behalf He performs this service.

What makes this understanding possible is the fact that antiquity regarded this task, which was most obviously that of the slave, as an expression of ultimate self-giving. Thus in 1 Βασ. 25:41 Abigail, when wooed by David, replies by inclining her face to the earth and saying : "Behold, let thine handmaid be a servant to wash the feet of the servants of my lord." Jos. Ant., 6, 308 sharpens even more the expression of readiness for service : ἡ δὲ ἀναξία μὲν εἶναι καὶ ποδῶν ἄψασθαι τῶν ἐκείνου ... ἔλεγεν. Hdt., VI, 19 contains a Delphic oracle on the overthrow of Miletus in which it is said : σαὶ δ' ἄλοχοι πολλοῖσι πόδας νίψουσι κομήταις, and the fulfilment of which it describes as follows : γυναῖκες καὶ τέκνα ἐν ἀνδραπόδων λόγῳ ἐγίνοντο. Plut. Pomp., 73 (I, 658d): θεραπεύων ὅσα δεσπότας δοῦλοι μέχρι νίψεως ποδῶν ... διετέλεσεν. [56]

When, therefore, Jn. 13:15 calls the act of foot-washing a ὑπόδειγμα (→ II, 33, 32 ff.), and charges the disciples (v. 14) with the same service in the same humility, the sending forth of the disciples to the world is thereby given the full dignity of the death and passion of Jesus.

In 1 Tm. 5:10 washing the feet of the ἅγιοι is one of the tasks laid on the widows of the community, → I, 788, 15 ff. This is to be construed in the same sense as the act in Jn. 13 and might well owe its origin to this tradition. [57]

7. The Cultic Uncovering of the Foot. Nowhere in the NT is there any command to do this, → 625, 17 ff.; 627, 5 ff. There is ref. to it only in the historical reminiscence in Ac. 7:33, where Stephen quotes Ex. 3:5.

Weiss

---

[55] Cf. Bu. J., 357, n. 5 on 13:10.
[56] For Rabb. writings cf. Str.-B., II, 557; I, 428.
[57] Suicerus, *s.v.* I, 2 adduces examples of the action and its understanding in the Gk. fathers.

```
┌─────────────────────────────────────────┐
│   πράσσω, πρᾶγμα, πραγματεία,           │
│ πραγματεύομαι, διαπραγματεύομαι,        │
│         πράκτωρ, πρᾶξις                  │
└─────────────────────────────────────────┘
```

† πράσσω.

Contents : A. Outside the New Testament : I. Secular Greek : 1. The Meaning of πράσσω ; 2. πράσσω of Acts of the Gods ; 3. πράσσω of Acts of Men ; II. The Septuagint ; III. Philo and Josephus : 1. Philo ; 2. Josephus. B. The New Testament : 1. Positive Evaluation ; 2. Negative Evaluation ; 3. πράσσω in Acts 26:31 etc. C. The Post-Apostolic Fathers.

A. Outside the New Testament.

I. Secular Greek.

1. The Meaning of πράσσω. The word derives from the Indo-Eur. root *per* and by way of πέρᾱ(ν), *πρᾱ-κο, *πρᾱκ-jω becomes Ionic πρήσσω and Attic πράττω. [1] It means "to get beyond," "to press on through," "to execute," "to do." a. The starting-point is the expression πρήσσειν ἅλα, κέλευθον, ὁδοῖο in epic poetry : "to cross" the sea (to the far shore), "to leave a way behind," "to traverse," "to advance," Hom. Od., 9, 491; Il., 14, 282; 24, 264 etc. This leads to the second sense b. "to travel a way in order to achieve something : κλέος ἔπραξεν, "he won renown," Pind. Isthm., 5, 8. c. With the transfer of the image of the way to abstract and total action, attention is diverted from the success achieved [2] to more or less intensive occupation with the matter in hand : "to busy oneself with something," "to be concerned about," "to pursue" : πράττειν τὰ [τὸ] ἑαυτοῦ, Plat. Charm., 162 etc.; πράττειν τὰ πολιτικὰ [πράγματα], Plat. Ap., 31d; πράττειν τί τινι [ὑπέρ τινος], "to prosecute a matter in the interests of someone," Demosth. Or., 19, 77; 26, 2; δράματα πράσσειν, "to analyse, study dramas," Suid., s.v. d. Of money, esp. public taxes and revenue : "to demand," "to collect" (also with the suggestion of unlawful practices): πράσσει με τόκον, "he collects taxes from me," Hom. Batrachomyomachia, 185, mostly mid.: πράττεσθαι χρήματα, μισθὸν κτλ., "to demand or agree upon a reward," Plat. Hi., I, 282c; pass.: ὑπὸ βασιλέως πεπραγμένος φόρους, "pressed by the king to pay the tribute," Thuc., VIII, 5, 5. e. When the intensity of concern is less prominent, we reach the abstract sense "to do," "to act": abs. often in the combination πράττειν καὶ λέγειν, while an added acc. of obj. defines the quality of the action : πράττειν δίκαια ἢ ἄδικα, Plat. Ap., 28b. f. The use with the adverb characterises the act by its moral worth on the one side : πράττειν [τι] ὀρθῶς, σωφρόνως, δικαίως, εὖ, "to act wisely etc.," "to do something rightly," Plat. Gorg., 488a; 507c; Alc., I, 116b c. Usually, however, the adv. expresses an outward or

---

π ρ ά σ σ ω κ τ λ. Pass., Liddell-Scott, Moult.-Mill., Preisigke Wört., Pr.-Bauer[4], s.v.; cf. also J. H. H. Schmidt, *Synonymik d. gr. Sprache*, I (1876), 397-423, which is still useful. For early Gk. poetry cf. O. Becker, "Das Bild des Weges u. verwandte Vorstellungen im früh-gr. Denken," *Hermes, Einzelschriften zur klass. Philologie*, 4 (1937), s.v.

[1] On the etym. Boisacq, 810; Hofmann, 282; Pokorny, 811.

[2] In earlier Gk. πράττειν denotes much more strongly a purposeful activity. Nevertheless B. Snell ("Aischylos u. das Handeln im Drama," *Philol. Supplementband*, 20 [1928], 11) goes too far when he says that the distinctive feature of πράττειν as compared with ποιεῖν is that it embraces completion. J. H. H. Schmidt, *Hndbch. d. lat. u. gr. Synonymik* (1889), 297 is nearer the mark when he says that in Attic πράττειν is used for "activity or industry directed to a specific goal in which the one who acts seems to be more or less claimed." For a full understanding it is important to distinguish between older and Attic usage [H. Schreckenberg].

inward situation : εὖ, καλῶς, κακῶς πράττω, "things go well or badly for me" (cf. "to do well"), Plat. Phaed., 58e; ὁ στόλος οὕτως ἔπρηξε, Hdt., III, 26. g. As a tt. in magical texts : "to perform a magical act," Preis. Zaub., I, 4, 951, 1396 f.; ποιεῖν, ibid., I, 5, 338. h. It is to be noted esp. that a bad sense appears early, esp. in history with ref. to treasonable proceedings : πράττειν τὴν πόλιν, "to betray the city," Polyb., 4, 17, 12; abs. οἱ πράσσοντες, "the traitors," Thuc., IV, 89, 2; 113, 1.

2. A general survey leads first to a negative conclusion of great significance. Only rarely is πράττειν employed for acts of the gods. The usage of Plato, which influences the centuries that follow, is esp. instructive. Among many hundred instances only three refer to a divine action, and these in a surprising way. Acc. to Plat. Resp., III, 391e one should not say anything prejudicial about the gods, for each will excuse himself for being bad if he is persuaded that the latest seed of the gods (sc. the gods themselves) also τοιαῦτα πράττουσί τε καὶ ἔπραττον. The same applies in Leg., X, 901b, which judges the act of him who is concerned about the great and neglects the small, εἴτε θεὸς εἴτ᾽ ἄνθρωπος. Even weaker is Phaedr., 247a, acc. to which each makes his own contribution to the festive dance of the gods, πράττων τὸ ἑαυτοῦ. In the account of the fashioning of the cosmos in Tim. the verbs ποιεῖν (→ 459, 5 ff.), ἐργάζεσθαι (→ II, 636, 8 f.), πλάττειν (→ 254, 26 ff.), δημιουργεῖν, γεννᾶν, γίγνεσθαι etc. are used for the work of the gods, but not πράττειν, cf. esp. Tim., 27d-42e. The situation is much the same in Xenoph. in the only place where he uses πράττειν for a divine action, Mem., IV, 3, 13. This says of the god who is behind all the gods and who ordains and sustains the whole world : οὗτος τὰ μέγιστα μὲν πράττων ὁρᾶται, τάδε δὲ οἰκονομῶν ἀόρατος ἡμῖν ἐστιν, "that he does the greatest things may be seen, but as the one who orders these things he is invisible to us." πράττειν here is a colourless term for the rule which as the epitome of the good guarantees everything to every man at the right time. Only incidentally, then, is the term related to the divine action which fashions and controls the cosmos. One might say that only in exceptional cases is πράττειν used for a divine action, and even then it does not suggest the creative action embraced by the term ποιεῖν, → 458, 36 ff. On the contrary, it is employed when the work of the gods is compared to human action, but as an abstract work it cannot be evaluated by man.

The same is true in older poetry. [3] Here, too, there are passages which refer naively to divine as well as human work : πρῆξαι δ᾽ ἔμπης οὔ τι δυνήσεαι, Hom. Il., I, 562 (cf. Aesch. Prom., 75; Soph. El., 200). Again, πράττειν may be preferred to δρᾶν, with which ethical judgments are associated, in order to indicate in a neutral way the divine planning and overruling which cannot be called in question ethically : (of Apollo) εἰς τὸ πᾶν ἔπραξας ὧν παναίτιος, Aesch. Eum., 200.

3. Even in respect of human πράττειν one may note a special distinction from ποιεῖν. The two groups overlap over a wide area in which they may be used interchangeably, but some par. expressions bring out the difference. Thus εἰρήνην ποιεῖν (→ II, 419, 8 ff., 29 ff.) means "to make peace," but περὶ εἰρήνης πράττειν "to exert oneself to make peace," Xenoph. Hist. Graec., VI, 3, 3, and εἰρήνην πράττειν, "to keep peace," ibid., III, 4, 6. It is thus evident that in later Gk. at least πράττειν denotes the activity as such rather than its successful outcome. The distinction between εὖ, καλῶς ποιεῖν τι, "to make a good job of," and εὖ, καλῶς πράττειν, "to be well," is also instructive in this connection. Cf. also Plat. Phaed., 60e-61a where Socrates is summoned by a dream : μουσικὴν ποίει καὶ ἐργάζου, "create musical art," which he finally does by composing poems. But earlier he had referred the summons to philosophy, of which he says : ὅπερ ἔπραττον, "in which I was already engaged." If this does not refer to the intensity of the occupation, it does not refer to the result either. In Plat. Charm., 163a-c Critias distinguishes between τὰ ἑαυτοῦ πράττειν in the sense of "doing what is right or good" and τὰ ἑαυτοῦ ποιεῖν, "the (manual) producing of objects for oneself (rather

---

[3] The ref. which follow are from a letter by H. Schreckenberg.

than others)." If Socrates rejects this sophistical distinction, he for his part uses πράττειν when he wants to define the character of the action by adverbs, *ibid.*, 163d-164c. These examples explain why πράττειν is an apt term in theoretical philosophical enquiry which considers human action apart from its content and objects. This is why πράττειν is so common in philosophical works as well as everyday speech. The ref. here is to the nature (καλῶς, ὀρθῶς, Symp., 180e-181a; Prot., 332a ff.) or purpose of the action (Gorg., 467c ff.). Action should take place for the sake of the good, Gorg., 499e. The problem of Gk. philosophy is esp. that of the knowledge which is the source of acts that lead to happiness (Plat. Charm., 173c d; Prot., 352c ff.) rather than the question whether there may be cleavage between knowledge and action, → ποιέω, 465, 35 ff. Behind defective action is a lack of ἐπιστήμη, ἀμαθία, rather than a lack of capacity or will, Prot., 357e; Gorg., 488a. With variations which need not be presented here this view persists in philosophy after Plato right on into Stoicism. Acc. to Epict. the good man does nothing for the sake of appearance but τοῦ πεπρᾶχθαι καλῶς ἕνεκα. For τὰ καλὰ καὶ δίκαια πράττειν is already the prize which is sought (Diss., III, 24, 50 f.), and the law of life of the man who is by nature capable of the good is τὸ ἀκόλουθον τῇ φύσει πράττειν, Diss., I, 26, 1. The sin in man, the anthesis between will and act (ποιεῖν), is perceived and overcome by knowledge which may be imparted, II, 26, 3-5. Though the statements about the antithesis between will and act sound like those in Paul, this is a radically different view of human action from that found in the apostle, → III, 51, 36 ff.

II. The Septuagint.

In the LXX πράσσειν [4] plays a much smaller part than ποιεῖν, → 467, 13 ff. It occurs here only 38 times, and is more common in the later books (e.g., once each in Gn. and Jos., 8 times each in Job and Prv.,[5] 7 times in 1-4 Macc.). For reasons no longer known to us πράσσειν is 5 times the transl. of עָשָׂה, 4 times of פָּעַל and twice of הָלַךְ. It is probably less prominent because its abstract sense is much too weak either for the creative work of God or for the human action characterised by personal obedience. Perhaps it also has too much of the sense of business. One may thus understand why an ethically negative implication clings to it. This is esp. true in the Wisdom literature: μετὰ ἀβουλίας, Prv. 14:17; cf. 25:28; πράσσειν τι ἐν ἔργοις ὕβρεως, Sir. 10:6; cf. 3 Macc. 2:3; πράσσειν ἄτοπα Job 27:6; 36:21; 2 Macc. 14:23; ἄδικα Job 36:23; κακά Prv. 10:23; 13:10, cf. πράσσειν ἀφρόνως Gn. 31:28; abs. Wis. 14:10. There is a striking connection with magic and with infanticide in mystical raving, Wis. 12:4. The fig. expression for the trade of the adulteress in Prv. 30:20 (she "eats") is rendered by the euphemistic ὅταν πράξῃ, cf. already Theocr. Idyll., 2, 143. The word undoubtedly has a positive sense only in the historical books: καλῶς πράσσειν, "to conduct oneself well," 4 Macc. 3:20; καλῶς καὶ ἀστείως πράττειν, "to act finely and nobly," 2 Macc. 12:43. In connection with αἱ πράξεις in the sense of *res gestae* we find τὸ πραχθέν in 1 Ἔσδρ. 1:31.[6] Of the many Gk. compounds the LXX adopts only διαπράσσειν and προσπράσσειν — which gives emphasis to the restraint.

The transl. of Symmachus (2nd cent. A.D.) diverges sharply from the LXX by using πράσσειν even for God's work in ψ 17:26; 118:126; cf. also ψ 45:9 : ἃ διεπράξατο κύριος.

---

[4] The form πραττ- occurs only in 2 and 4 Macc., Thackeray, 122 f.; Helbing, 19 f.

[5] The distinctive use of πράσσω in these two books lends support to the conjecture of G. Gerleman that they were transl. by the same hand ("Studies in the Septuagint. I. Book of Job," *Lunds Universitets Årsskrift*, NF, Avd. 1, Bd. 43, 2 [1946], 17), though many of his instances would apply to 2-4 Macc. as well [Katz].

[6] Cf. as source 2 Ch. 35:27, where W. Rudolph, *Die Chronikbücher, Hndbch. AT*, I, 21 (1955), *ad loc.* conjectures דְּרָכָיו rather than דְּבָרָיו.

III. Philo and Josephus.

1. Philo. The only statement of Philo about God's πράσσειν distinguishes pointedly between the purposeful act of the demiurge in creation (→ 461, 16 ff.) and his purposeless work in the present (πράσσειν). The mind of man enquires who the demiurge is καὶ τί διανοηθεὶς ἐποίει καὶ τί νῦν πράττει καὶ τίς αὐτῷ διαγωγὴ καὶ βίος, Abr., 163.

Human action includes not only the theoretical but also the practical art of virtue. Leg. All., I, 57 f. In accordance with the ideal of the Stoic sage the goal here is the harmony of thought, will and action, Poster. C., 85-88; Vit. Mos., I, 29 etc. This is why the variegated phrase πράττειν καὶ λέγειν occurs so often, Op. Mund., 144; Abr., 6; Decal., 101 etc. The normative court is always the OT love of God; piety consists in doing all things for the sake of God alone, Leg. All., III, 209; cf. 126. But there is no genuine confrontation in this demand, since God is constantly equated with φύσις in the Stoic sense: τὸ οἰκειότατον ἀνθρώπου φύσει τὸ εὖ καὶ βουλεύεσθαι καὶ πράττειν καὶ λέγειν, Mut. Nom., 197. Thus the philosophical concept of πράττειν stands decisively on Hell.-Stoic soil. The discrepancy between action on the one side and will and act on the other is at most a bad sign of sophistry; it is no problem for the wise man, Poster. C., 86. Those who do all things for their own sake rather than for the sake of their neighbour or God are possessed by an evil spirit, Deus Imm., 17.

2. Josephus. Joseph. uses both the simple πράττειν "to act" (e.g., Ant., 8, 252; 18, 264) and also various compounds such as ἀντι-, εἰσ-, κατα-, συμπράττω and such formations as ἀπραξία, εὐπραξία, κακοπραγία etc.

B. The New Testament.

In the NT one may see in even stronger form the tendency noted in secular Greek (→ 632, 10 ff.) and especially the LXX (→ 634, 22 ff.). Whereas the verbs ποιεῖν (Mk. 5:19; Mt. 19:4 etc. → 464, 10 ff.), ἐργάζεσθαι (Jn. 5:17 → II, 640, 13 ff.) and κατεργάζεσθαι (R. 15:18; 2 C. 12:12) are used for the work of God or Christ, there is no instance at all of any πράσσειν[7] of God. This colourless word is used only with reference to man's action, and a predominantly negative judgment is implied.

1. Positive Evaluation. With two exception (in John) the 39 instances are found only in the writings of Luke (Gospel 6 times, Acts 13) and Paul (18 times) and only rarely do they bear a positive evaluation. Ac. 26:20: ἄξια τῆς μετανοίας ἔργα πράσσοντας, is a weak rendering of the καρποὺς ποιεῖν of Mt. 3:8; Lk. 3:8. In R. 2:25 νόμον πράσσειν is found in combination with other verbs (φυλάσσειν v. 26; τελεῖν v. 27; ποιεῖν v. 14). Phil. 4:9 is a summons to imitate the apostle. Probably one might also refer to εὖ πράξετε in Ac. 15:29 in the sense of "you will do well," though this might also be a promise of blessing: "It will go well with you."[8] The latter would fit in well with common Gk. usage, cf. Eph. 6:21. But the former fits the preceding participle better and is found in Christian usage else-where.[9] A neutral use, either without evaluation or defined by ἀγαθὸν ἢ φαῦλον etc., may be seen in Ac. 5:35; R. 9:11; 2 C. 5:10. The same applies in Ac. 26:26 and 1 C. 9:17, where the emphasis is on the modal definition of the act rather than the act itself. 1 Th. 4:11 is another example of a neutral sense: πράσσειν τὰ ἴδια, "to be concerned about one's own affairs." Lk. 3:13 and 19:23 refer to the exacting of money.[10]

---

[7] The Attic form πραττ- occurs 5 times in textual variants: Lk. 3:13; Ac. 5:35; 17:7; 19:36; 1 Th. 4:11.

[8] Bengel; Zn. Ag.; Wdt. Ag.; Bau. Ag.

[9] Cf. the par. adduced in Haench. Ag. from Ign. Eph., 4, 2; Sm., 11, 3; Just. Apol., 28, 3.

[10] vl. on Lk. 19:23: ἀνέπραξα "to demand back" ΑΘ.

2. Negative Evaluation. In a good two thirds of the instances a negative judgment is associated with πράσσειν. This is usually made clear by the context. Thus τὰ περίεργα πράσσειν in Ac. 19:19 reminds us of the tt. in magic, → 633, 2 ff. A singular NT expression is μηδὲν πράξῃς σεαυτῷ κακόν[11] (Ac. 16:28; for similar phrases cf. Lk. 22:23; Ac. 17:7; 19:36; 1 C. 5:2; 2 C. 12:21; Gl. 5:21). When in Ac. 3:17 the concession is made to Peter's hearers : κατὰ ἄγνοιαν ἐπράξατε, this does not mean that a plea of psychologically mitigating circumstances is entered;[12] the act is still a guilty one, but it is set in relation to the transcendent mercy of God in the new age of revelation, as shown by the continuation in v. 18 f. and the parallels in Ac. 13:27; 17:30, → I, 116, 24 ff., 118, 12 ff. The negative aspect is brought out clearly when comparison is made with other verbs of action. To be sure, there is an area in which the terms may be used synonymously, cf. R. 2:25 (→ 635, 34 ff.); R. 13:4 : κακὸν πράσσειν = κακὸν ποιεῖν, or 1 C. 5:2 f.: ὁ πράξας[13] = ὁ κατεργασάμενος. On the other hand, there is in 1 Th. 4:11 no parallel between πράσσειν τὰ ἴδια and ἐργάζεσθαι.[14] The two passages in John point already to the fundamental difference. In Jn. 3:20 f. and 5:29 a sharp distinction is made between φαῦλα πράσσειν and ποιεῖν τὰ ἀγαθὰ or τὴν ἀλήθειαν. Even though Jn. can sometimes use ποιεῖν too in a negative sense (e.g., 8:34, 44; 13:27 → 481, 31 ff.), this is a little significance in view of its common use. πράσσειν, however, is employed only in a negative sense.

The distinction may be seen on another level in Paul. There is an intentional choice of words in R. 1:32-2:3. The οἱ πράσσοντες[15] of v. 32 refers to the mass of those who are rotting in the general swamp of pagan vices. On the other hand, the action of those who know God's righteous demands involves wilful transgression, and ποιεῖν is used for this.[16] The reference here is not just to philosophers and heathen rulers, who offer an example of greater offences. Paul already has Judaism in view since it is instructed by the Law. He speaks of this at greater length in 2:1 ff. Here, too, the ποιεῖν of v. 3 is differentiated by the accompanying knowledge of him who plays the judge from the imprecise πράσσειν of vv. 1-3, so that there is a crescendo in the passage. Even in the sphere of sinning πράσσειν has a more general sense as compared with the more definite ποιεῖν, just as encounter with the Law makes man more distinctly a sinner standing under judgment.

Possibly the distinction between πράσσειν and ποιεῖν in R. 7:15, 19 is to be understood in terms of this line of thought, → 481, 8 ff.; III, 50, 18 ff.[17] In view of v. 16 the will rather than the act is already at issue in v. 15b. Hence the act is in the first instance referred to only as a πράσσειν ("doing") which is not orientated to fulfilment.[18] For what is hated, however, the more sharply contoured

---

[11] The constr. πράττειν τινί τι is found only here in the NT; the sense calls for ποιεῖν (E) cf. Bl.-Debr., 157, 1 App.

[12] Wdt., Bau. and Haench. Ag.

[13] P46 BDG pm : ποιήσας.

[14] The Vulgate distinguishes fairly consistently between the abstract and general πράσσειν = agere, the productive ποιεῖν = facere, and the manual ἐργάζεσθαι = operari.

[15] The textual variants may be due to misunderstanding of the dat. part. πράσσουσιν. Nestle should be followed here.

[16] One may thus agree with Bengel's exposition of ποιεῖν (on R. 1:32 : etiam affectu et ratione) while disputing his understanding of πράσσειν (hoc verbum ... accurate exprimit petulantiam flagitiosorum divinae justitiae prorsus contrariam).

[17] For bibl. on R. 7 cf. W. G. Kümmel, R. 7 und die Bekehrung d. Pls. (1929), VII-XV; P. Althaus, Pls. u. Luther über den Menschen² (1951), 12; cf. also K. Barth K.D., IV, 1 (1953), 648-659 (C.D., IV, 1 [1956], 581 ff.); Mi. R., ad loc.

[18] The obi. of θέλειν, πράσσειν and ποιεῖν in v. 15 and κατεργάζεσθαι in v. 17 is

ποιεῖν is used, since a completed act is now is view. On the other hand, in 7:18-20 the κατεργάζεσθαι dominated by sin is examined. If from the standpoint of volition it seems that man is still in some sense autonomous, the sin which leads to the doing of evil is here the complete master, v. 18. In face of it the will to do what is good fails utterly, v. 20. The reversal of the verbs in v. 19 is to be understood in this light. The sharper ποιεῖν, which includes completion, gives emphasis to the serious situation in which the good which is willed is not done. Life is lived instead in the stupid doing of the evil which is not willed, and this is expressed by πράσσειν.

3. πράσσειν in Acts 26:31 etc. Special attention should be paid to the formulations in Ac. which assert Paul's innocence in the trial at Jerusalem and which culminate in the words of Festus to King Agrippa II : ὅτι οὐδὲν θανάτου ἢ δεσμῶν ἄξιον πράσσει ὁ ἄνθρωπος οὗτος, Ac. 26:31 cf. 25:11, 25; material parallels, though without the word πράσσειν, may be found in 23:9, 29; 25:18; 28:18. As the death of Stephen is deliberately compared with that of Jesus, so here there is a conscious parallel to the threefold declaration of the innocence of Jesus by Pilate in Lk. 23:4, 14 f., 22. [19]

> Lk. does not depict the matter thus merely because of a supposed tendency of his to blame the Jews and excuse the Roman state with a view to protecting infant Christianity thereby. [20] For 1. in these solemn declarations of innocence the Roman procurator and the Jewish king agree, Lk. 23:14 f.; Ac. 26:31. Again 2. the official decision of Pilate expressed by ἐπικρίνειν (Lk. 23:24) [21] is the true injustice of this Roman who was appointed to preserve justice. Similarly one may gather that the repeated ref. in Ac. to the imperial court (25:11 f., 21, 25; 26:32 etc.) is designed to increase rather decrease the responsibility of Rome for the death of the apostle, which is presupposed in the story (cf. Ac. 20:25). Finally 3. the innocence of Jesus is admitted not merely by the procurator but also by the centurion (Lk. 23:47) and esp. by the thief on His right hand (Lk. 23:41).
>
> In the third Gospel Jesus is the central character and His innocence is proclaimed by such dubious witnesses as the Roman and Jewish authorities and the malefactor on the cross. But this means that the legal question of responsibility for the death of Jesus cannot be decided by human computation. We are referred here to the strange righteousness of the divine δεῖ (→ II, 22, 41 ff.) in accordance with which the innocent One brings redemption to the guilty. [22] Similarly in Ac. it is Paul, the instrument of the exalted Christ, also declared innocent on all sides but still treated as guilty, who is the one to bring the Gospel to Rome. If Paul himself still proclaims that he earlier thought he had to do many things against the name of Jesus of Nazareth (Ac. 26:9), he is

---

the good or the evil, while in the thematic statement in v. 15a the unintelligible and unplanned total output of human conduct is at issue, cf. Bultmann Theol., 244. In his "R. 7 und die Anthropologie des Pls.," Imago Dei, Festschr. f. G. Krüger (1932), 60 f. Bultmann thinks that life and death are also obj. in v. 15.

[19] Cf. R. Morgenthaler, Die lk. Geschichtsschreibung als Zeugnis, I (1948), 182 f.

[20] Bau. Ag., 266; M. Dibelius, "Pls. in d. Ag.," Aufsätze zur Ag., ed. H. Greeven² (1953), 179 f. (acc. to Dibelius Lk. is also instructing Christians on how to act before the judgment-seat); H. Conzelmann, Die Mitte d. Zeit (1954), 117-124; Haench. Ag., 621 on Ac. 26:32; 664 f. Exoneration of Pilate is contested by, e.g., M. J. Lagrange, Evangile selon Saint Luc⁷ (1948), 575.

[21] ἐπικρίνειν denotes the official decision of the procurator, as against Conzelmann, op. cit., 71 f.; cf. 2 Macc. 4:47; 3 Macc. 4:2; Jos. Bell., 6, 416; Ant., 14, 192; Ditt. Or., II, 483, 1 ff.; Ac. 25:25.

[22] As against Conzelmann, 71 f., 120. All analogies to the innocent Jewish martyrs break down at this decisive point.

making clear his own distinction from Jesus, in whom alone his own innocence is grounded.

C. The Post-Apostolic Fathers.

In the post-apost. fathers, as in the NT, πράσσειν is used in many different ways, but the tendency here too is to use it mostly for bad conduct, cf. 1 Cl., 35, 6; 2 Cl., 4, 5; 10, 5; Herm. m., 3, 3 etc.

† πρᾶγμα.

1. πρᾶγμα is the concrete form of πρᾶξις, but is close to it in meaning. The following nuances call for consideration: a. Obligatory activity, "undertaking," "obligation," "business," "task": τὰ πολιτικά πράγματα, Plat. Ap., 31d; τὰ ἴδιά τε καὶ κοινὰ πράγματα, Philo Plant., 146; also negatively: πράγματα ἔχειν "to have burdensome tasks," "troubles," "worries"; τὸ μακάριον καὶ ἄφθαρτον (= the godhead) οὔτε αὐτὸ πράγματα ἔχει οὔτε ἄλλῳ παρέχει, Epic. Sententiae Selectae, 1; b. the object which can stand in manifold relation to human action, "cause," "affair," "thing": τὰ μετέωρα πράγματα "heavenly movements," Aristoph. Nu., 228; τὰ τῆς φύσεως πράγματα, "natural phenomena" of the cosmos, Philo Som., I, 53; πράγματα ἀσώματα, θεῖα, νοητά, Rer. Div. Her., 63, 66; τὰ τοῦ βίου πράγματα, Decal., 150 etc.; emphasising significance οὐ πρᾶγμά ἐστιν, οὐδὲν πρᾶγμα etc., "it is of no consequence," "there is nothing to it," Plat. Crat., 393d etc.; positively μέγιστον πρῆγμα, Hdt., III, 132; c. the result of activity, "what is effected," "act," "fact," "event," of historical deeds: τὴν ἱστορίαν τῶν πραγμάτων τούτων ἀναγράφειν, Jos. Vit., 40 etc.; d. things in their influence on man: "circumstances," "relations," "the situation": τὰ κοινὰ πράγματα, Eur. Iph. Taur., 1062; τὰ ἀνθρωπήϊα πρήγματα, Hdt., I, 207; Philo Som., I, 153 ff.; in a bad sense ἐν τοιούτοις πράγμασιν, "in such a difficult situation," Xenoph. An., II, 1, 16; e. specifically "legal process," "trial," πρᾶγμα ἔχειν πρός τινα, P. Oxy., IV, 743, 19 (1st cent. B.C.); Jos. Ap., 2, 177.

2. The LXX keeps to this sphere of general meaning. Of the 125 instances more than half are in the Gk. books of the Hell. period. In the others the usual original is דָּבָר in the sense of "matter," "affair."[1] Twice (ψ 63:4; Prv. 13:13) דָּבָר is rendered πρᾶγμα even though it obviously means "word." 3 Βασ. 10:22c: "Of the children of Israel Solomon gave none εἰς πρᾶγμα, i.e., "into slavery" (acc. to the context, cf. 2 Ch. 8:9). Qoh. 3:1, 17; 5:7; 8:6 have πρᾶγμα for חֵפֶץ "thing," "matter."[2] There are only odd instances of other equivalents.

It is worth noting, perhaps, that in some cases the ref. is to God's acts. But the instances show how random this is. Is. 25:1: ἐποίησας θαυμαστὰ πράγματα עָשִׂיתָ פֶּלֶא, "thou hast done wondrous things," a casual secondary form for τὰ θαυμάσια, which is used for פֶּלֶא in ψ 76:12, 15; 77:12; 87:11, 13; 88:6. There is a similar phrase in Is. 28:22: συντετελεσμένα καὶ συντετμημένα πράγματα "achieved and completed acts" (= כָּלָה וְנֶחֱרָצָה "destruction and punishment"). Cf. Is. 10:23, where λόγος συντετμημένος is used for the same Heb. phrase. ... πρᾶγμα ποιήσει μετὰ σοῦ ὁ θεός, Jdt. 11:6. The negative fixes the sense in Am. 3:7: οὐ μὴ ποιήσῃ κύριος ὁ θεὸς πρᾶγμα, cf. οὐδὲν πρᾶγμα for "nothing" in Gn. 19:22; Nu. 20:19; Dt. 24:5. In negative or conditional clauses πᾶν πρᾶγμα has the weak sense of "something," Lv. 5:2; Ju. 19:19 etc. The ref. is not to God's acts in the strict sense when acc. to Δα. 4:37a God alters

---

π ρ ᾶ γ μ α. [1] On the relation between ῥῆμα and πρᾶγμα in transl. of דָּבָר cf. E. Repo, *Der Begriff "Rhēma" im Biblisch-Griechischen I: "Rhēma" in der Septuaginta* (1951), 160 f., 190 f.
[2] As in later Heb., cf. Ges.-Buhl, *s.v.*

ὑπερμεγέθη or μεγάλα πράγματα in the life of a man, or when in Nu. 22:8 Balaam proclaims the πράγματα which the Lord speaks to him.

Certain detailed pts. call for notice. πρᾶγμα can also be used for "evil" in the LXX : πρᾶγμα ἀκάθαρτον, Lv. 7:21 etc.; πονηρόν, Dt. 17:5 A; παράνομον, ψ 100:3; ἄσχημον, Dt. 24:1; cf. also τὸ πρᾶγμα τοῦτο, Ju. 6:29 etc. In Macc. τὰ πράγματα often means "affairs of state," 2 Macc. 9:24 etc.; cf. Da. 2:48, 49, or "matter of government," 2 Macc. 3:38; 11:19 etc.; οἱ τεταγμένοι ἐπὶ πραγμάτων, "state officials," 3 Macc. 7:1; ὁ ἐπὶ τῶν πραγμάτων, "state administrator," 2 Macc. 3:7; 11:1 etc. The ref. in Jdt. 8:32; 11:16 is to "heroic deeds" and in 1 Macc. 10:35, 63 to "legal affairs."

3. In 6 of the 11 NT instances the meaning is neutral. Prayer will be heard as touching all possible "matters," Mt. 18:19. Similarly Paul asks that Phoebe be assisted in all her "business," R. 16:2. Lk. 1:1 calls the "events" that have taken place among us τὰ πεπληροφορημένα ἐν ἡμῖν πράγματα. These embrace the whole saving action up to the ascension as narrated in the Gospel. ³ In Hb. there is an echo of the πράγματα θεῖα, νοητά in Philo, → 638, 16 f. On two irrevocable "things," more precisely "events," "happenings" (Hb. 6:18), namely, the promise of God and His oath (6:13, 17), rests the assurance of receiving the blessings which are hoped for and which are already prepared. The Law contains only the shadow and not the reality of things, i.e., the fulfilment of salvation itself 10:1 → II, 395, 8 ff. Faith (→ 207, 6 ff.) is πραγμάτων ἔλεγχος οὐ βλεπομένων, Hb. 11:1. ⁴ This is not a subj. gen., ⁵ as though invisible things were their own proof. Though faith in Hb. is grounded wholly on God, faith is the subject which persuades, not God. ⁶ In contrast to Philonic and other philosophy, the "promised blessings of salvation" are again the things not seen. ⁷ It is impossible to construe πράγματα as "occurrence," "action," and to relate it to the priestly offering of Christ in heaven. ⁸

Condemnation is implied in Ac. 5:4 : "Why hast thou done this (evil) deed?" and 2 C. 7:11: "(bad) affair," but cf. J. 3:16 πᾶν φαῦλον πρᾶγμα, "every wickedness."

There are three possibilities at 1 Th. 4:6.

a. The defrauding is in "business" or "trade." ⁹ But this exposition, which is based on the Lat. transl., is barely tenable, since πρᾶγμα, though it is to some degree co-extensive with negotium, is not, like the latter, a tt. for business undertakings. ¹⁰ Even if one were to read enclitically ἔν τῳ πράγματι, ¹¹ πρᾶγμα would still have to have the very general sense "in any matter" with no restriction to commercial dealings.

b. The ref. may be to a "lawsuit," "dispute," "trial." ¹² Now πρᾶγμα is well attested in

---

³ So M. J. Lagrange, Ev. selon S. Luc⁷ (1948), ad loc.; Schl. Lk., ad loc. Zn. Lk., 50; Kl. Lk. and Hck. Lk., ad loc. also include the events of Ac.

⁴ On rhythmic grounds πραγμάτων is to be related to βλεπομένων, not ἐλπιζομένων (P¹³).

⁵ So Schl. Glaube, 524 f.

⁶ With Mi. Hb., ad loc. as against F. Büchsel (→ ἔλεγχος, II, 476, 10 ff.).

⁷ Acc. to J. Héring, L'Epître aux Hébreux (1954), ad loc. the ref. to the future world marks the decisive distinction from contemporary philosophy.

⁸ As against C. Spicq, L'épître aux Hébreux, II (1953), 339.

⁹ So already Jer. on Eph. 4:17 ff. (MPL, 26, 622); Dob. Th.; Wbg. Th.; Luther Bible ; J. Schneider, → V, 744, 16 ff.

¹⁰ The only instance in Moult.-Mill. (from Theadelphia) rests on a misunderstanding of the explanatory note in Mitteis-Wilcken, I, 2, 99, n. 1.

¹¹ Armenian (ἔν τινι cj Grotius).

¹² Cr.-Kö.; Dib. Th.; Delling, → 271, 11 ff.

this sense (→ 638, 24 f.), possibly even in Paul himself, 1 C. 6:1. [13] But this special sense always arises out of the context, whereas there is nothing to demand it here. Can one really say that Paul is simply calling for moderation in disputes and litigation and not issuing a basic summons to peace among the members of the community, as in 1 C. 6:7 f.? c. It is thus most natural to give to πρᾶγμα the general sense of "the matter" and to allow the contents to tell us what this is. It is then simplest to take the infinitives of v. 3 f., 6 as a final clause dependent on τὸ θέλημα, and the asyndetic relation of v. 6 shows that the ref. here is to the same matter as that treated previously. [14] ὑπερβαίνειν and πλεονεκτεῖν do not of themselves have any sexual connotation ; [15] they denote man's going beyond the measure due to him or transgressing the orders in which men are set in their life together. [16] In the context this ruthless over-reaching implies a breaking forth from one's own allotted sphere and an invasion of a brother's marriage. [17]

Here, then, πρᾶγμα is a euphemism for sex, which is elsewhere a par. of πράσσειν (→ 634, 34 ff.) and πρᾶξις (→ 643, 3 ff.). Thus one might freely translate the saying : Do not allow yourself any presumptuous infringement upon your brother in this matter, i.e., fornication. [18] Unity is thus given to the whole section 4:3-8. Sanctification is taken comprehensively and in this light one of the decisive questions of pagan society is set under the will of God. If the → σκεῦος of v. 4 means the wife, then the prohibition of free love is at issue in v. 3, the sanctity of one's own marriage in v. 4 and the protection of the brother's marriage in v. 6. Finally, v. 8 establishes once again that this is not just a question of intra-personal relations but of obedience to God, who has made the body an instrument of His Spirit.

4. Of the post-apost. fathers it is Herm. esp. who uses the word (19 times). He normally employs it in the colourless sense of "thing," "affair," "matter," e.g., τὰ βιωτικὰ πράγματα, v., 3, 11, 3; m., 5, 2, 2.

† πραγματεία.

1. From πραγματεύομαι : a. "Zealous prosecution of or concern with a matter" : πόνων πολλῶν καὶ πραγματείας εἶναι, Demosth. Or., 8, 48; ἀνθρώπων πραγματεία, "work" (or "affairs") of "men," Plat. Resp., VI, 500c; πραγματεία περί τινος or περί τι, "occupation with something," Epict. Diss., I, 7, 1 and 12; b. of the thing with which one is occupied : "business," "work" : ἡ τοῦ διαλέγεσθαι πραγματεία, Plat. Theaet., 161e; αἱ τοῦ βίου πραγματεῖαι, "the concerns of daily life," Philo Spec. Leg., II, 65, also "affairs of state" : αἱ πραγματεῖαι, "official duties," P. Tebt., I, 5, 143 etc.; c. "business" : ἡ τῶν ὑποζυγίων ζῴων ἡμῶν πραγματεία, "our trade in draught-animals," P. Oxy., IV, 806 (1st cent. B.C.); d. of the result, esp. of mental work : "treatise," "writing," esp. "historical works," Polyb., 1, 1, 4; 3, 1; Jos. Ant., 1, 5; 14, 218.

---

[13] Cf. L. Vischer, Die Auslegungsgeschichte v. 1 K. 6:1-11 (1955), 7-9.

[14] Bengel, ad loc.

[15] As against E. Klaar : "πλεονεξία, -έκτης, -εκτεῖν," ThZ, 10 (1954), 395-397.

[16] Delling (→ 267, 7 ff.; 268, 12 ff., 28 ff.; 270, 21 ff.) has plainly shown that πλεονεκτεῖν has this range in non-bibl. Gk. and Philo. Cf. the equation of πλεονεξία and ὑπερβῆναι τὸ δίκαιον in Dio Chrys. Or., 67, 12 (→ 268, 24 f.). For the same range in the NT (→ 271, 2 ff.) cf. esp. 2 C. 2:11.

[17] If in various NT passages, esp. lists of vices, avarice and fornication are mentioned together (1 C. 5:10; 6:9 f.; Eph. 4:19; 5:3, 5; Col. 3:5; 2 Pt. 2:14), this does not force us one-sidedly to limit the sense of πλεονεκτεῖν in 1 Th. 4:6 to "avarice."

[18] Chrys.; Bengel ; Schl. Erl.; W. Neil, The Epistle of Paul to the Thess., MNTC (1950); Moult.-Mill., s.v.; Zürich Bible.

2. The 8 LXX instances offer nothing new. a. "Zealous prosecution" may well be the sense in 3 Βασ. 9:1, esp. when one has in view the Heb. original חֵשֶׁק "hearty wish" or "desired object." Yet comparison with 3 Βασ. 10:22a (= 1 K. 9:19) pts. rather in the direction of b. "work prosecuted." For in spite of the Heb. background the ref. is more to the active work of Solomon than to his wishes. 3 Βασ. 7:19 (= 1 K. 7:33) is to be regarded as an error ; the transl. read חֵשֶׁק for חֶשֶׁק (spokes) and took it to refer to the work carried out. The "task to be carried out," "commission," is the sense at 1 Ch. 28:21 (מְלָאכָה) and Δα. 6:4, while 3 Βασ. 10:22a refers to the carrying out of forced labour (דְּבַר). πραγματείας for γραμματείας in ψ 70:15 (B) is a simple slip. c. "Historical work" is the meaning in 2 Macc. 2:31, cf. πολυπραγμονεῖν "to investigate closely" at 2:30.

3. In the Rabb. we find not only פְּרַגְמָטוֹטִיס for πραγματευτής [1] "business-man" but also the loan word פְּרַגְמָטְיָא (vl. פְּרַקְמָטְיָא) in the sense of "business," "trade," RH, 31b Bar.; BM, 42a. [2]

4. The word occurs in the NT only at 2 Tm. 2:4. Here the context does not require the special sense of "business as a means of livelihood," [3] → 640, 35 f., lines 12 ff. The meaning is the general one, → 640, 31 ff. The soldier does not become entangled in the varied "affairs of civilian life" which might stand in the way of his readiness to obey. [4] The difference from 1 C. 9:7 is that the main issue is not that of pay but of a radical turning aside from all the cheerful or sad demands of life and a turning to full readiness in relation to Christ. [5]

5. Only Hermas of the post-apost. fathers uses the term (10 times); it denotes the varied "affairs" of this aeon in m., 10, 1, 4b; s., 9, 20, 1 f.; "business" in v., 3, 6, 5; m., 10, 1, 4a.

† πραγματεύομαι, † διαπραγματεύομαι.

1. πραγματεύομαι mid. [1] "to pursue with vigor," "to be concerned about," "to be occupied with," περί τινος, ἐπί τινι etc., Hdt., II, 87; Xenoph. Mem., I, 3, 15; Philo Som., I, 53 etc.; Jos. Bell., 2, 594; Ant., 16, 180; 3 Βασ. 10:22a. There are three main lines : a. "to render political service," Da. 8:27: οἱ πραγματευόμενοι, "those charged with affairs of state," P. Petr., III, 36, verso 14; b. of intellectual pursuits, "to compose," "to treat of," "to write," esp. of historians : πραγματεύεσθαι τὰς πραγματείας, "to depict historical events," Polyb. 1, 4, 3 etc.; c. of business affairs, πραγματεύεσθαι ἀπὸ ἐμπορίας καὶ δανεισμῶν, "to do business in trade and moneylending," Plut. Cato Minor, 59 (I, 788c); οἱ πραγματευόμενοι, negotiatores, "traders," Ditt. Or., II, 532, 6; συμπραγματευόμενοι, "business partners," 3 Macc. 3:10.

The only NT instance (Lk. 19:13) demands the sense "do business," "make a profit" → lines 32 ff.

π ρ α γ μ α τ ε ί α. [1] πραγματευτής "business representative" (actor) from Plut.

[2] Str.-B., III, 657 on 2 Tm. 2:4; I, 592; M. Jastrow, A Dict. of the Targumim, the Talmud Babli and Yerushalmi and the Midrashic Literature, II (1950), 1214 f.

[3] Schl., Dib. Past.; J. Jeremias, Die Briefe an Timotheus u. Titus, NT Deutsch⁷ (1954); Bengel, ad loc.

[4] In Epict. Diss., III, 24, 34-36 the metaphor of the obedient soldier who watches for every signal from the general merges into that of the statesman who cannot concern himself too closely with domestic affairs (ὀλίγα μὲν δεῖ οἰκονομεῖν).

[5] Pr.-Bauer⁵, s.v.; Wbg. Past., ad loc. (the problems of life).

π ρ α γ μ α τ ε ύ ο μ α ι. [1] Directly from the stem πραγματ-; there is no πραγματεύς cf. Bl.-Debr. § 108, 5; Debr. Griech. Wortb. § 213-215.

2. διαπραγματεύομαι mid. "to deal with radically," "to investigate closely" → 641, 30 f.: τοῦτον τὸν λόγον, Plat. Phaed., 77d; τὴν αἰτίαν, 95e.

In the NT the word occurs only once at Lk. 19:15 and means "to handle," "to manage," → 641, 32 ff.

† πράκτωρ.

1. The ancient ending of the *nomen agentis* in -τωρ persisted in Attic (and Ionic) almost exclusively in the sacral and political sphere : [1] from πράσσειν "to exact" in the sacral sense "avenger," "recompenser" : πράκτωρ αἵματος, Aesch. Eum., 319; in the political sense a term for subordinate officials with various functions : [2] "one who executes judgment," "exactor" of judicial demands and penalties, [3] Antiphon. Or., VI, 49; Demosth. Or., 25, 28; Ditt. Or., II, 483, 7; in the Ptolemaic and esp. the Roman period : "collector of taxes" in money, wheat etc. : [4] πράκτωρ ἀργυρικῶν, BGU, II, 434, 3; b. from πράσσειν "to act" : πράκτορες ἀκουσίων, "involuntary actors or authors," Antiphon. Or., II, 2, 6. The term does not occur in Joseph.

2. In the LXX it is used at Is. 3:12 for נֹגֵשׂ "tyrannical government." [5] The Heb. word for its part is used for the exacting of tributes (2 K. 23:35) and the pressing of debtors (Dt. 15:2 f.).

3. The only NT occurrence is in the parable at Lk. 12:58. Here as compared with Mt. 5:25 f. the term is linguistically determined by assimilation to Roman judicial procedure and materially characterised by an eschatological orientation. Whereas in Mt. the issue is reconciliation on the way to an earthly judge, Lk. offers a pure parable. [6] The πράκτωρ is the "bailiff" who is in charge of the debtor's prison. [7] The parable calls for repentance before the imminent divine decision is made and the execution of the sentence takes its ineluctable course.

† πρᾶξις.

1. In profane Gk. the following special senses call for notice : a. In relation to what is or should be done : "action," "deed," "enterprise," "transaction" : πρῆξις δ' ἥδ' ἰδίη, οὐ δήμιος, Hom. Od., 3, 82; including the result, esp. in a good sense : "success," "favorable issue" : δὸς πόρον καὶ πρᾶξιν τῷ τόπῳ τούτῳ, Preis. Zaub., I, 4, 2366; b. in the abstract "action" : ἡ τῶν ἀγαθῶν πρᾶξις, Plat. Charm., 163e; ἡ πρᾶξις ἡ πολεμική, πολιτική, ποιητική, "art of war, politics, poetry." Plat. Resp., III, 399a etc.; c. "individual completed act," Soph. Oed. Tyr., 895; Isoc., 12, 127; in the plur. in the sense of *res gestae* : [1] πράξεις τε καὶ δωρεαὶ Σεβαστοῦ θεοῦ. [2] Οἱ τὰς κατὰ Πομπήιον πράξεις ἀναγράψαντες, Jos. Ant., 14, 68; d. par. to εὖ πράσσειν κτλ. "state," "situation," "condition" : εὐτυχὴς πρᾶξις, Soph. Trach., 294 etc.; κακαὶ πρά-

---

π ρ ά κ τ ω ρ. [1] Debr. Griech. Wortb. § 346, cf. E. Fraenkel, *Gesch. d. gr.* Nomina agentis, I (1910), 220; II (1912), 8 f., 49 f., 51.
[2] Preisigke Wört., III, 144a-147a; Pr.-Bauer⁵, *s.v.*
[3] Cf. Mitteis-Wilcken, II, 1, 19 f.
[4] *Ibid.*, I, 1, 185, 212 f.
[5] 'A has εἰσπράκτης or εἰσπράσσειν for נֹגֵשׂ cf. also Ex. 5:13; Job 3:18; 39:7; Zech. 10:4.
[6] J. Jeremias, *Die Gleichnisse Jesu*⁴ (1956), 32 f.; M. J. Lagrange, *Evangile selon Saint Luc*⁷ (1948), ad loc.
[7] In the Gk. φυλακή; πρακτόρειον occurs in Ditt. Or., II, 669, 15 and 17.
π ρ ᾶ ξ ι ς. [1] A. Wikenhauser, *Die Ag. u. ihr Geschichtswert* (1921), 94-104.
[2] Inscr. Graecae ad res Romanas pertinentes, ed. R. Cagnat, III (1906), No. 159.

ξεις, Soph. Ant., 1305; "experience," "condition," "destiny," Preis. Zaub., I, 4, 1227; with ποίησις, *ibid.,* I, 1, 141; f. in history also in a bad sense "cunning action," "deception," "treachery" : ἐπί τινα, Polyb., 2, 9, 2; 5, 96, 4; κατά τινος 4, 71, 6 etc.; g. in sayings where the context fixes the sense "sexual intercourse," Pind. Fr., 127; Aeschin. Tim., 158; Aristot. Hist. An., V, 2, p. 539b, 20.

2. The LXX, which is averse to abstract thought, uses πρᾶξις only rarely. More strongly than in the case of the verb its occurrence is concentrated in books influenced by Hellenism. Of 23 instances 3 have דֶּרֶךְ as the original, 3 have a neutral פֹּעַל and 2 (Sir. 11:10; 38:24) have the later Jewish עֵסֶק (or עֵשֶׂק) "business," "undertaking." In most cases the ref. is to an ordinary human "undertaking" or "project," Job 24:5; Prv. 13:13a; Jdt. 8:34. Once the sense is the "yielding of money," 2 Macc. 4:28. In 6 instances the ref. is to the completed acts (*res gestae*) of a ruler, 2 Ch. 12:15; 13:22; 27:7; 28:26; 1 Macc. 16:23; 2 Macc. subscriptio ; cf. 1 Ἐσδρ. 1:31. The LXX is palpably influenced by everyday Gk. usage and historical writing, but not by philosophy. On the other hand the sense of the Heb. דֶּרֶךְ is weakened in transl. Of interest is Sir. 35:22 : God repays man κατὰ τὰς πράξεις αὐτοῦ. Here πρᾶξις has for once the religious sense usually linked to ἔργον, → II, 637, 11 ff. The strong deviation of the son of Sirach from the common LXX line may be seen at this pt.

Symmachus departs even more drastically from the thought of the LXX. In the Ps. πράξεις is often used rather than ἔργα for פְּעָלִים, מַעֲשִׂים etc. God repays acc. to works, ψ 27:4. He will bring all works into judgment, Qoh. 12:14. He will prosper the work of men's hands, ψ 89:17. Symmachus also speaks of God's πράξεις, ψ 27:5; 65:5; 76:13 (cf. also ψ 142:5 ᾽Α). Here is a new wave of Hell. words with an OT content.

3. In Philo πρᾶξις is completely controlled by πράττειν. There is no ref. to God's πρᾶξις. Only rarely do we hear of human action in an abstract sense, cf. the allegorical exposition of the hand representing action in Leg. All., II, 89; Spec. Leg., IV, 138; cf. Vit. Mos., II, 130. When he has specific acts in view Phil. almost always has the plur.; OT influence may be seen here. But under this outward appearance one may detect the wisdom teaching of Stoicism, e.g., in the many schematic epithets such as καλαί, ἐπαινεταί, σπουδαῖαι, κατ᾽ ἀρετάς, κατὰ τὸν βίον, and in the orientation of the sayings to the ideal of the perfect sage. The greater importance of acts than words or theories is emphasised, Congr., 46; Det. Pot. Ins., 97; Mut. Nom., 243. But the main stress is on the unity of λόγοι, βουλαί, πράξεις, Poster. C., 85 ff.; Virt., 183 f.; Mut. Nom., 236 ff. Through the agreement of God's laws and the cosmos it is possible that in the sage the will of the law may be in harmony with the inner nature, Op. Mund., 3; cf. also the metaphor of the good works sown by God in the womb of virtue, Leg. All., III, 181 etc. Historical acts are παλαιαὶ πράξεις : παλαιῶν πράξεων ἱστορία, Cherub., 105; παλαιῶν πράξεων ὑπομνήματα, Vit. Mos., II, 48.

4. The 7 NT instances (three times each in Pl. and Lk., once in Mt.) do not give evidence of any uniform use, though there seems to be a derogatory nuance in most of them. The quotation in Mt. 16:27 is the counterpart to Sir. 35:22, where πρᾶξις in the sense of ἔργον ("work," "deed") is related to the divine judgment. [3] The Stoic unity of thought, will and act is echoed in Lk. 23:51 when Joseph of Arimathea does not agree with the decision of the Sanhedrin and its execution.

Paul's use is obviously abstract in R. 8:13 and Col. 3:9. To understand both verses it is important to remember 1. that πρᾶξις has above all the abstract sense (→ 642, 30 ff.) "action," "mode of action," "way of acting," and 2. that it has a strong inclination to the ethically negative side, → 643, 2 ff. Thus in R. 8:13 one

---

[3] The correction in אˣ F 1, 22, 28 etc. (τὰ ἔργα) is based more on ψ 61:13; Prv. 24:12 than on linguistic sense.

is not to think of deeds done by the body but of the indwelling evil nature of the man who lives κατὰ σάρκα. We are not to live after the flesh in an existence which is dominated by sin and which leads to death. In the spirit we are rather to mortify the evil actions of the body in order that we may live. The body as such is not to be put to death, but dedicated to the new Lord. [4] The situation is much the same in Col. 3:9. Here, however, the putting off of the old man with his wicked ways and practices, and the putting on of the new man, have already taken place. [5] As a parallel the turning to salvation which has happened in Christ runs through the whole chapter as the basis of present demands, cf. the οὖν of v. 5, 12, the νυνί of v. 8, and also v. 13, 15.

The πράξεις repented of in Ac. 19:18 might be "wicked acts" in general, since it is only in v. 19 that we read of some forsaking magic. Nevertheless, the whole context from v. 11 onwards (the mention of evil spirits in v. 12, incantations in vv. 13 ff.) forces us to adopt the technical sense of "magical arts or acts." Hence we have here the impressive depiction of a great victory of the name of Jesus over the broad sphere of ancient magic and conjuration.

The title of Acts, πράξεις ἀποστόλων, [6] does not come from Luke himself, [7] but probably from the 2nd cent.

Neither of the terms accords with the usage or purpose of Lk. [8] Lk. never has πράξεις in the sense of the *res gestae* of the OT or Hellenism (→ 642, 33 f.; 643, 12 ff.) and except at Ac. 14:4, 14 the ἀπόστολοι are for him simply the witnesses of the passion and resurrection of Jesus (Ac. 1:21 f.), which does not fit the chief charactes, Paul. Above all, Lk. ascribes the acts, not to the apostles, but to the exalted Lord through His Word, by means of which He moves from Jerusalem to the centre of the world, Rome. The emphasis on Christ's own action also makes it doubtful whether the suggested [9] rendering "acts and experiences" (→ 642, 34 ff.) is nearer the mark than a ref. to the *res gestae*.

5. In the post-apost. fathers πρᾶξις, like πρᾶγμα and πραγματεία, is most common in Herm. (47 times). The ref. is usually to human action in the sense of "deed," "act," m., 7, 1; 10, 2, 3, esp. in an ethically bad sense, m., 4, 2, 1; s., 4, 4. There are no peculiarities in this popular use.

Maurer

πραϋπάθεια → V, 939, 18 ff.

---

[4] In reading τῆς σαρκός, DEFG latt Ir^lat etc. confuse the person, who is here at issue, with the orientation of life to sin (understood as σάρξ).
[5] The aor. parts. do not have an imperative sense (Dib. Kol.) but express what has already taken place, Schl. Erl.; H. Rendtorff, *Der Brief an d. Kol.*, NT Deutsch, 8^7 (1955), *ad loc.*; C. Masson, *L'épitre de Saint Paul aux Coloss.* (1950), 143, n. 6.
[6] On the variants (πράξεις [τῶν] ἀποστόλων is the best attested reading, but we also find πράξεις; *actus, acta apostolorum*) cf. the editions and also Zn. Einl., II, 337, 395; Zn. Ag., 8; Bau. Ag., 16.
[7] So Zn. Ag., 7 f.; A. Wikenhauser, *op. cit.* (→ n. 1), 105 f.
[8] Cf. Bau. Ag., 16; Haench Ag., 91; W. Michaelis, *Einleitung in das NT*² (1954), 129.
[9] H. Hommel, "Neue Forschungen zur Areopagrede Ag. 17," ZNW, 49 (1955), 146.

† πραΰς, πραΰτης

Contents : A. Secular Greek : 1. πραΰς ; 2. πραΰτης. B. Septuagint and Hellenistic Judaism : 1. Old Testament ; 2. Philo ; 3. Josephus ; 4. Qumran Texts. C. New Testament : 1. Matthew ; 2. Paul ; 3. Pastoral Epistles ; 4. James. D. Post-Apostolic Fathers.

A. Secular Greek.

1. πραΰς.

πραΰς, [1] etym. related to *frijon, frionds, Freund,* friend, [2] denotes that which is "gentle" and pleasant. It is used a. of things : "mild" : φύσις (Plat. Resp., II, 375c), φωνή (Xenoph. Sym., I, 10), ἐν πραέσι λόγοις ... νουθετεῖν (Plat. Leg., X, 888a), also "soothing" : φάρμακον (Pind. Olymp., 13, 85), "allaying" (Xenoph. Eq., 9, 3); b. of animals : ἵπποι, Xenoph. Cyrop., II, 1, 29; ἰχθύων μεγάλων καὶ πραέων οὓς οἱ Σύροι θεοὺς ἐνόμιζον, An., I, 4, 9; ἡμεροῦν means to tame wild animals (ἄγρια), πραΰνειν "to calm" those that are irritated or excited, Xenoph. Mem., II, 3, 9; Eq., 9, 10; c. of persons : "mild," "friendly," "gentle," "pleasant" as opp. to "rough," "hard," "violent" χαλεπός, Plat. Resp., II, 375c; Isoc. Or., 3, 55; Plat. Resp., I, 354a (opp. χαλεπαίνειν); VI, 493b (opp. χαλεπός, ὀργή), or "angry," Epict. Diss., III, 20, 9 alongside ἀόργητος, ἀνεκτικός "patient," or "brutal" βίαιος, → lines 25 ff. It is a synonym of ἵλεως (Plat. Resp., VIII, 566e), δημοτικός "affable" (Plat. Euthyd., 303d), of ἥμερος and συγγνωμονικός (Epict. Diss., II, 22, 36), of ἄφθονος (Plat. Resp., VI, 500a), and of μεγαλόθυμος (II, 375c); d. of acts and feelings : agriculture as distinct from war is a φιλάνθρωπος καὶ πραεῖα τέχνη (Xenoph. Oec., 19, 17), of feelings ἡδοναὶ πραότεραι (Plat. Leg., VII, 815e). Plato speaks of λογισμὸς πρᾶος (Leg., I, 645a, opp. βίαιος); he expects agreement from one who is γεννάδας and πρᾶος τὸ ἦθος (Phaedr., 243c); milder punishments are in order for unpremeditated and sudden acts (Leg., IX, 867b, opp. χαλεπός). e. The adv. πράως is often used for the quiet and friendly composure which does not become embittered or angry at what is unpleasant, whether in the form of people (Epict. Ench., 42) or fate. This is an active attitude and deliberate acceptance, not just a passive submission, cf. Epict. Diss., III, 10, 6 : ἂν ἔτι ἐγὼ παρασκευάσωμαι πρὸς τὸ πράως φέρειν τὰ συμβαίνοντα, ὃ θέλει γινέσθω, IV, 7, 12; Xenoph. An., I, 5 and 14. Greatness of soul is demonstrated by this superior acceptance : μεγαλόθυμοι πράως εἰσί τινες ἡσυχῇ καὶ οἷον ἀοργήτως πράττοντες (Epict. Fr., 12), μεγαλοψυχίη τὸ φέρειν πραέως πλημμέλειαν, Democr. Fr., 46 (Diels⁷, II, 156, 3 f.). The sage is tranquil in relation to the acquisition of external goods

---

π ρ α ΰ ς,　π ρ α ΰ τ η ς. Note : F. Hauck prepared a draft for this art., and this has been partly revised and partly rewritten by S. Schulz. Bibl.: Cr.-Kö., 962-966; H. Birkeland, " 'Ani u. 'Anaw in den Ps.," *Skrifter utgitt av det Norske Videnskaps-Akademi* (1932); A. Harnack, "Sanftmut, Huld u. Demut in der alten Kirche," *Festgabe f. J. Kaftan* (1920), 113-129; E. Hatch, *Essays in Biblical Greek* (1889), 73-77; A. Rahlfs, עָנִי u. עָנָו in d. Ps. (1892); W. Sattler, "Die Anawim im Zeitalter Jesu," *Festg. f. A. Jülicher* (1927), 1-15; K. Thieme, *Die christliche Demut,* I (1906); also "Die ταπεινοφροσύνη Phil. 2 u. R. 12," ZNW, 8 (1907), esp. 29-41; Trench, 84-93, 239; A. Vögtle, "Die Tugend- u. Lasterkataloge im NT," *Nt.liche Abh.,* 16, 4/5 (1936), Index, *s.v.;* K. Winkler Art. "Clementia," RAC, III (1955), 206-231.
[1] On the forms πρᾶος and πραΰς — so always in the NT — cf. Kühner-Blass-Gerth, I, 532 f.; Bl.-Debr. § 26 App.; Thackeray, 180 f. In what follows the iota subscriptum is not used, though it occurs in some cod., cf. Liddell-Scott, *s.v.* πραΰς and Bl.-Debr. § 26 App.
[2] Walde-Pokorny, II, 87; Hofmann, 282 f.

and honours, but ἐρωτικῶς in relation to that of friends, Plat. Lys., 211e; Dio Cass., 43, 3, 6 (with φιλανθρώπως). In relation to the Stoic deity one reads: ἀλλ' ἔστιν εὐγνώμων ὁ θεός, ὡς θεός, οἶμαι, καὶ φέρει πράως τὴν τῶν πολλῶν ἄνοιαν, Dio Chrys. Or., 32, 50.

2. πραΰτης.

πραΰτης, "mild and gentle friendliness," is the opp. of roughness (ἀγριότης Plat. Symp., 197d), of bad temper (Aristot. Rhet., II, 3, p. 1380a, 6), of sudden anger (ὀργιλότης, Eth. Nic., IV, 11, p. 1125b, 26) and brusqueness (ἀποτομία, Plut. Lib. Educ., 187 [II, 13d]). It is close to the ἐπιείκεια which tempers stern law (→ II, 588, 34 ff.; Luc. Alex., 61; Somnium, 10; Dio Cass., 53, 6, 1), to φιλανθρωπία (Luc. Phalaris, I, 3), to the ἀνεξικακία which patiently endures discomfort (Plut. De Capienda ex Inimicis Utilitate, 9 [II, p. 90e]). It consists in μήτε κολαστικὸν εἶναι, μήτε τιμωρητικόν, ἀλλὰ ἵλεων καὶ εὐμενικὸν καὶ συγγνωμονικόν, Aristot. De Virtutibus et Vitiis, 8, p. 1251b, 31.

Among the Greeks gentle friendliness is highly prized as a social virtue in human relationships, though it needs compensation if it is not to be a fault. The Delphic oracle ὁμίλει πράως also has the more precise form τοῖς σεαυτοῦ πρᾶος ἴσθι, Diels[7], I, 63, 22, and the wise Chilon advises: μετὰ τῆς ἰσχύος τὴν πραότητα σῷζε, Stob., IV, 255, 2. It is fitting to show mildness to one's own people (οἰκεῖος, → V, 134, 16 ff.) and harshness to enemies. [3] Laws should be stern, but judges should punish with more leniency than the laws prescribe, Isaeus Fr., 33. Isoc. lauds the Athenians as the ἐλεημονέστατοι καὶ πραότατοι among all the Hellenes, also as the πραότατοι καὶ κοινωνότατοι, 15, 20 and 300. Demosth. says of them that they are πρᾶοι καὶ φιλάνθρωποι even in the popular assembly, 8, 33. But this gentleness, which is often stressed along with φιλανθρωπία (Dio C., 43, 3, 6), should not lead to self-abasement (πρᾶος ἔξω τοῦ ταπεινοῦ, 74, 5, 7. It is a mark of the high-minded (μεγαλόθυμος, Epict. Fr., 12) and noble (Plat. Phaedr., 243c; Leg., V, 731d), of the cultured (παιδευτικὸς ἄνθρωπος θέλων εἶναι ἄσκει πραότητα), [4] and therefore of the wise (with κόσμιος and ἡσύχιος in Stob., II, 115, 10), who remains calm even in face of abuse (Epict. Ench., 42); Socrates is a model here (Plat., Phaed., 116c). Hence the gentleness of leading citizens is constantly extolled in encomiums, [5] and it has a prominent place in depictions of rulers. [6] Rhetoric counts it among the *commoda animi.* [7] For Luc. it is an adornment of the soul like δικαιοσύνη, εὐσέβεια, ἐπιείκεια etc., Somnium, 10. It is one of the chief virtues in a woman, Plut. Praec. Coniug., 45 (II, 144e); consolatio ad uxorem, 2 (II, 608d). One finds it in feminine deities. [8] For Plato it is a mark of the ideal kingdom of Atlantis that there men, related to the divine, πραότητι μετὰ φρονήσεως πρός τε τὰς ἀεὶ συμβαινούσας τύχας καὶ πρὸς ἀλλήλους χρώμενοι, Critias, 120e. Individual and social ethics join forces here. The systematic thinker Aristot. places πραότης — as distinct from the διανοητικαί — among the ἠθικαὶ ἀρεταί, Eth. Nic., I, 13, p. 1103a, 4 ff. It is for him a mean between ὀργιλότης ("anger," "bad temper") and the spineless incompetence of ἀοργησία, Eth. M., I, 23, p. 1191b, 24. Since he sets a positive value on justifiable and moderate anger (Eth. Nic., II, 7, p. 1108a, 6), mildness is for him, with εὐόργητον, the laudable mean between the extremes of anger and indifference. [9]

---

[3] Plat. Resp., II, 375c; Tim., 17d-18a; Polyb., 18, 37, 7: πολεμοῦντας γὰρ δεῖ τοὺς ἀγαθοὺς ἄνδρας βαρεῖς εἶναι καὶ θυμικούς, ἡττωμένους δὲ γενναίους καὶ μεγαλόφρονας, νικῶντάς γε μὴν μετρίους καὶ πραεῖς καὶ φιλανθρώπους.

[4] *Pythagoreersprüche,* ed. Schenkl, *Wiener Studien,* 8 (1886), 84.

[5] Theon, Progymnasmata, 8 (Rhet. Graec., II, 111, 27 f.).

[6] Xenoph. Ag., 11, 2. 6. 20; Isoc. Or., 2, 23; Vögtle, 73-77; F. Wilhelm, "Der Regentenspiegel des Sopatros (Stob., IV, 215, 20 ff.; 217, 9)," *Rhein. Museum,* 72 (1917/18), 374-402, esp. 391-398.

[7] Aristot. Rhet., I, 9, p. 1366a, 1 ff.

[8] Artemis: Anthol. Pal., 6, 271 (cf. also 9, 525, 17); Leto: Plat. Crat., 406a.

[9] Eth. M., I, 7, p. 1186a, 23; cf. I, 25, p. 1191b, 36.

B. Septuagint and Hellenistic Judaism.

1. Old Testament. Here πραΰς occurs 12 times with a Heb. original in the Mas. text. It also occurs in Sir. 3:19; 10:14; Job 36:15; Jl. 3:10 and Δα. 4:19. In the 7 ref. in Ps. (ψ 24:9 twice ; 33:3; 36:11; 75:10; 146:6; 149:4) it is used for עָנָו, cf. also Nu. 12:3. Elsewhere it occurs 5 times for עָנָו, Job 24:4; Is. 26:6; Zech. 9:9; Sir. 10:14; Zeph. 3:12; only cod A has πολύν. πραΰτης is found 4 times in Sir. (3:17; 4:8; 10:28; 45:4) for עֲנָוָה, no Heb. at 36:23. It also occurs in ψ 44:5; 89:10; 131:1 and Est. 5:1ᵉ (no Heb.). Finally we find πραότης in Sir. 1:27 (with πραΰτης) and Est. 3:13b. [10]

If the rendering of the Heb. synonyms אֶבְיוֹן, דַּל, רָשׁ, עָנִי and עָנָו by πένης (→ 38, 35 ff.) → πτωχός, → ταπεινός and πραΰς is capricious, the last of these is obviously preferred for עָנָו. [11] עָנָו and עָנָו belong to the verb עָנָה "to find oneself in a stunted, humble, lowly position." [12] This is why πραΰς is never predicated of God in the OT, as distinct from profane Gk. [13] עָנִי is in the first instance a social and economic term like רָשׁ, דַּל, אֶבְיוֹן, "one who is in the position of a servant." It describes the man who has no property and who has thus to earn his bread by serving others, → 38, 41 ff. πένης. It then takes on the sense of "humble." עָנָו, too, means first "the one who is in subjection," though it then takes on the predominant sense of "one who feels that he is a servant in relation to God and who subjects himself to Him quietly and without resistance." [14] On this whole problem, however, cf. → πτωχός. Here, perhaps, is the reason why the translators of the LXX chose πραΰς as the best rendering of עָנָו, for the Gk. term often has the sense of the calm acceptance of fate or human injustice, → 645, 25 ff.

In the Pent. πραΰς (for עָנָו) is used only at Nu. 12:3 with ref. to Moses. The words are a more recent addition [15] possibly based on the later ideal of piety or the Hell. concept of the ideal ruler, cf. Sir. 45:4. There is nothing about the gentle and patient believer in pre-exilic prophecy. The only possible ref. here is Jl. 3:10. Here, however, there is no Heb. equivalent for πραΰς. It is customary to emend the Mas. acc. to the LXX, but the correction is dubious, since the root נוּחַ is not transl. by πραΰς etc. elsewhere ; עָנִי and עָנָו do not occur in Jl. Furthermore, Jl. might be post-exilic. [16] The prophet is calling for a holy war. The instruments of peace are to be refashioned into weapons of war and the gentle must become warriors. [17]

In the post-exilic period Zech. 9:9 f. depicts the king of salvation as the king of peace. Both metrically and materially (on the message of the herald cf. Is. 40:9 ff.) [18]

---

[10] The readings are not always certain.

[11] עָנָו 21 times in the OT, 8 times πραΰς, 4 times πτωχός, 5 ταπεινός (once as vl.) and 4 πένης. עָנָו 6 times various words (Ex. 22:24; Dt. 24:12; Ez. 18:17; Job 24:9; 36:15; Prv. 22:22). In 5 instances the LXX has another text or interpretation (Is. 10:30; Zech. 11:7, 11; Prv. 15:15; Job 24:14).

[12] On this cf. Birkeland, 7-10.

[13] The only instance (Ps. 18:35) rests on a doubtful original : 'A and Quinta have πραότης, LXX Θ παιδεία. In ψ 89:10 LXX Θ directly relate the (divine) πραότης and the παιδεύεσθαι of man. The LXX has πραΰνειν twice (ψ 93:13; Prv. 18:14), but not at all in the Gk. sense "to appease the gods"; cf. G. Bertram, "Der Begriff der Erziehung in d. gr. Bibel," Imago Dei, *Festschr. f. G. Krüger* (1932), 45 f.

[14] The reading עָנִי or עָנִי is debated.

[15] Cf. H. Holzinger, *Nu., Kurzer Hand-Comm. z. AT*, 4 (1903), and B. Baentsch, *Nu., Handcomm. z. AT*, II, 2 (1903), ad loc.; also Kautzsch, ad loc.; Rahlfs, 95-100. Cf. Moses in Ex. 2:12; 32:19 etc.

[16] Cf. O. Eissfeldt, *Einleitung in das AT²* (1956), 481 f.

[17] The original seems to be a slip ; perhaps the saying is an addition, cf. T. H. Robinson, *Die Zwölf Kleinen Propheten, Hndbch. AT*, 14 (1954); A. Weiser, *Das Buch der Zwölf Kleinen Propheten, AT Deutsch*, 24 (1949); Kautzsch, ad loc.

[18] Cf. A. Weiser, *Die Psalmen, NT Deutsch*, 14 (1950), ad loc.

the two verses stand apart from the context. The theme of the king of salvation riding on an ass belongs originally to a very ancient Messianic tradition [19] of Accadian derivation, but it has been reinterpreted here in a distinctive way. This new exposition is very plainly expressed in v. 10 : he sets aside weapons and chariots and proclaims peace to the peoples.

In ψ 44:5 πραΰτης, with truth and righteousness, is a characteristic of the royal hero, who is then called the prince of peace in v. 7 f. [20] πραΰς does not occur in the older proverbial wisdom (Prv.), i.e., the LXX here uses other terms for עָנִי and עָנָו. At Prv. 15:33 ולפני כבוד ענוה which LXX misunderstood, is practical wisdom in ΣΘ. The antithetical use of the same saying in 18:12 is clear evidence of the this-worldly character of the Heb. text. ΣΘ do, of course, take the saying first in a secular sense, but with the possibility of an eschatological interpretation : ἔμπροσθεν δόξης πραΰτης, cf. 18:12 (LXX πρὸ δόξης ταπεινοῦται [καρδία ἀνδρός]), cf. also 22:4 Σ : ὕστερον πραΰτητος φόβος κυρίου. Here, too, the ref. is plainly to earthly reward. On the other hand, Sir. values πραΰτης (the Heb. עֲנָוָה shines clearly through the Gk. dress); it is pleasing to God (1:27) who lifts up the πραεῖς (10:14) and is a quality of Moses (45:4). It adorns a woman (36:23), wins the love of one's fellows (3:17), befits the beggar (4:8) and is an antidote against arrogance (10:28).

In the early period the prophets castigated the sins of the wealthy. Later development gave the lowly the sense of being bearers of the divine promise, cf. Ps. 37:11. It was they who kept the requirements of God, Zeph. 2:3; 3:12 f. Hence for all their outward lowliness they are conscious of the divine good-pleasure. The quiet, patient, hopeful, expectant bearing of a severe destiny in exile without resistance or complaint, without vehement anger, is a sign of piety which stands out sharply from an earlier even disposition in times of national prosperity. The difference from profane usage is also plain. OT acceptance is rooted in God. Triumphant waiting on God rather than the superior aloofness of the sage is the correlate of mild acceptance, Is. 26:6. OT πραΰτης is based on the eschatological hope (Ps. 76:9) that God will judge (147:6; 149:4) and give the land to the lowly, i.e., to those who wait (37:9). Ps. 37:9-11 connects with this the promises of the land which were originally given to Abraham and his descendants and which the Psalmist now refers to his own age.

2. Philo. Philo, not knowing Hebrew nor the connection between עָנָו and πραΰς, is dependent on the LXX and the ethics of Gk. philosophy. He refers to God's judicial mildness [21] and depicts Moses as one who in the course of development daily "moderated" πάθη (ἐπράυνεν, Vit. Mos., I, 26), a particularly difficult achievement (Conf. Ling., 165), since only age lends ἐπιείκεια and πραΰτης τῶν παθῶν ἐπὶ πλέον ἡμερωθέντων, Op. Mund., 103. As a leader he lived up to the ideal when, sorely troubled by revolt, he still showed himself to be πραότατος and ἡμερώτατος, Vit. Mos., II, 279. As a law-giver he gave good laws to servants εἰς ὑπερησίαν φιλοδέσποτον, to masters εἰς ἠπιότητα καὶ πραότητα, δι' ὧν ἐξισοῦται τὸ ἄνισον (Decal., 167), to priests, for whom the appointed breast-plate ought to be a σύμβολον ... τῆς περὶ τὸν θυμὸν ἵλεω πραότητος (Spec. Leg., I, 145). High praise is deserved by the Jews who in persecution πάντων ἦσαν πραοπαθέστατοι, Leg. ad Gaj., 335.

3. Josephus. Joseph. uses πραΰνω (Ant., 3, 316), πραΰς (17, 212; 19, 330) and πράως (14, 46; 19, 33). He often speaks of friendly acceptance in the bearing of fate,

---

[19] Robinson, op. cit. (→ n. 17), ad loc.; cf. also the expression "from the river (Euphrates)."

[20] Weiser, op. cit., ad loc.; H. Schmidt, Die Psalmen, Hndbch. AT, 15 (1934), ad loc. and Kautzsch, ad loc.

[21] Det. Pot. Ins., 146 : κολάζων δὲ ἐπιεικῶς τε καὶ πράως ἅτε χρηστὸς ὤν.

3, 97; 5, 167; 7, 117. In the 2 passages in Test. XII in which πρᾷος and πραότης occur (Test. D. 6:9; Jud. 24:6) we seem to have Chr. interpolations. [22]

4. Qumran Texts. In the Qumran texts gentleness (עֲנָוָה) is common, e.g., 1 QS 2:24; 3:8; 4:3 etc. 10:26 is plainly based on the OT, → 648, 19 ff.: the humble and the faint-hearted. עֲנָוָה is demanded of members of the order and mentioned in the lists in 4:1 ff. in accordance with the dualistic view of power in which gentleness is constitutive for the sons of light.

C. New Testament.

In NT usage there is obviously a different distribution of the word in the different strata. Neither adjective nor noun occurs in Mark, Luke (Gospel and Acts), Hebrews or the Johannine writings, and the noun alone is found in Paul. This absence is connected especially with the particular Christology. Thus Mark and Luke emphasise more strongly the → υἱὸς θεοῦ or κύριος, John stresses the omnipotent → υἱός or υἱὸς τοῦ ἀνθρώπου, Paul speaks predominantly of the κύριος (→ III, 1088 ff.), and Hebrews presents the ἀρχιερεύς (→ III, 274 ff.) described in cultic categories.

1. Matthew. Of the Synoptists, then, only Mt. uses πραΰς (3 times at 5:5; 11:29; 21:5). Special significance attaches to the self-predication of Jesus in the tradition at 11:25-30 [23] which has not yet been explained in terms of comparative religion, → V, 992, 40 ff. Probably vv. 28-30 are modelled on the revelatory address in Prv. 8:4 ff.; Sir. 24:3-22; 51:23-30. [24] The mission of Jesus takes place on earth in lowliness and weakness (= πραΰς). His life is not a life at court; it charac-terises Him as the lowly in heart, i.e., the One who is fixed wholly on God (= ταπεινός). [25] But for that very reason He can invite with full authority (note the two imperatives δεῦτε and ἄρατε) and fulfil the promise contained in the invitation. In Mt. 21:5, with the help of the fulfilled prophecy of Zech. 9:9 (→ 647, 32 ff.), the entry of Jesus is depicted as that of a non-violent, non-warlike king of salvation and peace. In this respect Jesus stands radically opposed to the Zealots (→ II, 884, 23 ff.) and to all the champions of a political Messianism. In the beatitude in Mt. 5:5 [26] we read of the πραεῖς who on the basis of their oppressed situation acknowledge not their own will but the great and gracious will of God. To them Jesus promises the inheritance (→ III, 783, 6 ff.) of the coming aeon, which includes (cf. Mt. 19:29) secure dwelling in their own land. [27] In contrast to the first beatitude (Mt. 5:3), which mentions the related → πτωχοί, the emphasis in the third beatitude is on the future promise: Those who are now oppressed and bowed down will be rulers of the world in the eschaton.

---

[22] Cf. Kautzsch Apkr. u. Pseudepigr., II, 485.

[23] Cf. on this W. Grundmann, Jesus d. Galiläer (1940), 209-223; J. Bieneck, Sohn Gottes als Christusbezeichnung der Synpt. (1951), 75-87; W. Manson, Jesus the Messiah (1943), 71-76, esp. 73; E. Percy, Die Botschaft Jesu (1953), 108-110; W. D. Davies, "Knowledge in the Dead Sea Scrolls and Mt. 11:25-30," HThR, 46 (1953), 113-139; cf. also → ἐπι-γνώσκω, I, 713, 13 ff.; → ζυγός, II, 899, 34 ff.; → μανθάνω, IV, 409, 17 ff.; → νήπιος, IV, 920, 38 ff.

[24] H. Becker, "Die Reden des Joh.-Ev. u. der Stil der gnostischen Offenbarungsrede," FRL, NF, 50 (1956), 41-53; Bultmann Trad., 172.

[25] J. Schniewind, Das Ev. nach Mt., NT Deutsch, 2⁵ (1950), ad loc.

[26] In distinction from the other beatitudes this v. is a quotation (Ps. 37:11). Its position is textually uncertain; Wellh. Mt. and Kl. Mt., ad loc.

[27] Loh. Mt., ad loc.

2. Paul. In Paul's debate with the Corinthian pneumatics it is worth noting that the term πραΰτης [28] occurs twice. Paul had full reason to inveigh against the Corinthians on account of their disputatiousness and arrogance, but they would not make it impossible for him to bring the gentleness of Christ to bear against them, 2 C. 10:1. [29] This meekness has its basis in agape and it cannot therefore think in terms of harsh punishment even in relation to the disobedient, 1 C. 4:21. There can be no question of this course of action on the apostle's part being branded as softness or weakness, for it rests on the gentleness and love which Christ exemplified for the community during His life on earth. Hence it is also no virtue in the Greek Hellenistic sense, → 646, 14 ff. As Gl. 5:23 and 6:1 show, it is a gift of the Spirit. πραΰτης stands between πίστις and ἐγκράτεια (Gl. 5:23), [30] and it enables the Christian to correct the erring brother without arrogance, impatience, or anger, Gl. 6:1. According to Col. 3:12 meekness is one of the gifts of election, and in Eph. 4:2 it is one of the gifts of calling.

3. Pastoral Epistles. There are some moral features in the usage of the Pastorals. The servant of Christ should exercise meekness especially in correction of the lawless, for in this way they will perhaps be snatched away from Satan, 2 Tm. 2:25. [31] Meekness is commanded in relation to all in Tt. 3:2. When the authorities or others ask for an account of the Christian life of faith, it is to be given with meekness and kindness, even though injustice which has been suffered might cause indignation or defiance, 1 Pt. 3:16.

4. James. In Jm. 1:21 πραΰτης is contrasted with ὀργή (v. 20) and it refers to a meek and humble readiness to be taught by the Word of God without flaring up against the teacher. Gentleness is a mark of the true righteous who are inspired by divine wisdom (3:13: ἐν πραΰτητι σοφίας; v. 17: εἰρηνική, ἐπιεικής). It is demonstrated in the whole walk of the righteous and stands in pleasing contrast to bitter zeal and contentiousness, 3:14; cf. Sir. 3:17; also 1 Pt. 3:4.

D. Post-Apostolic Fathers.

Here [32] πραΰς and πραΰτης (or πραότης in Ign. and Herm.) are used in much the same way. πραΰς stands alone in Did., 3, 7, which has been influenced by Mt. 5:5 or perhaps ψ 36:11, and where the 2nd part of the sentence is obviously a quotation. Elsewhere the adj. occurs in lists or along with other virtues; 1 Cl., 13, 4 (with ἡσύχιος as in 1 Pt. 3:4) quotes Is. 66:2. πραΰς is more common in Herm. In m., 5, 2, 3 and 6, 2, 3 the combination of πραΰς with ἡσύχιος, which suggests some influence of Is. 66:2, has already become part of the language of edification. In m., 5, 2, 6 πραότης is found with ἡσυχία and in 12, 3, 1 with πίστις and other virtues. The noun also occurs in association with other virtues, e.g., ἐπιείκεια (cf. 2 C. 10:1) in 1 Cl., 30, 8, ὑπομονή in Did., 5, 2 and εἰρήνη in 1 Cl., 61, 2. Dg., 7, 4 seems to be based on 2 C. 10:1. For Ign. πραΰτης is an essential Chr. virtue, cf. Tr., 4, 2. This quality is also expected of a bishop, Tr., 3, 2; Pol., 2, 1; 6, 2. Did., 15, 1 also says that only ἄνδρες πραεῖς should be called as bishops and deacons (other attributes are ἀφιλαργύρους, ἀληθεῖς, δεδοκιμασμένους). In general a trend discernible already in the NT (→ lines 15 ff.) is now much plainer in

---

[28] Always πραΰτης in the NT, with πραότης (Ign. and Herm.) only as a variant.
[29] Allusion to a dominical saying (Thieme, 24 f.; Harnack, 113; Vögtle, 152) is very doubtful, cf. Wnd. 2 K., ad loc.
[30] Schlier Gl. on 5:23.
[31] Cf. on this Ign. Tr., 4, 2: χρήζω οὖν πραότητος, ἐν ᾗ καταλύεται ὁ ἄρχων τοῦ αἰῶνος τούτου.
[32] Notes by Schneemelcher have been used in this section.

the post-apost. fathers, namely, that πραΰτης should be regarded as an essential virtue. It is surprising that the example of Jesus plays no part in the exhortation to πραΰτης.

F. Hauck/S. Schulz

πρέσβυς, πρεσβύτερος, πρεσβύτης,
συμπρεσβύτερος, πρεσβυτέριον,
πρεσβεύω

---

† πρέσβυς, † πρεσβύτερος,
† συμπρεσβύτερος (→ II, 608 ff. ἐπίσκοπος), † πρεσβυτέριον.

Contents : A. Meaning and Occurrence. B. "Elders" in the Constitutional History of Israel and Judah : 1. In J and E ; 2. In the Time of the Judges and the Monarchy ; 3. In Deuteronomy ; 4. In the Exilic and Post-Exilic Period ; 5. "Elders" in the Sanhedrin at Jerusalem ; 6. זְקֵנִים as a Term for the Scribes ; 7. πρεσβύτεροι in the Local and Synagogal Government of Hellenistic Judaism. C. The παράδοσις τῶν πρεσβυτέρων in the Pro-

---

π ρ έ σ β υ ς κ τ λ. On A.: Liddell-Scott, *s.v.*; Preisigke Wört., II, 357; III, 147 f., 383, 405 f.; E. Ziebarth, *Das griech. Vereinswesen* (1896), Index, *s.v.*; F. Poland, *Geschichte d. gr. Vereinswesens* (1909), Index, *s.v.*; M. San Nicolò, *Ägypt. Vereinswesen zur Zeit der Ptolemäer u. Römer*, I (1913), 169-173; II (1915), 53-96. On B.: O. Seesemann, *Die Ältesten im AT* (1895); I. Benzinger, "Älteste in Israel," RE³, 1, 224-227; E. Meyer, *Die Israeliten u. ihre Nachbarstämme* (1906), 96 f.; W. Caspari, *Aufkommen u. Krise des isr. Königtums* (1906), 5-26, 67-75; A. Bertholet, *Kulturgeschichte Israels* (1919), *passim* ; M. Weber, *Gesammelte Aufsätze zur Religionssoziologie*, 3 (1921), 16-25; A. Alt, "Älteste," RLV, 1 (1924), 117 f.; P. Volz, *Bibl. Altertümer²* (1925), *v.* Index ; J. Pedersen, *Israel — Its Life and Culture*, I-II (1926); III-IV (1940), Index, *s.v.*; A. Causse, *Du groupe ethnique à la communauté religieuse* (1937), *passim* ; L. Rost, "Die Vorstufen von Kirche u. Synagoge im AT," BWANT, IV, 24 (1938), 60-76, esp. 61-64; W. H. Bennett, Art. "Elder (Semitic)," ERE, V (1912), 253-256; A. Menes, Art. "Älteste," EJ, II, 505-507; M. Weinberg, "Die Organisation d. jüd. Ortsgemeinden in talmudischer Zeit," MGWJ, NF, 5 (1897), 588-604, 639-660, 673-691; Schürer, II, 237-258, 497-516; also *Die Entstehung des Judt.* (1896), 132-135; G. Hölscher, *Sanhedrin u. Makkot* (1910), 15-24; J. Juster, *Les Juifs dans l'empire Romain* (1914), 440-447; G. La Piana, "The Roman Church at the End of the Second Century," HThR, 18 (1925), 201-277; also "Foreign Groups in Rome during the First Century of the Empire," HThR, 20 (1927), 183-403; J. B. Frey, "Les communautés juives à Rome aux premiers temps de l'église," *Recherches de Science Religieuse*, 21 (1931), 129-168; also Corpus Inscr. Judaicarum, I (1936); II (1952); H. Zucker, *Studien z. jüd. Selbstverwaltung im Altertum* (1936), 173-190; J. Jeremias, *Jerusalem z. Zeit Jesu*, II B (1937), 88-100; E. Lohse, *Die Ordination im Spätjudentum u. im NT* (1951), esp. 21-27, 50-60. On C.-E.: H. J. Holtzmann, *Die Pastoralbriefe* (1880), 207-221; E. Hatch-A. Harnack, *Die Gesellschaftsverfassung d. chr. Kirchen im Altertum* (1883), 51-78, 229-253; E. Kühl, *Die Gemeindeordnung in d. Past.* (1885), 7-28, 85-134; R. Sohm, *Kirchenrecht*, I (1892), 92-121, 137-151; E. v. Dobschütz, *Die urchr. Gemeinden* (1902), cf. Index ; R. Knopf, *Das nachapost. Zeitalter* (1905), 147-222; A. Harnack, *Entstehung u. Entwicklung d. Kirchenverfassung u. d. Kirchenrechts in d. ersten zwei Jhdt.* (1910), esp. 40-76; H. Lietzmann, "Zur altchr. Verfassungsgeschichte," ZwTh, 55 (1913), 97-153; K. Müller, "Beiträge z. Geschichte d. Verfassung in d. alten Kirche," AAB, 1922, 3 (1922), 3-5; also "Kleine Beiträge z. alten Kirchengeschichte, 16 : Die älteste Bischofswahl u. -weihe in Rom u. Alexandrien," ZNW, 28 (1929), 274-296; B. H. Streeter, *The Primitive Church* (1929), 67-97; O. Linton, *Das Problem der Urkirche in d. neueren Forschung* (1932), 110-113; A. C. Headlam/F. Gerke, "The Origin of the Christian Ministry," in A. C. Headlam-R. Donkerly, *The Ministry and the Sacraments* (1937), 326-367; E. J. Palmer, "A New Approach to an Old Problem : The Development of the Chr. Ministry," *ibid.*, 768 ff.; J. Michl, *Die 24 Ältesten in d. Apok. d. Hl. Johannes*

clamation of Jesus. D. Presbyters in the Primitive Christian Communities : 1. The First Jerusalem Church ; 2. The Pauline Churches ; 3. The Development of a Presbyteral Constitution under the Influence of the Synagogue of the Diaspora: a. James ; b. Acts ; c. 1 Peter ; d. Pastorals ; 4. The 24 πρεσβύτεροι in Revelation ; 5. The πρεσβύτερος in 2 and 3 John. E. "Elders" in the Post-Apostolic Fathers and the Early Church : 1. 1 Clement ; 2. Hermas ; 3. Ignatius ; 4. Polycarp of Smyrna ; 5. The "Presbyters" of Papias, Irenaeus, Clement of Alexandria and Origen ; 6. The Syrian Didascalia and the Church Order of Hippolytus.

A. Meaning and Occurrence.

1. πρεσβύτερος, comp. of πρέσβυς a. to denote greater age, esp. of men (Hom., inscr., pap., LXX, Philo, Jos., Chr. lit.). A common sense is that of "older" (of two): ὁ υἱὸς ὁ πρεσβύτερος (cf. Aelian. Var. Hist., 9, 42), Lk. 15:25; Barn., 13, 5; representatives of the older generation as compared to the younger (νεανίσκοι, νέοι, νεώτεροι etc.); though the comp. sense may fade[1] and the word simply mean "old," "the old," Jos. Ant., 13, 226 and 292; Herm. v., 3, 11, 3; 12, 2; thus the Church in Herm. v., 3, 10, 3 is a λίαν πρεσβυτέρα, cf. v., 3, 11, 2 and 2, 1, 3; 3, 1, 2 etc. In distinction from other terms for age (e.g., γέρων, παλαιός) this group has no negative implication (loss of powers etc.). Indeed, it contains from the very first the positive element of venerability.[2] This explains the distinction : ἐγὼ παλαιότατός εἰμι, σὺ δὲ πρεσβύτατος, Plut. Nicias, 15, 2 (I, 533b). Hence the gen. use of the comp. and superl. for that which is of weight or of supreme worth : τὰ τοῦ θεοῦ πρεσβύτερα ἐποιοῦντο ἢ τὰ τῶν ἀνθρώπων, Hdt., V, 63, cf. Eur. Fr., 959; Thuc., IV, 61; instructive also is Plat. Symp., 218d : ἐμοὶ μὲν γὰρ οὐδέν ἐστι πρεσβύτερον τοῦ ὡς ὅτι βέλτιστον ἐμὲ γενέσθαι. The counsel and wisdom of the aged are esp. emphasised : οἱ σοφοὶ καὶ πρεσβύτεροι, Aristot. Eth. Eud., I, 4, p. 1215a, 23 : βουλαὶ πρεσβύτεραι (the plans of the elder as distinct from the boldness of the younger) Pind. Pyth., 2, 65. The honour due the old or age is a favourite theme in popular ethical instruction : [ἀεί π]οτε μὲν πρεσβυτέ[ρους τιμῶν ὡς γονεῖ]ς, τοὺς δὲ καθήλικας ὡς ἀδελφούς, τοὺς δὲ [νεωτέρους ὡς παῖδας], Inscr. Priene (1st cent. B.C.), 117, 55 f.; τοῖς μὲν ἡλικιώταις προσφερόμενος ὡς ἀδελφός, τοῖς δὲ πρεσβυτέροις ὡς υἱός, // τοῖς δὲ παισὶν ὡς πατήρ, IPE, I, 22, 28 ff.; cf. also Plat. Apol., 31b; Iambl. Vit. Pyth., 8, 40;[3] also the blunt and witty apophthegm, Plut. Apophth. Lac., 12 (II, 232 f.): ἰδών τις ἐν ἀποχωρήσει θακέοντας ἐπὶ δίφρων ἀνθρώπους 'μὴ γένοιτο' εἶπεν 'ἐνταῦθα καθίσαι, ὅθεν οὐκ ἔστιν ἐξαναστῆναι πρεσβυτέρῳ'. Bibl. wisdom also refers frequently to the honouring of age, Prv. 20:29; Wis. 2:10; cf. Lv. 19:32. In praise of the wisdom, experience, judgment and fear of God of the aged cf. esp. Sir. 6:34; 25:4-6.

(1938); K. L. Schmidt, "Le ministère et les ministères dans l'église du NT," RHPhR, 17 (1937), 314-336; also "Amt u. Ämter im NT," ThZ, 1 (1945), 309-311; K. E. Kirk, The Apostolic Ministry (1946), v. Index ; E. Schweizer, Das Leben d. Herrn in d. Gemeinde u. ihren Diensten (1946), Index, s.v.; P. C. Spicq, "Les Epîtres pastorales," Etudes Bibl. (1947), p. XLIII-LI; R. Loewe, Die Ordnung in d. Kirche im Lichte d. Titusbriefes (1947), 26-37; T. W. Manson, The Church's Ministry (1948), 53-77; P. Menoud, L'Eglise et les ministères selon le NT (1949), 35-55, esp. 50-55; J. Brosch, Charismen u. Ämter in d. Urkirche (1951), 137-141; H. Schlier, Die Zeit d. Kirche (1956), 129-147; H. W. Beyer-H. Karpp, Art. "Bischof," RAC, II (1954), 394-407; W. Michaelis, Das Ältestenamt (1953); H. v. Campenhausen, Kirchliches Amt u. geistliche Vollmacht in d. ersten drei Jahrhunderten (1953), esp. 82-134; A. Ehrhardt, The Apostolic Succession (1953), Index s.v. "Elder," "Presbyter"; Dib. Past.[3], esp. 44-47, 60 f. Cf. also Bibl. on ἐπίσκοπος, → II, 608 f.

[1] Cf. Bl.-Debr. § 244, 2; Schwyzer, II, 184 f.; St. C. Caratzas, "Sur l'histoire du suffixe de comparatif -τερος (πρεσβύτερος, ἐξώτερος, νεώτερος)," Glotta, 32 (1953), 248-261; K. Jaberg, "Elation u. Komparation," Festschr. E. Tièche (1947), 56 f.

[2] On the etym. cf. Hofmann, s.v. πρέσβυς. On synon. J. H. H. Schmidt, Synonymik d. griech. Sprache, II (1878), 87 f.; IV (1886), 311.

[3] Cf. Deissmann LO, 263; Dib. Past.[3] on 1 Tm. 5:1.

b. Esp. important for bibl. usage is the fact that in the constitution of Sparta πρέσβυς occurs as a political title to denote the president of a college : τῶν ἐφόρων, IG, 5, 1, 51, 27; 6, 552, 11; νομοφυλάκων, 6, 555b, 19; βιδέων (ephebes), 6, 556, 6; συναρχίας (assembly of magistrates), 6, 504, 16. Quite independent is the use of πρεσβύτεροι as a title in Egypt inscr. and pap. (Ptolemaic and imperial period). [4] Here committees and colleges of various kinds are entitled πρεσβύτεροι : the freely elected board of associated national husbandmen (πρεσβύτεροι γεωργῶν), BGU, I, 85, 9 ff.; P. Tebt., I, 13, 5; 40, 17 f.; 43, 8; 50, 20; P. Gen., 42, 15; P. Lond., II, 255, 7, also corporations : πρεσβύτεροι τῶν ὀλυροκόπων (guild of millers in Alexandria, 6 πρεσβύτεροι with a ἱερεύς at their head, 3rd cent. B.C.). [5] πρεσβύτεροι also appear in village government : πρεσβύτεροι τῆς κώμης. [6] They have administrative and judicial functions. Their number varies (2, 4, even more than 10). Their period of office is limited to a year. It is important that πρεσβύτεροι is also a title among the priests of the "great god Socnopaios" (BGU, I, 16, 5 f.). The ref. is to an executive committee of 5 or 6 members alternating each yr. and charged with supervision of the finances and negotiations with the authorities. The members are not old men (the text speaks of presbyters of 45, 35 and 30 yrs. of age). [7] Rather different are the richly attested πρεσβύτεροι of Gk. societies. [8] Here the word is not a title ; the πρεσβύτεροι are not office-bearers but senior groups of various kinds (as distinct from junior groups), cf. the ὑμνῳδοὶ πρεσβύτεροι of an inscr. found in Radanovo [9] and the many clubs of men belonging to the senate. [10] Elsewhere πρεσβύτεροι is used to denote the age of one guild as compared to a younger one : [11] σύνοδος τῶν ἐν Ἀλεξανδρείᾳ πρεσβυτέρων ἐγδοχέων (carriers), Ditt. Or., I, 140, 7 ff.; πρεσβύτεροι γέρδιοι (weavers) [12] or τέκτονες πρεσβύτεροι. [13]

Egypt. usage deserves attention in view of the surprising LXX preference of πρεσβύτεροι (over γέροντες) for זְקֵנִים. On the other hand one has to take Jewish influence into account in the communities of the θεὸς ὕψιστος [14] concerning whose officials much light has been shed by the 1st-3rd cent. inscr. found in Crimea. [15] Here within the total membership we find narrower circles (of initiates) consisting of tested men who as

[4] Cf. Mitteis-Wilcken, I, 1, 275; Deissmann B., 153-155; Deissmann NB, 60-62; Deissmann LO, Index, s.v. πρεσβύτερος; Lietzmann, 117; Dib. Exc. on 1 Tm. 5:17; esp. San Nicolò, I, 169-173; II, 90-96 (examples esp. 94 f.).

[5] M. L. Strack, "Inschr. aus ptolemäischer Zeit," APF, 2 (1903), 544; also "Die Müllerinnung in Alexandrien," ZNW, 4 (1903), 213-234, with a list of older instances, 230 f.

[6] BGU, I, 195, 30; P. Oxy., XVII, 2121, 4; P. Zenon, III, 520, 4 (ed. C. C. Edgar, Catalogue Général des Antiquités égypt. du Musée du Caire, 85 [1928], 234); F. Bilabel, "Griech. Pap. (Urkunden, Briefe, Mumienetiketten)," Veröffentlichungen aus d. badischen Papyrussammlungen, Heft, 2 (1923), No. 32, 1; cf. H. Hauschildt, "ΠΡΕΣΒΥΤΕΡΟΙ in Ägypten im I.-III. Jhdt.," ZNW, 4 (1903), 235-242; L. Wenger, Die Stellvertretung im Rechte d. Pap. (1906), 113-115; R. Taubenschlag, The Law of Greco-Roman Egypt in the Light of the Pap.² (1955), 580 f.; Lietzmann, 117 f.

[7] W. Otto, Priester u. Tempel, I (1905), 47-52.

[8] Examples in Ziebarth and esp. Poland, passim.

[9] Ziebarth, 90; Poland, 556 (under B, 84).

[10] Elsewhere (and more commonly) γεραιοί, γερουσιασταί; Poland, 98-102; Lietzmann, 116 f.

[11] Ziebarth, 213; Poland, 171 f.; Lietzmann, 116 f.; Strack Müllerinnung, 232 thinks the πρεσβύτεροι are seniors in the trade concerned.

[12] Egypt Exploration Fund, III, Fayûm Towns and Their Pap. (1900), 64, Inscr. 6.

[13] Inscr. Graecae ad res Romanas pertinentes, ed. R. Cagnat, I (1911), No. 1155.

[14] On these E. Schürer, "Die Juden im bosporanischen Reiche u. d. Gemeinschaften der σεβόμενοι θεὸν ὕψιστον ebendaselbst," SAB (1897), 200-225; G. Bornkamm, Das Ende des Gesetzes (1952), 153-156.

[15] The inscr. in IPE, II, No. 437-467; on the constitution of these societies v. Lietzmann, 118-123.

distinct from the wider community of devotees are called εἰσποιητοὶ ἀδελφοί (adoptive brothers, sc. "sons of God"). At their head are πρεσβύτεροι; [16] there is no mention of any other office-bearers. This title is obviously taken from the synagogal constitution (→ συναγωγή). It is not used for one of the many offices of the total community but reserved for the conventicle. [17]

c. The peculiar problem of the use of πρεσβύτερος in Judaism and Christianity arises out of the twofold meaning of the word, which can be employed both as a designation of age and also as a title of office. The two meanings cannot always be distinguished with clarity, though age is plainly the only sense in Gn. 18:11 f.; 19:4, 31, 34; 24:1; 35:29 and many other passages. The word can still be used for this in Christian writings, Jn. 8:9; Ac. 2:17 (Jl. 2:28 opp. νεανίσκοι); 1 Tm. 5:1, 2; 1 Pt. 5:5 (opp. νεώτερος) etc.; cf. also πρεσβύτεροι for the forefathers in Hb. 11:2. On the other hand, passages like Mt. 15:2; Mk. 7:3, 5 (παράδοσις τῶν πρεσβυτέρων) show that πρεσβύτεροι can be bearers of the normative doctrinal tradition, and 1 Pt. 5:5; 1 Cl., 1, 3 are evidence that the term can denote a place of dignity in the community. The titular significance is no less clear when πρεσβύτεροι are members of a local authority (γερουσία), e.g., the Sanhedrin at Jerusalem (→ 658, 44 ff.), other governing bodies (→ 660, 27 ff.), or the synagogues (→ 660, 39 ff.), or when they are the leaders of the Christians churches duly appointed as such and charged with specific functions.

2. τὸ πρεσβυτέριον (always sing.) occurs in pre-Chr. literature only at Sus. 50 Θ: καὶ εἶπαν αὐτῷ οἱ πρεσβύτεροι Δεῦρο κάθισον ἐν μέσῳ ἡμῶν καὶ ἀνάγγειλον ἡμῖν· ὅτι σοὶ δέδωκεν ὁ θεὸς τὸ πρεσβυτέριον (B 88 410 πρεσβεῖον). What is meant is obviously the divinely given "dignity of elders" [18] in virtue of which the young (!) Daniel is qualified to speak in the council of the πρεσβύτεροι.

Elsewhere the term occurs only in Christian writings in the sense of a "college of elders" a. for the chief Jewish court in Jerusalem (usually συνέδριον) at Lk. 22:66; Ac. 22:5 (undoubtedly a Hellenistic Jewish and not just a Christian term), and b. for the council of elders in Christian congregations, so 1 Tm. 4:14 (→ 666, 14 ff.).

The word is surprisingly common in Ignatius (13 times, nowhere else in the post-apost. fathers). It occurs along with bishop and deacons, Eph., 2, 2; 4, 1; 20, 2; Mg., 2; Tr., 2, 2; 13, 2; Sm., 8, 1. Since acc. to Ign. the hierarchical position of the presbyters corresponds to that of the apostles, the ἀπόστολοι can be called the πρεσβυτέριον ἐκκλησίας in Phld., 5, 1. The presbytery is the council (συνέδριον) of the bishop (Phld., 8, 1), and since the latter stands "in the place of God," it is God's council, Tr., 3, 1.

3. ὁ συμπρεσβύτερος (only in Christian writings) is the "fellow-elder" in 1 Pt. 5:5; Iren. Ep. ad Victorem (in Eus. Hist. Eccl., V, 24, 14) and the antimontanist author in Eus. Hist. Eccl., V, 16, 5. Later, like συλλειτουργός, συμμύστης (and Latin equivalents), it is a common collegial form used by bishops in addressing their presbyters. [19]

---

[16] IPE, II, No. 450, 452, 456.

[17] So acc. to the convincing evidence in Lietzmann, 120-123. If the inscr. date only from the 3rd cent. A.D. the par. in 2 and 3 Jn. to a conventicle led by a presbyter should be noted, → 670, 10 ff.

[18] Cf. J. Jeremias, "ΠΡΕΣΒΥΤΕΡΙΟΝ ausserchristlich bezeugt," ZNW, 48 (1957), 127 f., where the textual question is also discussed.

[19] Cf. H. Achelis, Das Christentum in den ersten drei Jahrhunderten, II (1912), 16; E. G. Selwyn, The First Epistle of St. Peter (1955), 228; → n. 158.

B. "Elders" in the Constitutional History of Israel and Judah.

1. In J and E. In all strata of the OT tradition the elders (הַזְּקֵנִים) [20] are presupposed. Nowhere do we read of their appointment or of the establishment of their colleges. It is generally assumed that their origin lies in the most ancient patriarchal period when Israel was made up of tribes long before the settlement and national hegemony. As heads and representatives of the great families and clans the elders were leaders in the larger units which were then in process of formation. Nevertheless, even in the most ancient sources of the story of Israel's development as a nation, namely, J and E, there is now hardly a trace of their relation to the tribal constitution. [21] Always now the elders are representatives of the whole people, and they are this only in the sense of mere representation, not with any initiative or governing power, but along with and under leading figures like Moses and Joshua. [22] On important occasions affecting the whole people they are assembled to receive the will of Yahweh.

On the command of Yahweh Moses has to assemble the elders of Israel to declare to them, and thereby to the people in Egypt, the approaching emancipation (Ex. 3:16; 4:29), and then to go with them to Pharaoh (Ex. 3:18). It is their duty to supervise the slaying of the family offering to celebrate the Passover (Ex. 12:21). They keep a sacrificial feast with Jethro (Ex. 18:12) and at Sinai receive the revelation of Yahweh from the lips of Moses (Ex. 19:7). Some of the elders of Israel (Ex. 17:5) witness the miracle of the water at Horeb, and seventy elders see the glory of Yahweh in the story of the making of the covenant with Moses and his three companions at Sinai (Ex. 24:1, 9). As representatives of the whole people the elders go with Moses when he punishes Dathan and Abiram (Nu. 16:25). The elders also stand by Joshua when the theft of Achan is expiated (Jos. 7:6). [23] With Joshua they lead the people in the attack on Ai (Jos. 8:10). Joshua summons them when he calls all the people together to a national assembly at Shechem (Jos. 24:1; cf. 23:2). Instructive, if not uncontested historically, is the phrase "the elders of Israel" (Ex. 3:16, 18; 12:21; 18:12; 24:1, 9 etc.), [24] which is a favourite one in E and which presupposes the unity of the people even before the conquest. Instructive, too, is the unmistakable tendency to set the established authority of the elders, which needs neither validation nor legal definition, in the service of the guidance of the whole people. Naturally not all the elders shared in this leadership but only those chosen by Moses. This is the point of the (E ?) [25] narrative in Nu. 11:16 f., 24 f. which tells how Moses appointed 70 elders [26] at the command of Yahweh, how he shared his burdens with them, and how Yahweh endowed them with a portion of the spirit which rested on him. We seem to have here an aetiological story which developed under the influence of ecstatic prophetism [27] and which alters as well as adopts the earlier constitution of the elders, since Moses makes a selection and subordinates the 70 to himself as bearers of portions of his own spirit, thus validating them at the same time

---

[20] זָקֵן originally means one who wears a beard, i.e., a fully accredited adult in the national assembly, then an old man. Cf. Köhler-Baumg., s.v. זָקֵן. From the older men there are then chosen the narrower colleges of elders which represent the tribe, city, locality, or people. Cf. M. Noth, Geschichte Israels³ (1956), 104.

[21] Cf. also Ex. 12:21.

[22] M. Noth, Überlieferungsgeschichte d. Pent. (1948), 172-191 argues that in pre-Mosaic stories of the exodus and the Sinai revelation the elders were the original leaders and that they were demoted to the position of mere statistics or inactive supernumeraries only with the tendency to ascribe a leading role to Moses.

[23] The context Jos. 7:16-18 shows clearly that the tribes were made up of smaller clans.

[24] Cf. also זִקְנֵי בְנֵי יִשְׂרָאֵל in Ex. 4:29; זִקְנֵי הָעָם in Ex. 19:7; Nu. 11:16, 24.

[25] Noth, op. cit. (→ n. 22), 34 would say J.

[26] The number 70 seems to be Canaanite in origin (→ n. 37) a round number for an important aristocratic family, cf. Ju. 8:30; 9:2, 5; 12:14.

[27] On the concept of the spirit and the significance of the story of the elders in Nu. 11 cf. Noth, op. cit. (→ n. 22), 141-143.

as the bearers of an office. The story is clearly related to the J account of the making of the covenant at Sinai in Ex. 24:1, 9 (the manifestation of the glory of Yahweh to Moses and 70 of the elders of Israel). It is also another version of Ex. 18:13 ff., where on the advice of Jethro suitable men [28] are appointed as heads (שָׂרִים) of thousands, hundreds, fifties and tens and also as judges in minor cases. Finally Dt. 1:9-18 describes the same event in a very representative place in the parting discourse of Moses. [29] The fact that the various sources lay such emphasis on this choice and appointment of the elders shows that the story in Nu. 11:16 f., 24 f. is not recounting an isolated miracle like the related account of the giving of quails to eat. The real point is to tell of the appointment of office-bearers [30] and to ascribe their institution to Moses, even though they have as yet no official capacity. [31]

The two passages Ex. 24 and Nu. 11 exerted considerable influence on other parts of the Bible and on Jewish exegesis. In obvious dependence on Ex. 24:9 f. the late apc. in Is., depicting world judgment and the manifestation of the coming kingdom of Yahweh on Zion and in Jerusalem, closes with the words : "And before his elders is glory," Is. 24:23. The passage is a first example of the way in which apocalyptic likes to base its eschatological visions on sacred texts, so that it is itself to a large extent exegesis. [32] In relation to Is. 24:23, Rev. 4 follows the same pattern in its vision of the 24 elders before the throne of God, → 668, 9 ff. In Rabb. exegesis, too, Ex. 24 along with Is. 24 plays an important part, though now with the particular intention of bringing out the special honour of the elders both then and in the future world. Cf. S. Nu., 92 on 11:16 : "Not (just) in one place and not (just) in two does God give honour to the elders. But in every place where you find 'elders,' God gives honour to the elders." [33]

Nu. 11:16 f., 24 f. offers a model for the Sanhedrin and the number of its members, → 659, 18 ff. [34] It also offers scriptural support for Rabb. ordination. [35] The early Chr. church could also turn sometimes to this passage at the institution of presbyters. [36]

2. In the Time of the Judges and the Monarchy. If prior to the conquest the original data concerning the elders are difficult to discern, the picture changes after the occupation. Now for the first time we find elders who are leading members of the municipal nobility in various districts, no matter whether the towns are Israelite or not. [37] In the hands of these elders lie decisions in political,

---

[28] Ex. 18 does not refer, of course, to elders or to the choice of 70.

[29] Again there is no ref. to elders, but to the synon. "wise and understanding and perspicacious heads of your tribes," Dt. 1:13, 15. It is characteristic of Dt. to avoid the terms "elders of Israel"; Dt. refers only to local elders with limited judicial functions, → 657, 22 ff.

[30] In Nu. 11, then, the spirit is that of office, cf. Eichr. Theol. AT, II², 23, n. 7.

[31] Cf. the 70 elders as representatives of the whole people in Ez. 8:11.

[32] I owe this ref. to G. v. Rad.

[33] Cf. also Lv. r., 11 (113b) in Str.-B., III, 653 f.

[34] Colleges of 70 are also common. Thus Jos. appointed 70 elders over Galilee (Bell., 2, 570 f.); the Zealots set up a court of 70 members in Jerusalem (Bell., 4, 336 and 341); 70 distinguished men stand at the head of the Babylonian Jewish colony at Batanaea (Bell., 2, 482; Vit., 56) and also at the head of the Jewish community in Alexandria (jSukka, 5, 1 [55a, 70 f.]). The Ebionites also had a teaching college of 70 elders, Ep. Petri ad Jacobum, 1 and 2 (GCS, 42,1, p. 1 f.). Cf. H. J. Schoeps, Theol. u. Gesch. d. Judenchristentums (1949), 290.

[35] Cf. K. G. Kuhn, Sifre Numeri (1934), 247-251; Lohse, 21 f., 25-27.

[36] Church Order of Hipp., 32, 2 (ed. F. X. Funk, Didask. et Const. Ap., II [1905], 103). Cf. also Orig. Hom. in Nu. 22:4 (GCS, 30, 208).

[37] We read of elders of Moab and Midian already in Nu. 22:4, 7 (glosses), also of elders of Egypt (dignitaries) at the funeral of Joseph in Gn. 50:7. For elders in non-Isr. towns cf. Gibeon in Jos. 9:11, Succoth in Ju. 8:14, 16, Shechem in Ju. 9:2; in Isr. towns, the city and district of Gilead in Ju. 11:3-11, Jabesh in 1 S. 11:5-10, Bethlehem in 1 S. 16:4, the cities of Judah in 1 S. 30:26-31, cf. also Rt. 4.

military and judicial matters. [38] In addition to local elders, there seem to have elders (leading men) from districts and from many or all the tribes who met for common decisions (Ju. 11:5; 1 S. 30:26; 2 S. 19:12) and who were often called the elders of Israel (2 S. 3:17; 5:3 etc.). The history of the age of the judges and the monarchy shows what power lay in their hands especially in time of war and how advisable it was for ruling kings, or their opponents, to win them over.

The elders of Israel resolve to bring up the ark in the war against the Philistines, 1 S. 4:3. They demand that Samuel should appoint a king, 1 S. 8:4. Saul, when disgraced, asks to be reinstated before the elders of Israel, 1 S. 15:30. David, when Abner has won over the elders of Israel for him (2 S. 3:17), makes a treaty with them by which he attains to royal power, 2 S. 5:3. In the rebellion of Absalom the elders of Israel defect from David, 2 S. 17:4, 15. David can get back the kingdom only when he has won over the elders again, 2 S. 19:12. At the consecration of Solomon's temple the elders of Israel appear for the last time as the representatives of the whole people, 1 K. 8:1, 3. After the disruption they are representatives of the two sections, of the people of the land (1 K. 20:7 f.) or of individual towns (1 K. 21:8, 11; 2 K. 10:1, 5). When a royal bureaucracy was set up, the influence of the elders declined sharply. But they still had power, and the monarchy had to be able to count on this in critical situations (1 K. 20:7 f.) or in the carrying out of important decisions (1 K. 21:8, 11). 2 K. 6:32 and 10:1, 5 show that prophetic and political opposition to rulers sought and found support among the elders.

3. In Deuteronomy. Dt. accords to the elders certain clearly defined legal powers which are obviously based on ancient custom (cf. Rt. 4:2, 4, 9, 11). Nevertheless, it restricts these to the local sphere and associates judges and subordinate officials with the colleges of elders.

Matters allotted to the elders are casuistically delineated. The elders must deliver up to the blood-avenger a murderer who has fled to their city, Dt. 19:11-13. They must make atonement for an unsolved murder which has taken place in their area, 21:1-9. Acc. to detailed rules they must find concerning the complaint of parents against a refractory son (21:18-21) or of a husband against his erring wife (22:13-21). They must also supervise a levirate marriage, 25:5-10. Their judgment is given at the city gate, Dt. 22:15; 25:7; cf. Prv. 31:23. Apart from and along with the elders we read of special judges (שֹׁפְטִים Dt. 1:16; 25:2) and officials (שֹׁטְרִים Dt. 20:5, 8; both in 16:18; judges and elders in 21:2). The inter-relationship of the three groups seems to be as follows. The judges as individual officers (שֹׁפֵט is sing. in Dt. 25:2) and the subordinate officials had to be newly appointed (16:18), whereas the elders, where they had judicial functions as local colleges, now had an administrative character, but with limited powers. The authorisation of the elders in Nu. 11 is now transferred to the officials, Dt. 1:15 f.

Though the elders of Israel are less prominent in the Deuteronomic legislation, they still play an important role in the Deuteronomic histories, whether as those who share in the proclamation of the Law (Dt. 27:1), or as its responsible recipients (5:23; 31:9). They are also much to the fore in solemn assemblies when the whole people makes a committal (Dt. 29:9; 31:28; Jos. 8:33; 23:2; 24:1). Here, however, they are not an official corporation and usually there is mention of specific office-bearers along with them.

4. In the Exilic and Post-Exilic Period. In spite of the decay of the tribal organisation toward the end of the pre-exilic period and its collapse after the

---

[38] The question how far the Israelites took over the system of municipal elders from the Canaanites and how far they kept the tribal organisation after the conquest in more or less altered and adapted form is hard to answer ; certainly both possibilities have to be taken into account. There is evidence of aristocratic city government already in the Amarna period. Cf. J. A. Knudtzon, "Die El-Amarna-Tafeln," *Vorderasiatische Bibliothek,* 2 (1907), No. 59; 89, 48 f.

deportation, representation by elders continues both among those who remained at home and also among the exiles. At home a distinction must be made between country and capital. According to Jer. 26:17 the elders of the land (אַנְשִׁים מִזְקְנֵי הָאָרֶץ) oppose the judgment of the capital and plead for the prophet. In Ez. 8:11 f. we read of elders of Jerusalem who obviously represent the whole people (the prophet in a vision sees from Babylon the idolatrous practices of the 70 elders in Jerusalem). At the head of the community of exiles there are also elders, Jer. 29:1; Ez. 8:1; 14:1; 20:1, 3. Indeed, in exile, when all other political forms have been shattered, the elders take on enhanced significance as those who exercise limited self-government on behalf of the people. Nevertheless, their structure undergoes profound modification during and after the exile. With the dissolution of the tribal unions individual families (father's houses) [39] grow in importance. After the exile these are the foundation of the new community. Prominent families are also more important; their heads are the leaders of the people after the re-establishment of the community. Only now can one properly call the elders and the families from which they come an aristocracy. The patent of nobility which establishes the hereditary dignity of these families is officially documented membership of the Gola (Ezr. 8:1-14; Neh. 7:6-65, though the word זְקֵנִים is not used here). If previously the elders owed their authority to the position which they occupied in the clans and tribes, this is now based on the special position of their families within the people itself.

This change in structure is reflected in the vocabulary of post-exilic writings. The word וְקֵנִים, which is connected with the ancient and broken tribal constitution, is noticeably less prominent, [40] being replaced by other words (heads of families, captains, rulers). Though these are also called elders, the Aram. שָׂב is used, properly transl. πρεσβύτερος by the LXX, Ezr. 5:9; 6:7, 8, 14. These men stand at the head of the people and the Persian governor has dealings with them. With the "governor of the Jews" they rebuild the temple and reorganise the people. Their authority over the whole people was established with difficulty, as may be seen from the battle between Nehemiah and the "nobles and rulers" (הַחֹרִים וְהַסְּגָנִים) who were still powerful in the land, Neh. 2:16; 4:8, 13; 5:7; 7:5. Ezr. 10:7-17 also shows that the system of city elders (10:14) had not yet wholly perished. In conformity with the ancient constitution we read here of "judges and elders of cities" (וְזִקְנֵי עִיר וָעִיר) in connection with the resolve of the assembly of returned exiles in Jerusalem to excommunicate those guilty of mixed marriages. These men are to come to Jerusalem along with those affected by the law. They are not identical, however, with הַשָּׂרִים וְהַזְּקֵנִים of 10:18, who convene the assembly of exiles. [41] It should also be noted that Ezra appoints from among the heads of families the judicial commission which is charged with the execution of the decree, 10:16. There is obviously a trend towards setting the people under a leading centralised court made up of representatives of the aristocratic families in Jerusalem. These "senators" (הַסְּגָנִים) are daily guests at the governor's table, 150 in number, Neh. 5:17. The many synonyms and their large number show that this college is a chamber of notables rather than an official corporation.

5. "Elders" in the Sanhedrin at Jerusalem. As a clearly delineated supreme ruling body of the Jews with its seat in Jerusalem the "council of elders" is known

---

[39] On the term and its occurrence cf. Rost, 56-59.

[40] It is found in Ch. in the revision of older texts from S and K., but it is very rare in P, does not occur at all in Neh., and the only ref. in Ezr. are at 10:8, 14 (at 3:12 old men physically are meant), cf. Rost, 61-64.

[41] Only here do we find once again the archaic title זְקֵנִים for representatives of the whole people.

to us only from the time of the Seleucids (Antiochus III, 223-187 B.C.). But the beginnings of this aristocratic γερουσία, the later → συνέδριον, may be traced back to the Persian period. [42]

In the course of the fluctuating history of this body, which was dominated by party conflicts, the term πρεσβύτεροι undergoes a clear change. At the outset it is used for all the members of the γερουσία. [43] Only gradually does it become the special term for lay members as distinct from the representatives of the priestly families, from whom the high-priest and president of the Sanhedrin was chosen, and also from the theological group of the γραμματεῖς. It is obvious that the direction of the Sanhedrin never lay in the hands of the πρεσβύτεροι. Yet one may assume that the elders, as representatives of the privileged patrician families in Jerusalem, usually followed the lead of the priestly Sadducees. [44] Certainly the many synonyms used to describe the elders in Jos., NT and Talmud make it plain beyond question that the elders had a seat and a voice in the Sanhedrin as lay nobles. [45] Their weakness in relation to the other two groups may be seen from the NT, which usually calls the members of the Sanhedrin the ἀρχιερεῖς, γραμματεῖς, πρεσβύτεροι in this order (the ἀρχιερεῖς were still put first even when they had lost actual control to the γραμματεῖς). [46]

After the destruction of Jerusalem the great Sanhedrin found an heir and successor in the Sanhedrin of Jabneh (Jamnia), which derived its 72 elders from the council of elders appointed by Moses. As compared with the High Council at Jerusalem it has a different aspect, however, for all political powers have been taken away and only a limited judicial authority remains. Its members are made up exclusively of Pharisaic scribes; it no longer includes either priestly aristocracy or lay nobility. In this new form, as the supreme dogmatic court in exposition and application of the Law and as a higher school of scribal learning, this Sanhedrin soon became a normative authority for all Judaism.

6. זָקֵן as a Term for the Scribes. In view of this development, Jewish tradition, when it confers on leading older scholars [47] the honorary title זָקֵן, connects with this

---

[42] Jos. Ant., 12, 138-144. Cf. Schürer, II, 239.

[43] ἡ γερουσία = οἱ πρεσβύτεροι, cf. 2 Macc. 1:10; 4:44; 11:27 with 1 Macc. 7:33 and esp. 1 Macc. 12:6 with 14:20 etc.

[44] Jos. Ant., 18, 17 says expressly that the "nobles" belong to the Sadducean party. Sadducean control and the related lay nobility vanish with the destruction of the Jewish state in 70 A.D. This possibly explains the Rabb. emphasis on a special Beraka on the "elders" in the Prayer of Eighteen Benedictions, which must have found a place in some versions acc. to T. Ber., 4, 25. Cf. K. G. Kuhn, *Achtzehngebet u. Vaterunser u. der Reim* (1950), 18 f., 21 f.

[45] We learn quite a bit about the elders as a lay nobility from the synon. The chief of the people (Lk. 19:47 with ἀρχιερεῖς, γραμματεῖς); the chief of the city (Jos. Vit., 9); the leaders of the people (*ibid.*, 194); dignitaries (Jos. Bell., 2, 410); the powerful (*ibid.*, 2, 316 etc.). In Bell., 2, 411 the three groups are the powerful (δυνατοί), the chief priests and distinguished Pharisees. In the Talmud the lay members are constantly called "the great men of the generation," "the great men of Jerusalem," "the nobles of Jerusalem." For further instances cf. Jeremias, 88-100.

[46] Variation is possible, cf. Mk. 8:31 par.: πρεσβύτεροι, ἀρχιερεῖς, γραμματεῖς. There is no little fluctuation in describing members of the Sanhedrin in the first 3 Gospels. Thus Mk. often has ἀρχιερεῖς, γραμματεῖς, πρεσβύτεροι (11:27; 14:43, 53; 15:1, cf. Mt. 16:21; 27:41), but Mt. prefers the two-membered formula ἀρχιερεῖς καὶ οἱ πρεσβύτεροι (τοῦ λαοῦ) (21:23; 26:3; 27:1, 3, 12, 20; 28:11 f.). A notable feature in Mt. is his common omission of the γραμματεῖς. Lk. is obviously loosest in his description of the ruling body (cf. 7:3; 9:22; 20:1; 22:52). In Ac. we find ἄρχοντες, πρεσβύτεροι, γραμματεῖς (4:5); ἄρχοντες τοῦ λαοῦ καὶ πρεσβύτεροι (4:8); ἀρχιερεῖς, πρεσβύτεροι (4:23; 23:14; 25:15), cf. also 6:12; 24:1.

[47] Orla, 2, 5; Sukka, 2, 8 (Shammai); Ar., 9, 4; Shebi., 10, 3 (Hillel); their pupils are called בְּנֵי הַזְּקֵנִים, Sukka, 2, 7. Cf. Lohse, 50-52.

title the idea of their membership of the Sanhedrin. [48] Nevertheless, members of local corporations are also called זְקֵנִים. [49] Naturally a זָקֵן of this kind must always be authorised as a teacher : "Only he who has wisdom is a זָקֵן," Qidd., 32b. This helps us to understand the common use of זְקֵנִים for ordained scholars in the Mishnah. [50] It does not mean, however, that every חָכָם is eo ipso a זָקֵן; חָכָם is the broader term and זָקֵן a special honorary title almost equivalent to senator.

The way must have been prepared earlier for this assimilation of חֲכָמִים and זְקֵנִים in the Mishnah. It already underlies the LXX legend (1st half of the 1st cent. B.C., Ep. Ar., 32, 39, 46). Acc. to this account Ptolemy asks the high-priest Eleazar to appoint 72 elders of good scholarship and repute to undertake the work of translation. πρεσβύτεροι here is certainly not used as a title, for they are selected as scribes, not appointed elders. Nevertheless, the choice of 72 (6 from each of the 12 tribes) reflects the ancient representation of all Israel. πρεσβύτεροι is also used for scribes in Mk. 7:3 (παράδοσις τῶν πρεσβυτέρων) and Jos. Ant., 13, 292 (ἀκούομεν παρὰ τῶν πρεσβυτέρων).

The Dead Sea Scrolls have (as yet) little to offer on the history of the Jewish eldership. The Manual (1 QS 6:8-10) has one ref. to זְקֵנִים in the order of seating at a plenary session of the sect ; these are put behind the priests, who take the first place, and before the people, thus occupying the second rank. It is also laid down that the discussion of legal matters and community affairs is to be in the same order, though their precise function is obscure. It is possible that they are identical with the 12 men who acc. to 1 QS 8:1 are to act with 3 priests in deciding concerning transgressions of the Torah. At any rate they are lay representatives associated with and subordinate to the priests, cf. 1 QM 13:1. A consistory of judges, who must all be learned in the Law (from 25 to 60 yrs. old), is also mentioned in Damasc. (10:5 f. [11:2]: "4 from the tribe of Levi and Aaron and 6 from Israel"). This is subject to the Mᵉbaqqer (→ II, 618, 23 ff.) and it also acts with him in caring for the poor, 12:11-18 (14:12-16). [51]

7. πρεσβύτεροι in the Local and Synagogal Government of Hellenistic Judaism. The political importance of elders in the usage of Gk. speaking Judaism may be seen at once from the fact that the LXX uses both πρεσβύτεροι and γερουσία for the Heb. זְקֵנִים. [52] The situation in the age of the Maccabees is reflected in Jdt. and Macc. Here the patriarchal term πρεσβύτεροι is used as a designation of office both for the members of the supreme national court, the Jerusalem senate, [53] and also for local authorities. [54] In a broader sense, however, πρεσβύτεροι can be used for notables and distinguished from members of the council (3 Macc. 1:8, 23) and ἄρχοντες, 1 Macc. 1:26. We also find the sense of "the aged" (as distinct from "the young") in 1 Macc. 14:9; 2 Macc. 5:13; 8:30. πρεσβύτεροι is thus a broader term. The story of Susannah, which has ref. to the Babylonian dispersion, speaks expressly of elders who were appointed judges that year, Sus. 5 (Θ), 29, 34 (LXX).

The older communal order of the local Jewish community is continued in the constitution of the synagogue, → συναγωγή. To the local board, usually made up of 7 members, there corresponds in places with a separate Jewish cultic community the synagogal council. The title πρεσβύτεροι is also perpetuated for the leaders of the

---

[48] Cf. A. Sammter, Die sechs Ordnungen der Mischna, I² (1927), 181, n. 8a.
[49] Cf. S. Krauss, Synagogale Altertümer (1922), 143 f.
[50] Er., 3, 5; 8, 7; Sanh., 11, 1-4; AZ, 4, 7.
[51] Cf. B. Reicke, "Die Verfassung d. Urgemeinde im Lichte jüd. Dokumente," ThZ, 10 (1954), 95-112.
[52] γερουσία Ex. 3:16, 18; 4:29; 12:21; Lv. 9:1, 3; Nu. 22:4, 7; Dt. 5:23 etc. Ex. 24:9 B : ἐβδομήκοντα τῆς γερουσίας Ἰσραήλ, A : ἐβδομήκοντα τῶν πρεσβυτέρων Ἰσραήλ.
[53] 1 Macc. 1:26; 7:33; 11:23; 12:35; 13:36; 14:20; 2 Macc. 13:13; 14:37.
[54] The elders of Betylua (Jdt. 6:16, 21; 7:23; 8:10; 10:6) are distinguished from the Jerusalem γερουσία (4:8; 11:14; 15:8). πρεσβύτεροι τῆς χώρας, 1 Macc. 14:28. Lietzmann, 124-126.

community and the disciplinary body of the synagogue, cf. Lk. 7:3. [55] Yet it is worth noting that the titular use of πρεσβύτεροι is much less prominent in the synagogue of the *diaspora* in the first centuries A.D. The more frequent are titles common in Gk. constitutional usage (γερουσία, γερουσιάρχης, ἄρχοντες, φροντιστής, γραμματεύς, προστάτης). [56] In the numerous burial inscr. of the Jewish communities in Rome πρεσβύτερος is perhaps attested once in the first centuries. [57] More numerous, but late, are the instances from Asia Minor, Syria, and Palestine. [58] πρεσβύτερος here is not a term for officials, nor a simple designation of age, but an honorary title for the heads of leading families (cf. the Roman senator). [59] The families shared in the dignity of these senators, as may be seen from the adding of the title to the names of the fathers and forefathers of the deceased on funerary inscr., [60] and esp. from the use of πρεσβυτέρα for women [61] who are the wives of elders. [62] That the titular use is not more common in the first centuries is surprising. It is perhaps less due to the fact that πρεσβύτερος is an honorary title with no official standing [63] — this would have made it esp. well adapted for burial inscr. — than to the fact that it was not common as an honorary title in Gk. [64] The examples to hand show that it did not wholly die out in the Synagogue of the dispersion, esp. in the East. This is confirmed by the Codices Theodosianus and Justinianus in the 4th and 5th cent., which in many decrees refer to presbyters as members of the synagogal council. [65]

C. The παράδοσις τῶν πρεσβυτέρων in the Proclamation of Jesus.

In the debate about clean and unclean (Mk. 7:1-23; Mt. 15:1-20) [66] Jesus contrasts the commandment of God with the παράδοσις τῶν πρεσβυτέρων and He calls the latter a παράδοσις τῶν ἀνθρώπων, Mk. 7:8; cf. 9, 13 → II, 172, 10 ff.

---

[55] Very important is the occurrence of πρεσβύτεροι as an official title for synagogue leaders on a Jerusalem inscr. before 70 A.D., Suppl. Epigr. Graec., VIII, 170, 9; text and interpretation Deissmann LO, 378-380; Frey Corpus, II, No. 1404, with full bibl.

[56] Cf. Schürer, III, 91 f. To be noted are other constitutional terms like βουλή, βουλευτής, γραμματεὺς τῆς βουλῆς, συνέδριον, δικαστής, κριτής, δεκάπρωτος, ἐθνάρχης. These show to what degree even the Jewish community of the *diaspora* regarded itself as a people rather than a θίασος.

[57] [Μ]ητρό[δ]ωρος [πρεσβ]ύτερος [ἐνθάδε κε]ῖτε → Frey Corpus, I, No. 378, cf. p. LXXXVI f. For Lower Italy (Venosa) and Spain (Elcke) *ibid.,* No. 595, 663.

[58] *Ibid.,* II, No. 735, 739 : Ἡρηνοποι(ὸ)ς πρ(εσβύτερος) κ(αὶ) πατὴρ τοῦ στέμ[μ]ατος ... 790, 792, 800, 801, 803, 828, 829, 931, 1277, 1404. Cf. also the Heb. funerary inscr., *ibid.,* No. 1299 (Jerusalem): סבא (אבונה) שמעון סבא יהוסף ברה = πρεσβύτερος, though it is not clear whether this Simeon is being called an old man or the member of a corporation [the Sanhedrin ?]).

[59] In Lv. r., 2, 4 זקן is used for the Roman senator ; the common Gk. rendering of senator, however, is βουλευτής or γέρων, not πρεσβύτερος.

[60] Cf. T. Reinach, "Inscr. juive des environs de Constantinople," REJ, 26 (1893), 167-171; Frey Corpus, II, No. 792.

[61] *Ibid.,* I, No. 581, 590, 597 (3 examples from Venosa), 692 (Thrace).

[62] Possibly this title, like ἀρχισυνάγωγος and *pateressa* (= *mater synagogae*), was conferred on worthy women in analogy to Graeco-Rom. custom. Cf. Schürer, II, 512; III, 17, 95 f.; Frey Corpus, I, No. 606; E. Diehl, Inscr. Latinae christianae veteres, II (1927), No. 4900.

[63] So E. Schürer, *Die Gemeindeverfassung d. Juden in Rom* (1897), 19; Frey Corpus, I, p. LXXXVI f.

[64] On the use of πρεσβύτερος as a title of office in Egypt and the (political) use of the word in Gk. societies (esp. in Asia Minor) → 653, 1 ff., 17 ff.

[65] Examples in Schürer, III, 89 f.; Lietzmann, 130 f.

[66] "A disputation based on an ancient saying of Jesus and developed at such length because of its obvious importance for the readers of Mk.," Kl. Mk., 67. For analysis of the pericope cf. M. Dibelius, *Die Formgeschichte d. Evangeliums*² (1933), 222 f.; B. H. Branscomb, *Jesus and the Law of Moses* (1930), 156-182; W. G. Kümmel, "Jesus u. d. jüd. Traditionsgedanke," ZNW, 33 (1934), 105-130, esp. 122-125; Bultmann Trad., 15 f.

The use of πρεσβύτεροι is one which later became common in Judaism, = scribe, → 660, 2 ff.

Their tradition was associated with the Torah in Pharisaism and the Rabbinate, [67] whereas the Sadducees rejected any extension of the Torah. [68] Jesus' criticism is opposed to both groups, for He does not accept either Torah or tradition as formal authorities, but sets both under material criteria. For this reason He can sometimes appeal to the Law and the prophets against tradition (Mk. 7:6-13 etc.) and sometimes set the statutes of the Mosaic Torah in antithesis to the true command of God, cf. esp. Mk. 10:1-12, but also the saying in Mk. 7:15, which contests any defilement by meats, and thus actually affects not merely παράδοσις but also the cultic law of Moses. [69] On the other hand, the further development of the Torah is not criticised as such; indeed, it is taken for granted, [70] and Jesus can even make positive use of directions of the Halaka in disputation, [71] though in other instances (e.g., Mk. 7) He may attack them very sharply.

That this is Jesus' own attitude to the Law and tradition and not just the theology of the community may be seen from the fact that Mk. shows most emphatically that the antithesis between the ἐντολή of God and human παράδοσις is one of principle (7:9, 13) and that he also interprets the saying of 7:15 more precisely in terms of a Hell. list of vices (vv. 20-23), [72] whereas Mt., unable to abandon the Marcan original, contests defilement by unwashed hands (Mt. 15:20), but eliminates the declaration that all meats are clean (Mk. 7:19), and criticises, not the παράδοσις τῶν πρεσβυτέρων, nor the teaching office of the scribes as such (Mt. 23:2), [73] but simply the hypocritical exposition which leaves out of account the weightier matters of the Law. For him, therefore, the ceremonial law is not abolished; [74] it is subordinated to the law of love. [75]

D. Presbyters in the Primitive Christian Communities.

1. The First Jerusalem Church. According to Ac. [76] there were elders in the first church in Jerusalem. They are mentioned for the first time in relation to the collection at Antioch, which Paul and Barnabas brought to the πρεσβύτεροι at Jerusalem (11:30). They are then referred to in the account of the apostolic council and the formulation of the apostolic decree, 15:2, 4, 6, 22 f.; 16:4. We finally meet them again in the story of Paul's coming to Jerusalem and his discussion with James, 21:18. Comparison of the passages shows that only in 11:30 and 21:18 are the πρεσβύτεροι mentioned alone without the ἀπόστολοι, with whom they form a single body throughout c. 15 and in 16:4. Again, in 11:30 and 21:18 they are simply representatives of the Jerusalem congregation, and thus

---

[67] Shab., 31a; Ab., 1, 1; 3, 14; Sanh., 11, 3; Moore, I, 251-262.

[68] Jos. Ant., 13, 297 f.; Kl. Mk. Exc. on 2:16.

[69] For the theological significance of this cf. E. Käsemann, "Das Problem des historischen Jesus," ZThK, 51 (1954), esp. 144-148; G. Bornkamm, Jesus v. Nazareth² (1957), 88-92.

[70] E.g., Mt. 5:43.

[71] Mt. 12:11; for details cf. Kümmel, op. cit. (→ n. 66), 119 f.

[72] The Decalogue in Mt. 15:19.

[73] Mt. 5:23 f.; 17:24-27; 23:16-22; 24:20. Cf. G. Barth, Untersuchungen zum Gesetzesverständnis des Evangelisten Mt., Diss. Heidelberg (1955), 48-53.

[74] Cf. G. D. Kilpatrick, The Origins of the Gospel acc. to St. Matthew (1946), 108; E. Haenchen, "Matthäus 23," ZThK, 48 (1951), 38-63; Barth, op. cit. (→ n. 73), 44-48. Traditional rulings are expressly recognised in Mt. 23:23.

[75] The command of love as the sum of the Law and the prophets (7:12; 9:13; 12:7; 22:40) is already in view in Mt. 5:17-19, where the unrestricted validity of the Law is maintained in Jewish Chr. expressions; cf. E. Schweizer, "Mt. 5:17-20 — Anmerkungen zum Gesetzesverständnis des Mt.," ThLZ, 77 (1952), 479-484.

[76] In what follows the procedure is obviously open to historical criticism but it is adopted in order to obtain a better general view.

resemble a Jewish synagogue council. According to 21:8 they gather around James, who obviously presides. [77]

> These presbyters appear relatively late in the story of Ac. There is no mention of them up to 11:30 even though on not a few occasions the church meets representatively and makes decisions. Shortly after the ref. in 11:30 James is mentioned for the first time as the leader of the congregation, 12:17. The account of the bringing of the collection to the elders at Jerusalem seems to have been put too early by the author of Ac. (11:30). [78] 21:17-26 is undoubtedly based on an earlier tradition. The context here contains the most important critical argument against the description of the apostolic council and its supposed decree in Ac. 15, and it confirms Gl. 2, which says nothing about any such decree. The account in Paul also seems to conflict with the picture of the church's constitution in Ac. 15. The δοκοῦντες whom Paul meets in a special session in Gl. 2:2 are simply the three apostles here described as στῦλοι, 2:2, 6, 9; Ac., however, refers to ἀπόστολοι and πρεσβύτεροι, and it does so in a way which agrees neither with Gl. 2 nor indeed with Ac. 11:30; 21:18.

In Ac. 15; 16:4 the ἀπόστολοι and πρεσβύτεροι clearly function as a supreme court and normative teaching office for the whole Church. In the decree they come to a binding decision about the minimal demands of the Law so far as the Gentiles are concerned. In this instance the ἀπόστολοι and πρεσβύτεροι are patterned after the Jewish Sanhedrin (→ 658, 44 ff.) and not just the synagogue council (→ 660, 39 ff.). In keeping with this modification is the fact that the ἀπόστολοι and πρεσβύτεροι alone are mentioned (without the ἐκκλησία) in 15:2, 6, 23; 16:4, i.e., where they act as an authority for the whole Church (not in 15:4, 22).

> It may thus be seen that Ac. 15 is historically debatable, not merely in respect of the main result of the council (the decree), but also in respect of the body which reaches it. Though the literary and theological tendencies of the author are noticeable in this depiction (the grouping of the speakers, the harmonising bias of their speeches), nevertheless Lk. is here dependent on Jewish Christian tradition, of which he makes abundant use elsewhere in his historical writings. In this tradition the extension of the authority of the local Jerusalem presbytery into a Sanhedrin with teaching and judicial authority for the whole Church has already been effected.

The historical result of this analysis is that the formation of a body of elders, first after the synagogal model, then (probably in connection with the decree) with the same claim as the Sanhedrin, belongs only to the period of the increasing Judaising of the primitive community under James after the departure of Peter. There is a very clear picture of this situation in 21:17-26. Internal arguments all favour the hypothesis, e.g., the disappearance of the Twelve, the development of the ἀπόστολοι into an ideal, the growth of the church [79] and the existence of older and tested members who could serve as a presbytery.

> 2. The Pauline Churches. In contrast to the constitution of the first community after the Jewish pattern, the Hell. churches on the Pauline mission field present at first a very

---

[77] We need not pursue here the question how far the passage stylises the relation of James to the presbyters along the lines of a monarchically directed presbyterate. On the question of the caliphate or episcopate of James cf. E. Stauffer, "Zum Kalifat des Jakobus," Zeitschr. f. Religions- u. Geistesgeschichte, 4 (1952), 193-214; H. v. Campenhausen, "Die Nachfolge des Jakobus," ZKG, 63 (1950/51), 133-144; also "Lehrreihen u. Bischofsreihen im 2. Jhdt.," In Memoriam E. Lohmeyer (1951), 240-249; v. Campenhausen, 21 f. On Ac. 11:30 and 21:18 cf. Haench. Ag., 325, 544.

[78] The account is hard to reconcile with Gl. 1 and 2.

[79] Cf. the note in 21:20.

different picture. [80] In the uncontested Pauline epistles there is no ref. to presbyters, though there was no absence of organisation and offices in the Paul. congregations. Only rarely, however, does Paul confer any title on the office-bearers in a local church (διάκονος, → II, 89, 29 ff.; ἐπίσκοπος, → II, 615, 39 ff.). For the most part he refers to them in terms of their function in the congregation (R. 12:7 f.; 1 C. 12:28; 1 Th. 5:12): προϊστάμενοι (→ 701, 30), κοπιῶντες (→ III, 829, 40 ff.), men to whom the χάρισμα of ἀντίλημψις (→ I, 375, 35 ff.), κυβέρνησις (→ III, 1036, 14 ff.), διακονία (→ II, 89, 26 ff.) etc. is given. To them subordination is enjoined. Yet their authority derives from the ministry accepted and discharged by them, not from their status. Neither on the ground of age nor on that of length of membership in the community do they have authority. The constitutional principle in the congregation is that of plurality of *charismata,* not that of a naturally developed tradition which qualifies its bearers and sponsors to lead the church.

3. **The Development of a Presbyteral Constitution under the Influence of the Synagogue of the Diaspora.** For firm information on the development of a presbyteral constitution after the pattern of the synagogue of the *diaspora* we have to wait for the post-apostolic writings, which in other respects, too, are under the strong influence of Hellenistic Judaism. [81] The nearest approaches in the NT are as follows.

a. James. In the sphere of (Hellenistic) Jewish Christianity we have the Ep. of James, which mentions presbyters alone in 5:14. [82] In case of sickness one is to summon "the elders of the church" in order that they may cure the sick by prayer and anointing "in the name of the Lord," → I, 230, 9 ff.; II, 472, 38 ff. [83] Obviously these are office-bearers of the congregation (note the article) and not just charismatically endowed older men. Equally clearly they are regarded as endowed with the gift of efficacious prayer in virtue of their office. [84]

> Though these elders resemble the rulers of the synagogue, there is nothing in Judaism to correspond to the self-evident way in which they are all assumed to have the intrinsic gift of healing intercession. This presupposes the primitive Chr. experience of *charismata,* though these are now tied to the institution. Yet the later Jewish estimation of the elder as sage is close to the picture in Jm., cf. BB, 116a : "He who has a sick person in his house, let him go to a scribe, that he may pray for mercy on him." [85] Nowhere, however, is such an attribute ascribed to Jewish elders in general. Since Jm. 5:16 is not referring to confession of sins before presbyters, but to mutual confession and intercession and the efficacy of the prayer of the righteous, 5:14 does not allow us to draw any conclusions as to the position of presbyters as confessors [86] or their function as the leaders of the church's liturgy. [87]

---

[80] Cf. H. Greeven, "Propheten, Lehrer, Vorsteher bei Pls.," ZNW, 44 (1952/53), 1-43; v. Campenhausen, 59-81.

[81] Cf. Bultmann Theol., 448.

[82] Unfortunately we cannot say for certain what is the ecclesiastical provenance of Jm. Closeness to 1 Pt. and 1 Cl. has often been noted, but this rests, not on literary dependence, but on the use of a hortatory tradition which derives from the Judaism of the *diaspora* and which cannot be localised geographically, cf. Dib. Jk., 29-33.

[83] The action is meant to be an exorcism aiming at healing. There is no ref. to "extreme unction."

[84] Dib. Jk., *ad loc.*

[85] On the miraculous prayers and gifts of healing of some Rabb. cf. Ab. R. Nat., 41; Chag., 3a; jBer., 5, 6 (9d, 21); Ber., 34b (Str.-B., I, 526; II, 10, 441 etc.; IV, 534 f.). Cf. A. Meyer, *Das Rätsel des Jk.* (1930), 164 f.

[86] So B. Poschmann, Paenitentia secunda (1940), 54-62.

[87] So Knopf, 176 f.

b. Acts. The oldest passages which refer to presbyters as the leaders of Gentile Christian congregations are Acts 14:23; 20:17-38. Even if these are not referred to the Pauline period, they are still important, especially the second, for the light they shed on the significance and duties of presbyters in the post-apostolic churches. When Paul and Barnabas left the congregations, they selected elders everywhere in the churches and commended them to the Lord with prayer and fasting, 14:23. Above all, the great address of Paul to the Ephesian elders (20:18-35, esp. vv. 28 ff.) shows what significance attached to them. The Holy Spirit has appointed them to be overseers (bishops) and shepherds over the congregation and the apostle has made known to them the whole counsel of God. They have to administer the legacy of the apostle, to follow his example, and to protect the church against the danger of error which threatens from without (v. 29) and from within (v. 30) → IV, 310, 6 ff. λύκος. Here for the first time, then, they appear in corpore as guardians of the tradition of the apostles, who appointed them and entrusted the guidance of the community to them.

Constitutionally the designation of the πρεσβύτεροι as ἐπίσκοποι is of special interest, → II, 615, 47 ff. Though the title "presbyter" is common in Lk., the title "bishop" is not found elsewhere in his writings. It occurs only here (Ac. 20:28) and it is used to describe the work of presbyters. The current title, then, is always πρεσβύτεροι. Obviously Lk. adds the term ἐπίσκοποι, which comes from the Pauline mission field though it is not yet filled out by Paul to the same degree as here, "in order to equate those who bear it with the elders in his sense, and thus to fuse the two traditions."[88]

c. 1 Peter. The picture in 1 Pt. is essentially the same. Though perhaps writing from Rome, Peter, too, is addressing the churches in Paul's mission field in Asia Minor. Here πρεσβύτεροι occurs in the context of an admonition to the elders first (5:1-4), then to the younger members of the church (v. 5a), and finally to all the members (5b-9). The antithesis πρεσβύτεροι / νεώτεροι might suggest that the πρεσβύτεροι are a natural group such as we find elsewhere in the epistle, e.g., masters/slaves in 2:18 ff., wives/husbands in 3:1 ff. Nevertheless, this arrangement simply brings out the patriarchal character of the presbyterate; it does not call in question the fact that the elders here are a college entrusted with the guidance of the church, i.e., that they are office-bearers. In 1 Pt. 5:2, as in Ac. 20:28, their office is summed up as that of the shepherd. But the specific, if typical, admonitions in v. 2 f. give us a glimpse of certain details. Institution and obligation are obviously presupposed in the direction to discharge the office "not by constraint, but willingly." The fact that it might be a temptation to personal gain shows that the presbyters had charge of the community funds. Finally, the warning against love of power (v. 3) makes it clear that they had disciplinary powers. [89] Avoiding all abuse of their office, the elders are summoned to be examples to the flock and they are directed to Christ, the coming Chief Shepherd (→ 494, 1 ff.

---

[88] Cf. v. Campenhausen 88; Haench. Ag., 530 f., 535.

[89] κλῆροι is par. to ποίμνιον, v. 2 f. Hence it is not to be referred to material income and expenditure (Wbg. Pt., ad loc.) but to the entrusting of individual members to the elders for guidance, Wnd. Pt., ad loc. et al. → III, 764, 16 ff. This obviously does not mean that a diocese is divided up into parishes or a congregation into pastoral groups assigned to various presbyters. The plur. is perhaps due to the encyclical character of the epistle (ποίμνιον as an ecclesiological term cannot be put in the plur.); cf. Knopf, 175, n. 1. Though the word undoubtedly denotes the share allotted by God, it enables us to see clearly how the office could come to be regarded as a matter of power and possession. κλῆροι can hardly mean "the several parts of the spiritual κληρονομία" (1:4), so Selwyn, op. cit. (→ n. 19), on 1 Pt. 5:3.

ἀρχιποίμην), who will give an imperishable crown of glory to those who prove faithful, v. 4. Precautions are thus taken against any attempt to make the authority of the elders autonomous, e.g., on the basis of the weight of the implied natural and historical factors. The pastoral office is plainly subject to the authority of the Chief Shepherd, Christ, for whom alone the title ἐπίσκοπος (→ II, 615, 18 ff.) is reserved, 2:25. [90] But the emphasis with which the temptations implicit in the presbyteral office are dealt with here shows that the office was more developed and fixed than in the related verse in Ac. 20. Its dignity may be seen from Peter's self-designation as ὁ συμπρεσβύτερος, 5:1. It is true that the apostle is here setting himself alongside the presbyters with emphatic modesty. It is also true, however, that he is setting them alongside himself. It is worth noting that in 1 Pt. 5 the presbyteral office is not called the guardian of the apostolic tradition against error.

d. Pastorals. Already in Acts the fusing of what were at first different traditions regarding offices was rather more than a product of the theological and literary work of the author. It took place in various ways in the constitutional history of primitive Christianity. This may be seen especially in the Pastorals. [91] In the four passages in which πρεσβύτερος occurs here the usage is not quite consistent. In 1 Tm. 5:1 (cf. also v. 2) πρεσβύτερος is clearly a designation of age (opp. νεώτερος). Nevertheless, this should not be taken as a guide to the meaning in the other references. Elsewhere in the Past. πρεσβύτερος is plainly a tt. for the bearers of an office of leadership in the churches. The elders are a college (πρεσβυτέριον, 1 Tm. 4:14) which took part in the ordination of Timothy by the laying on of hands. [92] Titus was to appoint πρεσβύτεροι in the local congregations (κατὰ πόλιν) for the sake of order, Tt. 1:5. It is possible that 1 Tm. 5:22 is a warning to Timothy not to ordain too hastily. [93] According to 1 Tm. 5:19 the presbyters enjoy special disciplinary protection and according to 1 Tm. 5:17 those who discharge their office well are to receive double honour. Whether

---

[90] ἐπίσκοπος is not a term of office here, but there may be an allusion to the title of bishop. Cf. v. Campenhausen, 90, n. 4; A. M. Farrer, "The Ministry in the NT," in Kirk, 161-163.

[91] Cf. Spicq, Exc. XLIV-XLVII; Dib. Exc. on 1 Tm. 3:7 and 5:17.

[92] The traditional view that in 1 Tm. 4:14 the expression μετὰ ἐπιθέσεως τῶν χειρῶν τοῦ πρεσβυτερίου refers to the college of presbyters as an ordaining authority (subj. gen.) has recently been contested by D. Daube, "Evangelisten u. Rabbinen," ZNW, 48 (1957), 119-126, esp. 125 and Jeremias, op. cit. (→ n. 18). Both understand the phrase in terms of the Jewish formula סְמִיכַת זְקֵנִים as installation as an elder (final gen.). This disposes of the contradiction between 1 Tm. 4:14 and 2 Tm. 1:6. But 2 Tm. 1:6 itself shows (διὰ τῆς ἐπιθέσεως τῶν χειρῶν μου) that the gen. is a subj. gen., with ref. to one person here and to several in the other v. (cf. Ac. 8:18 : διὰ τῆς ἐπιθέσεως τῶν χειρῶν τῶν ἀποστόλων). Furthermore, there is no other ref. in the Past. to the presbyteral dignity of Timothy (or Titus), and in the lit. πρεσβυτέριον is always used of a body, → 654, 26 ff. The one instance (Sus. 50 Θ) of the word for the office (abstract) implies membership of a specific corporation and is thus unable to sustain the hypothesis. The difference between 1 Tm. 4:14 and 2 Tm. 1:6 is adequately explained by the difference in character between the two letters (congregational rule / apostolic testament), cf. Dib. Past.[3], 56 f.

[93] So many commentators, e.g., J. Jeremias, Die Briefe an Tm. u. Tt., NT Deutsch, 9[7] (1954), ad loc.; Lohse, 88; Michaelis, 77 f.; Schlier, 143. But one should put the break between v. 19 and 20 (note the plur. in v. 20) and then refer v. 22 more correctly to the readmission of penitent sinners. Cf. P. Galtier, "La réconciliation des pécheurs dans la première épître à Timothée," Recherches de science religieuse, 39 (1951/52), 317-320; W. Lock, A Critical and Exegetical Comm. on the Pastoral Epistles, ICC (1924), 63 f.; B. S. Easton, The Pastoral Epistles (1948), 160; v. Campenhausen, 160 f.; Dib. Past.[3], 62 f.

διπλῆς τιμῆς ἀξιούσθωσαν refers to a material reward or to "special honour" is debated. 1 Tm. 5:18 lends unconditional support to the former view.[94]

The functions of the elders may be known to some extent from 1 Tm. 5:17. The only uncertain point is the nature of the distinction between οἱ καλῶς προεστῶτες (→ 674, n. 140) and μάλιστα οἱ κοπιῶντες ἐν λόγῳ καὶ διδασκαλίᾳ. Does the former imply that within the college there is a group (or individual?) invested with a higher office, and that within this group again only the καλῶς προεστῶτες are singled out for double honour? Does the latter phrase mean that among these again there are some who are active in word and teaching? If so, we have four grades partly according to office and partly according to quality of achievement. But this is hardly possible. The associating of those who labour in word and doctrine with the καλῶς προεστῶτες shows that the ref. is to elders who discharge specific tasks in the congregation. οἱ καλῶς προεστῶτες is thus a recognition of those who are called κατασταθέντες in 1 Cl., 44, 3 and προϊστάμενοι πρεσβύτεροι in Herm. v., 2, 4, 3. Their special ministry and not just their special excellence in it is honoured. The patriarchal character of the Church's constitution is unaffected thereby. One may see from 1 Tm. 5:17 that the concrete requirements of the guiding and tending of the congregation brought with them quite naturally the choice and separation of specific presbyters even if not altogether within the framework of a collegial constitution.

A surprising point in the Pastorals is that the bishop plays an important part here as well as the presbyters (→ II, 617, 27 ff.) and that his functions are the same (cf. with 1 Tm. 5:17 προστῆναι in 3:5; διδακτικόν in 3:2; cf. also Tt. 1:9). It is thus natural to suppose that the offices are one and the same in the Pastorals. Only thus can one explain the fact that just after Titus is told to appoint elders (1:5) the portrait of a bishop is given (vv. 7 ff.). Yet one can hardly make a complete equation. This is proved by the simple fact that in the Pastorals ἐπίσκοπος is always in the singular while the πρεσβύτεροι form a college.[95]

Again, the passages which refer to the πρεσβύτεροι may be clearly distinguished from whose which treat of the ἐπίσκοπος (and διάκονος), 1 Tm. 3:1-7, 8-13. Only in Tt. 1:5 f., 7-9 do we have together the qualifications for presbyters and the bishop. But the change from plur. to sing. and the separate enumeration of qualifications are arguments against an equation of the titles. Since, however, the three offices of bishop, presbyters and deacons are never mentioned together, they cannot be interrelated along the lines of a three-tiered hierarchy.[96] On the contrary, one may affirm that the passages about the bishop reflect a different constitutional principle from those about presbyters and that already in the Past. there is a plain tendency for monarchical episcopate to merge with the presbyterate derived from Jewish tradition — a process which, at an earlier stage of development, one may see too in Ac. 20:17, 28 in relation to the same geographical area (Asia Minor), and which is also to be seen in respect of Rome in

---

[94] Michaelis, 112-119, who represents the others, has to excise v. 18 as a gloss on not very adequate grounds. His ref. to the fact that acc. to 3:4, 12 the officers of the congregation kept their secular jobs is no objection, for διπλῆ τιμή can indicate only an honorarium and not support for full-time work.

[95] For identification of bishops and presbyters in Roman Catholic scholarship cf. U. Holzmeister, "'Si quis episcopatum desiderat, bonum opus desiderat' (1 Tm. 3:1)," Biblica, 12 (1931), 41-69. An argument against a generic understanding of ἐπίσκοπος is that this is not the usage in relation to the other offices.

[96] Spicq, 91-96 thinks the ἐπίσκοπος is *primus inter pares*, not distinct from the πρεσβύτεροι in priestly dignity, but differentiated from the others as πρεσβύτερος κατ' ἐξοχήν by the καλὸν ἔργον (1 Tm. 3:1) of the οἰκοδομή of the community, through which he becomes a colleague and successor of the apostles.

1 Cl., → 672, 11 ff. [97] This process is easily explained by the fact that long since the πρεσβύτεροι had no longer been regarded as the natural representatives of the community but as the college of leaders appointed for the local churches by the apostles (Ac. 14:23) or their successors (Tt. 1:5), and it had become necessary to entrust certain administrative functions to individuals notwithstanding the patriarchal authority of all the presbyters. Within the total structure of the congregation, then, the bishops are to be seen as πρεσβύτεροι προεστῶτες (or ἐπισκοποῦντες). "At all events this is a developed identification, not one which was intrinsic from the very first." [98]

4. The 24 πρεσβύτεροι in Revelation. Special problems are raised by the passages in Rev. in which, in the visions of the divine, 24 elders surround the throne of God in heaven along with the four beasts, 4:4, 10; 5:6, 8, 11, 14; 7:11; 11:16; 14:3; 19:4. [99] The thrones on which they sit (4:4; 11:16), the white robes and the crowns which adorn them (4:4), show that they are heavenly beings, and the title πρεσβύτεροι suggests that they are God's council of elders. Yet there is no mention of God sitting in council with them nor do they seem to discharge a judicial office, cf. 20:4. Their function is not the exercising of their own dominion; it is simply adoration of the majesty of Him who sits on the throne (4:10; 19:4) and of the exalted Lamb (5:8-10) → θρόνος, III, 165, 21 ff. They sink to the ground, offer worship, and cast down their crowns before the throne of the eternal and omnipotent God (4:10) with songs of praise (4:11; 5:9 f.; 11:17 f.; 19:4 etc.). According to 5:8 they offer priestly ministry for the earthly community with harps and golden vials. Their divine service in heaven accompanies the events of redemption and judgment on earth, which the elders inaugurate and conclude with gesture and song.

There is no suggestion that these elders are redeemed and transfigured men. [100] They are plainly differentiated from the transfigured, 7 and 14. They are also distinguished from the angelic hosts (5:11; 7:11) which surround the throne, the four beasts and the 24 elders. But they are so only as a higher class of angels which is closer to the throne of God than the others and which is entrusted in a peculiar way with His secrets. "One of the elders" functions as *angelus interpres* (5:5; 7:13) and the seer addresses him by the title of majesty, κύριος, 7:14.

The depiction of these elders is based on the common OT and apoc. idea of the heavenly council of God, cf. 1 K. 22:19; Ps. 89:7; Job 1:6; 2:1; Da. 7:9 f.; En. 1:4, 9; 47:3 ff.; 60:2 etc. [101] The oldest and closest par. is Is. 24:23 : βασιλεύσει κύριος ἐν Σιων καὶ ἐν Ιερουσαλημ καὶ ἐνώπιον τῶν πρεσβυτέρων δοξασθήσεται, → 656, 12 ff. Worth nothing, however, is the number, which occurs only in Rev. It is possibly taken from astral ideas; acc. to Babylonian astrology 24 stars stand half to the north and half to the south of the Zodiac and are known as δικασταὶ τῶν ὅλων, [102] while in Test. Ad. 4:19 angelic powers offer worship and sacrifice all hours (24) of the day and night. [103] One may also recall the 24 Yazatas who acc. to Persian teaching constitute

---

[97] There is no reason to suppose that the bishop-ref. were interpolated later.
[98] Dib. Past.³, 46.
[99] Cf. Michl, who carefully surveys the history of interpretation.
[100] The thesis of Michl, 91-114 that the elders are the righteous of the old covenant viewed as the heavenly presbyters of the Chr. people seems to me to be quite untenable.
[101] In these passages, however, the word "elder" is never used. On the idea of the heavenly hosts around God's throne cf. Volz Esch., 276 f.
[102] Diod. S., 2, 31, 4; cf. H. Gunkel, *Zum religionsgeschichtlichen Verständnis des NT*³ (1930), 43; F. Boll, *Aus der Offenbarung Joh.* (1914), 35 f.
[103] J. Wellhausen, *Analyse d. Offenbarung Joh.* (1907), 9; Boll, *op. cit.,* 37; Boll, *Sphaira* (1903), 317.

the divine state of Ahura Mazda. [104] When it is considered that the contact of Judaism with oriental religions was precisely in the field of angelology, that the other numbers and symbols of Rev. pt. to this background, [105] and that the elders are depicted as heavenly beings, these religious par. take on considerable strength as possible sources of the concept of elders in Rev. But the original astral significance of these figures taken from an older tradition is completely effaced in Rev. In relation to the cultic functions of the elders we are thus to think in terms of the division of the priests and Levites into 24 classes (1 Ch. 24:5 ff.; 25:1 ff.), [106] esp. as the leaders of the former are called princes in 1 Ch. 24:5 [107] and elders in later Judaism [108] and the work of the temple singers ("who should prophesy with harps, with psalteries, and with cymbals," 1 Ch. 25:1) is closest to the functions of the elders in Rev. 5:8.

The chorus of 24 heavenly presbyters does not justify any conclusions as to the constitution either of a Jewish community or of the Christian churches from which Rev. derives and for which it is written. [109] On the contrary, Rev. presents the picture or fiction of a congregation which is guided spiritually and prophetically rather than acc. to fixed offices. There is no mentions of bishops, deacons, teachers, pastors, or congregational elders. Along with the apostles [110] the prophets [111] are the only authority. These are represented by the divine himself and all his "brethren that have the testimony of Jesus," i.e., the spirit of prophecy (19:10; 22:6). This prophecy is directed to the individual churches and to the whole Church ; there are no office-bearers to serve as intermediaries. [112]

If these remarks are true, a difficult question arises as to the constitutional position of the type of church found in Rev. That Ephesus and the other churches of Asia Minor, of Paul's old mission field, were still spiritual and prophetic communities and had no office-bearers towards the end of the 1st century is quite out of the question ; such a view cannot possibly be reconciled with the picture presented by Ac., Past., 1 Pt., Ign. and Pol. either contemporaneously or only a few decades later. One thing which is sure is that the structure of the churches in Rev. has nothing whatever to do with Paul himself. [113] The setting of the concept of the congregation in Rev. is rather to be sought in

---

[104] Bss. Apk., 247; Loh. Apk., ad loc. refers to the arithmetical speculations of the Pythagoreans for whom 24 was the no. of the cosmos (24 letters, 24 tones). But these abstract ideas bear little relation to the Apc.

[105] Boll, op. cit. (→ n. 102), esp. 16-29.

[106] Cf. Schürer, II, 286-290.

[107] שָׂרֵי קֹדֶשׁ וְשָׂרֵי הָאֱלֹהִים 1 Ch. 24:5; cf. שָׂרֵי הַכֹּהֲנִים Ezr. 8:24, 29; 10:5; 2 Ch. 36:14.

[108] Yoma, 1, 5; Tamid, 1, 1; Mid., 1, 8.

[109] Against Michl, 38 and v. Campenhausen, 90 : "But their work is undoubtedly to be reflected in the earthly presbytery of the Church, or in glowing colours it is at any rate drawn acc. to the same sketch." Again, in the fact that the 24 elders sit on thrones one is not to see a ref. to the liturgical seats of earthly presbyters, for these are the thrones of government (→ III, 166, 7 f., 167, 2 f.) and the insignia are those of rule (→ στέφανος).

[110] The view of the apostles is not uniform in Rev. In 2:2 the word is used of itinerant preachers unmasked as deceivers by the church, so that we have the extended sense of commissioned missionary. On the other hand in 21:14 the 12 names of the 12 apostles of the Lamb are written on the foundation stones of the New Jerusalem.

[111] Apostles and prophets are mentioned together in 18:20 and Eph. 2:20; 3:5 (in both Rev. and Eph. these are Chr. prophets, though cf. Loh. Apk. on 18:20); on Eph. cf. Dib. Gefbr., 72 f. In Rev. there is no ref. to OT prophets except as prototypes of Chr. prophets, 11:10, 18. The free and abundant use of NT prophecies (though not as Scripture) is in keeping with the prophetic style of Rev. That the prophets belong to the Church and their prophecy applies to it may be seen also in 1:3; 10:7; 16:6; 19:10; 22:6 f., 9, 18 f.

[112] We can learn no more about presbyters from the heavenly elders than about bishops from the ἄγγελοι of the letters, → I, 86, 32 ff.

[113] There is no reminiscence of Paul's work in Asia Minor or his founding of the church in Ephesus. Cf. W. Baurer, Rechtgläubigkeit u. Ketzerei (1934), 87 f.

specific conventicles of Jewish Christians [114] who obviously preserved an ancient apoc. tradition which derived from Palestine [115] and in the meantime had been further developed and assumed literary form. The origin of this tradition lies well back in a period when the spiritual and prophetic element still had a leading voice both theologically and constitutionally. Already Rev. and its view of the community have nothing in common with the type of church found in Jerusalem in the days of James or with the separate legalistic Jewish Christianity of a later time, which eradicated prophecy altogether. [116] The obvious preservation and development of the archaic apoc. tradition in Rev. is the immediate presupposition for the rise of Montanism in the 2nd half of the 2nd century. [117]

5. The πρεσβύτερος in 2 and 3 John. The open conflict between the holder of a congregational office viewed in terms of monarchical episcopacy and the representative of a free authority not restricted to any locality is reflected in 3 John. With no further definition, and no mention of any name, the author of 2 and 3 Jn. in the introduction calls himself ὁ πρεσβύτερος. In so doing he appeals to an authority which had hitherto been recognised not merely by the congregation addressed, but which was now contested by his opponent Diotrephes.

It is true that the term φιλοπρωτεύων (3 Jn. 9) plainly censures the presumption of the antagonist, but the statements about his conduct leave us in no doubt that he was already exercising and not just seeking the rights of monarchical leadership. He had kept from the church a letter addressed to it by the πρεσβύτερος. He had also repelled his messengers and excommunicated any who received them, v. 9 f. [118] Since there is no ref. to dogmatic differences — though there might well have been such [119] — and since the taking of disciplinary measures against others seems to be only for personal reasons, one is forced to describe this as a constitutional struggle. A local office-bearer, by slandering the presbyter and his envoys, is preventing, not without apparent success, any outside interference in his congregation. [120] One may assume that on the basis of his official authority he was resisting as unauthorised wandering apostles the men whom the elder himself said were in the service of the truth (3 Jn. 5-8) and whom he had sharply distinguished from the itinerant teachers of false doctrine (2 Jn. 10 f.).

What does the term πρεσβύτερος mean here? It can hardly refer to the age of the author, for it obviously expresses a special authority and dignity. Similarly, it cannot be regarded as a modest term for the apostolic dignity of the author, for the conduct of the opponent would have been quite impossible in relation to an

---

[114] Hence one cannot regard John and his book as typical of the Church of his age and district, cf. Bauer, op. cit., 81 f.

[115] Cf. on the close ties between Asia Minor and Palestine K. Holl, "Der Kirchenbegriff d. Pls. in seinem Verhältnis zu dem d. Urgemeinde," Ges. Aufsätze, II (1928), 66 f.; E. Schwartz, "Unzeitgemässe Betrachtungen zu den Clementinen," ZNW, 31 (1932), 191; H. Lietzmann, Gesch. d. Alten Kirche, I³ (1953), 198 f.; E. Hirsch, Studien z. vierten Ev. (1936), 149-152; esp. Bauer, op. cit. (→ n. 113), 89-92 (modifying the thesis of the others). The influence of Palestinian Jewish Christianity on Asia Minor in the 2nd cent. may be seen esp. in the Quartodecimans, cf. B. Lohse, Das Passafest der Quartadezimaner (1953), esp. 94-98.

[116] Cf. v. Campenhausen, 196-198.

[117] Cf. H. Kraft, "Die altkirchliche Prophetie u. d. Entstehung des Montanismus," ThZ, 11 (1955), 249-271, who thinks the emphasis on the bishop in Ign. is in opposition to the prophetic communities of Rev.

[118] Though φιλοπρωτεύων expresses obvious criticism, the position of Diotrephes is not contested but his conduct censured (slander, violation of hospitality). Hence the author is not defending presbyterianism against aspirations towards monarchical episcopacy.

[119] Bauer, op. cit., 97 wrongly calls Diotrephes a heretical leader.

[120] M. Goguel, L'église primitive (1947), 136 f.; v. Campenhausen, 132.

apostle, and in such a conflict the author would certainly not refrain from appealing to his apostolic status. Finally ὁ πρεσβύτερος cannot denote the member of a local presbytery.[121] Hence the title πρεσβύτερος in 2 Jn. 1; 3 Jn. 1 can be integrated into neither an episcopal nor a presbyterian form of government. The elder with his wishes and works is outside any ecclesiastical constitution.[122] He is to be regarded, not as an office-bearer, but as a specially valued teacher (→ 676, 10 ff.) or as a prophet of the older period, and his title is to be understood in the sense in which Papias and some later fathers (→ 676, 18 ff.) use it for pupils of the apostles and guarantors of the tradition which goes back to them.[123]

It is true that the reliability of this tradition is not worth much and that this circle also became the agent of wild teaching.[124] Did not Gnosticism commend itself by

---

[121] For the thesis that the author was calling himself a presbyter in the sense of an office-bearer in the local church, with far-reaching implications for the historical and political position of Jn. and the Johannine Epistles, cf. E. Käsemann, "Ketzer u. Zeuge," ZThK, 48 (1951), 292-311 (with good earlier bibl., esp. A. Harnack, "Über den 3. Joh.-Brief," TU, 15, 3b [1897]). Käsemann tries to show that the author of the Johannine writings (apart from Rev.) was a presbyter who had been excommunicated by the representative of monarchical episcopacy. In spite of the "verdict of orthodoxy" this presbyter "held on to his title and work and alongside the orthodox church he organised his own group with its own Gentile mission, though without letting go his hope and desire to reach an agreement with the opposite side," 301. The only problem is that this view is in contradiction with what the letters have to say about the position and work of the presbyter. Even the term presbyter and the absence of a name, which E. Schwartz, "Über den Tod der Söhne Zebedäi," AGG, 7, 5 (1904), 47 f. and Meyer Ursprung, III, 638 not very perspicaciously attribute to a later excision of the name (which in this case could not be John) with a view to the incorporation of the letters into the Johannine corpus, would be very odd for an office-bearer in a local congregation, since the dignity of the presbyter was always collegiate rather than individual. The argument that this presbyter was forced into isolation by excommunication is without force, for the author uses the same title in 2 Jn. where there is no trace of a conflict with Diotrephes or of any contesting of the authority of the author. Again, the presbyter exerts an influence through letters and envoys without restriction to a given place. He thus lays claim to an authority which could hardly be in accord with the title of a local presbyter. Nor do the epistles justify us in supposing that this was an emergency measure forced on him by excommunication. For the earlier letter mentioned in 3 Jn. 9 (2 Jn. ?) must have been written on the assumption that the church would receive both it and the brothers who had been sent. The messengers serve his solicitude for the churches. They are not just sent ad hoc to the congregation with which the elder finds himself at odds. These envoys are missionaries, moving from one church to another, bearing witness in each place (3 Jn. 7). They had already been received as accredited ministers by Gaius (v. 5 f.) and they thus had a right to expect hospitality and help for further missionary service (on προπεμφθῆναι cf. R. 15:24) — the very thing denied them by Diotrephes and his associates. Their return sparked the conflict between Diotrephes and the elder, or at least greatly exacerbated it. Yet nothing is said about the excommunication of the elder. Acc. to Käsemann this led to the exclusion of the elder from the congregation tyrannised by Diotrephes and to an emphasis on his disputed position. But if so, the author would hardly have asserted this in the second letter, which is composed in a spirit of peace. Or was this excommunication imposed in absentia ? But how could a local bishop, who certainly could not have been made the bishop of an orthodox catholic church transcending the local congregation, ever have excommunicated someone who was absent ? (ἐκβάλλειν means to expel from a local congregation.) In fact, even the non-resident envoys of the presbyter could not have been excommunicated ; acc. to 3 Jn. 10 the excommunication applies only to members of the congregation who wanted to entertain the envoys.

[122] v. Campenhausen, 132.

[123] Cf. C. H. Dodd, The Johannine Epistles (1947), 155 f.

[124] So Käsemann, op. cit., 300.

lavish appeal to apostolic traditions ? This explains quite adequately the discrediting of the dignity of the presbyter and the full-scale development of an official local authority of which the conduct of Diotrephes offers an example. The author of the three Epistles of John is best understood as a bearer of tradition, esp. of the Johannine traditions. [125] This is proved by a comparison of 1 Jn. esp. with John's Gospel. [126] No significance, of course, is attached here to the institutional office. Indeed, there is hardly any place for it. Nevertheless, it carried the day in the age which followed. Johannine Christianity, representing and defending an older type of community which had since been discredited, was forced into conventicles. [127]

E. The "Elders" in the Post-Apostolic Fathers and the Early Church.

1. Clement. Geographically and chronologically 1 Clement is close to 1 Pt. It is the most important document for the history of the presbyterate in the post-apost. age. On a broad basis it defends the rights and position of elders against a congregation which had been led by agitators to depose some of its presbyters. [128] The work says nothing about the nature of the opposition nor the alleged deficiencies of the elders. For 1 Cl. the deposition of a few is a revolt of the congregation against the presbyters as such, 44, 5; 47, 6; cf. also 54, 2; 57, 1.

The first and repeated argument of 1 Cl. against the Corinthian revolt is that it is a violation of the command to honour the aged. πρεσβύτεροι is used in this general way at the beginning of the letter (1, 3; 3, 3; 21, 6), whereas in later verses which deal more precisely with the dispute the πρεσβύτεροι are office-bearers in the congregation (44, 5; 47, 6; 54, 2; 57, 1). But the meanings overlap, for in 1, 3 and 21, 6 subjection to leaders (ἡγούμενοι) is the same as the honour due to the aged and in 3, 3 the events in Corinth are emphatically castigated as a rebellion of the young. Obviously this argument can be used only because the presbyters are in fact a patriarchal college and can thus claim the respect which is due to older members [129] of the church in general, → 665, 23 ff.

Within the college there are distinguished those office-bearers who are ordained to a sacrificial ministry (ἐπισκοπή, 44, 1 and 4). These are called "leaders" (ἡγούμενοι, 1, 3; προηγούμενοι, 21, 6). [130] They are also called ἐπίσκοποι (cf. 42, 4 f.; 44, 1 and

---

[125] The question whether the presbyter is identical with the elder John of Asia Minor, who is clearly attested to by Papias (Eus. Hist. Eccl., III, 39, 4), is not settled by this. All that may be said for certain is 1. that independently of the office-bearers there was an honorary group of elders, i.e., teachers, who were regarded as mediators and guarantors of the authentic tradition, 2. that these elders were peculiarly if not exclusively the normative guarantors of the Johannine tradition. In respect of the Johannine writings it should be noted that they nowhere claim to be the tradition of an apostle ; this concept plays no part in the Gospel or the Epistles.

[126] Cf. H. Conzelmann, " 'Was von Anfang war,' " Nt.liche Studien f. R. Bultmann (1954), 194-201. Here it is clearly shown (201, n. 22) that the antithesis between tradition and spirit (Käsemann, op. cit., 309) is off the pt.

[127] So Käsemann, 303. For all the material differences there is in this respect a sociological connection between Rev. and the other Johannine writings, → 669, 22 ff.

[128] The attempted explanations vary greatly : a revolt of enthusiastic Gnostics and pneumatics (Bauer, op. cit. [→ n. 113], 99-109; P. Meinhold, "Geschehen u. Deutung im 1 Cl.," ZKG, 58 [1939], 82-129); ambitious presbyters exceeding their lawful functions (though cf. 44, 3) (M. Goguel, La naissance du Christianisme [1946], 418 n.); generation gap (Lietzmann, op. cit. [→ n. 115], 201); party squabbling (A. v. Harnack, Einführung in d. Alte Kirchengeschichte [1929], 91).

[129] They are called ἔντιμοι, ἔνδοξοι, φρόνιμοι in 3, 3. Their status rests on long membership of the church as well as age, 1, 3; 63, 3.

[130] Knopf, 168 f. would number the prophets and teachers among the ἡγούμενοι, but these are not mentioned in 1 Cl.

6), and this is most important. [131] Acc. to this broad depiction, the office disputed in Corinth bears and represents the order willed and established by God. [132] Here for the first time the presbyteral office and the congregation are seen from this dominant standpt. The concept of order is so consistently stressed as to be elevated to the rank of a dogmatic principle. [133] The vital pt. is that the task of the presbyterate is no longer the safeguarding of the apostolic tradition. The institution itself is declared to be a basic element in the tradition. The impregnability of the office is established on this basis. For the office derives directly from the apostles, and through them from Christ and God, 42 and 44. In accordance with the idea of cosmic order and the divine ordering which gives the community its being as an organism and which ordains the time, place and personnel of its worship acc. to an inviolable and holy decree, the presbyters, too, have their assigned place. [134] 44, 3 tells us how the office was handed down : When this could no longer be by the apostles themselves or those immediately appointed to succeed them, it took place "by other eminent men, with the approval of the whole church." [135]

The ministry (λειτουργία, 40, 2; 44, 2 f., 6) [136] of the presbyters or bishops is a cultic ministry. Their task is to present the offerings of the congregation (44, 4); they are thus the cultic officers of the church's eucharist. 1 Cl., 40-43 places them expressly in the succession of the OT priests and thus constitutes them for the first time a clergy distinguished by peculiar rights and duties from the laity [137] in the congregation. The exclusive orientation of the presbyteral office to the cultus — there is no ref. to any teaching office — and the patent clericalising make it possible for 1 Cl. to proclaim the inviolability of the office-bearers and the lifelong nature of their office (44, 5) in so far as they are not guilty of neglect of their duties or unworthiness. Thus the conflict in Corinth can be settled only if the deposed are put back in office and the rebels submit to the presbyters (57, 1) [138] and voluntarily accept an exile fixed by the congregation (54), [139] so that the flock of Christ may live in peace together with the ordained presbyters, 54, 2.

2. Hermas. Written some decades later in Rome, the Shepherd of Hermas presents much the same picture as 1 Cl., though there is the distinction that here the office is not challenged and does not need to be given a basis. Furthermore, there is still free pro-

---

[131] "The ἐπίσκοποι are presbyters (44, 4 and 5), but not all presbyters are ἐπίσκοποι," Müller, "Bischofswahl," 275 : cf. Sohm, 95-103. The equation of titles shows that the presbyteral order has been permeated by elements of an episcopal order which was probably older in Rome, v. Campenhausen, 91. Both titles are used only in the plur. There is no monarchical episcopate in 1 Cl. Deacons are mentioned alongside the bishops, 42, 4 f.

[132] The concept of order in 1 Cl. derives from the Stoic doctrine of cosmos and state.

[133] This is rightly and emphatically stated by v. Campenhausen (102 f.) to be the true contribution of 1 Cl.

[134] Note the expression : μή τις αὐτοὺς μεταστήσῃ ἀπὸ τοῦ ἱδρυμένου αὐτοῖς τόπου, 44, 5.

[135] τοὺς οὖν κατασταθέντας ὑπ' ἐκείνων ἢ μεταξὺ ὑφ' ἑτέρων ἐλλογίμων ἀνδρῶν συνευδοκησάσης τῆς ἐκκλησίας πάσης, 44, 3. Analogy to the first generation demands that the later "eminent men" be official presbyters in the local church, cf. Müller, "Bischofswahl," 276. As against G. Dix, "The Ministry in the Early Church c. A.D. 90-410," Kirk, 257-266, the passage does not refer to the preservation of the local office but to the special ap. right of ordination, v. Campenhausen, 97, n. 2. The part of the congregation in the ordination of presbyters (συνευδοκεῖν) is most probably no more than agreement or acclamation.

[136] On λειτουργία cf. F. Gerke, "Die Stellung d. 1 Cl. innerhalb d. Entwicklung d. altkirchl. Gemeindeverfassung u. im Kirchenrecht," TU, 47, 1 (1931), 116-122 and → IV, 228, 25 ff.

[137] λαϊκός for the first time in 1 Cl., 40, 5 in distinction from the OT ministry but with a view to relations in the Chr. community, cf. Pr.-Bauer5, s.v.

[138] These cannot possibly be only those who still remained in office, as against Harnack, op. cit. [→ n. 128], 95.

[139] If the two passages are taken together it seems that the presbyters exercise the discipline but before the whole congregation. Cf. also 63, 1.

phesying directly to the saints (v., 3, 8, 11); this is represented by Hermas and is independent of the official ministry though not in opposition to it. The direction of the congregation is in the hands of a college of presbyters, v., 2, 4, 2 f.; 3, 1, 8. To this belong bishops and deacons, v., 3, 5, 1; s., 9, 26, 2; 27, 2. Both are responsible for seeing to the poor and supervising congregational finances. As leaders of the community the presbyters are called shepherds, which refers as always to a pastoral function, s., 9, 31, 5 f. They occupy the place of honour in congregational assemblies, v., 3, 9, 7. [140] Their high dignity may be seen from their association with the apostles, v., 3, 5, 1. [141] Their position in the church is unchallenged, though from the standpoint of the simple apostle and teacher they can be sharply censured for their petty jealousies, s., 8, 7, 4; v., 3, 9, 7 etc. [142] There is no hint anywhere of a conflict between prophets and office-bearers. [143] Prophecy continues in the congregation, but it is mostly false, and there is a strong warning against it. In spite of his apoc. writing, Herm. never calls himself a prophet and he directs that his book be given to the presbyters and read to the church in their presence, v., 2, 4, 2 f. The work is also to be sent to other congregations by a commissioned member of the presbytery, v., 2, 4, 3. [144] Rivalry between an official and a free prophetic ministry is thus avoided. To claim first place is eo ipso the mark of empty and arrogant prophecy, m., 11, 12; the true prophet is characterised by calm and humility, m., 11, 8. [145] Herm., then, offers us the picture of an established presbyteral order which is no longer threatened by prophecy though it is equally far removed from monarchical episcopacy.

3. Ignatius. Quite different is the position of the presbyters in Ign. Here they have a fixed place in an integrated hierarchy at whose head stands the bishop. The members of the presbytery stand around the bishop as his council (συνέδριον), Phld., 8, 1. [146] They are related to him in harmonious unity, as the strings belong to a zither, Eph., 4, 1. Nothing is said, however, about any presbyteral autonomy of power or ministry. The function of the presbyters is simply to be a finely woven spiritual crown for the bishop (Mg., 13, 1) to whom they are subordinate (Mg., 3, 1; Tr., 12, 2) but with whom they are associated as representatives of the hierarchy which culminates in him, [147] so that the church must obey them as a holy [148] and spiritual order, Eph., 2, 2; Mg., 7, 1; Tr., 2, 2;

---

[140] The expression in v., 2, 4, 3: μετὰ τῶν πρεσβυτέρων τῶν προϊσταμένων τῆς ἐκκλησίας (cf. 1 Tm. 5:17; 1 Cl., 54, 2) shows that a distinction is made between the official presbyters and a wider circle of those who are to be honoured.

[141] Here teachers as well as apostles are among the white four-cornered stones. Acc. to Herm. s., 9, 16, 5; 25, 2 these are ideal figures of the past who preached in all the world, not local office-bearers. Yet bishops and deacons are freely included among them.

[142] Cf. v. Campenhausen, 104 f.

[143] Dib. Herm., 454, 457, 635.

[144] Cl. is not expressly called a presbyter but only a secretary for the congregation ; the context (v., 2, 4, 2) shows, however, that he was unquestionably a member of the presbytery.

[145] In v., 3, 1, 8 f. Herm. is directed to take precedence of the presbyters to whom he would at first defer, and this seems to indicate that the pneumatic has the right to a seat, so Knopf, 185, who also lists the prophets among the leaders and presidents of v., 3, 9, 7 ff. and the bishops, teachers and deacons of 3, 5, 1. But the place of honour on the left hand — that on the right is for martyrs — is given to Herm. as a penitent Christian rather than a prophet. Cf. Dib. Herm., ad loc.; v. Campenhausen, 103 f.

[146] Ign. prefers the impersonal and hierarchical term πρεσβυτέριον (Eph., 2, 2; 4, 1; 20, 2; Mg., 2; Tr., 2, 2; 7, 2; 13, 2; Phld., 4; 5, 1; 7, 1; Sm., 8, 1; 12, 2), though οἱ πρεσβύτεροι is also common (Mg., 3, 1; 7, 1; Tr., 3, 1; 12, 2; Phld. inscr.; Pol., 6, 1). The liking for πρεσβυτέριον is the more noteworthy in that this word does not occur elsewhere in the post-apost. fathers.

[147] Not vice versa. It is nowhere said that the bishop is also presbyter. The Ignatian bishop could not be called a συμπρεσβύτερος → n. 158. Bau. Ign., ad loc. rightly transl. the τοῖς σὺν αὐτῷ πρεσβυτέροις καὶ διακόνοις of Phld. inscr. by "and the presbyters and deacons (united) with him."

[148] Cf. Mg., 3, 1: τοὺς ἁγίους πρεσβυτέρους.

Pol., 6, 1.[149] A vital pt. which characterises Ignatius' view of both Church and ministry is that the congregational duty of obedience is not based on the command to revere the elderly (as in 1 Pt.; 1 Cl.) nor on the constitutional arguments of appointment by the apostles or authority as bearers of the tradition but solely on the mystery of the unity of the Church which reflects the mystery of the hierarchy of God, Christ and the apostles and which is depicted as a cultic-aeonic reality.[150] The earthly hierarchy corresponds exactly to the heavenly hierarchy.[151] Hence the injunction: "Follow, all of you, the bishop, as Jesus Christ followed the Father, and the presbytery as the apostles; reverence the deacons as the commandment of God," Sm., 8, 1. That the "as" is more than a mere comparison and carries with it the idea of true representation is shown esp. by Mg., 6, 1: "... inasmuch as the bishop presides in the place of God (εἰς τόπον θεοῦ) and the presbyters in the place of the council of the apostles (εἰς τόπον συνεδρίου τῶν ἀποστόλων) ..."[152] The interrelating of presbytery and the apostles is common in Ign.[153] Hence his epistles present a radically different picture from the constitutional relations obtaining in Rome both at the time and also some decades later.[154]

4. Polycarp of Smyrna. The energy with which Ign. contends for a hierarchy of office and the position of the bishop shows that the order which he regarded as obligatory had not yet established itself throughout the churches of Asia Minor. This is confirmed by the letter of Polycarp, who is in many things so close to Ign. When one considers that in his letter to Polycarp, too, Ign. emphasises the unique position of the bishop (1, 2; 4, 1; 5, 2; 6, 1), it is the more surprising that in Polycarp's letter to the Philippians he neither says anything about this special position nor indeed mentions a bishop or bishops at all,[155] but refers only to deacons (5, 2) and presbyters (5, 3). To be sure, subjection to these two is stressed (5, 3) but the head of Ignatius' hierarchy is missing. This can hardly be explained by the theory that there were no bishops in Philippi, since we read of bishops and deacons there even in Paul's time, Phil. 1:1 → II, 616, 30 ff. Nor is there any indication that the bishop was not mentioned because he was a heretic.[156] The true explanation is that the bishops of Philippi, discharging a multiple office, had long since been absorbed into the wider body of presbyters,[157] and were not given their episcopal title because for Polycarp this denoted the monarchical bishop. He himself does not understand this episcopal office hierarchically but definitely puts himself on the same level as the presbyters.[158]

---

[149] The church is also to respect and obey the deacons though they always come third, do not properly discharge a spiritual office and are subordinate to the presbytery. They never form a unity with the bishop as the presbyters do, cf. Bau. Ign., 202.

[150] On this argument and the absence of the thought of law or tradition cf. v. Campenhausen, 106-112.

[151] The main job of the πρεσβυτέριον is to show forth the mystery of the divine hierarchy. On this is based the constant summons to subjection to the presbyters. This is why they are called συνέδριον θεοῦ καὶ σύνδεσμος ἀποστόλων (Tr., 3, 1) and the apostles πρεσβυτέριον ἐκκλησίας (Phld., 5, 1). Mg., 2 speaks of subjection to the bishop ὡς χάριτι θεοῦ and to the presbytery ὡς νόμῳ Ἰησοῦ Χριστοῦ.

[152] On the conjecture εἰς τύπον in both passages cf. Bau. Ign., ad loc.

[153] Cf. Tr., 2, 2; 3, 1; Phld., 5, 1 (here the apostles are the presbytery of the church).

[154] This difference is reflected in the fact that only in R. are there no ref. to the episcopal office. The bishops are mentioned expressly in all the other ep. except Phld., and this stresses the εἰς ἐπίσκοπος.

[155] Cf. H. v. Campenhausen, "Polykarp v. Smyrna u. d. Past.," SAH, 1951, Abh. 2 (1951), 33-36.

[156] So Bau., op. cit. (→ n. 113), 77 f.

[157] Presbyterianism, then, has absorbed the older order of the Pauline age, cf. v. Campenhausen, 130, n. 1.

[158] Cf. the greeting: Πολύκαρπος καὶ οἱ σὺν αὐτῷ πρεσβύτεροι, "Polycarp and the presbyters with him," to be taken in the same sense as ὁ συμπρεσβύτερος of 1 Pt. 5:1. The latter, attested elsewhere for Asia Minor (Eus. Hist. Eccl., V, 16, 5), became later (→ 654, 38 ff.) a common form for bishops in relation to their presbyters. For the meaning

We learn about the functions of presbyters in 6, 1 and esp. 11, 1 f. The deposed presbyter Valens (along with his wife, 11, 1 and 4) has forfeited the office committed to him [159] by embezzling congregational funds. Thus the duties of the presbyters include financial supervision and the administration of charity as well as disciplinary functions, pastoral care and the preaching of the word. [160] In all this Pol. agrees with Ac., 1 Pt. and esp. the Past., which are obviously closely related in time and place. [161] Like Pol. these show that in practice emerging monarchical episcopacy — with no ideas of hierarchical gradation — could merge quite smoothly with a presbyterian order. In distinction from the Past., however, episcopacy is present in Pol. only in fact and not in title.

5. The "Presbyters" of Papias, Irenaeus, Clement of Alexandria and Origen. From the constitutional use of πρεσβύτερος which has occupied us thus far a completely different employment of the term must be distinguished. This is richly illustrated esp. in Papias and Iren., but also in Cl. Al., Origen and Hipp. Here πρεσβύτερος (sing. and plur.) is not a title for office-bearers in the local congregation but a term for members of the older generation who are regarded as mediators of the authentic tradition and reliable teachers. The honorary title accorded them is best rendered by a word also current in Judaism, namely, "fathers," → V, 977, 18 ff. [162]

a. Papias. The most important passage in Papias is the much discussed quotation from his preface to the Expositions of the Dominical Oracles in Eus. Hist. Eccl., III, 39, 3 f. Here Papias assures his readers that he wants to assemble in his expositions everything that he had once learned and retained from the elders (παρὰ τῶν πρεσβυτέρων), and that in so doing he vouches for its truth. [163] Papias calls these elders his sponsors, though he claims to have known only their pupils and not the men themselves: [164] "And if anyone chanced to come who had actually been a follower of the elders (πρεσβύτεροι), I used to ask them concerning the words of the elders, what Andrew or what Peter said (εἶπεν), or what Philip, or what Thomas or James, or what John or Matthew or any other of the disciples of the Lord, and what Aristion and the elder John (ὁ πρεσβύτερος Ἰωάννης), the disciples of the Lord, say (λέγουσιν). For I was of the opinion that things taken from books would not be of so much value

---

of the expression cf. esp. v. Campenhausen, op. cit. (→ n. 155), 36; v. Campenhausen, 130, n. 1. The phrase in Polycarp is not to be carelessly equated with the similar sounding formula in Ign. Phld. inscriptio: ἐὰν ἐν ἑνὶ ὦσιν σὺν τῷ ἐπισκόπῳ καὶ τοῖς σὺν αὐτῷ πρεσβυτέροις καὶ διακόνοις. In Ign. the presbyters and deacons are the clergy associated with and subject to the bishop, whereas in Polyc. the presbyters are colleagues with whom the bishop modestly identifies himself as primus inter pares. The bishop's membership of presbytery is at first normative for his position and dignity. Iren. Ep. ad Victorem (Eus. Hist. Eccl., V, 24, 14-16) can still consistently call the bishop of Rome and his predecessors πρεσβύτεροι. Kraft, op. cit. (→ n. 117), 267 f. compares with this the emphatic stress on the episcopal dignity in the more or less contemporary letter of Polycrates of Ephesus (Eus. Hist. Eccl., V, 24, 2-7) and thinks there may be a constitutional bias behind the rather old-fashioned title used by bishop Iren., who came from Asia Minor and was friendly to the Montanists. But the relation of presbyter to bishop in Alexandria and Rome c. 200 is in keeping with his expression. Cf. Müller, "Beiträge," 29 f. and "Bischofswahl," 274-296.

[159] locus = τόπος as in Ign. Pol., 1, 2.

[160] There is no ref. to presiding at the eucharist, as in Ign.

[161] Cf. v. Campenhausen, op. cit.; the validity of his argument does not depend on acceptance or rejection of the special thesis that Polyc. or someone close to him was the author of the Past.

[162] So rightly Zahn Forsch., VI, 83; v. Campenhausen, 177 f., though v. Campenhausen's expression "leader of the church" is misleading, since it does not take into account the exclusive significance of these presbyters for the transmission of the teaching guaranteed by them.

[163] διαβεβαιούμενος ὑπὲρ αὐτῶν ἀλήθειαν is to be taken with the ἑρμηνεῖαι of Papias, not the teaching of the elders, cf. the context.

[164] The fragment itself says this; Eus. Hist. Eccl., III, 39, 2 is not making a tendentious statement in saying that Papias was not himself a pupil of the ap.

to me as those of a voice which lives and abides (τὰ παρὰ ζώσης φωνῆς καὶ μενούσης).'' The πρεσβύτεροι mentioned here can hardly be equated with the apostles who are adduced by name even if with no further designation. [165] On the contrary, they are to be regarded as pupils of the apostles, as Iren. later calls these elders, → line 26 f. With his appeal to these elders Papias expressly differentiates himself from heretical tradition and doctrine (Eus. Hist. Eccl., III, 39, 3), though his method of attaining to reliable teaching is quite similar to the practice of the competing Gnostics. In the latter we find an appeal to individual apostles and the teaching guaranteed by them and also the idea of the apostles as teachers around whom there gathered a school of pupils which passed on their doctrine and put in writing what was received orally. [166] The further examination by Eus. of the reports which Papias attributes to the elders leaves a distinct impression of this tradition, which was often fantastic but claimed to be authentic, and which included information on individual writings and also on the origin of Mk. and Mt. [167] From the verbs which Pap. uses to describe the relation of his sponsors to the elders and their coming (ἔρχεσθαι rather than παρακολουθεῖν, 39, 4 and 7) it is plain that the instruction given presupposes itinerant teachers. There is nothing to link the elders and their pupils with the offices of the organised congregation. The picture presented thus agrees with what we discovered in 2 and 3 Jn. (→ 670, 10 ff.), except that Papias stresses for the first time the special authority of the πρεσβύτεροι as pupils of the apostles and hence the legitimacy of their own pupils, whereas the elder of 2 and 3 Jn. does not think it necessary to establish the credentials of himself and his envoys. [168]

b. Irenaeus. The same school of presbyters whose beginnings we may trace in Papias meets us again in fully developed form [169] in Iren., who made copious use of the 5 books of the ἐξηγήσεις of Papias, and who expressly adduces a considerable number of doctrines as the teaching of the elders. Iren. calls these elders ἀποστόλων μαθηταί, Haer., V, 5, 1; 36, 2; Epid., 3. Acc. to Haer., II, 22, 5; V, 30, 1; 33, 3 they stood in personal relation to John, the Lord's disciple, [170] in Asia. Polycarp was one of them, ὁ μακάριος καὶ ἀποστολικὸς πρεσβύτερος, Ep. ad Florinum in Eus. Hist. Eccl., V, 20, 7. Iren. as a young man has heard him tell of his intimate converse with John and others who had seen the Lord, and of their reminiscences of the Lord's miracles and

---

[165] The plain distinction between the apostle John and the elder John, which is indicated by the change of tense and which Eus. notes without question (Hist. Eccl., III, 39, 5), should not be eliminated by the equation of the two which many have attempted.

[166] That Papias or his predecessors found an educational origin for the Gospels may be seen from what is said about Mk., who collected and wrote down from memory the instruction given by Peter (cf. W. Bousset, "Jüd.-chr. Schulbetrieb in Alexandrien u. Rom," FRL, NF, 6 [1915], 314); ἑρμηνευτὴς Πέτρου thus means that he is a mediator of the ap. διδασκαλίαι, → II, 663, n. 3.

[167] → n. 166. Acc. to Eus. Hist. Eccl., III, 39, 15 only what Papias says about Mk. is learned from the elder, but the same surely applies to Mt. too. Acc. to the context the elder can only be that of III, 39, 4, often called John thereafter ; cf. esp. III, 39, 14, which mentions Aristion's expositions (διηγήσεις) of the dominical sayings and the traditions (παραδόσεις) of the elder John.

[168] The singling out of John, who was still alive, above the other elders by the use of ὁ πρεσβύτερος by no means proves that he was the author of these epistles. Papias knew 1 Jn. and Rev., but there is no mention of the other epistles or the Gospel, and in the case of the latter this means either that he did not know it or that he intentionally did not refer to it, Bauer, op. cit. (→ n. 113), 189. Acc. to the quotations in Eus., who has a poor view of Papias but quotes him accurately (Hist. Eccl., III, 39, 14-17), the elder John simply vouches for the first two Gospels, → n. 167.

[169] The thesis of A. Harnack, Die Chronologie d. altkirchlichen Lit. bis Eus., I (1897), 334-340 and F. Loofs, "Theophilus v. Antiochien adversus Marcionem," TU, 46, 2 (1930), 310-338, namely, that Iren. took the whole tradition about the elders from Papias, seems to me to be without foundation.

[170] For Iren. the son of Zebedee.

teaching, Eus. Hist. Eccl., V, 20, 4 ff. [171] Papias too, though known to Iren. only from his works, is put in this circle as a hearer of John and companion of Polycarp ('Ιωάννου μὲν ἀκουστής, Πολυκάρπου δὲ ἑταῖρος γεγονώς), and he calls him ἀρχαῖος ἀνήρ (Haer., V, 33, 4), i.e., a man of old times.

In spite of the obvious role of literary mediator which Papias played for Iren. [172] the elders are adduced directly by Iren., and that not merely as sponsors for the accounts of the earthly Jesus and His sayings (Haer., II, 22, 5; V, 33, 3 f.) but also and chiefly as teaching authorities for the true exposition of Scripture and the doctrines, esp. eschatological, which were at issue in the fight against heresy, Haer., V, 30, 1; 33, 3 f.; 36, 1 f.; Epid., 61. Iren. obviously incorporated into his work one such address of the elders which defended at length against Marcion the unity of the Father of Jesus Christ and the Creator and the interrelationship of the testaments, Haer., IV, 27-32. [173] The many OT and NT quotations interwoven into this connected section show what a considerable part was played by these elders in the development of the Canon from Papias to Iren. Only in their school [174] could one learn the correct reading and exposition of Scripture which would establish the whole doctrine. [175] In the introduction to this address (IV, 26, 2) Iren. sharply distinguishes these elders from false presbyters and emphasises their authority and its claim to obedience by ascribing to them not only the apostolic succession of doctrine but also that of the episcopate. [176] His intention, of course, is not to distinguish an official *charisma* from that of truth or traditional teaching, [177] but the express identifying of elders and bishops in some passages [178] is undoubtedly an important new feature as compared with the relations found in Papias. The aim of Iren. in making this equation is the apologetical and polemical one of safeguarding the doctrine of the Church against heresy and its special traditions. [179] The equation is made possible by the double sense

---

[171] Eus. Hist. Eccl., V, 20, 6 f. refers to the instruction of Polycarp which Iren. did not write down but retained in his heart.

[172] Cf. Harnack, *op. cit.* (→ n. 169), 333-340; P. Corssen, "Warum ist das 4. Ev. für ein Werk des Ap. Joh. erklärt worden?" ZNW, 2 (1901), 202-227; Bss. Apk., 40 f.

[173] Adopting and modifying the thesis of Harnack ("Der Presbyter-Prediger des Iren.," *Philotesia Paul Kleinert* [1907], 1-38), Bousset, *op. cit.* (→ n. 166), 272-282 has shown that the homily of an elder underlies Haer., IV, 27-32. Cf. M. Widmann, "Iren. u. seine theol. Väter," ZThK, 54 (1957), 156-173.

[174] May we with tongue in cheek call them one of the first theological faculties in the form presupposed in Iren.? In this school Pl. is a recognised authority and John's Gospel has the same rank as the others. OT exposition is combined with that of the NT. In the fight against Marcion theology takes shape. For details of the Canon of this school, its doctrine of God, its Christology and its doctrine of the Spirit cf. Bousset, *Kyrios Christos*[3] (1926), 27, 192, n. 2, 225.

[175] Haer., IV, 32, 1: *post deinde et omnis sermo ei constabit, si et scripturas diligenter legerit apud eos, qui in ecclesia sunt presbyteri, apud quos est apostolica doctrina* ...

[176] IV, 26, 2: *Quapropter eis qui in ecclesia sunt, presbyteris obaudire oportet, his qui successionem habent ab apostolis, sicut ostendimus; qui cum episcopatus successione charisma veritatis ... acceperunt.*

[177] On *charisma veritatis* (→ n. 176) cf. K. Müller, "Kleine Beiträge zur alten Kirchengesch., 3: Das charisma veritatis u. der Episkopat d. Iren.," ZNW, 23 (1924), 216-222 and v. Campenhausen, 188. Cf. also the description of the true presbyter in Haer., IV, 26, 4: *qui et apostolorum, sicut praediximus, doctrinam custodiunt et cum presbyterii ordine sermonem sanum et conversationem sine offensa praestant ad confirmationem et correptionem reliquorum.* In what follows, on the basis of the prophecy already quoted in 1 Cl., 42, 5 (Is. 60:17), the presbyters are called the promised "bishops in righteousness" and true doctrine is attributed only to those *apud quos est ea quae est ab apostolis ecclesiae successio.* Then follows a characteristic summary of their teaching: *Hi enim et eam quae est in unum deum, qui omnia fecit, fidem nostram custodiunt: et eam quae est in filium dei dilectionem adaugent ... et scripturas sine periculo nobis exponunt neque deum blasphemantes neque patriarchas exhonorantes neque prophetas contemnentes,* 26, 5.

[178] Cf. not only Haer., IV, 26, 2 and 4 but also V, 20, 1 and 2.

[179] v. Campenhausen, 188.

of πρεσβύτερος as teacher of the older generation and holder of the chief congregational office, but esp. by the fact that what had originally been a free teaching position had now been clericalised. The pt. should not be missed that the teacher and bishop were brought together here to safeguard apostolic doctrine in a twofold way. The actual quotations from the elders do not refer to the episcopal office of these pupils of the apostles.

c. Clement of Alexandria. In contrast to the obvious tendency of Iren. to equate succession of teaching with that of office, the teaching office still retains its free form in Cl. Al. Cl., too, appeals to the elders as teachers of the past. : [180] "these preserved the true tradition of blessed doctrine which they had received from the holy apostles Peter and James, John and Paul, as children from the father ... and thus came with God's help even to us to plant that patriarchal and apostolic seed (in us)." [181] Here the πρεσβύτεροι are authorities for the collecting and transmission of stories of the apostles and for the correct exposition of the OT and NT Scriptures. [182] For Cl. πρεσβύτεροι is not just a term for pupils of the apostles. It is used for teachers of the preceding generation [183] to the degree that they pass on the apost. tradition and true knowledge, esp. Cl.'s own teacher Pantaenus, the μακάριος πρεσβύτερος. [184] Acc. to Ecl. Proph., 27 these elders passed on their traditions orally and left the writing to others, but the pledge they left demanded literary embodiment.

In essentials the πρεσβύτεροι of Cl. Al. are the same as those of Papias (→ 676, 18 ff.) and Iren. (→ 677, 23 ff.), [185] though there is a radical distinction from Iren. in that Cl., though he knew Iren., never couples the teaching succession of the elders with the episcopal succession. [186] The teaching office is free in relation to congregational offices, to which there are surprisingly few ref. Indeed, for Cl. Al. ecclesiastical offices are only types of the heavenly world. The true presbyter and deacon is for him the Gnostic, who, though he has no office, is set among the 24 elders in Rev. (→ 668, 9 ff.). [187] Acc. to the content and manner of their teaching the teachers of Cl. are in many respects close to those of Gnosticism, though by virtue of his acceptance of the OT and the NT Canon Cl. Al. can play an intensive part in the Church's battle against Gnosticism. [188]

As regards the position and function of the elders in Cl. Al. and his predecessors an analogy has rightly be seen with the Rabb. teaching succession, and the sayings of the elders have been understood after the manner of the Rabb. sayings of the fathers. [189]

---

[180] He says that it is a tradition of the oldest presbyters that the first Gospels are those with the genealogies ; then with slight changes there is an account of the origin of Mk. similar to that in Papias ; finally John is called the last and spiritual Gospel, cf. Cl. Al. Fr., 8 (Hypotyposeis).

[181] Strom., I, 11, 3 — noteworthy is the tracing back of true doctrine, as in Gnosticism, to a smaller circle of apostles, Hennecke, 138.

[182] Cl. Al. is the first to use "New Testament" to denote the Canon.

[183] The special place of πρεσβύτεροι in forming the tradition is stressed by attributes like οἱ ἀνέκαθεν πρεσβύτεροι, Cl. Al. Fr., 8 (Hypotyposeis); οἱ ἀρχαῖοι πρεσβύτεροι, Fr., 25 (de pascha), cf. Bauer, op. cit., 123, n. 2. Cl. Al. does not speak of pupils of the ap. though he claims emphatically that he is close to the ap. tradition, Eus. Hist. Eccl., VI, 13, 8 : περὶ ἑαυτοῦ δηλοῖ ὡς ἔγγιστα τῆς τῶν ἀποστόλων γενομένου διαδοχῆς.

[184] Cl. Al. Fr., 22 (Hypotyposeis); "the elder" might well be used for Pantaenus. Cl. Al. calls him the "Sicilian bee" because he sucked honey from the flowers of the prophetic and ap. meadow and planted pure knowledge in the souls of his hearers, Strom., I, 11, 2.

[185] We find the same type in Just. when in Dial., 3 he says he derived his doctrine from a παλαιός τις πρεσβύτης; from his Martyrdom (c. 3) we know that he himself taught in a special place in Rome. Cf. Bousset, op. cit. (→ n. 166), 282-308.

[186] v. Campenhausen, 221.

[187] Strom., VI, 103 ff., esp. 106, 2; Bousset, op. cit., 242 f. For other examples cf. v. Campenhausen, 220, n. 7.

[188] v. Campenhausen, 221-224.

[189] Hennecke, 130; Stauffer, op. cit. (→ n. 77), 207-214. One may see an obvious adoption of the Jewish teaching office into the order of the community in the Ps.-Clementines. Cf. C. Schmidt, "Studien zu d. Ps.-Clem.," TU, 46, 1 (1929), 314-334; H. J. Schoeps, Theol. u.

One also finds in the Chr. Alexandrians, as in Philo, a characteristic combining of the direct reading of Scripture with an appeal to the oral tradition of the fathers. [190]

d. Origen. Unlike Cl. Al., Origen no longer speaks of a free teaching office [191] independent of, though not in antithesis to, the clerical office. In him too, as in Cl. Al., there is an appeal to the exegesis of earlier men called πρεσβύτεροι, [192] but for Orig. it is important and self-evident that teachers should belong to the clergy and that the gulf between the two should be bridged. He was not satisfied with his own status as a non-ordained teacher in Alexandria but sought ordination as a clerical presbyter and finally achieved this in Caesarea. [193] Relations in Alexandria-Caesarea were thus following the same pattern as in Asia Minor. [194]

6. The Syrian Didascalia and the Church Order of Hippolytus. The Syr. Did. and the Church Order of Hipp. form something of a conclusion to the development. The former emphasises with solemn force the primacy of the bishop, like Ign., yet not on the basis of the mystery of the Church, but with stress on the legal foundation of his position and on his sacramental, administrative and sacramental functions. [195] The presbyters associated with and subordinate to the bishop, however, are also successors of the ap., though this dignity is not their own but accrues to them as apostles of the bishop. [196] The Church Order of Hipp., which arose in Rome but is based on the ecclesiastical orders of the East, [197] offers us finally the picture of a clergy which is graded by sacramental ordination and within which the bishop alone, as high-priest, has the authority to transmit office, [198] though the subordinate presbyters, as councillors and participants in the spirit of greatness (with express illusion to Nu. 11:16 f., 24 f.), also have priestly rank (32 and 33), which authorises them to baptise and to assist at the eucharist (administration of the cup and distribution of the bread), 46.

Gesch. des Judenchristentums (1949), 289-296. Here we find 70 presbyter-teachers as the college of elders set up by Moses, wholly after the manner of an authoritative academy of Jewish scribes. After a 7 year period of training and testing, followed by solemn ordination and dedication, true doctrine is transmitted to these presbyters alone, Diamartyria, 1, 2. 5 (GCS, 42, 1, p. 2 f. 4); Ep. Petr., 1-3 (ibid., p. 1 f.). Their ordination is by the bishop, to whom the teaching order is subordinate. The doctrine is expressly called secret (Diamartyria, 2. 5 ibid., p. 3 f.) to ensure its continuity and to protect it against corruption.

[190] Vita Mos., I, 4 : ἀλλ' ἔγωγε ... τὰ περὶ τὸν ἄνδρα μηνύσω, μαθὼν αὐτὰ κἀκ βίβλων τῶν ἱερῶν ... καὶ παρά τινων ἀπὸ τοῦ ἔθνους πρεσβυτέρων. τὰ γὰρ λεγόμενα τοῖς ἀναγινωσκομένοις ἀεὶ συνύφαινον. On the formulae with which Philo introduces such traditions cf. E. Bréhier, Les idées philosophiques et religieuses de Philon (1908), 55 f.; Bousset, op. cit., 44 f. The educational work of the philosophical schools offers an analogy, cf. Iambl. Vit. Pyth., 105 ff. and on this Bousset, 4 f.

[191] That Methodius of Olympus is of this type is shown by K. Quensell, Die wahre kirchliche Stellung u. Tätigkeit des fälschlich sog. Bischofs Methodius v. Olympus, Diss. Heidelberg (1953).

[192] For examples cf. A. Harnack, "Der kirchengeschichtliche Ertrag der exeget. Arbeiten des Orig." I, TU, 42, 3 (1918), 28; II, TU, 42, 4 (1919), 14; Zahn Forsch., VI, 60.

[193] v. Campenhausen, 274 f.; also Griech. Kirchenväter (1955), 56 f. On Orig.'s view of episcopacy and priesthood cf. Müller, "Bischofswahl," 285-293.

[194] Instructive are the appeals of Hipp. to the "elders" (cf. A. Hamel, Die Kirche bei Hipp. v. Rom [1951], 106 f.) as those who knew the ap. or their pupils (as in Papias, Iren., Cl. Al.). But the presbyters of Smyrna, as guardians of pure doctrine, exercised disciplinary power in excommunicating Noetus, unless πρεσβύτεροι in contra Noetum, 1 (ed. P. de Lagarde [1858]) reflects the older synonymity of ἐπίσκοποι and πρεσβύτεροι and as a judicial college refers specifically to bishops, Hamel, op. cit., 172 f.

[195] Cf. H. Achelis and J. Flemming, "Die syr. Didaskalia," TU, 25, 2 (1904), 270; v. Campenhausen, 264-272.

[196] Didasc., II, 28, 4 : nam et ipsi tamquam apostoli et conciliarii honorentur et corona ecclesiae ; sunt enim consilium et curia ecclesiae.

[197] Ed. F. X. Funk, Didask. et Const. Ap., II (1905).

[198] In relation to episcopal ordination we read : et presbyterium adstet quiescens, 68.

† πρεσβεύω.

1. In line with the basic sense of πρέσβυς (→ 652, 10 ff.) πρεσβεύω can mean "to be the older or the eldest" (most with gen. comp.), Soph. Oed. Col., 1422; Plat. Leg., XII, 951e etc.; "to occupy the first place" Soph. Ant., 720 or trans. "to honour (someone or something) very highly," Aesch. Eum., 1; Choeph., 488; Plat. Symp., 186b etc. Then in line with the special sense of πρέσβυς for "one who is sent" (→ 683, 18 ff.) "to be or to act as one who is sent," "to bring a message," "to negotiate" etc. In this political-legal sense πρεσβεύω is also common in the med. (corresponding to πρεσβευτής), Hdt., Thuc., Xen., Aristoph., Plat., inscr., pap., Philo, Jos. etc. The ambassador legally represents the political authority which sends him; his competence is acc. to its constitution. Athens had πρέσβεις αὐτοκράτορες who were entrusted with some freedom of action in detail but not with full authority to conclude treaties. [1] In the Rom. period πρεσβευτής is the Gk. equivalent of *legatus,* Polyb., 35, 4. 5; Plut. Mar., 7, 1 (I, 409a), etc. [2] It is commonly used for the imperial legates. [3] In the private sphere, too, the agent of another can be called πρεσβευτής, though not in the sense of a tt. for legally necessary or proxy representation. The one who gives the authority or commission is often introduced by ὑπέρ, e.g., Demosth. Or., 45, 64 (of a friend commissioned to negotiate): καὶ ὑπὲρ τούτου (Phormion) πρεσβευτὴς μὲν ᾤχετ' εἰς Βυζάντιον πλέων, ἡνίκ' ἐκεῖνοι τὰ πλοῖα τὰ τούτου κατέσχον ... For πρεσβεύω ὑπέρ τινος cf. also Ditt. Or., I, 339, 6; Syll.³, II, 656, 19; 805, 6; P. Lond., III, 1178, 14; P. Lips., 35, 12. In a transf. sense πρεσβεύω can be used gen. with acc. rei for "to represent something," Epict. Diss., IV, 8, 10; Luc. Piscator, 23; Gal. De bonis et malis sucis, 1, 10 (CMG, V, 4, 2, p. 391, 18), etc.

2. An important pt. for primitive Chr. usage is that the idea of the envoy is found fig. in the religious sphere. Thus πρεσβευτής is used for God's emissaries in Philo : for angels who deliver God's message to men (Abr., 115) and who represent men before God (Gig., 16), also for the mediatorial ministry of Moses (as ἀρχάγγελος and πρεσβύτατος λόγος): ὁ δ' αὐτὸς ἱκέτης μέν ἐστι τοῦ θνητοῦ κηραίνοντος ἀεὶ πρὸς τὸ ἄφθαρτον, πρεσβευτὴς δὲ τοῦ ἡγεμόνος πρὸς τὸ ὑπήκοον, Rer. Div. Her., 205. In particular the concept of the ambassador plays a dominant role in Gnostic texts to denote the heavenly origin and revelatory task of the Redeemer, [4] though πρεσβευτής and πρεσβεύω are seldom used; cf. the Redeemer as ὁ πρεσβευτὴς ὁ ἀπὸ τοῦ ὕψους ἀποσταλείς in Act. Thom., 10; ἐλθὲ ὁ πρεσβευτὴς τῶν πέντε μελῶν, [5] *ibid.,* 27, cf. 85. πρεσβευτής is a stock term for heavenly envoys in Manichaean texts, [6] also for

---

π ρ ε σ β ε ύ ω. [1] Cf. A. Heuss, "Abschluss u. Beurkundung des griech. u. röm. Staatsvertrages," *Clio,* 27 (1934), 14-53.

[2] On the duties, inviolability, privileges and rights of legates cf. A. v. Premerstein, Art. "Legatus," Pauly-W., 12 (1925), 1138.

[3] Examples in D. Magie, De Romanorum iuris publici sacrique vocabulis solemnibus in Graecum sermonem conversis (1905), 86-90.

[4] Cf. R. Bultmann, "Die Bedeutung d. neuerschlossenen mandäischen u. manichäischen Quellen f. das Verständnis d. Joh.-Ev.," ZNW, 24 (1925), 105 f.; Bu. J., 30, n. 3 etc.; H. Schlier, "Religionsgeschichtliche Untersuchungen zu d. Ignatiusbr.," Beih. z. ZNW, 8 (1929), 34-39; G. Bornkamm, *Mythos u. Legende in den apokryphen Thomasakten* (1933), 9 f.; G. Widengren, "Mesopotamian Elements in Manicheism," *Uppsala Universitets Årsskrift,* 1946, 3 (1946), 168-174; also "The Great Vohu Manah and the Apostle of God," *ibid.,* 1945, 5 (1945), *passim.* In Hb. 3:1 Christ is called ἀπόστολος and "as the unique messenger of God compared with the greatest instrument of revelation in the OT, Moses," Rgg. Hb., *ad loc.* For the Gnostic origin of the title cf. E. Käsemann, *Das wandernde Gottesvolk²* (1957), 95 f.

[5] For the reading πρεσβευτής in Act. Thom., 27 and the Manichean origin of the predication cf. W. Bousset, "Manichäisches in d. Thomas-Akten," ZNW, 18 (1917/18), 2; Bornkamm, *op. cit* (→ n. 4), 100-103.

[6] Cf. the index of Manichaean MSS in the A. Chester Beatty collection : I Man. Homilien, ed. H. J. Polotsky (1934); II A Man. Psalm-Book, ed. C. R. C. Allberry (1938); also Kephalaia I, ed. C. Schmidt (1940), 4, 34; 43, 15; 52, 20. 32; 56, 15. 19. 27; 57, 16 f. etc.

Mani himself and for those who proclaim Manichaean teaching.[7] The wandering Stoic-Cynic teachers of the Hell. period are also shown with the halo of a messenger and herald of God, → I, 408 ff.; III, 693, 2 ff.[8] In early Christianity, too, πρεσβευτής is used for the messenger of God. Thus Ign. Phld., 10, 1 asks the church to choose a διάκονος and to send him to Antioch εἰς τὸ πρεσβεῦσαι ἐκεῖ θεοῦ πρεσβείαν, cf. also Ign. Sm., 11, 2 : χειροτονῆσαι ... θεοπρεσβευτήν. The message which they have to pass on to the church in God's service is thereby said to be divinely authorised and inspired. In this usage it is everywhere evident that πρεσβευτής is not a title but denotes a specific function. This consists simply in the delivery of a divine message ; there is no ref. to the other duties of an envoy (in the secular political sense), e.g., negotiation with other parties, reporting to the sending authority etc., nor to his protection or legal status.[9]

3. As our review shows, Paul is making use of an established concept when in the important verse 2 C. 5:20, though only here,[10] he describes his preaching as an embassy: ὑπὲρ Χριστοῦ οὖν πρεσβεύομεν ὡς τοῦ θεοῦ παρακαλοῦντος δι' ἡμῶν· δεόμεθα ὑπὲρ Χριστοῦ, καταλλάγητε τῷ θεῷ. The use of the solemn official term πρεσβεύω is justified by the apostle (οὖν) on the ground that the divine act of reconciling the world in Christ entails also the institution of a ministry of reconciliation (διακονία τῆς καταλλαγῆς, λόγος τῆς καταλλαγῆς, 5:18 f.). The two belong indissolubly together and are interrelated in the parallel expressions τοῦ καταλλάξαντος ἡμᾶς ἑαυτῷ διὰ Χριστοῦ καὶ δόντος ἡμῖν τὴν διακονίαν τῆς καταλλαγῆς (5:18) and the ensuing elucidation of the divine act and the divine embassy (5:19). The preaching, then, is not just a later imparting of the news of the act of salvation ; it is an essential part of it. This is the only reason why Paul in 6:1 can use συνεργεῖν for his own work and proclaim the dawning of the day of eschatological salvation (along the lines of Is. 49:8) in the message of reconciliation, 6:2. 5:20 with its ὑπὲρ Χριστοῦ πρεσβεύειν very impressively sets forth this authoritative and official character of the proclamation.[11] That is, the authority of the message rests on the fact that Christ Himself speaks in the word of His ambassador, or — and it amounts to the same thing for the apostle — that God Himself uses the apostle as a mouthpiece to utter His own admonition. In the ministry and word of reconciliation the completed act of reconciliation is presented as a summons and invitation to the faith which appropriates this act. An important point here is that the interest of the statement is focused on the (material) authority of the message rather than the (formal) authority of an officer. Paul does not stress the latter even when defending his own apostleship, Gl. 1:8; 1 Th. 2:7.

---

[7] Cf. Man. Homilien (→ n. 6), 12, 18 ff.: "It (the πλάνη) killed the envoys who hastened there with the missives of the king."

[8] Wendland Hell. Kult., 88-96 rightly compares them with itinerant Chr. preachers. For further examples cf. Heinr. Sendschr., II on 2 C. 5:20; Wnd. 2 K. on 5:20; also H. Windisch, Pls. u. Christus (1934), 49-52 etc.; K. H. Rengstorf, → I, 408-413.

[9] How strongly the work of the ambassador and herald may predominate in the term πρεσβευτής may be seen in Poll. Onom., 8, 137: ὁ δὲ πρεσβευτής, εἴη ἂν ἄγγελος καὶ διάκονος· ἑτέρας δὲ χρείας, κῆρυξ καὶ σπονδοφόρος. πρεσβεύειν in the gen. sense "to be a messenger," "to bring news," occurs also in the pap., cf. P. Oxy., XII, 1477, 16; Preisigke Wört., s.v.

[10] In general it is surprising that Pl. does not think of himself in terms of the divine messenger of Hellenism and that he avoids the style of apodictic revelation (even in 2 C. 5).

[11] V. 20 a is formulated as a basic affirmation ; the delivery of the message itself follows in v. 20b.

ὑπὲρ Χριστοῦ occurs twice in 5:20a and 20b, but it is not in any circumstances to be given two different senses. [12] v. 20a provides the reason why the apostle can call his beseeching a beseeching for Christ's sake, namely, because in the word of the ambassador Christ Himself speaks. In this sense the apostle represents Christ. Hence it is inadequate to take the ὑπὲρ Χριστοῦ πρεσβεύομεν of 5:20 to mean "for the cause of Christ." [13] This does not do justice to the special feature of the embassy, i.e., the representation of Christ and the resultant authority of the message. [14] The meaning of "for Christ" is thus finely rendered by the A.V. "in Christ's stead" (Luther: an Christi Statt), though ὑπὲρ Χριστοῦ is not to be taken to imply the representing of someone absent (vice et loco) nor is the apostle's ministry to be regarded as a continuation of the work of Christ. [15]

Eph. 6:20 also refers to the apostle's preaching : ὑπὲρ οὗ (sc. τοῦ εὐαγγελίου) πρεσβεύω ἐν ἁλύσει. But here, in distinction from 2 C. 5:20, the Gospel takes the place of the person of the exalted Christ. Hence we no longer have the crucial point of 2 C. 5:20, namely, that another (God, Christ) speaks in the word of the apostle. Here, then, ὑπέρ should be rendered "for" (in the sense of "in favour of").

πρεσβύτης.

Paul calls himself πρεσβύτης in Phlm. 9. He almost certainly means "old man" here rather than "ambassador" as in 2 C. 5:20; Eph. 6:20. [1] This is linguistically possible since the two forms πρεσβύτης and πρεσβευτής both occur ; hence there is no need of conjecture. [2] In v. 8 f. Paul hesitates to make express assertion of his apostolic authority ; he thinks it enough to appeal to the love of Philemon, reinforcing this with a reference to his age, his bonds, and the fact that he is a spiritual father to Onesimus.

The ref. does not enable us to fix Paul's age with any exactitude. Acc. to Ps.-Hippocr. περὶ ἑβδομάδων (quoted by Philo Op. Mund., 105 et al.) πρεσβύτης denotes the 6th of the 7 ages of man (between ἀνήρ and γέρων), namely, 49-56 yrs. of age. [3]

Bornkamm

πρό

Contents : A. Linguistic Data : πρό in the New Testament : 1. Spatial ; 2. Temporal ; 3. Metaphorical. B. Biblical Theology : πρό in Salvation History : 1. The Old Testament ; 2. The New Testament ; 3. The Post-Apostolic Fathers.

Prep. with gen.: "before," related to παρά (→ V, 727 ff.), πρός etc., also Lat. prae, pro etc. Common from Hom., also found in the LXX some 260 times, in the NT only

---

[12] So K. H. Rengstorf, Apostolat u. Predigtamt² (1955), 19, n. 52 : "The second ὑπέρ probably goes beyond the first ..."
[13] So Ltzm. K., ad loc. etc.
[14] Cf. Bultmann Theol., 299 f.
[15] So mistakenly G. Sass, Apostelamt u. Kirche (1939), 81: "The apostle thus represents God as previously Christ did, as one who continues Christ's work"
[1] πρεσβύτης thus with others, Loh. Phil., ad loc.
[2] πρεσβύτης "envoy," "messenger," 2 Macc. 11:34; 2 Ch. 32:31 (B); 1 Macc. 14:22; 15:17 (א).
[3] Cf. F. Boll, "Die Lebensalter," N. Jbch. Kl. Alt., 31 (1913), 89-145, esp. 114-118; Dib. Gefbr., ad loc.; Pr.-Bauer⁵, s.v. πρεσβύτης.
π ρ ό. On A.: J. F. A. Procksch, "Zur Bdtg. v. πρό," Zschr. f. d. Gymnasial-Wesen, 32 (1878), 321-326; J. Golisch, "Zur Bdtg. der Präp. πρό," Jbch. f. Phil., 119 (1879), 806 f.;

48-49 times, the post-apost. fathers 21 times. Also in several compounds, e.g., προάγειν (→ I, 130, 13 ff.), etc.

A. Linguistic Data : πρό in the New Testament.

1. Spatial. πρὸ τῆς θύρας, "at the door," Ac. 12:6, also πρὸ τοῦ πυλῶνος, 12:14. A similar phrase fig. in Jm. 5:9 when the coming Judge is said to be "at the doors." The phrase πρὸ προσώπου τινός ("before someone") is OT (Heb. לִפְנֵי־), Mt. 11:10; Mk. 1:2; Lk. 7:27 (3 quotations from Mal. 3:1; cf. Ex. 23:20); also Lk. 9:52; 10:1 (Ac. 13:24 → 685, 39 ff.). [1]

Ac. 14:13: ὁ ἱερεὺς τοῦ Διὸς τοῦ ὄντος πρὸ τῆς πόλεως, is usually taken to refer to the priest of the Zeus who was, i.e., had his temple, before the city of Lystra. In analogy to instances where πρό expresses the thought of a protective deity, [2] however, it might be a reference to the Zeus who stood in front of the city as a protector, so that πρὸ τῆς πόλεως would be comparable with Πολιεύς ("protector of the city"), [3] an epithet which is characteristic of Zeus, though other deities are also protectors of cities. [4]

At all events the text of Codex D might mean "the priest of the local (ὄντος before the name of the god here) Zeus, the protector of the city" (πρὸ πόλεως without art.); a spatial "before the city" does not go too well with "local." The similar formula

---

P. Viereck, Sermo graecus (1888), 81; W. Schmid, Der Attizismus, III (1893), 287 f.; IV (1896), 464, 614, 629; W. Schmidt, "De Flavii Josephi elocutione observationes criticae," Jbch. f. class. Philologie, Suppl. Vol., 20 (1894), 395, 513 f.; A. N. Jannaris, An Historical Greek Grammar (1897) § 1644-1653; Kühner-Blass-Gerth, II, 1, 454-456; W. Schulze, "Graeca latina," Programm zur akademischen Preisverteilung Göttingen (1901), 14-18; E. A. Abbott, Johannine Grammar (1906), 227; J. H. Moulton, A Grammar of NT Greek, I (1906), 100 f.; J. Rouffiac, "Recherches sur les caractères du grec dans le NT d'après les inscr. de Priène," Bibliothèque de l'École des hautes études, Sciences religieuses, 24, 2 (1911), 29; P. Regard, Contributions à l'étude des prépositions dans la langue du NT (1918), 544-549; A. T. Robertson, A Grammar of the Gk. NT³ (1919), 620-622; Bau. J. on 12:1; Johannessohn, 184-198; F. M. Abel, Grammaire du grec biblique, Études bibliques (1927) § 46i; J. Wackernagel, Vorlesungen über Syntax², II (1928), 194-196, 211 f., 231-233, 237-240, 320 f.; Mayser, II, 1, 19 etc.; 2, 390-392 etc.; 3, 60; Schwyzer, II, 505-508; C. F. D. Moule, An Idiom Book of NT Greek (1953), 74; Pr.-Bauer⁵, s.v.; Bl.-Debr.⁹ § 213. 217, 1. 395. 403. 406, 3, also gen. bibl. on prep. in Pr.-Bauer, s.v. ἀνά and → II, 65 διά, Bibl.; → V, 727 παρά, Bibl. On B.: P. Lobstein, La notion de la préexistence du Fils de Dieu, Fragment de christologie expérimentale (1883), 11-124; H. Schumacher, Christus in seiner Präexistenz u. Kenose nach Phil. 2:5-8, I (1914), 131-232; II (1921), 95-266, 307-327, 388-397; E. Barnikol, "Mensch u. Messias. Der nichtpaulinische Ursprung der Präexistenz-Christologie," Forschungen z. Entstehung des Urchr., 6 (1932); J. Gross, "Le mystère de l'Homme-Dieu dans la théol. récente," Revue des Sciences Religieuses, 20 (1940), 379-397; J. Barbel, Christos Angelos. Die Anschauung von Christus als Bote u. Engel in der gelehrten u. volkstümlichen Lit. d. Altertums (1941), 37-311; O. Cullmann, Christus u. d. Zeit. Die urchr. Zeit- u. Geschichtsauffassung (1946), 13-189 (E.T. [1950], 17-174); H. Vogel, Christologie, I (1949), 79-218; G. Lindeskog, "Studien z. nt.lichen Schöpfungsgedanken," Uppsala Universitets Årsskrift, 1952, 11 (1952), 15-83, 163-272; E. Jenni, "Das Wort 'ōlām im AT," ZAW, 64 (1952), 197-248; 65 (1953), 1-35; O. Cullmann, D. Christologie d. NT (1957), 253-323; E.T., 247-314.

[1] In the post-apost. fathers we find πρὸ ὀφθαλμῶν ἔχειν or λαμβάνειν and πρὸ ὀφθαλμῶν τινος εἶναι, Mart. Pol., 2, 3; 1 Cl., 5, 3; 2, 1; 39, 3 (also in the LXX at Dt. 11:18; Job 4:16).

[2] Jannaris § 1648.

[3] G. Kruse, Art. "Polieus," Pauly-W., 21 (1952), 1376-1378.

[4] Cf. the list of protective deities for Nicaea in Bithynia in Dio Chrys. Or., 39, 8 : "I pray to Dionysus, the patron of this city, to Heracles, the founder of this city, to Zeus, the protector of this city (Πολιεύς), Athena, Aphrodite, Philia ... and the other gods."

῎Αρτεμις πρὸ πόλεως etc., which has been found in several MSS, [5] has been rendered by the editor of CIG by *ante urbem* [6] (previously *tutor urbis*), and later scholars have followed him in this. It should be considered, however, that the inscr. in question were not found outside the city and there is no proof that the temple was originally located outside. Indeed, in these inscr. the combination of the attribute πρὸ πόλεως with laudatory titles favours the view that these were protective deities. With ref. to Ac. 14:13 it should also be noted that the god is Zeus, who is often the protector of cities in Asia Minor. [7] It may thus be asked whether the usual text is not to be taken as a ref. to Zeus as a protective deity even though the connection with ὄντος and the art. show that πρὸ τῆς πόλεως is not an epithet. The material circumstances favour this solution. For if the ref. is to the city-god of Lystra, the prompt readiness of the people to identify Barnabas as Zeus and to offer sacrifices to him makes good sense. In view of the large-scale participation of the people in the sacrifice the temple is best sought either in the city or at the gate, and the gates before which sacrifice is made are either those of the temple [8] or of the city. In the first case "protector of the city" is the only possible rendering, while in the second we might have both this and also the spatial sense, since a god situated in front of the city gate might well be regarded as the protector of the city.

The relative rareness of a spatial πρό in the NT is connected with the fact that in Hellenistic Greek and also in the LXX figurative prepositions increasingly took over this function of πρό. [9] Thus in the NT a local πρό is usually replaced by ἔμπροσθεν, ἔναντι, ἐνώπιον and the like. [10]

2. Temporal. πρὸ τοῦ κατακλυσμοῦ, "before the flood," Mt. 24:38; similarly "before the meal," Lk. 11:38; "before the passover, the feast of the passover," Jn. 11:55; 13:1; "14 years ago," 2 C. 12:2; "before winter," 2 Tm. 4:21. πρό has a particularly important sense with reference to Christ and the election: "before the foundation of the world," Jn. 17:24; Eph. 1:4; 1 Pt. 1:20; "before the ages," 1 C. 2:7; "before eternal times," 2 Tm. 1:9; Tt. 1:2; "before all eternity," Jd. 25 etc., → 687, 21 ff. πρό is also used before a pronoun to constitute an attribute or an adverbial clause: τοὺς προφήτας τοὺς πρὸ ὑμῶν, "the prophets who lived before you," Mt. 5:12, cf. Ac. 7:4 vl.; πρὸ ἐμοῦ, Jn. 5:7 etc.; οἱ πρὸ ἐμοῦ, Gl. 1:17. Quite often, in analogy to many instances in the LXX, πρό is also used before the art. in the gen. and a following accus. with infin., mostly aor.; in such cases it means "before" (cf. πρίν and infin. without art.): πρὸ τοῦ ὑμᾶς αἰτῆσαι, "before you have asked," Mt. 6:8; cf. Lk. 2:21 etc.; πρὸ τοῦ γενέσθαι, "before it has happened," Jn. 13:19. In view of the aor. the (theoretically presupposed) completion of the action is to be noted in such cases. [11] Only once is the infin. in the pres.; [12] this expresses the permanence of the act: πρὸ τοῦ τὸν κόσμον εἶναι, "before the world existed," Jn. 17:5.

The Semitism πρό → προσώπου τινός (→ 684, 6 ff.) is on the border between a spatial and a temporal sense in Ac. 13:24: προκηρύξαντος ᾿Ιωάννου πρὸ προσώπου τῆς εἰσόδου αὐτοῦ, "when John preached first, before his (Jesus') coming." On the one

---

[5] Cf. CIG, II, 2462, 2963c, 2796, 3194, 3211, 3493; G. Radet, "Inscr. de Lydie," BCH, 11 (1887), 29, 5 (p. 469); T. Wiegand, *Milet, Ergebnisse d. Ausgrabungen u. Untersuchungen seit dem Jahre 1899*, I, 7 (1924), 299, No. 204a, 6.

[6] A. Boeckh, CIG, II (1843), 605 on 2963c.

[7] Examples: Sardis: ἀρχιερέα τῆς ᾿Ασίας ναῶν τῶν ἐν Λυδίᾳ Σαρδιανῶν, καὶ ἱερέα μεγίστου Πολίεως Διὸς δίς, CIG, II, 3461, 3; Ilium: προθύεσθαι τῷ Διὶ τῷ Πολιεῖ τὰ πέμματα, CIG, II, 3599, 24.

[8] W. M. Ramsay, *St. Paul the Traveller*[10] (1908), 118 f.

[9] Mayser, II, 2, 539; Johannessohn, 189-198.

[10] Bl.-Debr.[9] § 214.

[11] Mayser, II, 1, 152.

[12] Bl.-Debr.[9] § 403.

side, this Semitic expression is preferred here to a simple πρό in order to stress the spatial element in εἴσοδος : John goes before Jesus as one who prepares the way for Him, → V, 107, 3 ff., n. 13 εἴσοδος. On the other side, εἴσοδος undeniably expresses an event, so that the temporal aspect has to be taken into account.

The distinctive phrase πρὸ ἓξ ἡμερῶν τοῦ πάσχα in Jn. 12:1 literally means "six days before (from) the Passover."

Analogies with μετά and acc. show that the πρό here relates only to the first gen., while the second is to be taken as an abl.: μετὰ δέκα ἔτη τοῦ οἰκῆσαι Ἀβρὰμ ἐν γῇ Χανάαν, LXX Gn. 16:3; μετὰ ἡμέρας εἴκοσι τῆς προτέρας ὁράσεως, Herm. v., 4, 1, 1.[13] This form of expression occurs also in older Gk.[14] and cannot be originally a Latinism. There are also pre-Roman instances of similar expressions with πρό : πρὸ τριῶν ἡμερῶν τῆς τελευτῆς, Hippocr. Epid., VII, 51;[15] πρὸ δύο ἐτῶν τοῦ σεισμοῦ, LXX Am. 1:1 (cf. 4:7); πρὸ μιᾶς ἡμέρας τῆς Μαρδοχαϊκῆς ἡμέρας, 2 Macc. 15:36; πρὸ ἀμερᾶν δέκα τῶν μυστηρίων, Doric inscr. of Andania in Messenia, 91 B.C.[16] In gen. this became a popular expression only in the Roman period,[17] but it is not a true Latinism as was formerly maintained. Not even calendar formulae like πρὸ ἐννέα Καλανδῶν Σεπτεμβρίων ("on the 24th of August") in Ign. R., 10, 3 (cf. Mart. Pol., 21) are full Latinisms ; for one thing, cardinal numbers are used rather than ordinals as in Lat. (ante diem nonum),[18] and then again the basic day in the reckoning is in the gen. rather than the acc. (Lat. kalendas).[19] In all such instances the πρό has strictly an adv. sense : "before." Cf. πρὸ μιᾶς "one day before," Did., 7, 4; Herm. s., 6, 5, 3.[20]

3. Metaphorical. There are here 2 uses : a. to express preference, πρὸ πάντων, "above all," Jm. 5:12; 1 Pt. 4:8; Did., 10, 4; cf. πρὸ παντός, Pol., 5, 3; and b. to express protection, possibly Ac. 14:13 → 684, 9 ff.

B. Biblical Theology : πρό in Salvation History.

1. The Old Testament.

Since the OT has a special sense of historical relations (primitive history, the history of the people, eschatology), concepts like primeval time (→ I, 198-202 αἰών), priority, and antiquity play an important role in it. What was there at the beginning, or at least in ancient time, has special worth, cf. the patriarchs. In such contexts the words for "before," i.e., בְּטֶרֶם, לִפְנֵי and in the LXX πρό, take on theological significance. To be mentioned first are statements which emphasise the fact that God is before the world or even eternal, e.g., Ps. 90:2 : "Before the mountains were brought forth, or ever thou hadst formed the earth and the world, even from everlasting to everlasting, thou art God." In such sayings, which are

---

[13] In Ac. 1:5 there is a compressing of the expression by assimilation of case : οὐ μετὰ πολλὰς ταύτας ἡμέρας (for τούτων ἡμερῶν), cf. Vg : non post multos hos dies, Bl.-Debr.[9] § 226. Whether there may sometimes be such assimilation with πρό (Schmid, III, 287; IV, 614 speaks of case attraction in this connection) is hard to say, since πρό itself takes the gen.

[14] Schmid, IV, 458; Schulze, 15, 17.

[15] Littré, V, 420. This part of Hippocr. Epid. is not usually ascribed to Hippocr. himself, but it may be adduced as a pre-Roman work ; cf. Pr.-Bauer[5], s.v. ἡμέρα, 2; Bl.-Debr.[9] § 213 App.

[16] C. Michel, Recueil d'inscr. grecques (1901), No. 694, 70; Ditt. Syll.[3], II, 736, 70.

[17] Schulze, 15.

[18] Abel § 46i.

[19] For further material cf. Bl.-Debr.[9] § 213, 226 (App.); Schwyzer, II, 98c.

[20] Spatially, too, πρό can have this adv. function : πρὸ πολλοῦ τῆς πόλεως (abl.; Schwyzer, II, 96) : "a good way from the city," Dion. Hal. Ant. Rom., 9, 95, 5. Cf. ἀπό : οὐ γὰρ ἦσαν μακρὰν ἀπὸ τῆς γῆς, ἀλλὰ ὡς ἀπὸ πηχῶν διακοσίων, "not far from land, only some 200 cubits (away)," Jn. 21:8.

often liturgical in form, the majesty of God is stressed. In this connection the theological problem how God could exist before the world or time is not posed. This is not just because we are in the sphere of doxology. It is also due to the fact that for the OT there can be no antinomy here. For "eternity" is not understood philosophically as something timeless and abstract which has no content. It is quite simply the remotest conceivable time with its own specific content. [21] Again, God as the Lord of history is also the Lord of time, e.g., Is. 40:28. [22] Hence His eternity is co-incident with His never-ceasing power. [23] In analogy to statements concerning God's pre-existence are those about the pre-existence of wisdom, which was created before the whole world and which thus took part in creation. The most important passages here are Prv. 8:22-31 and Sir. 24:9 (14), where we have self-predications of wisdom connected with the educational ministry of teachers of wisdom. These sayings help to prepare the ground for NT statements concerning the pre-existence of Christ, → lines 21 ff. The word "before" also occurs in many other connections with reference to temporal relations in the development of the world, of the people of God, and of the individual. Here, too, the emphasis is often on God's sovereignty, e.g., Is. 42:9; Jer. 1:5, so that stress is laid on the position of God as Lord of time, → III, 459 f. καιρός.

2. The New Testament.

In the NT, too, the divine pre-existence is related, not to an abstract idea of timelessness, but to God's dominion over the world and history. [24] πρό occurs especially in the context of salvation history and the revelation of Christ when emphasis is put on the fact that God foreordained "before all times" or "before the foundation of the world" etc. the sending of His Son and the salvation which comes with Him, → 685, 24 ff. In this function πρό is found, of course, only in Jn., Pl. and the later Epistles. As glory is an attribute of God "before all eternity" (Jd. 25), so Jesus can say (Jn. 17:5, 24) that He possessed the divine glory even "before the foundation of the world." [25] In the Johannine Prologue about the Logos there is a theological exposition (Jn. 1:1-18) of the pre-existence of Christ and of His basic significance for creation; this reminds us of the OT ideas of wisdom already mentioned (→ lines 8 ff.), but πρό is not used. Even in the *kenosis* passage in Phil. 2:5-8, which is so significant in the study of Paul's pre-existence-Christology, πρό does not occur. On the other hand, one finds it in Col. 1:17a. According to this passage Christ existed "before all beings," and according to the context the universe was created by Him, the first-born of creation (v. 15), so that it both consists through Him and exists with a view to Him, v. 16, 17b. The pre-existence of Christ here is not a speculative theologoumenon but a dynamic expression of the unrestricted world dominion of Him to whom the Church is subject in its mission to the world. From another standpoint the foreordination of the mystery of Christ is stressed in 1 C. 2:7 (πρὸ τῶν αἰώνων)

---

[21] Jenni, 25, 50, 55 f.

[22] *Ibid.*, 67-70.

[23] *Ibid.*, 55 f.

[24] J. Jeremias, "Jesus als Weltvollender," BFTh, 33, 4 (1930), 8-12; Cullmann, *Zeit*, 55 (E.T. 63 f.): "Primitive Christianity knows nothing of a timeless God ... If we wish to grasp the Primitive Christian idea of eternity, we must strive above all to think in as unphilosophical a manner as possible."

[25] Whether or not He had a similar sense of pre-existence in the Synoptic Gospels depends on our understanding of the title Son of Man. Cf. also the question of the Son of David; G. H. Boobyer, "Mark xii. 35-37 and the Pre-Existence of Jesus in Mark," Exp. T., 51 (1939-40), 393 f.

and that of His passion in 1 Pt. 1:20 (πρὸ καταβολῆς κόσμου); hereby insight is given into the unending value of the *kerygma* which is only now proclaimed. The priority of divine grace is thus underlined, as also expressly in 2 Tm. 1:9 with reference to the apostle's calling (πρὸ χρόνων αἰωνίων) and in Tt. 1:2 with reference to the promise of eternal life (πρὸ χρόνων αἰωνίων). Common to the last four passages (1 C. 2:7; 1 Pt. 1:20; 2 Tm. 1:9; Tt. 1:2) is the fact that the context provides a specific contrast between pre-temporal concealment and present revelation. Man knows the eternal secret, not by speculation, but by an act of God in history which consists in the Christ event and the Christ *kerygma,* and which man may now experience through God's inestimable grace. In agreement with this special position of believers as the recipients of divine grace, Eph. 1:4 (πρὸ καταβολῆς κόσμου) refers to the pre-temporal election (→ IV, 144 ff. ἐκλέγομαι) of believers to fellowship with Christ, so that there is a hint here of the pre-existence of the Church, → III, 509 ff. ἐκκλησία (cf. προορισθέντες in v. 11; → V, 456, 12 ff. προορίζω).

πρό is also fairly common with a general reference to express the fact that God foreordains or foresees events. Thus God determines in advance the name of the child of Mary, Lk. 2:21. He knows what men need, Mt. 6:8. Jesus also knows things in advance according to Jn. 1:48; 13:19. [26] The events of salvation history follow a divine plan, so that one has to take place before the other, Lk. 21:12; 22:15. [27] According to God's saving plan man was a prisoner under the Law before the coming of faith, Gl. 3:23. Even evil spirits have an inkling of the planned nature of salvation history, but they get the plan wrong, so that they think the Son of God has come before the time (πρὸ καιροῦ), Mt. 8:29. The same expression occurs in 1 C. 4:5 : Believers are not to judge before the time, i.e., before the Lord comes. Another important point for Paul is whether one man has come to Christ or been called as an apostle before another, R. 16:7; Gl. 1:17; cf. what he says about the priority of the Jews in R. 3:1 f. etc. Also to be connected with a chronologically established plan of salvation is what is said about forerunners. Among such are the prophets (Mt. 5:12), the Baptist (Mt. 11:10; Mk. 1:2; Lk. 1:76 vl.; Ac. 13:24), and in part even the disciples in relation to the Lord of the Church (Lk. 9:52; 10:1). On the other hand those who lead the people astray, called thieves and robbers in Jn. 10:8, arose before Christ's coming quite outside the divine plan of salvation. Often in relation to predecessors the stronger πρὸ προσώπου is used (→ 684, 6 ff.); this gives to the concept of the forerunner a spatial nuance, → 685, 39 ff.

3. The Post-Apostolic Fathers.

The pre-existence of Christ is mentioned in Ign. Mg., 6, 1: "Who was with the Father before eternal ages," cf. Jn. 1:18. There is also a ref. to the Church's pre-existence in 2 Cl., 14, 1: "The first, spiritual Church which was founded before the sun and the moon," and in Ign. Eph. Praescr., where it is said of the church in Ephesus that it was foreordained "before eternal times" to attain to glory.

Reicke

---

[26] On the knowledge of Jesus cf. E. Gutwenger, "Das menschliche Wissen d. irdischen Jesus," *Zschr. f. katholische Theol.,* 76 (1954), 170-186.

[27] H. Conzelmann, *Die Mitte d. Zeit* (1954), 81 f., 112 f., 116, 128-133 etc. thinks the idea of a plan of salvation is peculiar to Lk. and is not much developed in the earlier Gospels. It is worth noting that the πρό of the Lucan passages finds no counterpart in the other Synoptists. Yet the concept of a plan of salvation occurs both in Mt. and Mk., e.g., Mt. 8:29 (→ lines 22 ff.); Mk. 14:41.

προάγω → I, 130, 13 ff.

---

† πρόβατον, † προβάτιον

A. The Word outside the New Testament.

1. The domestic sheep is to be distinguished from wild sheep, which live in herds on mountain ranges and steppes in all the continents. The value of the domestic sheep lies esp. in its yield of wool. [1] Climate and environment cause variations in the species of sheep. [2] In Palestine tending sheep is the most common occupation along with agriculture. Mutton is much sought after and greatly liked. [3] Sheep are also commonly used for sacrifice. Dressed sheep-pelts provide cloaks and over-garments for the shepherds, and the most important articles of clothing are made from the wool. [4]

2. The term πρόβατον is rare in older Gk. and does not occur at all in the tragic dramatists. The dimin. προβάτιον is also rare in Gk. In gen. πρόβατον means a. four-footed animals as distinct from those that swim or creep, esp. tame domestic animals, Hom. Il., 14, 124; Hdt., IV, 61; mares of Diomedes, Pind. Fr., 305; oxen, Hdt., IV, 61; horses, VI, 56; sacrificial animals, Hdt., I, 188, 207. πρόβατον soon comes to be used for small animals, so Hom. Il., 23, 550 (opp. ἵπποι); in Hdt., I, 133; VIII, 137 τὰ λεπτὰ τῶν προβάτων are sheep and goats. In Attic the ref. is esp. to sheep, Aristoph. Av., 714, so, too, the pap., P. Tebt., I, 53, 7; 64b, 16. Then πρόβατον means b. the simple man, Aristoph. Nu., 1203; c. a fish, Oppianos De Piscatione, I, 146; III, 139; [5] Ael. Nat. An., 9. 38. The Stoics often use πρόβατον to denote what is of lesser value or stupid, Epict. Diss., I, 23, 7 f.; 28, 15. In Epict. Ench., 46, 2 the proper active life of man is illustrated by natural processes like the growth of wool on sheep. It is taken for granted that shepherds become attached to their animals, Epict. Diss., III, 22, 35; here sheep are also an illustration of the men who must be guided by the Cynic.

3. The LXX mostly uses πρόβατον for the Heb. צֹאן, occasionally for שֶׂה, but very rarely for כֶּבֶשׂ, כַּבְשָׂה, כֶּשֶׂב, צֹנֶה and רָחֵל. In general πρόβατον is used for small cattle, Gn. 30:38, 40 f.; Lv. 1:2; Dt. 7:13; Is. 7:21; Am. 7:15; [6] Neh. 5:18 etc., and can then be used specifically for offerings, Gn. 22:7; Lv. 22:21; Nu. 15:3; Dt. 12:6; 16:2, for booty, Nu. 31:28 ff., and for a gift on the manumission of slaves, Dt. 15:14.

π ρ ό β α τ ο ν. Note: H. Preisker prepared the original MS of this art., which S. Schulz has had to revise and expand.

Etym.: "that which goes forward," movable property as distinct from κειμήλια "fixed possessions": Hom. Od., 2, 75; cf. Schwyzer, I, 499 [Debrunner].

[1] G. Dalman, Arbeit u. Sitte in Palästina, VI (1939), 184 f.

[2] Thus in the Aube valley in North Palestine Algerian shepherds tend black strong-boned sheep which have much softer wool than the sheep and goats in South Palestine, cf. E. Klippel, Wanderungen im Hl. Lande (1927), 253; Dalman, op. cit., 180.

[3] Dalman, op. cit., 194 f.

[4] Ibid., 195 f.

[5] Ed. F. S. Lehrs in Poetae Bucolici et Didactici (1862).

[6] Acc. to Am. 7:15 the prophet is taken by the Lord ἐκ τῶν προβάτων (Β ἐκ τῶν προφητῶν); the Mas. has צֹאן at 7:15, but at 7:14 בּוֹקֵר, which is associated with בָּקָר and rendered herdsman. But בּוֹקֵר comes from בקר, which is to be understood as a cultic tt. and which denotes a priestly function, cf. Lv. 13:36; 19:20; 27:33; 2 K. 16:15; Ps. 27:4; Prv. 20:25. Acc. to Ez. 34:11, 12 God is both priest and shepherd when He tests and inspects. Only in Sir. 11:7 do we have a purely secular usage. נֹקֵד in Am. 1:1, which is usually taken to mean 'herdsman," may also be understood as a cultic tt., cf. M. Bič, "Der Prophet Amos — ein Haepatoskopos," Vet. Test., 1 (1951), 293-296. The calling of Amos ἐκ τῶν προβάτων might thus mean that he is called away from a cultic office as tester of offerings and inspector of livers, and that he confronts the high-priest of Bethel in some sense as an expert [Bertram].

In a transf. sense πρόβατον is used to denote the people, 2 S. 24:17; ψ 76:21; 77:52; Is. 63:11; Ιερ. 13:20; 27:6; Ez. 34:2 ff. In Nu. 27:17 Moses asks Yahweh for a dedicated successor in order that the congregation of Yahweh should not be as πρόβατα, οἷς οὐκ ἔστιν ποιμήν. In the comforting prophecy of the exile it is said of Israel : πρόβατα νομῆς (Jer. 23:1 f. also ψ 73:1, cf. Zech. 9:16; 11:5 ff.), whose shepherd (→ 487, 3 ff.) is God Himself (Ps. 100:3). God has miraculously led and saved them out of the greatest distress, ψ 76:21; 77:52; Is. 63:11; Ez. 34:10 ff.; Zech. 9:16 etc. In the place of God the lawful shepherd of the sheep can also be the king (Jer. 13:10 → I, 566, 38 ff.) or Moses (ψ 76:21). This consolation is given to Israel because it is wandering about like a scattered flock (Ιερ. 23:1, 2; 27:17) and the sheep suffer severely at the hands of unfaithful shepherds, Ez. 34:23 ff.

The Psalmist in ψ 118:176 also cries out to God as a lost and straying sheep. In Is. 53:6 it is "we," the "many" (→ 537, 27 ff.), sinners, who heedlessly go astray like sheep. In Is. 53:7 the conduct of the Ebed Yahweh stands in sharp contrast to these straying sheep. The Ebed lets himself be led ὡς πρόβατον ἐπὶ σφαγήν. We see here the influence of the usage of the prophetic tradition (Jer. 11:19). But whereas the emphasis in Jer. 11:19 is on simplicity, in Is. 53:7 it is on dumb patience, cf. also Ps. 39:9. [7] Ez. promises the exiles that at the new creation of Israel (36:24, 36) the inhabitants will increase like πρόβατα (36:37); indeed, the πρόβατα ἀνθρώπων will become as large and numerous as the flocks of sheep which "used to be seen on feast-days in Jerusalem when they were driven in for sacrifice." [8]

4. Rabb. theology also speaks of flocks of sheep, Ex. r., 2 (68b); M. Ex., 21, 37 (95a), and it uses the flock as an image for the people of Israel, Pesikt. r., 26; Nu. r., 23 (193c). In the gt. vision in Eth. En. 89 and 90, the so-called sheep-apocalypse, the seer portrays men as a herd of cattle [9] and the word πρόβατον is used for great men, prophets and kings like Moses (89:16), Aaron (89:18), Samuel (89:41-50), Saul (89:42), David (89:45), Noah (89:1 f.), Abraham (89:10), also for the whole people of Israel or for Jews who are faithful to the Law (90:6). Distinction is made between deaf (90:7), blind (89:74) and dazzled sheep (90:26 f.) on the one side and white sheep (Jews faithful to the Law) on the other. The white sheep are the holy new community which has passed through many tribulations (90:32) and they will finally be venerated by all nations (90:30). God is thus the "Lord of the sheep" (89:16, 30 etc.). In Philo we find both the lit. use (Op. Mund., 85; Agr., 42; Spec. Leg., I, 163 [sacrificial animals]; IV, 11) and also a repeated allegorical use. Thus in Sacr. AC, 112 the law of Ex. 13:13 is construed as follows : ὁ πόνος is the equivalent of the ass and προκοπή of the sheep, and so πόνος is to be replaced by προκοπή. Acc. to Sacr. AC, 45 Νοῦς is the shepherd of the sheep, i.e., τῶν κατὰ ψυχὴν ἀλόγων δυνάμεων, cf. Mut. Nom., 110; Som., I, 199.

B. πρόβατον in the New Testament.

1. In the NT πρόβατον is often used in a literal sense. Thus Jesus in self-vindication appeals to the practical example of the sheep which falls into a well on the Sabbath and which is naturally brought up again, Mt. 12:11. Again, love and joy are shown in relation to the sheep which goes astray and is then found again, Mt. 18:12 and par. Sheep are amongst the most important imports to Rome according to Rev. 18:13. They are mentioned as offerings in Jn. 2:14 f. (cf. 1 Cl., 4, 1-6 quoting Gn. 4:3-8).

---

[7] P. Volz, *Jesaia*, II, *Komm. z. AT*, 9 (1932), *ad loc.*
[8] G. Fohrer, *Ezechiel, Handbuch z. AT*, I, 13 (1955), *ad loc.*
[9] Cf. 89:2 ff. and G. Beer in Kautzsch Apkr. u. Pseudepigr., *ad loc.*

2. Figuratively πρόβατον (note the ὡς) is used for sheep which have gone astray in the rhythmic tradition at 1 Pt. 2:21-25 with application to the readers in the lost wandering of their pre-Christian days, 1 Pt. 2:25; Ez. 34:5 serves as a model here. Elsewhere, too, OT usage is followed when sheep is used to denote God's people, → 690, 1 ff. These sheep are the true goal of the eschatological work of the Son of Man and of Jesus the King, who like a shepherd (ὥσπερ) will separate the sheep and the goats because the πρόβατα have wittingly or unwittingly done the will of God, Mt. 25:32 ff. Since the Jewish people is like a badly treated flock without a shepherd in the days of Jesus (Mk. 6:34 = Mt. 9:36), it needs to be taught and fed (Mk. 6:35-44) by the shepherd. In Mt. 10:16 the πρόβατα are the new disciples in the many afflictions of the present aeon. Their shepherd Jesus sends them out like defenceless sheep into a world full of ravening wolves. Behind the terrible scattering of the sheep there stands according to the saying of Jesus (Mk. 14:27 = Mt. 26:31, cf. Zech. 13:7 and Barn., 5, 12) the hand of God who in the crucifixion puts His own Shepherd to death and therewith scatters His sheep. In Mt. 7:15, however, the metaphorical saying about the sheep is also a first warning to the community of Jesus to keep itself from the corruption which is the more dangerous because it keeps up outward appearances. Jesus is especially near to the sons of God who are suffering under various afflictions (R. 8:36 on the basis of Ps. 44:22), and this is why He is called τὸν ποιμένα τῶν προβάτων τὸν μέγαν (Hb. 13:20). [10] After the death of Jesus the pastoral office is discharged towards the sheep (προβάτια) by the apostles who have become His disciples and who are the bearers of His Word and ἐξουσία, Jn. 21:16 f.

In the extended figure of Jn. 10:1 ff. (→ 494, 16 ff.) the relation between the Shepherd and the sheep is different. The Shepherd does not gather the people of God [11] but His own, who are lost in the world but to whom the Shepherd has the right of possession by pre-temporal predestination of the sheep even though they be of the most varied origin, 10:3 ff., 14, 16. This inter-relation of Shepherd and sheep finds expression in the call of the Shepherd and the hearing of the sheep (10:3), in their mutual knowledge and intimacy (10:14), in preceding and following (10:4), in the self-sacrifice of the Shepherd which brings life and fulness, in the readiness of the sheep to accept the One who rescues them from peril. The Shepherd is not the King and the sheep are not the people of God. He is the Son and the sheep are the community. If some of the features in the portrait of the Shepherd here correspond to the OT tradition, most of the analogies of thought and material parallels are to be found in non-Jewish, Gnostic-Hellenistic statements. [12]

Thus when πρόβατον is not used literally but figuratively and by way of illustration in the NT it is an image for the ancient people of God in its remoteness from God on the one side and for the new people of God in its eschatological situation of θλῖψις and σωτηρία and those who hear only the voice of the Good Shepherd on the other side. According to the tradition and preaching of the NT Jesus as Shepherd is both the royal Ruler of His people (= sheep) and also the true Revealer for His own (= sheep).

---

[10] E. Schweizer, "Das Leben des Herrn in der Gemeinde u. ihren Diensten," Abh. ThANT, 8 (1946), 22 f.

[11] There is a certain analogy of thought in Damasc. 13:9 f. (16:2 f.) (→ 489, 18 ff.; 498, 16 ff.).

[12] Cf. Bultmann J., 479 f., Bau. J., ad loc.; B. Noack, Zur joh. Tradition (1954), 55 f.

C. The Word in the Post-Apostolic Fathers.

In the post-apost. fathers it is hard to find any distinctive developments of either word or metaphor. If in Dt. 18:4 the first-fruits of the sheep belong to the priest, in Did., 13, 3 they are now to be given to the prophets as priests. In Ign., champion of episcopacy in the local church, the sheep follow the bishop as shepherd, Ign. Phld., 2, 1; only on the basis of the unity of the congregation can the bishop keep the wolves at bay, 2, 2. In Herm. s., 6, 1, 5 f.; 6, 2, 3 f.; 6, 2, 6; 6, 3, 2 f. gambolling sheep are a figure for men who are given up to the lusts of the world and who are then exposed to the torments of thickets of thorn, i.e., want, sickness, etc. For Herm., with his strong doctrine of retribution, exhausted sheep in the thorns without a shepherd are disobedient sheep which are punished in the thorns. In Herm. s., 9, 1, 9 and 9, 27, 1 sheep resting comfortably in the shade of trees are a figure of the poor who are sheltered by the bishops and hospitable members of the congregation. The term πρόβατον also occurs in many quotations: 1 Cl., 16, 7 (Is. 53); 59, 4 (ψ 99:3) in a prayer which may well be of Jewish origin; Barn., 5, 2 (Is. 53); 16, 5 (Eth. En. 89). This use is of particular significance since in these quotations the origin of the use of πρόβατον is in fact to be found in figurative speech. [13]

Preisker/Schulz

προγινώσκω → I, 715, 24 ff.

πρόγνωσις → I, 716, 10 ff.

προγράφω → I, 770, 37 ff.

πρόδρομος → τρέχω.

προελπίζω → II, 534, 27 ff.

προεπαγγέλλομαι → II, 586, 9 ff.

προετοιμάζω → II, 704, 17 ff.

προευαγγελίζομαι → II, 737, 30 ff.

---

† προέχομαι

1. Outside the New Testament.

Trans.: a. "to hold up before one": act. τὼ χεῖρε προέχειν, "to hold up one's hands for protection," Xenoph. Cyrop., II, 3, 10; also med.: πρὸ δὲ δούρατ' ἔχοντο, Hom. Il., 17, 355; fig. "to hold up as an excuse," "to plead," οὐ μὲν τάδ' ἂν προύχοι', Soph. Ant., 80; μάλιστα προύχονται ... μὴ ἂν γίγνεσθαι τὸν πόλεμον, Thuc., I, 140, 4; προέχεσθε τὰς ἐντεύξεις ὑμῶν εἰς μνημόσυνον, En. 99:3. b. "to have or to have received in advance": προέχων μὲν τῶν Ἀθηναίων οὐ φιλίας γνώμας, "having previously received hostile expressions of feeling from the Athenians," Hdt., IX, 4; ὑπολόγησον δ προέχουσιν, "consider what they have already obtained," P. Petr., II, 12, fr. 4 (p. 32).

Intrans. act.: a. "to stand out," "to be prominent," "to come into prominence": spatially of hills, cities, mountain ranges, Hom. Il., 22, 97; Hdt., IV, 177; in time: ἡμέρης ... ὁδῷ προέχοντας τῶν Περσέων, Hdt., IV, 120; in rank: οἱ προέχοντες, "the eminent," Thuc., V, 17, 1; πάντων προέχουσα ἐπιθυμία, "desire which surpasses all others," Herm. m., 12, 2, 1. b. With gen. of pers. and dat. of obj.: "to surpass," "to distinguish oneself," "to have the advantage over": ὁ προέχων "the one who has the advantage," Thuc., I, 39, 1; τέχνα γὰρ τέχνας ἑτέρας προύχει, Soph. Phil., 138 f., προέχω γὰρ αὐτέων τοσοῦτον ὅσον ὁ Ζεὺς τῶν ἄλλων θεῶν, Hdt., II, 136; ῥώμῃ προέχειν "to have the advantage of superior strength," Jos. Ant., 7, 237. Rarely with acc. of person: ἑνὶ μόνῳ προέχουσιν οἱ ἱππεῖς [ἡμᾶς], Xenoph. An., III, 2, 19; cf. the singular pass.: κατ' οὐθὲν προεχόμενοι ὑπὸ τοῦ Διός, "which was not surpassed by Zeus in anything," Plut. Stoic. Rep., 13 (II, 1038d).

---

[13] The last two sentences are by Schneemelcher.

π ρ ο έ χ ο μ α ι. Pass., Liddell-Scott, Moult.-Mill., Preisigke Wört., Pr.-Bauer[5], s.v.

In the LXX προέχειν occurs only in a vl. in Job 27:6 A : δικαιοσύνη δὲ προέχων, intrans. "achieving prominence in righteousness." Mas. refers to right, LXX in other readings to the righteousness to which Job would cling : προσέχων = רוח. Cf. Qoh. 10:10 Σ : προέχει δὲ ὁ γοργευσάμενος εἰς σοφίαν.

2. In the New Testament.

R. 3:9 is clearly to be read acc. to the Egyptian text :[1] τί οὖν; προεχόμεθα; οὐ πάντως. This is supported not merely by the outward attestation but also by the fact that the variants esp. in the Western text[2] are trying to overcome the difficulties of προεχόμεθα and thus presuppose it.

There are three possibilities of interpretation. The first a. is that, as in profane Greek, προεχόμεθα is to be taken as a med. in the sense of a trans. act., → 692, 25 f. In this case either the Jews are asking the apostle whether they may make any plea in face of God's judgment, which Paul radically rejects,[3] or Paul is the subject, meeting Jewish complaints of libertinism (v. 8) with the ironic statement : "Do I make excuses ? Not at all !"[4] Apart from the fact that the Jews would not ask this, and that Paul is on the offensive rather than the defensive, the med. trans. use of προέχεσθαι plainly demands an acc. object. Secondly b. a passive might be seen along the lines of the passage from Plutarch already mentioned (→ 692, 43 ff.): "Are we (sc. the Jews) surpassed ? Are we worse off (in respect of the imputation of sin)?"[5] But both linguistically and materially this solution is too difficult. Hence to-day c. the med. προεχόμεθα is generally taken in the sense of the intrans. act. (→ 692, 34 ff.):[6] "What then ? Have we an advantage ?" The absence of examples does not count so heavily when one remembers that this change of mood occurs elsewhere in the NT.[7] Having dealt with various objections and misunderstandings in vv. 8-8, Paul asks again whether the Jews have any advantage over the Gentiles (3:1) and he completely rejects the idea.[8] The promises of God do not in any way relieve the Jews of the guilt which alone is at issue in R. 2. Israel is not excused by the possession of the λόγια; it is more than ever put in the wrong, 3:2-4:19. The particular problem of the interrelation of God's gracious promise and Israel's guilt is set forth and solved only in R. 9-11.

Maurer

---

[1] With almost all the comm. against Bl.-Debr. § 433, 2.

[2] Τί οὖν [προ]κατέχομεν περισσόν; (omitting οὐ πάντως) "What advantage have we then ?" DG etc. with detailed variations, *v.* Ltzm. R., *ad loc.*

[3] R. A. Lipsius, *Der Brief an d. Römer, Hand-Comm. z. NT*[2] (1892), *ad loc.*; A. Jülicher, *Der Br. an d. Römer, Schriften d. NT*[3] (1917), *ad loc.*

[4] Pr.-Bauer[5], *s.v.* 2 (alternative to "to have an advantage").

[5] W. Sanday and A. C. Headlam, *A Crit. and Exegetical Comm. on the Ep. to the Romans,*[5] ICC (1925), *ad loc.*

[6] Cf. esp. Ltzm. R., *ad loc.*; M. J. Lagrange, *Saint Paul. Epitre aux Romains*[6] (1950), *ad loc.*; C. H. Dodd, *The Ep. of Paul to the Romans,* MNTC (1932), *ad loc.*; Mi. R., *ad loc.*

[7] Bl.-Debr. § 316. Thus the med. does not have the special nuance "we claim to be (rather than are) something special," as against Zn. R.; Schl. R.

[8] οὐ πάντως does not have here any restrictive sense ("not in any respect"), cf. Bl.-Debr., § 433, 2; Schl. R. as against Ltzm. R.; Mi. R.; Lagrange, *op. cit., ad loc.*; E. Gaugler, *Der Br. an d. Römer,* I (1945), *ad loc.*

προηγέομαι, → II, 908, 36 ff.   πρόθεσις → τίθημι.

| πρόθυμος, προθυμία |

πρόθυμος.

A. Usage outside the New Testament.

1. Common from the 5th cent.,[1] πρόθυμος means "ready," "willing," "eager," even "active," "passionate." In its use the adj. often cannot be distinguished from the part. of the (non-NT) verb προθυμέομαι. The neut. noun is close in meaning to προθυμία (→ 697, 26 ff.) or identical with this.

2. In the LXX (→ 698, 6 ff.) there is a clear relation to the stem נדב, and indeed to נָדִיב in the sense of "ready and willing," "joyfully ready" (1 Ch. 28:21; 2 Ch. 29:31); the activity and initiative implied in the attitude may be seen esp. in 2 Ch. 29:31.[2] 2 Macc. 4:14 misses the expected initiative in the sense of awareness of duty when it has to censure the priests because they are μηκέτι περὶ τὰς λειτουργίας πρόθυμοι. This kind of attitude, found in the righteous in difficult situations, arises out of attention to the Law and the prophets and recollection of earlier ἀγῶνες successfully overcome, 2 Macc. 15:9.[3] But example can also make a προθυμούμενος, 1 Ch. 29:1 ff. In both cases one may see again the voluntary element noted elsewhere, → 698, 32 ff. But passages like 2 Macc. 11:7; 15:9; 4 Macc. 16:16 show that πρόθυμος, like προθυμία (→ 698, 13 ff.), can also mean "resolute," "courageous," "brave," whether with ref. to battle or to death. Here one may see the connection of the content of the term with that of נדב (התנדב) in the Gk. Bible. This is esp. noteworthy in view of the fact that the word is used for this root only in 1 and 2 Ch.

3. If πρόθυμος and προθυμούμενος stand alongside one another in the LXX, this corresponds to the relation of נודבים and מתנדבים in the Dead Sea Scrolls,[4] and this

---

πρόθυμος. [1] For examples cf. the dict. On the derivation cf. Schwyzer, I, 435; II, 505: "the one whose θυμός is to the fore."

[2] כָּל־נְרִיב לֵב = πᾶς πρόθυμος τῇ καρδίᾳ → 698, 6 ff. on Sir. 45:23 and cf. 1 Ch. 29:9 [ἐν καρδίᾳ πλήρει προεθυμήθησαν]; 29:17). For נדיב־לב in this sense cf. also 1 QM 10:5: כול עתודי המלחמה נדיבי לב להחזיק בגבורת אל. Cf. also 1 Q 25:1, 7 (נדיבים); 28b (= 1 QSb) III, 27 (uncertain).

[3] For πρόθυμος with ἀγών cf. also 2 Macc. 6:28; 4 Macc. 16:16.

[4] Cf. 1 QS 1:7 f.: וזה 5:1, כול הנדבים לאמתו; 1:11: כול הנדבים לעשות חוקי אל בברית חסד הסרך לאנשי היחד המתנדבים לשוב מכול רע (cf. 6. 8. 10. 21. 22; 1 Q 14:10, 7; 31:1, 1 [uncertain]). In the first case the ref. is to candidates for the יחד אל who are still to be accepted or pledged; in the other it is to those who on the basis of their resolve have already been accepted into the יחד אל. Y. Yadin, The Scroll of the War of the Sons of Light against the Sons of Darkness (Heb.) (1955), 301b, rightly refers to 2 Ch. 17:16, where the LXX has προθυμούμενος for המתנדב. J. Licht, מושג הנדבה בכתוביה של כת מדבר יהודה (= The Concept of Nedabah in the Dead Sea Scrolls), in J. Liver, עיונים במגילות מדבר יהודה (= Studies in the Dead Sea Scrolls) (1957), 77-84 vocalises נדב as נְדָב rather נָדָב, and finds in the combination of נְדָב and מִתְנַדֵּב support for the view that the grammatical form of the term was not yet fixed when 1 QS was composed (op. cit., 80). Yet neither in bibl. nor Rabb. Heb. do we find a nif·al of נדב with the sense of a reflexive (cf. simply the common expression כָּל שֶׁהוּא נָדַר וְנָדַב, Meg., 1, 10 etc.), while in the latter even the act. נדב also occurs in the sense "to vow," e.g., bNed., 10a Bar. נָדַר וּמְקַיֵּם, "let him vow and keep it." This use of נדב seems to have developed out of the bibl. נדב לבו. Cf. the next note on the linguistic development of התנדב.

shows again from another angle that in the LXX both words are Semitically controlled in content even where there is no corresponding original. [5] In Rabb. Heb. התנדב has completely lost this specific sense and become a tt. for a votive offering (→ προθυμία, → 698, 25 ff.), [6] so that there is no need to pursue this usage.

4. In Philo πρόθυμος, combined with ἀγών (→ 694, 15 f. and I, 135) (Vit. Mos., I, 260), [7] means "courageous." [8] But the word can also mean "ready" (Abr., 109 : προθυμότατοι πρὸς τὰς τῶν ξενιζομένων ὑπηρεσίας), "willing" (Spec. Leg., I, 49; Virt., 83), "zealous" (Vit. Mos., I, 52), and sometimes in the superlative for "most willing" (Spec. Leg., IV, 170). Virt., 205 makes it quite clear that for Philo this denotes an attitude rather than a virtue, cf. esp. the adverbial use.

Joseph. uses the word as an adv. "willingly" (Ant., 6, 326; Bell., 2, 624, etc.), "gladly" (Ant., 20, 50; Vit., 142), "eagerly" (Ant., 7, 91: προθυμότερον = "with even greater zeal") and also — cf. 3 Macc. 5:26 — as a neuter noun in the same sense as προθυμία (→ 698, 22) = "readiness" (Ant., 4, 42; 6, 326), [9] "eagerness" (Ant., 4, 178) and occasionally even "solicitude" (Ant., 4, 213 : τὸ περὶ αὐτοὺς πρόθυμον τοῦ θεοῦ).

Β. πρόθυμος in the New Testament.

1. In the Garden of Gethsemane Jesus, turning to Peter, admonishes His tired and sleepy disciples to watch and pray in order that they should not enter into temptation, and He then adds in some sense as a reason [10] (→ 396, 24 ff.): τὸ μὲν πνεῦμα πρόθυμον, ἡ δὲ σὰρξ ἀσθενής (Mt. 26:41b = Mk. 14:38b). [11] The usual rendering of πρόθυμος here is "willing," but this hardly reproduces what is meant, especially as it does not do justice to the antithesis of ἀσθενής [12] demanded by the μέν ... δέ. The history of the term suggests the following interpretation : "The spirit indeed presses eagerly, but the flesh is powerless."

The authenticity of the saying has been much debated. It hardly fits the context stylistically and leaves the impression that the admonition has been adapted to instruction. [13] As a rule, however, criticism is aimed not merely at the second half but at the whole v. Thus the Evangelist is said to be pointing the moral of a story which always served to rouse and edify the community, [14] or the v. is described as an interpolation of Chr. edification. [15] Yet even on the critical side there have always been those who, [16] while regarding the whole verse as secondary in its present setting, do not on this account refuse to ascribe it to Jesus.

---

[5] The use of התנדב in the sense mentioned, which makes of מתנדבים a kind of "sworn member," may rest consciously on Ju. 5:2, 9; Neh. 11:2; 2 Ch. 17:16. This is all the more likely inasmuch as what the texts tell us about the organisation of the underlying movement suggests an intentional following of the great models in Israel's history. Prophetic influence is at work here (cf. O. Plöger, "Prophetisches Erbe in den Sekten d. frühen Judt.," ThLZ, 79 [1954], 291-296) — an aspect to which unfortunately little attention has been paid thus far.
[6] This is a typical development in the linguistic relation between the Rabb. writings and the Dead Sea Scrolls.
[7] The Israelites as εὐτολμότεροί τε καὶ ἀγωνισταὶ πρόθυμοι, cf. the whole context and also, e.g., Vit. Mos., I, 333.
[8] In Virt., 27 we find πρόθυμος with ἀκατάπληκτος.
[9] Cf. also Bell., 2, 466 : τὸ λίαν πρόθυμον ("too great readiness").
[10] There is, however, no γάρ as one would expect.
[11] Lk. leaves out the saying and shortens or alters his original in other ways.
[12] ἰσχυρός is the usual antonym of ἀσθενής, cf. 2 C. 10:10 and → I, 491, 21 f.
[13] E. Hirsch, Frühgeschichte d. Ev., I (1941), 158. Hirsch thinks the half-v. is the addition of a redactor (R). Cf. A. Pallis, Notes on St. Mark and St. Matthew[2] (1932), 101 f.
[14] J. Weiss, Das älteste Ev. (1903), 300; cf. also Hck. Mk., 173.
[15] Bultmann Trad., 288.
[16] So Wellh. Mk., ad loc.

The strongest objections to authenticity arise out of the antithesis of πνεῦμα and σάρξ found in the saying. This is thought by some [17] to be a Pauline way of speaking [18] (cf. Gl. 5:16 ff.) and also to involve a distinctively dualistic view of man whose roots the Dead Sea Scrolls seem to have exposed in the developed two-power thinking of the underlying sect. [19] Nevertheless, it must be conceded that Paul's view of the antithesis of spirit and flesh is different from that of the Gethsemane saying of Jesus [20] and also that the antithesis has nothing whatever to do with the juxtaposition of a good and bad impulse in Rabb. Judaism. [21], [22] Indeed, πνεῦμα has a very different meaning here. To προθυμ- corresponds the root √נדב. As the subj. of the process described by this, however, we find the "heart" both in Sir. 45:23 (→ 698, 6 ff.) and also in Ex. 25:2; 35:29 (לֵב), and though "spirit" (רוּחַ) is mentioned in Ex. 35:21, it occurs in immediate proximity to לֵב in such a way that here, too, the heart is to be regarded as the true subject. לֵב is transl. καρδία in Ex. 25:2; 35:21, [23] διάνοια in Ex. 35:29, [24] ψυχή in Sir. 45:23, while רוּחַ in Ex. 35:21 is ψυχή. This shows already that the borders of the concept are fluid. It also shows that לֵב and רוּחַ may be either φρόνησις or νοῦς in the LXX. Now it is true that the LXX never has πνεῦμα for לֵב but quite early לֵב and רוּחַ can be interchangeable (→ line 10 f.) and once at least LXX can use καρδία for רוּחַ Ez. 13:3. [25] This may be an accident, but it merits attention. [26] Two pts. at least should not be overlooked. On the one side the development of the use of καρδία in Jewish Gk. shows the increasing influence of Gk. rationalism to the degree that the word becomes with increasing clarity no more than a term for the physical organ which has as such no influence on spiritual processes. [27] On the other side רוּחַ/πνεῦμα and בָּשָׂר/σάρξ are traditional expressions to denote the limitation of man posited with his corporeality and hence also with his corruptibility, cf. Sir. 48:12. רוּחַ/πνεῦμα is esp. well adapted to emphasise that one must act acc. to objective standards and not just fancies or personal insights, 1 QS 9:15 : אִישׁ כְּרוּחוֹ כֵן לַעֲשׂוֹת מִשְׁפָּטוֹ. In such contexts רוּחַ/πνεῦμα is so close to לֵב/καρδία (cf. simply 1 K. 3:9) that one might get the impression they are to a large extent synonymous. Yet there is a greater degree of objectivity about רוּחַ/πνεῦμα even though one cannot talk about the endowment of the Spirit [28] in the Chr. sense. The decisive thing is what happens. The pt. is to be on the right way, and the spirit puts one there to the degree that it is πρόθυμον.

---

[17] Cf. already H. v. Soden, "Das Interesse d. apostolischen Zeitalters an d. evangelischen Geschichte," *Theol. Abhandlungen f. C. v. Weizsäcker* (1892), 144 : "... reminds us of Paul."

[18] E. Wendling, *Die Entstehung d. Mc.-Ev.* (1908), 171.

[19] K. G. Kuhn, "πειρασμός-ἁμαρτία-σάρξ im NT u. d. damit zusammenhängenden Vorstellungen," ZThK, 49 (1952), 200-222.

[20] Wellh. Mk., ad loc. and esp. F. Nötscher, *Zur theol. Terminologie der Qumran-Texte* (1956), 85 f.

[21] Str.-B., Exc.: "Der gute u. d. böse Trieb," IV, 466-483.

[22] As Str.-B. believes, I, 996 on Mt. 26:41.

[23] Cf. also Ju. 5:9; Ex. 35:5; 1 Ch. 29:9, 17; 2 Ch. 29:31.

[24] Cf. Ex. 35:22.

[25] But cf. Is. 66:2 Θ (καρδία) and ᾽Α (πνεῦμα) for רוּחַ.

[26] At Σιρ. 9:9 ἡ ψυχή σου (לֵב) and τὸ πνεῦμα σου are in parallelism. But the original is uncertain and no conclusions may be drawn. M. Z. Segal, ספר בן סירא השלם (1953), 48 thinks an original בדמך (αἵματι) has been corrupted to ברוחך (πνεύματι) (cf. V. Ryssel in Kautzsch Apkr. u. Pseudepigr., ad loc.).

[27] This is clearest in Joseph., who thus uses διάνοια for what is meant by לֵב, cf. Schl. Theol. d. Jdt., 21. At Dt. 6:5 B^r has διανοίας for καρδίας, cf. also Mk. 12:30 = Lk. 10:27.

[28] This is the by no means happy rendering of רוּחַ in 1 QS 2:20; 9:15 by G. Molin, *Die Söhne des Lichtes* (1954).

The question before the disciples in Gethsemane is that of the right way. In its context the saying tells us that this can be trodden only in orientation and commitment, not on the basis of inner movement alone. Where the latter is attempted, there is disclosed the limitation of man which causes him to fail. Hence the saying is a bridge from the disciples' declaration of solidarity with Jesus (Mt. 26:35 and par.) to their failure on the way with Him, and it shows us why failure was inevitable.

2. In R. 1:15 Paul claims it as τὸ κατ' ἐμὲ πρόθυμον, καὶ ὑμῖν τοῖς ἐν ᾽Ρώμῃ εὐαγγελίζεσθαι. Though the expression is difficult to us, it is good Greek. It combines τὸ πρόθυμον, corresponding to the noun ἡ προθυμία (→ 694, 7 ff.), with a current Hellenistic [29] use of κατά and accusative for the genitive μου or the possessive pronoun. [30] What Paul is saying is that it is his "resolve" to discharge his apostolic ministry to the Romans who are as yet unknown to him. [31] This is not because he saw here an attractive sphere of service, but because he had a sense of obligation to Rome also (and especially) within his calling as an apostle, R. 1:1, 5 f. [32]

C. The Usage in the Post-Apostolic Fathers.

The usage in the post-apost. fathers agrees with that of the NT. Here, too, πρόθυμος means "ready," "willing," "resolved," esp. for the good, 1 Cl., 34, 2 : εἰς ἀγαθοποιΐαν, Herm. m., 12, 5, 1: τὰς ἐντολὰς τοῦ θεοῦ φυλάσσειν, Herm. s., 9, 2, 4 : with ἱλαρός as a Chr. virtue. The adv. προθύμως is also used frequently, sometimes (Mart. Pol., 8, 13; 13, 1 with μετὰ σπουδῆς) with martyrdom as the goal, Herm. s., 9, 28, 2 (cf. also 4): προθύμως ἔπαθον ἐξ ὅλης τῆς καρδίας.

† προθυμία.

A. The Usage outside the New Testament.

1. This common word, derived from πρόθυμος (→ 694, 2 ff.), [1] has various nuances in non-bibl. and non-Chr. Gk. from "inclination," "readiness" (e.g., Hom. Il., 2, 588), by way of "wish," "desire" (Lys., 12, 99), to "resoluteness" (Plat. Leg., 3, 697d) and "zeal" (Hdt., IV, 98). No ethical evaluation attaches to the word as such, but the connection with θυμός, which relates to nature and manner of life (→ III, 167, 10 ff.), has an influence, albeit mostly unconscious. The word is esp. common in eulogies.

2. Philo follows this use. [2] In a series of passages the word acquires in him an emphasis in the direction of "self-awareness," "self-determination," [3] e.g., when it is sometimes more closely described as αὐτοκέλευστος (Vit. Mos., II, 137; Spec. Leg., I, 144) or ἐθελουργὸς καὶ αὐτοκέλευστος (Vit. Mos., I, 63; Mut. Nom., 270). In many instances in Philo the word is combined with the idea of the ἀγών, e.g., Decal., 146;

---

[29] Examples in Pr.-Bauer⁵, s.v. κατά II, 7b/c.
[30] Bl.-Debr. § 224, 1; Mi. R., 42, n. 3, ad loc.
[31] Cf. Zn. R., ad loc.
[32] d Or Ambst read the nom. masc. πρόθυμος (sc. εἰμι) for πρόθυμον; perhaps this is an ancient conjecture.

προθυμία. [1] For numerous examples from literature (Hom. on), inscr. and pap. cf. Pass., Moult.-Mill., Liddell-Scott, Pr.-Bauer⁵, s.v.
[2] It is used alongside σπουδή in Sacr. AC, 59; Spec. Leg., I, 144; Vit. Cont., 71; Migr. Abr., 218; τόλμη in Spec. Leg., IV, 111 (cf. Vit. Mos., I, 260); τάχος in Spec. Leg., II, 83.
[3] προθυμίαι καὶ τόλμαι are an explicit expression of καρτερία καὶ ἐγκράτεια in Spec. Leg., IV, 112. The image and the choice of word show that Philo is following the Gk. tradition here, cf. I. Heinemann, Philons gr. u. jüd. Bildung (1932), 162.

Vit. Mos., I, 315; Spec. Leg., IV, 111. [4] Along the same lines (cf. Agric., 165 where ἀγών is used again) it is called dangerous to rely on ἰδίᾳ προθυμίᾳ instead of the ἐπιφροσύνη θεοῦ and thus to try to attain by force what can only be received from God, Agric., 169. For Philo, then, there is a human προθυμία which must be rejected in so far as it is not in agreement with the divine will.

3. In the only LXX instance at Sir. 45:23 : ἐν ἀγαθότητι προθυμίας ψυχῆς αὐτοῦ, we seem to have at a first glance the common Gk. use and a deviation from bibl. psychology, for which the heart (→ III, 606, 10 ff. καρδία) is the locus and starting-point of all the spiritual processes in human life. In fact, however, this is not so, or is not meant to be so. This may be seen on the one side from the original : אשר נדבו לבו [5] in which the heart is the activating subject, and it is proved on the other side by the context of the LXX rendering, which does not detract in the least from the emphasised initiative of Aaron's grandson Phinehas (cf. Nu. 25:7 ff.). For the translator προθυμία refers to the "initiative" which is carried out here and which is the expression of "courage," "resolution," and "obedience" to the divine order. Yet the passage shows that προθυμ- is not properly adapted to render clearly what is meant by נדב. This may be seen from other LXX passages in which different words of the same stem occur, → 694, 9 ff.

4. In Joseph., who uses προθυμία a few times, the word means "inclination," "attraction" (Ant., 15, 193 : τὴν ἐμὴν προθυμίαν sc. πρὸς 'Αντώνιον), "impetuosity," "pressing onwards" in battle (Ant., 15, 124 : μετὰ πάσης προθυμίας, cf. 7, 236 : πάσῃ προθυμίᾳ χρωμένων) or (in the plur.) signs of (resolute) "readiness." For Joseph., too, the idea of an exercised initiative seems to be connected with the term, though again it is ill adapted to express this clearly. [6]

5. Rabbinic Judaism derives from the root נדב, the original of προθυμία in Heb. Sir. (→ lines 6 ff.), the word נְדָבָה, which is used for the voluntary offering (on the basis of a vow) as distinct from the obligatory offering, Men., 1, 1; Qinnim, 1, 1 ff. etc. But a soft, pleasant and fruitful rain can also be called גשם נדבה, Taan., 3, 8. Here (Ex. 35:29 etc.) and also in Ps. 68:9 (גשם נדבות, [7] plentiful rain) the usage of the OT is adopted. The common feature is the idea of non-regimentation, whether this be in the form of "voluntariness" or in that of "plenty." [8]

6. In the light of the connection between προθυμία and נדבה in Sir. 45:23 it is esp. important that נדבה also occurs in the Dead Sea Scrolls. In the so-called war scroll the sons of light are called אנשי נדבת מלחמה, i.e., volunteers (1 QM 7:5), for they fight willingly and not because they are forced to do so. [9] Significant is 1 QH 15:10 with the vow of the petitioner that in fulfilment of Dt. 6:5 he wants to love God בנדבה the בכל לב of the bibl. saying is obviously to be taken in the sense of "free surrender."

---

[4] Cf. also Vit. Mos., I, 260 (ἀγωνισταὶ πρόθυμοι).

[5] Ancient Heb.: Ex. 25:2; 35:29; cf. 35:21.

[6] A. Schalit in his comprehensive Heb. transl. of Ant. (קדמוניות היהודים, [2] II [1955], 249) has selected the very modern rendering בכל התלהבותם for the relevant expression in Ant., 7, 236 without alluding to the historical background of the term προθυμία.

[7] LXX has βροχὴ ἑκούσιος for this, ψ 67:10.

[8] Hence בִּנְדָבָה can mean "voluntary," Nu. 15:3; Ps. 54:7; 1 QS 9:24; 1 QH 15:10. Acc. to Taan., 6, 5 there were in the temple both collecting boxes for ear-marked gifts and also six boxes for gifts of money "for free use" (לִנְדָבָה).

[9] Yadin, op. cit. (→ 694, n. 4), 301b takes מרצונם to mean "voluntarily" in היינו המקריבים את עצמם למלחמת ה'. Cf. also Licht (→ 694, n. 4), 80, who finds the idea of free will behind נדבה. It should not be overlooked that already in older texts התנדב meant willingness for military service, Ju. 5:2 etc.

On the other hand, 1 QS 9:24 is too obscure to allow us to draw any great conclusions from it. [10] Esp. one should be on guard against finding here parallels to certain Stoic ideas which imply the ultimate futility of man's will when measured by God's. Attempts of this kind [11] will always be unsatisfactory and dubious. On the whole, however, the use of נדבה in the Dead Sea Scrolls leaves the impression that the word has in view an attitude which is the result of conversion and which is characterised by a willing and cheerful treading of the divine path entered upon at conversion. If so, נדבה is "the attitude of the man who in conversion has accepted God's will as his own, or cheerfully subordinated his own will to God's." If this is not more clearly expressed in the texts thus far published, it is because the interest of these texts is practical rather than theoretical. [12]

B. προθυμία in the New Testament.

The NT use is not uniform.

1. In Ac. 17:11 it is said of the Jews in Berea that under the influence of the preaching of Paul and his companion Silas ἐδέξαντο τὸν λόγον μετὰ πάσης προθυμίας. The expression adopts current formulae [13] and so far as these justify any conclusion (→ n. 2) it has in view the determined "zeal" which the hearers of the Gospel freely show in relation to this and to those who preach it.

2. In 2 C., discussing the love-offering initiated by him, Paul uses προθυμία three times to express the attitude in the matter which he hopes for and expects in the congregation at Corinth, 8:11, 12; 9:2. He also uses the term once for his own share in the collection, 8:19. His concern is for an attitude which will be more than a ready agreement with his project, which will be characterised by action as well as willingness, and which will thus rest on a consciously accepted obligation that is nevertheless free and not grounded in command or law. The mode of expression is clumsy and difficult. To understand it, one must realise that on the one side Paul does not want to compel and yet on the other side he must insist for the sake of the Corinthian church that it carry out the resolve which it has made, 8:11 f. The use of προθυμία is based on the need to say this

---

[10] H. Bardtke, *Die Handschriftenfunde vom Toten Meer* (1952), 103 is surely wrong when he suggests that נדבה here means "voluntary offering" (Rabb.; → 698, 25 ff.). A. Dupont-Sommer (*Évidences* No. 58 [June/July, 1956], 29) transl. the words כול הנעשה בו ירצה בנדבה by "en tout ce qui a été fait par Lui il se complaira de bon coeur," but this does not get the real pt.

[11] Licht, *op. cit.*, 82-84.

[12] Ps. 51:12 with its רוּחַ נְדִיבָה poses an exegetical and expository problem which this is not the place to discuss. The LXX has πνεῦμα ἡγεμονικόν, Vg *spiritus principalis*, both in the Jewish exegetical tradition, cf. Rashi, *ad loc.* Perhaps one should transl. "spirit of willingness" (for the good). Acc. to J. Schneider, "Πνεῦμα ἡγεμονικόν," ZNW, 34 (1935), 62-69 the LXX rendering rests on the fact that the translator took his phrase from the Hell. tradition that finds in the πνεῦμα the power which "in virtue of the reason immanent in it directs the whole spiritual life and continually shows me the right way," 69. But the ref. of ἡγεμονικόν is more likely to ὁδός/דֶּרֶךְ → 697, 1 ff. Against the theory of Stoic influence on Ps. 51:12 cf. P. Katz, Review of I. Soisalon-Soininen, *Die Textform der Septuaginta-Übers. des Richterbuches* (1951) in ThLZ, 77 (1952), 157.

[13] Jos. Ant., 15, 124: μετὰ πάσης προθυμίας, Philo Abr., 246: τὸν κλῆρον ... μετὰ προθυμίας πάσης ἀνεδέχετο (cf. Sacr. AC, 59; Migr. Abr., 218; Vit. Cont., 71), Ditt. Syll.³, I, 532, 6 f.: με[τὰ] πάσας προθυμ[ίας] τὰν ἀπόδεξιμ ποιουμένα. For further examples from inscr. cf. Pr.-Bauer⁵, *s.v.*; Jackson-Lake, I, 4, 248 (on Ac. 19:29). Cf. also 1 Cl., 33, 1: μετὰ προθυμίας.

clearly for all the required restraint. Hence the use of the same term for Paul himself in 8:19 serves to proclaim his solidarity with the Corinthian Christians in this matter. Their participation in the collection does not merely promote God's glory ; it also sustains the προθυμία of the apostle himself, which in turn works to the same end, 8:19. The whole section is closely related to Paul's testimony to freedom. [14] Herein also lies its closeness to the way in which the community of the Dead Sea Scrolls understands itself in respect of its task as God's community, → 698, 32 ff. In this light one may construe the προθυμία of 2 C. 8-9 as the "cheerful resolution" [15, 16] which cannot be separated as such from being a Christian. [17]

3. On the usage in the post-apost. fathers → n. 13 and also 1 Cl., 2, 3; Herm. s., 5, 3, 4; Dg., 1, 1 (always in bonam partem).

Rengstorf

<hr>

┌─────────────────┐
│ † προΐστημι   │
└─────────────────┘

1. In Gk. literature προΐστημι is copiously represented. Though the verb occurs only once in Hom. (→ line 16) and not at all in Hesiod, it is very common thereafter. Trans. it means "to put before," "to present" (e.g., Hom. Il., 4, 156; Polyb., 1, 33, 7; a meaning not found in the NT). The intr. med. προΐσταμαι (aor. προέστην, perf. προέστηκα) means "to put oneself at the head," "to go first," in the perf. "to preside." Only once (if the text has been correctly handed down) is there a wholly spatial sense : σὲ ... προὔστην, "I went on before thee," Soph. El., 1377 f. Elsewhere the verb is used in a transf. sense. The first fig. meaning is "to surpass," e.g., πάντων προστᾶσα, Plat. Tim., 25b. [1] But other metaphorical meanings are more important : a. The most important of all is "to preside" in the sense "to lead, conduct, direct, govern" : προεστάναι τῆς Ἑλλάδος, Hdt., I, 69; V, 49; προὔστη τῆς πόλεως, Thuc., II, 65, 5; προειστήκεσαν τῆς μεταβολῆς, Thuc., VIII, 75, 2; ὁ προεστηκὼς τοῦ οἴκου, 2 S. 13:17; cf. Prv. 23:5; Am. 6:10; Da. LXX Bel 8; πρόστητε τοῦ λαοῦ, "take over the direction of the people" 1 Macc. 5:19; δικαίως προστῆναι τοῦ πλήθους, Jos. Ant., 8, 300; τῷ μετὰ ταῦτα προϊσταμένῳ, Jos. Vit., 93; οἱ τοῦ πλήθους προεστῶτες, ibid., 168. [2] b. There is also the thought of standing or going before someone or something in protection : οἱ δορυφόροι οἱ Μασίστεω προέστησαν, Hdt., IX, 107. Out of this arises the sense "to assist," "to join with," more precisely defined as "to protect," "to

<hr>

[14] Cf. Schl. K., 596-599.

[15] Wnd. 2 K., 264 rightly perceives this when he renders πρὸς ... προθυμίαν ἡμῶν (8:19) by "to the heightening of our joy."

[16] Thus the Gk. word has here a content determined by נדב (התנדב) → 694, 9. On the discrepancy between the Gk. form and the Semitic content in the Pl. of 2 C. cf. for another section W. C. van Unnik, "Reisepläne u. Amen-Sagen, Zshg. u. Gedankenfolge in 2 K. 1:15-24," Studia Paulina in honorem Joh. de Zwaan (1953), 215-234.

[17] F. Delitzsch in his transl. of the NT into Heb. (ספרי הברית החדשה) [1883]) has rightly brought out the material connection between προθυμία in 2 C. 8-9 and נדב.

προΐστημι. Thes. Steph., Pass., Moult.-Mill., Preisigke Wört., Liddell-Scott, Pr.-Bauer⁵, s.v.; Δ. Δημητράκος, Μέγα λέξικον τῆς ἑλληνικῆς γλώσσης, 7 (1949), s.v.; A. Bailly, Dict. grec-français¹⁶ (1950), s.v.; Schwyzer, II, 505 f.; Mayser, I, 3, 230; II, 1, 98, 193 f., 215; II, 2, 211 f., 236; Dob. Th. on 1 Th. 5:12; H. Greeven, "Propheten, Lehrer, Vorsteher bei Pls. Zur Frage der 'Ämter' im Urchr.," ZNW, 44 (1952/53), 1-43.

[1] Cf. further Kühner-Blass-Gerth, II, 1 § 420, 2b.

[2] Also common in the pap. cf. Moulton-Mill., Preisigke, Mayser, II, 2, 236.

represent," "to care for," "to help," "to further" : τοιούτων ξένων προΰστητε, Eur. Heracl., 1036 f., cf. 306 : προΐστασθαι τῶν Ἑλλήνων καὶ ... τοῖς ἀδικουμένοις βοηθεῖν, Demosth. Or., 10, 46; τῆς εἰρήνης, Aeschin. Fals. Leg., 161; τῆς ἐναντίας γνώμης, "to represent," Polyb., 5, 5: 8; ἐν ταῖς ἁμαρτίαις σου ... προέστην σου, "in spite of thy sins ... I helped thee," Is. 43:24; προεστῶτες, "sponsors," "curators," Ep. Ar., 182 (masters of ceremonies at the Egypt. court who had to receive foreign embassies); θείου νόμου προεστήκασιν ἡμῶν οἱ δορυφόροι, "as representatives of a divine law the spearmen (in fact) assist us," 4 Macc. 11:27 (as in 11:12 the tyrant involuntarily helps the tortured and slain brothers to prove their fidelity by suffering); οἱ ἀμελῶς προστάντες τοῦ κοινῇ συμφέροντος, Jos. Ant., 5, 90; ὅπως ... ὁ ἀρχιερεὺς ... προΐσταται τῶν ἀδικουμένων, ibid., 14, 196; τὸν ... ἡμῶν ... προϊστάμενον (i.e., God), Epict. Diss., III, 24, 3; ὅπως ἐγδῶνταί με αὐτῷ προϊσταμένῳ, "in order that they (my parents) may give me to him in marriage as one who will look after me" (so that he will support the woman), BGU, IV, 1105, 5 f. (1st cent. A.D.); καλῶς ποιήσατε προϊστάντες Πετήσιος, "please receive Petesis," P. Fay., 13, 5 (2nd cent. A.D.). [3] c. There may be ref. simply to occupation with the relevant object without regard for the relation expressed by the πρό. Hence arises the sense "to care for," "to arrange," "to handle," "to execute" etc. (sometimes with ref. to a wholly contingent action): οὐκ ὀρθῶς σεωϋτοῦ προέστηκας, "you do not play your part properly," Hdt., II, 173; τοῖσιν ἐχθροῖς ... προὐστήτην φόνου, "they both committed murder on enemies," Soph. El., 979 f.; εἰ μόνον τοῦ ἑαυτοῦ βίου καλῶς προεστήκοι, "if only he looks after his own household well," Xenoph. Mem., III, 2, 2; ὁ προεστὼς ἀλλοτρίας κρίσεως, "he who concerns himself with the lawsuit of another," Prv. 26:17; [4] προΐστασθαι ἐργασίας, τέχνης, Plut. Pericl., 24, 5 (I, 165c); Athen., 13, 94; φιλοσοφίας, Philostr. Ep. Apollonii, 53 (I, 358, 8).

2. As concerns the LXX [5] it may be noted from the examples already given (→ 700, 25 ff.) that προΐστημι is used for various Heb. terms and that sometimes there is no direct equivalent in the Mas. In transl. each instance must be considered on its merits. From the pseudepigr. one may adduce Test. Jos. 2:6, where it is said of God that in all circumstances He προΐσταται, "grants protection."

3. The eight instances of προΐστημι in the NT contain only intransitive forms of the verb. They occur in the Pauline corpus and fall under the nuances a.-c. to which special attention has been directed above (→ 700, 22 ff.).

In most cases προΐστημι seems to have sense a. "to lead" (→ 700, 22 ff.) but the context shows in each case that one must also take into account sense b. "to care for" (→ 700, 29 ff.). This is explained by the fact that caring was the obligation of leading members of the infant Church. Thus Paul says in R. 12:8 : ὁ μεταδιδοὺς ἐν ἁπλότητι, ὁ προϊστάμενος ἐν σπουδῇ, ὁ ἐλεῶν ἐν ἱλαρότητι. Here the second expression is plainly analogous to the other two, which both refer to works of love. The meaning, then, is somewhat as follows : "He who gives let him do so with simplicity, he who cares with zeal, he who does good with cheerfulness." Yet the whole passage is speaking of the gifts of grace imparted to different office-bearers, so that οἱ προϊστάμενοι are a special group separated by the Spirit for the primary task of caring for others [6] (cf. ἀντιλήμψεις, κυβερνήσεις, 1 C. 12:28). The position is the same in 1 Th. 5:12 : εἰδέναι τοὺς κοπιών-

---

[3] For the pap. cf. Moult.-Mill., Preisigke, Mayser, II, 2, 211 f. with further examples of the meaning "to protect."

[4] Mas. עַל מִתְעַבֵּר, "one who is overzealous about."

[5] Helbing Kasussyntax, 187.

[6] M. J. Lagrange, Saint Paul, Épitre aux Romains (1922), ad loc.: "Ceux-là centralisent les dons, sont comme les intermédiaires entre les riches et les pauvres ou les malades ..."

τας ἐν ὑμῖν καὶ προϊσταμένους ὑμῶν ἐν κυρίῳ καὶ νουθετοῦντας ὑμᾶς. According to the context the task of the προϊστάμενοι is in large measure that of pastoral care, and the emphasis is not on their rank or authority but on their efforts for the eternal salvation of believers. [7] How far there is already reference to specific offices in these passages from R. and 1 Th. is a matter of lively debate ; the endowment with the Spirit presupposed in R. is no argument against this thesis, since Spirit and office are not antithetical in the NT, e.g., Mt. 7:29; Ac. 6:3. [8] In 1 Tm. again, where the verb and especially the participle occurs repeatedly, [9] the ideas of guiding and caring are both present. In this case the reference is quite definitely to official leaders in the churches. 1 Tm. 3:4 describes an acceptable bishop as a man who rules (προϊστάμενον) his own house well and can keep his children under control. We then read : "If a man know not how to rule (προστῆ-ναι) his own house, how shall he take care of (ἐπιμελήσεται) the church of God ?" v. 5. Here, then, "to rule" is the same as "to take care of." Cf. also 5:8 : "But if he provide not (προνοεῖ) for his own, and specially for those of his own house ..." Then 1 Tm. 3:12 describes good deacons as those who care well (προϊστάμενοι) for their own houses (families and servants). The author certainly has in view the authority of the head of the household (*patria potestas* → V, 949 ff., 961 ff., 1004 f.) but his attention is primarily directed, not to the exercise of power, but to the discretion and care to be shown therein. Finally, 1 Tm. 5:17 says that οἱ καλῶς προεστῶτες πρεσβύτεροι (→ 666, 26 ff.) are worthy of double reward, especially those who labour in the word and teaching. The context shows that the reference is not merely to elders who rule well but especially to those who exercise a sincere cure of souls. The second half of the verse makes their diligence in pastoral care the criterion. This is not to deny that here, too, the προϊστάμενοι have a special dignity and play a leading role as elders. [10] In all these instances, however, the verb has in the NT the primary senses of both "to lead" and "to care for," [11] and this agrees with the distinctive nature of office in the NT, since according to Lk. 22:26 the one who is chief (ὁ ἡγούμενος) is to be as he who serves. [12]

---

[7] Dob. Th. on 1 Th. 5:12; cf. F. J. A. Hort, *The Christian Ecclesia* (1897), 126 f. (the ref. is to office-bearers though not to a technical title); Greeven, 32, n. 74 (on R. 12:8 and 1 Th. 5:12 : care on the part of those in authority).

[8] O. Linton, "Das Problem der Urkirche in d. neueren Forschung," *Uppsala Universitets Årsskrift*, 1932, Teol. 2 (1932), 127, 195-211; G. Friedrich, "Geist und Amt," *Wort u. Dienst, Jbch. d. Theol. Schule Bethel*, NF, 3 (1952), 80, n. 65, 81-85; Greeven, 32-39, 42; H. v. Campenhausen, *Kirchliches Amt u. geistliche Vollmacht in den ersten drei Jahrhunderten* (1953), 323-332.

[9] C. Spicq, *Saint Paul, Les épîtres pastorales* (1947), 87 f.

[10] Dib. Past.³, *ad loc.* In Gk. societies ὁ προεστώς was a specific officer : F. Poland, *Gesch. des gr. Vereinswesens, Preisschriften der Fürstlichen Jablonowskischen Gesellschaft*, 38 (1909), Index, *s.v.* προεστώς; Greeven, 38, n. 91.

[11] Dob. Th. on 1 Th. 5:12 esp. has stressed that in NT usage προΐστασθαι tends to mean "to care for," and he has assembled many linguistic arguments in favour of this view. A. Harnack, "Κόπος (κοπιᾶν, οἱ κοπιῶντες) im frühchr. Sprachgebrauch," ZNW, 27 (1928), 1-10 agrees to the degree that the ref. is to a type of rule which involves caring (10), but he rightly emphasises against Dob. Th. that the men concerned are real office-bearers (8-10). The choice between "to lead" and "to care for" in these NT passages is not to be posed so sharply as in Pr.-Bauer⁵, *s.v.* Cf. also, e.g., E. Schweizer, "Das Leben des Herrn in der Gemeinde u. ihren Diensten," Abh. ThANT, 8 (1946), 56, n. 26.

[12] → ἐπίσκοπος, II, 610, 17 ff. ("protective care"); → 615, 15 ff.; → κυβέρνησις, III, 1036, 14 ff.; → ποιμήν, 490, 20 ff.

How significant the idea of care is in NT προΐσταμαι may be seen from the fact that προστάτις is the word for "protectress" or "patroness" in R. 16:2. [13] Similarly προστάτης, which does not occur in the NT, means "protector" in 1 Cl., 36, 1; 61, 3; 64; [14] it is always used here with ref. to Christ and in association with ἀρχιερεύς, so that again we have the twofold sense of leadership and care. [15]

Sense c. "to devote oneself to," "to execute" (→ 701, 16 ff.), occurs twice in Titus, where Christians are exhorted καλῶν ἔργων προΐστασθαι, "to devote themselves (in concert) to good works," [16], [17] Tt. 3:8, 14.

4. In the post-apost. fathers senses a. and b. are rare. Sense a. "to lead" (→ 700, 22 ff.) occurs in Herm. v., 2, 4, 3 : οἱ πρεσβύτεροι οἱ προϊστάμενοι τῆς ἐκκλησίας. Here there is no ref. to care but simply to the administrative function of elders, → 674, 2 ff. There is an instance of sense b. "to champion" (→ 700, 29 ff.) in Dg., 5, 3 : (Christians are not to withdraw from society) οὐδὲ δόγματος ἀνθρωπίνου προεστᾶσιν, "nor do they espouse a human teaching."

Reicke

προκαλέομαι → III, 496, 23 f.

προκαταγγέλλω → I, 73, 1 ff.

πρόκειμαι → III, 656, 10 ff.

προκηρύσσω → III, 717, 13 ff.

---

† προκοπή, † προκόπτω

(→ αὐξάνω, 281, 40 ff.; → περισσεύω, 61, 10 ff.; → πληθύνω, 279 ff.; → προάγω, I, 130, 30 ff. → τελειόω).

Contents : A. The Word Group in Greek : 1. History and Meaning of the Word ; 2. προκοπή as a Technical Term in Stoicism and Its Offshoots. B. The Idea of Progress in the Old Testament. C. The Word Group in the Writings of Hellenistic Judaism : 1. Septuagint and Symmachus, Testaments of the Twelve Patriarchs, Epistle of Aristeas and Josephus ; 2. προκοπή as an Ethical Concept in Philo. D. The Word Group in the New Testament : 1. Linguistic Data ; 2. The προκοπή of Individuals ; 3. The προκοπή of the Community and the Gospel ; 4. The προκοπή of Heresy ; 5. The προκοπή of the Aeons. E. The Word Group in the Older Post-NT Literature : 1. Post-Apostolic Fathers and Apologists ; 2. Clement of Alexandria.

---

[13] Pr.-Bauer⁵, *s.v.* προστάτις.
[14] Pr.-Bauer⁵, *s.v.* προστάτης with bibl. *s.v.* προστάτις. Cf. also Poland, *op. cit.*, 363-368 and Index, *s.v.* προστάτης; also Index, *s.v.* προεστώς.
[15] Cf. also προστατέω (Liddell-Scott, *s.v.*), which is not found in the NT.
[16] On good works in the Past. cf. B. Reicke, *The Disobedient Spirits and Christian Baptism* (1946), 177, 211-213, 223; Spicq, *op. cit.* (→ n. 9), on Tt. 3:8 with Exc.
[17] G. D. Kypke, Observationes sacrae in Novi Foederis libros, II (1755), 380 f.; W. Lock, *The Past. Epistles,* ICC (1952), on Tt. 3:8.

π ρ ο κ ο π ή, π ρ ο κ ό π τ ω. On A.: Pape, Pass., Liddell-Scott, Herwerden, Moult.-Mill., Preisigke Wört., *s.v.*; A. Bonhöffer, *Epiktet u. d. NT* (1911), 128; G. H. Putzner, *Die ethischen Systeme Platos u. der Stoa,* Diss. Leipzig (1913), 94-98; M. Pohlenz, *Die Stoa,* I (1948), 154 (also II² [1955], 83) etc.; also *Stoa u. Stoiker* (1950), 164-170; K. Ziegler, Art. "Plutarchos," Pauly-W., 21 (1952), 771 f.; P. Barth-A. Goedeckemeyer, *Die Stoa⁶* (1946), 34 f., 114 f., 202 f. etc. On C.: E. Turowski, *Die Widerspiegelung des stoischen Systems bei Philon v. Alexandreia,* Diss. Königsberg (1927), 42; W. Völker (= Völker I), *Fortschritt u. Vollendung bei Philo v. Alex.* (1938), 154-262, esp. 229-238; J. S. Boughton, *The Idea of Progress in Philo Iudaeus* (on the meaning of progress cf. p. VIII), Diss. New York (1932); E. Bréhier, *Les idées philosophiques et religieuses de Philon d.Alex.³* (1950), 250-310, esp. 302 f. On D.: G. Stählin, "Fortschritt u. Wachstum. Zur Herkunft u. Wandlung nt.licher Ausdrucksformen," *Festgabe f̶. J. Lortz,* II (1957), 13-25. On E.: W. Völker (= Völker II), *Der wahre Gnostiker nach Cl. Al.* (1952).

A. The Word Group in Greek.

1. History and Meaning of the Word.

a. Originally προκόπτω is probably a nautical tt. for "to make headway in spite of blows," [1] one of the many nautical metaphors in Gk. usage. Less likely is derivation from the work of the smith who "with the blow" of his hammer "lengthens out" iron. [2]

b. προκόπτω is originally used in a trans. sense : "to promote," "to further," e.g., Eur. Alc., 1079; Hec., 961; Xenoph. Eq. Mag., 6, 5; the med. is used accordingly for "to get on," Hdt., I, 190; III, 56. Already in Attic, [3] however, we find the intr. act. [4] which alone survives in post-class. usage and which means "to go ahead," "to make progress," "to thrive," cf. Aristot. De plantis, 3, p. 824b, 38 f.; also Thuc., VII, 56, 3; Sext. Emp. Math., 5, 71 etc.

The noun προκοπή occurs for the first time in the Hell. period ; [5] it is also common in the plur., esp. in Philo, also in fixed verbal combinations, e.g., λαμβάνω προκοπήν (Polyb., 8, 15, 6; 10, 47, 12; Philo Leg. All., III, 165 etc.), also in the fig. etym. προ-κοπὴν προκόπτω (Plut. De profectibus in virtute, 7 [II, 79b]; cf. the synon. αὔξησιν αὔξω in Col. 2:19).

c. προκόπτω and προκοπή are neutral as such. They may denote progress in evil (ἡ ἐπὶ τὸ χεῖρον προκοπή, Jos. Ant., 4, 59; 2 Tm. 3:13 → 715, 32 ff.; cf. Polyb., 5, 16, 9; T. Jud. 21:8 : ἐπὶ τὸ κακόν vl. ἐπὶ κακῷ, explained by the participial expression ἐν πλεονεξίᾳ ὑψούμενοι which follows) as well as good (ἡ ἐπὶ τὸ βέλτιον προκοπή, Polyb., I, 12, 7). [6] Like the word "progress," however, they are almost always taken a parte potiore (cf. Plut. De profectibus in virtute, 7 [II, 79b]: ἀληθὴς προκοπή). Thus προκοπή is found alongside, e.g., βελτίωσις (Philo Sacr. AC, 113; Mut. Nom., 19; Agric., 166; Aet. Mund., 43), ἀναθάλλωσις (P. Masp., I, 2, 3, 21), εὐημερία (P. Ryl., II, 233, 16; 2 Macc. 8:8 → 709, 8 ff.) and even συντέλεια (Polyb., 2, 37, 10), while with προκόπτω we find βελτιοῦμαι (Philo Poster. C., 78; Mut. Nom., 23 f.), ἔρρωμαι, ὑγιαίνω etc. (→ lines 29 ff.), also εἰς ἀνυπέρβλητον τύχην χωρέω (Vett. Val., IX, 1 [p. 332, 7]).

d. In this sense προκόπτω and προκοπή, often more or less equivalent to "blessing," "fortune," "success," are a common object of blessings and prayers (εὔχομαί σε ὑγιαί-

---

[1] Cf. Pass., s.v.; H. Blümner, "Die Metapher bei Herodotos," Jbch. f. Philol., 143 (1891), 45.

[2] Pape, s.v. A third derivation (first advocated by A. Coray, Anmerkungen zu Isoc., II [1807], 121 f., cf. also Liddell-Scott etc.) is from the movement of an army which "advances" in a wood "by hewing down" trees. This is, however, a type of popular etym., though προκόπτω can be used for moving forward on a road, e.g., Chion. Ep., 4, 2 (ed. R. Hercher, Epistolographi Graeci [1873], 196); Jos. Ant., 2, 133, 340; Suidas, s.v.; cf. also Babrius Fabulae, 111, 4 (ed. O. Crusius [1897]) and though προκόπτω here, as a kind of counter-part of ἐγκόπτω (→ III, 855, 29 f.), derives from the same sphere. The derivation is already discounted, however, by the fact that it is linked to the later intr. use of the verb.

[3] Plato avoids προκόπτω and uses ἐπιδίδωμι instead, as correctly noted by Luc. (Soloec., 6). The two verbs and the related nouns προκοπή and ἐπίδοσις are used as synon. (cf. Plut. De profectibus in virtute, 3 [II, 76d] and 10 [II, 81d]) or together (Just. Dial., 2, 6 → 717, 21 ff.; Jos. Vit., 8 → 705, 24 f.) in the post-class. period. Luc. himself does not hesitate to use προκόπτω acc. to contemporary usage, Hermot., 63; cf. also Amores, 21. He also has προκοπή (Alex., 22), not being pedantic in his Atticism ; cf. R. J. Deferrari, Lucian's Atticism, Diss. Princeton (1916).

[4] The use is often hard to determine, e.g., in προκόπτω οὐδέν (Alcaeus Fr., 91 [Diehl, I², 4, 135]; Xenoph. Hist. Graec., VII, 1, 6; Polyb., 27, 8, 14); this could well be a trans. use, hence, as often, with a neuter obj., cf. Liddell-Scott, s.v.

[5] Cf. C. A. Lobeck, Phrynichi Ecloga (1820), 85 : προκόπτειν λέγουσι (sc. the Atticists, but → n. 3), τὸ δὲ ὄνομα προκοπὴ οὐκ ἔστι παρ' αὐτοῖς, and on this W. G. Rutherford, The New Phrynichus (1881), 158.

[6] Cf. the twofold use of the synon. πορεύομαι in LXX 2 Βασ. 3:1.

νειν καὶ προκόπτειν, P. Gen., I, 74, 3; προκόπτειν εὔχομαι, P. Oxy., I, 122, 15; cf. P. Ryl., II, 233, 16; Ζεῦ Σαραθηνέ, προκοπὴν Ἀρχελάῳ Ἰουλίου, Ditt. Or., II, 627, 2) and also of astrological prophecies;[7] related is the use on an epitaph of the middle Ptolemy period:[8] ἐν προκοπαῖς, "in good circumstances"; προκοπὴ ζωῆς in T. Jud. 15:5 also has this broad sense. The ref. may be to economic prosperity, cf. Diod. S., 11, 87, 5 : ταῖς οὐσίαις, also T. Gad. 4:5 (→ n. 44), where προκοπή is the object of hatred and envy; Epict. Diss., I, 10, 9 : προκοπαί "possessions" etc. But it may also be to children (P. Masp., I, 2, 3, 21; Vett. Val., 12 [p. 179, 25]), vocational success (P. Oxy., XIV, 1631, 20; Diod. S., 1, 33, 9), promotion (BGU, II, 423, 17; Jos. Bell., 2, 27; 6, 142), precedence in rank, distinction, honour, regard[9] (δόξα καὶ προκοπή, Ep. Ar., 242; μείζονος προκοπῆς αἴτιος, Jos. Bell., 1, 195; προκόπτω ἐν ἀξίᾳ, Vett. Val., II, 4 [p. 60, 19];[10] cf. also Jos. Ant., 20, 205) etc. Special uses are for military success (e.g., εὐαγγελίζοντι τὰ τῆς νείκης αὐτοῦ καὶ προκοπῆς, P. Giess., 27, 2; 2 Macc. 8:8; ψ 44:5 Σ; cf. Vett. Val., II, 4 [p. 60, 15]: ἐν λαμπραῖς στρατείαις προκόψει, also V, 3 [p. 213, 1]) and for progress in healing.[11]

e. Alongside this use of προκοπή for progress and prosperity[12] in the physical, economic and social sphere, which is found esp. in everyday, non-literary Gk. the word has another important use in the literary speech of Hellenism, namely, in Stoic philosophy and its offshoots. Here the term denotes the process of moral and spiritual development in man.[13] This development can be more closely defined as progress in culture ([περὶ τὴν παι]δείαν προκόπτει;[14] [Pythagoras] προκεκοφὼς ἤδη ἐν παιδείᾳ, Diod. S., 10, 3, 1, also 17, 69, 4; εἰς μεγάλην παιδείας προύκοπτον ἐπίδοσιν Jos. Vit., 8; Cic. Att., 15, 16), in learning (... προύκοπτον ἐν τοῖς μαθήμασι, Luc. Hermot., 63; ἐπὶ πλέον ... προκόψαι ἐν ῥητορικῇ, M. Ant., I, 17), in philosophy (Diod. S., 16, 6, 3; νέῳ ... ἀνδρὶ γευσαμένῳ προκοπῆς ἀληθοῦς ἐν φιλοσοφίᾳ, Plut. De profectibus in virtute, 10 [II, 81d]), in religious knowledge (προκόπτειν μέχρι τᾶς τῶν Σεβαστῶν γνώσεως)[15] and esp. in virtue.[16] But in the abs., too, προκοπή obviously has here the sense of progress in intellectual and moral education (as an inseparable unity), e.g., in the pun of Bion (Diog. L., IV, 50) τὴν οἴησιν ἔλεγε προκοπῆς ἐγκοπήν (→ III,

---

[7] Planets in a specific conjunction ἀπὸ νεότητος τὰς προκοπὰς ἀποτελοῦσιν, P. Tebt., II, 276, 39; often in Vett. Val., e.g., I, 22 (p. 45, 36); with κτῆσις, I, 22 (p. 47, 26), ἀρχαί, τιμαί, τὰ ἀγαθά, II, 4 (p. 60, 3 f.); εὐτυχίαι, II, 37 (p. 116, 19 f.); πίστις, ὠφέλεια, μακαριότης, εὐεργεσία, VI, 1 (p. 247, 19 f.); cf. also II, 6 (p. 62, 27); IV, 16 (p. 185, 18 f.); V, 9 (p. 225, 28 f.); VII, 5 (p. 292, 16); IX, 1 (p. 331, 25 f.); the verb, too, in the same sense : ἐπὶ τῆς πρώτης ἡλικίας προκόψαντες καὶ τιμηθέντες ὑπὸ πολλῶν, II, 25 (p. 92, 16 f.); cf. also IV, 7 (p. 167, 1); IV, 11 (p. 178, 3).

[8] P. Jouguet, "Inscr. grecques d'Égypte," BCH, 20 (1896), 191, inscr. from Fayum (?), I, 12; the ed. transl. "dans leur fleur."

[9] In this sense the word passed into Rabb. usage (פְּרוֹקְפִּי or פְּרוֹקוֹפִּי, e.g., Ber. r., 12, 16 on 2, 4b); cf. Str.-B., III, 619 on Phil. 1:12; S. Krauss, Griech. u. lat. Lehnwörter im Talmud, Midrasch u. Targum, II (1899), 487a.

[10] In Vett. Val. one also finds προκοπτικός, "progressive," "favourable" (IV, 11 [p. 178, 2]; II, 21 [p. 84, 17]) and the opp. ἀπρόκοπος "without luck or success," II, 25 (p. 92, 30).

[11] E.g., Asclepiades Prusensis in Gal. De compositione medicamentorum secundum locos, I, 2 (Kühn, 12, 413); Herodotus Medicus in Oribasius, Collectionum medicarum reliquiae, 10, 8, 17 (CMG, VI, 1, 2, p. 54).

[12] It is worth noting that προκοπή, by nature a dynamic term, is often used statically : "prosperity," "possessions," "place of honour," "dignity," also "first stage" (→ 718, 21) and "climax" (→ 706, 4; 718, 1 ff.).

[13] The images of growth and progress are combined here, or rather, two images from different spheres are fully assimilated to one another, cf. Philo Fug., 176 : ... αἱ προκοπαὶ καὶ αὐξήσεις καὶ καρπῶν γενέσεις → Stählin, 18, → n. 77.

[14] P. Jandanae, 3, 5 (ed. K. Kalbfleisch [1912], 10 f.).

[15] IPE, I, 47, 6.

[16] Chrysipp. Fr., 217 (v. Arnim, III, 51, 37); cf. Cic. Fin., III, 14, 18 and esp. Plut. De profectibus in virtute (II, 75a-86a).

855, 27 f.) and the tractate of Epict. (Diss., I, 4) περὶ προκοπῆς, cf. also Ep. Socrati-corum, 27 [17] and the expression δι' ὑπερβολὴν εὐφυΐας καὶ σπουδῆς τῆς περὶ τὴν παίδευσιν καὶ σοφίας ἐν προκοπῇ γίνομαι in Jos. Ant., 10, 189. Finally, προκοπή can also denote the climax of the development. [18]

f. In all these forms of προκοπή the reference is to individual development. The use of προκοπή for the general progress of mankind or the world, as in the modern idea of progress, is for various reasons alien to antiquity. These reasons include the doctrine of eternal becoming and perishing (Heraclitus, Aristotle) and the thesis of cosmic perfection (Stoicism).

2. προκοπή as a Technical Term in Stoicism and Its Offshoots.

προκοπή plays a significant role in the system of Stoic ethics. It denotes the way from ἀφροσύνη to σοφία (cf. Chrysipp. Fr., 425 [v. Arnim, III, 104, 18]), from κακία to ἀρετή (Fr., 217 [III, 51, 37]; Fr. 530 [III, 142, 17 f.]; Fr., 532 [III, 142, 33 f.]), and hence from κακοδαιμονία to εὐδαιμονία (cf. Epict. Diss., I, 4, 3). This is the only προκοπή of real value, Epict. Diss., I, 4, 5. Yet in ancient Stoicism it is reckoned only among the μέσα (cf. Chrysipp. Fr., 538 [v. Arnim, III, 143, 35 f.]), the so-called inter-mediate virtues, the προηγμένα (preferred or relatively valuable things, cf. Fr., 126 f. [III, 30, 25 f.; 31, 2-5]; Fr., 136 [III, 32 f.]) which are of service to natural life (συμφώ-νως τῇ φύσει ζῆν, e.g., Epict. Diss., I, 4, 15). The προκόπτων, as ἠργμένος παιδεύ-εσθαι (Epict. Ench., 5), stands between the ἀπαίδευτος and the πεπαιδευμένος (Chrysipp. Fr., 543 [v. Arnim, III, 145, 5 ff.]), the ἰδιώτης (→ III, 215, 31 ff.) and the φιλόσοφος (Epict. Ench., 48). [19] But the doctrinaire strictness of older Stoicism, which unlike the Peripatetics recognises no middle ground between virtue and vice (Chrysipp. Fr., 536 [v. Arnim, III, 143, 15 f.]), sets even the προκόπτοντες among the ἀνόητοι καὶ μοχθηροί, the summe miseri and improbissimi (Fr., 539 [III, 144, 1]; Fr., 530 [III, 142, 34 f.]). [20] Even the one who had advanced furthest on the way of progress (ὁ ἐπ' ἄκρον προκόπτων = ad summa procedens, Sen. Ep., 71, 28 = qui non longe a sapientia abest, Chrysipp. Fr., 425 [v. Arnim, III, 104, 18]), who already fulfils and does not neglect τὰ καθήκοντα (→ III, 438, 13 ff. and n. 2), is not on this account happy, Fr., 510 (III, 137, 43-138, 3). Later Stoicism corrected this doctrine. Thus Sen. differen-tiated the προκόπτων (qui proficit) no less clearly from the stulti (though he is still one of these) than from the vir consummatae sapientiae, Ep., 75, 8; 72, 6. Hand in hand with this correction, however, the ideal of the true sage, still attainable acc. to Chrysipp. (Fr., 544-656 [v. Arnim, III, 146-164]), began to fade increasingly into the distance. [21] Even middle Stoicism concedes that one can find only the προκόπτων and not the sage. Thus Poseidonios places Socrates among the προκόπτοντες, [22] as Zeno had already set Plato, [23] and Sen. says of himself (Vita Beata, 17): non sum sapiens ... nec ero. The upshot — for all intermediary concepts have a levelling tendency — is that all men are regarded as προκόπτοντες. Yet Sen. (Ep., 75, 8) can still maintain: inter ipsos quoque proficientes sunt magna discrimina, and after the pattern of Chrysipp. he

---

[17] Ed. Hercher, op. cit. (→ n. 2), 627; there is a corresponding abs. use of the verb in Just. Dial., 2, 6: ... καὶ προέκοπτον καὶ πλεῖστον ὅσον ἑκάστης ἡμέρας ἐπεδίδουν.
[18] Thus in the summary of life: γέννα, ἀνατροφή, προκοπή, ἀποβίωσις (L. Sternbach, Fabularum Aesopiarum Sylloge [1894], 65) προκοπή has the sense of ἀκμή ("maturity"), cf. also the passages from Cl. Al. → 718, 1 ff.
[19] Cf. Plat. Symp., 204b, where the φιλόσοφος stands between the σοφός and the ἀμαθής, i.e., in the place which the προκόπτων occupies in Stoicism.
[20] In both passages we have the double comparison with those who will drown whether at one ell or 500 fathoms under the sea and with young dogs which have reached the pt. where they can almost see but are still as blind as those just born, Pohlenz, Stoa u. Stoiker, 165.
[21] Putzner, 95; cf. Pohlenz, op. cit., 170.
[22] Cf. Putzner, 97.
[23] Cf. Barth-Goedeckemeyer, 34.

divides them into three stages (Ep., 75, 9. 13. 14) corresponding to the division of the προηγμένα (→ 706, 18) into three groups (Ep., 66).

Stoicism finds in the disposition of man the decisive presupposition for an ἀξιόλογος προκοπή ... πρὸς τὰς ἀρετάς, Chrysipp. Fr., 217 [v. Arnim, III, 51, 37 f.]). Essential to their development, apart from nature, are the instruction (Fr., 532 [III, 142, 32 f.]) of philosophers, the help of friends, and esp. one's own will (ἡ προαίρεσις, Epict. Diss., I, 4, 18): *magna pars est profectus velle proficere* (Sen. Ep., 71, 36). Most important is constant orientation to προκοπή (cf. Seneca's confession concerning himself), [24] to self-perfection, to actualisation in life, Epict. Diss., I, 4, 11, cf. 17. Part of this is the daily self-examination by means of which Sen. observes his progress towards what is good. Hence τρέμειν and πενθεῖν are inseparable from προκοπή, Epict. Diss., I, 4, 12; cf. Phil. 2:12 f.; for there are also momentous regressions, Epict. Ench., 51, 2 : παρὰ μίαν ἧτταν καὶ ἔνδοσιν [25] καὶ ἀπόλλυται προκοπὴ καὶ σῴζεται. Self-knowledge on the part of the προκόπτων is followed by self-accusation, whereas the fool excuses himself and the wise man is guilty of no faults, Chrysipp. Fr., 543 (v. Arnim, III, 145, 6-9); Epict. Ench., 5. This gives us already one of the marks of the προκόπτων which were a concern of Zeno. [26] To these characteristics Plut. devotes the main part (c. 4-17) of his work *On the Recognisability of Progress in Virtue* [27] (De profectibus in virtute [II, 76f-86a]). Similarly Epict. (Ench., 48) enumerates the σημεῖα προκόπτοντος. He gives a description of the προκόπτων in Diss., I, 4, 18-21 and direction for προκοπή in Ench., 12 f. Both chapters begin : εἰ προκόψαι θέλεις, "if you would reach the goal of progress." [28] The goal is σοφία and ἀρετή in one, and hence *eo ipso* εὐδαιμονία and εὔροια, Epict. Diss., I, 4, 3, i.e., the complete personality, cf. I, 4, 24; Sen. Ben., VII, 1, 7 etc. The transition from προκοπή to τελειότης, though it involves a sudden μεταβολή (Plut. De profectibus in virtute, 1 [II, 75c]), takes place without the sage himself being aware of it (διαλεληθὼς σοφός). [29]

B. The Idea of Progress in the Old Testament.

1. The thinking of the OT is supremely historical. The event has absolute theological precedence over the logos. [30] Hence the idea of progress is a natural one here. The historical outlook of the individual sources which have come together in the historical books of the OT includes the thought of progress in salvation history. Yet this progress is never called προκοπή, and in detail the views of progressive salvation history vary a good deal. They do so already in respect of the event which is regarded both as the centre of salvation and also as the goal of the progress. Thus this might be the conquest in the Hexateuch and the Davidic monarchy in the Deuteronomistic view of history.

Nevertheless, there is a common conviction that a divine plan controls God's history. Insight into this naturally implies the thought of "the teleological tension of a history

---

[24] Cf. Pohlenz, *Stoa*, I, 318 f.

[25] ἔνδοσις does not fit too well. In view of ἀπόλλυται — σῴζεται one would expect a positive antithesis to ἧττα; perhaps we should read ἐπίδοσιν [Debrunner].

[26] He drew conclusions from the nature of dreams ; cf. Fr., 234 (v. Arnim, I, 56): ἠξίου ἀπὸ τῶν ὀνείρων ἕκαστον αὐτοῦ συναισθάνεσθαι προκόπτοντος, cf. Pohlenz, *Stoa u. Stoiker*, 164. For something similar cf. Plat. Resp., IX, 571c; Aristot. Eth. Nic., IX, 6, p. 1167b, 4 ff.

[27] As an answer to the assertion of Chrysipp., even the man who has become wise does not know that he is at the end of προκοπή, Plut. De prof. in virt., 1 (II, 75c).

[28] On this use of the aor. → 716, 22 f. and n. 85.

[29] Chrysipp. Fr., 539-541 (v. Arnim, III, 143 f.); Sen. Ep., 71, 4; 75, 9; Philo Agr., 161, 165 etc., cf. I. Heinemann in L. Cohn-I. Heinemann, *Die Werke Philos v. Alex. in deutscher Übers.*, IV (1923), 143, n. 1.

[30] G. v. Rad, *Theol. des AT*, I (1957), 121.

pressing on from promise to fulfilment." [31] Hence God's history does not stand still. In its movement it is like a fountain which catches, gathers and sends forth water in a steady flow, yet which wells up from an ultimate depth. [32] That is to say, all the decisive impulses in this onward movement are from God. They are acts of election and sending, of punishment and rejection in answer to the disobedience and apostasy of the people, but also of new blessings and renewals of the covenant. In particular the conclusions of the covenant are for the Hexateuch the decisive milestones in the progress of salvation history. [33]

The contribution of man to the progress of history is of a different kind. It is true that man is under a divine demand which necessarily impels him to advance positively, to be as God (Lv. 19:2). But this very goal, as the false promise of the tempter (Gn. 3:5), is for man the cause of progress in wickedness as J traces it from the fall of the first man (Gn. 3) to the fall of the sons of God and of all mankind (Gn. 6 and 11). Things are much the same in P (Gn. 6:11 f.) and the Deuteronomist (cf. the typical account in Ju. 2:11-23). [34]

2. Acc. to the historical understanding which controls the historical books historical progress in its various forms is mostly directed to the great goals of the past. At times, however, one also finds a future goal, cf. Ex. 32:34 E. P esp. finds such a goal in the reconstruction of the post-exilic community. Directing itself by the programme set forth in the Mosaic Law, the community advances towards the goal proclaimed in the past. It is in the historical understanding of the prophets, however, that everything is orientated to a future goal. [35] In the prophets, too, all things, all individual events, follow a great plan towards a final end (cf. Is. 10:12; 45:21) which will both vindicate and also give meaning to all that has gone before. This goal is not reached, however, by unbroken progress. It is attained only by a new creation. [36]

3. For the OT the history of the individual as well as that of the people is in movement from a whence to a whither. [37] Thus the stories of the patriarchs give illustrations of the purifying and walking of man before and under God. This is esp. true of Abraham and Jacob, [38] but also of others like Enoch and Noah who attain to a high degree of godliness, → n. 63. Even the later period offers examples like David and the psalmist of Ps. 32. But in most cases, as with the whole people, there is resistance which is overcome and set aside only by the saving intervention and forgiveness of God.

The wisdom of proverbs offers a supreme picture of the active man who seeks merit and progress and regards this as a task imposed by the Creator. [39] Wisdom often speaks of its ἀρχή, Prv. 1:7; 9:10; 15:33; Ps. 111:10. In so doing it also brings into view the goal, the path, and progress towards the goal. The goal here (→ 707, 22 ff.) is an all-round development of the personality, and Joseph, e.g., is the model. [40]

In spite of these in part basic theological ideas of the OT concerning both historical and individual progress, the general concept of a divinely directed προκοπή is never expressed here. This concept is ruled out by the fact that each

---

[31] For this definition of the προκοπή of salvation history in the OT cf. W. Zimmerli, "Das Menschenbild des AT," *Theol. Ex.*, NF, 14 (1949), 8.

[32] Cf. T. C. Vriezen, *An Outline of OT Theology* (1958), 29 ff.

[33] Cf. v. Rad, *op. cit.*, 135-140.

[34] Cf. Eichrodt Theol. AT, III², 99 f.; Zimmerli, *op. cit.*, 11.

[35] Cf. O. Eissfeldt, *Einleitung in d. AT²* (1956), 240 f., 245; Eichrodt Theol. AT, I⁵, 257; also v. Rad, *op. cit.*, 133 f.

[36] Cf. Eichrodt Theol. AT, I⁵, 230-263, esp. 256-260.

[37] Cf. Zimmerli, 10 f.

[38] Philo completely reinterprets the history of the patriarchs when he sees in it an example of humanistic προκοπή, even if in a Philonic sense, → 711, 23 f. and n. 63.

[39] Cf. Zimmerli, 20.

[40] Cf. v. Rad, 429-432; also "Josephsgeschichte u. ältere Chochma," VT Suppl., I (1953), 120-127.

individual event is interpreted *ad hoc*. [41] This is also why the OT does not use any term corresponding to the Greek προκοπή. Only once, not before Sir. (51:17), and here probably through faulty translation, [42] is προκοπή used as a tt. for the way of wisdom : προκοπὴ ἐγένετό μοι ἐν αὐτῇ (sc. τῇ σοφίᾳ), and even here it is doubtful whether the meaning is : "I succeeded in advancing in wisdom," or whether προκοπή should not be taken in the ordinary sense: "Blessing (→ 704, 29 ff.) was imparted to me through wisdom." The context makes it more probable that at least the translator and the readers of the Greek text would think in terms of progress in παιδεία (v. 16) and σοφία (v. 17b) → 713, 8 ff.

C. The Word Group in the Writings of Hellenistic Judaism.

1. Septuagint and Symmachus, Testaments of the Twelve Patriarchs, Epistle of Aristeas and Josephus.

Except at Sir. 51:17, προκοπή [43] occurs in the LXX only in 2 Macc., a work strongly influenced by Hell. thought, and here (8:8) ἔρχομαι εἰς προκοπήν means much the same as πυκνότερον ἐν ταῖς εὐημερίαις προβαίνω, the ref. being to military success, → 705, 12. The same applies to the only instance of προκόπτω in the OT sphere, namely, at ψ 44:5 Σ (LXX καθευοδοῦ).

In other Jewish works in Gk. the group has the same sense as elsewhere. προκόπτω means "to progress" in evil (T. Jud. 21:8 → 704, 19 f.; Jos. Bell., 6, 1; Ant., 4, 59 → 704, 18; 20, 214) or in good (Ant., 18, 340; 20, 205 → 712, 23 f.; Vit., 8), "to move on," Ant., 2, 340; "to reach the goal," Ant., 2, 133, while προκοπή is used in the sense of "progress," "development," Jos. Ant., 10, 189, → 706, 1 f.: γίνομαι ἐν προκοπῇ, "to make great progress," "to develop conspicuously"; "promotion," Bell., 2, 27; 6, 142; "regard," Ep. Ar., 242; Jos. Bell., 1, 195; "prosperity," T. Gad 4:5; [44] "fortune," T. Jud. 15:5 rec. A.

2. προκοπή as an Ethical Concept in Philo.

In some sense Philo stands apart, for he uses ὁ προκόπτων and ἡ προκοπή in a technical sense whose roots are undoubtedly in Stoicism. προκοπή and the προκόπτων (or the ψυχή [45] προκόπτουσα, Fug., 202, 213) are central concepts in his philosophical ethics. [46] In the first instance Philo's view of progress is wholly Hell. or individualistic, [47] and for this reason it is non-eschatological. [48] Though rather differently coloured, its sphere is the same as in Stoicism (→ 706, 11 ff.), and yet Philo transforms it by integrating

---

[41] Cf. v. Rad, *op. cit.* (→ n. 30), 123; also Eichrodt Theol. AT, I⁵, 256.

[42] R. Smend, *Die Weisheit des Jesus Sirach* (1906), 505, *ad loc.*; Str.-B., III, 652 on 1 Tm. 4:15.

[43] The verb does not occur in the LXX (for Σ → line 17; T. Jud. 21:8 → 704, 19 f. and cf. Jos.), though at 3 Macc. 5:18 LXX cod. A one should probably read προκοπτούσης (vl. προβαινούσης) τῆς ὁμιλίας for προσκοπτούσης; cf. Just. Dial., 11, 5 : προκοπτόντων ἡμῖν τῶν λόγων.

[44] (Of envy and hatred) ἐν προκοπῇ ἀκούων καὶ ὁρῶν πάντοτε ἀσθενεῖ, "he always becomes sick when he sees or hears of someone who is fortunate."

[45] But προκοπὴ ψυχῆς presupposes and includes προκοπὴ σώματος.

[46] On this section cf. esp. Völker I, 47-350.

[47] Cf. Völker I, *passim* ; Volz Esch., 59 f. The end of Exsecr. (164-172) is something of an exception, but here, too, non-eschatological and individualistic allegorising is in the background, cf. 172 and already 159-161. Similarly Philo regards τὰς πρὸς βελτίωσιν ἐπιδόσεις in the generation from Seth to Moses primarily as stages of development of the advancing soul, Poster. C., 174. There is a related impulse towards applying the thought of προκοπή to the whole race in Ebr., 34 (on this cf. M. Adler in Cohn-Heinemann, *op. cit.*, V [1929], 19, n. 3) but due to Philo's individualistic interest this is not followed up.

[48] The OT hope of a national future is all transferred to the individual in Philo, cf. Volz Esch., 60-62, 131 f. In place of the NT ἀνάστασις of θνητὰ σώματα (R. 8:11) Philo (Sacr. AC, 10) has ἡ πρὸς τὸν ὄντα μετανάστασις ψυχῆς τελείας, "the transition of the perfect soul to being."

it into the theocentric understanding of biblical thought, i.e., by contrasting προκοπαί (with αὐξήσεις and βελτιώσεις → 704, 23 ff.) as human with God as the ἴσος αὐτὸς ἑαυτῷ καὶ ὅμοιος, Aet. Mund., 43.

As the Stoa finds the source of προκοπή in φύσις, so for Philo the ἀρχὴ προκοπῆς is τὸ εὐφυές (Sacr. AC, 120) or εὐφυΐα. [49] This is the first member in the basic ethical triad : εὐφυΐα, [50] προκοπή, ἀρετὴ τελεία, Leg. All., III, 249. In Philo, however, φύσις is not just the starting-pt. It is also the *agens* of προκοπή to the degree that ἡ ἀρίστη φύσις is identical with God, Fug., 172. In fact Philo can say that the first and last source of all προκοπή is God Himself, [51] so Leg. All., II, 93 : The soul must admit that all its progress is from God and may not ascribe it to itself ; Agric., 168 : προκοπαί with εὐμάθειαι and τελειότητες are among the gifts of φύσις or indeed the gifts of God's grace (χάριτες), cf. 2 C. 9:8; Mut. Nom., 24 : The one who progresses reaches perfection (only) by divine beneficence, cf. also Poster. C., 154. On the other hand the human teacher of the προκόπτων (Fug., 172) [52] and the προκόπτων himself are most important for προκοπή. In the last resort Philo is in this matter, too, a champion of synergism. [53]

To these three main agents and promoters of προκοπή correspond the main impulses : to God εὐφυΐα, to the teacher μάθησις [54] or παραίνεσις (Leg. All., I, 93 f.) and διδασκαλία (Sacr. AC, 7), and to the man who makes progress ἄσκησις. [55] Part of this is the pitiless war against sin, πάθη and the world [56] and unceasing πόνος and κάματος which is tolerable only προκοπῆς χάριν (Sacr. AC, 113). But it is worth while when one can exchange πόνος for προκοπή (Sacr. AC, 112 and 114) and at the last τελειότης for προκοπαί (Ebr., 82); for the controlling urge in the προκόπτων is σπεύδειν ἀεὶ πρὸς ἀκρότητα, Mut. Nom., 2. The field of προκοπή is the whole sphere [57] of the good and the true, wisdom and virtue. Progress in knowledge, in θεωρήματα φρονήσεως (Agric., 158), always goes hand in hand with ethical progress, ἀρετή being commensurate with the given state of μάθησις. [58]

In virtue of all these efforts and achievements the προκόπτων is highly estimated in Philo, esp. when compared with the one who is only just entering the way of μάθησις. In contrast to the Stoa (e.g., Chrysipp. Fr., 510 [v. Arnim, III, 137 f.]) Philo can speak of the constancy, firmness and unswerving perseverance of the προκόπτων, whom he

---

[49] Cf. Chrysipp. Fr., 366 (v. Arnim, III, 89, 15 ff.); Fr., 136 (33, 14 ff.); Fr., 716 (180, 14 ff.). Acc. to Philo it consists of 3 elements : εὐθιξία, ἐπιμονή and μνήμη, Leg. All., I, 55; cf. Cher., 102; Som., II, 37.

[50] There is in Philo a εὐφυΐα which renders all προκοπή superfluous. Par. to the chief ways of προκοπή, i.e., ἄσκησις and μάθησις, it is thus ranked as the supreme way of perfection (in contrast 1 C. 12:31), so Poster. C., 130-169; Praem. Poen., 49-51; its type and representative is Isaac, *ibid.,* 31; Poster. C., 132-153 and → n. 63. This is one of the many cases in which Philo's statements are obviously full of tensions and obscurities in detail and he has not brought his rich allegorical interpretation of OT passages into a fully harmonious system, cf. Völker I, 1-12 etc., e.g., 121 f., 193 f.

[51] On this theme cf. Völker I, 117-121.

[52] Here Philo says that a teacher can produce προκοπαί but only God ἐπ' ἄκρον τελειότης.

[53] Cf. Völker I, 105-116.

[54] *Ibid.,* 158-198.

[55] *Ibid.,* 198-239.

[56] *Ibid.,* 105-154.

[57] Typical of this breadth is the wealth of genitives which Philo can combine with ὁ ἀσκητής (= ὁ προκόπτων), cf. Leg. All., III, 144 and 169; Poster. C., 78; Som., I, 152 etc.: on the one side σοφίας (Ebr., 48; Virt., 4), φρονήσεως (Leg. All., I, 80; Som., II, 65 and 134), ἐπιστήμης (Det. Pot. Ins., 3), φιλοσοφίας (Omn. Prob. Lib., 43; Vit. Cont., 69), τῆς ἀληθείας (Leg. All., III, 36), on the other τῆς ἀρετῆς (Som., II, 133), τῶν καλῶν (Migr. Abr., 153), καλῶν ἔργων καὶ λόγων (Abr., 37; cf. Det. Pot. Ins., 35), εὐσεβείας (Sobr., 40), ὁσιότητος (Spec. Leg., I, 271), καρτερίας (Det. Pot. Ins., 17; Leg. All., III, 11). In all these things the ἀσκητής or προκόπτων is concerned to progress.

[58] Cf. Völker I, 197 and n. 6.

ranks next after the σοφός, Som., II, 237. He extols the sure convictions of the προ-κεκοφότες in distinction from οἱ ἄρτι μανθάνειν ἀρχόμενοι, Det. Pot. Ins., 12. To this degree, again in contrast with Stoicism, he can reckon προκοπή, with διδασκαλία and προφητεῖαι on the one side, σπουδή and ἔρως τοῦ κατορθοῦν [59] on the other, among the ἀγαθά (Congr., 112), or, with εὐμάθειαι and τελειότητες, among the χάριτες, the gifts of God's grace, Agric., 168 → 710, 9 ff. If the προκόπτων sometimes comes close to the τέλειος here, the wide gulf between them is usually emphasised (cf. esp. Leg. All., III, 140-144), most pregnantly perhaps in the definition of προκοπή in Leg. All., III, 249 : ἀτελὲς ἐφιέμενον τοῦ τέλους, and again when Philo speaks of the προκόπτων as the ἀτελής (Agric., 160) or of the ἀτελέστερος καὶ ἐπιπόνῳ προ-κοπῇ χρώμενος, Det. Pot. Ins., 46. [60] To this essential "imperfection" corresponds his middle position, [61] which Philo, like the Stoa, depicts in various ways : μεθόριος ... ἁγίων καὶ βεβήλων "settled in the border territory between the sacred and the pro-fane") ... ἀποδιδράσκων μὲν τὰ φαῦλα, μήπω δ᾽ ἱκανὸς ὢν τελείοις συμβιοῦν ἀγαθοῖς, Fug., 213, or, in another image : he lives ἐν τῇ μεταξὺ χώρᾳ ζώντων καὶ τεθνηκότων, the living being those espoused to φρόνησις and the dead those espoused to ἀφροσύνη, Som., II, 234. Often Philo explicitly dwells on this middle position of the προκόπτων (μέσος, ἀσκητής) between φαῦλος (κακός) and τέλειος (σπουδαῖος, ἄριστος) (Som., II, 234-237; I, 151 f.; Mut. Nom., 19 and 23; Leg. All., I, 93), or, if προκοπή alone is in view, between the ἀρχόμενος (μανθάνειν) and the τετελειω-μένος (Agric., 159; cf. 160, 165; similarly προκοπαί are between ἀρχαί and τελειό-τητες, Agric., 157). [62]

These various stages Philo finds represented in many OT examples [63] with whose help he expounds the goal as well as the way of προκοπή. Concerning this goal he can say on one occasion that here the ψυχὴ προκόπτουσα becomes a φέγγος οὐράνιον and that then, like the full moon at the end of its παραύξησις, it will present the attained stages of perfection — perfect σοφία, ἀρετή and εὐδαιμονία (cf. Leg. All., III, 140, 147, 249; Abr., 58) — as a spotless sacrifice to God (Congr., 106).

---

[59] Like κατόρθωμα (Leg. All., I, 93) this is one of the tt. which Philo took from Stoicism.

[60] The προκόπτων for his part is imperfect in knowledge, Fug., 202 : οὔπω γάρ ἐστιν ἱκανὴ ψυχὴ προκόπτουσα τῷ σοφίας ἀκράτῳ ποτῷ χρῆσθαι, cf. 1 C. 3:1 f. He has al-ready the vision of the incorporeus intelligibilisque mundus (Quaest. in Gn., III, 42, cf. Völker I, 191-196; Bréhier, 152-157), but not that of God Himself, → n. 63, cf. Det. Pot. Ins., 31. On the other side he is also imperfect in his ethical life, only δεύτερος as com-pared with the θεοφιλής (Leg. All., II, 81), the τέλειος, who already has ἀπάθεια while the προκόπτων only has μετριοπάθεια (ibid., III, 131 f.; cf. Völker I, 134). He is still in danger of slipping back instead of going forward (Som., I, 152) and even in danger that the ἄλογος ὁρμή (→ V, 468, 35 ff. though cf. 468, 29 ff.) will completely "burn up" προ-κοπή again, Leg. All., 249.

[61] Völker I, 233 etc.

[62] The difference in the opening members (φαῦλος — ἀρχόμενος) means that a fourfold climax is possible (Leg. All., III, 159 : the φιλήδονος corresponds to the φαῦλος). Some-times Philo finds two stages of the τέλειοι, a definitive and a provisional. At the latter are those just perfected (Agric., 165) who are not even aware of their perfection (161, cf. the σοφὸς διαλεληθώς of Stoicism → 707, 26) and who are not yet confirmed in ἀρετή (160, 158; cf. Chrysipp. Fr., 510 [v. Arnim, III, 137 f.]). The twofold antithesis of the προ-κόπτων, to the φαῦλος and the τέλειος, yields a distinctive evaluation of the OT names for God : θεός corresponds to the προκόπτων, κύριος and δεσπότης to the φαῦλος, κύριος θεός to the ἄριστος καὶ τελειότατος, Mut. Nom., 19.

[63] The chief OT examples of προκοπή are Abraham, Jacob and Aaron (cf. Poster. C., 78), those of τελειότης Noah (Abr., 47), Isaac (e.g., Det. Pot. Ins., 46) and Moses (e.g., Leg. All., II, 81 and 91). Jacob, however, changes from a σύμβολον πόνου καὶ προκοπῆς (Sacr. AC, 120) to the paradigm of a τέλειος, as illustrated in the changing of his name to Israel (cf. Ebr., 82; Conf. Ling., 72; E. Stein in Cohn-Heinemann, V, 121, n. 1; M. Adler, ibid., 34, n. 4); for Philo derives this name from ראה and takes it to mean "he who beholds God" (→ III, 372, 10; V, 337, n. 113), θεωρία θεοῦ being the mark of the τέλειος as ἐξ ἀκοῆς καὶ ὑφηγήσεως μανθάνειν is of the προκόπτων, Sacr. AC, 7.

D. The Word Group in the New Testament.

1. Linguistic Data.

a. προκοπή and προκόπτω are not *voces biblicae* in the true sense. They belong to the definitely Hellenistic elements in NT Greek. It is thus worth noting that on the one side they occur only occasionally (nine times in all) and that on the other they are found only in authors who are more strongly influenced by the educated *koine* or even borrow more extensively from the language and thought-forms of the Cynic-Stoic diatribe: Paul (Gl. 1:14; R. 13:12; Phil. 1:12, 25) and his pupil Luke (Lk. 2:52), cf. also the Past. (1 Tm. 4:15; 2 Tm. 2:16; 3:9, 13). [64] In the transmission of the *logia* of Jesus, even in the later strata, the words do not occur, nor are they found in John, who at this point too shows that his true roots are not in a western-shaped Hellenism.

b. In part the authors take προκόπτω phrases and their use quite simply from everyday speech, cf. ἡ νὺξ προέκοψεν in R. 13:12 with ... τῆς νυκτὸς προκοπτούσης in Jos. Bell., 4, 298; ἡ ἡμέρα προκόπτει in Just. Dial., 56, 16. With οὐ προκόψουσιν ἐπὶ πλεῖον (the heretics) in 2 Tm. 3:9 cf. (Artaxerxes) οὐ βουλόμενος ... τὸν Εὐαγόραν ἐπὶ πλεῖον προκόπτειν ("be successful," "win power" → 704, 29 f.) in Diod. S., 14, 98, 3; ἐπὶ πλέον ... προκόψαι ἐν ῥητορικῇ in M. Ant., I, 17; (ἀλαζονεία) ... τὴν ἐπὶ πλέον παραύξησιν οὐ λαμβάνει in Philo Virt., 162; ἑώρων ἀβλαβεῖς ἐπὶ τὸ πολὺ προκεκοφότας in Jos. Ant., 2, 340; cf. also 18, 181 (προύκοπτεν ἐπὶ μέγα). With ἐπὶ πλεῖον ... προκόψουσιν ἀσεβείας in 2 Tm. 2:16 (→ n. 79) cf. Jos. Ant., 20, 205 : καθ᾽ ἑκάστην ἡμέραν ἐπὶ μέγα προύκοπτε δόξης. With πονηροὶ ἄνθρωποι καὶ γόητες προκόψουσιν ἐπὶ τὸ χεῖρον in 2 Tm. 3:13 cf. τὰ ... πάθη προύκοπτεν καθ᾽ ἡμέραν ἐπὶ τὸ χεῖρον in Jos. Bell., 6, 1; συνέβη τὴν πόλιν ἡμῶν νοσεῖν προκοπτόντων πάντων ἐπὶ τὸ χεῖρον in Ant., 20, 214; (the rebellion of Korah) χαλεπωτέραν ἐλάμβανε τῆς ἐπὶ τὸ χεῖρον προκοπῆς αἰτίαν in Ant., 4, 59; *v.* also (ἡ φύσις) πρὸς τὸ χεῖρον οἴχεται φερομένη in Plut. De profectibus in virtute, 3 (II, 76e).

c. Nevertheless, in three passages we catch echoes of popular Hell. philosophy, though these are none too distinct. With Ἰησοῦς προέκοπτεν ἐν τῇ σοφίᾳ καὶ ἡλικίᾳ κτλ. in Lk. 2:52 (→ 713, 14 ff.) and προέκοπτον ἐν τῷ Ἰουδαϊσμῷ in Gl. 1:14 cf. Plut. De profectibus in virtute, 10 (II, 81d) → 705, 24 f.; ἀνὴρ ἐν φιλοσοφίᾳ μεγάλην ἔχων προκοπήν in Diod. S., 16, 6, 3; Luc. Hermot., 63 → 705, 23; → n. 3; M. Ant., I, 17 → line 18; and esp. with Lk. 2:52 cf. προκόπτων τῇ ἡλικίᾳ in Apollonius, Vita Aeschinis, 4; [65] [τῇ] τε ἡλικίᾳ προκόπτων καὶ προαγόμενος εἰς τὸ θεοσεβεῖν in Ditt. Syll.³, II, 708, 18 (→ II, 942, 30 ff.): καθ᾽ ἡλικίας προκοπή in Cl. Al. Ecl. Proph., 18, 1. [66] With ταῦτα μελέτα, ἐν τούτοις ἴσθι, ἵνα σου ἡ προκοπή φανερὰ ᾖ πᾶσιν in 1 Tm. 4:15 cf. the personal use of προκοπή e.g.: σὺ οὖν ἐνταῦθά μοι δεῖξόν σου τὴν προκοπήν in Epict. Diss., I, 4, 12 (cf. Jm. 2:18).

d. With no recognisable external borrowing Paul himself seems to have coined the statements in Phil. 1:12 : τὰ κατ᾽ ἐμὲ μᾶλλον εἰς προκοπὴν τοῦ εὐαγγελίου ἐλήλυθεν (→ 715, 18 ff.) and v. 25 : μενῶ καὶ παραμενῶ πᾶσιν ὑμῖν εἰς τὴν ὑμῶν προκοπὴν καὶ χαρὰν τῆς πίστεως (→ 715, 1 ff.).

2. The προκοπή of Individuals.

a. In most instances, as in Hell. usage, προκοπή has a personal subj. in the NT : Lk. 2:52; Gl. 1:14; 2 Tm. 3:9, 13, probably also 2:16 (→ 716, 1 ff. and n. 79); 1 Tm. 4:15.

---

[64] Though cf. Bonhöffer, 128.
[65] Ed. F. Blass, Aeschinis Orationes² (1908), 6, 11.
[66] Cf. also the synon. expression προβαίνω τῇ ἡλικίᾳ, Vett. Val., II, 10 (p. 65, 21).

Only in a few instances (and only in Pl.) is the subj. material: ἡ νύξ in R. 13:12; τὸ εὐαγγέλιον in Phil. 1:12; probably ἡ πίστις (→ 715, 6 ff.) in Phil. 1:25.

b. The personal progress to which the NT refers is partly individual, as in Hellenism (→ 705, 17 ff.; 706, 5 ff.), and partly collective (2 Tm. 3:9, 13; 2:16; cf. Phil. 1:25). Closest to the widespread use in popular philosophy are the verses which speak of the personal progress of individuals (Lk. 2:52; 1 Tm. 4:15; at a somewhat greater distance Gl. 1:14).

What the Hellenist Luke says about Jesus in Lk. 2:52 (προέκοπτεν ἐν τῇ σοφίᾳ) sounds like a Hellenistic element, but it is not.

It was a common practice of the biographers and novelists of antiquity to emphasise the harmonious physical and intellectual development of their heroes and the favour which they received on every hand. Lk. appears to follow this practice in the three par. summaries (1:80; 2:40, 52) with which he rounds off three sections in his story. [67] If so, it is possible that προκόπτω ἐν σοφίᾳ was a current expression, though, so far as we know, the technical language of the philosophers and their friends [68] preferred to speak more cautiously only of progress in φιλοσοφία, μαθήματα, παιδεία (→ 705, 21 f.) and the like, → 706, 11 ff. Another possibility is that Lk. 2:52 is based on Sir. 51:17 (→ 709, 2 ff.), προκοπὴ γίνεταί μοι ἐν σοφίᾳ being regarded as obviously synon. to προκόπτω ἐν σοφίᾳ. This is at least just as convincing as an allusion to 1 S. 2:21, 26; 3:1; Prv. 3:1-4, in which the LXX uses neither προκόπτω, σοφία, ἡλικία, nor χάρις (the context is different in Prv. 3:3). [69] If this is correct, then it is an indication that the ref. is not to the wisdom of Hell. philosophy but to the chokma ideas of later Judaism, as in other instances of → σοφία in the Synoptic tradition, e.g., Lk. 7:35; 11:49. That the thought of Lk. 2:52 is in any case to be understood on Jewish presuppositions is supported by the Jewish Christian colouring of the introduction to Lk. which concludes with this v., and esp. by the definitely non-Hell. par. in 2:40 (and 1:80): ἐκραταιοῦτο (πνεύματι) πληρούμενον σοφίᾳ. Lk. has in view the σύνεσις of Jesus, of which he has just given an example (v. 47), [70] and also Jesus' own saying (11:31 Q) about His wisdom, which is greater than that of Solomon and which should evoke faith along with His κήρυγμα (= summons to repentance, v. 32). In the combination of προκόπτω (προκοπή) with ἡλικία, which is commonly attested elsewhere (→ 712, 33 ff.), the ref. is usually to age (→ II, 942, 30 ff.); in view of the par. to v. 40 it is possible that Lk. 2:52 has in view bodily stature (→ II, 943, 1) (προκόπτω ἡλικίᾳ = αὐξάνω). But it is even more probable that for Lk. ἡλικία (→ II, 942, 36) is spiritual maturity (cf. Eph. 4:13) (προκόπτω ἡλικίᾳ = κραταιοῦμαι πνεύματι in Lk. 1:80; 2:40 vl. cf. Eph. 3:16 → III, 913, 3 ff.). There is an obvious allusion to the OT in the third member, the twofold χάρις, favour with both God and man, cf. 1 S. 2:26; Prv. 3:4; [71] Sir. 45:1. Hence Lk. fills the biographical outline (→ line 10) with a very different content. Only 2:40, not 2:52, refers to physical growth. Even in 2:40 the emphasis is on spiritual progress, and this is the exclusive ref. in 2:52. In both verses divine χάρις replaces general popularity

---

[67] Cf. the passages adduced → 712, 29 ff. and n. 66, also Wettstein on Lk. 2:52; A. Fridrichsen, "Randbemerkungen zur Kindheitsgesch. des Lucas," *Symb. Osl.*, 6 (1928), 36-38 and the material presented there.

[68] But cf. the passage from Jos. Ant., 10, 189 → 706, 2 f., also Ael. Arist. Or., 46 (Dindorf, II, 405): προκοπὴ τῆς σοφίας.

[69] Luke's quotations, of course, seldom agree exactly with the LXX as we know it; even in 2:40 and 1:80 he has ηὔξανεν for ηὐξήθη.

[70] On the next occasion his sources (cf. Mk. 6:2) gave him the chance to speak of Jesus' wisdom Lk. has λόγοι τῆς χάριτος (4:22; → III, 38, 18 ff.). Like the other Evangelists he also emphasises that the strongest impression was made by Jesus' ἐξουσία, not His σοφία, 4:32.

[71] The LXX as we know it is not the original here either (1 S. 2:26 ἀγαθόν; Prv. 3:4 καλά). The combination of χάρις and σοφία might come from Prv. 3:4 Mas., but it occurs elsewhere in the NT, cf. Ac. 7:10; 6:8, 10; Eph. 1:8.

(→ n. 67), for χάρις παρ᾽ ἀνθρώποις is only an earthly reflection of being beloved of God, cf. 9:35.

Luke no more follows up these beginnings of the προκοπή of Jesus than do the other Evangelists. It is also questionable whether the sources justify us in speaking of the progress of Jesus in respect of awareness of His way and person, or indeed of His moral development (cf. at most Hb. 5:8 f.), as presupposed in so many reconstructions of His life. [72]

The NT concept is relatively closest to the Hellenistic in 1 Tm. 4:15. Timothy's προκοπή is the development of the χάρισμα imparted to him by the πρεσβυτέριον at ordination, v. 14. It is advance in faith and conduct (v. 12) and adjustment by παράκλησις and διδασκαλία (v. 13). It is to be visible, for he is to show himself hereby to be a τύπος for believers (v. 12) as a διάκονος Χριστοῦ Ἰησοῦ (v. 6), an ἄνθρωπος θεοῦ (6:11) and an εὐαγγελιστής (2 Tm. 4:5). Two points are significant here: 1. that the true spiritual progress of the Christian is visible to others as well as himself (→ 707, 17 ff. and n. 27), and 2. that although in the pastoral exhortation of this section προκοπή seems to be a matter of human effort (ταῦτα μελέτα, ἐν τούτοις ἴσθι), in the last resort, as the development of a grace, it is like all genuine NT προκοπή a gift of God, → 710, 9 ff.; 711, 6. [73]

In what is probably the oldest occurrence of προκόπτω in the NT at Gl. 1:14 Paul, reviewing his non-Christian past, [74] is speaking of his progress in becoming a full Jew (ἐν τῷ Ἰουδαϊσμῷ → III, 383, 18 f.). This was greater than that of his contemporaries. προκοπή is manifested here in theoretical and practical ζῆλος in the sphere of the ancestral religion (πατρικαὶ παραδόσεις). One may also conjecture that an additional element in προκοπή here is that of going ahead in a contest between several young Jews who are faithful to the Law (there is something of the same image in 1 Tm. 4:15, cf. v. 7 f.). At any rate, προκοπή has here, at least primarily, the character of a human achievement, so that it is for Paul the subject of human καύχημα, → III, 648, 20 ff., cf. Ac. 22:3 and on the other hand Phil. 1:25 f.; 1 C. 1:29, 31; 2 C. 10:15-17. But now (vv. 15 ff.) this προκόπτειν has almost an ironic undertone, [75] for it is the very opposite of what Paul to-day regards as προκοπή (cf. Phil. 1:12, 25; also 1 Tm. 4:15) and is more what 2 Tm. 2:16 calls an ἐπὶ πλεῖον προκόπτειν ἀσεβείας (R. 1:18; 5:6 with ref. to the Jews too), an ἐπὶ τὸ χεῖρον προκόπτειν (2 Tm. 3:13).

3. The προκοπή of the Community and the Gospel.

More plainly than the individual use of προκόπτω (προκοπή) in the NT the parallel use with reference to the community and the Gospel (Phil. 1:25, 12) gives evidence of a distinctive NT development of the term.

---

[72] Cf. as two different examples A. Schweitzer, Gesch. der Leben-Jesu-Forschung⁴ (1926), 392-443; M. Goguel, Das Leben Jesu (1934), 252-256. On the question of moral development cf. H. Strathmann, Der Brief an d. Hb., NT Deutsch, 9⁷ (1954) on 4:14-5:10.

[73] Cf. Stählin, 22 f. with n. 24. H. v. Campenhausen, Polykarp v. Smyrna u. die Past. (1951), 27 claims that this passage is closely related to Pol., 12, 3: ut fructus vester manifestus sit in omnibus, ut sitis in illo perfecti (retransl. by v. Campenhausen: ἵνα ὁ καρπὸς ὑμῶν φανερὸς ᾖ ἐν πᾶσιν). It is true that the characteristic thought of progress is here replaced by that of fruit. Like the whole letter, this saying of Polycarp is a web of NT reminiscences. On the par. concepts of progress and growth — fruit cf. Stählin, 14 f., 18 f., 20 f.

[74] Cf. E. Barnikol, Die vorchr. u. frühchr. Zeit d. Pls. (1929), 13, n. 2; also 31-46 (though the transl. of προκόπτω as "to come into prominence," "to outstrip," "to excel" is not quite accurate).

[75] When Paul looks back as a Christian his picture of the past becomes a kind of counterpart of the then greatly revered figure of the θεῖος ἀνήρ → III, 122, 17 ff.

In Phil. (1:25 → 712, 41 f.) two interpretations are possible. One can either take προκοπή abs. as personal προκοπή (as in 1 Tm. 4:15) in the sense of spiritual growth (→ 713, 34 ff.), or one can take it along with χαρά and relate it like this to πίστεως. In this case ὑμῶν goes with the total expression and thus acts, perhaps rather pleonastically, along with the immediately preceding ὑμῖν (though this is under the influence of the παρά in παραμενῶ). This understanding: "for a joyous furtherance of your life of faith," or (more freely): "for a cheerful advance in faith," is probably more in keeping with Paul's use of complex expressions and his line of thought elsewhere.

> Although there is only one faith (Eph. 4:5) which is the basis of salvation, Paul (→ 218, 34 ff.), like Jesus Himself (cf. Mk. 4:24b, 25a) can speak of different measures and stages of faith (R. 12:3; cf. Mt. 8:10; 15:28; 17:20; 1 C. 13:2, 7, also 1 Th. 3:10) and consequently of progress or growth in faith (cf. Lk. 17:5; 2 C. 10:15; 2 Th. 1:3, also Eph. 4:29 vl.). For Paul the *movens* of this προκοπή is the fact that he stays alive and can thus continue his work in the community (v. 26; R. 1:11 f.; 15:29). In short, it is his apostolic ministry. In the last resort, however, the ultimate force behind all genuine προκοπή is always for Paul the πνεῦμα. [76]

Phil. 1:12 is the counterpart of Phil. 1:25, → 712, 39 ff. As Paul's work serves the προκοπή of the life of faith of the congregation, his suffering serves the προκοπή of the Gospel. We can no longer say with certainty what were the detailed circumstances which Paul had in view. Obviously the mere fact of his imprisonment, which he suffers as a Christian, acts as a missionary *agens* among both pagans and Christians. That the Gospel advances does not mean only that it continues its victorious march through the world in spite of Paul's elimination; it means also that the power of the Gospel increasingly develops in the heart (v. 14), and that it does so in such a way as to become a missionary impulse and thus to serve the propagation of the Word, → III, 857, 14 ff. [77]

4. The προκοπή of Heresy.

The Pastorals, especially 2 Tm., speak of an antithesis to the προκοπή of the Gospel and God's community. This is the προκοπή of heresy and false teachers. Here, too, there is (at first) a προκοπή which is nourished by otherworldly powers. It can be compared to a growth, yet not to the organic growth of the fruit given by God, but to the vile growth of the cancer (2 Tm. 2:17). Its power is not that of the Word of God but the power of πλάνη which is effected by the πλάνος κατ' ἐξοχήν (cf. v. 26; 2 Jn. 7) and which continually gives rise to new πλάνη, 2 Tm. 3:13: false teachers are πλανῶντες καὶ πλανώμενοι. [78] This προ-

---

[76] Cf. Joh. W. 1 K., 72. The interpretation of προκοπή in Loh. Phil., *ad loc.* ("progress is … not to be diverted from the way of martyrdom but to tread it to the end with inner and outer steadfastness") expresses a genuine truth but it is too narrow in relation to Phil. 1:25.

[77] On the par. use of the metaphors of advance and growth with ref. to the Word or the Gospel (Ac. 6:7; 12:24; 19:20; Col. 1:6) cf. Stählin, 21; on the related idea of growth in general, *ibid.*, 13-16; → 281, 40 ff.; O. Bauernfeind, "Wachsen in allen Stücken," ZSTh, 14 (1937), 465-494. Jn., too, is perhaps referring to the progress of the Word in 8:37, cf. Pr.-Bauer[5], *s.v.* χωρέω, 2. The relation between mission and suffering hinted at in Phil. 1:12 may be seen throughout primitive Chr., cf. G. Stählin, Art. "Urchr. Mission," *Evangelisches Kirchenlex.*, II (1958), 1340.

[78] The punning expression "deceived deceivers" is not just conventional here (as against Dib. Past.[3], *ad loc.*; H. Braun, → 230, 30 f.; 249, 24); like δίκαιος καὶ δικαιῶν (R. 3:26) or the "redeemed redeemer" (cf. W. Schmithals, *Die Gnosis in Korinth* [1956], 82-134) it carries a full stress on both parts.

κοπή, then, is a constant increase in distance from God (2:16) [79] and to this extent in depth of perdition (3:13 : ἐπὶ τὸ χεῖρον). [80] The threefold use of προκόπτω a parto peiore (→ 704, 17 ff.) in a fairly short passage (2 Tm. 2:16-3:13) is perhaps the author's answer to the claim of heretics that they were progressive theologians (cf. the synon. προάγων in 2 Jn. 9 → I, 130, 39 ff.). [81] The progress of heresy is part of the πληθυνθῆναι of ἀνομία (Mt. 24:12) and hence of the pre-Messianic tribulation. [82] But like this (cf. Mt. 24:22, 13) the progress has a limit, 2 Tm. 3:9 : οὐ προκόψουσιν ἐπὶ πλεῖον.

5. The προκοπή of the Aeons.

What has been said thus far has shown that the use of προκοπή and προκόπτω in the NT, except when the reference is to individuals (esp. Lk. 2:52; Gl. 1:14), always has eschatological overtones. This is clearest in R. 13:12, where Paul clothes his view of the transition of the aeons, and his eschatological awareness of the rapid march of time (cf. v. 11), in the image of passing night (→ IV, 1125, 37 ff.) and dawning day (→ II, 953, 20 ff.) which he took from Rabbinic exposition of Is. 21:11 ff.: [83] ἡ νὺξ προέκοψεν, ἡ δὲ ἡμέρα ἤγγικεν. προκόπτω here, like ἐγγίζω, denotes the ambivalent interim [84] between the aeons which intersect in the Still of the one and the Not Yet of the other. The aorist προέκοψεν shows on the one side that the night is far spent. It is that time of night when especially deep darkness holds sway just before the dawn. Here is an illustration of mounting tribulation just before the end. Nevertheless — and this is the important side — this aorist [85] also carries with it the thought that the night is almost over; it is already time to wake up (v. 11). This note on the time is a decisive aspect of Paul's exhortation (v. 12b-14).

In this awareness of the progress of the divinely appointed times there is no room for any ideas of the progress of the human race in the history of this world. This is as remote from the NT as it is from the popular philosophy of the age,

---

[79] The gen. ἀσεβείας is perhaps directly dependent on προκόψουσιν (cf. Thuc., IV, 60, 2), in which case κενοφωνίαι is the subj.: "the empty babblings of the false teachers will constantly increase ungodliness." All the same 1. it is unlikely that this class. construction of προκόπτω and gen. ("to promote"), which is not found after Thuc., should be used in the NT, and 2. the continuation in v. 17 makes it even more probable that the heretics themselves are the subj.

[80] The connection between ungodliness and perdition is just as close as that between faith and salvation, cf. 1 Pt. 2:8. In view of the par. (→ 712, 20 ff., cf. also προκόπτω ἐπὶ τὸ βέλτιον, → 704, 20 f.) one may assume that προκόπτω ἐπὶ τὸ χεῖρον is a stereotyped phrase. The loose relationship of ἐπὶ τὸ χεῖρον suggested by Wbg. Past., ad loc. ("they will increase their following, but to their greater destruction") is thus not very likely.

[81] In 2 Jn. 9 we find the same antithesis between progressing and abiding as in 2 Tm. 3:13 f. Cf. W. Lütgert, Die Irrlehrer d. Past. (1909), 66.

[82] Jewish apc. often speaks of a step-like increase in eschatological afflictions, cf. S. Bar. 27 (12 stages); bSanh., 97a, 5 Bar. (Str.-B., IV, 981 f [λ] seven). For the eschatological increase of evil cf. also Jub. 23:22 f.; 4 Esr. 5:2, 10 and other ref. in Str.-B., IV, 982 etc.

[83] Cf. Str.-B., IV, 853 f., 855; III, 749, though the Rabb. took the passage differently : While it is day for Israel it is night for the Gentiles, cf. Str.-B., I, 164, 599 f.; IV, 248, 1028a, 3.

[84] It is the same element which characterises the προκόπτειν of the philosophers as an intermediary stage (ὁ προκόπτων = ὁ μέσος), → 706, 15 ff.; 711, 12 ff.

[85] This is also to be seen in Epict. (→ 707, 21 f.) cf. Diss., II, 17, 40 : ἐγγὺς ἐσόμεθα τοῦ προκόψαι, also III, 19, 3; IV, 2, 4; Ench., 51, 1 [Debrunner]. The perf. can have much the same sense, e.g., Jos. Ant., 2, 133 : τὴν ὁδὸν προκεκοφέναι, "to have reached the goal of the journey," cf. also Philo Det. Pot. Ins., 12 (→ 711, 1 f.) and also the ἤγγικεν corresponding to προέκοψεν in R. 13:12, cf. Mk. 1:15 and par.

though for very different reasons (→ 706, 5 ff., also 708, 38 ff.). On the biblical view history as "world" history is devoid of teleology and hence also of progress. [86] Only on the soil of the Gospel — and at a very different level — may one see a divinely ordained προκοπή in "history."

E. The Word Group in the Older Post-NT Literature.

1. Post-Apostolic Fathers and Apologists.

In post-NT Chr. writings there is at first no specific or theological use of the word group. In particular, the thought of the NT seems not to have had any noticeable influence at this as at many other points. The only use of προκόπτω in the post-apost. fathers is in 2 Cl., 17, 3 : ... πειρώμεθα προκόπτειν ἐν ταῖς ἐντολαῖς τοῦ κυρίου. In form (exhortation) as in content this reflects the legal understanding of the Chr. life common in the group. The means to the required progress are νουθετεῖσθαι ὑπὸ τῶν πρεσβυτέρων (in regular worship) and then (at home) μνημονεύειν τῶν τοῦ κυρίου ἐνταλμάτων; the danger is ἀντιπαρέλκεσθαι ἀπὸ τῶν κοσμικῶν ἐπιθυμιῶν; the mark πάντες τὸ αὐτὸ φρονοῦντες; the goal ἵνα ... συνηγμένοι [87] ὦμεν ἐπὶ τὴν ζωήν.

The use of προκόπτω in the extant works of the early Apologists is that of contemporary speech, Just. Dial., 11, 5 → n. 43; 56, 16 → 712, 14 f. Only in Just. Dial., 2, 6 do we find the usage of the popular philosophers of the day. Introduced by one such teacher to Platonic philosophy, Just. says about himself, προέκοπτον καὶ πλεῖστον ὅσον ἑκάστης ἡμέρας ἐπεδίδουν, → n. 3. This daily progress is due to the teacher (→ 707, 5 ff.; 710, 13 ff., 17 f.), his instruction, intercourse with him, and the τῶν ἀσωμάτων νόησις καὶ ἡ θεωρία τῶν ἰδεῶν thereby attained. The goal is the τέλος τῆς Πλάτωνος φιλοσοφίας : αὐτίκα κατόψεσθαι τὸν θεόν → 719, 19 f.; n. 63. On the other hand Iren. often speaks of προκόπτειν to God, e.g., IV, 11, 2; 38, 3; yet he fights against the concept of development taught by the Gnostics, who call themselves the progressives, → 716, 4 f. [88]

2. Clement of Alexandria.

Cl. Al. makes extensive and significant use of the verb προκόπτω and even more so of the noun προκοπή. With the works of Stoicism and those of Philo his writings are a third group in which προκοπή-προκόπτω are tt. for the whole system. As Philo draws on Stoicism, so does Cl. Al. on both. Yet (1) the idea of progress has even broader significance and finds even more varied use in Cl. Al. than in his predecessors and (2) it has a fuller bibl. content than in Philo. As always in Cl. Al. Stoic and Platonic ideas are here subject to the NT. [89] An important contribution is made to Cl.'s rich system of thought by a special development of the meaning of προκοπή. In Cl. this means not merely "progress," "ascent step by step" (e.g., Exc. Theod., [90] 15, 1: κατὰ

---

[86] Cf. K. Barth, K.D., IV, 1 (1953), 567 (C.D. [1956], 508): World history is Adamic ; it is Adam's history. It began in and with his history and will always correspond to it. This is God's Word and judgment on it. This is the reason why it is so terribly monotonous, why there can be no progress in it. *Ibid.*, 565 (506 f.): We have to accept the awful fact that, though progress in detail cannot be denied, the establishment of progress in world history as a whole, while often attempted, has always proved impossible ... In spite of all the changes in historical form and action, man himself is not "progressive."

[87] The eschatological sense of συνάγω is confirmed by what follows (cf. Mt. 3:12; 13:30; Did., 9, 4; Mart. Pol., 22, 3 etc.). Similar to the use of 2 Cl. is that of προκόπτω and προκοπή in Serapion of Thmuis, Sacramentarium (in Didascalia Constit. Apostolorum, ed. F. X. Funk, II [1905]), 3, 3; 11, 4. 6; 13, 15. 16. 19; 15, 2.

[88] Cf. W. Bousset, *Kyrios Christos*[2] (1921), 352-355.

[89] Cf. Stählin, *Die altchr. gr. Lit.* (1924), 1316; Völker II, 49, n. 2; 50, n. 2; 332-354; H. Chadwick, Art. "Clemens, Titus Flavius, v. Alex.," RGG[3], I, 1836.

[90] In Exc. Theod. one cannot always be certain whether the usage and thought are those of Cl. himself or of the Valentinian Theodotus, cf. (ed.) R. P. Casey, *The* Excerpta ex

προκοπήν [91] τελειούμενοι) but also the "step" and esp. the "highest step" (Exc. Theod., 12, 2; Strom., II, 75, 2 : ἡ μεγίστη πασῶν προκοπή, Fr., 24 on 1 Pt. 1:12 : *profectus perfectionis*), with approximation to the sense of "completed ascent," "stage of perfection" (*v.* also Strom., VI, 102, 5; cf. 103, 1; also Exc. Theod., 11, 1; 17, 3; 19, 3; Strom., VII, 68, 4). It can then mean "rank," "place of honour" (→ 705, 10 ff.; 719, 37 f.; Strom., VI, 107, 2 : αἱ ἐνταῦθα κατὰ τὴν ἐκκλησίαν προκοπαὶ ἐπισκόπων, πρεσβυτέρων, διακόνων), also in heaven (Strom., VII, 47, 7: κατὰ τὰς ὀφειλομένας ἐνθέους προκοπάς τε καὶ διοικήσεις, Exc. Theod., 11, 1 → 719, 3 f.). Indeed, it can denote Christ's *status exaltationis* (4, 1: ἵνα μάθῃ [sc. ἡ ἐκκλησία] τὴν προκοπὴν αὐτοῦ [sc. Christ] μετὰ τὴν ἐκ τῆς σαρκὸς ἔξοδον). More concretely προκοπαί (*profectus*) is then used with ref. to the angelic hierarchy in Fr., 24 on 1 Pt. 3:22 and Jd. 6.

Cl. Al. sees in endless [92] progress one of the divinely established basic principles of all creation. Strom., VI, 152, 3 : "Every creature has developed and still develops and thus continually advances to become a better being than it was" (προκόπτον εἰς τὸ αὐτοῦ ἄμεινον; [93] cf. also VI, 154, 1). [94] Cl. Al. values προκοπή so highly [95] that he believes it will continue in the world to come : eternal life must mean eternal progress, [96] → n. 103. For him progress is esp. a function of salvation history and it is thus a term which characterises his thinking in this sphere. The divine rule of the world (ἡ θεῖα διοίκησις, Strom., VI, 154, 1) embraces all mankind, Greeks and barbarians, philosophers and ἑτερόδοξοι (= the men of the Bible), in this progress towards the goal of salvation (Strom., VII, 11, 2 : from Gk. as from Jewish προκοπή [= preliminary stage] God leads to τελείωσις through the Chr. faith ; cf. also VI, 153, 1; 154, 1). In virtue of the goal προκοπή itself, including that of onetime pagans, can be called ζωή (II, 47, 2 on the basis of Lv. 18:5). [97] There thus follow successively, both οἰκονομικῶς (on the basis of the divine plan of salvation) δεδομέναι, the Law and the Gospel καθ' ἡλικίαν καὶ προκοπήν (according to the temporal stage of development), II, 29, 2; cf. IV, 130, 4. [98]

For Cl. Al. the starting-pt. of the human ascent is the longing to be different ; this is the first step to becoming, VI, 50, 6. At the early stages we also find φόβος (e.g., Ecl. Proph., 19, 1) and out of this ἀποχὴ τῶν κακῶν (= ἐπιβάθρα προκοπῆς μεγίστης, Strom., IV, 135, 1; cf. VII, 49, 1). [99] The decisive basis and power of all genuine προκοπή, however, is faith, Strom., VII, 55, 5. Progress first moves ἐκ πίστεως εἰς πίστιν (II, 126, 3), though it then moves beyond πίστις to γνῶσις (IV, 136, 5; Ecl. Proph., 19, 1). For the πιστός who has become the γνωστικός a new stage of ascent begins ; its starting-pt. is contemplation of the cosmos and its development, κοσμογονία, Strom., IV, 3, 1 f.

Bifurcation is even more evident in what is said about the means of progress. On the one side the means, as in Philo (→ 710, 17 ff.), are ἄσκησις καὶ διδασκαλία (Strom.,

---

Theodoto of *Clement of Alex.* (1934), esp. 98 f.; (ed.) F. Sagnard, *Clément d'Alex., Extraits de Théodote* (1948), 10, 59, n. 4 (προκοπή = mot charactéristique de Clément, hence used to distinguish Cl.'s maginal notes from the statements of Theod., *v.* p. 59, n. 2).

[91] This prepositional use is very common in Cl. Al. with various shades of meaning.

[92] The τέλειον is at least very far distant in Cl. Al.

[93] Though cf. O. Stählin in his transl. (Clement IV, *Bibliothek d. Kirchenväter* [1937]).

[94] Cf. Völker II, 89. In particular Cl. Al. "in a grand scheme views the whole of human existence as an unceasing development, an organic growth, which by a slow ascent leads to greater heights," Völker II, 388.

[95] In this evaluation of προκοπή Cl. Al. obviously differs from the Stoics, for whom it has only provisional worth (→ 706, 15 ff.), and also from Philo (→ 711, 12 ff.). Hence it is only partly true to say that in Cl. Al. the προκόπτων occupies a middle position similar to that in Philo and the Stoics (cf. Barth-Goedeckemeyer, 269), for with him the true Gnostic is the προκόπτων, the highest stage of humanity.

[96] J. Patrick, *Clement of Alexandria* (1914), 167.

[97] Cf. the different interpretation of Paul (Gl. 3:12), from whom Cl. Al. often diverges considerably.

[98] Cf. on this Völker II, 262-270.

[99] *Ibid.,* 299 f.

II, 75, 2), i.e., the work of the προκόπτων himself and that of his teachers. On the other side God, as in all creation, is the giver of progress, as expressed already in the phrase προκοπὴν (ἀπο)λαμβάνω (VII, 68, 4; Exc. Theod., 11, 1 → 704, 13) or the interpretation of the yoke of Mt. 11:30 in Strom., II, 126, 3 : Christ is the ἡνίοχος, "who drives each of us κατὰ προκοπήν to salvation." On these divine elements rests the "ethical optimism" [100] of the true Gnostic, namely, the conviction : εἰς τὸ ἄμεινον ἀεὶ τὴν προκοπὴν προϊέναι, Strom., VII, 45, 3. In terms of Cl.'s view of salvation history the chief means of advance on the Gk. side are general culture and philosophy (Strom., VI, 83, 1; I, 27, 2) and on the OT side the Law (→ 718, 28 ff.). But above both is the Gospel, the γνῶσις βάρβαρος, into whose teaching philosophy, too, must merge if it is to be προκόπτειν εἰς ἀλήθειαν (Strom., VI, 153, 1). For the Gospel is the true sphere of ascent for the true γνωστικός (IV, 130, 4; cf. II, 29, 2), since it is the source of γνῶσις, which is the power as well as the instrument and goal of true προκοπή, cf. VII, 49, 1; 66, 1; IV, 136, 5.

The goal of προκοπὴ γνωστική (Strom., IV, 170, 4) or the προκοπαὶ μυστικαί, to which γνῶσις leads man "by a light peculiar to itself" (VII, 57, 1), can be indicated and described in very different ways, whether simply and compendiously as αὐτὸ τὸ ἀγαθόν (VII, 45, 3), or with the Stoics as εὐδαιμονία (II, 126, 3) and ἀπάθεια (VII, 10, 1), or with Plato (and the mysteries) as the "vision of God" (VII, 68, 4; cf. 57, 1), or with the mystery cults as ἀπαθανατίζειν (IV, 160, 3 : "through the chain of births," beginning with baptism, "in a gradual ascent to immortality"), as θειότης [101] (V, 102, 2) and τελείωσις (cf. VI, 151, 1; VII, 11, 2), or with the Gnostics as γνῶσις (→ 718, 33 ff.), σύνεσις (VI, 154, 1) and ἀλήθεια (VI, 153, 1), also as the ἀνὴρ τέλειος (VI, 107, 2 : ἄχρις ἂν εἰς τέλειον ἄνδρα αὐξήσωσιν). Yet the last five terms (and also "vision of God") are also taken from the NT (ἀνὴρ τέλειος esp. usually bears a ref. to Eph. 4:13, Strom., e.g., VII, 10, 1). Thus for Cl. the goal of the mystical progress of the Gnostic can be the ἑνότης τῆς πίστεως (Eph. 4:13, VI, 87, 2), σωτηρία (II, 126, 3), υἱοθεσία (Ecl. Proph., 19, 1; called the μεγίστη πασῶν προκοπή in Strom., II, 75, 2), and the heavenly κληρονομία which can be both heavenly γνῶσις (Strom., VII, 10, 1) and heavenly ἀνάπαυσις, cf. VII, 57, 1. If Cl. seldom follows the NT use of προκοπή and προκόπτω (though cf. κατὰ προκοπὴν πίστεως, Strom., VII, 60, 2 with Phil. 1:25, also Exc. Theod., 61, 2), in his concept of the progress of the true Gnostic and its goal he is more influenced by the world of thought of the NT than anything else. The γνωστικός of Cl. Al., for all his significant Gnostic experiences in this world, is looking forward to the world to come in which further προκοπαί await him — προκοπαί not merely in the sense of progress but also in that of higher degrees and places of honour. [102] For in Cl. the heavenly destiny is not the same for all, cf. → III, 349, 21 ff. and esp. 350, n. 36. [103] It is manifold and graded κατὰ τὴν ἰδίαν προκοπήν (Ecl. Proph., 57, 2) or κατ' ἀξίαν (often, e.g., Strom., V, 102, 2). [104]

Stählin

---

[100] Cf. Völker II, 514 with n. 2.

[101] *Ibid.*, 597-609.

[102] *Ibid.*, 524 with n. 2, 3.

[103] Like much else, what is said about this gives evidence of inconsistency and tension in Cl. Al., → n. 50. The NT says nothing about προκοπή after death, though the eschatological term ζωή seems to imply dynamic development rather than static being. For an espousal of eschatological προκοπή cf. F. H. Brabant, *Time and Eternity in Christian Thought* (1936).

[104] These ideas of Cl. Al. are more broadly developed in his pupil Origen, cf. Princ., IV, 4, 10; also W. Völker, *Das Vollkommenheitsideal des Orig.* (1931), 62-75) and esp. in Greg. Nyss., whose προκοπή concept is regarded by many as the main element in his teaching (cf. W. Völker, *Greg. Nyss. als Mystiker* [1955], 186, n. 4 and 131-143, 186-195) and who, like Cl. Al., believes in ἀεὶ προκόπτειν, In Cantico Canticorum, 12 (MPG, 44, 1037 B). Even in the Western Church Christianised Stoic concepts of progress had a partial though not very profound influence, cf. Aug. De Officiis, II, 3; Ep., 167, 12 f.; Boethius De Consolatione Philosophiae, IV, 7, 15 (CSEL, 67, 105). They were then trans-

πρόκριμα → III, 953, 1 ff.	προνοέω → IV, 1009, 29 ff.
προκυρόω → III, 1100, 18 ff.	πρόνοια → IV, 1011, 3 ff.
προλαμβάνω → IV, 14, 30 ff.	προοράω → V, 381, 7 ff.
προμαρτύρομαι → IV, 512, 33 ff.	προορίζω → V, 456, 12 ff.
προμεριμνάω → IV, 589, 1 ff.	προπάσχω → V, 924, 24 ff.

πρός

Prep. with gen., dat. or acc., common from Hom., also in LXX; in NT once with gen., 6 times with dat., 679 with acc. As the epic (strictly pre-consonantal) form προτί shows, πρός derives from a (pre-vocalic) *προτj ; it is related to Sanskr. *práti* "over against" and Lat. *pretium* (cf. also *per* etc.).

The general sense of πρός is "(immediately) before"; with the gen., however, it expresses a going out "from," with the dat. being "before" or "by" something, with the acc. movement "to" something.[1] As an adv. in the sense "besides" it does not occur in the NT but is found in the post-apost. fathers, → 721, 9 f.

A. πρός with the Genitive.

In the NT πρός with gen. occurs only in a special instance in which with a noun in a predicative position it has the transferred sense of "to be essential for someone or something," namely, at Ac. 27:34 :[2] τοῦτο γὰρ πρὸς τῆς ὑμετέρας σωτηρίας ὑπάρχει, "for this (eating of the food blessed by Paul) is essential for (i.e., belongs to) your deliverance."[3]

There is a similar constr. in 1 Cl., 20, 10 : παρέχονται τοὺς πρὸς ζωῆς ἀνθρώποις μαζούς, "they (the sources) offer the breasts which are important for the life of men."

---

mitted through Scholasticism to Luther, who espoused them at least in his earlier works. Like the Stoics and Philo Luther distinguishes three (recognisable) stages in the *profectus* of the Chr. life, and like Greg. Nyss. he can speak of *infiniti gradus de claritate in claritatem, de virtute in virtutem, ex fide in fidem,* WA, 3, 512, 26. He finds scriptural support for his view of progress in sanctification at 2 C. 3:18; ψ 83:8; R. 1:17, also Jn. 1:16; 2 C. 4:16; Phil. 3:13. In his later works, however, Luther refers the same verses to progress in faith and to the advance from the old covenant to the new in salvation history ; cf. on this L. Pinomaa, "Die *profectio* bei Luther," *Gedenkschrift f. W. Elert* (1955), 119-127.

π ρ ό ς. Bibl. on prep → διά, II, 65; → εἰς, II, 420; → παρά, V, 727. More specifically : Z. Grundström, De usu praepositionis πρός apud Thuc. (1873); Kühner-Blass-Gerth, II, 1, 515-521; W. A. Lamberton, "πρός with the Acc.," *Publications of the Univ. of Pennsylvania, Series in Philology,* I, 3 (1891), 1-47; H. Jacobsohn, "Die Präp. πρός," *Zschr. f. vergleichende Sprachforschung,* 42 (1909), 277-286; Radermacher[2], 137-146; Johannessohn Präpos., 259 f.; Moult.-Mill., *s.v.*; A. T. Robertson, *A Grammar of the NT*[5] (1931), 622-626, cf. Index, 1281 f., 1441; Mayser, II, 2 § 127 (Bibl.); Schwyzer, I, 400 f.; II, 508 f.; Liddell-Scott, *s.v.*; Pr.-Bauer[5], *s.v.*; Bl.-Debr.[9] § 239 f.

[1] Schwyzer, I, 400 f.; II, 508-517; Pokorny, 815 f.
[2] B. Reicke, "Die Mahlzeit mit Pls. auf den Wellen des Mittelmeeres Act. 27:33-38," ThZ, 4 (1948), 401-410.
[3] Not final as, e.g., "serves your deliverance." As a linguistic form the final expression in Jos. Ant., 16, 313 has at root no connection with Ac. 27:34, though σωτηρία is the main word there too : πρὸς τῆς τοῦ βασιλεύοντος σωτηρίας, "with a view to the welfare of the king." Here the constr. is adverbial, whereas it is predicative in Ac. 27:34. The adv. form is secondarily related to the predicative, but strictly they are distinct, as against Moult.-Mill., 544. The sense in Jos. is explained by the fact that *mutatis mutandis* the Greek often says *ab oriente versus* instead of *ad orientem versus,* Kühner-Blass-Gerth, II, 1, 515, cf. Hdt., III, 101: πρὸς νότου ἀνέμου, "to the south" (lit. "reckoned by the south wind"). Transf. this gives the logical sense "with ref. to."

This is, of course, an attributive rather than a predicative expression, but one has only to put an ὄντας before μαζούς and there is an immediate kinship with Ac. 27:34. [4]

B. πρός with the Dative.

1. Spatial. a. To denote place, "before," "at," "by." Topographically πρὸς τῷ ὄρει Mk. 5:11; πρὸς τῇ θύρᾳ, πρὸς (vl. ἐν) τῷ μνημείῳ, Jn. 18:16; 20:11. Anatomically πρὸς τοῖς μαστοῖς, "about the breast," Rev. 1:13; [5] ἕνα πρὸς τῇ κεφαλῇ καὶ ἕνα πρὸς τοῖς ποσίν, Jn. 20:12. b. To denote direction, pleonastically with a dative verb: ἐγγίζοντος δὲ αὐτοῦ ἤδη πρὸς τῇ καταβάσει τοῦ ὄρους, "when he drew near to the descent of the mount," Lk. 19:37. On the other hand with transition to the acc.: προσκολληθήσεται πρὸς τὴν γυναῖκα αὐτοῦ, Mk. 10:7 vl.; Eph. 5:31.

2. Quantitatively : "besides." Not in the NT, but cf. 1 Cl., 17, 1: πρὸς τούτοις.

C. πρός with the Accusative.

This is very common and denotes movement "towards." In this case, which is also the most important theologically, πρός is almost par. to εἰς → II, 420 ff. A radical difference which is often overlooked is that with πρός the movement breaks off on the frontier of the object sought whereas with εἰς it is continued right on into the object.

1. Spatially, "to or towards someone or something," primarily with an intransitive or transitive verb expressing movement.

a. Intransitive : "to go" etc. The goal is usually a person, e.g., ἀναβαίνειν ... πρὸς τοὺς ἀποστόλους, "to," Ac. 15:2; ἔρχομαι πρὸς ὑμᾶς, 2 C. 13:1. At times the house of the person is in view : ἀπῆλθον οὖν πάλιν πρὸς αὐτούς, "to their home," Jn. 20:10. With verbs in εἰς denoting entry into a house etc. πρός is used for the final personal approach, εἰσῆλθεν πρὸς τὸν Πιλᾶτον, Mk. 15:43; ἦλθον πρὸς αὐτὸν εἰς τὴν ξενίαν, Ac. 28:23; cf. 11:3; 16:40; 1 Th. 1:9, also the theologically important verses Ac. 10:3 : ἄγγελον τοῦ θεοῦ εἰσελθόντα πρὸς αὐτόν (Cornelius); Rev. 3:20 : εἰσελεύσομαι πρὸς αὐτὸν καὶ δειπνήσω μετ' αὐτοῦ. προσαγωγή too (→ I, 133, 20 ff.; V, 1011, 25 ff.; 1012, 17 ff.) can be followed by a πρός : προσαγωγὴ πρὸς τὸν πατέρα, Eph. 2:18 (→ 722, 9 ff.). Here πρός denotes near approach without actual entry, while εἰς has a more "mystical" sense ; cf. how πρός in Jn. 7:33; 16:5 : ὑπάγω πρὸς τὸν πέμψαντά με, safeguards the person of God. The reference is often to the coming of someone to be received into religious fellowship (cf. the word "proselyte" → 727, 14 ff.).

E.g., ἐξεπορεύετο πρὸς αὐτὸν Ἱεροσόλυμα or πᾶσα ἡ Ἰουδαία χώρα, Mt. 3:5; Mk. 1:5; σὺ ἔρχῃ πρὸς μέ, Mt. 3:14; βλέπει τὸν Ἰησοῦν ἐρχόμενον πρὸς αὐτόν, Jn. 1:29; εἶδεν Ἰησοῦς τὸν Ναθαναὴλ ἐρχόμενον πρὸς αὐτόν, Jn. 1:47; οὐδεὶς δύναται ἐλθεῖν πρός με ἐὰν μὴ ὁ πατὴρ ... ἑλκύσῃ αὐτόν, Jn. 6:44, → 722, 7 ff.

---

[4] A similar πρός is found esp. in literary Gk., e.g., οὐ πρὸς τῆς ὑμετέρας δόξης τάδε, "this does not accord with your reputation," Thuc., III, 59, 1; οὐ γὰρ ἦν πρὸς τοῦ Κύρου τρόπου ἔχοντα μὴ ἀποδιδόναι, "for it was not the manner of Cyrus to have and not to pay," Xen. An., I, 2,11. This πρός simply amplifies the partitive gen. in cases like δοκεῖ ταῦτα καὶ δαπάνης μεγάλης καὶ πόνων πολλῶν καὶ πραγματείας εἶναι, "this seems to be combined with great expense as well as much toil and effort," Demosth. Or., 8, 48. Cf. Lat. alicuius esse in the sense "to be essential for someone or something." Kühner-Blass-Gerth, II, 1, 374, n. 2; Schwyzer, II, 515 f.; Bl.-Debr.[9] § 240, 1.

[5] In such instances we often find the dat. of relation, Bl.-Debr.[9] § 197.

b. Transitive: "to send," "to bring," "to lead," etc., e.g., ἤγαγον αὐτὸν (τὸν πῶλον) πρὸς τὸν Ἰησοῦν, Lk. 19:35; προσκόψῃς πρὸς λίθον τὸν πόδα σου, Mt. 4:6 par. Lk. 4:11. A definitely theological expression of this kind occurs in Jn. 12:32: πάντας ἑλκύσω πρὸς ἐμαυτόν. Jesus says here that after His lifting up He will win all men from the devil and draw them to Himself, i.e., bring them into fellowship with Him (cf. 10:16),[6] with reference both to the Church and also to heavenly glory. To the coming of the individual into religious fellowship (→ 721, 32 ff.) there thus corresponds his being drawn into fellowship, whether by Jesus as here, or by the Father as in Jn. 6:44, → 721, 36 f. This is also the point of προσαγωγή πρὸς τὸν πατέρα in Eph. 2:18 (→ 721, 28 ff.), where the chief word can be taken either intransitively or transitively. But the preposition can also be used of adherence to idols: πρὸς τὰ εἴδωλα ... ἤγεσθε ἀπαγόμενοι, 1 C. 12:2. The idea of adherence to the Lord is close to that of conversion to God or Christ: ἡνίκα ... ἐπιστρέψῃ πρὸς κύριον, 2 C. 3:16; ἐπεστρέψατε πρὸς τὸν θεὸν ἀπὸ τῶν εἰδώλων, 1 Th. 1:9; turning again to one's brother is a counterpart in Lk. 17:4: ἐὰν ... ἑπτάκις ἐπιστρέψῃ πρὸς σέ.

c. In passive forms of verbs of motion, which have the sense of the perfect and which are to be construed intransitively, πρός takes on the meaning of "with," "by," "before" someone or something even though it is used with the accusative, for the perfect expresses both the movement and also the ensuing state, and in this case the latter is the more important.

Examples: ἦν ὅλη ἡ πόλις ἐπισυνηγμένη πρὸς τὴν θύραν, "at the door," Mk. 1:33; δεδεμένον πρὸς θύραν, Mk. 11:4; ἐβέβλητο πρὸς τὸν πυλῶνα, "he lay at the door," Lk. 16:20; (συγ)καθήμενος ... πρὸς τὸ φῶς, Mk. 14:54 par. Lk. 22:56; ἡ ἀξίνη πρὸς τὴν ῥίζαν ... κεῖται, "lies at the root," Mt. 3:10 par. Lk. 3:9.

This construction can be loosely used in cases where there is no relation to a verb of motion.

Examples with εἶναι: πρὸς ἡμᾶς εἰσιν "among," Mt. 13:56; ἕως πότε πρὸς ὑμᾶς ἔσομαι, Mk. 9:19 (μεθ᾽ ὑμῶν in Mt. 17:17); ἦν πρὸς τὸν θεόν "with," Jn. 1:1 f. Cf. ἵνα ἡ ἀλήθεια ... διαμείνῃ πρὸς ὑμᾶς in Gl. 2:5 and also with a simple μένειν and various compounds.[7]

In some of these cases, however, movement to the object may be assumed even though on the surface πρός expresses only being "with" or "by" it. Cf. πρὸς σὲ (I come and) ποιῶ τὸ πάσχα, Mt. 26:18; ἕνεκα τοῦ φανερωθῆναι ... πρὸς ὑμᾶς, "in order that it might be manifest among you," 2 C. 7:12; μὴ πάλιν ἐλθόντος μου ταπεινώσῃ με ... πρὸς ὑμᾶς, 12:21; πρὸς ὃ δύνασθε ἀναγινώσκοντες νοῆσαι, "where you may (turn,) read and understand," Eph. 3:4; ἡ ἐμὴ παρουσία πάλιν πρὸς ὑμᾶς (with reference to both coming again and staying), Phil. 1:26; ἵνα ὁ λόγος ... τρέχῃ καὶ δοξάζηται καθὼς καὶ πρὸς ὑμᾶς, "even as with (when it came to) you," 2 Th. 3:1. Here one might have expected a dative; the accusative which replaces it is the result of attraction by the context.

Formulae: τὰ πρός τι, e.g., τὰ πρὸς τὴν θύραν, "what is toward the door," "the place before the door," Mk. 2:2; τὰ πρὸς τὸν θεόν, "that which pertains to God," R. 15:17; Hb. 2:17; 5:1; τί πρὸς ἡμᾶς; "what is that to do with us?" Mt. 27:4; τί πρὸς σέ; Jn. 21:22 f.

---

[6] B. Weiss, Das Ev. d. Joh., Krit.-exegetischer Komm. über d. NT[6] (1880), on Jn. 12:32.
[7] Cf. Pr.-Bauer[5], s.v., III, 7.

d. With ἀποστέλλω and πέμπω alongside a verb of speaking in the sense "to bring or impart a message," πρός denotes the recipient (Mt. 27:19; Mk. 3:31; Lk. 7:19; Jn. 1:19; Ac. 19:31); the verb of speaking may be left out (Ac. 10:33). This use is in accordance with the function of πρός with pure verbs of speaking, → lines 8 ff.

2. Psychologically, "to, towards," with verbs or nouns which express the movement of an intellectual content to a specific object.

a. With verbs of speaking: "to say or import something to someone." In a secular sense πρός is properly used instead of a simple dative only in authors who have certain connections with the dialogue form of Greek biography, namely, Luke and John (Lk. 1:13, 18 f. etc.; Ac. 1:7; 2:37 etc.; Jn. 2:3; 3:4 etc.). Only once do we find this use in Mt. (3:15 vl.), never in Mk., and rarely elsewhere (Phil. 4:6) if certain reflexive and reciprocal instances, which demand special attention, are not counted (cf. Mk. 9:33 f.). With these exceptions πρός τινα λέγειν and the like are reserved for the divine address and they do not mean only "to speak to someone" but "to direct a word to someone," "to cause him to be smitten by a word,"[8] e.g., πρὸς τὸν Ἰσραὴλ λέγει, R. 10:21; (λέγει) πρὸς τὸν υἱόν, Hb. 1:8 (cf. 1:7, 13; 5:5; 7:21; 11:18). Here the reference is unquestionably to God's direct address to Israel or Christ. Yet He is not just telling them something. He is giving them a special position or task in salvation history. The relevant Word of God has reference to them and has an effect on them.

For similar cases with OT quotations or parables of Jesus cf. πρὸς αὐτοὺς τὴν παραβολὴν εἶπε, Mt. 12:12; ὤμοσεν πρὸς Ἀβραάμ, Lk. 1:73; πρὸς ἡμᾶς τὴν παραβολὴν ... λέγεις ἢ καὶ πρὸς πάντας, "to" and also "with ref. to," 12:41; ἤρξατο πρὸς τὸν λαὸν λέγειν τὴν παραβολήν, 20:9; ἐκείνους ... πρὸς οὓς ὁ λόγος τοῦ θεοῦ ἐγένετο, "unto whom the word came," Jn. 10:35; τὴν πρὸς τοὺς πατέρας ἐπαγγελίαν γενομένην, Ac. 13:32 (cf. 26:6 vl.). With such verbs as "to pray," "to swear," "to blaspheme," God or Jesus can often be the recipient denoted by πρός, e.g., δεήθητε ... πρὸς τὸν κύριον, Ac. 8:24 (→ II, 807-808 [προσ]εύχομαι); βλασφημία (→ I, 622-624) πρὸς τὸν θεόν, Rev. 13:6.[9]

We also find λέγειν πρός τι, "with ref. to": ἔλεγεν παραβολὴν αὐτοῖς πρὸς τὸ δεῖν πάντοτε προσεύχεσθαι, "with ref. to the necessity," Lk. 18:1. Similarly, Lk. in a dialogue can say ἀποκρίνομαι πρός τινα (for τινί), Lk. 4:4; 6:3; Ac. 3:12; 25:16, also ἀνταποκριθῆναι πρὸς ταῦτα, "to reply to" (Lk. 14:6); cf. οὐκ ἀπεκρίθη αὐτῷ πρὸς οὐδὲ ἓν ῥῆμα, "he answered him to never a word" (Mt. 27:14).

b. With verbs and nouns which express an affective attitude to someone or something, whether friendly or hostile, and often in relation to God, one's neighbour, or the power of evil.

Friendly: πεποίθησιν, παρρησίαν ἔχειν πρός, 2 C. 3:4; 1 Jn. 3:21; πίστις πρὸς τὸν θεόν, 1 Th. 1:8; μακροθυμεῖν πρός, 5:14; ἤπιον εἶναι πρός, 2 Tm. 2:24; ἐνδείκνυσθαι πραΰτητα πρός, Tt. 3:2. Also of a friendly act: ἐργαζώμεθα τὸ ἀγαθὸν πρός, Gl. 6:10, or a friendly relation: διαθήκην διατίθεμαι πρός, Ac. 3:25; Hb. 10:16; εἰρήνην ἔχομεν πρὸς τὸν θεόν, Rev. 5:1; κοινωνία, συμφώνησις πρός, 2 C. 6:14 f.

Hostile: γογγύζω, γογγυσμὸς πρός, Lk. 5:30; Ac. 6:1; ἐν ἔχθρᾳ ὄντες πρὸς αὐτούς, Lk. 23:12; διακρίνομαι πρός, Ac. 11:2; εἴ τι ἔχοιεν πρὸς ἐμέ, "if they should

---

[8] After the pattern of the OT the divine Word is regarded as a mighty force, J. Pedersen, Israel, I/II (1920), 127 f.; L. Dürr, Die Wertung des göttlichen Wortes im AT u. im Alten Orient (1938), 123; H. Ringgren, Word and Wisdom (1947), 157-164; → IV, 92, 9 ff.; 107, 5 ff.; 118, 15 ff. λέγω.

[9] On the other hand πρὸς ἑαυτὸν προσηύχετο in Lk. 18:11 is analogous to πρὸς ἑαυτὸν λέγειν.

have anything to allege against me," 24:19; ἀσύμφωνοι πρὸς ἀλλήλους, 28:25; πρᾶγμα ἔχειν πρός, 1 C. 6:1; πάλη πρός, Eph. 6:12; μομφὴν (vl. ὀργὴν) ἔχειν πρός, Col. 3:13; πικραίνομαι πρός, 3:19; πρὸς τὴν ἁμαρτίαν ἀνταγωνιζόμενοι, Hb. 12:4.

The sense may also be neutral when the ref. is to non-blameworthy conduct towards someone : ἀσκῶ ἀπρόσκοπον συνείδησιν ἔχειν πρὸς τὸν θεὸν καὶ τοὺς ἀνθρώπους, "in relation to," Ac. 24:16; ἐν ἁγιότητι ... ἀνεστράφημεν ... πρός, 2 C. 1:12; ἐν σοφίᾳ περιπατεῖτε πρὸς τοὺς ἔξω, Col. 4:5.

3. Temporal : a. Of approach to a point in time : πρὸς ἑσπέραν, "toward evening," Lk. 24:29. b. Of duration up to the fulfilling of a given span : πρὸς καιρόν, "for a while," Lk. 8:13; 1 C. 7:5; πρὸς ὥραν, "for a certain time," Jn. 5:35; 2 C. 7:8; Gl. 2:5; Phlm. 15; πρὸς καιρὸν ὥρας, "for a period of time," 1 Th. 2:17; πρὸς ὀλίγας ἡμέρας, "for a few days," Hb. 12:10; πρὸς ὀλίγον, "for a moment," Jm. 4:14; πρὸς τὸ παρόν, "for the present," Hb. 12:11. This temporal πρός refers mostly to the future and is thus fairly close to πρός final (→ infra).

4. Final : a. Of the aim of a given action "with a view to," even "for the sake of" : ἡ ἀσθένεια οὐκ ἔστιν πρὸς θάνατον ἀλλ᾽ ὑπὲρ ... ἵνα ... "will not lead to death," Jn. 11:4; οὗτος ἦν ὁ πρὸς τὴν ἐλεημοσύνην καθήμενος, "for the sake of," "to acquire," Ac. 3:10. So probably πρὸς πᾶσαν συνείδησιν (acc.) ἀνθρώπων, "with a view to general agreement on the part of men," 2 C. 4:2; [10] ἐνδείκνυσθαι σπουδὴν πρὸς τὴν πληροφορίαν τῆς ἐλπίδος, "to show zeal for the full development of hope," Hb. 6:11. [11]

Other examples : πρὸς τὴν ἔνδειξιν τῆς δικαιοσύνης, "for the demonstration," R. 3:26; πρὸς οἰκοδομήν, R. 15:2; 1 C. 14:12, 26 etc.; πρὸς τὸ σύμφορον, εὔσχημον, εὐπάρεδρον, 1 C. 7:35; ἐγράφη πρὸς νουθεσίαν, 10:11; τῷ θεῷ πρὸς δόξαν, 2 C. 1:10. [12] The prep. often occurs with the inf.: πρὸς τὸ θεαθῆναι, Mt. 6:1; 23:5 etc.; [13] also with acc. and inf.: πρὸς τὸ μὴ ἀτενίσαι τοὺς υἱοὺς Ἰσραήλ, "that the children of Israel could not look," 2 C. 3:13. Dependent on an adj.: ἀγαθὸς πρός, Eph. 4:29; ἀδόκιμος πρός, Tt. 1:16 etc. [14]
Elliptic expressions : τὰ πρὸς εἰρήνην, "what belongs to peace," Lk. 14:32; 19:42; πρὸς τί; "to what end ?" Jn. 13:28; τὰ πρὸς τὰς χρείας, "what is necessary," Ac. 28:10; τὰ πρὸς ζωὴν καὶ εὐσέβειαν, "what is of service to life and piety," 2 Pt. 1:3.

b. Special modal sense : "up to" in the sense "to attain to," "to fulfil," "to correspond," i.e., "corresponding," "commensurate," "according." [15]

ποιεῖν πρὸς τὸ θέλημα αὐτοῦ, "to act acc. to his will," Lk. 12:47; πρὸς τὴν σκληροκαρδίαν ὑμῶν, "acc. to the degree of your hardness," Mt. 19:8 par. Mk. 10:5; πρὸς ἃ ἔπραξεν, "corresponding to what he has done," 2 C. 5:10; οὐκ ὀρθοποδοῦσιν [16] πρὸς τὴν ἀλήθειαν, "in agreement with," Gl. 2:14. Dependent on an adj.: οὐκ ἄξια τὰ παθήματα ... πρὸς τὴν μέλλουσαν δόξαν, "do not attain in significance," R. 8:18.

---

[10] Paul sets forth the truth everywhere in order to bring about a general assent of faith. On συνείδησις in the sense of "agreement" etc. (perhaps at 2 C. 5:11 too) cf. B. Reicke, The Disobedient Spirits and Christian Baptism (1946), 180; also "Syneidesis in R. 2:15," ThZ, 12 (1956), 157-161.
[11] Though cf. Pr.-Bauer[5], s.v., III, 6 for a different view.
[12] Cf. Pr.-Bauer[5], s.v., III, 3a c.
[13] Ibid., 3a for further examples.
[14] Ibid., 3c for further examples.
[15] Mayser, II, 2 § 127, 5.
[16] → V, 451 ὀρθοποδέω. C. H. Roberts, "A Note on Gl. 2:14," JThSt, 40 (1939), 55 f.; J. C. Winter, "Another Instance of ὀρθοποδεῖν," HThR, 34 (1941), 161 f.; G. D. Kilpatrick, "Gal. 2:14 ὀρθοποδοῦσιν," Nt.liche Studien f. R. Bultmann, Beih. ZNW, 21 (1954), 269-274.

5. Consecutive : "up to" a certain result, "so that" (in part Hebraic): λευκαί εἰσιν πρὸς θερισμόν, "are white enough for harvest," Jn. 4:35; ἅτινά ἐστιν ... πρὸς πλησμονὴν τῆς σαρκός, "which leads to the satisfaction of the flesh," Col. 2:23; [17] πρὸς φθόνον, "to the point of envy," "even with envy," Jm. 4:5; [18] ἁμαρτία πρὸς θάνατον, "so serious that it leads to death," 1 Jn. 5:16 f. With inf.: ὁ βλέπων γυναῖκα πρὸς τὸ ἐπιθυμῆσαι αὐτήν, "whosoever looks on a woman in such a way that he lusts after her," Mt. 5:28.

Reicke

προσάγω → I, 131, 3 ff.   προσδέομαι → II, 41, 43 ff.

προσαγωγή → I, 133, 20 ff.   προσδέχομαι → II, 57, 22 ff.

προσανατίθημι → I, 353, 27 ff.

---

† προσδοκάω, † προσδοκία

A. The Word Group outside the New Testament.

1. προσδοκάω, like δοκεύω from the root δεκ-, δοκ- (δέχομαι [1] = "to take, accept"), is usually construed with acc. of object or person or with (acc. and) inf.: "to wait for," "to expect," "to look for" someone or something. The tension of waiting as fear or as hope is very much to the fore. In a hopeful sense : μόχθου τέρμα, Aesch. Prom., 1026; κέρδος, Eur. Iph. Taur., 1311; (ἀγαθά) μέλλοντα καὶ προσδοκώμενα, [2] Philo Leg. All., III, 87; the gods as σωτῆρας, Plat. Theaet., 170b; τὰ βελτίω, Jos. Ant., 7, 114; God as σύμμαχον, Jos. Bell., 5, 403; of Nero : ὁ δὲ τῆς οἰκουμένης καὶ προσδοκηθεὶς καὶ ἐλπισθεὶς αὐτοκράτωρ, "the expected and hoped for emperor of the world," P. Oxy., VII, 1021, 6. Of anxious waiting : προσδοκῶντες ὀλέεσθαι, Hdt., VII, 156; φαῦλα, Jos. Bell., 5, 528. As vox media Lys., 19, 47; Epict. Ench., 48, 1 (twice).

προσδοκία, "expectation" : τῶν ἀγαθῶν, Xenoph. Cyrop., I, 6, 19; ἐλπὶς ... τῶν ἀγαθῶν οὖσα προσδοκία, Philo Poster. C., 26. But often of bad expectations : κακῶν etc. Plat. La., 198b; Philo Det. Pot. Ins., 140; Jos. Ant., 3, 219; in the sense of belief in providence, Jos. Ant., 5, 358.

2. In the LXX, where προσδοκᾶν occurs esp. in later writings, expectation is increasingly concentrated on God and His acts. Thus 6 of the 12 passages in which the verb is used speak of hoping in God Himself, ψ 103:27, in His salvation, ψ 118:166 (both for שבר pi), in His mercy, Wis. 12:22, in the victory given by Him, 2 Macc. 15:8, in the final resurrection, 2 Macc. 7:14; 12:44.

---

[17] B. Reicke, "Zum sprachlichen Verständnis v. Kol. 2:23," *Studia theologica,* 6 (1953), 39-53, though cf. R. Leaney, "Colossians II, 21-23. The Use of πρός," Exp. T., 64 (1952), 92.

[18] Analogies in Mayser, II, 2 § 127, 8.

π ρ ο σ δ ο κ ά ω, π ρ ο σ δ ο κ ί α. Pass., Liddell-Scott, Moult.-Mill., Pr.-Bauer⁵, *s.v.* Cr.-Kö., 286.

[1] Pokorny, 189 f.; on the forms ἔδεκτο, δέγμενος, δεδεγμένος in Hom., cf. A. Debrunner, "Δέγμενος, ἑσπόμενος, ἀρχόμενος," ΜΝΗΜΗΣ ΧΑΡΙΝ, *P. Kretschmer-Gedenkschr.* (1956), 77-81.

[2] On the relations between προσδοκάω and a psychologically understood ἐλπίζω in Philo → II, 529, 32 ff.

The use of προσδοκάω for OT hope is given emphasis by the extended employment of the verb in Aquila, Symmachus and Theodotion. More frequently than the LXX these use it for the Heb. קוה pi:[3] ψ 24:3 ᾽A (or ὑπομένοντες); ψ 68:7 Σ; Is. 49:23 Σ; 59:9, 11 Σ; Jer. 14:22 Σ; ψ 118:95 ΣΘ. Except in the last ref. God is always the direct or indirect obj.

This concentration is less evident in the case of προσδοκία. Among 9 LXX instances only 2 refer to God: Gn. 49:10 (the Messiah); ψ 118:116. In 4 instances the expectation is fearful: Sir. 40:2; 2 Macc. 3:21; 3 Macc. 5:41, 49.

B. The Word Group in the New Testament.

1. Like προσδέχομαι (→ II, 58, 12 ff.) προσδοκάω belongs to the sphere of NT expectation of salvation. This is quite unequivocally so in Q (5 times) and 2 Pt. (3 times). Among the other 8 instances, all in Lk., there is an echo of eschatological hope in Lk. 3:15; 8:40, but hardly a trace of it in Lk. 1:21; Ac. 3:5; 10:24; 27:33; 28:6 (twice).

a. Mt. 11:3 = Lk. 7:19, 20 refers to the contemporary hope of the coming Messiah, → II, 670, 12 ff. In face of the acts of Jesus, which recall the Messiah but which are ambiguous, the Baptist raises the question whether Jesus is really the fulfilment of this hope.[4]

b. Mt. 24:50 = Lk. 12:46 and esp. 2 Pt. 3:12-14 refer to the returning Christ. At issue in 2 Pt. is the basis of the Christian walk in view of the delay in the *parousia*. Inherited apocalyptic ideas of a coming world conflagration are only the background for the message that the community is moving towards the coming day of God (vv. 11-13) to which all other events are completely subordinate, δι᾽ ἥν v. 12b. The participles of v. 12a have an indicative and causal rather than an imperative character.[5] Because the community stands in possession of the hope given to it, in contrast to the mockers of v. 3 f. the very highest can be expected of it in face of the approaching cosmic catastrophe: "If all things are thus to be dissolved, what kind of people in respect of a holy walk are they[6] to be who have the hope which is given to them and the consequent striving[7] after the dawning of the day of God!" In v. 14, as in v. 12, 13, the participle has an indicative and causal rather than an imperative sense:[8] "Because, my beloved, you expect such great things ..." In 2 Pt., then, προσδοκᾶν is fully protected against psychologising disintegration and wholly orientated to hope as hope of salvation.

2. The two προσδοκία references have the same popular Hellenistic sense as the verb has in Lk. Lk. 21:26: ἀπὸ φόβου καὶ προσδοκίας τῶν ἐπερχομένων,

---

[3] LXX has προσδοκάω for קוה pi only at Lam. 2:16; it prefers ὑπομένω, → IV, 583, 15 ff.

[4] It is not necessary to take προσδοκῶμεν indicatively as does Schl. Mt., *ad loc.*

[5] Bengel, Schl. Erl., *ad loc.* The emphasis is not on the apocalyptic statements themselves as one head of instruction among others. The coming of the day of God is not just the centre of the eschatological statements as such but also the basis of the ethics of the present, as against E. Käsemann, "Eine Apologie der urchr. Eschatologie," ZThK, 49 (1952), 286 f.

[6] The ὑμᾶς is probably to be omitted with Vaticanus (+ AC ℵ etc.; ἡμᾶς ℵ* al.).

[7] σπεύδω τι can and must mean "to strive after, to aspire to," Pr.-Bauer[5], *s.v.* σπεύδω; Schl. Erl., *ad loc.* There is no thought of a hastening of the *parousia* by good works, Wnd. Pt., *ad loc.*; Käsemann, *op. cit.*, 283.

[8] Bengel, Schl. Erl., *ad loc.*

"for fearful expectation of things to come"; Ac. 12:11: the "hope" of the Jews who expect Peter to be put to death by Herod.

C. The Post-Apostolic Fathers.

There are 9 instances of προσδοκάω in the post-apost. fathers. Except at Herm. v., 3, 11, 3 and Dg., 9, 2 the hope or expectation is always of Chr. blessings : expectation of διδάσκαλος by the prophets in Ign. Mg., 9, 2; of the future Christ in 1 Cl., 23, 5; Ign. Pol., 3, 2 (to be referred to Christ rather than God). προσδοκία does not occur in the post-apost. fathers. Among the Apologists Justin alone uses the group to any marked degree (προσδοκάω some 30 times, προσδοκία 10 times), predominantly in connection with OT or NT promises, e.g., Dial., 52, 1 and 2; 120, 3.

Maurer

προσέρχομαι → II, 683, 3 ff.

προσεύχομαι, προσευχή → II, 807, 1 ff.

---

† προσήλυτος

Contents : A. Occurrence and Formation. B. The גֵּר in the Old Testament. C. προσή-λυτος/גֵּר in Post-OT Judaism : I. προσήλυτος in Hellenistic Judaism : 1. LXX; 2. Philo; 3. Josephus ; 4. Jewish Inscriptions ; II. προσήλυτος/גֵּר in Later Palestinian Judaism (apart from Rabbinic Writings): 1. The Oldest Examples of Proselytes ; 2. Apocrypha, Pseud-epigrapha and the Qumran Texts ; III. Rabbinic Judaism : 1. The Term ; 2. The Attitude

---

π ρ ο σ ή λ υ τ ο ς. On the whole subject : A. Bertholet, *Die Stellung d. Israeliten u. d. Juden zu den Fremden* (1896); Schürer, III, 150-188 (full older bibl.); G. F. Moore, *Judaism*, I (1927), 323-353; A. Geiger, *Urschrift u. Übers. d. Bibel*[2] (1928), 349-354; F. M. Derwacter, *Preparing the Way for Paul, The Proselyte Movement in Later Judaism* (1930); K. G. Kuhn, "Ursprung u. Wesen der talmudischen Einstellung zum Nichtjuden," FJFr, 3 (1939), 199-234; also "Das Problem der Mission in der Urchristenheit," *Evang. Missionszschr.*, 11 (1954), 161-168. On B.: E. v. Dobschütz, Art. "Proselyten 2 : Die Gerim im AT," RE[3], 16, 112-115; G. Rosen, *Juden u. Phönizier*, revised by F. Rosen and G. Bertram (1929); K. L. Schmidt, "Israels Stellung zu den Fremden u. Beisassen u. Israels Wissen um seine Fremdlings- u. Beisassenschaft," *Judaica*, 1 (1945/46), 269-296. On C.: W. C. Allen, "On the Meaning of προσήλυτος in the Septuagint," Exp., IV, 10 (1894), 264-275; K. Axenfeld, "Die jüd. Propaganda als Vorläuferin der urchr. Mission," *Missionswissenschaftliche Studien f. G. Warneck* (1904), 1-80; I. Lévi, *Le prosélytisme juif* (1905-1907); also "The Attitude of Talmud and Midrash toward Proselytism," REJ, 57 (1906), 1-29; J. Juster, *Les Juifs dans l'Empire Romain*, I (1914), 253-290; F. Kahn, *Die Juden als Rasse u. Kulturvolk* (1922); G. Polster, "Der kleine Talmudtraktat über die Proselyten," *Angelos*, II (1926), 1-38; F. Gavin, *The Jewish Antecedents of the Christian Sacraments* (1928); Str.-B., I, 924-931; II, 715-721; cf. also I, 102-112; A. Causse, *Les Dispersés d'Israel* (1929); F. Goldmann, Art. "Proselyt," Jüd. Lex., IV (1930), 1146-1151; S. Bialoblocki, *Die Beziehungen des Judt. zu Proselyten u. Proselytismus* (1930); Jackson-Lake, I, 5, 74-96; J. Jeremias, *Jerusalem z. Zeit Jesu*, II B (1937), 191-207; B. J. Bamberger, *Proselytism in the Talmudic Period* (1939); W. G. Braude, *Jewish Proselytising in the First Five Centuries of the Common Era, the Age of the Tannaim and Amoraim* (1940); M. Simon, "Verus Israel, Etude sur les relations entre Chrétiens et Juifs dans l'empire romain," *Bibliothèque des écoles françaises d'Athènes et de Rome* (1948); B. J. Bamberger, Art. "Proselyte," *The Universal Jewish Encycl.*, IX (1948), 1-3; F. M. Abel, *Hist. de la Palestine*, II (1952), 107-109; J. Jeremias, *Jesu Verheissung an die Völker* (1956), 9-16. On D.: M. Meinertz, *Jesus u. d. Heidenmission* (1925). The author is grateful to W. Eiss for his help with this art., particularly in the assembling and checking of materials, more esp. in relation to Philo, Joseph. and Jewish inscr.

to Proselytes ; 3. The Reception of Proselytes ; 4. The Legal Position of Proselytes ; 5. The גר־תושב and the ירא שמים. D. The New Testament : I. προσήλυτος ; II. σεβόμενοι or φοβούμενοι τὸν θεόν.

A. Occurrence and Formation.

προσήλυτος, formed from the stem -ελυ- (with extension -ηλυ-), a false abstraction from -ηλυσία etc.,[1] occurs only in Jewish and Chr. writings ; it has not been found elsewhere.[2] On the other hand, ἔπηλυς (from Aesch., Soph., Hdt.), ἐπηλύτης (from Thuc., I, 9, 2 or Xenoph. Oec., 11, 4), and ἐπήλυτος (Philo Som., I, 160) are common in the same sense in secular Gk. Corresponding to the Lat. *advena* these words were perhaps also used in the Isis cult. Cf. Apul. Met., XI, 26 : *eram cultor denique adsiduus, fani quidem advena, religionis autem indigena.*[3]

B. The גֵּר in the Old Testament.

In the OT there are two distinct classes of aliens in the land (→ V, 8, 13 ff. and 844, 13 ff.) and these are distinguished linguistically. First 1. there are foreigners present only for a time, e.g., travellers, and for these the word is נָכְרִי (Dt. 14:21 ; 15:3 ; 23:21 ; 29:21), as a Gentilic form בֶּן־(ה)נֵּכָר (Ex. 12:43 ; 2 S. 22:45 f. ; Ez. 44:9 etc. → I, 266, 15 f.). Then 2. there is the alien who resides temporarily or permanently in the land ; this is the גֵּר (Ex. 12:49 ; Dt. 23:8 ; 2 Ch. 2:16 : גֵּרִים).[4]

The נָכְרִי is outside the national and religious fellowship of Israel and is without rights or protection.[5] This position of the נָכְרִי in ancient Israel corresponds to that of foreigners among other peoples on the same cultural level.[6] Nevertheless, even in ancient Israel there are signs of a milder attitude to aliens such as is unusual at this level.[7]

The גֵּר corresponds to the μέτοικος in the Attic state.[8] He stands under a patron or the tribe within which he resides. The protection of the patron guarantees the necessary legal security of tenure but also lays upon him an obligation of dependence and service. In distinction from the slave, however, he preserves personal freedom[9] and can work his way up.[10] Yet he has no independent property nor can he ever attain this.[11] He is also exposed to the caprice of his patron.[12]

The oldest laws in favour of the גֵּר are in the Book of the Covenant. Cf. Ex. 22:20 ff.: ". . . if thou afflict him (the *ger*) in any wise, and he cry at all

---

[1] [Debrunner]. Cf. J. Wackernagel, "Studien z. gr. Perf.," *Kleine Schriften* (1953), 1015 ; E. Fraenkel, *Gesch. d. gr.* Nomina agentis, II (1912), 74.

[2] The ref. to Apoll. Rhod., 1, 834 in Pr.-Bauer[4], *s.v.* is an error, and is omitted in Pr.-Bauer[5]. This leaves no pre-Jewish or pre-Chr. instance. προσήλυτος was very probably coined by the Synagogue of the Dispersion as a rendering of גֵּר [Debrunner].

[3] Cf. Reitzenstein Hell. Myst., 193. In Apul. *advena* stands for ἐπήλυτος, not προσήλυτος, as Reitzenstein supposed [Debrunner].

[4] Cf. the verbal form גּוּר "to settle somewhere as an alien, a refugee." On (גר) תושב → 730, 6 ff. ; 740, 32 ff.

[5] Cf. the harshness and scorn for foreigners in the Song of Deborah in Ju. 5, also Gn. 4:14. On this cf. Bertholet, 9. Cf. also 2 S. 8:2 and Bertholet, 8-11.

[6] Bertholet, 9. The right of the foreigner to hospitality is highly estimated. Cf. Gn. 18, 19, 24 ; Ju. 19 ; 1 K. 17:7-13.

[7] Cf. in what follows passages like Ex. 22:20 ff. ; 23:9.

[8] Cf. Schürer, III, 175 ; Kuhn, "Ursprung," 201 f. ; Bertholet, 43-50.

[9] Unlike the slave he receives payment. Cf. Dt. 24:14, where the גֵּר can be a day-labourer.

[10] Bertholet, 39.

[11] Because he is not a fully enfranchised member of the tribe.

[12] Cf. Gn. 31, esp. v. 7, 39, 40.

unto me, I will surely hear his cry." Ex. 23:9 : "For ye know the heart of a גֵּר,
seeing ye were גֵּרִים in the land of Egypt." Especially important is the ordinance
in Ex. 20:10 and 23:12 that the גֵּר must keep the Sabbath. Here already in the
Book of the Covenant it is plain that the גֵּר stands in a specific religious relationship to Yahweh as the God of the people and tribe among whom he dwells.
Yet it is not this religious relationship which makes him a גֵּר. This is simply an
expression of the sociological fact that the גֵּר lives in an alien land and is thus
in the sphere of influence of the God to whom this land belongs.[13] With the
further development of the religion of Israel the religious position of the גֵּר also
changes. The tradition of election, which is renewed by the preaching of the
prophets, establishes a sense of uniqueness as compared with other nations. The
antithesis to other peoples is now no longer a mere national antithesis ; it is religious.[14] This religious attitude plays a decisive role in the legislation of Dt.
regarding the alien. It demands separation from every non-Jew, from the נָכְרִי.
But the גֵּר, who already has certain religious obligations, is increasingly drawn
into the religious fellowship of Israel. This inclusion of the גֵּר in the whole round
of religious duties may be seen most clearly in the laws concerning the keeping
of the great religious festivals (Dt. 5:14; 16:10 f.; 16:13 f.), as in Dt. 29:9-14 :
"Ye stand this day all of you before Yahweh your God ; your captains of your
tribes, your elders, and your officers . . . and thy stranger that is in thy camp . . ."

In P this line of development is continued and the גֵּר is as good as integrated
into the religious fellowship of the Jewish people. Basically the same religious
rights and duties apply to him as to full citizens.[15] The exception in relation
to the Passover, in which only the גֵּר who is circumcised may take part,[16] shows
that circumcision was expected if not required of the גֵּר as an external sign of
membership of the community of Israel. This alone completed his incorporation
into the religious union of the Jewish people. Thus גֵּר denotes the non-Israelite
who is almost or (with the exception of circumcision) wholly accepted into the
religious constitution of the Jewish people.[17] Religiously, then, the term comes
very close to the "proselyte" of later Judaism.[18]

It should be noted, however, that the גֵּר here is not simply any foreigner who
joins the Jewish religion but only the resident alien. Sociologically, then, the גֵּר
retains his ancient position and is not fully equivalent to the Israelite citizen.[19]
The reason for this is that the sociological structure presupposed by the Priestly
Code remains the same as before, namely, that of a compact national body around

---

[13] Bertholet, 67-78.

[14] The term גּוֹיִם, which originally meant "the nations" or "other nations" in general,
now came to mean "the Gentiles." In Talmudic Heb. a sing. גּוֹי "Gentile" is formed. Kuhn,
"Ursprung," 203, n. 2.

[15] Cf. Nu. 15:15 f.: "One ordinance shall be both for you and for the גֵּר, who resides
with you ; this is an eternal ordinance for all generations." Cf. also the collection of relevant
statutes in Bertholet, 168-171.

[16] Cf. Ex. 12:48, and on this Bertholet, 172 f.; Kuhn, "Ursprung," 205.

[17] Bertholet, 174; Kuhn, "Ursprung," 205.

[18] Cf. also Allen, 264-275.

[19] In P this finds expression in the fact that the גֵּר may not own any heritable landed
property.

Jerusalem in Palestine and predominantly rural. [20] The acceptance of the גֵּר into the religious fellowship by P is chiefly determined by the thought of the holiness and purity of the chosen people. This demands full differentiation from all foreigners. But this is not possible in relation to resident aliens and consequently these are accepted into the religious fellowship. [21]

In place of גֵּר in the original sense P thus uses the new term תּוֹשָׁב. This denotes the sociological structure of the resident alien as distinct from his religious allegiance, which is now the main point in גֵּר (for further details → 740, 32 ff.).

In the closing stages of the Jewish Law, then, גֵּר is wholly defined by the religious aspect but still harmonises with the national sociological structure of Palestinian Judaism. [22]

C. προσήλυτος/גֵּר in Post-OT Judaism.

I. προσήλυτος in Hellenistic Judaism.

The final development of "proselyte" as a tt. to denote the Gentile who becomes a full Jew by circumcision irrespective of his national or social position did not take place in Palestinian Judaism but in the Judaism of the Graeco-Roman *diaspora*. [23]

This provided the necessary presupposition of a different sociological structure. The dispersion of the Jewish people meant that the Jew no longer lived with his fellow-believers in a single area but now resided among non-Jews wherever his work took him. [24] He learned to know non-Jewish culture, esp. Hellenism, [25] and began to plead among non-Jews for his own conscious inheritance. There thus arose in the *diaspora* a lively Jewish mission. [26] This was part of the advance of all oriental religions at the turn of the epochs, but Jewish propaganda was distinguished from other religions by its preaching of the only true God who is invisible and not worshipped in images, the Creator of heaven and earth, and by its practical orientation to a happy and moral life. [27] Hence it had a special attraction. [28] There were, however, fewer instances of full conversion by the acceptance of circumcision. [29]

---

[20] Kuhn, "Ursprung," 206.

[21] Bertholet, 168.

[22] This is not refuted by Is. 56:1-8, where acceptance into the religious fellowship of Israel is promised to any בֶּן־הַנֵּכָר, "foreigner," not just the resident alien. Expressed here is the eschatological universalism of Dt. Is. and nothing needs to be said about the actual situation of the alien. Whether Bertholet, 176-178 is right to see a dissociation of the term from its sociological context in the Chronicler is open to question.

[23] Kuhn, "Ursprung," 207.

[24] Kuhn, "Ursprung," 207.

[25] On this *v.* esp. J. Wellhausen, *Isr. u. jüd. Geschichte*[8] (1921), 219-241; Schl. Gesch. Isr., 9-45, esp. 37-45; Schürer, III, 27-89; Bertholet, 196-207.

[26] Cf. Bousset-Gressm., 77-79; Axenfeld ; Jeremias, *Verheissung,* 9-16.

[27] These motifs are esp. plain in the 4th book of Sib., *v.* Schürer, III, 173; Bertholet, 257-302; P. Dalbert, "Die Theol. d. jüd.-hell. Missionslit.," *Theol. Forschungen,* 4 (1954), 106-123.

[28] Schürer, III, 155-162. For the gt. success of Jewish missions cf. Jos. Ap., 2, 123; 2, 284.

[29] This may be assumed on the basis of widespread anti-semitic feeling. Cf. also the story of King Izates of Adiabene (Jos. Ant., 20, 34-48), who wanted to accept Judaism but would not at first be circumcised for fear of losing his throne, since his subjects would not tolerate the rule of a true Jew over them.

Those who became full Jews by circumcision were described by the Greek Jewish tt. προσήλυτοι. This expression takes the place of the OT גֵּר and corresponds to it in respect of the religious position of the גֵּר but not the sociological. For those who go over to Judaism in this way are not resident aliens, and sociologically they are often much above native Jews. [30]

More numerous was the group of Gentiles who attended synagogue worship, believed in Jewish monotheism, and kept some part of the ceremonial law, but who did not take the step of full conversion to Judaism by circumcision. As distinct from proselytes these were called σεβόμενοι or φοβούμενοι τὸν θεόν → 732, 21 f.; 734, 5 ff.; 741, 15 ff.; 743, 12 ff. [31]

As regards the attitude of Jews of the dispersion to these God-fearers the saying of the Jewish missionary Ananias is typical. Speaking to King Izates of Adiabene, who has been won over to the Jewish religion and wants to join it, he says: Izates may worship God without circumcision if he will simply follow the liturgical practices of the Jews, which are much more important than circumcision, Jos. Ant., 20, 41 f. → 735, 7 ff.

The concern of Hellenistic Judaism in its missionary activity was not so much that Gentiles should accept circumcision and keep the cultic commandments but that they should believe in the one God and follow the basic ethical demands of the OT. [32]

1. LXX. In the LXX [33] προσήλυτος is used 77 times for the Heb. גֵּר, at least once (2 Ch. 15:9) for the verb גּוּר. In 14 instances the LXX has other words for גֵּר; in 11 of these the word is πάροικος (Gn. 15:13; 23:4; Ex. 2:22; 18:3; Dt. 14:21; 23:8; 2 Βασ. 1:13; 1 Ch. 29:15; Ps. 39:12; 119:19; Jer. 14:8), in 2 γ(ε)ιώρας, a Gk. form of Aram. גיורא = Heb. גֵּר (Ex. 12:19; Is. 14:1), and in 1 ξένος (Job 31:32). πάροικος is also the usual transl. of תּוֹשָׁב (Ex. 12:45; Lv. 22:10; 25:6, 23 etc.). The deviations in the transl. of גֵּר are in part to be explained by the fact that προσήλυτος was for the LXX translators a religious term and hence did not fit every OT instance of גֵּר, e.g., Gn. 15:13; 23:4; Ex. 2:22; 18:3; Dt. 14:21; 23:8; ψ 39:13; 119:9 etc. In such verses προσήλυτος is avoided and πάροικος used instead, or ξένος, e.g., Job 31:32. On the other hand, in Ex. 22:20; 23:9; Lv. 19:34; Dt. 10:19 the Jews are called προσήλυτοι in Egypt and not, as one might expect, πάροικοι. Only in a few instances, however, does προσήλυτος still have a sociological sense corresponding to the OT גֵּר, e.g., Lv. 19:10; Dt. 24:21; Jos. uses πένης instead in his account in Ant., 4, 231.

2. Philo. The new understanding of the OT term is fully developed in Philo. [34] For the Gentile converted to Judaism Philo uses not only προσήλυτος (Som., II, 273; Spec. Leg., I, 51; I, 308) but also — and more frequently — the terms ἔπηλυς (Flacc., 54; Exsecr., 152), ἐπηλύτης (Virt., 102, 103, 104, 182, 219; Spec. Leg., I, 52 f.) and ἐπήλυτος (Virt., 104; Spec. Leg., IV, 176 f.). Philo thus prefers words familiar to his pagan readers over the probably unfamiliar προσήλυτος, which he has first to explain to them, Spec.

---

[30] Cf. Izates of Adiabene, → n. 29.

[31] The σεβόμενοι τὸν θεόν are often wrongly called "a special class of proselytes" or "semi-proselytes." Against this misunderstanding cf. esp. Moore, I, 326 f. and 339. Acc. to Dalbert, op. cit., 22, n. 5 the expressions σεβόμενοι τὸν θεόν or φοβούμενοι τὸν θεόν and προσήλυτοι are used promiscue. But in fact (cf. the Jewish inscr. → 732, 33 ff.) the σεβόμενοι or φοβούμενοι τὸν θεόν on the one side and προσήλυτοι on the other are two sharply distinguished categories.

[32] Schürer, III, 173 and cf. Kuhn, "Problem der Mission," 162.

[33] Cf. Geiger, 353 f.; Allen, 264-275; Bertholet, 259-261; Schürer, III, 176, n.

[34] Cf. Bertholet, 285-290; Schürer, III, 176 f.

Leg., I, 51: τούτους δὲ καλεῖ προσηλύτους ἀπὸ τοῦ προσεληλυθέναι καινῇ καὶ φιλοθέῳ πολιτείᾳ. Even when quoting Dt. 10:17 f. he once has ἐπήλυτος (Spec. Leg., IV, 176 f.) though elsewhere he has προσήλυτος in the same quotation (Spec. Leg., I, 308), cf. the allusion to Dt. 26:13 in Som., II, 273). ἔπηλυς (Cher., 121; Flacc., 54 etc.) and ἐπήλυτος (Cher., 120, 121) can also be used for resident aliens as customarily in profane Gk., [35] i.e., as synon. of ξένος. [36] Philo defines προσήλυτος (Spec. Leg., I, 52, 309) as one who has left country, friends and relatives, also patriarchal customs, and set himself under the Jewish constitution. This applies only to the full proselyte. Circumcision is presupposed for the one who adopts Judaism as a proselyte, although, in a way typical of Hell. Judaism, it is said that the (true) proselyte is one "who is circumcised not merely in the foreskin but in lusts and desires and other passions of the soul." [37] Philo finds this understanding of the προσήλυτος in the OT passages which originally refer to resident aliens. Thus the *gerim* mentioned in the laws of poor relief along with widows and orphans (e.g., Dt. 10:18; 26:13) are taken to be those who "are sincerely attached to the truth and converted to piety." [38] Hence the term προσήλυτος does not describe a sociological status; it is a religious title. [39]

3. Josephus. Jos. [40] avoided προσήλυτος. He did this for the same reason as Philo. He was writing for pagans unfamiliar with the word. On the other hand in the use of the verb προσέρχεσθαι in Ant., 18, 82 there is a clear ref. to the term. Here Jos. describes the Roman lady Fulvia, who had come over to Judaism, as προσεληλυθυῖαν τοῖς 'Ιουδαϊκοῖς. [41] Jos. has σεβόμενος τὸν θεόν once in the technical sense (Ant., 14, 110): τῶν κατὰ τὴν οἰκουμένην 'Ιουδαίων καὶ σεβομένων τὸν θεόν, and perhaps θεοσεβής once (Ant., 20, 195): Νέρων ... τῇ γυναικὶ Ποππαίᾳ, θεοσεβὴς γὰρ ἦν, ὑπὲρ τῶν 'Ιουδαίων δεηθείσῃ χαριζόμενος. The pt. at issue in προσήλυτος and σεβόμενος τὸν θεόν is, of course, a common one in Jos. [42] To describe full conversion to Judaism (as a proselyte) Jos. uses the expressions τὰ 'Ιουδαίων ἔθη μεταλαβεῖν (Ant., 20, 139); μετέχειν τῶν ἡμετέρων (Ap., 2, 209); ὑπὸ τοὺς αὐτοὺς ἡμῖν νόμους ζῆν ὑπελθεῖν (Ap., 2, 210); εἰς τοὺς ἡμετέρους νόμους εἰσελθεῖν (Ap., 2, 123). The proselyte is in Jos. 'Ιουδαῖος (Ant., 20, 39), βέβαιος 'Ιουδαῖος (20, 38). Adherence to Judaism is generally described as τὸν θεὸν σέβειν (20, 34); τοῖς 'Ιουδαίων ἔθεσιν χαίρειν (20, 38); ἰουδαΐζειν (Bell., 2, 463, i.e., "to live acc. to Jewish customs and commandments," as in Gl. 2:14), also προσάγεσθαι ταῖς θρησκείαις (Bell., 7, 45).

4. Jewish Inscriptions. Jewish inscr. which refer to proselytes support the structure found in Philo. There are 2 of these from Jerusalem [43] and 8 (9) [44] from Italy, [45] of which 7 (8) are from Rome. As compared with the total no. of Jewish inscr. found in

[35] Liddell-Scott, s.v.; examples → 728, 7 f.
[36] Bertholet, 288.
[37] Fragmenta on Ex. 22:19 in Bibliotheca Sacra Patrum Ecclesiae Graec., II (1828), 241; Bertholet, 288. Cf. R. 2:28 f.
[38] Spec. Leg., I, 309 : ... γενόμενοι ἀτυφίας καὶ ἀληθείας ἐρασταὶ γνήσιοι, μετεχώρησαν πρὸς εὐσέβειαν, cf. also *ibid.*, IV, 177 f. and Virt., 102-104.
[39] Cf. Spec. Leg., I, 52 : ἰσοτιμίαν γοῦν ἅπασιν ἐπηλύταις διδοὺς καὶ χαρισάμενος ὅσα καὶ τοῖς αὐτόχθοσι. Cf. Bertholet, 289.
[40] Cf. also Schl. Mt., 675 f.; Bertholet, 291-294; Derwacter, 26.
[41] Elsewhere Jos. always uses προσέρχεσθαι lit. "to come to," cf. Bell., 5, 326 and 328; 6, 188 etc.
[42] Cf. also Derwacter, 26.
[43] 1. in J. Euting, "Nabatäische Inschr. aus Arabien," SAB (1885), 683, inscr. 64. 2. In J. B. Frey, Corpus Inscr. Iudaicarum, II (1952), 318, inscr. 1385.
[44] J. B. Frey, op. cit., I (1936), 28 suggests that inscr. 37 from the catacomb of the Via Nomentana in Rome should run προσηλύ]του πατήρ, but this is open to debate.
[45] Frey, I, inscr. 21, 68, 202, 222, 256, 462, 523. Inscr. 576 is from the Jewish catacomb of Venosa in Apulia.

Italy (554) the latter no. is surprisingly small. [46] On 533 Palestinian Jewish inscr. there is only 1 instance of προσήλυτος. [47] Almost all the inscr. from Rome which refer to proselytes are from Jewish catacombs. [48] There proselytes were buried with other Jews, in contrast to God-fearers who had not become full Jews and were thus buried among Gentiles. [49] This means that proselytes, like native Jews, separated themselves strictly from everything Gentile, since this was the pt. of Jewish catacombs. [50] It also means that proselytes were counted as full members of the community, whereas the God-fearers were in practice Gentiles. [51]

The full integration of proselytes into the Jewish congregation may be seen from the way they are described on individual inscr., cf. a 3½ yr. old girl on inscr. 21: Εἰρήνη θρεπτὴ προσήλυτος πατρὸς καὶ μητρὸς Εἰουδέα ᾿Ισδραηλίτης; by being a προσήλυτος she is also a Jewess and therewith an Israelitess, a member of God's chosen people; [52] also inscr. 68: Cresce(n)s Sinicerius Iud(a)eus prosel(y)tus. [53] Sometimes proselytes have a Jewish name instead of or along with their original pagan name. Thus in Aram. documents from Assuan (416 B.C.) an Egypt. proselyte is called As-Hor before being received into Judaism, but after his conversion he is Nathan. [54] In inscr. 523 [55] the proselyte Veturia bears the Jewish name Sara. [56] Θεοσεβής is also a common Jewish name of this kind. [57] In a Jewish ossuary inscr. from Jerusalem (1385) [58] there is ref. to a proselyte called Judas, son of Laganion: ᾿Ιούδατος Λαγανίωνος προσηλύτου; in distinction from his father, then, he bears a Hebrew name. Another Jerusalem inscr. mentions a proselyte Maria, [59] i.e., as a Jewess she bears the Heb. name Miriam. [60]

Of the Italian inscr. which mention proselytes 6 refer to women [61] and only 2 or 3 to men. [62] Another surprising pt. is that among the proselytes mentioned on these inscr. there is 1 slave, 1 female slave [63] and an adopted child (θρεπτή = alumna). [64] This is explained by the fact that conversion to Judaism was easier for women than for men,

---

[46] Frey, I, p. LXIII.

[47] This is the ossuary inscr. 1385; v. Frey, II, 318.

[48] 2 (3) from the catacomb of the Via Nomentana, Frey, I, inscr. 21, (37,) 68; 3 from the catacomb of the Via Appia, inscr. 202, 222, 256; 1 from the catacomb of Venosa, inscr. 576. In one (523) the exact location is uncertain. Cf. Frey, 384.

[49] Cf. J. B. Frey, "Inscr. inédites des catacombes juives de Rome," *Rivista di Archeologia Cristiana,* 7 (1930), 253 f.; also op. cit. → n. 44, p. CXXX. Cf. also Juster, I, 480; T. Mommsen, "Die Katakomben Roms," *Reden u. Aufsätze* (1905), 299.

[50] Frey, op. cit. (→ n. 44), p. LVI, CXXX.

[51] *Ibid.,* p. CXXX.

[52] → III, 360, 13 ff. ᾿Ισραήλ. Frey, op. cit. (→ n. 49), 254; op. cit. (→ n. 44), 19 f.

[53] Frey, op. cit. (→ n. 44), 41.

[54] Cf. Schürer, III, 185.

[55] Frey, op. cit. (→ n. 44), 384.

[56] This woman, who entered Judaism when advanced in yrs., is also called *mater synagogarum Campi.*

[57] Cf. the examples in Frey, op. cit. (→ n. 49), 256; cf. also op. cit. (→ n. 44), inscr. 202.

[58] Frey, op. cit. (→ n. 43), 318. Cf. E. L. Sukenik, *Jüd. Gräber Jerusalems um Christi Geburt* (1931), 18 and Plate 3.

[59] → n. 43, also S. Klein, Jüd.-päl. Corpus Inscr. (1920), 24-26.

[60] It is open to question whether in inscr. 462 in Frey, op. cit. (→ n. 44), 340 f. the fragment NVENN contains the second Jewish name (Nuemi, Noemi) or whether Felicitas is the Jewish name, cf. Frey, 341 and also the discussion in T. Reinach, "Le cimetière juif de Monteverde, à propos d'un livre récent," REJ, 71 (1920), 124.

[61] Frey, op. cit. (→ n. 44), inscr. 21: Irene; 202: Theosebes; 222: Crysis; 462: Felicitas; 523: Veturia Paula. Cf. also inscr. 72: Julia Irene Arista.

[62] Frey, op. cit. (→ n. 44), inscr. 68: Crescens Sinicerius; 256: Nicetas; uncertain 576: ᾿Αναστάσ(ι)ς (= Anastasios).

[63] Nicetas (Frey, I, inscr. 256) and Felicitas (inscr. 462).

[64] Irene (inscr. 21). Cf. also the inscr. of a Jewess Rufina of Smyrna for her adopted children (θρέμ[μ]ασιν), inscr. 255, n. 2.

since neither circumcision nor offering was demanded of women. Conversion also brought gt. advantages for slaves [65] and children would do as their adoptive parents decided. [66] Whether or how far the Jewish legislation of Hadrian and Antoninus Pius [67] was a reason for substantial restriction to the groups mentioned it is impossible to say. [68] "God-fearers" are referred to on 8 inscr. [69] either a. under the title θεοσεβής (inscr. 500, [70] an Ἀγρίππας Φούσκου Φαινήσιος [Rome]; inscr. 754, [71] an Εὐστάθιος [Dilelos near Philadelphia]; 748, [72] gen. τόπος < E > Ιουδ(αι)ων τῶν καὶ θεοσεβ(ῶ)ν [Miletus]), [73] or b. under the Lat. title metuens (Deum) for φοβούμενος (τὸν θεόν) (inscr. 5, [74] a 15 yr. old Roman knight Aemilius Valens [75] [Rome]).

II. προσήλυτος/גֵּר in Later Palestinian Judaism (apart from Rabbinic Writings).

In the usage of later Palestinian Judaism προσήλυτος corresponds exactly to גֵּר, which has now lost completely its sociological sense and become a purely religious tt. What προσήλυτος/גֵּר denotes, namely, conversion to Judaism by acceptance of circumcision, plays in Palestinian Judaism an essentially greater role than it does even in Hellenistic Judaism. In most cases the latter is content to win over Gentiles who with a certain pious zeal becomes adherents of the Jewish synagogue but who do not become full converts by circumcision. Palestinian Judaism, however, has a sense of the unconditional validity of all OT laws and is prepared to observe them consistently. It thus argues that he who wishes to come over to Judaism must accept the circumcision which the Law prescribes and submit to the Torah in its entirety. Otherwise he remains a Gentile who can be distinguished hardly, if at all, from any other non-Jew, → 741, 27 ff.

1. The Oldest Examples of Proselytes. In Palestinian Judaism the oldest examples date from the 2nd cent. B.C. to the 1st cent. A.D.

a. The house of Herod is to be numbered among the proselytes. For the Herod family was originally Idumean (Jos. Ant., 14, 8) and was compulsorily converted to Judaism by John Hyrcanus (13, 257). Since it was not acc. to Jewish custom that a non-native Jew should occupy the throne (14, 403), [76] the Herods were naturally regarded as usurpers. Herod the Gt. was contemptuously called ἡμιιουδαῖος and on this account regarded as unworthy of the kingly throne (14, 403). The story of his court historian Nicolas the Damascene that he descended from the first Jews to return from exile in Babylon (14, 9) is only an attempt to obscure his real descent for apologetic reasons. [77]

---

[65] Bertholet, 254.

[66] Frey, I, p. LXIV and Frey, op. cit. (→ n. 49), 255.

[67] Cf. Schürer, III, 118.

[68] Frey, op. cit. (→ n. 49), 255 and Frey, I, p. LXIII. Cf. also Simon, 330.

[69] Cf. also M. Levy, "Epigraphische Beiträge zur Gesch. d. Judt.," Jbch. f. d. Gesch. der Juden u. d. Judt., II (1861), 259-324.

[70] Frey, I, 365.

[71] Frey, II, 18 f.

[72] Ibid., 14 f.

[73] Cf. Deissmann LO, 391 f.; Schürer, III, 174.

[74] Frey, I, 9.

[75] Cf. Frey, op. cit. (→ n. 49), 252; also Frey, I, 285 : a Roman lady Larcia Quadratilla (Rome); ibid., inscr. 524 : Maionia Homeris (Rome); inscr. 529 : a lady whose name has not been preserved ... De]um metuens hic sita e(st) (cf. J. Bernays, "Die Gottesfürchtigen bei Juvenal," Commentationes philologae in honorem T. Mommseni [1877], 563-569; Frey, op. cit. [→ n. 49], 251-255); finally Frey, I, inscr. 642 : Aurelia Soter, with the addition : matri pientissimae religionis iud(a)eicae metuenti f(ilii) p(osuerunt) (Pola, Italy).

[76] Acc. to the Talmud (bBB, 3b) Rabb. exegesis bases this on Dt. 17:15 : "From among thy brethren shalt thou set a king over thee."

[77] Cf. Jos. Ant., 14, 9 : ταῦτα δὲ λέγει χαριζόμενος Ἡρώδῃ.

A Pharisaic scholar Shim'on stirred up the people against his grandson Agrippa I with the demand that as a non-Jew he should not be allowed access to the temple, i.e., the court of women and of Israelites (19, 332).[78] On the other hand, the ancient account in Sota, 7, 8[79] is typical of the conduct of Agrippa (I or II), namely, that with tears and confession of his own unworthiness for the throne (as איש נכרי acc. to Dt. 17:15) he sought to arouse the sympathy of the people, not without success.

b. The greatest achievement of Jewish missions was the winning over of King Izates of Adiabene, his mother Helena and his brother Monobazus as proselytes (Jos. Ant., 20, 34-38) in the days of the emperor Claudius.[80] The story of the king's conversion is an excellent illustration of the different attitudes of Palest. Judaism and the Judaism of the *diaspora* to the Gentile mission (20, 38-48). After the merchant Ananias (→ 731, 11 ff.), who was of the dispersion, a Palestinian Jew called El'azar[81] came and demanded that the king should not merely read the Law but also keep it, including the cultic and ceremonial statutes. Hence he had to be circumcised.[82] The requirement of El'azar was the occasion of the full conversion of Izates by circumcision.

c. In the first Jewish revolt ὁ (τοῦ) Γιώρα Σίμων (Jos. Bell., 2, 521 and 652; 5, 11; 7, 154) or υἱὸς Γιώρα (4, 503), often also just Σίμων (4, 353. 514. 516. 524 etc.) played a gt. role as a guerrilla, and then during the siege as the ruler of one part of Jerusalem and an opponent of John of Gischala. In Dio C., 66, 7, 1 we find the form Βαργιορᾶς and in Tac. Hist., V, 12 Bargiora ;[83] the original Aram. is שמעון בר־גיורא. Thus the father of Simon was a proselyte.

d. Ref. has been made already to proselytes on inscr. (→ 733, 18 ff.).

2. Apocrypha, Pseudepigrapha and the Qumran Texts. Here προσήλυτος/גֵּר occurs only once at Tob. 1:8; there are also 3 instances in Damasc. 6:21 (8:17); 14:4 (17:3) and 14:6 (17:4). In Tob. 1:8 acc. to some witnesses[84] the recipients of the alms of Tobit are orphans, widows and proselytes who have joined the children of Israel. The ref. to these 3 groups is based on Dt. 14:29 or 27:19 etc., though גֵּר is now used, not sociologically for the resident alien, but religiously for the proselyte, as shown by the words "who have joined" (Heb. הנלוים), which were used specifically for conversion to Judaism, cf. Est. 9:27. This means that the gifts were made only to Jews and not also to resident aliens as presupposed in the OT. This accords with the later Rabb. exegesis of the OT passages.[85] In Damasc. גֵּר occurs twice (14:4, 6 [17:3, 4]) in the context of the סרך מושב כל המחנות, the order of precedence in all establishments. This order runs as follows : הכהנים לראשונה והלוים שנים ובני ישראל שלשתם והגר רביע 14:4, 6 (17:3, 4). With it one may compare the order in the Essene Qumran community, 1 QS 2:19 f. and 6:8. There we find only the first three groups. Hence the fourth, the *gerim*, did not exist in Qumran but only in branch establishments of the Essene order (= מחנות). The religious

---

[78] Jeremias, *Jerusalem*, 205.

[79] *Ibid.*, 207.

[80] Cf. also Tac. Ann., 12. 13. 14 etc.; *v.* Schürer, III, 170, n. 59.

[81] The note in Jos. Ant., 20, 43 that El'azar πάνυ περὶ τὰ πάτρια δοκῶν ἀκριβὴς εἶναι προετρέψατο shows that he was a Pharisee, cf. the similar expressions in Ant., 17, 41; Bell., 2, 162; Ant., 19, 332; also M. Friedländer, *Die religiösen Bewegungen innerhalb d. Judt. im Zeitalter Jesu* (1905), 33; Derwacter, 47 f.

[82] Jos. Ant., 20, 44 : λανθάνεις ... ὦ βασιλεῦ, τὰ μέγιστα τοὺς νόμους καὶ δι' αὐτῶν τὸν θεὸν ἀδικῶν· οὐ γὰρ ἀναγινώσκειν σε δεῖ μόνον αὐτούς, ἀλλὰ καὶ πρότερον τὰ προστασσόμενα ποιεῖν ὑπ' αὐτῶν· μέχρι τίνος ἀπερίτμητος μένεις;

[83] Tac. erroneously gives this nickname to John of Gischala, *v.* Schürer, I, 621, n. 73.

[84] Cf. the text in R. H. Charles, *Apocrypha and Pseudepigrapha of the OT*, I (1913), 203.

[85] Cf. esp. S. Dt., 110 on 14:29, and on this Str.-B., IV, 678-681; Git., 5, 8 → 740, 25 ff.

division of the community into the 4 groups of priests, levites, Israelites and *gerim* corresponds to the Rabb. division of the people, cf. esp. Qid., 4, 1. The oldest instances from Rabb. Judaism are in Sheq. (1, 3 and 1, 6), whose traditions undoubtedly date from before 70 A.D. Here, too, גֵּרִים is a tt. like the προσήλυτοι of Hell. Judaism. This may be seen from the fact that they too, as Jews, must pay the temple tax, while non-Jews (נָכְרִים) and Samaritans do not, Sheq., 1, 5.

Damasc. 6:21 (8:17) is par. to Tob. 1:8. Here those who enter into covenant are obligated to support the poor and needy (cf. Ez. 16:49) and the גֵּר is an OT re-miniscence on the basis of the preceding עָנִי (cf. לְעָנִי וְלַגֵּר, Lv. 19:10; 23:22). It certainly does not mean the resident alien in the OT sense, i.e., the non-Jew living in the land. [86] It means a Jew, a proselyte who has been fully converted from paganism to Judaism.

The thing expressed by προσήλυτος may be seen in Syr. Bar. 41:4 which refers to those who have given up their vain life and found refuge beneath thy wings. The second part of the saying is a technical expression for conversion to Judaism as a proselyte, cf. Rt. 2:12 → 738, 21. Cf. also Syr. Bar. 42:5 : "Those who at first did not know life, but only came to know it later, and mingled with the holy seed of the people which separated itself, whose later time [87] will be regarded as something good."

III. Rabbinic Judaism.

1. The Term.

In Rabb. literature גֵּר always means a Gentile won over to Judaism ; it is a purely religious term, [88] and social position is of no consequence.

Along with the masc. גֵּר (bMen., 44a) we find the fem. גִּיוֹרֶת and Aram. גִּיּוֹרָא [89] also גִּירָא, jQid., 4, 1 (65b, 69) (also meaning "alien"). In the Heb. of the Mishnah the religious sense of גֵּר gives rise to the new verb הִתְגַּיֵּיר "to go over to Judaism," "to become a proselyte," and the corresponding act. form "to make a Jew." [90] הִתְיַהֵד (וְהַהוּדִי) has the same sense "to become a Jew," Est. 8:17.

Gentiles who became Jews out of worldly or impure motives were called גֵּרי (ה)שֶׁקֶר, "false proselytes." [91] These included Gentiles who became Jews [92] to be able to marry or to get the benefit of poor relief, [93] also the גֵּרי אֲרָיוֹת lit. "lion proselytes" (those converted for fear of lions, 2 K. 17:25 f.), among whom are esp. converted Samaritans and those converted for fear of the Jews in the days of Mordecai and Esther, also גֵּרי הַחֲלוֹמוֹת lit. "dream proselytes" (those converted as a result of dreams). [94] Common, too, is גֵּרים גְּרוּרים, [95] "proselytes who press in," cf. the Gibeonites in Jos. 9.

---

[86] Acc. to Damasc. 12:10 (14:11) to give a non-Jew of the fruits of the earth is forbidden.
[87] This refers to their days as Jews, *v.* Charles, *op. cit.*, 501.
[88] Cf. esp. the Mishnah passages Sheq., 1, 3 and 1, 6, where we have Levites, Israelites and proselytes on the one side, women, slaves and minors on the other.
[89] Cf. γ(ε)ιώρας in the LXX (Ex. 12:19; Is. 14:1) → 731, 24, also Philo Conf. Ling., 82. On this *v.* E. Nestle, "Zur aram. Bezeichnung der Proselyten," ZNW, 5 (1904), 263 f.; Just. Dial., 122 (γηόρας); Julius Africanus, Ep. ad Aristidem, 5 (MPG, 10, 61a); Euseb. Hist. Eccl., I, 7, 13; Jos. υἱὸς Γιώρα → 735, 17 ff.
[90] Cf. Moore, I, 329 f.
[91] Cf. jBM, 5, 7 (10c, 30); Str.-B., II, 717; Moore, I, 338. Cf. also M. Guttmann, *Das Judt. u. seine Umwelt*, I (1927), 76-78.
[92] bJeb., 24b; cf. Str.-B., II, 717.
[93] Jalqut Shim'oni, 1, 645 on Lv. 23:22, cf. Str.-B., II, 718.
[94] bJeb., 24b; Str.-B., II, 717.
[95] jQid., 4, 1 (65c, 53) in Str.-B., II, 718; also bAZ, 3b and 24a.

As compared with גרי (ה)שקר are גרי צדק, "true proselytes." [96] These are non-Jews who become Jews out of sincere religious conviction, "for God's sake" (לשום שמים,[97] not for outward advantage, [98] and who thus live acc. to God's will contained in the Torah. גר צדק is simply a precise term for what the Rabb. understand by גר in the true sense. [99] The term occurs in the 13th Beraka of the Prayer of Eighteen Benedictions in the Pal and Babyl. recension, [100] and then commonly in Rabb. writings. [101] It can also stand in contrast to גר תושב (M. Ex., 23, 12; bJeb., 48b Bar.; bSanh., 96b) [102] and ירא שמים (M. Ex., 22, 20; jMeg., 3, 2 [74a, 34]) [103] and thus denotes the real proselyte who has accepted the whole Torah as compared with Gentiles who simply attend divine service and keep the Noachic commandments. [104] Materially the term גרי אמת ("genuine proselytes") [105] means the same thing, i.e., those converted for authentic religious reasons as compared with גרי שקר. [106]

2. The Attitude to Proselytes.

The attitude to proselytes differs in individual Rabb. [107] Hillel advances the basic principle : "Be of the pupils of Aaron ..., loving men and bringing them to the Torah (i.e., the Jewish religion)." [108] As an instance of his mildness it is said of him in bShab., 31a Bar. that in contrast to Shammai he would receive a Gentile as a proselyte in spite of his deficient readiness to learn the oral Torah. [109] On the other hand, we already find in R. Eliezer b. Hyrcanos (c. 90 A.D.) the expression of a profound lack of trust in proselytes : They are by nature bad and their mind is always inclined to idolatry, [110] so that they relapse easily into paganism. [111] Very favourable statements about proselytes are found in traditions dating from the persecution under Hadrian (early 2nd cent.). [112] The prohibition of circumcision to Jews under Hadrian and to non-Jews under Antoninus Pius [113] made full conversion to Judaism impossible and put existing converts to a

---

96 Moore, I, 338; K. G. Kuhn, *Achtzehngebet u. Vaterunser und der Reim* (1950), 21.
97 Str.-B., II, 718; Gerim, 1, 7.
98 Moore, I, 338.
99 Cf. also Schürer, III, 177; Str.-B., II, 715; Bamberger, "Proselyte," 1. The older view (S. Deyling, "De σεβόμενος τὸν θεόν," Observationes sacrae, II [1737], 462-469; Schürer 1st ed.) was that גרי צדק was formed as the opp. of גרי השער "proselytes of the gate" (= σεβόμενοι τὸν θεόν) to denote true proselytes (= προσήλυτοι). But גר השער is only a medieval term first found in R. Bechai in the 13th cent. Cf. Moore, I, 341; Str.-B., II, 723; Schürer, III, 178, n. 75.
100 With the Israelites mentioned in the 13th Beraka the גרי הצדק stand in intentional antithesis to the apostates cursed in the preceding birkhat-ha-minim.
101 Cf. the examples in Str.-B., II, 717, esp. bJeb., 48b; bSanh., 96b; bBQ, 113b.
102 Str.-B., II, 717.
103 *Ibid.*, 719.
104 Cf. also Levy Wört., *s.v.* גֵּר; M. Ex. on 23:12 has the form גר צדיק as compared with גר תושב.
105 So also Str.-B., II, 716. גירי אמת bSanh., 85b, גרי אמת bNidda, 56b. Cf. the further instances in Str.-B., II, 719 and Moore, I, 338.
106 גירי אמת is also used for true proselytes in contrast to גרי אריות "lion proselytes" (→ 736, 29 ff.) in bSanh., 85b; bNidda, 56b: Acc. to the view of R. Meir (c. 150 A.D.) the Samaritans are not גרי אריות (so other scholars too) but גרי אמת, Str.-B., II, 719.
107 On this cf. also Str.-B., I, 924-931; Moore, 341-348; Lévi, 1-29; J. Klausner, *The Messianic Idea in Israel* (1955), 475-484.
108 Ab., 1, 12; *v.* Moore, I, 342; H. L. Strack, *Abot*4 (1915), 5.
109 Str.-B., I, 930 f.
110 So, too, bBM, 59b; bGit., 45b; cf. bBB, 10b.
111 Cf. also bAZ, 24a; on this Bacher Tannaiten, I, 106 f.
112 Cf. Moore, I, 345.
113 Juster, I, 266-268, Moore, I, 351, n. 5.

severe test which only those motivated by religious conviction could sustain. To this
period belongs esp. the midrash on Ex. 22:20 [114] acc. to which Abraham and David are
the gt. examples for proselytes, since they used גֵּר of themselves. [115] This kindly attitude
to the proselyte is based on Dt. 10:18, which says that God loves the גֵּר. Cf. the probably
ancient section Nu. r., 8 (on Nu. 5:6) with the parable of the stag which will not sleep
in the wilderness like others of its kind but goes into the fold with the cattle of the
king, so that the king holds it esp. dear. Similarly God loves the proselyte because he
has left his family, home, people and the Gentile nations and come to the Israelites.
One may also refer in this connection to the saying of R. Shim'on b. Gamaliel : "When
a foreigner comes to become a proselyte, one should stretch out a hand to him to bring
him under the wings of the shekinah," Lv. r., 2. Later we again find a more sceptical
attitude, cf. bMen., 44a; jSanh., 10, 2 (29b, 40). Typical is the Bar. in bJeb., 24b : In the
days of the Messiah no more proselytes will be received, for they do not keep the
Jewish Law out of conviction, and are thus in danger of falling away in the war against
Gog and Magog, bAZ, 3b Bar. [116] Cf. also the saying in bNidda, 13b Bar. that proselytes, reducing the required merits of Israel by their sins, delay the coming of the
Messiah. Nevertheless, the saying of R. Ḥelbos (3rd cent.) that proselytes are as big a
burden on Israel as leprosy [117] is only an isolated expression of strong antipathy and
is not typical of the general attitude of Talmudic Judaism to proselytes. [118]

3. The Reception of Proselytes.

In Rabb. writings the reception of proselytes is called קבל, [119] קרב תחת כנפי השכינה [120]
and נכנס לברית. The rite consists of three parts : circumcision, baptism, and the
offering of a sacrifice in the temple. [121]

    a. Circumcision מילה (→ 74, 30 ff.) as the oldest and decisive part is presupposed
already in the OT, → 729, 21 ff. It applies only to males.

    b. There is in the Rabb. writings no express account of the age, original meaning, or
most ancient form of proselyte baptism (טבילה) → I, 535, 23 ff. [122] To-day the oldest
historical instance is usually found [123] in the controversy between the followers of
Shammai and Hillel about the admission of a new proselyte to the Passover, Pes., 8, 8;
cf. Ed., 5, 2. Acc. to the school of Shammai a non-Jew who has become a proselyte the
evening before the Passover must take a bath (טבל) and may then take part. But acc.
to the school of Hillel such a proselyte may not take part, since the degree of his impurity (as a former Gentile) is equal to that of one made unclean by contact with a
grave, and hence (acc. to Nu. 19:16) he may cleanse himself only after 7 days (from
his conversion). Thus proselyte baptism is regarded as a setting aside of the cultic
impurity attaching to him as a former pagan. C. 90 A.D. it was the dominant view of
Rabb. scholars that both circumcision and baptism were indispensable for the reception
of a proselyte. This view was contested by R. Jehoshua b. Chananiah but definitively

---

[114] Gerim, 4, 2 ff.
[115] Acc. to Gn. r., 39 on 12:5 Abraham himself made many proselytes. Cf. Moore,
I, 344, n. 1.
[116] Str.-B., I, 929.
[117] bJeb., 47b; cf. 109b; bQid., 70b; bNidda, 13b.
[118] So also Moore, I, 346 f.; Bamberger, "Proselyte"; Simon, 319.
[119] E.g., Gerim, 1, 1; 1, 2.
[120] Acc. to Rt. 2:12, cf. Lv. r., 2 (134b), Str.-B., I, 927.
[121] All three together, e.g., S. Nu., 108 on 15:14; cf. Moore, I, 331, n. 5.
[122] Moore, I, 332.
[123] E.g., Schürer, III, 183; Billerbeck (Str.-B., I, 102); Jeremias, Jerusalem, 196; T. F.
Torrance, "Proselyte Baptism," NTSt, 1 (1954 f.), 154; G. Beer, Pesachim (1912), 176. Cf.
also T. M. Taylor, "The Beginnings of Jewish Proselyte Baptism," NTSt, 2 (1955 f.),
193-198.

established by R. Eliezer b. Hyrcanos on the basis of Ex. 19:10 (where the people are commanded to wash their clothes). [124] In the reign of Hadrian baptism had become a fixed rite of admission, as in the contemporary [125] ritual in bJeb., 46b Bar. (par. Gerim, 1). There is here no ref. to the washing having the character of cultic purification. [126] It is a legal act of reception into the religious fellowship of Judaism. It must take place in the presence of three witnesses [127] and instruction must be given in the Torah. Cf. also bJeb., 46b, which says that it must be administered by day, i.e., it has a public character. [128] In later testimonies, too, circumcision and baptism are the established rites of admission. Cf. bJeb., 46b (end of the 3rd cent.): One is a proselyte only when one has been circumcised and received baptism. [129] In Rabbi (end of the 2nd cent.) and then in the Talmud generally the following basis is laid down for baptism along with circumcision and an offering: As the Israelites in the wilderness had to fulfil three conditions before the conclusion of the covenant, namely, circumcision (cf. Ex. 12:48), sprinkling with water (Ex. 19:10) and an offering (Ex. 24:5), so proselytes must fulfil the same three conditions on entering the covenant. [130] Expressed here is the thought that a proselyte is an Israelite in every respect: "As the full (Israelite) citizen is a member of the covenant (בן ברית), so, too, a proselyte is a member of the covenant." [131]

c. An offering (הרצייה) had to be made in the temple by every convert to Judaism. This condition lapsed with the destruction of the Jerusalem temple.

The non-Jew received thus into Judaism was regarded after conversion "in every respect as a Jew," bJeb., 47b. This means in the first instance that like every Jew he is under obligation to keep the whole Jewish Law. In keeping is the saying of Paul in Gl. 5:3: μαρτύρομαι δὲ πάλιν παντὶ ἀνθρώπῳ περιτεμνομένῳ ὅτι ὀφειλέτης ἐστὶν ὅλον τὸν νόμον ποιῆσαι.

4. The Legal Position of Proselytes.

According to the dominant view of Rabbinic scholars the legal position of the proselyte is to be deduced from the principle that "the proselyte is like a newborn child." [132] This principle means that his former pagan life has no legal existence and he cannot be punished for transgressions of the Torah at that time. Jewish Law does not apply retrospectively to his Gentile life, but only to his life as a Jew. [133]

As regards inheritance this means that children begotten prior to his conversion are not blood relatives. They cannot be heirs even though they go over with him. [134] Only

---

[124] bJeb., 46b; v. Str.-B., I, 107.

[125] The dating rests on ref. to persecutions for the sake of circumcision.

[126] So also Moore, I, 334.

[127] The "fathers of baptism," bJeb., 47a etc.

[128] Cf. Torrance, op. cit., 151.

[129] Cf. also bAZ, 59a.

[130] bKerethoth, 81a; v. Str.-B., I, 107.

[131] S. Lv., 17, 15 (Perek, 12) in Moore, I, 334.

[132] Cf. esp. the discussion between R. Jochanan (d. 279 A.D.) and Resh Laqish in bJeb., 62a, Str.-B., II, 423; also bJeb., 22a; 97b; bBek., 47a.

[133] The principle that the proselyte is like a newborn child thus has a legal and not a religious sense. The act of admission into Judaism is not a religious new birth. Only later and occasionally (jBik., 3, 3 [65d, 1-4]) is it said that God forgives the proselyte all his sins (on conversion). The ref. here, however, is to the general meaning of the conversion rather than the special meaning of the baptism, though cf. J. Jeremias, Hat die Urkirche die Kindertaufe gekannt?² (1949), 21 f.

[134] Gerim, 3, 8; Jeremias, Jerusalem, 200. Roman law, too, says that a peregrinus cannot be the heir of a Roman citizen and therefore that an alien who obtains Roman citizenship while his son does not cannot have this son as heir, cf. Bertholet, 166.

children begotten after his conversion are descendants and heirs acc. to Jewish law. [135]
If he dies without heirs his property has no owner and can be appropriated by anyone. [136]
His slaves are free if of age. [137] The proselyte himself was allowed to inherit from his
Gentile father, though only such things as were not related to idolatry. [138]

Consistent application of the principle that the proselyte is as a newborn child would
have meant that on conversion he could not be accused of a marriage within the degrees
of consanguinity contrary to the OT law of incest (Lv. 18). Yet this was not pressed in
actual practice. [139] The proselyte was forbidden to have a wife who was a blood relative
on his mother's side, which was forbidden in paganism too. He could marry any wife to
whom he was related on his father's side. [140] Hence the OT laws of incest did not really
apply to the proselyte. In support of this judgment appeal was made to the principle that
the non-Jew has no father, [141] so that all (pagan) relationships on the father's side were
negated. In Judaism the proselyte might marry within all strata of the population [142]
apart from the priestly caste.

The ruling against priestly marriage was based on Lv. 21:13 f. Here the priest is
forbidden to marry "a widow, or a divorced woman, or profane, or a harlot; he shall
take only a virgin of his own people to wife." [143] Since only native Israelite girls were
here allowed to marry priests, marriage with a proselytess was ruled out. In the Rabbis,
however, the unsuitability of the proselytess for marriage with a priest is based on the
first part of the OT rule. The proselytess is regarded as a harlot, since as a former
Gentile she is under suspicion of having committed fornication, [144] so bJeb., 6, 5 etc. [145]
Acc. to bJeb., 60b, bQid., 78a etc. proselytesses who were converted when under three
years of age were regarded as eligible for marriage with priests, since there could then
be no grounds for suspecting fornication. But this is a relaxing of the ancient practice. [146]

The OT provisions for helping resident aliens (gleaning at harvest, poor relief and
alms) were reinterpreted by the Rabb. and applied to proselytes, [147] as quite expressly
in the exegesis of Lv. 19:10 in S. Lv., 19, 10 (348a), [148] which concludes as follows:
"Scripture teaches: To the poor, Lv. 19:10. As the poor is needy and a son of the
covenant, so must all (who share in the pea) be needy and sons of the covenant (full
Jews)." If gleaning and the pea are not forbidden to non-Israelites, it is simply "for the
sake of peace," Git., 5, 8.

5. The גר תושב and the ירא שמים (→ V, 850, 6 ff.).

In the OT (→ 730, 6 ff.) תּוֹשָׁב means the non-Jew in Israel standing in the sociological
relation of the resident alien but without the religious accent of גֵּר. As the Rabb. understand the OT תושב it is natural that as a non-Jew he must keep the commandments

---

[135] bJeb., 62a with ref. to the (double) portion of the firstborn.
[136] Gerim, 3, 8; bGit., 39a. Acc. to Gerim, 3, 9 ff. this applies to the whole estate except
for portions which provide for his wife or a creditor, cf. Gerim, 3, 11-12; Jeremias, *Jerusalem*,
200.
[137] Gerim, 3, 8.
[138] Jeremias, *Jerusalem*, 199 f.
[139] For the reason cf. bJeb., 22a: "That they might not be able to say they have come
from greater sanctity to lesser sanctity" (in so far as marriages previously forbidden are
now allowed in Judaism), v. Str.-B., III, 353 f.
[140] bJeb., 98a; bSanh., 57b Bar. and on this Rashi.
[141] Str.-B., III, 353.
[142] Jeremias, *Jerusalem*, 198.
[143] Cf. also Test. L. 9:10; 14:6; Jos. Ap., I, 31.
[144] Though cf. Bamberger, "Proselyte" 2.
[145] Jeremias, *Jerusalem*, 198.
[146] Cf. also bQid., 78b, acc. to which R. Jose b. Chalaphta (c. 150 A.D.) allows the
daughter of a proselyte marriage to marry a priest.
[147] → 735, 25 on Tob. 1:8.
[148] Cf. Str.-B., IV, 690.

laid on non-Jews too, namely, the seven Noachic commandments. In Rabb. writings, then, the term גר־) תושב) [149] comes to mean a non-Jew who keeps these seven commandments in distinction from the goy who does not. Cf. the dominant Rabb. definition (bAZ, 64b): "Who is a גר תושב?... The (Rabb.) scribes say: Any man who has accepted the seven commandments which the sons of Noah accepted." [150] As compared with this religious definition the older sociological definition of תושב fell into disuse, so that in a different way the same thing happened with תושב as had previously happened with גר. In Talmudic law the גר תושב falls under the category of non-Jews. Thus he may eat נבילות (i.e., that which has not been slaughtered ritually). [151] The Jew is forbidden *connubium* with him, [152] and he may be charged interest acc. to the Mishnah. [153] In view of the fact that the גר תושב keeps the seven Noachic commandments his position is in many respects unique as compared with other non-Jews. Thus separation from a goy is obligatory as from an idolater, but this is not necessary in relation to the גר תושב, since he observes the Noachic prohibition of idolatry. [154]

Among non-Jews who kept the Jewish commandments to a limited degree, who observed more strictly the Noachic commandments, but who had not been circumcised and hence in fact had not come over to Judaism but were גרי תושב, the Rabbis reckoned the σεβόμενοι τὸν θεόν. יְרְאֵי שָׁמַיִם is the term used for them in Rabbinic writings, i.e., those who fear God. φοβούμενοι τὸν θεόν is a literal semiticising rendering, σεβόμενοι τὸν θεόν a freer translation and better Greek. To these יראי שמים apply occasional sayings in the Talmud according to which there are righteous men among non-Jews, e.g., the saying of R. Jehoshua (c. 90 A.D.): "There are even among the peoples righteous men who have a share in the world to come" (T. Sanh., 13, 2; bSanh., 105a), or the well-known pronouncement of R. Meir (c. 150 A.D.): "A goy who keeps the Torah is of much greater value in God's sight even than the high-priest himself" (S. Lv., 18, 5 etc.). [155] Nevertheless, the predominant evaluation of the יראי שמים in Rabbinic Judaism is unfavourable. Unlike the Hellenistic Judaism of the *diaspora* (→ 731, 6 ff.), which was the true home of the יראי שמים, Talmudic Judaism, with its roots in the Palestinian tradition, was not content simply to have uncircumcised Gentiles as loose adherents. It would accord recognition only to those who came over to Judaism properly by circumcision. This outlook of Rabbinic Judaism finds typical expression in the answer of the proselyte Aquila to the objection to his conversion that he could have learned the Torah without being circumcised: "A man can never learn the Torah if he is not (already) circumcised." [156] With this demand for the full conversion of the σεβόμενος τὸν θεόν agrees that which is required of the תושב too: If twelve months after accepting the seven Noachic command-

---

[149] The usual term in Rabb. writings is גר־תושב (Lv. 25:47). In contrast to the proselyte (גר בן ברית or circumcised ger) he is the גר ערל (the uncircumcised ger). Tg. O. and Tg. J. I on Lv. 25:47 ערל תותב.

[150] For other explanations cf. Str.-B., II, 722 f. The differences in definition show that this group of non-Jews no longer existed in the Talmudic period so that nothing precise was known about them. Kuhn, "Ursprung," 218, n. 6.

[151] bAZ, 64b; cf. Str.-B., II, 722.

[152] Gerim, 3, 3.

[153] BM, 5, 6, though cf. Gerim, 3, 3. On this Polster, 9; Moore, I, 339.

[154] For this reason the produce of the גר תושב, e.g., may be declared clean, Gerim, 3, 2.

[155] For further examples cf. Str.-B., II, 719-721; Kuhn, "Ursprung," 219 f.

[156] Tanch., 92a, in Str.-B., III, 489 f.; cf. also the other examples in Str.-B., II, 719 f.

ments he does not take the further step of full conversion as a proselyte, he is again regarded as in every respect a goy. [157] This shows that the ירַאי שמים were placed under the category of the תושב.

At a later date there were no longer any σεβόμενοι τὸν θεόν and by the middle of the 3rd century the Rabbis were only partly aware of what was meant by the ירַאי שמים. [158] From then on they were incorrectly equated with proselytes. [159]

D. The New Testament.

I. προσήλυτος.

The term προσήλυτος occurs 4 times in the NT.

1. It is found first in Jesus' denunciation of the Pharisees in Mt. 23:15. The tremendous efforts made by the Pharisees to win even one proselyte are understandable in the light of the deep-seated distinction between the missionary work of Hellenistic Judaism, which was satisfied with the loose adherence of Gentiles as σεβόμενοι τὸν θεόν (→ 731, 11 ff.), and the mission of Palestinian Judaism, and especially the Pharisees, who regarded full conversion by circumcision as necessary to salvation and who demanded acceptance of the whole Jewish Law in their sense (→ 734, 17 ff.). Because the Pharisees make the convert to Judaism keep the Law as they themselves do, he becomes a ὑποκριτής as they are and therewith a υἱὸς γεέννης. [160]

2. In Ac. 2:11 we read of proselytes, alongside Ἰουδαῖοι (→ III, 379, 36 ff.), in the list of national groups of the Jewish dispersion who were present in Jerusalem for Pentecost. Unlike the other names on the list, these two terms do not denote geographical origin but the relation to Judaism. [161] Ἰουδαῖοί τε καὶ προσήλυτοι means "native Jews and those who have been converted to Judaism (= proselytes)." This sums up the religious position [162] of the groups just mentioned. [163] Since it can only come at the end, the Κρῆτες καὶ Ἄραβες which follows is to be regarded as a later addition, → 51, n. 44. [164]

3. In Ac. 6:5, in the list of members of the seven, Νικόλαος is differentiated from the others by the apposition προσήλυτος Ἀντιοχεύς. Since Ἑλληνισταί in 6:1 means Jews of Hellenistic origin living in Jerusalem (→ II, 511, 27 ff.; III, 389, 24 ff.), [165] and since Stephen was clearly a Jew according to the narrative which follows, the distinction can only imply that the other six were Jews by

---

[157] jJeb., 8, 1 (8d, 27 f.); cf. bAZ, 65a, v. Kuhn, "Ursprung," 220.

[158] Str.-B., II, 720 f.

[159] Cf. Gn. r., 8 (17d); Str.-B., II, 721.

[160] The saying does not mean that Jesus was condemning the Jewish mission (so Loh. Mt., 343) nor that He approved of it. It simply posits proselytising as a fact, and also the pride of Palest. Judaism in the results. Its main concern is with the consequences when the work is done by the Pharisees as the ὑποκριταί they are.

[161] Cf. Wdt. Ag., 81.

[162] Haench. Ag., 137.

[163] Some older comm. (in Wdt. Ag., 81) take Ἰουδαῖοί τε καὶ προσήλυτοι differently, namely, in apposition to Ῥωμαῖοι. In this case, however, it is a mystery why Roman proselytes should be mentioned and not those from other places too, cf. Wdt. Ag., 81.

[164] So also A. v. Harnack, Beitr. u. Einl. in d. NT, III : Die Ag. (1908), 65-67; Pr. Ag., 12; Wdt. Ag., 82; A. Loisy, Les actes des apôtres (1920), 190 f.; Haench. Ag., 137.

[165] So rightly Haench. Ag., 218, n. 1 as against H. J. Cadbury in Jackson-Lake, I, 4, 64; 5, 59-74, and E. Lohmeyer, "Das Abendmahl in d. Urgemeinde," JBL, 56 (1937), 236 f.

descent whereas Nicolaos had come over from paganism to Judaism by accepting circumcision, and he had come to Jerusalem from Antioch (and was thus a "Hellenist").

4. In Ac. 13:43 there is a reference to πολλοὶ τῶν Ἰουδαίων καὶ τῶν σεβομένων προσηλύτων. This more precise definition of προσήλυτοι is unique.[166] Since elsewhere in Acts the associated groups are always Ἰουδαῖοι or Ἰσραηλῖται and σεβόμενοι (φοβούμενοι) τὸν θεόν in the technical sense, i.e., Jews and Gentiles who came to synagogue worship, this must be the meaning here too. In other words σεβόμενοι is the tt. and the addition of προσήλυτοι is materially incorrect. An open question is whether the addition was a slip of Luke's or an ancient gloss.[167]

II. σεβόμενοι or φοβούμενοι τὸν θεόν.

These phrases occur only in Acts, φοβούμενοι τὸν θεόν in the first section, σεβόμενοι τὸν θεόν in the second.

1. The attitude of the primitive Palestinian community to σεβόμενοι τὸν θεόν was based on that of Palestinian Judaism. The only non-Jew to have a part in the salvation effected in Jesus was the one who had first become a member of the Jewish people by the acceptance of circumcision and of the obligation to keep the whole Jewish Torah. Otherwise the non-Jew remained a Gentile and as such he would fall victim to God's wrath in the Last Judgment. To attain to salvation it was not enough to be a σεβόμενος τὸν θεόν and as such to accept faith in Jesus. Typical of this attitude is the charge which the Jewish Christians brought against Peter in Ac. 11:3, namely, that he did not observe the required separation from non-Jews in the case of the Roman centurion Cornelius, who according to Ac. 10:2, 22 was a φοβούμενος τὸν θεόν and was particularly zealous as such in his adherence to the Jewish religion (v. 2),[168] cf. also v. 28, 45. According to the account in Acts the different attitude of Peter was due to a vision and the certainty which it imparted that God saves the Gentile, the φοβούμενος, without his conversion to Judaism and simply through his faith in Jesus, cf. 11:17 f.; 10:35. In accordance with the position of Palestinian Jewish Christianity the missionaries mentioned in Ac. 11:19 preach only to native Jews (Ἰουδαῖοι), whereas in Antioch those mentioned in 11:20 preach salvation in Jesus to (pious) Greeks as well (Ἕλληνες = σεβόμενοι τὸν θεόν).[169]

2. The missionary work of Paul is described in Acts as always beginning with preaching in Jewish synagogues, cf. 13:14; 14:1; 17:10; 17:17; 18:4 etc. As was to be expected in the synagogues of Hellenistic Judaism, Paul's hearers consisted not only of Ἰουδαῖοι, i.e., full members of the Jewish people by birth or conversion,[170] but also of Greeks (Ἕλληνες), who attended synagogue worship

[166] Cf. Wdt. Ag., 245.

[167] Haench. Ag., 361, n. 6 conjectures the latter. In post-NT writings προσήλυτος occurs only in Just. Dial., 13, 3.

[168] Like Cornelius, the centurion of Capernaum in Lk. 7:1-10 is a non-Jew who adheres to the Jewish religion with gt. zeal as σεβόμενος τὸν θεόν (though this term is not used in the context). He even gave money to build a synagogue.

[169] Cf. what follows, though also W. Michaelis, "Judaistische Heidenchristen," ZNW, 30 (1931), 93-99.

[170] With Ἰουδαῖοι in 13:50; 14:1 f.; 17:5, 17; 18:4 etc. we also find ἄνδρες Ἰσραηλῖται (13:16) and υἱοὶ γένους Ἀβραάμ (13:26) in the same sense.

but had not taken the step of proselyte conversion which would make them Ἰουδαῖοι. To denote the latter group we find not only Ἕλληνες (14:1; 18:4; 19:10) but also the more exact φοβούμενοι τὸν θεόν (13:16, 26) or σεβόμενοι τὸν θεόν (16:14; 17:17; 18:7), and once even σεβόμενοι Ἕλληνες (17:4). According to Acts Paul's missionary preaching enjoyed its greatest success among these σεβόμενοι τὸν θεόν, cf. the results in Pisidian Antioch (13:48), Thessalonica (17:4 : τῶν τε σεβομένων Ἑλλήνων πλῆθος πολύ), Berea (17:12), Iconium (14:1) and Corinth (18:4). This success among the σεβόμενοι τὸν θεόν is to be explained by the fact that Paul, unlike the Jewish Christians of Palestine, did not make conversion to Judaism by circumcision a condition of salvation. On the other hand, he is not satisfied with a mere confession of monotheism. He preaches faith in Jesus Christ as alone necessary to salvation, cf. 13:39. This explains the opposition of the Jews who according to 18:13 bring him before Gallio and accuse him of persuading men παρὰ τὸν νόμον σέβεσθαι τὸν θεόν. Rejection by native Jews causes Paul to preach exclusively to pious Gentiles or Ἕλληνες who had been attached to the Jewish synagogue as σεβόμενοι τὸν θεόν : ἐγὼ ἀπὸ τοῦ νῦν εἰς τὰ ἔθνη πορεύσομαι, 18:6. That the ἔθνη are these pious Gentiles is shown by the next verse which tells us that Paul went to the home of the σεβόμενος τὸν θεόν, Titius Justus.

As we have seen (→ 731, 1 ff.; 732, 33 ff.) contemporary Jewish usage differentiated sharply between προσήλυτοι who had become Jews by circumcision and the σεβόμενοι τὸν θεόν who in spite of their personal piety were still Gentiles according to Jewish estimation. It will thus be evident that the depiction of Paul's missionary work in Acts is always in exact agreement with the current situation. Since it is so true to life, there is no reason to doubt its historicity. [171]

Kuhn

---

[171] As against M. Dibelius, "Die Reden d. Ag. u. die antike Geschichtsschreibung," *Aufsätze z. Ag.*² (1953), 129; cf. Haench. Ag., 482.

---

† προσκόπτω, † πρόσκομμα,	→ λίθος, IV, 271, 24 ff. → πέτρα, 97, 38 ff.
† προσκοπή, † ἀπρόσκοπος	→ πίπτω κτλ., 161, 3 ff. → σκάνδαλον κτλ.

Contents : A. The Usage : I. προσκόπτω : 1. Literal ; 2. Transferred ; II. πρόσκομμα : 1. As nomen acti ; 2. As nomen actionis ; 3. As nomen causae ; III. προσκοπή ; IV. ἀπρόσκοπος. B. The Word Group in the Old Testament and in the Writings of Judaism : I. Hebrew Equivalents ; II. Metaphors ; III. Theological Use. C. The Word Group in the New Testament : I. Old Testament Basis ; II. Specific New Testament Use : 1. Jesus and Falling ; 2. Falling in Faith : a. Men as the Cause of Falling ; b. Christ as the Cause of Falling ; c. ἀπρόσκοπον εἶναι as an Eschatological Goal ; 3. Offence of Conscience. D. The Word Group in the Early Church.

A. The Usage.

With the exception of προσκόπτω itself, which is found already in Aristoph., Xenoph. and Aristot. (→ line 18 f.; n. 69), the words of the group are attested only from the Hellenistic period. [1] They all took on a specific biblical sense in the LXX and especially in the NT, → 751, 32 ff.

I. προσκόπτω.

1. Literal : "to strike, dash against," trans. τὸν δάκτυλον [τοῦ ποδός], Aristoph. Vesp., 275; μήποτε προσκόψῃς πρὸς λίθον τὸν πόδα σου, LXX ψ 90:12 (Mt. 4:6 par.); intrans. a. "to stumble against something (τινί, Xenoph. Eq., 7, 6; Aristot. Mot. An., 6, p. 700b, 13; R. 9:32 (fig. → 754, 21 ff. "to dash against," προσέκοψαν τῇ οἰκίᾳ ἐκείνῃ Mt. 7:27; (πρός τινα) "to give someone a push, jostle against" : προσκόψει τὸ παιδίον πρὸς τὸν πρεσβύτην, LXX Is. 3:5. b. Abs. (a) "to bump oneself"; (the blind Tobit went to the door) καὶ προσέκοπτεν, (b) "to stumble" : κἂν προσκόψῃ (sc. πτωχός), προσανατρέψουσιν (sc. all people) αὐτόν, "when he stumbles [2] they knock him down," Sir. 13:23 (cf. ψ 117:13; counterpart Ps. 37:24, in another fig. Is. 42:3 [Mt. 12:20]); Chrysipp. says that τὸ νοσῆσαι is οἷον προσκόψαι for the good, Plut. Stoic. Rep., 30 (II, 1048b), (c) "to slip," "to fall" ὁ δὲ πούς σου οὐ μὴ προσκόψῃ LXX Prv. 3:23, 6 vl.; (before it becomes dark round about) καὶ πρὸ τοῦ προσκόψαι πόδας ὑμῶν ἐπ' ὄρη σκοτεινά, "before your feet slip on the mountains by night," Jer. 13:16; αἱ δὲ ὁδοὶ τῶν ἀσεβῶν σκοτειναί, οὐκ οἴδασιν πῶς προσκόπτουσιν, Prv. 4:19; cf. Hos. 14:10 Σ; ψ 9:4 Σ; Is. 8:15 Σ; προσκόψομεν ἐν ἀορασίᾳ ὡς ἐν σκότῳ, ἀφανισμῷ, 59:10 Σ, probably also Jer. 18:23; ἐν ὁδῷ ἀντιπτώματος μὴ πορεύου, ἵνα μὴ προσκόψῃς ἐν λιθώδεσιν, "in order that you do not fall in stony places," [3] LXX Sir. 32(35):20; Jn. 11:9 f. → 752, 34 ff. (d) In a broader sense "to fall,"

προσκόπτω, πρόσκομμα. Cr.-Kö., 617-619; A. Bonhöffer, *Epiktet und d. NT* (1911), 128 f.; J. Lindblom, "Zum Begriff 'Anstoss' im NT," Strena Philologica Upsaliensis, *Festschr. f. Per Persson* (1922), 1-6; G. Stählin, *Skandalon* (1930), 95-97, 130 f., 261-265; K. Fullerton, "The Stone of Foundation," *Amer. Journal of Semitic Languages and Literatures,* 37 (1920/21), 1-50; V. Taylor, *The Names of Jesus* (1953), 93-97. προσκοπή. A. Bonhöffer, *Epiktet und die Stoa* (1890), 276; Bchm. 2 K., 277. ἀπρόσκοπος. Nägeli, 43; Lindblom, *op. cit.,* 3 f.; Loh. Phil., 33, n. 6.

[1] Though cf. Helbing, 114. Aristot. has once (Mechanica, 11, p. 852a, 32) the verbal noun πρόσκοψις ("rubbing," cf. *ibid.,* 8, p. 851b, 23).

[2] Lit. (as 13:21b), not (Lindblom, 2): "when he slips up in what he says."

[3] Though cf. Pr.-Bauer⁵, *s.v.* 2a; προσκόπτω ἔν τινι only in Sir. 30:13 and R. 14:21 for certain, → 746, 5.

"to succumb," Ju. 20:32 LXX A; Dt. 28:25 Σ (?) [4] → 749, 29 ff.; "to suffer hurt, misfortune" : καὶ προσκόψει (sc. the king of Syria) καὶ πεσεῖται καὶ οὐχ εὑρεθήσεται, Da. 11:14, 19 LXX; cf. also Ps. Sol. 3:5, 9; "to perish" (the understanding in the people) προσκόψουσι ῥομφαίᾳ, Da. 11:33; also : ἵνα μὴ ἐν τῇ ἀσχημοσύνῃ αὐτοῦ (sc. thy son's) προσκόψῃς, "in order that thou do not suffer pain through his shameful conduct," [5] Sir. 30:13; "to suffer spiritual hurt," R. 14:21 → 753, 9 ff.; 1 Pt. 2:8 → 756, 11 ff.

2. Transferred : a. Fig. starting-pt. "to give offence to another" (a) τινί : Polyb., 5, 49, 5 (with λυπέω); 7, 5, 6 (with δυσαρεστέω, "to cause displeasure") μᾶλλον ἀνθρώποις ἄφροσι ... προσκόψωμεν ἢ τῷ θεῷ, "we will cheerfully give offence to foolish men, but in no circumstances to God," [6] 1 Cl., 21, 5; cf. 1 Th. 2:4; προσκόψαι τῷ πατρί, Cl. Al. Strom., II, 53, 4; προσκεκοφὸς τῷ θεῷ, Synesios, Catastasis (MPG, 66, 1569 C) → 756, 16 ff. (b) abs.: καλλωπίζεσθαι ... τὸ σῶμα ... μέχρι τοῦ μὴ προσκόπτειν, "in so far as one will not give offence thereby," Epict. Diss., IV, 11, 33; cf. R. 13:14; μὴ ἀπληστεύου (with invitations) μήποτε προσκόψῃς, Sir. 31:17; cf. 30:13 cod. B → n. 5. b. Fig. starting-pt "to take offence at someone," [7] (a) τινί : οὐ προσκόψει οὐδενί, Epict. Diss., I, 28, 10; προσκόπτων ("to be annoyed at") τοῖς περὶ τὸν Λεόντιον, Polyb., 5, 7, 5; also the perf. Diod. S., 13, 80, 4; cf. προσκόψαντες ("to be enraged at") τῇ βαρύτητι (with δυσαρεστέω "to be dissatisfied"), Polyb., 1, 31, 7; ἐπὶ πλέον προσκόψαι ("to be even more incensed at") τοῖς λόγοις, Diod. S., 17, 30, 4; Aegeus when he saw the black sail went up to the castle καὶ διὰ τὴν ὑπερβολὴν τῆς λύπης προσκόψαντα τῷ ζῆν ("was beside himself about his life, despaired of it") ἑαυτὸν κατακρημνίσαι, Diod. S., 4, 61, 7. The med. too in the same sense, M. Ant., XI, 3, 6; Appian Bell. Civ., II, 27. (b) ἐπί τινι : ὅταν προσκόπτῃς ἐπί τινος ἁμαρτίᾳ, M. Ant., X, 30, 1. (c) abs. with δυσαρεστέω or δυσαρεστέομαι, "to experience displeasure," "to be vexed," Polyb., 6, 6, 3 and 6 : πάντες προσκόπτουσιν, sc. at the Cynic beggar, Epict. Diss., III, 22, 89; with ἐπισημαίνομαι "to declare one's displeasure," M. Ant., VI, 20, 1; with ἀγανακτέω, Diod. S., 1, 71, 2.

II. πρόσκομμα.

As a verbal noun in -μα [8] πρόσκομμα is properly a nomen acti ("result of falling," "destruction") but like other forms of this kind (e.g., αἰτίωμα Ac. 25:7, βάπτισμα → I, 545, 5 ff.; θέλημα → III, 52 ff.; κρίμα → III, 942, 10 ff.) it can also have the sense of a nomen actionis [9] ("stumbling," "falling" → 757, 3 ff.) and even that of a means (cf. ἄντλημα Jn. 4:11), "cause of falling" (nomen causae, cf. μέθυσμα, Herm. m., 8, 3).

1. As nomen acti. a. the "damage" or "wound" caused by stumbling, Athen., 3, 52 (97 f.) with ὑπώπιον the "bump" caused by a blow (cf. ὑπωπιάζω, 1 C. 9:27); b. "hurt," [10] "destruction," "ruin" : πολλοὺς ἀπώλεσεν ἡ πορνεία, for it brings shame to men καὶ πρόσκομμα τῷ Βελιαρ, "and destruction through (?) Beliar," Test. R. 4:7, but → n. 33; c. "(moral) fall," "sin" : ἐν προσκόμματι ὑπάρχω, "to live in sins," Const. Ap., II, 17, 1.

2. As nomen actionis : λίθος προσκόμματος, "the stone on which there is the stumbling, which leads to a fall," Is. 8:14 ᾽ΑΣΘ (LXX); R. 9:32 f.; 1 Pt. 2:8, also in the sense of a gen. of quality [11] as, e.g., ἡμέρα ἐπισκοπῆς, 1 Pt. 2:12; ἀκροατὴς ἐπι-

---

[4] Stählin, 130, n. 4.

[5] Cod B : προσκόψῃ, "that he may not ... cause offence."

[6] On this use of μᾶλλον ἤ cf. Ac. 4:19; 5:29; 20:35 (on this J. Jeremias, Unbekannte Jesusworte[2] [1951], 74 f.); 1 Tm. 1:4 (cf. Bl.-Debr. § 185, 2 App.); Pr.-Bauer[5], s.v. μᾶλλον 3c.

[7] Perhaps the use of προσκρούω (e.g., Demosth. Or., 21, 61; 24, 6) and of offendo had some influence here, cf. J. Hering, Lateinisches bei Appian, Diss. Leipzig (1935), 30.

[8] Cf. Bl.-Debr. § 109, 2.

[9] Cf. the par. use of πρόσκομμα and πτῶσις in LXX Sir. 34:16 → 749, 6 f.

[10] Hesych., s.v. takes πρόσκομμα in the sense of ζημία, βλάβη.

[11] Cf. Bl.-Debr. § 165.

λησμονῆς, Jm. 1:25 or a gen. epexegeticus : "a stone which is a cause of falling" (→ lines 5 ff.), as, e.g., ἀρραβὼν τοῦ πνεύματος, 2 C. 5:5; [12] also ξύλον προσκόμματος, [13] Sir. 31:7; God is φυλακὴ ἀπὸ προσκόμματος καὶ βοήθεια ἀπὸ πτώσεως, Sir. 34:16; perhaps also 31:30 → 751, 1 f.

3. As nomen causae. a. lit. (esp. in the metaphor of the way → 748, 37 ff.) "cause of falling," "(damaging) obstacle" : αἱ ὁδοὶ αὐτοῦ (sc. God's) τοῖς ὁσίοις εὐθεῖαι, οὕτως τοῖς ἀνόμοις προσκόμματα, "the ways of God will themselves set dangerous obstacles for the ungodly," Sir. 39:24; remove the προσκόμματα (LXX σκῶλα) from the way of my people, Is. 57:14 Σ; in the metaphor of the two ways ἡ στρεβλὴ ὁδός ... ἔχει ... ἀνοδίας καὶ προσκόμματα πολλά, Herm. m., 6, 1, 3. b. transf.: (a) "cause of hurt or misfortune," Ex. 23:33; 34:12; cf. εἰς πρόσκομμα, "to destruction," Jer. 3:3 → 749, 21 ff.; also Sir. 31:30. [14] (b) "Hindrance to faith," "cause of spiritual ruin," R. 14:13; 1 C. 8:9 → 753, 9 ff. (c) "Temptation," "seduction to a moral fall, to sin," Is. 29:21; Sir. 17:25 (?) → 750, 30 ff., also Herm. m., 2, 4.

III. προσκοπή.

The verbal noun προσκοπή ("stumbling") is rare and is found only in a transf. sense, usually 1. for "taking offence," "aversion," "irritation" : κατὰ προσκοπήν "as a result of taking offence," "out of aversion," Stob. Ecl., II, 93, 10 with φθόνος, Polyb., 6, 7, 8; with ἀλλοτριότης, "antipathy," 31, 10, 4; διδόναι προσκοπῆς καὶ δυσαρεστήσεως (→ 746, 24 f., 13, 18) ἀφορμάς, 27, 7, 10. To this context belongs the technical use of προσκοπή in Stoicism : [15] there is a sick inclination (νόσημα = aegrotatio) which is directed to what is not worth desiring as though it were, and also a sick aversion which arises through antipathy as the result of an offence (κατὰ προσκοπήν = ex offensione) and is directed against things which should not be spurned as if they ought to be, Cic. Tusc., IV, 26; cf. IV, 10, 25; εἶναι δέ τινα καὶ ἐναντία <τούτοις> τοῖς νοσήμασι κατὰ προσκοπὴν γινόμεναι οἷον μισογυνίαν, μισοινίαν, μισανθρωπίαν, Stob. Ecl., II, 93, 9 ff. [16] 2. Like πρόσκομμα (→ line 5 f.): "occasion of falling, of taking offence," also "reason for antipathy" : μηδεμίαν ἐν μηδενὶ διδόντες προσκοπήν, 2 C. 6:3; cf. ἀπρόσκοπος γίνομαι, 1 C. 10:32 → 753, 27 ff.

IV. ἀπρόσκοπος.

The verbal adj. ἀπρόσκοπος ("not causing to stumble") is rare and late in secular lit. → 748, 2 ff. It follows the various senses of the verb : [17] 1. (→ 745, 26 ff.) a. "what does not cause to fall" : μὴ πιστεύσῃς ἐν ὁδῷ ἀπροσκόπῳ (way without ἀντίπτωμα, v. 20 → 749, 6) "do not entrust yourself without caution to a way which seems to be without perils," or "do not believe there is a way without perils," Sir. 32:21; cf. v. 22 : ἀπὸ τῶν τέκνων σου φύλαξαι! b. "not falling" fig. of the ὀρθὴ ὁδός (→ 749, 2 ff.):

---

[12] The reversal of the relation of dependence at LXX Is. 8:14 (οὐχ ὡς λίθου προσκόμματι ... οὐδὲ ὡς πέτρας πτώματι) finds par. in the NT, e.g., ἐπὶ πλούτου ἀδηλότητι, 1 Tm. 6:17; διὰ ἀνακαινώσεως πνεύματος ἁγίου, Tt. 3:5; also R. 6:4; 7:6 and on this Winer, 34, 2.

[13] In the par. v. (7b) we read : ἁλώσεται ἐν αὐτῷ (sc. the gold); here, then, is the common pair of metaphors (→ σκάνδαλον): the stick without which one would fall, and the snares which entrap one, → 750, 10 ff.

[14] The par. v. suggests this interpretation (esp. προσποιῶν τραύματα); the sense "offensive action" (V. Ryssel in Kautzsch Apkr. u. Pseudepigr., ad loc.) does not occur in the LXX, cf. Stählin, 96, also → line 4.

[15] Cf. Bonhöffer, Epiktet u. die Stoa, 276.

[16] These instances are also in Chrysipp. Fr., 427 (v. Arnim, III, 104, 31-35), 424 (103, 21-28), 421 (102, 37-103, 2); Cic. and Stob. are obviously quoting these passages.

[17] In some sense προσκοπτικός is the anton. of ἀπρόσκοπος : 1. "offensive," "arousing aversion," Epict. Diss., I, 18, 9; 2. as a tt. in horoscopes "falling easily," "an unlucky person," Vett. Val., II, 10 (p. 65, 24 f.), 14 (68, 22); V, 3 (212, 21); also II, 16 (77, 7), where the context demands προσκοπτικοί in place of the προκοπτικοί of the text.

ὁμαλῶς περιπατοῦσι καὶ ἀπροσκόπως, "they journeyed on and did not stumble," Herm. m., 6, 1, 4; thanks be to all the gods ὅτι σε διαφυλάσσουσι ἀπρόσκοπον, "without suffering hurt or misfortune," "intact," "whole," P. Giess., I, 17, 7 (age of Hadrian); cf. 22, 9 : ἀπρόσ[κοπ]ος καὶ ἱλαρώτατος, "well and cheerful." 2. (→ 746, 7 ff.) "what does not give offence," a. "inoffensive," of an incorrect usage, Sext. Emp. Math., I, 195; ἵνα μετὰ φιλίας καὶ ἀπροσκόπως ἐξέλθωμεν ἀπ᾽ αὐτῶν ἐν ἀγαθῷ, "that we may be able to part from them on good terms, in friendship, and without vexing them," P. Giess., I, 79 col. IV, 8; b. "blameless" : ἔζησε ἀπρόσκοπος [18] ἔτη λς (36), IG, 14, 404; μιμούμενος (sc. θεόν) ἀπρόσκοπος (sc. for God) ἂν εἴης, Ep. Ar., 210; cf. Phil. 1:10 → 756, 11 ff.; τὴν λειτουργίαν αὐτῶν ἀπροσκόπως ἐπιτελοῦσιν, 1 Cl., 20, 10; in a prayer for temporal lords : εἰς τὸ διέπειν αὐτοὺς τὴν ... ἡγεμονίαν ἀπροσκόπως, "that they may exercise their lordship blamelessly," 1 Cl., 61, 1; also of the bishop : ἀμέμπτως καὶ ἀπροσκόπως ἐν τῇ ἐπισκοπῇ διατελείτω, "without giving offence," Sacramentarium Serapionis, 28, 2 [19] (cf. πρόσκομμα → 747, 12 ff.); 1 C. 10:32 → 753, 29 ff. 3. (→ 746, 15 ff.): "not taking offence," so perhaps Ac. 24:16: ἀπρόσκοπος συνείδησις → 757, 23 ff. and cf. Const. Ap., II, 9, 1: ἀπρόσκοπον εἶναι χρὴ τὸν ἐπίσκοπον in the sense of "having a conscience which takes no offence at, does not take exception to, his conduct," "which is clear," for the opp. in the following sentence is οὐκ εὐσυνείδητος ὑπάρχων.

B. The Word Group in the Old Testament and in the Writings of Judaism.

I. Hebrew Equivalents.

The first Heb. equivalent to the stem προσκοπ- is כשל (q and ni "to fall," hi "to cause to fall"); then we have תקל, taken from the Aram. Only rarely, however, does the LXX have προσκόπτω for כשל, Prv. 4:19; Da. 11:14, 19, 33. Σ seems to have it more often (Is. 5:27; 8:15; 59:10; Hos. 14:10; Ps. 9:3). In both the use is restricted to the prophets and writings. ᾽A has it only at Ps. 9:3; elsewhere he prefers √ σκανδαλ- (→ σκανδαλίζω). LXX and Σ show the same preference in the transl. of the noun מכשול, [20] (cf. 1 QS 2:12, 17). Apart from כשל, נגף (usually to "strike," also "to push") [21] is also rendered προσκόπτω, Ju. 20:32; ψ 90:12; Prv. 3:23; Jer. 13:16; once each in ᾽A : ψ 90:12 and Σ [?]: Dt. 28:25 → 749, 29 ff.). πρόσκομμα is also used once for נגף (Is. 8:14). The main original of LXX πρόσκομμα, however, is מוקש (Ex. 23:33; 34:12; probably also Jer. 3:3; [22] cf. also Is. 29:21: πρόσκομμα τίθημι for קוש = יקוש), which involves a remarkable shift of images between מוקש ("snare," "trap" = σκάνδαλον) and מכשול ("stumbling" = πρόσκομμα). [23] Finally, in Sir. προσκόπτω is mostly used for תקל ni (13:23; 30:13; 32:20) and πρόσκομμα for תקלה (31:7).

II. Metaphors.

The metaphors associated with the group fall into two classes : [24] 1. the metaphor of the way (→ ὁδός, V, 49, 37 ff. cf. Is. 8:14 LXX; 57:14 Σ; Sir. 31:7; 34:16; 39:24, also Herm. m., 6, 1, 3) and 2. that of the stone (→ λίθος IV, 274, 1 ff.; → πέτρα, 97, 38 ff.), which as such is definitely ambivalent (→ 754, 24 ff.) but which has a negative aspect here, Is. 8:14 = R. 9:33; 1 Pt. 2:8 → 754, 21 ff.; cf. Lk. 20:18; Barn., 6, 2. The images of the way and the stone, which are closely related in origin, are often combined (e.g.,

---

[18] The inscr. has the form ἀπρόσκοπος, not attested elsewhere, Nägeli, 43.

[19] Ed. F. X. Funk, Didasc. et Const. Ap., II (1905), 160.

[20] Cf. Stählin, 86 f., 130.

[21] For נגף the LXX has the synon. πταίω more often than προσκόπτω.

[22] Cf. Stählin, 53, 27 f.

[23] Ibid., 23-47, 53 f.

[24] In the Paul. use of Is. 8:14 (R. 9:32) there is combined with it 3. the metaphor of the contest, cf. Stählin, 197 → n. 57.

Prv. 4:12; Lam. 3:9; Mt. 16:23; 1 Jn. 2:10), esp. in the metaphor of the two ways (→ V, 53, 49 ff.; 57, 15 ff.; 70, 17 ff.), so Sir. 39:24 : God's ways (the things which He has ordained) are smooth for the righteous, with no stumbling-blocks (cf. Is. 57:14), but for the ungodly there are only προσκόμματα, "harmful obstacles."[25] Similarly a way can become a σκάνδαλον (ψ 48:14, not the HT) and hence a ὁδὸς ἀντιπτώματος, Sir. 32:20.[26] Cf. also Herm. m., 6, 1, 3, → V, 95, 32 ff.[27] On the other hand, on a different view controlled by the NT law of suffering προσκόμματα can be a mark of the right way, e.g., Chrys. Hom. Matth., 59 (MPG, 58, 574 C : κωλύματα), cf. Mt. 7:13 f., and cf. already Xenoph. Mem., II, 1, 23 : the way of κακία is ἡδίστη καὶ ῥᾴστη.

III. Theological Use.

1. In the OT translations the group προσκόπτω κτλ. and related terms (→ n. 28) are often used in connection with the doctrine of retribution. Stumbling, falling, suffering misfortune, is a punishment for sin, and often in such a way that the sin itself is the destruction ordained by God.

a. According to the Deuteronomistic theology of history the main cause of disaster in Israel is the worship of pagan gods, as in Ex. 23:33, where the Mas. says of idolatry and the LXX of the pagan gods themselves : οὗτοι ἔσονταί σοι πρόσκομμα,[28] or Ex. 34:12 : "Make no covenant with the inhabitants of the land (v. 11) lest they become a מוֹקֵשׁ ("snare") to thee," LXX : "that no πρόσκομμα arise in the midst of you," namely, in the form of idolatry (cf. v. 15 f.); cf. also Jer. 3:3 : ἔσχες ποιμένας πολλοὺς εἰς πρόσκομμα σεαυτῇ : the ποιμένες are the "lovers" of the apostate people, i.e., idols.[29]

It is thus easy to see how πρόσκομμα, like → σκάνδαλον (Hos. 4:17 LXX; Zeph. 1:3 Σ) can be used in the sense of "personified destruction" for false gods or idols (Ez. 20:7 Θ),[30] like Abaddon and Apollyon in Rev. 9:11, which both mean "destruction," "destroyer" (→ I, 4, 12 ff.; 397, 13 ff.). One may compare the par. use of גִּלּוּלִים "idols" and מִכְשׁוֹל עֲוֹנוֹ "cause of sin" (with obvious allusion to Ez. 14:3 f., 7) in 1 QS 2:12. 17, though both are used here in the fig. sense of "idolatrous, sinful thoughts."[31]

b. Even apart from the relation between idolatry and destruction falling is a punishment for the disobedience and ungodliness of the people : δῴη σε κύριος προσκόπτοντα ἐναντίον τῶν ἐχθρῶν σου, Dt. 28:25 Σ (?). In Is. 59:10 Σ, too, stumbling or falling is a metaphor for the many evils which God brings on His people as a penalty (cf. vv. 2-8), also Is. 8:15 Σ : "They shall stumble (προσκό-ψουσι), fall . . . and be snared and taken"; these are the same metaphors (→ n. 13) as in v. 14 (→ 746, 40 ff.), the only difference being that God Himself is now the secret destruction denoted by the metaphors, and especially by the λίθος προσκόμ-ματος, and visited on Israel and Judah because they do not count on God in their politics etc., but go their own independent and crooked ways. In the post-exilic period the same applies to the sins of ungodly individuals who are also

---

[25] Cf. V. Ryssel in Kautzsch Apkr. u. Pseudepigr., ad loc.; Stählin, 95 f.

[26] For a counterpart cf. Is. 49:11.

[27] Cf. also Ex. r., 30 (90b) and S. Dt., 11, 26 § 53 (86a) in Str.-B., I, 462.

[28] For the same thought the LXX also uses σκάνδαλον (Jos. 23:13; Ju. 2:3; 8:27; ψ 105:36; Wis. 14:11) and σκῶλον (Dt. 7:16).

[29] But cf. Stählin, 96, n. 1 (though ποιμένες can hardly refer to the false prophets and priests of the people themselves).

[30] Acc. to J. B. Pitra, Analecta sacra spicilegio Solesmensi parata, III (1883), 571; Stählin, 96.

[31] Cf. among others P. Wernberg-Møller, The Manual of Discipline (1957), 54 f. (n. 29 and 46).

enemies of the righteous. Thus in Prv. 4:19 LXX they will fall unsuspectingly because they fail to see the stumbling-blocks in the ungodly night of their ways, i.e., in their ignorance which is both guilty and disastrous, cf. Mt. 24:39, 50; Jn. 1:10; 2 Pt. 2:12 etc.

One might also refer to ψ 9:4 Σ; Hos. 14:10 Σ where προσκόπτω, like πρόσκομμα in Sir. 39:24 (→ 749, 2 ff.), denotes one of two possibilities which God's ways might mean for men, namely, salvation or ruin, → lines 16 ff.

c. In most of the passages adduced God Himself brings about the overthrow of the people or of the ungodly. Indeed, like the idols (→ 749, 23 ff.), He can be described as the personal cause of the overthrow. We find this most impressively in Is. 8:14 in the two images (→ n. 13) of the stone of stumbling (→ 748, 40 ff.) and the snare [32] (Hos. 13:7 is no less vivid : God as the lion and the panther). The metaphor of Is. 8:14 is the more significant in that elsewhere in the OT God is not only the One who keeps from stumbling and falling (cf. Ps. 91:11 f. → 752, 12 ff.; Sir. 34:16 → 747, 3 f.) but also the rock of refuge and salvation for His people (e.g., Is. 17:10; 26:4; Dt. 32:4, 15, 18 and often in the Ps.). Thus the metaphor of the stone can be a particularly significant expression for the OT message of the God of holy wrath and gracious faithfulness. It finds a NT counterpart in the application to Christ of the image of the stone which works in two ways, → 754, 24 ff. Both uses are simply variations on the no less biblical principle that God and His gifts can bring either salvation or perdition, e.g., Ps. 18:25-27; R. 7:10; 1 C. 1:23 f.; 11:27, 29.

d. Only outside the OT Canon is the devil expressly called the cause of destruction, as apparently [33] in Test. R. 4:7. Nevertheless, when pagan gods are called προσκόμματα and σκάνδαλα (→ line 9), this would suggest to the Greek translators the idea of the demonic background of idolatry. [34]

e. Only infrequently and only in the Wisdom literature is there no relation between destruction and a supernatural power, cf. Sir. 31:7, [35] 30 (→ 747, 3 f.), where ref. is made to the corrosive dangers of gold and wine.

2. It is a moot point (→ 747, 13) whether προσκόπτω κτλ. is used in the LXX for temptation to sin in the sense of falling into it.

Only in a few instances of πρόσκομμα does this transition of meaning call for consideration, e.g., Is. 29:21: πρόσκομμα τίθημί τινα par. ποιέω ἁμαρτεῖν τινα, i.e., "the judges in the gate led them astray into wrong"; [36] Sir. 17:25 : (δεήθητι κατὰ

---

[32] Cf. Stählin, 82 f.

[33] If the text suggested → 746, 36 ff. (Charles) is right : (ἡ πορνεία) ὀνειδισμὸν ... φέρει παρὰ τοὺς υἱοὺς τῶν ἀνθρώπων καὶ πρόσκομμα τῷ Βελίαρ. But perhaps one should read πρόσκωμμα "mocking" (= vl. γέλωτα); then both readings could be renderings of the same Heb. original (Charles). We possibly have the same interchanging of o and ω in Jdt. 8:22, though here we find ὄνειδος alongside πρόσκομμα and it would have to be transl. "cause of aversion" (Lindblom, 3) if original, cf. Stählin, 97, n. 3.

[34] On the further development of the idea of a relation between the devil and offence → σκάνδαλον and Stählin, 301-303.

[35] Only if ἐνθυσιάζουσιν (codd. Bℵ¹ A) is to be read instead of ἐνθουσιάζουσιν ℵ* etc. is idolatry regarded as a source of destruction.

[36] To do this one has to see here a difficult trans. construction of τίθημι πρόσκομμα analogous to the synon. → σκανδαλίζω. More likely in view of the use of πρόσκομμα elsewhere in the LXX is that (the ungodly through bribes) make all judges destruction (for the poor), cf. Sir. 7:6 (→ σκάνδαλον), cf. Stählin, 97.

πρόσωπον καὶ) σμίκρυνον πρόσκομμα par. ἀπόλειπε ἁμαρτίας, v. 25a;[37] 31:30 : πληθύνει μέθη θυμὸν ἄφρονος εἰς πρόσκομμα, "to a moral fall, so that he transgresses," → 747, 12 and n. 14. In one case προσκόπτω, too, may mean "to seduce into sin," namely, at Gr. En. 15:11, where προσκόπτοντα[38] are mentioned in a list of the attributes of πνεύματα τῶν γιγάντων, cf. Gn. 6:4.

On the other hand, in Rabb. writings the Heb. equivalents כָּשַׁל and תִּקְלָה (→ 748, 22 ff.) often have this sense, esp. הִכְשִׁיל and הֵבִיא תִּקְלָה לַחֲבֵרוֹ. The same is true of מִכְשׁוֹל in the Qumran texts, → 749, 26 f. This transition of sense undoubtedly has its basis in the biblical concept of the close causal relation between sin and disaster. This may be seen, e.g., in the Rabb. view that temptation to sin is a mortal sin. Even cattle (Sanh., 7, 4) and trees (bSanh., 55a) are to be destroyed for this, and "how much more does this apply to the man who leads another from the ways of life to the ways of death," loc. cit. Hence the Rabb. (often with appeal to Lv. 19:14 → σκάνδαλον) issue many warnings against tempting to sin,[39] which is viewed just as seriously and punished in the same way as the sin of the one who is tempted, S. Nu., 15 on 5:21,[40] and the righteous pray to God that no children of men may fall through them.[41] It can be said with full assurance, however, that God does not allow any offence to come through the righteous.[42]

C. The Word Group in the New Testament.

I. Old Testament Basis.

In its use of προσκόπτω κτλ. the NT follows the OT in two ways.

1. In the form of quotations : ψ 90:12 is quoted in Mt. 4:6 (Lk. 4:11) acc. to the LXX and Is. 8:14 in R. 9:32 f. and 1 Pt. 2:8 acc. to another (and later) rendering of the OT, → 746, 40 ff.

2. In usage, esp. in the form of similar expressions : προσκόπτω ἔν τινι in R. 14:21 as in Sir. 30:13 (→ 746, 4 ff.; cf. → n. 3); τίθημι πρόσκομμα (τινί) in R. 14:13 as in Is. 29:21 (though here with τινά → 750, 33 f.), πρόσκομμα γίνομαι in 1 C. 8:9 as in Ex. 23:33 (→ 749, 16 f.). New expressions are δίδωμι προσκοπήν in 2 C. 6:3 (though cf. Polyb., 27, 7, 10 : δίδωμι προσκοπῆς ἀφορμάς), and esp. (ἐσθίω) διὰ προσκόμματος in R. 14:20 (→ 756, 37 ff., but cf. Stob. Ecl., II, 93, 10 : κατὰ προσκοπήν, → 747, 17 ff.).

Nevertheless, even though the usage is the same and the same phrases are used word for word, there has been in part a vital change in meaning. This corresponds to the general distinction between the OT and the NT. For whereas disobedience, apostasy and ungodliness are the causes of temporal destruction in the OT, unbelief is the cause of spiritual hurt and eternal perdition in the NT. External injury is in view in the NT only in the quotation from the Psalms in Mt. 4:6 (→ 628, 21), though here προσκόπτω is ambiguous on the lips of the tempter, → 752, 18 ff. The same applies to the metaphorical use in Jn. 11:9 f., → 752, 34 ff.

---

[37] Better : "Lessen (through thy prayer or through turning from sin, v. 25a) what is destructive for thee" or "what gives offence to God," → 748, 8 f.; Stählin, 97.

[38] So the Gr Cod and the extract in Georgius Syncellus, Chronographia, 26 B, ed. W. Dindorf in Corpus Scriptorum Historiae Byzantinae, I (1829), 46, 17; the Eth. transl. presupposes ἀπρόσοπτα.

[39] Cf. BM, 5, 11 and ref. in Str.-B., III, 311 f.

[40] Cf. K. G. Kuhn, S. Nu. (1954), 56.

[41] Cf. bSota, 22 (Str.-B., III, 376); Ber., 4, 2 (ibid., I, 799).

[42] Cf. bChul., 5b = 7a (Str.-B., III, 225).

It also applies to the meaning "offence" ("to give" or "to take"), as in the reference to a conscience which "takes offence" at its own action (but also "suffers harm" thereby) in Ac. 24:16, → 757, 23 ff. and possibly also in R. 14:20, → 756, 37 ff. Superficially at least the meaning "offence" is also present in R. 14:13 (πρόσκομμα) and 21 (προσκόπτω, → 753, 9 ff.); 2 C. 6:3 (προσκοπή, → 754, 10 ff.); 1 C. 10:32 (ἀπρόσκοπος, → 753, 29 ff.), but in all these verses the primary reference is to spiritual injury, falling into unbelief (and therewith into sin), or eternal loss.

II. Specific New Testament Use.

1. Jesus and Falling.

a. The Goal of the Tempter, Mt. 4:6 and par.

It is a common biblical conviction that God keeps His own from falling into destruction. But when the tempter uses the promise of such protection by guardian angels in Ps. 91:11 f. (Mt. 4:6; Lk. 4:11; cf. → 34, 13 ff.) it is ambivalent and misleading. For, with all the other promises of the psalm, this promise of μὴ προσκόπτειν applies to the man who has made God his refuge (v. 2, 9). That is, it applies only to the man who treads the dangerous paths indicated in v. 11 f. in a true attitude of confidence in God. The tempter fails to mention this presupposition of the validity of the psalm. Indeed, he surreptitiously changes the presupposition into its opposite by seeking to make Jesus like himself, namely, a tempter of God, Mt. 4:7 and par. In so doing, he seeks to change the promise itself into its opposite in order to reach the primal goal of all temptation, namely, to bring about a fall. He also wants to use God Himself in the accomplishing of this devilish purpose by forcing Him to punish the abuse of His promise. Instead of preservation from falling there is to be a fall, perhaps even a fall to destruction in the literal sense, a fatal plunge, if the point of this second temptation (βάλε σεαυτὸν κάτω, Mt. 4:6) is to destroy Jesus even before He begins His work. Certainly, there is to be a fall in the transferred sense. The fall of Jesus would be deeper and, in the NT view, far more fateful even than that of Adam. Hence the tempter, by illegitimately claiming the biblical promise contained in the everyday metaphor of stumbling on a stone, betrays the basic purpose of the whole temptation, namely, to cause Jesus to fall before God. This helps us to understand why Luke puts this temptation at the end of the story as a kind of climax. [43]

b. Falling in the Night, Jn. 11:9 f.

The metaphor of the way is also present in the only instance of προσκόπτω in the Johannine writings, → 748, 38 f. [44] In Jn. 11:9 f. Jesus proclaims what seems to be an everyday truth. In the light of day there is no danger of stumbling and falling, but things are different at night. [45] John is here adopting the common OT

---

[43] Naturally there may be other reasons for making this temptation the climax, e.g., that the use of Scripture is the devil's most dangerous weapon or that the setting is the temple of God.

[44] Cf. on this cf. Bu. J., 271.

[45] The tacit presupposition is that if a man can see he avoids falling, but if he cannot see he cannot avoid falling, for he does not know where he is going (Jn. 12:35; 1 Jn. 2:11) and hence he does not know on what he might stumble, cf. Prv. 4:19. Other possibilities of falling even by daylight are not in view here.

relating of darkness and falling, cf. Jer. 13:16; Is. 59:10; Prv. 4:19 → 745, 28 ff. But he expands it along the lines of Johannine dualism [46] by making a positive statement about day, light, and not falling. When applied to the way of Jesus προσκόπτω takes on a wholly specific sense. The point of the metaphor is that Jesus is aware He has only a short time before His approaching fall, i.e., His death. In this context the term has a place in the group of Johannine passion pronouncements.

2. Falling in Faith.

a. Men as the Cause of Falling.

(a) The Danger to the Weak in Corinth and Rome, 1 C. 8:9; R. 14:13, 21. [47]

The ἐξουσία (→ II, 570, 10 ff.) of the strong, which is legitimate as such and which Paul himself shares, becomes a πρόσκομμα to the weak with their as yet unconquered bonds, 1 C. 8:9; R. 14:21. Both in Corinth (→ II, 693, 40 ff.) and Rome (→ IV, 66, 19 ff.), then, Paul issues admonitions, chiefly to the strong, 1 C. 8:9 : βλέπετε δὲ μή πως ἡ ἐξουσία ὑμῶν αὕτη πρόσκομμα γένηται τοῖς ἀσθενέσιν, and R. 14:13 : τοῦτο κρίνατε [48] μᾶλλον τὸ μὴ τιθέναι πρόσκομμα τῷ ἀδελφῷ ἢ σκάνδαλον. [49] The apparent compromise of the strong with paganism in Corinth and the conduct of a related group in the religious life of Rome [50] are a πρόσκομμα, however, only in so far as they cause genuine pain (R. 14:15, 21 vl.) or difficulty for the brother. [51] At issue in the question of πρόσκομμα are ultimate decisions, conscience and faith, sin and perdition. The decisive reason for avoiding πρόσκομμα is ἀγάπη, which in such cases demands renunciation of the ἐξουσία conferred by γνῶσις. If, then, the γνῶσις of the strong is the original source of the πρόσκομμα, of the κακόν (R. 14:20), ἀγάπη is the source of preservation therefrom, of the καλόν, v. 21. In this love which gives up freedom for the brother's sake (→ II, 501, 1 ff.) Paul is an example to his churches, cf. 1 C. 9, esp. v. 12.

(b) Not Giving Offence to Others as a Guiding Principle for Christians in General and the Apostles in Particular, 1 C. 10:32; 2 C. 6:3.

Summing up the lines which he has laid down for the two groups of the strong and the weak in 1 C. 8 and 10, Paul gives us in 1 C. 10:32 an admonition which applies to all Christians : ἀπρόσκοποι καὶ Ἰουδαίοις γίνεσθε καὶ Ἕλλησιν καὶ τῇ ἐκκλησίᾳ τοῦ θεοῦ. Thus the avoidance of πρόσκομμα must be a guiding

---

[46] Cf. Bultmann Theol., 361-379, esp. 364-367.

[47] Cf. the comm. on R. 14 and 1 C. 8, 10. On the many interrelations and common features in the two passages cf. also Stählin, 260.

[48] On the meaning of κρίνω in R. 14:13 → 757, 21 ff.

[49] Cod B and a Syr. text which is at least equally old read only τιθέναι σκάνδαλον. Similarly in v. 21 readings with and without ἢ σκανδαλίζεται ἢ ἀσθενεῖ are more or less equally well attested. Probably these differences express a different feel for language in the redactors (or scribes). It is obvious that the relation in sense between πρόσκομμα and σκάνδαλον or προσκόπτω and σκανδαλίζομαι was judged differently even then, just as it is still debated to-day. In R. 9:33 and 1 Pt. 2:8 this question is related to the no less debatable one of the relation between λίθος and πέτρα. Probably both pairs were regarded as synonymous by Paul and before him by the LXX (cf. Orig., In epistulam ad Romanos comment., 7, 19 [MPG, 14, 1156 B]; also Pr.-Bauer⁵, s.v. πέτρα, 2; Bertram → 99, 25 f. etc.). This is supported esp. by the parallelism in Is. 8:14; R. 9:33 and 1 Pt. 2:8 and the corresponding relation between πρόσκομμα and σκανδαλίζω in 1 C. 8:9, 13; cf. also Wettstein on R. 14:13, 21; Bengel on R. 14:21; Zn. R. on 14:13, 21; Stählin, 171 f., 261-265.

[50] Cf. Stählin, 255 f.

[51] προσκόπτω in R. 14:21 is almost synon. with ἀπόλλυμαι in 1 C. 8:11.

principle not only in relation to brethren in the congregation but also in relation to those who are outside as represented by the two groups of Ἰουδαῖοι and Ἕλληνες. The par. (καθώς) in v. 33 might suggest for ἀπρόσκοπος γίνομαι the sense of being inoffensive or pleasant towards all men. In fact, however, ἀπρόσκοπος γίνομαι is synon. with ἀρέσκω (cf. 1 C. 10:32 with R. 15:2), and ἀρέσκω has in Paul more than the common sense "to be pleasant, obliging," → I, 455, 15 ff., 26 f. The point of the ἀρέσκω of R. 15:2 and the ἀπρόσκοπος γίνομαι of 1 C. 10:32 is the avoidance of anything that might shake others in their faith (→ 753, 19 ff.) or keep them from faith and thus prevent their σύμφορον or salvation, v. 33. Probably in a rather different sense Paul lays down for himself as an apostle the principle: μηδεμίαν ἐν μηδενὶ διδόντες προσκοπήν, ἵνα μὴ μωμηθῇ ἡ διακονία, 2 C. 6:3. According to the context προσκοπὴν διδόναι has to be an act which makes reproach possible, and this Paul wants to avoid for the sake of the cause whether the offence be well-founded and justified or not, cf. the similar train of thought in 11:12 → V, 473, 8 ff. According to Paul's conviction, there ought not to be anything to cause offence at his ministry in the whole sphere of apostolic life so fully described in vv. 4-10. Here, then, προσκοπὴν δίδωμι has a rather different sense [52] from the πρόσκομμα τίθημι of R. 14:13. Here too, however, the ultimate concern is the salvation of the community, cf. the leitmotif of the section in v. 1: μὴ εἰς κενόν . . . (→ III, 660, 19 ff.).

b. Christ as the Cause of Falling, R. 9:32 f.; 1 Pt. 2:8. [53]

Paul (R. 9:32 f.) and 1 Pt. (2:6-8), which is close to him in many passages, combine two quotations from Isaiah in two very similar sections and apply them in analogous fashion to Christ: Christ is both the λίθος προσκόμματος (and πέτρα σκανδάλου) of Is. 8:14 and also the λίθος ἐκλεκτὸς ἀκρογωνιαῖος of Is. 28:16.

The starting-points and methods of the two combinations are, of course, quite different. Pl. is dealing with the destiny of Israel which stumbled on Christ, whereas 1 Pt. is dealing with the spiritual building in which Christ is the corner-stone. The ways in which the Is. quotations are combined are also different. [54] Pl. puts the decisive double expression from Is. 8:14 in the framework of Is. 28:16, so that here the elect and precious stone is replaced by its opposite. 1 Pt., however, puts a v. from the Ps. (ψ 117:22) between Is. 28:16 and 8:14 and joins this just as closely to the double expression from Is. 8:14 as Pl. in R. 9:33 joins this to Is. 28:16: οὗτος ἐγενήθη εἰς κεφαλὴν γωνίας καὶ λίθος προσκόμματος καὶ πέτρα σκανδάλου. The καί here is probably epexegetical (= "namely"). In other words, the expression κεφαλὴ γωνίας from ψ 117:22 is elucidated by the λίθος προσκόμματος κτλ., though in a loose construction as required by the quotations. Thus 1 Pt., following the interpretation of Ps. 118:22 in Lk. 20:17 f., finds the destructive effect of Christ on unbelievers not only in the stone of

---

[52] The same sense could be assumed only if God were the subj. of μωμᾶσθαι ("to blame") as applies to ἀμώμητος (from μωμάομαι), 2 Pt. 3:14; Phil. 2:15 vl. (→ IV, 831, 21 ff.), and as in the ref. to God's judgment in the predominantly eschatological use of the synon. ἄμωμος in the NT (→ IV, 831, 7 ff. though cf. → 830, 27 ff., 831, 4).

[53] Cf. → IV, 276, 19 ff.; VI, 97, 38 ff. H. J. Cadbury, "The Titles of Jesus in Acts," Jackson-Lake, I, 5, 373 f.; Fullerton; Taylor.

[54] For this reason there is little merit in the conjecture that the two verses are a quotation from a pre-Pauline hymn which on the basis of the OT verses addresses Christ as the stone, cf. E. G. Selwyn, The First Epistle of Peter[2] (1947), on 2:8.

Is. 8:14 (and in that of Da. 2:34 f., 44 f.: Lk. 20:18) but also in the stone of Ps. 118:22, though elsewhere the saving significance of Christ is seen in this, Mt. 21:42; Ac. 4:11. [55]

In accordance with the context, the element of ruin is predominant in R. 9 and that of salvation in 1 Pt. 2; the reverse in R. 9:33b (= Is. 28:16b) and 1 Pt. 2:7 f. (= ψ 117:22 + Is. 8:14) is only secondary. [56] In R. 9 the reason for the προσκόπτειν of the Jews is an erroneous view of the way of salvation on the one side and a failure to recognise the crucified Messiah on the other, 1 C. 1:23. Thus the stone of salvation becomes for them the stone of falling. [57] It is true that here, in distinction perhaps from 1 Pt. 2:8, προσκόπτω does not include eternal perdition. This may be seen from the further development of Paul's thought in R. 10 f. and especially from the adding of the inscription on the cornerstone (→ 96, 24 ff.): ὁ πιστεύων ἐπ' αὐτῷ οὐ καταισχυνθήσεται. In a different use of the metaphor (→ n. 55) 1 Pt. says the same as R. 9:32 f. The stone is the cornerstone which gives direction to the building and which supports it, but which is also a danger for the one who stumbles on it. There are only two possibilities: to let oneself be built (v. 5) into the divine building which rests on Christ, or to fall on it. This applies to all men to whom the call of the Gospel goes forth. In 1 Pt. 2:6-8 we have a particularly impressive statement of the inseparable interrelationship of

---

[55] To the material interpretation, which differs from the usual one, there corresponds in 1 Pt. (and probably also in Lk. 20:17 f. → 748, 40 ff.) a particularly concrete understanding of the κεφαλὴ γωνίας. It would seem that elsewhere the ref. of this, and of ἀκρογωνιαῖος (e.g., Eph. 2:20 f.), is to the final stone which crowns a building, and hence to Christ as the One who perfects the divine building, the eschatological community of salvation (→ I, 792, 5 ff., 22 ff.). Here, however, the κεφαλὴ γωνίας, like the λίθος προσκόμματος of Is. 28:16 (→ I, 792, 18 ff.), is the important lower cornerstone of a building on which one can suffer a grievous fall (→ I, 792, 33 ff.; VI, 98, 27 ff.). Some scholars, of course, think that the two terms always refer to the lower cornerstone in the NT; cf. Moult.-Mill., s.v.; Taylor, 94 and n. 4.

[56] Is. 28:16 at least was taken Messianically in pre-Chr. Judaism, cf. Tg. Is. 28:16 (→ IV, 272, 22 ff.; Str.-B., III, 276); on Ps. 118:22 cf. Str.-B., I, 875 f.; → IV, 273, 18 ff. On the other hand a Messianic interpretation of Is. 8:14 is not likely in the NT age. Tg. Is. 8:14 (Str.-B., III, 276) refers the stone to the Memra of Yahweh (cf. Bousset-Gressm., 347), but does not make the link between the Memra and the Messiah (cf. Str.-B., II, 329-333), which perhaps lies behind Jn. 1:1 ff. (cf. Cr.-Kö., 676 f.; Bau. J., 6; Bultmann J., 7 f.). bSanh., 38a, 3 (Str.-B., II, 139 f.; IV, 983) obviously refers Is. 8:14 to the Messiah and calls this a special mystery, but the strange scene does not take place until c. 200 A.D. (the two houses of Israel are the exilarchs in Babylon and the patriarchs in Palestine) and is undoubtedly unique in Rabb. writings. In view of these facts we may doubt whether the two Is. verses (and Ps. 118:22) were taken from a pre-Chr. collection, at least if the ref. were supposed to be grouped Messianically, though it is intrinsically possible that the theology of Judaism spoke of the twofold working of the Messiah to salvation and perdition, e.g., the one for Jews, the other for Gentiles. At most one might think in terms of an early Chr. pre-Paul. florilegium (?), cf. Stählin, 193 with bibl., esp. J. R. Harris Testimonies, I (1916), 26-32; O. Michel, Pls. u. seine Bibel (1929), 37-42, 53 f., 89 f., also Taylor, 96, → IV, 281, n. 11.

[57] How Christ is the destiny of the Jews Paul obviously shows in R. 9 in the metaphor of the contest, which he often used (cf. 1 C. 9:24 ff.; Phil. 3:12 ff.; 2 Tm. 4:7). Or, more accurately, he uses the technical terms from this sphere without actually using the metaphor. On this peculiarity of fig. usage cf. W. Straub, Die Bildersprache d. Ap. Pls. (1935). The Jews "chase" (διώκω cf. Phil. 3:12) after the goal of righteousness (R. 9:30) and erroneously think the fulfilment of the Law is their goal. But they do not "reach" the goal (φθάνω εἴς τι) because they do not "start" from faith but (run) as if they could start "with works" (v. 32a). Believing Gentiles, however, reach (καταλαμβάνω) the goal of righteousness in faith. The Jews "boast" of the stone which should be the goal of their running and they "fall." Because they have their eyes on the wrong goal they stumble over the right one, cf. Stählin, 196-200.

the three processes of "taking offence at Christ" (→ σκάνδαλον), "not believing," and "being destroyed." Because men stumble on Christ, they do not believe in Him, and as and because they do not believe in Him, they fall on Him.

Both passages emphasise, however, that this stone with its twofold effect has been laid by God Himself. [58] This means that the nature of Christ in His concealed revelation, and that of the Gospel with its justification of the sinner, correspond to God's will when they summon to faith and lead to salvation, yet can also lead to unbelief and thus to perdition. The divine appointment is stressed both by the reading τίθημι (R. 9:33; 1 Pt. 2:6), which diverges from Is. 28:16 LXX, and also by the concluding clause in 1 Pt. 2:8 (εἰς ὃ καὶ ἐτέθησαν). [59]

c. ἀπρόσκοπον εἶναι as an Eschatological Goal, Phil. 1:10.

The various lines in Paul's statements about man's stumbling and falling all converge in his petition in Phil. 1:10 : ἵνα ἦτε εἰλικρινεῖς καὶ ἀπρόσκοποι εἰς ἡμέραν Χριστοῦ. ἀπρόσκοπος here may be taken 1. in the sense of the usage which later became conventional and perhaps was so already in Paul's day (→ 754, 3 ff.; 758, 2 ff.), namely, "without blame," "free from spot," [60] 2. like ἀπρόσκοπος in Ep. Ar., 210 (→ 748, 8 f.) and Const. Ap., II, 25, 3 (ἀπρόσκοποι θεῷ γίνεσθε), or in the sense of προσκόπτω in 1 Cl., 21, 5 (→ 746, 8 ff.), perhaps also πρόσκομμα in Sir. 17:25 (→ n. 37): "without offence" for God. [61] Another possibility which best accords with Paul's use elsewhere is 3. that ἀπρόσκοπος expresses concern that the community reach the τέλος without falling in faith and consequently from grace (cf. Gl. 5:4); in this case ἄπταιστος and the context of Jd. 24 [62] would be most closely related. The eschatological context [63] makes it plain that ἀπρόσκοπος here hardly differs at all from σῳζόμενος (1 C. 1:18 etc.), for the man who does not fall now is one who stands in the judgment which is present already and will also stand in the future judgment, i.e., a σῳζόμενος. The ἵνα clause, like the parallel in v. 9, [64] is dependent on τοῦτο προσεύχομαι. Hence Paul's prayer to God is that he might not cause the Philippian Christians to stumble and fall on the path of faith. The prayer carries with it an admonition to the congregation so to walk that they will not slip and fall. Paul's concern in this twofold form of prayer and admonition stands, however, under 1. the διὰ Ἰησοῦ Χριστοῦ which goes with the καρπός of v. 11 — as justification is for Christ's sake, so abiding and the resultant conduct can only be through Christ or His Spirit — and then 2. under the concluding εἰς δόξαν καὶ ἔπαινον θεοῦ : he who attains the goal as ἀπρόσκοπος has to thank God alone.

3. Offence of Conscience, R. 14:20; Ac. 24:16.

a. The phrase κακὸν τῷ ἀνθρώπῳ τῷ διὰ προσκόμματος ἐσθίοντι in R. 14:20 does not fit too smoothly into the use of πρόσκομμα (and προσκόπτω)

---

[58] In Is. 50:7, appended to Barn., 6, 3 (→ 99, 24 ff.), God again "lays" the stone, cf. also κεῖται in Lk. 2:34; 1 C. 3:11; → III, 654, n. 1.

[59] → IV, 277, n. 71, though cf. Stählin, 197 f.

[60] So Loh. Phil., ad loc.

[61] ἀπρόσκοπον εἶναι would then correspond exactly to the important Pauline ἀρέσκειν θεῷ (→ 754, 4 ff.; cf. R. 8:8; 1 C. 7:32; 1 Th. 2:4, 15; 4:1) or εὐάρεστον εἶναι θεῷ (cf. R. 12:1 f.; 14:18; 2 C. 5:9; Eph. 5:10; Phil. 4:18; Col. 3:20).

[62] "(May God) keep you (to the end) as those who do not fall."

[63] εἰς ἡμέραν Χριστοῦ may mean "to the day of Christ" along the lines of imminent expectation, but it may also mean more generally "with a view to or for the day of Christ."

[64] Cf. Loh. Phil., ad loc.

elsewhere in Paul. The διά here certainly denotes the accompanying circumstance [65] (cf. 2 C. 2:4 and Gl. 4:13). The subject of the whole section is faith and conscience → 753, 9 ff. Hence there are two possibilities of interpretation. 1. The reference may be to falling in faith ; this takes place when a man acts contrary to his conviction and thus betrays it. In this case one should translate : "It is bad for a man if he eats, in case he stumbles inwardly." 2. The reference may be to offence of conscience : "It is bad for a man if he eats and offends his conscience by his act," i.e., "with a disturbed, resisting, bad conscience." On the first interpretation πρόσκομμα corresponds almost exactly to the προσκόπτω of the next verse (v. 21). But the second is more accurate, for in this context Paul seems to have the cleavage between conduct and conscience in view in his use of διάκρισις (v. 1) and διακρίνομαι (v. 23 → III, 947, 27 ff.). διὰ προσκόμματος in v. 20 is thus very close to the sense of διακρινόμενος in v. 23. In both the same cleavage is in view as in R. 2:15, which is again dealing with the witness of conscience. In the passage 1 C. 8 and 10, which are in part parallel to R. 14 even in detailed argument, Paul frequently refers to the distress of conscience suffered by the weak, 8:7, 10, 12; 10:27 ff. What he means by διὰ προσκόμματος in R. 14:20 corresponds in some sense to the τύπτεσθαι or μολύνεσθαι of συνείδησις in 1 C. 8:12, 7. If the meaning of πρόσκομμα in v. 20 diverges from that in v. 13 or the meaning of προσκόπτω in v. 21, this is in keeping with Paul's habits of speech. He can use the same word in two quite different senses in the same passage and even sometimes in the same verse, [66] cf. κρίνω in R. 14:13.

b. The probable thought of R. 14:20 is undoubtedly present in Ac. 24:16 : ἐν τούτῳ καὶ αὐτὸς ἀσκῶ ἀπρόσκοπον συνείδησιν ἔχειν πρὸς τὸν θεὸν καὶ τοὺς ἀνθρώπους διὰ παντός. Α συνείδησις ἀπρόσκοπος is either "a conscience which takes no offence" at one's own actions, "a quiet or clear conscience before God and man," or it is "a conscience which suffers no hurt" through one's acts, "an unharmed conscience." [67] Either way the sense is close to that of συνείδησις ἀγαθή in Ac. 23:1 or καθαρὰ συνείδησις in 2 Tm. 1:3. Whether one may rightly say that the theology of a good conscience [68] is a sign of lateness here is very doubtful in view of the genuine concern of Paul for conscience in 1 C. 8 and R. 14 → lines 2 ff.; 753, 19 ff.

D. The Word Group in the Early Church.

In the Chr. lit. of the ensuing period the NT uses of the group, with their theological and ethical focus, are less prominent. Instead there develop certain characteristic areas of usage. First the literal sense continues, e.g., in the favourite metaphor of the two ways (Herm. m., 6, 1, 3 f.) and in OT allusions, cf. Just. Apol., I, 52, 10 : ἐντελοῦμαι τῷ βορρᾷ φέρειν καὶ τῷ νότῳ μὴ προσκόπτειν, [69] "not to cause to fall," "not to impede" (cf. Is. 43:6 : καὶ τῷ λιβί [south-west wind]· μὴ κώλυε). The main use,

---

[65] Cf. Bl.-Debr. § 223, 3 with App.

[66] Cf. W. Stählin, "Zum Verständnis von 1 K. 2:6-8," *Verbum Dei manet in aeternum, Festschr. f. O. Schmitz* (1953), 94-102.

[67] Pr.-Bauer[5], *s.v.* suggests the meaning "not to take offence," "intact," "blameless," but the proper line of development is surely "not to fall," "not to suffer damage," "intact."

[68] Cf. Haench. Ag., 570.

[69] On the προσκόπτειν of winds cf. Mt. 7:27, also Ps.-Aristot. De Audibilibus, p. 801a, 14 f., also p. 802a, 26 f.; Aristot. Probl., 5, 17, p. 882b, 18 f.; 11, 45, p. 904a, 33 f. speaks, however of a προσκόπτειν τῷ ἀέρι.

however, is the transf. one (→ 746, 7 ff.) "(to give) offence," so 1 Cl., 21, 5; Herm. m., 2, 4 (πρόσκομμα πονηρόν); Cl. Al. Strom., II, 53, 4. In this sense ἀπρόσκοπος (→ 747, 30 ff.) is a standing expression for "blameless service" (e.g., 1 Cl., 20, 10 of winds) or "irreproachable discharge of office" (1 Cl., 61, 1 in a prayer for the authorities) or esp. the "blameless conduct" of spiritual office-bearers, as often in Const. Ap. (II, 9, 1; 25, 3; Sacramentarium Serapionis, 28, 2 → n. 19). [70] A typical pt. in this later usage is that attention is not directed so strongly as in the NT to the threat to the faith of those who are under guidance, but focuses instead on threats to the reputation of the office-bearers themselves.

Stählin

† προσκυνέω, † προσκυνητής	→ ἀσπάζομαι, I, 496, 9 ff.
	→ εὔχομαι, II, 775, 19 ff.
	→ πίπτω, 161 ff.

Contents : A. The Meaning of the Word for the Greeks. B. The Jewish Understanding of the Word : 1. The Septuagint ; 2. Josephus ; 3. Philo ; 4. Rabbinic Judaism. C. The New Testament. D. The Early Church.

† προσκυνέω.

The early history of the meaning of the word is obscure and contested. Etymologists [1] with few exceptions [2] connect the simple κυνέω to the Old High German *Kuss*, though through different intermediaries. [3] The oldest occurrence in Hom. (e.g., Il., 6, 474; Od., 23, 208) pts. to the same area of meaning.

---

[70] The Lat. equivalent is *sine scandalo gubernare* (e.g., Aug. Cresc., II, 11 [13] [CSEL, 52, 371]); cf. also Stählin, 295, 314, 329, 353.

προσκυνέω. A. Alföldi, "Die Ausgestaltung des monarchischen Zeremoniells am römischen Kaiserhofe," *Röm. Mitt.*, 49 (1934), 1-118; O. T. Allis, "The Comment on John IX 38 in the American Revised Version," *Princeton Theol. Review*, 17 (1919), 241-311; H. Bolkestein, "Theophrastos' Charakter der Deisidaimonia als religionsgeschichtliche Urkunde," RVV, 21, 2 (1929); L. Cerfaux and J. Tondrian, *Le culte des souverains* (1957), *s.v.* "proskynèse"; Cr.-Kö., *s.v.*; A. Delatte, "Le baiser, l'agenouillement et le prosternement de l'adoration (προσκύνησις) chez les Grecs," *Académie royale de Belgique, Bulletin de la Classe des Lettres et des Sciences morales et politiques*, 5, 37 (1951), 423-450; J. Horst, *Proskynein* (1933), older bibl. 4-8, historical material 10-14; Liddell-Scott, *s.v.*; B. M. Marti, "Proskynesis and adorare," *Language*, 12 (1936), 272-282; Moult.-Mill., *s.v.*; Pr.-Bauer[5], *s.v.*; Preisigke Wört., *s.v.*; P. Schnabel, "Die Begründung d. hell. Königskultes durch Alexander," *Klio*, 19 (1925), 113-127, esp. 118-120; L. R. Taylor, "The 'Proskynesis' and the Hell. Ruler Cult," JHS, 47 (1927), 53-62; also *The Divinity of the Roman Emperor* (1931), reviewed by A. D. Nock, *Gnomon*, 8 (1932), 513-518.

[1] Prellwitz Etym. Wört., 251; Boisacq, 535; Walde-Pok., I, 465, *s.v.* qu ; Hofmann, 165; Pokorny, 626; Delatte, 426.

[2] Cf. Horst, 12 f. Schwyzer, I, 692 takes κυνέω as a denominative of *κυνο- and compares Sanskr. *çunám* "hail."

[3] Lat. *adorare* has nothing to do with os (Walde-Pok., I, 182; Walde-Hofmann, 224; Pokorny, 781; Marti, 279 f.) and cannot be compared with προσκυνεῖν as against F. Heiler, *Das Gebet*[5] (1923), 104.

A. The Meaning of the Word for the Greeks.

It has been conjectured that the compound προσκυνέω [4] was "originally nothing more than the Greek term for a phenomenon of oriental life." [5] Since it appears first in the tragedians, the argument runs that Persian contacts are presupposed. There is not a single instance to refute this, [6] but there are many arguments against it. It would be strange if from a phenomenon of oriental life which they themselves rejected and regarded as undignified [7] the Gks. adopted the word for their own adoration of the gods. [8], [9] Again, there is as yet no sure answer to the debated issue whether the blown kiss to one of higher rank is an original part of the gesture of proskynesis or not. [10] On the other hand, there is no doubt at all that the element of casting oneself to the ground has a prominence which cannot be explained by the combination of the two components of the term. If προσκυνεῖν (in the first instance only "to kiss reverently") [11] had not already been used in a sense including prostration, the Gks. could not have described the offensive ceremonial in a way which disguised the true offence.

Now it should be remembered [12] that the adoration of chthonic deities offers a simple explanation of the development of the usual meaning of the term. The man who wants to honour an earth deity by kissing must stoop to do so. [13] Both Odysseus and Agamemnon prostrate themselves and kiss the earth after a happy landing. [14] It is here that we are to seek the religio-historical origin of the word. [15] Also evident is the fact that προσκυνεῖν as a tt. for adoration of the gods is of great antiquity, for worship of chthonic deities is probably older than that of the Olympians. [16] The apparent absence of the word in the pre-Persian period — if we restrict ourselves to the compound — may be an accident. [17] The extended use of the word for Gk. worship is also explained quite freely on this view.

At an early time the usage was transferred from the outward gesture to the inward attitude. The beginnings are to be sought in the tragedians. Thus Neoptolemos in Soph.

---

[4] Obviously προσκυνέω soon separated from κυνέω : προσκυνήσω, προσεκύνησα is usual from the very first (προσέκυσα only in Soph. and Aristoph.), while from the simple form κυνήσω, ἐκύνησα is rare and late [Debrunner].

[5] Cr.-Kö., 643.

[6] Horst refers to a choliambus of Hipponax. Fr., 37: παρ᾽ ὧι σὺ λευκόπεπλον ἡμέρην μείνας | πρὸς μὲν κυνήσειν τὸν Φλυησίων Ἑρμῆν (Diehl, III, 91). The age of Hipponax. (b. c. 575, G. A. Gerhard, Art. "Hipponax," Pauly-W., 8 [1913], 1891) does not rule out knowledge of Persian customs, cf. Horst, 14, n. 3; 15.

[7] Isoc., Panegyricus, 151 (ed. R. Rauchenstein[6] [1908]); Arrian, Anabasis, IV, 12 (ed. A. G. Roos [1907]).

[8] E.g., Aesch. Pers., 499; Soph. Oed. Col., 1654. Cf. Delatte, 436-441.

[9] So also Allis, 245; Horst, 21.

[10] For ref. and bibl. cf. Horst, 4-6; F. Altheim, Review of The Cambridge Ancient History, Vol. XII in Gnomon, 23 (1951), 93; cf. also passages like Xenoph. An., III, 2, 13 (with kiss?) and Isoc., Panegyricus, 151 (→ n. 7) (without kiss?).

[11] Delatte, 426 : "baiser avec ferveur."

[12] Horst, 18 and 24.

[13] A variant is the altar kiss, which acc. to F. J. Dölger, "Zu den Zeremonien der Messliturgie, II : der Altarkuss," Ant. Christ., II (1930), 217-221, was probably a pagan precursor of the liturgical practice in Christianity.

[14] Hom. Od., 4, 522; 5, 463; 13, 354; cf. also Pearson's conjecture on Soph. Phil., 533 f. (→ n. 18).

[15] Horst, 18.

[16] Cf. O. Kern, Die Religion d. Griechen, I (1926), 27-48.

[17] Cf. Allis, 245, n. 10 : σέβειν — σεβίζειν occur in Hom. only once, 4 times in Pind., not at all in Hes.

Phil., 656 f. expresses his respect for the bow of Heracles in the words : ἄρ' ἔστιν ὥστε κἀγγύθεν θέαν λαβεῖν, καὶ βαστάσαι με προσκύσαι θ' ὥσπερ θεόν. Again in 533 f. Philoctetes summons him to a solemn parting from his home : ἴωμεν, ὦ παῖ, προσκύσαντε τὴν ἔσω ἄοικον εἰσοίκησιν. [18] The word becomes more general later, though the original use persists. The deification of rulers which began from the time of Alexander the Gt. and culminated in the emperor cult of Rome undoubtedly had a decisive influence on the history of the word. [19] Cultic proskynesis is naturally predominant in inscr. Thus an Aesculapius (?) aretalogy of the 2nd (?) cent. A.D. opens an exact description of the process of healing in the words : αὐταῖς ταῖς ἡμέραις Γαΐῳ τινὶ τυφλῷ ἐχρημάτισεν (sc. ὁ θεός) ἐλθεῖν ἐπ[ὶ τὸ] ἱερὸν βῆμα καὶ προσκυνῆσαι (formal proskynesis) εἶ[τ]α ἀπὸ τοῦ δεξιοῦ ἐλθεῖν ἐπὶ τὸ ἀριστερὸν κτλ., Ditt. Syll.³, III, 1173. [20] On the other hand the sense in pap. of the 1st cent. A.D. is the very general one. Thus a female slave (?) at the beginning of the 2nd cent. writes to her master who had fallen sick on a journey : ὤφελον εἰ ἐδυνάμεθα πέτασθαι καὶ ἐλθεῖν καὶ προσκυνῆσαί σε, P. Giess., I, 17, 10 ff. A son asks his father to write him a letter so that he may again see with love and respect the familiar handwriting : ... ἵνα σου προσκυνήσω τὴν χέραν (= χεῖρα), BGU, II, 423, 15 f. (2nd cent. A.D.). [21] From the beginning of the imperial period assurance of intercession for the recipient is part of the introductory formula in letters : πρὸ μὲμ (sic !) πά[ν]των εὔχομαί σε ὑγιαίνειν, καὶ [τὸ] προσκύνημά σου ποιῶ παρὰ [τῷ] κυρίῳ Σαράπιδι, BGU, III, 843 (1st/2nd cent.). [22]

B. The Jewish Understanding of the Word.

1. The Septuagint. In the LXX προσκυνεῖν is virtually the only rendering of הִשְׁתַּחֲוָה [23] on the one side and סְגֵד [24] or סְגִד (Aram.) [25] on the other ; both words have the basic sense "to bow." It is also used once each for נָשַׁק [26] "to kiss," עָבַד "to serve," "to worship" Ps. 97:7, זוּע (Aram.) [27] "to tremble," and in 3 instances it is equivalent to כָּרַע ("to bow") with הִשְׁתַּחֲוָה, Est. 3:2 (twice), 5. προσκυνεῖν naturally suggested itself for הִשְׁתַּחֲוָה, since the Heb. word, originally denoting only a movement of the body, had

---

[18] So with C. Cavallin (1875), H. M. Blaydes (1908), R. C. Jebb (1908). Cf. W. Dindorf⁶ (1885): εἰς οἴκησιν, A. C. Pearson (1924): προσκύσαντε γῆν ἔσω | ἄοικον εἰς οἴκησιν.

[19] On this whole matter cf. Horst, 39-42.

[20] Cf. also Ditt. Or. Index, VIII, s.v. προσκυνέω and προσκύνημα; Preisigke Sammelbuch, II, 441, s.v. There is good material on proskynesis in Chr. and non-Chr. antiquity in F. J. Dölger, Sol Salutis (1925), Index, s.v. προσκυνέω, proskynesis.

[21] For several other examples v. Preisigke Wört., s.v. προσκυνέω.

[22] Cf. also Wendland Hell. Kult., 414; Dib. Th. on 1 Th. 1:2; Deissmann LO, 141, n. 12; W. Spiegelberg, "Pap. Erbach," Zschr. f. ägypt. Sprache u. Altertumskunde, 42 (1905), 54. On the προσκύνημα formula cf. F. X. J. Exler, A Study in Gk. Epistolography, Diss. Washington (1923), 108-112 [Debrunner].

[23] Of 171 instances of הִשְׁתַּחֲוָה 164 are rendered by προσκυνεῖν in the LXX, 1 by καταφιλεῖν (1 K. 2:19), 1 by ποιεῖν (1 K. 11:33), 5 no equivalent, though for 4 of these ᾽ΑΣΘ have προσκυνεῖν : Jos. 5:14; Is. 36:7; 60:14; Jer. 7:2; no text available for 1 S. 1:28. On the etym. and derivation of הִשְׁתַּחֲוָה cf. Ges.-Buhl, s.v., though also R. Meyer, Review of Köhler-Baumg. in ThLZ, 82 (1957), 425.

[24] 4 instances : Is. 44:15 (?), 17 προσκυνεῖν for הִשְׁתַּחֲוָה and סְגֵד ; Is. 44:19 προσκυνεῖν for סְגֵד alone ; 46:6 κύπτειν for סְגֵד.

[25] 12 instances in Da. 2:46; 3:5-7, 10-12, 14 f., 18, 28, all προσκυνεῖν in the LXX; Θ has no equivalent at 3:10.

[26] 1 K. 19:18; also Σ at Job 31:27 (LXX ἐφίλησα); Ps. 2:12 (LXX takes a different path → παιδεία, V, 610, 21 ff.); ᾽Α καταφιλήσατε; on cultic kisses cf. also Hos. 13:2.

[27] Da. 6:27 LXX; Θ : τρέμοντες.

become a cultic tt. The further definitions which often accompany it, e.g., "to the earth" [28] or "to do obeisance," [29] leave us in no doubt as to the meaning. [30] It makes no odds whether the proskynesis is to God or the gods or to men. That προσκυνεῖν can be used for (→ n. 26) or par. to נָשַׁק (Ex. 18:7) shows that the element of kissing, [31] including cultic kissing, was still present in the Gk. word at the time of the LXX. [32]

Almost three-quarters of the instances of προσκυνεῖν in the LXX relate to veneration and worship of the true God and Lord [33] or to that of false gods. [34] The angels, God's messengers, are also greeted in this way by the righteous. [35] Where προσκυνεῖν is used for the customary worship of God rather than a single act it often seems to be parallel to λατρεύειν (= עָבַד → IV, 60, 3 ff.). [36] What is appropriate to God is also appropriate to His elect. Thus the Egyptians are to fall at Moses' feet to ask for pardon and nations and kings lie in the dust before redeemed Zion. [37] Both word and thing also play quite a role in dealings between men ; the numinous background of power was perhaps of some significance here. Proskynesis is practised especially before the king or a superior. [38] Saul bows down before the shade of the prophet Samuel, the sons of the prophets and the Shunammite woman do the same before the prophet Elisha. [39] Even where προσκυνεῖν seems to be no more than a gesture of gratitude or affectionate regard, there is always expressed in the act a recognition that the one thus honoured is God's instrument. [40] Thus the way in which Abraham and Lot receive God's messengers (Gn. 18:2; 19:1) is not just politeness to important strangers ; in the ancient world the stranger was under divine protection or stood in mysterious relation to deity, cf. Hb. 13:2. Furthermore Abraham and Lot, by this not uncommon but specifically noted gesture, tell the reader, without being aware of it themselves, who is coming to them. The proskynesis of Abraham to the Hittites (Gn. 23:7, 12) seems to be a mere matter of etiquette, though the full observance of formalities serves to emphasise here the legality of Abraham's purchase. Protest against the form is

---

[28] אַרְצָה Gn. 18:2; 24:52; 33:3 etc. אַפַּיִם אַרְצָה Gn. 19:1; 42:6; 48:12 (43:26 LXX addition).

[29] קָדַד "to fall on one's knees" is close to הִשְׁתַּחֲוָה in all its 15 occurrences. The accompanying verb נָפַל "to fall down" is more common. Also found are כָּרַע "to bow down" (Ps. 22:29; 95:6; 2 Ch. 7:3; 29:29 cf. also → 760, 26 f. and סָגַד → n. 24). Apart from the last all these accompanying verbs are also found with the more precise definitions mentioned in → n. 28.

[30] Though the sense is none too clear, the mistransl. at Gn. 47:31 προσεκύνησεν Ἰσραὴλ ἐπὶ τὸ ἄκρον τῆς ῥάβδου αὐτοῦ (= Hb. 11:21) seems to be denoting a gesture of regard or respect, → n. 40.

[31] On προσκυνεῖν for the blown kiss cf. Horst, 60 f.

[32] The last sentence is by Bertram.

[33] Gn. 22:5; 24:26, 48, 52; Ex. 4:31; 24:1; Dt. 26:10; Ps. 5:7; 29:2 etc.

[34] Ex. 20:5; 23:24; 34:14; Dt. 4:19; 1 K. 22:54; 2 K. 5:18; Is. 2:8; 44:17 etc.

[35] Nu. 22:31; on Gn. 18:2; 19:1 → lines 20 ff.

[36] Ex. 20:5; 23:24; Dt. 4:19; 5:9; 8:19 etc.

[37] Ex. 11:8; Is. 45:14; 49:23.

[38] E.g., David before Saul 1 S. 24:9; Bathsheba and Nathan before David 1 K. 1:16, 23, 31; Jacob before Esau Gn. 33:3-7; Jacob's sons before Joseph Gn. 37:9, 10; 42:6; 43:26, 28; Ruth before Boaz Rt. 2:10.

[39] 1 S. 28:14; 2 K. 2:15; 4:37; Ex. 18:7 is to be classified with 1 K. 2:19 → n. 40.

[40] So David 3 times before Jonathan 1 S. 20:41; David before Solomon's ministers 1 K. 1:47 (probably Gn. 47:31 is similar → n. 30); Solomon before Bathsheba 1 K. 2:19; Moses before Jethro Ex. 18:7.

first voiced in Esther, [41] where Mordecai's refusal to do proskynesis before Haman is the true focus of the dramatic action. There is never any reason to doubt that the word denotes full proskynesis, i.e., bowing down low on the knee. The only exception is 4 Macc. 5:12, where we have the same weakening of sense as in the pagan Greek world : Antiochus tells the aged Eleazar to save his life by eating swine's flesh ... καὶ προσκυνήσας μου τὴν φιλάνθρωπον παρηγορίαν οἰκτιρήσεις τὸ σεαυτοῦ γῆρας.

As distinct from the usage in secular Gk., which almost always uses the trans., the LXX with few exceptions has the dat. or prepositional phrases rather than the acc. [42] This peculiarity is certainly due in part to the Heb. construction with לְ and לִפְנֵי, but there are also inner reasons. The starting-pt. of the trans. constr. is "to kiss," but this is hardly possible in worship without images.

2. Josephus. Jos. follows LXX usage in the main. For him, too, προσκυνεῖν denotes the worship of God or the gods and also respect for men. Yet there are unmistakable differences. In the conflict between Jewish and Gentile worship προσκυνεῖν is mostly used for the latter — perhaps the Gk. despising of proskynesis had a hand here — while σέβειν, θρησκεύειν and τιμᾶν are preferred for Jewish worship. [43] Again, though Jos. speaks just as freely as the LXX of proskynesis to king [44] or prophet [45] in his depiction of the monarchy in Israel, he avoids the gesture, or at least the word προσκυνεῖν, in relation to the Jews of his own day. [46] Almost certainly connected with this is the fact that in the Daniel story he softens the proskynesis of Nebuchadnezzar to Daniel (Da. 2:46 LXX and Θ προσεκύνησε): ... πεσὼν ἐπὶ πρόσωπον, ᾧ τρόπῳ τὸν θεὸν προσκυνοῦσι, τούτῳ τὸν Δανίηλον ἠσπάζετο. [47] New as compared with the LXX is the use of προσκυνεῖν in relation to the temple [48] or the Torah. [49] But when in his address to the besieged city of Jerusalem he pts. out that even the Romans respected the holy place from afar (προσκυνεῖν, Bell., 5, 402), one is to think in terms of respectful admiration rather than proskynesis towards the temple. [50]

3. Philo. The profane use of the word is more prominent in Philo than the purely religious use. Yet when he rejects the worship of wealth, the context shows that he is esp. against the religious fervour of this veneration, Spec. Leg., I, 24. Elsewhere he says of the tragic fate of those sold into slavery : μηδ' ὄναρ τὸ τῆς πατρίδος ἔδαφος ἔτι προσκυνήσοντας, ibid., IV, 17. Here it is uncertain whether he is depicting religious proskynesis or a spontaneous expression of love of country. Though in the attack on pagan polytheism he demands : τοὺς ἀδελφοὺς φύσει μὴ προσκυνῶμεν (Decal., 64), he finds no difficulty in using προσκυνεῖν, like the LXX, for respectful obeisance to men, e.g., the brothers to Joseph in Jos., 164 or the animals to Adam in Op. Mund., 83.

---

[41] Est. 3:2, 5. Cf. Horst, 121-125.

[42] Cf. Helbing Kasussyntax, 296-298; Bl.-Debr. § 151, 2 (with bibl.).

[43] Ant., 3, 91; 8, 248; 9, 133; Horst, 113 f.

[44] David before Saul Ant., 6, 285; Joab or Bathsheba before David Ant., 7, 187, 349, 354.

[45] Obadiah the governor of the palace to Elijah Ant., 8, 331. On the proskynesis of Alexander the Gt. before the ὄνομα (Ant., 11, 331 → I, 496, n. 4) cf. also Horst, 63 f.

[46] Bell., 2, 336 and 350, cf. 360; Horst, 127.

[47] Ant., 10, 211; Horst, 113 f., 126 f.

[48] E.g., Ant., 13, 54; 20, 49; Bell., 2, 341; 5, 381.

[49] Ant., 12, 114; Ep. Ar., 177 and 179 also tells us already that when the scrolls of the Law were brought by the envoys of Eleazar to Ptolemy Philadelphos he reverenced the holy books by sevenfold obeisance before greeting the envoys by a handclasp (→ line 19 f.), 179 cf. 173.

[50] In Jos. προσκυνεῖν usually takes the acc., more rarely the dat., Schl. Mt., 31. On this whole question cf. also Schl. Jos., 74.

If in contrast he calls proskynesis to the emperor a βαρβαρικὸν ἔθος which contradicts old Roman freedom, this is in keeping with his attempt to set in a favourable light the refusal of proskynesis by the Jewish embassy in Rome, Leg. Gaj., 116. Philo uses προσκυνεῖν fig. in relation to holy things like the temple, the day of atonement, or Holy Scripture, Leg. Gaj., 310; Vit. Mos., II, 23 and 40. But here, too, there is a corresponding idolatry and he censures men who have idolatrously yielded to the pomp and arrogance of city life, Decal., 4. [51]

4. Rabbinic Judaism. For Rabb. Judaism proskynesis is one of the gestures in prayer. The custom is to stand for prayer. [52] But it is recounted of R. Akiba (d. c. 135) that when praying alone rather than leading in prayer he often prostrated himself. [53] A later age distinguished between various kinds of prostration, one of which, called קִידָה, was said to be practised already by Rabban Shim'on ben Gamaliel (d. 70). [54] The Rabb. also refer to proskynesis to men. Nor do they simply expound and define the biblical accounts of proskynesis to the kings and great men of Israel. [55] One also hears of respect being shown to rabbis in this way. [56] Influential here, it would seem, is the idea that study of the Torah sets these men in a particularly close relation to God.

C. The New Testament.

1. When the NT uses προσκυνεῖν, the object is always something — truly or supposedly — divine. Mt. 18:26 : πεσὼν ... προσεκύνει αὐτῷ (v. 29 : πεσὼν ... παρεκάλει αὐτόν) is an exception only in appearance, for Mt. can hardly be using these words for the proskynesis of a slave to his master or to the king, → 163, 16. This is refuted not only by the use of προσκυνεῖν elsewhere in the NT but especially by the fact that Mt. has altered or expanded his Marcan original in no less than five passages in order to describe the gesture of those who approach Jesus explicitly as proskynesis : the leper in Mt. 8:2 cf. Mk. 1:40; Jairus in Mt. 9:18 cf. Mk. 5:22; His companions in the boat, Mt. 14:33 cf. Mk. 6:51; the woman of Canaan, Mt. 15:25 cf. Mk. 7:25; the mother of James and John, Mt. 20:20 cf. Mk. 10:35. The only instance to the contrary seems to point in the same direction, for it is very probable that Mt. 27:29 cut out the proskynesis of the soldiers (Mk. 15:19) because elsewhere the word always expresses true adoration for Mt. As regards Mt. 18:26 it may thus be concluded that the parable is not pure in Jülicher's sense but gives us a glimpse of God Himself behind the ἄνθρωπος βασιλεύς.

In view of the above movement from Mk. to Mt. [57] it is also not quite correct to say that when those who seek help fall down before the Jewish rabbi this is a secular proskynesis before Jesus which is no more than the customary form of respectful greeting. [58] This is certainly not true in Mt. Perhaps there was such

---

[51] Here we also find the combination with τεθηπέναι, which is common in Philo when the ref. is not to worship of God in the narrowest sense.

[52] Cf. Str.-B., II, 259 on Lk. 22:41 and the ref. adduced there.

[53] T. Ber., 3, 5 (6) (Str.-B., II, 260).

[54] bSukka, 53a Bar. (Str.-B., II, 261).

[55] bShebuoth, 16b Bar. (Str.-B., I, 78 on Mt. 2:2).

[56] bKet., 63a (before R. Akiba; Str.-B., I, 519 on Mt. 9:18); jPea, 1, 1 (15d, 28f) and bSanh., 27b (kissing the feet of R. Jonathan or Rab Papi, Str.-B., I, 996 on Mt. 26:49); Horst, 64; → I, 498, 22 ff.

[57] προσκυνεῖν occurs 13 times in Mt., twice in Mk. (5:6 and 15:19) and 7 times in Lk. (+ Ac).

[58] Horst, 186.

a form of greeting, → 763, 14 ff. But in Mt. the use of προσκυνεῖν shows that those who thus fall down already involuntarily and unconsciously declare by their attitude with whom they have to do. The proskynesis of the wise men (Mt. 2:2, 11, assumed in 2:8) is truly offered to the Ruler of the world. The ungodly totalitarian claim of the tempter finds expression in the fact that he asks for προσκυνεῖν which belongs to God alone, Mt. 4:9 f.; Lk. 4:7 f. [59] In comparison with suppliants there is little reference to proskynesis on the part of the disciples. Where this occurs it is especially motivated by dawning recognition of the divine sonship (Mt. 14:33 [→ III, 38, 6 ff.], cf. Jn. 9:38) or an appearance of the risen Lord (Mt. 28:9, 17; Lk. 24:52). [60]

In the NT, as in the world of Israelite-Jewish faith generally, [61] the thought of God's transcendence closed the door on the kind of devaluation of προσκυνεῖν which may be seen in pap. letters, → 760, 12 ff. Peter rejects the proskynesis of Cornelius with the words : "I too am a man," Ac. 10:25 f. Even the angel of Rev. points the divine to God when he falls down at his feet : ὅρα μή· σύνδουλός σού εἰμι καὶ τῶν ἀδελφῶν σου ..., Rev. 19:10; 22:9. The vivid idea of falling on the knees or the face remains unchanged. In many cases this gesture is expressly mentioned, e.g., Ac. 10:25 : πεσὼν ἐπὶ τοὺς πόδας, 1 C. 14:25 : ... ἐπὶ πρόσωπον, → 163 f.

2. The conversation of Jesus with the Samaritan woman in Jn. 4:20-24 [62] leaves an initial impression that προσκυνεῖν is used here in a wholly figurative sense, since Jesus speaks of προσκυνεῖν in spirit and in truth. But if prostrating oneself no longer plays any definite role, the reference in the statement and answer is to the place of worship. Furthermore, there obviously stands in the background the technical use of the word for the pilgrimage of Jews to Jerusalem, so also Jn. 12:20; Ac. 8:27; 24:11. If instead of naming a place to which the pilgrims should go to worship [63] Jesus says that the true place of worship is in the spirit and in truth this is an oxymoron. Undiluted προσκυνεῖν, the act of worship which is concrete in place and gesture, is lifted up to a new dimension : "spirit and truth." This is not a proclamation of God's omnipresence. The spiritualising of prayer [64] is neither demanded nor promised. This new reality into which the Son alone sets us is to control prayer, cf. → I, 246, 33 ff. There is no longer to be any exclusive place of worship, but prayer is still to take place at specific places and with specific gestures.

3. Here, then, the Fourth Evangelist joins hands with the divine of Rev., before whose eyes the worship of heaven involves constantly repeated proskynesis, Rev. 4:10; 5:14; 7:11; 11:16; 19:4. Here falling down is in each case specifically mentioned. On earth, too, those who fear God are προσκυνοῦντες on the one side

---

[59] προσκυνεῖν is used in the NT for the worship of ungodly powers at Ac. 7:43; Rev. 9:20; 13:4, 8, 12, 15; 14:9, 11; 16:2; 19:20; 20:4.

[60] If the words προσκυνήσαντες αὐτόν are part of the original.

[61] The only real exception here is to be found in Philo Jos., 164 : καὶ οἱ μὲν εἰς Αἴγυπτον ἐλθόντες ἐντυγχάνουσιν ὡς ἀλλοτρίῳ τἀδελφῷ καὶ τὴν περὶ αὐτὸν ἀξίωσιν καταπλαγέντες ἔθει παλαιῷ προσκυνοῦσιν ...; though here, too, ἔθει παλαιῷ sounds like an excuse.

[62] Cf. Horst, 293-307; Schl. J., 126; Bau. J., ad loc.; Bultmann J., ad loc.

[63] On Gerizim and Jerusalem as points to which prayer is directed cf. Dölger, op. cit. (→ n. 20), 186-189.

[64] Cf. also Bultmann J., 140, n. 3.

(Rev. 11:1; [65] 14:7), while the worshippers of the dragon and the beast are also called προσκυνοῦντες on the other (Rev. 13:4, 8, 12, 15; 14:9, 11; 16:2; 19:20; 20:4). At the end of the days, however, not only will all nations come and worship before God (Rev. 15:4) but those who serve Satan in Philadelphia will also come and worship before the angel of that church (Rev. 3:9). How strong is the reference to actual proskynesis may be seen from the repeated rejection of this gesture by the interpreting angel (Rev. 19:10; 22:8 f.). [66]

4. Statistics concerning προσκυνεῖν in the NT disclose the astonishing fact that the word is very common in the Gospels and Acts and then again in Rev., but that it is completely absent from the Epistles apart from two OT quotations in Hb. (1:6; 11:21) and one verse in Pl. (1 C. 14:25). Apart from Ac. 24:11, where προσκυνεῖν is a tt. for the worship of God in the temple (→ 764, 25 f.; 766, 6 ff.), the only instance of proskynesis in the primitive Christian community is at 1 C. 14:25. But here Paul seems to be using a particularly forceful expression for the unconditional subjection which the ἄπιστος confesses, and in so doing he is deliberately adopting OT usage. Elsewhere there is indeed reference to kneeling for prayer (Ac. 9:40; 20:36) or raising the hands in prayer (1 Tm. 2:8), [67] but the word προσκυνεῖν is not used. This is, however, a further proof of the concreteness of the term. Proskynesis demands visible majesty before which the worshipper bows. [68] The Son of God was visible to all on earth (the Gospels) and the exalted Lord will again be visible to His own when faith gives way to sight (Revelation).

D. The Early Church.

The data in the post-apost. fathers are much the same as in the NT. προσκυνεῖν is for the most part used only in the description of pagan worship. [69] Only in Mart. Pol., 17, 3 is it said of Chr. faith : τοῦτον (sc. τὸν Χριστόν) μὲν γὰρ υἱὸν ὄντα τοῦ θεοῦ προσκυνοῦμεν. This passage has, of course, a polemical emphasis. The veneration of Christ is to be strongly differentiated from that of martyrs. [70] Act. Phil., 42, on the other hand, says of a girl to whom the apostle promises healing : προσεκύνησεν αὐτῷ λέγουσα· προσκυνῶ τὸν ἐν σοὶ ἰατρόν. [71] Later the word undergoes notable restriction. The Seventh Ecumenical Council at Nicaea (787) distinguishes between a τιμητικὴ προσκύνησις which may be offered to icons and an ἀληθινὴ λατρεία which is to be paid only to the θεία φύσις. [72]

---

[65] So with Loh. Apk., ad loc.

[66] The formal contradiction between 3:9 and 19:10; 22:8 f. is resolved when one notes that the angel of the church is a messenger and instrument of God (Rev. 1:16, 20; 2:1; 3:1) and that the church represented in him will in the future stand around the throne of the Lamb (14:1, 3). Thus the proskynesis simply means that the church will share in the triumph of the Lamb over His enemies.

[67] κάμπτω τὰ γόνατά μου πρὸς τὸν πατέρα ..., ἵνα ... in Eph. 3:14 ff. (→ III, 595, 2 ff.) is in full material correspondence with προσκυνεῖν, but it is used as a figure of prayer, a watering down which προσκυνεῖν does not undergo in the NT.

[68] Cf. also Horst, 193, esp. n. 4.

[69] 2 Cl., 1, 6; 3, 1; Mart. Pol., 12, 2; Dg., 2, 4 f.

[70] Furthermore H. v. Campenhausen, "Bearbeitungen u. Interpolationen des Polykarpmartyriums," SAH, 1957, 3 (1957), 26-28, has shown that the clause is part of an interpolation, probably c. 200.

[71] [Nock.]

[72] J. D. Mansi, Sacrorum conciliorum ... collectio, VIII (1767), 377 D f.; cf. H. v. Campenhausen, "Die Bilderfrage als theol. Problem der alten Kirche," ZThK, 49 (1952), 56.

In constr. the older and better Gk. acc. is again more prominent as compared with the LXX. [73] But the dat. is still far more common. Prepositional phrases like ἐνώπιόν τινος are based on the LXX. It is impossible to discern any consistent difference of meaning between the acc. and the dat. [74]

† προσκυνητής.

1. Outside the NT this word occurs for the first time in an inscr. from Syria dated 3rd cent. A.D. (Ditt. Or., I, 262, 21). This contains a resolution in the interests of festal pilgrims (τοῖς ἀνιοῦσει προσκυνηταῖς) which was addressed to the emperor Augustus. It was not, then, under Chr. influence. All the familiar later examples are dependent on Jn. 4:23.

2. In the NT προσκυνητής occurs only at Jn. 4:23: οἱ ἀληθινοὶ προσκυνηταί. In the context of the conversation with the Samaritan woman it means "genuine worshippers." The words "to worship in spirit and in truth" offer a definition of "genuine." For further details → 764, 20 ff.

Greeven

προσλαμβάνομαι → IV, 15, 5 ff. **προσμένω** → IV, 579, 5 ff.
πρόσλημψις → IV, 15, 20 ff. **προστάσσω** → τάσσω.

---

† πρόσφατος, † προσφάτως

1. The etym. of the word is uncertain, [1] but the meaning is clear: "fresh," "new": a. of things exposed to decomposition and decay: "fresh," "uncorrupted": with ἐρσήεις ("dew-fresh") of the body of Hector, Hom.Il., 24, 757; cf. 419; of fish, Menand. Fr., 397, 4; of fruit and oil, Aristot. Probl., 20, 30, p. 926a, 30; 927a, 29; of blood, Hippocr. Epid., VII, 10 (Littré, V, 318); b. of fresh events or newly arrived people: "not there before," "new," "fresh": δίκαι, Aesch. Choeph., 804; ὀργή Lys., 18, 19; Jos. Ant., 1, 264; εὐεργεσίαι, Polyb., 2, 46, 1; μάρτυρες ... οἱ μὲν παλαιοὶ οἱ δὲ πρόσφατοι, Aristot. Rhet., I, 15, p. 1375b, 27.

The adv. προσφάτως, "newly," "lately," "recently": Ditt. Or., I, 315, 23; Jos. Bell., 1, 127; Ant., 10, 264.

2. In the LXX: a. "fresh," "new": σταφυλὴ πρόσφατος καὶ σταφίς, "fresh and dried grapes" (Heb. לַח) Nu. 6:3; of a new friend (= νέος, opp. ἀρχαῖος, παλαιο-)

---

[73] [Debrunner]; cf. Bl.-Debr. § 151, 2 (with bibl.).
[74] For attempts along these lines cf. E. A. Abbott, *Johannine Vocabulary* (1905), 133-142; also *Johannine Grammar* (1906), 78 f.; Loh. Apk., on 14:7; cf. Horst, 33-39.

π ρ ο σ κ υ ν η τ ή ς. Cr.-Kö., Pr.-Bauer⁵, *s.v.*; Bultmann J., 140, n. 7; Deissmann LO, 79 f.; J. Horst, *Proskynein* (1932), 306, n. 2; Preisigke Wört., II, 406.

π ρ ό σ φ α τ ο ς, π ρ ο σ φ ά τ ω ς. Pass., Liddell-Scott, Moult.-Mill., Pr.-Bauer⁵, *s.v.*
[1] πρός-φατος (θείνω, φονέω) = "freshly slaughtered (for the occasion)"? or from a πρόσφα (cf. μέσφα = μέχρι Schwyzer, I, 503, App. 2)? Derivations from πρόσ-φημι and προ-φθάνω are less likely, cf. Boisacq, 816; Hofmann, 285.

Sir. 19:10; b. with the subsidiary sense of the illegitimate as compared with the old-established: θεὸς πρόσφατος (with ἀλλότριος) = אֵל זָר ψ 80:10; for חֲדָשִׁים מִקָּרֹב: καινοὶ πρόσφατοι [θεοί], "new and alien gods," Dt. 32:17; c. of recent events: οὐκ ἔστιν πᾶν πρόσφατον ὑπὸ τὸν ἥλιον, there is nothing "new" under the sun (Heb. חָדָשׁ also transl. καινός in v. 10) Qoh. 1:9.

The adv. "just," "recently," Dt. 24:5; Jdt. 4:3, 5; 2 Macc. 14:36; Ez. 11:3 (for בְּקָרוֹב).

3. In the NT the adj. occurs only at Hb. 10:20: ἣν ἐνεκαίνισεν ἡμῖν ὁδὸν πρόσφατον καὶ ζῶσαν διὰ τοῦ καταπετάσματος, τοῦτ' ἔστιν τῆς σαρκὸς αὐτοῦ "which (access) he has newly established for us by a new and living way through the veil, i.e., his flesh," → V, 75, 30ff. The transition to the admonitory part of Hb. (vv. 19 ff.) sums up once again the results of the work of Christ. Through the definitive sacrifice of the High-priest Jesus the new community possesses a hitherto unrevealed (9:8) right [2] of access to the sanctuary, i.e., to God Himself (cf. 9:24), v. 19. The result of the work of Jesus is a newly made ὁδὸς πρόσφατος καὶ ζῶσα which is now open for use. [3] Two thoughts are here combined in πρόσφατος. In time the revelation in Christ is the new thing [4] compared with which the old way to the holy of holies has now been done away as a mere shadow of what was to come, cf. 8:13; 10:1. But there is also a qualitative aspect. [5] As the way is shown to be living by its powerful effects (cf. 4:12; 7:25), so πρόσφατος expresses the incorruptible freshness of the new revelation, so that the abandoned rites and ceremonies seem like dead works in comparison with the service of the living God, cf. 9:14. The compressed line of thought in v. 20, which is meant to be an elucidation of v. 19, contains a rather obscure parallel. The idea of ἐν τῷ αἵματι 'Ιησοῦ is taken up again in [διὰ] τῆς σαρκὸς αὐτοῦ and said to be the basis of the right of access. The new way no longer leads via the old offerings, i.e., through the veil of the temple. It is via the event of redemption in the person and death of Jesus, i.e., through His flesh. Jesus and the ancient veil are at one in granting access, the one to the holy of holies in the type, the other to the full presence of God. The idea that Christ's flesh is in some sense an obstacle on the way to God [6] is alien to Hb. [7] Nor is there any allusion to Mk. 15:38 and par.

The adv. "shortly before" occurs in Ac. 18:2, cf. Mart. Pol., 4.

Maurer

---

[2] παρρησία (→ V, 884, 4 ff.) is more than subj. confidence; it is an objectively given right to this.

[3] → ἐγκαινίζω III, 453, 32 ff.; Mi. Hb., ad loc.; C. Spicq, L'épître aux Hébreux (1953), ad loc.

[4] Much weaker, but in the same sense, Herm. s., 9, 2, 2 in contrast to παλαιός (old rock — newly inserted gate), cf. Dib. Herm., ad loc.: "The ancient city of God has become accessible only in the last times."

[5] Spicq, op. cit., 315: "c'est une propriété qu'elle (sc. la route neuve) gardera toujours, car rien ne vieillit dans la nouvelle alliance."

[6] Rgg., Hb.; J. Schneider (→ III, 630, 14 ff.); E. Käsemann, Das wandernde Gottesvolk² (1957), 145-147.

[7] J. Héring, L'épître aux Hébreux (1954), ad loc.

προσφέρω → φέρω.

προσφορά → φέρω.

πρόσωπον, εὐπροσωπέω,
προσωπολημψία, προσωπολήμπτης,
προσωπολημπτέω, ἀπροσωπολήμπτως

---

† πρόσωπον.

Contents : A. Greek Usage : 1. Face ; 2. Mask ; 3. Person. B. Septuagint and Later
Jewish Usage : I. Septuagint : 1. Face ; 2. Front Side ; 3. God's Countenance ; II. Later
Judaism : 1. Philo and Josephus ; 2. Pseudepigrapha and Rabbinic Writings. C. New
Testament Usage : 1. Face ; 2. Front Side ; 3. God's Countenance ; 4. Person. D. Early
Church Usage : 1. πρόσωπον in the Post-Apostolic Fathers ; 2. πρόσωπον in the Chris-
tology and Trinitarian Teaching of the Early Church.

A. Greek Usage.

The basic meaning of the word πρόσωπον is "face," "countenance." Cf. the def. in
Aristot. Hist. An., I, 8, p. 491b, 9 : τὸ δ' ὑπὸ τὸ κρανίον ὀνομάζεται πρόσωπον ...
προσώπου δὲ τὸ μὲν ὑπὸ τὸ βρέγμα (front of the head) μεταξὺ τῶν ὀμμάτων
μέτωπον. [1] Understanding of the other uses rests on this basic sense.

π ρ ό σ ω π ο ν. On A.: Preisigke Wört., II, 421 f.; Liddell-Scott, *s.v.*; Pr.-Bauer[5], *s.v.*;
K. Praechter, Πρόσωπον, *Philol.*, 63 (1904), 155 f.; S. Schlossmann, Persona u. ΠΡΟΣΩ-
ΠΟΝ *im Recht u. im chr. Dogma* (1906); A. Trendelenburg, "Zur Gesch. des Wortes
Person," *Kantstudien*, 13 (1908); R. Hirzel, "Die Person, Begriff u. Name derselben im
Altertum," S. A. Münch, 1914, 10 (1914); H. Rheinfelder, "Das Wort 'Persona,' Gesch.
seiner Bdtg. mit besonderer Berücksichtigung d. französischen u. italienischen Mittelalters,"
Beih. zur Zschr. f. Romanische Philologie, 77 (1928); F. Altheim, "Persona," ARW, 27
(1929), 35-52; M. Nédoncelle, "Prosopon et persona dans l'antiquité class.," *Revue des
Sciences Religieuses*, 22 (1948), 277-299; L. Malten, "Die Sprache des menschlichen Ant-
litzes in d. Antike," *Forschungen u. Fortschritte*, 27 (1953), 24-28. On B.: J. Boehmer,
"Gottes Angesicht," BFTh, 12 (1908), 321-347; W. W. Graf Baudissin, " 'Gott schauen' in
d. at.lichen Religion," ARW, 18 (1915), 173-239; E. G. Gulin, "Das Antlitz Jahwes im AT,"
Annales Academiae Scientiarum Fennicae, 17, 3 (1923); F. Nötscher, *"Das Angesicht Gottes
schauen," nach bibl. u. babyl. Auffassung* (1924); J. Morgenstern, "Moses with the Shining
Face," *Hebrew Union Coll. Ann.*, 2 (1925), 1-28; Johannessohn Präpos.; H. Middendorf,
Gott sieht, eine terminologische Studie über d. Schauen Gottes im AT, Diss. Freiburg (1935);
A. R. Johnson, *The Vitality of the Individual in the Thought of Ancient Israel* (1949), 42-46.
On C.: S. Antoniadis, Neotestamentica, I, Neophilologus, 14 (1929), 129-132. On D.:
Schlossmann ; A. Grillmeier, *Das Konzil v. Chalkedon*, I (1951), 49-52.

[1] One cannot accept the old explanation Thes. Steph., VI, 2048 : "πρόσωπον = *quod
est circa oculos ; Pars, quae est circa oculos* ; τὸ πρὸς τοῖς ὠψὶ μέρος." For hypostatisation
from προσ (earlier *προτj) -ωπ is certain, but the underlying idea is hard to fix ; it is
certainly not *circa oculos* (πρός does not mean *circa* ; the basic sense is "over against").
New attempts : "what is directed to the eyes (of another)," Schwyzer, II, 517, n. 1; πρόσωπα "the part of the head which is toward the eyes," F. Sommer, "Zur Gesch. d. gr.
Nominalkomposita," A. A. Münch, NF, 27 (1948), 115, n. 1 (though this fits only men and
not animals). [Debrunner]

1. Face.

The word πρόσωπον occurs first in Hom. and here it is almost always used in the plur, to denote the "face" or "countenance" of man : γρῆυς δὲ κατέσχετο χερσὶ πρόσωπα, Od., 19, 361; σπόγγῳ δ᾽ ἀμφὶ πρόσωπα ... ἀπομόργνυ, Il., 18, 414; also Od., 20, 352; Il., 7, 212, though also sing.: χαρίεν δ᾽ ᾔσχυνε πρόσωπον, Il., 18, 24. The plur. is also found occasionally in the tragedians : Electra says to Orestes : μή μ᾽ ἀποστερήσῃς τῶν σῶν προσώπων ἁδονὰν μεθέσθαι, Soph. El., 1277, cf. also Oed. Col., 314; Aesch. Ag., 794. The plural use shows "that not the organ of the eye ... is alone or predominantly felt to be that which controls expression but ... the 'part about the mouth'." For the Greeks the part about the eyes is dominant in the whole oval of the front side of the human head. [2] Already from an early period, however, there is a use in the sing. which later becomes the rule, Hes. Op., 594; Aesch. Ag., 639; Soph. Oed. Tyr., 448; Eur. Hipp., 280, 720; Aristoph. Av., 1321; Simonides, [3] 37, 12; Plat. Euthyd., 275e; Leg., IX, 854d; Xenoph. Cyrop., II, 2, 29; Demosth. Or., 18, 283; for the Hell. period cf. Wilcken Ptol., 70, 5; BGU, III, 909, 12; καὶ πολλὰ ἀσελγήματα λέγων εἰς πρόσωπόν μου, P. Oxy., VI, 903, 21. Normally the Gk. uses the term only for the face of men, though sometimes also for the face of gods (Eur. Ion, 1550), but not for that of animals : [4] τὸ δ᾽ ὑπὸ τὸ κρανίον ὀνομάζεται πρόσωπον ἐπὶ μόνου τῶν ἄλλων ζῴων ἀνθρώπου· ἰχθύος γὰρ καὶ βοὸς οὐ λέγεται πρόσωπον, Aristot. Hist. An., I, 8, p. 491b, 9. Yet there are occasional exceptions to this rule : of the ibis Hdt., II, 76; πρόσωπα (ἐλάφων), Aristot. Hist. An., VI, 29, p. 579a, 2; πρόσωπον τῆς ἵππου, ibid., IX, 47, p. 631a, 5.

Since the face controls the whole appearance πρόσωπον can sometimes be used for "form" or "figure" : εὐφυὲς πρόσωπον Eur. Med., 1198. The fixed combination κατὰ πρόσωπον serves to denote "personal presence" : τὴν κατὰ πρόσωπον ἔντευξιν "oral, personal converse," Plut. Caesar, 17 (I, 716a); κατὰ πρόσωπον λόγους ἐποιήσαντο, Inscr. Magn., 93b, 11; καὶ ἐπερωτηθεὶς παρ᾽ αὐτοῦ κατὰ πρόσωπον αὐτοῦ ὡμολόγησεν, "and asked by him he told him eye to eye," Preisigke Sammelb., I, 5174, 15. Cf. also Inschr. Priene, 41, 6; Ditt. Or., II, 441, 66; P. Oxy., VII, 1071, 1.

Fig. πρόσωπον is often used for "front" esp. in military contexts : τὴν κατὰ πρόσωπον τῆς φάλαγγος τάξιν, Xenoph. Cyrop., VI, 3, 35; ἐν τῇ κατὰ πρόσωπον πλευρᾷ, Polyb., 11, 23, 3; also Thuc., I, 106; Xenoph. Cyrop., I, 6, 43; Polyb., 11, 14, 6. Of the front of a building : κατὰ πρόσωπον τοῦ ἱεροῦ, P. Petr., III, 1 col. II, 8.

2. Mask.

The "mask" worn by actors resembles a human face and is thus called πρόσωπον : [5] τὰ τραγικὰ πρόσωπα, Aristot. Probl., 31, 7, p. 958a, 17; ἄνευ προσώπου κωμάζει, Demosth. Or., 19, 287; τὰ πρόσωπα τῶν θεῶν (sc. those who appear in the play), Luc. Jup. Trag., 41; πρόσωπον ὑπάργυρον κατάχρυσον, IG, I², 276, 6. [6] Later we also find προσωπεῖον (e.g., Jos. Bell., 4, 156) which is used exclusively for the actor's mask, though πρόσωπον is still found for this : ὥσπερ δὲ οἱ ἐν τοῖς θεάτροις δραμάτων τινῶν ὑποκριταὶ οὐχ ὅπερ λέγουσίν εἰσιν, οὐδ᾽ ὅπερ βλέπονται καθ᾽ ὃ περίκεινται πρόσωπον τοῦτο τυγχάνουσιν, Orig. Orat., 20, 2.

Fig. πρόσωπον can then mean the "part" played by the actor : τριῶν δ᾽ ὄντων προσώπων καθάπερ ἐν ταῖς κωμῳδίαις τοῦ διαβάλλοντος καὶ τοῦ διαβαλλομένου καὶ τοῦ πρὸς ὃν ἡ διαβολὴ γίνεται Luc. Calumniae, 6; πρόσελθε ἐν προσώ-

---

[2] Malten, 24 f.
[3] ed. T. Bergk, Poetae Lyrici Graeci, III (1882).
[4] Hirzel, 47.
[5] Schlossmann, 37; Hirzel, 40 f.
[6] Editio minor, ed. F. Hiller v. Gärtringen (1924).

πῳ τοιούτῳ, Epict. Diss., I, 29, 45; τοῦτό μοι τὸ πρόσωπον ἀνάλαβε, I, 29, 57.[7] Acc. to Epict. it is every man's business to play well in life the role assigned specifically to him : τὸ δοθὲν ὑποκρίνεσθαι πρόσωπον καλῶς, Ench., 17.

In the dialogues of the diatribe there was often presented the view of an anonymous opponent who was called κωφὸν πρόσωπον; the point was to present one's own view the more clearly in contrast : κωφὸν ὡς ἐπὶ σκηνῆς προσωπεῖον, Philo Flacc., 20; cf. also Plut. An Seni Sit Gerenda Res Publica, 15 (II, 791e).[8]

3. Person.

In the Hell. period πρόσωπον takes on the sense of "person" to denote man in his position in human society. [9] The face, "the eye is so distinctive for gods and men that a person is perceived in it." [10] πρόσωπον thus replaces other terms like → σῶμα which had previously been used in the sense of "person." [11]

Whether πρόσωπον already means "person" in Polyb. is debated and cannot be proved beyond dispute. For ἐζήτουν ἡγεμόνα καὶ πρόσωπον in Polyb., 5, 107, 3 means "they sought a leader and a man of esteem," while τὸ τῆς Ἑλλάδος ὄνομα καὶ πρόσωπον in 8, 13, 5 means "the name and face of Greece." Again, the ref. of τὸ τοῦ Ὀδυσσέως πρόσωπον in 12, 27, 10 is more to his "dramatic role," → 769, 43 ff. [12] On the other hand, πρόσωπον certainly means "person" in the following passages : ξένοις προσώποις, "foreign persons," P. Oxy., XIV, 1672, 4 (37-41 A.D.); μὴ κρῖνε πρόσωπον, Ps.-Phokylides, 10 (Diehl³, II, 92); ὁ φθόνος ἅπτεται μάλιστα τῶν χρηστῶν καὶ αὐξομένων πρὸς ἀρετὴν καὶ δόξαν καὶ ἠθῶν καὶ πρόσωπων, Plut. De Invidia et Odio, 6 (II, 537 f.); ἐξ Αἰγυπτιακῶν προσώπων, P. Oxy., II, 237 col. VII, 34; cf. also Dion. Hal. De Thucydide, 34; Epict. Diss., I, 2, 7; Plut. De Garrulitate, 13 (II, 509b); P. Ryl., 28, 8. Grammarians then used πρόσωπον for grammatical person, Dion. Thr. Art. Gramm., 638b, 4; Apollon. Dyscol. De Pronominis Appellationibus, 1c. [13] A technical use whereby πρόσωπον means a "person" legally is still not found in the first cent. A.D. [14] In the 2nd cent. Phrynichos [15] complains that orators often spoke of πρόσωπα in court and in so doing offended against correct Gk. But only later, probably under the influence of the Lat. persona → n. 7, did the word take on the technical sense which is then common in legal documents : οἱ τὸ σὸν πρόσωπον πληροῦντες, "the representatives of thy person," Preisigke Sammelb., I, 6000, II, line 13 (6th cent.); τὴν ὠνὴν τὴν γενομένην εἰς πρόσωπον τοῦ σοῦ εἰρημένου ἀδελφοῦ ("in the name of thy brother"), ibid., line 25; ἀναπληροῦντες τὸ πρόσωπον τοῦ ἁγίο[υ μοναστηρίου], ibid., I, 5114, 49 (7th cent.). One may not assume that the word had this sense in the NT period or the age of the early Church.

---

[7] The Gk. πρόσωπον is closely related to the Lat. persona, which can mean "mask," "role," "person," also "prominent personage," whereas the legal use of πρόσωπον, as will be shown, developed only later. Cf. Hirzel, 47 f. It is still a matter of debate whether or not the Lat. persona ("mask," "person") was borrowed from the Gk. πρόσωπον; if so, it could only be circuitously ; cf. Walde-Hofmann, 291 f. [Debrunner].

[8] Cf. Dib. Jk. on 2:18.

[9] Rheinfelder, 6-17 derives the use of πρόσωπον for "person" from the speech of the theatre : in the actor who plays Oedipus we see Oedipus. "Thus persona as the husk becomes the kernel of the matter," 8. But this is too restricted a derivation.

[10] Malten, 25.

[11] Hirzel, 5-19. In early times the term σῶμα could be used with no derogatory nuance. Only later did its stock decline so that it could be used for the slave with no sense of "person."

[12] On the disputed ref. in Polyb. cf. Hirzel, 44 f.

[13] Ed. R. Schneider-G. Uhlig in Grammatici Graeci, II, 1 (1878), 3, line 12.

[14] On the question of the legal use of πρόσωπον cf. Schlossmann.

[15] Ed. C. A. Lobeck (1820), 379.

B. Septuagint and Later Jewish Usage.

I. Septuagint.

πρόσωπον occurs in the LXX over 850 times, in by far the greatest no. of instances for Heb. פָּנִים. It is also the rendering of אַף in Gn. 2:7; מַרְאֶה in 1 Βασ. 16:7 A; עֵינַיִם in 1 Βασ. 16:7; Am. 9:4 A; פֶּה in ψ 54:22 and אַנְף in Da. 3:19 LXX Θ; [16] פָּנִים is connected with the verb "to turn" and means the "side turned to the fore," "the face" of man, "the front" of an inanimate obj. [17] The meaning of πρόσωπον in the LXX corresponds to this broad sense of the Heb. equivalent.

1. Face.

πρόσωπον is very commonly used for "face" in the LXX : εἶδεν Ιακωβ τὸ πρόσωπον τοῦ Λαβαν, Gn. 31:2; τὸ πρόσωπον τοῦ πατρός, Gn. 50:1; πρόσωπον τοῦ παιδαρίου, 4 Βασ. 4:29, 31; ἔπεσεν Αβραμ ἐπὶ πρόσωπον αὐτοῦ, Gn. 17:3 — a frequent expression for respectful greeting or veneration ; ἀπέστρεψεν ὁ βασιλεὺς τὸ πρόσωπον αὐτοῦ, 3 Βασ. 8:14. To see the face of a king is to be admitted to audience, so that οἱ ὁρῶντες τὸ πρόσωπον τοῦ βασιλέως can be a title for court officials, 4 Βασ. 25:19. [18] πρόσωπον πρὸς πρόσωπον (פָּנִים אֶל־פָּנִים) "face to face," Gn. 32:30; Ju. 6:22; [19] cf. also πρόσωπον κατὰ πρόσωπον, Dt. 34:10. Often πρόσωπον is used for the face of animals too, e.g., πρόσωπον λέοντος, Ez. 1:10; 41:19; 1 Ch. 12:9. Sometimes πρόσωπον means "features," "appearance" : συνέπεσεν (sc. Καιν) τῷ προσώπῳ, Gn. 4:5; poor appearance : τὰ πρόσωπα ὑμῶν σκυθρωπά, Gn. 40:7; appearance of a matter : τὸ πρόσωπον τοῦ ῥήματος τούτου, 2 Βασ. 14:20.

Sometimes the face of a man can be spoken of in such a way as to denote the whole man. Thus it is said of Absalom in 2 Βασ. 17:11: τὸ πρόσωπόν σου πορευόμενον ἐν μέσῳ αὐτῶν, i.e., Absalom should go forth among the Israelites in person. In this connection ref. might also be made to the Heb. of Dt. 7:10, which says that Yahweh will cause the one who hates him to undergo in his own person (אֶל־פָּנָיו LXX κατὰ πρόσωπον) retribution by destruction.

2. Front Side.

As the Heb. פָּנִים ("the side to the front") can be used of inanimate objects, so the LXX often uses πρόσωπον in this way : τὸ πρόσωπον τῆς γῆς, "the surface of the earth," Gn. 2:6; σκοπεύων πρόσωπον Δαμασκοῦ ("towards"), Cant. 7:5; πρόσωπον (sc. τοῦ σιδηρίου), "the edge of iron," Qoh. 10:10.

In the broad sense of the front side πρόσωπον is found in countless instances with prepositions denoting direction to or from : "Instead of simple prepositions the Semitic languages love to create fuller and more vivid expressions with the help of a noun which usually denotes a part of the body." [20] Like the Heb. original פָּנִים, πρόσωπον often serves simply to strengthen the prepos. on which it depends. [21]

---

[16] Prepositional combinations (ἀπὸ προσώπου etc.) and their Heb. originals are not counted.

[17] Cf. Koehler-Baumg., s.v. and Johnson, 42-46, with good material on OT usage. Johnson aptly remarks on the plur. form פָּנִים : "Indeed the fact that in Hebrew the use of this Semitic noun is restricted to the plur. form is sufficient to indicate the importance which was attached to what we should call one's 'features' ...," 42.

[18] Cf. Baudissin, 191; → V, 325, 20 f.

[19] Cf. ὀφθαλμοὶ πρὸς ὀφθαλμούς, Is. 52:8; στόμα πρὸς στόμα, 'Ιερ. 39(32):4.

[20] Johannessohn, 348.

[21] In this use we have definite Semitisms. Gk. knows only κατὰ πρόσωπον → 769, 24 ff.

a. ἀπό (τοῦ) [22] προσώπου (מִפְּנֵי etc.) "going out from," "away from": ἀπὸ προσώπου κυρίου τοῦ θεοῦ, Gn. 3:8; φύγωμεν ἀπὸ προσώπου Ισραηλ, Ex. 14:25; ἐφοβήθητε ἀπὸ προσώπου τοῦ πυρός, Dt. 5:5; also Dt. 9:5; 4 Βασ. 13:23; 1 Ch. 16:30; ψ 37:4; Jdt. 5:8 etc. The fact that with a prepos. πρόσωπον is almost always a simple expletive may be seen from the MS tradition at Job 1:12 LXX: אB ἐξῆλθεν ὁ διάβολος παρὰ τοῦ (A ἀπὸ προσώπου) κυρίου.

b. εἰς (τό) πρόσωπον (בִּפְנֵי, עַל־פְּנֵי etc.) "in or before the face": here πρόσωπον always means "face" or "front": οὐκέτι ὀφθήσομαί σοι εἰς πρόσωπον, Ex. 10:29; εἰς πρόσωπόν σε εὐλογήσει, Job 2:5; cf. also 3 Βασ. 8:8; 2 Ch. 5:9; Hos. 5:5. [23]

c. ἐκ (τοῦ) προσώπου (מִפְּנֵי etc.) "from": ἐὰν οὖν λάβητε καὶ τοῦτον ἐκ προσώπου μου, Gn. 44:29; ἔφυγον ἐκ προσώπου αὐτοῦ, 1 Βασ. 19:8; ἐκ προσώπου σου τὸ κρίμα μου ἐξέλθοι, ψ 16:2; cf. also 1 Βασ. 19:10; 21:11; 25:10; 31:1; 2 Βασ. 23:11 etc.

d. ἐν προσώπῳ (לִפְנֵי) "before": ταπεινῶσαί σε ἐν προσώπῳ δυνάστου, Prv. 25:7.

e. ἐπὶ προσώπου, ἐπὶ προσώπῳ, ἐπὶ (τὸ) πρόσωπον (עַל־פְּנֵי etc.) "on": ὃ ἦν ἐπὶ προσώπου πάσης τῆς γῆς, Gn. 7:23; cf. also Gn. 11:4; 41:56; Dt. 14:2; Ez. 34:6 etc. In the phrase ἐπὶ πρόσωπον the word πρόσωπον often has its true sense "face": ἔπεσεν Μωυσης καὶ Ααρων ἐπὶ πρόσωπον, Nu. 14:5; cf. Nu. 16:4, 22 etc.; ἤμην πεπτωκὼς ἐπὶ πρόσωπόν μου, Da. 10:9 LXX.

f. κατὰ πρόσωπον (לִפְנֵי etc.) "before," "over against": [24] κατὰ πρόσωπον πάντων τῶν ἀδελφῶν αὐτοῦ κατοικήσει, Gn. 16:12; κατὰ πρόσωπον τῆς πόλεως, Gn. 33:18; κατὰ πρόσωπον τοῦ ἱλαστηρίου, Lv. 16:14, 15; cf. also Nu. 3:38; Dt. 9:2; 11:25; Ἰερ. 18:17; 41(34):18. This is often used to denote geographical situation, e.g., ὅς ἐστιν κατὰ πρόσωπον Μαμβρη, Gn. 23:17; ἥ ἐστιν κατὰ πρόσωπον Αἰγύπτου, Gn. 25:18; κατὰ πρόσωπον τῆς Ἀραβίας, Jdt. 2:25.

g. μετὰ τοῦ προσώπου (אֶת־פָּנִים): πληρώσεις με εὐφροσύνης μετὰ τοῦ προσώπου σου ("with thee"), ψ 15:11.

h. πρὸ προσώπου (מִלִּפְנֵי, לִפְנֵי etc.) "before": [25] ἀποστέλλω τὸν ἄγγελόν μου πρὸ προσώπου σου, Ex. 23:20; cf. also Ex. 32:34; Nu. 14:42; Dt. 3:18; 30:1; Ἰερ. 21:8; Mal. 3:1; Jdt. 10:13; 2 Βασ. 6:14 Ἀ etc.

3. God's Countenance.

In many places in the LXX πρόσωπον, like the Heb. פָּנִים, is used to denote God's countenance, i.e., the side He turns to man.

a. Sometimes the manner of speech is anthropomorphic. When God lifts His countenance over man He has pity and gives peace: ἐπάραι κύριος τὸ πρόσωπον αὐτοῦ ἐπὶ σέ, Nu. 6:26. Prayer is made that He will cause His face to shine on the Israelites: ἐπιφάναι κύριος τὸ πρόσωπον αὐτοῦ ἐπὶ σέ, Nu. 6:25. When He hides His face He withdraws His grace: ἀποστρέψω τὸ πρόσωπόν μου,

---

[22] Since these are transl. of Semitic expressions, the art. may be left out. Cf. Bl.-Debr. § 259, 1.

[23] In a lit. rendering of the Heb. לִפְנֵי Ἀ Gn. 17:1 has περιπάτει εἰς πρόσωπόν μου. Cf. P. Katz, "Notes on the Septuagint," JThSt, 47 (1946), 31 f.

[24] The κατὰ πρόσωπον found in Gk. lit. never takes a dependent case except in later Egypt. pap: κατὰ πρόσωπον τοῦ ἱεροῦ, P. Petr., III, 1 col. II, 8 → 769, 33. Cf. κατὰ πρόσωπον τοῦ ναοῦ in Ez. 41:4. Materially cf. Johannessohn, 248, n. 2.

[25] πρὸ προσώπου does not occur in Gn.; instead we find ἐναντίον, ἔμπροσθεν and ἐνώπιον. Johannessohn, 190.

Dt. 32:20; cf. Mi. 3:4. Anxious prayer is made : ἕως πότε ἀποστρέψεις τὸ πρόσωπόν σου ἀπ᾽ ἐμοῦ; ψ 12:2; cf. 29:8; 43:25. If God has not turned away His countenance, grateful confession is made : οὐδὲ ἀπέστρεψεν τὸ πρόσωπον αὐτοῦ ἀπ᾽ ἐμοῦ, ψ 21:25. Prayer is also made to God μὴ ἀποστρέψῃς τὸ πρόσωπόν σου ἀπ᾽ ἐμοῦ, ψ 101:3; 142:7. In penal wrath God turns His face against those who do evil : πρόσωπον δὲ κυρίου ἐπὶ ποιοῦντας κακά, ψ 33:17. His wrathful glance smites transgressors of the Law : ἐπιστήσω τὸ πρόσωπόν μου ἐπὶ τὴν ψυχὴν τὴν ἔσθουσαν τὸ αἷμα καὶ ἀπολῶ αὐτὴν ἐκ τοῦ λαοῦ αὐτῆς, Lv. 17:10, cf. Lv. 20:3, 6; 26:17; Ez. 14:8; 15:7.

It is often said that men have seen the face of God : εἶδον γὰρ θεὸν πρόσωπον πρὸς πρόσωπον, Gn. 32:30; cf. Ju. 6:22. Because he had seen God face to face Jacob called the place of meeting פְּנִיאֵל, Gn. 32:30 f. LXX = εἶδος θεοῦ. [26] Seeing God involves the greatest peril, for man necessarily perishes before God's holiness. The OT does not dispute the fact that man may see God's face in certain circumstances, yet in general he may not do so, since the consuming holiness of God destroys man. [27] Thus Moses is warned οὐ δυνήσῃ ἰδεῖν μου τὸ πρόσωπον· οὐ γὰρ μὴ ἴδῃ ἄνθρωπος τὸ πρόσωπόν μου καὶ ζήσεται, Ex. 33:20. Moses can see only from behind when the glory of God passes by : ὄψῃ τὰ ὀπίσω μου, τὸ δὲ πρόσωπόν μου οὐκ ὀφθήσεταί σοι, Ex. 33:23. In distinction from the religion of the Greeks, according to which the gods can reveal themselves to the eye of man, the OT insists that God reveals Himself through the Word, not through seeing His face, → I, 217, 26 ff.

b. Alongside this use of "God's countenance" there is a second series of instances in which πρόσωπον (θεοῦ) is employed cultically. "To see God's face" is "to visit the cultic site." This expression was probably taken over from non-Israelite cults which had an idol in the temple for the veneration of worshippers. It then passed into OT usage in a transferred sense. [28] The yearning question is asked in prayer : πότε ἥξω καὶ ὀφθήσομαι τῷ προσώπῳ τοῦ θεοῦ; ψ 41:3; 94:2. Believers seek the face of the Lord and find it when they attend the temple : ἐκζητῆσαι τὸ πρόσωπον κυρίου, Zech. 8:21 f. [29] There is often reference to δεηθῆναι τοῦ προσώπου (God's), ψ 118:58; 4 Βασ. 13:4; Bar. 2:8; Zech. 8:21 Cf. ἐξιλάσκεσθε τὸ πρόσωπον τοῦ θεοῦ ὑμῶν, Mal. 1:9. In these expressions the accent is not on seeing. To see the face of God is to be certain of His presence and grace. Hence ψ 104:4 can say with reference to the everyday life of the righteous : ζητήσατε τὸ πρόσωπον αὐτοῦ (sc. God's) διὰ παντός. Here the expression breaks away from the cultic world and stresses the need to keep up a daily relation with God. When the Psalmist says : τὸ πρόσωπόν σου, κύριε,

---

[26] The place-name θεοῦ πρόσωπον (= פְּנֵי אֵל?) is used for the mountain rās shaḳḳa which juts out into the Mediterranean on the Lebanese coast, Strabo, 16, 754; Ps.-Skylax, Periplus, 104 (ed. C. Müller, Geographi Graeci Minores, I [1855], 78). Cf. on this K. Galling, "Die syrisch-palästinische Küste nach Ps.-Skylax," ZDPV, 61 (1938), 74 f.

[27] Cf. Baudissin, 184 f.; E. Fascher, "Deus invisibilis," Marburger Theol. Studien, I (1931), 41-77; R. Bultmann, "Untersuchungen zum Joh.-Ev., B. θεὸν οὐδεὶς ἑώρακεν πώποτε," ZNW, 29 (1930), 169-192 and what is said about seeing God in the art. → ὁράω V, 325, 7 ff., 331, 1 ff.

[28] Baudissin, 189-197; Gulin, 5-7; Nötscher, 88-95; G. Kittel, Religionsgeschichte u. Urchr. (1932), 100.

[29] The cultic phrase "to see God's face" was avoided later. Thus לִרְאוֹת פְּנַי in Is. 1:12 was read as לֵרָאוֹת פְּנַי, which was transl. ὀφθῆναί μοι in the LXX [J. Fichtner].

ζητήσω (ψ 26:8), he means that he wants to make Yahweh's grace and help a matter of supreme concern. [30]

It may be mentioned in conclusion that the shewbread is called ἄρτοι τοῦ προσώπου in 1 Βασ. 21:7 because it is kept in the holy place, the place of God's presence.

II. Later Judaism.

1. Philo and Josephus.

a. Philo describes τὸ πρόσωπον as σώματος ἡγεμονικόν, Leg. All., I, 39; cf. Fug., 182. At creation God blew into man πνοὴν ζωῆς εἰς τὸ τοῦ σώματος ἡγεμονικώτατον, τὸ πρόσωπον, Spec. Leg., IV, 123. Acc. to the will of God, then, the face is the most important part of the human body, Poster. C., 127; Leg. All., I, 28; for ἐν προσώπῳ τὰς αἰσθήσεις ἐδημιούργει, Leg. All., I, 39. Cf. Op. Mund., 139 : τὸ πρόσωπον, ἔνθα τῶν αἰσθήσεων ὁ τόπος. It is worth noting that the face is controlled by the significant number seven : τό τε ἡγεμονικώτατον τοῦ ζῴου πρόσωπον ἑπταχῆ κατατέτρηται, δυσὶν ὀφθαλμοῖς καὶ ὠσὶ δυσίν, ἴσοις μυκτῆρσιν, ἑβδόμῳ στόματι, Leg. All., I, 12. Ref. is often made to God's face : Cain must withdraw ἐκ προσώπου τοῦ θεοῦ, Poster. C., 12, 22 etc. God's Word goes forth ἐκ προσώπου θεοῦ, Deus Imm., 109; Plant., 63; Conf. Ling., 168; Mut. Nom., 39 etc. In Mut. Nom., 13 Philo speaks of a λόγιον ἐκ προσώπου θεσπισθὲν τοῦ τῶν ὅλων ἡγεμόνος. In harmony with the OT Philo also says that God's face is hidden from man. He takes the story in Ex. 33:12-23 to mean that the works of God may be seen but not His essential being, Poster. C., 169. [31] Cf. also Fug., 165 : αὔταρκες γάρ ἐστι σοφῷ τὰ ἀκόλουθα καὶ ἑπόμενα καὶ ὅσα μετὰ τὸν θεὸν γνῶναι, τὴν δ' ἡγεμονικὴν οὐσίαν ὁ βουλόμενος καταθεάσασθαι τῷ περιαυγεῖ τῶν ἀκτίνων πρὶν ἰδεῖν πηρὸς ἔσται. In Spec. Leg., I, 36-46 [32] Philo explains that Moses based his request that God would show Himself to him on the ground that only God Himself could reveal His essential being. When God could not accede to this request because man is incapable of such vision, Moses prayed that at least God would reveal His δόξα, the δυνάμεις which encircle Him in service. But even this petition was denied because the δυνάμεις are invisible and can be perceived only by God who is invisible.

Sometimes it would seem that πρόσωπον is used for "person" : τί δεῖ τὰς τῶν προσώπων ἀμυθήτους ἰδέας καταλέγεσθαι; Poster. C., 110; τὰ πράγματα καὶ τὰ πρόσωπα, ibid., 111; ἐπὶ τιμῇ προσώπων, Spec. Leg., I, 245.

b. In Joseph. πρόσωπον means "face" : πεσὼν (Hezekiah) ἐπὶ πρόσωπον τὸν θεὸν ἱκέτευσε, Ant., 10, 11. Cf. also Ant., 6, 285; 7, 95 and 114; 9, 11 and 269; 10, 211 for this expression. When the brother of a dead man refuses Levirate marriage, the rejected woman is to πτύειν εἰς πρόσωπον (cf. Dt. 25:8 f.), Ant., 4, 256; 5, 335. In Bell., 2, 29 πρόσωπον denotes the "features" : ἐπισχηματίζων τὸ πρόσωπον εἰς λύπην. The outside of the temple is called τὸ ἔξωθεν αὐτοῦ πρόσωπον in Bell., 5, 222. The sense "role" is found in Bell., I, 517. The common LXX combination κατὰ πρόσωπον with dependent case is also common in Jos.: κατὰ πρόσωπον τῆς τραπέζης, Ant., 3, 144; κατὰ πρόσωπον τοῦ ναοῦ, 9, 8; κατὰ πρόσωπον αὐτοῦ (of the king), 11, 235. Jos. refers to God's face only in explanation of the OT word Peniel : ἡσθεὶς δὲ τούτοις (sc. the encounter with God) Ἰάκωβος Φανούηλον ὀνομάζει τὸν τόπον ὃ σημαίνει θεοῦ πρόσωπον, Ant., 1, 334. πρόσωπον means "person" in Bell., 1, 263 : προλαβὼν Ἡρώδης μετὰ τῶν οἰκειοτάτων προσώπων ("with the persons most intimate with him," i.e., his closest relatives) νύκτωρ ἐπὶ Ἰδουμαίας ἐχώρει λάθρα τῶν πολεμίων.

---

[30] Cf. Nötscher, 136.
[31] I owe this ref. to G. Bertram.
[32] Cf. on this M. Pohlenz, "Pls. u. die Stoa," ZNW, 42 (1949), 71 f.

2. Pseudepigrapha and Rabbinic Writings.

It is not our task to give all the many examples of פָּנִים in Jewish literature. One still finds the OT senses (→ 771, 1 ff.) "forward side" : "face," "front," "surface," and also the combination with various prepos. → 771, 33 ff.

Apart from this the pseudepigr. speak of the face of the perfected righteous shining like the sun in the future world, since God will cause His light to shine on the face of the saints and the elect righteous, Eth. En. 38:4; cf. Da. 12:3; Eth. En. 39:7; 104:2. This means, however, that "they will be changed ... from beauty to splendour and from light to the radiance of glory," S. Bar. 51:10. Immediate proximity to God will be the lot of the righteous, S. Bar. 51:3. In 4 Esr. 7:97 the sixth joy granted to those who have kept the ways of the Most High is "that it will be shown to them how their face will one day shine as the sun." The seventh joy is that they exultantly press on "to see the face of Him whom they have served in life and from whom they will receive praise and reward," 7:98. [33] In the hour of death — so say the Rabbis — all men must see the face of God. Hence R. Jochanan b. Zakkai dies full of fears (→ II, 527, 23 ff.), Ab. R. Nat., 25; cf. bBer., 28b. The ungodly will see God's face to receive their punishment, Midr. Ps. 22 § 32 (99a). [34] But in the world to come the righteous will see the face of the shekinah as a reward for their deeds, bMen., 43b; bSota, 42a. [35] He who gives alms or does meritorious works will be made worthy thereby to greet the face of the shekinah, bBB, 10a.

In the form "to see or to greet the face of the shekinah" the Rabb. use the OT cultic formula "to see the face of God" not only for attending the temple but later for taking part in the worship of the synagogue as well, Dt. r., 7 (204a), [36] since this is the place where God draws near. It is also said of those who pray or study that they greet God's face, for God is near to those who pray and who apply themselves to the Torah, bSanh., 42a. [37]

πρόσωπον also came into Rabb. usage as a loan word and is of frequent occurrence : Heb. פרסוף/פרצוף or Aram. פרצופא. [38] Thus one reads in TBer., 7, 2 : אין פרוצופותיהין דומות זה לזה = "their (men's) faces are not like one another." [39]

C. New Testament Usage.

The use of πρόσωπον in the NT follows closely that of the LXX (→ 771, 1 ff.) and the word has the same range of meaning as in the OT → 771, 3 ff.

1. Face.

πρόσωπον is often used in the sense (→ 769, 1 ff., 771, 9 ff.) "face" (Mt. 6:16 f.; Ac. 6:15; Rev. 4:7; 9:7; Mk. 14:65; Mt. 26:67), εἰς πρόσωπον δέρειν, "to hit in the face," 2 C. 11:20. [40] Inclining (Lk. 24:5) or falling on one's face [41] (Mt. 17:6;

---

[33] On the vision of God in the pseudepig. and Rabb. writings cf. Str.-B., I, 206-214; → V, 339, 12 ff.

[34] Cf. Str.-B., I, 209.

[35] For further examples cf. Str.-B., I, 210-212.

[36] Ibid., 207.

[37] Ibid., 206 f.

[38] Cf. S. Krauss, Griech. u. lat. Lehnwörter im Talmud, Midrasch u. Targum, II (1899), 495.

[39] πρόσωπον in the sense of "person" is also a loan word in Syr.: O. Sol. 31:5 (ed. W. Bauer, Kl. T., 64 [1933]) פרצופה = "his person"; cf. also O. Sol. 17:4.

[40] To be taken fig. here, perhaps proverbially of bad treatment ; cf. Ltzm. K., ad loc.

[41] The art. may be left out in the phrase ἐπὶ πρόσωπον πίπτειν, cf. Bl.-Debr. § 255, 4.

26:39; Rev. 7:11; 11:16; without αὐτοῦ Lk. 5:12; 17:16; 1 C. 14:25) expresses respect and veneration, cf. the OT πίπτειν ἐπὶ (τὸ) πρόσωπον αὐτοῦ, → 771, 12 ff. Mention of the face of the angel (Rev. 10:1; cf. Ac. 6:15) or the face of Jesus (Mt. 17:2; Lk. 9:29) shining like the sun is a feature in the description of epiphanies.

On the basis of Ex. 34:29-35 Paul in a Christian midrash (2 C. 3:7-18) [42] refers to the radiant πρόσωπον of Moses which the Israelites could not look on because of its δόξα, v. 7. But the δόξα on the face of Moses was transitory, so that Moses had to cover his face lest the children of Israel should see it fade, v. 13. Paul abruptly adds a new thought. He speaks now, not of the cover on the face of Moses, but of that on the hearts of the Jews in virtue of which the OT is concealed from them and its true sense is closed to them, vv. 14 ff. [43] Christians, on the other hand, can see with uncovered face the δόξα κυρίου and experience the change ἀπὸ δόξης εἰς δόξαν which proceeds from the Lord of the Spirit, v. 18. [44] This line of thought is adopted again in 2 C. 4:6 where we are told that the δόξα of God shines for us in the face of Christ.

In a series of verses πρόσωπον denotes "personal presence" (→ 769, 24 ff.; 771, 14 ff.): ὁρᾶν τὸ πρόσωπόν τινος, "to see someone again" (Ac. 20:25, 38; Col. 2:1; 1 Th. 2:17b; 3:10 Hebraism, cf. Gn. 32:21; 43:3, 5); ἀπορφανισθέντες ἀφ' ὑμῶν ... προσώπῳ οὐ καρδίᾳ, 1 Th. 2:17a; ἀγνοούμενος τῷ προσώπῳ, "unknown personally," Gl. 1:22.

When Lk. 9:51 says of Jesus αὐτὸς τὸ πρόσωπον (αὐτοῦ) ἐστήρισεν τοῦ πορεύεσθαι εἰς Ἰερουσαλήμ, an OT form of expression is adopted (στηρίζειν τὸ πρόσωπον = שִׂים פָּנִים). [45] To turn one's face in a particular direction is to declare the firm intention of following this course without deviation. [46] The Hebraicising expression shows how significant to salvation history is the section which begins with the journey of Jesus from Galilee to Samaria and then on to Jerusalem → 50, 11 ff. With the τὸ πρόσωπον αὐτοῦ ἦν πορευόμενον εἰς Ἰερουσαλήμ of Lk. 9:53 one may compare the τὸ πρόσωπόν σου (Absalom's) πορευόμενον ἐν μέσῳ αὐτῶν of the OT model in 2 Βασ. 17:11, → 771, 22 ff. τὸ πρόσωπον here denotes the whole man : "He journeyed towards Jerusalem." [47]

Sometimes πρόσωπον does not denote the face but the "appearance" or "features" of a man or object. For τὸ πρόσωπον τῆς γενέσεως αὐτοῦ (sc. the man) in Jm. 1:23 one might have expected τὸ πρόσωπον αὐτοῦ; the reference is ob-

---

[42] Cf. Wnd. 2 K., 112; Ltzm. K., ad loc. In exposition → I, 454, 10 ff.; II, 251, 4 ff.; IV, 869, 10 ff.; S. Schulz, "Die Decke des Moses," ZNW, 49 (1958), 1-30.

[43] On the train of thought → III, 560 f.; V, 883, 5 ff.

[44] In exposition of the v. cf. J. Dupont, "Le Chrétien miroir de la gloire divine d'après II Cor. III 18," Rev. Bibl., 56 (1949), 392-411.

[45] Ἰερ. 3:12; 21:10 [24:6]; Ez. 6:2; 13:17; 14:8. Cf. also 4 Βασ. 12:18 : ἔταξεν Αζαηλ τὸ πρόσωπον αὐτοῦ ἀναβῆναι ἐπὶ Ἰερουσαλημ. Cf. A. Wifstrand, "Lukas och Septuaginta," Svensk Teologisk Kvartalskrift, 16 (1940), 247-249. Additional OT par.: τάξει τὸ πρόσωπον αὐτοῦ εἰσελθεῖν, Da. 11:17 Θ; ἐφίστημι τὸ πρόσωπόν μου τοῦ ἀπολέσαι, Ἰερ. 51(44):11 f.; ἔδωκεν Ιωσαφατ τὸ πρόσωπον αὐτοῦ ἐκζητῆσαι τὸν κύριον, 2 Ch. 20:3 [P. Katz].

[46] Cf. Schl. Lk., ad loc.; also Str.-B., II, 165, ad loc.; Dalman WJ, I, 24.

[47] Dalman WJ, I, 25 : This Lucan expression is an "incorrectly used Hebraism which cannot be imitated in Hebrew. Lk. 9:53 refers back to v. 51. The τὸ πρόσωπον αὐτοῦ ἐστήρισεν τοῦ πορεύεσθαι εἰς Ἰερουσαλήμ there ought properly to be repeated. The expression in v. 53 is an unskilful abbreviation of the full phrase."

viously to the kind of person he looks like. [48] ή εύπρέπεια τοῦ προσώπου αὐτοῦ is used of the outside of the flower in Jm. 1:11, while there is reference to the appearance of the sky in Mt. 16:3 (par. Lk. 12:56).

2. The Front Side.

As in the LXX (→ 771, 28 ff.) πρόσωπον can also mean the "front" or "surface" : ἐπὶ πρόσωπον πάσης τῆς γῆς, Lk. 21:35; ἐπὶ παντὸς προσώπου τῆς γῆς, Ac. 17:26. πρόσωπον is also used in dependence on prepositions [49] as in the LXX (→ 771, 33 ff.); here it mostly serves as a strengthening expletive.

a. ἀπὸ προσώπου : ἀπὸ προσώπου τοῦ κυρίου, "coming forth from the Lord," Ac. 3:19; ἀπὸ προσώπου τοῦ συνεδρίου, Ac. 5:41; also Ac. 7:45; 2 Th. 1:9; Rev. 6:16 (cf. Is. 2:10, 19, 21); 12:14 (to denote distance = "far from"); 20:11.

b. εἰς πρόσωπον : εἰς πρόσωπον τῶν ἐκκλησιῶν, "before the eyes of the (other) churches," 2 C. 8:24.

c. ἐν προσώπῳ : by means of ἐν προσώπῳ Χριστοῦ in 2 C. 2:10 Paul appeals to Christ as witness to the sincerity of his forgiveness. πρὸς τοὺς ἐν προσώπῳ καυχωμένους, "against those who boast of external things," 2 C. 5:12.

d. κατὰ πρόσωπον : without dependent case "personally present," "eye to eye" (→ 769, 24): Ac. 25:16; 2 C. 10:1; Gl. 2:11. τὰ κατὰ πρόσωπον, "what is before the eyes," 2 C. 10:7. With gen. following (as in LXX) κατὰ πρόσωπον occurs only in Luke : [50] κατὰ πρόσωπον πάντων τῶν λαῶν, [51] Lk. 2:31; κατὰ πρόσωπον Πιλάτου, Ac. 3:13.

e. μετὰ προσώπου : only in the quotation from ψ 15:11 in Ac. 2:28.

f. πρὸ προσώπου : ἀποστέλλω τὸν ἄγγελόν μου πρὸ προσώπου σου ("before thee") Mal. 3:1 = Mk. 1:2; Mt. 11:10; Lk. 7:27; ἀπέστειλεν ἀγγέλους πρὸ προσώπου αὐτοῦ, Lk. 9:52; cf. also Lk. 1:76 vl.; 10:1; πρὸ προσώπου τῆς εἰσόδου αὐτοῦ, "before his coming," Ac. 13:24.

3. God's Countenance.

Following an OT mode of speech the NT often refers to God's countenance (→ 772, 31 ff.), as in quotations from the OT : πρόσωπον δὲ κυρίου ἐπὶ ποιοῦντας κακά (ψ 33:17 = 1 Pt. 3:12; cf. also Ac. 2:28 = ψ 15:11). There is vision of the face of God only in the heavenly world : Christ has gone into the sanctuary, i.e., heaven, νῦν ἐμφανισθῆναι τῷ προσώπῳ τοῦ θεοῦ ὑπὲρ ἡμῶν, Hb. 9:24. Here the expression which the OT used for visiting the temple is transferred to the heavenly sanctuary. The guardian angels of the μικροί always see τὸ πρόσωπον τοῦ πατρός μου τοῦ ἐν οὐρανοῖς (Mt. 18:10) to whom the welfare of the smallest is especially dear. They are thus in the immediate presence of God. To see the divine countenance which is concealed from man will be granted to God's servants in the consummation, Rev. 22:4. Now we can only see through a glass obscurely (→ I, 178, 10 ff.), τότε δὲ πρόσωπον πρὸς πρόσωπον, 1 C. 13:12. This

---

[48] Cf. Dib. Jk., ad loc. On this difficult expression → I, 682, 37 ff.

[49] Cf. Bl.-Debr. § 217, 1.

[50] The common use of πρόσωπον in dependence on prep. in Luke is due to the fact that the author models his style on the LXX.

[51] πρόσωπον in the sing. in spite of the plur. which follows. Cf. Bl.-Debr. § 140.

means that what we see and say is now imperfect. There will be perfect vision and real knowledge only in the future consummation.

4. Person.

The sense "person" occurs in the NT at 2 C. 1:11. The Corinthians are to join the apostle in prayer in order that "thanks may be given for us by many persons" (ἐκ πολλῶν προσώπων). [52]

D. Early Church Usage.

1. πρόσωπον in the Post-Apostolic Fathers.

The usage of the post-apost. fathers reveals no peculiarities as compared with the NT. The word is very common in OT quotations. a. The meaning "face" occurs in 1 Cl., 4, 3 f. (Gn. 4:5 f.); 16, 3 (Is. 53:3); Barn., 5, 14 (Is. 50:6); Mart. Pol., 9, 2; 12, 1; Herm. v., 3, 10, 1. Of personal presence : ἐκζητεῖν τὰ πρόσωπα τῶν ἁγίων "to appear before the saints," Barn., 19, 10; Did., 4, 2; also Ign. R., 1, 1; Pol., 1, 1; Barn., 13, 4 (Gn. 48:11). b. The meaning "front," "surface" occurs in the quotation of ψ 1:4 in Barn., 11, 7: ... ὃν ἐκρίπτει ὁ ἄνεμος ἀπὸ προσώπου τῆς γῆς. πρόσωπον is common in dependence on prepos.: ἀπὸ προσώπου, 1 Cl., 4, 8. 10; 18:11 (ψ 50:13); 28, 3 (ψ 138:7); Barn., 6, 9; εἰς πρόσωπον, Ign. Pol., 2, 2; Herm. v., 3, 6, 3; κατὰ πρόσωπον, 1 Cl., 35, 10 (ψ 49:21). On κατὰ πρόσωπον for "personally present" cf. Barn., 15, 1; Pol., 3, 2. In Barn., 19, 7 and Did., 4, 10 κατὰ πρόσωπον in the abs. means "with partiality." πρὸ προσώπου, 1 Cl., 34, 3 (Is. 62:11); Ign. Eph., 15, 3. c. There is ref. to the "face of God" only in OT quotations in 1 Cl., 18, 9 (ψ 50:11); 22, 6 (ψ 33:17); 60, 3 (Nu. 6:25; ψ 66:2). d. Sometimes πρόσωπον means "person" : ὀλίγα πρόσωπα, 1 Cl., 1, 1; ἐν ἢ δύο πρόσωπα, 1 Cl., 47, 6; τὰ προγεγραμμένα πρόσωπα, "the afore-mentioned persons," Ign. Magn., 6, 1.

2. πρόσωπον in the Christology and Trinitarian Teaching of the Early Church.

In the theological disputes which produced the Christological and Trinitarian doctrine of the early Church the word πρόσωπον played a vital role. Since the legal sense has not yet been attested for the first two centuries A.D. (→ 770, 26 ff.), [53] one cannot understand the use of the term by the fathers in the light of this technical sense. [54] Content was given to the word only in the course of theological debate. The fathers adopted a word which had a wide range of meaning and could thus be given the more precise sense which it received in theological discussion. They were well aware that neither this nor any other word they might have adopted was able to express the mystery of the three divine persons in their unity and distinctness. [55] Cf. Aug. De Trinitate, VIII, 6, 11: *Quamquam et illi (sc. Graeci) si vellent, sicut dicunt tres substantias, tres hypostases, possunt dicere tres personas, tria prosopa.* Theodoret Dialogus, I (MPG, 83, 36 A): τὴν

---

[52] Cf. Wnd. 2 K.; Ltzm. K., *ad loc.*

[53] Sabellius used πρόσωπον in the sense of "face," "mask," so that when he spoke of τρία πρόσωπα he had in mind three different modes of revelation of the one God. Cf. Harnack Dg., I, 764.

[54] A. v. Harnack originally thought that Tert. took the words *substantia* and *persona* from the legal sphere, but in view of the convincing refutation of Schlossmann, 119-124 he abandoned this thesis, cf. Harnack Dg., I, 576, n. 2. On *persona* in the theology of Tert. cf. E. Evans, "Tertullian's Theological Terminology," *The Church Quarterly Review*, 139 (1944/45), 56-77; Grillmeier, 49-52.

[55] Cf. K. Barth K.D., I, 1 (1932), 375 f. (C.D., I, 1 [1936], 408 f.).

γὰρ ὑπόστασιν, καὶ τὸ πρόσωπον, καὶ τὴν ἰδιότητα, ταὐτὸν σημαίνειν φαμέν τοῖς τῶν ἁγίων πατέρων ὅροις ἀκολουθοῦντες. [56]

† εὐπροσωπέω.

From the adj. εὐπρόσωπος, [1] which derived from πρόσωπον but does not occur in the NT, there was later formed a verb εὐπροσωπέω, "to have a good appearance." It is found in a letter of 114 B.C.: ὅπως εὐπροσωπῶμεν, P. Tebt., I, 19, 12. [2]

In the NT εὐπροσωπέω is used only at Gl. 6:12 : ὅσοι θέλουσιν εὐπροσωπῆσαι ἐν σαρκί, "who want to stand well with men."

† προσωπολημψία, † προσωπολήμπτης,
† προσωπολημπτέω, † ἀπροσωπολήμπτως.

1. The expressions פָּנִים נָשָׂא = λαμβάνειν πρόσωπον or θαυμάζειν πρόσωπον and פָּנִים הִכִּיר = γιγνώσκειν πρόσωπον are common in the OT. They are to be explained in terms of the respectful oriental greeting in which one humbly turns one's face to the ground or sinks to the earth. If the person greeted thus raises the face of the man, this is a sign of recognition and esteem. The translation of פָּנִים נָשָׂא by λαμβάνειν πρόσωπον is modelled closely on the Hebrew expression. [1] In secular Greek, of course, λαμβάνειν means only "to take," "to accept," never "to raise up." But since נָשָׂא can mean "to take" as well as "to lift," λαμβάνειν was used for it in Greek. This rendering must have been virtually unintelligible to the Greek. [2] In the phrase θαυμάζειν πρόσωπον, θαυμάζειν means "to esteem," → III, 30, 1 ff., 41, 12 ff.

God does not respect persons : οὐ θαυμάζει πρόσωπον (Dt. 10:17; cf. 2 Ch. 19:7). Men, however, honour one another by humble greeting and lifting of the face. Thus Jacob before his meeting with Esau hopes : ἴσως γὰρ προσδέξεται τὸ πρόσωπόν μου, Gn. 32:21. But λαμβάνειν πρόσωπον may be partial when regard is hard for the person and there is unjust preference. Judges in particular are warned : οὐκ ἐπιγνώσῃ πρόσωπον ἐν κρίσει, Dt. 1:17, cf. also Lk. 19:15; Dt. 16:19. As there is no respect of persons with God, so the earthly judge must be incorruptible and return just verdicts.

2. The NT, following the usage of the OT, speaks of "respect of person" in the following expressions.

---

[56] The fact that πρόσωπον and ὑπόστασις were equivalents also finds expression in the confession of Bishop Flavian of Constantinople (A. Hahn, *Bibliothek der Symbole*³ [1897], 320 f.): ... ἐνανθρώπησιν ἐν μιᾷ ὑποστάσει καὶ ἐν ἑνὶ προσώπῳ, ἕνα Χριστόν, ἕνα υἱόν, ἕνα κύριον ὁμολογοῦμεν.

ε ὐ π ρ ο σ ω π έ ω. [1] = "with fair face," attested frequently from the 5th cent. Cf., e.g., LXX Gn. 12:11: Abraham tells the beautiful Sarah that he knows ὅτι γυνὴ εὐπρόσωπος εἶ.

[2] Cf. also Deissmann LO, 76 f.

π ρ ο σ ω π ο λ η μ ψ ί α κ τ λ. [1] The following sentences are based on a hint from Debrunner.

[2] Cf. J. Leipoldt-S. Morenz, *Heilige Schriften* (1953), 80.

βλέπειν εἰς πρόσωπον, Mk. 12:14 par. Mt. 22:16, λαμβάνειν πρόσωπον in Lk. 20:21. Jd. 16 refers to θαυμάζειν πρόσωπον (Gn. 19:21; Dt. 10:17; Ps. Sol. 2:18): false teachers in the congregations flatter the persons of men for the sake of gain.

πρόσωπον ὁ θεὸς ἀνθρώπου οὐ λαμβάνει (Gl. 2:6 cf. Dt. 10:17; Sir. 35:13): God is a judge who cannot be corrupted and who has no regard for persons.

From the Hebraism λαμβάνειν πρόσωπον the noun προσωπολημψία was formed (R. 2:11; Eph. 6:9; Col. 3:25; Jm. 2:1). This is found for the first time in the NT but was probably in use already in Hellenistic Judaism. [3] προσωπολημψία is often used with reference to God's judgment before which there is no respect of persons. Hence Jews and Gentiles are judged in the same way, R. 2:11. κύριοι who issue orders to slaves are reminded that over both slaves and masters there is a κύριος in heaven before whom there is no προσωπολημψία, Eph. 6:9. But δοῦλοι are to be obedient to their masters, realising that they serve the κύριος Χριστός. An evil-doer will receive his just deserts καὶ οὐκ ἔστιν προσωπολημψία, Col. 3:25. God is no προσωπολήμπτης. He does not single out the Jews. He also allows the Gentiles to come and receive salvation, Ac. 10:34. God judges ἀπροσωπολήμπτως; this gives to Christian exhortation its seriousness and gravity, 1 Pt. 1:17.

As God has no regard to persons, so there should be no προσωπολημψίαι in the Christian congregation. One cannot believe in Christ and at the same time show partiality, Jm. 2:1. How this may happen is shown by the example of the despising of the poor man and the favouring of the rich, Jm. 2:2-4. There is an impressive warning not to overlook this admonition: εἰ δὲ προσωπολημπτεῖτε, ἁμαρτίαν ἐργάζεσθε, ἐλεγχόμενοι ὑπὸ τοῦ νόμου ὡς παραβάται, Jm. 2:9.

3. In the post-apost. fathers there is ref. to regard for persons in the following places: λαμβάνειν πρόσωπον, Barn., 19, 4; Did., 4, 3; προσωπολημψία, Pol., 6, 1; ἀπροσωπολήμπτως, 1 Cl., 1, 3; Barn., 4, 12.

Lohse

---

[3] In Eph. 6:9 and Col. 3:25 the word occurs in household tables which contain an ancient hortatory tradition. Hence it would seem that the word probably has a Jewish origin. Cf. also Dib. Jk. on 2:1; Schl. R. on 2:11.

προτίθημι → τίθημι.

---

† προφήτης, † προφῆτις, † προφητεύω,
    † προφητεία, † προφητικός,
        † ψευδοπροφήτης

Contents : A. The Word Group in Profane Greek : I. Linguistic Aspects ; II. Material Aspects : 1. Oracle Prophets ; 2. The Poet as Prophet ; 3. The Broader Use ; 4. Summary. B. נָבִיא in the Old Testament : I. Derivation of the Word ; II. The Verb : 1. Older Texts ; 2. The Prophetic Books ; 3. The Chronicler ; III. The Noun : 1. Prophetic Groups ; 2. Individuals ; 3. The Transferring of the Term to Earlier Figures ; 4. נָבִיא in the Prophetic

---

π ρ ο φ ή τ η ς κ τ λ. On the whole or more than one part : J. Alizon, *Etude sur le prophétisme chrétien depuis les origines jusqu'à l'an 150* (1911); H. Bacht, "Wahres u. falsches Prophetentum," *Biblica,* 32 (1951), 237-262; Bau. J. on 1:21; J. Bénazech, *Le prophétisme chrétien depuis les origines jusqu'au Pasteur d'Hermas* (1901); A. Broek-Utne, "Eine schwierige Stelle in einer alten Gemeindeordnung (Did., 11, 11)," ZKG, 54 (1935), 576-581; N. Bonwetsch, "Die Prophetie im ap. u. nachap. Zeitalter," *Zschr. f. kirchliche Wissenschaft u. kirchliches Leben,* 5 (1884), 408-424, 460-477; H. Bruders, *Die Verfassung der Kirche von den ersten Jahrzehnten der ap. Wirksamkeit an bis zum Jahre 175 n. Chr.* (1904), 387-397; H. v. Campenhausen, "Kirchliches Amt u. geistliche Vollmacht in den ersten drei Jhdt.," *Beiträge zur hist. Theol.,* 14 (1953), 198-210; O. Cullmann, *Die Christologie d. NT* (1957), 11-49 (E.T. [1959], 13-50); G. Delling, *Der Gottesdienst im NT* (1952), 34-39; E. Fascher, ΠΡΟΦΗΤΗΣ (1927); A. Frövig, *Das Selbstbewusstsein Jesu als Lehrer u. Wundertäter nach Mk. u. der sog. Redequelle untersucht* (1918), 99-114; H. A. Guy, *NT Prophecy, Its Origin and Significance* (1947); H. Kraft, "Die altkirchliche Prophetie u. die Entstehung des Montanismus," ThZ, 11 (1955), 249-271; R. Meyer, *Der Prophet aus Galiläa* (1940); R. Schnackenburg, "Die Erwartung des Propheten nach dem NT u. den Qumran-Texten" in K. Aland and F. L. Cross, *Studia evangelica* ; H. J. Schoeps, *Theol. u. Gesch. des Judenchr.* (1949), 87-116; W. Staerk, "Soter, die bibl. Erlösererwartung als religionsgeschichtliches Problem, I," BFTh, II, 31 (1933), 61-72; Trench, 10-14; G. P. Wetter, *Der Sohn Gottes* (1916), 21-26. On A.: P. Amandry, *La mantique Apollinienne à Delphes* (1950), Index III, *s.v.;* E. R. Dodds, *The Greeks and the Irrational* (1951), Index, *s.v.;* E. Fraenkel, *Aeschylus Agamemnon* III (1950), 497 f.; H. Fournier, *Les verbes "dire" en grec ancien* (1946), 8-13; O. Kern, *Die Religion der Griechen,* I (1926); II (1935); III (1938), Index, *s.v.;* M. C. van der Kolf, Art. "Prophetes u. Prophetis," Pauly-W., 23, 1 (1957), 797-816; K. Latte, Art. "Orakel," *ibid.,* 18, 1 (1939), 829-854; J. Wackernagel, *Vorlesungen über Syntax,* II² (1928), 237-240. On B.: G. Fohrer, "Neuere Lit. z. at.lichen Prophetie," ThR, NF, 19 (1951), 277-346; 20 (1952), 193-271, 295-361; A. Guillaume, *Prophecy and Divination* (1938); A. Haldar, *Associations of Cult Prophets among the Ancient Semites* (1945); F. Häussermann, "Wortempfang u. Symbol in der at.lichen Prophetie," Beih. ZAW, 58 (1932); F. Hesse, "Wurzelt die prophetische Gerichtsrede im israelitischen Kult ?" ZAW, 65 (1953), 45-53; A. Jepsen, *Nabi* (1934); A. R. Johnson, *The Cultic Prophet in Ancient Israel* (1944); H. Junker, *Prophet u. Seher in Israel* (1927); S. Mowinckel, *Psalmenstudien, III : Kultprophetie u. prophetische Psalmen, Skrifter utgit av Videnskapsselskapet i Kristiania, II. Historisk-Filosofisk Klasse,* 1922, 1 (1923); also *Die Erkenntnis Gottes bei d. at.lichen Propheten* (1941); also *Prophecy and Tradition, Avhandlinger utgitt av det Norske Videnskaps-Akademi i Oslo, II. Historisk-Filosofisk Klasse,* 1946, 3 (1946); O. Plöger, "Priester u. Prophet," ZAW, 63 (1951), 157-192; G. Quell, "Wahre u. falsche Propheten," BFTh, 46, 1 (1952); G. v. Rad, "Die falschen Propheten," ZAW, 51 (1933), 109-120; H. H. Rowley, "Was Amos a nabi ?" *Festschr. O. Eissfeldt* (1947), 191-198; also *Studies in OT Prophecy, presented to T. H. Robinson* (1950); also "Ritual and the Hebrew Prophets," *Journal of Semitic Studies,* 1 (1956), 338-360; H. W. Wolff, "Hauptprobleme at.licher Prophetie," *Ev. Theol.,* 15 (1955), 446-468; E. Würthwein, "Amosstudien," ZAW, 62 (1949/50), 10-52; also "Der Ursprung der prophetischen Gerichtsrede," ZThK, 49 (1952), 1-16. On C.:

Books ; 5. The True Prophet and the False Prophet in Deuteronomy ; 6. נְבִיא in the Other
Works ; IV. Other Terms for the Prophet : 1. אִישׁ אֱלֹהִים; 2. רֹאֶה; 3. חֹזֶה; V. Form and
Content of Prophetic Proclamation ; VI. The Usage of the Septuagint. C. Prophecy and
Prophets in the Judaism of the Hellenistic-Roman Period : I. The Problem of Contemporary
Prophecy : 1. Non-Rabbinic Witness ; 2. The Rabbinic Tradition ; II. Historical Manifesta-
tions : 1. Prophetic Experience according to Palestinian Sources ; 2. Prophecy in the Light
of Alexandrian Theology ; 3. Seers and Prophets ; 4. The Ruler with the Threefold Office ;
5. Messianic Prophets ; III. The Apocalyptic Literature ; IV. The End of Prophecy.
D. Prophets and Prophecies in the New Testament : I. Occurrence and Meaning of the
Words ; II. The Old Testament Prophets ; III. Pre-Christian Prophets ; IV. John the
Baptist ; V. Jesus ; VI. Church Prophets : 1. The Nature of Primitive Christian Prophecy ;
2. Comparison with Old Testament Prophecy ; 3. The Most Important Charisma ; 4. Ecstasy
and Prophecy ; 5. Glossolalia and Prophecy ; 6. Prayer and Prophecy ; 7. Revelation and
Prophecy ; 8. Gnosis and Prophecy ; 9. Teaching and Prophecy ; 10. Evangelism and
Prophecy ; VII. False Prophets. E. Prophets in the Early Church : I. The Old Testament
Prophets ; II. Jesus as Prophet ; III. Church Prophets ; IV. False Prophets.

L. Finkelstein, *The Pharisees* (1938), Index, *s.v.* "Prophets"; H. A. Fischel, "Jewish Gnosticism in the Fourth Gospel," JBL, 65 (1946), 157-174; J. Giblet, "Prophétisme et attente
d'un Messie-Prophète dans le Judaisme," *L'attente du Messie* (1954), 85-130; Moore, Index,
s.v. "Prophets"; O. Michel, "Spätjüd. Prophetentum," *Nt.liche Studien f. R. Bultmann* (1954),
60-66; O. Plöger, "Prophetisches Erbe in den Sekten d. frühen Judt.," ThLZ, 79 (1954),
291-296; K. Schubert, *Die Religion d. nachbibl. Judt.* (1955), Index, *s.v.*; also "Die Messiaslehre in den Texten v. Chirbet Qumran," BZ, NF, 1 (1957), 177-197; H. M. Teeple, *The
Mosaic Eschatological Prophet,* JBL Monograph, 10 (1957); Volz Esch., 193-195; A. S.
van der Woude, "Die messianischen Vorstellungen der Gemeinde von Qumran," Studia
semitica Neerlandica, 3 (1957); F. W. Young, "Jesus the Prophet, A Reexamination," JBL,
68 (1949), 285-299. On D.: C. K. Barrett, *The Holy Spirit and the Gospel Tradition* (1954),
94-99; K. Bornhäuser, "Das Wirken des Christus durch Taten u. Worte," BFTh, II, 2
(1921); J. Brosch, Charismen u. Ämter in d. Urkirche (1951), 75-94; K. Burger, Art. "Prophetentum im NT," RE³, 16, 105-108; J. Daniélou, "Le Christe Prophète," *Vie Spirituelle,*
78 (1948), 154-170; also *Le mystère de l'Avent* (1948), 179-207; P. E. Davies, "Jesus and
the Role of the Prophet," JBL, 64 (1945), 241-254; C. H. Dodd, "Jesus as Teacher and
Prophet" in G. K. A. Bell and A. Deissmann, *Mysterium Christi* (1930), 69-86; H. Duesberg,
Jésus prophète et docteur de la Loi, Bible et vie chrétienne (1955); J. Dupont, *Gnosis, La
connaissance religieuse dans les épîtres de St. Paul,* Universitas Catholica Lovaniensis, Diss.
II, 40 (1949), 201-212; F. Gils, "Jésus Prophète d'après les Evang. synoptiques," Orientalia
et Biblica Lovaniensia, II (1957); L. Goppelt, "Typos. Die typologische Deutung d. AT im
NT," BFTh, II, 43 (1939), 70-97; H. Greeven, "Propheten, Lehrer, Vorsteher bei Pls.,"
ZNW, 44 (1952/53), 1-15; A. J. B. Higgins, "Jesus as Prophet," Exp. T., 57 (1945/46), 292-
294; O. Michel, "Prophet u. Märtyrer," BFTh, 37, 2 (1932); S. Munoz Iglesias, "Los pro-
fetas del NT comparados con los del Antiguo," *Estudios Bibl.,* 6 (1947), 307-337; I. M.
Nielen, *Gebet u. Gottesdienst im NT* (1937), 191-201; R. Otto, *Reich Gottes u. Menschen-
sohn²* (1940), 289-299; H. Riesenfeld, "Jesus als Prophet" in *Spiritus et Veritas, Mélanges
K. Kundzins* (1953), 135-148; H. Sasse, "Apostel, Propheten, Lehrer," *Luthertum* (1942),
3-16; H. Seventer, *De Christologie van het NT²* (1948), 38-47, 221-223; Schl. Gesch. d.
ersten Chr., 24-27; V. Taylor, *The Names of Jesus* (1954), 15-17; C. Weizsäcker, *Das ap.
Zeitalter²,³* (1902), Index, *s.v.* On E.: H. Bacht, "Die prophetische Inspiration in der kirch-
lichen Reflexion d. vormontanistischen Zeit," *Scholastik,* 19 (1944), 1-18; W. Bauer, "Rechtgläubigkeit u. Ketzerei im älteren Chr.," *Beiträge z. hist. Theologie,* 10 (1934), 182-185;
N. Bonwetsch, *Die Gesch. des Montanismus* (1881); Dib. Herm., 538-540; A. Harnack, *Die
Lehre d. 12 Ap.,* TU, 2, 1 (1884), 98-110, 119-131; R. Knopf, *Das nachapost. Zeitalter*
(1905), 250-252, 404 f.; E. Molland, "La thèse 'La prophétie n'est jamais venue de la volonté
de l'homme' (2 Pt. 1:21) et les Pseudoclémentines," *Studia theol.,* 9 (1955), 67-85; G. Strekker,
Das Judenchristentum in den Pseudoklementinen, TU, 70 (1958), 145-153; T. Zahn, *Der
Hirt d. Hermas* (1868), 102-117; also *Zur Gesch. d. nt.lichen Kanons u. d. altkirchlichen Lit.,*
III, Supplementum Clementinum (1884), 298-302; L. Zscharnack, *Der Dienst d. Frau in den
ersten Jhdt. d. chr. Kirche* (1902), 58-72, 156-187.

A. The Word Group in Profane Greek.

I. Linguistic Aspects.

1. προφήτης, attested from the 5th cent., is a nomen agentis [1] of the verbal stem φη- "to say," "to speak," with the prefix προ-. In the prefix lies the difficulty of determining the meaning of the noun. Since the actual verb πρόφημι is found only in the post-Chr. era [2] and can thus shed no light on the original meaning of προφήτης, one must start with the combination of προ- and early attested verbs of saying or speaking, [3] cf. Plat. Resp., X, 619c : τοῖς προρρηθεῖσιν ὑπὸ τοῦ προφήτου. Where the dependent obj. has no formal or material relation to the future, these verbs (προαγορεύω, -ερῶ, -εῖπον etc., προλέγω, the poetic προφωνέω) obviously mean "to declare openly," "to make known publicly," "to proclaim" etc., [4] e.g., Plat. Leg., IX, 871c : τὴν πρόρρησιν προαγορεύων, "making public declaration." This idea of publicly declaring and making known [5] gives προφήτης the sense of "one who proclaims," "speaker" [6] (Pind. Paean, 6, 6 of the poet : ἀοίδιμον Πιερίδων προφάταν, Eur. Ba., 211: ἐγὼ προφήτης σοι λόγων γενήσομαι) and in this compound one may detect in the root φη- the original religious ref. and the related emphatic tone. [7] Along with this sense, of course, there is soon found in προαγορεύω κτλ. the temporal meaning "in advance," "before," [8] plainly in Xenoph. Sym., 4, 5: προαγορεύειν, "to predict" par. προορᾶν [9] (cf. Hippocr. Progn., 15 [Kühlewein, I, 94]: πρόρρησις "prediction"). Whenever future forms (e.g., Hdt., I, 74, 2) [10] or τὰ μέλλοντα (Plat. Euthyphr., 3c) [11] are the obj. of these verbs,

---

[1] E. Fraenkel, *Gesch. d. gr. Nomina agentis,* I (1910), 34; Schwyzer, I, 499 f.; on the accent Debr. Griech. Wortb. § 349.

[2] Cf. the dict., *s.v.*

[3] Wackernagel, 238-240; Schwyzer, II, 505 f. The only example in Hom. (Od., 1, 37 ff.: πρό οἱ εἴπομεν ... μήτε ... κτείνειν μήτε μνάασθαι) brings to light the difficulties involved. Wackernagel, 239 takes this to mean that we had warned him in the sense of a divine direction or proclamation (also Fascher, 5; Kolf, 798), but Schwyzer, II, 505; Liddell-Scott, *s.v.* προεῖπον III take it temporally : we had warned him beforehand.

[4] προαγορεύω "to proclaim publicly," in the people's assembly, Hdt., III, 142, 3; Thuc., II, 13, 1; by a herald, Hdt., III, 61, 3; 62; of military leaders, Hdt., VIII, 83; Thuc., VII, 50, 3; of the declaration of war, Hdt., VII, 9 β; Thuc., I, 131, 1; Xenoph. Ag., 1, 17; Demosth. Or., 11, 20 (cf. προαγγέλλω, Polyb., 3, 20, 8), of the contents of the law, Plat. Crit., 51d; Xenoph. Resp. Lac., 12, 5. προλέγω "to declare openly" : Thuc., I, 139, 1 (ἐνηλότατα); Demosth. Or., 9, 13; "to proclaim an oracle," Hdt., VIII, 136, 3; with no ref. to the fut. Luc. Alex., 22 (to prescribe cures, means of healing). προφωνέω "to proclaim aloud," "to order publicly" : Soph. Oed. Tyr., 223 (par. ἐξερῶ, 219); Eur. Hipp., 956. Corresponding is the Lat. pro- in *pronuntiare, profiteri* etc.; *prodigium* "coming publicly into appearance and action out of concealment" (H. Kleinknecht, "Laokoon," Herm., 79 [1944], 110).

[5] Cf. also προφέρω "to publish an oracle," Aesch. Ag., 964; Hdt., IV, 151, 1; V, 63, 1.

[6] Trench, 11; Wackernagel, 239 f.; Fascher, 6; Kern, II, 112; Kolf, 798.

[7] Fournier, 8 : φημί orig. "proférer des paroles magiques ou sacrées," refers (8-12), along with προφήτης etc., to constructs like εὐφημέω "speak words of good omen" == "keep religious silence," φήμη "saying of the gods" (Xenoph. Cyrop., VIII, 7, 3; Sym., 4, 48), θέσφατος "decreed by God" (Homeric, poetic); he also notes (*ibid.,* 18, 38 f.) the emphatic note which φημί has before the inf. If there is the echo of an original identity (dissolved already in Indo-European) of the roots *bhā- "to shine" == Gk. φαίνομαι and *bhā "to speak" == Gk. φημί (cf. Walde-Hofmann, I, 438; Hofmann, 397; Fournier, 12 f.), hence an orig. meaning "to bring to light," "to make clear," "to indicate," this would be yet another pointer to the importance of the root φη- in προφήτης.

[8] Wackernagel, 238 f.; Schwyzer, II, 506; cf. also → III, 717, 15 ff. We need not consider here the common sense of going before in time, *v.* also → n. 3.

[9] Οἱ μάντεις (!) λέγονται ... ἄλλοις μὲν προαγορεύειν (προσ- BD) τὸ μέλλον, ἑαυτοῖς δὲ μὴ προορᾶν τὸ ἐπιόν.

[10] Τὴν μεταλλαγὴν ταύτην τῆς ἡμέρης Θαλῆς ... προηγόρευσε ἔσεσθαι.

[11] Ἐμοῦ ..., ὅταν τι λέγω ἐν τῇ ἐκκλησίᾳ περὶ τῶν θείων, προλέγων αὐτοῖς τὰ

it is possible that προ- is used not merely in the original sense of "forth" but also and even exclusively in the temporal sense of "fore." Logically, then, one has to grant that in the light of this derivation προφήτης κτλ. underwent a similar development in sense. Whether and how far this actually happened, however, can be shown only by interpretation of the individual instances.

2. προφῆτις, attested from the end of the 5th cent., is the regular fem. of προφήτης, [12] Eur. Ion, 42 : προφῆτις ἐσβαίνουσα μαντεῖον θεοῦ, cf. 92 f.: ἀείδουσ' "Ελλησι βοάς, ἃς ἂν 'Απόλλων κελαδήσῃ.

3. προφητεύω, attested from the 5th cent., is the denominative of προφήτης : [13] a. "to be a proclaimer, speaker," "to proclaim," Pind. Fr., 150 of the poet : μαντεύεο, Μοῖσα, προφατεύσω δ' ἐγώ, Ps.-Aristot. Mund., 1, p. 391a, 15 f. of the soul : τὰ θεῖα καταλαβομένη (vl.) τοῖς τε ἀνθρώποις προφητεύουσα; b. "to be an oracle prophet," "to occupy the office of an oracle prophet," IG, VII, 4155 : Θεωδώρω προφατεύοντος, CIG, II, 2854-2859 : προφητεύοντος ...

4. προφητεία, abstract of προφητεύω, [14] occurs in non-Jewish Gk. lit. only from the 2nd cent. A.D.: a. Luc. Alex., 40 : ἡ δὲ προφητείη δίης φρενός ἐστιν ἀπορρώξ, "ability to declare (the divine will), i.e., to give an oracle," is a portion of the divine spirit ; b. Heliodor. Aeth., II, 27, 1 "proclamation (of the divine will)," "answer by oracle"; c. Luc. Alex., 60 "prophetic office," [15] also Heliodor. Aeth., I, 22, 7; 33, 2 and inscr. from Asia Minor, Ditt. Or., II, 494, 8 f.; CIG, II, 2869, 2880 etc.

5. προφητικός, adj. of relation, [16] "belonging to the προφήτης," is, like προφητεία, attested for the first time outside Jewish lit. in Luc. Alex., 60 : προφητικὸν στέμμα "prophetic chaplet" of an oracle prophet ; Preis. Zaub., I, 1, 278 f.; I, 4, 933 (4th cent. A.D.): προφητικὸν σχῆμα, "prophetic garb, garment" as part of the prescribed equipment for magical invocation of the light-god Apollo or of light, ibid., I, 4, 957.

6. In the compound ψευδοπροφήτης, [17] not attested in secular Gk. B.C. outside the Jewish sphere, [18] the first part can be an obj. of the second, [19] "prophet of lies" (cf. Jer. 14:14 : ψευδῆ οἱ προφῆται προφητεύουσιν), or it can be taken as an adj., "false prophet." [20]

II. Material Aspects.

1. Oracle Prophets.

a. If the word group is attested only from the 5th century, the thing itself is much older and it is denoted not merely by προφήτης κτλ. but also by the com-

---

μέλλοντα, καταγελῶσιν ὡς μαινομένου· καίτοι οὐδὲν ὅτι οὐκ ἀληθὲς εἴρηκα ὧν προεῖπον. Cf. Plat. Phaedr., 244b.

[12] Debr. Griech. Wortb. § 382; Schwyzer, I, 464.

[13] Schwyzer, I, 730, 732 : -εύω == " 'to be' what the basic word says." Cf. ibid., I, 655 f.; Helbing, 79; Bl.-Debr. § 69, 4; Radermacher², 86.

[14] Debr. Griech. Wortb. § 287.

[15] Fascher, 53 f.

[16] Schwyzer, I, 497; Debr. Griech. Wortb. § 396.

[17] P. Corssen, "Über Bildung u. Bdtg. der Komposita ψευδοπροφήτης, ψευδόμαντις, ψευδόμαρτυς," Sokrates, NF, 6 (1918), 106-109; Debr. Griech. Wortb. § 114; Bl.-Debr. § 119, 5.

[18] Cf. the dict., s.v.

[19] As in ψευδάγγελος "proclaiming lies" (Hom. Il., 15, 159), ψευδολόγος "speaking lies" (Aristoph. Ran., 1521; 1 Tm. 4:2).

[20] As in ψευδαπόστολος "false apostle" (2 C. 11:13 → I, 445, 18 ff.).

pounds ὑποφήτης κτλ. [21] The oldest example, the only one before the 5th century, relates to the oldest oracle in Greece, the oracle of Zeus at Dodona in barbarian surroundings in Epirus. [22]

In a prayer to the Zeus of Dodona Hom. Il., 16, 234 f. says: ἀμφὶ δὲ Σελλοὶ σοὶ ναίουσ᾽ ὑποφῆται ἀνιπτόποδες χαμαιεῦναι, "messengers who do not wash their feet and who lie on the ground." While ὑποφῆται certainly refers to the oracle, the two epithets tell us nothing about the nature of the oracular activity [23] but denote a way of life which was primitive, [24] ascetic [25] and perhaps even barbaric. [26] This oldest account is unique in content [27] and thus leaves the impression of being non-Greek. The ὑποφῆται proclaim the will of the god who declares himself in the wafting of the wind from the rustling of the sacred oak (δρῦς, Hom. Od., 14, 328 = 19, 297; Aesch. Prom., 832; Soph. Trach., 1168; Plat. Phaedr., 275b; φηγός, Hes. Fr., 134; Soph. Trach., 171) and later (attested from the 4th cent.: FGH, III B No. 327 [Demon]; Fr. 20; Callim. Hymn., 4, 286) probably from the clanging of metal basins (χαλκίον, λέβης). [28] The divine will is thus intimated διά τινων συμβόλων (Strabo, 7 Fr. 1). [29] The task of the oracle prophets is to interpret it, i.e., to put it in human speech and to proclaim it to those seeking

---

[21] The prefix ὑπο- does not contain here an element of dependence or subordination (Fascher, 17, 28, 32) but means "from below." Thus in contrast to προ-, which denotes direction (whither? "out abroad"), it emphasises the origin (whence? "from concealment"); cf. ὑποκρίνομαι, orig. "to give one's view from the depth of the heart, from concealment" (Schwyzer, II, 524 f.; Hom. Il., 12, 228 : "to interpret" a portent, to bring out its hidden meaning ; Od., 19, 535, 555 : "to interpret" a dream ; Plat. Tim., 72b has τῆς δι᾽ αἰνιγμῶν φήμης καὶ φαντάσεως ὑποκριταί ("expositors") for προφῆται → 787, 34 ff.; cf. also A. Lesky, "Hypokrites," Studi in onore di U. E. Paoli [1955], 472 f. [H. Kleinknecht]). When the sea-demon Glaukos is called Νηρέως προφήτης in Eur. Or., 364 (5th cent. B.C.) or Νηρῆος ... ὑποφήτης in Apoll. Rhod., I, 1311 (3rd cent. B.C.), there is no more difference in content between προ- and ὑποφήτης than in Luc. Alex. (2nd cent. A.D.), where προφήτης (11, 22, 24, 43, 55) and ὑποφήτης (24, 26) are interchangeable. The group ὑποφήτης κτλ. ("he who brings and declares from concealment") thus means the same as προφήτης κτλ. : "messenger," "speaker" (Wackernagel, 239; cf. also Strabo, 7, 7, 12 : ὑποφήτας ..., ἐν οἷς τάττοιντο κἂν οἱ προφῆται) and the use of the two is par. The later distinction was artificial, e.g., Eustath. Thess. Comm. in Il., p. 1057, 63 f.: ὑποφῆται ὡς ὑποφητεύοντες προφητεύοντι τῷ ἐκεῖσε Διί, Zonaras Lex. (ed. J. A. H. Tittmann [1808], II, 1773): ἡ μὲν προφητεία πρὸ τοῦ γενέσθαι λέγει τὰ ὕστερον γενησόμενα, ἡ δὲ ὑποφητεία ... τὸ γενόμενον λέγει → 795, 32 ff.

[22] On this whole question cf. O. Kern, Art. "Dodona," Pauly-W., 5, 1 (1903), 1257-1264; Latte, 829 f.; Nilsson, I², 168, 423-427.

[23] To deduce incubation oracles (Eustath. Thess. Comm. in Il., p. 1057, 64 f.) from χαμαιεῦναι (Soph. Trach., 1166 χαμαικοῖται, Callim. Hymn., 4, 286 γηλεχέες) has rightly been opposed from Rohde on (I ⁹, ¹⁰, 122, n. 1).

[24] W. Kroll, "Unum exuta pedem," Glotta, 25 (1936), 153.

[25] P. Kretschmer, Einl. in d. Gesch. d. gr. Sprache (1896), 87 f.; Kern, op. cit. (→ n. 22), 1260.

[26] Nilsson, I², 427.

[27] ἀνιπτόποδες occurs on an inscr. from Tralles (ed. W. M. Ramsay, "Unedited Inscr. of Asia Minor," BCH, 7 [1883], 276, No. 19) with ref. to a non-Gk. Lydian practice. Kern, 1260; Latte, 840.

[28] The relation of the clanging of the basins to the giving of the oracle is not actually mentioned and Nilsson, I², 168 is thus sceptical. τρίποδες standing close together around the site of the oracle transmitted the sound on contact ; for the possibility of giving the oracle from this περίοδος τῆς ἠχῆς cf. F. Jacoby, FGH, IIIb, Suppl. I, 218 f. Acc. to a more likely version a metal tongue moved by the wind (ὑπὸ τοῦ πνεύματος) struck a bronze basin (FGH, III B, No. 327 [Demon], Fr. 20a, 19-33, cf. Strabo, 7, Fr. 3), while the rustling of leaves clarified the revelation given by the movement of the wind, Latte, 830. Ancient accounts of dove-oracles in Dodona (Hdt., II, 55; Soph. Trach., 171 f.; Strabo, 7, Fr. 1) are questionable. Nilsson, I², 424 f.; Latte, 830.

[29] Acc. to the continuation Strabo has in view the principle of revelation not the form of the answer imparted by the προφήτης.

advice.[30] The ὑποφήτης at Dodona, then, is both an "expositor"[31] of the signs of revelation and also a "proclaimer" of the divine revelation. The accounts do not permit us to say for certain what role was played in imparting the oracle by the priestesses who are first mentioned in Hdt., II, 55, who are obviously patterned on Delphi, and who are called προφήτιδες in Strabo, 7, 7, 12; 9, 2, 4, or what is the relation between ὑποφῆται and προφήτιδες.[32] Acc. to the clay tablets (πινάκια)[33] found in Dodona the inscribed questions of those who visited the oracle were addressed to men (οἱ Δωδωναῖοι), cf. the introductory formula of the answer of the prophets in Demosth. Or., 21, 53 : ὁ τοῦ Διὸς σημαίνει. The inscribed questions[34] always relate to a specific case and are either direct questions with the formula λῷον καὶ ἄμεινον etc.[35] to which the ὑποφήτης can usually answer only Yes or No, or they concern the name of a god whose favour is sought,[36] or very private matters[37] or new official foundations, esp. in the cultus, → lines 14 ff. Few written answers have been found, though those recorded in lit.[38] probably preserve in essentials the official form, cf. Demosth. Or., 21, 53 : ὁ τοῦ Διὸς σημαίνει ἐν Δωδώνῃ, Διονύσῳ δημοτελῆ ("at public expense") ἱερὰ τελεῖν καὶ κρατῆρα κεράσαι καὶ χοροὺς ἱστάναι, Ἀπόλλωνι Ἀποτροπαίῳ βοῦν θῦσαι, καὶ στεφανηφορεῖν ἐλευθέρους καὶ δούλους, καὶ ἐλινύειν ("rest") μίαν ἡμέραν· Διὶ Κτησίῳ βοῦν λευκόν. The oracle prophets of Dodona issue their answers in prose[39] as divine decisions and directions relating to the specific situation of those who come for counsel.

b. The oracle at Delphi[40] took on an importance surpassing that of all other Greek oracles by reason of the Apollonian manticism which came from Asia Minor at the beginning of the archaic period (→ 345, 6 f.), took possession of Delphi, and in essentials replaced the ancient oracle of lots by a speaking oracle.[41]

---

[30] Schol. Hom. Il., 16, 235 (ed. W. Dindorf, II [1875]): προφήτας γὰρ λέγουσι τοὺς περὶ τὰ χρηστήρια ἀσχολουμένους καὶ τὰς μαντείας τὰς γινομένας ὑπὸ τῶν ἱερέων ἐκφέροντας.

[31] M. Leumann, "Homerische Wörter," Schweizerische Beiträge z. Altertumswissenschaft, 3 (1950), 39 f.

[32] Kern, 1261 f.; Latte, 830; Nilsson, I², 424 f. Already in the 4th cent. B.C. an assimilation between Dodona and Delphi begins (Kolf, 814 f.), cf. Ephorus in Strabo, 9, 2, 4 (= FGH, II A, No. 70 [Ephorus] Fr. 119); the story of the προφῆτις Myrtila being cast in a hot cauldron is located in Dodona by Zenobius, II, 84 (CPG, I, 53) and in Delphi by Ps.-Plut. Proverbia, Alexandrinorum, 9 (II, 1253b). The confusion is palpable in Suid., s.v. προφητεία : καὶ ἡ διὰ δρυὸς Πυθία καὶ ἡ Δωδώνης ἱέρεια.

[33] For the inscr. cf. Amandry, 171, n. 1 for editions, Ditt. Syll.³, III, No. 1160-1166 for a selection. The πινάκια show that there was unbroken activity up to the 1st cent. B.C., Kern, III, 179.

[34] On what follows cf. Amandry, 171 f.; Latte, 841, 848 f.; Kern, II, 118.

[35] Ditt. Syll.³, III, 1165 : ἐρουτᾶι Κλεούτα(ς) τὸν Δία ... αἴ ἐστι αὐτοῖ προβατεύοντι ὄναιον καὶ ὠφέλιμον.

[36] Ibid., 1161: ἱστορεῖ Νικοκράτ[ει]α, τίνι θεῶν θύουσα λώϊον καὶ ἄμεινον πράσσοι καὶ τὰς νόσου παύσα(ι)το.

[37] Ibid., 1163 : ἐρωτῇ Λυσανίας Δία ..., ἦ οὐκ ἔστι ἐξ αὐτοῦ τὸ παιδάριον δ Ἀννύλα κύει.

[38] Indirectly Hdt., II, 52; Paus., VIII, 28, 6; directly Demosth. Or., 21, 53.

[39] Paus., VII, 25, 1; X, 12, 10, Macrob. Sat., I, 7, 28 speak of answers in hexameters, but this is due to confusion with Delphi, → n. 32.

[40] On this whole matter cf. Nilsson, I², 625-653; Amandry, and the review of H. Berve in Gnomon, 24 (1952), 5-12; G. Klaffenbach, "Das delphische Orakel," Wissenschaftliche Annalen, 3 (1954), 513-526; H. W. Parke-D. E. W. Wormell, The Delphic Oracle (1956), esp. I, 17-45.

[41] Nilsson, I², 170-173, 546, 625-628. The retention of the formula ἀνεῖλεν ὁ θεός in the sacral speech of Delphi pts. to the ancient oracle by lot. This could sometimes be used along with the speech oracle, cf. the alternative question on an inscr. of the mid-4th cent. B.C. (P. Amandry, "Convention religieuse conclue entre Delphes et Skiathos," BCH, 63 [1939], 184 = Amandry, 245, No. 16, cf. Nilsson, II, 99, n. 1) or at the nomination of a person,

It is here where the giving of oracles is διὰ λόγων (Strabo, 17, 1, 43) that the group προφήτης κτλ. finds its proper use.

(a) The Pythia who is stirred to mantic frenzy (→ 345, 8 ff.; 346, 13 ff.) in the oracle and whose official designation is πρόμαντις (Hdt., VI, 66, 2; VII, 141, 2; Thuc., V, 16, 2; Luc. Hermot., 60),[42] is called προφῆτις throughout antiquity,[43] first in Eur. Ion, 42 : προφῆτις ἐσβαίνουσα μαντεῖον θεοῦ, ibid., 321, 1322 : Φοίβου προφῆτις. The terms denote the same person but are not identical in content, → 790, 14 ff.[44] πρόμαντις has in view the disclosure of the future[45] (Plat. Charm., 173c-174a; Phaedr., 244b-c; Plut. Ei ap. Delph., 6 [II, 387b]) while προφῆτις means that the Pythia becomes the voice (→ 345, 31 ff.) or speaking-tube of the god which inspires her, cf. Eur. Ion, 92 f. Elected to her post by the native population (ibid., 1323 : πασῶν Δελφίδων ἐξαίρετος) she is the only woman in the oracle, the rest of the personnel consisting of men, Plut. Ei ap. Delph., 2 (II, 385c). Acc. to Plut. Def. Orac., 8 (II, 414b) two official prophetesses acted alternately, with a third in reserve, when the oracle was at its height. One was enough, however, in the 2nd cent. A.D. The term προφῆτις seems to imply that sometimes the Pythia herself could declare the answer of the god to those who sought counsel, Hdt., I, 47, 2; 65, 2; V, 92 β.[46]

(b) The oracle personnel included the προφήτης,[47] Hdt., VIII, 36 f.; Plut. Def. Orac., 51 (II, 438b); Berlin pap. 11, 517, 50 (2nd cent. A.D.).[48] Plut. Quaest. Graec., 9 (II, 292d); Quaest. Conv., VIII, 2 (II, 717d); Ael. Nat. An., X, 26 have the plur. In these accounts the oracle prophet is sometimes mentioned by name (Akeratos, Hdt., VIII, 37; Nikandros, Plut. Def. Orac., 51 [II, 438b]) but usually only incidentally with no specific ref. to the act of discovering and giving the oracle. There can be no doubt that he has something to do with declaring the oracle (Schol. Hom. Il., 16, 235 : προφήτας γὰρ λέγουσι τοὺς ... τὰς μαντείας ... ἐκφέροντας → n. 30) but it is a matter of probability at best what his special task was and in particular how it differed from that of the Pythia.[49] Plato's remarks about the nature of the Gk. oracle in Tim., 71e-72b relate implicitly to the practice at Delphi (→ 348, 3 ff.): the μαντικὴ ἔνθεος which the god grants only to human ἀφροσύνη is subjected to the criticism of an ἔμφρων whose task it is συννοῆσαι τὰ ῥηθέντα or τὰ φωνηθέντα κρίνειν. It is thus the custom τὸ τῶν προφητῶν γένος ἐπὶ ταῖς ἐνθέοις μαντείαις κριτὰς ἐπικαθιστάναι. For Plato, then, the distinctive feature of the oracle prophet at Delphi is that he understands and assesses critically the words which the Pythia utters in ecstasy, cf. Plat. Charm., 173c → 790, 18 ff. Then in Tim., 72b the oracle prophets are called τῆς δι' αἰνιγμῶν φήμης καὶ φαντάσεως ὑποκριταί, "interpreters or expositors of enigmatic statements and phenomena,"[50] and finally, in contrast to enthusiastic μάντεις, they are defined as προφῆται μαντευομένων, "interpreters of those who prophesy." The inner motif of

---

Plut. De Fraterno Amore, 21 (II, 492a/b), both by beans. Cf. also Amandry 25-36; Berve, op. cit. (→ n. 40), 6.

[42] G. Radke, Art. "Promantis, 2," Pauly-W., 23, 1 (1957), 647 with other examples.

[43] Cf. the instances in Kolf, 815, e.g., Plat. Phaedr., 244a; IG, XII, 3, No. 863; Strabo, 9, 3, 5; Diod. S., 14, 13, 3; 16, 26, 4; Plut. Pyth. Or., 7 (II, 397b); Iambl. Myst., III, 11 (p. 126, 4).

[44] Similarly of the prophetess of the oracle of Apollo in Argos, Ditt. Syll.[3], II, 735 (1st cent. B.C.) πρόμαντις, Paus., II, 24, 1 προφητεύουσα. Amandry, 121, n. 4.

[45] Cf. T. Hopfner, Art. "Μαντική," Pauly-W., 14, 1 (1928), 1258 f.

[46] Amandry, 121.

[47] Ibid., 118-123, 168, 233; Kolf, 808 f.

[48] Ed. W. Schubart, "Aus einer Apollon-Aretalogie," Herm., 55 (1920), 188-195 (ref. 191); Fascher, 41 f.

[49] Klaffenbach, op. cit. (→ n. 40), 525 f.; cf. Amandry, 119 f., 122.

[50] The whole passage includes a ref. to the visible phenomena of revelation (φαντάσματα, φανέντα) which naturally need interpreting to yield an oracle, e.g., dreams; cf. → n. 21 and Luc. Verae Historiae, II, 33 : τὸ μαντεῖον, οὗ προειστήκει προφητεύων Ἀντιφῶν ὁ τῶν ὀνείρων ὑποκριτής.

this description and evaluation of the σώφρων προφήτης is Plato's concept of the philosopher; for this reason one must exercise caution in drawing conclusions as to the actual practice at Delphi. What is clear is simply that Plato differentiates Pythia and prophet in respect of inspiration; whereas the one speaks under the constraint of divine ἐπίπνοια (→ 345, 8 ff.), the other uses rational discernment, λογισμός, *ibid.*, 72a. If the Pythia is sometimes called προφῆτις (→ 787, 3 ff.), the group προφήτης κτλ. is thus shown to be neutral in the question whether the person who bears the name is divinely inspired or not. The Delphic προφήτης would be an interpreter of the Pythia in the strict sense of ὑποκριτής (→ n. 21, 50) if the latter uttered only inarticulate cries or stammering whose hidden sense would have to be brought to light by the prophet. But the fact 1. that the whole tradition ascribes the main role to the Pythia rather than the prophet, 2. that, e.g., Plut. Def. Orac., 51 (II, 438b) plainly sets the ἀπόκρισις of the Pythia in contrast to κραυγὴ ἄσημος καὶ φοβερά uttered in wild frenzy, and 3. that the Pythia is also called προφῆτις, makes it probable that the Pythia speaks in ecstasy but διὰ λόγων. Then it is the prophet's task to put the Pythia's saying in official form without altering the content[51] and to declare it to him who seeks advice, ἐκφέρειν → 787, 23 ff. The questions presented either in writing[52] or by word of mouth have the same themes as those at Dodona (→ 786, 9 ff.) but they have a wider range; thus enquiry is made concerning the outcome of a war (Hdt., I, 53; VII, 220), the reason for the wrath of the gods at a time of public calamity (Hdt., I, 174; V, 82), the founding of a colony (IV, 150-159; Thuc., III, 92, 5), cleansing from blood-guiltiness (Thuc., I, 134, 4; Ael. Var. Hist., III, 43) etc. The answers[53] are given in hexameters or in prose (ἔμμετρά τε καὶ ἄμετρα, Strabo, 9, 3, 5); in Plut.'s time only in prose, Plut. Pyth. Or., 7 (II, 397c-d), cf. Cic. Divin., II, 56, 116. Use of the epic hexameter implies a claim to permanent memorising of the oracles and shows an intention not merely to answer the specific problem but to give more general directions on human conduct and to influence the whole mode of thought.[54] The best-known example is the answer given the Spartan Glaukos (Hdt., VI, 86γ) when he asked whether he could commit perjury and appropriate the money a stranger had left with him. The oracle stated that while this would bring an immediate advantage, since death awaits even the man who is faithful to his oath, nevertheless the oath has a son who pursues the perjurer until he has extirpated his whole house and race, so that the future advantage is with the house of the man who keeps his oath. The Delphic oracle formulates the generally recognised standard of conduct,[55] guarding tradition and cautiously giving it contemporary shape.[56] The language[57] of the Delphic prophets is often obscure; images and metaphors are used[58] and even full similitudes[59] borrowed from poetic riddles

---

[51] Amandry, 119 f.; Berve, 10 f.; Klaffenbach, 525 f.; Parke-Wormell, *op. cit.* (→ n. 40), I, 33 f.

[52] In contrast to Dodona (→ 786, 5 f.) no tablets with inscribed questions have thus far been found at Delphi; this may be due to the material used (wax tablets?); there was probably written questioning (cf. Schol. Aristoph. Pl., 39, ed. F. Dübner [1877]: οἱ μαντευόμενοι ἐγγράφῳ ἀνακοινώσει πρὸς τὸν θεὸν τὰς πεύσεις ἐποιοῦντο) when an official courier was sent, cf. Amandry, 149 f.

[53] Collected in Parke-Wormell, *op. cit.*, II: "The Oracular Responses." So far as we know the last enquiry at Delphi was under Julian, Kern, III, 181; Nilsson, II, 449, n. 11.

[54] Latte, 84 f. Similarly the philosopher Xenophanes at the end of the 6th cent. B.C. tries to capture public opinion as a rhapsodist by using the epic hexameter.

[55] K. Latte, *Heiliges Recht* (1920), 1. For the cult cf. Xenoph. Mem., I, 3, 1: ἡ Πυθία νόμῳ πόλεως ἀναιρεῖ ποιοῦντας εὐσεβῶς ἂν ποιεῖν.

[56] More incisive is the influence of the oracle on calendar reform through answers to sacral questions, cf. Nilsson, I², 644-647.

[57] Cf. U. Hölscher, "Der Logos bei Heraklit," *Varia Variorum, Festg. f. K. Reinhardt* (1952), 72 f.; Latte, 845 f. Heracl. Fr., 93 (Diels⁷, I, 172, 6 f.): ὁ ἄναξ, οὗ τὸ μαντεῖόν ἐστι τὸ ἐν Δελφοῖς, οὔτε λέγει οὔτε κρύπτει ἀλλὰ σημαίνει, Plat. Ap., 21b: ὁ θεὸς ... αἰνίττεται.

[58] E.g., Plut. Pyth. Or., 24 (II, 406e): "mountain-drinkers" = rivers.

[59] E.g., Hdt., V, 92β: "An eagle in the mountains is pregnant, it will bear a lion."

(e.g., Hdt., I, 67; III, 57). Sharpened by paradox [60] the oracle challenges the hearer not to take it in the first and simple sense but to seek by interpretation the true sense which is hinted at (ταῦτά νυν εὖ φράζεσθε, Hdt., V, 92β). Perception and understanding (γνῶναι, Hdt., III, 58) of the prophetic oracle is granted to man, though man is also shown his limits along the lines of the temple inscr. at Delphi Γνῶθι σεαυτόν (sc. ἄνθρωπον ὄντα), [61] so that an oracle like, e.g., Κροῖσος Ἅλυν διαβὰς μεγάλην ἀρχὴν καταλύσει (Aristot. Rhet., III, 5, p. 1407a, 37 f., cf. Hdt., I, 53) not only testifies to the prudent ambiguity (ἀμφίβολα Aristot., loc. cit.) of the oracle but also shows the challenge to the recipient correctly to evaluate his real situation and its possibilities.

(c) Apollo, the god of the oracle, is himself called Διὸς προφήτης in Aesch. Eum., 19. He is the true μάντις of the oracle, e.g., Aesch. Choeph., 559 : μάντις ἀψευδής. He is also the "spokesman" of Zeus, who for his part is called the μάντις ἀψευδέστατος among the gods, Archiloch. Fr., 84 (Diehl³, III, 37).

c. In relation to other Greek oracles [62] the use is essentially the same as described already.

We refer esp. to the oracles of Apollo, e.g., in Ptoion, [63] Corope, [64] Argos (προφῆτις → n. 44), Claros, [65] and Didyma, [66] to that of Zeus at Olympia (προφήτης Schol. Pind. Olymp., 6, 6b), [67] of Dionysus in Thrace (οἱ προφητεύοντες with πρόμαντις as in Delphi, Hdt., VII, 111, 2) etc. In the oracle of Zeus-Ammon in Libya προφήτης is again the name, perhaps through Interpretatio Graeca, for the priest (cf. first Ps.-Plat. Alc., II, 149b, 150a) who, as in Dodona, "interprets" the will of God διά τινων συμβόλων (Strabo, 7 Fr. 1), i.e., through the movements of the idol carried on the shoulders of the priests (νεύμασι καὶ συμβόλοις ... τοῦ προφήτου τὸν Δία ὑποκριναμένου) and who then "proclaims" the answer (ἀποκριθῆναι, Ps.-Plat. Alc., II, 149a, where the prophetic oracle begins : Ἀθηναίοις τάδε λέγει Ἄμμων).

d. If προφήτης here remains within the framework of its Greek use, a new and divergent content is plain in Lucian [68] in his satire on Alexandros of Abonoteichos (on the coast of Paphlagonia), who in the 2nd cent. A.D., exploiting the contemporary taste for oracles, established there an oracle of the god he preached, namely, Glykon, the new Aesculapius and the grandson of Apollo, ibid., 43.

It is true that ἄνευ ὑποφήτου, "without a special proclaimer of the oracle" (ibid., 26), is used in the strict Gk. sense, and the refusal of Luc. to call Alexandros a προφήτης when he visited the shrine (ibid., 55) may denote a feeling for the true meaning of the word in Gk. and not just opposition to the charlatan. Yet Alexandros' vaunting description of himself as a προφήτης or ὑποφήτης (11, 22, 24) contains elements alien to the oracular prophecy of Greece. Luc. calls his antagonist a γόης, "magician" (1, 25, also

---

[60] E.g., Hdt., V, 92β → n. 59; VII, 141, 3 : "wooden wall"; FGH, III B, No. 404 (Anaxandridas of Delphi), Fr. 1: "Take the head and thou hast the middle."
[61] Cf. K. Kerényi, Niobe (1949), 248 f.
[62] Cf. Kolf, 803-806, 809, 815 f.
[63] Boetia : Oracle through a προφήτης (Corinna Fr., 5, 68 f. [Diehl², I, 4, 198]) to a courier from abroad towards the end of the 5th cent. B.C. in "Carian" speech ; cf. Hdt., VIII, 135; Plut. Aristides, 19, 2 (I, 330c); Def. Orac., 5 (II, 412a).
[64] Magnesia ; προφήτης, Ditt. Syll.³, III, 1157, 22 (c. 100 B.C.); the inscr. gives an order of procedure for the oracle, Nilsson, II, 98 f.
[65] At Colophon : oracles through a προφήτης (Ditt. Or., II, 530 [132 A.D.]) who is inspired by drinking from the oracle well, cf. Tac. An., II, 54 (sacerdos); Iambl. Myst., III, 11 (p. 124, 9-126, 3); → 352, 6 ff.
[66] At Miletus : προφήτης from the leading priestly families ; later a προφῆτις as well, Iambl. Myst., III, 11 (p. 127, 12); the prophetic inscr. in T. Wiegand, Didyma II: Die Inschr., ed. A. Rehm and R. Harder (1958), 155-203 (No. 202-306).
[67] Ed. A. B. Drachmann, I (1903).
[68] Bibl. in Nilsson, II, 452, n. 3, esp. O. Weinreich, "Alexandros d. Lügenprophet u. seine Stellung in d. Religiosität d. II. Jhdt. n. Chr.," N. Jbch. Kl. Alt., 47 (1921), 129-151.

the pupil of a γόης, 5). He is thus one of the non-Gk. type of θεῖος ἄνθρωπος [69] who claims not merely to have predicted the future (προειπεῖν) and explained obscure events but also to have healed the sick and raised the dead, 24. He is an ecstatic seized by his god and foaming at the mouth, 12. He wears outlandish clothing, 11. In the mysteries associated with the oracle he extols himself as one born of God (38 f.) and claims to have begotten a daughter with the moon-goddess, 35. On the one side a servant of the god (θεράπων ὑποφήτης), προφήτης καὶ μαθητὴς τοῦ θεοῦ (24), he has a position far above that of ordinary oracle prophets, since the god ascribes particular importance to his intercession : ἔσται πάντα, ὁπόταν ἐθελήσω ἐγὼ καὶ Ἀλέξανδρος ὁ προφήτης μου δεηθῇ καὶ εὔξηται ὑπὲρ ὑμῶν, 22. The very different nature of the prophetic office of Alexandros may be seen esp. in the fact that he declares oracles unasked both to individuals (50) and to Italian towns (36), whereas the Gk. oracle prophet never gives the response of the god except on special enquiry.

e. προφήτης and μάντις are not synonyms. [70] While the functions of both e.g., Pind. Fr., 150 (→ 792, 35 ff.) are allotted to different persons, they may often fall to the same person, and in this case they denote different aspects : to the μάντις is given illumination, especially of the future, while the task of the προφήτης is to declare this knowledge. Theoretically the distinction is defined in Plat. Charm., 173c : τὴν μαντικὴν εἶναι ... ἐπιστήμην τοῦ μέλλοντος ἔσεσθαι, καὶ τὴν σωφροσύνην αὐτῆς ἐπιστατοῦσαν ... τοὺς ὡς ἀληθῶς μάντεις καθιστάναι ... προφήτας τῶν μελλόντων. Here the element of σωφροσύνη plainly differentiates the προφήτης from the μάντις on the one side, while on the other the addition of the genitive τῶν μελλόντων shows that the word denotes the speaker with no reference to any special content such as the future. In practice the distinction is plain at the Delphic oracle. Apollo is a μάντις (Aesch. Choeph., 559; Eum., 18) who has received his gift of divination from Zeus (17), but he is also Διὸς προφήτης (19), for he imparts the will of Zeus to the Pythia. The Pythia is a μάντις inspired by Apollo (29, 33), but she is also his προφῆτις when she becomes the voice of the god (→ 787, 9 ff.). Finally the προφήτης is the one who proclaims the ultimate oracle, → 788, 15 ff.

The twofold aspect of the usage is attested for the oracle of Apollo in Ptoion (πρόμαντις and προφήτης, Hdt., VIII, 135), in Argos (→ n. 44), and in Didyma (πρόμαντις Luc. Bis Accusatus, 1; προφῆτις Iambl. Myst., III, 11, p. 123, 15 f.). Apart from oracles, it is also found in 5th cent. poetry for the "seers" Teiresias (Pind. Nem., 1, 60 f.: Διὸς ὑψίστου προφάταν ... ὀρθόμαντιν), Amphiaraos (Aesch. Sept. c. Theb., 609 ff.) and Cassandra (Aesch. Ag. 1098 f.), and also for the sea-demon Glaukos (Eur. Or., 363 f.: μάντις ... Νηρέως προφήτης). That a sense of the distinction must have continued in the West to the 2nd cent. A.D. may be seen from Iren. Fr., 23 : [71] οὗτος οὐκέτι ὡς προφήτης, ἀλλ' ὡς μάντις λογισθήσεται, cf. Herm. m., 11, 2. [72] On the equation of the two terms in the East → 791, 10 ff.

f. Inspiration manticism, which is not found in Homer (→ 786, 22 f.) and was exercised by women in Greece but generally by men in Asia Minor, concerns only one aspect of oracular prophecy in Greece, though this is an important aspect. The agents of revelation are here ecstatically possessed in such a way that according to Plato's theory God takes away their understanding (ὁ θεὸς ἐξαιρούμενος ... τὸν νοῦν ... χρῆται ὑπηρέταις ... τοῖς χρησμῳδοῖς καὶ τοῖς μάντεσι τοῖς θείοις, Ion, 534c-d) and they ἐνθουσιῶντες λέγουσιν μὲν ἀληθῆ καὶ πολλά,

---

[69] Cf. Reitzenstein Hell. Myst., 26.
[70] Cf. on what follows Fraenkel, 498; Fascher, 13 f., 19, 42, 52-54; → 787, 6 ff.
[71] Ed. W. Harvey, II (1857), 491.
[72] Harnack Miss., I, 362, n. 2.

ἴσασι δὲ οὐδὲν ὧν λέγουσιν (Men., 99c, cf. Ap., 22c). In such descriptions the significance of the divine gift (μανία θεία δόσει διδομένη, Plat. Phaedr., 244a) is guaranteed, though it is worth noting that in these contexts Plato never speaks of προφῆται but of χρησμῳδοί and (θεο)μάντεις; [73] according to Plato a rational element is still intrinsic to prophets, cf. Tim., 71e-72b → 787, 27 ff. What Plato says very generally in Ion, 534c with his ὑπηρέτης of the god is developed by Plut. (→ 347, 42 ff.), who explains that the soul of the agent of revelation is an ὄργανον θεοῦ (Pyth. Or., 21 [II, 404b]), i.e., a zither of the god (Def. Orac., 50 [II, 437d]). Plut. also rules out reason (Def. Orac., 48 [II, 436e]) cf. → 350, 37 ff. In the Neo-Platonist Iamblichus, in some deviation from Greek usage, [74] προφήτης is then fully equated with the ecstatic μάντις who is ὄχημα ἢ ὄργανον τοῖς ἐπιπνέουσι θεοῖς (Myst., III, 4 [p. 109, 12]): the god χρῆται ὡς ὀργάνῳ τῷ προφήτῃ οὔτε ἑαυτοῦ ὄντι οὔτε παρακολουθοῦντι οὐδὲν οἷς λέγει ἢ ὅπου γῆς ἐστιν, ibid., 11 (p. 125, 10 ff.).

g. To summarise, the following points may be made concerning the use of the word group in relation to the Greek oracle. (a) It denotes appointed men and women and their work, which is to declare something whose content is not derived from themselves but from the god who reveals his will at the particular site. This revelation is through direct inspiration or through signs (σύμβολα) which stand in need of human interpretation, → 785, 9 ff.; 789, 19 ff. The distinction between the two forms of revelation is of no importance in the use of the group. [75] It does not affect the question of inspiration, which may be included, though it does not have to be. In the light of its use the group relates essentially to the public declaration of the divine will (previously concealed) to those who come for counsel, and it naturally includes a prior interpretation of the signs (ὑποκρίνεσθαι) or a conscious formulation of the oracle, → 788, 15 ff. The exact procedure in giving the oracle is not clear from the accounts. (b) The oracle prophet proclaims the will and counsel of the god in answer to questions and with reference to the particular situation of the one who asks for advice, → 786, 18 ff. In content the range of oracles extends to the whole sphere of private, political and cultic life, → 788, 17 ff. (c) The oracle prophets and prophetesses of Greece are chosen for their ministry by men and not by the god, → 787, 10 f. Human criteria control the choice. In inspiration manticism a certain psychical disposition has to be taken into account (→ 786, 21 ff.; 790, 41 ff.), but in general prophets come from the higher strata of the population, [76] e.g., from the ancient house of the Branchidae at Didyma. Not only in choice, however, does the initiative lie with man; the whole process is, as it were, only to order. [77] The prophet speaks only when a specific question is put to the oracle by an individual, [78] and even the inspiration is induced by human initiative, cf. → 344, 13 ff. Only once in Plut.'s time do we hear of a Pythia refusing to serve as the mouthpiece of the god,

---

[73] Only in Phaedr., 244a do we find the formula ἢ ἐν Δελφοῖς προφῆτις alongside the ἱέρειαι of Dodona.

[74] Cf. Nilsson, II, 431-435, also what is said about Alexandros of Abonoteichos → 789, 34 ff.

[75] The distinction between "intuitive" and "inductive" manticism (genus divinandi naturale and artificiosum, Cic. Divin., I, 49, 109 f.; II, 11, 26) is thus obscured in προφήτης κτλ.

[76] It seems to be an exception that a Pythia in Plut.'s time was a simple peasant girl (Pyth. Or., 22 [II, 405c]), cf. Amandry, 116; Berve, 10, n. 2.

[77] Bacht Prophetentum, 250.

[78] Fascher, 58 f.; Kolf, 799. When the prophet of the oracle of Ammon independently greets Alexander the Gt. as the son of Ammon (Plut. Alex., 27 [I, 680]) he is not pronouncing an oracle but officially greeting the new ruler of the land, cf. Nilsson, II, 138 f.

Def. Orac., 51 (II, 438a-c), → 350, 34 ff. (d) The oracle prophet enjoys such social esteem that he may be invited to fulfil representative functions like leading delegations and serving as spokesman for them. [79] The official character of his position is plain from the fact that it was common to name the year after his period of office, cf. esp. the inscr. of Dodona with the formulae ἐπὶ τοῦ προφήτου ... or προφητεύοντος ..., [80] where προφητεύω means "to hold the office of prophet to the oracle." (e) In Eur. Ion., 369 : οὐκ ἔστιν ὅστις σοι προφητεύσει τάδε, the verb includes the stating and presenting of the question to the god of the oracle, [81] → 793, 14 ff.

2. The Poet as Prophet.

a. Belief in a link between the divine Muse and the human poet [82] is found in the earliest Gk. poetry, where it is obviously traditional and finds its simplest expression in the appeal to the Muse, Hom. Il., 1, 1, esp. 2, 484-492 etc. The Homeric poet-singer feels that in his work he is dependent on the divine (θεὸς ... δῶκεν ἀοιδήν, Od., 8, 44); by contact therewith he is a θεῖος ἀοιδός, Od., 1, 336; 8, 43 etc. The gift sought from the Muse is not only song (τέρπειν Od., 8, 45) but also the content of the past which is to be depicted. The Muses have seen and know all things (ἴστε πάντα, Il., 2, 485) and they remind the singer (μνήσασθαι, 492), who is first the hearer and then the poet and speaker in the endowed power of presentation. [83] Continuing this view, but breaking free from the epic of chivalry, Hes. with a new claim to truth (ἀληθέα γηρύσασθαι, Theog., 28) finds the relation of the poet to the Muse in his personal experience of calling by the Muses, who breathe into him the divine voice, 22-34 → 350, 4 ff.

On the soil of this tradition Pind. [84] is the first Gk. poet to use the group προφήτης to describe the link with the Muses. He calls himself Πιερίδων προφάτας, "the spokesman of the Muses," Paean., 6, 6 (cf. the similar phrase in Bacchyl., 9, 3 : Μουσᾶν ... θεῖος προφάτας). In clear echo of Hom. Il., 2, 484-492 (→ lines 17 ff.) he calls upon the Muses in Paean., 6, 50-58 on the ground that they know all things (ἴστε ... πάντα, 54 f.) which mortals cannot otherwise discover ; their gift is εὐμαχανία ("discovery") and σοφία, Paean., 7b, 11-15. κῆρυξ is almost synon. with προφήτης in Dithyrambus, 2 (= Fr., 70b), 23 ff.; the Muse had raised up the poet in Hellas as the chosen and privileged herald of wise sayings ἐξαίρετον κάρυκα σοφῶν ἐπέων Μοῖσ᾽ ἀνέστασε (cf. ἄγγελος in Nem., 6, 57b). The essential content of this proclamation is the lauding of noble ἀρεταί and education in them. Pind. takes his description of the poet as προφήτης from the Delphic oracle and in Fr., 150 he defines his relation to the Muse more closely : μαντεύεο, Μοῖσα, προφατεύσω δ᾽ ἐγώ, "prophesy, Muse, and I will be thy speaker." Here the Muse has the place of the promantis and the poet that of the oracle prophet. What was the μνήσασθαι of the Muses in Hom. (→ line 18 f.) and their ἀληθέα γηρύσασθαι in Hes. (→ line 20) is now their μαντεύεσθαι. The analogy to the Delphic oracle shows that the prophet has of himself nothing to proclaim.

---

[79] Cf. M. Holleaux, "Fouilles au temple d'Apollon Ptoos," BCH, 14 (1890), 53 f.

[80] Cf. Rehm, op. cit. (→ n. 66), Indexes IV and V, s.v.

[81] In acc. with the relation μάντις-προφήτης (→ 790, 14 ff.) this usage may have been influenced by μαντεύομαι "to prophesy" (e.g., Plat. Tim., 72b) and "to consult an oracle," e.g., Plat. Ap., 21a, cf. Fascher, 15, n. 2.

[82] Cf. on what follows Dodds, 80 f.; W. F. Otto, Die Musen u. d. göttliche Ursprung des Singens u. Sagens (1954), 31-34; W. Schadewaldt, Von Homers Welt u. Werk² (1951), 76-83; K. Latte, "Hesiods Dichterweihe," Antike u. Abendland, 2 (1946), 152-163.

[83] Otto, op. cit. (→ n. 82), 34, cf. 85; Latte, op. cit. (→ n. 82), 159.

[84] Cf. Fascher, 12; Dodds, 82 and the review by G. Luck in Gnomon, 25 (1953), 364; H. Gundert, "Pind. u. sein Dichterberuf," Frankfurter Studien z. Religion u. Kultur d. Antike, 10 (1935), 62 f.; A. Sperduti, "The Divine Nature of Poetry in Antiquity," Transactions and Proceedings of the American Philol. Association, 81 (1950), 233-237; W. Kraus, Die Auffassung d. Dichterberufs im frühen Griechentum," Wiener Studien, 68 (1955), 85 f.; J. Duchemin, Pindare poète et prophète (1955), esp. 22-34, 337.

He mediates a divine task and divine knowledge. Nevertheless, self-awareness is expressed, for the poet offers himself as προφήτης. He can do so because his σοφία is inborn by divine favour, Pyth., 1, 41 f.; Olymp., 2, 86, cf. 9, 100. He thus commands a permanent creative ability. His own genius is essentially imparted when he speaks as προφήτης of the Muses. It is worth noting that in the idea of the μανία of the poet, which developed at the same time [85] though it is not attested until Democr. Fr., 17 f. (Diels⁷, II, 146, 5-15); Plat. Ion, 534a-e; Phaedr., 245a, 265b and acc. to which the poet does not know what he is saying (Plat. Ap., 22c; Men., 99c-d), the group προφήτης is patently avoided. [86] Hellenism then adopts the formulation coined by Pind. and using the epic ὑποφήτης (Hom. Il., 16, 235 → n. 21) it calls the poet Μουσάων ὑποφήτης, Theocr. Idyll., 16, 29; 17, 115, [87] cf. also in the post-Chr. period Dio Chrys. Or., 36, 42 : προφῆται τῶν Μουσῶν. Finally Ael. Arist. Or., 45, 12 (Dindorf) makes critical use of Pindar's analogy : the Muses are the μάντεις ἀληθεῖς, the poets their προφῆται.

b. While the predicate προφήτης describes the poet gen. as the one who declares to men what he has received from the divine Muses, there is sometimes a further use in which the poet becomes a spokesman for men. The analogy to the oracle prophet is still present (→ 792, 7 f.) when acc. to Ael. Arist. Or., 8, 48 (Dindorf) poets in their hymns return the thanks of men and in the προσαγορεύειν of the gods show themselves to be true προφῆται τῶν θεῶν, [88] "spokesmen to the gods." In Dio Chrys. Or., 7, 100 f. poets are the "spokesmen and advocates of men" (προφῆται αὐτῶν καὶ συνήγοροι) because they express public opinion.

3. The Broader Use.

From the earliest examples there may be seen a use of the group which goes beyond anything thus far mentioned.

a. In gen. religious usage (a) in Aesch. Ag., 409 δόμων προφῆται ("palace spokesmen") [89] deplore the adultery and flight of Helen. In Aristoph. Av., 972 a saying of Bacis mentions the προφήτης who "proclaims" and rightly "applies" such sayings (χρησμοί) to a situation. In Eur. Ba., 551 the Bacchics call themselves προφῆται of Dionysus because through frenzied singing and dancing they "proclaim" the nature of the new god who inspires them, ibid., 64-169, 416-433. In an eschatological myth in Plat. Resp., X, 617d-e a προφήτης ("spokesman," "herald") of Lachesis the goddess of fate, "proclaims" to the souls which begin a new earthly life, whose content they themselves must choose, the saying of the goddess which begins with the words Ἀνάγκης θυγατρὸς κόρης Λαχέσεως λόγος and which in 619c is described as τὰ προρρηθέντα ὑπὸ τοῦ προφήτου, "that which is proclaimed by the herald." In Plat., 262d the grasshoppers (cf. 258e) are τῶν Μουσῶν προφῆται because on the one side they transmit (ἐπιπνεῖν) the gift of the Muses to stirring speech with their song and on the other they tell (ἀπαγγέλλειν) the Muses after death who honours them on earth, 259c-d. (b) προφήτης shows syncretistic features in the 2nd cent. B.C. in the astrologist Vett. Val.: the one born under a certain constellation ἔσται μακάριος εὐσεβής, προφήτης μεγάλου θεοῦ καὶ ἐπακουσθήσεται ὡς θεός (II, 7 [p. 63, 18 f.]) or ἔσται προφήτης εὐτυχὴς πλούσιος ἔνδοξος, πολλῶν ἀγαθῶν κυριεύσει (II, 13

---

[85] Cf. P. Friedländer, Platon II² (1957), 297, n. 7.

[86] The group is not used for the "possessed" creative artist until the 3rd cent. A.D., Callistratus Descriptiones in C. L. Kayser, Flavii Philostrati Opera, II (1871), 422, 26 f. → 349, 17 ff.; of the plastic artist : his hands μετὰ μανίας προφητεύουσι τὰ ποιήματα.

[87] There is an appeal to the Muse on the model of Hom. and Pind. in Theocr. Idyll., 22, 116 : εἰπὲ θεά, σὺ γὰρ οἶσθα· ἐγὼ δ᾽ ἑτέρων ὑποφήτης φθέγξομαι, "will lift up my voice as a proclaimer to others"; cf. Callim. Hymn., 3, 186 : εἰπὲ θεὴ ... ἐγὼ δ᾽ ἑτέροισιν ἀείσω.

[88] Gen. like ἑτέρων ὑποφήτης → n. 87.

[89] Acc. to Fraenkel, II, 214 trusted persons called in, e.g., to interpret dreams, cf. δόμων ὀνειρόμαντις in Aesch. Choeph., 32; Kolf, 813 thinks they are servants who tell those outside what takes place in the house (→ 795, 1 ff.).

[p. 67, 22 f.]). Acc. to Luc. Pergr. Mort., 11 Peregrinus becomes προφήτης καὶ θιασάρ-χης (a leader in cultic purification) καὶ ξυναγωγεύς in a Chr. congregation. [90] Luc. probably regards him as a kind of γόης (→ 789, 36 ff.) who easily gains influence among Chr. with their hope of immortality, 13. [91]

b. From the 3rd cent. B.C. προφήτης is also attested as a transl. of the Egypt. priestly title ḥm-nṯr "servant of God," the term for those belonging to the upper priestly class. [92] Like all Egypt. priests these "prophets" are, with officials, nominated by the king ; [93] their special function in the ministry is not known but their honoured position in the hierarchy [94] and the possibility of hereditary succession [95] are plain. The following explanations of this usage have been advanced : transfer from the oracle of Ammon (→ 789, 19 ff.) [96] or direct transl. in the light of the honoured position of the Gk. oracle prophets, esp. as προφήτης gradually came to be used as a pure title in Gk. [97]

c. The use of the group for an office-bearer outside the oracle is also found on inscr. [98] from the 1st cent. B.C., e.g., IG, XII, 1, 833 : προφατεύσας ἐν τῷ ἄστει (Rhodes); IG, III, 1, 1169 (c. 200 A.D.) Φοίβου προφήτης as the title of an Attic leader of ephebes (κοσμήτωρ, loc. cit.), perhaps because he leads them at events in Delphi, e.g., on the occasion of the Pythiad. [99]

d. The group is used in philosophy and science from Plato ; here there is sometimes a religious overtone or the element of interpretation is suggested. Plat. Phileb., 28b-c : προφήτης "spokesman" who leads the enquiry out of a difficulty, also "spokesman" of (divine) νοῦς. Ps.-Aristot. Mund., 1, p. 391a, 15 f.: Under the guidance of νοῦς the soul is θείῳ ... ὄμματι τὰ θεῖα καταλαβομένη (vl.) τοῖς τε ἀνθρώποις προφη-τεύουσα. The Epicureans are "spokesmen" of their master (Ἐπικούρου προφῆται, Plut. Pyth. Or., 7 [II, 397c]) and "proclaimers" of his teaching (προφῆται ἀτόμων, Athen., V, 187b), cf. the sceptic Timon as προφήτης τῶν Πύρρωνος λόγων (Sext. Emp. Math., I, 53). In Dio Chrys. Or., 12, 47 the philosopher is λόγῳ ἐξηγητὴς καὶ προφήτης τῆς ἀθανάτου φύσεως (par. ἑρμηνεὺς καὶ διδάσκαλος, loc. cit.); Diogenes wants to be ἀληθείας καὶ παρρησίας προφήτης, i.e., "to teach," "to propagate" truth and candour as ethical values, Luc. Vit. Auct., 8. In Diod. S., I, 2, 2 the study and writing of history is the προφῆτις τῆς ἀληθείας which instructs in calocaga-thy (the deeds of the worthy are διαβοώμεναι τῷ θειοτάτῳ τῆς ἱστορίας στόματι, ibid., 2, 3) and in Sext. Emp. Math., I, 279 grammar is "exegesis" (προφῆτις) of the poets. Finally προφήτης can be used for the "specialist" in botany (Diosc. Mat. Med., I, 10) or ironically for the "quack" in medicine (Gal. in Hippocratis Prorrheticum, III, 23 [CMG, V, 9, 2, p. 134, 1 f.]), cf. also προφητεύω in Gal. in Hippocratis De Natura Hominis, II, 22 (CMG, V, 9, 1, p. 88, 2).

---

[90] Fascher, 205 : Luc. "lumps Christians, Jews and pagans together."

[91] προφήτης could also be understood in terms of the Egypt. priestly title (→ lines 5 ff.). If the continuation καὶ τῶν βίβλων τὰς μὲν ἐξηγεῖτο καὶ διεσάφει goes with προφήτης there is a Gk. element in the idea of exposition.

[92] W. Otto, Priester u. Tempel im hell. Ägypten, I (1905); II (1908), passim ; Fascher, 76-98; H. Bonnet, Reallex. d. ägypt. Religionsgesch. (1952), s.v. "Priester," esp. 604 f.; Kolf, 801 f., 809-811 (ref.). First found on inscr. in a decree of Canopos, 239/8 B.C. (Ditt. Or., I, 56, 3 f.) and in lit. in Manetho, quoted Jos. Ap., I, 249, cf. W. G. Waddell, Manetho with an English Transl.[2] (1948), Fr. 54.

[93] Bonnet, op. cit. (→ n. 92), 601 f.; H. Kees, Ägypten, Hndbch. AW, III, 1, 3, 1 (1933), 242, 252, 259.

[94] ἀρχιπροφήτης testifies to a further distinction in the class of prophets ; Fascher, 81; Kolf, 810 f.

[95] Cf. Fascher, 81.

[96] So Fascher, 96-98. The first mention of other Egypt. oracles is in the 2nd cent. A.D. in Luc. Deorum Concilium, 10 (Apis χρᾷ καὶ προφήτας ἔχει); Ps.-Luc. Syr. Dea, 36.

[97] So Kolf, 802.

[98] Ref. in Kolf, 811.

[99] F. Preisigke, Art. "Κοσμητής," Pauly-W., 11, 2 (1922), 1491; L. Deubner, Attische Feste (1932), 203.

e. Poetry can use the group either solemnly or humorously in the general sphere of life. The "heralds" who declare the victor in games are προφᾶται in Bacchyl., 10, 28 (cf. the trumpet as ὑποφᾶτις of war and peace in Anth. Pal., VI, 46, 1); Pind. Nem., 9, 50 calls the cup at the symposium the γλυκὺν κώμου προφάταν, "the sweet herald of comos," i.e., relaxed jollity ; [100] Antiphanes Fr., 217, 23 (CAF, II, 106) calls hunger δείπνου προφήτην, i.e., it tells us that it wants to be stilled by a meal ; in Plat. Comicus Fr., 184, 4 (CAF, I, 652) a skinny man is φθόης προφήτης, "a proclaimer of consumption." Eur. Ba., 211: ἐγὼ προφήτης σοι λόγων γενήσομαι, "I will tell you what transpires."

4. Summary.

a. προφήτης κτλ. is a group which is marked both by solemnity and also by lack of content ; [101] it simply expresses the formal function of declaring, proclaiming, making known. When it appears in the literature of the 5th century it has already a broad use for the oracle prophet (→ 786, 21 ff.), for the poet (→ 792, 23 ff.) and over a wider sphere not only for persons but also by poetic transference for things (→ lines 3 ff.). Yet in the light of the formation (→ 783, 3 ff.) and the Homeric ὑποφήτης (→ 784, 32 ff.) there can be no doubt but that προφήτης belongs to the religious sphere, where it denotes the one who speaks in the name of a god, declaring the divine will and counsel in the oracle, → 791, 15 ff. Historical seers and prophets not connected with an oracle are never called προφῆται but χρησμολόγοι or the like. On the other hand prophesying demons and gods may be called the προφήτης of a higher god as well as men (→ 790, 26 ff.), though it is worth noting that this does not apply to the supreme god Zeus. For every prophet declares something which is not his own ; hence κῆρυξ is the closest synonym, [102] for the κῆρυξ, too, declares what he receives from another, → III, 687, 21 ff. This parallelism (→ III, 691, 5 ff.) applies also to the occasional function of being a spokesman to the gods, → 790, 7 ff.; 792, 7 f.; 794, 1 ff. The prophet occupies a mediatorial role. He is the mouthpiece of the god and he is also man's spokesman to the god. The plain differentiation from μάντις on the one side (→ 790, 14 ff.) and the whole use of the term up to the 2nd cent. A.D. on the other make it plain that the prefix προ- never indicates the future. Only very much later, under Christian influence, does προφήτης take on the modern sense of "one who declares the future," e.g., Schol. Theocr., 22, 116 : προφήτης ἐστὶν ὁ προλέγων τι ἐσόμενον, ἤγουν ὁ τὰ μέλλοντα προλέγων. [103] b. The formal character of the word group explains its early transfer and use over a broad area. Yet even in the wider religious field the element of dependence is always clear, finding its strongest expression in the inspiration manticism of oracle prophecy (ὑπηρέτης, ὄργανον of the god, → 791, 5 ff.). At the same time, one may see a certain independence which is proper even to the oracle prophet as the one who interprets the signs and formulates the oracle, → 785, 9 ff.; 787, 34 ff.; 788, 15 ff.; 789, 21 ff. It is this above all which makes possible the self-designation of the poet as προφήτης (→ 792, 23 ff.) and the use of the group in philosophy and science (→ 794, 8 ff.). Here προφήτης approximates to ἐξηγητής or ἑρμηνεύς (→ 794, 26 f., 30) [104] on the one side and to διδάσκαλος (→ 794, 26 ff., cf. 788, 24 ff.; 792, 31 ff.) on the other. c. Because of its solemnity προφήτης

---

[100] Though cf. Fascher, 11 f.; Kolf, 813.
[101] Fascher, 51: "A skeletal word with no specific content."
[102] → 792, 29 ff.; 793, 30 f.; 795, 1 ff.; Anth. Pal., VII, 6, 1: ἡρώων κάρυκ' ἀρετᾶς, μακάρων δε προφήταν.
[103] Ed. F. Dübner (1849), 103; for further examples → n. 21.
[104] The poet as ἑρμηνεὺς τῶν θεῶν, Plat. Ion, 534e.

(προφητεύω) can become a formal title of office (→ 794, 13 ff.); its use in translation of a priestly Egyptian title is along these lines (→ 794, 5 ff.). d. The formal character of προφήτης makes it a good translation word well adapted to pick up the most diverse contents. Even in profane Greek the syncretism of the imperial period pours completely non-Greek contents into the term; this is most patent in the prophetic type represented by Alexandros of Abonoteichos (→ 789, 26 ff.), who is contemptuously described as γόης (→ n. 69).

Krämer

B. נָבִיא in the Old Testament.

The picture of the prophecy of Israel presented in the OT is by no means uniform. It embraces such different phenomena that it seems wellnigh impossible to bring it under a single common denominator. Even the attempt to write a history of OT prophecy can be only partially successful and leaves many open questions at decisive points. The difficulty arises at once in the sphere of terminology. Attention is focused almost exclusively on נָבִיא with its derived verbal forms, but this covers only one part of what is to be called prophecy in the OT and it is notably less prominent in the most important area, that of the so-called writing prophets. The material problem is chiefly that there are on the one side institutional prophets who appear in groups or individually and who are linked in all kinds of ways, but that on the other side the most striking prophetic figures are individuals who bear little or no discernible relationship to institutional prophecy. The sources often enable us to draw no very solid conclusions. In many cases one can only state what view the tradition had of a prophet at certain points without being able to ascertain the underlying historical data or to put them in their wider context.

I. Derivation of the Word.

The Heb. equivalent of προφήτης is almost always נָבִיא. The derivation and meaning of the term are contested. The Accadian *nabû* "to call," "to proclaim" and the Arab. *naba'a* "to impart" are usually adduced in explanation of the root נבא. Yet the word is not a genuine verbal root in Heb.; the verb forms ni and hitp are derived from the noun. For an understanding of the word נָבִיא the decisive question is whether the qatîl form is to be taken as act. or pass. Earlier it was almost universal to find an act. sense "speaker," "proclaimer" (→ II, 454, 15 ff.) [105] but more recently the pass. has claimed greater attention, [106] as proposed also for נָגִיד [107] and נָשִׂיא. [108] This view is more likely linguistically, esp. as it is supported by the Accad. *nabî'um,* "the called." [109] Materially, too, this understanding of נָבִיא seems to fit best the earliest OT instances. Yet there can

---

[105] J. Barth, *Die Nominalbildung in d. semitischen Sprachen*[2] (1894) § 125e; H. Zimmern, KAT, 400; C. Brockelmann, *Grundriss d. vergleichenden Grammatik d. semitischen Sprachen,* I (1908) § 138b; Ges.-K. § 84a, 1; more recently Häussermann, 8-12; Haldar, 109; Quell, 23, n. 2; H. J. Kraus, *Gottesdienst in Israel* (1954), 63, n. 111.

[106] H. Torczyner, "Das literarische Problem d. Bibel," ZDMG, 85 (1931), 322; Jepsen, 5, n. 1; W. F. Albright, *From the Stone Age to Christianity* (1946), 231 f., 332. Guillaume, 112 f.; Johnson, 24, n. 8.

[107] A. Alt, "Die Staatenbildung der Israeliten in Palästina," *Kleine Schriften z. Gesch. d. Volkes Israel,* II (1953), 23, n. 2.

[108] M. Noth, "Das System der zwölf Stämme Israels," BWANT, IV, 1 (1930), 162.

[109] Cf. W. v. Soden, *Grundriss d. akkadischen Grammatik* (1952) § 16, 1; J. J. Stamm, "Die akkad. Namengebung," *Mitteilungen d. vorderasiatisch-ägypt. Gesellschaft,* 44 (1939), 258, 2b.

be no doubt but that the word very quickly became a fixed term irrespective of its original meaning.

II. The Verb.

In sifting the examples we do best to begin with the verb. It is used in the ni and hitp. Both forms are derived from the noun and in the first instance mean "to show oneself or to act as a נָבִיא." But obviously distinctions were seen between the two verb forms. [110]

1. Older Texts. In the older texts the hitpael predominates. Ecstatic traits are almost always to the fore. In 1 S. 10:5 f., 10 ff. and 19:18 ff. there are two different aetiologies for the proverb "Is Saul also among the prophets?" Both refer to a group of נְבִיאִים who are in ecstasy, expressed by הִתְנַבֵּא. The רוּחַ (רוּחַ יהוה 10:6; רוּחַ אֱלֹהִים 10:10; 19:20, 23) seizes him who comes in contact with them and associates him, too, with the הִתְנַבֵּא. 10:5 mentions musical instruments which obviously help to bring on the state of ecstasy. The effect is depicted in 19:24. Saul takes off his clothes and lies naked a whole day and night. [111] In each of the texts there is a niphal form (10:11; 19:20). Both forms are part. [112] denoting the state reached by the הִתְנַבֵּא. That the ref. is again to ecstasy is shown by the fact that the state is visible. Saul's sudden attempt to kill David in 1 S. 18:10 f. is also attributed to a הִתְנַבֵּא of Saul, whose cause is a רוּחַ אֱלֹהִים רָעָה; the ref. is obviously to "raving." In 1 K. 18:29 this is the final stage in the attempt of the prophets of Baal to gain a hearing. It is connected with a cultic dance (v. 26) and with self-mutilation, v. 28. In Nu. 11:25-27 הִתְנַבֵּא as the effect of a materially understood רוּחַ denotes a purely ecstatic phenomenon. [113]

The ecstatic prophecy found in these texts is not peculiar to Israel; it may be seen in the religions of surrounding nations too. C. 1100 B.C. the Egypt. Wen-Amon at Byblos tells of similar prophetic speech in ecstasy. [114] In 1 K. 18:22 ff. there is ref. to 450 prophets of Baal (נְבִיאֵי הַבַּעַל) cf. also 2 K. 10:19) [115] whose conduct is depicted as ecstatic in v. 28 f. One might also recall Balaam (→ I, 524, 1 ff.), for his prophecy is ecstatic even though the word נָבִיא is not used; the רוּחַ אֱלֹהִים comes upon him (Nu. 24:2) and the two older sayings in Nu. 24:3-9, 15-19 open with the description of an ecstatic receiving of revelation. [116] Worth noting is the fact that the ecstatic of Byblos and Balaam are individuals. Hence one cannot regard group ecstasy as the historically original form from which prophetic individuals gradually emerged. There is at least no evidence for any such development. [117]

In 1 K. 22 one may see change and differentiation in the two verbal stems. In v. 10 we read מִתְנַבְּאִים לִפְנֵיהֶם — the hitp expresses the visible side supported by a symbolic action (v. 11). But in v. 12 it is said of the נְבִיאִים: נִבְּאִים כֵּן לֵאמֹר — the ni denotes their speech, their giving of the oracle, which is obviously possible on the basis of the pre-

---

[110] These distinctions are completely ignored by Ges.-Buhl and Köhler-Baumg., s.v., but cf. Jepsen, 5-11.

[111] 10:13 also says that the הִתְנַבֵּא is limited in time; when it is over Saul returns home and no one notes anything.

[112] As against Mandelkern the נִבָּא of 10:11 is to be taken as a part., as comparison with 19:20 shows.

[113] Acc. to M. Noth, *Überlieferungsgesch. d. Pent.* (1948), 141-143 the aim of the story of the elders in Nu. 11 is to authenticate ecstatic prophecy.

[114] Cf. AOT, 72.

[115] Acc. to A. Alt, "Das Gottesurteil auf dem Karmel," *Kleine Schriften z. Gesch. d. Volkes Israel,* II (1953), 137, n. 1 the ref. to them in v. 19 f. is not original; the same applies to the 400 נְבִיאֵי הָאֲשֵׁרָה in v. 19.

[116] Cf. R. Rendtorff, Art. "Bileam u. Bileamsprüche," RGG³, I, 1290 f.

[117] Plöger Priester, 165 f.

ceding הִתְנַבֵּא. On the other hand Ahab says of Micaiah ben Imlah : לֹא־יִתְנַבֵּא עָלַי טוֹב
(v. 8, 18); he uses the hitp for the speech (עַל), though in a patently derogatory sense. [118]

2. The Prophetic Books. In the prophetic books the distribution of the verb is very
uneven. It occurs only in Am., Jer., Ez., Jl. and Zech. This means that before the end
of the 7th cent. it is used only by Amos in the Northern Kingdom. Here it is in the
niphal and denotes the activity of the authentic prophet sent by Yahweh, 3:8; 7:15 f. [119]
The ref. is obviously to prophetic speech. Acc. to 3:8 הִנָּבֵא is a result of the דָּבָר
of Yahweh. In 7:16 לֹא תִנָּבֵא עַל־יִשְׂרָאֵל can only mean prophetic speech against Israel.
V. 15 is not so clear : לֵךְ הִנָּבֵא אֶל־עַמִּי יִשְׂרָאֵל. The אֶל makes possible the rendering :
"Speak as a prophet to my people ...," [120] but "Go to my people Israel as a prophet ..." [121] is also possible. Similarly there is no direct ref. to speech in v. 12 f. though
the context of 7:10-17 suggests this understanding. Ecstatic features are not mentioned.

The use of the verb in the later prophetic writings corresponds in essentials to the
picture in Amos. The niphal is easily predominant. Most of the Jer. ref. show at once
that speech is in view. The ni is used without distinction for the speech of both Jer.
and his opponents. Cf. 20:1: וַיִּשְׁמַע .... אֶת־יִרְמְיָהוּ נִבָּא אֶת־הַדְּבָרִים הָאֵלֶּה, [122] on the lips of
Jer. to Hananiah 28:6 : וְהָקֵם יהוה אֶת־דְּבָרֶיךָ אֲשֶׁר נִבֵּאתָ‖ with דָּבָר 23:16; [123] 26:12; 27:16,
with לֵאמֹר 23:25; 26:9; 32:3; 37:19; with וַיֹּאמֶר 26:18. Also with the prep. עַל (25:13; [124]
26:20; 28:8), אֶל (26:11, 12; 28:8) and לְ (14:16; 20:6; 23:16; 27:10, 14, 15, 16 twice;
29:9, 21, 31; 37:19) the aspect of speech is discernible. Words are also clearly meant
when the content of הִנָּבֵא is given : שֶׁקֶר (14:14; 23:25, 26; 27:10, 14, 16; 29:21), [125]
חֲלֹמוֹת שֶׁקֶר (23:32), or when it is said of the נְבִיאִים that they prophetically bring to pass
לְשָׁלוֹם (28:9), לַשֶּׁקֶר (27:15) or בַּשֶּׁקֶר (5:31; 20:6). Of the other instances of the ni 11:21
and 14:15 speak of the הִנָּבֵא בְּשֵׁם יהוה, which is to be taken in the sense of prophetic
speech acc. to 14:14; 23:25; 26:9, 20; 27:15; 29:9; the same applies to הִנָּבֵא בַּבַּעַל (2:8).
Finally in 19:14 the הִנָּבֵא pts. back to the sign in v. 10, 11a which is linked with a
saying. Ecstatic features are again absent, nor is there ref. to the רוּחַ. The hitpael is
often used in Jer. with disparaging ref. to the speech of opponents, cf. the saying of
Yahweh on the lips of Jer. (14:14; 23:13) or in the letter of Shemaiah concerning
Jer. (29:26 f.). In 29:26 the מִתְנַבֵּא is par. to מְשֻׁגָּע; certainly this contemptuous expression
does not permit us to draw any conclusions regarding ecstatic phenomena accompanying
the work of Jer. There is a striking use of the hitp in 26:20 : Urijah the son of Shemaiah
is called אִישׁ מִתְנַבֵּא בְּשֵׁם יהוה which is undoubtedly meant positively by the narrator ;
in the continuation וַיִּנָּבֵא עַל־הָעִיר וגו the ni is again used in the sense "to speak as a
prophet." Here the hitp seems to be understood as a larger and more general expression :
"to come forth as a prophet."

In Ez. the use of the niphal has become very formal and occurs chiefly in the intr.
to individual addresses : שִׂים פָּנֶיךָ (אֶל/עַל).... וְהִנָּבֵא עַל (אֶל) (6:2; 13:17; 21:2, 7; 25:2; 28:21;
29:2; 35:2; 38:2), וְאָמַרְתָּ ... בֶּן־אָדָם הִנָּבֵא (וְאַתָּה) [126] (13:2; [127] 21:14, 33; 30:2; 34:2;

---

[118] Cf. also Jepsen, 7.
[119] The word has also no derogatory ring on the lips of Amaziah in v. 12 f., cf. Würthwein, Amos-Studien, 20 f. 2:11 f. seem to be secondary.
[120] V. Maag, Text, Wortschatz u. Begriffswelt d. Buches Am. (1951), 104.
[121] Cf. Würthwein, Amos-Studien, 22, though his "as a nabi" gives it a specific emphasis.
[122] Cf. also 25:30; not by Jer. acc. to W. Rudolph, Jeremia, Hndbch. AT, I, 12 (1947).
[123] At 23:16 the verb is left out in LXX £.
[124] 25:13b β is a secondary heading for 25:15 ff. cf. LXX.
[125] 29:9 בְּשֶׁקֶר, though perhaps בְּ is to be excised cf. BH³.
[126] The assertion of Köhler-Baumg., s.v. that הִנָּבֵא וְאָמַרְתָּ shows that נִבָּא does not have
to mean speech" lacks cogency in view of an expression like דִּבֶּר...וְאָמַרְתָּ in Lv. 1:2 etc.
[127] In 13:2 one should perhaps read a second הִנָּבֵא (with the LXX) instead of הַנִּבָּאִים.

36:1; 39:1 cf. 11:4; 36:3, 6; 37:4, 9, 12; 38:14). The ni is again used for the prophetic speech of Ez. in 11:13; 12:27 and for that of his opponents in 13:16. [128] Only in 21:19 does וְאַתָּה בֶן־אָדָם הִנָּבֵא introduce an action of almost magical character rather than a saying. The form is perhaps to be vocalised as hitp הִנָּבֵא for the hitp is used in 37:10 and it there denotes a prophetic word which is intr. as that of Yahweh but does not, like v. 5 f., declare an act of Yahweh, containing instead a direct summons to the רוּחַ to come and awaken the dead to life ; this is an almost magical and very singular use of the prophetic word. For the rest the hitp occurs in Ez. only in 13:17 in disparaging ref. to the work of prophetesses, cf. Jer. 14:14; 23:13.

In later prophetic texts there are two other examples of opposing views. Jl. 2:28 believes that in the time of salvation there will be an outpouring of the רוּחַ, which will result in general הִנָּבֵא. Zech. 13:2 ff. (→ 812, 32 ff.), however, speaks of a time when Yahweh will root out the prophets with the רוּחַ טֻמְאָה, so that הִנָּבֵא is regarded as a disgrace and as a transgression worthy of death.

3. The Chronicler. In the Chronicler the verb in 2 Ch. 18:7, 9, 11, 17 is based on 1 K. 22:8, 10, 12, 18 with minor alterations. Noteworthy is the use of the hitpael in 2 Ch. 20:37, where it is said of a man called Eliezer : וַיִּתְנַבֵּא...עַל־יְהוֹשָׁפָט לֵאמֹר. Here the Chronicler has edited an ancient source. [129] In Ezr. 5:1 the Aram hitp is used for the work of Haggai and Zech. which takes place בְּשֵׁם אֱלָהּ יִשְׂרָאֵל; the עַל shows plainly that the ref. is to speech. There is a completely different use of the verb in 1 Ch. 25:1-3, where הִנָּבֵא is the work of the temple musicians. Acc. to the data now available no direct line can be traced from the use and understanding of the verb in pre-exilic texts to this usage of the Chronicler.

As a whole, then, the picture presented by the use of the verb is comparatively clear. In the oldest texts the hitp is used for ecstatic states. Then the ni appears to denote prophetic speech, while the hitp is used disparagingly. This distinction occurs yet again in the 7th and 6th cent. prophets, where the ni easily predominates. The verb is no longer employed for ecstatic phenomena.

III. The Noun.

The use of the noun נָבִיא is par. in part to that of the verb.

1. Prophetic Groups.

In the historical books there is often ref. to groups of נְבִיאִים. Thus the ecstatic groups in 1 S. 10 and 19 are called נְבִיאִים → 797, 9 ff.; II, 454, 31 ff. 1 K. 18 f. and 22 speak of נְבִיאֵי יהוה and contrast them with the נְבִיאֵי הַבַּעַל. In 1 K. 22 the נְבִיאִים are in close touch with the court. Ahab consults them (דרש v. 5, 7) before his campaign and they prophesy (הִנָּבֵא v. 12) success. In v. 22 f. the relation to the king is expressed by a personal suffix נְבִיאָיו v. 22, נְבִיאֶיךָ v. 23). One of this group validates his word by a preceding כֹּה־אָמַר יהוה, v. 11. Acc. to v. 24 the רוּחַ יהוה is the presupposition of a proper oracle. In relation to the work of the רוּחַ there is an obvious shift as compared with 1 S. 10 and 19, where ecstatic phenomena are induced. In 1 K. 20:35 ff.; 2 K. 2-9 we find בְּנֵי הַנְּבִיאִים, always in relation to Elisha, [130] who seems to be the head of the fellowship. They are located in various places (Bethel, Jericho 2 K. 2:3, 5, Gilgal 4:38). Certain things are known about their activity and manner of life. They have a common place of meeting in which they sit before Elisha, 2 K. 4:38; 6:1. They are dedicated to preserving certain traditions. There is also ref. to common meals, 4:38 ff., 42 ff. On the

---

[128] In the gloss 4:7 תָּכִין פָּנֶיךָ...וְנִבֵּאתָ denotes a mute gesture.

[129] Cf. M. Noth, Überlieferungsgesch. Studien, I (1943), 161, n. 4; W. Rudolph, Chronikbücher, Hndbch. AT, I, 21 (1955), ad loc.

[130] The independent tradition in 1 K. 20:35 ff. (cf. Noth, op. cit. [→ n. 129], 80) belongs materially to this context.

other hand a member of the group marries and has his own house, 4:1 ff. Their way of life is very modest (4:1 ff., 38 ff., 42 ff., cf. also 6:5 : the axe is borrowed). We may perhaps deduce from 1 K. 20:38, 41 that they bore a special mark on the forehead.

There is no mention of ecstatic features. Instead various sayings have come down from these circles. On the one side we have a group of crisp oracular pronouncements which give evidence of modest material hopes for the future, 1 K. 17:14; 2 K. 2:21; 3:16, 17; 4:43; 7:1.[131] Among these בְּנֵי הַנְּבִיאִים there seem to have been handed down eschatological expectations of limited scope which promise a permanent supply of elemental needs for the lower social orders. In the present context the sayings are intr. by כֹּה אָמַר יהוה. They thus claim to be sayings of Yahweh passed on to others by those who speak as commissioned by Yahweh. In this sphere we also find political sayings : One of the בְּנֵי הַנְּבִיאִים proclaims to the king of Israel with כֹּה־אָמַר יהוה the penalty for his breaking of the ban of Yahweh (1 K. 20:42), while another, on the order of Elisha, anoints Jehu king with the same formula (2 K. 9:3, 6, 12). In contrast to the נְבִיאִים of 1 K. 22 these בְּנֵי הַנְּבִיאִים are thus independent of the court. On the commission of Yahweh they oppose the king or even help to overthrow him by designating and anointing a successor. Amphictyonic traditions obviously stand behind this political activity. The ban is an integral part of the holy war and the anointing of Jehu opposes to the attempted establishment of a dynasty in the Northern Kingdom the concept of charismatic monarchy.[132]

During the later monarchy the sources no longer refer to נְבִיאִים as a group.[133] A history of this form of prophecy can hardly be reconstructed from the materials available. In particular there is no real evidence for the current thesis that these groups are connected with the cultus.[134]

2. Individuals.

The tradition concerning individuals described as נָבִיא is complex and conflicting. Only a few of these are linked with the groups already mentioned. Samuel is found among the נְבִיאִים in Ramah (1 S. 19:18-24), though he is obviously distinct from them. Elijah is the only survivor of the נְבִיאֵי יהוה whom Jezebel had had killed (1 K. 18:22; 19:10, 14). In 2 K. 2 Elijah, with Elisha, is connected with the בְּנֵי הַנְּבִיאִים. Finally Elisha is depicted as a leader of the groups of בְּנֵי הַנְּבִיאִים whom he assists with his miracles.[135] It is evident, however, that this covers only a part of the total picture which the tradition offers concerning these men. This part is much bigger in the case of Elisha than in that of Elijah or Samuel. But even in the case of Elisha it is worth noting that in other stories he acts very much as an individual or as a unique phenomenon in his circle. He is *the* נָבִיא in Samaria (2 K. 5:3) and indeed in Israel (5:8; 6:12).

Elsewhere in the tradition the נָבִיא is always an individual. When one considers the men to whom the title is given it is immediately apparent that there

---

[131] Cf. on this W. Reiser, "Eschatologische Gottessprüche in den Elisa-Legenden," ThZ, 9 (1953), 321-338.

[132] Cf. G. v. Rad, "Der Hl. Krieg im alten Israel," Abh. ThANT, 20 (1951), 13; A. Alt, "Das Königtum in den Reichen Israel u. Juda," Kl. Schriften z. Gesch. d. Volkes Israel, II (1953), 116-134.

[133] The special mention of the priests and נְבִיאִים in 2 K. 23:2 can hardly be original (cf. BH³) and it also tells us nothing about the role of the prophets presupposed here.

[134] Coming down from the בָּמָה (1 S. 10:5) and the fact that Ramah (1 S. 19:19), Gilgal (2 K. 2:1), Bethel (v. 3) and Jericho (v. 5) were cultic centres can hardly sustain the burden of proof (so, e.g., Mowinckel, *Psalmenstudien,* 17; Würthwein, *Amos-Studien,* 11; Plöger Priester, 176).

[135] The eschatological sayings from these circles are not given any particular emphasis by reason of the fact that the expectations expressed in them seem to be fulfilled in the person of Elisha, cf. Reiser, *op. cit.* (→ n. 131), 337.

can be no question of a single clearly delineated type. Particularly where the reference is to men of the age of the monarchy the most diverse features are connected with the title, → 803, 17 ff. Nevertheless, one common feature does begin to emerge in increasing measure, namely, that of speaking by Yahweh's commission. It is recognised that Samuel is instituted a נָבִיא לַיהוה because Yahweh does not let any of his words fall to the ground, 1 S. 3:19 f. All the prophets who follow use phrases like כֹּה אָמַר יהוה or דְּבַר יהוה, שָׁמַע, or it is said of them that Yahweh has sent forth His Word through them (1 K. 16:7, 12; 2 K. 14:25). In the case of many of them the fact that they come with a word from Yahweh is the only thing the tradition knows about them: Gad (1 S. 22:5; [136] 2 S. 24:11-13); Jehu (1 K. 16:1-4, 7, 12); Jonah (2 K. 14:25), the נְבִיאָה Huldah (2 K. 22:14-20), the anonymous נָבִיא in 1 K. 20 (v. 13 f., 22, 28). [137]

Only in the case of Gad and Nathan is there any obvious institutional connection. It is true that in 1 S. 22:5 Gad is only הַנָּבִיא, but in 2 S. 24:11 the term חֹזֵה דָוִד is also used, and this shows that he belonged to the entourage of the king. Nathan seems to be permanently present at court and plays a part in political affairs and even in court intrigue (cf. 2 S. 7:1 ff. and esp. 1 K. 1). [138] Nevertheless, he accuses David sharply (2 S. 12). Gad, too, proclaims the judgment of Yahweh on David. Hence the court connection does not entail dependence nor does it prejudice the freedom of the Word of Yahweh. The others individuals described as נָבִיא are completely independent even though some of them are actively related to the royal house, to whom their message applies in the first instance, cf. Elisha and Isaiah.

Of special significance are the Mari par. [139] In several texts there is ref. here to men who come unasked to the king with a message from the god Dagan which makes demands or sharply criticises the conduct of the king. The term for these messengers is muhhûm, which is closely related to the title mahhûm, used for a group of ecstatic priests. Yet there is no ref. to ecstatic phenomena on the receiving of revelation, and only once is a dream mentioned. The par. between the coming of these prophets in Mari and men like Gad and Nathan is palpable. One need only refer to the inscr. of King Zakir of Hamath, [140] which says in line 11 f. that the god Be'elšmain caused a word of salvation to come to the king "through seers (חֹזִין) and prophets (?)." It is a matter of debate how far one may also refer to Egypt. texts, in which there are no prophetic figures, but which contain formal and material par. to the prophetic sayings of the OT. [141]

For the most part the initiative in transmitting a word of Yahweh lies with the נָבִיא who hands on the דְּבַר יהוה which has come to him. Not infrequently there is reference to consulting Yahweh through the נָבִיא (1 S. 28:6; 1 K. 14:2; 22:5, 7; 2 K. 3:11; 22:13). In 2 K. 19:1 ff. the saying of Yahweh passed on by Isaiah is an answer to the request for intercession. Nevertheless, the נָבִיא usually comes unasked, so that it is not possible to see primarily in the נָבִיא a substitute for other possibilities of oracular consultation. [142] The freedom and independence of

---

[136] In 1 S. 22:5 there is no ref. to Gad speaking by Yahweh's commission.

[137] 1 K. 20:28 has אִישׁ הָאֱלֹהִים for נָבִיא, though with obvious ref. to the same prophet.

[138] 1 K. 1:34, 45 presupposes Nathan's sharing in the anointing of Solomon as king, though the priest Zadok is the only officiant in the account of the anointing itself, v. 39.

[139] Cf. M. Noth, "Gesch. u. Gotteswort im AT," Gesammelte Studien z. AT (1957), 230-247; W. v. Soden, "Verkündung des Gotteswillens durch prophetisches Wort in den altbabyl. Briefen aus Mari," Die Welt des Orients, I, 5 (1950), 397-403.

[140] Cf. AOT, 443 f.

[141] Cf. G. Lanczkowski, "Ägypt. Prophetismus im Lichte d. at.lichen," ZAW, 70 (1958), 31-38.

[142] So Jepsen, 149.

the prophet's work is a wholly new element. Declarations of judgment play a dominant role in the sayings of these independent individual prophets.

It is grounded in the character of the sources that these are directed mainly to the royal house (2 S. 12:1-15a; [143] 24:12 f.; 1 K. 11:29-39; [144] 14:7-16; 16:1-4; 20:38-42; 22:17-23; 2 K. 20:1, 16-18), though the judgment proclaimed often affects all Israel. In 2 K. 22:16 f. the judgment is on Jerusalem and Josiah is exempted, vv. 18-20. The story in 1 K. 13 (→ n. 192) contains a judgment on the altar of Bethel (v. 2 f.) whose execution is recorded in 2 K. 23:(15)16-18. Along with the judgments there are prophecies which speak of positive historical action on Yahweh's part. Thus Yahweh guarantees the permanence of the dynasty of David (2 S. 7) [145] and He also promises victory in various wars (1 K. 20:13, 28; 2 K. 19:6 f., 20-34). In 2 K. 20:5 f. Isaiah proclaims healing to Hezekiah in answer to the latter's prayer. The Deuteronomist ascribes a special function to the נְבִיא אִישׁ in Ju. 6:7-10, namely, to keep before the Israelites their backsliding from Yahweh. Acc. to 2 K. 17:13, 23 Yahweh constantly warns the Israelites and declares His judgments to them through the נְבִיאִים, [146] cf. 21:10-15; 24:2. In these summarised statements the נְבִיאִים are viewed as a continuous series and called Yahweh's עֲבָדִים, 17:23; 21:10; 24:2.

The question arises whether all the figures called נְבִיא are connected with one another, i.e., whether there is such a thing as an institutional office of נְבִיא. The institutional element is apparent at once in the נְבִיא groups. It is also present in the court prophets of David. But the attempt to relate the two runs into serious difficulties. [147] In the distinction between them one might perhaps see an indication of the differing relations in North and South. [148] The question still remains, however, whether these are not different forms of the same office, even if a negative answer seems to be suggested. Many of the later individuals do not fit too well, if at all, into the framework of an established office. The main reason why it is so hard to answer this question is that the sources do not provide the right kind of material for an institutional understanding. Any conjectures, then, must be advanced with caution. [149]

Nor do the texts throw much light on the very lively question as to the relation between such an office and the cultus.

Samuel was brought up in the sanctuary at Shiloh and received his first word from Yahweh there, 1 S. 3:1 ff. At the end of the ancient narrative 1 S. 1-3 [150] he is called נְבִיא לַיהוה, 3:20. But the circumstances under which he came to the shrine and esp. the emphasis on the extraordinary nature of this revelation (3:1, 21) hardly suggest a fixed office. Again, the note that he "blesses" (בֵּרַךְ) the offering at the beginning of the feast (1 S. 9:13) seems rather to denote his special position. David consults Nathan on his

---

[143] Acc. to the analysis of L. Rost, "Die Überlieferung v. d. Thronnachfolge Davids," BWANT, III, 6 (1926), 93-99 only vv. 1-7a and 13-15a are part of the original, to which two threatening oracles were later added.

[144] There are many Deuteronomistic additions in this passage.

[145] Cf. on this Rost, op. cit. (→ n. 143), 47-74; M. Noth, "David u. Israel in II Samuel," Mélanges Bibl., Gedenkschr. f. André Robert (1955), 122-130.

[146] At v. 13 read נְבִיאָו, dl כָּל־חֹזֶה, cf. BH³.

[147] Jepsen does not face squarely the question of the relation between the groups and individuals, so that there are many loose ends. This question is posed, however, by Plöger Priester, 166.

[148] So Jepsen, passim.

[149] For all the radical analysis Jepsen's book suffers too much from theorising based on a preconceived view of "nabism."

[150] Cf. Noth, op. cit. (→ n. 129), 60 f.

plan to build the temple, and Nathan brings him a word from Yahweh about this (2 S. 7:1 ff.), but this seems to be the extent of his connection with the cultus. Elijah's contest with the prophets of Baal takes place in the cultic sphere but sacrifice was not the privilege of certain cultic office-bearers in older times, [151] and the cultic battle is comparable to that recounted of Gideon in Ju. 6:25 ff. In 1 K. 19:10, 14 the overthrowing of altars and slaying of prophets are signs of apostasy from Yahweh, though far-reaching conclusions cannot be deduced therefrom. The most one can say even concerning Elisha is that acc. to 2 K. 4:23 he was consulted on the day of the new moon or the Sabbath. For the rest he is nowhere presented as a cultic prophet.

This review shows that there were points of contact between the older prophets and the cultus. Yet it is quite plain that the tradition nowhere regards the relation to the cultus as the characteristic feature of these prophets. Hence one can hardly say more than that according to the tradition the prophets of the 10th and 9th centuries stood in a more or less close positive relation to the cultus of their time. [152]

3. The Transferring of the Term to Earlier Figures.

The term נָבִיא was also transferred by the tradition to earlier figures. Thus Abraham is given this title in Gn. 20:7 (E). The characteristic feature here is intercession. In the patriarchal stories such unusual expressions as הָיָה דְבַר יהוה אֶל־אַבְרָם בַּ מַּחֲזֶה and וְהִנֵּה דְבַר־יהוה אֵלָיו (Gn. 15:1, 4) may well derive from this view of E, which is not developed elsewhere. Only in P (Ex. 7:1) is Aaron called נָבִיא. This takes up the statement in Ex. 4:16 that Aaron will be Moses' mouth and Moses will be Aaron's אֱלֹהִים, and changes it so that Moses is the אֱלֹהִים for Pharaoh and Aaron is his נָבִיא. For P, then, the נָבִיא is one who speaks on the commission of a superior. The observation in Ex. 15:20 that Miriam was a נְבִיאָה is probably older and is related to the ancient Song of the Red Sea in v. 21. If this is correct, cultic dancing and singing are the features which gave rise to the designation.

The expression נָבִיא is frequently used in relation to Moses. Reflection on his position in Nu. 12:6-8 emphatically places him above the נָבִיא. Yahweh speaks to the latter in visions and dreams but to Moses פֶּה אֶל־פֶּה (cf. Ex. 33:11: פָּנִים אֶל־פָּנִים). His extraordinary position is further emphasised by the designation עַבְדִּי, → V, 663, 19 ff. The story in Nu. 11:16 f., 24-26 may also be cited in this connection. The charisma of Moses is so incomparable that even a part of the רוּחַ resting upon him is enough to bring 70 men to הִתְנַבֵּא, v. 25 f. Another version finds in Moses the נָבִיא beyond compare with whom Yahweh deals פָּנִים אֶל־פָּנִים, Dt. 34:10. [153] It is expressly stated that no similar נָבִיא would arise though Joshua received the רוּחַ from Moses by laying on of hands. Hence the singularity of Moses is stressed here even though נָבִיא is used. In Dt. 18:15-19 Moses is regarded as the beginning of a נָבִיא-series. Yahweh will continually send a נָבִיא like Moses [154] who shall declare His will to the people. [155] The thought here is that of an established institution which is in some way institutionally connected by succession. The appearance of a נָבִיא is not viewed as a contingent and incalculable event but as

---

151 Cf. A. Wendel, *Das Opfer in d. altisraelitischen Religion* (1927), 10 f.

152 On this whole question cf. Rowley Ritual, *passim*.

153 It is uncertain to what source this belongs.

154 Acc. to the current view יָקִים in Dt. 18:15 or אָקִים in v. 18 is to be taken distributively : Yahweh will always raise up a נָבִיא.

155 Cf. on this v. Rad, 112 f.

something which can be counted on. Hence the task of this נָבִיא is not like that of prophets who shake up the people. His function is one of preservation. He is to keep the people in constant touch with the will of Yahweh so that it should not resort to pagan manticism, vv. 9-14. He is also to safeguard it against immediate exposure to the searing presence of Yahweh. There is a reference here to the events at Horeb where Moses was appointed a mediator to the same end. In the framework of Dt. this office is understood in terms of the Law, whose keeper, mediator, and authoritative interpreter this נָבִיא is to be. [156]

Finally the title נְבִיאָה in accorded in Ju. 4:4 to Deborah, who is also called a judge (שֹׁפְטָה). The tradition tells us that at the command of Yahweh she had Barak raise the levy, v. 6 f.

4. נָבִיא in the Prophetic Books.

a. נָבִיא can on occasion be used for the writing prophets. [157] In the older prophetic books this use is rare, though it increases later. Amos rejects the title, 7:14. [158] Hosea, however, uses it of himself in 9:7 f. [159] It is not used in this sense in Is., though 8:3 refers to the נְבִיאָה, obviously Isaiah's wife. [160] Jeremiah is called to be a נָבִיא לַגּוֹיִם 1:5. In the narrative sections (the Baruch narrative) he is always called a נָבִיא. [161] Ezekiel is emphatically called a נָבִיא in the vision at his calling (2:5) and then indirectly in 14:4. In Habakkuk, Haggai and Zechariah the term occurs both in the titles and then in the books themselves, Hab. 1:1; 3:1; Hag. 1:1, 3, 12; 2:1, 10; Zech. 1:1, 7, cf. also 8:9. It is thus clear that after the days of Jer. נָבִיא was used quite freely for the writing prophets. [162] The instances in Hos. and Is. also show that no difficulty was felt in relation to the term. Even Amos' refusal to be called a נָבִיא is not a refusal in principle, as the use of the verb in 7:15 shows. [163]

b. נָבִיא is used positively for others, mostly in the plural and with a past reference.

So first Hos.: [164] Yahweh "hews" through the נְבִיאִים (6:5); [165] He has spoken to them (12:11); through a נָבִיא. He led Israel out of Egypt and protected it (12:14). In

---

[156] Kraus, op. cit. (→ n. 105), 59-66 sees in Dt. 18:15 ff. an instance of the office of mediator of the covenant. The idea of a continuous series of נְבִיאִים occurs in Hos. (6:5; 12:11) → 804, 28 ff.

[157] The expression "writing prophets" is misleading since the sayings collected in the prophetic books undoubtedly derive in the main from oral proclamation and only later did the prophets or others assemble them. The term is retained here only to differentiate them from the "other" prophets.

[158] The traditional understanding of Am. 7:14 : "I am no נָבִיא," is to be kept, cf. E. Baumann, "Eine Einzelheit," ZAW, 64 (1952), 62.

[159] Though cf. E. Sellin, Das Zwölfprophetenbuch, Komm. z. AT, 12 [2, 3] (1929), ad loc.

[160] O. Procksch, Jesaia, I, Komm. z. AT, 9 (1930), ad loc.: "so that in this way he expressly acknowledges that he himself is a נָבִיא."

[161] As a rule, however, the LXX does not use the term.

[162] The statement of Jepsen, 141 that "here for the first time nabi is not a professional term but is used generally for 'God's spokesman'" rests on the petitio principii that נָבִיא is normally a fixed title of office and that the writing prophets are not among those who hold this office.

[163] There is no methodological justification for Jepsen's (6) express distinction between the use of the verb and "nabism."

[164] Am. 2:11 f.; 3:7 seem to be secondary.

[165] The meaning of the v. is contested. Many expositors emend it, while Sellin, op. cit. (→ n. 159), ad loc. transl. "Hence I have hewed among the prophets"; but cf. H. W. Wolff,

Jer. there is a positive evaluation of the נְבִיאִים in 5:13 f.: because the people despised them, Yahweh will make His words a fire on the lips of Jer. [166] In 28:8 Jer. is seen in a series with the נְבִיאִים before him מִן־הָעוֹלָם. In the parts of Jer. in Deuteronomistic style we often find the expression that Yahweh sent His servants the נְבִיאִים to warn Israel, 7:25; 25:4; 26:5; 29:19; 35:15; 44:4. Acc. to Ez. 38:17 Yahweh's servants the נְבִיאֵי יִשְׂרָאֵל intimated the coming of Gog and Magog. In the secondary parts of Amos the raising up of נְבִיאִים and נְזִרִים is called the gift of Yahweh and hampering them in the discharge of their office is censured, 2:11 f. Acc. to 3:7 Yahweh does nothing without making it known to His servants the נְבִיאִים. Zech. speaks of the נְבִיאִים רִאשׁוֹנִים who summoned the fathers to repentance and he calls them Yahweh's servants, 1:4-6; 7:7, 12. Mal. 3:23 expects the return of the נָבִיא Elijah. In the older period, then, a favourable ref. to other נְבִיאִים is found only in Hos., [167] and it becomes common only from Jer. on.

c. Most of what is said about the נְבִיאִים in the prophetic books is polemical, → III, 575, 1 ff.

It is true that this use is found only in one part. The first indication [168] of it is in Hos. 4:5, where a word of judgment on the priest is extended to cover the נָבִיא too. [169] In Is. the נָבִיא is mentioned among others in several judgment sayings, 3:1-3; 9:13 f.; 28:7 ff.; 29:10. Here concrete charges are made: the נָבִיא is מוֹרֶה־שֶׁקֶר (9:14); he is a drunkard and he scoffs at the hard sayings of the messengers of Yahweh, 28:7 ff. Micah attacks the נְבִיאִים who mislead the people by making various predictions for money, 3:5-7. The attack is most explicit in Jer. The most common charge is that they prophesy שֶׁקֶר, 5:31; 6:13; 8:10; 14:13 f.; 23:14, 25 f., 32; 27:9 f., 14-16; 29:8 f. They speak in the name of Yahweh even though He has not sent them, 14:14 f.; 23:21, 32; 27:15; 28:15; 29:9, 31. [170] Their words come from their own hearts, 14:14; 23:16, 26. They are dreams, 23:25, 27, 32; 29:8. His concrete reproach is that they proclaim שָׁלוֹם with no authority from Yahweh (6:13 f.; 8:10 f.; 14:13; 28:9), predicting success in the war or a speedy end to exile (14:13; 27:9, 14, 16; 29:8-10) when he himself proclaims the very opposite. Charges of adultery and other sins are also made, 23:14; 29:23. For this reason the judgment of Yahweh will smite them, 14:15; 23:15, 30-32; 28:16; 29:21 f. In intimations of judgment, however, the נְבִיאִים are more frequently mentioned along with others: the priests in 6:13; 8:10; 14:18; 23:11; priests and people in 23:33 f.; 26:7 f.; kings (princes), priests and נְבִיאִים in 2:26; 4:9; 8:1; 13:13. The only instance in Zeph. accuses a similar list of leaders (princes, judges, נְבִיאִים, priests) of perverting their office, 3:3 f. Finally, Ez. too attacks the נְבִיאִים. His charges are similar to those of Jer.: They prophesy out of their own heart and their own רוּחַ, 13:2 f., cf. v. 17; they speak vanity (שָׁוְא) and falsehood, 13:6-9; they say נְאֻם־יְהוָה even though Yahweh has not sent them, 13:6 f.; they falsely proclaim שָׁלוֹם (13:10, 16) and thus "whitewash" the true situation

---

Dodekapropheton, Bibl. Komm. AT, 14 (1957), ad loc.; also "Hoseas geistige Heimat," ThLZ, 81 (1956), 83-94.

[166] Cf. the charge of slaying the נְבִיאִים, 2:30.

[167] Cf. Wolff, "Hoseas geistige Heimat," passim.

[168] There is no polemic in the refusal of the title by Amos, cf. Würthwein, Amos-Studien, 22 f.

[169] Acc. to Sellin, op. cit. (→ n. 159), ad loc. the priest is Aaron and the נָבִיא Moses, cf. Ex. 32; Wolff, Dodekapropheton, ad loc. regards v. 5a β as a Jewish gloss.

[170] Only in relation to the early period is it said that they prophesied בַּבַּעַל (2:8), elsewhere stated only of the נְבִיאִים of Samaria, 23:13.

of the people, 13:10-15; 22:28. [171] For this reason judgment is declared against them (13:8 f., 11-16), and it will also smite the נָבִיא who gives a דָּבָר to a worshipper of idols, 14:9 f. In post-exilic prophecy the only negative assessment of נְבִיאִים is to be found in the radical repudiation in Zech. 13:2-6 → 799, 12 ff.

d. It is thus evident that the writing prophets from Isaiah to Ezekiel found themselves confronted by a majority of נְבִיאִים whose work they attacked. In answer to the question whether the נְבִיאִים against whom they thus inveighed occupied an official prophetic position one might begin by noting the common mention of prophets and priests, as is often done. [172] Nevertheless, most of the passages quoted in this connection do not prove that the נְבִיאִים were connected with the cultus.

It is natural that the prophet who proclaims the will of Yahweh and the priest who serves the sanctuary should be mentioned together. The decisive point, however, is that the prophet and priest are often referred to only along with other national leaders, cf. the series בָּבִיא, כֹּהֵן, שַׂר, מֶלֶךְ in Jer. 2:26; 4:9; 8:1; 13:13 without שַׂר; cf. also 18:18 נָבִיא, שַׂר, כֹּהֵן, [173] נָשִׂיא; נָבִיא, חָכָם, כֹּהֵן in Ez. 22:25-28. These passages show that the נָבִיא is simply one of the honoured leaders of the nation. Note should also be taken of passages in which the נָבִיא is mentioned with other officials but not the priest, e.g., Is. 3:2; 9:14; 29:10; [174] Jer. 27:9. Hence relationship to the priesthood is not an outstanding characteristic of the נָבִיא. The connection with the priests and the temple is plainer in Jer. 26, cf. also 23:11. But even here the simple equation נָבִיא = cultic prophet is hardly in keeping. The extent of the cultic connection is still open. That the נְבִיאִים discharged certain functions in the cultus is shown by the passages just mentioned, e.g., Jer. 29:26 f., where a priest is called "an overseer in the house of Yahweh over every מִתְנַבֵּא." [175] But what these functions were [176] and how close was the connection with the temple is not explained. It is very difficult to reach solid conclusions in this matter and great caution must be exercised. Nor is there any answer to the question of the institutional union of נְבִיאִים. Nothing forces us to assume that there is a prophetic profession in the full and exclusive sense. There is always the possibility of a free and charismatic prophecy even apart from the writing prophets. Thus there is nothing about the best-known opponent of Jer., namely Hananiah of Gibeon (Jer. 28), to suggest that he was the member of a definite profession.

e. This raises the further question: What was the relation of the writing prophets to the נְבִיאִים (→ II, 455, 5 ff.)? The use of נָבִיא (→ 804, 13 ff.) and the niphal form of the verb (→ 798, 13 ff.) have shown already that there can be no question of rigid distinction. [177] This is brought out even more clearly by the nature of the conflict, especially in Jer. Jer.'s opponents speak as he does בְּשֵׁם יהוה and they use the expression כֹּה אָמַר יהוה etc. There is obviously no distinction as regards presentation. The conflict is entirely about content. A passage like Jer. 14:13 f. shows that for Jer. himself the question of correct proclamation was a

---

[171] At 22:35 one should read אֲשֶׁר נְשִׂיאֶיהָ with the LXX.

[172] Cf. Mowinckel, *Psalmenstudien,* 17.

[173] Cf. BH³.

[174] 29:10 is textually uncertain.

[175] On the text cf. BH³. It is hardly true that "this says expressly that Jer. belonged to an organised corporation of temple prophets" (Würthwein, *Amos-Studien,* 15).

[176] Possibly one may think here of the prophetic office of intercession, cf. v. Rad, 114 f.

[177] So Jepsen, *passim.*

real problem. In the battle with Hananiah, in which one word from Yahweh confronted another, Jer. was obviously worsted in the first instance. He had to yield before his opponent's sense of mission until he himself received a new word from Yahweh, Jer. 28. [178] In the last resort what distinguishes Jer. from his adversary here is his different understanding of the judicial activity of Yahweh. He sees the will of Yahweh in the approaching debacle, while his antagonist clings to a message of salvation such as Isaiah had proclaimed a hundred years before. [179] This brings to light the peculiar and imponderable element in the writing prophets. They come with a message which claims the authority of a word of Yahweh even though it may sometimes conflict with the total tradition of faith in Israel. [180] Jer. has to proclaim his word without backing, while his opponent can appeal to tradition. A strong institutional connection may lie behind this appeal. But one cannot deduce therefrom the schema that the professional nabi is a prophet of salvation while the free prophet of Yahweh is a prophet of disaster. This is proved by the proclamation of Is. in the war between Syria and Ephraim (Is. 7:1-16), for here the writing prophet sides with tradition. [181] We also find other salvation sayings in the writing prophets whose authenticity there is no obvious reason to contest. [182] On the other hand Mi. 3:5 shows that the proclamation of catastrophe is possible among the נְבִיאִים too.

The problem of the relation between the writing prophets and the נְבִיאִים whom they opposed finds no solution, then, either in complete separation or in full integration. The writing prophets seem to be less institutionally committed but they were not completely isolated. In form and content their proclamation shows close relationship to that of the נְבִיאִים and yet at decisive points it is different. Their distinctiveness lies ultimately in the non-rational sphere of reception of the Word of Yahweh. This brings them into conflict with the popular view and thus establishes their unique position.

5. The True Prophet and the False Prophet in Deuteronomy.

Dt., too, discusses the question of the true prophet and the false prophet. Dt. 13:2-6 deals with the case of a נָבִיא who summons to the worship of other gods. He is to be regarded as an enemy of Yahweh and put to death. In 18:20 the threat of death is also suspended over the נָבִיא who speaks in Yahweh's name without any commission from Yahweh. The criterion is whether what he prophesies comes to pass or not, v. 22. This applies to any נָבִיא, but especially to the one whose message disturbs the people. The difference from Jer. 28:8 f. is obvious. There Jer. demands subsequent validation by fulfilment only from the prophet who proclaims salvation, whereas the prophet of calamity does not have to prove the correctness of his preaching.

---

[178] Cf. esp. Quell, 43-67.

[179] Cf. v. Rad, 119 f.

[180] Acc. to Würthwein Ursprung the declaration of judgment is a function of the cultic prophet, but → n. 200.

[181] Cf. v. Rad, op. cit. (→ n. 132), 56-58.

[182] Hence a false methodological presupposition lies behind the attempt of H. Bardtke, "Jer. d. Fremdvölkerprophet," ZAW, 53 (1935), 209-239; 54 (1936), 240-282 and Würthwein, Amos-Studien, 35-40, to divide up the work of Jer. or Amos into two periods acc. to the criterion of prophecy of salvation or destruction.

6. נָבִיא in the Other Works.

In the Ps. the title of 51 and 105:15 use נָבִיא for men of the older tradition (Nathan, Abraham). 74:9 complains that there is no longer any נָבִיא, i.e., acc. to the par. a man who knows how long the affliction will last, → 813, 35 ff. In Lam. 2 the depiction of the situation mentions נְבִיאִים along with the kings and princes; they now no longer receive any חָזוֹן (2:9) and in the description of the overthrow it is emphasised that priest and נָבִיא are slain in the sanctuary, 2:20. 2:14 accuses the נְבִיאִים of having seen vanity (שָׁוְא), whitewash and deception instead of bringing to light the guilt of Jerusalem, cf. also 4:13. Da. 9 refers in retrospect to the נְבִיאִים. In v. 6, 10 they are God's servants who gave warning; v. 2 speaks of Jer., through whom Yahweh revealed the no. of 70 yrs. which has now been "sealed," i.e., repealed by fulfilment, v. 24. The Chronicler is fond of the word נָבִיא. Along with some borrowing from his sources (1 Ch. 16:22; 17:1; [183] 2 Ch. 18; 32:20; 34:22) he has a wealth of instances. He often refers to the נְבִיאִים in general as those who are sent by Yahweh to warn, 2 Ch. 20:20; 36:16; Ezr. 9:11; Neh. 9:26, 30. Or else he speaks of individuals who proclaim the will of Yahweh in specific situations, 2 Ch. 12:5; 15:1-7, cf. 8; 21:12; 24:20; 25:15 f.; 28:9, cf. 36:12. He also adds to quotations from his sources ref. to the writings of various נְבִיאִים, 1 Ch. 29:29; 2 Ch. 9:29; 12:15; 13:22; 26:22; 32:32. Acc. to 2 Ch. 29:25 the music of the temple was set up by Yahweh through His נְבִיאִים. In the prayer of Neh. 9 the נְבִיאִים are mentioned along with the kings, princes, priests, fathers and the whole people, v. 32. In Ezr. 5:1 f.; 6:14 Hag. and Zech. are called נָבִיא. Acc. to Neh. 6:7, 14 there are נְבִיאִים who act on the instructions of political groups. The word נָבִיא occurs a few times in the Heb. text of Sir. [184] In 36:20 f. prayer is made to Yahweh: ‏והקם חזון דבר בשמך...ונביאיך יאמינו‎, "fulfil the prophecies which have been spoken in thy name ..., that thy prophets may be shown to be trustworthy." Elijah is called נָבִיא כְּאֵשׁ, "a prophet like fire" (48:1) and of Jer. it is said: ‏והוא מרחם נוצר נביא‎, "and he was made a prophet from his mother's womb" (49:6 f.). [185] In 44:3 נבואה is mentioned among the qualities of the fathers whom the hymn extols.

In non-bibl. Heb. the word occurs in the Lachish ostraca (588 B.C.). [186] The only certain instance, however, is in III, 20. [187] This refers to a letter which has come מאת הנבא. But acc. to the context the prophet cannot be the writer; he can only be the courier, since ספר טביהו in line 19 mentions another author. The statement in VI, 6 f. [188] that there are people who "make slack the hands of the land and the city" reminds us of the charge against Jer. (Jer. 38:4), though the prophet is not referred to here. [189]

---

[183] 17:1 = 2 S. 7:2.

[184] Text acc. to R. Smend, *Die Weisheit des Jesus Sirach* (1906).

[185] In 48:13 one should perhaps read נבא for נברא with the LXX; it is said of Elisha and refers to the raising of the dead by his corpse 2 K. 13:20 f., so that the meaning is "to work miracles."

[186] Ed. H. Torczyner etc., *Lachish*, I (tell ed duweir), *The Lachish Letters* (1938); cf. J. Hempel, "Die Ostraka v. Lakiš," ZAW, 56 (1938), 126-139; K. Galling, *Textbuch z. Gesch. Israels* (1950), 63-65.

[187] In Galling, *op. cit.*, No. 36; cf. D. W. Thomas, *"The Prophet" in the Lachish Ostraca* (1945), also "Again 'The Prophet' in the Lachish Ostraca," *Von Ugarit nach Qumran, Festschr. O. Eissfeldt*, Beih. ZAW, 77 (1958), 244-249.

[188] Galling, *op. cit.*, No. 39.

[189] In line 5 one cannot supply (הנבא) cf. Thomas, *op. cit.* (→ n. 187), 7 f.

All in all one gets the clear impression that prophecy did not play so large a role in the centuries after the exile, since it is almost always mentioned in retrospect. [190] The נְבִיאִים are now primarily the writing prophets.

IV. Other Terms for the Prophet.

1. אִישׁ (הָ)אֱלֹהִים. This is commonly used in contexts in which it has the same meaning as נָבִיא particularly when an אִישׁ אֱלֹהִים comes with a specific word from Yahweh, 1 S. 2:27 ff.; 1 K. 12:22; 13:1 ff.; 20:28, cf. → n. 137.

In the Elisha stories the terms alternate in the different strata. [191] Here Elisha is often differentiated as אִישׁ אֱלֹהִים from the circle of the בְּנֵי הַנְּבִיאִים, 2 K. 4:38 ff., 42 ff.; 6:1 ff. etc. The title thus seems to be regarded as a mark of special honour. Samuel and Elijah are also called this by others (1 S. 9:6-10; 1 K. 17:18, 24; 2 K. 1:9-13), but never by the narrator. A title again seems to be in view, and this explanation is supported by the use of the term for the (as yet unidentified) מַלְאָךְ in Ju. 13:6, 8 and for Moses in Dt. 33:1; Jos. 14:6; Ps. 90:1. Only in 1 K. 13 (cf. 2 K. 23:16-18) is there any discernible distinction between the two terms: the אִישׁ אֱלֹהִים of Judah who utters a threat against the altar at Bethel (vv. 1 ff.) is contrasted with the נָבִיא of Bethel. The latter says: גַּם־אֲנִי נָבִיא כָּמוֹךָ, "I am also a prophet as thou art," and thus equates the terms. One might be inclined to regard אִישׁ אֱלֹהִים as the title in Judah and נָבִיא as that in Northern Israel, but 1 K. 13 and 2 K. 23:16-18 are undoubtedly late [192] and the other instances do not support this distinction. It is not clear who is the אִישׁ אֱלֹהִים whose sons have a special chamber in the temple acc. to Jer. 35:4. The Chronicler not only borrows from 1 K. 12:22 (2 Ch. 11:2), but also uses the title for Moses (1 Ch. 23:14; Ezr. 3:2) and for David (2 Ch. 8:14; Neh. 12:24, 36) and introduces an anonymous אִישׁ אֱלֹהִים after the manner of a נָבִיא (2 Ch. 25:7, 9).

2. רֹאֶה. This is used for Samuel in 1 S. 9 (v. 9, 11, 18, 19). In v. 9 the narrator explains that it is an older expression for נָבִיא. There is no reason to question this, though one can hardly reconstruct an older office of the רֹאֶה on the basis of the note. The Chronicler also uses the word for Samuel (1 Ch. 9:22; 26:28; 29:29) and on one occasion he has it independently, 2 Ch. 16:7, 10. In Is. 30:10 it is a question whether the participle should be taken as a title or construed verbally.

3. חֹזֶה. This term often occurs as a title (→ V, 329, 13 ff.): first in 2 S. 24:11 for Gad, who is called חֹזֶה דָוִד as well as הַנָּבִיא obviously to denote his position at court; [193] then in the speech of Amaziah to Amos (Am. 7:12), where Amos himself takes it to be equivalent to נָבִיא, v. 14.

The other instances shed little light, esp. as the question always arises whether the part. q must be understood as a title (Is. 29:10; 30:10; Mi. 3:7; also Is. 47:13 of the astrologists of Babylon). [194] The Chronicler at 1 Ch. 21:9 takes the title from 2 S. 24:11

---

[190] Zech. 13:2-6 seems to show knowledge of ecstatic prophecy, → 813, 12 ff.

[191] Cf. Jepsen, 72-83.

[192] Acc. to Noth, op. cit. (→ n. 129), 81 they are a local tradition from the time of Josiah, while acc. to A. Jepsen, Die Quellen des Königsbuches (1953) they come from a "levitical redaction" at the end of the 6th cent.

[193] Jepsen's conjecture that the term was first introduced by Chronicles (Jepsen, 43, 95) is not very plausible. It is more likely that Chronicles adopted and extended an earlier usage.

[194] כָּל־חֹזֶה is probably an addition in 2 K. 17:13 (cf. → n. 146); Is. 28:15 is obscure.

for Gad (leaving out נָבִיא). He also uses it for Gad in 1 Ch. 29:29; 2 Ch. 29:25 and
then for others in 1 Ch. 25:5; 2 Ch. 9:29; 12:15; 19:2; 29:30; 33:18, 19; 35:15. The title
is often brought into connection here with the music of the temple, 1 Ch. 25:5; 2 Ch.
29:25, 30; 35:15. Perhaps there was a special office of the חֹזֶה, but it is no longer possible
to disentangle any details about this from the examples.

The fact that the terms רֹאֶה and חֹזֶה occurs in the tradition as well as נָבִיא
shows that in Israel prophecy was adopted in different forms from without.

V. Form and Content of Prophetic Proclamation.

The decisive feature in OT prophecy is the דָּבָר, the word (→ IV, 94 ff.). The
prophet has to pass on the דְּבַר יהוה which he receives. Jer. at his call becomes
certain that Yahweh has set His words on his lips, 1:9; cf. Ez. 3:1 ff. Yet He
does not have Yahweh's word at his disposal; he has to wait until it is given him,
cf. Jer. 28:11, 12. When he does, however, he has to speak it, Jer. 1:17; cf. Am. 3:8.
The judgment of Yahweh will fall on those who hinder him, Jer. 5:13 f.; cf.
Am. 7:16 f. The formal expression וַיְהִי דְבַר יהוה אֶל is often used to express the
receiving of the word of Yahweh, e.g., 2 S. 7:4; cf. 24:11. But above all the prophets use the formula כֹּה אָמַר יהוה to introduce their sayings. This is already
found in the tradition in relation to Moses (Ex. 4:22 etc.) and in the case of
Samuel it occurs in Deuteronomistic sections, 1 S. 10:18; 15:2. It comes into
general use from the time of Nathan (2 S. 7:5, 8; 12:7, 11) and Gad (2 S. 24:12). Its
distribution in the prophetic books varies greatly. It is most common in Jer. and
Ez., but does not occur in Hos., Jl., Jon., Hab. or Zeph. The formula is originally
used to denote a messenger (Gn. 32:5), so that it can be called a message-formula.
The prophet regards himself as a messenger of Yahweh, whose word he has to
pass on.

As in the case of the message (Gn. 32:5 f.; 45:9 ff.; 1 K. 20:3, 5 etc.) the content
of the word which is to be transmitted is mostly in the 1st person of the one who
gives the commission. In the prophets, then, it is formulated as a saying of Yahweh.
It often begins with הִנְנִי and following part., 2 S. 12:11; 1 K. 11:31; Am. 6:14 etc.
This shows that the saying of Yahweh is usually about an imminent action of
Yahweh. This action may mean salvation or destruction; hence the saying of
Yahweh is either promise or threat. The content of the word of promise may be
events in the immediate historical future (e.g., 1 K. 11:31; 20:13, 28; 2 K. 20:5 f.)
or more distant events (e.g., 2 S. 7:8 ff.). In the writing prophets the promises are
above all eschatological expectations in the broadest sense. Here we often find
introductory formulae like וְהָיָה בַּיּוֹם הַהוּא, הִנֵּה יָמִים בָּאִים, בַּיָּמִים הָהֵמָּה, בָּעֵת הַהִיא etc., → II,
943 ff. Messianic predictions (Jer. 11:1 ff.; Mi. 5:1 ff. → χριστός) should be men-
tioned in this connection. They have their root in the prophecy of Nathan in
2 S. 7. Threats, however, easily predominate. These are mostly against the people
as a whole, more rarely individuals, especially the king (e.g., 2 S. 12:7 ff.; 1 K.
20:42), or the priest and prophet (Am. 7:17; Jer. 28:16). The intimated calamity
is described in the most varied ways. In particular it takes the form of war,
devastation, exile, or such natural disasters as drought, poor crops, earthquake,
plague etc. To some degree one may see here connections with historical events
in which the prophets see the work of Yahweh; in other cases, e.g., in Amos,
a prophecy of disaster is proclaimed in a period of external peace and prosperity.

The prophets, however, do not merely pass on the word which they have
received from Yahweh. They are not involuntary instruments. They themselves are

responsible for the correct delivery of their message. They are appointed by Yahweh to be "examiners," Jer. 6:27. This finds expression especially in the fact that they often give a reason for the word of Yahweh. [195] The threat in particular is almost always provided with an explanation in which those addressed are shown their sin. This explanation is a word of accusation or rebuke. There is usually a very close connection between it and the calamity proclaimed. This connection is one of deed and consequence ; one is not to think in terms of "retribution." [196] The starting-point of the rebuke varies and is strongly influenced by the situation. In Amos and Micah the charge is predominantly that of disregarding what is right in God's eyes ; [197] in Hosea, Jeremiah and Ezekiel it is that of worshipping other gods ; in Isaiah it is that of false confidence in other powers. In most of the prophets there is also a sharp attack on the cultus. This cannot be regarded as a basic rejection of the cultus. In Hosea the evident charge is that the cultus is not really that of Yahweh but that of Baalim. In the main, however, the fault castigated by the prophets is that of false trust in the security supposedly found in the cultus. [198]

The responsible aspect of the prophets also finds expression in the fact that they do not just proclaim ineluctable judgment but also warn and admonish in order that judgment may be averted. Thus the word of admonition is one of the forms of prophetic address, e.g., Hos. 14:2; Am. 5:4 ff. In Ezekiel (3:17 etc.) the prophet is regarded as a watchman who has to warn the people entrusted to him in good time. Prophetic intercession may also be mentioned in this connection, Is. 37:1 ff.; Jer. 7:16 etc.; Am. 7:2, 5, cf. also Gn. 20:7; Ex. 32:31 f. etc. Possibly a cultic function of the נָבִיא may be discerned here, cf. Jer. 27:18. [199]

The specifically prophetic forms mentioned display great variety and may always be attributed to a secular situation or explained by the need to pass on the word of Yahweh in a way which is relevant. Hence one can hardly suppose that their original setting is a firmly rooted institutional prophetic office. The same point is brought out even more clearly by the fact that the prophets take many forms from other spheres of life : the disputation (e.g., Am. 3:3-6, 8; common in Dt. Is.), and the related forms of judgment (Is. 3:13 f.; Hos. 4:1 ff.), [200] Torah pronouncements, and other sacral formulations (Ez. 14:1 ff.; Am. 5:21 ff.). In Dt. Is. the cultic salvation oracle and elements of hymns are used on a very broad basis. [201] Songs of various kinds are also found, Is. 5:1 ff.; Am. 5:1 ff.

Along with the receiving of the word visions (→ V, 329, 27 ff.) are frequently mentioned, 1 K. 22:17 ff.; Jer. 1:11 ff. etc.; Ez. passim ; Am. 7:1 ff.; Zech. 1-6, cf. the visions at the calling of Is. (6:1 ff.), Jer. (1:4 ff.) and Ez. (1-3). Since these mostly

---

[195] Cf. H. W. Wolff, "Die Begründungen der prophetischen Heils- u. Unheilssprüche," ZAW, 52 (1934), 1-22.

[196] Cf. K. Koch, "Gibt es ein Vergeltungsdogma im AT ?" ZThK, 52 (1955), 1-42.

[197] Cf. Würthwein, Amos-Studien, 40-52; R. Bach, "Gottesrecht u. weltliches Recht in d. Verkündigung des Propheten Am.," Festschr. f. Günther Dehn (1957), 23-34.

[198] Cf. R. Rendtorff, "Priesterliche Kulttheologie u. prophetische Kultpolemik," ThLZ, 81 (1956), 339-342.

[199] v. Rad, 114 f.

[200] The attempt in Würthwein Ursprung to derive the "judgment" from the cultus is not very convincing ; understanding in terms of secular litigation is far more likely.

[201] H. E. v. Waldow, Anlass u. Hintergrund d. Verkündigung d. Deuterojesaja, Diss. Bonn (1953).

culminate in a word of Yahweh one has to take into account the possibility that the prophets commonly received the word of Yahweh within a vision.

Symbolic acts are a special aspect of prophecy, [202] 1 K. 11:29 ff.; 22:11; Is. 20:1 ff. etc. In them the prophet himself is completely drawn into his proclamation. Sometimes his personal life may be deeply affected, Jer. 16:1 ff.; Ez. 24:15 ff.; Hos. 1 and 3. Thus the prophet himself becomes a sign, Is. 8:18; 20:3. Personal involvement may finally take the form of martyrdom, Jer. 37 f. Thus Dt. finds in the prophet Moses (cf. 18:15, 18) one who suffers vicariously, 9:18 ff.; cf. 1:37; 4:21 f. [203] The picture of the Suffering Servant in Dt. Is. is related to this tradition, → V, 666 ff.

VI. The Usage of the Septuagint. [204]

1. In the LXX נָבִיא is always transl. προφήτης; there is not a single instance of any other word. The tradition vacillates only in so far as the LXX does not transl. נָבִיא in some passages or adds προφήτης in others. In Ch. the part. ὁ βλέπων (1 Ch. 9:22; 29:29) and ὁ ὁρῶν (1 Ch. 21:9; 2 Ch. 9:29; 12:15; 29:25; 33:18, 19; also ὁ ἀνακρουόμενος in 1 Ch. 25:5) may sometimes be used for רֹאֶה and חֹזֶה, but in several instances these are rendered προφήτης (רֹאֶה 1 Ch. 26:28; 2 Ch. 16:7, 10; cf. also Is. 30:10; חֹזֶה 2 Ch. 19:2; 29:30; 35:15). In 2 Ch. 36:15 מַלְאָךְ is transl. προφήτης. 2. προφῆτις is always used for the fem. נְבִיאָה. 3. προφητεία is mostly the rendering of the late noun נְבוּאָה, Neh. 6:12; Ezr. 6:14; 2 Ch. 9:29; 15:8. 4. The verb forms in the ni and hitp are rendered indiscriminately by προφητεύειν; only in 1 Ch. 25:1-3, where the ni denotes the work of the temple musicians, is ἀποφθέγγεσθαι (v. 1) or ἀνακρούεσθαι (v. 3) used for it. [205] Thus the LXX transl. follows the HT mechanically without attempting to reproduce the great distinctions in the original. 5. Only at one point is there an attempt at distinction. In Jer., esp. c. 26-29 (LXX 33-36), ψευδοπροφήτης is used for נָבִיא when the ref. is to the prophets who oppose Jer. (LXX 6:13; 33:7, 8, 11, 16; 34:9; 35:1; 36:1, 8; also Zech. 13:2). But this distinction is not made consistently, cf., e.g., 23:9 ff.

Rendtorff

C. Prophecy and Prophets in the Judaism of the Hellenistic-Roman Period.

I. The Problem of Contemporary Prophecy.

1. Non-Rabbinic Witness.

a. The most comprehensive post-exilic statement about contemporary prophecy is in the sayings in Zech. 13:2 f., 4 ff. (400-200 B.C. ?). [206] The first saying in 13:2 f. equates idols, [207] prophets and the spirit of uncleanness [208] and expects their extermination. It seems to be directed against the prophecy then current in Israel, [209] though its introduction as a saying of Yahweh Zebaot shows that

---

[202] Cf. G. Fohrer, "Die symbolischen Handlungen d. Propheten," Abh. ThANT, 25 (1953).
[203] Cf. G. v. Rad, Theol. d. AT, I (1957), 292 f.
[204] On this whole subject cf. Fascher, 102-108.
[205] In v. 2 the HT הַנִּבָּא is transl. ὁ προφήτης.
[206] Cf. T. H. Robinson-F. Horst, Die zwölf kleinen Proph., Hndbch. AT, 14 (1938), ad loc.; K. Elliger, Das Buch d. zwölf kleinen Proph., II, AT Deutsch, 25 (1950), ad loc.
[207] שְׁמוֹת הָ עֲצַבִּים in very loose allusion to Hos. 2:19 : שְׁמוֹת הַבְּעָלִים.
[208] רוּחַ הַטֻּמְאָה; cf. → n. 266.
[209] Hence Bousset-Gressm., 394 : "The author . . . is so convinced that there is no longer any prophet in Israel that he orders (sic !) that anyone who comes forth as a prophet

Zechariah himself claims to be a prophet. It is logical, then, that the LXX should describe those who are to be smitten by calamity as "false prophets." [210] The second saying in 13:4 ff. is not expressly stated to be a saying of Yahweh but the structure suggests this. Both formally and materially the two sayings are very closely related. They do not refer to the immediate future but to "that day" (→ II, 945, 34 ff.) when the age of salvation will dawn for Jerusalem. Only then will those who have come forth as prophets be pierced through by their parents because they have spoken lies in the name of Yahweh. [211] At the same time, according to the second saying, the prophets themselves will be ashamed of their vision and prophecy and will lay aside their hairy mantles. If anyone is found to be a prophet he will deny his calling and say that he has been a husbandman from his youth up. [212] Zech. 13:2 f., 4 ff. is directed against a contemporary ecstatic Yahweh prophecy whose proponents wear the prophetic cloak as a guild-sign and in their native dervish style reject all others in Israel as illegitimate, since their line goes back through Elijah to the days of Saul (→ 797, 8 ff.). This ecstaticism which Zech. so bitterly opposed found a descendant in NT days in Jesus ben Ananias, who emerged as a prophet of disaster a few years before the destruction of the temple, → 825, 6 ff.

The wilder side of post-exilic prophecy is not the only one to be deduced from Zech. 13:2-6. Its opposite is also to be found there. The reference to Dt. 13:5 f.; 18:20 (→ n. 211) and the distinctive use of Am. 7:14 (→ n. 212) give evidence of either an oracle-giving priesthood or a cultic prophecy anchored in the traditions of the temple and the post-exilic understanding of the Law. This circle, which naturally found in free ecstaticism a spirit of disorder and rebellion, [213] had predecessors in the pre-exilic period. In the Persian epoch — apart from the anonymous authors of sayings which have been incorporated into the canonical prophets [214] — the leading representatives of this group were Haggai, Zechariah and the anonymous Malachi, though the period which followed also had a prophetic priesthood or cultic prophets connected with the sanctuary or the sacred writings.

Thus in Zech. 13:2-6 we find two opposing prophetic groups who illustrate very plainly the difficult antithesis of true and false prophecy which had always been a problem for prophecy in Israel, → 805, 14 ff. Zech. 13:2-6 can hardly be invoked as a witness, however, either to the absence of the prophetic spirit or to the illegitimacy of the prophecy which arose in post-exilic Israel.

b. Ps. 74:9 is constantly referred to as another proof of the supposed drying up of prophecy: "We have not seen signs for us. No more prophet was there.

---

should be treated as a deceiver"; this completely overlooks the eschatological orientation of Zech. 13:2-6.

[210] LXX καὶ τοὺς ψευδοπροφήτας ... ἐξαρῶ, an obvious interpretation of the Heb. original.

[211] Zech. 13:3 with very free ref. to Dt. 13:5 f.; 18:20, though cf. Elliger, op. cit. (→ n. 206), ad loc. and Horst, op. cit. (→ n. 206), ad loc.

[212] Acc. to the conjecture of J. Wellhausen, Skizzen u. Vorarbeiten, V (1892), 192, ad loc.: אֲדָמָה קִנְיָנִי for Mas. אָדָם הִקְנַנִי (cf. BH³ on Zech. 13:5) with allusion to and re-interpreting Am. 7:14.

[213] Cf. already Am. 7:10-17 and conversely Micah's attack on the temple prophets at Jerusalem, Mi. 3:5-8.

[214] Special note should be taken of the fact that the Qumran texts contain fragments of non-canonical prophetic writings, DJD, I, 100 f.

None was with us who knew 'Till when?' " [215] The preceding description of the destruction of the temple (vv. 3-8) is on this view connected with 1 Macc. 4:38, [216] and the theme of the absence of a prophet is related to 1 Macc. 4:46; 9:27; 14:41. [217] In opposition to this interpretation, however, it is rightly pointed out that at decisive points Ps. 74:3-8 does not agree with 1 Macc. 4:38.

> Ps. 74:3 refers to "permanent ruins," [218] whereas acc. to 1 Macc. 4:38 the destruction and desecration of the temple lasted only 3 yrs. (167-164 B.C.). [219] Even if Ps. 74:3 is hyperbole it cannot be reconciled with 1 Macc. 4:38 when one considers that acc. to Ps. 74:7 the sanctuary went up in flames (cf. 2 K. 25:9), whereas 1 Macc. 4:38 says that the enemy laid the temple waste, desecrated the altar, burned the gates and destroyed the chambers. [220]

One is thus justified in supposing that the reference in Ps. 74 is not to the Maccabean period but to the destruction of Solomon's temple in 587 B.C. [221] This enables us to understand v. 9 properly. At the moment of destruction the prophets of salvation were necessarily silent, while even a prophet like Jer., though justified by events and officially rehabilitated by Nebuchadnezzar, was condemned to silence in this crisis ; [222] indeed, as Jer. 44:15 ff. shows, he might even be regarded as a prophet who was responsible for the disaster. In other words, it is quite possible to regard the period after the destruction of the Davidic monarchy as one which enjoyed neither signs nor prophets and which seemed to be completely hopeless. Thus among all the exegetical conjectures the most probable is that which sees in Ps. 74 an exilic national lament for the destruction of Solomon's temple and the resultant affliction. If this is true, Ps. 74:9 has no bearing on the question of post-exilic prophecy.

> c. Closely related to Ps. 74:9, it would seem, is the prayer of Azariah in Δα. 3:38 : "Also at this time we have neither king, prophet, leader, burnt offering, sacrifice, meal offering, incense, nor any place to bring thee the firstfruits and to find mercy." [223] Here again we have a theme of lamentation which as a whole does not seem to fit any post-exilic age right up to the destruction of the second temple. Obviously the exile is described. Thus Δα. 3:38, too, has no bearing on the question of prophecy in the Hell.-Roman period.

---

[215] Cf. the transl. of H. Schmidt, *Die Psalmen, Hndbch. AT,* 15 (1934), *ad loc.*

[216] Cf. R. Kittel, *Psalmen, Komm. AT,* 13 [5, 6] (1929), *ad loc.*

[217] So A. Bertholet in Kautzsch, *ad loc.*

[218] מַשְׁאוֹת נֶצַח; better perhaps "complete ruins" in the sense of definitive destruction, the נֶצַח being elative. Cf. D. W. Thomas, "The Use of נֶצַח as a Superlative in Hebrew," *Journal of Semitic Studies,* I (1956), 107.

[219] E. Bickermann, *Der Gott d. Makkabäer* (1937), 80-84.

[220] Furthermore 1 Macc. 4:38 mentions "plantations in the courts as in a forest or on a mountain." One may thus conclude with Bickermann, *op. cit.,* 110 f. that acc. to 1 Macc. 4:38 the temple was not destroyed by the Syrians but Zion was changed into the ancient Semitic type of sanctuary which was an open and planted place of sacrifice surrounded by a wall. This would also explain the "destructions" or better "structural alterations" to the temple, cf. M. Noth, *Gesch. Israels*[2] (1954), 332 f.

[221] So correctly Schmidt, *op. cit.* (→ n. 215), *ad loc.,* with bibl.

[222] Cf. Schmidt, *ad loc.*

[223] Cf. the transl. of W. Rothstein in Kautzsch Apkr. u. Pseudepigr., I, 180; on the literary character of the addition Da. 3:26-45 as a popular lament cf. O. Eissfeldt, *Einl.*[2] (1956), 730.

d. In the "Epistle of Baruch the son of Neriah to the nine and a half tribes" (S. Bar. 85:3) the appearance of "righteous men" and "prophets" is restricted to the ideal early period : "But now the righteous are gathered (to their fathers) and the prophets have fallen on sleep." [224] In this Apc., which is set against the historical background of the destruction of the second temple, we thus find the dogma of a canonical period of salvation as in Jos. Ap., I, 41 and the Rabb. Acc. to v. 1, however, the "righteous men" and "holy prophets" appear only as "helpers" in earlier times and previous generations, so that S. Bar. is in no sense ruling out the giving of oracles or the appearance of prophets under Vespasian. [225]

e. Particular note should be taken of 1 Macc. 4:46; 9:27; 14:41.

Acc. to 1 Macc. 4:43 ff. the desecrated altar was replaced by a new one when the temple was consecrated under Judas in 164 B.C. The stones of the old one were deposited in a suitable place on the temple hill "until a prophet should arise who would say what should be done with them." [226] If in the first instance this means only that the final decision as to what should be done with an unserviceable piece of cultic equipment was left to the chance prophet who might arise, 1 Macc. 4:46 takes on added significance in connection with the other verses. While 1 Macc. 4:46 stands at a climax in the whole story, 1 Macc. 9:27 introduces the darkest period in the Maccabean episode. Judas fell in 160 B.C. and his followers were delivered up to Bacchides : "Thus there came on Israel great tribulation such as had never arisen since the time when a prophet had last appeared among them." [227] It is an open question who was the last prophet acc. to the Hasmonean view of history but it would seem that 1 Macc. 9:27 is not just meant to be a dogmatic statement about the absence of prophecy in the present. Acc. to 1 Macc. 14:41 Simon was appointed commander and high-priest in 141 B.C. "Then the Jews and priests resolved that Simon should be their leader and high-priest for ever until an authentic prophet should arise." [228] The striking thing about this is that a ἕως τοῦ ἀναστῆναι προφήτην πιστόν follows the concluding statement εὐδόκησαν τοῦ εἶναι αὐτῶν Σίμωνα ἡγούμενον καὶ ἀρχιερέα εἰς τὸν αἰῶνα. From this it is concluded on the one side that the national decision would be in force until the extinguished prophetic gift should be kindled again in an authentic bearer of the Spirit and should perhaps call for a constitutional change, [229] while on the other there is seen behind 1 Macc. 14:41 the expectation of an eschatological prophet [230] who would come forth as προφήτης πιστός.

The general trend of 1 Macc., which is in essentials a single unit, [231] is against any such long-range expectation. The guiding thread in the book is the fluctuating rise of the Hasmoneans up to Simon ; [232] there then follows a new threat to the dynasty with the assassination of the priest-prince and his two older sons by a relative, but this is averted when John Hyrcanus arises and can be installed as the new priest-king, 1 Macc.

---

[224] Cf. the transl. of H. Gunkel in Kautzsch Apkr. u. Pseudepigr., II, 445 f.

[225] Thus S. Bar. 48:34-37 plainly refers to charismatic phenomena at the time of the destruction of the temple. The promises mentioned, some of which are confirmed while others are not, are allusions to contemporary prophecies of salvation and calamity. Bousset-Gressm., 394 is fundamentally wrong in his interpretation of S. Bar. 85:1, 3.

[226] 1 Macc. 4:46 : καὶ ἀπέθεντο τοὺς λίθους ... μέχρι τοῦ παραγενηθῆναι προφήτην τοῦ ἀποκριθῆναι περὶ αὐτῶν.

[227] 1 Macc. 9:27 : καὶ ἐγένετο θλῖψις μεγάλη ἐν τῷ Ἰσραηλ, ἥτις οὐκ ἐγένετο ἀφ' ἧς ἡμέρας οὐκ ὤφθη προφήτης αὐτοῖς. Acc. to the tendency in 1 Macc. "Israel" is to be taken in a specific party sense.

[228] Cf. the transl. and conjecture of E. Kautzsch in Kautzsch Apkr. u. Pseudepigr., I, 76.

[229] So Kautzsch, though the preceding formula εἰς τὸν αἰῶνα is against this.

[230] Volz Esch., 193; Schubert Religion, 66.

[231] Cf. K. D. Schunk, *Die Quellen d. I u. II Makkabäerbuches* (1954), 7-15 with bibl.

[232] Cf. esp. the hymn of praise in 1 Macc. 14:6-15.

16:11-22. John, who is the climax of the story of the fluctuating battle of faith and the rise of the Maccabeans, [233] has passed into history as the bearer of the *munus triplex*, → 825, 26 ff. The prophetic office of this ruler and high-priest would seem to give to 1 Macc. 9:27 and 14:41, and finally also to 4:46, a satisfying sense. If 1 Macc. 9:27 refers to the time when a prophet last appeared, now, after the days of affliction and conflict, a prophet has appeared again, and thus the age of salvation has come. [234] If again 1 Macc. 14:41 makes the national decision regarding a hereditary priestly monarchy dependent on its sanctioning by a prophet, now the royal dignity is confirmed by John Hyrcanus himself, since as a priestly ruler he bears the prophetic charisma, as even the Rabb. did not deny. If finally 1 Macc. 4:46 leaves the decision what to do with the desecrated altar to a future prophet, in John Hyrcanus there has now arisen for the Hasmonean party (→ Σαδδουκαῖος) a high-priest who is charismatically empowered to make valid decisions in temple matters. [235]

2. The Rabbinic Tradition.

Things are different in the sphere of Rabbinic tradition. Here one finds sophisticated theological deliberation aimed at restricting the rise of legitimate prophecy to an ideal classical period in the past. This speculation on the classical period of prophecy is closely linked with the development of the synagogal concept of the Canon (→ III, 978 ff.), which found its final and dogmatically binding form in the three groups of Law, Prophets and Writings in the first half of the 2nd century A.D.

The recognised class. period of the work of the Holy Spirit (→ 382, 16 ff.; 383, 29 ff.), who is equated with the Spirit of prophecy, [236] is the period in the history of Israel which concludes with the destruction of Solomon's temple in 587 B.C. This can be called the age of the "former prophets"; [237] Sota, 9, 12 : "When the former prophets were dead, the Urim and Thummim ceased." [238] All the prophets belong to this age apart from Haggai, Zech. and Mal. and their companions. [239] The destruction of Jerusalem, the burning of the temple, the exile and the fact that the Holy Spirit withdrew caused the prophet Jer. to sing his lamentations acc. to the Amoraean Jehoshua b. Levi (c. 250 A.D.). [240] Many believe that the Holy Spirit or the Spirit of prophecy is one of the five things which the second temple did not enjoy in contrast to Solomon's temple. [241] In the main, however, the age of prophecy is extended to cover the early post-exilic prophets, and the possibility of prophetic inspiration is not entirely ruled out even for the period which follows. In this case the ref. is to the "latter prophets" and then to

---

[233] In this 1 Macc. undoubtedly resembles the older historical writing of Israel, cf. also Noth, *op. cit.* (→ n. 220), 343 f.

[234] On the presence of "salvation" in the form of a favoured ruler cf. G. Widengren, *Sakrales Königtum im AT u. im Judt.* (1955), 17, who refers to the sacral nature of the Hasmonean monarchy but in my view goes too far when he finds here a restoration of pre-exilic relations.

[235] In antithesis is Alkimus, who had the wall of the inner court torn down and thus destroyed the works of the prophets (τὰ ἔργα τῶν προφητῶν), thereby falling victim to divine judgment, 1 Macc. 9:54 f.; cf. Schürer, I, 225 f.

[236] On the equation of the OT terms "Spirit of God," "Spirit of Yahweh," "Holy Spirit" with רוּחַ הַנְּבוּאָה cf. Str.-B., III, 27 ff. → 382, 4 ff.

[237] Not to be confused with the former and latter prophets of the Canon.

[238] Str.-B., III, 13.

[239] Bartenora, Mishnayyot, Seder Nashim (1863), 124 on Sota, 9, 12.

[240] Str.-B., II, 133.

[241] jTaan., 2, 1 (65a, 60 ff.) par.: "the last sanctuary had five things less than the first : the [heavenly altar-]fire, the ark, the Urim and Thummim, the anointing oil and the Holy Spirit"; author R. Acha (c. 320 A.D.); cf. Str.-B., II, 133.

the age which does not have the prophetic spirit in full measure but in which the divine will is declared through the Bat Qol ; [242] T. Sota, 13, 2 : "When Hagg., Zech. and Mal., the latter prophets (→ n. 237), were dead, the Holy Spirit departed from Israel (→ 385, 26 ff.), but the heavenly will was made known to them (the Israelites) by the Bat Qol." [243] Jos. has a similar dogmatic notion in Ap., 1, 38 ff. (→ III, 981, 33 ff.) when he maintains that the period from Moses to Artaxerxes I (464-424 B.C.) was one of unbroken development of the prophetic spirit, whereas there was no prophetic succession in the age which followed, though the work of the prophetic spirit is not ruled out in dogmatic principle. Within the developing schema of salvation history, which postulates a classical period of prophecy, the present, and a future age of salvation with a general outpouring of the Spirit, [244] the prophets are not in any sense the great individual representatives of the sovereign Spirit. For Pharisaic Rabbinism their work is understandable only in connection with an inner dependence on the Law (→ IV, 1054 ff.), which has a prototypical character along the lines of popular Platonic religious philosophy. That is to say, it contains already the whole of salvation history, whose individual stages are actualised in the world acc. to the measure of the time set for each by God. [245]

Thus we read in bMeg., 14a, Bar. : "Forty-eight prophets and seven prophetesses prophesied to Israel and they did not take from nor add to that which is written in the Torah with the exception of the reading of the scroll of Esther." [246] Acc. to Mar Shemuel (d. 254 A.D.) no prophet has any right to say anything which is not contained in the Torah, [247] and acc. to R. Jehoshua b. Levi (c. 250 A.D.) Moses spoke already all the words of the prophets and everything prophesied later derives from the prophecy of Moses. [248] How very speculative the Rabb. became at this pt. may be seen from a long passage in R. Jishaq (c. 300 A.D.), who has the prophet Is. say : "From the day that the Torah was given at Sinai I am there and I have received this prophecy ; only now, however, has God sent me and His Spirit. [249] Up to now authority was not given me to prophesy." [250] The prophets are thus the oldest expositors of the Law authorised by the Spirit, and they have their specific and limited task in the divine plan of salvation. [251] Hence it is emphasised continually that there was a plenitude of prophets in Israel. All the patriarchs and matriarchs were prophets. There were as many prophets as those

---

[242] Bat Qol (בַּת קוֹל), gen. used, means "echo," cf. Levy Wört., s.v. It then means the "word" (cf. Da. 9:23 : "At the beginning of thy supplications a word went forth") or "voice" (cf. S. Bar. 8:1 : "A voice from inside the temple") which usually goes forth from the heavenly sanctuary to inspire men in a specific situation. In this specific sense Bat Qol is better not transl. That we have here a widespread theologoumenon may be seen from Philo Rer. Div. Her., 258, acc. to which "another sounds forth" (ὑπηχοῦντος ἑτέρου) within the prophet during ecstasy → 822, 12 ff. For materials cf. Str.-B., Index s.v. "Himmelsstimme" and Schubert Religion, 211, n. 10 with a ref. to אינציקלופדיה תלמודית V (1953), 1-4.

[243] Cf. Str.-B., I, 127; the plur. here (משמיעין להן בבת קול) undoubtedly refers to angels who through the Bat Qol mediate to men the divine word for a specific situation or person. But cf. bSota, 48b Bar. (→ III, 970, 48 ff.) and par.; Str.-B., I, 133 and Schubert Religion, 6.

[244] Cf. Nu. r., 15, 25 on 11:17: "God said : In this world individuals have prophesied but in the world to come all Israelites will be prophets," cf. Str.-B., II, 134 and → 385, 6 ff.

[245] How popular such ideas may be can be seen in the exposition of Gn. 22:13 in the frescoes of Dura-Europos and the mosaic of Beth-Alpha, cf. R. Meyer, "Betrachtungen zu drei Fresken d. Synagoge v. Dura-Europos," ThLZ, 74 (1949), 30-34.

[246] No support was found in the Torah for reading Esther at Purim, cf. Str.-B., I, 601 f.

[247] With ref. to Lv. 27:34 acc. to bTem., 16a.

[248] Ex. r., 42, 8 on 32:7.

[249] Acc. to Is. 48:16.

[250] Ex. r., 28, 6 on 19:3 par.

[251] Lv. r., 15, 2 on 13:2 : Acc. to R. Acha the Holy Spirit rests on the prophet only acc. to the measure (במשקל) of his commission.

who came out of Egypt. Not a single city in Israel was without a prophet. Yet only those prophets whom the Law needed in its self-development were recorded and given a place in salvation history. [252]

On the basis of statements such as this, according to which the Law expounds itself in the prophets, it is obvious why in the Rabbinic view of Scripture the Prophets did not have anything like the same canonical validity as the Torah, → III, 986, 8 f. This also leads, however, to a second important principle. If the prophets of the classical period are at root no more than interpreters of the Law speaking with the authority of the Spirit and charged to unfold only what the Law contains, then they differ only in degree and not in kind from the wise. Both prophets and wise men belong to the same series, and there arises the chain of bearers of the "oral Law" [253] which is briefly summarised in Seder Olam rabba, 30 (→ III, 982, n. 80) as follows: "Up to now (the time of Alexander the Gt.) the prophets prophesied in the Holy Spirit. From now onwards incline thine ear and hear the words of the wise." How close can be the connection between the prophets and the wise men may be seen from the statement of the Aramaean Jishaq (c. 300 B.C.) quoted → 817, 24 ff., which closes with the words: "Yet not only did all the prophets receive their prophecy from Sinai but the wise men too who arise from generation to generation — each of them received what he had to say from Sinai."

This sheds a special light on the Bat Qol. It is not just a substitute for the lost spirit of prophecy but a legitimate continuation as the wise men were of the prophets. Thus, e.g., the victory of the school of Hillel over that of Shammai in the academy at Jamnia at the end of the 1st cent. A.D. is not attributed to rational historical reasons. It is traced back to the Bat Qol [254] and thus to divination. This theory, which the Rabb. used to justify themselves on the basis of prophecy, is religiously very interesting since it made possible the combining of two trends in Israel which were fundamentally different and even hostile. [255] For the prophet is primarily subject to the irrational, incalculable and often eruptive work of the Spirit, whereas the spirit of order, reason and prudence is embodied in the wise man. The two groups could be combined because the wise men — and not just those of Pharisaic persuasion [256] — became interpreters of the Law in the post-exilic period, and thus took up the role of the priest or cultic prophet. At the same time, acc. to the distant vision of the author of Zech. 13:2-6 (→ 813, 10 ff.), the prophetic spirit lost the element of the uncanny and incalculable, was tamed as a divinatory factor, and was integrated into and put in the service of the synagogal institution. [257]

History, of course, was stronger here than dogma. On the one side was the older rationalism of the wise men, hostile in principle to prophecy. Thus R. Chanina b. Dosa

---

[252] Seder Olam rabba, 21; for further material cf. Str.-B., II, 130 f.

[253] The dogmatic attempt to show a chain of tradition of this kind may be seen in Ab., cf. Schubert Religion, 6, 211, n. 11.

[254] Cf. jBer., 1, 7 (3b, 73 ff.) Bar.: The legal decisions of the schools of Hillel and Shammai were of equal merit, but a Bat Qol in the form of group inspiration decided for Hillel. Acc. to R. Jochanan (d. 279 A.D.) the academy of Jamnia was the place where the Bat Qol went forth (ביבנה יצאת בת קול).

[255] This fundamental opposition was just as true of early Judaism as of the pre-exilic period, though cf. J. Fichtner, "Jesaja unter den Weisen," ThLZ, 74 (1949), 75-80.

[256] Cf. on this R. Meyer, "Die Bdtg. d. Pharisäismus f. Gesch. u. Theol. d. Judt.," ThLZ, 77 (1952), 677-684, esp. 681 f.

[257] This is expressed in ordination by laying on of hands (סמיכה) which symbolises transmission of the Spirit from teacher to pupil, cf. Bousset-Gressm., 169; E. Lohse, Die Ordination im Spätjdt. u. im NT (1951), 54-56.

(c. 70 A.D.) tells how he refused recognition as a seer on the ground of an act of deliverance which he had accomplished through prayer and foreknowledge. [258] Similarly R. Eliezer b. Hyrcanos (c. 90 A.D.) did not want to be regarded as a prophet because of a prediction. [259] When Akiba joined Simon b. Koseba as a prophet at the beginning of the revolt under Hadrian (→ 824, 11 ff.) he immediately came up against the pessimistic rationalist Simon b. Torta, and it is undoubtedly in retrospect of bitter experiences in this tragic period in the history of his people that the Amoraean Jochanan b. Nappacha formulates the sarcastic saying: "From the days the sanctuary was destroyed prophecy has been taken from the prophets and given to fools and children." [260]

On the other side, however, the Spirit with all His incalculability cannot be imprisoned in a dogmatic and scribal schema; the revolts under Vespasian and Hadrian cannot be understood apart from a strong charismatic element. In face of this powerful eschatologically oriented charismatic element early Pharisaism was not only inwardly impotent; [261] at a decisive point it made its own contribution to it. [262] This means that a modern historical assessment cannot possibly point to the Rabbinic tradition as clear proof that Judaism in the time of Jesus and the apostles had no sense at all, or only a marginal sense, of the work of the prophetic charisma in its various forms. [263]

II. Historical Manifestations.

1. Prophetic Experience according to Palestinian Sources.

Express depiction of a pneumatic experience on the basis of a contemplative consideration of Scripture [264] may be found in Da. 9:1, 2 f., 20-27: [265] Daniel immerses himself in Jer. 25:11 f.; 29:10, which speak of the 70 yrs. to be fulfilled over the ruins of Jerusalem. To acquire true, i.e., pneumatic rather than rational insight into the meaning of the ancient prophetic sayings Daniel subjects himself to certain ascetic practices; he fasts [266] and prays and mourns in sackcloth and ashes. At the climax of these exercises the man Gabriel, known to him from earlier ecstatic experiences, appears to him and

---

[258] bJeb., 121b, Str.-B., II, 627.

[259] bErub., 63a, Str.-B., II, 627.

[260] bBB, 12b, though examples of prophecies from the lips of children have been added to the saying, cf. Str.-B., I, 607.

[261] This may be seen very dramatically and with great historical realism in Ac. 5:34 ff., where Gamaliel dare not condemn outright the charismatic element in the apostles, cf. on this Haench. Ag., ad loc.

[262] It is generally accepted that Zelotism, which had a strong charismatic element, developed out of the more moderate Pharisaism, → II, 884 ff.

[263] Cf. W. Förster, Nt.liche Zeitgeschichte, I² (1955), 16 f., 80.

[264] There is undoubtedly a reminiscence of the contemplative consideration of Scripture in the Rabb. concept מדרש to the degree that this is directed to exposition as such. It derives from the root דרש which in the sacral sphere denotes consulting the deity or oracle, cf. Ges.-Buhl and Köhler-Baumg., s.v.

[265] On what follows cf. Meyer, 43 f.

[266] In Rabbinism, too, we find mortification preparatory to ecstasy, though the tradition is already polemical, bSanh., 65b: When R. Akiba came to expound Dt. 18:10 f. he used to weep (and say): "If the spirit of uncleanness rests on the one who fasts in order that the spirit of uncleanness (רוח הטמאה; cf. Zech. 13:2) may rest upon him, how much more is this true of the one who fasts in order that the spirit of purity may rest upon him. But what can I do? For our sins have brought it about (that this does not happen)." Acc. to the par. S. Dt. § 173 on 18:12 Eleazar b. Azariah, an older contemporary of Akiba, was the author; cf. Str.-B., II, 133.

imparts a revelation, v. 22b, 23. As in the night visions of Zech. an angel mediates between the heavenly palace and the seer. In language which shows that the Rabb. were building on earlier tradition with their idea of a *Bat Qol* from the heavenly palace or sanctuary (→ n. 242), Daniel is granted a glimpse of the future. The 70 years are weeks of years. The last of these culminates in the sin of Antiochus Epiphanes IV and the setting up of the abomination of desolation between 167 and 164 B.C. Thus the meaning of an ancient prophecy is known and it takes on significance for the present, which is the last time. What Jer. could not possibly know has been revealed by God to Daniel through an angel. Daniel is not only in the same succession as the class. prophet; he is superior to him, for the granting of full understanding also means the fulfilment of the ancient prophecy.

1 Qp. Hab. 7:1-5 offers an exegesis of Hab. 2:2. The prophet is here a blind instrument of God who does not know what his prophecy is all about. But the commentator of Chirbet Qumran knows. Hab. 2:2 "refers to the teacher of righteousness to whom God has made known all the secrets of the words of His servants the prophets." [267] Since God has done this, revealing the eschatological meaning of the prophetic sayings, the Teacher of Righteousness is a legitimate successor of the ancient prophets as well as their charismatic or pneumatic expositor. Indeed, he is higher than they, for only now, through him, is the hidden content of the prophetic sayings brought to light. [268] This text also shows that too much emphasis should not be laid on the constantly repeated thesis that when the pneumatic broke forth in the post-exilic period, in consequence of the basic epigonal mood it necessarily had to remain anonymous, for the Teacher of Righteousness, perhaps an opponent of Alexander Jannaeus (103-76 B.C.), was undoubtedly a figure generally known and honoured in his community, and in him the time was fulfilled even though the final end (→ τέλος) had perhaps not been reached with his appearing.

A new light is thus cast on Jos. Bell., 2, 159. Here the Essenes are seers because they are occupied from youth up with the Holy Scriptures, with various purifications, and with the sayings of the prophets. In other words, they enter into the state of ecstasy on the basis of mortifications and a contemplative consideration of Scripture. [269] 1 Qp. Hab. 7:1-5 now shows us how these seers regarded themselves or what their contemporaries thought of them. This extra-Rabb. material also makes it plain that the Rabb. theory that the wise men were legitimate successors of the prophets was based historically on ideas which go far beyond the limits of Pharisaism.

Interpretation of dreams is another form of pneumatic experience. [270] Thus Jos. Ant., 17, 345 ff. (→ 823, 23 ff.) tells us that this was one expression of the divination of the Essenes, and here again Daniel is the basis. Thus in Da. 3:31-4:34 Daniel's interpretation of the dream of Nebuchadnezzar is an integral part of the story of the king's madness. This interpretation is given in a state of ecstasy. Daniel stands for a long time astonished and his thoughts frighten him. Under the power of the Spirit [271] he has to proclaim things which bring him pain and terror. There is a similar ref. in the Rabb.; acc. to

---

[267] On the Teacher of Righteousness cf. F. Nötscher, *Zur theol. Terminologie d. Qumran-Texte* (1956), Index, *s.v.*; van der Woude, *passim*; H. H. Rowley, "The Teacher of Righteousness and the Dead Sea Scrolls," *Bulletin of the John Rylands Library,* 40 (1957), 114-146.

[268] In appraising this seer of priestly descent (1 Qp. Hab. 9:4-7) from the standpoint of religious psychology it makes no basic difference whether he was — historically — right or wrong.

[269] Meyer, 43; Schubert Religion, 77 f. (with the Qumran ref.).

[270] On the dream as a "copy" (lit. "falling off" נוֹבֶלֶת) of prophecy cf. Gn. r., 17, 5 on 2:21 par. with R. Chanina b. Jishaq (early 4th cent.) as author. In the same passage deep sleep (תרדמה) can induce prophecy acc. to Rab (d. 247 A.D.).

[271] In Da. 4:5 f., 15 we read three times that "the spirit of the holy gods" (רוּחַ אֱלָהִין קַדִּישִׁין) was "in" him.

PREl, 39 R. Pinchas (c. 360 A.D.) said that Joseph interpreted Pharaoh's dream when the Holy Spirit rested upon him. [272]

Finally Jos. Bell., 6, 300 ff. tells the story of a rough ecstatic called Jesus b. Ananias whose appearance reminds us the type of prophecy reflected in the polemic of the twofold saying in Zech. 13:2-6, → 825, 6 ff.

2. Prophecy in the Light of Alexandrian Theology.

Whereas acc. to the theory of Pharisaic Rabbinism the Law develops in the prophets and their legitimate successors the wise men, in Alexandrian theology acc. to Sap. it is wisdom (→ σοφία), the cause of all things, which brings prophets into the world. Wisdom naturally exercises typical sway in the salvation history recorded in the Pentateuch, so that Moses appears as a holy prophet (Wis. 11:1; cf. 10:16). It continues its work in the history which follows, so that Solomon can say of it in Wis. 7:27: "Although only one, it can do everything, and remaining the same it renews all things, from generation to generation entering pure souls and equipping the friends of God and the prophets." [273] Thus the prophetic line continues in history, and basically everyone who possesses true wisdom is a prophet.

Philo did not merely reflect on the nature of prophecy; his writings also give insight into the content of the prophetic experience. For him, too, the Torah is the prototype and starting-pt. of the whole event of salvation. [274] It is wholly in keeping with this that men of the age of the patriarchs and Moses are presented as prophets in a special sense along with those from Israel's later history. [275] Furthermore several of the numerous statements about prophetic figures of the past have a special ref. to the present, so that from this, as from the appended general disquisitions on the nature of prophecy and ecstasy, Philo's own prophetic experience is brought to light. [276] In Philo Moses is a bearer of revelation in the full sense; he is king and legislator, priest and prophet, e.g., Vit. Mos., II, 292. When God gave him the commandments, He restricted Himself to the general laws of the Decalogue. He then promulgated more detailed laws through the most perfect of the prophets whom He chose as interpreter of revelations when He had filled him with the "divine Spirit," Decal., 175. Thus Moses is not just the ruler over a people which is chosen for a priestly ministry to the salvation of all mankind (Vit. Mos., I, 149) and which is also a people of prophets. Abraham is the father of this people, and from time immemorial Jewish tradition has connected him with the beginning of true knowledge of God. [277] Thus Philo in Abr., 98 with ref. to Gn. 12:10 ff. says that through the deliverance of Abraham and Sarah from Egypt a marriage was upheld from which "there was to proceed a whole people, and that the people dearest to God, to which, as it seems to me, the priestly and prophetic office was given for the salvation of the whole human race." [278]

Philo discusses the nature of prophecy with extraordinary frequency — a sign that he himself had inner pneumatic experience. Rer. Div. Her., 259, which says that acc. to Holy Scripture every wise man has the prophetic gift, reminds us of Wis. 7:27 and also of the Rabb. theory that the wise man is in the prophetic succession, → 818, 11 ff. [279] Since wisdom has also an ethical aspect acc. to the ancient Jewish view (→ σοφία),

---

[272] Meyer, 144, n. 24.

[273] Transl. J. Fichtner, Die Weisheit Sal., Hndbch. AT, II, 6 (1938), 30.

[274] On the agreement of "law" and the divine world-order → IV, 1053, 4 ff.

[275] Cf. the examples in Leisegang, s.v. προφήτης.

[276] Bousset-Gressm., 449-454.

[277] Ibid., Index, s.v. "Abraham."

[278] Cf. Hillel's saying in jShab., 19, 1 (17a, 4 ff.) acc. to which the Israelites are no longer prophets but sons of the prophets (בני נביאים), Str.-B., II, 627.

[279] Παντὶ δὲ ἀστείῳ προφητείαν ὁ ἱερὸς λόγος μαρτυρεῖ.

the righteous are also bearers of the prophetic spirit in Philo ;[280] in this connection it should be noted that the Rabb. can say the same of the just and of those who fear God, → 383, 5 ff. Among the righteous who acc. to Scripture are also prophets Philo lists Noah, Isaac, and, of course, Moses and Abraham, Rer. Div. Her., 260-266. Fundamentally, however, all these are only examples of every truly righteous man ; once the righteous man has reached the highest stage, he is a prophet.[281]

In Philo, too, the way to prophetic experience is *via* ecstasy. There are four stages of ecstasy acc. to Rer. Div. Her., 249. The first is raving which involves folly,[282] the second powerful stimulation by unexpected events[283] the third the quietness of the spirit which has withdrawn into rest,[284] the fourth the true pneumatic experience of divine seizure and inspiration enjoyed by the prophets : ἔνθεος κατοκωχή τε καὶ μανία, ἧ τὸ προφητικὸν γένος χρῆται. Standing at this high pt. of ecstasy the prophet has nothing of his own to say but only that of another, since it is another that speaks in him, Rer. Div. Her., 259 : προφήτης γὰρ ἴδιον μὲν οὐδὲν ἀποφθέγγεται, ἀλλότρια δὲ πάντα ὑπηχοῦντος ἑτέρου.[285] The prophet, then, is simply the instrument used by God to reveal His will. He has no awareness of what he is proclaiming (*ibid.*, 266) and certainly, when divinely seized, he does not understand what he says ; Spec. Leg., I, 65 : οὐδὲ γὰρ, εἰ λέγει, δύναται καταλαβεῖν ὅ γε κατεχόμενος ὄντως καὶ ἐνθουσιῶν. On the other hand, acc. to Spec. Leg., IV, 192 nothing is concealed from the prophet, since he bears within him a sun which can be perceived only spiritually and rays of light which have no shadow : προφήτῃ δ' οὐδὲν ἄγνωστον, ἔχοντι νοητὸν ἥλιον ἐν αὐτῷ καὶ ἀσκίους αὐγάς.

Philo depicts divine rapture — ἐνθουσιασμός — and inspiration — θεία μανία — in the language of Plato, who sublimated in his philosophy the ecstatic piety of Orphism.[286] But the terminology and experience of the contemporary mysteries may also be discerned in his statements.[287] He follows Plato when he rejects any kind of unbridled ecstaticism and espouses a refined ecstatic piety. Nevertheless, one is hardly justified in understanding Philo's view of prophecy solely in terms of the Hell. elements in his intellectual make-up and overlooking completely the understanding of prophecy and its manifestations current in contemporary Judaism. Though his statements echo, and are influenced by, Plato and the mysteries, they are in the last analysis tied to Scripture, which obviously was for him, psychologically, the basis of prophetic experience. He inveighs sharply against those who want to understand Holy Scripture literally.[288] This attack is not merely based on the fact that he champions the allegorical method in biblical exposition. It is ultimately based on the fact that he favours a contemplative consideration of Scripture, cf., e.g., Som., II, 252 : "The invisible spirit (τὸ

---

[280] Philo Rer. Div., 259 emphasises explicitly that only the wise man (σοφός) and not the sinner (φαῦλος) can partake of ἐνθουσιασμός.

[281] Cf. J. Cohn, "Der Erbe des Göttlichen," L. Cohn-J. Heinemann, *Die Werke Philos v. Alex.,* V (1929), 280, n. 2 with bibl., esp. H. Leisegang, *Der heilige Geist* (1919), 209-212.

[282] Rer. Div. Her., 249 : λύττα μανιώδης παράνοιαν ἐμποιοῦσα. This includes the crude ecstasy of Zech. 13:2-6 or a Jesus b. Ananias, → 825, 6 ff.

[283] *Loc. cit.*: ἡ δὲ σφοδρὰ κατάπληξις ἐπὶ τοῖς ἐξαπιναίως καὶ ἀπροσδοκήτως συμβαίνειν εἰωθόσιν, cf. possibly Da. 4:16.

[284] Cf. the deep sleep which acc. to Rab (d. 247 A.D.) leads to prophecy (תרדמת נבואה) → n. 270.

[285] Cf. also Praem. Poen., 55. Note the use of ὑπηχεῖν "to ring as an echo," which obviously brings us close to the original meaning of *Bat Qol* (→ n. 242). Philo, however, localises the spiritual experience within man, where Rabb. usage thinks in terms of the voice coming to the recipient from the heavenly sphere.

[286] The new thing in Philo as compared with Plato is the exclusion of νοῦς; Bousset-Gressm., 449.

[287] Bousset-Gressm., 451 f.

[288] Cf. Cher., 42; Bousset-Gressm., 451, n. 2.

πνεῦμα ἀόρατον), who is wont to act in me unnoticed, whispers to me again and says : O thou, thou dost seem to me to be ignorant of a great and weighty matter ; I will now instruct thee freely on this — for I have already taught thee betimes on many other things." There follows on the theme "the city of God" (Ps. 46:5) a spiritual exegesis which rests on higher inspiration. [289] It is true that Philo uses the language of the Gk. sages here, but materially there is no radical distinction between Philo and similar phenomena in Palestinian Judaism, though there is a fairly broad difference in vocabulary.

3. Seers and Prophets.

For all the paucity of sources there are several historical personages who either realised they were prophets in one of the various forms of pneumatic manifestation or who were reported to be prophets.

a. As already noted, the Essenes gloried in the reputation that they had seers and prophets among them, → 820, 26 ff. Thus Jos. Ant., 13, 311 ff. tells of a famous seer called Simon who was obviously the head of a whole prophetic school [290] and who prophesied the overthrow of the Hasmonean Antigonos, a son of John Hyrcanos I. Acc. to Jos. Ant., 15, 373 ff. the Essene seer Menachem, a contemporary of Hillel, had the gift of prediction. He is once said to have foretold to the young Herod his glittering rise but also his ungodliness, giving him a sign like a true prophet. [291] At the zenith of his power Herod remembered the seer, summoned him, questioned him further, and then dismissed him with respect. In this connection Jos. emphasises that Menachem was only one of many Essenes who because of their "excellence" [292] had insight into divine things. [293] Finally Jos. Ant., 17, 345 ff. (→ n. 291) tells of a seer Simon who through a dream predicted the imminent downfall of Archelaos of the house of Herod. It is also possible that the afore-mentioned Teacher of Righteousness (→ 820, 22 ff.) was a leading figure in this circle of Essene prophets. A sense of eschatological mission is particularly strongly developed in him and his followers.

b. The Pharisees also have prophets in their ranks. Thus Jos. Ant., 17, 43 ff. tells of a prophetic group of Pharisees at Herod's court ; they were among the opponents of the king. [294] Pharisaic or Pharisaic-Rabb. prophets are shown by the sources to have arisen esp. in the unsettled period between Vespasian and Hadrian. In the yrs. before the outbreak of the Roman war an oracle about the coming of a world ruler played an important role among the people acc. to Jos. Since this was supposed to be in Scripture, Da. 7:13 f. was probably in view. [295] The question was, of course, whether this meant good or evil for Israel. An answer was sought along pneumatic rather than rational lines. It is not surprising, then, that prophets of weal and woe were sharply divided in their interpretation of the oracle. Jos. in Bell., 3, 351 ff. numbers himself among the latter, who transcended the limits of nationalistic prophecy. He first dreamed of the imminent misfortune of the Jews and could then fix the meaning of the dream quite plainly on the basis of his biblical learning. In the hour of supreme danger, after the

---

[289] Cf. on this M. Adler, "Über d. Träume," J. Heinemann-M. Adler, *Die Werke Philos v. Alex.,* VI (1938), 269, n. 1 f.

[290] Judas was accompanied "by companions and friends who kept by him to learn predictions of the future," Meyer, 42 f., 143, n. 6; Schubert Religion, 78.

[291] Meyer, 44.

[292] Jos, speaks here in Hell. fashion of the καλοκαγαθία of the seer, Ant., 15, 379.

[293] Cf. 1 QS 11:5-9, which says of the members of the Qumran community that they possessed divine insight which was concealed from the masses and which united them with the angels (בני שמים).

[294] Meyer, 57 f.

[295] Ibid., 52-54.

capture of Jotapata in Galilee by the Romans, he remembered his dream. In the same moment he was transported into ecstasy and in this state saw that he had to proclaim world dominion to Vespasian. [296] There is a significant par. to the story in bGittin, 56a b : Here Jochanan b. Zakkai, by agreement with his nephew, the leader of the Zealots, leaves beleaguered Jerusalem in a coffin. On arrival in the Roman camp, he greets Vespasian as emperor, and shortly afterwards this prophetic acclamation is confirmed by a message from Rome. [297]

Acc. to the tradition the following are seers in different ways : [298] Gamaliel II (T. Pes., 1, 27 [c. 90 A.D.]), Samuel, [299] who like Jochanan b. Zakkai [300] saw the future in the hour of death, R. Akiba, [301] R. Meir, [302] and at the time of the suppression of the revolt under Hadrian R. Simon b. Jochai. [303] Of special political significance was the prophetic appearance of R. Akiba at the beginning of the Hadrian rebellion. [304] In a period of supreme political ferment Akiba, acc. to his pupil Simon b. Jochai, took Nu. 24:17 in such a way as to see a fulfilment of the ancient prophecy of a star out of Jacob in Ben Koseba. [305] From what we know of Akiba's ecstatic states we may assume that this recognition of the true and contemporary meaning of Nu. 24:17 was based on pneumatic insight. Only thus can one understand the inflammatory effect of his designation : "This is the king, the Messiah," [306] and all the fanaticism which led to certain destruction. A prophet exerts influence only when he evokes a response ; when cool reason prevails, his arguments are of no avail. Akiba had to learn this. His contemporary Simon b. Torta did not fall under the spell of his prophecy and opposed him : "Akiba, grass will grow on your jaw-bone but the Son of David will not yet have come." [307] The voice of reason which spoke here did not affect, of course, the enthusiastic word of that remarkable and forceful man who in his person — once a convinced 'Am ha-Ares [308] — combined rationalism, mysticism and prophecy, and who according to legend died for his faith with the confession of the one God.

c. Prophetic experiences are by no means limited to the Essenes and Pharisees. Prophets of good and evil are found in other circles too. [309] Thus Jos Bell., 6, 286 tells of

---

[296] Meyer, 55 f.

[297] Ibid., 56 f.

[298] On what follows cf. ibid., 58 f.

[299] T. Sota, 13, 4 par. Though a genuine prophetic experience is narrated, in an obvious dogmatic correction it is supposed that a Bat Qol was received in Jamnia which declared Simon the Less worthy of the Holy Spirit (ראוי לרוח הקודש). Cf. the same theme in relation to Hillel in 13, 3.

[300] jSota, 9, 17 (24c, 29 ff.) par.; Jochanan is regarded not merely as a prophet but also as a master of the contemplation of Scripture which leads to ecstasy, jChag., 2, 1 (77a, 49 ff.) par.

[301] Lv. r., 21, 8 on 16:3.

[302] jSota, 1, 4 (16d, 45 ff.) (c. 150 A.D.) in popular burlesque.

[303] jShebi, 9, 1 (38d, 37 ff.) par.

[304] On the revolt under Hadrian cf. H. Bietenhardt, "Die Freiheitskriege d. Juden unter d. Kaisern Trajan u. Hadrian u. d. messianische Tempelbau," Judaica, 4 (1948), 57-77, 81-108, 161-185; cf. also Noth, op. cit. (→ n. 220), 401-406 with bibl.

[305] The name acc. to two letters found in the Wadi Murabba'āt ; one of these bears the subscription שמעון בן בֹּן] כוסבה נסיא ישראל. For bibl. cf. H. Bardtke, "Bemerkungen zu den beiden Texten aus d. Bar Kochba-Aufstand," ThLZ, 79 (1954), 295-304; Noth, 403, n. 2.

[306] jTaan., 4, 8 (68d, 50): דין הוא מלכא משיחא, cf. Meyer, 79 f.

[307] jTaan., 4, 8 (68d, 51): עקיבה יעלו עשבים בלחייך ועדיין בן דוד לא יבא.

[308] bPes., 49b: "When I was still a 'Am ha-Ares, I thought : If only I had a scholar (תלמיד חכם) in my power I would bite him like an ass," cf. R. Meyer, "Der 'Am ha-Ares," Judaica, 3 (1947), 179.

[309] For this tension cf. S. Bar. 48:37 (→ n. 225).

Zealot prophets of salvation one of whom, in the final hours of the temple revolt, led 6000 to death who had assembled in a hall of the outer temple to await the signs of salvation. [310] To prophecy of disaster belongs the mass ecstasy which acc. to Jos. the priests experienced at Pentecost in the final yrs. of the revolt and in which they saw how the divine household left the temple with the cry : "We go hence." [311]

Among the prophets of disaster the uncultured countryman Jesus b. Ananias deserves special notice. At Tabernacles in 62 A.D. (Jos. Bell., 6, 300 ff.) he came to peaceful and prosperous Jerusalem and for no apparent reason proclaimed ceaselessly the following threat of catastrophe : "A voice from sunrise, a voice from sunset, a voice from the four winds : Woe to Jerusalem and the temple ! Woe to the bridegroom and the bride ! Woe to the whole people !" [312] Arrested by the Jewish authorities and handed over to the procurator Albinus as an agitator, he was dismissed by the latter as mad after severe but fruitless scourging. This strange prophet unsettled Jerusalem for seven yrs. and five months. During the siege he was killed by a missile after having added to his customary threat a "Woe is me !" Here we undoubtedly have the original and authentic form of ecstasy which Israel had known from the earliest times (→ 813, 12 ff.) and which was now found to be strange wherever sacred texts were the presupposition of sublime ecstasy in a contemplative consideration of Scripture.

4. The Ruler with the Threefold Office.

Along with seers and prophets there is found in the Hell.-Roman period the prophetically gifted ruler who as priest-prince also has the charisma of prophecy. Within the schema which finds correspondence between the first time and the last various models came together in his person, on the one side Moses, whose person ideally combines the qualities of the ruler, the priesthood and the prophetic office, [313] and on the other side the clearly mythical, primal-eschatological figure of the paradisial king. [314]

John Hyrcanos I (135-104 B.C.) passed into history as a charismatic ruler of this kind. [315] Acc. to Jos. Ant., 13, 299 Hyrcanos, when he died, "was regarded by God as worthy of the three offices : rule over the people, the dignity of the priesthood and the task of the prophet," cf. Bell., 1, 68. Acc. to Ant., 13, 300 he had the prophetic gift of foreseeing the future, and Ant., 13, 282 f. depicts him as a charismatically endowed high-priest who in the course of his sacral work in the temple received an audition which he then proclaimed to all the people. [316] The same figure probably underlies the Gk. version of Test. L. 8:11-17; 17:11-18:14. [317] But here he is already idealised and presented in the style of a contemplation of future history, i.e., in a method known to us not only

---

[310] Bell., 6, 283 ff.; Meyer, 54 f.

[311] Bell., 6, 299; Meyer, 50 f.

[312] On the transl. and what follows cf. Meyer, 46 f.

[313] Cf. Volz Esch., 192 and → 821, 24 ff.

[314] For material cf. Bousset-Gressm., 260 f.; Volz Esch., 191 f.

[315] On what follows cf. Meyer, 60-70.

[316] Φασὶν γάρ, ὅτι ... αὐτὸς ἐν τῷ ναῷ θυμιῶν μόνος ὢν ἀρχιερεὺς ἀκούσειε φωνῆς ... καὶ τοῦτο προελθὼν ἐκ τοῦ ναοῦ παντὶ τῷ πλήθει φανερὸν ἐποίησεν, cf. Lk. 1:8 ff.

[317] Cf. W. Bousset, "Die Test. XII, I. Die Ausscheidung d. chr. Interpolationen," ZNW, 1 (1900), 166; R. H. Charles, *The Greek Version of the Test. of the Twelve Patriarchs* (1908), 62-64; Meyer, 64. If on the basis of the Qumran discoveries it is fairly certain that the Test. XII are Zadokite in origin, this does not settle the question whether or how far, by secondary interpretation, they were used to justify the ideology of the Hasmonean court. In my view the par. traditions in Jos. and the Rabb. support an *interpretatio Hasmonaica* of this kind, though cf. K. G. Kuhn, "Die beiden Messias Aarons u. Israels," NTSt, 1 (1954/55), 168-179; van der Woude, 210-216. On 1 Q Levi cf. J. T. Milik, "Le Test. de Lévi en araméen," RB, 62 (1955), 398-406; DJD, I, 87-91 and bibl. Cf. also → Σαδδου- καῖος.

from the Sibylline lit., which was widespread throughout the Mediterranean world, but also from the apocalyptic depiction of history in Judaism. John Hyrcanos I is the bearer of the threefold office both as an eschatological counterpart of Moses and also as the paradisial king who restores the ideal state to mankind as a whole, Test. L. 18:9 ff. In opposition to the uniting of the three offices in the one person of a prophetically gifted priest-king is their presence alongside one another, which is the eschatological goal of the anti-Hasmonean community of Qumran. Acc. to 1 QS 9:7-11 the sons of Aaron, or more narrowly the sons of Zadok who had been driven out of Jerusalem (→ Σαδδου-καῖος), alone had the right of judgment in the community and also of administering the common property "until the coming of a prophet and of the anointed from Aaron and Israel." [318] This eschatological expectation was based on the early post-exilic period reflected in Zech. 4:14, where the prophet is a third person alongside the two anointed of Yahweh, the high-priest Joshua and the designated Davidic ruler Zerubbabel. Thus far the question of the role which 1 QS 9:11 sees for the prophet in the eschatology of the Zadokite community of Qumran, in which the high-priest takes precedence of the political ruler, has not yet been satisfactorily answered. Nevertheless, one may confidently assert at least that the prophet, to whom Dt. 18:15 ff. (→ 803, 38 ff.) is referred acc. to 4 Q Testimonia 5 ff., [319] is to be differentiated from the two Messianic figures. [320]

5. Messianic Prophets.

Whereas the charismatic priest-prince embodies present salvation in his person, the orientation of the Messianic prophet is to the immediate future. He and his followers expect a miracle of accreditation whereby the legitimacy of the prophet will be demonstrated and the age of salvation will open. These men and their groups are also convinced that events already enacted in the salvation history of Israel must be enacted afresh at the end of the present aeon. Thus their models are the ideal ruler Moses and Joshua, who according to the tradition led Israel out of the wilderness into the promised land.

Acc. to Jos. Ant., 18, 85 ff. there arose under Pontius Pilate in 35 A.D. a Samaritan who wanted to show his followers the temple vessels traditionally hidden by Moses on Gerizim. Apparently this miracle would prove that he was the initiator of the ideal Mosaic age marked by the "tabernacle." The procurator understood the movement thus and nipped it in the bud. [321] Under Fadus, acc. to Jos. Ant., 20, 97 f., Theudas, known to us from Ac. 5:36 (→ IV, 862, 4 ff.), came on the scene: "He said that he was a prophet and claimed that he would divide the river and make possible for them an easy passage." The miracle of accreditation which he promised the great crowd who had followed him to the Jordan with all their goods is an eschatological re-enactment of the crossing of the Jordan under Joshua, Jos., 3, 15 ff. On this basis Theudas as Joshua *redivivus* would then wrest the land and the capital from the Romans and seize them for God and His people. Cuspius Fadus took the fantastic enterprise quite seriously and destroyed Theudas and his followers. [322] As another instance among many (Ant.,

---

[318] 1 QS 9:11; עד בוא נביא ומשיחי אהרון וישראל. Cf. on this DJD, I, 121 f.; Kuhn, *op. cit.* (→ n. 317), 171; Nötscher, 50 f.

[319] J. M. Allegro, "Further Messianic Ref. in Qumran Literature," JBL, 75 (1956), 182-187.

[320] Cf. van der Woude, 186-189. It should be noted that Simon b. Koseba (→ 824, 11 ff.) is accompanied by a high-priest Eleazar, while R. Akiba obviously acts as prophet, so that there is a division of office here as in Zech. 4:14 and 1 QS 9:11. The difference is simply that in accordance with the historical situation Simon as secular ruler is to the fore, cf. also van der Woude, 116.

[321] Meyer, 82; Str.-B., II, 479 ff.

[322] Meyer, 83-85.

20, 167 f.; Bell., 2, 258 ff.) Jos. Ant., 20, 169 ff. mentions an Egypt. prophet who offered to repeat at Jerusalem Joshua's miraculous capture of Jericho (Jos. 6:16); from the Mt. of Olives he would show his followers "how at his behest the walls of Jerusalem would fall down. Hereby, he promised, he would make their entry into the city possible." This prophet, who arose under the procurator Felix (52-60 A.D.) and was arrested by him, seems to have commanded a considerable following. He escaped, and acc. to Ac. 21:38 it seems that the people expected his return. [323] Shortly after the suppression of the revolt under Vespasian (Jos. Bell., 7, 437 ff.) there appeared in Cyrene a *sicarius* called Jonathan, who persuaded the poorer Jews in the Libyan Pentapolis to follow him into the desert in order that he might perform miraculous signs for them. The richer Jews, concerned for life and property, reported the fanatic to the governor Catullus, who made short work of the unarmed crowd. In the case of Jonathan it is very clear that the prophet of the last time needed a miracle rather than weapons; hence the complete lack of arms among his supporters. [324]

In the time of Hadrian no Messianic prophet is recorded; Ben Koseba (→ 824, 11 ff.) sweeps all lovers of freedom into his train. In the period which followed, which was hostile to all forms of the charismatic, a Messianic prophet was officially quite inconceivable. But the spark lives on; thus the Byzantine church historian Socrates tells of a Messianic Jewish movement in Crete in the 5th cent. A.D. [325] Here a man came on the scene as Moses *redivivus*; returned from heaven, he sought to repeat the march through the Red Sea to the Holy Land, cf. Ex. 14:15-31. He found many to believe him and on the fixed day began the march through the sea. Many Jews plunged into the sea from the rocky coast of Crete and met with disaster. When they sought the false Moses, however, he had disappeared.

III. The Apocalyptic Literature.

The apoc. lit. (→ III, 577 f.), which survived in spite of the Pharisaic-Rabb. domination of the Synagogue, belongs to the Hell.-Rom. period and can thus be brought into connection with the seers and prophets of the time. It is a typical production of later post-exilic Judaism and is explicable only in terms of the current intellectual and religious situation. [326] Its roots lie for the most part outside Israel, namely, in Iran and the East Mediterranean world. True apoc. of Iranian origin offers "disclosures" about the rise and fall and change of world epochs. [327] Adopted by Judaism in the Persian-Hell. period and integrated into its own view of history, the doctrine of epochs finally led to the idea of two world epochs (→ I, 202 ff.), which was destined to outlast apocalyptic and to become an enduring principle of faith. [328]

A second basic element in Jewish apoc. is the regarding of history as *vaticinium ex eventu*. This "history in future form," which as prophecy leads up to the present, is probably based on the apoc. principle found in the Greek-Oriental lit. of the Sibylline oracles; this is found already in the 8th cent. B.C. and had an extraordinary influence in the age which followed. [329] One may even conjecture that the ancient prophetess at work through the centuries provided Judaism in the Hell.-Roman period with the impulse

---

[323] Meyer, 85 f.

[324] *Ibid.*, 86 f.

[325] Hist. Eccles., VII, 38 (ed. R. Hussey [1853], 822 ff.); Meyer, 87 f.

[326] Cf. Schürer, III, 258-370; Volz Esch., 1-62; Bousset-Gressm., Index, *s.v.* "Apokalyptik"; H. Ringgren, Art. "Apokalyptik, I, II," RGG³, I, 463-466 with bibl.

[327] G. Widengren, "Stand u. Aufgaben d. iranischen Religionsgeschichte, I," *Numen*, 1 (1954), 39-45; II, *ibid.*, 2 (1955), 107-110 with bibl.

[328] Cf. R. Meyer, Art. "Eschatologie, III Judt.," RGG³, II, 662-665.

[329] This lit. also had a formal influence on Judaism and Christianity, cf. J. Geffken in Hennecke, 399-422; Volz Esch., 53-58; Bousset-Gressm., 18 f.; Eissfeldt, *op. cit.* (→ n. 223), 761 f. The material influence, however, is what matters in this connection.

whereby it put such "prophecies" on the lips of figures from salvation history. It was all the easier to adopt this view of history and merge it with one's own ideas in view of the fact that from the very first the traditional writing prophets had offered prophetic reflections on history, though originally on a very different basis. Apart from these fundamental features, which are so important from the standpt. of theological history, Jewish apoc. provides us with speculations of the most diverse kinds. Sometimes seers speak who grant us an insight into their own contemplations and experiences, → 819, 21 ff. Viewed as a whole, this lit. with its learned speculative character is co-extensive with contemporary prophecy only to the degree that one learns from it something of the philosophical presuppositions of the men who acc. to the principle of correspondence between the first time and the last believed that they were summoned as Messianic prophets to usher in the new aeon.

IV. The End of Prophecy.

There never was in Israel a prophetic age in the sense of a fixed historical period. Prophecy was always accompanied and opposed by living and fruitful rational or anti-charismatic trends. Furthermore, it was always challenged from within by the question of its legitimacy. What distinguishes prophecy in Israel is its tremendous ability to live on in ever new forms. When the vivid prophetic manifestations of the post-exilic period finally had to give place to a nomistic rationalism, there were easily discernible historical reasons for this. After the death of Herod, prophecy was entangled in political developments as never before in Israel's history. After the overthrow of the hierocracy in Jerusalem, which was also a serious defeat for all charismatics, Pharisaic Rabbinism set to work creating a Palestinian patriarchate on a nomistic rational foundation. Thus the Canon was fixed (→ III, 981 ff.) and all movements which did not correspond or bow to the Pharisaic Rabb. norm were eliminated. At the same time all lit. which went beyond the new dogmatic limits was suppressed, and the schema triumphed whereby the wise men were the legitimate successors of the prophets, → 818, 7 ff. All the same, for all its consistency the nomistic trend was not strong enough to destroy at once the charismatic element, which was esp. dangerous in Zelotism. Hence the second revolt broke out, as it would appear, under the spiritual leadership of Akiba as prophet, → 824, 11 ff. The radical defeat and the Roman policy of extermination up to the edict of toleration under Antoninus Pius in 138 A.D. ended all spirit-effected manifestations. With gt. effort the Synagogue could be reconstructed, but now its official outlook was so strongly dominated by nomistic rationalism that soon there disappeared the whole of that colourful and tension-laden world which was the native soil of the preaching of Jesus and His apostles.

Meyer

D. Prophets and Prophecies in the New Testament.

I. Occurrence and Meaning of the Words.

1. In the NT the noun προφήτης is by far the most common term of the group. It occurs 144 times, 37 times in Mt., 29 in Lk., 30 in Ac., 14 in Jn., but only 6 in Mk. and only 10 in Paul unless one counts the 3 in Eph. and 1 in Past. By and large the NT understands by the prophet the biblical proclaimer of the divine, inspired message. If one disregards the reference to Balaam (→ I, 525, 1 ff.; 2 Pt. 2:16, cf. Nu. 22:18 with Nu. 24:1), the title is applied only once to a Gentile in the NT. The Cretan poet (→ 792, 10 ff.) Epimenides, who is called a prophet in Tt. 1:12, was reputed to have knowledge of divine things and to be able to predict future events. [330] Because of the revelation imparted to him by the Spirit, the

---

[330] Plat. Leg., I, 642d e; Cic. Divin., I, 18, 34; Plut. Solon, 12 (I, 84d).

biblical prophet has a special knowledge of the future. This is true of the NT prophets too (Ac. 11:28), but especially of those of the OT, → 832, 40 ff. The prophet also knows a man's past without prior information (Jn. 4:19), and he is able to look into the hearts of those who meet him (Lk. 7:39). In spite of this knowledge he is not a magician or soothsayer. The prophet is essentially a proclaimer of God's Word. This is especially true of the prophets in Paul's congregations, → line 24 f. Since the message of the OT prophets is contained in books, προφήτης can also denote the prophet's writing, → 832, 28 ff.

2. προφῆτις occurs only twice in the NT. Though some women in the primitive community had the spirit of prophecy (Ac. 2:17 f.; 21:9; 1 C. 11:5), they were not given this title, → lines 34 ff. The Jewess Anna, however, is called a prophetess in Lk. 2:36 (→ D, III, 4) and Jezebel the temptress bears the same title in Rev. 2:20 (→ III, 217, 34 ff.).

3. Whereas the noun προφήτης occurs chiefly in the Gospels and Acts and is rare in Paul, the verb προφητεύω is much more prominent in Paul. Of the 28 instances 11 are in the Pauline Epistles. Like προφήτης, προφητεύω has several meanings. a. Most comprehensively it can mean "to proclaim the revelation, the message of God, imparted to the prophet" (1 C. 11:4 f.; 13:9; 14:1, 4 f., 39). In content this may take various forms and hence we get the more detailed senses. b. Since the prophet knows the future, προφητεύω can have the special sense "to foretell." Thus according to the NT view the OT prophets (→ 832, 40 ff.) proclaim the future in advance (Mk. 7:6 par. Mt. 15:7; Mt. 11:13; 1 Pt. 1:10; Jd. 14). So, too, do Zacharias (Lk. 1:67), the high-priest Caiaphas (Jn. 11:51), [331] and John the Divine (Rev. 10:11). It is worth noting that Paul does not use the term in this sense. c. προφητεύω can also mean "to bring to light by prophetic speech something concealed," to impart to others what is outside the natural possibility of knowledge (Mk. 14:65 par. Mt. 26:68 and Lk. 22:64). [332] d. In Paul the word has a predominantly ethical and hortatory character. It denotes teaching, admonishing and comforting, 1 C. 14:3, 31. The one who prophesies utters the divine call of judgment and repentance which is burdensome and tormenting to many (Rev. 11:3, 10) but which convicts others of sin and leads them to the worship of God (1 C. 14:24 f.). e. In Ac. 19:6 the combination with λαλεῖν γλώσσαις shows that the reference of προφητεύω is to inspired and ecstatic magnifying of God, cf. Ac. 10:46. f. When the four daughters of Philip are called παρθένοι προφητεύουσαι (Ac. 21:9) this does not mean that they now spoke prophetically or proclaimed a divine revelation. No prophetic saying is here ascribed to them. More prominent is the sense "to have the gift of prophecy," "to be a prophet." There was obvious hesitation to ascribe the title prophetess to women; hence προφητεύω was chosen in designation of their function. g. προφητεύω might also mean "to act as a prophet" in Mt. 7:22. [333] More probable, however, is the general sense "to proclaim the revelation of God as a prophet." [334]

---

[331] E. Bammel, "ΑΡΧΙΕΡΕΥΣ ΠΡΟΦΗΤΕΥΩΝ," ThLZ, 79 (1954), 355.

[332] G. Friedrich, "Beobachtungen zur messianischen Hohepriestererwartung in d. Synpt.," ZThK, 53 (1956), 291 f., though cf. W. C. van Unnik, "Jesu Verhöhnung vor dem Synhedrium," ZNW, 29 (1930), 310.

[333] Fascher, 169.

[334] Pr.-Bauer⁵, s.v.

4. The occurrence of the abstract προφητεία is parallel to that of the verb. Of the 19 instances 7 are in Paul (not counting the 2 in Past.) and 7 in Rev., with only 1 in the Gospels. Various nuances may be discerned in προφητεία too. a. It is first the *charisma* of prophetic proclamation which God has granted to the primitive community by the Spirit. Only Paul speaks of this gift of prophecy, 1 C. 12:10; 13:2. Sometimes, as in 1 Th. 5:20, it is not clear whether the reference is to the prophetic gift or to a prophetic saying. προφητεία is expressly called a *charisma* in R. 12:6 but the addition κατὰ τὴν ἀναλογίαν τῆς πίστεως shows that the reference is also to the work and utterance of the prophet. b. προφητεία can also be the utterance of the prophet, the "prophetic word," 1 C. 14:6, 22. It is often found in the special sense of "prediction," Mt. 13:14; 2 Pt. 1:20 f.; Rev. 19:10; 22:7, 10, 18 f. This meaning occurs chiefly in Rev. In Rev. 1:3 one may render προφητεία expressly by "prophetic book," for there is reference here to ἀναγινώσκειν τοὺς λόγους τῆς προφητείας and τηρεῖν τὰ ἐν αὐτῇ γεγραμμένα. c. As a prophetic saying προφητεία need not refer exclusively to the future. It can also contain an "authoritative direction of the prophet," the "command transmitted through him," 1 Tm. 1:18; 4:14. d. In Rev. 11:6 the combination of προφητείας and τὰς ἡμέρας shows that προφητεία denotes the "work of the prophet" here. The same applies in 1 C. 13:8.

5. The adjective προφητικός occurs only twice in the NT. It qualifies γραφαί in R. 16:26 and λόγος in 2 Pt. 1:19. In both cases the reference is to the OT prophets.

6. The word ψευδοπροφήτης (→ D, VII) is not used by Paul. It occurs in all 11 times in the NT, of which 3 are in Mt. and 3 in Rev. The question whether the pseudo-prophet is a man who falsely pretends to be a prophet of God or a man who is thus styled because he proclaims what is false (→ 784, 26 ff.) must be answered according to context in the NT. In most cases pseudo-prophets are those who claim to be prophets without any truth. According to Mt. 7:15 they act like prophets but are liars by nature. In Mk. 13:22; Mt. 24:24; 1 Jn. 4:1 cf. 2:18 they are mentioned alongside ψευδόχριστοι. As the ψευδόχριστος is not a Christ who disseminates lies but one who falsely claims the title, [335] so the pseudo-prophet is primarily one who says he is a prophet when he is not. But 1 Jn. 4:1-3 shows that the pseudo-prophet is also a man who proclaims what is false. For he is shown up as a false prophet by the fact that he champions false doctrine. In 2 Pt. 2:1 the pseudo-prophets of the OT are compared with the false teachers who introduce destructive heresies. They are thus men who proclaim ψευδῆ. By and large, however, the pseudo-prophet is called this, not because his teaching and predictions are false, but because he raises without justification the claim to be a prophet. Because he is a false prophet it follows that in most cases he also says what is false, disseminating lies.

II. The Old Testament Prophets.

1. Several OT prophets are mentioned by name in the NT. Most frequently referred to is Isaiah, Mt. 3:3; 4:14; 8:17; 12:17; 13:14; 15:7; Mk. 1:2; 7:6; Lk. 3:4; 4:17; Jn. 1:23; 12:38; Ac. 8:28, 30; 28:25. One should also add passages in which Is. is mentioned but

---

[335] K. Holl, "Der ursprüngliche Sinn des Namens Märtyrer," N. Jbch. Kl. Alt., 37 (1916), 254.

there is no express use of the group προφήτης, Jn. 12:39, 41; R. 9:27, 29; 10:16, 20; 15:12, or in which Is. is not mentioned but is quoted as a prophet, Mt. 1:22; Jn. 6:45; Ac. 7:48. [336] Ref. is also made to Samuel, the last judge (Ac. 13:20) who is also the first prophet in the true sense (Ac. 3:24), so that the list of prophets begins with him. If the historical order is altered in Hb. 11:32 and David comes before Samuel, this is in expression of the fact that Samuel is reckoned with the prophets, esp. as he is linked to them by a καί, whereas David is linked by a τε to the previously mentioned warrior heroes of OT history. It is true that David is also regarded as a prophet in Ac. 2:30, cf. 1:16; 2:25; Mk. 12:36 par. Mt. 22:43. Balaam is called a prophet in 2 Pt. 2:16 (→ 828, 43 ff.) and in Jd. 14 f, προφητεύειν is used of Enoch (→ II, 559, 9 ff.; III, 988, 25 ff.), the seventh from Adam. Of the older prophets the title is accorded in the NT only once to Elisha, Lk. 4:27. [337] Jeremiah is mentioned by name only in Mt. and as a prophet strictly only in the quotation in Mt. 2:17, for there is a mistake in 27:9, → III, 218, 22 ff.; 220, 11 ff. [338] Of the other writing prophets only Daniel (Mt. 24:15), Joel (Ac. 2:16 cf. R. 10:13) and Jonah (Mt. 12:39) [339] are mentioned once each. With no ref. to their names the following are also quoted as prophets : Hosea in Mt. 2:15, [340] Amos in Ac. 7:42; 15:15, Micah in Mt. 2:5 cf. Jn. 7:42, Habakkuk in Ac. 13:40 cf. R. 1:17, and Zechariah in Mt. 21:4 cf. Jn. 12:15. [341]

2. The OT prophets are the mouth of God through which He speaks to men : ἐλάλησεν ὁ θεὸς διὰ στόματος τῶν ἁγίων ἀπ' αἰῶνος αὐτοῦ προφητῶν, Ac. 3:21 cf. Lk. 1:70 and Ac. 3:18. Mt. expresses this in the formula : τὸ ῥηθὲν ὑπὸ κυρίου διὰ τοῦ προφήτου λέγοντος, 1:22; 2:15. This corresponds to the OT "Thus saith Yahweh," → 810, 16 ff. The prophet is not the true speaker but God, who uses the prophet when He addresses the people. From the fact that Mt. 2:17 omits the words ὑπὸ κυρίου it has been deduced [342] that Mt. did not wish to present the slaughter of the innocents as an event willed and foretold by God. But the abbreviated formula occurs also in 2:23; 3:3; 4:14; 8:17; 12:17; 13:35; 21:4; 24:15; 27:9. Through the passive τὸ ῥηθέν it, too, gives expression to the fact that

---

[336] In the NT several quotations from Is. are also introduced very generally by γέγραπται or the like, e.g., Mk. 11:17 par.; Lk. 22:37; R. 2:24; 3:15; 10:15; 11:26; 14:11; 15:21; 1 C. 1:19; Gl. 4:27, λέγει ἡ γραφή, R. 10:11 cf. 2 C. 6:2, or λέγει κύριος, 2 C. 6:17 cf. Ac. 13:34; Hb. 2:12 f. Left out of account are the many NT allusions to this prophet.

[337] Elijah is often mentioned in the NT. After Moses, Abraham and David he is alluded to the most frequently, → II, 934, 23 ff. Rather oddly, however, he is never called a prophet. Probably at the time he was not regarded as a typical representative of prophecy. He was understood more as a precursor (→ II, 931, 16 ff.) or as a representative of the high-priest (→ II, 932, 24 ff.). Moses too (→ 803, 28; IV, 865, 3 ff.), though he wrote of Christ (Lk. 24:44; Jn. 1:45; 5:46; Ac. 3:22; 7:37; 26:22 f.; 28:33) and is a type of the Messianic prophet (→ 826, 25 ff.), is never expressly called a prophet in the NT except perhaps in Ac. 3:22 and 7:37, which refer to the prophet like Moses (Dt. 18:15). Even Lk. 24:27 hardly counts Moses among the prophets. It says that Jesus expounded to them what had been written by all the prophets, making a start with Moses, cf. Kl. Lk., ad loc. and J. Weiss Schr. NT, ad loc. The expression is imprecise, however, and what is meant is that He began with Moses and continued in all the prophets, cf. Hck. Lk., ad loc.

[338] Naturally Jer. is quoted more often, but without being explicitly called a prophet, e.g., 1 C. 1:31; Hb. 8:8 ff.; 10:16 f.

[339] Jonah is mentioned on other occasions in Mt. and Lk. but without being called a prophet, → III, 408, 1 ff.

[340] Cf. also Mt. 9:13; 12:7; R. 9:25 f.; 1 C. 15:55.

[341] There are also quotations from the other prophets, e.g., Ezekiel in 2 C. 6:16 f., Haggai in Hb. 12:26 f. and Malachi in Mk. 1:2; Lk. 1:17; Mt. 11:10; R. 9:13, but they are not mentioned by name nor called prophets.

[342] Zn. and Kl. Mt. and W. Michaelis, "Das Ev. nach Mt.," Prophezei (1948), ad loc.

God is the speaker, while the διὰ τοῦ προφήτου denotes that the prophet is His mouthpiece. [343] The same applies in the Pauline εὐαγγέλιον θεοῦ, ὃ προεπηγγείλατο διὰ τῶν προφητῶν αὐτοῦ, R. 1:1 f. The word of the prophet is God's own Word.

Whereas in the Synoptic Gospels God's speaking through the prophets is understood in the OT sense, things are different in Hb. and the Petrine Epistles. According to Hb. 1:1 God spoke to the fathers ἐν τοῖς προφήταις rather than διὰ τῶν προφητῶν. This ἐν can be taken instrumentally, of course, like the Hebrew בְּ. But according to the LXX "to say something through the prophets" is λαλεῖν ἐν χερσὶ [344] τῶν προφητῶν (Zech. 7:7; Ιερ. 26:13; 44:2) while λαλεῖν ἐν usually means "to speak with someone" (Zech. 1:9, 13 f., 17; 2:2, 7; 4:1 and passim). Probably the ἐν in Hb. 1:1 is to be taken more spatially. God dwells in the prophets and speaks forth from them, so that the statement is closer to the Hellenistic doctrine of inspiration found in 2 Pt. 1:21. The origin of prophecy is not in the will of man but in God. Men are involuntary instruments impelled by the Holy Spirit. The Spirit gives them words which they pronounce, but without fully knowing what they are saying, → 822, 12 ff. Thus every prophecy needs interpretation, → 856, 33 ff. In 1 Pt. 1:10 f. the prophets make their own words a theme of enquiry. They do not merely speak of Christ in their prophecies (→ 833, 4 ff.); according to 1 Pt. 1:11 the pre-existent Christ Himself speaks through them. For the Spirit of Christ dwells in them (→ 857, 1 ff.), inspires them, and causes them to utter their words. Perhaps Mt. 13:35 is to be understood along the same lines; as the Evangelist sees it, Christ is already speaking in ψ 77:2. According to Jn. 12:38 Christ is already complaining of the unbelief of the Jews in Is. 53:1. This corresponds to the apocryphal saying according to which Jesus says in the Gospel: ὁ λαλῶν ἐν τοῖς προφήταις ἰδοὺ πάρειμι, Epiph. Haer., 23, 5, 5; 41, 3, 2; 66, 42, 8; Ancoratus, 53, 4.

3. The prophets did not only preach; they also wrote down their words, or had them written. γέγραπται διὰ τοῦ προφήτου, Mt. 2:5 cf. Lk. 18:31; Jn. 1:45; αἱ γραφαὶ τῶν προφητῶν, Mt. 26:56; διὰ τῶν προφητῶν αὐτοῦ ἐν γραφαῖς ἁγίαις, R. 1:2; γέγραπται ἐν τῷ Ἠσαΐᾳ τῷ προφήτῃ, Mk. 1:2 or ἐν βίβλῳ λόγων Ἠσαΐου τοῦ προφήτου, Lk. 3:4 cf. 4:17; Ac. 7:42; ἐπροφήτευσεν Ἠσαΐας ... ὡς γέγραπται, Mk. 7:6 cf. Ac. 15:15; τὰς φωνὰς τῶν προφητῶν τὰς ... ἀναγινωσκομένας, Ac. 13:27. Hence the writings as well as the men are called prophets, Mk. 1:2. The Ethiopian eunuch reads the prophet Is. in Ac. 8:28, 30, 34. ἔστιν γεγραμμένον ἐν τοῖς προφήταις, Jn. 6:45 cf. Ac. 24:14. The ref. is to the prophetic writings in the formula the Law and the Prophets, Mt. 5:17; 7:12; 22:40; Lk. 16:16; Ac. 13:15; 24:14; Jn. 1:45; R. 3:21 or when we read of the Prophets and the Law (Mt. 11:13), Moses and the Prophets (Lk. 16:29, 31; 24:27 cf. Ac. 28:23) or the Prophets and Moses (Ac. 26:22) or the Law of Moses, the Prophets and the Psalms (Lk. 24:44). For Paul the OT prophets are Scripture, so that he usually introduces quotations with the words καθὼς γέγραπται.

4. In the NT the OT prophets are men who proclaimed in advance what was later fulfilled in Christ, → 295, 7 ff.; I, 758, 21 ff. It is said of them : προεπαγγέλ-

---

[343] It is worth noting, however, that in the massacre at Bethlehem in Mt. 2:17 and the purchase of the potter's field with Judas' 30 pieces of silver in Mt. 27:9 τότε ἐπληρώθη is used rather than the ἵνα πληρωθῇ of Mt. 1:22; 2:15; 4:14; 12:17; 21:4 or the ὅπως πληρωθῇ of Mt. 2:23; 8:17; 13:35. The use of an indication of time rather than a final clause shows that the event is not depicted as an immediate consequence of God's will.

[344] Cf. בְּיַד in Damasc. 3:21 (5:6); 4:13 (6:9).

λεσθαι (R. 1:2), προορᾶν (Ac. 2:31), προειπεῖν (R. 9:29; 2 Pt. 3:2 cf. Ac. 1:16), προκαταγγέλλειν (Ac. 3:18; 7:52), προμαρτύρεσθαι (1 Pt. 1:11). The προ- here does not mean "to publish something openly" (→ 783, 8 ff.); it has an unequivocal temporal sense, "to proclaim or tell in advance," → 783, 16 ff. According to the NT the predictions of the prophets refer to Jesus, Jn. 1:45; Ac. 28:23. The preaching of all the prophets from Samuel on is directed to the time of Christ, Ac. 3:24 cf. 8:34. He is the fulfilment of all the promises of God, 2 C. 1:20 (→ II, 584, 2 ff.). In Lk. 4:17 ff. Jesus refers Is. 61:1 f. to Himself. The prophetic saying is fulfilled in His person and work. Matthew especially shows that the prophets foretold many details in the life of Jesus. [345]

They foretold the virgin birth and related events (Mt. 1:23), the birth in Bethlehem (Mt. 2:5 f.), the return from Egypt (2:15), the slaughter of the innocents in Bethlehem (2:17 f.), the choice of Nazareth as a home (Mt. 2:23), the work of the Baptist (Mk. 1:2 par. Mt. 3:3), the stay in Capernaum (Mt. 4:14 ff.), the healings (Mt. 8:17), the work of Jesus in secret (Mt. 12:17 ff.), speaking in parables (Mt. 13:35), the entry into Jerusalem (Mt. 21:4 f.), the passion and death of Jesus (Mt. 26:56 cf. Lk. 18:31 ff.; 24:25, 44 ff.; Ac. 3:18; 13:27; 26:22 f.; 1 Pt. 1:11). Elsewhere we read that they predicted the resurrection (Lk. 18:31 ff.; 24:44 ff.; Ac. 2:30 f.; 26:22 f., 27), the glory of Jesus (Lk. 24:25 f.; 1 Pt. 1:11), Pentecost (Ac. 2:16), the acceptance of the Gentiles (Ac. 15:15 ff.), the parousia (2 Pt. 3:2), the judgment on the ungodly (Jd. 14 f.), the eschatological new order (Ac. 3:21).

Not just the salvation foretold by the prophets is actualised. So, too, is the rejection of the people which is referred to in the prophets. Is. spoke already of the hypocrisy (Mk. 7:6; Mt.15:7) and unbelief (Jn. 12:38) of Israel. When Jesus speaks in parables and is not understood there is fulfilled the prophecy of the hardening of Israel in Is. (Mt. 13:14 cf. Ac. 28:25). The purchase of the potter's field with Judas' thirty pieces of silver was also foretold, Mt. 27:9 → n. 343.

As the examples show, the passion and resurrection of Jesus are at the heart of the proof from prophecy as of primitive Christian preaching as a whole. But the Christian community also finds the other facts in the life, teaching and work of Jesus predicted in the OT. The prophets have to be read correctly, of course, and not arbitrarily, as by the false teachers. πᾶσα προφητεία γραφῆς ἰδίας ἐπιλύσεως οὐ γίνεται, 2 Pt. 1:20 (→ IV, 337, 24 ff.). As the prophecies do not owe their origin to the resolve of man, so their exposition is not left to human caprice. There can be true interpretation only through God Himself or through the Holy Spirit. Since prophecy as well as the message of the apostles treats of Christ, the two belong together. The promises of the OT prophets become the Gospel of the NT apostles, R. 1:1 f.; 1 Pt. 1:11 f. What the prophets saw and proclaimed beforehand but did not experience (Mt. 13:17 par. Lk. 10:24; 1 Pt. 1:11 f.) [346] has come to pass in Jesus Christ. According to Ac. 26:22 f. Paul says to Agrippa : οὐδὲν ἐκτὸς λέγων ὧν τε οἱ προφῆται ἐλάλησαν μελλόντων γίνεσθαι καὶ Μωϋσῆς, εἰ παθητὸς ὁ χριστός, εἰ πρῶτος ἐξ ἀναστάσεως νεκρῶν φῶς μέλλει καταγγέλλειν τῷ τε λαῷ καὶ τοῖς ἔθνεσιν.

---

[345] K. Weidel, "Studien über den Einfluss des Weissagungsbeweises auf die evangelische Gesch.," ThStKr, 83 (1910), 83-109, 163-195.

[346] They died as did Abraham, Jn. 8:52 f. The prophets, like the patriarchs, naturally belong to God's eschatological kingdom and with the many from the Gentile world will partake of the eschatological banquet, Lk. 13:28 f.

The words of the prophets do not usually take the form of open predictions (→ 857, 25 ff.) but often contain descriptions of existing situations or even deal with past events which the NT relates to the present, so that more is seen of advance depiction than of true prophecy. Thus the historical statement ἐξ Αἰγύπτου ἐκάλεσα τὸν υἱόν μου (Hos. 11:1 = Mt. 2:15), Rachel's mourning for the Jews led away into captivity (Jer. 31:15 = Mt. 2:17 f.), the proclamation of God's gracious acts in the history of the people Israel (Ps. 78:2 = Mt. 13:35), and the accusation of the prophet that the worship of God has been externalised by the people (Is. 29:13 = Mk. 7:6 par. Mt. 15:7 f.) or that his contemporaries do not believe (Is. 53:1 = Jn. 12:38) are all regarded as predictions. The NT sees no distinction between depiction and prophecy. It begins, not with the original meaning, but with the fact of fulfilment, and it then finds in the OT what it needs. The OT does not offer new knowledge. In the light of the fulfilment the NT authors find predictions in the statements of the OT. [347]

5. For the NT the OT prophets are not just men who proclaim future events. They are also adduced by the authors of the NT as authorities to support the truth of what is being maintained. Jesus when He takes action against the merchants and money-changers in the temple appeals to sayings in the prophets, Mk. 11:17 par. Jesus also uses Is. 54:13 to elucidate and back up His own statement that God will teach any man, Jn. 6:45. It is proved from the words of the prophets that Israel has been guilty of idolatry (Ac. 7:42), and that God does not dwell in the temple (Ac. 7:48). All the prophets emphatically proclaim forgiveness of sins through the name of Christ for all who believe, says Peter in the house of Cornelius (Ac. 10:43), and James appeals to the authority of the prophets to justify the receiving of Gentiles into the community (Ac. 15:15). In Antioch Paul warns the Jews that the word of the prophets is being fulfilled, Ac. 13:40. The words of the prophets are thus adduced to confirm important thoughts in preaching and to lend emphasis to proclamation.

6. With surprising frequency the NT refers to the persecution and putting to death of the prophets by the Jews, → V, 714, 8 ff. There are some OT references to the king or people harassing the prophets. [348] It was apparently in the apocryphal works, however, that the idea of the prophet as martyr was really popularised. [349] Primitive Christianity and possibly Jesus Himself took up the idea, cf. 1 Th. 2:15.

---

[347] R. Bultmann, "Weissagung u. Erfüllung," Glauben u. Verstehen, II (1952), 163-167; F. Baumgärtel, Verheissung (1952), 73-77.

[348] Urijah, the son of Shemaiah, was put to death by Jehoiakim, Jer. 26:20-23; Zechariah, the son of Jehoiada, was stoned in the temple at the command of king Joash, 2 Ch. 24:21; Jezebel killed the prophets, 1 K. 18:4, 13; Elijah complained that they "have slain thy prophets with the sword ; and I, even I only, am left ; and they seek my life, to take it away," 1 K. 19:10, 14; R. 11:3; Micaiah, the son of Imlah, was put in prison by Ahab in 1 K. 22:27 and Hanani by Asa in 2 Ch. 16:10; the men of Anathoth sought the life of Jer., Jer. 11:18-21; the priest Pashur, head of the temple police, had Jer. arrested and put in the stocks, Jer. 20:2; after his temple addresses priests, prophets and people seized Jer. and declared him worthy of death, Jer. 26:8-11; "the princes were wroth with Jeremiah, and smote him, and put him in prison ... so Jeremiah came into the vaulted cistern chamber, and remained there many days," Jer. 37:15 f. cf. 38:4-6; in addition there are the general statements : "Your own sword hath devoured your prophets" (Jer. 2:30), and : "They slew thy prophets" (Neh. 9:26).

[349] H. J. Schoeps, "Die jüd. Prophetenmorde," Aus frühchr. Zeit (1950), 126-143; H. A. Fischel, "Martyr and Prophet," JQR, 37 (1946), 265-280, 363-386; → V, 714, n. 470; 471.

It is the fate of the prophet — this seems to have been a current expression [350] — to die in Jerusalem, Lk. 13:33 f.; Mt. 23:37. The Jews are sons not only of the prophets and the covenant (Ac. 3:25) but also of those who slew the prophets (Mt. 23:31; Lk. 6:23; 11:47 f. cf. Mt. 21:35; 22:6; Hb. 11:36 f.). The disciples, when persecuted by the Jews, are in this respect descendants of the prophets, Mt. 5:12. The prophets, who did not flee from suffering but bore it patiently, are thus a model for the community, Jm. 5:10 cf. Hb. 11:32-38. In Mt. 23:34 par. Lk. 11:49 a saying from an apocryphal Wisdom writing concerning the martyrdom of prophets is quoted by the Evangelists, christianised in different ways, and referred to their own situation. The title of the Jewish work is better preserved in Lk., for in Mt. the saying is presented as a statement of Jesus. On the other hand, the wording is closer to the original in Mt., who speaks in Jewish fashion of prophets, wise men and scribes, for which Lk. has prophets and apostles. But Mt. too christianises the saying by interweaving the crucifixion in a reference to the death of Christ. [351] Mt. 23:29-35 par. Lk. 11:47-51 is a typical example of the way in which Christianity adopts Jewish sayings which are significant in relation to its own time of persecution. The connecting line from the killing of the prophets to the crucifixion of Jesus is drawn in Ac. 7:52 : "Which of the prophets have not your fathers persecuted? and they have slain them which shewed before of the coming of the Just One ; of whom ye have been now the betrayers and murderers."

III. Pre-Christian Prophets.

The NT does not refer only to OT prophets and primitive Christian prophets. In the infancy stories in Lk. Jewish men and women are either directly called prophets or shown to be such by the way they come on the scene and speak.

1. Ζαχαρίας ... ἐπλήσθη πνεύματος ἁγίου καὶ ἐπροφήτευσεν, Lk. 1:67. According to these introductory words the Benedictus is for Lk. neither the personal thanksgiving of a heart moved by joy nor a literary product taken from tradition but a prophecy inspired by the Holy Ghost. On the basis of the insight which he has been given into the mysteries of the divine counsel, Zacharias proclaims the saving will of God which will shortly be put into effect. The fact that we have here prophecies of the future is shown by the futures κληθήσῃ, προπορεύσῃ (v. 76), ἐπισκέψεται (v. 78).

2. In the account of the meeting between Elisabeth and Mary the word group προφητεύω is not used. But when it is said of Elisabeth as previously of Zacharias (→ lines 25 ff.): ἐπλήσθη πνεύματος ἁγίου, and when this is followed by ἀνεφώνησεν κραυγῇ μεγάλῃ (Lk. 1:41 f.), this obviously expresses the fact that Elisabeth spoke prophetically. Having the prophetic Spirit, she is able to know the past and see what is hidden without anyone telling her → n. 400. She thus greets Mary as the mother of the Messiah, just as the prophetess Anna later recognises the Redeemer in the child Jesus, → 836, 9 ff. She knows of the message of the angel and the faith of Mary, v. 45, 38.

3. The group προφητεύω is not used with ref. to Simeon. But there can be no doubt but that he is meant to be presented as a prophet : πνεῦμα ἦν ἅγιον ἐπ' αὐτόν (Lk. 2:25), i.e., the prophetic Spirit rested on him, Str.-B., II, 147. We also read that the

---

[350] Barrett, 97.
[351] E. Haenchen, "Mt. 23," ZThK, 48 (1951), 53 f.

Spirit told him he would not see death until he had seen the Lord's anointed, 2:26. Finally he goes ἐν τῷ πνεύματι into the temple, sees in Jesus the Messiah, and speaks about Him prophetically. This shows quite plainly that Lk. means to depict Simeon as a prophet.

4. In contrast to Zacharias, Elisabeth and Simeon, Anna is expressly called a prophetess, Lk. 2:36. Little more is said about her work as such. If she is called a prophetess, this does not mean that like the ancient prophet she came before the people with a message of grace and judgment. She was probably called a prophetess because she had the gift of foreseeing and foretelling the future. As a prophetess she sees the Messiah in the child Jesus when He is brought to the temple. Her praise and confession confirm the statements of Simeon. When she speaks of Jesus to all who await redemption in Jerusalem (Lk. 2:38), this means that she proclaims Jesus as the eschatological Saviour.

These men and women are not yet Christians; they are pious Jews. It is worth noting that they are all related in some way to the temple. Zacharias is a priest, discharges his priestly ministry, and prophesies at the circumcision of his son. Elisabeth is the wife of a priest. Simeon speaks at the presentation of Jesus in the temple. It is expressly said of Anna that she "departed not from the temple, but served God with fastings and prayers night and day," Lk. 2:37. Prophecy and temple are not opposed to one another in these pre-Christian prophets of Christ; they are in harmony. [352]

IV. John the Baptist.

1. In all strata of the Gospel tradition John the Baptist is called a prophet: in the historical source (Mk. 11:32 par. Mt. 21:26; Lk. 20:6), the Logia source (Mt. 11:9 par. Lk. 7:26), Matthew (14:5), Luke (1:76) and John (1:21, 25). According to the accounts very different people see in John a possible prophet. In Mk. 11:32 par. and Mt. 14:5 this is the general view of the people. In Jn. 1:21, 25 the investigating commission sent by the Sanhedrin even asks John himself. In Lk. 1:76 his father Zacharias calls him προφήτης ὑψίστου, and in Mt. 11:9 par. Jesus says of him that he is indeed more than a prophet, → 839, 3 ff.

2. The Synoptic Gospels describe the call, appearance and preaching of the Baptist wholly after the manner of the OT prophets.

Thus the call of Jer. is introduced by the saying τὸ ῥῆμα τοῦ θεοῦ ὃ ἐγένετο ἐπὶ Ιερεμιαν τὸν τοῦ Χελκιου and by a note of the date through ref. to the kings, Jer. 1:1 f. cf. Hos. 1:1; Jl. 1:1; Mi. 1:1; Zech. 1:1; 2 S. 7:4; 1 K. 17:2, 8. Similarly in Lk. 3:1 f. the account of the ministry of the Baptist opens with a note of the date through ref. to political and priestly rulers and with the familiar OT formula ἐγένετο ῥῆμα θεοῦ ἐπὶ ᾿Ιωάννην τὸν Ζαχαρίου υἱόν. Again, the preaching of the Baptist is like that of the prophets when he intimates God's wrathful judgment and demands radical conversion, → IV, 1000, 18 ff. Acc. to Mk. 1:2 par. he is the last prophet before the coming of the Messiah and he also fulfils the prophetic word. Before the ruler he acts as a genuine prophet of Israel acc. to the story in Mk. 6:17 ff. As Samuel spoke to Saul (1 S. 15:10 ff.), Nathan (2 S. 12:1 ff.) and Gad (2 S. 24:11) to David, Ahijah to the wife of Jeroboam (1 K. 14:7 ff.), Jehu to Baasha (1 K. 16:1 ff.) and Elijah to Ahab (1 K. 21:17 ff.) when they had done wrong, so John the Baptist speaks out when the king has transgressed

---

[352] Guy, 29.

God's commandments. He also shows himself to be a prophet in the Gospels by foretelling the future. He not only proclaims the imminent judgment of divine wrath (Mt. 3:7 ff.) but also prophesies the mighty One who will come after him, Mk. 1:7 f. Finally one may ask whether the baptism of John is not to be understood as a prophetic action, → 838, 6 ff. [353]

3. John the Baptist seems at first to have been not merely the forerunner of the Messiah. The sources leave the impression that he was more than an ordinary prophet (Mt. 11:9), that he was in fact a Messianic figure. His followers at least and perhaps a section of the Jews regarded him as the expected eschatological prophet, → 826, 7 ff.

a. The special nature of the Baptist may be seen clearly in the infancy stories in Lk. What Lk. 1:4 ff. says of him has a Messianic and eschatological character. The intimation of his birth is a gospel, Lk. 1:19, → II, 719, 14 f. His birth does not merely bring personal joy to his parents (χαρὰ καὶ ἀγαλλίασις → I, 20, 35 ff.) but has significance for the whole world: πολλοὶ ... χαρήσονται, Lk. 1:14 cf. 2:10. Of no prophet is it stated that he was filled with the Holy Ghost from his mother's womb, Lk. 1:15. Other prophets, even though God chose them prior to their birth (Jer. 1:5), were seized by the Spirit and given special tasks only as adults. John stands apart. He is a Spirit-filled prophet from the very first; he is the prophet. The expression μέγας ἐνώπιον κυρίου (Lk. 1:15 cf. v. 32) also bears a ref. to the special prophetic mission of the Baptist. μέγας does not denote the character of the man [354] but implies that he is a prophet. [355] If John is not merely μέγας but μέγας ἐνώπιον κυρίου, this expresses the fact that he is the prophet of Yahweh. The phrase means the same as προφήτης ὑψίστου in Lk. 1:76, [356] and acc. to Test. L. 8:15 "prophet of the Most High" is a term for the eschatological saviour. [357] Lk. 1:78 calls John the ἀνατολὴ ἐξ ὕψους. [358] He mediates deliverance to the people of salvation through the remission of sins and he brings light and peace into a world of darkness and strife. In the infancy stories in Lk. John is unambiguously described as the one who by his birth and word and work brings in the time of eschatological salvation for the people Israel, Lk. 1:16 f. (→ II, 719, 15 ff.).

b. Possibly John's baptising in the Jordan is to be regarded in the light of his work as an eschatological prophet. John's baptism was not proselyte baptism, for Jewish baptism was not eschatological, by it Gentiles were received into the cultic community, there was no baptiser, and it usually took place in a place for bathing, [359] → 600, 26 ff. Nor was John's baptism an Essene rite of purification, for running water was not esp.

---

[353] Barrett, 31; G. W. H. Lampe, *The Seal of the Spirit. A Study in the Doctrine of Baptism and Confirmation in the NT and the Fathers* (1951), 22; also "The Holy Spirit in the Writings of St. Luke," in D. E. Nineham, *Studies in the Gospels* (1955), 168; W. F. Flemington, *The NT Doctrine of Baptism* (1953), 22 f.

[354] H. J. Holtzmann, *Die Synpt., Handcomm. z. NT²* (1892), ad loc. referring to Gn. 10:9.

[355] K. H. Rengstorf, *Das Ev. nach Lk., NT Deutsch,* 3⁸ (1958), ad loc. Jos. Ant., 20, 97 says of Theudas προφήτης γὰρ ἔλεγεν εἶναι, cf. Ac. 5:36 D: λέγων εἶναί τινα μέγαν ἑαυτόν, also Ac. 8:9 of Simon Magus: λέγων εἶναί τινα ἑαυτὸν μέγαν.

[356] P. Vielhauer, "Das Benedictus d. Zacharias," ZThK, 49 (1952), 266.

[357] Cullmann, 20, cf. Test. B. 9:2: ἕως οὗ ὁ ὕψιστος ἀποστείλῃ τὸ σωτήριον αὐτοῦ ἐν ἐπισκοπῇ μονογενοῦς προφήτου.

[358] Vielhauer, *op. cit.,* 266.

[359] It is thought that proselyte baptism originated only at the end of the 1st or beginning of the 2nd cent., T. M. Taylor, "The Beginnings of Jewish Proselyte Baptism," NT St, 2 (1955/56), 193-198; cf. on this whole complex H. Sahlin, "Studien z. 3. Kp. d. Lk.," *Uppsala Univ. Årsskrift* (1949), 112 f.; J. Jeremias, "Proselytentaufe u. NT," ThZ, 5 (1949), 418-428; W. Michaelis, "Zum jüd. Hintergrund d. Johannestaufe," Judaica, 7 (1951), 81-120.

well adapted for ritual cleansing, → 600, 5 ff.; 612, 12 ff. John was not exclusive like
the sects. He turned to all and so long as they confessed their sins baptised them without
long preparation. [360] For him baptism was not a continually needed self-washing for the
attainment and maintaining of purity. It was a once-for-all action for those who received
the eschatological message of salvation as penitents. If this is noted, it is natural to see
in John's baptism the symbolical act of an eschatological prophet. As the Messianic
prophets led the people to the Jordan to perform an accrediting Messianic sign there
(→ 826, 32 ff.; II, 659, 15 ff.; IV, 862, 4 ff.), so John appeared at the Jordan with his
message and baptised there. The ref. to his food and clothing is perhaps to be viewed in
this light. Mk., who describes John's work very briefly and summarily, says explicitly
that he was clothed in camel's hair, wore a leather girdle, and ate the food of the desert,
Mk. 1:6. If he refers esp. to these apparently incidental matters, one may see from this
that they were important for him in interpreting and assessing the man. By his food
and clothing John makes it clear that he is a man of the desert, and Moses, the eschatological redeemer, comes from the desert (cf. Tg. on Ex. 12:42 [Neofiti I]: Moses arises
out of the wilderness). The baptism of John is a prophetic eschatological sign of a special
kind. It is worth noting that Paul, too, links baptism with the desert days of Israel in
1 C. 10:1 ff. This is the more surprising in that Paul, because of Moses' relation to the
Law, avoids the Moses-Messiah combination and refers to Moses more polemically than
typologically, → IV, 869, 34 ff. [361] If nevertheless he relates primitive Chr. baptism to
Moses this must go back to an ancient tradition which regarded baptism as a prophetic
eschatological act.

In Jn. 1:25 John's baptism is seen as proof of his Messianic work. For the
official Jewish commission asks John why he baptises if he is neither the anointed
one nor Elijah (→ II, 936, 3 ff.) nor the prophet. He was obviously regarded not
just as any prophetic figure. The question : "Art thou that prophet?" in Jn. 1:21
means strictly : "Art thou the prophet like Moses who is promised in Dt. 18:15
and who will come at the end of time to bring salvation?" (cf. Orig. Comm. in
Joh., 4, 7 and 15).

c. Herod, the local ruler, also regarded John as a dangerous eschatological prophet.
Acc. to Jos. Ant., 18, 117 ff. he did not put him to death for censuring his unlawful
marriage but because he feared John might instigate a rebellion. Since the Baptist's call
for repentance as reported in the Gospels provides no occasion for dynastic changes or
political revolution one must assume that for Herod John was not just a strict preacher
of morality but a Messianic prophet who was aiming at very different political relationships with his message. [362]

There is perhaps an echo of this view in Mk. 6:14 par. Mt. 14:2; Lk. 9:7, where
it is recorded that the people regarded Jesus as John come back again. If immediately after the Baptist's death the rumour spread that he had risen from the
dead, this can hardly be based on the popular belief that those slain without
cause come back to the earth. [363] There must have been a sense that John was
unique. If there was talk of the miraculous powers of the risen John and if a
comparison was drawn between this figure who had returned from the dead and

---

[360] 1 QS 3:4 f.: "He must not sanctify himself in lakes and rivers." Cf. K. Schubert, *Die
Gemeinde vom Toten Meer* (1958), 51 f., 112; M. Burrows, *More Light on the Dead Sea
Scrolls* (1958), 59.

[361] S. Schulz, "Die Decke des Moses," ZNW, 49 (1958), 21 f., 24, 28.

[362] Meyer, 90 f.

[363] Hck. Mk., *ad loc.*

Elijah *redivivus,* this means that there was seen in him an eschatological deliverer. [364]

d. The statements in Mt. 11:9, 11a, 13, which enshrine an ancient tradition, are significant for an understanding of the Baptist as an eschatological prophet. If according to v. 9 John is more than an ordinary prophet, the original point of this undoubtedly authentic saying of Jesus must be that he is the eschatological deliverer. [365] This is confirmed in v. 11a (par. Lk. 7:28), where John, in a saying which is difficult for the Christian, is called the greatest of those born of women. There is conflict as to the meaning of v. 13. Since the saying is put in a very different context in Lk. 16:16 it is to be regarded as a detached Q saying which, perhaps more accurately preserved by Mt., has been interwoven by him into the testimony concerning John. [366] Luke simplified and christianised the saying. [367] Mt. contains the exegetically difficult expression ἕως Ἰωάννου ἐπροφήτευσαν. The usual translation is that "all the prophets and the law prophesied until John," and the tacit supplement, which is not in the text, is along the lines of Luke: "With John the time of fulfilment has come." [368]

> In this exposition the whole emphasis is on that which is not in the text but is added. The meaning of προφητεύειν is deduced from the addition. The saying cannot be taken literally, for the prophets and the Law, which include the whole of Scripture, did not cease to prophesy only with the coming of John, but had long since ceased to do so. Nor can προφητεύειν mean that the Law and the Prophets could only prophesy up to John, [369] for this was still their task even after John. Nor can the original sense

---

[364] O. Cullmann, "Le problème littéraire et historique du roman pseudoclémentin," *Études d'histoire et de philosophie religieuses,* 23 (1930), 238; Cullmann, 33 f.; Riesenfeld, 142. The return of the Baptist can hardly be connected with the thesis that the Qumran sect expected the eschatological return of the Teacher of Righteousness, so Riesenfeld, 142. It is open to question whether Damasc. 6:10 f. (8:10) referred to the resurrection of the Teacher of Righteousness as supposed by G. Molin, "Die Rollen von En Fesha u. ihre Stellung in d. jüd. Religionsgeschichte," Judaica, 7 (1951), 202 f.; C. Rabin, *The Zadokite Documents* (1954), 23, 11, n. 2; J. M. Allegro, *The Dead Sea Scrolls* (1956), 148 f., 162; Schubert Messiaslehre, 180 f. *et al.* There are both linguistic and historical objections to this view. Elsewhere in Damasc. עמו does not mean "to rise again" but is synon. with בוא and means "to appear." If the Damascus community hoped for the return of the Teacher of Righteousness this should have been reflected more strongly in the Document. Cf. van der Woude, 71 f.

[365] Cullmann, 23; Cullmann, "Le problème ..." (→ n. 364), 237. If Lidz. Joh., 78, 2 f.; 80, 11 f., 25 f. says that John shall receive the Jordan and be called a prophet in Jerusalem, this is a reminiscence of the Jewish expectation of the eschatological prophet.

[366] A. Harnack, "Zwei Worte Jesu," SAB (1907), 956.

[367] But cf. M. Goguel, *Jean Baptiste* (1928), 66; E. Lohmeyer, *Das Urchr.* (1932), 20, n. 1; W. G. Kümmel, "Verheissung u. Erfüllung," Abh. ThANT, 6³ (1956), 115; J. Schmid, *Das Ev. nach Mt.*² (1952), ad loc. Lk. has the common ὁ νόμος καὶ οἱ προφῆται instead of the unusual πάντες οἱ προφῆται καὶ ὁ νόμος of Mt., → 832, 36 ff. The difficult ἐπροφήτευσαν is omitted by Lk. Thus the first part of the saying acquires a plain temporal sense: the period of the Law and the Prophets extends to John. He is at the turning-pt., but he belongs to the old period and is its corner-stone, → I, 612, 13 ff.; 613, 10 ff.; II, 719, 8 ff. Lk. then adds a second part in which he uses his favourite εὐαγγελίζομαι, cf. Harnack, *op. cit.* (→ n. 366), 947 f.; Dalman WJ, 116. ἀπὸ τότε means that after the days of John the Gospel was preached. The preaching of the Law, the Prophets and John was not yet εὐαγγέλιον.

[368] A. Merx, *Das Ev. Mt.* (1902), ad loc.; Schl. Erl., ad loc.; Lohmeyer, *op. cit.* (→ n. 367), 20; Otto, 79.

[369] Kl. Mt., ad loc.; Otto, 79.

be that the Prophets and the Law prophesied, including John. In that case one would expect: The Law and the Prophets prophesied up to John. But in spite of common usage v. 13 reverses the chronological order, probably to emphasise the prophesying function of the Law: the Law too, and the Law specifically, prophesied. But the note "including John" does not fit in with this. Since the literal sense of προφητεύειν does not offer a satisfactory interpretation, an attempt has been made to give the word the meaning: "to discharge the prophetic office, to act as a prophet." [370] But this meaning is not very common, → 829, 39 ff. It is also subject to the same material criticism as the translation "to proclaim prophecies." If one keeps to a temporal understanding of ἕως and to the corresponding supplementation, προφητεύειν ἕως can only mean "to declare unfulfilled prophecies up to this moment," "to be in the stage of prophecies which have not yet come to pass." But this meaning is a most unusual one for προφητεύειν. Hence it is better to take ἕως, not as a temporal preposition which sets the limit of προφητεύειν, but as the object of προφητεύειν. Elsewhere this can be expressed by εἰς, Ιερ. 35:8 f.; Ez. 12:27; Barn. 5:6. ἕως, with the gen., which can have a local sense, is used fig. like εἰς in Mt. 11:13. Since ἕως is sometimes combined with the preposition of orientation to a goal, [371] προφητεύειν ἕως means the same as προφητεύειν εἰς, "with reference to." [372]

Hence ἕως Ἰωάννου ἐπροφήτευσαν does not contain a temporal limitation which needs to be filled out by ἀπὸ τότε as in Lk. 16:16. It is a material saying: "All the prophets and the law prophesied with reference to John." He is the goal of their pronouncements, and he is thus the fulfilment of all the prophetic voices. As in Luke the Law and the Prophets predict Jesus (Lk. 24:27; Ac. 26:22; 28:23 cf. 3:24 and Jn. 1:45), so in this ancient Gospel saying they predict John. Luke could hardly use προφητεύειν since it did not fit in with his basic theological view. John, then, is not a prophet of future things who points forward to One who comes after. He himself brings salvation and ushers in the new time. [373]

e. The NT frequently inveighs against the evaluation of the Baptist which persisted among his disciples after his death. In the infancy stories Lk. expresses the superiority of Jesus to John, even though this might not have been in the original texts. [374] In the later primitive Chr. presentation there is no longer any ref. to John's possession of the Spirit, Mk. 1:8; Ac. 1:5; 19:2 → 837, 15 ff. [375] John has to be called as a prophet like the OT prophets, → 836, 33 ff. The title Kurios is now used of Christ, not God, Lk. 1:76. [376] Thus the one who prepares God's way becomes the precursor of Jesus. Acc. to Jn. 1:21, 23 cf. Ac. 13:25 John resolutely rejects the idea that he is *the* prophet. He is simply the voice of one who cries. In Mt. 11:10 ff. prophetic-Messianic claims are again rejected and John is declared to be Elijah *redivivus*. The saying that John is more than a prophet (Mt. 11:9) is explained in terms of Mal. 3:1. Since v. 11 runs on better from v. 9 and Lk. 7:26 D has this order and only then gives the quotation, one may assume that Mal. 3:1 was added later to check the Messianic claim of John's disciples. [377] The saying which set John above all men in v. 11a had also to be qualified.

---

[370] Schl. Erl. and Schl. Mt., *ad loc.*

[371] Pass., *s.v.*; Mayser, II, 2, 522, 525.

[372] J. Weiss, *Die Predigt Jesu vom Reiche Gottes²* (1900), 195; A. Fridrichsen, "Zu Mt. 11:11-15," ThZ, 2 (1946), 470.

[373] E. Käsemann, "Das Problem d. historischen Jesus," ZThK, 51 (1954), 149; G. Bornkamm, *Jesus v. Nazareth* (1956), 46.

[374] Vielhauer, *op. cit.*, 264 f.

[375] M. Dibelius, "Jungfrauensohn u. Krippenkind," *Botschaft u. Geschichte*, I (1953), 4.

[376] Cullmann, 24.

[377] M. Dibelius, *Die urchr. Überlieferung v. Joh. dem Täufer* (1911), 12; cf. Ps.-Clem. Recg., I, 60: *Et ecce unus ex discipulis Johannis adfirmabat, Christum Johannem fuisse, et*

Since 11b was already in Q the polemic against John must have been very early. Though he is the greatest of all men on earth, the least in the kingdom of heaven is greater than he. This means that John is still outside the eschatological fulfilment. There can be no question of his being the eschatological prophet, → II, 719, 12 ff. [378] Finally, the bold assertion in v. 13 that all Scripture with its prophecies has John in view is corrected in v. 14 by the restriction of the prophecies to John as the returning Elijah. As the words εἰ θέλετε δέξασθαι show, this is a special interpretation of John not found earlier, → II, 937, 27 ff. Allusions to the fact that John is the Elijah promised by Mal. occur in both the historical source (Mk. 9:13 par. Mt. 17:12) and the Logia source (Mt. 11:10 par. Lk. 7:27). But this is directly stated only in Mt. 11:14. Primitive Christianity does not reject John the Baptist. He is not, however, the eschatological prophet, the bringer of the Messianic age. He is the forerunner, the last prophet before the Messiah.

V. Jesus.

1. Statistically the description of Jesus as a prophet is not very common in the NT. In the historical source there are only two instances: Mk. 6:15 (par. Lk. 9:8) and Mk. 8:28 (par. Mt. 16:14; Lk. 9:19). Mk. 6:4 (par. Mt. 13:57; Lk. 4:24; Jn. 4:44) cannot be admitted since Jesus does not here call Himself a prophet [379] but in a proverbial saying compares His fate with that of a prophet. In Q Jesus is never presented as a prophet, but in the material peculiar to Mt. He is so twice (21:11, 46) and in Lk. He appears as a prophet with relative frequency (7:16, 39; 24:19; Ac. 3:22 f.; 7:37), and so, too, in Jn. (4:19; 6:14; 7:40; 9:17). Lk. 13:33 also calls for notice. Here Jesus says: "It cannot be that a prophet perish out of Jerusalem." It is true that in this saying, as in Mk. 6:4, Jesus is not describing Himself as a prophet but quoting a common view. Nevertheless, by not merely adopting the view but also preparing to exemplify it, Jesus numbers Himself among the prophets.

In most of the instances it is the people which calls Jesus a prophet, Mk. 6:15 and par.; 8:27 f. and par.; Mt. 21:11, 46; Lk. 7:16; Jn. 6:14; 7:40. Sometimes individuals do so, e.g., the Samaritan woman in Jn. 4:19, the man born blind in Jn. 9:17. Simon the Pharisee considers critically the report that Jesus is a prophet and reaches a negative conclusion, Lk. 7:39. In Jn. 7:52 the Pharisees definitely refuse to allow that Jesus is the prophet for theological reasons, → 846, 3 ff. On the other hand it is narrated in Lk. 24:19 that the disciples regarded Him as a prophet and in Ac. 3:22 Peter sees in Him the promised prophet of Dt. 18:15, cf. Stephen in Ac. 7:37. The four Evangelists do not use the title of Jesus when speaking in their own words, nor does He expressly call Himself a prophet except perhaps in Lk. 13:33, → lines 21 ff. This does not mean that originally the term was not used more commonly of Jesus than it now is in the Gospel testimonies. [380]

---

non Jesum; in tantum, inquit, ut et ipse Jesus omnibus hominibus et prophetis maiorem esse pronuntiaverit Johannem. Si ergo, inquit, maior est omnibus, sine dubio et Moyse et ipso Jesu maior habendus est. Quod si omnium maior est, ipse est Christus; I, 54: Ex discipulis Johannis, qui videbantur esse magni, segregarunt se a populo, et magistrum suum veluti Christum praedicarunt.

[378] Dibelius, op. cit. (→ n. 377), 13; Lohmeyer, op. cit. (→ n. 367), 19, n. 1; Michel (→ IV, 653, 16 ff.) and Cullmann, 23, n. 2, 31 have tried to promote the thesis of F. Dibelius, "Zwei Worte Jesu," ZNW, 11 (1910), 190 that the saying means that Jesus, who as a pupil of the Baptist is now the less, will be greater than John when the kingdom comes.
[379] But cf. Weiss, op. cit. (→ n. 372), 159 and Michaelis, op. cit. (→ n. 342), ad loc.
[380] Guy, 62.

2. Very different things were meant when Jesus was called a prophet. In Mk. 6:15 He is regarded as an ordinary prophet of the time (→ 823, 10 ff.) rather than an OT prophet [381] or the eschatological prophet [382] when the people says of Him ὅτι προφήτης ὡς εἷς τῶν προφητῶν. The εἷς here is not a cardinal number but is used for the indefinite τις. [383] In other words, Jesus is like one of the prophets then on the scene. Similarly the abbreviated εἷς τῶν προφητῶν of Mk. 8:28 (par. Mt. 16:14) does not mean that one of the biblical prophets was thought to have come back again. In this verse, too, εἷς is not a cardinal number. It does not mean "a specific prophet," i.e., the prophet predicted by Moses. [384] As in Mk. 6:15 it is synonymous with τις, so that Jesus is regarded as an ordinary prophet. [385] A prophet has the supernatural gift of knowing things which are concealed, → n. 400. When Jesus tells the woman of Samaria something out of her past, He is in her eyes a prophet, Jn. 4:19. Simon the Pharisee is more suspicious : "This man, if he were a prophet, would have known who and what manner of woman this is," Lk. 7:39. It is true that he gives Jesus the title διδάσκαλε, which is astonishing for a Pharisee. Yet he can hardly have regarded Jesus as the eschatological prophet who was to usher in the promised time of salvation. [386] He doubts whether Jesus is a prophet at all. In the conversation which follows Jesus shows him that He was well acquainted with the woman's past and that He could also see into Simon's own heart.

3. In some passages Jesus is compared with the OT prophets or even directly identified as one of them. Lk. 9:8 changes the ὡς εἷς τῶν προφητῶν of Mk. 6:15 into προφήτης τις τῶν ἀρχαίων. This lifts Jesus out of the company of contemporary prophets and sets Him alongside the classical prophets. Mk. 8:28 is similarly enhanced in Mt. 16:14 and Lk. 9:19. Luke again has προφήτης τις τῶν ἀρχαίων, while in Mt. 16:14 the people regards Jesus as Jeremiah (→ III, 220, 14 ff.) or ἕνα τῶν προφητῶν.

As the passages show, the comparison of Jesus with the OT prophets is secondary. It is natural, however, in view of the fact that Jesus, like the Baptist before Him (→ 836, 38 ff.), took up the prophetic call for conversion (→ IV, 1001, 25 ff.; Mk. 1:15; Mt. 4:17; 11:20; Lk. 5:32; 13:3, 5) and also appealed to prophets like Is. (Mk. 7:6 par. Mt. 15:7 cf. Mk. 12:1 par.), Hosea (Mt. 9:13; 12:7), Jer. and Dt. Is. (Mk. 11:17 par. Mt. 21:13; Lk. 19:46) and Jonah (Mt. 12:41 par. Lk. 11:32) in the conflict against the Jewish externalising of worship. [387] Jesus did not expound Scripture academically like the Rabb. He spoke to the people with God-given directness and power as the OT

---

[381] So Schl. Erl., J. Weiss Schr. NT, Loh. Mk. and J. Schmid, *Das Ev. nach Mk.*³ (1954), *ad loc.*; Cullmann, 33 f.

[382] So Cullmann, 33 f. He espouses the Western reading represented by D *et al.*; this leaves out ὡς and simply has εἷς τῶν προφητῶν. In this way Jesus is not compared with one of the prophets but identified with an OT prophet, though it is not said whether this is Moses, Enoch, Jer. or some other. In this case Jesus would be one of the gt. prophets come to earth as a Messianic saviour at the end of the time. But the Western text is hardly to be preferred as *lectio difficilior*.

[383] → IV, 858, n. 119; Gils, 21.

[384] So Bornhäuser, 129.

[385] Meyer, 11.

[386] So Schl. Lk., *ad loc.* The B reading ὁ προφήτης expresses this. But it is to be viewed as secondary since the other MSS would hardly introduce a lower estimation of Jesus.

[387] H. J. Cadbury, "Jesus and the Prophets," *Journal of Religion*, 5 (1925), 607-622.

prophets had done (→ II, 569, 19 ff.). Hence the people said that "he taught them as one having authority, and not as the scribes," Mt. 7:29; Mk. 1:22 cf. 1:27; Lk. 4:32, 36. The distinction between Him and the Rabb. was not one of degree as between different teachers. It was a fundamental one. He taught as one especially authorised by God, so that His Word was God's Word which men could not evade. The term ἐξουσία is not used of the work of the OT prophets. [388] But it expresses in the Gospels something similar to the "Thus saith Yahweh" of the OT. [389] In the OT the prophets introduce their sayings with this formula, while in the NT the people uses ἐξουσίαν ἔχων to describe its impression of the teaching of Jesus. In both cases what is expressed is divine authorisation, so that the word ἐξουσία is a ref. to the prophetic utterance of Jesus. [390] Acc. to the Gospel account the cursing of the fig-tree in Mk. 11:13 f., 20 f. par. Mt. 21:19 f. is a symbolical prophetic action on the part of Jesus [391] which expresses with figurative realism the rejection of Israel. [392] Perhaps we have here an original parable which the tradition later turned into a symbolical action corresponding to those of the OT prophets. [393]

When the passion and death of Jesus are viewed as the martyrdom of a prophet (Lk. 13:33), Jesus is equated with the persecuted prophets of the OT, → 834, 29 ff. Yet the superiority of Jesus to the OT prophets is continually stressed : "A greater than Jonas is here" (Mt. 12:41). Jesus is not to be set alongside the OT prophets. He is the One who brings the new age which the OT prophets had only foretold, → 832, 42 ff. "Many prophets and kings have desired to see those things which ye see, and have not seen them ; and to hear those things which ye hear, and have not heard them," Lk. 10:24 cf. Mt. 13:17. They knew only the hope and did not experience the fulfilment, 1 Pt. 1:10 f. Jesus is not just a prophet ; He is the One who fulfils the prophecies.

4. Reference may be made to several stories and sayings of Jesus which, even though they do not use the group προφητεύειν, contain features typical of the work of a prophet.

a. Like the OT prophets (→ 810, 31 ff. cf. also later Jesus b. Ananias → 825, 6 ff.), Jesus uttered promises and threats. [394] The Gospels record more invitations to salvation (e.g., Lk. 6:20 ff. par. Mt. 5:3 ff.; Lk. 10:23 par. Mt. 13:16 f.; Mk. 10:29 f.) than threats (Lk. 6:24 f.; Mt. 11:21 ff. par. Lk. 10:13 ff.; Mt. 23:13-29 par. Lk. 11:42-52).

b. Occasionally the Gospels suggest that Jesus had visions, auditions and ecstatic experiences, → II, 456 f. At His baptism He sees heaven opened and the Spirit come down like a dove ; He also hears a voice from heaven, Mk. 1:10 f. Acc. to Lk. 10:18 He sees Satan fall from heaven like lightning, [395] and acc. to Jn. 12:28 a φωνὴ ἐκ τοῦ

---

[388] Barrett, 96; Loh. Mk. on 1:22.

[389] Dodd, 74.

[390] Reitzenstein Poim., 48, n. 3; Zn. Lk. on 4:32; J. Weiss Schr. NT on Mk. 1:22; Str.-B. on Mt. 7:29; H. Huber, *Die Bergpredigt* (1932), 164 f.

[391] Cf. on the parabolic actions of Jesus Dodd, 77; Flemington, *op. cit.* (→ n. 353), 118 f.; G. Stählin, "Die Gleichnishandlungen Jesu," *Kosmos u. Ekklesia, Festschr. f. W. Stählin* (1953), 9-22; J. Jeremias, *Die Gleichnisse Jesu*[4] (1956), 192 f.

[392] R. Schnackenburg, "Die sittliche Botschaft d. NT," *Hndbch. d. Moraltheologie*, VI (1954), 14 f. cf. Schmid, *op. cit.* (→ n. 381), ad loc.

[393] Kl. Mk., *ad loc.*; J. Schniewind, *Das Ev. nach Mk., NT Deutsch*, 2[8] (1956), ad loc.

[394] Bultmann Trad., 113-124; H. Weinel, *Bibl. Theol. d. NT*[4] (1928), 107; Meyer, 13-16.

[395] This is taken to be a visionary experience by Hck. Lk., *ad loc.*; Kümmel, *op. cit.* (→ n. 367), 106 f.; Gils, 86. But the saying may be fig. or may express spiritual insight, cf. Wellh. Lk.; Rengstorf, *op. cit.* (→ n. 355); J. Schmid, *Das Ev. nach Lk.*[2] (1951), ad loc.; M. Goguel. "Pneumatisme et eschatologie dans le christianisme primitif," *Revue de l'hist. des religions*, 132 (1947), 154.

οὐρανοῦ rings forth as in the Jewish apoc. [396] When ἠγαλλιάσατο τῷ πνεύματι τῷ ἁγίῳ (→ I, 22, 6 ff.) is used of Jesus in Lk. 10:21 this means that He was seized by the Spirit and spoke by inspiration. [397] In the main the Gospel witness to the visions and ecstatic experiences of Jesus is sparse. [398] But there is the possibility that it was originally richer and that much of it was not accepted into the written form of the tradition because Jesus was not regarded merely as a prophet, and certainly not as an apocalyptist. [399]

c. Jesus does not display supernatural knowledge only in Lk. 7:39 ff. and Jn. 4:19 → 842, 11 ff. There are several examples in the Gospels of a prophetic scanning of the thoughts of men. [400] In the healing of the man let down through the roof Jesus perceives (ἰδών) the faith of those who brought him, Mk. 2:5; Mt. 9:2; Lk. 5:20. He also knows the thoughts of the scribes, ἐπιγνούς in Mk. 2:8; Lk. 5:22; εἰδώς in Mt. 9:4. He is aware of (ᾔδει) the thoughts of the scribes and Pharisees in Lk. 6:8; Mt. 12:25 par. Lk. 11:17. He knows the hypocrisy of the Pharisees and Herodians (εἰδώς Mk. 12:15; γνούς Mt. 22:18; κατανοήσας Lk. 20:23). He also knows (εἰδώς) what His disciples are thinking, Lk. 9:47. He can read the rich young ruler (Mk. 10:21) and Zacchaeus (Lk. 19:5). He also perceives the situation of the poor widow in Mk. 12:43. He has the ability to search the innermost impulses of the human heart, Jn. 2:24 f.

d. Jesus does not only see into those who meet Him. He also knows future events. The passion story esp. shows how much Jesus knew in advance. When He sends His disciples on He tells them all the details by virtue of His higher knowledge. The beast is a foal on which no one has yet sat and which is tied up, Mk. 11:2 par. Mt. 21:2; Lk. 19:30. In the preparation of the Passover He sees omnisciently that the disciples will meet a man carrying a pitcher of water whose master has a room which he will put at the disposal of Jesus, Mk. 14:13 ff. par. Lk. 22:10 ff. He also knows in advance that one of the disciples will betray Him, Mk. 14:18; Mt. 26:21; Lk. 22:21; Jn. 6:64, 70 f.; 13:11, 18 f. He knows also that all the disciples will fall away, Mk. 14:27 par. Mt. 26:31. He knows that Peter will deny Him, Mk. 14:30 par. Mt. 26:34; Lk. 22:34. He spoke in advance of His suffering, death and resurrection, Mk. 8:31 par.; 9:31 par.; 10:32 ff. par.; 14:27 f. par. In view of the vividness of the detail it would seem that the statements in their present form belong to the post-resurrection period. Nevertheless, one may see from Lk. 13:33 that in His lifetime Jesus expected to suffer a violent death in Jerusalem,

---

[396] Bau. J., ad loc.

[397] Schl. Erl., Kl. Lk., Hck. Lk., ad loc.; Barrett, 101 f.; Taylor, 15; Riesenfeld, 145; but cf. H. v. Baer, Der hl. Geist in d. Lk.-Schriften (1926), 73 f.

[398] It does not include the temptation or transfiguration (→ V, 353, 20 ff., 354, 3 ff.) nor the note on Jesus in Mk. 3:21, 30 cf. Barrett, 96.

[399] Bultmann Trad., 113; H. Windisch, "Jesus u. d. Geist nach synpt. Überlieferung," in S. J. Case, Studies in Early Christianity (1928), 235.

[400] Meyer, 12, 104; Guy, 57 f.; Gils, 87 f. That the prophet has the power of supernatural knowledge may be seen from the following examples: "When there came to one of the pupils of R. Akiba a message from home: 'Your daughter has become marriageable, come and marry her,' R. Akiba saw it in the Holy Spirit (i.e., by virtue of his prophetic gift) and said to his students: 'Let him who has a marriageable daughter go and marry her,'" Lv. r., 21 (120c) in Str.-B., II, 133. προφήτης δὲ ἀληθείας ἐστὶν ὁ πάντοτε πάντα εἰδώς, τὰ μὲν γεγονότα ὡς ἐγένετο, τὰ δὲ γινόμενα ὡς γίνεται, τὰ δὲ ἐσόμενα ὡς ἔσται, Ps.-Clem. Hom., 2, 6, 1; προφήτης δὲ ἀληθής ἐστιν ὁ πάντα πάντοτε εἰδώς, ἔτι δὲ καὶ τὰς πάντων ἐννοίας, Hom., 3, 11, 2; διὸ τεθαρρηκότως ἐξετίθετο περὶ τῶν μελλόντων ἔσεσθαι ... προφήτης γὰρ ὢν ἄπταιστος, ἀπείρῳ ψυχῆς ὀφθαλμῷ πάντα κατοπτεύων ἐπίσταται λανθάνων, Hom., 3, 13, 1 f.; προφητείαν δέ φησιν εἶναι τὴν τῶν μελλόντων προαγόρευσιν, λέγεσθαι δὲ καὶ τὸ τὰ ἐν πράξει ἤτοι καὶ βουλεύμασιν ἄδηλα ὄντα τοῖς πολλοῖς εἰπεῖν, ἀλλὰ μὴν καὶ τὸ τὰ παρεληλυθότα καὶ ἀγνοούμενα τοῖς πᾶσι δυνηθῆναι εἰπεῖν ὡς Μωϋσῆς διηγήσατο ἅπαντα, Theod. Mops. on 1 C. 12:10 in K. Staab, Pauluskomm. aus d. griech. Kirche, NT Abh., 15 (1933), 190.

→ V, 714, 5 ff. [401] In Jn. 14:29 He prophesies His return to the Father. In Jn. 16:4 He foretells persecutions. In Mt. 10:23 He promises that the Son of Man will come before the mission to Israel is completed. [402] In Mk. 9:1 par. Mt. 16:28; Lk. 9:27 He promises that some of His contemporaries will experience the coming of the kingdom of God in power. [403] Whether or not some of the apoc. sayings derive from Jesus, He certainly spoke of the coming kingdom of God. Nor can one legitimately excise all the sayings of Jesus about the future as *vaticinia ex eventu*, esp. since events do not always seem to be in agreement with the sayings. Mk. 13 uses material from Jewish apoc., the sayings of Jesus and the thinking of the community which reflects the experience of a later date. The prophecy of the destruction of the temple in v. 2, which is along the lines of OT prophecy of disaster, is certainly older than the event, → III, 245, 4 ff. [404] Jesus' saying about the sons of Zebedee in Mk. 10:39 is also an ancient prophecy. Since John probably did not die a martyr's death Mt. 20:22 omits the reference to the baptism of death. [405] These instances show how strongly the Evangelists are convinced of the foreknowledge of Jesus, and in fact Jesus must have predicted many things in prophetic vision.

5. In some verses in the NT Jesus is obviously regarded as the promised prophet of the last time, → 826, 19 ff.

a. Peter (Ac. 3:22) and Stephen (Ac. 7:37) in their addresses quote Dt. 18:15 (→ IV, 868, 10 ff.) with reference to Jesus. [406] The sayings in Jn. 7:40 and 6:14 are also based on expectation of the prophet like Moses. After the miracle of the loaves it is said : οὗτός ἐστιν ἀληθῶς ὁ προφήτης ὁ ἐρχόμενος εἰς τὸν κόσμον, Jn. 6:14, for what has been experienced is reminiscent of the miracle of the manna,

---

[401] Dodd, 73; Gils, 28.

[402] In view of the predicted nearness of the kingdom and the non-fulfilment when the Gospel was written one may attribute this saying to Jesus Himself, J. Weiss Schr. NT and Schniewind, *op. cit.* (→ n. 393), *ad loc.*; Kümmel, *op. cit.* (→ n. 367), 56 f.; J. Jeremias, *Jesu Verheissung f. d. Völker* (1956), 17 f., but cf. W. Bousset, *Kyrios Christos*[2] (1921), 10, n. 3; Bultmann Trad., 129: E. Grässer, "Das Problem der Parusieverzögerung in d. synpt. Ev. u. in d. Ag.," Beih. ZNW, 22 (1957), 138; P. Vielhauer, "Gottesreich u. Menschensohn in d. Verkündigung Jesu," *Festschr. f. G. Dehn* (1957), 58-61.

[403] This might be a saying of primitive Chr. prophecy which, designed to comfort and startle in a time of waning eschatological expectation, was then ascribed to Jesus. On this much debated and very difficult v. cf. the comm., also Bultmann Trad., 128; Otto, 111; W. Michaelis, *Der Herr verzieht nicht die Verheissung* (1942), 37 f.; G. Bornkamm, "Die Verzögerung d. Parusie," *In memoriam E. Lohmeyer* (1951), 118; R. Morgenthaler, *Kommendes Reich* (1952), 52 f.; Kümmel, *op. cit.*, 19-22; W. Michaelis, "Kennen d. Synpt. eine Verzögerung d. Parusie?" *Synpt. Studien, Wikenhauser-Festschr.* (1953), 116; E. Percy, "Die Botschaft Jesu," *Lunds Univ. Årsskrift*, NF, 49, 5 (1953), 177; H. Conzelmann, *Die Mitte d. Zeit, Beiträge z. hist. Theol.*, 17[2] (1957), 88 f.; W. Marxsen, "Der Evangelist Mk.," FRL, 67 (1956), 140, n. 1; Grässer, *op. cit.* (→ n. 402), 133 f.

[404] Apart from the comm. cf. the discussion in Meyer Urspr., I, 125, n. 1; Dodd, 76; J. Jeremias, "Jesus als Weltvollender," BFTh, 33, 4 (1930), 39 f.; M. Goguel, *Das Leben Jesu* (1932), 263 f.; G. Hölscher, "Der Ursprung d. Apokalypse Mk. 13," ThBl, 12 (1933), 192 f.; Otto, 290; F. Busch, "Zum Verständnis d. synpt. Eschatologie ; Mk. 13 neu untersucht," *NT.liche Forschungen*, IV, 2 (1938), 69; M. Meinertz, *Theol. d. NT*, I (1950), 58 f.; O. Cullmann, *Petrus* (1952), 222 f.; (E.T. [1962], 204 f.); G. Harder, "Das eschatologische Geschichtsbild d. sog. kleinen Apk. Mk. 13," *Theologia viatorum*, 4 (1952), 72; Kümmel, *op. cit.* (→ n. 367), 92-97; G. R. Beasley-Murray, *Jesus and the Future* (1954), 40; Marxsen, *op. cit.* (→ n. 403), 115.

[405] Dodd, 77; Otto, 291; J. Schniewind, *Das Ev. nach Mk., NT Deutsch*, I[8] (1958), *ad loc.*

[406] Staerk, 63 f.; Meyer, 24 f.; Schoeps, 89; C. Chavasse, "Jesus Christ and Moses," *Theology*, 54 (1951), 289; E. L. Allen, "Jesus and Moses in the NT," Exp. T., 67 (1955/56), 104; Haench. Ag., *ad loc.*

→ IV, 862, 26 ff. [407] In Jn. 7:40 the people says : οὗτός ἐστιν ἀληθῶς ὁ προφήτης, because it was expected that the prophet like Moses would repeat the miracle of the dispensing of water at Horeb. Probably ὁ προφήτης is also the reading in Jn. 7:52, so that what is contested is that the eschatological prophet will come from Galilee. [408] The Synoptists, too, seem to have the idea that Jesus is the eschatological prophet. Possibly the observation in Mk. 6:14 that Jesus is the Baptist come back again is to be understood thus, → 838, 37 ff. When on the entry into Jerusalem the people says : οὗτός ἐστιν ὁ προφήτης Ἰησοῦς ὁ ἀπὸ Ναζαρέθ (Mt. 21:11), it is not referring to a known prophet from Nazareth but because of the Messianic character of the whole event — it has called Him the Son of David and the One who comes in the name of the Lord (v. 9) — it is thinking of the prophet of the last time : "This is the prophet, Jesus of Nazareth." [409] Luke does not use the expression ὁ προφήτης because it would mean nothing to his readers. The Emmaus disciples call Jesus ἀνὴρ προφήτης, Lk. 24:19. Even after death has removed Jesus, they still think of Him as a great prophetic personality. They had hoped He would be more ; He had once shown Himself to be mighty in deed and word like Moses (Ac. 7:22 → II, 300, 10 ff.). They had thus hoped He would redeem Israel (Lk. 24:21) as Moses had been sent by God as a redeemer (Ac. 7:35). [410] Lk. 7:16, too, refers to the Messianic prophet. Jesus is not called ὁ προφήτης but the word μέγας places Him above the other prophets. The crowd at the raising of the young man in Nain is also under the impress of eschatological events, as shown by what is said about God visiting His people (→ n. 357), which takes place at the end of the time, Lk. 1:68, 78. [411] The two clauses ὅτι προφήτης μέγας ἠγέρθη ἐν ἡμῖν and ὅτι ἐπεσκέψατο ὁ θεὸς τὸν λαὸν αὐτοῦ (Lk. 7:16) supplement one another.

b. The fact that Jesus is the prophet promised in Dt. 18:15 is reflected in many stories even though the word ὁ προφήτης is not used.

Esp. in Mt. the story of Jesus is told in obvious parallelism to that of Moses. [412] The intimation of His birth by astrologers, the slaughter of the innocents and the saving of the child through a warning given to His father in a dream (Mt. 2:2-16) are based on the Jewish Moses legend, → IV, 870, 21 ff. The same words are used to describe Moses' return to Egypt in Ex. 4:19 and that of Jesus to Palestine in Mt. 2:20. As Moses in Ex. 34:28; Dt. 9:9, 18 stayed 40 days and nights on the Mount of God without tasting food, so Jesus fasted in the wilderness 40 days and nights in Mt. 4:2. [413] As Moses received God's commandments on Sinai, so Jesus proclaimed God's will from the mount,

---

[407] J. Jeremias, *Das Ev. nach J.* (1931), *ad loc.*; Meyer, 26; Davies, 244; Riesenfeld, 143; Taylor, 16; Cullmann, 35; H. Strathmann, *Das Ev. nach J., NT Deutsch,* 4⁸ (1955), *ad loc.*; van der Woude, 80, though cf. Bultmann J., *ad loc.*; Fischel, 158.

[408] On Jn. 7:40 cf. Staerk, 66; Schl. Erl. ,*ad loc.*; Schl. J. on 7:38; J. Jeremias, *Golgotha* (1926), 83; Bultmann J., *ad loc.*; on Jn. 7:52 cf. E. R. Smothers, "Two Readings in Papyrus Bodmer II," HThR, 51 (1958), 109-111. The data do not accord with the idea that no prophet arises in Galilee — the Jonah of 2 K. 14:25 is from Galilee and acc. to Rabb. tradition (cf. Str.-B., *ad loc.*) a prophet was supposed to have sprung from every tribe in Israel. It has thus been conjectured that one should read ὁ προφήτης, cf. Bultmann J. and Strathmann, *op. cit.* (→ n. 407), *ad loc.* P⁶⁶ supports this.

[409] On Mt., Schl. Mt., Loh. Mt., *ad loc.*; Meyer, 19 f.; Cullmann, 34.

[410] Meyer, 21 f.; Gils, 29.

[411] Rengstorf, *op. cit.* (→ n. 355) on Lk. 7:16; but cf. Cullmann, 29.

[412] P. Dabeck, "Siehe, es erschienen Moses u. Elias," Biblica, 23 (1942), 176.

[413] Cf. Schl. Mt., *ad loc.*; Bornhäuser, 30.

Mt. 5:1 ff. When the Pharisees demanded a sign from Jesus, they wanted a miracle of Messianic accreditation (→ 826, 30 ff.) which would prove Him to be the eschatological prophet, Mk. 8:11 par. Mt. 12:38; Lk. 11:16. [414] Miracles were performed, but not in the way expected by the Jews. When, questioned by envoys from the Baptist, Jesus pts. out that the blind see, the lame walk, lepers are cleansed, the deaf hear and the dead are raised (Mt. 11:5), He lets it be known that He is the Messianic prophet who brings in the paradisial conditions of the wilderness period, for acc. to the Rabb. there were then, prior to the sin with the golden calf, none with fluxes, no lepers, no dumb, blind, or deaf, no imbeciles, and even death was ruled out. [415] Perhaps the quoting of Dt. 18:15 in the account of the transfiguration in Mk. 9:7 par. Mt. 17:5; Lk. 9:35 is also a ref. to the promised prophet like Moses. [416]

If Jesus is depicted as the second Moses, this is for the most part in antithetical typology. We see this in the discourse on the bread in Jn. 6:32 ff. We also see it in Mt. 5. Jesus is not here a law-giver who lays on man a "thou shalt." He is the Messianic prophet who brings the Law to eschatological fulfilment so that it can be done, Mt. 5:17. The power and authority of the eschatological prophet may be seen in the "I say unto you" as contrasted with the "thou shalt" of Moses, Mt. 5:22, 28, 32, 34, 39, 44. Jesus as prophet is not just God's mouthpiece so that He has to introduce His preaching with a "thus saith Yahweh." His ἐγὼ δὲ λέγω ὑμῖν sets Him directly at the side of God, → II, 156, 7 f.; 348, 13 ff. [417] After the Sermon on the Mount ten miracles follow in Mt. 8-9, just as Moses wrought ten miracles in Egypt, → 858, 23 ff. cf. Ab., 5, 4. But there is again a difference. The acts of Moses were penal acts which brought sickness and death to men. The acts of Jesus, the eschatological prophet, are healings which banish sickness and distress.

c. As in Judaism Messianic titles and functions cannot be sharply separated nor the picture of the eschatological prophet drawn with accuracy (→ 825, 20 ff.), [418] since many hopes combine in eschatological expectation, so various concepts of Jesus merge into one another in the NT. [419] In Jn. 6:14 f. and Mt. 21:9-11 (→ 846, 7 ff.) Jesus is the kingly as well as the prophetic Messiah. The Emmaus disciples also expect the prophet to be a political liberator, Lk. 24:19 (→ 846, 15 ff.). Peter's temple address refers to the Christ as well as the prophet (Ac. 3:18-22) [420] and in Mt. 24:24 ψευδό-

---

[414] Meyer, 121 f.; Schl. Mt., ad loc.

[415] Lv. r., 18 (118a) cf. Str.-B., I, 595 f.; Meyer, 27 f.; Friedrich, op. cit. (→ n. 332), 278; cf. Ps.-Clem. Recg., V, 10 : Hic ergo est verus propheta ... qui stans publice sola iussione faciebat coecos videre, surdos audire, fugabat daemones, aegris sanitatem reddebat et mortuis vitam.

[416] Kl., Loh. Mk., ad loc.; Schniewind Mk. (→ n. 405), ad loc.; Rengstorf Lk. (→ n. 355), ad loc.; Goppelt, 73; H. Riesenfeld, Jésus transfiguré (1947), 270; Friedrich, op. cit., 309.

[417] This is not a common Rabb. formula, cf. I. Abrahams, Studies in Pharisaism and the Gospels, I (1917), 16 f.; M. Smith, Tannaitic Parallels to the Gospels (1951), 27-30, but more, cf. W. G. Kümmel, "Jesus u. d. jüd. Traditionsgedanke," ZNW, 33 (1934), 126, n. 77; Percy, op. cit. (→ n. 403), 124, n. 3; R. Schnackenburg, Die sittliche Botschaft d. NT (1954), 37; cf. also Guy, 53 and Käsemann, op. cit. (→ n. 373), 144 f., who sees the words in the light of the Messiahship of Jesus, while H. Braun, Spätjüdisch-häretischer u. frühchr. Radikalismus, II. Die Synoptiker, Beiträge zur historischen Theol., 24 (1957), 5 and 9 regards the ἐγὼ δὲ λέγω ὑμῖν as the secondary work of Mt. and does not think that the sharper form contains even a latent Messianic claim. It should be noted, however, that in Mt. 5 there is more than a sharpening of the Law as in the theologians of Qumran. The rejection of oaths in Mt. 5:33 ff. and revenge in 5:38 ff. and the injunction to love one's enemies in 5:43 ff. are opposed to the Torah, cf. Percy, 163 f.

[418] van der Woude, 83, 248 f.

[419] Friedrich, op. cit. (→ n. 332), 305-311.

[420] Meyer, 109.

χριστοί and ψευδοπροφῆται are mentioned together. The prophetic motif is very closely interwoven into other Messianic expectations in the NT.

d. The fact that Jesus never explicitly calls Himself the eschatological prophet cannot be regarded as proof that He did not view Himself as such. [421] It is in keeping with His guarding of the Messianic secret elsewhere. Directly He neither declared Himself to be the apocalyptic Son of Man nor claimed any other Messianic title. But He certainly spoke and acted like a prophet. There were several reasons why the primitive community did not portray Jesus more strongly as a prophet. Pl. does not call Jesus a prophet on polemical grounds, since the term was used by Jewish Christians (→ 858, 31 ff.) who adhered to the Law and for whom Jesus was the second Moses. [422] Again, primitive Christianity did not think the title prophet corresponded to the uniqueness of Jesus, since there were pagan, Jewish and early Christian prophets. [423] The greatness and dignity of Jesus were better brought out by titles like Son of Man, Kurios, Christ and Son of God, and the concept of the Servant of the Lord more vividly expressed the significance of the crucifixion than that of the persecuted prophet, → 834, 33 ff. Originally the tradition of Jesus as Prophet was probably much richer, for it is more likely that many statements about Him as Prophet were changed into statements about Him as Son of God, Son of Man, or Messiah than that the idea of Jesus as prophet was imported later. [424] As titles such as Rabbi and Teacher fell out of use, so it may well be that the idea of Jesus as Prophet fairly quickly retreated into the background.

VI. Church Prophets.

1. The Nature of Primitive Christian Prophecy.

Primitive Christian prophecy is the inspired speech of charismatic preachers through whom God's plan of salvation for the world and the community and His will for the life of individual Christians are made known. The prophet knows something of the divine mysteries (1 C. 13:2 → IV, 822, 26 ff.). God's saving will for the Gentiles is known to him, Eph. 3:5 f. According to Rev. 22:6 f. one of his chief concerns is to declare imminent eschatological events. He also knows other aspects of the future. Thus Agabus prophesies the great famine which will come on the world, Ac. 11:28. [425] Paul predicts the fate which awaits him in Jerusalem, Ac. 21:10 f. Nevertheless, primitive Christian prophecy does not consist only in the disclosure of future events. Nor is it concerned merely to keep expectation of the parousia alive in the community. The prophet speaks out on contemporary issues, → 855, 5 ff. He does not say only what God intends to do; he also proclaims what God would have done by men. Barnabas and Paul are separated for missionary work by prophecy, Ac. 13:1 ff. Timothy is ordained to the ministry by prophecy, 1 Tm. 1:18; 4:14. The prophet admonishes the indolent and weary and consoles (→ V, 822, 35 ff.) and encourages those under assault, 1 C. 14:3; Ac. 15:32. Through his preaching he brings to light the secret wickedness of men, 1 C. 14:25. Since he speaks with a sense of God-given authority, he gives authoritative instruction, though he is not above criticism, → 855, 44 ff.

---

[421] Cullmann, 35.

[422] Chavasse, op. cit. (→ n. 406), 290.

[423] Davies, 254; Taylor, 17.

[424] Fascher, 178.

[425] Perhaps λιμός did not originally denote an ordinary famine but one of the eschatological terrors which would shake the earth, Mk. 13:8 par. Mt. 24:7 and Lk. 21:11; Rev. 6:6. If so, Lk. de-eschatologises and historicises the eschatological prophecy of Agabus.

2. Comparison with Old Testament Prophecy.

The prophets of the NT have much in common with those of the OT and they rightly bear the same name. Ac. 2:17 says that the utterance of the apostles at Pentecost is a fulfilment of the prophesying promised for the last times. Agabus, like the OT prophets (→ 812, 3 ff.), uses a symbolical action to intimate Paul's imprisonment. He also introduces his prophecy in the style of the OT (→ 810, 16 ff.) except that the Holy Ghost takes the place of Yahweh: τάδε λέγει τὸ πνεῦμα τὸ ἅγιον, Ac. 21:10 f. Apart from Ac. Rev. esp. (→ lines 40 ff.) brings out the similarity between primitive Chr. prophecy and that of the OT. The vision of prophetic calling in Rev. 1:9 ff. reminds us of the visions of the OT prophets in Is. 6:1 ff.; Ez. 1:1 ff. The divine, like Ez. (2:8-3:3), has to swallow a small book (10:8-11), and in a symbolical action he has to measure the temple with a reed, Rev. 11:1.

But there are also differences between NT prophecy and that of the OT and Judaism. In the OT and Judaism only a few were called to be prophets apart from the prophetic groups mentioned in the historical books of the OT, → 799, 32 ff. Now some NT prophets are given prominence, e.g., Agabus in Ac. 11:28; 21:10 f., Barnabas and Silas in Ac. 15:32, the four daughters of Philip in Ac. 21:9. Several prophets at Antioch are also mentioned by name in Ac. 13:1. [426] Again, the prophets are esp. gifted leaders in the congregation acc. to R. 12:6; 1 C. 12:10, 28 f.; Eph. 2:20; 3:5; 4:11; Rev. 10:7; 11:18; 16:6 ;18:20, 24; 22:9 → 850, 9 ff. Fundamentally, however, prophecy is not restricted to a few men and women in primitive Christianity. Acc. to Ac. 2:4; 4:31 all are filled with the prophetic Spirit and acc. to Ac. 2:16 ff. it is a specific mark of the age of fulfilment that the Spirit does not only lay hold of individuals but that all members of the eschatological community without distinction are called to prophesy. In Corinth there was obviously a greater number of prophets, for those who spoke at divine service had to be limited to two or three, 1 C. 14:29. In spite of this, Paul urges the Corinthians to strive after the *charisma* of prophecy, 1 C. 14:1, 5, 12, 39. It is not a gift for the chosen few. It can be imparted to any man even though in practice it may be limited to a comparatively small circle. [427]

In comparison with OT prophecy the work of the NT prophets has undergone both an extension and a restriction. The broader basis of prophetic powers has not entailed a disappearance of prophetic insight. The NT prophets make known to the community things hidden from all former generations, Eph. 3:5. On the other hand the NT prophet does not enjoy such unlimited authority as the Jewish prophet. Since in Judaism, as distinct from the primitive Chr. community, the prophet alone has the Spirit, he has greater power over men and they sometimes follow him blindly, → 826, 35 ff. The Chr. prophet, too, declares God's will with authority, → 848, 34 ff. But he is not an unrestricted ruler over others. He is subject to their judgment, → 855, 44 ff. He does not stand above the community ; like all the rest, he is a member of it. [428]

Closest to Jewish prophecy in this regard is the prophet of Rev., → 853, 21 ff. Here there can be no question of testing the correctness of his sayings (→ 855, 44 ff.) since they are declared to be reliable and true by the supreme authority, God Himself, Rev. 21:5; 22:6. The divine claims for himself an authority (→ 850, 15) which can be compared only with that of the apostles. His proclamation is the Word of God and testimony of Jesus Christ, Rev. 1:2; 19:9. Hence it has decisive significance : μακάριος ὁ ἀναγινώσκων καὶ οἱ ἀκούοντες τοὺς λόγους τῆς προφητείας καὶ τηροῦντες τὰ ἐν αὐτῇ γεγραμμένα, 1:3 cf. 22:7. Criticism of what he says is impossible. The eternal

---

[426] Acc. to H. J. Holtzmann, *Die Ag., Handcomm. z. NT,* I² (1892) and Harnack Miss., 349, n. 2 the use of the part. shows that Barnabas, Simon and Lucius are prophets, Manaen and Saul teachers.

[427] Greeven, 4-8; cf. Nu. r., 15 (180c): "In this world few have prophesied, but in the future world all Israelites will be prophets," Str.-B., II, 134.

[428] Schl. Gesch. d. erst. Chr., 25 and Schl. Mt. on 7:16.

destiny of men depends on whether they accept it, or corrupt and reject it. The conclusion runs: Μαρτυρῶ ἐγὼ παντὶ τῷ ἀκούοντι τοὺς λόγους τῆς προφητείας τοῦ βιβλίου τούτου· ἐάν τις ἐπιθῇ ἐπ᾽ αὐτά, ἐπιθήσει ὁ θεὸς ἐπ᾽ αὐτὸν τὰς πληγὰς τὰς γεγραμμένας ἐν τῷ βιβλίῳ τούτῳ· καὶ ἐάν τις ἀφέλη ἀπὸ τῶν λόγων τοῦ βιβλίου τῆς προφητείας ταύτης, ἀφελεῖ ὁ θεὸς τὸ μέρος αὐτοῦ ἀπὸ τοῦ ξύλου τῆς ζωῆς καὶ ἐκ τῆς πόλεως τῆς ἁγίας, τῶν γεγραμμένων ἐν τῷ βιβλίῳ τούτῳ, Rev. 22:18 f.

3. The Most Important Charisma.

Paul gives preference to prophecy over all other gifts of grace, 1 C. 14:1. The prophets are repeatedly mentioned directly after the apostles, 1 C. 12:28 f.; Eph. 2:20; 3:5; 4:11; Rev. 18:20; evangelists, pastors and teachers are put behind the prophets, Eph. 4:11; Ac. 13:1; R. 12:6 ff.; 1 C. 12:28 f. It is said expressly of the prophets Barnabas and Silas that they were leaders in the church at Jerusalem, Ac. 15:22, 32. According to Eph. 2:20 the prophets are with the apostles the foundation of the Church, → I, 792, 22 ff. The prophets also occupy a prominent position in Rev. → 849, 43 and 669, 17 ff. [429] In Rev. 11:18; 16:6; 18:24 (→ I, 110, 19 ff.) they are distinguished from ordinary members of the congregation and put before the saints as a special group. The prophet has a much more direct relation to God, to Christ and to the angels than others. In relation to God he is almost on the same level as the angel, who is a fellow-servant of the prophet, so that the divine need not bow down to him, 22:9. Prophecy is the revelation and testimony of Jesus Christ; it is the Word of God, 1:1 f. (→ II, 28, 26 ff., IV, 500, 36 ff.).

Ac. might seem to suggest (cf. also Mt. 10:41) that the prophets were wandering preachers. Barnabas and Silas are at work in Jerusalem in Ac. 15:22 and in Antioch in Ac. 15:32. Agabus is found first in Jerusalem, then in Antioch (11:27 f.), and finally in Caesarea (21:10). But these statements should not be generalised. One may see from R. 12:6; 1 C. 12:10, 28; 14:1 ff.; Eph. 4:11 that originally each congregation had members who had been endowed with the prophetic *charisma*.

Though prophecy stood in such high esteem in the primitive community, and though Paul rated it highly, it was still something inadequate and transitory, 1 C. 13:8 f., 12. In the consummation the community will no longer be referred to prophecy, since it will no longer need fragmentary revelation, comfort and admonition.

Paul never calls himself a prophet but always an apostle. Yet he says that he spoke prophetically to the churches, 1 C. 14:6. He did this by declaring to them the mysteries of God and by admonishing and comforting them. In R. 11:25 ff. he reveals to the church that after the conversion of the Gentiles the Jews, who are now hardened, will attain to salvation. In 1 C. 15:51 ff. he proclaims the transforming of Christians at the *parousia,* and in v. 23 ff. the events of the resurrection and consummation, cf. 1 Th. 4:13 ff. In Ac. he predicts detailed events. He tells the Ephesian elders in 20:22 f. that sufferings await him, and in 20:29 f. he warns them that false teachers will ravage the congregation. During the storm on the journey to Rome Paul predicts than none of those on board will be lost, 27:22 ff. His epistles are exhortations, R. 12:1 ff.; 1 C. 1:10 ff.; 1 Th. 4:1 ff. They contain admonitions and promises. They are prophetic proclamation which serves the edification of the community.

---

[429] Bss. Apk., 138.

4. Ecstasy and Prophecy.

It is not always possible to make a sharp distinction between ecstasy, inspiration by Spirit-possession, and prophetic revelation, → II, 450, 40 ff. There is in the NT no exclusion of the individual ego, no replacement of the human ego by divine, prophetic rapture. Expressions like μάντις (→ 790, 14 ff.), χρησμολόγος, μαίνομαι (→ IV, 360, 21 ff.) and ἐνθουσιασμός are not used for primitive Chr. prophecy. [430] This does not mean that NT prophets did not have ecstatic experiences. That they did may be deduced from the narratives in Ac. which speak of believers being filled with the Spirit, Ac. 2:4, 17; 4:31; 10:44 ff.; 11:15; 19:6. Here the manifestations of prophecy are similar to those of glossolalia, → lines 38 ff. The prophecy of John the divine also has ecstatic features. The words ἐγενόμην ἐν πνεύματι are used in Rev. 1:10 and 4:2, and the words ἀπήνεγκέν με ἐν πνεύματι in 17:3 and 21:10, to denote the ecstatic rapture in which he hears and sees what is beyond the senses. The many visions and auditions make him more of an apocalyptic seer than a primitive Chr. prophet, → 853, 21 ff.

The prophet is very different in Paul. He certainly receives revelations (→ 853, 14 ff.) but he is not characterised by visions and auditions which transport him out of the world. His chief mark is the Word which God has given him to proclaim. The prophet in the Pauline congregations is not the seer but the recipient and preacher of the Word. He is not one who, possessed by God, has no control over his senses and has to do what the indwelling power orders. Alienation and raving are foreign to him. The primitive Christian prophet is a man of full self-awareness. When he is speaking he can break off if a revelation is given to someone else. When two or three prophets have spoken in the congregation others may remain silent even though something is revealed to them, 1 C. 14:29 ff. They cannot influence the revelation itself. This comes from God with no co-operation on their part. But the proclamation of what is revealed to them is according to their own will and it does not have to follow at once. Revelation does not cause a cleavage of personality which makes man an involuntary instrument, → 822, 12 ff.; 861, 25 ff. The responsible personhood of the prophet remains intact even though the whole man with his understanding and will stands under the operation of the Spirit. [431] Perhaps this is what is being expressed in the difficult statement that prophecy is to be κατὰ τὴν ἀναλογίαν τῆς πίστεως (R. 12:6), → I, 347, 21 ff. The reference here is to the limit and scope of the personal responsibility of the prophet. Paul is speaking against enthusiastic pneumatics who do not stay on the sober ground of faith. God gives the measure of faith (v. 3) and the charisma (v. 6). When Paul speaks of the analogy of faith, πίστις is experienced χάρις. God gives, and man must make responsible use of the gift.

5. Glossolalia and Prophecy.

Prophecy and speaking in tongues have much in common, since both are in a special way the work of the Spirit. They are obviously related in Ac.: ἐπλήσθησαν

---

[430] Trench, 10 f.; Fascher, 166 f.; Bacht Scholastik, 8 f.; Bacht Biblica, 253 f. In the LXX the word group μαντεύομαι is almost always used of pagan soothsayers and false prophets (the exception is Prv. 16:10 : μαντεῖον ἐπὶ χείλεσιν βασιλέως) and in the NT it is used for the girl with a spirit of soothsaying at Philippi, Ac. 16:16. Cf. Chrys. Hom. in 1 C., 29 (MPG, 61 [1862], 241): τοῦτο γὰρ μάντεως ἴδιον, τὸ ἐξεστηκέναι, τὸ ἀνάγκην ὑπομένειν, τὸ ὠθεῖσθαι, τὸ ἕλκεσθαι, τὸ σύρεσθαι, ὥσπερ μαινόμενον. ὁ δὲ προφήτης οὐχ οὕτως, ἀλλὰ μετὰ διανοίας νηφούσης καὶ σωφρονούσης καταστάσεως καὶ εἰδὼς ἃ φθέγγεται, φησὶν ἅπαντα· ὥστε καὶ πρὸ τῆς ἐκβάσεως κἀντεῦθεν γνώριζε τὸν μάντιν καὶ τὸν προφήτην.

[431] Schl. Gesch. d. erst. Chr., 25 f.

πάντες πνεύματος ἁγίου, καὶ ἤρξαντο λαλεῖν ἑτέραις γλώσσαις καθὼς τὸ πνεῦμα ἐδίδου ἀποφθέγγεσθαι αὐτοῖς, 2:4. This speaking is called προφητεύειν in Ac. 2:17. The parallelism is clear in Ac. 19:6. When Paul has laid hands on the baptised disciples of John, ἦλθε τὸ πνεῦμα τὸ ἅγιον ἐπ' αὐτούς, ἐλάλουν τε γλώσσαις καὶ ἐπροφήτευον.

In contrast to Ac. Paul differentiates more sharply between prophecy and glossolalia. His concern is to show the Corinthians that prophecy is more important and ranks higher than speaking with tongues, 1 C. 14:1, 5, 39 → 348, 28 ff. Both have to do with μυστήρια. For the prophet the secret counsels of God are revealed (1 C. 13:2; Eph. 3:5) and he declares them to the community through his preaching. In the case of the man who speaks with tongues, however, what he says is a mystery to the hearers (→ IV, 822, 26 ff.), since it is like the sound of a foreign language, 1 C. 14:11, 16. [432] Another similarity and distinction between the prophet and the man who speaks with tongues is that they are not alone in the congregation but have other members of the church at their side. The man who speaks with tongues has an interpreter (→ I, 722, 24 ff.) who puts what is said into intelligible words, 1 C. 14:27. The prophet has the examiner who assesses what is said by him, → 855, 44 ff. A difference is that the man who speaks with tongues may interpret his own words (→ II, 665, 20 ff.), whereas the prophet cannot examine himself. Another similarity arises in relation to the effect, namely, the edification of men, 1 C. 14:3, 4. Yet οἰκοδομή also brings out the distinction between the two charismata. Whereas speaking with tongues is of profit only for the one who speaks (→ I, 722, 15 f.), the prophet edifies the whole community. The prophet's message is for all the members, while the man who speaks with tongues speaks to God and does not profit the whole body, 1 C. 14:2 f. It is true that human volition is not ruled out in the case of the man who speaks with tongues. When Paul himself does this, he is master of his actions, 1 C. 14:19. The man who speaks with tongues does not have to speak if he does not want, so that the number of those who speak with tongues at divine service may be fixed, 1 C. 14:27. But the understanding has no part (1 C. 14:14), and to those outside the man who speaks with tongues seems like a maniac, 1 C. 14:23 → IV, 959, 7 ff. Prophecy, on the other hand, is intelligible speech. The spiritual experience is worked out and presented by the prophet in intelligible form, so that what is said may be understood by all, including outsiders as well as members, 1 C. 14:24 f. → V, 141, 21 ff.

6. Prayer and Prophecy.

Already in the OT the prophets are great men of prayer, → 803, 18 f. Similarly it is stressed that Anna the prophetess engages in constant prayer, → 836, 18 ff. In primitive Christianity, too, there is a direct connection between prayer and prophecy, for both are in a special sense works of the Spirit. In Antioch the prophets and teachers hold a service of prayer, → IV, 226, 29 ff. 1 C. 11:4 deals with prayer (i.e., public prayer in the congregation) and prophecy in relation to men, 1 C. 11:5 with prayer and prophecy in relation to women. It is certainly no accident that prayer and prophecy are brought together in 1 Th. 5:17-20. When

---

[432] Bonwetsch Prophetie, 414; H. Leisegang, "Pneuma hagion. Der Ursprung des Geistbegriffes d. synpt. Ev. aus d. griech. Mystik," Veröffentlichungen des Forschungsinstituts f. vergleichende Religionsgeschichte an d. Universität Leipzig, 4 (1922), 114-119.

one surveys the lists of gifts of the Spirit in R. 12:6 ff.; 1 C. 12:8 ff., 28 ff., it is striking that prayer is nowhere mentioned as a *charisma* in the community. Probably prayer, to which the congregation says Amen, is one of the tasks of the prophets. [433] The interrelation between prayer and prophecy is apparent in 1 C. 14. [434] The theme of the whole chapter is the difference between prophecy and tongues, cf. v. 1 and v. 39. What is said about prayer in vv. 13-19 is not an excursus. It is an integral part of the comparison. The προσεύχεσθαι γλώσσῃ (v. 14) and προσεύχεσθαι τῷ πνεύματι (v. 15) correspond to λαλεῖν γλώσσῃ (v. 13). It would seem, then, that προσεύχεσθαι τῷ νοΐ (v. 15) is ascribed to the prophet, especially as this form of prayer clearly leads to edification (v. 17), which is described as the work of prophecy in this chapter (v. 3 f., 12). Prophecy and prayer are not the same, but they belong very closely together.

7. Revelation and Prophecy.

All prophecy rests on revelation, 1 C. 14:30. The prophet does not declare what he has taken from tradition or what he has thought up himself. He declares what has been revealed to him. The ἀποκάλυψις of 1 C. 14:26 is the revelation which is imparted to the prophet and which is to become prophetic proclamation in the congregation, 1 C. 14:26-30. Thus prophecy is very closely related to revelation, 1 C. 14:6, 30; Eph. 3:5; 1 Pt. 1:10-12. God is the subject in revelation, but only indirectly the subject in prophecy.

Rev. is a transition from prophecy to apocalyptic, → 851, 10 ff. If it is never easy to draw the boundary between these, [435] this is esp. so in Rev. Rev. calls itself ἀποκάλυψις Ἰησοῦ Χριστοῦ; hence the tt. apocalyptic, → III, 578, 11 ff. It contains many of the features typical of apoc. The explanation appended to ἀποκάλυψις Ἰησοῦ Χριστοῦ, namely, "to show his servants what will shortly take place" (1:1), states the apoc. theme of the book : the disclosure of the course of the world and its end, the destruction of ungodly powers, the setting up of the new world. Other apoc. traits may also be seen, e.g., the angel as the mediator of revelation, the visions with their obscure images, cryptic numbers, the book which is written and read in place of concrete prophetic address. [436] Nevertheless, acc. to its own testimony Rev. is meant to be genuine prophecy, 1:3; 10:11; 22:7, 19 → III, 588, 38 ff. For Jn. prophecy includes much more than simply foretelling the future. This may be seen in the description of the two witnesses, whose prophetic preaching is a summons to repentance, 11:3. The letters to the churches are also to be regarded as admonition and comfort, 2-3. All the same, the view of prophecy is patently different from that of Paul. For the prophets of the Pauline Epistles exhortation is paramount and predictions are mentioned only incidentally ; in Rev. prediction is central and the exhortations are more or less on the margin.

8. Gnosis and Prophecy.

As 1 C. 14 deals with prophecy and tongues, so 1 C. 13:8-12 deals with prophecy and *gnosis*. Both are *charismata,* both are concerned with the knowledge of

---

[433] On the intercession of the prophets in Judaism cf. J. Jeremias, *Heiligengräber in Jesu Umwelt* (1958), 136 f. In Did., 10, 7 the prophet may give thanks extemporaneously. Did., 15, 1 alludes to the ministry of prophets in the congregation and in view of Did., 10, 7 this would seem to include prayer as well as preaching, cf. Kn. Did. on 15:1.

[434] Though cf. Greeven, 10.

[435] H. Ringgren, Art. "Jüd. Apokalyptik," RGG³, I, 464.

[436] G. Gloege, "Mythologie u. Luthertum," *Luthertum,* 5 (1952), 110-119.

mysteries, and both are fragmentary rather than definitive or perfect. *Gnosis* is not set above prophecy in 1 C. 13:2, for prophecy rather than *gnosis* is for Paul the supreme gift of grace, → 850, 9 ff. They differ in the way that the knowledge of mysteries is attained and in the use to which this knowledge is put. *Gnosis* is one of the "rational gifts of the Spirit." [437] It is attained speculatively, by thinking about the mysteries of faith, → I, 708, 9 f. In contrast, prophecy rests on inspiration. Knowledge is given to it by sudden revelation. The prophetic thought or image strikes the prophet from without, → 853, 14 ff. The point of *gnosis* as a *charisma* is also that what is known may be confessed in the congregation. Hence we read expressly of the λόγος γνώσεως (1 C. 12:8) and of λαλεῖν ἐν γνώσει (1 C. 14:6). But as distinct from prophecy *gnosis* is individualistic. Prophecy, on the other hand, is by its very meaning and nature concerned with proclaiming to others, with impartation to the community. Hence it can be said that *gnosis* puffs up (1 C. 8:1) but prophecy edifies (1 C. 14:3 f.).

9. Teaching and Prophecy.

Prophets and teachers (→ II, 157, 30 ff.) are frequently mentioned as the most significant preachers of the Word in the community, Ac. 13:1; 1 C. 12:28 f.; Eph. 4:11; R. 12:6 f. The prophets, too, mediate knowledge, so that one can learn from them, 1 C. 14:31; Rev. 2:20; cf. Did., 11, 10 f. Yet prophecy is not the same as teaching. Whereas teachers expound Scripture, cherish the tradition about Jesus and explain the fundamentals of the catechism, [438] the prophets, not bound by Scripture or tradition, speak to the congregation on the basis of revelations, → 853, 14 ff. διδασκαλία is instruction, προφητεία deals with specific situations, → 848, 33 ff.; 855, 5 ff. The teacher considers the past, and gives direction for the present on the basis of what took place or what was said then. The gaze of the prophet is directed to the future, and he fixes the path of the community from this angle. The correctness of doctrine depends on agreement with Scripture and tradition. For the reliability of prophecy there is no objective criterion; it is grounded in the divinely given prophetic proclamation itself, → 855, 46 ff.

10. Evangelism and Prophecy.

Like evangelism, prophecy is proclamation. It is distinguished from evangelism, however, by the hearers whom it addresses and the message which it transmits. Evangelism is addressed in the main to unbelievers who have not yet heard or accepted the message of Jesus Christ, → II, 719, 34 ff. Prophecy, on the other hand, is in the first instance God's message to existing believers in the congregation, 1 C. 14:3 f., 29 ff. It serves the οἰκοδομή of Christians, 1 C. 14:3 f., 12 (→ V, 141, 20 ff.). Nevertheless, the two types of preaching cannot be too sharply differentiated as regards the listeners. Evangelism does not merely create the community; it also preserves it by constantly preaching Christ, → II, 720, 1 ff., 734, 40 ff. Similarly, prophecy is not addressed solely to Christians; it also has missionary significance. The προφητεύειν at Pentecost (Ac. 2:17 f.) is a διαμαρτύρεσθαι and παρακαλεῖν: "Save yourselves from this untoward generation," Ac. 2:40. The words of the prophets lead non-Christians to recognition of their guilt and to worship of God, 1 C. 14:24 f. Normally, how-

---

[437] Delling, 35.
[438] Greeven, 22 f.

ever, prophecy is preaching to the congregation and evangelism is missionary preaching. There is a similar distinction in content. Whereas evangelism proclaims God's dominion by preaching God's great acts in Christ (→ II, 720, 6 ff., 730, 14 ff.), prophecy sets forth God's will for the world and for individual believers, → 848, 33 ff. The prophet is the Spirit-endowed counsellor of the community who tells it what to do in specific situations, who blames and praises, whose preaching contains admonition and comfort, the call for repentance and promise, 1 C. 14:3.

As the examples in the Did. show, the injunctions of the prophets deal very concretely with everyday matters. Thus they ask for money for particular causes (Did., 11, 12) or for support (11, 9). One cannot say for certain whether people came to the prophets for information and advice when they did not know God's will for them, as in the case of the prophets of Greece (→ 786, 6 ff.) and Israel (→ 801, 35 ff.). In any case, the Chr. prophet did not have a pat answer to all questions; he could give help only when the Spirit gave him a revelation, → 853, 14 ff. Acc. to Herm. m., 11, 5 f. it is the false prophet who lets himself be consulted, → 861, 1.

VII. False Prophets.

1. In the NT the term ψευδοπροφήτης covers various kinds of false prophets.

The ref. in Lk. 6:26 and 2 Pt. 2:1 is to Jewish prophets of the past. In Ac. 13:6 a contemporary of Paul, the Jewish magician Bar-jesus at the court of the deputy Sergius Paulus, is given the title. This man was probably regarded as a prophet by many because he claimed to see the future and to know hidden mysteries. In fact he was a false prophet because he did not act by God's commission but was a son of the devil, an enemy of all righteousness and full of deceit and all wickedness, Ac. 13:10. Balaam is called a prophet rather than a false prophet in 2 Pt. 2:16 even though, along the lines of Jewish tradition, he is quoted there as a representative of false prophecy, → I, 524, 13 ff. In particular there are false Chr. prophets, teachers who belong to the community or have come out of it, and who disturb the congregation by their teaching of abominable heresies. In 2 Pt. 2:1 these followers of the false prophets of the OT are called ψευδοδιδάσκαλοι, while in 2 Jn. 7 they are πλάνοι and in 1 Jn. 2:18 ἀντίχριστοι cf. 1 Jn. 4:1 ff. Jezebel calls herself a prophetess but is in reality a pseudo-prophetess, Rev. 2:20 (→ III, 217, 34 ff.). False prophets are esp. expected in the last days, Mt. 24:11. At their head is the assistant of antichrist (Rev. 16:13; 19:30; 20:10), the second beast (Rev. 13:11 ff.) which has two horns like a lamb but speaks like a dragon. This man puts on a pious act (→ III, 135, 18 ff.) and tries to imitate Elijah, the forerunner of the Messiah. He is not, however, a Chr. prophet who perverts the Gospel. He is rather a false prophet because he seduces men to the false religion of totalitarianism by miracles and brute force.

2. As in the OT (→ III, 575, 7 ff.), so in the NT criteria are given whereby the false prophet may be known (→ III, 589, 33 ff.). One is not to follow any prophet without reservation. All prophecy must be examined, 1 Jn. 4:1; 1 Th. 5:21. This cannot be done rationally; it can be done only spiritually and charismatically. All rational attempts to unmask the false prophet break down, for there are no generally trustworthy criteria by which to tell whether a man is a false prophet or not. Only he who has the spirit or gift of discernment (1 C. 12:10) can judge whether what is said comes from God or whether it is alloyed. According to 1 C. 14:29 prophets are judged by other prophets. [439] In 1 C. 14:37 Paul expects that

---

[439] But cf. L. Lerle, *Diakrisis Pneumaton bei Pls.*, Diss. Heidelberg (1947), 89 f.

the prophets in Corinth will agree with his presentation. Only prophets can see to it that human opinion is not proclaimed as God's Word in the congregation.

When the Spirit departed from the community and the *charisma* of discernment disappeared, but the work of false teachers increased, general standards were sought whereby false prophets could be detected. Miracles could not serve as accrediting signs [440] because the false prophets of the last days use miracles as a means of seduction, Mk. 13:22 par. Mt. 24:24; Rev. 13:13; 16:13 f.; 19:20. Thus note was taken of the teaching and conduct of the prophets. A presupposition of genuine prophecy is a right confession of Jesus Christ : "Hereby know ye the Spirit of God : every spirit that confesseth that Jesus Christ is come in the flesh is of God : and every spirit that confesseth not that Jesus Christ is come in the flesh is not of God," 1 Jn. 4:2 f. cf. 1 C. 12:3. But agreement with the christological confession of the Church (→ V, 210, n. 34) is hardly a sufficient confirmation of genuine prophecy. False prophets, too, can confess Jesus Christ, prophesy in His name (Mt. 7:22) and play the role of true preachers so perfectly that it is hard to see that they are liars. Hence their conduct must be scrutinised. The detailed meaning of the καρπός of Mt. 7:16 is hard to determine. In the case of Jezebel (→ 250, 5 ff.; III, 217, 34 ff.) the fruits are the results of her work : she leads Christians into immorality and the eating of sacrificial meat, Rev. 2:20. [441] Primitive Christianity was firmly convinced that in the last analysis the true nature of false prophets would come to light for all their pious garb. Their destiny is sure : "Every tree that bringeth not forth good fruit is hewn down, and cast into the fire," Mt. 7:19. Hard though it may be in detail to unmask the false prophet as such, the work of the true prophet is plain. His preaching effects οἰκοδομή, παράκλησις, παραμυθία, 1 C. 14:3. It brings conviction of sin and humbling before God, 1 C. 14:25.

E. Prophets in the Early Church.

I. The Old Testament Prophets.

1. Barnabas often quotes the OT prophets in a proof from prophecy, → 833, 5 ff. They are of gt. importance to him since they promote a true knowledge of the past (the incarnation and passion of Christ) and an understanding of the present (the rise and persecution of the Chr. community). They also offer a foretaste of the future, which has already begun to come to pass, 1, 7. Yet they cannot be understood at once by anyone, → 857, 25 ff. Their sayings are often enigmatic and can be properly interpreted only by the man who is wise and skilled and who loves the Lord, 6, 10. For the man of insight the OT is prophecy of Christ, 5, 6; 6, 2. 4 (cf. Ign. Phld., 5, 2; 9, 2; Mg., 9, 2). Moses as a prophet intimated the coming of Jesus in the flesh, 6, 8 f. David prophesied that Jesus is not the son of a man but the Son of God, 12, 10. In particular the sufferings of Christ (5, 5 ff.; 6, 6 f.), the drinking of vinegar (7, 4) and the crucifixion (5, 13 f.; 12, 1-4) are foretold. But the prophets speak of Christians as well as Christ, namely, of baptism (11, 1-8), and of the regeneration in the last time (6, 13 f.). Israel was not worthy to receive the covenant, 14, 1 ff. But there is fulfilled in Christians what the prophets said about the circumcision of the ears and the hearing of the Word, 9, 1-3. The inheritance now passes to Christians, 13, 1 ff. They are the holy people of the

---

[440] Cf. S. Dt., 18, 19 § 177 (108a) cf. Str.-B., I, 727: "If a prophet who begins to prophesy gives a sign and wonder one must listen to him ; but if not one need not listen to him."

[441] Guy, 114.

covenant, 14, 6 ff. All this is predicted in the OT and is now coming to pass. The prophets had the grace of Christ, (→ 832, 20 ff.), 5, 6 (Ign. Mg., 8, 2 : οἱ γὰρ θειότατοι προφῆται κατὰ Χριστὸν ᾿Ιησοῦν ἔζησαν ... ἐνπνεόμενοι ὑπὸ τῆς χάριτος αὐτοῦ, 9, 2 : οἱ προφῆται μαθηταὶ ὄντες τῷ πνεύματι, cf. also the apocr. 3 C. 3:10).

2. The proof from prophecy is even more explicit in Justin than in Barn. The OT prophets are older than all so-called philosophers. Their statements are absolutely reliable, for they proclaim only what, filled by the Holy Spirit, they have heard and seen, and they do so without fear of man or desire for renown, Dial., 7. God (Apol., 37) or Christ (38) speaks through these prophets. The oldest is Moses (32), on whom all Gk. philosophy is based : "All that philosophers and poets have said about the immortality of the soul, punishment after death, the contemplation of heavenly things and similar doctrines, they have been able to know and have developed only on the basis of suggestions received from the prophets," Apol., 44, 8 ff. The statement of Plato that God created the world by transforming shapeless matter comes from Moses, 59, 1. The myths and legends invented by the poets are an imitation of the prophetic history of Christ and owe their origin to evil spirits who wanted to make the stories of Christ seem incredible, 54; Dial., 69 f. The prophets foretold future events before they happened, Apol., 31, 1. In proof of the divine sonship of Christ they are thus more important than the apostles and teachers, who can only maintain their views, whereas the course of history vindicates the prophets. One can see with one's own eyes the fulfilment of their prophecies, Apol., 30. Since so many predictions have already been fulfilled, the others will be fulfilled too, 52.

When Just. speaks of προφητικαὶ γραφαί, he has in view not merely the prophetic writings in the strict sense but the whole of the OT, since for him this all deals with Christ, Dial., 32. Not all prophecies may be immediately recognised as such, → 856, 33 ff. Many are intentionally very obscure so that the Jews will not understand them easily, Dial., 52. The prophets clothe their thoughts in enigmatic sayings, parables and symbolic actions so that those who want to find and know them will exert themselves, 68, 90. Many actions are models for future events. Often the prophets do not use the future tense but speak of future things as though they were already coming to pass or had already done so, 114. In reality, however, they speak of Christ. The divine Logos, to utter prophecies, can also use the mouth of nations which respond to the Lord and His Father, Apol., 36, 2. The OT reader must know this method of OT prophecy, Dial., 114. It is also to be noted that there are various stages of prophecy. Later prophets are more precise and often expound older prophecies, 68. Many mysterious promises can be understood properly only when Christ opens the eyes, 76. Christ is the exegete of prophecies which are not understood, Apol., 32, 2.

Most prophecies refer to Christ, whom the Holy Spirit has fully intimated in advance through the prophets, Apol., 61, 13. The schema prophecy/fulfilment is a motif in Justin's presentation of the Gospel. He gives little biographies of Jesus compiled from the standpt. of fulfilled prophecy, Apol., 31, 7 f. The prophets knew in advance even the details of the story of Jesus. They refer to the place of His birth (Apol., 34, 1), the virgin birth (31, 7; 32, 9 ff.; 33, 1; Dial., 54, 63, 76, 84), His miracles (Apol., 31, 7; 48, 1), the entry into Jerusalem (32, 5 f.; 35, 10 f.), the Lord's Supper (Dial., 70), the passion (Apol., 32, 7; Dial., 76, 106), the bloody sweat in Gethsemane, the arrest, and the flight of the disciples (Dial., 103), the silence before Pilate (102 f.), the agreement between Herod, Pilate and the Jews (Apol., 40, 5 f.), the transferring from Pilate to Herod (Dial., 103), the mocking (Apol., 35, 6; Dial., 101), the crucifixion (Apol., 31, 7; 32, 6; 35; Dial., 73, 97), the gambling for His clothes (Dial., 104), His death (Apol., 31, 7; 48, 4), His resurrection (Apol., 31, 7; Dial., 73, 97, 100, 118), His ascension (Apol., 31, 7; 45; 51, 6), His rule as King (Apol., 41; Dial., 76), His return in glory with the resurrection of the dead and the Last Judgment (Apol., 50, 1 f.; 51, 8; 52, 3 f.; Dial., 52).

II. Jesus as Prophet.

In the early Church Jesus was still regarded as a prophet in Jewish Christianity. A definite doctrine of the prophet is developed in the Kerygmata of Peter. The Ps.-Clem. refer to Jesus as the teacher, Hom., 2, 51, 1; 3, 12, 3; Recg., II, 28; VI, 5, the Kurios, Hom., 11, 35, 3; Recg., III, 5, 3, the Christ, Recg., I, 59 f. But the truly characteristic title for Jesus is prophet. This is so much a christological predicate that Peter refuses to be described thus: προφήτου ἀληθοῦς μαθητὴς ὤν, οὐ προφήτης, Hom., 18, 7, 6 cf. Recg., III, 45 and Hom., 7, 11, 3. Jesus is called ὁ προφήτης, Hom., 3, 13, 1; 10, 4, 3; 11, 26, 2; 11, 35, 3; 13, 14, 3: Recg., I, 37, 2 f. or more precisely ὁ ἀληθὴς προφήτης, Hom., 3, 13, 2; 10, 3, 3; Recg., III, 41, 4; V, 2, 5. 9. 10; VI, 14, ὁ τῆς ἀληθείας προφήτης, Hom., 7, 6, 2; 11, 19, 1; 12, 29, 1; Recg., I, 44, 5 f.; cf. Hom., 8, 22, 4; even more sharply ὁ τῆς ἀληθείας μόνος προφήτης, Hom., 7, 8, 1 or ὁ δέξιος αὐτοῦ (θεοῦ) προφήτης, Hom., 7, 11, 3; ὁ ἀψευδὴς προφήτης, Hom., 11, 33, 1 cf. 3, 30, 2, ὁ ἀγαθὸς προφήτης, Recg., I, 40, 1, ὁ εἷς προφήτης, Recg., I, 50, 7; 54, 5, unus verus propheta, Recg., I, 54; IV, 35, solus fidelis ac verus propheta, Recg., IV, 36, iustus et verus propheta, IX, 29.

The Jewish influence on the concept may be seen in the constant emphasis on the fact that Jesus is the promised prophet of Dt. 18:15, Recg., I, 36, 2; 39, 1; 40, 4; 49, 1; 54, 5; 56, 2; 57; II, 48. "They (the Jews) often sent to us (the disciples) and asked us to speak with them about Jesus, whether he is the prophet whom Moses foretold, who is the Christus aeternus," Recg., I, 43. Acc. to Hom., 3, 53, 3 Jesus Himself said: ἐγώ εἰμι περὶ οὗ Μωυσῆς προεφήτευσεν εἰπών· προφήτην ἐγερεῖ ὑμῖν κύριος ὁ θεός ... Since Jesus did signs and wonders like Moses, there is no doubt but that He is the prophet promised by Moses. The similarity of the signs is shown in Recg., I, 57. Whereas the ungodly mocked and crucified Jesus in spite of His miracles of healing (I, 40 f.), the disciples found confirmation of their faith not merely in His works. The symbolical actions of Moses and the patriarch Jacob were fulfilled in Him as well as the OT prophecies, V, 10. For all the agreement there are differences between Moses and Christ. Jesus is not just like Moses; He is greater. Moses was a prophet as Jesus also is. But Jesus is also Christ, as Moses was not, I, 52, 2 f.

That Jesus is the Christian prophet is clearly expressed in the Ps.-Clem. by repeated allusions to Gospel sayings and stories, e.g., the temptation in Hom., 11, 35, 3, the parable of the royal marriage in 8, 22, 4. The prophet first chose 12 apostles and then 72 disciples, Recg., I, 40, 4. He sent them out to preach the Word, IV, 36. Gospel sayings are adduced as pronouncements of the prophet. The true prophet has said: I am the door of life; come to me, all you who are weary; my sheep hear my voice; seek and you shall find, Hom., 3, 52, 2 f.; verily I say to you, if you are not born again of the Spirit by living water in the name of the Father, the Son and the Holy Ghost, you cannot enter into the kingdom of heaven, 11, 26, 2 cf. Recg., VI, 9; I have not come to bring peace on earth but the sword, Recg., II, 28; seek first his righteousness and all these things will be added unto you, III, 41, 4; verily I say to you, if you have faith as a grain of mustard seed ..., V, 2; no man can serve two masters ..., V, 9; be merciful as your heavenly Father is merciful, V, 13; the queen of the south will rise up with this generation ..., VI, 14; Hom., 11, 33, 1. Jesus, the true prophet, rejects sacrifices and the temple and practises baptism for the remission of sins, Recg., I, 36 f. 39. 54.

Added to these OT and Christian aspects of the prophet are other elements which derive from Gnosticism or are influenced by its ideas: τῆς δὲ γνώσεως οὐκ ἄλλως τυχεῖν ἔστιν, ἐὰν μὴ πρότερόν τις τὸν τῆς ἀληθείας προφήτην ἐπιγνῷ· προφήτης δὲ ἀληθείας ἐστὶν ὁ πάντοτε πάντα εἰδώς, Hom., 2, 5, 3 f. cf. 3, 11, 1; 3, 13, 2; Recg., III, 45. Though Jesus is regarded as the prophet promised by Moses, He is not the eschatological Deliverer as in the NT but the Preacher of truth in more Gnostic fashion. He is certainly the one true prophet alongside whom there is no other, → lines 12 ff. But the figure of the true prophet is not equated exactly with the person of Jesus. The true prophet was there before Jesus. He was incarnate in Adam, the first man, Hom.,

8, 10, 1, so that Adam is also called μόνος ἀληθὴς προφήτης, 3, 21, 1. The true prophet appeared to Abraham (Recg., I, 33) and Moses (I, 34). He is at work through the centuries from the very beginning, changing name and form until he comes to the proper times and finds lasting rest, Hom., 20, 2; Recg., I, 52; II, 22. His task is to bring men to the truth. Without him saving truth cannot be attained, Hom., 2, 4, 3; 3, 54. One has to seek this true prophet, for he is the only one who knows all things and who knows what each seeks and why, Recg., VIII, 59. The world with its sins and errors is like a house filled with smoke. Even the friends of truth must cry out for help in order that someone outside may come and open the door and let in the light of the sun. This man who can bring help is the true prophet who alone can illumine the soul of men, Hom., 1, 18 f.

III. Church Prophets.

At the beginning of the post-apost. period the prophets are still held in high esteem in the churches. This may be seen from the Did., where the prophets enjoy great repute. They stand above other leaders in the congregation and occupy a special position. In Did., 13, 1-7 they are called high-priests to whom belong all the firstfruits of the wine-press and threshing floor, of oxen and sheep, of baking, of wine and oil, of money and raiment and every chattel as seems appropriate, so that they need have no material worries. Supporting the prophets is more important than caring for the poor, to whom firstfruits are paid only if there are no prophets in the congregation. Whereas other Christians must keep to the set liturgy, the prophet may give thanks freely, for as a pneumatic he is not tied either to the wording or the extent of the usual prayers, 10, 7. How high was this regard for the prophet may be seen from the fact that he was not tested or judged on whether he spoke in the Spirit. Whereas Paul demands that prophets be examined (→ 855, 39 ff.), the Did., in spite of the false prophets who threaten the community (→ 860, 37 ff.), views it as an unforgivable sin to adopt a critical attitude to prophets who speak in the Spirit, 11, 7. From what the Did. says one may conclude that the number of prophets was already dwindling. It is assumed that there will not be a prophet in every church, 13, 4. If there are not enough prophetic men in a congregation, the bishops and deacons are to take over the ministry of the prophets and teachers and to conduct divine worship. How highly the prophets were valued in this period of transition from a pneumatic to an institutional ministry may be seen from the fact that the churches are not too willing to hand over the work of the prophets to the church officers. They are thus reminded that the bishops and deacons are also honoured among them, 15, 1-2.

Hermas, who had revelations, does not call himself a prophet. Nor does he number the prophets among the worthies of the Church like the apostles, bishops, teachers and deacons, v. 3, 5, 1. But he is still acquainted with prophets who have τὸ πνεῦμα τὸ θεῖον and who speak as filled by the angel of the prophetic Spirit, m., 11, 9. True prophets do not have special secret seats for the giving of knowledge. They are not consulted like soothsayers and the givers of oracles, m., 11, 5. 8. They must wait until the Spirit reveals to them what takes place when the congregation prays, m., 11, 9. The Holy Spirit speaks when God decides, not man, m., 11, 8 f. He has the δύναμις τῆς θεότητος, for he comes from the power of the divine Spirit, m., 11, 5.

The regard still enjoyed by prophets in many circles right up to 300 A.D. may be seen from the following saying : τὸ γὰρ προφητικὸν πνεῦμα τὸ σωματεῖόν ἐστιν τῆς προφητικῆς τάξεως, ὅ ἐστιν τὸ σῶμα τῆς σαρκὸς Ἰησοῦ Χριστοῦ τὸ μιγὲν τῇ ἀνθρωπότητι διὰ Μαρίας, P. Oxy., I, 5, 9 ff. There is a college of prophets which is the body of Jesus Christ. [442] In the main, however, congregational prophets become

---

[442] A. Harnack, "Über 2 von Grenfell u. Hunt entdeckte u. publicierte altchr. Fragmente," SAB, 1898 (1898), 516-520.

increasingly less prominent in the post-apost. period. There are two reasons for this. First, pneumatic powers fade out in the Church, so that the office-bearers and Scripture take the place of the prophets, → 859, 29 f.; line 20. Secondly, false prophets are abroad and these undermine the authority and repute of true prophets, nor is the Church able to guard against them, since it does not have the *charisma* of discernment, → 856, 3 ff. Many a prophet is rejected as a false prophet because there is distrust of all prophecy, → 861, 16 ff. Iren. issues a warning that true prophecy is being suppressed in the battle against the false prophets, Haer., III, 11, 9. The prophets did not vanish at a stroke. Ign. is possibly claiming prophetic gifts when he refers to the revelation granted to him in Eph., 20, 2. For him, however, the responsible men are the bishops, presbyters and deacons, Phld., 7, 1. Polycarp, too, had prophetic gifts, Mart. Pol., 16, 2 cf. 5, 2; 12, 3. So did Melito of Sardis, Hier. De viris illustribus, 24 (MPL, 23 [1883], 677 n.); Eus. Hist. Eccl., V, 24, 5; cf. 2. Justin pts. out that the Church, as distinct from Judaism, contains men who have the spirit of prophecy, Dial., 39, 2; 82, 1 cf. 88, 1. But the prophets no longer seem to have played a decisive role in the churches. That the number of prominent prophets was never very gt. in the early Church may be seen from the fact that in the debate with the Montanists only Quadratus and Ammia were mentioned as examples of Chr. prophets apart from those referred to in the NT, Eus. Hist. Eccl., V, 17, 2. 4 cf. III, 37, 1.

Already in 2 Pt. there are no longer any primitive prophets. In defence of eschatology the author quotes Scripture rather than congregational prophets. [443] Similarly Orig. in his later battle against pagan prophecy appeals to the OT prophets rather than Chr. prophets, Cels., VII, 3 f.; VIII, 45 f. Whether Iren. knew prophecy at first hand is doubtful, Haer., V, 6, 1. Tert., who values the Montanist prophets (De anima, 9 [CSEL, 20, 310]), does not mention any prophets in his list of prominent persons in the community, Praescr. Haer., 3 (CSEL, 70, 4). Orig. is aware that prophecies are given, but denies that prophets play any decisive role in the congregations, cf. Cels., I, 46. In the days of Celsus there cannot have been any prophets comparable with the original ones ; otherwise the hearers would have written down their prophecies as they had done earlier, Cels., VII, 11. When Miltiades says δεῖν γὰρ εἶναι τὸ προφητικὸν χάρισμα ἐν πάσῃ τῇ ἐκκλησίᾳ μέχρι τῆς τελείας παρουσίας ὁ ἀπόστολος ἀξιοῖ, Eus. Hist. Eccl., V, 17, 4, this is a basic principle of theological tradition and bears no ref. to actual prophets in the community. The dogma that there are Chr. prophets survived longer than prophecy itself. With the repudiation of Montanism prophecy came to an end in the Church.

IV. False Prophets.

False prophets caused the early Church a good deal of trouble. The Did. lays down the following rule for unmasking them : οὐ πᾶς δὲ ὁ λαλῶν ἐν πνεύματι προφήτης ἐστίν, ἀλλ᾽ ἐὰν ἔχῃ τοὺς τρόπους κυρίου· ἀπὸ οῦν τῶν τρόπων γνωσθήσεται ὁ ψευδοπροφήτης καὶ ὁ προφήτης, 11, 8. Consistency of teaching and conduct is a mark of the true prophet. He who does not practise what he preaches is a false prophet, 11, 10. Above all, complete unselfishness is required of the prophet. If a man orders a table for selfish reasons (11, 9) or asks for money etc. to meet his personal needs (11, 12), he is a lying prophet. The number of these will increase in the last days, 16, 3.

Even more concrete is the depiction of false prophets in Herm. : μηδεμίαν ἔχων ἐν ἑαυτῷ δύναμιν πνεύματος θείου, m., 11, 2, his πνεῦμα ... ἐπίγειόν ἐστιν καὶ ἐλαφρόν, δύναμιν μὴ ἔχον, m., 11, 6 cf. 11; more strongly still ὁ γὰρ διάβολος πληροῖ αὐτὸν τῷ αὐτοῦ πνεύματι, m., 11, 3 cf. 17. The criteria for distinguishing between true and false prophets are purely moral. The true prophet is mild, peaceful and humble, He steers clear of all wickedness and vain desire. But the false prophet is

---

[443] E. Käsemann, "Eine Apologie d. urchr. Eschatologie," ZThK, 49 (1952), 289.

arrogant, ambitious, bold, shameless, talkative, licentious and deceitful, m., 11, 12. He need not wait for revelation but acts as if he knew everything. He avoids divine service, where he will be unmasked by the prayer of Christians. Instead he gives information in secret (m., 11, 13 f.) and is consulted like a soothsayer (m., 11, 2. 4. 6). His main concern is his fee, m., 11, 12. He thus tells those who ask what they want to hear, m., 11, 2. 6. 13. If he receives no payment he does not prophesy, m., 11, 12. Work and life are the decisive criteria for knowing true prophets and false, m., 11, 16. ἀπὸ τῆς ζωῆς δοκίμαζε τὸν ἄνθρωπον τὸν ἔχοντα τὸ πνεῦμα τὸ θεῖον, m., 11, 7.

Acc. to the view of the main body the Montanist prophets, who called themselves νέα προφητεία, Eus. Hist. Eccl., V, 16, 4; 19, 2; Tert. De ieiunio adversus psychicos, 1 (CSEL, 20, 274), [444] were false prophets. Montanus came forward with the claim that he was a prophet. He was accompanied by Prisca, Maximilla and other prophetesses, Epiph. Haer., 48, 1, 3; 49, 2, 3; Tert. De anima, 9 (CSEL, 20, 310). There was tense expectation of the end, Epiph. Haer., 48, 2, 4. It was believed that the heavenly Jerusalem would come down in the Phrygian towns of Pepuza and Tymion, where all Christians were to gather, ibid., 48, 14, 1; 49, 1, 2 f.; Eus. Hist. Eccl., V, 18, 2. In the fight against Montanism it was stressed that Jesus Himself had said there would be no more prophets after John, Filastrius De haeresibus, 78 (CSEL, 38, 40), though in principle Church prophecy was accepted, → 860, 30 ff. Appeal was made to the OT criterion that a prophet must give evidence by miracles and that what he prophesies must come to pass, Epiph. Haer., 48, 2, 5 ff.; Eus. Hist. Eccl., V, 18, 10. Since the wars predicted did not take place, Montanist prophecy was shown to be false, Eus. Hist. Eccl., V, 16, 18. Ecstasy was attacked. Anon. in Eus. Hist. Eccl., V, 16, 7 describes the first ecstatic trance of Montanus, how, seized by the spirit, he began to rave and utter strange sounds, cf. V, 16, 9. Montanus describes himself as an involuntary instrument of the Holy Spirit who causes the prophet to speak as the plectron causes the lyre to sound forth. A man falls asleep ; he loses consciousness and an alien power seizes possession of him, Epiph. Haer., 48, 4, 1 cf. Eus. Hist. Eccl., V, 17, 2. Montanus maintained that the Father came down to men in him, Epiph. Haer., 48, 11, 1. 6. 9. In opposition to the Montanist prophets Miltiades advances the basic principle μὴ δεῖν προφήτην ἐν ἐκστάσει λαλεῖν, Eus. Hist. Eccl., V, 17, 1. In this he could appeal to Pl., but hardly to the NT as a whole, → 851, 2 ff. Where there was no polemic against the Montanists ecstasy was not rejected in principle, Athenag. Suppl., 7, 9; Hipp. De Antichristo, 2 (GCS, 1, 2, p. 4). Above all the mode of life of the new prophets was criticised ; they accepted money, gifts and costly clothes, Eus. Hist. Eccl., V, 18, 2. 4. 11, and this even from the poor, widows and orphans, Eus. Hist. Eccl., V, 18, 7. They dyed their hair and adorned said δεῖ γὰρ τοὺς καρποὺς δοκιμάζεσθαι τοῦ προφήτου, V, 18, 8 cf. 11. Ecstasy and a mode of life which is not in keeping with moral requirements point to false prophecy. What was true and false in the Montanists, what was calumny and what real aberration, it is hard to say. It should be noted that Tert. always spoke of the Montanist prophets with gt. respect. Most people hesitated to join the movement because they seemed to be too ascetic and rigorous, De ieiunio adv. psychicos, 1 (CSEL, 20, 274). Even Epiph. Haer., 48, 1, 4 writes that he has nothing against the Montanists dogmatically : περὶ δὲ πατρὸς καὶ υἱοῦ καὶ ἁγίου πνεύματος ὁμοίως φρονοῦσι τῇ ἁγίᾳ καθολικῇ ἐκκλησίᾳ. Montanism was the last great flare up of prophecy in the Church. When it was resisted and vanquished, the institutional office gained a decisive victory over the charisma.

Friedrich

---

[444] For further examples cf. W. Schepelern, *Der Montanismus u. die phrygischen Kulte* (1929), 10.

---

† προχειρίζω

1. προχειρίζω is not a compound of the simple χειρίζω [1] but comes from the adj. πρόχειρος, "to have or to find readily, to hand" etc. This is used both of things ("ready," "always at one's disposal," e.g. Aesch. Prom., 54; Soph. El., 1116) and also of persons ("ready," "resolved," "bold," e.g., τῇ φυγῇ Eur. Herc. Fur., 161, ἐν ταῖς ὁμιλίαις, Polyb., 23, 5, 7). [2] προχειρίζω, very rare act. ("to hand over," also "to hold ready" in, e.g., Polyb., 3, 107, 10), is common as a dep. mid. "to take into one's hand," "to handle," "to prepare," e.g., "to equip" ships etc., Polyb., 3, 97, 2; 1, 16, 2; with ref. to people "to choose," "to appoint" : δημαγωγούς, Isocr., 8, 122, ἄρχοντα, Ditt. Syll.[3], II, 873, 14 f. (2nd cent. B.C.), τοὺς τὴν πίστιν εὐσεβῶς τε καὶ δικαίως τηρήσαντας, Ditt. Or., I, 339, 46 f. (2nd cent. B.C.), with double acc. of obj. and predicate, Diod. S., 12, 27, 1. In this sense often pass., aor. or perf. part. : προχειρισθεὶς ... ἀγωνοθέτης, Ditt. Or., I, 268, 4 (3rd cent. B.C.), προχειρισθεὶς καὶ ὑφ' ὑμῶν πρεσβεῦσαι, Ditt. Syll.[3], II, 601, 5 (193 B.C.), ἱερέως προκεχειρισμένου, BGU, IV, 1198, 2 f. (1st cent. B.C.), προχειρισθέντες ἀντιστρατηγοί, Polyb., 3, 106, 2; cf. ὁ προκεχειρισμένος ἐν τῷ νῦν λόγος, "the speech intended and even begun," Plat. Leg., I, 643a. In the pap. we find the med. but the use of the pass. part. in the sense "appointed," "arranged," is predominant. [3]

2. In the LXX the adj. πρόχειρος occurs once in Prv. 11:3 : πρόχειρος δὲ γίνεται καὶ ἐπίχαρτος ἀσεβῶν ἀπώλεια. If the rest of the line is based on HT 11:10b, πρόχειρος has no Mas. equivalent either there or in 11:3. The meaning is either "lying to hand" = "before one's eyes," "following already," or "following at once," "to be expected immediately." προχειρίζω is common, med. in the sense "to elect," "to name," Ex. 4:13 (שׁלח); Jos. 3:12 (לקח); προχειρισάμενος 2 Macc. 3:7 (προχειρησάμενος A; itacistic error); 8:9 (ἐπέλεξεν in the par. 1 Macc. 3:38, also Jos. Ant., 12, 298); 14:12 (A again προχειρησάμενος, vl. προσκαλεσάμενος), pass. part. aor. Da. LXX 3:22 (no Mas.). [4]

3. Philo uses the adj. πρόχειρος 17 times (also comp. and superl.), esp. in the sense "close at hand," "on the surface," of ideas or conceptions, e.g., Det. Pot. Ins., 155; Som., I, 127; Post. C., 1; Ebr., 65; Dec., 69; Conf. Ling., 190; Deus Imm., 133, "at the first glance," Sacr. AC, 35; Det. Pot. Ins., 47; "easy," Agric., 3; Sobr., 33. He does not have

---

προχειρίζω. [1] χειρίζω, "to have in or under one's hands," "to treat" (e.g., of the doctor), is also used transf. esp. in the sense "to rule" (common in Polyb., e.g., 1, 20, 4; 2, 36, 1); also LXX τὰ πράγματα χειρίζειν, "to conduct state business," Est. 8:12e. χειρίζω does not occur in the NT, early Chr. writings, or the Apologists.

[2] Also pap. (2nd/3rd cent. A.D.). Cf. Preisigke Wört., II, 428 (with examples of πρόχειρον for "hand-bag," "strong-box").

[3] For numerous instances (from the 2nd cent. B.C.) cf. Preisigke Wört., II, 420; III, 151; Moult.-Mill., 556; Mayser, I, 3, 144; II, 1, 93; II, 2, 486. Noun προχειρισμός "equipping," "training" : ὁ δεῖνα ἡγεμὼν τῶν ἐν προχειρισμῷ, "master of recruits," "training officer," P. Amh., 39, 1 (2nd cent. B.C.).

[4] At Prv. 8:23 Θ and Σ have προχείρισμαι (נסך ni ; LXX ἐθεμελίωσέν με); cf. Field, II, 326.

the verb.[5] Nor does Joseph. (cf. → 862, 25), though he has the adj. πρόχειρος in Ant., 8, 214; Ap., 1, 24; Bell., 4, 85 and the adv. προχείρως in Bell., 2, 463 "swiftly resolved" (the verb προχειρόομαι in Bell., 4, 444 "to be subjugated before" does not come from πρόχειρος but is a compound of χειρόω).

4. In the NT only the verb προχειρίζω is used (med. and pass.) and this only 3 times by Luke in Ac. In the second and third accounts[6] of the conversion of the apostle Paul (Ac. 22:14; 26:16)[7] it means "to ordain," "to choose," "to appoint."[8]

> The use of προχειρίζεσθαι for appointment to a military function in the examples from 2 Macc. (→ 862, 24 ff.) and the pap. (→ n. 3) is not so different from the ordinary use as to affect the employment of the term in Ac. 22:14; 26:16, esp. as the words μάρτυς (→ IV, 493, 24 ff.) and → ὑπηρέτης show clearly enough what is the point of the ordination and for their part bear no affinity to the concept of the *militia Christi*. The idea that once a decision has been made it is binding may be very much to the fore in military appointments but it is also present in other fields. Hence the desire to express the binding nature of the decision made about Paul may have influenced the choice of προχειρίζεσθαι.

The verb, in accordance with its etymology, does not suggest the foreordination of God or Christ. The main reference is to the function to which Paul is appointed. In Ac. 22:14 the appointment is already made (the point of the aor.), while in 26:16 it is made as Paul is addressed. In Ac. 3:20, too, the meaning is "to ordain," "to appoint," rather than "to foreordain."[9, 10] After healing the lame man Peter tells the people to repent and to seek remission of sins ὅπως ἄν ... ἀποστεί-

---

[5] At least not acc. to Leisegang. Cf. Cl. Al., who also has the adj. but not the verb (Index, *s.v.* [GCS, 39, 690]).

[6] There is no par. in the first account in Ac. 9 because there the directions to Paul are much shorter, cf. also what Ananias says in 9:17 as compared with 22:14-16. But the thought expressed by προχειρίζεσθαι in 22:14; 26:16 finds a material par. in the σκεῦος ἐκλογῆς of Ac. 9:15 (→ IV, 179, 3 ff.).

[7] On the constr. with double acc. in Ac. 26:16 → 862, 11. 22:14 has acc. of obj. with inf., which does not seem to occur elsewhere and certainly not in the LXX. In the sense "to plan," "to resolve," προχειρίζομαι is used with the inf., e.g., πέμπειν Πόπλιον, Polyb., 3, 40, 2 and there is an acc. c. inf. in this sense : Ditt. Syll.³, I, 457, 14 ff. (3rd cent. B.C.), cf. Liddell-Scott, *s.v.*, II, 4. But the meaning in Ac. 22:14 is not "has resolved that ..." (acc. c. inf.) but "has ordained you to ..." (σε is acc. obj. and the final inf. shows what Paul is ordained to do, cf. Pr.-Bauer⁵, *s.v.*).

[8] Bau. Ag. transl. 22:14 "chosen" (251) and 26:16 "to appoint" (267). There are similar variations in other renderings, but since Lk. has related the two passages it seems best to stick to one translation.

[9] As against Pr. Ag., *ad loc.* The vl. προκεκηρυγμένον, in which προ- means "before," cannot be adduced in favour of the sense "to foreordain." Though perhaps promoted by the twofold if differently meant προ-, this is influenced by προκηρύσσω in Ac. 13:24 (→ III, 717, 32 ff.). Yet the ref. of the reading can hardly be to John the Baptist (cf. 13:24); it is materially based on προκαταγγέλλω in Ac. 3:18 (→ I, 73, 2 f., 5 ff.). Wettstein, II, 474 f., who on Ac. 3:20 has adduced several non-bibl. instances of προχειρίζομαι, notes that minusc. 46 reads προκεχρισμένον. This seems to be a mere slip, not a play on the χριστόν which follows. The reading must have been fairly widespread since Tisch. NT, II, 27, *ad loc.* observes that it appears in the Ethiop. transl., and this can hardly have been influenced by minusc. 46 alone.

[10] Among the compounds with προ- adduced in support of Luke's idea of a divine plan (cf. H. Conzelmann, *Die Mitte d. Zeit*² [1957], 130) one can hardly list προχειρίζομαι along with προοράω, προορίζω etc. unless it is assumed with Haench. Ag., 172, n. 5 that in defiance of the etym. Lk. uses the word in a temporal sense (but would Lk. do this?). Cf. also Zn. Ag., 155 f., n. 65.

λῃ (God as the κύριος already mentioned) τὸν προκεχειρισμένον ὑμῖν χριστὸν Ἰησοῦν. Jesus is the Messiah whom God appointed and provided for the Jews, [11] though it is not clear whether He is appointed with the *parousia,* with His earthly ministry (Ac. 2:22; 13:23), after the resurrection (Ac. 3:13, 15), or from the very beginning. If Luke has worked over an older text in Ac. 3:20 [12] one may see from Ac. 22:14; 26:16 that in using προχειρίζεσθαι he introduced a word which was of significance for him elsewhere.

5. προχειρίζω does not occur in early Chr. writings outside the NT.

Michaelis

---

[11] ὑμῖν is a *dat. commodi* as in Jos. 3:12 except that there it relates to the subj. of προχειρίζεσθαι. The comment of H. W. Beyer, *Die Ag., NT Deutsch,* 5⁸ (1957), *ad loc.* that Pt. is showing the Jews "how this Jesus has been appointed 'Christ for you'" wrongly separates the ὑμῖν from the verb and brings in something which is not in the Gk. Wdt. Ag., 106, *ad loc.* refers to the ὑμῖν in Ac. 2:39.

[12] Cf. the hypothesis in Bau. Ag., 66-68 that Lk. in Ac. 3:20 f. is using a Jewish original referring to Elijah *redivivus.* As regards προκεχειρισμένος he recalls נכון in Sir. 48:10, which acc. to the conjecture of R. Smend, *Die Weisheit d. Jesus Sir.* (1906), 460 was at first transl. ἕτοιμος (rather than the present ἐν ἐλεγμοῖς) in the LXX: "perhaps Lk. found a similar word and substituted for it the more solemn προκεχειρισμένος" (66; cf. 68: "he probably substituted προκεχειρισμένος for a more colourless and less suitable word, e.g., ἕτοιμος"). This thesis can hardly be accepted in full, but it should be noted that Hesych., *s.v.* has ἑτοίμως, ταχέως, ὀξέως in elucidation of προχείρως and προβεβλημένον, ἡτοιμασμένον in elucidation of προκεχειρισμένον.

πρῶτος, πρῶτον, πρωτοκαθεδρία, πρωτοκλισία,
πρωτότοκος, πρωτοτοκεῖα, πρωτεύω

πρῶτος.

1. From Hom. πρῶτος, "the first," developed along three lines : a. spatially "the front," e.g., Hom. Il., 15, 340; this meaning became less common later ; b. the first in time and no., e.g., Hdt., 7, 168; Hom. Od., 9, 449; c. the first in rank and value, "the most eminent, important" etc., e.g., Hom. Od., 6, 60; Thuc., 6, 28. [1]

2. In the LXX πρῶτος occurs some 240 times, half of these in Gn.-Neh., 25 in Macc. Where there is an original it is usually רִאשׁוֹן, רִאשׁ. Most of the ref. are to number, but a third are indications of time, and the idea of rank is also found, e.g., Est. 1:14, of the angelic hierarchy Da. LXX Θ 10:13, a court title (πρῶτος φίλος etc.) 1 Ch. 27:33; 1 Macc. 10:65; 11:27; 2 Macc. 8:9, ἱερεὺς πρῶτος "chief priest" (→ III, 266, 12) 3 Βασ. 2:35; 4 Βασ. 25:18 = Ἰερ. 52:24; 2 Ch. 26:20; cf. 22:46. In the derisive question to Job in 15:7a: μὴ πρῶτος ἀνθρώπων ἐγενήθης; the ref. is not to the primal man who was in God's counsels (cf. 15:8) but to Adam (cf. the mention of creation in 15:7b). On God as the πρῶτος cf. Is. 41:4; 44:6; 48:12 (→ I, 1, 27 ff.; on the influence on the NT → 867, n. 9). רִאשׁוֹן in Is. 41:27 as a significant term for the prophet is only weakly rendered (by ἀρχή) in the LXX (so also מְבַשֵּׂר loc. cit.). [2] But cf. → 866, 5 f.; 867, n. 11.

3. πρῶτος is used in many connections in Philo. [3] πρῶτος θεός is a common term for God, Poster. C., 183 (πρῶτος καὶ μόνος); Migr. Abr., 181; Abr., 115; Vit. Mos., II (III), 205. Acc. to Decal., 59 only ἀπόνοια can give this title to other entities. In Abr., 75, 88 Philo attacks the idea that the visible cosmos (→ III, 877, 31 ff.) can be regarded as πρῶτος θεός. The cosmos is rather ἔργον τοῦ πρώτου θεοῦ καὶ τοῦ συμπάντων πατρός, 75 (cf. Migr. Abr., 194). In connection with the description of the logos as δεύτερος θεός (→ IV, 89, 9 ff.), πρῶτος θεός obviously does not occur, which is not surprising, since the title is designed to express the uniqueness of God and there is no thought of enumeration behind it. Hence Philo can say in Leg. All., III, 207 that the logos (as God's ἑρμηνεύς) is indeed θεός for the ἀτελεῖς but only ὁ πρῶτος (God Himself) is truly God for the σοφοί and τέλειοι. When Philo calls God πρῶτος καὶ μέγας βασιλεύς (Op. Mund., 88 etc.; cf. also πρῶτος τῶν ὅλων καὶ μόνος βασιλεύς in Poster. C., 101) he is perhaps using a fixed expression of Stoic origin. [4]

π ρ ῶ τ ο ς. [1] Pass., Liddell-Scott, s.v. In inscr. πρῶτος esp. denotes rank and it is also a title (cf. Index in Ditt. Syll.[3] and Ditt. Or.); in the pap. though rarely, it can denote office or military rank, cf. Preisigke Wört., III, 153, 215; Moult.-Mill., s.v.

[2] Cf. J. Schniewind, Euangelion, I (1927), 35 f., 67 f. The Rabb. referred the v. to the Messiah (e.g., Ex. r., 15, 2) and made רִאשׁוֹן a Mess. title (Str.-B., I, 65).

[3] Cf. Leisegang, s.v., and on πρῶτος ἄνθρωπος s.v., ἄνθρωπος, 8.

[4] Cf. the description of the supreme god as πρῶτος καὶ μέγιστος βασιλεύς, e.g., Dio Chrys. Or., 2, 72 ff.; 19, 35 ff.; 36, 11; 64, 21 [H. Kleinknecht]. It may be noted that πρῶτος had a long and important history in the Gk. world as a predicate of God, e.g., Ζεὺς πρῶτος γένετο in the Orphic hymn to Zeus in Ps.-Aristot. Mund., 7, p. 401a, 28; the earthly king as ζαλωτὸς τῷ πράτῳ θεῷ, Stob. Ecl., IV, 270, 14.

There seems to be no corresponding usage in Joseph. [5] Joseph. often has οἱ πρῶτοι (ἄνδρες) for the leading men of a tribe, the people, the priesthood, etc., Ant., 4, 140 and 174; 10, 71 and 213; 11, 141; 13, 146; 18, 7 and 64; 20, 125. 132. 135; Vit., 185, 381 etc.; sing. Ant., 13, 85; 20, 130. When Ezra is called πρῶτος ἱερεὺς τοῦ θεοῦ in Ant., 11, 121, which goes beyond the preceding ἀρχιερεύς, this is hardly based on 1 Εσδρ. 8:2; 2 Εσδρ. 7:5, since there πρῶτος, referring to Aaron, means the first in time. The sense "former," "preceding" is also found in Ant., 1, 81; 2, 86; 16, 1. 68. 258; 19, 323; hence it is open to question whether πρῶτος βασιλεύς in 7, 85 means that Saul was the first king or the predecessor of David. On Adam as πρῶτος ἐκ γῆς γενόμενος in Ant., 1, 67 cf. also 82; 20, 259.

4. πρῶτος occurs over 90 times in the NT. The distribution of the various senses is most uneven.

a. The rare spatial sense (→ 865, 4 f.) occurs only in the description of the tabernacle in Hb. 9:2, 6, 8 : πρώτη → σκηνή.

b. More numerous are instances of "the first in time, number, sequence." [6]

The first day of the Passover plays a role in the passion story, Mk. 14:12 par. Mt. 26:17, → II, 902, 18 ff.; → n. 7. In the inauthentic Marcan ending Easter Day is called πρώτη σαββάτου (16:9), μία σαββάτων in Mt. 28:1 par. Lk. 24:1, cf. also Jn. 20:1, → II, 434, n. 1; 950, 14 ff. Even in Ac. 20:7; 1 C. 16:2, which are important in relation to the Lord's Day (→ III, 1096, 16 ff.), we find μία τῶν σαββάτων or σαββάτου.

Very common is the use of πρῶτος for "earlier," "preceding," which develops out of a comparison between past and present. [7] τὰ πρῶτα ἔργα ποίησον in Rev. 2:5 means : Become as you were earlier, τὴν ἀγάπην σου τὴν πρώτην ἀφῆκας in 2:4 : the love which you had and showed earlier but now have and show no more. In 1 Tm. 5:12 : τὴν πρώτην πίστιν ἠθέτησαν, the opposite is not a different faith but ἀπιστία, cf. 5:8. In this connection it may be noted that in Hb. the πρώτη διαθήκη (8:7, 13; 9:1, 15, 18) is contrasted with the καινὴ διαθήκη (8:8, 13; 9:15), or the νέα διαθήκη (12:24). Only in 8:7 is the new διαθήκη described as δευτέρα, cf. 10:9; on the other hand, the πρώτη διαθήκη is not the παλαιὰ διαθήκη in Hb. because πρώτη itself is the equivalent of old, antiquated, outdated, cf. 8:13 → II, 132, 8 ff. The same expression is used in a comparison of the past (or present) and the future in Rev. 21:1, where πρῶτος οὐρανός and πρώτη γῆ are the opposite of οὐρανὸς καινός and γῆ καινή (→ I, 678, 26 ff.; V, 515, 4 ff.), and also in Rev. 21:4, 5, where the τὰ πρῶτα ἀπῆλθαν of v. 4 is followed by the ἰδοὺ καινὰ ποιῶ πάντα of v. 5, → III, 449, 1 ff. [8]

---

[5] There is nothing in Schl. Theol. d. Jdt.

[6] Cf. the review in Pr.-Bauer⁵, s.v. On πρῶτος or πρῶτον for πρότερος or πρότερον cf. also Bl.-Debr. § 62.

[7] Hardly convincing is the attempt of C. N. Ghiaouroff, "Le jour de la Sainte-Cène," Annuaire de l'Acad. de Théol. St. Clement d'Ochrida, Sofia, II (XXVIII) (1951-1952), 145-186 to reconcile the difference between the Synoptic and Johannine chronology of the passion week with the help of the thesis that τῇ πρώτῃ ἡμέρᾳ τῶν ἀζύμων in Mk. 14:12 and par. is to be transl. "on the day which preceded the feast of unleavened bread." Neither in bibl. nor non-bibl. Gk. is there a single instance to show that πρῶτος (or πρότερος) with a note of time in the gen. can mean that that denoted by πρῶτος does not belong to the time indicated but precedes it. The author expressly appeals to Ju. 20:22 (163), but this is no real help, for, although the ref. is to the day before and the LXX has ἐν τῇ ἡμέρᾳ τῇ πρώτῃ, there is no gen. Cf. the review of this essay by W. Michaelis in Kirchenblatt f. d. reformierte Schweiz, 110 (1954), 12.

[8] Used somewhat differently, but in clear comparison of the beginning and the end (the present is also included in Rev. 21:1, 4 and πρῶτος can thus mean "present" too), the word

A more common antithesis in the NT is πρῶτος/ἔσχατος. The exalted Christ is ὁ πρῶτος καὶ ὁ ἔσχατος in Rev. 1:17; 2:8; 22:13; the reference here is to the beginning and the end. [9] ὁ πρῶτος refers to pre-existence, being in eternity before all time, [10] while ὁ ἔσχατος refers to being in eternity after all time. The use of πρῶτος/ἔσχατος is different in Mt. 12:45 par. Lk. 11:26; Mt. 27:64; 2 Pt. 2:20; Rev. 2:19. Here πρῶτος means "the earlier" and ἔσχατος "the later," "the last in time," i.e., "the present." [11] The expressions πρῶτος and ἔσχατος Ἀδάμ in 1 C. 15:45 (→ I, 142, 13 ff., 25 ff.) may also be cited in this connection.

πρῶτος Ἀδάμ refers, not to pre-existence, but to the creation of Adam, → II, 542, 4 ff. But the ἔσχατος Ἀδάμ is not just expected in the future, for Paul can already look back to the resurrection of Christ — it is to this rather than the parousia that the ἐξ οὐρανοῦ of 15:47 and hence the statement in 15:45b refer. Thus the sense of "former/ present," to which ref. has already been made → line 6 f., underlies the use of πρῶτος/ ἔσχατος Ἀδάμ here. Christ, the initiator of the new humanity, is contrasted with Adam, the beginner of the old. Both are called Ἀδάμ or ἄνθρωπος, Adam being the πρῶτος Ἀδάμ in 1 C. 15:45 = πρῶτος ἄνθρωπος in 15:47, Christ the δεύτερος ἄνθρωπος in 15:47 but not the δεύτερος Ἀδάμ in 15:45, where Paul, esp. since no τρίτος Ἀδάμ etc. can follow, prefers ἔσχατος Ἀδάμ, i.e., the last in time, the present Adam, or, since there are only two, the second (new) Adam. [12]

---

also occurs in Barn., 6, 13 : ἰδοὺ ποιῶ τὰ ἔσχατα ὡς τὰ πρῶτα. It is open to question whether the ref. here is to a true "return of the same thing," so R. Bultmann, "Ursprung u. Sinn d. Typologie als hermeneutische Methode," ThLZ, 75 (1950), 205. Another possible sense is that God creates both τὰ πρῶτα and τὰ ἔσχατα. Quoting Is. 43:18 f., J. Hempel, "Mensch u. Gott im AT," BWANT, III, 2 (1926), 52, also emphasises the fact that the "sameness of the personality of the Creator" is important in Barn., 6, 13. Cf. Wnd. Barn., ad loc.

[9] The influence of the corresponding divine predicate in Dt. Is., esp. 44:6 but also 41:4; 48:12, is patent. By using ἔσχατος, which the LXX intentionally avoided (→ I, 1, 28 ff.), Rev. is closer to the HT. It is of no significance, and unrelated to the previously mentioned hesitation of the LXX to use ἔσχατος of God, that πρῶτος/ἔσχατος is in Rev. referred only to Christ and not to God, esp. as the related expressions τὸ ἄλφα καὶ τὸ ὦ and ἡ ἀρχὴ καὶ τὸ τέλος can be used of both in Rev., → I, 1, 3 ff. On the possibility that A and O may be based on Is. 44:5 f. cf. W. Michaelis, "Zeichen, Siegel, Kreuz," ThZ, 12 (1956), 516, n. 31.

[10] πρῶτος (= πρότερος) constr. with the gen. helps to give Jn. 1:15 a ref. to pre-existence.

[11] Cf. the corresponding use of πρῶτος/ἔσχατος in the LXX : Rt. 3:10; 2 Βασ. 13:16; Hag. 2:9.

[12] Cf. O. Cullmann, Die Christologie d. NT² (1958), 171: Paul coined ἔσχατος Ἀδάμ in simple analogy to πρῶτος Ἀδάμ. In this antithesis it has something of the sense of "second man." But cf., e.g., J. Jeremias (→ I, 143, 17 ff.), for whom Christ's eschatological role gave rise to the term ἔσχατος Ἀδάμ, and (even more sharply) K. H. Rengstorf, Die Auferstehung Jesu³ (1955), 65, who renders ἔσχατος Ἀδάμ by "Adam of the last time" (cf. E. Hirsch, "Zur paul. Christologie," ZSTh, 7 [1929], 618, n. 28) and "Adam of the new aeon." In other words, he takes ἔσχατος to mean "eschatological." Now the word may bear this sense acc. to context, → II, 697, 24 ff. But it is open to question whether it ever does so directly in the NT (on αἰώνιος = "eschatological" cf. W. Michaelis, Die Versöhnung d. Alls [1950], 47). That Christ is in truth the first in relation to Adam (K. Barth, KD, IV, 1 [1953], 52 f., 572, C.D., IV, 1 [1956], 50, 512 f.; cf. → I, 142, n. 10; 143, 11 ff.) is intrinsically correct but sheds no light on the use of πρῶτος/ἔσχατος in 1 C. 15:45. On the influence of ideas of the primal man (cf. the first Adam in 3 Esr. 3:21, Vis. I, 4, 5 Violet) cf. Cullmann, op. cit., 144-146, 169-171; E. Schweizer, "Erniedrigung u. Erhöhung bei Jesus u. seinen Nachfolgern," Abh. ThANT, 28 (1955), 159 f.; W. Schmithals, "Die Gnosis in Korinth," FRL, NF, 48 (1956), 105 f.

c. πρῶτος/ἔσχατος is also used hierarchically. This is plain in the saying: πολλοὶ δὲ ἔσονται πρῶτοι ἔσχατοι καὶ οἱ ἔσχατοι πρῶτοι, Mk. 10:31 par. Mt. 19:30, which is also found in slightly altered form in Mt. 20:16 and Lk. 13:30. Now it is true that there is a temporal use of πρῶτος in Mt. 20:8, 10 and of ἔσχατος in 20:8, 12, 14. But this meaning has obviously fallen into the background in 20:16 and given place to the hierarchical sense, as in 19:30. [13] The ref. in the logion is not just to the conversion of the first and of others who are expected to follow. The point is that those who are regarded as rejected and without hope of admittance will be accepted into the kingdom of God, but those who are regarded as the only ones qualified will be shut out, cf. Lk. 13:28 f. par. Mt. 8:11 f. [14] In the sense "the first in rank" πρῶτος (synon. with μέγας in Mk. 10:43 par. Mt. 20:26 or μείζων in Lk. 22:26) is a catchword in the disciples' squabbling for pre-eminence and the firm rebukes of Jesus, Mk. 10:44 par. Mt. 20:27; Mk. 9:35. The antonyms here are δοῦλος or διάκονος in Mk. 10:43 f. par. Mt. 20:26 f. and ἔσχατος in Mk. 9:35 → II, 84, 16 ff.; 85, 29 ff.; 278, n. 114; 698, 16 ff. On the question of the ἐντολὴ πρώτη πάντων (Mk. 12:28 par. ἐντολὴ μεγάλη in Mt. 22:36) and the expression πρώτη or δευτέρα ἐντολή in Jesus' answer (Mk. 12:29 f. par. Mt. 22:38 f. → II, 549, 16 ff.; IV, 535, 17 ff.), and on πρώτη ἐντολή (Eph. 6:2), → II, 552, 32 ff. οἱ πρῶτοι for "the leading men" (→ 866, 1 ff.) occurs in Mk. 6:21; Lk. 19:47; Ac. 13:50; 25:2; 28:7 (sing.), 17. [15]

5. In the post-apost. fathers it may be noted that the pre-existent Church is ἡ ἐκκλησία ἡ πρώτη in 2 Cl., 14, 1 (→ III, 533, 36 ff.; cf. Herm. v., 2, 4, 1) and that the archangels are οἱ ἄγγελοι οἱ πρῶτοι (i.e., before the others) κτισθέντες, Herm. m., 3, 4, 1 cf. s., 5, 5, 3. On Barn., 6, 13 → n. 8.

πρῶτον.

1. The neut. πρῶτον as adv. means "first," "at first," "in the first instance," "before," e.g., Hes. Theog., 34 (the most common sense in the NT), "earlier" (= πρότερον), e.g., Xenoph. Hist. Graec., V, 4, 1. The plur. πρῶτα means the same, Hom. Od., 14, 158, though it does not occur as an adv. in the LXX and NT. We also find the word with the art. τὸ πρῶτον, τὰ πρῶτα, "the first time," e.g., Hom. Il., 4, 267, NT only Jn. 10:40; 19:39 and in the sense "at the first" 12:16. [1] In the LXX the adv. πρῶτον is plainly attested only 8 times and in single MSS another 6; of the total of 14 there are 4 each in Is. and Macc. and 2 each in 1 Βασ., Tob. and Sir. The meaning is "first" in lists, e.g., 2 Macc. 14:8 (so often in the NT), "at first," e.g., 1 Βασ. 2:16. In the admonition in

---

[13] Whether this difference in meaning necessarily calls in question the original relation of Mt. 20:16 to the parable in 20:1 ff. is doubtful in spite of J. Jeremias, Die Gleichnisse Jesu⁴ (1956), 25. Cf. W. Michaelis, Die Gleichnisse Jesu³ (1956), 180 f. (on 260, n. 120 cf. 257, n. 85).

[14] A primary question is whether application to the Jews and the Gentiles, though this occurs only in Lk. 13:30, does not emphasise the temporal aspect, → 869, 5 ff. If this was originally an independent saying or if it belonged elsewhere, one may ask whether the pt. is not that the two groups are on exactly the same footing. Cf. 4 Esr. 5:42, Vis. II, 4, 2 Violet: "As the last cannot be too late, so the first cannot be too early" (Violet).

[15] In spite of the temporal sense of πρῶτος in 1 Tm. 1:16 one cannot assume that it bears a similar sense in v. 15, so A. Kirchgässner, Erlösung u. Sünde im NT (1950), 169.

π ρ ῶ τ ο ν. [1] Pass. and Liddell-Scott, s.v. Preisigke Wört., II, 422 f. notes that τὸ πρῶτον can mean "above all things" in the pap. (from the 1st cent. A.D.); cf. also Mayser, II, 2, 327 and Moult.-Mill., s.v.

Tob. 4:12 AB the meaning is "above all." Jos. has πρῶτον in the sense "first" in Ant., 12, 92; 14, 15; Bell., 6, 37. 51. ²

2. There are over 60 instances in the NT and of these a few deserve special mention.

a. In the sense "first" πρῶτον is used by Paul in R. 1:16, where to παντὶ τῷ πιστεύοντι he adds Ἰουδαίῳ τε πρῶτον καὶ Ἕλληνι. The apostle wants to emphasise that the Gospel of salvation is offered to the Jews first, → II, 514, 4 ff. cf. πρῶτον in Ac. 3:26; 13:46. In R. 2:9 f. πρῶτον is again designed to strengthen the twofold reference to the Jew before the Greek. ³ Of particular seriousness is the πρῶτον ἀφ' ἡμῶν in the announcement of judgment in 1 Pt. 4:17. This takes up the preceding ἄρξασθαι ἀπὸ τοῦ οἴκου τοῦ θεοῦ and its temporal significance is thereby established, → III, 939, 14 ff.; V, 127, 12 ff.

b. In the sense "first of all" πρῶτον denotes the priority of certain demands of Jesus, e.g., first to be reconciled with one's brother (Mt. 5:24), first to pull out the beam from one's own eye (Mt. 7:5 par. Lk. 6:42), ⁴ first to count the cost (Lk. 14:28, 31). What is not so urgent for disciples may be seen from the men who first wanted to bury their father or say farewell before they would follow Jesus, Mt. 8:21 par. Lk. 9:59; Lk. 9:61. In the same sense πρῶτον often serves to emphasise the observance of the divinely established sequence of eschatological events: Elias must come first (Mk. 9:11 f. par. Mt. 17:10 → II, 936, 3 ff.); the Son of Man must first be rejected (Lk. 17:25); apostasy must first come and the antichrist must first be manifested, 2 Th. 2:3 cf. Lk. 21:9. ⁵

There is much to be said in favour of a similar meaning in Mk. 13:10: εἰς πάντα τὰ ἔθνη πρῶτον δεῖ κηρυχθῆναι τὸ εὐαγγέλιον, esp. as this is the thought in the par. Mt. 24:14, in which πρῶτον is not used but καὶ τότε follows → n. 4. A further pt. in support of this sense is the importance of the missionary principle which results, and which does not merely cancel the Jewish rule: "First Israel, then the Gentiles," but even goes beyond the OT equation of Israel and the Gentiles as recipients of the message. ⁶ Yet to construe Mk. 13:10 thus is to tear it from its context (v. 11 is certainly connected with v. 9) and to treat it as an isolated saying. The same objection arises if one takes εἰς πάντα τὰ ἔθνη with πρῶτον and gives it the sense "above all," as though the saying were emphasising the obligation to engage in worldwide mission to the nations. In the sense "above all" πρῶτον can, of course, be connected with κηρυχθῆναι τὸ εὐαγγέλιον, so that the saying is related to the situation denoted in 13:9, 11. Witness

---

² פרוטי seems to have been a not very common loan word in the Rabb., cf. S. Krauss, Gr. u. lat. Lehnwörter in Talmud, Midrasch u. Targum, II (1899), 485. But the link with πρῶτον is by no means certain since there may be textual corruption, cf. J. Fürst, Glossarium Graeco-Hebraeum (1891), 71a.

³ Though this is based on the previous singling out of the Jews (cf. Schl. R., ad loc.), πρῶτον does not mean "above all," "especially," but relates to the sequence, as against Pr.-Bauer⁵, s.v. → III, 381, 32 ff.

⁴ In the instances previously mentioned a καὶ τότε follows the πρῶτον in the next clause. Cf. also Mk. 3:27 par. Mt. 12:29.

⁵ In view of the comparatively small no. of examples it is doubtful whether one can really say that this πρῶτον is "a typically Lucan connecting word, esp. in eschatological contexts," "a pre-Lucan catchword denoting the eschatological commencement" whose use Lk. extended. H. Conzelmann, Die Mitte d. Zeit² (1957), 106, n. 1. On πρῶτον in Ac. 15:14 cf. Haench. Ag., 393.

⁶ Cf. F. Busch, Zum Verständnis d. synpt. Eschatologie ; Mk. 13 neu untersucht (1938), 89.

to the Gospel is to have priority even in pagan courts. It is for this rather than the answering of questions put by the courts that the help of the Holy Ghost is promised in 13:11. [7] The fact that the sense "above all" is comparatively rare (→ 869, 1 f. and n. 1) is no real argument against this explanation of Mk. 13:10.

c. Unless one includes R. 2:9 f. (→ n. 3), the sense "above all" occurs elsewhere in the NT only at Mt. 6:33. The meaning here cannot be that one must first seek after God's kingdom (→ I, 583, 7; 588, 4 f.) and then after other things. "Above all" is the only meaning which corresponds to the central position which orientation to the kingdom of God has in the proclamation of Jesus. Indeed, πρῶτον is so exclusive here that it carries the implication of "only." [8]

† πρωτοκαθεδρία, † πρωτοκλισία.

πρωτοκαθεδρία and πρωτοκλισία occur together in the saying in Mk. 12:39 par. Mt. 23:6; Lk. 20:46 (always plur. except for πρωτοκλισία in Mt. 23:6). πρωτοκαθεδρία also occurs in the doublet Lk. 11:43 (sing.) and πρωτοκλισία in Lk. 14:7 f. (plur. and sing.). Both words, though of fairly common construction, [1] are very rare outside the NT. [2] In the NT instances their meaning is established by the context. πρωτοκαθεδρία is "the first place," "the place of honour," and this ἐν ταῖς συναγωγαῖς, where there are several such places, as the plur. shows. [3]

---

[7] In this case Mk. 13:10 has nothing to do with the problem of the delay in the *parousia*. Even if the meaning is "first" it is not necessarily dealing with this problem, not even in the version in Mt. 24:14, though cf. E. Grässer, "Das Problem d. Parusieverzögerung in d. synpt. Ev. u. in d. Ag.," Beih. ZNW, 22 (1957), 158 f., 169, 202.

[8] Cf. πλήν in the par. Lk. 12:31 (πλήν ζητεῖτε as the opp. of μὴ ζητεῖτε 12:29); πλήν in Lk. 11:41 also corresponds to πρῶτον in Mt. 23:26.

π ρ ω τ ο κ α θ ε δ ρ ί α, π ρ ω τ ο κ λ ι σ ί α. [1] πρωτοκαθεδρία presupposes a non-attested πρωτοκάθεδρος and πρωτοκλισία a non-attested πρωτοκλίτης, just as πρωτο-λογία (LXX) is related to πρωτολόγος and πρωτοστασία to πρωτοστάτης (Ac. 24:5). Perhaps both words are formed after the analogy of the many derivations in -ία with πρωτο-, e.g., πρωτολογία [Debrunner].

[2] πρωτοκαθεδρία, though not thus far attested in non-christian works, can hardly be a Chr. construct. Pr.-Bauer⁵, *s.v.* refers to the Schol. on Eur. Or., 93 (Schol. in Eur. ed. E. Schwartz, I [1887], 106 f.), but this does not contain πρωτοκαθεδρία, only προσεδρία. Under NT influence the word is used in Herm. (→ n. 6) and the fathers, e.g., Cl. Al. Strom., VI, 106, 7; VII, 98, 2. The example from Theoph., 163, 26 quoted in Pr.-Bauer⁵, *s.v.* is late. πρωτοεδρία, too, occurs for the first time only in the Byzantine grammarian John Tzetzes (12th cent. A.D.). The adj. πρωτοθρόνιος, however, is found in Paus., 10, 38, 6 and πρωτόθρονος even earlier, Liddell-Scott, *s.v.* πρωτοκλισία has been found on a Delos inscr. of the 2nd cent. B.C. ("An Unpublished Decree of a Delian Association," JHS, 54 [1934], 142, line 33 f.) (= κλισία ἔντιμος or κλισία ἡ πρώτη elsewhere, cf. *ibid.,* 151, n. 53). The post-apost. fathers and Apologists do not use it. Cf. Cl. Al. Strom., VII, 98, 2. Suid., *s.v.*: πρωτοκλισία· ἡ πρώτη καθέδρα. τὰ πρωτοκλίσια occurs (only) in 2 Macc. 4:21 in the obvious sense of "accession." Pass., *s.v.* adduces πρωτοκλήσια in Cod. A in the sense "the first call," but one might also think of πρωτοκλήσια as a ceremonial name, cf. Polyb., 18, 55, 3; 28, 12, 8 and Liddell-Scott, *s.v.* πρωτοκλίναρχος in a pap. of the 5th cent. A.D. (U. Wilcken, "Heidnisches u. Christliches aus Ägypten," APF, 1 [1901], 413) is a title ; cf. Preisigke Wört., III, 152; Moult.-Mill., 557.

[3] καθέδρα, used in Mk. 11:15 par. Mt. 21:12 of the seats of the merchants in the temple, became a loan word in the Rabb., cf. S. Krauss, *Gr. u. lat. Lehnwörter in Talmud, Midrasch u. Targum,* II (1899), 572 on קתדרא. It denoted a chair with arms and back such as was offered to welcome guests at meals and to famous people, esp. scholars, for sitting ; it was also used by women, cf. S. Krauss, *Talmudische Archäol.,* I (1910), 62, 384, n. 62, 385,

πρωτοκλισία is "the first place," "the place of honour," ἐν τοῖς δείπνοις; [4] obviously there were several such seats of honour, esp. at larger banquets. [5] In Mk. 12:39 and par. Jesus is castigating the vain and self-satisfied manner of the Pharisees who everywhere, whether in the synagogues or in private houses, want to occupy the places of honour. [6] He also warns His disciples against self-exaltation by the examples which are given in Lk. 14:8 ff. and which are also intended as parables.

† πρωτότοκος, † πρωτοτοκεῖα.

A. The Word Group outside the New Testament.

1. πρωτότοκος, "firstborn," is rare outside the Bible and does not occur at all prior to the LXX. Better attested and earlier (Hom.) is the act. form πρωτοτόκος, "bearing for the first time," of animals and men. Also common in the sense of "firstborn" from Hom. on is πρωτόγονος, which can also mean "first in rank"; in this instance the act. form is rare and late (Polyb.). [1] Thus far the earliest instance of πρωτότοκος [2] is a

---

n. 67 f. But there is also ref. to the use of קתדרא in synagogues, cf. Str.-B., I, 909 on Mt. 23:2: ἐπὶ τῆς Μωϋσέως καθέδρας; E. L. Sukenik, *Ancient Synagogues in Palestine and Greece* (1934), 57-61; Stauffer Theol., Ill. 99. It may be gathered from Mt. 23:2 that teaching was given from these chairs, of which there was one in each synagogue (Ditt. Syll.³, II, 845, 2 f.: ὁ ... ἐπὶ τῆς καθέδρας σοφιστής [3rd cent. B.C.] is a good secular par.). But the ref. in Mt. 23:6 is to places of honour, since the plur. cannot mean that the Pharisees coveted the one seat, the *cathedra Mosis,* in all the synagogues. Cf. also Str.-B., I, 915 f., *ad loc.*

⁴ One reclined at table, → III, 654, 17 ff. Cf. κλίνη Mk. 7:4 vl.; κλισία Lk. 9:14; κατακλίνω cf. Pr.-Bauer⁵, *s.v.*

⁵ Cf. Str.-B., IV, 618 : In every group of guests the place on the middle couch was the place of honour. Lk. 14:8 refers in the sing. to the only πρωτοκλισία at a wedding-feast, perhaps in antithesis to the sing. ἔσχατος τόπος. In other ways, too, the antithesis is much sharper than in the Rabb. par. in Str.-B., II, 204, *ad loc.* and I, 916 on Mt. 23:6. The πρωτοκλισία in Lk. 14:8 is not necessarily taken first by the guest of honour but may be reserved for him. Acc. to the description in 1 QS 6:8 the priests take their seats as the first (ישבו לרשונה).

⁶ Herm. v., 3, 9, 7 has πρωτοκαθεδρῖται (after προηγούμενοι), but not critically as in Mt. 23:6 and par. Cf. Dib. Herm., 476, *ad loc.*; H. Campenhausen, *Kirchliches Amt u. geistliche Vollmacht in d. ersten 3 Jhdt.* (1953), 91. But this term, perhaps because of the unfavourable judgment of Mt. 23:6, apparently did not become widespread ; it is not found among the many ecclesiastical titles in πρωτο- listed, e.g., in Suic. Thes., *s.v.* When θέλει πρωτοκαθεδρίαν ἔχειν is put on the lips of the false prophet in Herm. m., 11, 12, this suggests [Schneemelcher] that the word was perhaps more common than our present material shows, but here again one sees the direct influence of Mt. 23:6.

π ρ ω τ ό τ ο κ ο ς, π ρ ω τ ο τ ο κ ε ῖ α. Cr.-Kö., *s.v.*; A. Durand, "Le Christ 'premier-né'," *Recherches de science religieuse,* 1 (1910), 56-66; J. Gewiess, *Christus u. das Heil nach d. Kol.,* Diss. Breslau (1932), 31-48 (with a review of patristic exposition); E. Käsemann, *Das wandernde Gottesvolk,*² FRL, NF, 37 (1957) = Käsemann I; also "Eine urchr. Taufliturgie," *Festschr. R. Bultmann* (1949), 133-148 = Käsemann II ; Mi. Hb. on 1:6; W. Michaelis, "Die bibl. Vorstellung v. Christus als dem Erstgeborenen," ZSTh, 23 (1954), 137-157.

¹ The two developments can hardly be independent. Since πρωτόγονος was available in the pass. there was no need to promote πρωτότοκος, and τεκ-τόκος leads more easily to an act., γεν-γόνος more easily to a pass.

² In the inscr. Ditt. Syll.³, III, 1024, 17 (200 B.C.), which is adduced by Moult.-Mill., 557 the true reading is ὄν ἐνκύμονα πρωτοτόκον : "a sow which is pregnant and will give birth for the first time."

Jewish burial inscr. (5 B.C.) from Tell el Jehudieh (Leontopolis), which reads (line 5 f.):
ὠδεῖνι δὲ Μοῖρα πρωτοτόκου με τέκνου πρὸς τέλος ἦγε βίου, "in the travail at
the birth of the first child destiny brought me to the end of life." [3] Though this inscr.,
like others from the same site, is composed in distichs and bears other marks of non-
biblical influence, the LXX is probably responsible for the use of πρωτότοκος rather
than the more common πρωτόγονος. [4] This is out of the question for the Trachonitis
inscr. for a pagan high-priest: ἱερεὺς γάρ εἰμι πρωτοτόκων ἐκ τελεθ[ῶν?] (= τελε-
τῶν?), Epigr. Graec., 460, 4. Unfortunately this cannot be dated, but it is unlikely to
be older than the former inscr. or the LXX. Nor is the sense clear. [5] Most of the other
examples refer to animals, e.g., P. Osl., I, 1, 312 (4th cent. A.D.), Preis. Zaub., I, 4,
1092 f., 1101 f., 3149 (4th cent. A.D.), Anth. Pal., VIII, 34 (allusion to OT usage). Part.
note should be taken of the deed of adoption in P. Lips., 28, 15 (381 A.D.): πρὸς τὸ
εἶναι σοῦ υἱὸν γνήσιον καὶ πρωτότοκον ὡς ἐξ ἰδίου αἵματος γενηθέντα σοι (cf.
the par. in line 15 f.). This shows that outside the Bible the word πρωτότοκος has a
more general sense. The -τοκος element is less prominent and privilege rather than
birthright is denoted, cf. πρωτόγονος → 871, 15. [6] Cf. Schol. on Eur. Or., 12 : [7] Thyestes
as πρωτότοκος and Atreus as δεύτερος.

2. In the LXX, whose latest examples are older than the earliest outside the Bible,
πρωτότοκος occurs some 130 times. Of these instances 74 are in Gn.-Dt. and 29 in
1 Ch., usually in legal enactments or genealogies.

a. In 111 cases the Heb. is בְּכוֹר or בְּכֹר. In another 6 we find Heb. words of the
same group and in 5 there is no equivalent, while 3 more are in works outside the Mas.
With very few exceptions (παιδίον in Dt. 25:6; πρεσβύτερος in Job 1:13, 18), בְּכוֹר
itself is always transl. πρωτότοκος, so that the two are clear equivalents. πρωτότοκος
is used of animals in Gn. 4:4; Ex. 34:19 f. etc. and of men and animals together in
Ex. 11:5; 12:12; Nu. 18:15 etc., also often as a neut. sing. noun (πᾶν πρωτότοκον,
Ex. 12:29 etc., frequently with the addition διανοῖγον τὴν μήτραν etc., e.g., Ex. 13:2; [8]
cf. also Lk. 2:23), also plur. (so Hb. 11:28 referring to Ex. 12:12 f.). Of men alone
πρωτότοκος is either an adj. with υἱός, Gn. 25:25; 27:32 etc., or a noun without υἱός
but with the proper name, Gn. 10:15; 22:21; 25:13 etc.

b. The examples of בְּכוֹר or πρωτότοκος and related terms (→ 874, 26 ff.) express
the great importance which the firstborn had in the experience both of antiquity in general
and of the men of the OT in particular. Because the land belongs to God, God has a
claim to the firstfruits and the firstborn of animals and men. [9] Presentation of the first-

---

[3] Cf. C. C. Edgar, "More Tomb-Stones from Tell el Yahoudieh," *Annales du service
des antiquités de l'Égypte*, 22 (1922), 9 f. = Preisigke Sammelbuch, 6647 → n. 36.

[4] In the LXX only Mi. 7:1; Σιρ. 36:11 (→ 873, 27 ff.); in the NT not at all.

[5] Cf. Deissmann LO, 71. The metrical inscr. for a 2 yr. old child (Epigr. Graec., 730, 3
= CIG, IV, 9727, 3) is Christian (2nd/3rd cent. A.D.).

[6] If in such texts a preference for the firstborn may be seen (Mitteis-Wilcken, II, 1, 234),
he is called πρεσβύτερος or πρεσβύτατος υἱός, not πρωτότοκος. Cf. BGU, I, 136, 6 f.;
U. Wilcken, "Zu d. Pap. d. Münchner Bibliothek," APF, 1 (1901), 479.

[7] Ed. E. Schwartz, I (1887), 98.

[8] Probably there lies behind this closer definition the need in polygamy to distinguish
between the firstborn of the father and the firstborn of the mother, H. Haag, Art. "Erst-
geburt," *Bibel-Lex.* [1956], 422). The formulations are, of course, more general and do not
bring out the distinction, a matriarchal background being no longer apparent, cf. J. Hempel,
"Das Ethos d. AT," Beih. ZAW, 67 (1928), 68. On the other hand it is evident that in
polygamy the firstborn (or firstbegotten) of the father must occupy a special position as the
"רֵאשִׁית of his power" (Gn. 49:3; Dt. 21:17).

[9] Cf. V. Ryssel, Art. "Erstlinge u. Erstlingsopfer," RE³, 5, 482-484; O. Eissfeldt, *Erstlinge
u. Zehnten im AT* (1917); also Art. "Erstlinge," RGG², II, 293 f.; A. Wendel, Art. "Erst-

born of cattle as a sacrifice, and later as a gift to the priests, plays an important role in the religion of Israel and Judah, as does also the offering of the firstfruits. For this the LXX uses πρωτογέννημα or more correctly πρωτογέννημα, almost always plur. and usually for בְּכוּרִים. All the male firstborn of men and animals are holy to the Lord, Ex. 22:28 f.; 34:19 f.; Nu. 18:15 ff. (cf. Lk. 2:23 f.); Dt. 15:19 ff. [10] In the family the firstborn son took precedence, cf. Gn. 25:29 ff.; 49:3; 2 Ch. 21:3 and also the echo of this in the laws of inheritance. The advantage of the firstborn is then the presupposition of the transf. use of בְּכוֹר and of πρωτότοκος in the LXX. An important question here is whether and to what extent the equation of the latter with בְּכוֹר influenced the history of its meaning. [11]

c. From the standpt. of πρωτότοκος the transf. use might be affected by -τοκος and thus restricted to cases in which the idea of birth is at least fig. present, or this idea might retreat into the background and the transf. sense rest exclusively on πρωτο-. בְּכוֹר is impartial here, since the root can denote the earlier or older as well as the first-born. If it is hard to determine which of the two by no means identical ideas is the older, [12] this does not mean, of course, that there is doubt as to which of the meanings was present to the minds of the LXX translators. A positive starting-pt. here is that etym. בְּכוֹר etc. is neither connected with the Heb. words for "to give birth" ⏤ it can thus be used for fruits etc. as well ⏤ nor is it related to the words for "one," "first," nor the similar word for "head," "chief," → n. 10. Since בְּכוֹר is thus etym. equally far removed from both the main components of πρωτότοκος, it was quite possible that as an equivalent of בְּכוֹר this might become increasingly remote and even detached altogether from the idea of birth or the whole question of origin. To the concept which it was designed to express there did not necessarily belong a comparison with other things of the same kind, since the first might also be the only one. [13] Do the LXX data support this conclusion?

d. When Ex. 4:22 says: υἱὸς πρωτότοκός μου Ἰσραήλ, and Σιρ. 36:11 also says: Ἰσραὴλ ὃν πρωτογόνῳ (weakly attested vl. πρωτοτόκῳ) ὡμοίωσας, this designation as firstborn, which is almost a title in Ex. 4:22 (it is applied to Ephraim in Ἰερ. 38:9), expresses the particularly close relation in which God stands to Israel. Though something is said about God's relations to other peoples in, e.g., Dt. 32:8 f. LXX; Am. 9:7; Is. 19:25, this expression does not suggest that other nations or all the other

---

linge," RGG³, II, 609 f. On the possibility of a typological or representative significance of the laws concerning the offering of the firstborn cf. M. Barth, *Die Taufe ein Sakrament?* (1951), 291; W. Michaelis, *Versöhnung des Alls* (1950), 34 f.

[10] The fem. בְּכִירָה occurs only in Gn. 19:31, 33 f., 37; 29:26; 1 S. 14:49. The opp. in 1 S. 14:49 is קְטַנָּה, elsewhere צְעִירָה. The LXX has πρωτότοκος and δευτέρα in 1 S. 14:49, πρεσβυτέρα and νεωτέρα elsewhere. We usually transl. "the elder" and in so doing acknowledge that etym. the Heb. word group is not connected either with a word "to give birth" or with one for "one," "first," → lines 17 ff. Nevertheless, it is clear that the rendering "firstborn" (influenced perhaps by LXX πρωτότοκος and Lat. *primogenitus*?) cannot be regarded as inappropriate or even erroneous for the easily predominant masc. בְּכוֹר.

[11] Cf. W. Michaelis, "Der Beitrag d. LXX zur Bedeutungsgeschichte von πρωτότοκος," *Sprachgesch. u. Wortbedeutung, Festschr. A. Debrunner* (1954), 313-320.

[12] On the history of the meaning of בְּכוֹר and nouns and verbs related to the root in Heb. and other Semitic languages cf. J. J. Stamm in Michaelis, *op. cit.,* 317 f.

[13] Cf. the corresponding development outside the Bible (→ 872, 11 ff.) and the emergence of the sense "first in rank" in the case of πρωτόγονος, → 871, 15.

nations are also God's sons, [14] the more so since this idea is not attested at all elsewhere in the OT. [15] The firstborn here is not seen, then, in relation to other brothers but solely as an object of the special love of his father. [16] Cf. also Ps. Sol. 13:9 : νουθετήσει δίκαιον ὡς υἱὸν ἀγαπήσεως καὶ ἡ παιδεία αὐτοῦ ὡς πρωτοτόκου, 18:4 : ἡ παιδεία σου ἐφ' ἡμᾶς ὡς υἱὸν πρωτότοκον μονογενῆ. It is true that πρωτότοκος and μονογενής are not fully synon. → 876, 22 ff. but if they are par. here this is possible only on the assumption of the uniqueness of the position of the πρωτότοκος. [17] The use of πρωτότοκος for the king in ψ 88:28 is also to be understood in this sense : κἀγὼ πρωτότοκον θήσομαι αὐτὸν ὑψηλὸν παρὰ τοῖς βασιλεῦσιν τῆς γῆς. Directly before v. 27 refers to the close relation of the king to God : αὐτὸς ἐπικαλέσεταί με Πατήρ μου εἶ σύ, and the obvious pt. is that only the πρωτότοκος can speak thus ; the kings of the earth do not have God as Father in this sense and it is not in relation to them that the king is called the firstborn, but as the elect and beloved of God who as such is thus set above the kings of the earth. The king is not *primus inter pares* ; between him and the kings of the earth there is an antithesis, cf. Ps. 2:7, 10.

The idea of even a figurative birth or begetting [18] is no longer a clear element in πρωτότοκος in these passages. It is nowhere set forth and in ψ 88:28 it is in fact ruled out by θήσομαι, which rather suggests adoption, cf. also Ps. 2:7. The idea of priority in time over other sons is also remote. The orientation of the word is no longer to the presence of other sons. It expresses the fact that the people, the individual, or the king is especially dear to God. [19] This nuance, found already in the OT, is impressively expressed in the synonyms of the title which, on the basis of the OT, 4 Esr. 6:58 accords to Israel : "(my) firstborn, only one, elect and beloved." [20]

e. Along with πρωτότοκος — πρωτοτόκος does not occur — we also find in the LXX the following words not previously attested : πρωτοτοκέω "to give birth for the first time" of animals in 1 Βασ. 6:7, 10, a woman in Jer. 4:31; [21] πρωτοτοκεύω with

---

[14] So E. Wechssler, *Hellas im Ev.* (1936), 318 : "that all peoples stem from this father but Israel may boast of being his firstborn son" (with appeal to J. Klausner, *Jesus v. Nazareth* [1930], 524 on Ex. 4:22).

[15] This is also true from the standpt. that God is Father only for Israel (e.g., Jer. 31:9) or that this exclusiveness is only very hesitantly transcended in the OT, → V, 972, 3 ff., 26 ff.; 973, 1 ff. Cf. Gewiess, 33, n. 4; W. Twisselmann, "Die Gotteskindschaft der Christen nach d. NT," BFTh, 41, 1 (1939), 26, n. 2.

[16] This is not altered by the fact that the youngest son too, the son of old age, may be esp. dear (cf. Joseph in Gn. 37:3, Benjamin in Gn. 42 f.) or that Yahweh may set aside the right of primogeniture and choose the younger (Jacob, Ephraim, David).

[17] Cf. Durand, 60 f. יָחִיד and בְּכוֹר are also par. in Zech. 12:10, where the LXX has ἀγαπητός and πρωτότοκος, not missing the aspect of uniqueness in יָחִיד since ἀγαπητός (cf. υἱὸς ἀγαπήσεως Ps. Sol. 13:9 → line 4) means the only-beloved → 879, 11 ff.; IV, 739, 3 ff.; Zn. Mt. on 3:17, n. 68. The transl. of Mt. 3:16 f. par. in Ev. Hebr. (*filius meus primogenitus* instead of ἀγαπητός) betrays later influence, cf. Hier. in Is. 11:2 (MPL, 24 [1845], 1458). Cf. A. Seeberg, *Das Ev. Christi* (1905), 21.

[18] Only rarely, even fig., does the OT speak of begetting by deity, → I, 668, 17 ff.

[19] The designation of the Messiah as firstborn is based on Mess. interpretation of ψ 88:28 → 875, 36 f.

[20] The Heb. acc. to B. Violet (GCS, 32, 64 f.) is בְּכוֹרִי יְחִידִי בְּחִירִי יְדִידִי = πρωτότοκον μονογενῆ ἐκλεκτὸν ἀγαπητόν σου (μου), though → IV, 739, 3 ff. Cf. also W. Turner, "Ο ΥΙΟΣ ΜΟΥ Ο ΑΓΑΠΗΤΟΣ," JThSt, 27 (1926), 112-129; P. Winter, "ΜΟΝΟΓΕΝΗΣ ΠΑΡΑ ΠΑΤΡΟΣ," *Zeitschr. f. Religions- u. Geistesgesch.*, 5 (1953), 347, cf. 340.

[21] Quoted in 1QH 3:8. Cf. H. Bardtke, "Die Loblieder v. Qumran, II," ThLZ, 81 (1956), 592 and n. 66 f., *ibid.* 80 (1955), 692; M. Burrows, *More Light on the Dead Sea Scrolls* (1958), 317 f.

dat. "to grant the right of a firstborn," Dt. 21:16, also Lv. 27:26 'Α; τὰ πρωτοτοκεῖα "the right of the firstborn," Gn. 25:31-34; 27:36; Dt. 21:17; 1 Ch. 5:1 (always for בְּכֹרָה) Cf. Hb. 12:16 in transl. of Gn. 25:33 f.: Ἠσαῦ ὃς ἀντὶ βρώσεως μιᾶς ἀπέδοτο τὰ πρωτοτοκεῖα ἑαυτοῦ. [22] In Gn. 43:33 Αλλ ἡ πρωτοτοκία is used for בְּכֹרָה, while the LXX has τὰ πρεσβεῖα. This noun — read either πρωτοτοκία (= being πρωτότοκος) or πρωτοτοκεία (= πρωτοτοκεύειν) also occurs in Gn. 25:34; Dt. 21:17 'Α, [23] Dt. 21:17 also ΘΣ. At Ex. 13:2 (HT only בְּכוֹר) πρωτότοκος is strengthened by an added πρωτογενής; this word also occurs in Prv. 31:2 : πρωτογενές, σοὶ λέγω, υἱέ. [24] In Wis. 7:1; 10:1 Adam is called πρωτόπλαστος.

3. Philo often uses πρωτότοκος as adj. and noun both of men and animals, almost always on an OT basis. [25] The only instance of independent use is in Cher., 54. In Cher., 53 Philo raises the question why in the case of Cain's birth in Gn. 4:1, unlike that of Seth in 4:25, it is not expressly noted that Eve bore and named a son, but Cain, the γεννηθεὶς πρῶτος ἐξ ἀνθρώπων, is introduced at once by name. In this connection he calls Cain in Cher., 54 πρωτότοκος, ὃς ἦν ἀρχὴ τῆς ἐξ ἀλλήλων γενέσεως ἀνθρώποις : Cain is the first man who came into the world by begetting and birth, whereas Adam and Eve must be regarded as φύντες ἐκ γῆς, Cher., 53. [26] The idea of firstborn is thus very much to the fore in Philo. This is why he four times calls the *logos* πρωτόγονος but never [27] πρωτότοκος.

Joseph. uses πρωτότοκος on an OT basis for the firstfruits of flocks (Ant., 1, 54 cf. Gn. 4:4), the firstborn of men and cattle (2, 313 cf. Ex. 12:12). On the other hand in 4, 71, unlike Nu. 18:15, he alternates between πρωτότοκος ἄνθρωπος and (in the case of cattle) ἀπαρχή (4, 70 f.) or τὸ γεννηθὲν πρῶτον (4, 70). In his version of Jos. 6:26 Joseph. (Ant., 5, 31) has πρῶτος παῖς and νεώτερος for πρωτότοκος and ἐλάχιστος.

4. In the pseudepigr. the OT use is continued, cf. Jub. 24:3 ff. (Gn. 25:29 ff.); 26:27 (Gn. 27:19); 36:14 f.; 41:3. Going beyond Gn. 22:16 LXX Jub. 18:15 calls Isaac Abraham's firstborn son ; in Jub. 18:2 = Gn. 22:2 firstborn is equivalent to beloved. The same stress on the special position of the firstborn may be seen in Jub. 19:28 : God as Jacob's father, Jacob as God's firstborn son. Ex. 4:22 is obviously in view and behind Jub. 2:20 is the concept of the sole election of Israel : "I have chosen the seed of Jacob from all that I have seen and have inscribed him as my firstborn son" etc. (cf. Heb. En. 44:10). On 4 Esr. 6:58 → 874, 21 ff. If בְּכוֹר is the original of the Lat. *primogenitus*, 4 Esr. 6:55 is also referring to Israel rather than the world as the firstborn. [28]

5. On the basis of Ex. 4:22 Rabb. Judaism used the term firstborn esp. for Israel or Jacob, though it is also applied to the Torah, sometimes to Adam, and in Ex. r., 19 (81a); Pesikt. r., 34 (159b) to the Messiah-King on the basis of Ps. 89:27 and Jer. 31:9 (Ephraim

---

[22] πρωτοτοκεῖα is better than πρωτοτόκια, which most MSS have in the LXX and at Hb. 12:16. -εῖα par. -εύω is common for distinction, cf. τὰ πρεσβεῖα, τὰ ἀριστεῖα, τὰ πρωτεῖα. In these cases -ια is impossible. Bl.-Debr. § 120, 1 is to be corrected here. [Debrunner] → n. 25.

[23] In this form 'Α seems to be attempting a more exact reproduction of the Heb. sing. בְּכֹרָה [P. Katz].

[24] No Mas., though this is to be supplied from the LXX, cf. BHK³.

[25] Cf. Leisegang, *s.v.* τὰ πρωτοτόκια (*sic !* → n. 22) also occurs a few times.

[26] Michaelis, *op. cit.*, 320 on Cher., 54 stands in need of correction here, cf. Michaelis, 155. → n. 30.

[27] Cf. W. Staerk, *Die Erlösererwartung in d. östlichen Religionen* (1938), 72 f.

[28] In S. Bar. 44:1 "my (i.e., Baruch's) firstborn son" possibly rests on בְּנִי הַגָּדוֹל (e.g., Gn. 27:1), cf. B. Violet, *ad loc.* (GCS, 32, 261).

as a pet name for the Messiah).[29] The term expresses the love and regard which God shows a man[30] and it can also refer to the special qualities of a man.[31]

B. The Word Group in the New Testament.

In the NT πρωτότοκος, which occurs in the plural in Hb. 11:28 (→ 872, 28); 12:23 (→ 881, 1 ff.), always refers in the singular to Jesus Christ.

1. Lk. 2:7 says of Mary, the mother of Jesus : καὶ ἔτεκεν τὸν υἱὸν αὐτῆς τὸν πρωτότοκον. This is the only instance in the NT where, through the paronomastic use of τίκτειν, πρωτότοκος refers unequivocally to the process of birth, and this in the natural sense. It is hard to say what the special point of describing the new-born child as πρωτότοκος is. It is unlikely that 2:7 is simply preparing the way for 2:22 ff., for though express reference is made to Ex. 13 in the story of the presentation the word πρωτότοκος, suggested by Ex. 13:2 (not 13:12), is not used there.[32] One may conjecture that the stress on the fact that Jesus was the firstborn son of His mother is related to the emphatic reference to the virginity of Mary in 1:27, 34.[33] If so, the main point of the πρωτότοκος is "to rule out earlier children" rather than "to contrast the child Jesus with later children of Mary."[34] If we did not have other accounts of the fact that Jesus had brothers and sisters (→ I, 144, 16 ff.) the wording of Lk. 2:7 would hardly be enough to warrant the latter conclusion, for the firstborn is called πρωτότοκος because he is the first, whether or not other children follow later. On the other hand πρωτότοκος does very generally include the possibility and even the expectation that other children will follow, → V, 834, 16 ff.[35] Hence πρωτότοκος in Lk. 2:7 cannot

---

[29] Cf. Str.-B., III, 256-258 on R. 8:29; 626 on Col. 1:15; 677 on Hb. 1:6; Mi. Hb. on 1:6 (52 and n. 2).

[30] Str.-B., III, 626. That Adam, though not born but created, can be called the "firstborn of the world" in Nu. r., 4 (141c) shows how remote must have been the idea of birth. Priority in time is not meant except in relation to the Torah and Gn. 1:1; Str.-B., III, 257. Cf. Staerk, op. cit., 14; → n. 46, 53.

[31] Str.-B., III, 258. "Firstborn" can also be used in malam partem : the most dangerous or dreadful of its kind (ibid., 258 f.); cf. already Job 18:13 (Mas.): "firstborn of death" for a bad illness. Cf. also πρωτότοκος τοῦ σατανᾶ for a heretic, Pol., 7, 1; cf. Mart. Pol. epil., 3; Iren. Haer., III, 3, 4. Cf. W. Bauer, Rechtgläubigkeit u. Ketzerei im ältesten Christentum (1939), 74, 237. The Aram. proper name פֶּטְרוֹס (on the various ways of writing it cf. Str.-B., I, 530 on Mt. 10:2) may be connected with פטר and if so means the διανοίγων τὴν μήτραν → 872, 27, the firstborn. Cf. → 101, n. 8; O. Cullmann, Petrus (1952), 13 and n. 11; 14, n. 13 (ET [1953], 19, n. 11, 13); O. Betz, "Felsenmann u. Felsengemeinde," ZNW, 48 (1957), 65, n. 48.

[32] Cf. Zn. Lk., ad loc. If πρωτότοκος is an adj. in Lk. 2:7 it cannot be a "Christ-predicate" in the sense of, e.g., Col. 1:15, cf. G. Erdmann, "Die Vorgeschichten des Lk.-u. Mt.-Ev. u. Vergils 4. Ekloge," FRL, NF, 30 (1932), 41 f., → Michaelis, 137 f.

[33] This connection is completely ruled out, of course, if Lk. 2:1 ff. was not originally a continuation of 1:26 ff. but an independent narrative in which Joseph and Mary were married and Jesus was the child of this marriage, cf. M. Dibelius, "Jungfrauensohn u. Krippenkind," SAH, 1931/32, 4 (1932), esp. 55-57.

[34] Kl. Lk., ad loc., though with the opposite emphasis ; cf. Zn. Lk., ad loc.

[35] If Jesus had not had brothers and sisters the πρωτότοκος of Lk. 2:7 would perhaps not have gone undisputed and even become later a vl. at Mt. 1:25. The only child is called μονογενής, cf. Lk. 7:12; 8:42; 9:38; Hb. 11:17. John the Baptist is not called πρωτότοκος even though it is perhaps significant that he was the first child of his parents. P. Winter, "The Proto-Source of Lk. 1," Nov. Test., 2 (1956), 190 f. finds a par. in Samson, but he, too, is not described in this way in Ju. 13:24.

have the sense of μονογενής (→ IV, 737, 22 ff.) or rule out the possibility that Mary had other children. [36]

2. The metaphor of the firstborn among brethren is used by Paul in R. 8:29 : οὓς προέγνω, καὶ προώρισεν συμμόρφους τῆς εἰκόνος τοῦ υἱοῦ αὐτοῦ, εἰς τὸ εἶναι αὐτὸν πρωτότοκον ἐν πολλοῖς ἀδελφοῖς. The reference is to eschatological transfiguration. [37] The resurrection is not in view, and πρωτότοκος is not to be understood along the lines of the πρωτότοκος ἐκ τῶν νεκρῶν in Col. 1:18. [38] Paul is thinking rather of perfected fellowship with Christ which begins with the resurrection on the Last Day and which presupposes being made like Him, cf. ὅμοιοι αὐτῷ ἐσόμεθα, 1 Jn. 3:2. In this perfected fellowship with Christ transfigured believers are regarded as brothers of Christ, just as they enter into their inheritance (R. 8:17) and attain to eschatological υἱοθεσία as συγκληρονόμοι Χριστοῦ (8:23). He is thus the πρωτότοκος, like them but above them in rank and dignity, since He remains their Lord. [39]

3. As there is no great emphasis on -τοκος in the πρωτότοκος of R. 8:29, so it is also in Col. 1:18, where Christ is called πρωτότοκος ἐκ τῶν νεκρῶν. [40] The expressions ἀπαρχὴ τῶν κεκοιμημένων in 1 C. 15:20 and πρῶτος ἐξ ἀναστάσεως νεκρῶν in Ac. 26:23 are close parallels which show that what is denoted here is that Christ is the first to have risen from the dead. Nevertheless, priority in time is not the only important aspect ; included, too, is the significance which

---

[36] J. B. Frey, "La signification du terme πρωτότοκος d'après une inscr. juive," Biblica, 11 (1930), 373-390 (cf. also Haag, op. cit. [→ n. 8], 422) has incorrectly argued that πρωτότοκος and μονογενής are full synonyms on the basis of the burial inscr. of Tell el Jehudieh mentioned → 872, 1 ff. Now it is true that the child born to Arsinoe, who acc. to this inscr. died in childbirth, remained the only child of his mother. But he is called πρωτότοκον τέκνον, not for this reason, but because he was the first child. Cf. also H. Koch, Virgo Eva — Virgo Maria (1937), 102-106 (App. 5); 46-60 for details on Lk. 2:7 in the fathers, esp. Iren. and Tert.

[37] "εἰκών denotes the transfigured body after the resurrection," Ltzm. R., ad loc.; → II, 397, 5 ff. Cf. also 1 C. 15:49; Phil. 3:21. The ref. is not to the historical Jesus as though discipleship were in view in συμμόρφους τῆς εἰκόνος, Zn. R., ad loc. To claim εἰκών for this is a modern but not a NT idea. Nor does 2 C. 3:18 refer to a present event ; it relates εἰκών to the form of existence of the risen Lord, cf. Käsemann II, 138. This is true in spite of the fact (T. W. Manson) that the divine sonship of believers is a present possession in R. 8:14 ff.; 1 Jn. 3:2. Nor does the μορφή of Phil. 2:7 support the idea that σύμμορφος is non-eschatological in R. 8:29. Even if it is not expressly stated, the idea that Christ is "image," "the image of God" (2 C. 4:4; Col. 1:15), lies behind R. 8:29. The ἐδόξασεν at the end of the various aor. in R. 8:29 f. may pt. to a relation between the eschatological statement and some event in the present life of the Christian, but this does not alter the eschatological orientation of the context (→ II, 397, 15 ff.; 250, 38 ff.), certainly as regards the εἰς clause and already in respect of συμμόρφους etc. as well.

[38] → III, 18, 23 ff. Cf. E. Brunner, Das Ewige als Zukunft u. Gegenwart (1953), 184, by rising again on the third day Christ became the firstborn among many brethren, but only proleptically, since they will rise only on the Last Day.

[39] Cf. Mich. Ph. on 3:21. It is not likely that in R. 8:29 Paul is adopting πρωτότοκος as a Jewish Mess. title (Schl. R., ad loc.), since this carries no ref. to brethren and has in view only the relation to God, → 875, 36 ff.

[40] Nowhere in the NT is the resurrection viewed as generation. Zn. Ac. on 2:24 suggests that θάνατος (vl. ᾅδης) suffered labour in yielding up the dead Jesus and relates πρωτότοκος ἐκ τῶν νεκρῶν to this idea. But θάνατος and ᾅδης are masc. and in spite of ὠδῖνας δὲ αὐτῶν ἔλυσας in Job 39:2 and the odd Rabb. interpretation of Is. 18:4 (Str.-B., II, 617 f. on Ac. 2:24) λύσας τὰς ὠδῖνας does not mean birth-pangs but sorrows generally (so also ψ 114:3). Cf. further Haench. Ag., 148, n. 5.

the resurrection of Christ has as the prelude to the general resurrection at the Last Day. [41] Finally, this carries with it a reference to the superior rank and dignity of Christ, the more so as the succeeding ἵνα clause (→ 882, 8 ff.) has this implication, the preceding ἀρχή points in the same direction, [42] and the parallel πρωτότοκος saying in 1:15 (→ lines 19 ff.) supports a hierarchical understanding. As Christ from all creation bears the rank of a πρωτότοκος in relation to every creature, so He does also and especially as the risen Lord, [43] → line 28 f.; 879, 6 ff.

4. In Rev. 1:5 πρωτότοκος τῶν νεκρῶν does not simply refer to priority in time. The succeeding ὁ ἄρχων τῶν βασιλέων τῆς γῆς is reminiscent of ψ 88:28b and ὁ μάρτυς ὁ πιστός echoes already the ὁ μάρτυς ἐν οὐρανῷ πιστός of ψ 88:38 (→ IV, 495, 32 ff.). Hence πρωτότοκος is related to the κἀγὼ πρωτότοκον θήσομαι αὐτόν of ψ 88:28a (→ 874, 7 ff.) and refers not merely to priority in time but more particularly to the rank of firstborn which accrues to Jesus with His resurrection. The strong dependence on ψ 88 supports the view that this statement is not just catching up Col. 1:18, where there is no such dependence, but is either a phrase with its own prior history or an independent formulation of the author.

5. The description of Christ as πρωτότοκος πάσης κτίσεως in Col. 1:15 obviously finds in the ὅτι clause of v. 16 its more precise basis and explanation: Christ is the Mediator at creation to whom all creatures without exception owe their creation, → V, 894, 28 ff., 37 ff. Hence πρωτότοκος πάσης κτίσεως does not simply denote the priority in time of the pre-existent Lord. [44] If the expression refers to the mediation of creation through Christ, it cannot be saying at the same time [45] that He was created as the first creature. [46] The decisive objection to this view, which sees in the πάση κτίσεως a partitive genitive, is that it would demand emphasis on the -τοκος, whereas with the exception of Lk. 2:7 (→ 876, 6 ff.), which refers to literal birth, the -τοκος is never emphasised in the NT in passages which speak of Christ, especially Col. 1:18 (→ 877, 15 ff.). A further point is that this view would bring -τοκος into tension with κτίσις (and κτίζεσθαι in 1:16), for creation and birth are different concepts and πρωτότοκος cannot be regarded

---

[41] → I, 371, 4 ff. O. Cullmann, "Unsterblichkeit d. Seele u. Auferstehung der Toten," ThZ, 12 (1956), esp. 144-148. This is also the pt. in Ac. 26:23; cf. H. Conzelmann, *Die Mitte d. Zeit²* (1957), 179, 202. For interpretation along Gnostic lines cf. Käsemann I, 66, n. 2, 72 f.; II, 139, and more soberly Mi. Hb. Exc. on 1:6 and 2:10.

[42] ἀρχή in parallelism with the statements in Col. 1:15 f., → I, 483, 38 ff., though related to the resurrection in → I, 371, 7 ff.; Dib. Gefbr.³, *ad loc.*; Durand, 64.

[43] Michaelis, 144-146.

[44] Dib. Gefbr.³, *ad loc.* ("firstborn before all creatures"). Even the phrase קַדְמוֹנוֹ שֶׁל עוֹלָם "the One who is before the world," which is used of God and which acc. to Str.-B., III, 626, *ad loc.* is closest to Paul's expression, is not a true par. if this does not refer merely to pre-temporality. On the description of God Himself as the Firstborn in later Judaism cf. the reservations of Durand, 60 and n. 2. Dib., *op. cit.* relates the comp. use of πρῶτος or πρῶτον in Jn. 1:15, 30; 15:18 to πρωτότοκος, but there is no valid basis for this in Radermacher², 68, 70 or Bl.-Debr. § 62 (cf. § 185, 1). πρωτότοκος means "the one born first"; it does not have to mean "the one born before (another)."

[45] Pre-temporality and mediation of creation are mentioned one after the other in Jn. 1:1, 3. But this is not to say that πρωτότοκος covers both.

[46] Hence the description of Adam as "the firstborn of the world" (→ n. 30; Käsemann I, 128) is not a close par.

as a simple synonym of πρωτόκτιστος. [47] The only remaining possibility [48] is to take πρωτότοκος hierarchically (→ line 7 f.). What is meant is the unique supremacy of Christ over all creatures as the Mediator of their creation. The succeeding statement in 1:17a : αὐτός ἐστιν πρὸ πάντων, emphasises the same supremacy, [49] while 1:17b draws the conclusion from 1:16.

If πρωτότοκος is selected in Col. 1:15 and then again in 1:18 to express this supremacy, this is because of the great importance which the term "firstborn" took on as a word for rank in the OT and then retained in later Judaism, → 873, 27 ff.; 875, 35 ff. It is true that this term denotes the relation to God, which is not in view in Col. 1:15, and this distinction is to be upheld in face of the intrinsically noteworthy observation that the relation to God is described just before in v. 13 by the phrase υἱὸς τῆς ἀγάπης αὐτοῦ and that υἱὸς ἀγαπήσεως and πρωτότοκος are related in Ps. Sol. 13:9, → 874, 3. [50] On the other hand, if Col. 1:15 refers to the relation of Christ to all creatures as the Mediator of their creation, this finds no basis in the relevant OT and Jewish material. Though Jewish σοφία speculation is important in relation to the NT (→ IV, 136, 12 ff.), even Prv. 8:22 : κύριος ἔκτισέν με (i.e., σοφία) ἀρχὴν ὁδῶν αὐτοῦ, cannot have had any direct influence, since there is no express thought of mediation in creation here.

From another angle, it is surprising that a rare NT word like πρωτότοκος should occur twice in Col. 1:15-20, and that, coming each time in the second statement of the two parts of the hymn, it should help to determine the structure, so that the two occurrences are not unrelated. [51] This singular use does not have to be based on an older tradition ; it may go back to Paul himself. It is unlikely that the saying in 1:18 came first and provided the impulse for that in 1:15, as though the use in relation to the resurrection were more common or easier to attain, for the fact is that 1:15 comes first and the use in relation to the resurrection is no more frequent (on Rev. 1:5 → 878, 9 ff.; on Hb. 1:6 → 880, 7 ff.). On the contrary, the saying in 1:15 came first and then led to that in 1:18, unless the two arose independently, though on common presuppositions. The thesis that such presuppositions are to be sought in the doctrine of the primal man or the Gnostic idea of the redeemed redeemer [52] deserves serious consideration but it cannot be regarded as proved, esp. as the concept of the firstborn is not very prominent in Gnosticism (prior to Col.) and even where it does occur it may be traced back in part to the OT. [53] All told, then, it is inadvisable to explain the use of the

---

[47] Cf. Durand, 62. Nor can the antithesis between πρωτότοκος and κτίσις be eliminated by expounding as follows : "But Christ is the πρωτότοκος of all creation because He and He alone is begotten of the Father, while all others are created by Him through the Son," Koch, op. cit. (→ n. 36), 56 n. If stress is laid on the -τοκος, πρωτότοκος cannot possibly mean the "only-begotten," and if by equating τίκτειν and γεννᾶν it is given the sense of "first-begotten" we again have the contradiction that the creatures, being called κτίσις, are made, not begotten. The idea in 1 Jn. 5:18 (but not Jn. 1:13 → I, 671, 25 ff.), whereby Christ is begotten of God, has no bearing on πρωτότοκος here, nor does the use of Ps. 2:7 in the NT, cf. Michaelis, 145 f., 147-149. In the Bible the distinction between γεννᾶν and τίκτειν is upheld, at any rate in relation to God's work.
[48] To be rejected also are all attempts to relate the passage to the καινὴ κτίσις or to read πρωτοτόκος. Cf. Gewiess, 32; W. Staerk, Soter, I (1933), 155; J. Héring, "Die bibl. Grundlagen d. chr. Humanismus," Abh. ThANT (1946), 7, n. 4; E. Fascher, Textgeschichte als hermeneutisches Problem (1953), 103, n. 1.
[49] Even Dib. Gefbr.³, ad loc. thinks rank is "at least included" ; Gewiess, 36 more correctly thinks there is only slight ref. to the temporal aspect. Cf. → III, 680, 42 ff.; 681, 24 ff.
[50] Cf. also Käsemann II, 140.
[51] Ibid., 134.
[52] Ibid., I, 58-61, 66, n. 2, 72 f., 98-105, 128, 136 f., 139.
[53] On Adam as the firstborn (Käsemann I, 128; II, 137) → n. 30; on πρωτόγονος in Philo, Käsemann II, 137, 147, n. 29. Angels or archangels as πρωτόκτιστοι (Käsemann

term in Col. along Gnostic lines. [54] Since methodologically it is not absolutely necessary to seek a common derivation for all the aspects of the phrase πρωτότοκος πάσης κτίσεως, it is not impossible that the idea of the pre-existent Christ as the Mediator of creation had an earlier history unrelated to the term πρωτότοκος, while the latter is based on an older use, like that in the OT and later Judaism (→ 879, 7 f.), which adequately prepared it for its later employment in Christology. [55]

6. As regards Hb. 1:6 : ὅταν δὲ πάλιν εἰσαγάγῃ τὸν πρωτότοκον εἰς τὴν οἰκουμένην, both the context (1:3) and the content of the quotation (Dt. 32:43 LXX ; ψ 96:7) which follows support the view that it refers to the enthronement of the exalted Christ at the *parousia*. If this is correct the designation of Christ as πρωτότοκος here is like that of Col. 1:18 (→ 877, 15 ff.) and Rev. 1:5 (→ 878, 9 ff.) and adds to the instances of the risen or exalted Lord being regarded as πρωτότοκος. [56] In Hb. 1:6, however, there is no addition like (ἐκ) τῶν νεκρῶν (Col. 1:18; Rev. 1:5). Again without the addition ἡ μέλλουσα (cf. 2:5) ἡ οἰκουμένη does not, perhaps, denote the heavenly world. Finally, εἰσάγω also fits the incarnation and πάλιν can be equivalent to the πάλιν of 1:5. In view of all this, precedence must be given to a relating of the statement to the situation of the incarnation of the pre-existent Lord. In this case, πρωτότοκος corresponds to the earlier υἱός of 1:2 and the quotations in 1:5a b (cf. also 1:8), and along with it refers to the unique relation of sonship in which Christ, primarily if not exclusively as the pre-existent One, stands to God.

The thesis that the expression derives from the γεγέννηκά σε of Ps. 2:7 used in 1:5a cannot be sustained (→ n. 47), esp. as the quotation is not adduced for the sake of this phrase but is meant to illustrate rather than explain the uniqueness of the sonship, like 2 S. 7:14 in 1:5b. Nor can one argue that the Son is πρωτότοκος in comparison with the angels, since the context does not accord this relation of sonship to the angels. [57] It seems as though we have here a title which was not fashioned *ad hoc* but which was already firmly established and probably known to the readers. There can be no saying, however, from what older tradition the author took it, whether from that behind Col. 1:15 or some other. [58] In 12:23, too, the author uses πρωτότοκος in a way for which there is no par. in the NT.

I, 28, 126; Cl. Al. Exc. Theod., 27, 3 ff.; J. Barbel, "Christos Angelos," *Theophanie,* 3 [1941], esp. 199-201; W. Lueken, *Michael* [1898], 111-117, cf. 38 : Rabb. par.) are no par. to Col. 1:15, since this does not assume that the pre-existent Christ was created, → 878, 23 ff.

[54] Mi. Hb. on 1:6. These reservations in respect of Gnostic derivation are valid irrespective of whether or not Käsemann II is thought to have proved that a primitive baptismal liturgy has been worked over in Col. 1:15-20 and that this in turn derives from a pre-Chr. hymn (on this cf. W. Michaelis, *Einl. in das NT*² [1954], 215). "Firstborn" (also "First" → I, 2, n. 6) is a mythological concept in the Mandaeans, e.g., Lidz. Ginza R., 5, 1; Lidz. Liturg., 28, 11; 123, 8 f. (Cain as the first firstborn → 875, 13 ff.).

[55] Michaelis, 146-152.

[56] Cf. Käsemann I, 58-61, 131, n. 2; 136 f.; Mi. Hb. on 1:6; F. J. Schierse, *Verheissung u. Heilsvollendung. Zur theol. Grundfrage d. Hb.* (1955), 96; G. Schille, "Die Basis d. Hb.," ZNW, 48 (1957), 275. But G. Widengren, "Mesopotamian Elements in Manicheism," *Uppsala Univ. Årsskrift,* 1946, 3 (1946), 24, n. 1 lays stronger emphasis on the connection between the Hb. saying and the OT-Jewish legacy.

[57] Cr.-Kö., *s.v.*; Mi. Hb. on 1:6 (n. 2). Nor is there in 1:6 any comparison with the υἱοί of 2:10, though intrinsically there is acc. to Hb. a connection between the sonship of Jesus and that of believers.

[58] Even though it is correctly observed that Ps. 2:7; 2 S. 7:14 and πρωτότοκος from Ps. 89:27 "stand in a direct exegetical connection (Mi. Hb. on 1:6, cf. also Durand, 60), it is questionable whether this alone adequately explains the derivation of πρωτότοκος in Hb. 1:6. It should be noted that though the author heaps up quotations and adduces ψ 2:7

7. Hb. 12:23 speaks of an ἐκκλησία πρωτοτόκων ἀναγεγραμμένων ἐν οὐρανοῖς. The πρωτότοκοι who take part in this heavenly convocation (→ III, 513, 12 ff.) but who are obviously not yet in heaven, whose names are rather written in the heavenly book of life (→ I, 619, 26 ff.), are certainly not the angels, who in any case are mentioned already in 12:22. [59] Nor does the reference seem to be to the OT community nor to the witnesses of faith of c. 11. The author clearly has in view the saved community of the NT. [60] How this isolated use of πρωτότοκος fits in with the use elsewhere in the NT it is hard to say. That the relation of believers to Christ as πρωτότοκος is a basis [61] is not suggested by R. 8:29 (→ 877, 3 ff.) since the πρωτότοκος there strictly rules out any transfer to the ἀδελφοί. [62] It is also unlikely that the expression refers to the relation between the community and the rest of creation (cf. Jm. 1:18 : εἰς τὸ εἶναι ἡμᾶς ἀπαρχήν τινα τῶν αὐτοῦ κτισμάτων), [63] since the context does not seem to point in this direction.

On πρωτότοκα in Hb. 11:28 → 872, 25, on πρωτοτοκεῖα in 12:16 → 875, 3 f. [64]

† πρωτεύω.

1. πρωτεύω, from Isoc., Xenoph., Plat. "to be the first" (in rank); the person below one may be added in the gen., e.g., Xenoph. Ag., 1, 3, or with prep., e.g., Xenoph. Cyrop., VIII, 2, 28, the sphere in which one is first in the dat. (Xenoph. Ag., 10, 1) or with ἐν, e.g., πρωτεύειν ἐν ἕδρᾳ, Xenoph. Cyrop., VIII, 4, 5; σπεύδοντες τοὺς παῖδας ἐν πᾶσι τάχιον πρωτεῦσαι, Plut. Lib. Educ., 13 (II, 9b). [1] Cf. also inscr. in Ditt. Or., II, 529, 24 (1st cent. A.D.); II, 563, 6 (2nd cent. A.D.) and pap., Preis. Zaub., I, 4, 244 : τοῦτό ἐστιν τὸ πρωτεῦον ὄνομα τοῦ Τυφῶνος (4th cent. A.D.). [2]

2. In the LXX πρωτεύω occurs at Est. 5:11: πρωτεύειν καὶ ἡγεῖσθαι τῆς βασιλείας cf. 4:8 : Αμαν ὁ δευτερεύων τῷ βασιλεῖ, 2 Macc. 6:18 : Ελεάζαρός τις τῶν πρωτευόντων γραμματέων, 13:15 : τὸν πρωτεύοντα τῶν ἐλεφάντων. אֶת־הָאֶבֶן הָרֹאשָׁה in Zech. 4:7 is also transl. τὸν λίθον τὸν πρωτεύοντα by ᾽Α (LXX τὸν λίθον τῆς κληρονομίας, Σ τὸν λίθον τὸν ἄκρον, Θ τὸν λίθον τὸν πρῶτον). Joseph. often has

---

and 2 S. 7:14 in 1:5a b, he does not quote ψ 88:28. Is this omission really explained by the observation ? Also correct is the observation that πρωτότοκος in Hb. 1:6 is a more general designation, since there is no "addition or interpretation" as in R. 8:29; Col. 1:15, 18; Rev. 1:5. Yet it is still open to question whether the additions in R. 8:29 etc. may thus be regarded as the "intentional limitation of an originally broader Messianic formula" which is found in ψ 88:28 and echoed in Hb. 1:6, Mi. Hb. on 1:6. What we have in R. 8:29 etc. are rather contextual applications of the concept to specific christological data.

[59] As against Käsemann I, 28, 126. There is not even a reminiscence of πρωτόκτιστος as a term for angels (→ n. 53), cf. also Mi. Hb. on 1:6.

[60] J. Schneider, Hb. (1954), 122. Cf. → I, 620, 5 ff. One cannot refer the term only to dead Christians if those denoted are not yet in heaven, → lines 3 ff.

[61] Mi. Hb. on 12:23 : "The 'Firstborn' and the 'firstborn' are closely related like the 'Son' and the 'sons' (R. 8:29).''

[62] This cannot be just an apocalyptic title for the community (Mi. Hb. on 12:23) since, as the plur. shows, the term is not used for the community as such (cf. Ex. 4:22 and its later history → 873, 7 ff.; 875, 30, 35) but for individual believers.

[63] Cr.-Kö., 1076.

[64] Post-apost. fathers : on Pol., 7, 1 → n. 31; also Barn., 13, 5 (= Gn. 48:18); 1 Cl. 4:1 (= Gn. 4:4).

π ρ ω τ ε ύ ω. [1] Cf. Pass., Liddell-Scott, s.v.

[2] In pap., though only later, an official and military title, cf. Preisigke Wört., II, 431; III, 152, 218; Moult.-Mill., 556 f.

οἱ πρωτεύοντες for "chief men," "leaders" (= οἱ πρῶτοι → 866, 1 f.), usually with gen. τοῦ πλήθους, Ant., 9, 167; τῆς γερουσίας, Bell., 7, 412; τῶν Γαλιλαίων, Vit., 305; cf. Ant., 12, 181; 20, 182; Vit., 313. Seldom sing. part.: πρωτεύων τῆς πόλεως, Vit., 124; cf. also Ephesus as πόλις πρωτεύουσα τῆς ᾿Ασίας, Ant., 14, 224. Cf. too Ant., 19, 209; 20, 100. 147. 173; Bell., 1, 123. Ep. Ar. uses πρωτεύω in 275 with ref. to precedence at table, which is acc. to age in 187. εὐσέβεια is described as καλλονὴ πρωτεύουσα in 229.

3. In Col. 1:18 there is added to ὅς ἐστιν ἀρχή, πρωτότοκος ἐκ τῶν νεκρῶν : the final clause which mentions the divine aim : ἵνα γένηται ἐν πᾶσιν αὐτὸς πρωτεύων. As elsewhere the reference is to rank, especially as πρωτότοκος ἐκ τῶν νεκρῶν is also to be construed thus, → 877, 15 ff. The clause sums up, intensifies and rounds off what was said in 1:15 : Christ is πρωτότοκος πάσης κτίσεως (→ 878, 19 ff.), He is πρὸ πάντων (→ 879, 3 f.), He is κεφαλὴ τοῦ σώματος, τῆς ἐκκλησίας. In all these things He is πρωτεύων, but He would not be so ἐν πᾶσιν, in an unrestricted sense, if He were not also ἀρχή (→ 878, 4) and πρωτότοκος ἐκ τῶν νεκρῶν. [3]

Michaelis

---

[3] On γίνεσθαι with part. cf. Bl.-Debr. § 354 (the ἵνα clause is not eschatologically orientated). αὐτός as well as ἐν πᾶσιν is stressed (cf. Bl.-Debr. § 277, 3) and with these emphases the statement meets the theses of the false teachers in Colossae. πρωτεύων cannot be a title here, since the verbal function of the saying is evident, as against E. Käsemann, *Das wandernde Gottesvolk*[2], FRL, NF, 37 (1957), 72; hence "First" as a Jewish Mess. title has not influenced it. On φιλοπρωτεύω in 3 Jn. 9 cf. Pr.-Bauer[5], *s.v.*

† πταίω

1. The etym. of this word, found from Pind., also inscr., pap. and LXX, is uncertain. It is possibly related [1] to πετ-, πτη, "to fall" (→ 161, 8 ff.). [2] The basic meanings are certainly much the same, though the nuance in πταίω is that of "to stumble against." As compared with the rare trans. use "to collide with," "cause something to fall, move" the intr. use is the customary one, as in the following expressions: [3] πταίειν πρὸς τὰς πέτρας, Xenoph. An., IV, 2, 3; μὴ δὶς πρὸς τὸν αὐτὸν λίθον πταίειν (proverb), Polyb., 31, 11, 5; 12, 1, and cf. the transf. sense "to run against," "to stumble," "to fall," e.g., πταίσας δὲ τῷδε πρὸς κακῷ, Aesch. Prom., 926. Often also "to suffer a reverse, misfortune," e.g., μὴ περὶ Μαρδονίῳ πταίσῃ ἡ Ἑλλάς, (it was feared) Greece would be ruined by Mardonius, Hdt., IX, 101. Fig. "to err," "to sin," e.g., μὴ πταίων τῇ διανοίᾳ, Plat. Theaet., 160d; abs. ἴδιον ἀνθρώπου φιλεῖν καὶ τοὺς πταίοντας, M. Ant., VII, 22; cf. P. Oxy., VIII, 1165, 11; Ep. Ar., 230.

2. In the LXX the word occurs only once at Sir. 37:12 in the fig. sense "to slip," "to stumble," "to sin." Cf. Dt. 7:25, where πταίω corresponds to the ni of יקש "to be entangled," "led astray." Elsewhere πταίω means "to be beaten" (of an army) and corresponds to the Heb. נגף ni in 1 Βασ. 4:2, 10; 7:10; 2 Βασ. 2:17; 10:15, 19; 18:7; 3 Βασ. 8:33; 4 Βασ. 14:12; 1 Ch. 19:19 (also 2 Macc. 14:17 with no Heb.). Cf. also Sir. 2:8 : οὐ μὴ πταίσῃ ὁ μισθὸς ὑμῶν, "your reward will not be lost." 1 Βασ. 4:3 uses πταίω = q of נגף in the rare trans. sense "to push," "to strike."

3. The usage of Philo is in the main the same as that of the NT. Sometimes, as in Spec. Leg., IV, 70; Leg. All., III, 16; III, 66 (ἡ δέ γε ὁμολογεῖ πταῖσαι, "she [Eve] admits having sinned"); III, 149 (πταίοντας περὶ τὴν τῆς γαστρὸς ἐπιθυμίαν, "those who pander to the desire of the stomach"), means "to stumble" = "to sin," while in other passages, like Jos., 144 (πταίεις πολλάκις, χρηστὰ ἔλπιζε, "thou hast suffered much misfortune but art still of good hope"); Spec. Leg., IV, 18 (λαβόντες οἶκτον τῶν ἐπταικότων, "those who sympathise with the unfortunate, i.e., slaves"), it means "to suffer a reverse, misfortune."

4. In the NT, where there are 5 instances, the main meaning is fig. "to slip," "to err," "to sin" : ὅστις ... ὅλον τὸν νόμον (→ IV, 1081, 16 ff.) τηρήσῃ, πταίσῃ δὲ ἐν ἑνί, γέγονεν πάντων ἔνοχος, Jm. 2:10; [4] also πολλὰ ... πταίομεν (abs.) ἅπαντες· εἴ τις ἐν λόγῳ οὐ πταίει, Jm. 3:2; also ταῦτα ... ποιοῦντες (i.e., if you endeavour to make your calling and election sure) οὐ μὴ πταίσητε (Vg

---

π τ α ί ω. This art. was prepared for press by S. Schulz, who made some additions and alterations.

[1] Perhaps we are to assume a root form πτει-, πτι- with Hofmann, 287, though Walde-Pok., II, 21 has reservations.

[2] Cf. Schwyzer, I, 325 and 676; Prellwitz Etym. Wört. thinks πταίω is related to τὸ πτῶμα as ψαίω to ὁ ψωμός.

[3] Cf. Pape and Pr.-Bauer[5], s.v.

[4] Acc. to Dib. Jk., ad loc. this saying is demonstrably of Jewish derivation, cf. also Wnd. Jk.[3], ad loc. and esp. Str.-B., III, 755; IV, 1 and 22. The Stoics, starting with the solidarity of virtues (and vices), also teach that he who transgresses one virtue transgresses all, v. Dib. Jk., ad loc.

peccabitis), 2 Pt. 1:10. This passage is perhaps unique in that the sense "to suffer a reverse, misfortune," found in Greek writings, also calls for consideration. [5]

The true sense of the original term is still to be seen quite clearly in R. 11:11: μὴ ἔπταισαν (sc. the hardened Jews) ἵνα πέσωσιν; Vg : *numquid sic offenderunt ut caderent*? Luther : "Sind sie darum abgelaufen damit sie zu Fall kommen?" A.V. : "Have they stumbled that they should fall?" Most expositors take it here in the sense "to stumble." [6] πταίω in R. 11:11 is thus equated with προσκόπτω (→ 754, 22 ff.) in R. 9:32 : προσέκοψαν τῷ λίθῳ τοῦ προσκόμματος. For a proper understanding of R. 11:11 it is perhaps not so essential to distinguish narrowly between πταίω and πίπτω (→ 164, 21 ff.). Perhaps all that is being said is that stumbling or falling is not to be regarded as an end in itself. But perhaps there is a certain crescendo from stumbling to falling, for the one who stumbles may get up again, pull himself together and stand on his feet, or he may fall and lie on the ground. Falling as a possible result of stumbling is perhaps a figure for the eternal ruin which threatens to overtake the Jews through their stumbling. [7, 8]

5. In the post-apost. fathers the term occurs only in 1 Cl., 51, 1: [9] ὅσα ... ἐπταίσαμεν διά τινας παρεμπτώσεις τοῦ ἀντικειμένου, ἀξιώσωμεν ἀφεθῆναι ἡμῖν, "We would beseech forgiveness for that which we have done amiss through the cunning snares of the adversary."

K. L. Schmidt

πτερύγιον → III, 236, 3 ff.
πτῶμα   → 166, 14 ff.
πτῶσις → 168, 3 ff.

---

[5] Wnd. Kath. Br.[3], *ad loc.* refers to the material par. in Test. R. 4:5 : φυλάξατε πάντα ὅσα ἐντέλλομαι ὑμῖν καὶ οὐ μὴ ἁμάρτητε.

[6] Cf. the transl. and comm., also Liddell-Scott and Moult.-Mill., *s.v.*

[7] The fullest and most valuable exposition is in B. Weiss, *Der Brief an d. Römer, Krit.-exeget. Komm. über d. NT*[6] (1881), 527 f. Other interpretations are rightly set aside. On the philological problem cf. W. Sanday-A. C. Headlam, *The Ep. to the Romans,* ICC[5] (1902), *ad loc.*

[8] More recent translators and exegetes have allowed for this by putting a "finally" or "definitively" in the ἵνα clause ; cf. C. H. Dodd, *The Ep. of Paul to the Romans,* MNTC (1932), 176 : "Israel has indeed stumbled, but not to their (final) ruin"; acc. to Mi. R., *ad loc.* there is something to be said for both views (final or consecutive sense).

[9] Probably a conjecture, cf. O. v. Gebhardt-A. v. Harnack-T. Zahn, Patrum Apostolicorum Opera[6] (1920), 28.

---

† πτωχός, † πτωχεία, † πτωχεύω

Contents : A. πτωχός in the Greek World : I. Meaning. II. View of Poverty. B. The Poor in the Old Testament : I. Hebrew Equivalents ; II. Attitude to the Poor : 1. Early Period ; 2. Older Prophecy ; 3. Deuteronomy ; 4. Psalms ; 5. Prophecy of the Exilic Period ; 6. Wisdom Literature. C. Later Judaism : I. Usage in the Rabbis, Josephus and Philo ; II. View of the Poor in the Apocrypha and Pseudepigrapha ; III. Qumran : 1. The Poor in the Individual Writings ; 2. Attitude to Possessions ; IV. Position of the Poor in Palestinian Judaism : 1. The Social Structure ; 2. The Interpretation of the Poor Law ; 3. Voluntary Philanthropy ; 4. Social Care of the Poor. V. Judgment of the Rabbis. D. The New Testament : I. The Gospels : 1. Mark ; 2. Matthew ; 3. Luke ; 4. John ; II. Community Theology, Jesus, John the Baptist ; III. Paul ; IV. James ; V. Revelation ; VI. The Primitive Community. E. The Post-Apostolic Age : I. Later Jewish Christianity ; II. The Post-Apostolic Fathers.

π τ ω χ ό ς κ τ λ. Bibl. → πένης and πλοῦτος. Gen. J. Leipoldt, *Der soziale Gedanke in d. urchr. Kirche* (1952); E. Percy, "Die Botschaft Jesus," *Lunds Univ. Årsskrift*, 49, 5 (1953), 40-108; A. Gelin, *Les pauvres de Yahvé* (1953). On A.: J. Hemelrijk, Πενία en Πλοῦτος, Diss. Utrecht (1925); J. J. van Manen, Πενία en Πλοῦτος *in de periode na Alexander*, Diss. Utrecht (1931); H. Bolkestein, "De Armen in de moraal, de politiek en de religio van de voor-christelijke oudheid," *Verhandelingen der koninklijke Akad. van Wetenschappen te Amsterdam, Afdeeling Letterkunde*, NR, 12, 2 (1939); also *Wohltätigkeit u. Armenpflege im vorchr. Altertum* (1939) (cf. the review by W. Bauer in GGA, 202 [1940], 358-368). On B.: H. Graetz, *Krit. Komm. z. d. Ps.* (1882), 20-37; A. Rahlfs, *'Anî u. 'Anāw in d. Ps.* (1892); I. Loeb, *La littérature des pauvres dans la Bible* (1892); W. W. Graf Baudissin, "Die at.liche Religion u. d. Armen," *Pr. Jahrb.*, 149 (1912), 193-231; A. Bertholet, *Kulturgeschichte Israels* (1919), 170-174; F. Wilke, "Der Sozialismus im hbr. Altertum," *Religion u. Sozialismus, Festschr. d. ev.-theol. Fakultät in Wien* (1921), 9-40; H. Schmökel. *D. angewandte Recht im AT*, Diss. Breslau (1930); H. Birkeland, *'Anî u. 'Anāw in d. Ps.* (1933) (= Birkeland I); *D. Feinde d. Individuums in d. isr. Psalmenlit.* (1933), 317-320 (= Birkeland II); N. Peters, *D. soziale Fürsorge im AT* (1936); P. A. Munch, "Einige Bemerkungen zu 'anijjîm u. den resā'im in d. Ps.," *Le monde oriental*, 30 (1936), 13-26; A. Causse, *Du groupe ethnique à la communauté religieuse* (1937), 243-258; J. Hempel, *D. Ethos d. AT*, Beih. ZAW, 67 (1938), Index, *s.v.*; A. Kuschke, "Arm u. reich im AT mit bes. Berücksichtigung d. nachexilischen Zeit," ZAW, NF, 16 (1939), 31-57; J. v. d. Ploeg, "Les pauvres d'Israël et leur piété," *Oudtest. Studiën*, 7 (1950), 236-270; P. Humbert, "Le mot biblique 'ebyôn'," RevHPhR, 32 (1952), 1-6; C. van d. Leeuwen, *Le développement du sens social en Israël avant l'ère chrétienne*," *St. Semitica Neerlandica*, 1 (1955); H. J. Kraus, *Psalmen, Bibl. Komm. AT*, 15, 2 (1958), 82 f. On C.: J. Hamburger, *Real-Enc. d. Judt.*, I (1874), *s.v.* "Almosen"; "Arme"; "Wohltätigkeit"; "Zehent"; M. Lazarus, *Die Ethik d. Judt.* (1898); K. Kohler, "Zum Kapitel d. jüd. Wohltätigkeitspflege," *Festschr. A. Berliner* (1903), 195-203; M. Weinberg, *Die Organisation d. jüd. Ortsgemeinden*, E. 3 : "Die Almosenpflege," MGWJ, 41 (1896/97), 678-681; S. Krauss, *Talmudische Archäologie*, III (1912), 63-74; I. Abrahams, *Studies in Pharisaism and the Gospels*, I (1917), 113-117; J. Jeremias, *Jerusalem z. Zeit Jesu*² 1958, II A: "Reich u. Arm"; M. Katz, "Protection of the Weak in the Talmud," *Columbia Univ. Oriental Studies*, 24 (1925), 78-82; A. Marmorstein, Art. "Armut im Talmud," EJ, III (1929), 370-374; C. Tchernowitz, "רמא'"," *Jewish Studies in Memory of G. A. Kohut* (1935), 46-58; A. Cronbach, "The Social Ideas of the Apocrypha and Pseudepigrapha," *Hebrew Union Coll.*, 18 (1944), 119-156; S. W. Baron, *A Social and Religious History of the Jews*, II (1952), 69-74; E. E. Urbach, מגמות דתיות וחברתיות בתורת הצדקה של חז"ל ציון, 16 (1951), 1-27. On D : J. Weiss, *Die Predigt Jesu vom Reiche Gottes*² (1900), 128-132, 179-

A. πτωχός in the Greek World.

I. Meaning.

1. πτωχός, etym. related to πτώσσειν (Hom. Od., 18, 363; Hes. Op., 395), [1] "to bow down timidly," means as an adj. "destitute," "mendicant," πτωχὸς ἀνὴρ ἀλαλήμενος ἐλθών, Hom. Od., 21, 327; πτωχοὺς ἀλᾶσθαι παῖδας, Eur. Med., 515; πτωχὸς δίαιτα, "begged bread," Soph. Oed. Col., 751; P. Petr., III, 36a, 17 (3rd cent. B.C.); comp. Timocles Fr., 6, 10 (CAF, II, 453); proverbially : πτωχότερος κίγκλου (water-wagtail, of which it was assumed that it had no nest of its own), Menand. Fr., 190; Plut. Apophth. Aristides, 4 (II, 186b); Epict. Diss., III, 9, 16; πτωχίστερος, Aristoph. Ach., 425; superl. Anth. Pal., 10, 50, 4. Much more common, esp. in prose, as a noun, Hom. Od., 18, 1; καὶ κεραμεὺς κεραμεῖ κοτέει καὶ τέκτονι τέκτων, καὶ πτωχός πτωχῷ φθονέει καὶ ἀοιδὸς ἀοιδῷ, Hes. Op., 25 f.; proverbially of the insatiable πτωχῶν οὐλὰς ἀεὶ κενεή, Callim. Fr., 724.

2. πτωχεύω intr. "to be destitute," "to lead the life of a beggar," Hom. Od., 15, 309; 19, 73; Tyrtaeus Fr., 6, 4; [2] Ps.-Plat. Eryx., 394b; Luc. Nec., 17; ἀλᾶσθαι καὶ πτω-χεύειν ἐν Λιβύῃ, Plut. Titus, 21, 12 (I, 381d); fig. Polyb., 7, 7, 6 (πραγμάτων). Trans. "to beg" δαῖτα, Hom. Od., 17, 11 and 19; with acc. of person, "to beg from someone," Theogn., I, 922 (Diehl[3], II, 56).

3. πτωχεία, "begging" ἐς πτωχηΐην ἀπίκται, Hdt., III, 14, 10; "destitution," "the life of a beggar," εἰς πτωχείαν τὴν ἐσχάτην ἐλθεῖν, Plat. Leg., XI, 936b; τυραννίδας ... εἰς πενίας τε καὶ φυγὰς καὶ εἰς πτωχείας τελευτώσας, Resp., X, 618a.

Whereas πένης denotes one who has to earn his living because he has no property (→ 37, 4 ff.) πτωχός denotes the complete destitution which forces the poor to seek the help of others by begging. [3] Marc. Aurel. has the definition : ὁ ἐνδεὴς ἑτέρου καὶ μὴ πάντα ἔχων παρ' ἑαυτοῦ τὰ εἰς τὸν βίον χρήσιμα, M. Ant., IV, 29, 2. It is the fate of a πτωχός to have nothing οὐδὲν ἔχων, Isocr. Or., 14, 46; Hdt., III, 14, 7, but that of a πένης to live frugally. [4] In Aristoph. Pl., 548 πενία firmly refuses to be identified with πτωχεία, which is her sister but which represents a much greater degree

---

187; also Das Urchr. (1917), 47-56, 269-272; J. Leipoldt, "Jesus u.d. Armen," NkZ, 28 (1917), 784-810; R. A. Hoffmann, "Besitz u. Recht in d. Gedankenwelt d. Urchr.," Religion u. Sozialismus, Festschr. d. ev.-theol. Fakultät in Wien (1921), 41-63; A. Steinmann, Jesus u.d. soziale Frage (1925); H. v. Campenhausen, Die Askese im Urchr. (1949), 5-20; H. Preisker, Das Ethos d. Urchr.² (1949), 102-105; B. Reicke, "Diakonie, Festfreude u. Zelos," Uppsala Univ. Årsskrift, 1951, 5 (1951), 21-50, 167-185; M. Dibelius, "Das soziale Motiv im NT," Botschaft u. Gesch., I (1953), 178-203; A. George, "Le Dieu des pauvres," Évangile, 9 (1953); R. Schnackenburg, Die sittliche Botschaft d. NT (1954), 79-86; J. Dupont, Les Béatitudes (1954), 184-244; Dib. Jk.⁸, 37-44; R. Koch, "Die Wertung d. Reichtums im Lk.," Biblica, 38 (1957), 151-169. On E: A. Bigelmair, "Zur Frage des Sozialismus u. Kommunismus im Christentum der ersten drei Jhdt.," Beiträge z. Gesch. des chr. Altertums u. d. byzantinischen Lit. (1922), 73-93.

[1] πτη- Homeric, "cowering," πτήσσειν, "to be afraid," πτώξ, "timid," πτοεῖν "to shrink," Walde-Pok., II, 19; Boisacq, 822 f.

[2] Diehl³, I, 11.

[3] Fr. adespota, 284, 2 (TGF, 893), the πένης can keep himself, but not so the πτωχός, a πλανήτης. Ps.-Ammon Adfin. Vocab. Diff., s.v. πένης (p. 108): πένης καὶ πτωχὸς διαφέρει· πένης μὲν γάρ, ὁ ἀπὸ τοῦ ἐργάζεσθαι καὶ πονεῖν ποριζόμενος τὸν βίον· πτωχὸς δέ, ὁ ἐπαίτης, ὁ τοῦ ἔχειν ἐκπεπτωκώς. Suidas, s.v.: πτωχός· ὁ ἐκπεπτωκώς τοῦ ἔχειν, ἐπαίτης. Cf. Poll. Onom., III, 109 f.: πλούσιος ... τὰ δ᾽ ἐναντία πένης ... πτωχός, VI, 197: ἔνιοι δὲ πένητα τὸν πτωχὸν καὶ πτωχείαν τὴν πενίαν (ὀνομά-ζουσιν). Cf. also G. Meyer, Laudes inopiae, Diss. Göttingen (1915), 11 f.

[4] Aristoph. Pl., 552 ff.: πτωχοῦ μὲν γὰρ βίος, ὃν σὺ λέγεις, ζῆν ἐστι μηδὲν ἔχοντα, τοῦ δὲ πένητος ζῆν φειδόμενον καὶ τοῖς ἔργοις προσέχοντα, περιγίγνεσθαι δ᾽ αὐτῷ μηδέν, μὴ μέντοι μηδ᾽ ἐπιλείπειν, cf. Bolkestein Wohltätigkeit, 184.

of poverty. [5] As a social group or class the πένητες are the antithesis of the πλούσιοι or εὔποροι, but the πτωχοί are at the opposite pole altogether, cf. the common phrase πλούσιος ἐκ πτωχοῦ γεγονώς, Demosth. Or., 18, 131; 3, 29; 8, 66; 10, 68 and *vice versa*. Luc. Nec., 17 calls it an extreme reversal of fortune when kings and satraps are beggars in the hereafter.

II. View of Poverty.

From an aristocratic standpt. Hom. in Od., 18, 1 ff. describes the permanent beggar who will not work (14, 226 f.; 18, 363; cf. Hes. Op., 381 f., 496) and who preys on the well-to-do, not letting any others into his settled sphere, Od., 18, 49. But there is also the uprooted beggar who for various reasons has lost all native rights and in great unhappiness wanders about begging, Od., 21, 327; 17, 10 and 18 f.; 19, 74; Eur. Med., 515, even though he was once an ὄλβιος in a fine house, Od., 19, 76. The guilt and destiny of the two types are assessed very differently (Theogn., 1, 155 [Diehl³, II, 12]) and there can even be sympathy for the latter (Od., 6, 208), though in general the beggar is despised, Od., 17, 18; ἀνιηρός, 17, 377.

Naturally the beggar is given a small gift (Od., 17, 420) but to give alms is never regarded as a virtue even from a religious standpoint. [6] Sometimes Homer can say that strangers and beggars come from God (Od., 6, 207 f.; 14, 57 f.; cf. 17, 475) and also that the gods appear in humble form, but the idea that the very poor are under special divine protection is quite alien to the Greek world. Zeus is called ξένιος and ἱκετήσιος but never πτώχιος. [7]

There was no system of state poor relief in the Greek world. [8] Beneficence (εὐεργετεῖν, εὖ ποιεῖν) is not giving alms but rendering services which benefit society, → II, 654, 18 ff. [9] If orphans are looked after, the aim is to protect their inheritance rather than relieve their poverty. Distributions of grain and the like are for citizens, not specifically for the poor. [10] ἐλευθεριότης and φιλανθρωπία are highly rated as social virtues, but the poor of the city are not their object. It is expected that citizens will aid the indigent, but especially those rendered poor by misfortune, Stob., IV, 152, 9 ff. There is in the Greek world no moral or religious glorifying of poverty; on the contrary, in social conflicts the poor could not even invoke the help of the gods. [11]

On the position of Plato, Aristot., the Cynics and the Stoics → πένης, 38, 16 ff. and → πλούσιος, 320, 26 ff.

† *Hauck*

---

[5] Bolkestein Wohltätigkeit, 549; it should be noted, however, that this distinction is not always made. Thus Hemelrijk, 34 f. adduces many passages from the comedians in which πτωχός = πένης, cf. also van Manen, 19.

[6] ἐλεημοσύνη is a late construct of the Hell. Orient; → II, 486, 7 ff. and n. 4; 478, n. 8; Bolkestein, *op. cit.*, 146.

[7] Bolkestein, *op. cit.*, 177 and 179 on Hom. Od., 6, 207.

[8] There was organised relief only in societies, cf. B. Laum, *Stiftungen in d. griech. u. röm. Antike*, I (1914), 96 ff.; Bolkestein, *op. cit.*, 235-241.

[9] Bolkestein, 213; class. Gk. has no word for alms.

[10] For examples *v.* Bolkestein, 164, 312-320.

[11] Bolkestein, 181.

B. The Poor in the Old Testament.

I. Hebrew Equivalents.

1. The main Heb. equivalent of πτωχός, which occurs some 100 times in the LXX, is עָנִי.[12] πτωχεία is used 10 times for עָנִי.[13] עָנִי from the stem עָנָה denotes the situation of answering and readiness for this ; in the more developed form it then describes the position of inferiority in the face of the one who demands the answer. עָנִי, then, is concretely the hearer, the dependent.[14] Primarily the word expresses a relation rather than a state of social distress. When עָנִי is used for an economic position, it is in the first instance combined with דַּל (Ps. 82:3) or אֶבְיוֹן (Dt. 24:14; Ex. 16:49; 18:12; 22:29). Only in a more developed usage does עָנִי denote a state of lowliness or distress and hence a man in a state of reduced competence and lesser worth.[15] In this case the ref. is predominantly to poverty. Relatively close to the basic meaning is the common sense in the Pent. "without inheritance of one's own," Ex. 22:24; Lv. 19:10; 23:22; Dt. 15:11; 24:12, 14, 15.[16] The antonym of עָנִי is not עָשִׁיר — which is the antonym of רָשׁ (and אֶבְיוֹן in Ps. 49:2) — but "violent" (עוֹשֵׁק, פָּרִיץ, רָשָׁע), and this is another pointer to the original meaning. The fact that עָנִי denotes one who is "wrongfully impoverished or dispossessed" — the term is not used for deserved poverty — helps us to understand why Yahweh can be presented as the protector of such עֲנָיִים. As the man who is really Yahweh's עָנָו confidently draws near to Him, עָנִי takes on religious significance : "humble" and even "pious" (Ps. 18:27 ταπεινός). The Aram. and later Heb. secondary form עָנָו, which might originally have had the same sense as עָנִי,[17] mostly has a religious nuance in its special biblical use (always plur.)[18] and was unhesitatingly construed thus by the Masoretes.[19] The LXX usually has πραΰς for עָנָו (→ 647, 3 ff.) and thus emphasises the ethical aspect.[20] But ταπεινός, πένης and πτωχός are also found.

2. In 22 instances, 7 in Prv., 8 in Am., Is. and Jer., πτωχός is used for דַּל, while πτωχεύειν occurs 3 times for דָּלַל. Ju. 6:6; Ps. 79:8; Prv. 23:21. דַּל is used a. of physical weakness, Gn. 41:19; 2 S. 13:4 (ἀσθενής); b. of social status, "lowly," "poor," "wretched," "insignificant," Lv. 19:15; 1 S. 2:8 etc. דַּלַּת עַם־הָאָרֶץ in 2 K. 24:14; 25:12; cf. Jer. 40:7; 52:15 f.; 39:10 denotes the lower orders. In part the LXX substitutes the sense "humble" (ταπεινός), so Is. 25:4; 26:6 (11:4); esp. Zeph. 3:12.

3. In 11 instances πτωχός is used for אֶבְיוֹן.[21] From the stem אבה, "to will," "to be willing" (Arab. "to desire"), this word originally denotes "the one who seeks alms," "the beggar." The word then comes to be used more gen. for "the poor man,"[22] and

---

[12] 37 times, 20 in Ps., 12 in the combination עָנִי וְאֶבְיוֹן.

[13] → ταπείνωσις is more common for עֳנִי (19 times).

[14] At least עָנָה I and II are related.

[15] Birkeland I, 6 and 8 only begins with this sense.

[16] Cf. Ges.-Buhl, s.v.

[17] So Birkeland I, 16. Late development is supported by 1 QIsᵃ 61:1, which reads עֲנוּים, though עָנִיים (incorrect transcription in Burrows, ad loc.) at 11:4; 14:32; 29:19. The distribution of forms fits in with the thesis of P. Kahle, Die hbr. Handschriften aus d. Höhle (1951), 72 f. that 1 QIsᵃ had two Heb. originals. Is. LXX seems to have had the same original.

[18] Nu. 12:3 is a slip, cf. Birkeland I, 19 f.

[19] Rahlfs, 54 f.

[20] T. Häring, "Die עֲנִיים u. עֲנָוִים im AT," Theol. Studien aus Württemberg, 5 (1884), 157-161; Rahlfs, 57.

[21] LXX mostly has πένης for this (always in Am. and Jer.) → 38, 36 ff.

[22] So also Birkeland II, 317 f. On the Mas. understanding cf. Rahlfs, 54.

hence [23] it is never associated with רָשׁ. Where the sense is not fig. the word is often used for the very poor, "those with no roof over their heads" etc., 1 S. 2:8 etc. Like עָנִי it often has a religious nuance. This is esp. true of the notable double form עָנִי וְאֶבְיוֹן which, apparently pre-Israelite, is the regular expression in the Ps. for the attitude of him who prays to God, [24] Ps. 35:10; 37:14; 40:17; 70:5; 74:21; 86:1; 109:16, 22. Except at Ps. 109:16 the LXX has πτωχός καὶ πένης. Sometimes the two words are parallel, Am. 8:4 etc.

4. רָשׁ, part. of רוּשׁ, "to be poor, needy, famished," in an exclusively social and economic sense, is a favourite word in the Wisdom lit., to which the fable in 2 S. 12:3 belongs. In Prv. πτωχός is easily the most common transl. (11 times), usually in express antithesis to "rich." → πένης also occurs (7 times) and → ταπεινός once at 1 S. 18:23. πτωχεύειν is used for רָשׁ in Ps. 34:10 and πτωχίζω for the part. hi at 1 S. 2:7.

5. מִסְכֵּן [25] means the "dependent" [26] and then the "socially inferior." Even to-day the oriental beggar styles himself thus. It came into the later OT books when עָנִי had long since lost its older sense. LXX has → πένης at Qoh. 4:13; 9:15 f. and πτωχός at Sir. 30:14 (προσδεόμενος at Sir. 4:3); cf. also πτωχεία for מִסְכֵּנָת at Dt. 8:9 (redactor).

6. At ψ 9:35 πτωχός is used for the uncertain חֵלְכָה (πένης at ψ 9:29).

The main Heb. words are עָנִי, דַּל and אֶבְיוֹן. Often they are synon. like the Gk. → πένης and πτωχός. [27] In many passages, however, where two words are par. or linked by ו, there are distinctions in the transl., Am. 8:6; Is. 26:6; 41:17 etc., even antithesis Is. 11:4 (?); 14:30; 32:7 etc. In gen. constructions [28] or double forms this tendency on the part of the transl. is esp. noticeable.

II. Attitude to the Poor.

1. The nomadic and semi-nomadic mode of life of the Isr. tribes prior to the conquest knew no sharp or rigid distinction between rich and poor. [29] Members of the tribe had more or less equal rights and status as defenders of the community. The settled life which commenced with the conquest brought to every Israelite a hereditary portion in the divinely given land, → III, 770, 27 ff. But it also led to contact with the Canaanites, who in part already lived in towns and had established social differences. The presence of the conquered, who can only partially be regarded as גֵּרִים but who merge into the less successful among the conquerors, gives rise to the problem of the poor. [30] In opposition to this new development the Book of the Covenant [31] declares it to be Yahweh's will

---

[23] Though cf. Humbert, 2.

[24] Originally the idea is that the one who prays belongs to God (עָנִי) and thus comes to him as a suppliant (אֶבְיוֹן). As Ps. 107:41 shows, this sense was completely lost and the two expressions were used as par., cf. also 86:1 f. etc. Birkeland II, 319 thinks there is the distinction that עָנִי emphasises need while אֶבְיוֹן denotes helplessness before God.

[25] Cf. also Akkadian muškenu, which denotes the act of subjection and then possession of a lease in return for certain obligations. Cf. E. A. Speiser, "The muškênum," Orientalia, NF, 27 (1958), 19-28. But cf. F. R. Kraus, Ein Edikt d. Königs Ammi-Ṣaduqa v. Babylon (1958), 147, 150 f., 154 f.

[26] Hence עָרֵי מִסְכְּנוֹת "cities built by forced labour," Ex. 1:11.

[27] E.g., Prv. 22:22. On the par. use of πένης, πτωχός and ταπεινός in Ps. cf. E. Hatch, Essays in Biblical Greek (1889), 73-79; also E. Sellin, Beiträge z. isr. u. jüd. Religionsgeschichte, II (1897), 284-291, 294-299.

[28] Thus at Is. 10:2; 29:19 the transl. diverges from normal usage.

[29] Bertholet, 170.

[30] Humbert, 3 f. thinks אֶבְיוֹן was adopted into Heb. only at this period.

[31] On the date of the Book of the Covenant cf. O. Eissfeldt, Einl. in d. AT² (1957), 260 f.

as Ruler that there should be no permanent or hopeless poverty in the community. If a man has to be sold into slavery because of need, he must be liberated after 6 yrs, Ex. 21:2. In the fallow yr. that which grows of itself belongs to the poor, Ex. 23:10 f. אֶבְיוֹן or πτωχός. Exploitation of the poor fellow-countryman is forbidden, Ex. 22:24 עָנִי or πενιχρός. Yahweh is against the oppression of the poor in the courts, Ex. 23:6 אֶבְיוֹן or πένης. Already in the fundamental laws, which on the one side, at least for the 7th yr., restore the normal state of Yahweh's own exclusive right to the land, [32] and on the other grant lasting protection to the poor, Yahweh, unlike the Gk. gods (→ 887, 17 f.), is the protector of the poor [33] — a thought which was to endure throughout the history of Isr.

2. The economic development of the monarchy created new classes and thus accentuated social distinctions, and this, combined with the fact that landowners, who alone had civil rights, also functioned as judges, worsened the position of the poor. Hence the older prophets (→ 39, 12 ff.; 324, 6 ff.) took up the cause of the poor in the name of Yahweh and protected them as צַדִּיקִים. [34] They accused the socially strong of oppression, Am. 2:7; 4:1; 5:11, דַּל or πτωχός. They castigated their merciless desire to increase their riches, Am. 8:4; Is. 3:15. By large-scale acquisitions of property they were driving the poor — the "inheritance" of Ps. 94:5 — out of their portions in the land of Yahweh, Is. 5:8 f.; Mi. 2:2. The wrongdoing of the wealthy will inevitably bring down God's judgment on the whole people (Am. 2:6 ff.), on the people which He Himself formerly delivered as a poor people out of Egypt (Am. 2:10; cf. Ex. 22:20; 23:9 גֵּר). The perversion is so gt. that in striking counterpoint to Am. 2:6 one can even find phrases which seem to equate the poor and the people of God, Is. 10:2 עֲנִיֵּי עַמִּי; cf. Is. 3:15; 14:32; Damasc. 6:16 (8:13). The basic thought is not that the poor are specially elected — no prophet identifies himself completely with them. [35] It is that of legal principle, commitment to ancient law [36] (cf. Is. 22:15 ff.), which is violated by the oppressions. [37] Only in Zeph. 3:12 is there as yet a true religious estimation of the poor; here God will leave only a עַם עָנִי וָדָל (λαὸς πραΰς καὶ ταπεινός), and this will trust in Him. [38]

3. Dt. represents both a par. to prophetic criticism [39] and also a particularly influential depiction of the social order in the wilderness age, [40] though πτωχός does not occur at all in the book. [41] The land which Yahweh gave His people as an inheritance

---

[32] A. Alt, "Die Ursprünge d. isr. Rechts," *Kleine Schriften z. Gesch. des Volkes Israel,* I (1953), 327 f.

[33] The thought is soon added that in case of oppression the poor may by prayer and cursing invoke Yahweh's special protection (Ex. 22:26), cf. Hempel, 129, 144.

[34] Cf. v. d. Ploeg, 244 f.

[35] So correctly v. d. Ploeg, 269.

[36] E. Tröltsch, "Das Ethos d. hbr. Propheten," *Logos,* 6 (1916/17), 18.

[37] Cf. Kuschke, 40, though for another view *v.* Wilke, 22. There is no strict equating of צַדִּיק and אֶבְיוֹן (so U. Türck, *Die sittlichen Forderungen d. isr. Propheten im 8. Jhdt.,* Diss. Göttingen [1935], 24, n. 19). Correct though it is not to claim the prophets as social reformers (cf. M. Lurje, "Studien z. Gesch. d. wirtschaftlichen u. sozialen Verhältnisse im isr.-jüd. Reich," Beih. z. ZAW, 45 [1927], 60), it is going too far to say that their position reduces social problems to social ethics, Bertholet, 172.

[38] A pre-exilic date is disputed, however, by L. P. Smith and E. R. Lachemann, "The Authorship of the Book of Zephaniah," *Journal of Near Eastern Studies,* 9 (1950), 141.

[39] Cf. A. Alt, "Die Heimat d. Dt.," *Kleine Schr. z. Gesch. d. Volkes Israel,* II (1953), 268 f.

[40] The Rechabite movement (Ju. 13:7, 14) was a more radical protest against the new economic structure, cf. Wilke, 13-15.

[41] A system of guarantees to protect the weak at the expense of the rich and strong, E. Renan, *Gesch. d. Volkes Israel,* III (1894), 226.

(נַחֲלָה) is a land of plenty and wealth, in which there should be no one in want (15:4 ἐνδεής) and hence no πτωχεία is necessary, 8:9. The promise is to Israel as a whole; hence all have a portion in the land. This is the basis of the poor law. Its aim is to help the victims of human injustice, 15:7-11. Above all its protective measures alleviate and provide for impoverished brethren (אָח tt.), 15:1 ff., 12 ff.; 23:20, 25 f.; 24:6, 14 ff.; cf. the Holiness Code, [42] Lv. 19:9 f.; 23:22; 25:25; Ex. 22:24c; 23:11. [43] Apart from the law of the sabbatical year in Lv. 25:8 ff., [44] these go far beyond the original legislation. [45] Dt., of course, met with little success in practice. [46] The tension between its laws and the actual situation, the increasing addition of גֵּרִים etc., which had not been envisaged by the older prophets, the deterioration of the social situation [47] and finally the collapse of the Jewish state, which was regarded as a punishment for the oppression of the עָנִי וְאֶבְיוֹן (Ez. 22:29 πτωχὸς καὶ πένης), all necessarily helped to perpetuate the problem of poverty.

4. The *topos* "poor" has an established place in the ancient cultic psalm of the Orient. Poverty here is not merely a divine punishment. [48] God is also extolled as the One who extends His protection to the poor in a special way. [49] דַּל, עָנִי and אֶבְיוֹן are used in this objective [50] manner in the royal psalms prior to the exile, Ps. 72:2, 4, 12, 13; 132:15, [51] cf. also Ps. 18:27 (עַם עָנִי). Ps. 82 may be regarded as a testimony to the appropriation of oriental ideas, for here a strong reproach is levelled against the divine world for not caring about the poor (רָשׁ, דַּל). [52]

---

[42] Only עָנִי is used (אֶבְיוֹן does not occur in the priestly code at all). A supplementary word is דַּל, not found in Dt. or the Book of the Covenant, cf. Baudissin, 204, n. 1.

[43] In part revisions of rules which arose for other reasons, v. H. Schmidt, "Das Bodenrecht im Verfassungsentwurf des Esr.," *Hallische Universitätsreden,* 56 (1932), 26.

[44] Perhaps the relic of a communal economy, J. Wellhausen, *Prolegomena z. Gesch. Israels,*⁵ (1899), 115. On the historical problem v. Alt, op. cit. (→ n. 32), 328, n. 1.

[45] Cf. H. Bruppacher, *Die Beurteilung der Armut im AT* (1924), 41 f.; related is the fact that stealing, a typical crime of the poor, is punished relatively leniently in this part of the tradition of Isr., Hempel, 128. Cf. also on this F. Horst, "Der Diebstahl im AT," *Studien z. Gesch. des Nahen u. Fernen Ostens, Festschr. P. Kahle* (1935), 19-28.

[46] Kuschke, 44; M. Weber, "Das antike Judt.," *Ges. Aufsätze z. Religionssoziologie,* III (1921), 73 : Based on exhortation rather than valid law ; Baudissin, 203 is more positive. The alleviations laid down in the priestly code in Lv. 5:7, 11; 12:8; 14:21; 27:8 were naturally carried out. Ez. is the first to sketch a Utopia (an equal and inalienable share for all). Ezr. also sought a new distribution of property each year of jubilee but this was not carried out.

[47] Cf. the harsher view of stealing, Hempel, 244, n. 183.

[48] A. Falkenstein-W. v. Soden, *Sumerische u. akkad. Hymnen u. Gebete* (1953), 263, 270.

[49] E. Ebeling, *Keilschrifttexte aus Assur religiösen Inhalts* (1919), 355, 12; J. Pinckert, *Hymnen u. Gebete an Nebo* (1920), 10, 55; A. Schollmeyer, *Sumerisch-bab. Hymnen* (1917), 84, 20 f.; J. Hehn, *Hymnen u. Gebete an Marduk* (1903), 357, 4; cf. G. Widengren, *The Akkadian and Hebrew Psalms of Lamentation as Religious Documents,* Diss. Uppsala (1936), 45 f., 54.

[50] The use in 1 S. 2:8 is different unless (Birkeland II, 43) a king is here speaking of himself as a אֶבְיוֹן and דַּל. Cf. on this the ZKR inscr. where acc. to E. Sachsse, " 'Anī als Ehrenbezeichnung in inschr. Beleuchtung," *Festschr. E. Sellin* (1927), 108 the king calls himself אִישׁ עָנִי אָנִי = אשׁ ענה אנה.

[51] עָנִי in Ps. 68:10 (cf. v. 6 f.) is stylistically related to the royal psalms. On the date of Ps. 68 cf. S. Mowinckel, *Psalmenstud.,* I, "Awän u. d. individuellen Klagepsalmen," *Skrifter utgit av videnskapsselskapet i Kristiana, historisk-filosofisk klasse* (1921), 144; also "Der 68. Ps.," *Avhandlinger utgitt av det Norske Videnskaps-Akad. i Oslo* (1953), 72 f. (cf. 29 f.).

[52] On the date of Ps. 82 cf. O. Eissfeldt, "El and Yahweh," *Journal of Semitic Studies,* 1 (1956), 29 f.

Another situation is that in which the poor man is confronted by enemies, Ps. 9:12, 18; 10:2, 9, 17 etc. In an otherwise hopeless conflict he turns to God, who he knows has promised to help the poor, and whose assistance is now claimed. [53] In individual songs of petition and thanksgiving there is then an equation of the petitioner and the poor man אֲנִי עָנִי וְאֶבְיוֹן (Ps. 40:17; 86:1; 109:22; cf. 69:29 and 25:16) in a way which is not yet evident in the royal psalms. [54] Ps. 9:34 and 140 go even further when they regard what happens to the individual as typical of a group. Hence we have a collective use of עָנִי in Ps. 74:19, 21; 140:12; 37:14; 10:2, 9; cf. 68:10, where the situation of need is depicted more generally. The fact that עָנִי is almost always sing. is an indication of original reference to actual experiences.

The adversaries of the poor are esp. the רְשָׁעִים, who are to be regarded only in part as political enemies. [55] In many cases, e.g., Ps. 69:29; 86:1; 88:15 the ref. seems to be to situations of acute distress [56] to which the poor are exposed through their opponents, e.g., sickness, magic, foreign enemies. Material poverty is often the cause or the result. [57] Elsewhere social poverty, i.e., belonging to an oppressed class, is obviously intended, e.g., Ps. 35:10; 37:14 (cf. v. 16); 22:27 (?). That those who are not poor in any lit. sense also try to achieve this relation of protection leads to an extension of meaning and of the blessings of salvation sought. From the very outset the term carries with it a complementary religious and ethical content in so far as the poor are considered in their divinely willed fulness of life. This is developed in the individual Ps. of complaint. The prospect of material reward maintains the link with the lit. sense. Since the adversary is called רָשָׁע, there is also a dimension of class, and the social element is emphasised in עָנִי.

The subsidiary form עָנָו (→ 888, 20 ff.) occurs only in later Ps., Ps. 9:19; 10:16; 22:26; 34:2; 37:11; 69:32; 76:9 עַנְוֵי־אָרֶץ 147:6; 149:4. [58] Possibly it is not always original, in 22:26; 35:9; [59] 69:32 [60] it might well be an addition. Up to Ps. (76;) 147; 149 it always occurs in contexts in which we also find עָנִי or אֶבְיוֹן, though עָנִי is the chief term. A formal distinction is that the related words are always in the plur., though there is no difference in content. Hymns celebrate deliverances of the עֲנָוִים whose greatness may be seen from the fate of God's enemies. The individual is not called עָנָו in prayers and thanksgivings. The usage is so distinctive that, since there is no original difference from עָנִי, one can only think that an established term was adopted from real life. The description

---

[53] But not against the רְשָׁעִים except perhaps in the late Ps. 109:16, so Mowinckel, op. cit. (→ n. 51), 116; Kuschke, 49, n. 2. Cf. the Egypt. par.: "Amon, lend thine ear to one who stands alone in the judgment, who is poor and his (opponent) is rich," A. Erman, Lit. d. Ägypter (1923), 380 and oriental conjurations, e.g., E. Ebeling, Die akkad. Gebetsserie "Handerhebung" (1953), 17: "I ... am ... wretched ... before thee ... bowed down ..., through thy mouth I might go forth whole," cf. also the instances referred to in Birkeland I, 103 f.

[54] But → n. 50. On the poor and righteous in the Ps. cf. J. J. Stamm, "Ein Vierteljahrhundert Psalmenforschung," ThR, 23 (1955), 55-60 and the books discussed there.

[55] So Birkeland I and II passim.

[56] "Real distress" (Percy, 63; S. Mowinckel, Psalmenstudien, VI. "Die Psalmendichter," op. cit. [n. 51] [1924], 61); cf. already Rahlfs, 76 f. It should be noted, however, that the affliction is esp. emphasised because it leads to prayer.

[57] Either view qualifies the thesis of Mowinckel, Birkeland and Percy (49, 63). Ps. 22:6 f. is no argument against a social background since it is only the intensification of inner and outer sufferings shared in part with others (cf. v. 26) which isolates the psalmist, as against Birkeland I, 42.

[58] Ps. 149 Maccabean; Ps. 69. 147 revised in the Maccabean age.

[59] Grätz, ad loc.; H. Gunkel, Die Ps., Handkomm. AT, II, 2 (1926), ad loc. read אֶבְיוֹנִים.

[60] An interpolation here as distinct from Ps. 22:22 f. (beginning of the song of thanksgiving) and Ps. 31:23 f. (end of the song).

of a movement of עֲנִיִּים or humble pious, called עֲנָוִים in Aram., has thus made its way primarily or secondarily into the Psalms. [61] It would seem that the sing. עָנִי was no longer adequate to denote a group. Along with supplementary forms like עַם־עָנִי in Ps. 18:27 [62] and the rise of עָנָו, אֶבְיוֹן replaced it (cf. the plur. in 1 QIs a 26:6; 32:7).

5. The tragedy of the exile led to a collective use of עָנִי etc. outside the Ps. It is worth noting that this first occurs in hymns where Jerusalem is addressed as עֲנִיָּה, Is. 54:11 cf. 51:21, also עָנִיו as a par. to עַמּוֹ in 49:13. The equation resulted from the situation, so that the religious element is less developed than in the Ps. Another reason for this may be that the passages contain divine promises, not human petitions. God will deliver the soul of the אֶבְיוֹן, Jer. 20:13. עֲנָוִים [63] is used instead in Is. 29:19; 61:1, and the context suggests emphasis on the religious sense of עָנִי. But the thought is never pressed to the pt. of hinting that deliverance is regarded as imminent because the people is in the (ideal) state of poverty. [64] In keeping is the fact that the ref. is usually material, [65] the attack on the exploitation of the poor by Israel continues, and דַּל even has a negative sense in Jer. 5:4. Though it became significant later, עָנִי as the people's term for itself still represents a fleeting mood based on the Ps., and it has as yet no very formative influence. The solution to the problem of poverty is also the same as in the Ps.: a final balancing, which is, of course, understood semi-eschatologically, Is. 11:4 f. etc.

6. Except for the Ps., most of the statements about poverty are in the Wisdom lit., → 39, 15 ff.; 324, 29 ff. There are certain common features. Biblical wisdom as distinct from that of the surrounding oriental world [66] relates its thoughts on poverty more closely to God, and, unlike the social criticism of Stoicism, it accepts in principle a hierarchical social order. [67] Sometimes wealth is self-evidently approved, Sir. 40:18; 47:18. Hence poverty lies under a deep shadow. It is regarded as the result of man's own acts — a thought alien to both the Ps. and the prophets. Laziness (Prv. 6:6-11), pleasure-seeking (21:17; Sir. 18:32 f.), frivolity (Prv. 23:21) and even envy lead to poverty, Ps.-Menander, 85. [68] Hence even the sage despises the beggar, Sir. 25:2; cf. 40:30; Ps.-Menander, 64. The beggar's life is not really worth living, Sir. 41:1-4; cf. 38:19 vl.; Ps.-Menander, 94. [69] Better die than beg, Sir. 40:28; Ps.-Menander, 19. But there is also criticism of the rich (Sir. 13:24a; 26:29) and understanding for the poor ; it is better to be poor and righteous than rich and a liar, Prv. 19:22; 28:6; cf. Sir. 30:14. It is known that the rich lay burdens on the poor, Sir. 13:3 ff.; this kindles understanding for the life of the poor. The loneliness which afflicts him (Prv. 14:20; 19:4, 7), his restlessness (Sir. 31:4 though cf. 29:22), his humiliation (Prv. 18:23), the non-recognition of his merits (Qoh. 9:16) are all perceived and deplored. Thus the despising of poverty is attacked, Ps.-Menander, 16. It is even possible to laud the poor for his understanding, Sir. 10:30. [70] It is esp. concluded that one should help to improve the lot of the poor by benevolence (Ep. Ar., 290), or that one should at least be kind to him, Sir. 4:8. It is true that צְדָקָה is not to be used of all but

---

[61] Though cf. Birkeland I, 94; Percy, 55-62.

[62] Gunkel, op. cit. (→ n. 59), 67 favours a late date for this.

[63] Birkeland I, 15 f.

[64] This idea is introduced by Is. LXX by using πτωχός for עָנָו and עָנִי rather than the customary ταπεινός when the context is eschatological, 29:19; 41:17; 61:1; also 14:30.

[65] Always in Ez., so also perhaps Zech. 9:9.

[66] Cf. Amenemope, 6 : Better poverty in the hand of God than riches in store, AOT², 40. In gen. oriental wisdom is not greatly concerned about the poor.

[67] Emphasised by G. Wohlenberg, "Jesus Sir. u. d. soziale Frage," NkZ, 8 (1897), 332.

[68] Ed. J. Land, Anecdota Syriaca, I (1852).

[69] With a contemporary ref. Cf. Achikar, 105 (ed. A. Cowley [1923], 216): There is nothing more bitter than poverty (עֲנוּה).

[70] Cf. R. Smend, Die Weisheit d. Jesus Sirach (1906), 101.

only of the poor and worthy of Israel, Sir. 12:4; 29:20; 41:21; Tob. 4:6 f. Of 42 instances in Prv. 33 are from the pre-exilic collections II and V, [71] whose basic thrust is still to be seen in post-exilic verses like 30:14; 31:9. The difference from the Ps. in vocabulary and understanding is shaped by genre rather than age. Since the rules are taken from life, the situation of the poor is in part depicted neutrally (esp. by רָשׁ == πτωχός), though the obligation towards the poor is not forgotten ; indeed, this is in view: πλούσιος καὶ πτωχός ... ἀμφοτέρους δὲ ὁ κύριος ἐποίησεν, Prv. 22:2; cf. 14:31; 17:5; 29:13. In later wisdom there is shift and a relativising : πτωχεία καὶ πλοῦτος παρὰ κυρίου ἐστίν, Sir. 11:14; cf. v. 21; Qoh. 4:13; Sir. 13:3, 24. They are both contingent and hence not eternal, Ps.-Menander, 16. Other categories are introduced in estimation of a man, Sir. 10:22, 23. In Prv. one may note an increasing permeation by the poor law of Dt. and a corresponding admonition of the rich (not the poor). In Sir. there is a gentle and thoughtful appeal.

The practical orientation of Prv. did not leave scope for prospects of recompense for the poor. In Job the non-rewarding of benevolence to the poor (29:12, 16; 30:25; 31:16, 19 etc.) — the righteous Job is no longer the starting-pt. [72] — and the delivering up of the poor to oppressors (24:4, 9, 14) are a riddle whose solution is sought after the manner of the Psalmist, 5:15; 34:19, 28; 36:6, 15, [73] though to some degree in more muted tones (21:10, 19 ff.). Sir. ethicised the problem in part : μὴ δῷς τόπον ἀνθρώπῳ καταράσασθαί σε ... τῆς δεήσεως αὐτοῦ ἐπακούσεται ὁ ποιήσας αὐτόν (4:5 f.; cf. 21:5), though in the main he ignored it.

C. Later Judaism.

I. Usage in the Rabbis, Josephus and Philo.

1. The Rabb. know all the terms for "poor," [74] but in practice they make little use of most of them. אֶבְיוֹן disappears altogether ; [75] אֶבְיוֹנוּת is found in formal liturgical contexts. [76] דַּל is also rare and the usage shows a tendency to abstraction (hence mostly in comparisons), but with no religious element. רָשׁ is weakly attested. מִסְכֵּן and מִסְכְּנוּת are rather more common, esp. in Aram., in the Tg. commonly for אֶבְיוֹן, עָנִי, רָשׁ; also חֶלְכָה. When an adequate word is sought for beggar, for which Heb. has no specific term, מִסְכֵּן is used, jBM, 4, 2 (9d, 3 [Rab]); cf. jPea, 8, 9 (21b, 13); Lv. r., 34, 10 on 25:39. The normal term is עָנִי, Aram. עֲנְיָא. But the meaning is more restricted : עָנִי simply denotes the poor man, Shebi., 9, 7; Ter., 9, 2; Shab., 1, 1; Ab., 1, 5 etc., the socially poor. [77] Like עָנִי, עָנָו has completely lost any religious nuance in the Rabb. and it is used almost exclusively for "meek," "humble." [78]

2. In translations πτωχός and πένης are mostly used interchangeably. [79] Only in better Gk. is there differentiation [80] and a partial avoidance of πτωχός, e.g., Ep. Ar.

---

[71] All the רָשׁ passages are from this complex (אֶבְיוֹן only once). This shatters the thesis of Kuschke, 45 f., 53.

[72] The poor and the righteous are not equated, cf. v. d. Ploeg, 253.

[73] Cf. G. Hölscher, Das Buch Hi., Hndbch. AT, I, 17 (1937), ad loc.

[74] Lv. r., 34, 6 on 25:39; Str.-B., I, 825 f.

[75] bBM, 111b, where the use of a verse of Scripture demands it.

[76] Teh. Ps. 70 (ed. S. Buber [1891], 322, line 12).

[77] In a semi-transf. sense bBB, 43a.

[78] Explanation in S. Nu. § 101 (27a) on 12:3, cf. K. G. Kuhn, Tannaitische Midraschim, II SNu (1933), 264, 135. עֲנָוָה is more common, a virtue in Hb. En. 41:3, an angelic power 8:1 f. On humility in the Rabb. cf. P. Fiebig, "Jesu Bergpredigt," FRL, 37 (1924), 2 f.

[79] Cf. Test. Job 10:6 f.; 11; 12:1 (ed. J. A. Robinson, TSt, V, 1 [1899]).

[80] Joseph and Asenath 10:11-13 (ed. P. Batiffol, Studia Patristica [1889 f.]): law of development.

In Lat. πτωχός is often given the special sense *mendicus*, though one also finds *pauper*, *egens*. Joseph. has πτωχός only in Bell., 5, 570, πτωχεία in Ant., 11, 8; 12, 224. He has πένης more frequently to describe a man as the member of a social stratum, [81] Ant., 4, 269 (also πένομαι); 10, 155; Bell., 2, 585 — the πτωχός seems not to be in any stratum. He also uses πενία to denote economic status (Ant., 17, 307 on Herod). The abstract vocabulary of Philo is not concerned about the phenomena of poverty and hence πτωχός is not used at all. The term occurs only in a quotation in Euseb. → n. 139.

II. View of the Poor in the Apocrypha and Pseudepigrapha.

1. The evidence in the apocr. and pseudepigr. lit. is not uniform. One part of the apocalyptic writings avoids not only πτωχός but also any ref. to the social situation either in this or the future age (Mart. Is., Gr. Bar., Vit. Ad., parts of Test. XII etc.) except for marginal ref. in some instances (e.g., Ps.-Philo). Other works are full of complaints, though πτωχός is not used and the antithesis to the rich is not suggested in any other form.

2. Another group follows the Wisdom lit. (→ 893, 20 ff.) by referring to the life of the poor (Test. Jud. 15:5 : πτωχεία; Test. R. 4:7: πένης), demanding pity (Test. Iss. 5:2 πένης καὶ ἀσθενής) and the giving of alms (Tob. 4:7, 16 : πτωχός/πεινῶν) and even in one instance addressing the poor. [82] πτωχός comes at the beginning of a list of services in Ps.-Phocylides. [83] Examples of generosity are given : Isaac (Test. Isaac 10:8 [→ n. 82]); Issachar (Test. Iss. 7:5 : πτωχός cf. Ep. Ar., 290), Joseph (Test. Jos. 3:5), and Asenath (Jos. and Asenath 10:12 : πτωχός [→ n. 80]). The Test. of Job occupies a special place here. [84] What is stressed is not the wealth of Job but the way he uses it in διακονία. [85] Attention is directed to his earlier days and the focus is on his dealings with the poor. In Test. Is. 8:9 (→ n. 82) it is suggested that there be an anniversary when the poor are fed. Consideration is given to the value of liberality and its reward as compared with other virtues and vices (Test. A. 2:5 : πτωχός). [86] This stream debouches almost unchanged in the Rabb. writings.

3. Other works mention the poor only in an eschatological connection. In the new aeon πενία will vanish, Sib., 3, 378 cf. 8, 208, οἱ πτωχοὶ πλουτισθήσονται, Test. Jud. 25:4 cf. Test. Sol. 10:12. The people which follows the harlot Babylon will then bear the mark *misera* and is threatened with wretchedness and *paupertas*. [87] If the end is near, the man of God should lift up the poor, 4 Esr. 14:13. This view of the future which is kindly to the poor is preceded by the neutral depiction of an eschatological stage when the poor will be in conflict with the rich and beggars with princes, Jub. 23:19. This yields to a final period when the poor will be set above the rich, though this is understood as an age of confusion, S. Bar. 70:4. In this respect S. Bar. is close to the Rabb. The Rabb. certainly preserve the tradition that there will be no poor in the next aeon, [88] but it is already expressly rejected in the Amoraean period, bShab., 151b, Bar. Rabb. exegesis of Dt. 15:4, 11 is exclusively ethical in orientation, S. Dt. on 15:11; Tg. J. I on

---

[81] Not Ant., 1, 134; 14, 31, in each case elucidated by another adj.

[82] Testamentum Isaac 8:12 (cf. the transl. of W. E. Barnes, TSt, II, 2 [1892]).

[83] vv. 22 ff. (Diehl³, II, 93). The first 2 members are from Is. 58:7; but πτωχός is made autonomous and given emphasis by the context.

[84] πτωχός 13-14 times (50:1 vl.; 10:7 addition ?), πένης 8-10 times (9:7; 50:1 vl.), ἀδύνατος 5 times.

[85] More and other than in the Rabb.

[86] For material cf. Cronbach, 139-143.

[87] 6 Esr. 1:47-51 (ed. O. F. Fritzsche, Libri apocr. Veteris Testamenti [1871]).

[88] bShab., 151b, Bar. and even more precisely Yirmya in exposition of Zech. 14:21 כען עני for כנעני, bPes., 50a.

Dt. 15:4; bBer., 34b (Shemuel b. Nachman), and עַם־עָנִי in Ps. 18:27 is understood only in terms of individual recompense. [89]

4. In a fourth group of texts — always short proverbs interwoven into other works — the poor themselves speak. They make violent complaints against the rich (Eth. En. 94:7; 96:4 ff.; 97:8 f.; cf. 63:10) in which the accusers portray themselves as the victims of infringements of the *pauperum bonorum comestores*, [90] as עֲנָוִים and צַדִּיקִים who are oppressed, Eth. En. 96:5, 8. The indirect statement of Sir. 13:15-19 (20) goes even further. The constitutive antithesis of πτωχός and πλούσιος is made quite irreconcilable by further definition, and the terms πτωχός and εὐσεβής are interfused and employed in the service of an aggressive view of past and present.

5. A special position is occupied by Ps. Sol. 5:2, 11; 10:6; 15:1; 18:2 inasmuch as the predicate "poor" is here used exclusively for man as an obj. of God's dealings, cf. esp. 10:6a b. This corresponds to the עָנִי of the later Ps. (→ 892, 24 ff.), but the diction is less formal. Materially πτωχός is here identical with δίκαιος and ὅσιος and denotes more of an inner quality, esp. when used in confrontation with adversaries. Where used, πτωχός is always the chief term and it thus represents an essential aspect in the self-understanding of the community which expresses itself in the Ps. Since this is undergoing various forms of affliction, πτωχός can include material poverty, [91] though this is not the essential characteristic of the community nor does the climax of the statement lie here. πτωχός is in this sense the relic that brings to light a piety which is seeking release from a powerful ideology of poverty. [92]

At some points the poor groups are permeated by a martyr theology which integrates poverty — harder to bear than physical sufferings acc. to the Rabb. view (→ C.V.) — into the divine dealings in history. The passive mood which shaped this view seized upon this theology (Ps. Sol. 15; Ass. Mos. 9) and also upon the theology of poverty, and thus prevented the development of an active poor movement. The epilogue to Eth. En. extols the עֲנוּי־רוּחַ (108:7), transl. *pios* by the Syr. translation of 4 Esr. 14:13. Both are further from the original concrete sense of πτωχός than is Ps. Sol. The range of the term from an emphasising of the content of עָנִי to its evaporation can in fact work itself out only in different generations, so that historically one cannot speak of a continuous poor party but only of a wave-like movement of social tensions in which various aspects of the OT terminology of poverty are adopted.

III. Qumran.

1. The Poor in the Individual Writings. The mood of the Ps. is unmistakable in one part of the Hodayot. In the individual thanksgivings the author — probably the Teacher of Righteousness [93] — calls himself an עָנִי, נפש עני ורש, 1 QH 5:1, אביון, 5:13 f., 16, 18. God has helped the נפש אביון 2:32 cf. Jer. 20:13; Ps. 82:3. There is no clear distinction between the terms. In other songs of praise a larger no. of men are called עָנוִים, 5:21;

---

[89] Cf. Str.-B., I, 136. Material from the Targums in Rahlfs, 93.

[90] Ass. Mos. 7:8. A. Hilgenfeld, *Messias Judaeorum* (1869), 449 transl. πτωχῶν ἀγαθῶν καταφαγάδες.

[91] If πενία bears a negative sense in 4:6; 16:13 f., this is of little account since the corpus is not of uniform origin.

[92] It is also detaching itself from the Rabb. understanding of עֲנָוה as a virtue. For this reason a derivation of Ps. Sol. from a Qumran-type community is to be preferred to a Pharisaic origin.

[93] So, e.g., H. Bardtke, *Die Handschriftenfunde am Toten Meer* (1953), 159; S. Glanzman, "Sectarian Psalms from the Dead Sea," *Theol. Studies*, 13 (1952), 490; Sukenik, 34; J. P. Hyatt, "The View of Man in the Qumran 'Hodayot'," NTSt, 2 (1955/56), 277. But cf. H. Bardtke, "Das Ich des Meisters in d. Hodajot Qumrān," *Wissenschaftliche Ztschr. d. Karl-Marx-Universität Leipzig*, 6 (1956/57), 93-104.

18:14 or אביונים, 18:22; in the first instance the terms are simply metaphors, cf. 1:36, but they are then used with a specific emphasis and denote a group. [94] We often find the same usage in the War Scroll. There the בני אור are עני רוח, 1 QM 14:7, cf. also נכאי רוח, in 11:10 [95] and תמימי רוח in 7:5. [96] Above all the poor are at decisive pts. the objects of God's dealings. God acts עם אביונים (13:13 f.); by the hand of the poor of His redemption [כה]ביד אביוני פדות the hosts of Belial are smitten down (11:9). Enemies from all lands will be delivered up into the hand of the poor ביד אביונים (11:13). In the last passage a par. of אביונים is כורעי עפר, "those bowed in the dust," and in 14:5 ff. the sons of light are called "those who stumble" כושלים. The situation is the same in the Habakkuk commentary. The ungodly priest has attacked the poor גמל על אביונים (1 QpH 12:3); he tried to destroy them זמם לכלות אביונים (12:6); he plundered their goods גזל הון אביונים (12:10). In all three writings "poor" is a title of honour along with others. It should be noted, however, that in the typical expressions of the group אביון replaces all other terms for poor — there are attacks on the עמים in 1 QpH 8:12; 9:5 f. and on the אביונים — and that אביון is the most frequently used title, so that it seems to occupy a privileged place as compared with others. This is certainly true in the comm. on Ps. 37. [97] If the text says that the קואי יהוה or ענוים (Ps. 37:9, 11) shall inherit the earth, this is referred in the comm. to the עדת בחירו first and then to the עדת אביונים [98] (col. 1, 5. 9). [99] In this respect we have more than a continuation of the traditional bibl. terminology. [100] At a specific point in time [101] "community of the poor" seems to have become the favourite term for the Qumran community or for a part of it or for a related group. [102] Thus far, however, the material does not enable us to draw from the general use of the

---

[94] That this usage is not just taken from the OT is clear from the fact that חלכאים, which in Ps. 10:10 refers to helpless men who are to be approved as such, denotes here the opponents of the נפש אביון, 1 QS 3:25; cf. 38:25, 35. Cf. E. L. Sukenik, מגילות גנוזות II (1950), 39, 47 for an appreciation of the meaning of the term.

[95] Cf. 1 QH 18:15. Y. Yadin, מלחמת בני אור בבני חושך (1955), 341 f. thinks the usage is coloured by the OT: "Hence it is hard to build up the theory that it (the Qumran community) is a sect of the Ebionites"; cf. H. J. Schoeps, Urgemeinde, Judenchristentum, Gnosis (1956), 71.

[96] Other characteristic expressions are נמוגי ברכים in 14:6, כושלים in 14:5, מכים and תמימי דרך in 14:7. Cf. the similar usage in the 2nd of the apocr. psalms preserved in Syr. and possibly from the Qumran circle, where the קהל הרבים calls itself אביונים (trans. M. Noth, "Die fünf syr. überlieferten apokr. Ps.," ZAW, 48 [1930], 18); cf. M. Delcor, "Cinq nouveaux Psalmes esséniens?" Revue de Qumran, 1 (1958), 89.

[97] Cf. J. M. Allegro, "A Newly Discovered Fragment of a Comm. on Ps. 37 from Qumran (4 Qp Ps. 37:8-11, 19b-26)," Palestine Exploration Quarterly, 86 (1954), 71; also "Further Light on the History of the Qumran Sect," JBL, 75 (1956), 94; the expressions which are decisive in this context are in the first ref.

[98] עדת is supplied, but its validity is established by 4 QpPs 37 col. 2, 10.

[99] The poor man is tested and freed. But then the fr. breaks off, so that one cannot say whether a formula for taking possession of the earth follows, but cf. col. 2, 10.

[100] A link with this is unmistakable; C. Rabin, The Zadokite Documents² (1958), 40, n. 15 sees in Prv. 19:22 the model, though the precise counterformulation איש הכזב does not occur there.

[101] If the general dating is still uncertain, a beginning has only been made with the order of the works, the inner chronology and the sifting out of alien matter, so that conclusions can be drawn only with great caution.

[102] To be distinguished is 1 QSb 5:21 f., where to the נשיא העדה is given the task of ruling the ענוי ארץ. In origin (cf. Is. 11:4) and context (cf. DJD, I, 128 f.) the phrase is eschatological, but it is not impossible that the order of the time of salvation was practised already in the community.

words any conclusions as to various groups in the Qumran movement. The Damascus Document castigates the exploitation of the עניי עמו by the priestly opponents of the community, 6:16 (8:13). They are summoned to aid עני ואביון וגר 6:21 (8:17).[103] An injunction in the second part directs that at least two days' wages a month be set aside in favour of the עני ואביון (obviously a double term) amongst others, 14:14 (18:3); the ref. here is mainly to adherents of the community,[104] whereas others are in view in 6:21 (8:17).[105] On the other hand the community identifies itself in 19:9 (9:10) with the עניי הצון, who will be preserved through persecution.[106]

2. Attitude to Possessions. The Qumran fellowship, as laid down in its regulations, is characterised by renunciation of private property; the member is a יחד...בהון, 1 QS 5:2. In the first yr. the novice is legally outside the community, but in the second he places הון ומלאכה[107] at the disposal of the community, though not yet in the common pool, 6:19. The latter takes place only when he is definitively received into the community after the second yr., 6:22. Control is exercised by the sons of Aaron, 9:7. There are severe penalties for false statements regarding private property (6:25)[108] and for mis-appropriation of community property, 7:6. For the member of the fellowship[109] every possession is הון חמס, 10:19.[110] Property as such is not wrong. Only when the wilder-ness period begins should it be left behind, 9:22.[111] Prior to this the community itself is a comprehensive economic unit.[112] It is a fellowship which erases the distinctions between rich and poor, attempting to reflect the form of life which God will establish with the coming age.[113] In the Damascus Document, however, private property[114] is

---

[103] The text from 6:14b (8:12) mentions conditions for the reinstatement of fellowship with the Jerusalem priests, and it does so in the form which is also a catechism for those outside, though cf. P. Kahle, "Die Gemeinde d. Neuen Bundes u. d. hbr. Handschriften aus d. Höhle," ThLZ, 77 (1952), 405 f. The words quoted are not in the fr. from 6 Q (ed. M. Baillet, "Fragments du document de Damas Qumran Grotte 6," Rev. Bibl., 63 [1956], 520.

[104] Caring for the ישבה לגוי (14:15 [18:4]) may have been necessary too, since this is distinguished from the corresponding formulae precisely by the regard for עני ואביון.

[105] אח in 6:20 (8:17) is not to be related to members, cf. 6:21 (8:18).

[106] This is the older par. (B) to the judgment address in the first part; it shows that before special terms came into use for the fellowship, along with the appropriate bibl. ref., one group in the community understood itself in the light of Zech. 11:11 — עני for אביון under the influence of the quotation.

[107] = ὑπάρχοντα καὶ ἴδια? ממון for הון in 1 QS 6:2 supports this.

[108] There is uncertainty as to whether the ref. is to false declarations as a witness (P. Wernberg-Møller, "The Manual of Discipline," Studies on the Texts of the Desert of Judah, I [1957], 111) or in one's own cause (S. E. Johnson, "The Dead Sea Man. of Discipline and the Jerusalem Church of Acts," ZAW, 66 [1954], 108 f.).

[109] This decisive pt. is missed by H. Braun, Spätjüd.-häretischer u. frühchristlicher Radi-kalismus (1957), I, 36.

[110] C. Rabin, "Qumran Studies," Scripta Judaica, II, ed. A. A. Altmann (1957), 22-36, thinks there was private property at Qumran. But he wrongly applies the analogy of Damascus, builds on conjectures on 1 QS 7:6, and can only suggest the possibility.

[111] It is uncertain whether the ref. is to community property or to the private property of those called forth; probably the former.

[112] W. R. Farmer, "The Economic Basis of the Qumran Community," ThZ, 11 (1955), 295-308.

[113] So rightly F. M. Cross, The Ancient Library of Qumran and Modern Biblical Studies (1958), 62. On the other hand S. Segert, "Die Gütergemeinschaft d. Essäer," Studia Antiqua A. Salač oblata (1955), 73, thinks that the striving for purity led to community of goods. Similar conditions are presupposed in 4 QpPs 37 (→ n. 97) where members of the community put נחלת כול (col. 2, 10) in the common chest, cf. T. H. Gaster, The Scriptures of the Dead Sea Sect (1957), 244. The sustaining in רעב col., 2, 4 and the overthrow of the wicked are eschatological but seem to presuppose the actuality of hunger.

[114] Cf. Braun, op. cit. (→ n. 109), 121 f.; Rabin, op. cit. (→ n. 110), 23.

undoubtedly presupposed (cf. 13:15 [16:8]; 16:16 [20:12]) as well as community property (14:14 [18:3 f.]). Capricious use of this is forbidden by the rules of the fellowship (14:17 ff. [18:6 ff.]) and living in special quarters מחנות is restricted, 14:3 (17:1 f.). Those only loosely associated with the community [115] even have slaves and business relations with Gentiles, 12:9 f. (14:10 f.). Only the unlawfully acquired property of the Jerusalem priests is regarded as הון הרשע, 8:5 (9:15); [116] moderate seeking of possessions is permissible, 8:7 (9:17).

Acc. to available accounts the Essenes are closest to the Damascus community. They may have been the same or a similar group. Philo and Joseph. emphasise their sharing of goods, Philo Omn. Prob. Lib., 84 f.; Jos. Ap., 4: ὥστε ἐν ἅπασιν μήτε πενίας ταπεινότητα φαίνεσθαι μήθ' ὑπεροχὴν πλούτου, Bell., 2, 122; Ant., 18, 20. [117] But both make statements which seem to suggest that private property was allowed within limits. [118] The Therapeutae gave their οὐσία to relatives and friends and lived without χρήματα and κτήματα, Philo Vit. Cont., 13, 16. In view of the strongly rhetorical character of Philo's description [119] one cannot say whether their form of life was strictly communistic or not.

IV. Position of the Poor in Palestinian Judaism.

1. The Social Structure. From the Maccabean age Judaism was plagued by gt. social tensions. After the climax of unrest under Gabinius more settled conditions came in the age of Herod. At this period the interest of the Pharisees in the masses, and their connection with them, declined. [120] On the other hand new extremist movements found support among the dregs of the people. The distress caused by the two wars created a kind of ethos of poverty. Akiba declared : Beautiful is the poverty of the daughter of Jacob like a red necklace on the neck of a white horse. [121] He drew the legal conclusion that even the poorest of Israel are to be regarded as free men who have lost their property, BQ, 8, 6. The saying that God loves the poor אלוהים אהב עניים (cf. bBB, 10a) must have been circulating at this period. Even the rabbis were poor after the catastrophe. [122] But there were well-to-do rabbis again soon after. [123] Social cleavages deepened afresh. Typical are the relations in Sepphoris, where the scholars regarded the am haarez with open contempt, supporting them neither regularly nor in times of famine (bSanh., 92a; bBB, 8a) and avoiding all dealings with them. For this reason the

---

[115] 12:9-12 (14:9 ff.) seems to be a rule for those loosely attached to the fellowship, though cf. K. G. Kuhn, "Zur Bedeutung d. neuen palästinischen Handschriftenfunde f. d. nt.liche Wissenschaft," ThLZ, 75 (1950), 85.

[116] Though cf. L. Rost, "Qumranprobleme. Eine Übersicht," Ev. Theol., 18 (1958), 107.

[117] Cf. Plin. Hist. Nat., 5, 17, 4 : sine pecunia ; Philastrius De Haeresibus, 9 (CSEL, 38, 5). For further details Braun, op. cit. (→ n. 109), 77-80.

[118] Philo Omn. Prob. Lib., 85 f. (cf. W. Bauer, Art. "Essener," Pauly-W., Suppl. 4 [1924], 423); Jos. Bell., 2, 124 and 127 (garbled in Hipp. Ref., 9, 20), 134 (v. Bauer, 403). It should be noted that Philo interprets along the lines of his philosophical ideal, whereas Jos. gives a short summary.

[119] H. Lewy, "Sobria Ebrietas," Beih. ZNW, 9 (1929), 31, n. 4; I. Heinemann, Art. "Therapeutai," Pauly-W., 5 A (1934), 2340-2345.

[120] A mark of this is Hillel's introduction of the prosbol, Shebi., 10, 3 f.; S. Dt., 113 on 15:3.

[121] Cf. the par. formulae in BM, 2, 11; bSanh., 110a; Sota, 9, 15; bGit., 62a; bSukka, 38b; bQid., 32b.

[122] jPea, 8, 8 (21b, 2 ff.); bBB, 75a cf. bShab., 151b. On their standard of life there is a good deal of material in A. Büchler, "The Economic Conditions of Judaea after the Destruction of the Second Temple," Jew. College Publications, 4 (1912), 48-50; cf. also Jeremias, 31.

[123] Tarphon bHor., 33; Nechuniah bMeg., 28a; Gamaliel II BM, 5, 8. On Jehuda v. S. Klein, "The Estates of R. Judah ha-Nasi," JQR, 2 (1911/12), 545-556; also בעקבות האריסות הגדולה בסביבות לוד. ספר היובל לש" קרויס (1936), 69-79.

am haarez hated scholars more than non-Jews. [124] Tensions were so great at this time that sometimes the poor seized the goods of others, bSukka, 44b. These tensions remained and played a considerable part in the rise of Jewish sects, esp. the Karaite movement. [125] In these we find the ancient glorifying of the poor, with whom the sectaries identified themselves, in exposition of verses like Zeph. 3:12; Is. 29:19; 32:7; Zech. 11:11. [126]

2. The Interpretation of the Poor Law. The legal situation of the poor is characterised by the fact that although they must make certain offerings acc. to religious law — even the עָנִי must pay the temple tex (Sheq., 1, 7; 2, 5) and even the πένης must pay the tax for the firstborn (Philo De praemiis sacerdotum, 1) [127] — relief and aid are provided for them. The poor tax based on Dt. 14:29; 26:12; [128] Tob. 1:8 א, is for the προσήλυτος, ὀρφανός, χήρα. Jos. mentions only widows and orphans, Ant., 4, 240. The term מַעֲשֵׂר עָנִי occurs for the first time in the Mishnah period, Pea, 8, 2; Demai, 3, 4; cf. jSota, 3, 4 (19a, 40): מעשר מסכינין. For the most part, however, this tax was a dead letter. [129] On the other hand the Pharisaic fellowships made loyal observance of it a duty, jMS, 5, 9 (56d, 26 ff.). In the Rabb. one may note a tendency to limit the 1st tithe. [130] The result was that the poor tax gradually became more important than it had been prior to 70 A.D., [131] but also that priests and Levites — poor priest is now a tt. — derive support from it, Pea, 8, 5. Perhaps the new description of the tithe is linked with the partial establishment of Pharisaic principles after 70 A.D. To the poor was allotted the pea, the forgotten sheaf, gleanings, [132] what grows in the sabbatical yr. (Shebi., 5, 3; bTaan., 19b, Bar.) and the right to pickings in the fields and in oliveyards and vineyards. Mishnah law hardly improved the legal status of the poor. It is true that an indispensable minimum is secured for them in Pea, 1, 2 and that additional decisions brought some amelioration, [133] though in view of the modest value of the pea the change was not great. [134] Above all, only limited credibility was ascribed to the statements of the poor (BB, 43a), and the appointment of the court as their advocate (BQ, 36b) was only theoretical.

3. Voluntary Philanthropy. This was more important. [135] Like the poor [136] tithe this is firmly rooted in established customs : the distributions to the אביונים at the feast of Purim (Est. 9:22; Meg., 1, 4) and the gifts to the poor on the night of the Passover (Pes., 9, 11; 10, 1). It was also the practice to give to charity one part of the 2nd tithe which was to be spent in Jerusalem, so that swarms of beggars were attracted to the holy city. The

---

[124] bPes., 49b. Cf. A. Büchler, "Political and Social Leaders of the Jewish Community of Sepphoris in the Second and Third Century," *Jew. College Publications,* 1 (1909), 61.

[125] Cf. R. Mahler, קאראימער (1947), 294 ff.

[126] Cf. N. Wieder, "The Qumran Sectaries and the Karaites," JQR, 47 (1956/57), 283-289.

[127] Ed. K. E. Richter, IV (1828), 315.

[128] Cf. O. Eissfeldt, "Erstlinge u. Zehnten im AT," BWANT, 22 (1917), 162; Schürer, II, 307; Str.-B., IV, 680-682; G. Lisowsky, *Jadajim* (1956), 5.

[129] Sir. 7:32; Ab., 5, 9. The picture presented in A. Geiger, *Urschrift u. Übers. d. Bibel* (1857), 179 is quite misleading.

[130] Cf. in the statement in bSota, 48a (on the additional character of this *v.* R. Meyer, "Das angebliche Demaj-Gesetz Hyrkans, I," ZNW, 38 [1939], 125 f.) the restriction of beneficiaries (bSanh., 90b) and the secondary view that the priestly tithes are for the poor or for poor priests (bJeb., 86b).

[131] Jub. 32 says nothing about it.

[132] This is also for the Gentile poor : Git., 5, 8 (later addition ?), though cf. the restriction in T. Pea, 3, 1 (20, 30 f.).

[133] On exceeding the minimum *v.* jPea, 1, 2 (16b, 61-68); on extension beyond Palestine bChul., 137b.

[134] As against Katz, 80 the omission of the 2nd tithe in the 3rd and 6th yr. did not essentially increase the value of the 3rd tithe.

[135] Cf. Str.-B., IV, 536-610.

[136] Cf. Eissfeldt, *op. cit.* (→ n. 128), 157.

giving of alms to the poor (T. Pea, 4, 19 [24, 26 f.]) became a more or less common habit. In Pea, 1, 1 generosity (גְמִילוּת חֲסָדִים)[137] is extolled as a virtue which brings fruits in this world and whose capital remains intact for the world to come.[138] Jos. has a different Gk.-Jewish schema acc. to which it is a duty πᾶσι παρέχειν τοῖς δεομένοις πῦρ ὕδωρ τροφήν, Ap., 2, 211. Philo defines those who seek assistance more precisely as πτωχοὶ καὶ πηροί.[139] The ref. display different trends in the commending of benevolence. Thus it is an established concept in missionary preaching that as the sin-offerings bring atonement for Israel so does philanthropy for the Gentiles, BB, 10b, Bar. Hence the demand for this plays no inconsiderable role in works of propaganda.[140] For the Israelites it is more an *opus superadditum*. If commended, it is not absolutely necessary, though certainly adapted to bear weight with God, bBB, 10a. Only after the destruction of the temple is there a change : "So long as the temple still stood, one brought a shekel and received atonement ; but now when the temple is no longer standing one exercises charity and all is well," bBB, 9a; cf. AbRNat., 4 (Jochanan b. Zakkai). Before 70 benevolence exceeding law and custom was largely restricted to individuals [141] and special circles. Pharisaic communities (jMS, 5, 9 [56d, 26 ff.]), Essenes, societies of Hell. Jews in Jerusalem and other fellowships made it a duty. The idea of works of love, which were rated above almsgiving, was developed here. The objects were mostly the poor in the broader sense. Feeding the poor [142] and clothing the naked are esp. mentioned, though not in the first place.

4. Social Care of the Poor. After the Jewish War there came into being an official system of poor relief such as seems to have existed earlier only in the *diaspora*.[143] In the developed form the synagogue had several officers charged with the task. Money came in partly through taxation and partly through voluntary gifts. The income was divided into two funds, the קוּפָּה for weekly care of the local poor and the תמחוי [144] for relief of the poor who passed through daily. In relation to this hospices were set up in the synagogues.[145] The system sometimes evoked the astonishment of those outside, cf. Jul. Ep., 30 and 49. Yet there is no trace of any desire to eliminate social distinctions.

V. Judgment of the Rabbis.

In the period after the exile a negative attitude to the poor predominated in normative circles. Job is said to have prayed that God would send suffering rather than poverty,

---

[137] New Rabb. construct to distinguish voluntary philanthropy from duty. Sir. and Da. use חסד in a different sense. In Gk. ἔλεος, ἐλεημοσύνη and δικαιοσύνη shade into one another.

[138] An ancient rule repeated in bShab., 127a and bKidd., 40a.

[139] In Eus. Praep. Ev., VIII, 7, 6 (GCS, 43, 1, p. 430, 21). The two passages are related. J. Bernays, *Ges. Abh.*, I (1885), 277-282 has shown the relation of the latter to the bizygic curses of the Attic cult. D. Daube, *The NT and Rabb. Judaism* (1956), 138-140 has pointed out that the first is a minor modification of the schema in the proselyte catechism.

[140] Monobazus, the prototype of the proselyte, boasts of his acts of generosity to the עניים, T. Pea, 4, 18 (24, 15). Acc. to bJeb., 47a, Bar. the saying is : "Go forth and sell all that thou hast and become a proselyte." On the special requirement that proselytes fulfil legal duties to the poor cf. Gerim, 1, 3; *v.* G. Polster, "Der kleine Talmudtraktat über d. Proselyten," *Angelos*, 2 (1926), 2-38. On fixing the time of the rite *v.* D. Chwolson in a letter in A. Seeberg, *Das Ev. Christi* (1905), 99 f.

[141] Recollection of, e.g., Nicodemus influenced the synagogue, bKet., 66b.

[142] jPea, 1 (15d, 8 f.); Simon bYochai ; jQid., 1, 7 (61b, 47); Pesikt. r., 23/24 (122b); Str.-B., I, 707 f.; Sl. En. 51:1. Usually they are called the hungry (πεινῶν/רָעֵב; cf. the alternation in bBB, 10a) or there is ref. to hospitality (הכנסת אורחים) or some other paraphrase is used (Ab RN, 7[3c]). Clothing the naked, however, is a fixed expression.

[143] Cf. the recommendation or injunction to receive an orphan in Est. r., 6, 1 on 2:5; cf. Bacher Tannaiten, I, 188, n. 4.

[144] For details Str.-B., II, 643-647.

[145] bPes., 101a. In bSota, 10a and Gn. r., 54 on 21:33 there is allusion to the Rabb. interpretation of Gn. 21:33 as a hospice.

Ex. r., 31, 12 on 22:24. The modest sacrifies of the poor were scorned by the priests. [146]
Even after 70 the view was current that the heavenly judgment would not recognise the
excuse of the poor that because of his poverty he could not engage in study of the Law,
bYoma, 35b, Bar. In a saying attributed to Jehoshua b. Levi the poor were regarded as
non-existent for society, being classified with the dead along with and before lepers,
the blind and the childless, bNed., 64b; jNed., 9, 2 (41c, 8 ff.). Judaism realises that
earthly possessions [147] are fickle and that poverty is a misfortune, bMQ, 28a; bBer., 5b.
But even though many Palest. Tannaites were poor, they branded poverty as poverty
in the Torah, [148] saw in it a curse, quoted Prv. 15:15 (bKet., 110b; bSanh., 100b), and
thus judged it more harshly than Babyl. Judaism. [149] The Rabbinate was only lightly
influenced by the ideology of poverty and related it only to Israel as a whole, Gn. r.,
71, 1 on 29:31. In fact poverty was puzzling even for Akiba, → 899, 22 ff. The attempt
to view it as a chastisement [150] takes from it, as from martyrdom, its own theological
value. In the second century, which also saw the full development of rejection of the *am-
haarez*, [151] the eschatology of poverty was checked, the persistent anti-ascetic tendency
was extended to the sphere of poor relief, [152] and ancient sayings regarding the poor
were reinterpreted. [153] Perhaps the estimation of the עָנָוה [154] is connected with this
rethinking of a questionable theologoumenon. Only in popular tradition and more moderate statements does one still see an awareness that the poor (עֲנִיִּים) are the primary
objects of the divine mercy, Ex. r., 31, 13 on 22:24.

D. The New Testament.

In the NT πτωχός and not πένης (→ 40, 9 ff.) [155] is the usual term for the poor. [156]
The word occurs 31-35 times. It is most common in the Gospels, esp. the Synoptics
(Mk. 4-5 times, Mt. 4-5, Lk. 10). [157] This is in acc. with the contents. Outside these the
distribution is fairly even. The only surprising factor is the complete absence of the
word from Ac., [158] esp. in comparison with the common use in Lk. (6 times in material
peculiar to Lk.).

I. The Gospels.

1. Mark. In the three complexes in Mk. the use is literal. Mk. 12:41 ff. is
attacking the γραμματεῖς who devour widows' houses. The χήρα πτωχή of
v. 42 f. has a right to be supported and the tiny gift she puts in the treasury is
worth more than the big gifts of the πλούσιοι. In Mk. 10:17 ff. the life of the
poor is commended to the landowner ; he is summoned to distribute all his posses-

---

[146] Lv. r., 3, 5 on 2:1; cf. Jeremias, 24, who is sceptical as to the historicity.
[147] bShab., 151b. For details cf. Kittel Probleme, 142-149.
[148] Ab., 4, 9; Ab RN, 30; cf. bNed., 41a: עֲנִי בַּדֵּעָה. Cf. also Lv. r., 34 on 25:39.
[149] Marmorstein, 370 f.
[150] Str.-B., I, 819-822.
[151] A. Büchler, *Der galiläische 'Am-ha 'Areṣ d. 2. Jhdt.* (1906), 4 f.
[152] By limitation of alms to 20% of the ὑπάρχοντα. Cf. bBer., 61b, Bar.
[153] E.g., Test. Gad 7:6; ἀφθόνως seems to be a Jewish gloss.
[154] Most strongly in bAZ, 20b (Jehoshua b. Levi), also bAr., 16b.
[155] πένης in 2 C. 9:9 is based on the quotation, which Pl. follows closely, cf. H. Vollmer,
Die at.lichen Zitate bei Pls. (1895), 59, n. 3. There is no longer any discernible distinction
between πτωχός and πένης in the NT; in part. the element of beseeching is no longer
present in πτωχός, cf. R. Kabisch, "Die erste Seligpreisung," ThStKr, 69 (1896), 203.
[156] ἐνδεής occurs in Ac. 4:34 and the emphatic πενιχρός in Lk. 21:2, perhaps for stylistic
variety.
[157] On Lk. 1:53 → n. 215.
[158] The absence from Hb., 1 and 2 Pt., Jd. and the Joh. Ep. may well be accidental.

sions [159] to the πτωχοί. It would not seem, however, that the author has any intention of exalting the poor as such or in principle. [160] The most important πτωχός passage in Mk. is at 14:5, 7: πάντοτε γὰρ τοὺς πτωχοὺς ἔχετε μεθ' ἑαυτῶν ... ἐμὲ δὲ οὐ πάντοτε ἔχετε. The answer, which seems to depreciate almsgiving, is softened by the explanatory circumstances. [161] Mark has made the indignant disciples of the original into an indefinite group [162] and thereby lifted from the twelve and the Christian community the problem put by Jesus. This feature shows again that Mk. is not concerned about the problem of poverty. The point of the story lies elsewhere.

2. Matthew. Mt. takes 2 πτωχός passages from Mk. and adds 2 others. In 19:21 he gives the direction to the rich young ruler a different turn by calling the giving away of possessions — and only ὑπάρχοντα [163] — a task of the τέλειος. [164] This makes the requirement more than an individual instance but also restricts it to a higher stage of morality. Relations in the community seem to be reflected here. [165] In 26:11 the formulation in Mk. is tightened, but with no change of sense. In Mt. 11:5 the last part of Jesus' answer to the Baptist's question runs : πτωχοὶ εὐαγγελίζονται. [166] Coming at the end [167] this carries a special emphasis,

---

[159] As the unanimously reported reaction of the rich man shows, we do not have here the broader use of ὅσα ἔχεις πώλησον, Leipoldt Jesus u. d. Armen, 199; Leipoldt Gedanken, 95 f.; cf. also Jeremias, 42.

[160] The context from v. 13 on deals with those who are near the kingdom, cf. v. 23. There is no independent saying about the poor unless one extends the thesis of J. A. Montgomery ("Notes from the Samaritan," JBL, 25 [1906], 53) to Mk. 10:14. But this would mean regarding the lovingly constructed setting (v. 14a, 16a, cf. 22a b) as secondary to v. 23. In any case the complex is directed to those who have this or that which they must renounce for the βασιλεία. It is true that the first part of the passage attacks the rich, but the theme of the poor is not developed. The original used by Mk. might well have taken this form up to v. 22, cf. Bultmann Trad., 20. Percy, 91-93 builds up his understanding on the essential unity of vv. 17-27. Cf. also W. Grundmann, Geschichte Jesu (1956), 173. Was v. 23 added prior to Mk.'s day ? The theme of possessions is both developed in v. 23, 29 and relativised in v. 24, 27, as though the problem were not now so important. In the tradition it would seem that there were two settings, the attack on the rich in v. 23, 25 and the understanding of history along the lines of the Jewish doctrine of merit. v. 21d does not fit the context acc. to E. Hirsch, Frühgeschichte d. Evangeliums, I² (1951), 111 f. and it is not in Ev. Hebr.

[161] Mk. 14 contains a Judaising (A. Daube, op. cit. [→ n. 139], 312-324; also "Evangelisten u. Rabbinen," ZNW, 48 [1957], 122) and theologising interpretation and is not original acc. to Loh. Mk., ad loc., though cf. Hirsch, op. cit. (→ n. 160), 151. Perhaps it is based on the understanding of καλὸν ἔργον in v. 6 as a commandment of love, though this interpretation does not meet the situation if v. 7 has a specific sense (for another view cf. J. Jeremias, "Die Salbungsgeschichte Mk. 14:3-9," ZNW, 35 [1936], 75-82). v. 8 is thus to be ascribed to the community, v. 9 to the Evangelist.

[162] In the Western text μαθηταί has been added from Mt. (cf. A. Merx, Die vier kanon. Ev., II, 2 : "Die Ev. d. Mk. u. Lk." [1905], 148). On the other hand, it is hard to see why Mt. himself should have added it ; perhaps this more precise definition was taken by him from the tradition attested also in Jn.

[163] In interpretation cf. K. Bornhäuser, Der Christ u. seine Habe nach d. NT (1936), 30-43.

[164] Cf. Mt. 10:9; Lk. 9:3; 10:4 in contrast to Mk. 6:8.

[165] Cf. Hirsch, op. cit. (→ n. 160), II, 311. Later cf. Act. Joh. Fr., 5 (ed. T. v. Zahn [1880], 235 f.).

[166] Not in sys k Clem or the Tatian reading in Ephr. Evangelii concordantis expositio (ed. P. B. Aucher-G. Mösinger [1876], 100), cf. F. C. Burkitt, Evangelion da-Mepharreshe, II (1904), 238.

[167] νεκροὶ ἐγείρονται is put at the end in syc Θφ, also the quotation in Adamantius, Dialogus de recta in Deum fide, GCS, 4, p. 52, 7. We have here a secondary arrangement acc. to the greatness of the miracles.

→ II, 718, 2 ff. The saying stands in correlation to the work of the disciples sent out in c. 10. This is true of all the members. [168] Hence the answer of Jesus is a summary of events already known to the Baptist. [169] The individual signs of salvation stand under the givenness of the εὐαγγέλιον (9:35) or culminate in proclamation (11:5). [170] In 5:3 Mt. puts the beatitude concerning the πτωχοὶ τῷ πνεύματι (→ 401, 5 ff.) at the beginning of the Sermon on the Mount. Even in the Greek translation [171] this stands in close relation to 5:5, and this is even clearer if one translates back into Aramaic — עניים or עניי־רוח in both cases. [172] It is possible that one and the same beatitude underlies both verses and that this blessing of the poor [173] contains the two different additions which together display the full breadth of anawim piety from purely earthly hopes [174] to pure eschatology. [175] At any rate the emphasis is shifted from the material sphere [176] to the spiritual and hence the religious sphere, → 401, 11 ff. [177] The beatitude is the first and programmatic πτωχοί saying of the Evangelist; it shows that he is not greatly interested in the problems of actual want.

---

[168] Acc. to Mt., who interweaves materials from different sources, εὐαγγελίζονται corresponds to the preaching of ἤγγικεν ἡ βασιλεία τῶν οὐρανῶν (10:7), which is expressly called εὐαγγέλιον in 9:35. The πτωχοί are the πρόβατα τὰ ἀπολωλότα οἴκου Ἰσραήλ in 10:6. 10:8 sums up the other members. This is more natural than the commonly adduced (cf. K. L. Schmidt, Rahmen d. Gesch. Jesu [1919], 117) ref. to the miracles of Jesus, in depicting which Mt. mentions all of them up to raising the dead (9:18 ff.). (Addressing the poor, however, is not specifically in view.) Lk. substitutes 7:21 for this ref.

[169] Does Mt. assume that the disciples are already back and John has heard of their work?

[170] This is not, however, to be taken merely abstractly. The link with the other members shows that amelioration of the material lot of the πτωχοί is also envisaged; cf. Schl. Mt., ad loc.

[171] If one transl. "poor in knowledge" (H. Huber, Die Bergpredigt [1932], 22, 27), in knowledge of the Torah (עניי בדעת), then this beatitude and the second are not conditions of sharing salvation like the others (cf. H. H. Wendt, Die Lehre Jesu, I [1886], 55) and it is hard to find any uniform architectonic principle. It is impossible to think, however, that the sequence is broken at the very outset. In the mind of the redactor, which is identical with that of the Evangelist, τῷ πνεύματι thus denotes a quality, the self-awareness (this element, though ruled out by Percy, 42, is demanded by the context) of poverty of spirit and perhaps of longing for the πνεῦμα ἅγιον. Behind this, of course, is the simpler sense of "voluntary poverty." K. Schubert, "Bergpredigt u. Texte von En Fešha," Theol. Quart., 135 (1955), 327; also Die Gemeinde vom Toten Meer (1958), 119 f., argues for this, but without being able to distinguish the various strata.

[172] The practical need for differentiation demands עניים for עניי הרוח (v. 3), so F. Delitzsch, ספרי הברית החדשה (1880). Zn. Mt.[4], 180 f. adopts the same transl. back, since he regards the beatitudes as a unity from the very first. Yet one cannot rule out a connection with Lk. (so J. Rezevskis, "Die Makarismen bei Mt. u. Lk., ihr Verhältnis zueinander u. ihr historischer Hintergrund," Studia Theologica, I [1935], 164). Cf. Wellh. Mt., ad loc.

[173] On the common one-membered macarism with no word of comfort → IV, 363 f.

[174] As against Heinrici, Beiträge z. Gesch. u. Erklärung d. NT, III (1905), 25 f.

[175] It is thus erroneous to regard τῷ πνεύματι as an addition (so K. A. Credner, Beiträge z. Einleitung in d. bibl. Schriften, I (1832), 307 etc.). Mt. has simply put into Gk. the content of עניים (perhaps already with an explanatory רוח). On the other hand it is going too far to regard Mt.'s emphasis as self evident, Kittel Probleme, 54; P. Gächter, Review of J. Dupont, "Les Béatitudes," in Ztschr. f. kath. Theol., 77 (1955), 343.

[176] The interpretation of F. Nägelsbach, Der Schlüssel zum Verständnis d. Bergpredigt (1916), 16 and Loh. Mt., ad loc.: "voluntary poor," is rendered improbable by the Qumran par. → 897, 3 f.

[177] Cf. Zn. Mt.[4], 183.

3. Luke. No less than 5 of the 9 complexes in which Lk. uses πτωχός are peculiar to the author. [178] This is the more noteworthy in that he does not have one of the πτωχός passages common to Mt. and Mk. Lk. 21:3 is par. to Mk. 12:43, [179] but elsewhere shifts of accent may be perceived.

In Lk. 18:22 the command to sell possessions and give to the poor — understood as a general command if the ἔτι, which corrects Mt. 19:20, is to be taken strictly [180] — is given emphasis by a πάντα (cf. τὰ ἴδια in v. 28) [181] and a whole class (v. 18 ἄρχων) is accused of not fulfilling it, → 328, 30 ff. The τυφλοὶ ... πτωχοὶ εὐαγγελίζονται of 7:22 is not anchored in the context and is thus part of the story, v. 21. On the other hand, the blessing of the poor (6:20) which opens the Sermon on the Plain, like the Sermon on the Mount, is the only one of the four beatitudes in Luke which fits the situation as he has depicted it. [182, 183]

The eight-membered passage is not uniform, nor does the form of the first beatitude go back to Lk., so that only in a modified way can one use it as evidence of his social attitude. This does not settle the question of the priority of Mt. over Lk. [184] or *vice versa*. [185] The possibility has been discussed that they go back to two independent sources, and hypothetically these might derive from the primitive community, since the formula עֲנִיֵּי־רוּחַ = πτωχοὶ τῷ πνεύματι, whose absence was often regarded as the decisive argument for the greater fidelity of the Lucan form, [186] is now attested,

---

[178] An interesting but unproved thesis is that Lk. 21:1-4 has its origin in the material peculiar to Lk. and has then been interpolated into Mk. (Schmidt, *op. cit.* [→ n. 168], 277 following the example of J. Weiss, *Das älteste Ev.* [1903], 273).

[179] πενιχρά is put for πτωχή in v. 2 simply on stylistic grounds, unless Lk. is using a version close to D.

[180] So correctly W. M. L. de Wette, *Erklärung der Ev. d. Lk. u. Mk.*² (1839), 111.

[181] Materially there is no distinction from Mk./Mt. (→ n. 159) but the content has been given a new profile in the tradition used by Lk. In the context of the Gospel the requiremen⁺ has greater emphasis than in Mk. and Mt., cf. 11:41; 12:33. The Jewish argument, on the basis of Mt. 19:21, that the Chr. law is harder to keep than the Jewish, which demands only a tithe (J. Truki, חיזוק אמונה ed. D. Deutsch [1873], I, 19, 49 f.; II, 19), would thus seem to have, historically, more support in the Lucan text.

[182] The sequence 6:19 to 6:20 corresponds to that of 7:21 to 7:22. Jesus speaks only as He also acts. There are slight variations in 7:21 and 7:22.

[183] The orientation of 2-4 is eschatological; hence they do not fit the context of the demonstration of the power of Jesus.

[184] So first C. G. Wilke, *Der Urevangelist* (1838), 685; then, e.g., D. F. Strauss, *Das Leben Jesu*, I⁴ (1840), 603; A. Hilgenfeld, *Die Ev. nach ihrer Entwicklung u. gesch. Bdtg.* (1854), 173; B. Weiss, *Das Mt.-Ev. und seine Lk.-Par.* (1876), 134 f.; C. Weizsäcker, *Untersuchungen über d. evang. Gesch.*² (1901), 218; P. Feine, "Über d. gegenseitige Verhältnis d. Texte d. Bergpredigt bei Mt. u. bei Lk.," *Jbch. pr. Th.*, 11 (1885), 14; H. Leisegang, *Pneuma Hagion* (1922), 134-139; H. Huber, *op. cit.* (→ n. 171), 16 f., 18; T. Soiron, *Die Bergpredigt Jesu* (1941), 142 f.

[185] So, e.g., A. Ritschl, *Das Ev. Marcions* (1846), 237-241; H. J. Holtzmann, *Die synpt. Ev.* (1863), 76 f.; Wendt, *op. cit.* (→ n. 171), I, 54-56; H. v. Soden, *Die wichtigsten Fragen f. ein Leben Jesu*² (1907), 46; A. v. Harnack, *Sprüche u. Reden Jesu* (1907), 38; J. Weiss, "Die drei älteren Ev.," *Schr. NT*², I, 259; Wellh. Mt., *ad loc.*; K. Köhler, "Die ursprüngliche Form d. Seligpreisungen," *ThStKr*, 91 (1918), 170; W. Bussmann, *Synopt. Studien*, II (1929), 43; Bultmann Trad., 114; F. Hauck, → IV, 368, 20 f.; Hirsch, *op. cit.* (→ n. 160), 83; M. Dibelius, *Die Bergpredigt, Botschaft u. Geschichte*, I (1953), 120; G. D. Kilpatrick, *The Origins of the Gospel acc. to St. Matthew* (1946), 15; Percy, 41-45; Braun, *op. cit.* (→ n. 109), II, 73.

[186] Heinrici, *op. cit.* (→ n. 174), II, 28 f. and esp. Kittel Probleme, 53 f. C. Rabin, "The Dead Sea Scrolls and the History of the OT Text," *JThSt*, 6 (1955), 178 discusses whether Is. 66:2 (עָנִי וּנְכֵה־רוּחַ), which is behind Mt. 5:3, is a mixture of two readings.

→ 897, 3 ff. [187] Hence one has to take into account the circulation of various blessings of the poor — four have come down to us, Mt. 5:3, 5; Lk. 6:20; Pol., 2, 3 — though, as only three contain πτωχοί in Gk., one cannot be sure whether the original is always עני and not אביון. [188] Another open question is whether they all carry an additional clause. The early popularity of πτωχοί beatitudes makes it difficult to find the basis of these formulae in a saying of Jesus. [189] Most of them, and their incompleteness as shown by the need for additions, are quite understandable if they are seen as part of the broad stream of later Jewish sayings about the poor. [190]

Lk. introduces the theme of rich and poor in the infancy stories. For him the preaching of Jesus opens, not with the blessing of the poor, but with the themati-cally used quotation from Is. 61:1, which makes εὐαγγελίσασθαι πτωχοῖς the specific task of Jesus 4:18a, and which thus sums up in advance the individual forms of its execution (18b). In the address on feasts the host is commanded to invite πτωχοί, ἀνάπηροι, χωλοί, τυφλοί, 14:13. In the parable of the great supper which follows almost [191] the same words are used in 14:21 to denote the groups of substitute guests. There is a formal distinction here from 7:22 and a material distinction from 4:18 in that there is no political element. [192] Luke took both passages to refer to the eschatological banquet, v. 15. Both human transgression and the divine purpose mean that only the marginal phenomena of human society — πτωχοί is the key term for these and it refers primarily to the Gentile world according to 4:24, 27 — will partake of this feast. The thought is radicalised in 16:19-31, where torment is to be the lot of the rich man as such, whereas felicity will be the lot of Lazarus as πτωχός, v. 20, 22. There is no indication either of special guilt on the part of Dives or special merit on that of Lazarus. [193] In this story, which is intrinsically pre-NT, the poor man is as such the heir of an extra-ordinary visitation of divine grace. The point of the story, then, is not the failure of the rich man in relation to the poor [194] but the ineluctable [195] alienation of his life, and that of all rich men, from the sphere of God. The hope of the poor man — a metaphorical interpretation is not suggested — is in the world to come, though not entirely. In Lk. 19:1 ff. a πλούσιος and ἁμαρτωλός gives half of his wealth

---

[187] It was certainly not coined by Mt. with ref. to "a rich city community," Kilpatrick, op. cit., 125.

[188] The transl. back of Mt. 5:3 is more or less guaranteed by 1 QM 14:7 (→ 897, 3 f.), but אביון might lie behind Lk. 6:20.

[189] This way of relating the βασιλεία to a specific circle, as in 5:3b, does not correspond to the preaching of Jesus. On the question of authenticity cf. E. Käsemann, "Das Problem d. hist. Jesus," ZThK, 51 (1954), 144; Braun, op. cit., (→ n. 109), II, 55; E. Fuchs, "Jesu Selbstzeugnis nach Mt. 5," ZThK, 51 (1954), 28; also Bultmann Trad., 114.

[190] But this rules out a primitive harmonising of variants, cf. Weiss, op. cit. (→ n. 184), 134. Bultmann Trad., 133 also considers the possibility of a Jewish origin.

[191] In 14:21 the two members are joined by a καί. Hirsch, op. cit. (→ n. 160), II, 137 thinks this is original and sees the editorial hand of the Evangelist in the enumeration without καί. sypbo have only poor, impotent, blind in 14:21, but follow the versio graeca in v. 13.

[192] This is brought in by sys : despised. As compared with Mt. it does not occur in the setting either (vv. 15 ff.).

[193] Unless with Hirsch, II, 145, one finds in v. 14 f. the original introduction to the parable. It is hardly possible to follow K. Bornhäuser, Studien z. Sondergut d. Lk. (1934), 138-160.

[194] So Wellh. Lk., 91; Schl. Lk., ad loc.

[195] Hence one cannot see a demand for repentance in what seems to be the "unchristian" v. 31 (Wellh. Lk., 91; Hirsch, II, 226), though cf. Hauck Lk., ad loc. Wellh., loc. cit. : "perhaps absolute." Moses and the prophets are at the disposal of the rich man but cannot change him. Whether or not the poor man follows these authorities is left uncertain.

to the πτωχοί, v. 8. Zacchaeus, quite overcome, makes a vow which far exceeds what is customary in such cases. [196] His action is thus exemplary for Lk. and causes him to appear in a favourable light. [197]

If this implies a conditional recognition of wealth, the other passages are shot through by a patent rejection of the rich which corresponds to the addressing of the message to the poor. Highly polemical are Lk. 6:24 f.; 8:14; 12:15, 21, 33 f.; 14:33; 16:10-12; 18:25, and more moderately so 16:9; 18:24. Perhaps intentionally, the two trends are not fully harmonised by the author. [198] Where he himself speaks, he inclines to the second. If the rich man will part with his wealth, his salvation is possible, 14:33. [199] The parable of the unjust steward is forced into this context, 16:9. [200] The parable of the great supper is also made into an example of hospitality, [201] and the preceding 16:17 serves as a counterpoise to 16:19 ff. [202] The ambivalent story of the anointing is left out. Everything possible must be done for the πτωχός, and yet, though he is the first [203] heir of the βασιλεία, he is not the only one. The word πτωχός is not important in Lk. It does not occur in the redactional material, cf. the absence in Ac. Lk. neither thinks from the standpt. of the poor nor really seeks to address them. He does not address the penniless (cf. 18:18) and yet he believes that wealth more than other ἐπιθυμίαι rivets to this world. [204] The partial or total renunciation he demands is less for the sake of the poor than for that of the salvation of the owner; this trend towards a new Pharisaism may be seen most plainly in 16:9. The *anawim* mood has vanished. Dominant instead is a semi-asceticism in which the *anawim* criticism of riches is adopted but also given a legal setting.

4. John. Jn. tells the story of the anointing in a free form. Only Judas of the disciples grumbles at the waste, and impure motives are ascribed to his concern for the πτωχοί (12:5, 6). In most of the tradition, and the best forms, [205] the answer of Jesus (v. 8) contains the saying about the poor as we have it in Mt. Since it is now only a reply to the objection of the traitor, it loses something of its unconditional character. 13:29 [206] refers to the fact that Judas kept the purse. When Jesus sent him out, this gave rise to the misunderstanding on the part of the disciples, based on the custom of giving to the poor on the night of the Passover, [207] that he had been given the commission τοῖς πτωχοῖς ἵνα τι δῷ.

II. Community Theology, Jesus, John the Baptist.

Ref. to the theme of rich and poor are very common in Lk. 14-18 or 19, a complex which bears at other pts. too the strong impress of a separate tradition. [208] In this Gospel the

---

[196] Str.-B., II, 250.

[197] Vv. 8-9a, 10 are an addition.

[198] Uncritically Koch, 151-169.

[199] Redactional, cf. J. Jeremias, *Die Gleichnisse Jesu*[4] (1956), 94.

[200] Cf. esp. O. Pfleiderer, *Urchr.*[2] (1902), 459; Merx, *op. cit.* (→ n. 162), 329 f.; Jeremias, *op. cit.* (→ n. 199), 35 f.

[201] Cf. Jeremias, *op. cit.*, 34, 82.

[202] In exegesis cf. E. Bammel, "Is Lk. 16:16-18 of Baptist's Provenience?" HThR, 51 (1958), 101-106.

[203] Thus the followers of Jesus are put in groups. The disciple gives up πάντα, 5:11, 28. He who will not do this is not in the inner circle.

[204] Cf. the concentrated reproduction of Mk. 4:19 in Lk. 8:14.

[205] Not in D br sy[s]. P[66], which is fairly close to D, has the words. Bultmann Trad., *ad loc.* regards them as a marginal gloss which later made its way into the text.

[206] On the not very convincing interpolation hypotheses cf. Bau. J., *ad loc.*

[207] Cf. J. Jeremias, *Die Abendmahlsworte Jesu*[2] (1949), 29. One cannot deduce from this that the disciples gave regularly to the poor.

[208] Cf. Hck. Lk., 6 f. ("Leitquelle"); Bultmann Trad., 387.

problem must have played a dominant part. [209] Woe is pronounced on the rich man, who is the representative of Judaism, → 328, 22 ff. The group behind the work, which identified itself with the poor, the lost, the little people, widows, sinners etc., [210] was thus separating itself from the mother community. It is worth noting that when we get down to bed-rock the πτωχός is introduced (16:20) and this term precedes the others, 14:21. One might see in this work the first, the most consistent and in the last resort the only true Ebionite Gospel. A moot pt. is whether Lk. 4:18 belongs to this corpus, for here the author seems to stress more strongly than elsewhere in the Gospel the political relevance of the message to the poor. Mt. 11:5 / Lk. 7:22 finds a model in many Jewish formulae, but the mention of [211] and stress upon the poor as the true possessors of the Gospel is new and represents a deliberate correction of the usual Jewish tradition. In this form it might well derive from disciples of the Baptist who had become Christians. [212] Jesus occasionally uses πτωχός, Lk. 14:13; Mk. 12:43; 10:21. His only distinctive saying about the poor is a refusal to let Himself be tied down to a social principle, Mk. 14:7. He realises that He is one with the tired and lowly, Mt. 11:28. Yet He does not use the catchword which denotes their situation and hopes, [213] obviously because it was too specialised and too distorted by glowing expectations. [214] It is true that in the preaching of John the Baptist, which was rich in social overtones, as the rudimentary tradition still enables us to see, πτωχός has not been preserved. [215] Nevertheless, we do find related terms, and there is much to be said for the conjecture that he addressed the πτωχοί. The influence of a theology of poverty in certain circles connected with John may well be traced to the master himself.

III. Paul.

The Pauline material is notably ambivalent. On the one side Paul uses πτωχός infrequently. When he refers to social tensions in his congregations he uses other words, R. 12:7 f.; 2 C. 8:14; Gl. 6:10. When he extols the removal of distinctions in Christ (Gl. 3:27 f.), or when he demands this (Col. 3:11), he does not mention the difference between rich and poor. [216] On the other hand, the 4-5 passages in which the word occurs are central ones and call for special treatment.

---

[209] 14:21 (πτωχοί); 14:33 (renunciation); 15:7 (opp. δίκαιος); 16:10 (πιστὸς ἐν ἐλαχίστῳ); 16:13 (opp. δουλεύοντες μαμωνᾷ); 16:15 (δικαιοῦντες ἑαυτούς); 16:19 f. (πλούσιος/πτωχός); 17:2 (μικροί); 17:12 (λεπροί); 18:3 (χήρα); 18:11 (τελώνης/δίκαιος).

[210] Meyer Ursprung, I, 223 f. and Hirsch, II, 143 f. have made various points concerning the popular character of the special material in Lk. II.

[211] Chronologically uncertain par. are 5 Esr. 2:18-20 (ed. Fritzsche, op. cit. [→ n. 87]) and Slav. Jos. Bell., 1, 364 ff. (transl. A. Berendts and K. Grass, Acta et Commentationes Univ. Tartuensis [Dorpatensis] [1924 ff.], 24-42).

[212] The question of the Baptist is obviously historical; the core of Jesus' reply is in Lk. 7:23/Mt. 11:6.

[213] He addresses them as the πραεῖς and ταπεινοί; the authenticity of Mt. 11:29b has been contested.

[214] The attempt of W. Sattler, "Die Anawim im Zeitalter Jesu Christi," Festg. f. A. Jülicher (1927), 1-15 and W. Grundmann, Jesus d. Galiläer (1940), passim, to explain the self-consciousness of Jesus in terms of anawim piety can hardly be regarded as successful.

[215] In sy^cs Lk. 1:53 runs: "He hath filled the poor with his goodness and despised the rich, since they are empty," A. Merx, D. vier kanon. Ev., I: "Übers." (1897), 106. Burkitt, op. cit. (→ n. 166), ad loc., thinks the second half is corrupt. The opus imperfectum from Italy also reads: pauperes implevit bonis, MPG, 56 (1859), 809. The spiritualising reading is not secondary but it may be a par. version reaching back to an early period (cf. Rev. 3:17), perhaps pre-Chr.

[216] Cf. R. Eleazar (270 A.D.): Before God they are all equal, women and slaves, poor (עניים) and rich, Ex. r., 21, 4 on 14:15; cf. Rev. 13:16 and S. Dt., 48, 84b.

Gl. 2:10 and R. 15:26 are materially related, for in both the recipients of the collection, which Paul energetically promoted and also mentions elsewhere, [217] are called the πτωχοί or the πτωχοὶ τῶν ἁγίων τῶν ἐν Ἰερουσαλήμ. In connection with the decisions reached at the Apostolic Council [218] Paul refers to a duty which he had accepted : [219] τῶν πτωχῶν ἵνα μνημονεύωμεν, Gl. 2:10 → IV, 682, 39 ff.

This is not to be regarded as a Chr. substitute for the temple tax → 414, 23 ff. It is analogous rather to the voluntary gifts which even non-proselytes made in Jerusalem. There must have been a special reason for Paul's enjoining this as an obligation, and it may be discerned in Ac. 24:16 f. The collection has partly come into the hands of the Jewish leaders and it is designed to alleviate the widespread suffering in the primitive church. The alternation of terms, the lack of ref. to personal initiative in R. 15:27, and the narrow circumscribing of the goal make it likely that Paul was using a concealed form of speech. [220] He could do this the more easily in that ἅγιοι had a general signification [221] which did not entirely rule out non-Chr. Jerusalem. Similarly the ref. in the supporting argument in 15:27b is to the Jerusalem of the OT. [222]

Though ἅγιοι (R. 15:26) is not to be regarded as a term for the community, [223] the same does not apply to πτωχοί, for πτωχοί in the sense of the poor of Jerusalem can hardly explain the continuation of the collection when the emergency had passed. Gl. 2:10 is probably quoting a formula emanating from Jerusalem. [224] R. 15:26, however, deviates from Pauline usage elsewhere. Since πτωχοί can be regarded as a short form of the solemn πτωχοί τῶν ἁγίων τῶν ἐν Ἰερουσαλήμ = אביונים ועניים בירושלים one may assume that the phrase is not Paul's but is a self-designation or title of the primitive community. [225] In Gl. 4:9 Paul speaks of the ἀσθενῆ καὶ πτωχὰ στοιχεῖα to which the Galatians are in danger of falling victim afresh. → στοιχεῖον is undoubtedly a term used in the debate between Jew and Gentile. The same seems to be true of ἀσθενῆ καὶ πτωχά, a phrase which does not directly deny the existence of pagan deities but which describes their power as weak and their operations as beggarly. At the end of Paul's self-defence in 2 C. 6:3 ff. we find seven paradoxes describing the nature of apostolic life and

---

217 1 C. 16:1; 2 C. 8:4; 9:1 f., 12; R. 12:13 (cf. Mi. R., ad loc.); perhaps also 2 C. 12:16-18 (v. Ltzm. K., ad loc.) and 1 C. 16:15.

218 Cf. H. Mosbech, "Apostolos in the NT," Studia Theologica, 2 (1948), 193.

219 Marcion reads : ut meminissent egenorum. This "can only be taken to mean that Barnabas was absent and the duty of caring for the poor devolved on the original apostles as on Paul. Marcion is thus avoiding the appearance of a special injunction laid on Paul alone," A. v. Harnack, Marcion² (1924), 71.

220 So K. Holl, "Der Kirchenbegriff d. Pls. in seinem Verhältnis zu dem d. Urgemeinde," Ges. Aufsätze z. Kirchengesch., II : Der Osten (1928), 59, though he himself does not accept this.

221 The term denotes not only the true Israel but also the cultically pure place (Mt. 4:5; 27:53; 1 Macc. 2:7; 2 Macc. 1:12; 9:14; 3 Macc. 6:5; Tob. 13:10) and cultically pure men (Jos. Bell., 6, 425; bAZ, 50a : Menachem as בנן של קדושים), esp. the inhabitants of Jerusalem (bBer., 9b: Jose bEliaqim [heretic ?] on the קהלא קדישא דבירושלים). On the place in Paul cf. F. Kattenbusch, "Die Vorzugsstellung des Petrus u. d. Charakter der Urgemeinde zu Jerusalem," Festg. f. K. Müller (1922), 345. The thesis of S. Safrai, "The Holy Assembly of Jerusalem," ציון, 22 (1957), 183-193 is hazardous and cannot apply to Paul's day.

222 It should be noted that the στῦλοι rather than the ἅγιοι enjoined Pl. to make the collection.

223 Cf. R. Asting, Heiligkeit im Urchr. (1930), 154, 157.

224 In Gl. 2:7-9b Paul interprets the decree given in 2:9c-10a.

225 Not the only one, as at Qumran.

ministry. The next to the last of these is ὡς πτωχοὶ πολλοὺς δὲ πλουτίζοντες, v. 10 → 329, 22 ff. Though the second half is figurative, [226] one can hardly say the same of the first. If this alone distinguishes the saying from the first antitheses, a greater point of difference is that it is the only one to transcend the sphere of the personal. [227]

1 C. 15:10 vl. says that the grace of God to the apostle was not πτωχή. Textually this "highly distinctive" [228] reading has much in its favour. [229] It also fits in well with the context with its many partly positive and partly negative formulae. [230] In this case Pl. counters the description of his work as πτωχή with the assertion, which is fairly general and which does not have to be a response to κενή, that he has achieved [231] more than they all.

In each instance the use of πτωχός is either based on the literary tradition or suggested by the situation. The apostle never has it in a free formulation of his own thoughts. Hence it is not part of his own true vocabulary. [232] This does not mean that Paul ignored the problem of poverty in his churches. The Corinthian church was composed in the main of the despised, the poor, and the humble, 1 C. 1:27. Things seem to have been much the same in other places too, 2 C. 8:2. Poor relief of various kinds was thus established, [233] though sharing of goods was not attempted. Paul himself, however, does not devote particular attention to these matters, cf. 1 C. 11:21 f. His eschatological orientation is too strong to allow him to seek amelioration of conditions which are in any way tolerable. [234]

For this reason there is also no theological transvaluation of poverty. πτωχός is not used as a title for the Pauline communities nor is πτωχεία a figurative term for the Christian life. In 2 C. 8:9 (→ III, 328, 11 ff.), which might seem to be an exception, the usage is suggested by 2 C. 8:2, which tells how the churches in Macedonia gave liberally in spite of their extreme πτωχεία. Furthermore, the word forms a simple contrast to πλούσιος or πλουτέω (→ 328, 48 ff.) with no content of its own. [235] A theological development of the "poverty of Christ," which adopts pre-Pauline usage, [236] is linked up with → ταπεινοφροσύνη. [237]

---

[226] Cf. Wnd. 2 K., ad loc.; yet not to be taken eschatologically.

[227] In vv. 3-10 Paul has almost word for word a Stoic schema (v. Wnd., ad loc.; Joh. W. 1 K. on 3:21), though this does not seem to view πολλοὺς πλουτίζειν as a possibility of the πτωχός. It would appear that though we have well-known terms (esp. Phil. Omn. Prob. Lib., 77 [ἀχρήματοι ... πλουσιώτατοι], that πτωχός does not occur may be accidental) there is a deviation which shatters the principle of individual perfection in Stoic ethics and christianises the antitheses. This is taken up in Dg., 5, 15.

[228] Joh. W. 1 K., ad loc.

[229] We find πτωχή in the group D* FG deg Ambst (E. Diehl, "Zur Textgesch. d. lat. Pls.," ZNW, 20 [1921], 106, 122), also Ambr, Orosius, Hier, Pelag, got. The par. Phil. 2:16; 1 Th. 3:5; Is. 49:4 pushed πτωχή into the background. As the more difficult reading it is to be preferred.

[230] Cf. E. Bammel, "Herkunft u. Funktion d. Traditionselemente in 1 Kor. 15:1-11," ThZ, 11 (1955), 401-419. Cf. G. Björck, "Nochmals Pls. abortivus," Coni. Neot., 3 (1938), 7 f.

[231] This is how Joh. W. 1 K., ad loc. understands ἐκοπίασα.

[232] It should be noted that πένης occurs only once in 2 C. 9:9 (quoting Ps. 112:9), and ἐνδεής not at all.

[233] R. 12:7 f.; 1 Th. 1:3; the love-feasts may also be regarded as such. For renunciation of property cf. 1 C. 13:3.

[234] Thus he does not go as far as the Jews in helping slaves, v. 1 C. 7:21.

[235] Cf. Ltzm. K., ad loc.

[236] Cf. E. Lohmeyer, "Kyrios Jesus," SAH (1927/28), 32 f.

[237] It should be noted that both go back to the same Hebrew root and concept. Poverty is more commonly used later, e.g., Treasure Cave, 46, 12.

IV. James.

James contains a running attack on the rich both inside and outside the community, [238] → 330, 5 ff. The opposite of the rich man is the → ταπεινός [239] or the πτωχός (2:2), though one cannot assume that the latter is as such characteristic of the environment of author and readers. [240] A reason for the repudiation of the wealthy is that God has chosen the πτωχοὶ τῷ κόσμῳ (2:5), the poor before the world. [241] Since these are also called πλούσιοι ἐν πίστει, a religious quality is obviously attached to πτωχός. The attitude of the community is not at all one of identification with the poor, and the author can only hope that it will incline back to solidarity with the oppressed. Though he himself is a friend of the poor, this fact does not control his thinking. Hence the section cannot be regarded as documenting Christian Ebionitism. [242] It is scarcely Jewish either, [243] and seems to be the product of a later time when the themes of a piety of poverty could be adopted without any direct genealogical connection with this. [244] As far as the situation in James is concerned one can merely say that the rich were beginning to seek entry into the church and the poor had already come to be esteemed less highly (ἠτιμάσατε τὸν πτωχόν, [245] 2:6) → III, 948, 1 ff. [246]

V. Revelation.

In Rev. 13:16, which describes mankind according to classes, πτωχός and πλούσιος are used literally. On the other hand in 2:9 the spiritual wealth of the church of Smyrna is contrasted with its material poverty (πτωχεία) and its persecution. In 3:17 both concepts are used figuratively: the supposed wealth of Laodicaea [247] is unmasked as poverty. [248]

The formula ταλαίπωρος καὶ ἐλεεινὸς καὶ πτωχὸς καὶ τυφλὸς καὶ γυμνός is not attested as such. [249] It would appear that the first two adj. are in antithesis to v. 17a and the last three are added by association to lead on to the injunction of v. 18. Materially v. 17b, 18 are no longer in strict relation to the church but apply to the whole city with its characteristic activities (banking, medical school, manufacturing). [250]

---

[238] Cf. Dib. Jk., ad loc.

[239] 1:9; 4:6 (10); cf. πραΰτης 1:21; 3:13.

[240] On the fixed rhetorical style of 2:1 ff. cf. Dib. Jk., ad loc. Reicke, 338, 342-344 boldly tries to relate the passage to successful ambitus before the cultic community, though in this case one would have thought that δίκαιος would be a better antonym, cf. 5:6.

[241] On this transl. cf. Hck. Jk., ad loc.; Dib. Jk., ad loc.; Schl. Jk., ad loc., though H. J. Schoeps, Theol. u. Gesch. des Judenchristentums (1949), 350, n. 1, takes a different tack. 2:5 seems to be composed of two familiar formulae: πτωχὸς πλούσιος ἐν πίστει and πτωχὸς τῷ κόσμῳ κληρονόμος τῆς βασιλείας. There seems to be no evidence of dependence on 1 C. 1:27.

[242] So Wnd. Jk.¹, 34; ², 36 (more cautiously).

[243] Percy, 70-73.

[244] Hence one may speak only in a limited sense of the "revival of the mood of poverty" (Dib. Jk., 43). For further points v. Schoeps, op. cit. (→ n. 241), 347.

[245] Used collectively; it is noteworthy that one finds here neither theological embellishment (v. 5) nor rhetorical example.

[246] The duty of benevolence is strictly enjoined in 2:16.

[247] πλούσιός εἰμι καὶ πεπλούτηκα καὶ οὐδὲν χρείαν ἔχω = have no need of repentance, so Bornhäuser, op. cit. (→ n. 163), 28. πέπτωχα for πεπλούτηκα in 2329 is an error due to misunderstanding of the tense form.

[248] The par. being γυμνός is shameful in 3:18; hence the state of the πτωχός is no ideal.

[249] But cf. Tob. 7:6 S ταλαίπωρος, τυφλόω, ἐλεημοσύνη.

[250] So correctly R. H. Charles, The Rev. of St. John, ICC (1920), I, 93.

VI. The Primitive Community.

When Ac. tells of the sharing of goods in the primitive community the key words are κοινός, κοινωνία, ἰδιώτης (= עַם הָאָרֶץ?) and ἐνδεής, but not πτωχός. But since these are not part of the original tradition [251] it is better to start with R. 15:26. If πτωχός here is a title (→ 909, 17 ff.) and not just a factual ref. to the results of mismanagement it expresses an awareness that all members of the community are comprehended by the term. In keeping is the fact that very early on the church in Jerusalem developed a structure which did away with social distinctions. The common meals, the responsibility of the δώδεκα for διακονεῖν (→ II, 84, 40 ff.), [252] the benefits of this ministry to the members and the individual instances of surrender of property [253] all give evidence of a community which went far beyond the synagogue in its care for the poor. How far relations in the band of disciples were simply transferred to the wider circle, and how far the influence of the Baptist might have played a part, it is no longer possible to say for certain. It seems, however, that the seven appointed at Qumran [254] played quite a role in the development of the social order, and that under this influence there took place a considerable modification of the order and of poor relief (also practised outside the community?), whose operations were soon afterwards affected by the outbreak of persecution.

In spite of the enigmatic nature of the sources it is evident that later Jewish enthusiasm for the poor, which had its basis in the OT and which manifested itself spasmodically rather than continuously, found its way into the primitive Church and there exerted a general influence at first and later had a more enduring effect in specific circles. This phenomenon is recorded for the most part in the non-Palestinian epistles and the expression which it has also found in Palestinian sources hardly does justice to the historical events.

E. The Post-Apostolic Age.

I. Later Jewish Christianity.

In the Jewish Chr. sphere אֶבְיוֹן is used just as centrally as πτωχός is avoided over a broad area. The name אֶבְיוֹנִים is only insecurely attested in Hbr. lit. [255] The Gk. form Ἐβιωναῖοι, Ἐβιωνῖται or Ebionaei is first found in Iren. Haer., I, 26, 2; III, 11, 17; 21:1; IV, 33, 4; V, 1, 3. The caricaturing explanation of the term is not attested prior to Orig.: οἱ πτωχοὶ Ἐβιωναῖοι τῆς πτωχείας διανοίᾳ ἐπώνυμοι, Princ., IV, 3, 8 (GCS, 22, 334); Comm. in Mt. 16:12 (40, 512); Comm. in Gn. 3:5 (29, 44). It is common later. [256] Since Orig. also gives the true derivation in Cels., II, 1 (2, 126) one may

---

[251] So J. Jeremias, "Untersuchungen zum Quellenproblem d. Ag.," ZNW, 36 (1937), 207 and cf. Wdt. Ag., ad loc. The author of Ac. has put the details handed on to him in the framework of a concept of righteous order (v. F. Hauck, Die Stellung d. Urchr. z. Arbeit u. Geld [1921], 99 and → III, 796, 10 f.) and esp. the idea of a restoration of original equality (the expression πάντα κοινά does not occur in the OT but is a catchword in Gk. proverbs and philosophical circles, v. Hauck, loc. cit.). He has thus made actual relations into a normative principle.
[252] Cf. E. Lohmeyer, "Das Abendmahl in d. Urgemeinde," JBL, 56 (1937), 232 f. Reicke, 25-28 sees a combination of liturgy and poor relief.
[253] These are reliable as compared with the summaries acc. to Jeremias, op. cit. (→ n. 251), 206 f.
[254] Cf. O. Cullmann, "The Significance of the Qumran Texts for Research into the Beginnings of Christianity," JBL, 74 (1955), 220-224.
[255] MN, "Über zwei im Talmud vorkommende Chr. Sekten," Der Orient, Lit.-Blatt, 6 (1845), 1-5 wrongly conjectured אֶבְיוֹנִי for אֲבִידָן, in bShab., 116a. One is rather to suppose that the אֶבְיוֹנֵי located in Babylon (bBQ, 117a) is a place of Ebionite worship, cf. S. Krauss, Synagogale Altertümer (1922), 32. Cf. also Schoeps, op. cit. (→ n. 241), 21 f.
[256] Epiph. Haer., 30, 17, 1 f. (GCS, 25, 355); Hier. In Is. 1:3 (MPL, 24 [1845], 27); 66:20 (672 B); Ps.-Ign. Philad., 6 (ed. W. Cureton [1849], 95), cf. Eus. Hist. Eccl., X, 27, 6 where the name is also associated with the Christology of the group.

assume that the frivolous interpretation is designed to replace an older and honourable understanding. It was once a title which the community used for itself [257] and its reinterpretation seems to have been undertaken in the Gk. world and then to have caused the avoidance of the transl. πτωχοί among Jewish Chr. themselves → 913, 10 ff. If, then, אביונים pts. to an earlier stage of Jewish Christianity, there is a fairly obvious link with the primitive community called πτωχοί. [258] The possibility of Essene influences early in the 2nd century [259] certainly cannot be ruled out. Perhaps these led to the preferring of this term above others [260] and made it the characteristic term for a greater fellowship.

Symmachus [261] almost always has πτωχός in transl. of עָנִי (exceptions are Is. 41:17; Jer. 22:16), while אֶבְיוֹן is consistently rendered πένης. [262] At Qoh. 12:5 he has ἐπίπονος for אֲבִיּוֹנָה. [263] There is method here as compared with the LXX, the aim being not to equate either אֶבְיוֹן and πτωχός or עָנִי and πένης. Since there is no discernible interest in the latter [264] and ἐπίπονος is for Symmachos a title, the reason is to be sought in the first alternative. [265] Since the group called itself אֶבְיוֹנִים Symmachus wanted to dissociate the word πτωχός from it. It seems that he was not just carrying through consistently a previous mode of transl. but undertaking an innovation. The discredited word πτωχός is passed on to Jews who identified themselves with the עֲנִיִּים.

Things are much the same in the Ps.-Clementine corpus. In the oldest part adopted by the basic author [266] the blessing of the πτωχοί [267] is still mentioned and defended, [268] Ps.-Clem. Recg., 1, 61, 2. But already in Recg., 2, 28, 3 Jesus is called τοὺς πένητας μακαρίζων and in Hom., 15, 10, 4 it is explained that the beatitude refers neither to the πτωχοί nor the πένητες [269] as such but refers to the πιστοὶ πένητες. [270] Apart

---

257 So correctly W. Brandt, *Elchasai* (1912), 56; the non-use of אביון in Aram. rules out its rise as a term of derision; cf. E. Schwartz, "Unzeitgemässe Beobachtungen z. d. Clementinen," ZNW, 31 (1932), 190. Harnack Miss., 412 f. also regards Chr. derivation as more probable, though cf. Schoeps, *op. cit.*, 402f.

258 Cf. Epiph. Haer., 30, 17, 2 (GCS, 25, 356): αὐτοὶ δὲ δῆθεν σεμνύνονται ἑαυτοὺς φάσκοντες πτωχοὺς διὰ τὸ ... ἐν χρόνοις τῶν ἀποστόλων πωλεῖν τὰ αὐτῶν ὑπάρχοντα. The Church identified it with the heresies combatted by Paul, so Tert. Praescr. Haer., 4, 3 (CSEL, 70, 5).

259 First suggested by Credner, *op. cit.* (→ n. 175), 366, then adopted by A. Ritschl, "Über die Essener," *Theol. Jbch.*, 14 (1855), 315-356, also *Die Entstehung der altkatholischen Kirche* (1857), 210 and more recently O. Cullmann, "Die neuentdeckten Qumran-Texte u. d. Judenchristentum d. Pseudoklementinen," *Bultmann-Festschr. Beih.* ZNW, 21 (1954), 50 f.

260 So Credner, *op. cit.*, 366.

261 On his relation to Jewish Christianity cf. E. Schwartz, *op. cit.* (→ n. 257), 193; Schoeps, *op. cit.*, 33-37; also *Aus frühchr. Zeit* (1950), 82-88. But R. Bultmann is sceptical, Review of H. J. Schoeps, *Theol. u. Gesch. d. Judenchristentums*, in *Gnomon*, 26 (1954), 180.

262 Schoeps, *op. cit.*, 352 f.

263 Possibly the self-designation of a Jewish Chr. fellowship, v. Schoeps, *op. cit.*, 355-360. Prv. 15:15 (πᾶσαι αἱ ἡμέραι τοῦ πτωχοῦ [= עָנִי = τῶν κακῶν ο'] πονηραί [= προσδέχονται κακά ο']), which gives a negative twist to πτωχός, is not to be construed thus.

264 עָנִי was never a self-designation of the community but it was a title in contemporary Judaism.

265 Schoeps, 250-260, takes a different view but illogically regards ἐπίπονος as a title for the community close to Symmachus.

266 Cf. G. Strecker, "Das Judenchristentum d. Pseudoklem.," TU, 70 (1958), 41; H. J. Schoeps, "Die Pseudoklem. u. d. Urchr.," *Zschr. f. Religions- u. Geistesgesch.*, 10 (1958), 4-7.

267 πτωχός is probably original, though one cannot rule out πένης.

268 Not without reinterpretation of the prophetic witness, to which ref. is also made.

269 This does not prevent a life as πένης being regarded as proper and exemplary for the Christian in Ps.-Clem. Hom., 2, 20, 12; 12, 6, 7.

270 It is worth noting that in both ref. ἐπιθυμία is used in elucidation; the aim of the

from this πτωχός does not occur in the group. This is more than an abandonment of the word; there is a certain aloofness from the ideal of external poverty. [271]

In the scanty remnants of Jewish Chr. Gospels note should be taken of the command to the rich young ruler with its mention of the sons of Abraham who are dying of hunger. [272] The man with the withered hand asks for healing *ne turpiter mendicem cibos,* Hier. in Mt. 12:13 (MPL, 26 [1884], 80 D). The first beatitude is given in a form close to that in Lk. [273] and a special Woe against the rich who do not remember the ἐνδεεῖς is quoted in Ps.-Clem. Recg., 2, 29, 2.

II. The Post-Apostolic Fathers.

Early exhortation first commends benevolence in a form found in Dispersion Judaism, namely, that of sayings about the two ways. In contrast are the οὐκ ἐλεοῦντες πτωχόν, ... ἀποστρεφόμενοι τὸν ἐνδεόμενον, ... πενήτων ἄνομοι κριταί, Did., 5, 2 = Barn., 20, 2. If the catechism presupposes social distinction, nevertheless in the ideal of the πραεῖς and the demand to observe it with the ταπεινοὶ καὶ δίκαιοι (= עֲנָוִים וְצַדִּיקִים, Did., 3, 9; cf. Barn., 19, 6) one may see the influence of enthusiasm for the poor, which has, of course, become a matter of ethical disposition (cf. Barn., 14, 9 : εὐαγγελίσασθαι ταπεινοῖς) and which thus regards the πτωχοί, understood as the socially poor, as objects of the desire to help. A special position is ascribed to the poor only in so far as their prayer is thought to be esp. efficacious, Herm. s., 2, 5-8; 1 Cl., 15, 6 = ψ 11:6. [274] Only Marcion, who finds the *proprietas* of Jesus' preaching in the Beatitudes, emphasises the relation between the Gospel and the poor. [275] There is a direct equation of Christians and *pauperes* only in Minucius Felix, Octavius, 36; [276] this may well have its source, however, in pagan polemics. [277]

Benevolence is exercised through almsgiving on the one side (2 Cl., 16, 4; Pol., 10, 2; Did., 15, 4) and the *ministerium pauperum* [278] on the other. The latter finds a place in the church orders (Const. Ap., VII, 29, 2; Herm. s., 5, 3, 7) and also in apologetic depictions of the life of the churches. [279] The Jewish tradition of works of love is obviously adopted here, cf. Aristid. Apol., 14, 3 and 15, 7 f. In Jewish Chr. circles it is not very clearly associated with a reinterpretation of the OT tithe, Const. Ap., VII, 29, 2; Did., 13, 4.

---

beatitude is to free from this, Ps.-Clem. Recg., 2, 28, 3; it does not apply to the πτωχοί, since ἐπιθυμεῖν need not be suppressed in them, Hom., 15, 10, 4. A narrowing down is thus discernible. The ref. come from circles which are not plainly identifiable as Jewish Chr., cf. Strecker, *op. cit.,* 215. Schoeps, 52, thinks they were.

[271] This includes sharing with the needy even to the pt. of one's own πενία (Ps.-Clem. Hom., 12, 32, 3) and indeed an abhorrence of possessions (τὰ κτήματα ἁμαρτήματα, 15, 9, 3).

[272] Orig. Comm. in Ev. Mt. 15:14 (text in E. Klostermann and E. Benz, "Zur Überlieferung d. Matthäuserklärung d. Orig.," TU, 47, 2 [1931], 91, 33 ff.); cf. A. Schmidtke, "Neue Untersuchungen zu d. judenchr. Ev.," TU, 37, 1 (1911), 290.

[273] μακαρίζων τοὺς πτωχούς, Ps.-Clem. Recg., 1, 61, 2; on the underlying special tradition *v.* H. Waitz, "Eine Par. zu den Seligpreisungen aus einem ausserkanon. Ev.," ZNW, 4 (1903), 335-340; τοὺς πένητας μακαρίζων, Ps.-Clem. Recg., 2, 28, 3.

[274] This is the presupposition of the theory of recompense which Herm. develops here and whose starting-pt. is soon (cf. 2 Cl., 16, 4) lost sight of.

[275] Harnack, *Marcion,* 127.

[276] Ed. J. Martin (1930).

[277] Jews as beggars : Juv. Sat., 3, 16; 6, 543; Schol. on Juv., 4, 116 (ed. P. Wessner [1931], 64). Since there is nothing Jewish in the counterpolemic, it is more likely that a Jewish source has been copied which transfers the reproach to Christians.

[278] A term in Act. Pt., 17 for the ministry to *viduae, orfani, pauperi* (cf. Pol., 6, 1).

[279] Aristid. Apol., 15, 8 f.: Burial for the πένης (on the uncertainty of the Gk. transl. *v.* J. Geffcken, *Zwei gr. Apologeten* [1907], 82, n. 1). Aid (even to the pt. of fasting) for δοῦλος and πένης, freeing of prisoners. Cf. Just. Apol., I, 67; Tert. Apol., 39, 6.

Ascetic [280] tendencies in the early Church led to opposition to property, though this did promote interest in or help for the poor. [281] It is true that the abstemious as such are called the πενίην ποθέοντες (Sib., 8, 281), and in Chr. Syr. עני becomes a word for the ascetic, but in general the term is not used in description of the ideal. [282] The blessing of the poor is not preserved in the ascetic beatitudes of Act. Pl. et Thecl. Above all, the social problem is recast : want of desire is true wealth, [283] and true poverty is ignorance concerning oneself. [284] The logic of this leads to the esteeming of gifts to martyrs more highly than gifts to the poor, Const. Ap., VI, 1, 4 App.

In the ordinary theology of the Church wealth is not an evil, only attachment to it, cf. Mk. 10:29 vl. and Iren. Haer., IV, 30. Similarly, poverty is not glorified ; it, too, can stand in the way of knowledge of God, Cl. Al. Paed., III, 35, 1; Strom., IV, 21, 1. The more earnestly, then, almsgiving is commended, yet less for the sake of the poor [285] than for the salvation of the giver. [286] This view gradually gained ground and found pregnant expression in the testamentary counsels of the later fathers [287] to the effect that the soul, i.e., the poor, be remembered either before or equally with the body, i.e., progeny. [288] This principle was most influential and the related adoption of Gk. schemata almost completely obscured the legacy of the OT and later Jewish view of the poor.

Bammel

---

† πυγμή, † πυκτεύω

1. Like the adverbial πύξ ("with the fist") and πυκτής ("boxer"), πυγμή comes from the stem *peug-*, also found in the Lat. *pugneus, pugna, pugnare, pungere* etc. [1] It is attested from Hom. In the LXX it is used for אֶגְרֹף in Ex. 21:18; [2] Is. 58:4. Its meaning from early times is "a fight with fists," so in πυγμῇ νικᾶν, e.g., Hom. Il., 23, 669, and πυγμὴν ἀσκεῖν, e.g., Plat. Leg., VII, 795b. [3] We also find the more gen. sense "fight," "affray," in Jos. Ant., 14, 210; cf. ἐν μέσῳ τῆς πυγμῆς, Barn., 12, 2 (with ref. to the battle between Israel and Amalek in Ex. 17:8 ff.). [4]

---

[280] Things are much the same in Gnostic circles. On the aversion of the Copt. Gospel of Thomas to wealth cf. J. Leipoldt, "Ein neues Ev. ? Das kopt. Thomasev. übers. u. erklärt," ThLZ, 83 (1958), 496.

[281] This also applies to the Sentences of Sextus, which are not really favourable to the poor but influenced rather by the Stoic ideal of ἐγκράτεια, ed. A. Elter (1892), 18, 49, 82b, 137, 267, 294.

[282] An exception is Test. D. 5:13 (Chr. interpolation).

[283] πλοῦτος ἄριστος ἡ τῶν ἐπιθυμιῶν πενία Cl. Al. (K. Holl, "Fragm. vornicänischer Kirchenväter," TU, 20, 2 [1899], 86, No. 189).

[284] H. G. E. White, *The Sayings of Jesus* (1920), 31 (attempted reconstruction).

[285] Only an isolated optimism could expect the abolition of poverty thus, Doctrina Petri, Holl, *op. cit.* (→ n. 283), 234, No. 503 καὶ οὐδεὶς ἔσται πένης.

[286] In contrast there is an unusual externalising in Act. Pt., 30, which regards the moral worthiness of the giver as irrelevant.

[287] Here πένης, δεόμενος, etc. seem to be preferred to πτωχός. πτωχός has on the whole a slight edge in the 2nd cent.

[288] For material cf. E. F. Bruck, *Kirchenväter u. soziales Erbrecht* (1956), 30-41, 72-75; also *Totenteil u. Seelgerät* (1926), 315 f.

πυγμή κτλ. Note : This art. was prepared for press by S. Schulz.

[1] Cf. Walde-Pok., II, 828 (*peug-*); Schwyzer, I, 620.

[2] Par. to stone, elsewhere mattock, pickaxe acc. to Köhler-Baumg., *s.v.*

[3] Cf. Pass., Pape, Liddell-Scott, Preisigke Wört.

[4] It is to be noted that the LXX has ἐπολέμει, not a form of πυκτεύω, which it never uses.

In Mk. 7:3 : ἐὰν μὴ πυγμῇ νίψωνται τὰς χεῖρας, πυγμῇ is textually uncertain [5] and exegetically difficult. [6] The meaning seems to be the intrinsically established one of "fist." [7] If πυγμή is to be retained on critical grounds, the following mode of washing the hands is in view : one clenched fist (πυγμή) rubbing in the hollow hand, or up to the elbow or joint of the hand, [8] or "with a handful," i.e., of water, [9] unless with poetic licence the reference is simply to dry rubbing with the hand. [10] The original Aram. might well have been : אן לא נטלין ידיהין בטפח. טפח can mean both "hand's breadth" and also "jug" (cf. bYoma, 30a). Thus the true sense of the Aram. was probably : "Unless they wash their hands in a (special) jug (= טפיח)." [11]

In the Apol. the only occurrences are in Tat. Or. Graec., 4, 1 and 26, 3 : ὥσπερ (ὡς) ἐν πυγμῇ συγκρούειν, apart from Just. Dial., 15, 3 quoting Is. 58:4.

2. Of the many derivates of πυγμή in the realm of ancient boxing the only one found in the NT is πυκτεύω, which is common from Xenoph., Plat., and which means "to practise the art of the πύκτης," "to box," "to fight as a boxer," [12] cf. τίς ἐς σὸν κρᾶτ᾽ ἐπύκτευσεν, Eur. Cyc., 229; πυκτεύειν καὶ παγκρατιάζειν, Plat. Gorg., 456d.

Since this sport, this εἶδος γυμνασίου καὶ παλαίστρας, [13] was a favourite one, it is not surprising that πυκτεύειν can be used fig. as in 1 C. 9:26 : οὕτως πυκτεύω ὡς οὐκ ἀέρα δέρων, "so I box (and) not as one who beats the air." [14] From an early period exegetes have been divided as to whether πυκτεύειν as an εἰς ἀέρα δέρειν implies the presence of an opponent or not. [15] There are in fact two ways in which the metaphor may be understood. a. The fighter whom Paul does not wish to emulate does not hit his opponent because he is a poor boxer who misses and beats the air ; he has no success. [16] b. The boxer whom Paul does not wish to emulate beats the air because he does not want a match and has no

[5] A. E. J. Rawlinson, St. Mark (1925) on 7:3 : ". . . it seems likely that the text is corrupt." The vl. πυκνά in Cod א is presupposed in Vg (crebro) and other ancient versions, while others leave out the debatable term (Pr.-Bauer[5], s.v. and the textual apparatus in C. Tischendorf, NT Graece, ed. octava critica maior, I [1869], ad loc.). But the vl., which means "frequently" (cf. Lk. 5:33 : νηστεύουσιν πυκνά, and on this F. Schulthess, "Zur Sprache d. Ev.," ZNW, 21 [1922], 232; critically Str.-B., II, 13 f.), is obviously an easier reading and is thus no help. Conjectures have been attempted ; for a critical assessment of these cf. Loh. Mk., ad loc.
[6] Wellh. Mk., ad loc.: "What πυγμή is supposed to mean it is impossible to say."
[7] The ancient lexicographers give the following def.: ἐὰν συγκλείσῃς τὴν χεῖρα, τὸ μὲν ἔξωθεν καλεῖται πυγμή, Poll. Onom., II, 147; πάλη, σύγκλεισις δακτύλων, γρόνθος, Phot. Lex., s.v.
[8] So J. Lightfoot, Horae hebraicae et talmudicae, I (1675), 618.
[9] So Kl. Mk.; Hck. Mk. ("the πυγμή of Mk., which is not found in the Rabb., does not mean 'with the fist' — this was forbidden, Str.-B., I, 698 f. — but 'with a handful' "); J. Schniewind, Das Ev. nach Mk., NT Deutsch, 1[7] (1956), ad loc.
[10] So Schulthess, op. cit., 233.
[11] Cf. P. R. Weis, "A Note on ΠΥΓΜΗΙ," NTSt, 3 (1957), 233-236.
[12] Pass., Pape, s.v.
[13] Suid., s.v.; earlier Phot. Lex., s.v.
[14] So Ltzm. 1 K., ad loc. and others, cf. Luther ; O. Holtzmann NT; H. D. Wendland, Die Briefe an d. Korinther, NT Deutsch, 7 (1954); J. Moffatt, The First Ep. of Paul to the Cor., MNTC (1954), ad loc.: "I do not plant my blows upon the empty air — no."
[15] Twice we have ὡς οὐ . . . rather than οὐχ ὡς . . . and the exact sense is to be gleaned from the par. οὐκ ἀδήλως. Thus "I run as one who is not without a sure goal (i.e., who has a precise goal), I fight as one who does not swing aimlessly in the air" (but I train systematically). [Debrunner.] On the history of exegesis Heinr. 1 K., ad loc.
[16] Cf. Joh. W. 1 K., ad loc.: "A boxer who instead of hitting his opponent δέρει (flays) the air is unskilful, careless, undisciplined ; this corresponds to ἀδήλως τρέχειν."

opponent ; he is not a serious fighter ; he prefers σκιαμαχία, shadow-boxing, either at home or in the gymnasium, not real boxing in the ring ; perhaps he even fights his own shadow in mere pretence. [17] Lack of seriousness may still be true even when there is an opponent if the two boxers have not yet begun to fight seriously but are only engaged in preliminary sparring. [18] In contrast the apostle does not want to be a boxer of this kind. He is not content with mere swings, mere lunging in the air. He has no time for an initial lack of seriousness. The question whether success or seriousness is primary for Paul cannot be decided with any certainty. A point in favour of the actual presence of an opponent, which would favour the first explanation, is the fact that in v. 27, in a distinctive development of the image, the target which is not to be missed is mentioned ; it is his own body. Vivid though Paul's use of the metaphor is, however, one cannot be certain as to one or the other meaning, since there are parallels for each of the two possibilities in antiquity. [19]

Photius has two fine formal and material par. In his Ep., II, 100 (MPG, 102 [1860], 916B) he says : οὔτε κατὰ φίλων, ἀλλ' οὐδὲ κατ' ἐχθρῶν ὡπλισάμεθα βέλη καὶ τόξα καὶ παρατάξεις· καὶ πολεμίους καὶ ἀσπίδας ὀνειρώττοντες, ὥσπερ οἱ πρὸς ἀέρα πυκτεύοντες (qui cum aëre depugnant)· ἀλλ' ὑπὲρ φίλων ἐπαρρησιασάμεθα. Ibid., 39 (853 G): καὶ ὑπὲρ μὲν σαυτοῦ εἰς ἀέρα δέρων ἐπύκτευσας (aërem verberans concertas), καθ' ἡμῶν δὲ ὀξὺν μὲν καὶ σφοδρὸν τὸν δρόμον, ἀλλ' ἐπισφαλῆ καὶ ἀναίτιον διηγώνισαι. Phot. is probably directly dependent on Pauline usage, for he quotes 1 C. 9:26 f. literally in Epist., II, 99 (912 A). [20]

K. L. Schmidt

---

† πύθων

1. πύθων is attested in two senses in Gk. (1) It is the name of the snake which guards the Delphic oracle, and which Apollo is supposed to have slain, → V, 569, n. 47. Delphi seems to have been originally an earth oracle. [1] But only Hyginus says that the snake πύθων itself imparted the oracle : Python Terrae filius draco ingens ; hic ante

---

[17] Cf. Bchm. 1 K., ad loc.: ... a boxer ... who in no clear relation to an opponent plants his blows in the air (not misses his opponent). This is however, the linguistic meaning of the term. Cf. Eustath. Thessal. Comm. in Il., 7, 39 (II, 139, 36 f.): ὁ μόνος ὡς ἐν σκιαμα- χίᾳ μαχόμενος καὶ ὅ φασιν ἀέρα δαίρων."

[18] Thus rather like the formalities at a duel. Cf. Bengel, ad loc.: Pugilatum cursui prae ceteris certandi generibus adjicit Paulus — ὡς οὐκ ἀέρα δέρων, non quasi aërem verberans. In sciamachia, quae certamini serio praemitteretur, solebant aërem verberare.

[19] Cf. the par. collected by Wettstein, ad loc.; in addition to the Eustathius passages (→ n. 17) adduced by Bchm. 1 K., ad loc., these include further examples from this comm. on Homer and other instances.

[20] Thes. Steph., s.v. uses figurate of the first two, but not of the Pauline quotation.

π ύ θ ω ν. J. Tambornino, "De antiquorum daemonismo," RVV, VII, 3 (1909), 59 f.; A. Wikenhauser, "Die Ag. u. ihr Geschichtswert," NT Abh., 8, 3/5 (1921), 401-407; H. Leisegang, Pneuma hagion (1922), 36 f.; T. Hopfner, Griech.-ägypt. Offenbarungszauber (1924), § 276, 364; E. Fascher, Προφήτης (1927), 166 f.; F. Cumont, L'Égypte des astrologues (1937), 161, n. 4; J. H. Waszink, Tertulliani De Anima (1947), 363, 582 f.; P. Amandry, "La mantique apollinienne à Delphes," Bibliothèque des écoles françaises d'Athènes et de Rome, 170 (1950), 64 f. Comm. on Ac. 16:16.

[1] H. W. Parke and D. E. W. Wormell, The Delphic Oracle, I (1956), 3-16.

Apollinem ex oraculo in monte Parnasso responsa dare solitus erat,[2] though this is also presupposed in Schol. on Pind.[3] These passages agree with the rest of the tradition that from time immemorial Python had been dead and Apollo had given the oracle.[4] Hence Ac. 16:16 cannot be explained along these lines.

(2) From the beginning of the Roman imperial period πύθων was also used for a ventriloquist. The earliest instance is Erotianus grammaticus (age of Nero), who says in elucidation of Hippocr. Epid., V, 63, 7: ἐγγαστρίμυθοι· οὓς πύθωνάς τινες καλοῦσιν· ἔστι δὲ τῶν ἅπαξ εἰρημένων,[5] also Plut. Def. Orac., 9 (II, 414e): εὔηθες γάρ ἐστι καὶ παιδικὸν κομιδῇ τὸ οἴεσθαι τὸν θεὸν αὐτὸν ὥσπερ (εἰς) τοὺς ἐγγαστριμύθους, Εὐρυκλέας πάλαι νυνὶ δὲ Πύθωνας προσαγορευομένους, ἐνδυόμενον εἰς τὰ σώματα τῶν προφητῶν ὑποφθέγγεσθαι, τοῖς ἐκείνων στόμασι καὶ φωναῖς χρώμενον ὀργάνοις. In both these passages the ἐγγαστρίμυθος = πύθων is the ventriloquist himself, though for many, as Plut.'s refutation shows, a god speaks through him. The ventriloquist is again directly equated with the πύθων by Augustine, who groups *pythones* with *sortilegi* and *mathematici,*[6] cf. also Schol. on Plat. Soph.,[7] Hesych.,[8] and Suid.[9] In the last two we also find the later view that πύθων is a spirit of soothsaying. In the first cent. of the Empire, however, the πύθων is the ventriloquist, not a spirit speaking through him. Ventriloquism has to be learned, but is in fact mastered and produced at will only by a few.[10] The first ventriloquist mentioned in Gk. antiquity is a Eurycles in the days of Plato and Aristoph. Plato says of some philosophers whose ideas are contradicted by their acts that they always have with them what is said by others as an enemy and opponent, and that they thus bear it around as one who speaks secretly within them, like the strange Eurycles, Soph., 252c. This comparison presupposes that Plato and his readers thought Eurycles did not control his strange utterances. In this regard Aristoph. says that at first he published his pieces under another name and that in so doing he imitated the prophecy and purpose of Eurycles, entering into the bellies of others and pouring forth much that was comical.[11] This again presupposes that someone else had entered into Eurycles and was speaking from him, and also that this was prophecy, the same view as that of Plut. in the passages already mentioned → lines 8 ff. The great regard in which Eurycles was had may be seen from the fact that the Athenians put up a monument to him.[12] That ventriloquists were viewed as soothsayers may be seen also in Cl. Al., who sets alongside the various oracles ἀλευρομάντεις, κριθομάν-

---

[2] Hyginus Fabulae, 140 (ed. H. J. Rose [1933]).

[3] Schol. on Pind. Pyth. (ed. A. B. Drachmann, II [1910], 2): εἶτα ἔρχεται (sc. Apollo) ἐπὶ τὸ μαντεῖον, ἐν ᾧ πρώτη Νὺξ ἐχρησμῴδευσεν, εἶτα Θέμις. Πύθωνος δὲ τότε κυριεύσαντος τοῦ προφητικοῦ τρίποδος, ἐν ᾧ πρῶτος Διόνυσος ἐθεμίστευσε.

[4] Only Lucian De astrologia, 23 says that the Python-snake still imparted the oracle: δράκων ὑπὸ τῷ τρίποδι φθέγγεται.

[5] Erotianus grammaticus Fr., 21 (ed. E. Nachmann [1918], 105, 19 f.).

[6] Enarratio in Ps. 91:10 (MPL, 37 [1841], 1178); cf. Eus. Praep. Ev., V, 25, 4.

[7] Schol. on Plat. Soph., 252c (ed. G.C. Greene [1938], 44): τοῦτον καὶ ἐγγαστρίμαντιν νῦν τινες Πύθωνά φασι, Σοφοκλῆς δὲ στερνόμαντιν.

[8] Hesych., *s.v.* Πύθων: ὁ ἐγγαστρίμυθος ἢ ἐγγαστρίμαντις, *s.v.* πύθων: δαιμόνιον μαντικόν, *s.v.* ἐγγαστρίμυθος: τοῦτον ἡμεῖς Πύθωνα νῦν καλοῦμεν.

[9] Suid., *s.v.* Πύθωνος: δαιμονίου μαντικοῦ, *s.v.* ἐγγαστρίμυθος: ἐγγαστρίμαντις· ὃν νῦν τινες Πύθωνα, cf. Cyril of Alexandria comm. in Isaiam prophetam, IV, 2 (MPG, 70 [1864], 944 C): ἐγγαστριμύθους φησὶ τοὺς ψευδομάντεις ἤτοι πυθωνικούς.

[10] R. Luchsinger and G. E. Arnold, *Lehrbuch d. Stimm- u. Sprachheilkunde* (1949), 73: "Ventriloquism is a peculiar projection of the voice which ... even in the immediate vicinity of the artist can create an illusion as to the place from which one or many voices are supposed to come."

[11] Vesp., 1019 f.: μιμησάμενος τὴν Εὐρυκλέους μαντείαν καὶ διάνοιαν εἰς ἀλλοτρίας γαστέρας ἐνδὺς κωμῳδικὰ πολλὰ χέασθαι.

[12] Athen., I, 35 (19e). Since θαυματοποιοί are mentioned in the context, the Eurycles here is the ventriloquist rather than the statesman of this name.

τεις καὶ τοὺς εἰσέτι παρὰ τοῖς πολλοῖς τετιμημένους ἐγγαστριμύθους. [13] This connection was based not merely on the fact that the ventriloquist spoke with a second voice but also on the fact that this second voice had an unusual sound, as noted already by Hippocr. [14] How the equation ἐγγαστρίμυθος = πύθων arose can only be conjectured. Probably different forces were at work. Like a ventriloquist the Pythia in Delphi spoke in strange sounds which needed interpretation. As the god of the oracle Apollo is called "the pythian," and though the Python-snake had been supplanted by him ages before the snake was still the mantic animal, → V, 569, 22 ff. Ref. may also be made to the etymologically concocted idea that the Pythia was inspired by the odours of corruption from the dead body of the Python. [15] In the 1st cent. of imperial Rome there is no evidence for the view that πύθων was a spirit of soothsaying which inspired soothsayers.

2. The LXX used ἐγγαστρίμυθος for the Heb. אוֹב either alone or in various combinations. [16] The meaning of the Heb. word is uncertain. [17] The Gk. takes it to mean ventriloquist. Only once in 1 Βασ. 28:8 : μάντευσαι δή μοι ἐν τῷ ἐγγαστριμύθῳ, is there possible ref. to an evil spirit, though this is suggested only by the connection with the HT.

3. The fact that that there is a conjuring up of the dead in the story of the witch of Endor led Joseph. to use ἐγγαστρίμυθοι gen. for those who practise soothsaying by conjuration of the dead. [18] Along these lines a common Tannaitic tradition explains the bibl. בַּעַל אוֹב by פִּיתוֹם = πύθων, elucidates it by הַמְדַבֵּר מִשֶּׁחְיוֹ or בֵּין פְּרָקִים, and treats it in context as דּוֹרֵשׁ הַמֵּתִים. [19] Vg renders אוֹב by magus, [20] python, or pythonicus spiritus. [21] One can at least ask whether the בַּדִּין of the Targum is not also the same as πύθων. [22] When the fathers expound the story of the witch of Endor a primary

---

[13] Prot., II, 11, 1 f. Philo Som., I, 220 mentions as Αἰγύπτου πάντες σοφισταί : οἰωνομάντεις, ἐγγαστρίμυθοι, τερατοσκόποι, δεινοὶ παλεῦσαι καὶ κατεπᾶσαι καὶ γοητεῦσαι.

[14] Hippocr. Epid., V, 63, 12 (ed. É. Littré, V [1846], 242, 12): a sick woman ἐκ τοῦ στήθεος ὑπεψόφεεν, ὥσπερ αἱ ἐγγαστρίμυθοι λεγόμεναι.

[15] Amandry, 65 pts. out that the altering of the name of ἐγγαστρίμυθοι coincides with a broad extension of the tradition that the odour of the decomposed body of the snake inspires the Pythia. In antiquity Python was often derived from the verb πύθω, ibid., n. 3. This idea occurs in Chrys. In epist. I ad Corinth. homilia, 29, 1 (MPG, 61 [1862], 242) in the rather different form of an evil spirit from the abyss entering the womb of the Pythia.

[16] אוֹב = ἐγγαστρίμυθος, Lv. 19:31; 20:6; 1 Βασ. 28:3, 9; 1 Ch. 10:13; 2 Ch. 33:6; שָׁאַל אוֹב = ἐγγαστρίμυθος, Dt. 18:11; אֵשֶׁת בַּעֲלַת־אוֹב = γυνὴ ἐγγαστρίμυθος, 1 Βασ. 28:7; אוֹב מֵאֶרֶץ = οἱ φωνοῦντες ἐκ τῆς γῆς, Is. 29:4 (Σ: ἐγγαστρίμυθος); אוֹב = θελητής (erroneous derivation from the Heb. אָבָה), 4 Βασ. 21:6; 23:24 (Σ + ᾽Α : ἐγγαστρίμυθος); אִישׁ אוֹ־אִשָּׁה כִּי־יִהְיֶה בָהֶם אוֹב אוֹ יִדְּעֹנִי = ἀνὴρ ἢ γυνή, ὃς ἂν γένηται αὐτῶν ἐγγαστρίμυθος ἢ ἐπαοιδός, Lv. 20:27. On 1 Βασ. 28:8 → line 15 f. οἱ ἀπὸ (ἐκ) τῆς γῆς φωνοῦντες = אוֹבוֹת are distinguished from ἐγγαστρίμυθοι (יִדְּעֹנִים) in Is. 8:19; 19:3. In Dt. 18:11 necromancy is separated from the שָׁאַל אוֹב = ἐγγαστρίμυθος. ἐγγαστρίμυθος = בַּדִּים in Is. 44:25; no HT 2 Ch. 35:19a.

[17] Mostly shade of the dead → 364, 30 ff. H. Schmid, "אוֹב," Festschr. K. Marti (1925), 253-261 regards אוֹב as an instrument of magic, the whirring piece of wood.

[18] Ant., 6, 330 : τὸ γὰρ τῶν ἐγγαστριμύθων γένος ἀνάγον τὰς τῶν νεκρῶν ψυχὰς δι᾽ αὐτῶν προλέγει τοῖς δεομένοις τὰ ἀποβησόμενα.

[19] Sanh., 7, 2: בַּעַל אוֹב זֶה פִּיתוֹם הַמְדַבֵּר מִשֶּׁחְיוֹ; bSanh., 65b (הַמְדַבֵּר בֵּין פְּרָקִים); T. Sanh., 10, 6; S. Dt. § 172 on 18:11; S. Lv. on 20:27; Str.-B., II, 743.

[20] Lv. 19:31; 20:6; 1 S. 28:3, 9; 2 Ch. 33:6.

[21] Dt. 18:11; 1 S. 28:7 f.; 1 Ch. 10:13 (pythonissa); Is. 8:19; 19:3; 29:4; 2 K. 21:6; 23:24. pythonicus spiritus : Lv. 20:27.

[22] Str.-B., II, 743.

concern is whether the ἐγγαστρίμυθος could really conjure up the shade of Samuel and hence utter true prophecies. [23] The link between ventriloquism and conjuring up the dead is at first based on the LXX alone and only later did it become more general. [24] In Sib., 3, 226 ἐγγαστρίμυθοι are mentioned with many other forms of soothsaying and magic among the various pagan peoples, cf. also Test. Jud. 23:1; there is no discernible relation to necromancy.

4. In Ac. 16:16 the reading πνεῦμα πύθωνος [25] is an obvious simplification and is materially impossible, for no matter how the word be construed there is no instance of spirits going forth from πύθων. It is hard to decide whether to take πύθωνα as apposition : [26] a spirit, namely a πύθων, or named Python, or to translate the whole expression by "a Pythonian spirit." The peculiar feature of the phrase is that the girl is said to have had a spirit called πύθων. This idea occurs elsewhere only in the fathers (→ lines 27 ff.) and perhaps (→ 919, 13 ff.) the LXX, who equate πύθων or ἐγγαστρίμυθος with the spirit which speaks from the ventriloquist. [27] This equation of demon and demonic is also found in the Gospels at Mk. 5:7 ff. and the Lucan par. It perhaps led the author of Acts and later the fathers to transfer the expression πύθων from the ventriloquist to the spirit who spoke out of her. At any rate Ac. 16:16 tells us that the girl was a soothsayer-ventriloquist and that she thus stood in relation to the demonic.

When Ac. 16:17 uses κράζειν for her speech, this does not fit in too well with ventriloquism, though there are examples of loud ventriloquists. [28] A more serious difficulty is that ventriloquism is possible at will, so that all ventriloquists who claimed to be prophets were frauds and there could be no question of exorcism as in Ac. 16:16. We must assume, however, that for this girl, as for those mentioned by Origen (→ line 30 f.), the art of ventriloquism was inseparably connected with a (supposed or authentic) gift of soothsaying.

5. In the fathers πύθων does not denote the ventriloquist but the spirit which speaks from him. Ps.-Clem. Hom., 9, 16, 3 : οὐ γὰρ εἴ τι μαντεύεται, θεός ἐστιν· ὅτι καὶ πύθωνες μαντεύονται, ἀλλ᾽ ὑφ᾽ ἡμῶν ὡς δαίμονες ὁρκιζόμενοι φυγαδεύονται. Orig. Princ., III, 3, 5 : alii a prima aetate daemonem, quem Pythonem nominant, id est ventriloquum, passi sunt ; the same view seems to lie behind Hier. in Is. 8:20 (MPL, 24 [1845] 123 A): quaerite ventriloquos, quos pythonas intellegimus ... et qui de terra loquuntur, quod in evocatione animarum magi se facere pollicentur, for the first part of the sentence says that "we" have unmasked ventriloquists as Python-demons, cf. also → n. 8, 9.

Foerster

---

[23] Examples in Wikenhauser, 405 f. and Waszink, 582 f. Just. Dial., 105, 4 : ὅτι μένουσιν αἱ ψυχαὶ ἀπέδειξα ὑμῖν ἐκ τοῦ καὶ τὴν Σαμουὴλ ψυχὴν κληθῆναι ὑπὸ τῆς ἐγγαστριμύθου. But cf. Act. Pionii, 14, 2 ff. (R. Knopf and G. Krüger, *Ausgewählte Märtyrerakten*[3] [1929]).

[24] Suid., *s.v.* ἐγγαστρίμυθος : αὗται (sc. γυναῖκες ἐγγαστρίμυθοι) τὰς τῶν τεθνηκότων ψυχὰς ἐξεκαλοῦντο. μιᾷ δὲ αὐτῶν ἐχρήσατο Σαούλ.

[25] P[45] E and *koine* witnesses.

[26] πύθωνα as apposition Pr. Ag., *ad loc.*; F. F. Bruce, *The Acts of the Apostles* (1952), *ad loc.*; Haench. Ag., *ad loc.* "Spirit named Python," Zn. Ag. Pr.-Bauer[5], *s.v.* refers to the ἄνθρωπος βασιλεύς of the Gospels. Bl.-Debr.[9] § 242 : "Pythonian spirit like ἄνδρες Ἀθηναῖοι = Athenian men : proper names used as adj.

[27] Act. Pionii, 14, 7: πῶς ἠδύνατο ἡ ἄδικος ἐγγαστρίμυθος, ἡ δαίμων, ἀναγαγεῖν τὴν τοῦ ἁγίου προφήτου ψυχήν ... ;

[28] T. S. Flatau and H. Gutzmann, *Die Bauchrednerkunst* (1894), 65.

πυκτεύω, → 916, 13 ff.

| † πύλη, † πυλῶν | → θύρα, III, 173 ff.; κλείς, → III, 744 ff.

Contents : A. πύλη and πυλών in the Literal Sense. B. The Narrow Gate of Mt. 7:13 f. C. The Gates of Hades in Mt. 16:18.

A. πύλη and πυλών in the Literal Sense.

Lit. ἡ πύλη in the NT[1] means (a) "city gate," Hb. 13:12 (Jerusalem); Lk. 7:12 (Nain); Ac. 9:24 (Damascus); 16:13 (Philippi). Mention of a gate shows that the town or place concerned — even little Nain[2] — was protected by fortifications. (b) Temple-gate, Ac. 3:10 : ἡ ὡραία πύλη (probably the Nicanor gate between the Israelites' court and the women's court).[3] (c) Prison-gate, Ac. 12:10 : ἡ πύλη ἡ σιδηρᾶ. On the prison-gate which opens of itself in a miracle of liberation → III, 175 f.

In distinction from ἡ πύλη, ὁ πυλών denotes the gate-way (a) of a city wall (the Jerusalem which comes down from heaven has twelve gates, Rev. 21:12 f., 15, 21, 25; 22:14); (b) of a temple (cf. Ac. 14:13); c. of a house, or complex of houses, Mt. 26:71; Lk. 16:20; Ac. 10:17; 12:13 f.; in the latter case the πυλών is separated from the house or houses by a court.

What is said about πύλη in Hb. is important from the standpoint of biblical theology. Hb. 13:12 says with reference to Jesus : ἵνα ἁγιάσῃ διὰ τοῦ ἰδίου αἵματος τὸν λαόν, ἔξω τῆς πύλης ἔπαθεν. In the Gospels, too, we learn that in accordance with Roman[4] and oriental[5] custom the crucifixion of Jesus took place outside the wall of Jerusalem.[6] This fact is used by Hb. to illustrate the

---

π ύ λ η, π υ λ ώ ν. Pr.-Bauer⁵, s.v. On C : W. Köhler, "Die Schlüssel des Petrus," ARW, 8 (1905), 214-243, esp. 222-224; A. Dell, "Matthäus 16:17-19," ZNW, 15 (1914), 1-49, esp. 27-33; O. Immisch, "Matthäus 16:18," ZNW, 17 (1916), 18-26; A. v. Harnack, "Der Spruch über Petrus als den Felsen d. Kirche," SAB, 32 (1918), 637-654; S. Euringer, "Der locus classicus des Primates (Mt. 16:18) u. d. Diatessarontext d. hl. Ephräm," Beiträge z. Gesch. d. chr. Altertums u. d. byzantinischen Lit., Festg. A. Ehrhard, ed. A. M. Koeniger (1922), 141-179; Str.-B., I, 736; IV, 1087, 1089; Joach. Jeremias, Golgotha (1926), 34-88, esp. 68-77; O. Weinreich, "Gebet u. Wunder," Tübinger Beiträge z. Altertumswissenschaft, 5 (1929), 316-320, 424, 436-445; Bultmann Trad., 148 f.; J. Kroll, "Gott u. Hölle. Der Mythos vom Descensuskampfe," Studien d. Bibliothek Warburg, 20 (1932); A. Oepke, "Der Herrnspruch über d. Kirche Mt. 16:17-19 in d. neuesten Forschung," Studia Theol., 2 (1948), 110-165; J. Ludwig, "Die Primatworte Mt. 16:18, 19 in d. altkirchlichen Exegese," NT Abh., 19, 4 (1952), 44, 66, 70; O. Betz, "Felsenmann u. Felsengemeinde," ZNW, 48 (1957), 49-77; comm. on Mt. 16:18. On πύλη as a term for Christ in early Chr. lit. → III, 179, n. 80.
[1] As regards pre-NT use πύλη is etym. obscure (Boisacq, 826); it is always plur. in Hom. and mostly so later (for "the two leaves of a door," Schwyzer, II, 44; also → III, 174, n. 8). [A. Debrunner.]
[2] On Nain cf. G. Dalman, Orte u. Wege Jesu³, BFTh, II, 1 (1924), 206 f.; C. Kopp, Die heiligen Stätten d. Ev. (1959), 295.
[3] E. Stauffer, "Das Tor des Nikanor," ZNW, 44 (1952-53), 64, n. 72; acc. to Stauffer this gate is to the east of the court of women rather than the west (as in → III, 173, n. 5).
[4] E.g., Plaut. Miles gloriosus, 359 f.: crucifixion extra portam.
[5] Lv. 24:14, 23; Nu. 15:35 f.; Dt. 17:5; Jos. Ant., 4, 264; Bell., 4, 360; Lk. 4:29; Ac. 7:58; bSanh., 42b-43a; S. Lv., 24, 14; S. Dt., 149 on 17:5; 242 on 22:24. This custom still prevails, cf. the executions outside the Jaffa gate at the end of the 19th cent. and those outside the Jaffa and Damascus gates during the first world war.
[6] Jn. 19:20 cf. Mk. 15:20; Mt. 27:32; Jn. 19:17, cf. Jeremias, 1-33. Cf. also Mt. 21:39 par. Lk. 20:15, though here the christological interpretation brings about a reversal of the older order (slaying — casting out of the vineyard, Mk. 12:8). That is to say, in Mk. 12:8 the son is slain in the vineyard and then his body is thrown over the wall in contempt, whereas in

complete separation of Christianity from Judaism. No matter how θυσιαστήριον be construed in v. 10 (→ III, 185, 22 ff.) the v. emphasises this separation. The priests, who represent the Jewish community, have no part in the altar of the Christian community. In v. 11 f. proof is adduced from Scripture in favour of this separation : Lv. 16:27 ordained that on the day of atonement the carcases of the bull and goat of the sin-offering, whose blood had been used for sprinkling in the Holy of Holies, should be burnt outside the camp ; this ordinance was fulfilled, says Hb. 13:12, when Jesus as the sin-offering of the new covenant died ἔξω τῆς πύλης, i.e., outside the holy city and the sacred precincts. The community is thus summoned to take upon itself the shame of Jesus by exodus from the camp, i.e., Judaism, v. 13. The execution of Jesus outside the gate of Jerusalem is interpreted, then, in two ways. First, it is part of His saving work. For according to the Halakah the Palestinian counterpart of the "outside the camp" of wilderness days (v. 11, 13) was the area outside the walls of Jerusalem, [7] and the two sacrificial beasts of the day of atonement were burnt outside the gates of Jerusalem, bYoma, 68a b. Hence the execution of Jesus outside the gates represents the true offering of the day of atonement. Secondly, the execution outside the gate was part of the shame. Jesus is classified with the blasphemer (Lv. 24:14) and the sabbath-breaker (Nu. 15:35) who were to be stoned outside the camp. The fact that He had to die as One rejected by His people gave added bitterness to His death. Readiness to bear this shame is part of following Jesus.

B. The Narrow Gate of Mt. 7:13 f.

As regards the text of Mt. 7:13 f., it is customary in some circles to cut out ἡ πύλη in 7:13b with א* a b c h k m Cl Al Orig Eus Cyprian [8] on the ground that it is an interpolation from v. 14. In 113 544 h k m Cl Al Orig Eus Cyprian, however, ἡ πύλη is also left out in v. 14, so that we should either omit it from both verses, [9] which is not to be commended in view of the weak support, or keep it in both verses, [10] which is backed by the antithetical parallelism in v. 13 bc and v. 14.

As regards the metaphor in v. 13 f., the twofold sequence πύλη-ὁδός (πλατεῖα ἡ πύλη καὶ εὐρύχωρος ἡ ὁδός ... στενὴ ἡ πύλη καὶ τεθλιμμένη ἡ ὁδός) should not lead us to seek the gates at the beginning of the ways [11, 12] or to regard πύλη (= תֶּרְעָא) as a passage on the way, [13] since the parallel in Lk. 13:23 f. makes

---

Mt. and Lk. the son is cast out first and then done to death. The son was taken to be the Messiah and so the story was adapted to the passion, cf. J. Jeremias, *Die Gleichnisse Jesu*[5] (1958), 61 f.

[7] S. Nu., 1 on 5:3; T. Kelim Baba Qamma, 1, 12; bZeb., 116b; Nu. r., 7 on 5:3. Tradition arranged the desert camp in three concentric circles : the Levites had their tents around the tabernacle (God's camp), and the people had theirs around the Levites. The three degrees of holiness within the walls of Jerusalem corresponded to these circles, cf. G. Dalman, "Der zweite Tempel z. Jerusalem," PJB, 5 (1909), 33; also *op. cit.*, (→ n. 2), 305 f.

[8] Wellh. Mt., *ad loc.*; Kl. Mt., *ad loc.*; P. Joüon, "L'Év. de Notre-Seigneur Jésus-Christ," Verbum Salutis, V (1930), 42; A. Huck-H. Lietzmann, *Synopse d. drei ersten Ev.*[9] (1936), *ad loc.*; Nestle[23] has ἡ πύλη in square brackets.

[9] So, e.g., Bultmann Trad., 81.

[10] So, e.g., Schl. Mt., *ad loc.*; → V, 71, 12 ff. and n. 100.

[11] Cf. the gate in 1 Cl., 48, 2-4 which has no connection with Mt. 7:13 f.: Those who walk in holiness and righteousness will go through the gate of righteousness, Ps. 118:19.

[12] K. Bornhäuser, "Die Bergpredigt," BFTh, II, 7 (1923), 177, 180; Kl. Mt. and Schl. Mt., *ad loc.*

[13] Joüon, 42 f. The double εἰσέρχεσθαι in v. 13 is against this.

it plain that the image of the gates has an eschatological character. The narrow and broad gates are the gates to eternal life and eternal perdition, and the sequence πύλη-ὁδός is to be regarded as a popular hysteron-proteron. [14] In fact, comparison of entrance into the kingdom of God with a city gate, the gate of the eschatological Jerusalem, is quite common in eschatological usage. [15] The idea that hell also has an entrance is parallel. [16]

The narrowness of the way and gate to life as compared with the broadness of the way and gate to perdition expresses the fact that eternal life is difficult to obtain. The way thereto demands sacrifice and self-denial. [17] The number of those attaining to life is thus small, cf. Lk. 13:23 f. [18] By the twofold metaphor of the gate, then, Jesus makes it plain to His disciples that they must have the courage to break away from the masses and from the nation which rejects Jesus, and to accept the way of suffering with the little flock, if they are to reach the gate of the future city of God. [19]

The metaphor is different in the par. Lk. 13:23 f. Instead of the πύλη to the future city of God we find the θύρα to the banqueting hall where the eschatological banquet is held, → III, 178, 7 ff. Another pt. in Lk. is that there are not two gates to which two ways lead but a single door which is now open but will soon (v. 25) be closed. Like the metaphor, the emphasis is also different in Lk. If Mt. 7:13 f. demands the courage to choose the way of the small company which is going to the city of God, Lk. 13:23 f. demands that every effort be made to find entry into the banqueting hall while there is still time. In Lk. the saying reflects more strongly the critical situation of the imminent coming of God's rule with its threatening "too late." The eschatological note is less clear in Mt., where the saying is perhaps developed pedagogically with the help of the schema of the two ways, → V, 43 ff., 53 ff., 57 ff., 61 ff. [20]

---

[14] 4 Esr. 7:6-8 puts the way before the gate : "(Place yourself before) a city ... Access to it is narrow and skirts an abyss with fire threatening on the right and water on the left. There is only one small path between the fire and the water, and this path is so narrow that it can hold the track of only one man." The hysteron-proteron of Mt. 7:13 f. might be due to the combination of two synon. metaphors (way and gate) into a double metaphor, → lines 23 ff.; → V, 71, 22 ff.

[15] 4 Esr. 7:6-8 → n. 14; Pesikt., 179b (Str.-B., I, 463): "Through which gate פּיילִיּ (πυλών) is there access to the life of the world to come ?" Rev. 22:4 : ἵνα ... τοῖς πυλῶσιν εἰσέλθωσιν εἰς τὴν πόλιν, cf. 21:12ab; 13abcd, 15, 21ab; Herm. s., 9, 12, 5 : εἰ οὖν τὴν πόλιν οὐ δύνῃ εἰσελθεῖν εἰ μὴ διὰ τῆς πύλης αὐτῆς, οὕτω, φησί, καὶ εἰς τὴν βασιλείαν τοῦ θεοῦ ἄλλως εἰσελθεῖν οὐ δύναται ἄνθρωπος εἰ μὴ διὰ τοῦ ὀνόματος τοῦ υἱοῦ αὐτοῦ (God's). Comparison of access to salvation with a city gate also occurs in Ceb. Tab., 17, 2; 18, 1; 20, 2 and Luc. Hermot., 22 ff. (H. Windisch, "Die Sprüche vom Eingehen in das Reich Gottes," ZNW, 27 [1928] 189-192), though salvation here is thought of idealistically rather than eschatologically.

[16] bSukka, 32b; bEr., 19a (Str.-B., IV, 1115); cf. S. Bar. 59:10 : "mouth of hell," cf. also → III, 746, n. 26.

[17] Cf. 4 Esr. 7:12, 14; Pesikt., 179b (Str.-B., I, 463); → V, 74, n. 113.

[18] 'Ολίγοι εἰσὶν οἱ εὑρίσκοντες αὐτήν (Mt. 7:14). Grammatically αὐτήν might go with ζωή as well as πύλη or ὁδός, but the conclusion of v. 13 (πολλοί εἰσιν οἱ εἰσερχόμενοι δι' αὐτῆς), where the διά shows that δι' αὐτῆς must go with πύλη, establishes a similar ref. in v. 14.

[19] Schl. Mt., ad loc.

[20] W. Grundmann, Die Frage d. ältesten Gestalt u. des urspr. Sinnes der Bergrede Jesu (1939), 5, n. 2; T. W. Manson, The Sayings of Jesus (1950), 175. A linguistic pt. is whether or not Jesus would use the simple εἰς τὴν ζωήν of Mt. 7:14, Dalman WJ, I, 131. For de-eschatologising in the Hell. world cf. Sib., 2, 150 : τοῦτο πύλη ζωῆς καὶ εἴσοδος ἀθανασίης, where ζωή (Mt. 7:14) has lost its eschatological significance and become a synon. of ἀθανασία.

C. The Gates of Hades in Mt. 16:18.

Many peoples in antiquity viewed the underworld as a land, city, fortress, or prison with strong gates which prevented escape and barred access to invaders.[21] Thus there is ref. in Babylon to the gate of the land of no return into which Ishtar forces entry.[22] The Egyptian underworld is also guarded by a gate.[23] Gk. lit. from Hom.[24] speaks of the πύλαι ἄδου and their keys, → III, 745, 18 ff. These gates are made of the strongest steel (Preis. Zaub., 4, 2720) and only by force or in return for gifts do they open to gods and heroes seeking entry into the underworld.[25] They also have a part in magic; thus Menippos (Luc. Nec., 6) says of the Persian magicians that through their arts they can ἀνοίγειν τε τοῦ Ἅιδου τὰς πύλας.[26]

In view of the Semitic character of Mt. 16:17-19[27] OT and later Jewish par. are more important for an understanding of Mt. 16:18. In the OT we find the phrase שַׁעֲרֵי שְׁאוֹל ("gates of the world of the dead") only in Hezekiah's song of thanksgiving in Is. 38:10,[28] but materially similar are phrases like שַׁעֲרֵי מָוֶת "the gates of death" in Ps. 9:13; 107:18; Job 38:17a,[29] שַׁעֲרֵי צַלְמָוֶת "the gates of darkness" in Job 38:17b,[30] and בַּדֵּי שְׁאֹל "the bars of the world of the dead" in Job 17:16.[31] All these metaphors are perhaps based on the myth of the creation conflict.[32] Later "gates of the world of the dead" is a common phrase:

Sir. 51:9 Heb.: "I lifted up my voice from the earth
And from the gates of the world of the dead (משערי שאול) my cry for help,"

Wis. 16:13: σὺ γὰρ ζωῆς καὶ θανάτου ἐξουσίαν ἔχεις καὶ κατάγεις εἰς πύλας ἄδου καὶ ἀνάγεις,[33]

Ps. Sol. 16:2: παρ᾽ ὀλίγον ἐξεχύθη ἡ ψυχή μου εἰς θάνατον σύνεγγυς πυλῶν ἄδου μετὰ ἁμαρτωλοῦ,[34]

3 Macc. 5:51: ἀνεβόησαν φωνῇ μεγάλῃ σφόδρα τὸν τῆς ἀπάσης δυνάμεως δυνάστην ἱκετεύοντες οἰκτῖραι μετὰ ἐπιφανείας αὐτοὺς ἤδη πρὸς πύλαις ἄδου καθεστῶτας. Slav. En. 42:1 A: "And I (Enoch) saw the keepers and watchers of the gates of Hades standing like gt. snakes and their faces like extinguished lamps and their

---

[21] For bibl. cf. Köhler, 222, n. 1; Weinreich, 437, n. 64. Cf. also Dell, 27-33; Str.-B., IV, 1087, 1089 f.; good material in Kroll.

[22] A. Jeremias, "Hölle u. Paradies bei den Babyloniern²," AO, 1, 3 (1903), 18-20; E. Lehmann-H. Haas, *Textbuch z. Religionsgeschichte²* (1922), 297; AOT, I, 207; Kroll, 206-214.

[23] Kroll, 194-197.

[24] Il., 5, 646; 9, 312; Od., 14, 156: πύλαι ᾽Αΐδαο. On the plur. in class. Gk. v. Bl.-Debr. 141, 4 and → n. 1.

[25] Weinreich, 437; cf. Kroll, 363-522.

[26] For additional material cf. Köhler, 223 f.; Kroll, 466-511. The Mandaean texts depict the redeemer opening the gate of the prison of souls, Kroll, 292-296, though the prison here is gen. located in the planetary spheres, 297. In astrology ἄδου πύλη is the area under the horoscope, Liddell-Scott, s.v. Ἅιδης.

[27] Jeremias, 69; → 925, 17 ff.; 927, 4 ff.

[28] פְּקַדְתִּי יֶתֶר שְׁנוֹתָי (LXX ἐν πύλαις ἄδου) בְּשַׁעֲרֵי שְׁאוֹל "I was sent to the gates of the dead for the rest of my years," cf. J. Begrich, "Der Psalm d. Hiskia," FRL, NF, 25 (1926), 23.

[29] LXX αἱ πύλαι τοῦ θανάτου (Job 38:17a no art. πύλαι θανάτου).

[30] LXX πυλωροὶ ἄδου → n. 36.

[31] LXX εἰς ἄδην. Cf. Kroll, 316-362, esp. 322-348 on "descent" in the OT.

[32] Cf. Job 38:8, 10 [Bertram].

[33] The context (Wis. 16:14) shows plainly that ἀνάγεις means "thou savest out of (not keepest from) the realm of the dead."

[34] Here ἄδης, cf. Ps. Sol. 14:9; 15:10, is the realm of the ungodly dead (→ I, 147, 12 ff.), as may be seen from the last words μετὰ ἁμαρτωλοῦ.

eyes fiery and their teeth bared to the breast." [35] Vivid terms are used to depict the security of the brass gates of Hades. [36]

Rabb. lit. has the idea, but the phrase תַּרְעֵי שְׁאוֹל seems to occur only in Tg. Is. 38:10. This is due to the fact that from the middle of the 1st cent. A.D. sheol is no longer used academically as a tt., but is replaced by Gehinnom. [37] Hence the Rabb. speak only of the entrance (also plur.) and gates of Gehinnom, and one has to decide from the context whether the ref. is to the intermediate Gehinnom (= ᾅδης → I, 146, 34 ff.) [38] or the final Gehinnom (= γέεννα → I, 657, 22 ff.). [39] To the πύλαι ᾅδου correspond the gates (שְׁעָרִים) or portals (פְּתָחִים) of Gehinnom, of which we find one (jChag., 77d, 50; bChag., 15b → n. 42), two [40] or seven [41] in the case of the intermediate Gehinnom, with a door-keeper to keep watch over them. [42]

A feature of the later Jewish usage of the pre-Chr. period is that πύλαι ᾅδου is always fig. except in Slav. En. 42:1 A (→ 924, 28 ff.). The expression denotes delivering up to death (Is. 38:10; Wis. 16:13), supreme danger of death (Sir. 51:9; Ps. Sol. 16:2; 3 Macc. 5:51; cf. Ps. 9:13; 107:18; Job 17:16) and unravelling the deepest mysteries. [43] In this sense πύλαι ᾅδου may be a *pars-pro-toto* term for ᾅδης itself. [44]

In the NT the expression occurs only in Mt. 16:18c : καὶ πύλαι ᾅδου οὐ κατισχύσουσιν αὐτῆς. [45] The noteworthy omission of the art. before πύλαι ᾅδου

---

[35] Cf. also Eth. En. 56:8 : "In those days (the days of the last assault of the Gentiles on Jerusalem) sheol will open its throat wide ... sheol will swallow up sinners before the face of the elect," and 4 Esr. 4:7, where one of the questions man cannot answer is that as to the exits of sheol (Syr., Eth., Arab., Arm., not Lat.).

[36] The security of the gates, Anon. Apc. 6:18-20 (ed. G. Steindorff, *Apk. Eliae* [1899], 45); Sib., 2, 228. The door-keepers LXX Job 38:17b: πυλωροὶ ᾅδου (שׁערי) read as שֹׁעֲרֵי, perhaps correctly); Slav. En. 42:1 A → 924, 28 ff.; bChag., 15b → n. 42.

[37] Str.-B., IV, 1022, 1032 f.

[38] Entry into the intermediate Gehinnom bBB, 84a (in the far west); bShab., 39a (the springs of Tiberias flow by it); Gn. r., 48 on 18:1 (Abraham sits at the entrance and does not let any circumcised Israelite in); Cant. r. on 8:10 (Isaac at the entrance to save his children from the judgment of Gehinnom). The opening of this Gehinnom Nu. r., 10 on 6:2; bMen., 99b (narrow). Gates → n. 39-42.

[39] Entrance to the final Gehinnom → n. 16.

[40] Pesikt. r., 24 (ed. M. Friedmann [1880], 124b): an outer and an inner gate. Those prematurely cut off from life fill up their years around the outer gate, Str.-B., IV, 1089.

[41] PREl, 53 (Prague [1784], 31d): "Seven gates of Gehinnom." Absalom had already gone through five when recalled by David's five-fold cry.

[42] bChag., 15b: "Even the door-keeper did not stand before thee, our teacher," is the boast concerning R. Jochanan, who after death redeemed the apostate Acher (= Elisha bAbuiah) from the intermediate Gehinnom, → n. 36.

[43] Cf. Job 38:17a: "Have the gates of the realm of the dead (→ 924, 15 f.) been opened unto thee ?"

[44] Sometimes שַׁעַר means more than "gate" in the OT ; thus שַׁעֲרֵי צִיּוֹן in Ps. 87:2, שַׁעַר־עַמִּי in Ob. 13; Mi. 1:9, דַּלְתוֹת הָעַמִּים in Ez. 26:2 = Jerusalem. Here as elsewhere in lofty speech, e.g., Gn. 22:17; 24:60; Is. 14:31; Jer. 14:2; 15:7, שַׁעַר means "fortified place" or city, Joüon, 106. As concerns the corresponding use of πύλαι ᾅδου for Hades one may compare Wis. 16:13 : κατάγεις εἰς πύλας ᾅδου καὶ ἀνάγεις, with the underlying 1 Βασ. 2:6 : κατάγει εἰς ᾅδου καὶ ἀνάγει (Tob. 13:2 BA κατάγει εἰς ᾅδην καὶ ἀνάγει); πύλαι ᾅδου and ᾅδης can thus alternate without change of sense. One may also compare LXX Is. 38:10 : ἐν πύλαις ᾅδου καταλείψω τὰ ἔτη τὰ ἐπίλοιπα, where πύλαι ᾅδου = ᾅδης, cf. too Ps. Sol. 16:2 → 924, 24 f.

[45] The text is beyond dispute. Euringer, 141-156 has cogently refuted the thesis of Harnack, 647-649 that the Diatessaron does not have the saying about building the Church (16:18b) and that it read σοῦ (not αὐτῆς) as the last word in v. 18c. He has shown that in the Diatessaron as known to Ephr. and Aphraates the text of Mt. 16:18 was the same as the canonical text apart from "bars" for "gates." Cf. also the examples from Ephr. in

finds par. in Jewish Gk. (→ 924, 22 ff.) and may be explained by the underlying Heb. status constructus שַׁעֲרֵי שְׁאוֹל; it is thus a Semitism. Interpretations of Mt. 16:18c vary widely according to the understanding of ᾅδης as the realm of the dead or the underworld, [46] the construing of πύλαι as literal or figurative, the rendering of κατισχύειν as "to be a match" or "to overpower" (so correctly → III, 398, 23 ff.), and the referring of αὐτῆς to πέτρα or ἐκκλησία, → n. 64.

Of these questions the first concerning the meaning of ᾅδης is fundamental to correct exegesis. A negative pt. relating to it is that interpretations which refer ᾅδης strictly to the realm of the dead are subject to serious difficulties. Of the many proposals the most important are 1. πύλαι ᾅδου denotes lit. the gates of the underworld. On this view the meaning is that these gates cannot resist the pressure of the community to get back its members [47] (but where does the idea of the community's descensus ad inferos come from ?). Another possibility is that the gates cannot arrest the exodus of the community on the descent of Jesus [48] or the resurrection [49] (but the community is not imprisoned in Hades). [50] 2. πύλαι ᾅδου means fig. the realm of the dead. Further interpretation will then depend on whether (οὐ κατισχύσουσιν) αὐτῆς is related to πέτρα or ἐκκλησία. a. If the former, Mt. 16:18c is a promise that Peter will not die before the parousia. [51] This understanding can appeal to πύλαι ᾅδου (or τοῦ θανάτου) in Is. 38:10; Ps. 9:13; 107:18; Sir. 51:9; Ps. Sol. 16:2; 3 Macc. 5:51, since the ref. in all these is to being preserved from death, → 924, 12 ff. It can also adduce in its favour the earliest exegesis of Mt. 16:18c. [52] b. If, however, αὐτῆς is taken to refer to ἐκκλησία the pt. is either that death has no power over members of the community or, since ᾅδης in NT days often denotes the realm of the ungodly dead (→ I, 147, 29 f.), that members of the community will not in death share the fate of the ungodly. [53] An objection to both 2 a. and 2 b. is

---

C. A. Kneller, "Über d. 'ursprüngliche' Form v. Mt. 16:18 f.," Zschr. f. kathol. Theol., 44 (1920), 147-169, also Ludwig, 22 f.
[46] The ref. is not to hell (the dominant exegesis up to 1918, Harnack, 639), since the NT always differentiates clearly between → ᾅδης and → γέεννα.
[47] J. Grill, Der Primat d. Petrus (1904), 13; L. E. Sullivan, "The Gates of Hell (Mt. 16:18s.)," Theol. Studies, 10 (1949), 62 ff. → 107, 24 ff.
[48] Dell, 31-33; W. Bousset, Kyrios Christos² (1921), 30.
[49] Schl. Mt., ad loc.; O. J. F. Seitz, "Upon this Rock," JBL, 69 (1950), 337 (he compares Ac. 2:24); O. Cullmann, Petrus (1952), 226-228 (ET [1962], 207-210).
[50] Cf. Bultmann Trad., 148, n. 2. Another objection to these two interpretations is that they depict the community as aggressors → 927, 20 ff.
[51] Harnack, 638-647; Windisch, op. cit. (→ n. 15), 187.
[52] The pagan (probably Porphyrius, d. c. 304) in Macarius Magnes (c. 400), III, 22 (A. v. Harnack, Porphyrius "Gg. die Christen" [1916], No. 26, p. 56) thinks Mt. 16:18c is a promise that Peter will not die: ἱστορεῖται ... ὁ Πέτρος ἐσταυρῶσθαι, εἰρηκότος τοῦ Ἰησοῦ τὰς ᾅδου πύλας μὴ κατισχύσειν αὐτοῦ. If this testimony is of doubtful value because it is polemical (Ludwig, 70), that of Orig. Comm. in Mt. 12, 33 on 16:28 (GCS, 40, 145, 11 ff.) is more telling: ἀκόλουθον οὖν ἦν τῷ Πέτρῳ, οὗ "πύλαι ᾅδου οὐ κατισχύσουσι," τὸ μηδὲ γεύσασθαι θανάτου, ἐπεὶ τότε γεύεταί τις θανάτου καὶ ἐσθίει θανάτου, ὅτε "πύλαι ᾅδου" κατισχύουσιν αὐτοῦ, cf. also Ambr. Expositio Ev. Lc., 7, 5 on 9:27 (CSEL, 32, 4, 284, 1-3): neque enim Petrus mortuus est, cui iuxta dominicam sententiam inferi porta praeualere non potuit. If both Orig. (cf. J. Sickenberger, "Eine neue Deutung d. Primatstelle Mt. 16:18," Theol. Revue, 19 [1920], 1-7; Ludwig, 44) and Ambr. have in view the preservation of Peter from spiritual death this might be a way of finding a fulfilment for the prophecy of Mt. 16:18c. It may be noted that in the Arab. version of the Vita of Shenute of Atripe we find the following saying of unknown provenance: "For the Lord Christ has said (to Peter): Verily, in eternity thine eye will never be closed for the light of this world," L. E. Iselin, "Eine bisher unbekannte Version d. ersten Teiles der 'Apostellehre,' " TU, 13, 1b (1895), 26.
[53] Ref. in W. Bieder, "Die Vorstellung v. d. Höllenfahrt Jesu Christi," Abh. ThANT, 19 (1949), 46, n. 97.

that no matter how αὐτῆς be taken full justice is not done to the eschatological character of the fut. οὐ κατισχύσουσιν → lines 23 f. None of the views which restrict ᾅδης to the realm of the dead is thus adequate.

Exegesis must take the structure of the section Mt. 16:17-19 as its starting-point. Each of the three verses (v. 17, 18, 19) consists of three lines (tetrameter). [54] In each case the first line states the theme while the second and third elucidate it in antithetical parallelism. The theme of v. 18 is the naming of Peter as the rock. What Jesus means by this is explained in v. 18b c. On this rock Jesus will build His ἐκκλησία (→ III, 518, 29 ff.) and the gates of hell will not overcome it (the rock or the Church).

The saying uses the symbol of the cosmic rock (→ 96, 13 ff.) which is the top of the hollow world-mountain and which has a double function, first, to support the sanctuary, and secondly, to close the underworld which is inside the mountain, which embraces the realm of the dead and the prison of spirits, and from which the primal floods stream forth. [55] Later Judaism applies this symbol not merely to the rock in the Holy of Holies [56] and to the altar of burnt offering [57] but also to persons. Thus Abraham is called the rock (פֶּטְרָא → 99, 14 ff., cf. Is. 51:1), for he carries all creation on the one side and can resist the primal waters on the other, [58] cf. also the patriarchs. [59]

Within this concept πύλαι ᾅδου is a *pars-pro-toto* term (→ 925, 16) for the ungodly powers of the underworld which assail the rock. [60] This interpretation is supported by the linguistic consideration that κατισχύειν when followed by a genitive is always active ("to vanquish") in Jewish Greek. [61] Hence the πύλαι ᾅδου are the aggressors. Since the two futures in Mt. 16:18 (οἰκοδομήσω, οὐ κατισχύσουσιν) are also meant eschatologically [62] the reference is to the final attack of the powers of the underworld along the lines of the descriptions in Rev. (6:8; 9:1 ff.; 20:3, 7 f. → I, 4, 13 ff.; 10, 3 ff.; III, 746, 5 ff.) and the Qumran psalm 1 QH 5:20 ff. [63] Even the last and most terrible assault of the forces of the underworld will not be able to overcome the rock and the ἐκκλησία erected upon it. [64], [65]

---

[54] C. F. Burney, *The Poetry of Our Lord* (1925), 117. Jesus favoured the tetrameter when teaching the disciples, *ibid.*, 124.

[55] Jeremias, 66-68. Cf. E. Lohmeyer, *Kultus u. Evangelium* (1942), 76.

[56] Jeremias, 51-58.

[57] *Ibid.*, 58-65.

[58] Jalqut Shimoni, I, § 766 on Nu. 23:9 (ed. Vilna [1898], p. 530), transl. Str.-B., I, 733 and Jeremias, 73 f.

[59] Ex. r., 15, 8 on 12:2, Jeremias, 74.

[60] C. Weizsäcker, *Untersuchungen über d. evang. Geschichte* (1864), 494; Jeremias, 73; H. Schmidt, *Der heilige Fels in Jerusalem* (1933), 100; Betz, 70 f. (power of chaos).

[61] So always in the Gk. OT: LXX Jer. 15:18; Θ Da. 11:21; Σ ψ 90(91):10. Also Wis. 7:30 (reading uncertain); Test. R. 4:11; D. 5:2; Jos. 6:7. Cf. Helbing Kasussyntax, 119.

[62] For οἰκοδομήσω cf. Mk. 14:58, hence also for the antithetical par. οὐ κατισχύσουσιν. Yet these futures, though both eschatological, are not contemporary, since the building of the new temple precedes the attack of the powers of the underworld.

[63] In the raging of the waters of Tehom (6:23 f.) and in face of the gates of death (6:24 : שַׁעֲרֵי מָוֶת), the worshipper is delivered in a strong fortified city surrounded by a wall (6:25) and built on a rock (6:26). Cf. Betz, 55 f.

[64] Αὐτῆς (οὐ κατισχύσουσιν αὐτῆς) in Mt. 16:18c refers formally to πέτρα but materially to the ἐκκλησία erected upon it (cf. the alternation of plur. and sing. in the related Lk. 22:31 f.).

[65] This is how Ephr. took the v. (Diatessaron Comm., 14, 3 Arm.): Tu es, *ait*, petra, *illa petra quam erexit ut offenderet per eam Satanas* (L. Leloir, *Saint Éphrem. Comm. de l'év. concordant. Version arménienne*, Corp. Script. Christ. Or., 145 [1954], 134, 24 f.); Euringer,

Later πύλαι ᾅδου figured especially in statements about the descent into Hades. [66] The fact that Christ has power over the gates of Hades is emphasised already in Rev. 1:18, which says of the exalted Christ : ἔχω τὰς κλεῖς τοῦ θανάτου καὶ τοῦ ᾅδου, → III, 746, 11 ff.

J. Jeremias

| πῦρ, πυρόω, πύρωσις, |
| πύρινος, πυρρός |

† πῦρ.

Contents : A. Fire in the Greek and Hellenistic World : I. General Usage : 1. Literal ; 2. Transferred. II. Fire in Philosophy. III. Fire in Religion. B. Persian Fire Worship. C. Fire in the Old Testament, Later Judaism and Gnosticism : I. The Old Testament : 1. Statistics ; 2. Technical Use ; 3. Transferred Use ; 4. Fire in Relation to God : a. Fire

---

146, 151, 177; Jeremias, 75-77. Cf. Zn. Mt., *ad loc.*; J. Weiss-W. Bousset, *Die drei älteren Ev., Schr. NT*³, I, *ad loc.*; C. A. Bernoulli, *Joh. d. Täufer u. d. Urgemeinde* (1918), 280; T. Hermann, "Zu Mt. 16:18 u. 19," *Theol. Bl.*, 5 (1926), 203-207; Bultmann Trad., 148; Stauffer Theol.⁴, 16 f. and n. 482; R. Bohren, *Das Problem der Kirchenzucht im NT* (1952), 63 f.; Betz, 72 f.

[66] Kroll, 46 f., 48, 57, 68, 81 etc.

πῦρ. Gen.: Thes. Steph., VI, *s.v.*; S. Mühsam, *Das Feuer in Bibel u. Talmud* (1869); A. Kuhn, *Die Herabkunft des Feuers u. des Göttertranks* (1886); E. Goblet d'Alviella, *Histoire religieuse du feu* (1887); O. Höfer, Art. "Pyr" in Roscher, III, 3332-3334; J. Patrick, Art. "Fire" in Hastings DB, II; E. G. Hirsch, Art. "Fire" in Jew. Enc., V, 391-393; A. E. Crawley, Art. "Fire" in ERE, VI, 26-30; P. Saintyves, *Essais du Folklore Biblique*. I. "Le feu qui descend du ciel et le renouvellement du feu sacré" (1922), 1-58; H. Fuchs, Art. "Feuer" in Jüd. Lex., II; O. Rühle, Art. "Feuer" in RGG², II, 569 f.; J. G. Frazer, *Myths of the Origin of Fire* (1930); H. Freudenthal, *Das Feuer im deutschen Glauben u. Brauch* (1931); O. C. de C. Ellis, *A History of Fire and Flame* (1932); Thes. Ling. Lat., VII, 1, *s.v. ignis*; C. M.Edsman, "Le baptême de feu," Acta Seminarii Neotestamentici Upsaliensis, 9 (1940); also "Ignis divinus. Le feu comme moyen de rajeunissement et d'immortalité : contes, légendes, mythes et rites," Skrifter utgivna av Vetenskaps-Sozieteten i Lund, 34 (1949); T. Blasius, *Das himmlische Feuer*, Diss. Bonn (1949); F. Lang, *Das Feuer im Sprachgebrauch d. Bibel, dargestellt auf dem Hintergrund der Feuervorstellungen in d. Umwelt*, Diss. Tübingen (1950); E. Pax, ΕΠΙΦΑΝΕΙΑ, Münchener Theol. Stud., I, 10 (1955), Index, *s.v.* "Feuerepiphanien"; C. M. Edsman, Art. "Feuer" RGG³, II, 927 f. On A.: M. P. Nilsson, "Der Flammentod d. Herakles auf dem Oite," ARW, 21 (1922), 310-316; also "Fire Festivals in Ancient Greece," JHS, 43 (1923), 144-148; S. Eitrem, "Die vier Elemente in d. Mysterienweihe," Symb. Osl., 4 (1926), 39-59; 5 (1927), 39-59; A. D. Nock, "Cremation and Burial in the Roman Empire," HThR, 25 (1932), 321-359; O. Huth, "Der Feuerkult d. Germanen," ARW, 36 (1939), 108-134; K. Reinhardt, "Heraklits Lehre vom Feuer," Hermes, 77 (1942), 1-27; O. Huth, "Vesta. Untersuchungen z. idg. Feuerkult," Beih. z. ARW, 2 (1943); F. Cumont, *Lux perpetua* (1949). On B.: J. Hertel, "Die arische Feuerlehre, I u. II," *Indo-iran. Quellen u. Forschungen*, 6, 7 (1925/31); also "Die awestischen Herrschafts- u. Siegesfeuer," ASG, 41, 6 (1931); J. C. Tavadia, "Ein alter Feuerritus bei den Zoroastriern in Iran," ARW, 36 (1939), 256-276; K. Erdmann, *Das iranische Feuerheiligtum* (1941); S. Wikander, *Feuerpriester in Kleinasien u. Iran* (1946); J. Duchesne-Guillemin, *Zoroastre* (1948), 27 f. On C.: E. Böklen, *Die Verwandtschaft der jüd.-chr. mit d. parsischen Eschatologie* (1902), 115-135; W. Bousset, *Hauptprobleme d. Gnosis* (1907), Index, *s.v.*; Bousset-Gressm., 275-286 and *passim*; Volz Esch., 309-340 and *passim*; S. Aalen, "D. Begriffe Licht u. Finsternis im AT, im Spätjudt. u. im Rabbinismus," *Skrifter utgitt av Det Norske Videnskaps-Akademi i Oslo*, II, Historisk-Filosofisk Klasse, 1 (1951), 73-78; R. Mayer, "Die bibl. Vorstellung vom Weltenbrand," *Bonner Orientalistische Stud.*, NF, 4 (1956), esp. 79-136. On

in Theophany; b. Fire as a Means of Divine Judgment; c. Fire as a Sign of Gracious Visitation; d. Fire as a Term for God. II. Development in Later Judaism: 1. Apocalyptic; 2. The Rabbis; 3. The Qumran Sect; 4. Hellenistic Judaism. III. Gnostic Usage: 1. The Hermetic Writings; 2. Coptic Gnostic Works; 3. The Mandaean Literature. D. Fire in the New Testament: I. The Earthly Phenomenon. II. Figurative and Transferred Usage. III. Theological Use: 1. Fire at Theophanies; 2. Fire as a Means of Divine Judgment: a. The Symbol; b. The Eschatological Fire of Judgment; c. The Fire of Hell; 3. Fire as a Sign of Heavenly Glory. E. Fire in the Post-Apostolic Fathers: I. The Biblical Tradition. II. Alien Influences.

A. Fire in the Greek and Hellenistic World.

I. General Usage.

1. Literal.

πῦρ [1] is used from Hom. for fire in its various forms both in nature and as used by man. The three distinctive functions, burning, lighting and warming, have influenced the usage and help us to understand the individual nuances: (1) the fire of the funeral pile ὄφρα πυρός με ... λελάχωσι θανόντα, Hom. Il., 7, 79 f.; (2) the fire of sacrifice ἐν πυρὶ βάλλε θυηλάς, Hom. Il., 9, 220; κατὰ τοῦ πυρὸς σπένδοντες, Plat. Critias, 120a; (3) hearth-fire πυρὸς ἐσχάραι, Hom. Il., 10, 418; ἐπ’ ἐσχάρᾳ πυρός, Aesch. Eum., 108; (4) manufacturing πῦρ μαγειρικόν, τεκτονικόν, χαλκευτικόν, χρυσοχοϊκόν, Aristot. Spir., 9, p. 485a, 34 f., esp. the smithy fire χαλκὸν δ’ ἐν πυρὶ βάλλεν, Hom. Il., 18, 474; (5) fire of torches τὸ φέγγος ὁρμάσθω πυρός, Aesch. Eum., 1029; (6) lightning, forced παλτῷ ῥιπτεῖ πυρί, Soph. Ant., 131, divine fire θείῳ πυρὶ παμφαής, Soph. Phil., 728; (7) sunshine εὐάλιον πῦρ, Eur. Iph. Taur., 1139 and the shining of the stars πῦρ πνεόντων ... ἄστρων, Soph. Ant., 1146 f.; (8) glance of the eyes πυρὶ δ’ ὄσσε δεδήειν, Hom. Il., 12, 466; (9) summer heat πυρὸς ἢ χειμῶνος προσβολῇ, Plat. Leg., IX, 865b; (10) fever = πυρετός, Aristoph. Fr., 690 (CAF, I, 561). Cf. also τὰ πυρά (τοῖς πυροῖς) the watch-fire, Hom. Il., 8, 509; Thuc., VII, 80, 1 and ἡ πυρά the place where fire is kindled, esp. the funeral pile, Hom. Il., 1, 52. [2]

Fire has for man a double character. It is both a beneficent and civilising [3] power and also a terrifying and destructive force. Along with the uses already mentioned it is employed esp. in war to destroy cities, ships etc. [4] and also as a signal, Aesch. Ag., 9, 282; Thuc., IV, 111, 2. Another use is for the purifying of noble metals βασανίζειν ... χρυσὸν ἐν πυρί, Plat. Resp., III, 413e, cf. Polit., 303e, for purgation πῦρ καθάρσιον, Eur. Iph. Aul., 1112, and as a test, a kind of divine judgment, to prove innocence, Soph. Ant., 265. There is also very occasional ref. to the bonfire πῦρ καὶ φῶς ἐπ’ ἐλευθερίᾳ δαίων, Aesch. Choeph., 863 f.

2. Transferred.

Fig. fire denotes violence and irresistibility πτόλεμος ... ἄγριος ἠΰτε πῦρ, Hom. Il., 17, 736 f.; μάρναντο δέμας πυρὸς αἰθομένοιο, 11, 596; anarchy, Eur. Hec., 607 f.; wickedness, Aristoph. Lys., 1015. It is also used for the fury of battle, Hom. Il., 17, 565,

---

D.: A. Fridrichsen, "Würzung mit Feuer," Symb. Osl., 4 (1926), 36-38; also "Johannes vattendop och det messianska elddopet," Uppsala Univ. Årsskrift, 73 (1941), 1-14; H. Bietenhard, "Kennt d. NT die Vorstellung vom Fegefeuer?" ThZ, 3 (1947), 101-122; J. Gnilka, Ist 1 Kor. 3:10-15 ein Schriftzeugnis f. d. Fegefeuer? Eine exegetisch-historische Untersuchung (1955); G. Delling, "βάπτισμα βαπτισθῆναι," Nov. Test., 2 (1957), 92-115.

[1] Etym. related to Feuer, fire, Arm. hur etc. Probably connected with the root peu "to purify," "to cleanse," "to sift," cf. Lat. purus. Walde-Pok., II, 14 f.; Pokorny, 828; Boisacq, 828 f.; Hofmann, 291.

[2] On the declension cf. Schwyzer, I, 582e.

[3] Cf. the story of Prometheus, Aesch. Prom. and W. Kraus, Art. "Prometheus" in Pauly-W., 23 (1957), 653-702.

[4] "Flame-throwers," Xenoph. An., V, 2, 14.

for vaunting courage πῦρ πνεῖν, "to breathe out fire," Xenoph. Hist. Graec., VII, 5, 12; also personally: ὦ πῦρ σὺ καὶ πᾶν δεῖμα, Soph. Phil., 927. The term can denote various emotions like yearning hope (Soph. El., 888) or the desire of love (Callim. Epigr., 27, 5; cf. 45, 2).

The destructive aspect of fire is expressed in proverbial expressions like ἐν πυρὶ γενέσθαι = "to perish," Hom. Il., 2, 340, φεύγων καπνὸν (δουλείας) εἰς πῦρ (δεσποτείας) ἐμπεπτωκώς = "out of the frying-pan into the fire," Plat. Resp., VIII, 569b, πῦρ ἐπὶ πῦρ ὀχετεύειν = "to pour oil on the flames," Plat. Leg., II, 666a, διὰ πυρὸς ἰέναι μετά τινος = "to share every danger with someone," Xenoph. Sym., 4, 16, but διὰ πυρὸς μολεῖν τινι = "to act cruelly to someone," Eur. El., 1183, εἰς πῦρ ξαίνειν, Plat. Leg., VI, 780c. The rare expression πῦρ ἐναύειν τινί = "to act with friendliness towards someone" in Hdt., VII, 231 is connected with the fire on the hearth.

II. Fire in Philosophy.

In philosophy [5] πῦρ usually denotes the element, whether it be one of two (πῦρ and γῆ, Parmen. A, 7 [Diels[7], I, 219, 36]), three (γῆ, πῦρ ὕδωρ, Orphic. A, 1 [Diels[7], I, 1, n. 10]), four (πῦρ, ὕδωρ, γαῖα, ἠήρ, Emped. Fr., 17, 18 [I, 316, 12]; Plat. Tim., 32b etc.) or five elements (αἰθήρ, πῦρ, ἀήρ, ὕδωρ, γῆ, Aristot. Cael., III, 1, p. 298b, 6).[6] Heraclitus of Ephesus (c. 500 B.C.) exercised a decisive influence on all later development; for him fire was the basic material. The world is the play of fire in constant process of change (πυρός τε ἀνταμοιβὴ τὰ πάντα καὶ πῦρ ἁπάντων, Heracl. Fr., 90 [Diels[7], I, 171, 6 f.]): "This world order, the same for all beings, was created neither by a god nor a man; it always was and is and will be eternally living fire (πῦρ ἀείζωον), flaring up and dying down by measure," Fr., 30 (I, 157, 11 ff.). In its change the original being, identified with the deity or *logos*, assumes three basic forms, πυρὸς τροπαί, Fr., 31 (I, 158, 6). Fire becomes water and water earth (in a downward movement, Fr., 60 [I, 164, 5]); in the reverse upward movement earth becomes water and water fire. After a cosmic epoch everything returns in conflagration to the original fire in order that the world may be set up anew. The formation of the world is a lack (χρησμοσύνη), the conflagration is satisfaction (κόρος, Fr., 65 [I, 165, 4]). As the original fire is endowed with reason and is the cause of all world government (Fr., 64 [I, 165, 1 ff.]), so the soul of man consists of fire. The drier it is, the wiser and better, Fr., 118 (I, 177, 4 f.). This pantheistic view of God and the fiery universe, of world reason and the spirit of man, recurs later esp. in Stoicism.

The Stoics regarded all reality as physical, Chrysipp. Fr., 363 (v. Arnim, II, 123, 31 f.). It is true that they perceived two principles, τὸ πάσχον and τὸ ποιοῦν, equating the former with matter and the latter with indwelling reason or deity, Fr., 300 (II, 111, 8 ff.). Yet this distinction is only relative, for even what is active is bodily, though in finer form. This purest substance (= θεός, Fr., 1035 [II, 307, 15 ff.]; ὁ λόγος τοῦ θεοῦ, Fr., 1051 [II, 310, 16 ff.]) is fiery (νοῦς κόσμου πύρινος, Zeno Fr., 157 [I, 42, 7 f.]; cf. Chrysipp. Fr., 1026 [II, 306, 12 ff.], 1032 [II, 307, 4 ff.]). It is a rational fire-like breath (πνεῦμα νοερὸν καὶ πυρῶδες, Chrysipp. Fr., 1009 [II, 299, 11 ff.]), a fire which shapes things for different ends like an artist (πῦρ τεχνικόν, Fr., 1027 [II, 306, 20]). As the world soul and guiding principle it overrules and upholds all things normatively and providentially, and it contains within itself the individual rational seed-forms (τοὺς σπερματικοὺς λόγους, Fr., 1027 [II, 306, 19 ff.]). As in Heracl. the process of forming the world is a change in the primal fire. By ἐκπύρωσις (Fr., 626 [II, 190, 38]) all things return to the original state from which the world then develops again in exactly the same way in an endless cycle. The human soul is a part of the fiery spirit of deity, Zeno Fr., 135 (I, 38, 3 f.); Chrysipp. Fr., 885 (II, 238, 32). It can also be described simply

---

[5] For the Pre-Socratics cf. the index, *s.v.* πῦρ, Diels[7], III, 380-384.

[6] Theophrast. (c. 300 B.C.), the pupil of Aristot., wrote a special work on fire along the line of his master's teaching on the elements, cf. Theophrast. περὶ πυρός, ed. A. Gercke, Univ. Greifswald (1896).

as fire, Zeno Fr., 134 (I, 38, 2); Chrysipp. Fr., 775 (II, 217, 19). It continues after death, but only up to the cosmic conflagration, when it returns to the primal fire, Chrysipp. Fr., 809 (II, 223, 17 ff.). Cleanthes thought all souls continued thus, Chrysipp. only the souls of the wise, Cleanthes Fr., 522 (I, 118, 3 ff.).

III. Fire in Religion.

1. In the pre-deistic stage fire is an antidote to evil influences and a means of ritual purification, → IV, 17 ff. Thus Odysseus cleanses his house with fire and brimstone, Hom. Od., 22, 492 ff. In case of death the polluted fire must be put out and new fire brought from others, Plut. Quaest. Graec., 24 (II, 297a). The cleansing function of fire may also be seen at the lustration after the birth of a child (Suid., *s.v.* ἀμφιδρόμια), [7] in the sacrifices of purification (περίστια) before assemblies (Suid., *s.v.* περιστίαρ-χος), [8] and in the Rom. *parilia,* a festival of purification for the herdsmen in spring, [9] Varro Fr. in Schol. Persius Sat., I, 72 : [10] *ut ... ignem magnum transsiliant Parilibus.* In the world of magic we find the so-called annual fires. At the Laphria festival of Artemis in Patrai [11] all kinds of living animals are burnt on a funeral pyre, Paus., VII, 18, 11 ff. Such fires were usually on the tops of hills. At the gt. Daidala festival [12] the Boeotians and Plataeans set up an altar on the top of the Cithaeron and burnt it with fire along with the images solemnly laid on it, Paus., IX, 3, 1 ff. In the cult of the dead the custom of cremation [13] brought by Gk. immigrants did not completely suppress older concepts of the continued life of the dead. At any rate, it was a common belief that fire cannot destroy the soul, Aesch. Choeph., 323-325.

2. In the worship of the gods Hephaistos (Vulcanus) and Hestia (Vesta) are associated with fire. The pre-Gk. god Hephaistos [14] is originally the god of the earth-fire, volcanoes. The myth of his plunge from heaven recalls this, Hom. Il., 1, 590 ff., cf. 18, 395 ff. He bears the nicknames αἰθαλόεις, αἴθων, πυρίπνοος, πυρίτης, πυρόεις, πυρσοφόρος, σελασφόρος. [15] His worship as the divine smith is also related hereto, Hom. Il., 18, 369 ff. Hephaistos could then be used for fire generally, Diod. S., 1, 12, 3; "flame of Hephaistos," Hom. Il., 9, 468; 17, 88; 23, 33; Od., 24, 71; the crackling of fire as his laughter, Aristot. Meteor., II, 9, p. 369a, 32. The Stoics in allegorising myths took Hephaistos to signify fire, Zeno Fr., 169 (v. Arnim, I, 43, 30); Chrysipp. Fr., 1076 (II, 315, 14 f.). The ancient Gk. goddess Hestia [16] is protectress of the hearth fire and embodies the centre of domestic society, of the state (Thuc., II, 5), of a district (Paus., VIII, 53, 9) and of an alliance (altar of Hestia in Aigion at the centre of the Achaian alliance). The Pythagoreans regard the central fire as the hearth of the cosmos πῦρ ἐν μέσῳ περὶ τὸ κέντρον ὅπερ ἑστίαν τοῦ παντὸς καλεῖ, Philolaos A, 16 (Diels⁷, I, 403, 14). On the sacred national hearth in the Prytaneion there burned the undying flame, [17] Paus., V, 15, 5; Aesch. Choeph., 1037; τὸ πῦρ τὸ ἄσβεστον, Poll. Onom., I, 7; Plut. Numa, 9 (I, 666); τὸ πῦρ τὸ ἀθάνατον, Plut. Ei ap. Delph., 2 (II, 385c). From the Prytaneion of the mother city colonists took fire for the hearth in new settlements, cf. Hdt., I, 146 and Etym. M., 694, 28. Other divinities were also linked with fire. [18] The Orphics say of Zeus: Ζεὺς πνοιὴ πάντων, Ζεὺς ἀκαμάτου πυρὸς ὁρμή,

---

[7] P. Stengel, Art. "Amphidromia" in Pauly-W., 1 (1894), 1901 f.
[8] K. Hanell, Art. "Peristiarchos" in Pauly-W., 19 (1937), 859.
[9] Bertholet-Leh., II, 425.
[10] Ed. G. Némethy (1903), 88.
[11] W. Kroll, Art. "Laphria" in Pauly-W., 12 (1924), 766-768.
[12] V. v. Schoeffer, Art. "Daidala, 6" in Pauly-W., 4 (1901), 1991-1993.
[13] Bertholet-Leh., II, 296; cf. Nilsson, I², 174-178, 374-378.
[14] L. Malten, Art. "Hephaistos" in Pauly-W., 8 (1912), 311-366, esp. 327-342.
[15] C. F. H. Bruchmann, Epitheta Deorum ... (1893), 155 f.
[16] W. Süss, Art. "Hestia" in Pauly-W., 8 (1912), 1257-1304.
[17] Cf. the sacred undying fire (*ignis aeternus,* Cic. Pro M. Fonteio Or., 47) which the Vestals had to guard in Rome, Bertholet-Leh., II, 449.
[18] [H. Kleinknecht.]

Fr., 21a (Kern, 91) and in the Stoic hymn to Zeus : ἔχεις ... πυρόεντα ... κεραυνόν, Cleanthes Fr., 537 (v. Arnim, I, 122, 5 f.). With Prometheus (→ 929, n. 3) Hermes was regarded as the first to give fire and fire-vessels to men, Hom. Hymn. Merc., 111. Dionysos, saved from the bosom of Semele when she was smitten by the lightning of Zeus, is called the one born of fire πυριγενής, Diod. S., 4, 5, 1, [19] or the fiery one πυρόεις, Nonnus Dionys., 21, 222. [20] Proteus changes into fire in Verg. Georgicon, IV, 442 and Thetis in Schol. on Pind. Nem., III, 60. [21], [22] At the epiphany of gods [23] fire-phenomena are often mentioned as an expression of glory. When Aphrodite appeared to Anchises she wore a garment φαεινότερον πυρὸς αὐγῆς, Hom. Hymn. Ven., 86. At the epiphany of Dionysos on the death of Pentheus πρὸς οὐρανὸν καὶ γαῖαν ἐστήριζε φῶς σεμνοῦ πυρός, Eur. Ba., 1083 f. In the pious legend of the transfer of the cult of the god Sarapis from Sinope to Alexandria the visionary divine figure rises up to heaven igne plurimo, Tac. Hist., IV, 83. Fiery phenomena are also omens, [24] e.g., bloody fire falls to the earth, Plin. Nat. Hist., II, 27. In descriptions of the underworld [25] there is ref. to much fire and violent rivers of fire, Plat. Phaed., 111d. The third of the four gt. rivers of the underworld, which debouches into a broad region burning with a gt. fire and finally plunges into Tartarus, is called Pyriphlegethon. It is regarded as a source of mountains which spew out fire rather than as a place of torment, Phaed., 113a b. But we also find the idea of a purgation of souls by fire [26] along with water and wind : aliae panduntur inanes suspensae ad ventos, aliis sub gurgite vasto infectum eluitur scelus, aut exuritur igni, Verg. Aen., VI, 740 ff.

3. In the mysteries fire plays a notable part in the rites of purification before initiation (cf. Suid., s.v. Μίθρου) and esp. as a source of light symbolising the deity as heavenly light and the new nature of the initiate, [27] → IV, 19 f. Acc. to Hippolyt. the Eleusinian mysteries were celebrated ὑπὸ πολλῷ πυρί, Ref., V, 8, 40. By the change from darkness to light the participant experienced the horror of darkness and the blessedness of the hereafter. [28] In the wild Bacchanalia at Rome raving women plunged burning torches into the Tiber, Liv., 39, 13. In the oriental-Hell. mysteries fire was often used to produce light-effects at initiation. [29] In the Mithras liturgy the initiate is born again by the spirit to wonder at the sacred fire, ἵνα θαυμάσω τὸ ἱερὸν πῦρ, Mithr. Liturg., 4, 15. He is to view "with immortal spirit the immortal Aeon and Lord of the fiery crowns," 4, 21 f. This fire-god Aeon [30] is given the following titles in prayer : "Hear me ..., Lord, who with thy breath hast closed the fiery locks of heaven, thou ruler of fire (πυρίπολε), breather of fire (πυρίπνοε), strong in fire (πυρίθυμε), joyous in fire (πυριχαρῆ), having a body of fire (πυρισώματε), sowing fire (πυρισπόρε), fire-roaring (πυρικλόνε), fire-whirling (πυριδῖνα), receptacle of fire (ἐνπυρισχησίφως)," 8, 17 ff. After initiation the sun-god Helios is seen with fiery locks (πυρινότριχα) in white raiment and a scarlet mantle with a fiery crown, and he greets the initiate with a greeting of fire, 10, 28 ff.

---

[19] Ovid Fast., III, 503 : ortus in igne Bacchus.
[20] W. F. Otto, Dionysos (1933), 136.
[21] Ed. A. B. Drachmann, III (1927), 51 f.
[22] In mythology fabulous beasts also breathe out fire : Diomedis equi spirantes naribus ignem, Lucretius De Rerum Natura, V, 29 (ed. J. Martin [1953], 176); tauri, Verg. Georgicon, II, 140.
[23] F. Pfister, Art. "Epiphanie" in Pauly-W. Suppl., 4 (1924), 315; Pax, 26, 30.
[24] Cf. the Prodigiorum liber of Julius Obsequens, ed. O. Rossbach (1910), 153-181.
[25] Cf. L. Radermacher, Das Jenseits im Mythos d. Hellenen (1903), 96.
[26] E. Norden, P. Vergilius Maro, Aen. Buch VI² (1916), 28.
[27] Acc. to Eitrem, 4, 52 ff.; 5, 39, 54 ff., there is in the initiation of the mysteries an elemental regeneration, a reconstruction of the new man by the pure primal elements when he has been purged of the hylic elements and is thus ready for the divine vision. The Persian doctrine of the elements seems to have had some influence here, cf. Hdt., I, 131.
[28] O. Kern, Art. "Mysterien" in Pauly-W., 16 (1935), 1243.
[29] T. Hopfner, Art. "Die orientalisch-hell. Mysterien" in Pauly-W., 16 (1935), 1334.
[30] Cf. A. Dieterich, Abraxas (1891), 48-62.

In the Gk. world fire, for all its destructive effects in detail, is in the main valued as most refined, most active and yet also most constant element, and it is connected with deity (cf. Plat. Tim., 40a) and spirit.

B. Persian Fire Worship.

Fire is worshipped throughout the earth, but esp. by the Indo-Eur. peoples. In the bibl. world [31] the Persians call for special notice here. The ancient Gks. were already aware that fire was worshipped as divine by the Persians, Hdt., I, 131, cf. III, 16 : Πέρσαι γὰρ θεὸν νομίζουσι εἶναι τὸ πῦρ, cf. Diog. L. Prooimion, 6; Luc. Jup. Trag., 42 ; Strabo, 15, 3, 13 f., 16; Diod. S., 17, 114, 4.

In the cosmological and ethical dualism of the Mazda doctrine of Zarathustra truth (Aša) and falsehood (Drug) are embodied in the fire and the snake. Reflected here is the primal ancient Iranian myth of the conflict between Atar (fire) and Aži Dahaka (the dragon). Men play an inescapable role in this battle through their conduct. Either they fight for a good outlook, for truth and life, by caring for good things (e.g., oxen, fire and earth), or they strengthen the forces of evil. Fire is here on the good side. It belongs to the kingdom of Ahura Mazda, whose body is always a fiery one in Persian orthodoxy, a flame blazing forth in uncreated light. Fire is very often addressed as the son of the wise Lord, Yasna, 1, 38; 2, 18, 48; 3, 26, 52 etc. [32] Fire is the earthly embodiment of Aša vahišta, the genius of truth or best righteousness, who is regarded as one of the Spenta, the immortal holy ones. The nature and dominion of Ahura Mazda are focused and worked out in these. They are in some sense hypostases of his attributes and have both physical and moral significance. Their job is to preserve life and further the world's interests. Thus fire is the most important element of purity, the most beneficial force of life in the divine kingdom of truth, Yasna, 46, 7.

Worship is paid to the pure element itself as an embodiment of this spiritual divine power. This may be seen from the fact that there is no development of a personified fire-god. All things connected with death, deformity, or diminution of life render unclean and are not in any circumstances to come into contact with fire. Esp. connected herewith is the mode of burial. Corpses are to pollute fire, water and earth as little as possible. They are thus exposed naked in "towers of silence" (dakhmas) to the beasts of prey, which embody the world of the evil spirit. Cremation is an abominable offence, Vendidad, 8, 229 ff. [33]

In eschatology fire is a means of final testing at the last judgment. [34] Already in the Gathas we read : "Therefore, wise Lord, when decision is made by thy holy spirit and fire thou wilt apportion (reward and punishment) acc. to guilt and merit with the help of Armaiti and Aša," Yasna, 47, 6. The typical concept of a stream of fiery metal to sift the evil from the good is also found in the Gathas where the aim of this testing by the red fire of Ahura Mazda is more closely defined as impressing a sign on consciences by the molten metal, to the hurt of false believers and the good of true believers, Yasna, 51, 9. The later Bundahish (9th cent. A.D.) has an even fuller depiction of this act of purifying : "When Gocihar in heaven falls to earth from a moonbeam, earth will be as agitated as a sheep when attacked by a wolf. Then fire and ... the metal of Shatvair (archangel of metals) melt in the mountains and hills, and are as a river on the earth. Then all men will go into the molten metal and be purged. If a man is righteous it will be as though he went continuously in warm milk ; but if he is ungodly it will be as though he went continuously in the world in molten metal," 30, 18-20. [35] Finally, Ahura

---

[31] On the Egypt. view of fire cf. O. Clemen, Fontes religionis aegyptiacae (1925), Index, s.v. ignis ; Lang, 23-26.

[32] Ed. F. Spiegel (1859).

[33] Ed. F. Spiegel (1852), 153.

[34] Mayer, 1-79 traces the development from the eschatological ordeal by fire in Zarathustra to the world conflagration in Middle Persian writings.

[35] Ed. K. F. Geldner (1926).

Mazda overcomes the two last enemies, Ahriman and Az (the snake-like demon of greed) and definitively cleanses hell itself by the power of fire. The renewed earth [36] will be an ice-free plain with no unevenness, Bundahish, 30, 30-33. Fire is the refuge of the good divine order of life and the antithesis of the ungodly and demonic powers which dwell in darkness and icy wastes. In principle the devil and hell have no part in fire in this system.

Whereas in the early period of the Achaemenidae worship of Ahura Mazda took place before a flaming altar under the open sky (Hdt., I, 131 f.), later a special temple of fire came into use, [37] like the temples of the modern Parsees. In the innermost chamber, the holy of holies, which is enclosed and darkened, the sacred fire burns on a quadratic stone in a metal vessel, and no human hand may touch it nor human breath defile it. Hence the priests of the fire [38] must wear mittens and gags and tend the fire, which is continually nourished by ritually purified wood, with tongs and ladles. [39] Every new fire which is to burn in the houses is fetched from this sacred hearth. [40]

C. Fire in the Old Testament, Later Judaism and Gnosticism.

I. The Old Testament.

1. Statistics.

In by far the most instances πῦρ is used for Heb. אֵשׁ (some 350 times) in Da. for Aram. נוּר (LXX 12 times, Theodotion 16). In the LXX πῦρ occurs about 490 times, some 100 of these being in writings only in Gk. ἡ πυρά is found only in the Apocrypha (8 times). Other Heb. originals for πῦρ are rare, e.g., אוּר in Is. 44:16; 47:14; Ez. 5:2; שְׂרֵפָה in Gn. 11:3; Am. 4:11; אִשֶּׁה in 1 S. 2:28; בְּעֵרָה in Ex. 22:5; לֶהָבָה in Is. 10:17; cf. Ex. 3:2; רֶשֶׁף in Ps. 78:48. אֵשׁ is only infrequently rendered by other Gk. words, Lv. 2:14 קָלוּי בָּאֵשׁ = πεφρυγμένος, cf. Ez. 23:47; Is. 54:16 : נָפַח בָּאֵשׁ = φυσᾶν; Job 18:5 : שְׁבִיב אֵשׁ = φλόξ; Nu. 18:9 read הָאִשֶּׁה = κάρπωμα "sacrifice."

2. Technical Use.

It is not necessary to record in detail the many occurrences of fire in creation or the human sphere. At this pt. there is nothing peculiar about OT usage. A bare summary of the most important areas will suffice : cooking, Ex. 12:8; 2 Ch. 35:13; Jer. 7:18 etc.; heating, Is. 44:15 f.; Jer. 36:22; manufacture, e.g., Gn. 11:3, esp. metal-work, Jer. 6:29; Sir. 38:28 etc.; destruction in war, e.g., Dt. 13:17; Ju. 20:48; Am. 1:4; Jer. 21:10; Ps. 46:10. Kindling fires was prohibited on the Sabbath, Ex. 35:3. Fire serves as a source of light in Jdt. 13:13.

In the cultus fire is esp. used in sacrifices, Lv. 1:7 ff. The fire of the altar is to be kept burning with the daily burnt-offerings and is never to go out, Lv. 6:2, 6. It is thus called perpetual fire later, πῦρ ἐνδελεχές, 1 Εσδρ. 6:23. [41] Strictly forbidden is the offering of sacrifices with fire not from the altar. A non-cultic sacrifice of this kind is called אֵשׁ זָרָה = πῦρ ἀλλότριον, Lv. 10:1; Nu. 3:4. The offering of children to

[36] On fire as a means of cosmic consummation cf. Mayer, 55 f.

[37] On the basis of excavated remains Erdmann has reconstructed the architectural development of the fire-temple.

[38] On the relation of the Persian fire-cult to worship of the goddess Anahita, cf. Wikander, esp. 52-101.

[39] Bertholet-Leh., II, 236 f.

[40] On the fire-cult cf. also H. H. v. d. Osten, *Die Welt d. Perser*[2] (1956), Index, 294 [K. H. Rengstorf].

[41] At the exile, acc. to an apocr. account, the sacred fire was hidden in a well. It was then rediscovered under Neh. and by a miraculous kindling of the well-water restored to the new altar of the returned exiles. The custom of a special feast of fire rests on this, 2 Macc. 1:18 ff.

Moloch was condemned by the Law as a pagan abomination, Lv. 20:2; Dt. 12:31; 18:10. Nevertheless, in the days of Ahaz (2 K. 16:3) and esp. Manasseh (2 K. 21:6) such sacrifices were made in the Vale of Hinnom (cf. Jer. 7:31), the tt. for these being "to cause sons or daughters to pass through the fire" הֶעֱבִיר בָּאֵשׁ = διάγειν ἐν πυρί, 2 K. 17:17; 21:6. [42] In the cultus fire is also a means of ritual purification (→ III, 416, 22 ff.), Lv. 13:52; Nu. 31:23; Is. 6:6 → 936, 12 ff. It may be used to destroy what is sanctified to keep it from profanation, Ex. 12:10; 29:34; Lv. 4:12 etc., probably also Nu. 6:18. Cremation is practised only in the case of transgressors, Gn. 38:24; Lv. 20:14; 21:9; Jos. 7:15. [43] A possible factor here is the keeping of the people clean as in the case of the destruction of pagan altars and images by fire, Dt. 7:5, 25; 2 K. 23:11; 1 Ch. 14:12 etc., or the devoting of enemies and their goods to radical destruction by fire and sword, Dt. 13:17; Jos. 6:24; 1 S. 15.

As a natural phenomenon fire is found esp. for lightning. As thunder is God's voice, lightning is God's fire, Job 1:16; 2 K. 1:12; cf. the fire of Yahweh in Nu. 11:1; 1 K. 18:38. This meaning is esp. clear when fire is mentioned along with other phenomena like thunder in Ex. 9:28; Ps. 29:7, hail in Ex. 9:24; Ps. 78:48; 105:32, storm and bad weather in Is. 29:6, wind in Ps. 104:4, and snow and ice in Ps. 148:8. In a couple of instances the context shows that אֵשׁ means summer heat or gt. drought, Am. 7:4; Jl. 1:19. In Job 28:5 (כְּמוֹ־אֵשׁ; Theodotion ὡσεὶ πῦρ) mining is compared to volcanic activity, though the original reading is probably "with fire" and refers to what is called firing, an ancient practice whereby hard rocks are prized loose in the shaft by a fire of wood. [44]

3. Transferred Use.

Predominant here is the consuming power of fire. In the Wisdom lit. all kinds of destructive human passions are compared to fire: calumniation and contentiousness, Prv. 26:20 f., anger, Sir. 28:10 f., shedding of blood, Sir. 11:32; 22:24, love and lust, Sir. 9:8; 23:17, adultery, Job 31:12; Prv. 6:27 f. (compared to walking on hot coals), sin, Sir. 3:30; 8:10. Primarily, however, fire is a common image for the judicial wrath of God, Jer. 4:4; 5:14; 21:12; Ez. 21:36; 22:21, 31; 38:19; Zeph. 1:18; 3:8; Na. 1:6; Ps. 79:5; 89:46. In detail various ideas lie behind the usage, the forest fire in Jer. 21:14, the fiery oven in Ps. 21:9, the pile of wood in Is. 30:33, the refining fire in Mal. 3:2, lightning in Lam. 1:13. What is depicted is mostly the irresistible power of destruction, though sometimes also the tendency to spread (cf. the forest fire), the insatiability (Prv. 30:16), the refining function, or occasionally the inconstancy of oppressors (fire of thorns, Ps. 118:12). Proverbially we find "like a brand plucked out of the burning" (Am. 4:11; Zech. 3:2) for someone who has escaped gt. danger, and "as wax melts before the fire" (Mi. 1:4; Ps. 68:2; 97:5) for a radical and relentless process of dissolution. Common, too, is the metaphor of the refiner's fire for purifying in suffering or judgment, Is. 1:22, 25; Jer. 6:27 f.; Ez. 22:17-22; Mal. 3:2; Prv. 17:3; Sir. 2:5; Zech. 13:9.

In contrast the function of illumination plays only a small role in the fig. or transf. use of fire, Na. 2:4; 1 Macc. 6:39.

4. Fire in Relation to God.

a. Fire in Theophany.

In almost all the OT theophanies fire appears as a way of representing the unapproachable sanctity and overpowering glory of Yahweh. Behind all later depictions lies the theophany at Sinai in Ex. 19, where the details suggest a thunder-storm accompanied by a volcanic eruption and earthquake. But the theophany is not always within the setting of natural phenomena of this kind. In the vision at the call of Moses

---

[42] At Dt. 18:10 LXX transl. מַעֲבִיר ...בָּאֵשׁ by περικαθαίρων ... ἐν πυρί.
[43] In the case of Saul and his sons in 1 S. 31:12 we do not have ordinary cremation but a special form of burial, BR, 239.
[44] Cf. G. Hölscher, *Das Buch Hiob, Hndbch. AT* (1937), ad loc.; Galling, BR, 98.

Yahweh appears in a burning bush (Ex. 3:2) and in the case of Gideon He appears in
a flame of fire from the rock (Ju. 6:21). Fire is a means whereby God reveals His
presence, and it represents the mystery of the glory of Yahweh, the כְּבוֹד יהוה, Ex. 24:17
(→ II, 240, 27 ff.). The pillar of cloud and fire which went before Israel in the wilderness
(Ex. 13:21 f.; 14:24; Nu. 14:14; cf. Neh. 9:12, 19) shows that the God who came down
in fire on Sinai is not restricted to that place but leads and protects His people on their
further wanderings.

In later theophanies a progressive theological separation from the element may be
noted. When God appears to Elijah at Horeb it is stated expressly that "the Lord was
not in the fire" (1 K. 19:12). God's being is not made up of the elements; He is Lord
and Ruler of the forces of nature, cf. Ps. 104:4. True revelation is by the Word, 1 K. 19:13;
cf. Ex. 3:4 ff. and 19:21 ff. At the call of Isaiah, where the vision takes cultic forms,
fire is used to purge unclean lips for service as God's messenger, Is. 6:6. The vision of
the prophet Ez. in c. 1, which has some features in common with Is. 6, is dominated
by a heavenly throne scene with four throne-carrying creatures which bear witness on
every hand to the active omnipotence of Yahweh even in the exile. [45] Fire here expresses
the divine radiance and glory, the כְּבוֹד יהוה, Ez. 1:28. In Da. 7 fire is a current image
for the heavenly radiance proper to the angels as well as God, cf. Da. 10:6.

b. Fire as a Means of Divine Judgment.

A primary concern in the OT is Yahweh's judicial intervention in the course
of history. As the Sinai revelation influenced theophanies, so the destruction of
Sodom and Gomorrah by fire and brimstone (Gn. 19:24) exerted a strong influence
on subsequent ideas of divine judgment. Similarly the motif of the ten plagues of
Egypt, of which the seventh is flaming fire mixed with hail (Ex. 9:24), left a
mark which is still to be seen in eschatological depictions, cf. Rev. 8:7. Certain
formal expressions are used for Yahweh's intervention in judgment: "There went
out fire from Yahweh" (Lv. 10:2), "there came down fire from heaven" (2 K. 1:10),
"the fire of Yahweh burnt among them" (Nu. 11:1). In the prophets fire is one
of the most common means of divine judgment. It smites both the vain-glorious
enemies of Israel (Am. 1:4, 7, 10, 12, 14; 2:2; Jer. 43:12; Na. 3:13 etc.) and also the
disobedient people of Israel itself (Am. 2:5; Hos. 8:14; Jer. 11:16; 17:27; 21:14;
22:7; Ez. 15:7; 16:41; 24:9 etc.). The close relation between images of judgment
and theophany expresses the fact that fire is understood, not as a blindly raging
natural force, but as an instrument of punishment in the hand of the divine Judge.

The same is true of the fire of eschatological judgment found from the time of
the prophets. Here biblical thinking centres on the coming of Yahweh to judgment,
not on the manner of the world's destruction or the changing of the elements, as,
e.g., in the doctrine of the cosmic conflagration in Stoicism. Fire has especially
three roles in the eschatological drama. 1. It is a sign of the day of Yahweh,
Jl. 2:30. 2. Yahweh will execute the judgment of eschatological destruction with
fire on all His enemies, Mal. 3:19; Is. 66:15 f.; Ez. 38:22; 39:6. [46] 3. The damned
fall victim to eternal torment by fire. This idea is found for the first time in the

---

[45] W. Zimmerli, *Ezechiel, Bibl. Komm. AT,* 13 (1956), 46-70 has attempted to distinguish
between an original depiction and the adding of the idea of throne-chariots in the "school"
of Ezekiel.

[46] In pre-exilic times the ref. is usually to partial judgments; only Zeph. 1:18; 3:8 speak
fig. of a judgment of fire on the whole earth. After the exile, however, the scene of fiery
judgment was greatly extended, e.g., Is. 33:11 f.; Jl. 2:3; Zech. 12:6. There is no clear-cut
instance of a world conflagration in the OT. In distinction from Parseeism the judgment of
fire is not connected with the concept of the ordeal, Mayer, 132.

post-exilic period and is not uninfluenced by ideas from outside Israel. The most significant OT text in this connection is Is. 66:24 in which the worm and fire denote an unceasing process of torment and corruption, cf. Is. 34:10; Jdt. 16:17; Sir. 21:9 f. "Eternal fire" is not yet a term for hell in the OT.

c. Fire as a Sign of Gracious Visitation.

Though much less frequently, fire can also be a sign of divine grace. This use is normally found in relation to the acceptance of sacrifices. By an appearance of fire Yahweh indicates His pleasure in the sacrifice and His saving presence, Gn. 15:17; Lv. 9:23 f.; Ju. 6:21; 1 K. 18:38; 1 Ch. 21:26; 2 Ch. 7:1.[47] Fire also plays a role in the taking up of esp. eminent men into heaven (a chariot and horses of fire in the case of Elijah in 2 K. 2:11). Fiery phenomena are often signs of divine guidance (the pillar of cloud and fire in the wilderness, → 936, 4 ff.) and divine protection, 2 K. 6:17. In Zech. 2:9 (LXX) Yahweh is a protective wall of fire without[48] and a light within. In the eschatological age of salvation the presence of God is mostly expressed in terms of light, cf. Is. 58:10; 60:1 f., 19 f. Only in Is. 4:5 is the image of fire used to depict the dwelling of the Lord in the perfected city of God.

d. Fire as a Term for God.

When God is called a consuming fire (אֵשׁ אֹכְלָה) in the OT (Dt. 4:24; 9:3; Is. 33:14), He is not understood as a personified element (cf. the Indian fire-god Agni) or as the original substance of all being and becoming (Heraclit. and Stoicism → 930, 18 ff.). In the OT this designation denotes the majestic being of God embracing both grace and judgment. It points to the judicial work of Yahweh. With fiery zeal He watches over obedience to His will. The explanatory addition "a zealous God" in Dt. 4:24 makes this sufficiently plain, and it is demanded by the whole concept of God in the OT. In this sense light and fire can denote the God who acts in grace and judgment: "And the light of Israel shall be for a fire, and his Holy One for a flame," Is. 10:17.

If the cosmologically and philosophically oriented understanding of fire in the surrounding world is predominantly concerned with the element, by contrast fire is viewed theocentrically in the OT as a representation of the mysterious, unapproachable, terrifying and yet gracious glory of Yahweh in revelation, and also as a means and established image of His judicial action.

II. Development in Later Judaism.

1. Apocalyptic.

Whereas the OT mentions the stars only in relation to day and night, in apoc. they are often described as fiery bodies: the sun in Eth. En. 72:4 f.; Gr. Bar. 6 and 8; the stars as great burning hills, Eth. En. 18:13. The idea of disobedient stars in Eth. En. 18:15 is linked with that of fallen angels, 19:1-3. 4 Esr. echoes the doctrine of the four elements in which man is a microcosm made up of earth, water, air and fire, 4 Esr. 4:10 f., 8:8.[49] Fire is very significant in eschatology: a final judgment with fire, Eth. En. 102:1; S. Bar. 37:1; 48:39, 43; 4 Esr. 13:10 f.; Ps. Sol. 15:4 f.; Jub. 9:15; 36:10; Sib. 3, 53 f., 71 f., 542, 618, 673 f., 761; 4, 159 f.; Apc. Eliae 40:17 ff. We find the idea of a world con-

---

[47] In the very first sacrifice in the Bible Theodotion (Gn. 4:4: ἐνεπύρισεν; Heb. וַיִּשַׁע; LXX ἐπεῖδεν) interprets Yahweh's kindly acceptance of Abel and His gift as a consuming with fire.

[48] The idea in Lact. Inst., II, 12, 19 (CSEL, 19, 158): *ipsumque Paradisum igni circumvallavit (Deus)*, is obviously based on Gn. 3:24 and Zech. 2:9. Cf. F. J. Dölger, *Sol Salutis* (1925), 227, n. 3; A. Jeremias, *Das AT im Lichte des alten Orients*[3] (1916), 100, 358 [G. Bertram].

[49] In inspiration the Spirit is depicted as a cup of water "whose colour was like fire," 4 Esr. 14:39.

flagration esp. in Sib., [50] cf. 2, 186 ff., 238 ff., 315 ff.; 3, 83 ff.; 4, 172 ff.; 5, 158 ff., 211 ff., 512-531. Here the motifs of a fiery stream of metal and a falling star pt. to Iranian influence. With increasing dualism, fire has a double form in apoc.: (a) as a means of eternal torment in hell, Eth. En. 91:9; 100:9; 103:8; 4 Esr. 7:38; S. Bar. 44:15; 59:2; eternal fire, Gr. Bar. 4:16; Test. Zeb. 10:3, cf. Test. Jud. 25:3; 4 Macc. 12:12; fiery abyss, Eth. En. 90:24; Gr. En. 10:13 (χάος τοῦ πυρός); pool of fire, Eth. En. 90:25; [51] Gr. En. 10:6 (ἐμπυρισμός); pillars of fire, Eth. En. 18:11; 21:7; 90:26; lake of fire, Apc. of Sophonias 7:2, 3; fiery oven, Eth. En. 54:6; 98:3; 4 Esr. 7:36; cf. Vis. Esr. 48; fiery instruments of torture, Apc. Esr. 4:9 ff., 16 ff.; Vis. Esr. 13 ff., 19, 45 f.; Apc. of Sophonias 5:1; 15:6; Sib., 2, 286 ff., 295, (b) as a sign of the heavenly world of light, Eth. En. 14:9-25; 71:1-12; Apc. Abr. 18 : Vit. Ad. 25; angels as fiery beings, Sl. En. 1:5; 29:3; 4 Esr. 8:21; S. Bar. 21:6; Apc. of Sophonias 9:4; Apc. Abr. 19:5-9; angels of the spirit of fire, Jub. 2:2.

2. The Rabbis.

There were various views as to the temporal origin of fire. The Midr. lists it among the three elements which existed before the world, Ex. r., 15 on 12:12. Acc. to a widespread view it was created on the second day of creation, acc. to another view on the day of preparation for the Sabbath or at the end of the Sabbath, bPes., 54a. The Rabb. refer to six forms of fire. The first consumes but does not drink : ordinary fire which is quenched by water ; the second drinks but does not consume : fever, bShab., 67a; bJeb., 71b; the third consumes and drinks : the fire of Elijah, 1 K. 18:38; the fourth consumes both what is moist and what is dry : the fire of the altar ; the fifth drives back other fire : the fire of the angel Gabriel who cooled the fiery furnace in Da. 3:25; the sixth consumes other fire : the fire of deity, for the master said, He burnt the rebellious angels (fiery beings) with His finger, bJoma, 21b, Bar. Cultic worship of fire is rejected by the Rabb.; those who worship fire (חַבְּרִים) are compared to the angels of perdition, bQid., 72a.

On the basis of the Sinai story the Torah was often associated with fire. The Law itself consisted of fire, its skin of white fire, the letters of black fire, jSota, 8, 4 (22d, 32 ff.). It is called fire in Dt. 33:2 (Midr.: "On his right hand was the fire of the Law"). [52] The two fires of the Torah are the written and the oral Law, Cant. r., 2, 5. In this light it is easy to understand why there are ref. to fiery phenomena in the study and reading of the Law [53] and finally why the scholar wholly dedicated to the Torah is also said to consist of fire : the fire of hell has no power over scribes, "whose whole body is fire," bChag., 27a.

In eschatology Rabbinism, like apoc., chiefly developed the ideas of heaven and hell, with some Babyl. and Iranian influences. [54] From the 2nd cent. B.C. sheol, originally the dark abode of all the dead, becomes increasingly the place of fiery punishment for the ungodly, [55] → I, 146, 36 ff.; 657, 22 ff., usually called Gehinnom by the Rabb. In the days of Jesus sheol is still regarded as the intermediate place of punishment alongside the final place, Gehinnom. [56] But after the famous saying of R. Jochanan b. Zakkai (c. 20 A.D.) about the two ways to Gan Eden and Gehinnom (bBer., 28b → V, 59, 13 ff.) Gehinnom gradually replaced sheol in the Rabb. even as the intermediate place of punishment.

---

[50] But cf. Eth. En. 1:6 ff.; Vit. Ad. 49 f.; Apc. Eliae 43:5 f.; Ps.-Sophocles, 2, 1-6 (Riessler, 1046).

[51] Cf. A. Dieterich, *Nekyia²* (1913), 218-221. In Eth. En. 90:25 we may assume that λίμνη was the Gk. text [P. Katz].

[52] Str.-B., IV, 1068.

[53] *Ibid.*, 603 f.

[54] We do not find the idea of a world conflagration in the Rabb. apart from an odd comparing of the flood of water and that of fire, M. Ex., 18, 1 (64b); Str.-B., III, 773.

[55] Str.-B., IV, 1075 f.

[56] *Ibid.*, 1023.

In the intermediate Gehinnom men suffer the torments of fire, bChag., 15b. From the 2nd century A.D. atoning and purifying power is ascribed to the fire of the intermediate Gehinnom. This corresponds, then, to the purgatory of Roman Catholicism. Those who remain may alleviate or shorten it by intercession and almsgiving, bQid., 31b; Pesikt. r., 20, 95b. [57] Apart from the eternally rejected on a special list (Sanh., 10, 1-3) all the transgressors of Israel will pass through this purifying phase to the salvation of the world to come. The Mishnah hands down a saying of R. Akiba that the intermediate fire of purgatory lasts for 12 months, Ed., 2, 10. Some 3rd century scholars see two successive periods of heat and cold; the ungodly suffer for 6 months in fire and for 6 months in snow, jSanh., 10, 3 (29b, 71 ff.). [58]

By means of exegetical combinations the Rabb. could make the most astonishing statements about the penal fire of the final and intermediate Gehinnom. [59] It never goes out, bPes., 54a. It burns 60 times as hot as ordinary fire, bBer., 57b. Its intensity increases with depth, Midr. Ps. 84 § 3. It is heated with coals which maintain their heat for a long time, Midr. Ps. 120 § 4. Those whose merits and demerits are equally balanced at the Last Judgment must first purge their sins in the fire of hell acc. to the school of Shammai, whereas according to the school of Hillel they may enter into the future world at once by the grace of God, bRH, 16b, Bar. [60]

Since fire expresses the glory of God and His sphere, it is also the matter of the heavenly world acc. to the Rabb. God's finger (bSanh., 38b) and the angels (Pesikt. r., 57a) are composed of flaming fire. [61] Acc. to a widespread view the angels are created out of the river of fire נְהַר דִּי־נוּר (Da. 7:10) which consists of the sweat of the four living creatures before the throne of God, e.g., Gn. r., 78 on 32:26. [62] The divinely given models acc. to which Moses was to make the ark, table and lights (Ex. 25:40) were composed of fire as the building material of heaven, bMen., 29a. [63]

3. The Qumran Sect.

The Dead Sea Scrolls [64] share the idea that the last act will bring God's fiery judgment on His foes. 1 Qp Hab. 10:5: God will judge the house of judgment with fiery brimstone (באש גופרית, Sodom motif); 10:13: The enemies of the elect of God will come into fiery judgment (למשפטי אש): 1 QS 2:15: May God's wrath and the zeal of His judgments burn him to eternal destruction (יבערו בו לכלת עולמים), cf. 1 QH 6:18 f. They are also acquainted with the idea of eternal hell-fire. 1 QS 2:8: May you be cursed in the darkness of eternal fire (באפלת אש עולמים); 1 QS 4:13: The shame of destruction in the fire of dark places (כלמת כלה באש מחשכים); 1 QH 17:13: Fire in the depths of sheol. In this respect they are wholly within the framework of apoc. usage. Fig., too, fire denotes judgment and affliction, 1 QH 4:33; 6:25; 8:20, 30. In the desciption of the last time in the Hymn Scroll there are traces of the idea of a world conflagration (1 QH 3:29-33 as in the Sib. → 937, 41 ff. In spite of a strong dualism we do not find in the Scrolls the Gnostic view of matter as fire.

4. Hellenistic Judaism.

a. In Philo there is an obvious conflict between the Greek cosmological view of fire and the Jewish eschatological view. Philo adopts the four-element teaching (Det. Pot.

---

[57] Str.-B., IV, 1043-1059.
[58] Ibid., 1058, 1061.
[59] Ibid., 1075-1083.
[60] Ibid., 1033, 1050.
[61] III, 678.
[62] I, 977.
[63] III, 702 f.
[64] Cf. Delling, 106.

Ins., 8) and describes the nature and properties of fire wholly after the manner of Gk. philosophy. Fire is what is warm by nature θερμόν (Rer. Div. Her., 135), light κοῦφον (Aet. Mund., 115), fine λεπτομερές (Rer. Div. Her., 134), porous μανόν (Aet. Mund., 105). It has a threefold form as coal, flame and light (Aet. Mund., 86). It has three essential functions, to give light φωτίζειν (Decal., 48), to burn καίειν (Leg. All., I, 5) and to warm ἀλεαίνειν (Spec. Leg., IV, 56). Gk., too, is the strong emphasis on the cultural significance of fire, Vit. Mos., II, 219 f.; Spec. Leg., II, 65.

Anthropologically Philo differs from the ancient Stoic equation of spirit and fire when he insists on the unknowability of the human spirit (Mut. Nom., 10) and the world soul or deity (Leg. All., I, 91), though he shows some dependence on this in his expressions : ὁ νοῦς, ἔνθερμον καὶ πεπυρωμένον πνεῦμα, Fug., 133; ἔνθερμον καὶ πυρώδη λόγον Cher., 30. The same applies to his critical discussion of the Gk. doctrine of a world conflagration, Aet. Mund., 79-103.

It is worth noting that for him the penal judgment with fire on Nadab and Abihu (Lv. 10:2) means transition to fellowship with God (Leg. All., II, 57; Fug., 59; Rer. Div. Her., 309), just as the vision of God is connected with fire (Praem. Poen., 37-39), hellfire playing only a minor part. Also worth noting is the fact that allegorical interpretation enables him to set the cultic fire of the altar in the service of philosophical ethics, Spec. Leg., I, 285-288. But with his stress on the ineffability and transcendence of God he gets beyond the rationalistic fire monism of the older Stoa.

b. Joseph. uses πῦρ in the lit. sense in Ant., 10, 95; πολλὰ πυρά, 12, 306; πυρὶ ἐκκαθαρθῆναι τὰ ἄγια, Bell., 4, 323, cf. also πυρεῖον "fuel" in Ant., 5, 238 and πυρετός "fever" [65] in Ant., 13, 398; Bell., 1, 106; Vit., 48. [66]

III. Gnostic Usage.

The anti-cosmic dualism of Gnosticism finds expression in the antithesis light/darkness. In this connection fire is an alternative for darkness, and it is thus diametrically opposed to the supreme God, who is light.

1. The Hermetic Writings.

In the Corp. Herm. fire denotes the material cosmos (1, 4), the planetary and demonic sphere (10, 16) and the sensual passions in man (10, 20). The demiurge is ὁ ἐπικείμενος ἐπὶ τοῦ πυρός, 1, 13. The impulse to earthly corporeality is the real evil, 1, 19; 7, 2 f. When the soul ascends to the higher world, vices are given back to the individual spheres, 1, 25.

2. Coptic Gnostic Works.

In the cosmology of the Pistis Sophia the sub-lunar world is surrounded by three spheres (12-14) ruled by fiery archons (c. 27). These also represent Egypt or matter, c. 18. When the soul ascends to the sphere of light of the 13th aeon it must pass through the fire zone of the archons. Thanks to the mysteries of light it is kept safe there (c. 143) when otherwise it would fall victim to the judicial power of fire. Fiery punishments vary in nature and duration acc. to the deeds of sinners, c. 144-147. Here the most diverse concepts of hell-fire are combined with the fiery region of the archons in the air. The Gnostic baptism of fire, along with water and Spirit baptism, is described in the so-called Book of Jeû.

3. The Mandaean Literature.

In the Ginza living fire and consuming fire are often contrasted, 76, 10 f.; 91, 37 f.; 264, 39; 267, 11 ff.; 294, 3. This is the same antithesis as that of light and darkness or truth and falsehood. One example will illustrate the sense : "They left living fire and

---

[65] Cf. LXX Dt. 28:22 (Heb. קַדַּחַת).
[66] I owe these Jos.-ref. to K. H. Rengstorf.

went and loved consuming fire," 69, 22 f. Often water == "living fire" and fire == "consuming fire," Lidz. Liturg., 24, 3-8. Positively evaluated, fire belongs to the eternal, victorious king of light and glory, Lidz. Ginza, 73, 10 ff. The emissaries of light wear a "garment of living fire" (91, 17) or a "crown of living fire" (79, 11) at a glimpse of which the demons are afraid (83, 6). The soul of man is also living fire, 246, 6. Negatively we find two expressions which are often par. [67] For the most part, however, "consuming fire" refers to life in the material cosmos while "flaming fire" refers to judgment after death. Consuming fire controls the realm of the planets (Lidz. Ginza, 53, 27 f.; 248, 6) and the whole earthly and material world. This world of darkness, falsehood and death (14, 30-37), of wickedness and corruptibility (78, 9 f.), is full of consuming fire (33, 4 f.). This is also a mark of false prophets (29, 7 and 17; 47, 9 and 17-22; Lidz. Liturg., 154) and demons (Lidz. Ginza, 67, 29 f.). In anthropology consuming fire denotes the material body (91, 35 ff.), the "filthy, stinking, wasting, corruptible body" (430, 17 f.), and human passions (94, 4 f.; 132, 20 f.; 278, 7 f.). Flaming fire usually, if not always, represents the eschatological fire of judgment, Lidz. Ginza, 19, 5 f.; 54, 5; 225, 22; 299, 3; Lidz. Joh., 63, 11 and 19 ff. Here hell is connected with the region of fire in the air and current ideas of the punishments of hell are adopted. With some schematisation it may be said that he who loves consuming fire (matter) in life will fall victim to flaming fire (judgment) when the soul ascends.

In the work Ἀπόφασις μεγάλη (Hipp. Ref., VI, 9, 4 ff.), which is ascribed to Simon Magus, fire is the basic element in all cosmic development. It is "the root of all," though one may discern dualism in the double nature of fire (κρυπτόν — φανερὸν πῦρ). [68] Visible fire arises out of invisible. Everything corporeal is dissolved again in the world conflagration. In Gnosticism, then, fire is either twofold in acc. with the idea that the same elements can be pure and impure, [69] or, in distinction from Parseeism, it is the evil principle, often in antithesis to water as the good element. [70]

D. Fire in the New Testament.

I. The Earthly Phenomenon.

The use of πῦρ for the earthly phenomenon is within the bounds of general usage. Only rarely is the ref. to a phenomenon of nature. In the quotation from Ps. 104:4 in Hb. 1:7 πυρὸς φλόγα, with πνεύματα, denotes lightning. The context of Rev. 16:8 (cf. v. 9) suggests the heat of the sun. Often the ref. is to fire as used by man. In Mk. 9:22 (par. Mt. 17:15) the fire is that of the house or daily village life. The epileptic boy incurs risks when he falls into fire or water in his fits. Acc. to Lk. 22:55 the Jewish servants in the court of the high-priest's house lit a kind of watch-fire to warm themselves. The connection of this with φῶς (v. 56) is explained by the fact that it was night-time. The ref. in Ac. 28:5 is to the previously mentioned fire (cf. ἡ πυρά in v. 2 f.); Paul shakes off the viper into this. In Hb. 11:34 fire is a last impotent weapon of torture and execution used against the heroes of faith, and in Rev. 17:16; 18:8 it is a weapon of fighting and destruction in war. The absence of ref. to the fire of the altar or sacrifice is in keeping with the new concept of priest and offering. The fire of the heavenly altar is mentioned in Rev. 8:5. In distinction from the Gk. world the NT has no place for fire as an element or a cultural factor.

II. Figurative and Transferred Usage.

1. On an OT basis fire is common especially as a figure of divine judgment, → 935, 27 ff. The metaphors are mostly taken from the agricultural sphere: the

---

[67] Cf. the Index, s.v. in Lidz. Ginza, 606.

[68] Bousset, 230-232.

[69] Cf. the five elements of light and darkness in Manicheanism.

[70] The antithesis of water and fire plays a part esp. in Gnostic baptismal circles, Epiph. Haer., 19, 3, 7; Ps.-Clem. Hom., 11, 26, 4; 20, 9, 4. Cf. Bousset, 156 f.; H. Schlier, Religionsgeschichtliche Untersuchungen z. d. Ignatiusbriefen (1929), 146 f.

burning of unfruitful trees (Mt. 3:10 par. Lk. 3:9; Mt. 7:19), of chaff (Mt. 3:12; [71]
Lk. 3:17), of tares (Mt. 13:40), of the unfruitful branches of the vine (Jn. 15:6).
The reference in the Synoptists is always to eschatological judgment. [72] In Jm. 5:3
there is a closer interweaving of image and reality and the metaphor describes the
consuming severity of judgment on the rich who are guilty towards their neighbours because they heap up transitory wealth even though the last time has already broken in, → III, 335, 24 ff. The proverbial saying about gold tried in the
fire (cf. Prv. 17:3; 27:21; Sir. 2:5; Wis. 3:6) is applied in 1 Pt. 1:7 to the keeping of
hope and faith in the sorrows of this world, → II, 259, 3 ff., while in Rev. 3:18
it is a summons to repentance directed against the lukewarmness and self-confidence of the faith of the church of Laodicea.

2. In transferred usage the term is mostly used *in malam partem* as in the OT
(→ 935, 22 ff.) and the Greek world (→ 929, 37 ff.). In Jm. 3:5 f. the destructive
power of the tongue is called a fire (cf. Sir. 28:22) and the image of the world
conflagration, common in the diatribe and Philo, [73] is used. The saying of Jesus in
Lk. 12:49 is set in a context which yields the transferred meaning: "fire of
discord" (cf. διαμερισμόν in v. 51 and Mt. 10:34).

III. Theological Use.

The main influence here is that of the OT and the Jewish apocalyptic tradition.

1. Fire at Theophanies.

Sometimes there is reference to the familiar OT theophanies in fire. In Stephen's
speech (Ac. 7:30) the appearance to Moses in the burning bush (Ex. 3:2) [74] is
mentioned; the wording varies only slightly from the LXX account. Hb. 12:18 ff.
alludes to the divine self-revelation at Sinai. Explicitly there are no new theophanies in the NT. Fire is no longer mentioned in this connection. When Christ
appears to Paul outside Damascus there is reference only to a light from heaven,
Ac. 9:3.

2. Fire as a Means of Divine Judgment.

In temporal judgments fire occurs only in allusions to OT scenes. Lk. 9:54
refers to 2 K. 1:10, 12, and the addition ὡς καὶ Ἡλίας ἐποίησεν underlines this.
Fire from heaven denotes a miraculous penal intervention on God's part. As
compared with this the question of a natural sub-stratum is secondary. [75] In
Lk. 17:26-30 the unexpected coming of judgment in the days of Noah and Lot
is compared to the day of the Son of Man. V. 29 quotes Gn. 19:24 (גָּפְרִית וָאֵשׁ)
and is thus to be taken transitively: "He (God) caused fire and brimstone (πῦρ
καὶ θεῖον) to rain down from heaven" (cf. הִמְטִיר).

Mostly fire is found in an eschatological context.

---

[71] Here the addition of ἀσβέστῳ to πυρί detaches the image from the reality: the
coming One will deliver up the impenitent to the fire of eternal perdition.
[72] In Jn. the ref. is to the judgment which takes place with the present decision of faith,
Bultmann J. on 15:6.
[73] On the use of the world conflagration motif cf. Dib. Jk., *ad loc.* Cf. the threats of
judgment in Is. 9:17; 10:17 ff.; Jer. 21:14; Ez. 21:3; Ps. 83:14 [Fohrer].
[74] With B we are to read ἐν πυρὶ φλογός. On the readings cf. P. Katz, "'Εν πυρὶ
φλογός," ZNW, 46 (1955), 133-138.
[75] Hck. Lk., *ad loc.* suggests a flash of lightning.

a. The Symbol.

It is especially in Revelation, which makes considerable use of the images of Jewish apocalyptic, that fire occurs among the signs and judgments which precede the final act. The punishments on the sounding of the seventh trumpet are in part analogous to the plagues of Egypt. The combination of fire and hail in the judgment on the earth (Rev. 8:7) reminds us of the seventh plague, Ex. 9:24. It is hard to say for certain whether the expression "as it were a great mountain burning with fire" (8:8) has in view a volcanic eruption [76] or a star. [77] The horses of the judgment of the sixth trumpet are painted in mythological colours and spew out fire, smoke and brimstone (9:17 f.); they are thereby characterised as hellish monsters spreading destruction. The two witnesses (11:3) are eschatological precursors of the Messiah and are Moses and Elijah according to v. 6, → II, 938, 23 ff.; IV, 863, 21 ff. In a traditional phrase (2 Βασ. 22:9) it is said of them that "fire proceedeth out of their mouth, and devoureth their enemies" (v. 5). This means that they stand under the protection of God's mighty judgment. Those who attack them have to reckon with God, like the opponents of Moses and Elijah. The scene in 2 K. 1:10 was linked with Elijah in the tradition, as may be seen from the description of Elijah as προφήτης ὡς πῦρ in Sir. 48:1 and also from Lk. 9:54. Part of the satanic seduction of the last days is that the pseudo-prophet can even make "fire come down from heaven on the earth in the sight of men" (13:13) as a sign of divine validation, cf. 4 Esr. 5:4 ff.; Mk. 13:22; 2 Th. 2:9. In Rev. 14:18 a special angel of fire (ἔχων ἐξουσίαν ἐπὶ τοῦ πυρός) comes forth from the heavenly temple with the command to execute judgment (according to the image of the vintage). In Jewish apocalyptic angels are the representatives of mankind (the nations) and of all the natural orders (Eth. En. 60:12-22; angel of water, Rev. 16:5; of wind, 7:1; of fire, Jub. 2:2). [78] In the sermon at Pentecost (Ac. 2:19) the promise of Jl. 2:30 is regarded as fulfilled by the outpouring of the Spirit.

b. The Eschatological Fire of Judgment. Fire plays a vital role in the NT as the eschatological fire of judgment.

(a) In the Messianic preaching of John the Baptist the final judgment is portrayed already as a baptism of fire. The Q text (Mt. 3:11; Lk. 3:16) is closer to the original here. [79] The logion describes the gathering of the eschatological community in grace and judgment (cf. the purging of the floor in Mt. 3:12). The coming Messiah will give penitents the Spirit promised for the last time (cf. 1 QS 4:20-22) and judge the recalcitrant with fire.

(b) In the sayings of Jesus the fire of the Last Judgment is less prominent than eternal hell-fire. Yet one must presuppose acquaintance with the idea of an eschatological judgment of fire found in the OT and apocalyptic. This is the best starting-point for an interpretation of the difficult sayings Mk. 9:49 and Lk. 12:49. The obscure saying in Mk. 9:49 : πᾶς γὰρ πυρὶ ἁλισθήσεται, [80] is to

---

[76] Had. Apk. and Zn. Apk., ad loc.: eruption of Vesuvius.

[77] Loh. Apk., ad loc.

[78] For the Rabb. cf. Str.-B., III, 820. In the Midr. Gabriel is the angel of fire, Nu. r., 12 on 7:1; cf. bPes., 118a.

[79] Bultmann Trad., 263; cf. H. J. Flowers, "ἐν πνεύματι ἁγίῳ καὶ πυρί," Exp. T., 64 (1952/53), 155 f.

[80] Lohmeyer on the basis of the African text proposes πᾶσα δὲ οὐσία ἀναλωθήσεται (Loh. Mk., ad loc.) but this disrupts the relation between ἁλισθήσεται in v. 49 and τὸ ἅλας in v. 50.

be regarded as a paradoxical riddle. [81] Salt and fire are antithetical concepts. Salt has a purifying, flavouring and preservative power, → I, 228 f. Fire is a fixed metaphor for God's judgment, → I, 658, 35 ff. The combination of these antithetical concepts gives the saying its paradoxical edge. The way to fellowship with God is by judgment of the old man. [82] He who does not accept this now by denial of self falls victim to the wrath to come. Thus the saying is a material parallel to Mt. 10:39 and to the similar riddle in Mk. 10:25 ff. The double saying in Lk. 12:49 f., which is not from Q, since Mt. does not have it, comprehensively describes the mission of Jesus as a fulfilment of the promise of the Baptist, yet in such a way that the One who baptises with the Spirit and fire must first tread the path of suffering Himself. The fig. use of baptism (→ I, 538, 28 ff.) for severe affliction (cf. Mk. 10:38 and Ps. 11:6) [83] is related in v. 50 to Jesus' own death and passion whereby He founds the eschatological community. The parallel forms of v. 49 and v. 50 suggest material correspondence too. Thus v. 49 says that Jesus will bring a judgment of fire on the earth in which He Himself will be implicated. The meaning of πῦρ here is controlled by the basic sense of the eschatological judgment of fire, but the judgment is present in and with Jesus. The attitude to Jesus decides between fellowship with God and alienation from Him. The eschatological possibilities of judgment (πῦρ) and salvation (βασιλεία) are brought home to the dwellers on earth by the coming of Jesus. [84]

(c) πῦρ occurs in 3 passages in Paul, 1 C. 3:13, 15 (3 times); 2 Th. 1:8; R. 12:20. The reference in each case is to the eschatological judgment of fire. In 1 C. 3:13 Paul adopts in his argument the idea that the Lord will execute the last judgment with fire. The coming day will decide concerning the work of preachers, "for it shall appear with fire." The eschatological judgment of fire will test the quality of every work. The good builder whose work is fire-proof will receive a reward. The poor builder whose work burns up will suffer loss, but not eternal damnation : "he shall be saved, yet so as through fire," v. 15b. The difficult concluding clause does not describe the punishment as a purging by fire [85] but uses a proverbial saying to make the point that only with the skin of his teeth, and not without great peril, will the one concerned attain to eternal salvation. Paul is here bringing four current ideas into loose connection without following them through consistently : 1. the theme of the house on fire, which derives logically from the metaphorical description of preaching as building ; 2. the expectation that the coming Lord will appear with fire (2 Th. 1:8); 3. the idea of an eschatological refining by fire (Mal. 3:2); and 4. the proverbial expression about being saved through fire, i.e., having a narrow escape → 935, 34 ff. The stress is on the incorruptibility and definitiveness of the Last Judgment. In 2 Th. 1:7 f. the *parousia* of Jesus is depicted in OT terms as both judgment and redemption. The revelation of the Lord will be in flaming fire, Ex. 3:2 B → n. 74. What is said about Yahweh in the OT (Is. 66:15) is here transferred to Jesus. There is no hint of the idea

---

[81] J. Schniewind, *Das Ev. nach Mk., NT Deutsch,* 1⁸ (1958), ad loc.

[82] Cf. the same thought in another theological form in Paul (2 C. 5:17) and John (3:3, 4, 7).

[83] Delling, 102-112.

[84] The pt. is the same in the apocr. saying of Jesus in Orig. in Jer. hom. lat., 3, 3 (ed. A. Baehrens [1925], 312): *Qui iuxta me est, iuxta ignem est ; qui longe est a me, longe est a regno.* Cf. J. Jeremias, *Unbekannte Jesusworte* (1951), 53-55.

[85] Orig. was the first to introduce this idea in connection with the doctrine of a cosmic conflagration, Gnilka, 126; cf. G. Anrich, "Clemens u. Orig. als Begründer d. Lehre vom Fegfeuer," *Holtzmann-Festschr.* (1902), 97-120.

of a world conflagration. Fire is essentially a means of punishment used by the Lord when He comes for the Last Judgment. In R. 12:20 Paul uses the quotation from Prv. 25:21 f. to back up his admonition to renounce all revenge. The OT proverb [86] calls for reconciliation in the paradoxical form : "If you want revenge, avenge yourself by helping." [87] In this way you will overcome your enemy by doing good. Paul sets the metaphor in the context of eschatological judgment, v. 19. Hence the coals of fire acquire a secondary reference to the judgment of fire. If your enemy does not react to your acts of kindness by a change of heart, i.e., if he now dodges the coals of fire on his head, he will not escape the fire of the wrath to come. [88]

(d) In the other NT writings πῦρ refers plainly to the eschatological judgment of fire in Hb. 10:27: ἐκδοχὴ κρίσεως καὶ πυρὸς ζῆλος ἐσθίειν μέλλοντος τοὺς ὑπεναντίους. In Hb. 12:29 the OT definition of God as a consuming fire (πῦρ καταναλίσκον, Dt. 4:24; 9:3) is set in an eschatological context, v. 27. Rev. 20:9 uses a traditional formula (2 K. 1:10) to describe the annihilating fiery judgment of God on the nations Gog and Magog in the final struggle. In 2 Pt. 3:7 the disaster of the flood is compared with a second destruction of the world by fire. The present heaven and earth are being kept for the fire by the same Word of God (τεθησαυρισμένοι ... πυρί). The description which follows makes it clear that a world conflagration is meant. On the day of the Lord "the heavens shall pass away with a great noise, and the elements shall melt in the fire," v. 10. This late passage is the only one in the NT in which the doctrine of a world conflagration, current in Babylonia, Persia and Greece, is distinctly combined with the apocalyptic concept of judgment.

c. The Fire of Hell. In the NT, as in apocalyptic, we find not only the fire of eschatological judgment but also eternal hell-fire, the unceasing fiery torment of the damned in the final Gehinnom. In many cases the two ideas merge into one another with no clear-cut frontier between them. Hell-fire occurs chiefly in Mark/ Matthew (13 times) and Rev. (7 times).

(a) In the sayings and parables of Jesus πῦρ is for the most part the opposite of βασιλεία or ζωή, Mt. 13:42; 18:8 f.; 25:41; Mk. 9:43, 45, 47. βασιλεία or ζωή and πῦρ or σκότος represent here the two eschatological possibilities of salvation or perdition. [89] In Mk. 9:48 [90] hell-fire is described in terms of a quotation which Judaism had already used for the same purpose, namely, Is. 66:24 : ὅπου ὁ σκώληξ αὐτῶν οὐ τελευτᾷ καὶ τὸ πῦρ οὐ σβέννυται. This also explains the use of τὸ πῦρ τὸ ἄσβεστον for the eternal torments of hell (Mk. 9:43; [91] cf. Mt. 3:12; Lk. 3:17), which is found in the main in Mk. Mt. uses τὸ πῦρ τὸ αἰώνιον for this (Mt. 18:8; 25:41) and describes hell-fire as ἡ γέεννα τοῦ πυρός [92] (5:22; 18:9) [93]

---

[86] Behind the proverbial saying about coals of fire on the head there might well stand an Egypt. change-of-heart rite consisting of carrying glowing embers on a layer of ashes in a basin on one's head. This gives rise to the transf. sense in the proverb : to bring about a change of heart in one's enemy by acts of kindness, v. S. Morenz, "Feurige Kohlen auf dem Haupt," ThLZ, 78 (1953), 187-192.

[87] P. Volz, Hi. u. Weisheit, Schr. AT, ad loc.

[88] Schl. R., ad loc.

[89] The combination of πῦρ and σκότος for the place of perdition reflects the fact that dark sheol and fiery Gehinnom had now merged into a single concept.

[90] In later MSS the quotation was introduced from v. 48 into v. 44 and 46 as well.

[91] In v. 45 εἰς τὸ πῦρ τὸ ἄσβεστον is a later addition.

[92] In later witnesses τοῦ πυρός was added in Mk. 9:47 to give another instance.

[93] D omits τοῦ πυρός.

or ἡ κάμινος τοῦ πυρός (13:42, 50). The fiery furnace which is a place of earthly torment in the OT (Da. 3:6 ff.) had already become a current term for the place of perdition in later Judaism, → 938, 8.

(b) According to Jd. 7 the wicked inhabitants of Sodom and Gomorrha already suffer the punishment of eternal fire. According to a later Jewish view the fire of judgment depicted in Gn. 19:24 f. still burns on as the subterranean fire of hell. The Dead Sea with its remarkable fiery phenomena offers to all who live in the area a terrifying illustration of the punishment of hell. [94] The idea of eternal hell-fire seems to stand behind the phrase σῴζετε ἐκ πυρὸς ἁρπάζοντες in Jd. 23. This echoes the proverbial phrase for being rescued from great danger (Am. 4:11 → 935, 34 ff.), but in the light of v. 7 πῦρ is to be related here, too, to the fire of judgment. [95]

(c) In Rev. the reference of fire and brimstone is usually to eternal damnation in hell. Those who worship the beast and his image fall victim to the endless torments of fire and brimstone in the presence of the holy angels and the Lamb, 14:10. [96] For hell we find not only ἄβυσσος in 20:3 etc. but also the image of the sulphurous lake of fire : εἰς τὴν λίμνην τοῦ πυρὸς τῆς καιομένης [97] ἐν θείῳ (19:20); εἰς τὴν λίμνην τοῦ πυρὸς καὶ θείου (20:10); ἐν τῇ λίμνῃ τῇ καιομένῃ πυρὶ καὶ θείῳ (21:8); ἡ λίμνη τοῦ πυρός (20:14 f. 3 times). The term "lake of fire" (cf. Eth. En. 90:25), which corresponds materially to the Synoptic ἡ γέεννα τοῦ πυρός, is obviously based on the punishment of Sodom and the view that the Dead Sea is the place where evil spirits and the Sodomites are punished. This may be seen from the combination of fire and brimstone and the concept of the lake ; lakes are often holy in pagan cults. [98]

(d) The almost complete absence of any ref. to fire in the Gospel and Epistles of John is connected with the strong emphasis on the present decision of faith regarding Jesus Christ and the lesser prominence of apocalyptic ideas, though expectation of the return of Christ is not abandoned. John opposes the biblical view of the Creator to the Gnostic idea that matter is fire, → 940, 29 ff.

3. Fire as a Sign of Heavenly Glory.

Fire was already regarded as a sign of heavenly glory in Jewish apocalyptic, and it retains this significance in the NT, though the judicial aspect is more prominent. As might be expected, Rev. yields the most instances. In the vision of the call of the divine in Rev. 1:9 ff. the appearance of the Son of Man is described with traits drawn from Da. 7 and 10, the attributes of God being transferred to Jesus. Christ is characterised as a royal high-priest in v. 13. The images which follow express "the heavenly δόξα which is manifest in Jesus." [99] "Eyes as a flame of fire" (v. 14; cf. Da. 10:6; 7:9; Slav. En. 1:5) and "feet like unto fine brass, as if it were burned in a furnace" [100] (v. 15; cf. Da. 10:6; Ez. 1:27) are current apocalyptic expressions to denote heavenly glory. Most of the attributes in this vision of Christ recur in the individual letters in a certain material order

---

[94] For the fiery phenomena cf. Philo Abr., 140 f.; Vit. Mos., II, 56. For the paradigmatic aspect of the judgment on Sodom cf. 3 Macc. 2:5.
[95] Kn. Pt. on Jd. 23.
[96] Heaven and hell are thus within sight of one another, cf. Lk. 16:19 ff.
[97] Loh. Apk., ad loc.
[98] Dionysus is called Λιμναῖος in Aristoph. Ra., 210 f.; Thuc., II, 15, 4; Paus., II, 37, 5.
[99] Had. Apk., ad loc.
[100] πεπυρωμένης is a grammatical slip for πεπυρωμένῳ, Loh. Apk., ad loc.

with a view to emphasising the authority of the exalted Lord who speaks. The flaming eyes and glowing feet are mentioned in 2:18 in the letter to the church of Thyatira, which has to be sharply rebuked. Implied here is the judicial element, [101] cf. Christ coming for the Last Judgment in 19:12. The symbols of fire or light are not restricted to God or Christ but may be ascribed to the angels too as dwellers in the heavenly sphere. The angel who comes down from heaven in 10:1 has "feet as pillars of fire." This does not apply to a specific angel like Gabriel but is a general characteristic of angels as beings which share the heavenly glory. Another reference to the angels as fiery figures of light is the equation of the seven burning torches before the throne with the seven spirits of God, 4:5; cf. S. Bar. 21:6. In this connection fire expresses the splendour of the heavenly glory; the closer to the throne, the greater the δόξα, cf. Eth. En. 14:22. Objects as well as persons may be invested with the attribute of fire to show that they belong to the world of light. The crystal sea before the throne of God (4:6) is to be regarded as a heavenly counterpart to the molten sea (1 K. 7:23; 2 Ch. 4:2) in the priests' court. The addition μεμιγμένην πυρί (Rev. 15:2), which is parallel to the ὁμοία κρυστάλλῳ of 4:6, shows that this belongs to the heavenly sphere.

To the context of this apocalyptic usage, and not to the tradition of the Greek-Stoic equation of spirit and fire, belong the tongues of fire of the story of Pentecost in Ac. 2:3. [102] The comparison with fire (γλῶσσαι ὡσεὶ πυρός) indicates the heavenly origin of the Spirit and the nature of the event, which can be explained only by a miraculous intervention on God's part and not by forces immanent in the world.

In the main fire is in the NT a metaphorical term for the divine wrath and a means of divine judgment in the final act and in eternal hell-fire. But it also denotes the glory of heavenly light along the lines of the apocalyptic tradition. It thus covers both aspects of the eschatological denouement, whether in hell on the one side or heaven on the other.

E. Fire in the Post-Apostolic Fathers.

I. The Biblical Tradition.

In an overwhelming majority of instances the use of the term in the post-apostolic fathers is controlled by the biblical tradition.

Direct quotations from the Bible should be mentioned in this connection. As distinct from Mk. 9:48, 2 Cl., 7, 6 and 17, 5 quote Is. 66:24 lit. acc. to the LXX. 2 Cl., 5, 4 is closer to Lk. 12:4 f. than Mt. 10:28. In 1 Cl., 36, 3 Ps. 104:4 is given acc. to Hb. 1:7 rather than the LXX. Predominant here is the eschatological fire of judgment and perdition: τὸ πῦρ τὸ ἄσβεστον, Ign. Eph., 16, 2 cf. Mk. 9:43; ἡ κάμινος τοῦ πυρός, 2 Cl., 8, 2 cf. Mt. 13:50; ὡς κλίβανος καιόμενος, 2 Cl., 16, 3 cf. Mal. 3:19; the righteous see the torments of the damned δειναῖς βασάνοις πυρὶ ἀσβέστῳ, 2 Cl., 17, 7 cf. Lk. 16:28; eternal fire in contrast to temporal fire: τὸ πῦρ τὸ αἰώνιον — τὸ πῦρ τὸ πρόσκαιρον, Dg., 10, 7 f. cf. Mt. 18:8; 25:41; τὸ τῆς μελλούσης κρίσεως καὶ αἰωνίου κολάσεως τοῖς ἀσεβέσι τηρούμενον πῦρ, Mart. Pol., 11, 2 cf. 2 Pt. 3:7; Herm. v., 3, 7, 2 cf. Mt. 13:42; polemic against the Stoic interrelating of fire and deity in the light of the bibl. idea of hell-fire, Dg., 8, 2.

---

[101] Echoed perhaps in 2:23 is the idea of the flame which penetrates all things and in v. 27 the advance which shatters all resistance.

[102] This may be seen from the addition of the apoc. ὡσεί, and it is the more probable in view of the fact that Lk. was using older traditions in his account of Pentecost, Bau. Ag., ad loc.

The doctrine of a world conflagration occurs only in 2 Cl. and Herm. In this respect Iranian-Bab. and Gk. influences permeated later Judaism and from the beginning of the 2nd cent. A.D. may be seen occasionally in the Church too, until the doctrine was finally given dogmatic shape in Cl. and Orig. Bibl. passages obviously influenced the post-apost. fathers, cf. 2 Pt. 3:10 and Is. 34:4 B in 2 Cl., 16, 3 and Jl. 2:30; Is. 66:16 in Herm. v., 4, 3, 3.

The idea of fire as a means of earthly punishment and torment is also based on OT tradition. The punishment of Sodom (1 Cl., 11, 1 cf. Gn. 19:24 ff.) and the three men in the burning fiery furnace (1 Cl., 45, 7 cf. Da. 3:19 ff.) are mentioned as examples. When the state persecuted Christians many were put to death by fire, Ign. R., 5, 3; Sm., 4, 2. Mart. Pol. gives a description of one such execution by fire with many bibl. traits (15-16, 1) which show that the fire cannot finally harm believers, Da. 3:19 ff.; 1 Macc. 2:59; Hb. 11:34. For the righteous martyrs the tormentor's fire was cold, Mart. Pol., 2, 3 cf. 4 Macc. 11:26. The common image of the fiery test is also found : in the life of faith, Herm. v., 4, 3, 4 cf. 1 Pt. 1:7; Rev. 3:18; in the last time, Did., 16, 4 f. cf. 1 Pt. 4:12; Mt. 24:10, 24.

II. Alien Influences.

In spite of the strong reliance on the biblical tradition ideas from other world-views are sometimes found.

Dualistic Gnostic usage may be seen in Ign. In Ign. R., 7, 2 : οὐκ ἔστιν ἐν ἐμοὶ πῦρ φιλόϋλον· ὕδωρ δὲ ζῶν καὶ λαλοῦν ἐν ἐμοί, the train of thought is influenced by the antithesis of fire and water current in all Gnostic baptismal circles → 941, n. 70. πῦρ φιλόϋλον (cf. Ign. R., 6, 2) denotes love of the world, the impulse towards matter (ὕλη), which is the abominable thing, cf. Corp. Herm., 1, 18 ff. The Gk. doctrine of the elements has had some influence on Dg. Fire is part of the cosmos along with heaven, earth, sea, air and abyss, 7, 2.

On the whole, however, the ideas of fire found in the post-apostolic fathers are still predominantly rooted in the soil of the biblical tradition.

† πυρόω. [1]

A. In the Greek World.

The word occurs from Pind., also on inscr.

1. Lit. Use. a. "to burn, destroy with fire" all kinds of combustible things (ὁ ... χρυσὸς μόνος οὐ πυροῦται, Aristot. Meteor., III, 6, p. 378b, 4), in war (πυρωθέντων Τρώων, Pind. Pyth., XI, 33) and in daily life (ναοὺς πυρώσων ἦλθε, Soph. Ant., 286). This leads to the specific sense to burn in the sacrificial fire ὀσφῦν, Aesch. Prom., 497, σώματα, Eur. Herc. Fur., 244, corpses on the funeral pyre ἣν πεπύρωκαν (sic !) ἐγώ, inscr. from Tell el Yehudieh, 20, 4; [2] b. "to treat with fire" domestically and industrially, e.g., "to bake" τὸ σταῖς, Aristot. Probl., 21, 10, p. 927b, 39, "to roast," Hippocr. De victu, II, 56 (Littré, VI, 566), "to cause to glow," Aristot. De coloribus, 2, p. 792a, 12, "to smoke out" the house, δῶμα θεείῳ, Theocr. Idyll., 24, 96, "to smelt" metal, IG, VII, 303, 15; c. rarely abs. "to make fire," φλόγα ποιεῖν καὶ πυροῦν, Aristot. Part. An., II, 2, p. 649b, 5, pass. "to become fire," Aristot. Cael., III, 8, p. 307a, 24; d. medically πυροῦν τὴν γεῦσιν, "to be hot to the taste," Diosc. Mat. Med., I, 16, 2; IV, 170, 2, πυροῦσθαι, "to suffer heartburn," Herodotus Medicus in Aet., 9, 2. [3]

π υ ρ ό ω. [1] E. Fraenkel, Gr. Denominativa (1906), 97, 153 [A. Debrunner].
[2] Ed. H. Lietzmann, "Jüd.-gr. Inschr. aus Tell el Yehudieh," ZNW, 22 (1923), 282.
[3] Ed. S. Zerbos, ᾿Αθηνᾶ, 23 (1911), 278, 14.

2. Transf. Use. Mostly pass. "to become enflamed," "annoyed," παραγγέλμασι ...
πυρωθεὶς καρδίαν, Aesch. Ag., 480 f., τινί, "to be seized with love for someone,"
Anth. Graec., 12, 87.

B. In Judaism.

1. In the LXX the lit. use, predominant in Gk., is late, mainly in Macc. 2 Macc. 10:3 :
"to get fire" from stones ; 4 Macc. 9:17: "to burn" the flesh of martyrs ; 4 Macc. 11:19 :
"to make lances hot" for torture. [4] The same applies to the transf. use in the pass. "to
be seized" by emotions, esp. anger πυρωθεὶς τοῖς θυμοῖς, 2 Macc. 4:38; cf. 10:35; 14:45,
and grief στεναγμοῖς πεπυρωμένης ... τῆς καρδίας, 3 Macc. 4:2. The most common
use of the term for "to refine," "to prove" (Heb. צָרַף), is usually related to the image
of the metal-smelter, common from the time of the prophets. The main ref. of the verb
is to the refining of precious metals in the fire, Job 22:25; Zech. 13:9; Ps. 12:6; 66:10;
Prv. 10:20, and it is then used fig. for the testing of men by God's dispensations, Is. 1:25;
Jdt. 8:27; Ps. 105:19; Da. 12:10, often synon. with δοκιμάζειν, Ps. 17:3; 26:2; 66:10;
Jer. 9:6, or πειράζειν, Ps. 26:2. That which withstands the fiery test is certified, so esp.
the Word of God, 2 S. 22:31; Ps. 18:29; 119:140; Prv. 30:5. Only occasionally does the
idea of illuminating by fire determine the sense, Est. 5:1d; Lam. 4:7 B.

2. Philo has the word only in the pass. He knows the lit. sense, "to be burned"
(ὁ κόσμος ὁ πυρωθείς, Aet. Mund., 102; the golden calf = the body, Poster. C., 158),
also "to be glowing with heat," Som., I, 31; Ebr., 147. But he usually employs the term
fig. for "to be enflamed" with emotion, whether favourably or unfavourably. The friend
of virtue is enflamed (πυρωθείς) by the radiance of the beautiful and burns up (κατα-
φλέγει) bodily lusts (Poster. C., 159), which are described elsewhere as fiery desires
πεπυρωμένας ἐπιθυμίας, Rer. Div. Her., 65. The confessor is aglow with thanksgiving
to God πεπυρωμένος ἐν εὐχαριστίᾳ θεοῦ (Leg. All., I, 84), aflame with zeal (Spec.
Leg., III, 126), with righteous indignation (Vit. Mos., II, 280). Typical of Philo is that he
combines the bibl. image of the refining of metals in the fire with the Stoic concept of
fiery reason : ἡ φρόνησις, ἣν εἴκασε χρυσίῳ, ἀδόλῳ καὶ καθαρᾷ καὶ πεπυρωμένῃ
καὶ δεδοκιμασμένῃ καὶ τιμίᾳ φύσει, Leg. All., I, 77. He calls the immutable, wholly
pure mind (γνώμη) τὴν ἄτρεπτον καὶ πεπυρωμένην καὶ δόκιμον φύσιν, Leg. All.,
II, 67. In this Stoic sense he also speaks of the πεπυρωμένος καὶ ἀνίκητος λόγος,
Sacr. AC. 87 and understands the νοῦς as ἔνθερμον καὶ πεπυρωμένον πνεῦμα,
Fug., 134.

Joseph. has the verb only in the lit. sense "to burn," Ant., 5, 65 act.; Bell., 7, 316 pass.,
also πυρπολεῖν "to set on fire," Ant., 7, 191; 9, 159; 20, 123; Ap., 2, 212.

3. In the desert community of Qumran the OT idea of refining in the fire was applied
to the opposition of the children of light to enemies of the sect : "Wonderfully hast thou
dealt with the poor, and thou hast brought him under the oppression of the enemy, into
the works of fire, and (hast treated him) like silver, purified in the smelting furnace of
the firers, to refine it seven times," 1 QH 5:15 f. [5]

C. In the New Testament.

The six NT passages in which πυρόομαι occurs fit into the pattern of usage
indicated thus far.

1. Paul uses the term only in a transf. sense and only in the passive for being
enflamed by emotions. In 1 C. 7:9 he advises the unmarried and widows that it is
better to marry than to burn up with desire. The context yields the clear sense

---

[4] We also find in Macc. the compounds ἐκ- 2 Macc. 7:3, 4, δια- 4 Macc. 3:15 and
προσπυρόω 2 Macc. 14:11.
[5] H. Bardtke, Die Handschriftenfunde am Toten Meer (1958), 240.

"to be consumed with the fire of sexual desire," which is attested also in the Gk. world. [6] In 2 C. 11:29 the reference of πυρόομαι is to the sympathetic sorrow of the apostle when a member of the community is offended. Any attack on the community is an attack on the apostle too. He burns "with sympathy and a desire to help." [7]

2. The armour of the Christian includes in Eph. 6:16 "the shield of faith, wherewith ye shall be able to quench all the fiery darts of the wicked," → V, 300, 20 ff.

Both Greeks and Jews used flaming arrows in war. [8] But this expression is not taken directly from the military sphere, cf. also 2 Macc. 10:30. The OT has various words for flaming arrows (Is. 50:11 זִיקוֹת; Prv. 26:18 זִקִּים) but these are not rendered by the present verb in the LXX. Ps. 7:13 uses flaming arrows as a metaphor for the fate which will befall false accusers. In Eph., however, the addition "of the wicked" (→ 559, 4 ff.) shows that the expression comes from a dualistic background in which the children of light are engaged in conflict with the hosts of Belial. It is to be regarded as closely par. to a passage in the Hymn Scroll of Qumran : "They have surrounded me with all their weapons of war, and arrows destroy with none to help, and the spear-blade is in a fire which devours trees," 1 QH 2:25 f. [9]

3. The word is used lit. for "to be destroyed by fire" in 2 Pt. 3:12 : "The heavens shall be dissolved in fire, and the elements shall melt with fervent heat," namely, in the final world conflagration.

4. Rev. adopts the OT metaphor (→ 949, 9 ff.) of the testing of precious metals. In 3:18 the gold which is purified in the fire is a phrase for Christ's attested gift of salvation and genuine faith in contrast to appearance. [10] This plain use of the metaphor helps us to understand 1:15 : "His feet were like unto fine brass, as if it were refined in the furnace." The many variants are best explained if πεπυρωμένης is original, but is a grammatical error for πεπυρωμένῳ, which is to be related to χαλκολιβάνῳ. An argument against taking it with κάμινος is that in the LXX we find only κάμινος καιομένη (Job 41:12), not πεπυρωμένη.

D. In the Post-Apostolic Fathers.

In Mart. Pol., 15, 2 the ref. of πυρούμενος is to the metals, not the furnace : ὡς χρυσὸς καὶ ἄργυρος ἐν καμίνῳ πυρούμενος. [11] Herm. v., 4, 3, 4 regards the traditional image of the testing of gold in the fire as a summons to make oneself useful in building the tower.

† πύρωσις.

1. Nomen actionis of πυρόω, esp. in Aristot. and his followers, also pap. Lit. use : "burning," Theophr. Hist. Plant., V, 9, 1; Archelaos A, 4 (Diels[7], II, 46, 11), treating with fire, e.g., "baking," Aristot. Probl., 21, 12, p. 928a, 24, "boiling," Aristot. Meteor., IV, 3, p. 380b, 28, "flame," ibid., II, 9, p. 369b, 6; transf.: "burning desire," Schol. Aristoph.

---

[6] Anacreontea, 10, 15 (ed. T. Bergk, Poetae Lyrici Graeci, III [1882], 303).
[7] Wnd. 2 K., ad loc.
[8] For details cf. Amm. Marc., 23, 4.
[9] Bardtke, op. cit. (→ n. 5), 236.
[10] Cf. ψ 17:31; Ps. Sol. 17:43; 1 Pt. 1:7, though cf. also πεπυρωμένος σίδηρος as an instrument of punishment in Apc. Pt. 28.
[11] Cf. Da. LXX 3:46 : ἡ κάμινος ἦν διάπυρος, and 3 Macc. 6:6 [G. Bertram].

Pl., 974; [1] medical : "fever," Sext. Emp. Pyrrh. Hyp., II, 240, "inflammation" στομάχου, Diosc. Mat. Med., II, 124.

2. The word is rare in the LXX (twice). In Prv. 27:21, par. to the predominant use of πυρόω in the OT, it means the testing of gold in the fire (δοκίμιον ἀργύρῳ καὶ χρυσῷ πύρωσις [בּוּר]). In Am. 4:9 it has the special sense of the blasting of crops (as a result of hot winds).

3. Jos. has the word for the divine punishment of Sodom in Ant., 1, 203 : γῆν ... πυρώσει ἀφανίζων. It does not occur in Philo.

4. The word occurs three times in the NT and the usage is the same as that of the LXX and Jos. In Rev. 18:9, 18 it denotes the destruction of the city of Babylon by fire. πύρωσις is passive : the smoke which rises up from her being burnt (τὸν καπνὸν τῆς πυρώσεως αὐτῆς). The use in 1 Pt. 4:12 is plainly based on the OT metaphor of the refining of metals, applied here to the sufferings which God sends to test believers. Suffering is essential to the Christian as a participation in the παθήματα τοῦ Χριστοῦ, v. 13. Hence "do not be surprised by the fiery heat present among you (in the form of suffering), which comes upon you (from God) as a test (of faith)." The thought is obviously linked with the coming of the last time, 4:7, 17.

5. The same idea lives on in the post-apost. fathers, though the fiery trial (Did., 16, 5 : ἡ πύρωσις τῆς δοκιμασίας) is now in the fut. rather than the present and is linked with the raging of antichrist in the last time before the coming of the Lord.

† πύρινος.

1. With a short υ in distinction from πῡρινος, which is derived from ὁ πῡρός ("wheat"), this means "fiery," "of fire," and is used in Gk. from the pre-Socratics lit. of all bodies or things which acc. to the ancient view are composed of fire : ὁ οὐρανός, Heracl. A, 10 (Diels⁷, I, 146, 23), ὁ ἥλιος Anaxim. A, 15 (I, 93, 40), τὰ ἄστρα, ibid., 7 (I, 92, 12); Aristot. Cael., II, 7, p. 289a, 16, or which are fiery hot : πύριναι νύμφαι, hot springs, Anth. Pal., 14, 52; transf. like πῦρ for great violence : πύρινος πόλεμος, Polyb., 35, 1, 6. [1]

2. The adj. is seldom used in the LXX (3 times). [2] It refers here to the radiance of paradisial or heavenly phenomena, Ez. 28:14, 16 : λίθοι πύρινοι; [3] Sir. 48:9 : Elijah was taken up into heaven ἐν ἅρματι ἵππων πυρίνων. [4] Joseph. has πυρώδης "like fire" in Bell., 5, 222 : of the splendour of the temple.

3. In the NT πύρινος occurs only once at Rev. 9:17. After the loosing of the four angels mythical riders rage over the earth (ἔχοντας θώρακας πυρίνους καὶ ὑακινθίνους καὶ θειώδεις). It is hard to say for certain whether the various colours of the breastplates correspond to the horses and these are grouped in three squadrons [5] or whether they refer to the fire, smoke and brimstone [6] which proceed from the horses' mouths, v. 18. In any case the equipment of the horsemen

---

π ύ ρ ω σ ι ς. [1] Ed. J. F. Dübner (1855).

π ύ ρ ι ν ο ς. [1] Positively πύρινον ἀσπαστικόν, Preis. Zaub., 4, 639.

[2] Also 3 times in Symmachus Dt. 33:2; πύρινος νόμος cf. ψ 103:4; Cant. 8:6.

[3] Better בְּנֵי אֵשׁ == angel, A. Bertholet, Hesekiel, Hndbch. AT, 13 (1936), ad loc.

[4] But cf. the fiery swords from heaven (Sib., 3, 673) as eschatological instruments of punishment.

[5] Loh. Apk., ad loc.

[6] H. J. Holtzmann, Ev., Briefe u. Offenbarung d. Joh., Hand-Comm. z. NT³ (1908), ad loc.

shows that they are demonic beings bringing destruction. Similarly, the fiery locusts (Herm. v., 4, 1, 6) are demonic beings of the last times, cf. Rev. 9:3.

† πυρρός. [1]

1. Older and poetically πυρσός, from Aesch., also inscr. and pap.: "fiery red," "flame-coloured," is for Plato a mixture of yellow and gray πυρρὸν ... ξανθοῦ τε καὶ φαιοῦ κράσει γίγνεται (Tim., 68c) and embraces the various shades of glowing red χλανίς (Hdt., III, 139), ῥόδον (Moschus, I, 70) [2] by way of brown to bright yellow ᾠοῦ τὸ πυρρόν (Hippocr. Mul., II, 171, Littré, VIII, 352). It is esp. used of hair, of gods in Xenophanes Fr., 16 (Diels[7], I, 133, 7), men ἔθνος ... πυρρόν (Hdt., IV, 108); οἱ πυρροὶ ἄγαν πανοῦργοι (Aristot. Physiognomonica, 6, p. 812a, 16); οἱ τὴν θάλατταν ἐργαζόμενοι πυρροί εἰσιν (Aristot. Probl., 2, p. 966b, 26), esp. the first beard (Eur. Phoen., 32), and animals, e.g., lions (Eur. Herc. Fur., 361); λέοντες πυρροὶ πάντες (Aristot. Gen. An., 6, p. 785b, 17 f.), oxen (Plut. Is. et Os., 31 [II, 363a]), horses ὑπὲρ τοῦ πυρροῦ ἵππου (P. Oxy., VI, 922, 8), goats (P. Hibeh, I, 120, 6), dogs (Ps.-Xenoph. Cyn., 4, 7). Sometimes there is a special ref. to blushing for shame (Aristoph. Eq., 900) or to the blood-shot eyes of dogs (Eur. Hec., 1265).

2. The LXX always uses πυρρός for אָדֹם "red" Gn. 25:30 : ἔψεμα πυρρόν mess of pottage ; Nu. 19:2 : red heifer without blemish ; 2 K. 3:22 : water red like blood ; Cant. 5:10 : the beloved white and red, i.e., looking healthy like milk and blood. Among the four-coloured horses of the visions of Zech. are ἵπποι πυρροί along with the black and white and speckled horses, 1:8; 6:2 ff. As the horses are connected with the four winds, so the colours are connected with the four quarters of heaven, red being the east, black the north, white the west and speckled the south, cf. 6:6. [3] The task of these horsemen is to see what is going on in the world, to report on this, and sometimes to execute special missions.

3. Philo does not use the word but Jos. has it in Ant., 1, 34.

4. In the NT the colours of the Four Horsemen of the Apocalypse (6:1-8) are based on those of the horses in Zech. → lines 19 ff. Whereas the order in Zech. is red, black, white, speckled, it is changed in Rev. to white, red, black, pale. The second rider on the red horse (v. 4 : ἄλλος ἵππος πυρρός) causes war and bloodshed. The original connection of the colour with the quarter of heaven is here replaced by a reference to the sword and "red" murder. Similarly, the colour of the great fiery red dragon (12:3) depicts his bellicose and bloodthirsty character. Ancient tradition might also lie behind this. [4]

5. In the post-apost. fathers the expression in 1 Cl., 8, 3 : ἁμαρτίαι ... πυρρότεραι κόκκου, is based on Is. 1:18, though the LXX does not have πυρρός here, cf. 1 Cl., 8, 4. But the expression is also proverbial in Gk. (ἐρυθρότερον κόκκου, Athen., VI, 240D). The source of the whole quotation is not known.

Lang

π υ ρ ρ ό ς. [1] E. Wunderlich, "Die Bdtg. d. roten Farbe im Kultus d. Griechen u. Römer," RVV, 20, 1 (1925). [H. Kleinknecht.]
[2] Ed. H. L. Ahrens (1909), 105.
[3] T. H. Robinson-F. Horst, *Die zwölf kl. Propheten*, Hndbch. AT, 14² (1954), 219 f., 237.
[4] Cf. the red colour of the Bab. Mušruššu and the Egypt. Typhon, Loh. Apk., *ad loc.*

† πύργος

1. πύργος can hardly be a Germanic word which in pre-historic times passed into Gk. by way of a North Balkan people (Illyrians or Macedonians), cf. the German *Burg*. [1] It is wholly Pelasgic [2] and originally in the Indo-European world it must have denoted an inhabited walled fortress or place of refuge. [3] Among the Gks., however, it came to be used for the "tower" taken over from the previous inhabitants of Greece. [4] This was the beginning of its development in Gk. It denotes the tower, the wall with towers, the fortress, the movable tower in sieges, the column of an army, also the castle and then any high (private) building, cf. πύργος ἰδιωτικός, Hdt., IV, 164 (many derivates are military or architectural tt.). [5] Often in the pap. the best rendering is "out-buildings" in the sense of independent buildings connected with a dwelling. [6]

2. πύργος occurs some 80 times in the LXX. It is almost always used for מִגְדָּל, which is almost always rendered πύργος (1 Εσδρ. 9:42; 2 Εσδρ. 18:4 = Neh. 8:4 βῆμα; [7] Prv. 18:10 μεγαλωσύνη, though ᾿ΑΘ πύργος → n. 7). The usual meaning is a "fortified tower" or "castle," "citadel," often with no inner rooms, as part of a larger

---

π ύ ρ γ ο ς. [1] So with full arguments P. Kretschmer, "Nordische Lehnwörter im Altgriechischen," *Glotta*, 22 (1934), 100-122. But if it derived from the Germanic one would expect βυργ- or πυρκ- [Debrunner].

[2] Acc. to V. Georgiev, *Vorgr. Sprachwissenschaft*, I (1941), 96 Indo-Eur. *bhrgh-> brgh-> Pelasgic πύργ-; from the same Indo-Eur. root also <*bhergh-, Germ. *Burg, bergen*. Cf. also A. J. van Windekens, *Le pélasgique* (1952), 131 f. [Risch].

[3] Kretschmer, *op. cit.*, 107-110; C. Schuchhardt, "Hof, Burg u. Stadt bei Germanen u. Griechen," N. Jbch. Kl. Alt., 11 (1908), 305-321; also "Urspr. u. Wanderung des Wohnturms," SAB (1929), 437-469.

[4] Kretschmer, 112 f.

[5] Cf. Pass. and Liddell-Scott, *s.v.* In inscr. often with τεῖχος and πύλη, cf. Ditt. Syll.³, Index, *s.v.* The watch-tower on Astyages hill in Ephesus, later called φυλακὴ Παύλου, cf. W. Michaelis, "Das 'Gefängnis d. Paulus' in Ephesus," *Byzantinisch-Neugriech. Jahrbücher,* 6 (1928), 1-18, is also called πύργος in the related deed (3rd cent. B.C.), cf. Michaelis, 7; Ditt. Syll.³, III, 936 nota. Hesych.: πύργος· προμαχεών, τεῖχος ... καὶ τάξις ἐν τετραγώνῳ ὁπλιτῶν ... καὶ πολεμιστήριον ὄργανον, Suid.: πύργοι· τάξεις.

[6] F. Preisigke, "Die Begriffe πύργος u. στέγη bei d. Hausanlage," Herm., 54 (1919), 423-432 argues that in the pap. πύργος means out-buildings, cf. also the examples in Preisigke Wört., II, 437; Moult.-Mill., 560, *s.v.* E. Meyer supports him, "ΠΥΡΓΟΣ 'Wirtschaftsgebäude'," Herm., 55 (1920), 100-102, also Meyer Ursprung, I, 217, n. 1. But the latter's ref. to the "completely unequivocal witness" of the NT to this usage is rightly qualified by A. Alt, "Noch einmal ΠΥΡΓΟΣ 'Wirtschaftsgebäude'," Herm., 55 (1920), 334-336. The thesis is also accepted by J. Hasebroek, "Nochmals ΠΥΡΓΟΣ 'Wirtschaftsgebäude'," ibid., 57 (1922), 621-623; P. Kretschmer, "Literaturbericht f. d. Jahre 1919 u. 1920," Glotta, 12 (1923), 195 f.; P. M. Meyer, "Juristischer Papyrusbericht, II," Zschr. f. vergleichende Rechtswissenschaft, 40 (1923), 207. For a summary cf. U. Wilcken, "Pap.-Urkunden," IX," APF, 7 (1924), 92 (on P. Strassb., II, 110, 6 [3rd cent. B.C.]). Against we may mention W. Crönert's review of Radermacher² (1925) in Gnomon, 4 (1928), 80 : The transl. "outbuildings" is wrong ; we should simply render "tower," for field-tower, watch-tower, and threshing-tower miss the habitable aspect, and block-house the tower-like aspect ; A. Pallis, *Notes on St. Mark and St. Matthew*² (1932), 41: ἔπαυλις is farm-building, but πύργος is "a country villa with an upper storey" (as in modern Gk.).

[7] In 1 Εσδρ. 1:52, however, πύργος = אַרְמוֹן ("palace," βασίλειον, Prv. 18:19). In the par. 2 Ch. 36:19 LXX has βάρις, often used for אַרְמוֹן (mostly = θεμέλιον). In ψ 121:7 the hapax legomenon πυργόβαρις occurs for אַרְמוֹן. In Ez. 29:10; 30:6 LXX takes מִגְדָּל as a proper name ; ᾿ΑΣ again have πύργος [Bertram]. For אַצֶּה סֹפֵר אֶת־הַמִּגְדָּלִים in Is. 33:18 (the conjecture in BHK³ is unnecessary, cf. ψ 47:13) LXX has ποῦ ἐστιν ὁ ἀριθμῶν τοὺς τρεφομένους (vl. συστρεφομένους or ἀναστρεφομένους). מִגְדָּלִים is here regarded as a part. of גדל pi, cf. Nu. 6:5 LXX; Da. 1:5 Θ.

fortification or city wall, [8] but also an isolated "watch-tower" (cf. 4 Βασ. 17:9; 18:8; 1 Ch. 27:25), [9] esp. a tower for the supervision and protection of flocks: מִגְדַּל־עֵדֶר in Gn. 35:21, LXX πύργος Γάδερ, and Mi. 4:8, LXX πύργος ποιμνίου, 2 Ch. 26:10. In Is. 5:2 the watch-tower in a vineyard is מִגְדָּל or πύργος; the ref. is to a small building with no inner chamber and with an outside stair from the top of which the watchman may look out; the סֻכָּה בְכֶרֶם of Is. 1:8 is where the keeper lodges, LXX → σκηνὴ ἐν ἀμπελῶνι, cf. מְלוּנָה בְמִקְשָׁה, loc. cit. [10] Transf. πύργος means shelter in ψ 60:4 (cf. Hom. Od., 11, 556) and it symbolises the world powers in Is. 30:25; cf. also Sir. 26:22.

3. Philo uses πύργος in exposition of Gn. 11:4 f., briefly in Poster. C., 53 and at greater length in Conf. Ling. (he also refers to Ju. 8:8 f., 17 in 128-130). The tower of Babel is a symbol of the ἄνοια of men, Conf. Ling., 5, of their μεγαλαυχία, 5 and 113, and their κακία, 83, 113, 115, in short their ἀθεότης, 196, combined with the αἰσθήσεις in 133, → V, 591, 8 ff. and n. 3. Jos., too, uses πύργος on the basis of the OT, e.g., Ant., 1, 114 f., 118 (Gn. 11:4 f.), 7, 142 (Ju. 9:51 f.), 11, 45 (1 Εσδρ. 4:4). More often still he goes beyond OT usage and calls fortresses πύργοι, e.g., Ant., 9, 122 (cf. 4 Βασ. 9:30 ff.), 10, 134 (4 Βασ. 25:1 f.), 13, 16. 26. 57. 202 (cf. 1 Macc. 9:50 f., 62; 10:45; 13:10), cf. 8, 150. The building and use of towers is often mentioned in accounts of military measures, e.g., Ant., 14, 466; 15, 324; 18, 147; Bell., 1, 99 f., 147, 344; 2, 435 f., 441. Jos. devotes special attention to the towers of the third wall of Jerusalem, esp. the gt. towers (Bell., 5, 156 ff.), the Phasael tower (cf. also Ant., 16, 144; Bell., 1, 418; 2, 46), the Hippicus tower (5, 144 and 147). In their gigantic proportions and with the dwellings on

---

[8] J. Benzinger, Art. "Kriegswesen bei d. Hebräern," RE³, 11, 117; K. Galling, Art. "Migdal," BR, 381 f. O. E. Ravn, "Der Turm zu Babel," ZDMG, 91 (1937), 353-370, esp. 359 f., 368 f., has proposed that the πύργος of Gn. 11:4 f. (also with no Mas. 11:8) is a fortified tower, but in spite of the support of E. Sellin in his epilogue, ibid., 370-372, this is most improbable. Perhaps the מִגְדָּל of Gn. 11:4 f. is a temple-tower or step-tower like the step-pyramids of Bab. Cf. also K. Galling, Art. "Babylon, 2," BR, 72-75.

[9] In Heb. we find the same development as in Gk. from the refuge to the high, solid building, esp. in the case of מָעוֹז. This word means "retreat," "refuge," and concretely "mountain fortress" or "mountain-top." Inaccessibility rather than artificial fortification is the primary idea. Such places of refuge have been found in Palestine, e.g., on the kurūn hattīn near the site where Saladin decisively beat the Crusaders in 1187, in Galilee from Neolithic times, also at Mashkena between Tiberias and Zippori, cf. C. Watzinger, Denkmäler Palästinas, I (1933), 25; G. Dalman Orte, 121; also "Die Zeltreise," PJB, 10 (1916), 41. In the history of Israel flight to the mountains was often required, cf. Ju. 6:2. There and elsewhere different words are used. In Gk., too, the range is broad, esp. as מָעוֹז can often be used fig. for refuge in God (fortress, rock), Ps. 27:1; 28:7; 31:2 etc.; Prv. 10:29; Is. 17:10; 25:4; Jer. 16:19 etc., with different LXX transl. At Prv. 10:29 the gracious saying of the HT: "Yahweh is a defence to him who walks in innocence," becomes in the LXX an expression of Pharisaical self-righteousness: "The piety of the righteous guarantees his security" (ὀχύρωμα ὁσίου φόβος κυρίου). ὀχύρωμα (→ V, 590, 32 ff.) and πύργος (and their Heb. originals) overlap. Thus Prv. 10:15; 18:11, 19; 21:22 speak of the πόλις ὀχυρά in the same sense as ψ 60:4 speaks of the πύργος ἰσχύος (cf. πύργος ὀχυρός in Ju. 9:51 A). Cf. G. Bertram, "Der Sprachschatz d. LXX u. der des hbr. AT," ZAW, 57 (1939), esp. 93-98 [Bertram].

[10] Cf. H. Schick, "Baugeschichte d. Stadt Jerusalem," ZDPV, 16 (1893), 236 f. In Rabb. times, too, the towers of watchers in the fields are called מגדל, while the hut is שמרה, cf. S. Krauss, Talmudische Archäologie, I (1910), 8, 280, n. 101; II (1911), 185, 203; Str.-B., I, 868 f. Field-towers may still be seen in Palestine, cf. also L. Bauer, Volksleben im Lande d. Bibel² (1903), 132 (App.). As the loan word פרגוס, πύργος was adopted by the Rabb. in the sense "tower," cf. S. Krauss, Griech. u. lat. Lehnwörter in Talmud, Midr. u. Tg., II (1898), 477, though בורגין "tower," "strong-point," "watch-post," is not, as Krauss supposes (143 f.), connected with φρούριον, nor indeed with πύργος ("a military term of Germanic origin may be in the background," 144).

the massive sub-structure these towers are compared to palaces. Bell., 5, 168 : ὡς μηδὲν ἐνδέοι τῷ πύργῳ βασίλειον δοκεῖν. For the tower later built on the castle Antonia, in which the high-priestly vesture was kept, Jos. uses βᾶρις rather than πύργος Ant., 18, 91 f. He could call the tower-like dovecots in the royal park towers (πύργοι πελειάδων) in Bell., 5, 181. [11] In Ant., 13, 309; 15, 293; 19, 343; Bell., 1, 77, 156, 408 there is ref. to the Στράτωνος πύργος, known in the NT only by the name Καισάρεια given to it by Herod the Gt. Ep. Ar. in its description of Jerusalem mentions the πύργοι of the fortress (ἄκρα, 101 f.) and those of the city wall, 105.

Towers are mentioned in the pseudepigr. in Jub. 10:18 ff. (cf. Gn. 11:4 f.); 11:2, and in characterisation of the perilous sojourning of the patriarchs among the Gentiles 29:16, 19 (Lat. baris); 31:6; 37:16 f.; Or. Sib., 3, 98 ff. (cf. Gn. 11:4 f.); 4, 69. 105 f.; 5, 424; 11, 10; Eth. En. 87:3, also 89:50, 54, 66 f., 73; Gr. Bar. 2 f.; Test. L. 2:3 (unrighteousness builds walls for itself and ἐπὶ πύργους ἡ ἀνομία κάθηται); Test. Jud. 5:5. The Qumran settlement had a tower as well as walls, so that wall and tower are common metaphors in the Scrolls. [12]

4. In the NT πύργος occurs at Mk. 12:1 par. Mt. 21:33 at the beginning of the parable of the wicked husbandmen : ᾠκοδόμησεν πύργον. Since this is in the opening section and the expression is plainly reminiscent of Is. 5:2, [13] the reference, as there (→ 954, 4 ff.), is to a field-tower. [14] In Lk. 13:4 ὁ πύργος ἐν τῷ Σιλωάμ is mentioned. Since this tower, not known to us from contemporary sources, buried 18 men when it collapsed, it must have been a considerable structure. [15] In Lk. 14:28 Jesus asks : τίς γὰρ ἐξ ὑμῶν θέλων πύργον οἰκοδομῆσαι οὐχὶ πρῶτον καθίσας ψηφίζει τὴν δαπάνην, εἰ ἔχει εἰς ἀπαρτισμόν. As ἐξ ὑμῶν shows, the reference is not to a public structure (a fortified tower or tower on the ramparts). Yet this can hardly be a simple field-tower, as in Mk. 12:1 and par., since in v. 29 the laying of the foundation is mentioned as a separate part of the work and a field-tower would not in any case have entailed so great an expenditure. The reference would seem to be, then, to a tower-like private house of many storeys, unless the sense of "out-buildings (→ 953, 10 ff.) calls for consideration here too. [16]

---

[11] Cf. Krauss Archäol., II, 138 (examples of מגדל in this sense, 525, n. 975).

[12] Many examples in O. Betz, "Felsenmann u. Felsengemeinde," ZNW, 48 (1957), 52, 65 and n. 47, 66, also n. 49, 69. Cf. H. Bardtke, "Die Kriegsrolle v. Qumran übers.," ThLZ, 80 (1955), 410, n. 100. Str.-B., Index, s.v. "Turm" refers only to III, 325: expositions of Is. 33:18 (→ n. 7), bChag., 15b etc.

[13] At Lk. 20:9 the quotation is abbreviated and the term does not occur. This version, even though πύργος is not essential to interpretation of the parable, is not original, since the use of the quotation demands that it be recognised, and this in turn demands that it be explicit, cf. W. Michaelis, Die Gleichnisse Jesu³ (1956), 116.

[14] Since the מִגְדָּל of Is. 5:2 is transl. πύργος, it is hard to see why Loh. Mk., ad loc. regards the word πύργος as one of the features which are "incidental and even artificial." The usage of the LXX demolishes his argument ("πύργος and migdal are equivalent only in the sense 'tower,' which is not appropriate here"). The ref. is not to an out-building even on a large estate, since the vineyard is let out to many smallholders, cf. Alt, op. cit. (→ n. 6), 335.

[15] It may be conjectured that the tower, which can hardly have borne the name Siloam as seems to be suggested by E. Stauffer, Jesus. Gestalt u. Gesch. (1957), 48 (the "tower Siloam"), was part of the water system, and that an accident occurred during repairs, cf. Hck. and Kl. Lk., ad loc.; G. Bornkamm, Jesus v. Nazareth (1956), 79; Str.-B., II, 197. Jos. Bell., 5, 292 tells how one of the towers which Titus was building on the siege ramparts before Jerusalem collapsed one midnight πεσεῖν αὐτομάτως (ἔπεσεν is also used in Lk. 13:3 → 162, 28 f.). E. Hirsch, Frühgesch. d. Ev., II (1941), 217, thinks that the ref. is to the collapse of a tower on the wall.

[16] Cf. Hck. Lk., ad loc.; Alt, 335; Bornkamm, op. cit., 135, 191, n. 5; A. Sizoo, Die antike Welt u. d. NT (1955), 48 f.

5. In the post-apost. fathers Barn., 16, 5 has πύργος in a "Scripture" quotation from Eth. En. 89:56 ff. (→ 955, 12 f.). The context suggests a tower for flocks, → 954, 2 ff. In the allegory of the tower in Herm. v., 3, 2, 4 ff. and 3, 1-7, 6, cf. also s., 8, 2, 1 ff.; 9, 3, 1-9, 31 the ἐκκλησία is depicted under the figure of the πύργος (149 times in all). [17]

Michaelis

---

† πυρέσσω, † πυρετός

1. All popular descriptions of sickness tend to describe a symptom which in most cases does not cover the true nature of the sickness. [1] Similarly, πυρετός denotes in the first instance no more than a high temperature, [2] while ῥῖγος and φρίξ emphasise other symptoms behind which various illnesses might be concealed. From the time of Hippocr., however, the Greeks investigated the nature of πυρετοί and there are many descriptions of kinds, causes and cures. Thus we find already a distinction which is still accepted to-day between ἀμφημερινὸς πυρετός (quotidian), τριταῖος πυρετός (tertian), τεταρταῖος πυρετός (quartan) and ἡμιτριταῖος πυρετός (a duplication of tertian and quartan). [3] At that stage of medical research into fevers the causes were understandably sought in natural circumstances, the atmosphere, exhalations of water or the earth, or secretions of the inward organs. Mythical medicine is still to be found as well. This recognises gods who are to be invoked for special sicknesses. It believes that demons and heroes can both cure and also cause illness. It has magical ways of exorcising the spirits which bring sickness. [4] In the Hell. period we find again the divisions mentioned or others like them. [5] The separation into πυρετὸς μέγας and πυρετὸς μικρός should be mentioned in view of Lk. 4:38 f., though the examples are

---

[17] Cf. Dib. Herm., 459 f. (Exc. "Die Turm-Allegorie"), 587 ff. (Exc. "Die Allegorie vom Weidenbaum," esp. 589), 604 ff. (Exc. "Der Fels u. d. Berge," esp. 605 f.); R. Knopf, "Die Himmelsstadt," Nt.liche Studien G. Heinrici dargebracht, UNT, 6 (1914), 213-219, esp. 216-218. Cf. Stauffer Theol. Abb., 93 f. Rev. 21:10 ff. does not refer to the towers of the heavenly Jerusalem and ideas of a heavenly tower find no echo in the NT. Even the building of the tower in Gn. 11 finds in Ac. 2 only a very indirect theological counterpoise. W. Schmithals, "Die Gnosis in Korinth," FRL, NF, 48 (1956), 133 f. tries to show that in Herm. v., 3; s., 9 the obvious basis is the idea of the redeemed redeemer, the cosmic primal man. Under the influence of Verg. Aen., VI, 517 (Helen, standing with a torch in her hand on the πύργος of Troy, invites the Greeks into the city), Gnostics, esp. the Simonians, developed the idea of the goddess Helena displaying the primal light to the lowly archons of chaos (Epiph. Haer., 21, 3, 2); on this cf. G. Quispel, Gnosis als Weltreligion (1951), 64, 66-69.

πυρέσσω κτλ. Pr.-Bauer⁵, Pass., Liddell-Scott, Moult.-Mill., s.v.; A. Debrunner, "Zu den konsonantischen io-Präsentien im Gr.," Idg. Forschungen 21 (1907), 228, 254 f.
[1] For the NT cf. H. Seng, Die Heilungen Jesu in medizinischer Beleuchtung² (1926), 10.
[2] Cf. Aristot. Probl., 1, 20, p. 861b, 38 f.
[3] For details cf. M. Neuburger, Handbuch d. Gesch. d. Medizin, I (1902), 251 f. Other non-specific differentiations relate to duration (σύνοχοι, πυκνοί and πλάνητες πυρετοί), symptoms (ἠπίαλος πυρετός = ῥιγοπύρετος "chill," καῦσος "hot fever," λήθαργος πυρετός "lethargic," λειπυρία = ἀσώδης πυρετός "vomiting," κνημώδης πυρετός, "itching," λυγγώδης πυρετός, "hiccuping"), or degree (χλιαρὸς πυρετός, "lukewarm," περικαὴς πυρετός, "burning"). For good specialised bibl. cf. Neuburger, op. cit.
[4] Cf. Neuburger, 167 f. with examples. On scientific and mythical medicine in the history of the peoples of antiquity and on their interrelationship → III, 195, 25 ff.
[5] P. Oxy., VIII, 924, 2 ff.; 1151, 34 ff.; BGU, III, 956, 3 f.; Audollent Def. Tab., 74, 6; Cels. Med., III, 3. Jos. Ant., 13, 398 and Bell., 1, 106 tell how Alexander Jannaeus died of a quartan fever.

post-NT. [6] Galen's criticism of this [7] suggests that it is a simplification and popularisation of the classical division, to which he himself opposes his own division into πυρετοὶ περικαέες ("hot"), δεινοί, βληχροί ("weak") and πρηέες ("mild"). [8] Such distinctions are of little help in getting at the true nature of a given fever, since these endemic malaria fevers are peculiar to a sub-tropical rather than a temperate zone. [9] It is obvious, of course, that a demonic explanation of fever holds the field. [10] This even increased under the influence of eastern religions [11] and, as is known, made its way unchecked into Chr. writings. [12]

2. Like the Gk. word, the OT terms for fever are derivates of roots meaning "to burn," "to catch fire," cf. קַדַּחַת in Lv. 26:16; Dt. 28:22 and דַּלֶּקֶת in Dt. 28:22. [13] It is hard to say whether Ibn Ezra [14] is right in referring these to quotidian/tertian or quartan fevers, or Sa'adiah [15] in referring them to tropical and quartan malaria. There is no way of singling out the types of fever intended. The important pt. is that they are here threatened as divine judgments or described as precursors of the divine coming in judgment. They are thus set in the context of sickness and sin, of which the OT offers many typical examples, → III, 200. The LXX uses πυρετός only for the קַדַּחַת of Dt. 28:22. [16] Apart from ῥῖγος ("spasm of fever") in the same v. the LXX has no other word for fever. πυρέσσω does not occur at all.

3. The Rabb. use for fever either the same words as the Mas. or their contemporary or Aram. equivalents. Other terms are all derivates of roots denoting "burning," "fire," etc.: שִׁמְשָׁא, צִימְרָא, אֶשָׁתָא, חַרְחוּרָא, חַמְתָה. [17] The Rabb. know the distinctions of Gk. medicine (→ 956, 12 ff.) and the natural causes and remedies. [18] For the most part fever is regarded as demonic, [19] though also as a divine punishment. [20] Indeed, it was in Judaism that this idea was first developed on a large scale, → III, 201, 7 ff.; IV, 1094, 8 ff. Incantations and magical practices help against demonic influence. [21] What is true of

---

[6] Gal. De differentiis febrium, 1 (Kühn, 7, 273-277); Gal. De curandi ratione per venaesectionem, 6 (11, 269 f.); Aret. De curatione acutorum morborum, I, 10, 1. 19 (CMG, II, 113, 27 f.; 118, 13); Alex. Aphr. De febribus libellus, 18. 31 (ed. J. L. Ideler, Physici et medici graeci minores, I [1841]); Cels. Med., IV, 14, 1. Cf. J. Schuster, "Zwei neue medizingeschichtliche Quellen zum 'Grossen Fieber' Lk. 4:38," BZ, 13 (1915), 338-343.

[7] → n. 6, esp. Gal. De differentiis febrium, 1 (Kühn, 7, 274 f.).

[8] Cf. Schuster, op. cit. (→ n. 6). The list in P. Oxy., VI, 924, 6 closes with λεπτὸς πυρετός.

[9] Neuburger, 251. Philo diagnoses fever by heat in Sobr., 45 and in Leg. Gaj., 125 attributes it to breathing in hot and tainted air: τὸ λεγόμενον κατὰ τὴν παροιμίαν πῦρ ἐπιφέρων πυρί, i.e., bodily warmth.

[10] Cf. Audollent Def. Tab., 74, 6; Pliny (the Elder) Hist. Nat., II, 16: ideoque etiam publice Febris fanum in Palatio dicatum est ... and the story of the stoning of the fever demon in Philostr. Vit. Ap., IV, 10. A. Harnack, "Medizinisches aus der ältesten Kirchengeschichte," TU, 8, 4 (1892), 107 f. and 129-132.

[11] Cf. P. Diepgen, Gesch. d. Medizin, I² (1923), 50.

[12] Cf. also the apoc. of Gregory Thaumaturgos Cod. Paris, 2316, fol. 433r, to which there is ref. in Reitzenstein Poim., 18, n. 8: κύριε, δεῖξόν μοι τὸν ἄγγελον τοῦ ῥιγοπυρετοῦ· καὶ εἶπέν μοι τὸ ὄνομα αὐτοῦ. Συχαὴλ καλεῖται κτλ.

[13] Cf. J. Preuss, Bibl.-Talmudische Medizin (1911), 182-187.

[14] Loc. cit. from jTer., 8, 5 (45c, 71).

[15] Cf. Dalman Arbeit, I, 107.

[16] Lv. 26:16 ἴκτερος ("jaundice").

[17] A full list in Str.-B., I, 479. In bBer., 32a fever is said to be a fire of the bones.

[18] bGit., 67b and jShab., 4b, 28 in Str.-B., I, 479. Preuss, op. cit. (→ n. 13), 184-187.

[19] Str.-B., I, 479 from bNed., 41a; bGit., 70a: אֲחִילוּ results from dancing in the moonlight from Tammuz to Elul. Cf. F. Fenner, Die Krankheit im NT (1930), 22.

[20] Cf. Philo's list of illnesses which are to be regarded as divine chastisements in Exsecr., 143, where πυρετός and ῥῖγος come first. On the integration or non-integrated presence of the two views cf. Str.-B., IV, 522.

[21] Str.-B., I, 479 from bGit., 67b and bShab., 66b; Jos. Ant., 8, 45-49; Preuss, op. cit.

fevers is, of course, true of sickness generally. [22] Study of the bedouins and fellaheen now resident in the Holy Land shows that these ideas are still current, and they are an integral part of the religion of all peoples. [23]

4. The NT mentions πυρετός three times among the sicknesses healed by Jesus or the apostles. Peter's mother-in-law (Mk. 1:30 f.; Mt. 8:14 f.; [24] Lk. 4:38 f.), the nobleman's son (Jn. 4:52) and the father of Publius, the most prominent man in Malta (Ac. 28:8), all suffered from it.

The question which kind of fever can be answered only in the last instance. [25] Lk. says that the father of Publius lay sick πυρετοῖς καὶ δυσεντερίῳ συνεχόμενος, Ac. 28:8. From medical works from Hippocr. to Gal. [26] it appears that we have here the medically sound definition of feverish dysentery. In Lk. 4:38 Peter's mother-in-law is said to suffer from πυρετὸς μέγας, but this is too popular a description (→ 956, 21 ff.) to allow of any assured conclusions. The value of the description is indeed purely literary, as may be seen from a comparison with Mk. 1:30 f. and Mt. 8:14 f., which simply have πυρέσσειν and πυρετός. Lk. with his sense of style tries to be more vivid, or, as is more likely, he gives added weight to the story by pointing out how serious the fever was. [27] There is also no indication of the type of fever in the case of the nobleman's son, Jn. 4:52. If this boy is the same as the servant of the centurion of Capernaum in Q (Mt. 8:5 ff.; Lk. 7:1 ff.), he was a παραλυτικός acc. to Mt. But there is nothing to suggest that the Fourth Evangelist regards the boy as paralysed or is describing a kind of fever which accompanies paralysis.

In contrast, it is quite plain that in all three passages the causes of fever are sought in the sphere of influence of supernatural or, better, religious forces. That is, the fevers are regarded as of demonic origin or divine (as a punishment for sin). It need hardly be proved that the idea that sickness is demonic in origin and nature is a common one in the NT, → I, 493, 8 f.; III, 204, 3 ff. The NT also regards it as self-evident that sickness is a punishment which God imposes, → I, 493, 10; III, 204, 8; IV, 1094, 30 ff. [28] In the case of the fevered patients of the present stories the demonic character may be seen from the ἀφῆκεν αὐτὴν (αὐτὸν) ὁ πυρετός, Mk. 1:31; Mt. 8:15; Jn. 4:52. In Lk. it is indisputable that the healing of Peter's mother-in-law is understood as an exorcism; the καὶ ἐπιστὰς ἐπάνω αὐτῆς ἐπετίμησεν τῷ πυρετῷ καὶ ἀφῆκεν αὐτήν (4:39) cannot be taken in any other way. The healing of the father of Publius, however, is differently described in Ac. 28:8: πρὸς ὃν ὁ Παῦλος εἰσελθὼν καὶ προσευξάμενος, ἐπιθεὶς τὰς χεῖρας αὐτῷ ἰάσατο αὐτόν. The account is more sober. Yet the assessment of the fever is no less clear than in the other story. It is conquered by invocation of the Father of Jesus Christ or of the Lord Himself. Hence it can have had only a supernatural cause, whether this be found in divine punishment or wicked demons. Both these can be set aside in the power of Him who took upon Himself the penalties of sin and who drove out demons by the finger of God, Lk. 11:20,

---

[22] Str.-B., IV, 524e.

[23] T. Canaan, "Dämonenglaube im Lande d. Bibel," Morgenland, 21 (1929), 45 and the works listed → I, 493, n. 20.

[24] Mk. 1:30 f. and Mt. 8:14 f. are the only passages in primitive Chr. lit. which have the verb (in the form πυρέσσουσα[ν]).

[25] Cf. Dalman Arbeit, I, 107: The fever of Peter's mother-in-law and the nobleman's son cannot be specified.

[26] Cf. W. K. Hobart, The Medical Language of St. Luke (1892), 52 f.

[27] The attempts of W. Ebstein, Die Medizin im NT u. im Talmud (1903), 103 f. and Fenner, op. cit., 52 to attribute the fever here and in Ac. 28:8 to hysterical or nervous causes find no support in the text and are simply made to serve their total view of Jesus' healings.

[28] Cf. Fenner, 21-26.

cf. 13:16. Where, then, the NT refers to fever, the main reason is to demonstrate the dominion of Jesus over sin and the devil, or, as in the healing of the man born blind in Jn. 9:3, ἵνα φανερωθῇ τὰ ἔργα τοῦ θεοῦ. The banishing of fever is a σημεῖον which awakens faith, Jn. 4:53 f. This is faith in the Messianic salvation which has come with Jesus, Mt. 11:4 f.; 12:23. It is faith in the dawning of God's eschatological rule. Further reflection on the meaning of healing for the healed or for the demonised cosmos as a whole, i.e., liberation from the bonds of sin and restoration of the state of creation (→ III, 212, 18 f.; IV, 1094, 31 ff.), is suggested only in Mk. 1:31 and par., where Peter's mother-in-law resumes the daily round when cured of the fever. Elsewhere the texts offer no occasion for such considerations.

Weiss

πύρινος → 951, 22 ff.

πυρόω → 948, 29 ff.

πυρρός → 952, 3 ff.

πύρωσις → 950, 35 ff.

---

† πῶλος

1. ὁ πῶλος, related to "foal," Germ. *Fohlen*, means "foal," the young of the horse or ass. It is attested already for the young of both horse and ass in the Cnossian tablets,[1] cf. also young horses in Hom. Il., 11, 681 f.; Aristot. Hist. An., VI, 18, p. 572a, 28; VI, 23, p. 577a, 9; VIII, 24, p. 605a, 3 and 7; Part. An., IV, 10, p. 686b, 15, and the foals of asses in Aristot. Mirabilia, 10, p. 831a, 23 and 25; Aristot. Geoponica, 16, 21, 6;[2] P. Lille, I, 8, 9; P. Osl., II, 134, 11; BGU, II, 373, 7. It is then used for the young of other animals too,[3] e.g., the elephant in Aristot. Hist. An., IX, 1, p. 610a, 33; Ael. Nat. An., 3, 46, the camel in Aristot. Hist. An., IX, 47, p. 630b, 34; BGU, III, 768, 2, the ox in Phot. Lex., *s.v.* πῶλος, the gazelle in Ael. Nat. An., 7, 47, the dog in Anth. Graec., 12, 238, 2, the dove in Alexander Trallianus, V, 6,[4] the swallow in Schol. on Oppian, Halieutica, V, 57a[5] and the grasshopper in Schol. on Theocr., V, 34c.[6] There even develops a usage which equates πῶλος (πωλίον) and ἵππος, e.g., Ps.-Callisth., II, 14, 2; II, 15, 9; III, 22, 3. Fig. πῶλος can also be used of men and denotes the young girl (Anacr., 88, 1 [Diehl², I, 4, 187]) or the youth (Aesch. Choeph., 794; Eur. Phoen., 947; Rhes., 386). A Corinthian coin bears the image of Pegasus and thus comes to be called simply πῶλος, Eur. Fr., 675 (TGF, 572 f.); Poll. Onom., IX, 75. ἱερὸς πῶλος Ἴσιδος is the title of an Egypt. priest,

---

π ῶ λ ο ς. Cf. Pass., Liddell-Scott, Moult.-Mill., Pr.-Bauer⁵, Preisigke Wört., Levy Chald. Wört. and M. Jastrow, *A Dict. of the Targumim, the Talmud Babli and Yerushalmi and the Midrashic Lit.* (1950), *s.v.* Cf. also W. Bauer, "The 'Colt' of Palm Sunday," JBL, 72 (1953), 220-229; H. W. Kuhn, "Das Reittier Jesu in d. Einzugsgeschichte d. Mk.," ZNW, 50 (1959), 82-92.

[1] M. Ventris-J. Chadwick, *Documents in Mycenean Greek* (1956), No. 82 (c. 895) [Risch].
[2] Ed. H. Beckh (1895).
[3] Cf. on what follows Bauer, *op. cit.*, 221 f.
[4] Ed. T. Puschmann, II (1879), 215.
[5] Ed. U. C. Bussemaker (1849), 363.
[6] Ed. C. Wendel (1914), 165.

Ditt. Or., II, 739, 8, [7] cf. also IG, 5, 1, No. 1444. Sometimes Πῶλος is found as a man's proper name, e.g., Plat. Gorg., 448a, Xenoph. An., VII, 2, 5. Πώλου πεδίον is also a geographical designation in Paus., VIII, 35, 10.

2. In the OT we find together in a list in Gn. 32:16 ὄνους εἴκοσι καὶ πώλους δέκα, she-asses and young asses (עַיִר) acc. to the context. The list of sheep, camels, oxen and she-asses reminds us of Job 1:3 and might belong to the same cultural background. Ju. 10:4 and 12:14 presuppose that young asses were used for riding in the days of the Judges, and the narrator sees a close linguistic relation between the name Jair and the word עַיִר (πῶλος). For the LXX πῶλος is the Gk. rendering of עַיִר, and no gen. is needed to show that the ref. is to the young ass. In the prophecy in Gn. 49:11, later understood Messianically, the words עַיִר and בֶּן אֲתֹנוֹ are synon. (πῶλος or πῶλος τῆς ὄνου αὐτοῦ). [8] The distinction is due to poetic parallelism and should not be misunderstood. Here in oriental usage, then, πῶλος (= עַיִר) is simply the young ass. The same is true in Zech. 9:9, which echoes Gn. 49:11: πραῢς καὶ ἐπιβεβηκὼς ἐπὶ ὑποζύγιον καὶ πῶλον νέον. ὑποζύγιον is strictly the yoked animal in Thuc., II, 3, 2 and in Xenoph. Oec., 18, 4 it means both ox and ass, but from Aristot. Hist. An., IX, 24, p. 604b, 28 and Theophr. Char., 14, 4 it is restricted to the ass. [9] The Gk. text is quite plain: "He rides on an ass, and indeed [10] on a young animal which was not used previously." A distinctive use is that in Prv. 5:19, which says of the wife: ἔλαφος φιλίας καὶ πῶλος σῶν χαρίτων ὁμιλείτω σοι. Comparison with the Gk. use of πῶλος for "young girl" (→ 959, 30) is no gt. help. The Heb. יַעֲלָה, transl. πῶλος here, has in view the image of the chamois. [11]

3. Later Rabb. tradition has several words for the young ass or foal of the ass. From the Heb. עוּל comes the Aram. עִילָא "young" (pullus) = πῶλος. [12] The Tg. always have this for the OT עַיִר, cf. Tg. on Job 11:12; Ju. 12:14; Gn. 32:16. In later Heb. we find סָיָח, bBB, 78b: "foal," "young ass," which is etym. related to the noun שִׂיחָה "speech," "address." On the basis of the Gk. γαῦδαρον or γαϊδάριον the loan word גַּיִּידוֹר קָטָן was formed meaning "small, young ass," jBM, 6, 3 (11a, 24). [13] Undoubtedly עַיִר became Aram. עִילָא = πῶλος even in the OT period. According to an ancient Rabb. tradition (c. 150 A.D.) the bull and the ass are Messianic images, Gn. r., 75 (48c), on 32:6.

4. Mk. 11:2, 4, 5, 7 emphasises that Jesus entered Jerusalem on a young ass (πῶλος = Aram. עִילָא). In this regard Mk. follows LXX usage, which equates πῶλος and עַיִר. According to Gn. 49:11 πῶλος δεδεμένος is in keeping with the Messianic character of the story. Lk. 19:30, 33, 35 follows Mk. in using πῶλος, though elsewhere he can use ὄνος and κτῆνος. Mt. 21:2, 5, 7 refers to both a she-ass and a colt (on the basis of Zech. 9:9 LXX); the Evangelist seems to be thinking of an oriental throne above two animals. Jn. 12:15 quotes Zech. 9:9 LXX according to an independent tradition from a florilegium. [14] καθήμενος ἐπὶ πῶλον

---

[7] Cf. also T. Reinach, Papyrus grecs et démotiques (1905), Pap., 10, 5; B. P. Grenfell and A. S. Hunt, New Classical Fr. and Other Greek and Latin Pap. (1897), Pap., 20, 5.

[8] The later pun עַיִר and עִיר (= the city of Jerusalem) is based on Gn. 49:11: God binds Himself to Israel and Jerusalem, Gn. r., 98 (62a), on 49:11; cf. Str.-B., I, 842.

[9] Mayser, II, 1 § 31, 1.

[10] Bl.-Debr. § 442, 9.

[11] Bauer, op. cit., 227, suggests that the LXX rendering πῶλος in Prv. 5:19 is a guess and that the animal name in Heb. was already causing trouble.

[12] Levy Chald. Wört., s.v. gives as examples Gn. 32:16; Ju. 12:14; Is. 30:6; Job 11:12; bShab., 155a: עִילֵי זוּטְרֵי "small foals."

[13] Jastrow, I, 237; Str.-B., I, 842.

[14] Cf. C. K. Barrett, The Gospel acc. to St. John (1956), 348 f.

ὄνου denotes here kingly session on a young animal, → V, 286, 8 ff. The diminutive in Jn. 12:14 thus corresponds also to the Aram. עִילָא. The NT use of πῶλος lies, then, within the circle of the LXX and of further developments in Aramaic and later Hebrew.

Michel

πωρόω, πώρωσις → V, 1025, 25 ff.

Ραάβ → III, 3, 13 ff.

† ῥαββί, ῥαββουνί

A. רַבִּי, רַבּוּנִי in Judaism.

1. רַב "great" is a term for someone who occupies a high and respected position. [1] Cf. רַב־טַבָּחִים 2 K. 25:8; Jer. 39:13, "the chief of the guard"; רַב־מָג Jer. 39:3, 13, "the chief magician"; רַב־בֵּיתוֹ Est. 1:8 "officer of his household"; רַב־סָרִיס 2 K. 18:17; Jer. 39:3, 13 or רַב־סָרִיסִים Da. 1:3 "lord high chamberlain." רַבִּי [2] or רַבֵּינוּ, "my/our great one or lord," is a respectful term of address for the high official by those under him, → II, 153, n. 36. The one called רַבִּי is recognised thereby to be higher in rank than the speaker: [3] the prince by the people, [4] the master by the slave (Pes., 8, 2), the master craftsman by his associates (bAZ, 17b), the robber captain by his accomplices (bBM, 84a). רַבִּי can also be used on occasion for the prophet Elijah (bBer., 3a), the Messiah, [5] and God. [6] Above

---

ῥ α β β ί. Schürer, II, 375 f. (older bibl., 376, n. 9); J. Braydé *et al.,* Art. "Rabbi" in Jew. Enc., X, 294-297; Dalman WJ, I, 272-280; Str.-B., I, 916 f.; Moore, III, 15-17; A. J. Feldmann, *The Rabbi and His Early Ministry* (1941); E. Lohse, *Die Ordination im Spät-judt. u. im NT* (1951), 52; M. Kadushin, *The Rabbinic Mind* (1952); G. Schrenk, "Rabb. Charakterköpfe im nt.lichen Zeitalter," *Studien zu Pls., Abh.* ThANT, 26 (1954), 9-45; Pr.-Bauer⁴, s.v.

[1] Cf. Levy Wört., IV, 409.

[2] רַבִּי could later be pronounced ribbi or rebbi as well. Cf. the inscr. in CIJ, I, 568, 611; II, 893, 951, 1052. Cf. *infra* → n. 27, 30, 31.

[3] Dalman, 275.

[4] T. Sanh., 4, 4; cf. Dalman, 274.

[5] bSanh., 98a; cf. Dalman, 268.

[6] The Samaritans addressed God as Rabbi, Dalman, 275. Rabbi is also used in address to God in Islam. Cf. W. W. Graf Baudissin, *Kyrios,* II (1929), 35-37; III, 590, 688. רב, רבא or the fem. רבת is an epithet for Syr., Arab., Phoenician, Punic, Palmyrenian and Nabataean deities, *ibid.,* III, 60-65 [Bertram].

all, it was a custom for the pupil to address his teacher thus. [7] Derived from רַב, the intensified form רַבָּן "lord" is a title for the outstanding scribe. [8] רַבָּן obviously served also as "the older Jewish designation for the head of the Jews recognised by the Roman government." [9] Since Palest. Aram. often has the ending -on for -an, [10] we also find the form רַבּוֹן, later often רִבּוֹן. [11] In the Tg. רִבּוֹן is used in address to men, [12] but elsewhere it is reserved almost exclusively for God, esp. in the phrase "Lord of the world," רִבּוֹנוֹ שֶׁל עוֹלָם or רִבּוֹנֵיהּ דְּעָלְמָא. [13] In the Palest. Pentateuch Tg. רַבּוּנִי [14] occurs with the suffix of the 1st person. [15]

2. רַב is already used for "teacher" in the saying handed down by Jehoshua bPerachiah (c. 110 B.C.): "Get a teacher (רַב) and find a fellow-student." [16] The saying shows that a student had to try to gain admittance into the circle of a respected teacher and to engage in the study of Scripture and tradition in this fellowship. If the teacher acceded to his request the תַּלְמִיד could enter the school and in daily contact with his master he could get to know the Torah, and the tradition tested thereby, from his decisions and teachings. [17] The pupil followed his teacher with obedience and respect and expressed this by addressing him as רַבִּי, "my master" but also "my teacher." [18] Since the student-teacher relation is determined by respect, and this is as gt. as the respect accorded to heaven (= God, Ab., 4, 12), the student was bound to his teacher for the rest of his life. [19] When after several yrs. of association with his master he had become familiar with the oral tradition he would be called תַּלְמִיד־חָכָם and allowed to teach himself and to be addressed as Rabbi, → IV, 432 f. [20] Nor did the scribes receive this respectful appellation only from their pupils; theologians were held in such high esteem by the people that everybody greeted them with this title. Thus we read in the Talmudic

---

[7] For examples → n. 16-30.

[8] Levy Wört., IV, 416.

[9] Dalman, 273; Str.-B., I, 917; Levy Wört., 416. נְשִׂיא later replaces this title.

[10] Dalman, 275.

[11] Dalman Gr. § 35, 2.

[12] Examples in Str.-B., II, 25.

[13] Str.-B., II, 25, 176; III, 671 f.

[14] On רַבּוּנִי cf. E. Kautzsch, Grammatik d. bibl. Aram. (1884), 10; Schürer, II, 377; Dalman, 267, 279; G. Dalman, Jesus Jeschua (1922), 17; Str.-B., II, 25; Pr.-Bauer⁵, s.v.

[15] Though this term, found in Mk. 10:51 and Jn. 20:16, is not attested in Rabb. Aram. texts, rabbuni is common in the Palest. Pentateuch Tg., cf. the Fr. on Gn. 32:19 published by P. Kahle, also Kahle's Masoreten des Westens, II (1930), 10 and The Cairo Geniza (1947), 129. The discovery of new and more complete MSS of the Pent. Tg. in Rome has given enhanced importance to this work in relation to the language of Jesus, cf. M. Black, "The Recovery of the Language of Jesus," NT Studies, 3 (1956/57), 305-314; also "Die Erforschung der Muttersprache Jesu," ThLZ, 82 (1957), 661; P. Kahle, "Zehn Jahre Entdeckungen in d. Wüste Juda," ThLZ, 82 (1957), 648; also "D. paläst. Pentateuchtg. u. das zur Zeit Jesu gesprochene Aram.," ZNW, 49 (1958), 111, 115.

[16] Ab., 1, 6. Cf. Str.-B., I, 916. Cf. also the saying of Rabban Gamliel: "If you take a teacher (רַב), you will rise above doubt," Ab., 1, 16.

[17] On the Jewish institution of the תַּלְמִיד cf. esp. the art. μαθητής, → IV, 432 ff.

[18] רַבִּי as an address in the Mishnah, RH, 2, 9; Ned., 9, 5; BQ, 8, 6; רַבֵּינוּ as the address of several pupils to their teacher, Ber., 2, 5-7.

[19] Thus, e.g., R. El'azar b Azariah addresses his teacher R. Jochanan b Zakkai (d. c. 80 A.D.) as רַבִּי "my teacher" when he visits him on the death of his son, AbRN, 14, cf. Str.-B., I, 971.

[20] Lohse, 41 f.

tradition: "When King Jehoshaphat saw a תַּלְמִיד־חָכָם, he rose up from his throne, embraced and kissed him, and addressed him as 'my father, my father' (אָבִי, אָבִי), 'my teacher, my teacher' (רַבִּי, רַבִּי), 'my lord, my lord' (מָרִי, מָרִי)."[21] Since the scribes were generally called רַבִּי and referred to as such in the presence of others,[22] רַבִּי[23] gradually became the exclusive term for those who had completed their studies and been ordained as teachers of the Law.[24] From the middle of the 1st cent. A.D. the suffix increasingly lost its pronominal significance[25] and examples of רַבִּי as a general title begin to appear.[26] From the end of the 1st cent. A.D. רַבִּי as a title occurs on many Jewish inscr., esp. burial inscr., in Palestine,[27] Syria,[28] Cyprus,[29] and Italy.[30] Along with the common use of the title in Rabb. lit., these bear witness to the general employment and recognition of רַבִּי as a way of showing respect to the scribe throughout Judaism.

---

[21] bMak., 24a par. bKet., 103b; cf. Str.-B., I, 919.

[22] R. Jochanan (c. 250 A.D.) said, Gehazi was punished because in the presence of the king (2 K. 8:5) he simply called his teacher Elisha by name, bSanh., 100a, cf. Dalman, 274, n. 1. This example shows that it was customary for the pupil to call his teacher Rabbi in the presence of a third person.

[23] Scribes were called רַבִּי in Palestine, but addressed as רַב in Babylonia. Cf. Str.-B., I, 917; examples in Levy Wört., IV, 409. רַב is also attested in Palestine. Cf. the Joppa inscr. (CIJ, II, 900) → n. 27; N. Avigad, "Excavations at Beth She'arim 1953," *Israel Exploration Journal*, 4 (1954), 104 f.

[24] Ordination carried with it the right to be called רַבִּי. Cf. bBM, 85a; J. Jeremias, *Jerusalem z. Zeit Jesu²*, II B (1958), 104; J. Bonsirven, *Le Judaisme Palest. au temps de Jésus-Christ*, I (1954), 272-275; Lohse, 52.

[25] Cf. Str.-B., I, 916 f.

[26] The oldest example which can be dated with certainty is on a Jerusalem ossuary from the period before 70 A.D. which has διδάσκαλος and the name of the deceased. Cf. E. L. Sukenik, *Jüd. Gräber Jerusalems um Christi Geburt* (1931), 17 f.; K. H. Rengstorf → II, 151, 28 ff.; Lohse, 52; CIJ, II, 1266; W. F. Albright "Recent Discoveries in Palestine and the Gospel of St. John," *The Background of the NT and Its Eschatology, Studies in Honour of C. H. Dodd* (1956), 158; cf. also the inscr. from Jerusalem ossuaries in CIJ, II, 1218, 1268 and 1269.

[27] CIJ, II, 892 Joppa: רבי; II, 893 Joppa בירריבי = contraction of בִּיר ריבי (sic! c. n. 2) = "son of the rabbi"; II, 900 Joppa: bilingual PAB/רב; II, 951 Joppa βηρεβι (cf. on No. 893); II, 979 Er-Rama: רבי; II, 989 Sepphoris: רבי; II, 994 Beth-Shearim: רבי; II, 1042 Beth-Shearim: ברריבי; II, 1052 Beth-Shearim: bilingual וברב]י/PIBBI; II, 1055 Beth-Shearim: רבי; II, 1165 Beth-Alpha synagogue: רבי; for Jerusalem → n. 26, and II, 1410: רבי; II, 1414: 'Ραββί. Excavations since 1953 at Beth-Shearim, which was the seat of the Sanhedrin in the time of the patriarch Jehuda I, have brought to light other graves and burial inscr. of rabbis (2nd-4th cent. A.D.) which bear witness to the title Rabbi. Cf. the accounts in N. Avigad, "Excavations at Beth She'arim 1953," *Israel Explor. Journal*, 4 (1954), 88-107; "Excavations at Beth She'arim 1954," *ibid.*, 5 (1955), 205-239; "Excavations at Beth She'arim 1955," *ibid.*, 7 (1957), 73-92; "Excavations at Beth She'arim 1955, II," *ibid.*, 7 (1957), 239-255; also "The Necropolis of Beth She'arim," *Archaeology* 8 (1955), 236-244.

[28] CIJ, II, 857 El Hammeh: רב.

[29] CIJ, II, 736 Lapethos/Cyprus: a pillar bears the name of its donor: εὐχὴ ῥαββ(ὶ) 'Αττικοῦ. Cf. on this T. Reinach, "Une inscr. juive de Chypre," REJ, 48 (1904), 191-196; S. Krauss, *Synagogale Altertümer* (1922), 238 f.

[30] CIJ, I, 113 Rome: νομομαθής; I, 193 Rome: νομομαθής; I, 201 Rome: νομοδιδάσκαλος; I, 333 Rome: διδάσκαλος; I, 594 Venosa διδάσκαλος. Rebbi is also found, I, 568 Salerno: *filia Rebbitis Abundanti(i)*; I, 611 Venosa: *duo rebbites*. Cf. → n. 2.

B. ραββί, ραββουνί in the New Testament.

1. In the NT ραββί [31] occurs only in the Gospels. Mt. 23:7 alludes to the fact that scribes [32] were generally addressed as Rabbi and it censures their desire to be greeted with respect and called ραββί. According to Jn. 3:26 John the Baptist was called ραββί by his disciples ; this shows that as his pupils they paid him respect and obedience.

2. In all the other instances of ραββί in the Gospels it is Jesus who is respectfully addressed thus. [33] In Mk. 9:5 and 11:21 Peter calls Him ραββί, and at the betrayal and arrest Judas greets Him as ραββί, Mk. 14:45. [34] The Evangelists often have διδάσκαλος when Jesus is addressed, and here, too, one may assume that the original was רַבִּי, e.g., Mk. 4:38; 9:17, 38; 10:17, 20, 35; 12:14, 19. Following Palestinian tradition, Jn. has ραββί more frequently. Two of the disciples of John call Jesus ραββί in Jn. 1:38, and the Evangelist correctly explains to his readers that the Hebrew word means διδάσκαλος. Similarly Jesus is greeted by Nathanael as ραββί (Jn. 1:49), [35] then again by Nicodemus (3:2), the crowd (6:25), and the disciples (4:31; 9:2; 11:8). Twice we find ραββουνί, [36] which does not differ significantly from ραββί : [37] at Mk. 10:51 [38] on the lips of the blind man at Jericho, and at Jn. 20:16 as the term with which Mary addresses the Risen Lord.

When Jesus is called ραββί by His disciples and others, this shows that He conducted Himself like the Jewish scribes, → II, 139 ff.; 153 ff. [39] In the synagogues before His disciples and others who listened to His addresses He supported His teaching from Scripture. His disciples stood to Him in the relation of students to their master, and showed him the respect due by calling Him ραββί. Jesus was also a teacher for the common people, and was greeted by them with respect and

---

[31] Also written ραββεί, though always pronounced Rabbi. ι and ει are often interchangeable, cf. Bl.-Debr. § 38 and E. Nestle, "Rabbi," ZNW, 7 (1906), 184. If Ribbi also occurs on Palest. inscr., this shows that the title was not always pronounced the same in Palestine. Cf. N. Avigad, "Excavations at Beth She'arim 1953," Israel Explor. Journal, 4 (1954), 104 f.; B. Mazar, Beth She'arim, I² (1958), 136 [Rengstorf].

[32] V. 7 applies only to them and not to the Pharisees mentioned in v. 2. Cf. Jeremias, → I, 741, 22 ff.

[33] The name of Barabbas Mk. 15:7 par., which is a Gk. form of בַּר אַבָּא "son of the father," was explained to be בַּר רַבָּן in the Gospel of the Hebrews acc. to Hier. (in Mt. 27:16): Barrabas ... in evangelio, quod scribitur iuxta Hebraeos, filius magistri eorum interpretatur, qui propter seditionem et homicidium fuerit condemnatus. Cf. E. Klostermann, Apocrypha II, Kl. T., 8³ (1929), 10; Loh. Mk. on 15:7.

[34] Double in the Imperial Text, cf. (→ 962, 23 ff.) the example from bMak., 24a par. bKet., 103a (→ n. 21).

[35] Cf. the apocr. Gospel Fr. Berlin Pap., 11710, which records the witness of Nathanael as follows : ὡμολ]όγησεν καὶ εἶπε· ραμβιοὺ κύριε, σὺ εἶ ὁ υἱὸς θεοῦ. (ἀπεκρίθη αὐτῷ) ὁ ραμβὶς καὶ εἶπε· Ναθαναήλ, [α] πορεύου ἐν τῷ ἡλίῳ. ἀπεκρίθη αὐτῷ Ναθαναήλ καὶ εἶπεν· ραμβιοὺ κύριε, σὺ εἶ ὁ ἀμνὸς τοῦ θεοῦ, ὁ αἴρων τὰς ἁμ<α>ρ<τί>α<ς> τοῦ κόσμου. ἀπεκρίθη αὐτῷ ὁ ραμβὶς καὶ εἶπεν. ὁ ραμβίς, vocative ραμβιού, is a rendering of ραββί (μβ for ββ). Cf. H. Lietzmann, "Notizen," ZNW, 22 (1923), 153 f.

[36] → n. 14. Also written ραββουνεί, ραββονί, ραββονεί, but always pronounced rabbuni, → n. 31. Cf. Kautzsch, op. cit. (→ n. 14), 10 and Pr.-Bauer⁵, s.v.

[37] Dalman, 275, 279.

[38] D κύριε ραββί. Cf. Mt. 20:33; Lk. 18:41 κύριε.

[39] Cf. also E. Fascher, "Jesus der Lehrer," ThLZ, 79 (1954), 325-342.

addressed as ραββί. On the other hand, there was a basic difference between the relation of Jesus to His disciples and that of scribes to their pupils, for Jesus had called them to discipleship and was thus their Lord. His teaching did not contain the explication and development of traditional material which had to be proved by scriptural exegesis. Jesus preached with ἐξουσία and opposed His authoritative ἐγὼ δὲ λέγω ὑμῖν (Mt. 5:21-48 and par.) to the Law and tradition. Hence the Gospels often note the astonishment of the crowd that Jesus did not teach as the γραμματεῖς but with ἐξουσία, Mk. 1:22 and par.; Mt. 7:29. Since Jesus preaches with prophetic authority (→ 841 ff.), His disciples do not take up the study which, when successfully completed, will qualify them to end their training and become rabbis, → IV, 444 ff. They remain μαθηταί and Jesus remains their διδάσκαλος. They are expressly forbidden to call themselves ραββί, εἷς γάρ ἐστιν ὑμῶν ὁ διδάσκαλος, πάντες δὲ ὑμεῖς ἀδελφοί ἐστε, Mt. 23:8. If, then, Jesus is called διδάσκαλος and ραββί in the Gospels, this denotes a different relation of the disciples to Him than that between the Jewish תַּלְמִיד and his teacher. For this reason the Evangelists not only translate ραββί in many instances as διδάσκαλος but also use other terms for ραββί which better bring out the majesty of Jesus for the Christian community. Whereas the Fourth Evangelist does not avoid the offence that the teacher and rabbi Jesus of Nazareth is the Son of God, Lk. never uses ραββί, which his Hellenistic readers would not understand, but employs the Greek word ἐπιστάτης instead, Mk. 9:5 = Lk. 9:33. [40] Mt. keeps ραββί as an address to Jesus on the lips of the traitor Judas, Mt. 26:25, 49. [41] The disciples, however, call Him κύριε rather than ραββί (Mt. 17:4 for ραββί in Mk. 9:5). [42] Mt. 20:33 has κύριε for the ραββουνί of Mk. 10:51 [43] and Mt. 8:25 has the same for the διδάσκαλε of Mk. 4:38. [44] By avoiding ραββί or διδάσκαλε on the lips of the disciples [45] and always using κύριε instead, Mt. is obviously seeking to emphasise that Jesus is not a διδάσκαλος in the Jewish sense but the Lord of His people. As far as the disciples are concerned the title "master" is not enough ; only κύριος will suffice. [46]

3. ραββί does not occur elsewhere in early Chr. writings. This is a sign that the Palestinian tradition became less prominent and that the title Teacher played only a subsidiary role as compared with other Christological designations, → II, 156.

Lohse

---

[40] Cf. also Mk. 4:38 διδάσκαλε = Lk. 8:24 ἐπιστάτα, cf. Mk. 9:38 = Lk. 9:49; also Lk. 5:5; 8:45; 17:13. Cf. O. Glombitza, "Die Titel διδάσκαλος u. ἐπιστάτης f. Jesus bei Lukas," ZNW, 49 (1958), 275-278 : "Jesus Christ is a teacher or rabbi only in the eyes of strangers and for strangers, not for His own," 276.

[41] Here, then, Mt. sticks to the tradition, cf. Loh. Mt., *ad loc.*

[42] At Mt. 21:20 = Mk. 11:21 (ραββί) Mt. leaves out the address altogether.

[43] Cf. Lk. 18:41 κύριε.

[44] Judas says ραββί in Mt. 26:25, but the other disciples κύριε in 26:22.

[45] Those outside say to the disciples ὁ διδάσκαλος ὑμῶν in Mt. 9:11; 17:24, and the disciples introduce Jesus to others as διδάσκαλος in Mt. 26:18. Cf. G. Bornkamm, "Enderwartung u. Kirche im NT," *The Background of the NT and Its Eschatology, in Honour of C. H. Dodd* (1956), 250 f.

[46] Cf. Bornkamm, *op. cit.*, 250 f.

ῥάβδος, ῥαβδίζω, ῥαβδοῦχος

† ῥάβδος.

Etym. the basic meaning of ἡ ῥάβδος is "flexible twig," "switch," "rod." It is related to ῥάμνος, Lat. *verbera* (only plur.), Lith. *virbas*, Lett. *virbs*.

A. ῥάβδος outside the New Testament.

I. The Meaning in Greek.

1. "Staff," "rod." Orig. only the flexible cane in contrast to σκῆπτρον, but the two soon became interchangeable, Pind. Olymp., 9, 33; P. Tebt., I, 44, 20 etc. As compared with βακτηρία, not found in the NT, ῥάβδος is lighter and more supple, Xenoph. Eq., 11, 4. 2. "Stick" for beating, plur. "blows," esp. in relation to slaves or in school, Plat. Leg., III, 700c; Xenoph. Eq., 8, 4 (with μάστιξ); 11, 4; Plut. Alex., 51, 2 (I, 694a); Herodian. Hist., VII, 9, 6. A rod to punish the less serious offences of the Vestal virgins [1] Dion. Hal. Ant. Rom., 2, 67, 3; Plut. Numa, 10, 7 and 8 (I, 67a). 3. "Herdsman's staff" to drive oxen or keep off dogs, Anth. Graec., 11, 153; Anthologia Planudea, IV, 200. [2] 4. "Riding switch," Xenoph. Eq., 8, 4. 5. "Magician's rod," e.g., of Circe, Hermes or Athena, Hom. Il., 24, 343; Od., 10, 238, 293, 319, 389; 13, 429; 16, 172, 456; Hom. Hymn. Merc., 529; θεία ῥάβδος Ps.-Plut. De nobilitate, 17 (II, 967a). This can be of gold and with its help the god or a magician may change, blind, protect against misfortune, restore lost youth; we also read of wishing wands among the Scythians, Hdt., IV, 67. 6. "Oracular staff." The simplest form of ῥαβδομαντεία or ῥάβδοις μαντεύεσθαι was the writing of yes and no on two rods which were then drawn. But there were also more complicated forms, [3] Iambl. Myst., III, 17 (p. 141, 13 ff.) 7. "Staves" carried by the gods, e.g., the ῥάβδοι of Aesculapius of Cos, whose ἀνάληψις was celebrated each year in Cos by a festival and procession, [4] Ps.-Hippocr. Epist. Ad Abderitas (Kühn, III, 778), the staff of Dike on the ark of Cypselos, [5] originally probably a judge's penal rod,

---

ῥ ά β δ ο ς κτλ. Liddell-Scott, *s.v.*; Walde-Pok., I, 275; Preisigke Wört., III, 153; Mayser, I, 3, p. 167, 34 f.; Wilke-Grimm, *s.v.*; Pr.-Bauer⁵, *s.v.*; F. de Waele, Art. "Stab," Pauly-W., 3a (1929), 1894-1923; E. Thalheim, Art. "ῥαβδοφόροι," *ibid.*, 1a (1920), 18 f.; E. Kalt, Art. "Stab," *Bibl. Reallex.*, II (1937-1939), 745 f.; F. J. Doelger, "Die Auspeitschung einer Frau auf einer Reliefplatte d. Prätextat-Katakombe in Rom," *Ant. Christ.*, III (1932), 214 f.; S. Krauss, *Talmudische Archaeol.*, II (1911), 312-314; also "Die Instruktion Jesu an die Ap.," *Angelos*, 1 (1925), 96-102; T. W. Manson, *The Sayings of Jesus* (1949), 181-183; T. Mommsen, "Die Rechtsverhältnisse d. Ap. Pls.," ZNW, 2 (1901), 81-96; Nilsson, I², 509 f.; P. Saintyves, *Essai de folklore biblique* (1923), 59-137; F. Schulthess, "Zur Sprache d. Ev.," ZNW, 21 (1922), 234; P. Stengel, *Die griech. Kultusaltertümer³* (1920), 194; F. de Waele, *The Magic Staff or Rod in Graeco-Italian Antiquity* (1927); comm. on relevant verses.

[1] T. Mommsen, *Röm. Strafrecht* (1899), 928; E. Brasstoff, "Die Rechtsstellung d. Vestalin," *Zeitschr. f. vergleichende Rechtswissenschaft*, 22 (1908), 140 f.

[2] Ed. F. Dübner, *Anthologia Palatina*, II (1887), 568.

[3] M. Gundel, Art. "ῥαβδομαντεία" in Pauly-W., 1a (1920), 13-18; Nilsson, I², 167-171.

[4] M. Gundel, Art. "ῥάβδου ἀνάληψις" in Pauly-W., 1a (1920), 18; the festival is not mentioned, however, in the calendar ed. by R. Herzog, Ditt. Syll.³, III, 1025-1027.

[5] R. Hirzel, *Themis, Dike u. Verwandtes* (1907), 100-102. Archaeologically Dike usually carries a sword, more rarely scales.

Paus., V, 18, 2, the kerukeion of Hermes, Hom. Il., 24, 343 etc. 8. "Sceptre," Hom. Od., 16, 172; Pind. Olymp., 9, 33; Ps.-Plat. Ax., 367a. 9. "Rod" of the judge, umpire, police official, esp. αἱ ῥάβδοι for the Roman *fasces*, Polyb., 11, 29, 6; Dion. Hal. Ant. Rom., 4, 11, 6; 5, 2, 1; Strabo, 5, 2, 2; Epict. Diss., IV, 1, 57; 20, 21; Plut. Quaest. Rom., 82 (II, 283e); Herodian., VII, 6, 2. 10. "Staff" of the rhapsodist, Callim. Fr., 138; Paus., IX, 30, 3. 11. Angler's "rod," Hom. Od., 12, 251; "lime-twig" to catch birds, Aristoph. Av., 527, Lat. *viscata virga,* Ovid Metam., 15, 474. 12. "Mineral vein," Diod. S., 5, 37; Theophr. De causis plantarum, IV, 12, 7. 13. "Spike," "metal plate," perhaps interchangeable with ῥαφή, Hom. Il., 12, 297. 14. "Stripe" in clothes, Poll. Onom., VII, 53; on animals' skins, Aristot. Hist. An., IV, 1, p. 525a, 12; Clearchus Fr., 73 (FHG, II, 325); in heaven, Ps.-Arist. Mund., 4, p. 395a, 31. 15. "Spear-shaft," Ps.-Xenoph. Cyn., 10, 3 and 16. 16. "Shoot" of a tree, Ion Fr., 40 (TGF, 740); Theophr. Hist. Plant., II, 1, 2. 17. "Ray of light," Aristot. Meteor., III, 6, p. 377a, 30. 18. "Line," "verse," Schol. on Pind. Isthm., IV, 63a. [6]

II. The Word in the Septuagint.

1. "Staff," "rod," gen. for מַקֵּל Gn. 30:37 ff.; Jer. 48:17; for חֹטֶר Is. 11:1; for עֵץ Ez. 37:16 f.; for מִשְׁעֶנֶת, esp. as a "wand," 2 K. 18:21; Is. 36:6; Ez. 29:6; for מַטֶּה Ez. 7:10; 19:11 ff. 2. "Stick" for beating, for שֵׁבֶט Ex. 21:20; 2 S. 7:14; 1 Ch. 11:23; ψ 88:33; Prv. 10:13; 22:15; 23:13 f.; 26:3; Job 9:34; Is. 10:5 (fig. τοῦ θυμοῦ); Is. 10:15, 24; Lam. 3:1; Ez. 20:37; Mi. 4:14; for מַטֶּה Is. 9:3; 28:27. 3. "Shepherd's staff," for שֵׁבֶט Lv. 27:32; Ps. 2:9; ψ 22:4; Mi. 7:14; for מַקֵּל 1 S. 17:43; Zech. 11:7 ff. 4. "Staff" as a support for travellers, old men and the sick, for מַקֵּל Gn. 32:11; for מַטֶּה Gn. 38:18, 25; for מִשְׁעֶנֶת Ex. 21:19; Zech. 8:4. 5. "Magician's rod," for מַטֶּה Ex. 7:9-12. 6. "Oracular rods," for מַטֶּה Nu. 17:17; for מַקֵּל Hos. 4:12. 7. "Wands" as carried by angels, for מִשְׁעֶנֶת Ju. 6:21. 8. "Sceptre," also fig. for rule, for מַטֶּה ψ 109:2; for שֵׁבֶט ψ 44:7; 124:3; Ju. 5:14 B; for מַקֵּל Ez. 39:9; for שַׁרְבִיט Est. 4:11; 5:2; 8:4. 9. "Rods" of Moses and Aaron, for מַטֶּה Ex. 4:2, 4, 17, 20; 7:9 ff.; 8:13; 10:13; 14:16; 17:5, 9; Nu. 20:8 f.; of Balaam, for מַקֵּל Nu. 22:27.

With no distinction of meaning LXX (more rarely) uses βακτηρία as well as ῥάβδος. The only pt. worth noting is the ascribing of a βακτηρία to the prophet in 2 K. 4:29 ff. [7]

B. ῥάβδος in the New Testament.

1. Staff of reed or wood to measure a specific but undefined length, Rev. 11:1. On the basis of Ez. 40:3 ff., and perhaps also 2 S. 8:2, the divine has the experience of a rod being handed to him to measure a portion of the temple precincts (→ IV, 634, 31 ff.) into which the enemies of God will not penetrate. [8]

Related are the many accounts of the measuring of areas at the founding of colonies or of places of asylum in temple enclosures. Throughout antiquity staves are used for measuring along with strings and strips of skin. [9]

---

[6] Ed. A. B. Drachmann, III (1927), 232.

[7] L. Köhler, *Kleine Lichter* (1945), 25-27.

[8] The unit of measure in Ez. 40:5; 43:13 is the royal ell of 52,5 cm.; this, then, is the length of the instrument.

[9] On measuring in antiquity cf. esp. Vitruvius De Architectura (ed. F. Krohn [1912]); F. Hultsch, Metrologici (1864); H. Nissen, *Griech. u. röm. Metrologie*² (1892); also *Das Templum* (1869), 22-53 (on the measuring of the precincts). For Palest. materials cf. J. Benzinger, *Hbr. Archaeologie*³ (1927), 190-204.

If the verse is accepted as original — and there are good grounds for this — then it carries with it the constant promise of Rev. that the true community of God will come unscathed through all the terrors of the last time. If it is regarded as an intrusion, the most natural suggestion is that it comes from a Zealot pamphlet of the period when Roman troops were already in Jerusalem but there was hope that the inner part of the temple would still be saved. [10]

2. Stick for beating. In 1 C. 4:21 Paul, on the basis of v. 15, portrays himself as a Greek schoolmaster or pedagogue who can come either ἐν ἀγάπῃ or with a stick. [11]

Since the Jewish schoolmaster (סופר) used a strap (רצועה) rather than a stick, [12] it is obvious that Paul has the Hell. school in view. According to the principle ὁ μὴ δαρεὶς ἄνθρωπος οὐ παιδεύεται in Menand. Monosticha, 422 [13] beatings were common here ; both in lit. and art the pedagogue's rod plays an important role. Also important in the pedagogic lit. of Hellenism and late antiquity is the question at issue, namely, whether better results are achieved by kindness or blows. [14]

3. Shepherd's staff. Messianically understood, Ps. 2:9 is referred to Christ in Rev. 2:27; 12:5; 19:15; Christ will feed the nations with an iron rod. [15]

There is nothing intrinsically impossible about the metaphor. Shepherd's staves with iron points to keep the animals together and to hurt them if need be are common (κέντρον → III, 663, 1 ff.). The shepherd's staff already carries a threat with it in Hom. Il., 23, 845 ff. In Rabb. lit. we find rods completely of iron or with iron clasps. [16] It is possible, however, that the LXX confused תִּרְעֵם "thou wilt feed" with תְּרֹעֵם "thou wilt smash"; if so, Rev. followed it. But there are serious objections against this conjecture. רעע is an Aramaism, and the delivering up of subjects to destruction would be pointless. "To feed" commonly means "to rule" (→ 487, 3 ff.) (Vg transl. regere). [17] A special problem in Rev. 2:27 is that this alone quotes the second half-verse of Ps. 2:9 but in a form which deviates markedly from the LXX, [18] and that here alone the saying is not taken in a strict Messianic sense but is referred to the one who follows Christ

---

[10] For authenticity cf. Loh. Apk., ad loc.; J. Behm, Die Offenbarung d. Joh., NT Deutsch, 11[7] (1956), ad loc.; Had. Apk., ad loc.; against R. H. Charles, The Rev. of St. John, ICC (1950), ad loc.; Bss. Apk., ad loc.

[11] On the instrumental ἐν (based on v. 15) cf. Schwyzer, II, 435; Bl.-Debr. § 219.

[12] A. Klostermann, "Das Schulwesen im alten Israel," Theol. Studien. Zahn-Festschr. (1908), 193-232.

[13] Ed. A. Meinecke, Fr. Comicorum Graecorum, IV (1841), 352. Cf. also on the peda-gogue Herond. Mim., 3; Mart., 10, 62; 14, 80; W. Helbig, Wandgemälde der vom Vesuv verschütteten Städte Campaniens (1868), No. 1492; M. P. Nilsson, Die hell. Schule (1955); J. Keil, "Das Unterrichtswesen im antiken Ephesos," Anzeiger d. österreichischen Akademie, philosophisch-historische Klasse, 88 (1952); H. I. Marrou, Gesch. d. Erziehung im klass. Altertum (1957).

[14] Cf. esp. Plut. Lib. Educ. (II, 1 ff.) and in the OT Prv. 13:24; 23:14; 29:17; Sir. 30:12.

[15] On Ps. 2:9 R. Kittel, Die Psalmen, Komm. z. AT, 13[5, 6] (1929); H. Gunkel, Psalmen, Handkomm. AT, 14[4] (1926); W. E. Barnes, The Psalms (1931); W. O. E. Oesterley, The Psalms (1939), ad loc.; on the further development of the Messianic image in the early Church M. A. Veyries, Les figures criophores. Bibliothèque des écoles françaises d'Athènes et de Rome, 39 (1884); L. Clausnitzer, Die Hirtenbilder in d. altchr. Kunst, Diss. Halle (1904).

[16] Nu. r., 12, 3; Lam. r., 1, 3; Kelim, 11, 6; bSanh., 102a.

[17] Cf. H. Schmidt, Die Psalmen, Hndbch. AT (1934), ad loc.

[18] Expositions in the catenae equate ὡς and ἵνα [Bertram]. But this is ruled out by the parallelism and is an obvious evasion of the difficulty. Nor is it possible to harmonise "feed" and "smash" by way of "rule."

"to the end." This disciple has the same authority as Christ Himself. At Rev. 19:15 ῥάβδος has sometimes been understood as a sword from the time of H. Grotius (on the basis of Jewish use of the saying). But this is ruled out by the fact that Rev. combines two rural images, that of the shepherd and that of the one who treads the winepress.

In the post-apost. fathers ῥάβδος is the shepherd's rod in Herm. v., 5, 1; s., 6, 2, 5.

4. Traveller's staff. In Mk. 6:8 Jesus allows His disciples to take a ῥάβδος for the way, though Mt. 10:10 and Lk. 9:3 forbid this. Lk. 22:35 does not refer to a stick, → 120, 11 ff. [19] Mk., supported by Lk. 22:35, is probably the original. In antiquity one could not take long journeys on eastern roads without a staff. Jewish Christian rigorism might have altered the saying to conform to the rule that no one must walk on the temple hill with staff, sandals or girdle. [20]

In general the staff is part of the equipment of Gk. and Jewish itinerant teachers. The staff, the satchel, and the practical Cynic cloak were marks of the wandering Cynic missionaries; after the death of Peregrinus Proteus an admirer paid a whole talent for his staff. [21] To indicate discipleship of Heracles the staff often took the form of a club (σκυτάλη). Itinerant rabbis also carried staffs. The itinerant rabbi Jeremiah orders that when he dies his staff should be put in his hand and his sandals on his feet. [22] To give a traveller's staff to the dead is an Egypt. custom. [23]

5. Staff for the support of an old man. Hb. 11:21 follows the LXX in putting מַטֶּה ("staff") for מִטָּה ("bed") at Gn. 47:31. As the author sees it, the fact that Jacob leans on his staff when he makes his last prayer is a sign of special humility before God. [24]

The staff is an indispensable feature of old age on all Gk. vases depicting old men, also in the riddle of the sphinx at Thebes etc. [25] Rabb. writings too (bShab., 66a, Bar.) speak of מַקֵּל שֶׁל זְקֵנִים.

6. The budding rod of Aaron (Nu. 17:16-26) was in the ark according to Hb. 9:4. But the author does not ask what function the prototype of the rod has in the heavenly temple, so that the field was open for later Christian speculation on this question.

This rod is also mentioned in Philo Vit. Mos., II, 178-180; Joseph. Ant., 4, 63-66. So far as is known, however, there is no other testimony to its being in the ark. Acc. to

---

[19] Wellh. Mk. on 6:8 tries to harmonise the two versions by assuming that the simple לֹא is read for אֶלָּא in Mk. 6:8. But this is unlikely. Nor does a textual alteration of the very strong Gk. εἰ μή ... μόνον offer any help. Cf. on this J. Lagrange, Év. selon Saint Marc[5] (1929), 151 and Loh. Mk., ad loc.

[20] Ber., 9, 5, cf. Manson, 181-183.

[21] Luc. Indoct., 14; Epict. Diss., III, 22, 50; Dio Chrys. Or., 34, 2.

[22] Gn. r., 100, 2 on 49:33; Schl. Mt. on 10:10. Cf. bBB, 133b; Jeb., 16, 7; Kelim, 17, 16; Tohorot, 8, 9; T. Meg., 4, 30; Lev. r., 25, 1 on 19:25. On the other hand, the prophet does not necessarily carry a staff, Zech. 13:4; 2 K. 1:8.

[23] R. Reitzenstein, Hell. Wundererzählungen (1906), 112; on the other hand the customary long staffs depicted on the graves of Egypt. officials are simply marks of rank.

[24] On the gesture cf. F. Heiler, "Die Körperhaltung beim Gebet," Orientalistische Studien, II (1918), 168.

[25] Examples in E. Buschor, Griech. Vasen (1940), Ill. 178 (Duris), 180 (Brygos), 187 (Cleophrades), 228 (Cleophon).

the Jewish Midr., which combines Nu. 17:25 and Ex. 16:33, it was in the holy of holies (Yoma, 3, 7) before the ark (Tg. O. Nu. 17:25), and it is elsewhere mentioned in connection with the ark. [26] It was created on the evening of the first Sabbath, served as a sceptre for the kings, and will come back again in the Messianic kingdom. [27] The motif of a budding rod is very common. [28] In religion it is associated with Dionysus, cf. the budding mast in the Homeric Dionysus hymn, depicted on the Munich Exekias bowl. [29] It is also associated with Attis, the budding stone-pine being a symbol of resurrection. [30]

In post-NT Chr. writings 1 Cl., 43, 2-5 uses another Haggadic version. Herm. s., 8 mixes several motifs. [31] The rod becomes the budding wood of the cross ξύλον, Ign. Trall., 11, 2; Sib., 5, 257. On the basis of Acta Pilati, 19 the Middle Ages identify allegorically the tree of Paradise, the budding rod of Aaron and the cross. [32] In connection with this development the budding rod finally becomes in the Tannhäuser saga the sign of God's pardoning grace, the blossoming rod a symbol of Joseph, and the sprouting rod a symbol of Christophoros. [33]

7. Sceptre. According to Hb. 1:8 (on the basis of ψ 44:7) Christ as ruler of the world holds the sceptre of God in expression of His legitimate divine government. [34]

> Throughout antiquity the sceptre is an expression of the legitimate rule which demands respect, cf. Paus., II, 8, 7; IX, 40, 11 f.

8. Magician's staff or oracular staff. There is no mention of either of these in the NT, though cf. Herm. v., 3, 2, 4; s., 9, 6, 3 and catacomb art, which gives Jesus a magician's rod at the miracles of feeding and raising the dead, like Moses when he brought forth water out of the rock. [35]

† ῥαβδίζω.

1. The verb occurs in Gk. in the following senses: a. "to strike with a stick," Aristoph. Lys., 587; Pherecrates Fr., 50 (CAF, I, 159); b. "to scourge" as a transl. of virgis caedere for the Roman punishment (verberatio and fustuarium), Diod. S., 19, 101; [1] c. "to thresh," P. Ryl., II, 148, 20, cf. the derived nouns ῥαβδισμός, P. Tebt., I, 119, 46, and ῥαβδιστής, BGU, I, 115, 1, 15; d. "to beat down" olives or fruit from the trees with long sticks, Theophr. De causis plantarum, I, 19, 4; V, 4, 2.

---

[26] jSota, 8, 3 (22c, 7 ff.); Ab. R. Nat., 41, but not bBB, 14a b.

[27] M. Ex., 16, 32 f. (59b); Str.-B., III, 739 f.

[28] A. Jeremias, Das AT im Lichte d. alten Orients (1930), 444; W. Henry, Art. "Bâton" in DAC, 2, 1 (1925), 621.

[29] J. Leipoldt, "Dionysos," Angelos-Beih., III (1937), 7. Cf. Hom. Hymn. Bacch., 38-40; Philostr. Imagines, I, 19, 3 (ed. O. Benndorf and C. Schenkl [1893], 39).

[30] H. Hepding, Attis (1903), 149-151; F. Cumont, Die orient. Religionen im röm. Heidentum³ (1931), 44, 52 f.; also Lux perpetua (1949), 261.

[31] Herm. has a gt. liking for staffs of all kinds, v., 3, 2, 4; 5, 1; s., 6, 2, 5; 9, 6, 3.

[32] F. Kampers, Mittelalterliche Sagen von dem Paradiesbaum u. d. Holz des Kreuzes Christi (1897).

[33] J. Braun, Tracht u. Attribute der Heiligen (1943), 171 f., 185 f.

[34] On the Messianic use of the Ps. cf. Str.-B., III, 679 f.

[35] J. Wilpert, Die Malereien der Katakomben Roms (1903), 292-314; O. Wulff, Die altchr. Kunst von ihren Anfängen bis zur Mitte d. ersten Jahrtausends (1914), 75-119 (sculpture), 123 f., 185 (ivory).

ῥ α β δ ί ζ ω. [1] Dölger, 214 f.; ῥαβδίζω is always used for Roman scourging in the NT, μαστίζω, μαστιγόω being used for the synagogue punishment, → IV, 516, 7 ff.

2. In the LXX only for חָבַט "to thresh," Ju. 6:11; Rt. 2:17, also in ᾽ΑΣΘ with ref. to the harvest of the Last Judgment in Is. 27:12 (cf. also 28:27); the LXX alters the thought here under the influence of the second half of the v.

3. In the NT the word is used only for the Roman punishment of scourging. Paul tells us that as an apostle he suffered this three times, 2 C. 11:25. Ac. 16:22 describes one of these occasions. Denounced by the Jews, Paul had his clothes ripped off by the police of Philippi and was beaten. This scourging is to be re-garded as a means of police coercion rather than torture, → IV, 517, 17 ff. The local magistrates (στρατηγοί) had wide powers in a military colony. According to the Lex Porcia de tergo civium Paul as a Roman citizen should not have been scourged. He made use of the privilege, however, only after the scourging so as not to give the impression that he wanted to avoid suffering for Christ's sake. It may be assumed that the scourging was public — on the main square before the bema. [2]

† ῥαβδοῦχος.

ῥαβδοῦχος, from ῥάβδος and ἔχω, is used in Gk. as follows : of police with cudgels who have the right and duty to use force if needed, Aristoph. Pax, 734; Thuc., V, 50, 31; P. Oxy., XIV, 1626, 9 and 21; 1750, 12; of referees, Plat. Prot., 338a; of supervisors in temples and at religious festivals, Ditt. Syll.[3], II, 736, 147 ff.; in Andania 20 ῥαβδοφόροι were chosen from among the ἱεροί for this office, IG, IX, 2, No. 1109, 23 f.; in Magnesia they had not to be under 30, cf. CIG, II, 3599; of the ladies accompanying a princess, Polyb., 15, 29, 13 (though perhaps they are cultic officials of the Thesmophoreion). The word is the transl. of the Rom. lictor in official circles, Polyb., 5, 26, 10; Polyb. Fr., 74; Diod. S., 5, 40; 17, 77; Herodian, VII, 8, 10; Plut. Quaest. Rom., 67 (II, 280a).

The related verb ῥαβδουχέω, the noun ῥαβδουχία and the synon. ῥαβδοφόρος do not occur in the NT, nor are any of these words found in the LXX.

In Ac. 16:35, 38 Paul is led by the city police to the boundary of the city when he has proved to the στρατηγοί that he is a Roman citizen. Usually two lictors accompany the municipal στρατηγοί. [1] The escort is less to protect Paul than to excuse the illegal conduct of the magistrates by a mark of respect.

C. Schneider

---

[2] Worth noting, though not very likely in view of the lack of corroboration, is the suggestion of Jackson-Lake, I, 5, 272 f. that the στρατηγοί tore their own clothes as a sign of condemnation.

ῥ α β δ ο ῦ χ ο ς. [1] J. Marquardt, Röm. Staatsverwaltung, I² (1881), 175; E. Samter, Art. "Fasces" in Pauly-W., 6 (1909), 2002-2004; E. Kübler, Art. "Lictor" in Pauly-W., 13 (1927), 507-518; on the pre-Roman office of στρατηγοί in Philippi cf. H. Bengtson, Die Strategie in d. hell. Zeit, II (1944), 400 f.

```
† ῥᾳδιούργημα, † ῥᾳδιουργία
```

The compound ῥᾳδιουργός (from Xenoph.) and derivates all come from ῥᾴδιος in the sense "unburdened" (Eur. Hipp., 1116), "light." [1] The ref. might well be to the neutral basic sense of "ready accomplishment" in Luc. Hermot., 71, where a supraterrestrial power, Εὐχή, is the subj. of the action : ... ἡ θεὸς ... ῥᾳδιουργεῖ. [2] Nevertheless, the θεός only builds castles in the air, so that an element of disparagement is plain to see. Acc. to the degree of disparagement intended the ῥᾳδιο- can take on more or less of its specific sense.

The adj. ῥᾳδιουργός is used in Xenoph. Sym., 8, 9 for offerings in which one is not too particular (opp. θυσίαι ... ἁγνότεραι). A man who is called ῥᾳδιουργός is without self-discipline, Aristot. De virtutibus et vitiis, 6, p. 1251a, 20. Nevertheless, the more lenient element strictly contained in ῥᾴδιος [3] is often less prominent ; in Philo Det. Pot. Ins., 165 (→ V, 726, 14); Poster. C., 43; Som., II, 148 there is no discernible difference between ῥᾳδιουργός and πανοῦργος (→ V, 722 ff.). [4] In Xenoph. Cyrop., I, 6, 8 ῥᾳδιουργέω is synon. with ἀπονώτερον διάγειν (opp. προνοεῖν καὶ φιλοπονεῖν), "unconcerned and planless drifting." The usual ref., however, is to the careless neglect of ethical demands, e.g., truthfulness, Philostr. Imagines, I, 12, cf. also the intentional falsifying of documents, Jos. Vit. (vl. ῥᾳδιουργόν).

ʽΡᾳδιούργημα is the result of ῥᾳδιουργεῖν, e.g., falsification in Plut. Pyrrhus, 6, 7 (I, 460a), or some other deception, or even sexual transgression, Dion. Hal. Ant. Rom., I, 77, 3; the word becomes a general term for offences of all kinds, Ps.-Luc. De calumniis, 20 : ... καὶ ἄλλα μυρία ῥᾳδιουργήματα. The verbal abstr. ῥᾳδιουργία, corresponding to the verb, describes the attitude of the man who "takes life too lightly," Suid., s.v., for whom serious πονεῖν is a painful matter, Xenoph. Cyrop., VII, 5, 74. [5] Acc. to Xenoph. Cyrop., I, 6, 34 the dangers arising from ἐπιθυμίαι increase incalculably where there is ῥᾳδιουργία. The word is also used for "negligence" in office in Plut. Cato Minor, 16, 3 (I, 914c) and gen. for "unscrupulousness," whether in the falsifications of

---

ῥᾳδιούργημα, ῥᾳδιουργία. Moult.-Mill., 562; Preisigke Wört., II, 439; W. J. Goodrich, "A Passage of Pindar Reconsidered," *Class. Quarterly,* 2 (1908), 31-33; H. Richards, "The Minor Works of Xenophon," Class. Rev., 11 (1897), 134bf, 334a.

[1] In his discussion of the right mean of ἐλευθεριότης ("generosity") Aristot. Eth. Nic., IV, 1, 9, p. 1120a, 17 says that it is easier simply to refuse passively to take the goods of others than actively to give up possessions of one's own (καὶ ῥᾷον τὸ μὴ λαβεῖν τοῦ δοῦναι). Yet the more difficult active course corresponds better to ἀρετή (→ (I, 458, 20 ff.) than the easier passive course (τῆς γὰρ ἀρετῆς μᾶλλον τὸ εὖ ποιεῖν ἢ τὸ εὖ πάσχειν, *ibid.,* 1120a, 11 f.). These statements show esp. clearly why the neutral concept ῥᾴδιος (Aristot. Rhet., I, 6, 27, p. 1363a, 23 : ῥᾴδια δὲ ὅσα ἢ ἄνευ λύπης ἢ ἐν ὀλίγῳ χρόνῳ, "anything is easy which can be done without effort or in a short space of time") can be used disparagingly in our group. On the adv. ῥᾳδίως cf. Thuc., I, 73, 1: ὅπως μὴ ῥᾳδίως περὶ μεγάλων πραγμάτων ... χεῖρον βουλεύσησθε, "in order that you may not casually make a wrong decision in so important a matter." ʽΡᾳδίως βουλεύσησθε contains a sharper warning than the preceding ταχέως βουλευτέον, I, 72, 1.

[2] Cf. Liddell-Scott, *s.v.*

[3] Cf. for the mitigating element "light-hearted" (Germ. *leichtfertig, leichtsinnig*), though also "light-minded."

[4] In the list of vices of the φιλήδονος which begins with πανοῦργος and also contains αἰσχρουργός (Philo Eacr. AC, 32 → V, 726, 18) ῥᾳδιουργός describes the inner attitude between ἐνεδρευτικός and ἀδιόρθωτος in the sense of "cunning," "crafty" [Bertram].

[5] ʽΡᾳδιουργία is used here along with ἡδυπάθεια τῶν κακῶν ἀνθρώπων, "the good living of the dissolute man," so also in Xenoph. Mem., II, 2, 20; cf. E. C. Marchant, Review of W. Müller, *Xenoph. Cyrop.* (1914), Class. Rev., 30 (1916), 165 f.

worthless historians (Polyb., 12, 25e) [6] or in trespasses (P. Magd., 35). [7] Hence it is hardly a milder term for "wickedness," Philo Cher., 80. In P. Oxy., II, 237, col. VIII, 12 and 15 ῥᾳδιουργία and πανουργία (→ V, 723, 21 ff.) are synon.

In Acts, the only NT work to use the group, ῥᾳδιο- has its developed sense in the two relevant passages, though in different ways. In Ac. 18:14 there is a legal distinction. Not every villainy, but only that which is definitely wicked, a ῥᾳδιούργημα πονηρόν, is a matter for the proconsul. In Ac. 13:10, however, the choice [8] of ῥᾳδιουργία is theological, though not in the sense of mitigation. The "wickedness" of Elymas implies a loosening of all [9] ethical restraints as a result of connection with the διάβολος, magic, and pseudo-prophecy.

Bauernfeind

| † ῥακά | → κενός, III, 659 f.; → μωρός, IV, 839 ff.

Contents : 1. Derivation ; 2. רֵיקָא; 3. Matthew 5:22.

1. Derivation.

ῥακά (vl. ῥαχά) [1] is a transcription of the Aram. insult רֵיקָא. [2] It is a NT hapax legomenon (only Mt. 5:22); in pre-NT Gk. it is found only on a Zeno pap. of 257 B.C.: Ἀντίοχον τὸν ῥαχᾶν. [3] The double α raises a difficulty in respect of derivation from

---

[6] Cf. the verb in the same sense in Strabo, 11, 6, 4.

[7] Cf. T. Reinach, "Les juifs d'Alexandronèse," *Mélanges Nicole* (1905), 451-459; O. Guéraud, Ἐντεύξεις = *Publications de la société royale égypt. de papyrologie, Textes et Documents*, I (1931), 83-85.

[8] This is the only word in the v. not found also in the LXX, cf. Haench. Ag., 349.

[9] Πάσης before ῥᾳδιουργίας is probably original ; we do not have here, as in 18:14, a differentiation, but ῥᾳδιουργία affects all spheres of life.

ῥ α κ ά. F. Blass, "Textkrit. Bemerkungen z. Mt.," BFTh, 4 (1900), 13 f.; Dalman Gr., 173 f.; K. Köhler, "Zu Mt. 5:22," ZNW, 19 (1919-1920), 91-95; G. Dalman, *Jesus-Jeschua* (1922), 13, 71; F. Schulthess, "Zur Sprache der Ev.," ZNW, 21 (1922), 241-243; P. Fiebig, *Jesu Bergpredigt* (1924), 34-38; P. Joüon, *L'Évangile de Notre-Seigneur Jésus-Christ* (1930), 25; C. C. Edgar, "A New Group of Zenon Pap.," *Bulletin of the John Rylands Library*, 18 (1934), 111-130; E. C. Colwell, "Has Raka a Parallel in the Pap. ?" JBL, 53 (1934), 351-354; A. Fridrichsen, "Exegetisches z. NT," *Symb. Osl.*, 13 (1934), 38-40; C. C. Torrey, *The Four Gospels*[2] (1947), 290 f.; Pr.-Bauer[5], *s.v.*

[1] The sparsely attested variant ῥαχά (א* DW lat Tert Cypr) offers a form found already in the Zeno pap. → n. 3. There can be no doubt but that it is the same word → n. 5. Nor does it contradict a derivation from רֵיקָא. It is true that ק is usually κ, but the NT MSS often vacillate between κ and χ for ק and codex א has instances of χ : Nu. 13:22, 28 Ἐνάχ rather than Ἐνάκ, Αἰνάκ (A); Mt. 1:14 Σαδώχ for Σαδώκ; 27:46 σαβαχθάνει for σαβακθάνει (on the vacillation in transcribing שְׁבַקְתַּנִי cf. Dalman Gr., 365, n. 1; Bl.-Debr. § 39, 2 App.); Ac. 1:19 Ἀχελδαμάχ for Ἀκελδαμάχ. Hence ῥαχά is to be regarded as a dialectical or orthographical variant of ῥακά.

[2] So already older exegesis, cf. Ps.-Chrys., Opus imperfectum in Mt., Hom. XI (MPG, 56 [1859], 690): *Racha quidem dicitur hebraice vacuus* ; for further examples cf. Zn. Mt. on 5:22; most modern exegetes agree.

[3] Edgar, 112 f., No. 2; also Preisigke Sammelbuch, 5, No. 7638, 7; P. Ryl., IV, No. 555. On the pap. cf. esp. Colwell, 351-354.

רֵיקָא (one would expect ῥηκά). The first α has led some to contest the derivation from רֵיקָא [4] and to make other suggestions. [5] The difficulty vanishes, however, when one takes into account the influence of the Syr. *raqa* as a call to servants : "Hi there, you idiot !" [6] The argument that there has been Syr. influence on the vowels has far more in its favour than the suggestion that the first α is based on the Gk. τὸ ῥάκος ("rags" [Mk. 2:21 par.], "tatters," sometimes of persons), [7] for it is natural to turn to Syria first.

The fact that ῥακά is not accompanied by a translation in Mt. 5:22 has an important bearing on the provenance of the Gospel. Matthew is writing for readers who, though they speak Greek, can understand an oriental term of abuse without further ado. This points to Syria, for after 70 A.D. it was only in Syrian cities that one would find Greek-speaking Christians in an oriental setting.

2. רֵיקָא.

The Aram. רֵיקָא is connected with the Heb. adj. רֵיק (Aram. רֵיקָן) "empty" (in the head); [8] this has been given a vocative ending -a. [9]

The great number of Rabb. instances of רֵיקָא [10] enables us to fix the implication of the word with some precision. It expresses vexed disparagement which may be accompanied by displeasure, anger, or contempt, and which is usually addressed to a foolish, thoughtless, or presumptuous person. The insult was regarded as harmless : "blockhead," "donkey."

---

[4] Blass, 13 f.; Wellh. Mt. on 5:22; Zn. Mt. on 5:22; S. Krauss, "Drei palästin. Stadtnamen," OLZ, 22 (1919), 63; Schulthess, 241-243; Loh. Mt., ad loc.

[5] Schulthess, 242 f., starting with ῥαχά, would derive it from the Heb. רַךְ ("fine," "tender") in the sense of "weakling," but this sense is not attested. Torrey, 291 suggests derivation of ῥακά from the Heb. part. רָקִיע, but there are no instances of this. Edgar, 113 proposes that the τὸν ῥαχᾶν of the Zeno pap. is an abbreviation of ῥαχιστής ("braggart") and Colwell, 351-354, Loh. Mt., ad loc. and P. Benoit, "Papyrologie," Rev. Bibl., NS, 61 (1954), 478 (hesitantly) extend this to the NT ῥαχά, but the sparseness of Gk. examples (only 2) is against a Gk. derivation, esp. as the ref. in Mt. 5:22 must have been to a common term of abuse.

[6] Chrys. Hom., 16, 7 in Mt. (MPG, 57 [1862], 248): τὸ δὲ ʿΡακὰ τοῦτο, οὐ μεγάλης ἐστὶν ὕβρεως ῥῆμα, ἀλλὰ μᾶλλον καταφρονήσεως καὶ ὀλιγωρίας τινὸς τοῦ λέγοντος, καθάπερ γὰρ ἡμεῖς, ἢ οἰκέταις ἤ τισι τῶν καταδεεστέρων ἐπιτάττοντες λέγομεν· ἄπελθε σύ, εἰπὲ τῷ δεῖνι σύ· οὕτω καὶ οἱ τῇ Σύρων κεχρημένοι γλώττῃ ʿΡακὰ λέγουσιν, ἀντὶ τοῦ, σύ, τοῦτο τιθέντες, "for as we say: 'You, be off,'" or : "'You, tell NN,' when we give an order to a servant or a poor person, in Syriac they say 'Raka' where we say 'you'." Bas. Regulae brevius tractatae, 51 (MPG, 31 [1885], 1117 A): τί ἐστι ῥακά; ἐπιχώριον ῥῆμα ἠπιωτέρας ὕβρεως, πρὸς τοὺς οἰκειοτέρους λαμβανόμενον, "a harmless, familiar word of abuse used by the native population."

[7] Antiphilius Byzantius (1st cent. A.D.) Anth. Graec., 9, 242 of an old sailor: ἁλίοιο βίου ῥάκος ("a derelict of life at sea"). For this explanation of the α cf. Dalman Gr., 173, n. 2; Dalman Jesus, 71.

[8] Dalman Gr., 173, n. 2 (like E. Kautzsch, Grammatik d. Bibl.-Aram. [1884], 10) first regarded רֵיקָא as a short form of רֵיקָן, but then in Jesus, 71 decided in favour of a link with the Heb. רֵיק.

[9] On the vocative ending -a cf. C. Brockelmann, Grundriss d. vergleichenden Grammatik d. semitischen Sprachen, II (1913), § 19.

[10] J. Lightfoot, Horae Hebraicae et Talmudicae in Ev. Mt. ad 5:22, Opera omnia II (1686), 286; A. Wünsche, Neue Beiträge z. Erläuterung d. Ev. aus Talmud u. Midr. (1878), 47 f.; Dalman Jesus, 71; Fiebig, 34-38; esp. Str.-B., I, 278 f., 286, 385, 900; II, 586, 714; III, 271, 851.

Next to רֵיקָא the Heb. שׁוֹטֶה / Aram. שָׁטְיָא is the most common term of abuse. A def. of the word [11] shows that it corresponds to "idiot." Though the meaning of μωρέ in Mt. 5:22c is debated (→ IV, 839 f.), it is most likely based on שָׁטְיָא,[12] so that in ῥακά and μωρέ (Mt. 5:22) the two most common terms of abuse in the days of Jesus are associated.

3. Matthew 5:22.

Mt. 5:22 acquires its true edge only against the contemporary background.

Linguistically it should be noted that like the Hb. חַיָּב the Aram. אִתְחַיַּב, which lies behind the fourfold ἔνοχος (→ II, 828, 30 ff.), is not followed by a ref. to the specific court [13] but to the penalty to which one is subject (or the obligation or guilt incurred). This is supported by a second linguistic observation, namely, that neither ἡ κρίσις nor the original Aram. דִּינָא means "court" or even "local court"; [14] דִּינָא means "trial," "verdict," "penalty," so that ἔνοχος ἔσται τῇ κρίσει (Mt. 5:21b) does not mean, as commonly thought, that "(the murderer) is subject to local justice" but that "(the murderer) comes under (capital) [15] sentence," cf. Ex. 21:12; Lv. 24:17. The phrase has the same meaning in Mt. 5:22a and similarly ἔνοχος ἔσται τῷ συνεδρίῳ in Mt. 5:22b means that "he deserves the death sentence from the supreme court" and ἔνοχος ἔσται εἰς τὴν γέενναν τοῦ πυρός that "he deserves (to be cast) into hell." Mt. 5:21b is thus a continuation of the bibl. quotation in 21a and the three phrases which follow in 5:22a-c do not refer to three different courts, the local, the supreme, and the divine (hell), but are simply three expressions for the death penalty in a kind of crescendo. [16] If, as is likely, ὀργιζόμενος refers to the expression of anger in the word (→ IV, 841, 32 ff.), [17] the first three parallel phrases in Mt. 5:22 all refer to the sin of the tongue against one's brother, while the second three all refer to the death penalty.

The following translation is thus suggested: (21) "You have heard (in the reading of Scripture) that God said to the fathers: 'Thou shalt do no murder; the murderer shall be punished (with death).' (22) But I say unto you:

> Any man who is angry with his brother
> deserves to be punished (with death).
> He who says to his brother 'Thou blockhead!'
> deserves to be condemned (to death) by the supreme court.
> He who says: 'Thou idiot!'
> deserves to suffer (death) in hell."

Jesus establishes a new divine law when He opposes His ἐγὼ δὲ λέγω ὑμῖν to the Word of Scripture and proclaims in threefold repetition that the term of abuse which is regarded as harmless though spoken in ill-humour is an offence worthy of death. It is on the same level as murder and deserves the same and

---

[11] jTer., 1, 1 (40b, 24): "Marks of the שׁוֹטֶה: he runs about by night, sleeps in burial grounds, tears his clothes, and destroys what is given him."

[12] A. Merx, *Das Ev. Mt.* (1902), 89; Wellh. Mt., 20; Dalman Jesus, 71 f.; Schl. Mt., 169.

[13] Dalman Jesus, 67.

[14] Joüon, 24 f. In Da. 7:10, 26, too, דִּינָא does not denote justice in the abstract but is an abbreviation for the "members of the בֵּית דִּין."

[15] In the same way "to death" has to be supplied in Tg. J. I O. Nu. 35:21: כַּד אִתְחַיַּב לֵיהּ "as soon as he was condemned (to death)." Cf. also Jos. Ant., 1, 102: (God says) παραινῶ ... καθαρεύειν φόνου τοὺς δράσαντάς τι τοιοῦτον κολάζοντας (sc. with death).

[16] That there is at least a climax in the second three clauses in Mt. 5:22 can hardly be missed, though → IV, 841, 41 ff.

[17] So already Köhler, 95.

indeed a severer punishment, namely, the imposing of the death penalty by the supreme court (which obviously carries with it expulsion from the national fellowship) [18] and even the penalty of eternal death. This paradox of unparalleled sharpness [19] is designed to bring home to the hearers the terrible seriousness of sins of the tongue in God's eyes and hence to save them from having on their consciences the everyday ill feelings towards their brothers which might appear innocuous but in fact poison relationships. Membership of the coming kingdom of God and its order is demonstrated by taking sin seriously in this way.

As regards authenticity, attempts have been made to show that 5:22c is secondary as an extension of 22b, [20] or 5:22b β, c α (as an accretion to 22b α, c β) [21] or more commonly 5:22bc as an elucidation of 22a. [22] In answer to the main objections that there is no crescendo from wrath to insult and that the Sanhedrin is not a higher authority than the local court [23] one should consider what is said about ὀργιζόμενος → 975, 22 f., κρίσις → 975, 11 ff. and συνέδριον → line 2 f. In addition to what is noted → IV, 841, 32 ff. one may also observe that in any case the speech (ῥακά, συνέδριον, γέεννα, γέεννα τοῦ πυρός [gen. for adj]), style (parallelism) and outlook (→ 974, 16 ff.; → συνέδριον) of 5:22bc are all distinctly Palestinian, and that Jesus judges sins of the tongue with similar severity elsewhere (e.g., Mt. 12:36 f.), even regarding them as the very epitome of uncleanness in Mk. 7:15b.

J. Jeremias

---

† ῥαντίζω, † ῥαντισμός

A. Meaning in Greek.

1. ῥαντίζω is a subsidiary form of ῥαίνω which is late and rare outside the Bible. Even in the LXX it is much less common than ῥαίνω, though in the NT ῥαντίζω alone is used. It is not possible to establish any distinction of meaning between the two verbs, so that instances of ῥαίνω may be introduced to clarify the meaning. ῥαίνω/ ῥαντίζω is used in two ways: a. τί τινι "to spray or sprinkle something with something," Aristot. Hist. An., VI, 13, p. 567b, 4 f., b. τὶ ἐπί τι, e.g., *ibid.*, VI, 13, p. 567b, 5 f.

---

[18] Dalman Jesus, 74.

[19] The paradoxical character of Mt. 5:22 is particularly clear in comparison with contemporary punishments for abuse, cf. bQid., 28a Bar., Str.-B., I, 280; 1 QS 7:4 f.

[20] Fridrichsen, 38 f.

[21] Köhler, 94; G. D. Kilpatrick, *The Origins of the Gospel acc. to St. Mt.* (1946), 18, 25.

[22] Kl. Mt., *ad loc.*; Bultmann Trad., 142; Fridrichsen, 39 f.; T. W. Manson, *The Sayings of Jesus* (1950), 155; cf. M. Weise, "Mt. 5:21 f. — ein Zeugnis sakraler Rechtsprechung in der Urgemeinde," ZNW, 49 (1958), 116-123, though he thinks Mt. 5:22b c might be an original independent logion.

[23] Bultmann Trad., 142.

ῥαντίζω, ῥαντισμός. Cr.-Kö., Liddell-Scott, Pr.-Bauer⁵, *s.v.*; O. Schmitz, *Die Opferanschauung d. späteren Judt. u. d. Opferaussagen d. NT* (1910), esp. 196-318; H. Wenschkewitz, *Die Spiritualisierung der Kultusbegriffe Tempel, Priester u. Opfer im NT, Angelos Beih.*, 4 (1932); T. C. Vriezen, "The Term Hizza: Lustration and Consecration," *Oudtestamentische Studiën*, 7 (1950), 201-235; L. Koep, Art. "Besprengung" in RAC, II, 185-194; E. Lohse, "Märtyrer u. Gottesknecht, Untersuchungen zur urchr. Verkündigung vom Sühntod Jesu Christi," FRL, NF, 46 (1955), esp. 162-187; W. Nauck, *Die Tradition u. d. Charakter d. 1 Jn. Zugleich ein Beitrag zur Taufe im Urchr. u. in d. alten Kirche* (1957), 56-59.

or εἰς, e.g., Aristoph. Ra., 1440 f. etc. "to spray or sprinkle something on something." Various fluids may be mentioned as the thing sprinkled, e.g., water in Hom. Od., 20, 150; Theocr. Idyll., 24, 98 etc.; oil in Hippocr. De Fracturis, 21 (ἔλαιον); Polyb., 30, 25, 17 (μύρον); vinegar in Aristoph. Ra., 1440 f.; blood in Hom. Od., 20, 354; Pind. Isthm., VIII, 50; granular solids are also mentioned on occasion, dust in Hom. Il., 11, 282;[1] salt in Aristot. Hist. An., VIII, 10, p. 596a, 27; grain ;[2] fig., e.g., sleep in Pind. Pyth., VIII, 57.

2. ῥαντισμός "sprinkling" has not been found thus far in non-biblical usage.

B. The Word Group in the Old Testament.

I. Linguistic Data.

1. ῥαντίζω occurs only 3 times in the LXX at Lv. 6:20; 4 Βασ. 9:33; ψ 50:9; the compounds ἐπιρραντίζω (Lv. 6:20) and περιρραντίζω (Nu. 19:13, 20; Ez. 43:20 vl.) also call for consideration. Much more common is ῥαίνω, which occurs 13 times, also διαρραίνω once at Prv. 7:17, ἐπιρραίνω once at 2 Macc. 1:21, περιρραίνω 6 times and προσραίνω twice. There is no difference in sense; all the verbs are used interchangeably.[3] But ῥαίνω (with compounds) is preferred, esp. in the cultic sphere; ῥαντίζω (with compounds) is used only in exceptional cases.[4] Syntactically the main construction has the material sprinkled in the acc. and the obj. with ἐπί and acc. (Lv. 16:15 etc.) or πρός and acc. (4 Βασ. 9:33 etc.), so that the meaning is "to sprinkle something on something," → 976, 28 f. In this respect the LXX follows the construction in the original Heb., → lines 29 ff. Only in 5 instances do we find "to sprinkle something with something" (→ 976, 27) and these are the exceptional cases in which the Gk. group is used for the Heb. חטא pi (ψ 50:9; Ez. 43:20 vl.) or נטף (Prv. 7:17 → n. 12) plus 2 Macc. 1:21 (a Gk. work) and Nu. 8:7, where the highly unusual double acc. suggests a slip in the Gk. tradition. Various fluids are mentioned as the material sprinkled, blood (usually cultically → 979, 39 ff. though not always → 979, 2 ff.), oil (always cultically → 979, 32 ff.), water (usually in expiation → 979, 20 ff. cf. also Ez. 36:25 → 980, 21 ff. and 2 Macc. 1:21 → 979, 10 ff.), once a solid (→ line 5 f.): saffron and cinnamon, Prv. 7:17; once fig. (→ line 6 f.), righteousness, Is. 45:8 → 980, 27 ff.

2. The Heb. equivalent for the Gk. group is usually נזה hi with acc. and עַל or לִפְנֵי etc.:[5] "to spray or sprinkle something on something." But the equation is not uniform. Another Gk. verb is used for נזה once at Is. 52:15, and the group ῥαντίζω can be used for other Heb. verbs as well as נזה.

a. In the 19 instances in which נזה hi is used and cultic sprinkling is denoted it is rendered by ῥαίνω and compounds, not ῥαντίζω. In 4 instances we find נזה q "to be sprinkled" (intr.) "to sprinkle," always non-cultically (→ 979, 2 ff.), and in 3 cases it is transl. by pass. ῥαντίζω or ἐπιρραντίζω (Lv. 6:20 twice; 4 Βασ. 9:33), while in the 4th the LXX shows a marked divergence, Is. 63:3.[6] A v. apart is Is. 52:15:

---

[1] Philostr. De Gymnastica, 56 (ed. J. Jüthner [1909], 182, 2).

[2] Oppianus Anazarbensis Halieutica, II, 100 (ed. F. S. Lehrs, Poetae Bucolici et Didactici[2] [1862], 58).

[3] Cf. the fully synon. use of ἐπιρραντίζω and ῥαντίζω in Lv. 6:20b α/β, of προσραίνω and ῥαίνω in Lv. 4:6/4:17, and of περιρραίνω and περιρραντίζω in Nu. 19:13, 18, 19, 20, 21 (on the basis of the alternation of נזה and זרק in the HT).

[4] On the transl. of נזה q → lines 34 ff., חטא pi → 978, 10 f., זרק pu → 978, 6 ff.

[5] With the predominant עַל (13 times) and the equivalent אֶל, e.g., Lv. 14:51 cf. לִפְנֵי in Lv. 14:16, עַל־פְּנֵי in Lv. 16:14, אֶת־פְּנֵי in Lv. 4:6, אֶל־נֹכַח פְּנֵי in Nu. 19:4.

[6] Only in later witnesses is there assimilation to the Mas. by addition, and נזה is then transl. by ῥαντίζω pass., cf. J. Ziegler, Isaias, Septuaginta, 14 (1939), ad loc. The Heb. tradition is also uncertain. 1 QIsa omits the whole passage, while 1 QIsb is the same as the Mas.

כֵּן יַזֶּה גּוֹיִם רַבִּים. In default of emendation [7] it is best [8] to take the hi here as a genuine causative of q נזה and to transl. "to cause to sprinkle," "to bring to sprinkling": the Servant of God brings it about that many nations spray (out). [9] The LXX (θαυμάσονται ἔθνη πολλὰ ἐπ' αὐτῷ) is either based on a different text or — more likely — is a free rendering of a v. which was not properly understood.

b. Other Heb. equivalents of ῥαίνω/ῥαντίζω: זרק pu = περιρραντίζω (pass.) Nu. 19:13, 20. In the immediate context נזה hi is used 3 times as a synon., and for this the LXX, noting the alternation of the Heb. words, has περιρραίνω at Nu. 19:18, 19, 21; [10] זרק pi = ῥαίνω at Ez. 36:25 "to gush out," sc. pure water for cleansing, as God's promise; חטא pi = ῥαντίζω ψ 50:9 or περιρραντίζω Ez. 43:20 vl.: "to sprinkle," sc. in expiation; נזל q [11] = ῥαίνω Is. 45:8, "to pour forth," fig. of clouds which are to cause righteousness to gush out; נטף q [12] = διαρραίνω Prv. 7:17 "to strew," sc. the bed with saffron (or myrrh Mas.). With no Heb. equivalent ἐπιρραίνω in 2 Macc. 1:21 means "to moisten," sc. wood with water.

3. ῥαντισμός in the LXX is used only in the expression ὕδωρ ῥαντισμοῦ "water of sprinkling" for מֵי נִדָּה or מֵי הַנִּדָּה "water for uncleanness," "water of cleansing," Nu. 19:9, 13, 20, 21 (twice); this is a tt. for the water mixed with the ashes of a red heifer which is used for sprinkling in cases of uncleanness through contact with a corpse. The Heb. expression has the purpose of the water in view (against uncleanness), while the Gk. denotes the process (sprinkling). The terms נִדָּה and ῥαντισμός bear no intrinsic relation to one another, and elsewhere נִדָּה is always transl. by other Gk. words. [13] Apart from Nu. 19 we find מֵי נִדָּה only in Nu. 31:23, where the LXX has ὕδωρ ἁγνισμοῦ (used for מֵי חַטָּאת in Nu. 8:7).

---

[7] The Mas. is supported not only by 1 QIs[b] but also by 1QIs[a] (where we simply have the slip וקפצו for יקפצו and עליו is thus related to what precedes as in the LXX).

[8] With Vriezen, 203-205.

[9] Cf. the Tg. (ed. J. F. Stenning [1949]): יבדר "he scatters." The Peshitta, however, takes יַזֶּה to mean "he sprinkles," though this is against the ordinary use of נזה hi (→ 977, 30 f.), and transl. מדכא "he cleanses," the idea being that of a purifying cultic sprinkling of the nations by the Servant of God. This thought might also lie behind 'A (ῥαντίσει) unless 'A is simply following the principle of always having the same Gk. word for the same Heb. — he always has ῥαντίζω for נזה hi elsewhere. The NT does not exploit this possibility of interpreting the v. Cf. H. Hegermann, Js. 53 in Hexapla, Tg. u. Peschitta (1954), 33, 69, 96 f.

[10] To some degree the meaning of זרק q is the same as that of נזה hi. In most instances the ref. of זרק too is to fluids, blood 25 times, always cultically. Yet this word is never rendered by the ῥαίνω/ῥαντίζω group in the LXX but always by προσχέω (except for περιχέω at 2 Ch. 29:22c and κατασκεδάννυμι at Ez. 24:8). It is a sacrificial tt. for the spilling of the blood on the altar, or the people in Ex. 24:8 → 980, 30 ff. It denotes the spilling of all the blood, whereas in the case of נזה hi only a part (cf. Lv. 5:9 מִדַּם "some blood") is sprinkled with the finger (Lv. 16:19 etc.). Thus the use of προσχέω for זרק is to the pt. זרק can also be used of water and in this case ῥαίνω or περιρραντίζω is the right transl., → lines 6 ff. It can also refer to solids like ashes, grain etc. (Ex. 9:8, 10; Is. 28:25; Ez. 10:2; Job 2:12; 2 Ch. 34:4); in this case different Gk. verbs are used.

[11] There is a very different reading in 1 QIs[a].

[12] For the unintelligible HT נפתי we should read נטפתי, BHK, ad loc.

[13] In the longer secondary addition at Zech. 13:1, which brings the LXX into line with the Mas., לְנִדָּה is transl. εἰς τὸν ῥαντισμόν in many witnesses (B א* χωρισμόν), cf. J. Ziegler, Duodecim Prophetae, Septuaginta, 13 (1943), ad loc.; this reading probably comes from 'A.

II. Material Aspects.

1. The profane use of the group plays only a minor role in the OT. At 4 Βασ. 9:33 (נזה q = ῥαντίζομαι) Jezebel falls from the window and her blood sprays the walls and horses. At Is. 63:3 (נזה q → n. 6) the clothing of Yahweh is sprinkled with blood when He has trampled Edom as in a winepress. Lv. 6:20 (twice) (נזה q / [ἐπιρ]ῥαντί- ζομαι) refers to the blood of sacrifice, yet not in the sense of cultic sprinkling, but rather the inadvertent splashing of clothing. In Is. 52:15 (נזה hi / θαυμάζομαι) the Servant of the Lord causes the peoples to spray out, → 977, 37 ff. In Prv. 7:17 (נטף → n. 12 / διαρραίνω) the adulteress strews her bed with myrrh, aloes and cinammon (LXX saffron). In 2 Macc. 1:21 (ἐπιρραίνω) Nehemiah, like Elijah in 3 Βασ. 18:34, has water poured on the prepared sacrifice, which then catches fire miraculously; this again is not cultic sprinkling in the true sense.

2. The cultic use of the word group is always to the fore in the OT. Cultic sprinklings take place in many ways. Different materials are used, namely, prepared water, oil, or blood. Different objects are sprinkled, namely, the sanctuary, men, or things. Different purposes are in view, namely, the consecration of the fluid sprinkled, the cleansing or dedication of the object sprinkled. Different occasions call for sprinkling, namely, contact with the dead, leprosy, the consecration of priests, sacrifice for sin, the day of atonement, the conclusion of the covenant.

a. When water is used, it is usually qualified cultically by some addition. Thus the water of purification (מֵי נִדָּה = ὕδωρ ῥαντισμοῦ → 978, 15 ff.) acc. to Nu. 19:2-10 is water mixed with the ashes of a red heifer or other substances like cedar, hyssop, or crimson; it is used when a man (Nu. 19:13, 18, 19, 20), a house, or a vessel (Nu. 19:18) is made unclean by contact with a corpse; sprinkling with the water of purification purges (חטא pi Nu. 19:19) the unclean person. [14] In the case of leprosy spring-water mixed with the blood of a slain bird is sprinkled on the cured person and his house and cultic purity is thus restored, Lv. 14:7, 51 (טהר pi 14:7, חטא pi 14:49, 52). Only in Nu. 8:7 is unmixed water used as the water of purification (מֵי חַטָּאת). The Levites are sprinkled and purified (טהר pi 8:6 f.) by this (in an abbreviated form of the washing at the consecration of priests, 8:6). In each of these instances sprinkling cleanses and purifies.

b. When Aaron and his sons are consecrated priests they and their clothing undergo sprinkling with oil mixed with the blood of sacrifice, Ex. 29:21; Lv. 8:30. On this occasion the altar is also sprinkled with oil, Lv. 8:11. The sprinkling sanctifies what is sprinkled (קדש pi Lv. 8:11, 30). The meaning is different, however, when in Lv. 14:16, 27 some of the oil used to anoint a cured leper is sprinkled seven times לִפְנֵי יהוה by the priest with his finger; this sprinkling before Yahweh (i.e., towards the holy of holies) is a con- secration of the oil, which acquires its cultic power thereby.

c. Sacrificial blood is also sprinkled towards the holy of holies (before Yahweh) [15] (→ III, 307, 15 ff.) on the offering of the sin-offering (Lv. 4:6, 17; 5:9) and the slaying of the red heifer (Nu. 19:4). But this is not on behalf of the object sprinkled, so that it is not true sprinkling. It is on behalf of the blood or the sacrifice of which a part (pars pro toto) is sprinkled. Yet blood is also used to sprinkle objects which are to be purified. In this connection one may refer esp. to the ritual of the great Day of Atonement, → III, 308, 26 ff. Here some of the blood of the bullock (Lv. 16:14) and the goat (v. 15)

---

[14] In QS 3:4, 9 (cf. 4:21 → n. 21) מי נדה obviously does not have the technical sense of Nu. 19 but refers to everyday cultic baths, though cf. J. Bowman, "Did the Qumran Sect Burn the Red Heifer?" Revue de Qumran, 1 (1958/59), 73-84.

[15] This formula does not, of course, recur in the context but it yields the best inter- pretation.

is sprinkled with the finger towards and seven times before the cover (כַּפֹּרֶת) of the ark of the covenant in the holy of holies, and then the altar before the sanctuary is sprinkled seven times with the blood of both beasts, v. 19. If literary analysis suggests that the rite on the Day of Atonement was meant as a consecration of the sacrificial blood (→ 979, 35 ff., 39 ff.), [16] in the present context of Lv. 16 it is plainly interpreted as a purifying of the sanctuary, v. 16, 18, 19, 20 (כפר pi, טהר pi, קדשׁ pi). Sprinkling with sacrificial blood brings the power of the sacrifice to bear on the objects sprinkled. In this connection one may also refer to the aforementioned rites in which water (Lv. 14:7, 51) or oil (Ex. 29:21; Lv. 8:30) mixed with sacrificial blood is used to sprinkle men or objects.

As the verbs (→ 979, 20 ff.) which are parallel to נזה hi and which interpret it show, it is evident that the predominant thought connected with sprinkling is that of cleansing and expiation, as in the leading chapters Lv. 16 and Nu. 19. This explains why ῥαντίζω is so firmly linked to the thought of expiation that it can sometimes be used in translation of חטא pi, ψ 50:9, → lines 16 ff., cf. also Ez. 43:20 vl.

3. In ψ 50:9 (חטא pi / ῥαντίζω): "Cleanse me (by sprinkling) with (a bunch of) [17] hyssop that I may be clean," there obviously stands in the background a specific cultic rite of the ordeal type, to which allusion is possibly made in Is. 1:18 too. [18] It is very doubtful, however, whether the psalmist has the actual performance of the rite in view. It seems more likely that he is referring figuratively to the purifying sprinkling. [19] Separated from the cultus, the concept expresses God's forgiving action. In an obvious figure of speech Ez. 36:25 (זרק q / ῥαίνω) speaks of God's eschatological action : "I will sprinkle pure water [20] on you that ye may be clean." Like the restoration of Israel (v. 24), the gift of a new heart of flesh (v. 26) and the gift of the Spirit (v. 27), God's cleansing sprinkling is an act of eschatological re-creation of the people of God. [21]

In an eschatological promise, though with no relation to cultic sprinkling, there is a transf. use of ῥαίνω (Heb. נזל) in Is. 45:8 (→ n. 11): "the clouds shall pour down righteousness."

4. Though neither נזה hi nor the group is used, ref. must finally be made to the sprinkling of blood in Ex. 24:8 (זרק q / κατασκεδάννυμι): [22] when the covenant is

---

[16] Vriezen, 219-233.

[17] This is the obvious meaning of בְּאֵזוֹב after the analogy of Nu. 19:18, though H. Schmidt, *Die Psalmen, Hndbch. AT,* I, 15 (1934), ad loc. suggests water mixed with burnt hyssop, cf. Nu. 19:6 (yet hyssop here is only one element among others → 979, 22 f.).

[18] R. Press, "Das Ordal im alten Israel," ZAW, 51 (1933), 243 f.; Schmidt, op. cit., ad loc.; S. Mowinckel, *Offersang og sangoffer* (1951), 271 f.

[19] O. Eissfeldt, *Einl. in d. AT²* (1956), 140 f.; A. Weiser, *Die Psalmen,* I⁴, AT Deutsch, 14 (1955), ad loc.; R. Press, "Die eschatologische Ausrichtung d. 51. Ps.," ThZ, 11 (1955), 241-249 (esp. 246); H. J. Kraus, *Psalmen, Bibl. Komm. AT,* 15 (1958 ff.), 388, ad loc.

[20] מַיִם טְהוֹרִים is not attested in strict cultic usage ; at most one may compare מֵי נִדָּה → 978, 15 ff.

[21] Cf. G. Fohrer, *Ezechiel, Hndbch. AT,* I, 13 (1955), ad loc. Reminiscent of Ez. 36:25 is the depiction of God's eschatological action in 1 QS 4:21: ויז עליו רוח אמת כמי נדה, "and God will sprinkle the spirit of truth on them like cleansing water."

[22] The fact that the tt. is not used here may be linked with the ascription of Ex. 24:3-8 to E and all the ref. → 979, 20 ff. to P. In Rabb. texts זרק in Ex. 24:8 is repeatedly equated with נזה hi, e.g., bKer., 9a; cf. also Hb. 9:18-21, → 982, 6 ff. In Tg. O. and Tg. J. I however, because of the verb זרק the sprinkling of the people becomes a spraying of blood on the altar, cf. Str.-B., III, 742.

made at Sinai Moses sprays half the blood of the sacrifices on the altar and then after the reading of the book of the covenant he sprinkles the people with the rest of the blood and the people subjects itself to him. This blood is expressly called דַּם־הַבְּרִית "the blood of the covenant." The sprinkling establishes fellowship between the covenant partners and seals the conclusion of the covenant.

C. The Word Group in the New Testament.

1. Apart from two probably secondary readings in Mk. 7:4 [23] and Rev. 19:13 [24] the group is limited in the NT to Hb. (5 times) and 1 Pt. (once). Of the verbs we find only ραντίζω in Hb. 9:13, 19, 21; 10:22 with the sprinkled object in the acc. and the material in the dat., i.e., "to sprinkle something with something," → 976, 27, LXX usually the reverse, → 977, 16 ff. The noun ραντισμός "sprinkling" (Hb. 12:24; 1 Pt. 1:2) is no longer restricted, as in the OT → 978, 15 ff., to the phrase ὕδωρ ραντισμοῦ. On the other hand, αἷμα ραντισμοῦ in Hb. 12:24 (cf. also Barn., 5, 1) is to be explained as analogous to ὕδωρ ραντισμοῦ.

2. The use of the group in the NT is controlled by the cultic use of the OT → 979, 13 ff. Sprinkling with the blood of Christ is compared with the OT rites of sprinkling. In Hb. 12:24 the blood of Christ [25] is called αἷμα ραντισμοῦ. This expression cannot be understood merely in terms of the immediate context: "the blood of sprinkling which cries better [26] than the (blood) of Abel," [27] for though the innocently shed blood of Abel [28] may be compared with that of Christ the

---

[23] In Mk. 7:4 ραντίσωνται has ancient support but only from Egypt. witnesses (ℵ sa), so that in comparison with βαπτίσωνται (ADWΘλφℜ latt sy^s.p bo) it may be regarded as a secondary Egypt. reading. Material arguments also favour this. In Mk. 7:3 f. a redactional parenthesis explains the Jewish rules of ritual cleansing. Washing the hands is at issue in both 3a and 4a. In 4a, though "market wares," "food," is in itself a possible sense of ἀπ' ἀγορᾶς (cf. Pr.-Bauer⁵, s.v. ἀγορά), this is ruled out both linguistically (mid. verb) and materially (ritual washing of food is unknown), though cf. V. Taylor, The Gospel acc. to St. Mark (1952), ad loc.; the addition ὅταν ἔλθωσιν (D it) is materially on the right track, Pr.-Bauer⁵, s.v. ἀγορά; Kl. Mk. and Loh. Mk., ad loc. The combination of νίψωνται τὰς χεῖρας in v. 3 and βαπτίσωνται in v. 4a corresponds exactly to the Jewish distinction between נטל, the pouring of water over the hands, and טבל, the dipping of the hands in a quantity of water. In the LXX טבל is almost always rendered βάπτω or βαπτίζω. Cf. materially Str.-B., I, 695-704; → I, 529 ff.; III, 421 f.; IV, 946 ff. On the other hand, since the verb cannot mean "to bathe" (Loh. Mk., ad loc.), it is hard to link ραντίσωνται with any known Jewish rite; this form is thus to be regarded as an emendation due to the fact that βαπτίζομαι had in the meantime been qualified by Chr. baptism.

[24] In Rev. 19:13 (Christ appears περιβεβλημένος ἱμάτιον βεβαμμένον αἵματι) it is hardly possible to reach any decision in view of the textual confusion. We find the readings βεβαμμένον (A ℜ 1 pl), ῥεραμμένον (1611), ἐρραμμένον (Or), ῥεραντισμένον (P 2329), περιρεραμμένον (ℵ* Ir.); a verb of the group ραντίζω is presupposed in Lat sy^h. Since there is obvious allusion to the blood-sprinkled garment of Yahweh in Is. 63:3 (→ 979, 4 f.) one of the forms of ραντίζω might be original and βεβαμμένον might be due to a slip. On the other hand an original βάπτω (cf. Mk. 7:4 → n. 23) might have been replaced by various forms of the group ραντίζω whose co-existence can be explained only in this way.

[25] On the meaning of the blood of Christ cf. → I, 174 ff.; Lohse, 138-141; W. Nauck, Art. "Blut Christi im NT," RGG³, I, 1329 f.

[26] κρεῖσσον, i.e., for forgiveness, not revenge, cf. the comm., ad loc.; Nauck, 59.

[27] Read παρὰ τὸ Ἄβελ with P⁴⁶ L al; in Hb., which puts the art. before proper names only when needed for the sake of clarity, παρὰ τὸν Ἄβελ is most unlikely, cf., e.g., Hb. 11:4.

[28] Cf. Hb. 11:4 and Mt. 23:35 → I, 6 f.

motif of sprinkling finds nothing to correspond to it in the case of Abel. The expression αἷμα ῥαντισμοῦ is not, then, fashioned *ad hoc* but is a formula. It is based formally on the OT ὕδωρ ῥαντισμοῦ (→ 978, 15 ff.) but materially it embraces a reference to many OT rites, as may be seen more precisely from Hb. 9:13 f., 18-21.

Hb. 9:18-21 refers to the conclusion of the covenant at Sinai (Ex. 24:3-8 → 980, 30 ff. This is described with some variations from the OT text not attested elsewhere. Moses takes the blood of the young bullock [29] along with water, red wool and hyssop [30] and with these he sprinkles the book from which he has read God's Law, [31] the whole people, the tabernacle, and the cultic vessels. [32] The fact that the πρώτη διαθήκη was not established χωρὶς αἵματος is for the author of Hb. an indication of the fundamental significance of the death of Jesus for the καινὴ διαθήκη (→ II, 132, 8 ff.) whose μεσίτης He is, 9:15, cf. 12:24 → II, 131, 18 ff. The naming of the blood with which Moses sprinkled the people as τὸ αἷμα τῆς διαθήκης (Ex. 24:8) is expressly quoted in Hb. 9:20. [33] Contrasted with it is the blood of Christ as τὸ αἷμα διαθήκης αἰωνίου, 13:20, cf. 10:29. As sprinkling with the sacrificial blood gave a share in the first covenant, so sprinkling with the blood of Christ gives a share in the new covenant.

Hb. 9:13 f. (→ III, 426, 1 ff.) has in view primarily (cf. 9:7) the great Day of Atonement in Lv. 16 (→ 979, 44 ff.). The blood of bulls and goats which is limited in its efficacy to the cleansing of the σάρξ [34] is contrasted with the blood of Christ which is able to purge our conscience (by sprinkling, 10:22 → 983, 13 ff.). It should be noted, however, that on the Day of Atonement only the cultic vessels are cleansed by sprinkling; there is no sprinkling of the people, which is the primary concern in Hb. To introduce the element of sprinkling another OT rite is mentioned in which there is sprinkling of men, though not with blood, i.e., the sprinkling with the water of purification of those defiled (here κεκοινωμένοι) by a corpse, Nu. 19 → 979, 21 ff. Thus the cleansing ashes of the red heifer [35] are a symbol of Christ's blood as well as the atoning blood of the sacrifices of the Day of Atonement.

The same typological schema lies behind all these statements. There is sprinkling in the NT community as in that of the OT. In the OT the blood of sacrificial

---

[29] μόσχοι corresponds to the Hb. פָּרִים "bullocks" (Ex. 24:5), μοσχάρια in the LXX. The additional mention of the τράγοι, to which there is no ref. in Ex. 24, is an assimilation to Hb. 9:12, 13; 10:4 and probably secondary, since the best attested reading simply has τῶν μόσχων (P⁴⁶ KL 1739 pm sy), and the various positions of the addition in other MSS make it suspect.

[30] These three elements are not mentioned in Ex. 24 but have been brought in from Lv. 14:4-7 (→ 979, 25 ff.) or Nu. 19:6 (→ 979, 21 ff.).

[31] There is no sprinkling of the book of the covenant in Ex. 24.

[32] Not in Ex. 24, and probably under the influence of Nu. 19:4 (→ 979, 40) and Lv. 16:14-19 (→ 979, 44 ff.).

[33] In the form τοῦτο τὸ αἷμα κτλ., which deviates from both Mas. (הִנֵּה) and LXX (ἰδού) and is obviously influenced by the eucharistic formula, cf. C. Spicq, *L'Épître aux Hébreux*, II² (1953), 264, *ad loc.*; J. Héring, *Épître aux Hb., Comm. du NT*, 12 (1954), *ad loc.*; Lohse, 177, n. 5; Mi. Hb., *ad loc.*

[34] Behind this lies the judgment of Hb. 10:4 (ἀδύνατον αἷμα ταύρων καὶ τράγων ἀφαιρεῖν ἁμαρτίας) which is impossible for OT and Jewish thought. The OT cultus claims that it mediates not just external cleansing but purity before God by the remission of guilt, cf. Wenschkewitz, 134; G. v. Rad, *Theol. d. AT*, I (1957), 249-271.

[35] The ashes here, as a decisive component, denote the purifying water as a whole.

beasts and the ashes of the red heifer were sprinkled; in the NT the blood of Christ is sprinkled. In the OT the sprinkling conferred a part in the old covenant; in the NT it confers a part in the new covenant which is superior in every way to the old. In the OT the flesh was purified; in the NT the conscience is purified. In this contrast Hb. adopts in ῥαντίζω / ῥαντισμός a cultic term, but by transferring it to the blood of Christ removes it from true cultic use and employs it figuratively. [36] We have already found a figurative use in Ez. 36:25 and 1 QS 4:21 (→ 980, 22 ff. and n. 21), where sprinkling is a metaphor for the eschatological action of God which grants perfect purity. In Hb., however, this sprinkling occurs already for the community of the heavenly High-priest who by His own blood purifies His people and gives them a share in the new covenant.

According to Hb. 10:22b sprinkling with Christ's blood takes place in baptism: ῥεραντισμένοι τὰς καρδίας ἀπὸ συνειδήσεως πονηρᾶς καὶ λελουσμένοι τὸ σῶμα ὕδατι καθαρῷ.

That the ref. in 22b α is to sprinkling with the blood of Christ [37] may be seen not only from Hb. 12:24 (and 1 Pt. 1:2; Barn., 5, 1) or indirectly from Hb. 9:18-21 (cf. 10:29; 13:20) but also from 9:13 f. too. Here the ashes of the red heifer, or the water of purification attained therefrom, is an antitype of the blood of Christ, and the statement in v. 14: καθαριεῖ τὴν συνείδησιν ἡμῶν ἀπὸ νεκρῶν ἔργων, is closely related to 10:22b α. The ref. of 10:22b β to baptism hardly needs demonstration, → IV, 304, 18 ff. [38] Now the two par. clauses in 22b can hardly be separated from one another as though 22b β were speaking of baptism and 22b α of something else. [39] This is ruled out at once by the fact that baptism could hardly be described as a mere washing of the body. 22b β and 22b α describe two aspects of one and the same thing. As the body is washed with water, so the heart is cleansed and freed from a bad conscience. [40]

The idea of sprinkling with the blood of Christ belongs, then, to baptismal theology. It is an interpretation of the event of baptism. In baptism the candidate receives a share in the atoning, purifying and covenant-making power of the blood of Christ.

3. On this basis one may assume that 1 Pt. 1:2 is also referring to baptism, → IV, 303, 23 ff. [41] The parallel expressions ἐν ἁγιασμῷ πνεύματος, εἰς ὑπακοήν and (εἰς) ῥαντισμὸν αἵματος Ἰησοῦ Χριστοῦ are probably describing different acts in the ceremony: the imparting of the Spirit (which in one branch of early Church tradition preceded water baptism), [42] the commitment to obedience (cf. 1 Pt. 1:22; Did., 7, 1), and the act of baptism in the strict sense. The putting of ὑπακοή before ῥαντισμός, [43] which might seem strange at first, is perhaps to

---

[36] Wenschkewitz, 162-166; → I, 175, 22 ff.

[37] Schmitz, 276; Wenschkewitz, 144; O. Kuss, "Zur paul. u. nachpaul. Tauflehre im NT," Theologie u. Glaube, 42 (1952), 401-425 (esp. 420); H. Strathmann, Der Br. an d. Hebräer, NT Deutsch, 9⁶ (1953), ad loc.; Lohse, 176, n. 1; Mi. Hb., ad loc., though cf. Pr.-Bauer⁵, s.v. ῥαντίζω 2b.

[38] It is disputed in M. Barth, Die Taufe — ein Sakrament? (1951), 478.

[39] So Rgg. Hb., ad loc.; Strathmann, ad loc.; Héring, ad loc. Wnd. Hb., ad loc. also inclines to this view.

[40] Kuss, op. cit., 420; Spicq, II, 317, ad loc.; Lohse, 175 f.; Mi. Hb., ad loc.

[41] The introduction to 1 Pt. is thus oriented already to the baptismal homily which follows in 1:3, cf. Nauck, 57, n. 1.

[42] Ac. 10:44-48 and in the ancient Syr. rite, cf. T. W. Manson, "Entry into Membership of the Early Church," JThSt, 48 (1947), 25-32; Nauck, 155-159.

[43] Wnd. Kath. Br., ad loc. and Lohse, 183 refer to Ex. 24:3-8, where sprinkling with the blood of the covenant is preceded by the reading of the book of the covenant.

be explained in terms of the liturgical order. At any rate 1 Pt. 1:2 shows that the idea of sprinkling with the blood of Christ is not peculiar to Hb. but is part of a widespread baptismal tradition in the primitive Church. [44]

D. The Post-Apostolic Fathers.

In the post-apost. fathers the phrase "blood of sprinkling" occurs only in Barn., 5, 1: ἵνα τῇ ἀφέσει τῶν ἁμαρτιῶν ἁγνισθῶμεν, ὅ ἐστιν ἐν τῷ αἵματι τοῦ ῥαντίσματος αὐτοῦ. [45] The fact that the term ῥάντισμα is not explained more precisely indicates formal use. There is no express ref. to baptism ; it is perhaps suggested in ἄφεσις τῶν ἁμαρτιῶν (cf. Mk. 1:4 and par.; Ac. 2:38) and ἁγνίζω (cf. 1 Pt. 1:22), though cf. 8, 1, 3 f. In Barn., 8 we have a typological interpretation of Nu. 19, → 979, 21 ff. If in 8, 1 the sprinkling relates to the whole people (ῥαντίζειν ... καθ' ἕνα τὸν λαόν) and brings cleansing from sins (ἵνα ἁγνίζωνται ἀπὸ τῶν ἁμαρτιῶν), other OT texts and the interpretation have a hand in this. The heifer represents Jesus (8, 2 : ὁ μόσχος ὁ Ἰησοῦς ἐστιν) and the παιδία who do the sprinkling are the apostles οἱ εὐαγγελισάμενοι ἡμῖν τὴν ἄφεσιν τῶν ἁμαρτιῶν καὶ τὸν ἁγνισμὸν τῆς καρδίας, 8, 3. The sprinkling, then, accomplishes remission of sins and cleansing of the heart, cf. Hb. 9:14; 10:22 (→ 983, 12 ff.). But the process of sprinkling seems to be equated with preaching rather than baptism. ῥαντίζω also occurs in 1 Cl., 18, 7 quoting ψ 50:3-19 (→ 980, 16 ff.) and ῥαίνω is used in a profane sense in Herm. s., 9, 10, 3 (ἔρραναν ὕδωρ sc. for cleaning).

Hunzinger

Ῥαχάβ → III, 1 ff.
ῥῆμα → IV, 69, 21 ff.

---

[44] Other verses in which there is ref. to Christ's blood without mention of sprinkling might also be related to baptismal traditions, cf. esp. Eph. 1:7; 2:13; 1 Pt. 1:18 f.; 1 Jn. 1:7; Rev. 1:5; 7:14, Nauck, 50-52. In relation to 1 Jn. 5:8 (not 5:6) one may thus ask whether all three terms (πνεῦμα, ὕδωρ, αἷμα) do not refer to baptism, cf. Nauck, 147-182, though, following Manson, *op. cit.,* 28, he prefers to relate αἷμα to the eucharist held within the baptismal service. At all events, the αἷμα motif is closely related to baptism as well as the Lord's Supper.

[45] Reading with א; C (11th cent.) and the Lat. transl., in assimilation to the preceding τῇ ἀφέσει κτλ., read ἐν τῷ ῥαντίσματι αὐτοῦ τοῦ αἵματος.

| ῥίζα, ῥιζόω, ἐκριζόω |

† ῥίζα.

1. Profane Greek.

ῥίζα root ϝρδ- [1] (in ῥίζα from *ϝραδja), with other vowels ϝραδ- (in the rare ῥάδ-αμνος), Old High German *wurz*, Lat. *radix* (from *vrad-*) "root" a. lit. of plants, Hom. Od., 10, 304, b. transf. of other things, "point" of the quill, Plat. Phaedr., 251b; "foot" of the mountain, Aesch. Prom., 365; ῥίζαν ἀπείρου τρίταν of Libya as the third "root" of the mainland, Pind. Pyth., IX, 8; c. historically and genealogically, Cyrene as ἀστέων ῥίζα, the "starting-point" for the founding of towns round about, Pind. Pyth., IV, 15; "origin" or "stem" of a family ἀπ' εὐγενοῦς ῥίζης, Eur. Iph. Taur., 610; also of a later member of the family offering the hope of progeny, Soph. Ant., 600; d. fig. ῥίζα κακῶν, Eur. Fr., 912, 11 (TGF, 655); ἀρχὴ καὶ ῥίζα παντὸς ἀγαθοῦ, Epic. Fr., 409; e. cosmologically and theologically : ῥίζα πάντων καὶ βάσις ἁ γᾶ, "the earth as the origin and basis of all things," Tim. Locr., 97e; [2] the soul which comes from above and makes man a heavenly growth is κεφαλὴ καὶ ῥίζα ἡμῶν, "our head and origin," Plat. Tim., 90a.

2. The Septuagint.

a. In the OT שֹׁרֶשׁ and ῥίζα are equivalents with few exceptions. Only in 4 of the 57 LXX instances is the ref. to plants, Job 8:12; 14:8; 30:4; Wis. 7:20. With transf. ref. to other things the word is also seldom used : ῥίζα τῶν ποδῶν, "footprint," Job 13:27; "foot" of the mountain, Jdt. 6:13; 7:12; ῥιζώματα (!) τῆς θαλάσσης, "depths of the sea," Job 36:30. The common expression ἐκ ῥιζῶν, "root and branch," might also be mentioned in this connection, Job 28:9; 31:12. In most of the other ref. the use is fig. whether in simple metaphors or broader allegories. The polar combination "root and fruit (or blossom, twig)" is often used to denote the totality of a man or people, Job 18:16; Am. 2:9 etc. [3]

b. Since the flora of Palestine is often threatened by heat or drought, special attention is directed to the root as the part of the plant which guarantees the existence of the whole. This comes out in several expressions. The root gives purchase and stability. The whole is affected, then, if the roots of the righteous are not torn up (Prv. 12:3), if the root of a good mind does not perish (Wis. 3:15), or if the root of unrighteous judges is as dust, Is. 5:24. The same applies to ῥίζαν βάλλειν, διδόναι, Hos. 14:6; Wis. 4:3 ff. The natural extension of the metaphor is also in keeping with OT thought. The life mediated by the root is dependent on the soil which sustains the root, whether this be firm ground (Prv. 12:12), water which may be reached in the earth (Job 29:19; Jer. 17:8; Ez. 31:7), the crag which can support only a feeble shoot (Sir. 40:15), or the parched earth (Is. 53:2). In the post-exilic passages, which constitute about four fifths of the whole, the metaphor is usually applied individually to the ungodly or the righteous. This is, however, a mere variation on the older theme that Israel as a people is planted in good soil. The song of the vineyard in Is. 5:1-7 and the statements that God has planted the Israelites on the hill of His inheritance in Ex. 15:17; 2 S. 7:10 are the oldest examples of this. Special note should be taken here of the image of Israel as a vine which God has planted in the good earth of Canaan, ψ 79:9-12 etc. (→ I, 342, 14 ff.). Another use is with ref. to the royal house of Judah, Ez. 17. Since the later OT state-

---

ῥίζα. Pass., Liddell-Scott, Preisigke Wört., Moult.-Mill., Pr.-Bauer[5], *s.v.*
[1] Etym. cf. Boisacq, 831, 1121; Hofmann, 293; Schwyzer, I, 359.
[2] Ed. F. Hermann, IV (1856), 412.
[3] A. E. Rüthy, *Die Pflanze u. ihre Teile im bibl.-hbr. Sprachgebrauch,* Diss. Basel (1942), 44 f.

ments draw on the earlier, one may expect the image of Israel in its totality to have a definite influence later even in apparently incidental details. Thus Mal. 4:1 may well echo the living recollection of Israel as a plant when it says that "it shall leave them neither root nor branch."

c. The visible plant grows out of the root as its origin. Tob. 5:14; Δα. 11:7, 20 refer to origins genealogically. Ez. 16:3 speaks of the historical origin of Israel : ἡ ῥίζα⁴ σου καὶ γένεσίς σου ἐκ γῆς Χανααν. ῥίζα σοφίας in Sir. 1:6 has in view the first begetting ; wisdom was created first by God, v. 6, 9. When the word is used fig. in the spiritual sphere, origin and innermost being are one and the same : ῥίζα σοφίας φοβεῖσθαι τὸν κύριον, Sir. 1:20, ⁵ cf. ἀρχὴ σοφία φόβος κυρίου, ψ 110:10; Prv. 1:7; 9:10.

d. From the root a fallen tree can renew itself and put forth fresh shoots, Job 14:7-9. The root, then, is the hope of a new beginning after catastrophe. Twice the thought of the holy remnant is expressed in the metaphor of the abiding root ; one catches here an echo of the sacred stem of Is. 6:13 Mas. The only root of Nebuchadnezzar's tree of life which is left in the earth intimates the rising up again of the ruler, Δα. 4:15, 26 ff. Ezra's prayer (Ezr. 9:6 ff.) glorifies the faithfulness of God which in merited and annihilating judgment has left a remnant and which thus sponsors the hope of Israel's future. Surprisingly only the transl. of 1 Εσδρ. takes up the term ῥίζα in 8:75, 84, 85. The par. 2 Εσδρ. 9:8, 13-15 transl. the Heb. expressions הַשְׁאִיר [נָתַן] פְּלֵיטָה lit. by καταλεί-πειν εἰς σωτηρίαν [διδόναι σωτηρίαν]. In 1 Εσδρ. one may perhaps detect the influence of Is. 11:1, 10 where the hope of Israel in a Messianic sense is connected with ῥίζα. A complete digging up of the roots and hence of all existence is proclaimed to the king in Ez. 17:9, to the nations in Sir. 10:15, to Ephraim in Hos. 9:16, to the proud in Israel in Mal. 4:1 Mas. In the last of these passages the LXX obviously read זָרִים = ἀλλογενεῖς for זֵדִים "the proud," which yields a surprising expression in the context.

e. Special attention is merited by Is. 11:1, 10 ⁶ which speaks of the root of Jesse in a Messianic sense. Is. 11:1: וְיָצָא חֹטֶר מִגֶּזַע יִשָׁי וְנֵצֶר מִשָּׁרָשָׁיו יִפְרֶה = καὶ ἐξελεύσεται ῥάβδος ἐκ τῆς ῥίζης Ιεσσαι, καὶ ἄνθος ἐκ τῆς ῥίζης ἀναβήσεται. ⁷ From the pitiable remnant of the house of Jesse there will come forth, as from the remaining stump of a tree, a new shoot which will establish the coming kingdom of peace and righteousness. גֶּזַע ("stump of a tree," "root-stem"), like שֹׁרֶשׁ, denotes both the relic of past glory and also the hopeful starting-point for a better future. The later editorial addition in v. 10 brings out yet another aspect of ῥίζα : .... וְהָיָה בַיּוֹם הַהוּא שֹׁרֶשׁ יִשַׁי אֲשֶׁר עֹמֵד לְנֵס עַמִּים אֵלָיו גּוֹיִם יִדְרֹשׁוּ = καὶ ἔσται ἐν τῇ ἡμέρᾳ ἐκείνῃ ἡ ῥίζα τοῦ Ιεσσαι καὶ ὁ ἀνιστάμενος ἄρχειν ἐθνῶν, ἐπ' αὐτῷ ἔθνη ἐλπιοῦσιν ... In v. 1 ῥίζα Ιεσσαι is to be construed as a genitive of apposition or explication : "the root which is called Jesse." In v. 10, however, the genitive is one of origin : ἡ ῥίζα τοῦ Ιεσσαι = "the root which comes forth from Jesse." In the former v. the root is the origin of the new shoot, while in the latter v. it is the shoot itself. The transition is naturally facilitated by the idea that the root as pars pro toto includes the shoot.

Comparison of the Mas. and LXX yields a further decisive point. In the HT שֹׁרֶשׁ יִשַׁי is the subj. (as casus pendens), and two statements are made about it, the one in part. form, the other with a finite verb. By transl. אֲשֶׁר as καί, LXX understands ὁ ἀνιστά-

---

⁴ Worth noting is that ῥίζα is here the transl. of מְכוּרָה "descent."
⁵ R. Smend, Die Weisheit des Jesus Sirach (1906), ad loc.
⁶ Cf. J. Ziegler, Untersuchungen zur Septuaginta des Buches Isaias (1934), 140 f.
⁷ LXX seems to read יִפְרַח for יִפְרֶה.

μενος ἄρχειν ἐθνῶν as a second Messianic title. ἔσται = "he will be," "will come forth," is then to be taken as a predicate to which is added the further statement that the Gentiles will hope in Him. This shows that ἡ ῥίζα τοῦ Ιεσσαι has already become a fixed formula, an independent Messianic title. In this light one may ask whether there is a Messianic undertone in Sir. 47:22: ἔδωκεν ... τῷ Δαυιδ ἐξ αὐτοῦ (sc. Solomon) ῥίζαν. The par. κατάλειμμα in 22c and ἔκγονα in 22b again display the twofold significance of ῥίζα as both "remnant" and also "possibility of new beginning."

The shift of meaning from the act. sense of ῥίζα (root which brings forth) to the pass. sense (shoot which is brought forth) may be noted elsewhere in the OT with no Messianic implication. Dt. 29:17 LXX speaks of a shoot which comes up (ἄνω φύουσα intrans.) in gall and bitterness, whereas the Mas. has in view a root which produces (פֹּרֶה trans.) [8] poison and wormwood. Antiochus Epiphanes is ῥίζα ἁμαρτωλός, "a sinful shoot, scion," 1 Macc. 1:10. On the other hand, in Is. 14:29, 30 LXX cannot use ῥίζα twice for שֹׁרֶשׁ but selects σπέρμα, since the ref. in the latter v. is obviously to descendants. This shows that there are limits to the use of ῥίζα in a pass. sense.

Is. 53:2 perhaps carries with it the Messianic sense of Is. 11:10 → V, 676, 27 ff. Acc. to the traditional LXX text (ἀνηγγείλαμεν) the comparison with the shoot and the root does not relate to the figure of the Servant of the Lord but to proclamation concerning Him: "We proclaim in his presence as a child (proclaims), as a root pines in the dry ground." [9] But there has probably been corruption in the Gk. and one may conjecture ἀνέτειλεν [10] and construe like the Mas.: "He (sc. the Servant of the Lord) grew up before him (sc. Yahweh) like a child, like a shoot in the dry ground."

3. Later Judaism.

We may restrict ourselves here to the aspects which are most important for the NT.

a. The concept of Israel as God's plant is common. [11] God will transform the apostate people into a plant of righteousness, Jub. 1:16. Israel is the plant of righteousness and truth, Eth. En. 10:16; 93:10. The planting of the righteous, the trees of life, is firmly rooted in eternity, Ps. Sol. 14:3 f. This planting goes back to Abraham who is their root. Abraham knew that the plants of righteousness would go forth from him, Jub. 16:26. He says the same of Isaac, 21:24. He is himself the plant of righteous judgment and after him comes the eternal plant of righteousness, Eth. En. 93:2, 5. Israel is the race of the elect root, 93:8. These images from Hell. and apoc. Judaism are given a noteworthy turn in the few Rabb. instances. The two beautiful sprigs which God engrafted into Abraham are Ruth and Naomi, who let themselves be planted into Israel as proselytes, bJeb., 63a. [12] When Acher, i.e., Elisha bAbuya, "hews down the plantings," the ref. is to the work of this apostate, through whom several Israelites were cut off from their community, bChag., 15a. Very plain is the late passage Midr. Cant. 6:2: God will plant the righteous Gentiles in Israel, cf. jBer., 5c, 2-10. [13] Acc. to Philo God in the Messianic age will greatly honour the stranger who comes over to Judaism, but He will repel runagate Jews. This will show that virtue even of lowly origin is welcome to God. He is not concerned about the roots, but will accept the healthy shoot because it has changed into a good one, Exsecr., 152. [14]

---

[8] Perhaps LXX read פֶּרַח in the original, cf. Is. 11:1; Hos. 10:4.

[9] K. F. Euler, Die Verkündigung vom leidenden Gottesknecht aus Js. 53 in d. gr. Bibel (1934), 14, 22 f., 53-56.

[10] J. Ziegler, Isaias, Septuaginta, 14 (1939), ad loc. and 99.

[11] Str.-B., I, 720 f.; III, 290-292.

[12] Ibid., I, 26.

[13] Ibid., I, 21.

[14] If the common ref. to Dt. 28:13, 44 connects Exsecr., 152 with Jub. 1:16 (→ line 25 f.), the shared concept of Israel as God's plant may come from older tradition.

In all later Judaism there thus lives on the varied concept of Israel as a plant of God which stems from Abraham and into which the Gentiles may be grafted.

b. The idea that the Messiah is the root of Jesse is common in the Synagogue. In this connection שׁרֶשׁ is always related to the descendant of Jesse in the sense of shoot, Tg. Pro. Is. on 11:1, [15] → 986, 27 ff. This is supported by the general replacement of שׁרֶשׁ by the unequivocal צֶמַח "shoot," Tg. Pro. Jer. on 23:5; 33:15; Zech. 3:8; 6:12. [16] From the fact that it is the Gentiles who ask after the Messiah in Is. 11:10, the strange conclusion is later reached that Israel itself, having the Torah, does not need the teaching of the Messiah. Gn. r., 98 on 49:11; Midr., 21 § 1 on Ps. 21:2. [17] The absence of Messianic expectation in Philo may be seen in the fact that he never quotes Is. 11:1, 10. The state of peace acc. to Is. 11:6 ff. is described in Praem. Poen., 89 f., but there is no mention of the Davidic shoot. Philo often uses the metaphor of the root, but it is for him a stylistic device like other figures of speech. This may be seen in his use of the formula καθάπερ ἐκ (ἀπὸ) ῥίζης in Sacr. AC, 40; Poster. C., 129; Rer. Div. Her., 279 etc., and also in his varied use of the comparison: The Ten Commandments are the ῥίζα καὶ ἀρχαὶ <καὶ> πηγή of the individual statutes, Congr., 120; φύσις is the root and basis of the arts and sciences, Rer. Div. Her., 116 etc. Joseph. has the word only in the lit. sense, e.g., Ant., 8, 47; 18, 9 ff.; Bell., 7, 180.

4. In the New Testament.

The 17 instances, including 4 Synoptic par., are distributed as follows: 8 (or 4) in the Synoptic Gospels, 6 in Paul (including Past.), 1 in Hb. and 2 in Rev. The use is always within the limits set by the OT. Apart from the fig-tree which withers to the very roots in Mk. 11:20, the occurrence is always fig. or in comparisons.

a. In the parable of the Sower (Mk. 4:6 / Mt. 13:6) the root which needs good ground is the source of sap for the plant. The interpretation of the parable (Mk. 4:17 / Mt. 13:21 / Lk. 8:13) applies the idea of having a root to men. By leaving out ἐν ἑαυτοῖς Lk. emphasises more strongly than Mk. or Mt. the fact that what matters is not man himself but his rooting in the soil outside. [18] Mt. 3:10 / Lk. 3:9 is to be set against the background of Mal. 3-4. Mal. 3:23 defines the whole work and preaching of the Baptist as that of the returning Elijah. Furthermore, Mal. 4:1 is the basis of the idea of a fiery judgment which leaves neither root nor branch. When the axe [19] is laid to the roots to hew down the whole tree and throw it into the fire, this is not just a general comparison. Like Mal. 4:1, this passage is illumined by the common view of Israel as God's plant. The reference is to Israel as a whole; it is threatened with complete destruction if it does not repent.

b. R. 11:16 ff. (→ III, 720, 33 ff.) is a warning to Gentile Christians not to give up the fallen Jews. The argument which begins in v. 16 unfolds the premiss for the deduction a minore ad maius in v. 15. The premiss for the fact that the eschatological acceptance of Israel will bring with it the general resurrection and the coming of God's kingdom is that in all circumstances Israel maintains a special holiness. This is stated in v. 16. As the heave offering of Nu. 15:17-21 declares the whole dough and harvest to be God's (→ I, 485, 23 ff.), so the holiness of the root means that the branches are holy. One may thus conclude that the new

---

[15] Str.-B., I, 28.
[16] Ibid., I, 93 f.; cf. II, 113 for further examples.
[17] Ibid., II, 438.
[18] Already at 8:6 Lk. put ἰκμάς for ῥίζα.
[19] This may go back to Is. 10:34 Mas. (LXX transl. בַּבַּרְזֶל by τῇ μαχαίρᾳ).

train of thought begins with v. 16a and not just with v. 16b or v. 17. No longer, as in v. 15, will the future position of the nations be deduced from the Jews. The reference now is to the holiness of the Jews in general, and especially in the present. ῥίζα has sometimes been referred to the firstfruits of Jewish Christians by whom non-believing Jews are sanctified. [20] But this would carry with it too abrupt a break in the movement of thought from v. 16b to v. 17, since Jewish Christians are obviously among the remaining branches in v. 17. It is best to take the common view of exegetes that v. 16a has in mind the historical origin of Israel, the patriarchs. This agrees with the Jewish concept of Abraham as the holy root of Israel, → 987, 28 ff., cf. esp. Eth. En. 93:5, 8. [21] R. 11:28 proves that Paul is thinking of the fathers. The holiness of the patriarchs, which is the basis of that of Israel, consists from the very first in the fact that they were chosen and fashioned by God with a view to the work of salvation accomplished in Christ. [22] This holiness, which is grounded in the act of God encompassing the whole existence and history of Israel, cannot be set aside by even the most radical and culpable perversion. V. 17 refers to the present unhappy situation. Gentile Christians have been grafted in as wild shoots in place of the Jewish branches broken off by their own guilt. The horticultural impossibility of this process is to be viewed in the light of the Jewish idea that the wild Gentiles will be planted into the good tree of Israel, → III, 721, n. 5; cf. esp. bJeb., 63a; Philo Exsecr., 152 → 987, 33 f., 38 ff. Theologically this deliberately unnatural comparison corresponds exactly to what happens when the Gentile παρὰ φύσιν is grafted into the holy people (v. 24) and the irrevocable calling of God (v. 29) demands and promotes the planting in again of the good branches which had been broken off. The patriarchs are a rich root [23] as bearers of the promise fulfilled in Christ. Boasting against the branches which are broken off is shown up for what it is by the nature of the root which sustains the branches. Since this is determined by God's saving action even in relation to the branches which are temporarily broken off, any scorning of the Jews by Gentile Christians is a scorning of their root. This entails a cutting off that is hopeless and final, v. 22.

c. R. 15:12 has the Messianic title from Is. 11:10 (→ 986, 33 ff.): ἡ ῥίζα τοῦ Ιεσσαι. [24] The quotation from the LXX emphasises the fact that it is the "servant of the circumcision" (v. 8) in whom the Gentiles hope and that for this reason Jews and Gentiles may join in common praise. The modified Messianic title ἡ ῥίζα Δαυίδ is solemnly emphasised in Rev. 5:5; 22:16. The par. γένος "descendant" in 22:16 shows plainly that the reference is again to Is. 11:10 rather than 11:1. It must be translated "shoot (out) of David." The various Messianic titles overlap.

---

[20] E. Gaugler, Der Römerbrief, II (1952), 191. Ltzm. R., ad loc., though not ruling out a ref. to the patriarchs, relates v. 16a to Gentile Christians and v. 16b quite definitely to the patriarchs.

[21] Mi. R., 243 : 'The two comparisons are established traditions which Pl. quotes in v. 16 and presupposes in vv. 17 ff. They are treated like quotations from Scripture."

[22] The metaphor must not be overpressed to the point of equating the holy root with Christ as in patristic exegesis and K. Barth, K.D., II, 2 (1942), 314 (E.T. [1957], 285 f.). A distinction has to be made between the root and the "soil" which fashions it.

[23] The addition of a καί after ῥίζης (AΧpl vg sy Or) and the omission of τῆς ῥίζης (P46 D*G it Ir) are later attempts to make the text easier.

[24] As in Is. 11:10 this is a gen. of derivation, not explication, so Schl. R., ad loc.

d. 1 Tm. and Hb. each have an instance of figurative usage. 1 Tm. 6:10 : ῥίζα γὰρ πάντων τῶν κακῶν ἐστιν ἡ φιλαργυρία. That the desire for money is the origin of all evil is a widespread dictum, → 270, 40 and 271, n. 17. [25] Hb. 12:15 is a quotation from Dt. 29:17 LXX. [26] Here, as there, the reference is not to the root but to a new shoot. [27] The bitter root springs from apostasy from God's grace and involves strife which besmirches the community by destruction of peace, v. 14 f. It may be doubted whether there is any reference to an anti-christian counterpart to Messianic expection. [28]

5. The Post-Apostolic Fathers.

The post-apost. fathers use the word in its broad sense : αἱ ῥίζαι τοῦ ὄρους, "the feet" of the mountain (→ 985, 7 and 22), Herm. s., 9, 30, 1 f.; plants whose roots are withered even though the upper parts are still green signify doubters and purely nominal believers, 9, 1, 6; 21, 1 f. The expression ἡ βεβαία τῆς πίστεως ὑμῶν ῥίζα in Pol., 1, 2 is the positive counterpart to 1 Tm. 6:10 (→ lines 1 ff.), cf. Sir. 1:6, 20 → 986, 7 ff. 1 Cl. and Barn. use ῥίζα only in OT quotations.

† ῥιζόω.

1. ῥιζόω "to cause to take root," act. metaph.: Poseidon roots in the sea-floor the ship which has been changed into a rock, Hom. Od., 13, 163; τὴν τυραννίδα, Hdt., I, 64; pass. of plants "to take or strike root(s)," Xenoph. Oec., 19, 9; of a planted garden : ἀλωὴ ἐρρίζωνται, Hom. Od., 7, 122; mid.: αἱ πίνναι (mussels) ἐρρίζωνται, Aristot. Hist. An., V, 17, p. 548a, 5; ἐξ ... ἀμαθίας πάντα κακὰ ἐρρίζωται, Plat. Ep., 7, 336b; of building : ὁδὸς χαλκοῖς βάθροισιν γῆθεν ἐρριζωμένος, "the threshold (to Hades) rooted in the earth with bronze steps," Soph. Oed. Col., 1591; of a bridge : αἰώνιος ἐρρίζωται, Epigr. Graec., 1087, 7; παρέσχε ῥιζῶσαι καὶ καταστῆσαι τὴν πόλιν, Plut. De fortuna Romanorum, 9 (II, 321d).

2. In the LXX "to take root" act. of the plant of unrighteousness in Sir. 3:28, of the wisdom rooted in Israel in Sir. 24:12; pass. of the root of princes in Is. 40:24 and the ungodly in Jer. 12:2.

3. Philo refers to rooted virtue in Leg. All., I, 45 and 89 and to the planted and rooted cosmos in Plant., 11.

4. In the NT the word occurs only in two related passages which both refer to the personal rootage of Christians. Col. 2:7: ἐρριζωμένοι καὶ ἐποικοδομούμενοι ἐν αὐτῷ (sc. Χριστῷ); Eph. 3:17: ἐν ἀγάπῃ [1] ἐρριζωμένοι καὶ τεθεμελιωμένοι. In both the figure of speech is linked with that of building used elsewhere of the community ; on ἐποικοδομεῖν (→ V, 147, 22 ff.) cf. Eph. 2:20 f.; 4:12, 16 etc.; on θεμελιοῦν (→ III, 63, 19 ff.) cf. Col. 1:23; Eph. 2:20; 1 C. 3:10 ff. etc. In the light of this one may naturally think of the parallels mentioned → lines 22 ff. The point is the close rooting in Christ, the lifegiving soil and sustaining foundation.

---

[25] Examples in Dib. Past.[3], ad loc. and C. Spicq, Les Épitres Pastorales (1947), ad loc.
[26] On the textual relation between Hb. and Dt. cf. P. Katz, Review of B. Roberts, The Old Testament Text and Versions in ThLZ, 76 (1951), 537; also P. Katz, "Οὐ μή σε ἀνῶ, οὐδ' οὐ μή σε ἐγκαταλίπω (Hb. 13:5), The Biblical Source of the Quotation," Biblica, 33 (1952), 525, n. 1.
[27] Wnd. Hb.; Mi. Hb., ad loc.
[28] Mi. Hb., ad loc.
ῥιζόω. [1] The ref. in the context can only be to God's love.

† ἐκριζόω.

ἐκριζόω, "to tear out by the root," "to uproot," Lk. 17:6 literally, Mt. 13:29 of weeds in the parable. On the model of Wis. 4:4 and Δα. 4:14, 26 the reference in Mt. 15:13 and Jd. 12 is to judgment on the Pharisees and false teachers.

For the extirpation of great peoples by jealousy and strife cf. 1 Cl., 6, 4; doubt wrests believers from their faith, Herm. m., 9, 9.

Maurer

ῥίπτω, ἐπιρίπτω, † ἀπορίπτω

A. Greek Usage.

ῥίπτω means a. "throwing" things, stones at Pentheus, Eur. Ba., 1097, a writing tablet to the ground, Eur. Iph. Aul., 39, a shield in the battle, Aristoph. Nu., 353; b. "casting to the ground" of persons, Heracles throws the bringer of the garment of Nessus on the rock, Soph. Trach., 780; ἐρριμμένους καὶ μεθύοντας πάντας in Polyb., 5, 48, 2 for those who are overcome by drunkenness and who thus lie around; Heracles casts himself to the ground in his grief (χθονὶ ῥίπτων ἑαυτόν, Soph. Trach., 790); c. "throwing away" to get rid of something, Jason throws off his cloak to do heroic deeds, Pind. Pyth., IV, 232; in Plato Resp., 474a throwing off clothes expresses the resolve of opponents to resist Plato's doctrine of the state; d. "casting off" (rejecting) people, Zeus can cast the presumptuous into Tartarus, Hom. Il., 14, 257; 8, 13; Oedipus in Soph. Oed. Tyr., 719 and Philoctetus in Soph. Phil., 265 are banished and Myrtilus is thrown into the sea in Soph. El., 512; the ἀπερριμμένοι are the banished in Demosth. Or., 18, 48; the goddess Aphrodite can be rejected by men, Aesch. Eum., 215; "even though your parents had suspected you would (later) maintain such wicked things they would not have cast you out" (οὐκ ἄν σε ἔρριψαν), Epict. Diss., I, 23, 10; e. "throwing on or towards," in a gesture of supplication in prayer ῥίπτειν ὀρθὰς ὠλένας πρὸς οὐρανόν, Eur. Hel., 1095 f.

B. Old Testament Usage.

1. The Translation of Hebrew Words.

In 61 instances ῥίπτω is used for שלך, in 11 for other Heb. words (נפל, שלח, רמה, ירט hi, ירה). שלך is 20 times rendered by ἀπορίπτω, which is also used 19 times for other Heb. terms. ἐπιρίπτω occurs 14 times (12 for שלך, 2 for נפל). ἐκρίπτω also occurs 15 times, διαρίπτω twice, καταρρίπτω twice, παραρρίπτω 3 times, ὑπορρίπτω once.

2. God's Throwing.

a. God throws stones at Israel's enemies, Jos. 10:11; the shorn hairs of lady Jerusalem will be thrown away, Jer. 7:29; Jehoiakim is to be cast out of the city, Jer. 22:19. b. God casts away, i.e., banishes to Babylon in Jer. 22:26; Is. 22:18. The king of Babylon in Is. 14:19 and the king of Tyre in Ez. 28:17 will be thrown far from the grave or cast down. This leads to the sense c. "to reject" Jer. 7:15; 4 Βασ. 17:20; 24:20. The psalmist experiences God's repelling: ἀπέρριμμαι ἄρα ἀπὸ προσώπου τῶν ὀφθαλμῶν σου ψ 30:23; ἀπέρριψάς με εἰς βάθη καρδίας θαλάσσης Jon. 2:4; ἀπέρριψάς με ἀπὸ σωτηρίας Job 30:22 LXX; he hopes not to be rejected ψ 50:13; 70:9. d. God casts sins behind Him: ἀπέρριψας ὀπίσω μου πάσας τὰς ἁμαρτίας μου Is. 38:17; He casts them into the depths of the sea ἀπορριφήσονται (sc. αἱ ἀδικίαι), εἰς τὰ βάθη τῆς θαλάσσης, Mi. 7:19.

3. Man's Throwing.

a. Lit. sense: the brothers cast Joseph into the well, Gn. 37:20; cf. Jos. 8:29; 10:27; 2 Βασ. 18:17; 4 Βασ. 9:25; 10:25. The throwing is often despairing (Gn. 21:15; Ez. 7:19) or resolute (4 Βασ. 2:21) but may be for a humanitarian end (4 Βασ. 2:21). When the dust of overthrown altars is cast in the water this act symbolises firm renunciation of idolatry, Dt. 9:21; 4 Βασ. 23:6, 12. b. Transf. sense: God accuses Jeroboam of rejecting Him καὶ ἐμὲ ἔρριψας ὀπίσω σώματός σου, 3 Βασ. 14:9. Israel's fathers cast the Law of Yahweh behind their backs ἔρριψαν τὸν νόμον σου ὀπίσω σώματος αὐτῶν, 2 Εσδρ. 19:26; cf. Ez. 23:35. ἐρρίφη χαμαὶ ἡ δικαιοσύνη, Da. 8:12. The righteous man casts his care (ψ 54:23), his pitiable condition (Da. 9:18), like a burden on the Lord.

C. New Testament Usage.

1. ῥίπτω.

Mt. has the act. of ῥίπτειν twice. In 15:30 men cast the sick at the feet of Jesus, → 630, 6 ff. The thought here is more that of casting offerings before the altar [1] than that of desperation. When Judas threw the money into the temple and hanged himself, this is the act of a desperate man (Mt. 27:5 → 991, 14 f.). In Lk. 4:35 the word is used to describe an exorcism. In Lk. 17:2 the threat of destruction hangs over the man who harms the little one: ἔρριπται εἰς τὴν θάλασσαν. The casting off of clothes in Ac. 22:23 expresses the resolve of opponents to use every possible means. In Mt. 9:36 ἐρριμμένοι goes with ὡσεὶ πρόβατα; the house of Israel is compared to sheep lying on the ground with no shepherd.

2. ἐπιρίπτω.

1 Pt. 5:7 echoes ψ 54:23 (→ 992, 15 f.). But the reference is no longer individual as in the psalm. The admonition applies to the whole community. The added πᾶσαν denotes radicalisation. Subjection to God's lordship is demonstrated in the fact that the community casts all its care on the Lord and is thus relieved of its burden.

3. ἀπορίπτω.

This verb is used intrans. in Ac. 27:43 "to cast oneself." It has here no theological significance.

D. Usage in the Post-Apostolic Fathers.

ἔριψεν τὰς δύο πλάκας ἐκ τῶν χειρῶν αὐτοῦ in Barn., 4, 8 is modelled on Ex. 32:19, which is quoted in Barn., 14, 3. In his building metaphors Herm. speaks of the throwing away of stones, v., 3, 2, 7; s., 9, 7, 2; the term symbolises rejection. In the similitude of the vine and the elm in s., 2, 3 ῥίπτω is used to express the fact that the vine will lie

---

ῥίπτω κτλ. [1] Loh. Mt., ad loc.

on the ground without the elm's support (ἐρριμμένη χαμαί). ² Dg., 5, 6 uses ῥίπτω for the exposing of infants.

Bieder

---

† ῥομφαία

A. Usage outside the New Testament.

1. ῥομφαία ¹ is acc. to Hesych., *s.v.* a Thracian weapon, μάχαιρα, ξίφος or ἀκόντιον μακρόν ("large javelin") being suggested as the meaning, cf. also Suid., *s.v.*: ῥομφαία τὸ μακρὸν ἀκόντιον, ἢ μάχαιρα. It is first said to be a Thracian weapon in Plut. Aem., 18, 3 (I, 316), which says in description of Thracian equipment: ὀρθὰς ῥομφαίας βαρυσιδήρους ἀπὸ τῶν δεξιῶν ὤμων ἐπισείοντες. ² Though from the way these Thracian ῥομφαῖαι were carried it would seem that they were lances, spears, or javelins, not swords, ³ the latter became the dominant sense, esp. as the word soon passed into Lat. ⁴ in this sense and the note in Suic. Thes., II, 908 : ῥομφαῖαι *etiam vocantur hastae quas tenebant principes honoratissimi ad latus Imperatoris stantes ... et* ῥομφαιοκράτορες *dicebantur,* seems to represent a late and rare usage. Gk. has several terms for swords and lances. ⁵ ῥομφαία never came to be accepted as a full equivalent among these and is very rare in non-bibl. Gk. ⁶

2. The more surprising it is, then, to find it so often in the LXX (over 230 times). In some 200 instances it corresponds to the Heb. חֶרֶב, (410 times), which (→ IV, 524, 24 ff.) is rather less commonly transl. μάχαιρα, only 8 times ξίφος, 4 times ἐγχειρίδιον and once at Job 41:18 λόγχη (→ n. 24). ῥομφαία corresponds almost exclusively to חֶרֶב. Once it is used for מַאֲכֶלֶת (Ju. 19:29 B, secondary as compared with μάχαιρα in A) and 3 times (1 Ch. 11:11, 20; ψ 34:3) for חֲנִית. But in view of the small no. of examples the fact that ῥομφαία can = חֲנִית and חֶרֶב λόγχη ⁷ does not justify the conclusion

---

² Dib. Herm., *ad loc.*: "since it then cringes to the ground."

ῥ ο μ φ α ί α. ¹ The etym. is contested, cf. A. J. Reinach, Art. "Rhomphaea" in Darembg.-Saglio, IV, 2 (1912), 865, n. 1. Boisacq and Walde-Pok. do not discuss it. If it comes from Thrace it might have moved from Macedonia to Egypt and passed into Gk. there, hence into the LXX. Cf. O. Fiebiger, Art. "ῥομφαία" in Pauly-W., 1a (1914), 1072 f.

² Thrace is also suggested by Arrian Fr., 103 (FGH, II, 871). The oldest instance is in the historian Phylarch. (3rd cent. B.C.) Fr., 57 (FGH, II, 181): ἡ γὰρ ῥομφαία βαρβαρικόν ἐστιν ὅπλον, ὡς ἱστορεῖ Φύλαρχος. Cf. also Plut. Cleomenes, 26 (I, 817c): κόπτων ξύλοις μεγάλοις εἰς σχῆμα ῥομφαίας ἀπειργασμένοις [Debrunner].

³ ὀρθάς here means "straight up" rather than just "straight" [Kleinknecht] → n. 30.

⁴ ῥομφαία is a loan word in Lat. from Liv., 31, 39, 11. Cf. the examples in Fiebiger, *op. cit.* and Reinach, *op. cit.* For Chr. Lat. cf. also H. Rönsch, *Itala u. Vulgata* (1875), 245. Apart from *rhomphaea* and *romphaea* we also find subsidiary forms like *rumpia* (reminiscent of *rumpere*).

⁵ Cf. E. Breulier, Art. "Gladius (ξίφος)" in Darembg.-Saglio, II, 2 (1896), 1600 f.; art. "Hasta (δόρυ)," *ibid.,* III, 1 (1900), 33, also O. Fiebiger, Art. "Gladius" in Pauly-W., 7 (1912), 1372-1376; art. "Hasta, 2," *ibid.,* 2503-2507.

⁶ Cf. Pass., Liddell-Scott, *s.v.* Nor does ῥομφαία occur in inscr. or pap.

⁷ In the LXX חֲנִית is mostly transl. δόρυ, רֹמַח δόρυ and λόγχη. This shows that ῥομφαία for חֲנִית and λόγχη for חֶרֶב are exceptional. Cf. → n. 18.

that ῥομφαία may denote the lance or spear when used for חֶרֶב. The statistics over-whelmingly support the equation ῥομφαία = חֶרֶב = "sword," and this is the sense even where there is no Mas. [8] Since ῥομφαία and μάχαιρα do not differ in sense as transl. of חֶרֶב, and there may sometimes be alternation in the MSS for this reason (e.g., Ju. 1:8; 19:29; Jos. 8:24), one may ask what principles governed the selection of one or the other term. ῥομφαία is obviously a larger sword, e.g., that of the Cherubim at the gate of Paradise in Gn. 3:24 or that of Goliath in 1 S. 17:45, 47, 51; 21:10; 22:10. Furthermore some translators evidently preferred the one term or the other. [9] Cf. → n. 18, 21, 24, 26.

3. Philo Cher. is influenced by the LXX (περὶ τῶν Χερουβιμ καὶ τῆς φλογίνης ῥομφαίας κτλ.) when in exposition of Gn. 3:24 (→ line 6 f.) he often uses ῥομφαία, cf. 1. 11. 20 f. 25 etc. When it is said in Cher., 31 that Abraham, on the occasion of the sacrifice of Isaac, took πῦρ καὶ μάχαιραν (Gn. 22:6) as μίμημα τῆς φλογίνης ῥομφαίας, Philo, though μάχαιρα means here the sacrificial knife rather than a sword, has the meaning "sword" in view in order to be able to make this combination. Then in Cher., 32, having quoted Nu. 22:29, he replaces μάχαιρα by ξίφος in his exposi-tion. [10]

Joseph., too, is often dependent on the LXX in his use of ῥομφαία, e.g., Ant., 6, 187 (1 S. 17:45), 244 (1 S. 21:9 f.), 254 (1 S. 22:10), 370 (1 S. 31:4 f.), cf. also 7, 299 (not based on 2 S. 21:16). Jos. also has ῥομφαία as a synon. in 7, 12 though 2 S. 2:16 uses only μάχαιρα, while in his rendering of 1 S. 17:51 in Ant., 6, 190 the meaning of the explanatory addition μάχαιραν οὐκ ἔχων αὐτός can only be that David did not even have a μάχαιρα, let alone a ῥομφαία like Goliath's. In the description of the weapons of the Roman army in Bell., 3, 94 ff. Jos. calls the sword of the infantry ξίφος and that of the cavalry μάχαιρα; ξίφος and ῥομφαία are differentiated, however, in 3, 386 and 6, 86 and 88. Cf. also Bell., 6, 289.

In the pseudepigr. it may be noted that Gr. En. 99:16 has ἀπολεῖ πάντας ὑμᾶς ἐν ῥομφαίᾳ. Sib. (e.g., 3, 673) also uses ῥομφαία (on 3, 316; 5, 260 → 995, 18 ff.). Test. XII has ῥομφαία along with the less common μάχαιρα (Test. B. 7:1 f.; Jos. 6:2; Jud. 5:5; 6:3; L. 6:5; Zeb. 1:6; 4:9) and with no discernible distinction, cf. Test. Jud. 23:3; L. 5:3; 18:10; S. 5:4; Zeb. 4:11; ξίφος also occurs in Test. D. 1:7. Where there is no Gk. (Eth. En. 63:11; on 4 Esr. 13:10 → n. 31) there is no pt. in trying to decide which would be the Gk. term. This applies also to the Qumran Scrolls, in which, along with other weapons (→ V, 300, 7 ff.), we find חֶרֶב fairly often, 1 Qp Hab. I, 17; 1 QM 6:3; [11] 12:2

---

[8] On the lance in Israel and Judah cf. P. Thomsen, Art. "Lanze C. Palästina-Syrien" in RLV, 7 (1926), 231-233; K. Galling, Art. "Lanze" in BR, 353-355; on the sword cf. the bibl. → IV, 524, n. 2.

[9] ʼΑ, Σ and Θ use ῥομφαία and μάχαιρα in the proportion 1 to 3. In view of the common use of ῥομφαία its dominance in some works is worth noting : 1 Βασ. 23 times, μάχαιρα once ; 4 Βασ. 8 times, μάχαιρα once ; Ps. 19 times, μάχαιρα twice ; Minor Prophets 31 times, μάχαιρα once ; Jdt. 7 times to none ; 1 Macc. 11 times, μάχαιρα 3; 3 Βασ. 9 times, μάχαιρα 3; 1 Ch. 9 times, μάχαιρα 4; Ez. 46 times, μάχαιρα 38. Cf. J. Herrmann, "Die LXX zu Ez. das Werk dreier Übersetzer" in J. Herrmann-F. Baumgärtel, Beiträge zur Entstehungsgesch. d. LXX, BWANT, NF, 5 (1923), 9 and 15. In Ju., too, ῥομφαία is more common than μάχαιρα, though the better A text favours μάχαιρα. μάχαιρα is more common in Is. (18 times to 1) and Jer. (49 to 14). It alone occurs in Job (3) and Prv. (4 times).

[10] Leisegang lists ῥομφαία only under Cher.; μάχαιρα does not occur at all and ξίφος carries 7 ref.

[11] Cf. on this K. G. Kuhn, "Beiträge zum Verständnis d. Kriegsrolle von Qumrān," ThLZ, 81 (1956), 28; cf. also ibid., 29 f. on כידן 1 QM 5:7, 11 f., 14. Kuhn defends the idea of a sickle sword. Cf. also H. Molin, "What is a Kidon ?" Journal of Semitic Studies, 1 (1956), 334-337. But cf. also M. Burrows, More Light on the Dead Sea Scrolls (1958), 242 (acc. to Driver etc. we are to think in terms of the sica or curved dagger).

(based on 1 S. 17:45, cf. 17:47: חֶרֶב and חֲנִית, LXX ρομφαία and δόρυ); 11:11 (cf. Is. 31:8; LXX μάχαιρα); 12:11; 15:3; 16:1; 19:4; 1 QH 5:10, 13, 15; 6:28 f.; 1 Q 38 (DJD I, 142); Damasc. 1:4 (1:3), 17 (1:12), 20 (1:16); 3:11 (4:9); 19:7 (9:3); 7:13 (9:4); 19:13 (9:11 f.); 4 Qp Ps. 37 col. 4:1 f. [12] (Ps. 37:14 f.: LXX ρομφαία); 4 Qp Na. 9 [13] (Na. 2:14 : LXX ρομφαία).

In Rabb. writings ρομφαία, unlike μάχαιρα, ξίφος and σπάθη, [14] does not occur as a loan word.

B. New Testament Usage.

1. If the NT not only has μάχαιρα 27 times (→ IV, 525, 7 ff.), but also ρομφαία 7 times, [15] this is unquestionably, as in Philo (→ 994, 10 ff.) and Josephus (→ 994, 18 ff.), due to the influence of the common occurrence of this rare word in the LXX → 993, 18 ff. [16] The saying of the aged Simeon to the mother of Jesus in Lk. 2:34 f. contains in v. 35a the parenthetical statement : [17] καὶ σοῦ δὲ αὐτῆς τὴν ψυχὴν διελεύσεται ρομφαία. This intimation, influenced by OT diction (→ 996, 2 ff.), looks ahead to the later fate of Jesus [18] and to the maternal sorrow which Mary will not be spared but which will not lead her astray from God's gracious guidance. [19]

The (metrically badly transmitted) saying in Sib., 3, 316 about the fate of Egypt when invaded by Antiochus Epiphanes : ρομφαία γὰρ διελεύσεται διὰ μέσον σεῖο, bears a strong kinship to Lk. 2:35a, though this is only formal. The notable occurrence of ρομφαία and διελεύσεται in both passages should not perhaps lead us to overlook the fact that the ref. in Sib. is to the political and geographical rending of a country

---

[12] Ed. J. M. Allegro, JBL, 75 (1956), 94.

[13] Ibid., 91.

[14] Cf. S. Krauss, Talmudische Archäologie, II (1911), 311, 313 f.

[15] ξίφος (ξιφίδιον) and σπάθη do not occur in the NT. On λόγχη → n. 18. On πελεκίζω in Rev. 20:4 cf. Loh. Apk., 159, ad loc.

[16] The reading in Cod D at Lk. 21:24, which has στόματι ρομφαίας for στόματι μαχαίρης (cf. also minusc. 1241), is also to be explained thus, esp. as ἐν στόματι ρομφαίας is more common in the LXX than ἐν στόματι μαχαίρης.

[17] J. M. Creed, The Gospel acc. to St. Luke (1930), 42, following Loisy, discusses the possibility that the parenthesis is an interpolation of Luke's and that by means of the interpolation (and the introduction in 2:34) a general saying is addressed specifically to Mary. With its OT colouring however (→ line 14) the statement in 2:35a fits in well with the character of the original or the tradition which is to be presupposed in this part of the infancy story in Lk. Furthermore, Lk. always uses μάχαιρα in the material peculiar to him, 21:24; 22:36, 38, 49; cf. Ac. 12:2; 16:27.

[18] Though Lk. has nothing corresponding to Jn. 19:25 ff. one has also and esp. to think of the death of Jesus in 2:35a in view of what Simeon says elsewhere. There is, of course, no connection with Jn. 19:34 (λόγχη). Even Zn. Lk., 158, n. 85 does not consider this, though he thinks "spear" is "more suitable" for ρομφαία in Lk. 2:35a. His ref. to LXX instances of ρομφαία for חֲנִית is, however, a misreading of LXX usage → 993, 18 ff. Nor is it of decisive importance that e.g., at ψ 34:3 (→ 993, 23) 'Α Θ Σ Quinta have λόγχη or that Cod e at Lk. 2:35a (for gladius) has famea = framea, esp. as framea mostly means "sword" in Chr. Lat., cf. O. Fiebiger, Art. "Framea" in Pauly-W., 7 (1910), 81 f.; Reinach, op. cit., n. 15; Rönsch, 313 (→ n. 30).

[19] Cf. K. H. Rengstorf, Das Ev. nach Lk., NT Deutsch, 3⁸ (1958), 47, ad loc. Hck. Lk., 44 ad loc. suggests that "εἰς ἀνάστασιν, which does not fit smoothly into the figure of speech, might have been added later as a ray of hope." It should be noted, however, that εὐλόγησεν in 2:34 pts. in the same direction and indicates the ultimate meaning of Simeon's statement. Rightly most modern comm. are against the idea that there is any ref. to Mary's future doubts concerning Jesus' mission.

during military hostilities whereas in Lk. we have a figure of speech for sorrow of soul, cf. μάχαιρα in Sib., 5, 260. This difference comes out the more strongly when it is noted that Sib., 3, 316 is obviously influenced by Ez. 14:17: ἦ καὶ ῥομφαίαν ἐὰν ἐπάγω ἐπὶ τὴν γῆν ἐκείνην καὶ εἴπω· ʿΡομφαία διελθάτω διὰ τῆς γῆς. This connection is the more certain in view of the no less plain reference to Ez. 14:21 in Sib., 3, 317. Of the four plagues in Ez. (cf. the use of Ez. 14:21 in Rev. 6:8 → line 23) ῥομφαία is not mentioned because it is referred to already in Sib., 3, 316. For all the formal similarity, and apart from all questions of date, any dependence of Lk. on Sib. is shown to be quite improbable simply by the difference in spheres of use. [20] What separates Lk. from Sib., however, also separates Lk. from Ez. Hence one should not postulate any direct relation between Lk. 2:35a and Ez. 14:21. This makes it all the more possible that ψ 36:15 : ἡ ῥομφαία αὐτῶν εἰσέλθοι εἰς τὴν καρδίαν (vl. ψυχὴν ℵ) αὐτῶν, has influenced the formulation in Lk. [21]

2. Apart from Lk. 2:35a ῥομφαία occurs 6 times in Rev., which also uses μάχαιρα in 6:4; 13:10, 14. The only literal use is in 6:8, which says of the Fourth Horseman of the Apocalypse that he was given power to slay a fourth part of the human race by sword and famine, pestilence and wild beasts. The influence of Ez. 14:21 on the fourfold series (→ line 22 f.) carried with it the use of ῥομφαία too and plainly distinguishes 6:8 from 6:4, where there is reference to the μάχαιρα μεγάλη of the Second Horseman. [22] It is thus possible that unlike 6:4, where μάχαιρα is the opposite of εἰρήνη, i.e., war, [23] 6:8 has murder in view. [24]

6:8 is unmistakably influenced by the fourfold series λιμός, θηρία πονηρά, θάνατος, αἷμα in Ez. 5:17 and esp. ῥομφαία, λιμός, θηρία πονηρά, θάνατος in Ez. 14:21, cf. also Lv. 26:22 ff. (θηρία, μάχαιρα, famine, murder). But one is also reminded of the threefold series λιμός, ῥομφαία, θάνατος in Ps. Sol. 15:7 and the many similar instances of μάχαιρα, λιμός and θάνατος in Jer. (14:12; 21:7; 24:10 etc., cf. also 15:2). ῥομφαία and λιμός also occur together in Ιερ. 45(38):2; 49(42):22; 51(44):18; Lam. 2:21; cf. Bar. 2:25 and also ψ 75:4; Sir. 40:9. [25]

The other five passages in Rev. 1:16; 2:12, 16; 19:15, 21 are interrelated in that all refer to the ῥομφαία which proceeds from the mouth of Christ. It is true that in the introduction to the letter to Pergamos in 2:12 we simply read : τάδε λέγει ὁ ἔχων τὴν ῥομφαίαν τὴν δίστομον τὴν ὀξεῖαν, but the phrase ἐν τῇ ῥομφαίᾳ

---

[20] Cf. Hck. Lk., 41; Clemen, 211. H. Sahlin, "Der Messias u. d. Gottesvolk," Acta Seminarii Neotest. Upsaliensis, 12 (1945), 273 refutes the view of G. Erdmann, "Die Vorgeschichte d. Lk.- u. Mt.-Ev. u. Vergils 4. Ekloge," FRLANT, NF, 30 (1932), 13, that Lk. is dependent on Sib. But Sahlin's own ref. of ῥομφαία to the sword of the Word (279) is not satisfying. Cf. T. Gallus, "De sensu verborum Lk. 2:35 eorumque momento mariologico," Biblica, 29 (1948), 220-239.

[21] Suic. Thes., II, 908 pointed already to this par., which is wrongly overlooked in modern works. Wettstein, ad loc. refers to ψ 104:18 : σίδηρον διῆλθεν ἡ ψυχὴ αὐτοῦ. Cf. also the Rabb. par. in Str.-B., II, 140.

[22] For other reasons we cannot regard the series in 6:8 as a summary of the plagues of all Four Horsemen and refer back ἐν ῥομφαίᾳ to 6:4. αὐτοῖς does not refer to the four but to the Fourth Horseman and his companions. Cf. Clemen, 386.

[23] → II, 412, 3 (6:4 is meant); IV, 526, 1 f.

[24] LXX often transl. חֶרֶב by φόνος, so Ex. 5:3 (ʾΑ μάχαιρα, Θ ῥομφαία); Lv. 26:7 (Αλλ. ῥομφαία); Dt. 28:22. At Jer. 14:15, too, LXX paraphrased sword by ἐν θανάτῳ νοσερῷ (ʾΑΘ have ῥομφαία) [Bertram].

[25] Though the Fourth Horseman in Rev. 6:8 is death, the many OT ref. adduced do not allow us to conclude from the mention of the ῥομφαία that death is a horseman bearing a sword, as against A. Dieterich, Abraxas (1891), 95.

τοῦ στόματός μου in 2:16 shows that what is meant in 2:12 is not that the Speaker holds the sword in His hand but that here as elsewhere it is presupposed that the sword goes forth from His mouth. How is the surprising feature in 1:16: καὶ ἐκ τοῦ στόματος αὐτοῦ ρομφαία δίστομος ὀξεῖα ἐκπορευομένη, to be explained?

Since the description in 1:13-15 is shot through with OT reminiscences and the same style is maintained in 1:16b, it is natural to suppose that this is also true in v. 16a. To a limited degree this is so. Thus the description of the ρομφαία as δίστομος and ὀξεῖα, which is characteristically repeated in 2:12 (cf. also 19:15 → lines 19 ff.), finds precedents in the OT. [26] But the features are not combined there and they might simply be qualities which experience has learned to find in a good ρομφαία. Nor was much influence exerted by passages like Is. 11:4; Ps. Sol. 17:24, 25; Hos., 6:5, which certainly see in the Word (λόγος or ῥῆμα) an instrument of punishment and destruction, but do not plainly call it a weapon, let alone a sword. Though μάχαιρα is used, Is. 49:2 would seem to be more important: ἔθηκεν τὸ στόμα μου ὡσεὶ μάχαιραν ὀξεῖαν. One may also recall that the tongue is a μάχαιρα in ψ 56:5; Prv. 24:22c and a ρομφαία in ψ 63:4, while ψ 58:8 says: ρομφαία ἐν τοῖς χείλεσιν αὐτῶν. Not by a long way, however, do these passages actually say that a sword proceeds out of the mouth.

The idea in Rev. 1:16a is to be regarded as a peculiarity of the author or of the vision vouchsafed to him. [27] The fact that this idea influences not only 2:12, 16 but also 19:15, 21 shows how constitutive it was felt to be. The author must have known that it was surprising and even strained; he intended it to be so. [28] 2:16 shows what is at issue in 1:16. In distinction from the μάχαιρα passage in Hb. 4:12 (→ IV, 526, 25 ff.), Christ is here the Judge who watches over His churches and where necessary judges and punishes by His Word. Thus 2:16 announces to the adherents of the Nicolaitans: πολεμήσω μετ' αὐτῶν ἐν τῇ ρομφαίᾳ τοῦ στόματός μου. The statement in 19:15: καὶ ἐκ τοῦ στόματος αὐτοῦ ἐκπορεύεται ρομφαία ὀξεῖα, lies within a description no less vivid than that of 1:13 ff. Christ is the eschatological Judge of the nations (19:11 ff.) and He is depicted as the Rider on the white horse advancing at the head of His armies as the heavenly King and Kurios. [29] In 19:21 [30] there is another reference to this: καὶ οἱ λοιποὶ ἀπεκτάνθησαν ἐν τῇ ρομφαίᾳ τοῦ καθημένου ἐπὶ τοῦ ἵππου τῇ ἐξελθούσῃ ἐκ τοῦ στόματος αὐτοῦ. This statement can apply to a real event like the great slaughter of 6:8 (→ 996, 15 ff.) and within the realism of the apocalyptically visionary depiction this is undoubtedly the intention. Nevertheless, with 19:15, this statement has also to be fitted into the totality of the concept of a ρομφαία

---

[26] δίστομος is found with ρομφαία in ψ 149:6; Sir. 21:3, with μάχαιρα in Ju. 3:16; Prv. 5:4. ὀξεῖα occurs with ρομφαῖα in Ez. 5:1, with μάχαιρα in ψ 56:5; Is. 49:2. Cf. also ξίφος ὀξύ in Wis. 18:15 (of the λόγος), also Ez. 21:14 f.; Wis. 5:20. Cf. A. Strobel, "Die Passa-Erwartung als urchr. Problem in Lk. 17:20 f.," ZNW, 49 (1958), 177 f.

[27] That the divine must have been acquainted with a pagan depiction of a god bearing a sword in his mouth (Clemen, 373) is not a satisfactory solution.

[28] The judgment of Bss. Apk., ad loc. that a fig. expression is here awkwardly applied to a real phenomenon contributes little to understanding. C. Schneider, Die Erlebnisechtheit der Apk. d. Joh. (1930), 46 rightly stresses the fact that the divine obviously saw all this in a vision. The concept is not mental but visionary.

[29] The image of the shepherd, which in 19:15 is suggested by the phrase ποιμανεῖ αὐτοὺς ἐν ῥάβδῳ σιδηρᾷ (ψ 2:9), cannot claim any independent significance → 494, 13 f. and n. 87; W. Jost, ΠΟΙΜΗΝ (1939), 43.

[30] It is by no means evident that 19:15 provides a basis for transl. ρομφαία by lance on the ground that the royal lance was an ancient symbol of the royal dominion of Christ as Victor-King [Kleinknecht].

proceeding from the mouth of Christ, and this may mean that, although the severity of judgment is emphasised in 19:15, 21 as well as 2:16, what is brought out in both cases is that the only weapon used by Christ is the Word. [31] In the total view of 2:16 and 19:21 the same admonition is given to the community as in 1 Pt. 4:17, namely, that judgment begins in the house of God. It is characteristic that the great number of literal ῥομφαία passages in the OT, which often speak of violence and vengeance, has influenced the NT only in Rev., and directly even here only in 6:8.

C. The Post-Apostolic Fathers.

In the post-apost. fathers ῥομφαία occurs only in Barn., 5, 13 (quoting ψ 21:21). Among the Apologists only Justin has the term (6 times, always in OT quotations). This confirms the fact that ῥομφαία remained a rare word even in the post-NT period.

Michaelis

Ῥούθ → III, 1 ff.

---

† ῥύομαι

Contents: A. Basic Meaning of the Greek Verb and Its Hebrew Equivalents. B. Use of the Verb: I. In the Greek World; II. In the Old Testament: 1. Similarity with Profane Greek Usage; 2. Distinctiveness of Old Testament Usage; III. In the New Testament.

A. Basic Meaning of the Greek Verb and Its Hebrew Equivalents.

1. The verb belongs to an Indo-Europ. group with the basic sense "to guard," "to protect." Its original sense is plain in the ancient Nordic *waru* "the circle of stones around a grave," also in the Avestic *var* "castle," Sanskr. *varutar* "protector," Gothic *warjan* ("resist"), Old High German *weren* ("defend"). In Gk., formed from the root ϝρυ,

---

[31] Cf. J. Behm, *Die Offenbarung des Johannes,* NT Deutsch, II⁷ (1956), on 19:15. It is the chief motif in Wis. 18:22: ἐνίκησεν δὲ τὸν χόλον οὐκ ἰσχύι τοῦ σώματος, οὐχ ὅπλων ἐνεργείᾳ, ἀλλὰ λόγῳ τὸν κολάζοντα ὑπέταξεν. The absence of the sword in 4 Esr. 13:10 is for a different reason: the stream of fire and scorching breath with which the Messiah there destroys His enemies in the final conflict has (in spite of 13:4) nothing whatever to do with the Word of judgment but is an exaggerated depiction of a real sword.

ῥύομαι. Note: On the death of A. Oepke W. Kasch worked over the incomplete MS which he had left to produce the present art. On A.: Boisacq, Frisk, *s.v.* ἐρύω 568 f.; M. Leumann, "σάος u. σῶς" in ΜΝΗΜΗΣ ΧΑΡΙΝ, *Gedenkschr. P. Kretschmar,* II (1957), 8 f.; Liddell-Scott, *s.v.* ῥύομαι; Pass., *s.v.*; Preisigke Wört.; Prellwitz Etym. Wört., *s.v.*; Pokorny, 1080; Walde-Pok., I, 282; Bl.-Debr. § 101; 311, 2. On B. III: F. H. Chase, *The Lord's Prayer, Texts and Studies in the Early Church,* I, 3 (1891), 71-73; A. Kirchgässner, *Erlösung u. Sünde im NT* (1950), 66-69, 170 f.; K. G. Kuhn, "πειρασμός — ἁμαρτία — σάρξ," ZThK, 49 (1952), 200-222; E. Lohmeyer, *Das Vater unser* (1946), 147-162; T. W. Manson, *The Lord's Prayer* (1955), 99-113; C. G. Sherwood, *The Lord's Prayer, A Study in Sources* (1940/41), 119 f.

Ϝερυ,[1] the term appears (from Hom. Il. in epic Ionic poetry) as ἔρυμαι, ῥύομαι, εἴρυμαι in the senses "to ward off," Hom. Il., 5, 538; Od., 24, 524; "to guard," Il., 15, 257 and 290, "to save," Il., 17, 645 etc., "to protect," Il., 9, 396, "to keep," Il., 23, 819, cf. also the derivates ἔρυμα "protection," "bulwark," Il., 4, 137; Hes. Op., 536; Xenoph. Cyrop., IV, 3 and 9, ἐρυμνότης "defensive power," "strength," Xenoph. Cyrop., VI, 1 and 23; Aristot. Pol., VII, 11, p. 1330b, 18, ῥυτήρ, Hom. Od., 17, 187 and 223 or ῥύτωρ, "protector," "guardian," Aesch. Sept. c. Theb., 318, ῥύσιος "liberating," "saving," Aesch. Suppl., 150, ῥῦσις "deliverance," Sir. 51:9 and ῥῦμα "protection," Aesch. Suppl., 85; Soph. Ai., 159; Eur. Heracl., 260. In acc. with the basic sense it denotes the keeping intact of men or possessions through the exercise of divine, human, technical or magical force. Compared with σώζω the word is comparatively uncommon. It is found in Hom., e.g., Il., 15, 141; Od., 12, 107 etc.; Hes. Theog., 662; Hdt., I, 86, 2; IV, 187, 3 etc.; not too frequently in the tragedians and Aristoph., in Attic prose only in Thuc., V, 63 in the phrase ῥύσεσθαι ἔργῳ ἀγαθῷ τὰς αἰτίας, "to square off charges by a good act"; not in the pre-Socratics, Plat., Aristot., the Cynics, the Stoics, or Philo, but in Plut., e.g., Vit. Dec. Orat., 2 (II, 834e), inscr. IG, 5, 1 No. 1328, 12[2] and P. Oxy., XII, 1424, 10. It is distinguished from → σώζω[3] by a narrower range of sense which derives from the basic meaning, which persists throughout the story of the term as followed here, and which results in the fact that σώζω can always be used for it whereas ῥύομαι is a synon. of σώζω only where the latter has the special sense "to deliver," "to protect."

2. Yet the LXX saw a certain distinction between σώζω and ῥύομαι, for out of 141 instances it uses it 84 times for the Heb. hi of נצל "to save," 4 times for the ni "to save oneself or someone," and 2 times for the ho,[4] whereas σώζω, though much more common than ῥύομαι in the Gk. Bible, occurs only 23 times for נצל. In 12 instances ῥύομαι is used for גאל "to release," "to buy back," also of God who redeems His people; σώζω is not used for this. In 10 cases ῥύομαι is used for פלט pi "to bring to safety," "to save" (σώζω once). On 7 occasions ישע hi is the original, "to deliver," "to free," "to help out of distress" (σώζω 138 times). ῥύομαι also occurs 6 times for מלט pi "to deliver" (σώζω 11 times), and twice for the ni of the same stem, "to escape," "to save oneself" (σώζω 33 times). Occasionally (in all 14 times) ῥύομαι is also the transl. of פדה "to redeem," "to free," חלץ pi and ni "to save" and "to be saved," נצר "to watch," "to keep," "to guard," פצה "to snatch from," "to deliver," Aram. שיזב "to free."

B. Use of the Verb.

I. In the Greek.

In acc. with the basic sense of the Gk. term ῥύομαι is used for the "deliverance and keeping of men by the gods." "Father Zeus," prays Ajax, "O save the Achaians from the dark night," Hom. Il., 17, 645. "Only Zeus and the other gods saved thee," cries Achilles to Aeneas in an exchange of words before the battle, 20, 194. "Then grant me protection and lead me hence with the gods," prays Priam to the divine messenger Hermes, 24, 430. Apollo comforts the sorrowing Hector: "Apollo protected thee and Ilion's towering fortress," 15, 257 cf. 15, 290. It is not only in battle, however, that the

---

[1] One can hardly agree with Boisacq and Pass. that ῥύομαι is formed from ἐρύω "to draw away, to oneself" ("out of danger" = "to save") for in this case the derivates would be hard to understand.

[2] Cf. H. Collitz, Sammlung gr. Dialektinschr., IV (1884 ff.), 4438, 4.

[3] Cf. Leumann, 8 f.; Pokorny, 1080; Walde-Pok., I, 706.

[4] ἐρύω roughly corresponds to נָצַל qal. The LXX thus regarded ῥύομαι as formed from ἐρύω.

gods protect and save. Man hopes that they will keep him in dangers and afflictions and death. "If you will keep Damis from poverty, as recently from the sea, he will offer thee a kid, goddess with the golden horn," Anth. Graec., VI, 231, [5] cf. VI, 191, where deliverance is sought ἐκ νόσου καὶ πενίης. A young girl tormented by an old woman can say : τῆς δὲ γεραιῆς ῥύεο τὴν κούρην, πρίν τι κακὸν παθέειν, Anth. Graec., V, 288, 12. In Hdt., I, 87 deliverance is sought ἐκ τοῦ κακοῦ, in V, 49; IX, 76 ἐκ δουλοσύνης, in IV, 187 ἐκ νόσου, in Eur. Or., 1563 ἐκ χερῶν μιαιφόνων in Soph. Oed. Tyr., 1352 ἀπὸ φόνου, in Eur. Or., 598 ἐκ θανάτου (cf. Eur. Alc., 11; Hdt., VII, 11), in Eur. Alc., 770 κακῶν μυρίων. Pind. Pyth., 12, 18 f. says that a goddess ἐκ τούτων φίλον ἄνδρα πόνων ἐρρύσατο. The gods may protect and save not only men but also things which men need for life or security. The walls of a city in Hdt., VI, 7 and the land in Hdt., VII, 217 are objects of divine protection and deliverance.

2. What is true of the gods is also true of men. Princes protect cities and countries, Hom. Il., 9, 396. Ilion's warriors protect the wives and infants of Troy from the martial peoples of Argos, 17, 224. Priests may bring deliverance by prayer and sacrifice, Soph. Oed. Tyr., 312. A nation gives protection to the outcast, Soph. Oed. Col., 285. Friend keeps and protects friend, Theogn., 103 (Diehl[3], II, 8). It is worth noting that Odysseus could not save companions who became guilty, Hom. Od., 1, 6. In everyday life guards protect an army against enemy surprise, Il., 10, 417. Finally things can also guard and protect man and thus keep him intact. Walls protect, Il., 18, 515. Helmets protect the heads of youngsters, 10, 259. Armour keeps from injury, 23, 819. In Od., 6, 129 a twig protects the shame of the naked Odysseus from Nausicaa and her companions. The central sense of the verb is particularly evident in the last example. The pt. is always the keeping intact of man's control over himself and his world. This is why the protection which men and gods can give is limited. Odysseus cannot save his comrades because they have already destroyed themselves by their sin, Od., 1, 6 f. Similarly, the gods can save man only within the limits of his destiny. Athene in the council of the Olympians says that "it is impossible to save all mortal men from death in battle," Il., 15, 141. For the gods, too, there are limits they cannot pass : "Even Poseidon himself did not save thee from disaster (sc. Charybdis)," Od., 12, 107. This means that man prays to the deity with anxious questioning : "Who, god or goddess, will save us ?" Aesch. Sept. c. Theb., 91. Salvation and protection by the gods, men, or things is projected and controlled anthropologically. Even in estimating divine possibilities man's experience, the indwelling possibility of ontological knowledge, is the measure of things.

II. In the Old Testament.

1. Similarity with Profane Greek Usage.

a. In individual instances there is hardly any difference between the OT use of ῥύομαι and that of profane Gk. Yahweh replaces the Olympian gods, → 999, 36 ff. He saves both His people (e.g., Ex. 6:6; 14:30; Ju. 6:9 B; 8:34; 4 Βασ. 18:32; 2 Εσδρ. 8:31; Mi. 4:10; 5:5; Is. 36:15; 44:6; 48:17; 49:7, 26; 54:5, 8; Ez. 13:21, 23; 1 Macc. 16:2 etc.) and also individuals (cf. 2 Βασ. 12:7; 22:18, 44, 49; Job 5:20; 22:30; 33:17; ψ 6:5; 24:20; 7:2; 16:13 etc.; Δα. 3:88 etc.). He delivers His people out of the hand of the Egyptians, Ex. 14:30; Ju. 6:9 B; out of bondage, Ex. 6:6; out of the hand of all their enemies, Ju. 8:34; out of the hand of Assyria, 4 Βασ. 18:32; Mi. 5:5; Is. 36:15; out of captivity, Mi. 4:10; out of all these evils, Est. 10:3 f.; 3 Macc. 2:12; from false prophets, Ez. 13:21, 23. He saves the individual out of the hand of Saul (David), 2 Βασ. 12:7; from the strong enemy, 22:18 cf. 3 Macc. 6:10; from persecutors, ψ 7:2; from wicked neighbours, ψ 33:5; from false and evil men, ψ 42:1; Is. 25:4; from those that hate him, ψ 68:15; from attempted murder, ψ 17:30; from blood, ψ 50:16; from the sword, ψ 21:21;

---

[5] Cf. H. Beckby in Anth. Graec. (1957).

from burning fire, Da. LXX 3:88; from destruction, Job 33:17; from the snares of the fowler, ψ 90:3; from death and famine, ψ 32:18 f. cf. Job 5:20; from the realm of the dead, ψ 85:13 cf. ψ 55:14; Hos. 13:14; from the ungodly, ψ 16:13 cf. 58:3; 70:4; 96:10; from tribulations, ψ 33:18, 20; from sins, ψ 38:9; 39:14; 78:9.

b. As in profane Gk. (→ 1000, 13 ff.), there are also human deliverers in the OT. Moses saves the daughters of the priest of Midian in Ex. 2:17, 19. Gideon is called the saviour of Israel in Ju. 9:17 B and the king in 2 Βασ. 19:10. The king saves a woman in 2 Βασ. 14:16. In ψ 81:4 judges are commanded to save the poor and needy out of the hand of the ungodly. Sir. 40:24 refers to the significance of the brother and companion as a possible saviour. A thief can save himself if he gives up his own possessions along with what he has stolen, Prv. 6:31. Finally a man can save himself by giving money, 3 Macc. 2:32.

2. Distinctiveness of Old Testament Usage.

a. The picture is different when the total OT use of ῥύομαι is considered. For a theocentric understanding replaces the basic anthropocentric understanding within which the possibilities of the meaning of the word are developed in Gk. The nature and possibility of salvation are no longer determined by laws of being which obtain for both gods and men and which are known from experience. They are determined by the creating and sustaining will of Yahweh for whom the salvation of the people and the individual is part of His creative action in the salvation history commenced by Him. Because He is the sovereign Lord of this history, the nature, range and possibility of deliverance are wholly dependent on Him and His will. He thus saves "according to his great mercy" (Neh. 9:8), "according to his mercy" (ψ 32:18 f.; 33:8; 85:13), "for his name's sake" (ψ 78:9). Yahweh saves "because he wanted me" (ψ 17:20). Acc. to the OT all salvation, even that through men, comes from Him and is thus to His glory and honour. "There is no god who can save thus," confesses Nebuchadnezzar in Δα. Θ 3:96. "The gods of the peoples have not delivered their lands," 4 Βασ. 18:33 (cf. Is. 36:19). But Yahweh can do this. No powers or laws can limit Him and His will to save. "He made the depths of the sea a way for the ransomed to pass over," Is. 51:10. Thus the word Deliverer is a name for Him, ῥῦσαι ἡμᾶς, ἀπ' ἀρχῆς τὸ ὄνομά σου ἐφ' ἡμᾶς ἐστιν, Is. 63:16.

b. If, however, Yahweh is the only Saviour, a personal understanding of salvation replaces the magical substantial view of the Gk. world (the keeping of the object intact by magical or technical means). Salvation in the OT is preservation from being snatched out of the sphere of salvation established by Yahweh. Since this sphere is not magical but historical, salvation can meaningfully extend only to historical beings, i.e., persons. The examples already quoted show this. They refer always to the salvation of men either socially or as individuals. Salvation is almost always from situations caused by the hostile intent of other persons. How self-evident is this personal understanding may be seen from the fact that Moses dares to reproach God because deliverance has not come : "For since I came to Pharaoh to speak in thy name, he hath done evil to this people ; neither hast thou delivered thy people at all," Ex. 5:23 cf. 3 Macc. 6:11.

c. If salvation is keeping man in the sphere of the saving presence of Yahweh, faith in Yahweh must correspond to deliverance on man's side. We can thus read : "Our fathers trusted in thee, and thou didst deliver them," ψ 21:5, 9; "he saves them that fear him and hope in his mercy," ψ 32:18 f.; 33:8. Unbelief is a denial of the ability of Yahweh to save : "If the righteous is a son of God he will accept him and save him out of the hand of his enemies. With abuse and ill-usage let us put him to the test ... Let us condemn him to a shameful death ; for according to his words protection will be given him," Wis. 2:18, 19a, 20 cf. Is. 36:14-20. But the religious and ethical understanding of salvation goes even deeper. Trust that Yahweh saves has ethical implications. It cannot go hand in hand with disobedience to His will. We thus read that Yahweh delivers only the innocent (Job 22:30 cf. 1 Macc. 2:60), the righteous (ψ 33:20 cf.

Ez. 14:20), the one who has regard to the weak (ψ 40:2 cf. Sir. 40:24). Conversely, He abandons the people when it is disobedient to Him, Ju. 8:34.

When finally man acknowledges that he is guilty before Yahweh, the basis of his salvation is Yahweh's mercy (ψ 30:2; 70:2 cf. 32:18 f.; 33:8; 85:13) and the real act of salvation is the restoration of a relationship with God undisturbed by man's guilt. Thus the righteous man prays : "Deliver me from all my transgressions," ψ 38:9 cf. 39:13 f.; 78:9.

d. Linguistically the data thus far presented show that the variety of the word in the Gk. world narrows down almost exclusively to the sense "to save" in the LXX. For the understanding of salvation in terms of will and person, with a constant reference to the mind or disposition of the one who acts, expunges the distinction between "to guard," "to keep," "to protect" on the one side and "to save," "to liberate," "to redeem" on the other, since this distinction has ref. only to the concrete situation of the one who needs salvation and not to the mind of the saviour, in terms of which the event denoted by ῥύομαι is seen in the OT. A further pt. is that (except in 3 Macc. 2:32) we never read of deliverance by technical means (castle, walls, weapons, money), though the soldiers of Israel took these just as much for granted as did those of Greece. For in contrast to the magico-cosmological thinking of the Greeks, which emphasises the category of substance and can ascribe independent functions to things, the OT faith in God produces thinking in terms of will and person in which things are so much the instruments of him who acts that no saving function can be ascribed to them and hence they cannot be said to save, etc.[6]

III. In the New Testament.

1. When one considers the use of the term in the NT the first pt. to attract attention is its infrequency. In the Gospels it occurs only in the Lord's Prayer at Mt. 6:13, in the contemptuous saying of the rulers at Mt. 27:43 and in the Benedictus at Lk. 1:74. It is found three times in R. at 7:24; 11:26; 15:31, three times in 2 C. 1:10, once each in Col. 1:13; 1 Th. 1:10; 2 Th. 3:2; 2 Tm. 3:11; 4:17, 18; 2 Pt. 2:7, 9. As compared with σῴζω, which is used more than 100 times, ῥύομαι is rare.

2. In content it always means "to save," men are always the object, and God is always the author of salvation. In this respect the usage is fully dependent on that of the OT, → 1000, 35 ff. Dependence on the OT may also be seen in the fact that in 7 of the 15 instances we have either OT quotations or material derivation from the OT. Thus Mt. 27:43 : πέποιθεν ἐπὶ τὸν θεόν, ῥυσάσθω νῦν εἰ θέλει αὐτόν, is a conflation of ψ 21:9 and Wis. 2:13, 18-20, and here, as in the OT, the blasphemous character of what is done is brought out by the word of derision. Lk. 1:73 f.: ὅρκον ὃν ὤμοσεν ... τοῦ δοῦναι ἡμῖν ... ἐκ χειρὸς ἐχθρῶν ῥυσθέντας λατρεύειν αὐτῷ, is based on ψ 17:1 (cf. 3 Macc. 6:10; 2 Βασ. 22:18; Ju. 8:34). R. 11:26 : ἥξει ἐκ Σιὼν ὁ ῥυόμενος, is a quotation from Is. 59:20. Similarly dependent on the OT are 2 C. 1:10 : ῥύεσθαι ἐκ θανάτου (cf. ψ 55:14; Job 5:20), 2 Th. 3:2 : ῥύεσθαι ἀπὸ τῶν ... πονηρῶν ἀνθρώπων (cf. Is. 25:4 LXX), 2 Tm. 3:11: καὶ ἐκ πάντων με διωγμῶν ἐρρύσατο ὁ κύριος (cf. ψ 33:20), 2 Tm. 4:17: ἐρρύσθην ἐκ στόματος λέοντος (cf. 1 Macc. 2:60).

---

[6] Only in the Wisdom lit. do we find vv. in which salvation is neither directly nor indirectly ascribed to God but is regarded as accomplished by men, Prv. 6:31; 13:17; 32:23; 23:14; 24:11; Sir. 40:24. In place of Yahweh wisdom (Prv. 2:12; Wis. 10:6, 9, 13, 15) or righteousness (Prv. 10:2; 11:6; 12:6) is repeatedly said to deliver men here. Finally there is a spiritualising and individualising understanding of salvation not found elsewhere in the OT : "Do no violence to the wretched, for he is poor, and do not act unjustly against the righteous. For the Lord will uphold his right and thou wilt save thy soul (only) if it is unspotted," Prv. 22:22 f. LXX cf. 14:25; 23:14.

3. In one respect, of course, the content of the meaning of ῥύομαι is extended in the NT. The word is used eschatologically. Thus one reads in Mt. 6:13 : ἀλλὰ ῥῦσαι ἡμᾶς ἀπὸ τοῦ πονηροῦ, R. 11:26 : ἥξει ἐκ Σιὼν ὁ ῥυόμενος, ἀποστρέψει ἀσεβείας ἀπὸ ᾿Ιακώβ, Col. 1:13 : ὃς ἐρρύσατο ἡμᾶς ἐκ τῆς ἐξουσίας τοῦ σκότους καὶ μετέστησεν εἰς τὴν βασιλείαν τοῦ υἱοῦ τῆς ἀγάπης αὐτοῦ, 1 Th. 1:10 : ᾿Ιησοῦν τὸν ῥυόμενον ἡμᾶς ἐκ τῆς ὀργῆς τῆς ἐρχομένης, 2 Tm. 4:18 : ῥύσεταί με ὁ κύριος ἀπὸ παντὸς ἔργου πονηροῦ καὶ σώσει εἰς τὴν βασιλείαν αὐτοῦ, 2 Pt. 2:9 : οἶδεν κύριος εὐσεβεῖς ἐκ πειρασμοῦ ῥύεσθαι. If one is to understand the meaning of ῥύομαι in these verses one must follow the line leading up from the OT. Thus Is. 59:20 f. reads : καὶ ἥξει ἕνεκεν Σιων ὁ ῥυόμενος καὶ ἀποστρέψει ἀσεβείας ἀπὸ Ιακωβ. It is noteworthy that the noun here is a part. of ῥύομαι, not σωτήρ. The Saviour does not actually bring in the time of salvation but does the preliminary work which is its presupposition, namely, that of abolishing ungodliness. When this is seen in relation to the NT passages quoted, it implies that ῥύομαι, used eschatologically, denotes final preservation from being snatched out of the eternal salvation which God has promised. Moreover the bearing is not just future. For eternal preservation necessarily has consequences in the present. [7] The NT extension of the meaning of ῥύομαι thus corresponds exactly to what we find in the Dead Sea Scrolls. [8] The NT, like the apocalyptic Qumran sect, bases its understanding of salvation on the theologically most central passages of the OT in which prayer is made for salvation from sin, ψ 38:9; 39:13 f.; 78:9. But it goes further in tracing man's sinfulness not only to man himself but to the power of evil which reigns in this aeon, which in relation to the imminent final struggle seeks to drag man down to eternal perdition, and which man himself has no power to resist. This is the point of the question in R. 7:24 : τίς με ῥύσεται ἐκ τοῦ σώματος τοῦ θανάτου τούτου, to which Col. 1:13 gives the answer that it is God ὃς ἐρρύσατο ἡμᾶς ἐκ τῆς ἐξουσίας τοῦ σκότους καὶ μετέστησεν εἰς τὴν βασιλείαν τοῦ υἱοῦ τῆς ἀγάπης αὐτοῦ, and God by ᾿Ιησοῦν τὸν ῥυόμενον ἡμᾶς ἐκ τῆς ὀργῆς τῆς ἐρχομένης, 1 Th. 1:10 cf. R. 5:9. This all casts a bright light on the most important of all the verses in which ῥύομαι occurs, namely, Mt. 6:13 : ῥῦσαι ἡμᾶς ἀπὸ τοῦ πονηροῦ. No matter whether ἀπὸ τοῦ πονηροῦ (→ 560, 14 ff.) be taken as a masculine or a neuter, [9] the point of this petition in the Lord's Prayer is that prayer is made to God for final deliverance from the power of evil which in the last conflict will plunge man into eternal perdition and against which he cannot protect himself. In this petition however — and this concludes the development of ῥύομαι — God is acknowledged to be not merely the Creator, Sustainer and Saviour of the natural historical life of His people and all men but also the eternal Lord who impresses even evil into His service. But this means that in the very prayer for deliverance evil is overcome by the acknowledgment of God's majesty and the divinely conferred affirmation of His will.

Kasch

---

[7] Cf. Kuhn, 218-221.

[8] Thus 1 Qp Hab. 8:1-3 speaks of being saved by God from the house of judgment, the comm. on Micah 1:5-7 1 Qp Mi. (DJD, I, 78, 8-10) of the elect (of God who keep the Law) in the community of unity who will be delivered from the day (of judgment), cf. 1 QH 6:4; 7:17; 17:11; also negatively of idols, 1 Qp Hab. 12:14. Cf. H. Bardtke, *Die Handschriftenfunde am Toten Meer. Die Sekte von Qumran* (1958), 293.

[9] Cf. on this esp. Lohmeyer, 149-153.